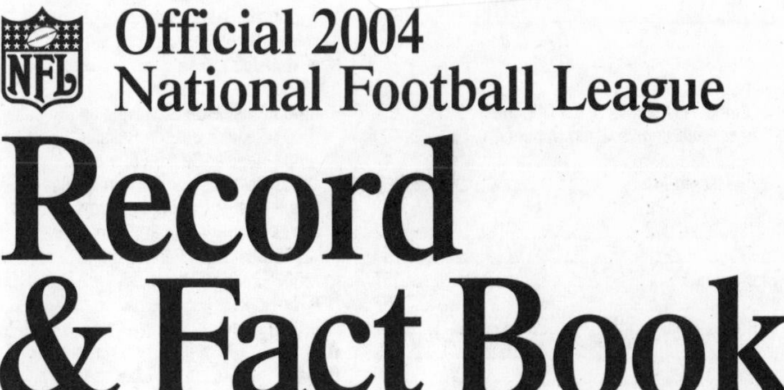

Official 2004 National Football League Record & Fact Book

National Football League
280 Park Avenue, New York, N.Y. 10017 (212) 450-2000. NFL Internet Address: http://www.NFL.com

Printed in the United States of America.

A National Football League Book.

Compiled by the NFL Communications Department and Seymour Siwoff, Elias Sports Bureau.

Edited by Randall Liu, NFL Communications Department, and Matt Marini. Layout by William Tham. Cover design by John Thelian.
Statistics by Elias Sports Bureau.
Produced by NFL Communications Department.

Cover photograph of Tom Brady by Robert E. Klein/NFL Photos.

Time Inc. Home Entertainment
1271 Avenue of the Americas, New York, N.Y. 10020
Manufactured in the United States of America.
First printing, July 2004.
10 9 8 7 6 5 4 3 2 1

A National Football League Book
Time Inc. Home Entertainment

INDEX

2004 SCHEDULE AND NOTE CALENDAR

All times ET. Dates and times subject to change.
Nationally televised games indicated by network in parentheses.

	Monday, August 9	AFC-NFC Pro Football Hall of Fame Game at Canton, Ohio Denver _____ vs. Washington _____	(ABC) 8:00
PRESEASON/FIRST WEEK	**Thursday, August 12**	Atlanta _____ at Baltimore _____	(ESPN) 8:00
		Chicago _____ at St. Louis _____	8:00
	Friday, August 13	Philadelphia _____ at New England _____	8:00
		New York Jets _____ at New Orleans _____	8:00
		Kansas City _____ at New York Giants _____	8:00
	Saturday, August 14	Cincinnati _____ at Tampa Bay _____	7:00
		Pittsburgh _____ at Detroit _____	7:30
		Jacksonville _____ at Miami _____	7:30
		Cleveland _____ at Tennessee _____	8:00
		Dallas _____ at Houston _____	8:00
		Arizona _____ at Minnesota _____	8:00
		Oakland _____ at San Francisco _____	8:00
		Carolina _____ at Washington _____	8:00
		Indianapolis _____ at San Diego _____	10:00
	Sunday, August 15	Denver _____ at Buffalo _____	(NFLN) 7:00
	Monday, August 16	Seattle _____ at Green Bay _____	(ESPN) 8:00
PRESEASON/SECOND WEEK	**Thursday, August 19**	New York Giants _____ at Carolina _____	(FOX) 8:00
	Friday, August 20	Minnesota _____ at Atlanta _____	7:30
		Tampa Bay _____ at Jacksonville _____	7:30
		Baltimore _____ at Philadelphia _____	(CBS) 8:00
	Saturday, August 21	Detroit _____ at Cleveland _____	(NFLN) 4:30
		Tennessee _____ at Buffalo _____	7:00
		New England _____ at Cincinnati _____	7:30
		Washington _____ at Miami _____	7:30
		Houston _____ at Pittsburgh _____	7:30
		New Orleans _____ at Green Bay _____	8:00
		New York Jets _____ at Indianapolis _____	(ESPN) 8:00
		San Francisco _____ at Chicago _____	8:30
		Dallas _____ at Oakland _____	9:00
		San Diego _____ at Arizona _____	10:00
		Denver _____ at Seattle _____	10:00
	Monday, August 23	St. Louis _____ at Kansas City _____	(ABC) 8:00
PRESEASON/THIRD WEEK	**Thursday, August 26**	Pittsburgh _____ at Philadelphia _____	(ESPN) 8:00
	Friday, August 27	New York Giants _____ at New York Jets _____	7:00
		Green Bay _____ at Jacksonville _____	8:00
		San Francisco _____ at Minnesota _____	8:00
		Washington _____ at St. Louis _____	(FOX) 8:00
		New Orleans _____ at Chicago _____	8:30
		Houston _____ at Denver _____	9:00
		Seattle _____ at San Diego _____	10:00
	Saturday, August 28	Miami _____ at Tampa Bay _____	7:00
		Cincinnati _____ at Atlanta _____	7:30
		Detroit _____ at Baltimore _____	8:00
		New England _____ at Carolina _____	(CBS) 8:00
		Buffalo _____ at Indianapolis _____	8:00
		Cleveland _____ at Kansas City _____	8:00
		Oakland _____ at Arizona _____	10:00
	Monday, August 30	Tennessee _____ at Dallas _____	(ABC) 8:00

PRESEASON/FOURTH WEEK	**Thursday, September 2**	Jacksonville ____ at New England ____	(NFLN) 6:45
		Baltimore ____ at New York Giants ____	7:00
		Carolina ____ at Pittsburgh ____	7:00
		Kansas City ____ at Dallas ____	8:00
		Buffalo ____ at Detroit ____	8:00
		Tampa Bay ____ at Houston ____	8:00
		Arizona ____ at Denver ____	9:00
		Minnesota ____ at Seattle ____	9:00
		St. Louis ____ at Oakland ____	10:00
		San Diego ____ at San Francisco ____	11:00
	Friday, September 3	Philadelphia ____ at New York Jets ____	7:00
		Atlanta ____ at Washington ____	7:00
		Indianapolis ____ at Cincinnati ____	7:30
		Chicago ____ at Cleveland ____	8:00
		Miami ____ at New Orleans ____	8:00
		Green Bay ____ at Tennessee ____	8:00
FIRST WEEKEND	**Thursday, September 9**	Indianapolis ____ at New England ____	(ABC) 9:00
	Sunday, September 12	Jacksonville ____ at Buffalo ____	1:00
	FOX-TV National Weekend	Detroit ____ at Chicago ____	1:00
		Baltimore ____ at Cleveland ____	1:00
		San Diego ____ at Houston ____	1:00
		Tennessee ____ at Miami ____	1:00
		Seattle ____ at New Orleans ____	1:00
		Cincinnati ____ at New York Jets ____	1:00
		Oakland ____ at Pittsburgh ____	1:00
		Arizona ____ at St. Louis ____	1:00
		Tampa Bay ____ at Washington ____	1:00
		Dallas ____ at Minnesota ____	4:15
		New York Giants ____ at Philadelphia ____	4:15
		Atlanta ____ at San Francisco ____	4:15
		Kansas City ____ at Denver ____	(ESPN) 8:30
	Monday, September 13	Green Bay ____ at Carolina ____	(ABC) 9:00
SECOND WEEKEND	**Sunday, September 19**	St. Louis ____ at Atlanta ____	1:00
	CBS-TV National Weekend	Pittsburgh ____ at Baltimore ____	1:00
		Houston ____ at Detroit ____	1:00
		Chicago ____ at Green Bay ____	1:00
		Denver ____ at Jacksonville ____	1:00
		Carolina ____ at Kansas City ____	1:00
		San Francisco ____ at New Orleans ____	1:00
		Washington ____ at New York Giants ____	1:00
		Indianapolis ____ at Tennessee ____	1:00
		Seattle ____ at Tampa Bay ____	4:05
		New England ____ at Arizona ____	4:15
		Cleveland ____ at Dallas ____	4:15
		Buffalo ____ at Oakland ____	4:15
		New York Jets ____ at San Diego ____	4:15
		Miami ____ at Cincinnati ____	(ESPN) 8:30
	Monday, September 20	Minnesota ____ at Philadelphia ____	(ABC) 9:00
THIRD WEEKEND	**Sunday, September 26**	Arizona ____ at Atlanta ____	1:00
Open Dates:	**FOX-TV National Weekend**	Baltimore ____ at Cincinnati ____	1:00
Buffalo, Carolina, New England, New York Jets		Philadelphia ____ at Detroit ____	1:00
		Houston ____ at Kansas City ____	1:00
		Pittsburgh ____ at Miami ____	1:00
		Chicago ____ at Minnesota ____	1:00
		Cleveland ____ at New York Giants ____	1:00
		New Orleans ____ at St. Louis ____	1:00
		Jacksonville ____ at Tennessee ____	1:00
		San Diego ____ at Denver ____	4:05
		Green Bay ____ at Indianapolis ____	4:15
		San Francisco ____ at Seattle ____	4:15
		Tampa Bay ____ at Oakland ____	(ESPN) 8:30
	Monday, September 27	Dallas ____ at Washington ____	(ABC) 9:00

2004 SCHEDULE AND NOTE CALENDAR

FOURTH WEEKEND
Open Dates:
Dallas, Detroit, Minnesota, Seattle

Sunday, October 3	New England _____ at Buffalo _____	1:00
CBS-TV National Weekend	Philadelphia _____ at Chicago _____	1:00
	Washington _____ at Cleveland _____	1:00
	New York Giants _____ at Green Bay _____	1:00
	Oakland _____ at Houston _____	1:00
	Indianapolis _____ at Jacksonville _____	1:00
	Cincinnati _____ at Pittsburgh _____	1:00
	New Orleans _____ at Arizona _____	4:05
	Atlanta _____ at Carolina _____	4:05
	New York Jets _____ at Miami _____	4:15
	Tennessee _____ at San Diego _____	4:15
	Denver _____ at Tampa Bay _____	4:15
	St. Louis _____ at San Francisco _____	(ESPN) 8:30
Monday, October 4	Kansas City _____ at Baltimore _____	(ABC) 9:00

FIFTH WEEKEND
Open Dates:
Chicago, Cincinnati, Kansas City, Philadelphia

Sunday, October 10	Detroit _____ at Atlanta _____	1:00
FOX-TV National Weekend	New York Giants _____ at Dallas _____	1:00
	Minnesota _____ at Houston _____	1:00
	Oakland _____ at Indianapolis _____	1:00
	Miami _____ at New England _____	1:00
	Tampa Bay _____ at New Orleans _____	1:00
	Cleveland _____ at Pittsburgh _____	1:00
	Buffalo _____ at New York Jets _____	4:05
	Jacksonville _____ at San Diego _____	4:05
	Carolina _____ at Denver _____	4:15
	Arizona _____ at San Francisco _____	4:15
	St. Louis _____ at Seattle _____	4:15
	Baltimore _____ at Washington _____	(ESPN) 8:30
Monday, October 11	Tennessee _____ at Green Bay _____	(ABC) 9:00

SIXTH WEEKEND
Open Dates:
Arizona, Baltimore, Indianapolis, New York Giants

Sunday, October 17	San Diego _____ at Atlanta _____	1:00
CBS-TV National Weekend	Miami _____ at Buffalo _____	1:00
	Washington _____ at Chicago _____	1:00
	Cincinnati _____ at Cleveland _____	1:00
	Green Bay _____ at Detroit _____	1:00
	Kansas City _____ at Jacksonville _____	1:00
	Seattle _____ at New England _____	1:00
	San Francisco _____ at New York Jets _____	1:00
	Carolina _____ at Philadelphia _____	1:00
	Houston _____ at Tennessee _____	1:00
	Pittsburgh _____ at Dallas _____	4:15
	Denver _____ at Oakland _____	4:15
	Minnesota _____ at New Orleans _____	(ESPN) 8:30
Monday, October 18	Tampa Bay _____ at St. Louis _____	(ABC) 9:00

SEVENTH WEEKEND
Open Dates:
Houston, Pittsburgh, San Francisco, Washington

Sunday, October 24	Buffalo _____ at Baltimore _____	1:00
FOX-TV National Weekend	San Diego _____ at Carolina _____	1:00
	Philadelphia _____ at Cleveland _____	1:00
	Jacksonville _____ at Indianapolis _____	1:00
	Atlanta _____ at Kansas City _____	1:00
	St. Louis _____ at Miami _____	1:00
	Tennessee _____ at Minnesota _____	1:00
	Detroit _____ at New York Giants _____	1:00
	Chicago _____ at Tampa Bay _____	1:00
	New York Jets _____ at New England _____	4:05
	Seattle _____ at Arizona _____	4:15
	Dallas _____ at Green Bay _____	4:15
	New Orleans _____ at Oakland _____	4:15
Monday, October 25	Denver _____ at Cincinnati _____	(ABC) 9:00

EIGHTH WEEKEND
Open Dates:
Cleveland, New Orleans, St. Louis, Tampa Bay

Sunday, October 31	Arizona _____ at Buffalo _____	1:00
CBS-TV National Weekend	Detroit _____ at Dallas _____	1:00
	Jacksonville _____ at Houston _____	1:00
	Indianapolis _____ at Kansas City _____	1:00
	New York Giants _____ at Minnesota _____	1:00
	Baltimore _____ at Philadelphia _____	1:00
	Cincinnati _____ at Tennessee _____	1:00
	Green Bay _____ at Washington _____	1:00
	Atlanta _____ at Denver _____	4:05
	Carolina _____ at Seattle _____	4:05
	New England _____ at Pittsburgh _____	4:15
	Oakland _____ at San Diego _____	4:15
	San Francisco _____ at Chicago _____	(ESPN) 8:30
Monday, November 1	Miami _____ at New York Jets _____	(ABC) 9:00

NINTH WEEKEND
Open Dates:
Atlanta, Green Bay, Jacksonville, Tennessee

Sunday, November 7	New York Jets _____ at Buffalo _____	1:00
CBS-TV National Weekend	Oakland _____ at Carolina _____	1:00
	Dallas _____ at Cincinnati _____	1:00
	Washington _____ at Detroit _____	1:00
	Arizona _____ at Miami _____	1:00
	Philadelphia _____ at Pittsburgh _____	1:00
	Kansas City _____ at Tampa Bay _____	1:00
	Chicago _____ at New York Giants _____	4:05
	New Orleans _____ at San Diego _____	4:05
	Seattle _____ at San Francisco _____	4:05
	Houston _____ at Denver _____	4:15
	New England _____ at St. Louis _____	4:15
	Cleveland _____ at Baltimore _____	(ESPN) 8:30
Monday, November 8	Minnesota _____ at Indianapolis _____	(ABC) 9:00

TENTH WEEKEND
Open Dates:
Denver, Miami, Oakland, San Diego

Sunday, November 14	Tampa Bay _____ at Atlanta _____	1:00
FOX-TV National Weekend	Pittsburgh _____ at Cleveland _____	1:00
	Houston _____ at Indianapolis _____	1:00
	Detroit _____ at Jacksonville _____	1:00
	Kansas City _____ at New Orleans _____	1:00
	Baltimore _____ at New York Jets _____	1:00
	Seattle _____ at St. Louis _____	1:00
	Chicago _____ at Tennessee _____	1:00
	Cincinnati _____ at Washington _____	4:05
	New York Giants _____ at Arizona _____	4:15
	Minnesota _____ at Green Bay _____	4:15
	Carolina _____ at San Francisco _____	4:15
	Buffalo _____ at New England _____	(ESPN) 8:30
Monday, November 15	Philadelphia _____ at Dallas _____	(ABC) 9:00

ELEVENTH WEEKEND

Sunday, November 21	Dallas _____ at Baltimore _____	1:00
FOX-TV National Weekend	St. Louis _____ at Buffalo _____	1:00
	Arizona _____ at Carolina _____	1:00
	Indianapolis _____ at Chicago _____	1:00
	Pittsburgh _____ at Cincinnati _____	1:00
	New York Jets _____ at Cleveland _____	1:00
	Tennessee _____ at Jacksonville _____	1:00
	Detroit _____ at Minnesota _____	1:00
	Denver _____ at New Orleans _____	1:00
	San Francisco _____ at Tampa Bay _____	1:00
	San Diego _____ at Oakland _____	4:05
	Miami _____ at Seattle _____	4:05
	Atlanta _____ at New York Giants _____	4:15
	Washington _____ at Philadelphia _____	4:15
	Green Bay _____ at Houston _____	(ESPN) 8:30
Monday, November 22	New England _____ at Kansas City _____	(ABC) 9:00

Weekend	Date	Game	Time
TWELFTH WEEKEND	**Thursday, November 25**	Indianapolis _____ at Detroit _____	(CBS) 12:30
		Chicago _____ at Dallas _____	(FOX) 4:15
	Sunday, November 28	Tampa Bay _____ at Carolina _____	1:00
	CBS-TV National Weekend	Cleveland _____ at Cincinnati _____	1:00
		Tennessee _____ at Houston _____	1:00
		San Diego _____ at Kansas City _____	1:00
		Jacksonville _____ at Minnesota _____	1:00
		Baltimore _____ at New England _____	1:00
		Philadelphia _____ at New York Giants _____	1:00
		Washington _____ at Pittsburgh _____	1:00
		New Orleans _____ at Atlanta _____	4:05
		New York Jets _____ at Arizona _____	4:15
		Miami _____ at San Francisco _____	4:15
		Buffalo _____ at Seattle _____	4:15
		Oakland _____ at Denver _____	(ESPN) 8:30
	Monday, November 29	St. Louis _____ at Green Bay _____	(ABC) 9:00
THIRTEENTH WEEKEND	**Sunday, December 5**	Cincinnati _____ at Baltimore _____	1:00
	FOX-TV National Weekend	Minnesota _____ at Chicago _____	1:00
		New England _____ at Cleveland _____	1:00
		Arizona _____ at Detroit _____	1:00
		Tennessee _____ at Indianapolis _____	1:00
		Buffalo _____ at Miami _____	1:00
		Carolina _____ at New Orleans _____	1:00
		Houston _____ at New York Jets _____	1:00
		San Francisco _____ at St. Louis _____	1:00
		Atlanta _____ at Tampa Bay _____	1:00
		Kansas City _____ at Oakland _____	4:05
		Denver _____ at San Diego _____	4:05
		Green Bay _____ at Philadelphia _____	4:15
		New York Giants _____ at Washington _____	4:15
		Pittsburgh _____ at Jacksonville _____	(ESPN) 8:30
	Monday, December 6	Dallas _____ at Seattle _____	(ABC) 9:00
FOURTEENTH WEEKEND	**Sunday, December 12**	Oakland _____ at Atlanta _____	1:00
	FOX-TV National Weekend	New York Giants _____ at Baltimore _____	1:00
		Cleveland _____ at Buffalo _____	1:00
		New Orleans _____ at Dallas _____	1:00
		Detroit _____ at Green Bay _____	1:00
		Indianapolis _____ at Houston _____	1:00
		Chicago _____ at Jacksonville _____	1:00
		Seattle _____ at Minnesota _____	1:00
		Cincinnati _____ at New England _____	1:00
		Miami _____ at Denver _____	4:05
		New York Jets _____ at Pittsburgh _____	4:05
		San Francisco _____ at Arizona _____	4:15
		St. Louis _____ at Carolina _____	4:15
		Tampa Bay _____ at San Diego _____	4:15
		Philadelphia _____ at Washington _____	(ESPN) 8:30
	Monday, December 13	Kansas City _____ at Tennessee _____	(ABC) 9:00
FIFTEENTH WEEKEND	**Saturday, December 18**	Pittsburgh _____ at New York Giants _____	(CBS) 1:30
		Washington _____ at San Francisco _____	(FOX) 5:00
		Carolina _____ at Atlanta _____	(ESPN) 8:30
	Sunday, December 19	Houston _____ at Chicago _____	1:00
	CBS-TV National Weekend	Buffalo _____ at Cincinnati _____	1:00
		Jacksonville _____ at Green Bay _____	1:00
		Minnesota _____ at Detroit _____	1:00
		San Diego _____ at Cleveland _____	1:00
		Seattle _____ at New York Jets _____	1:00
		Dallas _____ at Philadelphia _____	1:00
		St. Louis _____ at Arizona _____	4:05
		New Orleans _____ at Tampa Bay _____	4:05
		Denver _____ at Kansas City _____	4:15
		Tennessee _____ at Oakland _____	4:15
		Baltimore _____ at Indianapolis _____	(ESPN) 8:30
	Monday, December 20	New England _____ at Miami _____	(ABC) 9:00

SIXTEENTH WEEKEND

Friday, December 24	Green Bay _____	at Minnesota _____	(FOX) 3:00
Saturday, December 25	Oakland _____	at Kansas City _____	(CBS) 5:00
	Denver _____	at Tennessee _____	(ESPN) 8:30
Sunday, December 26	New York Giants _____	at Cincinnati _____	1:00
FOX-TV National Weekend	Chicago _____	at Detroit _____	1:00
	San Diego _____	at Indianapolis _____	1:00
	Houston _____	at Jacksonville _____	1:00
	Atlanta _____	at New Orleans _____	1:00
	Baltimore _____	at Pittsburgh _____	1:00
	Carolina _____	at Tampa Bay _____	1:00
	New England _____	at New York Jets _____	4:05
	Buffalo _____	at San Francisco _____	4:05
	Washington _____	at Dallas _____	4:15
	Arizona _____	at Seattle _____	4:15
	Cleveland _____	at Miami _____	(ESPN) 8:30
Monday, December 27	Philadelphia _____	at St. Louis _____	(ABC) 9:00

SEVENTEENTH WEEKEND

Sunday, January 2	Miami _____	at Baltimore _____	1:00
CBS-TV National Weekend	Pittsburgh _____	at Buffalo _____	1:00
	New Orleans _____	at Carolina _____	1:00
	Green Bay _____	at Chicago _____	1:00
	Cleveland _____	at Houston _____	1:00
	San Francisco _____	at New England _____	1:00
	Cincinnati _____	at Philadelphia _____	1:00
	New York Jets _____	at St. Louis _____	1:00
	Detroit _____	at Tennessee _____	1:00
	Minnesota _____	at Washington _____	1:00
	Tampa Bay _____	at Arizona _____	4:05
	Atlanta _____	at Seattle _____	4:05
	Indianapolis _____	at Denver _____	4:15
	Jacksonville _____	at Oakland _____	4:15
	Kansas City _____	at San Diego _____	4:15
	Dallas _____	at New York Giants _____	(ESPN) 8:30

Wild Card Playoff Games
Site Priorities
Two Wild Card teams (division non-champions with best two records) from each conference and the division champions with the third and fourth-best record in each conference will enter the first round of the playoffs. The division champion with the third-best record will play host to the Wild Card team with the second-best record. The division champion with the fourth-best record will play host to the Wild Card team with the best record. There are no restrictions on intra-division games.

Saturday, January 8, 2005

American Football Conference

_______________ at _______________ (ABC)

National Football Conference

_______________ at _______________ (ABC)

Sunday, January 9, 2005

American Football Conference

_______________ at _______________ (CBS)

National Football Conference

_______________ at _______________ (FOX)

Divisional Playoff Games
Site Priorities
In each conference, the two division champions with the highest won-lost-tied percentage during the regular season will play host to the Wild Card winners. The division champion with the best record in each conference is assured of playing the lowest seeded Wild Card survivor. There are no restrictions on intra-division games.

Saturday, January 15, 2005

American Football Conference

_______________ at _______________ (CBS)

National Football Conference

_______________ at _______________ (FOX)

Sunday, January 16, 2005

American Football Conference

_______________ at _______________ (CBS)

National Football Conference

_______________ at _______________ (FOX)

Championship Games **Site Priorities for Championship Games** The home teams will be the surviving playoff winners with the best won-lost-tied percentage during the regular season. A Wild Card team cannot play host unless two Wild Card teams are in the game, in which case the Wild Card team that was seeded highest in the first round of the playoffs will be the home team.	**Sunday, January 23, 2005**	American Football Conference __________ at __________ (CBS) National Football Conference __________ at __________ (FOX)
Super Bowl XXXIX	**Sunday, February 6, 2005**	Super Bowl XXXIX at ALLTEL Stadium, Jacksonville, Florida __________ vs. __________ (FOX)
AFC-NFC Pro Bowl	**Sunday, February 13, 2005**	AFC-NFC Pro Bowl at Aloha Stadium, Honolulu, Hawaii AFC__________ vs. NFC __________ (ESPN)

POSTSEASON GAMES

Saturday, January 8	AFC and NFC Wild Card Playoffs (ABC)
Sunday, January 9	AFC and NFC Wild Card Playoffs (CBS and FOX)
Saturday, January 15	AFC and NFC Divisional Playoffs (CBS and FOX)
Sunday, January 16	AFC and NFC Divisional Playoffs (CBS and FOX)
Sunday, January 23	AFC and NFC Championship Games (CBS and FOX)
Sunday, February 6	Super Bowl XXXIX at ALLTEL Stadium, Jacksonville, Florida (FOX)
Sunday, February 13	AFC-NFC Pro Bowl at Aloha Stadium, Honolulu, Hawaii (ESPN)

2004 NATIONALLY TELEVISED GAMES AT A GLANCE

All times ET.

Thursday, September 9	Indianapolis at New England (ABC)	9:00 P.M.
Sunday, September 12	Kansas City at Denver (ESPN)	8:30 P.M.
Monday, September 13	Green Bay at Carolina (ABC)	9:00 P.M.
Sunday, September 19	Miami at Cincinnati (ESPN)	8:30 P.M.
Monday, September 20	Minnesota at Philadelphia (ABC)	9:00 P.M.
Sunday, September 26	Tampa Bay at Oakland (ESPN)	8:30 P.M.
Monday, September 27	Dallas at Washington (ABC)	9:00 P.M.
Sunday, October 3	St. Louis at San Francisco (ESPN)	8:30 P.M.
Monday, October 4	Kansas City at Baltimore (ABC)	9:00 P.M.
Sunday, October 10	Baltimore at Washington (ESPN)	8:30 P.M.
Monday, October 11	Tennessee at Green Bay (ABC)	9:00 P.M.
Sunday, October 17	Minnesota at New Orleans (ESPN)	8:30 P.M.
Monday, October 18	Tampa Bay at St. Louis (ABC)	9:00 P.M.
Monday, October 25	Denver at Cincinnati (ABC)	9:00 P.M.
Sunday, October 31	San Francisco at Chicago (ESPN)	8:30 P.M.
Monday, November 1	Miami at New York Jets (ABC)	9:00 P.M.
Sunday, November 7	Cleveland at Baltimore (ESPN)	8:30 P.M.
Monday, November 8	Minnesota at Indianapolis (ABC)	9:00 P.M.
Sunday, November 14	Buffalo at New England (ESPN)	8:30 P.M.
Monday, November 15	Philadelphia at Dallas (ABC)	9:00 P.M.
Sunday, November 21	Green Bay at Houston (ESPN)	8:30 P.M.
Monday, November 22	New England at Kansas City (ABC)	9:00 P.M.
Thursday, November 25	Indianapolis at Detroit (CBS)	12:30 P.M.
	Chicago at Dallas (FOX)	4:15 P.M.
Sunday, November 28	Oakland at Denver (ESPN)	8:30 P.M.
Monday, November 29	St. Louis at Green Bay (ABC)	9:00 P.M.
Sunday, December 5	Pittsburgh at Jacksonville (ESPN)	8:30 P.M.
Monday, December 6	Dallas at Seattle (ABC)	9:00 P.M.
Sunday, December 12	Philadelphia at Washington (ESPN)	8:30 P.M.
Monday, December 13	Kansas City at Tennessee (ABC)	9:00 P.M.
Saturday, December 18	Pittsburgh at New York Giants (CBS)	1:30 P.M.
	Washington at San Francisco (FOX)	5:00 P.M.
	Carolina at Atlanta (ESPN)	8:30 P.M.
Sunday, December 19	Baltimore at Indianapolis (ESPN)	8:30 P.M.
Monday, December 20	New England at Miami (ABC)	9:00 P.M.
Friday, December 24	Green Bay at Minnesota (FOX)	3:00 P.M.
Saturday, December 25	Oakland at Kansas City (CBS)	5:00 P.M.
	Denver at Tennessee (ESPN)	8:30 P.M.
Sunday, December 26	Cleveland at Miami (ESPN)	8:30 P.M.
Monday, December 27	Philadelphia at St. Louis (ABC)	9:00 P.M.
Sunday, January 2	Dallas at New York Giants (ESPN)	8:30 P.M.

IMPORTANT DATES

2004

July 6 — Claiming period of 24 hours begins in waiver system.

Mid-July — Preseason training camps open. Clubs not permitted to open official preseason camp earlier than July 5. Veteran players cannot be required to report earlier than 15 days prior to club's first preseason game.

July 22# — Signing period ends at 4 P.M., New York time, for Unrestricted Free Agents to whom a June 1 tender was made by Old Club, and for Transition Players. After this date and through 4 P.M., New York time, on November 11, Old Club has exclusive negotiating rights to these players.
#or the first scheduled day of the first NFL training camp, whichever is later.

August 7-9 — Hall of Fame Weekend.

August 9 — Pro Football Hall of Fame Game, Canton, Ohio:
Denver vs. Washington

August 10 — If a Drafted Rookie has not signed with his club by this date, he may not be traded to any other club in 2004.

August 10 — Deadline for players under contract to report to earn a season of free-agency credit.

August 12-16 — First Preseason Weekend.

August 14-18 — Deadline for club to provide written notice to certain unsigned players and the NFLPA of its intent to place them on the Exempt List if they fail to report no later than one day prior to the club's second preseason game. Any player who fails to report prior to the deadline will be ineligible to play or receive compensation for at least three games (preseason or regular season) from the time that he reports.

August 31 — Roster cut-down to maximum of 65 players on Active List by 4 P.M., New York time.

September 1 — All tryouts on this date and for the remainder of the season must be reported to the League office.

September 5 — Roster cut-down to maximum of 53 players on Active/Inactive List by 4 P.M., New York time. Clubs may dress minimum of 42 and maximum of 45 players and Third Quarterback for each regular-season and postseason game.

September 5 — Simultaneously with the cut-down to 53, clubs that have players in the categories of Active/Physically Unable to Perform or Active/Non-Football Injury or Illness must take one of the following options: place player on Reserve/Physically Unable to Perform or Reserve/Non-Football Injury or Illness, whichever is applicable; ask waivers; terminate; trade; or continue to count him on Active List.

September 6 — After 12 noon, New York time, clubs may establish a Practice Squad of five players by signing free agents who do not have an accrued season of free-agency credit or who were on the 45-player Active List for less than nine regular-season games during their only Accrued Season(s). A player cannot participate on the Practice Squad for more than two seasons.

September 7 — All clubs are required to file a personnel (injury) report with their conference Director of Information by 1 P.M., New York time, on this Tuesday and thereafter on each Wednesday before a regular-season game. Such report is to be updated by 1 P.M., New York time, each Thursday. An update must also be reported if there is any change in a player's condition after Thursday.

September 8 — Beginning at 4 P.M., New York time, Team Salary includes all players receiving compensation under their 2004 contracts. Top 51 rule is no longer in effect.

September 9-13 — Regular Season opens.

September 9-14 — Beginning on these dates vested veterans terminated from the Active List or Inactive List (and from Reserve/Injured if the player is placed on Reserve/Injured after the beginning of the regular season) are entitled to receive, after the end of the regular-season schedule, Termination Pay pursuant to the terms of the 1993 CBA.

September 28 — Priority on multiple waiver claims is now based on the current season's standing.

October 19 — Beginning the day after the conclusion of the sixth regular-season weekend and continuing through the day after the conclusion of the ninth regular-season weekend, clubs are permitted to begin practicing players on Reserve/Physically Unable to Perform and Reserve/Non-Football Injury or Illness for a period not to exceed 21 days. Players may be activated during the 21-day practice period or until 4 P.M., New York time, on the day after the conclusion of the 21-day period.

October 19 — All trading ends at 4 P.M., New York time.

October 20 — Players with at least four previous pension-credited seasons are subject to the waiver system for the remainder of the regular season and postseason.

November 8 — Deadline at 4 P.M., New York time, for an increase in a player's 2004 Salary to be counted as Salary for the current year. Any notice of an increase in a player's 2004 Salary received by the NFLMC after this deadline will be treated as a Signing Bonus.

November 16 — Signing period ends at 4 P.M., New York time, for Franchise Players who are eligible to receive Offer Sheets.

November 16 — Deadline for clubs to sign by 4 P.M., New York time, their unsigned Franchise and Transition Players, including Franchise Players who were eligible to receive Offer Sheets until this date. If still unsigned after this date, such players are prohibited from playing in NFL in 2004.

November 16 — Deadline for clubs to sign by 4 P.M., New York time, their Unrestricted Free Agents to whom June 1 tender was made. If still unsigned after this date, such players are prohibited from playing in NFL in 2004.

November 16 — Deadline for clubs to sign by 4 P.M., New York time, their Restricted Free Agents to whom June 1 tender was made. If such players remain unsigned, they are prohibited from playing in NFL in 2004.

November 16 — Deadline for clubs to sign Drafted players by 4 P.M., New York time. If such players remain unsigned, they are prohibited from playing in NFL in 2004.

December 3 — Deadline for reinstatement of players in Reserve List categories of Retired, Did Not Report, and Exclusive Rights, and of players who were placed on Reserve/Left Squad in a previous season.

December 31 — Deadline for waiver requests in 2004, except for "special waiver requests," which have a 10-day claiming period, with termination or assignment delayed until after the Super Bowl.

January 3 — Clubs may begin signing free-agent players for the 2005 season.

2005

January 8-9 — Wild Card Playoff Games.

January 15-16 — Divisional Playoff Games.

January 23 — AFC and NFC Championship Games.

January 29 — Senior Bowl, Mobile, Alabama.

February 6 — Super Bowl XXXIX ALLTEL Stadium, Jacksonville, Florida.

February 8* — First day clubs can designate Franchise or Transition players.

February 13 — AFC-NFC Pro Bowl, Honolulu, Hawaii.

February 22* — Waiver system begins for 2005. Waivers will expire on the first business day of the new League Year. Players with at least four previous pension-credited seasons that a club desires to terminate are not subject to the waiver system until after the trading deadline.

February 22* — Deadline at 4 P.M., New York time, for clubs to designate Franchise and Transition Players.

Feb. 23-March 1 — Combine Timing and Testing, RCA Dome, Indianapolis, Indiana.

March 1* — Expiration date of all player contracts due to expire in 2005.

March 1* — Deadline for exercising options for 2005 on all players who have option clauses in their 2004 contracts.

March 1* — Deadline for submission of Qualifying Offers by clubs to their Restricted Free Agents whose contracts have expired and to whom they desire to retain a Right of First Refusal/Compensation.

March 1* — Deadline for clubs to submit offer of minimum salary to retain exclusive negotiating rights to their players with fewer than three seasons of free-agency credit whose contracts have expired.

March 2* — Free Agency period begins.

March 2* — Trading period begins for 2005 after expiration of all 2004 contracts.

March 2* — A claiming period of three business days is in effect for waiver requests made prior to May 1.

March 20-23 — NFL Annual Meeting, Ritz-Carlton Maui, Hawaii.

April 15 — Deadline for signing of Offer Sheets by Restricted Free Agents.

April 22 — Deadline for Old Club to exercise Right of First Refusal to Restricted Free Agents.

April 23-24 — Annual Player Selection Meeting, New York, N.Y.

May 2 — Claiming period of 10 calendar days begins in waiver system.

May 16 — Except for a three-day mini-camp held within 15 days of the draft, this is the first day that players eligible for the 2005 Draft are permitted to participate in mini-camps, practices, or meetings. If final examinations at a player's school conclude after this date, the player is prohibited from participating in any activities until after the player's final day of examinations. If the player has left or leaves school, he is prohibited from participating in any club activities until after the final day of examinations at his school.

May 23-26 — NFL Spring Meeting.

June 1 — Deadline for Old Club to send tender to its unsigned Restricted Free Agents or to extend Qualifying Offer, whichever is greater, in order to retain rights.

June 1 — Deadline for Old Club to send tender to its unsigned Unrestricted Free Agents to retain rights if player is not signed by another club by July 22.

June 2 — Any unamortized signing bonus amounts will be included in the succeeding year's Team Salary for any players removed from the team's roster other than by trade.

June 15 — Deadline for club to withdraw Qualifying Offer to Restricted Free Agents and still retain exclusive negotiating rights by substituting tender of one-year contract at 110 percent of previous year's Paragraph 5 salary (with all other terms carried forward unchanged).

2006

February 5 — Super Bowl XL, Ford Field, Detroit, Michigan.

2007

February 4 — Super Bowl XLI, Pro Player Stadium, Miami, Florida.

2008

February 3 — Super Bowl XLII, Cardinals Stadium, Glendale, Arizona.

*Tentative

NFL ON THE INTERNET

The NFL is online to provide fans and media quick and easy access to all the latest professional football information.

NFL.COM—(http://NFL.com or AOL Keyword: NFL.com)
NFL.com, the league's year-round home page on the Internet, enters its eighth season in cyberspace. The site provides NFL information during the regular season, postseason, and offseason, including:

NEWS/STATS: Up-to-the-minute news from around the league, plus game previews, injury reports, and player and team stats.

TEAM AREAS: Customized areas for all 32 clubs, featuring updated rosters, depth carts, and all the latest news from the teams.

GAMEDAY COVERAGE: Live game coverage with play-by-play, scores, and statistics, including graphical drive charts and comprehensive scoreboard that does not require reloading to get the latest information.

VIDEO HIGHLIGHTS: The site showcases NFL Films video highlights of the previous week's games as well as upcoming matchups. Video also supports feature stories and team highlight clips from every game last season.

SUPERBOWL.COM—(http://SuperBowl.com)
Look for SuperBowl.com in late December for complete coverage of the playoffs and Super Bowl XXXIX. The multimedia site follows all postseason action and features audio and video clips of past Super Bowls.

During the week leading up to Super Bowl XXXIX, the site will go 'live' from Jacksonville, providing coverage of events, press conferences, and chats with Super Bowl players and coaches.

On Super Bowl Sunday, SuperBowl.com will showcase a live Internet cybercast, complete with online commentators calling the action. The site also features digital photos from the game, live public address audio and press-box announcements, and live audio from foreign broadcasts.

NFLEUROPE.COM—(http://NFLEurope.com)
The official site of NFL Europe League provides in-depth information on the six teams and their players, and weekly video highlights of game action. In addition, the site includes weekly player diaries from NFL allocated players, as well as a complete league stats package.

PLAYFOOTBALL.COM—(http://playfootball.com)
Play Football.com is the NFL's official Website for kids. It offers boys and girls an interactive sports destination where kids and their families can get actively involved with the NFL, including information on national youth football programs such as Punt, Pass & Kick, and NFL Flag. Youths also can find profiles on NFL players and people behind the scenes of the NFL, vote on weekly MVPs and Plays of the Week, play challenging games, and learn about football strategy and skill.

NFLHS.COM—(http://NFLHS.com)
The League's Website dedicated to high school and youth football. NFLHS.com covers high school football on a nation-wide basis and also looks into the high school careers of current and former NFL players and coaches. NFLHS.com goes behind the scenes at major NFL events, such as the Super Bowl and the Draft, and provides coverage from a high school perspective. The site is packed with tips and drills, health and safety information, academic tips and news on the NFL's and its teams' efforts in the community. Whatever you are looking for regarding high school football, we've got it!

JOINTHETEAM.com—(http://JoinTheTeam.com)
JointheTeam.com is the official Website dedicated to the off-the-field community work of the NFL and the member clubs. The site provides news and information regarding how the NFL gives back and serves as a useful tool for individuals who are looking for a way to make a difference in their communities. As part of the NFL's Join The Team platform, the site encourages people to unite with NFL teams, players and partners to give back to communities across America. Join The Team is a "call to action" —a way for everyone to come together and make a difference through community involvement.

PROFOOTBALLHOF.com—(http://profootballhof.com)
Profootballhof.com is the official site of the Pro Football Hall of Fame in Canton, Ohio. In addition to a complete visitor's guide to the Hall, the site features bios, stories and Q & A's with Hall of Fame inductees, a detailed archive of football history, and information on appearances by members of the Hall.

OFFICIAL NFL TEAM SITES

In addition to a dedicated area on NFL.com, all 32 teams have their own Websites, which have separate URLs, and are linked from NFL.com.

Arizona Cardinals (www.azcardinals.com)
Atlanta Falcons (www.atlantafalcons.com)
Baltimore Ravens (www.baltimoreravens.com)
Buffalo Bills (www.buffalobills.com)
Carolina Panthers (www.panthers.com)
Chicago Bears (www.chicagobears.com)
Cincinnati Bengals (www.bengals.com)
Cleveland Browns (www.clevelandbrowns.com)
Dallas Cowboys (www.dallascowboys.com)
Denver Broncos (www.denverbroncos.com)
Detroit Lions (www.detroitlions.com)
Green Bay Packers (www.packers.com)
Houston Texans (www.houstontexans.com)
Indianapolis Colts (www.colts.com)
Jacksonville Jaguars (www.jaguars.com)
Kansas City Chiefs (www.kcchiefs.com)
Miami Dolphins (www.miamidolphins.com)
Minnesota Vikings (www.vikings.com)
New England Patriots (www.patriots.com)
New Orleans Saints (www.neworleanssaints.com)
New York Giants (www.giants.com)
New York Jets (www.newyorkjets.com)
Oakland Raiders (www.raiders.com)
Philadelphia Eagles (www.philadelphiaeagles.com)
Pittsburgh Steelers (www.steelers.com)
St. Louis Rams (www.stlouisrams.com)
San Diego Chargers (www.chargers.com)
San Francisco 49ers (www.sf49ers.com)
Seattle Seahawks (www.seahawks.com)
Tampa Bay Buccaneers (www.buccaneers.com)
Tennessee Titans (www.titansonline.com)
Washington Redskins (www.redskins.com)

NFL Network provides fans with a network to call their own.

Seven days a week, 24 hours a day, 365 days a year, fans turn to NFL Network to receive information and insight straight from team headquarters, league offices and wherever the NFL is making news.

NFL Network gives fans unprecedented year-round access to all NFL events, including the preseason, regular season, playoffs, Super Bowl, Pro Bowl, Scouting Combine, league meetings, Schedule Announcement Show, NFL Draft, mini-camps and training camps.

NFL Network is available on cable and satellite television through your local service provider. DirecTV carries NFL Network nationally to all its subscribers on Channel 212. If your provider doesn't currently offer NFL Network, please call (866) NFL-NETWORK to make them aware of your interest in receiving it.

KEY PROGRAMMING

NFL TOTAL ACCESS

NFL Network's signature show is uniquely structured to see the game through the participants' eyes, airing at 7:00 PM ET/PT every Monday through Saturday and hosted by Rich Eisen.

Covering all 32 teams, ***NFL Total Access*** is the most comprehensive and informative show dedicated to the NFL. Using the most advanced technology, *NFL Total Access* has the ability to go live to any NFL team headquarters at any time.

NFL NETWORK GAME OF THE WEEK

Every Wednesday and Thursday recent and classic NFL games are featured on ***NFL Network Game of the Week***, a 60-minute condensed version of a full-game game airing at 9:00 PM ET/PT.

Much more than a three-minute recap, the series takes fans inside an NFL game, explaining outstanding performances and crucial plays.

During the season, *NFL Network Game of the Week* enables fans to relive Sunday's most interesting game(s). In the off-season the series will showcase match-ups from years past.

IN THEIR OWN WORDS

In a stark departure from classic documentary style, NFL Network lets the NFL's most successful and intriguing coaches and players tell their own stories on a show called ***In Their Own Words***, airing Tuesday's at 9 PM ET/PT.

The series uses rare interviews, archival action footage and exclusive sound captured on the field, on the sidelines and in the locker room, to let the subject tell a story *in his own words*, without the use of a host or narration.

In Their Own Words gives fans unprecedented access to NFL personalities as they reveal their intensity, humor, competitiveness and humanity in each one-hour episode.

OTHER PROGRAMMING HIGHLIGHTS

NFL Network also airs preseason and NFL Europe games during the spring and summer months.

PRESEASON GAMES: NFL Network is the only place on television where fans can view the majority of NFL preseason games. NFL Network televises every game that does not appear on the four NFL broadcast partners (ABC, CBS, FOX, and ESPN) during the preseason, more than 50 games each summer.

NFL EUROPE: From April to June, pro football fans can watch young players compete for a World Bowl championship on NFL Network, which televises two primetime games each week during the NFL Europe season, 22 games in all.

Log on to www.NFL.com/NFLnetwork for more information on NFL Network.

SCHEDULING FORMULA

The NFL expanded to 32 teams in 2002 with the addition of the Houston Texans. In addition, the NFL realigned for the first time since 1970—into eight divisions of four teams each—and the scheduling formula that was introduced guarantees for the first time that all teams play each other on a regular, rotating basis. Although the number of teams has increased to 32, the number of playoff teams remains the same at 12.

Under the NFL scheduling formula, every team within a division plays 16 games as follows:

- Home and away against its three division opponents (6 games).
- The four teams from another division within its conference on a rotating three-year cycle (4 games).
- The four teams from a division in the other conference on a rotating four-year cycle (4 games).
- Two intraconference games based on the prior year's standings (2 games). These games will match a first-place team against the first-place teams in the two same-conference divisions the team is not scheduled to play that season. The second-place, third-place, and fourth-place teams in a conference will be matched in the same way each year.

"The scheduling formula is one of the most positive aspects of realignment," says NFL Commissioner Paul Tagliabue. "The formula guarantees that NFL fans will see every team play each other on a regular, rotating basis. The formula will eliminate the many aberrations of the past in which teams either did not play for long periods of time or did not play in another team's stadium for many years."

The schedule format takes each team through a cycle of games—home and away—against every other team in the league. From 2002-2009, every team will play every other team at least twice—once home and once away. After the 2009 season, a decision will be made on whether to continue with the same rotation or modify it.

In determining how to begin the divisional rotation in 2002, the displacement of teams from their old divisions in the new alignment was taken into account. Preference was given to scheduling games with former division rivals and other regional opponents for clubs realigned from otherwise intact divisions.

The scheduling format includes the following elements:

- There is an increased common-opponent emphasis with every team in a division playing against 14 common opponents.
- All teams play each other on a regular basis, home and away, for a more consistent presentation of attractive games, eliminating the many schedule aberrations of the past.
- Teams are guaranteed to play all non-division opponents in their conference at least once every three years, and at home at least once every six years.
- Every AFC team plays every NFC team once every four years, and at home once every eight years.
- A team's record from the previous year has less of a bearing on its schedule, with only two (rather than four) opponents being based on the previous year's standing. Thus, the so-called "easy" fifth-place schedules are eliminated.
- The division in which a team resides is less of a factor in a team's won-loss record with 10 of 16 games each year being against non-division teams.

FUTURE SCHEDULING ROTATION

		2004	2005	2006	2007	2008	2009
AFC EAST	Intraconference	AFCN	AFCW	AFCS	AFCN	AFCW	AFCS
	Interconference	NFCW	NFCS	NFCN	NFCE	NFCW	NFCS
AFC NORTH	Intraconference	AFCE	AFCS	AFCW	AFCE	AFCS	AFCW
	Interconference	NFCE	NFCN	NFCS	NFCW	NFCE	NFCN
AFC SOUTH	Intraconference	AFCW	AFCN	AFCE	AFCW	AFCN	AFCE
	Interconference	NFCN	NFCW	NFCE	NFCS	NFCN	NFCW
AFC WEST	Intraconference	AFCS	AFCE	AFCN	AFCS	AFCE	AFCN
	Interconference	NFCS	NFCE	NFCW	NFCN	NFCS	NFCE
NFC EAST	Intraconference	NFCN	NFCW	NFCS	NFCN	NFCW	NFCS
	Interconference	AFCN	AFCW	AFCS	AFCE	AFCN	AFCW
NFC NORTH	Intraconference	NFCE	NFCS	NFCW	NFCE	NFCS	NFCW
	Interconference	AFCS	AFCN	AFCE	AFCW	AFCS	AFCN
NFC SOUTH	Intraconference	NFCW	NFCN	NFCE	NFCW	NFCN	NFCE
	Interconference	AFCW	AFCE	AFCN	AFCS	AFCW	AFCE
NFC WEST	Intraconference	NFCS	NFCE	NFCN	NFCS	NFCE	NFCN
	Interconference	AFCE	AFCS	AFCW	AFCN	AFCE	AFCS

AFC EAST NON-DIVISIONAL OPPONENTS 2004-2009

BUFFALO BILLS

	2004 Home	2004 Away	2005 Home	2005 Away	2006 Home	2006 Away
Intraconference by Division	CLE	BALT	DEN	OAK	JAX	HOU
	PITT	CIN	KC	SD	TENN	IND
Interconference by Division	ARIZ	SF	ATL	NO	GB	CHI
	STL	SEA	CAR	TB	MINN	DET
Intraconference by Position	AFCS	AFCW	AFCS	AFCN	AFCW	AFCN

	2007 Home	2007 Away	2008 Home	2008 Away	2009 Home	2009 Away
Intraconference by Division	BALT	CLE	OAK	DEN	HOU	JAX
	CIN	PITT	SD	KC	IND	TENN
Interconference by Division	DALL	PHIL	SF	ARIZ	NO	ATL
	NYG	WASH	SEA	STL	TB	CAR
Intraconference by Position	AFCW	AFCS	AFCN	AFCS	AFCN	AFCW

MIAMI DOLPHINS

	2004 Home	2004 Away	2005 Home	2005 Away	2006 Home	2006 Away
Intraconference by Division	CLE	BALT	DEN	OAK	JAX	HOU
	PITT	CIN	KC	SD	TENN	IND
Interconference by Division	ARIZ	SF	ATL	NO	GB	CHI
	STL	SEA	CAR	TB	MINN	DET
Intraconference by Position	AFCS	AFCW	AFCS	AFCN	AFCW	AFCN

	2007 Home	2007 Away	2008 Home	2008 Away	2009 Home	2009 Away
Intraconference by Division	BALT	CLE	OAK	DEN	HOU	JAX
	CIN	PITT	SD	KC	IND	TENN
Interconference by Division	DALL	PHIL	SF	ARIZ	NO	ATL
	NYG	WASH	SEA	STL	TB	CAR
Intraconference by Position	AFCW	AFCS	AFCN	AFCS	AFCN	AFCW

NEW ENGLAND PATRIOTS

	2004 Home	2004 Away	2005 Home	2005 Away	2006 Home	2006 Away
Intraconference by Division	BALT	CLE	OAK	DEN	HOU	JAX
	CIN	PITT	SD	KC	IND	TENN
Interconference by Division	SF	ARIZ	NO	ATL	CHI	GB
	SEA	STL	TB	CAR	DET	MINN
Intraconference by Position	AFCS	AFCW	AFCS	AFCN	AFCW	AFCN

	2007 Home	2007 Away	2008 Home	2008 Away	2009 Home	2009 Away
Intraconference by Division	CLE	BALT	DEN	OAK	JAX	HOU
	PITT	CIN	KC	SD	TENN	IND
Interconference by Division	PHIL	DALL	ARIZ	SF	ATL	NO
	WASH	NYG	STL	SEA	CAR	TB
Intraconference by Position	AFCW	AFCS	AFCN	AFCS	AFCN	AFCW

NEW YORK JETS

	2004 Home	2004 Away	2005 Home	2005 Away	2006 Home	2006 Away
Intraconference by Division	BALT	CLE	OAK	DEN	HOU	JAX
	CIN	PITT	SD	KC	IND	TENN
Interconference by Division	SF	ARIZ	NO	ATL	CHI	GB
	SEA	STL	TB	CAR	DET	MINN
Intraconference by Position	AFCS	AFCW	AFCS	AFCN	AFCW	AFCN

	2007 Home	2007 Away	2008 Home	2008 Away	2009 Home	2009 Away
Intraconference by Division	CLE	BALT	DEN	OAK	JAX	HOU
	PITT	CIN	KC	SD	TENN	IND
Interconference by Division	PHIL	DALL	ARIZ	SF	ATL	NO
	WASH	NYG	STL	SEA	CAR	TB
Intraconference by Position	AFCW	AFCS	AFCN	AFCS	AFCN	AFCW

SCHEDULING FORMULA

AFC NORTH NON-DIVISIONAL OPPONENTS 2004-2009

BALTIMORE RAVENS

	2004 Home	2004 Away	2005 Home	2005 Away	2006 Home	2006 Away
Intraconference by Division	BUFF	NE	HOU	JAX	OAK	DEN
	MIA	NYJ	IND	TENN	SD	KC
Interconference by Division	DALL	PHIL	GB	CHI	ATL	NO
	NYG	WASH	MINN	DET	CAR	TB
Intraconference by Position	AFCW	AFCS	AFCE	AFCW	AFCE	AFCS

	2007 Home	2007 Away	2008 Home	2008 Away	2009 Home	2009 Away
Intraconference by Division	NE	BUFF	JAX	HOU	DEN	OAK
	NYJ	MIA	TENN	IND	KC	SD
Interconference by Division	ARIZ	SF	PHIL	DALL	CHI	GB
	STL	SEA	WASH	NYG	DET	MINN
Intraconference by Position	AFCS	AFCW	AFCW	AFCE	AFCS	AFCE

CINCINNATI BENGALS

	2004 Home	2004 Away	2005 Home	2005 Away	2006 Home	2006 Away
Intraconference by Division	BUFF	NE	HOU	JAX	OAK	DEN
	MIA	NYJ	IND	TENN	SD	KC
Interconference by Division	DALL	PHIL	GB	CHI	ATL	NO
	NYG	WASH	MINN	DET	CAR	TB
Intraconference by Position	AFCW	AFCS	AFCE	AFCW	AFCE	AFCS

	2007 Home	2007 Away	2008 Home	2008 Away	2009 Home	2009 Away
Intraconference by Division	NE	BUFF	JAX	HOU	DEN	OAK
	NYJ	MIA	TENN	IND	KC	SD
Interconference by Division	ARIZ	SF	PHIL	DALL	CHI	GB
	STL	SEA	WASH	NYG	DET	MINN
Intraconference by Position	AFCS	AFCW	AFCW	AFCE	AFCS	AFCE

CLEVELAND BROWNS

	2004 Home	2004 Away	2005 Home	2005 Away	2006 Home	2006 Away
Intraconference by Division	NE	BUFF	JAX	HOU	DEN	OAK
	NYJ	MIA	TENN	IND	KC	SD
Interconference by Division	PHIL	DALL	CHI	GB	NO	ATL
	WASH	NYG	DET	MINN	TB	CAR
Intraconference by Position	AFCW	AFCS	AFCE	AFCW	AFCE	AFCS

	2007 Home	2007 Away	2008 Home	2008 Away	2009 Home	2009 Away
Intraconference by Division	BUFF	NE	HOU	JAX	OAK	DEN
	MIA	NYJ	IND	TENN	SD	KC
Interconference by Division	SF	ARIZ	DALL	PHIL	GB	CHI
	SEA	STL	NYG	WASH	MINN	DET
Intraconference by Position	AFCS	AFCW	AFCW	AFCE	AFCS	AFCE

PITTSBURGH STEELERS

	2004 Home	2004 Away	2005 Home	2005 Away	2006 Home	2006 Away
Intraconference by Division	NE	BUFF	JAX	HOU	DEN	OAK
	NYJ	MIA	TENN	IND	KC	SD
Interconference by Division	PHIL	DALL	CHI	GB	NO	ATL
	WASH	NYG	DET	MINN	TB	CAR
Intraconference by Position	AFCW	AFCS	AFCE	AFCW	AFCE	AFCS

	2007 Home	2007 Away	2008 Home	2008 Away	2009 Home	2009 Away
Intraconference by Division	BUFF	NE	HOU	JAX	OAK	DEN
	MIA	NYJ	IND	TENN	SD	KC
Interconference by Division	SF	ARIZ	DALL	PHIL	GB	CHI
	SEA	STL	NYG	WASH	MINN	DET
Intraconference by Position	AFCS	AFCW	AFCW	AFCE	AFCS	AFCE

AFC SOUTH NON-DIVISIONAL OPPONENTS 2004-2009

HOUSTON TEXANS

	2004 Home	2004 Away	2005 Home	2005 Away	2006 Home	2006 Away
Intraconference by Division	OAK	DEN	CLE	BALT	BUFF	NE
	SD	KC	PITT	CIN	MIA	NYJ
Interconference by Division	GB	CHI	ARIZ	SF	PHIL	DALL
	MINN	DET	STL	SEA	WASH	NYG
Intraconference by Position	AFCN	AFCE	AFCW	AFCE	AFCN	AFCW

	2007 Home	2007 Away	2008 Home	2008 Away	2009 Home	2009 Away
Intraconference by Division	DEN	OAK	BALT	CLE	NE	BUFF
	KC	SD	CIN	PITT	NYJ	MIA
Interconference by Division	NO	ATL	CHI	GB	SF	ARIZ
	TB	CAR	DET	MINN	SEA	STL
Intraconference by Position	AFCE	AFCN	AFCE	AFCW	AFCW	AFCN

INDIANAPOLIS COLTS

	2004 Home	2004 Away	2005 Home	2005 Away	2006 Home	2006 Away
Intraconference by Division	OAK	DEN	CLE	BALT	BUFF	NE
	SD	KC	PITT	CIN	MIA	NYJ
Interconference by Division	GB	CHI	ARIZ	SF	PHIL	DALL
	MINN	DET	STL	SEA	WASH	NYG
Intraconference by Position	AFCN	AFCE	AFCW	AFCE	AFCN	AFCW

	2007 Home	2007 Away	2008 Home	2008 Away	2009 Home	2009 Away
Intraconference by Division	DEN	OAK	BALT	CLE	NE	BUFF
	KC	SD	CIN	PITT	NYJ	MIA
Interconference by Division	NO	ATL	CHI	GB	SF	ARIZ
	TB	CAR	DET	MINN	SEA	STL
Intraconference by Position	AFCE	AFCN	AFCE	AFCW	AFCW	AFCN

JACKSONVILLE JAGUARS

	2004 Home	2004 Away	2005 Home	2005 Away	2006 Home	2006 Away
Intraconference by Division	DEN	OAK	BALT	CLE	NE	BUFF
	KC	SD	CIN	PITT	NYJ	MIA
Interconference by Division	CHI	GB	SF	ARIZ	DALL	PHIL
	DET	MINN	SEA	STL	NYG	WASH
Intraconference by Position	AFCN	AFCE	AFCW	AFCE	AFCN	AFCW

	2007 Home	2007 Away	2008 Home	2008 Away	2009 Home	2009 Away
Intraconference by Division	OAK	DEN	CLE	BALT	BUFF	NE
	SD	KC	PITT	CIN	MIA	NYJ
Interconference by Division	ATL	NO	GB	CHI	ARIZ	SF
	CAR	TB	MINN	DET	STL	SEA
Intraconference by Position	AFCE	AFCN	AFCE	AFCW	AFCW	AFCN

TENNESSEE TITANS

	2004 Home	2004 Away	2005 Home	2005 Away	2006 Home	2006 Away
Intraconference by Division	DEN	OAK	BALT	CLE	NE	BUFF
	KC	SD	CIN	PITT	NYJ	MIA
Interconference by Division	CHI	GB	SF	ARIZ	DALL	PHIL
	DET	MINN	SEA	STL	NYG	WASH
Intraconference by Position	AFCN	AFCE	AFCW	AFCE	AFCN	AFCW

	2007 Home	2007 Away	2008 Home	2008 Away	2009 Home	2009 Away
Intraconference by Division	OAK	DEN	CLE	BALT	BUFF	NE
	SD	KC	PITT	CIN	MIA	NYJ
Interconference by Division	ATL	NO	GB	CHI	ARIZ	SF
	CAR	TB	MINN	DET	STL	SEA
Intraconference by Position	AFCE	AFCN	AFCE	AFCW	AFCW	AFCN

SCHEDULING FORMULA

AFC WEST NON-DIVISIONAL OPPONENTS 2004-2009

DENVER BRONCOS

	2004 Home	2004 Away	2005 Home	2005 Away	2006 Home	2006 Away
Intraconference by Division	HOU	JAX	NE	BUFF	BALT	CLE
	IND	TENN	NYJ	MIA	CIN	PITT
Interconference by Division	ATL	NO	PHIL	DALL	SF	ARIZ
	CAR	TB	WASH	NYG	SEA	STL
Intraconference by Position	AFCE	AFCN	AFCN	AFCS	AFCS	AFCE

	2007 Home	2007 Away	2008 Home	2008 Away	2009 Home	2009 Away
Intraconference by Division	JAX	HOU	BUFF	NE	CLE	BALT
	TENN	IND	MIA	NYJ	PITT	CIN
Interconference by Division	GB	CHI	NO	ATL	DALL	PHIL
	MINN	DET	TB	CAR	NYG	WASH
Intraconference by Position	AFCN	AFCE	AFCS	AFCN	AFCE	AFCS

KANSAS CITY CHIEFS

	2004 Home	2004 Away	2005 Home	2005 Away	2006 Home	2006 Away
Intraconference by Division	HOU	JAX	NE	BUFF	BALT	CLE
	IND	TENN	NYJ	MIA	CIN	PITT
Interconference by Division	ATL	NO	PHIL	DALL	SF	ARIZ
	CAR	TB	WASH	NYG	SEA	STL
Intraconference by Position	AFCE	AFCN	AFCN	AFCS	AFCS	AFCE

	2007 Home	2007 Away	2008 Home	2008 Away	2009 Home	2009 Away
Intraconference by Division	JAX	HOU	BUFF	NE	CLE	BALT
	TENN	IND	MIA	NYJ	PITT	CIN
Interconference by Division	GB	CHI	NO	ATL	DALL	PHIL
	MINN	DET	TB	CAR	NYG	WASH
Intraconference by Position	AFCN	AFCE	AFCS	AFCN	AFCE	AFCS

OAKLAND RAIDERS

	2004 Home	2004 Away	2005 Home	2005 Away	2006 Home	2006 Away
Intraconference by Division	JAX	HOU	BUFF	NE	CLE	BALT
	TENN	IND	MIA	NYJ	PITT	CIN
Interconference by Division	NO	ATL	DALL	PHIL	ARIZ	SF
	TB	CAR	NYG	WASH	STL	SEA
Intraconference by Position	AFCE	AFCN	AFCN	AFCS	AFCS	AFCE

	2007 Home	2007 Away	2008 Home	2008 Away	2009 Home	2009 Away
Intraconference by Division	HOU	JAX	NE	BUFF	BALT	CLE
	IND	TENN	NYJ	MIA	CIN	PITT
Interconference by Division	CHI	GB	ATL	NO	PHIL	DALL
	DET	MINN	CAR	TB	WASH	NYG
Intraconference by Position	AFCN	AFCE	AFCS	AFCN	AFCE	AFCS

SAN DIEGO CHARGERS

	2004 Home	2004 Away	2005 Home	2005 Away	2006 Home	2006 Away
Intraconference by Division	JAX	HOU	BUFF	NE	CLE	BALT
	TENN	IND	MIA	NYJ	PITT	CIN
Interconference by Division	NO	ATL	DALL	PHIL	ARIZ	SF
	TB	CAR	NYG	WASH	STL	SEA
Intraconference by Position	AFCE	AFCN	AFCN	AFCS	AFCS	AFCE

	2007 Home	2007 Away	2008 Home	2008 Away	2009 Home	2009 Away
Intraconference by Division	HOU	JAX	NE	BUFF	BALT	CLE
	IND	TENN	NYJ	MIA	CIN	PITT
Interconference by Division	CHI	GB	ATL	NO	PHIL	DALL
	DET	MINN	CAR	TB	WASH	NYG
Intraconference by Position	AFCN	AFCE	AFCS	AFCN	AFCE	AFCS

NFC EAST NON-DIVISIONAL OPPONENTS 2004-2009

DALLAS COWBOYS

	2004 Home	2004 Away	2005 Home	2005 Away	2006 Home	2006 Away
Intraconference by Division	CHI	GB	ARIZ	SF	NO	ATL
	DET	MINN	STL	SEA	TB	CAR
Interconference by Division	CLE	BALT	DEN	OAK	HOU	JAX
	PITT	CIN	KC	SD	IND	TENN
Intraconference by Position	NFCS	NFCW	NFCN	NFCS	NFCN	NFCW

	2007 Home	2007 Away	2008 Home	2008 Away	2009 Home	2009 Away
Intraconference by Division	GB	CHI	SF	ARIZ	ATL	NO
	MINN	DET	SEA	STL	CAR	TB
Interconference by Division	NE	BUFF	BALT	CLE	OAK	DEN
	NYJ	MIA	CIN	PITT	SD	KC
Intraconference by Position	NFCW	NFCS	NFCS	NFCN	NFCW	NFCN

NEW YORK GIANTS

	2004 Home	2004 Away	2005 Home	2005 Away	2006 Home	2006 Away
Intraconference by Division	CHI	GB	ARIZ	SF	NO	ATL
	DET	MINN	STL	SEA	TB	CAR
Interconference by Division	CLE	BALT	DEN	OAK	HOU	JAX
	PITT	CIN	KC	SD	IND	TENN
Intraconference by Position	NFCS	NFCW	NFCN	NFCS	NFCN	NFCW

	2007 Home	2007 Away	2008 Home	2008 Away	2009 Home	2009 Away
Intraconference by Division	GB	CHI	SF	ARIZ	ATL	NO
	MINN	DET	SEA	STL	CAR	TB
Interconference by Division	NE	BUFF	BALT	CLE	OAK	DEN
	NYJ	MIA	CIN	PITT	SD	KC
Intraconference by Position	NFCW	NFCS	NFCS	NFCN	NFCW	NFCN

PHILADELPHIA EAGLES

	2004 Home	2004 Away	2005 Home	2005 Away	2006 Home	2006 Away
Intraconference by Division	GB	CHI	SF	ARIZ	ATL	NO
	MINN	DET	SEA	STL	CAR	TB
Interconference by Division	BALT	CLE	OAK	DEN	JAX	HOU
	CIN	PITT	SD	KC	TENN	IND
Intraconference by Position	NFCS	NFCW	NFCN	NFCS	NFCN	NFCW

	2007 Home	2007 Away	2008 Home	2008 Away	2009 Home	2009 Away
Intraconference by Division	CHI	GB	ARIZ	SF	NO	ATL
	DET	MINN	STL	SEA	TB	CAR
Interconference by Division	BUFF	NE	CLE	BALT	DEN	OAK
	MIA	NYJ	PITT	CIN	KC	SD
Intraconference by Position	NFCW	NFCS	NFCS	NFCN	NFCW	NFCN

WASHINGTON REDSKINS

	2004 Home	2004 Away	2005 Home	2005 Away	2006 Home	2006 Away
Intraconference by Division	GB	CHI	SF	ARIZ	ATL	NO
	MINN	DET	SEA	STL	CAR	TB
Interconference by Division	BALT	CLE	OAK	DEN	JAX	HOU
	CIN	PITT	SD	KC	TENN	IND
Intraconference by Position	NFCS	NFCW	NFCN	NFCS	NFCN	NFCW

	2007 Home	2007 Away	2008 Home	2008 Away	2009 Home	2009 Away
Intraconference by Division	CHI	GB	ARIZ	SF	NO	ATL
	DET	MINN	STL	SEA	TB	CAR
Interconference by Division	BUFF	NE	CLE	BALT	DEN	OAK
	MIA	NYJ	PITT	CIN	KC	SD
Intraconference by Position	NFCW	NFCS	NFCS	NFCN	NFCW	NFCN

SCHEDULING FORMULA

NFC NORTH NON-DIVISIONAL OPPONENTS 2004-2009

CHICAGO BEARS

	2004		2005		2006	
	Home	**Away**	**Home**	**Away**	**Home**	**Away**
Intraconference by Division	PHIL	DALL	ATL	NO	SF	ARIZ
	WASH	NYG	CAR	TB	SEA	STL
Interconference by Division	HOU	JAX	BALT	CLE	BUFF	NE
	IND	TENN	CIN	PITT	MIA	NYJ
Intraconference by Position	NFCW	NFCS	NFCW	NFCE	NFCS	NFCE

	2007		2008		2009	
	Home	**Away**	**Home**	**Away**	**Home**	**Away**
Intraconference by Division	DALL	PHIL	NO	ATL	ARIZ	SF
	NYG	WASH	TB	CAR	STL	SEA
Interconference by Division	DEN	OAK	JAX	HOU	CLE	BALT
	KC	SD	TENN	IND	PITT	CIN
Intraconference by Position	NFCS	NFCW	NFCE	NFCW	NFCE	NFCS

DETROIT LIONS

	2004		2005		2006	
	Home	**Away**	**Home**	**Away**	**Home**	**Away**
Intraconference by Division	PHIL	DALL	ATL	NO	SF	ARIZ
	WASH	NYG	CAR	TB	SEA	STL
Interconference by Division	HOU	JAX	BALT	CLE	BUFF	NE
	IND	TENN	CIN	PITT	MIA	NYJ
Intraconference by Position	NFCW	NFCS	NFCW	NFCE	NFCS	NFCE

	2007		2008		2009	
	Home	**Away**	**Home**	**Away**	**Home**	**Away**
Intraconference by Division	DALL	PHIL	NO	ATL	ARIZ	SF
	NYG	WASH	TB	CAR	STL	SEA
Interconference by Division	DEN	OAK	JAX	HOU	CLE	BALT
	KC	SD	TENN	IND	PITT	CIN
Intraconference by Position	NFCS	NFCW	NFCE	NFCW	NFCE	NFCS

GREEN BAY PACKERS

	2004		2005		2006	
	Home	**Away**	**Home**	**Away**	**Home**	**Away**
Intraconference by Division	DALL	PHIL	NO	ATL	ARIZ	SF
	NYG	WASH	TB	CAR	STL	SEA
Interconference by Division	JAX	HOU	CLE	BALT	NE	BUFF
	TENN	IND	PITT	CIN	NYJ	MIA
Intraconference by Position	NFCW	NFCS	NFCW	NFCE	NFCS	NFCE

	2007		2008		2009	
	Home	**Away**	**Home**	**Away**	**Home**	**Away**
Intraconference by Division	PHIL	DALL	ATL	NO	SF	ARIZ
	WASH	NYG	CAR	TB	SEA	STL
Interconference by Division	OAK	DEN	HOU	JAX	BALT	CLE
	SD	KC	IND	TENN	CIN	PITT
Intraconference by Position	NFCS	NFCW	NFCE	NFCW	NFCE	NFCS

MINNESOTA VIKINGS

	2004		2005		2006	
	Home	**Away**	**Home**	**Away**	**Home**	**Away**
Intraconference by Division	DALL	PHIL	NO	ATL	ARIZ	SF
	NYG	WASH	TB	CAR	STL	SEA
Interconference by Division	DJAX	HOU	CLE	BALT	NE	BUFF
	TENN	IND	PITT	CIN	NYJ	MIA
Intraconference by Position	NFCW	NFCS	NFCW	NFCE	NFCS	NFCE

	2007		2008		2009	
	Home	**Away**	**Home**	**Away**	**Home**	**Away**
Intraconference by Division	PHIL	DALL	ATL	NO	SF	ARIZ
	WASH	NYG	CAR	TB	SEA	STL
Interconference by Division	OAK	DEN	HOU	JAX	BALT	CLE
	SD	KC	IND	TENN	CIN	PITT
Intraconference by Position	NFCS	NFCW	NFCE	NFCW	NFCE	NFCS

NFC SOUTH NON-DIVISIONAL OPPONENTS 2004-2009

ATLANTA FALCONS

	2004 Home	2004 Away	2005 Home	2005 Away	2006 Home	2006 Away
Intraconference by Division	ARIZ	SF	GB	CHI	DALL	PHIL
	STL	SEA	MINN	DET	NYG	WASH
Interconference by Division	OAK	DEN	NE	BUFF	CLE	BALT
	SD	KC	NYJ	MIA	PITT	CIN
Intraconference by Position	NFCN	NFCE	NFCE	NFCW	NFCW	NFCN

	2007 Home	2007 Away	2008 Home	2008 Away	2009 Home	2009 Away
Intraconference by Division	SF	ARIZ	CHI	GB	PHIL	DALL
	SEA	STL	DET	MINN	WASH	NYG
Interconference by Division	HOU	JAX	DEN	OAK	BUFF	NE
	IND	TENN	KC	SD	MIA	NYJ
Intraconference by Position	NFCE	NFCN	NFCW	NFCE	NFCN	NFCW

CAROLINA PANTHERS

	2004 Home	2004 Away	2005 Home	2005 Away	2006 Home	2006 Away
Intraconference by Division	ARIZ	SF	GB	CHI	DALL	PHIL
	STL	SEA	MINN	DET	NYG	WASH
Interconference by Division	OAK	DEN	NE	BUFF	CLE	BALT
	SD	KC	NYJ	MIA	PITT	CIN
Intraconference by Position	NFCN	NFCE	NFCE	NFCW	NFCW	NFCN

	2007 Home	2007 Away	2008 Home	2008 Away	2009 Home	2009 Away
Intraconference by Division	SF	ARIZ	CHI	GB	PHIL	DALL
	SEA	STL	DET	MINN	WASH	NYG
Interconference by Division	HOU	JAX	DEN	OAK	BUFF	NE
	IND	TENN	KC	SD	MIA	NYJ
Intraconference by Position	NFCE	NFCN	NFCW	NFCE	NFCN	NFCW

NEW ORLEANS SAINTS

	2004 Home	2004 Away	2005 Home	2005 Away	2006 Home	2006 Away
Intraconference by Division	SF	ARIZ	CHI	GB	PHIL	DALL
	SEA	STL	DET	MINN	WASH	NYG
Interconference by Division	DEN	OAK	BUFF	NE	BALT	CLE
	KC	SD	MIA	NYJ	CIN	PITT
Intraconference by Position	NFCN	NFCE	NFCE	NFCW	NFCW	NFCN

	2007 Home	2007 Away	2008 Home	2008 Away	2009 Home	2009 Away
Intraconference by Division	ARIZ	SF	GB	CHI	DALL	PHIL
	STL	SEA	MINN	DET	NYG	WASH
Interconference by Division	JAX	HOU	OAK	DEN	NE	BUFF
	TENN	IND	SD	KC	NYJ	MIA
Intraconference by Position	NFCE	NFCN	NFCW	NFCE	NFCN	NFCW

TAMPA BAY BUCCANEERS

	2004 Home	2004 Away	2005 Home	2005 Away	2006 Home	2006 Away
Intraconference by Division	SF	ARIZ	CHI	GB	PHIL	DALL
	SEA	STL	DET	MINN	WASH	NYG
Interconference by Division	DEN	OAK	BUFF	NE	BALT	CLE
	KC	SD	MIA	NYJ	CIN	PITT
Intraconference by Position	NFCN	NFCE	NFCE	NFCW	NFCW	NFCN

	2007 Home	2007 Away	2008 Home	2008 Away	2009 Home	2009 Away
Intraconference by Division	ARIZ	SF	GB	CHI	DALL	PHIL
	STL	SEA	MINN	DET	NYG	WASH
Interconference by Division	JAX	HOU	OAK	DEN	NE	BUFF
	TENN	IND	SD	KC	NYJ	MIA
Intraconference by Position	NFCE	NFCN	NFCW	NFCE	NFCN	NFCW

SCHEDULING FORMULA

NFC WEST NON-DIVISIONAL OPPONENTS 2004-2009

ARIZONA CARDINALS

	2004		2005		2006	
	Home	**Away**	**Home**	**Away**	**Home**	**Away**
Intraconference by Division	NO	ATL	PHIL	DALL	CHI	GB
	TB	CAR	WASH	NYG	DET	MINN
Interconference by Division	NE	BUFF	JAX	HOU	DEN	OAK
	NYJ	MIA	TENN	IND	KC	SD
Intraconference by Position	NFCE	NFCN	NFCS	NFCN	NFCE	NFCS

	2007		2008		2009	
	Home	**Away**	**Home**	**Away**	**Home**	**Away**
Intraconference by Division	ATL	NO	DALL	PHIL	GB	CHI
	CAR	TB	NYG	WASH	MINN	DET
Interconference by Division	CLE	BALT	BUFF	NE	HOU	JAX
	PITT	CIN	MIA	NYJ	IND	TENN
Intraconference by Position	NFCN	NFCE	NFCN	NFCS	NFCS	NFCE

ST. LOUIS RAMS

	2004		2005		2006	
	Home	**Away**	**Home**	**Away**	**Home**	**Away**
Intraconference by Division	NO	ATL	PHIL	DALL	CHI	GB
	TB	CAR	WASH	NYG	DET	MINN
Interconference by Division	NE	BUFF	JAX	HOU	DEN	OAK
	NYJ	MIA	TENN	IND	KC	SD
Intraconference by Position	NFCE	NFCN	NFCS	NFCN	NFCE	NFCS

	2007		2008		2009	
	Home	**Away**	**Home**	**Away**	**Home**	**Away**
Intraconference by Division	ATL	NO	DALL	PHIL	GB	CHI
	CAR	TB	NYG	WASH	MINN	DET
Interconference by Division	CLE	BALT	BUFF	NE	HOU	JAX
	PITT	CIN	MIA	NYJ	IND	TENN
Intraconference by Position	NFCN	NFCE	NFCN	NFCS	NFCS	NFCE

SAN FRANCISCO 49ERS

	2004		2005		2006	
	Home	**Away**	**Home**	**Away**	**Home**	**Away**
Intraconference by Division	ATL	NO	DALL	PHIL	GB	CHI
	CAR	TB	NYG	WASH	MINN	DET
Interconference by Division	BUFF	NE	HOU	JAX	OAK	DEN
	MIA	NYJ	IND	TENN	SD	KC
Intraconference by Position	NFCE	NFCN	NFCS	NFCN	NFCE	NFCS

	2007		2008		2009	
	Home	**Away**	**Home**	**Away**	**Home**	**Away**
Intraconference by Division	NO	ATL	PHIL	DALL	CHI	GB
	TB	CAR	WASH	NYG	DET	MINN
Interconference by Division	BALT	CLE	NE	BUFF	JAX	HOU
	CIN	PITT	NYJ	MIA	TENN	IND
Intraconference by Position	NFCN	NFCE	NFCN	NFCS	NFCS	NFCE

SEATTLE SEAHAWKS

	2004		2005		2006	
	Home	**Away**	**Home**	**Away**	**Home**	**Away**
Intraconference by Division	CATL	NO	DALL	PHIL	GB	CHI
	CAR	TB	NYG	WASH	MINN	DET
Interconference by Division	BUFF	NE	HOU	JAX	OAK	DEN
	MIA	NYJ	IND	TENN	SD	KC
Intraconference by Position	NFCE	NFCN	NFCS	NFCN	NFCE	NFCS

	2007		2008		2009	
	Home	**Away**	**Home**	**Away**	**Home**	**Away**
Intraconference by Division	NO	ATL	PHIL	DALL	CHI	GB
	TB	CAR	WASH	NYG	DET	MINN
Interconference by Division	BALT	CLE	NE	BUFF	JAX	HOU
	CIN	PITT	NYJ	MIA	TENN	IND
Intraconference by Position	NFCN	NFCE	NFCN	NFCS	NFCS	NFCE

TOP ACTIVE PASSERS

1,000 or more attempts

		Yrs.	Att.	Comp.	Pct. Comp.	Yards	TD	Pct. TD	Had Int.	Pct. Int.	Ratings Pts.
1.	Kurt Warner, *	6	1,688	1,121	66.4	14,447	102	6.0	65	3.9	97.2
2.	Jeff Garcia, Cle.	5	2,360	1,449	61.4	16,408	113	4.8	56	2.4	88.3
3.	Peyton Manning, Ind.	6	3,383	2,128	62.9	24,885	167	4.9	110	3.3	88.1
4.	Daunte Culpepper, Minn.	5	1,843	1,160	62.9	13,881	90	4.9	63	3.4	88.0
5.	Brett Favre, G.B.	13	6,464	3,960	61.3	45,646	346	5.4	209	3.2	86.9
6.	Trent Green, K.C.	6	2,266	1,336	59.0	17,016	106	4.7	65	2.9	86.1
7.	Tom Brady, N.E.	4	1,544	955	61.9	10,233	69	4.5	38	2.5	85.9
8.	Mark Brunell, Wash.	10	3,643	2,196	60.3	25,793	144	4.0	86	2.4	85.2
9.	Rich Gannon, Oak.	15	4,138	2,492	60.2	28,219	177	4.3	102	2.5	84.7
10.	Brad Johnson, T.B.	10	3,401	2,101	61.8	23,239	140	4.1	95	2.8	84.1
11.	Steve McNair, Tenn.	9	3,180	1,884	59.2	22,637	132	4.2	83	2.6	84.1
12.	Matt Hasselbeck, Sea.	5	1,282	769	60.0	9,084	50	3.9	33	2.6	83.9
13.	Brian Griese, T.B.	6	1,808	1,118	61.8	12,576	76	4.2	59	3.3	83.0
14.	Aaron Brooks, N.O.	4	1,798	1,014	56.4	12,464	86	4.8	51	2.8	82.1
15.	Neil O'Donnell, *	13	3,229	1,865	57.8	21,690	120	3.7	68	2.1	81.8
16.	Steve Beuerlein, Den.	15	3,328	1,894	56.9	24,046	147	4.4	112	3.4	80.3
17.	Chris Chandler, St.L.	16	3,943	2,293	58.2	28,021	168	4.3	138	3.5	79.8
18.	Donovan McNabb, Phil.	5	2,117	1,207	57.0	13,051	87	4.1	49	2.3	79.3
19.	Jeff Blake, Phil.	11	3,195	1,801	56.4	21,530	132	4.1	98	3.1	78.1
20.	Jay Fiedler, Mia.	6	1,514	899	59.4	10,551	61	4.0	58	3.8	78.1
21.	Charlie Batch, Pitt.	6	1,334	747	56.0	9,063	49	3.7	40	3.0	76.8
22.	Drew Bledsoe, Buff.	11	5,599	3,193	57.0	36,876	201	3.6	165	2.9	76.7
23.	Doug Flutie, S.D.	10	2,103	1,152	54.8	14,410	85	4.0	68	3.2	76.3
24.	Gus Frerotte, Minn.	10	2,140	1,169	54.6	15,097	77	3.6	66	3.1	76.1
25.	Jon Kitna, Cin.	7	2,704	1,589	58.8	17,537	103	3.8	98	3.6	75.7
26.	Vinny Testaverde, *	17	5,925	3,334	56.3	40,943	251	4.2	235	4.0	75.4
27.	Tim Couch, Cle.	5	1,714	1,025	59.8	11,131	64	3.7	67	3.9	75.1
28.	Tommy Maddox, Pitt.	7	1,069	622	58.2	7,352	45	4.2	48	4.5	74.5
29.	Rodney Peete, Car.	15	2,345	1,343	57.3	16,335	76	3.2	92	3.9	73.3
30.	Kerry Collins, Oak.	9	4,004	2,235	55.8	26,383	132	3.3	134	3.3	73.1

TOP ACTIVE SCORERS

(number in paranteses represents 2-point conversions scored)

		Yrs.	TD	FG	PAT	TP
1.	Gary Anderson, *	22	0	521	783	2,346
2.	Morten Andersen, K.C.	22	0	502	753	2,259
3.	John Carney, N.O.	16	0	343	404	1,433
4.	Steve Christie, *	14	0	314	435	1,377
5.	Matt Stover, Balt.	13	0	321	401	1,364
6.	Jason Elam, Den.	11	0	288	449	1,313
7.	Jerry Rice, Oak.	19	205	0	(4)	1,238
8.	Jason Hanson, Det.	12	0	284	384	1,236
9.	John Kasay, Car.	13	0	265	305	1,100
10.	Emmitt Smith, Ari.	14	166	0	(1)	998
11.	Jeff Wilkins, St.L.	10	0	205	367	982
12.	Adam Vinatieri, N.E.	8	0	212	279 (1)	917
13.	Mike Hollis, *	9	0	200	279	879
14.	Todd Peterson, S.F.	10	0	194	280	862
15.	Ryan Longwell, G.B.	7	0	182	298	844
16.	Doug Brien, NYJ	10	0	182	254	800
17.	Marshall Faulk, St.L.	10	131	0	(4)	794
18.	Olindo Mare, Mia.	7	0	182	240	786
19.	Mike Vanderjagt, Ind.	6	0	174	233	755
20.	John Hall, Was.	7	0	174	231	753
21.	Tim Brown, Oak.	16	104	0	(1)	626
22.	Joe Nedney, Tenn.	8	0	127	191	572
23.	Martín Gramatica, T.B.	5	0	126	160	538
24.	Marvin Harrison, Ind.	8	83	0	(5)	508
25.	Terrell Owens, Phil.	8	83	0	(2)	502
26.	David Akers, Phil.	6	0	112	160	496
27.	Curtis Martin, NYJ	9	81	0	(3)	492
28.	Kris Brown, Hous.	5	0	115	143	488
29.	Randy Moss, Minn.	6	78	0	(3)	474
30.	Eddie George, Tenn.	8	74	0	(3)	450

**Free agent; subject to developments.*

TOP ACTIVE RUSHERS

		Yrs.	Att.	Yards	TD
1.	Emmitt Smith, Ariz.	14	4,142	17,418	155
2.	Jerome Bettis, Pitt.	11	3,119	12,353	69
3.	Curtis Martin, NYJ	9	2,927	11,669	73
4.	Marshall Faulk, St.L.	10	2,576	11,213	97
5.	Eddie George, Tenn.	8	2,733	10,009	64
6.	Corey Dillon, Cin.	7	1,865	8,061	45
7.	Garrison Hearst, Den.	11	1,811	7,885	29
8.	Stephen Davis, Car.	8	1,701	7,234	53
9.	Charlie Garner, T.B.	10	1,507	6,986	39
10.	Priest Holmes, K.C.	7	1,419	6,692	66
11.	Fred Taylor, Jax.	6	1,377	6,356	46
12.	Ricky Williams, Mia.	5	1,589	6,354	41
13.	Edgerrin James, Ind.	5	1,494	6,172	42
14.	Ahman Green, G.B.	6	1,269	6,014	42
15.	James Stewart, *	9	1,478	5,841	48
16.	Warrick Dunn, Atl.	7	1,425	5,799	27
17.	Antowain Smith, N.E.	6	1,481	5,713	47
18.	Tiki Barber, NYG	7	1,211	5,409	28
19.	Lamar Smith, N.O.	10	1,322	4,853	38
20.	Duce Staley, Pitt.	7	1,200	4,807	22
21.	Jamal Lewis, Balt.	3	1,004	4,757	26
22.	Tyrone Wheatley, Oak.	9	1,185	4,635	36
23.	Mike Alstott, T.B.	8	1,198	4,607	47
24.	LaDainian Tomlinson, S.D.	3	1,024	4,564	37
25.	Dorsey Levens, *	10	1,149	4,545	32
26.	Shaun Alexander, Sea.	4	994	4,241	46
27.	Travis Henry, Buf.	3	869	3,523	27
28.	Michael Pittman, T.B.	6	909	3,414	12
29.	Steve McNair, Tenn.	9	559	3,172	34
30.	Deuce McAllister, N.O.	3	692	3,120	22

NFL ACTIVE STATISTICAL LEADERS

TOP ACTIVE PASS RECEIVERS

		Yrs.	No.	Yards	TD
1.	Jerry Rice, Oak.	19	1,519	22,466	194
2.	Tim Brown, Oak.	16	1,070	14,734	99
3.	Larry Centers, *	14	827	6,797	28
4.	Shannon Sharpe, *	14	815	10,060	62
5.	Marvin Harrison, Ind.	8	759	10,072	83
6.	Keenan McCardell, T.B.	12	724	9,370	52
7.	Jimmy Smith, Jax.	10	718	10,092	55
8.	Isaac Bruce, St.L.	10	688	10,461	68
9.	Marshall Faulk, St.L.	10	673	6,274	34
10.	Rod Smith, Den.	9	633	8,628	52
11.	Ricky Proehl, Car.	14	607	7,910	50
12.	Keyshawn Johnson, Dall.	8	603	7,936	48
13.	Terrell Owens, Phi.	8	592	8,572	81
14.	Curtis Conway, S.F.	11	556	7,827	49
15.	Johnnie Morton, K.C.	10	548	7,636	40
16.	Wayne Chrebet, NYJ	9	534	6,815	40
17.	Randy Moss, Minn.	6	525	8,375	77
18.	Frank Sanders, Balt.	9	507	6,749	24
19.	Eric Moulds, Buff.	7	506	7,237	39
20.	Frank Wycheck, *	11	505	5,126	28
21.	Emmitt Smith, Ariz.	14	500	3,119	11
22.	Muhsin Muhammad, Car.	8	485	6,346	28
23.	Antonio Freeman, *	9	477	7,251	61
24.	Shawn Jefferson, *	13	470	7,023	29
25.	Tony Gonzalez, K.C.	7	468	5,647	47
26.	Troy Brown, N.E.	11	458	5,332	24
27.	Wesley Walls, G.B.	14	450	5,291	54
28.	Terry Glenn, Dall.	8	437	6,240	29
29.	Joey Galloway, T.B.	9	434	6,798	49
30.	Hines Ward, Pitt.	6	425	5,051	37

TOP ACTIVE INTERCEPTORS

		Yrs.	No.	Yards	TD
1.	Rod Woodson, Oak.	17	71	1,483	12
2.	Aeneas Williams, St.L.	13	55	807	9
3.	Terrell Buckley, *	12	47	763	6
4.	Ray Buchanan, Oak.	11	46	800	4
5.	Troy Vincent, Buff.	12	42	625	3
6.	Ashley Ambrose, N.O.	12	39	493	3
7.	Donnie Abraham, NYJ	8	36	402	2
8.	Ty Law, N.E.	9	35	583	6
9.	Darren Sharper, G.B.	7	32	580	3
10.	Sammy Knight, Mia.	7	31	562	4
	Ryan McNeil, Den.	11	31	312	2
12.	Aaron Glenn, Hous.	10	30	475	5
13.	Rodney Harrison, N.E.	10	29	345	2
	Sam Madison, Mia.	7	29	476	2
	Otis Smith, N.E.	13	29	645	7
	Dewayne Washington, Jax.	10	29	569	5
17.	Doug Evans, Det.	11	28	323	2
	Brock Marion, Det.	11	28	484	3
19.	Dexter McCleon, K.C.	7	26	137	0
	Jimmy Spencer, Den.	12	26	209	2
21.	Victor Green, *	11	25	643	3
	Kwanie Lassiter, S.D.	9	25	356	2
	Patrick Surtain, Mia.	6	25	296	2
	Willie Williams, *	11	25	302	4
25.	Jay Bellamy, N.O.	10	24	286	1
	Dale Carter, *	11	24	256	1
	Tony Parrish, S.F.	6	24	572	1
28.	John Lynch, Den.	11	23	200	0
	Darren Woodson, Dall.	12	23	271	2
30.	Marcus Coleman, Hous.	8	22	354	1
	Robert Griffith, Cle.	10	22	171	0
	Tory James, Cin.	7	22	262	0
	Samari Rolle, Tenn.	6	22	349	1
	Duane Starks, Ariz.	6	22	199	1

TOP ACTIVE PUNT RETURNERS

40 or more punt returns

		Yrs.	No.	Yards	Avg.	TD
1.	Santana Moss, NYJ	3	61	827	13.6	2
2.	Phillip Buchanon, Oak.	2	51	669	13.1	3
3.	Dante Hall, K.C.	4	96	1,134	11.8	4
4.	Reggie Swinton, Det.	3	74	873	11.8	2
5.	Az-Zahir Hakim, Det.	6	131	1,513	11.5	3
6.	Jermaine Lewis, Jax.	8	272	3,055	11.2	6
7.	Michael Lewis, N.O.	3	88	981	11.1	1
8.	Troy Brown, N.E.	11	225	2,441	10.8	3
9.	Brian Mitchell, NYG	14	463	4,999	10.8	9
10.	Karl Wiliams, Ariz.	8	213	2,279	10.7	5
11.	Allen Rossum, Atl.	6	153	1,627	10.6	2
12.	Jeff Burris, *	10	105	1,103	10.5	0
13.	Jimmy Williams, S.F.	3	55	576	10.5	1
14.	Charlie Rogers, Mia.	5	120	1,248	10.4	1
15.	Reggie Barlow, *	8	158	1,639	10.4	2
16.	Hank Poteat, Car.	4	76	788	10.4	1
17.	Deltha O'Neal, Cin.	4	128	1,325	10.4	2
18.	Bobby Engram, Sea.	8	90	926	10.3	2
19.	Joey Galloway, T.B.	9	116	1,190	10.3	4
20.	Tim Brown, Oak.	16	320	3,272	10.2	3
21.	Dennis Northcutt, Cle.	4	103	1,037	10.1	2
22.	Tim Dwight, S.D.	6	129	1,294	10.0	3
23.	Eddie Kennison, K.C.	8	141	1,413	10.0	3
24.	Lamont Brightful, Balt.	2	60	592	9.9	1
25.	Antwaan Randle El, Pitt.	2	82	799	9.7	2
26.	Peter Warrick, Cin.	4	54	526	9.7	2
27.	Amani Toomer, NYG	8	109	1,060	9.7	3
28.	Tiki Barber, NYG	7	122	1,181	9.7	1
29.	Steve Smith, Car.	3	133	1,273	9.6	4
30.	Chad Morton, Wash.	4	66	630	9.5	0

TOP ACTIVE KICKOFF RETURNERS

40 or more kickoff returns

		Yrs.	No.	Yards	Avg.	TD
1.	Jerry Azumah, Chi.	5	45	1,256	27.9	2
2.	MarTay Jenkins, Den.	5	151	3,865	25.6	2
3.	Darrick Vaughn, Hous.	4	103	2,620	25.4	4
4.	Tim Brown, Oak.	16	49	1,235	25.2	1
5.	Terry Fair, Pitt.	6	101	2,516	24.9	2
6.	Steve Smith, Car.	3	93	2,311	24.8	2
7.	Michael Lewis, N.O.	3	147	3,637	24.7	2
8.	Eddie Drummond, Det.	2	61	1,508	24.7	0
9.	Kevin Kasper, Ariz.	3	74	1,808	24.4	0
10.	Michael Bates, Dall.	11	373	9,110	24.4	5
11.	Deuce McAllister, N.O.	3	45	1,091	24.2	0
12.	Chad Morton, Wash.	4	158	3,814	24.1	3
13.	Duce Staley, Pitt.	7	48	1,158	24.1	0
14.	Reggie Swinton, Det.	3	127	3,053	24.0	2
15.	Brock Marion, Det.	11	123	2,951	24.0	0
16.	Ronney Jenkins, N.O.	4	190	4,550	23.9	3
17.	Dante Hall, K.C.	4	174	4,159	23.9	3
18.	John Avery, Minn.	3	68	1,623	23.9	0
19.	Kevin Mathis, Atl.	7	51	1,216	23.8	0
20.	Aaron Stecker, N.O.	4	100	2,376	23.8	0
21.	Chris Cole, Oak.	4	89	2,105	23.7	0
22.	Corey Harris, *	12	238	5,528	23.2	1
23.	Aaron Glenn, Hou.	10	111	2,578	23.2	1
24.	Reggie Barlow, *	8	80	1,855	23.2	1
25.	Rod Smart, Car.	3	41	947	23.1	1
26.	Brian Mitchell, *	14	607	14,014	23.1	4
27.	Allen Rossum, Atl.	6	286	6,601	23.1	3
28.	James Thrash, Wash.	7	104	2,400	23.1	1
29.	Josh Scobey, Ariz.	1	73	1,684	23.1	1
30.	Arlen Harris, St.L.	1	51	1,175	23.0	0

TOP ACTIVE PUNTERS

50 or more punts

		Yrs.	No.	Avg.	LG
1.	Shane Lechler, Oak.	4	287	45.7	73
2.	Todd Sauerbrun, Car.	9	684	44.0	73
3.	Darren Bennett, Minn.	8	771	43.8	66
4.	Chris Hanson, Jax.	4	190	43.8	64
5.	Tom Rouen, Sea.	11	723	43.6	76
6.	Seah Landeta, St.L.	19	1,327	43.3	74
7.	Tom Tupa, Wash.	15	770	43.3	73
8.	Mitch Berger, N.O.	9	554	43.2	75
9.	Josh Miller, N.E.	8	572	42.9	75
10.	Chris Gardocki, Pitt.	13	978	42.9	72
11.	Hunter Smith, Ind.	5	319	42.9	69
12.	Craig Hentrich, Ten.	10	745	42.9	78
13.	Brian Moorman, Buff.	3	231	42.8	84
14.	Leo Araguz, Minn.	6	304	42.8	64
15.	Scott Player, Ariz.	6	477	42.7	67
16.	Matt Turk, Mia.	9	692	42.5	77
17.	John Jett, *	11	756	42.4	62
18.	Bryan Barker, *	14	1,016	42.2	83
19.	Mark Royals, Jax.	14	1,116	42.1	69
20.	Brad Maynard, Chi.	7	633	42.0	75
21.	Toby Gowin, NYJ	7	549	41.7	72
22.	Jeff Feagles, NYG	16	1,290	41.6	77
23.	Micah Knorr, Den.	4	275	41.4	62
24.	Dave Zastudil, Balt.	2	170	41.3	67
25.	Kyle Richardson, Cin.	7	494	41.1	67
26.	Josh Bidwell, T.B.	4	308	41.1	68
27.	Chad Stanley, Hou.	5	368	40.7	70
28.	Filip Filipovic, S.F.	2	65	40.6	60
29.	Chris Mohr, S.F.	14	1,076	40.4	80
30.	Dirk Johnson, Phil.	2	87	40.4	60

TOP ACTIVE QUARTERBACK SACKERS

		Yrs.	No.
1.	Bruce Smith, *	19	200.0
2.	John Randle, *	14	137.5
3.	Michael Strahan, NYG	11	114.0
4.	Trace Armstrong, *	15	106.0
5.	Robert Porcher, Det.	12	95.5
6.	Simeon Rice, T.B.	8	93.0
7.	Kevin Carter, Tenn.	9	80.0
8.	Chad Brown, Sea.	11	77.0
	Hugh Douglas, Jax.	9	77.0
	Jason Gildon, *	10	77.0
	Warren Sapp, Oak.	9	77.0
12.	Rob Burnett, *	14	73.0
13.	Jason Taylor, Mia.	7	71.0
14.	Peter Boulware, Balt.	7	67.5
15.	Bryant Young, S.F.	10	66.5
16.	Willie McGinest, N.E.	10	62.5
17.	Marco Coleman, Den.	12	62.0
18.	La'Roi Glover, Dall.	8	61.5
19.	Trevor Pryce, Den.	7	60.0
20.	Anthony Pleasant, *	14	58.0
21.	Chad Bratzke, *	10	56.5
22.	Tony Brackens, Jax.	8	55.0
23.	Dana Stubblefield, *	11	53.5
24.	Joe Johnson, G.B.	9	52.5
	Mo Lewis, *	13	52.5
26.	Lance Johnstone, Minn.	8	51.5
27.	Chester McGlockton, *	12	51.0
28.	Junior Seau, Mia.	14	50.0
	Dan Wilkinson, Det.	10	50.0
30.	Ellis Johnson, Atl.	9	48.0

COACHES RECORDS

ACTIVE COACHES' CAREER RECORDS (Order Based on Career Victories)
Start of 2004 Season

			Regular Season				Postseason			Career			
Coach	**Team(s)**	**Yrs.**	**Won**	**Lost**	**Tied**	**Pct.**	**Won**	**Lost**	**Pct.**	**Won**	**Lost**	**Tied**	**Pct.**
Marty Schottenheimer	Cleveland Browns, Kansas City Chiefs, Washington Redskins, San Diego Chargers	18	165	113	1	.593	5	11	.313	170	124	1	.578
Bill Parcells	New York Giants, New England Patriots, New York Jets, Dallas Cowboys	16	148	106	1	.582	11	7	.611	159	113	1	.584
Joe Gibbs	Washington Redskins	12	124	60	0	.674	16	5	.762	140	65	0	.683
Mike Holmgren	Green Bay Packers, Seattle Seahawks	12	116	76	0	.604	9	7	.563	125	83	0	.601
Bill Cowher	Pittsburgh Steelers	12	115	76	1	.602	7	8	.467	122	84	1	.592
Dick Vermeil	Philadelphia Eagles, St. Louis Rams, Kansas City Chiefs	13	103	94	0	.523	6	5	.545	109	99	0	.524
Mike Shanahan	Los Angeles Raiders, Denver Broncos	11	99	65	0	.604	7	3	.700	106	68	0	.609
Dennis Green	Minnesota Vikings, Arizona Cardinals	10	97	62	0	.610	4	8	.333	101	70	0	.591
Jeff Fisher	Tennessee Titans	9	88	62	0	.587	5	4	.556	93	66	0	.585
Dave Wannstedt	Chicago Bears, Miami Dolphins	10	81	79	0	.506	2	3	.400	83	82	0	.503
Bill Belichick	Cleveland Browns, New England Patriots	9	75	69	0	.521	7	1	.875	82	70	0	.539
Tony Dungy	Tampa Bay Buccaneers, Indianapolis Colts	8	76	52	0	.594	4	6	.400	80	58	0	.580
Tom Coughlin	Jacksonville Jaguars, New York Giants	8	68	60	0	.531	4	4	.500	72	64	0	.529
Steve Mariucci	San Francisco 49ers, Detroit Lions	7	62	50	0	.554	3	4	.429	65	54	0	.546
Jon Gruden	Oakland Raiders, Tampa Bay Buccaneers	6	57	39	0	.594	5	2	.714	62	41	0	.602
Andy Reid	Philadelphia Eagles	5	51	29	0	.638	5	4	.556	56	33	0	.629
Brian Billick	Baltimore Ravens	5	47	33	0	.588	5	2	.714	52	35	0	.598
Norv Turner	Washington Redskins, Oakland Raiders	7	49	59	1	.454	1	1	.500	50	60	1	.455
Mike Martz	St. Louis Rams	4	43	21	0	.672	2	3	.400	45	24	0	.652
Mike Sherman	Green Bay Packers	4	43	21	0	.672	2	3	.400	45	24	0	.652
Dom Capers	Carolina Panthers, Houston Texans	6	39	57	0	.406	1	1	.500	40	58	0	.408
Dennis Erickson	Seattle Seahawks, San Francisco 49ers	5	38	42	0	.475	0	0	.000	38	42	0	.475
Jim Haslett	New Orleans Saints	4	34	30	0	.531	1	1	.500	35	31	0	.530
Herman Edwards	New York Jets	3	25	23	0	.521	1	2	.333	26	25	0	.510
John Fox	Carolina Panthers	2	18	14	0	.563	3	1	.750	21	15	0	.583
Butch Davis	Cleveland Browns	3	21	27	0	.438	0	1	.000	21	28	0	.429
Mike Tice	Minnesota Vikings	3	15	18	0	.455	0	0	.000	15	18	0	.455
Marvin Lewis	Cincinnati Bengals	1	8	8	0	.500	0	0	.000	8	8	0	.500
Jack Del Rio	Jacksonville Jaguars	1	5	11	0	.313	0	0	.000	5	11	0	.313
Jim Mora	Atlanta Falcons	0	0	0	0	.000	0	0	.000	0	0	0	.000
Mike Mularkey	Buffalo Bills	0	0	0	0	.000	0	0	.000	0	0	0	.000
Lovie Smith	Chicago Bears	0	0	0	0	.000	0	0	.000	0	0	0	.000

COACHES WITH 100 CAREER VICTORIES (Order Based on Career Victories)
Start of 2004 Season

			Regular Season				Postseason			Career			
Coach	**Team(s)**	**Yrs.**	**Won**	**Lost**	**Tied**	**Pct.**	**Won**	**Lost**	**Pct.**	**Won**	**Lost**	**Tied**	**Pct.**
Don Shula	Baltimore Colts, Miami Dolphins	33	328	156	6	.677	19	17	.528	347	173	6	.666
George Halas	Chicago Bears	40	318	148	31	.682	6	3	.667	324	151	31	.682
Tom Landry	Dallas Cowboys	29	250	162	6	.607	20	16	.556	270	178	6	.603
Earl (Curly) Lambeau	Green Bay Packers, Chicago Cardinals, Washington Redskins	33	226	132	22	.631	3	2	.600	229	134	22	.631
Chuck Noll	Pittsburgh Steelers	23	193	148	1	.566	16	8	.667	209	156	1	.572
Dan Reeves	Denver Broncos, New York Giants, Atlanta Falcons	23	190	165	2	.535	11	9	.550	201	174	2	.536
Chuck Knox	Los Angeles Rams, Buffalo Bills, Seattle Seahawks	22	186	147	1	.558	7	11	.389	193	158	1	.550
Paul Brown	Cleveland Browns, Cincinnati Bengals	21	166	100	6	.624	4	8	.333	170	108	6	.612
Marty Schottenheimer	Cleveland Browns, Kansas City Chiefs, Washington Redskins, San Diego Chargers	18	165	113	1	.593	5	11	.313	170	124	1	.578
Bud Grant	Minnesota Vikings	18	158	96	5	.621	10	12	.455	168	108	5	.608
Bill Parcells	New York Giants, New England Patriots, New York Jets, Dallas Cowboys	16	148	106	1	.582	11	7	.611	159	113	1	.584
Marv Levy	Kansas City Chiefs, Buffalo Bills	17	143	112	0	.561	11	8	.579	154	120	0	.562
Steve Owen	New York Giants	23	151	100	17	.602	2	8	.200	153	108	17	.586
Joe Gibbs	Washington Redskins	12	124	60	0	.674	16	5	.762	140	65	0	.683
Hank Stram	Kansas City Chiefs, New Orleans Saints	17	131	97	10	.574	5	3	.625	136	100	10	.576
Weeb Ewbank	Baltimore Colts, New York Jets	20	130	129	7	.502	4	1	.800	134	130	7	.508
Mike Ditka	Chicago Bears, New Orleans Saints	14	121	95	0	.560	6	6	.500	127	101	0	.557
Mike Holmgren	Green Bay Packers, Seattle Seahawks	12	116	76	0	.604	9	7	.563	125	83	0	.601
Jim Mora	New Orleans Saints, Indianapolis Colts	15	125	106	0	.541	0	6	.000	125	112	0	.527
George Seifert	San Francisco 49ers, Carolina Panthers	11	114	62	0	.648	10	5	.667	124	67	0	.649
Sid Gillman	Los Angeles Rams, Los Angeles-San Diego Chargers, Houston Oilers	18	122	99	7	.552	1	5	.167	123	104	7	.542
Bill Cowher	Pittsburgh Steelers	12	115	76	1	.602	7	8	.467	122	84	1	.592
George Allen	Los Angeles Rams, Washington Redskins	12	116	47	5	.712	2	7	.222	118	54	5	.686
Don Coryell	St. Louis Cardinals, San Diego Chargers	14	111	83	1	.572	3	6	.333	114	89	1	.561
John Madden	Oakland Raiders	10	103	32	7	.759	9	7	.563	112	39	7	.739
Ray (Buddy) Parker	Chicago Cardinals, Detroit Lions, Pittsburgh Steelers	15	104	75	9	.581	3	1	.750	107	76	9	.585
Dick Vermeil	Philadelphia Eagles, St. Louis Rams, Kansas City Chiefs	13	103	94	0	.523	6	5	.545	109	99	0	.524
Mike Shanahan	Los Angeles Raiders, Denver Broncos	11	99	65	0	.604	7	3	.700	106	68	0	.609
Vince Lombardi	Green Bay Packers, Washington Redskins	10	96	34	6	.739	9	1	.900	105	35	6	.750
Tom Flores	Oakland-Los Angeles Raiders, Seattle Seahawks	12	97	87	0	.527	8	3	.727	105	90	0	.538
Bill Walsh	San Francisco 49ers	10	92	59	1	.609	10	4	.714	102	63	1	.617
Dennis Green	Minnesota Vikings, Arizona Cardinals	10	97	62	0	.610	4	8	.333	101	70	0	.591

Active coaches in bold.

WHAT TO LOOK FOR IN 2004

The **New England Patriots** have won 15 consecutive games (including playoffs) and need four wins in a row to set the NFL record (18, held by five teams) for the most consecutive wins (regular season and playoffs).

The **Chicago Bears** need nine regular season victories to become the first team with 650 regular season victories.

The **New York Giants** need 13 victories to become the third team (Chicago Bears, 655 and Green Bay Packers, 626) with 600 total victories.

The **Washington Redskins** need one regular season victory to reach 500 regular season victories.

The **St. Louis Rams** need six victories to reach 500 total victories.

The **Pittsburgh Steelers** need eight victories to reach 500 total victories.

The **New York Jets** need six regular season victories to reach 300 regular season victories.

The **San Francisco 49ers** have scored in 418 consecutive games, the longest streak in NFL history.

Marty Schottenheimer, San Diego, needs one victory to pass Paul Brown (170) to move into sole possession of eighth place all-time in career victories (see Parcells note) In 18 seasons, Schottenheimer has 170 career victories.

Bill Parcells, Dallas, needs 12 victories to pass Bud Grant (168), Paul Brown (170) and Marty Schottenheimer (170) to move into eighth place all-time in career victories (see Schottenheimer note). In 16 seasons, Parcells has 159 career victories.

Joe Gibbs, Washington, needs 10 victories to reach 150 career victories. In 12 seasons, Gibbs has 140 career victories.

Mike Shanahan, Denver, needs one regular season victory to reach 100 regular season victories. In 11 seasons, Shanahan has 99 regular season victories.

Dennis Green, Arizona, needs three regular season victories to reach 100 regular season victories. In 10 seasons, Green has 97 regular season victories.

Jeff Fisher, Tennessee, needs seven victories to reach 100 career victories. In nine seasons, Fisher has 93 career victories.

Brett Favre, Green Bay, needs 3,680 yards to pass Fran Tarkenton (47,003) and Warren Moon (49,325) to move into third place all-time. In 13 seasons, Favre has passed for 45,646 yards.

Favre has passed for 3,000 yards in a season 12 times in his 13-year career and can tie Dan Marino (13) for first all-time with his next 3,000-yard passing season. Favre holds the record for the most consecutive seasons with 3,000 passing yards with 12 (active).

Favre has thrown 346 touchdown passes, second-most all-time, in 13 seasons and needs four to become the second player in NFL history with 350 career touchdown passes.

Favre has led the league in touchdown passes four times in his 13-year career and can pass Johnny Unitas, Len Dawson and Steve Young (4) for the most seasons leading the league in touchdown passes.

Favre needs 20 touchdown passes to pass Dan Marino (10) for the most consecutive seasons with 20 touchdown passes. Favre has thrown for 20 touchdowns in 10 consecutive seasons.

Favre has thrown a touchdown pass in 25 consecutive games and needs to throw a touchdown in six games in a row to pass Peyton Manning (27), Dave Krieg (28) and Dan Marino (30) to move into second place all-time.

Favre needs 164 completions to pass Warren Moon (3,988) and John Elway (4,123) to move into second place all-time. Favre has completed 3,960 passes in 13 seasons.

Favre needs 360 passing attempts to pass Fran Tarkenton (6,467) and Warren Moon (6,823) to move into third place all-time. In 13 seasons, Favre has 6,464 passing attempts.

Favre has 125 career victories in his 13-year career and needs one to pass Fran Tarkenton (125) to move into sole possession of third place all-time.

Favre has started an NFL quarterback record 189 consecutive games and needs 11 starts in a row to become the first quarterback in NFL history to start 200 consecutive games.

Peyton Manning, Indianapolis, needs 4,000 passing yards to become the first player in NFL history with six consecutive 4,000-yard passing seasons. Manning is the only player to pass for 4,000 yards in five consecutive seasons. Manning needs 4,000 passing yards to tie Dan Marino (6) for the most career 4,000-yard passing seasons.

Manning has passed for 24,885 yards in 96 career games and needs 115 yards to reach 25,000 career passing yards in the second-fewest games (Dan Marino, 92). The current mark for the second-fewest games is 107 (Brett Favre and Warren Moon).

Manning needs 25 touchdown passes to become the first player in NFL history with seven consecutive seasons having 25 touchdown passes. Manning is the only player to have six consecutive seasons with 25 touchdown passes.

Manning has thrown 68 touchdown passes to wide receiver Marvin Harrison and the duo needs 12 touchdowns to pass Dan Marino-Mark Clayton (79) for the second-most touchdowns by an NFL quarterback-receiver tandem.

Manning and Harrison have combined for 621 completions and 8,331 yards and the duo needs 43 completions and 1,208 yards to pass Jim Kelly-Andre Reed (663 completions, 9,538 yards) for the most in NFL history.

Steve McNair, Tennessee, needs 3,000 passing yards and 400 rushing yards this season to pass Daunte Culpepper, Randall Cunningham and Steve Young (3) to become the first quarterback in NFL history with four seasons with 3,000 passing yards and 400 rushing yards (see Culpepper note).

Daunte Culpepper, Minnesota, needs 3,000 passing yards and 400 rushing yards this season to pass Randall Cunningham, Steve McNair and Steve Young (3) to become the first quarterback in NFL history with four seasons with 3,000 passing yards and 400 rushing yards (see McNair note).

Emmitt Smith, Arizona, needs 582 rushing yards to become the first player in history to rush for 18,000 yards. In 14 seasons, Smith, the NFL's all-time leading rusher, has 17,418 yards.

Smith has 76 career 100-yard rushing games in 14 seasons and needs two to pass Barry Sanders (76) and Walter Payton (77) for the most all-time.

Smith needs 463 combined yards to join Brian Mitchell (23,330), Jerry Rice (23,117) and Walter Payton (21,803) as the only players in NFL history with 21,000 combined yards. Smith has gained 20,537 combined yards in his 14-year career.

Smith has 20,537 scrimmage yards in 14 seasons and needs 728 yards from scrimmage to pass Walter Payton (21,264) to move into second place all-time. Smith needs 463 total yards from scrimmage to join Jerry Rice (23,111) and Payton as the only players in NFL history with 21,000 total scrimmage yards.

Jerome Bettis, Pittsburgh, has rushed for 12,353 yards in 11 seasons. Bettis needs 907 rushing yards to pass Tony Dorsett (12,739) and Eric Dickerson (13,259) to move into fourth place all-time (see Martin note).

Bettis needs 1,000 rushing yards to move into sole possession of fifth place all-time in career 1,000-yard seasons. In 11 seasons, Bettis has rushed for 1,000 yards eight times, tied with Tony Dorsett, Franco Harris and Thurman Thomas.

Curtis Martin, New York Jets, needs 1,000 rushing yards to become the second player in NFL history (Barry Sanders, 10) to rush for 1,000 yards in each of his first 10 seasons.

Martin needs 1,000 rushing yards to become the third player in NFL history (Emmitt Smith, 11 and Barry Sanders, 10) to rush for 1,000 yards in 10 consecutive seasons.

Martin needs 1,000 rushing yards to tie Walter Payton and Barry Sanders (10) for second place all-time in career 1,000-yard seasons. In nine seasons, Martin has rushed for 1,000 yards nine times.

In his nine-year career, Martin has rushed for 11,669 yards and needs 1,071 yards to pass Thurman Thomas (12,074), Franco Harris (12,120), Marcus Allen (12,243), Jim Brown (12,312), Jerome Bettis (12,353) and Tony Dorsett (12,739) to move into fifth place all-time (see Bettis note).

Martin needs 250 carries to become the second player in NFL history (Emmitt Smith, 12) to record 10 consecutive seasons with 250 rushing attempts. Martin needs 250 carries to become the first player in NFL history to begin his career with 10 consecutive seasons with 250 rushing attempts.

Marshall Faulk, St. Louis, needs 15 touchdowns to pass Cris Carter (131) and Marcus Allen (145) to move into third place all-time. In 10 seasons, Faulk has scored 131 touchdowns.

Faulk has rushed for 97 touchdowns in his 10-year career and needs 3 to become the sixth player in NFL history to rush for 100 touchdowns. Faulk needs 14 rushing touchdowns to pass John Riggins (104), Jim Brown (106) and Walter Payton (110) to move into third place all-time.

Faulk needs 1,812 total yards from scrimmage to pass (17,654) and Barry Sanders (18,190) to move into fourth place all-time. In 10 seasons, Faulk has 17,487 total scrimmage yards.

Faulk needs 787 rushing yards and 726 receiving yards to become the first player in NFL history with 12,000 rushing yards and 7,000 receiving yards. In 10 seasons, Faulk has 11,213 rushing yards and 6,274 receiving yards.

Priest Holmes, Kansas City, needs 20 touchdowns to become the first player in NFL history to record three consecutive seasons with 20 total touchdowns. Holmes needs 20 rushing touchdowns to become the only player to rush for 20 touchdowns three years in a row.

Holmes needs 2,000 scrimmage yards to become the second player in NFL history (Marshall Faulk, 4) with four consecutive seasons with 2,000 yards from scrimmage.

Eddie George, Tennessee, needs 300 carries to extend his streak of consecutive seasons with 300 carries to nine, the most in NFL history.

Clinton Portis, Washington, needs 1,500 rushing yards to become the first player in NFL history to rush for 1,500 yards in each of his first three seasons.

LaDainian Tomlinson, San Diego, needs 100 receptions to become the only running back in NFL history with 100 catches in consecutive seasons. Tomlinson is the only player in NFL history to post 100 receptions and rush for 1,000 yards in the same season.

Jerry Rice, Oakland, needs six receiving touchdowns to become the first player in NFL history with 200 career touchdown receptions. In 19 seasons, Rice has scored 194 touchdown receptions, the most in NFL history.

In 19 seasons, Rice has 1,519 receptions, the most in NFL history, and needs 81 to become the first player with 1,600 career receptions.

Rice needs 100 receptions to pass Marvin Harrison (4) to become the first player in NFL history with five 100-catch seasons (see Harrison note). In 19 seasons, Rice has four seasons with 100 receptions.

Rice needs 534 receiving yards to become the first player in NFL history with 23,000 receiving yards. Rice has gained an NFL-best 22,466 receiving yards in 19 seasons.

Rice has led the league in receiving yards six times in his 19-year career and can tie Don Hutson (7) for the most seasons leading the league in receiving yards.

Rice has gained 1,000 yards in a season 14 times in his 19-year career and needs one 1,000-yard season to become the first player in NFL history with 15 career 1,000-yard receiving seasons.

Rice needs 214 combined yards to pass Brian Mitchell (23,330) and become the all-time leader in combined yards (see Mitchell note). In 19 seasons, Rice has gained 23,117 combined yards and needs 883 combined yards to become the first player in NFL history with 24,000 combined yards.

Rice needs 889 total yards from scrimmage to become the first player in NFL history to reach 24,000 scrimmage yards. In 19 seasons, Rice has gained an NFL-record 23,111 total yards from scrimmage.

Tim Brown, Oakland, needs 32 receptions to pass Cris Carter (1,101) to move into second place all-time. Brown has 1,070 receptions in 16 seasons.

Brown needs 1,000 receiving yards to become the second player in NFL history (Jerry Rice, 14) with double-digit 1,000-yard seasons. Brown has nine 1,000-yard receiving seasons in his 16-year career.

In 16 seasons, Brown has 43 100-yard receiving games and needs eight to pass Marvin Harrison (43), James Lofton (43), Michael Irvin (47) and Don Maynard (50) to move into second place all-time (see Harrison note).

Brown needs 266 receiving yards to become the second player in NFL history (Jerry Rice, 22,466) with 15,000 career receiving yards. In 16 seasons, Brown has 14,734 receiving yards.

Brown has 99 touchdown receptions in 16 seasons and needs two to pass Steve Largent (100) to move into third place all-time. With one touchdown reception, Brown would become the fourth player in NFL history (Jerry Rice, 192, Cris Carter, 130 and Steve Largent, 100) with 100 career touchdown receptions.

Brown needs 566 combined yards to become the fourth player in NFL history with 20,000 combined yards. In 16 seasons, Brown has 19,434 combined yards and needs 1,104 combined yards to pass Emmitt Smith (20,537) to move into fourth place all-time (see Smith note).

Randy Moss, Minnesota, needs 1,000 receiving yards to become the first player in NFL history with 1,000 receiving yards in each of his first seven seasons. Moss is the only player in NFL history with 1,000 receiving yards in each of his first six seasons.

Marvin Harrison, Indianapolis, needs 100 receptions to pass Jerry Rice (4) to become the first player in NFL history with five 100-catch seasons (see Rice note). In eight seasons, Harrison has four seasons with 100 receptions.

Harrison has 759 career receptions in his first eight seasons and already has more catches than any player in NFL history had in their first nine.

Harrison has three 1,500-receiving yard seasons in his eight-year career and needs 1,500 receiving yards to tie Jerry Rice (4) for the most 1,500-receiving yard seasons.

In nine seasons, Harrison has 43 100-yard receiving games and needs eight to pass Tim Brown (43), James Lofton (43), Michael Irvin (47) and Don Maynard (50) to move into second place all-time (see Brown note).

Jimmy Smith, Jacksonville, needs 1,000 receiving yards to tie Cris Carter and Steve Largent (8) for third place all-time in 1,000-yard receiving seasons. In 11 seasons, Smith has seven 1,000-yard seasons.

Brian Mitchell has 23,330 combined yards in 14 seasons, the most in NFL history (see Rice note). Mitchell needs 670 yards to become the first player in NFL history to gain 24,000 combined yards.

Mitchell has gained 4,999 yards on punt returns, the most all-time, and needs one punt return yard to become the first player in NFL history with 5,000 punt return yards.

Mitchell needs two punt return touchdowns to pass Eric Metcalf (10) for the most punt return touchdowns in NFL history. In 14 seasons, Mitchell has returned nine punts for touchdowns.

Mitchell has gained 14,014 yards on kickoff returns, the most all-time, and needs 986 kickoff return yards to become the first player in NFL history with 15,000 kickoff return yards.

Mitchell has gained 19,013 total yards on kick returns (kickoff and punt), the most all-time, and needs 987 yards to become the first player in NFL history with 20,000 kick return yards.

Rod Woodson, Oakland, needs four interceptions to become the third person in NFL history (Paul Krause, 81 and Emlen Tunnell, 79) with 75 interceptions. In 17 seasons, Woodson has 71 interceptions.

Woodson has 1,483 interception return yards, the most all-time, and needs 17 interception return yards to become the first player in NFL history with 1,500 interception return yards.

Aeneas Williams, St. Louis, needs one interception return for a touchdown to pass Ken Houston (9) to move into second place all-time. In 13 seasons, Williams has nine interception returns for touchdowns.

Morten Andersen, Kansas City, has scored 2,259 points in his 22-year career and needs 88 points to pass Gary Anderson (2,346) for the most in NFL history.

DRAFT LIST FOR 2004

69th Annual NFL Draft, April 24-25, 2004
*Denotes Compensatory Selection

ARIZONA CARDINALS
1. Larry Fitzgerald—3, WR, Pittsburgh
2. Karlos Dansby—33, LB, Auburn
3. Darnell Dockett—64, DT, Florida State
4. Alex Stepanovich—100, C, Ohio State
5. Antonio Smith—135, DE, Oklahoma State
6. Nick Leckey—167, G, Kansas State
7. John Navarre—202, QB, Michigan

ATLANTA FALCONS
1. DeAngelo Hall—8, DB, Virginia Tech
   Michael Jenkins—29, WR, Ohio State, from Indianapolis
3. Matt Schaub—90, QB, Virginia, from Indianapolis
4. Demorrio Williams—101, LB, Nebraska
5. Chad Lavalais—142, DT, Louisiana State
6. Etric Pruitt—186, DB, Southern Mississippi, from Miami
7. Quincy Wilson—219, RB, West Virginia, from New Orleans through Miami

BALTIMORE RAVENS
2. Dwan Edwards—51, DT, Oregon State
3. Devard Darling—82, WR, Washington State, from Minnesota
5. Roderick Green—153, LB, Central Missouri, from Green Bay through Miami
6. Josh Harris—187, QB, Bowling Green
   * Clarence Moore—199, WR, Northern Arizona
7.* Derek Abney—244, WR, Kentucky
   * Brian Rimpf—246, T, East Carolina

BUFFALO BILLS
1. Lee Evans—13, WR, Wisconsin
   J.P. Losman—22, QB, Tulane, from Dallas
3. Tim Anderson—74, DT, Ohio State
4. Tim Euhus—109, TE, Oregon State
7. Dylan McFarland—207, T, Montana, from Detroit
   Jonathan Smith—214, WR, Georgia Tech

CAROLINA PANTHERS
1. Chris Gamble—28, DB, Ohio State, from Philadelphia through San Francisco
2. Keary Colbert—62, WR, Southern California
3. Travelle Wharton—94, T, South Carolina
5. Drew Carter—163, WR, Ohio State
6. Sean Tufts—196, LB, Colorado
7. Michael Gaines—232, TE, Central Florida

CHICAGO BEARS
1. Tommie Harris—14, DT, Oklahoma
2. Terry Johnson—47, DT, Washington
3. Bernard Berrian—78, WR, Fresno State
4. Nathan Vasher—110, DB, Texas
   Leon Joe—112, LB, Maryland, from San Francisco
5. Claude Harriott—147, DE, Pittsburgh, from San Francisco
   Craig Krenzel—148, QB, Ohio State
7. Alfonso Marshall—215, DB, Miami

CINCINNATI BENGALS
1. Chris Perry—26, RB, Michigan, from St. Louis
2. Keiwan Ratliff—49, DB, Florida
   Madieu Williams—56, DB, Maryland, from Miami through New England
3. Caleb Miller—80, LB, Arkansas
   * Landon Johnson—96, LB, Purdue
4. Matthias Askew—114, DT, Michigan State
   Robert Geathers—117, DE, Georgia, from Denver
   Stacy Andrews—123, T, Mississippi, from St. Louis
5. Maurice Mann—149, WR, Nevada
6. Greg Brooks—183, DB, Southern Mississippi
7. Casey Bramlet—218, QB, Wyoming

CLEVELAND BROWNS
1. Kellen Winslow—6, TE, Miami, from Detroit
2. Sean Jones—59, DB, Georgia, from Indianapolis
4. Luke McCown—106, QB, Louisiana Tech
5. Amon Gordon—161, DT, Stanford, from Indianapolis
6. Kirk Chambers—176, T, Stanford, from Buffalo
7. Adimchinobe Echemandu—208, RB, California

DALLAS COWBOYS
2. Julius Jones—43, RB, Notre Dame, from Buffalo
   Jacob Rogers—52, T, Southern California
3. Stephen Peterman—83, G, Louisiana State
4. Bruce Thornton—121, DB, Georgia
5. Sean Ryan—144, TE, Boston College, from Buffalo
7. Nathan Jones—205, DB, Rutgers, from Oakland
   Patrick Crayton—216, WR, Northwestern Oklahoma State, from Tampa Bay
   Jacques Reeves—223, DB, Purdue, reacquired from Oakland

DENVER BRONCOS
1. D.J. Williams—17, LB, Miami, from Cincinnati
2. Tatum Bell—41, RB, Oklahoma State, from Washington
   Darius Watts—54, WR, Marshall
3. Jeremy LeSueur—85, DB, Michigan
5. Jeff Shoate—152, DB, San Diego State
6. Triandos Luke—171, WR, Alabama, from Washington
   Josh Sewell—190, C, Nebraska
7. Matt Mauck—225, QB, Louisiana State
   * Brandon Miree—247, RB, Pittsburgh
   * Bradlee Van Pelt—250, QB, Colorado State

DETROIT LIONS
1. Roy Williams—7, WR, Texas, from Cleveland
   Kevin Jones—30, RB, Virginia Tech, from Kansas City
2. Teddy Lehman—37, LB, Oklahoma, from Cleveland
3. Keith Smith—73, DB, McNeese State
5. Alex Lewis—140, LB, Wisconsin
6. Kelly Butler—172, T, Purdue

GREEN BAY PACKERS
1. Ahmad Carroll—25, DB, Arkansas
3. Joey Thomas—70, DB, Montana State, from Jacksonville
   Donnell Washington—72, DT, Clemson, from Washington through Jacksonville
   B.J. Sander—87, P, Ohio State, from Miami
6. Corey Williams—179, DT, Arkansas State, from San Francisco
7.* Scott Wells—251, C, Tennessee

HOUSTON TEXANS
1. Dunta Robinson—10, DB, South Carolina
   Jason Babin—27, LB, Western Michigan, from Tennessee
2. Tony Hollings—RB, Georgia Tech
   (2003 Supplemental Selection, from Oakland)
4. Glenn Earl—122, DB, Notre Dame, from Indianapolis
6. Vontez Duff—170, DB, Notre Dame
   Jammal Lord—175, DB, Nebraska, from Jacksonville
   * Charlie Anderson—200, LB, Mississippi
7. Raheem Orr—210, LB, Rutgers, from Jacksonville
   Sloan Thomas—211, WR, Texas
   * B.J. Symons—248, QB, Texas Tech

INDIANAPOLIS COLTS
2. Bob Sanders—44, DB, Iowa, from Pittsburgh
3. Ben Hartsock—68, TE, Ohio State, from Cleveland
   Gilbert Gardner—69, LB, Purdue, from Atlanta
4. Kendyll Pope—107, LB, Florida State, from Pittsburgh
   Jason David—125, DB, Washington State,
   from Philadelphia through Atlanta
5. Jake Scott—141, T, Idaho, from Cleveland
6. Von Hutchins—173, DB, Mississippi, from Cleveland
   Jim Sorgi—193, QB, Wisconsin
7. David Kimball—229, K, Penn State, from St. Louis

JACKSONVILLE JAGUARS
1. Reggie Williams—9, WR, Washington
2. Daryl Smith—39, LB, Georgia Tech
   Greg Jones—55, RB, Florida State, from Green Bay
3. Jorge Cordova—86, LB, Nevada, from Green Bay
4. Anthony Maddox—118, DT, Delta State, from Green Bay
   Ernest Wilford—120, WR, Virginia Tech, from Baltimore
5. Josh Scobee—137, K, Louisiana Tech
   Chris Thompson—150, DB, Nicholls State,
   from New Orleans
   Sean Bubin—159, T, Illinois,
   from Tennessee through Houston
7.* Bobby McCray—249, DE, Florida

KANSAS CITY CHIEFS
2. Junior Siavii—36, DT, Oregon, from Detroit
   Kris Wilson—61, TE, Pittsburgh
3. Keyaron Fox—93, LB, Georgia Tech
4. Samie Parker—105, WR, Oregon, from Detroit
   Jared Allen—126, DE, Idaho State
6. Jeris McIntyre—195, WR, Auburn
7. Kevin Sampson—231, T, Syracuse

MIAMI DOLPHINS
1. Vernon Carey—19, T, Miami, from Minnesota
4. Will Poole—102, DB, Southern California
   from Jacksonville through Green Bay
5. Tony Bua—160, LB, Arkansas
   from Philadelphia through Baltimore
6. Rex Hadnot—174, G, Houston, from Atlanta
7. Tony Pape—221, T, Michigan
   Derrick Pope—222, LB, Alabama, from Baltimore

MINNESOTA VIKINGS
1. Kenechi Udeze—20, DE, Southern California, from Miami
2. Dontarrious Thomas—48, LB, Auburn, from New Orleans
3. Darrion Scott—88, DE, Ohio State, from Baltimore
4. Nat Dorsey—115, T, Georgia Tech
   Mewelde Moore—119, RB, Tulane, from Miami
5. Rod Davis—155, LB, Southern Mississippi, from Baltimore
6. Deandre Eiland—184, DB, South Carolina
7. Jeff Dugan—220, TE, Maryland

NEW ENGLAND PATRIOTS
1. Vince Wilfork—21, DT, Miami, from Baltimore
   Ben Watson—32, TE, Georgia
2. Marquise Hill—63, DE, Louisiana State
3. Guss Scott—95, DB, Florida
4. Dexter Reid—113, DB, North Carolina, from New Orleans
   Cedric Cobbs—128, RB, Arkansas
5. P.K. Sam—164, WR, Florida State
7. Christian Morton—233, DB, Illinois

NEW ORLEANS SAINTS
1. Will Smith—18, DE, Ohio State
2. Devery Henderson—50, WR, Louisiana State
   from Minnesota
   Courtney Watson—60, LB, Notre Dame, from St. Louis
5. Rodney Leisle—139, DT, UCLA, from Washington
   Mike Karney—156, RB, Arizona State, from Dallas
7.* Colby Bockwoldt—240, LB, Brigham Young

NEW YORK GIANTS
1. Philip Rivers—4, QB, North Carolina State
2. Chris Snee—34, G, Boston College
4. Reggie Torbor—97, LB, Auburn
5. Gibril Wilson—136, DB, Tennessee
6. Jamaar Taylor—168, WR, Texas A&M
7. Drew Strojny—203, T, Duke
   * Isaac Hilton—253, DE, Hampton

NEW YORK JETS
1. Jonathan Vilma—12, LB, Miami
3. Derrick Strait—76, DB, Oklahoma
4. Jerricho Cotchery—108, WR, North Carolina State
   * Adrian Jones—132, T, Kansas
5. Erik Coleman—143, DB, Washington State
6. Marko Cavka—178, T, Sacramento State
7. Darrell McClover—213, LB, Miami
   * Trevor Johnson—234, DE, Nebraska
   * Derrick Ward—235, RB, Ottawa (Kan.)
   * Rashad Washington—236, DB, Kansas State

OAKLAND RAIDERS
1. Robert Gallery—2, T, Iowa
2. Jake Grove—45, C, Virginia Tech, from Tampa Bay
3. Stuart Schweigert—67, DB, Purdue
4. Carlos Francis—99, WR, Texas Tech
5. Johnnie Morant—134, WR, Syracuse
6. Shawn Johnson—166, DE, Delaware
   Cody Spencer—182, LB, North Texas,
   from New Orleans through Dallas
7.* Courtney Anderson—245, TE, San Jose State
   * Andre Sommersell—255, LB, Colorado State

PHILADELPHIA EAGLES
1. Shawn Andrews—16, T, Arkansas, from San Francisco
3. Matt Ware—89, DB, UCLA
4.* J.R. Reed—129, DB, South Florida
   * Trey Darilek—131, T, Texas-El Paso
5. Thomas Tapeh—162, RB, Minnesota, from Kansas City
6. Andy Hall—185, QB, Delaware, from Green Bay
   Dexter Wynn—192, DB, Colorado State
7. Adrien Clarke—227, G, Ohio State
   * Bruce Perry—242, RB, Maryland
   * Dominic Furio—243, C, Nevada-Las Vegas

DRAFT LIST FOR 2004

PITTSBURGH STEELERS
1. Ben Roethlisberger—11, QB, Miami (Ohio)
2. Ricardo Colclough—38, DB, Tusculum (Tenn.)
   from Atlanta through Indianapolis
3. Max Starks—75, T, Florida
5. Nathaniel Adibi—145, LB, Virginia Tech
6. Bo Lacy—177, T, Arkansas
   Matt Kranchick—194, TE, Penn State, from St. Louis
   Drew Caylor—197, C, Stanford, from New England
7. Eric Taylor—212, DT, Memphis

ST. LOUIS RAMS
1. Steven Jackson—24, RB, Oregon State,
   from Denver through Cincinnati
3. Tony Hargrove—91, DE, Georgia Tech
4. * Brandon Chillar—130, LB, UCLA
5. Jason Shivers—158, DB, Arizona State
6. * Jeff Smoker—201, QB, Michigan State
7. * Erik Jensen—237, TE, Iowa
   * Larry Turner—238, C, Eastern Kentucky

SAN DIEGO CHARGERS
1. Eli Manning—1, QB, Mississippi
2. Igor Olshansky—35, DT, Oregon
3. Nate Kaeding—65, K, Iowa, from N.Y. Giants
   Nick Hardwick—66, C, Purdue
4. Shaun Phillips—98, LB, Purdue
5. Dave Ball—133, DE, UCLA
   Michael Turner—154, RB, Northern Illinois, from Miami
6. Ryan Krause—169, TE, Nebraska-Omaha
7. Ryon Bingham—204, DT, Nebraska
   Shane Olivea—209, T, Ohio State, from Atlanta
   * Carlos Joseph—254, T, Miami

SAN FRANCISCO 49ERS
1. Rashaun Woods—31, WR, Oklahoma State, from Carolina
2. Justin Smiley—46, G, Alabama
   Shawntae Spencer—58, DB, Pittsburgh, from Philadelphia
3. Derrick Hamilton—77, WR, Clemson
4. Isaac Sopoaga—104, DT, Hawaii,
   from Washington through New England and Chicago
   Richard Seigler—127, LB, Oregon State, from Carolina
6. Andy Lee—188, P, Pittsburgh,
   from Dallas through Green Bay
   * Keith Lewis—198, DB, Oregon
7. Cody Pickett—217, QB, Washington
   Christian Ferrara—226, DT, Syracuse, from Green Bay

SEATTLE SEAHAWKS
1. Marcus Tubbs—23, DT, Texas
2. Michael Boulware—53, DB, Florida State
3. Sean Locklear—84, G, North Carolina State
4. Niko Koutouvides—116, LB, Purdue
5. D.J. Hackett—157, WR, Colorado
6. Craig Terrill—189, DT, Purdue
7. Donnie Jones—224, P, Louisiana State

TAMPA BAY BUCCANEERS
1. Michael Clayton—15, WR, Louisiana State
3. Marquis Cooper—79, LB, Washington
4. Will Allen—111, DB, Ohio State
5. Jeb Terry—146, G, North Carolina
6. Nate Lawrie—181, TE, Yale
7. Mark Jones—206, WR, Tennessee,
   from Washington through New Orleans and Dallas
   Casey Cramer—228, RB, Dartmouth, from Indianapolis
   * Lenny Williams—252, DB, Southern

TENNESSEE TITANS
2. Ben Troupe—40, TE, Florida, from Houston
   Travis LaBoy—42, DE, Hawaii, from N.Y. Jets
   Antwan Odom—57, DE, Alabama
3. Randy Starks—71, DT, Maryland, from Houston
   Rich Gardner—92, DB, Penn State
4. Bo Schobel—103, DE, TCU, from Houston
   Michael Waddell—124, DB, North Carolina
5. Jacob Bell—138, T, Miami (Ohio), from Houston
   * Robert Reynolds—165, LB, Ohio State
6. Troy Fleming—191, RB, Tennessee
7. Jared Clauss—230, DT, Iowa
   * Eugene Amano—239, C, Southeast Missouri State
   * Sean McHugh—241, RB, Penn State

WASHINGTON REDSKINS
1. Sean Taylor—5, DB, Miami
3. Chris Cooley—81, TE, Utah State, from New Orleans
5. Mark Wilson—151, T, California,
   from Minnesota through New Orleans
6. Jim Molinaro—180, T, Notre Dame

NUMBER OF PLAYERS DRAFTED—2004

BY POSITION:

Defensive Backs....48
Linebackers....36
Wide Receivers....31
Tackles....26
Defensive Tackles....23
Running Backs....19
Defensive Ends....17
Quarterbacks....17
Tight Ends....15
Centers....9
Guards....8
Kickers....3
Punters....3

BY COLLEGE:

Ohio State....14
Miami....9
Purdue....9
Louisiana State....7
Arkansas....6
Pittsburgh....6
Florida....5
Florida State....5
Georgia Tech....5
Iowa....5
Maryland....5
Nebraska....5
Notre Dame....5
Virginia Tech....5
Alabama....4
Auburn....4
Georgia....4
Michigan....4
Mississippi....4
Oregon....4
Oregon State....4
Penn State....4
Southern California....4
Tennessee....4
Texas....4
UCLA....4
Washington....4
Colorado State....3
North Carolina....3
North Carolina State....3
Oklahoma....3
Oklahoma State....3
South Carolina....3
Southern Mississippi....3
Stanford....3
Syracuse....3
Washington State....3
Wisconsin....3
Arizona State....2
Boston College....2
California....2
Clemson....2
Colorado....2
Delaware....2
Hawaii....2
Illinois....2
Kansas State....2
Louisiana Tech....2
Miami (Ohio)....2
Michigan State....2
Nevada....2
Rutgers....2
Texas Tech....2
Tulane....2
Arkansas State....1
Bowling Green....1
Brigham Young....1
Central Florida....1
Cetnral Missouri....1
Dartmouth....1
Delta State....1
Duke....1
East Carolina....1
Eastern Kentucky....1
Fresno State....1
Hampton....1
Houston....1
Idaho....1
Idaho State....1
Kansas....1
Kentucky....1
Marshall....1
McNeese State....1
Memphis....1
Minnesota....1
Montana....1
Montana State....1
Nebraska-Omaha....1
Nevada-Las Vegas....1
Nicholls State....1
North Texas....1
Northern Arizona....1
Northern Illinois....1
Northwestern Oklahoma State....1
Ottawa (Kan.)....1
Sacramento State....1
San Diego State....1
San Jose State....1
South Florida....1
Southeast Missouri State....1
Southern....1
TCU....1
Texas A&M....1
Texas-El Paso....1
Tusculum (Tenn.)....1
Utah State....1
Virginia....1
West Virginia....1
Western Michigan....1
Wyoming....1
Yale....1

BY CONFERENCE:

Big Ten....44
Southeastern....42
Pacific 10....30
Big East....28
Atlantic Coast....25
Big 12....23
Conference USA....10
Western Athletic....9
Mid-American....7
Mountain West....7
Big Sky....5
Independent....5
Sun Belt....4
Atlantic 10....2
Ivy League....2
Ohio Valley....2
Southland....2
Central States Football League....1
Gulf South....1
Kansas Collegiate Athletic....1
Mid-America Intercollegiate Athletic....1
Mid-Eastern Athletic....1
North Central Intercollegiate Athletic....1
South Atlantic....1
Southwestern Athletic....1

UNDERCLASSMEN IN THE DRAFT

Year	Entered	Drafted	In Top 10
1989	25	12	3
1990	38	18	5
1991	33	22	2
1992	48	25	5
1993	46	24	5
1994	43	26	6
1995	42	22	2
1996	46	21	4
1997	44	27	7
1998	41	20	3
1999	42	27	5
2000	31	20	4
2001	54	31	5
2002	43	26	5
2003	54	32	5
2004	44	35	5

WAIVERS

The waiver system is a procedure by which player contracts or NFL rights to players are made available by a club to other clubs in the League. During the procedure, the 31 other clubs either file claims to obtain the players or waive the opportunity to do so—thus the term "waiver." Claiming clubs are assigned players on a priority based on the inverse of won-and-lost standing. The claiming period is three business days from the beginning of the League Year through April 30, 10 calendar days from May 1 through the last business day before July 4, and 24 hours after July 4 through the conclusion of the regular season. If a player passes through waivers unclaimed, he becomes a free agent. All waivers are no recall and no withdrawal. Under the Collective Bargaining Agreement, from the beginning of the waiver system each year through the trading deadline (October 19, 2004), any veteran who has acquired four years of pension credit is not subject to the waiver system if the club desires to release him. After the trading deadline, such players are subject to the waiver system.

ACTIVE/INACTIVE LIST

The Active/Inactive List is the principal status for players participating for a club. It consists of all players under contract who are eligible for preseason, regular-season, and postseason games. Teams are permitted to open training camp with no more than 80 players under contract and thereafter must meet two mandatory roster reductions prior to the season opener. Teams will be permitted an Active List of 45 players and an Inactive List of eight players for each regular-season and postseason game. Provided that a club has two quarterbacks on its 45-player Active List, a third quarterback from its Inactive List is permitted to dress for the game, but if he enters the game during the first three quarters, the other two quarterbacks are thereafter prohibited from playing. Teams also are permitted to establish Practice Squads of up to five players who are eligible to participate in practice, but these players remain free agents and are eligible to sign with any other team in the league.

August 31 .... Roster reduction to 65 players
September 5 .... Roster reduction to 53 players
September 6 .... Teams establish a Practice Squad of up to five players

In addition to the squad limits described above, the overall roster limit of 80 players remains in effect throughout the regular season and postseason. The overall limit is applicable to players on a team's Active, Inactive, and certain Exempt Lists, players on the Practice Squad, and players on the Reserve List as Injured, Physically Unable to Perform, Non-Football Illness/Injury, and Suspended by Club.

RESERVE LIST

The Reserve List is a status for players who, for reasons of injury, retirement, military service, or other circumstances, are not immediately available for participation with a club. Players on Reserve/Injured are not eligible to practice or return to the Active/Inactive List in the same season that they are placed on Reserve. Players in the category of Reserve/Retired, Reserve/Did Not Report, Reserve/Exclusive Rights, and players who were placed in the category of Reserve/Left Squad in a previous season may not be reinstated during the period from 30 days before the end of the regular season through the postseason.

TRADES

Unrestricted trading between the AFC and NFC is allowed in 2004 through October 19, after which trading will end until 2005.

ANNUAL ACTIVE PLAYER LIMITS

NFL

Year(s)	Limit
1991-2004	45**
1985-90	45
1983-84	49
1982	45†-49
1978-81	45
1975-77	43
1974	47
1964-73	40
1963	37
1961-62	36
1960	38
1959	36
1957-58	35
1951-56	33
1949-50	32
1948	35
1947	35*-34
1945-46	33
1943-44	28
1940-42	33
1938-39	30
1936-37	25
1935	24
1930-34	20
1926-29	18
1925	16

** 45 plus a third quarterback
† 45 for first two games
* 35 for first three games

AFL

Year(s)	Limit
1966-69	40
1965	38
1964	34
1962-63	33
1960-61	35

NFL FREE AGENCY MOVEMENT

The following chart details veteran free agents who signed with new teams:

	Unrestricted	Restricted	Transition	Franchise	TOTALS
1993	100	8	4	1	113
1994	101	0	4	0	105
1995	154	6	2	1	163
1996	100	4	2	0	106
1997	86	2	2	0	90
1998	112	4	1	2	119
1999	115	2	1	0	118
2000	107	4	0	1	112
2001	93	4	0	2	99
2002	130	1	0	0	131
2003	111	5	1	0	117

The following procedures will be used to break standings ties for postseason playoffs and to determine regular-season schedules.

Note: Tie games count as one-half win and one-half loss for both clubs.

TO BREAK A TIE WITHIN A DIVISION

If, at the end of the regular season, two or more clubs in the same division finish with the best won-lost-tied percentage, the following steps will be taken until a champion is determined:

TWO CLUBS

1. Head-to-head (best won-lost-tied percentage in games between the clubs.)
2. Best won-lost-tied percentage in games played within the division.
3. Best won-lost-tied percentage in common games.
4. Best won-lost-tied percentage in games played within the conference.
5. Strength of victory.
6. Strength of schedule.
7. Best combined ranking among conference teams in points scored and points allowed.
8. Best combined ranking among all teams in points scored and points allowed.
9. Best net points in common games.
10. Best net points in all games.
11. Best net touchdowns in all games
12. Coin toss.

THREE OR MORE CLUBS

(Note: If two clubs remain tied after a third club is eliminated during any step, tie-breaker reverts to Step 1 of the two-club format.)

1. Head-to-head (best won-lost-tied percentage in games among the clubs.)
2. Best won-lost-tied percentage in games played within the division.
3. Best won-lost-tied percentage in common games.
4. Best won-lost-tied percentage in games played within the conference.
5. Strength of victory.
6. Strength of schedule.
7. Best combined ranking among conference teams in points scored and points allowed.
8. Best combined ranking among all teams in points scored and points allowed.
9. Best net points in common games.
10. Best net points in all games.
11. Best net touchdowns in all games.
12. Coin toss.

TO BREAK A TIE FOR THE WILD-CARD TEAM

If it is necessary to break ties to determine the two Wild Card clubs from each conference, the following steps will be taken:

A. If all the tied clubs are from the same division, apply division tie-breaker.

B. If the tied clubs are from different divisions, apply the following steps:

TWO CLUBS

1. Head-to-head, if applicable.
2. Best won-lost-tied percentage in the games played within the conference.
3. Best won-lost-tied percentage in common games, minimum of four.
4. Strength of victory.
5. Strength of schedule.
6. Best combined ranking among conference teams in points scored and points allowed.
7. Best combined ranking among all teams in points scored and points allowed.
8. Best net points in conference games.
9. Best net points in all games.
10. Best net touchdowns in all games.
11. Coin toss.

THREE OR MORE CLUBS

1. Apply division tie-breaker to eliminate all but highest ranked club in each division prior to proceeding to Step 2. The original seeding within a division upon application of the division tie-breaker remains the same for all subsequent applications of the procedure that are necessary to identify the Wild Card participants.
2. Head-to-head sweep (apply only if one club has defeated each of the others or one club has lost to each of the others).
3. Best won-lost-tied percentage in games played within the conference.
4. Best won-lost-tied percentage in common games, minimum of four.
5. Strength of victory.
6. Strength of schedule.
7. Best combined ranking among conference teams in points scored and points allowed.
8. Best combined ranking among all teams in points scored and points allowed.
9. Best net points in conference games.
10. Best net points in all games.
11. Best net touchdowns in all games.
12. Coin toss.

When the first Wild Card team has been identified, the procedure is repeated to name the second Wild Card (i.e., eliminate all but the highest ranked club in each division prior to proceeding to Step 2.) In situations where three teams from the same division are involved in the procedure, the original seeding of the teams remains the same for subsequent applications of the tie-breaker if the top-ranked team in that division qualifies for a Wild Card berth.

OTHER TIE-BREAKING PROCEDURES

1. Only one club advances to the playoffs in any tie-breaking step. Remaining tied clubs revert to the first step of the applicable division or Wild Card tie-breakers. As an example, if two clubs remain tied in any tie-breaker step after all other clubs have been eliminated, the procedure reverts to Step 1 of the two-club format to determine the winner. When one club wins the tie-breaker, all other clubs revert to Step 1 of the applicable two-club or three-club format.
2. In comparing records against common opponents among tied teams, the best won-lost-tied percentage is the deciding factor since teams may have played an unequal number of games.
3. To determine home-field priority among division-titlists, apply Wild Card tie-breakers.
4. To determine home-field priority for Wild Card qualifiers, apply division tie-breakers (if teams are from the same division) or Wild Card tie-breakers (if teams are from different divisions).

TIE-BREAKING PROCEDURE FOR SELECTION MEETING

If two or more clubs are tied in the selection order, the strength-of-schedule tie-breaker is applied, subject to the following exceptions for playoff clubs:

1. The Super Bowl winner is last and the Super Bowl loser next-to-last.
2. Any non-Super Bowl playoff club involved in a tie shall be assigned priority within its segment below that of non-playoff clubs and in the order that the playoff club exited from the playoffs. Thus, within a tied segment a playoff club that loses in the Wild Card game will have priority over a playoff club that loses in the Divisional playoff game, which in turn will have priority over a club that loses in the Conference Championship game. If two tied clubs exited the playoffs in the same round, the tie is broken by strength of schedule.

If any ties cannot be broken by strength of schedule, the divisional or conference tie-breakers, whichever are applicable, are applied. Any ties that still exist are broken by a coin flip.

INSTANT REPLAY

For the 2004-08 seasons, the NFL will continue to employ a system of Referee Replay Review to aid officiating.

Prior to the two-minute warning of each half, a Coaches' Challenge System will be in effect. After the two-minute warning, and throughout any overtime period, a Referee Review will be initiated by a Replay Assistant from a Replay Booth.

The following procedures will be used:

REVIEWS BY REFEREE: All Replay Reviews will be conducted by the Referee on a field-level monitor after consultation with the other covering official(s), prior to review. A decision will be reversed only when the Referee has *indisputable visual evidence* available to him that warrants the change.

COACHES' CHALLENGE: In each game, a team will be permitted two challenges that will initiate Referee Replay reviews. Each challenge will require the use of a team time out. If a challenge is upheld, the time out will be restored to the challenging team. If both challenges are upheld, a third challenge will be awarded to the challenging team. No challenges will be recognized from a team that has exhausted its time outs.

REPLAY ASSISTANT'S REQUEST FOR REVIEW: After the two-minute warning of each half, and throughout any overtime period, any review will be initiated by a Replay Assistant. There is no limit to the number of reviews that may be initiated by the Replay Assistant. His ability to initiate a review will be unrelated to the number of time outs that either team has remaining, and no time out will be charged for any review initiated by the Replay Assistant.

TIME LIMIT: Each review will be a maximum of 90 seconds in length, timed from when the Referee begins his review of the replay at the field-level monitor.

REVIEWABLE PLAYS: The Replay System will cover the following play situations only:

A) PLAYS GOVERNED BY SIDELINE, GOAL LINE, END ZONE, AND END LINE:
1. Scoring plays, including a runner breaking the plane of the goal line.
2. Pass complete/incomplete/intercepted at sideline, goal line, end zone, and end line.
3. Runner/receiver in or out of bounds.
4. Recovery of loose ball in or out of bounds.

B) PASSING PLAYS:
1. Pass ruled complete/incomplete/intercepted in the field of play.
2. Touching of a forward pass by an ineligible receiver.
3. Touching of a forward pass by a defensive player.
4. Quarterback (Passer) forward pass or fumble.
5. Illegal forward pass beyond line of scrimmage.
6. Illegal forward pass after change of possession.
7. Forward or backward pass thrown from behind line of scrimmage.

C) OTHER DETECTABLE INFRACTIONS:
1. Runner ruled not down by defensive contact.
2. Forward progress with respect to first down.
3. Touching of a kick.
4. Number of players on the field.

INSTANT REPLAY HISTORY

From 1986-1991, a limited system of Instant Replay was used on a year-by-year basis. Replay also was experimented with during the 1996 and 1998 preseasons. For the 1999 season, the NFL introduced a system of Referee Replay Review to aid officiating. That system was extended on a one-year basis for the 2000 season and and then approved for the next three years through 2003. In March 2004, the system was extended for five seasons through 2008.

Following are the results of the different systems:

REGULAR SEASON, 1986-1991

Year	Games	Plays Closely Reviewed	Reversals
1986	224	374	38
1987	210	490	57
1988	224	537	53
1989	224	492	65
1990	224	504	73
1991	224	570	90
TOTAL	1,330	2,967	376

PRESEASON, 1996, 1998

Year	Games	Challenges	Reversals
1996	10	13	3
1998	10	10	3
TOTAL	20	23	6

REGULAR SEASON, 1999-2003

Year	Games	Total Replay Reviews	Challenges	Reversals
1999	248	195	133	57
2000	248	247	179	84
2001	248	258	191	89
2002	256	294	208	94
2003	256	255	184	66
TOTAL	1,256	1,249	895	390

The AFC

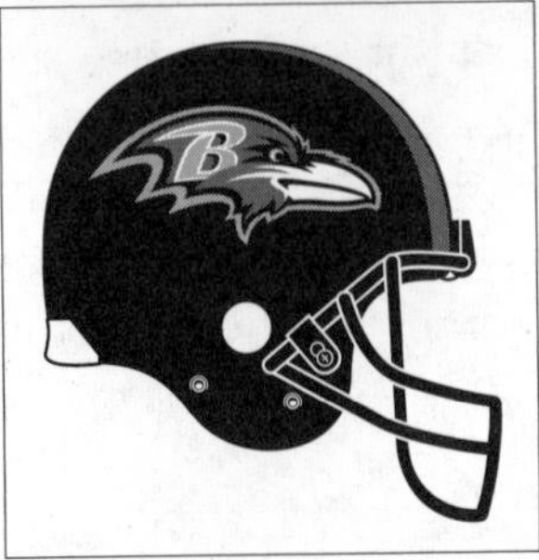

American Football Conference
North Division
Team Colors: Black, Purple, and Metallic Gold
11001 Owings Mills Boulevard
Owings Mills, Maryland 21117
Telephone: (410) 654-6200

2004 SCHEDULE

PRESEASON — **Baltimore time**

Date	Opponent	Time
Aug. 12	**Atlanta**	8:00
Aug. 20	at Philadelphia	8:00
Aug. 28	**Detroit**	8:00
Sept. 2	at New York Giants	7:00

REGULAR SEASON

Date	Opponent	Time
Sept. 12	at Cleveland	1:00
Sept. 19	**Pittsburgh**	1:00
Sept. 26	at Cincinnati	1:00
Oct. 4	**Kansas City** (Mon.)	9:00
Oct. 10	at Washington	8:30
Oct. 17	Open Date	
Oct. 24	**Buffalo**	1:00
Oct. 31	at Philadelphia	1:00
Nov. 7	**Cleveland**	8:30
Nov. 14	at New York Jets	1:00
Nov. 21	**Dallas**	1:00
Nov. 28	at New England	1:00
Dec. 5	**Cincinnati**	1:00
Dec. 12	**New York Giants**	1:00
Dec. 19	at Indianapolis	8:30
Dec. 26	at Pittsburgh	1:00
Jan. 2	**Miami**	1:00

Stadium: M&T Bank Stadium (opened in 1998)
• **Capacity:** 69,084
1101 Russell Street
Baltimore, Maryland 21230
Playing Surface: Sportexe Momentum
Training Camp: McDaniel College
2 College Hill
Westminster, Maryland 21157

M&T BANK STADIUM

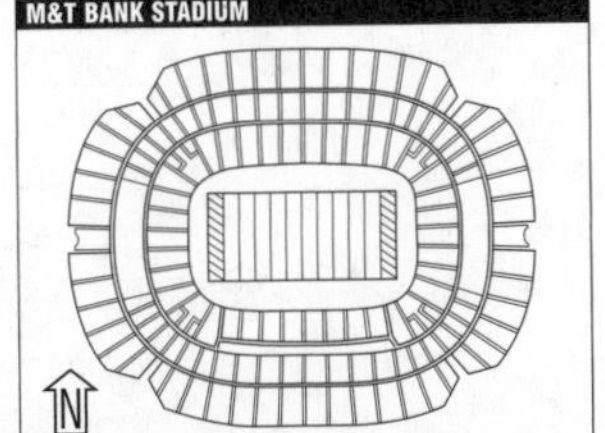

CLUB OFFICIALS

Owner: Steve Bisciotti
President: Dick Cass
Executive Vice President/General Manager: Ozzie Newsome
Senior Vice President/Public and Community Relations: Kevin Byrne
Senior Vice President/Business Ventures: Dennis Mannion
Chief Financial Officer: Jeff Goering
Director of Player Personnel: Phil Savage
Director of Football Administration: Pat Moriarty
Director of Operations: Bob Eller
Director of Publications/Assistant Director of Public Relations: Francine Lubera
Director of Pro Personnel: George Kokinis
Director of College Scouting: Eric DeCosta
Director of Player Programs: O.J. Brigance
Assistant Director of Pro Personnel: Vince Newsome
Scouts: Chad Alexander, Joe Douglas, Joe Hortiz, Ron Marciniak, T.J. McCreight
Head Trainer: Bill Tessendorf
Equipment Manager: Ed Carroll
Video Director: Jon Dubé
Senior Director, Finance: Jeff Goering
Senior Director, Business Development: Mark Burdett
Senior Director, Stadium Operations: Roy Sommerhof
Senior Director of Broadcasting and Video Production: Larry Rosen
Director of Premium Services: Theresa Abato
Director, Ticket Sales and Operations: Baker Koppelman
Director, Corporate Sales: Ed Burchell
Director, Corporate Sales: Kevin Rochlitz
Director, Consumer Marketing: Lisa Dixon

COACHING HISTORY
(68-66-1)

Years	Coach	Record
1996-98	Ted Marchibroda	16-31-1
1999-2003	Brian Billick	52-35-0

ATTENDANCE

Home 546,614 Away 458,750
Total 1,005,364
Single-game home record, 69,638 (10/27/02)
Single-season home record, 549,531 (1998)

2004 DRAFT CHOICES

Round	Name	Pos.	College
2	Dwan Edwards	DT	Oregon State
3	Devard Darling	WR	Washington St.
5	Roderick Green	LB	Central Missouri
6	Josh Harris	QB	Bowling Green
	Clarence Moore	WR	Northern Arizona
7	Derek Abney	WR	Kentucky
	Brian Rimpf	T	East Carolina

BALTIMORE RAVENS

2003 TEAM RECORD

PRESEASON (1-3)

Date	Result	Opponent
8/9	L 19-20	Buffalo
8/16	W 13-10	at Atlanta
8/23	L 3-24	at Washington
8/28	L 24-30	New York Giants

REGULAR SEASON (10-6)

Date	Result	Opponent	Att.
9/7	L 15-34	at Pittsburgh	63,157
9/14	W 33-13	Cleveland	69,473
9/21	W 24-10	at San Diego	52,028
9/28	L 10-17	Kansas City	69,459
10/12	W 26-18	at Arizona	24,193
10/19	L 26-34	at Cincinnati	53,553
10/26	W 26-6	Denver	69,721
11/2	W 24-17	Jacksonville	69,486
11/9	L 22-33	at St. Louis	66,085
11/16	L 6-9	at Miami (OT)	73,333
11/23	W 44-41	Seattle (OT)	69,477
11/30	W 44-6	San Francisco	69,549
12/7	W 31-13	Cincinnati	69,468
12/14	L 12-20	at Oakland	45,398
12/21	W 35-0	at Cleveland	72,548
12/28	W 13-10	Pittsburgh (OT)	70,001

(OT) Overtime

POSTSEASON (0-1)

Date	Result	Opponent	Att.
1/3	L 17-20	Tennessee	69,452

SCORE BY PERIODS

Ravens	61	90	84	150	6	— 391
Opponents	63	73	77	65	3	— 281

2003 TEAM STATISTICS

	Ravens	Opp.
Total First Downs	259	248
Rushing	115	78
Passing	121	144
Penalty	23	26
3rd Down: Made/Att	72/226	69/235
3rd Down Pct.	31.9	29.4
4th Down: Made/Att	7/11	5/17
4th Down Pct.	63.6	29.4
Possession Avg.	30:14	29:46
Total Net Yards	4929	4341
Avg. Per Game	308.1	271.3
Total Plays	1,009	1,026
Avg. Per Play	4.9	4.2
Net Yards Rushing	2,674	1,536
Avg. Per Game	167.1	96.0
Total Rushes	552	448
Net Yards Passing	2,255	2,805
Avg. Per Game	140.9	175.3
Sacked/Yards Lost	42/262	47/353
Gross Yards	2,517	3,158
Att./Completions	415/217	531/296
Completion Pct.	52.3	55.7
Had Intercepted	19	24
Punts/Average	91/40.8	105/40.1
Net Punting Avg.	91/34.9	105/34.7
Penalties/Yards	126/970	106/935
Fumbles/Ball Lost	37/19	29/17
Touchdowns	41	28
Rushing	18	6
Passing	16	19
Returns	7	3

2003 INDIVIDUAL STATISTICS

PASSING	Att.	Comp.	Yds.	Pct.	TD	Int.	Tkld.	Rate
Boller	224	116	1,260	51.8	7	9	17/92	62.4
Wright	178	94	1,199	52.8	9	8	19/125	72.3
Redman	13	7	58	53.8	0	2	6/45	26.0
Ravens	415	217	2,517	52.3	16	19	42/262	64.7
Opponents	531	296	3,158	55.7	19	24	47/353	66.4

SCORING	TD R	TD P	TD Rt	PAT	FG	Saf	PTS
Stover	0	0	0	35/35	33/38	0	134
J. Lewis	14	0	0	0/0	0/0	0	84
Robinson	0	6	0	0/0	0/0	0	36
Heap	0	3	0	0/0	0/0	0	26
T. Jones	0	3	0	0/0	0/0	0	18
Reed	0	0	3	0/0	0/0	0	18
T. Taylor	0	3	0	0/0	0/0	0	18
M. Smith	2	0	0	0/0	0/0	0	12
C. Taylor	2	0	0	0/0	0/0	0	12
R. Lewis	0	0	1	0/0	0/0	0	6
McAlister	0	0	1	0/0	0/0	0	6
Ogden	0	1	0	0/0	0/0	0	6
Ricard	0	0	1	0/0	0/0	0	6
Williams	0	0	1	0/0	0/0	0	6
Richey	0	0	0	0/0	1/2	0	3
Ravens	18	16	7	35/35	34/40	0	391
Opponents	6	19	3	27/27	28/31	0	281

2-Pt. Conversions: Heap 4.
Ravens 4-6, Opponents 1-1.

RUSHING	Att.	Yds.	Avg.	LG	TD
J. Lewis	387	2,066	5.3	82t	14
C. Taylor	63	276	4.4	32	2
Ricard	19	79	4.2	30	0
Wright	28	73	2.6	17	0
Boller	30	62	2.1	15	0
T. Taylor	11	62	5.6	16	0
M. Smith	9	31	3.4	11t	2
Heap	3	21	7.0	9	0
Redman	2	4	2.0	4	0
Ravens	552	2,674	4.8	82t	18
Opponents	448	1,536	3.4	36	6

RECEIVING	No.	Yds.	Avg.	LG	TD
Heap	57	693	12.2	33t	3
T. Taylor	39	632	16.2	73t	3
Robinson	31	451	14.5	50t	6
J. Lewis	26	205	7.9	26	0
C. Taylor	20	132	6.6	23	0
T. Jones	19	159	8.4	25	3
Sanders	14	170	12.1	44	0
Ricard	9	62	6.9	15	0
R. Johnson	1	12	12.0	12	0
Ogden	1	1	1.0	1t	1
Ravens	217	2,517	11.6	73t	16
Opponents	296	3,158	10.7	82t	19

INTERCEPTIONS	No.	Yds.	Avg.	LG	TD
Reed	7	132	18.9	54t	1
R. Lewis	6	99	16.5	37	1
McAlister	3	93	31.0	83t	1
Baxter	3	41	13.7	34	0
Demps	2	57	28.5	54	0
Williams	1	52	52.0	52t	1
Hartwell	1	26	26.0	26	0
Suggs	1	11	11.0	11	0
Ravens	24	511	21.3	83t	4
Opponents	19	269	14.2	45	0

PUNTING	No.	Yds.	Avg.	In 20	LG
Zastudil	89	3,649	41.0	21	67
Boller	1	29	29.0	0	29
Stover	1	34	34.0	0	34
Ravens	91	3,712	40.8	21	67
Opponents	105	4,211	40.1	28	68

PUNT RETURNS	No.	FC	Yds.	Avg.	LG	TD
Brightful	45	20	351	7.8	44	0
Reed	5	3	33	6.6	19	0
Ward	3	0	26	8.7	16	0
Ravens	53	23	410	7.7	44	0
Opponents	42	18	354	8.4	44	0

KICKOFF RETURNS	No.	Yds	Avg	LG	TD
Brightful	29	716	24.7	75	0
C. Taylor	23	448	19.5	29	0
M. Smith	2	17	8.5	15	0
A. Thomas	1	21	21.0	21	0
Walls	1	0	0.0	0	0
Ward	1	20	20.0	20	0
Ravens	57	1,222	21.4	75	0
Opponents	70	1,495	21.4	97t	1

FIELD GOALS	1-19	20-29	30-39	40-49	50+
Stover	0/0	16/16	6/6	11/14	0/2
Richey	0/0	0/0	0/0	0/0	1/2
Ravens	0/0	16/16	6/6	11/14	1/4
Opponents	0/0	9/9	5/6	13/14	1/2

SACKS	No.
Suggs	12.0
Boulware	8.5
Weaver	5.0
Douglas	4.5
A. Thomas	4.0
Gregg	3.0
Hartwell	3.0
R. Lewis	1.5
Baxter	1.0
C. Brown	1.0
Kemoeatu	1.0
Reed	1.0
Williams	1.0
Knight	0.5
Ravens	47.0
Opponents	42.0

RECORD HOLDERS

INDIVIDUAL RECORDS—CAREER

Category	Name	Performance
Rushing (Yds.)	Jamal Lewis, 2000-03	4,757
Passing (Yds.)	Vinny Testaverde, 1996-97	7,148
Passing (TDs)	Vinny Testaverde, 1996-97	51
Receiving (No.)	Qadry Ismail, 1999-2001	191
Receiving (Yds.)	Qadry Ismail, 1999-2001	2,819
Interceptions	Rod Woodson, 1998-2001	20
	Duane Starks, 1998-2001	20
	Ray Lewis, 1996-2003	20
Punting (Avg.)	Greg Montgomery, 1996-97	43.2
Punt Return (Avg.)	Jermaine Lewis, 1996-2001	11.8
Kickoff Return (Avg.)	Corey Harris, 1998-2001	23.9
Field Goals	Matt Stover, 1996-2003	213
Touchdowns (Tot.)	Jamal Lewis, 2000-03	27
Points	Matt Stover, 1996-2003	884

INDIVIDUAL RECORDS—SINGLE SEASON

Category	Name	Performance
Rushing (Yds.)	Jamal Lewis, 2003	2,066
Passing (Yds.)	Vinny Testaverde, 1996	4,177
Passing (TDs)	Vinny Testaverde, 1996	33
Receiving (No.)	Michael Jackson, 1996	76
Receiving (Yds.)	Michael Jackson, 1996	1,201
Interceptions	Rod Woodson, 1999	7
	Ed Reed, 2003	7
Punting (Avg.)	Kyle Richardson, 1998	43.9
Punt Return (Avg.)	Jermaine Lewis, 2000	16.1
Kickoff Return (Avg.)	Corey Harris, 1998	27.6
Field Goals	Matt Stover, 2000	35
Touchdowns (Tot.)	Michael Jackson, 1996	14
	Jamal Lewis, 2003	14
Points	Matt Stover, 2000	135

INDIVIDUAL RECORDS—SINGLE GAME

Category	Name	Performance
Rushing (Yds.)	Jamal Lewis, 9-14-03	*295
Passing (Yds.)	Vinny Testaverde, 10-27-96	429
Passing (TDs)	Tony Banks, 9-10-00	5
Receiving (No.)	Priest Holmes, 10-11-98	13
Receiving (Yds.)	Qadry Ismail, 12-12-99	268
Interceptions	Many times	2
	Last time by Ed Reed, 9-14-03	
Field Goals	Matt Stover, 9-21-97, 12-26-99, 10-28-00	5
Touchdowns (Tot.)	Marcus Robinson, 11-23-03	4
Points	Marcus Robinson, 11-23-03	24

*NFL Record

BALTIMORE RAVENS

2004 VETERAN ROSTER

No.	Name	Pos.	Ht.	Wt.	Birthdate	NFL Exp.	College	Hometown	How Acq.	'03 Games/ Starts
66	Anderson, Bennie	G	6-5	345	2/17/77	4	Tennessee State	St. Louis, Mo.	FA-'01	15/15
28	Baxter, Gary	DB	6-2	204	11/24/78	4	Baylor	Tyler, Texas	D2-'01	16/16
7	Boller, Kyle	QB	6-3	220	6/17/81	2	California	Newhall, Calif.	D1b-'03	11/9
58	Boulware, Peter	LB	6-4	255	12/18/74	8	Florida State	Columbia, S.C.	D1-'97	15/15
45	Brightful, Lamont	DB-KR	5-10	160	1/29/79	3	Eastern Washington	Oak Harbor, Wash.	D6a-'02	16/0
77	Brooks, Ethan	T	6-6	310	4/27/72	6	Williams College	Simsbury, Conn.	FA-'02	15/3
90	Brown, Cornell	LB	6-0	240	3/15/75	7	Virginia Tech	Lynchburg, Va.	FA-'02	16/3
78	Brown, Orlando	T	6-7	360	12/12/70	9	South Carolina State	Washington, D.C.	FA-'03	16/13
72	Cook, Damion	T	6-5	335	4/16/79	3	Bethune-Cookman	Fort Lauderdale, Fla.	FA-'02	1/0
47	Demps, Will	S	6-0	205	11/7/79	3	San Diego State	Palmdale, Calif.	FA-'02	16/8
94	Douglas, Marques	DE	6-2	280	3/5/77	5	Howard	Greensboro, N.C.	FA-'01	16/16
62	Flynn, Mike	C	6-3	305	6/15/74	7	Maine	Springfield, Mass.	FA-'97	16/16
91	Franklin, Aubrayo	DT	6-1	320	8/27/80	2	Tennessee	Johnson City, Tenn.	D5a-'03	1/0
26	Fuller, Corey	CB	5-10	220	5/1/71	10	Florida State	Rickards, Fla.	UFA(Cle)-'03	14/10
97	Gregg, Kelly	DT	6-0	310	11/1/76	5	Oklahoma	Edmond, Okla.	FA-'00	16/15
56 †	Hartwell, Edgerton	LB	6-1	250	5/27/78	4	Western Illinois	Las Vegas, Nev.	D4-'01	16/15
86	Heap, Todd	TE	6-5	252	3/16/80	4	Arizona State	Mesa, Ariz.	D1-'01	16/16
84	Hunter, Javin	WR	5-11	190	5/9/80	3	Notre Dame	Detroit, Mich.	D6b-'02	0*
80	Hymes, Randy	WR	6-3	211	8/7/79	3	Grambling State	Galveston, Texas	FA-'02	0*
95	Johnson, Jarret	DE	6-3	285	8/14/81	2	Alabama	Chiefland, Fla.	D4a-'03	15/1
85 t-	Johnson, Kevin	WR	5-11	195	7/15/76	6	Syracuse	Hamilton Township, N.J.	T(Jax)-'04	15/9*
83	Johnson, Ron	WR	6-2	225	5/23/80	3	Minnesota	Detroit, Mich.	D4b-'02	6/0
82	Jones Jr., Terry	TE	6-3	265	12/3/79	3	Alabama	Tuscaloosa, Ala.	D5-'02	16/13
92	Kemoeatu, Maake	DT	6-5	335	1/10/79	3	Utah	Kahuku, Hawaii	FA-'02	15/0
31	Lewis, Jamal	RB	5-11	240	8/29/79	5	Tennessee	Atlanta, Ga.	D1a-'00	16/16
52	Lewis, Ray	LB	6-1	245	5/15/75	9	Miami	Lakeland, Fla.	D1b-'96	16/16
59 †	Maese, Joe	LS	6-0	241	12/2/78	4	New Mexico	Phoenix, Ariz.	D6-'01	16/0
21	McAlister, Chris	CB	6-1	206	6/14/77	6	Arizona	Pasadena, Calif.	D1-'99	15/15
33	Morrow, Harold	FB	5-11	232	2/24/73	10	Auburn	Maplesville, Ala.	FA-'03	14/0
34	Mughelli, Ovie	FB	6-1	260	6/10/80	2	Wake Forest	Charleston, S.C.	D4b-'03	6/0
64	Mulitalo, Edwin	G	6-3	345	9/1/74	6	Arizona	Daly City, Calif.	D4b-'99	15/15
75	Ogden, Jonathan	T	6-9	340	7/31/74	9	UCLA	Washington, D.C.	D1a-'96	16/16
79	Pashos, Tony	T	6-6	337	8/3/80	2	Illinois	Palos Heights, Ill.	D5b-'03	0*
61	Rabach, Casey	G-C	6-4	301	9/24/77	4	Wisconsin	Sturgeon Bay, Wis.	D3-'01	14/2
20	Reed, Ed	S	5-11	200	9/11/78	3	Miami	St. Rose, La.	D1-'02	16/16
39 †	Ricard, Alan	FB	5-11	237	1/17/77	4	Northeast Louisiana	Amite, La.	FA-'00	16/3
9	Richey, Wade	K	6-3	205	5/19/76	7	Louisiana State	Lafayette, La.	FA-'03	15/0
27	Sapp, Gerome	S	6-1	216	2/8/81	2	Notre Dame	Houston, Texas	D6-'03	14/0
57	Scott, Bart	LB	6-2	235	8/18/80	3	Southern Illinois	Detroit, Mich.	FA-'02	16/0
53	Slaughter, T.J.	LB	6-0	233	2/20/77	5	Southern Mississippi	Birmingham, Ala.	FA-'03	7/0
32	Smith, Musa	RB	6-0	232	5/31/82	2	Georgia	Elliottsburg, Pa.	D3-'03	11/0
88	Smith, Trent	TE	6-5	245	9/15/79	2	Oklahoma	Norman, Okla.	D7a-'03	0*
43	Solwold, Mike	LS	6-6	244	9/30/77	4	Wisconsin	Hartland, Wis.	FA-'03	0*
3	Stover, Matt	K	5-11	178	1/27/68	15	Louisiana Tech	Dallas, Texas	PB(NYG)-'91	16/0
55	Suggs, Terrell	LB	6-3	260	10/11/82	2	Arizona State	Chandler, Ariz.	D1a-'03	16/1
29	Taylor, Chester	RB	5-11	213	9/22/79	3	Toledo	River Rouge, Mich.	D6c-'02	16/1
89	Taylor, Travis	WR	6-1	210	3/30/78	5	Florida	Jacksonville, Fla.	D1b-'00	16/16
96	Thomas, Adalius	LB	6-2	270	8/18/77	5	Southern Mississippi	Equality, Ala.	D6a-'00	13/11
38	Walls, Raymond	CB	5-10	188	7/24/79	4	Southern Mississippi	Kentwood, La.	FA-'03	10/0
98	Weaver, Anthony	DE	6-3	290	7/28/80	3	Notre Dame	Saratoga Springs, N.Y.	D2-'02	15/15
49	Williams, Chad	S	5-9	207	1/22/79	3	Southern Mississippi	Birmingham, Ala.	D6d-'02	16/1
2	Wright, Anthony	QB	6-1	211	2/14/76	6	South Carolina	Vanceboro, N.C.	FA-'02	7/7
15	Zastudil, Dave	P	6-3	210	10/26/78	3	Ohio	Bay Village, Ohio	D4a-'02	16/0

* Hunter missed '03 season because of injury; Hymes missed '03 season because of injury; K. Johnson played 9 games with Cleveland and 6 games with Jacksonville in '03; Pashos missed '03 season because of injury; T. Smith missed '03 season because of injury; Solwold inactive for 4 games.

† Unrestricted free agent; subject to developments.

t- Ravens traded for Kev. Johnson (Jax).

Traded—WR Terrell Owens (15 games in '03 with San Francisco) to Philadelphia.

Players lost through free agency (3): TE John Jones (Mia; 11 games in '03), CB Tom Knight (TB; 10), WR Marcus Robinson (Minn; 15).

Also played with Ravens in '03—DE Riddick Parker (6), QB Chris Redman (2), WR Frank Sanders (13).

2004 FIRST-YEAR ROSTER

Name	Pos.	Ht.	Wt.	Birthdate	College	Hometown	How Acq.
Abney, Derek	WR-KR	5-9	180	12/19/80	Kentucky	Scholfield, Wis.	D7a
Allmond, Marcell	CB	6-0	209	5/28/81	Southern California	Santa Fe Springs, Calif.	FA
Barnes, Brandon	LB	6-2	235	6/12/81	Missouri	Columbia, Mo.	FA
Colas, Cols	LB	6-0	233	5/16/80	Virginia Tech	Plantation, Fla.	FA
Crittenden, Monreko	G	6-4	358	3/14/80	Auburn	Montgomery, Ala.	FA
Darling, Devard	WR	6-1	213	4/16/82	Washington State	Houston, Texas	D3
Devoe, Todd (1)	WR	6-2	198	4/5/80	Central Missouri State	Fort Lauderdale, Fla.	FA-'03
Dumas, Eric	T	6-5	316	4/30/81	Maryland	Atlanta, Ga.	FA
Edwards, Dwan	DT	6-3	315	5/16/81	Oregon State	Columbus, Mont.	D2
Eller, Nick	TE	6-3	262	3/27/81	Eastern Illinois	Charleston, Ill.	FA
Frazier, Lance	CB	5-10	183	5/23/81	West Virginia	Delray Beach, Fla.	FA
Gaither, Brian	QB	6-1	221	12/21/79	Western Carolina	Winston Salem, N.C.	FA
Garrett, John	LB	5-11	243	7/4/81	Baylor	Mart, Texas	FA
Goodwin, Douglas	DT	6-1	289	2/28/82	Boston College	Freeport, N.Y.	FA
Greathouse, Clinton	P	5-10	221	5/28/80	Texas Tech	Coppell, Texas	FA
Green, Roderick	LB	6-2	245	4/26/82	Central Missouri State	Brenham, Texas	D5
Harris, Josh	QB	6-1	238	9/9/82	Bowling Green	Westerville, Ohio	D6a
Harrison, James (1)	LB	6-0	240	5/4/78	Kent State	Akron, Ohio	FA
Kelly, Kareem (1)	WR	6-0	186	4/1/81	Southern California	Long Beach, Calif.	FA-'03
Massey, Sam	CB	6-2	205	3/17/81	Morgan State	Camden, Ga.	FA
Mitchell, Jesse	DT	6-0	273	12/27/81	Mississippi	Oxford, Miss.	FA
Moore, Cecil (1)	WR	6-1	210	12/30/80	East Tennessee State	Morristown, Tenn.	FA
Moore, Clarence	WR	6-6	211	9/24/82	Northern Arizona	Buena Park, Calif.	D6b
Muhlbach, Don	LS	6-5	262	8/17/81	Texas A&M	Lufkin, Texas	FA
Norton, Zach	CB	5-11	183	11/19/81	Cincinnati	Lloyd, Fla.	FA
Pierce, Brett	TE	6-5	250	1/7/81	Stanford	Vancouver, Wash.	FA
Quiroga, Robert	WR	6-2	188	2/7/82	Baylor	Waco, Texas	FA
Revill, Dave	S	5-11	203	10/28/80	Utah	Salt Lake City, Utah	FA
Rimpf, Brian	G	6-5	319	2/11/81	East Carolina	Raleigh, N.C.	D7b
Sams, BJ	RB	5-10	187	10/29/80	McNeese State	Mandeville, La.	FA
Smith, Phil	LB	6-1	259	2/17/81	Miami (Ohio)	Oxford, Ohio	FA
Vandermade, Lenny	C	6-2	291	1/3/81	Southern California	Santa Ana, Calif.	FA
Zielinski, Matt	DT	6-2	302	12/2/80	Duke	Amherst, N.Y.	FA

The term NFL Rookie is defined as a player who is in his first season of professional football and has not been on the roster of another professional football team for any regular-season or postseason games. A Rookie is designated by an "R" on NFL rosters. Players who have been active in another professional football league or players who have NFL experience, including either preseason training camp or being on an Active List or Inactive List, or on Reserve/Injured or Reserve/Physically Unable to Perform for fewer than six regular-season games, are termed NFL First-Year Players. An NFL First-Year Player is designated by a "1" on NFL rosters. Thereafter, a player is credited with an additional year of experience for each season in which he accumulates six games on the Active List or Inactive List, or on Reserve/Injured or Reserve/Physically Unable to Perform.

Log on to www.baltimoreravens.com for an up-to-date roster.

BALTIMORE RAVENS

COACHING STAFF

Head Coach,
Brian Billick

Pro Career: Brian Billick, who was named the second head coach in Baltimore Ravens history on January 19, 1999, has compiled a 52-35 record (.598) after his first five years as the Ravens' head coach. Billick has led his team to the playoffs in three of his five seasons, including the Super Bowl XXXV title following the 2000 season. Baltimore defeated the New York giants, 34-7, in Super Bowl XXXV, highlighted by its record-setting defense. Prior to joining the Ravens, Billick coached for the Minnesota Vikings (1992-98), where as offensive coordinator in 1998, the Vikings' offense scored an NFL record for most points in a season (556). In 2000, Billick's defense surrendered only 165 points, the fewest allowed in a 16-game season and also became the first team since 1978 to allow fewer than 1,000 rushing yards (970) in a regular season. Career record: 52-35.

Background: Billick was a honorable mention All-America in 1976 as a tight end at Brigham Young. Played linebacker at Air Force before transferring to Brigham Young. Drafted by the 49ers in the eleventh round of the 1977 draft, was released, and had a brief stint with the Cowboys, but did not play. Coached collegiately at Redlands (1977), Brigham Young (1978), San Diego State (1981-85), Utah State (1986-88), and Stanford (1989-1991). Was the 49ers' assistant director of public relations (1979-1980).

Personal: Born February 28, 1954 in Fairborne, Ohio. He and his wife Kim have two daughters—Aubree and Keegan.

ASSISTANT COACHES

Matt Cavanaugh, offensive coordinator; born October 27, 1956, Youngstown, Ohio. Quarterback Pittsburgh 1974-77. Pro quarterback New England Patriots 1978-1982, San Francisco 49ers 1983-85, Philadelphia Eagles 1986-89, New York Giants 1990-91. College coach: Pittsburgh 1993. Pro coach: Arizona Cardinals 1994-95, San Francisco 49ers 1996, Chicago Bears 1997-98, joined Ravens in 1999.

Jim Colletto, offensive line; born October 2, 1944, San Francisco. Fullback-linebacker UCLA 1964-67. No pro playing experience. College coach: UCLA 1967-68, Brown 1969, Xavier 1970-71, Pacific 1972-74, Cal State-Fullerton 1975-79 (head coach), UCLA 1980-1981, Purdue 1982-84, Arizona State 1985-87, Ohio State 1988-1990, Purdue 1991-96 (head coach), Notre Dame 1997-98. Pro coach: Joined Ravens in 1999.

Jim Fassel, senior consultant; born August 31, 1949, Anaheim, Calif. Quarterback Fullerton College 1967-68, USC 1969-1972. No pro game experience. College coach: Fullerton College 1973, Utah 1976, 1985-89, Weber State 1977-78, Stanford 1979-1983. Pro coach: Hawaii Hawaiians (World League) 1974, New Orleans Breakers (USFL) 1984, New York Giants 1991-92, Denver Broncos 1993-94, Oakland Raiders 1995, Arizona Cardinals 1996, New York Giants 1997-2003, joined Ravens in 2004.

Jedd Fisch, offensive assistant; born May 5, 1976, Livingston, N.J. Attended Florida. No college or pro playing experience. College coach: Florida 1999-2000. Pro coach: Houston Texans 2001-2003, joined Ravens in 2004.

Jeff FitzGerald, outside linebackers; born April 18, 1960, Burbank, Calif. Linebacker Oregon State. No pro player experience. College coach: Cincinnati 1985-86, Alabama 1987-89, San Diego State 1994-97. Pro coach: Tampa Bay Buccaneers 1990-93, Washington Redskins 1998-99, Arizona Cardinals 2000-2003, joined Ravens in 2004.

Jeff Friday, strength and conditioning; born October 11, 1966, Milwaukee, Wis. Attended Wisconsin-Milwaukee. No college or pro playing experience. College coach: Illinois State 1991-92, Northwestern 1992-95. Pro coach: Minnesota Vikings 1996-98, joined Ravens in 1999.

Wade Harman, tight ends/asst. offensive line; born October 1, 1963, Corydon, Iowa. Linebacker Drake 1985, Utah State 1986. No pro playing experience. College coach: Utah State 1987-1991, Pacific 1992-95, Morningside 1996. Pro coach: Minnesota Vikings 1997-98, joined Ravens in 1999.

Johnnie Lynn, secondary; born December 19, 1956, Los Angeles. Defensive back UCLA 1975-78. Pro defensive back New York Jets 1979-1986. College coach: Arizona 1988-1993. Pro coach: Tampa Bay Buccaneers 1994-95, San Francisco 49ers 1996, New York Giants 1997-2003, joined Ravens in 2004.

Mike Nolan, defensive coordinator; born March 7, 1959, Baltimore. Safety Oregon 1978-1980. No pro playing experience. College coach: Oregon 1981, Stanford 1982-83, Rice 1984-85, Louisiana State 1986. Pro coach: Denver Broncos 1987-1992, New York Giants 1993-96, Washington Redskins 1997-99, New York Jets 2000, joined Ravens in 2001.

Mike Pettine, coaching assistant/quality control; born September 25, 1966, Doylestown, Pa. Safety Virginia 1984-87. No pro playing experience. College coach: Pittsburgh 1993-94. Pro coach: Joined Ravens in 2002.

Paul Ricci, asst. strength and conditioning; born November 15, 1969, Elmer, N.J. Offensive lineman Penn State 1988-89. Pro coach: Seattle Seahawks 1993, Philadelphia Eagles 1995-96, Arizona Cardinals 1996-97, joined Ravens in 2002.

Rex Ryan, defensive line; born December 13, 1962, Ardmore, Okla. Defensive end Southwest Oklahoma State 1983-86. No pro playing experience. College coach: Eastern Kentucky 1987-88, New Mexico Highlands 1989, Morehead State 1990-93, Cincinnati 1996-97, Oklahoma 1998. Pro coach: Arizona Cardinals 1994-95, joined Ravens in 1999.

David Shaw, quarterbacks/receivers; born July 31, 1972, San Diego. Wide receiver Stanford 1990-94. No pro playing experience. College coach: Western Washington University 1995-96. Pro coach: Philadelphia Eagles 1997, Oakland Raiders 1998-2001, joined Ravens in 2002.

Matt Simon, running backs; born December 6, 1953, Akron, Ohio. Linebacker Eastern New Mexico 1972-75. No pro playing experience. College coach: Washington 1982-1991, New Mexico 1992-94, North Texas 1994-97 (head coach). Pro coach: Denver Broncos 1998, joined Ravens in 1999.

Mike Singletary, inside linebackers; born October 9, 1958, Houston. Linebacker Baylor 1977-1980. Pro linebacker Chicago Bears 1981-1992. Inducted into Pro Football Hall of Fame 1998. Pro coach: Joined Ravens in 2003.

Bennie Thompson, asst. special teams; born February 10, 1963, New Orleans. Safety Grambling State 1981-84. Pro safety New Orleans 1989-1991, Kansas City Chiefs 1992-93, Cleveland Browns 1994-95, Baltimore Ravens 1996-99. Pro coach: Joined Ravens in 2000.

Dennis Thurman, secondary; born April 13, 1956, Santa Monica, Calif. Safety Southern California 1974-77. Pro defensive back Dallas Cowboys 1978-1985, St. Louis Cardinals 1986. College coach: Southern California 1993-2000. Pro coach: Phoenix Cardinals 1988-89, joined Ravens in 2002.

Phil Zacharias, defensive assistant/outside linebackers; born February 12, 1959, Sewickley, Pa. Running back-linebacker Salem College (W. Va.) 1978-1981. No pro playing experience. College coach: Georgetown College 1981, St. Paul College 1982-84, North Carolina 1985, Morehead State 1986-88, Eastern Michigan 1989-1990, Rutgers 1991-93, Stanford 1995-2001. Pro coach: Joined Ravens in 2002.

Gary Zauner, special teams coordinator; born November 2, 1950, Milwaukee. Punter Wisconsin-La Crosse 1968-1972. No pro playing experience. College coach: Brigham Young 1979-1980, San Diego State 1981-86, New Mexico 1987-88, Long Beach State 1990-91. Pro coach: Minnesota Vikings 1994-2001, joined Ravens in 2002.

American Football Conference
East Division
Team Colors: Dark Navy, Red, Royal, and Nickel
One Bills Drive
Orchard Park, New York 14127-2296
Telephone: (716) 648-1800

2004 SCHEDULE

PRESEASON		Buffalo time
Aug. 15	**Denver**	7:00
Aug. 21	**Tennessee**	7:00
Aug. 28	at Indianapolis	8:00
Sept. 2	at Detroit	8:00

REGULAR SEASON		
Sept. 12	**Jacksonville**	1:00
Sept. 19	at Oakland	4:15
Sept. 26	Open Date	
Oct. 3	**New England**	1:00
Oct. 10	at New York Jets	4:05
Oct. 17	**Miami**	1:00
Oct. 24	at Baltimore	1:00
Oct. 31	**Arizona**	1:00
Nov. 7	**New York Jets**	1:00
Nov. 14	at New England	8:30
Nov. 21	**St. Louis**	1:00
Nov. 28	at Seattle	4:15
Dec. 5	at Miami	1:00
Dec. 12	**Cleveland**	1:00
Dec. 19	at Cincinnati	1:00
Dec. 26	at San Francisco	4:05
Jan. 2	**Pittsburgh**	1:00

Stadium: Ralph Wilson Stadium (opened in 1973) • **Capacity:** 73,967
One Bills Drive
Orchard Park, New York
14127-2296
Playing Surface: AstroPlay
Training Camp: St. John Fisher College
Rochester, New York
14618

RALPH WILSON STADIUM

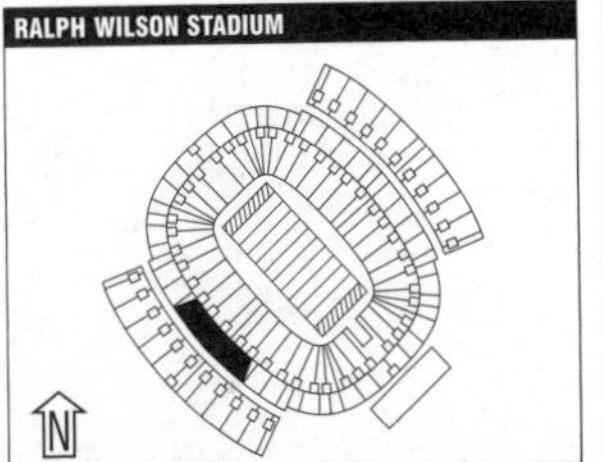

CLUB OFFICIALS

Owner: Ralph C. Wilson, Jr.
President/General Manager: Tom Donahoe
Asst. General Manager: Tom Modrak
Corporate V.P.: Linda Bogdan
Treasurer: Jeffrey C. Littmann
Vice President/Communications: Scott Berchtold
Vice President/Business Development and Marketing: Russ Brandon
Vice President/Operations: Bill Munson
Vice President/Business Administration: Jim Overdorf
Director of Pro Personnel: John Guy
Consultant: Christy Wilson Hofmann
Executive Director/Marketing: Marc Honan
Executive Director/Sales: Pete Guelli
Executive Director/Business Development: Karen Marsch
Director of Merchandising: Julie Regan
Director of Ticket Operations and Customer Service: David Wheat
Director of Archives: Denny Lynch
Director of Community Programs: Gretchen Geitter
Director of Player Programs: Paul Lancaster
Director of Information Technology: Dan Evans
Director of Guest Services & Event Management: Jan Eberle
Director of Stadium Operations: Joseph Frandina
Director of Security: Bill Bambach
Business Manager: Don Purdy
Controller: Frank Wojnicki
Equipment Manager: Dave Hojnowski
Asst. Equipment Manager: Randy Ribbeck
Director of Physical Development and Asst. to the Head Coach: Rusty Jones
Conditioning Assistant: John Allaire
Athletic Trainers: Bud Carpenter, Corey Bennett, Chris Fischetti, Greg McMillen
Video Director: Henry Kunttu
Asst. Video Director: Greg Estes
Scouts: Brad Forsyth, Joe Haering, David Hinson, Doug Majeski, Marc Ross, Bob Ryan, George (Chink) Sengel, David G. Smith, David W. Smith

COACHING HISTORY
(327-354-8)

1960-61	Buster Ramsey	11-16-1
1962-65	Lou Saban	38-18-3
1966-68	Joe Collier*	13-17-1
1968	Harvey Johnson	1-10-1
1969-1970	John Rauch	7-20-1
1971	Harvey Johnson	1-13-0
1972-76	Lou Saban**	32-29-1
1976-77	Jim Ringo	3-20-0
1978-1982	Chuck Knox	38-38-0
1983-85	Kay Stephenson***	10-26-0
1985-86	Hank Bullough****	4-17-0
1986-1997	Marv Levy	123-78-0
1998-2000	Wade Phillips	29-21-0
2001-03	Gregg Williams	17-31-0

*Released after two games in 1968
**Resigned after five games in 1976
***Released after four games in 1985
****Released after nine games in 1986

ATTENDANCE

Home 572,887 Away 568,457
Total 1,141,344
Single-game home record, 80,368 (10/4/92)
Single-season home record, 635,889 (1991)

2004 DRAFT CHOICES

Round	Name	Pos.	College
1	Lee Evans	WR	Wisconsin
	J.P. Losman	QB	Tulane
3	Tim Anderson	DT	Ohio State
4	Tim Euhus	TE	Oregon State
7	Dylan McFarland	T	Montana
	Jonathan Smith	WR	Georgia Tech

BUFFALO BILLS

2003 TEAM RECORD

PRESEASON (3-1)

Date	Result	Opponent
8/9	W 20-19	at Baltimore
8/16	L 24-37	at Tennessee
8/23	W 28-24	St. Louis
8/28	W 22-16	Detroit

REGULAR SEASON (6-10)

Date	Result	Opponent	Att.
9/7	W 31-0	New England	73,262
9/14	W 38-17	at Jacksonville	58,613
9/21	L 7-17	at Miami	73,458
9/28	L 13-23	Philadelphia	73,305
10/5	W 22-16	Cincinnati (OT)	72,615
10/12	L 3-30	at New York Jets	77,740
10/19	W 24-7	Washington	73,149
10/26	L 5-38	at Kansas City	78,689
11/9	L 6-10	at Dallas	63,770
11/16	L 10-12	Houston	72,677
11/23	L 14-17	Indianapolis	73,004
11/30	W 24-7	at New York Giants	78,481
12/7	W 17-6	New York Jets	72,791
12/14	L 26-28	at Tennessee	68,809
12/21	L 3-20	Miami	73,319
12/27	L 0-31	at New England	68,436

(OT) Overtime

SCORE BY PERIODS

Bills	34	81	58	64	6	— 243
Opponents	54	93	54	78	0	— 279

2003 TEAM STATISTICS

	Bills	Opp.
Total First Downs	268	270
Rushing	96	92
Passing	150	153
Penalty	22	25
3rd Down: Made/Att	67/212	86/225
3rd Down Pct.	31.6	38.2
4th Down: Made/Att	13/25	7/13
4th Down Pct.	52.0	53.8
Possession Avg.	29:40	30:20
Total Net Yards	4,348	4,313
Avg. Per Game	271.8	269.6
Total Plays	980	1,010
Avg. Per Play	4.4	4.3
Net Yards Rushing	1,664	1,606
Avg. Per Game	104.0	100.4
Total Rushes	427	464
Net Yards Passing	2,684	2,707
Avg. Per Game	167.8	169.2
Sacked/Yards Lost	51/385	38/231
Gross Yards	3,069	2,938
Att./Completions	502/293	508/285
Completion Pct.	58.4	56.1
Had Intercepted	17	10
Punts/Average	85/44.6	93/38.2
Net Punting Avg.	85/37.1	93/34.2
Penalties/Yards	106/891	110/996
Fumbles/Ball Lost	36/17	22/8
Touchdowns	27	30
Rushing	13	11
Passing	11	18
Returns	3	1

2003 INDIVIDUAL STATISTICS

PASSING	Att.	Comp.	Yds.	Pct.	TD	Int.	Tkld.	Rate
Bledsoe	471	274	2,860	58.2	11	12	49/371	73.0
T. Brown	18	14	160	77.8	0	1	1/7	80.6
Van Pelt	12	5	49	41.7	0	3	1/7	14.2
Henry	1	0	0	0.0	0	1	0/0	0.0
Bills	502	293	3,069	58.4	11	17	51/385	69.4
Opponents	508	285	2,938	56.1	18	10	38/231	76.5

SCORING	TD R	TD P	TD Rt	PAT	FG	Saf	PTS
Lindell	0	0	0	24/24	17/24	0	75
Henry	10	1	0	0/0	0/0	0	66
Shaw	0	4	0	0/0	0/0	0	24
Bledsoe	2	0	0	0/0	0/0	0	12
Moore	0	2	0	0/0	0/0	0	12
Reed	0	2	0	0/0	0/0	0	12
Adams	0	0	1	0/0	0/0	0	6
Campbell	0	1	0	0/0	0/0	0	6
Clements	0	0	1	0/0	0/0	0	6
Morris	1	0	0	0/0	0/0	0	6
Moulds	0	1	0	0/0	0/0	0	6
P. Williams	0	0	1	0/0	0/0	0	6
Prioleau	0	0	0	0/0	0/0	1	2
Bills	13	11	3	24/24	17/24	3	243
Opponents	11	18	1	26/26	23/31	0	279

2-Pt. Conversions: None.
Bills 0-2, Opponents 2-4.

RUSHING	Att.	Yds.	Avg.	LG	TD
Henry	331	1,356	4.1	64	10
Burns	39	113	2.9	12	0
Morris	19	70	3.7	12	1
Reed	3	38	12.7	16	0
Bledsoe	24	29	1.2	11	2
Moorman	1	21	21.0	21	0
A. Brown	1	17	17.0	17	0
Neufeld	1	14	14.0	14	0
T. Brown	1	5	5.0	5	0
Simonton	2	4	2.0	2	0
Gash	1	3	3.0	3	0
Van Pelt	4	-6	-1.5	-1	0
Bills	427	1,664	3.9	64	13
Opponents	464	1,606	3.5	62t	11

RECEIVING	No.	Yds.	Avg.	LG	TD
Moulds	64	780	12.2	49	1
Reed	58	588	10.1	26	2
Shaw	56	732	13.1	54t	4
Campbell	34	339	10.0	31	1
Henry	28	158	5.6	18	1
Morris	14	100	7.1	24	0
Gash	11	83	7.5	18	0
Coleman	8	69	8.6	12	0
Moore	7	82	11.7	28	2
Burns	7	62	8.9	14	0
Neufeld	3	41	13.7	25	0
Aiken	3	35	11.7	19	0
Bills	293	3,069	10.5	54t	11
Opponents	285	2,938	10.3	77t	18

INTERCEPTIONS	No.	Yds.	Avg.	LG	TD
Clements	3	54	18.0	54t	1
McGee	2	5	2.5	3	0
Spikes	2	1	0.5	1	0
Adams	1	37	37.0	37t	1
Winfield	1	11	11.0	11	0
Schobel	1	6	6.0	6	0
Bills	10	114	11.4	54t	2
Opponents	17	186	10.9	74t	1

PUNTING	No.	Yds.	Avg.	In 20	LG
Moorman	85	3,788	44.6	20	71
Bills	85	3,788	44.6	20	71
Opponents	93	3,553	38.2	24	53

PUNT RETURNS	No.	FC	Yds.	Avg.	LG	TD
A. Brown	25	10	111	4.4	18	0
Clements	14	11	137	9.8	35	0
Prioleau	1	0	0	0.0	0	0
Winfield	1	0	0	0.0	0	0
Bills	41	21	248	6.0	35	0
Opponents	52	8	577	11.1	48	0

KICKOFF RETURNS	No.	Yds.	Avg.	LG	TD
A. Brown	48	1,046	21.8	75	0
McGee	8	160	20.0	26	0
Morris	6	146	24.3	52	0
Burns	1	17	17.0	17	0
Bills	63	1,369	21.7	75	0
Opponents	55	1,080	19.6	35	0

FIELD GOALS	1-19	20-29	30-39	40-49	50+
Lindell	0/0	11/12	3/3	3/7	0/2
Bills	0/0	11/12	3/3	3/7	0/2
Opponents	0/0	8/9	9/9	5/8	1/5

SACKS	No.
Schobel	11.5
Posey	5.5
Adams	5.0
Denney	3.5
Milloy	3.0
Fletcher	2.0
Spikes	2.0
McGee	1.0
Winfield	1.0
Wire	1.0
Edwards	0.5
Prioleau	0.5
K. Thomas	0.5
Bills	38.0
Opponents	51.0

RECORD HOLDERS

INDIVIDUAL RECORDS—CAREER

Category	Name	Performance
Rushing (Yds.)	Thurman Thomas, 1988-1999	11,938
Passing (Yds.)	Jim Kelly, 1986-1996	35,467
Passing (TDs)	Jim Kelly, 1986-1996	237
Receiving (No.)	Andre Reed, 1985-1999	941
Receiving (Yds.)	Andre Reed, 1985-1999	13,095
Interceptions	George (Butch) Byrd, 1964-1970	40
Punting (Avg.)	Brian Moorman, 2001-03	42.8
Punt Return (Avg.)	Clifford Hicks, 1990-92	12.2
Kickoff Return (Avg.)	O.J. Simpson, 1969-1977	30.0
Field Goals	Steve Christie, 1992-2000	234
Touchdowns (Tot.)	Andre Reed, 1985-1999	87
	Thurman Thomas, 1988-1999	87
Points	Steve Christie, 1992-2000	1,011

INDIVIDUAL RECORDS—SINGLE SEASON

Category	Name	Performance
Rushing (Yds.)	O.J. Simpson, 1973	2,003
Passing (Yds.)	Drew Bledsoe, 2002	4,359
Passing (TDs)	Jim Kelly, 1991	33
Receiving (No.)	Eric Moulds, 2002	100
Receiving (Yds.)	Eric Moulds, 1998	1,368
Interceptions	Billy Atkins, 1961	10
	Tom Janik, 1967	10
Punting (Avg.)	Paul Maguire, 1969	44.5
Punt Return (Avg.)	Keith Moody, 1977	13.1
Kickoff Return (Avg.)	Ed Rutkowski, 1963	30.2
Field Goals	Steve Christie, 1998	33
Touchdowns (Tot.)	O.J. Simpson, 1975	23
Points	Steve Christie, 1998	140

INDIVIDUAL RECORDS—SINGLE GAME

Category	Name	Performance
Rushing (Yds.)	O.J. Simpson, 11-25-76	273
Passing (Yds.)	Drew Bledsoe, 9-15-02	463
Passing (TDs)	Jim Kelly, 9-8-91	6
Receiving (No.)	Andre Reed, 11-20-94	15
Receiving (Yds.)	Jerry Butler, 9-23-79	255
Interceptions	Many times	3
	Last time by Nate Clements, 10-20-02	
Field Goals	Steve Christie, 10-20-96	6
Touchdowns (Tot.)	Cookie Gilchrist, 12-8-63	5
Points	Cookie Gilchrist, 12-8-63	30

BUFFALO BILLS

2004 VETERAN ROSTER

No.	Name	Pos.	Ht.	Wt.	Birthdate	NFL Exp.	College	Hometown	How Acq.	'03 Games/ Starts
95	Adams, Sam	DT	6-4	335	6/13/73	11	Texas A&M	Houston, Texas	UFA(Oak)-'03	15/15
89	Aiken, Sam	WR	6-2	204	12/14/80	2	North Carolina	Kenansville, N.C.	D4b-'03	5/0
97	Bannan, Justin	DT	6-3	305	4/18/79	3	Colorado	Organerale, Calif.	D5-'02	14/1
11	Bledsoe, Drew	QB	6-5	238	2/14/72	12	Washington State	Ellensburg, Wash.	T(NE)-'02	16/16
86	Brown, Antonio	WR	5-10	175	3/3/78	2	West Virginia	Miami, Fla.	FA-'03	16/0
5	Brown, Travis	QB	6-3	215	7/17/77	5	Northern Arizona	Phoenix, Ariz.	FA-'03	2/0
35	Burns, Joe	RB	5-9	215	9/15/79	3	Georgia Tech	Thomasville, Ga.	FA-'02	16/1
83	Campbell, Mark	TE	6-6	255	12/6/75	6	Michigan	Clawson, Mich.	T(Cle)-'03	16/11
22	Clements, Nate	CB	6-0	209	12/12/79	4	Ohio State	Shaker Heights, Ohio	D1-'01	16/16
85	Coleman, Clarence	WR	5-10	193	6/4/80	2	Ferris State	Miami, Fla.	FA-'02	14/0
55	Crowell, Angelo	LB	6-1	235	8/16/81	2	Virginia	Winston-Salem, N.C.	D3-'03	6/0
92	Denney, Ryan	DE	6-7	275	6/15/77	3	Brigham Young	Thornton, Colo.	D2b-'02	16/13
54	Dorenbos, Jon	LS	6-0	250	7/21/80	2	Texas-El Paso	Garden Grove, Calif.	FA-'03	16/0
98	Edwards, Ron	DT	6-3	320	7/12/79	4	Texas A&M	Houston, Texas	D3a-'01	5/0
59	Fletcher, London	LB	5-10	245	5/19/75	7	John Carroll	Cleveland, Ohio	UFA(StL)-'02	16/16
99	Gibson, Oliver	DT	6-2	310	3/15/72	9	Notre Dame	Chicago, Ill.	FA-'04	16/0*
53	Haggan, Mario	LB	6-3	248	3/3/80	2	Mississippi State	Clarksdale, Miss.	D7-'03	2/0
20	Henry, Travis	RB	5-9	215	10/29/78	4	Tennessee	Frostproof, Fla.	D2b-'01	15/15
75	Jennings, Jonas	T	6-3	325	11/21/77	4	Georgia	College Park, Ga.	D3b-'01	11/11
90	Kelsay, Chris	DE	6-4	275	10/31/79	2	Nebraska	Auburn, Neb.	D2-'03	16/0
9	Lindell, Rian	K	6-3	235	1/20/77	5	Washington State	Vancouver, Wash.	UFA(Sea)-'03	16/0
21	McGahee, Willis	RB	6-0	228	10/21/81	2	Miami	Miami, Fla.	D1-'03	0*
24	McGee, Terrence	CB	5-9	195	10/14/80	2	Northwestern State (La.)	Athens, Texas	D4a-'03	14/2
91	McKenzie, Keith	DE	6-3	267	10/17/73	9	Ball State	Highland Park, Mich.	UFA(GB)-'03	6/0
36	Milloy, Lawyer	S	6-0	190	11/14/73	9	Washington	Tacoma, Wash.	UFA(NE)-'03	16/16
8	Moorman, Brian	P	6-0	175	2/5/76	4	Pittsburg State	Sedgwick, Kan.	FA-'01	16/0
80	Moulds, Eric	WR	6-2	210	7/17/73	9	Mississippi State	Lucedale, Miss.	D1-'96	13/13
88	Neufeld, Ryan	TE	6-4	250	11/22/75	4	UCLA	Morgan Hill, Calif.	FA-'03	16/1
96	Posey, Jeff	LB	6-4	241	8/14/75	7	Southern Mississippi	Bassfield, Miss.	UFA(Hou)-'03	16/16
73	Price, Marcus	T	6-4	310	3/3/72	7	Louisiana State	Port Arthur, Texas	UFA(NO)-'02	16/4
25	Prioleau, Pierson	S	5-11	188	8/6/77	6	Virginia Tech	Alvin, S.C.	UFA(SF)-'01	16/6
61	Pucillo, Mike	G	6-4	311	7/14/79	3	Auburn	Brandon, Fla.	D7a-'02	13/12
82	Reed, Josh	WR	5-10	208	5/1/80	3	Louisiana State	Rayne, La.	D2a-'02	16/16
43	Reese, Izell	S	6-2	195	5/7/74	7	Alabama-Birmingham	Dothan, Ala.	UFA(Den)-'03	13/9
60	Robertson, Bernard	T	6-3	310	6/9/79	3	Tulane	New Orleans, La.	FA-'03	0*
66	Sape, Lauvale	DT	6-1	296	8/29/80	2	Utah	Leilehua, Hawaii	D6-'03	2/0
94	Schobel, Aaron	DE	6-4	262	9/1/77	4	TCU	Columbus, Texas	D2a-'01	16/16
81	Shaw, Bobby	WR	6-1	185	4/23/73	7	California	San Fransico, Calif.	UFA(Jax)-'03	16/7
31	Shelton, Daimon	RB	6-0	262	9/15/72	7	Sacramento State	Duarte, Calif.	FA-'04	0*
30	Simonton, Ken	RB	5-9	191	6/7/79	2	Oregon State	Pittsburg, Calif.	FA-'03	2/0
64	Sobieski, Ben	OT	6-5	315	5/3/79	2	Iowa	Mahtomedi, Minn.	D5-'03	1/0
51	Spikes, Takeo	LB	6-2	242	12/17/76	7	Auburn	Sandersville, Ga.	UFA(Cin)-'03	16/16
57	Stamer, Josh	LB	6-2	238	10/11/77	2	South Dakota	Sutherland, Iowa	FA-'03	16/0
50	Stevenson, Dominique	LB	6-0	235	12/28/77	3	Tennessee	Gaffney, S.C.	D7d-'02	16/0
74	Sullivan, Marques	T	6-5	325	2/2/78	4	Illinois	Chicago, Ill.	D5-'01	6/4
70	Teague, Trey	C	6-5	300	12/27/74	7	Tennessee	Jackson, Tenn.	UFA(Den)-'02	16/16
28	Thomas, Kevin	CB	6-0	182	7/28/78	3	Nevada-Las Vegas	Sacramento, Calif.	D6-'02	6/1
65	Tucker, Ross	G	6-4	316	3/2/79	4	Princeton	Wyomissing, Pa.	W(Dall)-'03	12/5
58	Villarial, Chris	G	6-3	318	6/9/73	9	Indiana (Pa.)	Hershey, Pa.	UFA(Chi)-'04	13/13*
23	Vincent, Troy	CB	6-1	200	6/8/71	13	Wisconson	Trenton, N.J.	UFA(Phil)-'04	13/13*
68	Williams, Mike	T	6-6	360	1/11/80	3	Texas	The Colony, Texas	D1-'02	13/13
93	Williams, Pat	DT	6-3	317	10/24/72	8	Texas A&M	Monroe, La.	FA-'97	16/16
27	Wire, Coy	S	6-0	205	11/7/78	3	Stanford	Camp Hill, Pa.	D3-'02	16/1

* Gibson played 16 games with Cincinnati in '03; McGahee was on the Reserve/Non-football injury list for 8 games and inactive for 8 games; Robertson was inactive for 1 game and did not play for 1 game; Shelton last played with Chicago in '02; Villarial played 13 games with Chicago; Vincent played 13 games with Philadelphia.

Players lost through free agency (5): FB Sam Gash (NO; 16 games in '03), RB Sammy Morris (Mia; 9), LB DaShon Polk (Hou; 16), CB Dainon Sidney (Det; 2), CB Antoine Winfield (Minn; 16).

Also played with Bills in '03—G Ruben Brown (15 games), RB Phil Crosby (3), TE Dave Moore (15), QB Alex Van Pelt (6).

2004 FIRST-YEAR ROSTER

Name	Pos.	Ht.	Wt.	Birthdate	College	Hometown	How Acq.
Acholonu, Dilibe	LB	6-2	239	10/17/80	Washington State	Seattle, Wash.	FA
Anderson, Tim	DT	6-3	304	11/22/80	Ohio State	Clyde, Ohio	D3
Baker, Rashad	CB-S	5-10	198	2/22/82	Tennessee	Camden, N.J.	FA
Beard, Kevin	WR	6-2	173	1/20/81	Miami	Plantation, Fla.	FA
Bonner, Cedric (1)	WR	5-11	181	12/14/78	Texas A&M-Commerce	Dallas, Texas	FA-'03
Case, Tony	G	6-2	285	7/10/82	Adams State	Colorado Springs, Colo.	FA
Chandler, Nathan	QB	6-6	257	10/24/80	Iowa	Southlake, Texas	FA
Euhus, Tim	TE	6-5	249	10/2/80	Oregon State	Eugene, Ore.	D4
Evans, Lee	WR	5-10	197	3/11/81	Wisconsin	Bedford, Ohio	D1a
Giddens, Deon	CB	5-10	181	6/23/81	Tennessee State	Nashville, Tenn.	FA
Graham, Mark	S	6-0	204	10/29/80	Buffalo	Detroit, Mich.	FA
Greer, Jabari	CB	5-11	169	2/11/82	Tennessee	Jackson, Tenn.	FA
Lamar, Johnny	CB	5-10	181	12/6/80	Florida	Ft. Lauderdale, Fla.	FA
Lawton, Luke	FB	5-11	248	8/26/80	McNeese State	Lafayette, La.	FA
Losman, J.P.	QB	6-2	217	3/12/81	Tulane	Venice, Calif.	D1b
McFarland, Dylan	T	6-5	290	7/11/80	Montana	Kalispell, Mont.	D7a
Mitchell, Isaac	RB	5-10	220	1/14/81	Idaho State	Pocatello, Idaho	FA
Myers, Jerel (1)	WR	5-10	180	7/18/81	Louisiana State	Houston, Texas	FA-'03
Peters, Jason	TE-T	6-4	324	1/22/82	Arkansas	Queen City, Texas	FA
Phillips, David	T	6-4	292	9/11/80	Stephen F. Austin	Midland, Texas	FA
Porter, David (1)	T	6-6	311	2/23/80	Iowa	Belleville, Ill.	FA-'03
Richardson, Lawrence	CB	5-9	184	6/17/81	Arkansas	Galveston, Texas	FA
Ritzmann, Constantin	DE	6-3	254	12/20/79	Tennessee	Mellensee, Germany	FA
Seals, Richard (1)	T-G	6-3	308	3/18/76	Utah	Houston, Texas	FA-'03
Sigler, Kurt	C	6-4	306	8/24/80	Eastern Washington	Coeur d'Alene, Idaho	FA
Smith, Jonathan	WR	5-10	194	11/28/81	Georgia Tech	Argyle, Ga.	D7b
Smith, Lawrence (1)	T	6-3	295	8/16/79	Tennessee State	Atlanta, Ga.	FA
Spicer, Michale	DE	6-1	255	6/30/82	Western Carolina	Goldsboro, N.C.	FA
Towns, Darryl	LB	6-0	236	9/21/82	Nevada	Pasadena, Calif.	FA
Trafford, Rod (1)	TE	6-3	250	11/28/78	South Carolina	Morristown, NJ.	FA-'03
Williams, Shaud	RB	5-7	193	10/02/80	Alabama	Andrews, Texas	FA

The term NFL Rookie is defined as a player who is in his first season of professional football and has not been on the roster of another professional football team for any regular-season or postseason games. A Rookie is designated by an "R" on NFL rosters. Players who have been active in another professional football league or players who have NFL experience, including either preseason training camp or being on an Active List or Inactive List, or on Reserve/Injured or Reserve/Physically Unable to Perform for fewer than six regular-season games, are termed NFL First-Year Players. An NFL First-Year Player is designated by a "1" on NFL rosters. Thereafter, a player is credited with an additional year of experience for each season in which he accumulates six games on the Active List or Inactive List, or on Reserve/Injured or Reserve/Physically Unable to Perform.

Log on to www.buffalobills.com for an up-to-date roster.

BUFFALO BILLS

COACHING STAFF

Head Coach,
Mike Mularkey

Pro Career: Enters his first season with the Bills after being named as the thirteenth coach in franchise history on January 14, 2004. Mularkey comes to Buffalo with 10 years experience as an NFL assistant coach and another nine as an NFL player. He spent the last three seasons as the offensive coordinator for the Pittsburgh Steelers (2001-03), who ranked among the NFL's top five overall offenses in two of those three years. In 2001, Mularkey's first as coordinator, Pittsburgh had the league's number one-ranked rushing attack and the third-ranked overall offense. That year, the Steelers posted a 13-3 regular season record, won the AFC Central title, and advanced to the AFC Championship Game. The next year, Pittsburgh had the league's fifth-ranked overall offense and again won the division crown as well as a first-round playoff game before falling 34-31 in overtime to Tennessee in a Divisional Playoff game. Mularkey was named Pittsburgh's offensive coordinator on January 5, 2001 after five seasons as Pittsburgh's tight ends coach. He broke into coaching at Concordia College in 1993 before spending the next two seasons as an assistant with the Tampa Bay Buccaneers. He was selected in the ninth round of the 1983 draft by San Francisco and went on to spend nine seasons as an NFL tight end with the Minnesota Vikings (1983-88) and Pittsburgh Steelers (1989-91). His career statistics include 102 catches for 1,222 yards and 9 touchdowns. Career record: 0-0.
Background: Played collegiately at Florida and finished his Gator career with 55 catches for 628 yards and 3 touchdowns. He later earned a dual degree in kinesiology and sociology from Minnesota.
Personal: Born November 19, 1961 in Fort Lauderdale, Fla. He and his wife, Betsy, have two sons, Shane and Patrick.

ASSISTANT COACHES

Bobby April, special teams coordinator; born April 15, 1963, New Orleans. Linebacker-defensive end Nicholls State 1972-75. No pro playing experience. College coach: Southern Mississippi 1978, Tulane 1979, Arizona 1980-86, Southern California 1987-1990. Pro coach: Atlanta Falcons 1991-93, Pittsburgh Steelers 1994-95, New Orleans Saints 1996-99, St. Louis Rams 2001-02, joined Bills in 2004.
Don Blackmon, linebackers; born March 14, 1958, Pompano Beach, Fla. Linebacker Tulsa 1977-1980. Pro linebacker New England Patriots 1981-87. Pro coach: New England Patriots 1988-1990, Cleveland Browns 1991-92, New York Giants 1993-96, Atlanta Falcons 1997-2001, joined Bills in 2003.
Tom Clements, offensive coordinator; born June 18, 1953, McKees Rocks, Pa. Quarterback Notre Dame 1972-74. Pro quarterback Ottawa Rough Riders (CFL) 1975-78, Hamilton Tiger-Cats (CFL) 1979, 1981-82, Kansas City Chiefs 1980, Winnipeg Blue Bombers (CFL) 1983-87, College coach: Notre Dame 1992-95. Pro coach: New Orleans Saints 1997-99, Kansas City Chiefs 2000, Pittsburgh Steelers 2001-03, joined Bills in 2004.
Jerry Gray, defensive coordinator; born December 16, 1962, Lubbock, Texas. Safety Texas 1981-84. Pro defensive back Los Angeles Rams 1985-1991, Houston Oilers 1992, Tampa Bay Buccaneers 1993. College coach: Southern Methodist 1995-96. Pro coach: Tennessee Titans 1997-2000, joined Bills in 2001.
Rusty Jones, director of physical development and asst. to the head coach; born August 14, 1953, Berwick, Maine. Attended Springfield College. No college or pro playing experience. College coach: Springfield College 1978-79. Pro coach: Pittsburgh Maulers (USFL) 1983-84, joined Bills in 1985.
Tim Krumrie, defensive line; born May 20, 1960, Menomonie, Wis. Defensive tackle Wisconsin 1979-1982. Pro defensive tackle Cincinnati Bengals 1983-1994. No college coaching experience. Pro coach: Cincinnati Bengals 1995-2002, joined Bills in 2003.
Chuck Lester, defensive assistant; born May 18, 1955, Chicago. Linebacker Oklahoma 1974. No pro playing experience. College coach: Iowa State 1980-81, Oklahoma 1982-84. Pro coach: Kansas City Chiefs 1984-86 (scout), joined Bills in 1987.
Jim McNally, offensive line; born December 13, 1943, Buffalo. Guard Buffalo 1961-65. No pro playing experience. College coach: Buffalo 1966-1970, Marshall 1971-74, Boston College 1975-77, Wake Forest 1978-79. Pro coach: Cincinnati Bengals 1980-94, Carolina Panthers 1995-98, New York Giants 1999-2003, joined Bills in 2004.
Mike Miller, tight ends/offensive quality control; born April 9, 1970, Plum Borough, Pa. No college or pro playing experience. College coach: Robert Morris 1997-98. Pro coach: Pittsburgh Steelers 1999-2003, joined Bills in 2004.
Brad Roll, strength & conditioning; born July 4, 1958, Houston. Center Blinn (Tex.) J.C. 1976-77, Stephen F. Austin 1978-79. No pro playing experience. College coach: Stephen F. Austin 1980, Southwestern Louisiana 1981-86, Kansas 1987-88, Miami 1989-1992. Pro coach: Tampa Bay Buccaneers 1993-95, Miami Dolphins 1996-2003, joined Bills in 2004.
Eric Studesville, running backs; born May 29, 1967, Madison, Wis. Defensive back Wisconsin-Whitewater 1985-88. No pro playing experience. College coach: Wingate 1994, Kent State 1995-96. Pro coach: Chicago Bears 1997-2000, New York Giants 2001-03, joined Bills in 2004.
Steve Szabo, defensive backs; born September 11, 1943, Chicago. Halfback-defensive back Navy 1961-64. No pro playing experience. College coach: Johns Hopkins 1969, Toledo 1970, Iowa 1971-73, Syracuse 1974-76, Iowa State 1977-78, Ohio State 1979-1981, Western Michigan 1982-84, Edinboro 1985-87 (head coach), Northern Iowa 1988, Colorado State 1989-1990, Boston College 1991-93. Pro coach: Jacksonville 1995-2002, joined Bills in 2004.
Tyke Tolbert, wide receivers; born September 15, 1967, Conroe, Texas. Wide receiver Louisiana State 1988-90. No pro playing experience. College coach: Louisiana-Monroe 1994-97, Auburn 1998, Louisiana-Lafayette 1999-2001, Florida 2002. Pro coach: Arizona Cardinals 2003, joined Bills in 2004.
Frank Verducci, asst. offensive line/tight ends; born March 17, 1957, Glen Ridge, N.J. Tight end-fullback U.S. Merchant Marine Academy-Kings Point 1975. No pro playing experience. College coach: Colorado State 1980, Maryland 1981-83, Northern Illinois 1984, Iowa 1985-86, 1989-1998, Northwestern 1987-88. Pro coach: Cincinnati Bengals 1999-2001, Dallas Cowboys 2002, joined Bills in 2004.
Sam Wyche, quarterbacks; born January 5, 1945, Atlanta. Quarterback Furman 1963-65. Pro quarterback Cincinnati Bengals 1968-1970, Washington Redskins 1971-73, Detroit Lions 1974, St. Louis Cardinals 1976, Buffalo Bills 1976. College coach: South Carolina 1967, Indiana 1983 (head coach). Pro coach: San Francisco 49ers 1979-1982, Cincinnati 1984-1991 (head coach), Tampa Bay Buccaneers 1992-95 (head coach), joined Bills in 2004.

American Football Conference
North Division
Team Colors: Black, Orange, and White
One Paul Brown Stadium
Cincinnati, Ohio 45202-3492
Telephone: (513) 621-3550
Ticket Office (513) 621-TDTD (8383)

2004 SCHEDULE

PRESEASON — **Cincinnati time**

Aug. 14	at Tampa Bay	7:00
Aug. 21	**New England**	7:30
Aug. 28	at Atlanta	7:30
Sept. 3	**Indianapolis**	7:30

REGULAR SEASON

Sept. 12	at New York Jets	1:00
Sept. 19	**Miami**	8:30
Sept. 26	**Baltimore**	1:00
Oct. 3	at Pittsburgh	1:00
Oct. 10	Open Date	
Oct. 17	at Cleveland	1:00
Oct. 25	**Denver** (Mon.)	9:00
Oct. 31	at Tennessee	1:00
Nov. 7	**Dallas**	1:00
Nov. 14	at Washington	4:05
Nov. 21	**Pittsburgh**	1:00
Nov. 28	**Cleveland**	1:00
Dec. 5	at Baltimore	1:00
Dec. 12	at New England	1:00
Dec. 19	**Buffalo**	1:00
Dec. 26	**New York Giants**	1:00
Jan. 2	at Philadelphia	1:00

Stadium: Paul Brown Stadium (opened in 2000) • **Capacity:** 65,327
One Paul Brown Stadium
Cincinnati, Ohio 45202-3492
Playing Surface: Grass
Training Camp: Georgetown College
Georgetown, Kentucky
40324

PAUL BROWN STADIUM

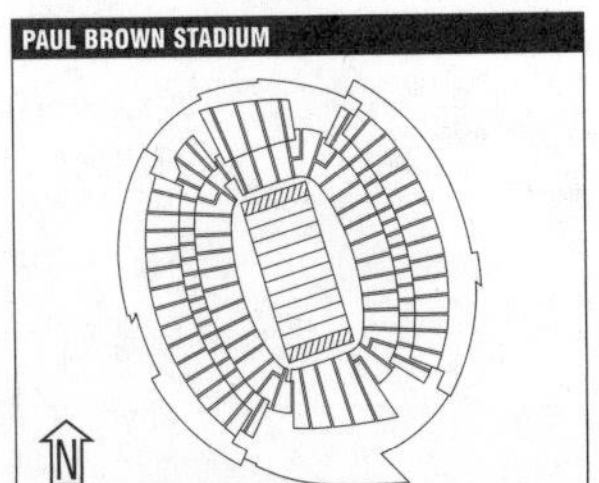

CLUB OFFICIALS

President: Mike Brown
Senior Vice President: Pete Brown
Executive Vice President: Katie Blackburn
Vice President: Paul Brown
Vice President: John Sawyer
Business Development: Troy Blackburn
Business Manager: Bill Connelly
Chief Financial Officer: Bill Scanlon
Controller: Johanna Kappner
Managing Director of Paul Brown Stadium: Eric Brown
Director of Technology: Jo Ann Ralstin
Bengals.com Editor: Geoff Hobson
Director of Sales and Public Affairs: Jeff Berding
Director of Corporate Sales and Marketing: Vince Cicero
Ticket Manager: Tim Kelly
Director of Ticket Sales: Kevin Lane
Director of Player Relations: Eric Ball
Director of Football Operations: Jim Lippincott
Director of Player Personnel: Duke Tobin
Public Relations Director: Jack Brennan
Athletic Trainer: Paul Sparling
Equipment Manager: Rob Recker
Video Director: Travis Brammer

COACHING HISTORY
(239-320-1)

1968-1975	Paul Brown	55-59-1
1976-78	Bill Johnson*	18-15-0
1978-79	Homer Rice	8-19-0
1980-83	Forrest Gregg	34-27-0
1984-1991	Sam Wyche	64-68-0
1992-96	Dave Shula**	19-52-0
1996-2000	Bruce Coslet***	21-39-0
2000-02	Dick LeBeau	12-33-0
2003	Marvin Lewis	8-8-0

* Resigned after five games in 1978
** Released after seven games in 1996
*** Resigned after three games in 2000

ATTENDANCE

Home 468,420 Away 477,613
Total 946,033
Single-game home record, 65,362 (12/28/03)
Single-season home record, 473,288 (1990)

2004 DRAFT CHOICES

Round	Name	Pos.	College
1	Chris Perry	RB	Michigan
2	Keiwan Ratliff	DB	Florida
	Madieu Williams	DB	Maryland
3	Caleb Miller	LB	Arkansas
	Landon Johnson	LB	Purdue
4	Matthias Askew	DT	Michigan State
	Robert Geathers	DE	Georgia
	Stacy Andrews	T	Mississippi
5	Maurice Mann	WR	Nevada
6	Greg Brooks	DB	So. Mississippi
7	Casey Bramlet	QB	Wyoming

CINCINNATI BENGALS

2003 TEAM RECORD

PRESEASON (1-3)

Date	Result	Opponent
8/10	L 13-28	at New York Jets
8/16	W 23-10	Detroit
8/23	L 15-23	Tennessee
8/29	L 20-21	at Indianapolis

REGULAR SEASON (8-8)

Date	Result	Opponent	Att.
9/7	L 10-30	Denver	63,820
9/14	L 20-23	at Oakland	50,135
9/21	L 10-17	Pittsburgh	64,596
9/28	W 21-14	at Cleveland	73,428
10/5	L 16-22	at Buffalo (OT)	72,615
10/19	W 34-26	Baltimore	53,553
10/26	W 27-24	Seattle	52,131
11/2	L 14-17	at Arizona	23,531
11/9	W 34-27	Houston	50,437
11/16	W 24-19	Kansas City	64,923
11/23	W 34-27	at San Diego	52,069
11/30	W 24-20	at Pittsburgh	58,797
12/7	L 13-31	at Baltimore	69,468
12/14	W 41-38	San Francisco	64,666
12/21	L 10-27	at St. Louis	66,061
12/28	L 14-22	Cleveland	65,362

(OT) Overtime

SCORE BY PERIODS

Bengals	83	115	49	99	0 —	346
Opponents	71	117	74	116	6 —	384

2003 TEAM STATISTICS

	Bengals	Opp.
Total First Downs	313	320
Rushing	101	119
Passing	181	177
Penalty	31	24
3rd Down: Made/Att	102/228	85/206
3rd Down Pct.	44.7	41.3
4th Down: Made/Att	5/11	9/14
4th Down Pct.	45.5	64.3
Possession Avg.	30:52	29:08
Total Net Yards	5,329	5,620
Avg. Per Game	333.1	351.3
Total Plays	1,038	999
Avg. Per Play	5.1	5.6
Net Yards Rushing	1,987	2,218
Avg. Per Game	124.2	138.6
Total Rushes	481	461
Net Yards Passing	3,342	3,402
Avg. Per Game	208.9	212.6
Sacked/Yards Lost	37/249	30/196
Gross Yards	3,591	3,598
Att./Completions	520/324	508/297
Completion Pct.	62.3	58.5
Had Intercepted	15	14
Punts/Average	77/39.5	67/42.5
Net Punting Avg.	77/32.2	67/35.1
Penalties/Yards	107/846	108/921
Fumbles/Ball Lost	16/7	26/10
Touchdowns	40	43
Rushing	12	18
Passing	26	23
Returns	2	2

2003 INDIVIDUAL STATISTICS

PASSING	Att.	Comp.	Yds.	Pct.	TD	Int.	Tkld.	Rate
Kitna	520	324	3,591	62.3	26	15	37/249	87.4
Bengals	520	324	3,591	62.3	26	15	37/249	87.4
Opponents	508	297	3,598	58.5	23	14	30/196	83.9

SCORING	TD R	TD P	TD Rt	PAT	FG	Saf	PTS
Graham	0	0	0	40/40	22/25	0	106
C. Johnson	0	10	0	0/0	0/0	0	60
Ru. Johnson	9	0	0	0/0	0/0	0	54
Warrick	0	7	1	0/0	0/0	0	48
Washington	0	4	0	0/0	0/0	0	24
Dillon	2	0	0	0/0	0/0	0	12
J. Johnson	1	1	0	0/0	0/0	0	12
Schobel	0	2	0	0/0	0/0	0	12
Bennett	0	1	0	0/0	0/0	0	6
Hardy	0	0	1	0/0	0/0	0	6
Kelly	0	1	0	0/0	0/0	0	6
Bengals	12	26	2	40/40	22/25	0	346
Opponents	18	23	2	38/38	28/33	0	384

2-Pt. Conversions: None.
Bengals 0-0, Opponents 2-4.

RUSHING	No.	Yds	Avg	LG	TD
Ru. Johnson	215	957	4.5	54	9
Dillon	138	541	3.9	39	2
Bennett	56	173	3.1	19	0
Warrick	18	157	8.7	50	0
Kitna	38	113	3.0	15	0
J. Johnson	15	41	2.7	12	1
Washington	1	5	5.0	5	0
Bengals	481	1,987	4.1	54	12
Opponents	461	2,218	4.8	78t	18

RECEIVING	No.	Yds	Avg	LG	TD
C. Johnson	90	1,355	15.1	82t	10
Warrick	79	819	10.4	77t	7
Bennett	25	176	7.0	16	1
Schobel	24	332	13.8	45t	2
Washington	22	299	13.6	51t	4
Stewart	21	212	10.1	21	0
Ru. Johnson	21	146	7.0	17	0
J. Johnson	15	82	5.5	16	1
Kelly	13	81	6.2	13	1
Dillon	11	71	6.5	14	0
Walter	3	18	6.0	9	0
Bengals	324	3,591	11.1	82t	26
Opponents	297	3,598	12.1	73t	23

INTERCEPTIONS	No.	Yds	Avg	LG	TD
James	4	56	14.0	31	0
Burris	2	17	8.5	17	0
Simmons	2	14	7.0	13	0
Beckett	2	11	5.5	11	0
Kaesviharn	1	10	10.0	10	0
Hawkins	1	8	8.0	8	0
Roberts	1	6	6.0	6	0
Roman	1	1	1.0	1	0
Bengals	14	123	8.8	31	0
Opponents	15	225	15.0	83t	2

PUNTING	No.	Yds.	Avg.	In 20	LG
Richardson	49	1,961	40.0	9	58
Harris	28	1,084	38.7	5	53
Bengals	77	3,045	39.5	14	58
Opponents	67	2,845	42.5	21	72

PUNT RETURNS	Ret	FC	Yds	Avg	LG	TD
Warrick	25	8	273	10.9	68t	1
Burris	5	0	58	11.6	34	0
Bengals	30	8	331	11.0	68t	1
Opponents	47	7	403	8.6	37	0

KICKOFF RETURNS	No.	Yds	Avg	LG	TD
Bennett	53	1,146	21.6	46	0
Roberts	7	128	18.3	23	0
Watson	7	113	16.1	27	0
Ru. Johnson	2	23	11.5	15	0
Powell	2	33	16.5	20	0
J. Johnson	1	16	16.0	16	0
Steele	1	2	2.0	2	0
Stewart	1	13	13.0	13	0
Bengals	74	1,474	19.9	46	0
Opponents	71	1,470	20.7	45	0

FIELD GOALS	1-19	20-29	30-39	40-49	50+
Graham	0/0	5/5	10/10	7/8	0/2
Bengals	0/0	5/5	10/10	7/8	0/2
Opponents	1/1	11/12	9/11	5/7	2/2

SACKS	No.
Clemons	6.0
Thornton	6.0
J. Smith	5.0
Beckett	3.0
Williams	2.0
Hardy	1.5
Simmons	1.5
James	1.0
Kaesviharn	1.0
Roberts	1.0
Gibson	0.5
Powell	0.5
Roman	0.5
Steele	0.5
Bengals	30.0
Opponents	37.0

RECORD HOLDERS

INDIVIDUAL RECORDS—CAREER

Category	Name	Performance
Rushing (Yds.)	Corey Dillon, 1997-2003	8,061
Passing (Yds.)	Ken Anderson, 1971-1986	32,838
Passing (TDs)	Ken Anderson, 1971-1986	197
Receiving (No.)	Carl Pickens, 1992-99	530
Receiving (Yds.)	Isaac Curtis, 1973-1984	7,101
Interceptions	Ken Riley, 1969-1983	65
Punting (Avg.)	Dave Lewis, 1970-73	43.8
Punt Return (Avg.)	Mike Martin, 1983-89	9.9
Kickoff Return (Avg.)	Lemar Parrish, 1970-77	24.7
Field Goals	Jim Breech, 1980-1992	225
Touchdowns (Tot.)	Pete Johnson, 1977-1983	70
Points	Jim Breech, 1980-1992	1,151

INDIVIDUAL RECORDS—SINGLE SEASON

Category	Name	Performance
Rushing (Yds.)	Corey Dillon, 2000	1,435
Passing (Yds.)	Boomer Esiason, 1986	3,959
Passing (TDs)	Ken Anderson, 1981	29
Receiving (No.)	Carl Pickens, 1996	100
Receiving (Yds.)	Chad Johnson, 2003	1,355
Interceptions	Ken Riley, 1976	9
Punting (Avg.)	Dave Lewis, 1970	46.2
Punt Return (Avg.)	Lemar Parrish, 1974	18.8
Kickoff Return (Avg.)	Tremain Mack, 1999	27.1
Field Goals	Doug Pelfrey, 1995	29
Touchdowns (Tot.)	Carl Pickens, 1995	17
Points	Doug Pelfrey, 1995	121

INDIVIDUAL RECORDS—SINGLE GAME

Category	Name	Performance
Rushing (Yds.)	Corey Dillon, 10-22-00	278
Passing (Yds.)	Boomer Esiason, 10-7-90	490
Passing (TDs)	Boomer Esiason, 12-21-86	5
	Boomer Esiason, 10-29-89	5
Receiving (No.)	Carl Pickens, 10-11-98	13
Receiving (Yds.)	Eddie Brown, 11-6-88	216
Interceptions	Many times	3
	Last time by David Fulcher, 12-17-89	
Field Goals	Doug Pelfrey, 11-6-94	6
Touchdowns (Tot.)	Larry Kinnebrew, 10-28-84	4
	Corey Dillon, 12-4-97	4
Points	Larry Kinnebrew, 10-28-84	24
	Corey Dillon, 12-4-97	24

*NFL Record

CINCINNATI BENGALS

2004 VETERAN ROSTER

No.	Name	Pos.	Ht.	Wt.	Birthdate	NFL Exp.	College	Hometown	How Acq.	'03 Games/ Starts
53	Abdullah, Khalid	LB	6-2	227	3/6/79	2	Mars Hill	Jacksonville Beach, Fla.	D5-'03	16/0
71	Anderson, Willie	T	6-5	340	7/11/75	9	Auburn	Whistler, Ala.	D1-'96	16/16
45	Beckett, Rogers	S	6-2	207	1/31/77	5	Marshall	Apopka, Fla.	W(SD)-'03	16/9
74	Braham, Rich	C	6-4	305	11/6/70	11	West Virginia	Morgantown, W.Va.	W(Ariz)-'94	16/15
55	Chamberlin, Frank	LB	6-1	238	1/2/78	4	Boston College	Mahwah, N.J.	FA-'03	5/0
92	Clemons, Duane	DE	6-5	275	5/23/74	9	California	Riverside, Calif.	FA-'03	16/13
29	Goodman, Herbert	RB	5-11	205	8/31/77	3	Graceland College	Homestead, Fla.	FA-'04	0*
17	Graham, Shayne	K	6-0	197	12/9/77	4	Virginia Tech	Dublin, Va.	W(Car)-'03	16/0
51	Hardy, Kevin	LB	6-4	259	7/24/73	9	Illinois	Evansville, Ind.	UFA(Dall)-'03	16/16
22	Herring, Kim	S	6-0	200	9/10/75	8	Penn State	Solon, Ohio	FA-'04	0*
38	Hicks, Skip	RB	6-0	230	10/13/74	5	UCLA	Burkburnett, Texas	FA-'04	0*
84	Houshmandzadeh, T.J.	WR	6-1	197	9/26/77	4	Oregon State	Barstow, Calif.	D7-'01	2/0
95	Jackson, LaDairis	LB	6-2	260	6/16/79	3	Oregon State	Gardena, Calif.	FA-'04	0*
20	James, Tory	CB	6-2	186	5/18/73	9	Louisiana State	Marrero, La.	FA-'03	16/16
85	Johnson, Chad	WR	6-1	192	1/9/78	4	Oregon State	Miami, Fla.	D2-'01	16/14
31	Johnson, Jeremi	FB	5-11	265	9/4/80	2	Western Kentucky	Louisville, Ky.	D4b-'03	16/13
88	Johnson, Patrick	WR	5-10	196	8/10/76	7	Oregon	Gainesville, Ga.	UFA(Wash)-'04	16/2*
32	Johnson, Rudi	RB	5-10	220	10/1/79	4	Auburn	Ettrick, Va.	D4-'01	13/5
76	Jones, Levi	T	6-5	310	8/24/79	3	Arizona State	Eloy, Ariz.	D1-'02	16/16
42	Joseph, Ricot	S	6-0	195	6/16/78	2	Central Florida	Lake Worth, Fla.	FA-'04	0*
34	Kaesviharn, Kevin	S	6-1	194	8/29/76	4	Augustana (S.D.)	Lakeville, Minn.	FA-'01	16/7
82	Kelly, Reggie	TE	6-4	255	2/22/77	6	Mississippi State	Aberdeen, Miss.	UFA(Atl)-'03	12/11
3	Kitna, Jon	QB	6-2	220	9/21/72	8	Central Washington	Tacoma, Wash.	UFA(Sea)-'01	16/16
75	Kooistra, Scott	T	6-6	320	10/14/80	2	North Carolina State	Cary, N.C.	D7a-'03	8/0
52	Levels, Dwayne	LB	6-2	248	5/9/79	2	Oklahoma State	Richardson, Texas	FA-'02	13/1
77	Leyva, Victor	G	6-4	307	12/18/77	4	Arizona State	Porterville, Calif.	D5-'01	0*
44	Manuel, Marquand	S	6-0	209	7/11/79	3	Florida	Miami, Fla.	D6-'02	13/1
6	#Matthews, Shane	QB	6-3	199	6/1/70	11	Florida	Pascagoula, Miss.	FA-'03	0*
69	McCleary, Norris	DT	6-6	305	5/10/77	2	East Carolina	Shelby, N.C.	FA-'04	0*
50	Moore, Larry	C	6-2	309	6/1/75	7	Brigham Young	La Mesa, Calif.	FA-'04	9/8*
37	Myles, Reggie	CB	5-11	185	10/10/79	3	Alabama	Pascagoula, Miss.	FA-'02	16/0
24	t-O'Neal, Deltha	CB	5-11	190	1/30/77	5	California	Milpitas, Calif.	T(Den)-'04	13/6*
9	Palmer, Carson	QB	6-5	230	12/27/79	2	Southern California	Laguna Hills, Calif.	D1-'03	0*
98	Patterson, Elton	DE	6-2	271	6/3/81	2	Central Florida	Tallahassee, Fla.	D7b-'03	0*
21	Porter, Alvin	CB	5-11	175	5/10/77	3	Oklahoma State	Dallas, Texas	FA-'04	1/0*
72	Powell, Carl	DE	6-2	285	1/4/74	6	Louisville	Detroit, Mich.	UFA(Wash)-'03	16/3
10	Richardson, Kyle	P	6-2	210	3/2/73	7	Arkansas State	Farmington, Mo.	FA-'03	11/0
30	Roberts, Terrell	CB	5-10	197	4/7/81	2	Oregon State	Richmond, Calif.	FA-'03	12/0
57	Ross, Adrian	LB	6-2	245	2/19/75	7	Colorado State	San Jose, Calif.	FA-'98	15/12
48	St. Louis, Brad	LS-TE	6-3	247	8/19/76	5	Southwest Missouri State	Belton, Mo.	D7-'00	16/0
89	Schobel, Matt	TE	6-5	257	11/4/78	3	TCU	Columbus, Texas	D3-'02	15/1
93	Scott, Greg	DE	6-4	293	10/2/79	2	Hampton	Courtland, Va.	FA-'04	0*
56	Simmons, Brian	LB	6-3	244	6/21/75	7	North Carolina	New Bern, N.C.	D1b-'98	16/16
90	Smith, Justin	DE	6-4	270	9/30/79	4	Missouri	Holt's Summit, Mo.	D1-'01	16/16
70	#Steele, Glen	DT	6-4	300	10/4/74	7	Michigan	Ligonier, Ind.	D4-'98	16/0
65	Steinbach, Eric	G	6-6	297	4/4/80	2	Iowa	Lockport, Ill.	D2-'03	15/15
86	Stewart, Tony	TE	6-5	260	8/9/79	4	Penn State	Allentown, Pa.	W(Phil)-'02	16/7
62	Sulfsted, Alex	G	6-3	320	12/21/77	3	Miami (Ohio)	Cincinnati, Ohio	FA-'03	0*
66	Szalay, Thatcher	C	6-4	303	1/18/79	2	Montana	Whitefish, Mont.	FA-'03	0*
97	Thornton, John	DT	6-3	297	10/2/76	6	West Virginia	Philadelphia, Pa.	UFA(Tenn)-'03	16/16
83	Walter, Kevin	WR	6-3	218	8/4/81	2	Eastern Michigan	Libertyville, Ill.	W(NYG)-'03	11/0
80	Warrick, Peter	WR-PR	5-11	192	6/19/77	5	Florida State	Bradenton, Fla.	D1-'00	15/14
87	Washington, Kelley	WR	6-3	218	8/21/79	2	Tennessee	Stephens City, Va.	D3-'03	16/3
33	Watson, Kenny	RB	5-11	218	3/13/78	3	Penn State	Harrisburg, Pa.	FA-'03	8/0
23	Weathersby, Dennis	CB	6-1	204	6/16/80	2	Oregon State	Duarte, Calif.	D4a-'03	4/0
58	Webster, Nate	LB	6-0	230	11/29/77	5	Miami	Miami, Fla.	UFA(TB)-'04	15/5*
63	Williams, Bobbie	G	6-3	320	9/25/76	5	Arkansas	Jefferson, Texas	UFA(Phil)-'04	16/11*
94	Williams, Tony	DT	6-2	296	7/9/75	8	Memphis	Memphis, Tenn.	UFA(Minn)-'01	16/16

* Goodman last active with Green Bay in '01; Herring missed '03 season because of injury with St. Louis; Hicks last active with Carolina '02; Jackson did not play in 1 game with Washington; P. Johnson played 16 games for Washington in '03; Joseph last active with Washington in '02; Leyva inactive for 10 games and did not play in 6 games; Matthews did not play in 9 games and inactive for 7 games; McCleary last active with Seattle in '02; Moore played 9 games with Washington; O'Neal played 13 games with Denver; Palmer inactive for 9 games and did not play in 7 games; Patterson inactive for 16 games; Porter played 1 game with Baltimore; Scott last active with Washington in '02; Sulfsted inactive for 3 games; Szalay inactive for 1 game with Cincinnati; Webster played 15 games with Tampa Bay; B. Williams played 16 games with Philadelphia.

\# Unrestricted free agent; subject to developments.

t- Bengals traded for O'Neal (Den).

Players lost through free agency (4): RB Brandon Bennett (TB; 16 games in '03), G Mike Goff (SD; 16), G Matt O'Dwyer (TB; 4), S Mark Roman (GB; 16).

Also played with Bengals in '03—CB Jeff Burris (13 games), RB Corey Dillon (13), FB Chris Edmonds (4), DT Oliver Gibson (16), WR Lawrence Hamilton (5), P Nick Harris (5), CB Artrell Hawkins (14), LB Riall Johnson (13), G Scott Rehberg (16).

2004 FIRST-YEAR ROSTER

Name	Pos.	Ht.	Wt.	Birthdate	College	Hometown	How Acq.
Andrews, Stacy	T	6-6	342	6/2/81	Mississippi	Camden, Ark.	D4c
Askew, Matthias	DT	6-5	308	7/1/82	Michigan State	Ft. Lauderdale, Fla.	D4a
Ayers, Nick	RB	5-10	236	7/16/80	Georgetown (Ky.)	Cincinnati, Ohio	FA
Bramlet, Casey	QB	6-4	225	4/2/81	Wyoming	Wheatland, Wyo.	D7
Brooks, Greg	CB	5-11	177	12/16/80	Southern Mississippi	New Orleans, La.	D6
Broussard, Jamall	WR	5-9	172	8/19/81	San Jose State	Kingwood, Texas	FA
Crawford, Derrick	DE	6-3	279	9/13/78	Texas A&M-Commerce	Avon Park, Fla.	FA
Dickerson, Mondre	DT	6-4	316	7/1/82	Tennessee	Memphis, Tenn.	FA
Geathers, Robert	DE	6-3	271	8/11/83	Georgia	Georgetown, S.C.	D4b
Jackson, Kenny (1)	LB	6-2	253	9/30/76	Nevada	Santa Monica, Calif.	FA
Johnson, Belton (1)	T	6-6	303	7/23/80	Mississippi	Coffeeville, Miss.	FA
Johnson, Landon	LB	6-2	227	3/13/81	Purdue	Lubbock, Texas	D3b
Larson, Kyle	P	6-1	204	9/2/80	Nebraska	Funk, Neb.	FA
Lougheed, Pete (1)	T	6-5	300	1/5/79	Purdue	Fort Wayne, Ind.	FA
Lynch, James (1)	FB	5-11	276	6/17/82	Maryland	Washington, D.C.	FA
Mabry, Mike (1)	C	6-1	300	4/26/80	Central Florida	Dayton, Texas	FA
Mann, Maurice	WR	6-2	191	9/14/82	Nevada	Seaside, Calif.	D5
Mays, Marlus	WR	6-0	204	10/10/80	Northern Iowa	Kansas City, Mo.	FA
Miller, Caleb	LB	6-3	225	9/3/80	Arkansas	Sulphur Springs, Texas	D3a
Moore, Langston (1)	DT	6-1	303	7/17/81	South Carolina	Charleston, S.C.	FA-'03
Perry, Chris	RB	6-0	224	12/27/81	Michigan	Advance, N.C.	D1
Pritchett, Jonathan	TE	6-3	252	6/6/80	Houston	Friendswood, Texas	FA
Ratliff, Keiwan	CB	5-10	194	4/19/81	Florida	Columbus, Ohio	D2a
Rislov, Scott	QB	6-1	224	6/29/80	San Jose State	Pierre, S.D.	FA
Sands, Justin (1)	T	6-7	315	4/3/80	Kansas	Lawton, Iowa	FA
Siofele, Joe	LB	6-2	245	4/15/81	Arizona	Waipahu, Hawaii	FA
Stevens, Larry	LB	6-2	241	1/22/82	Michigan	Tacoma, Wash.	FA
Wade, Alex	FB	6-0	248	2/12/81	Duke	Newtown, Pa.	FA
Walker, Michael	TE	6-5	245	5/6/79	Minnesota-Morris	Scottsdale, Ariz.	FA
Williams, Madieu	S	6-1	193	10/18/81	Maryland	Lanham, Md.	D2b
Williams, Wendell	S	6-1	215	10/20/81	Louisiana-Lafayette	Baton Rouge, La.	FA
Woolridge, Michael	TE	6-1	237	7/2/82	Eastern Kentucky	Columbus, Ga.	FA
Young, Lance	WR	6-1	181	6/8/81	Iowa State	St. Louis, Mo.	FA
Ziesel, Adam (1)	WR	6-2	194	4/16/81	Missouri Western	St. Joseph, Mo.	FA

The term NFL Rookie is defined as a player who is in his first season of professional football and has not been on the roster of another professional football team for any regular-season or postseason games. A Rookie is designated by an "R" on NFL rosters. Players who have been active in another professional football league or players who have NFL experience, including either preseason training camp or being on an Active List or Inactive List, or on Reserve/Injured or Reserve/Physically Unable to Perform for fewer than six regular-season games, are termed NFL First-Year Players. An NFL First-Year Player is designated by a "1" on NFL rosters. Thereafter, a player is credited with an additional year of experience for each season in which he accumulates six games on the Active List or Inactive List, or on Reserve/Injured or Reserve/Physically Unable to Perform.

Log on to www.bengals.com for an up-to-date roster.

COACHING STAFF

Head Coach,
Marvin Lewis

Pro Career: A record-setting NFL defensive coordinator, Lewis was named the ninth head coach in Bengals history on January 14, 2003. In his first season as head coach, Lewis guided the Bengals to an 8-8 record, a six-game improvement over the previous season. Cincinnati posted its best record since 1996 and its second-place finish in the AFC North was the club's best since 1995. Lewis was named rookie coach of the year by *Football Digest*. Lewis directed the NFL's fifth-ranked defensive unit in 2002 with the Washington Redskins, serving as assistant head coach in addition to his coordinator's role. He spent six seasons (1996-2001) as defensive coordinator with the Baltimore Ravens, a tenure that included a Super Bowl victory following the 2000 season. In the 2000 regular season, Lewis' Baltimore defense set the NFL record for fewest points allowed in a 16-game campaign (165). It also finished first in the NFL in rushing yards allowed (970), rushing average allowed (2.7), total takeaways (49), fumble recoveries (26), and shutouts (4). Lewis' 2000 defensive unit has been widely considered as one of the best NFL defenses of all time. The 970 rushing yards allowed was the fewest in NFL history for a 16-game season. The Ravens' four shutouts were the most by an NFL team since Pittsburgh had five in 1976. Lewis has 22 years of coaching experience. Prior to his tenure with the Ravens, he spent four seasons (1992-95) with the Pittsburgh Steelers as linebackers coach. He taught some of the NFL's best linebackers, including Pro Bowl selections Kevin Greene, Chad Brown, Levon Kirkland, and Greg Lloyd. Lewis began his coaching career working four seasons (1981-84) with the linebackers at his alma mater, Idaho State. Also nicknamed the Bengals, Idaho State finished 12-1 during Lewis' first season and won the NCAA Division I-AA championship. Lewis was also a linebackers coach at Long Beach State (1985-86), New Mexico (1987-89), and Pittsburgh (1990-91). Career record: 8-8.

Background: Lewis earned All-Big Sky Conference honors as a linebacker at Idaho State for three consecutive years (1978-1980), and he also saw action at quarterback and free safety. He received his bachelor's degree in physical education from Idaho State in 1981, and earned his Master's degree in athletic administration from the school in 1982. He was inducted into Idaho State's Hall of Fame in 2001.

Personal: Born Sept. 23, 1958, McDonald, Pa. Lewis and his wife, Peggy, have a daughter, Whitney, and a son, Marcus.

ASSISTANT COACHES

Paul Alexander, asst. head coach/offensive line; born February 12, 1960, Rochester, N.Y. Tackle Cortland State 1979-1981. No pro playing experience. College coach: Penn State 1982-84, Michigan 1985-86, Central Michigan 1987-1991. Pro coach: New York Jets 1992-93, joined Bengals in 1994.

Jim Anderson, running backs; born March 27, 1948, Harrisburg, Pa. Linebacker-defensive end California Western 1967-1970. No pro playing experience. College coach: California Western 1970-71, Scottsdale (Ariz.) C.C. 1973, Nevada-Las Vegas 1974-75, Southern Methodist 1976-1980, Stanford 1981-83. Pro coach: Joined Bengals in 1984.

Bob Bratkowski, offensive coordinator; born December 22, 1995, San Angelo, Texas. Wide receiver Washington State. No pro playing experience. College coach: Missouri 1978-1980, Weber State 1981-85, Wyoming 1986, Washington State 1987-88, Miami 1989-1991. Pro coach: Seattle Seahawks 1992-98, Pittsburgh Steelers 1999-2000, joined Bengals in 2001.

Chuck Bresnahan, assistant; born September 8, 1960, Springfield, Mass. Linebacker Navy 1979-1982. No pro playing experience. College coach: Navy 1983, 1986, Georgia Tech 1987-1991, Maine 1992-93. Pro coach: Cleveland Browns 1994-95, Indianapolis Colts 1996-97, Oakland Raiders 1998-2003, joined Bengals in 2004.

Louie Cioffi, asst. defensive backs; born September 21, 1973, Greenlawn, N.Y. Attended SUNY-Stony Brook. No college or pro playing experience. College coach: C.W. Post 1995-96. Pro coach: New York Jets 1993-94, joined Bengals in 1997.

Kevin Coyle, defensive backs; born January 14, 1956, Staten Island, N.Y. Defensive back Massachusetts 1975-77. No pro playing experience. College coach: Cincinnati 1978-79, Arkansas 1980, U.S. Merchant Marine Academy 1981, Holy Cross 1982-1990, Syracuse 1991-93, Maryland 1994-96, Fresno State 1997-2000. Pro coach: Joined Bengals in 2001.

Leslie Frazier, defensive coordinator; born April 3, 1959, Columbus, Miss. Defensive back Alcorn State 1979-1980. Pro defensive back Chicago Bears 1981-86. College coach: Trinity (Ill.) College 1988-1996 (head coach), Illinois 1997-98. Pro coach: Philadelphia Eagles 1999-2002, joined Bengals in 2003.

Jay Hayes, defensive line; born March 3, 1960, South Fayette, Pa. Defensive end Idaho 1978-1981. Pro defensive end-linebacker Michigan Panthers (USFL) 1984, Memphis Showboats (USFL) 1985. College coach: Notre Dame 1988-1991, California 1992-94, Wisconsin 1995-98. Pro coach: Pittsburgh Steelers 1999-2001, Minnesota Vikings 2002, joined Bengals in 2003.

Jonathan Hayes, tight ends; born Aug. 11, 1962, South Fayette, Pa. Linebacker-tight end Iowa 1981-84. Pro tight end Kansas City Chiefs 1985-1993, Pittsburgh Steelers 1994-96. College coach: Oklahoma 1999-2002. Pro coach: Joined Bengals in 2003.

Ricky Hunley, linebackers; born November 11, 1961, Petersburg, Va. Linebacker Arizona 1980-83. Pro linebacker Denver Broncos 1984-87, Los Angeles Raiders 1989-1990. College coach: Southern California 1992-93, Missouri 1994-2000, Florida 2001. Pro coach: Washington Redskins 2002, joined Bengals in 2003.

Hue Jackson, wide receivers; born October 22, 1965, Los Angeles. Quarterback Pacific 1985-86. No pro playing experience. College coach: Pacific 1987-89, Cal State-Fullerton 1990, Arizona State 1992-95, California 1996, Southern California 1997-2000. Pro coach: London Monarchs (WFL) 1991, Washington Redskins 2001-03, joined Bengals in 2004.

Chip Morton, strength and conditioning; born November 27, 1962, Hamden, Conn. Attended North Carolina. No college or pro playing experience. College coach: Ohio State 1985-86, Penn State 1987-1991. Pro coach: San Diego Chargers 1992-94, Carolina Panthers 1995-98, Baltimore Ravens 1999-2001, Washington Redskins 2002, joined Bengals in 2003.

Ray Oliver, asst. strength and conditioning; born June 6, 1961, Cincinnati. Defensive back Ohio State 1980-81. College coach: Pittsburgh 1985-88, Kentucky 1989-1991, South Carolina 1993-95, Memphis 2001-03. Pro coach: Tampa Bay Buccaneers 1992, New Jersey Nets (NBA) 1996-97, joined Bengals in 2004.

Darrin Simmons, special teams; born April 9, 1973, Elkhart, Kan. Punter Kansas 1993-95. No pro playing experience. College coach: Kansas 1996, Minnesota 1997. Pro coach: Baltimore Ravens 1998, Carolina Panthers 1999-2002, joined Bengals in 2003.

Bob Surace, offensive assistant; born April 25, 1968, Harrisburg, Pa. Center Princeton 1987-89. No pro playing experience. College coach: Springfield College 1990-91, Maine Maritime Academy 1992-93, Rensselaer Polytechnic Institute 1995, Western Connecticut State 1996-2001 (head coach 2000-01). Pro coach: Shreveport Pirates (CFL) 1994, joined Bengals in 2002.

Ken Zampese, quarterbacks; born July 19, 1967, Santa Maria, Calif. Wide receiver San Diego 1985-88. No pro playing experience. College coach: San Diego 1989, Southern California 1990-91, Northern Arizona 1992-95, Miami (Ohio) 1996-97. Pro coach: Philadelphia Eagles 1998, Green Bay Packers 1999, St. Louis Rams 2000-02, joined Bengals in 2003.

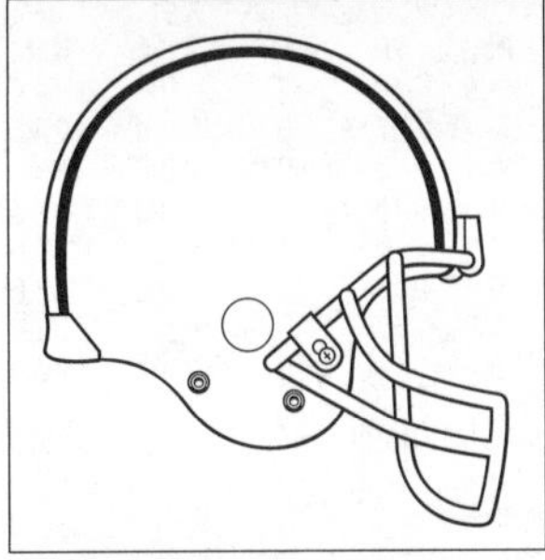

American Football Conference
North Division
Team Colors: Brown, Orange, and White
76 Lou Groza Blvd.
Berea, Ohio 44017
Telephone: (440) 891-5000

2004 SCHEDULE

PRESEASON		Cleveland time
Aug. 14	at Tennessee	8:00
Aug. 21	**Detroit**	4:30
Aug. 28	at Kansas City	8:00
Sept. 3	**Chicago**	8:00

REGULAR SEASON		
Sept. 12	**Baltimore**	1:00
Sept. 19	at Dallas	4:15
Sept. 26	at New York Giants	1:00
Oct. 3	**Washington**	1:00
Oct. 10	at Pittsburgh	1:00
Oct. 17	**Cincinnati**	1:00
Oct. 24	**Philadelphia**	1:00
Oct. 31	Open Date	
Nov. 7	at Baltimore	8:30
Nov. 14	**Pittsburgh**	1:00
Nov. 21	**New York Jets**	1:00
Nov. 28	at Cincinnati	1:00
Dec. 5	**New England**	1:00
Dec. 12	at Buffalo	1:00
Dec. 19	**San Diego**	1:00
Dec. 26	at Miami	8:30
Jan. 2	at Houston	1:00

Stadium: Cleveland Browns Stadium (opened in 1999) • **Capacity:** 73,300
100 Alfred Lerner Way
Cleveland, Ohio 44114
Playing Surface: Grass
Headquarters/Training Camp:
76 Lou Groza Boulevard
Berea, Ohio 44017

CLEVELAND BROWNS STADIUM

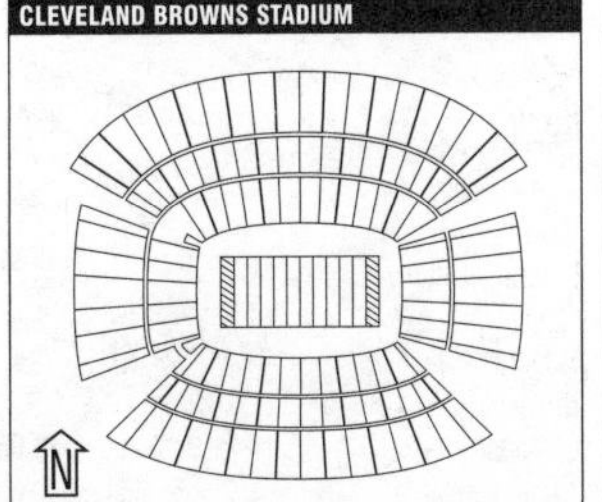

CLUB OFFICIALS

Owner: Randy Lerner
President and Chief Executive Officer: John Collins
Executive Vice President, Finance: Doug Jacobs
Executive Vice President, Stadium and Security: Lew Merletti
Vice President, Player Personnel and Football Development: Pete Garcia
Vice President, Operations: Bill Hampton
Vice President, Marketing and Development: Bruce Popko
Director, College Personnel: Phil Neri
Director, Pro Personnel: Jeremy Green
Executive Director, Communications/Media Relations: Todd Stewart
Director, Community Relations and Asst. Director, Foundation: Renee Zidan
Director, Ticket Operations: John Schulze
Director, Stadium Operations: Diane Downing
Director, Cleveland Browns Foundation: Judge George White
Manager, Publicity/Media Relations: Ken Mather
Manager, New Media: Amy Gretsinger
Manager, Berea Facilities: Greg Hipp
Head Athletic Trainer: Mike Colello
Equipment Manager: Bobby Monica
Video Director: Pat Dolan
Head Groundskeeper: Chris Powell

COACHING HISTORY
(411-340-10)

1950-1962	Paul Brown	115-49-5
1963-1970	Blanton Collier	79-38-2
1971-74	Nick Skorich	30-26-2
1975-77	Forrest Gregg*	18-23-0
1977	Dick Modzelewski	0-1-0
1978-1984	Sam Rutigliano**	47-52-0
1984-88	Marty Schottenheimer	46-31-0
1989-1990	Bud Carson***	12-14-1
1990	Jim Shofner	1-6-0
1991-95	Bill Belichick	37-45-0
1999-2000	Chris Palmer	5-27-0
2001-03	Butch Davis	21-28-0

*Resigned after 13 games in 1977
**Released after eight games in 1984
***Released after nine games in 1990

ATTENDANCE

Home 567,731 Away 545,709
Total 1,113,440
Single-game home record, 85,073 (9/21/70)
Single-season home record, 620,496 (1980)

2004 DRAFT CHOICES

Round	Name	Pos.	College
1	Kellen Winslow	TE	Miami
2	Sean Jones	DB	Georgia
4	Luke McCown	QB	Louisiana Tech
5	Amon Gordon	DT	Stanford
6	Kirk Chambers	T	Stanford
7	Adimchinobe Echemandu	RB	California

CLEVELAND BROWNS

2003 TEAM RECORD

PRESEASON (1-3)

Date	Result		Opponent
8/9	L	6-10	at Tennessee
8/15	L	31-38	Green Bay
8/23	L	17-38	at Detroit
8/28	W	20-9	Atlanta

REGULAR SEASON (5-11)

Date	Result		Opponent	Att.
9/7	L	6-9	Indianapolis	73,358
9/14	L	13-33	at Baltimore	69,473
9/21	W	13-12	at San Francisco	67,412
9/28	L	14-21	Cincinnati	73,428
10/5	W	33-13	at Pittsburgh	64,595
10/12	W	13-7	Oakland	73,318
10/19	L	20-26	San Diego	73,238
10/26	L	3-9	at New England	68,436
11/9	L	20-41	at Kansas City	78,560
11/16	W	44-6	Arizona	72,908
11/23	L	6-13	Pittsburgh	73,658
11/30	L	7-34	at Seattle	64,680
12/8	L	20-26	St. Louis	73,108
12/14	L	20-23	at Denver (OT)	75,358
12/21	L	0-35	Baltimore	72,548
12/28	W	22-14	at Cincinnati	65,362

(OT) Overtime

SCORE BY PERIODS

Browns	46	79	50	79	0 —	254
Opponents	74	102	59	84	3 —	322

2003 TEAM STATISTICS

	Browns	Opp.
Total First Downs	276	283
Rushing	91	100
Passing	153	160
Penalty	32	23
3rd Down: Made/Att	74/202	87/222
3rd Down Pct.	36.6	39.2
4th Down: Made/Att	6/18	8/13
4th Down Pct.	33.3	61.5
Possession Avg.	29:21	30:39
Total Net Yards	4,504	4,959
Avg. Per Game	281.5	309.9
Total Plays	961	994
Avg. Per Play	4.7	5.0
Net Yards Rushing	1,670	2,113
Avg. Per Game	104.4	132.1
Total Rushes	412	457
Net Yards Passing	2,834	2,846
Avg. Per Game	177.1	177.9
Sacked/Yards Lost	40/282	35/203
Gross Yards	3,116	3,049
Att./Completions	509/313	502/297
Completion Pct.	61.5	59.2
Had Intercepted	18	15
Punts/Average	73/41.8	76/41.4
Net Punting Avg.	73/34.7	76/35.3
Penalties/Yards	98/767	141/1,095
Fumbles/Ball Lost	32/15	24/7
Touchdowns	27	31
Rushing	8	14
Passing	17	13
Returns	2	4

2003 INDIVIDUAL STATISTICS

PASSING	Att.	Comp.	Yds.	Pct.	TD	Int.	Tkld.	Rate
Holcomb	302	193	1,797	63.9	10	12	21/166	74.6
Couch	203	120	1,319	59.1	7	6	19/116	77.6
Boyer	1	0	0	0.0	0	0	0/0	39.6
F. Jackson	1	0	0	0.0	0	0	0/0	39.6
Johnson	1	0	0	0.0	0	0	0/0	39.6
Northcutt	1	0	0	0.0	0	0	0/0	39.6
Browns	509	313	3,116	61.5	17	18	40/282	75.2
Opponents	502	297	3,049	59.2	13	15	35/203	72.9

SCORING	TD R	TD P	TD Rt	PAT	FG	Saf	PTS
Dawson	0	0	0	20/21	18/21	0	74
Andre Davis	0	5	0	0/0	0/0	0	30
Conway	0	0	0	3/3	5/7	0	18
J. Jackson	3	0	0	0/0	0/0	0	18
Morgan	0	3	0	0/0	0/0	0	18
Heinrich	0	2	0	0/0	0/0	0	12
Johnson	0	2	0	0/0	0/0	0	12
Northcutt	0	2	0	0/0	0/0	0	12
Suggs	2	0	0	0/0	0/0	0	12
White	1	1	0	0/0	0/0	0	12
Bowers	0	1	0	0/0	0/0	0	6
Couch	1	0	0	0/0	0/0	0	6
Green	1	0	0	0/0	0/0	0	6
King	0	0	1	0/0	0/0	0	6
McCutcheon	0	0	1	0/0	0/0	0	6
D. Sanders	0	1	0	0/0	0/0	0	6
Browns	8	17	2	23/24	23/28	0	254
Opponents	14	13	4	31/31	35/43	0	322

2-Pt. Conversions: None.
Browns 0-3, Opponents 0-0.

RUSHING	No.	Yds	Avg	LG	TD
Green	142	559	3.9	26	1
J. Jackson	102	382	3.7	18	3
Suggs	56	289	5.2	78t	2
White	70	266	3.8	23	1
Northcutt	12	83	6.9	23	0
Couch	11	39	3.5	17	1
Andre Davis	5	28	5.6	7	0
Dawson	1	14	14.0	14	0
Boyer	1	7	7.0	7	0
Holcomb	8	7	0.9	6	0
Faine	1	0	0.0	0	0
Morgan	3	-4	-1.3	2	0
Browns	412	1,670	4.1	78t	8
Opponents	457	2,113	4.6	82t	14

RECEIVING	No.	Yds	Avg	LG	TD
Northcutt	62	729	11.8	44	2
White	46	303	6.6	22	1
Johnson	41	381	9.3	41	2
Andre Davis	40	576	14.4	49	5
Morgan	38	516	13.6	71t	3
Heiden	18	134	7.4	17	0
D. Sanders	15	95	6.3	12	1
J. Jackson	14	114	8.1	18	0
Green	10	50	5.0	12	0
King	9	88	9.8	28	0
Heinrich	8	64	8.0	17	2
Mustard	4	29	7.3	12	0
F. Jackson	2	29	14.5	19	0
Shea	2	9	4.5	7	0
Suggs	2	0	0.0	1	0
Bowers	1	2	2.0	2t	1
Couch	1	-3	-3.0	-3	0
Browns	313	3,116	10.0	71t	17
Opponents	297	3,049	10.3	55t	13

INTERCEPTIONS	No.	Yds	Avg	LG	TD
Little	6	41	6.8	21	0
Griffith	2	3	1.5	3	0
McCutcheon	1	75	75.0	75t	1
Bentley	1	25	25.0	25	0
Henry	1	19	19.0	19	0
Boyer	1	4	4.0	4	0
Bodden	1	1	1.0	1	0
Lang	1	0	0.0	0	0
Taylor	1	0	0.0	0	0
Browns	15	168	11.2	75t	1
Opponents	18	391	21.7	54t	4

PUNTING	No.	Yds.	Avg.	In 20	LG
Gardocki	72	3,019	41.9	18	60
Dawson	1	29	29.0	1	29
Browns	73	3,048	41.8	19	60
Opponents	76	3,146	41.4	18	592

PUNT RETURNS	Ret	FC	Yds	Avg	LG	TD
Northcutt	36	10	295	8.2	38	0
Andre Davis	1	1	7	7.0	7	0
Browns	37	11	302	8.2	38	0
Opponents	33	9	316	9.6	49	0

KICKOFF RETURNS	No.	Yds	Avg	LG	TD
Andre Davis	38	803	21.1	69	0
Suggs	14	318	22.7	42	0
King	9	172	19.1	30	0
Maddox	3	58	19.3	26	0
Morgan	2	67	33.5	47	0
White	2	2	1.0	2	0
J. Jackson	1	68	68.0	39	0
Mustard	1	6	6.0	6	0
Stokes	1	7	7.0	7	0
Browns	71	1,501	21.1	69	0
Opponents	60	1,231	20.5	77	0

FIELD GOALS	1-19	20-29	30-39	40-49	50+
Dawson	2/2	7/7	4/5	3/5	2/2
Conway	1/1	0/0	1/3	3/3	0/0
Browns	3/3	7/7	5/8	6/8	2/2
Opponents	0/0	13/13	9/10	10/16	3/4

SACKS	No.
Lang	8.0
Brown	6.0
Warren	5.5
Andra Davis	5.0
Word	4.0
Myers	3.0
Roye	1.5
Rogers	1.0
Browns	35.0
Opponents	40.0

RECORD HOLDERS

INDIVIDUAL RECORDS—CAREER

Category	Name	Performance
Rushing (Yds.)	Jim Brown, 1957-1965	12,312
Passing (Yds.)	Brian Sipe, 1974-1983	23,713
Passing (TDs)	Brian Sipe, 1974-1983	154
Receiving (No.)	Ozzie Newsome, 1978-1990	662
Receiving (Yds.)	Ozzie Newsome, 1978-1990	7,980
Interceptions	Thom Darden, 1972-74, 1976-1981	45
Punting (Avg.)	Horace Gillom, 1950-56	43.8
Punt Return (Avg.)	Greg Pruitt, 1973-1981	11.8
Kickoff Return (Avg.)	Greg Pruitt, 1973-1981	26.3
Field Goals	Lou Groza, 1950-59, 1961-67	234
Touchdowns (Tot.)	Jim Brown, 1957-1965	126
Points	Lou Groza, 1950-59, 1961-67	1,349

INDIVIDUAL RECORDS—SINGLE SEASON

Category	Name	Performance
Rushing (Yds.)	Jim Brown, 1963	1,863
Passing (Yds.)	Brian Sipe, 1980	4,132
Passing (TDs)	Brian Sipe, 1980	30
Receiving (No.)	Ozzie Newsome, 1983	89
	Ozzie Newsome, 1984	89
Receiving (Yds.)	Webster Slaughter, 1989	1,236
Interceptions	Thom Darden, 1978	10
	Anthony Henry, 2001	10
Punting (Avg.)	Gary Collins, 1965	46.7
Punt Return (Avg.)	Leroy Kelly, 1965	15.6
Kickoff Return (Avg.)	Billy Lefear, 1975	31.7
Field Goals	Matt Stover, 1995	29
Touchdowns (Tot.)	Jim Brown, 1965	21
Points	Jim Brown, 1965	126

INDIVIDUAL RECORDS—SINGLE GAME

Category	Name	Performance
Rushing (Yds.)	Jim Brown, 11-24-57	237
	Jim Brown, 11-19-61	237
Passing (Yds.)	Brian Sipe, 10-25-81	444
Passing (TDs)	Frank Ryan, 12-12-64	5
	Bill Nelsen, 11-2-69	5
	Brian Sipe, 10-7-79	5
Receiving (No.)	Ozzie Newsome, 10-14-84	14
Receiving (Yds.)	Ozzie Newsome, 10-14-84	191
Interceptions	Many times	3
	Last time by Anthony Henry, 11-18-01	
Field Goals	Don Cockroft, 10-19-75	5
	Matt Stover, 10-29-95	5
Touchdowns (Tot.)	Dub Jones, 11-25-51	*6
Points	Dub Jones, 11-25-51	36

*NFL Record

CLEVELAND BROWNS

2004 VETERAN ROSTER

No.	Name	Pos.	Ht.	Wt.	Birthdate	NFL Exp.	College	Hometown	How Acq.	'03 Games/ Starts
68	Beasley, Chad	G-T	6-5	300	11/13/78	3	Virginia Tech	Gate City, Va.	FA-'02	8/3
59	Bentley, Kevin	LB	6-1	245	12/29/79	3	Northwestern	North Hills, Calif.	D4a-'02	16/15
28	Bodden, Leigh	CB	6-1	195	9/24/81	2	Duquesne	Upper Marlborough, Md.	FA-'03	13/1
52	Boyer, Brant	LB	6-1	240	6/27/71	11	Arizona	Ogden, Utah	UFA(Jax)-'01	15/7
92	Brown, Courtney	DE	6-4	280	2/14/78	5	Penn State	Alvin, S.C.	D1-'00	13/13
91	Claybrooks, Felipe	DE	6-5	275	1/22/78	3	Georgia Tech	Decatur, Ga.	FA-'01	7/0
56	Coates, Sherrod	LB	6-2	225	12/22/78	2	Western Kentucky	Boynton Beach, Fla.	FA-'03	16/0
2	Couch, Tim	QB	6-4	220	7/31/77	6	Kentucky	Hyden, Ky.	D1-'99	10/8
25	Crocker, Chris	S	5-11	194	3/9/80	2	Marshall	Chesapeake, Va.	D3-'03	16/1
54	Davis, Andra	LB	6-1	255	12/23/78	3	Florida	Live Oak, Fla.	D5-'02	16/16
87	Davis, Andre'	WR	6-1	195	6/12/79	3	Virginia Tech	Niskayuna, N.Y.	D2-'02	16/8
4	Dawson, Phil	K	5-11	195	1/23/75	6	Texas	Dallas, Texas	FA-'99	13/0
70	DeMar, Enoch	G	6-4	317	9/7/80	2	Indiana	Indianapolis, Ind.	FA-'03	5/2
98	Ekuban, Ebenezer	DE	6-3	265	5/29/76	6	North Carolina	Ghana, Africa	UFA(Dall)-'04	15/14*
50	Faine, Jeff	C	6-3	303	4/6/81	2	Notre Dame	Milwaukee, Ore.	D1-'03	9/9
67	Fowler, Melvin	G-C	6-3	310	3/31/79	3	Maryland	Wheatley Heights, N.Y.	D3-'02	14/10
95	Garay, Antonio	DE-DT	6-4	300	11/30/79	2	Boston College	Rahway, N.J.	D6-'03	4/0
5	Garcia, Jeff	QB	6-1	195	2/24/70	6	San Jose State	Gilroy, Calif.	FA-'04	13/13*
55	Gardner, Barry	LB	6-1	245	12/13/76	6	Northwestern	Harvey, Ill.	UFA(Phil)-'03	16/0
63	Garmon, Kelvin	T-G	6-2	350	10/26/76	6	Baylor	Fort Worth, Texas	UFA(SD)-'04	16/16*
73	Gonzalez, Joaquin	T	6-5	310	9/7/79	3	Miami	Miami, Fla.	D7-'02	16/3
31	Green, William	RB	6-0	215	12/17/79	3	Boston College	Atlantic City, N.J.	D1-'02	7/7
24	Griffith, Robert	S	5-11	197	11/30/70	11	San Diego State	San Diego, Calif.	UFA(Minn)-'02	16/16
82	Heiden, Steve	TE	6-5	265	9/21/76	6	South Dakota State	Rushford, Minn.	T(SD)-'02	9/9
49	Heinrich, Keith	HB	6-5	265	3/19/79	3	Sam Houston State	Tomball, Texas	FA-'03	7/3
37	Henry, Anthony	CB	6-1	205	11/3/76	4	South Florida	Fort Myers, Fla.	D4-'01	14/13
10	Holcomb, Kelly	QB	6-2	212	7/9/73	8	Middle Tennessee State	Fayetteville, Tenn.	FA-'01	10/8
57	Holdman, Warrick	LB	6-1	234	11/22/75	6	Texas A&M	Arlief, Texas	FA-'04	13/13*
7	Husak, Todd	QB	6-3	216	7/6/78	3	Stanford	Bellflower, Calif.	FA-'04	0*
8	Hybl, Nate	QB	6-4	222	5/1/80	2	Oklahoma	Hazelhurst, Ga.	FA-'03	0*
88	Jackson, Frisman	WR	6-3	215	6/12/79	3	Western Illinois	Chicago, Ill.	FA-'02	5/0
21	Jackson, James	RB	5-10	215	8/4/76	4	Miami	Bella Glade, Fla.	D3-'01	12/6
22	Jameson, Michael	S	5-11	205	7/14/79	4	Texas A&M	Killeen, Texas	D6-'01	15/0
85	Jones, C.J.	WR	5-11	192	9/20/80	2	Iowa	Boynton Beach, Fla.	FA-'03	0*
84	King, Andre	WR	5-11	195	11/26/73	4	Miami	Fort Lauderdale, Fla.	D7b-'01	15/0
96	Lang, Kenard	DE	6-3	280	1/31/75	8	Miami	Orlando, Fla.	UFA(Wash)-'02	15/15
39	Lehan, Michael	CB	6-0	190	11/25/79	2	Minnesota	Hopkins, Minn.	D5b-'03	12/2
20	Little, Earl	S	6-1	200	3/10/73	7	Miami	Miami, Fla.	W(NO)-'99	16/16
33	McCutcheon, Daylon	CB	5-10	190	12/9/76	6	Southern California	La Puente, Calif.	D3a-'99	15/14
97	McKinley, Alvin	DE-DT	6-3	310	6/9/78	5	Mississippi State	Jackson, Miss.	FA-'01	9/0
81	Morgan, Quincy	WR	6-1	210	9/23/77	4	Kansas State	Garland, Texas	D2-'01	16/15
83	Mustard, Chad	TE	6-6	288	10/8/77	2	North Dakota	Columbus, Neb.	FA-'03	10/0
93	Myers, Michael	DT	6-2	292	1/20/76	7	Alabama	Vicksburg, Miss.	FA-'03	7/1
	Nix, John	DT	6-1	313	11/24/76	3	Southern Mississippi	Lucedale, Miss.	FA-'03	0*
86	Northcutt, Dennis	WR	5-11	175	12/22/77	5	Arizona	Los Angeles, Calif.	D2-'00	15/6
62	Osika, Craig	C	6-3	293	12/4/79	3	Indiana	Valparaiso, Ind.	FA-'03	1/0
64	Pontbriand, Ryan	LS	6-2	255	10/1/79	2	Rice	Houston, Texas	D5a-'03	16/0
99	Roye, Orpheus	DT	6-4	320	1/21/73	9	Florida State	Carrol City, Fla.	UFA(Pitt)-'00	16/15
89	Sanders, Darnell	TE	6-6	270	3/16/79	3	Ohio State	Warrensville Heights, Ohio	D4c-'02	16/12
	Scott, Cedric	DE-DT	6-5	290	10/19/77	3	Southern Mississippi	Gulfport, Miss.	FA-'04	0*
80	Shea, Aaron	TE	6-3	255	12/5/76	5	Michigan	Ottawa, Ill.	D4b-'00	4/2
42	Smith, Terrelle	FB	6-0	246	3/12/78	5	Arizona State	West Covina, Calif.	UFA(NO)-'04	15/10*
44	Suggs, Lee	RB	6-0	205	8/11/80	2	Virginia Tech	Roanoke, Va.	D4-'03	7/0
58	Taylor, Ben	LB	6-2	245	8/31/78	3	Virginia Tech	Bellaire, Ohio	D4b-'02	13/8
51	Thompson, Chaun	LB	6-2	250	5/22/80	2	West Texas A&M	Mt. Pleasant, Texas	D2-'03	16/0
72	Tucker, Ryan	T	6-6	325	6/12/75	8	Texas Christian	Midland, Texas	UFA(StL)-'02	16/16
77	Verba, Ross	G	6-4	308	10/31/73	8	Iowa	Des Moines, Iowa	UFA(GB)-'01	0*
61	Warren, Gerard	DT	6-4	325	7/25/78	4	Florida	Radford, Fla.	D1-'01	16/15
27	Williams, Roosevelt	CB	6-1	205	9/10/78	3	Tuskegee	Jacksonville, Fla.	FA-'03	7/3
90	Word, Mark	DE-DT	6-5	305	11/23/75	4	Jacksonville State	Miami, Fla.	FA-'01	16/2
66	Zukauskas, Paul	G	6-5	320	7/12/79	4	Boston College	Boston, Mass.	D7a-'01	12/10

* Ekuban played 15 games with Dallas in '03; Garcia played 13 games with San Francisco; Garmon played 16 games with San Diego; Holdman played 13 games with Chicago; Husak last active with N.Y. Jets in '02; Hybl inactive for 11 games and did not play in 2 games; Jones inactive for 11 games; Nix did not play in 1 game; Scott last active with Cleveland in '02; Smith played 15 games with New Orleans; Verba missed '03 season because of injury.

Players lost through free agency (4): P Chris Gardocki (Pitt; 16 games in '03), G Shaun O'Hara (NYG; 14), T Barry Stokes (NYG; 13), CB-S Lewis Sanders (Jax; 9).

Also played with Browns in '03—RB R.J. Bowers (1 game), K Brett Conway (3), RB Nick Maddox (1), DE Tyrone Rogers (8), LB Mason Unck (1), RB Jamel White (16).

2004 FIRST-YEAR ROSTER

Name	Pos.	Ht.	Wt.	Birthdate	College	Hometown	How Acq.
Alston, Richard (1)	WR	5-11	215	11/20/80	East Carolina	Warrenton, N.C.	FA
Browden, Terrell	FB	6-3	260	1/12/82	Southern Mississippi	Baton Rouge, La.	FA
Buhl, Josh	LB	6-0	210	5/4/81	Kansas State	Mesquite, Texas	FA
Chambers, Kirk	OL	6-7	313	3/19/79	Stanford	Provo, Utah	D6
Curry, Kentrell	DB	6-1	198	5/11/81	Georgia	Toccoa, Ga.	FA
Dawson, Lewis	OL	6-5	320	2/25/81	The Citadel	Fayetteville, N.C.	FA
Dutton, Ryan (1)	P	6-4	213	12/27/77	Minnesota State-Mankato	Oshkosh, Wis.	FA
Echemandu, Adimchinobe	RB	5-10	226	11/21/80	California	Lagos, Nigeria	D7
Frost, Derrick (1)	K	6-4	200	11/25/80	Northern Iowa	St. Louis, Mo.	FA-'03
Galles, Eddie	WR	6-2	190	4/21/81	Northern Iowa	Mankato, Minn.	FA
Geathers, Jason	WR	6-3	208	9/8/80	Miami	Delray Beach, Fla.	FA
Gordon, Amon	OL	6-2	302	10/13/81	Stanford	San Diego, Calif.	D5
Grant, Michael	DB	6-1	205	7/10/80	Mars Hill	Asheville, N.C.	FA
Harris, Sterling	OL	6-6	310	8/17/81	Southern Methodist	Dallas, Texas	FA
Hickman, Bryan	LB	6-3	220	1/18/81	Kansas State	Mesquite, Texas	FA
Jackson, Corey (1)	DL	6-6	255	11/6/78	Nevada	Cassatt, S.C.	FA-'03
Jones, Sean	DB	6-1	212	3/2/82	Georgia	Atlanta, Ga.	D2
Klabo, Chuck (1)	OL	6-6	310	9/12/79	North Dakota State	Maryville, N.D.	FA-'03
Maddox, Nick (1)	RB	5-11	209	12/11/80	Florida State	Shelby, N.C.	FA-'03
McCown, Luke	QB	6-3	208	7/12/81	Louisiana Tech	Jacksonville, Texas	D4
Miller, Ben (1)	FB	6-3	250	8/18/79	Air Force	Colulmbia Station, Ohio	FA-'02
Oakley, Anthony	OL	6-4	295	8/16/81	Western Kentucky	Little Rock, Ark.	FA
Osborne, Scot (1)	OL	6-4	298	10/30/77	William & Mary	Asheville, N.C.	FA-'03
Osunde, Uyi	DL	6-3	248	2/28/82	Connecticut	Bloomsburg, Pa.	FA
Pittman, Chris	WR	6-0	192	6/6/81	Colorado State	San Diego, Calif.	FA
Reynolds, Joffrey (1)	RB	5-10	221	11/26/79	Houston	Houston, Texas	FA
Schorejs, Derek (1)	K	6-0	220	5/14/73	Bowling Green	Westerville, Ohio	FA
Sharpe, Ricky (1)	DB	6-1	190	1/23/80	San Diego State	San Diego, Calif.	FA
Unck, Mason (1)	LB	6-3	235	9/7/80	Arizona State	Ogden, Utah	FA-'03
Winslow, Kellen	TE	6-4	243	7/21/83	Miami	San Diego, Calif.	D1
Young, David (1)	DB	6-1	209	5/17/79	Georgia Southern	Columbia, S.C.	FA-'03

The term NFL Rookie is defined as a player who is in his first season of professional football and has not been on the roster of another professional football team for any regular-season or postseason games. A Rookie is designated by an "R" on NFL rosters. Players who have been active in another professional football league or players who have NFL experience, including either preseason training camp or being on an Active List or Inactive List, or on Reserve/Injured or Reserve/Physically Unable to Perform for fewer than six regular-season games, are termed NFL First-Year Players. An NFL First-Year Player is designated by a "1" on NFL rosters. Thereafter, a player is credited with an additional year of experience for each season in which he accumulates six games on the Active List or Inactive List, or on Reserve/Injured or Reserve/Physically Unable to Perform.

Log on to www.clevelandbrowns.com for an up-to-date roster.

CLEVELAND BROWNS

COACHING STAFF

Head Coach,
Butch Davis

Pro Career: Named head coach of the Browns on January 30, 2001, and is entering his fourth season as head coach. In 2002, Davis led the Browns to the club's first postseason appearance since 1994 with a 9-7 record in his second year as head coach. Davis came to Cleveland from the University of Miami where Davis rebuilt the Hurricanes program. Davis returned the program back to the college football elite status as Miami defeated Florida in the 2001 Nokia Sugar Bowl, and finished second in both the Associated Press and ESPN/*USA Today* rankings. Davis won two Super Bowl championships with the Dallas Cowboys (1992 and 1993) and, at the collegiate level, he won a national championship with Miami (1987). He was the head coach at Miami (1995-2000), where he compiled a 51-20 record, including a 4-0 mark in bowl games. He joined Miami after six years (1989-1994) with the Cowboys, serving as the defensive line coach for four years and the last two seasons as the Cowboys' defensive coordinator. His 1993 defense won Super Bowl XXVIII and allowed just one offensive touchdown or less in 12 of 16 games. Career record: 21-28.

Background: Davis spent five seasons (1984-88) as the defensive line coach for Miami, including the Hurricanes' 1987 national championship team. Davis started as an assistant on Jimmy Johnson's Oklahoma State teams (1979-1983). Davis was the head coach at Rogers High School in Tulsa, Okla., for one season (1978) after spending time as an assistant at two high schools in Oklahoma and one in Arkansas where he taught biology, anatomy, and physiology. Davis played defensive end for Arkansas (1971-74).

Personal: Born Paul Hilton Davis in Tahlequah, Okla., on November 17, 1951. Earned his bachelor's degree in biology and life science from Arkansas. Davis and his wife Tammy have one son, Andrew.

ASSISTANT COACHES

Phil Banko, defensive assistant; born August 9, 1964, Belle Chasse, La. Linebacker Northeast Louisiana 1982. College coach: Miami 1998-2000. Pro coach: Joined Browns in 2001.

Todd Bowles, defensive backs; born November 18, 1963, Elizabeth, N.J. Defensive back Temple 1982-85. Pro defensive back Washington 1986-1990, 1991-93, San Francisco 1990. College coach: Morehouse College 1997, Grambling State 1998-99. Pro coach: New York Jets 2000, joined Browns in 2001.

Dave Campo, defensive coordinator; born July 18, 1947, Groton, Conn. Defensive back Central Connecticut State 1967-1970. No pro playing experience. College coach: Central Connecticut State 1971-72, Albany 1973, Bridgeport 1974, Pittsburgh 1975, Washington State 1976, Boise State 1977-79, Oregon State 1980, Weber State 1981-82, Iowa State 1983, Syracuse 1984-86, Miami 1987-88. Pro coach: Dallas Cowboys 1989-2002 (head coach 2000-2002), joined Browns in 2003.

Rob Chudzinski, tight ends: born May 12, 1968, Toledo, Ohio. Tight end Miami 1986-1990. No pro playing experience. College coach: Miami 1994-2003. Pro coach: Joined Browns in 2004.

George Edwards, linebackers: born January 16, 1967, Siler City, N.C. Linebacker Duke 1985-89. No pro playing experience. College coach: Florida 1990-91, Appalachian State 1992-95, Duke 1996, Georgia 1997. Pro coach: Dallas Cowboys 1998-2001, Washington Redskins 2002-03, joined Browns in 2004.

Fred Graves, wide receivers: born March 2, 1950, Los Angeles. Halfback-split end Utah 1968-1970. Pro wide receiver Chicago Bears 1971. College coach: Northeast Missouri State 1975-76, Western Illinois 1977-78, New Mexico State 1979-1981, Utah 1982-2000. Pro coach: Buffalo Bills 2001-03, joined Browns in 2004.

Steve Hagen, quarterbacks; born September 15, 1961. Tight end Cal Lutheran 1979-1982. Pro tight end Boston Breakers (USFL) 1983. College coach: Northern Arizona 1987-88, Notre Dame 1989-1990, Kent State 1991, Nevada 1992-93, Nevada-Las Vegas 1994-95, Wartburg (Iowa) 1996, San Jose State 1997-98, California 1999-2000. Pro coach: Joined Browns in 2001.

Taver Johnson, asst. special teams; born July 8, 1972, Cincinnati. No pro playing experience. College coach: Wittenberg (Ohio) 1994-95, Millikin (Ill.) 1996-98, Notre Dame 1999, Miami (Ohio) 2000-03. Pro coach: Joined Browns in 2004.

Buddy Morris, head strength and conditioning; born September 29, 1957, South Park, Pa. Attended Pittsburgh. No college or pro playing experience. College coach: Pittsburgh 1980-89, 1997-2001. Pro coach: Joined Browns in 2002.

Tom Myslinski, asst. strength and conditioning; born December 7, 1968, Rome, N.Y. Guard Tennessee 1989-1992. Guard Chicago Bears 1993-94, Pittsburgh Steelers 1996-97, 2000, Indianapolis Colts 1998. College coach: North Florida 1996, Pittsburgh 1998-2001. Pro coach: Joined Browns in 2004.

Chuck Pagano, secondary; born October 2, 1960, Boulder, Colo. Safety Wyoming 1980-83. No pro playing experience. College coach: Southern California 1984-85, Miami 1986, Boise State 1987-88, East Carolina 1989, Nevada-Las Vegas 1990-91, East Carolina 1992-94, Miami 1995-2000. Pro coach: Joined Browns in 2001.

Andre Patterson, defensive line; born June 12, 1960, Camdon, Ark. Offensive lineman Contra Costa (Calif.) J.C. 1978-1980, Montana 1981. No pro playing experience. College coach: Montana 1982, Weber State 1988, Cornell 1990-91, Washington State 1992-93, Cal Poly-San Luis Obispo 1994-96. Pro coach: New England Patriots 1997, Minnesota Vikings 1998-99, Dallas Cowboys 2000-02, joined Browns in 2003.

Rob Phillips, senior asst. strength and conditioning; born December 3, 1971, Ft. Wayne, Ind. Attended Tennessee. No college or pro playing experience. College coach: Western Carolina 1997-98, Miami 1999-2000. Pro coach: Joined Browns in 2001.

Kennedy Pola, running backs; born November 22, 1963, Pago Pago, American Samoa. Fullback Southern California 1982-85. No pro playing experience. College coach: UCLA 1992-93, San Diego State 1994-96, Colorado 1997-98, San Diego State, 1999, Southern California 2000-03. Pro coach: Joined Browns in 2004.

Terry Robiskie, offensive coordinator; born November 12, 1954, New Orleans. Running back Louisiana State 1973-76. Pro running back Oakland Raiders 1977-79, Miami Dolphins 1980-81. Pro coach: Los Angeles Raiders 1982-1993, Washington Redskins 1994-2000 (head coach 2000), joined Browns in 2001.

Jerry Rosburg, special teams coordinator; born November 24, 1955, Fairmont, Minn. Linebacker North Dakota State 1974-77. No college or pro playing experience. College coach: Northern Michigan 1981-86, Western Michigan 1987-91, Cincinnati 1992-95, Minnesota 1996, Boston College 1997-98, Notre Dame 1999-2000. Pro coach: Joined Browns in 2001.

Mike Sullivan, offensive assistant; born December 22, 1967, Chicago. Offensive lineman Miami 1986-1990. Pro offensive lineman Dallas Cowboys 1991, Tampa Bay Buccaneers 1992-95. College coach: Miami 2000. Pro coach: Joined Browns in 2001.

Larry Zierlein, offensive line; born July 12, 1945, Lenora, Kan. Attended Fort Hays (Kan.) State College. No college or pro playing experience. College coach: Fort Hays (Kan.) State College 1970-71, Houston 1978-1986, Tulane 1988-1990, 1995-96, Louisiana State 1993-94, Cincinnati 1997-2000. Pro coach: Washington Commandos (Arena League) 1987, New York/New Jersey Knights (WLAF) 1991-92, joined Browns in 2001.

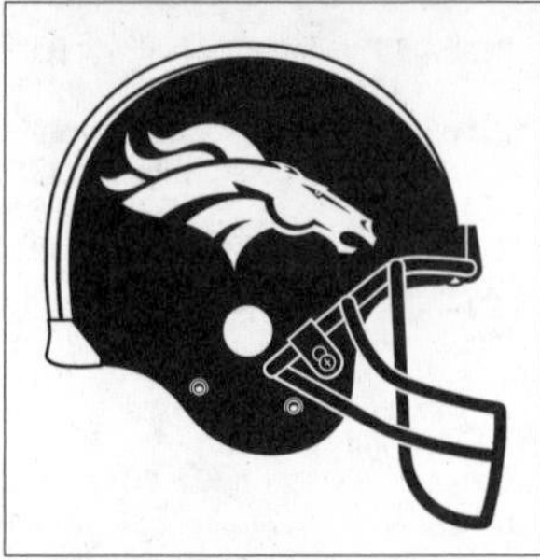

American Football Conference
West Division
Team Colors: Orange, Broncos Navy Blue, and White
13655 Broncos Parkway
Englewood, Colorado 80112
Telephone: (303) 649-9000

2004 SCHEDULE

PRESEASON		**Denver time**
Aug. 9	vs. Washington, Canton, OH	6:00
Aug. 15	at Buffalo	5:00
Aug. 21	at Seattle	8:00
Aug. 27	**Houston**	7:00
Sept. 2	**Arizona**	7:00

REGULAR SEASON		
Sept. 12	**Kansas City**	6:30
Sept. 19	at Jacksonville	11:00*
Sept. 26	**San Diego**	2:00
Oct. 3	at Tampa Bay	2:15
Oct. 10	**Carolina**	2:15
Oct. 17	at Oakland	2:15
Oct. 25	at Cincinnati (Mon.)	7:00
Oct. 31	**Atlanta**	2:05
Nov. 7	**Houston**	2:15
Nov. 14	Open Date	
Nov. 21	at New Orleans	11:00*
Nov. 28	**Oakland**	6:30
Dec. 5	at San Diego	2:05
Dec. 12	**Miami**	2:05
Dec. 19	at Kansas City	2:15
Dec. 25	at Tennessee (Sat.)	6:30
Jan. 2	**Indianapolis**	2:15

*A.M.

Stadium: INVESCO Field at Mile High (opened in 2001)
•**Capacity:** 76,125
1701 Bryant Street
Denver, Colorado 80204
Playing Surface: Grass (PAT)
Training Camp: 13655 Broncos Parkway
Englewood, Colorado 80112

INVESCO FIELD AT MILE HIGH

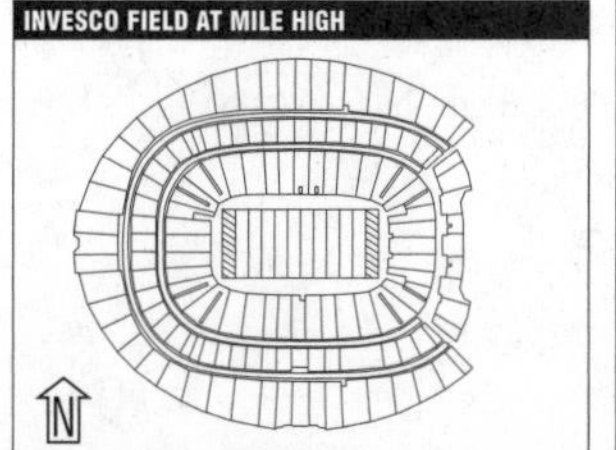

CLUB OFFICIALS
President-Chief Executive Officer: Pat Bowlen
Executive Vice President of Football Operations/ Head Coach: Mike Shanahan
Executive Vice President of Business Operations: Joe Ellis

FOOTBALL STAFF
General Manager: Ted Sundquist
Director of Pro Scouting: Rick Smith
Director of College Scouting: Jim Goodman
Coordinator of Football Administration: Mike Bluem
Trainer: Steve Antonopulos
Equipment Manager: Chris Valenti
Video Director: Kent Erickson

BUSINESS STAFF
General Counsel/Senior Vice President of Administration: Rich Slivka
Vice President of Public Relations: Jim Saccomano
Vice President of Ticket Operations/ Business Development: Rick Nichols
Vice President of Marketing: Greg Carney
Vice President of Finance: Jim Barlow
Senior Director of Community Development: Cindy Galloway

STADIUM MANAGEMENT COMPANY
Vice President and General Manager: Mac Freeman

COACHING HISTORY
(355-324-10)

1960-61	Frank Filchock	7-20-1
1962-61	Jack Faulkner*	9-22-1
1964-66	Mac Speedie**	6-19-1
1966	Ray Malavasi	4-8-0
1967-1971	Lou Saban***	20-42-3
1971	Jerry Smith	2-3-0
1972-76	John Ralston	34-33-3
1977-1980	Robert (Red) Miller	42-25-0
1981-1992	Dan Reeves	117-79-1
1993-94	Wade Phillips	16-17-0
1995-2003	Mike Shanahan	98-56-0

*Released after four games in 1964
**Resigned after two games in 1966
***Resigned after nine games in 1971

ATTENDANCE
Home 593,770 Away 521,329
Total 1,115,099
Single-game home record, 76,643 (11/11/00)
Single-season home record, 594,813 (2000)

2004 DRAFT CHOICES

Round	Name	Pos.	College
1	D.J. Williams	LB	Miami
2	Tatum Bell	RB	Oklahoma State
	Darius Watts	WR	Marshall
3	Jeremy LeSueur	DB	Michigan
5	Jeff Shoate	DB	San Diego State
6	Triandos Luke	WR	Alabama
	Josh Sewell	C	Nebraska
7	Matt Mauck	QB	Louisiana State
	Brandon Miree	RB	Pittsburgh
	Bradlee Van Pelt	QB	Colorado State

DENVER BRONCOS

2003 TEAM RECORD

PRESEASON (3-1)

Date	Result	Opponent
8/10	W 27-3	at Chicago
8/19	L 7-12	San Francisco
8/24	W 19-13	at Arizona
8/29	W 31-0	Seattle

REGULAR SEASON (10-6)

Date	Result	Opponent	Att.
9/7	W 30-10	at Cincinnati	63,820
9/14	W 37-13	at San Diego	65,445
9/22	W 31-10	Oakland	76,753
9/28	W 20-16	Detroit	75,719
10/5	L 23-24	at Kansas City	78,903
10/12	W 17-14	Pittsburgh	75,974
10/19	L 20-28	at Minnesota	64,381
10/26	L 6-26	at Baltimore	69,721
11/3	L 26-30	New England	76,203
11/16	W 37-8	San Diego	75,217
11/23	L 10-19	Chicago	75,540
11/30	W 22-8	at Oakland	57,201
12/7	W 45-27	Kansas City	76,403
12/14	W 23-20	Cleveland (OT)	75,358
12/21	W 31-17	at Indianapolis	57,149
12/28	L 3-31	at Green Bay	70,299

(OT) Overtime

POSTSEASON (0-1)

Date	Result	Opponent	
1/4	L 10-41	at Indianapolis	56,586

SCORE BY PERIODS

Broncos	110	122	74	72	3	—	381
Opponents	63	87	45	106	0	—	301

2003 TEAM STATISTICS

	Broncos	Opp.
Total First Downs	334	241
Rushing	133	77
Passing	162	141
Penalty	39	23
3rd Down: Made/Att	82/211	61/207
3rd Down Pct.	38.9	29.5
4th Down: Made/Att	3/13	12/25
4th Down Pct.	23.1	48.0
Possession Avg.	33:53	26:07
Total Net Yards	5598	4433
Avg. Per Game	349.9	277.1
Total Plays	1047	910
Avg. Per Play	5.3	4.9
Net Yards Rushing	2629	1605
Avg. Per Game	164.3	100.3
Total Rushes	543	379
Net Yards Passing	2969	2828
Avg. Per Game	185.6	176.8
Sacked/Yards Lost	25/157	36/221
Gross Yards	3126	3049
Att./Completions	479/280	495/265
Completion Pct.	58.5	53.5
Had Intercepted	18	9
Punts/Average	70/42.0	85/43.1
Net Punting Avg.	70/32.2	85/35.5
Penalties/Yards	107/922	137/1031
Fumbles/Ball Lost	24/6	27/11
Touchdowns	42	32
Rushing	20	11
Passing	19	17
Returns	3	4

2003 INDIVIDUAL STATISTICS

PASSING	Att.	Comp.	Yds.	Pct.	TD	Int.	Tkld.	Rate
Plummer	302	189	2,182	62.6	15	7	14/73	91.2
Kanell	103	53	442	51.5	2	5	2/24	49.1
Beuerlein	63	33	389	52.4	2	5	9/60	49.0
J. Jackson	9	4	41	44.4	0	1	0/0	18.5
Knorr	1	0	0	0.0	0	0	0/0	39.6
Smith	1	1	72	100.0	0	0	0/0	118.8
Broncos	479	280	3,126	58.5	19	18	25/157	75.6
Opponents	495	265	3,049	53.5	17	9	36/221	76.2

SCORING	TD R	TD P	TD Rt	PAT	FG	Saf	PTS
Elam	0	0	0	39/39	27/31	0	120
Portis	14	0	0	0/0	0/0	0	86
Sharpe	0	8	0	0/0	0/0	0	48
Anderson	3	2	0	0/0	0/0	0	30
Smith	0	3	1	0/0	0/0	0	24
Plummer	3	0	0	0/0	0/0	0	18
Droughns	0	2	0	0/0	0/0	0	12
Lelie	0	2	0	0/0	0/0	0	12
Carlisle	0	1	0	0/0	0/0	0	6
D. Carswell	0	1	0	0/0	0/0	0	6
Gold	0	0	1	0/0	0/0	0	6
O'Neal	0	0	1	0/0	0/0	0	6
Knorr	0	0	0	2/2	1/1	0	5
Broncos	20	19	3	41/41	28/32	1	381
Opponents	11	17	4	28/29	25/28	1	301

2-Pt. Conversions: None.
Portis, Broncos 1-1, Opponents 2-3.

RUSHING	No.	Yds	Avg	LG	TD
Portis	290	1,591	5.5	65t	14
Griffin	94	345	3.7	23	0
Anderson	70	257	3.7	44	3
Plummer	37	205	5.5	40	3
Smith	10	98	9.8	26	0
Lelie	8	43	5.4	13	0
Sapp	12	31	2.6	5	0
Droughns	6	14	2.3	12	0
Beuerlein	5	13	2.6	7	0
Madise	1	10	10.0	10	0
J. Jackson	1	9	9.0	9	0
Cole	2	8	4.0	8	0
Kanell	6	5	0.8	9	0
O'Neal	1	0	0.0	0	0
Broncos	543	2,629	4.8	65t	20
Opponents	379	1,605	4.2	98t	11

RECEIVING	No.	Yds	Avg	LG	TD
Smith	74	845	11.4	38	3
Sharpe	62	770	12.4	28	8
Portis	38	314	8.3	72	0
Lelie	37	628	17.0	60	2
McCaffrey	19	195	10.3	23	0
Anderson	12	53	4.4	18	2
Droughns	9	87	9.7	15	2
Griffin	8	61	7.6	24	0
D. Carswell	6	53	8.8	19	1
Putzier	4	34	8.5	13	0
Cole	3	36	12.0	18	0
Hape	3	30	10.0	12	0
Madise	2	10	5.0	5	0
O'Neal	2	4	2.0	3	0
Carlisle	1	6	6.0	6t	1
Broncos	280	3,126	11.2	72	19
Opponents	265	3,049	11.5	66t	17

INTERCEPTIONS	No.	Yds	Avg	LG	TD
K. Herndon	3	19	6.3	16	0
Gold	2	14	7.0	12t	1
O'Neal	1	6	6.0	6	0
Brandon	1	0	0.0	0	0
Kennedy	1	0	0.0	0	0
Walls	1	0	0.0	0	0
Broncos	9	39	4.3	16	1
Opponents	18	319	17.7	41	2

PUNTING	No.	Yds.	Avg.	In 20	LG
Knorr	68	2,937	43.2	14	62
Broncos	70	2,937	42.0	14	62
Opponents	85	3,663	43.1	19	64

PUNT RETURNS	Ret	FC	Yds	Avg	LG	TD
O'Neal	33	10	315	9.5	57t	1
Smith	6	8	127	21.2	65t	1
Broncos	39	18	442	11.3	65t	2
Opponents	46	5	560	12.2	93t	1

KICKOFF RETURNS	No.	Yds	Avg	LG	TD
Cole	30	714	23.8	34	0
Droughns	12	293	24.4	36	0
O'Neal	8	128	16.0	24	0
Madise	5	137	27.4	83	0
Anderson	2	14	7.0	14	0
Fatafehi	1	0	0.0	0	0
Putzier	1	16	16.0	16	0
Broncos	59	1,302	22.1	83	0
Opponents	73	1,679	23.0	63	0

FIELD GOALS	1-19	20-29	30-39	40-49	50+
Elam	0/0	10/11	6/6	9/11	2/3
Knorr	0/0	1/1	0/0	0/0	0/0
Broncos	0/0	11/12	6/6	9/11	2/3
Opponents	1/1	10/10	4/5	8/10	2/2

SACKS	No.
Berry	11.5
Hayward	8.5
Pryce	8.5
Fatafehi	2.5
Ferguson	1.0
Kennedy	1.0
Pope	1.0
Wilson	1.0
Broncos	36.0
Opponents	25.0

RECORD HOLDERS

INDIVIDUAL RECORDS—CAREER

Category	Name	Performance
Rushing (Yds.)	Terrell Davis, 1995-2001	7,607
Passing (Yds.)	John Elway, 1983-1998	51,475
Passing (TDs)	John Elway, 1983-1998	300
Receiving (No.)	Shannon Sharpe, 1990-99, 2002-03	675
Receiving (Yds.)	Rod Smith, 1995-2003	8,628
Interceptions	Steve Foley, 1976-1986	44
Punting (Avg.)	Jim Fraser, 1962-64	45.2
Punt Return (Avg.)	Darrien Gordon, 1997-98	12.5
Kickoff Return (Avg.)	Abner Haynes, 1965-66	26.3
Field Goals	Jason Elam, 1993-2003	288
Touchdowns (Tot.)	Terrell Davis, 1995-2001	65
Points	Jason Elam, 1993-2003	1,313

INDIVIDUAL RECORDS—SINGLE SEASON

Category	Name	Performance
Rushing (Yds.)	Terrell Davis, 1998	2,008
Passing (Yds.)	John Elway, 1993	4,030
Passing (TDs)	John Elway, 1997	27
Receiving (No.)	Rod Smith, 2001	113
Receiving (Yds.)	Rod Smith, 2000	1,602
Interceptions	Goose Gonsoulin, 1960	11
Punting (Avg.)	Tom Rouen, 1998	46.9
Punt Return (Avg.)	Floyd Little, 1967	16.9
Kickoff Return (Avg.)	Bill Thompson, 1969	28.5
Field Goals	Jason Elam, 1995, 2001	31
Touchdowns (Tot.)	Terrell Davis, 1998	23
Points	Terrell Davis, 1998	138

INDIVIDUAL RECORDS—SINGLE GAME

Category	Name	Performance
Rushing (Yds.)	Mike Anderson, 12-3-00	251
Passing (Yds.)	Gus Frerotte, 11-19-00	462
Passing (TDs)	Frank Tripucka, 10-28-62	5
	John Elway, 11-18-84	5
	Gus Frerotte, 11-19-00	5
Receiving (No.)	Rod Smith, 9-23-01	14
Receiving (Yds.)	Shannon Sharpe, 10-20-02	214
Interceptions	Goose Gonsoulin, 9-18-60	*4
	Willie Brown, 11-15-64	*4
	Deltha O'Neal, 10-7-01	*4
Field Goals	Gene Mingo, 10-6-63	5
	Rich Karlis, 11-20-83	5
	Jason Elam, 9-3-95, 10-13-02	5
Touchdowns (Tot.)	Mike Anderson, 12-3-00	4
Points	Mike Anderson, 12-3-00	24

*NFL Record

DENVER BRONCOS

2004 VETERAN ROSTER

No.	Name	Pos.	Ht.	Wt.	Birthdate	NFL Exp.	College	Hometown	How Acq.	'03 Games/ Starts
12	Adams, Charlie	WR	6-2	190	10/23/79	2	Hofstra	Camp Hill, Pa.	FA-'02	4/0
69	Alexander, P.J.	T	6-4	297	12/23/78	2	Syracuse	Tallahassee, Fla.	FA-'03	0*
76	Almanzar, Luis	DT	6-3	295	12/15/76	2	Southwest Missouri State	Jersey City, N.J.	FA-'03	0*
38	Anderson, Mike	RB	6-0	230	9/21/73	5	Utah	Winnsboro, S.C.	D6-'00	12/5
24	Bailey, Champ	CB	6-0	192	6/22/78	6	Georgia	Folkston, Ga.	T(Wash)-'04	16/16*
11	Beuerlein, Steve	QB	6-3	220	3/7/65	18	Notre Dame	Anaheim, Calif.	FA-'01	4/2
42	Brandon, Sam	S	6-2	200	7/5/79	3	Nevada-Las Vegas	Riverside, Calif.	D4-'02	16/10
65	Carlisle, Cooper	G-T	6-5	295	8/11/77	5	Florida	McComb, Miss.	D4b-'00	16/2
89	Carswell, Dwayne	TE	6-3	260	1/18/72	11	Liberty	Jacksonville, Fla.	FA-'94	16/10
	Chamberlain, Byron	TE	6-1	242	10/17/71	9	Wayne State	Fort Worth, Texas	FA-'04	4/1*
55	Chukwurah, Patrick	LB	6-1	250	3/1/79	4	Wyoming	Irving, Texas	FA-'04	0*
92	Coleman, Marco	DE	6-3	270	12/18/69	13	Georgia Tech	Dayton, Ohio	UFA(Phil)-'04	13/0*
61	Collins, Calvin	G	6-2	310	1/5/74	6	Texas A&M	Beaumont, Texas	FA-'04	0*
96	Davis, Dorsett	DT	6-5	305	1/24/79	3	Mississippi State	Cleveland, Miss.	D3-'02	14/0
34	Droughns, Reuben	RB	5-11	207	8/21/78	5	Oregon	Anaheim, Calif.	FA-'02	15/4
97	Eason, Nick	DT	6-3	301	5/29/80	2	Clemson	Lyons, Ga.	D4b-'03	0*
1	Elam, Jason	K	5-11	200	3/8/70	12	Hawaii	Ft. Walton Beach, Fla.	D3b-'93	16/0
94	Elliss, Luther	DT	6-5	318	3/22/73	10	Utah	Mancos, Colo.	FA-'04	5/0*
6	Epstein, Hayden	P	6-2	206	11/16/80	2	Michigan	San Diego, Calif.	FA-'04	0*
68	Fatafehi, Mario	DT	6-2	300	1/27/79	4	Kansas State	Honolulu, Hawaii	FA-'03	16/9
25	Ferguson, Nick	S	5-11	201	11/24/74	5	Georgia Tech	Miami, Fla.	FA-'03	15/10
72	Foster, George	T	6-5	338	6/9/80	2	Georgia	Macon, Ga.	D1-'03	1/0
27	Galloway, Ahmaad	RB	5-11	223	3/10/80	2	Alabama	Millington, Tenn.	D7b-'03	0*
74	Green, Cornell	T	6-6	315	8/25/76	5	Central Florida	St. Petersburg, Fla.	UFA(TB)-'04	8/5*
22	Griffin, Quentin	RB	5-7	195	1/12/81	2	Oklahoma	Houston, Texas	D4a-'03	10/1
50	Hamilton, Ben	C-G	6-4	283	8/18/77	4	Minnesota	Minneapolis, Minn.	D4a-'01	16/16
86	Hape, Patrick	TE	6-4	262	6/6/74	8	Alabama	Killen, Ala.	UFA(TB)-'01	16/0
19	Harris, Atnaf	WR	6-1	182	2/27/79	2	Cal State-Northridge	Fresno, Calif.	FA-'03	0*
98	Hayward, Reggie	DE	6-5	270	3/14/79	4	Iowa State	Dolton, Ill.	D3-'01	16/2
20	Hearst, Garrison	RB	5-11	215	1/4/71	12	Georgia	Lincolnton, Ga.	FA-'04	12/12*
31	Herndon, Kelly	CB	5-10	180	11/3/76	3	Toledo	Twinsburg, Ohio	FA-'01	15/11
90	Holland, Darius	DT	6-5	330	11/10/73	9	Colorado	Las Cruces, N.M.	FA-'03	16/14
36	Israel, Ron	S	6-0	204	1/5/78	2	Notre Dame	Haddon Heights, N.J.	FA-'04	0*
41	Jackson, Jarious	QB	6-0	228	5/3/77	5	Notre Dame	Tupelo, Miss.	FA-'03	1/1
14	Jackson, Nate	WR	6-3	223	6/4/79	2	Menlo	San Jose, Calif.	T(SF)-'03	1/0
81	Jackson, Willie	WR	6-1	212	8/16/71	10	Florida	Gainesville, Fla.	FA-'04	0*
15	Jenkins, MarTay	WR	6-0	206	2/28/75	5	Nebraska-Omaha	Des Moines, Iowa	FA-'04	0*
39	Johnson, Kyle	FB	6-0	242	12/15/78	2	Syracuse	Woodbridge, N.J.	FA-'03	0*
99	Johnson, Raylee	DE	6-3	272	6/1/70	12	Arkansas	Fordyce, Ark.	FA-'04	9/1*
13	Kanell, Danny	QB	6-3	218	11/21/73	7	Florida State	Fort Lauderdale, Fla.	FA-'03	5/2
28	Kennedy, Kenoy	S	6-1	215	11/15/77	5	Arkansas	Terrell, Texas	D2b-'00	13/12
4	Knorr, Micah	P-K	6-2	199	1/9/75	5	Utah State	Orange, Calif.	FA-'02	16/0
83	Leach, Mike	TE-LS	6-2	245	10/18/76	5	William & Mary	Jefferson Township, N.J.	FA-'02	16/0
85	Lelie, Ashley	WR	6-3	200	2/16/80	3	Hawaii	Honolulu, Hawaii	D1-'02	16/10
78	Lepsis, Matt	T	6-4	290	1/13/74	8	Colorado	Conroe, Texas	FA-'97	16/16
47	Lynch, John	S	6-2	220	9/25/71	12	Stanford	Del Mar, Calif.	FA-'04	14/14*
82	Madise, Adrian	WR	5-11	215	3/23/80	2	Texas Christian	Lancaster, Texas	D5b-'03	11/0
91	McNeal, Bryant	DE	6-4	248	7/13/79	2	Clemson	Swansea, S.C.	D4c-'03	0*
23	Middlebrooks, Willie	CB	6-1	200	2/12/79	4	Minnesota	Homestead, Fla.	D1-'01	16/0
95	Mitchell, Clint	DE	6-6	257	9/21/80	2	Florida	Clearwater, Fla.	D7a-'03	0*
51	Mobley, John	LB	6-1	236	10/10/73	9	Kutztown	Chester, Pa.	D1-'96	8/7
66	Nalen, Tom	C	6-3	286	5/13/71	11	Boston College	Foxboro, Mass.	D7c-'94	16/16
62	Neil, Dan	G	6-2	285	10/21/73	8	Texas	Cypress Creek, Texas	D3-'97	14/14
58	Pierce, Terry	LB	6-1	251	6/21/81	2	Kansas State	Fort Worth, Texas	D2-'03	3/0
16	Plummer, Jake	QB	6-2	212	12/19/74	8	Arizona State	Boise, Idaho	UFA(Ariz)-'03	11/11
75	Pope, Monsanto	DT	6-3	300	1/27/78	3	Virginia	Hopewell, Va.	D7b-'02	16/5
93	Pryce, Trevor	DE	6-5	295	8/3/75	8	Clemson	Winter Park, Fla.	D1-'97	16/16
88	Putzier, Jeb	TE	6-4	256	1/20/79	3	Boise State	Eagle, Idaho	D6-'02	4/0
	Quinn, Mike	QB	6-4	216	4/15/74	7	Stephen F. Austin	Houston, Texas	UFA(Hou)-'04	0*
	Santiago, O.J.	TE	6-7	265	3/4/74	7	Kent State	Toronto, Ontario, Canada	UFA(Oak)-'04	12/7*
37	Sapp, Cecil	RB	5-11	229	12/23/78	2	Colorado State	Miami, Fla.	FA-'03	1/0
80	Smith, Rod	WR	6-0	200	5/15/70	10	Missouri Southern	Texarkana, Ark.	FA-'94	15/15
33	Spencer, Jimmy	CB	5-9	188	3/29/69	13	Florida	Belle Glade, Fla.	FA-'00	16/2
59	Spragan, Donnie	LB	6-3	239	7/12/76	3	Stanford	Union City, Calif.	FA-'01	16/8
	Stephens, Jamain	T	6-6	374	1/9/74	8	North Carolina A&T	Lumberton, N.C.	FA-'04	0*

No.	Name	Pos.	Ht.	Wt.	Birthdate	NFL Exp.	College	Hometown	How Acq.	'03 Games/ Starts
29	Stephens, Reggie	CB	5-9	200	2/21/75	5	Rutgers	Santa Cruz, Calif.	FA-'04	0*
57	Sykes, Jashon	LB	6-2	236	9/25/79	2	Colorado	Los Angeles, Calif.	FA-'02	16/8
21	Turner, Scott	CB	5-10	190	2/26/72	9	Illinois	Richardson, Texas	FA-'03	9/0
35	Walls, Lenny	CB	6-4	192	9/26/79	3	Boston College	San Francisco, Calif.	FA-'02	16/16
87	Weaver, Jed	TE	6-4	258	8/11/76	6	Oregon	Bend, Ore.	UFA(SF)-'04	16/15*
56	Wilson, Al	LB	6-0	240	6/21/77	6	Tennessee	Jackson, Tenn.	D1-'99	16/16
32	Young, Chris	S	6-0	210	1/23/80	2	Georgia Tech	Senoia, Ga.	D7a-'02	11/0

* Alexander inactive for 4 games with New Orleans in '03; Almanzar inactive for 4 games; Bailey played 16 games with Washington, Chamberlain played 4 games with Washington; Chukwurah last active with Minnesota in '02; Coleman played 13 games with Philadelphia; Collins last active with Minnesota in '01; Eason missed '03 season because of injury; Elliss played 5 games with Detroit; Epstein last active with Jacksonville in '02; Galloway missed '03 season because of injury; Green played 5 games with Tampa Bay; Harris last active with Houston in '02; Hearst played 12 games with San Francisco; Israel inactive with Cleveland for 2 games; Jackson last active with Washington in '02; Jenkins last active with Arizona in '02; K. Johnson inactive for 3 games; R. Johnson played 9 games with San Diego; Lynch played 14 games with Tampa Bay; McNeal missed '03 season because of injury; Mitchell missed '03 season because of injury; Quinn inactive for 3 games and did not play in 1 game with Houston; Santiago played 12 games with Oakland; J. Stephens last active with Cincinnati in '01; R. Stephens did not play in 2 games with N.Y. Giants; Weaver played 16 games with San Francisco.

t- Broncos traded for Bailey (Wash).

Traded—CB Deltha O'Neal (Cin; 13 games in '03); RB Clinton Portis (Wash; 13).

Retired—Ed McCaffrey, 13-year wide receiver, 12 games in '03; Shannon Sharpe, 14-year tight end, 15 games in '03.

Players lost through free agency (4): DE Bertrand Berry (Ariz; 16 games in '03), LB Keith Burns (TB; 16), WR Chris Cole (Oak; 11), LB Ian Gold (TB; 6).

Also played with Broncos in '03—T Blake Brockermeyer (16 games), DT Daryl Gardener (5), G Steve Herndon (2), CB Ryan McNeil (4), LB Johnny Rutledge (6), T Ephraim Salaam (14).

2004 FIRST-YEAR ROSTER

Name	Pos.	Ht.	Wt.	Birthdate	College	Hometown	How Acq.
Alexander, Roc	CB	5-10	186	9/23/81	Washington	Colorado Springs, Colo.	FA
Bell, Tatum	RB	5-11	213	3/2/81	Oklahoma State	Dallas, Texas	D2a
Campbell, Darrell	DT	6-3	302	7/6/81	Notre Dame	South Holland, Ill.	FA
Clabo, Tyson	G	6-6	314	10/17/81	Wake Forest	Knoxville, Tenn.	FA
Crenshaw, Romar	WR	6-0	185	9/22/80	Southeast Oklahoma State	Broken Bow, Okla.	FA
Green, Louis (1)	LB	6-3	228	9/23/79	Alcorn State	Vicksburg, Miss.	FA-'03
Johnson, B.J.	WR	5-11	207	8/4/82	Texas	Grand Prairie, Texas	FA
Kennedy, Brandon	DT	5-10	315	10/20/81	North Texas	Terrell, Texas	FA
LeSueur, Jeremy	CB	6-0	197	10/5/80	Michigan	Holly Springs, Miss.	D3
Luke, Triandos	WR	5-10	189	12/24/81	Alabama	Phenix City, Ala.	D6a
Mauck, Matt	QB	6-1	213	2/12/79	Louisiana State	Jasper, Ind.	D7a
Miree, Brandon	RB	5-11	237	4/14/81	Pittsburgh	Cincinnati, Ohio	D7b
Pittman, Thomas (1)	DT	6-4	295	11/2/79	Florida	Garyville, La.	FA
Sewell, Josh	C-G	6-2	300	7/26/81	Nebraska	Lincoln, Neb.	D6b
Shoate, Jeff	CB	5-10	189	3/23/81	San Diego State	San Diego, Calif.	D5
Snell, Shannon	G	6-2	310	4/27/82	Florida	Tampa, Fla.	FA
Van Pelt, Bradlee	QB	6-2	231	7/3/80	Colorado State	Santa Barbara, Calif.	D7c
Watton, Chris (1)	G-C	6-3	305	10/6/77	Baylor	Sioux Falls, S.D.	FA-'03
Watts, Darius	WR	6-2	181	12/19/81	Marshall	Atlanta, Ga.	D2b
Williams, D.J.	LB	6-1	242	7/20/82	Miami	Pittsburg, Calif.	D1

The term NFL Rookie is defined as a player who is in his first season of professional football and has not been on the roster of another professional football team for any regular-season or postseason games. A Rookie is designated by an "R" on NFL rosters. Players who have been active in another professional football league or players who have NFL experience, including either preseason training camp or being on an Active List or Inactive List, or on Reserve/Injured or Reserve/Physically Unable to Perform for fewer than six regular-season games, are termed NFL First-Year Players. An NFL First-Year Player is designated by a "1" on NFL rosters. Thereafter, a player is credited with an additional year of experience for each season in which he accumulates six games on the Active List or Inactive List, or on Reserve/Injured or Reserve/Physically Unable to Perform.

Log on to www.denverbroncos.com for an up-to-date roster.

COACHING STAFF

Head Coach,
Mike Shanahan

Pro Career: Became the eleventh head coach in Broncos history on January 31, 1995. Mike Shanahan led the Broncos to back-to-back Super Bowl championships in 1997 and 1998, becoming just the fifth head coach to accomplish that feat, and is the only coach to win seven consecutive postseason games in a two-year period. No NFL head coach has won more game than Mike Shanhan's 98 victories since the start of the 1995 season. During his NFL career, Shanahan has been a part of teams that have played in nine conference championship games and six Super Bowls. His .700 winning percentage (7-3) as a head coach in postseason games is second only to Vince Lombardi (9-1, .900) among coaches with more than five playoff victories. In 26 seasons as a pro and college coach, Shanahan's teams ahve participated in postseason or bowl games 21 times. Under Shanahan's guidance, Denver has set and NFL record by posting the most victories in both a two-year (33, 1997-98) and three-year (46, 1996-98) period. In the last twelve years (nine with Denver and three as offensive coordinator with the San Francisco 49ers), Shanahan's offenses have finished number one in the NFL four times, second twice, and third twice. Shanahan was an assistant with Denver (1984-87, 1989-1991) and San Francisco (1992-94). Returned to Denver as quarterbacks coach on October 16, 1989, after posting 8-12 record as the Los Angeles Raiders' head coach. Career record: 106-68.

Background: Shanahan coached at Oklahoma (1975-76), Northern Arizona (1977), Eastern Illinois (1978), Minnesota (1979), and Florida (1980-83).

Personal: Born in Oak Park, Illinois, on August 24, 1952. He was a wishbone quarterback-defensive back at Eastern Illinois. Mike and his wife, Peggy, have two children—Kyle and Krystal.

ASSISTANT COACHES

Ronnie Bradford, special teams; born October 1, 1970, Minot, N.D. Defensive back Colorado 1989-1992. Pro defensive back Denver Broncos 1993-95, Arizona Cardinals 1996, Atlanta Falcons 1997-2001, Minnesota Vikings 2002. Pro coach: Joined Broncos in 2003.

Jacob Burney, defensive line; born January 24, 1959, Chattanooga, Tenn. Defensive tackle Tennessee-Chattanooga 1977-1980. No pro playing experience. College coach: New Mexico 1983-86, Tulsa 1987, Mississippi State 1988, Wisconsin 1989, UCLA 1990-92, Tennessee 1993. Pro coach: Cleveland Browns/Baltimore Ravens 1994-98, Carolina Panthers 1999-2001, joined Broncos in 2002.

Troy Calhoun, offensive assistant/special teams; born September 26, 1966, McMinnville, Ore. Quarterback Air Force 1986-89. No pro playing experience. College coach: Air Force 1989, 1993-94, Ohio University 1994-2000, Wake Forest 2001-02. Pro coach: Joined Broncos in 2003.

Larry Coyer, defensive coordinator; born April 19, 1943, Huntington, W. Va. Linebacker Marshall 1962-64. No pro playing experience. College coach: Marshall 1965-67, Iowa 1974-77, Oklahoma State 1978, Iowa State 1979-1983, 1995-96, UCLA 1987-89, Houston 1990, Ohio State 1991-92, East Carolina 1993, Pittsburgh 1997-99. Pro coach: Michigan Panthers (USFL) 1984-85, Memphis Showboats (USFL) 1986, New York Jets 1994, joined Broncos in 2000.

Rick Dennison, offensive line; born June 22, 1958, in Kalispell, Mont. Tight end Colorado State 1976-79. Pro linebacker Denver Broncos 1982-1990. Pro coach: Joined Broncos in 1995.

Kirk Doll, defensive assistant-special teams; born September 24, 1951, Wichita, Kan. Defensive end-tackle East Carolina 1971-72. No pro playing experience. College coach: Wichita State 1975-76, Iowa State 1979, Tulsa 1980-84, Arizona State 1985-87, Texas A&M 1988-1994, Notre Dame 1994-2001, Louisiana State 2002-03. Pro coach: Joined Broncos in 2004.

David Gibbs, defensive backs; born January 10, 1968, Mount Airy, N.C. Defensive back Colorado 1986-1990. No pro playing experience. College coach: Oklahoma 1991-92, Colorado 1993-94, Kansas 1995-96, Minnesota 1997-2000. Pro coach: Joined Broncos in 2001.

Gary Kubiak, offensive coordinator; born August 15, 1961, Houston, Texas. Quarterback Texas A&M 1979-1982. Pro quarterback Denver Broncos 1983-1991. College coach: Texas A&M 1992-93. Pro coach: San Francisco 49ers 1994, joined Broncos in 1995.

Pat McPherson, quarterbacks; born April 15, 1969, Santa Clara, Calif. Linebacker Santa Clara 1991-92. No pro playing experience. Pro coach: Joined Broncos in 1998.

Keith Millard; asst. defensive line/pass rush specialist; born March 18, 1962, Pleasanton, Calif. Defensive lineman Washington State 1980-84. Pro defensive lineman Minnesota Vikings 1985-1991, Seattle Seahawks 1992, Green Bay Packers 1992, Philadelphia Eagles 1993. College coach: Fort Lewis 1996, Menlo College 1997-2000. Pro coach: San Francisco Demons (XFL) 2001, joined Broncos in 2002.

Brian Pariani, tight ends; born July 2, 1965, San Francisco. No college or pro playing experience. College coach: UCLA 1989. Pro coach: San Francisco 49ers 1991-94, joined Broncos in 1995.

Greg Saporta, asst. strength and conditioning; born February 2, 1957, New York, N.Y., lives in Englewood, Colo. Wide receiver Buffalo State 1977-79. No pro playing experience. College coach: Florida 1981-88, 1993-94, North Carolina 1989-1992. Pro coach: Joined Broncos in 1995.

Cedric Smith, asst. strength and conditioning; born May 27, 1968, Enterprise, Ala. Running back Florida 1986-89. Pro fullback Minnesota Vikings 1990, New Orleans Saints 1991, Washington Redskins 1994-95, Arizona Cardinals 1996-98. Pro coach: Joined Broncos in 2001.

Jimmy Spencer, player/asst. defensive backs; born March 29, 1969, Manning, S.C. Cornerback Florida 1988-1990. Pro cornerback Washington Redskins 1991, New Orleans Saints 1992-95, Cincinnati Bengals 1996-97, San Diego Chargers 1998-99, Denver Broncos 2000-current. Pro coach: Joined Broncos in 2003.

Bobby Turner, running backs; born May 6, 1949, East Chicago, Ind. Defensive back Indiana State 1968-1971. No pro playing experience. College coach: Indiana State 1975-1982, Fresno State 1983-88, Ohio State 1989-1990, Purdue 1991-94. Pro coach: Joined Broncos in 1995.

Rich Tuten, strength and conditioning; born December 30, 1953, Columbia, S.C. Nose guard Clemson 1976-78. No pro playing experience. College coach: Florida 1979-1988, 1993-94, North Carolina 1989-1992. Pro coach: Joined Broncos in 1995.

Steve Watson, wide receivers; born May 28, 1957, Baltimore. Wide receiver Temple 1975-78. Pro wide receiver Denver 1979-1987. Pro coach: Joined Broncos in 2001.

American Football Conference
South Division
Team Colors: Deep Steel Blue, Battle Red, and Liberty White
Two Reliant Park
Houston, Texas 77054
Telephone: (832) 667-2000

2004 SCHEDULE

PRESEASON		**Houston time**
Aug. 14	**Dallas**	7:00
Aug. 21	at Pittsburgh	6:30
Aug. 27	at Denver	8:00
Sept. 2	**Tampa Bay**	7:00

REGULAR SEASON		
Sept 12	**San Diego**	12:00
Sept. 19	at Detroit	12:00
Sept. 26	at Kansas City	12:00
Oct. 3	**Oakland**	12:00
Oct. 10	**Minnesota**	12:00
Oct. 17	at Tennessee	12:00
Oct. 24	Open Date	
Oct. 31	**Jacksonville**	12:00
Nov. 7	at Denver	3:15
Nov. 14	at Indianapolis	12:00
Nov. 21	**Green Bay**	7:30
Nov. 28	**Tennessee**	12:00
Dec. 5	at New York Jets	12:00
Dec. 12	**Indianapolis**	12:00
Dec. 19	at Chicago	12:00
Dec. 26	at Jacksonville	12:00
Jan. 2	**Cleveland**	12:00

Stadium: Reliant Stadium (opened in 2002) • **Capacity:** 71,054 Houston, Texas 77054
Playing Surface: Grass
Training Camp: Reliant Park Practice Facility

RELIANT STADIUM

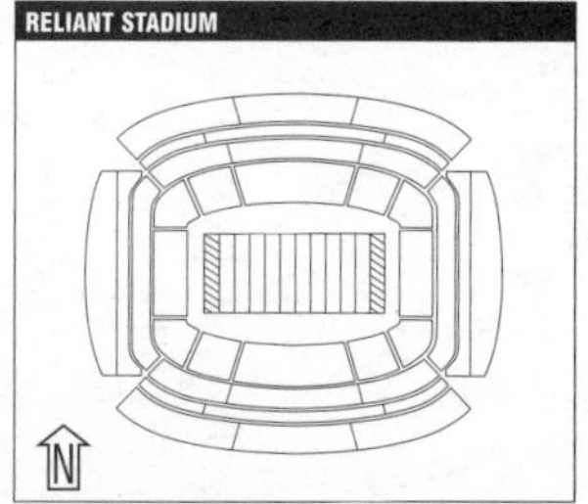

CLUB OFFICIALS

Chairman and CEO: Robert C. McNair
Vice Chairman: Philip Burguieres
Senior Vice President and General Manager/Football Operations: Charley Casserly
Senior Vice President/Chief Sales & Marketing Officer: Jamey Rootes
Senior Vice President/Treasurer and Chief Financial Officer: Scott Schwinger
Senior Vice President/General Counsel and Chief Administrative Officer: Suzie Thomas
Vice President/Ticket Operations: John Schriever
Vice President/Communications: Tony Wyllie
Vice President/Corporate Sales: David Peart
Controller: Marilan Logan
Director of Negotiations: Dan Ferens
Director of Pro Scouting: Chuck Banker
Associate Directors of Pro Scouting: Bobby Grier, Miller McCalmon, Rob Keisel
Coordinator of College Scouting: Mike Maccagnan
National Scout: George Saimes
College Scouts: Larry Bryan, Eugene Armstrong, Pete Russell, Dave Sears, Rob Lohman, Tom Throckmorton
Director of Operations: Barry Asimos
Director of Marketing: Kim Babiak
Director of Corporate Sales: Patrick Streko
Director of Security: Ryan Reichert
Director of Community Relations: Regina Woolfolk
Director of Internet Services & Publications: Carter Toole
Media Relations Manager: Rocky Harris
Director of Player Programs: Marcus Heard
Director of Information Technology: Nick Ignatiev
Executive Director, Houston Texans Foundation: Joanie Haley
Human Resources Administrator: Glenda Morrison
Head Athletic Trainer: Kevin Bastin
Coordinator of Rehabilitation: Tom Colt
Assistant Athletic Trainer: John Ishop
Director of Equipment Services: Jay Brunetti
Assistant Equipment Managers: Matt Grupp, Greg Read
Video Director: Ken Sparacino
Assistant Video Director: Joe Malota
Video Assistant: Robert Wells

COACHING HISTORY
(9-23-0)

2002-03 Dom Capers 9-23-0

ATTENDANCE

Home 553,360 Away 496,847
Total 1,050,207
Single-game home record, 70,758 (12/21/03)
Single-season home record,

553,360 (2003)

2004 DRAFT CHOICES

Round	Name	Pos.	College
1	Dunta Robinson	DB	South Carolina
	Jason Babin	LB	Western Michigan
4	Glenn Earl	DB	Notre Dame
6	Vontez Duff	DB	Notre Dame
	Jammal Lord	DB	Nebraska
	Charlie Anderson	LB	Mississippi
7	Raheem Orr	LB	Rutgers
	Sloan Thomas	WR	Texas
	B.J. Symons	QB	Texas Tech

HOUSTON TEXANS

2003 TEAM RECORD

PRESEASON (0-4)

Date	Result		Opponent
8/9	L	12-20	Denver
8/15	L	6-34	at Dallas
8/23	L	17-19	San Diego
8/28	L	3-34	at Tampa Bay

REGULAR SEASON (5-11)

Date	Result		Opponent	Att.
9/7	W	21-20	at Miami	73,010
9/14	L	10-31	at New Orleans	68,390
9/21	L	14-42	Kansas City	70,487
9/28	W	24-20	Jacksonville	70,041
10/12	L	17-38	at Tennessee	68,809
10/19	L	14-19	New York Jets	70,623
10/26	L	21-30	at Indianapolis	56,132
11/2	W	14-10	Carolina	70,052
11/9	L	27-34	at Cincinnati	50,437
11/16	W	12-10	at Buffalo	72,677
11/23	L	20-23	New England (OT)	70,719
11/30	W	17-13	Atlanta	70,388
12/7	L	0-27	at Jacksonville	43,363
12/14	L	3-16	at Tampa Bay	65,124
12/21	L	24-27	Tennessee	70,758
12/28	L	17-20	Indianapolis	70,680

(OT) Overtime

SCORE BY PERIODS

Texans	23	87	84	61	0 —	255
Opponents	64	115	73	125	3 —	380

2003 TEAM STATISTICS

	Texans	Opp.
Total First Downs	237	336
Rushing	86	130
Passing	127	179
Penalty	24	27
3rd Down: Made/Att	63/204	89/222
3rd Down Pct.	30.9	40.1
4th Down: Made/Att	9/14	10/14
4th Down Pct.	64.3	71.4
Possession Avg.	27:39	32:21
Total Net Yards	4,306	6,082
Avg. Per Game	269.1	380.1
Total Plays	896	1,054
Avg. Per Play	4.8	5.8
Net Yards Rushing	1,651	2,370
Avg. Per Game	103.2	148.1
Total Rushes	421	533
Net Yards Passing	2,655	3,712
Avg. Per Game	165.9	232.0
Sacked/Yards Lost	36/186	19/123
Gross Yards	2,841	3,835
Att./Completions	439/248	502/297
Completion Pct.	56.5	59.2
Had Intercepted	18	14
Punts/Average	97/41.5	75/41.7
Net Punting Avg.	97/36.7	75/35.8
Penalties/Yards	121/961	96/767
Fumbles/Ball Lost	18/9	18/8
Touchdowns	29	42
Rushing	14	15
Passing	14	22
Returns	1	5

2003 INDIVIDUAL STATISTICS

PASSING	Att.	Comp.	Yds.	Pct.	TD	Int.	Tkld.	Rate
Carr	295	167	2,013	56.6	9	13	15/90	69.5
Banks	102	61	693	59.8	5	3	13/57	84.3
Ragone	40	20	135	50.0	0	1	8/39	47.4
Gaffney	1	0	0	0.0	0	0	0/0	39.6
Mack	1	0	0	0.0	0	1	0/0	0.0
Texans	439	248	2,841	56.5	14	18	36/186	69.7
Opponents	502	297	3,835	59.2	22	14	19/123	86.2

SCORING	TD R	TD P	TD Rt	PAT	FG	Saf	PTS
K. Brown	0	0	0	27/27	18/22	0	81
D. Davis	8	0	0	0/0	0/0	0	48
Bradford	0	4	0	0/0	0/0	0	24
Johnson	0	4	0	0/0	0/0	0	24
Mack	4	0	0	0/0	0/0	0	24
Miller	0	3	0	0/0	0/0	0	18
Carr	2	0	0	0/0	0/0	0	12
Gaffney	0	2	0	0/0	0/0	0	12
Armstrong	0	1	0	0/0	0/0	0	6
McCree	0	0	1	0/0	0/0	0	6
Texans	14	14	1	27/27	18/22	0	255
Opponents	15	22	5	40/40	28/35	2	380

2-Pt. Conversions: None.
Texans 0-2, Opponents 0-2.

RUSHING	No.	Yds	Avg	LG	TD
D. Davis	238	1,031	4.3	51	8
Mack	93	253	2.7	13	4
Carr	27	151	5.6	36	2
Hollings	38	102	2.7	17	0
Ragone	6	51	8.5	14	0
Banks	6	27	4.5	13	0
Wells	5	14	2.8	10	0
Gaffney	1	13	13.0	13	0
Stanley	1	12	12.0	12	0
Simmons	1	7	7.0	7	0
Johnson	5	-10	-2.0	11	0
Texans	421	1,651	3.9	51	14
Opponents	533	2,370	4.4	64	15

RECEIVING	No.	Yds	Avg	LG	TD
Johnson	66	976	14.8	46t	4
D. Davis	47	351	7.5	17	0
Miller	40	355	8.9	25	3
Gaffney	34	402	11.8	33	2
Bradford	24	460	19.2	78t	4
Mack	9	55	6.1	10	0
Holloway	8	84	10.5	33	0
Armstrong	7	75	10.7	18	1
Norris	7	40	5.7	11	0
Hollings	2	25	12.5	19	0
Wells	2	17	8.5	12	0
Coleman	1	6	6.0	6	0
Ragone	1	-5	-5.0	-5	0
Texans	248	2,841	11.5	78t	14
Opponents	297	3,835	12.9	84t	22

INTERCEPTIONS	No.	Yds	Avg	LG	TD
Coleman	7	95	13.6	41	0
Wright	3	-2	-0.7	0	0
McCree	1	95	95.0	95t	1
Stevens	1	12	12.0	12	0
E. Brown	1	5	5.0	5	0
Glenn	1	0	0.0	0	0
Texans	14	205	14.6	95t	1
Opponents	18	207	11.5	51t	3

PUNTING	No.	Yds.	Avg.	In 20	LG
Stanley	97	4,028	41.5	36	58
Texans	97	4,028	41.5	36	58
Opponents	75	3,130	41.7	20	59

PUNT RETURNS	Ret	FC	Yds	Avg	LG	TD
Moses	36	7	244	6.8	40	0
Gaffney	4	1	22	5.5	15	0
Texans	40	8	266	6.7	40	0
Opponents	43	37	407	9.5	73t	1

KICKOFF RETURNS	No.	Yds	Avg	LG	TD
Moses	58	1,355	23.4	70	0
Hollings	8	142	17.8	30	0
Norris	5	71	14.2	19	0
D. Davis	3	61	20.3	28	0
Vaughn	3	47	15.7	22	0
Wells	2	24	12.0	14	0
T. Martin	1	0	0.0	0	0
Texans	80	1,700	21.3	70	0
Opponents	53	1,149	21.7	49	0

FIELD GOALS	1-19	20-29	30-39	40-49	50+
K. Brown	1/1	3/3	8/8	5/6	1/4
Texans	1/1	3/3	8/8	5/6	1/4
Opponents	0/0	13/14	10/12	5/9	0/0

SACKS	No.
Sharper	4.0
Wong	3.0
Foreman	2.0
Orr	2.0
Clemons	1.0
Foley	1.0
S. Martin	1.0
Payne	1.0
Peek	1.0
Sears	1.0
Wright	1.0
E. Brown	0.5
Ioane	0.5
Texans	19.0
Opponents	36.0

RECORD HOLDERS

INDIVIDUAL RECORDS—CAREER

Category	Name	Performance
Rushing (Yds.)	Domanick Davis, 2003	1,031
Passing (Yds.)	David Carr, 2002-03	4,605
Passing (TDs)	David Carr, 2002-03	18
Receiving (No.)	Billy Miller, 2002-03	91
Receiving (Yds.)	Corey Bradford, 2002-03	1,157
Interceptions	Marcus Coleman, 2002-03	8
Punting (Avg.)	Chad Stanley, 2002-03	41.4
Punt Return (Avg.)	Avion Black, 2002	13.4
Kickoff Return (Avg.)	J.J. Moses, 2003	23.4
Field Goals	Kris Brown, 2002-03	35
Touchdowns (Tot.)	Corey Bradford, 2002-03	10
Points	Kris Brown, 2002-03	152

INDIVIDUAL RECORDS—SINGLE SEASON

Category	Name	Performance
Rushing (Yds.)	Domanick Davis, 2003	1,031
Passing (Yds.)	David Carr, 2002	2,592
Passing (TDs)	David Carr, 2002, 2003	9
Receiving (No.)	Andre Johnson, 2003	66
Receiving (Yds.)	Andre Johnson, 2003	976
Interceptions	Marcus Coleman, 2003	7
Punting (Avg.)	Chad Stanley, 2003	41.5
Punt Return (Avg.)	Avion Black, 2002	13.4
Kickoff Return (Avg.)	J.J. Moses, 2003	23.4
Field Goals	Kris Brown, 2003	18
Touchdowns (Tot.)	Domanick Davis, 2003	8
Points	Kris Brown, 2003	81

INDIVIDUAL RECORDS—SINGLE GAME

Category	Name	Performance
Rushing (Yds.)	Domanick Davis, 10-19-03	129
Passing (Yds.)	David Carr, 10-12-03	371
Passing (TDs)	David Carr, 9-8-02, 9-29-02, 10-12-03, 11-9-03	2
	Tony Banks, 11-23-03	2
Receiving (No.)	James Allen, 12-1-02	10
Receiving (Yds.)	Corey Bradford, 10-12-03	127
Interceptions	Aaron Glenn, 12-8-02	2
	Marcus Coleman, 9-7-03	2
	Kenny Wright, 9-28-03	2
Field Goals	Kris Brown, 9-7-03	5
Touchdowns (Tot.)	Corey Bradford, 9-29-02	2
	David Carr, 11-17-02	2
	Andre Johnson, 9-21-03	2
	Stacey Mack, 10-19-03	2
	Domanick Davis, 10-26-03, 11-30-03, 12-28-03	2
Points	Kris Brown, 9-7-03	15

HOUSTON TEXANS

2004 VETERAN ROSTER

No.	Name	Pos.	Ht.	Wt.	Birthdate	NFL Exp.	College	Hometown	How Acq.	'03 Games/ Starts
87	Armstrong, Derick	WR	6-2	196	4/2/79	2	Arkansas-Monticello	Dallas, Texas	FA-'03	9/1
12	Banks, Tony	QB	6-4	230	4/5/73	8	Michigan State	San Diego, Calif.	FA-'02	7/3
47	Baxter, Jarrod	FB	6-1	245	3/9/79	3	New Mexico	Albuquerque, N.M.	D5a-'02	0*
33	Bell, Jason	CB	6-0	182	4/1/78	4	UCLA	Long Beach, Calif.	W(Dall)-'02	13/0
57	Bell, Marcus	LB	6-1	245	7/19/77	4	Arizona	St. John's, Ariz.	FA-'04	0*
85	Bradford, Corey	WR	6-1	197	12/8/75	7	Jackson State	Clinton, La.	UFA(GB)-'02	16/6
24	Brown, Eric	S	6-1	210	3/20/75	7	Mississippi State	San Antonio, Texas	FA-'02	16/16
3	Brown, Kris	K	5-11	206	12/23/76	6	Nebraska	Southlake, Texas	RFA(Pitt)-'02	16/0
67	Brown, Milford	G	6-4	320	8/15/80	3	Florida State	Montgomery, Ala.	SD6-'02	4/2
88	Bruener, Mark	TE	6-4	260	9/16/72	10	Washington	Olympia, Wash.	FA-'04	14/0*
8	Carr, David	QB	6-3	223	7/21/79	3	Fresno State	Bakersfield, Calif.	D1-'02	12/11
9	Charles, Terry	WR	6-3	207	7/18/79	2	Portland State	Long Beach, Calif.	FA-'04	0*
50	Clemons, Charlie	LB	6-2	250	7/4/72	8	Georgia	Griffin, Ga.	UFA(NO)-'03	9/8
42	Coleman, Marcus	CB	6-2	210	5/24/74	9	Texas Tech	Dallas, Texas	ED(NYJ)-'02	15/15
37	Davis, Domanick	RB	5-9	216	10/1/80	2	Louisiana State	Breaux Bridge, La.	D4-'03	14/10
95	Deloach, Jerry	DE	6-2	315	7/17/77	4	California	Valley, Calif.	T(Wash)-'02	16/16
16	Dugans, Ron	WR	6-2	205	4/27/77	4	Florida State	Tallahassee, Fla.	FA-'04	0*
54	Evans, Troy	LB	6-1	230	12/3/77	3	Cincinnati	Cincinnati, Ohio	FA-'02	15/0
38	Faggins, Demarcus	CB	5-10	178	6/13/79	3	Kansas State	Irving, Texas	D6a-'02	8/1
56	Foreman, Jay	LB	6-1	240	2/18/76	6	Nebraska	Eden Prairie, Minn.	T(Buff)-'02	16/16
86	Gaffney, Jabar	WR	6-1	193	12/1/80	3	Florida	Jacksonville, Fla.	D2-'02	16/11
31	Glenn, Aaron	CB	5-9	185	7/16/72	11	Texas A&M	Humble, Texas	ED(NYJ)-'02	11/11
25	Hollings, Tony	RB	5-10	216	12/1/81	2	Georgia Tech	Jeffersonville, Ga.	SD2-'03	14/1
89	Holloway, Jabari	TE	6-2	260	12/18/78	4	Notre Dame	Tyrone, Ga.	W(NE)-'02	15/9
94	Ioane, Junior	DT	6-4	320	7/21/77	5	Arizona State	Mt. Pleasant, Utah	W(Oak)-'03	13/4
80	Johnson, Andre	WR	6-3	227	7/11/81	2	Miami	Miami, Fla.	D1-'03	16/16
73	Jones, Garrick	T	6-5	306	12/2/78	2	Arkansas State	Little Rock, Ark.	W(KC)-'03	0*
83	Joppru, Bennie	TE	6-4	262	1/5/80	2	Michigan	Minnetonka, Minn.	D2-'03	0*
90	Martin, Terrance	DE	6-2	290	7/16/79	2	North Carolina State	Toano, Va.	FA-'03	12/1
29	McCree, Marlon	S	5-11	198	3/17/77	4	Kentucky	Daytona Beach, Fla.	W(Jax)-'03	13/11
76	McKinney, Steve	C	6-4	295	10/15/75	7	Texas A&M	Friendswood, Texas	UFA(Ind)-'02	16/16
82	Miller, Billy	TE	6-3	230	4/24/77	6	Southern California	Westlake Village, Calif.	FA-'02	16/5
84	Moses, J.J.	WR	5-6	178	9/12/79	3	Iowa State	Waterloo, Iowa	FA-'03	15/0
81	Murphy, Matt	TE	6-5	260	2/23/80	2	Maryland	New Haven, Mich.	FA-'03	1/0
44	Norris, Moran	FB	6-1	250	6/16/78	4	Kansas	Houston, Texas	W(NO)-'02	16/10
53	Orr, Shantee	LB	6-0	250	5/28/81	2	Michigan	Detroit, Mich.	FA-'03	6/0
91	Payne, Seth	DT	6-4	303	2/12/75	8	Cornell	Victor, N.Y.	ED(Jax)-'02	2/2
98	Peek, Antwan	LB	6-3	243	10/29/79	2	Cincinnati	Cincinnati, Ohio	D3-'03	10/4
48	Pittman, Bryan	LS	6-3	270	1/20/77	2	Washington	Auburn, Wash.	FA-'03	16/0
69	Pitts, Chester	T	6-4	320	6/26/79	3	San Diego State	Inglewood, Calif.	D2-'02	16/16
51	Polk, DaShon	LB	6-2	240	3/13/77	5	Arizona	Pacoima, Calif.	UFA(Buff)-'04	16/0*
4	Ragone, Dave	QB	6-3	245	10/3/79	2	Louisville	Middleberg, Ohio	D3-'03	2/2
92	Sears, Corey	DE	6-3	319	4/15/73	6	Mississippi State	Converse, Texas	FA-'02	16/13
55	Sharper, Jamie	LB	6-3	240	11/23/74	8	Virginia	Richmond, Va.	ED(Balt)-'02	16/16
66	Silvers, Elliot	T	6-7	320	2/19/78	2	Washington	Agoura, Calif.	FA-'04	0*
30	Simmons, Jason	CB	5-9	198	3/30/76	7	Arizona State	Lawndale, Calif.	UFA(Pitt)-'02	16/2
79	Slechta, Jeremy	DT	6-6	285	5/12/80	2	Nebraska	LaVista, Neb.	FA-'03	2/0
99	Smith, Robaire	DE	6-4	315	11/15/77	5	Michigan State	Flint, Mich.	UFA(Tenn)-'04	16/15*
7	Stanley, Chad	P	6-3	205	1/29/76	5	Stephen F. Austin	Ore City, Texas	FA-'02	16/0
21	Vaughn, Darrick	CB	5-11	193	10/2/78	4	Southwest Texas State	Aldine, Texas	FA-'03	16/0
71	Wade, Todd	T	6-8	315	10/30/76	5	Mississippi	Jackson, Miss.	UFA(Mia)-'04	16/16*
96	Walker, Gary	DE	6-2	305	2/28/73	10	Auburn	Royston, Ga.	ED(Jax)-'02	4/4
41	Walker, Ramon	S	6-0	197	11/8/79	3	Pittsburgh	Akron, Ohio	D5b-'02	11/0
78	Wand, Seth	T	6-7	327	8/6/79	2	Northwest Missouri State	Springfield, Mo.	D3-'03	16/2
77	Washington, Todd	C	6-3	310	7/19/76	7	Virginia Tech	Melfa, Va.	FA-'03	16/14
70	Weary, Fred	G	6-4	308	9/30/77	3	Tennessee	Montgomery, Ala.	D3-'02	14/2
32	Wells, Jonathan	RB	6-1	243	7/21/79	3	Ohio State	River Ridge, La.	D4-'02	13/0
72	Wiegert, Zach	G-T	6-5	309	8/16/72	10	Nebraska	Fremont, Neb.	UFA(Jax)-'03	14/14
52	Wong, Kailee	LB	6-2	250	5/23/76	6	Stanford	Eugene, Ore.	UFA(Minn)-'02	16/16
43	Wright, Kenny	CB	6-1	205	9/14/77	6	Northwestern State (La.)	Ruston, La.	W(Minn)-'02	15/5

* Baxter missed '03 because of injury; M. Bell last played with Arizona in '02; Bruner played 14 games with Pittsburgh in '03; Charles missed '02 season with San Diego because of injury; Dugans last active with Cincinnati '02; Jones inactive for 11 games; Joppru missed '03 season because of injury; Polk played 16 games with Buffalo; Silvers last played with San Diego in '01; Smith played 16 games with Tennessee; Wade played 16 games with Miami.

Players lost through free agency (5): FB Greg Comella (TB; 5 games in '03), LB Steve Foley (SD; 13), DT Steve Martin (Minn; 14), QB Mike Quinn (Den; 0), T Greg Randall (SF; 16 games in '03).

Also played with Texans in '03—TE Rashod Kent (7 games), RB Stacey Mack (8), LB Jimmy McClain (8), LB Armegis Spearman (1), S Matt Stevens (12).

2004 FIRST-YEAR ROSTER

Name	Pos.	Ht.	Wt.	Birthdate	College	Hometown	How Acq.
Anderson, Charlie	LB	6-4	240	12/8/81	Mississippi	Jackoson, Miss.	D6c
Anderson, Jason (1)	RB	6-0	205	4/39/80	South Dakota	Palmdale, Calif.	FA
Babin, Jason	LB	6-2	260	5/24/80	Western Michigan	Kalamazoo, Mich.	D1b
Bachman, Ryan	T	6-6	300	7/28/80	Kearney State	Ponca, Neb.	FA
Burns, Curry (1)	S	6-0	212	2/12/81	Louisville	Miami, Fla.	D7a-'03
Carroll, Travis (1)	LB	6-4	240	10/26/78	Florida	Jacksonville, Fla.	FA-'03
Cheek, Steve (1)	P	6-4	205	4/18/77	Humboldt State	Westfield, N.J.	FA
Davis, Jason (1)	DE	6-3	290	9/12/80	West Virginia	Ft. Lauderdale, Fla.	FA-'03
Dawson, Curry (1)	T	6-6	290	8/4/79	Angelo State	Water Valley, Texas	FA-'03
Deronde, Kevin (1)	LB	6-4	258	8/15/78	Iowa State	Pella, Iowa	FA-'03
Duff, Vontez	CB	5-11	198	3/8/82	Notre Dame	Copperas Cove, Texas	D6a
Dunn, Anthony (1)	LB	6-2	250	7/1/80	Northern Colorado	Denver, Colo.	FA
Earl, Glenn	S	6-1	222	6/10/81	Notre Dame	Naperville, Ill.	D4
Freeman, Rober' (1)	CB	5-9	182	8/28/81	Clark Atlanta	Atlanta, Ga.	FA-'03
Johnson, Albert (1)	WR	5-9	190	11/11/77	Southern Methodist	Houston, Texas	FA-'03
Lekkerkerker, Brad	T	6-7	330	5/8/78	California-Davis	Chino, Calif.	FA
Lewis, Jermaine (1)	WR	6-4	209	11/1/79	Western Michigan	Kalamazoo, Mich.	FA
Lord, Jammal	S	6-2	219	1/10/82	Nebraska	Bayonne, N.J.	D6b
Martin, Andrew	C	6-3	290	6/26/81	Northern Colorado	Boulder, Colo.	FA
Orr, Raheem	LB	6-3	258	11/8/80	Rutgers	Elizabeth, N.J.	D7a
Pili, Ifo	DT	6-3	310	12/7/79	Brigham Young	Provo, Utah	FA
Powell, Jamal (1)	C	6-3	311	4/10/81	TCU	Channelview, Texas	FA-'03
Renteria, D.J.	DE	6-3	282	1/15/81	New Mexico	Roswell, N.M.	FA
Robinson, Dunta	CB	5-10	186	4/11/82	South Carolina	Athens, Ga.	D1a
Sievers, Todd (1)	K	6-2	215	4/1/80	Miami	Ankeny, Iowa	FA
Stansbury, Ed (1)	FB	6-0	257	5/3/79	UCLA	El Paso, Texas	FA
Starling, Kendrick	WR	6-0	193	5/3/79	San Jose State	Marshall, Texas	FA
Stephens, Travis (1)	RB	5-7	195	6/26/78	Tennessee	Clarksville, Tenn.	FA-'03
Symons, B.J.	QB	6-1	210	11/19/80	Texas Tech	Cypress, Texas	D7c
Taylor, Chris (1)	WR	5-10	183	4/25/79	Texas A&M	Madisonville, Texas	FA
Thomas, Sloan	WR	6-1	203	12/22/81	Texas	Klein, Texas	D7b

The term NFL Rookie is defined as a player who is in his first season of professional football and has not been on the roster of another professional football team for any regular-season or postseason games. A Rookie is designated by an "R" on NFL rosters. Players who have been active in another professional football league or players who have NFL experience, including either preseason training camp or being on an Active List or Inactive List, or on Reserve/Injured or Reserve/Physically Unable to Perform for fewer than six regular-season games, are termed NFL First-Year Players. An NFL First-Year Player is designated by a "1" on NFL rosters. Thereafter, a player is credited with an additional year of experience for each season in which he accumulates six games on the Active List or Inactive List, or on Reserve/Injured or Reserve/Physically Unable to Perform.

Log on to www.houstontexans.com for an up-to-date roster.

HOUSTON TEXANS

COACHING STAFF

Head Coach,

Dom Capers

Pro Career: The Texans introduced Capers as their first head coach on January 21, 2001. The 2002 Texans finished 4-12, tied for the second-most victories by an expansion team (Jacksonville, 1995). The Texans finished 5-11 in 2003. Capers previously spent four seasons (1995-98) as head coach of the Carolina Panthers, guiding that expansion franchise from its infancy to a playoff berth in its second season. Capers compiled a 31-35 record in four seasons as the Panthers' head coach. In 1995, the Panthers' 7-9 record set an NFL mark for most victories by an expansion team. Carolina also posted the first four-game winning streak in expansion history, the first winning home record by an expansion club, and the first win over a defending Super Bowl champion (San Francisco) in expansion annals. In 1996, Capers won coach of the year as the Panthers posted a 12-4 record and won the NFC West title. Carolina then defeated defending Super Bowl champion Dallas in the divisional playoffs before losing to Green Bay in the NFC Championship Game. Capers has been a professional assistant coach for the USFL's Philadelphia/Baltimore Stars (1984-85), New Orleans Saints (1986-1991), Pittsburgh Steelers (1992-94), and Jacksonville Jaguars (1999-2000). Career record: 40-58.

Background: Capers played safety and linebacker at Mount Union College (1968-1971). Capers coached collegiately at Kent State (1972-74), Hawaii (1975-76), San Jose State (1977), California (1978-79), Tennessee (1980-81), and Ohio State (1982-83).

Personal: Born August 7, 1950 in Cambridge, Ohio. He and his wife Karen live in Houston.

ASSISTANT COACHES

Kippy Brown, wide receivers; born March 6, 1955, Sweetwater, Tenn. Quarterback Memphis State 1974-77. No pro playing experience. College coach: Memphis State 1978-1980, Louisville 1982, Tennessee 1983-89, 1993-94. Pro coach: New York Jets 1990-92, Tampa Bay Buccaneers 1995, Miami Dolphins 1996-99, Green Bay Packers 2000, Memphis Maniax (XFL, head coach) 2001, joined Texans 2002.

Vic Fangio, defensive coordinator; born August 22, 1958, Dunmore, Pa. East Stroudsburg State University. No pro playing experience. College coach: North Carolina 1983. Pro coach: Philadelphia/Baltimore Stars (USFL) 1984-85, New Orleans Saints 1986-1994, Carolina Panthers 1995-98, Indianapolis Colts 1999-2001, joined Texans in 2002.

Todd Grantham, defensive line; born September 13, 1966, Pulaski, Va. Guard-tackle Virginia Tech 1984-88. No pro playing experience. College coach: Virginia Tech 1990-95, Michigan State 1996-98. Pro coach: Indianapolis Colts 1999-2001, joined Texans in 2002.

Chick Harris, running backs; born September 21, 1945, Durham, N.C. Running back Northern Arizona 1966-69. No pro playing experience. College coach: Colorado State 1970-71, Long Beach State 1972-73, Washington 1975-1980. Pro coach: Detroit Wheels (WFL) 1974, Buffalo Bills 1981-82, Seattle Seahawks 1983-1991, Los Angeles Rams 1992-94, Carolina Panthers 1995-2001, joined Texans in 2002.

Jon Hoke, defensive backs; born January 24, 1957, Kettering, Ohio. Defensive back Ball State 1976-1979. Pro defensive back Chicago Bears 1980. College coach: Bowling Green 1983-86, San Diego State 1987-88, Kent State 1989-1993, Missouri 1994-98, Florida 1999-2001. Pro coach: Joined Texans in 2002.

Joe Marciano, special teams coordinator; born February 10, 1954, Dunmore, Pa. Quarterback Temple 1972-75. No pro playing experience. College coach: East Stroudsburg 1977, Rhode Island 1978-79, Villanova 1980, Penn State 1981, Temple 1982. Pro coach: Philadelphia/Baltimore Stars (USFL) 1983-85, New Orleans Saints 1986-1995, Tampa Bay Buccaneers 1996-2001, joined Texans in 2002.

Tony Marciano, tight ends; born June 14, 1956, Scranton, Pa. Offensive line Indiana University (Pa.) 1975-77. No pro playing experience. College coach: Texas Christian 1978-1980, Southern Methodist 1981-87, Brown 1987-88, Richmond 1989-1990, Kent State 1991-92. Pro coach: Toronto Argonauts (CFL) 1994, Calgary Stampeders (CFL) 1995-97, Indianapolis Colts 1998-2001, joined Texans in 2002.

Steve Marshall, offensive line (tackles); born June 20, 1956, Hartford, Conn. Guard-tight end Louisville 1976-78. No pro playing experience. College coach: Plymouth State 1979, Tennessee 1980-81, Marshall 1982-83, Louisville 1984, Murray State 1985-86, Virginia Tech 1987-1992, Tennessee 1993-95, UCLA 1996, Texas A&M 1997, North Carolina 1998-99, Colorado 2000-2001. Pro coach: Joined Texans in 2002.

Tony Oden, defensive assistant/asst. defensive backs; born June 30, 1973, Cleveland. Linebacker Baldwin-Wallace College 1991-95. No pro playing experience. College coach: Millersville (Penn.) 1996, Boston College 1997, Army 1998-99, East Carolina 2000-02, Eastern Michigan 2003. Pro coach: Joined Texans in 2004.

Tom Olivadotti, linebackers; born September 22, 1945, Long Beach, N.J. Defensive back-wide receiver Upsala College 1963-66. No pro playing experience. College coach: Princeton 1976-77, Boston College 1978-79, Miami 1980-83. Pro coach: Washington Federals (USFL) 1984, Cleveland Browns 1985-86, Miami Dolphins 1987-1995, Minnesota Vikings 1996-99, New York Giants 2000-03, joined Texans in 2004.

Chris Palmer, offensive coordinator; born September 23, 1949, Brewster, N.Y. Quarterback Southern Connecticut State 1968-1971. No pro playing experience. College coach: Connecticut 1972-74, Lehigh 1975, Colgate 1976-1982, New Haven 1986-87 (head coach), Boston 1988-89 (head coach). Pro coach: Montreal Concordes (CFL) 1983, New Jersey Generals (USFL) 1984-85, Houston Oilers 1990-92, New England Patriots 1993-96, Jacksonville Jaguars 1997-98, Cleveland Browns 1999-2000 (head coach), joined Texans in 2001.

Joe Pendry, offensive line (centers-guards); born August 5, 1947, Welch, W. Va. Tight end West Virginia 1965-66. No pro playing experience. College coach: West Virginia 1969-1974 1976-77, Kansas State 1975, Pittsburgh 1978-79, Michigan State 1980-81, Southwest Missouri State 2003. Pro coach: Philadelphia Stars (USFL) 1983, Pittsburgh Maulers (USFL) 1984, Cleveland Browns 1985-88, Kansas City Chiefs 1989-1992, Chicago Bears 1993-94, Carolina Panthers 1995-97, Buffalo Bills 1998-2000, Washington Redskins 2001, joined Texans in 2004.

Dan Riley, strength and conditioning; born October 19, 1949, Syracuse, N.Y. Attended Keene State. No college or pro playing experience. College coach: Army 1974-77, Penn State 1977-1981. Pro coach: Washington Redskins 1982-2000, joined Texans 2001.

Greg Roman, quarterbacks; born August 19, 1972, Atlantic City, N.J. Defensive line-linebacker John Carroll 1990-94. No pro playing experience. Pro coach: Carolina 1995-2001, joined Texans in 2002.

Eric Sutulovich, asst. special teams; born February 28, 1974, Kansas City, Kan. Tight end Louisiana Tech 1993-95. No pro playing experience. College coach: Louisiana Tech 1997-99, Pittsburgh 2000, Fort Scott 2001. Pro coach: Joined Texans in 2002.

Ray Wright, asst. strength and conditioning; born December 30, 1971, Cleveland. Running back-wide receiver Duke 1990-95. No pro playing experience. College coach: Cornell 1999, Maryland 2001. Pro coach: Joined Texans in 2002.

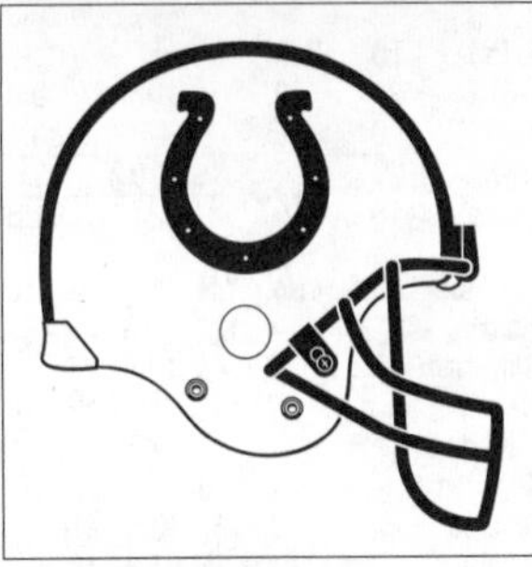

American Football Conference
South Division
Team Colors: Royal Blue and White
P.O. Box 535000
Indianapolis, Indiana 46253
Telephone: (317) 297-2658

2004 SCHEDULE

PRESEASON		Indianapolis time
Aug. 14	at San Diego	9:00
Aug. 21	**New York Jets**	7:00
Aug. 28	**Buffalo**	7:00
Sept. 3	at Cincinnati	6:30

REGULAR SEASON

Sept. 9	at New England (Thu.)	9:00
Sept. 19	at Tennessee	12:00
Sept. 26	**Green Bay**	3:15
Oct. 3	at Jacksonville	12:00
Oct. 10	**Oakland**	12:00
Oct. 17	Open Date	
Oct. 24	**Jacksonville**	12:00
Oct. 31	at Kansas City	1:00
Nov. 8	**Minnesota** (Mon.)	9:00
Nov. 14	**Houston**	1:00
Nov. 21	at Chicago	1:00
Nov. 25	at Detroit (Thu.)	1:30
Dec. 5	**Tennessee**	1:00
Dec. 12	at Houston	1:00
Dec. 19	**Baltimore**	8:30
Dec. 26	**San Diego**	1:00
Jan. 2	at Denver	4:15

Stadium: RCA Dome (opened in 1983)
•**Capacity:** 55,506
100 South Capitol Avenue
Indianapolis, Indiana 46225
Playing Surface: AstroTurf
Training Camp: Rose-Hulman Institute
5500 Wabash Avenue
Terre Haute, Indiana
47803

RCA DOME

CLUB OFFICIALS

Owner and CEO: James Irsay
President: Bill Polian
Head Coach: Tony Dungy
Senior Executive Vice President: Pete Ward
Executive Vice President: Bob Terpening
Senior Vice President-Sales and Marketing: Ray Compton
Director of Football Operations: Dom Anile
Vice President-Finance: Kurt Humphrey
Vice President-Ticket Operations: Larry Hall
Vice President-Public Relations: Craig Kelley
Vice President-Business Development: Tom Zupancic
Director of Pro Player Personnel: Clyde Powers
Director of College Scouting: Mike Butler
Assistant Director of Football Operations: Chris Polian
Director of Player Development: Steve Champlin
Executive Director of Administration: Bill Brooks
Executive Director of Sponsorship Sales: Jay Souers
Director of Ticket Sales/Marketing: Greg Hylton
Director of Community Relations/Marketing: Nicole Duncan
Equipment Manager: Jon Scott
Video Director: Marty Heckscher
Head Trainer: Hunter Smith
Assistant Director of Public Relations: Vernon Cheek
Assistant Equipment Manager: Mike Mays
Assistant Trainers: Dave Hammer, Dave Walston
Assistant Video Director: John Starliper
Purchasing Administrator: Dave Filar

COACHING HISTORY

Baltimore 1953-1983
(376-385-7)

1953	Keith Molesworth	3-9-0
1954-1962	Weeb Ewbank	61-52-1
1963-69	Don Shula	73-26-4
1970-72	Don McCafferty*	26-11-1
1972	John Sandusky	4-5-0
1973-74	Howard Schnellenberger**	4-13-0
1974	Joe Thomas	2-9-0
1975-79	Ted Marchibroda	41-36-0
1980-81	Mike McCormack	9-23-0
1982-84	Frank Kush***	11-28-1
1984	Hal Hunter	0-1-0
1985-86	Rod Dowhower****	5-24-0
1986-1991	Ron Meyer#	36-36-0
1991	Rick Venturi	1-10-0
1992-95	Ted Marchibroda	32-35-0
1996-97	Lindy Infante	12-21-0
1998-2001	Jim Mora	32-34-0
2002-03	Tony Dungy	24-12-0

*Released after five games in 1972
**Released after three games in 1974
***Resigned after 15 games in 1984
****Released after 13 games in 1986
#Released after five games in 1991

ATTENDANCE

Home 438,733 Away 538,773
Total 977,506
Single-game home record, 61,139 (10/20/97)
Single-season home record, 481,305 (1984)

2004 DRAFT CHOICES

Round	Name	Pos.	College
2	Bob Sanders	DB	Iowa
3	Ben Hartsock	TE	Ohio State
	Gilbert Gardner	LB	Purdue
4	Kendyll Pope	LB	Florida State
	Jason David	DB	Washington St.
5	Jake Scott	T	Idaho
6	Von Hutchins	DB	Mississippi
	Jim Sorgi	QB	Wisconsin
7	David Kimball	K	Penn State

INDIANAPOLIS COLTS

2003 TEAM RECORD

PRESEASON (3-1)

Date	Result		Opponent
8/9	L	18-20	at Chicago
8/15	W	21-7	Seattle
8/25	W	28-23	at Denver
8/29	W	21-20	Cincinnati

REGULAR SEASON (12-4)

Date	Result		Opponent	Att.
9/7	W	9-6	at Cleveland	73,358
9/14	W	33-7	Tennessee	56,999
9/21	W	23-13	Jacksonville	55,770
9/28	W	55-21	at New Orleans	70,020
10/6	W	38-35	at Tampa Bay (OT)	65,647
10/12	L	20-23	Carolina (OT)	57,082
10/26	W	30-21	Houston	56,132
11/2	W	23-17	at Miami	73,258
11/9	L	23-28	at Jacksonville	45,037
11/16	W	38-31	New York Jets	56,801
11/23	W	17-14	at Buffalo	73,004
11/30	L	34-38	New England	57,102
12/7	W	29-27	at Tennessee	68,809
12/14	W	38-7	Atlanta	57,103
12/21	L	17-31	Denver	57,149
12/28	W	20-17	at Houston	70,680

(OT) Overtime

POSTSEASON (2-1)

Date	Result		Opponent	Att.
1/4	W	41-10	Denver	56,586
1/11	W	38-31	at Kansas City	79,159
1/18	L	14-24	at New England	68,436

SCORE BY PERIODS

Colts	61	135	130	118	3	—	447
Opponents	75	89	83	86	3	—	336

2003 TEAM STATISTICS

	Colts	Opp.
Total First Downs	348	279
Rushing	104	117
Passing	212	138
Penalty	32	24
3rd Down: Made/Att	91/217	72/188
3rd Down Pct.	41.9	38.3
4th Down: Made/Att	11/17	6/11
4th Down Pct.	64.7	54.5
Possession Avg.	30:54	29:06
Total Net Yards	5,874	4,789
Avg. Per Game	367.1	299.3
Total Plays	1,041	913
Avg. Per Play	5.6	5.2
Net Yards Rushing	1,695	1,980
Avg. Per Game	105.9	123.8
Total Rushes	453	437
Net Yards Passing	4,179	2,809
Avg. Per Game	261.2	175.6
Sacked/Yards Lost	19/110	31/225
Gross Yards	4,289	3,034
Att./Completions	569/381	445/277
Completion Pct.	67.0	62.2
Had Intercepted	10	15
Punts/Average	64/41.3	74/42.1
Net Punting Avg.	64/35.4	74/37.8
Penalties/Yards	92/662	123/1,005
Fumbles/Ball Lost	25/10	30/15
Touchdowns	48	41
Rushing	16	19
Passing	29	18
Returns	3	4

2003 INDIVIDUAL STATISTICS

PASSING	Att.	Comp.	Yds.	Pct.	TD	Int.	Tkld.	Rate
Manning	566	379	4,267	67.0	29	10	18/107	99.0
Huard	3	2	22	66.7	0	0	1/3	88.2
Colts	569	381	4,289	67.0	29	10	19/110	99.0
Opponents	445	277	3,034	62.2	18	15	31/225	81.8

SCORING	TD R	TD P	TD Rt	PAT	FG	Saf	PTS
Vanderjagt	0	0	0	46/46	37/37	0	157
James	11	0	0	0/0	0/0	0	66
Harrison	0	10	0	0/0	0/0	0	60
Wayne	0	7	0	0/0	0/0	0	42
Pollard	0	3	0	0/0	0/0	0	18
Stokley	0	3	0	0/0	0/0	0	18
Walters	0	3	0	0/0	0/0	0	18
R. Williams	2	1	0	0/0	0/0	0	18
Mungro	2	0	0	0/0	0/0	0	14
Brackett	0	0	1	0/0	0/0	0	6
Clark	0	1	0	0/0	0/0	0	6
Freeney	0	0	1	0/0	0/0	0	6
Harper	0	0	1	0/0	0/0	0	6
Rhodes	0	1	0	0/0	0/0	0	6
H. Smith	1	0	0	0/0	0/0	0	6
Colts	16	29	3	46/46	37/37	0	447
Opponents	19	18	4	38/38	16/21	0	336

2-Pt. Conversions: Mungro.
Colts 1-2, Opponents 2-3.

RUSHING	No.	Yds	Avg	LG	TD
James	310	1,259	4.1	43	11
Rhodes	37	157	4.2	25	0
R. Williams	48	155	3.2	19	2
Mungro	24	60	2.5	9	2
Manning	28	26	0.9	10	0
H. Smith	1	21	21.0	21t	1
Huard	3	8	2.7	9	0
Walters	1	6	6.0	6	0
Harrison	1	3	3.0	3	0
Colts	453	1,695	3.7	43	16
Opponents	437	1,980	4.5	42	19

RECEIVING	No.	Yds	Avg	LG	TD
Harrison	94	1,272	13.5	79t	10
Wayne	68	838	12.3	57t	7
James	51	292	5.7	17	0
Pollard	40	541	13.5	70	3
Walters	36	456	12.7	46t	3
Clark	29	340	11.7	42	1
Stokley	22	211	9.6	37t	3
R. Williams	22	157	7.1	17t	1
Moorehead	7	101	14.4	35	0
Rhodes	6	62	10.3	27	1
Davenport	3	23	7.7	9	0
Pyatt	1	2	2.0	2	0
Manning	1	-2	-2.0	-2	0
Mungro	1	-4	-4.0	-4	0
Colts	381	4,289	11.3	79t	29
Opponents	277	3,034	11.0	74t	18

INTERCEPTIONS	No.	Yds	Avg	LG	TD
Harper	4	121	30.3	75t	1
Strickland	2	43	21.5	24	0
Nelson	2	22	11.0	12	0
Bashir	2	9	4.5	9	0
Thornton	2	3	1.5	2	0
Brackett	1	31	31.0	31t	1
Doss	1	15	15.0	15	0
Macklin	1	0	0.0	0	0
Colts	15	244	16.3	75t	2
Opponents	10	125	12.5	41	1

PUNTING	No.	Yds.	Avg.	In 20	LG
H. Smith	62	2,617	42.2	20	55
Vanderjagt	1	29	29.0	1	29
Colts	64	2,646	41.3	21	55
Opponents	74	3,115	42.1	32	64

PUNT RETURNS	Ret	FC	Yds	Avg	LG	TD
Pyatt	12	8	110	9.2	21	0
Walters	11	7	105	9.5	26	0
Wilkins	7	0	25	3.6	16	0
Macklin	1	0	0	0.0	0	0
Harrison	0	1	0	—	—	0
Colts	31	16	240	7.7	26	0
Opponents	32	15	319	10.0	36	0

KICKOFF RETURNS	No.	Yds	Avg	LG	TD
Pyatt	19	544	28.6	90	0
Rhodes	16	411	25.7	49	0
Wilkins	14	325	23.2	42	0
Walters	6	126	21.0	34	0
R. Williams	4	67	16.8	23	0
Mungro	2	7	3.5	5	0
Allen	1	6	6.0	6	0
Pollard	1	9	9.0	9	0
D. Smith	1	15	15.0	15	0
Colts	64	1,510	23.6	90	0
Opponents	93	1,999	21.5	92t	2

FIELD GOALS	1-19	20-29	30-39	40-49	50+
Vanderjagt	0/0	17/17	7/7	12/12	1/1
Colts	0/0	17/17	7/7	12/12	1/1
Opponents	1/1	5/5	3/3	7/10	0/2

SACKS	No.
Freeney	11.0
Washington	6.0
Mathis	3.5
Bratzke	3.0
Brock	2.0
Brackett	1.0
Thornton	1.0
Tripplett	1.0
J. Williams	1.0
Reagor	0.5
Colts	31.0
Opponents	19.0

RECORD HOLDERS

INDIVIDUAL RECORDS—CAREER

Category	Name	Performance
Rushing (Yds.)	Edgerrin James, 1999-2003	6,172
Passing (Yds.)	Johnny Unitas, 1956-1972	39,768
Passing (TDs)	Johnny Unitas, 1956-1972	287
Receiving (No.)	Marvin Harrison, 1996-2003	759
Receiving (Yds.)	Marvin Harrison, 1996-2003	10,072
Interceptions	Bob Boyd, 1960-68	57
Punting (Avg.)	Chris Gardocki, 1994-98	44.8
Punt Return (Avg.)	Ron Gardin, 1970-71	13.5
Kickoff Return (Avg.)	Jim Duncan, 1969-1971	32.5
Field Goals	Dean Biasucci 1984, 1986-1994	176
Touchdowns (Tot.)	Lenny Moore, 1956-1967	113
Points	Dean Biasucci, 1984, 1986-1994	783

INDIVIDUAL RECORDS—SINGLE SEASON

Category	Name	Performance
Rushing (Yds.)	Edgerrin James, 2000	1,709
Passing (Yds.)	Peyton Manning, 2000	4,413
Passing (TDs)	Peyton Manning, 2000	33
Receiving (No.)	Marvin Harrison, 2002	*143
Receiving (Yds.)	Marvin Harrison, 2002	1,722
Interceptions	Tom Keane, 1953	11
Punting (Avg.)	Rohn Stark, 1985	45.9
Punt Return (Avg.)	Clarence Verdin, 1989	12.9
Kickoff Return (Avg.)	Jim Duncan, 1970	35.4
Field Goals	Cary Blanchard, 1996	36
Touchdowns (Tot.)	Lenny Moore, 1964	20
Points	Mike Vanderjagt, 2003	157

INDIVIDUAL RECORDS—SINGLE GAME

Category	Name	Performance
Rushing (Yds.)	Edgerrin James, 10-15-00	219
Passing (Yds.)	Peyton Manning, 9-25-00	440
Passing (TDs)	Peyton Manning, 9-28-03	6
Receiving (No.)	Marvin Harrison, 12-26-99, 11-17-02	14
Receiving (Yds.)	Raymond Berry, 11-10-57	224
Interceptions	Many times Last time by Mike Prior, 12-20-92	3
Field Goals	Many times Last time by Mike Vanderjagt, 12-7-03	5
Touchdowns (Tot.)	Many times Last time by Eric Dickerson, 10-31-88	4
Points	Many times Last time by Eric Dickerson, 10-31-88	24

*NFL Record

INDIANAPOLIS COLTS

2004 VETERAN ROSTER

No.	Name	Pos.	Ht.	Wt.	Birthdate	NFL Exp.	College	Hometown	How Acq.	'03 Games/ Starts
34	Allen, Brian	RB	5-9	205	4/20/80	3	Stanford	Ontario, Calif.	FA-'04	4/0
28	Bashir, Idrees	S-CB	6-2	198	12/7/78	4	Memphis	Decatur, Ga.	D2a-'01	9/9
41	Bird, Cory	CB-S	5-10	213	8/10/78	4	Virginia Tech	Atlantic City, N.J.	D3b-'01	12/0
58	Brackett, Gary	LB	5-11	235	5/23/80	2	Rutgers	Glassboro, N.J.	FA-'03	16/0
79	Brock, Raheem	DE	6-4	274	6/10/78	3	Temple	Philadelphia, Pa.	FA-'02	16/16
44	Clark, Dallas	TE-FB	6-3	252	6/12/79	2	Iowa	Livermore, Iowa	D1-'03	10/10
64	Demulling, Rick	G	6-4	304	7/21/77	4	Idaho	Cheney, Wash.	D7-'01	16/16
71	Diem, Ryan	T	6-6	331	7/1/79	4	Northern Illinois	Carol Stream, Ill.	D4-'01	13/13
20	Doss, Mike	S	5-10	207	3/24/81	2	Ohio State	Canton, Ohio	D2-'03	15/15
39	Floyd, Anthony	CB-S	5-10	202	2/1/81	2	Louisville	Youngstown, Ohio	FA-'03	6/0
93	Freeney, Dwight	DE	6-1	268	2/19/80	3	Syracuse	Hartford, Conn.	D1-'02	15/13
76	Freitas, Makoa	T	6-4	307	11/23/79	2	Arizona	Honolulu, Hawaii	D6c-'03	12/6
78	Glenn, Tarik	T	6-5	332	5/25/76	8	California	Oakland, Calif.	D1-'97	10/10
25	Harper, Nick	CB-S	5-10	182	9/10/74	4	Ft. Valley State	Baldwin, Ga.	FA-'01	16/13
88	Harrison, Marvin	WR	6-0	175	8/25/72	9	Syracuse	Philadelphia, Pa.	D1-'96	15/15
32	James, Edgerrin	RB	6-0	214	8/1/78	6	Miami	Immokalee, Fla.	D1-'99	13/13
29	Jefferson, Joseph	CB-S	6-1	202	2/15/80	3	Western Kentucky	Adairville, Ky.	D3-'02	0*
59	June, Cato	LB	6-0	227	11/18/79	2	Michigan	Washington, Calif.	D6a-'03	11/0
36	Lopienski, Tom	RB	6-0	246	6/12/79	2	Notre Dame	Parkersburg, W.Va.	FA-'03	4/0
18	Manning, Peyton	QB	6-5	230	3/24/76	7	Tennessee	New Orleans, La.	D1-'98	16/16
98	Mathis, Robert	DE	6-2	235	2/26/81	2	Alabama A&M	Atlanta, Ga.	D5a-'03	16/0
85	Moorehead, Aaron	WR	6-3	200	11/5/80	2	Illinois	Deerfield, Ill.	FA-'03	7/0
94	Morris, Rob	LB	6-2	243	1/18/75	5	Brigham Young	Nampa, Idaho	D1-'00	16/16
23	Mungro, James	RB	5-9	214	2/13/78	3	Syracuse	E. Stroudsburg, Pa.	W(Det)-'02	7/0
57	Nelson, Jim	LB	6-1	234	4/16/75	6	Penn State	West Chester, Pa.	UFA(Minn)-'03	7/0
56	Peko, Tupe	C-G	6-4	305	9/19/78	3	Michigan State	Whittier, Calif.	FA-'02	16/1
81	Pollard, Marcus	TE	6-3	247	2/8/72	10	Bradley	Valley, Ala.	FA-'95	14/13
95	Pugh, David	DT	6-2	270	7/24/79	2	Virginia Tech	Madison Heights, Va.	D6a-'02	0*
84	Pyatt, Brad	WR	5-11	195	4/16/80	2	Northern Colorado	Arvada, Colo.	FA-'03	8/0
90	Reagor, Montae	DT	6-3	285	6/29/77	6	Texas Tech	Waxahachie, Texas	UFA(Den)-'03	13/12
33	Rhodes, Dominic	RB	5-9	203	1/17/79	4	Midwestern State	Abilene, Texas	FA-'01	11/0
63	Saturday, Jeff	C	6-2	295	6/8/75	6	North Carolina	Tucker, Ga.	FA-'99	16/16
16	Sauter, Cory	QB	6-4	216	11/21/74	7	Minnesota	Hutchinson, Minn.	FA-'03	0*
99	Scioli, Brad	DE	6-3	280	9/6/76	6	Penn State	Bridgeport, Pa.	D5-'99	16/0
74	Sciullo, Steve	G	6-5	325	8/27/80	2	Marshall	Pittsburgh, Pa.	D4-'03	13/13
17	Smith, Hunter	P	6-2	209	8/9/77	6	Notre Dame	Sherman, Texas	D7a-'99	16/0
48	Snow, Justin	TE	6-3	240	12/21/76	5	Baylor	Abilene, Texas	FA-'00	16/0
83	Stokley, Brandon	WR	5-11	197	6/23/76	6	Southwestern Louisiana	Dallas, Texas	UFA(Balt)-'03	6/3
30	Strickland, Donald	CB	5-10	187	11/24/80	2	Colorado	Redwood City, Calif.	D3-'03	11/8
50	Thornton, David	LB	6-2	230	11/1/78	3	North Carolina	Goldsboro, N.C.	D4-'02	16/16
75	Tripplett, Larry	DT	6-2	295	1/18/79	3	Washington	Los Angeles, Calif.	D2-'02	16/16
13	Vanderjagt, Mike	K	6-5	211	3/24/70	7	West Virginia	Oakville, Ontario, Canada	FA-'98	16/0
86	Walters, Troy	WR	5-7	172	12/15/76	5	Stanford	College Station, Texas	W(Minn)-'02	15/4
87	Wayne, Reggie	WR	6-0	198	11/17/78	4	Miami	New Orleans, La.	D1b-'01	16/16
52	Whiteside, Keyon	LB	6-0	229	1/31/80	2	Tennessee	Forest City, N.C.	FA-'03	5/0
96	Williams, Josh	DT	6-3	285	8/9/76	5	Michigan	Houston, Texas	D4-'00	16/4

* Jefferson inactive for 9 games; Pugh missed '03 season because of injury; Sauter inactive for 7 games.

Players lost through free agency (3): CB David Macklin (Ariz; 16 games in '03), LB Marcus Washington (Wash; 16), WR Terrence Wilkins (Mia; 3).

Also played with Colts in '03—DE Chad Bratzke (16 games), S-CB Cliff Crosby (14), TE Joe Dean Davenport (16), CB Jason Doering (16), CB Walt Harris (16), DT Brandon Hicks (4), QB Brock Huard (2), T Adam Meadows (12), T Jim Newton (3), DB Detron Smith (11), RB Ricky Williams (13).

2004 FIRST-YEAR ROSTER

Name	Pos.	Ht.	Wt.	Birthdate	College	Hometown	How Acq.
Arth, Tom (1)	QB	6-4	235	5/11/81	John Carroll	Westlake, Ohio	FA
Ayeni, Louis	DB	5-11	213	2/5/81	Northwestern	Woodbury, Minn.	FA
Bacon, Waine (1)	DB	5-10	191	4/11/79	Alabama	Ft. Washington, Md.	FA
Bartoszek, Chad (1)	TE	6-6	255	9/12/81	Buffalo	Salamanca, N.Y.	FA
Beard, Brett	DT	6-4	296	11/22/80	Southeast Louisiana	Birmingham, Ala.	FA
Bernard, Chris	WR	6-0	190	2/1/82	Kentucky	Mission Viejo, Calif.	FA
Carthon, Ran	RB	6-0	213	2/10/81	Florida	Key West, Fla.	FA
Caudill, Jeremy	DT	6-3	305	11/22/81	Kentucky	Martin, Ky.	FA
Clemons, Crance (1)	DB	5-9	175	12/20/79	Texas-El Paso	Houston, Texas	FA
Crow, Antonio	LB	6-0	236	7/10/80	Louisiana Tech	Minden, La.	FA
David, Jason	DB	5-8	172	6/12/82	Washington State	Covina, Calif.	D4b
Davis, Carey	RB	5-9	223	3/27/81	Illinois	St. Louis, Mo.	FA
Davis, Daniel	RB	5-11	228	3/21/80	Kansas State	Stafford, Va.	FA
Dixon, Daryl	DB	5-10	193	9/6/80	Florida	Oak Hill, Fla.	FA
Fletcher, Bryan (1)	TE	6-5	238	3/23/79	UCLA	Florrisant, Mo.	FA
Fulton, Skyler	WR	6-0	218	6/17/82	Arizona State	Olympia, Wash.	FA
Gardner, Gilbert	LB	6-1	228	5/9/82	Purdue	Angleton, Texas	D3b
Griebel, Matt	G	6-2	298	7/15/81	Indiana State	Cresthill, Ill.	FA
Hall, Antonio	T	6-3	316	3/28/82	Kentucky	Canton, Ohio	FA
Hartsock, Ben	TE	6-4	262	7/5/80	Ohio State	Chillicothe, Ohio	D3a
Hicks, Elgin	WR	5-11	178	6/13/81	South Florida	Punta Gorda, Fla.	FA
Hill, Eric	WR	6-0	190	5/22/80	Colorado State	Denver, Colo.	FA
Houchin, Thomas	DE	6-3	254	10/7/80	Kansas State	Sanger, Texas	FA
Hutchins, Von	DB	5-9	181	2/14/81	Mississippi	Natchez, Miss.	D6a
Hutton, Trevor	G	6-5	305	2/28/80	Utah State	Santa Maria, Calif.	FA
Iorio, Joe (1)	C	6-2	302	7/7/81	Penn State	Sylvania, Ohio	FA
Kennard, Derek	DT	6-0	282	3/19/82	Nevada	Phoenix, Ariz	FA
Kimball, David	K	6-1	209	1/13/82	Penn State	State College, Pa.	D7
Mahdavi, Ben (1)	LB	6-2	236	2/27/80	Washington	Shoreline, Wash.	FA
Mckay-Loesher, Nautyn	DE	6-3	260	12/9/80	Alabama	Toronto, Ontario, Canada	FA
Miles, Willie (1)	DB	6-0	186	12/29/79	Tennessee	Fort Worth, Texas	FA
Newton, Jim (1)	T	6-9	297	10/13/78	Utah State	Omaha, Neb.	FA
Pope, Kendyll	LB	6-1	220	5/9/81	Florida State	Fort White, Fla.	D4a
Reese, Tank (1)	DT	5-10	294	10/10/80	Kansas State	Auburndale, Fla.	FA
Richards, Rex (1)	G	6-4	315	10/17/80	Texas Tech	Midland, Texas	FA
Rideaux, Darrell (1)	DB	5-9	171	12/27/79	Southern California	Long Beach, Calif.	FA
Roundtree, Durand (1)	DT	6-3	263	2/16/80	Maryland	Baltimore, Md.	FA
Rubin, Deandrew (1)	WR	5-11	175	10/9/78	South Florida	St. Petersburg, Fla.	FA
Samuels, Stanford	DB	5-10	190	7/27/80	Florida State	Miami, Fla.	FA
Sanders, Bob	DB	5-8	206	2/24/81	Iowa	Erie, Pa.	D2
Save, Bryan	DT	6-1	316	12/16/81	Colorado State	Santa Ana, Calif.	FA
Scott, Jake	T	6-5	280	4/16/81	Idaho	Lewiston, Idaho	D5
Sorgi, Jim	QB	6-5	196	12/3/80	Wisconsin	Fraser, Mich.	D6b
Thomas, Josh	DE	6-5	271	6/26/81	Syracuse	Orchard Park, N.Y.	FA
Utecht, Ben	TE	6-6	251	6/30/81	Minnesota	Hastings, Minn.	FA
Ward, Eli	DB	5-11	204	12/6/80	Minnesota	Akron, Ohio	FA
Wright, Keith (1)	DT-DE	6-2	275	6/8/80	Missouri	Santa Clara, Calif.	FA

The term NFL Rookie is defined as a player who is in his first season of professional football and has not been on the roster of another professional football team for any regular-season or postseason games. A Rookie is designated by an "R" on NFL rosters. Players who have been active in another professional football league or players who have NFL experience, including either preseason training camp or being on an Active List or Inactive List, or on Reserve/Injured or Reserve/Physically Unable to Perform for fewer than six regular-season games, are termed NFL First-Year Players. An NFL First-Year Player is designated by a "1" on NFL rosters. Thereafter, a player is credited with an additional year of experience for each season in which he accumulates six games on the Active List or Inactive List, or on Reserve/Injured or Reserve/Physically Unable to Perform.

Log on to www.colts.com for an up-to-date roster.

INDIANAPOLIS COLTS

COACHING STAFF

Head Coach,
Tony Dungy

Pro Career: Tony Dungy enters his third season as head coach of the Indianapolis Colts. Dungy was named head coach of the club on January 22, 2002. This season marks his ninth as an NFL head coach. He has directed the Colts to 10-6 and 12-4 records in 2002 and 2003, guiding the club to the AFC Championship game in his second year. Dungy has directed six of his eight Colts and Buccaneers teams to the playoffs, twice being a conference finalist. He has produced five career double-digit victory totals and joins Don McCafferty and Ted Marchibroda as the only Colts coaches to produce double-digit victory totals and playoff appearances in the first two years with the team. His mark of 52-28 over the past five seasons is second-best in the NFL, and he is the only coach to defeat all 32 NFL teams. From 1996-2001, Dungy served as head coach at Tampa Bay. He was the most successful head coach in franchise history, compiling a 56-46 record and leading the club to the playoffs four times. Dungy's defenses at Tampa Bay ranked no lower than eleventh in his six seasons. At 25, Dungy was the NFL's youngest assistant coach when hired by the Pittsburgh Steelers in 1981. In 1982, he was promoted from defensive assistant to defensive backs coach, before becoming the league's youngest defensive coordinator in 1984 at age 28. He served as defensive backs coach at Kansas City (1989-1991) and as defensive coordinator at Minnesota (1992-95). Dungy signed with Pittsburgh as a free agent in 1977 and played safety for two seasons. He had 9 interceptions in 30 games for Pittsburgh and played in the club's Super Bowl XIII victory over Dallas. He was traded to San Francisco in 1979 and played 15 games for 49ers. Career record: 80-58.

Background: Starred as a quarterback at University of Minnesota from 1973-76. Finished career as school's all-time leader in attempts, completions, passing yards, and touchdown passes. Two-time team most valuable player, played in Hula Bowl, East-West Shrine Game and Japan Bowl. Attended Parkside High School in Jackson, Michigan.

Personal: Born October 6, 1955, in Jackson, Michigan. Tony and his wife Lauren have five children—daughters Tiara and Jade, and sons James, Eric and, Jordan.

ASSISTANT COACHES

Jim Caldwell, quarterbacks; born January 16, 1955, Beloit, Wis. Defensive back Iowa 1973-76. No pro playing experience. College coach: Iowa 1977, Southern Illinois 1978-1980, Northwestern 1981, Colorado 1982-84, Louisville 1985, Penn State 1986-1992, Wake Forest 1993-2000. Pro coach: Tampa Bay Buccaneers 2001, joined Colts in 2002.

Clyde Christensen, wide receivers; born January 28, 1958, Covina, Calif. Quarterback Fresno (Calif.) J.C. 1975, North Carolina 1976-78. No pro playing experience. College coach: East Tennessee State 1980-82, Temple 1983-85, East Carolina 1986-88, Holy Cross 1989-90, South Carolina 1991, Maryland 1992-93, Clemson 1994-95. Pro coach: Tampa Bay Buccaneers 1996-2001, joined Colts in 2002.

Richard Howell, asst. strength and conditioning; born February 19, 1972, Bladenboro, N.C. Quarterback Davidson 1990-93. No pro playing experience. College coach: Davidson 1994-97, North Carolina 1998-99. Pro coach: Barcelona Dragons (NFL Europe) 1999, joined Colts in 2000.

Gene Huey, running backs; born July 20, 1947, Uniontown, Pa. Defensive back-wide receiver Wyoming 1966-69. Pro running back San Diego Chargers 1969. College coach: Wyoming 1970-74, New Mexico 1975-77, Nebraska 1978-1986, Arizona State 1987, Ohio State 1988-1991. Pro coach: Joined Colts in 1992.

Ron Meeks, defensive coordinator; born August 27, 1954, Jacksonville, Fla. Defensive back Arkansas State 1975-76. Pro defensive back Hamilton Tiger-Cats (CFL) 1977-79, Ottawa Rough Riders (CFL) 1979, Toronto Argonauts (CFL) 1980-81. College coach: Arkansas State 1984-85, Miami 1986-87, New Mexico State 1988, Fresno State 1989-1990. Pro coach: Dallas Cowboys 1991, Cincinnati Bengals 1992-96, Atlanta Falcons 1997-99, Washington Redskins 2000, St. Louis Rams 2001, joined Colts in 2002.

Pete Metzelaars, offensive quality control; born May 24, 1960, Three Rivers, Mich. Tight end Wabash College 1978-1982. Pro tight end Seattle Seahawks 1982-84, Buffalo Bills 1985-1994, Carolina Panthers 1995, Detroit Lions 1996-97. College coach: Wingate 2003. Pro coach: Joined Colts in 2004.

Tom Moore, offensive coordinator; born November 7, 1938, Owatanna, Minn. Quarterback Iowa 1957-60. No pro playing experience. College coach: Iowa 1961-62, Dayton 1965-68, Wake Forest 1969, Georgia Tech 1970-71, Minnesota 1972-73, 1975-76. Pro coach: New York Stars (WFL) 1974, Pittsburgh Steelers 1977-1989, Minnesota Vikings 1990-93, Detroit Lions 1994-96, New Orleans Saints 1997, joined Colts in 1998.

Howard Mudd, offensive line; born February 10, 1942, Midland, Mich. Guard Hillsdale (Mich.) College 1960-63. Pro offensive lineman San Francisco 49ers 1964-69, Chicago Bears 1969-1970. College coach: California 1972-73. Pro coach: San Diego Chargers 1974-76, San Francisco 49ers 1977, Seattle Seahawks 1978-1982, 1993-97, Cleveland Browns 1983-88, Kansas City Chiefs 1989-1992, joined Colts in 1998.

Mike Murphy, linebackers; born September 25, 1944, New York, N.Y. Guard-linebacker Huron (S.D.) 1963-66. No pro playing experience. College coach: Vermont 1970-73, Idaho State 1974-76, Western Illinois 1977-78. Pro coach: Saskatchewan Rough Riders (CFL) 1979-1983, Chicago Blitz (USFL) 1984, Detroit Lions 1985-89, Arizona Cardinals 1990-93, Seattle Seahawks 1995-97, joined Colts in 1998.

Russ Purnell, special teams; born June 12, 1948, Chicago. Center Orange Coast (Calif.) J.C. 1966-67, Whittier College 1968-69. No pro playing experience. College coach: Whittier College 1970-71, Southern California 1982-84. Pro coach: Seattle Seahawks 1986-1994, Tennessee Oilers 1995, Baltimore Ravens 1999-2001, joined Colts in 2002.

Diron Reynolds, defensive assistant; born February 23, 1971, Aiken, S.C. Linebacker Wake Forest 1989-1993. No pro playing experience. College coach: Wake Forest 1997-2000; Indiana 2001. Pro coach: Joined Colts in 2002.

John Teerlinck, defensive line; born April 9, 1951, Rochester, N.Y. Defensive lineman Western Illinois 1970-73. Pro defensive tackle San Diego Chargers 1974-76. College coach: Iowa Lakes J.C. 1977, Eastern Illinois 1978-79, Illinois 1980-82. Pro coach: Chicago Blitz (USFL) 1983, Arizona Wranglers/Outlaws (USFL) 1984-85, Cleveland Browns 1989-1990, Los Angeles Rams 1991, Minnesota Vikings 1992-94, Detroit Lions 1995-96, Denver Broncos 1997-2001, joined Colts in 2002.

Ricky Thomas, tight ends; born March 29, 1965, London, England. Safety Alabama 1983-86. Pro safety Seattle Seahawks 1987. College coach: Kentucky 1996, Gardner-Webb 1996. Pro coach: Tampa Bay Buccaneers 1997-2001, joined Colts in 2002.

Jon Torine, strength and conditioning; born November 16, 1973, Livingston, N.J. Linebacker Springfield (Mass.) College 1991. No pro playing experience. Pro coach: Buffalo Bills 1995-97, joined Colts in 1998.

Alan Williams, defensive assistant; born November 4, 1969, Norfolk, Va. Running back William & Mary 1988-1991. No pro playing experience. College coach: William & Mary 1996-2000. Pro coach: Tampa Bay Buccaneers 2001, joined Colts in 2002.

American Football Conference
South Division
Team Colors: Teal, Black, and Gold
ALLTEL Stadium
One ALLTEL Stadium Place
Jacksonville, Florida 32202
Telephone: (904) 633-6000

2004 SCHEDULE

PRESEASON		Jacksonville time
Aug. 14	at Miami	7:30
Aug. 20	**Tampa Bay**	7:30
Aug. 27	**Green Bay**	8:00
Sept. 2	at New England	6:45

REGULAR SEASON		
Sept. 12	at Buffalo	1:00
Sept. 19	**Denver**	1:00
Sept. 26	at Tennessee	1:00
Oct. 3	**Indianapolis**	1:00
Oct. 10	at San Diego	1:05
Oct. 17	**Kansas City**	1:00
Oct. 24	at Indianapolis	1:00
Oct. 31	at Houston	1:00
Nov. 7	Open Date	
Nov. 14	**Detroit**	1:00
Nov. 21	**Tennessee**	1:00
Nov. 28	at Minnesota	1:00
Dec. 5	**Pittsburgh**	8:30
Dec. 12	**Chicago**	1:00
Dec. 19	at Green Bay	1:00
Dec. 26	**Houston**	1:00
Jan. 2	at Oakland	4:05

Stadium: ALLTEL Stadium (opened in 1995) • **Capacity:** 76,877
One ALLTEL Stadium Place
Jacksonville, Florida 32202
Playing Surface: Grass
Training Camp: ALLTEL Stadium
One ALLTEL Stadium Place
Jacksonville, Florida 32202

ALLTEL STADIUM

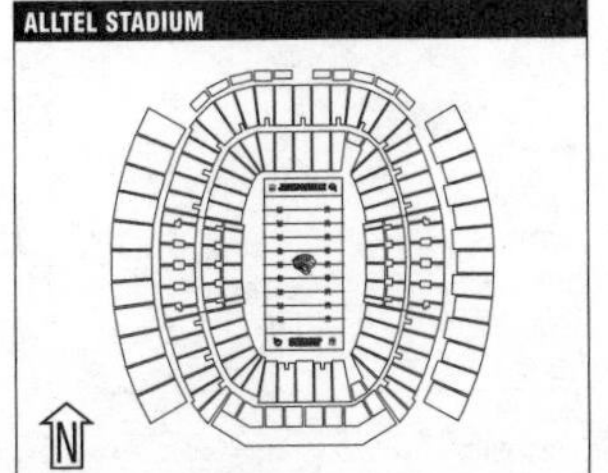

CLUB OFFICIALS

Chairman and Chief Executive Officer: Wayne Weaver
Senior Vice President/Football Operations: Paul Vance
Senior Vice President/Marketing: Dan Connell
Senior Vice President/Chief Financial Officer: Bill Prescott
Vice President/Player Personnel: James Harris
Vice President/Communications and Media: Dan Edwards
Vice President/Development: Tim Connolly
Executive Director of Ticket Sales and Service: Scott Loft
Director of Pro Personnel: Charles Bailey
Director of College Scouting: Gene Smith
Director of Football Operations: Skip Richardson
Director of Information Technology: Bruce Swindell
Director of Corporate Sponsorship: Macky Weaver
Director of Ticket Operations: Tim Bishko
Director of Special Events and Promotions: Bo Reed
Director of Creative Services: Jennifer Johnston
Director of Finance: Edwina Britton
Director of Broadcasting: Chris Sinclair
Associate General Counsel: Joe Pierce
Head Athletic Trainer: Michael Ryan
Video Director: Mike Perkins
Equipment Manager: Drew Hampton
Assistant Director of Pro Personnel: Louis Clark
Executive Scouts: Terry McDonough, Tim Mingey
Regional Scouts: Andy Dengler, Chris Driggers, Art Perkins
BLESTO Representative: David Dougherty
Scouts: Marty Miller, Larry Wright
Scouting Assistant: Chris Prescott
Coordinator, Communications: Hunter Robinson
Assistant Coordinator, Communications: Steven Drummond
Executive Assistant, Communications and Media: Alisa Abbott
Chair & Chief Executive Officer, Jaguars Foundation: Delores Barr Weaver
Executive Director: Peter Racine

COACHING HISTORY
(77-75-0)

1995-2002	Tom Coughlin	72-64-0
2003	Jack Del Rio	5-11-0

ATTENDANCE
Home 482,269 Away 541,863
Total 1,024,132
Single-game home record, 74,143 (12/28/98)
Single-season home record, 561,472 (1998)

2004 DRAFT CHOICES

Round	Name	Pos.	College
1	Reggie Williams	WR	Washington
2	Daryl Smith	LB	Georgia Tech
	Greg Jones	RB	Florida State
3	Jorge Cordova	LB	Nevada
4	Anthony Maddox	DT	Delta State
	Ernest Wilford	WR	Virginia Tech
5	Josh Scobee	K	Louisiana Tech
	Chris Thompson	DB	Nicholls State
	Sean Bubin	T	Illinois
7	Bobby McCray	DE	Florida

JACKSONVILLE JAGUARS

2003 TEAM RECORD

PRESEASON (3-1)

Date	Result	Opponent
8/9	W 16-14	at Minnesota
8/15	W 27-23	Miami
8/23	L 6-10	at Tampa Bay
8/28	W 17-15	Washington

REGULAR SEASON (5-11)

Date	Result	Opponent	Att.
9/7	L 23-24	at Carolina	72,134
9/14	L 17-38	Buffalo	58,613
9/21	L 13-23	at Indianapolis	55,770
9/28	L 20-24	at Houston	70,041
10/5	W 27-21	San Diego	48,954
10/12	L 10-24	Miami	66,437
10/26	L 17-30	Tennessee	55,918
11/2	L 17-24	at Baltimore	69,486
11/9	W 28-23	Indianapolis	45,037
11/16	L 3-10	at Tennessee	68,809
11/23	L 10-13	at New York Jets	77,614
11/30	W 17-10	Tampa Bay	60,543
12/7	W 27-0	Houston	43,363
12/14	L 13-27	at New England	68,436
12/21	W 20-19	New Orleans	49,207
12/28	L 14-21	at Atlanta	70,266

SCORE BY PERIODS

Jaguars	34	93	57	92	0	—	276
Opponents	85	81	57	108	0	—	331

2003 TEAM STATISTICS

	Jaguars	Opp.
Total First Downs	305	276
Rushing	118	84
Passing	163	172
Penalty	24	20
3rd Down: Made/Att	80/216	92/218
3rd Down Pct.	37.0	42.2
4th Down: Made/Att	13/26	7/14
4th Down Pct.	50.0	50.0
Possession Avg.	30:09	29:51
Total Net Yards	5,358	4,657
Avg. Per Game	334.9	291.1
Total Plays	1,024	976
Avg. Per Play	5.2	4.8
Net Yards Rushing	2,073	1,406
Avg. Per Game	129.6	87.9
Total Rushes	481	442
Net Yards Passing	3,285	3,251
Avg. Per Game	205.3	203.2
Sacked/Yards Lost	28/136	24/134
Gross Yards	3421	3385
Att./Completions	515/303	510/303
Completion Pct.	58.8	59.4
Had Intercepted	17	15
Punts/Average	69/41.3	75/41.0
Net Punting Avg.	69/33.5	75/34.1
Penalties/Yards	108/895	103/881
Fumbles/Ball Lost	27/14	26/12
Touchdowns	31	37
Rushing	13	12
Passing	17	23
Returns	1	2

2003 INDIVIDUAL STATISTICS

PASSING	Att.	Comp.	Yds.	Pct.	TD	Int.	Tkld.	Rate
Leftwich	418	239	2,819	57.2	14	16	19/90	73.0
Brunell	82	54	484	65.9	2	0	9/46	89.7
Garrard	12	9	86	75.0	1	0	0/0	122.2
Toefield	2	1	32	50.0	0	0	0/0	95.8
Royals	1	0	0	0.0	0	1	0/0	0.0
Jaguars	515	303	3,421	58.8	17	17	28/136	76.0
Opponents	510	303	3,385	59.4	23	15	24/134	82.0

SCORING	TD R	TD P	TD Rt	PAT	FG	Saf	PTS
Marler	0	0	0	30/30	20/33	0	90
F. Taylor	6	1	0	0/0	0/0	0	42
Ji. Smith	0	4	0	0/0	0/0	0	24
T. Edwards	0	3	0	0/0	0/0	0	18
Toefield	2	1	0	0/0	0/0	0	18
Hatchette	0	2	0	0/0	0/0	0	12
Leftwich	2	0	0	0/0	0/0	0	12
Wrighster	0	2	0	0/0	0/0	0	12
Allen	0	1	0	0/0	0/0	0	6
Ayodele	0	0	1	0/0	0/0	0	6
Brady	0	1	0	0/0	0/0	0	6
Brunell	1	0	0	0/0	0/0	0	6
M. Edwards	1	0	0	0/0	0/0	0	6
Fuamatu-Ma'afala	1	0	0	0/0	0/0	0	6
Johnson	0	1	0	0/0	0/0	0	6
Lewis	0	1	0	0/0	0/0	0	6
Jaguars	13	17	1	30/30	20/33	0	276
Opponents	12	23	2	33/34	24/27	1	331

2-Pt. Conversions: None.
Jaguars 0-1, Opponents 1-3.

RUSHING	No.	Yds	Avg	LG	TD
F. Taylor	345	1,572	4.6	62	6
Toefield	53	212	4.0	30	2
Fuamatu-Ma'afala	35	144	4.1	18	1
Leftwich	25	108	4.3	18	2
Brunell	8	19	2.4	12	1
M. Edwards	7	13	1.9	3	1
Allen	4	8	2.0	6	0
Lewis	1	6	6.0	6	0
T. Edwards	3	-9	-3.0	4	0
Jaguars	481	2,073	4.3	62	13
Opponents	442	1,406	3.2	29t	12

RECEIVING	No.	Yds	Avg	LG	TD
Ji. Smith	54	805	14.9	67	4
F. Taylor	48	370	7.7	60t	1
T. Edwards	35	487	13.9	84t	3
M. Edwards	31	226	7.3	32	0
Brady	29	281	9.7	26	1
Johnson	17	253	14.9	28	1
Hankton	17	166	9.8	22	0
Hatchette	15	203	13.5	45	2
Toefield	14	105	7.5	16	1
Wrighster	13	150	11.5	30	2
Stokes	13	116	8.9	22	0
Allen	6	60	10.0	31	1
Lewis	4	100	25.0	65t	1
Redmond	3	67	22.3	29	0
Luzar	3	30	10.0	21	0
Fuamatu-Ma'afala	1	2	2.0	2	0
Jaguars	303	3,421	11.3	84t	17
Opponents	303	3,385	11.2	75t	23

INTERCEPTIONS	No.	Yds	Avg	LG	TD
Peterson	3	8	2.7	7	0
Craft	2	29	14.5	21	0
Ayodele	2	15	7.5	13	0
Mathis	2	0	0.0	0	0
Cooper	1	12	12.0	12	0
Brackens	1	4	4.0	4	0
Darius	1	4	4.0	4	0
Trapp	1	4	4.0	4	0
Spicer	1	2	2.0	2	0
Bryant	1	0	0.0	0	0
Jaguars	15	78	5.2	21	0
Opponents	17	198	11.6	52	1

PUNTING	No.	Yds.	Avg.	In 20	LG
Royals	45	1,852	41.2	9	51
Hanson	23	1,001	43.5	4	58
Jaguars	69	2,853	41.3	13	58
Opponents	75	3,077	41.0	24	58

PUNT RETURNS	Ret	FC	Yds	Avg	LG	TD
Allen	27	15	324	12.0	52	0
Lewis	5	0	45	9.0	14	0
Mathis	2	3	7	3.5	6	0
Jaguars	34	18	376	11.1	52	0
Opponents	40	3	420	10.5	40	0

KICKOFF RETURNS	No.	Yds	Avg	LG	TD
Allen	41	831	20.3	61	0
Toefield	14	272	19.4	35	0
Lewis	6	111	18.5	26	0
M. Edwards	2	44	22.0	24	0
Brady	1	10	10.0	10	0
T. Edwards	1	20	20.0	20	0
Mathis	1	7	7.0	7	0
Redmond	1	21	21.0	21	0
Jaguars	67	1,316	19.6	61	0
Opponents	58	1,227	21.2	58	0

FIELD GOALS	1-19	20-29	30-39	40-49	50+
Marler	0/0	10/11	4/8	5/12	1/2
Jaguars	0/0	10/11	4/8	5/12	1/2
Opponents	0/0	8/8	9/9	6/8	1/2

SACKS	No.
Brackens	6.0
Stroud	4.5
Douglas	3.5
Henderson	3.5
Meier	1.5
Ayodele	1.0
Barnes	1.0
Peterson	1.0
Slaughter	1.0
Thomas	1.0
Jaguars	24.0
Opponents	28.0

RECORD HOLDERS

INDIVIDUAL RECORDS—CAREER

Category	Name	Performance
Rushing (Yds.)	Fred Taylor, 1998-2003	6,356
Passing (Yds.)	Mark Brunell, 1995-2003	25,698
Passing (TDs)	Mark Brunell, 1995-2003	144
Receiving (No.)	Jimmy Smith, 1995-2003	718
Receiving (Yds.)	Jimmy Smith, 1995-2003	10,092
Interceptions	Aaron Beasley, 1996-2001	15
Punting (Avg.)	Chris Hanson, 2001-2003	43.9
Punt Return (Avg.)	Chris Hudson, 1995-98	10.9
Kickoff Return (Avg.)	Reggie Barlow, 1997-2000	23.3
Field Goals	Mike Hollis, 1995-2001	175
Touchdowns (Tot.)	Jimmy Smith, 1995-2003	57
Points	Mike Hollis, 1995-2001	764

INDIVIDUAL RECORDS—SINGLE SEASON

Category	Name	Performance
Rushing (Yds.)	Fred Taylor, 2003	1,572
Passing (Yds.)	Mark Brunell, 1996	4,367
Passing (TDs)	Mark Brunell, 1998	20
Receiving (No.)	Jimmy Smith, 1999	116
Receiving (Yds.)	Jimmy Smith, 1999	1,636
Interceptions	Aaron Beasley, 1999	6
	Marlon McCree, 2002	6
Punting (Avg.)	Bryan Barker, 1998	45.0
Punt Return (Avg.)	Reggie Barlow, 1998	12.9
Kickoff Return (Avg.)	Reggie Barlow, 1998	24.9
Field Goals	Mike Hollis, 1997, 1999	31
Touchdowns (Tot.)	Fred Taylor, 1998	17
Points	Mike Hollis, 1997	134

INDIVIDUAL RECORDS—SINGLE GAME

Category	Name	Performance
Rushing (Yds.)	Fred Taylor, 11-19-00	234
Passing (Yds.)	Mark Brunell, 9-22-96	432
Passing (TDs)	Mark Brunell, 11-29-98	4
Receiving (No.)	Keenan McCardell, 10-20-96	16
Receiving (Yds.)	Jimmy Smith, 9-10-00	291
Interceptions	Deon Figures, 8-31-97	2
	Aaron Beasley, 9-12-99	2
	Rayna Stewart, 9-10-00	2
	Marlon McCree, 9-15-02	2
Field Goals	Mike Hollis, 12-1-96, 11-30-97, 9-10-00	5
Touchdowns (Tot.)	James Stewart, 10-12-97	5
Points	James Stewart, 10-12-97	30

JACKSONVILLE JAGUARS

2004 VETERAN ROSTER

No.	Name	Pos.	Ht.	Wt.	Birthdate	NFL Exp.	College	Hometown	How Acq.	'03 Games/ Starts
26	Adams, Blue	CB	5-10	184	10/15/79	2	Cincinnati	Miami, Fla.	W(TB)-'03	9/0
47	Akbar, Hakim	LB	6-0	222	8/11/80	3	Washington	Riverside, Calif.	W(TB)-'03	0*
32	Allen, David	RB-KR	5-9	195	2/5/78	2	Kansas State	Liberty, Mo.	FA-'02	14/0
51	Ayodele, Akin	LB	6-2	251	9/17/79	3	Purdue	Grand Prairie, Texas	D3-'02	16/16
94	Barnes, Lionel	DE	6-5	260	4/19/76	4	Louisiana-Monroe	Bossier, La.	FA-'03	13/0
21	Bolden, Juran	CB	6-2	207	6/27/74	7	Mississippi Delta	Tampa, Fla.	UFA(Atl)-'04	8/8*
90	Brackens, Tony	DE	6-4	266	12/26/74	9	Texas	Fairfield, Texas	D2a-'96	15/15
80	Brady, Kyle	TE	6-6	278	1/14/72	10	Penn State	New Cumberland, Pa.	UFA(NYJ)-'99	16/15
49	Bullard, Courtland	LB	6-3	234	9/2/78	3	Ohio State	Miami, Fla.	FA-'04	9/0*
3	Chandler, Jeff	K	6-2	218	6/18/79	2	Florida	Jacksonville, Fla.	FA-'04	2/0*
79	Compton, Mike	G-T	6-6	310	9/18/70	12	West Virginia	Richlands, Va.	UFA(NE)-'04	2/2*
35	Cooper, Deke	S	6-2	210	10/18/77	3	Notre Dame	Evansville, Ind.	FA-'03	14/10
20	Darius, Donovin	S	6-1	225	8/12/75	7	Syracuse	Camden, N.J.	D1b-'98	16/16
53	Douglas, Hugh	DE	6-2	281	8/23/71	10	Central State (Ohio)	Fayetteville, Ga.	UFA(Phil)-'03	16/16
44	Edwards, Marc	FB	6-0	249	11/17/74	8	Notre Dame	Cincinnati, Ohio	UFA(NE)-'03	16/16
16	Edwards, Troy	WR	5-10	195	4/7/77	6	Louisiana Tech	Shreveport, La.	FA-'03	13/11
55	Favors, Greg	LB	6-1	244	9/30/74	6	Mississippi State	Atlanta, Ga.	UFA(Car)-'04	16/12*
68	Fletcher, Derrick	G	6-6	350	9/9/75	4	Baylor	Houston, Texas	FA-'04	0*
45	Fuamatu-Ma'afala, Chris	RB	6-0	252	3/4/77	7	Utah	Honolulu, Hawaii	FA-'03	13/0
9	Garrard, David	QB	6-1	244	2/14/78	3	East Carolina	Durham, N.C.	D4a-'02	2/0
50	Gilbert, Tony	LB	6-0	244	10/16/79	2	Georgia	Macon, Ga.	W(Ariz)-'03	8/0
37	Grant, Deon	S	6-2	210	3/14/79	5	Tennessee	Augusta, Ga.	UFA(Car)-'04	16/16*
97	Green, Brandon	DE	6-3	264	9/5/80	2	Rice	Vanderbilt, Texas	D6a-'03	0*
85	Hankton, Cortez	WR	6-0	200	1/20/81	2	Texas Southern	New Orleans, La.	FA-'03	16/0
2	Hanson, Chris	P	6-2	223	10/25/76	4	Marshall	Riverdale, Ga.	FA-'01	5/0
81	Hatchette, Matthew	WR	6-3	202	5/1/74	7	Langston	Cleveland, Ohio	FA-'03	6/4
98	Henderson, John	DT	6-7	328	1/9/79	3	Tennessee	Nashville, Tenn.	D1-'02	16/16
57	Hendricks, Tommy	LB	6-2	235	10/23/78	5	Michigan	Houston, Texas	UFA(Mia)-'04	16/2*
56	Humphrey, Deon	LB	6-3	245	5/7/76	4	Florida State	Lake Worth, Fla.	FA-'03	8/0
12	Johnson, Doug	QB	6-2	225	10/27/77	5	Florida	Gainesville, Fla.	UFA(Atl)-'04	10/8*
7	Leftwich, Byron	QB	6-5	245	1/14/80	2	Marshall	Washington D.C.	D1-'03	15/13
96	Leonard, Matt	DT	6-3	301	11/7/79	2	Stanford	Agua Dolce, Calif.	FA-'03	4/0
84	Lewis, Jermaine	WR-KR	5-7	183	10/16/74	9	Maryland	Lanham, Md.	FA-'03	2/0
89	Luzar, Chris	TE	6-7	262	2/12/79	3	Virginia	Williamsburg, Va.	D4b-'02	11/1
67	Manuwai, Vince	G	6-2	312	7/12/80	2	Hawaii	Honolulu, Hawaii	D3-'03	15/14
6	Marler, Seth	K	6-1	200	3/27/81	2	Tulane	Lilburn, Ga.	FA-'03	16/0
27	Mathis, Rashean	CB	6-1	200	8/27/80	2	Bethune-Cookman	Jacksonville, Fla.	D2-'03	16/16
48	McClain, Jimmy	LB	6-0	231	7/23/80	3	Troy State	Enterprise, Ala.	FA-'04	9/0*
63	Meester, Brad	C	6-3	300	3/23/77	5	Northern Iowa	Parkersburg, Iowa	D2-'00	16/16
92	Meier, Rob	DT	6-5	293	8/29/77	5	Washington State	W. Vancouver, B.C.	D7b-'00	16/0
42	Mitchell, Anthony	S	6-1	198	12/13/74	5	Tuskegee	Atlanta, Ga.	T(Balt)-'03	16/2
65	Naeole, Chris	G	6-3	320	12/25/74	8	Colorado	Kaaava, Hawaii	UFA(NO)-'02	16/16
77	Ogden, Marques	T-G	6-5	312	11/15/80	2	Howard	Washington D.C.	D6c-'03	0*
72	Pearson, Mike	T	6-7	297	8/22/80	3	Florida	Seffner, Fla.	D2-'02	16/16
54	Peterson, Mike	LB	6-1	230	6/17/76	6	Florida	Gainesville, Fla.	UFA(Ind)-'03	16/16
17	Redmond, Jimmy	WR	6-0	190	8/18/77	3	McNeese State	Blue Springs, Mo.	FA-'02	12/0
66	Romberg, Brett	C	6-2	293	10/10/79	2	Miami	Windsor, Ontario, Canada	FA-'03	0*
76	Salaam, Ephraim	T	6-7	295	6/19/76	7	San Diego State	Sacramento, Calif.	FA-'04	14/14
25	Sanders, Lewis	CB-S	6-1	210	6/22/78	5	Maryland	Staten Island, N.Y.	UFA(Clev)-'04	9/0*
82	Smith, Jimmy	WR	6-1	208	2/9/69	12	Jackson State	Jackson, Miss.	FA-'95	12/12
41	Sorensen, Nick	S	6-3	210	7/31/78	4	Virginia Tech	Vienna, Va.	FA-'03	14/0
95	Spicer, Paul	DE	6-4	287	8/18/75	5	Saginaw Valley State	Indianapolis, Ind.	FA-'00	16/1
99	Stroud, Marcus	DT	6-6	312	6/25/78	4	Georgia	Barney, Ga.	D1-'01	16/16
28	Taylor, Fred	RB	6-1	234	1/27/76	7	Florida	Belle Glade, Fla.	D1a-'98	16/16
24	Thomas, Kiwaukee	CB	5-11	192	6/19/77	5	Georgia Southern	Perry, Ga.	D5-'00	11/1
22	Toefield, LaBrandon	RB	5-11	232	9/24/80	2	Louisiana State	Independence, La.	D4b-'03	16/0
30	Washington, Dewayne	CB	5-11	193	12/27/72	10	North Carolina State	Durham, N.C.	FA-'04	16/12*
74	Williams, Maurice	T	6-5	310	1/26/79	4	Michigan	Detroit, Mich.	D2-'01	16/16
60	Williams, Sammy	T-G	6-5	310	12/14/74	7	Oklahoma	Harvey, Ill.	FA-'03	0*
87	Wrighster, George	TE	6-3	260	4/1/81	2	Oregon	Van Nuys, Calif.	D4a-'03	15/1
46	Yoder, Todd	TE	6-4	250	3/18/78	5	Vanderbilt	New Palestine, Ind.	UFA(TB)-'04	16/1*
88	Zelenka, Joe	TE-LS	6-3	270	3/9/76	6	Wake Forest	Cleveland, Ohio	FA-'01	16/0

* Akbar inactive for 2 games; Bolden played 8 games with Atlanta in '03; Bullard played 9 games with St. Louis; Chandler played in 2 games with San Francisco; Favors played 16 games with Carolina; Fletcher last active with Carolina in '02; Grant played 16 games with Carolina; Green missed '03 season because of injury; Hendricks played 16 games with Miami; Johnson played 10 games with Atlanta; McClain played 9 games with Houston; Ogden inactive for 16 games; Romberg inactive for 6 games and did not play in 1 game; Sanders played 9 games with Cleveland; Washington played 16 games with Pittsburgh; S. Williams inactive for 14 games and did not play in 1 game; Yoder played 16 games for Tampa Bay.

Traded—QB Mark Brunell (3 games in '03) to Washington; CB Jason Craft (7 games) to New Orleans; WR Kevin Johnson (15 games, 6 with Jaguars) to Baltimore.

Players lost through free agency (4): CB Fernando Bryant (Det; 16 games in '03), LB Danny Clark (Oak; 16), T Leander Jordan (SD; 6), G Jamar Nesbit (NO; 16).

Also played with Jaguars in '03—CB Brad Franklin (4 games), FB Malaefoe MacKenzie (1), S Marlon McCree (2), LB Keith Mitchell (4), WR Micah Ross (1), P Mark Royals (14), LB T.J. Slaughter (6), WR J.J. Stokes (6), LB Shannon Taylor (2), S-CB James Trapp (5), LB Eric Westmoreland (2).

2004 FIRST-YEAR ROSTER

Name	Pos.	Ht.	Wt.	Birthdate	College	Hometown	How Acq.
Alexis, Rich	RB	6-0	213	3/6/81	Washington	Coral Springs, Fla.	FA
Ball, Matt	DE	6-6	286	1/4/81	UCLA	Dixon, Calif.	FA
Brown, Chris (1)	CB	6-1	196	5/9/78	Alabama-Birmingham	Atlanta, Ga.	FA-'03
Bubin, Sean	T	6-6	308	1/26/81	Illinois	Rantoul, Ill.	D5c
Cherry, Matt	WR	6-1	203	12/14/81	Akron	Chicago, Ill.	FA
Cordova, Jorge	DE/LB	6-1	241	9/25/81	Nevada	Murrieta, Calif.	D3
Dean, Konrad (1)	G	6-4	303	6/6/79	Akron	Jackson, N.J.	FA
Gomez, Mike	LS	6-6	235	4/23/82	Illinois	Miami, Fla.	FA
Gray, Quinn (1)	QB	6-3	246	5/21/79	Florida A&M	Fort Lauderdale, Fla.	FA-'03
Hage, Marwan	C	6-2	291	9/14/81	Colorado	Montreal, Quebec	FA
Jones, Brian	TE	6-3	235	8/23/81	Arkansas-Pine Bluff	Bastrop, La.	FA
Jones, Greg	RB	6-1	250	4/4/81	Florida State	Beaufort, S.C.	D2b
Maddox, Anthony	DT	6-1	295	11/22/78	Delta State	Funston, Ga.	D4a
Mccray, Bobby	DE	6-6	251	11/1/81	Florida	Miami, Fla.	D7
Perryman, Ray (1)	S	5-11	195	11/27/78	Northern Arizona	Phoenix, Ariz.	FA-'03
Randall, Curtis (1)	LB	6-2	221	8/6/79	Louisiana Tech	Morgan City, La.	FA-'03
Richardson, David	CB	6-0	202	9/9/81	Cal Poly-SLO	Los Angeles, Calif.	FA
Scobee, Josh	PK	6-1	190	6/23/82	Louisiana Tech	Longview, Texas	D5a
Smith, Daryl	LB	6-2	234	4/14/82	Georgia Tech	Albany, Ga.	D2a
Smith, Joe (1)	RB	6-1	224	8/26/79	Louisiana Tech	Cleveland, Texas	FA-'03
Smith, Linnis	DT	6-4	299	2/9/82	Texas A&M	Tyler, Texas	FA
Street, Lacorey	DT	6-6	334	3/26/81	Louisiana Tech	Lucedale, Miss.	FA
Suber, Allen	WR	5-9	189	10/21/81	Bethune-Cookman	Tampa, Fla.	FA
Tate, Joe	G	6-5	291	12/30/80	Michigan State	Southfield, Mich.	FA
Thompson, Chris	CB	6-0	187	5/19/82	Nicholls State	New Orleans, La.	D5b
Wilford, Ernest	WR	6-4	223	1/14/79	Virginia Tech	Richmond, Va.	D4b
Williams, Reggie	WR	6-4	223	5/17/83	Washington	Tacoma, Wash.	D1

The term NFL Rookie is defined as a player who is in his first season of professional football and has not been on the roster of another professional football team for any regular-season or postseason games. A Rookie is designated by an "R" on NFL rosters. Players who have been active in another professional football league or players who have NFL experience, including either preseason training camp or being on an Active List or Inactive List, or on Reserve/Injured or Reserve/Physically Unable to Perform for fewer than six regular-season games, are termed NFL First-Year Players. An NFL First-Year Player is designated by a "1" on NFL rosters. Thereafter, a player is credited with an additional year of experience for each season in which he accumulates six games on the Active List or Inactive List, or on Reserve/Injured or Reserve/Physically Unable to Perform.

Log on to www.jaguars.com for an up-to-date roster.

JACKSONVILLE JAGUARS

COACHING STAFF

Head Coach,
Jack Del Rio

Pro Career: Jack Del Rio was named head coach of the Jaguars on January 17, 2003, becoming the second head coach in franchise history. In his first season, the Jaguars posted a 5-11 record, with six losses coming by seven points or less and a defense that ranked sixth in the NFL. Del Rio was the defensive coordinator for the Carolina Panthers in 2002, his sixth season as an NFL assistant coach. He previously spent 11 years as an NFL linebacker. At 41, Del Rio is the second-youngest head coach in the NFL (Jon Gruden is the youngest). In his only season with Carolina, the team's defense ranked second in the league after finishing thirty-first in 2001. From 1999-2001, he was the linebackers coach for the Baltimore Ravens, helping the team win Super Bowl XXXV. The Ravens finished second in total defense in each of those three seasons. During the Ravens' Super Bowl championship season in 2000, Baltimore's defense set the NFL 16-game record by allowing only 165 points. Del Rio coached two seasons in New Orleans, as the linebackers coach in 1998 and the assistant strength coach in 1997. In 1985, he was a third-round choice of the New Orleans Saints and was named to the NFL's All-Rookie team. Del Rio also played for the Kansas City Chiefs (1987-88), Dallas Cowboys (1989-1991), and Minnesota Vikings (1992-95). He played in the Pro Bowl following the 1994 season. Career record: 5-11.

Background: Four-year starter at linebacker from 1981-84 at Southern California, where he earned consensus All-America honors as a senior and was runner-up for the Lombardi Award. He was co-MVP of the 1985 Rose Bowl. Drafted by baseball's Toronto Blue Jays in 1981, Del Rio batted .340 while playing catcher on USC's baseball team in 1983 and 1984 with future stars Randy Johnson and Mark McGwire. He has a political science degree from Kansas.

Personal: Born April 4, 1963 in Castro Valley, Calif. Jack and his wife, Linda, live in Jacksonville, and have three daughters, Lauren, Hope, and Aubrey, and a son, Luke.

ASSISTANT COACHES

Ken Anderson, wide receivers; born February 15, 1949, Batavia, Ill. Quarterback Augustana (Ill.) 1967-1970. Pro quarterback Cincinnati Bengals 1971-1986. Pro coach: Cincinnati Bengals 1992-2002, joined Jaguars in 2003.

Mark Asanovich, strength and conditioning; born May 20, 1959, Duluth, Minn. Attended St. Cloud State. No college or pro playing experience. College coach: Ohio State 1984-85, The Citadel 1986. Pro coach: Minnesota Vikings 1995, Tampa Bay Buccaneers 1996-2001, Baltimore Ravens 2002, joined Jaguars in 2003.

Paul Boudreau, offensive line; born December 30, 1949, Arlington, Mass. Offensive lineman Boston College 1971-73. No pro playing experience. College coach: Boston College 1974-75, Maine 1976-78, Dartmouth 1979-1981, Navy 1982. Pro coach: Edmonton Eskimos (CFL) 1983-86, New Orleans Saints 1987-1993, Detroit Lions 1994-96, New England Patriots 1997-98, Miami Dolphins 1999-2000, Carolina Panthers 2001-02, joined Jaguars in 2003.

Les Ebert, asst. strength and conditioning coach, born October 1, 1972, Brainerd, Minn. Attended Minnesota-Duluth. No college or pro playing experience. Pro coach: Tampa Bay Buccaneers 1999-2002, joined Jaguars in 2003.

Mike Haluchak, linebackers; born November 28, 1949, Concord, Calif. Linebacker Southern California 1967-1970. No pro playing experience. College coach: Southern California 1976-77, Cal State-Fullerton 1978, Pacific 1979-1980, California 1981, North Carolina State 1982. Pro coach: Oakland Invaders (USFL) 1983-85, San Diego Chargers 1986-1991, Cincinnati Bengals 1992-93, Washington Redskins 1994-96, New York Giants 1997-99, St. Louis Rams 2000-02, joined Jaguars in 2003.

Ray Hamilton, defensive line; born January 20, 1951, Omaha, Neb. Nose tackle Oklahoma 1969-1972. Pro defensive lineman New England Patriots 1973-1981. College coach: Tennessee 1992. Pro coach: New England Patriots 1985-89, Tampa Bay Buccaneers 1991, Los Angeles Raiders 1993-94, New York Jets 1994-96, 2000, New England Patriots 1997-99, Cleveland Browns 2001-02, joined Jaguars in 2003.

Andy Heck, offensive assistant, born January 1, 1967, Fargo, N.D. Tackle Notre Dame 1985-88. Pro tackle Seattle 1989-1993, Chicago 1994-98, Washington 1999-2000. College coach: Virginia 2001-03. Pro coach: Joined Jaguars in 2003.

Todd Howard, defensive assistant; born February 18, 1965, Bryan, Texas. Linebacker Texas A&M 1983-86. Pro linebacker Kansas City Chiefs 1987-88, Barcelona Dragons (WLAF) 1991-92. College coach: Texas A&M 1991-93, Grinnell 1994-97, Louisiana Tech 2000-02. Pro coach: St. Louis Rams 1998-99, joined Jaguars in 2003.

Bob Ligashesky, asst. special teams, born June 2, 1962. Linebacker Indiana (Pa.) 1983-84. No pro playing experience. College coach: Wake Forest 1985, Arizona State 1986-89, Kent State 1990, Bowling Green 1991-99, Pittsburgh 2000-03. Pro coach: Joined Jaguars in 2004.

Anthony Lynn, running backs; born December 21, 1968, McKinney, Texas. Fullback Texas Tech 1987-1990. Pro fullback Denver Broncos 1993, 1997-99, San Francisco 49ers 1995-96. Pro coach: Denver Broncos 2000-02, joined Jaguars in 2003.

Bill Musgrave, offensive coordinator, quarterbacks; born November 11, 1967, Grand Junction, Colo. Quarterback Oregon 1987-1990. Pro quarterback San Francisco 49ers 1991-94, Denver Broncos 1995-96. College coach: Virginia 2001-02. Pro coach Oakland Raiders 1997, Philadelphia Eagles 1998, Carolina Panthers 1999-2000, joined Jaguars in 2003.

Alvin Reynolds, defensive backs; born June 24, 1959, Pineville, La. Safety Indiana State 1978-1981. No pro playing experience. College coach: Indiana State 1982-1992. Pro coach: Denver Broncos 1993-95, Baltimore Ravens 1996-98, Carolina Panthers 1999-2002, joined Jaguars in 2003.

Alfredo Roberts, tight ends; born March 17, 1965, Fort Lauderdale, Fla. Tight end Miami 1983-87. Pro tight end Kansas City Chiefs 1988-1990, Dallas Cowboys 1991-93. College coach: Florida Atlantic 1999-2002. Pro coach: Joined Jaguars in 2003.

Pete Rodriguez, special teams coordinator, born July 25, 1940, Chicago. Guard-linebacker Denver 1959-1960, Western State (Colo.) 1961-63. College coach: Arizona 1968-69, Western Illinois 1970-73, 1979-1982 (head coach, 1979-1982), Florida State 1974-75, Iowa State 1976-78, Northern Iowa 1986. Pro coach: Michigan Panthers (USFL) 1983-84, Denver Gold (USFL) 1985, Jacksonville Bulls (USFL) 1986, Ottawa Rough Riders (CFL) 1987, Los Angeles Raiders 1988-89, Phoenix Cardinals 1990-93, Washington Redskins 1994-97, Seattle Seahawks 1998-2003, joined Jaguars in 2004.

Steve Shafer, asst. head coach; born December 8, 1940, Glendale, Calif. Quarterback-defensive back Utah State 1961-62. Pro defensive back British Columbia Lions (CFL) 1963-67. College coach: San Mateo (Calif.) J.C. 1968-1974 (head coach 1973-74), San Diego State 1975-1982, 1994. Pro coach: Los Angeles Rams 1983-1990, Tampa Bay Buccaneers 1991-93, Oakland Raiders 1995-97, Carolina Panthers 1998, Baltimore Ravens 1999-2001, joined Jaguars in 2003.

Mike Smith, defensive coordinator; born November 30, 1959, Chicago. Linebacker East Tennessee 1977-1981. Pro linebacker Winnipeg Blue Bombers (CFL) 1982. College coach: San Diego State 1982-85, Morehead State (Ky.) 1986, Tennessee Tech 1987-1998. Pro coach: Baltimore Ravens 1999-2002, joined Jaguars in 2003.

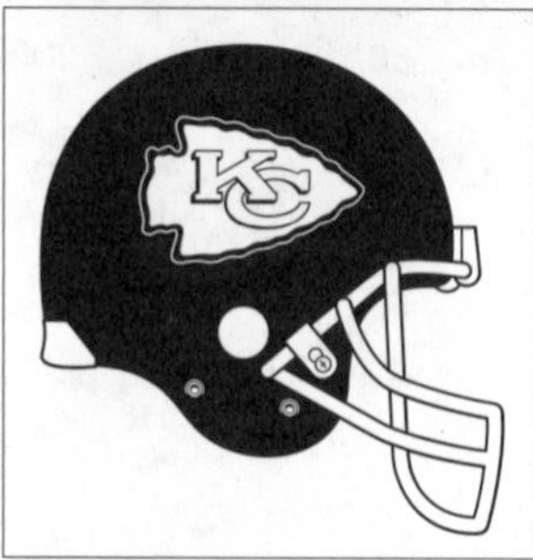

American Football Conference
West Division
Team Colors: Red, Gold, and White
One Arrowhead Drive
Kansas City, Missouri 64129
Telephone: (816) 920-9300

2004 SCHEDULE

PRESEASON		**Kansas City time**
Aug. 13	at New York Giants	7:00
Aug. 23	**St. Louis**	7:00
Aug. 28	**Cleveland**	7:00
Sept. 2	at Dallas	7:00

REGULAR SEASON		
Sept. 12	at Denver	7:30
Sept. 19	**Carolina**	12:00
Sept. 26	**Houston**	12:00
Oct. 4	at Baltimore (Mon.)	8:00
Oct. 10	Open Date	
Oct. 17	at Jacksonville	12:00
Oct. 24	**Atlanta**	12:00
Oct. 31	**Indianapolis**	12:00
Nov. 7	at Tampa Bay	12:00
Nov. 14	at New Orleans	12:00
Nov. 22	**New England** (Mon.)	8:00
Nov. 28	**San Diego**	12:00
Dec. 5	at Oakland	3:05
Dec. 13	at Tennessee (Mon.)	8:00
Dec. 19	**Denver**	3:15
Dec. 25	**Oakland** (Sat.)	4:00
Jan. 2	at San Diego	3:15

Stadium: Arrowhead Stadium (opened in 1972) • **Capacity:** 79,451
One Arrowhead Drive
Kansas City, Missouri 64129
Playing Surface: Grass
Training Camp: University of Wisconsin-River Falls
River Falls, Wisconsin 54022

ARROWHEAD STADIUM

N

CLUB OFFICIALS

Founder: Lamar Hunt
Chairman of the Board: Jack Steadman
Vice Chairman of the Board: Clark Hunt
President: Carl Peterson
Executive Vice President/Assistant General Manager: Dennis Thum
Vice President of Football Operations/Player Personnel: Lynn Stiles
Secretary: Jim Seigfreid
Director of Finance/Treasurer: Dale Young
Vice President of Sales and Marketing: Wallace Bennett
Vice President of Pro Personnel: Bill Kuharich
Director of College Scouting: Chuck Cook
Director of Public Relations: Bob Moore
Associate Director of Public Relations: Pete Moris
Director of Stadium Operations: Steve Schneider
Director of Development: Ken Blume
Director of Corporate Sponsorship: Anita Bailey
Director of Sales: Gary Spani
Director of Player Development: Lamonte Winston
Director of Community Relations: Brenda Sniezek
Director of Ticket Operations: Doug Hopkins
Director of Special Events: Annette Teson
Equipment Manager: Mike Davidson
Asst. Equipment Managers: Allen Wright, Chris Shropshire
Head Athletic Trainer: Dave Kendall
Assistant Trainers: Bud Epps, Keith Abrams
Director of Video Operations: Mike Portz
Video Assistants: Todd Weger, Andrew Hearne

COACHING HISTORY

Dallas Texans 1960-62
(357-311-12)

1960-1974	Hank Stram	129-79-10
1975-77	Paul Wiggin*	11-24-0
1977	Tom Bettis	1-6-0
1978-1982	Marv Levy	31-42-0
1983-86	John Mackovic	30-35-0
1987-88	Frank Gansz	8-22-1
1989-1998	Marty Schottenheimer	104-65-1
1999-2000	Gunther Cunningham	16-16-0
2001-03	Dick Vermeil	27-22-0

*Released after seven games in 1977

ATTENDANCE

Home 627,981 Away 536,840
Total 1,164,821
Single-game home record, 82,893* (10/2/00)
Single-season home record, 629,569 (1999)
*Arrowhead Stadium attendance: 78,502; Kauffman Stadium attendance: 4,391

2004 DRAFT CHOICES

Round	Name	Pos.	College
2	Junior Siavii	DT	Oregon
	Kris Wilson	TE	Pittsburgh
3	Keyaron Fox	LB	Georgia Tech
4	Samie Parker	WR	Oregon
	Jared Allen	DE	Idaho State
6	Jeris McIntyre	WR	Auburn
7	Kevin Sampson	T	Syracuse

KANSAS CITY CHIEFS

2003 TEAM RECORD

PRESEASON (3-2)

Date	Result		Opponent
8/4	W	9-0	vs. Green Bay at Canton, Ohio
8/9	L	6-24	San Francisco
8/16	W	26-16	Minnesota
8/23	L	31-42	at Seattle
8/28	W	22-6	at St Louis

REGULAR SEASON (13-3)

Date	Result		Opponent	Att.
9/7	W	27-14	San Diego	78,048
9/14	W	41-20	Pittsburgh	78,416
9/21	W	42-14	at Houston	70,487
9/28	W	17-10	at Baltimore	69,459
10/5	W	24-23	Denver	78,903
10/12	W	40-34	at Green Bay (OT)	70,407
10/20	W	17-10	at Oakland	62,391
10/26	W	38-5	Buffalo	78,689
11/9	W	41-20	Cleveland	78,560
11/16	L	19-24	at Cincinnati	64,923
11/23	W	27-24	Oakland	78,889
11/30	W	28-24	at San Diego	57,671
12/7	L	27-45	at Denver	76,403
12/14	W	45-17	Detroit	77,922
12/20	L	20-45	at Minnesota	64,291
12/28	W	31-3	Chicago	78,413

(OT) Overtime

POSTSEASON (0-1)

Date	Result		Opponent	Att.
1/11	L	31-38	Indianapolis	79,159

SCORE BY PERIODS

	1	2	3	4	OT		Total
Chiefs	112	153	82	131	6	—	484
Opponents	57	94	85	96	0	—	332

2003 TEAM STATISTICS

	Chiefs	Opp.
Total First Downs	348	322
Rushing	120	120
Passing	201	184
Penalty	27	18
3rd Down: Made/Att	84/201	78/213
3rd Down Pct.	41.8	36.6
4th Down: Made/Att	6/10	10/23
4th Down Pct.	60.0	43.5
Possession Avg.	29:23	30:37
Total Net Yards	5,910	5,707
Avg. Per Game	369.4	356.7
Total Plays	1,003	1,054
Avg. Per Play	5.9	5.4
Net Yards Rushing	1,929	2,344
Avg. Per Game	120.6	146.5
Total Rushes	446	453
Net Yards Passing	3,981	3,363
Avg. Per Game	248.8	210.2
Sacked/Yards Lost	21/132	36/251
Gross Yards	4,113	3,614
Att./Completions	536/339	565/332
Completion Pct.	63.2	58.8
Had Intercepted	12	25
Punts/Average	81/39.0	73/40.7
Net Punting Avg.	81/33.2	73/31.4
Penalties/Yards	79/698	95/781
Fumbles/Ball Lost	13/6	21/12
Touchdowns	63	39
Rushing	32	18
Passing	24	19
Returns	7	2

2003 INDIVIDUAL STATISTICS

PASSING	Att.	Comp.	Yds.	Pct.	TD	Int.	Tkld.	Rate
Green	523	330	4,039	63.1	24	12	20/130	92.6
Collins	12	9	74	75.0	0	0	0/0	90.3
Holmes	1	0	0	0.0	0	0	0/0	39.6
Hall	0	0	0	—	0	0	1/2	—
Chiefs	536	339	4,113	63.2	24	12	21/132	92.4
Opponents	565	332	3,614	58.8	19	25	36/251	70.5

SCORING	TD R	TD P	TD Rt	PAT	FG	Saf	PTS
Holmes	27	0	0	0/0	0/0	0	162
M. Andersen	0	0	0	58/59	16/20	0	106
Gonzalez	0	10	0	0/0	0/0	0	60
Hall	0	1	4	0/0	0/0	0	30
Kennison	0	5	0	0/0	0/0	0	30
Morton	0	4	0	0/0	0/0	0	24
Blaylock	2	1	0	0/0	0/0	0	18
Dunn	0	3	0	0/0	0/0	0	18
Green	2	0	0	0/0	0/0	0	12
Woods	0	0	2	0/0	0/0	0	12
Harts	0	0	1	0/0	0/0	0	6
L. Johnson	1	0	0	0/0	0/0	0	6
Chiefs	32	24	7	58/59	16/20	0	484
Opponents	18	19	2	39/39	19/25	1	332

2-Pt. Conversions: None.
Chiefs 0-3, Opponents 0-0.

RUSHING	No.	Yds	Avg	LG	TD
Holmes	320	1,420	4.4	31t	27
Blaylock	22	112	5.1	25t	2
Morton	8	94	11.8	39	0
L. Johnson	20	85	4.3	15	1
Green	26	83	3.2	14	2
Hall	16	73	4.6	16	0
Richardson	24	60	2.5	8	0
Kennison	2	9	4.5	5	0
Collins	8	-7	-0.9	0	0
Chiefs	446	1,929	4.3	39	32
Opponents	453	2,344	5.2	65t	18

RECEIVING	No.	Yds	Avg	LG	TD
Holmes	74	690	9.3	36	0
Gonzalez	71	916	12.9	67	10
Kennison	56	853	15.2	51t	5
Morton	50	740	14.8	50	4
Hall	40	423	10.6	67t	1
Blaylock	15	181	12.1	63t	1
Richardson	12	76	6.3	14	0
Boerigter	11	158	14.4	30	0
Dunn	5	35	7.0	15	3
Easy	3	19	6.3	8	0
Baber	1	20	20.0	20	0
L. Johnson	1	2	2.0	2	0
Chiefs	339	4,113	12.1	67t	24
Opponents	332	3,614	10.9	77t	19

INTERCEPTIONS	No.	Yds	Avg	LG	TD
Wesley	6	63	10.5	27	0
McCleon	6	-3	-0.5	0	0
Warfield	4	39	9.8	20	0
Woods	3	125	41.7	79t	2
Harts	2	39	19.5	39t	1
Barber	1	28	28.0	28	0
Fujita	1	8	8.0	8	0
Sims	1	8	8.0	8	0
Mitchell	1	3	3.0	3	0
Chiefs	25	310	12.4	79t	3
Opponents	12	150	12.5	50	1

PUNTING	No.	Yds.	Avg.	In 20	LG
J. Baker	80	3,156	39.5	21	68
Chiefs	81	3,156	39.0	21	68
Opponents	73	2,974	40.7	22	71

PUNT RETURNS	Ret	FC	Yds	Avg	LG	TD
Hall	29	14	472	16.3	93t	2
Kennison	3	0	70	23.3	46	0
Bartee	1	0	0	0.0	0	0
Chiefs	33	14	542	16.4	93t	2
Opponents	38	18	327	8.6	68t	1

KICKOFF RETURNS	No.	Yds	Avg	LG	TD
Hall	57	1,478	25.9	100t	2
Blaylock	1	32	32.0	32	0
Boerigter	1	44	44.0	44	0
D. Johnson	1	12	12.0	12	0
Ward	1	11	11.0	11	0
Wilkerson	1	0	0.0	0	0
Chiefs	62	1,577	25.4	100t	2
Opponents	87	2,043	23.5	60	0

FIELD GOALS	1-19	20-29	30-39	40-49	50+
M. Andersen	0/0	3/3	8/8	5/8	0/1
Chiefs	0/0	3/3	8/8	5/8	0/1
Opponents	0/0	10/10	0/0	6/10	3/5

SACKS	No.
Holliday	5.5
Barber	5.0
Hicks	5.0
Truluck	5.0
Fujita	4.0
Sims	3.0
Stills	3.0
Wesley	2.0
Beisel	1.0
Sharpe	1.0
Warfield	1.0
Browning	0.5
Chiefs	36.0
Opponents	21.0

RECORD HOLDERS

INDIVIDUAL RECORDS—CAREER

Category	Name	Performance
Rushing (Yds.)	Christian Okoye, 1987-1992	4,897
Passing (Yds.)	Len Dawson, 1962-1975	28,507
Passing (TDs)	Len Dawson, 1962-1975	237
Receiving (No.)	Tony Gonzalez, 1997-2003	468
Receiving (Yds.)	Otis Taylor, 1965-1975	7,306
Interceptions	Emmitt Thomas, 1966-1978	58
Punting (Avg.)	Jerrel Wilson, 1963-1977	43.4
Punt Return (Avg.)	Dante Hall, 2000-03	11.8
Kickoff Return (Avg.)	Noland Smith, 1967-69	26.8
Field Goals	Nick Lowery, 1980-1993	329
Touchdowns (Tot.)	Priest Holmes, 2001-03	61
Points	Nick Lowery, 1980-1993	1,466

INDIVIDUAL RECORDS—SINGLE SEASON

Category	Name	Performance
Rushing (Yds.)	Priest Holmes, 2002	1,615
Passing (Yds.)	Bill Kenney, 1983	4,348
Passing (TDs)	Len Dawson, 1964	30
Receiving (No.)	Tony Gonzalez, 2000	93
Receiving (Yds.)	Derrick Alexander, 2000	1,391
Interceptions	Emmitt Thomas, 1974	12
Punting (Avg.)	Jerrel Wilson, 1965	45.4
Punt Return (Avg.)	Dante Hall, 2003	16.3
Kickoff Return (Avg.)	Dave Grayson, 1962	29.7
Field Goals	Nick Lowery, 1990	34
Touchdowns (Tot.)	Priest Holmes, 2003	*27
Points	Priest Holmes, 2003	162

INDIVIDUAL RECORDS—SINGLE GAME

Category	Name	Performance
Rushing (Yds.)	Barry Word, 10-14-90	200
Passing (Yds.)	Elvis Grbac, 11-5-00	504
Passing (TDs)	Len Dawson, 11-1-64	6
Receiving (No.)	Ed Podolak, 10-7-73	12
Receiving (Yds.)	Stephone Paige, 12-22-85	309
Interceptions	Bobby Ply, 12-16-62	*4
	Bobby Hunt, 10-4-64	*4
	Deron Cherry, 9-29-85	*4
Field Goals	Many times	5
	Last time by Nick Lowery, 9-20-93	
Touchdowns (Tot.)	Abner Haynes, 11-26-61	5
Points	Abner Haynes, 11-26-61	30

*NFL Record

KANSAS CITY CHIEFS

2004 VETERAN ROSTER

No.	Name	Pos.	Ht.	Wt.	Birthdate	NFL Exp.	College	Hometown	How Acq.	'03 Games/ Starts
72	Alford, Darnell	G	6-4	325	6/11/77	4	Boston College	Fredericksburg, Va.	FA-'02	0*
8	Andersen, Morten	K	6-2	217	8/19/60	23	Michigan State	Indianapolis, Ind.	UFA(NYG)-'02	16/0
45	Baber, Billy	TE	6-3	255	1/17/79	3	Virginia	Crozet, Va.	D5a-'01	16/0
9	Baker, Jason	P	6-1	201	5/17/78	4	Iowa	Fort Wayne, Ind.	FA-'03	16/0
59	Barber, Shawn	LB	6-2	245	1/14/75	7	Richmond	Richmond, Va.	UFA(Phil)-'03	16/16
24	Bartee, William	CB	6-1	200	6/25/77	5	Oklahoma	Daytona Beach, Fla.	D2-'00	11/1
26	Battle, Julian	CB	6-2	205	7/11/81	2	Tennessee	West Palm Beach, Fla.	D3-'03	14/0
56	Beisel, Monty	LB	6-3	254	8/20/78	4	Kansas State	Douglass, Kan.	D4a-'01	12/0
65	Black, Jordan	T	6-5	314	1/28/80	2	Notre Dame	Mesquite, Texas	D5-'03	0*
23	Blaylock, Derrick	RB	5-9	205	8/23/79	4	Stephen F. Austin	Atlanta, Texas	D5b-'01	16/0
67	Bober, Chris	T	6-5	305	12/24/76	5	Nebraska-Omaha	Omaha, Neb.	UFA(NYG)-'04	16/16*
85	Boerigter, Marc	WR	6-3	220	5/4/78	3	Hastings	Hastings, Neb.	FA-'02	15/0
93	Browning, John	DT	6-4	297	9/30/73	9	West Virginia	Miami, Fla.	D3-'96	16/16
13	Burford, Seth	QB	6-3	236	3/11/79	2	Cal Poly-San Luis Obispo	Oakdale, Calif.	FA-'04	0*
52	Caver, Quinton	LB	6-4	241	8/22/78	4	Arkansas	Anniston, Ala.	FA-'03	12/0
15	Collins, Todd	QB	6-4	225	11/5/71	10	Michigan	Walpole, Mass.	W(Buff)-'98	5/0
75	Dalton, Lional	DT	6-1	315	2/21/75	7	Eastern Michigan	Detroit, Mich.	FA-'04	12/9*
92	Downing, Eric	DT	6-3	315	9/16/78	4	Syracuse	Paterson, N.J.	D3a-'01	14/0
89	Dunn, Jason	TE	6-6	276	11/15/73	8	Eastern Kentucky	Harrodsburg, Ky.	FA-'00	16/4
43	Easy, Omar	FB	6-1	245	10/29/77	3	Penn State	Everett, Mass.	D4-'02	15/0
71	Freeman, Eddie	DE	6-5	307	1/4/78	3	Alabama-Birmingham	Mobile, Ala.	D2-'02	5/0
51	Fujita, Scott	LB	6-5	247	4/28/79	3	California	Rio Mesa, Calif.	D5-'02	16/16
83	Gammon, Kendall	TE	6-4	255	10/23/68	13	Pittsburg State	Rose Hill, Kan.	UFA(NO)-'00	16/0
88	Gonzalez, Tony	TE	6-4	248	2/27/76	8	California	Huntington Beach, Calif.	D1-'97	16/16
10	Green, Trent	QB	6-3	217	7/9/70	11	Indiana	St. Louis, Mo.	T(StL)-'01	16/16
82	Hall, Dante	WR	5-8	187	9/21/78	5	Texas A&M	Houston, Texas	D5a-'00	16/2
42	Harts, Shaunard	S	6-0	207	8/4/78	3	Boise State	Pittsburg, Calif.	D7a-'01	16/0
17	Haygood, Herb	WR	5-11	193	12/30/77	2	Michigan State	Sarasota, Fla.	FA-'04	0*
98	Hicks, Eric	DE	6-6	280	6/17/76	7	Maryland	Erie, Pa.	FA-'98	16/16
99	Holliday, Vonnie	DE	6-5	290	12/11/75	7	North Carolina	Camden, S.C.	UFA(GB)-'03	16/16
31	Holmes, Priest	RB	5-9	213	10/7/73	8	Texas	San Antonio, Texas	UFA(Balt)-'01	16/16
81	Horn, Chris	WR	5-11	195	7/13/77	2	Rocky Mountain	Caldwell, Idaho	FA-'04	0*
27	Johnson, Larry	RB	6-1	228	11/19/79	2	Penn State	State College, Pa.	D1-'03	6/0
53	Jones, Fred	LB	6-2	247	10/18/77	4	Colorado	San Diego, Calif.	FA-'03	11/0
87	Kennison, Eddie	WR	6-1	201	1/20/73	9	Louisiana State	Lake Charles, La.	FA-'01	16/16
57	Maslowski, Mike	LB	6-1	243	7/11/74	6	Wisconsin-La Crosse	Thorp, Wis.	FA-'99	10/10
22	McCleon, Dexter	CB	5-10	195	10/9/73	8	Clemson	Meridian, Miss.	FA-'03	16/16
50	Mitchell, Kawika	LB	6-0	253	10/10/79	2	South Florida	Lake Howell, Fla.	D2-'03	12/6
80	Morton, Johnnie	WR	6-0	190	10/7/71	11	Southern California	Torrance, Calif.	FA-'02	16/16
49	Richardson, Tony	FB	6-1	232	12/17/71	10	Auburn	Daleville, Ala.	FA-'95	16/10
77	Roaf, Willie	T	6-5	320	4/18/70	12	Louisiana Tech	Pine Bluff, Ark.	T(NO)-'02	16/16
61	Sharpe, Montique	DT	6-2	296	3/10/80	2	Wake Forest	Washington, D.C.	D7a-'03	5/0
39	Shields, Scott	S	6-4	230	3/29/76	3	Weber State	Chula Vista, Calif.	FA-'04	0*
68	Shields, Will	G	6-3	315	9/15/71	12	Nebraska	Lawton, Okla.	D3-'93	16/16
90	Sims, Ryan	DT	6-4	315	5/4/80	3	North Carolina	Spartanburg, S.C.	D1-'02	16/16
70	Spears, Marcus	T	6-4	320	9/28/71	11	Northwestern State (La.)	Scotlandville, La.	FA-'97	16/0
55	Stills, Gary	DE	6-2	244	7/11/74	6	West Virginia	Valley Forge, Pa.	D3a-'99	16/0
91	Truluck, R-Kal	DE	6-4	255	9/30/74	3	SUNY-Cortland	Rockland County, N.Y.	FA-'02	14/0
44	Warfield, Eric	CB	6-0	200	3/3/76	7	Nebraska	Texarkana, Ark.	D7a-'98	15/15
54	Waters, Brian	G	6-3	318	2/18/77	5	North Texas	Waxahachie, Texas	FA-'00	16/16
76	t- Welbourn, John	G-T	6-5	318	3/30/76	6	California	Rolling Hills, Calif.	T(Phil)-'04	13/13*
25	Wesley, Greg	S	6-2	206	3/19/78	5	Arkansas-Pine Bluff	England, Ark.	D3-'00	16/16
30	West, Lyle	S	6-0	210	12/20/76	5	San Jose State	Fremont, Ga.	FA-'02	13/0
62	Wiegmann, Casey	C	6-2	285	7/20/73	9	Iowa	Parkersburg, Iowa	UFA(Chi)-'01	16/16
66	Wilkerson, Jimmy	DE	6-2	271	1/4/81	2	Oklahoma	Omaha, Texas	D6-'03	12/0
74	Williams, Brett	T	6-5	321	5/2/80	2	Florida State	Kissimmee, Fla.	D4-'03	0*
60	Willis, Donald	G	6-3	325	7/15/73	7	North Carolina A&T	Lompoc, Calif.	FA-'00	16/0
21	Woods, Jerome	S	6-2	210	3/17/73	9	Memphis	Memphis, Tenn.	D1-'96	16/16

* Alford last active with Kansas City in '02; Black inactive for 16 games; Bober played 16 games for N.Y. Giants in '03; Burford last active with San Diego in '02; Dalton played 12 games with Washington; Haygood last active with Denver in '02; Horn inactive for 7 games; S. Shields last active with Pittsburgh in '00; Welbourn played 13 games with Philadelphia; Williams inactive for 16 games.

t- Chiefs traded for Welbourn (Phil).

Players lost through free agency (1): T John Tait (Chi; 16 games in '03).

Also played with Chiefs in '03—CB Corey Harris (3 games), CB Darrius Johnson (2), DT Allen Reese (2).

2004 FIRST-YEAR ROSTER

Name	Pos.	Ht.	Wt.	Birthdate	College	Hometown	How Acq.
Allen, Jared	DE	6-6	265	4/3/82	Idaho State	Los Gatos, Calif.	D4b
Barnett, Thomas (1)	T	6-4	314	10/21/78	Kansas State	Oklahoma City, Okla.	FA
Booth, John	WR	6-0	196	7/22/82	Mid-America Nazarene	Miami, Fla.	FA
Childs, Henri (1)	RB	6-1	215	1/15/80	Colorado State	Kansas City, Mo.	FA
Clausen, Casey	QB	6-3	215	1/9/81	Tennessee	Westlake, Calif.	FA
Connot, Scott	S	6-3	216	6/24/81	South Dakota State	O'Niell, Neb.	FA
Cruz, Ronnie	RB	6-0	237	6/11/81	Northern State	Long Beach, Calif.	FA
Dunn, Marc (1)	QB	6-3	209	4/27/78	Kansas State	Oakland, Calif.	FA
Farmer, Kirk (1)	QB	6-4	216	8/27/79	Missouri	Columbia, Mo.	FA
Finley, Clint (1)	S	6-0	210	3/27/77	Nebraska	Andrews, Texas	FA
Fletcher, Zach	WR	6-3	196	3/8/81	Alabama	Decatour, Ala.	FA
Ford, Willie (1)	CB	6-2	200	5/12/78	Syracuse	San Francisco, Calif.	FA
Fox, Keyaron	LB	6-2	227	1/24/82	Georgia Tech	Atlanta, Ga.	D3
Golliday, Aaron (1)	TE	6-3	282	12/3/79	Nebraska	Topeka, Kan.	FA
Hall, Joe (1)	FB	6-1	300	11/3/79	Kansas State	Lakewood, Calif.	FA
Ingram, Jonathan (1)	C	6-2	300	9/20/80	San Diego State	Indio, Calif.	FA
Kazar, Jason (1)	LB	5-11	219	4/17/78	Kansas State	Stuttgart, Germany	FA
Klemic, Dave (1)	WR	5-11	186	6/16/78	Northeastern	Philadelphia, Pa.	FA
Lilja, Ryan	C	6-2	285	10/15/81	Kansas State	Shawnee, Kan.	FA
McIntyre, Jeris	WR	5-11	203	7/4/81	Auburn	Tampa, Fla.	D6
Miller, Matt	G	6-4	321	2/15/81	Louisiana College	Bossier, La.	FA
Parker, Samie	WR	5-10	179	3/25/81	Oregon	Long Beach, Calif.	D4a
Pile, Willie (1)	S	6-2	206	5/25/80	Virginia Tech	Alexandria, Va.	FA
Pinkard, Mike (1)	TE	6-4	259	12/27/79	Arizona State	Thornton, Colo.	FA
Sampson, Kevin	T	6-4	312	6/19/81	Syracuse	Westwood, N.J.	D7
Sapp, Benny	CB	5-9	182	1/20/81	Northern Iowa	Ft. Lauderdale, Fla.	FA
Scanlon, Rich	LB	6-1	249	12/23/80	Syracuse	Myack, N.J.	FA
Siavii, Junior	DT	6-4	344	11/14/79	Oregon	Pago Pago, American Samoa	D2a
Smith, Jonathan	RB	5-8	193	10/19/81	Washington State	Gardena, Calif.	FA
Smith, Richard	WR	5-10	191	7/16/80	Arkansas	Shreveport, La.	FA
Tynes, Lawrence (1)	K	6-0	188	5/3/78	Troy State	Greenock, Scotland	FA
Walker, Demetrios	DE	6-2	261	4/21/81	Middle Tennessee State	Kansas City, Mo.	FA
Ward, LaShaun (1)	WR	5-11	198	9/22/80	California	Pasadena, Calif.	FA
Weston, Sean	CB	5-8	181	5/26/81	Texas A&M	Inglewood, Calif.	FA
White, Isaac (1)	LB	6-2	235	7/10/77	Oregon State	Honolulu, Hawaii	FA
Wilson, Kris	TE	6-2	248	8/22/81	Pittsburgh	Lancaster, Pa.	D2b

The term NFL Rookie is defined as a player who is in his first season of professional football and has not been on the roster of another professional football team for any regular-season or postseason games. A Rookie is designated by an "R" on NFL rosters. Players who have been active in another professional football league or players who have NFL experience, including either preseason training camp or being on an Active List or Inactive List, or on Reserve/Injured or Reserve/Physically Unable to Perform for fewer than six regular-season games, are termed NFL First-Year Players. An NFL First-Year Player is designated by a "1" on NFL rosters. Thereafter, a player is credited with an additional year of experience for each season in which he accumulates six games on the Active List or Inactive List, or on Reserve/Injured or Reserve/Physically Unable to Perform.

Log on to www.kcchiefs.com for an up-to-date roster.

KANSAS CITY CHIEFS

COACHING STAFF

Head Coach,
Dick Vermeil

Pro Career: Dick Vermeil was named the ninth head coach in Chiefs franchise history on January 12, 2001. Vermeil joins Bill Parcells, Dan Reeves, and Don Shula as the only coaches in NFL history to guide two different teams to the Super Bowl. In 1999, he led St. Louis to a win in Super Bowl XXXIV and guided Philadelphia to Super Bowl XV after the 1980 season. Was head coach of the Philadelphia Eagles from 1976-1982. Named NFL coach of the year in 1980 and 1999. Entered league as the first special teams coach in NFL history with the L.A. Rams (1969). Career record: 109-99.

Background: Vermeil played quarterback at San Jose State (1956-57) after transferring from Napa (Calif.) J.C. Was named "Coach of the Year" on four levels: high school, junior college, NCAA Division I, and the NFL. Is the only coach to post victories in the Super Bowl (Rams, XXXIV) and the Rose Bowl (UCLA, Jan. 1976). Was head coach at UCLA from 1974-75.

Personal: Born October 30, 1936 in Calistoga, Calif. Vermeil and his wife Carol have three children and 11 grandchildren.

ASSISTANT COACHES

Gunther Cunningham, defensive coordinator; born June 19, 1946, Munich, Germany. Linebacker-placekicker Oregon 1966-68. No pro playing experience. College coach: Oregon 1969-1971, Arkansas 1972, Stanford 1973-76, California 1977-1980. Pro coach: Hamilton Tiger-Cats (CFL) 1981, Baltimore/Indianapolis Colts 1982-84, San Diego Chargers 1985-1990, L.A. Raiders 1991-94, Kansas City Chiefs 1995-2000 (head coach 1999-2000), Tennessee Titans 2001-03, rejoined Chiefs in 2004.

Vernon Dean, asst. defensive backs; born May 5, 1959, Houston. Cornerback Los Angeles Valley J.C. 1977-78, U.S. International 1979, San Diego State 1980-81. Pro cornerback Washington Redskins 1982-87, Seattle Seahawks 1988. College coach: Georgetown 1990-93, Western Oregon 2000-01, Western Illinois 2002. Pro coach: Joined Chiefs in 2003.

Irv Eatman, asst. offensive line; born January 1, 1961, Birmingham, Ala. Defensive end-offensive tackle UCLA 1979-1982. Pro offensive tackle Philadelphia/Baltimore Stars (USFL) 1983-85, Kansas City Chiefs 1986-1990, New York Jets 1991-92, L.A. Rams 1993, Atlanta Falcons 1994, Houston Oilers 1995-96. Pro coach: Green Bay Packers 1999, Pittsburgh Steelers 2000, joined Chiefs in 2001.

Frank Gansz, Jr., special teams; born August 8, 1962, Greenville, S.C. Defensive back The Citadel 1981-84. No pro playing experience. College coach: Kansas 1987, Pittsburgh 1988-89, Army 1990-91, Houston 1993-97. Pro coach: New York-New Jersey Knights (WLAF) 1992, Oakland Raiders 1998-99, joined Chiefs in 2001.

Peter Giunta, defensive backs; born August 11, 1956, Salem, Mass. Running back-defensive back Northeastern 1974-77. No pro playing experience. College coach: Penn State 1981-83, Brown 1984-87, Lehigh 1988-1990. Pro coach: Philadelphia Eagles 1991-94, N.Y. Jets 1995-96, St. Louis Rams 1997-2000, joined Chiefs in 2001.

Carl Hairston, defensive line; born December 15, 1952, Martinsville, Va. Defensive end Maryland-Eastern Shore 1972-75. Pro defensive end Philadelphia Eagles 1976-1983, Cleveland Browns 1984-89, Phoenix Cardinals 1990. Pro coach: Kansas City Chiefs 1995-96, St. Louis Rams 1997-2000, rejoined Chiefs in 2001.

Jeff Hurd, strength and conditioning; born April 24, 1958, Pomona, Calif. Attended Fort Hays State. No college or pro playing experience. College coach: Fort Hays State 1984, Delta State 1985-86, Clemson 1986-87, Western Michigan 1987-1993, Tulsa 1994. Pro coach: Jacksonville Jaguars 1995-97, joined Chiefs in 1998.

Charlie Joiner, receivers; born October 14, 1947, Many, La. Wide receiver Grambling State 1965-68. Pro defensive back-wide receiver Houston Oilers 1969-1972, Cincinnati Bengals 1972-75, San Diego Chargers 1976-1986. Inducted into Pro Football Hall of Fame 1996. Pro coach: San Diego Chargers 1987-1991, Buffalo Bills 1992-2000, joined the Chiefs in 2001.

Bob Karmelowicz, defensive line; born July 22, 1949, New Britain, Conn. Nose tackle Bridgeport 1968-1971. No pro playing experience. College coach: Arizona State 1975-79, Massachusetts 1980, Texas-El Paso 1981, Nevada-Las Vegas 1982, Illinois 1983-86, Washington State 1987-88, Miami 1989-1991. Pro coach: Cincinnati Bengals 1992-93, Washington Redskins 1994-96, joined Chiefs in 1997.

Billy Long, asst. strength and conditioning coach; born June 23, 1959, Phenix City, Ala. College coach: Alabama State 1981-86, Arkansas-Pine Bluff 1987-1991, Southern 1992-2000. Pro coach: Joined Chiefs in 2001.

Chad O'Shea, asst. special teams; born Dec. 18, 1972, Houston. Quarterback Marshall 1991-93, Houston 1994-95. No pro playing experience. College coach: Houston 1996-99, Southern Mississippi 2000-03. Pro coach: Joined Chiefs in 2004.

Fred Pagac, linebackers; born April 26, 1952, Richeyville, Penn. Tight end Ohio State 1971-73. Pro tight end Chicago Bears 1974, Tampa Bay Buccaneers 1976. College coach: Ohio State 1982-2000. Pro coach: Oakland Raiders 2001-03, joined Chiefs in 2004.

Keith Rowen, tight ends; born September 2, 1952, New York, N.Y. Offensive tackle Stanford 1972-74. No pro playing experience. College coach: Stanford 1975-76, Long Beach State 1977-78, Arizona 1979-1982. Pro coach: Boston/New Orleans Breakers (USFL) 1983-84, Cleveland Browns 1984, Indianapolis Colts 1985-88, New England Patriots 1989, Atlanta Falcons 1990-93, Minnesota Vikings 1994-96, Oakland Raiders 1997-98, joined Chiefs in 1999.

Al Saunders, asst. head coach/offensive coordinator; born February 1, 1947, London, England. Wide receiver-defensive back San Jose State 1966-68. No pro playing experience. College coach: Southern California 1970-71, Missouri 1972, Utah State 1973-75, California 1976-1981, Tennessee 1982. Pro coach: San Diego Chargers 1983-88 (head coach 1986-88), Kansas City Chiefs 1989-1998, St. Louis Rams 1999-2000, rejoined Chiefs in 2001.

Bob Saunders, offensive assistant/quality control; born Nov. 21, 1976, Walnut Creek, Calif. Wide receiver-defensive back Southern Methodist 1995. No pro playing experience. Pro coach: Joined Chiefs in 2004.

James Saxon, running backs; born March 23, 1966, Beaufort, S.C. Running back American River J.C. (S.C.) 1985, San Jose State 1986-87. Pro running back Kansas City Chiefs 1988-1991, Miami Dolphins 1992-94, Philadelphia Eagles 1995. College coach: Rutgers 1997-98, Menlo College 1999. Pro coach: Buffalo Bills 2000, joined Chiefs in 2001.

Mike Solari, offensive line; born January 16, 1955, Daly City, Calif. Offensive lineman San Diego State 1975-76. No pro playing experience. College coach: Mira Vista (Calif.) J.C. 1978, U.S. International 1979, Boise State 1980, Cincinnati 1981-82, Kansas 1983-85, Pittsburgh 1986, Alabama 1990-91. Pro coach: Dallas Cowboys 1987-88, Phoenix Cardinals 1989, San Francisco 49ers 1992-96, joined Chiefs in 1997.

Jason Verduzco, quarterbacks; born April 3, 1970, Walnut Creek, Calif. Quarterback Illinois 1989-1992. Pro quarterback: British Columbia Lions (CFL) 1993. College coach: Hamilton College (N.Y.) 1994-96, Illinois 1997-99. Pro coach: Washington Redskins 2000, joined Chiefs in 2001.

Darvin Wallis, defensive assistant/quality control; born February 14, 1949, Ft. Branch, Ind. Defensive end Arizona 1970-71. No pro playing experience. College coach: Adams State 1976-77, Tulane 1978-79, Mississippi 1980-81. Pro coach: Cleveland Browns 1982-88, joined Chiefs in 1989.

Mike White, director of football administration; born January 4, 1936, Berkeley, Calif. Offensive end California 1955-57. No pro playing experience. College coach: California 1958-1963, 1972-77 (head coach 1972-77), Stanford 1964-1971, Illinois 1980-87 (head coach). Pro coach: San Francisco 49ers 1978-79, Los Angeles-Oakland Raiders 1990-96 (head coach 1995-96), St. Louis Rams 1997-99, joined Chiefs in 2001.

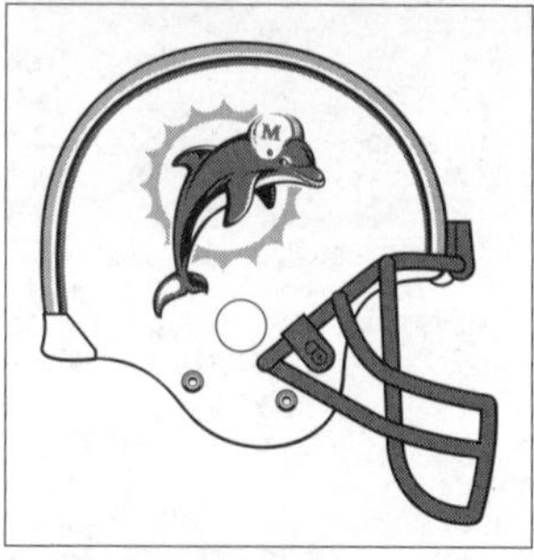

American Football Conference
East Division
Team Colors: Aqua, Coral, Blue, and White
7500 S.W. 30th Street
Davie, Florida 33314
Telephone: (954) 452-7000

2004 SCHEDULE

PRESEASON		Miami time
Aug. 14	**Jacksonville**	7:30
Aug. 21	**Washington**	7:30
Aug. 28	at Tampa Bay	7:00
Sept. 3	at New Orleans	8:00

REGULAR SEASON		
Sept. 12	**Tennessee**	1:00
Sept. 19	at Cincinnati	8:30
Sept. 26	**Pittsburgh**	1:00
Oct. 3	**New York Jets**	4:15
Oct. 10	at New England	1:00
Oct. 17	at Buffalo	1:00
Oct. 24	**St. Louis**	1:00
Nov. 1	at New York Jets (Mon.)	9:00
Nov. 7	**Arizona**	1:00
Nov. 14	Open Date	
Nov. 21	at Seattle	1:05
Nov. 28	at San Francisco	1:15
Dec. 5	**Buffalo**	1:00
Dec. 12	at Denver	2:05
Dec. 20	**New England** (Mon.)	9:00
Dec. 26	**Cleveland**	8:30
Jan. 2	at Baltimore	1:00

Stadium: Pro Player Stadium (opened in 1987)
• **Capacity:** 75,192
2269 Dan Marino Blvd.
Miami, Florida 33056
Playing Surface: Grass (PAT)
Training Camp: Nova Southeastern University
7500 S.W. 30th Street
Davie, Florida 33314

PRO PLAYER STADIUM

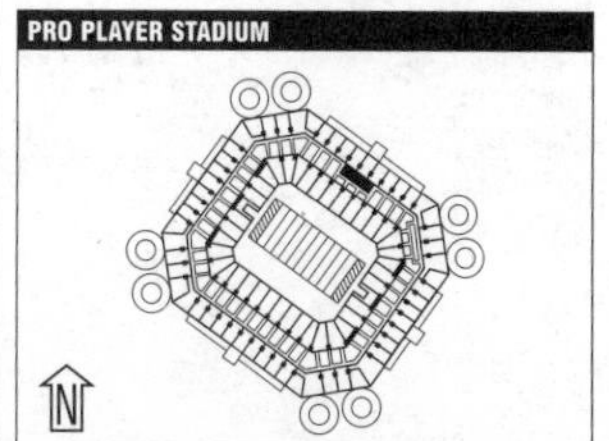

CLUB OFFICIALS

Owner/Chairman of the Board: H. Wayne Huizenga
President: Eddie J. Jones
Head Coach: Dave Wannstedt
General Manager: Rick Spielman
Executive Vice President & Chief Operating Officer: Bryan Wiedmeier
Senior Vice President-Finance & Administration: Jill R. Strafaci
Senior Vice President-Operations: Bill Galante
Senior Vice President-Media Relations: Harvey Greene
Senior Vice President-Sales & Marketing: Jim Ross
Director of Pro Personnel: George Paton
Director of College Scouting: Ron Labadie
Staff Counsel: Matt Thomas
Senior Director of Community & Alumni Relations: Fudge Browne
Senior Director of Ticket Operations: Andy Major
Senior Director of Business Development: Jim Frevola
Director of Player Programs: Jamie Allen
Director of Media Relations: Neal Gulkis
Senior Director of Internet & Publications: Scott Stone
Director of Operations: Rhett Ticconi
Director of Information Technology: Tery Howard
Director of Cheerleaders & Event Entertainment: Dorie Grogan
Director of Special Events & Television Programming: Jeff Griffith
Director of Records & Archives: Kristin Hingston
Head Athletic Trainer: Kevin O'Neill
Equipment Manager: Tony Egues
Video Director: Dave Hack
Team Security Investigator: Stuart Weinstein

COACHING HISTORY
(369-242-4)

1966-69	George Wilson	15-39-2
1970-1995	Don Shula	274-147-2
1996-99	Jimmy Johnson	38-31-0
2000-03	Dave Wannstedt	42-25-0

ATTENDANCE

Home 587,787 Away *493,972
Total 1,081,759*
Single-game home record, 75,283 (10/27/96)
Single-season home record, 592,161 (1999)
**The Week 8 Miami at San Diego game is not included. The game was moved to Arizona due to the San Diego wildfires and tickets were distributed at no charge.*

2004 DRAFT CHOICES

Round	Name	Pos.	College
1	Vernon Carey	T	Miami
4	Will Poole	DB	Southern California
5	Tony Bua	LB	Arkansas
6	Rex Hadnot	G	Houston
7	Tony Pape	T	Michigan
	Derrick Pope	LB	Alabama

MIAMI DOLPHINS

2003 TEAM RECORD

PRESEASON (2-2)

Date	Result	Opponent
8/8	L 19-20	Tampa Bay
8/15	L 23-27	at Jacksonville
8/22	W 30-21	Atlanta
8/28	W 24-10	at New Orleans

REGULAR SEASON (10-6)

Date	Result	Opponent	Att.
9/7	L 20-21	Houston	73,010
9/14	W 21-10	at New York Jets	77,461
9/21	W 17-7	Buffalo	73,458
10/5	W 23-10	at New York Giants	78,863
10/12	W 24-10	at Jacksonville	66,437
10/19	L 13-19	New England (OT)	73,650
10/27	W 26-10	at San Diego	73,014
11/2	L 17-23	Indianapolis	73,258
11/9	L 7-31	at Tennessee	68,809
11/16	W 9-6	Baltimore (OT)	73,333
11/23	W 24-23	Washington	73,578
11/27	W 40-21	at Dallas	64,110
12/7	L 0-12	at New England	68,436
12/15	L 27-34	Philadelphia	73,780
12/21	W 20-3	at Buffalo	73,319
12/28	W 23-21	New York Jets	73,720

(OT) Overtime

SCORE BY PERIODS

Dolphins	68	124	44	72	3 —	311
Opponents	49	86	48	72	6 -	261

2003 TEAM STATISTICS

	Dolphins	Opp.
Total First Downs	266	283
Rushing	99	82
Passing	145	171
Penalty	22	30
3rd Down: Made/Att	67/205	81/222
3rd Down Pct.	32.7	36.5
4th Down: Made/Att	5/10	2/12
4th Down Pct.	50.0	16.7
Possession Avg.	29:49	30:11
Total Net Yards	4,609	4,787
Avg. Per Game	288.1	299.2
Total Plays	968	1,014
Avg. Per Play	4.8	4.7
Net Yards Rushing	1,817	1,452
Avg. Per Game	113.6	90.8
Total Rushes	487	441
Net Yards Passing	2,792	3,335
Avg. Per Game	174.5	208.4
Sacked/Yards Lost	31/209	44/253
Gross Yards	3,001	3,588
Att./Completions	450/257	529/319
Completion Pct.	57.1	60.3
Had Intercepted	19	22
Punts/Average	84/39.0	80/41.2
Net Punting Avg.	84/34.9	80/36.1
Penalties/Yards	103/913	98/766
Fumbles/Ball Lost	26/15	26/14
Touchdowns	35	26
Rushing	14	11
Passing	17	12
Returns	4	3

2003 INDIVIDUAL STATISTICS

PASSING	Att.	Comp.	Yds.	Pct.	TD	Int.	Tkld.	Rate
Fiedler	314	179	2,138	57.0	11	13	19/126	72.4
Griese	130	74	813	56.9	5	6	12/83	69.2
Rosenfels	6	4	50	66.7	1	0	0/0	131.9
Dolphins	450	257	3,001	57.1	17	19	31/209	72.5
Opponents	529	319	3,588	60.3	12	22	44/253	70.8

SCORING	TD R	TD P	TD Rt	PAT	FG	Saf	PTS
Mare	0	0	0	33/34	22/29	0	99
Chambers	0	11	0	0/0	0/0	0	66
R. Williams	9	1	0	0/0	0/0	0	60
Fiedler	3	0	0	0/0	0/0	0	18
McKnight	1	2	0	0/0	0/0	0	18
McMichael	0	2	1	0/0	0/0	0	18
Taylor	0	0	1	0/0	0/0	1	8
Buckley	0	0	1	0/0	0/0	0	6
Lee	0	1	0	0/0	0/0	0	6
Madison	0	0	1	0/0	0/0	0	6
Minor	1	0	0	0/0	0/0	0	6
Dolphins	14	17	4	33/34	22/29	1	311
Opponents	11	12	3	23/23	26/31	2	261

2-Pt. Conversions: None.
Dolphins 0-1, Opponents 0-2.

RUSHING	No.	Yds	Avg	LG	TD
R. Williams	392	1,372	3.5	45	9
Minor	41	193	4.7	26	1
Fiedler	34	88	2.6	14	3
McKnight	2	75	37.5	68t	1
Chambers	4	30	7.5	12	0
Turk	3	30	10.0	23	0
Konrad	4	17	4.3	11	0
Griese	5	15	3.0	9	0
Rosenfels	1	-1	-1.0	-1	0
O. Ayanbadejo	1	-2	-2.0	-2	0
Dolphins	487	1,817	3.7	68t	14
Opponents	441	1,452	3.3	28	11

RECEIVING	No.	Yds	Avg	LG	TD
Chambers	64	963	15.0	57t	11
R. Williams	50	351	7.0	59	1
McMichael	49	598	12.2	46	2
Thompson	26	359	13.8	31	0
McKnight	23	285	12.4	80t	2
Konrad	16	166	10.4	25	0
O. Ayanbadejo	12	53	4.4	12	0
Lee	7	110	15.7	25	1
Gadsden	4	48	12.0	23	0
Minor	4	13	3.3	12	0
Newson	2	55	27.5	37	0
Dolphins	257	3,001	11.7	80t	17
Opponents	319	3,588	11.2	82t	12

INTERCEPTIONS	No.	Yds	Avg	LG	TD
Surtain	7	59	8.4	32	0
Knight	3	98	32.7	70	0
Madison	3	82	27.3	36	1
Thomas	3	21	7.0	19	0
Marion	3	3	1.0	3	0
Buckley	2	75	37.5	74t	1
Zgonina	1	0	0.0	0	0
Dolphins	22	338	15.4	74t	2
Opponents	19	194	10.2	54t	3

PUNTING	No.	Yds.	Avg.	In 20	LG
Turk	68	2,631	38.7	23	57
Royals	16	643	40.2	5	50
Dolphins	84	3,274	39.0	28	57
Opponents	80	3,294	41.2	25	64

PUNT RETURNS	Ret	FC	Yds	Avg	LG	TD
Rogers	21	13	186	8.9	48	0
Simmons	8	6	100	12.5	32	0
Buckley	1	0	2	2.0	2	0
Newson	1	0	0	0.0	0	0
Dolphins	31	19	288	9.3	48	0
Opponents	29	26	185	6.4	26	0

KICKOFF RETURNS	No.	Yds	Avg	LG	TD
Minor	34	727	21.4	49	0
Rogers	19	383	20.2	33	0
Simmons	3	64	21.3	34	0
Lee	1	0	0.0	0	0
McKnight	0	28	—	28	0
Dolphins	57	1,202	21.1	49	0
Opponents	47	1,010	21.5	73	0

FIELD GOALS	1-19	20-29	30-39	40-49	50+
Mare	0/0	9/9	3/6	6/8	4/6
Dolphins	0/0	9/9	3/6	6/8	4/6
Opponents	0/0	10/11	8/9	5/6	3/5

SACKS	No.
Ogunleye	15.0
Taylor	13.0
Seau	3.0
Zgonina	3.0
J. Williams	2.5
T. Bowens	2.0
Burnett	2.0
D. Bowens	1.0
Freeman	1.0
Thomas	1.0
Greenwood	0.5
Dolphins	44.0
Opponents	31.0

RECORD HOLDERS

INDIVIDUAL RECORDS—CAREER

Category	Name	Performance
Rushing (Yds.)	Larry Csonka, 1968-1974, 1979	6,737
Passing (Yds.)	Dan Marino, 1983-1999	*61,361
Passing (TDs)	Dan Marino, 1983-1999	*420
Receiving (No.)	Mark Clayton, 1983-1992	550
Receiving (Yds.)	Mark Duper, 1982-1992	8,869
Interceptions	Jake Scott, 1970-75	35
Punting (Avg.)	John Kidd, 1994-97	44.2
Punt Return (Avg.)	Jeff Ogden, 2000-01	13.7
Kickoff Return (Avg.)	Mercury Morris, 1969-1975	26.5
Field Goals	Olindo Mare, 1997-2003	182
Touchdowns (Tot.)	Mark Clayton, 1983-1992	82
Points	Garo Yepremian, 1970-78	830

INDIVIDUAL RECORDS—SINGLE SEASON

Category	Name	Performance
Rushing (Yds.)	Ricky Williams, 2002	1,853
Passing (Yds.)	Dan Marino, 1984	*5,084
Passing (TDs)	Dan Marino, 1984	*48
Receiving (No.)	O.J. McDuffie, 1998	90
Receiving (Yds.)	Mark Clayton, 1984	1,389
Interceptions	Dick Westmoreland, 1967	10
Punting (Avg.)	John Kidd, 1996	46.3
Punt Return (Avg.)	Jeff Ogden, 2000	17.0
Kickoff Return (Avg.)	Duriel Harris, 1976	32.9
Field Goals	Olindo Mare, 1999	*39
Touchdowns (Tot.)	Mark Clayton, 1984	18
Points	Olindo Mare, 1999	144

INDIVIDUAL RECORDS—SINGLE GAME

Category	Name	Performance
Rushing (Yds.)	Ricky Williams, 12-1-02	228
Passing (Yds.)	Dan Marino, 10-23-88	521
Passing (TDs)	Bob Griese, 11-24-77	6
	Dan Marino, 9-21-86	6
Receiving (No.)	Jim Jensen, 11-6-88	12
Receiving (Yds.)	Mark Duper, 11-10-85	217
Interceptions	Dick Anderson, 12-3-73	*4
Field Goals	Olindo Mare, 10-17-99	6
Touchdowns (Tot.)	Paul Warfield, 12-15-73	4
	Mark Ingram, 11-27-94	4
Points	Paul Warfield, 12-15-73	24
	Mark Ingram, 11-27-94	24

*NFL Record

MIAMI DOLPHINS

2004 VETERAN ROSTER

No.	Name	Pos.	Ht.	Wt.	Birthdate	NFL Exp.	College	Hometown	How Acq.	'03 Games/ Starts
36	Akins, Chris	S	5-11	200	11/29/76	6	Arkansas-Pine Bluff	Little Rock, Ark.	UFA(NE)-'04	12/0*
50	Ayanbadejo, Brendon	LB	6-1	230	9/6/76	2	UCLA	Santa Cruz, Calif.	FA-'03	16/0
63	Bedell, Brad	G	6-4	302	2/12/77	4	Colorado	Arcadia, Calif.	FA-'03	0*
80	t- Boston, David	WR	6-2	240	8/19/78	6	Ohio State	Humble, Texas	T(SD)-'04	14/14*
96	Bowens, David	DE	6-3	260	7/3/77	5	Western Illinois	Detroit, Mich.	FA-'01	4/0
95	Bowens, Tim	DT	6-4	325	2/7/73	11	Mississippi	Okolona, Miss.	D1-'94	13/13
	#Buckley, Terrell	CB	5-10	180	6/7/71	13	Florida State	Pascagoula, Miss.	UFA(NE)-'03	16/5
	#Burnett, Rob	DE	6-4	267	8/27/67	15	Syracuse	Selden, N.Y.	FA-'02	12/0
84	Chambers, Chris	WR	5-11	210	8/12/78	4	Wisconsin	Cleveland, Ohio	D2-'01	16/16
64	Chester, Larry	DT	6-2	325	10/17/75	7	Temple	Hammond, La.	UFA(Car)-'02	15/15
16	Davis, Nick	WR	6-0	182	10/6/79	3	Wisconsin	Manchester, Mich.	FA-'04	1/0*
21	Edwards, Antuan	S	6-1	210	5/26/77	6	Clemson	Starkville, Miss.	UFA(GB)-'04	10/10*
7	t- Feeley, A.J.	QB	6-3	225	5/16/77	4	Oregon	Ontario, Ore.	T(Phil)-'04	0*
9	Fiedler, Jay	QB	6-2	225	12/29/71	9	Dartmouth	Oceanside, N.Y.	UFA(Jax)-'00	12/11
79	Flemons, Ronald	DE	6-6	276	10/20/79	3	Texas A&M	San Antonio, Texas	FA-'04	0*
20	Freeman, Arturo	S	6-1	200	10/27/76	5	South Carolina	Orangeburg, S.C.	D5-'00	16/0
	#Gadsden, Oronde	WR	6-2	215	8/20/71	7	Winston-Salem State	Charleston, S.C.	FA-'98	6/0
67	Goodspeed, Dan	T	6-6	300	5/20/77	2	Kent State	Uniontown, Ohio	FA-'04	0*
52	Greenwood, Morlon	LB	6-0	238	7/17/78	4	Syracuse	Freeport, N.Y.	D3b-'01	16/11
98	Grigsby, Otis	DE	6-3	260	11/19/80	2	Kentucky	Converse, Texas	FA-'03	0*
26	Henry, Leonard	RB	6-1	210	1/5/78	2	East Carolina	Clinton, N.C.	D7-'02	0*
25	Howard, Reggie	CB	6-0	190	5/17/77	5	Memphis	Memphis, Tenn.	UFA(Car)-'04	15/15*
78	James, Jeno	G	6-3	310	1/12/77	5	Auburn	Montgomery, Ala.	UFA(Car)-'04	16/16*
57	Jenkins, Corey	LB	6-0	222	8/25/76	2	South Carolina	Columbia, S.C.	D6a-'03	16/0
60	Jerman, Greg	G	6-5	310	1/24/79	3	Baylor	El Paso, Texas	FA-'02	8/1
49	Jones, John	TE	6-4	255	4/4/75	5	Indiana (Pa.)	Cleveland, Ohio	UFA(Balt)-'04	11/0*
24	Knight, Sammy	S	6-0	215	9/10/75	8	Southern California	Riverside, Calif.	UFA(NO)-'04	16/16
44	Konrad, Rob	FB	6-3	255	11/12/76	6	Syracuse	Andover, Mass.	D2b-'99	14/12
85	Lee, Donald	TE	6-3	255	8/31/80	2	Mississippi State	Maben, Miss.	D5a-'03	16/5
29	Madison, Sam	CB	5-11	185	4/23/74	8	Louisville	Monticello, Fla.	D2-'97	16/16
56	Mallard, Josh	DE	6-2	259	3/21/80	2	Georgia	Savannah, Ga.	FA-'04	0*
10	Mare, Olindo	K	5-10	190	6/6/73	8	Syracuse	Cooper City, Fla.	FA-'97	16/0
77	McIntosh, Damion	T	6-4	325	3/25/77	5	Kansas State	Hollywood, Fla.	UFA(SD)-'04	13/13*
68	McKinney, Seth	C	6-3	305	6/12/79	3	Texas A&M	Austin, Texas	D3-'02	16/3
81	McMichael, Randy	TE	6-3	250	6/28/79	3	Georgia	Fort Valley, Ga.	D4-'02	16/16
19	Minnis, Snoop	WR	6-1	170	2/6/77	3	Florida State	Miami, Fla.	FA-'04	0*
28	Minor, Travis	RB	5-10	205	6/30/79	4	Florida State	Baton Rouge, La.	D3a-'01	16/0
58	Moore, Eddie	LB	6-0	230	7/5/80	2	Tennesssee	S. Pittsburg, Tenn.	D2-'03	0*
31	Morris, Sammy	RB	6-0	220	3/23/77	5	Texas Tech	San Antonio, Texas	UFA(Buff)-'04	9/0*
	#Nails, Jamie	G	6-6	330	6/3/77	7	Florida A&M	Baxley, Ga.	FA-'02	15/15
82	Newson, Kendall	WR	6-1	198	3/5/80	2	Middle Tennessee State	Decatur, Ga.	FA-'03	6/0
93	† Ogunleye, Adewale	DE	6-4	260	8/9/77	4	Indiana	Staten Island, N.Y.	FA-'00	16/16
89	Perry, Ed	TE	6-4	265	9/1/74	9	James Madison	Richmond, Va.	D6d-'97	0*
	#Rogers, Charlie	KR-RB	5-9	180	6/19/76	6	Georgia Tech	Cliffwood, N.J.	UFA(Buff)-'03	11/0
94	Romero, Dario	DT	6-3	305	4/13/78	3	Eastern Washington	Spokane, Wash.	FA-'02	8/1
18	Rosenfels, Sage	QB	6-4	222	3/6/78	4	Iowa State	Maquoketa, Iowa	T(Wash)-'02	2/0
55	Seau, Junior	LB	6-3	250	1/19/69	15	Southern California	Oceanside, Calif.	T(SD)-'03	15/15
83	Simmons, Sam	WR	5-9	200	11/25/79	3	Northwestern	Kansas City, Kan.	D5b-'02	11/0
74	Smith, Wade	T	6-4	300	4/26/81	2	Memphis	Dallas, Texas	D3a-'03	16/16
70	St. Clair, John	T	6-4	315	7/31/78	5	Virginia	Roanoke, Va.	UFA(StL)-'04	16/0*
5	Stoerner, Clint	QB	6-2	225	12/29/77	4	Arkansas	Baytown, Texas	FA-'04	0*
23	Surtain, Patrick	CB	5-11	192	6/19/76	7	Southern Mississippi	New Orleans, La.	D2a-'98	15/15
99	Taylor, Jason	DE	6-6	255	9/1/74	8	Akron	Woodland Hills, Pa.	D3a-'97	16/16
54	Thomas, Zach	LB	5-11	230	9/1/73	9	Texas Tech	Pampa, Texas	D5c-'96	15/15
88	Thompson, Derrius	WR	6-2	220	7/5/77	6	Baylor	Cedar Hill, Texas	UFA(Wash)-'03	16/12
87	Tolver, J.R.	WR	6-1	200	1/13/80	2	San Diego State	San Diego, Calif.	D5b-'03	0*
1	Turk, Matt	P	6-5	250	6/16/68	10	Wisconsin-Whitewater	Greenfield, Wis.	FA-'03	13/0
69	Whitley, Taylor	G	6-4	315	2/21/80	2	Texas A&M	Sudan, Texas	D3b-'03	0*
86	Wilkins, Terrence	WR	5-10	180	7/29/75	6	Virginia	Arlington, Va.	UFA(Ind)-'04	3/0*
91	Williams, Jay	DE	6-3	275	10/13/71	10	Wake Forest	Washington, D.C.	T(Car)-'02	16/0
34	Williams, Ricky	RB	5-10	226	5/21/77	6	Texas	San Diego, Calif.	T(NO)-'02	16/16
22	Wooden, Shawn	S	5-11	205	10/23/73	9	Notre Dame	Abington, Pa.	D6-'02	15/0
	#Wyrick, Jimmy	CB	5-9	170	12/31/76	4	Minnesota	DeSoto, Texas	FA-'03	7/1*
73	Yates, Billy	C-G	6-2	305	4/15/80	2	Texas A&M	Corsicana, Texas	FA-'03	3/0
90	Zgonina, Jeff	DT	6-2	285	5/24/70	12	Purdue	Mundelein, Ill.	UFA(StL)-'03	16/3

* Akins played 12 games with New England in '03; Bedell inactive for 7 games; Boston played 14 games with San Diego; Davis played 1 game with Minnesota; Edwards played 10 games with Green Bay; Feeley inactive for 16 games with Philadelphia; Flemons last active with Atlanta in '02; Goodspeed last active with N.Y. Jets in '01; Grigsby inactive for 16 games; Henry inactive for 13 games; Howard played 15 games with Carolina; James played 16 games with Carolina; Jones played 11 games with Baltimore; Mallard last active with Indianapolis in '02; McIntosh played 13 games with San Diego; Minnis inactive with Tampa Bay for 2 games; Moore missed '03 season because of injury; S. Morris played 9 games with Buffalo; Perry missed '03 season because of injury; St. Clair played 16 games with St. Louis; Stoerner last active with Dallas in '01; Tolver inactive for 10 games; Whitley inactive for 16 games; Wilkins played 3 games with Indianapolis; Wyrick played 7 games with Detroit.

Unrestricted free agent; subject to developments.

† Restricted free agent; subject to developments.

Traded—CB Jamar Fletcher (11 games in '03) to San Diego.

t- Dolphins traded for Boston (SD); Feeley (Phil).

Players lost through free agency (3): FB Obafemi Ayanbadejo (Ariz; 16 games in '03); LB Tommy Hendricks (Jax; 16); T Todd Wade (Hou; 16).

Also played with Dolphins in '03—S Trent Gamble (9 games), LS Jeff Grau (11), QB Brian Griese (5), S Brock Marion (16), LS Sean McDermott (5), WR James McKnight (15), G Todd Perry (15), P Mark Royals (3), C Tim Ruddy (14).

2004 FIRST-YEAR ROSTER

Name	Pos.	Ht.	Wt.	Birthdate	College	Hometown	How Acq.
Banks, Korey (1)	CB	5-10	188	8/15/79	Mississippi State	Boynton Beach, Fla.	FA
Bell, Yeremiah (1)	S	6-1	200	3/3/78	Eastern Kentucky	Winchester, Ky.	D6c-'03
Bellamy, Ronald (1)	WR	6-0	200	12/28/81	Michigan	New Orleans, La.	FA
Bolling, Nate (1)	DT	6-4	288	1/10/79	Wake Forest	Swanton, Ohio	FA
Brown, Tony (1)	DE	6-1	280	9/29/80	Memphis	Chattanooga, Tenn.	FA-'03
Bua, Tony	LB	5-11	212	2/11/80	Arkansas	River Ridge, La.	D5
Carey, Vernon	T	6-5	333	7/31/81	Miami	Miami, Fla.	D1
Delahoussaye, William	LS	6-2	242	5/7/80	Louisiana-Lafayette	Crowley, La.	FA
Easlick, Doug	FB	5-11	243	12/4/80	Virginia Tech	Marlton, N.J.	FA
Givan, Brenden (1)	LB	6-2	252	5/8/80	Stillman	Birmingham, Ala.	FA
Hadnot, Rex	C	6-2	323	1/28/82	Houston	Lufkin, Texas	D6
Hunt, Aaron (1)	DE	6-3	259	6/19/80	Texas Tech	Denison, Texas	FA
Jones, Derek	P	6-5	234	3/26/81	Nevada	Reno, Nev.	FA
Louisdor, Mesene (1)	CB	5-10	179	12/3/75	Central Michigan	Miami, Fla.	FA
Lynch, Shawn (1)	CB	6-4	289	7/25/79	Duke	West Palm Beach, Fla.	FA
Millhouse, Kelvin	CB	6-1	208	1/7/81	Hawaii	Santa Ana, Calif.	FA
Mitchell, Kevin	LB	5-11	218	10/2/80	Oregon	Orange, Calif.	FA
Moa, Ben	FB	6-2	256	4/22/81	Utah	Ogden, Utah	FA
Morris, Carl (1)	WR	6-3	213	3/3/81	Harvard	Sterling, Va.	FA
Pape, Tony	T	6-6	324	9/29/81	Michigan	Clarendon Hills, Ill.	D7a
Poole, Will	CB	5-10	193	7/24/81	Southern California	Queens, N.Y.	D4
Pope, Derrick	LB	5-11	233	5/4/82	Alabama	Galveston, Texas	D7b
Roundtree, Alphonso (1)	S	6-0	190	7/7/77	Tulane	Bradenton, Fla.	FA-'03
Russell, Fred	RB	5-7	191	9/14/80	Iowa	Romulus, Mich.	FA
Stevens, Jerome	DT	6-1	303	10/19/80	Washington	Oxnard, Calif.	FA
Taylor, Winston	LB	6-1	241	10/10/81	Illinois	Decatur, Ill.	FA
Turner, Hart	TE	6-4	243	11/17/81	South Carolina	Spartanburg, S.C.	FA
Wagstrom, Andy	G	6-4	296	9/18/80	South Dakota State	Faribault, Minn.	FA
Williams, Quintin	S	5-11	204	9/24/82	Wake Forest	Goldsboro, N.C.	FA
Works, Renaldo	RB	6-0	216	12/10/81	Oklahoma	Tulsa, Okla.	FA

The term NFL Rookie is defined as a player who is in his first season of professional football and has not been on the roster of another professional football team for any regular-season or postseason games. A Rookie is designated by an "R" on NFL rosters. Players who have been active in another professional football league or players who have NFL experience, including either preseason training camp or being on an Active List or Inactive List, or on Reserve/Injured or Reserve/Physically Unable to Perform for fewer than six regular-season games, are termed NFL First-Year Players. An NFL First-Year Player is designated by a "1" on NFL rosters. Thereafter, a player is credited with an additional year of experience for each season in which he accumulates six games on the Active List or Inactive List, or on Reserve/Injured or Reserve/Physically Unable to Perform.

Log on to www.miamidolphins.com for an up-to-date roster.

COACHING STAFF
Head Coach,
Dave Wannstedt

Pro Career: Was named the fourth head coach in Miami history on January 16, 2000. In his four seasons, has led the Dolphins to a regular-season record of 41-23 and a pair of playoff appearances. The team's 22-10 regular-season mark in the first two seasons under Wannstedt was the best by the Dolphins in consecutive seasons since 1984-85. In 2000, Wannstedt guided the Dolphins to the team's first AFC East title since 1994. Led the Chicago Bears to a 41-57 record in six seasons (1993-98) as head coach, and in 1994 was named NFC coach of the year. Served as the Dolphins' assistant head coach in 1999. Began his NFL coaching career as linebackers coach with the Dolphins in 1989. Spent seven weeks in that post during the offseason before hired in Dallas as the Cowboys' defensive coordinator prior to the 1989 season. In 1992 the Cowboys led the league in total defense as they went on to capture the first of two straight Super Bowl titles. Career record: 83-82.

Background: Wannstedt coached collegiately at Pittsburgh (1975-78), Oklahoma State (1979-1982), Southern California (1983-85), and Miami (1986-88). Wannstedt lettered three seasons (1971-73) as an offensive lineman at Pittsburgh. Wannstedt was selected by Green Bay in the fifteenth round of the 1974 NFL Draft.

Personal: Born in Pittsburgh on May 21, 1952. He and his wife, Jan, have two daughters, Keri and Jami.

ASSISTANT COACHES

Keith Armstrong, special teams; born December 15, 1963, Trenton, N.J. Running back-defensive back Temple 1983-86. No pro playing experience. College coach: Temple 1986, Miami 1987-88, Oklahoma State 1990-92, Notre Dame 1993. Pro coach: Atlanta Falcons 1994-96, Chicago Bears 1997-2000, joined Dolphins in 2001.

Jim Bates, defensive coordinator; born May 31, 1946, Pontiac, Mich. Linebacker Tennessee 1964-67. No pro playing experience. College coach: Tennessee 1968, Southern Mississippi 1972, Villanova 1973-74, Kansas State 1975-76, West Virginia 1977, Texas Tech 1978-1983, Tennessee 1989, Florida 1990. Pro coach: San Antonio Gunslingers (USFL) 1984-85 (head coach 1985), Arizona Outlaws (USFL) 1986, Detroit Drive (AFL) 1988, Cleveland Browns 1991-93, 1995, Atlanta Falcons 1994, Dallas Cowboys 1996-99, joined Dolphins in 2000.

Clarence Brooks, defensive line; born May 20, 1951, New York, N.Y. Guard Massachusetts 1970-73. No pro playing experience. College coach: Massachusetts 1976-1980, Syracuse 1981-89, Arizona 1990-92. Pro coach: Chicago Bears 1993-98, Cleveland Browns 1999, joined Dolphins in 2000.

Joel Collier, running backs; born December 25, 1963, Buffalo. Linebacker Northern Colorado 1984-87. No pro playing experience. College coach: Syracuse 1988-89. Pro coach: Tampa Bay Buccaneers 1990, New England Patriots 1991-93, joined Dolphins in 1994.

Jeff Dellenbach, offensive assistant/asst. special teams; born February 14, 1963, Wausau, Wis. Offensive lineman Wisconsin 1981-84. Pro offensive lineman Miami Dolphins 1985-1994, New England Patriots 1995-96, Green Bay Packers 1996-98, Philadelphia Eagles 1999. Pro coach: Joined Dolphins in 2004.

Eric Fears, asst. strength and conditioning; born December 12, 1960, Tallahassee, Fla. Running back Virginia 1981-83. No pro playing experience. College coach: Virginia 1984-86, 1994-95, The Citadel 1987, South Carolina 1988-1992, Washington State 1993, Georgia 1996-2003. Pro coach: Joined Dolphins in 2004.

Chris Foerster, offensive coordinator; born October 12, 1961 in Milwaukee, Wis. Center Colorado State 1979-1982. No pro playing experience. College coach: Colorado State 1983-87, Stanford 1988-1991, Minnesota 1992. Pro coach: Minnesota Vikings 1993-95, Tampa Bay Buccaneers 1996-2001, Indianapolis Colts 2002-03, joined Dolphins in 2004.

John Gamble, strength and conditioning; born June 26, 1957, Richmond, Va. Linebacker Hampton Institute 1975-78. No pro playing experience. College coach: Virginia 1982-1993. Pro coach: Joined Dolphins in 1994.

Judd Garrett, offensive quality control/wide receivers; born June 25, 1967, Abington, Pa. Running back Princeton 1987-89. Pro running back London Monarchs (WLAF) 1991-92, Dallas Cowboys 1993, Las Vegas Posse (CFL) 1994, San Antonio Texans (CFL) 1995. College coach: Princeton 1990. Pro coach: New Orleans Saints 1997-99, joined Dolphins in 2000.

Bill Lewis, defensive nickel package; born August 5, 1941, Bristol, Pa. Quarterback East Stroudsburg State 1959-1962. No pro playing experience. College coach: East Stroudsburg State 1963-65, Pittsburgh 1966-68, Wake Forest 1969-1970, Georgia Tech 1971-72, 1992-94 (head coach), Arkansas 1973-76, Wyoming 1977-79, Georgia 1980-88, East Carolina 1989-1991 (head coach). Pro coach: Joined Dolphins in 1996.

Bernie Parmalee, tight ends; born September 16, 1967, Jersey City, N.J. Running back Ball State 1987-1990. Pro running back Miami Dolphins 1992-98, New York Jets 1999-2000. Pro coach: Joined Dolphins in 2002.

Mel Phillips, secondary; born January 6, 1942, Shelby, N.C. Defensive back-running back North Carolina A&T 1964-65. Pro defensive back San Francisco 49ers 1966-1977. Pro coach: Detroit Lions 1980-84, joined Dolphins in 1985.

Glenn Pires, asst. defensive line; born September 13, 1958, New Bedford, Mass. Offensive lineman Springfield College 1976-79. No pro playing experience. College coach: Dartmouth 1985-88, Syracuse 1989-1994, Michigan State 1995. Pro coach: Arizona Cardinals 1996-2000, Detroit Lions 2001-02, joined Dolphins in 2003.

Bob Sanders, linebackers; born December 5, 1953, Jacksonville, N.C. Linebacker Davidson College 1973-75. No pro playing experience. College coach: Georgia Tech 1978, East Carolina 1980-82, Richmond 1983-84, Duke 1985-89, Florida 1990-2000. Pro coach: Joined Dolphins in 2001.

Jerry Sullivan, wide receivers; born July 13, 1944, Miami. Quarterback Florida State 1963-64. No pro playing experience. College coach: Kansas State 1971-72, Texas Tech 1973-75, South Carolina 1976-1982, Indiana 1983, Louisiana State 1984-1990, Ohio State 1991. Pro coach: San Diego Chargers 1992-96, Detroit Lions 1997-2000, Arizona Cardinals 2001-03, joined Dolphins in 2004.

Marc Trestman, asst. head coach/quarterbacks; born January 15, 1956 in Minneapolis. Quarterback Minnesota 1974-75, Moorehead (Minn.) State 1977. No pro playing experience. College coach: Miami 1981-84. Pro coach: Minnesota Vikings 1985-86, 1990-91, Tampa Bay Buccaneers 1987, Cleveland Browns 1988-89, San Francisco 49ers 1995-96, Detroit Lions 1997, Arizona Cardinals 1998-2000, Oakland Raiders 2001-03, joined Dolphins in 2004.

Tony Wise, offensive line; born December 28, 1951, Albany, N.Y. Offensive lineman Ithaca College 1971-72. No pro playing experience. College coach: Albany State 1973, Bridgeport 1974, Central Connecticut State 1975, Washington State 1976, Pittsburgh 1977-78, Oklahoma State 1979-1983, Syracuse 1984, Miami 1985-88. Pro coach: Dallas Cowboys 1989-1992, Chicago Bears 1993-98, Carolina Panthers 1999-2000, joined Dolphins in 2001.

American Football Conference
East Division
Team Colors: Blue, Red, Silver, and White
Gillette Stadium
One Patriot Place
Foxborough, Massachusetts 02035
Telephone: (508) 543-8200

2004 SCHEDULE

PRESEASON		New England time
Aug. 13	**Philadelphia**	8:00
Aug. 21	at Cincinnati	7:30
Aug. 28	at Carolina	8:00
Sept. 2	**Jacksonville**	6:45

REGULAR SEASON		
Sept. 9	**Indianapolis** (Thu.)	9:00
Sept. 19	at Arizona	4:15
Sept. 26	Open Date	
Oct. 3	at Buffalo	1:00
Oct. 10	**Miami**	1:00
Oct. 17	**Seattle**	1:00
Oct. 24	**New York Jets**	4:05
Oct. 31	at Pittsburgh	4:15
Nov. 7	at St. Louis	4:15
Nov. 14	**Buffalo**	8:30
Nov. 22	at Kansas City (Mon.)	9:00
Nov. 28	**Baltimore**	1:00
Dec. 5	at Cleveland	1:00
Dec. 12	**Cincinnati**	1:00
Dec. 20	at Miami (Mon.)	9:00
Dec. 26	at New York Jets	4:05
Jan. 2	**San Francisco**	1:00

Stadium: Gillette Stadium (opened in 2002)
•**Capacity:** 68,436
One Patriot Place
Foxborough, Massachusetts 02035
Playing Surface: Grass
Training Camp: Gillette Stadium
Foxborough,
Massachusetts 02035

GILLETTE STADIUM

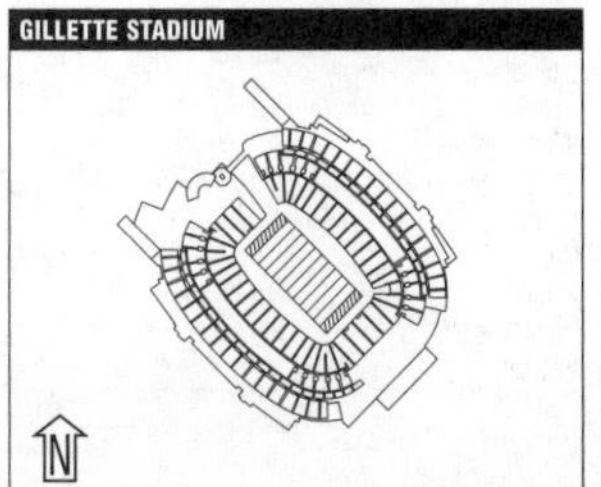

CLUB OFFICIALS

Owner and Chairman: Robert K. Kraft
Vice Chairman: Jonathan A. Kraft
Senior Vice President and COO: Andy Wasynczuk
Vice President, Player Personnel: Scott Pioli
Vice President, Finance: Jim Hausmann
Vice President, Chief Marketing Officer: Lou Imbriano
Vice President, Community Affairs and Corporate Philanthropy: Rena Clark
Chief Administrative Counsel: Jack Mula
Executive Director of Corporate Development: David Pearlstein
Executive Director of Marketing Operations: Jennifer Ferron
Executive Director of Media Relations: Stacey James
Executive Director of Sales: Murray Kohl
Executive Director of Security and Front of House Operations: Mark Briggs
Director of Cheerleaders: Tracy Sormanti
Director of College Scouting: Thomas Dimitroff
Director of Customer and Sponsor Services: Gail Titus
Director of Entertainment and Broadcast Production: Gary Grodecki
Director of Finance: Jim Wilson
Director of Football Development and Promotions for Community Affairs: Andre Tippett
Director of Human Resources: Joanne Nichols
Director of Premium Seating Services: Bill Nelsen
Director of Pro Personnel: Nick Caserio
Director of Suite Services: Melissa Aghjayan
Director of Research: Richard Miller
Director of Retail Operations: Ken Flanders
Director of Sales: Jon Levy
Director of Sales: Joe Mariani
Director of Ticketing: Maryruth Hughey
Equipment Manager: Don Brocher
Head Athletic Trainer: Jim Whalen
Video Director: Jimmy Dee
Kraft Group, Vice President of Information Technology: Pat Curley
Gillette Stadium, Vice President of Business Development and External Affairs: Dan Murphy
Gillette Stadium, Vice President of Operations: Jim Nolan

COACHING HISTORY

Boston 1960-1970
(327-347-9)

1960-61	Lou Saban*	7-12-0
1961-68	Mike Holovak	53-47-9
1969-1970	Clive Rush**	5-16-0
1970-72	John Mazur***	9-21-0
1972	Phil Bengtson	1-4-0
1973-78	Chuck Fairbanks****	46-41-0
1978	Hank Bullough-Ron Erhardt#	0-1-0
1979-1981	Ron Erhardt	21-27-0
1981-84	Ron Meyer##	18-16-0
1984-89	Raymond Berry	51-41-0
1990	Rod Rust	1-15-0
1991-92	Dick MacPherson	8-24-0
1993-96	Bill Parcells	34-34-0
1997-99	Pete Carroll	28-23-0
2000-03	Bill Belichick	45-25-0

*Released after five games in 1961
**Released after seven games in 1970
***Resigned after nine games in 1972
****Suspended for final regular-season game in 1978
#Co-coaches
##Released after eight games in 1984

ATTENDANCE

Home 538,707 Away 571,984
Total 1,110,691
Single-game home record, 68,436 (last time: 12/29/02)
Single-season home record, 538,707 (2003)

2004 DRAFT CHOICES

Round	Name	Pos.	College
1	Vince Wilfork	DT	Miami
	Ben Watson	TE	Georgia
2	Marquise Hill	DE	Louisiana State
3	Guss Scott	DB	Florida
4	Dexter Reid	DB	North Carolina
	Cedric Cobbs	RB	Arkansas
5	P.K. Sam	WR	Florida State
7	Christian Morton	DB	Illinois

NEW ENGLAND PATRIOTS

2003 TEAM RECORD

PRESEASON (4-0)

Date	Result	Opponent
8/7	W 26-6	N.Y. Giants
8/16	W 20-13	at Washington
8/22	W 24-12	at Philadelphia
8/27	W 38-23	Chicago

REGULAR SEASON (14-2)

Date	Result	Opponent	Att.
9/7	L 0-31	at Buffalo	73,262
9/14	W 31-10	at Philadelphia	67,624
9/21	W 23-16	New York Jets	68,436
9/28	L 17-20	at Washington	83,632
10/5	W 38-30	Tennessee	68,436
10/12	W 17-6	New York Giants	68,436
10/19	W 19-13	at Miami (OT)	73,650
10/26	W 9-3	Cleveland	68,436
11/3	W 30-26	at Denver	76,203
11/16	W 12-0	Dallas	68,436
11/23	W 23-20	at Houston (OT)	70,719
11/30	W 38-34	at Indianapolis	57,102
12/7	W 12-0	Miami	68,436
12/14	W 27-13	Jacksonville	68,436
12/20	W 21-16	at New York Jets	77,835
12/27	W 31-0	Buffalo	68,436

(OT) Overtime

POSTSEASON (3-0)

Date	Result	Opponent	
1/10	W 17-14	Tennessee	68,436
1/18	W 24-14	Indianapolis	68,436
2/1	W 32-29	vs. Carolina at Houston	71,525

SCORE BY PERIODS

Patriots	80	83	79	97	9	— 348
Opponents	42	73	51	72	0	— 238

2003 TEAM STATISTICS

	Patriots	Opp.
Total First Downs	294	293
Rushing	91	91
Passing	177	177
Penalty	26	25
3rd Down: Made/Att	84/227	81/235
3rd Down Pct.	37.0	34.5
4th Down: Made/Att	6/14	6/16
4th Down Pct.	42.9	37.5
Possession Avg.	30:50	29:10
Total Net Yards	5,039	4,666
Avg. Per Game	314.9	291.6
Total Plays	1,042	1,060
Avg. Per Play	4.8	4.4
Net Yards Rushing	1,607	1,434
Avg. Per Game	100.4	89.6
Total Rushes	473	401
Net Yards Passing	3,432	3,232
Avg. Per Game	214.5	202.0
Sacked/Yards Lost	32/219	41/253
Gross Yards	3,651	3,485
Att./Completions	537/320	618/328
Completion Pct.	59.6	53.1
Had Intercepted	13	29
Punts/Average	88/37.1	90/40.6
Net Punting Avg.	88/33.5	90/34.4
Penalties/Yards	111/998	107/845
Fumbles/Ball Lost	25/11	31/12
Touchdowns	39	23
Rushing	9	10
Passing	23	11
Returns	7	2

2003 INDIVIDUAL STATISTICS

PASSING	Att.	Comp.	Yds.	Pct.	TD	Int.	Tkld.	Rate
Brady	527	317	3,620	60.2	23	12	32/219	85.9
Davey	7	3	31	42.9	0	0	0/0	56.3
Faulk	1	0	0	0.0	0	0	0/0	39.6
Givens	1	0	0	0.0	0	1	0/0	0.0
Huard	1	0	0	0.0	0	0	0/0	39.6
Patriots	537	320	3,651	59.6	23	13	32/219	84.3
Opponents	618	328	3,485	53.1	11	29	41/253	56.2

SCORING	TD R	TD P	TD Rt	PAT	FG	Saf	PTS
Vinatieri	0	0	0	37/38	25/34	0	112
Givens	0	6	0	0/0	0/0	0	36
Cloud	5	0	0	0/0	0/0	0	30
T. Brown	0	4	0	0/0	0/0	0	24
Graham	0	4	0	0/0	0/0	0	24
Branch	0	3	0	0/0	0/0	0	18
B. Johnson	0	2	1	0/0	0/0	0	18
Smith	3	0	0	0/0	0/0	0	18
Bruschi	0	0	2	0/0	0/0	0	12
Fauria	0	2	0	0/0	0/0	0	12
Brady	1	0	0	0/0	0/0	0	6
Centers	0	1	0	0/0	0/0	0	6
Chatham	0	0	1	0/0	0/0	0	6
Law	0	0	1	0/0	0/0	0	6
McGinest	0	0	1	0/0	0/0	0	6
Samuel	0	0	1	0/0	0/0	0	6
Ward	0	1	0	0/0	0/0	0	6
Patriots	9	23	7	37/38	25/34	1	348
Opponents	10	11	2	21/21	25/35	1	238

2-Pt. Conversions: None.
Patriots 0-0, Opponents 1-2.

RUSHING	No.	Yds	Avg	LG	TD
Smith	182	642	3.5	30	3
Faulk	178	638	3.6	23	0
Cloud	27	118	4.4	42	5
Centers	21	82	3.9	13	0
Brady	42	63	1.5	11	1
T. Brown	6	27	4.5	11	0
Pass	6	27	4.5	11	0
Branch	1	11	11.0	11	0
Klecko	2	5	2.5	5	0
Patten	1	4	4.0	4	0
McCrary	3	3	1.0	4	0
Walter	2	0	0.0	0	0
Huard	1	-1	-1.0	-1	0
B. Johnson	1	-12	-12.0	-12	0
Patriots	473	1,607	3.4	42	9
Opponents	401	1,434	3.6	23	10

RECEIVING	No.	Yds	Avg	LG	TD
Branch	57	803	14.1	66t	3
Faulk	48	440	9.2	27	0
T. Brown	40	472	11.8	82t	4
Graham	38	409	10.8	38	4
Givens	34	510	15.0	57	6
Fauria	28	285	10.2	28	2
Centers	19	106	5.6	14	1
B. Johnson	16	209	13.1	45	2
Smith	14	92	6.6	16	0
Patten	9	140	15.6	42	0
Ward	7	106	15.1	31t	1
Pass	4	21	5.3	11	0
Stokes	2	38	19.0	31	0
McCrary	2	12	6.0	9	0
Cloud	1	8	8.0	8	0
Andruzzi	1	0	0.0	0	0
Patriots	320	3,651	11.4	82t	23
Opponents	328	3,485	10.6	67	11

INTERCEPTIONS	No.	Yds	Avg	LG	TD
Law	6	112	18.7	65t	1
Poole	6	81	13.5	44	0
Wilson	4	18	4.5	10	0
Bruschi	3	26	8.7	18t	2
Harrison	3	0	0.0	2	0
Samuel	2	55	27.5	55t	1
Vrabel	2	18	9.0	14	0
Morris	1	33	33.0	33	0
McGinest	1	15	15.0	15t	1
Izzo	1	0	0.0	0	0
Patriots	29	358	12.3	65t	5
Opponents	13	122	9.4	37t	1

PUNTING	No.	Yds.	Avg.	In 20	LG
Walter	76	2,865	37.7	25	52
Barnard	10	365	36.5	4	49
Brady	1	36	36.0	1	36
Patriots	88	3,266	37.1	30	52
Opponents	90	3,658	40.6	21	71

PUNT RETURNS	Ret	FC	Yds	Avg	LG	TD
T. Brown	29	13	293	10.1	23	0
Poole	11	3	75	6.8	18	0
Faulk	5	6	66	13.2	19	0
Branch	4	1	26	6.5	11	0
B. Johnson	1	0	2	2.0	2	0
Ward	0	2	0	—	—	0
Patriots	50	25	462	9.2	23	0
Opponents	38	11	240	6.3	57t	1

KICKOFF RETURNS	No.	Yds	Avg	LG	TD
B. Johnson	30	847	28.2	92t	1
Pass	11	254	23.1	36	0
Faulk	10	207	20.7	30	0
Cloud	2	38	19.0	19	0
Givens	2	31	15.5	20	0
Klecko	2	20	10.0	10	0
Vrabel	2	22	11.0	14	0
Bruschi	1	9	9.0	9	0
Patriots	60	1,428	23.8	92t	1
Opponents	77	1,623	21.1	75	0

FIELD GOALS	1-19	20-29	30-39	40-49	50+
Vinatieri	0/0	16/17	4/8	5/8	0/1
Patriots	0/0	16/17	4/8	5/8	0/1
Opponents	1/1	8/8	8/11	7/14	1/1

SACKS	No.
Vrabel	9.5
Seymour	8.0
McGinest	5.5
Harrison	3.0
Bruschi	2.0
Colvin	2.0
Green	2.0
Washington	2.0
Chatham	1.5
Klecko	1.5
Banta-Cain	1.0
Cherry	1.0
Pleasant	1.0
Warren	1.0
Patriots	41.0
Opponents	32.0

RECORD HOLDERS

INDIVIDUAL RECORDS—CAREER

Category	Name	Performance
Rushing (Yds.)	Sam Cunningham, 1973-79, 1981-82	5,453
Passing (Yds.)	Drew Bledsoe, 1993-2001	29,657
Passing (TDs)	Steve Grogan, 1975-1990	182
Receiving (No.)	Stanley Morgan, 1977-1989	534
Receiving (Yds.)	Stanley Morgan, 1977-1989	10,352
Interceptions	Raymond Clayborn, 1977-1989	36
Punting (Avg.)	Tom Tupa, 1996-98	44.7
Punt Return (Avg.)	Mack Herron, 1973-75	12.0
Kickoff Return (Avg.)	Allen Carter, 1975-76	27.2
Field Goals	Adam Vinatieri, 1996-2003	212
Touchdowns (Tot.)	Stanley Morgan, 1977-1989	68
Points	Gino Cappelletti, 1960-1970	1,130

INDIVIDUAL RECORDS—SINGLE SEASON

Category	Name	Performance
Rushing (Yds.)	Curtis Martin, 1995	1,487
Passing (Yds.)	Drew Bledsoe, 1994	4,555
Passing (TDs)	Vito (Babe) Parilli, 1964	31
Receiving (No.)	Troy Brown, 2001	101
Receiving (Yds.)	Stanley Morgan, 1986	1,491
Interceptions	Ron Hall, 1964	11
Punting (Avg.)	Tom Tupa, 1997	45.8
Punt Return (Avg.)	Mack Herron, 1974	14.8
Kickoff Return (Avg.)	Raymond Clayborn, 1977	31.0
Field Goals	Tony Franklin, 1986	32
Touchdowns (Tot.)	Curtis Martin, 1996	17
Points	Gino Cappelletti, 1964	155

INDIVIDUAL RECORDS—SINGLE GAME

Category	Name	Performance
Rushing (Yds.)	Tony Collins, 9-18-83	212
Passing (Yds.)	Drew Bledsoe, 11-13-94	426
Passing (TDs)	Vito (Babe) Parilli, 11-15-64	5
	Vito (Babe) Parilli, 10-15-67	5
	Steve Grogan, 9-9-79	5
Receiving (No.)	Troy Brown, 9-22-02	16
Receiving (Yds.)	Terry Glenn, 10-3-99	214
Interceptions	Many times	3
	Last time by Roland James, 10-23-83	
Field Goals	Gino Cappelletti, 10-4-64	6
Touchdowns (Tot.)	Many times	3
	Last time by Antowain Smith, 11-3-02	
Points	Gino Cappelletti, 12-18-65	28

NEW ENGLAND PATRIOTS

2004 VETERAN ROSTER

No.	Name	Pos.	Ht.	Wt.	Birthdate	NFL Exp.	College	Hometown	How Acq.	'03 Games/ Starts
63	Andruzzi, Joe	G	6-3	312	8/23/75	8	Southern Connecticut State	Staten Island, N.Y.	FA-'00	16/16
68	Ashworth, Tom	T	6-6	305	10/10/77	3	Colorado	Englewood, Colo.	FA-'01	16/13
96	Bailey, Rodney	DE-DT	6-3	300	10/7/79	4	Ohio State	Cleveland, Ohio	RFA(Pitt)-'04	16/0*
48	Banta-Cain, Tully	LB	6-2	250	8/28/80	2	California	Sunnyvale, Calif.	D7b-'03	9/0
12	Brady, Tom	QB	6-4	225	8/3/77	5	Michigan	San Mateo, Calif.	D6b-'00	16/16
83	Branch, Deion	WR	5-9	193	7/18/79	3	Louisville	Albany, Ga.	D2-'02	15/11
80	Brown, Troy	WR	5-10	196	7/2/71	12	Marshall	Blackville, S.C.	D8-'93	12/10
60	Brown, Wilbert	G	6-2	320	5/9/77	4	Houston	Hooks, Texas	W(Wash)-'03	2/0
54	Bruschi, Tedy	LB	6-1	247	6/9/73	9	Arizona	Roseville, Calif.	D3-'96	16/16
27	Burris, Jeff	DB	6-0	190	6/7/72	11	Notre Dame	Rock Hill, S.C.	FA-'04	13/8*
58	Chatham, Matt	LB	6-4	250	6/28/77	5	South Dakota	Sioux City, Iowa	W(StL)-'00	16/4
30	Cherry, Je'Rod	S	6-1	210	5/30/73	9	California	Berkeley, Calif.	FA-'01	11/0
21	Cloud, Michael	RB	5-10	205	7/1/75	6	Boston College	Portsmouth, R.I.	UFA(KC)-'03	5/1
59	Colvin, Rosevelt	LB	6-3	250	9/5/77	6	Purdue	Indianapolis, Ind.	UFA(Chi)-'03	2/2
41	Crosby, Phillip	FB	6-0	242	11/5/76	4	Tennessee	Bessemer City, N.C.	FA-'04	3/0*
6	Davey, Rohan	QB	6-2	245	4/14/78	3	Louisiana State	Miami, Fla.	D4a-'02	1/0
51	Davis, Don	LB	6-1	235	12/17/72	9	Kansas	Olathe, Kan.	UFA(StL)-'03	15/0
28	t-Dillon, Corey	RB	6-1	225	10/24/74	8	Washington	Seattle, Wash.	T(Cin)-'04	13/11*
33	Faulk, Kevin	RB	5-8	202	6/5/76	6	Louisiana State	Carencro, La.	D2-'99	15/8
88	Fauria, Christian	TE	6-4	250	9/22/71	10	Colorado	Encino, Calif.	UFA(Sea)-'02	16/13
87	Givens, David	WR	6-0	212	8/16/80	3	Notre Dame	Humble, Texas	D7b-'02	13/5
76	Gorin, Brandon	T	6-6	308	7/17/78	3	Purdue	Muncie, Ind.	FA-'03	6/0
82	Graham, Daniel	TE	6-3	257	11/16/78	3	Colorado	Denver, Colo.	D1-'02	14/9
97	Green, Jarvis	DT-DE	6-3	290	1/12/79	3	Louisiana State	Donaldsonville, La.	D4b-'02	16/7
37	Harrison, Rodney	S	6-1	220	12/15/72	11	Western Illinois	Chicago, Ill.	FA-'03	16/16
71	Hochstein, Russ	G	6-4	305	10/7/77	4	Nebraska	Hartington, Neb.	FA-'02	15/1
53	Izzo, Larry	LB	5-10	228	9/26/74	9	Rice	Houston, Texas	UFA(Mia)-'01	16/0
81	Johnson, Bethel	WR	5-11	200	2/11/79	2	Texas A&M	Corsicana, Texas	D2b-'03	15/5
52	Johnson, Ted	LB	6-4	253	12/4/72	10	Colorado	Alameda, Calif.	D2-'95	8/2
16	Kingsbury, Kliff	QB	6-3	220	8/9/79	2	Texas Tech	New Braunfels, Texas	D6-'03	0*
90	Klecko, Dan	DT-DE	5-11	283	1/12/81	2	Temple	Colts Neck, N.J.	D4a-'03	13/1
70	Klemm, Adrian	T	6-3	312	5/21/77	5	Hawaii	Los Angeles, Calif.	D2-'00	3/3
67	Koppen, Dan	C	6-2	296	9/12/79	2	Boston College	Whitehall, Pa.	D5-'03	16/15
47	Kurpeikis, Justin	LB	6-3	254	7/17/77	3	Penn State	Allison Park, Pa.	FA-'04	0*
24	Law, Ty	CB	5-11	200	2/10/74	10	Michigan	Aliquippa, Pa.	D1-'95	15/15
72	Light, Matt	T	6-4	305	6/23/78	4	Purdue	Greenville, Ohio	D2-'01	16/16
23	Mayer, Shawn	S	6-0	202	3/4/79	2	Penn State	Hillsborough, N.J.	FA-'03	9/0
44	McCrary, Fred	FB	6-0	247	9/19/72	8	Mississippi State	Naples, Fla.	FA-'03	6/3
49	McDermott, Sean	LS	6-4	250	12/5/76	4	Kansas	Lufkin, Texas	FA-'03	6/0*
55	McGinest, Willie	LB	6-5	270	12/11/71	11	Southern California	Long Beach, Calif.	D1-'94	14/11
8	Miller, Josh	P	6-4	220	7/14/70	9	Arizona	Rockway, N.Y.	FA-'04	16/0*
43	Moreau, Frank	RB	6-0	223	9/6/76	3	Louisville	Elizabethtown, Ky.	FA-'04	0*
64	Mruczkowski, Gene	T-G	6-2	305	6/6/80	2	Purdue	Cleveland, Ohio	FA-'03	0*
61	Neal, Stephen	G	6-4	305	10/9/76	3	Cal State-Bakersfield	San Diego, Calif.	FA-'01	0*
35	Pass, Patrick	FB	5-10	217	12/31/77	5	Georgia	Tucker, Ga.	D7b-'00	13/1
86	Patten, David	WR	5-10	190	8/19/74	8	Western Carolina	Hopkins, S.C.	UFA(Cle)-'01	6/5
66	Paxton, Lonie	LS	6-2	260	3/13/78	5	Sacramento State	Corona, Calif.	FA-'00	13/0
	Perry, Jason	S	6-0	200	8/1/76	5	North Carolina State	Passaic, N.J.	FA-'04	0*
95	Phifer, Roman	LB	6-2	248	3/5/68	14	UCLA	Pineville, N.C.	FA-'01	16/15
38	Poole, Tyrone	CB	5-8	188	2/3/72	9	Fort Valley State	LaGrange, Ga.	UFA(Den)-'03	16/16
22	Samuel, Asante	CB	5-10	185	1/6/81	2	Central Florida	Ft. Lauderdale, Fla.	D4b-'03	16/1
93	Seymour, Richard	DT-DE	6-6	310	10/6/79	4	Georgia	Gadsden, S.C.	D1-'01	15/14
45	Smith, Otis	CB	5-11	198	10/22/65	15	Missouri	New Orleans, La.	FA-'04	16/13*
85	Stokes, J.J.	WR	6-4	225	10/6/72	10	UCLA	San Diego, Calif.	FA-'03	8/3*
98	Traylor, Keith	DT	6-2	340	9/3/69	13	Central State (Okla.)	Little Rock, Ark.	FA-'04	10/10*
4	Vinatieri, Adam	K	6-0	202	12/28/72	9	South Dakota State	Rapid City, S.D.	FA-'96	16/0
50	Vrabel, Mike	LB	6-4	261	8/14/75	8	Ohio State	Akron, Ohio	UFA(Pitt)-'01	13/9
94	Warren, Ty	DT-DE	6-5	300	2/6/81	2	Texas A&M	Bryan, Texas	D1-'03	16/4
26	Wilson, Eugene	S	5-10	195	8/17/80	2	Illinois	Merrillville, Ill.	D2a-'03	16/15

* Bailey played 16 games with Pittsburgh in '03; Burris played 13 games with Cincinnati; Crosby played 3 games with Buffalo; Dillon played 13 games with Cincinnati; Kingsbury missed '03 season because of injury; Kurpeikis last active with Pittsburgh in '02; McDermott played 5 games with Miami and 1 with New England; Miller played 16 games with Pittsburgh; Moreau last active with Jacksonville in '01; Mruczkowski missed '03 season because of injury; Neal missed '03 season because of injury; Perry last active with Cincinnati in '02; Smith played 16 games with Detroit; Stokes played 6 games with Jacksonville and 2 with New England; Traylor played 10 games with Chicago.

t- Patriots traded for Dillon (Cin).

Players lost through free agency (4): S Chris Akins (Mia; 12 games in '03), G-C Mike Compton (Jax; 2), NT Ted Washington (Oak; 10), G-C Damien Woody (Det; 14).

Also played with Patriots in '03—P Brooks Barnard (1 game), TE Fred Baxter (12), FB Larry Centers (9), WR Jamin Elliott (1), DE Bobby Hamilton (16), S-CB Antwan Harris (13), QB Damon Huard (2), LS Brian Kinchen (2), DT-DE Rick Lyle (8), S Aric Morris (4), DE Anthony Pleasant (7), RB Antowain Smith (13), P Ken Walter (15), WR Dedric Ward (4).

2004 FIRST-YEAR ROSTER

Name	Pos.	Ht.	Wt.	Birthdate	College	Hometown	How Acq.
Alexander, Eric	LB	6-2	223	2/8/82	Louisiana State	Port Arthur, Texas	FA
Bryant, Ricky	WR	6-0	173	3/24/81	Hofstra	Farmington Hills, Mich.	FA
Cobbs, Cedric	RB	6-0	221	1/9/81	Arkansas	Little Rock, Ark.	D4b
Dorsey, Quinn	LB	6-4	270	4/1/80	Oregon	Denver, Colo.	FA
Fadule, Jack (1)	T	6-5	316	9/11/80	Harvard	Mission Viejo, Calif.	FA
Farley, Scott (1)	DB	6-0	212	4/24/80	Williams	Williamstown, Mass.	FA
Flugence, Lawrence (1)	LB	6-1	239	1/19/80	Texas Tech	Klein, Texas	FA
Gachelin, Louis	DT	6-1	284	12/26/80	Syracuse	Miami, Fla.	FA
Gay, Randall	CB	5-11	186	5/5/82	Louisiana State	Brusly, La.	FA
Gessner, Chas (1)	WR	6-4	215	8/17/81	Brown	Hyattsville, Md.	FA-'03
Hill, Marquise	DE	6-6	297	8/7/82	Louisiana State	New Orleans, La.	D2
Jennings, Michael (1)	WR	5-11	170	9/7/79	Florida State	Jacksonville, Fla.	FA
Kelley, Ethan (1)	DT	6-2	303	2/12/80	Baylor	Sugar Land, Texas	D7c-'03
Mackenzie, Malaefou (1)	RB	5-10	233	7/24/79	Southern California	Mission Viejo, Calif.	FA
Mignery, Andy	TE	6-3	250	9/12/80	Michigan	Hamilton, Ohio	FA
Morton, Christian	CB	6-0	188	4/28/81	Illinois	St. Louis, Mo.	D7
Provost, Tim (1)	T	6-5	300	8/24/80	San Jose State	Downey, Calif.	FA-'03
Pruce, David (1)	T	6-8	295	6/1/78	Buffalo	Chardon, Ohio	FA
Rasmussen, Buck (1)	DL	6-4	285	10/1/78	Nebraska-Omaha	Tekamah, Neb.	FA
Reid, Dexter	S	5-11	203	3/18/81	North Carolina	Norfolk, Va.	D4a
Sam, P.K.	WR	6-3	210	12/16/83	Florida State	Buford, Ga.	D5
Sawyer, Brian	LS	6-2	246	5/7/81	Florida State	Cordele, Ga.	FA
Scates, Cody	P-K	6-1	197	12/8/81	Texas A&M	Tyler, Texas	FA
Scott, Guss	S	5-10	198	5/21/82	Florida	Jacksonville, Fla.	D3
Soriano, Jamil (1)	G-T	6-4	310	5/11/81	Harvard	Plainview, N.Y.	FA-'03
Steen, Grant	LB-LS	6-2	242	10/22/80	Iowa	Emmetsburg, Iowa	FA
Walker, Marquise (1)	WR	6-2	219	12/11/78	Michigan	Syracuse, N.Y.	FA
Watson, Benjamin	TE	6-3	253	12/17/80	Georgia	Rock Hill, S.C.	D1b
Wilfork, Vince	DL	6-2	344	11/4/81	Miami	Boynton Beach, Fla.	D1a

The term NFL Rookie is defined as a player who is in his first season of professional football and has not been on the roster of another professional football team for any regular-season or postseason games. A Rookie is designated by an "R" on NFL rosters. Players who have been active in another professional football league or players who have NFL experience, including either preseason training camp or being on an Active List or Inactive List, or on Reserve/Injured or Reserve/Physically Unable to Perform for fewer than six regular-season games, are termed NFL First-Year Players. An NFL First-Year Player is designated by a "1" on NFL rosters. Thereafter, a player is credited with an additional year of experience for each season in which he accumulates six games on the Active List or Inactive List, or on Reserve/Injured or Reserve/Physically Unable to Perform.

Log on to www.patriots.com for an up-to-date roster.

NEW ENGLAND PATRIOTS

COACHING STAFF

Head Coach,
Bill Belichick

Pro Career: Bill Belichick returned to New England when Patriots owner Robert Kraft named him the fourteenth head coach in Patriots history on January 27, 2000. Belichick, who was a defensive assistant for the Patriots when the team won a conference title in 1996, took over and quickly molded the Patriots into one of the elite teams in the NFL, winning two Super Bowls in the past three seasons. Since 2001, Belichick has directed the Patriots to a 40-14 (.741) record heading into the 2004 season, the best mark in the NFL over the past three seasons. The most successful run in franchise history includes a 6-0 postseason record and the first two league titles in the club's 44-year history. In 2003, Belichick led the Patriots to one of the finest seasons in pro football annals, compiling a 17-2 mark that culminated in a victory over the Carolina Panthers in Super Bowl XXXVIII. The Patriots became the first team in 31 years and just the second club ever to win 15 consecutive games en route to the championship. Only the 1972 Miami Dolphins won more consecutive games in a season. By 2001, just his second season at the helm in New England, he had reversed the course of the team and returned it to NFL prominence. The Patriots closed out the 2001 season by winning nine consecutive games, including a victory in Super Bowl XXXVI against the Rams to claim the first league championship in franchise history. In addition to his two Super Bowl titles as a head coach, Belichick owns a 7-1 (.875) mark in the postseason, second only to Vince Lombardi (9-1) in NFL history. Long renowned as one of the league's premier defensive coaches after years as a defensive assistant, Belichick is now recognized as one of the NFL's premier game strategists. His contributions as a head coach and an assistant coach have led to four Super Bowl titles, five conference championships and seven division titles since 1986. Now entering his 30th season as an NFL coach, Belichick has spent more seasons in the league than any other NFL head coach. He launched his career in 1975 as a special assistant with the Baltimore Colts, then became an assistant special teams coach with Detroit (1976-77) and Denver (1978). In 1979, he joined the New York Giants as the special teams coach, and by 1981 he was also working with the linebackers. In 1985, he was named defensive coordinator and contributed to the Giants winning Super Bowl titles in 1986 and again in 1990. Following Super Bowl XXV, Belichick was named head coach of the Cleveland Browns in 1991, becoming the youngest head coach in the NFL at age 37. By 1994, Belichick brought the Browns back to the playoffs, finishing 11-5 and advancing to the second round of the playoffs, while allowing a league-low 204 total points. In 1996, Belichick joined New England and was a key contributor to the team's rebound from a 6-10 season in 1995 to an 11-5 season and the team's first division title in 10 years en route to Super Bowl XXXI against Green Bay. Belichick then spent three seasons with the New York Jets from 1997 to 1999, helping New York improve from a 1-15 season in 1996 to an appearance in the AFC Championship Game in 1998. Career record: 82-70.

Background: Belichick was a center/tight end at Wesleyan 1971-74.

Personal: Born April 16, 1952, Nashville. Bill and his wife, Debby, have three children—Amanda, Stephen, and Brian.

ASSISTANT COACHES

Romeo Crennel, defensive coordinator; born June 18, 1947, Lynchburgh, Va. Offensive-defensive tackle, linebacker Western Kentucky 1966-69. No pro playing experience. College coach: Western Kentucky 1970-74, Texas Tech 1975-77, Mississippi 1978-79, Georgia Tech 1980. Pro coach: New York Giants 1981-1992, New England Patriots 1993-96, New York Jets 1997-99, Cleveland Browns 2000, rejoined Patriots in 2001.

Brian Daboll, wide receivers; born Welland, Ontario. Safety Rochester 1994-96. No pro playing experience. College coach: William & Mary 1997, Michigan State 1998-99. Pro coach: Joined Patriots in 2000.

Jeff Davidson, asst. offensive line-tight ends; born October 3, 1967, Akron, Ohio. Offensive lineman Ohio State 1986-89. Pro offensive lineman Denver Broncos 1990-92, New Orleans Saints 1994. Pro coach: New Orleans Saints 1995-96, joined Patriots in 1997.

Ivan Fears, running backs; born November 15, 1954, Portsmouth, Va. Running back William & Mary 1973-75. No pro playing experience. College coach: William & Mary 1977-1980, Syracuse 1981-1990. Pro coach: New England Patriots 1991-92, Chicago Bears 1993-98, rejoined Patriots in 1999.

Pepper Johnson, defensive line; born July 29, 1964, Detroit. Linebacker Ohio State 1982-85. Pro linebacker New York Giants 1986-1992, Cleveland Browns 1993-95, Detroit Lions 1996, New York Jets 1997-98. Pro coach: Joined Patriots in 2000.

Eric Mangini, defensive backs; born January 10, 1971, Hartford, Conn. Nose tackle Wesleyan (Conn.) 1989-1990, 1992-93. No pro playing experience. Pro coach: Cleveland Browns 1995, Baltimore Ravens 1996, New York Jets 1997-99, joined Patriots in 2000.

Josh McDainels, quarterbacks; born April 22, 1976, in Canton, Ohio. Wide receiver John Carroll University, 1995-98. No pro playing experience. College coach: Michigan State 1999-2000. Pro coach: Joined Patriots in 2001.

Markus Paul, asst. strength and conditioning; born April 1, 1966, Orlando, Fla. Safety Syracuse 1984-88. Pro safety Chicago Bears 1989-1993, Tampa Bay Buccaneers 1993. Pro coach: New Orleans 1998-99, joined Patriots in 2000.

Dean Pees, linebackers; born September 4, 1949, Dunkirk, Ohio. Attended Bowling Green. No college or pro playing experience. College coach: Findlay 1979-1982, Miami (Ohio) 1983-86, Navy 1987-89, Toledo 1990-93, Notre Dame 1994, Michigan State 1995-97, Kent State 1998-2003. Pro coach: Joined Patriots in 2004.

Dante Scarnecchia, asst. head coach-offensive line; born February 15, 1948, Los Angeles. Center-guard California Western (now U.S. International) 1968-1970. No pro playing experience. College coach: California Western 1970-72, Iowa State 1973-74, Southern Methodist 1975-76, 1980-81, Pacific 1977-78, Northern Arizona 1979. Pro coach: New England Patriots 1982-88, Indianapolis Colts 1989-1990, rejoined Patriots in 1991.

Brad Seely, special teams; born September 6, 1956, Vinton, Iowa. Tackle-guard South Dakota State 1974-77. No pro playing experience. College coach: Colorado State 1980, Southern Methodist 1981, North Carolina State 1982, Pacific 1983, Oklahoma State 1984-88. Pro coach: Indianapolis Colts 1989-1993, New York Jets 1994, Carolina Panthers 1995-98, joined Patriots in 1999.

Charlie Weis, offensive coordinator; born March 30, 1956, Trenton, N.J. Attended Notre Dame. No college or pro playing experience. College coach: South Carolina 1985-88. Pro coach: New York Giants 1988-1992, New England Patriots 1993-96, New York Jets 1997-99, rejoined Patriots in 2000.

Mike Woicik, strength and conditioning; born September 26, 1956, Baltimore. Attended Boston College. No college or pro playing experience. College coach: Springfield College 1978-79, Syracuse 1980-89. Pro coach: Dallas Cowboys 1990-96, New Orleans Saints 1997-99, joined Patriots in 2000.

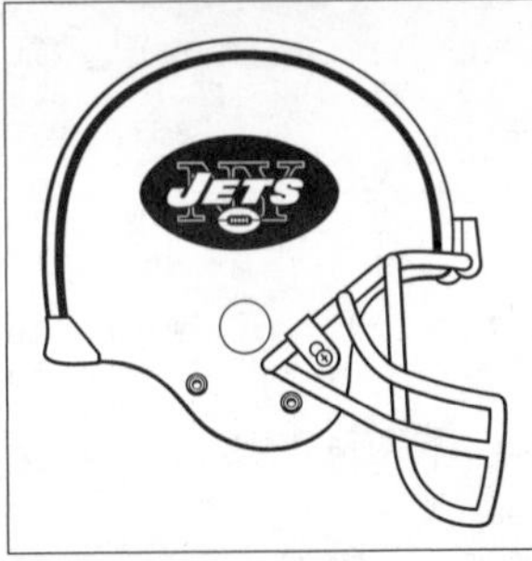

American Football Conference
East Division
Team Colors: Green and White
1000 Fulton Avenue
Hempstead, New York 11550
Telephone: (516) 560-8100

2004 SCHEDULE

PRESEASON		New York time
Aug. 13	at New Orleans	8:00
Aug. 21	at Indianapolis	8:00
Aug. 27	**New York Giants**	7:00
Sept. 3	**Philadelphia**	7:00

REGULAR SEASON		
Sept. 12	**Cincinnati**	1:00
Sept. 19	at San Diego	4:15
Sept. 26	Open Date	
Oct. 3	at Miami	4:15
Oct. 10	**Buffalo**	4:05
Oct. 17	**San Francisco**	1:00
Oct. 24	at New England	4:05
Nov. 1	**Miami** (Mon.)	9:00
Nov. 7	at Buffalo	1:00
Nov. 14	**Baltimore**	1:00
Nov. 21	at Cleveland	1:00
Nov. 28	at Arizona	4:15
Dec. 5	**Houston**	1:00
Dec. 12	at Pittsburgh	4:05
Dec. 19	**Seattle**	1:00
Dec. 26	**New England**	4:05
Jan. 2	at St. Louis	1:00

Stadium: Meadowlands
(opened in 1976)
• **Capacity:** 79,466
East Rutherford, New Jersey
07073
Playing Surface: FieldTurf
Training Camp: 1000 Fulton Avenue
Hempstead, New York
11550

MEADOWLANDS

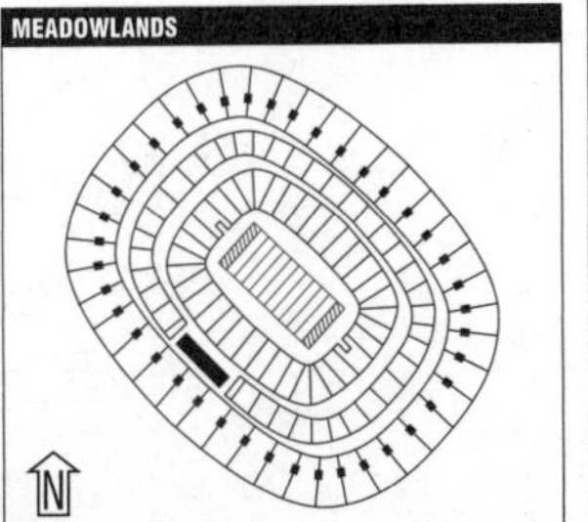

CLUB OFFICIALS

Owner and CEO: Robert Wood Johnson IV
President: Jay Cross
G.M./Executive Vice President: Terry Bradway
Senior V.P., Football Operations: Mike Tannenbaum
Senior V.P., Design & Construction: Bill Senn
Senior V.P., Marketing and Sales: Lee Stacey
Vice President, Public Relations: Ron Colangelo
Vice President, Finance and CFO: Michael Gerstle
Vice President, Operations: Michael Kensil
Vice President, Business Operations: Robert Parente
Vice President, Corporate Sales Marc Riccio
Vice President, Stadium Development: Thad Sheely
Senior Pro Scout/AFC: JoJo Wooden
Pro Scout/NFC: Brian Gaine
Salary Cap Analyst/Pro Personnel Assistant: Dawn Aponte
Pro Personnel Assistant: Chris Shea
Director of College Scouting: Jessie Kaye
National Scout: Joey Clinkscales
Consultant: Dick Haley
Scouting Coordinator: John Griffin
Personnel Scouts: Jeff Bauer, Joe Bommarito, Ron Brockington, Jim Cochran, Michael Davis, Sid Hall, Brendan Prophett, Bob Schmitz, Gary Smith
Head Athletic Trainer: David Price
Assistant Head Athletic Trainer: John Mellody
Assistant Head Athletic Trainer: Bill Peters
Controller: Mike Minarczyk
Director of Media Relations: Douglas P. Miller
Director, Video: Jim Space
Senior Director of Player & Community Relations: Kevin Winston
Director of Security: Steve Yarnell
Equipment Manager: Clay Hampton
Assistant Equipment Manager: Gus Granneman
Director of Internet and Publications: Ken Ilchuk
Director of Ticket Operations: John Buschhorn

COACHING HISTORY

New York Titans 1960-62
(301-367-8)

1960-61	Sammy Baugh	14-14-0
1962	Clyde (Bulldog) Turner	5-9-0
1963-1973	Weeb Ewbank	73-78-6
1974-75	Charley Winner*	9-14-0
1975	Ken Shipp	1-4-0
1976	Lou Holtz**	3-10-0
1976	Mike Holovak	0-1-0
1977-1982	Walt Michaels	41-49-1
1983-89	Joe Walton	54-59-1
1990-93	Bruce Coslet	26-39-0
1994	Pete Carroll	6-10-0
1995-96	Rich Kotite	4-28-0
1997-99	Bill Parcells	30-20-0
2000	Al Groh	9-7-0
2001-03	Herman Edwards	26-25-0

*Released after nine games in 1975
**Resigned after 13 games in 1976

ATTENDANCE

Home 622,781 Away 535,953
Total 1,158,734
Single-game home record, 78,920 (11/10/02)
Single-season home record, 628,773 (2002)

2004 DRAFT CHOICES

Round	Name	Pos.	College
1	Jonathan Vilma	LB	Miami
3	Derrick Strait	DB	Oklahoma
4	Jerricho Cotchery	WR	North Carolina St.
	Adrian Jones	T	Kansas
5	Erik Coleman	DB	Washington St.
6	Marko Cavka	T	Sacramento St.
7	Darrell McClover	LB	Miami
	Trevor Johnson	DE	Nebraska
	Derrick Ward	FB	Ottawa (Kan.)
	Rashad Washington	DB	Kansas State

NEW YORK JETS

2003 TEAM RECORD

PRESEASON (3-2)

Date	Result	Opponent
8/2	L 14-30	vs. Tampa Bay at Tokyo
8/10	W 28-13	Cincinnati
8/16	L 17-22	New Orleans
8/23	W 15-14	at N.Y. Giants
8/28	W 17-9	at Philadelphia

REGULAR SEASON (6-10)

Date	Result	Opponent	Att.
9/4	L 13-16	at Washington	85,420
9/14	L 10-21	Miami	77,461
9/21	L 16-23	at New England	68,436
9/28	L 6-17	Dallas	77,863
10/12	W 30-3	Buffalo	77,740
10/19	W 19-14	at Houston	70,623
10/26	L 17-24	at Philadelphia	67,853
11/2	L 28-31	N.Y. Giants (OT)	78,132
11/9	W 27-24	at Oakland (OT)	51,909
11/16	L 31-38	at Indianapolis	56,801
11/23	W 13-10	Jacksonville	77,614
12/1	W 24-17	Tennessee	77,710
12/7	L 6-17	at Buffalo	72,791
12/14	W 6-0	Pittsburgh	77,900
12/20	L 16-21	New England	77,835
12/28	L 21-23	at Miami	73,720

(OT) Overtime

SCORE BY PERIODS

Jets	70	48	76	86	3	— 283
Opponents	64	130	48	54	3	— 299

2003 TEAM STATISTICS

	Jets	Opp.
Total First Downs	274	316
Rushing	78	134
Passing	181	168
Penalty	15	14
3rd Down: Made/Att	82/206	84/207
3rd Down Pct.	39.8	40.6
4th Down: Made/Att	6/13	10/22
4th Down Pct.	46.2	45.5
Possession Avg.	27:50	32:10
Total Net Yards	4,951	5,319
Avg. Per Game	309.4	332.4
Total Plays	936	1,032
Avg. Per Play	5.3	5.2
Net Yards Rushing	1,635	2,294
Avg. Per Game	102.2	143.4
Total Rushes	409	542
Net Yards Passing	3,316	3,025
Avg. Per Game	207.3	189.1
Sacked/Yards Lost	31/208	35/218
Gross Yards	3,524	3,243
Att./Completions	496/312	455/281
Completion Pct.	62.9	61.8
Had Intercepted	14	11
Punts/Average	72/36.9	66/38.2
Net Punting Avg.	72/31.3	66/32.2
Penalties/Yards	69/550	79/620
Fumbles/Ball Lost	18/6	17/9
Touchdowns	29	34
Rushing	8	17
Passing	20	14
Returns	1	3

2003 INDIVIDUAL STATISTICS

PASSING	Att.	Comp.	Yds.	Pct.	TD	Int.	Tkld.	Rate
Pennington	297	189	2,139	63.6	13	12	25/160	82.9
Testaverde	198	123	1,385	62.1	7	2	6/48	90.6
Stryzinski	1	0	0	0.0	0	0	0/0	39.6
Jets	496	312	3,524	62.9	20	14	31/208	85.8
Opponents	455	281	3,243	61.8	14	11	35/218	83.4

SCORING	TD R	TD P	TD Rt	PAT	FG	Saf	PTS
Brien	0	0	0	24/24	27/32	0	105
Moss	0	10	0	0/0	0/0	0	60
Becht	0	4	0	0/0	0/0	0	26
Jordan	4	0	0	0/0	0/0	0	24
J. Carter	0	1	1	0/0	0/0	0	12
Conway	0	2	0	0/0	0/0	0	12
C. Martin	2	0	0	0/0	0/0	0	12
Pennington	2	0	0	0/0	0/0	0	12
Chrebet	0	1	0	0/0	0/0	0	6
Sowell	0	1	0	0/0	0/0	0	6
Swayne	0	1	0	0/0	0/0	0	6
Jets	8	20	1	24/24	27/32	1	283
Opponents	17	14	3	33/33	20/27	0	299

2-Pt. Conversions: Becht.
Jets 1-5, Opponents 1-1.

RUSHING	No.	Yds	Avg	LG	TD
C. Martin	323	1,308	4.0	56	2
Jordan	46	190	4.1	39	4
Moss	10	67	6.7	25	0
Pennington	21	42	2.0	10t	2
Testaverde	6	17	2.8	13	0
Askew	2	9	4.5	6	0
Sowell	1	2	2.0	2	0
Jets	409	1,635	4.0	56	8
Opponents	542	2,294	4.2	31t	17

RECEIVING	No.	Yds	Avg	LG	TD
Moss	74	1,105	14.9	65t	10
Sowell	47	436	9.3	44	1
Conway	46	640	13.9	45	2
C. Martin	42	262	6.2	29	0
Becht	40	356	8.9	29	4
Chrebet	27	289	10.7	29t	1
Baker	14	137	9.8	24	0
Jordan	11	101	9.2	25	0
Lockett	5	76	15.2	23	0
J. Carter	4	93	23.3	62t	1
Swayne	2	29	14.5	27t	1
Jets	312	3,524	11.3	65t	20
Opponents	281	3,243	11.5	59t	14

INTERCEPTIONS	No.	Yds	Avg	LG	TD
Beasley	3	64	21.3	39	0
T. Carter	2	37	18.5	23	0
Mickens	2	16	8.0	16	0
Garnes	2	0	0.0	0	0
Hobson	1	26	26.0	26	0
D. Abraham	1	12	12.0	12	0
Jets	11	155	14.1	39	0
Opponents	14	164	11.7	55t	2

PUNTING	No.	Yds.	Avg.	In 20	LG
Stryzinski	71	2,655	37.4	22	55
Jets	72	2,655	36.9	22	55
Opponents	66	2,518	38.2	31	56

PUNT RETURNS	Ret	FC	Yds	Avg	LG	TD
Moss	30	18	332	11.1	47	0
Jets	30	18	332	11.1	47	0
Opponents	22	26	322	14.6	78t	1

KICKOFF RETURNS	No.	Yds	Avg	LG	TD
Bates	22	596	27.1	48	0
J. Carter	18	517	28.7	90t	1
Jordan	11	209	19.0	25	0
Swayne	3	48	16.0	23	0
Baker	2	6	3.0	4	0
Johnson	2	50	25.0	29	0
Askew	1	27	27.0	27	0
Machado	1	8	8.0	8	0
Jets	60	1,461	24.4	90t	1
Opponents	71	1,496	21.1	63	0

FIELD GOALS	1-19	20-29	30-39	40-49	50+
Brien	0/0	5/5	15/15	7/8	0/4
Jets	0/0	5/5	15/15	7/8	0/4
Opponents	0/0	9/10	7/9	3/4	1/4

SACKS	No.
Ellis	12.5
J. Abraham	6.0
Ferguson	4.5
Cowart	2.0
Hobson	2.0
Robertson	1.5
Evans	1.0
McGlockton	1.0
Reed	1.0
Thomas	1.0
Garnes	0.5
Jets	35.0
Opponents	31.0

RECORD HOLDERS

INDIVIDUAL RECORDS—CAREER

Category	Name	Performance
Rushing (Yds.)	Freeman McNeil, 1981-1992	8,074
Passing (Yds.)	Joe Namath, 1965-1976	27,057
Passing (TDs)	Joe Namath, 1965-1976	170
Receiving (No.)	Don Maynard, 1960-1972	627
Receiving (Yds.)	Don Maynard, 1960-1972	11,732
Interceptions	Bill Baird, 1963-69	34
Punting (Avg.)	Tom Tupa, 1999-2001	43.1
Punt Return (Avg.)	Dick Christy, 1961-63	16.2
Kickoff Return (Avg.)	Chad Morton, 2001-02	25.0
Field Goals	Pat Leahy, 1974-1991	304
Touchdowns (Tot.)	Don Maynard, 1960-1972	88
Points	Pat Leahy, 1974-1991	1,470

INDIVIDUAL RECORDS—SINGLE SEASON

Category	Name	Performance
Rushing (Yds.)	Curtis Martin, 2001	1,513
Passing (Yds.)	Joe Namath, 1967	4,007
Passing (TDs)	Vinny Testaverde, 1998	29
Receiving (No.)	Al Toon, 1988	93
Receiving (Yds.)	Don Maynard, 1967	1,434
Interceptions	Dainard Paulson, 1964	12
Punting (Avg.)	Curley Johnson, 1965	45.3
Punt Return (Avg.)	Dick Christy, 1961	21.3
Kickoff Return (Avg.)	Bobby Humphery, 1984	30.7
Field Goals	Jim Turner, 1968	34
Touchdowns (Tot.)	Art Powell, 1960	14
	Don Maynard, 1965	14
	Emerson Boozer, 1972	14
Points	Jim Turner, 1968	145

INDIVIDUAL RECORDS—SINGLE GAME

Category	Name	Performance
Rushing (Yds.)	Curtis Martin, 12-3-00	203
Passing (Yds.)	Joe Namath, 9-24-72	496
Passing (TDs)	Joe Namath, 9-24-72	6
Receiving (No.)	Clark Gaines, 9-21-80	17
Receiving (Yds.)	Don Maynard, 11-17-68	228
Interceptions	Many times	3
	Last time by Marcus Coleman, 10-23-00	
Field Goals	Jim Turner, 11-3-68	6
	Bobby Howfield, 12-3-72	6
Touchdowns (Tot.)	Wesley Walker, 9-21-86	4
Points	Wesley Walker, 9-21-86	24

NEW YORK JETS

2004 VETERAN ROSTER

No.	Name	Pos.	Ht.	Wt.	Birthdate	NFL Exp.	College	Hometown	How Acq.	'03 Games/ Starts
29	Abraham, Donnie	CB	5-10	192	10/8/73	9	East Tennessee State	Orangeburg, S.C.	UFA(TB)-'02	8/2
94	Abraham, John	DE	6-4	256	5/6/78	5	South Carolina	Lamar, S.C.	D1b-'00	7/5
35	Askew, B.J.	FB	6-3	233	8/19/80	2	Michigan	Cincinnati, Ohio	D3-'03	16/0
86	Baker, Chris	TE	6-3	258	11/18/79	3	Michigan State	Queens, N.Y.	D3-'02	16/0
36	Barrett, David	CB	5-10	195	12/22/77	5	Arkansas	Osceola, Ark.	UFA(Ariz)-'04	16/16*
50	Barton, Eric	LB	6-2	245	9/29/77	6	Maryland	Alexandria, Va.	UFA(Oak)-'04	16/16*
88	Becht, Anthony	TE	6-5	272	8/8/77	5	West Virginia	Drexel Hill, Pa.	D1d-'00	16/16
5	Bollinger, Brooks	QB	6-0	205	11/15/79	2	Wisconsin	Grand Forks, N.D.	D6-'03	0*
6	Brien, Doug	K	6-0	180	11/24/70	11	California	Danville, Calif.	FA-'03	16/0
84	Carter, Jonathan	WR-KR	6-0	180	3/20/79	3	Troy State	Lineville, Ala.	W(NYG)-'02	9/0
66	Chevrier, Randy	DT-LS	6-2	291	6/6/76	2	McGill	Quebec, Canada	FA-'04	0*
80	Chrebet, Wayne	WR	5-10	188	8/14/73	10	Hofstra	Garfield, N.J.	FA-'95	7/5
56	Cowart, Sam	LB	6-2	245	2/26/75	7	Florida State	Jacksonville, Fla.	UFA(Buff)-'02	15/15
85	Dearth, James	TE-LS	6-4	270	1/22/76	4	Tarleton State	Scurry, Texas	FA-'01	16/0
9	Dominguez, Matt	WR	6-2	220	6/27/78	2	Sam Houston State	Georgetown, Texas	FA-'04	0*
92	Ellis, Shaun	DE	6-5	294	6/24/77	5	Tennessee	Anderson, S.C.	D1a-'00	16/16
91	Evans, Josh	DT	6-3	280	9/6/72	9	Alabama-Birmingham	West Shaumut, Ala.	UFA(Tenn)-'02	6/0
69	Fabini, Jason	T	6-7	304	8/25/74	7	Cincinnati	Ft. Wayne, Ind.	D4-'98	16/16
72	Ferguson, Jason	DT	6-3	305	11/28/74	8	Georgia	Nettleton, Miss.	D7b-'97	16/16
58	Glenn, Jason	LB	6-0	231	8/20/79	4	Texas A&M	Humble, Texas	W(Det)-'01	14/1
78	Goodwin, Jonathan	G	6-3	318	12/2/78	3	Michigan	Columbia, S.C.	D5-'02	15/0
4	Gowin, Toby	P	5-10	167	3/30/75	8	North Texas	Coppell, Texas	FA-'04	16/0*
87	Hamilton, Lawrence	WR	6-2	204	8/31/80	2	Stephen F. Austin	Marshall, Texas	FA-'03	5/1
98	Harper, Alan	DT	6-1	285	9/6/79	3	Fresno State	Fontana, Calif.	FA-'03	0*
23	Henderson, Jamie	CB	6-2	202	1/1/79	4	Georgia	Carrollton, Ga.	D4-'01	14/0
54	Hobson, Victor	LB	6-0	252	2/3/80	2	Michigan	Mt. Laurel, N.J.	D2-'03	16/1
34	Jordan, LaMont	RB-KR	5-10	230	11/11/78	4	Maryland	Forestville, Md.	D2-'01	16/0
21	Lowe, Omare	CB	6-1	195	4/20/78	3	Washington	Seattle, Wash.	FA-'03	2/0
28	Martin, Curtis	RB	5-11	205	5/1/73	10	Pittsburgh	Pittsburgh, Pa.	RFA(NE)-'98	16/16
68	Mawae, Kevin	C	6-4	305	1/23/71	11	Louisiana State	Leesville, La.	UFA(Sea)-'98	16/16
81	t-McCareins, Justin	WR	6-2	215	12/11/78	4	Northern Illinois	Naperville, Ill.	T(Tenn)-'04	16/10
38	McGraw, Jon	S	6-3	206	4/2/79	3	Kansas State	Manhattan, Kan.	D2-'02	6/6
67	McKenzie, Kareem	T	6-6	327	5/24/79	4	Penn State	Willingboro, N.J.	D3-'01	16/16
24	Mickens, Ray	CB	5-8	180	1/4/73	9	Texas A&M	El Paso, Texas	D3-'96	16/14
65	Moore, Brandon	G	6-3	295	6/3/80	2	Illinois	Gary, Ind.	FA-'03	3/1
83	Moss, Santana	WR-KR	5-10	185	6/1/79	4	Miami	Miami, Fla.	D1-'01	16/12
70	Nimmo, Lance	T	6-5	303	9/13/79	2	West Virginia	New Castle, Pa.	W(TB)-'03	0*
20	Pagel, Derek	S	6-1	208	10/24/79	2	Iowa	Plainfield, Iowa	D5a-'03	14/0
10	Pennington, Chad	QB	6-3	225	6/26/76	5	Marshall	Knoxville, Tenn.	D1c-'00	10/9
82	Rambo, Ken-Yon	WR-KR	6-1	195	10/4/78	3	Ohio State	Long Beach, Calif.	FA-'03	0*
93	Reed, James	DT	6-0	286	2/3/77	4	Iowa State	Saginaw, Mich.	D7a-'01	16/0
63	Robertson, Dewayne	DT	6-1	317	10/16/81	2	Kentucky	Memphis, Tenn.	D1-'03	16/16
74	Smith, Brent	G-T	6-5	305	11/21/73	8	Mississippi State	Pontotoc, Miss.	UFA(Mia)-'03	16/16
33	Sowell, Jerald	FB	6-0	237	1/21/74	8	Tulane	Baker, La.	W(GB)-'97	16/16
51	Stewart, Quincy	LB	6-1	234	3/27/78	4	Louisiana Tech	Tyler, Texas	FA-'03	12/0
99	Thomas, Bryan	DE	6-4	266	6/7/79	3	Alabama Birmingham	Birmingham, Ala.	D1-'02	16/10
25	Tongue, Reggie	S	6-0	204	4/11/73	9	Oregon State	Baltimore, Md.	UFA(Sea)-'04	14/14*
95	Walters, Matt	DE	6-5	272	8/22/79	2	Miami	Melbourne, Fla.	D5b-'03	11/0
52	Wright, Kenyatta	LB	6-0	240	2/19/78	4	Oklahoma State	Vian, Okla.	FA-'03	16/0
64	Yovanovits, Dave	G	6-3	294	3/6/81	2	Temple	Stanhope, N.J.	D7-'03	0*

* Barrett played 16 games with Arizona in '03; Barton played 16 games with Oakland; Bollinger did not play in 6 games; Chevrier last with Cincinnati in '01; Dominguez last with Denver in '02; Gowin played 16 games with Dallas; Harper inactive for 7 games; Nimmo inactive for 16 games; Rambo inactive for 3 games; Tongue played 14 games with Seattle; Yovanovits inactive for 16 games.

t- Jets traded for McCareins (Tenn).

Retired—Dave Szott, 14-year guard, 15 games in '03.

Also played for Jets in '03—KR Michael Bates (8 games), CB Aaron Beasley (16), LB Khary Campbell (4), S Tyrone Carter (16), WR Curtis Conway (16), S Sam Garnes (16), LB Marvin Jones (16), LB Mo Lewis (15), WR Kevin Lockett (3), C J.P. Machado (16), DT Chester McGlockton (16), CB Jacoby Shepherd (4), P Dan Stryzinski (16), WR Kevin Swayne (15), QB Vinny Testaverde (7), S David Young (5).

2004 FIRST-YEAR ROSTER

Name	Pos.	Ht.	Wt.	Birthdate	College	Hometown	How Acq.
Bautovich, Wes (1)	LB	6-2	210	8/18/79	Texas A&M	Arlington, Texas	FA
Brinker, Chad (1)	RB-KR	5-10	205	11/5/79	Ohio	Martins Ferry, Ohio	FA
Brown, Mark (1)	LB	6-0	238	5/19/80	Auburn	Germantown, Tenn.	FA-'03
Carter, Michael	TE	6-2	251	12/3/80	Chapman	Reno Valley, Calif.	FA
Cavka, Marko	T	6-7	294	4/4/81	Sacramento State	Cypress, Calif.	D6
Coleman, Erik	S	5-10	200	5/6/82	Washington State	Spokane, Wash.	D5
Cotchery, Jerricho	WR	6-0	207	6/16/82	North Carolina State	Birmingham, Ala.	D4a
Davis, Josh	RB	5-10	200	10/11/80	Nebraska	Loveland, Colo.	FA
Evans, Joey (1)	DE	6-4	279	8/22/79	North Carolina	Fayetteville, N.C.	FA
Finlen, Chris (1)	QB	6-3	200	5/19/79	Northern Illinois	Roscoe, Ill.	FA
Flowers, Little John (1)	RB	6-0	215	1/31/80	Michigan State	Kalamazoo, Mich.	FA
Foschi, John Paul	TE	6-4	268	5/19/82	Georgia Tech	Atlanta, Ga.	FA
Fuata, Lui (1)	C-G	6-2	313	7/18/80	Hawaii	Honolulu, Hawaii	FA-'03
Johnson, Trevor	DE	6-4	260	2/26/81	Nebraska	Lincoln, Neb.	D7b
Jones, Adrian	T	6-4	296	6/10/81	Kansas	Dallas, Texas	D4b
Kearney, Carl	WR	6-1	213	2/16/81	Georgia Southern	Griffin, Ga.	FA
Keith, Kenton	RB	5-11	189	6/14/80	New Mexico State	Omaha, Neb.	FA
Klein, Kory	DT	6-2	288	6/4/81	Oklahoma	Tulsa, Okla.	FA
Knutson, Matt (1)	T	6-7	315	6/14/79	North Dakota	Minot, N.D.	FA
Lee, Derrick	WR	6-5	215	9/26/81	Tennessee Tech	Atlanta, Ga.	FA
McClover, Darrell	LB	6-2	226	8/25/81	Miami	Fort Lauderdale, Fla.	D7a
Moore, Muneer (1)	WR	6-1	200	3/15/77	Richmond	Yonkers, N.Y.	FA
Morgan, Donovan	WR	6-3	195	7/29/82	Pearl River (Miss.) C.C.	New Orleans, La.	FA
Myers, Ryan	LB	6-2	245	2/27/80	Akron	Wallington, Ohio	FA
Nerys, Jason	G	6-3	305	6/16/81	Delaware	Waldwick, N.J.	FA
Pendergrass, Jon (1)	S	6-1	215	10/7/78	Southern Illinois	Torrejon, Spain	FA
Ray, Ricky (1)	QB	6-3	210	10/22/79	Sacramento State	Shasta, Calif.	FA
Reese, Johnathan (1)	RB	6-1	220	4/15/80	Columbia	St. Louis, Mo.	FA
Roderick, Bryant	CB	6-1	185	2/17/81	Idaho	Washington, D.C.	FA
Shuler, Alonzo (1)	DT	6-3	310	7/19/77	Benedict	Newark, N.J.	FA
Simnjanovski, Brian (1)	P	6-3	205	5/29/81	San Diego State	Escondido, Calif.	FA
Smart, Ian (1)	RB-KR	5-8	192	2/28/80	C.W. Post	Wyandanch, N.Y.	FA
Strait, Derrick	CB	5-11	189	8/27/80	Oklahoma	Austin, Texas	D3
Stubbs, Terrance	WR	5-11	190	3/25/80	Temple	Chesapeake, Va.	FA
Sykes, Gerald	G	6-2	310	2/23/81	San Diego State	San Diego, Calif.	FA
Thomas, Art	CB	6-2	205	9/24/79	Virginia	Mechanicsburg, Pa.	FA
Vilma, Jonathan	LB	6-0	223	4/16/82	Miami	South Miami, Fla.	D1
Ward, Derrick	RB	5-11	233	8/30/80	Ottawa (Kan.)	Los Angeles, Calif.	D7c
Washington, Rashad	S	6-1	217	3/15/80	Kansas State	Wichita, Kan.	D7d
Weaver, Jerrell	S	6-3	205	12/28/80	Miami	Miami, Fla.	FA
Westbrook, Brandon	G-T	6-5	320	12/17/80	Middle Tennessee State	Cummings, Ga.	FA
Young, Sean	T-G	6-6	317	12/1/81	Tennessee	Cohutta, Ga.	FA

The term NFL Rookie is defined as a player who is in his first season of professional football and has not been on the roster of another professional football team for any regular-season or postseason games. A Rookie is designated by an "R" on NFL rosters. Players who have been active in another professional football league or players who have NFL experience, including either preseason training camp or being on an Active List or Inactive List, or on Reserve/Injured or Reserve/Physically Unable to Perform for fewer than six regular-season games, are termed NFL First-Year Players. An NFL First-Year Player is designated by a "1" on NFL rosters. Thereafter, a player is credited with an additional year of experience for each season in which he accumulates six games on the Active List or Inactive List, or on Reserve/Injured or Reserve/Physically Unable to Perform.

Log on to www.newyorkjets.com for an up-to-date roster.

NEW YORK JETS

COACHING STAFF

Head Coach,
Herman Edwards

Pro Career: On January 28, 2001, Edwards was named the Jets' thirteenth full-time head coach. Edwards previously served as the assistant head coach-defensive backs coach for Tampa Bay (1996-2000). Last season, the Jets won the AFC East and posted the biggest post-season victory (41-0) in club history. In 2001, he led the Jets to a 10-6 regular-season mark and became the first head coach in team history to make the play-offs in his first season. Before joining Tampa Bay, Edwards worked for the Kansas City Chiefs for six seasons (1990-95) in several different roles. He began his pro coaching career as a participant of the NFL's Minority Coaching Fellowship program with the Kansas City Chiefs in the summer of 1989. Career record: 26-25.

Background: Played cornerback collegiately for California (1972, 1974), Monterrey Peninsula (Calif.) J.C. (1973), and San Diego State (1975-76). Played in NFL for Philadelphia Eagles (1977-1985), Los Angeles Rams (1986), and Atlanta Falcons (1986). He was defensive backs coach at San Jose State (1987-89).

Personal: Born April 27, 1954, Monmouth, N.J. Edwards and his wife Lia have one son, Marcus.

ASSISTANT COACHES

Sal Alosi, asst. strength and conditioning; born May 11, 1977, Massapequa, N.Y. Linebacker Hofstra 1996-2000. No pro playing experience. College coach: Hofstra 2001. Pro coach: Joined Jets in 2002.

Tim Berbenich, offensive assistant; born December 19, 1979, Huntington, N.Y. Wide receiver Hamilton College 1998-2001. No pro playing experience. Pro coach: Joined Jets in 2003.

Corwin Brown, asst. special teams/asst. defensive backs; born April 25, 1970, Chicago. Safety Michigan 1989-1992. Pro safety New England Patriots 1993-96, New York Jets 1997-98, Detroit Lions 1999-2000. College coach: Virginia 2001-03. Pro coach: Joined Jets in 2004.

Bob Casullo, tight ends; born March 24, 1951, Little Falls, N.Y. Running back Brockport State College 1970-73. No pro playing experience. College coach: Syracuse 1985-1994, Georgia Tech 1995-98, Michigan State 1999. Pro coach: Oakland Raiders 2000-03, joined Jets in 2004.

Dick Curl, senior offensive assistant/special projects; born May 4, 1940, Chester, Pa. Quarterback Richmond 1959-62. No pro playing experience. College coach: Trenton State 1973-74 (head coach 1974), Rutgers 1975-79, 1982-88, Virginia 1980-81, Boston College 1989-1990. Pro coach: Barcelona Dragons (NFLEL) 1991-97, Frankfurt Galaxy (NFLEL) 1998-99 (head coach), joined Jets in 2003.

Doug Graber, defensive backs; born September 26, 1944, Detroit. Defensive back Wayne State 1963-66. No pro playing experience. College coach: Michigan Tech 1969-1971, Eastern Michigan 1972-75, Ball State 1976-77, Wisconsin 1978-1981, Montana State 1982 (head coach), Rutgers 1990-95 (head coach). Pro coach: Kansas City Chiefs 1983-86, Tampa Bay Buccaneers 1987-89, Frankfurt Galaxy (NFLEL) 2001-03 (head coach), joined Jets in 2004.

Paul Hackett, offensive coordinator; born July 5, 1947, Burlington, Vt. Quarterback Cal-Davis 1965-68. No pro playing experience. College coach: Cal-Davis 1969-1971, California 1972-75, Southern California 1976-1980, 1998-2000 (head coach 1998-2000), Pittsburgh 1989-1992 (head coach 1990-92). Pro coach: Cleveland Browns 1981-82, San Francisco 49ers 1983-85, Dallas Cowboys 1986-88, Kansas City Chiefs 1993-97, joined Jets in 2001.

Pep Hamilton, offensive quality control; born September 19, 1974, Charlotte. Quarterback Howard 1993-96. No pro playing experience. College coach: Howard 1997-2002. Pro coach: Joined Jets in 2003.

Bishop Harris, running backs; born November 23, 1941, Phenix City, Ala. Running back-defensive back North Carolina College 1960-63. No pro playing experience. College coach: Duke 1972-75, North Carolina State 1977-79, Louisiana State 1980-83, Notre Dame 1984-85, Minnesota 1986-1990, North Carolina Central 1991-92 (head coach). Pro coach: Denver Broncos 1993-94, Oakland Raiders 1995-97, Buffalo Bills 1998-99, joined Jets in 2001.

Donnie Henderson, defensive coordinator; born May 17, 1957, Baltimore. Defensive back Utah State 1978-79. No pro playing experience. College coach: Utah State 1983-88, Idaho 1989, California 1990-91, Arizona State 1992-97, Houston 1998. Pro coach: Baltimore Ravens 1999-2003, joined Jets in 2004.

Jim Hostler, quarterbacks; born November 11, 1966, Pittsburgh. Defensive back Indiana (Penn.) 1986-89. No pro playing experience. College coach: Indiana (Penn.) 1990-92, 1994-99, Juanita (Penn.) 1993. Pro coach: Kansas City Chiefs 2000, New Orleans Saints 2001-02, joined Jets in 2003.

John Lott, strength and conditioning; born May 9, 1964, Denton, Texas. Offensive lineman North Texas 1983-86. Pro offensive lineman Pittsburgh Steelers 1987. College coach: North Texas 1990, Houston 1991-96. Pro coach: Joined Jets in 1997.

Denny Marcin, defensive line; born April 24, 1942, Cleveland. Defensive-offensive lineman Miami (Ohio) 1960-63. No pro playing experience. College coach: Miami (Ohio) 1974-77, North Carolina 1978-1987, Illinois 1988-1996. Pro coach: New York Giants 1997-2003, joined Jets in 2004.

Doug Marrone, offensive line; born July 25, 1964, Bronx, N.Y. Offensive lineman Syracuse 1982-86. Pro offensive lineman Miami Dolphins 1987, New Orleans Saints 1989, London Monarchs (NFLE) 1992. College coach: Cortland State 1992, U.S. Coast Guard 1993, Northeastern 1994, Georgia Tech 1995-99, Georgia 2000, Tennessee 2001. Pro coach: Joined Jets in 2002.

Bob Sutton, linebackers; born January 28, 1951, Ypsilanti, Mich. Attended Eastern Michigan. No college or pro playing experience. College coach: Michigan 1972-73, Syracuse 1974, Western Michigan 1975-76, 1980-81, Illinois 1977-79, North Carolina State 1982, Army 1983-1999 (head coach 1991-99). Pro coach: Joined Jets in 2000.

Nate Wainwright, asst. coach; born July 28, 1975, Iowa City, Iowa. Attended Iowa. No college or pro playing experience. Pro coach: Joined Jets in 2002.

Mike Westhoff, asst. head coach/special teams coordinator; born January 10, 1948, Pittsburgh. Center-linebacker Wichita State 1967-69. No pro playing experience. College coach: Indiana 1974-75, Dayton 1976, Indiana State 1977, Northwestern 1978-1980, Texas Christian 1981. Pro coach: Baltimore/Indianapolis Colts 1982-84, Arizona Outlaws (USFL) 1985, Miami Dolphins 1986-2000, joined Jets in 2001.

American Football Conference
West Division
Team Colors: Silver and Black
1220 Harbor Bay Parkway
Alameda, California 94502
Telephone: (510) 864-5000

2004 SCHEDULE

PRESEASON		Oakland time
Aug. 14	at San Francisco	5:00
Aug. 21	**Dallas**	6:00
Aug. 28	at Arizona	7:00
Sept. 2	**St. Louis**	7:00

REGULAR SEASON		
Sept. 12	at Pittsburgh	10:00*
Sept. 19	**Buffalo**	1:15
Sept. 26	**Tampa Bay**	5:30
Oct. 3	at Houston	10:00*
Oct. 10	at Indianapolis	1:05
Oct. 17	**Denver**	1:15
Oct. 24	**New Orleans**	1:15
Oct. 31	at San Diego	1:15
Nov. 7	at Carolina	10:00*
Nov. 14	Open Date	
Nov. 21	**San Diego**	1:05
Nov. 28	at Denver	5:30
Dec. 5	**Kansas City**	1:05
Dec. 12	at Atlanta	10:00*
Dec. 19	**Tennessee**	1:15
Dec. 25	at Kansas City (Sat.)	2:00
Jan. 2	**Jacksonville**	1:15

*A.M.

Stadium: Network Associates Coliseum (opened in 1966)
• **Capacity:** 63,132
7000 Coliseum Way
Oakland, CA 94621-1917
Playing Surface: Grass
Training Camp: Napa Valley Marriott
Napa, California 94558

NETWORK ASSOCIATES COLISEUM

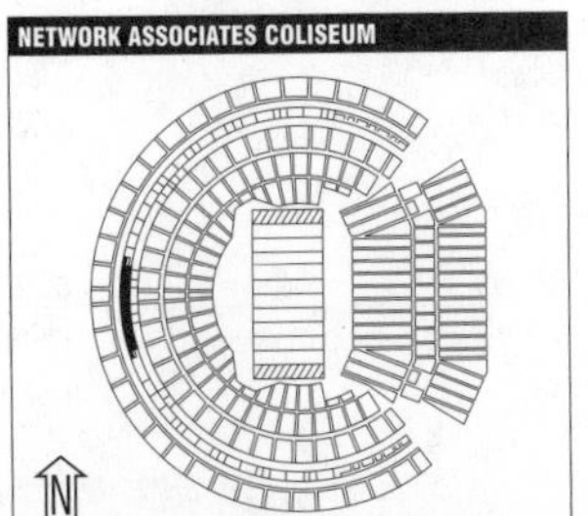

CLUB OFFICIALS

Owner: Al Davis
Chief Executive: Amy Trask
Personnel Executive: Mike Lombardi
General Counsel: Jeff Birren
Finance: Marc Badain, Tom Blanda, Derek Person, Ed Villanueva
Special Projects: Jim Otto
Senior Executive: John Herrera
Public Relations: Mike Taylor, Craig Long, Zac Emmons
Ticket Operations: Peter Eiges
Hispanic Initiatives: Patty Herrera, Elena Valenzuela
Internet: Jerry Knaak
Suites: Andrea Stamps, Mattie Lindsey
Marketing/Promotions/Community/ Business Relations: Morris Bradshaw, Dawn Roberts, Scott Fink, Karen Kovac
Trainers: H. Rod Martin, Scott Touchet, Mark Mayer
Equipment: Bob Romanski, Dick Romanski, Danny Molina
Video Operations: Dave Nash, Jim Otten, John Otten

COACHING HISTORY

Oakland 1960-1981
Los Angeles 1982-1994
(410-282-11)

1960-61	Eddie Erdelatz*	6-10-0
1961-62	Marty Feldman**	2-15-0
1962	Red Conkright	1-8-0
1963-65	Al Davis	23-16-3
1966-68	John Rauch	35-10-1
1969-1978	John Madden	112-39-7
1979-1987	Tom Flores	91-56-0
1988-89	Mike Shanahan***	8-12-0
1989-1994	Art Shell	56-41-0
1995-96	Mike White	15-17-0
1997	Joe Bugel	4-12-0
1998-2001	Jon Gruden	40-28-0
2002-03	Bill Callahan	17-18-0

*Released after two games in 1961
**Released after five games in 1962
***Released after four games in 1989

ATTENDANCE

Home 425,503 Away 545,420
Total 970,923
Single-game home record, 62,660 (11/3/02)
Single-season home record, 471,151 (2002)

2004 DRAFT CHOICES

Round	Name	Pos.	College
1	Robert Gallery	T	Iowa
2	Jake Grove	C	Virginia Tech
3	Stuart Schweigert	DB	Purdue
4	Carlos Francis	WR	Texas Tech
5	Johnnie Morant	WR	Syracuse
6	Shawn Johnson	DE	Delaware
	Cody Spencer	LB	North Texas
7	Courtney Anderson	TE	San Jose State
	Andre Sommersell	LB	Colorado State

OAKLAND RAIDERS

2003 TEAM RECORD

PRESEASON (1-3)

Date	Result	Opponent
8/8	W 7-6	St. Louis
8/14	L 10-14	at San Francisco
8/22	L 6-21	Minnesota
8/28	L 13-52	at Dallas

REGULAR SEASON (4-12)

Date	Result	Opponent	Att.
9/7	L 20-25	at Tennessee	68,809
9/14	W 23-20	Cincinnati	50,135
9/22	L 10-31	at Denver	76,753
9/28	W 34-31	San Diego (OT)	54,078
10/5	L 21-24	at Chicago	61,099
10/12	L 7-13	at Cleveland	73,318
10/20	L 10-17	Kansas City	62,391
11/2	L 13-23	at Detroit	61,561
11/9	L 24-27	New York Jets (OT)	51,909
11/16	W 28-18	Minnesota	56,653
11/23	L 24-27	at Kansas City	78,889
11/30	L 8-22	Denver	57,201
12/7	L 7-27	at Pittsburgh	53,079
12/14	W 20-12	Baltimore	45,398
12/22	L 7-41	Green Bay	62,298
12/28	L 14-21	at San Diego	62,222

(OT) Overtime

SCORE BY PERIODS

Raiders	76	81	31	79	3	— 270
Opponents	99	110	59	108	3	— 379

2003 TEAM STATISTICS

	Raiders	Opp.
Total First Downs	258	317
Rushing	98	127
Passing	140	159
Penalty	20	31
3rd Down: Made/Att	66/217	80/215
3rd Down Pct.	30.4	37.2
4th Down: Made/Att	14/25	8/14
4th Down Pct.	56.0	57.1
Possession Avg.	27:41	32:19
Total Net Yards	4,573	5,904
Avg. Per Game	285.8	369.0
Total Plays	987	1,036
Avg. Per Play	4.6	5.7
Net Yards Rushing	1,822	2,510
Avg. Per Game	113.9	156.9
Total Rushes	423	544
Net Yards Passing	2,751	3,394
Avg. Per Game	171.9	212.1
Sacked/Yards Lost	43/237	25/162
Gross Yards	2,988	3,556
Att./Completions	521/278	467/286
Completion Pct.	53.4	61.2
Had Intercepted	14	14
Punts/Average	96/46.9	82/39.9
Net Punting Avg.	96/37.2	82/31.0
Penalties/Yards	134/1,120	115/981
Fumbles/Ball Lost	25/12	24/11
Touchdowns	29	42
Rushing	15	21
Passing	9	21
Returns	5	0

2003 INDIVIDUAL STATISTICS

PASSING	Att.	Comp.	Yds.	Pct.	TD	Int.	Tkld.	Rate
Gannon	225	125	1,274	55.6	6	4	17/90	73.5
Mirer	221	116	1,267	52.5	3	5	22/122	64.8
Tuiasosopo	45	25	324	55.6	0	3	2/14	50.6
Martin	16	6	69	37.5	0	1	1/5	25.3
R. Johnson	13	6	54	46.2	0	1	1/6	25.8
Rice	1	0	0	0.0	0	0	0/0	39.6
Raiders	521	278	2,988	53.4	9	14	43/237	65.0
Opponents	467	286	3,556	61.2	21	14	25/162	87.3

SCORING	TD R	TD P	TD Rt	PAT	FG	Saf	PTS
Janikowski	0	0	0	28/29	22/25	0	94
Crockett	7	0	0	0/0	0/0	0	42
Buchanon	0	0	4	0/0	0/0	0	24
Garner	3	1	0	0/0	0/0	0	24
Wheatley	4	0	0	0/0	0/0	0	24
Brown	0	2	0	0/0	0/0	0	12
Rice	0	2	0	0/0	0/0	0	12
Gabriel	0	0	1	0/0	0/0	0	6
Te. Johnson	0	1	0	0/0	0/0	0	6
Jolley	0	1	0	0/0	0/0	0	6
Mirer	1	0	0	0/0	0/0	0	6
Porter	0	1	0	0/0	0/0	0	6
Whitted	0	1	0	0/0	0/0	0	6
Raiders	15	9	5	28/29	22/25	1	270
Opponents	21	21	0	35/36	28/34	0	379

2-Pt. Conversions: None.
Raiders 0-0, Opponents 4-6.

RUSHING	No.	Yds	Avg	LG	TD
Wheatley	159	678	4.3	41	4
Garner	120	553	4.6	33	3
Fargas	40	203	5.1	53	0
Crockett	48	145	3.0	44	7
Mirer	20	83	4.2	20	1
Whitted	6	37	6.2	16	0
Redmond	9	30	3.3	9	0
Martin	5	28	5.6	8	0
Tuiasosopo	6	22	3.7	8	0
Gannon	6	18	3.0	6	0
R. Johnson	2	15	7.5	14	0
Porter	1	10	10.0	10	0
Curry	1	0	0.0	0	0
Raiders	423	1,822	4.3	53	15
Opponents	544	2,510	4.6	55t	21

RECEIVING	No.	Yds	Avg	LG	TD
Rice	63	869	13.8	47t	2
Brown	52	567	10.9	36t	2
Garner	48	386	8.0	46t	1
Jolley	31	250	8.1	26	1
Porter	28	361	12.9	35	1
Te. Johnson	14	128	9.1	21	1
Wheatley	12	120	10.0	25	0
Whitted	7	106	15.1	36t	1
Crockett	7	53	7.6	16	0
Santiago	5	69	13.8	36	0
Curry	5	31	6.2	16	0
Hetherington	2	23	11.5	17	0
Fargas	2	2	1.0	6	0
Gabriel	1	17	17.0	17	0
Redmond	1	6	6.0	6	0
Raiders	278	2,988	10.7	47t	9
Opponents	286	3,556	12.4	65t	21

INTERCEPTIONS	No.	Yds	Avg	LG	TD
Buchanon	6	176	29.3	83t	2
C. Woodson	3	67	22.3	51	0
R. Woodson	2	18	9.0	13	0
Gibson	2	16	8.0	11	0
E. Johnson	1	3	3.0	3	0
Raiders	14	280	20.0	83t	2
Opponents	14	132	9.4	43	0

PUNTING	No.	Yds.	Avg.	In 20	LG
Lechler	96	4,503	46.9	27	73
Raiders	96	4,503	46.9	27	73
Opponents	82	3,271	39.9	22	61

PUNT RETURNS	Ret	FC	Yds	Avg	LG	TD
Buchanon	36	14	491	13.6	80t	2
Dorsett	1	0	0	0.0	0	0
E. Johnson	1	0	1	1.0	1	0
Raiders	38	14	492	12.9	80t	2
Opponents	52	14	669	12.9	54	0

KICKOFF RETURNS	No.	Yds	Avg	LG	TD
Gabriel	29	646	22.3	85t	1
Jenkins	25	553	22.1	33	0
Fargas	16	315	19.7	32	0
Whitted	4	48	12.0	18	0
Buchanon	2	25	12.5	17	0
Santiago	1	9	9.0	9	0
Raiders	77	1,596	20.7	85t	1
Opponents	57	1,474	25.9	61	0

FIELD GOALS	1-19	20-29	30-39	40-49	50+
Janikowski	0/0	6/6	6/6	9/10	1/3
Raiders	0/0	6/6	6/6	9/10	1/3
Opponents	0/0	4/4	13/14	7/10	4/6

SACKS	No.
Coleman	5.5
Armstrong	3.0
Brayton	2.5
Cooper	2.5
Bromell	2.0
Harris	2.0
Romanowski	2.0
Gbaja-Biamila	1.0
Gibson	1.0
Grant	1.0
Smith	1.0
C. Woodson	1.0
Barton	0.5
Raiders	25.0
Opponents	43.0

RECORD HOLDERS

INDIVIDUAL RECORDS—CAREER

Category	Name	Performance
Rushing (Yds.)	Marcus Allen, 1982-1992	8,545
Passing (Yds.)	Ken Stabler, 1970-79	19,078
Passing (TDs)	Ken Stabler, 1970-79	150
Receiving (No.)	Tim Brown, 1988-2003	1,070
Receiving (Yds.)	Tim Brown, 1988-2003	14,734
Interceptions	Willie Brown, 1967-1978	39
	Lester Hayes, 1977-1986	39
Punting (Avg.)	Shane Lechler, 2000-03	45.7
Punt Return (Avg.)	Claude Gibson, 1963-65	12.6
Kickoff Return (Avg.)	Jack Larscheid, 1960-61	28.4
Field Goals	Chris Bahr, 1980-88	162
Touchdowns (Tot.)	Tim Brown, 1988-2003	104
Points	George Blanda, 1967-1975	863

INDIVIDUAL RECORDS—SINGLE SEASON

Category	Name	Performance
Rushing (Yds.)	Marcus Allen, 1985	1,759
Passing (Yds.)	Rich Gannon, 2002	4,689
Passing (TDs)	Daryle Lamonica, 1969	34
Receiving (No.)	Tim Brown 1997	104
Receiving (Yds.)	Tim Brown, 1997	1,408
Interceptions	Lester Hayes, 1980	13
Punting (Avg.)	Shane Lechler, 2003	46.9
Punt Return (Avg.)	Claude Gibson, 1964	14.4
Kickoff Return (Avg.)	Harold Hart, 1975	30.5
Field Goals	Jeff Jaeger, 1993	35
Touchdowns (Tot.)	Marcus Allen, 1984	18
Points	Jeff Jaeger, 1993	132

INDIVIDUAL RECORDS—SINGLE GAME

Category	Name	Performance
Rushing (Yds.)	Napoleon Kaufman, 10-19-97	227
Passing (Yds.)	Cotton Davidson, 10-25-64	427
Passing (TDs)	Tom Flores, 12-22-63	6
	Daryle Lamonica, 10-19-69	6
Receiving (No.)	Tim Brown, 12-21-97	14
Receiving (Yds.)	Art Powell, 12-22-63	247
Interceptions	Many times	3
	Last time by Rod Woodson, 9-29-02	
Field Goals	Jeff Jaeger, 12-11-94	5
	Sebastian Janikowski, 10-29-00	5
Touchdowns (Tot.)	Art Powell, 12-22-63	4
	Marcus Allen, 9-24-84	4
	Harvey Williams, 11-16-97	4
Points	Art Powell, 12-22-63	24
	Marcus Allen, 9-24-84	24
	Harvey Williams, 11-16-97	24

OAKLAND RAIDERS

2004 VETERAN ROSTER

No.	Name	Pos.	Ht.	Wt.	Birthdate	NFL Exp.	College	Hometown	How Acq.	'03 Games/ Starts
21	Asomugha, Nnamdi	CB	6-2	210	7/6/81	2	California	Los Angeles, Calif.	D1-'03	15/1
70	Badger, Brad	G-T	6-4	320	1/11/75	8	Stanford	Corvallis, Ore.	UFA(Minn)-'02	16/11
91	Brayton, Tyler	DE	6-6	280	11/20/79	2	Colorado	Pasco, Wash.	D1-'03	16/16
	Brooks, Bobby	LB	6-2	240	3/3/76	3	Fresno State	Vallejo, Calif.	FA-'04	0*
81	Brown, Tim	WR	6-0	195	7/22/66	17	Notre Dame	Dallas, Texas	D1-'88	16/15
34	Buchanan, Ray	CB-S	5-9	185	9/29/71	12	Louisville	Chicago, Ill.	FA-'04	15/8*
31	Buchanon, Philip	CB	5-10	185	9/19/80	3	Miami	Miami, Fla.	D1-'02	16/11
23	Charlton, Ike	CB	6-0	205	10/6/77	5	Virginia Tech	Orlando, Fla.	UFA(NYG)-'04	7/2*
55	Clark, Danny	LB	6-2	245	5/9/77	5	Illinois	Blue Island, Ill.	UFA(Jax)-'04	16/8*
16	Cole, Chris	WR	6-0	195	11/12/77	5	Texas A&M	Orange, Texas	UFA(Den)-'04	11/0*
5	Collins, Kerry	QB	6-5	245	12/30/72	10	Penn State	Lebanon, Pa.	FA-'04	13/13*
79	Collins, Mo	G	6-4	325	9/22/76	7	Florida	Charlotte, N.C.	D1-'98	10/10
75	Cooper, Chris	DT	6-5	275	12/27/77	4	Nebraska-Omaha	Lincoln, Neb.	D6-'01	16/9
32	Crockett, Zack	FB	6-2	240	12/2/72	10	Florida State	Pompano Beach, Fla.	UFA(Jax)-'99	16/7
89	Curry, Ronald	WR	6-2	220	5/28/79	2	North Carolina	Hampton, Va.	D7-'02	16/2
20	Fargas, Justin	RB	6-1	220	1/25/80	2	Southern California	Sherman Oaks, Calif.	D3-'03	10/1
85	Gabriel, Doug	WR	6-2	215	8/27/80	2	Central Florida	Orlando, Fla.	D5-'03	12/0
12	Gannon, Rich	QB	6-3	210	12/20/65	17	Delaware	Philadelphia, Pa.	UFA(KC)-'99	7/7
98	Gbaja-Biamila, Akbar	DE	6-5	270	5/6/79	2	San Diego State	Los Angeles, Calif.	FA-'03	14/0
36	Gibson, Derrick	S	6-2	215	3/22/79	4	Florida State	Miami, Fla.	D1-'01	15/14
59	Grant, DeLawrence	LB	6-3	280	11/18/79	4	Oregon State	Compton, Calif.	D3-'01	13/4
52	Green, Donny	LB	6-2	240	9/18/77	2	Virginia	Hampton, Va.	FA-'04	0*
	Hambrick, Troy	RB	6-1	235	11/6/76	5	Savannah State	Pasco, Fla.	FA-'04	16/16*
58	Harris, Napoleon	LB	6-2	255	2/25/79	3	Northwestern	Dixmoor, Ill.	D1-'02	16/16
44	Hetherington, Chris	FB	6-3	245	11/27/72	9	Yale	North Branford, Conn.	FA-'03	14/0
71	Hulsey, Corey	G-T	6-4	325	7/21/77	3	Clemson	Gainsville, Ga.	FA-'03	4/0
96	Irons, Grant	DE	6-5	275	7/7/79	3	Notre Dame	The Woodlands, Texas	FA-'03	1/0
11	Janikowski, Sebastian	K	6-2	250	3/3/78	5	Florida State	Daytona Beach, Fla.	D1-'00	16/0
82	Johnson, Teyo	TE	6-6	260	11/29/81	2	Stanford	San Diego, Calif.	D2-'03	16/5
51	Johnson, Tim	LB	6-0	245	2/7/78	3	Youngstown State	Fairfield, Ala.	FA-'03	12/3
88	Jolley, Doug	TE	6-4	250	1/2/79	3	Brigham Young	St. George, Utah	D2-'02	16/10
72	Kennedy, Lincoln	T	6-6	335	2/12/71	12	Washington	San Diego, Calif.	T(Atl)-'96	12/10
9	Lechler, Shane	P	6-2	225	8/7/76	5	Texas A&M	East Bernard, Texas	D5-'00	16/0
38	Love, Clarence	CB	5-10	180	6/16/76	5	Toledo	Jackson, Mich.	FA-'02	13/0
17	Martin, Tee	QB	6-2	225	7/25/78	4	Tennessee	Mobile, Ala.	FA-'03	2/0
73	Middleton, Frank	G	6-4	330	10/25/74	8	Arizona	Beaumont, Texas	UFA(TB)-'01	10/8
40	Niklos, J.R.	RB	6-2	240	6/19/79	2	Western Illinois	Worthington, Ohio	FA-'04	0*
	Nugent, David	DE	6-5	300	10/27/77	4	Purdue	Collierville, Tenn.	FA-'04	0*
97	Parrella, John	DT	6-3	300	11/22/69	12	Nebraska	Topeka, Kan.	UFA(SD)-'02	5/5
50	Pierson, Shurron	LB	6-2	250	5/31/82	2	South Florida	Wildwood, Fla.	D4-'03	6/0
84	Porter, Jerry	WR	6-2	220	7/14/78	5	West Virginia	Washington, D.C.	D2-'00	9/1
27	Redmond, J.R.	RB	5-11	215	9/28/77	5	Arizona State	Los Angeles, Calif.	FA-'03	1/0
80	Rice, Jerry	WR	6-2	200	10/13/62	20	Mississippi Valley State	Crawford, Miss.	FA-'01	16/15
63	Robbins, Barret	C	6-3	320	8/26/73	10	TCU	Houston, Texas	D2-'95	9/9
57	Rudd, Dwayne	LB	6-2	235	2/3/76	8	Alabama	Batesville, Miss.	FA-'04	16/2*
90	Sands, Terdell	DT	6-7	335	10/31/79	2	Tennessee-Chattanooga	Chattanooga, Tenn.	FA-'03	3/1
99	Sapp, Warren	DT	6-2	300	12/19/72	10	Miami	Apopka, Fla.	UFA(TB)-'04	15/15*
37	Scott, Carey	S	5-11	210	8/11/78	3	Kentucky State	Savannah, Ga.	FA-'03	5/0
	Setzer, Bobby	DE	6-4	275	6/16/76	3	Boise State	Walnut Creek, Calif.	FA-'04	0*
22	Shepherd, Jacoby	CB	6-2	205	8/31/79	4	Oklahoma State	Lufkin, Texas	UFA(Det)-'04	8/4*
65	Sims, Barry	T	6-5	300	12/1/74	6	Utah	Park City, Utah	FA-'99	16/16
78	Slaughter, Chad	T	6-8	340	6/4/78	4	Alcorn State	Dallas, Texas	FA-'02	9/1
56	Smith, Travian	LB	6-4	240	8/26/75	7	Oklahoma	Tatum, Texas	D5-'98	10/7
67	Stone, Ron	G	6-5	325	7/20/71	12	Boston College	Boston, Mass.	UFA(SF)-'04	13/13*
	Terrell, David	S	6-0	190	7/8/75	5	Texas-El Paso	Sweetwater, Texas	UFA(Wash)-'04	13/0*
62	Treu, Adam	C	6-5	300	6/24/74	8	Nebraska	Lincoln, Neb.	D3-'97	16/4
8	Tuiasosopo, Marques	QB	6-1	220	3/22/79	4	Washington	Woodinville, Wash.	D2-'01	4/1
25	Walker, Denard	CB	6-1	190	8/9/73	8	Louisiana State	Dallas, Texas	FA-'04	16/8*
66	Walker, Langston	T	6-8	345	9/3/79	3	California	Oakland, Calif.	D2-'02	16/8
92	Washington, Ted	DT	6-5	365	4/13/68	13	Louisville	Tampa, Fla.	UFA(NE)-'04	10/10*
47	Wheatley, Tyrone	RB	6-0	235	1/19/72	10	Michigan	Inkster, Mich.	FA-'99	15/4
87	Whitted, Alvis	WR	6-0	185	9/4/74	7	North Carolina State	Hillsborough, N.C.	FA-'02	16/1
86	Williams, Roland	TE	6-5	265	4/27/75	7	Syracuse	Rochester, N.Y.	UFA(TB)-'04	1/0*
54	Williams, Sam	LB	6-5	265	7/28/80	2	Fresno State	Clayton, Calif.	D3-'03	1/0
77	Wong, Joe	G-T	6-6	315	2/24/76	3	Brigham Young	Honolulu, Hawaii	FA-'03	2/0

24	Woodson, Charles	CB	6-0	200	10/7/76	7	Michigan	Fremont, Ohio	D1-'98	15/15
26	Woodson, Rod	S	6-2	205	3/10/65	18	Purdue	Ft. Wayne, Ind.	FA-'02	15/15
28	Zereoue, Amos	RB	5-8	205	10/8/76	6	West Virginia	Hempstead, N.Y.	FA-'04	16/6*

* Brooks last active with Jacksonville in '02; R. Buchanan played 15 games with Atlanta in '03; Charlton played 7 games with N.Y. Giants; Clark played 16 games with Jacksonville; Cole played 11 games with Denver; K. Collins played 13 games with N.Y. Giants; Green last active with Jacksonville in '01; Hambrick played 16 games with Dallas; Niklos last active with St. Louis in '02; Nugent last active with Baltimore in '02; Rudd played 16 games for Tampa Bay; Sapp played 15 games with Tampa Bay; Setzer last active with Chicago in '02; Shepherd played 8 games with Houston; Stone played 13 games with San Francisco; Terrell played 13 games with Washington; D. Walker played 16 games with Minnesota; Washington played 10 games with New England; R. Williams played 1 game with Tampa Bay; Zereoue played 16 games with Pittsburgh.

Players lost through free agency (9): LB Eric Barton (NYJ; 16 games in '03), DE Lorenzo Bromell (NYG; 6), DT Rod Coleman (Atl; 16), RB Charlie Garner (TB; 14), LB-S Eric Johnson (Atl; 16), QB Rick Mirer (Det; 9), TE O.J. Santiago (Den; 12), CB Terrance Shaw (Car; 16), T-G Matt Stinchcomb (TB; 6).

Also played with Raiders in '03—DE Trace Armstrong (10 games), LB Larry Atkins (1), S Anthony Dorsett (14), DT Sean Gilbert (6), RB-KR Ronney Jenkins (7), QB Rob Johnson (1), LB Bill Romanowski (3), S Siddeeq Shabazz (4), DT Dana Stubblefield (8).

2004 FIRST-YEAR ROSTER

Name	Pos.	Ht.	Wt.	Birthdate	College	Hometown	How Acq.
Adkisson, James (1)	WR	6-5	230	1/11/80	South Carolina	St. Louis. Mo.	FA
Anderson, Courtney	TE	6-6	270	11/19/80	San Jose State	Richmond, Calif.	D7a
Bethea, James	CB	5-10	190	9/24/82	California	Reseda, Calif.	FA
Burnell, Keith (1)	RB	5-11	205	1/8/79	Delaware	Chesapeake, Va.	FA
Campion, Pete (1)	C	6-4	305	12/3/79	North Dakota State	Fergus Falls, Minn.	FA
Chapman, Robert (1)	LB	6-3	240	1/19/79	Southern	Houma, La.	FA
Downs, Chris (1)	RB	5-8	195	3/26/79	Maryland	Philadelphia, Pa.	FA
Engemann, Brett (1)	QB	6-5	235	12/7/77	Brigham Young	Provo, Utah	FA
Evero, Ejiro	S	6-0	195	1/6/81	California-Davis	Rancho Cucamonga, Calif.	FA
Francis, Carlos	WR	5-10	190	1/3/81	Texas Tech	Fort Worth, Texas	D4
Gallery, Robert	T	6-7	320	7/26/80	Iowa	Masonville, Iowa	D1
Green, DeJuan	RB	5-11	205	5/13/80	South Florida	Jacksonville, Fla.	FA
Grove, Jake	C	6-4	300	1/22/80	Virginia Tech	Forest, Va.	D2
Johnson, Shawn	DE	6-5	275	3/21/80	Delaware	Rochester, N.Y.	D6a
Kelly, Tommy	DT	6-5	300	12/27/80	Mississippi State	Jackson, Miss.	FA
Morant, Johnnie	WR	6-4	215	12/7/81	Syracuse	Parsippany, N.J.	D5
Nash, Keyon (1)	S	6-3	215	3/11/79	Albany State	Colquitt, Ga.	D6-'02
Newman, David (1)	TE	6-6	265	8/6/78	Louisiana Tech	St. Joseph, La.	FA
Saipaia, Blaine (1)	C	6-3	310	8/25/78	Colorado State	Channel Islands, Calif.	FA-'03
Schweigert, Stuart	S	6-1	210	6/21/81	Purdue	Saginaw, Mich.	D3
Sommersell, Andre	LB	6-2	230	6/26/80	Colorado State	Fountain Valley, Calif.	D7b
Spencer, Cody	LB	6-2	245	6/1/81	North Texas	Port Lavaca, Texas	D6b
Stone, John (1)	WR	5-11	180	7/7/79	Wake Forest	Linwood, N.J.	FA-'03
Wike, Todd (1)	G	6-3	305	11/18/79	Maryland	Lebanon, Pa.	FA

The term NFL Rookie is defined as a player who is in his first season of professional football and has not been on the roster of another professional football team for any regular-season or postseason games. A Rookie is designated by an "R" on NFL rosters. Players who have been active in another professional football league or players who have NFL experience, including either preseason training camp or being on an Active List or Inactive List, or on Reserve/Injured or Reserve/Physically Unable to Perform for fewer than six regular-season games, are termed NFL First-Year Players. An NFL First-Year Player is designated by a "1" on NFL rosters. Thereafter, a player is credited with an additional year of experience for each season in which he accumulates six games on the Active List or Inactive List, or on Reserve/Injured or Reserve/Physically Unable to Perform.

Log on to www.raiders.com for an up-to-date roster.

OAKLAND RAIDERS

COACHING STAFF

Head Coach,
Norv Turner

Pro career: Norv Turner became the fourteenth head coach in Raiders history on January 26, 2004. Turner was head coach of the Washington Redskins from 1994-2000. Turner posted a winning record in four of his seven seasons with the Redskins, including two in a row in 1999 and 2000. His 1999 Redskins claimed their first NFC Eastern Division title since 1991. Washington then defeated Detroit, 27-13, in an NFC first-round playoff game before dropping a one-point decision (14-13) at Tampa Bay in the divisional round. That season, the Redskins' offense finished the year as the league's second-ranked unit. He guided the Redskins to a record of 7-6 in 2000 before being released with three games to play in the season. The Redskins' final three losses under Turner were by a total of six points, while their six losses over these first 13 games came by an average of less than four points. Turner spent the past two seasons (2002-03) as assistant head coach/offensive coordinator for the Miami Dolphins. In his first season with the Dolphins, Miami ranked second in the NFL in rushing. The 2,502 total rushing yards were the third-highest total in Dolphins history. In 2001, Turner was the assistant head coach/offensive coordinator with the San Diego Chargers. Under Turner's guidance, the Chargers' offense improved to the eleventh-best unit in the NFL after having finished twenty-eighth hte previous season. Turner was offensive coordinator for Dallas from 1991-93, and helped lead the Cowboys to two straight Super Bowl titles (XXVII and XXVIII). Turner began his NFL coaching career as an assistant with the Los Angeles Rams (1985-1990). Career record: 50-60-1.
Background: Turner was a three-year letterman (1972-74) as a quarterback at the Oregon, spending two seasons behind NFL Hall of Fame quarterback Dan Fouts. Turner coached collegiately at Oregon (1975) and the University of Southern California (1976-1984). where the Trojans won four Rose Bowl games and claimed the 1978 National Championship.
Personal: Born in LeJeune, N.C. on May 17, 1952. Turner and his wife, Nancy, have three children—Scott, Stephanie. and Drew.

ASSISTANT COACHES

Joe Avezzano, special teams; born November 17, 1943, Yonkers, N.Y. Guard Florida State 1961-65. Pro center Boston Patriots 1966. College coach: Florida State 1968, Iowa State 1969-1972, Pittsburgh 1973-76, Tennessee 1977-79, Oregon State 1980-84 (head coach), Texas 1985-88. Pro coach: Dallas Cowboys 1990-2002, Dallas Desperados (AFL) 2002-03 (head coach), joined Raiders in 2004.
Martin Bayless, specials teams asst.; born October 11, 1962, Dayton, Ohio. Defensive back Bowling Green 1981-83. Pro defensive back St. Louis Cardinals 1984, Buffalo Bills 1984-86, San Diego Chargers 1987-1991, Kansas City Chiefs 1992-93, 1995-96, Washington Redskins 1994. College coach: North Carolina 2001 Pro coach: Amsterdam Admirals (NFLE) 2002-03, Carolina Panthers 2003, joined Raiders in 2004.
Fred Biletnikoff, wide receivers; born February 23, 1943, Erie, Pa. Receiver Florida State 1962-64. Pro wide receiver Oakland Raiders 1965-1978, Montreal Alouettes (CFL) 1980. Inducted into Pro Football Hall of Fame in 1988. College coach: Palomar (Calif.) J.C. 1983, Diablo Valley (Calif.) J.C. 1984, 1986. Pro coach: Oakland Invaders (USFL) 1985, Calgary Stampeders (CFL) 1987-88, joined Raiders in 1989.
Willie Brown, squad development; born December 2, 1940, Yazoo City, Miss., Defensive back Grambling State 1959-1962. Pro defensive back Denver Broncos 1963-66, Oakland Raiders 1967-78. Inducted into Pro Football Hall of Fame in 1984. College coach: Long Beach State 1990-91 (head coach 1991). Pro coach: Oakland/Los Angeles Raiders 1979-1988, rejoined Raiders in 1995.
Sam Clancy, defensive line; born May 29, 1958, Pittsburgh. No college playing experience. Pro defensive lineman Seattle Seahawks 1982-83, Pittsburgh Maulers (USFL) 1984-85, Cleveland Browns 1985-88, Indianapolis Colts 1989-1993. Pro coach: Barcelona Dragons (NFLE) 1995-99, New Orleans Saints 2000-03, joined Raiders in 2004.
Jeff Fish, strength & conditioning; born June 6, 1966, Ithaca, N.Y. Wide receiver Western Carolina 1986-88. No pro playing experience. College coach: Clemson 1991-92, Kent State 1993-94, Tulsa 1995-96, Missouri 2001-02. Pro coach: Tampa Bay Buccaneers 1997, Kansas City Chiefs 1998-2000, joined Raiders in 2004.
Chris Griswold, quality control, defense; born February 23, 1973, Hornell, N.Y. Defensive lineman Hobart College 1992-96. No pro playing experience. College coach: Allegheny 1998, Princeton 1999-2001. Pro coach: Joined Raiders in 2002.
Pat Jones, outside linebackers; born November 4, 1947, Memphis, Tenn. Nose guard Arkansas Tech 1965, line backer-nose guard Arkansas 1966-1967. No pro playing experience. College coach: Arkansas 1974-75, Southern Methodist 1976-77, Pittsburgh 1978, Oklahoma State 1979-1994 (head coach 1984-1994). Pro coach: Miami Dolphins 1996-2003, joined Raiders in 2004.
Aaron Kromer, offensive line; born April 30, 1967, Sandusky, Ohio. Offensive tackle Miami (Ohio) 1986-89. No pro playing experience. College coach: Miami (Ohio) 1990-98, Northwestern 1999-2000. Pro coach: Joined Raiders in 2001.
Clayton Lopez, defensive backs; born May 26, 1971, Los Angeles. Safety Nevada 1991-94. No pro playing experience. College coach: Nevada 1995-98. Pro coach: Seattle Seahawks 1999-2003, joined Raiders in 2004.
Don Martindale, inside linebackers, born May 19, 1963, Dayton, Ohio. Linebacker Defiance College 1984-86. No pro playing experience. College coach: Defiance 1987, Notre Dame 1994-95, Cincinnati 1996-98, Western Illinois 1999, Western Kentucky 2000-02. Pro coach: Joined Raiders in 2004.
John Morton, tight ends; born September 24, 1969, Pontiac, Mich. Wide receiver Grand Rapids (Mich.) C.C. 1989-1990, Western Michigan 1991-92. Pro wide receiver Los Angeles Raiders 1993-94, Toronto Argonauts (CFL) 1995-96, Frankfurt Galaxy (WLAF) 1997. Pro coach: Joined Raiders in 1998.
Skip Peete, running backs; born January 30, 1963, Mesa, Ariz. Wide receiver Arizona 1981-82, Kansas 1984-85. Pro wide receiver New York Jets 1987. College coach: Pittsburgh 1988-1992, Michigan State 1993-94, Rutgers 1995, UCLA 1996-97. Pro coach: Joined Raiders in 1998.
Jimmy Raye, offensive coordinator; born March 26, 1946, Fayetteville, N.C. Quarterback Michigan State 1965-67. Pro defensive back Philadelphia Eagles 1969. College coach: Michigan State 1971-75, Wyoming 1976. Pro coach: San Francisco 49ers 1977, Detroit Lions 1978-79, Atlanta Falcons 1980-82, 1987-89, Los Angeles Rams 1983-84, 1991, Tampa Bay Buccaneers 1985-86, New England Patriots1990, Kansas City Chiefs 1992-2000, Washington Redskins 2001, New York Jets 2002-03, joined Raiders in 2004.
Rob Ryan, defensive coordinator; born December 13, 1962, Ardmore, Okla. Linebacker Oklahoma State 1984, Southwestern Oklahoma State 1985-86. No pro playing experience. College coach: Western Kentucky 1987, Ohio State 1988, Tennessee State 1989-1993, Hutchinson (Kan.) C.C. 1996, Oklahoma State 1997-99. Pro coach; Arizona Cardinals 1994-95, New England Patriots 2000-03, joined Raiders in 2004.
Steve Sarkisian, quarterbacks, born March 8, 1974, Torrance, Calif. Quarterback El Camino (Calif.) J.C. 1993-94, Brigham Young 1995-96. Pro quarterback Saskatchewan (CFL) 1997-99. College coach: El Camino (Calif.) J.C. 2000, Southern California 2001-03. Pro coach: Joined Raiders in 2004.
Chris Turner, offensive assistant; born February 28, 1969, Fairfield, Calif. No pro playing experience. College coach: San Jose State 1993, Notre Dame 1994, Bucknell 1995-2001. Pro coach: Joined Raiders in 2002.

American Football Conference
North Division
Team Colors: Black and Gold
3400 South Water Street
Pittsburgh, Pennsylvania 15203
Telephone: (412) 432-7800

2004 SCHEDULE

PRESEASON		Pittsburgh time
Aug. 14	at Detroit	7:30
Aug. 21	**Houston**	7:30
Aug. 26	at Philadelphia	8:00
Sept. 2	**Carolina**	7:00

REGULAR SEASON		
Sept. 12	**Oakland**	1:00
Sept. 19	at Baltimore	1:00
Sept. 26	at Miami	1:00
Oct. 3	**Cincinnati**	1:00
Oct. 10	**Cleveland**	1:00
Oct. 17	at Dallas	4:15
Oct. 24	Open Date	
Oct. 31	**New England**	4:15
Nov. 7	**Philadelphia**	1:00
Nov. 14	at Cleveland	1:00
Nov. 21	at Cincinnati	1:00
Nov. 28	**Washington**	1:00
Dec. 5	at Jacksonville	8:30
Dec. 12	**New York Jets**	4:05
Dec. 18	at N.Y. Giants (Sat.)	1:30
Dec. 26	**Baltimore**	1:00
Jan. 2	at Buffalo	1:00

Stadium: Heinz Field (opened in 2001)
•**Capacity:** 64,350
100 Art Rooney Avenue
Pittsburgh, Pennsylvania 15212
Playing Surface: DD GrassMaster
Training Camp: St. Vincent College
Latrobe, Pennsylvania
15650

HEINZ FIELD

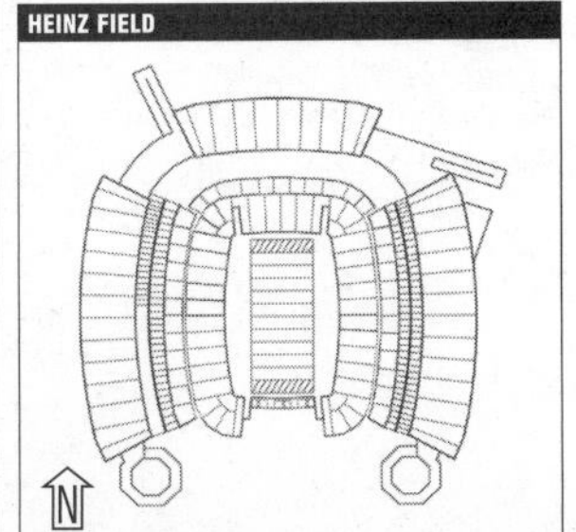

CLUB OFFICIALS

Chairman: Daniel M. Rooney
President: Arthur J. Rooney II
Vice President: John R. McGinley
Vice President: Arthur J. Rooney Jr.
Administration Advisor: Charles H. Noll
Director of Business: Mark Hart
Business Operations: Omar Khan
Director of Football Operations: Kevin Colbert
College Scouting Coordinator: Ron Hughes
Pro Scouting Coordinator: Doug Whaley
Head Athletic Trainer: John Norwig
Director of Marketing: Tony Quatrini
Communications Coordinator: Ron Wahl
Public Relations/Media Manager: Dave Lockett
Director of Stadium Management: Jim Sacco
Video Coordinator: Bob McCartney
Human Relations/Office Coordinator: Geraldine Glenn
Ticket Manager: Ben Lentz

COACHING HISTORY

Pittsburgh Pirates 1933-1940
(492-496-21)

1933	Forrest (Jap) Douds	3-6-2
1934	Luby DiMelio	2-10-0
1935-36	Joe Bach	10-14-0
1937-39	Johnny (Blood) McNally*	6-19-0
1939-1940	Walt Kiesling	3-13-3
1941	Bert Bell**	0-2-0
	Aldo (Buff) Donelli***	0-5-0
1941-44	Walt Kiesling****	13-20-2
1945	Jim Leonard	2-8-0
1946-47	Jock Sutherland	13-10-1
1948-1951	Johnny Michelosen	20-26-2
1952-53	Joe Bach	11-13-0
1954-56	Walt Kiesling	14-22-0
1957-1964	Raymond (Buddy) Parker	51-48-6
1965	Mike Nixon	2-12-0
1966-68	Bill Austin	11-28-3
1969-1991	Chuck Noll	209-156-1
1992-2003	Bill Cowher	122-84-1

*Released after three games in 1939
**Resigned after two games in 1941
***Released after five games in 1941
****Co-coach with Earle (Greasy) Neale in Philadelphia-Pittsburgh merger in 1943 and with Phil Handler in Chicago Cardinals-Pittsburgh merger in 1944

ATTENDANCE

Home 507,224 Away 567,252
Total 1,074,476
Single-game home record, 63,763 (10/29/01)
Single-season home record, 507,433 (2002)

2004 DRAFT CHOICES

Round	Name	Pos.	College
1	Ben Roethlisberger	QB	Miami (Ohio)
2	Ricardo Colclough	DB	Tusculum (Tenn.)
3	Max Starks	T	Florida
5	Nathaniel Adibi	LB	Virignia Tech
6	Bo Lacy	T	Arkansas
	Matt Kranchick	TE	Penn State
	Drew Caylor	C	Stanford
7	Eric Taylor	DT	Memphis

PITTSBURGH STEELERS

2003 TEAM RECORD

PRESEASON (1-3)

Date	Result	Opponent
8/9	L 13-26	at Detroit
8/16	L 16-21	Philadelphia
8/21	W 15-14	Dallas
8/29	L 14-21	at Carolina

REGULAR SEASON (6-10)

Date	Result	Opponent	Att.
9/7	W 34-15	Baltimore	63,157
9/14	L 20-41	at Kansas City	78,416
9/21	W 17-10	at Cincinnati	64,596
9/28	L 13-30	Tennessee	63,244
10/5	L 13-33	Cleveland	64,595
10/12	L 14-17	at Denver	75,974
10/26	L 21-33	St. Louis	62,665
11/2	L 16-23	at Seattle	66,507
11/9	W 28-15	Arizona	59,520
11/17	L 14-30	at San Francisco	67,877
11/23	W 13-6	at Cleveland	73,658
11/30	L 20-24	Cincinnati	58,797
12/7	W 27-7	Oakland	53,079
12/14	L 0-6	at New York Jets	77,900
12/21	W 40-24	San Diego	52,527
12/28	L 10-13	at Baltimore (OT)	70,001

(OT) Overtime

SCORE BY PERIODS

	1	2	3	4	OT	Total
Steelers	50	94	93	63	0	— 300
Opponents	61	98	71	94	3	— 327

2003 TEAM STATISTICS

	Steelers	Opp.
Total First Downs	343	279
Total First Downs	275	270
Rushing	77	89
Passing	174	155
Penalty	24	26
3rd Down: Made/Att	82/227	71/209
3rd Down Pct.	36.1	34.0
4th Down: Made/Att	11/22	7/16
4th Down Pct.	50.0	43.8
Possession Avg.	30:42	29:18
Total Net Yards	4,792	4,783
Avg. Per Game	299.5	298.9
Total Plays	1,020	968
Avg. Per Play	4.7	4.9
Net Yards Rushing	1,488	1,741
Avg. Per Game	93.0	108.8
Total Rushes	446	449
Net Yards Passing	3,304	3,042
Avg. Per Game	206.5	190.1
Sacked/Yards Lost	42/244	35/203
Gross Yards	3,548	3,245
Att./Completions	532/306	484/294
Completion Pct.	57.5	60.7
Had Intercepted	17	14
Punts/Average	85/41.4	91/40.6
Net Punting Avg.	85/36.0	91/32.1
Penalties/Yards	111/1,005	96/709
Fumbles/Ball Lost	24/11	24/11
Touchdowns	33	38
Rushing	10	14
Passing	19	20
Returns	4	4

2003 INDIVIDUAL STATISTICS

PASSING	Att.	Comp.	Yds.	Pct.	TD	Int.	Tkld.	Rate
Maddox	519	298	3,414	57.4	18	17	41/242	75.3
Batch	8	4	47	50.0	0	0	1/2	68.2
Randle El	4	3	6	75.0	0	0	0/0	77.1
Miller	1	1	81	100.0	1	0	0/0	158.3
Steelers	532	306	3,548	57.5	19	17	42/244	76.4
Opponents	484	294	3,245	60.7	20	14	35/203	82.4

SCORING	TD R	TD P	TD Rt	PAT	FG	Saf	PTS
Reed	0	0	0	31/32	23/32	0	100
Ward	0	10	0	0/0	0/0	0	60
Bettis	7	0	0	0/0	0/0	0	44
Burress	0	4	0	0/0	0/0	0	24
Randle El	0	1	2	0/0	0/0	0	18
Zereoue	2	0	0	0/0	0/0	0	12
Bruener	0	1	0	0/0	0/0	0	6
Doering	0	1	0	0/0	0/0	0	6
Hope	0	1	0	0/0	0/0	0	6
Kreider	1	0	0	0/0	0/0	0	6
Riemersma	0	1	0	0/0	0/0	0	6
Scott	0	0	1	0/0	0/0	0	6
Townsend	0	0	1	0/0	0/0	0	6
Steelers	10	19	4	31/32	23/32	0	300
Opponents	14	20	4	32/35	21/24	1	327

2-Pt. Conversions: Bettis.
Steelers 1-1, Opponents 1-3.

RUSHING	No.	Yds	Avg	LG	TD
Bettis	246	811	3.3	21	7
Zereoue	132	433	3.3	22	2
Randle El	15	75	5.0	32	0
Haynes	20	63	3.2	15	0
Ward	11	61	5.5	25	0
Kreider	7	29	4.1	9	1
Maddox	13	12	0.9	6	0
Batch	1	11	11.0	11	0
Burress	1	-7	-7.0	-7	0
Steelers	446	1,488	3.3	32	10
Opponents	449	1,741	3.9	78t	14

RECEIVING	No.	Yds	Avg	LG	TD
Ward	95	1,163	12.2	50	10
Burress	60	860	14.3	47	4
Zereoue	40	310	7.8	29	0
Randle El	37	364	9.8	32t	1
Doering	18	240	13.3	53	1
Bettis	13	86	6.6	16	0
Tuman	12	113	9.4	23	0
Riemersma	10	138	13.8	24	1
Kreider	9	107	11.9	26	0
Haynes	7	57	8.1	13	0
Mays	2	17	8.5	9	0
Bruener	2	12	6.0	11	1
Hope	1	81	81.0	81t	1
Steelers	306	3,548	11.6	81t	19
Opponents	294	3,245	11.0	61t	20

INTERCEPTIONS	No.	Yds	Avg	LG	TD
Alexander	4	63	15.8	34	0
Scott	3	50	16.7	26t	1
Townsend	3	24	8.0	25t	1
Bell	1	61	61.0	42	0
Farrior	1	9	9.0	9	0
Washington	1	7	7.0	7	0
Gildon	1	1	1.0	1	0
Steelers	14	215	15.4	42	2
Opponents	17	386	22.7	75t	3

PUNTING	No.	Yds	Avg	In 20	Lg
Miller	84	3,521	41.9	27	72
Steelers	85	3,521	41.4	27	72
Opponents	91	3,694	40.6	23	61

PUNT RETURNS	Ret	FC	Yds	Avg	LG	TD
Randle El	45	12	542	12.0	84t	2
Doering	0	0	9	—	9	0
Steelers	45	12	551	12.2	84t	2
Opponents	47	12	299	6.4	45	0

KICKOFF RETURNS	No.	Yds	Avg	LG	TD
Taylor	37	831	22.5	53	0
Randle El	24	466	19.4	34	0
Mays	4	79	19.8	27	0
Kreider	3	29	9.7	15	0
Steelers	68	1,405	20.7	53	0
Opponents	66	1,359	20.6	100t	1

FIELD GOALS	1-19	20-29	30-39	40-49	50+
Reed	0/0	9/12	6/7	7/12	1/1
Steelers	0/0	9/12	6/7	7/12	1/1
Opponents	1/1	7/7	5/5	8/9	0/2

SACKS	No.
von Oelhoffen	8.0
Gildon	6.0
Bell	5.0
Porter	5.0
Bailey	2.0
Polamalu	2.0
A. Smith	2.0
Alexander	1.0
Haggans	1.0
Hampton	1.0
Logan	1.0
Townsend	1.0
Steelers	35.0
Opponents	42.0

RECORD HOLDERS

INDIVIDUAL RECORDS—CAREER

Category	Name	Performance
Rushing (Yds.)	Franco Harris, 1972-1983	11,950
Passing (Yds.)	Terry Bradshaw, 1970-1983	27,989
Passing (TDs)	Terry Bradshaw, 1970-1983	212
Receiving (No.)	John Stallworth, 1974-1987	537
Receiving (Yds.)	John Stallworth, 1974-1987	8,723
Interceptions	Mel Blount, 1970-1983	57
Punting (Avg.)	Bobby Joe Green, 1960-61	45.7
Punt Return (Avg.)	Bobby Gage, 1949-1950	14.9
Kickoff Return (Avg.)	Lynn Chandnois, 1950-56	29.6
Field Goals	Gary Anderson, 1982-1994	309
Touchdowns (Tot.)	Franco Harris, 1972-1983	100
Points	Gary Anderson, 1982-1994	1,343

INDIVIDUAL RECORDS—SINGLE SEASON

Category	Name	Performance
Rushing (Yds.)	Barry Foster, 1992	1,690
Passing (Yds.)	Terry Bradshaw, 1979	3,724
Passing (TDs)	Terry Bradshaw, 1978	28
Receiving (No.)	Hines Ward, 2002	112
Receiving (Yds.)	Yancey Thigpen, 1997	1,398
Interceptions	Mel Blount, 1975	11
Punting (Avg.)	Bobby Joe Green, 1961	47.0
Punt Return (Avg.)	Bobby Gage, 1949	16.0
Kickoff Return (Avg.)	Lynn Chandnois, 1952	35.2
Field Goals	Norm Johnson, 1995	34
Touchdowns (Tot.)	Louis Lipps, 1985	15
Points	Norm Johnson, 1995	141

INDIVIDUAL RECORDS—SINGLE GAME

Category	Name	Performance
Rushing (Yds.)	John Fuqua, 12-20-70	218
Passing (Yds.)	Tommy Maddox, 11-10-02	473
Passing (TDs)	Terry Bradshaw, 11-15-81	5
	Mark Malone, 9-8-85	5
Receiving (No.)	Courtney Hawkins, 11-1-98	14
Receiving (Yds.)	Plaxico Burress, 11-10-02	253
Interceptions	Jack Butler, 12-13-53	*4
Field Goals	Gary Anderson, 10-23-88	6
	Jeff Reed, 12-1-02	6
Touchdowns (Tot.)	Ray Mathews, 10-17-54	4
	Roy Jefferson, 11-3-68	4
Points	Ray Mathews, 10-17-54	24
	Roy Jefferson, 11-3-68	24

*NFL Record

PITTSBURGH STEELERS

2004 VETERAN ROSTER

No.	Name	Pos.	Ht.	Wt.	Birthdate	NFL Exp.	College	Hometown	How Acq.	'03 Games/ Starts
16	Batch, Charlie	QB	6-2	220	12/5/74	7	Eastern Michigan	Pittsburgh, Pa.	FA-'03	3/0
97	Bell, Kendrell	LB	6-1	254	7/2/78	4	Georgia	Augusta, Ga.	D2-'01	16/16
36	Bettis, Jerome	RB	5-11	252	2/16/72	12	Notre Dame	Detroit, Mich.	T(StL)-'96	16/10
72	Brooks, Barrett	T	6-4	325	5/5/72	9	Kansas State	Florissant, Mo.	FA-'03	0*
46	Brown, Dante	RB	6-1	218	7/28/80	2	Memphis	Cincinnati, Ohio	FA-'03	0*
80	Burress, Plaxico	WR	6-5	226	8/12/77	5	Michigan State	Virginia Beach, Va.	D1-'00	16/16
96	Clancy, Kendrick	NT	6-1	292	9/17/78	5	Mississippi	Tuscaloosa, Ala.	D3a-'00	12/0
48	Cushing, Matt	TE	6-4	255	7/2/75	6	Illinois	South Bend, Ind.	FA-'03	4/0
83	Doering, Chris	WR	6-4	202	5/19/73	7	Florida	Gainesville, Fla.	FA-'03	16/0
23	Fair, Terry	DB	5-9	193	7/20/76	6	Tennessee	Phoenix, Ariz.	FA-'04	0/*
66	Faneca, Alan	G	6-5	312	12/7/76	7	Louisiana State	New Orleans, La.	D1-'98	16/16
51	Farrior, James	LB	6-2	242	1/6/75	8	Virginia	Ettrick, Va.	UFA(NYJ)-'02	16/16
50	Foote, Larry	LB	6-0	234	6/12/80	3	Michigan	Detroit, Mich.	D4-'02	16/0
71	Fordham, Todd	T	6-5	320	10/9/73	8	Florida State	Tifton, Ga.	UFA(Jax)-'03	11/6
17	Gardocki, Chris	P	6-1	200	2/7/70	14	Clemson	Stone Mountain, Ga.	UFA(Cle)-'04	16/0*
53	Haggans, Clark	LB	6-3	251	1/10/77	5	Colorado State	Torrance, Calif.	D5a-'00	16/2
98	Hampton, Casey	DT	6-1	320	9/3/77	4	Texas	Galveston, Texas	D1-'01	16/16
64	Hartings, Jeff	C	6-3	301	9/7/72	9	Penn State	St. Henry, Ohio	UFA(Det)-'01	16/16
34	Haynes, Verron	RB	5-9	224	2/17/79	3	Georgia	Bronx, N.Y.	D5-'02	12/0
76	Hoke, Chris	DT	6-3	296	4/6/76	4	Brigham Young	Long Beach, Calif.	FA-'02	0*
28	Hope, Chris	S	6-0	214	9/29/80	3	Florida State	Rock Hill, S.C.	D3-'02	16/0
29	Iwuoma, Chidi	CB	5-8	184	2/19/78	4	California	Pasadena, Calif.	FA-'02	15/0
95	Jackson, Alonzo	LB	6-4	262	9/15/80	2	Florida State	Americus, Ga.	D2-'03	2/0
99	Keisel, Brett	DE	6-5	290	9/19/78	2	Brigham Young	Greybull, Wyo.	D7b-'02	0*
90	Kirschke, Travis	DT	6-3	286	9/6/74	8	UCLA	Highland Ranch, Colo.	UFA(SF)-'04	15/15*
35	Kreider, Dan	FB	5-11	246	3/11/77	5	New Hampshire	Mount Joy, Pa.	FA-'00	16/12
57	Kriewaldt, Clint	LB	6-1	242	3/16/76	6	Wisc-Stevens Point	Shiocton, Wis.	UFA(Det)-'03	15/0
31	Logan, Mike	S-CB	6-0	212	9/15/74	8	West Virginia	McKeesport, Pa.	UFA(Jax)-'01	16/15
8	Maddox, Tommy	QB	6-4	220	9/2/71	8	UCLA	Hurst, Texas	FA-'01	16/16
89	Mays, Lee	WR	6-2	200	9/18/78	3	Texas-El Paso	Houston, Texas	D6-'02	16/0
81	Milons, Freddie	WR	5-11	190	6/27/80	3	Alabama	Starksville, Miss.	T(Phil)-'03	0*
56	Okobi, Chukky	C-G	6-1	310	10/18/78	4	Purdue	Pittsburgh, Pa.	D5-'01	16/0
43	Polamalu, Troy	S	5-10	213	4/19/81	2	Southern California	Roseburg, Ore.	D1-'03	16/0
55	Porter, Joey	LB	6-2	250	3/22/77	6	Colorado State	Bakersfield, Calif.	D3a-'99	14/14
82	Randle El, Antwaan	WR	5-10	186	8/17/79	3	Indiana	Markham, Ill.	D2-'02	16/1
3	Reed, Jeff	K	5-11	226	4/9/79	3	North Carolina	Charlotte, N.C.	FA-'02	16/0
85	Riemersma, Jay	TE	6-5	255	5/17/73	9	Michigan	Evansville, Ind.	UFA(Buff)-'03	11/8
79	Ross, Oliver	T-G	6-5	317	9/27/74	7	Iowa State	Culver City, Calif.	FA-'00	16/11
54	Schneck, Mike	LS	6-0	246	8/4/77	6	Wisconsin	Whitefish Bay, Wis.	FA-'99	16/0
30	Scott, Chad	CB	6-1	205	9/6/74	8	Maryland	Capitol Heights, Md.	D1-'97	12/12
73	Simmons, Kendall	G	6-3	313	3/11/79	3	Auburn	Ripley, Miss.	D1-'02	16/16
91	Smith, Aaron	DE	6-5	300	4/9/76	6	Northern Colorado	Colo. Springs, Colo.	D4-'99	16/16
77	Smith, Marvel	T	6-5	310	8/6/78	5	Arizona State	Oakland, Calif.	D2-'00	6/6
2	St. Pierre, Brian	QB	6-2	220	11/28/79	2	Boston College	Danvers, Mass.	D5-'03	0*
22	Staley, Duce	RB	5-11	220	2/27/75	8	South Carolina	Columbia, S.C.	UFA(Phil)-'04	16/4*
33	Stuvaints, Russell	S	6-0	200	8/28/80	2	Youngstown State	McKeesport, Pa.	FA-'03	4/0
24	Taylor, Ike	CB	6-0	195	5/5/80	2	Louisiana-Lafayette	Gretna, La.	D4-'03	16/1
26	Townsend, Deshea	CB	5-9	191	9/8/75	7	Alabama	Batesville, Miss.	D4a-'98	16/8
25	Tucker, B.J.	CB	5-11	188	10/12/80	2	Wisconsin	Milwaukee, Wis.	FA-'03	0*
84	Tuman, Jerame	TE	6-4	255	3/24/76	6	Michigan	Liberal, Kan.	FA-'03	16/11
68	Vincent, Keydrick	G	6-5	330	4/13/78	4	Mississippi	Bartow, Fla.	FA-'01	10/9
67	von Oelhoffen, Kimo	DT-DE	6-4	300	1/30/71	11	Boise State	Kaunakakai, Hawaii	UFA(Cin)-'00	16/16
86	Ward, Hines	WR	6-0	205	3/8/76	7	Georgia	Forest Park, Ga.	D3b-'98	16/16

* Brooks did not play in 1 game; Brown did not play in 1 game; Fair last active with Carolina in '02; Gardocki played 16 games with Cleveland in '03; Hoke did not play in 1 game; Keisel missed '03 season because of injury; Kirschke played 15 games with San Francisco; Milons did not play in 1 game; St. Pierre did not play in 1 game; Staley played 16 games with Philadelphia; Tucker did not play in 1 game.

Players lost through free agency (1): DE Rodney Bailey (NE; 16 games in '03).

Also played with Steelers in '03—S Brent Alexander (16 games), RB Dee Brown (2), TE Mark Bruener (14), LB Jason Gildon (16), P Josh Miller (16), T Mathias Nkwenti (1), CD Dewayne Washington (16), RB Amos Zereoue (16).

2004 FIRST-YEAR ROSTER

Name	Pos.	Ht.	Wt.	Birthdate	College	Hometown	How Acq.
Adibi, Nathaniel	LB	6-3	255	1/25/81	Virginia Tech	Hampton, Va.	D5
Augustin, Allen	LB	6-0	225	6/12/81	Florida State	Miami, Fla.	FA
Barr, Mike (1)	P	6-2	230	12/8/78	Rutgers	Lynchburg, Va.	FA
Blizzard, Robert	TE	6-4	265	3/22/80	North Carolina	Hampton, Va.	FA
Burr, Josh (1)	T	6-9	320	9/8/76	South Dakota	Dubuque, Iowa	FA-'03
Calton, Brandon	DE	6-2	291	7/3/80	East Tennessee State	Pennington Gap, Va.	FA
Caylor, Drew	C-LS	6-5	288	1/27/81	Stanford	Kensington, Md.	D6c
Cobb, Zamir	WR	5-11	180	6/11/81	Temple	Washington, D.C.	FA
Colclough, Ricardo	CB	5-11	195	4/18/82	Tusculum	Sumter, S.C.	D2
Dyer, Nashville (1)	CB-S	5-10	180	11/6/79	Kent State	St. Catherine, Jamaica	FA
Jones, Jim (1)	G	6-2	310	1/27/78	Notre Dame	Chicago, Ill.	FA
Kennedy, Darryl	FB	6-0	230	6/24/80	Syracuse	Plainfield, N.J.	FA
Kranchick, Matt	TE	6-7	255	12/13/79	Penn State	Carlisle, Pa.	D6b
Lacy, Bo	T	6-4	303	11/22/80	Arkansas	New Port, Ark.	D6a
Markham, John (1)	K	6-0	212	4/27/79	Vanderbilt	Brentwood, Tenn.	FA
Martinez, Glenn	WR	6-2	182	11/30/81	Saginaw Valley State	Auburndale, Fla.	FA
McNeil, Nick	LB	6-2	244	8/19/81	Western Carolina	Leland, N.C.	FA
Parker, Willie	RB	5-10	208	11/11/80	North Carolina	Clinton, N.C.	FA
Parrish, Josh	G	6-6	337	4/25/80	Washington State	Chewelah, Wash.	FA
Patton, Janssen	S	5-11	191	4/15/82	Bowling Green	Stone Mountain, Ga.	FA
Pearce, Chance (1)	LS	6-2	246	5/11/80	Texas A&M	Brownwood, Texas	FA
Pears, Morgan (1)	T	6-6	325	5/4/80	Colorado State	Denver, Colo.	FA-'03
Pugh, Jimond (1)	C	6-2	300	7/28/80	Memphis	Atlanta, Ga.	FA-'03
Robinson, Brian (1)	WR	6-3	205	6/24/79	Houston	Daytona Beach, Fla.	FA
Roethlisberger, Ben	QB	6-5	242	3/2/81	Miami (Ohio)	Findlay, Ohio	D1
Roper, Dedrick	LB	6-2	256	7/31/81	Northwood	Milpitas, Calif.	FA
Starks, Max	T	6-7	343	1/10/82	Florida	Orlando, Fla.	D3
Taylor, Eric	DE	6-3	302	12/14/81	Memphis	Winchester, Tenn.	D7
Upchurch, David (1)	DT	6-3	285	5/12/80	West Virginia	Syracuse, N.Y.	FA-'03
Wall, J.T. (1)	FB	6-0	265	9/12/79	Georgia	Milledgeville, Ga.	FA-'03
Whittaker, Huey	WR	6-4	234	6/19/81	South Florida	Spring Hill, Fla.	FA
Yisrael, Yaacov	S	5-11	198	8/17/81	Penn State	Palatine, Ill.	FA

The term NFL Rookie is defined as a player who is in his first season of professional football and has not been on the roster of another professional football team for any regular-season or postseason games. A Rookie is designated by an "R" on NFL rosters. Players who have been active in another professional football league or players who have NFL experience, including either preseason training camp or being on an Active List or Inactive List, or on Reserve/Injured or Reserve/Physically Unable to Perform for fewer than six regular-season games, are termed NFL First-Year Players. An NFL First-Year Player is designated by a "1" on NFL rosters. Thereafter, a player is credited with an additional year of experience for each season in which he accumulates six games on the Active List or Inactive List, or on Reserve/Injured or Reserve/Physically Unable to Perform.

Log on to www.steelers.com for an up-to-date roster.

PITTSBURGH STEELERS

COACHING STAFF

Head Coach,
Bill Cowher

Pro Career: Became the fifteenth head coach in Steelers history when he replaced Chuck Noll on January 21, 1992. In 1995, at age 38, he became the youngest coach to lead his team to a Super Bowl. Cowher is only the second coach in NFL history to lead his team to the playoffs in each of his first six seasons as head coach, joining Pro Football Hall of Fame member Paul Brown. During Cowher's 18-year coaching career, teams he has been associated with have made the postseason 14 times. Began his NFL career as a free-agent linebacker with the Philadelphia Eagles in 1979, and then signed with the Cleveland Browns the following year. Cowher played three seasons (1980-82) in Cleveland before being traded back to the Eagles, where he played two more years (1983-84). Cowher began his coaching career in 1985 at age 28 under Marty Schottenheimer with the Browns. He was the Browns' special teams coach in 1985-86 and secondary coach in 1987-88 before following Schottenheimer to the Kansas City Chiefs in 1989 as defensive coordinator. Career record: 122-84-1.

Background: Excelled in football, basketball, and track for Carlynton High in Crafton, Pa. Was a three-year starter at linebacker for North Carolina State, serving as captain and earning team MVP honors as a senior. Graduated in 1979 with education degree.

Personal: Born in Pittsburgh, on May 8, 1957. His wife Kaye, also a North Carolina State graduate, played professional basketball for the New York Stars of the Women's Professional Basketball League with twin sister Faye. Bill and Kaye live in Pittsburgh and have three daughters—Meagan Lyn, Lauren Marie, and Lindsay Morgan.

ASSISTANT COACHES

Bruce Arians, wide receivers; born October 3, 1952, Paterson, N.J. Quarterback Virginia Tech 1970-74. No pro playing experience. College coach: Virginia Tech 1975-77, Mississippi State 1978-1980, Alabama 1981-82, Temple 1983-88 (head coach), Mississippi State 1993-95, Alabama 1997. Pro coach: Kansas City Chiefs 1989-1992, New Orleans Saints 1996, Indianapolis Colts 1998-2000, Cleveland Browns 2001-03, joined Steelers in 2004.

Keith Butler, linebackers; born May 16, 1956, Anniston, Ala. Linebacker Memphis 1974-77. Pro linebacker Seattle Seahawks 1978-1987. College coach: Memphis 1990-97, Arkansas State 1998. Pro coach: Cleveland Browns 1999-2002, joined Steelers in 2003.

James Daniel, tight ends; born January 17, 1953, Wetumpka, Ala. Guard Alabama State 1970-73. No pro playing experience. College coach: Auburn 1981-1992. Pro coach: New York Giants 1993-96, Atlanta Falcons 1997-2003, joined Steelers in 2004.

Russ Grimm, offensive line; born May 2, 1959, Scottdale, Pa. Center Pittsburgh 1977-1980. Pro guard Washington Redskins 1981-1991. Pro coach: Washington Redskins 1992-2000, joined Steelers in 2001.

Dick Hoak, running backs; born December 8, 1939, Jeannette, Pa. Halfback-quarterback Penn State 1958-1960. Pro running back Pittsburgh Steelers 1961-1970. Pro coach: Joined Steelers in 1972.

Ray Horton, asst. defensive backs; born April 12, 1960, Tacoma, Wash. Defensive back Washington 1979-1982. Pro defensive back Cincinnati Bengals 1983-88, Dallas Cowboys 1989-1992. Pro coach: Washington Redskins 1994-96, Cincinnati Bengals 1997-2001, Detroit Lions 2002-03, joined Steelers in 2004.

Dick LeBeau, defensive coordinator; born September 9, 1937, London, Ohio. Defensive back Ohio State 1955-58. Pro cornerback Detroit Lions 1959-1972. Pro coach: Philadelphia Eagles 1973-75, Green Bay Packers 1976-79, Cincinnati Bengals 1980-1991, 1997-2002 (head coach 2000-02), Pittsburgh Steelers 1992-96, Buffalo Bills 2003, re-joined Steelers in 2004.

John Mitchell, defensive line; born October 14, 1951, Mobile, Ala. Defensive end Eastern Arizona J.C. 1969-1970, Alabama 1971-72. No pro playing experience. College coach: Alabama 1973-76, Arkansas 1977-1982, Temple 1986, Louisiana State 1987-1990. Pro coach: Birmingham Stallions (USFL) 1983-85, Cleveland Browns 1991-93, joined Steelers in 1994.

Darren Perry, asst. defensive backs; born December 29, 1968, Chesapeake, Va. Safety Penn State 1987-1991. Pro safety Pittsburgh Steelers 1992-98, New Orleans Saints 2000. Pro coach: Cincinnati Bengals 2002, joined Steelers in 2003.

Kevin Spencer, special teams; born November 2, 1953, Queens, N.Y. Outside linebacker Springfield College 1971. No pro playing experience. College coach: SUNY-Cortland 1975-76, Cornell 1979-1980, Ithaca 1981-86, Wesleyan 1978-1991. Pro coach: Cleveland Browns 1991-94, Oakland Raiders 1995-97, Indianapolis Colts 1998-2001, joined Steelers in 2002.

Mark Whipple, quarterbacks; born April 1, 1957, Tarrytown, N.Y. Quarterback Brown 1976-78. No pro playing experience. College coach: St. Lawrence 1980, Union College 1981-82, Brown 1983, New Hampshire 1986-87, New Haven 1988-1993 (head coach), Brown 1994-97 (head coach), Massachusetts 1998-2003 (head coach). Pro coach: Arizona Wranglers 1984 (USFL), joined Steelers in 2004.

Ken Whisenhunt, offensive coordinator; born February 28, 1962, Atlanta. Tight end-quarterback Georgia Tech 1980-84. Pro tight end Atlanta Falcons 1985-88, Washington Redskins 1989-1990, New York Jets 1991-93. College coach: Vanderbilt 1995-96. Pro coach: Baltimore Ravens 1997-98, Cleveland Browns 1999, New York Jets 2000, joined Steelers in 2001.

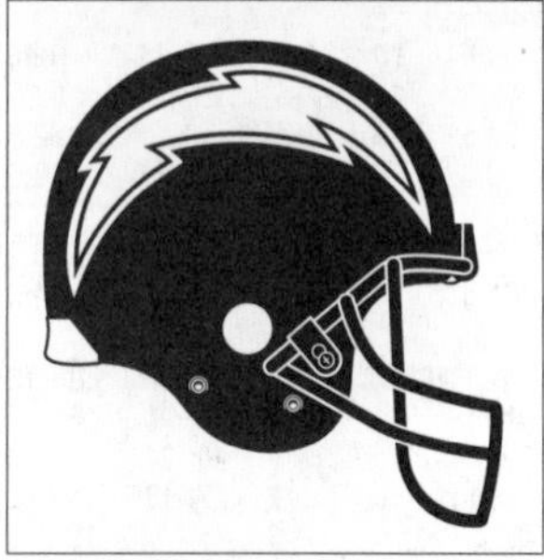

American Football Conference
West Division
Team Colors: Navy Blue, White, and Gold
P.O. Box 609609
San Diego, California 92160-9609
Telephone: (858) 874-4500

2004 SCHEDULE

PRESEASON		**San Diego time**
Aug. 14	**Indianapolis**	7:00
Aug. 21	at Arizona	7:00
Aug. 27	**Seattle**	7:00
Sept. 2	at San Francisco	8:00

REGULAR SEASON

Sept. 12	at Houston	10:00*
Sept. 19	**New York Jets**	1:15
Sept. 26	at Denver	1:05
Oct. 3	**Tennessee**	1:15
Oct. 10	**Jacksonville**	1:05
Oct. 17	at Atlanta	10:00*
Oct. 24	at Carolina	10:00*
Oct. 31	**Oakland**	1:15
Nov. 7	**New Orleans**	1:05
Nov. 14	Open Date	
Nov. 21	at Oakland	1:05
Nov. 28	at Kansas City	10:00*
Dec. 5	**Denver**	1:05
Dec. 12	**Tampa Bay**	1:15
Dec. 19	at Cleveland	10:00*
Dec. 26	at Indianapolis	10:00*
Jan. 2	**Kansas City**	1:15

*A.M.

Stadium: Qualcomm Stadium
(opened in 1967)
• **Capacity:** 70,000
9449 Friars Road
San Diego, California 92108
Playing Surface: Grass
Training Camp: The Home Depot
National Training Center
18400 Avalon Blvd.
Suite 500
Carson, CA 90746

QUALCOMM STADIUM

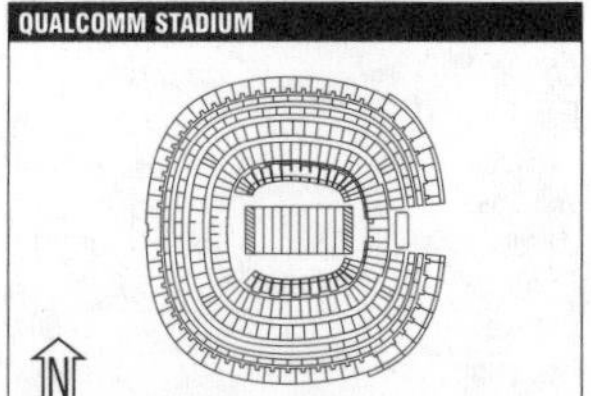

CLUB OFFICIALS

Owner: Alex G. Spanos
President/CEO: Dean A. Spanos
Executive Vice President: Michael A. Spanos
Executive Vice President & General Manager: A.J. Smith
Executive Vice President-Finance: Jeremiah T. Murphy
Vice President of Football Operations: Ed McGuire
Vice President-Chief Financial & Administrative Officer: Jeanne M. Bonk
Vice President & Chief Marketing Officer: Ken Derrett
Assistant General Manager & Director of Player Personnel: Buddy Nix
Director of College Scouting: Jimmy Raye
Director of Pro Scouting: Fran Foley
Assistant Director of Pro Scouting: Dennis Abraham
Head Athletic Trainer: James Collins
Director of Video Operations: Brian Duddy
Equipment Manager: Bob Wick
Director of Player Development: Ron George
Senior Director of Marketing Partnerships: Dennis O'Leary
Director of Marketing Programs and Business Development: A.G. Spanos
Director of Business & Stadium Operations: John Hinek
Director of Public Relations: Bill Johnston
Director of Public Affairs & Corporate/Community Relations: Kimberley Layton
Director of Security: Dick Lewis
Senior Director of Ticket Sales and Service: Todd Poulsen
Director of Marketing & Events: Sean O'Connor
Controller: Marsha Wells

COACHING HISTORY

Los Angeles 1960
(315-352-11)

1960-69	Sid Gillman*	83-51-6
1969-1970	Charlie Waller	9-7-3
1971	Sid Gillman**	4-6-0
1971-73	Harland Svare***	7-17-2
1973	Ron Waller	1-5-0
1974-78	Tommy Prothro****	21-39-0
1978-1986	Don Coryell#	72-60-0
1986-88	Al Saunders	17-22-0
1989-1991	Dan Henning	16-32-0
1992-96	Bobby Ross	50-36-0
1997-98	Kevin Gilbride	6-16-0
1998	June Jones	3-7-0
1999-2001	Mike Riley	14-34-0
2002-03	Marty Schottenheimer	12-20-0

*Retired after nine games in 1969
**Resigned after 10 games in 1971
***Resigned after eight games in 1973
****Resigned after four games in 1978
#Resigned after eight games in 1986
##Released after six games in 1998

ATTENDANCE

Home 476,681* Away 515,767
Total 992,448*
Single-game home record, 69,288 (11/7/99)
Single-season home record, 546,533 (1999)
**The Week 8 Miami at San Diego game is not included. The game was moved to Arizona due to the San Diego wildfires and tickets were distributed at no charge.*

2004 DRAFT CHOICES

Round	Name	Pos.	College
1	Eli Manning	QB	Mississippi
2	Igor Olshansky	DT	Oregon
3	Nate Kaeding	K	Iowa
	Nick Hardwick	C	Purdue
4	Shaun Phillips	LB	Purdue
5	Dave Ball	DE	UCLA
	Michael Turner	RB	Northern Illinois
6	Ryan Krause	TE	Nebraska-Omaha
7	Ryon Bingham	DT	Nebraska
	Shane Olivea	T	Ohio State
	Carlos Joseph	T	Miami

SAN DIEGO CHARGERS

2003 TEAM RECORD

PRESEASON (2-2)

Date	Result	Opponent
8/9	L 7-20	at Seattle
8/16	L 10-16	Arizona
8/23	W 19-17	at Houston
8/29	W 24-3	San Francisco

REGULAR SEASON (4-12)

Date	Result	Opponent	Att.
9/7	L 14-27	at Kansas City	78,048
9/14	L 13-37	Denver	65,445
9/21	L 10-24	Baltimore	52,028
9/28	L 31-34	at Oakland (OT)	54,078
10/5	L 21-27	at Jacksonville	48,954
10/19	W 26-20	at Cleveland	73,238
10/27	L 10-26	Miami	73,014
11/2	L 7-20	at Chicago	61,500
11/9	W 42-28	Minnesota	64,738
11/16	L 8-37	at Denver	75,217
11/23	L 27-34	Cincinnati	52,069
11/30	L 24-28	Kansas City	57,671
12/7	W 14-7	at Detroit	61,544
12/14	L 21-38	Green Bay	64,978
12/21	L 24-40	at Pittsburgh	52,527
12/28	W 21-14	Oakland	62,222

(OT) Overtime

SCORE BY PERIODS

Chargers	60	86	50	117	0	— 313
Opponents	121	140	60	117	3	— 441

2003 TEAM STATISTICS

	Chargers	Opp.
Total First Downs	290	326
Rushing	117	124
Passing	146	178
Penalty	27	24
3rd Down: Made/Att	62/197	97/231
3rd Down Pct.	31.5	42.0
4th Down: Made/Att	10/19	10/18
4th Down Pct.	52.6	55.6
Possession Avg.	27:52	32:08
Total Net Yards	5,167	5,593
Avg. Per Game	322.9	349.6
Total Plays	971	1,072
Avg. Per Play	5.3	5.2
Net Yards Rushing	2,146	2,218
Avg. Per Game	134.1	138.6
Total Rushes	417	518
Net Yards Passing	3,021	3,375
Avg. Per Game	188.8	210.9
Sacked/Yards Lost	29/205	30/200
Gross Yards	3,226	3,575
Att./Completions	525/297	524/322
Completion Pct.	56.6	61.5
Had Intercepted	19	13
Punts/Average	83/41.6	74/42.7
Net Punting Avg.	83/36.0	74/36.4
Penalties/Yards	126/1,016	110/1,006
Fumbles/Ball Lost	20/12	22/7
Touchdowns	38	53
Rushing	16	12
Passing	21	36
Returns	1	5

2003 INDIVIDUAL STATISTICS

PASSING	Att.	Comp.	Yds.	Pct.	TD	Int.	Tkld.	Rate
Brees	356	205	2,108	57.6	11	15	21/178	67.5
Flutie	167	91	1,097	54.5	9	4	8/27	82.8
Bennett	1	0	0	0.0	0	0	0/0	39.6
Tomlinson	1	1	21	100.0	1	0	0/0	158.3
Chargers	525	297	3,226	56.6	21	19	29/205	73.1
Opponents	524	322	3,575	61.5	36	13	30/200	94.3

SCORING	TD R	TD P	TD Rt	PAT	FG	Saf	PTS
Tomlinson	13	4	0	0/0	0/0	0	102
Christie	0	0	0	36/36	15/20	0	81
Boston	0	7	0	0/0	0/0	0	44
E. Parker	0	3	0	0/0	0/0	0	18
Flutie	2	0	0	0/0	0/0	0	12
Gates	0	2	0	0/0	0/0	0	12
Osgood	0	2	0	0/0	0/0	0	12
Brees	0	1	0	0/0	0/0	0	6
Lassiter	0	0	1	0/0	0/0	0	6
Neal	1	0	0	0/0	0/0	0	6
Norman	0	1	0	0/0	0/0	0	6
Peelle	0	1	0	0/0	0/0	0	6
Alexander	0	0	0	0/0	0/0	0	2
Chargers	16	21	1	36/36	15/20	0	313
Opponents	12	36	5	52/53	23/26	1	441

2-Pt. Conversions: Alexander, Boston. Chargers 2-2, Opponents 0-0.

RUSHING	No.	Yds	Avg	LG	TD
Tomlinson	313	1,645	5.3	73t	13
Flutie	33	168	5.1	17	2
Dwight	9	88	9.8	20	0
Brees	21	84	4.0	18	0
Neal	18	40	2.2	7	1
Caldwell	5	39	7.8	14	0
L. Johnson	4	26	6.5	18	0
E. Parker	3	21	7.0	13	0
Boston	3	18	6.0	13	0
Chatman	8	17	2.1	6	0
Chargers	417	2,146	5.1	73t	16
Opponents	518	2,218	4.3	58	12

RECEIVING	No.	Yds	Avg	LG	TD
Tomlinson	100	725	7.3	73t	4
Boston	70	880	12.6	46t	7
Gates	24	389	16.2	48	2
E. Parker	18	244	13.6	33t	3
Peelle	16	133	8.3	24	1
Neal	16	62	3.9	11	0
Dwight	14	193	13.8	32	0
Osgood	13	278	21.4	57t	2
Caldwell	8	80	10.0	15	0
Gilliam	6	95	15.8	37	0
Norman	6	72	12.0	21t	1
Chatman	5	54	10.8	23	0
Brees	1	21	21.0	21t	1
Chargers	297	3,226	10.9	73t	21
Opponents	322	3,575	11.1	60t	36

INTERCEPTIONS	No.	Yds	Avg	LG	TD
Jammer	4	6	1.5	6	0
Davis	2	48	24.0	41	0
Edwards	2	27	13.5	15	0
Kiel	2	15	7.5	15	0
Lassiter	1	38	38.0	38t	1
Cooper	1	25	25.0	25	0
Wilson	1	-2	-2.0	-2	0
Chargers	13	157	12.1	41	1
Opponents	19	196	10.3	32	1

PUNTING	No.	Yds.	Avg.	In 20	LG
Bennett	82	3,436	41.9	28	56
Christie	1	20	20.0	1	20
Chargers	83	3,456	41.6	29	56
Opponents	74	3,162	42.7	16	73

PUNT RETURNS	Ret	FC	Yds	Avg	LG	TD
L. Johnson	24	5	184	7.7	21	0
E. Parker	23	2	207	9.0	49	0
Dwight	2	2	0	0.0	2	0
Chargers	49	9	391	8.0	49	0
Opponents	38	20	409	10.8	80t	2

KICKOFF RETURNS	No.	Yds	Avg	LG	TD
L. Johnson	50	1,151	23.0	60	0
Dwight	22	488	22.2	32	0
Florence	4	47	11.8	24	0
Chatman	2	31	15.5	23	0
Pinnock	2	50	25.0	41	0
Carson	1	13	13.0	13	0
Neal	1	1	1.0	1	0
Peelle	1	14	14.0	14	0
Scott	1	9	9.0	9	0
Chargers	84	1,804	21.5	60	0
Opponents	67	1,437	21.4	85t	1

FIELD GOALS	1-19	20-29	30-39	40-49	50+
Christie	1/1	6/6	3/3	3/7	2/3
Chargers	1/1	6/6	3/3	3/7	2/3
Opponents	0/0	5/6	5/6	12/13	1/1

SACKS	No.
Scott	6.5
Dingle	6.0
R. Johnson	4.0
Leber	3.0
Wiley	3.0
Moreno	2.0
Cooper	1.0
Fisk	1.0
Leverette	1.0
Williams	1.0
Wilson	1.0
Edwards	0.5
Chargers	30.0
Opponents	29.0

RECORD HOLDERS

INDIVIDUAL RECORDS—CAREER

Category	Name	Performance
Rushing (Yds.)	Paul Lowe, 1960-67	4,972
Passing (Yds.)	Dan Fouts, 1973-1987	43,040
Passing (TDs)	Dan Fouts, 1973-1987	254
Receiving (No.)	Charlie Joiner, 1976-1986	586
Receiving (Yds.)	Lance Alworth, 1962-1970	9,585
Interceptions	Gill Byrd, 1983-1992	42
Punting (Avg.)	Darren Bennett, 1995-2003	43.8
Punt Return (Avg.)	Darrien Gordon, 1993-96	13.6
Kickoff Return (Avg.)	Leslie (Speedy) Duncan, 1964-1970	25.3
Field Goals	John Carney, 1990-2000	261
Touchdowns (Tot.)	Lance Alworth, 1962-1970	83
Points	John Carney, 1990-2000	1,076

INDIVIDUAL RECORDS—SINGLE SEASON

Category	Name	Performance
Rushing (Yds.)	LaDainian Tomlinson, 2002	1,683
Passing (Yds.)	Dan Fouts, 1981	4,802
Passing (TDs)	Dan Fouts, 1981	33
Receiving (No.)	LaDainian Tomlinson, 2003	100
Receiving (Yds.)	Lance Alworth, 1965	1,602
Interceptions	Charlie McNeil, 1961	9
Punting (Avg.)	Darren Bennett, 2000	46.2
Punt Return (Avg.)	Leslie (Speedy) Duncan, 1965	15.5
Kickoff Return (Avg.)	Keith Lincoln, 1962	28.4
Field Goals	John Carney, 1994	34
Touchdowns (Tot.)	Chuck Muncie, 1981	19
Points	John Carney, 1994	135

INDIVIDUAL RECORDS—SINGLE GAME

Category	Name	Performance
Rushing (Yds.)	LaDainian Tomlinson, 12-28-03	243
Passing (Yds.)	Dan Fouts, 10-19-80, 12-11-82	444
Passing (TDs)	Dan Fouts, 11-22-81	6
Receiving (No.)	Kellen Winslow, 10-7-84	15
Receiving (Yds.)	Wes Chandler, 12-20-82	260
Interceptions	Many times	3
	Last time by Dwayne Harper, 11-27-95	
Field Goals	John Carney, 9-5-93, 9-18-93	6
	Greg Davis, 10-5-97	6
Touchdowns (Tot.)	Kellen Winslow, 11-22-81	5
Points	Kellen Winslow, 11-22-81	30

SAN DIEGO CHARGERS

2004 VETERAN ROSTER

No.	Name	Pos.	Ht.	Wt.	Birthdate	NFL Exp.	College	Hometown	How Acq.	'03 Games/ Starts
60 †	Ball, Jason	C	6-2	301	3/21/79	3	New Hampshire	Londonderry, N.H.	FA-'02	8/8
98	Ballard, Clenton	DT	6-3	308	4/17/79	2	Southwest Texas State	San Antonio, Texas	FA-'03	0*
50	Binn, David	LS	6-3	223	2/6/72	11	California	San Mateo, Calif.	FA-'94	16/0
64	Bogle, Phil	T	6-2	332	9/27/79	2	New Haven	Spring Valley, N.Y.	FA-'03	15/13
65	Brandt, David	C-G	6-4	311	9/25/77	3	Michigan	Jenison, Mich.	FA-'03	0*
9	Brees, Drew	QB	6-0	209	1/15/79	4	Purdue	Austin, Texas	D2-'01	11/11
82	Caldwell, Reche	WR	6-0	215	3/28/79	3	Florida	Tampa, Fla.	D2b-'02	9/4
74	Cesaire, Jacques	DT	6-2	295	8/30/80	2	Southern Connecticut St.	Gardner, Mass.	FA-'03	4/0
28	Chapman, Doug	RB	5-10	218	8/22/77	5	Marshall	Chesterfield, Va.	FA-'04	4/0*
24 †	Chatman, Jesse	RB	5-8	247	9/22/79	3	Eastern Washington	Seattle, Wash.	FA-'02	16/0
54	Cooper, Stephen	LB	6-1	235	6/19/79	2	Maine	Wareham, Mass.	FA-'03	16/0
22	Davis, Sammy	CB	6-0	190	4/8/80	2	Texas A&M	Humble, Texas	D1-'03	16/16
68	Dielman, Kris	G	6-4	310	2/3/81	2	Indiana	Troy, Ohio	FA-'03	6/0
90	Dingle, Adrian	DE	6-3	296	6/25/77	6	Clemson	Holly Hill, S.C.	D5a-'99	16/16
87	Dwight, Tim	WR	5-8	180	7/13/75	7	Iowa	Iowa City, Iowa	T(Atl)-'01	9/3
80	Dyson, Kevin	WR	6-2	212	6/23/75	7	Utah	Clearfield, Utah	UFA(Car)-'04	1/0*
59	Edwards, Donnie	LB	6-2	227	4/6/73	9	UCLA	Chula Vista, Calif.	UFA(KC)-'02	16/16
92	Fisk, Jason	DT	6-3	295	9/4/72	10	Stanford	Davis, Calif.	UFA(Tenn)-'02	16/16
25 t-	Fletcher, Jamar	CB	5-10	186	8/28/79	4	Wisconsin	St. Louis, Mo.	T(Mia)-'04	11/0*
29	Florence, Drayton	CB	6-0	195	12/19/80	2	Tuskegee	Ocala, Fla.	D2a-'03	16/0
7	Flutie, Doug	QB	5-10	180	10/23/62	11	Boston College	Natick, Mass.	UFA(Buff)-'01	7/5
53	Foley, Steve	LB	6-4	265	9/11/75	7	Northeast Louisiana	Little Rock, Ark.	UFA(Hous)-'04	13/3*
77	Fonoti, Toniu	G	6-4	350	11/26/81	3	Nebraska	Hauula, Hawaii	D2a-'02	0*
36	Fox, Vernon	S	5-10	200	10/9/79	3	Fresno State	Las Vegas, Nev.	FA-'02	12/2
85	Gates, Antonio	TE	6-4	260	6/18/80	2	Kent State	Detroit, Mich.	FA-'03	15/11
58	Godfrey, Randall	LB	6-2	245	4/6/73	9	Georgia	Valdosta, Ga.	UFA(Sea)-'04	15/14*
79	Goff, Mike	G	6-5	311	1/6/76	7	Iowa	Peru, Ill.	UFA(Cin)-'04	16/16*
32	House, Kevin	CB	6-0	185	1/9/79	3	South Carolina	Tampa, Fla.	FA-'02	15/0
23	Jammer, Quentin	CB	6-0	204	6/19/79	3	Texas	Angleton, Texas	D1-'02	16/16
35	Johnson, Leon	RB-KR	6-0	232	7/13/74	7	North Carolina	Morgantown, N.C.	FA-'03	14/0
75	Jordan, Leander	G-T	6-4	316	9/15/77	5	Indiana (Pa.)	Pittsburgh, Pa.	UFA(Jax)-'04	6/0*
48	Kiel, Terrence	S	5-11	207	11/24/80	2	Texas A&M	Lufkin, Texas	D2b-'03	16/8
42	Lassiter, Kwamie	S	6-0	207	12/3/69	10	Kansas	Newport News, Va.	UFA(Ariz)-'03	10/10
51	Leber, Ben	LB	6-3	244	12/7/78	3	Kansas State	Vermillion, S.D.	D3-'02	16/16
93	Leverette, Otis	DE	6-7	278	5/31/78	4	Alabama-Birmingham	Americus, Ga.	W(Wash)-'02	7/0
86	Mattos, Grant	WR	6-2	220	3/12/81	2	Southern California	Mountain View, Calif.	FA-'03	6/0
31	Milligan, Hanik	S	6-3	200	11/3/79	2	Houston	Coconut Creek, Fla.	D6-'03	0*
57	Moreno, Zeke	LB	6-2	235	10/10/78	4	Southern California	Chula Vista, Calif.	D5b-'01	16/12
41	Neal, Lorenzo	FB	5-11	255	12/27/70	12	Fresno State	Hanford, Calif.	UFA(Cin)-'03	16/15
83	Norman, Josh	TE	6-2	259	7/27/80	3	Oklahoma	Midland, Texas	FA-'02	7/1
34	Okanlawon, Tony	S	5-11	187	3/4/79	3	Maryland	Forestville, Md.	FA-'03	1/0
81	Osgood, Kassim	WR	6-5	209	5/20/80	2	San Diego State	Salinas, Calif.	FA-'03	16/2
88 †	Parker, Eric	WR	6-0	180	4/14/79	3	Tennessee	Shorewood, Ill.	FA-'02	8/4
84	Peelle, Justin	TE	6-4	255	3/15/79	3	Oregon	Dublin, Calif.	D4-'02	15/9
30	Pinnock, Andrew	FB-RB	5-10	260	3/12/80	2	South Carolina	Bloomfield, Conn.	D7-'03	16/0
52	Polk, Carlos	LB	6-2	262	2/22/77	4	Nebraska	Rockford, Ill.	D4-'01	16/0
11	Ross, Micah	WR	6-2	219	1/13/76	4	Jacksonville	Jacksonville, Fla.	FA-'03	7/0*
5	Scifres, Mike	P	6-2	236	10/8/80	2	Western Illinois	Destrehan, La.	D5-'03	6/0
78 †	Scott, DeQuincy	DT	6-1	260	3/5/78	3	Southern Mississippi	LaPlace, La.	FA-'01	16/0
21	Tomlinson, LaDainian	RB	5-10	221	6/23/79	4	Texas Christian	Waco, Texas	D1-'01	16/16
72	Van Buren, Courtney	T	6-5	350	2/22/80	2	Arkansas-Pine Bluff	St. Louis, Mo.	D3-'03	8/7
56	Wilhelm, Matt	LB	6-2	254	2/2/81	2	Ohio State	Elryia, Ohio	D4-'03	2/0
76	Williams, Jamal	DT	6-3	348	4/28/76	7	Oklahoma State	Washington, D.C.	D2(Supp)-'98	15/15
20	Wilson, Jerry	S	5-11	190	7/17/73	9	Southern	Lake Charles, La.	FA-'02	16/16

* Ballard inactive for 16 games with Jacksonville in '02; Brandt did not play in 7 games and inactive for 4 games; Chapman played 4 games with Minnesota in '03; Dyson played 1 game with Carolina; Fletcher played 11 games with Miami; Foley played 13 games with Houston; Fonoti missed '03 season because of injury; Godfrey played 15 games with Seattle; Goff played 16 games with Cincinnati; Jordan played 6 games with Jacksonville; Milligan missed '03 season because of injury; Ross played 1 game with Jacksonville.

† Unrestricted free agent; subject to developments.

t- Chargers traded for Fletcher (Mia).

Traded—WR David Boston (14 games in '03) to Miami.

Players lost through free agency (6): P Darren Bennett (Minn; 16 games in '03), T Ed Ellis (NYG; 2), G Kelvin Garmon (Cle; 16), C Bob Hallen (NE; 3), T Damion McIntosh (Mia; 13), DT Joe Salave'a (Wash; 9).

Also played with Chargers in '03—TE Stephen Alexander (3 games), G Kevin Breedlove (1), DT Leonardo Carson (5), K Steve Christie (16), CB Tay Cody (16), WR Dondre Gilliam (5), DE Raylee Johnson (9), T Michael Keathley (8), T Solomon Page (8), T Vaughn Parker (3), C Cory Raymer (15), DE Marcellus Wiley (16).

2004 FIRST-YEAR ROSTER

Name	Pos.	Ht.	Wt.	Birthdate	College	Hometown	How Acq.
Ball, Dave	DE	6-5	277	1/4/81	UCLA	Dixon, Calif.	D5a
Bingham, Ryon	DT	6-3	303	6/6/81	Nebraska	Sandy, Utah	D7a
Butler, Robb	S	6-0	217	9/14/81	Robert Morris	Pittsburgh, Pa.	FA
Cox, Jonathan	CB	5-10	185	2/16/82	Georgia Tech	Chicago, Ill.	FA
Edwards, Brock	TE	6-4	250	11/13/81	Texas	Fort Worth, Texas	FA
Evans, Jerton (1)	S	5-11	202	11/25/80	Virginia	Forest, Va.	FA
Floyd, Malcom	WR	6-5	201	9/8/81	Wyoming	Sacramento, Calif.	FA
Garrison, Jeremiah	LB	6-1	233	8/1/82	South Carolina	Belton, S.C.	FA
Hackett, Jay	CB	6-0	195	10/24/79	Montana State	San Diego, Calif.	FA
Hand, Omari (1)	DE	6-4	265	7/3/80	Tennessee	Tallahassee, Fla.	FA-'03
Hardwick, Nick	C	6-4	295	9/12/81	Purdue	Indianapolis, Ind.	D3b
Hoambrecker, Mackenzie (1)	K	6-1	200	6/13/80	Northern Iowa	Davenport, Iowa	FA-'03
Hodges, Howard	LB	6-2	255	5/29/81	Iowa	Copperas Cove, Texas	FA
Jordan, Randy	CB	6-1	175	4/25/82	Kansas State	Tulare, Calif.	FA
Joseph, Carlos	T	6-6	342	7/14/80	Miami	Miami, Fla.	D7c
Kaeding, Nate	K	6-0	187	3/26/82	Iowa	Coralville, Iowa	D3a
Krause, Ryan	TE	6-3	256	6/16/81	Nebraska-Omaha	Omaha, Neb.	D6
Lemon, Cleo (1)	QB	6-2	215	8/16/79	Arkansas State	Greenwood, Miss.	FA-'03
Lenzmeier, Jason	T	6-5	312	2/2/81	New Mexico	Frisco, Texas	FA
Martin, Ruvell	WR	6-4	215	8/10/82	Saginaw Valley State	Muskegon, Pa.	FA
Murray, Calvin	RB	5-10	198	4/19/81	Miami (Ohio)	Dublin, Ohio	FA
Myers, Ty	LB	6-4	240	1/13/81	Illinois	Springfield, Ohio	FA
Olivea, Shane	G-T	6-3	312	10/7/81	Ohio State	Cedarhurst, N.Y.	D7b
Olshansky, Igor	DT	6-6	309	5/3/82	Oregon	San Francisco, Calif.	D2
Phillips, Shaun	LB	6-3	262	5/13/81	Purdue	Willingboro, N.J.	D4
Pippens, Jerrell	S	6-3	205	6/30/80	Nebraska	Philadelphia, Pa.	FA
Pollard, Robert	DE	6-2	278	6/28/81	Texas Christian	Beaumont, Texas	FA
Powell, Luke	WR	5-8	175	2/22/81	Stanford	Smyrna, Tenn.	FA
Riley, Justin	LB	6-2	250	2/9/81	Ball State	Elkhart, Ind.	FA
Rivers, Philip	QB	6-5	228	12/8/81	North Carolina State	Athens, Ala.	T(NYG)
Ross, Isaiah	G	6-3	322	11/6/81	Nevada	Sacramento, Calif.	FA
Skinner, Jon	G	6-6	325	12/12/80	Montana	Dillon, Mont.	FA
Terry, James	WR	6-4	180	9/6/81	Kansas State	Homestead, Fla.	FA
Turner, Michael	RB	5-10	237	2/13/82	Northern Illinois	North Chicago, Ill.	D5b
Veal, Ken	DT	6-1	305	4/14/80	Georgia	Cedartown, Ga.	FA
Ward, Chad (1)	G	6-4	320	1/12/77	Washington	Finley, Wash.	FA
Welker, Wes	WR	5-9	190	5/1/81	Texas Tech	Oklahoma City, Okla.	FA
Wilson, Travis	FB	6-3	257	5/31/81	Kansas State	Howell, Mich.	FA

The term NFL Rookie is defined as a player who is in his first season of professional football and has not been on the roster of another professional football team for any regular-season or postseason games. A Rookie is designated by an "R" on NFL rosters. Players who have been active in another professional football league or players who have NFL experience, including either preseason training camp or being on an Active List or Inactive List, or on Reserve/Injured or Reserve/Physically Unable to Perform for fewer than six regular-season games, are termed NFL First-Year Players. An NFL First-Year Player is designated by a "1" on NFL rosters. Thereafter, a player is credited with an additional year of experience for each season in which he accumulates six games on the Active List or Inactive List, or on Reserve/Injured or Reserve/Physically Unable to Perform.

Log on to www.chargers.com for an up-to-date roster.

SAN DIEGO CHARGERS

COACHING STAFF

Head Coach,
Marty Schottenheimer

Pro Career: Marty Schottenheimer was named the thirteenth head coach in Chargers history on January 29, 2002. In 17 full seasons as a head coach in the NFL, Schottenheimer has led his teams to 12 winning seasons. He is ninth on the NFL's all-time list with 165 regular-season wins. Schottenheimer is 12-20 in two seasons as head coach of the Chargers. He spent 2001 as the Washington Redskins head coach and director of football operations. In his 10 years as head coach of the Kansas City Chiefs (1989-1998), he had a record of 104-65-1 and advanced to the playoffs seven times. The Cleveland Browns went to the playoffs all four full seasons (1985-88) he was coach. In 1986, Schottenheimer was the consensus AFC coach of the year. He coached with the Portland Storm (WFL) in 1974, New York Giants (1975-77), and Detroit Lions (1978-79), and Cleveland Browns (1980-84). In 1984, he took over as the Browns' head coach midway through the season. Played linebacker for Buffalo (1965-68) and Boston Patriots (1969-1970). Career record: 170-124-1.

Background: Schottenheimer was an All-America linebacker at Pittsburgh (1962-64). After leaving the Chiefs in 1998, he joined ESPN as a pro football analyst.

Personal: Born September 23, 1943 in Canonsburg, Pa. Marty and his wife Patricia have one daughter, Kristen, one son, Brian, who is the Chargers' quarterbacks coach, and one grandchild, Brandon.

ASSISTANT COACHES

Tim Brewster, asst. head coach/tight ends; born October 13, 1960, Phillipsburg, N.J. Tight end Illinois 1980-83. No pro playing experience. College coach: Purdue 1986, North Carolina 1989-1997, Texas 1998-2001. Pro coach: Joined Chargers in 2002.

Cam Cameron, offensive coordinator; born February 6, 1961, Chapel Hill, N.C. Quarterback Indiana 1980-83. No pro playing experience. College coach: Michigan 1984-1993, Indiana 1997-2001 (head coach). Pro coach: Washington Redskins 1994-96, joined Chargers in 2002.

Pete Carmichael Jr., offensive assistant/quality control; born October 6, 1971, Farmingham, Mass. Attended Boston College. No college or pro playing experience. College coach: New Hampshire 1994, Louisiana Tech 1995-99. Pro coach: Cleveland Browns 2000, Washington Redskins 2001, joined Chargers in 2002.

Steve Crosby, special teams; born July 3, 1950, Great Bend, Kan. Running back Fort Hayes State 1970-73. Pro running back New York Giants 1974-76. College coach: Vanderbilt 1998-2001. Pro coach: Miami Dolphins 1979-1982, Atlanta Falcons 1983-84, 1986-89, Cleveland Browns 1985, 1991-95, New England Patriots 1990, joined Chargers in 2002.

Hudson Houck, offensive line; born January 7, 1943, Los Angeles. Center Southern California 1962-64. No pro playing experience. College coach: Southern California 1970-72, 1976-1982, Stanford 1973-75. Pro coach: Los Angeles Rams 1983-1991, Seattle Seahawks 1992, Dallas Cowboys 1993-2001, joined Chargers in 2002.

James Lofton, wide receivers; born July 5, 1956, Fort Ord, Calif. Wide receiver Stanford 1975-77. Pro wide receiver Green Bay Packers 1978-1986, Los Angeles Raiders 1987-88, Buffalo Bills 1989-1992, Los Angeles Rams 1993, Philadelphia Eagles 1993. Pro coach: Joined Chargers in 2002.

Greg Manusky, linebackers; born August 12, 1966, Wilkes-Barre, Pa. Linebacker Colgate 1983-87. Pro linebacker Washington Redskins 1988-1990, Minnesota Vikings 1991-93, Kansas City Chiefs 1994-99. Pro coach: Washington Redskins 2001, joined Chargers in 2002.

Wayne Nunnely, defensive line; born March 29, 1952, Los Angeles. Fullback Nevada-Las Vegas 1972-75. No pro playing experience. College coach: Nevada-Las Vegas 1976, 1982-89 (head coach 1986-89), Cal Poly-Pomona 1977-78, Cal State-Fullerton 1979, Pacific 1980-81, Southern California 1991-92, UCLA 1993-94. Pro coach: New Orleans Saints 1995-96, joined Chargers in 1997.

John Pagano, defensive assistant/quality control; born March 30, 1967, Boulder, Colo. Linebacker Mesa State College 1985-88. No pro playing experience. College coach: Mesa State College 1989, Nevada-Las Vegas 1990-91, Louisiana Tech 1994, Mississippi 1995. Pro coach: New Orleans Saints 1996-97, Indianapolis Colts 1998-2001, joined Chargers in 2002.

Wade Phillips, defensive coordinator; born June 21, 1947, Orange, Texas. Linebacker Houston 1966-68. No pro playing experience. College coach: Houston 1969, Oklahoma State 1973-74, Kansas 1975. Pro coach: Houston 1976-1980, New Orleans 1981-85 (head coach of last four games in 1985), Philadelphia 1986-88, Denver 1989-1994 (head coach 1993-94), Buffalo 1995-2000 (head coach 1998-2000), Atlanta 2002-03 (head coach last three games of 2003), joined Chargers in 2004.

Dave Redding, strength and conditioning; born June 14, 1952, North Platte, Neb. Defensive end Nebraska 1972-75. No pro playing experience. College coach: Nebraska 1976, Washington State 1977, Missouri 1978-1981. Pro coach: Cleveland Browns 1982-88, Kansas City Chiefs 1989-1997, Washington Redskins 2001, joined Chargers in 2002.

Matt Schiotz, asst. strength and conditioning; born June 8, 1971, Menomonie, Wis. Attended Wisconsin-La Crosse. No college or pro playing experience. College coach: Kansas 1995-96, Southern California 1998-2000. Pro coach: Kansas City Chiefs 1997, Washington Redskins 2001, joined Chargers in 2002.

Brian Schottenheimer, quarterbacks; born October 16, 1973, Denver. Quarterback Kansas 1992, Florida 1993-96. No pro playing experience. College coach: Syracuse 1999, Southern California 2000. Pro coach: St. Louis Rams 1997, Kansas City Chiefs 1998, Washington Redskins 2001, joined Chargers in 2002.

Clarence Shelmon, running backs; born September 17, 1952, Bossier City, La. Running back Houston 1971-75. No pro playing experience. College coach: Army 1978-1980, Indiana 1981-83, Arizona 1984-86, Southern California 1987-1990. Pro coach: Los Angeles Rams 1991, Seattle Seahawks 1992-97, Dallas Cowboys 1998-2001, joined Chargers in 2002.

Brian Stewart, secondary; born December 4, 1964, San Diego. Cornerback Northern Arizona 1983, 1986-87, Santa Monica City College 1984-85. No pro playing experience. College coach: Cal Poly-San Luis Obispo 1993-94, Northern Arizona 1995, Missouri 1996, 1999-2000, San Jose State 1997-98, Syracuse 2001. Pro coach: Houston 2002-03, joined Chargers in 2004.

John Wuehrmann, coaching administrator; born January 21, 1956, Chicago. Attended Wyoming. No college or pro playing experience. Pro coach: Joined Chargers in 2003.

American Football Conference
South Division
Team Colors: Navy, Titans Blue, Red, Silver
460 Great Circle Road
Nashville, Tennessee 37228
Telephone: (615) 565-4000

2004 SCHEDULE

PRESEASON	**Nashville time**
Aug. 14 **Cleveland**	7:00
Aug. 21 at Buffalo	6:00
Aug. 30 at Dallas	7:00
Sept. 3 **Green Bay**	7:00

REGULAR SEASON

Sept. 12 at Miami	12:00
Sept. 19 **Indianapolis**	12:00
Sept. 26 **Jacksonville**	12:00
Oct. 3 at San Diego	3:15
Oct. 11 at Green Bay (Mon.)	8:00
Oct. 17 **Houston**	12:00
Oct. 24 at Minnesota	12:00
Oct. 31 **Cincinnati**	12:00
Nov. 7 Open Date	
Nov. 14 **Chicago**	12:00
Nov. 21 at Jacksonville	12:00
Nov. 28 at Houston	12:00
Dec. 5 at Indianapolis	12:00
Dec. 13 **Kansas City** (Mon.)	8:00
Dec. 19 at Oakland	3:15
Dec. 25 **Denver** (Sat.)	7:30
Jan. 2 **Detroit**	12:00

Stadium: The Coliseum (opened in 1999) • **Capacity:** 68,809
One Titans Way
Nashville, Tennessee 37213
Playing Surface: Natural Grass
Training Camp: Baptist Sports Park
460 Great Circle Road
Nashville, Tennessee
37228

THE COLISEUM

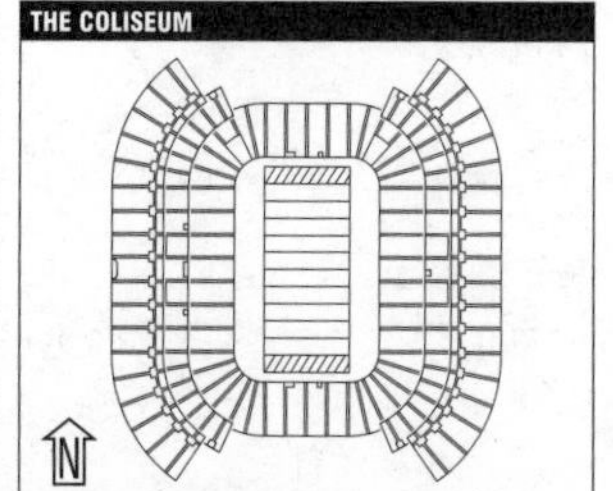

CLUB OFFICIALS

Owner/Chairman of the Board/CEO/President: K.S. (Bud) Adams, Jr.
Executive V.P./General Manager and Director Of Football Operations: Floyd Reese
Executive V.P. of Administration/Facilities: Don MacLachlan
Executive V.P./General Counsel: Steve Underwood
Asst. General Counsel: Elza Bullock
Vice President/Finance: Robert McBurnett
Vice President/Community Affairs: Bob Hyde
Director of Player Personnel: Rich Snead
Director of College Scouting: Mike Ackerley
Director of Sales and Operations: Stuart Spears
Asst. Director of Sales and Operations: Brent Akers
Director of Broadcasting: Mike Keith
Director of Marketing: Ralph Ockenfels
Controller: Jenneen Kaufman
Director of Information Systems: Russ Hudson
Director of Internet Operations/Publications: Gary Glenn
Director of Media Relations: Robbie Bohren
Asst. Director of Media Relations: William Bryant
Director of Security: Steve Berk
Director of Ticket Operations: Marty Collins
Director of Pro Personnel: Al Smith
Director of Player Development: Marcus Robertson
Director of Cheerleading and Entertainment: Meeka Winn
Director of Suite and Club Services: Bill Wainwright
Head Athletic Trainer: Brad Brown
Assistant Athletic Trainers: Don Moseley, Geoff Kaplan
Equipment Manager: Paul Noska
Video Director: Anthony Pastrana

COACHING HISTORY

Houston 1960-1996
(337-348-6)

1960-61	Lou Rymkus*	12-7-1
1961	Wally Lemm	10-0-0
1962-63	Frank (Pop) Ivy	17-12-0
1964	Sammy Baugh	4-10-0
1965	Hugh Taylor	4-10-0
1966-1970	Wally Lemm	28-40-4
1971	Ed Hughes	4-9-1
1972-73	Bill Peterson**	1-18-0
1973-74	Sid Gillman	8-15-0
1975-1980	O.A. (Bum) Phillips	59-38-0
1981-83	Ed Biles***	8-23-0
1983	Chuck Studley	2-8-0
1984-85	Hugh Campbell****	8-22-0
1985-89	Jerry Glanville	35-35-0
1990-94	Jack Pardee#	44-35-0
1994-2003	Jeff Fisher	93-66-0

* Released after five games in 1961
** Released after five games in 1973
*** Resigned after six games in 1983
**** Released after 14 games in 1985
# Released after 10 games in 1994

ATTENDANCE

Home 536,830 Away 534,177
Total 1,071,007
Single-game home record, 68,809, many times, last (12/28/03)
Single-season home record, 537,496 (2001)

2004 DRAFT CHOICES

Round	Name	Pos.	College
2	Ben Troupe	TE	Florida
	Travis LaBoy	DE	Hawaii
	Antwan Odom	DE	Alabama
3	Randy Starks	DT	Maryland
	Rich Gardner	DB	Penn State
4	Bo Schobel	DE	TCU
	Michael Waddell	DB	North Carolina
5	Jacob Bell	T	Miami (Ohio)
	Robert Reynolds	LB	Ohio State
6	Troy Fleming	RB	Tennessee
7	Jared Clauss	DT	Iowa
	Eugene Amano	C	Southeast Missouri St.
	Sean McHugh	RB	Penn State

TENNESSEE TITANS

2003 TEAM RECORD

PRESEASON (4-0)

Date	Result	Opponent
8/9	W 10-6	Cleveland
8/16	W 37-24	Buffalo
8/23	W 23-15	at Cincinnati
8/28	W 27-3	at Green Bay

REGULAR SEASON (12-4)

Date	Result	Opponent	Att.
9/7	W 25-20	Oakland	68,809
9/14	L 7-33	at Indianapolis	56,999
9/21	W 27-12	New Orleans	68,809
9/28	W 30-13	at Pittsburgh	63,244
10/5	L 30-38	at New England	68,436
10/12	W 38-17	Houston	68,809
10/19	W 37-17	at Carolina	72,851
10/26	W 30-17	at Jacksonville	55,918
11/9	W 31-7	Miami	68,809
11/16	W 10-3	Jacksonville	68,809
11/23	W 38-31	at Atlanta	70,891
12/1	L 17-24	at New York Jets	77,710
12/7	L 27-29	Indianapolis	68,809
12/14	W 28-26	Buffalo	68,809
12/21	W 27-24	at Houston	70,758
12/28	W 33-13	Tampa Bay	68,809

POSTSEASON (1-1)

Date	Result	Opponent	Att.
1/3	W 20-17	Baltimore	69,452
1/10	L 14-17	at New England	68,436

SCORE BY PERIODS

	1	2	3	4	OT		Total
Titans	103	120	82	130	0	—	435
Opponents	52	75	75	122	0	—	324

2003 TEAM STATISTICS

	Titans	Opp.
Total First Downs	310	275
Rushing	84	79
Passing	211	167
Penalty	15	29
3rd Down: Made/Att	86/211	51/184
3rd Down Pct.	40.8	27.7
4th Down: Made/Att	6/14	11/18
4th Down Pct.	42.9	61.1
Possession Avg.	32:52	27:08
Total Net Yards	5,501	4,901
Avg. Per Game	343.8	306.3
Total Plays	1,013	926
Avg. Per Play	5.4	5.3
Net Yards Rushing	1,623	1,295
Avg. Per Game	101.4	80.9
Total Rushes	486	342
Net Yards Passing	3,878	3,606
Avg. Per Game	242.4	225.4
Sacked/Yards Lost	25/153	38/223
Gross Yards	4,031	3,829
Att./Completions	502/315	546/332
Completion Pct.	62.7	60.8
Had Intercepted	9	21
Punts/Average	71/43.9	78/42.2
Net Punting Avg.	71/37.8	78/35.9
Penalties/Yards	110/887	96/793
Fumbles/Ball Lost	24/12	21/13
Touchdowns	48	35
Rushing	11	10
Passing	30	20
Returns	7	5

2003 INDIVIDUAL STATISTICS

PASSING	Att.	Comp.	Yds.	Pct.	TD	Int.	Tkld.	Rate
McNair	400	250	3,215	62.5	24	7	19/108	100.4
Volek	69	44	545	63.8	4	1	6/45	101.4
O'Donnell	27	18	232	66.7	2	1	0/0	102.7
Hentrich	5	2	25	40.0	0	0	0/0	56.3
Bennett	1	1	14	100.0	0	0	0/0	118.8
Titans	502	315	4,031	62.7	30	9	25/153	100.3
Opponents	546	332	3,829	60.8	20	21	38/223	78.2

SCORING	TD R	TD P	TD Rt	PAT	FG	Saf	PTS
Anderson	0	0	0	42/42	27/31	0	123
Mason	0	8	0	0/0	0/0	0	48
McCareins	0	7	1	0/0	0/0	0	48
George	5	0	0	0/0	0/0	0	30
Calico	0	4	0	0/0	0/0	0	26
McNair	4	0	0	0/0	0/0	0	26
Bennett	0	4	0	0/0	0/0	0	24
Kinney	0	3	1	0/0	0/0	0	24
Holcombe	1	1	0	0/0	0/0	0	14
Hentrich	0	0	0	1/1	4/5	0	13
Dyson	0	0	2	0/0	0/0	0	12
Wycheck	0	2	0	0/0	0/0	0	12
Boiman	0	0	1	0/0	0/0	1	8
Berlin	0	1	0	0/0	0/0	0	6
Bulluck	0	0	1	0/0	0/0	0	6
Rolle	0	0	1	0/0	0/0	0	6
Volek	1	0	0	0/0	0/0	0	6
Nedney	0	0	0	0/1	1/1	0	3
Titans	11	30	7	43/44	32/37	1	435
Opponents	10	20	5	34/34	26/30	1	324

2-Pt. Conversions: Calico, Holcombe, McNair. Titans 3-4, Opponents 0-1.

RUSHING	No.	Yds	Avg	LG	TD
George	312	1,031	3.3	27	5
Brown	56	221	3.9	28	0
Holcombe	63	201	3.2	21	1
McNair	38	138	3.6	23	4
McCareins	1	13	13.0	13	0
Mason	3	11	3.7	7	0
Calico	1	5	5.0	5	0
Volek	11	4	0.4	5	1
O'Donnell	1	-1	-1.0	-1	0
Titans	486	1,623	3.3	28	11
Opponents	342	1,295	3.8	42	10

RECEIVING	No.	Yds	Avg	LG	TD
Mason	95	1,303	13.7	50t	8
McCareins	47	813	17.3	73	7
Kinney	41	381	9.3	28	3
Bennett	32	504	15.8	48	4
George	22	163	7.4	22	0
Holcombe	19	121	6.4	11	1
Calico	18	297	16.5	45	4
Wycheck	17	165	9.7	25	2
Meier	13	159	12.2	27	0
Brown	8	61	7.6	11	0
Berlin	1	50	50.0	50t	1
McGarrahan	1	10	10.0	10	0
McNair	1	4	4.0	4	0
Titans	315	4,031	12.8	73	30
Opponents	332	3,829	11.5	86t	20

INTERCEPTIONS	No.	Yds	Avg	LG	TD
Rolle	6	141	23.5	52	0
Dyson	4	62	15.5	51t	2
Boiman	2	70	35.0	60t	1
Calmus	2	26	13.0	15	0
Bulluck	2	9	4.5	9	0
Ta. Williams	2	0	0.0	0	0
Woolfolk	1	4	4.0	4	0
Beckham	1	0	0.0	0	0
Kearse	1	0	0.0	0	0
Titans	21	312	14.9	60t	3
Opponents	9	264	29.3	95t	3

PUNTING	No.	Yds.	Avg.	In 20	LG
Hentrich	71	3,117	43.9	26	58
Titans	71	3,117	43.9	26	58
Opponents	78	3,290	42.2	24	65

PUNT RETURNS	Ret	FC	Yds	Avg	LG	TD
McCareins	29	17	330	11.4	58t	1
Mason	8	5	99	12.4	21	0
Titans	37	22	429	11.6	58t	1
Opponents	30	13	276	9.2	59t	1

KICKOFF RETURNS	No.	Yds	Avg	LG	TD
Schifino	35	703	20.1	39	0
McCareins	13	256	19.7	25	0
Mason	5	106	21.2	34	0
Berlin	4	73	18.3	25	0
Holcombe	4	38	9.5	20	0
Jackson	3	77	25.7	31	0
Kinney	3	37	12.3	17	0
Meier	1	9	9.0	9	0
Titans	68	1,299	19.1	39	0
Opponents	81	1,521	18.8	71	0

FIELD GOALS	1-19	20-29	30-39	40-49	50+
Anderson	0/0	5/5	12/12	10/14	0/0
Hentrich	0/0	0/0	2/2	2/2	0/1
Nedney	0/0	0/0	0/0	0/0	1/1
Titans	0/0	5/5	14/14	12/16	1/2
Opponents	0/0	11/11	6/9	8/9	1/1

SACKS	No.
Kearse	9.5
Carter	5.5
Smith	4.5
Thomas	4.0
Bulluck	3.0
Hall	3.0
Haynesworth	2.5
Boiman	1.5
Calmus	1.0
Long	1.0
McGarrahan	1.0
Schulters	1.0
Ta. Williams	0.5
Titans	38.0
Opponents	25.0

RECORD HOLDERS

INDIVIDUAL RECORDS—CAREER

Category	Name	Performance
Rushing (Yds.)	Eddie George, 1996-2003	10,009
Passing (Yds.)	Warren Moon, 1984-1993	33,685
Passing (TDs)	Warren Moon, 1984-1993	196
Receiving (No.)	Ernest Givins, 1986-1994	542
Receiving (Yds.)	Ernest Givins, 1986-1994	7,935
Interceptions	Jim Norton, 1960-68	45
Punting (Avg.)	Greg Montgomery, 1988-1993	43.6
Punt Return (Avg.)	Billy Johnson, 1974-1980	13.2
Kickoff Return (Avg.)	Bobby Jancik, 1962-67	26.5
Field Goals	Al Del Greco, 1991-2000	246
Touchdowns (Tot.)	Eddie George, 1996-2003	74
Points	Al Del Greco, 1991-2000	1,060

INDIVIDUAL RECORDS—SINGLE SEASON

Category	Name	Performance
Rushing (Yds.)	Earl Campbell, 1980	1,934
Passing (Yds.)	Warren Moon, 1991	4,690
Passing (TDs)	George Blanda, 1961	36
Receiving (No.)	Charley Hennigan, 1964	101
Receiving (Yds.)	Charley Hennigan, 1961	1,746
Interceptions	Fred Glick, 1963	12
	Mike Reinfeldt, 1979	12
Punting (Avg.)	Craig Hentrich, 1998	47.2
Punt Return (Avg.)	Billy Johnson, 1977	15.4
Kickoff Return (Avg.)	Ken Hall, 1960	31.3
Field Goals	Al Del Greco, 1998	36
Touchdowns (Tot.)	Earl Campbell, 1979	19
Points	Al Del Greco, 1998	136

INDIVIDUAL RECORDS—SINGLE GAME

Category	Name	Performance
Rushing (Yds.)	Billy Cannon, 12-10-61	216
	Eddie George, 8-31-97	216
Passing (Yds.)	Warren Moon, 12-16-90	527
Passing (TDs)	George Blanda, 11-19-61	*7
Receiving (No.)	Charley Hennigan, 10-13-61	13
	Haywood Jeffires, 10-13-91	13
Receiving (Yds.)	Charley Hennigan, 10-13-61	272
Interceptions	Many times	3
	Last time by Samari Rolle, 12-26-99	
Field Goals	Roy Gerela, 9-28-69	5
	Al Del Greco, 12-3-00	5
Touchdowns (Tot.)	Billy Cannon, 12-10-61	5
Points	Billy Cannon, 12-10-61	30

*NFL Record

TENNESSEE TITANS

2004 VETERAN ROSTER

No.	Name	Pos.	Ht.	Wt.	Birthdate	NFL Exp.	College	Hometown	How Acq.	'03 Games/ Starts
58	Amato, Ken	LS	6-2	245	5/18/77	2	Montana State	Miami, Fla.	FA-'03	16/0
96	Atkins, James	DT	6-5	325	6/23/78	2	Virginia Union	Yonkers, N.Y.	FA-'02	13/4
24	Beckham, Tony	CB	6-1	187	10/1/78	3	Wisconsin-Stout	Ocala, Fla.	D4b-'02	16/2
83	Bennett, Drew	WR	6-5	206	8/26/78	4	UCLA	Orinda, Calif.	FA-'01	12/8
82	Berlin, Eddie	WR	5-11	195	1/14/78	4	Northern Iowa	Urbandale, Iowa	D5-'01	14/0
50	Boiman, Rocky	LB	6-4	236	1/24/80	3	Notre Dame	Cincinnati, Ohio	D4c-'02	16/3
29	Brown, Chris	RB	6-3	219	4/17/81	2	Colorado	Naperville, Ill.	D3-'03	11/0
53	Bulluck, Keith	LB	6-3	235	4/4/77	5	Syracuse	New City, N.Y.	D1-'00	16/16
87	Calico, Tyrone	WR	6-4	222	11/9/80	2	Middle Tennessee State	Memphis, Tenn.	D2-'03	14/2
54	Calmus, Rocky	LB	6-3	238	8/1/79	3	Oklahoma	Jenks, Okla.	D3-'02	10/8
93	Carter, Kevin	DE	6-5	290	9/21/73	10	Florida	Tallahassee, Fla.	T(StL)-'01	16/16
22	Dyson, Andre	CB	5-10	183	5/25/79	4	Utah	Clearfield, Utah	D2-'01	16/16
20	Echols, Mike	CB	5-10	185	10/13/78	3	Wisconsin	Youngstown, Ohio	D4a-'02	5/0
27	George, Eddie	RB	6-3	235	9/24/73	9	Ohio State	Philadelphia, Pa.	D1-'96	16/16
13	Gesser, Jason	QB	6-1	204	5/31/79	2	Washington State	Honolulu, Hawaii	FA-'03	0*
97	Hall, Carlos	DE	6-4	261	1/16/79	3	Arkansas	Moro, Ark.	D7b-'02	16/4
77	Hartwig, Justin	C-G	6-4	305	11/21/78	3	Kansas	West Des Moines, Iowa	D6-'02	16/16
92	Haynesworth, Albert	DT	6-6	320	6/17/81	3	Tennessee	Hartsville, S.C.	D1-'02	12/11
15	Hentrich, Craig	P-K	6-3	213	5/18/71	11	Notre Dame	Alton, Ill.	UFA(GB)-'98	16/0
80	Hill, Darrell	WR	6-3	200	6/19/79	3	Northern Illinois	Chicago, Ill.	D7a-'02	12/0
35	Holcombe, Robert	RB	5-11	208	12/11/75	7	Illinois	Mesa, Ariz.	UFA(StL)-'02	15/0
72	Hopkins, Brad	T	6-3	305	9/5/70	12	Illinois	Moline, Ill.	D1-'93	16/16
55	Kassell, Brad	LB	6-3	242	1/7/80	3	North Texas	Llano, Texas	FA-'02	16/4
88	Kinney, Erron	TE	6-5	275	7/28/77	5	Florida	Ashland, Va.	D3a-'00	16/16
57	Kramer, Jordan	LB	6-1	230	12/7/79	2	Idaho	Parma, Idaho	FA-'03	2/0
99	Long, Rien	DT	6-6	300	8/7/81	2	Washington State	Anacortes, Wash.	D4-'03	8/0
68	Martin, Matt	T	6-6	300	10/12/79	2	Kansas State	Huntington Beach, Calif.	FA-'02	0*
85	Mason, Derrick	WR	5-10	190	1/17/74	8	Michigan State	Detroit, Mich.	D4a-'97	16/16
76	Mathews, Jason	T	6-5	285	2/9/71	11	Texas A&M	Orange, Texas	FA-'98	16/0
42	#McGarrahan, Scott	S	6-1	200	2/12/74	7	New Mexico	Arlington, Texas	FA-'03	16/2
9	McNair, Steve	QB	6-2	235	2/14/73	10	Alcorn State	Mt. Olive, Miss.	D1-'95	14/14
84	Meier, Shad	TE	6-4	255	6/7/78	4	Kansas State	Pittsburg, Kan.	D3-'01	15/6
71	Miller, Fred	T	6-7	320	2/6/73	9	Baylor	Houston, Texas	UFA(StL)-'00	16/16
6	Nedney, Joe	K	6-5	225	3/22/73	9	San Jose State	San Jose, Calif.	UFA(Car)-'01	1/0
23	Nickey, Donnie	S	6-3	215	4/25/80	2	Ohio State	Plain City, Ohio	D5-'03	13/0
75	Olson, Benji	G	6-4	320	6/5/75	7	Washington	Port Orchard, Wash.	D5-'98	16/16
69	Piller, Zach	G	6-5	321	5/2/76	6	Florida	Tallahassee, Fla.	D3-'99	16/16
21	Rolle, Samari	CB	6-0	175	8/10/76	7	Florida State	Miami, Fla.	D2-'98	13/13
81	Schifino, Jake	WR	6-1	201	11/15/79	3	Akron	Pittsburgh, Pa.	D5-'02	13/0
31	Schulters, Lance	S	6-2	202	5/27/75	7	Hofstra	Brooklyn, N.Y.	UFA-'02	16/16
59	Sirmon, Peter	LB	6-2	237	2/18/77	5	Oregon	Walla Walla, Wash.	D4b-'00	14/14
94	Thomas, Juqua	DE	6-2	250	5/15/78	4	Oklahoma State	Houston, Texas	FA-'01	15/0
28	Thompson, Lamont	S	6-1	220	7/30/78	3	Washington State	Richmond, Calif.	FA-'03	16/0
7	Volek, Billy	QB	6-2	214	4/28/76	5	Fresno State	Fresno, Calif.	FA-'00	7/1
56	Wells, Ray	LB	6-1	234	8/20/80	2	Arizona	San Diego, Calif.	W(SF)-'03	16/0
25	Williams, Tank	S	6-3	223	6/30/80	3	Stanford	Bay St. Louis, Miss.	D2-'02	16/16
78	Williams, Todd	G-T	6-5	330	4/9/78	2	Florida State	Bradenton, Fla.	D7-'03	0*
26	Woolfolk, Andre	CB	6-2	197	1/26/80	2	Oklahoma	Denver, Colo.	D1-'03	6/2
	Wright, Thomas	S	6-2	201	7/3/81	2	Michigan State	Lake Wales, Fla.	FA-'03	0*

* Gesser inactive for 16 games in '03; Martin did not play in 1 game; Todd Williams inactive for 16 games; Wright missed '03 season because of injury.

\# Unrestricted free agent; subject to developments.

Retired—Gary Anderson, 22-year kicker, 15 games in '03; Neil O'Donnell, 12-year quarterback,1 game; Frank Wycheck, 11-year tight end, 10 games.

Traded—WR Justin McCareins (NYJ; 16 games in '03).

Players lost through free agency (2): DE Jevon Kearse (Phil; 14 games in '03); DT Robaire Smith (Hou; 16).

Also played with Titans in '03—C-G Tom Ackerman (16 games), DE Anthony Dunn (2), RB Dwone Hicks (3).

2004 FIRST-YEAR ROSTER

Name	Pos.	Ht.	Wt.	Birthdate	College	Hometown	How Acq.
Alexander, Dennis	G	6-4	326	9/28/81	Alabama	Memphis, Tenn.	FA
Amano, Eugene	C	6-3	295	8/1/82	Southeast Missouri State	San Diego, Calif.	D7
Bell, Jacob	G-T	6-4	306	3/2/81	Miami (Ohio)	Cleveland, Ohio	D5
Bishop, Bryce	G	6-2	310	8/20/81	Ohio State	Miami, Fla.	FA
Blakley, Dwayne (1)	TE	6-4	257	8/10/79	Missouri	St. Joseph, Mo.	FA-'03
Bowman, Grant	DT	6-0	298	5/13/80	Michigan	Columbus, Ohio	FA
Branch, Mario (1)	T	6-7	310	8/13/79	Mississippi Valley State	Greenwood, Miss.	FA-'03
Brantley, Kellen	LB	6-2	238	3/22/81	Wake Forest	Miami, Fla.	FA
Clauss, Jared	DT	6-4	294	4/7/81	Iowa	West Des Moines, Iowa	D7
Douglas, Tramon	WR	5-10	204	7/6/82	Grambling State	Baton Rouge, La.	FA
Fleming, Troy	FB	6-0	230	10/1/80	Tennessee	Franklin, Tenn.	D6
Frank, Chris	G	6-3	310	6/8/80	Sacramento State	Moreno Valley, Calif.	FA
Gardner, Rich	CB	5-10	199	2/1/81	Penn State	Chicago, Ill.	D3
Grant, Akil	S	5-10	195	4/16/82	Northern Illinois	Kankakee, Ill.	FA
Jackson, Ray (1)	RB	6-1	227	8/1/78	Cincinnati	Indianapolis, Ind.	FA-'03
Kent, Robert	QB	6-4	222	10/6/80	Jackson State	Indianola, Miss.	FA
King, Vick	RB	5-10	215	2/4/80	McNeese State	Cutoff, La.	FA
LaBoy, Travis	DE	6-3	253	8/10/81	Hawaii	San Rafael, Calif.	D2
Leake, John	LB	6-0	230	8/28/81	Clemson	Plano, Texas	FA
Lucas, Chad	WR	6-0	201	11/7/81	Alabama State	Tuskegee, Ala.	FA
Lynch, Brandon	S	5-11	192	1/31/82	Middle Tennessee State	Hephzibah, Ga.	FA
McClendon, Ronald	RB	5-8	196	4/2/81	Mississippi	Ponchatoula, La.	FA
McConnell, Aaron	DT	6-2	297	7/8/80	Pittsburg State	Midwest City, Okla.	FA
McHugh, Sean	TE	6-5	264	5/27/82	Penn State	Chargin Falls, Ohio	D7
Musinski, Richard	WR	5-11	199	10/12/80	William & Mary	W. Pittston, Pa.	FA
Odom, Antwan	DE	6-4	277	9/24/81	Alabama	Bayou LaBatre, Ala.	D2
Payton, Jarrett	RB	6-0	220	12/26/80	Miami	Arlington, Ill.	FA
Peters, Mickey	WR	6-2	203	8/17/80	Texas Tech	Weatherford, Texas	FA
Portis, Marico (1)	G	6-2	313	11/29/79	Alabama	Prichard, Ala.	FA-'03
Reilly, Hugh	C	6-4	285	11/24/80	Georgia Tech	Roswell, Ga.	FA
Reynolds, Rob	LB	6-3	242	5/20/81	Ohio State	Bowling Green, Ky.	D5
Roberts, Jake	WR	6-3	196	5/19/80	Central Washington	Spokane, Wash.	FA
Rutledge, Jonas	CB	5-10	184	10/23/80	Southern Methodist	Gainesville, Fla.	FA
Sandy, Justin	S	6-0	214	2/22/82	Northern Iowa	Sioux City, Iowa	FA
Schobel, Bo	DE	6-5	264	3/24/81	TCU	Columbus, Texas	D4
Sonnier, Maurice	LB	6-2	238	10/17/82	Louisiana-Monroe	Part Barre, La.	FA
Smith, Steve (1)	S	6-1	204	6/28/79	Oregon	San Pedro, Calif.	FA-'03
Starks, Randy	DT	6-3	307	12/14/83	Maryland	Waldorf, Md.	D3
Stovall, K.T.	DE	6-2	244	12/20/80	Appalachian State	Fayetteville, N.C.	FA
Troupe, Ben	TE	6-4	262	9/1/82	Florida	Augusta, Ga.	D2
Waddell, Michael	CB	5-10	187	1/9/81	North Carolina	Ellerbe, N.C.	D4
Washburn, Brady (1)	T	6-5	305	10/2/79	Appalachian State	Fayetteville, Ark.	FA
Wolcott, Kevin	WR	6-2	190	10/15/81	Tusculum	Cumberland, Tenn.	FA

The term NFL Rookie is defined as a player who is in his first season of professional football and has not been on the roster of another professional football team for any regular-season or postseason games. A Rookie is designated by an "R" on NFL rosters. Players who have been active in another professional football league or players who have NFL experience, including either preseason training camp or being on an Active List or Inactive List, or on Reserve/Injured or Reserve/Physically Unable to Perform for fewer than six regular-season games, are termed NFL First-Year Players. An NFL First-Year Player is designated by a "1" on NFL rosters. Thereafter, a player is credited with an additional year of experience for each season in which he accumulates six games on the Active List or Inactive List, or on Reserve/Injured or Reserve/Physically Unable to Perform.

Log on to www.titansonline.com for an up-to-date roster.

TENNESSEE TITANS

COACHING STAFF

Head Coach,
Jeff Fisher

Pro Career: Became the franchise's fifteenth head coach on January 5, 1995 after closing his first campaign as head coach/defensive coordinator. He replaced Jack Pardee on November 14, 1994, serving the remaining six games as head coach. Fisher is the winningest coach in the NFL during the last five seasons, compiling 56 victories, and is the winningest head coach in franchise history with 93 wins. Last year he became the fourth youngest coach (45) since 1960 to reach 80 regular-season victories (Don Shula, John Madden, and Bill Cowher). Throughout the past five seasons, Fisher has led the Titans to four playoff appearances, two AFC Championship Games, two division titles, and a berth in Super Bowl XXXIV. In 2000, Fisher became only the fifth coach in NFL history to lead his team to consecutive 13-win seasons, joining Mike Holmgren, George Seifert, Marv Levy, and Mike Ditka. Fisher originally joined the Oilers in 1994 as the defensive coordinator after serving as defensive backs coach for the San Francisco 49ers (1992-93). Prior to heading up the 49ers' secondary, Fisher served as the defensive coordinator for the Los Angeles Rams (1991). He began his coaching career with the Philadelphia Eagles in 1986, where he handled defensive backs until becoming the NFL's youngest defensive coordinator in 1988. Drafted by Chicago in the seventh round in 1981, he spent five seasons as a cornerback and kick returner for the Bears (1981-85). Assisted defensive coordinator Buddy Ryan in Bears' 1985 Super Bowl championship season after being placed on injured reserve with ankle injury. Career record: 93-66.

Background: Played at Southern California (1977-1980) for John Robinson in a star-studded defensive backfield that included Ronnie Lott, Dennis Smith, and Joey Browner. Member of the USC team that won the national championship in 1978. Also served as the Trojans' backup placekicker and was a Pac-10 All-Academic selection in 1980.

Personal: Born February 25, 1958, in Culver City, Calif. Jeff and his wife, Juli, have three children, sons Brandon and Trenton, and daughter Tara. The family resides in Franklin, Tenn.

ASSISTANT COACHES

Chuck Cecil, asst. coach/safeties and nickel backs; born November 8, 1964, Red Bluff, Calif. Defensive back Arizona 1983-87. Pro safety Green Bay Packers 1988-1992, Phoenix Cardinals 1993, Houston Oilers 1995. Pro coach: Joined Titans in 2001.

Mike Heimerdinger, offensive coordinator; born October 13, 1952, DeKalb, Ill. Wide receiver Eastern Illinois 1970-74. No pro playing experience. College coach: Florida 1980, Air Force 1981, North Texas State 1982, Florida 1983-87, Cal State-Fullerton 1988, Rice 1989-1993, Duke 1994. Pro coach: Denver Broncos 1995-99, joined Titans in 2000.

George Henshaw, asst. head coach; born January 22, 1948, Richmond, Va. Defensive tackle West Virginia 1967-69. No pro playing experience. College coach: West Virginia 1970-75, Florida State 1976-1982, Alabama 1983-86, Tulsa 1987 (head coach). Pro coach: Denver Broncos 1988-1992, New York Giants 1993-96, joined Titans/Oilers in 1997.

Ned James, offensive assistant/quality control; born January 18, 1964, Syracuse, N.Y. Quarterback New Mexico 1985-86. Pro quarterback Dallas Texans (Arena League) 1990. College coach: Arizona State 1987, Long Beach State 1988, Texas Christian 1989-1990, Winona State 1992-94, Indiana 2000, New Mexico 2001. Pro coach: London Monarchs (WLAF) 1992, Seattle Seahawks 1995-97, New Orleans Saints 1998-99, New Jersey Gladiators (Arena League) 2001, joined Titans in 2002.

Craig Johnson, quarterbacks; born March 3, 1960, Rome, N.Y. Quarterback Wyoming 1978-1982. No pro playing experience. College coach: Wyoming 1983, Arkansas 1984, Army 1985, Rutgers 1986-88, Virginia Military Institute 1989-1991, Northwestern 1992-96, Maryland 1997-99. Pro coach: Joined Titans in 2000.

Alan Lowry, special teams; born November 21, 1950, Miami, Okla. Defensive back-quarterback Texas 1970-72. No pro playing experience. College coach: Virginia Tech 1974, Wyoming 1975, Texas 1977-1981. Pro coach: Dallas Cowboys 1982-1990, Tampa Bay Buccaneers 1991, San Francisco 49ers 1992-95, joined Titans/Oilers in 1996.

Dave McGinnis, asst. head coach/linebackers, born August 7, 1951, Independence, Kan. Defensive back Texas Christian 1970-72. No pro playing experience. College coach: Texas Christian 1973-74, 1982, Missouri 1975-77, Indiana State 1978, 1980-81, Kansas State 1983-85. Pro coach: Chicago Bears 1986-1995, Arizona Cardinals 1996-2003 (head coach 2000-2003), joined Titans in 2004.

Mike Munchak, offensive line; born March 5, 1960, Scranton, Pa. Guard-tackle Penn State 1979-1981. Pro guard Houston Oilers 1982-1993. Inducted into Pro Football Hall of Fame 2001. Pro coach: Joined Titans/Oilers in 1994.

Jim Schwartz, defensive coordinator; born June 2, 1966, Baltimore. Linebacker Georgetown 1984-88. No pro playing experience. College coach: Maryland 1989, Minnesota 1990, North Carolina Central 1991, Colgate 1992. Pro coach: Cleveland Browns/Baltimore Ravens 1995-98, joined Titans in 1999.

Sherman Smith, running backs; born November 1, 1954, Youngstown, Ohio. Quarterback Miami (Ohio) 1972-75. Pro running back Seattle Seahawks 1976-1982, San Diego Chargers 1983-84. College coach: Miami (Ohio) 1990-91, Illinois 1992-94. Pro coach: Joined Titans/Oilers in 1995.

Steve Walters, wide receivers; born June 16, 1948, Jonesboro, Ark. Quarterback-defensive back Arkansas 1967-1970. No pro playing experience. College coach: Tampa 1973, Northeastern Louisana 1974-75, Morehead State 1976, Tulsa 1977-78, Memphis State 1979, Southern Methodist 1980-81, Alabama 1985. Pro coach: New England Patriots 1982-84, 1997-98, New Orleans 1986-1996, joined Titans in 1999.

Jim Washburn, defensive line; born December 2, 1949, Shelby, N.C. Offensive lineman Gardner-Webb 1969-1973. No pro playing experience. College coach: Southern Methodist 1976, Lees McRae J.C. 1977-78, Livingston 1979, New Mexico 1980-82, South Carolina 1983-88, Purdue 1989, Arkansas 1994-97, Houston 1998. Pro coach: London Monarchs (WLAF) 1991, Charlotte Rage (AFL) 1993, joined Titans in 1999.

Steve Watterson, strength and rehabilitation; born November 27, 1956, Newport, R.I. Attended Rhode Island. No college or pro playing experience. Pro coach: Philadelphia Eagles 1984-85, joined Titans/Oilers in 1986.

Everett Withers, defensive backs; born June 15, 1963, Charlotte. Defensive back Appalachian State 1981-85. No pro playing experience. College coach: Austin Peay 1988-1990, Tulane 1991, Southern Mississippi 1992-93, Louisville 1995-97, Texas 1998-2000. Pro coach: New Orleans Saints 1994, joined Titans in 2001.

The NFC

National Football Conference
West Division
Team Colors: Cardinal Red, Black, and White
P.O. Box 888
Phoenix, Arizona 85001-0888
Telephone: (602) 379-0101

2004 SCHEDULE

PRESEASON — **Phoenix Time**

Aug. 14	at Minnesota	5:00
Aug. 21	**San Diego**	7:00
Aug. 28	**Oakland**	7:00
Sept. 2	at Denver	6:00

REGULAR SEASON

Sept. 12	at St. Louis	10:00*
Sept. 19	**New England**	1:15
Sept. 26	at Atlanta	10:00*
Oct. 3	**New Orleans**	1:05
Oct. 10	at San Francisco	1:15
Oct. 17	Open Date	
Oct. 24	**Seattle**	1:15
Oct. 31	at Buffalo	11:00*
Nov. 7	at Miami	11:00*
Nov. 14	**New York Giants**	2:15
Nov. 21	at Carolina	11:00*
Nov. 28	**New York Jets**	2:15
Dec. 5	at Detroit	11:00*
Dec. 12	**San Francisco**	2:15
Dec. 19	**St. Louis**	2:05
Dec. 26	at Seattle	2:15
Jan. 2	**Tampa Bay**	2:05

*A.M.

Stadium: Sun Devil Stadium
•**Capacity:** 73,014
Fifth Street
Tempe, Arizona 85287
Playing Surface: Grass
Training Camp: Northern Arizona University
Flagstaff, Arizona 86011

SUN DEVIL STADIUM

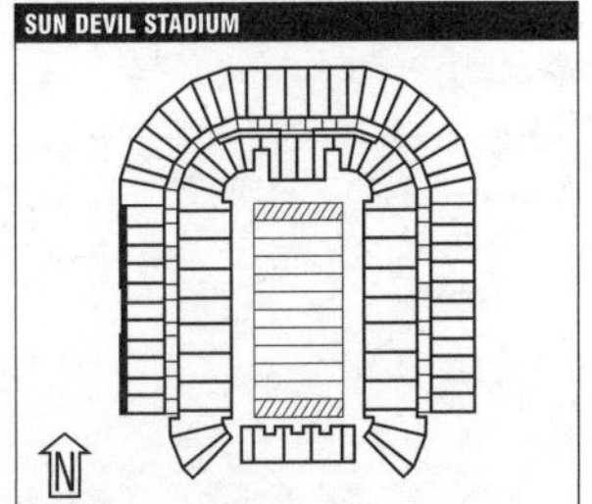

CLUB OFFICIALS

President: William V. Bidwill
Vice Chairman: Thomas J. Guilfoil
Vice President: William V. Bidwill, Jr.
Vice President/General Counsel: Michael Bidwill
Vice President-Football Operations: Rod Graves
Vice President-Sales and Marketing: Ron Minegar
Treasurer and Chief Financial Officer: Charley Schlegel
Public Relations Director: Mark Dalton
Media Coordinator: Greg Gladysiewski
Director of Players Programs: Anthony Edwards
Director of Community Relations: Luis Zendejas
Director of Security: Rick Knight
Director of Operations: Steve Walsh
Director of Cardinals Charities: Pat Tankersley
Information Services Director: Mark Feller
Broadcast Manager/Executive Producer: Tom Hanny
Director of Ticketing: Steve Bomar
Director of Ticket Sales: Jamie Brandt
Director of Group Sales: Scott Bull
Director of Corporate Sales: Steve Ryan
Senior Director of Marketing and Promotions: Lisa Manning
Director of Cheerleading: Heather Shrake
Marketing Communications Coordinator: Chrissy Mauck
Trainer: John Omohundro
Assistant Trainers: Jim Shearer, Jeff Herndon, Freddie Carbajal
Equipment Manager: Mark Ahlemeier
Assistant Equipment Managers: Steve Christensen, Chris Collins

COACHING HISTORY

Chicago 1920-1959, St. Louis 1960-1987 (442-632-39)

1920-22	John (Paddy) Driscoll	17-8-4
1923-24	Arnold Horween	13-8-1
1925-26	Norman Barry	16-8-2
1927	Guy Chamberlin	3-7-1
1928	Fred Gillies	1-5-0
1929	Dewey Scanlon	6-6-1
1930	Ernie Nevers	5-6-2
1931	LeRoy Andrews*	0-1-0
1931	Ernie Nevers	5-3-0
1932	Jack Chevigny	2-6-2
1933-34	Paul Schissler	6-15-1
1935-38	Milan Creighton	16-26-4
1939	Ernie Nevers	1-10-0
1940-42	Jimmy Conzelman	8-22-3
1943-45	Phil Handler**	1-29-0
1946-48	Jimmy Conzelman	27-10-0
1949	Phil Handler-Buddy Parker***	2-4-0
1949	Raymond (Buddy) Parker	4-1-1
1950-51	Earl (Curly) Lambeau****	7-15-0
1951	Phil Handler-Cecil Isbell#	1-1-0
1952	Joe Kuharich	4-8-0
1953-54	Joe Stydahar	3-20-1
1955-57	Ray Richards	14-21-1
1958-1961	Frank (Pop) Ivy##	15-31-2
1961	Chuck Drulis-Ray Prochaska-Ray Willsey###	2-0-0
1962-65	Wally Lemm	27-26-3
1966-1970	Charley Winner	35-30-5
1971-72	Bob Hollway	8-18-2
1973-77	Don Coryell	42-29-1
1978-79	Bud Wilkinson####	9-20-0
1979	Larry Wilson	2-1-0
1980-85	Jim Hanifan	39-50-1
1986-89	Gene Stallings@	23-34-1
1989	Hank Kuhlmann	0-5-0
1990-93	Joe Bugel	20-44-0
1994-95	Buddy Ryan	12-20-0
1996-2000	Vince Tobin@@	29-44-00
2000-03	Dave McGinnis	17-40-0

* Resigned after one game in 1931
** Co-coach with Walt Kiesling in Chicago Cardinals-Pittsburgh merger in 1944
*** Co-coaches for first six games in 1949
**** Resigned after 10 games in 1951
\# Co-coaches
\## Resigned after 12 games in 1961
\### Co-coaches
\#### Released after 13 games in 1979
@ Released after 11 games in 1989
@@ Released after seven games in 2000

ATTENDANCE

Home 288,567 Away 511,250
Total 799,817
Single-game home record, 73,025 (9/19/93)
Single-season home record, 497,330 (1994)

2004 DRAFT CHOICES

Round	Name	Pos.	College
1	Larry Fitzgerald	WR	Pittsburgh
2	Karlos Dansby	LB	Auburn
3	Darnell Dockett	DT	Florida State
4	Alex Stepanovich	C	Ohio State
5	Antonio Smith	DE	Oklahoma State
6	Nick Leckey	G	Kansas State
7	John Navarre	QB	Michigan

ARIZONA CARDINALS

2003 TEAM RECORD

PRESEASON (4-0)

Date	Result	Opponent
8/9	W 13-0	Dallas
8/16	W 16-10	at San Diego
8/22	W 27-17	Chicago
8/28	W 31-27	at Minnesota

REGULAR SEASON (4-12)

Date	Result	Opponent	Att.
9/7	L 24-42	at Detroit	60,691
9/14	L 0-38	Seattle	23,127
9/21	W 20-13	Green Bay	58,784
9/28	L 13-37	at St. Louis	65,758
10/5	L 7-24	at Dallas	63,601
10/12	L 18-26	Baltimore	24,193
10/26	W 16-13	San Francisco (OT)	40,824
11/2	W 17-14	Cincinnati	23,531
11/9	L 15-28	at Pittsburgh	59,520
11/16	L 6-44	at Cleveland	72,908
11/23	L 27-30	St. Louis (OT)	42,089
11/30	L 3-28	at Chicago	61,550
12/7	L 14-50	at San Francisco	66,975
12/14	L 17-20	Carolina	23,217
12/21	L 10-28	at Seattle	64,899
12/28	W 18-17	Minnesota	52,734

(OT) Overtime

SCORE BY PERIODS

Cardinals	55	55	52	60	3	— 225
Opponents	117	117	99	116	3	— 452

2003 TEAM STATISTICS

	Cardinals	Opp.
Total First Downs	256	326
Rushing	80	120
Passing	147	184
Penalty	29	22
3rd Down: Made/Att	83/222	92/199
3rd Down Pct.	37.4	46.2
4th Down: Made/Att	10/22	3/8
4th Down Pct.	45.5	37.5
Possession Avg.	29:41	30:19
Total Net Yards	4,490	5,504
Avg. Per Game	280.6	344.0
Total Plays	981	993
Avg. Per Play	4.6	5.5
Net Yards Rushing	1,531	1,915
Avg. Per Game	95.7	119.7
Total Rushes	403	475
Net Yards Passing	2,959	3,589
Avg. Per Game	184.9	224.3
Sacked/Yards Lost	44/306	21/97
Gross Yards	3,265	3,686
Att./Completions	534/303	497/311
Completion Pct.	56.7	62.6
Had Intercepted	22	13
Punts/Average	83/42.3	67/40.0
Net Punting Avg.	83/34.4	67/36.4
Penalties/Yards	98/761	86/754
Fumbles/Ball Lost	29/14	21/10
Touchdowns	25	55
Rushing	5	17
Passing	18	29
Returns	2	9

2003 INDIVIDUAL STATISTICS

PASSING	Att.	Comp.	Yds.	Pct.	TD	Int.	Tkld.	Rate
Blake	367	208	2,247	56.7	13	15	19/132	69.6
McCown	166	95	1,018	57.2	5	6	25/174	70.3
Boldin	1	0	0	0.0	0	1	0/0	0.0
Cardinals	534	303	3,265	56.7	18	22	44/306	68.9
Opponents	497	311	3,686	62.6	29	13	21/97	93.7

SCORING	TD R	TD P	TD Rt	PAT	FG	Saf	PTS
Boldin	0	8	0	0/0	0/0	0	48
Rackers	0	0	0	8/8	9/12	0	35
Duncan	0	0	0	5/6	6/10	0	23
Jones	0	3	0	0/0	0/0	0	18
Gramatica	0	0	0	6/6	3/4	0	15
Blake	2	0	0	0/0	0/0	0	14
Gilmore	0	2	0	0/0	0/0	0	12
Hodgins	0	2	0	0/0	0/0	0	12
Smith	2	0	0	0/0	0/0	0	12
Bush	0	1	0	0/0	0/0	0	6
Hill	0	0	1	0/0	0/0	0	6
B. Johnson	0	1	0	0/0	0/0	0	6
McCown	1	0	0	0/0	0/0	0	6
Poole	0	1	0	0/0	0/0	0	6
Scobey	0	0	1	0/0	0/0	0	6
Cardinals	5	18	2	19/20	18/26	0	225
Opponents	17	29	9	53/53	21/28	3	452

2-Pt. Conversions: Blake.
Cardinals 1-5, Opponents 0-2.

RUSHING	Att.	Yds.	Avg.	LG	TD
Shipp	228	830	3.6	36	0
Smith	90	256	2.8	22	2
Blake	30	177	5.9	19	2
McCown	28	158	5.6	16t	1
Anderson	18	68	3.8	17	0
Boldin	5	40	8.0	23	0
Hodgins	2	6	3.0	3	0
Gilmore	1	0	0.0	0	0
Kasper	1	-4	-4.0	-4	0
Cardinals	403	1,531	3.8	36	5
Opponents	475	1,915	4.0	52	17

RECEIVING	No.	Yds	Avg	LG	TD
Boldin	101	1,377	13.6	71t	8
Jones	55	517	9.4	34	3
B. Johnson	35	438	12.5	54t	1
Shipp	30	184	6.1	34	0
Gilmore	17	208	12.2	32	2
Smith	14	107	7.6	36	0
Hodgins	14	58	4.1	9	2
Poole	13	177	13.6	37	1
Bush	11	71	6.5	14	1
Anderson	6	36	6.0	11	0
McAddley	4	53	13.3	25	0
Kasper	1	23	23.0	23	0
Scobey	1	9	9.0	9	0
Foster	1	7	7.0	7	0
Cardinals	303	3,265	10.8	71t	18
Opponents	311	3,686	11.9	68t	29

INTERCEPTIONS	No.	Yds	Avg	LG	TD
Jackson	6	122	20.3	30	0
Hill	5	119	23.8	70t	1
Barrett	1	25	25.0	25	0
Rhinehart	1	5	5.0	5	0
Cardinals	13	271	20.8	70t	1
Opponents	22	418	19.0	83t	4

PUNTING	No.	Yds.	Avg.	In 20	LG
Player	82	3,511	42.8	19	64
Cardinals	83	3,511	42.3	19	64
Opponents	67	2,679	40.0	21	59

PUNT RETURNS	Ret	FC	Yds	Avg	LG	TD
Boldin	20	12	130	6.5	19	0
Goss	1	0	7	7.0	7	0
B. Johnson	1	3	3	3.0	3	0
Cardinals	22	15	140	6.4	19	0
Opponents	41	12	472	11.5	57t	2

KICKOFF RETURNS	No.	Yds	Avg	LG	TD
Scobey	73	1,684	23.1	100t	1
Kasper	5	136	27.2	37	0
Anderson	2	31	15.5	16	0
Garcia	1	17	17.0	17	0
Hodgins	1	13	13.0	13	0
Cardinals	82	1,881	22.9	100t	1
Opponents	48	1,042	21.7	47	0

FIELD GOALS	1-19	20-29	30-39	40-49	50+
Rackers	0/0	5/5	1/4	3/3	0/0
Duncan	0/0	2/2	2/4	1/2	1/2
Gramatica	0/0	1/1	2/2	0/0	0/1
Cardinals	0/0	8/8	5/10	4/5	1/3
Opponents	0/0	8/9	7/9	5/9	1/1

SACKS	No.
D. Johnson	3.0
Thompson	3.0
Darling	2.0
Hill	2.0
King	2.0
McKinnon	2.0
Bell	1.0
R. Davis	1.0
Fisher	1.0
Pace	1.0
Tanner	1.0
Wakefield	1.0
Woods	1.0
Cardinals	21.0
Opponents	44.0

RECORD HOLDERS

INDIVIDUAL RECORDS—CAREER

Category	Name	Performance
Rushing (Yds.)	Ottis Anderson, 1979-1986	7,999
Passing (Yds.)	Jim Hart, 1966-1983	34,639
Passing (TDs)	Jim Hart, 1966-1983	209
Receiving (No.)	Larry Centers, 1990-98	535
Receiving (Yds.)	Roy Green, 1979-1990	8,497
Interceptions	Larry Wilson, 1960-1972	52
Punting (Avg.)	Jerry Norton, 1959-1961	44.9
Punt Return (Avg.)	Charley Trippi, 1947-1955	13.7
Kickoff Return (Avg.)	Ollie Matson, 1952, 1954-58	28.5
Field Goals	Jim Bakken, 1962-1978	282
Touchdowns (Tot.)	Roy Green, 1979-1990	70
Points	Jim Bakken, 1962-1978	1,380

INDIVIDUAL RECORDS—SINGLE SEASON

Category	Name	Performance
Rushing (Yds.)	Ottis Anderson, 1979	1,605
Passing (Yds.)	Neil Lomax, 1984	4,614
Passing (TDs)	Charley Johnson, 1963	28
	Neil Lomax, 1984	28
Receiving (No.)	Larry Centers, 1995	101
	Anquan Boldin, 2003	101
Receiving (Yds.)	David Boston, 2001	1,598
Interceptions	Bob Nussbaumer, 1949	12
Punting (Avg.)	Jerry Norton, 1960	45.6
Punt Return (Avg.)	John (Red) Cochran, 1949	20.9
Kickoff Return (Avg.)	Ollie Matson, 1958	35.5
Field Goals	Greg Davis, 1995	30
Touchdowns (Tot.)	John David Crow, 1962	17
Points	Jim Bakken, 1967	117
	Neil O'Donoghue, 1984	117

INDIVIDUAL RECORDS—SINGLE GAME

Category	Name	Performance
Rushing (Yds.)	LeShon Johnson, 9-22-96	214
Passing (Yds.)	Boomer Esiason, 11-10-96 (OT)	522
Passing (TDs)	Jim Hardy, 10-2-50	6
	Charley Johnson, 9-26-65, 11-2-69	6
Receiving (No.)	Sonny Randle, 11-4-62	16
Receiving (Yds.)	Sonny Randle, 11-4-62	256
Interceptions	Bob Nussbaumer, 11-13-49	*4
	Jerry Norton, 11-20-60	*4
	Kwamie Lassiter, 12-27-98	*4
Field Goals	Jim Bakken, 9-24-67	*7
Touchdowns (Tot.)	Ernie Nevers, 11-28-29	*6
Points	Ernie Nevers, 11-28-29	*40

*NFL Record

ARIZONA CARDINALS

2004 VETERAN ROSTER

No.	Name	Pos.	Ht.	Wt.	Birthdate	NFL Exp.	College	Hometown	How Acq.	'03 Games/ Starts
20	Anderson, Damien	RB	5-11	212	7/17/79	3	Northwestern	Wilmington, Ill.	FA-'02	16/0
30	Ayanbadejo, Obafemi	FB	6-2	235	3/5/75	6	San Diego State	San Jose, Calif.	UFA(Mia)-'04	16/2*
84	Banks, Mike	TE	6-4	262	11/5/79	3	Iowa State	Boone, Iowa	D7-'02	6/0
94	Bell, Marcus	DT	6-2	339	6/1/79	4	Memphis	Memphis, Tenn.	D4b-'01	13/10
92	Berry, Bertrand	DE	6-3	250	8/15/75	7	Notre Dame	Houston, Texas	UFA(Den)-'04	16/16*
81	Boldin, Anquan	WR	6-1	218	10/3/80	2	Florida State	Pahokee, Fla.	D3-'03	16/16
91	Bryant, Wendell	DT	6-5	303	9/12/80	3	Wisconsin	St. Louis, Mo.	D1-'02	12/5
87	Bush, Steve	TE-LS	6-3	280	7/4/74	8	Arizona State	Paradise Valley, Ariz.	FA-'01	16/4
35	Carter, Dyshod	CB	5-10	195	6/18/78	2	Kansas State	Denver, Colo.	FA-'04	0*
65	Clement, Anthony	T	6-8	333	4/10/76	7	Southwestern Louisiana	Lafayette, La.	D2b-'98	16/16
51	Darling, James	LB	6-1	247	12/29/74	8	Washington State	Kettle Falls, Wash.	UFA(NYJ)-'03	16/0
75	Davis, Leonard	G	6-6	384	9/5/78	4	Texas	Wortham, Texas	D1-'01	14/14
98	Davis, Russell	DT	6-4	314	3/28/75	6	North Carolina	Fayetteville, N.C.	W(Chi)-'00	15/15
52	Fisher, Levar	LB	6-1	239	7/2/79	3	North Carolina State	Beaufort, N.C.	D2-'02	16/15
63	Garcia, Frank	C-G	6-2	290	1/28/72	10	Washington	Phoenix, Ariz.	UFA(StL)-'03	8/3
86	Gilmore, Bryan	WR	6-0	200	7/21/78	4	Midwestern State	Lufkin, Texas	FA-'00	14/10
25	Goss, Jason	CB	5-10	185	10/4/79	2	Texas Christian	Fort Worth, Texas	W(Chi)-'03	4/0
64	Grace, Steve	C	6-3	292	2/13/79	2	Arizona	Honolulu, Hawaii	FA-'02	0*
29	Harris, Quentin	S	6-1	214	1/26/77	3	Syracuse	Wilkes-Barre, Pa.	FA-'02	16/1
54	Hayes, Gerald	LB	6-1	237	10/10/80	2	Pittsburgh	Paterson, N.J.	D3-'03	12/2
21	Hill, Renaldo	CB	5-11	194	11/12/78	4	Michigan State	Detroit, Mich.	D7a-'01	14/14
48	Hodel, Nathan	LS	6-2	249	11/12/77	3	Illinois	Fairfield Heights, Ill.	FA-'01	16/0
42	Hodgins, James	FB	6-1	274	4/30/77	6	San Jose State	San Jose, Calif.	UFA(StL)-'03	16/8
34	Jackson, Dexter	S	6-0	205	7/28/77	6	Florida State	Quincy, Fla.	UFA(TB)-'03	16/16
83	Johnson, Bryant	WR	6-2	214	3/7/81	2	Penn State	Baltimore, Md.	D1a-'03	15/8
96	Johnson, Dennis	DE	6-5	269	12/4/79	3	Kentucky	Harrodsburg, Ky.	D3b-'02	15/10
47	Johnson, Riall	LB	6-3	245	4/20/78	4	Stanford	Lynwood, Wash.	UFA(Cin)-'01	13/1*
85	Jones, Freddie	TE	6-4	260	9/16/74	8	North Carolina	Landover, Md.	UFA(SD)-'02	16/16
38	Joyce, Eric	CB	5-10	200	1/21/78	2	Tennessee State	Nashville, Tenn.	FA-'04	0*
82	Kasper, Kevin	WR	6-1	197	12/23/77	4	Iowa	Hinsdale, Ill.	W(Sea)-'02	7/0
66	Kendall, Pete	G	6-5	279	7/9/73	9	Boston College	Weymouth, Mass.	UFA(Sea)-'01	14/13
58	Keys, Isaac	LB	6-3	245	6/6/78	2	Morehouse	St. Louis, Mo.	FA-'04	0*
95	King, Kenny	DE	6-3	285	4/23/81	2	Alabama	Daphne, Ala.	D5-'03	11/1
4	King, Shaun	QB	6-1	215	5/29/77	6	Tulane	St. Petersburg, Fla.	UFA(TB)-'04	3/0*
72	Kolodziej, Ross	DT	6-2	295	5/11/78	4	Wisconsin	Stevens Point, Wis.	FA-'04	0*
41	Lucas, Justin	S	5-10	211	7/15/76	6	Abilene Christian	Victoria, Texas	FA-'99	11/0
27	Macklin, David	CB	5-9	196	7/14/78	5	Penn State	Newport News, Va.	UFA(Ind)-'04	16/4*
80	McAddley, Jason	WR	6-2	200	7/28/79	3	Alabama	Oak Ridge, Tenn.	D5-'02	2/0
12	McCown, Josh	QB	6-4	212	7/4/79	3	Sam Houston State	Jacksonville, Texas	D3a-'02	8/3
57	McKinnon, Ronald	LB	6-0	245	9/20/73	9	North Alabama	Elba, Ala.	FA-'96	16/16
79	Pace, Calvin	DE	6-4	262	10/28/80	2	Wake Forest	Douglasville, Ga.	D1b-'03	16/16
15	Parsons, Preston	QB	6-4	232	2/19/79	3	Northern Arizona	Beaverton. Ore.	FA-'02	0*
10	Player, Scott	P	6-1	213	12/17/69	7	Florida State	St. Augustine, Fla.	FA-'98	16/0
89	Poole, Nathan	WR	6-2	210	2/1/77	3	Marshall	Danville, Va.	FA-'02	15/1
1	Rackers, Neil	K	6-0	205	8/16/76	5	Illinois	St. Louis, Mo.	FA-'03	7/0
23	Rhinehart, Coby	CB	5-11	198	2/7/77	6	Southern Methodist	Dallas, Texas	D6a-'99	16/2
78	Rogers, Kendrick	T	6-5	311	10/10/76	2	Alabama A&M	Mobile, Ala.	FA-'02	0*
73	Roundtree, Raleigh	G-T	6-5	344	8/31/75	8	South Carolina State	Augusta, Ga.	FA-'02	0*
33	Scobey, Josh	RB	6-0	222	12/11/79	2	Kansas State	Oklahoma City, Okla.	D6-'02	15/0
70	Shelton, L.J.	T	6-6	335	3/21/76	6	Eastern Michigan	Rochester Hills, Mich.	D1b-'99	15/15
31	Shipp, Marcel	RB	5-11	230	8/8/78	4	Massachusetts	Paterson, N.J.	FA-'01	16/11
22	Smith, Emmitt	RB	5-10	221	5/15/69	15	Florida	Escambia, Fla.	UFA(Dall)-'03	10/5
76	Spikes, Cameron	G	6-4	325	11/6/76	6	Texas A&M	Madisonville, Texas	UFA(Hous)-'03	16/16
28	Starks, Duane	CB	5-10	174	5/23/74	6	Miami	Miami, Fla.	UFA(Balt)-'02	0*
44	Stone, Michael	CB	5-11	199	2/13/78	3	Memphis	Southfield, Mich.	D2b-'01	0*
92	Tanner, Barron	DT	6-3	360	9/14/73	7	Oklahoma	Athens, Texas	FA-'00	14/2
26	Tate, Robert	CB	5-10	193	10/19/73	7	Cincinnati	Harrisburg, Pa.	FA-'04	0*
55	Thompson, Ray	LB	6-3	224	11/21/77	5	Tennessee	New Orleans, La.	D2-'00	12/12
93	Vanden Bosch, Kyle	DE	6-4	282	11/17/78	3	Nebraska	Larchwood, Iowa	D2-'01	0*
97	Wakefield, Fred	DE	6-7	288	9/17/78	4	Illinois	Tuscola, Ill.	FA-'01	10/5
74	Wells, Reggie	T	6-4	298	11/3/80	2	Clarion (Pa.)	Liberty, Pa.	D6a-'03	15/1
19	Williams, Karl	WR	5-11	177	4/10/71	9	Texas A&M-Kingsville	Garland, Texas	FA-'04	13/0*
24	Wilson, Adrian	DB	6-3	222	10/12/79	4	North Carolina State	High Point, N.C.	D3-'01	16/15
56	Woods, LeVar	LB	6-3	244	3/15/78	4	Iowa	Larchwood, Iowa	FA-'01	16/3
68	Wragge, Tony	G	6-4	320	6/1/78	2	New Mexico State	Creighton, Neb.	FA-'02	0*
53	Young, Michael	LB	6-2	245	6/1/78	3	Illinois	St. Louis, Mo.	FA-'01	6/0

* Ayanbadejo played 16 games with Miami in '03; Berry played 16 games with Denver; Carter last active with Cleveland in '01; Grace last active with Arizona in '02; R. Johnson played 13 games with Cincinnati; Joyce last active with Chicago in '02; Keys missed '01 season with Minnesota because of injury; S. King played 3 games with Tampa Bay; Kolodziej inactive for 4 games with San Francisco; Macklin played 16 games with Indianapolis; Parsons inactive for 15 games and did not play in 1 game; Rogers inactive for 5 games and did not play in 3 games; Roundtree inactive for 4 games and did not play in 4 games; Starks missed '03 season because of injury; Stone missed '03 season because of injury; Tate last active with Baltimore in '02; Vanden Bosch missed '03 season because of injury; Williams played 13 games with Tampa Bay; Wragge missed '03 season because of injury.

Players lost through free agency (1): S David Barrett (NYJ; 16 games in '03).

Also played with Cardinals in '03—QB Jeff Blake (13 games), G Chris Dishman (14), K Tim Duncan (5), WR Larry Foster (1), K Bill Gramatica (4), CB Emmanuel McDaniel (15), DT Derrick Ransom (5), C Jason Starkey (4).

2004 FIRST-YEAR ROSTER

Name	Pos.	Ht.	Wt.	Birthdate	College	Hometown	How Acq.
Alexander, Vince (1)	LB	6-0	224	11/21/81	Pennsylvania	Southfield, Mich.	FA
Bryant, Rhomby	WR	6-1	183	12/21/79	Tulsa	Oklahoma City, Okla.	FA
Croom, Larry	RB	5-10	205	10/29/81	Nevada-Las Vegas	Long Beach, Calif.	FA
Dansby, Karlos	LB	6-4	243	11/3/81	Auburn	Birmingham, Ala.	D2
Diamond, Lorenzo (1)	TE	6-3	256	12/15/79	Auburn	Biloxi, Miss.	FA-'03
Dockett, Darnell	DT	6-4	301	5/27/81	Florida State	Burtonsville, Md.	D3
Edwards, Eric	TE	6-5	256	8/4/80	Louisiana State	Monroe, La.	FAa
Fitzgerald, Larry	WR	6-3	223	8/31/83	Pittsburgh	Minneapolis, Minn.	D1
Fordyce, Matt	K	6-0	196	9/21/80	Fordham	Mentor, Ohio	FA
Leckey, Nick	G	6-3	286	3/12/82	Kansas State	Grapevine, Texas	D6
Mayes, Adrian	S	6-1	215	11/17/80	Louisiana State	Houston, Texas	FA
Navarre, John	QB	6-6	250	9/9/80	Michigan	Cudahy, Wis.	D7
Newhouse, Reggie (1)	WR	6-1	191	2/16/81	Baylor	Dallas, Texas	FA
Rue, Joshua (1)	FB	6-4	245	8/19/79	Duquesne	Pittsburgh, Pa.	FA
Smith, Antonio	DE	6-4	272	10/21/81	Oklahoma State	Oklahoma City, Okla.	D5
Stepanovich, Alex	C	6-4	301	9/25/81	Ohio State	Berea, Ohio	D4
Thomas, Rodney (1)	LB	6-1	226	10/16/80	Clemson	Dublin, Ga.	FA

The term NFL Rookie is defined as a player who is in his first season of professional football and has not been on the roster of another professional football team for any regular-season or postseason games. A Rookie is designated by an "R" on NFL rosters. Players who have been active in another professional football league or players who have NFL experience, including either preseason training camp or being on an Active List or Inactive List, or on Reserve/Injured or Reserve/Physically Unable to Perform for fewer than six regular-season games, are termed NFL First-Year Players. An NFL First-Year Player is designated by a "1" on NFL rosters. Thereafter, a player is credited with an additional year of experience for each season in which he accumulates six games on the Active List or Inactive List, or on Reserve/Injured or Reserve/Physically Unable to Perform.

Log on to www.azcardinals.com for an up-to-date roster.

ARIZONA CARDINALS

COACHING STAFF
Head Coach,
Dennis Green

Pro Career: Named the thirty-third head coach of the Arizona Cardinals on January 7, 2004. Posted 101-70 (.591) composite record in 10 seasons (1992-2001) as head coach of the Minnesota Vikings. Led club to eight postseason berths (four NFC Central Division titles) and two NFC championship games. Green is one of three NFL coaches to achieve a 15-victory season (15-1 in 1998), joining Bill Walsh (San Francisco, 1984) and Mike Ditka (Chicago, 1985), and is one of just eight coaches in NFL history to lead his team to the playoffs in each of his first three seasons (1992-94) as an NFL head coach. Green's eight postseason appearances with the Vikings were accomplished with seven different quarterbacks—Sean Salisbury (1992), Jim McMahon (1993), Warren Moon (1994), Brad Johnson (1996), Randall Cunningham (1997-98), Jeff George (1999), and Daunte Culpepper (2000). The Vikings were the only NFL team to qualify for the playoffs each season from 1996-2000 and posted the NFL's best winning percentage (.639, 92-52) from 1992-2000. Green's first professional coaching opportunity came as special teams coach for San Francisco in 1979. Career record: 101-70.

Background: Green was an all-Pennsylvania running back at John Harris High School in Harrisburg, Pa. before attending Iowa where he started for one season as a flanker (1968) followed by two at running back (1969-70 where he was honorable mention all-Big Ten both years) for the Hawkeyes. Green played defensive back briefly for the British Columbia Lions of the Canadian Football League in 1971. Green was a college assistant coach at Iowa (1972, 1974-76), Dayton (1973), and Stanford (1977-78, 1980). During his six seasons (1981-85) as head coach at Northwestern, he was named Big Ten Conference coach-of-the-year in 1982. As head coach at Stanford from 1989-1991, Green led the Cardinal to the 1991 Aloha Bowl.

Personal: Born February 17, 1949 in Harrisburg, Pa., Green earned his degree in recreation from Iowa. He and his wife, Marie, have a daughter, Vanessa, and son ,Zachary. Green also has a daughter, Patti, and a son, Jeremy.

ASSISTANT COACHES

Frank Bush, linebackers; born January 10, 1963, Athens, Ga. Linebacker North Carolina State 1981-84. Pro linebacker Houston Oilers 1985-86. Pro coach: Houston Oilers 1987-1991 (scout), 1992-94, Denver Broncos 1995-2003, joined Cardinals in 2004.

Ryan Capretta, asst. strength and conditioning; born June 25, 1977, Westlake Village, Calif. Wide receiver Santa Barbara City College 1995-96, Indiana State 1997-99. No pro playing experience. College coach: Indiana State 1999, Stanford 2002-03. Pro coach: Baltimore Ravens 2000-01, joined Cardinals in 2003.

Rick Courtright, defensive quality control; born Jan. 4, 1961, Miami. Linebacker Wheaton College 1980-83. No pro playing experience. College coach: Washington 1991-92, Minnesota-Morris 1993, Ohio 1994, Idaho State 1995, Idaho 1996-99, Murray State 2000, Western Illinois 2001-03. Pro coach: Joined Cardinals in 2004.

Robert Ford, wide receivers; born June 21, 1951, Belton, Texas. Wide receiver Houston 1970-72. No pro playing experience. College coach: Western Illinois 1974-76, New Mexico 1977-79, Oregon State 1980-81, Mississippi State 1982-83, Kansas 1986, Texas Tech 1987-88, Texas A&M 1989-1990. Pro coach: Houston Gamblers (USFL) 1985, Dallas Cowboys 1991-97, Miami Dolphins 1998-2003, joined Cardinlas in 2004.

Bill Khayat, offensive quality control; born March 26, 1973, York, Pa. Tight end Duke 1992-95. Pro tight end Kansas City Chiefs 1996, Carolina Panthers 1997, Barcelona Dragons (NFL Europe) 1998. College coach: Tennessee State 2000-03. Pro coach: Joined Cardinals in 2004.

Mike Kruczek, quarterbacks; born March 15, 1953, Washington, D.C. Quarterback Boston College 1973-75. Pro quarterback Pittsburgh Steelers 1976-79, Washington Redskins 1980. College coach: Florida State 1982-83 Central Florida 1985-2003 (head coach 1998-2003). Pro coach: Jacksonville Bulls (USFL) 1984, joined Cardinals in 2004.

Daryl Lawrence, asst. strength and conditioning; born October 20, 1965, Chicago Heights, Ill. Attended Illinois State. No college or pro playing experience. College coach: Illinois State 1995-96, Army 1998-99. Pro coach: Minnesota Vikings 1997, 2000-03, joined Cardinals in 2004.

Kevin O'Dea, special teams; born June 9, 1960, Williamsport, Pa. Wide receiver-defensive back Lock Haven 1983-85. No pro playing experience. College coach: Lock Haven 1986, Cornell 1987, Virginia 1988-1990, Penn State 1991-93. Pro coach: San Diego Chargers 1994-95, Tampa Bay Buccaneers 1996-2001, Detroit Lions 2002-03, joined Cardinals in 2004.

Clancy Pendergast, defensive coordinator; born November 29, 1967, Phoenix. Attended Arizona. No college or pro playing experience. College coach: Mississippi State 1991, Southern California 1992, Oklahoma 1993-94, Alabama-Birmingham 1995. Pro coach: Houston Oilers 1995, Dallas Cowboys 1996-2002, Cleveland Browns 2003, joined Cardinals in 2004.

Donald 'Deek' Pollard, defensive line; born September 16, 1939, Roodhouse, Ill. Defensive back Western Illinois 1957-1961. No pro playing experience. College coach: Western Illinois 1971-73, Florida State 1974-75, Oklahoma State 1976-78, Central Florida 1990-93, Boston College 1994, Syracuse 1998-99. Pro coach: New York Giants 1979-1981, Denver Gold (USFL) 1983, Arizona Wranglers (USFL) 1984-85, Cleveland Browns 1989, St. Louis Rams 1995–96, joined Cardinals in 2004.

Richard Solomon, defensive backs; born, December 8, 1949, New Orleans. Running back-defensive back Iowa 1970-72. No pro playing experience. College coach: Dubuque 1973-75, Southern Illinois 1976, Iowa 1977-78, Syracuse 1979, Illinois 1980-86, Western Illinois 2003. Pro coach: New York Giants 1987-1991 (scout), Minnesota Vikings 1992-2001, joined Cardinals in 2004.

Steve Wetzel, strength and conditioning; born May 11, 1963, Washington, D.C. Attended Slippery Rock. No college or pro playing experience. College coach: Maryland 1985-89, George Mason 1990. Pro coach: Washington Redskins 1990-91, Minnesota Vikings 1991-2003, joined Cardinals in 2004.

Kirby Wilson, running backs; born August 24, 1961, Los Angeles, Calif. Running back-wide receiver Pasadena (Calif.) C.C. 1979-1980, Illinois 1981-82. Pro cornerback Winnipeg Blue Bombers (CFL) 1983, Toronto Argonauts (CFL) 1984. College coach: Pasadena (Calif.) C.C. 1989-1990, Southern Illinois 1991-92, Wyoming 1993-94, Iowa State 1995-96, Southern California 2001. Pro coach: New England Patriots 1997-99, Washington Redskins 2000, Tampa Bay Buccaneers 2002-03, joined Cardinals in 2004.

Mike Wilson, tight ends; born December 19, 1958, Los Angeles, Calif. Wide receiver Washington State 1978-1980. Pro wide receiver San Francisco 49ers 1981-1990. College coach: Stanford 1992-94, Southern California 1997-2000. Pro coach: Oakland Raiders 1995-96, joined Cardinals in 2004.

Alex Wood, offensive coordinator; born March 14, 1955, Massilon, Ohio. Running back Iowa 1974-77, No pro playing experience. College coach: Iowa 1978, Kent State 1979-1980, Southern Illinois 1981, Southern 1982-84, Wyoming 1985-86, Washington State 1987-88, Miami 1989-1992, Wake Forest 1993-94, James Madison 1995-98 (head coach). Pro coach: Minnesota Vikings 1999-2002, Cincinnati Bengals 2003, joined Cardinals in 2004.

Bob Wylie, offensive line; born February 16, 1951, West Warwick, R.I. Linebacker Colorado 1969-1971. No pro playing experience. College coach: Brown 1980-82, Holy Cross 1983-84, Ohio 1985-87, Colorado State 1988-89, Cincinnati 1996. Pro coach: New York Jets 1990-91, Tampa Bay Buccaneers 1992-95, Cincinnati Bengals 1997-98, Chicago Bears 1999-2003, joined Cardinals in 2004.

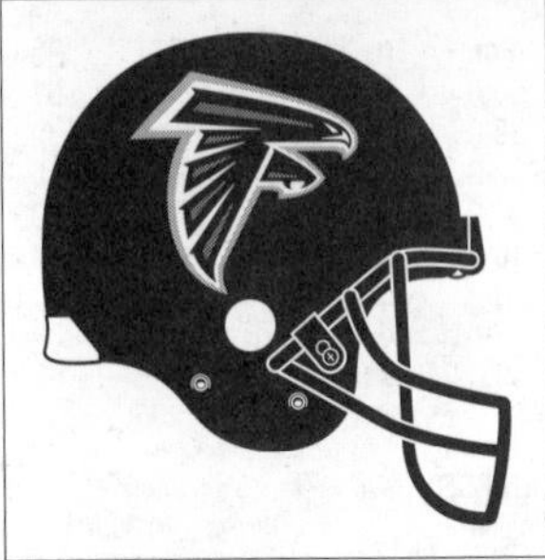

National Football Conference
South Division
Team Colors: Black, Red, Silver, and White
4400 Falcon Parkway
Flowery Beach, Georgia 30542
Telephone: (770) 965-3115

2004 SCHEDULE

PRESEASON		Atlanta time
Aug. 12	at Baltimore	8:00
Aug. 20	**Minnesota**	7:30
Aug. 28	**Cincinnati**	7:30
Sept. 3	at Washington	7:00

REGULAR SEASON		
Sept. 12	at San Francisco	4:15
Sept. 19	**St. Louis**	1:00
Sept 26	**Arizona**	1:00
Oct. 3	at Carolina	4:05
Oct. 10	**Detroit**	1:00
Oct. 17	**San Diego**	1:00
Oct. 24	at Kansas City	1:00
Oct. 31	at Denver	4:05
Nov. 7	Open Date	
Nov. 14	**Tampa Bay**	1:00
Nov. 21	at New York Giants	4:15
Nov. 28	**New Orleans**	4:05
Dec. 5	at Tampa Bay	1:00
Dec. 12	**Oakland**	1:00
Dec. 18	**Carolina** (Sat.)	8:30
Dec. 26	at New Orleans	1:00
Jan. 2	at Seattle	4:05

Stadium: Georgia Dome (opened in 1992) • **Capacity:** 71,228
One Georgia Dome Drive
Atlanta, Georgia 30313
Playing Surface: FieldTurf
Training Camp: Furman University
3300 Poinsett Highway
Greenville, South Carolina 29613

GEORGIA DOME

CLUB OFFICIALS

Owner & CEO: Arthur M. Blank
President-General Manager: Rich McKay
Executive Vice President-Head Coach: Jim Mora
Executive Vice President-Chief Administrative Officer: Ray Anderson
Executive Vice President-Marketing: Dick Sullivan
Executive Vice President-People & Organization Development: Wayne Luke
Assistant General Manager: Tim Ruskell
Vice President of Football Operations: Ron Hill
Vice President & CFO: Greg Beadles
Controller: Wallace Norman
Vice President of Corporate Development: Tommy Nobis
Director of Corporate Sales and Sponsorships: Mark Fuhrman
Operations/Special Events Coordinator: Spencer Treadwell
Vice President of Communications and Community Relations: Susan Bass
Director of Communications: Aaron Salkin
Director of Media Relations: Frank Kleha
Director of Ticket Operations: Jack Ragsdale
Assistant Director of Ticket Operations: Brent Coleman
Coordinator-Program Development/ Player Outreach: Chris Demos
Player Programs Coordinator: Billy (White Shoes) Johnson
Director of Football Administration: Brian Xanders
Director of Information Systems: Donald Zullick
Director of Player Personnel/Pro: Les Sneed
Director of Player Personnel/College: Reed Johnson
Director of College Scouting: Paul Emery
Area Scouts: Matt Berry, Billy Campfield, Dick Corrick, Boyd Dowler, Bill Groman, Bob Harrison, Mark Olson
Head Athletic Trainer: Ron Medlin
Assistant Athletic Trainers: Harold King, Thomas Reed
Video Director: Mike Crews
Assistant Video Director: Jonah Bassett, Charles Sabbatini
Equipment Manager: Brian Boigner
Senior Equipment Director/Gameday Coordinator: Horace Daniel

COACHING HISTORY
(231-351-6)

1966-68	Norb Hecker*	4-26-1
1968-1974	Norm Van Brocklin**	37-49-3
1974-76	Marion Campbell***	6-19-0
1976	Pat Peppler	3-6-0
1977-1982	Leeman Bennett	47-44-0
1983-86	Dan Henning	22-41-1
1987-89	Marion Campbell****	11-32-0
1989	Jim Hanifan	0-4-0
1990-93	Jerry Glanville	28-38-0
1994-96	June Jones	19-30-0
1997-2003	Dan Reeves#	52-61-1
2003	Wade Phillips	2-1-0

*Released after three games in 1968
**Released after eight games in 1974
***Released after five games in 1976
****Retired after 12 games in 1989
#Released after 13 games in 2003

ATTENDANCE

Home 549,263 Away 531,185
Total 1,080,448
Single-game home record, 70,452 (11/11/01)
Single-season home record, 553,979 (1992)

2004 DRAFT CHOICES

Round	Name	Pos.	College
1	DeAngelo Hall	DB	Virginia Tech
	Michael Jenkins	WR	Ohio State
3	Matt Schaub	QB	Virginia
4	Demorrio Williams	LB	Nebraska
5	Chad Lavalais	DT	Louisiana State
6	Etric Pruitt	DB	So. Mississippi
7	Quincy Wilson	RB	West Virginia

ATLANTA FALCONS

2003 TEAM RECORD

PRESEASON (0-4)

Date	Result	Opponent
8/9	L 21-27	Green Bay
8/16	L 10-13	Baltimore
8/22	L 21-30	at Miami
8/28	L 9-20	at Cleveland

REGULAR SEASON (5-11)

Date	Result	Opponent	Att.
9/7	W 27-13	at Dallas	64,104
9/14	L 31-33	Washington	70,241
9/21	L 10-31	Tampa Bay	70,871
9/28	L 3-23	at Carolina	72,765
10/5	L 26-39	Minnesota	70,427
10/13	L 0-36	at St. Louis	66,075
10/19	L 17-45	New Orleans	70,837
11/2	L 16-23	Philadelphia	70,064
11/9	W 27-7	at New York Giants	78,813
11/16	L 20-23	at New Orleans (OT)	68,432
11/23	L 31-38	Tennessee	70,891
11/30	L 13-17	at Houston	70,388
12/7	W 20-14	Carolina (OT)	70,079
12/14	L 7-38	at Indianapolis	57,103
12/20	W 30-28	at Tampa Bay	65,572
12/28	W 21-14	Jacksonville	70,266

(OT) Overtime

SCORE BY PERIODS

Falcons	88	99	50	56	6	— 299
Opponents	65	132	116	106	3	— 422

2003 TEAM STATISTICS

	Falcons	Opp.
Total First Downs	252	333
Rushing	99	122
Passing	127	187
Penalty	26	24
3rd Down: Made/Att	58/194	86/216
3rd Down Pct.	29.9	39.8
4th Down: Made/Att	6/11	5/14
4th Down Pct.	54.5	35.7
Possession Avg.	27:38	32:22
Total Net Yards	4,357	6,108
Avg. Per Game	272.3	381.8
Total Plays	930	1,043
Avg. Per Play	4.7	5.9
Net Yards Rushing	1,949	2,308
Avg. Per Game	121.8	144.3
Total Rushes	435	499
Net Yards Passing	2,408	3,800
Avg. Per Game	150.5	237.5
Sacked/Yards Lost	35/223	36/205
Gross Yards	2,631	4,005
Att./Completions	460/230	508/323
Completion Pct.	50.0	63.6
Had Intercepted	21	15
Punts/Average	87/39.9	82/43.4
Net Punting Avg.	87/36.0	82/34.0
Penalties/Yards	90/790	130/1,001
Fumbles/Ball Lost	22/10	33/16
Touchdowns	35	51
Rushing	17	21
Passing	14	28
Returns	4	2

2003 INDIVIDUAL STATISTICS

PASSING	Att.	Comp.	Yds.	Pct.	TD	Int.	Tkld.	Rate
D. Johnson	243	136	1,655	56.0	8	12	19/121	67.5
Kittner	114	44	391	38.6	2	6	5/30	32.5
Vick	100	50	585	50.0	4	3	9/64	69.0
Dantzler	1	0	0	0.0	0	0	1/5	39.6
Duckett	1	0	0	0.0	0	0	0/0	39.6
Mohr	1	0	0	0.0	0	0	0/0	39.6
Dunn	0	0	0	—	0	0	1/3	—
Falcons	460	230	2,631	50.0	14	21	35/223	58.7
Opponents	508	323	4,005	63.6	28	15	36/205	94.0

SCORING	TD R	TD P	TD Rt	PAT	FG	Saf	PTS
Feely	0	0	0	32/33	19/27	0	89
Duckett	11	0	0	0/0	0/0	0	66
Dunn	3	2	0	0/0	0/0	0	30
Crumpler	0	3	0	0/0	0/0	0	18
Price	0	3	0	0/0	0/0	0	18
Farris	0	2	0	0/0	0/0	0	12
Finneran	0	2	0	0/0	0/0	0	12
Griffith	0	2	0	0/0	0/0	0	12
Bolden	0	0	1	0/0	0/0	0	6
Dantzler	1	0	0	0/0	0/0	0	6
D. Johnson	1	0	0	0/0	0/0	0	6
Mathis	0	0	1	0/0	0/0	0	6
McBride	0	0	1	0/0	0/0	0	6
Rossum	0	0	1	0/0	0/0	0	6
Vick	1	0	0	0/0	0/0	0	6
Falcons	17	14	4	32/33	19/27	0	299
Opponents	21	28	2	47/48	19/25	4	422

2-Pt. Conversions: None.
Falcons 0-1, Opponents 2-3.

RUSHING	Att.	Yds.	Avg.	LG	TD
Duckett	197	779	4.0	55	11
Dunn	125	672	5.4	69t	3
Vick	40	255	6.4	43	1
Griffith	38	168	4.4	15	0
Dantzler	8	21	2.6	12	1
D. Johnson	14	21	1.5	13	1
Layne	1	15	15.0	15	0
Kittner	8	13	1.6	7	0
Price	2	3	1.5	5	0
McCord	2	2	1.0	1	0
Falcons	435	1,949	4.5	69t	17
Opponents	499	2,308	4.6	63t	21

RECEIVING	No.	Yds.	Avg.	LG	TD
Price	64	838	13.1	49	3
Crumpler	44	552	12.5	63	3
Dunn	37	336	9.1	86t	2
Finneran	26	368	14.2	38	2
Griffith	21	122	5.8	24	2
Duckett	11	94	8.5	21	0
Kozlowski	10	87	8.7	19	0
McCord	9	121	13.4	33	0
Farris	6	100	16.7	42t	2
Edwards	1	10	10.0	10	0
Layne	1	3	3.0	3	0
Falcons	230	2,631	11.4	86t	14
Opponents	323	4,005	12.4	76t	28

INTERCEPTIONS	No.	Yds	Avg	LG	TD
Bolden	3	61	20.3	41t	1
McBride	3	44	14.7	25	1
Carpenter	3	22	7.3	14	0
Scott	2	3	1.5	3	0
Mathis	1	32	32.0	32t	1
Newman	1	29	29.0	29	0
Draft	1	4	4.0	4	0
Buchanan	1	2	2.0	2	0
Falcons	15	197	13.1	41t	3
Opponents	21	310	14.8	78	1

PUNTING	No.	Yds.	Avg.	In 20	LG
Mohr	87	3,473	39.9	19	54
Falcons	87	3,473	39.9	19	54
Opponents	82	3,557	43.4	23	60

PUNT RETURNS	No.	FC	Yds.	Avg.	LG	TD
Rossum	39	11	545	14.0	72	1
Bolden	1	0	14	14.0	14	0
Dantzler	1	0	6	6.0	6	0
Edwards	1	0	2	2.0	2	0
McCord	1	0	46	46.0	46	0
Falcons	43	11	613	14.3	72	1
Opponents	35	33	301	8.6	58t	1

KICKOFF RETURNS	No.	Yds.	Avg.	LG	TD
Rossum	62	1,291	20.8	52	0
Dantzler	7	136	19.4	29	0
Jervey	7	118	16.9	25	0
Kozlowski	3	27	9.0	12	0
Falcons	79	1,572	19.9	52	0
Opponents	62	1,204	19.4	44	0

FIELD GOALS	1-19	20-29	30-39	40-49	50+
Feely	0/0	6/6	9/11	4/7	0/3
Falcons	0/0	6/6	9/11	4/7	0/3
Opponents	0/0	9/9	4/6	4/6	2/4

SACKS	No.
E. Johnson	8.0
Kerney	6.5
T. Hall	5.0
Smith	4.0
Jasper	3.0
Stewart	2.5
Draft	2.0
Newman	2.0
Mathis	1.0
McCadam	1.0
Rogers	1.0
Falcons	36.0
Opponents	35.0

RECORD HOLDERS

INDIVIDUAL RECORDS—CAREER

Category	Name	Performance
Rushing (Yds.)	Gerald Riggs, 1982-88	6,631
Passing (Yds.)	Steve Bartkowski, 1975-1985	23,468
Passing (TDs)	Steve Bartkowski, 1975-1985	154
Receiving (No.)	Terance Mathis, 1994-2001	573
Receiving (Yds.)	Terance Mathis, 1994-2001	7,349
Interceptions	Rolland Lawrence, 1973-1980	39
Punting (Avg.)	Rick Donnelly, 1985-89	42.6
Punt Return (Avg.)	Darrien Gordon, 2001	14.1
Kickoff Return (Avg.)	Darrick Vaughn, 2000-01	25.7
Field Goals	Morten Andersen, 1995-2000	139
Touchdowns (Tot.)	Terance Mathis, 1994-2001	57
Points	Morten Andersen, 1995-2000	620

INDIVIDUAL RECORDS—SINGLE SEASON

Category	Name	Performance
Rushing (Yds.)	Jamal Anderson, 1998	1,846
Passing (Yds.)	Jeff George, 1995	4,143
Passing (TDs)	Steve Bartkowski, 1980	31
Receiving (No.)	Terance Mathis, 1994	111
Receiving (Yds.)	Alfred Jenkins, 1981	1,358
Interceptions	Scott Case, 1988	10
Punting (Avg.)	Billy Lothridge, 1968	44.3
Punt Return (Avg.)	Darrien Gordon, 2001	14.1
Kickoff Return (Avg.)	Darrick Vaughn, 2000	27.7
Field Goals	Jay Feely, 2002	32
Touchdowns (Tot.)	Jamal Anderson, 1998	16
Points	Jay Feely, 2002	138

INDIVIDUAL RECORDS—SINGLE GAME

Category	Name	Performance
Rushing (Yds.)	Gerald Riggs, 9-2-84	202
Passing (Yds.)	Steve Bartkowski, 11-15-81	416
Passing (TDs)	Wade Wilson, 12-13-92	5
Receiving (No.)	William Andrews, 11-15-81	15
Receiving (Yds.)	Terance Mathis, 12-13-98	198
Interceptions	Many times Last time by Ashley Ambrose, 11-18-01	2
Field Goals	Norm Johnson, 11-13-94	6
Touchdowns (Tot.)	Many times Last time by Jamal Anderson, 11-1-98	3
Points	Norm Johnson, 11-13-94	20

ATLANTA FALCONS

2004 VETERAN ROSTER

No.	Name	Pos.	Ht.	Wt.	Birthdate	NFL Exp.	College	Hometown	How Acq.	'03 Games/ Starts
22	Beasley, Aaron	CB	6-0	205	7/7/73	9	West Virginia	Pottstown, Pa.	FA-'04	16/16*
79	Beverly, Eric	G	6-3	300	3/28/74	7	Miami (Ohio)	Bedford Heights, Ohio	UFA(Det)-'04	13/13*
64	Bibla, Martin	G	6-3	306	10/4/79	3	Miami	Mountaintop, Pa.	D4-'02	10/2
88	Brewer, Sean	TE	6-4	255	10/5/77	4	San Jose State	Riverside, Calif.	W(Cin)-'03	9/0
56	Brooking, Keith	LB	6-2	245	10/30/75	7	Georgia Tech	Senoia, Ga.	D1-'98	16/16
35	Brown, Dee	RB	5-10	215	5/12/78	4	Syracuse	Clearwater, Fla.	FA-'04	2/0*
29	Carpenter, Keion	S	5-11	205	10/31/77	6	Virginia Tech	Baltimore, Md.	UFA(Buff)-'02	15/8
75	Coleman, Rod	DT	6-2	285	8/16/76	6	East Carolina	Vicksburg, Miss.	UFA(Oak)-'04	16/12*
83	Crumpler, Alge	TE	6-2	262	12/23/77	4	North Carolina	Wilmington, N.C.	D2-'01	16/16
84	Dantzler, Woodrow	WR	5-10	209	10/4/79	3	Clemson	Orangeburg, S.C.	W(Dall)-'03	9/0
14	Detmer, Ty	QB	6-0	189	10/30/67	13	Brigham Young	San Antonio, Texas	UFA(Det)-'04	1/0*
54	Draft, Chris	LB	5-11	232	2/26/76	6	Stanford	Anaheim, Calif.	W(SF)-'00	16/16
45	Duckett, T.J.	RB	6-0	254	2/17/81	3	Michigan State	Kalamazoo, Mich.	D1-'02	16/10
82	Dunbar, LaTarence	WR	5-11	196	8/15/80	2	Texas Christian	Dallas, Texas	D6a-'03	5/0
53	Duncan, Jamie	LB	6-1	238	7/20/75	7	Vanderbilt	Wilmington, Del.	FA-'04	16/6*
28	Dunn, Warrick	RB	5-9	180	1/5/75	8	Florida State	Baton Rouge, La.	UFA(TB)-'02	11/6
80	Edwards, Terrence	WR	6-0	176	4/29/79	2	Georgia	Tennille, Ga.	FA-'03	6/0
87	Farris, Jimmy	WR	6-0	200	4/13/78	2	Montana	Lewiston, Idaho	FA-'02	16/0
4	Feely, Jay	K	5-10	206	5/23/76	4	Michigan	Odessa, Fla.	FA-'01	16/0
30	Fenderson, James	RB	5-9	200	10/24/76	4	Hawaii	Oahu, Hawaii	FA-'04	9/0*
86	Finneran, Brian	WR	6-5	210	1/31/76	6	Villanova	Mission Viejo, Calif.	FA-'00	12/10
65	Forney, Kynan	G	6-3	307	9/8/78	4	Hawaii	Nacogdoches, Texas	D7b-'01	16/16
63	Garza, Roberto	G-C	6-2	296	3/26/79	4	Texas A&M-Kingsville	Rio Hondo, Texas	D4a-'01	14/8
33	Griffith, Justin	FB	5-11	232	4/13/81	2	Mississippi State	Magee, Miss.	D4-'03	16/11
27	Hall, Cory	S	6-0	213	12/5/76	6	Fresno State	Bakersfield, Calif.	UFA(Cin)-'03	11/10
98	Hall, Travis	DE	6-5	295	8/3/72	10	Brigham Young	Kenai, Alaska	D6-'95	15/2
73	Herndon, Steve	G	6-4	292	5/25/77	4	Georgia	LaGrange, Ga.	FA-'04	2/0*
93	House, Raymond	DE	6-2	277	10/7/80	2	Arkansas	Little Rock, Ark.	FA-'03	0*
95	Jasper, Ed	DT	6-2	293	1/18/73	8	Texas A&M	Tyler, Texas	FA-'99	14/14
61	Johnson, Ellis	DT	6-2	288	10/30/73	10	Florida	Wildwood, Fla.	FA-'02	16/3
55	Johnson, Eric	LB	6-0	210	4/30/76	5	Nebraska	Phoenix, Ariz.	UFA(Oak)-'04	16/2*
59	Johnson, J.R.	LB	6-0	240	6/20/79	2	Syracuse	Los Angeles, Calif.	FA-'04	0*
97	Kerney, Patrick	DE	6-5	273	12/30/76	6	Virginia	Newtown, N.J.	D1-'99	16/16
96	Lake, Antwan	DE	6-4	308	7/10/79	2	West Virginia	Seaforo, Del.	FA-'03	0*
38	Layne, George	FB	5-11	250	10/9/78	4	Texas Christian	Alvin, Texas	FA-'03	3/0
23	Mathis, Kevin	CB	5-9	185	4/29/74	8	Texas A&M-Commerce	Gainesville, Texas	FA-'02	14/3
32	McBride, Tod	CB	6-1	208	1/26/76	6	UCLA	Los Angeles, Calif.	UFA(GB)-'03	12/9
47	McCadam, Kevin	S	6-1	219	3/6/79	3	Virginia Tech	Lakeside, Calif.	D5a-'02	12/3
62	McClure, Todd	C	6-1	286	2/16/77	6	Louisiana State	Baton Rouge, La.	D7-'99	16/16
13	Mohr, Chris	P	6-5	215	5/11/66	15	Alabama	Atlanta, Ga.	FA-'01	16/0
67	Moore, Michael	G	6-2	318	11/1/76	3	Troy State	Fayette, Ala.	FA-'03	16/0
90	Overstreet, Will	DE	6-2	259	10/7/79	3	Tennessee	Jackson, Miss.	D3-'02	2/0
81	Price, Peerless	WR	5-11	190	10/27/76	6	Tennessee	Dayton, Ohio	T(Buff)-'03	4/2
48	Rackley, Derek	TE	6-4	250	7/18/77	5	Minnesota	Apple Valley, Minn.	FA-'00	16/15
92	Riley, Karon	DE	6-2	268	8/23/78	4	Minnesota	Detroit, Mich.	FA-'02	16/1
53	Robinson, Terrence	LB	6-2	245	3/12/80	2	Oklahoma State	Tyler, Texas	FA-'03	16/0
34	Ross, Derek	CB	5-10	197	1/5/80	3	Ohio State	Rock Hill, S.C.	W(Dall)-'03	1/0
20	Rossum, Allen	CB	5-8	178	10/22/75	7	Notre Dame	Dallas, Texas	UFA(GB)-'02	2/1
24	Scott, Bryan	S	6-1	219	4/3/81	2	Penn State	Warrington, Pa.	D2-'03	16/0
26	Shabazz, Siddeeq	S	5-11	200	2/5/81	2	New Mexico State	Anthony, N.M.	W(Oak)-'03	15/6
76	Shaffer, Kevin	T	6-5	290	3/2/80	3	Tulsa	Leola, Pa.	D7b-'02	11/0
91	Smith, Brady	DE	6-5	274	6/5/73	9	Colorado State	Barrington, Ill.	UFA(NO)-'00	16/8
52	Stewart, Matt	LB	6-3	232	8/31/79	4	Vanderbilt	Columbus, Ohio	D4b-'01	16/14
50	Ulmer, Artie	LB	6-3	247	7/30/73	7	Valdosta State	Rincon, Ga.	FA-'01	16/16
99	Veal, Demetrin	DE	6-2	288	8/11/81	2	Tennessee	Paramount, Calif.	D7-'03	16/0
7	Vick, Michael	QB	6-0	215	6/26/80	4	Virginia Tech	Newport News, Va.	D1-'01	3/0
36	Webster, Jason	CB	5-9	187	9/8/77	5	Texas A&M	Houston, Texas	UFA(SF)-'04	5/4
74	Weiner, Todd	T	6-4	297	9/16/75	7	Kansas State	Coral Springs, Fla.	UFA(Sea)-'02	10/5*
89	White, Dez	WR	6-1	215	8/23/79	5	Georgia Tech	Jacksonville, Fla.	UFA(Chi)-'04	16/16
70	Whitfield, Bob	T	6-5	310	10/18/71	13	Stanford	Carson, Calif.	D1a-'92	15/11*
25	Williams, Brandon	CB	5-11	186	11/17/80	2	Michigan	Omaha, Neb.	FA-'03	8/8
37	Williams, Tyrone	CB	5-11	193	5/31/73	9	Nebraska	Bradenton, Fla.	UFA(GB)-'03	0*

* Beasley played 16 games with N.Y. Jets in '03; Beverly played 13 games with Detroit; Brown played 2 games with Pittsburgh; Coleman played 16 games with Oakland; Detmer played 1 game with Detroit; Duncan played 16 games with St. Louis; Fenderson played 9 games with New Orleans; Herdon played 2 games with Denver; House did not play in 1 game and inactive for 1 game; Eric Johnson played 16 games with Oakland; J.R. Johnson last active with New Orleans in '02; Lake last active with Detroit in '02; Webster played 10 games with San Francsico; White played 15 games with Chicago; B. Williams inactive for 1 game.

Players lost through free agency (4): CB Juran Bolden (Jax; 8 games in '03), G Travis Claridge (Car; 6), QB Doug Johnson (Jax; 10), TE Brian Kozlowski (Wash; 10).

Also played with Falcons in '03—CB Ray Buchanan (15 games), RB Travis Jervey (15), QB Kurt Kittner (7), S Gerald McBurrows (13), WR Quentin McCord (9), G-T Dwayen Morgan (5), LB Keith Newman (12), S Travaris Robinson (5), LB Sam Rogers (2), LB Twan Russell (16).

2004 FIRST-YEAR ROSTER

Name	Pos.	Ht.	Wt.	Birthdate	College	Hometown	How Acq.
Allen, Jeremy (1)	FB	5-11	239	9/5/79	Iowa	Indianapolis, Ind.	FA-'03
Alston, Charles (1)	DE	6-5	272	6/8/78	Bowie State	Washington, D.C.	FA-'03
Ashkinaz, David	C	6-4	300	3/2/81	Central Florida	San Jose, Calif.	FA
Cox, Curome	CB	6-1	199	2/28/81	Maryland	Washington, D.C.	FA
Duval, Damon (1)	K	5-11	195	4/13/80	Auburn	Chattanooga, Tenn.	FA-'03
Hall, DeAngelo	CB	5-10	197	11/19/83	Virginia Tech	Cheapeake, Va.	D1a
Henry, William	T	6-4	295	10/16/81	Clemson	Greenville, S.C.	FA
House, Raymond (1)	DE	6-2	277	10/7/80	Arkansas	Little Rock, Ark.	FA-'03
Jenkins, Michael	WR	6-4	217	6/18/82	Ohio State	Tampa, Fla.	D1b
Johnson, Brandon	FB	6-1	234	12/30/79	Auburn	Bayou La Batre, La.	FA
Jowers, Jason (1)	T	6-6	324	9/9/80	Wisconsin	Libertyville, Ill.	FA-'03
Lavalais, Chad	DT	6-1	293	4/15/79	Louisiana State	Marksville, La.	D5
Melton, Terrence (1)	LB	6-1	235	1/1/77	Rice	Houston, Texas	FA
Mosley, Kendrick	WR	6-2	197	7/21/81	Western Michigan	Pahokee, Fla.	FA
Pakulak, Glenn (1)	P	6-2	226	4/9/80	Kentucky	Pontiac, Mich.	FA
Peck, Jared (1)	T	6-5	290	5/6/79	North Dakota State	Bloomington, Minn.	FA-'03
Pruitt, Etric	S	6-0	196	8/16/81	Southern Mississippi	Theodore, Ala.	D6
Quinnie, Willie (1)	WR	6-2	180	10/2/80	Alabama-Birmingham	Birmingham, Ala.	FA-'03
Rader, Jason	TE	6-4	274	4/12/81	Marshall	St. Albans, W. Va.	FA
Reed, Rodney	G	6-4	280	8/17/80	Louisiana State	Baton Rouge, La.	FA
Ricketts, Pat	CB	5-11	180	8/2/80	Nebraska	Omaha, Neb.	FA
Robinson, Terrence (1)	LB	6-2	245	3/12/80	Oklahoma State	Tyler, Texas	FA-'03
Royal, Roderick	LB	6 -1	241	12/22/81	McNeese State	Zachary, La.	FA
Schaub, Matt	QB	6-5	237	6/25/81	Virginia	West Chester, Pa.	D3
Stewart, Steve	T	6-4	309	11/12/80	Michigan State	East Lansing, Mich.	FA
Toles, Deryck	LB	5-11	224	12/30/80	Penn State	Warren, Ohio	FA
Williams, Brandon (1)	CB	5-11	186	11/17/80	Michigan	Omaha, Neb.	FA-'03
Williams, Demorrio	LB	6-0	232	7/6/80	Nebraska	Beckville, Texas	D4
Wilson, Quincy	RB	5-9	225	4/26/81	West Virginia	Weirton, W. Va.	D7
Youngblood, Kevin	WR	6-4	221	11/22/80	Clemson	Jacksonville, Fla.	FA

The term NFL Rookie is defined as a player who is in his first season of professional football and has not been on the roster of another professional football team for any regular-season or postseason games. A Rookie is designated by an "R" on NFL rosters. Players who have been active in another professional football league or players who have NFL experience, including either preseason training camp or being on an Active List or Inactive List, or on Reserve/Injured or Reserve/Physically Unable to Perform for fewer than six regular-season games, are termed NFL First-Year Players. An NFL First-Year Player is designated by a "1" on NFL rosters. Thereafter, a player is credited with an additional year of experience for each season in which he accumulates six games on the Active List or Inactive List, or on Reserve/Injured or Reserve/Physically Unable to Perform.

Log on to www.atlantafalcons.com for an up-to-date roster.

ATLANTA FALCONS

COACHING STAFF

Executive Vice President/Head Coach, Jim Mora

Pro Career: First-time head coach Jim Mora was hired by the Falcons on January 9, 2004. In 2003, in his fifth season as defensive coordinator of the San Francisco 49ers, Mora's unit finished fourth in the NFC in total defense and ninth in the NFL in rushing defense. San Francisco's 42 quarterback sacks finished tied for fourth in the NFL. Despite a rash of injuries, the 49ers gave a solid effort on defense in 2002, finishing seventh in the NFL against the run and 14th in total defense. The 49ers defense was truly a team effort as four starters earned NFC Player-of-the-Week honors during the season. In 2001, the defense ranked sixth in the NFL in scoring defense, allowing only 16.3 points per game. The team also registered three shutouts, the most in 49ers history. Mora served as the 49ers' secondary coach (1997-98). He was named as the secondary coach for the Saints in 1992. During his five years in New Orleans (1992-96), the team twice led the NFL in fewest passing yards allowed (1992-93). Mora spent seven seasons in the Chargers' organization as a member of the pro personnel department (1985), defensive assistant in the secondary (1986-88), and defensive backs coach (1989-1991). Career record: 0-0.

Background: Mora played defensive back for Washington (1980-83), appearing in two Rose Bowls. He served as an assistant for one season (1984) on Don James' staff, helping the squad earn a berth in the Orange Bowl.

Personal: Born November 19, 1961 in Los Angeles. Mora attended Interlake High in Bellevue, Wash. He is the son of former NFL head coach Jim Mora. He and his wife, Shannon, have four children: Cole (1-7-95), Lillia (8-19-96), Ryder (1-11-99), and Trey (10-4-02).

ASSISTANT COACHES

Dennis Allen, defensive assistant; born September 22, 1972, Hurst, Texas. Safety Texas A&M 1992-95. No pro playing experience. College coach: Texas A&M 1996-99, Tulsa 2000-01. Pro coach: Joined Falcons in 2002.

Clancy Barone, asst. offensive line; born July 26, 1963, San Andreas, Calif. Attended Cal State-Sacramento. No college or pro playing experience. College coach: American River (Calif.) J.C. 1987-1989, Cal State-Sacramento 1990-92, Texas A&M 1993, Eastern Illinois 1994-96, Wyoming 1997-1999, Houston 2000-02, Texas State 2003. Pro coach: Joined Falcons in 2004.

Chris Beake, linebackers; born September 10, 1972, Kansas City, Missouri. Attended Air Force. No college or pro playing experience. College coach: Air Force 1994-95. Pro coach: San Francisco 49ers 1999-2003, joined Falcons in 2004.

Rocky Colburn, asst. strength and conditioning; born May 24, 1963, Dallas, Ore. Safety Alabama 1981-83. No pro playing experience. College coach: Alabama 1984, 1987-1992, Samford 1986. Pro coach: Joined Falcons in 1999.

Joe DeCamillis, special teams coordinator; born June 29, 1965, Arvada, Colo. Attended Wyoming. No college or pro playing experience. College coach: Wyoming 1988. Pro coach: Denver Broncos 1989, Miami Dolphins 1990, New York Giants 1993-96, joined Falcons in 1997.

Ed Donatell, defensive coordinator; born February 4, 1957, Akron, Ohio. Defensive back Glenville (W. Va.) State 1975-78. College coach: Kent State 1979-1980, Washington 1981-82, Pacific 1983-85, Idaho 1986-88, Cal State-Fullerton 1989. Pro coach: New York Jets 1990-94, Denver Broncos 1995-99, Green Bay Packers 2000-03, joined Falcons in 2004.

Alex Gibbs, asst. head coach/offensive line; born February 22, 1941 Morganton, N.C. Running back-defensive back Davidson College 1959-1963. No pro playing experience. College coach: Duke 1969-1970, Kentucky 1971-72, West Virginia 1973-74, Ohio State 1975-78, Auburn 1979-1981, Georgia 1982-83.. Pro coach: Denver Broncos 1984-87, Oakland Raiders 1988-89, San Diego Chargers 1990-91, Indianapolis Colts 1992, Kansas City Chiefs 1993-94, Denver Broncos 1995-2003, joined Falcons in 2004.

Jeff Jagodzinski, tight ends; born October 12, 1963, Milwaukee, Wis. Fullback Wisconsin-Whitewater 1981-84. No pro playing experience. College coach: Wisconsin-Whitewater 1985, Northern Illinois 1986, Louisiana State 1987-88, East Carolina 1989-1996, Boston College 1997-98. Pro coach: Green Bay Packers 1999-2003, joined Falcons in 2004.

Bill Johnson, defensive line; born June 23, 1955, Monroe, Louisiana. Defensive lineman Northwestern (La.) State 1976-79. No pro playing experience. College coach: Northwestern (La.) State 1980-81, McNeese State 1985-86, Miami 1987, Louisiana Tech 1988-89, Arkansas 1990-91, 2000, Texas A&M 1992-99. Pro coach: Joined Falcons in 2001.

Mike Johnson, quarterbacks; born May 2, 1967, Los Angeles. Quarterback Arizona State 1985-86, Akron 1988-89. Pro quarterback Arizona Cardinals 1990, San Antonio Riders (World League) 1991-92, British Columbia Lions (CFL) 1992-93, Shreveport Pirates (CFL) 1994-95. College coach: Oregon State 1997-99. Pro coach: San Diego Chargers 2000-01, joined Falcons in 2002.

Greg Knapp, offensive coordinator; born March 5, 1963, Long Beach, Calif. Quarterback Cal State-Sacramento 1982-85. No pro playing experience. College coach: Cal State-Sacramento 1986-1994. Pro coach: San Francisco 49ers 1995-2003, joined Falcons in 2004.

Brett Maxie, defensive backs; born January 13, 1962, Dallas. Safety Texas Southern 1982-85. Pro safety New Orleans Saints 1985-1993, Atlanta Falcons 1994, Carolina Panthers 1995-96, San Francisco 49ers 1997. Pro coach: Carolina Panthers 1998, San Francisco 49ers 1999-2003, joined Falcons in 2004.

Al Miller, strength and conditioning; born August 29, 1947, El Dorado, Ark. Wide receiver Northeast Louisiana 1965-69. No pro playing experience. College coach: Northwestern State (La.) 1974-78, Mississippi State 1980, Northeast Louisiana 1981, Alabama 1982-84. Pro coach: Denver Broncos 1987-92, New York Giants 1993-96, joined Falcons in 1997.

Robert Prince, offensive assistant; born May 8, 1965, Okinawa, Japan. Attended Humboldt State. No college or pro playing experience. College coach: Humboldt State 1989-1990, Montana State 1991, Cal State-Sacramento 1992-93, Fort Lewis College 1994-95, Recruit Seagulls (X League Japan) 1996-97, Portland State 1998-2000, Boise State 2001-03. Pro coach: Joined Falcons in 2004.

George Stewart, wide receivers; born December 29, 1958, Little Rock, Ark. Guard Arkansas 1977-1980. No pro playing experience. College coach: Minnesota 1984-85, Notre Dame 1986-88. Pro coach: Pittsburgh Steelers 1989-1991, Tampa Bay Buccaneers 1992-95, San Francisco 49ers 1996-2002, joined Falcons in 2003.

Emmitt Thomas, senior defensive assistant/secondary; born June 3, 1943, Angleton, Texas. Quarterback-receiver Bishop (Texas) College 1963-65. Pro defensive back Kansas City Chiefs 1966-1978. College coach: Central Missouri State 1979-1980. Pro coach: St. Louis Cardinals 1981-85, Washington Redskins 1986-1994, Philadelphia Eagles 1995-98, Green Bay Packers 1999, Minnesota Vikings 2000-01, joined Falcons in 2002.

Ollie Wilson, running backs; born March 3, 1951, Worcester, Mass. Wide receiver Springfield 1971-73. No pro playing experience. College coach: Springfield 1975, Northeastern 1976-1982, California 1983-1990. Pro coach: Atlanta Falcons 1991-96, San Diego Chargers 1997-2001, rejoined Falcons in 2002.

National Football Conference
South Division
Team Colors: Black, Panther Blue, and Silver
800 South Mint Street
Charlotte, North Carolina 28202-1502
Telephone: (704) 358-7000

2004 SCHEDULE

PRESEASON — **Charlotte time**

Aug. 14	at Washington	8:00
Aug. 19	**New York Giants**	8:00
Aug. 28	**New England**	8:00
Sept. 2	at Pittsburgh	7:00

REGULAR SEASON

Sept. 13	**Green Bay** (Mon.)	9:00
Sept. 19	at Kansas City	1:00
Sept. 26	Open Date	
Oct. 3	**Atlanta**	4:05
Oct. 10	at Denver	4:15
Oct. 17	at Philadelphia	1:00
Oct. 24	**San Diego**	1:00
Oct. 31	at Seattle	4:05
Nov. 7	**Oakland**	1:00
Nov. 14	at San Francisco	4:15
Nov. 21	**Arizona**	1:00
Nov. 28	**Tampa Bay**	1:00
Dec. 5	at New Orleans	1:00
Dec. 12	**St. Louis**	4:15
Dec. 18	at Atlanta (Sat.)	8:30
Dec. 26	at Tampa Bay	1:00
Jan. 2	**New Orleans**	1:00

Stadium: Bank of America Stadium (opened in 1996) • **Capacity:** 73,250
Charlotte, North Carolina 28202-1502
Playing Surface: Grass
Training Camp: Wofford College
Spartanburg, South Carolina 29303

BANK OF AMERICA STADIUM

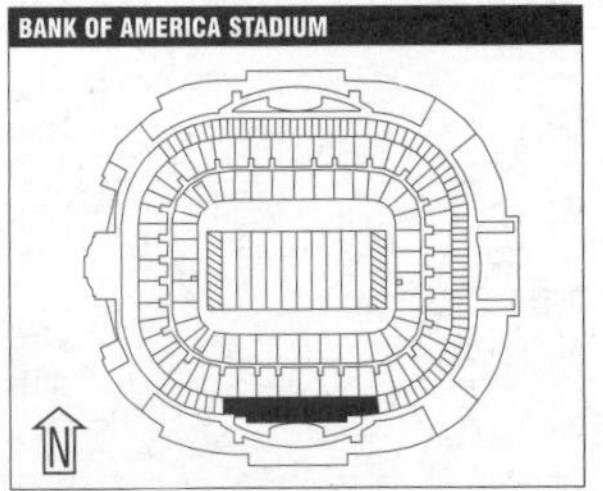

CLUB OFFICIALS

Owner/Founder: Jerry Richardson
President, Carolina Panthers: Mark Richardson
President Carolinas Stadium Corp.: Jon Richardson
General Manager: Marty Hurney
General Counsel: Richard Thigpen
Chief Financial Officer: Dave Olsen
Controller: Mike Dudan
Director of Player Personnel: Jack Bushofsky
Director of Pro Scouting: Mark Koncz
Pro Scouts: Hal Hunter
Director of College Scouting: Tony Softli
College Scouts: Brian Adams, Kevin Beck, Bucky Brooks, Ryan Cowden, Jeff Morrow, Mike Szabo, Joe Schoen, Khary Darlington
Director of Communications: Charlie Dayton
Communications Assistant: Bruce Speight
Public Relations Assistant: Deedee Mills
Media Relations Assistant: Ted Crews
Director of Ticket Sales: Phil Youtsey
Director of Player Relations: Donnie Shell
Director of Community Relations/Family Programs: Riley Fields
Director of Entertainment and Cheerleaders: Leslie Matz
Director of Sales and Sponsor Services: Kyle Caddell
Director of Broadcast Administration: Henry Thomas
Executive Producer-Television: Greg Brannon
Executive Producer-Radio: David Langton
Director of Information Systems: Roger Goss
Salary Cap Analyst/Negotiatior: Rob Rogers
Video Director: Mark Hobbs
Assistant Video Director: Jeff Mueller
Head Trainer: Ryan Vermillion
Assistant Trainers: Mark Shermansky, Reggie Scott
Equipment Manager: Jackie Miles
Assistant Equipment Manager: Don Toner
Director of Security: Gene Brown
Stadium Operations Manager: Scott Paul
Scoreboard Manager: Kyle Ritchie
Facilities Manager: Matthew Getz
Head Groundskeeper: Tom Vaughan
Human Resources/Office Manager: Jackie Jeffries

COACHING HISTORY
(68-82-0)

1995-98	Dom Capers	31-35-0
1999-2001	George Seifert	16-32-0
2002-03	John Fox	21-15-0

ATTENDANCE

Home 573,041 Away 485,137
Total 1,058,178
Single-game home record, 76,136 (12/10/95)
Single-season home record, 573,041 (2003)

2004 DRAFT CHOICES

Round	Name	Pos.	College
1	Chris Gamble	DB	Ohio State
2	Keary Colbert	WR	Southern California
3	Travelle Wharton	T	South Carolina
5	Drew Carter	WR	Ohio State
6	Sean Tufts	LB	Colorado
7	Michael Gaines	TE	Central Florida

CAROLINA PANTHERS

2003 TEAM RECORD

PRESEASON (4-0)

8/9	W	20-0	Washington
8/15	W	20-10	at N.Y. Giants
8/23	W	20-7	at Green Bay
8/29	W	21-14	Pittsburgh

REGULAR SEASON (11-5)

Date	Result		Opponent	Att.
9/7	W	24-23	Jacksonville	72,134
9/14	L	12-9	at Tampa Bay (OT)	65,621
9/28	W	23-3	Atlanta	72,765
10/5	W	19-13	New Orleans	72,496
10/12	W	23-20	at Indianapolis (OT)	57,082
10/19	L	17-37	Tennessee	72,851
10/26	W	23-20	at New Orleans (OT)	68,370
11/2	L	10-14	at Houston	70,052
11/9	W	27-24	Tampa Bay	73,245
11/16	W	20-17	Washington	73,263
11/23	L	20-24	at Dallas	63,871
11/30	L	16-25	Philadelphia	72,977
12/7	L	14-20	at Atlanta (OT)	70,079
12/14	W	20-17	at Arizona	23,217
12/21	W	20-14	Detroit	72,835
12/28	W	37-24	at New York Giants	78,130

POSTSEASON (3-1)

1/3	W	29-10	Dallas	73,014
1/10	W	29-23	at St. Louis (2OT)	66,165
1/18	W	14-3	at Philadelphia	67,707
2/1	L	29-32	vs. New England, at Houston	71,525

(OT) Overtime

SCORE BY PERIODS

Panthers	73	70	87	86	9	— 325
Opponents	41	94	44	119	6	— 304

2003 TEAM STATISTICS

	Panthers	Opp.
Total First Downs	284	274
Rushing	114	83
Passing	146	161
Penalty	24	30
3rd Down: Made/Att	78/219	78/225
3rd Down Pct.	35.6	34.7
4th Down: Made/Att	6/11	5/16
4th Down Pct.	54.5	31.3
Possession Avg.	30:27	29:33
Total Net Yards	5,141	4,725
Avg. Per Game	321.3	295.3
Total Plays	1,008	996
Avg. Per Play	5.1	4.7
Net Yards Rushing	2,091	1,722
Avg. Per Game	130.7	107.6
Total Rushes	522	434
Net Yards Passing	3,050	3,003
Avg. Per Game	190.6	187.7
Sacked/Yards Lost	26/188	40/212
Gross Yards	3,238	3,215
Att./Completions	460/270	522/299
Completion Pct.	58.7	57.3
Had Intercepted	16	16
Punts/Average	81/42.8	90/42.0
Net Punting Avg.	81/35.6	90/35.8
Penalties/Yards	116/966	111/1,011
Fumbles/Ball Lost	33/15	20/10
Touchdowns	33	35
Rushing	9	10
Passing	19	19
Returns	5	6

2003 INDIVIDUAL STATISTICS

PASSING	Att.	Comp.	Yds.	Pct.	TD	Int.	Tkld.	Rate
Delhomme	449	266	3,219	59.2	19	16	23/168	80.6
Peete	10	4	19	40.0	0	0	3/20	47.9
Sauerbrun	1	0	0	0.0	0	0	0/0	39.6
Panthers	460	270	3,238	58.7	19	16	26/188	79.6
Opponents	522	299	3,215	57.3	19	16	40/212	74.8

SCORING	TD R	TD P	TD Rt	PAT	FG	Saf	PTS
Kasay	0	0	0	29/30	32/38	0	125
Davis	8	0	0	0/0	0/0	0	48
S. Smith	0	7	1	0/0	0/0	0	48
Proehl	0	4	0	0/0	0/0	0	24
Muhammad	0	3	0	0/0	0/0	0	18
Foster	0	2	0	0/0	0/0	0	12
Minter	0	0	2	0/0	0/0	0	12
Delhomme	1	0	0	0/0	0/0	0	6
Goings	0	1	0	0/0	0/0	0	6
Hoover	0	1	0	0/0	0/0	0	6
Manning	0	0	1	0/0	0/0	0	6
Smart	0	0	1	0/0	0/0	0	6
Wiggins	0	1	0	0/0	0/0	0	6
Panthers	9	19	5	29/30	32/38	1	325
Opponents	10	19	6	31/32	21/32	0	304

2-Pt. Conversions: None.
Panthers 0-3, Opponents 0-2.

RUSHING	Att.	Yds.	Avg.	LG	TD
Davis	318	1,444	4.5	40	8
Foster	113	429	3.8	21	0
Goings	10	69	6.9	17	0
Smart	20	49	2.5	6	0
S. Smith	11	42	3.8	14	0
Delhomme	42	39	0.9	9	1
Hoover	6	21	3.5	5	0
Muhammad	2	-2	-1.0	0	0
Panthers	522	2,091	4.0	40	9
Opponents	434	1,722	4.0	43	10

RECEIVING	No.	Yds.	Avg.	LG	TD
S. Smith	88	1,110	12.6	67t	7
Muhammad	54	837	15.5	60	3
Proehl	27	389	14.4	66t	4
Foster	26	207	8.0	47	2
Mangum	17	199	11.7	34	0
Davis	14	159	11.4	25	0
Goings	12	97	8.1	14	1
Hoover	12	72	6.0	17	1
Wiggins	8	80	10.0	23	1
Seidman	5	35	7.0	14	0
Smart	3	11	3.7	5	0
Hankton	2	27	13.5	15	0
Dyson	2	15	7.5	9	0
Panthers	270	3,238	12.0	67t	19
Opponents	299	3,215	10.8	65t	19

INTERCEPTIONS	No.	Yds.	Avg.	LG	TD
Minter	3	100	33.3	35t	2
Manning	3	33	11.0	27t	1
Grant	3	25	8.3	25	0
Wallace	2	58	29.0	53	0
Howard	2	2	1.0	2	0
Burton	1	10	10.0	10	0
Witherspoon	1	10	10.0	10	0
Rucker	1	0	0.0	0	0
Panthers	16	238	14.9	53	3
Opponents	16	225	14.1	44	2

PUNTING	No.	Yds.	Avg.	In 20	LG
Sauerbrun	77	3,433	44.6	22	64
Kasay	1	33	33.0	1	33
Panthers	81	3,466	42.8	23	64
Opponents	90	3,778	42.0	31	59

PUNT RETURNS	No.	FC	Yds.	Avg.	LG	TD
S. Smith	44	14	439	10.0	53t	1
Dyson	1	1	14	14.0	14	0
Panthers	45	15	453	10.1	53t	1
Opponents	35	12	402	11.5	89t	1

KICKOFF RETURNS	No.	Yds.	Avg.	LG	TD
Smart	41	947	23.1	100t	1
S. Smith	11	309	28.1	42	0
Proehl	2	34	17.0	19	0
Seidman	2	24	12.0	17	0
Hoover	1	0	0.0	0	0
Muhammad	1	2	2.0	2	0
Rasmussen	1	16	16.0	16	0
Wallace	1	13	13.0	13	0
Wiggins	0	0	0.0	0	0
Panthers	60	1,345	22.4	100t	1
Opponents	70	1,425	20.4	53	0

FIELD GOALS	1-19	20-29	30-39	40-49	50+
Kasay	0/0	13/13	6/8	11/13	2/4
Panthers	0/0	13/13	6/8	11/13	2/4
Opponents	0/0	7/7	7/11	7/11	0/3

SACKS	No.
Rucker	12.0
Peppers	7.0
Jenkins	5.0
Wallace	5.0
Burton	2.0
Cousin	2.0
Allen	1.0
Grant	1.0
Rasmussen	1.0
Wesley	1.0
Witherspoon	1.0
Buckner	0.5
Howard	0.5
Panthers	40.0
Opponents	26.0

RECORD HOLDERS

INDIVIDUAL RECORDS—CAREER

Category	Name	Performance
Rushing (Yds.)	Tshimanga Biakabutuka, 1996-2001	2,530
Passing (Yds.)	Steve Beuerlein, 1996-2000	12,690
Passing (TDs)	Steve Beuerlein, 1996-2000	86
Receiving (No.)	Muhsin Muhammad, 1996-2003	485
Receiving (Yds.)	Muhsin Muhammad, 1996-2003	6,346
Interceptions	Eric Davis, 1996-2000	25
Punting (Avg.)	Todd Sauerbrun, 2001-03	45.9
Punt Return (Avg.)	Winslow Oliver, 1996-98	10.7
Kickoff Return (Avg.)	Michael Bates, 1996-2000	25.7
Field Goals	John Kasay, 1995-2003	183
Touchdowns (Tot.)	Wesley Walls, 1996-2002	44
Points	John Kasay, 1995-2003	759

INDIVIDUAL RECORDS—SINGLE SEASON

Category	Name	Performance
Rushing (Yds.)	Stephen Davis, 2003	1,444
Passing (Yds.)	Steve Beuerlein, 1999	4,436
Passing (TDs)	Steve Beuerlein, 1999	36
Receiving (No.)	Muhsin Muhammad, 2000	102
Receiving (Yds.)	Muhsin Muhammad, 1999	1,253
Interceptions	Doug Evans, 2001	8
Punting (Avg.)	Todd Sauerbrun, 2001	47.5
Punt Return (Avg.)	Winslow Oliver, 1996	11.5
Kickoff Return (Avg.)	Michael Bates, 1996	30.2
Field Goals	John Kasay, 1996	37
Touchdowns (Tot.)	Wesley Walls, 1999	12
	Patrick Jeffers, 1999	12
Points	John Kasay, 1996	145

INDIVIDUAL RECORDS—SINGLE GAME

Category	Name	Performance
Rushing (Yds.)	Stephen Davis, 10-26-03	178
Passing (Yds.)	Steve Beuerlein, 12-12-99	373
Passing (TDs)	Steve Beuerlein, 1-2-00	5
Receiving (No.)	Muhsin Muhammad, 12-18-99, 11-27-00	11
Receiving (Yds.)	Muhsin Muhammad, 9-13-98	192
Interceptions	Deon Grant, 9-22-02	3
Field Goals	John Kasay, 9-1-96, 9-8-96	5
Touchdowns (Tot.)	Fred Lane, 11-2-97	3
	Tshimanga Biakabutuka, 10-3-99	3
	Muhsin Muhammad, 12-18-99	3
	Steve Smith, 12-8-02	3
Points	Fred Lane, 11-2-97	18
	Tshimanga Biakabutuka, 10-3-99	18
	Muhsin Muhammad, 12-18-99	18
	Steve Smith, 12-8-02	18

CAROLINA PANTHERS

2004 VETERAN ROSTER

No.	Name	Pos.	Ht.	Wt.	Birthdate	NFL Exp.	College	Hometown	How Acq.	'03 Games/ Starts
52	Allen, Brian	LB	6-0	232	4/1/78	4	Florida State	Lake City, Fla.	W(Hou)-'02	14/4
59	Armstead, Jessie	LB	6-1	237	10/26/70	12	Miami	Dallas, Texas	FA-'04	16/5*
80	Baker, Eugene	WR	6-2	183	3/18/76	3	Kent State	Pittsburgh, Pa.	FA-'03	1/0
47	#Battaglia, Marco	TE	6-3	250	1/25/73	9	Rutgers	Queens, N.Y.	FA-'03	2/0
28	Branch, Colin	S	5-11	205	3/2/80	2	Stanford	Carlsbad, Calif.	D4-'03	16/0
79	Brzezinski, Doug	G	6-4	305	3/11/76	6	Boston College	Redford, Mich.	UFA(Phil)-'03	1/0
99	Buckner, Brentson	DT	6-2	310	9/30/71	11	Clemson	Columbus, Ga.	UFA(SF)-'01	12/12
98	Burton, Shane	DT	6-6	305	1/18/74	9	Tennessee	Catawba, N.C.	FA-'02	16/4
50	Ciurciu, Vinny	LB	6-0	235	5/2/80	2	Boston College	Paramus, N.J.	FA-'03	2/0
75	Claridge, Travis	G	6-5	300	3/23/78	5	Southern California	Fort Vancouver, Wash.	UFA(Atl)-'04	6/6*
40	Cooper, Jarrod	S	6-0	215	3/31/78	4	Kansas State	Pearland, Texas	D5-'01	12/0
48	Davis, Stephen	RB	6-0	230	3/1/74	9	Auburn	Spartanburg, S.C.	FA-'03	14/14
17	Delhomme, Jake	QB	6-2	215	1/10/75	6	Louisiana-Lafayette	Lafayette, La.	UFA(NO)-'03	16/15
58	Fields, Mark	LB	6-2	244	11/9/72	10	Washington State	Los Angeles, Calif.	FA-'02	0*
36	Floyd, Marcus	CB	5-9	188	10/12/78	2	Indiana	Bartow, Fla.	FA-'04	0*
26	Foster, DeShaun	RB	6-0	222	1/10/80	3	UCLA	Tustin, Calif.	D2-'02	14/2
37	Goings, Nick	RB	6-0	225	1/26/78	4	Pittsburgh	Dublin, Ohio	FA-'01	15/0
69	Gross, Jordan	T	6-4	300	7/20/80	2	Utah	Fruitland, Idaho	D1-'03	16/16
31	Hampton, William	CB	5-10	190	3/7/75	3	Murray State	Little Rock, Ark.	FA-'03	5/0
88	Hankton, Karl	WR	6-2	202	7/24/70	6	Trinity College (Ill.)	New Orleans, La.	FA-'00	14/0
27	Hawkins, Artrell	CB	5-10	190	11/24/76	7	Cincinnati	Johnstown, Pa.	FA-'04	14/9*
84	Hayes, Donald	WR	6-4	220	7/13/75	7	Wisconsin	Century, Fla.	FA-'04	0*
45	Hoover, Brad	FB	6-0	245	11/11/76	5	Western Carolina	Thomasville, N.C.	FA-'00	16/9
68	Houghton, Mike	T	6-3	315	12/01/79	2	San Diego State	San Diego, Calif.	FA-'03	0*
77	Jenkins, Kris	DT	6-4	335	8/3/79	4	Maryland	Ypsilanti, Mich.	D2-'01	16/16
61	Kadela, Dave	T	6-6	304	5/6/78	2	Virginia Tech	Dearborn, Mich.	FA-'04	0*
4	Kasay, John	K	5-10	198	10/27/69	14	Georgia	Athens, Ga.	UFA(Sea)-'95	16/0
56	Kyle, Jason	LB	6-3	242	5/12/72	10	Arizona State	Tempe, Ariz.	UFA(SF)-'01	16/0
86	Mangum, Kris	TE	6-4	252	8/15/73	7	Mississippi	Magee, Miss.	D7-'97	16/11
24	Manning Jr., Ricky	CB	5-8	185	11/18/80	2	UCLA	Fresno, Calif.	D3b-'03	16/7
78	Meadows, Adam	T	6-5	290	1/25/74	8	Georgia	Powder Springs, Ga.	FA-'04	12/5*
30	Minter, Mike	S	5-10	195	1/15/74	8	Nebraska	Lawton, Okla.	D2-'97	16/16
60	Mitchell, Jeff	C	6-4	300	1/29/74	9	Florida	Dallas, Texas	UFA(Balt)-'01	15/15
33	Moore, Casey	FB	6-1	240	7/26/80	2	Stanford	St. Petersburg, Fla.	D7b-'03	0*
94	Moorehead, Kindal	DT	6-2	285	10/14/78	2	Alabama	Memphis, Tenn.	D5-'03	14
55	Morgan, Dan	LB	6-2	245	12/19/78	4	Miami	Coral Springs, Fla.	D1-'01	11/11
87	Muhammad, Muhsin	WR	6-2	217	5/5/73	9	Michigan State	Lansing, Mich.	D2-'96	15/15
72	Nelson, Bruce	G	6-5	301	5/12/79	2	Iowa	Emmetsburg, Iowa	D2-'03	15/1
9	Peete, Rodney	QB	6-0	230	3/16/66	16	Southern California	Shawnee Mission, Kan.	UFA(Oak)-'02	1/1
90	Peppers, Julius	DE	6-6	283	1/18/80	3	North Carolina	Bailey, N.C.	D1-'02	16/16
92	Pittman, Kavika	DE	6-6	273	10/9/74	9	McNeese State	Frankfurt, Germany	FA-'03	2/0
22	Poteat, Hank	CB	5-10	192	8/30/77	4	Pittsburgh	Harrisburg, Pa.	FA-'04	1/0*
81	Proehl, Ricky	WR	6-0	190	3/7/68	15	Wake Forest	Hillsborough, N.J.	UFA(StL)-'03	16/2
97	Rasmussen, Kemp	DE	6-3	265	5/25/79	3	Indiana	Hadley, Mich.	FA-'02	13/0
76	Reyes, Tutan	G-T	6-3	305	10/28/77	5	Mississippi	Queens, N.Y.	W(TB)-'02	0*
39	Richardson, Damien	S	6-1	210	4/3/76	7	Arizona State	Fresno, Calif.	D6-'98	0*
93	Rucker, Micheal	DE	6-5	275	2/28/75	6	Nebraska	St. Joseph, Mo.	D2b-'99	14/14
10	Sauerbrun, Todd	P	5-10	215	1/4/73	10	West Virginia	Garden City, N.Y.	FA-'01	16/0
82	Seidman, Mike	TE	6-4	261	2/11/81	2	UCLA	Westlake Village, Calif.	D3a-'03	12/5
23	Shaw, Terrance	CB	6-0	200	1/11/73	10	Stephen F. Austin	Marshall, Texas	UFA(Oak)-'04	16/8*
53	Short, Brandon	LB	6-3	253	7/11/77	5	Penn State	McKeesport, Pa.	UFA(NYG)-'04	16/12*
32	Smart, Rod	RB	5-11	201	1/9/77	4	Western Kentucky	Lakeland, Fla.	W(Phil)-'02	16/0
89	Smith, Steve	WR	5-9	185	5/12/79	4	Utah	Lynwood, Calif.	D3-'01	16/11
42	Tillman, Travares	S	6-1	190	10/8/77	4	Georgia Tech	Lyons, Ga.	W(Hou)-'03	7/0
57	#Towns, Lester	LB	6-1	245	8/28/77	5	Washington	Pasadena, Calif.	D7-'00	15/1
73	Tuten, Melvin	T	6-7	320	11/11/71	8	Syracuse	Washington, D.C.	W(Den)-'00	0*
65	Tylski, Rich	G	6-4	305	2/27/71	7	Utah State	San Diego, Calif.	FA-'04	0*
95	Walker, Rod	DT	6-3	320	2/4/76	4	Troy State	Milton, Fla.	FA-'04	7/1
96	Wallace, Al	DE	6-5	275	3/25/74	5	Maryland	W. Palm Beach, Fla.	T(Mia)-'02	16/2
16	Weinke, Chris	QB	6-4	232	7/31/72	4	Florida State	St. Paul, Minn.	D4-'01	0*
21	Wesley, Dante	CB	6-0	211	4/5/79	3	Arkansas-Pine Bluff	Pine Bluff, Ark.	D4-'02	16/1
71	Willig, Matt	T	6-8	315	1/21/69	12	Southern California	Santa Fe Springs, Calif.	FA-'03	13/0
54	Witherspoon, Will	LB	6-1	231	8/19/80	2	Georgia	Panama City, Fla.	D3-'02	16/16
83	Young, Walter	WR	6-4	220	12/7/79	2	Illinois	Park Forest, Ill.	D7a-'03	7/0

* Armstead played 16 games with Washington in '03; Claridge played 6 games with Atlanta; Fields missed '03 season because of injury; Floyd last active with Buffalo in '02; Hawkins played 14 games with Cincinnati; Hayes last active with New England in '02; Houghton last active with Buffalo in '02; Kadela inactive for Jacksonville in '02; Meadows played 12 games with Indianapolis; Moore missed '03 season because of injury; Poteat played 1 game with Tampa Bay; Reyes inactive for 16 games; Richardson missed '03 season because of injury; Shaw played 16 games with Oakland; Short played 16 games with N.Y. Giants; Tuten missed '03 season because of injury; Tylski last active with Pittsburgh in '01; Weinke inactive for 16 games.

Unrestricted free agent, subject to developments.

Retired—Kevin Donnalley, guard, 13-year guard, 16 games in '03.

Players lost through free agency (6): WR Kevin Dyson (SD; 1 game in '03), LB Greg Favors (Jax; 16), S Deon Grant (Jax; 16), CB Reggie Howard (Mia; 15), G Jeno James (Mia; 16), TE Jermaine Wiggins (Minn; 16).

Also played with Carolina in '03—TE Marco Battaglia (2 games), LB Mike Caldwell (9), CB Terry Cousin (13), G Kevin Donnalley (16), T Todd Steussie (16), LB Lester Towns (15).

2004 FIRST-YEAR ROSTER

Name	Pos.	Ht.	Wt.	Birthdate	College	Hometown	How Acq.
Adamson, Rob (1)	QB	6-4	210	12/20/79	Mount Union	Akron, Ohio	FA
Bennett, Billy	K	5-7	174	8/16/82	Georgia	Athens, Ga.	FA
Carstens, Jordan	DT	6-5	300	1/22/81	Iowa State	Bagley, Iowa	FA
Carter, Drew	WR	6-3	200	9/5/81	Ohio State	Solon, Ohio	D5
Cecil, Toby	C	6-4	290	12/26/80	Texas Tech	Richardson, Texas	FA
Colbert, Keary	WR	5-10	193	5/21/82	Southern California	Oxnard, Calif.	D2
Dubuc, Deitan (1)	TE	6-4	248	2/4/77	Michigan	Fabreville, Quebec, Canada	FA-'03
Duckett, Damane	DT	6-6	300	1/21/81	East Carolina	Clemmons, N.C.	FA
Gaines, Michael	TE	6-3	280	3/30/80	Central Florida	Tallahassee, Fla.	D7
Gamble, Chris	CB	6-1	181	3/11/83	Ohio State	Sunrise, Fla.	D1
Harrell, Jonathan	LB	6-1	245	6/19/80	Northern Iowa	Montgomery, Ala.	FA
Harris, Joey	RB	5-10	205	12/18/80	Purdue	Tomball, Texas	FA
Hayes, Mike (1)	P	6-3	225	4/19/76	Akron	Elyria, Ohio	FA
Herrell, Ben	T	6-7	316	7/28/80	Miami (Ohio)	Middleton, Wis.	FA
Hugo, James (1)	TE	6-6	265	9/28/79	Arizona	The Woodlands, Texas	FA
Jackson, Eddie	CB	6-0	190	12/19/80	Arkansas	Richardson, Texas	FA
Johnson, Adam	LS	6-5	213	11/11/79	Buffalo	Alta Loma, Calif.	FA
Jordan, Omari (1)	DT	6-4	315	4/15/78	Buffalo	Cleveland, Ohio	FA-'03
King, Brian	CB	5-11	183	10/8/80	West Virginia	Damascus, Md.	FA
Knight, Derrick	RB	5-9	209	4/3/81	Boston College	Westwood, Mass.	FA
Olinger, Jon (1)	WR	6-3	222	8/24/80	Cincinnati	Hazard, Ky.	FA
Price, Shawn (1)	LB	6-0	233	2/26/80	North Carolina State	Haddon Heights, N.J.	FA
Rutherford, Roderick	QB	6-2	223	12/12/80	Pittsburgh	Pittsburgh, Pa.	FA
Strong, Derrick	DE	6-4	261	4/16/82	Illinois	Chicago, Ill.	FA
Tufts, Sean	LB	6-3	236	3/26/82	Colorado	Englewood, Colo.	D6
Wharton, Travelle	T	6-4	312	5/19/81	South Carolina	Simpsonville, S.C.	D3

The term NFL Rookie is defined as a player who is in his first season of professional football and has not been on the roster of another professional football team for any regular-season or postseason games. A Rookie is designated by an "R" on NFL rosters. Players who have been active in another professional football league or players who have NFL experience, including either preseason training camp or being on an Active List or Inactive List, or on Reserve/Injured or Reserve/Physically Unable to Perform for fewer than six regular-season games, are termed NFL First-Year Players. An NFL First-Year Player is designated by a "1" on NFL rosters. Thereafter, a player is credited with an additional year of experience for each season in which he accumulates six games on the Active List or Inactive List, or on Reserve/Injured or Reserve/Physically Unable to Perform.

Log on to www.panthers.com for an up-to-date roster.

CAROLINA PANTHERS

COACHING STAFF

Head Coach,

John Fox

Pro Career: Became third coach in Carolina Panthers history on January 25, 2002. In 2003, guided Panthers to Super Bowl XXXVIII two years after inheriting team that won one game in 2001. Joined Vince Lombardi and Bill Parcells as the only coaches in NFL history to inherit a one-win team and guide it to the playoffs in their second season. In 2002, engineered a six-game turn-around that ranks second for rookie head coaches since the NFL went to 16-game schedule in 1978. In 2002, the Panthers became the only team since the NFL merger to improve from thirty-first to second in total defense in one season. Prior to joining Carolina he served as the defensive coordinator for the New York Giants (1997-2001). In 2000, Fox helped the Giants reach Super Bowl XXXV. In the NFC Championship Game, the Giants' 41-0 victory over Minnesota was the first shutout in a conference title game since 1986. Before joining the Giants, Fox was a consultant for the Rams (1996), defensive coordinator for the Raiders (1994-95), and defensive backs coach for the Chargers (1992-93) and Steelers (1989-1991). Career record: 21-15.

Background: Defensive back at San Diego State (1976-77). Coached at San Diego State (1978), U.S. International (1979) Boise State (1980), Long Beach State (1981), Utah (1982), Kansas (1983), Iowa State (1984), and Pittsburgh (1986-88). Fox entered the pro ranks in 1985 as the secondary coach for the Los Angeles Express (USFL). Received bachelor's degree in physical education and earned a teaching credential from San Diego State.

Personal: Born February 8, 1955, in Virginia Beach, Va. He and his wife, Robin, have four children—Mathew, Mark, Cody, and Halle—and live in Charlotte, N.C.

ASSISTANT COACHES

Danny Crossman, special teams assistant; born January 17, 1967, El Paso, Texas. Defensive back Kansas 1985, Pittsburgh 1987-89. Pro defensive back Washington Redskins 1990, Detroit Lions 1991-92. College coach: U.S. Coast Guard Academy 1993, Western Kentucky 1994-96, Central Florida 1997-98, Georgia Tech 1999-2001, Michigan State 2002. Pro coach: Joined Panthers in 2003.

Ken Flajole, linebackers/defensive assistant; born October 4, 1954, Seattle. Linebacker Wenatchee Valley (Wash) C.C. 1973-74, Pacific Lutheran 1975-76. No pro playing experience. College coach: Pacific Lutheran 1977-78, Washington 1979, Montana 1980-85, Texas-El Paso 1986-88, Missouri 1989-1993, Richmond 1994, Hawaii 1995, Nevada 1996-97. Pro coach: Green Bay Packers 1998, Seattle Seahawks 1999-2002, joined Panthers in 2003.

Mike Gillhamer, defensive asisstant-secondary; born February 20, 1956, Oakland. Defensive back Carrol College 1972, Wenatchee (Wash.) J.C. 1973, Humboldt State 1974-75. No pro playing experience. College coach: College of the Sequoias 1979-1983, Weber State 1984, Utah 1985-89, San Jose State 1990-93, Nevada 1994-95, Oregon 2001-02, Louisville 2003. Pro coach: New York Giants 1997-2000, joined Panthers in 2004.

Dan Henning, offensive coordinator/quarterbacks; born June 21, 1942, Bronx, N.Y. Quarterback William & Mary 1962-64. Pro quarterback San Diego Chargers 1964, 1966-67. College coach: Florida State 1968-1970, 1974, Virginia Tech 1971, 1973, Boston College 1994-96 (head coach). Pro coach: Houston Oilers 1972, New York Jets 1976-78, 1998-2000, Miami Dolphins 1979-1980, Washington Redskins 1981-1982, 1987-88, Atlanta Falcons 1983-86 (head coach), San Diego Chargers 1989-1991 (head coach), Detroit Lions 1992-93, Buffalo Bills 1997, joined Panthers in 2002.

David Magazu, tight ends; born June 10, 1957, Taunton Mass. Defensive tackle Springfield College 1976-79. No pro playing experience. College coach: Ithaca 1980, Western Michigan 1981, Eastern Michigan 1982, Michigan 1983, Northern Illinois 1984, Ball State 1985-86, Navy 1987-89, Indiana State 1990-91, Colorado State 1992-94, Kentucky 1995-96, Memphis 1997-98, Boston College 1999-2002. Pro coach: Joined Panthers in 2003.

Mike Maser, offensive line; born March 2, 1947, Clayton N.Y. Guard Buffalo 1967-1970. No pro playing experience. College coach: Marshall 1973, Bluefield State College 1974-78, Maine 1979-1980, Boston College 1981-1993. Pro coach: Jacksonville Jaguars 1995-2002, joined Panthers in 2003.

Mike McCoy, offensive assistant; born April 1, 1972, San Francisco. Quarterback Long Beach State 1990-91, Utah 1992-94. Pro quarterback Amsterdam Admirals (NFLE) 1997, Calgary Stampeders (CFL) 1999. Pro coach: Joined Panthers in 1999.

Sam Mills, linebackers; born June 3, 1959, Neptune, N.J. Linebacker Montclair State 1977-1980. Pro linebacker Philadelphia/Baltimore Stars (USFL) 1983-85, New Orleans Saints 1986-1994, Carolina Panthers 1995-97. Pro coach: Joined Panthers in 1999.

Scott O'Brien, asst. head coach/special teams; born June 25, 1957, Superior, Wis. Defensive end Wisconsin-Superior 1975-78. Pro defensive end Green Bay Packers 1979, Toronto Argonauts (CFL) 1979. College coach: Wisconsin-Superior 1980-82, Nevada-Las Vegas 1983-85, Rice 1986, Pittsburgh 1987-1990. Pro coach: Cleveland Browns/Baltimore Ravens 1991-98, joined Panthers in 1999.

Rod Perry, secondary; born September 11, 1953, Fresno, Calif. Defensive back Colorado 1972-74. Pro cornerback Los Angeles Rams 1975-1982, Cleveland Browns 1983-84. College coach: Columbia 1985, Fresno City College 1986, Fresno State 1987-88. Pro coach: Seattle Seahawks 1989-1991, Los Angeles Rams 1992-94, Houston Oilers 1995-96, San Diego Chargers 1997-2001, joined Panthers in 2002.

Jerry Simmons, strength and conditioning; born June 15, 1954, Elkhart, Kan. Linebacker Fort Hays State 1976-77. No pro playing experience. College coach: Fort Hays State 1978, Clemson 1980, Rice 1981-82, Southern California 1983-87. Pro coach: New England Patriots 1988-1990, Cleveland Browns/Baltimore Ravens 1991-98, joined Panthers in 1999.

Jim Skipper, running backs; born January 23, 1949, Breaux Bridge, La. Defensive back Whittier College 1971-72. No pro playing experience. College coach: Cal Poly-Pomona 1974-76, San Jose State 1977-78, Pacific 1979, Oregon 1980-82. Pro coach: Philadelphia/Baltimore Stars (USFL) 1983-85, New Orleans Saints 1986-1995, Arizona Cardinals 1996, New York Giants 1997-2000, San Francisco Demons (XFL) 2001 (head coach), joined Panthers in 2002.

Sal Sunseri, defensive line; born August 1, 1959, Pittsburgh. Linebacker Pittsburgh 1979-1981. College coach: Pittsburgh 1985-1992, Iowa Wesleyan 1993, Louisville 1995-97, Alabama A&M 1998-99, Louisiana State 2000, Michigan State 2001. Pro coach: Joined Panthers in 2002.

Mike Trgovac, defensive coordinator; born February 27, 1959, Youngstown, Ohio. Defensive lineman Michigan 1977-1980. No pro playing experience. College coach: Michigan 1984-85, Ball State 1986-88, Navy 1989, Colorado State 1990-91, Notre Dame 1992-94. Pro coach: Philadelphia Eagles 1995-98, Green Bay Packers 1999, Washington Redskins 2000-01, joined Panthers in 2002.

Richard Williamson, wide receivers; born April 13, 1941, Ft. Deposit, Ala. Receiver Alabama 1961-62. No pro playing experience. College coach: Alabama 1963-67, 1970-71, Arkansas 1968-69, 1972-74, Memphis State 1975-1980 (head coach). Pro coach: Kansas City Chiefs 1983-86, Tampa Bay Buccaneers 1987-1991 (interim head coach 1990, head coach 1991), Cincinnati Bengals 1992-94, joined Panthers in 1995.

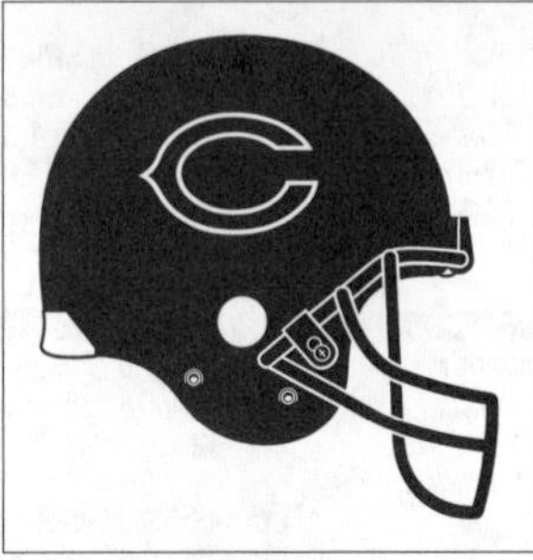

National Football Conference
North Division
Team Colors: Navy Blue, Orange, and White
Halas Hall at Conway Park
1000 Football Drive
Lake Forest, Illinois 60045
Telephone: (847) 295-6600

2004 SCHEDULE

PRESEASON		**Chicago time**
Aug. 12	at St. Louis	7:00
Aug. 21	**San Francisco**	7:30
Aug. 27	**New Orleans**	7:30
Sept. 3	at Cleveland	7:00

REGULAR SEASON		
Sept. 12	**Detroit**	12:00
Sept. 19	at Green Bay	12:00
Sept. 26	at Minnesota	12:00
Oct. 3	**Philadelphia**	12:00
Oct. 10	Open Date	
Oct. 17	**Washington**	12:00
Oct. 24	at Tampa Bay	12:00
Oct. 31	**San Francisco**	7:30
Nov. 7	at New York Giants	3:05
Nov. 14	at Tennessee	12:00
Nov. 21	**Indianapolis**	12:00
Nov. 25	at Dallas (Thu.)	3:15
Dec. 5	**Minnesota**	12:00
Dec. 12	at Jacksonville	12:00
Dec. 19	**Houston**	12:00
Dec. 26	at Detroit	12:00
Jan. 2	**Green Bay**	12:00

Stadium: Soldier Field
(opened in 1924)
• **Capacity:** 61,500
1410 S. Museum Campus Dr.
Chicago, Illinois 60605
Playing Surface: Natural Grass
Training Camp: Olivet-Nazarene University
Bourbonnais, Illinois 60901

SOLDIER FIELD

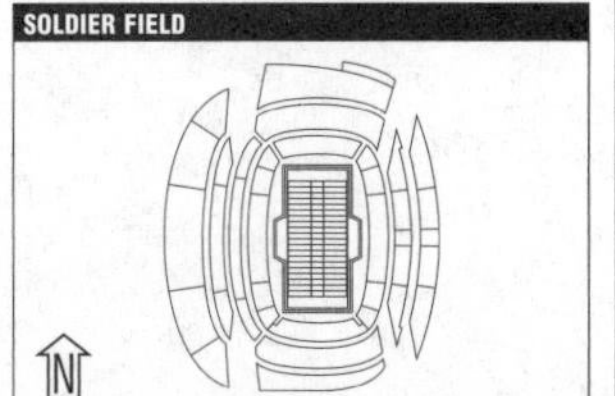

CLUB OFFICIALS

Chairman of the Board: Michael B. McCaskey
Secretary: Virginia H. McCaskey
President and CEO: Ted Phillips
General Manager: Jerry Angelo
Vice President: Tim McCaskey
Senior Director of Administration: John Bostrom
Senior Director of Corporate Communications: Scott Hagel
Senior Director of Corporate Sales & Marketing: Dave Greeley
Senior Director of Business Development & Alumni Relations: Brian McCaskey
Senior Director of Ticket Operations: George McCaskey
Senior Director of Finance & Treasurer: Karen Murphy
Director of Pro Personnel: Bobby DePaul
Director of College Scouting: Greg Gabriel
Director of Player Contracts and Legal Affairs: Cliff Stein
Assistant Director of Pro Personnel: Morocco Brown
Director of Player Development: Dwayne Joseph
Director of Special Projects: Pat McCaskey
Director of Community Relations: Caroline Guip
Director of Broadcasting: Greg Miller
Media Services Manager: Jim Christman
Media Information Manager: Roger Hacker
Media Relations Assistant: Brian Hardin
Video Director: Dean Pope
Assistant Video Directors: Dave Hendrickson, Dan Tuohy
Head Athletic Trainer: Tim Bream
Assistant Trainers: Reggie Barnes, Chris Hanks
Director of Rehabilitation: Bobby Slater
Strength Coach: Russ Riederer
Head Equipment Manager: Tony Medlin
Assistant Equipment Managers: Carl Piekarski, Kenico Hines
Scouts: Chris Ballard, Marty Barrett, Phil Emery, Ted Monago, Pat Roberts, Jeff Shiver

COACHING HISTORY

Decatur Staleys 1920,
Chicago Staleys 1921
(655-478-42)

1920-29	George Halas	84-31-19
1930-32	Ralph Jones	24-10-7
1933-1942	George Halas*	88-24-4
1942-45	Hunk Anderson-Luke Johnsos**	24-12-2
1946-1955	George Halas	76-43-2
1956-57	John (Paddy) Driscoll	14-10-1
1958-1967	George Halas	76-53-6
1968-1971	Jim Dooley	20-36-0
1972-74	Abe Gibron	11-30-1
1975-77	Jack Pardee	20-23-0
1978-1981	Neill Armstrong	30-35-0
1982-1992	Mike Ditka	112-68-0
1993-98	Dave Wannstedt	41-57-0
1999-2003	Dick Jauron	35-46-0

*Retired after five games to enter U.S. Navy
**Co-coaches

ATTENDANCE

Home 479,857 Away 544,641
Total 1,024,498
Single-game home record, 66,900 (9/5/93)
Single-season home record, 527,769 (1999)

2004 DRAFT CHOICES

Round	Name	Pos.	College
1	Tommie Harris	DT	Oklahoma
2	Terry Johnson	DT	Washington
3	Bernard Berrian	WR	Fresno State
4	Nathan Vasher	DB	Texas
	Leon Joe	LB	Maryland
5	Claude Harriott	DE	Pittsburgh
	Craig Krenzel	QB	Ohio State
7	Alfonso Marshall	DB	Miami

CHICAGO BEARS

2003 TEAM RECORD

PRESEASON (1-3)

Date	Result	Opponent
8/9	W 20-18	Indianapolis
8/16	L 10-15	Denver
8/22	L 17-27	at Arizona
8/27	L 23-38	at New England

REGULAR SEASON (7-9)

Date	Result	Opponent	Att.
9/7	L 7-49	at San Francisco	67,554
9/14	L 13-24	at Minnesota	64,144
9/29	L 23-38	Green Bay	61,500
10/5	W 24-21	Oakland	61,099
10/12	L 13-20	at New Orleans	68,390
10/19	L 17-24	at Seattle	65,671
10/26	W 24-16	Detroit	61,428
11/2	W 20-7	San Diego	61,500
11/9	L 10-12	at Detroit	61,492
11/16	L 21-23	St. Louis	61,820
11/23	W 19-10	at Denver	75,540
11/30	W 28-3	Arizona	61,550
12/7	L 21-34	at Green Bay	70,458
12/14	W 13-10	Minnesota	61,804
12/21	W 27-24	Washington	61,719
12/28	L 3-31	at Kansas City	78,413

SCORE BY PERIODS

Bears	46	76	53	108	0 —	283
Opponents	69	109	50	118	0 —	346

2003 Team Statistics

	Bears	Opp.
Total First Downs	264	289
Rushing	104	104
Passing	143	156
Penalty	17	29
3rd Down: Made/Att	77/228	84/213
3rd Down Pct.	33.8	39.4
4th Down: Made/Att	15/23	6/15
4th Down Pct.	65.2	40.0
Possession Avg.	29:39	30:21
Total Net Yards	4,380	4,947
Avg. Per Game	273.8	309.2
Total Plays	1,001	992
Avg. Per Play	4.4	5.0
Net Yards Rushing	1,763	1,865
Avg. Per Game	110.2	116.6
Total Rushes	443	449
Net Yards Passing	2,617	3,082
Avg. Per Game	163.6	192.6
Sacked/Yards Lost	43/288	18/105
Gross Yards	2,905	3,187
Att./Completions	515/271	525/326
Completion Pct.	52.6	62.1
Had Intercepted	20	15
Punts/Average	81/40.2	76/40.4
Net Punting Avg.	81/34.6	76/33.3
Penalties/Yards	92/806	93/746
Fumbles/Ball Lost	25/9	19/5
Touchdowns	29	36
Rushing	13	13
Passing	12	20
Returns	4	3

2003 INDIVIDUAL STATISTICS

PASSING	Att.	Comp.	Yds.	Pct.	TD	Int.	Tkld.	Rate
Stewart	251	126	1,418	50.2	7	12	25/146	56.8
Chandler	192	107	1,050	55.7	3	7	14/101	61.3
Grossman	72	38	437	52.8	2	1	4/41	74.8
Bears	515	271	2,905	52.6	12	20	43/288	61.0
Opponents	525	326	3,187	62.1	20	15	18/105	79.9

SCORING	TD R	TD P	TD Rt	PAT	FG	Saf	PTS
Edinger	0	0	0	27/27	26/36	0	105
Thomas	6	0	0	0/0	0/0	0	36
Booker	0	4	0	0/0	0/0	0	24
Stewart	3	0	0	0/0	0/0	0	20
White	0	3	0	0/0	0/0	0	18
Azumah	0	0	2	0/0	0/0	0	12
Clark	0	2	0	0/0	0/0	0	12
Forsey	2	0	0	0/0	0/0	0	12
Gage	0	2	0	0/0	0/0	0	12
Pritchett	2	0	0	0/0	0/0	0	12
Briggs	0	0	1	0/0	0/0	0	6
McQuarters	0	0	1	0/0	0/0	0	6
Terrell	0	1	0	0/0	0/0	0	6
Chandler	0	0	0	0/0	0/0	0	2
Bears	13	12	4	27/27	26/36	0	283
Opponents	13	20	3	31/33	31/38	0	346

2-Pt. Conversions: Chandler, Stewart
Bears 2-2, Opponents 3-3

RUSHING	Att.	Yds.	Avg.	LG	TD
Thomas	244	1,024	4.2	67t	6
Stewart	59	290	4.9	25	3
Forsey	50	191	3.8	17	2
Pritchett	21	93	4.4	18	2
Peterson	22	70	3.2	10	0
Abdullah	18	37	2.1	10	0
Chandler	14	35	2.5	11	0
Wade	5	14	2.8	6	0
White	2	13	6.5	12	0
Terrell	1	4	4.0	4	0
Maynard	1	0	0.0	0	0
Grossman	3	-1	-0.3	0	0
Booker	3	-7	-2.3	1	0
Bears	443	1,763	4.0	67t	13
Opponents	449	1,865	4.2	60t	13

RECEIVING	No.	Yds.	Avg.	LG	TD
Booker	52	715	13.8	61t	4
White	49	583	11.9	49	3
Clark	44	433	9.8	31	2
Terrell	43	361	8.4	35	1
Pritchett	18	83	4.6	20	0
Gage	17	338	19.9	57	2
Wade	12	137	11.4	24	0
Lyman	11	80	7.3	12	0
Thomas	9	36	4.0	9	0
Abdullah	8	55	6.9	17	0
Merritt	3	50	16.7	25	0
Forsey	3	37	12.3	22	0
Peterson	1	5	5.0	5	0
Kreutz	1	-8	-8.0	-8	0
Bears	271	2,905	10.7	61t	12
Opponents	326	3,187	9.8	51	20

INTERCEPTIONS	No.	Yds.	Avg.	LG	TD
Azumah	4	44	11.0	25	0
Tillman	4	27	6.8	32	0
McQuarters	2	72	36.0	43	0
M. Brown	2	0	0.0	0	0
Briggs	1	45	45.0	45t	1
Green	1	3	3.0	3	0
A. Brown	1	0	0.0	0	0
Bears	15	191	12.7	45t	1
Opponents	20	390	19.5	90t	2

PUNTING	No.	Yds.	Avg.	In 20	LG
Maynard	79	3,258	41.2	23	53
Bears	81	3,258	40.2	23	53
Opponents	76	3,073	40.4	21	62

PUNT RETURNS	No.	FC	Yds.	Avg.	LG	TD
McQuarters	37	12	452	12.2	60t	1
Wade	2	1	9	4.5	10	0
Bears	39	13	461	11.8	60t	1
Opponents	36	13	277	7.7	35	0

KICKOFF RETURN	No.	Yds.	Avg.	LG	TD
Azumah	41	1,191	29.0	89t	2
Merritt	20	405	20.3	35	0
Abdullah	5	62	12.4	17	0
Tafoya	4	55	13.8	19	0
Gilmore	3	25	8.3	11	0
Bears	73	1,738	23.8	89t	2
Opponents	64	1,367	21.4	96t	1

FIELD GOALS	1-19	20-29	30-39	40-49	50+
Edinger	1/1	4/4	9/13	9/14	3/4
Bears	1/1	4/4	9/13	9/14	3/4
Opponents	0/0	12/12	12/14	6/9	1/3

SACKS	No.
A. Brown	5.5
Daniels	2.5
Urlacher	2.5
Haynes	2.0
Azumah	1.0
Boone	1.0
Gray	1.0
Robinson	1.0
Tillman	1.0
Green	0.5
Bears	18.0
Opponents	43.0

RECORD HOLDERS

INDIVIDUAL RECORDS—CAREER

Category	Name	Performance
Rushing (Yds.)	Walter Payton, 1975-1987	16,726
Passing (Yds.)	Sid Luckman, 1939-1950	14,686
Passing (TDs)	Sid Luckman, 1939-1950	137
Receiving (No.)	Walter Payton, 1975-1987	492
Receiving (Yds.)	Johnny Morris, 1958-1967	5,059
Interceptions	Gary Fencik, 1976-1987	38
Punting (Avg.)	George Gulyanics, 1947-1952	44.5
Punt Return (Avg.)	George McAfee, 1940-41, 1945-1950	*12.8
Kickoff Return (Avg.)	Gale Sayers, 1965-1971	*30.6
Field Goals	Kevin Butler, 1985-1995	243
Touchdowns (Tot.)	Walter Payton, 1975-1987	125
Points	Kevin Butler, 1985-1995	1,116

INDIVIDUAL RECORDS—SINGLE SEASON

Category	Name	Performance
Rushing (Yds.)	Walter Payton, 1977	1,852
Passing (Yds.)	Erik Kramer, 1995	3,838
Passing (TDs)	Erik Kramer, 1995	29
Receiving (No.)	Marty Booker, 2001	100
Receiving (Yds.)	Marcus Robinson, 1999	1,400
Interceptions	Mark Carrier, 1990	10
Punting (Avg.)	Bobby Joe Green, 1963	46.5
Punt Return (Avg.)	Harry Clark, 1943	15.8
Kickoff Return (Avg.)	Gale Sayers, 1967	37.7
Field Goals	Kevin Butler, 1985	31
Touchdowns (Tot.)	Gale Sayers, 1965	22
Points	Kevin Butler, 1985	144

INDIVIDUAL RECORDS—SINGLE GAME

Category	Name	Performance
Rushing (Yds.)	Walter Payton, 11-20-77	275
Passing (Yds.)	Johnny Lujack, 12-11-49	468
Passing (TDs)	Sid Luckman, 11-14-43	*7
Receiving (No.)	Jim Keane, 10-23-49	14
Receiving (Yds.)	Harlon Hill, 10-31-54	214
Interceptions	Many times	3
	Last time by Mark Carrier, 12-9-90	
Field Goals	Roger LeClerc, 12-3-61	5
	Mac Percival, 10-20-68	5
Touchdowns (Tot.)	Gale Sayers, 12-12-65	*6
Points	Gale Sayers, 12-12-65	36

*NFL Record

CHICAGO BEARS

2004 VETERAN ROSTER

No.	Name	Pos.	Ht.	Wt.	Birthdate	NFL Exp.	College	Hometown	How Acq.	'03 Games/ Starts
27	Abdullah, Rabih	RB	6-0	220	4/27/75	7	Lehigh	Roselle, N.J.	UFA(TB)-'02	15/0
49	Anelli, Mark	TE	6-3	245	6/5/79	3	Wisconsin	Melrose Park, Ill.	FA-'03	0*
23	Azumah, Jerry	CB	5-10	195	9/1/77	6	New Hampshire	Worcester, Mass.	D5c-'99	16/13
16	Barnard, Brooks	P	6-3	195	11/4/79	2	Maryland	Arnold, Md.	FA-'03	1/0*
86	Booker, Marty	WR	6-0	212	7/31/76	6	Northeast Louisiana	Jonesboro-Hodge, La.	D3c-'99	13/13
70	Boone, Alfonso	DT	6-4	328	1/11/76	4	Mt. San Antonio (Calif.) J.C.	Saginaw, Mich.	FA-'00	16/6
55	Briggs, Lance	LB	6-1	245	11/12/80	2	Arizona	Sacramento, Calif.	D3-'03	16/13
96	Brown, Alex	DE	6-3	272	6/4/79	3	Florida	White Springs, Fla.	D4-'02	16/16
30	Brown, Mike	S	5-10	212	2/13/78	5	Nebraska	Scottsdale, Ariz.	D2-'00	16/16
74	Brown, Ruben	G	6-3	304	2/13/72	10	Pittsburgh	Lynchburg, Va.	FA-'04	15/15*
88	Clark, Desmond	TE	6-3	255	4/20/77	6	Wake Forest	Lakeland, Fla.	UFA(Mia)-'03	15/15
75	Colombo, Marc	T	6-8	325	10/8/78	3	Boston College	Bridgewater, Mass.	D1-'02	0*
2	Edinger, Paul	K	5-8	175	1/17/78	5	Michigan State	Lakeland, Fla.	D6b-'00	16/0
79	Edwards, Steve	T	6-5	340	2/20/79	2	Central Florida	Chicago, Ill.	FA-'03	16/16
14	Elliott, Jamin	WR	5-11	195	10/5/79	3	Delaware	Portsmouth, Va.	D6b-'02	1/0*
44	Forsey, Brock	RB	5-11	203	2/11/80	2	Boise State	Meridian, Idaho	D6b-'03	9/2
87	Gage, Justin	WR	6-4	208	1/25/81	2	Missouri	Jefferson City, Mo.	D5b-'03	10/3
69	Gandy, Mike	G	6-4	325	1/3/79	4	Notre Dame	Garland, Texas	D3-'01	14/14
78	Gibson, Aaron	G-T	6-6	375	9/27/77	6	Wisconsin	Indianapolis, Ind.	FA-'02	16/16
85	Gilmore, John	TE	6-4	260	9/21/79	3	Penn State	West Lawn, Pa.	FA-'02	15/1
25	Gray, Bobby	S	6-0	212	4/30/78	3	Louisiana Tech	Aldine, Texas	D5a-'02	16/9
43	Green, Mike	S	6-0	195	12/6/76	5	Northwestern State (La.)	Ruston, La.	D7b-'00	10/8
8	Grossman, Rex	QB	6-1	222	8/23/80	2	Florida	Bloomington, Ind.	D1b-'03	3/3
97	Haynes, Michael	DE	6-3	281	9/13/80	2	Penn State	Columbus, N.J.	D1a-'03	16/0
38	Hicks, Dwone	RB	5-9	222	4/25/81	2	East Tennessee State	Huntsville, Ala.	W(Tenn)-'03	3/0*
63	Hill, Charles	DT	6-2	293	11/1/80	2	Maryland	Palmer Park, Md.	FA-'03	0*
92	Hillenmeyer, Hunter	LB	6-4	238	10/28/80	2	Vanderbilt	Nashville, Tenn.	FA-'03	13/0
47	Johnson, Bryan	FB	6-1	245	1/18/78	4	Boise State	Pocatello, Idaho	T(Wash)-'04	16/11*
82	Johnson, Robert	TE	6-6	270	6/20/80	2	Auburn	Montgomery, Ala.	W(Atl)-'03	1/0
32	Johnson, Todd	FS	6-1	200	12/18/78	2	Florida	Sarasota, Fla.	D4a-'03	0*
18	Jones, Daryl	WR	5-9	190	2/2/79	2	Miami	Dallas, Texas	FA-'03	0*
20	Jones, Thomas	RB	5-10	220	8/19/78	5	Virginia	Big Stone Gap, Va.	UFA(TB)-'04	16/3*
58	Keathley, Michael	G	6-4	296	3/9/78	4	Texas Christian	Glen Rose, Texas	FA-'04	8/2*
90	Knight, Bryan	LB	6-2	238	1/22/79	3	Pittsburgh	Buffalo, N.Y.	D5b-'02	16/2
57	Kreutz, Olin	C	6-2	292	6/9/77	7	Washington	Honolulu, Hawaii	D3-'98	16/16
73	LaFavor, Tron	DT	6-2	290	11/27/79	2	Florida	Ft. Lauderdale, Fla.	D5c-'03	4/0
89	Lyman, Dustin	TE	6-4	245	8/5/76	5	Wake Forest	Boulder, Colo.	D3b-'00	9/1
65	Mannelly, Patrick	T-LS	6-5	265	4/18/75	7	Duke	Atlanta, Ga.	D6b-'98	16/0
4	Maynard, Brad	P	6-1	186	2/9/74	8	Ball State	Sheridan, Ind.	UFA(NYG)-'01	16/0
37	McKie, Jason	FB	5-11	231	5/22/80	3	Temple	Gulf Breeze, Fla.	FA-'03	6/0
26	McMillon, Todd	CB	5-11	188	9/26/74	5	Northern Arizona	Bellflower, Calif.	FA-'00	13/0
21	McQuarters, R.W.	CB	5-10	198	12/21/76	7	Oklahoma State	Tulsa, Okla.	T(SF)-'00	16/6
81	Merritt, Ahmad	WR	5-10	195	2/5/77	4	Wisconsin	Chicago, Ill.	FA-'00	15/1
60	Metcalf, Terrence	G-T	6-3	325	1/28/78	3	Mississippi	Clarksdale, Miss.	D3-'02	8/2
72	Mitchell, Qasim	T	6-6	355	12/3/79	2	North Carolina A&T	Jacksonville, N.C.	FA-'03	3/2
59	Odom, Joe	LB	6-1	238	12/14/79	2	Purdue	Bethalto, Ill.	D6a-'03	10/3
29	Peterson, Adrian	RB	5-10	210	7/1/79	3	Georgia Southern	Alachua, Fla.	D6a-'02	6/1
36	Pritchett, Stanley	FB	6-2	250	12/22/72	9	South Carolina	Atlanta, Ga.	FA-'01	16/10
12	Quinn, Jonathan	QB	6-6	240	2/27/75	7	Middle Tennessee State	Nashville, Tenn.	UFA(KC)-'04	0*
48	Reid, Gabe	TE	6-4	260	5/28/77	2	Brigham Young	American Samoa	W(Tenn)-'03	1/0
98	Robinson, Bryan	DE	6-4	305	6/22/74	8	Fresno State	Toledo, Ohio	FA-'98	16/16
95	Scott, Ian	DT	6-2	315	11/8/81	2	Florida	Gainesville, Fla.	D4b-'03	6/0
99	Tafoya, Joe	DE	6-4	278	9/6/77	4	Arizona	Pittsburg, Calif.	FA-'01	16/0
76	Tait, John	T	6-6	323	1/26/75	6	Brigham Young	Tempe, Ariz.	TFA(KC)-'04	16/16*
83	Terrell, David	WR	6-3	215	3/13/79	4	Michigan	Richmond, Va.	D1-'01	16/8
35	Thomas, Anthony	RB	6-2	228	11/11/77	4	Michigan	Winnfield, La.	D2-'01	13/13
33	Tillman, Charles	CB	6-1	196	2/23/81	2	Louisiana-Lafayette	Copperas Cove, Texas	D2-'03	16/13
64	Tucker, Rex	G	6-5	320	12/20/76	6	Texas A&M	Midland, Texas	D3a-'99	0*
54	Urlacher, Brian	LB	6-4	258	5/25/78	5	New Mexico	Lovington, N.M.	D1-'00	16/16
84	Wade, Bobby	WR	5-10	193	2/25/81	2	Arizona	Phoenix, Ariz.	D5a-'03	12/0
67	Warner, Josh	T	6-5	320	5/15/79	2	SUNY-Brockport	Cato, N.Y.	FA-'03	10/0
22	Williams, Brock	CB	5-10	195	8/11/79	3	Notre Dame	Hammond, La.	W(Oak)-'03	10/0
24	Worrell, Cameron	S	5-11	199	12/14/79	2	Fresno State	Chowchilla, Calif.	FA-'03	14/0

* Anelli missed '02 season because of injury with San Francisco; Barnard played 1 game with New England in '03; R. Brown played 15 games with Buffalo; Columbo missed '03 season because of injury; Elliott played 1 game with New England; Golden played 4 games with Tampa Bay; Hicks played 3 games with Tennessee; Hill last active with Houston in '02; B. Johnson played 16 games with Washington; T. Johnson missed '03 season because of injury; D. Jones inactive for 1 game; T. Jones played 16 games with Tampa Bay; Keathley played 8 games with San Diego, Quinn was third quarterback for 16 games with Kansas City; Tait played 16 games with Kansas City; Tucker missed '03 season because of injury.

Players lost through free agency (3): DT Keith Traylor (NE; 10 games in '03), T-G Chris Villarrial (Buff; 13), WR Dez White (Atl; 15).

Also played with Bears in '03—QB Chris Chandler (8 games), DE Phillip Daniels (16), LB Warrick Holdman (13), LB Bobbie Howard (3), G-T Corbin Lacina (7), QB Kordell Stewart (9).

2004 FIRST-YEAR ROSTER

Name	Pos.	Ht.	Wt.	Birthdate	College	Hometown	How Acq.
Aiello, Sam	T	6-5	306	2/27/81	Iowa	Streamwood, Ill.	FA
Anderson, Bryan (1)	G	6-4	325	3/30/80	Pittsburgh	Philadelphia, Penn.	D7-'03
Ballard, Derrick	S	6-1	205	12/8/81	Memphis	Madison, Ga.	FA
Berrian, Bernard	WR	6-1	183	12/27/80	Fresno State	Winton, Calif.	D3
Boone, Aaron (1)	WR	6-2	204	1/13/78	Kentucky	Fillmore, Utah	W(Dall)-'03
Cain, Jeremy	LB	6-1	231	4/24/80	Massachusetts	Ft. Lauderdale, Fla.	FA
Campbell, Darrell	DT	6-4	304	7/6/81	Notre Dame	South Holland, Ill.	FA
Dinwiddie, Ryan	QB	6-1	176	11/27/80	Boise State	Elk Grove, Calif.	FA
Droege, Rob	T	6-6	302	2/15/81	Missouri	St. Louis, Mo.	FA
Forde, Andre (1)	WR	5-10	207	10/29/80	Buffalo	Coral Springs, Fla.	W(Ind)-'03
Fryzel, Jimmy (1)	WR	5-11	195	4/21/81	Central Florida	Lakeland, Fla.	FA
Harriott, Claude	DE	6-4	252	4/8/81	Pittsburgh	Belle Glade, Fla.	D5
Harris, Tommie	DT	6-3	292	4/29/83	Oklahoma	Killeen, Tex.	D1
Hicks, Dwone (1)	RB	5-9	222	4/25/81	Middle Tennessee State	Huntsville, Ala.	W(Tenn)-'03
Idonije, Israel (1)	DT	6-7	290	11/17/80	Manitoba	Brandon, Manitoba, Canada	W(Cle)-'03
Joe, Leon	LB	6-1	233	10/26/81	Maryland	Fort Washington, Md.	D4
Johnson, Terry "Tank"	DT	6-3	302	12/7/81	Washington	Tempe, Ariz.	D2
Kashama, Alain	DE	6-4	256	12/8/79	Michigan	Montreal, Quebec, Canada	FA
Krenzel, Craig	QB	6-4	228	7/1/81	Ohio State	Sterling Heights, Mich.	D5
Marshall, Alfonso	CB	6-0	185	1/17/81	Miami	Clewiston, Fla.	D7
Minkins, Josh	CB	5-10	185	5/23/80	Louisville	Willingboro, N.J.	FA
O'Donnell, Joe (1)	K	5-10	215	2/11/75	Maryland	Fox Chapel, Penn.	W(Oak)
Pare, Brian	LS	6-2	255	2/9/82	Florida Atlantic	Boca Raton, Fla.	FA
Reese, Marcus (1)	LB	6-1	233	6/15/81	UCLA	San Jose, Calif.	W(SF)-'03
Rumishek, Dan (1)	DT	6-4	284	6/6/80	Michigan	Addison Trail, Ill.	W(Pitt)
Schumacher, Jerry (1)	LB	6-2	245	12/19/80	Illinois	Chicago, Ill.	FA
Vasher, Nathan	CB	5-10	180	11/17/81	Texas	Texarkana, Texas	D4
Washburn, Cliff (1)	DE	6-5	285	1/25/80	The Citadel	Shelby, N.C.	W(NYG)-'03
Williams, Virgil	S	6-1	195	11/28/80	Washington State	Tacoma, Wash.	FA

The term NFL Rookie is defined as a player who is in his first season of professional football and has not been on the roster of another professional football team for any regular-season or postseason games. A Rookie is designated by an "R" on NFL rosters. Players who have been active in another professional football league or players who have NFL experience, including either preseason training camp or being on an Active List or Inactive List, or on Reserve/Injured or Reserve/Physically Unable to Perform for fewer than six regular-season games, are termed NFL First-Year Players. An NFL First-Year Player is designated by a "1" on NFL rosters. Thereafter, a player is credited with an additional year of experience for each season in which he accumulates six games on the Active List or Inactive List, or on Reserve/Injured or Reserve/Physically Unable to Perform.

Log on to www.chicagobears.com for an up-to-date roster.

CHICAGO BEARS

COACHING STAFF

Head Coach,
Lovie Smith

Pro Career: Named the thirteenth head coach in Chicago Bears history on January 15, 2004. Smith comes to the Bears from St. Louis where he engineered a dramatic turnaround as the defensive coordinator of the Rams over the last three seasons. In Smith's first season as an NFL defensive coordinator with St. Louis in 2001, he helped the Rams return to the Super Bowl after missing the playoffs the previous season. Smith has coached on playoff teams in four of the last five campaigns and in five of his eight NFL seasons. Smith previously coached the linebackers for the Tampa Bay Buccaneers (1996-2000). Known for his attacking style on defense, Smith orchestrated one of the NFL's most productive units in takeaways, defensive touchdowns and sacks in 2003. St. Louis led the NFL with 46 takeaways while tying for fourth with 24 interceptions and leading the NFL with 22 fumble recoveries. The 46 takeaways for the Rams equals the 1999 Eagles for the second-highest single-season total in the NFL since 1993. While in Tampa Bay, he helped improve a Buccaneers' defense that had not ranked above twentieth in the NFL in the four seasons prior to Smith's arrival under head coach Tony Dungy and defensive coordinator Monte Kiffin. However, the Buccaneers ranked eleventh in 1996, third in 1997, second in 1998, third in 1999, and ninth in 2000. Career record: 0-0.

Background: Played at Tulsa (1976-79), where he played linebacker as a freshman before being switched to strong safety for the remainder of his collegiate career. Smith was a two-time All-America and three-time All-Missouri Conference defensive back. Attended high school in Big Sandy, Texas, where the Wildcats won three consecutive state championships where he earned all-state honors three years as an end and linebacker. Smith has spent 21 years in coaching at the collegiate and professional levels. He began his coaching career at his hometown high school in 1980 before moving to Cascia Hall Prep in Tulsa the following year. Two years later Smith made the jump to the college ranks at his alma mater of Tulsa University as linebackers coach (1983-86). He also coached linebackers at Wisconsin (1987), Arizona State (1988-91), and Kentucky (1992). Smith was the defensive backs coach at Tennessee (1993-94) and Ohio State (1995).

Personal: Born May 8, 1958, Gladewater, Texas. Lovie and his wife MaryAnne have three sons—Mikal, Matthew and Miles and twin grandsons—Malachi and Noah.

ASSISTANT COACHES

Bob Babich, linebackers; born February 20, 1961, Aliquippa, Pa. Linebacker Mesa (Colo.) C.C. 1979-1980, Tulsa 1981-82. No pro playing experience. College coach: Tulsa 1984-87, 1990, Wisconsin 1988-89, Bowling Green 1991, East Carolina 1992-93, Pittsburgh 1994-96, North Dakota State (head coach) 1997-2002. Pro coach: St. Louis Rams 2003, joined Bears in 2004.

Mike Bajakian, offensive quality control; born August 4, 1974, River Vale, N.J. Quarterback Williams College 1993-96. No pro playing experience. College coach: Rutgers 1998-99, Sacred Heart 2000, Michigan 2000-01, Central Michigan 2002-03. Pro coach: Joined Bears in 2004.

Vance Bedford, defensive backs; born August 20, 1958, Houston. Defensive back Texas 1977-79, 1981. Pro defensive back St. Louis Cardinals 1982, Oklahoma Outlaws (USFL) 1984. College coach: Navarro (Texas) J.C. 1986, Colorado State 1987-1992, Oklahoma State 1993-94, Michigan 1995-98. Pro coach: Joined Bears in 1999.

Rob Boras, tight ends; born September 30, 1970, Glen Ellyn, Ill. Center DePauw 1988-1991. No pro playing experience. College coach: DePauw 1992-93, Texas 1994-97, Benedictine 1998 (head coach), Nevada-Las Vegas 1999-2003. Pro coach: Joined Bears in 2004.

Charlie Coiner, asst. special teams; born Waynesboro, Va. Attended Catawba College, Appalachian State. No college or pro playing experience. College coach: Appalachian State 1983-86, Minnesota 1987, Louisville 1995-97, Tennessee-Chattanooga 1998, Louisiana State 1999, Texas Southern 2000. Pro coach: Joined Bears in 2001.

Darryl Drake, wide receivers; born December 11, 1956, Louisville, Ky. Wide receiver Western Kentucky 1975-78. Pro wide receiver Washington Redskins 1979, Ottawa Roughriders (CFL) 1981, Cincinnati Bengals 1983. College coach: Western Kentucky 1983-1991, Georgia 1992-96, Baylor 1997, Texas 1998-2003. Pro coach: Joined Bears in 2004.

Karl Dunbar, defensive line; born May 18, 1967, Plaisance, La. Defensive lineman Louisiana State 1986-89. Pro defensive lineman Pittsburgh Steelers 1990, Orlando Thunder (World League) 1992, New Orleans Saints 1992-93, Rhein Fire (World League) 1995. College coach: Nicholls State 1998-99, Louisiana State 2000-01, Oklahoma State 2002-03. Pro coach: Joined Bears in 2004.

Harold Goodwin, asst. offensive line; born November 14, 1973, Columbia, S.C. Offensive lineman Michigan 1992-94. No pro playing experience. College coach: Eastern Michigan 1998-99, Central Michigan 2000-03. Pro coach: Joined Bears in 2004.

Torrian Gray, asst. defensive backs; born March 18, 1974, Lakeland, Fla. Safety Virginia Tech 1993-96. Pro safety Minnesota Vikings 1997-99. College coach: Maine 2000-01, Connecticut 2002-03. Pro coach: Joined Bears in 2004.

Pete Hoener, offensive line; born June 14, 1951, Peoria, Ill. Tight end-defensive end Bradley 1969-1970. No pro playing experience. College coach: Missouri 1975-76, Illinois State 1977, Indiana State 1978-1984, Illinois 1986-88, Purdue 1989-1991, Texas Christian 1991-97, Iowa State 1998-99, Texas A&M 2000. Pro coach: St. Louis Cardinals 1985-86, Arizona Cardinals 2003, joined Bears in 2004.

Lloyd Lee, defensive quality control; born August 10, 1976, Minneapolis. Safety Dartmouth 1994-98. Pro safety San Diego Chargers 1998-99. Pro coach: Tampa Bay Buccaneers (scout) 2001-03, joined Bears in 2004.

Ron Rivera, defensive coordinator; born January 7, 1962, Fort Ord, Calif. Linebacker California 1980-83. Pro linebacker Chicago Bears 1984-1992. Pro coach: Chicago Bears 1997-98, Philadelphia Eagles 1999-2003, re-joined Bears in 2004.

Terry Shea, offensive coordinator; born June 12, 1946, San Mateo, Calif. Quarterback Oregon 1965-67. No pro playing experience. College coach: Oregon 1968-69, Mt. Hood (Ore.) J.C. 1970-75, Utah State 1976-1981, San Jose State 1984-86, 1990-91 (head coach 1990-91), California 1987-89, Stanford 1992-94, Rutgers (head coach) 1996-2000. Pro coach: British Columbia Lions (CFL) 1995, Kansas City Chiefs 2001-03, joined Bears in 2004.

Tim Spencer, running backs; born December 10, 1960, Martin Ferry, Ohio. Running back Ohio State 1979-1982. Pro running back Chicago Blitz (USFL) 1983, Arizona Wranglers (USFL) 1984, Memphis Showboats (USFL) 1985, San Diego Chargers 1985-1990. College coach: Ohio State 1994-2003. Pro coach: Joined Bears in 2004.

Dave Toub, special teams coordinator; born June 1, 1962, Ossining, N.Y. Offensive lineman Springfield College 1980-81, Texas-El Paso 1983-84. No pro playing experience. College coach: Texas El-Paso 1987-89, Missouri 1989-2000. Pro coach: Philadelphia Eagles 2001-03, joined Bears in 2004.

Wade Wilson, quarterbacks; born February 1, 1959, Commerce, Texas. Quarterback East Texas State 1977-1980. Pro quarterback Minnesota Vikings 1981-1991, Atlanta Falcons 1992, New Orleans Saints 1993-94, Dallas Cowboys 1995-97, Oakland Raiders 1998-99. Pro coach: Dallas Cowboys 2000-02, joined Bears in 2004.

National Football Conference
East Division
Team Colors: Royal Blue, Metallic Silver Blue, and White
Cowboys Center
One Cowboys Parkway
Irving, Texas 75063
Telephone: (972) 556-9900

2004 SCHEDULE

PRESEASON		**Dallas time**
Aug. 14	at Houston	7:00
Aug. 21	at Oakland	8:00
Aug. 30	**Tennessee**	7:00
Sept. 2	**Kansas City**	7:00

REGULAR SEASON

Sept. 12	at Minnesota	3:15
Sept. 19	**Cleveland**	3:15
Sept. 27	at Washington (Mon.)	8:00
Oct. 3	Open Date	
Oct. 10	**New York Giants**	12:00
Oct. 17	**Pittsburgh**	3:15
Oct. 24	at Green Bay	3:15
Oct. 31	**Detroit**	12:00
Nov. 7	at Cincinnati	12:00
Nov. 15	**Philadelphia** (Mon.)	8:00
Nov. 21	at Baltimore	12:00
Nov. 25	**Chicago** (Thu.)	3:15
Dec. 6	at Seattle (Mon.)	8:00
Dec. 12	**New Orleans**	12:00
Dec. 19	at Philadelphia	12:00
Dec. 26	**Washington**	3:15
Jan. 2	at New York Giants	7:30

Stadium: Texas Stadium (opened in 1971) • **Capacity:** 65,529
2401 E. Airport Freeway
Irving, Texas 75062
Playing Surface: Sportfield Realgrass
Training Camp: Marriott Residence Inn
Oxnard, California 93030

TEXAS STADIUM

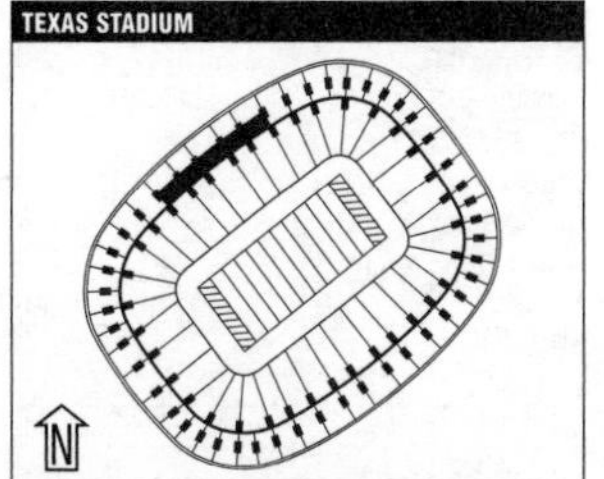

CLUB OFFICIALS

Owner/President/General Manager: Jerry Jones
Chief Operating Officer/Executive Vice President-Player Personnel: Stephen Jones
Vice President/Director of Charities and Special Events: Charlotte Anderson
Chief Sales and Marketing Officer/Vice President/General Counsel: Jerry Jones Jr.
CFO: George Mitchell
Director of Public Relations: Rich Dalrymple
Director of Corporate Communications: Brett Daniels
Director of Community Relations: Emily Robbins
Director of College and Pro Scouting: Larry Lacewell
Assistant Director of College Scouting: Tom Ciskowski
Assistant Director of Pro Scouting: Bryan Broaddus
Director of Operations: Bruce Mays
Director of Player Development: Steve Carichoff
Chief Human Resources and Diversity Officer: Vincent Thompson
Director of Information Technology: Derek Eagleton
Director of Ticket Operations: Carol Padgett
Director of Sales, Promotions and Advertising: Joel Finglass
Head Athletic Trainer: Jim Maurer
Equipment Manager: Mike McCord
Video Director: Robert Blackwell
Cheerleader Director: Kelli Finglass

COACHING HISTORY
(409-297-6)

1960-1988	Tom Landry	270-178-6
1989-1993	Jimmy Johnson	51-37-0
1994-97	Barry Switzer	45-26-0
1998-99	Chan Gailey	18-16-0
2000-02	Dave Campo	15-33-0
2003	Bill Parcells	10-7-0

ATTENDANCE
Home 496,506 Away 567,803
Total 1,064,309
Single-game home record, 65,180 (11/12/95)
Single-season home record, 518,167 (1995)

2004 DRAFT CHOICES

Round	Name	Pos.	College
2	Julius Jones	RB	Notre Dame
	Jacob Rogers	T	Southern California
3	Stephen Peterman	G	Louisiana State
4	Bruce Thornton	DB	Georgia
5	Sean Ryan	TE	Boston College
7	Nathan Jones	DB	Rutgers
	Patrick Crayton	WR	Northwestern Oklahoma St.
	Jacques Reeves	DB	Purdue

DALLAS COWBOYS

2003 TEAM RECORD

PRESEASON (2-2)

Date	Result	Opponent
8/9	L 0-13	at Arizona
8/15	W 34-6	Houston
8/21	L 14-15	at Pittsburgh
8/28	W 52-13	Oakland

REGULAR SEASON (10-6)

Date	Result	Opponent	Att.
9/7	L 13-27	Atlanta	64,104
9/15	W 35-32	at N.Y. Giants (OT)	78,907
9/28	W 17-6	at New York Jets	77,863
10/5	W 24-7	Arizona	63,601
10/12	W 23-21	Philadelphia	63,648
10/19	W 38-7	at Detroit	61,160
10/26	L 0-16	at Tampa Bay	65,602
11/2	W 21-14	Washington	64,002
11/9	W 10-6	Buffalo	63,770
11/16	L 0-12	at New England	68,436
11/23	W 24-20	Carolina	63,871
11/27	L 21-40	Miami	64,110
12/7	L 10-36	at Philadelphia	69,773
12/14	W 27-0	at Washington	70,284
12/21	W 19-3	New York Giants	64,118
12/28	L 7-13	at New Orleans	68,451

(OT) Overtime

POSTSEASON (0-1)

Date	Result	Opponent	Att.
1/3	L 10-29	at Carolina	73,014

SCORE BY PERIODS

	1	2	3	4	OT		Total
Cowboys	72	106	57	51	3	—	289
Opponents	52	69	70	69	0	—	260

2003 TEAM STATISTICS

	Cowboys	Opp.
Total First Downs	286	228
Rushing	115	68
Passing	149	127
Penalty	22	33
3rd Down: Made/Att	88/241	69/227
3rd Down Pct.	36.5	30.4
4th Down: Made/Att	4/12	7/15
4th Down Pct.	33.3	46.7
Possession Avg.	32:34	27:26
Total Net Yards	5,161	4,056
Avg. Per Game	322.6	253.5
Total Plays	1,062	937
Avg. Per Play	4.9	4.3
Net Yards Rushing	1,999	1,425
Avg. Per Game	124.9	89.1
Total Rushes	515	413
Net Yards Passing	3,162	2,631
Avg. Per Game	197.6	164.4
Sacked/Yards Lost	37/185	32/189
Gross Yards	3,347	2,820
Att./Completions	510/294	492/239
Completion Pct.	57.6	48.6
Had Intercepted	21	13
Punts/Average	95/38.9	105/42.6
Net Punting Avg.	95/34.6	105/37.5
Penalties/Yards	98/837	88/763
Fumbles/Ball Lost	26/8	24/12
Touchdowns	31	28
Rushing	11	7
Passing	17	18
Returns	3	3

2003 INDIVIDUAL STATISTICS

PASSING	Att.	Comp.	Yds.	Pct.	TD	Int.	Tkld.	Rate
Carter	505	292	3,302	57.8	17	21	37/185	71.4
Hutchinson	2	1	8	50.0	0	0	0/0	60.4
Anderson	1	0	0	0.0	0	0	0/0	39.6
Cason	1	1	37	100.0	0	0	0/0	118.8
Glenn	1	0	0	0.0	0	0	0/0	39.6
Cowboys	510	294	3,347	57.6	17	21	37/185	71.4
Opponents	492	239	2,820	48.6	18	13	32/189	67.6

SCORING	TD R	TD P	TD Rt	PAT	FG	Saf	PTS
Cundiff	0	0	0	30/31	23/29	0	99
Anderson	1	4	0	0/0	0/0	0	30
Glenn	0	5	0	0/0	0/0	0	30
Hambrick	5	0	0	0/0	0/0	0	30
Bryant	0	2	0	0/0	0/0	0	12
Carter	2	0	0	0/0	0/0	0	12
Cason	2	0	0	0/0	0/0	0	12
Galloway	0	2	0	0/0	0/0	0	12
Robinson	0	2	0	0/0	0/0	0	12
Bickerstaff	1	0	0	0/0	0/0	0	6
Campbell	0	1	0	0/0	0/0	0	6
Edwards	0	0	1	0/0	0/0	0	6
Singleton	0	0	1	0/0	0/0	0	6
Ra. Williams	0	0	1	0/0	0/0	0	6
Witten	0	1	0	0/0	0/0	0	6
Coleman	0	0	0	0/0	0/0	1	2
Glover	0	0	0	0/0	0/0	1	2
Cowboys	11	17	3	30/31	23/29	2	289
Opponents	7	18	3	23/26	21/23	1	260

2-Pt. Conversions: None.
Cowboys 0-0, Opponents 2-2.

RUSHING	No.	Yds	Avg	LG	TD
Hambrick	275	972	3.5	42	5
Anderson	70	306	4.4	19	1
Carter	68	257	3.8	19	2
Cason	40	220	5.5	63t	2
Murrell	28	107	3.8	17	0
Bickerstaff	19	56	2.9	9	1
Glenn	3	55	18.3	47	0
Galloway	4	22	5.5	10	0
Ja. Martin	4	7	1.8	3	0
Bryant	2	0	0.0	2	0
Hutchinson	2	-3	-1.5	-1	0
Cowboys	515	1,999	3.9	63t	11
Opponents	413	1,425	3.5	64t	7

RECEIVING	No.	Yds	Avg	LG	TD
Anderson	69	493	7.1	37	4
Glenn	52	754	14.5	51t	5
Bryant	39	550	14.1	54	2
Witten	35	347	9.9	36t	1
Galloway	34	672	19.8	64	2
Campbell	20	195	9.8	23	1
Cason	17	142	8.4	28	0
Hambrick	17	99	5.8	13	0
Murrell	4	32	8.0	14	0
Smith	3	46	15.3	32	0
Ja. Martin	2	9	4.5	6	0
Robinson	2	8	4.0	5t	2
Cowboys	294	3,347	11.4	64	17
Opponents	239	2,820	11.8	76t	18

INTERCEPTIONS	No.	Yds	Avg	LG	TD
Newman	4	23	5.8	25	0
Ro. Williams	2	69	34.5	39	0
Singleton	2	42	21.0	41t	1
Edwards	1	27	27.0	27t	1
Coakley	1	24	24.0	24	0
Hunter	1	0	0.0	0	0
Ross	1	0	0.0	0	0
Woodson	1	-2	-2.0	-2	0
Cowboys	13	183	14.1	41t	2
Opponents	21	285	13.6	70	1

PUNTING	No.	Yds.	Avg.	In 20	LG
Gowin	94	3,665	39.0	25	59
Cundiff	1	32	32.0	0	32
Cowboys	95	3,697	38.9	25	59
Opponents	105	4,471	42.6	33	60

PUNT RETURNS	Ret	FC	Yds	Avg	LG	TD
Smith	30	13	212	7.1	46	0
Galloway	20	8	178	8.9	36	0
Swinton	1	3	0	0.0	0	0
Cowboys	51	24	390	7.6	46	0
Opponents	34	26	227	6.7	19	0

KICKOFF RETURNS	No.	Yds	Avg	LG	TD
Smith	23	495	21.5	54	0
Ross	18	434	24.1	37	0
Cason	5	81	16.2	19	0
Bates	4	90	22.5	30	0
Swinton	3	65	21.7	25	0
Bickerstaff	2	24	12.0	15	0
Galloway	2	38	19.0	22	0
Ra. Williams	2	60	30.0	37t	1
Ogbogu	1	5	5.0	5	0
Cowboys	60	1,292	21.5	54	1
Opponents	66	1,448	21.9	63	0

FIELD GOALS	1-19	20-29	30-39	40-49	50+
Cundiff	0/0	11/11	5/6	4/7	3/5
Cowboys	0/0	11/11	5/6	4/7	3/5
Opponents	0/0	9/9	7/7	4/5	1/2

SACKS	No.
Ellis	8.0
Glover	5.0
Ogbogu	3.5
Ekuban	2.5
Nguyen	2.0
Ro. Williams	2.0
Carson	1.5
Stewart	1.5
Blade	1.0
Coakley	1.0
Coleman	1.0
Newman	1.0
Singleton	1.0
Woodson	1.0
Cowboys	2.0
Opponents	37.0

RECORD HOLDERS

INDIVIDUAL RECORDS—CAREER

Category	Name	Performance
Rushing (Yds.)	Emmitt Smith, 1990-2002	*17,162
Passing (Yds.)	Troy Aikman, 1989-2000	32,942
Passing (TDs)	Troy Aikman, 1989-2000	165
Receiving (No.)	Michael Irvin, 1988-1999	750
Receiving (Yds.)	Michael Irvin, 1988-1999	11,904
Interceptions	Mel Renfro, 1964-1977	52
Punting (Avg.)	Toby Gowin, 1997-99, 2003	41.7
Punt Return (Avg.)	Deion Sanders, 1995-99	13.3
Kickoff Return (Avg.)	Mel Renfro, 1964-1977	26.4
Field Goals	Rafael Septien, 1978-1986	162
Touchdowns (Tot.)	Emmitt Smith, 1990-2002	164
Points	Emmitt Smith, 1990-2002	986

INDIVIDUAL RECORDS—SINGLE SEASON

Category	Name	Performance
Rushing (Yds.)	Emmitt Smith, 1995	1,773
Passing (Yds.)	Danny White, 1983	3,980
Passing (TDs)	Danny White, 1983	29
Receiving (No.)	Michael Irvin, 1995	111
Receiving (Yds.)	Michael Irvin, 1995	1,603
Interceptions	Everson Walls, 1981	11
Punting (Avg.)	Sam Baker, 1962	45.4
Punt Return (Avg.)	Bob Hayes, 1968	20.8
Kickoff Return (Avg.)	Mel Renfro, 1965	30.0
Field Goals	Richie Cunningham, 1997	34
Touchdowns (Tot.)	Emmitt Smith, 1995	25
Points	Emmitt Smith, 1995	150

INDIVIDUAL RECORDS—SINGLE GAME

Category	Name	Performance
Rushing (Yds.)	Emmitt Smith, 10-31-93	237
Passing (Yds.)	Don Meredith, 11-10-63	460
Passing (TDs)	Many times	5
	Last time by Troy Aikman, 9-12-99	
Receiving (No.)	Lance Rentzel, 11-19-67	13
Receiving (Yds.)	Bob Hayes, 11-13-66	246
Interceptions	Many times	3
	Last time by Terance Newman, 12-14-03	
Field Goals	Chris Boniol, 11-18-96	*7
	Billy Cundiff, 9-15-03	*7
Touchdowns (Tot.)	Many times	4
	Last time by Emmitt Smith, 9-4-95	
Points	Many times	24
	Last time by Emmitt Smith, 9-4-95	

*NFL Record

DALLAS COWBOYS

2004 VETERAN ROSTER

No.	Name	Pos.	Ht.	Wt.	Birthdate	NFL Exp.	College	Hometown	How Acq.	'03 Games/ Starts
76	Adams, Flozell	T	6-7	357	5/18/75	7	Michigan State	Bellwood, Ill.	D2-'98	16/16
73	Allen, Larry	G	6-3	335	11/27/71	11	Sonoma State	Compton, Calif.	D2-'94	16/16
20	Anderson, Richie	FB	6-2	230	9/13/71	12	Penn State	Sandy Spring, Md.	UFA(NYJ)-'03	15/8
36	t- Barnes, Darian	FB	6-2	250	2/28/80	3	Hampton	Toms River, N.J.	T(TB)-'04	14/0*
29	#Bates, Michael	WR	5-10	189	12/19/69	12	Arizona	Tucson, Ariz.	W(NYJ)-'03	9/0*
46	Bickerstaff, Erik	RB	6-0	230	7/25/80	2	Wisconsin	Waukesha, Wis.	FA-'03	4/0
99	Blade, Willie	DT	6-3	315	2/7/79	3	Mississippi State	Warner Robins, Ga.	FA-'03	15/15
50	Brooks, Jamal	LB	6-2	240	11/9/76	4	Hampton	Grenada Hills, Calif.	FA-'03	0*
88	Bryant, Antonio	WR	6-1	192	3/9/81	3	Pittsburgh	Miami, Fla.	D2b-'02	16/5
86	Campbell, Dan	TE	6-5	263	4/13/76	6	Texas A&M	Glen Rose, Texas	UFA(NYG)-'03	16/16
91	Carson, Leonardo	DT	6-2	305	2/11/77	5	Auburn	Mobile, Ala.	FA-'03	8/0
17	Carter, Quincy	QB	6-2	213	10/13/77	4	Georgia	Decatur, Ga.	D2a-'01	16/16
23	Cason, Aveion	RB	5-10	204	7/12/79	4	Illinois State	St. Petersburg, Fla.	T(Det)-'03	10/0
52	Coakley, Dexter	LB	5-10	236	10/20/72	8	Appalachian State	Mt. Pleasant, S.C.	D3a-'97	16/16
93	Coleman, Kenyon	DE	6-5	285	4/10/79	3	UCLA	Alta Loma, Calif.	T(Oak)-'03	16/0
70	Collins, Javiar	T	6-6	322	4/13/78	4	Northwestern	St. Paul, Minn.	FA-'01	1/0
3	Cundiff, Billy	K	6-1	201	3/30/80	3	Drake	Harlan, Iowa	FA-'02	15/0
29	Davis, Keith	CB	5-10	201	12/30/78	2	Sam Houston State	Italy, Texas	FA-'04	0*
26	Davison, Andrew	CB	5-11	185	12/19/79	3	Kansas	Detroit, Mich.	FA-'03	4/0
63	DiNapoli, Gennaro	C	6-3	287	5/25/75	7	Virginia Tech	Manhassat, N.Y.	FA-'03	7/0
24	Dixon, Tony	S	6-1	213	6/18/79	4	Alabama	Reform, Ala.	D2b-'01	16/0
98	Ellis, Greg	DE	6-6	277	8/14/75	7	North Carolina	Wendell, N.C.	D1-'98	16/16
83	Glenn, Terry	WR	5-11	195	7/23/74	9	Ohio State	Columbus, Ohio	T(GB)-'03	16/14
97	Glover, La'Roi	DT	6-2	285	7/4/74	9	San Diego State	San, Diego, Calif.	UFA(NO)-'02	16/16
61	Graham, DeMingo	G-T	6-3	310	9/10/73	6	Hofstra	Newark, N.J.	FA-'04	0*
65	Gurode, Andre	G	6-4	326	3/6/78	3	Colorado	Houston, Texas	D2a-'02	16/15
47	Hunter, Pete	CB	6-2	212	5/25/80	3	Virginia Union	Atlantic City, N.J.	D5-'02	16/0
7	Hutchinson, Chad	QB	6-5	237	2/21/77	3	Stanford	Del Mar, Calif.	FA-'02	1/0
56	James, Bradie	LB	6-2	243	1/17/81	2	Louisiana State	Monroe, La.	D4-'03	14/0
80	James, Cedric	WR	6-1	197	3/19/79	3	TCU	Kennedale, Texas	FA-'03	0*
62	Johnson, Al	C	6-5	303	1/27/79	1	Wisconsin	Brussels, Wis.	D2-'03	0*
19	t- Johnson, Keyshawn	WR	6-4	212	7/22/72	9	Southern California	Los Angeles, Calif.	T(TB)-'04	10/10*
68	Lehr, Matt	C	6-2	304	4/25/79	4	Virginia Tech	Woodbridge, Va.	D5-'01	16/16
34	Martin, Jamar	FB	5-11	256	4/12/80	2	Ohio State	Canton, Ohio	D4-'02	14/1
30	Mitchell, Donald	CB	5-10	182	12/14/76	5	Southern Methodist	Beaumont, Texas	UFA(Tenn)-'03	0*
41	Newman, Terence	CB	5-11	188	9/4/78	2	Kansas State	Salina, Kan.	D1-'03	16/16
59	Nguyen, Dat	LB	5-11	243	9/25/75	6	Texas A&M	Rockport, Texas	D3-'99	16/16
90	Ogbogu, Eric	DE	6-4	270	7/18/75	7	Maryland	Irvington, N.Y.	FA-'03	16/2
54	O'Neil, Keith	LB	6-0	230	8/26/80	2	Northern Arizona	Amherst, N.Y.	FA-'03	15/0
25	Powell, Jemeel	CB	6-0	186	8/29/80	2	California	Los Angeles, Calif.	W(Det)-'03	3/0
85	Robinson, Jeff	TE	6-4	264	2/20/70	12	Idaho	Spokane, Wash.	UFA(StL)-'02	16/0
9	Romo, Tony	QB	6-2	227	4/21/80	2	Eastern Illinois	Burlington, Wis.	FA-'03	0*
38	Scott, Lynn	S	6-0	221	6/23/77	4	Northwestern Oklahoma St.	Turpin, Okla.	FA-'01	16/0
58	Shanle, Scott	LB	6-2	245	11/23/79	2	Nebraska	St. Edward, Neb.	W(StL)-'03	6/0*
51	Singleton, Al	LB	6-2	228	8/7/75	8	Temple	Irvington, N.J.	UFA(TB)-'03	16/16
84	Smith, Zuriel	WR	5-11	166	1/15/80	2	Hampton	Mechanicsville, Va.	D6b-'03	9/0
55	Steele, Markus	LB	6-3	240	7/24/79	4	Southern California	New Bedford, Ohio	D4-'01	15/0
64	Stewart, Daleroy	DT	6-4	327	11/2/78	3	Southern Mississippi	Vero Beach, Fla.	D6-'01	15/1
77	Tucker, Torrin	T	6-6	329	12/25/79	2	Southern Mississippi	Meridian, Miss.	FA-'03	7/1
78	Vollers, Kurt	T	6-7	317	4/4/79	3	Notre Dame	Whittier, Calif.	FA-'02	13/8
71	Walter, Tyson	G-C	6-4	310	3/17/78	3	Ohio State	Bainbridge, Ohio	D6a-'02	16/0
81	Whalen, James	TE	6-2	244	12/11/77	4	Kentucky	Portland, Ore.	FA-'00	7/0
75	Wiley, Marcellus	DE	6-4	280	11/30/74	8	Columbia	Santa Monica, Calif.	FA-'04	16/16*
89	Williams, Randal	WR	6-3	220	5/21/78	4	New Hampshire	Bronx, N.Y.	W(Jax)-'01	15/0
31	Williams, Roy	S	6-0	235	8/14/80	3	Oklahoma	Union City, Calif.	D1-'02	16/16
82	Witten, Jason	TE	6-5	257	5/6/82	2	Tennessee	Elizabethton, Tenn.	D3-'03	15/7
28	Woodson, Darren	S	6-1	219	4/25/69	13	Arizona State	Phoenix, Ariz.	D2b-'92	16/16

* Barnes played 14 games with Tampa Bay in '03; Bates played 8 games with N.Y. Jets and 1 game with Dallas; Davis last active with Dallas in '02; Graham last active with Houston in '02; C. James inactive for 1 game; A. Johnson missed '03 season because of injury; K. Johnson played 10 games with Tampa Bay; Mitchell missed '03 season because of injury; Romo inactive for 16 games; Shanle played 6 games with St. Louis; Wiley played 16 games with San Diego.

t - Cowboys traded for Barnes (TB) and K. Johnson (TB).

Traded—WR Joey Galloway (15 games in '03) to Tampa Bay.

Players lost through free agency (2): CB Mario Edwards (TB; 16 games in '03); DE Ebenezer Ekuban (Cle; 16).

Also played with Cowboys in '03—P Toby Gowin (16 games), RB Troy Hambrick (16), TE Tony McGee (1), RB Adrian Murrell (3), DT Michael Myers (1), CB Derek Ross (8), CB Jeff Sanchez (1), WR Reggie Swinton (1), T Ryan Young (11).

2004 FIRST-YEAR ROSTER

Name	Pos.	Ht.	Wt.	Birthdate	College	Hometown	How Acq.
Boies, Josh (1)	P	6-4	225	12/14/74	Temple	Santa Fe, N.M.	FA
Brooks, Jermaine (1)	DT	6-3	290	4/11/79	Arkansas	Rancho Cucamonga, Calif.	FA-'03
Cargile, Steve	S	6-1	205	6/2/82	Columbia	Cleveland, Ohio	FA
Copper, Terrance	WR	6-0	204	3/12/82	East Carolina	Washington, N.C.	FA
Crayton, Patrick	WR	6-0	210	4/7/79	Northwestern Oklahoma St.	DeSoto, Texas	D7b
Crowder, Tom	S	6-1	203	1/21/81	Arkansas	Camden, Ark.	FA
Emanuel, Kevin	DE	6-4	259	12/6/79	Florida State	Waco, Texas	FA
Flinn, Ryan	P	6-5	205	2/14/80	Central Florida	Lehigh Acres, Fla.	FA
Fowler, Ryan	LB	6-3	243	5/20/82	Duke	Redington Shores, Fla.	FA
Henson, Drew	QB	6-4	230	2/13/80	Michigan	Brighton, Mich.	T(Hou)
Hilliard, Cedric	DT	6-2	307	11/19/80	Notre Dame	Arlington, Texas	FA
Jones, Julius	RB	5-10	217	8/14/81	Notre Dame	Big Stone Gap, Va.	D2a
Jones, Nathan	CB	5-10	187	6/13/82	Rutgers	Scotch Plains, N.J.	D7a
Lee, Darrell	DE	6-4	273	6/28/82	Florida	Kirkwood, Mo.	FA
Lee, ReShard (1)	RB	5-10	232	10/12/80	Middle Tennessee State	Brunswick, Ga.	FA-'03
McBriar, Mat (1)	P	6-1	202	7/8/79	Hawaii	East Brighton, Australia	FA
McCauley, Tango	G	6-4	307	10/27/78	Alabama State	Oklahoma City, Okla.	FA
Middleton, Brandon	WR	5-10	190	1/2/81	Houston	Houston, Texas	FA
Newson, James	WR	6-1	219	12/21/79	Oregon State	Stockton, Calif.	FA
Peterman, Stephen	G	6-4	317	1/11/82	Louisiana State	Waveland, Miss.	D3
Polite, Lousaka	FB	6-0	246	9/14/81	Pittsburgh	North Braddock, Pa.	FA
Reeves, Jacques	CB	5-11	188	10/8/82	Purdue	Lancaster, Texas	D7c
Rogers, Jacob	T	6-6	305	8/17/81	Southern California	Oxnard, Calif.	D2b
Ruffin, Jonathan (1)	K	5-11	174	8/1/81	Cincinnati	Metairie, La.	FA
Ryan, Sean	TE	6-5	266	3/27/80	Boston College	Buffalo, N.Y.	D5
Sanders, Darrick	T	6-4	312	10/15/80	Arkansas-Monticello	Pine Bluff, Ark.	FA
Smith, Shaun (1)	DT	6-2	320	8/19/81	South Carolina	Brooklyn, N.Y.	FA-'03
Thornton, Bruce	CB	5-10	197	1/31/80	Georgia	LaGrange, Ga.	D4
Thornton, Kalen	LB	6-3	245	5/12/82	Texas	Dallas, Texas	FA
Volk, Dave (1)	T	6-5	300	8/1/78	Nebraska	Battle Creek, Neb.	FA-'03
Wingrove, Ryan (1)	DE	6-3	250	7/3/79	Bowling Green	Parkersburg, W.Va.	FA

The term NFL Rookie is defined as a player who is in his first season of professional football and has not been on the roster of another professional football team for any regular-season or postseason games. A Rookie is designated by an "R" on NFL rosters. Players who have been active in another professional football league or players who have NFL experience, including either preseason training camp or being on an Active List or Inactive List, or on Reserve/Injured or Reserve/Physically Unable to Perform for fewer than six regular-season games, are termed NFL First-Year Players. An NFL First-Year Player is designated by a "1" on NFL rosters. Thereafter, a player is credited with an additional year of experience for each season in which he accumulates six games on the Active List or Inactive List, or on Reserve/Injured or Reserve/Physically Unable to Perform.

Log on to www.dallascowboys.com for an up-to-date roster.

COACHING STAFF

Head Coach,
Bill Parcells

Pro Career: Named head coach on January 2, 2003, Parcells has accumulated a 159-113-1 record, including two Super Bowl victories (XXI and XXV with the Giants) and another Super Bowl appearance (XXXI with New England) in 16 seasons as an NFL head coach. His 159 career victories make him the second winningest active coach in the NFL, trailing only Marty Schottenheimer (170). Parcells has guided his teams to 11 winning seasons, nine playoff berths, and posted an 11-7 postseason record. Parcells-led teams have finished in either first or second place in their division ten times. With the Cowboys' postseason appearance in 2003, Parcells became the first coach in NFL history to lead four different teams to the playoffs. He is one of only four coaches (Don Shula, Reeves, and Dick Vermeil) in NFL history to have led two separate teams to the Super Bowl. Parcells, Denver's Mike Shanahan, Washington's Joe Gibbs, and New England's Bill Belichick are the only active coaches to have claimed two Super Bowl titles, and he is one of just eight active coaches to have ever won a Super Bowl title. In his first season at the helm in Dallas, Parcells took a team that had posted three consecutive 5-11 seasons and posted a 10-6 mark in the regular seaon, as well as an NFC Wild Card playoff berth. Under his direction, the N.Y. Jets (1997-99)—who won a combined four games the two seasons prior to his arrival—improved to 9-7 his first season and 12-4 with a trip to the AFC Championship Game his second season. This success marked the first time in NFL history that a team had won one game and within two years was playing for a conference championship. He took over the New England Patriots (1993-96) following a 2-14 season by the Patriots. Within two years, Parcells coached the team to a 10-6 mark and its first playoff game in eight years. In his fourth year, the Patriots went 11-5 and advanced to Super Bowl XXXI against Green Bay. Parcells began his NFL head coaching career with the N.Y. Giants (1983-1990), who had posted one winning season in its previous 10 years. After an initial campaign of 3-12-1, he improved the club's victory total to 9, 10, 14, 10, 12, and 13 between 1984 and 1990. In the process, the Giants were able to win two Super Bowl titles—Super Bowl XXI over Denver and Super Bowl XXV over Buffalo. During his time at the Giants helm, the club won two Super Bowls, three division titles, and had only one losing season. For his accomplishment, Parcells was honored with NFL Coach of the Year honors in both 1986 and 1989. Career record: 159-113-1.

Background: Played linebacker at Wichita State 1961-63. Served as college coach at: Hastings (Neb.) 1964, Wichita State 1965, Army 1966-69, Florida State 1970-72, Vanderbilt 1973-74, Texas Tech 1975-77, and was head coach at Air Force in 1978.

Personal: Born August 22, 1941, in Englewood, N.J. Parcells resides in Irving, Texas. He has three daughters—Suzy, Jill, and Dallas.

ASSISTANT COACHES

Maurice Carthon, offensive coordinator-running backs; born April 24, 1961, Chicago. Running back Arkansas State 1979-1982. Pro running back New Jersey Generals (USFL) 1983-85, New York Giants 1985-1991, Indianapolis Colts 1992. Pro coach: New England Patriots 1994-96, New York Jets 1997-2000, Detroit Lions 2001-02, joined Cowboys in 2003.

Bruce DeHaven, special teams; born September 6, 1948, Trousdale, Kan. Attended Southwestern (Kan.) College. No pro playing experience. College coach: Kansas 1979-1981, New Mexico State 1982. Pro coach: New Jersey Generals (USFL) 1983, Pittsburgh Maulers (USFL) 1984, Orlando Renegades (USFL) 1985, Buffalo Bills 1987-1999, San Francisco 49ers 2000-02, joined Cowboys in 2003.

Gary Gibbs, linebackers; born August 13, 1952, Beaumont, Texas. Linebacker Oklahoma 1972-74. No pro playing experience. College coach: Oklahoma 1975-1994 (head coach 1989-1994), Georgia 2000, Louisiana State 2001. Pro coach: Joined Cowboys in 2002.

Todd Haley, wide receivers; born February 28, 1967, Atlanta. Attended Florida and Miami. No college or pro playing experience. Pro coach: New York Jets 1996-2000, Chicago Bears 2001-2003, joined Cowboys in 2004.

Steve Hoffman, kickers/defensive quality control; born September 8, 1958, Camden, N.J. Quarterback-running back-wide receiver Dickinson College 1977-1980. Pro punter Washington Federals (USFL) 1983. College coach: Miami 1985-87. Pro coach: Joined Cowboys in 1989.

Jim Jeffcoat, defensive ends; born April 1, 1961, Cliffwood, N.J. Defensive end Arizona State 1979-1982. Pro defensive end Dallas Cowboys 1983-1994, Buffalo Bills 1995-97. Pro coach: Joined Cowboys in 1998.

Joe Juraszek, strength and conditioning; born June 8, 1958, Chicago. Linebacker-defensive end New Mexico 1976-1980. No pro playing experience. College coach: Oklahoma 1981-86, 1993-96, Texas Tech 1987-1992. Pro coach: Joined Cowboys in 1997.

David Lee, offensive assistant; born July 2, 1953, Cape Girardeau, Mo. Quarterback Vanderbilt 1971-74. No pro playing experience. College coach: Tennessee-Martin 1975-76, Vanderbilt 1977, Mississippi 1978-1982, New Mexico 1983, Arkansas 1984-88, 2001-02, Texas-El Paso 1989-1993 (head coach), Rice 1994-2000. Pro coach: Joined Cowboys in 2003.

Mike MacIntyre, asst. secondary; born March 14, 1965, Miami. Safety Vanderbilt 1985-86, Georgia Tech 1987-88. No pro playing experience. College coach: Georgia 1990-91, Davidson 1992, Tennessee-Martin 1993-96, Temple 1997-98, Mississippi 1999-2002. Pro coach: Joined Cowboys in 2003.

Sean Payton, asst. head coach-quarterbacks; born December 29, 1963, San Mateo, Calif. Quarterback Eastern Illinois 1982-86. Pro quarterback Ottawa Rough Riders (CFL) 1987, Chicago Bears 1987. College coach: San Diego State 1988-89, 1992-93, Indiana State 1990-91, Miami (Ohio) 1994-95, Illinois 1996. Pro coach: Philadelphia Eagles 1997-98, New York Giants 1999-2002, joined Cowboys in 2003.

Kacy Rodgers, defensive tackles; born June 24, 1969, Humboldt, Tenn. Linebacker-defensive end Tennessee 1988-1991. Pro linebacker Shreveport Pirates (CFL) 1994. College coach: Tennesse-Martin 1994-97, Louisiana-Monroe 1998, Middle Tennessee State 1999-2001, Arkansas 2002. Pro coach: Joined Cowboys in 2003.

Tony Sparano, tight ends; born October 7, 1961, West Haven, Conn. Center New Haven 1978-1981. No pro playing experience. College coach: New Haven 1984-87, 1994-98 (head coach 1994-98), Boston University 1988-1993. Pro coach: Cleveland Browns 1999-2000, Washington Redskins 2001, Jacksonville Jaguars 2002, joined Cowboys in 2003.

George Warhop, offensive line; born September 19, 1961, Riverside, Calif. Guard Mt. San Jacinto (Calif.) J.C. 1979-1980, center Cincinnati 1981-82. No pro playing experience. College coach: Cincinnati 1983, Kansas 1984-86, Vanderbilt 1987-89, New Mexico 1990, Southern Methodist 1993, Boston College 1994-95. Pro coach: London Monarchs (World League) 1991-92, St. Louis Rams 1996-97, Arizona Cardinals 1998-2002, joined Cowboys in 2003.

Mike Zimmer, defensive coordinator; born June 5, 1956, Peoria, Ill. Quarterback-linebacker Illinois State 1974-76. No pro playing experience. College coach: Missouri 1979-1980, Weber State 1981-88, Washington State 1989-1993. Pro coach: Joined Cowboys in 1994.

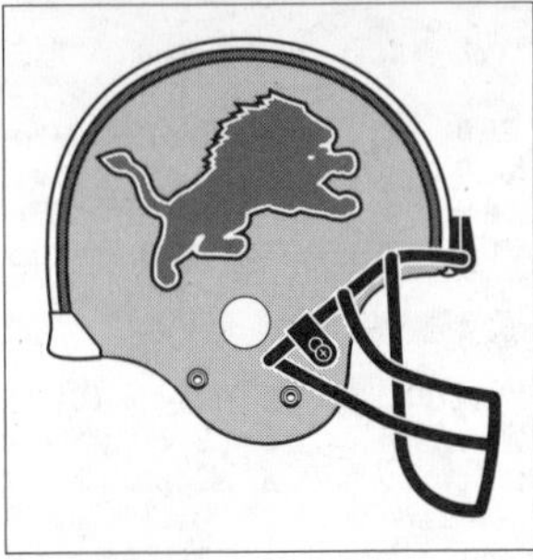

National Football Conference
North Division
Team Colors: Honolulu Blue and Silver
Detroit Lions Practice & Training Facility
222 Republic Drive
Allen Park, Michigan 48101
Telephone: (313) 216-4000

2003 SCHEDULE

PRESEASON		Detroit time
Aug. 14	**Pittsburgh**	7:30
Aug. 21	at Cleveland	4:30
Aug. 28	at Baltimore	8:00
Sept. 2	**Buffalo**	8:00

REGULAR SEASON		
Sept. 12	at Chicago	12:00
Sept. 19	**Houston**	1:00
Sept. 26	**Philadelphia**	1:00
Oct. 3	Open Date	
Oct. 10	at Atlanta	1:00
Oct. 17	**Green Bay**	1:00
Oct. 24	at New York Giants	1:00
Oct. 31	at Dallas	12:00
Nov. 7	**Washington**	1:00
Nov. 14	at Jacksonville	1:00
Nov. 21	at Minnesota	12:00
Nov. 25	**Indianapolis** (Thu.)	12:30
Dec. 5	**Arizona**	1:00
Dec. 12	at Green Bay	12:00
Dec. 19	**Minnesota**	1:00
Dec. 26	**Chicago**	1:00
Jan. 2	at Tennessee	12:00

Stadium: Ford Field (opened in 2002)
•**Capacity:** 64,500
2000 Brush Street
Detroit, Michigan 48226
Playing Surface: FieldTurf
Training Camp: 222 Republic Drive
Allen Park, Michigan
48101

FORD FIELD

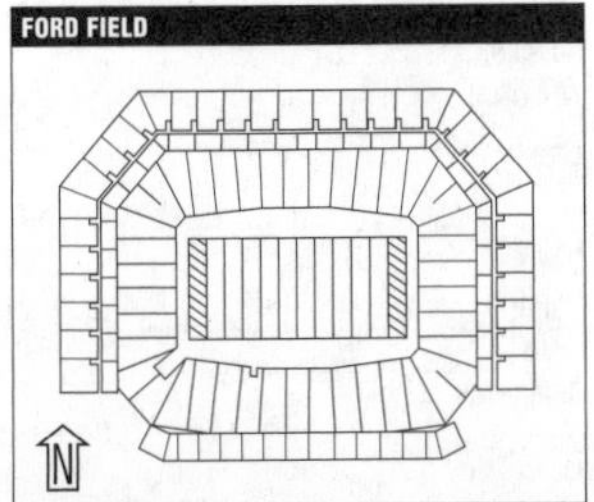

CLUB OFFICIALS

Chairman and Owner: William Clay Ford
Vice Chairman: William Clay Ford Jr.
President and CEO: Matt Millen
Executive Vice President/COO: Tom Lewand
Senior Vice President: Bill Keenist
Senior Vice President: Martin Mayhew
Senior Vice President/CFO: Tom Lesnau
Secretary: David Hempstead
Senior Director of Community Affairs: Tim Pendell
Director of Media Relations: Matt Barnhart
Director of Pro Personnel: Sheldon White
Director of College Scouting: Scott McEwen
Scouts: Bob Beers, Russ Bolinger, Dennis Gentry, Hessley Hempstead, Chad Henry, Silas McKinnie, Dennis Murphy, Lance Newmark, Charlie Sanders, Dave Uryus
Director of Broadcasting and New Media: Bryan Bender
Director of Ticket Operations: Mark Graham
Head Athletic Trainer: Al Bellamy
Equipment Manager: Tim O'Neill
Video Director: Steve Hermans

COACHING HISTORY

Portsmouth Spartans 1930-33
(474-520-32)

1930	Hal (Tubby) Griffen	5-6-3
1931-36	George (Potsy) Clark	49-20-6
1937-38	Earl (Dutch) Clark	14-8-0
1939	Elmer (Gus) Henderson	6-5-0
1940	George (Potsy) Clark	5-5-1
1941-42	Bill Edwards*	4-9-1
1942	John Karcis	0-8-0
1943-47	Charles (Gus) Dorais	20-31-2
1948-1950	Alvin (Bo) McMillin	12-24-0
1951-56	Raymond (Buddy) Parker	50-24-2
1957-1964	George Wilson	55-45-6
1965-66	Harry Gilmer	10-16-2
1967-1972	Joe Schmidt	43-35-7
1973	Don McCafferty	6-7-1
1974-76	Rick Forzano**	15-17-0
1976-77	Tommy Hudspeth	11-13-0
1978-1984	Monte Clark	43-63-1
1985-88	Darryl Rogers***	18-40-0
1988-1996	Wayne Fontes	67-71-0
1997-2000	Bobby Ross****	27-32-0
2000	Gary Moeller	4-3-0
2001-02	Marty Mornhinweg	5-27-0
2003	Steve Mariucci	5-11-0

*Released after three games in 1942
**Resigned after four games in 1976
***Released after 11 games in 1988
****Resigned after nine games in 2000

ATTENDANCE

Home 490,448 Away 547,706
Total 1,038,154
Single-game home record, 80,444 (12/20/81)
Single-season home record, 644,904 (1980)

2004 DRAFT CHOICES

Round	Name	Pos.	College
1	Roy Williams	WR	Texas
	Kevin Jones	RB	Virginia Tech
2	Teddy Lehman	LB	Oklahoma
3	Keith Smith	DB	McNeese State
5	Alex Lewis	LB	Wisconsin
6	Kelly Butler	T	Purdue

DETROIT LIONS

2003 TEAM RECORD

PRESEASON (2-2)

Date	Result	Opponent
8/9	W 26-13	Pittsburgh
8/16	L 10-23	at Cincinnati
8/23	W 38-17	Cleveland
8/28	L 16-22	at Buffalo

REGULAR SEASON (5-11)

Date	Result	Opponent	Att.
9/7	W 42-24	Arizona	60,691
9/14	L 6-31	at Green Bay	70,244
9/21	L 13-23	Minnesota	60,865
9/28	L 16-20	at Denver	75,719
10/5	L 17-24	at San Francisco	67,365
10/19	L 7-38	Dallas	61,160
10/26	L 16-24	at Chicago	61,428
11/2	W 23-13	Oakland	61,561
11/9	W 12-10	Chicago	61,492
11/16	L 14-35	at Seattle	65,865
11/23	L 14-24	at Minnesota	63,946
11/27	W 22-14	Green Bay	62,123
12/7	L 7-14	San Diego	61,544
12/14	L 17-45	at Kansas City	77,922
12/21	L 14-20	at Carolina	72,835
12/28	W 30-20	St. Louis	61,006

SCORE BY PERIODS

Lions	64	56	66	84	0	— 270
Opponents	94	156	96	33	0	— 379

2003 TEAM STATISTICS

	Lions	Opp.
Total First Downs	250	298
Rushing	69	105
Passing	152	166
Penalty	29	27
3rd Down: Made/Att	80/228	87/214
3rd Down Pct.	35.1	40.7
4th Down: Made/Att	8/20	8/13
4th Down Pct.	40.0	61.5
Possession Avg.	28:21	31:39
Total Net Yards	4,262	5,360
Avg. Per Game	266.4	335.0
Total Plays	975	997
Avg. Per Play	4.4	5.4
Net Yards Rushing	1,338	1,782
Avg. Per Game	83.6	111.4
Total Rushes	376	447
Net Yards Passing	2,924	3,578
Avg. Per Game	182.8	223.6
Sacked/Yards Lost	11/64	28/182
Gross Yards	2,988	3,760
Att./Completions	588/319	522/331
Completion Pct.	54.3	63.4
Had Intercepted	24	15
Punts/Average	96/39.5	84/42.5
Net Punting Avg.	96/33.8	84/34.0
Penalties/Yards	107/859	119/953
Fumbles/Ball Lost	18/4	32/13
Touchdowns	29	47
Rushing	5	14
Passing	17	26
Returns	7	7

2003 INDIVIDUAL STATISTICS

PASSING	Att.	Comp.	Yds.	Pct.	TD	Int.	Tkld.	Rate
Harrington	554	309	2,880	55.8	17	22	9/55	63.9
McMahon	31	9	87	29.0	0	2	2/9	12.7
Hakim	1	1	21	100.0	0	0	0/0	118.8
N. Harris	1	0	0	0.0	0	0	0/0	39.6
Schroeder	1	0	0	0.0	0	0	0/0	39.6
Lions	588	319	2,988	54.3	17	24	11/64	61.1
Opponents	522	331	3,760	63.4	26	15	28/182	89.6

SCORING	TD R	TD P	TD Rt	PAT	FG	Saf	PTS
Hanson	0	0	0	26/27	22/23	0	92
Hakim	0	4	0	0/0	0/0	0	26
Bryson	3	0	0	0/0	0/0	0	18
C. Rogers	0	3	0	0/0	0/0	0	18
Anderson	0	2	0	0/0	0/0	0	14
Bly	0	0	2	0/0	0/0	0	12
Fitzsimmons	0	2	0	0/0	0/0	0	12
Gary	2	0	0	0/0	0/0	0	12
Ricks	0	2	0	0/0	0/0	0	12
Schlesinger	0	2	0	0/0	0/0	0	12
Schroeder	0	2	0	0/0	0/0	0	12
Swinton	0	0	2	0/0	0/0	0	12
Bailey	0	0	1	0/0	0/0	0	6
Drummond	0	0	1	0/0	0/0	0	6
C. Harris	0	0	1	0/0	0/0	0	6
Lions	5	17	7	26/27	22/23	0	270
Opponents	14	26	7	46/46	17/24	0	379

2-Pt. Conversions: Anderson, Hakim.
Lions 2-2, Opponents 0-1.

RUSHING	No.	Yds	Avg	LG	TD
Bryson	158	606	3.8	39	3
Gary	113	384	3.4	27	2
Pinner	39	99	2.5	12	0
Harrington	30	86	2.9	26	0
Hakim	3	51	17.0	35	0
McMahon	5	32	6.4	12	0
Cobourne	10	27	2.7	19	0
C. Rogers	2	17	8.5	12	0
Schlesinger	9	16	1.8	4	0
Swinton	3	11	3.7	9	0
P. Smith	2	5	2.5	3	0
Jefferson	1	3	3.0	3	0
Drummond	1	1	1.0	1	0
Lions	376	1,338	3.6	39	5
Opponents	447	1,782	4.0	65t	14

RECEIVING	No.	Yds	Avg	LG	TD
Bryson	54	340	6.3	26	0
Hakim	49	449	9.2	28	4
Ricks	37	434	11.7	38	2
Schroeder	36	397	11.0	26	2
Schlesinger	34	247	7.3	33t	2
Fitzsimmons	23	160	7.0	22	2
C. Rogers	22	243	11.0	33t	3
Anderson	17	325	19.1	72t	2
Gary	13	69	5.3	13	0
Swinton	9	100	11.1	25	0
Jefferson	6	46	7.7	13	0
P. Smith	5	45	9.0	12	0
Pinner	5	40	8.0	21	0
Cobourne	4	30	7.5	13	0
Kircus	3	53	17.7	19	0
Harrington	1	8	8.0	8	0
Trejo	1	2	2.0	2	0
Lions	319	2,988	9.4	72t	17
Opponents	331	3,760	11.4	73t	26

INTERCEPTIONS	No.	Yds	Avg	LG	TD
Bly	6	89	14.8	48t	1
Holt	3	42	14.0	30	0
Bri. Walker	2	0	0.0	0	0
Evans	1	2	2.0	2	0
O. Smith	1	0	0.0	0	0
C. Harris	1	-1	-1.0	-1	0
Bailey	1	-2	-2.0	-2	0
Lions	15	130	8.7	48t	1
Opponents	24	377	15.7	56t	4

PUNTING	No.	Yds.	Avg.	In 20	LG
N. Harris	63	2,531	40.2	11	51
Jett	25	995	39.8	8	58
Hanson	7	264	37.7	1	50
Lions	96	3,790	39.5	20	58
Opponents	84	3,574	42.5	20	61

PUNT RETURNS	Ret	FC	Yds	Avg	LG	TD
Swinton	23	9	318	13.8	89t	1
Drummond	12	4	151	12.6	57t	1
Hakim	9	0	85	9.4	20	0
Bly	3	0	22	7.3	14	0
Lions	47	13	576	12.3	89t	2
Opponents	59	15	390	6.6	83t	1

KICKOFF RETURNS	No.	Yds	Avg	LG	TD
Swinton	40	964	24.1	96t	1
Drummond	21	469	22.3	38	0
Cobourne	7	123	17.6	22	0
Redding	1	5	5.0	5	0
Schlesinger	1	23	23.0	23	0
Lions	70	1,584	22.6	96t	1
Opponents	53	1,313	24.8	89t	1

FIELD GOALS	1-19	20-29	30-39	40-49	50+
Hanson	0/0	7/7	6/6	5/6	4/4
Lions	0/0	7/7	6/6	5/6	4/4
Opponents	0/0	4/4	5/8	6/9	2/3

SACKS	
Hall	4.5
Porcher	4.5
S. Rogers	4.0
Green	3.0
Edwards	2.0
Holmes	2.0
Wilkinson	2.0
Bailey	1.5
O. Smith	1.5
Bly	1.0
DeVries	1.0
C. Harris	1.0
Lions	28.0
Opponents	11.0

RECORD HOLDERS

INDIVIDUAL RECORDS—CAREER

Category	Name	Performance
Rushing (Yds.)	Barry Sanders, 1989-1998	15,269
Passing (Yds.)	Bobby Layne, 1950-58	15,710
Passing (TDs)	Bobby Layne, 1950-58	118
Receiving (No.)	Herman Moore, 1991-2001	670
Receiving (Yds.)	Herman Moore, 1991-2001	9,174
Interceptions	Dick LeBeau, 1959-1972	62
Punting (Avg.)	Yale Lary, 1952-53, 1956-1964	44.3
Punt Return (Avg.)	Jack Christiansen, 1951-58	12.8
Kickoff Return (Avg.)	Pat Studstill, 1961-67	25.7
Field Goals	Jason Hanson, 1992-2003	284
Touchdowns (Tot.)	Barry Sanders, 1989-1998	109
Points	Jason Hanson, 1992-2003	1,236

INDIVIDUAL RECORDS—SINGLE SEASON

Category	Name	Performance
Rushing (Yds.)	Barry Sanders, 1997	2,053
Passing (Yds.)	Scott Mitchell, 1995	4,338
Passing (TDs)	Scott Mitchell, 1995	32
Receiving (No.)	Herman Moore, 1995	123
Receiving (Yds.)	Herman Moore, 1995	1,686
Interceptions	Don Doll, 1950	12
	Jack Christiansen, 1953	12
Punting (Avg.)	Yale Lary, 1963	48.9
Punt Return (Avg.)	Pat Studstill, 1962	15.8
Kickoff Return (Avg.)	Mel Gray, 1994	28.4
Field Goals	Jason Hanson, 1993	34
Touchdowns (Tot.)	Barry Sanders, 1991	17
Points	Jason Hanson, 1995	132

INDIVIDUAL RECORDS—SINGLE GAME

Category	Name	Performance
Rushing (Yds.)	Barry Sanders, 11-13-94	237
Passing (Yds.)	Charlie Batch, 11-18-01	436
Passing (TDs)	Gary Danielson, 12-9-78	5
Receiving (No.)	Herman Moore, 12-4-95	14
Receiving (Yds.)	Cloyce Box, 12-3-50	302
Interceptions	Don Doll, 10-23-49	*4
Field Goals	Garo Yepremian, 11-13-66	6
	Jason Hanson, 10-17-99	6
Touchdowns (Tot.)	Dutch Clark, 10-22-34	4
	Cloyce Box, 12-3-50	4
	Barry Sanders, 11-24-91	4
Points	Dutch Clark, 10-22-34	24
	Cloyce Box, 12-3-50	24
	Barry Sanders, 11-24-91	24

*NFL Record

DETROIT LIONS

2004 VETERAN ROSTER

No.	Name	Pos.	Ht.	Wt.	Birthdate	NFL Exp.	College	Hometown	How Acq.	'03 Games/ Starts
88	Anderson, Scotty	WR	6-2	191	11/24/79	4	Grambling State	Jonesboro, La.	D5a-'01	9/0
26	Babers, Roderick	CB	5-9	192	10/6/80	2	Texas	Houston, Texas	W(NYG)-'03	5/0
76	Backus, Jeff	T	6-5	305	9/21/77	4	Michigan	Norcross, Ga.	D1-'01	16/16
97	Bailey, Boss	LB	6-3	233	10/14/79	2	Georgia	Folkston, Ga.	D2-'03	16/16
89	Banta, Bradford	TE	6-6	253	12/14/70	11	Southern California	Baton Rouge, La.	UFA(NYJ)-'01	13/0
32	Bly, Dré	CB	5-9	185	5/22/77	6	North Carolina	Chesapeake, Va.	UFA(StL)-'03	14/14
25	Bryant, Fernando	CB	5-11	178	3/26/77	6	Alabama	Murfeesboro, Tenn.	UFA(Jax)-'04	16/16*
24	Bryson, Shawn	RB	6-1	228	11/30/76	6	Tennessee	Franklin, N.C.	UFA(Buff)-'03	16/13
29	Cash, Chris	CB	5-11	170	7/13/80	3	Southern California	Stockton, Calif.	D6-'02	0*
23	Cobourne, Avon	RB	5-8	205	3/6/79	2	West Virginia	Camden, N.J.	FA-'03	7/0
55	Curry, Donté	LB	6-1	233	7/22/78	4	Morris Brown	College Park, Ga.	W(Wash)-'02	11/0
52	Davis, James	LB	6-1	221	4/26/79	2	West Virginia	Stuart, Fla.	D5b-'03	8/1
95	DeVries, Jared	DE	6-4	272	6/11/76	6	Iowa	Aplington, Iowa	D3-'99	13/2
18	Drummond, Eddie	WR	5-9	185	4/12/80	3	Penn State	Pittsburgh, Pa.	FA-'02	6/0
98	Edwards, Kalimba	DE	6-5	264	12/26/79	3	South Carolina	Atlanta, Ga.	D2-'02	15/0
82	FitzSimmons, Casey	TE	6-3	250	10/10/80	2	Carroll College (Mont.)	Helena, Mont.	FA-'03	16/11
33	Gary, Olandis	RB	5-11	218	5/18/75	6	Georgia	Washington, D.C.	T(Buff)-'03	13/1
15	Gaylor, Trevor	WR	6-3	195	11/3/77	4	Miami (Ohio)	St. Louis, Mo.	FA-'04	0*
35	Goodman, André	CB	5-10	185	8/11/78	3	South Carolina	Greenville, S.C.	D3-'02	3/3
81	Hakim, Az-Zahir	WR	5-10	189	6/3/77	7	San Diego State	Los Angeles, Calif.	UFA(StL)-'02	14/12
96	Hall, James	DE	6-2	270	2/4/77	5	Michigan	New Orleans, La.	FA-'00	16/16
4	Hanson, Jason	K	5-11	182	6/17/70	13	Washington State	Spokane, Wash.	D2b-'92	16/0
3	Harrington, Joey	QB	6-4	220	10/21/78	3	Oregon	Portland, Ore.	D1-'02	16/16
2	Harris, Nick	P	6-2	218	7/23/78	4	California	Avondale, Ariz.	W(Cin)-'03	11/0
50	Holmes, Earl	LB	6-2	242	4/28/73	9	Florida A&M	Tallahassee, Fla.	UFA(Cle)-'03	16/13
42	Holt, Terrence	S	6-2	208	3/5/80	2	North Carolina State	Raleigh, N.C.	D5a-'03	11/2
75	Joyce, Matt	T	6-7	300	3/30/72	10	Richmond	Scottsdale, Ariz.	UFA(Ariz)-'01	13/3
87	Kircus, David	WR	6-1	185	2/19/80	2	Grand Valley State	Imlay City, Mich.	D6-'03	5/2
57	Littleton, Jody	LB	6-1	235	10/23/74	2	Baylor	Brighton, Colo.	FA-'03	3/0
70	Lovelady, Josh	G	6-3	330	1/28/78	3	Houston	Midfield, Texas	FA-'01	12/0
62	Loverne, David	G	6-3	299	5/22/76	7	San Jose State	Concord, Calif.	UFA(StL)-'04	1/0*
31	Marion, Brock	S	5-11	200	6/11/70	13	Nevada	Bakersfield, Calif.	FA-'04	16/16*
73	McDougle, Stockar	T	6-6	335	1/11/77	4	Oklahoma	Deerfield Beach, Fla.	D1-'00	16/16
8	McMahon, Mike	QB	6-2	208	2/8/79	3	Rutgers	Wexford, Pa.	D5b-'01	3/0
5	Mirer, Rick	QB	6-3	210	3/19/70	12	Notre Dame	Goshen, Ind.	UFA(Oak)-'04	9/8*
65	Noa, Kaulana	G	6-3	317	12/29/76	2	Hawaii	Honoka, Hawaii	FA-'03	0*
83	Owens, John	TE	6-3	266	1/10/80	3	Notre Dame	Washington, D.C.	D5-'02	7/1
21	Pinner, Artose	RB	5-9	229	1/5/78	2	Kentucky	Hopkinsville, Ky.	D4-'03	3/2
91	Porcher, Robert	DE	6-3	266	7/30/69	13	South Carolina State	Wando, S.C.	D1-'92	14/14
93	Pritchett, Kelvin	DT	6-3	322	10/24/69	14	Mississippi	Atlanta, Ga.	UFA(Jax)-'99	13/0
58	Rainer, Wali	LB	6-2	247	4/19/77	6	Virginia	Rockingham, N.C.	UFA(Jax)-'03	16/0
51	Raiola, Dominic	C	6-1	295	12/30/78	4	Nebraska	Honolulu, Hawaii	D2a-'01	16/16
78	Redding, Cory	DE	6-4	285	11/15/80	2	Texas	Austin, Texas	D3-'03	9/0
86	Ricks, Mikhael	TE	6-5	260	11/14/74	7	Stephen F. Austin	Anahuac, Texas	UFA(KC)-'02	16/5
80	Rogers, Charles	WR	6-2	202	5/23/81	2	Michigan State	Saginaw, Mich.	D1-'03	5/5
92	Rogers, Shaun	DT	6-4	357	3/12/79	4	Texas	LaPorte, Texas	D2b-'01	16/16
71	Rogers, Victor	T	6-6	331	11/10/78	3	Colorado	Federal Way, Wash.	D7c-'02	0*
30	Schlesinger, Cory	FB	6-0	247	6/23/72	10	Nebraska	Duncan, Neb.	D6b-'95	16/10
47	Sidney, Dainon	CB	6-0	197	5/30/75	7	Alabama-Birmingham	Atlanta, Ga.	UFA(Buff)-'04	2/0*
40	Smith, Paul	RB	5-11	234	1/31/78	5	Texas-El Paso	El Paso, Texas	FA-'03	7/0
84	Streets, Tai	WR	6-3	207	4/20/77	6	Michigan	Matteson, Ill.	UFA(SF)-'04	16/16*
10	Swinton, Reggie	WR	6-0	186	7/24/75	4	Murray State	Little Rock, Ark.	W(GB)-'03	11/1
36	Trejo, Stephen	FB	6-2	254	11/20/77	4	Arizona State	Casa Grande, Ariz.	FA-'01	16/0
28	Walker, Bracy	S	6-0	210	10/28/70	11	North Carolina	Lake Villa, Ill.	UFA(KC)-'02	16/1
45	Walker, Brian	S	6-1	205	5/31/72	9	Washington State	Widefield, Colo.	UFA(Mia)-'02	16/16
72	Wilkinson, Dan	DT	6-4	353	3/13/73	11	Ohio State	Dayton, Ohio	FA-'03	16/16
65	Woody, Damien	G	6-3	325	11/3/77	6	Boston College	Beaverdam, Va.	UFA(NE)-'04	14/14*

* Bryant played 16 games with Jacksonville in '03; Cash missed '03 season because of injury; Gaylor last active with Atlanta in '02; Loverne played 1 game with St. Louis; Marion played 16 games with Miami; Mirer played 9 games with Oakland; Noa inactive with St. Louis in '01; V. Rogers missed '03 season because of injury; Sidney played 2 games with Buffalo; Streets played 16 games with San Francisco; Woody played 14 games with New England.

Retired—John Jett, 11-year punter, 4 games in '03.

Players lost through free agency (5): G Eric Beverly (Wash; 13 games in '03), QB Ty Detmer (Atl; 1), LB Jeff Gooch (TB; 16), LB Barrett Green (NYG; 16), CB Otis Smith (NE; 16).

Also played with Lions in '03—G Kerlin Blaise (3 games), G Ray Brown (16), DT Luther Elliss (5), CB Doug Evans (9), S Corey Harris (13), WR Shawn Jefferson (7), CB Alex Molden (2), CB Leonard Myers (1), WR Bill Schroeder (16), CB Jacoby Sheppard (4), WR James Williams (1), CB Jimmy Wyrick (7).

2004 FIRST-YEAR ROSTER

Name	Pos.	Ht.	Wt.	Birthdate	College	Hometown	How Acq.
Ansel, Curtis	P	6-0	210	5/1/80	Kansas	Lakin, Kan.	FA
Battle, Andrew	LB	6-4	235	7/21/81	Indiana (Pa.)	Allentown, Pa.	FA
Belton, Keith	FB	6-0	232	6/1/81	Syracuse	Charlotte, N.C.	FA
Brandt, Matt	TE	6-5	248	12/7/79	Miami (Ohio)	Toronto, Ontario, Canada	FA
Butler, Kelly	T	6-7	324	7/24/82	Purdue	Grand Rapids, Mich.	D6
Childress, Ahmad	DT	6-6	331	6/15/81	Alabama	Nashville, Tenn.	FA
Cole, Colin (1)	DT	6-2	299	6/24/80	Iowa	Ft. Lauderdale, Fla.	FA-'03
Curry, Julius (1)	S	6-0	195	5/17/79	Michigan	Detroit, Mich.	FA-'03
Drake, Charles (1)	DB	6-1	208	9/25/81	Michigan	Los Angeles, Calif.	FA-'03
Fife, Jason	QB	6-3	222	1/23/81	Oregon	Lake Elsinore, Calif.	FA
Genord, Scott	LB	6-2	245	7/28/81	Fullerton (Calif.) J.C.	Detroit, Mich.	FA
Hall, Branden	G	6-3	329	2/19/82	Troy State	Auburn, Ala.	FA
Heatly, Kenny	CB	5-11	180	3/28/82	Bethune-Cookman	St. Petersburg, Fla.	FA
Johnson, Ben (1)	T	6-6	329	4/7/80	Wisconsin	Brussels, Wis.	D7a-'03
Johnson, Clifford	S	6-3	215	1/18/81	Morgan State	Baltimore, Md.	FA
Jones, Kevin	RB	6-0	227	8/21/82	Virginia Tech	Chester, Pa.	D1b
Kabongo, Patrick	DE	6-6	315	6/27/79	Nebraska	Montreal, Quebec, Canada	FA
Kern, Chris (1)	DB	5-11	196	5/16/79	Mount Union	Fairbault, Minn.	FA-'03
Lehman, Teddy	LB	6-1	240	11/18/81	Oklahoma	Fort Gibson, Okla.	D2
Lewis, Alex	LB	6-0	228	6/11/81	Wisconsin	Delran, N.J.	D5
McCoy, Matt	T	6-8	290	8/13/81	Ferris State	Charlotte, Mich.	FA
Miller, David (1)	G	6-3	322	2/24/80	Ball State	Goshen, Ind.	FA-'03
Pearson, Dave	C	6-3	297	3/29/81	Michigan	Brighton, Mich.	FA
Shull, Andrew	DE	6-5	260	4/2/81	Kansas State	Webb City, Mo.	FA
Smith, Keith	CB	6-0	200	3/20/80	McNeese State	Leesville, La.	D3
Snyder, Chris	K	6-0	204	11/7/81	Montana	Spokane, Wash.	FA
Williams, Roy	WR	6-2	212	12/20/81	Texas	Odessa, Texas	D1a
Wilson, George	WR	6-1	210	3/14/81	Arkansas	Paducah, Ky.	FA

The term NFL Rookie is defined as a player who is in his first season of professional football and has not been on the roster of another professional football team for any regular-season or postseason games. A Rookie is designated by an "R" on NFL rosters. Players who have been active in another professional football league or players who have NFL experience, including either preseason training camp or being on an Active List or Inactive List, or on Reserve/Injured or Reserve/Physically Unable to Perform for fewer than six regular-season games, are termed NFL First-Year Players. An NFL First-Year Player is designated by a "1" on NFL rosters. Thereafter, a player is credited with an additional year of experience for each season in which he accumulates six games on the Active List or Inactive List, or on Reserve/Injured or Reserve/Physically Unable to Perform.

Log on to www.detroitlions.com for an up-to-date roster.

DETROIT LIONS

COACHING STAFF

Head Coach,
Steve Mariucci

Pro Career: Named the Lions' twenty-second head coach February 4, 2003. Joined the Lions after spending six years as the head coach for San Francisco 49ers (1997-2002). He compiled a 60-43 (.583) record, while his teams earned playoff berths four times (1997, 1998, 2001, and 2002). One of thirteen head coaches since the NFL-AFL merger in 1970 to lead his team to a division title in his first season. He established an NFL mark for consecutive wins by a rookie head coach with an 11-game winning streak. He served as quarterbacks coach for the Green Bay Packers (1992-95). His first pro position was in 1985 when he was a receivers coach for the USFL's Orlando Renegades. Later that fall, he had a brief stint with the Los Angeles Rams as quality control coach. Career record: 65-54.

Background: Three-time All-America quarterback at Northern Michigan. Began his coaching career at his alma mater (1978-79), and moved to Cal State-Fullerton (1980-82), and Louisville (1983-84). Joined the Southern California staff in 1986, then moved to California in 1987. In 1990-91, he served as the Bears' offensive coordinator. Became the head coach at California in 1996 and guided the squad to a 5-0 start and a berth in the Aloha Bowl.

Personal: Born November 4, 1955, in Iron Mountain, Mich. He and his wife, Gayle, have four children—Tyler, Adam, Stephen, and Brielle.

ASSISTANT COACHES

Jason Arapoff, strength and conditioning; born July, 8 1965, Weymouth, Mass. Defensive back Springfield College 1985-88. No college or pro playing experience. Pro coach: Washington Redskins 1992-2000, joined Lions in 2001.

Malcolm Blacken, asst. strength and conditioning; born October 12, 1965, Richmond, Va. Running back Virginia Tech 1984-88. No pro playing experience. College coach: South Carolina 1990-91, George Mason 1992-94, Virginia 1995. Pro coach: Washington Redskins 1996-2000, joined Lions in 2001.

Larry Brooks, defensive line; born June 10 1950 in Prince George, Va. Defensive lineman Virginia State 1968-1971. Pro defensive tackle Los Angeles Rams 1972-1982. College coach: Virginia State 1992-93. Pro coach: Los Angeles Rams 1983-1990, Green Bay Packers 1994-98, Seattle Seahawks 1999-2002, Chicago Bears 2003, joined Lions in 2004.

George Catavolos, defensive backs; born May 8, 1945 in Chicago. Defensive back Purdue 1964-67. No pro playing experience. College coach: Purdue 1967-68, 1971-76, Middle Tennessee State 1969, Louisville 1970, Kentucky 1977-1981, Tennessee 1982-83. Pro coach: Indianapolis Colts 1984-1994, 1998-2001, Carolina Panthers 1995-97, Washington Redskins 2002-03, joined Lions in 2004.

Don Clemons, defensive assistant/quality control; born February 15, 1954, Newark, N.J. Defensive end Muhlenberg (Pa.) 1973-76. No pro playing experience. College coach: Kutztown State 1977-78, New Mexico 1979, Arizona State 1980-84. Pro coach: Joined Lions in 1985.

Kevin Higgins, wide receivers; born December 1, 1955, New York City. Defensive back West Chester (Pa.) 1973-76. No pro playing experience. College coach: Gettysburg College 1981-84, Richmond 1985-87, Lehigh 1988-2000 (head coach 1994-2000). Pro coach: Joined Lions in 2001.

Johnny Holland, defensive assistant; born March 11, 1965, Belleville, Texas. Linebacker Texas A&M 1983-86. Pro linebacker Green Bay Packers 1987-1993. Pro coach: Green Bay Packers 1995-99, Seattle Seahawks 2000-02, joined Lions in 2003.

Dick Jauron, defensive coordinator; born October 7, 1950 in Peoria, Ill. Running back Yale 1970-72. Pro defensive back Detroit Lions 1973-77, Cincinnati Bengals 1978-1980. Pro coach: Buffalo Bills 1985, Green Bay Packers 1986-1994, Jacksonville Jaguars 1995-98, Chicago Bears 1999-2003 (head coach), joined Lions in 2004.

Sean Kugler, asst. offensive line/tight ends; born August 9, 1966, Lockport, N.Y. Offensive lineman Texas-El Paso 1985-88. Pro offensive lineman Sacramento Surge (WLAF) 1991. College coach: Texas-El Paso 1993-2000. Pro coach: Joined Lions in 2001.

Stan Kwan, special teams assistant/offensive assistant; born November 2, 1967, Phoenix. No college or pro playing experience. Pro coach: San Diego Chargers 1991-96, Detroit Lions 1997-2000, Arizona Cardinals 2001-2003, re-joined Lions in 2004.

Sherman Lewis, offensive coordinator; born June 29, 1942, Louisville, Ky. Running back Michigan State 1960-63. Pro running back Toronto Argonauts (CFL) 1964-65, New York Jets 1966. College coach: Michigan State 1969-1982. Pro coach: San Francisco 49ers 1983-1991, Green Bay Packers 1992-99, Minnesota Vikings 2000-01, joined Lions in 2002.

Pat Morris, offensive line; born April 7, 1954 in Cleveland. Offensive lineman Southern California 1972-75. No pro playing experience. College coach: Southern California 1976-77, 1983-86, Northern Arizona 1978, Minnesota 1979-1982, Michigan State 1987-1994, Stanford 1995-96. Pro coach: San Francisco 49ers 1997-2003, joined Lions in 2004.

Greg Olson, quarterbacks; born March 1, 1963, Richland, Wash. Quarterback Central Washington 1983-86. No pro playing experience. College coach: Washington State 1987-89, Central Washington 1990-93, Idaho 1994-96, Purdue 1997-2000, 2002. Pro coach: San Francisco 49ers 2001, Chicago Bears 2003, joined Lions in 2004.

Chuck Priefer, special teams; born July 26, 1944, Cleveland. Attended John Carroll. No college or pro playing experience. College coach: Miami (Ohio) 1977, North Carolina 1978-1983, Kent State 1986, Georgia Tech 1987-1991. Pro coach: Green Bay Packers 1984-85, San Diego Chargers 1992-96, joined Lions in 1997.

Tom Rathman, running backs; born October 7, 1962, Grand Island, Neb. Running back Nebraska 1983-85. Pro running back San Francisco 49ers 1986-1993, Los Angeles Raiders 1994. College coach: Menlo College 1996. Pro coach: San Francisco 49ers 1997-2002, joined Lions in 2003.

Richard Smith, asst. head coach/linebackers; born October 17, 1955, Los Angeles. Offensive lineman Rio Hondo (Calif.) J.C. 1975-76, Fresno State 1977-78. No pro playing experience. College coach: Rio Hondo (Calif.) J.C. 1979-1980, Cal State-Fullerton 1981-83, California 1984-86, Arizona 1987. Pro coach: Houston Oilers 1988-1992, Denver Broncos 1993-96, San Francisco 49ers 1997-2002, joined Lions in 2003.

Andy Sugarman, tight ends; born May 23, 1972, San Francisco. Attended California. No college or pro playing experience. College coach: California 1990-1997. Pro coach: San Francisco 49ers 1998-2002, joined Lions in 2003.

National Football Conference
North Division
Team Colors: Dark Green, Gold, and White
Lambeau Field Atrium
1265 Lombardi Avenue
Green Bay, Wisconsin 54304
Telephone: (920) 569-7500

2004 SCHEDULE

PRESEASON		Green Bay time
Aug. 16	**Seattle**	7:00
Aug. 21	**New Orleans**	7:00
Aug. 27	at Jacksonville	7:00
Sept. 3	at Tennessee	7:00

REGULAR SEASON		
Sept. 13	at Carolina (Mon.)	8:00
Sept. 19	**Chicago**	12:00
Sept. 26	at Indianapolis	3:15
Oct. 3	**New York Giants**	12:00
Oct. 11	**Tennessee** (Mon.)	8:00
Oct. 17	at Detroit	12:00
Oct. 24	**Dallas**	3:15
Oct. 31	at Washington	12:00
Nov. 7	Open Date	
Nov. 14	**Minnesota**	3:15
Nov. 21	at Houston	7:30
Nov. 29	**St. Louis** (Mon.)	8:00
Dec. 5	at Philadelphia	3:15
Dec. 12	**Detroit**	12:00
Dec. 19	**Jacksonville**	12:00
Dec. 24	at Minnesota (Fri.)	2:00
Jan. 2	at Chicago	12:00

Stadium: Lambeau Field (opened in 1957)
•**Capacity:** 72,569
1265 Lombardi Avenue
Green Bay, Wisconsin 54304
Playing Surface: Grass
Training Camp: St. Norbert College
De Pere, Wisconsin 54115

LAMBEAU FIELD

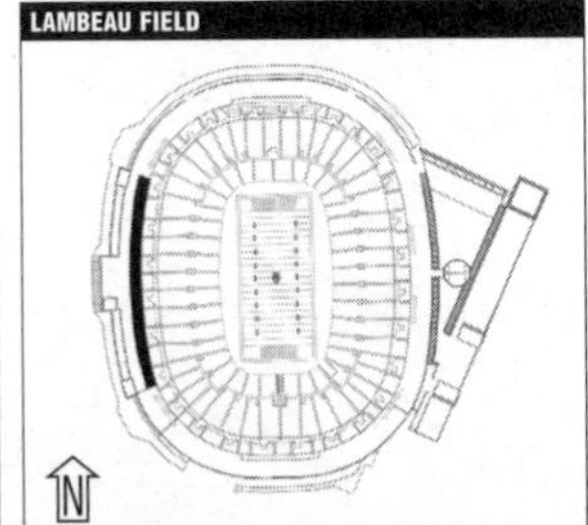

CLUB OFFICIALS

President and CEO: Bob Harlan
Vice President: John Fabry
Secretary: Peter Platten
Treasurer: John Underwood
Exec. V.P./General Manager/Head Coach: Mike Sherman
Executive Vice President and Chief Operating Officer: John Jones
Vice President of Football Operations: Mark Hatley
Vice President of Player Finance/General Counsel: Andrew Brandt
Dir. of College Scouting: John Dorsey
Dir. of Pro Personnel: Reggie McKenzie
Personnel Analyst to General Manager: John Schneider
Assistant to GM/Director of Football Administration: Bruce Warwick
Director of Player Development: Edgar Bennett
Director of Public Relations: Jeff Blumb
Assistant Director of Public Relations-Broadcasting/Corporate Communications: Aaron Popkey
Assistant Director of Public Relations-Football Communications: Zak Gilbert
Public Relations Coordinators: Sarah Koenig, Adam Woullard
Ticket Director: Mark Wagner
Director of Marketing and Corporate Sales: Craig Benzel
Director of Premium Guest Services: Jennifer Ark
Director of Atrium Business Development: Steve Klegon
Director of Retail Operations: Kate Hogan
Team Historian: Lee Remmel
Director of Administrative Affairs: Mark Schiefelbein
Director of Finance: Vicki Vannieuwenhoven
Director of Information Technology: Wayne Wichlacz
Director of Facility Operations: Ted Eisenreich
Director of Corporate Security: Jerry Parins
Assistant Director of Security: Doug Collins
Corporate Counsel: Jason Wied
Salary Cap Analyst: Melanie Marohl
Staff Development Consultant: Betsy Mitchell
Manager of Community Relations: Cathy Dworak
Assistant Director of College Scouting: Shaun Herock
College Scouts: Lee Gissendaner, Brian Gutekunst, Alonzo Highsmith, Lenny McGill, Sam Seale, Red Cochran
Scouting Coordinator: Danny Mock
Pro Personnel Assistant: Marc Lillibridge
Personnel Assistant: Eliot Wolf
Director of Research and Development: Mike Eayrs
Video Director: Bob Eckberg
Head Trainer: Pepper Burruss
Equipment Manager: Gordon (Red) Batty

COACHING HISTORY
(626-487-36)

1921-1949	Earl (Curly) Lambeau	212-106-21
1950-53	Gene Ronzani*	14-31-1
1953	Hugh Devore- Ray (Scooter) McLean**	0-2-0
1954-57	Lisle Blackbourn	17-31-0
1958	Ray (Scooter) McLean	1-10-1
1959-1967	Vince Lombardi	98-30-4
1968-1970	Phil Bengtson	20-21-1
1971-74	Dan Devine	25-28-4
1975-1983	Bart Starr	53-77-3
1984-87	Forrest Gregg	25-37-1
1988-1991	Lindy Infante	24-40-0
1992-98	Mike Holmgren	84-42-0
1999	Ray Rhodes	8-8-0
2000-03	Mike Sherman	45-24-0

*Resigned after 10 games in 1953
**Co-coaches

ATTENDANCE

Home 562,819 Away 501,551
Total 1,064,370
Single-game home record, 70,505 (9/7/03)
Single-season home record, 562,819 (2003)

2004 DRAFT CHOICES

Round	Name	Pos.	College
1	Ahmad Carroll	DB	Arkansas
3	Joey Thomas	DB	Montana State
	Donnell Washington	DT	Clemson
	B.J. Sander	P	Ohio State
6	Corey Williams	DT	Arkansas State
7	Scott Wells	C	Tennessee

GREEN BAY PACKERS

2003 TEAM RECORD

PRESEASON (2-3)

Date	Result		Opponent
8/4	L	0-9	vs. Kansas City, in Canton, Ohio
8/9	W	27-21	at Atlanta
8/15	W	38-31	at Cleveland
8/23	L	7-20	Carolina
8/28	L	3-27	Tennessee

REGULAR SEASON (10-6)

Date	Result		Opponent	Att.
9/7	L	25-30	Minnesota	70,505
9/14	W	31-6	Detroit	70,244
9/21	L	13-20	at Arizona	58,784
9/29	W	38-23	at Chicago	61,500
10/5	W	35-13	Seattle	70,365
10/12	L	34-40	Kansas City (OT)	70,407
10/19	L	24-34	at St. Louis	66,201
11/2	W	30-27	at Minnesota	64,482
11/10	L	14-17	Philadelphia	70,291
11/16	W	20-13	at Tampa Bay	65,614
11/23	W	20-10	San Francisco	70,250
11/27	L	14-22	at Detroit	62,123
12/7	W	34-21	Chicago	70,458
12/14	W	38-21	at San Diego	64,978
12/22	W	41-7	at Oakland	62,298
12/28	W	31-3	Denver	70,299

POSTSEASON (1-1)

Date	Result		Opponent	Att.
1/4	W	33-27	Seattle (OT)	71,457
1/11	L	17-20	at Philadelphia (OT)	67,707

(OT) Overtime

SCORE BY PERIODS

Packers	103	138	69	132	0	— 442
Opponents	86	64	49	102	6	— 307

2003 TEAM STATISTICS

	Packers	Opp.
Total First Downs	315	288
Rushing	127	91
Passing	166	172
Penalty	22	25
3rd Down: Made/Att	85/207	85/228
3rd Down Pct.	41.1	37.3
4th Down: Made/Att	4/7	4/17
4th Down Pct.	57.1	23.5
Possession Avg.	30:52	29:08
Total Net Yards	5,798	5,101
Avg. Per Game	362.4	318.8
Total Plays	999	1,036
Avg. Per Play	5.8	4.9
Net Yards Rushing	2,558	1,701
Avg. Per Game	159.9	106.3
Total Rushes	507	413
Net Yards Passing	3,240	3,400
Avg. Per Game	202.5	212.5
Sacked/Yards Lost	19/137	34/200
Gross Yards	3,377	3,600
Att./Completions	473/310	589/326
Completion Pct.	65.5	55.3
Had Intercepted	21	21
Punts/Average	71/41.3	83/41.0
Net Punting Avg.	71/34.6	83/35.0
Penalties/Yards	88/699	97/767
Fumbles/Ball Lost	19/11	21/11
Touchdowns	53	31
Rushing	18	10
Passing	32	18
Returns	3	3

2003 INDIVIDUAL STATISTICS

PASSING	Att.	Comp.	Yds.	Pct.	TD	Int.	Tkld.	Rate
Favre	471	308	3,361	65.4	32	21	19/137	90.4
Pederson	2	2	16	100.0	0	0	0/0	100.0
Packers	473	310	3,377	65.5	32	21	19/137	90.5
Opponents	589	326	3,600	55.3	18	21	34/200	69.0

SCORING	TD R	TD P	TD Rt	PAT	FG	Saf	PTS
Green	15	5	0	0/0	0/0	0	120
Longwell	0	0	0	51/51	23/26	0	120
J. Walker	0	9	0	0/0	0/0	0	54
Franks	0	4	0	0/0	0/0	0	28
Ferguson	0	4	0	0/0	0/0	0	24
Fisher	1	2	0	0/0	0/0	0	18
Henderson	0	3	0	0/0	0/0	0	18
Davenport	2	0	0	0/0	0/0	0	12
Driver	0	2	0	0/0	0/0	0	12
Martin	0	2	0	0/0	0/0	0	12
Harris	0	0	1	0/0	0/0	0	6
McKenzie	0	0	1	0/0	0/0	0	6
Walls	0	1	0	0/0	0/0	0	6
Wilkins	0	0	1	0/0	0/0	0	6
Packers	18	32	3	51/51	23/26	0	442
Opponents	10	18	3	29/29	30/33	0	307

2-Pt. Conversions: Franks 2.
Packers 2-2, Opponents 1-1.

RUSHING	No.	Yds	Avg	LG	TD
Green	355	1,883	5.3	98t	15
Davenport	77	420	5.5	76t	2
Fisher	40	200	5.0	19	1
Driver	5	51	10.2	45	0
Favre	18	15	0.8	7	0
Luchey	1	3	3.0	3	0
J. Walker	2	1	0.5	1	0
Nall	2	-2	-1.0	-1	0
Pederson	6	-5	-0.8	0	0
Ferguson	1	-8	-8.0	-8	0
Packers	507	2,558	5.0	98t	18
Opponents	413	1,701	4.1	67t	10

RECEIVING	No.	Yds	Avg	LG	TD
Driver	52	621	11.9	41	2
Green	50	367	7.3	27	5
J. Walker	41	716	17.5	66t	9
Ferguson	38	520	13.7	47	4
Franks	30	241	8.0	24	4
Henderson	24	214	8.9	22	3
Fisher	21	206	9.8	32	2
Walls	20	222	11.1	36	1
Freeman	14	141	10.1	15	0
Martin	13	79	6.1	14	2
Davenport	6	38	6.3	12	0
Luchey	1	12	12.0	12	0
Packers	310	3,377	10.9	66t	32
Opponents	326	3,600	11.0	68t	18

INTERCEPTIONS	No.	Yds	Avg	LG	TD
Sharper	5	78	15.6	50	0
McKenzie	4	98	24.5	90t	1
Harris	3	89	29.7	56t	1
Barnett	3	21	7.0	14	0
Diggs	2	13	6.5	13	0
Hawthorne	2	8	4.0	8	0
Edwards	1	5	5.0	5	0
Anderson	1	3	3.0	3	0
Packers	21	315	15.0	90t	2
Opponents	21	429	20.4	79t	2

PUNTING	No.	Yds.	Avg.	In 20	LG
Bidwell	69	2,875	41.7	16	60
Longwell	2	58	29.0	1	30
Packers	71	2,933	41.3	17	60
Opponents	83	3,399	41.0	23	62

PUNT RETURNS	Ret	FC	Yds	Avg	LG	TD
Chatman	33	18	277	8.4	33	0
Harris	1	0	0	0.0	0	0
Wilkins	1	0	0	0.0	0	0
Packers	35	18	277	7.9	33	0
Opponents	32	15	316	9.9	32	0

KICKOFF RETURNS	No.	Yds	Avg	LG	TD
Chatman	36	804	22.3	46	0
Davenport	16	505	31.6	60	0
Ferguson	7	148	21.1	31	0
Henderson	3	33	11.0	15	0
Luchey	2	21	10.5	12	0
Packers	64	1,511	23.6	60	0
Opponents	82	1,707	20.8	88t	1

FIELD GOALS	1-19	20-29	30-39	40-49	50+
Longwell	0/0	5/5	11/11	6/9	1/1
Packers	0/0	5/5	11/11	6/9	1/1
Opponents	0/0	10/11	10/10	8/10	2/2

SACKS	No.
Gbaja-Biamila	10.0
Hunt	4.0
G. Jackson	2.5
Nwokorie	2.5
Barnett	2.0
Kampman	2.0
Sharper	2.0
Jue	1.5
Smith	1.5
Diggs	1.0
Edwards	1.0
Hawthorne	1.0
Marshall	1.0
Navies	1.0
Packers	34.0
Opponents	19.0

RECORD HOLDERS

INDIVIDUAL RECORDS—CAREER

Category	Name	Performance
Rushing (Yds.)	Jim Taylor, 1958-1966	8,207
Passing (Yds.)	Brett Favre, 1992-2003	45,646
Passing (TDs)	Brett Favre, 1992-2003	346
Receiving (No.)	Sterling Sharpe, 1988-1994	595
Receiving (Yds.)	James Lofton, 1978-1986	9,656
Interceptions	Bobby Dillon, 1952-59	52
Punting (Avg.)	Craig Hentrich, 1994-97	42.8
Punt Return (Avg.)	Desmond Howard, 1996, 1999	13.8
Kickoff Return (Avg.)	Travis Williams, 1967-1970	26.7
Field Goals	Ryan Longwell, 1997-2003	182
Touchdowns (Tot.)	Don Hutson, 1935-1945	105
Points	Ryan Longwell, 1997-2003	844

INDIVIDUAL RECORDS—SINGLE SEASON

Category	Name	Performance
Rushing (Yds.)	Ahman Green, 2003	1,883
Passing (Yds.)	Lynn Dickey, 1983	4,458
Passing (TDs)	Brett Favre, 1996	39
Receiving (No.)	Sterling Sharpe, 1993	112
Receiving (Yds.)	Robert Brooks, 1995	1,497
Interceptions	Irv Comp, 1943	10
Punting (Avg.)	Craig Hentrich, 1997	45.0
Punt Return (Avg.)	Billy Grimes, 1950	19.1
Kickoff Return (Avg.)	Travis Williams, 1967	*41.1
Field Goals	Chester Marcol, 1972	33
	Ryan Longwell, 2000	33
Touchdowns (Tot.)	Ahman Green, 2003	20
Points	Paul Hornung, 1960	*176

INDIVIDUAL RECORDS—SINGLE GAME

Category	Name	Performance
Rushing (Yds.)	Ahman Green, 12-28-03	218
Passing (Yds.)	Lynn Dickey, 10-12-80	418
Passing (TDs)	Many times	5
	Last time by Brett Favre, 9-27-98	
Receiving (No.)	Don Hutson, 11-22-42	14
Receiving (Yds.)	Billy Howton, 10-21-56	257
Interceptions	Bobby Dillon, 11-26-53	*4
	Willie Buchanon, 9-24-78	*4
Field Goals	Chris Jacke, 11-11-90, 10-14-96	5
	Ryan Longwell, 9-24-00	5
Touchdowns (Tot.)	Paul Hornung, 12-12-65	5
Points	Paul Hornung, 10-8-61	33

*NFL Record

GREEN BAY PACKERS

2004 VETERAN ROSTER

No.	Name	Pos.	Ht.	Wt.	Birthdate	NFL Exp.	College	Hometown	How Acq.	'03 Games/ Starts
20	Anderson, Marques	S	5-11	207	5/26/79	3	UCLA	Long Beach, Calif.	D3-'02	16/7
56	Barnett, Nick	LB	6-2	240	5/27/81	2	Oregon State	Fontana, Calif.	D1-'03	15/15
71	Barry, Kevin	T	6-4	330	7/20/79	3	Arizona	Racine, Wis.	FA-'02	16/1
83	Chatman, Antonio	WR-KR	5-9	177	2/12/79	2	Cincinnati	Los Angeles, Calif.	FA-'03	16/0
76	Clifton, Chad	T	6-5	330	6/26/76	5	Tennessee	Martin, Tenn.	D2-'00	16/16
79	Cochran, Earl	DE	6-5	270	4/19/81	2	Alabama State	Bessemer, Ala.	FA-'03	0*
45	Combs, Derek	CB	6-0	185	2/28/79	2	Ohio State	Urbancrest, Ohio	T(KC)-'03	8/0
69	Curtin, Brennan	T	6-9	315	6/30/80	2	Notre Dame	Palm Beach, Fla.	D6-'03	0*
44	Davenport, Najeh	RB	6-1	245	2/8/79	3	Miami	Miami, Fla.	D4-'02	15/0
60	Davis, Rob	LS	6-3	284	12/10/68	9	Shippensburg	Greenbelt, Md.	FA-'97	16/0
	Davis, Shockmain	WR	6-0	206	8/20/77	2	Angelo State	Port Arthur, Texas	FA-'04	0*
59	Diggs, Na'il	LB	6-4	238	7/8/78	5	Ohio State	Los Angeles, Calif.	D4a-'00	16/16
10	Dorsch, Travis	P	6-6	221	9/4/79	2	Purdue	Bozeman, Mont.	FA-'03	0*
80	Driver, Donald	WR	6-0	188	2/2/75	6	Alcorn State	Houston, Texas	D7b-'99	15/15
4	Favre, Brett	QB	6-2	225	10/10/69	14	Southern Mississippi	Kiln, Miss.	T(Atl)-'92	16/16
89	Ferguson, Robert	WR	6-1	209	12/17/79	4	Texas A&M	Houston, Texas	D2-'01	15/12
40	Fisher, Tony	RB	6-1	222	10/12/79	3	Notre Dame	Euclid, Ohio	FA-'02	15/0
58	Flanagan, Mike	CB	6-5	297	11/10/73	9	UCLA	Sacramento, Calif.	D3a-'96	16/16
86	Ford, Carl	WR	6-0	179	10/8/80	2	Toledo	Monroe, Mich.	D7c-'03	0*
88	Franks, Bubba	TE	6-6	263	1/6/78	5	Miami	Big Spring, Texas	D1-'00	16/15
29	Fuller, Curtis	S	5-10	191	7/25/78	4	Texas Christian	Fort Worth, Texas	W(Sea)-'03	9/0
94	Gbaja-Biamila, Kabeer	DE	6-4	255	9/24/77	5	San Diego State	Los Angeles, Calif.	FA-'00	16/16
30	Green, Ahman	RB	6-0	217	2/16/77	7	Nebraska	Omaha, Neb.	T(Sea)-'00	16/16
31	Harris, Al	CB	6-1	185	12/7/74	7	Texas A&M-Kingsville	Pompano Beach, Fla.	T(Phil)-'03	16/16
27	Hawthorne, Michael	CB-S	6-3	200	1/26/77	5	Purdue	Sarasota, Fla.	FA-'03	14/2
33	Henderson, William	FB	6-1	249	2/19/71	10	North Carolina	Chester, Va.	D3b-'95	16/12
97	Hunt, Cletidus	DT	6-4	305	1/2/76	6	Kentucky State	Memphis, Tenn.	D3b-'99	16/16
75	Jackson, Grady	DT	6-2	350	1/21/73	8	Knoxville	Greensboro, Ala.	W(NO)-'03	8/1
37	Johnson, Chris	CB	5-11	195	9/25/79	2	Louisville	Longview, Texas	D7a-'03	0*
91	Johnson, Joe	DE	6-4	275	7/11/72	11	Louisville	St. Louis, Mo.	UFA(NO)-'02	6/6
21	Jue, Bhawoh	S-CB	6-0	200	5/24/79	4	Penn State	Chantilly, Va.	D3a-'01	16/0
74	Kampman, Aaron	DE	6-4	286	11/30/79	3	Iowa	Parkersburg, Iowa	D5a-'02	12/10
64	Lee, James	DT	6-5	325	3/12/80	2	Oregon State	Salem, Ore.	D5a-'03	0*
53	Lenon, Paris	LB	6-2	240	11/26/77	3	Richmond	Lynchburg, Va.	FA-'02	16/0
82	Lewis, Devin	WR	6-2	210	7/22/79	2	Southern	New Orleans, La.	FA-'03	0*
8	Longwell, Ryan	K	6-0	199	8/16/74	8	California	Bend, Ore.	W(SF)-'97	16/0
22	Luchey, Nick	FB	6-2	270	3/30/77	6	Miami	Farmington Hills, Mich.	UFA(Cin)-'03	11/2
51	Marshall, Torrance	LB	6-2	255	6/12/77	4	Oklahoma	Miami, Fla.	D3b-'01	12/1
87	Martin, David	TE	6-4	260	3/13/79	4	Tennessee	Norfolk, Va.	D6-'01	16/3
34	McKenzie, Mike	CB	6-0	194	4/26/76	6	Memphis	Miami, Fla.	D3a-'99	14/14
16	Nall, Craig	QB	6-3	230	4/21/79	3	Northwestern State (La.)	Alexandria, La.	D5b-'02	1/0
50	Navies, Hannibal	LB	6-3	247	7/19/77	6	Colorado	Berkeley, Calif.	UFA(Car)-'03	16/16
90	Nwokorie, Chukie	DE	6-3	288	7/10/75	6	Purdue	Lafayette, Ind.	UFA(Ind)-'03	14/0
18	Pederson, Doug	QB	6-3	220	1/31/68	12	Northeast Louisiana	Ferndale, Wash.	FA-'01	16/0
98	Peterson, Kenny	DT	6-3	300	11/21/78	2	Ohio State	Canton, Ohio	D3-'03	9/0
99	Reynolds, Jamal	DE	6-3	260	2/20/79	4	Florida State	Aiken, S.C.	D1-'01	5/0
62	Rivera, Marco	G	6-4	310	4/26/72	9	Penn State	Elmont, N.Y.	D6-'96	16/16
23	Roman, Mark	S	5-11	200	3/26/77	5	Louisiana State	New Iberia, La.	UFA(Cin)-'04	16/16*
67	Ruegamer, Grey	C-G	6-4	310	6/11/76	6	Arizona State	Las Vegas, Nev.	UFA(NE)-'03	15/0
42	Sharper, Darren	S	6-2	210	11/3/75	8	William & Mary	Richmond, Va.	D2-'97	15/15
96	Smith, Larry	DT-DE	6-5	310	12/4/74	6	Florida State	Valley Forge, Pa.	FA-'03	10/0
52	Spearman, Armegis	LB	6-2	251	4/5/78	4	Mississippi	Bruce, Miss.	FA-'04	1/0*
26	Swiney, Erwin	CB	6-0	192	10/8/78	2	Nebraska	Lincoln, Neb.	FA-'02	6/0
65	Tauscher, Mark	T	6-4	320	6/17/77	5	Wisconsin	Auburndale, Wis.	D7a-'00	16/16
68	Wahle, Mike	G	6-6	307	3/29/77	7	Navy	Lake Arrowhead, Calif.	SD2-'98	16/16
84	Walker, Javon	WR	6-3	220	10/14/78	3	Florida State	Lafayette, La.	D1-'02	16/3
85	#Walls, Wesley	TE	6-5	240	3/26/66	16	Mississippi	Pontotoc, Miss.	FA-'03	14/1
43	Watson, Chris	CB	6-1	197	6/30/77	5	Eastern Illinois	Chicago, Ill.	FA-'04	0*
32	Westbrook, Bryant	S	6-0	205	12/19/74	8	Texas	Oceanside, Calif.	FA-'02	0*
25	Whitley, James	S-CB	5-11	190	5/13/79	2	Michigan	Norfolk, Va.	FA-'03	3/0
55	Wilkins, Marcus	LB	6-2	235	1/2/80	3	Texas	Austin, Texas	FA-'02	7/0

* Cochran missed '03 season because of injury; Curtin inactive for 16 games; S. Davis last active with New England in '00; Dorsch last active with Cincinnati in '02; Ford missed '03 season because of injury; C. Johnson missed '03 season because of injury; Lee missed '03 season because of injury; Lewis missed '03 season because of injury; Roman played 16 games with Cincinnati in '03; Spearman played 1 game with Houston; Watson last active with Buffalo in '02; Westbrook missed '03 season because of injury.

Unrestricted free agent; subject to developments.

Players lost through free agency (2): P Josh Bidwell (TB; 16 games in '03), S Antuan Edwards (Mia; 10).

Also played with Packers in '03—WR Karsten Bailey (1 game), DT Gilbert Brown (14), WR Antonio Freeman (15), WR Chris Jackson (1), DT Terdell Sands (1), LB T.J. Slaughter (1), T Marcus Spriggs (2), NT Rod Walker (11).

2004 FIRST-YEAR ROSTER

Name	Pos.	Ht.	Wt.	Birthdate	College	Hometown	How Acq.
Breeden, Sam	WR	6-4	207	7/12/79	Northwestern Oklahoma State	Hamlet, N.C.	FA
Briggs, Kris (1)	FB	5-11	234	4/17/81	Southern Methodist	Carthage, Texas	FA
Broyles, James (1)	G	6-4	303	5/18/79	Southwest Missouri	Rensselaer, Ind.	FA
Carroll, Ahmad	CB	5-10	195	8/4/82	Arkansas	Atlanta, Ga.	D1
Crouch, Eric (1)	S	6-0	203	11/16/78	Nebraska	Omaha, Neb.	W(StL)-'03
Diedrick, Dahrran (1)	RB	6-0	225	1/11/79	Nebraska	Scarborough, Ontario, Canada	FA
Donald, Tony (1)	TE	6-3	245	6/4/79	Western State (Colo.)	Fountain, Colo.	FA
Glymph, Junior	DE	6-5	277	9/9/80	Carson Newman	Newberry, S.C.	FA
Hilliard, Jason	T	6-6	333	6/1/81	Louisville	Jeffersonville, Ind.	FA
Horton, Jason (1)	CB	6-0	183	2/16/80	North Carolina A&T	Ahoskie, N.C.	FA
Jackson, Kevin	LB	6-4	241	11/10/81	Hawaii	Moreno Valley, Calif.	FA
Jenkins, Cullen (1)	DE	6-3	292	1/20/81	Central Michigan	Belleville, Mich.	FA
Jimenez, Jason (1)	T	6-7	310	5/1/80	Southern Mississippi	Orlando, Fla.	FA
Jones, Maurice	LB	6-1	246	3/15/81	South Florida	Sarasota, Fla.	FA
Josue, Steve (1)	LB	6-2	222	4/5/80	Carson-Newman	Miami, Fla.	FA
Leach, Vonta	FB	6-0	241	11/6/81	East Carolina	Rowland, N.C.	FA
McBrien, Scott	QB	6-0	189	2/1780	Maryland	Hyattsville, Md.	FA
Morley, Steve (1)	G-T	6-7	326	8/18/81	St. Mary's (Canada)	Halifax, Nova Scotia, Canada	FA
Powell, Eric (1)	DE	6-3	268	11/16/79	Florida State	Orlando, Fla.	FA
Rice, Frank (1)	WR	6-0	181	2/2/78	Colorado State	Serra, Calif.	FA
Sander, B.J.	P	6-4	219	7/29/80	Ohio State	Cincinnati, Ohio	D3c
Shreve, Chris	WR	6-0	184	7/15/81	Virginia Tech	Independence, Va.	FA
Taylor, Jermaine	LB	5-10	220	11/29/81	Bridgewater (Va.)	Miramar, Fla.	FA
Thomas, Joey	CB	6-1	195	8/29/80	Montana St.	Seattle, Wash.	D3a
Thomas, Wilson (1)	WR	6-5	207	10/21/79	Nebraska	Omaha, Neb.	FA
Vance, Forest	G-C	6-4	298	4/16/81	California-Davis	Colfax, Calif.	FA
Vines, Scottie (1)	WR	6-2	203	4/17/79	Wyoming	Alexander City, Ala.	FA
Washington, Donnell	DT	6-6	323	2/6/81	Clemson	Beaufort, S.C.	D3b
Wells, Scott	C	6-2	300	1/17/81	Tennessee	Brentwood, Tenn.	D7
White, Mitch (1)	T	6-4	312	3/25/78	Oregon State	San Diego, Calif.	FA
Williams, Corey	DT	6-4	313	8/17/80	Arkansas State	Camden, Ark.	D6
Williams, Walter (1)	RB	6-1	206	9/8/77	Grambling State	Brusly, La.	FA
Willis, Keith	TE	6-6	250	12/14/80	Virginia Tech	Norfolk, Va.	FA

The term NFL Rookie is defined as a player who is in his first season of professional football and has not been on the roster of another professional football team for any regular-season or postseason games. A Rookie is designated by an "R" on NFL rosters. Players who have been active in another professional football league or players who have NFL experience, including either preseason training camp or being on an Active List or Inactive List, or on Reserve/Injured or Reserve/Physically Unable to Perform for fewer than six regular-season games, are termed NFL First-Year Players. An NFL First-Year Player is designated by a "1" on NFL rosters. Thereafter, a player is credited with an additional year of experience for each season in which he accumulates six games on the Active List or Inactive List, or on Reserve/Injured or Reserve/Physically Unable to Perform.

Log on to www.packers.com for an up-to-date roster.

GREEN BAY PACKERS

COACHING STAFF

Executive Vice President/ General Manager/Head Coach, Mike Sherman

Pro Career: Named the thirteenth head coach in Packers history January 18, 2000. Added general manager responsibilities in 2001 following the retirement of Ron Wolf. Sherman has led Green Bay to four consecutive winning seasons and back-to-back division titles. Joins Pro Football Hall of Fame members Curly Lambeau and Vince Lombardi, along with Mike Holmgren, as the only head coaches in team history to post a winning record. Previously had served as Green Bay's tight ends coach (1997-98) before following Holmgren to Seattle in 1999 to serve as the Seahawks' offensive coordinator-tight ends coach. Career record: 45-24.

Background: Played guard, tackle, and linebacker at Central Connecticut State (1974, 1976-77), where he holds a bachelor's degree in English. Coached high school football (1978-1980) before collegiately coaching at Pittsburgh (1981-82), Tulane (1983-84), Holy Cross (1985-88), Texas A&M (1989-1993, 1995-96), and UCLA (1994).

Personal: Born December 19, 1954, in Norwood, Mass. He and his wife, Karen, have five children—Sarah, Emily, Matthew, Benjamin, and Selena.

ASSISTANT COACHES

Larry Beightol, offensive line; born November 21, 1942, Pittsburgh. Guard-linebacker Catawba College 1960-63. No pro playing experience. College coach: William & Mary 1968-1971, North Carolina State 1972-75, Auburn 1976, Arkansas 1977-78, 1980-82, Louisiana Tech 1979 (head coach), Missouri 1983-84. Pro coach: Atlanta Falcons 1985-86, Tampa Bay Buccaneers 1987-88, San Diego Chargers 1989, New York Jets 1990-94, Houston Oilers 1995, Miami Dolphins 1996-98, joined Packers in 1999.

Darrell Bevell, quarterbacks; born January 6, 1970, Yuma, Ariz. Quarterback Northern Arizona 1989, Wisconsin 1992-95. No pro playing experience. College coach: Westmar 1996, Iowa State 1997, Connecticut 1998-99. Pro coach: Joined Packers in 2000.

John Bonamego, special teams coordinator; born August 14, 1963, Waynesboro, Pa. Wide receiver-quarterback Central Michigan 1985-86. No pro playing experience. College coach: Maine 1988-1991, Lehigh 1992, Army 1993-98. Pro coach: Jacksonville Jaguars 1999-2002, joined Packers in 2003.

James Campen, asst. offensive line/quality control; born June 11, 1964, Sacramento, Calif. Center Sacramento (Calif.) City J.C. 1982-83, Tulane 1984-85. Pro center New Orleans Saints 1987-88, Green Bay Packers 1989-1993. Pro coach: Joined Packers in 2004.

Mark Duffner, linebackers; born July 19, 1953, Annandale, Va. Defensive lineman William & Mary 1972-74. No pro playing experience. College coach: Ohio State 1975-76, Cincinnati 1977-1980, Holy Cross 1981-1991 (head coach 1986-1991), Maryland 1992-96 (head coach). Pro coach: Cincinnati Bengals 1997-2002, joined Packers in 2003.

Jethro Franklin, defensive line; born October 25, 1965, St. Lazaire, France. Defensive end San Jose (Calif.) C.C. 1984-85, Fresno State 1986-87. Pro defensive end Seattle Seahawks 1989. College coach: Fresno State 1991-98, UCLA 1999. Pro coach: Joined Packers in 2000.

Brad Miller, asst. defensive line; born May 30, 1963, Pasadena, Calif. Tight end-safety Oregon State 1981-84. No pro playing experience. College coach: Riverside (Calif.) C.C. 1986-1993, Portland State 1994. Pro coach: Birmingham Barracudas (CFL) 1995, Edmonton Eskimos (CFL) 1996-2000, joined Packers in 2001.

Frank Novak, special teams consultant; born May 18, 1938, Leominster, Mass. Quarterback Northern Michigan 1959-1961. No pro playing experience. College coach: Northern Michigan 1966-1972, East Carolina 1973, Virginia 1974-75, Western Illinois 1976-77, Holy Cross 1978-1983, Missouri 1988. Pro coach: Oklahoma Outlaws (USFL) 1984, Birmingham Stallions (USFL) 1985, Houston Oilers 1989-1994, Detroit Lions 1995-96, San Diego Chargers 1997-98, joined Packers in 2000.

Joe Philbin, tight ends/asst. offensive line; born July 2, 1961, Springfield, Mass. Tight end Washington & Jefferson 1980. No pro playing experience. College coach: Tulane 1984-85, Worcester Tech 1986-87, U.S. Merchant Marine Academy 1988-89, Allegheny 1990-93, Ohio University 1994, Northeastern 1995-96, Harvard 1997-98, Iowa 1999-2002. Pro coach: Joined Packers in 2003.

Johnny Roland, running backs; born May 21, 1943, Corpus Christi, Texas. Running back Missouri 1961-65. Pro running back St. Louis Cardinals 1966-1972, New York Giants 1973. College coach: Notre Dame 1975. Pro coach: Green Bay Packers 1974, Philadelphia Eagles 1976-78, Chicago Bears 1983-1992, New York Jets 1993-94, St. Louis Rams 1995-96, Arizona Cardinals 1997-2003, re-joined Packers in 2004.

Tom Rossley, offensive coordinator; born August 9, 1946, Painesville, Ohio. Wide receiver Cincinnati 1966-68. No pro playing experience. College coach: Arkansas 1972, Rice 1976, 1978-1981, Cincinnati 1977, Holy Cross 1986-87, Southern Methodist 1988-89, 1991-96 (head coach 1991-96). Pro coach: Montreal Concorde (CFL) 1982-84, San Antonio Gunslingers (USFL) 1985, Denver Dynamite (Arena) 1987, Atlanta Falcons 1990, Chicago Bears 1997-98, Kansas City Chiefs 1999, joined Packers in 2000.

Barry Rubin, strength and conditioning; born June 25, 1957, Monroe, La. Running back-punter Louisiana State 1976-77, tight end-punter Northwestern (La.) State 1978-1980. No pro playing experience. College coach: Northeast Louisiana 1981-83, 1987-1990, 1994, Louisiana State 1984-85. Pro coach: Joined Packers in 1995.

Kurt Schottenheimer, defensive backs; born October 1, 1949, McDonald, Pa. Quarterback Coffeyville (Kan.) J.C. 1967-68, defensive back Miami 1969-1970. No pro playing experience. College coach: William Paterson 1974, Michigan State 1978-1982, Tulane 1983, Louisiana State 1984-85, Notre Dame 1986. Pro coach: Cleveland Browns 1987-88, Kansas City Chiefs 1989-2000, Washington Redskins 2001, Detroit Lions 2002-03, joined Packers in 2004.

Ray Sherman, wide receivers; born November 27, 1951, Berkeley, Calif. Wide receiver Laney (Calif.) J.C. 1969-1970, Fresno State 1971-72. No pro playing experience. College coach: San Jose State 1974, California 1975, 1981, Michigan State 1976-77, Wake Forest 1978-1980, Purdue 1982-85, Georgia 1986-87. Pro coach: Houston Oilers 1988-89, Atlanta Falcons 1990, San Francisco 49ers 1991-93, New York Jets 1994, Minnesota Vikings 1995-97, 1999, Pittsburgh Steelers 1998, joined Packers in 2000.

Bob Slowik, defensive coordinator; born May 16, 1954, Pittsburgh. Defensive back Delaware 1973-76. No pro playing experience. College coach: Delaware 1977-78, Florida 1979-1982, Drake 1983, Rutgers 1984-89, East Carolina 1990-91. Pro coach: Dallas Cowboys 1992, Chicago Bears 1993-98, Cleveland Browns 1999, joined Packers in 2000.

Vince Tobin, special assistant; born September 29, 1943, Burlington Junction, Mo. Defensive back Missouri 1961-64. No pro playing experience. College coach: Missouri, 1965, 1967-1976. Pro coach: British Columbia Lions (CFL) 1977-1982, Philadelphia/Baltimore Stars (USFL) 1983-85, Chicago Bears 1986-1992, Indianapolis Colts 1994-95, Arizona Cardinals 1996-2000 (head coach), Detroit Lions 2001, joined Packers in 2004.

Lionel Washington, asst. defensive backs; born October 21, 1960, New Orleans. Defensive back Tulane 1979-1982. Pro defensive back St. Louis Cardinals 1983-86, Los Angeles/Oakland Raiders 1987-1994, 1997, Denver Broncos 1995-96. Pro coach: Joined Packers in 1999.

National Football Conference
North Division
Team Colors: Purple, Gold, and White
9520 Viking Drive
Eden Prairie, Minnesota 55344
Telephone: (952) 828-6500

2004 SCHEDULE

PRESEASON		**Minneapolis time**
Aug. 14	**Arizona**	7:00
Aug. 20	at Atlanta	6:30
Aug. 27	**San Francisco**	7:00
Sept. 2	at Seattle	8:00

REGULAR SEASON

Sept. 12	**Dallas**	3:15
Sept. 20	at Philadelphia (Mon.)	8:00
Sept. 26	**Chicago**	12:00
Oct. 3	Open Date	
Oct. 10	at Houston	12:00
Oct. 17	at New Orleans	7:30
Oct. 24	**Tennessee**	12:00
Oct. 31	**New York Giants**	12:00
Nov. 8	at Indianapolis (Mon.)	8:00
Nov. 14	at Green Bay	3:15
Nov. 21	**Detroit**	12:00
Nov. 28	**Jacksonville**	12:00
Dec. 5	at Chicago	12:00
Dec. 12	**Seattle**	12:00
Dec. 19	at Detroit	12:00
Dec. 24	**Green Bay** (Fri.)	2:00
Jan. 2	at Washington	12:00

Stadium: Hubert H. Humphrey Metrodome (opened in 1982)
•**Capacity:** 64,121
500 11th Avenue South
Minneapolis, Minnesota 55415
Playing Surface: FieldTurf
Training Camp: Minnesota State-Mankato
Mankato, Minnesota
56001

HUBERT H. HUMPHREY METRODOME

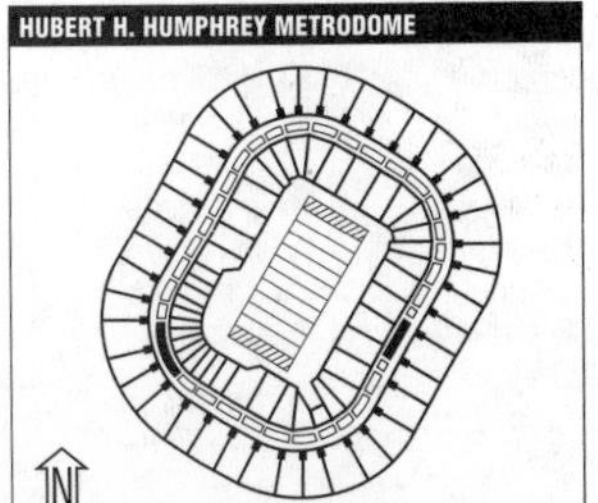

CLUB OFFICIALS

Owners: Red & Charline McCombs
President: Gary Woods
Executive Vice President: Mike Kelly
Vice President of Football Operations: Rob Brzezinski
Vice President of Sales and Marketing: Steve LaCroix
Vice President of Finance: Steve Poppen
Director of Football Administration: Dave Blando
Director of Pro Scouting: Paul Wiggin
Director of College Scouting: Scott Studwell
Senior Consultant/Player Personnel: Frank Gilliam
Director of Public Relations: Bob Hagan
Director of Community Relations: Brad Madson
Director of Research and Development: Chad Ostlund
Director of Operations: Breck Spinner
Director of Ticket Sales: Phil Huebner
Director of Video: Bob Marcus
Equipment Manager: Dennis Ryan
Head Athletic Trainer: Chuck Barta
Senior Consultant/Medical Services: Fred Zamberletti

COACHING HISTORY

(371-306-9)

1961-66	Norm Van Brocklin	29-51-4
1967-1983	Bud Grant	161-99-5
1984	Les Steckel	3-13-0
1985	Bud Grant	7-9-0
1986-1991	Jerry Burns	55-46-0
1992-2001	Dennis Green*	101-70-0
2001-03	Mike Tice	15-18-0

*Resigned after 15 games in 2001

ATTENDANCE

Home 499,837 Away 500,436
Total 1,000,273
Single-game home record, 64,482 (11/2/03)
Single-season home record, 510,741 (1998)

2004 DRAFT CHOICES

Round	Name	Pos.	College
1	Kenechi Udeze	DE	Southern California
2	Dontarrious Thomas	LB	Auburn
3	Darrion Scott	DE	Ohio State
4	Nat Dorsey	T	Georgia Tech
	Mewelde Moore	RB	Tulane
5	Rod Davis	LB	So. Mississippi
6	Deandré Eiland	DB	South Carolina
7	Jeff Dugan	TE	Maryland

MINNESOTA VIKINGS

2003 TEAM RECORD

PRESEASON (1-3)

Date	Result	Opponent
8/9	L 14-16	Jacksonville
8/16	L 16-26	at Kansas City
8/22	W 21-6	at Oakland
8/28	L 27-31	Arizona

REGULAR SEASON (9-7)

Date	Result	Opponent	Att.
9/7	W 30-25	at Green Bay	70,505
9/14	W 24-13	Chicago	64,144
9/21	W 23-13	at Detroit	60,865
9/28	W 35-7	San Francisco	64,111
10/5	W 39-26	at Atlanta	70,427
10/19	W 28-20	Denver	64,381
10/26	L 17-29	New York Giants	64,114
11/2	L 27-30	Green Bay	64,482
11/9	L 28-42	at San Diego	64,738
11/16	L 18-28	at Oakland	56,653
11/23	W 24-14	Detroit	63,946
11/30	L 17-48	at St. Louis	66,134
12/7	W 34-7	Seattle	63,968
12/14	L 10-13	at Chicago	61,804
12/20	W 45-20	Kansas City	64,291
12/28	L 17-18	at Arizona	52,734

SCORE BY PERIODS

Vikings	76	136	84	120	0	— 416
Opponents	69	92	72	120	0	— 353

2003 TEAM STATISTICS

	Vikings	Opp.
Total First Downs	336	316
Rushing	124	94
Passing	194	186
Penalty	18	36
3rd Down: Made/Att	102/219	70/182
3rd Down Pct.	46.6	38.5
4th Down: Made/Att	8/20	6/14
4th Down Pct.	40.0	42.9
Possession Avg.	32:52	27:08
Total Net Yards	6,294	5,356
Avg. Per Game	393.4	334.8
Total Plays	1,055	955
Avg. Per Play	6.0	5.6
Net Yards Rushing	2,343	1,879
Avg. Per Game	146.4	117.4
Total Rushes	493	387
Net Yards Passing	3,951	3,477
Avg. Per Game	246.9	217.3
Sacked/Yards Lost	42/218	37/245
Gross Yards	4,169	3,722
Att./Completions	520/333	531/311
Completion Pct.	64.0	58.6
Had Intercepted	13	28
Punts/Average	64/38.5	64/40.3
Net Punting Avg.	64/32.1	64/35.8
Penalties/Yards	127/1,029	90/720
Fumbles/Ball Lost	31/11	28/7
Touchdowns	51	42
Rushing	15	22
Passing	32	17
Returns	4	3

2003 INDIVIDUAL STATISTICS

PASSING	Att.	Comp.	Yds.	Pct.	TD	Int.	Tkld.	Rate
Culpepper	454	295	3,479	65.0	25	11	37/196	96.4
Frerotte	65	38	690	58.5	7	2	5/22	118.1
Moss	1	0	0	0.0	0	0	0/0	39.6
Patriots	520	333	4,169	64.0	32	13	42/218	99.0
Opponents	531	311	3,722	58.6	17	28	37/245	68.8

SCORING	TD R	TD P	TD Rt	PAT	FG	Saf	PTS
Elling	0	0	0	48/48	18/25	0	102
Moss	0	17	0	0/0	0/0	0	102
M. Williams	5	3	0	0/0	0/0	0	48
O. Smith	5	0	0	0/0	0/0	0	32
Campbell	0	4	0	0/0	0/0	0	24
Culpepper	4	0	0	0/0	0/0	0	24
Kleinsasser	0	4	0	0/0	0/0	0	24
Burleson	0	2	0	0/0	0/0	0	12
Avery	0	1	0	0/0	0/0	0	6
Bates	0	1	0	0/0	0/0	0	6
Bennett	1	0	0	0/0	0/0	0	6
Chavous	0	0	1	0/0	0/0	0	6
Johnstone	0	0	1	0/0	0/0	0	6
Nattiel	0	0	1	0/0	0/0	0	6
B. Williams	0	0	1	0/0	0/0	0	6
Goodwin	0	0	0	0/0	0/0	0	2
Vikings	15	32	4	48/48	18/25	2	416
Opponents	22	17	3	36/36	21/26	0	353

2-Pt. Conversions: Goodwin, O. Smith.
Vikings 2-3, Opponents 1-6

RUSHING	No.	Yds	Avg	LG	TD
M. Williams	174	745	4.3	61	5
O. Smith	107	579	5.4	47	5
Bennett	90	447	5.0	28	1
Culpepper	73	422	5.8	42	4
Campbell	10	71	7.1	19	0
Chapman	15	33	2.2	6	0
Moss	6	18	3.0	11	0
Johnson	2	15	7.5	15	0
Kleinsasser	2	15	7.5	12	0
Avery	1	0	0.0	0	0
Stackhouse	1	0	0.0	0	0
Frerotte	12	-2	-0.2	4	0
Vikings	493	2,343	4.8	61	15
Opponents	387	1,879	4.9	73t	22

RECEIVING	No.	Yds	Avg	LG	TD
Moss	111	1,632	14.7	72	17
M. Williams	65	644	9.9	42	3
Kleinsasser	46	401	8.7	19	4
Burleson	29	455	15.7	52	2
Campbell	25	522	20.9	72t	4
Bates	15	151	10.1	18	1
O. Smith	15	129	8.6	20	0
Bennett	12	132	11.0	40	0
Stackhouse	6	30	5.0	10	0
Goodwin	4	26	6.5	12	0
Avery	2	24	12.0	13	1
Howry	2	15	7.5	8	0
Chapman	1	8	8.0	8	0
Vikings	333	4,169	12.5	72t	32
Opponents	311	3,722	12.0	51	17

INTERCEPTIONS	No.	Yds	Avg	LG	TD
Russell	9	185	20.6	50	0
Chavous	8	143	17.9	39	1
B. Williams	5	205	41.0	77	1
Nattiel	1	80	80.0	80t	1
Johnstone	1	33	33.0	33t	1
Claiborne	1	3	3.0	3	0
K. Williams	1	3	3.0	3	0
Irvin	1	1	1.0	1	0
Walker	1	0	0.0	0	0
E. Kelly	0	40	—	40	0
Vikings	28	693	24.8	80t	4
Opponents	13	149	11.5	64t	1

PUNTING	No.	Yds.	Avg.	In 20	LG
Johnson	56	2,191	39.1	12	55
Araguz	7	271	38.7	1	44
Vikings	64	2,462	38.5	13	55
Opponents	64	2,576	40.3	19	53

PUNT RETURNS	Ret	FC	Yds	Avg	LG	TD
Howry	35	16	247	7.1	52	0
Burleson	1	0	0	0.0	0	0
Vikings	36	16	247	6.9	52	0
Opponents	29	19	310	10.7	46	0

KICKOFF RETURNS	No.	Yds	Avg	LG	TD
O. Smith	27	588	21.8	46	0
Avery	16	346	21.6	48	0
Howry	12	271	22.6	42	0
Campbell	5	101	20.2	23	0
Chapman	4	51	12.8	20	0
Clark	2	33	16.5	21	0
Berton	1	7	7.0	7	0
Henderson	1	0	0.0	0	0
Moss	1	22	22.0	22	0
Rogers	1	1	1.0	1	0
Withrow	1	8	8.0	8	0
Vikings	71	1,428	20.1	48	0
Opponents	75	1,608	21.4	56	0

FIELD GOALS	1-19	20-29	30-39	40-49	50+
Elling	0/0	7/7	6/8	4/7	1/3
Vikings	0/0	7/7	6/8	4/7	1/3
Opponents	0/0	9/9	5/5	6/9	1/3

SACKS	No.
K. Williams	10.5
Johnstone	10.0
Mixon	5.0
Claiborne	3.0
B. Williams	3.0
Hovan	2.0
Biekert	1.0
Russell	1.0
Wiley	1.0
Robbins	0.5
Vikings	37.0
Opponents	42.0

RECORD HOLDERS

INDIVIDUAL RECORDS—CAREER

Category	Name	Performance
Rushing (Yds.)	Robert Smith, 1993-2000	6,818
Passing (Yds.)	Fran Tarkenton, 1961-66, 1972-78	33,098
Passing (TDs)	Fran Tarkenton, 1961-66, 1972-78	239
Receiving (No.)	Cris Carter, 1990-2001	1,004
Receiving (Yds.)	Cris Carter, 1990-2001	12,383
Interceptions	Paul Krause, 1968-1979	53
Punting (Avg.)	Harry Newsome, 1990-93	43.8
Punt Return (Avg.)	David Palmer, 1994-2000	9.4
Kickoff Return (Avg.)	Charlie West, 1968-1973	25.5
Field Goals	Fred Cox, 1963-1977	282
Touchdowns (Tot.)	Cris Carter, 1990-2001	110
Points	Fred Cox, 1963-1977	1,365

INDIVIDUAL RECORDS—SINGLE SEASON

Category	Name	Performance
Rushing (Yds.)	Robert Smith, 2000	1,521
Passing (Yds.)	Warren Moon, 1994	4,264
Passing (TDs)	Randall Cunningham, 1998	34
Receiving (No.)	Cris Carter, 1994, 1995	122
Receiving (Yds.)	Randy Moss, 2003	1,632
Interceptions	Paul Krause, 1975	10
Punting (Avg.)	Bobby Walden, 1964	46.4
Punt Return (Avg.)	David Palmer, 1995	13.2
Kickoff Return (Avg.)	John Gilliam, 1972	26.3
Field Goals	Gary Anderson, 1998	35
Touchdowns (Tot.)	Chuck Foreman, 1975	22
Points	Gary Anderson, 1998	164

INDIVIDUAL RECORDS—SINGLE GAME

Category	Name	Performance
Rushing (Yds.)	Chuck Foreman, 10-24-76	200
Passing (Yds.)	Tommy Kramer, 11-2-86	490
Passing (TDs)	Joe Kapp, 9-28-69	*7
Receiving (No.)	Rickey Young, 12-16-79	15
Receiving (Yds.)	Sammy White, 11-7-76	210
Interceptions	Many Times	3
	Last time by Brian Williams, 11-23-03	
Field Goals	Rich Karlis, 11-5-89	*7
Touchdowns (Tot.)	Chuck Foreman, 12-20-75	4
	Ahmad Rashad, 9-2-79	4
Points	Chuck Foreman, 12-20-75	24
	Ahmad Rashad, 9-2-79	24

*NFL Record

MINNESOTA VIKINGS

2004 VETERAN ROSTER

No.	Name	Pos.	Ht.	Wt.	Birthdate	NFL Exp.	College	Hometown	How Acq.	'03 Games/ Starts
86	Angulo, Richard	TE	6-8	283	11/13/80	2	Western New Mexico	Albuquerque, N.M.	W(StL)-'03	6/0
2	Bennett, Darren	P	6-5	235	1/9/65	10	No College	Perth, Australia	UFA(SD)-'04	16/0*
23	Bennett, Michael	RB	5-9	211	8/13/78	4	Wisconsin	Milwaukee, Wis.	D1-'01	8/7
44	Berton, Sean	TE	6-4	272	10/31/79	2	North Carolina State	Greensburg, Pa.	FA-'03	16/0
78	Birk, Matt	C	6-4	308	7/23/76	7	Harvard	St. Paul, Minn.	D6-'98	16/16
81	Burleson, Nate	WR	6-0	192	8/19/81	2	Nevada	Seattle, Wash.	D3-'03	16/9
16	Campbell, Kelly	WR	5-10	171	7/23/80	3	Georgia Tech	Atlanta, Ga.	FA-'02	6/2
41	Carter, Tyrone	S	5-8	190	3/31/76	5	Minnesota	Pompano Beach, Fla.	FA-'04	16/10*
21	Chavous, Corey	S	6-1	206	1/5/76	7	Vanderbilt	Petticoat Junction, S.C.	UFA(Ariz)-'02	16/16
55	Claiborne, Chris	LB	6-3	258	7/26/78	6	Southern California	Riverside, Calif.	UFA(Det)-'03	12/12
89	Clark, Kenny	WR	6-1	227	5/14/78	2	Central Florida	Ocala, Fla.	FA-'01	1/0
11	Culpepper, Daunte	QB	6-4	260	1/28/77	6	Central Florida	Ocala, Fla.	D1a-'99	14/14
71	Dixon, David	G	6-5	359	1/5/69	11	Arizona State	Auckland, New Zealand	FA-'94	16/16
8	Elling, Aaron	K	6-2	201	5/31/78	2	Wyoming	Lander, Wyo.	FA-'03	16/0
48	Farmer, Steve	TE	6-4	253	2/24/80	2	Tennessee State	Michigan City, Ind.	FA-'03	0*
12	Frerotte, Gus	QB	6-3	225	7/3/71	11	Tulsa	Ford City, Pa.	UFA(Cin)-'03	16/2
72	Haayer, Adam	T	6-6	306	2/22/77	3	Minnesota	Forest Lake, Minn.	W(Tenn)-'02	0*
56	Henderson, E.J.	LB	6-1	245	8/3/80	2	Maryland	Aberdeen, Md.	D2-'03	16/0
13	Hill, Shaun	QB	6-3	223	1/9/80	3	Maryland	Parsons, Kan.	FA-'02	0*
99	Hovan, Chris	DT	6-2	294	5/12/78	5	Boston College	Rocky River, Ohio	D1-'00	16/16
82	Howry, Keenan	WR	5-10	172	6/17/81	2	Oregon	Los Alamitos, Calif.	D7-'03	16/1
22	Irvin, Ken	CB	5-11	186	7/11/72	10	Memphis	Lindale, Ga.	UFA(NO)-'03	16/8
4	Johnson, Eddie	P	6-3	236	3/2/81	2	Idaho State	Newport Beach, Calif.	D6a-'03	14/0
51	Johnstone, Lance	DE	6-4	253	6/11/73	8	Temple	Germantown, Pa.	FA-'01	16/16
31	Jones, Rushen	CB	5-10	194	4/4/80	2	Vanderbilt	Memphis, Tenn.	FA-'03	11/0
25	Kelly, Eric	CB	5-10	197	1/15/77	4	Kentucky	Panama, Fla.	D3-'01	16/0
61	Kelly, Lewis	G	6-4	306	4/21/77	5	South Carolina State	Lithonia, Ga.	D7c-'00	6/0
40	Kleinsasser, Jim	TE	6-3	274	1/31/77	6	North Dakota	Carrington, N.D.	D2-'99	16/16
43	Liddiard, Brody	LS	6-4	234	6/12/77	5	Colorado	San Diego, Calif.	FA-'01	16/0
62 #	Lindsay, Everett	G	6-4	305	9/8/70	11	Mississippi	Raleigh, N.C.	T(Cle)-'01	12/0
76	Liwienski, Chris	G	6-5	321	8/2/75	6	Indiana	Sterling Heights, Mich.	FA-'99	16/16
96	Lyon, Billy	DT	6-5	295	12/10/73	7	Marshall	Erlanger, Ky.	UFA(GB)-'03	13/0
90	Martin, Steve	DT	6-4	292	5/31/74	9	Missouri	Jefferson City, Mo.	UFA(Hou)-'04	14/8*
74	McKinnie, Bryant	T	6-8	343	9/23/79	3	Miami	Woodbury, N.J.	D1-'02	16/16
79	Mixon, Kenny	DE	6-4	275	5/31/75	7	Louisiana State	Pineville, La.	UFA(Mia)-'02	16/16
84	Moss, Randy	WR	6-4	204	2/13/77	7	Marshall	Rand, W.Va.	D1-'98	16/16
59	Nattiel, Mike	LB	6-0	227	11/8/80	2	Florida	Archer, Fla.	D6b-'03	16/0
38	Nelson, Rhett	CB	6-0	201	2/16/80	2	Colorado State	Littleton, Colo.	FA-'03	3/0
24	Offord, Willie	S	6-1	215	12/22/78	3	South Carolina	Palatka, Fla.	D3-'02	16/0
87	Robinson, Marcus	WR	6-3	215	2/27/75	8	South Carolina	Fort Valley, Ga.	UFA(Balt)-'04	15/5*
58	Rogers, Nick	DE	6-2	251	5/31/79	3	Georgia Tech	East Point, Ga.	D6-'02	16/0
75	Rosenthal, Mike	T	6-7	315	6/10/77	6	Notre Dame	Mishawaka, Ind.	UFA(NYG)-'03	16/16
27	Russell, Brian	S	6-2	204	2/5/78	3	San Diego State	West Covina, Calif.	FA-'01	16/16
32	Smith, Onterrio	RB	5-10	214	12/8/80	2	Oregon	Sacramento, Calif.	D4-'03	15/3
57	Smith, Raonall	LB	6-2	244	10/22/78	3	Washington State	Gig Harbor, Wash.	D2-'02	7/0
85	Wiggins, Jermaine	TE	6-2	260	1/18/75	5	Georgia	East Boston, Mass.	UFA(Car)-'04	16/11*
94	Wiley, Chuck	DE	6-5	277	3/6/75	7	Louisiana State	Baton Rouge, La.	UFA(Atl)-'02	7/4
29	Williams, Brian	CB	5-11	207	7/2/79	3	North Carolina State	High Point, N.C.	D4a-'02	16/16
93	Williams, Kevin	DT	6-5	311	8/16/80	2	Oklahoma State	Fordyce, Ark.	D1-'03	16/16
20	Williams, Moe	RB	6-1	210	7/26/74	9	Kentucky	Columbus, Ga.	UFA(Balt)-'02	16/7
26	Winfield, Antoine	CB	5-9	180	6/24/77	6	Ohio State	Akron, Ohio	UFA(Buff)-'04	16/16*
60	Withrow, Cory	C	6-2	287	4/5/75	5	Washington State	Spokane, Wash.	FA-'99	8/0

* Bennett played 16 games for San Diego in '03; Carter played 16 games for N.Y. Jets; Farmer missed '03 season because of injury; Haayer last active with Minnesota in '02; Hill inactive for 15 games; Martin played 14 games for Houston; Robinson played 15 games for Baltimore; Wiggins played 16 games for Carolina; Winfield played 16 games for Buffalo.

\# Unrestricted free agent; subject to developments.

Players lost through free agency (1): DT Fred Robbins (NYG; 16 games in '03).

Retired—Greg Biekert, 11-year linebacker, 16 games in '03.

Also played with Vikings in '03—P Leo Araguz (2 games), RB John Avery (3), WR D'Wayne Bates (10), S Jack Brewer (6), RB Doug Chapman (4), K José Cortez (2), LB Henri Crockett (16), WR Nick Davis (1), TE Hunter Goodwin (16), S Ron Israel (1), DE Talance Sawyer (3), FB Charles Stackhouse (14), CB Denard Walker (16).

2004 FIRST-YEAR ROSTER

Name	Pos.	Ht.	Wt.	Birthdate	College	Hometown	How Acq.
Anderson, Kane (1)	TE	6-4	257	9/12/80	New Hampshire	Bomoseen, Vt.	FA
Capone, Gino	LB	6-2	238	10/16/80	Penn State	Ashland, Pa.	FA
Cottrell, T.J.	TE	6-5	245	5/3/82	Buffalo State	Buffalo, N.Y.	FA
Danielsen, Lane	WR	6-0	197	5/20/81	Iowa State	Dike, Iowa	FA
Davis, Rod	LB	6-2	239	4/2/81	Southern Mississippi	Gulfport, Miss.	D5
Dorsey, Nat	T	6-7	322	9/9/83	Georgia Tech	New Orleans, La.	D4a
Dugan, Jeff	TE	6-4	258	4/8/81	Maryland	Pittsburgh, Pa.	D7
Eiland, Deandré	CB	5-11	202	6/4/82	South Carolina	Tupelo, Miss.	D6
Elliott, Blake	WR	6-2	215	2/19/81	St. John's (Minn.)	Melrose, Minn.	FA
Goldberg, Adam (1)	T	6-7	330	8/12/80	Wyoming	Edina, Minn.	FA
Herrera, Anthony	G	6-2	315	6/14/80	Tennessee	Naples, Fla.	FA
Hosack, Aaron	WR	6-5	210	11/28/81	Minnesota	Chino, Calif.	FA
Jenkins, Omar	WR	6-1	204	5/8/81	Notre Dame	Dallas, Texas	FA
Johnson, Spencer	DT	6-3	286	12/12/81	Auburn	Silas, Ala.	FA
Kegel, Matt	QB	6-4	242	8/1/80	Washington State	Havre, Mont.	FA
Loeffler, Cullen	LS	6-5	241	1/27/81	Texas	Ingram, Texas	FA
Mack, Jeff	LB	6-0	241	2/20/81	Wisconsin	Madison, Wis.	FA
Mays, Jermaine (1)	WR	5-11	200	7/13/79	Minnesota	Miami, Fla.	FA
Moore, Mewelde	RB	5-11	209	7/24/82	Tulane	Baton Rouge, La.	D4b
Nauman, Ben	S	6-1	200	12/10/80	Augustana	Rochester, Minn.	FA
Ned, Larry (1)	RB	5-11	217	8/23/78	San Diego State	Moreno Valley, Calif.	FA
Nelson, Ben (1)	WR	6-2	185	8/21/79	St. Cloud State	Anoka, Minn.	FA
Orner, Dan	K	5-8	170	10/17/80	North Carolina	Warwick, N.Y.	FA
Owens, Richard	TE	6-4	273	11/4/80	Louisville	Middleburgh, Fla.	FA
Reuber, Alan	T	6-6	323	1/26/81	Texas A&M	Plano, Texas	FA
Scott, Darrion	DE	6-3	289	10/25/81	Ohio State	Charleston, W.Va.	D3
Steele, Ben (1)	TE	6-5	241	5/27/78	Mesa State	Palisade, Colo.	FA
Thomas, Dontarrious	LB	6-2	241	9/2/80	Auburn	Perry, Ala.	D2
Udeze, Kenechi	DE	6-3	281	3/5/83	Southern California	Los Angeles, Calif.	D1
Wallace, Butchie	RB	5-10	205	12/24/80	Marshall	Myrtle Beach, S.C.	FA
Wiley, Grant	LB	6-0	229	3/11/81	West Virginia	Trappe, Pa.	FA
Willis, Horace (1)	CB	6-0	198	7/11/79	Auburn	Marietta, Ga.	FA
Womble, Jeff	DT	6-1	313	2/13/81	Florida State	Dunwoody, Ga.	FA
Yates, Max (1)	LB	6-3	228	10/30/79	Marshall	Newport News, Va.	FA

The term NFL Rookie is defined as a player who is in his first season of professional football and has not been on the roster of another professional football team for any regular-season or postseason games. A Rookie is designated by an "R" on NFL rosters. Players who have been active in another professional football league or players who have NFL experience, including either preseason training camp or being on an Active List or Inactive List, or on Reserve/Injured or Reserve/Physically Unable to Perform for fewer than six regular-season games, are termed NFL First-Year Players. An NFL First-Year Player is designated by a "1" on NFL rosters. Thereafter, a player is credited with an additional year of experience for each season in which he accumulates six games on the Active List or Inactive List, or on Reserve/Injured or Reserve/Physically Unable to Perform.

Log on to www.vikings.com for an up-to-date roster.

COACHING STAFF

Head Coach,
Mike Tice

Pro Career: Named the Vikings' sixth head coach on January 10, 2002. Led the team to a 9-7 record in his second season at the helm. Guided the team to a nine-game winning streak in 2002-03, tied for third-best in team history. Led the team to three consecutive wins to end the 2002 season and a 6-0 start in 2003. Tice has been associated with the team since 1992, playing tight end from 1992-93 and 1995, coaching the tight ends in 1996 and the offensive line from 1997-2001. Tice added the title of assistant head coach for the 2001 season and was made the interim head coach for the Vikings' last regular season game of the 2001 season against Baltimore. Tice is the first Vikings alumni player to hold the title of the franchise's head coach. In five seasons coaching the offensive line, Tice guided five different players—Matt Birk, Jeff Christy, Randall McDaniel, Todd Steussie, Korey Stringer—to 10 Pro Bowl appearances. In 1998, the offensive line paved the way for numerous NFL and Vikings records including a League record for points scored in a season (556) and set Vikings records for total yards (6,264) and fewest sacks allowed in a 16-game season (25). Career record: 15-18.

Background: Played quarterback at the University of Maryland from 1977-1980. Tice completed 71 of 140 passes for 928 yards with 5 touchdowns as a senior and 896 yards and 5 touchdowns as a junior. Over his 14-year NFL career, Tice caught 107 passes for 894 yards and 11 touchdowns and blocked for running backs that rushed for over 1,000 yards in a season five times. Tice played three seasons with the Vikings (1992-93, 1995), 10 years with the Seattle Seahawks (1981-88, 1990-91), and one season with the Washington Redskins (1989) and made 109 starts in 177 games played.

Personal: Born February 2, 1959 in Bayshore, N.Y. Attended Central Islip High School on Long Island. He and wife Diane have two children, Adrienne and Nathan, and live in Edina, Minn.

ASSISTANT COACHES

Charlie Baggett, wide receivers; born January 21, 1953, Fayetteville, N.C. Quarterback Michigan State 1972-75. No pro playing experience. College coach: Bowling Green 1977-1980, Minnesota 1981-82, Michigan State 1983-1992, 1995-98. Pro coach: Houston Oilers 1993-94, Green Bay Packers 1999, joined Vikings in 2000.

Brian Baker, defensive line; born June 20, 1962, Baltimore. Linebacker Maryland 1980-83. No pro playing experience. College coach: Maryland 1984-85, Army 1986, Georgia Tech 1987-1995. Pro coach: San Diego Chargers 1996, Detroit Lions 1997-2000, joined Vikings in 2001.

Pete Bercich, defensive assistant/asst. linebackers; born December 23, 1971, Joliet, Ill. Linebacker Notre Dame 1990-93. Pro linebacker Minnesota Vikings 1994-2000. Pro coach: Joined Vikings in 2002.

Ted Cottrell, defensive coordinator/linebackers; born June 13, 1947, Chester, Pa. Linebacker Delaware Valley College 1966-68. Pro linebacker Atlanta Falcons 1969-1970, Winnipeg Blue Bombers (CFL) 1971. College coach: Rutgers 1973-1980, 1983. Pro coach: Kansas City Chiefs 1981-82, New Jersey Generals (USFL) 1983-84, Buffalo Bills 1986-89, 1995-2000, Arizona Cardinals 1990-94, New York Jets 2001-03, joined Vikings in 2004.

Dean Dalton, running backs; born July 27, 1963, Platteville, Wis. Defensive back Air Force Academy 1981-82, Western Illinois 1983-84. No pro playing experience. College coach: Western Illinois 1984-85, Wisconsin 1986-87, Texas Southern 1988-89, Purdue 1990. Pro coach: Joined Vikings in 1999.

Mark Ellis, asst. strength and conditioning; born December 18, 1969, Littlefield, Texas. Defensive back Temple 1990-91. College coach: Lackawanna (Pa.) J.C. 1993, Navarro College 1994, Fort Scott (Kan.) C.C. 1995. Pro coach: Joined Vikings in 2004.

Randy Hanson, offensive quality control; born January 17, 1968, Sacramento, Calif. Quarterback Pacific 1990-92. No pro playing experience. College coach: Eastern Washington 1993-95, 1998-99, Washington 1996-97, Portland State 2000-02. Pro coach: Joined Vikings in 2003.

Chuck Knox Jr., secondary; born February 19, 1965, Englewood, N.J. Running back Arizona 1984-88. No pro playing experience. Pro coach: Los Angeles Rams 1993-94, Philadelphia Eagles 1995-98, Green Bay Packers 1999, joined Vikings in 2000.

Scott Linehan, offensive coordinator-quarterbacks; born September 17, 1963, Sunnyside, Wash. Quarterback Idaho 1982-86. No pro playing experience. College coach: Idaho 1988-1990, Nevada-Las Vegas 1991, Idaho 1992-93, Washington 1994-98, Louisville 1999-2001. Pro coach: Joined Vikings in 2002.

Steve Loney, offensive line; born April 26, 1952, Marshalltown, Iowa. Offensive line Iowa State 1970-73. No pro playing experience. College coach: Missouri Western College 1975-76, Moorhead State 1979-1983, The Citadel 1984-86, Colorado State 1989-1992, Connecticut 1994, Iowa State 1995-97, 2000-01, Minnesota 1998-99. Pro coach: Phoenix Cardinals 1993, joined Vikings in 2002.

Jim Panagos, defensive quality control; born March 23, 1971, Brooklyn, N.Y. Defensive line Maryland 1989-1992. No pro playing experience. College coach: Maryland 1993. Pro coach: Joined Vikings in 2002.

Kevin Ross, asst. secondary; born January 16, 1962, Camden, N.J. Defensive back Temple 1980-83. Pro defensive back Kansas City Chiefs 1984-1993, Atlanta Falcons 1994-95, San Diego Chargers 1996. Pro coach: Joined Vikings in 2003.

Kurtis Shultz, strength and conditioning; born March 10, 1972, Baltimore. Attended Maryland. No college or pro playing experience. College coach: Loyola (Md.) 1995-97, Maryland and Johns Hopkins 1999-2002. Pro coach: Cincinnati Bengals 2003, joined Vikings in 2004.

John Tice, tight ends/asst. offensive line; born June 22, 1960, Bayshore, N.Y. Tight end Maryland 1978-1982. Pro tight end New Orleans Saints 1983-1992. Pro coach: Joined Vikings in 1999.

Rusty Tillman, special teams; born February 27, 1946, Beloit, Wis. Tight end-linebacker-defensive end-punter Northern Arizona 1967-69. Pro linebacker Washington Redskins 1970-77. Pro coach: Seattle Seahawks 1979-1994, Tampa Bay Buccaneers 1995, Oakland Raiders 1996-97, Indianapolis Colts 1998, New York/New Jersey Hitmen (XFL) (head coach) 2001, joined Vikings in 2003.

National Football Conference
South Division
Team Colors: Old Gold, Black, and White
5800 Airline Drive
Metairie, Louisiana 70003
Telephone: (504) 733-0255

2004 SCHEDULE

PRESEASON		New Orleans time
Aug. 13	**New York Jets**	7:00
Aug. 21	at Green Bay	7:00
Aug. 27	at Chicago	7:30
Sept. 3	**Miami**	7:00

REGULAR SEASON		
Sept. 12	**Seattle**	12:00
Sept. 19	**San Francisco**	12:00
Sept. 26	at St. Louis	12:00
Oct. 3	at Arizona	3:05
Oct. 10	**Tampa Bay**	12:00
Oct. 17	**Minnesota**	7:30
Oct. 24	at Oakland	3:15
Oct. 31	Open Date	
Nov. 7	at San Diego	3:05
Nov. 14	**Kansas City**	12:00
Nov. 21	**Denver**	12:00
Nov. 28	at Atlanta	3:05
Dec. 5	**Carolina**	12:00
Dec. 12	at Dallas	12:00
Dec. 19	at Tampa Bay	3:05
Dec. 26	**Atlanta**	12:00
Jan. 2	at Carolina	12:00

Stadium: Louisiana Superdome (opened in 1975)
•**Capacity:** 68,390
1500 Poydras Street
New Orleans, Louisiana 70112
Playing Surface: Sportexe Momentum
Training Camp: New Orleans Saints Training Facility

LOUISIANA SUPERDOME

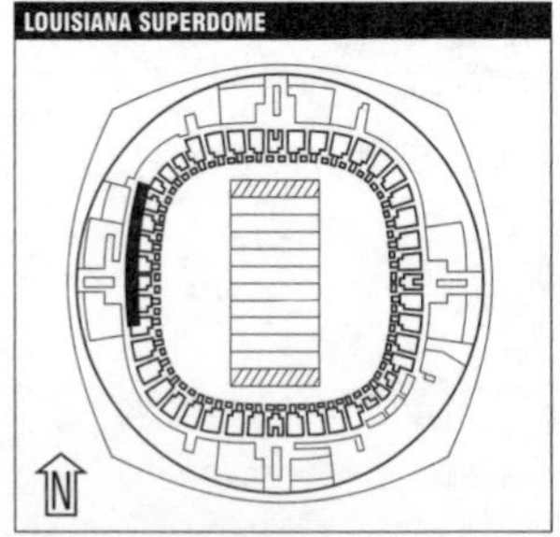

CLUB OFFICIALS

Owner: Tom Benson
Owner/Executive: Rita Benson LeBlanc
Executive Vice President/General Manager: Mickey Loomis
Executive Vice President/Administration: Arnold D. Fielkow
Executive Vice President/Chief Financial Officer: Dennis Lauscha
Director of Player Personnel: Rick Mueller
Senior Football Administrator: Russ Ball
Director of Operations: James Nagaoka
College Scouting Coordinator: Rick Thompson
Regional Scout: Mike Faulkiner
Area/Pro Scout: Bill Quinter
Pro Scouts: Mike Baugh, Grant Neill
Area Scouts: Tim Heffelfinger, Mark Sadowski, James Jefferson, Andrew Weidl, Barrett Wiley
Player Personnel Assistant: Ryan Pace
Equipment Manager: Dan Simmons
Assistant Equipment Manager: Glennon (Silky) Powell
Equipment Assistants: Nolan Castex, Eddie Falgout
Head Athletic Trainer: Scottie B. Patton
Assistant Athletic Trainers: Duane Brooks, Kevin Mangum
Training Assistant: Reggie Stone
Video Director: Dave Desposito
Director of Player Development: Ricky Porter
Defensive Assistant/Special Projects: Joe Alley
Director of Media & Public Relations: Greg Bensel
Assistant Director of Media & Public Relations: Ricky Zeller
Media & Public Relations Manager: Justin Macione
Media & Public Relations Assistant: Nicholas Karl
Director of Security: Geoff Santini
Director of Photography: Michael C. Hebert
Director of Community Affairs/Director of Business Public Relations: Paul Corliss
Senior Director of Marketing & Business Development: Conrad Kowal
Director of Ticket Sales & Operation Services: Michael Stanfield
Director of New Media: Chris Pika
Director of Information Technologies: Jeff Huffman
Facilities Manager: Terry Ashburn

COACHING HISTORY
(227-336-5)

1967-70	Tom Fears*	13-34-2
1970-72	J.D. Roberts	7-25-3
1973-75	John North**	11-23-0
1975	Ernie Hefferle	1-7-0
1976-77	Hank Stram	7-21-0
1978-80	Dick Nolan***	15-29-0
1980	Dick Stanfel	1-3-0
1981-85	O.A. (Bum) Phillips****	27-42-0
1985	Wade Phillips	1-3-0
1986-96	Jim Mora#	93-78-0
1996	Rick Venturi	1-7-0
1997-99	Mike Ditka	15-33-0
2000-03	Jim Haslett	35-31-0

*Released after seven games in 1970
**Released after six games in 1975
***Released after 12 games in 1980
****Resigned after 12 games in 1985
#Resigned after eight games in 1996

ATTENDANCE

Home 529,856 Away 528,418
Total 1,058,178
Single-game home record, 70,940 (9/2/79)
Single-season home record, 548,728 (1992)

2004 DRAFT CHOICES

Round	Name	Pos.	College
1	Will Smith	DE	Ohio State
2	Devery Henderson	WR	Louisiana State
	Courtney Watson	LB	Notre Dame
5	Rodney Leisle	DT	UCLA
	Mike Karney	FB	Arizona State
7	Colby Bockwoldt	LB	Brigham Young

NEW ORLEANS SAINTS

2003 TEAM RECORD

PRESEASON (1-3)

Date	Result	Opponent
8/11	L 17-27	Philadelphia
8/16	W 22-17	at N.Y. Jets
8/23	L 12-27	at San Francisco
8/28	L 10-24	Miami

REGULAR SEASON (8-8)

Date	Result	Opponent	Att.
9/7	L 10-27	at Seattle	52,250
9/14	W 31-10	Houston	68,390
9/21	L 12-27	at Tennessee	68,809
9/28	L 21-55	Indianapolis	70,020
10/5	L 13-19	at Carolina	72,496
10/12	W 20-13	Chicago	68,390
10/19	W 45-17	at Atlanta	70,837
10/26	L 20-23	Carolina (OT)	68,370
11/2	W 17-14	at Tampa Bay	65,524
11/16	W 23-20	Atlanta (OT)	68,432
11/23	L 20-33	at Philadelphia	67,802
11/30	W 24-20	at Washington	76,821
12/7	L 7-14	Tampa Bay	68,442
12/14	W 45-7	New York Giants	68,399
12/21	L 19-20	at Jacksonville	49,207
12/28	L 13-7	Dallas	68,451

(OT) Overtime

SCORE BY PERIODS

Saints	52	112	78	95	3 —	340
Opponents	64	140	55	64	3 —	326

2003 TEAM STATISTICS

	Saints	Opp.
Total First Downs	302	298
Rushing	100	109
Passing	177	165
Penalty	25	24
3rd Down: Made/Att	106/229	79/208
3rd Down Pct.	46.3	38.0
4th Down: Made/Att	5/19	9/16
4th Down Pct.	26.3	56.3
Possession Avg.	30:18	29:42
Total Net Yards	5,438	5,234
Avg. Per Game	339.9	327.1
Total Plays	1,019	997
Avg. Per Play	5.3	5.2
Net Yards Rushing	2,000	2,241
Avg. Per Game	125.0	140.1
Total Rushes	448	480
Net Yards Passing	3,438	2,993
Avg. Per Game	214.9	187.1
Sacked/Yards Lost	36/203	32/171
Gross Yards	3,641	3,164
Att./Completions	535/314	485/264
Completion Pct.	58.7	54.4
Had Intercepted	8	14
Punts/Average	72/43.7	76/41.9
Net Punting Avg.	72/38.2	76/36.4
Penalties/Yards	103/878	101/1,012
Fumbles/Ball Lost	33/20	29/13
Touchdowns	39	36
Rushing	11	12
Passing	25	20
Returns	3	4

2003 INDIVIDUAL STATISTICS

PASSING	Att.	Comp.	Yds.	Pct.	TD	Int.	Tkld.	Rate
Brooks	518	306	3,546	59.1	24	8	34/195	88.8
Bouman	13	7	81	53.8	1	0	2/8	98.6
McAllister	2	0	0	0.0	0	0	0/0	39.6
Berger	1	0	0	0.0	0	0	0/0	39.6
Horn	1	1	14	100.0	0	0	0/0	118.8
Saints	535	314	3,641	58.7	25	8	36/203	88.7
Opponents	485	264	3,164	54.4	20	14	32/171	76.3

SCORING	TD R	TD P	TD Rt	PAT	FG	Saf	PTS
Carney	0	0	0	36/37	22/30	0	102
Horn	0	10	0	0/0	0/0	0	60
McAllister	8	0	0	0/0	0/0	0	48
B. Williams	0	5	0	0/0	0/0	0	30
Pathon	0	4	0	0/0	0/0	0	24
Stallworth	0	3	0	0/0	0/0	0	18
Brooks	2	0	0	0/0	0/0	0	12
Conwell	0	2	0	0/0	0/0	0	12
Ambrose	0	0	1	0/0	0/0	0	6
K. Carter	1	0	0	0/0	0/0	0	6
M. Lewis	0	1	0	0/0	0/0	0	6
Rodgers	0	0	1	0/0	0/0	0	6
Thomas	0	0	1	0/0	0/0	0	6
J. Allen	0	0	0	0/0	0/0	1	2
Fenderson	0	0	0	0/0	0/0	0	2
Saints	11	25	3	36/37	22/30	1	340
Opponents	12	20	4	35/35	25/31	0	326

2-Pt. Conversions: Fenderson.
Saints 1-2, Opponents 0-1.

RUSHING	No.	Yds	Avg	LG	TD
McAllister	351	1,641	4.7	76t	8
Brooks	54	175	3.2	15	2
K. Carter	19	72	3.8	31	1
L. Smith	11	61	5.5	17	0
Horn	2	15	7.5	13	0
Fenderson	4	14	3.5	6	0
McAfee	1	13	13.0	13	0
Carney	1	3	3.0	3	0
Stallworth	1	3	3.0	3	0
M. Lewis	1	2	2.0	2	0
Bouman	3	1	0.3	2	0
Saints	448	2,000	4.5	76t	11
Opponents	480	2,241	4.7	69t	12

RECEIVING	No.	Yds	Avg	LG	TD
Horn	78	973	12.5	50t	10
McAllister	69	516	7.5	39	0
Pathon	44	578	13.1	40	4
B. Williams	41	436	10.6	31t	5
Conwell	26	290	11.2	32	2
Stallworth	25	485	19.4	76t	3
M. Lewis	12	226	18.8	39	1
Rasby	6	55	9.2	17	0
T. Smith	6	28	4.7	8	0
Gardner	3	29	9.7	11	0
K. Carter	1	11	11.0	11	0
D. Lewis	1	7	7.0	7	0
Fenderson	1	5	5.0	5	0
L. Smith	1	2	2.0	2	0
Saints	314	3,641	11.6	76t	25
Opponents	264	3,164	12.0	79t	20

INTERCEPTIONS	No.	Yds	Avg	LG	TD
Thomas	4	47	11.8	20	0
Ambrose	3	78	26.0	73t	1
Bellamy	3	19	6.3	10	0
Rodgers	1	40	40.0	40t	1
D. Smith	1	9	9.0	9	0
Ruff	1	7	7.0	7	0
Jones	1	2	2.0	2	0
V. Green	0	24	—	24	0
Saints	14	226	16.1	73t	2
Opponents	8	104	13.0	20	1

PUNTING	No.	Yds.	Avg.	In 20	LG
Berger	71	3,144	44.3	28	59
Saints	72	3,144	43.7	28	59
Opponents	76	3,183	41.9	21	60

PUNT RETURNS	Ret	FC	Yds	Avg	LG	TD
M. Lewis	30	10	275	9.2	27	0
Stallworth	5	1	44	8.8	18	0
Craver	2	1	22	11.0	19	0
V. Green	2	0	15	7.5	9	0
Thomas	1	0	4	4.0	4	0
Saints	40	12	360	9.0	27	0
Opponents	36	18	294	8.2	46	0

KICKOFF RETURNS	No.	Yds	Avg	LG	TD
M. Lewis	45	1,068	23.7	53	0
McAfee	9	140	15.6	23	0
Stallworth	8	171	21.4	28	0
Craver	5	128	25.6	52	0
Rasby	2	9	4.5	6	0
M. Williams	2	0	0.0	0	0
J. Allen	1	8	8.0	8	0
Saints	72	1,524	21.2	53	0
Opponents	67	1,587	23.7	100t	2

FIELD GOALS	1-19	20-29	30-39	40-49	50+
Carney	0/0	6/6	10/12	5/9	1/3
Saints	0/0	6/6	10/12	5/9	1/3
Opponents	0/0	8/9	8/10	9/11	0/1

SACKS	No.
Ch. Grant	10.0
Whitehead	5.5
Howard	5.0
Jackson	3.5
Bellamy	1.0
D. Carter	1.0
Hodge	1.0
D. Smith	1.0
K. Smith	1.0
Sullivan	1.0
Thomas	1.0
Saints	32.0
Opponents	36.0

RECORD HOLDERS

INDIVIDUAL RECORDS—CAREER

Category	Name	Performance
Rushing (Yds.)	George Rogers, 1981-84	4,267
Passing (Yds.)	Archie Manning, 1971-1982	21,734
Passing (TDs)	Archie Manning, 1971-1982	115
Receiving (No.)	Eric Martin, 1985-1993	532
Receiving (Yds.)	Eric Martin, 1985-1993	7,854
Interceptions	Dave Waymer, 1980-89	37
Punting (Avg.)	Mark Royals, 1997-98	45.7
Punt Return (Avg.)	Mel Gray, 1986-88	13.4
Kickoff Return (Avg.)	Walter Roberts, 1967	26.3
Field Goals	Morten Andersen, 1982-1994	302
Touchdowns (Tot.)	Dalton Hilliard, 1986-1993	53
Points	Morten Andersen, 1982-1994	1,318

INDIVIDUAL RECORDS—SINGLE SEASON

Category	Name	Performance
Rushing (Yds.)	George Rogers, 1981	1,674
Passing (Yds.)	Jim Everett, 1995	3,970
Passing (TDs)	Aaron Brooks, 2002	27
Receiving (No.)	Joe Horn, 2000	94
Receiving (Yds.)	Joe Horn, 2000	1,340
Interceptions	Dave Whitsell, 1967	10
Punting (Avg.)	Mark Royals, 1997	45.9
Punt Return (Avg.)	Mel Gray, 1987	14.7
Kickoff Return (Avg.)	Don Shy, 1969	27.9
	Mel Gray, 1986	27.9
Field Goals	Morten Andersen, 1985	31
	John Carney, 2002	31
Touchdowns (Tot.)	Dalton Hilliard, 1989	18
Points	John Carney, 2002	130

INDIVIDUAL RECORDS—SINGLE GAME

Category	Name	Performance
Rushing (Yds.)	George Rogers, 9-4-83	206
Passing (Yds.)	Aaron Brooks, 12-3-00	441
Passing (TDs)	Billy Kilmer, 11-2-69	6
Receiving (No.)	Tony Galbreath, 9-10-78	14
Receiving (Yds.)	Wes Chandler, 9-2-79	205
Interceptions	Tommy Myers, 9-3-78	3
	Dave Waymer, 10-6-85	3
	Reggie Sutton, 10-18-87	3
	Gene Atkins, 12-22-91	3
	Sammy Knight, 9-9-01	3
Field Goals	Many times	5
	Last time by John Carney, 10-28-01	
Touchdowns (Tot.)	Joe Horn, 12-14-03	4
Points	Joe Horn, 12-14-03	24

NEW ORLEANS SAINTS

2004 VETERAN ROSTER

No.	Name	Pos.	Ht.	Wt.	Birthdate	NFL Exp.	College	Hometown	How Acq.	'03 Games/ Starts
50	Allen, James	LB	6-2	240	11/11/79	3	Oregon State	Portland, Ore.	D3-'02	15/1
99	Allen, Kenderick	DT	6-6	318	9/14/78	2	Louisiana State	Bogalusa, La.	FA-'03	10/1
33	Ambrose, Ashley	CB	5-11	190	9/17/70	13	Mississippi Valley State	New Orleans, La.	FA-'03	16/12
31	Banks, Tavian	RB	5-10	208	2/17/74	3	Iowa	Bettendorf, Iowa.	FA-'04	0*
20	Bellamy, Jay	S	5-11	200	7/8/72	11	Rutgers	Aberdeen, N.J.	UFA(Sea)-'01	16/16
65	Bentley, LeCharles	G-C	6-2	299	11/7/79	3	Ohio State	Cleveland, Ohio	D2-'02	13/13
17	Berger, Mitch	P	6-4	220	6/24/72	10	Colorado	Karnloops, B.C., Canada	UFA(StL)-'03	16/0
16	Black, Nathan	WR	6-0	190	6/20/78	2	Northwestern State	Baton Rouge, La.	FA-'04	0*
4	Bouman, Todd	QB	6-2	229	8/1/72	7	St. Cloud State	Ruthton, Minn.	T(Minn)-'03	4/0
2	Brooks, Aaron	QB	6-4	205	3/24/76	6	Virginia	Newport News, Va.	T(GB)-'00	16/16
41	Brooks, Ahmad	CB	5-8	180	2/13/80	2	Texas	Abilene, Texas	FA-'04	0*
35	Brown, Fakhir	CB	5-11	192	9/21/77	5	Grambling State	Mansfield, La.	FA-'02	16/0
92	Bryant, Tony	DE	6-6	275	9/3/76	5	Florida State	Marathon, Fla.	FA-'03	0*
3	Carney, John	K	5-11	180	4/20/64	15	Notre Dame	West Palm Beach, Fla.	UFA(SD)-'01	16/0
85	Conwell, Ernie	TE	6-2	265	8/17/72	9	Washington	Kent, Wash.	UFA(StL)-'03	10/10
21 t-	Craft, Jason	CB	5-10	179	2/13/76	6	Colorado State	Denver, Colo.	T(Jax)-'04	7/6*
29	Craver, Keyuo	CB	5-10	195	8/22/80	3	Nebraska	Harleton, Texas	D4-'02	12/0
86	Crowell, Germane	WR	6-3	222	9/13/76	6	Virginia	Winston-Salem, N.C.	FA-'04	0*
77	Draper, Shawn	G-T	6-3	275	4/5/79	2	Alabama	Huntsville, Ala.	FA-'04	0*
71	Folau, Spencer	T	6-5	315	4/5/73	8	Idaho	Redwood City, Calif.	UFA(Mia)-'02	14/1
62	Fontenot, Jerry	C	6-3	300	11/21/66	16	Texas A&M	Lafayette, La.	UFA(Chi)-'97	16/16
72	Gandy, Wayne	T	6-4	308	2/10/71	11	Auburn	Haines City, Fla.	UFA(Pitt)-'03	16/16
88	Gardner, Talman	WR	6-1	205	3/10/80	2	Florida State	New Orleans, La.	D7-03	10/1
23	Gash, Sam	FB	6-0	242	3/7/69	13	Penn State	Hendersonville, N.C.	UFA(Buff)-'04	16/10*
37	Gleason, Steve	S	5-11	215	3/19/77	4	Washington State	Gonzaga, Calif.	FA-'01	16/0
94	Grant, Charles	DE	6-3	282	9/3/78	3	Georgia	Colquitt, Ga.	D1b-'02	16/16
58	Grant, Cie	LB	6-0	228	11/27/79	2	Ohio State	New Philadelphia, Ohio	D3-'03	7/0
95	Green, Howard	DT	6-2	331	1/12/79	2	Louisiana State	Donaldsonville, La.	FA-'03	4/0
28	Harper, Deveron	S	5-11	187	11/15/77	4	Notre Dame	Orangeburg, S.C.	FA-'03	14/0
81	Hilton, Zachary	TE	6-8	262	7/2/80	2	North Carolina	Silver Springs, Md.	FA-'03	3/0
52	Hodge, Sedrick	LB	6-4	244	9/13/78	4	North Carolina	Atlanta, Ga.	D3a-'01	9/9
61	Holland, Montrae	G	6-2	333	5/21/80	2	Florida State	Ore City, Texas	D4-'03	16/7
87	Horn, Joe	WR	6-1	206	1/16/72	9	Itawamba (Miss.) J.C.	Fayetteville, N.C.	UFA(KC)-'00	15/14
47	Houser, Kevin	LS	6-2	250	8/23/77	5	Ohio State	Westlake, Ohio	D7-'00	16/0
93	Howard, Darren	DE	6-3	281	11/19/76	5	Kansas State	St. Petersburg, Fla.	D2-'00	8/8
64	Jacox, Kendyl	C-G	6-2	330	6/10/75	7	Kansas State	Dallas, Texas	UFA(SD)-'02	12/11
38	Jenkins, Ronney	RB	5-11	190	5/25/77	5	Northern Arizona	Los Angeles, Calif.	FA-'04	7/0*
34	Jones, Tebucky	S	6-2	218	10/6/74	7	Syracuse	New Britain, Conn.	T(NE)-'03	15/15
53	Knight, Roger	LB	6-0	245	10/11/78	3	Wisconsin	Brooklyn, N.Y.	FA-'01	16/2
89	Lewis, Derrick	WR	6-2	185	10/30/75	2	San Diego State	New Orleans, La.	FA-'02	3/0
84	Lewis, Michael	WR	5-8	165	11/14/71	4	No College	New Orleans, La.	FA-'01	13/1
26	McAllister, Deuce	RB	6-1	221	12/27/78	4	Mississippi	Lena, Miss	D1-'01	16/16
40	Mitchell, Mel	S	6-1	220	2/10/79	3	Western Kentucky	Rockledge, Fla	D5-'02	0*
67	Nesbit, Jamar	G	6-4	329	12/17/76	6	South Carolina	Summersville, S.C.	UFA(Jax)-'04	16/2*
14	O'Sullivan, J.T.	QB	6-2	220	8/25/79	3	Cal-Davis	Carmichael, Calif.	D6a-'02	0*
80	Pathon, Jerome	WR	6-0	182	12/16/75	7	Washington	North Vancouver, B.C., Canada	UFA(Ind)-'02	16/12
68	Riley, Victor	T	6-5	328	11/4/74	7	Auburn	Swansea, S.C.	UFA(KC)-'02	16/16
59	Rodgers, Derrick	LB	6-0	230	10/14/71	8	Arizona State	New Orleans, La.	T(Mia)-'03	15/15
56	Ruff, Orlando	LB	6-3	250	9/28/76	6	Furman	Winnsboro, S.C.	UFA(SD)-'03	16/10
54	Smith, Darrin	LB	6-1	236	4/15/70	12	Miami	Miami, Fla.	FA-'00	14/10
90	Smith, Kenny	DT-DE	6-4	295	9/8/77	4	Alabama	Meridian, Miss.	D3b-'01	15/9
36	Smith, Lamar	RB	5-11	230	11/29/70	11	Houston	Fort Wayne, Ind.	FA-'03	4/0
83	Stallworth, Donte'	WR	6-0	197	11/10/80	3	Tennessee	Sacramento, Calif.	D1a-'02	11/3
27	Stecker, Aaron	RB	5-10	205	11/13/75	5	Western Illinois	Green Bay, Wis.	UFA(TB)-'04	16/1*
78	Stinchcomb, Jon	T	6-5	302	8/27/79	2	Georgia	Lilburn, Ga.	D2-'03	6/0
97	Sullivan, Johnathan	DT	6-3	313	1/21/81	2	Georgia	Griffin, Ga.	D1-'03	14/13
22	Thomas, Fred	CB	5-9	184	9/11/73	9	Tennessee-Martin	Bruce, Miss.	UFA(Sea)-'00	16/14
98	Whitehead, Willie	DE	6-3	285	1/26/73	6	Auburn	Tuskegee, Ala.	FA-'99	11/10
82	Williams, Boo	TE	6-4	245	6/22/79	4	Arkansas	Tallahassee, Fla.	FA-'01	16/6
96	Williams, Melvin	DE	6-2	269	2/2/79	2	Kansas State	St. Louis, Mo.	D5-'03	14/2
66	Young, Brian	DT	6-2	290	7/8/77	5	Texas-El Paso	El Paso, Texas	UFA(StL)-'04	16/12*

* Banks last active with Jacksonville in '99; Black last active with Carolina in '02; Ahmad Brooks last active with Buffalo in '02; Bryant inactive for 1 game; Craft played 7 games with Jacksonville; Crowell last active with Detroit in '02; Draper did not play 1 game with Carolina in '02; Gash played 16 games with Buffalo; Jenkins played 7 games with Oakland; Mitchell missed '03 season because of injury; Nesbit played 16 games with Jacksonville; O'Sullivan inactive for 16 games; Stecker played 16 games with Tampa Bay; Young played 16 games with St. Louis.

t- Saints traded for Craft (Jax).

Players lost to free agency (2): TE Walter Rasby (Wash; 16 games in '03); FB Terrell Smith (Cle; 15).

Also played with Saints in '03—LB Travis Carroll (1 game), CB Dale Carter (8), RB Ki-Jana Carter (8), RB James Fenderson (9), DT Henry Ford (4), S Victor Green (13), DT Grady Jackson (7), RB Fred McAfee (14), TE David Sloan (4).

2004 FIRST-YEAR ROSTER

Name	Pos.	Ht.	Wt.	Birthdate	College	Hometown	How Acq.
Acker, Kyle	TE	6-3	255	8/28/82	Salisbury State	Annapolis, Md.	FA
Archibald, Ben (1)	T	6-3	317	8/26/78	Brigham Young	Tacoma, Wash.	FA
Bockwoldt, Colby	LB	6-1	230	4/14/81	Brigham Young	Sunset, Utah	D7
Booker, Fred (1)	CB	5-9	185	6/4/78	Louisiana State	Independence, La.	FA
Cook, Kerwin (1)	WR	6-1	185	12/21/79	Tulane	Ferriday, La.	FA
Curley, Danny (1)	TE	6-4	250	9/25/78	Eastern Washington	Tacoma, Wash.	FA
Frederick, Spencer (1)	TE	6-2	250	4/28/79	Montana	Skobey, Mont.	FA-'03
Hafford, Brent	S	6-0	185	9/20/81	Stephen F. Austin	Jasper, Texas	FA
Henderson, Devery	WR	5-11	191	3/26/82	Louisiana State	Opelousas, La.	D2a
Hoffmann, Augie	G	6-2	307	2/23/81	Boston College	Park Ridge, N.J.	FA
Karney, Mike	FB	5-11	254	7/6/81	Arizona State	Kent, Wash.	D5b
Leisle, Rodney	DT	6-3	309	2/5/81	UCLA	Bakersfield, Calif.	D5a
Mariscal, Mark (1)	P	6-2	200	9/10/79	Colorado	Tallahassee, Fla.	FA
McDonald, LaMarcus (1)	LB	6-1	228	2/25/81	Texas Christian	Waco, Texas	FA
McGeoghan, Phil (1)	WR	6-2	224	7/8/79	Maine	Feeding Hills, Mass.	FA-'03
McKelvy, Chris	G	6-4	327	7/7/81	Penn State	Lansdale, Pa.	FA
Schurman, Nate	FB	6-2	247	11/8/81	Southwest Missouri State	St. Joseph, Mo.	FA
Setterstrom, Chad (1)	G	6-3	309	6/13/80	Northern Iowa	Northfield, Minn.	FA-'03
Smith, Will	DE	6-3	267	8/4/81	Ohio State	Utica, N.Y.	D1
Sorahan, Ryan	QB	6-4	240	1/8/81	Arkansas	Los Gatos, Calif.	FA
Tucker, Maurice (1)	CB	5-11	185	11/10/79	South Florida	Bartow, Fla.	FA
Vance, Chris	WR	6-0	189	9/13/80	Ohio State	Fort Myers, Fla.	FA
Wagner, Terence (1)	C	6-2	290	5/26/79	Sacramento State	Carmichael, Calif.	FA
Watson, Courtney	LB	6-1	238	9/18/80	Notre Dame	Sarasota, Fla.	D2b

The term NFL Rookie is defined as a player who is in his first season of professional football and has not been on the roster of another professional football team for any regular-season or postseason games. A Rookie is designated by an "R" on NFL rosters. Players who have been active in another professional football league or players who have NFL experience, including either preseason training camp or being on an Active List or Inactive List, or on Reserve/Injured or Reserve/Physically Unable to Perform for fewer than six regular-season games, are termed NFL First-Year Players. An NFL First-Year Player is designated by a "1" on NFL rosters. Thereafter, a player is credited with an additional year of experience for each season in which he accumulates six games on the Active List or Inactive List, or on Reserve/Injured or Reserve/Physically Unable to Perform.

Log on to www.neworleanssaints.com for an up-to-date roster.

NEW ORLEANS SAINTS

COACHING STAFF

Head Coach,
Jim Haslett

Pro Career: Named the thirteenth head coach in Saints history on February 3, 2000. Owns second-best winning percentage (.530) in club history and in 2000 earned NFL coach of the year honors, won a division title, and led Saints to their first-ever playoff victory. Joined the Saints after three-year stint as defensive coordinator of the Pittsburgh Steelers (1997-99). Previously coached with the Saints (1995-96), Los Angeles Raiders (1993-94), and NFL Europe's Sacramento Surge (1991-92). Career record: 35-31.

Background: Three-time defensive end All-America at Indiana University (Penn.) from 1975-78, and was inducted into College Football Hall of Fame in 2001. Second-round pick of the Buffalo Bills and was voted as *Associated Press* defensive rookie of the year (1979) and as an All-Pro in 1981. Played nine NFL seasons (Buffalo 1979-1986, N.Y. Jets 1987). Began his coaching career at the University of Buffalo (1988-1990).

Personal: Born December 9, 1955 in Pittsburgh. He and his wife Beth, have three children—Kelsey, Elizabeth, and Chase.

ASSISTANT COACHES

Dave Atkins, running backs; born May 18, 1949, Victoria, Texas. Running back Texas-El Paso 1970-72. Pro running back San Francisco 49ers 1973, Honolulu Hawaiians (WFL) 1974, San Diego Chargers 1975. College coach: Texas El-Paso 1979-1980, San Diego State 1981-85. Pro coach: Philadelphia Eagles 1986-1992, New England Patriots 1993, Arizona Cardinals 1994-95, New Orleans Saints 1996, Minnesota Vikings 1997-99, rejoined Saints in 2000.

Joe Baker, secondary; born June 29, 1969, Glen Ridge, N.J. Wide receiver Princeton 1987-1990. No pro playing experience. College coach: East Stroudsburg 1991, Samford 1993, Wisconsin 1999. Pro coach: Birmingham Fire (WFL) 1992, Jacksonville Jaguars 1994-98, joined Saints in 2000.

Chip Beake, offensive assistant/quality control; born May 27, 1969, Kansas City, Mo. Quarterback South Carolina 1990-1992. No pro playing experience. College coach: Kentucky 1993-94, MacPherson College (Kan.) 1998, Colorado School of Mines 1999. Pro coach: Barcelona Dragons (NFLE) 1995-2000, joined Saints in 2000.

Greg Brown, secondary-cornerbacks; born October 10, 1957, Denver. Defensive back Glendale (Ariz.) C.C. 1976-77, Texas-El Paso 1978-79. No pro playing experience. College coach: Wyoming 1987-88, Purdue 1989-1990, Colorado 1991-93. Pro coach: Tampa Bay Buccaneers 1984-86, Atlanta Falcons 1994, San Diego Chargers 1995-96, Tennessee Oilers 1997-98, San Francisco 49ers 1999, Atlanta Falcons 2000-01, joined Saints in 2002.

Al Everest, special teams coordinator; born August 22, 1950, Santa Barbara, Calif. Safety Southern Methodist 1970-71. No pro playing experience. College coach: Southern Methodist 1972, North Texas State 1973-74, Cameron (Okla.) 1974-75, U.S. International 1981-87. Pro coach: Arkansas Miners (PSFL) 1991-92, Birmingham Barracudas (CFL) 1995, Arizona Cardinals 1996-99, joined Saints in 2000.

Rock Gullickson, strength and conditioning; born April 11, 1955, Moorhead, Minn. Guard Moorhead (Minn.) State 1973-76. College coach: Moorhead State 1978, Mayville (N.D.) State 1979-1980, South Dakota State 1981, Montana State 1982-89, Rutgers 1990-92, Texas 1993-97, Louisville 1998-99. Pro coach: Joined Saints in 2000.

John (Jack) Henry, offensive line; born March 14, 1946, Wilmerding, Pa. Linebacker Penn State 1964-65, guard Indiana (Penn.) 1967-68. No pro playing experience. College coach: West Virginia 1970, 1978-79, Edinboro 1973, Louisville 1974, Millersville 1975-76, Southern Illinois 1977, Appalachian State 1980, Wake Forest 1981-85, Indiana (Penn.) 1986-89, Pittsburgh 1993-95. Pro coach: Pittsburgh Steelers 1990-91, San Diego Chargers 1996, Detroit Lions 1997-99, joined Saints in 2000.

Ty Knott, defensive assistant/quality control; born December 9, 1965, Los Angeles, Defensive back Oregon Tech 1988-89. No pro playing experience. College coach: Whittier College 1994-95, Indiana University (Pa.) 1997-99, Mt. San Antonio (Calif.) J.C. 2000, Greenville 2001. Pro coach: Jacksonville Jaguars 2002, joined Saints in 2003.

Danny Langsdorf, asst. special teams-asst. wide receivers; born June 28, 1972, Fargo, N.D. Quarterback Boise State 1991-93, Linfield College 1994-95. No pro playing experience. College coach: Cal Lutheran 1996, Oregon State 1997-98. Pro coach: Edmonton Eskimos (CFL) 1999-2001, joined Saints in 2002.

Ben McAdoo, offensive administrative assistant-quality control; born July 7, 1977, Homer City, Pa.. Attended Indiana University (Penn.). No college or pro playing experience. College coach: Michigan State 2001-02, Fairfield 2002, Akron 2003, Pittsburgh 2003. Pro coach: Joined Saints in 2004.

Mike McCarthy, offensive coordinator; born November 10, 1963, Pittsburgh. Tight end Baker 1985-86. No pro playing experience. College coach: Fort Hays State 1987-88, Pittsburgh 1989-1992. Pro coach: Kansas City Chiefs 1993-98, Green Bay Packers 1999, joined Saints in 2000.

Winston Moss, linebackers; born December 24, 1965, Miami. Linebacker Miami 1983-86. Pro linebacker Tampa Bay Buccaneers 1987-1990, Los Angeles Raiders 1991-94, Seattle Seahawks 1995-97. Pro coach: Seattle Seahawks 1998, joined Saints in 2000.

Bob Palcic, tight ends; born July 2, 1948, Gownada, N.Y. Linebacker Dayton 1968-1970. No pro playing experience. College coach: Dayton 1974-75, Ball State 1976-77, Wisconsin 1978-1981, Arizona 1984-85, Ohio State 1986-1991, Southern California 1992, UCLA 1993. Pro coach: Atlanta Falcons 1994-96, Detroit Lions 1997-98, Cleveland Browns 1999, joined Saints in 2000.

John Pease, defensive line; born October 14, 1943, Pittsburgh. Wingback Utah 1963-64. No pro playing experience. College coach: Fullerton (Calif.) J.C. 1970-73, Long Beach State 1974-76, Utah 1977, Washington 1978-1983. Pro coach: Philadelphia/Baltimore Stars (USFL) 1983-85, New Orleans Saints 1986-94, Jacksonville Jaguars 1995-2002, re-joined Saints in 2004.

Jimmy Robinson, wide receivers; born January 3, 1953, Atlanta. Wide receiver Georgia Tech 1972-74. Pro wide receiver Atlanta Falcons, 1975, New York Giants 1976-79, San Francisco 49ers 1980, Denver Broncos 1981. College coach: Georgia Tech 1986-89. Pro coach: Memphis Showboats (USFL) 1984-85, Atlanta Falcons 1990-93, Indianapolis Colts 1994-97, New York Giants 1998-2003, joined Saints in 2004.

Mike Sheppard, quarterbacks; born October 29, 1951, Tulsa, Okla. Wide receiver Cal Lutheran 1969-1972. No pro playing experience. College coach: Cal Lutheran 1974-76, Brigham Young 1977-78, U.S. International 1979, Idaho State 1980-81, Long Beach State 1982, 1984-86, Kansas 1983, New Mexico 1987-1991, California 1992. Pro coach: Cleveland Browns 1993-95, Baltimore Ravens 1996, San Diego Chargers 1997-98, Seattle Seahawks 1999-2000, Buffalo Bills 2001, joined Saints in 2002.

Mark Smith, asst. strength and conditioning; born October 16, 1964, Kannapolis, N.C. Linebacker North Carolina State 1983-87. No pro playing experience. College coach: North Carolina State 1993-97, Florida 1998-2001, Kansas 2002. Pro coach: Washington Redskins 2003, joined Saints in 2004.

Rick Venturi, defensive coordinator; born February 23, 1946, Taylorville, Ill. Quarterback-defensive back Northwestern 1965-67. No pro playing experience. College coach: Northwestern 1968-1972, 1978-1980 (head coach), Purdue 1973-76, Illinois 1977. Pro coach: Hamilton Tiger-Cats (CFL) 1981, Indianapolis Colts 1982-1993 (interim head coach for final 11 games of 1991), Cleveland Browns 1994-95, joined Saints in 1996 (interim head coach for final eight games of 1996).

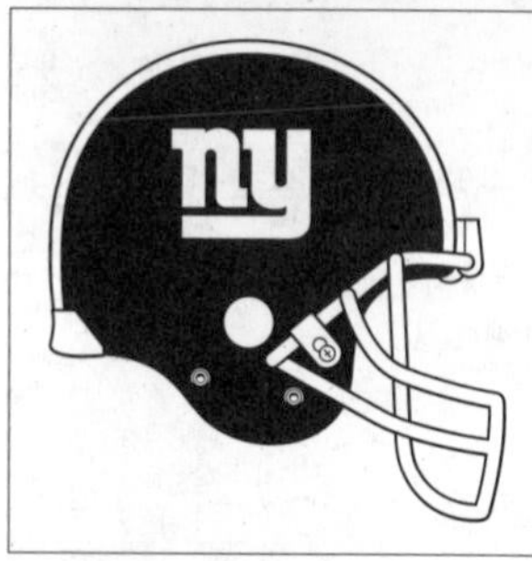

National Football Conference
East Division
Team Colors: Blue, Red, and White
Giants Stadium
East Rutherford, New Jersey 07073
Telephone: (201) 935-8111

2004 SCHEDULE

PRESEASON		**New York time**
Aug. 13	**Kansas City**	8:00
Aug. 19	at Carolina	8:00
Aug. 27	at New York Jets	7:00
Sept. 2	**Baltimore**	7:00

REGULAR SEASON

Sept. 12	at Philadelphia	4:15
Sept. 19	**Washington**	1:00
Sept. 26	**Cleveland**	1:00
Oct. 3	at Green Bay	1:00
Oct. 10	at Dallas	1:00
Oct. 17	Open Date	
Oct. 24	**Detroit**	1:00
Oct. 31	at Minnesota	1:00
Nov. 7	**Chicago**	4:05
Nov. 14	at Arizona	4:15
Nov. 21	**Atlanta**	4:15
Nov. 28	**Philadelphia**	1:00
Dec. 5	at Washington	4:15
Dec. 12	at Baltimore	1:00
Dec. 18	**Pittsburgh** (Sat.)	1:30
Dec. 26	at Cincinnati	1:00
Jan. 2	**Dallas**	8:30

Stadium: Giants Stadium (opened in 1976) • **Capacity:** 80,242 East Rutherford, New Jersey 07073
Playing Surface: FieldTurf
Training Camp: University at Albany
1400 Washington Avenue
Albany, New York 12222

GIANTS STADIUM

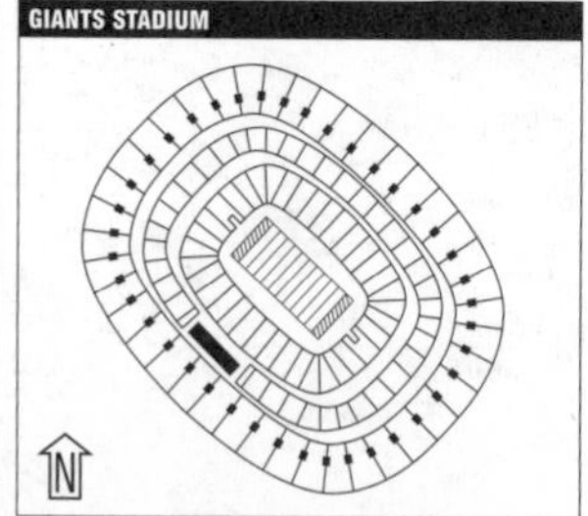

CLUB OFFICIALS

President/Co-CEO: Wellington T. Mara
Chairman/Co-CEO: Preston Robert Tisch
Executive Vice President and Chief Operating Officer/General Counsel: John K. Mara, Esq.
Treasurer: Jonathan Tisch
Senior Vice President-General Manager: Ernie Accorsi
Vice President-Player Evalutions: Chris Mara
Vice President-Chief Financial Officer: Christine Procops
Vice President-Marketing: Rusty Hawley
Vice President of Medical Services: Ronnie Barnes
Vice-President-Communications: Pat Hanlon
Assistant General Manager: Kevin Abrams
Director of Player Personnel: Jerry Reese
Director of Pro Player Personnel: David Gettleman
Assistant Director of Pro Player Personnel: Ken Sternfeld
Director of College Scouting: Jerry Shay
Director of Research and Development: Raymond J. Walsh, Jr.
Director of Player Development: Charles Way
Director of Marketing Partnerships: Glenn Todd
Pro Personnel Assistants: Geoff Mazza, Tom Polifroni
Director of Promotions: Frank Mara
Ticket Manager: John Gorman
Director of Administration: Jim Phelan
Controller: Steven Hamrahi
Director of Community Relations: Allison Stangeby
Director of Creative Services: Doug Murphy
Director of Public Relations: Peter John-Baptiste
Assistant Director of Communications: Avis Roper
Head Athletic Trainer: Ronnie Barnes
Assistant Athletic Trainers: John Johnson, Steve Kennelly, Byron Hansen
Equipment Manager: Ed Wagner, Jr.
Assistant Equipment Managers: Joseph Skiba, Ed Skiba, Tim Slaman
Video Director: Dave Maltese
Assistant Video Directors: Carmen Pizzano, Ed Triggs
Community Relations/Player Development Coordinator: Lauren Zidel
Community Relations Coordinator: Ethan Medley

COACHING HISTORY
(587-498-33)

1925	Bob Folwell	8-4-0
1926	Joe Alexander	8-4-1
1927-28	Earl Potteiger	15-8-3
1929-1930	LeRoy Andrews*	24-5-1
1930	Benny Friedman-Steve Owen	2-0-0
1931-1953	Steve Owen	153-108-17
1954-1960	Jim Lee Howell	55-29-4
1961-68	Allie Sherman	57-54-4
1969-1973	Alex Webster	29-40-1
1974-76	Bill Arnsparger**	7-28-0
1976-78	John McVay	14-23-0
1979-1982	Ray Perkins	24-35-0
1983-1990	Bill Parcells	85-52-1
1991-92	Ray Handley	14-18-0
1993-96	Dan Reeves	32-34-0
1997-2003	Jim Fassel	60-56-1

*Released after 15 games in 1930
**Released after seven games in 1976

ATTENDANCE

Home 628,962 Away 550,195
Total 1,179,157
Single-game home record, 78,907 (9/15/03)
Single-season home record, 629,213 (2002)

2004 DRAFT CHOICES

Round	Name	Pos.	College
1	Philip Rivers	QB	North Carolina St.
2	Chris Snee	G	Boston College
4	Reggie Torbor	LB	Auburn
5	Gibril Wilson	DB	Tennessee
6	Jamaar Taylor	WR	Texas A&M
7	Drew Strojny	T	Duke
	Isaac Hilton	DE	Hampton

NEW YORK GIANTS

2003 TEAM RECORD

PRESEASON (1-3)

Date	Result		Opponent
8/7	L	6-26	New England
8/15	L	10-20	Carolina
8/23	L	14-15	N.Y. Jets
8/28	W	30-24	at Baltimore

REGULAR SEASON (4-12)

Date	Result		Opponent	Att.
9/7	W	23-13	St. Louis	78,666
9/15	L	32-35	Dallas (OT)	78,907
9/21	W	24-21	at Washington (OT)	84,856
10/5	L	10-23	Miami	78,863
10/12	L	6-17	at New England	68,436
10/19	L	10-14	Philadelphia	78,883
10/26	W	29-17	at Minnesota	64,114
11/2	W	31-28	at N.Y. Jets (OT)	78,132
11/9	L	7-27	Atlanta	78,813
11/16	L	10-28	at Philadelphia	67,867
11/24	L	13-19	at Tampa Bay	65,648
11/30	L	7-24	Buffalo	78,481
12/7	L	7-20	Washington	78,217
12/14	L	7-45	at New Orleans	68,399
12/21	L	3-19	at Dallas	64,118
12/28	L	24-37	Carolina	78,130

(OT) Overtime

SCORE BY PERIODS

Giants	44	83	47	63	6	— 243
Opponents	91	111	98	84	3	— 387

2003 TEAM STATISTICS

	Giants	Opp.
Total First Downs	300	314
Rushing	90	102
Passing	184	178
Penalty	26	34
3rd Down: Made/Att	73/218	85/225
3rd Down Pct.	33.5	37.8
4th Down: Made/Att	2/17	5/11
4th Down Pct.	11.8	45.5
Possession Avg.	28:04	31:56
Total Net Yards	4,942	5,320
Avg. Per Game	308.9	332.5
Total Plays	1,047	1,060
Avg. Per Play	4.7	5.0
Net Yards Rushing	1,559	1,908
Avg. Per Game	97.4	119.3
Total Rushes	387	496
Net Yards Passing	3,383	3,412
Avg. Per Game	211.4	213.3
Sacked/Yards Lost	44/259	45/298
Gross Yards	3,642	3,710
Att./Completions	616/344	519/309
Completion Pct.	55.8	59.5
Had Intercepted	20	10
Punts/Average	91/40.0	82/35.6
Net Punting Avg.	91/33.9	82/32.9
Penalties/Yards	127/1,090	118/983
Fumbles/Ball Lost	35/18	31/12
Touchdowns	26	43
Rushing	6	12
Passing	16	25
Returns	4	6

2003 INDIVIDUAL STATISTICS

PASSING	Att.	Comp.	Yds.	Pct.	TD	Int.	Tkld.	Rate
Collins	500	284	3,110	56.8	13	16	28/164	70.7
Palmer	116	60	532	51.7	3	4	16/95	58.5
Giants	616	344	3,642	55.8	16	20	44/259	68.4
Opponents	519	309	3,710	59.5	25	10	45/298	89.5

SCORING	TD R	TD P	TD Rt	PAT	FG	Saf	PTS
Bryant	0	0	0	17/17	11/14	0	50
Hilliard	0	6	0	0/0	0/0	0	36
Conway	0	0	0	6/6	9/12	0	33
Toomer	0	5	0	0/0	0/0	0	30
Barber	2	1	0	0/0	0/0	0	20
Levens	3	0	0	0/0	0/0	0	18
Shiancoe	0	2	0	0/0	0/0	0	12
Shockey	0	2	0	0/0	0/0	0	12
Brown	0	0	1	0/0	0/0	0	6
Holmes	0	0	1	0/0	0/0	0	6
Mitchell	1	0	0	0/0	0/0	0	6
Walker	0	0	1	0/0	0/0	0	6
Washington	0	0	1	0/0	0/0	0	6
Collins	0	0	0	0/0	0/0	0	2
Feagles	0	0	0	0/0	0/1	0	0
Giants	6	16	4	23/23	20/27	0	243
Opponents	12	25	6	41/42	28/37	1	387

2-Pt. Conversions: Barber, Collins.
Giants 2-3, Opponents 1-1.

RUSHING	No.	Yds	Avg	LG	TD
Barber	278	1,216	4.4	27	2
Levens	68	197	2.9	17	3
Collins	17	49	2.9	22	0
Joyce	11	39	3.5	8	0
Palmer	4	23	5.8	26	0
Mitchell	4	20	5.0	18	1
Hilliard	2	19	9.5	13	0
Toomer	1	5	5.0	5	0
Feagles	1	0	0.0	0	0
Tyree	1	-9	-9.0	-9	0
Giants	387	1,559	4.0	27	6
Opponents	496	1,908	3.8	68t	12

RECEIVING	No.	Yds	Avg	LG	TD
Barber	69	461	6.7	36	1
Toomer	63	1,057	16.8	77t	5
Hilliard	60	608	10.1	38	6
Shockey	48	535	11.1	46	2
Carter	26	309	11.9	30	0
Rivers	17	155	9.1	27	0
Tyree	16	211	13.2	48	0
Finn	14	115	8.2	27	0
Shiancoe	10	56	5.6	10	2
Ponder	7	35	5.0	16	0
Levens	5	39	7.8	11	0
Mitchell	4	38	9.5	11	0
Joyce	3	7	2.3	5	0
Dinkins	2	16	8.0	10	0
Giants	344	3,642	10.6	77t	16
Opponents	309	3,710	12.0	64	25

INTERCEPTIONS	No.	Yds	Avg	LG	TD
Walker	2	74	37.0	56t	1
Brown	2	51	25.5	29t	1
W. Allen	2	23	11.5	22	0
Harris	2	3	1.5	3	0
Stoutmire	1	34	34.0	34	0
Williams	1	14	14.0	14	0
Giants	10	199	19.9	56t	2
Opponents	20	169	8.5	41t	2

PUNTING	No.	Yds.	Avg.	In 20	LG
Feagles	90	3,641	40.5	31	59
Giants	91	3,641	40.0	31	59
Opponents	82	2,922	35.6	25	57

PUNT RETURNS	Ret	FC	Yds	Avg	LG	TD
Mitchell	29	14	154	5.3	15	0
Joyce	2	1	9	4.5	8	0
Stoutmire	1	0	0	0.0	0	0
Giants	32	15	163	5.1	15	0
Opponents	40	20	432	10.8	84t	2

KICKOFF RETURNS	No.	Yds	Avg	LG	TD
Mitchell	55	1,117	20.3	29	0
Joyce	15	309	20.6	36	0
Greisen	2	26	13.0	13	0
Carter	1	9	9.0	9	0
Finn	1	19	19.0	19	0
Rivers	1	12	12.0	12	0
Giants	75	1,492	19.9	36	0
Opponents	56	1,128	20.1	50	0

FIELD GOALS	1-19	20-29	30-39	40-49	50+
Bryant	0/0	3/4	4/5	4/5	0/0
Conway	0/0	3/3	5/6	1/3	0/0
Feagles	0/0	0/1	0/0	0/0	0/0
Giants	0/0	6/8	9/11	5/8	0/0
Opponents	0/0	10/10	7/8	9/12	2/7

SACKS	No.
Strahan	18.5
Holmes	5.5
Jones	3.0
Short	3.0
Barrow	2.0
Legree	2.0
Hamilton	1.5
Williams	1.5
Brown	1.0
Clark	1.0
Griffin	1.0
Joseph	1.0
Stoutmire	1.0
Umenyiora	1.0
Washington	1.0
Giants	45.0
Opponents	44.0

RECORD HOLDERS

INDIVIDUAL RECORDS—CAREER

Category	Name	Performance
Rushing (Yds.)	Rodney Hampton, 1990-97	6,897
Passing (Yds.)	Phil Simms, 1979-1993	33,462
Passing (TDs)	Phil Simms, 1979-1993	199
Receiving (No.)	Joe Morrison, 1959-1972	395
Receiving (Yds.)	Frank Gifford, 1952-1964	5,434
Interceptions	Emlen Tunnell, 1948-1958	74
Punting (Avg.)	Don Chandler, 1956-1964	43.8
Punt Return (Avg.)	Ward Cuff, 1941-45	12.1
Kickoff Return (Avg.)	Rocky Thompson, 1971-73	27.2
Field Goals	Pete Gogolak, 1966-1974	126
Touchdowns (Tot.)	Frank Gifford, 1952-1964	78
Points	Pete Gogolak, 1966-1974	646

INDIVIDUAL RECORDS—SINGLE SEASON

Category	Name	Performance
Rushing (Yds.)	Joe Morris, 1986	1,516
Passing (Yds.)	Kerry Collins, 2002	4,073
Passing (TDs)	Y.A. Tittle, 1963	36
Receiving (No.)	Amani Toomer, 2002	82
Receiving (Yds.)	Amani Toomer, 2002	1,343
Interceptions	Otto Schnellbacher, 1951	11
	Jim Patton, 1958	11
Punting (Avg.)	Don Chandler, 1959	46.6
Punt Return (Avg.)	Merle Hapes, 1942	15.5
Kickoff Return (Avg.)	John Salscheider, 1949	31.6
Field Goals	Ali Haji-Sheikh, 1983	35
Touchdowns (Tot.)	Joe Morris, 1985	21
Points	Ali Haji-Sheikh, 1983	127

INDIVIDUAL RECORDS—SINGLE GAME

Category	Name	Performance
Rushing (Yds.)	Gene Roberts, 11-12-50	218
Passing (Yds.)	Phil Simms, 10-13-85	513
Passing (TDs)	Y.A. Tittle, 10-28-62	*7
Receiving (No.)	Tiki Barber, 1-2-00	13
Receiving (Yds.)	Del Shofner, 10-28-62	269
Interceptions	Many times	3
	Last time by Terry Kinard, 9-20-87	
Field Goals	Joe Danelo, 10-18-81	6
Touchdowns (Tot.)	Ron Johnson, 10-2-72	4
	Earnest Gray, 9-7-80	4
	Rodney Hampton, 9-24-95	4
Points	Ron Johnson, 10-2-72	24
	Earnest Gray, 9-7-80	24
	Rodney Hampton, 9-24-95	24

*NFL Record

NEW YORK GIANTS

2004 VETERAN ROSTER

No.	Name	Pos.	Ht.	Wt.	Birthdate	NFL Exp.	College	Hometown	How Acq.	'03 Games/ Starts
74	Allen, Ian	T	6-4	310	7/22/78	3	Purdue	Atlanta, Ga.	FA-'02	16/11
25	Allen, Will	CB	5-10	196	8/5/78	4	Syracuse	Syracuse, N.Y.	D1-'01	12/12
21	Barber, Tiki	RB	5-10	200	4/7/75	8	Virginia	Roanoke, Va.	D2-'97	16/16
31	Brewer, Jack	S	6-0	194	1/8/79	3	Minnesota	Grapevine, Texas	W(Minn)-'04	6/0*
91	Bromell, Lorenzo	DE	6-6	260	9/23/75	7	Clemson	Georgetown, S.C.	UFA(Oak)-'04	6/4*
8	Bryant, Matt	PK	5-9	200	5/29/75	3	Baylor	Orange, Texas	FA-'02	11/0
84	Carter, Tim	WR	6-0	200	9/21/79	3	Auburn	Lakewood, Fla.	D2-'02	12/2
97	Chase, Martin	DT	6-2	310	12/19/74	7	Oklahoma	Lawton, Okla.	UFA(Wash)-'04	13/2*
39	Clark, Ryan	S	5-11	200	10/12/79	3	Louisiana State	Marrero, La.	FA-'02	16/4
22	Cousin, Terry	CB	5-9	185	4/11/75	8	South Carolina	Miami, Fla.	FA-'04	13/13*
57	Dach, Carson	LS	6-1	253	9/29/80	2	Eastern Michigan	Grand Blanc, Mich.	W(Chi)-'03	16/0
27	Dayne, Ron	RB	5-10	245	3/14/78	5	Wisconsin	Berlin, N.J.	D1-'00	0*
66	Diehl, David	G	6-5	315	9/15/80	2	Illinois	Oak Lawn, Ill.	D5-'03	16/16
89	Dinkins, Darnell	TE	6-3	255	1/20/77	3	Pittsburgh	Pittsburgh, Pa.	FA-'03	7/0
76	Ellis, Ed	T	6-5	325	10/13/75	7	Buffalo	Hamden, Conn.	UFA(SD)-'04	2/1*
51	Emmons, Carlos	LB	6-5	250	9/3/73	9	Arkansas State	Greenwood, Miss.	UFA(Phil)-'04	15/15*
17	Feagles, Jeff	P	6-1	215	3/7/66	17	Miami	Phoenix, Ariz.	UFA(Sea)-'03	16/0
20	Finn, Jim	FB	6-0	245	12/2/76	5	Pennsylvania	Fair Lawn, N.J.	UFA(Ind)-'03	15/10
12	Gramatica, Bill	K	5-10	189	7/10/78	4	South Florida	LaBelle, Fla.	FA-'03	4/0*
52	Green, Barrett	LB	6-0	225	10/29/77	5	West Virginia	West Palm Beach, Fla.	UFA(Det)-'04	16/16*
29	Green, Ray	CB	6-3	195	3/22/77	5	South Carolina	Charleston, S.C.	FA-'03	2/0
54	Greisen, Nick	LB	6-1	245	8/10/79	3	Wisconsin	Sturgeon Bay, Wis.	D5-'02	15/0
95	Hand, Norman	DT	6-3	310	9/4/72	10	Mississippi	Walterboro, S.C.	FA-'04	6/5*
88	Hilliard, Ike	WR	5-11	210	4/5/76	8	Florida	Patterson, La.	D1-'97	13/12
94	Joseph, William	DT	6-5	315	9/3/79	2	Miami	Miami, Fla.	D1-'03	14/0
33	Joyce, Delvin	RB	5-7	195	9/21/78	3	James Madison	Martinsville, Va.	FA-'02	16/0
90	Kuehl, Ryan	LS	6-5	280	1/18/72	8	Virginia	Potomac, Md.	UFA(Cle)-'03	0*
35	LeBlanc, Clarence	S	6-3	210	3/26/77	4	Louisiana State	River Ridge, La.	FA-'03	4/0
70	Legree, Lance	DT	6-1	300	12/22/77	4	Notre Dame	St. Stephens, S.C.	FA-'01	16/2
59	Lewis, Kevin	LB	6-1	235	10/6/78	5	Duke	Orlando, Fla.	FA-'01	16/0
62	Lucier, Wayne	C	6-3	300	12/5/79	2	Colorado	Salem, N.H.	D7b-'03	12/11
53	Mallard, Wesly	LB	6-1	230	11/21/78	3	Oregon	Columbus, Ga.	D6-'02	15/0
96	Monds, Mario	DT	6-3	325	11/10/76	3	Cincinnati	Fort Pierce, Fla.	FA-'04	0*
93	Monk, Quincy	LB	6-3	250	1/30/79	3	North Carolina	Jacksonville, N.C.	D7b-'02	4/0
60	O'Hara, Shaun	C-G	6-3	306	6/23/77	5	Rutgers	Hillsborough, N.J.	UFA(Cle)-'04	14/14*
3	Palmer, Jesse	QB	6-2	225	10/5/78	4	Florida	Toronto, Ontario, Canada	D4b-'01	6/3
63	Peters, Scott	C	6-3	300	11/23/78	2	Arizona State	Pleasanton, Calif.	FA-'03	7/4
24	Peterson, Will	CB	6-0	200	6/15/79	4	Western Illinois	Uniontown, Pa.	D3-'01	5/5
77	Petitgout, Luke	T	6-6	310	6/16/76	6	Notre Dame	Georgetown, Del.	D1-'99	10/10
87	Ponder, Willie	WR	6-0	205	2/14/80	2	Southeast Missouri State	Tulsa, Okla.	D6a-'03	4/0
83	Rivers, Marcellus	TE	6-4	250	10/26/78	4	Oklahoma State	Oklahoma City, Okla.	FA-'01	12/5
98	Robbins, Fred	DT	6-4	325	3/25/77	5	Wake Forest	Pensacola, Fla.	UFA(Minn)-'04	16/12*
73	Roehl, Jeff	T	6-4	300	5/18/80	2	Northwestern	Orland Park, Ill.	FA-'03	12/2
64	Scott, Travis	G	6-6	300	8/9/79	2	Arizona State	Mesa, Ariz.	FA-'04	0*
69	Seubert, Rich	G	6-5	305	3/30/79	4	Western Illinois	Rozellville, Wis.	FA-'01	6/6
82	Shiancoe, Visanthe	TE	6-4	250	6/18/80	2	Morgan State	Laurel, Md.	D3-'03	16/7
80	Shockey, Jeremy	TE	6-5	253	8/18/80	3	Miami	Ada, Okla.	D1-'02	9/9
68	Smith, Omar	C	6-2	295	9/8/77	3	Kentucky	Miramar, Fla.	FA-'03	4/0
79	Stokes, Barry	T-G	6-4	310	12/20/73	7	Eastern Michigan	Flint, Mich.	UFA(Cle)-'04	14/13*
23	Stoutmire, Omar	S	5-11	205	7/9/74	8	Fresno State	Long Beach, Calif.	FA-'00	16/16
92	Strahan, Michael	DE	6-5	275	11/21/71	12	Texas Southern	Westbury, Texas	D2-'93	16/16
81	Toomer, Amani	WR	6-3	208	9/8/74	9	Michigan	Berkeley, Calif.	D2-'96	16/16
85	Tyree, David	WR	6-0	205	1/3/80	2	Syracuse	Montclair, N.J.	D6c-'03	16/3
72	Umenyiora, Osi	DE	6-3	280	11/16/80	2	Troy State	Auburn, Ala.	D2-'03	13/1
41	Walker, Frank	CB	5-10	198	8/6/80	2	Tuskegee	Tuskegee, Ala.	D6b-'03	10/7
99	Washington, Keith	DE	6-4	285	12/18/72	10	Nevada-Las Vegas	Dallas, Texas	UFA(Den)-'03	14/6
36	Williams, Shaun	S	6-2	218	10/10/76	7	UCLA	Encino, Calif.	D1-'98	10/10
47	Womack, Antwoine	RB	5-11	225	3/20/78	2	Virginia	Hampton, Va.	FA-'04	0*

* Brewer played 6 games with Minnesota in '03; Bromell played 6 games with Oakland; Chase played 13 games with Washington; Cousin played 13 games with Carolina; Dayne inactive for 16 games; Ellis played 2 games with San Diego; Emmons played 15 games with Philadelphia; Gramatica played 4 games with Arizona; Green played 16 games with Detroit; Hand played 6 games with Seattle; Kuehl missed '03 season because of injury; Monds last active with Cincinnati in '01; O'Hara played 14 games with Cleveland; Robbins played 16 games with Minnesota; Scott missed '02 season with St. Louis because of injury; Stokes played 14 games with Cleveland; Womack missed '02 season with New England because of injury.

Players lost through free agency (7): C-T Chris Bober (KC; 16 games in '03), CB Ralph Brown (Wash; 11), CB Ike Charlton (Oak; 7), QB Jason Garrett (TB; 0), DT Cornelius Griffin (Wash; 15), LB Dhani Jones (Phil; 16), LB Brandon Short (Car; 16).

Also played with Giants in '03—QB Kerry Collins (13 games), K Brett Conway (5), DE Frank Ferrara (2), DT Keith Hamilton (15), S Johnnie Harris (14), T Jeff Hatch (4), DE Kenny Holmes (9), RB Dorsey Levens (11), TE Tony McGee (3), RB Brian Mitchell (16), CB Kato Serwanga (13).

2004 FIRST-YEAR ROSTER

Name	Pos.	Ht.	Wt.	Birthdate	College	Hometown	How Acq.
Cash, Ataveus (1)	WR	6-1	205	5/2/79	Hampton	Washington, D.C.	FA-'03
Cervantes, Edgar	FB	6-1	250	9/19/81	Iowa	Maywood, Calif.	FA
Davis, Chris	WR	6-0	182	10/9/81	Southern	Greensburg, La.	FA
Deloatch, Curtis	CB	6-2	217	10/4/81	North Carolina A&T	Murfreesboro, N.C.	FA
Douglas, Chris	RB	5-10	200	2/13/81	Duke	Sherrillsford, N.C.	FA
Ellerbe, Dewitt	CB	6-0	190	4/1/81	South Carolina State	Lamar, S.C.	FA
France, Todd (1)	K	6-3	185	2/13/80	Toledo	Maumee, Ohio	FA
Fullerton, Beau	TE	6-2	247	7/3/80	Tennessee Tech	Petersburgh, La.	FA
Gould, Mark	P	6-2	214	1/17/81	Northern Arizona	Boise, Idaho	FA
Guthrie, Sean (1)	DE	6-4	269	7/14/79	Boston College	Miami, Fla.	FA
Hilton, Isaac	DE	6-3	251	2/26/81	Hampton	Charleston, S.C.	D7b
Hoag, Ryan (1)	WR	6-2	200	11/23/79	Gustavus Adolphus	Minneapolis, Minn.	FA
Hollowell, T.J.	LB	6-0	235	4/8/81	Nebraska	Copperas Cove, Texas	FA
Inkrott, Mark (1)	TE	6-4	255	12/13/78	Findlay	Ottawa, Ohio	FA-'03
Jones, Charles	CB	5-10	182	2/3/81	Alabama	Waynesboro, Ga.	FA
Kincade, Keylon	RB	5-11	204	8/20/82	Southern Methodist	Troup, Texas	FA
Lorenzen, Jared	QB	6-3	288	2/14/81	Kentucky	Ft. Thomas, Ky.	FA
Madarieta, Levi	LB	6-2	241	3/20/80	Brigham Young	Weiser, Idaho	FA
Manning, Eli	QB	6-4	218	1/3/81	Mississippi	New Orleans, La.	T(SD)
Maxwell, James	LB	6-4	242	8/8/81	Gardner Webb	Johnsonville, S.C.	FA
Meredith, Dion (1)	T	6-3	314	6/15/78	Morris Brown	Atlanta, Ga.	FA-'03
Moore, Lewis	LB	6-1	247	10/14/80	Pittsburgh	Cape May Courthouse, N.J.	FA
Peace, Robert	LB	6-2	237	10/2/80	Tennessee	Ruston, La.	FA
Saffer, Michael (1)	T	6-5	302	4/25/79	UCLA	Tucson, Ariz.	FA-'03
Snee, Chris	G	6-3	314	1/8/82	Boston College	Montrose, Pa.	D2
Sprague, Jake (1)	DT	6-2	274	10/1/79	Wisconsin	Oak Creek, Wis.	FA
Strojny, Drew	T	6-7	327	6/30/81	Duke	Westwood, Mass.	D7a
Taylor, Jamaar	WR	6-0	197	2/25/81	Texas A&M	Mission, Texas	D6
Thurman, Andrae	WR	5-11	192	10/25/80	Southern Oregon	Avondale, Ariz.	FA
Torbor, Reggie	LB	6-2	254	1/25/81	Auburn	Baton Rouge, La.	D4
Van Dyke, Ryan (1)	QB	6-5	240	2/13/80	Michigan State	Marshall, Mich.	FA
Vaughn, Khaleed	DE	6-4	276	5/20/81	Clemson	Atlanta, Ga.	FA
Wilson, Gibril	S	6-0	197	11/12/81	Tennessee	San Jose, Calif.	D5

The term NFL Rookie is defined as a player who is in his first season of professional football and has not been on the roster of another professional football team for any regular-season or postseason games. A Rookie is designated by an "R" on NFL rosters. Players who have been active in another professional football league or players who have NFL experience, including either preseason training camp or being on an Active List or Inactive List, or on Reserve/Injured or Reserve/Physically Unable to Perform for fewer than six regular-season games, are termed NFL First-Year Players. An NFL First-Year Player is designated by a "1" on NFL rosters. Thereafter, a player is credited with an additional year of experience for each season in which he accumulates six games on the Active List or Inactive List, or on Reserve/Injured or Reserve/Physically Unable to Perform.

Log on to www.giants.com for an up-to-date roster.

COACHING STAFF

Head Coach, Tom Coughlin

Pro Career: Was named the sixteenth head coach in Giants history on January 6, 2004. Coughlin previously spent eight years (1995-2002) with the Jacksonville Jaguars. Under Coughlin, the Jaguars had the most victories of any NFL expansion team in its first seven seasons. They were also the only expansion team in NFL history to advance to the playoffs four times in their first five seasons. Coughlin's team went 9-7 in year two on the way to the AFC Championship Game, and was 11-5 and earned playoff berths in both 1997 and 1998. In 1999, Coughlin posted an NFL-best 14-2 mark in the regular season and a second AFC Championship Game appearance. Coughlin became the first head coach of the Jaguars on February 21, 1994. Coughlin previously coached wide receivers for the Philadelphia Eagles (1984-85), Green Bay Packers (1986-87), and New York Giants (1988-1990). He was a member of the Giants' Super Bowl XXV champion coaching staff. Career record: 68-60.

Background: Served as head coach at Boston College (1991-93), where he posted a 21-13-1 record, and coached at Syracuse (1969, 1974-1980), Rochester Institute of Technology 1970-73 (head coach), and Boston College (1981-83). Played wingback for Syracuse (1965-67), with teammates Larry Csonka and Floyd Little. Received Syracuse 1967 Orange Key Award as outstanding scholar athlete, and graduated with bachelor's degree in education (1968) and master's degree in education from Syracuse (1969).

Personal: Born August 31, 1947, Waterloo, N.Y. Tom and his wife, Judy, have two daughters, Keli and Katie, two sons, Brian and Tim, a daughter-in-law, Andrea (Tim's wife), and two grandchildren, Emma Rose and Dylan.

ASSISTANT COACHES

Andy Barnett, asst. strength and conditioning; born January 12, 1960, Des Moines, Iowa. Attended Wyoming and Calgary. College coach: Wyoming 1988-1991, Calgary 1993-95, Olympic Training Center, Calgary 1995-2000, International Performance Institute 2000-2003. Pro coach: Joined Giants in 2004.

Billy Davis, linebackers; born November 5, 1965, Youngstown, Ohio. Quarterback Cincinnati 1984-88. No pro playing experience. College coach: Michigan State 1990-91. Pro coach: Pittsburgh Steelers 1992-94, Carolina Panthers 1995-98, Cleveland Browns 1999, Green Bay Packers 2000, Atlanta Falcons, 2001-03, joined Giants in 2004.

Dave DeGuglielmo, asst. offensive line/quality control; born July 15, 1968, Cambridge, Mass. Attended Boston University. College coach: Boston College 1991-92, Boston University 1993-96, Connecticut 1997-98, South Carolina 1999-2003. Pro coach: Joined Giants in 2004.

Pat Flaherty, offensive line; born April 27, 1956, Hanover, Pa. Center East Stroudsburg 1974-77. No pro playing experience. College coach: East Stroudsburg 1980-81, Penn State 1982-83, Rutgers 1984-1991, East Carolina 1992, Wake Forest 1993-98, Iowa 1999. Pro coach: Washington Redskins 2000, Chicago Bears 2001-03, joined Giants in 2004.

Kevin Gilbride, quarterbacks, born August 27, 1951, New Haven, Conn. Quarterback-tight end Southern Connecticut State 1971-73. No pro playing experience. College coach: Idaho State 1974-75, Tufts 1976-77, American International 1978-79. Southern Connecticut State 1980-84, East Carolina 1987-88. Pro coach: Ottawa Rough Riders (CFL) 1985-86, Houston Oilers 1989-1994, Jacksonville Jaguars 1995-96, San Diego Chargers 1997-98, Pittsburgh Steelers 1999-2000, Buffalo Bills 2002-2003, joined Giants 2004.

John Hufnagel, offensive coordinator; born September 13, 1951, Pittsburgh. Quarterback Penn State 1969-1972. Pro quarterback Denver Broncos 1973-75, Calgary Stampeders (CFL) 1976-79, Saskatchewan Roughriders (CFL) 1980-83, 1987, Winnipeg Blue Bombers (CFL) 1984-86. Pro coach: Saskatchewan Roughriders (CFL) 1988, Calgary Stampeders (CFL) 1990-96, New Jersey Red Dogs (Arena League) 1997-98, Cleveland Browns 1999-2000, Indianapolis Colts 2001, Jacksonville Jaguars 2002, New England Patriots 2003, joined Giants in 2004.

Jerald Ingram, running backs; born December 24, 1960, Dayton, Ohio. Fullback Michigan 1979-1983. College coach: Michigan 1984, Ball State 1985-1990, Boston College, 1991-93. Pro coach: Jacksonville Jaguars 1994-2002, joined Giants in 2004.

Tim Lewis, defensive coordinator; born December 18, 1961, Quakertown, Pa. Defensive back Pittsburgh 1979-1982. Pro cornerback Green Bay Packers 1983-86. College coach: Texas A&M 1987-88, Southern Methodist 1989-1992, Pittsburgh 1993-94. Pro coach: Pittsburgh Steelers 1995-2003, joined Giants in 2004.

David Merritt Sr., defensive assistant-quality control; born September 8, 1971, Raleigh, N.C. Linebacker North Carolina State 1989-1992. Pro linebacker Miami Dolphins 1993, Arizona Cardinals 1993-96, Rhein Fire (NFLE) 1997. College coach: Chattanooga 1997, Virginia Military Institute 1998-2000. Pro coach: New York Jets 2001-2003, joined Giants in 2004.

Ron Milus, defensive secondary; born November 25, 1963, Tacoma, Wash. Cornerback-punt returner Washington 1982-1985. No pro playing experience. College coach: Washington 1991-98, Texas A&M 1999. Pro coach: Denver Broncos 2000-02, Arizona Cardinals 2003, joined Giants in 2004.

Jerry Palmieri, strength and conditioning; born October 30, 1958, Englewood, N.J. Attended Montclair State. No college or pro playing experience. College coach: North Carolina 1982-83, Oklahoma State 1984-86, Kansas State 1987-1992, Boston College 1993-94. Pro coach: Jacksonville Jaguars 1995-2002, New Orleans Saints 2003, joined Giants in 2004.

Michael Pope, tight ends; born March 15, 1942, Monroe, N.C. Quarterback Lenoir-Rhyne 1962-64. No pro playing experience. College coach: Florida State 1970-74, Texas Tech 1975-77, Mississippi 1978-1982. Pro coach: New York Giants 1983-1991, Cincinnati Bengals 1992-93, New England Patriots 1994-96, Washington Redskins 1997-99, rejoined Giants in 2000.

Mike Priefer, asst. special teams; born August 21, 1966, Cleveland. Attended U.S. Naval Academy. No college or pro playing experience. College coach: U.S. Naval Academy 1994-96, Youngstown State 1997-98, Virginia Military Institute 1999, Northern Illinois 2000-01. Pro coach: Jacksonville Jaguars 2002, joined Giants in 2003.

Mike Sullivan, wide receivers; born January 28, 1967, Santa Maria, Calif. Defensive back Army 1987-88. No pro playing experience. College coach: Mt. San Jacinto (Calif.) J.C. 1993, Humboldt State 1993-94, Army 1995-96, 1999-2000, Youngstown State 1997-98, Ohio 2001. Pro coach: Jacksonville Jaguars 2002-03, joined Giants 2004.

Mike Sweatman, special teams coordinator; born October 23, 1946, Kansas City, Mo. Linebacker Kansas 1964-67. Linebacker Quantico Marines 1969. College coach: Kansas 1973-74, 1979-1982, Coffeyville (Kan.) C.C. 1975-76, Tulsa 1977-78, Tennessee 1983. Pro coach: Okinawa Devil Dogs 1970, Quantico Marines 1971-72, Minnesota Vikings 1984, New York Giants 1985-1992, New England Patriots 1993-96, New York Jets 1997-2000, Chicago Bears 2001-2003, rejoined Giants in 2004.

Mike Waufle, defensive line; born June 27, 1954, Hornell, N.Y. U.S. Marines 1972-75. Defensive lineman Bakersfield (Calif.) J.C. 1975-76, Utah State 1977-78. No pro playing experience. College coach: Alfred 1979, Utah State 1980-84, Fresno State 1985-88, UCLA 1989, Oregon State 1990-91, California 1992-97. Pro coach: Oakland Raiders 1998-2003, joined Giants in 2004.

National Football Conference
East Division
Team Colors: Midnight Green, Silver, Black, and White
NovaCare Complex
One NovaCare Way
Philadelphia, Pennsylvania 19145
Telephone: (215) 463-2500

2004 SCHEDULE

PRESEASON		**Philadelphia time**
Aug. 13	at New England	8:00
Aug. 20	**Baltimore**	8:00
Aug. 26	**Pittsburgh**	8:00
Sept. 3	at New York Jets	7:00

REGULAR SEASON

Sept. 12	**New York Giants**	4:15
Sept. 20	**Minnesota** (Mon.)	9:00
Sept. 26	at Detroit	1:00
Oct. 3	at Chicago	1:00
Oct. 10	Open Date	
Oct. 17	**Carolina**	1:00
Oct. 24	at Cleveland	1:00
Oct. 31	**Baltimore**	1:00
Nov. 7	at Pittsburgh	1:00
Nov. 15	at Dallas (Mon.)	9:00
Nov. 21	**Washington**	4:15
Nov. 28	at New York Giants	1:00
Dec. 5	**Green Bay**	4:15
Dec. 12	at Washington	8:30
Dec. 19	**Dallas**	1:00
Dec. 27	at St. Louis (Mon.)	9:00
Jan. 2	**Cincinnati**	1:00

Stadium: Lincoln Financial Field (opened in 2003)
•**Capacity:** 68,400
One Lincoln Financial Field Way
Philadelphia, Pennsylvania 19148
Playing Surface: Natural Grass
Training Camp: Lehigh University
Bethlehem, Pennsylvania
18015

LINCOLN FINANCIAL FIELD

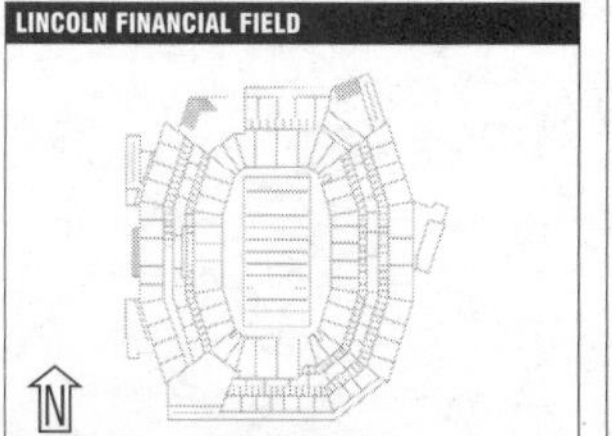

CLUB OFFICIALS

Chairman/Chief Executive Officer: Jeffrey Lurie
President: Joe Banner
Head Coach/Executive Vice President of Football Operations: Andy Reid
Vice President of Player Personnel: Tom Heckert
Senior Vice President of Business Operations: Mark Donovan
Senior Vice President/Chief Financial Officer: Don Smolenski
Vice President, Sales: Jason Gonella
Vice President of Stadium Operations and Facility Management: Scott Jenkins
Executive Director of Eagles Youth Partnership: Sarah Martinez-Helfman
Director of Pro Personnel: Scott Cohen
Director of College Scouting: Marc Ross
Director of Football Media Relations: Derek Boyko
Assistant Director of Football Media Services: Rich Burg, Bob Lange
Senior Director of Marketing: Tim McDermott
Manager of Community Relations: Julie Dubin
Director of Human Resources: Eric Newman
Director of Stadium Operations: Dave Duernberger
Director, Broadcasting: Rob Alberino
Ticket Manager: Leo Carlin
Director of Merchandise: Steve Strawbridge
Travel Coordinator: Tracey Detweiler
Director of Team Security: Anthony (Butch) Buchanico
Director of Facility and Stadium Security: Victor Cooper
Head Athletic Trainer: Rick Burkholder
Asst. Athletic Trainers: Eric Sugarman, Chris Peduzzi
Video Director: Mike Dougherty
Head Equipment Manager: John Hatfield

COACHING HISTORY
(456-512-25)

1933-35	Lud Wray	9-21-1
1936-1940	Bert Bell	10-44-2
1941-1950	Earle (Greasy) Neale*	66-44-5
1951	Alvin (Bo) McMillin**	2-0-0
1951	Wayne Millner	2-8-0
1952-55	Jim Trimble	25-20-3
1956-57	Hugh Devore	7-16-1
1958-1960	Lawrence (Buck) Shaw	20-16-1
1961-63	Nick Skorich	15-24-3
1964-68	Joe Kuharich	28-41-1
1969-1971	Jerry Williams***	7-22-2
1971-72	Ed Khayat	8-15-2
1973-75	Mike McCormack	16-25-1
1976-1982	Dick Vermeil	57-51-0
1983-85	Marion Campbell****	17-29-1
1985	Fred Bruney	1-0-0
1986-1990	Buddy Ryan	43-38-1
1991-94	Rich Kotite	37-29-0
1995-98	Ray Rhodes	30-36-1
1999-2003	Andy Reid	56-33-0

*Co-coach with Walt Kiesling in Philadelphia-Pittsburgh merger in 1943
**Retired after two games in 1951
***Released after three games in 1971
****Released after 15 games in 1985

ATTENDANCE

Home 532,888 Away 580,492
Total 1,113,380
Single-game home record, 72,111 (11/1/81)
Single-season home record, 557,325 (1980)

2004 DRAFT CHOICES

Round	Name	Pos.	College
1	Shawn Andrews	T	Arkansas
3	Matt Ware	DB	UCLA
4	J.R. Reed	DB	South Florida
	Trey Darilek	T	Texas-El Paso
5	Thomas Tapeh	RB	Minnesota
6	Andy Hall	QB	Delaware
	Dexter Wynn	DB	Colorado State
7	Adrien Clarke	G	Ohio State
	Bruce Perry	RB	Maryland
	Dominic Furio	C	Nevada-Las Vegas

PHILADELPHIA EAGLES

2003 TEAM RECORD

PRESEASON (2-2)

Date	Result	Opponent
8/11	W 27-17	at New Orleans
8/16	W 21-16	at Pittsburgh
8/22	L 12-24	New England
8/28	L 9-17	New York Jets

REGULAR SEASON (12-4)

Date	Result	Opponent	Att.
9/8	L 0-17	Tampa Bay	67,772
9/14	L 10-31	New England	67,624
9/28	W 23-13	at Buffalo	73,305
10/5	W 27-25	Washington	67,792
10/12	L 21-23	at Dallas	63,648
10/19	W 14-10	at New York Giants	78,883
10/26	W 24-17	New York Jets	67,853
11/2	W 23-16	at Atlanta	70,064
11/10	W 17-14	at Green Bay	70,291
11/16	W 28-10	New York Giants	67,867
11/23	W 33-20	New Orleans	67,802
11/30	W 25-16	at Carolina	72,977
12/7	W 36-10	Dallas	69,773
12/15	W 34-27	at Miami	73,780
12/21	L 28-31	San Francisco (OT)	67,886
12/27	W 31-7	at Washington	76,766

(OT) Overtime

POSTSEASON (1-1)

Date	Result	Opponent	Att.
1/11	W 20-17	Green Bay (OT)	67,707
1/18	L 3-14	Carolina	67,862

SCORE BY PERIODS

Eagles	82	102	59	131	0 —	374
Opponents	43	91	62	88	3 —	287

2003 TEAM STATISTICS

	Eagles	Opp.
Total First Downs	302	306
Rushing	105	116
Passing	156	171
Penalty	41	19
3rd Down: Made/Att	69/190	78/221
3rd Down Pct.	36.3	35.3
4th Down: Made/Att	3/7	8/22
4th Down Pct.	42.9	36.4
Possession Avg.	28:17	31:43
Total Net Yards	5,035	5,307
Avg. Per Game	314.7	331.7
Total Plays	944	1,058
Avg. Per Play	5.3	5.0
Net Yards Rushing	2,015	2,071
Avg. Per Game	125.9	129.4
Total Rushes	417	461
Net Yards Passing	3,020	3,236
Avg. Per Game	188.8	202.3
Sacked/Yards Lost	43/253	38/248
Gross Yards	3,273	3,484
Att./Completions	484/279	559/337
Completion Pct.	57.6	60.3
Had Intercepted	11	13
Punts/Average	79/40.6	78/38.9
Net Punting Avg.	79/34.6	78/33.6
Penalties/Yards	96/817	129/1,105
Fumbles/Ball Lost	21/11	26/13
Touchdowns	43	32
Rushing	23	13
Passing	17	17
Returns	3	2

2003 INDIVIDUAL STATISTICS

PASSING	Att.	Comp.	Yds.	Pct.	TD	Int.	Tkld.	Rate
McNabb	478	275	3,216	57.5	16	11	43/253	79.6
Detmer	5	3	32	60.0	0	0	0/0	78.8
Mitchell	1	1	25	100.0	1	0	0/0	158.3
Eagles	484	279	3,273	57.6	17	11	43/253	80.5
Opponents	559	337	3,484	60.3	17	13	38/248	78.7

SCORING	TD R	TD P	TD Rt	PAT	FG	Saf	PTS
Akers	0	0	0	42/42	24/29	0	114
Westbrook	7	4	2	0/0	0/0	0	78
Buckhalter	8	1	0	0/0	0/0	0	54
Staley	5	2	0	0/0	0/0	0	42
McNabb	3	0	0	0/0	0/0	0	18
Ritchie	0	3	0	0/0	0/0	0	18
Mitchell	0	2	0	0/0	0/0	0	12
Pinkston	0	2	0	0/0	0/0	0	12
Kalu	0	0	1	0/0	0/0	0	6
C. Lewis	0	1	0	0/0	0/0	0	6
Smith	0	1	0	0/0	0/0	0	6
Thrash	0	1	0	0/0	0/0	0	6
Eagles	23	17	3	42/42	24/29	1	374
Opponents	13	17	2	27/28	22/30	0	287

2-Pt. Conversions: None.
Eagles 0-1, Opponents 1-4.

RUSHING	No.	Yds	Avg	LG	TD
Westbrook	117	613	5.2	62t	7
Buckhalter	126	542	4.3	64t	8
Staley	96	463	4.8	22	5
McNabb	71	355	5.0	34	3
Thrash	5	52	10.4	47	0
Ritchie	1	1	1.0	1	0
Pinkston	1	-11	-11.0	-11	0
Eagles	417	2,015	4.8	64t	23
Opponents	461	2,071	4.5	76t	13

RECEIVING	No.	Yds	Avg	LG	TD
Thrash	49	558	11.4	51	1
Westbrook	37	332	9.0	38	4
Pinkston	36	575	16.0	59	2
Staley	36	382	10.6	52t	2
Mitchell	35	498	14.2	39	2
Smith	27	321	11.9	36	1
C. Lewis	23	293	12.7	29	1
Ritchie	17	86	5.1	12	3
Buckhalter	10	133	13.3	27	1
G. Lewis	6	95	15.8	25	0
Mahe	1	5	5.0	5	0
McMullen	1	2	2.0	2	0
McNabb	1	-7	-7.0	-7	0
Eagles	279	3,273	11.7	59	17
Opponents	337	3,484	10.3	60t	17

INTERCEPTIONS	No.	Yds	Avg	LG	TD
M. Lewis	3	31	10.3	23	0
Vincent	3	28	9.3	28	0
Sheppard	1	34	34.0	34	0
Wayne	1	33	33.0	33	0
Kalu	1	15	15.0	15t	1
Brown	1	10	10.0	10	0
Hood	1	5	5.0	5	0
Taylor	1	2	2.0	2	0
Dawkins	1	0	0.0	0	0
Eagles	13	158	12.2	34	1
Opponents	11	161	14.6	34	1

PUNTING	No.	Yds.	Avg.	In 20	LG
D. Johnson	79	3,207	40.6	27	60
Eagles	79	3,207	40.6	27	60
Opponents	78	3,037	38.9	20	69

PUNT RETURNS	Ret	FC	Yds	Avg	LG	TD
Westbrook	20	16	306	15.3	84t	2
Mahe	6	6	55	9.2	17	0
Sheppard	4	1	15	3.8	5	0
Thrash	1	1	2	2.0	2	0
Eagles	31	24	378	12.2	84t	2
Opponents	35	15	272	7.8	72	0

KICKOFF RETURNS	No.	Yds	Avg	LG	TD
Thrash	34	815	24.0	54	0
Westbrook	23	487	21.2	47	0
Morey	7	93	13.3	24	0
Mitchell	1	-8	-8.0	-8	0
Eagles	65	1,387	21.3	54	0
Opponents	74	1,590	21.5	54	1

FIELD GOALS	1-19	20-29	30-39	40-49	50+
Akers	0/0	9/9	7/7	6/10	2/3
Eagles	0/0	9/9	7/7	6/10	2/3
Opponents	0/0	10/10	5/7	4/7	3/6

SACKS	No.
Simon	7.5
Walker	6.0
Kalu	5.5
Wayne	3.0
M. Lewis	2.0
Rayburn	2.0
Simoneau	2.0
Whiting	2.0
Brown	1.0
Grasmanis	1.0
Hart	1.0
Reese	1.0
Coleman	0.5
Dawkins	0.5
Eagles	38.0
Opponents	43.0

RECORD HOLDERS

INDIVIDUAL RECORDS—CAREER

Category	Name	Performance
Rushing (Yds.)	Wilbert Montgomery, 1977-1984	6,538
Passing (Yds.)	Ron Jaworski, 1977-1986	26,963
Passing (TDs)	Ron Jaworski, 1977-1986	175
Receiving (No.)	Harold Carmichael, 1971-1983	589
Receiving (Yds.)	Harold Carmichael, 1971-1983	8,978
Interceptions	Bill Bradley, 1969-1976	34
	Eric Allen, 1988-1994	34
Punting (Avg.)	Joe Muha, 1946-1950	42.9
Punt Return (Avg.)	Brian Westbrook, 2002-03	15.3
Kickoff Return (Avg.)	Steve Van Buren, 1944-1951	26.7
Field Goals	David Akers, 1999-2003	112
Touchdowns (Tot.)	Harold Carmichael, 1971-1983	79
Points	Bobby Walston, 1951-1962	881

INDIVIDUAL RECORDS—SINGLE SEASON

Category	Name	Performance
Rushing (Yds.)	Wilbert Montgomery, 1979	1,512
Passing (Yds.)	Randall Cunningham, 1988	3,808
Passing (TDs)	Sonny Jurgensen, 1961	32
Receiving (No.)	Irving Fryar, 1996	88
Receiving (Yds.)	Mike Quick, 1983	1,409
Interceptions	Bill Bradley, 1971	11
Punting (Avg.)	Joe Muha, 1948	47.2
Punt Return (Avg.)	Steve Van Buren, 1944	15.3
Kickoff Return (Avg.)	Al Nelson, 1972	29.1
Field Goals	Paul McFadden, 1984	30
	David Akers, 2002	30
Touchdowns (Tot.)	Steve Van Buren, 1945	18
Points	David Akers, 2002	133

INDIVIDUAL RECORDS—SINGLE GAME

Category	Name	Performance
Rushing (Yds.)	Steve Van Buren, 11-27-49	205
Passing (Yds.)	Randall Cunningham, 9-17-89	447
Passing (TDs)	Adrian Burk, 10-17-54	*7
Receiving (No.)	Don Looney, 12-1-40	14
Receiving (Yds.)	Tommy McDonald, 12-10-60	237
Interceptions	Russ Craft, 9-24-50	*4
Field Goals	Tom Dempsey, 11-12-72	6
Touchdowns (Tot.)	Many times	4
	Last time by Irving Fryar, 10-20-96	
Points	Bobby Walston, 10-17-54	25

*NFL Record

PHILADELPHIA EAGLES

2004 VETERAN ROSTER

No.	Name	Pos.	Ht.	Wt.	Birthdate	NFL Exp.	College	Hometown	How Acq.	'03 Games/ Starts
57	Adams, Keith	LB	5-11	223	11/21/75	4	Clemson	Atlanta, Ga.	W(Dall)-'02	15/0
2	Akers, David	K	5-10	200	12/8/70	6	Louisville	Lexington, Ky.	FA-'99	16/0
88	Bartrum, Mike	TE-LS	6-4	245	6/23/70	11	Marshall	Pomeroy, Ohio	FA-'00	16/0
	Blake, Jeff	QB	6-1	223	12/4/70	13	East Carolina	Orlando, Fla.	FA-'04	13/13*
74	Bridges, Jeremy	T-G	6-4	301	4/19/80	2	Southern Mississippi	McComb, Miss.	D6-'03	0*
24	Brown, Sheldon	CB	5-10	196	3/19/79	3	South Carolina	Ft. Lawn, S.C.	D2b-'02	16/3
28	Buckhalter, Correll	RB	6-0	222	10/6/78	4	Nebraska	Collins, Miss.	D4-'01	15/5
56	Burgess, Derrick	LB-DE	6-2	266	8/12/78	4	Mississippi	Greenbelt, Md.	D3-'01	0*
20	Dawkins, Brian	S	6-0	210	10/13/73	9	Clemson	Jacksonville, Fla.	D2b-'96	7/7
10	Detmer, Koy	QB	6-1	195	7/5/73	8	Colorado	San Antonio, Texas	D7a-'97	16/0
6	Duncan, Tim	K	6-2	210	6/12/79	2	Oklahoma	Clinton, Okla.	FA-'04	5/0*
59	Ena, Justin	LB	6-3	247	11/20/77	3	Brigham Young	Shelton, Wash.	FA-'02	16/0
50	Ephraim, Alonzo	C	6-4	312	11/8/81	2	Alabama	Birmingham, Ala.	FA-'03	16/0
63	Fraley, Hank	C-G	6-2	300	9/21/77	5	Robert Morris	Gaithersburg, Md.	W(Pitt)-'00	16/16
96	Grasmanis, Paul	DT	6-3	298	8/2/74	9	Notre Dame	Jenison, Mich.	UFA(Den)-'00	2/0
65	Green, Jamaal	DE	6-2	272	6/5/80	2	Miami	Camden, N.J.	D4-'03	0*
51	Harrison, Tyreo	LB	6-2	238	5/15/80	3	Notre Dame	Sulphur Springs, Texas	D6-'02	12/0
33	Hart, Clinton	S	6-0	205	7/20/77	2	Central Florida C.C.	Bushnell, Fla.	FA-'02	16/9
77	Hicks, Artis	T	6-4	320	11/28/78	3	Memphis	Jackson, Tenn.	FA-'02	10/4
29	Hood, Roderick	CB	5-11	196	10/3/81	2	Auburn	Columbus, Ga.	FA-'03	14/0
8	Johnson, Dirk	P	6-0	205	6/1/75	2	Northern Colorado	Montrose, Colo.	FA-'03	16/0
62	Johnson, Ron	DE	6-5	255	10/23/79	2	Shippensburg	York, Pa.	FA-'03	3/0
55	Jones, Dhani	LB	6-1	240	2/22/78	5	Michigan	Potomac, Md.	UFA(NYG)-'04	16/16*
94	Kalu, N.D.	DE	6-3	265	8/3/75	8	Rice	San Antonio, Texas	UFA(Wash)-'01	16/16
93	Kearse, Jevon	DE	6-4	265	9/3/76	6	Florida	Ft. Myers, Fla.	UFA(Tenn)-'04	14/14*
68	Lavergne, Damian	T	6-6	328	4/22/80	2	Louisiana Tech	Baton Rouge, La.	FA-'03	0*
89	Lewis, Chad	TE	6-6	252	10/5/71	7	Brigham Young	Orem, Utah	W(StL)-'99	16/14
83	Lewis, Greg	WR	6-0	180	2/12/80	2	Illinois	Matteson, Ill.	FA-'03	11/0
32	Lewis, Michael	S	6-1	211	4/29/80	3	Colorado	Richmond, Texas	D2a-'02	16/16
34	Mahe, Reno	RB	5-10	212	6/3/80	2	Brigham Young	Salt Lake City, Utah	FA-'03	2/0
71	Mayberry, Jermane	G-T	6-4	325	8/29/73	9	Texas A&M-Kingsville	Floresville, Texas	D1-'96	5/5
95	McDougle, Jerome	DE	6-2	264	12/15/78	2	Miami	Pompano Beach, Fla.	D1-'03	8/0
80	McMullen, Billy	WR	6-4	210	3/8/80	2	Virginia	Richmond, Va.	D3-'03	5/0
5	McNabb, Donovan	QB	6-2	240	11/25/76	6	Syracuse	Chicago, Ill.	D1-'99	16/16
46	Mikell, Quintin	S	5-10	206	9/16/80	2	Boise State	Eugene, Ore.	FA-'03	16/0
84	Mitchell, Freddie	WR	5-11	184	11/28/78	4	UCLA	Lakeland, Fla.	D1-'01	16/6
85	Morey, Sean	WR	5-11	200	2/26/76	3	Brown	Marshfield, Mass.	FA-'03	16/0
81	t-Owens, Terrell	WR	6-3	226	12/7/73	9	Tennessee-Chattanooga	Alexander City, Ala.	T(Balt)-'04	15/15*
87	Pinkston, Todd	WR	6-2	174	4/23/77	5	Southern Mississippi	Forest, Miss.	D2a-'00	16/15
91	Rayburn, Sam	DT	6-3	303	10/20/80	2	Tulsa	Chickasha, Okla.	FA-'03	10/0
58	Reese, Ike	LB	6-2	222	10/16/73	7	Michigan State	Cincinnati, Ohio	D5-'98	16/1
48	Ritchie, Jon	FB	6-2	250	9/4/74	7	Stanford	Mechanicsburg, Pa.	UFA(Oak)-'03	16/7
69	Runyan, Jon	T	6-7	330	11/27/73	9	Michigan	Flint, Mich.	UFA(Tenn)-'00	16/16
26	Sheppard, Lito	CB	5-10	194	4/8/81	3	Florida	Jacksonville, Fla.	D1-'02	16/9
90	Simon, Corey	DT	6-2	293	3/2/77	5	Florida State	Pompano Beach, Fla.	D1-'00	16/16
53	Simoneau, Mark	LB	6-0	234	1/16/77	5	Kansas State	Smith Center, Kan.	T(Atl)-'03	16/16
82	Smith, L.J.	TE	6-3	258	5/13/80	2	Rutgers	Highland Park, N.J.	D2-'03	15/5
78	Thomas, Hollis	DT	6-0	306	1/10/74	9	Northern Illinois	St. Louis, Mo.	FA-'96	7/2
72	Thomas, Tra	T	6-7	349	11/20/74	7	Florida State	Deland, Fla.	D1-'98	15/15
97	Walker, Darwin	DT	6-3	294	6/15/77	5	Tennessee	Walterboro, S.C.	W(Ariz)-'00	16/16
54	Wayne, Nate	LB	6-0	237	1/12/75	7	Mississippi	Macon, Miss.	FA-'03	16/16
36	Westbrook, Brian	RB-KR	5-10	205	9/2/79	3	Villanova	Ft. Washington, Md.	D3-'02	15/8

* Blake played 13 games with Arizona in '03; Bridges inactive for 16 games; Burgess missed '03 season because of injury; Duncan played 5 games with Arizona; Green missed '03 season because of injury; Jones played 16 games with N.Y. Giants; Kearse played 14 games with Tennessee; Lavergne missed '03 season because of injury; Owens played 15 games with San Francisco.

t- Eagles traded for Owens (Balt).

\# Unrestricted free agent; subject to developments.

Traded—QB A.J. Feeley (0 games in '03) to Miami, WR James Thrash (16) to Washington, G John Welbourn (13) to Kansas City, DE Brandon Whiting (14) to San Francisco.

Players lost through free agency (6): DE Marco Coleman (Den; 13 games in '03), LB Carlos Emmons (NYG; 15), RB Duce Staley (Pitt; 16), CB Bobby Taylor (Sea; 7), CB Troy Vincent (Buff; 13), G Bobbie Williams (Cin; 16).

Also played with Eagles in '03—CB Daryon Brutley (1 game), DT Jim Flanigan (6).

2004 FIRST-YEAR ROSTER

Name	Pos.	Ht.	Wt.	Birthdate	College	Hometown	How Acq.
Andrews, Shawn	T-G	6-4	340	12/25/82	Arkansas	Camden, Ark.	D1
Bartosic, Mark	WR	6-1	195	10/30/80	Susquehanna	Northumberland, Pa.	FA
Bradley, Jon	DT	6-0	301	1/13/81	Arkansas State	Barton, Ark.	FA
Brantley, Yardon	WR	6-1	180	7/8/82	Duquense	Reading, Pa.	FA
Clark, Howard (1)	LB	6-1	227	2/8/80	Miami	Pennsauken, N.J.	FA
Clarke, Adrian	G	6-5	330	3/26/81	Ohio State	Shaker Heights, Ohio	D7a
Crawford, Regis	C	6-2	316	1/28/81	Arizona State	San Diego, Calif.	FA
Darilek, Trey	T-G	6-5	310	4/23/81	Texas-El Paso	San Antonio, Texas	D4b
Dickerson, Kori (1)	TE	6-4	240	12/6/78	Southern California	Los Angeles, Calif.	FA-'02
Ellington, Dante (1)	T	6-6	330	2/29/80	Alabama	Leighton, Ala.	FA-'03
Foli, Anthony	C	6-5	280	3/6/80	San Diego State	Newbury Park, Calif.	FA
Furio, Dominic	C	6-3	305	6/4/81	Nevada-Las Vegas	San Pedro, Calif.	D7c
Ghent, Ronnie	TE	6-2	253	1/5/80	Louisville	Lakeland, Fla.	FA
Hall, Andy	QB	6-3	218	11/26/80	Delaware	Cheraw, S.C.	D6a
Haw, Brandon	CB	6-0	185	9/24/80	Rutgers	Cheverly, Md.	FA
Jackson, Jamaal (1)	G-C	6-4	330	5/8/80	Delaware State	Miami, Fla.	FA-'03
Jenkins, Justin	WR	6-0	213	12/10/80	Mississippi State	Pearl, Miss.	FA
Labinjo, Mike	LB	6-0	241	7/8/80	Michigan State	Toronto, Ontario, Canada	FA
LeJeune, Norman (1)	S	6-0	200	5/10/80	Louisiana State	Brusly, La.	D7-'03
Leslie, Jerome	WR	6-3	205	5/23/80	Virginia Union	Lake Carmel, N.Y.	FA
McCoo, Eric (1)	RB	5-10	210	9/6/80	Penn State	Red Bank, N.J.	FA-'03
McMullen, Scott	QB	6-3	217	11/18/80	Ohio State	Granville, Ohio	FA
Murphy, Nick (1)	P	5-11	188	10/22/79	Arizona State	Scottsdale, Ariz.	FA
Parry, Josh (1)	FB	6-2	250	4/5/78	San Jose State	Sonora, Calif.	FA-'01
Perez, Carlos	WR	5-11	193	9/15/80	Florida	Hoboken, N.J.	FA
Perry, Bruce	RB	5-9	200	3/22/81	Maryland	Philadelphia, Pa.	D7b
Pinderhughes, Brandon	S	5-11	195	8/21/82	Nebraska-Omaha	St. Paul, Minn.	FA
Pope, Jeremiah	WR	5-11	185	1/11/81	C.W. Post	Floral Park, N.Y.	FA
Reed, J.R.	S	5-11	202	2/11/82	South Florida	Tampa, Fla.	D4a
Richmond, Greg	LB	6-1	233	7/15/81	Oklahoma State	Oklahoma City, Okla.	FA
Short, Jason (1)	LB	6-4	254	7/15/78	Eastern Michigan	Painesville, Ohio	FA-'03
Tapeh, Thomas	FB	6-1	243	3/28/80	Minnesota	St. Paul, Minn.	D5
Ware, Matt	CB	6-2	210	12/2/82	UCLA	Malibu, Calif.	D3
Wynn, Dexter	CB	5-9	177	2/25/81	Colorado State	Colorado Springs, Colo.	D6b

The term NFL Rookie is defined as a player who is in his first season of professional football and has not been on the roster of another professional football team for any regular-season or postseason games. A Rookie is designated by an "R" on NFL rosters. Players who have been active in another professional football league or players who have NFL experience, including either preseason training camp or being on an Active List or Inactive List, or on Reserve/Injured or Reserve/Physically Unable to Perform for fewer than six regular-season games, are termed NFL First-Year Players. An NFL First-Year Player is designated by a "1" on NFL rosters. Thereafter, a player is credited with an additional year of experience for each season in which he accumulates six games on the Active List or Inactive List, or on Reserve/Injured or Reserve/Physically Unable to Perform.

Log on to www.philadelphiaeagles.com for an up-to-date roster.

PHILADELPHIA EAGLES

COACHING STAFF

Head Coach/Executive Vice President of Football Operations, Andy Reid

Pro Career: Reid was named the twentieh head coach in franchise history on January 11, 1999 and was promoted to head coach/executive vice president of football operations in 2001. He has been masterful in transforming the Eagles into one of the NFL's elite teams. Under Reid, the Eagles have captured three consecutive NFC East division titles for the first time in team history and have made three consecutive trips to the NFC Championship Game. The NFL coach of the year in 2000 and 2002, Reid has the most playoff wins (5) in Eagles history and has the highest winning percentage of any Eagles head coach (.629). In his 12-year pro coaching career, Reid's teams have made the playoffs 10 times. He has coached in the Super Bowl twice and the NFC Championship Game six times. Reid joined the Eagles after a seven-year stint as an assistant coach with Green Bay (1992-98) under Mike Holmgren. With Green Bay, Reid helped the Packers earn a Super XXXI victory over the New England Patriots. Career record: 43-28.

Background: Coached at Brigham Young (1982), San Francisco State (1983-85), Northern Arizona (1986), Texas-El Paso (1987-88), and Missori (1989-1991). Reid first met Holmgren, who was a member of BYU's coaching staff, when Reid was an offensive tackle and guard on three Cougar Holiday Bowl teams. Reid graduated with a bachelor's degree in physical education. He also received a master's degree in professional leadership in physical education and athletics.

Personal: Born in Los Angeles on March 19, 1958, Reid and his wife Tammy have five children—Garrett, Britt, Crosby, Drew Ann, and Spencer.

ASSISTANT COACHES

Tommy Brasher, defensive line; born Dec. 30, 1940, El Dorado, Ark.. Linebacker Arkansas 1962-63. No pro playing experience. College coach: Arkansas 1970, Virginia Tech 1971, Northeast Louisiana 1974, 1976, Southern Methodist 1977-1981. Pro coach: Shreveport Steamer (WFL) 1975, New England Patriots 1982-84, Philadelphia Eagles 1985, Atlanta Falcons 1986-89, Tampa Bay Buccaneers 1990, Seattle Seahawks 1992-98, rejoined Eagles in 1999.

Juan Castillo, offensive line; born October 8, 1959, Port Isabel, Texas. Linebacker Texas A&I (now Texas A&M-Kingsville) 1978-1980. Pro linebacker San Antonio Gunslingers (USFL) 1984-85. College coach: Texas A&M-Kingsville 1982-85, 1990-94. Pro coach: Joined Eagles in 1995.

Brad Childress, offensive coordinator; born June 27, 1956, Aurora, Ill. Eastern Illinois 1975-78. No pro playing experience. College coach: Illinois 1978-1984, Northern Arizona 1986-89, Utah 1990, Wisconsin 1991-98. Pro coach: Indianapolis Colts 1985, joined Eagles in 1999.

David Culley, wide receivers; born September 17, 1955, Sparta, Tenn. Quarterback Vanderbilt 1973-77. No pro playing experience. College coach: Austin Peay 1978, Vanderbilt 1979-1981, Middle Tennessee State 1982, Tennessee-Chattanooga 1983, Western Kentucky 1984, Southwestern Louisiana 1985-88, Texas-El Paso 1989-1990, Texas A&M 1991-93. Pro coach: Tampa Bay Buccaneers 1994-95, Pittsburgh Steelers 1996-1998, joined Eagles in 1999.

Ted Daisher, special teams quality control; born February 2, 1955, Taylor, Mich. Wide receiver-defensive back Western Michigan 1975-77. No pro playing experience. College coach: Illinois 1979, Northern Illinois 1980-84, Eastern Michigan 1985-88, Cincinnati 1989-1992, Army 1995-97, Indiana 1998-2000, East Carolina 2001-2002. Pro coach: Joined Eagles in 2004.

John Harbaugh, special teams; born September 23, 1962, Perrysburg, Ohio. Defensive back Miami (Ohio) 1980-83. No pro playing experience. College coach: Western Michigan 1984-86, Pittsburgh 1987, Morehead State 1988, Cincinnati 1989-1996, Indiana 1997. Pro coach: Joined Eagles in 1998.

Jim Johnson, defensive coordinator; born May 26, 1941, Maywood, Ill. Quarterback Missouri 1959-1962. Pro tight end Buffalo Bills 1963-64. College coach: Missouri Southern 1967-68 (head coach), Drake 1969-1972, Indiana 1973-76, Notre Dame 1977-1980. Pro coach: Oklahoma Outlaws (USFL) 1984, Jacksonville Bulls (USFL) 1985, Phoenix Cardinals 1986-1993, Indianapolis Colts 1994-97, Seattle Seahawks 1998, joined Eagles in 1999.

Sean McDermott, secondary/safeties; born March 21, 1974, Omaha, Neb. Safety William & Mary 1994-97. No pro playing experience. College coach: William & Mary 1998. Pro coach: Joined Eagles in 1998.

Tom Melvin, tight ends; born October 1, 1961, Redwood City, Calif. Offensive lineman San Francisco State 1982-83. No pro playing experience. College coach: San Francisco State 1984-85, Northern Arizona 1986-87, California-Santa Barbara 1988-1990, Occidental College 1991-98. Pro coach: Joined Eagles in 1999.

Marty Mornhinweg, senior assistant; born March 29, 1962, Edmond, Okla.. Quarterback Montana 1981-84. Pro quarterback Denver Dynamite (Arena Football League) 1987. College coach: Montana 1985, Texas-El Paso 1986-87, Northern Arizona 1988, 1994, Southeast Missouri State 1989-1990, Missouri 1991-93. Pro coach: Green Bay Packers 1995-96, San Francisco 49ers 1997-2000, Detroit Lions 2001-02 (head coach), joined Eagles in 2003.

Mike Reed, defensive assistant/quality control; born August 16, 1972, Wilmington, Del. Defensive back Boston College 1991-94. Pro defensive back Carolina Panthers 1995-96, Frankfurt Galaxy (NFL Europe) 1998-99. College coach: Richmond 2000-02. Pro coach: Joined Eagles in 2003.

Bill Shuey, offensive assistant/quality control; born October 5, 1974, Bethlehem, Pa. Attended Slippery Rock. No college or pro playing experience. Pro coach: Joined Eagles in 2003.

Pat Shurmur, quarterbacks; born April 14, 1965, Dearborn Heights, Mich. Center Michigan State 1983-87. No pro playing experience. College coach: Michigan State 1988-1997, Stanford 1998. Pro coach: Joined Eagles in 1999.

Steve Spagnuolo, linebackers; born December 21, 1959, Witinsville, Mass. Wide receiver Springfield College 1979-1981. No pro playing experience. College coach: Massachusetts 1982-83, Lafayette 1984-86, Connecticut 1987-1991, Maine 1993, Rutgers 1994-95, Bowling Green 1996-97. Pro coach: Barcelona Dragons (World League) 1992, Frankfurt Galaxy (NFL Europe) 1998, joined Eagles in 1999.

Trent Walters, secondary; born November 20. 1943, Knoxville, Tenn. Defensive back Indiana 1963-65. Pro defensive back Edmonton Eskimos (CFL) 1966-67. College coach: Indiana 1968-1971, Louisville 1972, 1986-1990, Indiana 1973-1980, Washington 1981-83, Pittsburgh 1985, Texas A&M 1991-93, Notre Dame 2002-03. Pro coach: Cincinnati Bengals 1984, Minnesota Vikings 1994-2001, joined Eagles in 2004.

Ted Williams, running backs; born November 17, 1943, Lyons, Texas. Attended Cal Poly-Pomona. No college or pro playing experience. College coach: UCLA 1980-89, Washington State 1991-93, Arizona 1994. Pro coach: Joined Eagles in 1995.

Mike Wolf, strength and conditioning; born May 15, 1965, Allentown, Pa. Center Penn State 1983-87. No pro playing experience. College coach: Vanderbilt 1988-89, Lehigh 1990, Penn State 1991. Pro coach: Minnesota Vikings 1992-94, joined Eagles in 1995.

National Football Conference
West Division
Team Colors: New Century Gold, Millennium Blue, and White
One Rams Way
St. Louis, Missouri 63045
Telephone: (314) 982-7267

2004 SCHEDULE

PRESEASON		St. Louis time
Aug. 12	**Chicago**	7:00
Aug. 23	at Kansas City	7:00
Aug. 27	**Washington**	7:00
Sept. 2	at Oakland	9:00

REGULAR SEASON

Sept. 12	**Arizona**	12:00
Sept. 19	at Atlanta	12:00
Sept. 26	**New Orleans**	12:00
Oct. 3	at San Francisco	7:30
Oct. 10	at Seattle	3:15
Oct. 18	**Tampa Bay** (Mon.)	8:00
Oct. 24	at Miami	12:00
Oct. 31	Open Date	
Nov. 7	**New England**	3:15
Nov. 14	**Seattle**	12:00
Nov. 21	at Buffalo	12:00
Nov. 29	at Green Bay (Mon.)	8:00
Dec. 5	**San Francisco**	12:00
Dec. 12	at Carolina	3:15
Dec. 19	at Arizona	3:05
Dec. 27	**Philadelphia** (Mon.)	8:00
Jan. 2	**New York Jets**	12:00

Stadium: Edward Jones Dome (opened in 1995) • **Capacity:** 66,000
701 Convention Plaza
St. Louis, Missouri 63101
Playing Surface: AstroTurf
Training Camp: Western Illinois University
Thompson Hall
Macomb, Illinois 61455

EDWARD JONES DOME

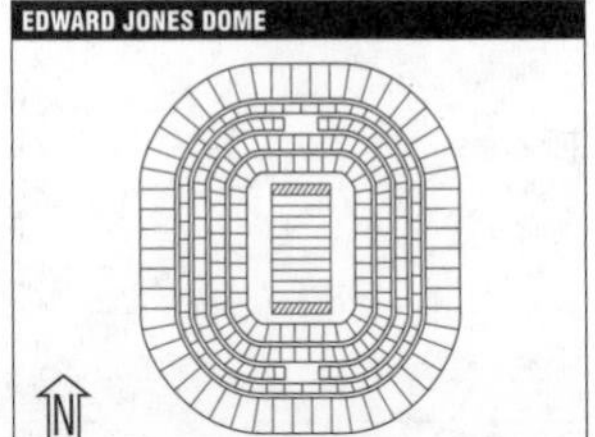

CLUB OFFICIALS
Owner/Chairman: Georgia Frontiere
Owner/Vice Chairman: Stan Kroenke
President: John Shaw
President-Football Operations: Jay Zygmunt
Executive Vice President: Bob Wallace
Treasurer: Jeff Brewer
Vice President-Finance: Adrian Bracy
General Manager: Charley Armey
Vice President-Sales and Marketing: Phil Thomas
Director-Player Personnel: Lawrence McCutcheon
Vice President-Ticket Operations: Michael T. Naughton
Vice President-Operations: John Oswald
Director-Football Administration: Samir Suleiman
Director-Football Media: Duane Lewis
Head Trainer: Jim Anderson
Assistant Trainers: Dake Walden, Ron DuBuque
Equipment Manager: Todd Hewitt
Scouts: Dick Daniels, Mel Foels, Tom Marino, John Mancini, David Razzano

COACHING HISTORY
Cleveland 1937-1945,
Los Angeles 1946-1994
(494-438-20)

1937-38	Hugo Bezdek*	1-13-0
1938	Art Lewis	4-4-0
1939-1942	Earl (Dutch) Clark	16-26-2
1944	Aldo (Buff) Donelli	4-6-0
1945-46	Adam Walsh	16-5-1
1947	Bob Snyder	6-6-0
1948-49	Clark Shaughnessy	14-8-3
1950-52	Joe Stydahar**	19-9-0
1952-54	Hamp Pool	23-11-2
1955-59	Sid Gillman	28-32-1
1960-62	Bob Waterfield***	9-24-1
1962-65	Harland Svare	14-31-3
1966-1970	George Allen	49-19-4
1971-72	Tommy Prothro	14-12-2
1973-77	Chuck Knox	57-20-1
1978-1982	Ray Malavasi	43-36-0
1983-1991	John Robinson	79-74-0
1992-94	Chuck Knox	15-33-0
1995-96	Rich Brooks	13-19-0
1997-99	Dick Vermeil	25-26-0
2000-03	Mike Martz	45-24-0

*Released after three games in 1938
**Resigned after one game in 1952
***Resigned after eight games in 1962

ATTENDANCE
Home 515,747 Away 508,330
Total 1,024,077
Single-game home record, 66,273 (12/10/00)
Single-season home record, 520,926 (1999)

2004 DRAFT CHOICES

Round	Name	Pos.	College
1	Steven Jackson	RB	Oregon State
3	Tony Hargrove	DE	Georgia Tech
4	Brandon Chillar	LB	UCLA
5	Jason Shivers	DB	Arizona State
6	Jeff Smoker	QB	Michigan State
7	Erik Jensen	TE	Iowa
	Larry Turner	C	Eastern Kentucky

ST. LOUIS RAMS

2003 TEAM RECORD

PRESEASON (1-3)

Date	Result	Opponent
8/8	L 6-7	at Oakland
8/18	W 26-16	Tampa Bay
8/23	L 24-28	at Buffalo
8/28	L 6-22	at Kansas City

REGULAR SEASON (12-4)

Date	Result	Opponent	Att.
9/7	L 13-23	at New York Giants	78,666
9/14	W 27-24	San Francisco (OT)	65,990
9/21	L 23-24	at Seattle	65,841
9/28	W 37-13	Arizona	65,758
10/13	W 36-0	Atlanta	66,075
10/19	W 34-24	Green Bay	66,201
10/26	W 33-21	at Pittsburgh	62,665
11/2	L 10-30	at San Francisco	67,812
11/9	W 33-22	Baltimore	66,085
11/16	W 23-21	at Chicago	61,820
11/23	W 30-27	at Arizona (OT)	42,089
11/30	W 48-17	Minnesota	66,134
12/8	W 26-20	at Cleveland	73,108
12/14	W 27-22	Seattle	66,152
12/21	W 27-10	Cincinnati	66,061
12/28	L 20-30	at Detroit	61,006

(OT) Overtime

POSTSEASON (0-1)

Date	Result	Opponent	
1/10	L 23-29	Carolina (2OT)	66,135

SCORE BY PERIODS

Rams	123	120	76	122	6 —	447
Opponents	67	117	82	62	0 —	328

2003 TEAM STATISTICS

	Rams	Opp.
Total First Downs	335	272
Rushing	97	92
Passing	211	164
Penalty	27	16
3rd Down: Made/Att	92/216	75/209
3rd Down Pct.	42.6	35.9
4th Down: Made/Att	7/15	9/21
4th Down Pct.	46.7	42.9
Possession Avg.	31:53	28:07
Total Net Yards	5457	5052
Avg. Per Game	341.1	315.8
Total Plays	1054	964
Avg. Per Play	5.2	5.2
Net Yards Rushing	1496	1980
Avg. Per Game	93.5	123.8
Total Rushes	411	412
Net Yards Passing	3961	3072
Avg. Per Game	247.6	192.0
Sacked/Yards Lost	43/326	42/291
Gross Yards	4287	3363
Att./Completions	600/377	510/296
Completion Pct.	62.8	58.0
Had Intercepted	23	24
Punts/Average	59/42.8	74/41.4
Net Punting Avg.	59/32.9	74/34.6
Penalties/Yards	92/667	114/882
Fumbles/Ball Lost	33/16	31/22
Touchdowns	47	39
Rushing	19	9
Passing	23	23
Returns	5	7

2003 INDIVIDUAL STATISTICS

PASSING	Att.	Comp.	Yds.	Pct.	TD	Int.	Tkld.	Rate
Bulger	532	336	3,845	63.2	22	22	37/288	81.4
Warner	65	38	365	58.5	1	1	6/38	72.9
Bruce	2	2	66	100.0	0	0	0/0	118.8
Looker	1	1	11	100.0	0	0	0/0	112.5
Rams	600	377	4,287	62.8	23	23	43/326	81.0
Opponents	510	296	3,363	58.0	23	24	42/291	73.3

SCORING	TD R	TD P	TD Rt	PAT	FG	Saf	PTS
Wilkins	0	0	0	46/46	39/42	0	163
Holt	0	12	0	0/0	0/0	0	72
M. Faulk	10	1	0	0/0	0/0	0	66
Bruce	0	5	0	0/0	0/0	0	30
Bulger	4	0	0	0/0	0/0	0	24
Harris	4	0	0	0/0	0/0	0	24
Looker	0	3	0	0/0	0/0	0	18
T. Fisher	0	0	2	0/0	0/0	0	12
Manumaleuna	0	2	0	0/0	0/0	0	12
A. Williams	0	0	2	0/0	0/0	0	12
Archuleta	0	0	1	0/0	0/0	0	6
Gordon	1	0	0	0/0	0/0	0	6
Wistrom	0	0	0	0/0	0/0	1	2
Rams	19	23	5	46/46	39/42	1	447
Opponents	9	23	7	35/36	19/24	1	328

2-Pt. Conversions: None.
Rams 0-1, Opponents 0-3.

RUSHING	No.	Yds	Avg	LG	TD
M. Faulk	209	818	3.9	52	10
Gordon	71	298	4.2	20	1
Harris	85	255	3.0	18	4
Bulger	29	75	2.6	28	4
Bruce	2	17	8.5	14	0
Manumaleuna	4	15	3.8	8	0
McDonald	2	7	3.5	5	0
Wilkins	1	7	7.0	7	0
Furrey	3	5	1.7	2	0
Holt	1	5	5.0	5	0
Warner	1	0	0.0	0	0
Massey	1	-1	-1.0	-1	0
Cleeland	2	-5	-2.5	0	0
Rams	411	1,496	3.6	52	19
Opponents	412	1,980	4.8	76t	9

RECEIVING	No.	Yds	Avg	LG	TD
Holt	117	1,696	14.5	48	12
Bruce	69	981	14.2	41	5
Looker	47	495	10.5	41	3
M. Faulk	45	290	6.4	30	1
Manumaleuna	29	238	8.2	39	2
Furrey	20	189	9.5	24	0
Harris	15	102	6.8	26	0
Cleeland	10	145	14.5	29	0
McDonald	10	62	6.2	13	0
Gordon	8	59	7.4	21	0
Curtis	4	13	3.3	8	0
St. Clair	1	18	18.0	18	0
Nead	1	6	6.0	6	0
Timmerman	1	-7	-7.0	-7	0
Rams	377	4,287	11.4	48	23
Opponents	296	3,363	11.4	77	23

INTERCEPTIONS	No.	Yds	Avg	LG	TD
T. Fisher	4	205	51.3	74t	2
A. Williams	4	82	20.5	46t	1
Butler	4	72	18.0	45	0
Polley	4	32	8.0	22	0
Tinoisamoa	3	46	15.3	29	0
Little	1	28	28.0	28	0
Archuleta	1	22	22.0	22	0
Jackson	1	11	11.0	11	0
Groce	1	7	7.0	7	0
Duncan	1	0	0.0	0	0
Rams	24	505	21.0	74t	3
Opponents	23	300	13.0	70t	1

PUNTING	No.	Yds.	Avg.	In 20	LG
Landeta	59	2,525	42.8	14	57
Rams	59	2,525	42.8	14	57
Opponents	74	3,061	41.4	19	61

PUNT RETURNS	Ret	FC	Yds	Avg	LG	TD
Groce	19	3	135	7.1	19	0
Furrey	11	7	119	10.8	28	0
Harris	7	0	36	5.1	13	0
Looker	2	1	47	23.5	44	0
Rams	39	11	337	8.6	44	0
Opponents	32	12	484	15.1	84t	2

KICKOFF RETURNS	No.	Yds	Avg	LG	TD
Harris	51	1,175	23.0	42	0
Furrey	7	140	20.0	27	0
Reynolds	6	109	18.2	25	0
Nead	2	27	13.5	20	0
Coady	1	0	0.0	0	0
Goodspeed	1	1	1.0	1	0
Groce	1	33	33.0	25	0
St. Clair	1	3	3.0	3	0
Rams	70	1,488	21.3	42	0
Opponents	83	1,985	23.9	100t	2

FIELD GOALS	1-19	20-29	30-39	40-49	50+
Wilkins	0/0	16/16	11/13	8/9	4/4
Rams	0/0	16/16	11/13	8/9	4/4
Opponents	0/0	5/5	7/9	6/7	1/3

SACKS	No.
Little	12.5
Wistrom	7.5
Jackson	5.5
Archuleta	5.0
B. Fisher	2.0
Thomas	2.0
Tinoisamoa	2.0
Young	2.0
Duncan	1.0
Pickett	1.0
A. Williams	1.0
Lewis	0.5
Rams	42.0
Opponents	43.0

RECORD HOLDERS

INDIVIDUAL RECORDS—CAREER

Category	Name	Performance
Rushing (Yds.)	Eric Dickerson, 1983-87	7,245
Passing (Yds.)	Jim Everett, 1986-1993	23,758
Passing (TDs)	Roman Gabriel, 1962-1972	154
Receiving (No.)	Isaac Bruce, 1994-2003	688
Receiving (Yds.)	Isaac Bruce, 1994-2003	10,461
Interceptions	Ed Meador, 1959-1970	46
Punting (Avg.)	Danny Villanueva, 1960-64	44.3
Punt Return (Avg.)	Az-Zahir Hakim, 1998-2001	11.4
Kickoff Return (Avg.)	Ron Brown, 1984-89, 1991	26.3
Field Goals	Jeff Wilkins, 1997-2003	163
Touchdowns (Tot.)	Marshall Faulk, 1999-2003	80
Points	Mike Lansford, 1982-1990	789
	Jeff Wilkins, 1997-2003	789

INDIVIDUAL RECORDS—SINGLE SEASON

Category	Name	Performance
Rushing (Yds.)	Eric Dickerson, 1984	*2,105
Passing (Yds.)	Kurt Warner, 2001	4,830
Passing (TDs)	Kurt Warner, 1999	41
Receiving (No.)	Isaac Bruce, 1995	119
Receiving (Yds.)	Isaac Bruce, 1995	1,781
Interceptions	Dick (Night Train) Lane, 1952	*14
Punting (Avg.)	Danny Villanueva, 1962	45.5
Punt Return (Avg.)	Woodley Lewis, 1952	18.5
Kickoff Return (Avg.)	Verda (Vitamin T) Smith, 1950	33.7
Field Goals	Jeff Wilkins, 2003	39
Touchdowns (Tot.)	Marshall Faulk, 2000	*26
Points	Jeff Wilkins, 2003	163

INDIVIDUAL RECORDS—SINGLE GAME

Category	Name	Performance
Rushing (Yds.)	Willie Ellison, 12-5-71	247
Passing (Yds.)	Norm Van Brocklin, 9-28-51	*554
Passing (TDs)	Many times	5
	Last time by Kurt Warner, 10-10-99	
Receiving (No.)	Tom Fears, 12-3-50	18
Receiving (Yds.)	Willie Anderson, 11-26-89	*336
Interceptions	Many times	3
	Last time by Keith Lyle, 12-15-96	
Field Goals	Bob Waterfield, 12-9-51	5
	Jeff Wilkins, 10-1-00	5
Touchdowns (Tot.)	Many times	4
	Last time by Marshall Faulk, 10-20-02	
Points	Many times	24
	Last time by Marshall Faulk, 10-20-02	

*NFL Record

ST. LOUIS RAMS

2004 VETERAN ROSTER

No.	Name	Pos.	Ht.	Wt.	Birthdate	NFL Exp.	College	Hometown	How Acq.	'03 Games/ Starts
31	Archuleta, Adam	S	6-0	223	11/27/77	4	Arizona State	Chandler, Ariz.	D1b-'01	13/13
80	Bruce, Isaac	WR	6-0	188	11/10/72	11	Memphis State	Fort Lauderdale, Fla.	D2a-'94	15/15
10	Bulger, Marc	QB	6-3	215	4/5/77	4	West Virginia	Pittsburgh, Pa.	FA-'01	15/15
23	Butler, Jerametrius	CB	5-10	181	11/28/78	4	Kansas State	Dallas, Texas	D5-'01	16/15
12	Chandler, Chris	QB	6-4	224	10/12/65	17	Washington	Everett, Wash.	FA-'04	8/6*
25	Coady, Rich	S	6-1	210	1/26/76	6	Texas A&M	Dallas, Texas	T(Ind)-'03	13/5
83	Curtis, Kevin	WR	5-11	186	7/17/78	2	Utah State	South Jordan, Utah	D3-'03	4/1
58	Eby, Andy	C	6-3	300	4/26/79	3	Kansas State	Olathe, Kan.	FA-'02	0*
28	Faulk, Marshall	RB	5-10	211	2/26/73	11	San Diego State	New Orleans, La.	T(Ind)-'99	11/11
57	Faulk, Trev	LB	6-3	254	8/6/81	3	Louisiana State	Lafayette, La.	FA-'03	0*
94	Fisher, Bryce	DE	6-3	272	5/12/77	4	Air Force	Renton, Wash.	W(Buff)-'02	16/1
22	Fisher, Travis	CB	5-10	189	9/12/79	3	Central Florida	Tallahassee, Fla.	D2-'02	15/15
96	Flowers, Erik	DE	6-4	273	3/1/78	5	Arizona State	San Antonio, Texas	FA-'03	4/0
82	Furrey, Mike	WR	6-0	185	5/12/77	2	Northern Iowa	Hilliard, Ohio	FA-'03	13/0
21	Garrett, Kevin	CB	5-10	194	7/29/80	2	Southern Methodist	Brazoria, Texas	D5c-'03	9/0
44	Goodspeed, Joey	RB	6-1	247	2/22/78	3	Notre Dame	Oswego, Ill.	FA-'03	8/4
34	Gordon, Lamar	RB	6-1	228	1/7/80	3	North Dakota State	Milwaukee, Wis.	D3a-'02	10/4
24	Groce, DeJuan	CB	5-10	192	2/17/80	2	Nebraska	Garfield Heights, Ohio	D4b-'03	16/1
33	Harris, Arlen	RB	5-10	212	4/22/80	2	Virginia	Downingtown, Pa.	FA-'03	16/2
81	Holt, Torry	WR	6-0	190	6/5/76	6	North Carolina State	Greensboro, N.C.	D1-'99	16/15
97	Jackson, Tyoka	DT	6-2	280	11/22/71	10	Penn State	Forrestville, Md.	UFA(TB)-'01	16/3
73	Kennedy, Jimmy	DT	6-4	320	11/15/79	2	Penn State	Yonkers, N.Y.	D1-'03	13/0
65	King, Andy	G	6-4	310	11/9/78	3	Illinois State	Lincoln, Ill.	FA-'02	1/0
5	Landeta, Sean	P	6-0	215	1/6/62	20	Towson State	Towson, Md.	UFA(Phil)-'03	16/0
92	Lewis, Damione	DT	6-2	301	3/1/78	4	Miami	Sulphur Springs, Texas	D1a-'01	12/7
91	Little, Leonard	DE	6-3	261	10/19/74	7	Tennessee	Asheville, N.C.	D3-'98	12/12
89	Looker, Dane	WR	6-0	194	5/5/76	4	Washington	Puyallup, Wash.	FA-'02	16/2
56	Loyd, Jeremy	LB	6-2	235	7/30/80	2	Iowa State	Pittsburg, Texas	FA-'03	10/0
86	Manumaleuna, Brandon	TE	6-2	288	1/4/80	4	Arizona	Lomita, Calif.	D4b-'01	16/15
45	Massey, Chris	RB	6-0	245	8/21/79	3	Marshall	Chesapeake, W. Va.	D7-'02	16/0
67	McCollum, Andy	G	6-4	300	6/2/70	11	Toledo	Richfield, Ohio	UFA(NO)-'99	16/16
84	McDonald, Shaun	WR	5-10	183	6/13/81	2	Arizona State	Phoenix, Ariz.	D4a-'03	8/1
99	Moran, Sean	DE	6-4	275	6/5/73	9	Colorado State	Aurora, Colo.	FA-'04	16/0*
47	Nead, Spencer	TE	6-4	259	11/3/77	2	Brigham Young	Driggs, Idaho	FA-'04	10/0
51	Newson, Tony	LB	6-1	247	9/11/79	2	Utah State	Las Vegas, Nev.	FA-'04	0*
76 †	Pace, Orlando	T	6-7	325	11/4/75	8	Ohio State	Sandusky, Ohio	D1-'97	16/16
79	Pickett, Ryan	DT	6-2	310	10/8/79	4	Ohio State	Zephyrhills, Fla.	D1c-'01	16/13
52	Polley, Tommy	LB	6-3	240	1/18/78	4	Florida State	Baltimore, Md.	D2-'01	14/14
53	Smith, Justin	LB	6-0	221	6/5/79	3	Indiana	Indianapolis, Ind.	FA-'03	3/0
59	Spoon, Brandon	LB	6-2	240	7/5/78	3	North Carolina	Burlington, N.C.	FA-'04	0*
63	Tercero, Scott	G	6-4	303	10/28/81	2	California	Pico Rivera, Calif.	FA-'03	0*
55	Thomas, Robert	LB	6-1	237	7/17/80	3	UCLA	Imperial, Calif.	D1-'02	12/9
62	Timmerman, Adam	G	6-4	310	8/14/71	10	South Dakota State	Cherokee, Iowa	UFA(GB)-'99	16/16
50	Tinoisamoa, Pisa	LB	6-1	235	7/15/81	2	Hawaii	Vista, Calif.	D2-'03	16/15
68	Turley, Kyle	T	6-5	309	9/24/75	7	San Diego State	Moreno Valley, Calif.	T(NO)-'03	16/16
38	Walton, Shane	S	5-11	195	10/9/79	2	Notre Dame	San Diego, Calif.	D5b-'03	4/0
14	Wilkins, Jeff	K	6-2	205	4/19/72	11	Youngstown State	Austintown, Ohio	RFA(SF)-'97	16/0
35	Williams, Aeneas	S	5-11	200	1/29/68	14	Southern	New Orleans, La.	T(Ariz)-'01	16/16
77	Williams, Grant	T	6-7	320	5/10/74	9	Louisiana Tech	Clinton, Miss.	T(NE)-'02	16/0
64	Wohlabaugh, Dave	C	6-3	302	4/13/72	10	Syracuse	Hamburg, N.Y.	FA-'03	16/16

* Chandler played 8 games with Chicago in '03; Eby missed '03 season because of injury; T. Faulk with St. Louis only in postseason; Moran played 16 games with San Francisco; Newson last active with Kansas City in '02; Spoon last active with Buffalo in '02; Tercero inactive for 3 games.

† Franchise player; subject to developments.

Players lost through free agency (4): G David Loverne (Det; 1 game in '03), T John St. Clair (Mia; 16), DE Grant Wistrom (Sea; 16), DT Brian Young (NO; 16).

Also played with Rams in '03—RB Dan Alexander (1 game), TE Richard Angulo (6), LB Courtland Bullard (9), TE Cameron Cleeland (16), TE Dan Curley (1), LB Jamie Duncan (16), RB Joffrey Reynolds (4), S Jason Sehorn (10), LB Scott Shanle (5), DT Jeremy Staat (3), QB Kurt Warner (2), CB Fred Weary (11), CB James Whitley (3).

2004 FIRST-YEAR ROSTER

Name	Pos.	Ht.	Wt.	Birthdate	College	Hometown	How Acq.
Anderson, Dwight	CB	5-10	172	7/5/81	South Dakota	Bluefield, Conn.	FA
Brake, Mike	TE	6-4	256	5/6/80	Akron	Hilliard, Ohio	FA
Burley, Nick (1)	DE	6-3	243	3/31/80	Fresno State	Mountain View, Calif.	FA
Chillar, Brandon	LB	6-3	253	10/21/82	UCLA	Carlsbad, Calif.	D4
Coleman, Michael (1)	WR	6-0	190	9/7/80	Widener	Wilmington, Del.	FA
Copeland, Shedrick	S	6-1	216	9/14/80	Florida A&M	Miami, Fla.	FA
Frieser, John	TE	6-4	260	12/10/81	Colgate	Endwell, N.Y.	FA
Hargrove, Anthony	DE	6-3	269	7/20/83	Georgia Tech	Punta Gorda, Fla.	D3
Hofmann, Joel	T	6-7	300	7/27/81	Ball State	Liberty, Ind.	FA
Howard, Brian	DT	6-4	278	9/9/81	Idaho	Kent, Wash.	FA
Jackson, Steven	RB	6-2	231	7/22/83	Oregon State	Las Vegas, Nev.	D1
Jensen, Erik	TE	6-2	253	10/11/80	Iowa	Appleton, Wis.	D7a
Jensen, Mark (1)	K	6-2	205	7/11/76	California	Pleasant Grove, Utah	FA
Jones, Jamal	WR	5-11	212	4/24/81	North Carolina A&T	Washington, D.C.	FA
Kight, Kelvin	WR	6-0	213	7/2/82	Florida	Lithonia, Ga.	FA
Matthews, Adam	RB	5-10	205	10/3/81	Northern Colorado	Northglenn, Colo.	FA
McCoy, Derek	WR	6-3	210	11/13/80	Colorado	Thornton, Colo.	FA
McGrorty, Dusty	RB	5-10	218	5/9/81	Southern Oregon	Warrenton, Ore.	FA
McGuffey, Ryan	WR	6-2	210	2/19/81	Wyoming	Riverton, Wyo.	FA
McWilliams, Jason (1)	LB	6-0	224	8/31/79	Western Illinois	Detroit, Mich.	FA
Miller, Fred	LB	6-0	219	1/11/82	Eastern Illinois	Fort Lauderdale, Fla.	FA
Miner, Jimmy	P	6-0	206	1/6/82	Wofford	Kennesaw, Ga.	FA
Morgan, Matt	T	6-6	304	12/3/80	Pittsburgh	Plum, Pa.	FA
Narcisse, Nick	WR	5-11	178	12/24/80	Tulane	Slidell, La.	FA
Phillips, Jeremy	T	6-4	315	8/5/80	Lenoir-Rhyne	Eden, N.C.	FA
Ruffin, Jeff	DT	6-3	295	2/6/81	Illinois	Aurora, Ill.	FA
Shivers, Jason	S	6-0	201	11/4/82	Arizona State	Phoenix, Ariz.	D5
Smoker, Jeff	QB	6-3	223	6/13/81	Michigan State	Manheim, Pa.	D6
Stephens, Brandon	T	6-6	282	12/7/79	Brigham Young	Logan, Utah	FA
Thompson, David (1)	DT	6-5	295	8/23/79	Ohio State	Paterson, N.J.	FA
Turner, Larry	C	6-2	290	3/8/82	Eastern Kentucky	Huber Heights, Ohio	D7b
Williams, Kailan	S	6-1	194	11/17/81	Southwest Missouri State	Tucson, Ariz.	FA
Worthy, Kevin	LB	6-0	233	10/14/81	Iowa	Attalla, Ala.	FA
Yates, Corey	CB	5-9	177	7/17/79	Southern Mississippi	Holly Springs, Miss.	FA

The term NFL Rookie is defined as a player who is in his first season of professional football and has not been on the roster of another professional football team for any regular-season or postseason games. A Rookie is designated by an "R" on NFL rosters. Players who have been active in another professional football league or players who have NFL experience, including either preseason training camp or being on an Active List or Inactive List, or on Reserve/Injured or Reserve/Physically Unable to Perform for fewer than six regular-season games, are termed NFL First-Year Players. An NFL First-Year Player is designated by a "1" on NFL rosters. Thereafter, a player is credited with an additional year of experience for each season in which he accumulates six games on the Active List or Inactive List, or on Reserve/Injured or Reserve/Physically Unable to Perform.

Log on to www.stlouisrams.com for an up-to-date roster.

ST. LOUIS RAMS

COACHING STAFF

Head Coach,
Mike Martz

Pro Career: Named twenty-first head coach of the Rams on February 2, 2000. Led Rams to two division titles and three playoff berths in his four seasons as head coach, including berth in Super Bowl XXXVI. In 2003, he led the Rams to their second division title in three years. In 2002, he became only second coach in NFL history to lead team to five consecutive wins after an 0-5 start. Offensive mastermind behind one of the most explosive offenses in NFL history, as Rams are the only franchise in league history to score at least 500 points in three different seasons (526 in 1999, 540 in 2000, 503 in 2001). Since he rejoined the Rams as offensive coordinator in 1999, the Rams have scored more points (2,332), gained more total yards (31,193), and accumulated more passing yards (22,363) than in any club during a five-year span in NFL history. The Rams also produced three consecutive NFL most valuable players (quarterback Kurt Warner 1999 and 2001, running back Marshall Faulk 2000). Martz rejoined Rams in 1999 after two seasons as quarterbacks coach of Washington Redskins. He began his NFL career with the Rams, where he coached tight ends, receivers, and quarterbacks (1992-96). Career record: 45-24.

Background: Played tight end at Fresno State (1972) after transferring from the University of California-Santa Barbara. Began coaching career in 1973 at Bullard High in Fresno, California, before coaching collegiately at San Diego Mesa Community College (1974, 1976-77), San Jose State (1975), and Santa Ana College (1978), Fresno State (1979), Pacific (1980-81), Minnesota (1982), and Arizona State (1983-1991), where he served as the Sun Devils' offensive coordinator the final five seasons.

Personal: Born May 13, 1951 in Sioux Falls, S.D. Graduated summa cum laude from Fresno State (1973). Lives with wife Julie and has three sons and one daughter.

ASSISTANT COACHES

Bob Babich, linebackers; born February 20, 1961, Aliquippa, Pa. Linebacker Mesa (Colo.) C.C. 1979-1980, Tulsa 1981-82. No pro playing experience. College coach: Tulsa 1984-87, 1990, Wisconsin 1988-89, Bowling Green 1991, East Carolina 1992-93, Pittsburgh 1994-96, North Dakota State 1997-2002 (head coach). Pro coach: Joined Rams in 2003.

John Benton, asst. offensive line, born December 13, 1963, Los Angeles. Offensive lineman Colorado State 1986-1990. No pro playing experience. College coach: California University (Penn.)_ 1990-94, Colorado State 1996-2003. Pro coach: Joined Rams in 2004.

Gill Byrd, defensive assistant; born February 20, 1961, San Francisco. Cornerback San Jose 1979-1982. Pro cornerback San Diego Chargers 1983-1992. Pro coach: Joined Rams in 2003.

Chris Clausen, strength and conditioning coordinator; born February 21, 1958, Evergreen Park, Ill. Cornerback Indiana 1976-79. No pro playing experience. College coach: San Diego State 1987-88. Pro coach: San Diego Chargers 1989-1991, joined Rams in 1992.

Henry Ellard, wide receivers; born July 21, 1961, Fresno, Calif. Wide receiver Fresno State 1979-1982. Pro wide receiver-punt returner Los Angeles Rams 1983-1993, Washington Redskins 1994-97, New England Patriots 1998, Washington Redskins 1998. College coach: Fresno State 2000. Pro coach: Joined Rams in 2001.

Steve Fairchild, offensive coordinator; born June 21, 1958, Decatur, Ill. Quarterback Colorado State 1980-81. No pro playing experience. College coach: Mesa (Colo.) C.C. 1982-83, Ferris State 1984-85, San Diego State 1991-92, Colorado State 1997-2000. Pro coach: Buffalo Bills 2001-02, joined Rams in 2003.

Frank Falks, tight ends; born March 9, 1943, Tampa. Linebacker Joplin (Mo.) J.C. 1963-64, Parsons College 1965-66. No pro playing experience. College coach: Parsons College 1967-69, Kansas State 1970-72, Arkansas 1973-77, Wyoming 1978-79, San Diego State 1980, Oklahoma State 1981-82, Southern California 1983-86, Arizona State 1987-1991, Ohio State 1992-93. Pro coach: San Diego Chargers 1994-96, Detroit Lions 1997-2000, joined Rams in 2003.

Perry Fewell, secondary; born November 7, 1962, Gastonia, N.C. Defensive back Lenoir-Ryhne 1981-84. No pro playing experience: College coach: Army 1987, 1992-94, Kent State 1988-1991, Vanderbilt 1995-97. Pro coach: Jacksonville Jaguars 1998-2002, joined Rams in 2003.

Bill Kollar, defensive line; born November 27, 1952, Warren, Ohio. Defensive end Montana State 1971-74. Pro defensive end Cincinnati Bengals 1974-76, Tampa Bay Buccaneers 1977-1981. College coach: Illinois 1985-87, Purdue 1988-89. Pro coach: Tampa Bay Buccaneers 1984, Atlanta Falcons 1990-2000, joined Rams in 2001.

Dana LeDuc, strength and conditioning; born March 22, 1953, Tacoma, Wash. Attended Texas. No college or pro playing experience. College coach: Texas 1977-1992, Miami 1993-94. Pro coach: Seattle Seahawks 1995-98, joined Rams in 1999.

Larry Marmie, defensive coordinator, born October 17, 1942, Barnesville, Ohio. Quarterback Eastern Kentucky 1962-65. No pro playing experience. College coach: Eastern Kentucky 1967-68, 1972-76, Morehead State 1968-1971, Tulsa 1977-78, North Carolina 1979-1982, Tennessee 1983-84, 1992-94, Arizona State 1988-91 (head coach), UCLA 1995. Pro coach: Arizona Cardinals 1996-2003, joined Rams in 2004.

John Matsko, associate head coach/offensive line; born February 2, 1951, Cleveland. Fullback Kent State 1970-73. No pro playing experience. College coach Kent State 1973, Miami (Ohio) 1974-75, 1977, North Carolina 1978-1984, Navy 1985, Arizona 1986, Southern California 1987-1991. Pro coach: Phoenix Cardinals 1992-93, New Orleans Saints 1994-96, New York Giants 1997-98, joined Rams in 1999.

Wilbert Montgomery, running backs; born September 16, 1954, Greenville, Miss. Running back Abilene Christian 1973-76. Pro running back Philadelphia Eagles 1977-1984, Detroit Lions 1985-86. Pro coach: Joined Rams in 1997.

John Ramsdell, quarterbacks; born August 16, 1954, Lafayette, Ind. Running back Springfield (Mass.) College 1972-75. No pro playing experience. College coach: San Francisco State 1976-77, Long Beach State 1978, Pacific 1979-1982, Oregon 1983-1994. Pro coach: Joined Rams in 1995.

Matt Sheldon, special assistant/special teams; born February 26, 1969, Berwyn, Ill. Cornerback Minnesota 1987-1991. No pro playing experience. College coach: Wisconsin 1997-99. Pro coach: Joined Rams in 2001.

Mike Stock, special teams, born September 29, 1939, Baberton, Ohio. Fullback Northwestern 1957-1960. Pro running back Saskatchewan Roughriders (CFL) 1961. College coach: Northwestern 1961, Buffalo 1966-67, Navy 1968, Notre Dame 1969-1974, 1984-86, Wisconsin 1975-78, Eastern Michigan 1979-1983 (head coach), Ohio State 1992-94. Pro coach: Cincinnati Bengals 1987-1991, Kansas City Chiefs 1995-2000, Washington Redskins 2001-2003, joined Rams in 2004.

Joe Vitt, asst. head coach/linebackers, born August 23, 1954, Syracuse, N.Y. Linebacker Towson State 1973-75. No pro playing experience. Pro coach: Baltimore Colts 1979-1981, Seattle Seahawks 1982-1991, L.A. Rams 1992-94, Philadelphia Eagles 1995-98, Green Bay Packers 1999, Kansas City Chiefs 2000-2003, Joined Rams in 2004.

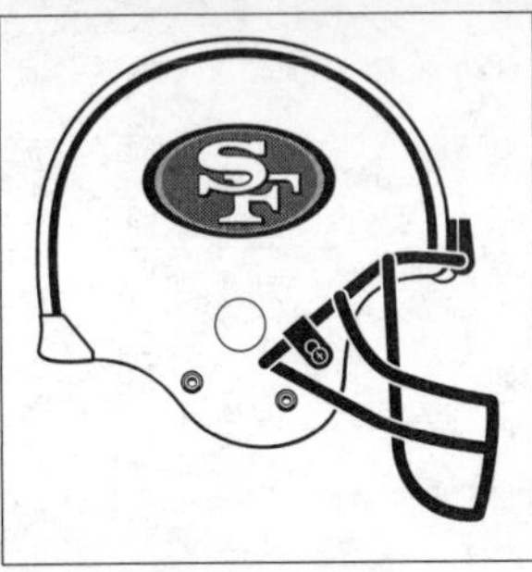

National Football Conference
West Division
Team Colors: Metalllic Gold, Cardinal Red, and Beige
4949 Centennial Boulevard
Santa Clara, California 95054
Telephone: (408) 562-4949

2004 SCHEDULE

PRESEASON — **San Francisco time**

Aug. 14	**Oakland**	5:00
Aug. 21	at Chicago	5:30
Aug. 27	at Minnesota	5:00
Sept. 2	**San Diego**	8:00

REGULAR SEASON

Sept. 12	**Atlanta**	1:15
Sept. 19	at New Orleans	10:00*
Sept. 26	at Seattle	1:15
Oct. 3	**St. Louis**	5:30
Oct. 10	**Arizona**	1:15
Oct. 17	at New York Jets	10:00*
Oct. 24	Open Date	
Oct. 31	at Chicago	5:30
Nov. 7	**Seattle**	1:05
Nov. 14	**Carolina**	1:15
Nov. 21	at Tampa Bay	10:00*
Nov. 28	**Miami**	1:15
Dec. 5	at St. Louis	10:00*
Dec. 12	at Arizona	1:15
Dec. 18	**Washington** (Sat.)	2:00
Dec. 26	**Buffalo**	1:05
Jan. 2	at New England	10:00*

*A.M.

Stadium: 3Com Park (opened in 1958)
•**Capacity:** 69,734
San Francisco, California
94124
Playing Surface: Grass
Training Camp: 49ers Facility
4949 Centennial Boulevard
Santa Clara, California
95054

3COM PARK

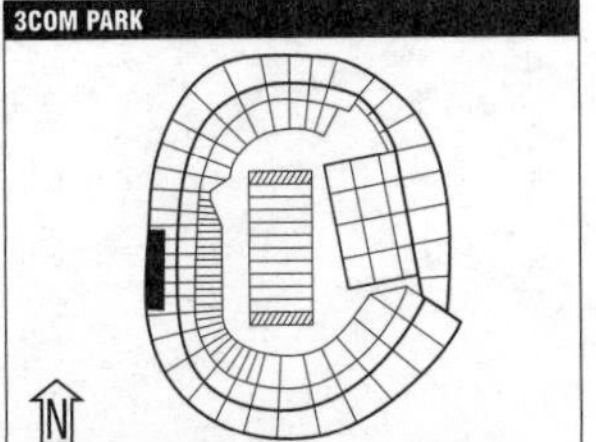

CLUB OFFICIALS

Owner: Denise DeBartolo York
Owner: Dr. John York
Owner: The DeBartolo Corporation
General Manager: Terry Donahue
CFO: Larry MacNeil
President/CEO: Peter Harris
Asst. Director of Football Operations/ Salary Cap: Dominic Corsell
Vice President/Operations: Murlan Fowell
Director of Player Personnel: Bill Rees
Vice President of Business Affairs/ General Counsel: Ed Goines
Personnel Consultant: Bill McPherson
Asst. Director of Football Administration: Terry Turney
Ticket Manager: Lynn Carrozzi
Director of Security: Fred Formosa
Director of Public Relations: Kirk Reynolds
Equipment Manager: Steve Urbaniak
Head Athletic Trainer: Todd Lazenby
Video Director: Robert Yanagi

COACHING HISTORY
(457-350-13)

1950-54	Lawrence (Buck) Shaw	33-25-2
1955	Norman (Red) Strader	4-8-0
1956-58	Frankie Albert	19-17-1
1959-1963	Howard (Red) Hickey*	27-27-1
1963-67	Jack Christiansen	26-38-3
1968-1975	Dick Nolan	56-56-5
1976	Monte Clark	8-6-0
1977	Ken Meyer	5-9-0
1978	Pete McCulley**	1-8-0
1978	Fred O'Connor	1-6-0
1979-1988	Bill Walsh	102-63-1
1989-1996	George Seifert	108-35-0
1997-2002	Steve Mariucci	60-43-0
2003	Dennis Erickson	7-9-0

*Resigned after three games in 1963
**Released after nine games in 1978

ATTENDANCE

Home 540,644 Away 501,299
Total 1,041,943
Single-game home record, 69,014 (11/13/94)
Single-season home record, 544,228 (1999)

2004 DRAFT CHOICES

Round	Name	Pos.	College
1	Rashaun Woods	WR	Oklahoma St.
2	Justin Smiley	G	Alabama
	Shawntae Spencer	DB	Pittsburgh
3	Derrick Hamilton	WR	Clemson
4	Isaac Sopoaga	DT	Hawaii
	Richard Seigler	LB	Oregon State
6	Andy Lee	P	Pittsburgh
	Keith Lewis	DB	Oregon
7	Cody Pickett	QB	Washington
	Christian Ferrara	DT	Syracuse

SAN FRANCISCO 49ERS

2003 TEAM RECORD

PRESEASON (3-1)

Date	Result	Opponent
8/9	W 24-6	at Kansas City
8/14	W 14-10	Oakland
8/23	W 27-12	New Orleans
8/29	L 3-24	at San Diego

REGULAR SEASON (7-9)

Date	Result	Opponent	Att.
9/7	W 49-7	Chicago	67,554
9/14	L 24-27	at St. Louis (OT)	65,990
9/21	L 12-13	Cleveland	67,412
9/28	L 7-35	at Minnesota	+4,111
10/5	W 24-17	Detroit	67,365
10/12	L 19-20	at Seattle	66,437
10/19	W 24-7	Tampa Bay	67,809
10/26	L 13-16	at Arizona (OT)	40,824
11/2	W 30-10	St. Louis	67,812
11/17	W 30-14	Pittsburgh	67,877
11/23	L 10-20	at Green Bay	70,250
11/30	L 6-44	at Baltimore	69,549
12/7	W 50-14	Arizona	66,975
12/14	L 38-41	at Cincinnati	64,666
12/21	W 31-28	at Philadelphia (OT)	67,866
12/27	L 17-24	Seattle	67,840

(OT) Overtime

SCORE BY PERIODS

49ers	85	133	78	85	3	— 384
Opponents	66	113	48	104	6	— 337

2003 TEAM STATISTICS

	49ers	Opp.
Total First Downs	313	292
Rushing	118	99
Passing	172	165
Penalty	23	28
3rd Down: Made/Att	86/215	85/209
3rd Down Pct.	40.0	40.7
4th Down: Made/Att	5/19	7/12
4th Down Pct.	26.3	58.3
Possession Avg.	30:54	29:06
Total Net Yards	5,687	4,928
Avg. Per Game	355.4	308.0
Total Plays	1,038	976
Avg. Per Play	5.5	5.0
Net Yards Rushing	2,279	1,690
Avg. Per Game	142.4	105.6
Total Rushes	499	420
Net Yards Passing	3,408	3,238
Avg. Per Game	213.0	202.4
Sacked/Yards Lost	28/158	42/306
Gross Yards	3,566	3,544
Att./Completions	511/299	514/310
Completion Pct.	58.5	60.3
Had Intercepted	15	23
Punts/Average	69/38.1	76/39.1
Net Punting Avg.	69/33.5	76/34.7
Penalties/Yards	104/807	78/720
Fumbles/Ball Lost	24/10	23/14
Touchdowns	44	41
Rushing	16	13
Passing	25	25
Returns	3	3

2003 INDIVIDUAL STATISTICS

PASSING	Att.	Comp.	Yds.	Pct.	TD	Int.	Tkld.	Rate
Garcia	392	225	2,704	57.4	18	13	21/104	80.1
Rattay	118	73	856	61.9	7	2	7/54	96.6
Wilson	1	1	6	100.0	0	0	0/0	91.7
49ers	511	299	3,566	58.5	25	15	28/158	84.0
Opponents	514	310	3,544	60.3	25	23	42/306	78.6

SCORING	TD R	TD P	TD Rt	PAT	FG	Saf	PTS
T. Peterson	0	0	0	22/23	12/15	0	58
Owens	0	9	0	0/0	0/0	0	54
Barlow	6	1	0	0/0	0/0	0	42
Garcia	7	0	0	0/0	0/0	0	42
Streets	0	7	0	0/0	0/0	0	42
Pochman	0	0	0	9/10	8/15	0	33
Chandler	0	0	0	7/8	6/7	0	25
Hearst	3	1	0	0/0	0/0	0	24
Wilson	0	2	1	0/0	0/0	0	18
Lloyd	0	2	0	0/0	0/0	0	14
Beasley	0	1	0	0/0	0/0	0	6
Harris	0	0	1	0/0	0/0	0	6
Plummer	0	0	1	0/0	0/0	0	6
Walker	0	1	0	0/0	0/0	0	6
Weaver	0	1	0	0/0	0/0	0	6
Ulbrich	0	0	0	0/0	0/0	1	2
49ers	16	25	3	38/41	26/37	1	384
Opponents	13	25	3	40/40	17/26	0	337

2-Pt. Conversions: Lloyd.
49ers 1-3, Opponents 0-1.

RUSHING	No.	Yds	Avg	LG	TD
Barlow	201	1,024	5.1	78t	6
Hearst	178	768	4.3	36	3
Garcia	56	319	5.7	21t	7
Robertson	32	136	4.3	23	0
Beasley	17	24	1.4	5	0
Battle	2	14	7.0	9	0
Lafleur	1	0	0.0	0	0
Rattay	8	0	0.0	6	0
Owens	3	-2	-0.7	3	0
Wilson	1	-4	-4.0	-4	0
49ers	499	2,279	4.6	78t	16
Opponents	420	1,690	4.0	49t	13

RECEIVING	No.	Yds	Avg	LG	TD
Owens	80	1,102	13.8	75t	9
Streets	47	595	12.7	41t	7
Weaver	35	437	12.5	30	1
Wilson	35	396	11.3	29	2
Barlow	35	307	8.8	48	1
Hearst	25	211	8.4	26	1
Beasley	19	184	9.7	32	1
Lloyd	14	212	15.1	44	2
Walker	8	116	14.5	26	1
Garcia	1	6	6.0	6	0
49ers	299	3,566	11.9	75t	25
Opponents	310	3,544	11.4	75t	25

INTERCEPTIONS	No.	Yds	Avg	LG	TD
Parrish	9	202	22.4	49	0
Plummer	4	85	21.3	68t	1
Rumph	3	19	6.3	12	0
J. Peterson	2	31	15.5	31	0
Bronson	1	22	22.0	22	0
Webster	1	17	17.0	17	0
Ulbrich	1	7	7.0	7	0
J. Williams	1	6	6.0	6	0
Heard	1	0	0.0	0	0
49ers	23	389	16.9	68t	1
Opponents	15	291	19.4	65	1

PUNTING	No.	Yds.	Avg.	In 20	LG
Lafleur	68	2,629	38.7	17	56
49ers	69	2,629	38.1	17	56
Opponents	76	2,975	39.1	16	58

PUNT RETURNS	Ret	FC	Yds	Avg	LG	TD
J. Williams	35	10	240	6.9	20	0
Bruce	4	2	24	6.0	18	0
Wilson	1	3	12	12.0	12	0
49ers	40	15	276	6.9	20	0
Opponents	28	15	258	9.2	81t	1

KICKOFF RETURNS	No.	Yds	Avg	LG	TD
Wilson	37	836	22.6	95t	1
J. Williams	11	207	18.8	41	0
Bruce	6	125	20.8	29	0
Battle	5	88	17.6	21	0
Lloyd	2	32	16.0	21	0
Moran	2	35	17.5	19	0
Gutierrez	1	4	4.0	4	0
49ers	64	1,327	20.7	95t	1
Opponents	77	1,641	21.3	75	0

FIELD GOALS	1-19	20-29	30-39	40-49	50+
T. Peterson	0/0	5/7	3/3	4/4	0/1
Pochman	0/0	1/1	3/8	4/5	0/1
Chandler	0/0	5/5	1/1	0/1	0/0
49ers	0/0	11/13	7/12	8/10	0/2
Opponents	0/0	6/6	8/9	2/9	1/2

SACKS	No.
J. Peterson	7.0
Carter	6.5
Engelberger	4.5
Ahanotu	4.0
Smith	3.5
Young	3.5
Winborn	3.0
Ulbrich	2.5
Rumph	2.0
Adams	1.5
Kirschke	1.5
Moran	1.5
Heard	0.5
Parrish	0.5
49ers	42.0
Opponents	28.0

RECORD HOLDERS

INDIVIDUAL RECORDS—CAREER

Category	Name	Performance
Rushing (Yds.)	Joe Perry, 1950-1960, 1963	7,344
Passing (Yds.)	Joe Montana, 1979-1992	35,124
Passing (TDs)	Joe Montana, 1979-1992	244
Receiving (No.)	Jerry Rice, 1985-2000	1,281
Receiving (Yds.)	Jerry Rice, 1985-2000	19,247
Interceptions	Ronnie Lott, 1981-1990	51
Punting (Avg.)	Tommy Davis, 1959-1969	44.7
Punt Return (Avg.)	Dana McLemore, 1982-87	10.8
Kickoff Return (Avg.)	Abe Woodson, 1958-1964	29.4
Field Goals	Ray Wersching, 1977-1987	190
Touchdowns (Tot.)	Jerry Rice, 1985-2000	187
Points	Jerry Rice, 1985-2000	1,130

INDIVIDUAL RECORDS—SINGLE SEASON

Category	Name	Performance
Rushing (Yds.)	Garrison Hearst, 1998	1,570
Passing (Yds.)	Jeff Garcia, 2000	4,278
Passing (TDs)	Steve Young, 1998	36
Receiving (No.)	Jerry Rice, 1995	122
Receiving (Yds.)	Jerry Rice, 1995	*1,848
Interceptions	Dave Baker, 1960	10
	Ronnie Lott, 1986	10
Punting (Avg.)	Tommy Davis, 1965	45.8
Punt Return (Avg.)	Dana McLemore, 1982	22.3
Kickoff Return (Avg.)	Joe Arenas, 1953	34.4
Field Goals	Jeff Wilkins, 1996	30
Touchdowns (Tot.)	Jerry Rice, 1987	23
Points	Jerry Rice, 1987	138

INDIVIDUAL RECORDS—SINGLE GAME

Category	Name	Performance
Rushing (Yds.)	Charlie Garner, 9-24-00	201
Passing (Yds.)	Joe Montana, 10-14-90	476
Passing (TDs)	Joe Montana, 10-14-90	6
Receiving (No.)	Terrell Owens, 12-17-00	*20
Receiving (Yds.)	Jerry Rice, 12-18-95	289
Interceptions	Dave Baker, 12-4-60	*4
Field Goals	Ray Wersching, 10-16-83	6
	Jeff Wilkins, 9-29-96	6
Touchdowns (Tot.)	Jerry Rice, 10-14-90	5
Points	Jerry Rice, 10-14-90	30

*NFL Record

SAN FRANCISCO 49ERS

2004 VETERAN ROSTER

No.	Name	Pos.	Ht.	Wt.	Birthdate	NFL Exp.	College	Hometown	How Acq.	'03 Games/ Starts
91	Adams, Anthony	DT	6-0	300	8/18/80	2	Penn State	Detroit, Mich.	D2-'03	14/1
32	† Barlow, Kevan	RB	6-1	238	1/7/79	4	Pittsburgh	Pittsburgh, Pa.	D3-'01	16/4
83	Battle, Arnaz	WR	6-1	217	2/22/80	2	Notre Dame	Dallas, Texas	D6-'03	8/0
40	Beasley, Fred	FB	6-0	246	9/18/74	7	Auburn	Montgomery, Ala.	D6-'98	16/11
9	Boyd, Danny	K	5-11	220	6/1/78	2	Louisiana State	Bradenton, Fla.	FA-'04	0*
31	Bronson, Zack	S	6-1	204	1/28/74	8	McNeese State	Jasper, Texas	FA-'97	12/12
35	Carpenter, Dwaine	S	6-1	203	11/4/76	2	North Carolina A&T	Pinehurst, N.C.	FA-'03	15/2
96	Carter, Andre	DE	6-4	265	5/12/79	4	California	San Jose, Calif.	D1-'01	15/15
	Conway, Curtis	WR	6-1	196	1/13/71	12	Southern California	Hawthorne, Calif.	FA-'04	16/15*
76	Davis, Jerome	T	6-5	290	2/4/74	3	Minnesota	Detroit, Mich.	FA-'03	2/0
75	Demaree, Chris	DE	6-3	265	3/12/80	2	Kentucky	Louisville, Ky.	FA-'04	0*
11	Doman, Brandon	QB	6-1	210	12/29/76	2	Brigham Young	Salt Lake City, Utah	FA-'04	0*
7	Dorsey, Ken	QB	6-4	205	4/22/81	2	Miami	Orinda, Calif.	D7-'03	0*
95	#Engelberger, John	DE	6-4	268	10/18/76	5	Virginia Tech	Green Bay, Wis.	D2a-'00	16/16
78	Gragg, Scott	T	6-8	315	2/28/72	10	Montana	Silverton, Ore.	UFA(NYG)-'00	15/14
52	Gutierrez, Brock	C	6-3	304	9/25/73	8	Central Michigan	Charlotte, Mich.	FA-'03	13/0
77	Harris, Kwame	T	6-7	310	3/15/82	2	Stanford	Jamaica	D1-'03	14/5
38	#Heard, Ronnie	S	6-3	215	10/5/76	5	Mississippi	Bay City, Texas	FA-'03	12/1
66	Heitmann, Eric	G	6-3	305	2/24/80	3	Stanford	Katy, Texas	D7a-'02	9/8
41	Isom, Jasen	FB	6-0	240	1/7/77	2	Western Illinois	Wheatley Heights, Md.	FA-'02	1/0
22	Jackson, Terry	FB	6-0	232	1/10/76	6	Florida	Gainesville, Fla.	D5-'99	16/0
86	#Jennings, Brian	TE-LS	6-5	245	10/14/76	5	Arizona State	Mesa, Ariz.	D7b-'00	16/0
82	† Johnson, Eric	TE	6-3	256	9/15/79	4	Yale	Needham, Mass.	D7b-'01	0*
18	Jordan, James	WR	6-2	225	6/11/78	2	Louisiana Tech	Kenner, La.	FA-'03	1/0
69	Kosier, Kyle	T	6-5	293	1/27/78	3	Arizona State	Peoria, Ariz.	D7b-'02	16/12
67	Ledford, Dwayne	C	6-4	300	11/2/76	3	East Carolina	Marion, N.C.	FA-'03	8/1
85	Lloyd, Brandon	WR	6-0	184	7/5/81	2	Illinois	Kansas City, Mo.	D4-'03	16/1
72	Mitrione, Matt	DT	6-2	295	7/15/78	2	Purdue	Springfield, Ill.	FA-'04	0*
56	Moore, Brandon	LB	6-1	242	1/16/79	3	Oklahoma	Baldwin, N.Y.	FA-'02	15/1
68	Murphy, Rob	C-G	6-5	310	1/18/77	3	Ohio State	Cincinnati, Ohio	FA-'03	1/0
62	Newberry, Jeremy	C	6-5	310	3/23/76	7	California	Antioch, Calif.	D2-'98	16/16
33	Parrish, Tony	S	6-0	210	11/23/75	7	Washington	Huntington Beach, Wash.	UFA(Chi)-'02	16/16
98	Peterson, Julian	LB	6-3	235	7/28/78	5	Michigan State	Hillcrest Heights, Ohio	D1a-'00	16/16
2	Peterson, Todd	K	5-11	177	2/4/70	11	Georgia	Washington, D.C.	FA-'03	8/0
29	#Plummer, Ahmed	CB	6-0	191	3/26/76	5	Ohio State	Wyoming, Ohio	D1b-'00	15/15
64	#Randall, Greg	T	6-5	322	6/23/78	5	Michigan State	Galveston, Texas	UFA(Hou)-'04	16/16*
51	Rasheed, Saleem	LB	6-2	229	6/15/81	3	Alabama	Birmingham, Ala.	D3-'02	16/1
13	Rattay, Tim	QB	6-0	200	3/15/77	5	Louisiana Tech	Elyria, Ohio	D7a-'00	11/3
60	#Rehberg, Scott	T-G	6-8	325	11/17/73	8	Central Michigan	Kalamazoo, Mich.	FA-'04	16/1
25	Robertson, Jamal	RB	5-10	210	1/10/77	3	Ohio Northern	Dayton, Ohio	FA-'02	9/0
24	Rumph, Mike	CB	6-2	205	11/8/79	3	Miami	Boynton Beach, Fla.	D1-'02	15/13
92	Shaw, Josh	DT	6-2	290	9/7/79	2	Michigan State	Fort Lauderdale, Fla.	FA-'04	0*
50	Smith, Derek	LB	6-2	245	1/18/75	8	Arizona State	American Fork, Utah	UFA(Wash)-'01	16/16
53	Ulbrich, Jeff	LB	6-0	249	2/17/77	5	Hawaii	San Jose, Calif.	D3b-'00	15/15
49	Walker, Aaron	TE	6-6	252	3/14/80	2	Florida	Titusville, Fla.	D5-'03	16/2
94	t- Whiting, Brandon	DE	6-3	285	7/30/76	7	California	Long Beach, Calif.	T(Phil)-'04	14/14
99	Williams, Andrew	DE	6-2	263	4/18/79	2	Miami	Tampa, Fla.	D3-'03	2/0
23	† Williams, Jimmy	CB	5-11	190	3/10/79	4	Vanderbilt	Baton Rouge, La.	FA-'01	15/0
84	† Wilson, Cedrick	WR	5-10	183	12/17/78	4	Tennessee	Memphis, Tenn.	D6a-'01	16/4
55	Winborn, Jamie	LB	5-11	242	5/14/79	4	Vanderbilt	Wetumpka, Ala.	D2-'01	9/0
97	Young, Bryant	DT	6-3	291	1/27/72	11	Notre Dame	Chicago Heights, Ill.	D1-'94	16/16

* Boyd last played with Jacksonville in '02; Conway played 16 games with N.Y. Jets in '03; Demaree last active with San Diego in '02; Doman inactive for 16 games for San Francisco in '02; Dorsey inactive for 13 games; Johnson missed '03 season because of injury; Mitrione last active with N.Y. Giants in '02; Randall played 16 games with Houston; Shaw last active with San Francisco in '02.

\# Restricted free agent; subject to developments.

† Unrestricted free agent; subject to developments.

t- 49ers traded for Whiting (Phil).

Traded—WR Terrell Owens (15 games in '03) to Baltimore.

Players lost through free agency (4): DT Travis Kirschke (Pitt; 15 games in '03), WR Tai Streets(Det; 16), TE Jed Weaver (Den; 16), CB Jason Webster (Atl; 5).

Also played with 49ers in '03—DE Chidi Ahanotu (16 games), LB Cornelius Anthony (7), WR Arland Bruce (2), K Jeff Chandler (2), LB Devone Claybrooks (3), T Derrick Deese (11), QB Jeff Garcia (13), RB Garrison Hearst (12), CB Rashad Holman (14), S John Keith (8), P Bill LaFleur (16), DE Sean Moran (16), K Owen Pochman (6), G Ron Stone (13).

2004 FIRST-YEAR ROSTER

Name	Pos.	Ht.	Wt.	Birthdate	College	Hometown	How Acq.
Adams, Mike	CB	5-11	193	3/24/81	Delaware	Paterson, N.J.	FA
Allen, Bosley (1)	WR	6-1	195	6/7/80	Sam Houston State	Tallahassee, Fla.	FA
Amundson, Allan (1)	CB	5-9	186	9/9/80	Oregon	Kentfield, Calif.	FA
Bruce, Arland (1)	WR-KR	5-10	193	11/23/77	Minnesota	Kansas City, Kan.	FA-'03
Carlyle, Calvin (1)	CB	6-0	192	9/12/79	Oregon State	Los Angeles, Calif.	FA
Carothers, Greg	LB	6-2	230	7/13/81	Washington	Helena, Mont.	FA
Cooper, Josh	DE	6-3	261	12/5/80	Mississippi	Marietta, Ga.	FA
Crecion, Gabe (1)	TE	6-5	255	7/9/77	UCLA	Westhills, Calif.	FA
Cunningham, Alonzo (1)	G	6-4	315	5/21/79	Iowa	Iowa City, Iowa	FA-'03
Drew, Randee	CB	5-9	192	1/22/81	Northern Illinois	Milwaukee, Wis.	FA
Ferrara, Christian	DT	6-4	295	2/21/81	Syracuse	Livingston, N.J.	D7b
Fikse, Nate (1)	P	5-9	195	8/11/81	UCLA	Anaheim, Calif.	FA
Fleck, P.J.	WR	5-10	191	11/29/80	Northern Illinois	Sugar Grove, Ill.	FA
Groom, Andy (1)	P	6-1	198	9/10/79	Ohio State	Columbus, Ohio	FA
Hamilton, Derrick	WR	6-4	203	11/30/81	Clemson	Dillon, S.C.	D3
Hanson, Joselio (1)	CB	5-9	175	8/13/81	Texas Tech	Los Angeles, Calif.	FA
Helfman, Marcus (1)	TE-LS	6-5	255	1/8/80	San Jose State	Agoura Hills, Calif.	FA
Herzing, Adam (1)	WR	6-3	205	9/23/80	Cal Poly	San Jose, Calif.	FA
Hicks, Maurice (1)	RB	5-11	200	7/22/78	North Carolina A&T	Emporia, Va.	FA
Hill, Kahlil (1)	WR	6-2	200	3/18/79	Iowa	Iowa City, Iowa	FA
Jackson, Pasha	LB	6-2	247	8/9/82	Oklahoma	Hayward, Calif.	FA
Johnson, Tony	WR	5-11	202	3/12/82	Penn State	State College, Pa.	FA
Jones, Ronald	DE	6-4	284	9/17/81	Southern Mississippi	Gulfport, Miss.	FA
Katnik, Norm	C	6-4	298	7/2/81	Southern California	Santa Ana, Calif.	FA
Landry, Michael (1)	DE	6-3	267	12/12/78	Southern	Donaldsonville, La.	FA
Lee, Andy	P	6-0	206	8/11/82	Pittsburgh	Westminster, N.C.	D6a
Lewis, Keith	S	6-0	202	10/20/81	Oregon	Sacramento, Calif.	D6b
Maxie, Demetrious (1)	LB	6-2	280	10/18/73	Texas-El Paso	Downey, Calif.	FA
Pickett, Cody	QB	6-3	227	6/30/80	Washington	Caldwell, Idaho	D7a
Poli-Dixon, Brian (1)	WR	6-5	210	4/21/79	UCLA	Tucson, Ariz.	FA
Reed, Rayshun	CB	5-10	185	4/10/81	Troy State	Columbus, Ga.	FA
Seigler, Richard	LB	6-2	238	10/19/80	Oregon State	Las Vegas, Nev.	D4b
Simmons, Antuan (1)	CB	5-9	185	3/31/79	Southern California	Sacramento, Calif.	FA
Smiley, Justin	G	6-3	301	11/11/81	Alabama	Ellabel, Ga.	D2a
Sopoaga, Issac	DT	6-2	321	9/4/81	Hawaii	Pago, Pago, American Samoa	D4a
Spencer, Shawntae	CB	6-1	181	2/22/82	Pittsburgh	Rankin, Pa.	D2b
Stamps, Fred	WR	6-0	190	12/10/80	Louisiana-Lafayette	New Orleans, La.	FA
Stanley, Matt (1)	FB	6-3	245	4/27/79	UCLA	Columbus, Ohio	FA
Swaggert, Brent	T	6-4	293	4/7/81	Montana State	Buffalo, Minn.	FA
Woods, Rashaun	WR	6-2	202	10/17/80	Oklahoma State	Oklahoma City, Okla.	D1
Wright, Jason	RB	5-10	211	7/12/82	Northwestern	Diamond Bar, Calif.	FA
Yliniemi, Kirk	K	6-1	207	11/21/80	Oregon State	Independence, Ore.	FA
Zureki, Kevin	TE	6-2	267	11/3/80	Eastern Michigan	Dearborn, Mich.	FA

The term NFL Rookie is defined as a player who is in his first season of professional football and has not been on the roster of another professional football team for any regular-season or postseason games. A Rookie is designated by an "R" on NFL rosters. Players who have been active in another professional football league or players who have NFL experience, including either preseason training camp or being on an Active List or Inactive List, or on Reserve/Injured or Reserve/Physically Unable to Perform for fewer than six regular-season games, are termed NFL First-Year Players. An NFL First-Year Player is designated by a "1" on NFL rosters. Thereafter, a player is credited with an additional year of experience for each season in which he accumulates six games on the Active List or Inactive List, or on Reserve/Injured or Reserve/Physically Unable to Perform.

Log on to www.sf49ers.com for an up-to-date roster.

SAN FRANCISCO 49ERS

COACHING STAFF
Head Coach,
Dennis Erickson

Pro Career: Named the fourteenth head coach in 49ers history on February 12, 2003. Erickson previously spent four seasons (1995-98) with Seattle, where he coached the Seahawks to a 31-33 record and helped the franchise bounce back from four consecutive losing seasons. Seattle enjoyed its most productive season on offense under Erickson in 1997, leading the NFL in passing offense (274.4 yards/game) and finishing third overall. The defense improved as well, placing eighth in the NFL, making Seattle one of only four teams to place in the top 10 on both sides of the ball. Career record: 38-42.

Background: Two-time first-team All-Big Sky Conference quarterback at Montana State. Erickson began his coaching career as an assistant at his alma mater (1971-73), Idaho (1974-75), Fresno State (1976-78), and San Jose State (1979-1981). He was named head coach at Idaho (1982-85), where he posted a 32-15 record. Erickson spent one season at Wyoming (1986) and two years as head coach at Washington State (1987-88), before moving on to Miami (1989-1994). Erickson won two National Championships (1989 and 1991) with the Hurricanes, becoming one of 15 college coaches to win multiple titles. His 63-9 (.875) record at Miami was the best in the nation during his six-year tenure. Erickson took over the Oregon State program in 1999, leading the Beavers to their first-ever 11-win season in 2000, earning a share of the Pac-10 Conference Championship, a berth in the Fiesta Bowl, and a number four national ranking. His 144 career coaching victories at the collegiate level ranked him ninth among active coaches prior to accepting the position with the 49ers.

Personal: Born March 24, 1947 in Everett, Wash. He and wife, Marilyn, have two sons—Bryce and Ryan.

ASSISTANT COACHES

Jerry Attaway, physical development coordinator; born January 3, 1946, Susanville, Calif. Defensive back Yuba (Calif.) J.C. 1964-65, U.C. Davis 1967. No pro playing experience. College coach: U.C. Davis 1970-71, Idaho 1972-74, Utah State 1975-77, Southern California 1978-1982. Pro coach: Joined 49ers in 1983.

Jamie Christian, defensive quality control; born February 10, 1972, Auburn, Wash. Fullback Fresno State 1990-93, running back Central Washington 1995. College coach: Oregon State 2000-01, Northern Arizona 2002. Pro coach: Joined 49ers in 2003.

Dan Cozzetto, tight ends; born May 26, 1955, Spokane, Wash. Tight end-linebacker-guard Idaho 1976-79. No college or pro playing experience. College coach: Idaho 1979-1989, California 1990-92, Arizona State 1993-99, Oregon State 2000-01, Washington 2003. Pro coach: Joined 49ers in 2004.

Terrell Jones, strength development coordinator; born April 25, 1961, Chicago. Attended San Jose State. No college or pro playing experience. College coach: San Jose (Calif.) C.C. 1998-2000. Pro coach: Joined 49ers in 2000.

Tim Lappano, running backs; born October 14, 1956, Spokane, Wash. Running back Idaho 1976-79. College coach: Idaho 1982-85, Wyoming 1986, 1996, Washington State 1987-1991, California 1992-95, Purdue 1997, Oregon State 1999-2002. Pro coach: Seattle Seahawks 1998, joined 49ers in 2003.

Ron Lynn; secondary; born December 6, 1944, Youngstown, Ohio. Quarterback Mt. Union College 1962-66. College coach: San Jose State 1977-78, Pacific 1979, California 1980-82. Pro coach: San Diego Chargers 1986-1991, Cincinnati Bengals 1992-93, Washington Redskins 1994-96, New England Patriots 1997-99, Oakland Raiders 2000-03, joined 49ers in 2004.

Larry Mac Duff, special teams coordinator; born June 22, 1948, Clinton, Iowa. Defensive end Fullerton (Calif.) J.C. 1966-67, Oklahoma 1968-69. College coach: Stanford 1980-83, Hawaii 1984-86, Arizona 1987-1996, 2001-02. Pro coach: New York Giants 1997-2000, joined 49ers in 2003.

Greg McMackin, asst. head coach/linebackers; born April 24, 1947, Springfield, Ore. College coach: Western Oregon 1974-76, Idaho 1977-78, San Jose State 1979-1983, Stanford 1984, Oregon Tech 1986-89 (head coach), Utah 1990-91, Navy 1992, Miami 1993-94, Hawaii 1999, Texas Tech 2000-02. Pro coach: Denver Gold (USFL) 1985-86, Seattle Seahawks 1995-98, joined 49ers in 2003.

Rich Olson, quarterbacks; born July 7, 1948 in Los Angeles. Quarterback-free safety Washington State 1968-69. College coach: Washington State 1970, Fresno State 1971, 1984-1991, Southern California 1977, Southern Methodist 1978-1980, Arkansas 1981-83. Pro coach: Seattle Seahawks 1995-98, Washington Redskins 1999-2000, Arizona Cardinals 2002, joined 49ers in 2004.

Dan Quinn, defensive line; born September 11, 1970, Orange, N.J. Defensive lineman Salisbury State 1990-93. No pro playing experience. College coach: William & Mary 1994, Virginia Military Institute 1995, Hofstra 1997-2000. Pro coach: Joined 49ers in 2001.

Willy Robinson, defensive coordinator; born February 10, 1956 in Ft. Carson, Colo. Defensive back Fresno State 1976-77. College coach: Fresno State 1978, 1980-1993, San Jose State 1979, Miami 1994, Oregon State 1999. Pro coach: Seattle Seahawks 1995-98, Pittsburgh Steelers 2000-03, joined 49ers in 2004.

Jeff Rodgers, special teams quality control; born January 12, 1978, St. Paul, Minn. Linebacker North Texas 1997-2000. No pro playing experience. College coach: Arizona 2001-02. Pro coach: Joined 49ers in 2003.

Al Simmons, secondary; born December 6, 1962, Oakland. Safety Cal State-Hayward 1982-85. No pro playing experience. College coach: Cal State-Hayward 1986-1993, San Francisco State 1994, Montana State 1995-96, Idaho State 1997, California 1998-2000, Oregon State 2001-02. Pro coach: Joined the 49ers in 2003.

Gregg Smith, asst. head coach/offensive line; born October 28, 1946, Oklahoma City, Okla. Tight end Idaho 1965. No pro playing experience. College coach: Idaho 1982-85, Wyoming 1986, Washington State 1987-88, Miami 1989-1994, Oregon State 1999-2002. Pro coach: Seattle Seahawks 1995-98, joined 49ers in 2003.

Scott Swartz, offensive quality control; born August 11, 1975, San Jose, Calif. Quarterback De Anza Community College 1994-95, Cal State-Northridge 1996. College coach: San Jose State 1997-98, Oregon State 1999-2001, Northern Arizona 2002-03. Pro coach: Joined 49ers in 2004.

Jason Tarver, asst. running backs/offensive assistant; born August 28, 1974, Stanford, Calif. Defensive back West Valley College 1994-95. No pro playing experience. College coach: West Valley College 1996-97, UCLA 1998-2000. Pro coach: Joined 49ers in 2001.

Ted Tollner, offensive coordinator; born May 29, 1940, San Francisco. Quarterback Cal Poly-San Luis Obispo 1959-1961. No pro playing experience. College coach: College of San Mateo 1971-72 (head coach), San Diego State 1973-1980, 1994-2001 (head coach 1994-2001), Brigham Young 1981, Southern California 1982-86 (head coach 1983-86). Pro coach: Buffalo Bills 1987-88, San Diego Chargers 1989-1991, joined 49ers in 2002.

Eric Yarber, wide receivers; born September 22, 1964, Chicago. Wide receiver Los Angeles Valley 1982-83, Idaho 1984-85. Pro wide receiver Washington Redskins 1986-88. College coach: Idaho 1996, Nevada-Las Vegas 1997, Oregon State 1999-2002. Pro coach: Seattle Seahawks 1998, joined 49ers in 2003.

National Football Conference
West Division
Team Colors: Seahawks Blue, Seahawks Navy, Seahawks Bright Green
11220 N.E. 53RD Street
Kirkland, Washington, 98033
Telephone: (425) 827-9777

2004 SCHEDULE

PRESEASON		Seattle time
Aug. 16	at Green Bay	5:00
Aug. 21	**Denver**	7:00
Aug. 27	at San Diego	7:00
Sept. 2	**Minnesota**	6:00

REGULAR SEASON		
Sept. 12	at New Orleans	10:00*
Sept. 19	at Tampa Bay	1:05
Sept. 26	**San Francisco**	1:15
Oct. 3	Open Date	
Oct. 10	**St. Louis**	1:15
Oct. 17	at New England	10:00*
Oct. 24	at Arizona	1:15p
Oct. 31	**Carolina**	1:05
Nov. 7	at San Francisco	1:05
Nov. 14	at St. Louis	10:00*
Nov. 21	**Miami**	1:05
Nov. 28	**Buffalo**	1:15
Dec. 6	**Dallas** (Mon.)	6:00
Dec. 12	at Minnesota	10:00*
Dec. 19	at New York Jets	10:00*
Dec. 26	**Arizona**	1:15
Jan. 2	**Atlanta**	1:05

*A.M.

Stadium: Seahawks Stadium (opened in 2002)
•**Capacity:** 67,000
Playing Surface: FieldTurf
Training Camp: Eastern Washington Univ. Cheney, Washington 99004

SEAHAWKS STADIUM

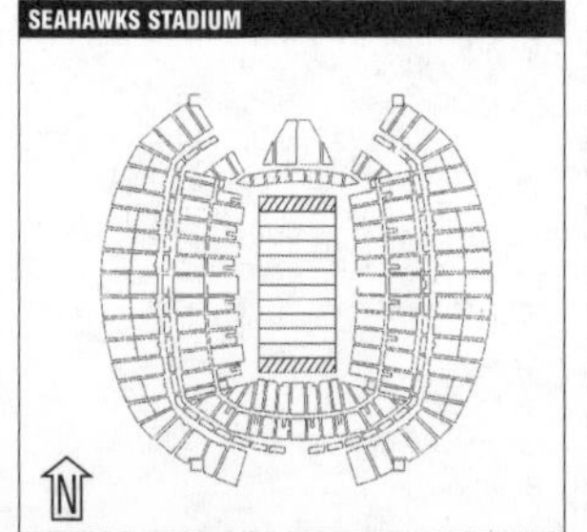

CLUB OFFICIALS

Chairman: Paul Allen
President: Bob Whitsitt
CEO: Tod Leiweke
Executive VP of Football Operations/ Head Coach: Mike Holmgren
General Manager: Bob Ferguson
VP/Community Outreach: Mike Flood
VP/Corporate Partnership/Legal Affairs: Lance Lopes
VP/Football Operations: Ted Thompson
VP/Corporate Sales: Scott Patrick
VP/Administration: Gary Wright
Director of Marketing, Suite Sales and Service: Ron Jenkins
Director of Pro Personnel: Will Lewis
Director of College Scouting: Scot McCloughan
Director of Communications and Broadcasting: Dave Pearson
Asst. Director of Public Relations: Lane Gammel
Director of Community Outreach: Sandy Gregory
Director of Player Programs: Nesby Glasgow
Director of Ticket Sales/Operations: Chuck Arnold
Gameday Presentation: Rick Crawford
Football Operations Coordinator/Team Travel: Bill Nayes
Video Director Football: Thom Fermstad
Head Athletic Trainer: Paul Federici
Equipment Manager: Erik Kennedy

COACHING HISTORY
(208-237-0)

1976-1982	Jack Patera*	35-59-0
1982	Mike McCormack	4-3-0
1983-1991	Chuck Knox	83-67-0
1992-94	Tom Flores	14-34-0
1995-98	Dennis Erickson	31-33-0
1999-2003	Mike Holmgren	41-41-0

*Released after two games in 1982

ATTENDANCE

Home 500,102 Away 490,725
Total 990,827
Single-game home record, 68,681 (12/16/00)
Single-season home record, 522,656 (1999)

2004 DRAFT CHOICES

Round	Name	Pos.	College
1	Marcus Tubbs	DT	Texas
2	Michael Boulware	DB	Florida State
3	Sean Locklear	G	North Carolina St.
4	Niko Koutouvides	LB	Purdue
5	D.J. Hackett	WR	Colorado
6	Craig Terrill	DT	Purdue
7	Donnie Jones	P	Louisiana State

SEATTLE SEAHAWKS

2003 TEAM RECORD

PRESEASON (2-2)

Date	Result	Opponent
8/9	W 20-7	San Diego
8/15	L 7-21	at Indianapolis
8/23	W 42-31	Kansas City
8/29	L 3-20	at Denver

REGULAR SEASON (10-6)

Date	Result	Opponent	Att.
9/7	W 27-10	New Orleans	52,250
9/14	W 38-0	at Arizona	23,127
9/21	W 24-23	St. Louis	65,841
10/5	L 13-35	at Green Bay	70,365
10/12	W 20-19	San Francisco	66,437
10/19	W 24-17	Chicago	65,671
10/26	L 24-27	at Cincinnati	52,131
11/2	W 23-16	Pittsburgh	66,507
11/9	L 20-27	at Washington	80,728
11/16	W 35-14	Detroit	65,865
11/23	L 41-44	at Baltimore (OT)	69,477
11/30	W 34-7	Cleveland	64,680
12/7	L 7-34	at Minnesota	63,968
12/14	L 22-27	at St. Louis	66,152
12/21	W 28-10	Arizona	64,899
12/27	W 24-17	at San Francisco	67,840

POSTSEASON (0-1)

Date	Result	Opponent
1/4	L 27-33	at Green Bay (OT)

(OT) Overtime

SCORE BY PERIODS

Seahawks	89	166	67	82	0 —	404
Opponents	51	104	73	96	3 —	327

2003 TEAM STATISTICS

	Seahawks	Opp.
Total First Downs	338	304
Rushing	121	93
Passing	190	183
Penalty	27	28
3rd Down: Made/Att	96/205	99/235
3rd Down Pct.	46.8	42.1
4th Down: Made/Att	2/7	7/18
4th Down Pct.	28.6	38.9
Possession Avg.	28:33	31:27
Total Net Yards	5,627	5,239
Avg. Per Game	351.7	327.4
Total Plays	1,017	1,069
Avg. Per Play	5.5	4.9
Net Yards Rushing	2,009	1,759
Avg. Per Game	125.6	109.9
Total Rushes	453	456
Net Yards Passing	3,618	3,480
Avg. Per Game	226.1	217.5
Sacked/Yards Lost	43/254	40/248
Gross Yards	3,872	3,728
Att./Completions	521/317	573/343
Completion Pct.	60.8	59.9
Had Intercepted	16	16
Punts/Average	69/40.0	76/39.8
Net Punting Avg.	69/37.1	76/34.1
Penalties/Yards	91/777	105/825
Fumbles/Ball Lost	23/13	25/12
Touchdowns	48	36
Rushing	17	9
Passing	27	24
Returns	4	3

2003 INDIVIDUAL STATISTICS

PASSING	Att.	Comp.	Yds.	Pct.	TD	Int.	Tkld.	Rate
Hasselbeck	513	313	3,841	61.0	26	15	42/246	88.8
Dilfer	8	4	31	50.0	1	1	1/8	59.9
Seahawks	521	317	3,872	60.8	27	16	43/254	88.2
Opponents	573	343	3,728	59.9	24	16	40/248	81.4

SCORING	TD R	TD P	TD Rt	PAT	FG	Saf	PTS
J. Brown	0	0	0	48/48	22/30	0	114
Alexander	14	2	0	0/0	0/0	0	96
Jackson	0	9	0	0/0	0/0	0	54
Engram	0	6	1	0/0	0/0	0	42
K. Robinson	0	4	1	0/0	0/0	0	30
Mili	0	4	0	0/0	0/0	0	24
Hasselbeck	2	0	0	0/0	0/0	0	12
Huff	0	0	1	0/0	0/0	1	8
Bannister	0	1	0	0/0	0/0	0	6
Godfrey	0	0	1	0/0	0/0	0	6
Morris	0	1	0	0/0	0/0	0	6
Strong	1	0	0	0/0	0/0	0	6
Seahawks	17	27	4	48/48	22/30	1	404
Opponents	9	24	3	34/35	25/31	0	327

2-Pt. Conversions: None.
Seahawks 0-0, Opponents 1-1.

RUSHING	No.	Yds	Avg	LG	TD
Alexander	326	1,435	4.4	55	14
Morris	38	239	6.3	43	0
Strong	37	174	4.7	21t	1
Hasselbeck	36	125	3.5	18	2
H. Evans	7	24	3.4	8	0
K. Robinson	4	15	3.8	16	0
Dilfer	2	-1	-0.5	0	0
Carter	3	-2	-0.7	1	0
Seahawks	453	2,009	4.4	55	17
Opponents	456	1,759	3.9	50	9

RECEIVING	No.	Yds	Avg	LG	TD
Jackson	68	1,137	16.7	80t	9
K. Robinson	65	896	13.8	38t	4
Engram	52	637	12.3	34t	6
Mili	46	492	10.7	46t	4
Alexander	42	295	7.0	22	2
Strong	29	216	7.4	32	0
Stevens	6	72	12.0	26	0
Morris	4	32	8.0	13	1
Bannister	3	61	20.3	31t	1
H. Evans	2	34	17.0	20	0
Seahawks	317	3,872	12.2	80t	27
Opponents	343	3,728	10.9	72t	24

INTERCEPTIONS	No.	Yds	Avg	LG	TD
Tongue	4	11	2.8	10	0
Simmons	3	38	12.7	33	0
Trufant	2	21	10.5	15	0
Lucas	1	27	27.0	27	0
D. Robinson	1	26	26.0	26	0
Okeafor	1	18	18.0	18	0
Springs	1	8	8.0	8	0
Godfrey	1	7	7.0	7	0
Hamlin	1	2	2.0	2	0
C. Brown	1	-1	-1.0	-1	0
Seahawks	16	157	9.8	33	0
Opponents	16	164	10.3	80t	1

PUNTING	No.	Yds.	Avg.	In 20	LG
Rouen	67	2,762	41.2	29	61
Seahawks	69	2,762	40.0	29	61
Opponents	76	3,028	39.8	19	64

PUNT RETURNS	Ret	FC	Yds	Avg	LG	TD
Engram	31	22	320	10.3	83t	1
Lucas	1	0	0	0.0	0	0
Richard	1	0	0	0.0	0	0
D. Robinson	1	0	0	0.0	0	0
Seahawks	34	22	320	9.4	83t	1
Opponents	29	22	140	4.8	19	0

KICKOFF RETURNS	No.	Yds	Avg	LG	TD
Morris	47	1,007	21.4	56	0
Carter	8	185	23.1	33	0
Strong	3	60	20.0	27	0
Engram	1	18	18.0	18	0
H. Evans	1	14	14.0	14	0
Hannam	1	17	17.0	17	0
Palepoi	1	14	14.0	14	0
Womack	1	11	11.0	11	0
Wunsch	1	10	10.0	10	0
Seahawks	64	1,336	20.9	56	0
Opponents	79	1,626	20.6	52	0

FIELD GOALS	1-19	20-29	30-39	40-49	50+
J. Brown	0/0	5/5	10/11	6/11	1/3
Seahawks	0/0	5/5	10/11	6/11	1/3
Opponents	0/0	5/6	12/15	7/8	1/2

SACKS	No.
Okeafor	8.0
C. Brown	7.0
Randle	5.5
King	3.0
Mitchell	3.0
Simmons	3.0
Bernard	2.0
Tongue	2.0
Springs	1.5
Cochran	1.0
Hand	1.0
Huff	1.0
Moore	1.0
Richard	1.0
Seahawks	40.0
Opponents	43.0

RECORD HOLDERS

INDIVIDUAL RECORDS—CAREER

Category	Name	Performance
Rushing (Yds.)	Chris Warren, 1990-97	6,706
Passing (Yds.)	Dave Krieg, 1980-1991	26,132
Passing (TDs)	Dave Krieg, 1980-1991	195
Receiving (No.)	Steve Largent, 1976-1989	819
Receiving (Yds.)	Steve Largent, 1976-1989	13,089
Interceptions	Dave Brown, 1976-1986	50
Punting (Avg.)	Rick Tuten, 1991-97	43.8
Punt Return (Avg.)	Charlie Rogers, 1999-2001	12.7
Kickoff Return (Avg.)	Steve Broussard, 1995-98	23.2
Field Goals	Norm Johnson, 1982-1990	159
Touchdowns (Tot.)	Steve Largent, 1976-1989	101
Points	Norm Johnson, 1982-1990	810

INDIVIDUAL RECORDS—SINGLE SEASON

Category	Name	Performance
Rushing (Yds.)	Chris Warren, 1994	1,545
Passing (Yds.)	Matt Hasselbeck, 2003	3,841
Passing (TDs)	Dave Krieg, 1984	32
Receiving (No.)	Brian Blades, 1994	81
Receiving (Yds.)	Steve Largent, 1985	1,287
Interceptions	John Harris, 1981	10
	Kenny Easley, 1984	10
Punting (Avg.)	Rick Tuten, 1995	45.0
Punt Return (Avg.)	Charlie Rogers, 1999	14.5
Kickoff Return (Avg.)	Charlie Rogers, 2000	24.9
Field Goals	Todd Peterson, 1999	34
Touchdowns (Tot.)	Shaun Alexander, 2002	18
Points	Todd Peterson, 1999	134

INDIVIDUAL RECORDS—SINGLE GAME

Category	Name	Performance
Rushing (Yds.)	Shaun Alexander, 11-11-01	266
Passing (Yds.)	Matt Hasselbeck, 12-29-02	449
Passing (TDs)	Dave Krieg, 12-2-84, 9-15-85, 11-28-88	5
	Warren Moon, 10-26-97	5
	Matt Hasselbeck, 11-23-03	5
Receiving (No.)	Steve Largent, 10-18-87	15
Receiving (Yds.)	Steve Largent, 10-18-87	261
Interceptions	Kenny Easley, 9-3-84	3
	Eugene Robinson, 12-6-92	3
	Darryl Williams, 9-21-97	3
Field Goals	Norm Johnson, 9-20-87, 12-18-88	5
Touchdowns (Tot.)	Shaun Alexander, 9-29-02	5
Points	Shaun Alexander, 9-29-02	30

SEATTLE SEAHAWKS

2004 VETERAN ROSTER

No.	Name	Pos.	Ht.	Wt.	Birthdate	NFL Exp.	College	Hometown	How Acq.	'03 Games/ Starts
37	Alexander, Shaun	RB	5-11	225	8/30/77	5	Alabama	Florence, Ky.	D1a-'00	16/15
85	Bannister, Alex	WR	6-5	207	4/23/79	4	Eastern Kentucky	Cincinnati, Ohio	D5-'01	16/2
50	Bates, Solomon	LB	6-1	243	4/18/82	2	Arizona State	Moreno Valley, Calif.	D4b-'03	7/0
99	Bernard, Rocky	DT	6-3	293	4/19/79	3	Texas A&M	Baytown, Texas	D5a-'02	12/0
34	Bierria, Terreal	S	6-3	211	10/10/80	3	Georgia	Slidell, La.	D4-'02	0*
94	Brown, Chad	LB	6-2	245	7/12/70	12	Colorado	Altadena, Calif.	UFA(Pitt)-'97	14/14
3	Brown, Josh	K	6-0	202	4/29/79	2	Nebraska	Foyil, Okla.	D7a-'03	16/0
32	Carter, Kerry	RB	6-1	238	12/19/80	2	Stanford	Vaughn, Ontario	FA-'03	16/0
78	Cochran, Antonio	DE	6-4	299	6/21/76	6	Georgia	Montezuma, Ga.	D4-'99	15/7
52	Darche, Jean-Philippe	LS	6-0	246	2/28/75	5	McGill	Montreal, Quebec, Canada	FA-'00	16/0
35	Davis, Chris	FB	5-11	235	11/8/79	2	Syracuse	Tampa, Fla.	D5-'03	1/0
4	Dilfer, Trent	QB	6-4	225	3/13/72	11	Fresno State	Santa Cruz, Calif.	UFA(Balt)-'01	5/0
84	Engram, Bobby	WR	5-10	188	1/7/73	9	Penn State	Camden, S.C.	UFA(Chi)-'01	16/7
44	Evans, Heath	FB	6-0	245	12/30/78	4	Auburn	W. Palm Beach, Fla.	D3-'01	14/0
62	Gray, Chris	G	6-4	308	6/19/70	12	Auburn	Birmingham, Ala.	UFA(Chi)-'98	16/16
26	Hamlin, Ken	S	6-2	209	1/20/81	2	Arkansas	Memphis, Tenn.	D2-'03	16/14
83	Hannam, Ryan	TE	6-2	248	2/24/80	3	Northern Iowa	St. Ansgar, Iowa	D5b-'02	5/0
8	Hasselbeck, Matt	QB	6-4	223	9/25/75	6	Boston College	Westwood, Mass.	T(GB)-'01	16/16
74	Hill, Matt	T	6-6	304	11/10/78	3	Boise State	Grangeville, Idaho	D5c-'02	13/2
7	Huard, Brock	QB	6-4	232	4/15/76	6	Washington	Puyallup, Wash.	FA-'04	2/0*
57	Huff, Orlando	LB	6-2	250	8/14/78	4	Fresno State	Upland, Calif.	D4a-'01	11/2
73	Hunter, Wayne	T	6-5	303	7/2/81	2	Hawaii	Honolulu, Hawaii	D3-'03	0*
76	Hutchinson, Steve	G	6-5	313	11/1/77	4	Michigan	Ft. Lauderdale, Fla.	D1b-'01	16/16
82	Jackson, Darrell	WR	6-0	201	12/6/78	5	Florida	Tampa, Fla.	D3-'00	16/16
71	Jones, Walter	T	6-5	315	1/19/74	8	Florida State	Aliceville, Ala.	D1b-'97	16/16
58	Kacyvenski, Isaiah	LB	6-1	252	10/3/77	5	Harvard	Endicott, N.Y.	D4b-'00	14/0
54	Lewis, D.D.	LB	6-1	241	1/8/79	3	Texas	Houston, Texas	FA-'02	15/5
21	Lucas, Ken	CB	6-0	205	1/23/79	4	Mississippi	Cleveland, Miss.	D2-'01	14/7
88	Mili, Itula	TE	6-4	260	4/20/73	8	Brigham Young	Laie, Hawaii	D6-'97	16/12
97	Mitchell, Brandon	DE	6-3	290	6/19/75	8	Texas A&M	Abbeville, La.	UFA(NE)-'02	14/6
95	Moore, Rashad	DT	6-3	324	3/16/79	2	Tennessee	Huntsville, Ala.	D6-'03	14/6
20	Morris, Maurice	RB	5-11	202	12/1/79	3	Oregon	Chester, S.C.	D2a-'02	16/1
68	Norman, Dennis	C	6-5	312	1/26/80	4	Princeton	Marlton, N.J.	D7b-'01	1/0
56	Okeafor, Chike	DE	6-4	265	3/27/76	6	Purdue	Grand Rapids, Mich.	UFA(SF)-'03	16/16
91	Palepoi, Anton	DE	6-3	283	11/19/78	3	Nevada-Las Vegas	Salt Lake City, Utah	D2b-'02	7/0
42	Richard, Kris	CB	5-11	190	10/28/78	3	Southern California	Carson, Calif.	D3-'02	15/1
22	Robinson, Damien	S	6-2	223	12/23/73	8	Iowa	Dallas, Texas	UFA(NYJ)-'03	15/4
81	Robinson, Koren	WR	6-1	205	3/19/80	4	North Carolina State	Belmont, N.C.	D1a-'01	15/15
16	Rouen, Tom	P	6-3	225	6/9/68	12	Colorado	Littleton, Colo.	UFA(Pitt)-'03	16/0
51	Simmons, Anthony	LB	6-0	240	6/20/76	7	Clemson	Spartanburg, S.C.	D1-'98	13/13
86	Stevens, Jerramy	TE	6-7	260	11/13/79	3	Washington	Olympia, Wash.	D1-'02	16/3
38	Strong, Mack	FB	6-0	245	9/11/71	12	Georgia	Columbus, Ga.	FA-'93	16/9
25	Taylor, Bobby	CB	6-3	216	12/28/73	10	Notre Dame	Houston, Texas	UFA(Phil)-'04	7/7*
72	Terry, Chris	T	6-5	295	8/8/75	6	Georgia	Jacksonville, Fla.	W(Car)-'02	12/10
61	Tobeck, Robbie	C	6-4	297	3/6/70	11	Washington State	Tarpon Springs, Fla.	UFA(Atl)-'00	16/16
23	Trufant, Marcus	CB	5-11	199	12/25/80	2	Washington State	Tacoma, Wash.	D1-'03	16/16
89	Urban, Jerheme	WR	6-3	212	11/26/80	2	Trinity	Victoria, Texas	FA-'03	0*
15	Wallace, Seneca	QB	5-11	196	8/6/80	2	Iowa State	Sacramento, Calif.	D4a-'03	0*
87	Wallace, Taco	WR	6-1	190	4/14/81	2	Kansas State	Los Angeles, Calif.	D7b-'03	1/0
59	White, Tracy	LB	6-0	230	4/14/81	2	Howard	St. Stephens, S.C.	FA-'03	11/0
48	Whitman, Josh	TE	6-4	245	8/5/78	4	Illinois	Lafayette, Ind.	FA-'04	0*
96	Wistrom, Grant	DE	6-4	272	7/3/76	6	Nebraska	Webb City, Mo.	UFA(StL)-'04	16/16*
77	Womack, Floyd	T	6-4	333	11/15/78	4	Mississippi State	Cleveland, Miss.	D4c-'01	10/4
98	Woodard, Cedric	DT	6-2	310	9/5/77	5	Texas	Sweeny, Texas	W(Balt)-'00	16/12
70	Wunsch, Jerry	T-G	6-6	339	1/21/74	8	Wisconsin	Eau Claire, Wis.	UFA(TB)-'02	12/0

* Bierria missed '03 season because of injury; Huard played 2 games with Indianapolis; Hunter inactive for 16 games; Taylor played 7 games with Philadelphia; Urban inactive for 1 game; S. Wallace inactive for 16 games; Whitman inactive for 1 game with Miami; Wistrom played 16 games with St. Louis.

Players lost through free agency (3): LB Randall Godfrey (SD; 15 games in '03), CB Shawn Springs (Wash; 12), S Reggie Tongue (NYJ; 14).

Retired—John Randle, 14-year defensive tackle, 16 games in '03.

Also played with Seahawks in '03—DT Norman Hand (6 games), DE Lamar King (9), CB Willie Williams (15).

2004 FIRST-YEAR ROSTER

Name	Pos.	Ht.	Wt.	Birthdate	College	Hometown	How Acq.
Babineaux, Jordan	S	6-0	200	8/31/82	Southern Arkansas	Port Arthur, Texas	FA
Bernard, Walter (1)	S	6-2	200	5/3/78	New Mexico	San Diego, Calif.	FA-'02
Boulware, Michael	S	6-3	223	9/17/81	Florida State	Columbia, S.C.	D2
Brown, Isaac	LB	6-3	222	10/13/81	Washington State	Upland, Calif.	FA
Davis, Marque	WR	5-11	190	1/15/81	Fresno State	Dos Palos, Calif.	FA
Farmer, Clarence	RB	6-0	218	10/16/81	Arizona	Houston, Texas	FA
Fredrickson, Tyler	K	6-3	220	2/26/81	California	Santa Barbara, Calif.	FA
Gilford, Jernaro	CB	6-1	185	5/6/80	Brigham Young	Hawthorne, Calif.	FA
Hackett, D.J.	WR	6-2	199	7/31/81	Colorado	Ontario, Calif.	D5
Harden, Michael	CB	5-11	190	10/20/81	Missouri	Kansas City, Mo.	FA
Herring, Issac (1)	T	6-5	305	5/20/80	Brigham Young	Mapleton, Utah	FA
Jones, Donnie	P	6-2	222	7/5/80	Louisiana State	Baton Rouge, La.	D7
Koutouvides, Niko	LB	6-2	238	3/25/81	Purdue	Plainville, Conn.	D4
Kroeker, Dustin (1)	T	6-5	312	10/4/78	Cal Poly-San Luis Obispo	Shafter, Calif.	FA-'03
Locklear, Sean	G	6-4	301	5/29/81	North Carolina State	Lumberton, N.C.	D3
Luke, R.J. (1)	TE	6-3	256	5/25/79	Western Illinois	Aurora, Ill.	FA
Moore, Sammy	WR	5-11	194	2/6/81	Washington State	Mesa, Ariz.	FA
Nazel, Omar	DE	6-5	245	3/9/81	Southern California	Oakland, Calif.	FA
Nyenhuis, Gabe	DE	6-4	275	6/26/81	Colorado	St. Charles, Ill.	FA
Parker, Arnold	S	6-2	210	7/1/81	Utah	Las Vegas, Nev.	FA
Poppinga, Casey (1)	TE	6-5	256	10/15/77	Utah State	Evanston, Wyo.	FA-'03
Roberson, Clayton	LB	6-1	234	3/10/81	North Carolina	Bethel, N.C.	FA
Tatum, Derrick (1)	CB	5-11	190	2/7/81	Kentucky	Cleveland, Ohio.	FA
Terrill, Craig	DT	6-2	290	6/27/80	Purdue	Lebanon, Ind.	D6
Tubbs, Marcus	DT	6-4	320	5/16/81	Texas	DeSoto, Texas	D1

The term NFL Rookie is defined as a player who is in his first season of professional football and has not been on the roster of another professional football team for any regular-season or postseason games. A Rookie is designated by an "R" on NFL rosters. Players who have been active in another professional football league or players who have NFL experience, including either preseason training camp or being on an Active List or Inactive List, or on Reserve/Injured or Reserve/Physically Unable to Perform for fewer than six regular-season games, are termed NFL First-Year Players. An NFL First-Year Player is designated by a "1" on NFL rosters. Thereafter, a player is credited with an additional year of experience for each season in which he accumulates six games on the Active List or Inactive List, or on Reserve/Injured or Reserve/Physically Unable to Perform.

Log on to www.seahawks.com for an up-to-date roster.

SEATTLE SEAHAWKS

COACHING STAFF

Executive Vice President of Football Operations/Head Coach, Mike Holmgren

Pro Career: Named as the Seahawks' sixth head coach on January 8, 1999. Under Holmgren's tutelage in 2003, the Seahawks posted their first double-digit victory total since 1986. In his first season, Holmgren guided the Seahawks to their first postseason appearance since 1988. Holmgren joined Seattle after serving as the head coach of the Green Bay Packers (1992-98). By winning at least one game in five consecutive postseasons (1993-97) Holmgren joined John Madden (1973-77) as the only coaches in league history to accomplish that feat. In 18 NFL seasons (1999-2003 head coach, 1992-98 head coach Green Bay, 1986-1991 assistant coach San Francisco) Holmgren's teams have a 187-100-1 (.651) record, posted double-digit win totals 11 times, made the postseason 13 times, won three Super Bowls (XXIII, XXIV, and XXXI), and reached another (XXXII). Career record: 125-83.

Background: Quarterback at Southern California (1966-69) and was drafted by the St. Louis Cardinals in the eighth round of the 1970 NFL Draft. He served as an assistant coach at San Francisco State (1981) and Brigham Young (1982-85). Earned his bachelor degree in business finance at Southern California.

Personal: Born June 15, 1948, in San Francisco. He and his wife, Kathy, live in Mercer Island, Wash., and have four daughters—Calla, Jenny, Emily, and Gretchen.

ASSISTANT COACHES

Teryl Austin, defensive backs; born March 3, 1965, Sharon, Pa. Defensive back Pittsburgh 1984-87. Pro defensive back Montreal Machine (WLAF) 1991. College coach: Penn State 1991-92, Wake Forest 1993-95, Syracuse 1996-98, Michigan 1999-2002. Pro coach: Joined Seahawks in 2003.

Dwaine Board, defensive line; born November 29, 1956, Rocky Mount, Va. Defensive lineman North Carolina A&T 1974-77. Pro defensive lineman San Francisco 49ers 1979-1987, New Orleans Saints 1988. Pro coach: San Francisco 49ers 1990-2002, joined Seahawks in 2003.

Mike Clark, strength and conditioning; born August 22, 1954, Wichita, Kan. Linebacker Ottawa College 1973-77. No pro playing experience. College coach: Kansas 1977-78, 1982, Wyoming 1981, Oregon 1983-88, Southern California 1988-89, Texas A&M 2000-2003, joined Seahawks in 2004.

Nolan Cromwell, wide receivers; born January 30, 1955, Smith Center, Kan. Quarterback-safety Kansas 1973-76. Pro defensive back Los Angeles Rams 1977-1987. Pro coach: Los Angeles Rams 1991, Green Bay Packers 1992-98, joined Seahawks in 1999.

Gil Haskell, offensive coordinator; born September 24, 1943, San Francisco. Defensive back San Francisco State 1961, 1963-65. No pro playing experience. College coach: Southern California 1978-1982. Pro coach: Los Angeles Rams 1983-1991, Green Bay Packers 1992-97, Carolina Panthers 1998-99, joined Seahawks in 2000.

Darren Krein, asst. strength & conditioning; born July 7, 1971, Aurora, Colo. Linebacker-defensive end Miami 1989-1993. Pro linebacker San Diego Chargers 1994, Barcelona Dragons (NFLEL) 1996. Pro coach: Seattle 1997-98, rejoined Seahawks in 2002.

Bill Laveroni, offensive line; born July 20, 1948, San Francisco. Center California 1967-69. No pro playing experience. College coach: California 1970, 1978, 1983-89, San Francisco 1971, Utah State 1979-1982, San Jose State 1990-94, Rutgers 1996-2000, Vanderbilt 2001. Pro coach: San Jose Sabercats (Arena League) 1995, joined Seahawks in 2002.

Jim Lind, tight ends; born Novemeber 11, 1947, Isle, Minn. Linebacker Bethel College 1965-66, defensive back Bemidji State 1971-72. No pro playing experience. College coach: St. Cloud State 1977-78, St. John's (Minn.) 1979-1980, Brigham Young 1981-82, Minnesota-Morris 1983-86 (head coach), Wisconsin-Eau Claire 1987-1991 (head coach). Pro coach: Green Bay Packers 1992-98, joined Seahawks in 1999.

John Marshall, linebackers; born October 2, 1945, Arroyo Grande, Calif. Linebacker Washington State 1964. No pro playing experience. College coach: Oregon 1970-76, Southern California 1977-79. Pro coach: Green Bay Packers 1980-82, Indianapolis Colts 1986-88, San Francisco 49ers 1989-1998, Carolina Panthers 1999-2001, Detroit Lions 2002, joined Seahawks in 2003.

Mark Michaels, special teams; born August 15, 1963, Kingston, Pa. Defensive lineman Connecticut 1983-86. No pro playing experience. College coach: New Haven 1987-1990, Brown 1993-97, Massachusetts 1998. Pro coach: Helsinki Roosters (Finnish Maple League) 1991, Utah Pioneers (Professional Spring Football Leauge) 1992, Cleveland Browns 1999-2000, joined Seahawks in 2001.

Stump Mitchell, running backs; born March 15, 1959, St. Mary's, Ga. Tailback The Citadel 1977-1980. Running back St. Louis/Phoenix Cardinals 1981-89. College coach: Morgan State 1995-98 (head coach 1996-98). Pro coach: San Antonio Rough Riders (WLAF) 1991, joined Seahawks in 1999.

Gary Reynolds, offensive assistant/quality control; born October 15, 1966, Boston. Attended Texas A&M. No college or pro playing experience. College coach: Texas A&M 1991, Tennessee 1992. Pro coach: Green Bay Packers 1996-98, joined Seahawks in 1999.

Ray Rhodes, defensive coordinator; born October 20, 1950, Mexia, Texas. Running back Texas Christian 1969-1970, wide receiver-defensive back-kick returner Tulsa 1972-73. Pro wide receiver-defensive back New York Giants 1974-79, San Francisco 49ers 1980. Pro coach: San Francisco 49ers 1981-1991, 1994, Green Bay Packers 1992-93, 1999 (head coach 1999), Philadelphia Eagles 1995-98 (head coach), Washington Redskins 2000, Denver Broncos 2001-02, joined Seahawks in 2003.

Zerick Rollins, defensive assistant; born June 20, 1975, Houston. Defensive end Texas A&M 1995-97. No pro playing experience. Graduate assistant Texas A&M 1997-2000. Pro coach: Joined seahawks in 2001.

Jim Zorn, quarterbacks; born May 10, 1953, Whittier, Calif. Quarterback Cal Poly-Pomona 1973-75. Pro quarterback Seattle Seahawks 1975-1984, Green Bay Packers 1985, Winnipeg Blue Bombers (CFL) 1986, Tampa Bay Buccaneers 1987. College coach: Boise State 1989-1991, Utah State 1992-94, Minnesota 1995-96. Pro coach: Seattle Seahawks 1997, Detroit Lions 1998-2000, rejoined Seahawks in 2001.

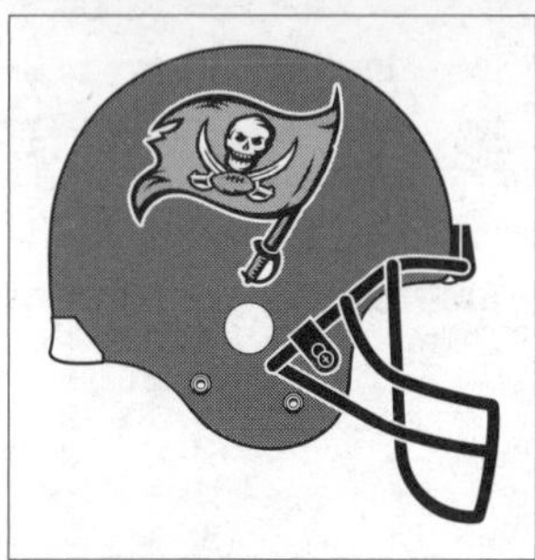

National Football Conference
South Division
Team Colors: Buccaneer Red, Pewter, Black, and Orange
One Buccaneer Place
Tampa, Florida 33607
Telephone: (813) 870-2700

2004 SCHEDULE

PRESEASON		Tampa time
Aug. 14	**Cincinnati**	7:00
Aug. 20	at Jacksonville	7:30
Aug. 28	**Miami**	7:00
Sept. 2	at Houston	8:00

REGULAR SEASON		
Sept. 12	at Washington	1:00
Sept. 19	**Seattle**	4:05
Sept. 26	at Oakland	8:30
Oct. 3	**Denver**	4:15
Oct. 10	at New Orleans	1:00
Oct. 18	at St. Louis (Mon.)	9:00
Oct. 24	**Chicago**	1:00
Oct. 31	Open Date	
Nov. 7	**Kansas City**	1:00
Nov. 14	at Atlanta	1:00
Nov. 21	**San Francisco**	1:00
Nov. 28	at Carolina	1:00
Dec. 5	**Atlanta**	1:00
Dec. 12	at San Diego	4:15
Dec. 19	**New Orleans**	4:05
Dec. 26	**Carolina**	1:00
Jan. 2	at Arizona	4:05

Stadium: Raymond James Stadium (opened in 1998) • **Capacity:** 65,657 Tampa, Florida 33607
Playing Surface: Grass
Training Camp: Disney's Wide World of Sports Lake Buena Vista, Florida 92830

RAYMOND JAMES STADIUM

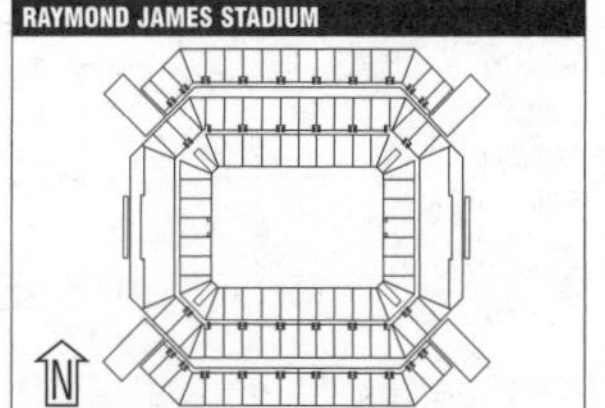

CLUB OFFICIALS

Owner/President: Malcolm Glazer
Executive Vice President: Bryan Glazer
Executive Vice President: Joel Glazer
Executive Vice President: Edward Glazer
General Manager: Bruce Allen
Senior Director of Business Administration: Mike Newquist
Director of Football Operations: Mark Arteaga
Director of College Scouting: Ruston Webster
Director of Pro Personnel: Mark Dominik
Personnel Executive: Doug Williams
General Counsel: Roxanne Kosarzycki
Director of Player Development: Cedric Saunders
Director of Football Technology: Michael Lamberson
College Scouts: Frank Dorazio, Dennis Hickey, Mike Phair, Mike Yowarsky
National Combine Scout: Seth Turner
Director of Human Resources/Sales: Michael Pocchiari
Director of Marketing: Jeff Ajluni
Director of Public Relations: Jeff Kamis
Director of Security/Facilities: Andre Trescastro
Director of Team Services: Tom Szubka
Director of Ticketing and Customer Relations: Jeff Leinen
Internet Manager: Scott Smith
Public Relations Manager: Zack Bolno
Trainer: Todd Toriscelli
Director of Rehabilitation: Shannon Merrick
Equipment Manager: Tim Sain
Assistant Equipment Manager: Mark Meschede
Video Director: Dave Levy
Assistant Video Director: Pat Brazil

COACHING HISTORY (173-275-1)

1976-1984	John McKay	45-91-1
1985-86	Leeman Bennett	4-28-0
1987-1990	Ray Perkins*	19-41-0
1990-91	Richard Williamson	4-15-0
1992-95	Sam Wyche	23-41-0
1996-2001	Tony Dungy	56-46-0
2002-03	Jon Gruden	22-13-0

*Released after 13 games in 1990

ATTENDANCE

Home 510,736 Away 560,019
Total 1,070,755
Single-game home record, 73,523 (12/7/97)
Single-season home record, 545,980 (1979)

2004 DRAFT CHOICES

Round	Name	Pos.	College
1	Michael Clayton	WR	Louisiana St.
3	Marquis Cooper	LB	Washington
4	Will Allen	DB	Ohio State
5	Jeb Terry	G	North Carolina
6	Nate Lawrie	TE	Yale
7	Mark Jones	WR	Tennessee
	Casey Cramer	FB	Dartmouth
	Lenny Williams	DB	Southern

TAMPA BAY BUCCANEERS

2003 TEAM RECORD

PRESEASON (4-1)

Date	Result	Opponent
8/2	W 30-14	New York Jets, at Tokyo
8/8	W 20-19	Miami
8/18	L 16-26	at St. Louis
8/23	W 10-6	Jacksonville
8/28	W 34-3	Houston

REGULAR SEASON (7-9)

Date	Result	Opponent	Att.
9/8	W 17-0	at Philadelphia	67,772
9/14	L 9-12	Carolina (OT)	65,621
9/21	W 31-10	at Atlanta	70,871
10/6	L 35-38	Indianapolis (OT)	65,647
10/12	W 35-13	at Washington	85,490
10/19	L 7-24	at San Francisco	67,809
10/26	W 16-0	Dallas	,65,602
11/2	L 14-17	New Orleans	65,524
11/9	L 24-27	at Carolina	73,245
11/16	L 13-20	Green Bay	65,614
11/24	W 19-13	New York Giants	65,648
11/30	L 10-17	at Jacksonville	60,543
12/7	W 14-7	at New Orleans	68,442
12/14	W 16-3	Houston	65,124
12/20	L 28-30	Atlanta	65,572
12/28	L 13-33	at Tennessee	68,809

(OT) Overtime

SCORE BY PERIODS

Buccaneers	34	105	60	102	0 —	301
Opponents	50	83	56	69	6 —	264

2003 TEAM STATISTICS

	Buccaneers	Opp.
Total First Downs	307	249
Rushing	86	89
Passing	190	140
Penalty	31	20
3rd Down: Made/Att	78/220	68/214
3rd Down Pct.	35.5	31.8
4th Down: Made/Att	8/15	7/18
4th Down Pct.	53.3	38.9
Possession Avg.	31:36	28:24
Total Net Yards	5,453	4,466
Avg. Per Game	340.8	279.1
Total Plays	1,036	962
Avg. Per Play	5.3	4.6
Net Yards Rushing	1,648	1,756
Avg. Per Game	103.0	109.8
Total Rushes	421	451
Net Yards Passing	3,805	2,710
Avg. Per Game	237.8	169.4
Sacked/Yards Lost	23/136	36/234
Gross Yards	3,941	2,944
Att./Completions	592/369	475/274
Completion Pct.	62.3	57.7
Had Intercepted	22	20
Punts/Average	83/43.3	82/43.4
Net Punting Avg.	83/35.9	82/38.0
Penalties/Yards	117/1,104	104/817
Fumbles/Ball Lost	23/9	29/13
Touchdowns	36	27
Rushing	5	6
Passing	27	16
Returns	4	5

2003 INDIVIDUAL STATISTICS

PASSING	Att.	Comp.	Yds.	Pct.	TD	Int.	Tkld.	Rate
B. Johnson	570	354	3,811	62.1	26	21	20/111	81.5
S. King	22	15	130	68.2	1	1	3/25	79.7
Buccaneers	592	369	3,941	62.3	27	22	23/136	81.5
Opponents	475	274	2,944	57.7	16	20	36/234	69.7

SCORING	TD R	TD P	TD Rt	PAT	FG	Saf	PTS
Gramatica	0	0	0	33/34	16/26	0	81
McCardell	0	8	1	0/0	0/0	0	54
K. Johnson	0	3	0	0/0	0/0	0	18
Jones	3	0	0	0/0	0/0	0	18
Alstott	2	0	0	0/0	0/0	0	12
Jurevicius	0	2	0	0/0	0/0	0	12
Lee	0	2	0	0/0	0/0	0	12
Pittman	0	2	0	0/0	0/0	0	12
Sapp	0	2	0	0/0	0/0	0	12
Yoder	0	2	0	0/0	0/0	0	12
Barber	0	0	1	0/0	0/0	0	6
Barlow	0	1	0	0/0	0/0	0	6
Brooks	0	0	1	0/0	0/0	0	6
Cook	0	1	0	0/0	0/0	0	6
Dilger	0	1	0	0/0	0/0	0	6
Dudley	0	1	0	0/0	0/0	0	6
Heller	0	1	0	0/0	0/0	0	6
Stecker	0	1	0	0/0	0/0	0	6
Wansley	0	0	1	0/0	0/0	0	6
K. Williams	0	0	0	0/0	0/0	0	2
Buccaneers	5	27	4	33/34	16/26	1	301
Opponents	6	16	5	27/27	25/34	0	264

2-Pt. Conversions: K. Williams.
Buccaneers 1-2, Opponents 0-0

RUSHING	No.	Yds	Avg	LG	TD
Pittman	187	751	4.0	17	0
Jones	137	627	4.6	61	3
Stecker	37	125	3.4	15	0
Alstott	27	77	2.9	29	2
B. Johnson	25	33	1.3	13	0
S. King	4	20	5.0	12	0
Lee	2	14	7.0	8	0
K. Williams	1	2	2.0	2	0
Cook	1	-1	-1.0	-1	0
Buccaneers	421	1,648	3.9	61	5
Opponents	451	1,756	3.9	47	6

RECEIVING	No.	Yds	Avg	LG	TD
McCardell	84	1,174	14.0	76t	8
Pittman	75	597	8.0	68t	2
K. Johnson	45	600	13.3	39t	3
Lee	33	432	13.1	72	2
Jones	24	180	7.5	29	0
Dilger	22	244	11.1	48	1
Cook	20	120	6.0	19	1
Jurevicius	12	118	9.8	22	2
Alstott	10	83	8.3	17	0
Stecker	9	48	5.3	14t	1
K. Williams	7	114	16.3	43	0
Yoder	7	68	9.7	20	2
Dudley	7	42	6.0	9	1
Sapp	4	39	9.8	18	2
Shepherd	4	38	9.5	14	0
Barlow	3	27	9.0	13	1
Heller	2	15	7.5	11	1
Barnes	1	6	6.0	6	0
Coleman	0	1	—	1	0
B. Johnson	0	-2	—	-2	0
Green	0	-3	—	-3	0
Buccaneers	369	3,941	10.7	76t	27
Opponents	274	2,944	10.7	75t	16

INTERCEPTIONS	No.	Yds	Avg	LG	TD
D. Smith	5	3	0.6	3	0
Brooks	2	56	28.0	44t	1
Barber	2	53	26.5	29t	1
Wansley	2	38	19.0	23t	1
Lynch	2	18	9.0	18	0
Rice	2	12	6.0	12	0
Phillips	1	41	41.0	41	0
Robinson	1	6	6.0	6	0
Nece	1	2	2.0	2	0
Kelly	1	0	0.0	0	0
McFarland	1	0	0.0	0	0
Buccaneers	20	229	11.5	44t	3
Opponents	22	394	17.9	73t	4

PUNTING	No.	Yds.	Avg.	In 20	LG
Tupa	83	3,590	43.3	26	60
Buccaneers	83	3,590	43.3	26	60
Opponents	82	3,559	43.4	22	58

PUNT RETURNS	Ret	FC	Yds	Avg	LG	TD
K. Williams	15	10	110	7.3	19	0
Barlow	12	6	58	4.8	17	0
Wansley	8	2	74	9.3	12	0
Buccaneers	35	18	242	6.9	19	0
Opponents	39	12	489	12.5	52	0

KICKOFF RETURNS	No.	Yds	Avg	LG	TD
Stecker	25	520	20.8	44	0
Jones	17	271	15.9	25	0
Barlow	10	221	22.1	32	0
White	1	7	7.0	7	0
K. Williams	1	15	15.0	15	0
Yoder	1	8	8.0	8	0
Barnes	0	0	0.0	0	0
Buccaneers	55	1,042	18.9	44	0
Opponents	59	1,393	23.6	90	0

FIELD GOALS	1-19	20-29	30-39	40-49	50+
Gramatica	0/0	9/9	3/6	3/8	1/3
Buccaneers	0/0	9/9	3/6	3/8	1/3
Opponents	0/0	8/8	11/14	5/10	1/2

SACKS	No.
Rice	15.0
Sapp	5.0
Spires	3.5
McFarland	2.5
Darby	2.0
Wyms	2.0
Barber	1.5
Brooks	1.0
Pinkney	1.0
Webster	1.0
Lynch	0.5
Buccaneers	36.0
Opponents	23.0

RECORD HOLDERS

INDIVIDUAL RECORDS—CAREER

Category	Name	Performance
Rushing (Yds.)	James Wilder, 1981-89	5,957
Passing (Yds.)	Vinny Testaverde, 1987-1992	14,820
Passing (TDs)	Vinny Testaverde, 1987-1992	77
Receiving (No.)	James Wilder, 1981-89	430
Receiving (Yds.)	Mark Carrier, 1987-1992	5,018
Interceptions	Donnie Abraham, 1996-2001	31
Punting (Avg.)	Tom Tupa, 2002-03	43.0
Punt Return (Avg.)	Jacquez Green, 1998-2001	12.0
Kickoff Return (Avg.)	Aaron Stecker, 2000-03	23.8
Field Goals	Martín Gramatica, 1999-2003	126
Touchdowns (Tot.)	Mike Alstott, 1996-2003	59
Points	Martín Gramatica, 1999-2003	538

INDIVIDUAL RECORDS—SINGLE SEASON

Category	Name	Performance
Rushing (Yds.)	James Wilder, 1984	1,544
Passing (Yds.)	Brad Johnson, 2003	3,811
Passing (TDs)	Brad Johnson, 2003	26
Receiving (No.)	Keyshawn Johnson, 2001	106
Receiving (Yds.)	Mark Carrier, 1989	1,422
Interceptions	Ronde Barber, 2001	10
Punting (Avg.)	Tom Tupa, 2003	43.3
Punt Return (Avg.)	Karl Williams, 1996	21.1
Kickoff Return (Avg.)	Karl Williams, 1996	27.4
Field Goals	Martín Gramatica, 2002	32
Touchdowns (Tot.)	James Wilder, 1984	13
Points	Martín Gramatica, 2002	128

INDIVIDUAL RECORDS—SINGLE GAME

Category	Name	Performance
Rushing (Yds.)	James Wilder, 11-6-83	219
Passing (Yds.)	Doug Williams, 11-16-80	486
Passing (TDs)	Steve DeBerg, 9-13-87	5
	Brad Johnson, 11-3-02	5
Receiving (No.)	James Wilder, 9-15-85	13
Receiving (Yds.)	Mark Carrier, 12-6-87	212
Interceptions	Ronde Barber, 12-23-01	3
Field Goals	Martín Gramatica, 12-29-02	5
Touchdowns (Tot.)	Jimmie Giles, 10-20-85	4
Points	Jimmie Giles, 10-20-85	24

TAMPA BAY BUCCANEERS

2004 VETERAN ROSTER

No.	Name	Pos.	Ht.	Wt.	Birthdate	NFL Exp.	College	Hometown	How Acq.	'03 Games/ Starts
40	Alstott, Mike	FB	6-1	248	12/21/73	9	Purdue	Joliet, Ill.	D2-'96	4/3
20	Barber, Ronde	CB	5-10	184	4/7/75	8	Virginia	Roanoke, Va.	D3b-'97	16/16
66	Benjamin, Ryan	LS	6-1	242	11/11/77	3	South Florida	New Port Richey, Fla.	FA-'02	16/0
36	Bennett, Brandon	RB	5-11	220	2/3/73	6	South Carolina	Taylors, S.C.	UFA(Cin)-'04	16/0*
9	Bidwell, Josh	P	6-3	220	3/13/76	5	Oregon	Winston, Ore.	UFA(GB)-'04	16/0*
55	Brooks, Derrick	LB	6-0	235	4/18/73	10	Florida State	Pensacola, Fla.	D1b-'95	16/16
51	Burns, Keith	LB	6-2	235	6/16/72	11	Oklahoma State	Alexandria, Va.	UFA(Den)-'04	16/0*
60	Coleman, Cosey	G	6-4	322	10/27/78	5	Tennessee	Clarkston, Ga.	D2-'00	16/16
34	Comella, Greg	FB	6-1	248	7/29/75	7	Stanford	Wellesly, Mass.	UFA(Hou)-'04	5/0*
43	Cook, Jameel	FB	5-10	237	2/8/79	4	Illinois	Miami, Fla.	D6a-'01	14/8
93	Cowsette, Delbert	DT	6-1	296	9/3/77	3	Maryland	Cleveland, Ohio	FA-'04	0*
24	Cox, Torrie	CB	5-10	181	10/29/80	2	Pittsburgh	Miami, Fla.	D6-'03	0*
91	Darby, Chartric	DT	6-0	270	10/22/75	4	South Carolina State	North, S.C.	FA-'00	16/1
70	Deese, Derrick	T	6-3	289	5/17/70	13	Southern California	Culver City, Calif.	FA-'04	11/11*
85	Dilger, Ken	TE	6-5	250	2/2/71	10	Illinois	Mariah Hill, Ill.	FA-'02	15/15
88	Dudley, Rickey	TE	6-6	255	7/15/72	9	Ohio State	Henderson, Texas	FA-'02	7/2
44	Dyer, Deon	FB	5-11	255	10/2/77	4	North Carolina	Chesapeake, Va.	FA-'04	0*
37	Edwards, Mario	CB	6-0	199	12/1/75	5	Florida State	Pascagoula, Miss.	UFA(Dall)-'04	16/16*
11	Farmer, Danny	WR	6-3	215	5/21/77	4	UCLA	Los Angeles, Calif.	FA-'04	0*
21	Frost, Scott	S	6-3	218	1/4/75	7	Nebraska	Wood River, Neb.	FA-'03	4/0
84	t-Galloway, Joey	WR	5-11	197	11/20/71	10	Ohio State	Bellaire, Ohio	T(Dall)-'04	15/14*
30	Garner, Charlie	RB	5-10	190	2/13/72	11	Tennessee	Fairfax, Va.	UFA(Oak)-'04	14/9*
17	Garrett, Jason	QB	6-2	205	3/28/66	12	Princeton	Chagrin, Ohio	UFA(NYG)-'04	0*
52	Gold, Ian	LB	6-0	223	8/23/78	5	Michigan	Belleville, Mich.	FA-'04	6/6*
50	Gooch, Jeff	LB	5-11	226	10/31/74	9	Austin Peay	Nashville, Tenn.	UFA(Det)-'04	16/0*
10	Gramatica, Martin	K	5-8	170	11/27/75	6	Kansas State	LaBelle, Fla.	D3-'99	16/0
78	Gregory, Damian	DT	6-2	305	1/21/77	4	Illinois State	Lansing, Mich.	FA-'04	0*
8	Griese, Brian	QB	6-3	214	3/18/75	7	Michigan	Miami, Fla.	FA-'04	5/5*
89	Heller, Will	TE	6-6	250	2/28/81	2	Georgia Tech	Dunwoody, Ga.	FA-'03	9/1
38	Howell, John	S	5-11	210	4/28/78	4	Colorado State	Mullen, Neb.	D4-'01	8/0
35	Ivy, Corey	CB	5-8	183	3/29/77	3	Oklahoma	Moore, Okla.	FA-'01	16/2
71	Jenkins, Kerry	G	6-5	305	9/6/73	7	Troy State	Tuscaloosa, Ala.	FA-'02	16/11
14	Johnson, Brad	QB	6-5	226	9/13/68	13	Florida State	Black Mountain, N.C.	UFA(Wash)-'01	16/16
83	Jurevicius, Joe	WR	6-5	230	12/23/74	7	Penn State	Mentor Lake, Ohio	UFA(NYG)-'02	5/2
25	Kelly, Brian	CB	5-11	193	1/14/76	7	Southern California	Aurora, Colo.	D2b-'98	5/5
62	King, Austin	C	6-5	303	4/11/81	2	Northwestern	Cincinnati, Ohio	D4b-'03	0*
15	Knight, Marcus	WR	6-1	180	6/19/78	3	Michigan	Sylacauga, Ala.	FA-'04	0*
27	Knight, Tom	CB	6-0	202	12/29/74	7	Iowa	Marlton, N.J.	UFA(Balt)-'04	10/1*
82	Lee, Charles	WR	6-3	227	11/19/77	5	Central Florida	Homestead, Fla.	FA-'02	8/5
79	Mahan, Sean	G	6-3	301	5/28/80	2	Notre Dame	Jenks, Okla.	D5-'03	9/0
87	McCardell, Keenan	WR	6-1	191	1/6/70	13	Nevada-Las Vegas	Houston, Texas	FA-'02	16/16
92	McFarland, Anthony	DT	6-0	300	12/18/77	6	Louisiana State	Winnsboro, La.	D1-'99	16/16
81	Moore, Dave	TE	6-2	250	11/11/69	13	Pittsburgh	Succasunna, N.J.	FA-'04	15/6*
16	Morris, Sylvester	WR	6-3	212	10/6/77	5	Jackson State	New Orleans, La.	FA-'04	0*
5	Murphy, Frank	WR	6-0	206	2/11/77	4	Kansas State	Jacksonville, Fla.	FA-'04	0*
56	Nece, Ryan	LB	6-3	224	2/24/79	3	UCLA	San Bernardino, Calif.	FA-'02	15/10
72	Oben, Roman	T	6-4	305	10/9/72	9	Louisville	Washington, D.C.	FA-'02	15/13
73	O'Dwyer, Matt	G	6-5	305	9/1/72	10	Northwestern	Lincolnshire, Ill.	UFA(Cin)-'04	4/1*
23	Phillips, Jermaine	S	6-1	214	3/27/79	3	Georgia	Roswell, Ga.	D5-'02	14/8
61	Pinkney, Cleveland	DT	6-1	300	9/14/77	2	South Carolina	Sumter, S.C.	FA-'03	4/0
32	Pittman, Michael	RB	6-0	218	8/14/75	7	Fresno State	San Diego, Calif.	UFA(Ariz)-'02	16/13
53	Quarles, Shelton	LB	6-1	225	9/11/71	8	Vanderbilt	Whites Creek, Tenn.	FA-'97	11/11
97	Rice, Simeon	DE	6-5	268	2/24/74	9	Illinois	Chicago, Ill.	UFA(Ariz)-'01	16/16
28	Robinson, Travaris	S	5-10	193	9/1/81	2	Auburn	Miami, Fla.	W(Atl)-'03	9/1*
98	Russell, Darrell	DT	6-5	325	5/27/76	7	Southern California	San Diego, Calif.	UFA(Wash)-'04	8/0*
86	Shepherd, Edell	WR	6-1	175	5/18/80	2	San Jose State	Los Angeles, Calif.	FA-'03	3/0
2	Simms, Chris	QB	6-4	220	8/29/80	2	Texas	Ramapo, N.J.	D3-'03	0*
12	Skaggs, Justin	WR	6-2	202	4/22/79	2	Evangel	Wentzville, Mo.	FA-'04	0*
98	Smith, Corey	DE	6-2	250	10/2/79	3	North Carolina State	Richmond, Va.	FA-'02	1/0
26	Smith, Dwight	DB	5-10	201	8/13/78	4	Akron	Detroit, Mich.	D3-'01	16/16
94	Spires, Greg	DE	6-1	265	8/12/74	7	Florida State	Cape Coral, Fla.	UFA(Cle)-'02	15/15
75	Steussie, Todd	T	6-6	308	12/1/70	11	California	Aguora, Calif.	FA-'04	16/16*
78	Stinchcomb, Matt	T-G	6-6	310	6/3/77	6	Georgia	Lilburn, Ga.	UFA (Oak)-'04	6/4*
59	Thomas, Edward	LB	6-1	228	9/27/74	3	Georgia Southern	Thomasville, Ga.	FA-'04	0*
76	Wade, John	C	6-5	299	1/25/75	7	Marshall	Harrisonburg, Va.	UFA(Jax)-'03	16/16

67	Walker, Kenyatta	T	6-5	302	2/1/79	4	Florida	Meridian, Miss.	D1-'01	14/14
29	Whitaker, Ronyell	CB	5-9	196	3/19/79	2	Virginia Tech	Norfolk, Va.	FA-'03	4/1
90	White, Dewayne	DE	6-2	273	10/19/79	2	Louisville	Marbury, Ala.	D2-'03	12/1
22	White, Jamel	RB	5-9	222	2/11/78	5	South Dakota	Los Angeles, Calif.	FA-'04	16/3*
65	Whittle, Jason	G	6-4	305	3/7/75	7	Southwest Missouri State	Camdenton, Mo.	UFA(NYG)-'03	16/5
95	Wilson, Reinard	DE	6-2	265	12/14/73	7	Florida State	Lake City, Fla.	FA-'03	0*
96	Wyms, Ellis	DE	6-3	279	4/12/79	4	Mississippi State	Indianola, Miss.	D6b-'01	13/0
68	Ziemann, Chris	T	6-7	307	9/20/76	2	Michigan	Aurora, Ill.	FA-'04	0*

* Bennett played 16 games with Cincinnati in '03; Bidwell played 16 games with Green Bay; Burns played 16 games with Denver; Comella played 5 games with Houston; Cowsette last active with Washington in '02; Cox missed '03 season because of injury; Deese played 11 games with San Francisco; Dyer last active with Miami in '02; Edwards played 16 games with Dallas; Farmer last active with Cincinnati in '02; Galloway played 15 games with Dallas; Garner played 14 games with Oakland; Garrett inactive for 16 games with N.Y. Giants; Gold played 6 games with Denver; Gooch played 16 games with Detroit; Gregory last active with Cleveland in '02; Griese played 5 games with Miami; King inactive for 16 games; M. Knight last active with Oakland in '02; T. Knight played 10 games with Baltimore; Moore played 15 games with Buffalo; Morris last active with Kansas City in '00; Murphy last active with Houston in '02; O'Dwyer played 4 games with Cincinnati; Robinson played 5 games with Atlanta; Russell played 8 games with Washington; Simms inactive for 16 games; Skaggs last active with Washington in '02; Steussie played 16 games with Carolina; Stinchcomb played 16 games with Oakland; Thomas last active with Jacksonville in '02; J. White played 16 games with Cleveland; Wilson inactive for 2 games; Ziemann last active with N.Y. Giants in '00.

t- Buccaneers traded for Galloway (Dall).

Traded—FB Darian Barnes (14 games in '03) to Dallas; WR Keyshawn Johnson (10) to Dallas.

Players lost through free agency (8)—T Cornell Green (Den; 8 games in '03), RB Thomas Jones (Chi; 16), QB Shaun King (Ariz; 3), DT Warren Sapp (Oak; 15), RB Aaron Stecker (NO; 16), P Tom Tupa (Wash; 16), LB Nate Webster (Cin; 15), TE Todd Yoder (Jax; 16).

Also played with Buccaneers in '03—WR Reggie Barlow (11 games), LB Vinny Ciurciu (8), S David Gibson (9), LB Jack Golden (4), S John Lynch (14), FB Cecil Martin (1), CB Hank Poteat (1), LB Dwayne Rudd (16), LB Justin Smith (2), CB Tim Wansley (12), DE Ron Warner (4), TE Daniel Wilcox (2), WR Karl Williams (13), TE Roland Williams (1).

2004 FIRST-YEAR ROSTER

Name	Pos.	Ht.	Wt.	Birthdate	College	Hometown	How Acq.
Allen, Will	S	6-1	193	6/17/82	Ohio State	Dayton, Ohio	D4
Breedlove, Kevin (1)	G	6-4	326	6/25/80	Georgia	Arlington, Texas	FA-'03
Brown, Michael (1)	LB	5-10	220	1/16/80	Louisville	Louisville, Ky.	FA-'03
Claxton, Ben (1)	C	6-2	301	7/30/80	Mississippi	Dublin, Ga.	FA-'03
Clayton, Michael	WR	6-4	197	10/13/82	Louisiana State	Baton Rouge, La.	D1
Collins, Chris	WR	6-0	192	8/16/82	Mississippi	Gloster, Miss.	FA
Cooper, Marquis	LB	6-3	213	3/11/82	Washington	Gilbert, Ariz.	D3
Cramer, Casey	FB	6-2	250	1/5/82	Dartmouth	Middleton, Wis.	D7b
Davis, Anthony (1)	T	6-4	322	3/27/80	Virginia Tech	Victoria, Va.	FA-'03
Davis, Fabian (1)	WR	5-11	180	12/7/78	Wake Forest	Greenville, S.C.	FA-'03
Elpheage, Lynaris (1)	DB	5-9	179	10/8/82	Tulane	New Orleans, La.	FA
Garrison, John (1)	C-LS	6-5	288	7/7/80	Nebraska	Clarksburg, W.Va.	FA
Graham, Earnest (1)	RB	5-9	215	1/15/80	Florida	Naples, Fla.	FA
Jackson, Scott	C	6-4	300	1/19/79	Brigham Young	Rancho Palos Verdes, Calif.	FA
Jones, Mark	WR	5-9	185	11/3/80	Tennessee	Wallingford, Pa.	D7a
Lawrie, Nate	TE	6-7	256	10/17/81	Yale	Indianapolis, Ind.	D6
Pearson, Kalvin (1)	DB	5-10	190	10/22/78	Grambling State	Town Creek, Ala.	FA
Savage, Josh	DE	6-4	276	9/28/80	Utah	Salt Lake City, Utah	FA
Terry, Jeb	G	6-5	311	4/10/81	North Carolina	Dallas, Texas	D5
Williams, Lenny	CB	5-10	190	12/16/81	Southern	Lake Charles, La.	D7c
Zeigler, Doug (1)	TE	6-3	257	10/20/79	Mississippi	Wilmington, Ohio	FA

The term NFL Rookie is defined as a player who is in his first season of professional football and has not been on the roster of another professional football team for any regular-season or postseason games. A Rookie is designated by an "R" on NFL rosters. Players who have been active in another professional football league or players who have NFL experience, including either preseason training camp or being on an Active List or Inactive List, or on Reserve/Injured or Reserve/Physically Unable to Perform for fewer than six regular-season games, are termed NFL First-Year Players. An NFL First-Year Player is designated by a "1" on NFL rosters. Thereafter, a player is credited with an additional year of experience for each season in which he accumulates six games on the Active List or Inactive List, or on Reserve/Injured or Reserve/Physically Unable to Perform.

Log on to www.buccaneers.com for an up-to-date roster.

TAMPA BAY BUCCANEERS

COACHING STAFF

Head Coach,
Jon Gruden

Pro Career: Gruden was named the seventh head coach in Buccaneers history on February 18, 2002, when he signed a five-year contract. Gruden, the NFL's youngest head coach at 40, led Tampa Bay to its first Super Bowl title in his first season as head coach in 2002. Gruden became the youngest head coach in NFL history to win a Super Bowl, and he was also the first veteran head coach in the history of the NFL to lead his team to the Super Bowl in his first season with a new team. Prior to joining the Buccaneers, Gruden guided the Oakland Raiders to division titles in each of his final two seasons as head coach. He steered the Raiders to a 40-28 mark in four seasons (1998-2001) with the club, including postseason appearances in 2000 and 2001. Under Gruden, the Raiders advanced to the AFC title game in 2000 and lost in 2001 in a divisional playoff game to eventual Super Bowl champion New England. Gruden's offenses have finished among the league's Top 10 in four of the last past seasons, including fifth in 1999. Prior to his four seasons in Oakland, Gruden spent 1995-97 as offensive coordinator for the Philadelphia Eagles and three years (1992-94) as wide receivers coach for Green Bay Packers. He worked as offensive assistant for the San Francisco 49ers in 1990. Career record: 62-41.

Background: Quarterback at Dayton (1982-84), graduating with a degree in communications. The Flyers had a 24-7 record in Gruden's three varsity seasons. Coach collegiately at Tennessee (1986-87), Southeast Missouri State (1988), Pacific (1989), and Pittsburgh (1991).

Personal: Born August 17, 1963 in Sandusky, Ohio. Jon and his wife Cindy, have three sons, Jon II, Michael, and Jayson.

ASSISTANT COACHES

Joe Barry, linebackers; born July 5, 1970, Boulder, Colo. Linebacker Southern California 1991-93. No pro playing experience. College coach: Southern California 1994-95, Northern Arizona 1996-98, Nevada-Las Vegas 1999. Pro coach: San Francisco 49ers 2000, joined Buccaneers in 2001.

Jeremy Bates, asst. quarterbacks; born August 27, 1976, Sevierville, Tenn. Quarterback Tennessee 1995, Rice 1996-99. No pro playing experience. Pro coach: Joined Buccaneers in 2002.

Richard Bisaccia, special teams; born June 3, 1960, Yonkers, N.Y. Defensive back Yankton College 1979-1982, Philadelphia Stars (USFL) 1983. College coach: Wayne State College 1983-87, South Carolina 1988-1993, Clemson 1994-98, Mississippi 1999-2001. Pro coach: Joined Buccaneers in 2002.

Garrett Giemont, strength and conditioning coordinator; born August 31, 1957, Fullerton, Calif. Attended Fullerton College. No college or pro playing experience. Pro coach: Los Angeles Rams 1978-1991, Oakland Raiders 1995-2002, joined Buccaneers in 2003.

Jay Gruden, offensive assistant; born March 4, 1967. Quarterback Louisville 1985-88. Pro quarterback Tampa Bay Storm (Arena League) 1991-96, Orlando Predators (Arena League) 2002-03. Pro coach: Nashville Kats (Arena League) 1997, Orlando Predators (Arena League) 1998-2001, joined Buccaneers in 2002.

Monte Kiffin, defensive coordinator; born February 29, 1940, Lexington, Neb. Offensive/defensive tackle Nebraska 1959-63. Pro defensive end Winnipeg Blue Bombers (CFL) 1965. College coach: Nebraska 1966-76, Arkansas 1977-79, North Carolina State 1980-82 (head coach). Pro coach: Green Bay Packers 1983, Buffalo Bills 1984-85, Minnesota Vikings 1986-89, 1991-94, New York Jets 1990, New Orleans Saints 1995, joined Buccaneers in 1996.

Richard Mann, wide receivers; born April 20, 1947, Aliquippa, Pa. Wide receiver Arizona State 1966-68. No pro playing experience. College coach: Arizona State 1974-79, Louisville 1980-81. Pro coach: Baltimore/Indianapolis Colts 1982-84, Cleveland Browns 1985-1993, New York Jets 1994-96, Baltimore Ravens 1997-98, Kansas City Chiefs 1999-2000, Washington Redskins 2001, joined Buccaneers in 2002.

Rod Marinelli, asst. head coach/defensive line; born July 13, 1949, Rosemead, Calif. Offensive/defensive tackle Utah 1968, offensive tackle California Lutheran 1970-72 (military service 1969-70). No pro playing experience. College coach: Utah State 1976-82, California 1983-91, Arizona State 1992-94, Southern California 1995. Pro coach: Joined Buccaneers in 1996.

Ron Middleton, tight ends/asst. special teams; born July 17, 1965, Atmore, Ala. Tight end Auburn 1982-85. Pro tight end Atlanta Falcons 1986-87, Washington Redskins 1988, 1990-93, Cleveland Browns 1989, Los Angeles Rams 1994, San Diego Chargers 1995. College coach: Troy State 1997-98, Mississippi 1999-2003. Pro coach: Joined Buccaneers in 2004.

Mike Morris, asst. strength and conditioning; born May 7, 1964, Ayer, Mass. Wide receiver Syracuse 1981-85. No pro playing experience. Pro coach: New England Patriots 1997-99, joined Buccaneers in 2002.

Raheem Morris, asst. defensive backs; born September 3, 1976, Irvington, N.J. Safety Hofstra 1994-97. No pro playing experience. College coach: Hofstra 1998, 2000-2001, Cornell 1999. Pro coach: New York Jets 2001, joined Buccaneers in 2002.

Bill Muir, offensive coordinator/offensive line; born October 26, 1942, Pittsburgh, Pa. Tackle Susquehanna 1962-64. No pro playing experience. College coach: Susquehanna 1965, Delaware Valley 1966-67, Rhode Island 1970-71, Idaho State 1972-73, Southern Methodist 1976-77. Pro coach: Orlando (Continental Football League) 1968-69, Houston Shreveport Steamer (WFL) 1975, New England Patriots 1982-88, Indianapolis Colts 1989-1991, Philadelphia Eagles 1992-94, New York Jets 1995-2001, joined Buccaneers in 2002.

Jim Pyne, offensive quality control; born November 23, 1971, Milford, Mass. Center Virginia Tech 1990-93. Pro center-guard Tampa Bay Buccaneers 1994-97, Detroit Lions 1998, Cleveland Browns 1999-2000, Philadelphia Eagles 2001. Pro coach: Joined Buccaneers in 2003.

Kyle Shanahan, offensive quality control; born December 14, 1979, Minneapolis. Wide receiver Duke 1998-99, Texas 2000-02. No pro playing experience. College coach: UCLA 2003. Pro coach: Joined Buccaneers in 2004.

John Shoop, quarterbacks; born August 1, 1969, Pittsburgh. Quarterback University of South 1987-1990. No pro playing experience. College coach: Dartmouth 1991, Vanderbilt 1992-94. Pro coach: Carolina Panthers 1995-98, Chicago Bears 1999-2003, joined Buccaneers in 2004.

Mike Tomlin, defensive backs; born March 15, 1972, Hampton, Va. Wide receiver William & Mary 1991-94. No pro playing experience. College coach: Virginia Military Institute 1995, Memphis 1996, Tennessee-Martin 1997, Arkansas State 1997-98, Cincinnati 1999-2000. Pro coach: Joined Buccaneers in 2001.

Art Valero, running backs; born May 12, 1958, Whittier, Calif. Offensive lineman Boise State 1979-1980. No pro playing experience. College coach: Boise State 1981-82, Iowa State 1983, Long Beach State 1984-86, New Mexico 1987-89, Idaho 1990-94, Louisville 1998-2001. Pro coach: Kansas City Chiefs 1994, Buffalo Bills 1996, joined Buccaneers in 2002.

Joe Woods, defensive quality control; born June 25, 1970, Natrona Heights, Pa.. Safety Illinois State 1988-92. No pro playing experience. College coach: Muskingum 1992, Eastern Michigan 1993-94, Northwestern State 1994, Grand Valley State 1994-97, Kent State 1997, Hofstra 1998-2000, Western Michigan 2001-03. Pro coach: Joined Buccaneers in 2004.

National Football Conference
East Division
Team Colors: Burgundy and Gold
Redskin Park
21300 Redskin Park Drive
Ashburn, Virginia 20147
Telephone: (703) 726-7000

2004 SCHEDULE

PRESEASON **Washington, D.C. time**

Aug. 9	vs. Denver, Canton, OH	8:00
Aug. 14	**Carolina**	8:00
Aug. 21	at Miami	7:30
Aug. 27	at St. Louis	8:00
Sept. 3	**Atlanta**	7:00

REGULAR SEASON

Sept. 12	**Tampa Bay**	1:00
Sept. 19	at New York Giants	1:00
Sept. 27	**Dallas** (Mon.)	9:00
Oct. 3	at Cleveland	1:00
Oct. 10	**Baltimore**	8:30
Oct. 17	at Chicago	1:00
Oct. 24	Open Date	
Oct. 31	**Green Bay**	1:00
Nov. 7	at Detroit	1:00
Nov. 14	**Cincinnati**	4:05
Nov. 21	at Philadelphia	4:15
Nov. 28	at Pittsburgh	1:00
Dec. 5	**New York Giants**	4:15
Dec. 12	**Philadelphia**	8:30
Dec. 18	at San Francisco (Sat.)	4:00
Dec. 26	at Dallas	4:15
Jan. 2	**Minnesota**	1:00

Stadium: FedExField (opened in 1997)
• **Capacity:** 86,484
1600 FedEx Way
Landover, Maryland 20785
Playing Surface: Natural Grass
Training Camp: Redskins Park
Ashburn, Virginia 20147

FEDEXFIELD

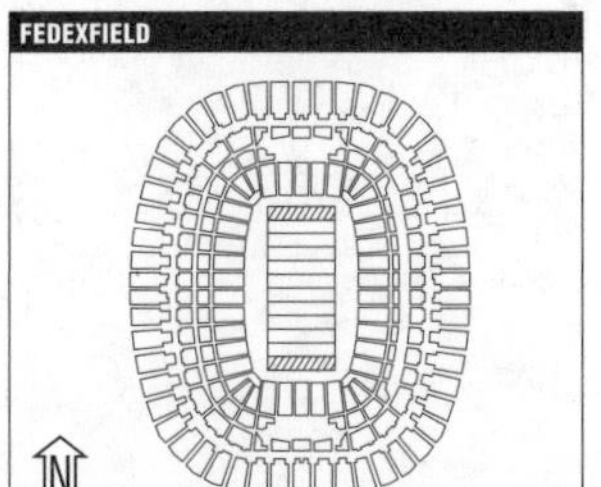

CLUB OFFICIALS

Owner: Daniel M. Snyder
Chief Operating Officer: David Pauken
Chief Financial Officer: Jay Sloan
General Counsel: Norm Chirite
Senior Vice President: Karl Swanson
Senior Vice President, Marketing: Mike Stevens
Senior Vice President, Stadium Operations: Michael Dillow
Director of Ticket Operations: Jeff Ritter
Vice President, Football Operations: Vinny Cerrato
Vice President, Football Operations: Pepper Rodgers
Director of Pro Personnel: Scott Campbell
Pro Scouts: Mike Kelly, Louis Riddick
Personnel Assistant: Mike Rutenberg
College Scouting Coordinator: Trent Baalke
College Scouts: Tim Gribble, Shemy Schembechler, Foge Fazio
National Scout: Joel Patten
Contracts Manger: Eric Schaffer
Director of Player Development: John "JJ" Jefferson
Director of Public Relations: Michelle Tessier
Leadership Council/Community Affairs: Charlene Lefkowitz, Alex Hahn
Video Director: Mike Bracken
Video Department: Steve Pratti, Matt Shea
Director of Sports Medicine: Bubba Tyer
Head Athletic Trainer: John Burrell
Assistant Athletic Trainers: Eric Steward, Larry Hess
Equipment Manager: Brad Berlin
Assistant Equipment Manager: Anders Beutel

COACHING HISTORY

Boston 1932-36
(521-467-27)

1932	Lud Wray	4-4-2
1933-34	William (Lone Star) Dietz	11-11-2
1935	Eddie Casey	2-8-1
1936-1942	Ray Flaherty	56-23-3
1943	Arthur (Dutch) Bergman	7-4-1
1944-45	Dudley DeGroot	14-6-1
1946-48	Glen (Turk) Edwards	16-18-1
1949	John Whelchel*	3-3-1
1949-1951	Herman Ball**	4-16-0
1951	Dick Todd	5-4-0
1952-53	Earl (Curly) Lambeau	10-13-1
1954-58	Joe Kuharich	26-32-2
1959-1960	Mike Nixon	4-18-2
1961-65	Bill McPeak	21-46-3
1966-68	Otto Graham	17-22-3
1969	Vince Lombardi	7-5-2
1970	Bill Austin	6-8-0
1971-77	George Allen	69-35-1
1978-1980	Jack Pardee	24-24-0
1981-1992	Joe Gibbs	140-65-0
1993	Richie Petitbon	4-12-0
1994-2000	Norv Turner***	50-60-1
2000	Terry Robiskie	1-2-0
2001	Marty Schottenheimer	8-8-0
2002-03	Steve Spurrier	12-20-0

*Released after seven games in 1949
**Released after three games in 1951
***Released after 13 games in 2000

ATTENDANCE

Home 667,033 Away 553,691
Total 1,220,724
Single-game home record, 85,490 (10/12/03)
Single-season home record, 667,033 (2003)

2004 DRAFT CHOICES

Round	Name	Pos.	College
1	Sean Taylor	S	Miami
3	Chris Cooley	TE	Utah State
5	Mark Wilson	T	California
6	Jim Molinaro	T	Notre Dame

WASHINGTON REDSKINS

2003 TEAM RECORD

PRESEASON (1-3)

Date	Result	Opponent
8/9	L 0-20	at Carolina
8/16	L 13-20	New England
8/23	W 24-3	Baltimore
8/28	L 15-17	at Jacksonville

REGULAR SEASON (5-11)

Date	Result	Opponent	Att.
9/4	W 16-13	New York Jets	85,420
9/14	W 33-31	at Atlanta	70,241
9/21	L 21-24	N.Y. Giants (OT)	84,856
9/28	W 20-17	New England	83,632
10/5	L 25-27	at Philadelphia	67,792
10/12	L 13-35	Tampa Bay	85,490
10/19	L 7-24	at Buffalo	73,149
11/2	L 14-21	at Dallas	64,002
11/9	W 27-20	Seattle	80,728
11/16	L 17-20	at Carolina	73,263
11/23	L 23-24	at Miami	73,578
11/30	L 20-24	New Orleans	76,821
12/7	W 20-7	at New York Giants	78,217
12/14	L 0-27	Dallas	70,284
12/21	L 24-27	at Chicago	61,719
12/27	L 7-31	Philadelphia	76,766

(OT) Overtime

SCORE BY PERIODS

	1	2	3	4	OT	Total
Redskins	40	113	59	75	0 —	287
Opponents	78	106	76	109	3 —	372

2003 TEAM STATISTICS

	Redskins	Opp.
Total First Downs	272	325
Rushing	95	122
Passing	156	176
Penalty	21	27
3rd Down: Made/Att	73/215	84/209
3rd Down Pct.	34.0	40.2
4th Down: Made/Att	8/14	8/11
4th Down Pct.	57.1	72.7
Possession Avg.	28:45	31:15
Total Net Yards	4,659	5,412
Avg. Per Game	291.2	338.3
Total Plays	991	1,014
Avg. Per Play	4.7	5.3
Net Yards Rushing	1,653	2,217
Avg. Per Game	103.3	138.6
Total Rushes	421	504
Net Yards Passing	3,006	3,195
Avg. Per Game	187.9	199.7
Sacked/Yards Lost	43/267	27/159
Gross Yards	3,273	3,354
Att./Completions	527/283	483/285
Completion Pct.	53.7	59.0
Had Intercepted	16	17
Punts/Average	84/40.2	71/42.2
Net Punting Avg.	84/34.3	71/36.5
Penalties/Yards	124/1,038	95/835
Fumbles/Ball Lost	21/12	26/13
Touchdowns	30	45
Rushing	8	20
Passing	21	23
Returns	1	2

2003 INDIVIDUAL STATISTICS

PASSING	Att.	Comp.	Yds.	Pct.	TD	Int.	Tkld.	Rate
Ramsey	337	179	2,166	53.1	14	9	30/206	75.8
Hasselbeck	177	95	1,012	53.7	5	7	9/44	63.6
R. Johnson	7	5	39	71.4	0	0	3/15	84.8
Gardner	3	2	46	66.7	2	0	0/0	149.3
Hamdan	2	1	7	50.0	0	0	1/2	58.3
Barker	1	1	3	100.0	0	0	0/0	79.2
Redskins	527	283	3,273	53.7	21	16	43/267	73.3
Opponents	483	285	3,354	59.0	23	17	27/159	81.4

SCORING	TD R	TD P	TD Rt	PAT	FG	Saf	PTS
Hall	0	0	0	26/27	25/33	0	101
McCants	0	6	0	0/0	0/0	0	40
Coles	0	6	0	0/0	0/0	0	36
Gardner	0	5	0	0/0	0/0	0	30
Cartwright	4	0	0	0/0	0/0	0	24
Betts	2	0	0	0/0	0/0	0	12
Canidate	1	1	0	0/0	0/0	0	12
Morton	0	1	1	0/0	0/0	0	12
Jacobs	0	1	0	0/0	0/0	0	6
P. Johnson	0	1	0	0/0	0/0	0	6
Ramsey	1	0	0	0/0	0/0	0	6
Armstead	0	0	0	0/0	0/0	1	2
Redskins	8	21	1	26/27	25/33	1	287
Opponents	20	23	2	45/45	19/31	0	372

2-Pt. Conversions: McCants 2.
Redskins 2-3, Opponents 0-0.

RUSHING	No.	Yds	Avg	LG	TD
Canidate	142	600	4.2	38	1
Cartwright	107	411	3.8	22	4
Betts	77	255	3.3	13t	2
Morton	48	216	4.5	27	0
Ramsey	15	62	4.1	24	1
Hasselbeck	15	41	2.7	11	0
Coles	10	39	3.9	23	0
McCullough	1	9	9.0	9	0
Simon	3	9	3.0	6	0
R. Johnson	1	6	6.0	6	0
B. Johnson	2	5	2.5	4	0
Redskins	421	1,653	3.9	38	8
Opponents	504	2,217	4.4	52	20

RECEIVING	No.	Yds	Avg	LG	TD
Coles	82	1,204	14.7	64	6
Gardner	59	600	10.2	35	5
McCants	27	360	13.3	32t	6
Cartwright	18	176	9.8	40	0
Morton	15	187	12.5	36t	1
P. Johnson	15	170	11.3	31	1
Betts	15	167	11.1	34	0
Canidate	10	71	7.1	25	1
Flemister	9	89	9.9	18	0
B. Johnson	9	71	7.9	19	0
Royal	5	48	9.6	20	0
Chamberlain	4	29	7.3	15	0
Jacobs	3	37	12.3	19t	1
Simon	3	21	7.0	12	0
Ware	3	17	5.7	7	0
McCullough	3	13	4.3	8	0
C. Russell	2	10	5.0	7	0
Ohalete	1	3	3.0	3	0
Redskins	283	3,273	11.6	64	21
Opponents	285	3,354	11.8	80t	23

INTERCEPTIONS	No.	Yds	Avg	LG	TD
Smoot	4	35	8.8	35	0
Ohalete	3	60	20.0	30	0
Bowen	3	44	14.7	44	0
Dav. Terrell	2	21	10.5	20	0
Bailey	2	2	1.0	2	0
Bauman	2	1	0.5	1	0
Trotter	1	21	21.0	21	0
Redskins	17	184	10.8	44	0
Opponents	16	178	11.1	44t	2

PUNTING	No.	Yds.	Avg.	In 20	LG
Barker	84	3,377	40.2	24	69
Redskins	84	3,377	40.2	24	69
Opponents	71	2,997	42.2	20	59

PUNT RETURNS	Ret	FC	Yds	Avg	LG	TD
Morton	19	16	188	9.9	28	0
P. Johnson	3	3	17	5.7	11	0
Redskins	22	19	205	9.3	28	0
Opponents	40	16	393	9.8	36	0

KICKOFF RETURNS	No.	Yds	Avg	LG	TD
Morton	44	1,029	23.4	94t	1
P. Johnson	13	310	23.8	50	0
Betts	3	59	19.7	26	0
Cartwright	2	26	13.0	13	0
Flemister	2	22	11.0	11	0
B. Johnson	1	15	15.0	15	0
Simon	1	21	21.0	21	0
Redskins	66	1,482	22.5	94t	1
Opponents	60	1,238	20.6	52	0

FIELD GOALS	1-19	20-29	30-39	40-49	50+
Hall	0/0	8/8	7/9	6/9	4/7
Redskins	0/0	8/8	7/9	6/9	4/7
Opponents	1/1	9/10	4/7	3/8	2/5

SACKS	No.
Armstead	6.5
Arrington	6.0
B. Smith	5.0
Holsey	2.5
Wynn	2.0
Trotter	1.5
Dalton	1.0
Upshaw	1.0
Zellner	1.0
Marshall	0.5
Redskins	27.0
Opponents	43.0

RECORD HOLDERS

INDIVIDUAL RECORDS—CAREER

Category	Name	Performance
Rushing (Yds.)	John Riggins, 1976-79, 1981-85	7,472
Passing (Yds.)	Joe Theismann, 1974-1985	25,206
Passing (TDs)	Sammy Baugh, 1937-1952	187
Receiving (No.)	Art Monk, 1980-1993	888
Receiving (Yds.)	Art Monk, 1980-1993	12,028
Interceptions	Darrell Green, 1983-2001	54
Punting (Avg.)	Sammy Baugh, 1937-1952	*45.1
Punt Return (Avg.)	Johnny Williams, 1952-53	12.8
Kickoff Return (Avg.)	Bobby Mitchell, 1962-68	28.5
Field Goals	Mark Moseley, 1974-1986	263
Touchdowns (Tot.)	Charley Taylor, 1964-1977	90
Points	Mark Moseley, 1974-1986	1,206

INDIVIDUAL RECORDS—SINGLE SEASON

Category	Name	Performance
Rushing (Yds.)	Stephen Davis, 2001	1,432
Passing (Yds.)	Jay Schroeder, 1986	4,109
Passing (TDs)	Sonny Jurgensen, 1967	31
Receiving (No.)	Art Monk, 1984	106
Receiving (Yds.)	Bobby Mitchell, 1963	1,436
Interceptions	Dan Sandifer, 1948	13
Punting (Avg.)	Sammy Baugh, 1940	*51.4
Punt Return (Avg.)	Johnny Williams, 1952	15.3
Kickoff Return (Avg.)	Mike Nelms, 1981	29.7
Field Goals	Mark Moseley, 1983	33
Touchdowns (Tot.)	John Riggins, 1983	24
Points	Mark Moseley, 1983	161

INDIVIDUAL RECORDS—SINGLE GAME

Category	Name	Performance
Rushing (Yds.)	Gerald Riggs, 9-17-89	221
Passing (Yds.)	Sammy Baugh, 10-31-43	446
Passing (TDs)	Sammy Baugh, 10-31-43, 11-23-47	6
	Mark Rypien, 11-10-91	6
Receiving (No.)	Art Monk, 12-15-85, 11-4-90	13
	Kelvin Bryant, 12-7-86	13
Receiving (Yds.)	Anthony Allen, 10-4-87	255
Interceptions	Sammy Baugh, 11-14-43	*4
	Dan Sandifer, 10-31-48	*4
Field Goals	Many times	5
	Last time by Chip Lohmiller, 10-25-92	
Touchdowns (Tot.)	Dick James, 12-17-61	4
	Larry Brown, 12-16-73	4
Points	Dick James, 12-17-61	24
	Larry Brown, 12-16-73	24

*NFL Record

WASHINGTON REDSKINS

2004 VETERAN ROSTER

No.	Name	Pos.	Ht.	Wt.	Birthdate	NFL Exp.	College	Hometown	How Acq.	'03 Games/ Starts
71	Albright, Ethan	LS	6-5	265	6/20/78	10	North Carolina	Greensboro, N.C.	UFA(Buff)-'01	16/0
56	Arrington, LaVar	LB	6-3	253	5/7/79	5	Penn State	Pittsburgh, Pa.	D1-'00	16/16
59	Barrow, Michael	LB	6-2	245	4/19/70	12	Miami	Homestead, Fla.	UFA(NYG)-'04	16/16*
25	Bauman, Rashad	CB	5-8	184	8/27/79	3	Oregon	Phoenix, Ariz.	D3-'02	12/2
46	Betts, Ladell	RB	5-10	222	11/12/76	3	Iowa	Blue Springs, Mo.	D2-'02	9/1
41	Bowen, Matt	S	6-1	207	9/16/78	5	Iowa	Glen Ellyn, Ill.	RFA(GB)-'03	16/16
32	Brown, Ralph	CB	5-10	185	9/17/70	4	Nebraska	Hacienda Heights, Calif.	UFA(NYG)-'04	11/7*
8	t- Brunell, Mark	QB	6-1	217	4/4/79	11	Washington	Santa Maria, Calif.	T(Jax)-'04	3/3*
40	Cartwright, Rock	FB	5-7	223	10/30/81	3	Kansas State	Conroe, Texas	D7-'02	15/3
80	Coles, Laveranues	WR	5-11	193	10/31/80	5	Florida State	Jacksonville, Fla.	RFA(NYJ)-'03	16/16
93	Daniels, Phillip	DL	6-3	288	9/7/80	9	Georgia	Donalson, Ga.	UFA(Chi)-'04	16/16*
66	Dockery, Derrick	T-G	6-6	345	9/22/78	2	Texas	Lakeview, Texas	D3-'03	16/13
79	Elisara, Pita	T	6-4	305	8/10/74	2	Indiana	Tafuna, American Samoa	FA-'03	0*
63	Ferrario, Bill	G-T	6-2	315	4/12/76	3	Wisconsin	Scranton, Pa.	FA-'04	0*
74	Fiore, Dave	G	6-4	293	8/13/76	7	Hofstra	Waldwick, N.J.	FA-'03	3/3
29	Franz, Todd	DB	6-0	202	10/26/77	3	Tulsa	Enid, Okla.	FA-'02	16/2
64	Friedman, Lennie	G-C	6-3	283	12/3/76	5	Duke	Livingston, N.J.	FA-'03	16/8
87	Gardner, Rod	WR	6-2	213	2/13/73	4	Clemson	Jacksonville, Fla.	D1-'01	16/16
96	Griffin, Cornelius	DT	6-3	300	3/17/74	5	Alabama	Brundidge, Ala.	UFA(NYG)-'04	15/15*
10	Hall, John	K	6-3	240	2/8/81	8	Wisconsin	Port Charlotte, Fla.	UFA(NYJ)-'03	6/5
2	Hamdan, Gibran	QB	6-4	208	4/6/78	2	Indiana	North Potomac, Md.	D7-'03	1/0
37	Harris, Walt	CB	5-11	192	5/30/81	9	Mississippi State	LaGrange, Ga.	UFA(Ind)-'04	16/15*
4	Hasselbeck, Tim	QB	6-1	211	1/28/76	3	Boston College	Westwood, Mass.	FA-'03	7/5
84	Jacobs, Taylor	WR	6-0	198	4/18/80	2	Florida	Tallahassee, Fla.	D2-'03	8/0
76	Jansen, Jon	T	6-6	305	1/18/79	6	Michigan	Clawson, Mich.	D2-'99	16/16
73	Jones, Kenyatta	T	6-3	307	10/4/70	3	South Florida	Gainesville, Fla.	FA-'03	0*
78	Killings, Cedric	DT	6-2	290	4/1/78	3	Carson-Newman	Miami, Fla.	FA-'03	4/0*
34	Lott, Andre	DB	5-10	196	8/1/78	3	Tennessee	Memphis, Tenn.	D5-'02	11/0
98	Marshall, Lemar	LB	6-2	227	2/12/80	3	Michigan State	Cincinnati, Ohio	FA-'01	12/0
85	McCants, Darnerien	WR	6-3	214	12/16/76	3	Delaware State	Odenton, Md.	D5-'01	15/1
55	Mitchell, Kevin	LB	6-1	258	6/1/75	11	Syracuse	Harrisburg, Pa.	UFA(NO)-'00	16/0
20	Morton, Chad	RB-KR	5-8	203	4/10/74	5	Southern California	South Torrance, Calif.	RFA(NYJ)-'03	15/2
75	Noble, Brandon	DT	6-2	304	5/27/80	5	Penn State	Virginia Beach, Va.	UFA(Dall)-'03	0*
26	Ohalete, Ifeanyi	DB	6-2	222	10/26/78	4	Southern California	Springfield, Ill.	FA-'01	15/15
58	Pierce, Antonio	LB	6-1	240	9/1/81	4	Arizona	Long Beach, Calif.	FA-'01	15/0
6	t- Portis, Clinton	RB	5-11	205	2/14/79	3	Miami	Gainesville, Fla.	T(Den)-'04	13/13*
11	Ramsey, Patrick	QB	6-2	217	9/7/72	3	Tulane	Ruston, La.	D1-'02	11/11
86	Rasby, Walter	TE	6-3	252	3/3/73	10	Wake Forest	Washington, N.C.	UFA(NO)-'04	16/6*
52	Raymer, Cory	C	6-3	300	5/15/79	9	Wisconsin	Fond du Lac, Wis.	UFA(SD)-'04	15/8*
88	Royal, Robert	TE	6-4	257	2/8/79	2	Louisiana State	New Orleans, La.	D5-'02	6/6
83	Russell, Cliff	WR	5-11	193	3/25/75	2	Utah	Ewa Beach, Hawaii	D3-'02	3/0
95	Salave'a, Joe	DT-DE	6-3	295	7/28/77	6	Arizona	Leone, American Samoa	FA-'04	9/1*
60	Samuels, Chris	T	6-5	310	6/2/78	5	Alabama	Mobile, Ala.	D1-'00	13/13
45	Sellers, Mike	FB	6-3	260	7/21/75	5	Walla Walla (Wash.) C.C.	North Thurston, Wash.	FA-'04	0*
31	Simon, John	RB	5-11	202	12/11/78	3	Louisiana Tech	Baton Rouge, La.	FA-'03	4/0
21	Smoot, Fred	CB	5-11	174	4/17/79	4	Mississippi State	Jackson, Miss.	D2-'01	15/14
24	Springs, Shawn	CB	6-0	204	3/11/75	8	Ohio State	Silver Spring, Md.	UFA(Sea)-'04	12/8*
	Stephens, Leonard	TE	6-3	258	7/9/78	3	Howard	Princeton, N.J.	FA-'04	0*
67	Terrell, Daryl	T-G	6-4	327	1/25/75	7	Southern Miss	Vossburg, Miss.	FA-'04	3/0
77	Thomas, Randy	G	6-5	306	1/19/76	6	Mississippi State	East Point, Ga.	UFA(NYJ)-'03	16/16
3	t- Thrash, James	WR	6-0	200	4/28/75	8	Missouri Southern	Wewoka, Okla.	T(Phil)-'04	16/16*
19	Tupa, Tom	P	6-4	225	2/6/66	16	Ohio State	Cleveland, Ohio	UFA(TB)-'04	16/0*
91	Upshaw, Regan	DE	6-4	265	8/12/75	9	California	Pittsburg, Calif.	FA-'03	16/8
48	Ware, Kevin	TE	6-3	259	9/30/80	2	Washington	Spring, Texas	FA-'03	11/2
94	Warner, Ron	DE	6-3	270	9/26/75	3	Kansas	Independence, Kan.	FA-03	1/0
53	Washington, Marcus	LB	6-3	247	10/17/76	5	Auburn	Auburn, Ala.	UFA(Ind)-'04	16/16*
68	Winey, Brandon	T	6-7	315	1/27/78	2	Louisiana State	Lake Charles, La.	FA-'03	11/3
97	Wynn, Renaldo	DL	6-3	292	9/3/74	8	Notre Dame	Chicago, Ill.	UFA(Jax)-'02	16/16

* Barrow played 16 games with N.Y. Giants in '03; Brown played 11 games with N.Y. Giants; Brunell played 3 games with Jacksonville; Daniels played 16 games with Chicago; Elisara did not play in 8 games; Ferrario last active with Green Bay in '02; Griffin played 15 games with N.Y. Giants; Harris played 16 games with Indianapolis; Jones missed '03 season because of injury; Killings played 4 games with Carolina; Noble missed '03 season because of injury; Portis played 13 games with Denver; Rasby played 16 games with New Orleans; Raymer played 15 games with San Diego; Salave'a played 9 games with San Diego; Sellers last active with Cleveland in '02; Springs played 12 games with Seattle; Stephens last active with Washington in '02; Thrash played 16 games with Philadelphia; Tupa played 16 games with Tampa Bay; Washington played 16 games with Indianapolis.

t – Redskins traded for Brunell (Jax), Portis (Den), Thrash (Phil).

Traded—CB Champ Bailey (16 games in '03) to Denver; FB Bryan Johnson (16) to Chicago.

Retired—Bruce Smith, 19-year defensive end; 16 games in '03.

Players lost through free agency (4): DE-DT Martin Chase (NYG; 13 games in '03), WR Patrick Johnson (Cin; 16), DT Darrell Russell (TB; 8), S David Terrell (Oak; 13).

Also played with Redskins in '03—LB Jessie Armstead (16 games), P Bryan Barker (16), RB Trung Canidate (11), TE Byron Chamberlain (4), TE Zeron Flemister (12), LB Orantes Grant (1), DE-DT Bernard Holsey (16), DE Ladairis Jackson (1), QB Rob Johnson (2), C Larry Moore (9), LB Jeremiah Trotter (16), DE Peppi Zellner (16).

2004 FIRST-YEAR ROSTER

Name	Pos.	Ht.	Wt.	Birthdate	College	Hometown	How Acq.
Boschetti, Ryan	DT	6-4	295	10/7/81	UCLA	San Mateo, Calif.	FA
Brewer, Jonathan	WR	6-0	175	5/21/80	Howard	Charlotte, N.C.	FA
Brown, Rufus	CB	5-9	188	7/18/80	Florida State	El Paso, Texas	FA
Campbell, Khary (1)	LB	6-3	230	3/3/77	Bowling Green	Toledo, Ohio	FA
Christensen, Quinn	OL	6-5	312	2/13/80	Brigham Young	Idaho Falls, Idaho	FA
Clemons, Chris (1)	LB	6-3	234	11/6/75	Georgia	Griffin, Ga.	FA-'03
Clemons, Nic (1)	DL	6-6	278	12/29/77	Georgia	Griffin, Ga.	FA-'03
Cloman, Scott (1)	WR	6-3	214	3/4/73	Southern	Compton, Calif.	FA-'03
Cooley, Chris	TE	6-3	265	7/11/82	Utah State	Powell, Utah	D3
Dillard, Sean (1)	WR	5-10	172	11/16/76	Temple	Stone Mountain, Ga.	FA
Hall, Michael (1)	DB	5-10	175	4/22/81	Illinois	Tehachapi, Calif.	FA
Heuer, Norman	DL	6-5	288	12/6/80	Michigan	Peoria, Ariz.	FA
Jimoh, Ade (1)	DB	6-1	190	12/14/77	Utah State	Woodland Hills, Calif.	FA-'03
Lemons, Devin (1)	LB	6-2	232	12/17/76	Texas Tech	Bryan, Texas	FA
McCullough, Sultan (1)	RB	6-0	197	1/1/71	Southern California	Pasadena, Calif.	FA-'03
Molinaro, Jim	OL	6-6	309	4/27/81	Notre Dame	Bethlehem, Pa.	D7
Nowland, Ben (1)	C	6-3	298	5/22/79	Auburn	Ponte Verde Beach, Fla.	FA-'03
Smith, Clifton (1)	LB	6-3	255	7/21/80	Syracuse	Freeport, N.Y.	FA-'03
Standeford, John	WR	6-4	206	4/15/82	Purdue	Monrovia, Ind.	FA
Stemke, Kevin (1)	P	6-2	194	11/23/78	Wisconsin	Green Bay, Wis.	FA
Strother, Billy	LB	6-0	230	1/8/82	New Mexico	Evansville, Ind.	FA
Taylor, Sean	S	6-2	231	4/1/83	Miami	Miami, Fla.	D1
White, Greg (1)	DL	6-3	268	7/25/79	Minnesota	Newark, N.J.	FA-'03
Wilds, Garnell	CB	5-11	196	6/8/81	Virginia Tech	Tampa, Fla.	FA
Williams, Jafar	WR	6-2	210	7/21/80	Maryland	Philadelphia, Pa.	FA
Wilson, Dennard	S	5-10	189	3/31/82	Maryland	Upper Marlboro, Md.	FA
Wilson, Mark	OL	6-6	295	11/11/80	California	San Jose, Calif.	D5

The term NFL Rookie is defined as a player who is in his first season of professional football and has not been on the roster of another professional football team for any regular-season or postseason games. A Rookie is designated by an "R" on NFL rosters. Players who have been active in another professional football league or players who have NFL experience, including either preseason training camp or being on an Active List or Inactive List, or on Reserve/Injured or Reserve/Physically Unable to Perform for fewer than six regular-season games, are termed NFL First-Year Players. An NFL First-Year Player is designated by a "1" on NFL rosters. Thereafter, a player is credited with an additional year of experience for each season in which he accumulates six games on the Active List or Inactive List, or on Reserve/Injured or Reserve/Physically Unable to Perform.

Log on to www.redskins.com for an up-to-date roster.

WASHINGTON REDSKINS

COACHING STAFF

Head Coach,
Joe Gibbs

Pro Career: On January 7, 2004 Joe Gibbs made his return to the Washington Redskins as head coach and team president. The most successful coach in Redskins history, Gibbs, who coached the team from 1981-1992, led the Redskins to four Super Bowls (XVI, XVII, XXII, and XXVI). He is the only coach to win three Super Bowls with three different quarterbacks. His 140 wins ranks 14th in NFL history, and his .683 win percentage is the best among all NFL coaches with more than 125 wins. Gibbs coached with the St. Louis Cardinals (1973-1977), Tampa Bay Buccaneers (1978), and San Diego Chargers (1979-1980), before joining the Redskins in 1981. Career record: 140-65.
Background: Played tight end, offensive guard and linebacker at San Diego State. Coached at San Diego State (1964-66), Florida State (1967-1968), USC (1969-1970), and Arkansas (1971-1972).
Personal: Born November 25, 1940 in Mocksville, N.C,. lives in Charlotte, with wife Pat. They have two sons: JD and Coy.

ASSISTANT COACHES

Greg Blache, defensive coordinator-defensive line; born March 9, 1949, New Orleans. Attended Notre Dame. No college or pro playing experience. College coach: Notre Dame 1972-75, 1981-83, Tulane 1976-1980, Southern 1986, Kansas 1987. Pro coach: Jacksonville Bulls (USFL) 1984-85, Green Bay Packers 1988-1993, Indianapolis Colts 1994-98, Chicago Bears 1999-2003, joined Redskins in 2004.
Don Breaux, offensive coordinator; born August 3, 1940, Jennings, La. Quarterback McNeese State 1959-1961. Pro quarterback Denver Broncos 1963, San Diego Chargers 1964-65. College coach: Florida State 1966-67, Arkansas 1968-1971, 1977-1980, Florida 1973-74, Texas 1975-76. Pro coach: Houston Oilers 1972, Washington Redskins 1981-1993, New York Jets 1994, Carolina Panthers 1995-2001, re-joined Redskins in 2004.
Joe Bugel, asst. head coach-offense; born March 10, 1940, Pittsburgh. Guard-linebacker Western Kentucky 1960-63. No pro playing experience. College coach: Western Kentucky 1964-1968, Navy 1969-1972, Iowa State 1973, Ohio State 1974. Pro coach: Detroit Lions 1975-76, Houston Oilers 1977-1980, Washington Redskins 1981-89, Phoenix Cardinals 1990-1993 (head coach), Oakland Raiders 1995-97 (head coach 1997), San Diego Chargers 1998-2001, re-joined Redskins in 2004.
Jack Burns, quarterbacks; born January 3, 1949, Tampa, Fla. Safety Florida 1967-1970. No pro playing experience. College coach: Florida 1971-73, 1975, Louisville 1974, 1985-88, Texas 1976, Vanderbilt 1977-78, Auburn 1979-1980. Pro coach: Tampa Bay Bandits (USFL) 1983, Washington Redskins 1989-1991, Minnesota Vikings 1992-93, Atlanta Falcons 1997-2002, re-joined Redskins in 2004.
Earnest Byner, running backs; born September 15, 1962, Milledgeville, Ga. Running back East Carolina 1980-83. Pro running back Cleveland Browns 1984-88, 1994-95, Washington Redskins 1989-93, Baltimore Ravens 1996-97. Pro coach: Joined Redskins in 2004.
Bobby Crumpler, strength and conditioning; born April 23, 1965, Newton Grove, N.C. Running back North Carolina State 1983-87. No pro playing experience. College coach: North Carolina State 1989, 1992-96, 2000-01, Kansas 2002. Pro coach: Joined Redskins in 2003.
John Dunn, head strength and conditioning; born July 22, 1956, Wayne, N.J. Guard Penn State 1974-77. No pro playing experience. College coach: Penn State 1978. Pro coach: Washington Redskins 1984-86, Los Angeles Raiders 1987-89, San Diego Chargers 1990-96, New York Giants 1997-2003, re-joined Redskins in 2004.
Coy Gibbs, quality control-offense; born December 9, 1972, Little Rock, Ark. Linebacker Stanford 1991-94. No pro playing experience. Pro coach: Joined Redskins in 2004.
John Hastings, strength and conditioning; born July 5, 1964, Newport News, Va.. Attended Ohio University. No college or pro playing experience. Pro coach: San Diego Chargers 1990-2001, joined Redskins in 2002.
Stan Hixon, wide receivers; born July 24, 1957, Lakeland, Fla. Wide receiver Iowa State 1975-78. No pro playing experience. College coach: Morehead State 1980-82, Appalachian State 1983-88, South Carolina 1989-1992, Wake Forest 1993-94, Georgia Tech 1995-99, Louisiana State 2000-03. Pro coach: Joined Redskins in 2004.
Steve Jackson, third down-safeties; born April 8, 1969, Houston. Defensive back Purdue 1987-1990. Pro defensive back Houston Oilers/Tennessee Titans 1991-1999. Pro coach: Buffalo Bills 2001-03, joined Redskins in 2004.
Bill Lazor, offensive assistant; born June 14, 1972, Scranton, Pa. Quarterback Cornell 1991-93. No pro playing experience. College coach: Cornell 1995-2000, Buffalo 2001-02. Pro coach: Atlanta Falcons 2003, joined Redskins in 2004.
Dale Lindsey, linebackers; born January 18, 1943, Bedford, Ind. Linebacker Western Kentucky 1961-64. Pro linebacker Cleveland Browns 1965-1973. College coach: Southern Methodist 1988-89. Pro coach: Green Bay Packers 1986-87, New England Patriots 1990, Tampa Bay Buccaneers 1991, San Diego Chargers 1992-96, 2002-03, Washington Redskins 1997-98, Chicago Bears 1999-2001, re-joined Redskins in 2004.
Kirk Olivadotti, asst. defensive backs; born January 1, 1974, Wilmington, Del. Wide receiver Purdue 1992-1996. No pro playing experience. College coach: Maine Maritime Academy 1997, Indiana State 1998-99. Pro coach: Joined Redskins in 2000.
Warren (Rennie) Simmons, tight end; born February 25, 1942, Poughkeepsie, N.Y. Center San Diego State 1961-65. No pro playing experience. College coach: Cal State-Fullerton 1974-78, Cerritos (Calif.) J.C. 1978-1980, Vanderbilt 1995. Pro coach: Washington Redskins 1981-1993, Los Angeles Rams 1994, Houston Oilers 1996, Atlanta Falcons 1997-2003, re-joined Redskins in 2004.
Danny Smith, special teams; born September 7, 1953, Pittsburgh. Defensive back Edinboro State 1972-75. No pro playing experience. College coach: Edinboro State 1976, Clemson 1979, William & Mary 1980-83, The Citadel 1984-86, Georgia Tech 1987-1994. Pro coach: Philadelphia Eagles 1995-98, Detroit Lions 1999-2000, Buffalo Bills 2001-03, joined Redskins in 2004.
DeWayne Walker, secondary-cornerbacks; born December 3, 1960. Cornerback Pasadena (Calif.) C.C. 1978-79, Minnesota 1980-81. Pro cornerback Edmonton Eskimos (CFL) 1982, Oakland Invaders (USFL) 1985. College coach: Mt. San Antonio (Calif.) C.C. 1988-1992, Utah State 1993, Brigham Young 1994, Oklahoma State 1995, California 1996-97, Southern California 2001. Pro coach: New England Patriots 1998-2000, New York Giants 2002-03, joined Redskins in 2004.
Gregg Williams, asst. head coach/defense; born July 15, 1958, Excelsior Springs, Mo. Quarterback Northeast Missouri State 1976-79. No pro playing experience. College coach: Houston 1988-89. Pro coach: Houston Oilers/Tennessee Titans 1990-2000, Buffalo Bills (head coach) 2001-03, joined Redskins in 2004.
Ernie Zampese, offensive consultant; born March 12, 1936, Santa Barbara, Calif. Running back USC 1956-58. No pro playing experience. College coach: Hancock (Calif.) J.C. 1962-65, Cal Poly-San Luis Obispo 1966, San Diego State 1967-1975. Pro coach: San Diego Chargers 1976, 1979-1986, Los Angeles Rams 1987-1993, Dallas Cowboys 1994-1997, New England Patriots 1998-1999, St. Louis Rams 2002, joined Redskins in 2004.

2003 Season in Review

2003 TRADES

Tight end **Mark Campbell** from Cleveland to Buffalo for an unannounced future selection choice. (2/28)

Wide receiver **Terry Glenn** from Green Bay to Dallas for an unannounced future selection choice. (2/28)

Running back **Trung Canidate** from St. Louis to Washington for guard **David Loverne** and a fourth-round selection in 2003 (DB **Dejuan Groce**). (2/28)

Defensive back **Al Harris** and a fourth-round selection in 2003 (#127) from Philadelphia to Green Bay for a second-round selection in 2003 (#62). (3/3)

Linebacker **Mark Simoneau** from Atlanta to Philadelphia for a sixth-round (DB **Waine Bacon**) draft choice and an unannounced future selection choice. (3/4)

Tackle **Greg Randall** from New England to Houston for a fifth-round supplemental selection in 2003 (#154). (3/6)

New England's third-round selection in 2003 (T **Derrick Dockery**) and Dallas' fifth-round selection in 2003 (#140) from New England to Washington for Washington's third-round selection in 2003 (#75) and an unannounced future selection choice. (3/6)

Wide receiver **Peerless Price** from Buffalo to Atlanta for Buffalo's first-round selection in 2003 (RB **Willis McGahee**). (3/7)

Quarterback **Todd Bouman** from Minnesota to New Orleans for the Saints' sixth-round selection in 2003 (LB **Mike Nattiel**). (3/13)

Tackle **Kyle Turley** from New Orleans to St. Louis for an unannounced future selection choice. (3/24)

Guard **David Brandt** from Washington to Green Bay for an unannounced future selection choice. (4/1)

Tackle **Michael Thompson** from Atlanta to Seattle for an unannounced future selection choice. (4/10)

Defensive back **Tebucky Jones** from New England to New Orleans for the Chiefs' third-round selection in 2003 (#78), the Colts' seventh-round selection in 2003 (LB **Tully Banta-Cain**), and an unannounced future selection choice. (4/14)

Linebacker **Junior Seau** from San Diego to Miami for an unannounced future selection choice. (4/16)

Defensive back **Derek Combs** from Kansas City to Green Bay for an unannounced future selection choice. (4/24)

Kansas City's third-round selection in 2003 (T **Wade Smith**) from New England to Miami for an unannounced future selection choice. (4/25)

Chicago's first-round selection in 2003 (DT **Dewayne Robertson**) from Chicago to the New York Jets for the Redskins' first-round selection in 2003 (#13), the Jets' first-round selection in 2003 (QB **Rex Grossman**), and the Jets' fourth-round selection in 2003 (DT **Ian Scott**). (4/26)

Arizona's first-round selection in 2003 (DT **Johnathan Sullivan**), second-round selection in 2003 (T **Jon Stinchcomb**), and fourth-round seleciton in 2003 (G **Montrae Holland**) from Arizona to New Orleans for the Saints' first-round selection in 2003 (WR **Bryant Johnson**), the Dolphins' first-round selection in 2003 (DE **Calvin Pace**), and the Saints' second-round selection in 2003 (WR **Anquan Boldin**). (4/26)

Washington's first-round selection in 2003 (DT **Ty Warren**) from Chicago to New England for Buffalo's first-round selection in 2003 (DE **Michael Haynes**) and the Patriots' sixth-round selection in 2003 (#193). (4/26)

Philadelphia's first-round selection in 2003 (DB **Sammy Davis**) and the Packers' second-round selection in 2003 (DB **Terrence Kiel**) from Philadelphia to San Diego for the Chargers' first-round selection in 2003 (DE **Jerome McDougle**). (4/26)

Kansas City's first-round selection in 2003 (DB **Troy Polamalu**) from Kansas City to Pittsburgh for the Steelers' first-round selection in 2003 (RB **Larry Johnson**), the Steelers' third-round selection in 2003 (DB **Julian Battle**), and the Steelers' sixth-round selection in 2003 (#200). (4/26)

Baltimore's second-round selection in 2003 (#41) and first-round selection in 2004 (DT **Vince Wilfork**) from Baltimore to New England for the Patriots' first-round selection in 2003 (QB **Kyle Boller**). (4/26)

Houston's second-round selection in 2003 (DB **Eugene Wilson**) and the Texans' fourth-round supplemental selection in 2003 (DT **Dan Klecko**) from Houston to New England for the Ravens' second-round selection in 2003 (TE **Bennie Joppru**) and the Redskins' third-round selection (T **Seth Wand**). (4/26)

Carolina's second-round selection in 2003 (WR **Bethel Johnson**) from Carolina to New England for the Patriots' second-round selection in 2003 (C **Bruce Nelson**) and the Patriots' fourth-round selection in 2003 (#120). (4/26)

Buffalo's third-round selection in 2003 (DT **Kenny Peterson**) from Buffalo to Green Bay for the Packers' third-round selection in 2003 (LB **Angelo Crowell**) and the Eagles' fourth-round selection in 2003 (WR **Sam Aiken**). (4/26)

Carolina's fourth-round selection in 2003 (RB **Quentin Griffin**), the Patriots' fourth-round selection in 2003 (#120) and the Panthers' seventh-round selection in 2003 (DE **Clint Mitchell**) from Carolina to Denver for the Broncos' third-round selection in 2003 (DB **Ricky Manning Jr.**). (4/26)

Houston's third-round supplemental selection in 2003 (LB **Sam Williams**) and the Texans' seventh-round supplemental selection in 2003 (WR **Ryan Hoag**) from Houston to Oakland for the Raiders' second-round selection in 2004 (RB **Tony Hollings**). (4/26)

New England's fourth-round selection in 2003 (DB **Asante Samuel**) from Denver to New England for the Packers' fourth-round selection in 2003 (DE **Bryant McNeal**) and the Patriots' fifth-round selection in 2003 (C **Ben Claxton**). (4/27)

Houston's fifth-round selection in 2003 (DE **Robert Mathis**) from Houston to Indianapolis for the Colts' fourth-round selection in 2004 (DB **Glenn Earl**). (4/27)

Jacksonville's fifth-round selection in 2003 (WR **Justin Gage**) from Jacksonville to Chicago for the Bears' sixth-round selection in 2003 (DE **Brandon Green**), the Patriots' sixth-round selection in 2003 (T **Marques Ogden**), and the Bears' seventh-round selection in 2003 (RB **Malaefou MacKenzie**). (4/27)

Green Bay's fifth-round selection in 2003 (RB **Chris Davis**) and the Packers' sixth-round selection in 2003 (#203) from Green Bay to Seattle for the Seahawks' fifth-round selection in 2003 (DT **James Lee**). (4/27)

Kansas City's fifth-round selection in 2003 (DT **Matt Walters**) and the Steelers' sixth-round selection in 2003 (QB **Brooks Bollinger**) from Kansas City to New York Jets for the Jets' fifth-round selection in 2003 (T **Jordan Black**) and the Jets' sixth-round selection in 2003 (DE **Jimmy Wilkerson**). (4/27)

Houston's fifth-round supplemental selection in 2003 (DB **Donnie Nickey**) and the Rams' seventh-round selection in 2003 (G **Todd Williams**) from New England to Tennessee for the Titans' fifth-round selection in 2003 (C **Dan Koppen**), the Titans' sixth-round selection in 2003 (QB **Kliff Kingsbury**), and the Titans' seventh-round selection in 2003 (NT **Ethan Kelley**). (4/27)

Philadelphia's fifth-round selection in 2003 (LB **Hunter Hillenmeyer**) from Philadelphia to Green Bay for the Redskins' sixth-round selection in 2003 (T **Jeremy Bridges**) and the Packers' seventh-round selection in 2003 (DB **Norman LeJeune**). (4/27)

Carolina's sixth-round selection in 2003 (DB **Corey Jenkins**) from Carolina to Miami for the Redskins' seventh-round selection in 2003 (WR **Walter Young**) and the Buccaneers' seventh-round selection in 2003 (RB **Casey Moore**). (4/27)

Defensive tackle **Norman Hand** from New Orleans to Seattle for the Packers' sixth-round selection in 2003 (WR **Kareem Kelly**). (4/27)

Wide receiver **Larry Foster** from Detroit to Arizona for the Cardinals' seventh-round selection in 2003 (DB **Blue Adams**). (4/27)

Running back **Avion Cason** from Detroit to Dallas for the Browns' seventh-round selection in 2003 (RB **Brandon Drumm**). (4/27)

Philadelphia's seventh-round selection in 2003 (DB **Chris Johnson**) from Philadelphia to Green Bay for the Packers' sixth-round selection in 2004 (QB **Andy Hall**). (4/27)

Linebacker **Derrick Rodgers** from Miami to New Orleans for an unannounced future selection choice. (5/27)

Running back **Thomas Jones** from Arizona to Tampa Bay for wide receiver **Marquise Walker**. (6/17)

Tight end **Jeff Grau** from Dallas to Tampa Bay for an unannounced future selection choice. (8/7)

Wide receiver **Nate Jackson** from San Francisco to Denver for an unannounced future selection choice. (8/13)

Running back **Deon Dyer** from Miami to Houston for an unannounced future selection choice. (8/19)

Defensive tackle **Ted Washington** from Chicago to New England for an unannounced future selection choice. (8/20)

Defensive tackle **Martin Chase** from New Orleans to Washington for an unannounced future selection choice. (8/20)

Punter **Mat McBriar** from Denver to Seattle for an unannounced future selection choice. (8/23)

Defensive back **Scott McGarrahan** from Miami to Green Bay for an unannounced future selection choice. (8/25)

Guard **Jamil Soriano** from Chicago to New England for an unannounced future selection choice. (8/25)

Defensive tackle **Lional Dalton** from Denver to Washington for an unannounced future selection choice. (8/26)

Defensive back **Anthony Mitchell** from Baltimore to Jacksonville for an unannounced future selection choice. (8/26)

Wide receiver **Freddie Milons** from Philadelphia to Pittsburgh for an unannounced future selection choice. (8/30)

Running back **Olandis Gary** from Buffalo to Detroit for an unannounced future selection choice. (8/31)

Defensive back **Rich Coady** from Indianapolis to St. Louis for an unannounced future selection choice. (8/31)

Defensive end **Kenyon Coleman** from Oakland to Dallas for an unannounced future selection choice. (8/31)

Wide receiver **Reginald Swinton** from Dallas to Green Bay for an unannounced future selection choice. (9/30)

2004 TRADES

Quarterback **A.J. Feeley** from Philadelphia to Miami for an unannounced future selection choice. (3/3)

Quarterback **Mark Brunell** from Jacksonville to Washington for the Redskins' third-round selection in 2004 (#72). (3/3)

Running back **Clinton Portis** from Denver to Washington for cornerback **Champ Bailey** and the Redskins' second-round selection in 2004 (RB **Tatum Bell**). (3/4)

Wide receiver **Terrell Owens** from San Francisco to Baltimore for the Ravens' second-round selection in 2004 (#51). (3/4)

Wide receiver **Justin McCareins** from Tennessee to New York Jets for the Jets' second-round selection in 2004 (DE **Travis LaBoy**). (3/8)

Wide receiver **Terrell Owens** from Baltimore to Philadelphia. Defensive tackle **Brandon Whiting** from Philadelphia to San Francisco. Baltimore's second-round selection (#51) from San Francisco to Baltimore. Philadelphia's fifth-round selection (#160) from Philadelphia to Baltimore. (3/16)

Defensive back **Jamar Fletcher** and an unannounced future selection choice from Miami to San Diego for wide receiver **David Boston**. (3/16)

Quarterback **Drew Henson** from Houston to Dallas for an unannounced future selection choice. (3/19)

Wide receiver **Joey Galloway** from Dallas to Tampa Bay for wide receiver **Keyshawn Johnson**. (3/22)

Running back **Bryan Johnson** from Washington to Chicago for the Bears' sixth-round selection in 2004 (#180). (3/29)

Wide receiver **James Thrash** from Philadelphia to Washington for an unannounced future selection choice. (3/31)

Defensive back **Jason Craft** from Jacksonville to New Orleans for the Saints' fifth-round selection in 2004 (DB **Chris Thompson**). (4/8)

Defensive back **Deltha O'Neal** and the Broncos' first-round selection in 2004 (#17) and fourth-round selection (DE **Robert Geathers**) from Denver to Cincinnati for the Bengals' first-round selection in 2004 (LB **D.J. Williams**). (4/9)

Running back **Corey Dillon** from Cincinnati to New England for the Dolphins' second-round selection in 2004 (DB **Madieu Williams**). (4/20)

Quarterback **Eli Manning** from San Diego to New York Giants for quarterback **Philip Rivers** and the Giants' third-round selection in 2004 (K **Nate Keading**) and first-round and fifth-round selections in 2005. (4/24)

Cleveland's first-round selection in 2004 (WR **Roy Williams**) and second-round selection in 2004 (LB **Teddy Lehman**) from Cleveland to Detroit for the Lions' first-round selection in 2004 (TE **Kellen Winslow**). (4/24)

Philadelphia's first-round selection in 2004 (#28) and second-round selection in 2004 (DB **Shawntae Spencer**) from Philadelphia to San Francisco for the 49ers' first-round selection in 2004 (T **Shawn Andrews**). (4/24)

Miami's first-round selection in 2004 (DE **Kenechi Udeze**) and fourth-round selection in 2004 (RB **Mewelde Moore**) from Miami to Minnesota for the Vikings' first-round selection in 2004 (T **Vernon Carey**). (4/24)

Buffalo's second-round selection in 2004 (RB **Julius Jones**), fifth-round selection in 2004 (TE **Sean Ryan**), and first-round selection in 2005 from Buffalo to Dallas for the Cowboys' first-round selection in 2004 (QB **J.P. Losman**). (4/24)

Denver's first-round selection in 2004 (RB **Steven Jackson**) from Cincinnati to St. Louis for the Rams' first-round selection in 2004 (RB **Chris Perry**) and fourth-round selection in 2004 (T **Stacy Andrews**). (4/24)

Houston's second-round selection in 2004 (TE **Ben Troupe**), third-round selection in 2004 (DT **Randy Starks**), fourth-round selection in 2004 (DE **Bo Schobel**) and fifth-round selection in 2004 (T **Jacob Bell**) from Houston to Tennessee for the Titans' first-round selection in 2004 (LB **Jason Babin**) and fifth-round selection in 2004 (#159). (4/24)

Carolina's first-round selection in 2004 (WR **Rashaun Woods**) and fourth-round selection in 2004 (LB **Richard Seigler**) from Carolina to San Francisco for the Eagles' first-round selection in 2004 (DB **Chris Gamble**). (4/24)

Atlanta's second-round selection in 2004 (#38), third-round selection in 2004 (LB **Gilbert Gardner**), and the Eagles' fourth-round selection in 2004 (DB **Jason David**) from Atlanta to Indianapolis for the Colts' first-round selection in 2004 (WR **Michael Jenkins**) and third-round selection in 2004 (QB **Matt Schaub**). (4/24)

Detroit's second-round selection in 2004 (DT **Junior Siavii**), fourth-round selection in 2004 (WR **Samie Parker**), and fifth-round selection in 2005 from Detroit to Kansas City for the Chiefs' first-round selection in 2004 (RB **Kevin Jones**). (4/24)

Atlanta's second-round selection in 2004 (DB **Ricardo Colclough**) from Indianapolis to Pittsburgh for the Steelers' second-round selection in 2004 (DB **Bob Sanders**) and fourth-round selection in 2004 (LB **Kendyll Pope**). (4/24)

Minnesota's second-round selection in 2004 (WR **Devery Henderson**) and fifth-round selection in 2004 (#151) from Minnesota to New Orleans for the Saints' second-round selection in 2004 (LB **Dontarrious Thomas**). (4/24)

Green Bay's second-round selection in 2004 (RB **Greg Jones**) from Green Bay to Jacksonville for the Jaguars' third-round selection in 2004 (DB **Joey Thomas**) and fourth-round selection in 2004 (#102). (4/24)

Cleveland's third-round selection in 2004 (TE **Ben Hartsock**), fifth-round selection in 2004 (T **Jake Scott**), and sixth-round selection in 2004 (DB **Von Hutchins**) from Cleveland to Indianapolis for the Colts' second-round selection in 2004 (DB **Sean Jones**) and fifth-round selection in 2004 (DT **Amon Gordon**). (4/24)

Green Bay's third-round selection in 2004 (LB **Jorge Cordova**) and fourth-round selection in 2004 (DT **Anthony Maddox**) from Green Bay to Jacksonville for the Redskins' third-round selection in 2004 (DT **Donnell Washington**). (4/24)

New Orleans' third-round selection in 2004 (TE **Chris Cooley**) and the Vikings' fifth-round selection in 2004 (T **Mark Wilson**) from New Orleans to Washington for the Redskins' fifth-round selection in 2004 (DT **Rodney Leisle**) and second-round selection in 2005. (4/24)

Baltimore's third-round selection in 2004 (DE **Darrion Scott**) and fifth-round selection in 2004 (LB **Rod Davis**) from Baltimore to Minnesota for the Vikings' third-round selection in 2004 (WR **Devard Darling**). (4/24)

Jacksonville's fourth-round selection in 2004 (DB **Will Poole**) and fifth-round selection in 2004 (#153) from Green Bay to Miami for the Dolphins' third-round selection in 2004 (P **B.J. Sander**). (4/24)

Washington's fourth-round selection in 2004 (DT **Isaac Sopoaga**) from Chicago to San Francisco for the 49ers' fourth-round selection in 2004 (LB **Leon Joe**) and fifth-round selection in 2004 (DE **Claude Harriet**). (4/25)

Wide receiver **Kevin Johnson** from Jacksonville to Baltimore for the Ravens' fourth-round selection in 2004 (WR **Ernest Wilford**). (4/25)

Philadelphia's fifth-round selection in 2004 (LB **Tony Bua**) and seventh-round selection (LB **Derrick Pope**) from Baltimore to Miami for the Packers' fifth-round selection in 2004 (LB **Roderick Green**). (4/25)

Dallas' fifth-round selection in 2004 (RB **Mike Karney**) from Dallas to New Orleans for the Saints' sixth-round selection in 2004 (#182) and the Redskins' seventh-round selection in 2004 (#206). (4/25)

Guard **John Welbourn** from Philadelphia to Kansas City for the Chiefs' fifth-round selection in 2004 (RB **Thomas Tapeh**) and fourth-round selection in 2005. (4/25)

Tennessee's fifth-round selection in 2004 (T **Sean Bubin**) from Houston to Jacksonville for the Jaguars' sixth-round selection in 2004 (DB **Jammal Lord**) and seventh-round selection in 2004 (LB **Raheem Orr**). (4/25)

Atlanta's sixth-round selection in 2004 (G **Rex Hadnot**) from Atlanta to Miami for the Dolphins' sixth-round selection in 2004 (DB **Etric Pruitt**) and the Saints' seventh-round selection in 2004 (RB **Quincy WIlson**). (4/25).

Dallas' sixth-round selection in 2004 (P **Andy Lee**) and seventh-round selection in 2004 (DT **Christian Ferrara**) from Green Bay to San Francisco for the 49ers' sixth-round selection in 2004 (DT **Corey Williams**). (4/25)

Dallas' sixth-round selection in 2004 via New Orleans (LB **Cody Spencer**) from Dallas to Oakland for the Raiders' sixth-round selection in 2004 (DB **Nathan Jones**) and the Cowboys' seventh-round selection in 2004 (DB **Jacques Reeves**). (4/25)

Running back **Darian Barnes** and the Buccaneers' seventh-round selection in 2004 (WR **Patrick Clayton**) from Tampa Bay to Dallas for the Cowboys' seventh-round selection in 2004 (WR **Mark Jones**). (4/25)

** Draft choice number is listed if club later traded the pick.*

2003 PRESEASON STANDINGS/RESULTS

PRESEASON STANDINGS

AMERICAN FOOTBALL CONFERENCE

East Division

	W	L	T	Pct.	Pts.	OP
New England	4	0	0	1.000	108	54
Buffalo	3	1	0	.750	94	96
N.Y. Jets	3	2	0	.600	91	88
Miami	2	2	0	.500	96	78

North Division

	W	L	T	Pct.	Pts.	OP
Baltimore	1	3	0	.250	59	84
Cincinnati	1	3	0	.250	71	82
Cleveland	1	3	0	.250	74	95
Pittsburgh	1	3	0	.250	58	82

South Division

	W	L	T	Pct.	Pts.	OP
Tennessee	4	0	0	1.000	97	48
Indianapolis	3	1	0	.750	88	70
Jacksonville	3	1	0	.750	66	62
Houston	0	4	0	.000	38	107

West Division

	W	L	T	Pct.	Pts.	OP
Denver	3	1	0	.750	78	53
Kansas City	3	2	0	.600	94	88
San Diego	2	2	0	.500	60	56
Oakland	1	3	0	.250	36	93

AFC PRESEASON RECORDS—TEAM BY TEAM

East Division

BUFFALO (3-1)

20	at Baltimore	19
24	at Tennessee	37
28	St. Louis	24
22	Detroit	16
94		96

MIAMI (2-2)

19	Tampa Bay	20
23	at Jacksonville	27
30	Atlanta	21
24	at New Orleans	10
96		78

NEW ENGLAND (4-0)

26	N.Y. Giants	6
20	at Washington	13
24	at Philadelphia	12
38	Chicago	23
108		54

N.Y. JETS (3-2)

14	vs. Tampa Bay (a)	30
28	Cincinnati	13
17	New Orleans	22
15	at N.Y. Giants	14
17	at Philadelphia	9
91		88

North Division

BALTIMORE (1-3)

19	Buffalo	20
13	at Atlanta	10
3	at Washington	24
24	N.Y. Giants	30
59		84

CINCINNATI (1-3)

13	at N.Y. Jets	28
23	Detroit	10
15	Tennessee	23
20	at Indianapolis	21
71		82

CLEVELAND (1-3)

6	at Tennessee	10
31	Green Bay	38
17	at Detroit	38
20	Atlanta	9
74		95

PITTSBURGH (1-3)

13	at Detroit	26
16	Philadelphia	21
15	Dallas	14
14	at Carolina	21
58		82

South Division

HOUSTON (0-4)

12	Denver	20
6	at Dallas	34
17	San Diego	19
3	at Tampa Bay	34
38		107

INDIANAPOLIS (3-1)

18	at Chicago	20
21	Seattle	7
28	at Denver	23
21	Cincinnati	20
88		70

JACKSONVILLE (3-1)

16	at Minnesota	14
27	Miami	23
6	at Tampa Bay	10
17	Washington	15
66		62

TENNESSEE (4-0)

10	Cleveland	6
37	Buffalo	24
23	at Cincinnati	15
27	at Green Bay	3
97		48

West Division

DENVER (3-1)

20	at Houston	12
15	at Chicago	10
23	Indianapolis	28
20	Seattle	3
78		53

KANSAS CITY (3-2)

9	Green Bay (b)	0
6	San Francisco	24
26	Minnesota	16
31	at Seattle	42
22	at St. Louis	6
94		88

OAKLAND (1-3)

7	St. Louis	6
10	at San Francisco	14
6	Minnesota	21
13	at Dallas	52
36		93

SAN DIEGO (2-2)

7	at Seattle	20
10	Arizona	16
19	at Houston	17
24	San Francisco	3
60		56

(a) American Bowl at Tokyo, Japan
(b) Pro Football Hall of Fame Game at Canton, Ohio

NFC PRESEASON RECORDS—TEAM BY TEAM

East Division

DALLAS (2-2)

0	At Arizona	13
34	Houston	6
14	At Pittsburgh	15
52	Oakland	13
100		47

N.Y. GIANTS (1-3)

6	At New England	26
10	Carolina	20
14	N.Y. Jets	15
30	At Baltimore	24
60		85

PHILADELPHIA (2-2)

27	at New Orleans	17
21	At Pittsburgh	16
12	New England	24
9	N.Y. Jets	17
69		74

WASHINGTON (1-3)

0	At Carolina	20
13	New England	20
24	Baltimore	3
15	At Jacksonville	17
52		60

North Division

CHICAGO (1-3)

20	Indianapolis	18
10	Denver	15
17	At Arizona	27
23	At New England	38
70		98

DETROIT (2-2)

26	Pittsburgh	13
10	At Cincinnati	23
38	Cleveland	17
16	At Buffalo	22
90		75

GREEN BAY (2-3)

0	Kansas City (b)	9
27	At Atlanta	21
38	At Cleveland	31
7	Carolina	20
3	Tennessee	27
75		108

MINNESOTA (1-3)

14	Jacksonville	16
16	At Kansas City	26
21	At Oakland	6
27	Arizona	31
78		79

South Division

ATLANTA (0-4)

21	Green Bay	27
10	Baltimore	13
21	At Miami	30
9	At Cleveland	20
61		90

CAROLINA (4-0)

20	Washington	0
20	At N.Y. Giants	10
20	At Green Bay	7
21	Pittsburgh	14
81		31

NEW ORLEANS (1-3)

17	Philadelphia	27
22	At N.Y. Jets	17
12	At San Francisco	27
10	Miami	24
61		95

TAMPA BAY (4-1)

30	vs. N.Y. Jets (a)	14
20	At Miami	19
16	At St. Louis	26
10	Jacksonville	6
34	Houston	3
110		68

West Division

ARIZONA (4-0)

13	Dallas	0
16	At San Diego	10
27	Chicago	17
31	At Minnesota	27
87		54

ST. LOUIS (1-3)

6	At Oakland	7
26	Tampa Bay	16
24	At Buffalo	28
6	Kansas City	22
62		73

SAN FRANCISCO (3-1)

24	At Kansas City	6
14	Oakland	10
27	New Orleans	12
3	At San Diego	24
68		52

SEATTLE (2-2)

20	San Diego	7
7	At Indianapolis	21
42	Kansas City	31
3	At Denver	20
72		79

(a) American Bowl at Tokyo, Japan
(b) Pro Football Hall of Fame Game at Canton, Ohio

PRESEASON STANDINGS

NATIONAL FOOTBALL CONFERENCE

East Division

	W	L	T	Pct.	Pts.	OP
Dallas	2	2	0	.500	100	47
Philadelphia	2	2	0	.500	69	74
N.Y. Giants	1	3	0	.250	60	85
Washington	1	3	0	.250	52	60

North Division

	W	L	T	Pct.	Pts.	OP
Detroit	2	2	0	.500	90	75
Green Bay	2	3	0	.400	75	108
Chicago	1	3	0	.250	70	98
Minnesota	1	3	0	.250	78	79

South Division

	W	L	T	Pct.	Pts.	OP
Carolina	4	0	0	1.000	81	31
Tampa Bay	4	1	0	.800	110	68
New Orleans	1	3	0	.250	61	95
Atlanta	0	4	0	.000	61	90

West Division

	W	L	T	Pct.	Pts.	OP
Arizona	4	0	0	1.000	87	54
San Francisco	3	1	0	.750	68	52
Seattle	2	2	0	.500	72	79
St. Louis	1	3	0	.250	62	73

2003 AFC RESULTS

AMERICAN FOOTBALL CONFERENCE

BALTIMORE (10-6)

15	at Pittsburgh	34
33	CLEVELAND	13
24	at San Diego	10
10	KANSAS CITY	17
26	at Arizona	18
26	at Cincinnati	34
26	DENVER	6
24	JACKSONVILLE	17
22	at St. Louis	33
6	at Miami (OT)	9
44	SEATTLE (OT)	41
44	SAN FRANCISCO	6
31	CINCINNATI	13
12	at Oakland	20
35	at Cleveland	0
13	PITTSBURGH (OT)	10
391		281

BUFFALO (6-10)

31	NEW ENGLAND	0
38	at Jacksonville	17
7	at Miami	17
13	PHILADELPHIA	23
22	CINCINNATI (OT)	16
3	at New York Jets	30
24	WASHINGTON	7
5	at Kansas City	38
6	at Dallas	10
10	HOUSTON	12
14	INDIANAPOLIS	17
24	at New York Giants	7
17	NEW YORK JETS	6
26	at Tennessee	28
3	MIAMI	20
0	at New England	31
243		279

CINCINNATI (8-8)

10	DENVER	30
20	at Oakland	23
10	PITTSBURGH	17
21	at Cleveland	14
16	at Buffalo (OT)	22
34	BALTIMORE	26
27	SEATTLE	24
14	at Arizona	17
34	HOUSTON	27
24	KANSAS CITY	19
34	at San Diego	27
24	at Pittsburgh	20
13	at Baltimore	31
41	SAN FRANCISCO	38
10	at St. Louis	27
14	CLEVELAND	22
346		384

CLEVELAND (5-11)

6	INDIANAPOLIS	9
13	at Baltimore	33
13	at San Francisco	12
14	CINCINNATI	21
33	at Pittsburgh	13
13	OAKLAND	7
20	SAN DIEGO	26
3	at New England	9
20	at Kansas City	41
44	ARIZONA	6
6	PITTSBURGH	13
7	at Seattle	34
20	ST. LOUIS	26
20	at Denver (OT)	23
0	BALTIMORE	35
22	at Cincinnati	14
254		322

DENVER (10-6)

30	at Cincinnati	10
37	at San Diego	13
31	OAKLAND	10
20	DETROIT	16
23	at Kansas City	24
17	PITTSBURGH	14
20	at Minnesota	28
6	at Baltimore	26
26	NEW ENGLAND	30
37	SAN DIEGO	8
10	CHICAGO	19
22	at Oakland	8
45	KANSAS CITY	27
23	CLEVELAND (OT)	20
31	at Indianapolis	17
3	at Green Bay	31
381		301

HOUSTON (5-11)

21	at Miami	20
10	at New Orleans	31
14	KANSAS CITY	42
24	JACKSONVILLE	20
17	at Tennessee	38
14	NEW YORK JETS	19
21	at Indianapolis	30
14	CAROLINA	10
27	at Cincinnati	34
12	at Buffalo	10
20	NEW ENGLAND (OT)	23
17	ATLANTA	13
0	at Jacksonville	27
3	at Tampa Bay	16
24	TENNESSEE	27
17	INDIANAPOLIS	20
255		380

INDIANAPOLIS (12-4)

9	at Cleveland	6
33	TENNESSEE	7
23	JACKSONVILLE	13
55	at New Orleans	21
38	at Tampa Bay (OT)	35
20	CAROLINA (OT)	23
30	HOUSTON	21
23	at Miami	17
23	at Jacksonville	28
38	NEW YORK JETS	31
17	at Buffalo	14
34	NEW ENGLAND	38
29	at Tennessee	27
38	ATLANTA	7
17	DENVER	31
20	at Houston	17
447		336

JACKSONVILLE (5-11)

23	at Carolina	24
17	BUFFALO	38
13	at Indianapolis	23
20	at Houston	24
27	SAN DIEGO	21
10	MIAMI	24
17	TENNESSEE	30
17	at Baltimore	24
28	INDIANAPOLIS	23
3	at Tennessee	10
10	at New York Jets	13
17	TAMPA BAY	10
27	HOUSTON	0
13	at New England	27
20	NEW ORLEANS	19
14	at Atlanta	21
276		331

KANSAS CITY (13-3)

27	SAN DIEGO	14
41	PITTSBURGH	20
42	at Houston	14
17	at Baltimore	10
24	DENVER	23
40	at Green Bay (OT)	34
17	at Oakland	10
38	BUFFALO	5
41	CLEVELAND	20
19	at Cincinnati	24
27	OAKLAND	24
28	at San Diego	24
27	at Denver	45
45	DETROIT	17
20	at Minnesota	45
31	CHICAGO	3
484		332

MIAMI (10-6)

20	HOUSTON	21
21	at New York Jets	10
17	BUFFALO	7
23	at New York Giants	10
24	at Jacksonville	10
13	NEW ENGLAND (OT)	19
26	at San Diego	10
17	INDIANAPOLIS	23
7	at Tennessee	31
9	BALTIMORE (OT)	6
24	WASHINGTON	23
40	at Dallas	21
0	at New England	12
27	PHILADELPHIA	34
20	at Buffalo	3
23	NEW YORK JETS	21
311		261

NEW ENGLAND (14-2)

0	at Buffalo	31
31	at Philadelphia	10
23	NEW YORK JETS	16
17	at Washington	20
38	TENNESSEE	30
17	NEW YORK GIANTS	6
19	at Miami (OT)	13
9	CLEVELAND	3
30	at Denver	26
12	DALLAS	0
23	at Houston (OT)	20
38	at Indianapolis	34
12	MIAMI	0
27	JACKSONVILLE	13
21	at New York Jets	16
31	BUFFALO	0
348		238

NEW YORK JETS (6-10)

13	at Washington	16
10	MIAMI	21
16	at New England	23
6	DALLAS	17
30	BUFFALO	3
19	at Houston	14
17	at Philadelphia	24
28	NEW YORK GIANTS (OT)	31
27	at Oakland (OT)	24
31	at Indianapolis	38
13	JACKSONVILLE	10
24	TENNESSEE	17
6	at Buffalo	17
6	PITTSBURGH	0
16	NEW ENGLAND	21
21	at Miami	23
283		299

OAKLAND (4-12)

20	at Tennessee	25
23	CINCINNATI	20
10	at Denver	31
34	SAN DIEGO (OT)	31
21	at Chicago	24
7	at Cleveland	13
10	KANSAS CITY	17
13	at Detroit	23
24	NEW YORK JETS (OT)	27
28	MINNESOTA	18
24	at Kansas City	27
8	DENVER	22
7	at Pittsburgh	27
20	BALTIMORE	12
7	GREEN BAY	41
14	at San Diego	21
270		379

PITTSBURGH (6-10)

34	BALTIMORE	15
20	at Kansas City	41
17	at Cincinnati	10
13	TENNESSEE	30
13	CLEVELAND	33
14	at Denver	17
21	ST. LOUIS	33
16	at Seattle	23
28	ARIZONA	15
14	at San Francisco	30
13	at Cleveland	6
20	CINCINNATI	24
27	OAKLAND	7
0	at New York Jets	6
40	SAN DIEGO	24
10	at Baltimore (OT)	13
300		327

SAN DIEGO (4-12)

14	at Kansas City	27
13	DENVER	37
10	BALTIMORE	24
31	at Oakland (OT)	34
21	at Jacksonville	27
26	at Cleveland	20
10	MIAMI	26
7	at Chicago	20
42	MINNESOTA	28
8	at Denver	37
27	CINCINNATI	34
24	KANSAS CITY	28
14	at Detroit	7
21	GREEN BAY	38
24	at Pittsburgh	40
21	OAKLAND	14
313		441

TENNESSEE (12-4)

25	OAKLAND	20
7	at Indianapolis	33
27	NEW ORLEANS	12
30	at Pittsburgh	13
30	at New England	38
38	HOUSTON	17
37	at Carolina	17
30	at Jacksonville	17
31	MIAMI	7
10	JACKSONVILLE	3
38	at Atlanta	31
17	at New York Jets	24
27	INDIANAPOLIS	29
28	BUFFALO	26
27	at Houston	24
33	TAMPA BAY	13
435		324

NATIONAL FOOTBALL CONFERENCE

ARIZONA (4-12)

24	at Detroit	42
0	SEATTLE	38
20	GREEN BAY	13
13	at St. Louis	37
7	at Dallas	24
18	BALTIMORE	26
16	SAN FRANCISCO (OT)	13
17	CINCINNATI	14
15	at Pittsburgh	28
6	at Cleveland	44
27	ST. LOUIS (OT)	30
3	at Chicago	28
14	at San Francisco	50
17	CAROLINA	20
10	at Seattle	28
18	MINNESOTA	17
225		452

ATLANTA (5-11)

27	at Dallas	13
31	WASHINGTON	33
10	TAMPA BAY	31
3	at Carolina	23
26	MINNESOTA	39
0	at St. Louis	36
17	NEW ORLEANS	45
16	PHILADELPHIA	23
27	at New York Giants	7
20	at New Orleans (OT)	23
31	TENNESSEE	38
13	at Houston	17
20	CAROLINA (OT)	14
7	at Indianapolis	38
30	at Tampa Bay	28
21	JACKSONVILLE	14
299		422

CAROLINA (11-5)

24	JACKSONVILLE	23
12	at Tampa Bay (OT)	9
23	ATLANTA	3
19	NEW ORLEANS	13
23	at Indianapolis (OT)	20
17	TENNESSEE	37
23	at New Orleans (OT)	20
10	at Houston	14
27	TAMPA BAY	24
20	WASHINGTON	17
20	at Dallas	24
16	PHILADELPHIA	25
14	at Atlanta (OT)	20
20	at Arizona	17
20	DETROIT	14
37	at New York Giants	24
325		304

CHICAGO (7-9)

7	at San Francisco	49
13	at Minnesota	24
23	GREEN BAY	38
24	OAKLAND	21
13	at New Orleans	20
17	at Seattle	24
24	DETROIT	16
20	SAN DIEGO	7
10	at Detroit	12
21	ST. LOUIS	23
19	at Denver	10
28	ARIZONA	3
21	at Green Bay	34
13	MINNESOTA	10
27	WASHINGTON	24
3	at Kansas City	31
283		346

DALLAS (10-6)

13	ATLANTA	27
35	at New York Giants (OT)	32
17	at New York Jets	6
24	ARIZONA	7
23	PHILADELPHIA	21
38	at Detroit	7
0	at Tampa Bay	16
21	WASHINGTON	14
10	BUFFALO	6
0	at New England	12
24	CAROLINA	20
21	MIAMI	40
10	at Philadelphia	36
27	at Washington	0
19	NEW YORK GIANTS	3
7	at New Orleans	13
289		260

DETROIT (5-11)

42	ARIZONA	24
6	at Green Bay	31
13	MINNESOTA	23
16	at Denver	20
17	at San Francisco	24
7	DALLAS	38
16	at Chicago	24
23	OAKLAND	13
12	CHICAGO	10
14	at Seattle	35
14	at Minnesota	24
22	GREEN BAY	14
7	SAN DIEGO	14
17	at Kansas City	45
14	at Carolina	20
30	ST. LOUIS	20
270		379

GREEN BAY (10-6)

25	MINNESOTA	30
31	DETROIT	6
13	at Arizona	20
38	at Chicago	23
35	SEATTLE	13
34	KANSAS CITY (OT)	40
24	at St. Louis	34
30	at Minnesota	27
14	PHILADELPHIA	17
20	at Tampa Bay	13
20	SAN FRANCISCO	10
14	at Detroit	22
34	CHICAGO	21
38	at San Diego	21
41	at Oakland	7
31	DENVER	3
442		307

MINNESOTA (9-7)

30	at Green Bay	25
24	CHICAGO	13
23	at Detroit	13
35	SAN FRANCISCO	7
39	at Atlanta	26
28	DENVER	20
17	NEW YORK GIANTS	29
27	GREEN BAY	30
28	at San Diego	42
18	at Oakland	28
24	DETROIT	14
17	at St. Louis	48
34	SEATTLE	7
10	at Chicago	13
45	KANSAS CITY	20
17	at Arizona	18
416		353

NEW ORLEANS (8-8)

10	at Seattle	27
31	HOUSTON	10
12	at Tennessee	27
21	INDIANAPOLIS	55
13	at Carolina	19
20	CHICAGO	13
45	at Atlanta	17
20	CAROLINA (OT)	23
17	at Tampa Bay	14
23	ATLANTA (OT)	20
20	at Philadelphia	33
24	at Washington	20
7	TAMPA BAY	14
45	NEW YORK GIANTS	7
19	at Jacksonville	20
13	DALLAS	7
340		326

NEW YORK GIANTS (4-12)

23	ST. LOUIS	13
32	DALLAS (OT)	35
24	at Washington (OT)	21
10	MIAMI	23
6	at New England	17
10	PHILADELPHIA	14
29	at Minnesota	17
31	at New York Jets (OT)	28
7	ATLANTA	27
10	at Philadelphia	28
13	at Tampa Bay	19
7	BUFFALO	24
7	WASHINGTON	20
7	at New Orleans	45
3	at Dallas	19
24	CAROLINA	37
243		387

PHILADELPHIA (12-4)

0	TAMPA BAY	17
10	NEW ENGLAND	31
23	at Buffalo	13
27	WASHINGTON	25
21	at Dallas	23
14	at New York Giants	10
24	NEW YORK JETS	17
23	at Atlanta	16
17	at Green Bay	14
28	NEW YORK GIANTS	10
33	NEW ORLEANS	20
25	at Carolina	16
36	DALLAS	10
34	at Miami	27
28	SAN FRANCISCO (OT)	31
31	at Washington	7
374		287

ST. LOUIS (12-4)

13	at New York Giants	23
27	SAN FRANCISCO (OT)	24
23	at Seattle	24
37	ARIZONA	13
36	ATLANTA	0
34	GREEN BAY	24
33	at Pittsburgh	21
10	at San Francisco	30
33	BALTIMORE	22
23	at Chicago	21
30	at Arizona (OT)	27
48	MINNESOTA	17
26	at Cleveland	20
27	SEATTLE	22
27	CINCINNATI	10
20	at Detroit	30
447		328

SAN FRANCISCO (7-9)

49	CHICAGO	7
24	at St. Louis (OT)	27
12	CLEVELAND	13
7	at Minnesota	35
24	DETROIT	17
19	at Seattle	20
24	TAMPA BAY	7
13	at Arizona (OT)	16
30	ST. LOUIS	10
30	PITTSBURGH	14
10	at Green Bay	20
6	at Baltimore	44
50	ARIZONA	14
38	at Cincinnati	41
31	at Philadelphia (OT)	28
17	SEATTLE	24
384		337

SEATTLE (10-6)

27	NEW ORLEANS	10
38	at Arizona	0
24	ST. LOUIS	23
13	at Green Bay	35
20	SAN FRANCISCO	19
24	CHICAGO	17
24	at Cincinnati	27
23	PITTSBURGH	16
20	at Washington	27
35	DETROIT	14
41	at Baltimore (OT)	44
34	CLEVELAND	7
7	at Minnesota	34
22	at St. Louis	27
28	ARIZONA	10
24	at San Francisco	17
404		327

TAMPA BAY (7-9)

17	at Philadelphia	0
9	CAROLINA (OT)	12
31	at Atlanta	10
35	INDIANAPOLIS (OT)	38
35	at Washington	13
7	at San Francisco	24
16	DALLAS	0
14	NEW ORLEANS	17
24	at Carolina	27
13	GREEN BAY	20
19	NEW YORK GIANTS	13
10	at Jacksonville	17
14	at New Orleans	7
16	HOUSTON	3
28	ATLANTA	30
13	at Tennessee	33
301		264

WASHINGTON (5-11)

16	NEW YORK JETS	13
33	at Atlanta	31
21	NEW YORK GIANTS (OT)	24
20	NEW ENGLAND	17
25	at Philadelphia	27
13	TAMPA BAY	35
7	at Buffalo	24
14	at Dallas	21
27	SEATTLE	20
17	at Carolina	20
23	at Miami	24
20	NEW ORLEANS	24
20	at New York Giants	7
0	DALLAS	27
24	at Chicago	27
7	PHILADELPHIA	31
287		372

2003 NFL STANDINGS

FINAL STANDINGS

AMERICAN FOOTBALL CONFERENCE

East Division	W	L	T	Pct.	Pts.	OP
New England#	14	2	0	.875	348	238
Miami	10	6	0	.625	311	261
Buffalo	6	10	0	.375	243	279
N.Y. Jets	6	10	0	.375	283	299
North Division						
Baltimore	10	6	0	.625	391	281
Cincinnati	8	8	0	.500	346	384
Pittsburgh	6	10	0	.375	300	327
Cleveland	5	11	0	.313	254	322
South Division						
Indianapolis	12	4	0	.750	447	336
Tennessee*	12	4	0	.750	435	324
Houston	5	11	0	.313	255	380
Jacksonville	5	11	0	.313	276	331
West Division						
Kansas City	13	3	0	.813	484	332
Denver*	10	6	0	.625	381	301
Oakland	4	12	0	.250	270	379
San Diego	4	12	0	.250	313	441

NATIONAL FOOTBALL CONFERENCE

East Division	W	L	T	Pct.	Pts.	OP
Philadelphia#	12	4	0	.750	374	287
Dallas*	10	6	0	.625	289	260
Washington	5	11	0	.313	287	372
N.Y. Giants	4	12	0	.250	243	387
North Division						
Green Bay	10	6	0	.625	442	307
Minnesota	9	7	0	.563	416	353
Chicago	7	9	0	.438	283	346
Detroit	5	11	0	.313	270	379
South Division						
Carolina	11	5	0	.688	325	304
New Orleans	8	8	0	.500	340	326
Tampa Bay	7	9	0	.438	301	264
Atlanta	5	11	0	.313	299	422
West Division						
St. Louis	12	4	0	.750	447	328
Seattle*	10	6	0	.625	404	327
San Francisco	7	9	0	.438	384	337
Arizona	4	12	0	.250	225	452

**Wild-Card qualifier for playoffs*
#Top playoff seed in conference

Buffalo finished ahead of New York Jets based on better division record (2-4 to 1-5). Indianapolis finished ahead of Tennessee based on head-to-head sweep (2-0). Jacksonville finished ahead of Houston based on better division record (2-4 to 1-5). Denver finished ahead of Miami based on better conference record (9-3 to 7-5). Oakland finished ahead of San Diego based on better conference record (3-9 to 2-10). Philadelphia finished ahead of St. Louis based on better conference record (9-3 to 8-4). Seattle finished ahead of Dallas based on better strength of victory (65-95 to 62-98).

WILD-CARD PLAYOFFS

AFC

Tennessee 20, BALTIMORE 17
INDIANAPOLIS 41, Denver 10

NFC

CAROLINA 29, Dallas 10
GREEN BAY 33, Seattle 27 (OT)

DIVISIONAL PLAYOFFS

AFC

NEW ENGLAND 17, Tennessee 14
Indianapolis 38, KANSAS CITY 31

NFC

Carolina 29, ST. LOUIS 23 (2OT)
PHILADELPHIA 20, Green Bay 17 (OT)

CHAMPIONSHIP GAMES

AFC

NEW ENGLAND 24, Indianapolis 14

NFC

Carolina 14, PHILADELPHIA 3

SUPER BOWL XXXVIII

New England (AFC) 32, Carolina (NFC) 29
at Reliant Stadium, Houston, Texas

AFC-NFC PRO BOWL

NFC 55, AFC 52
at Aloha Stadium, Honolulu, Hawaii

Home teams in playoff games are indicated in CAPS.

FIRST WEEK SUMMARIES

American Football Conference

East Division	W	L	T	Pct.	Pts.	OP
Buffalo	1	0	0	1.000	31	0
Miami	0	1	0	.000	20	21
New England	0	1	0	.000	0	31
N.Y. Jets	0	1	0	.000	13	16
North Division	**W**	**L**	**T**	**Pct.**	**Pts.**	**OP**
Pittsburgh	1	0	0	1.000	34	15
Baltimore	0	1	0	.000	15	34
Cincinnati	0	1	0	.000	10	30
Cleveland	0	1	0	.000	6	9
South Division	**W**	**L**	**T**	**Pct.**	**Pts.**	**OP**
Houston	1	0	0	1.000	21	20
Indianapolis	1	0	0	1.000	9	6
Tennessee	1	0	0	1.000	25	20
Jacksonville	0	1	0	.000	23	24
West Division	**W**	**L**	**T**	**Pct.**	**Pts.**	**OP**
Denver	1	0	0	1.000	30	10
Kansas City	1	0	0	1.000	27	14
Oakland	0	1	0	.000	20	25
San Diego	0	1	0	.000	14	27

National Football Conference

East Division	W	L	T	Pct.	Pts.	OP
N.Y. Giants	1	0	0	1.000	23	13
Washington	1	0	0	1.000	16	13
Dallas	0	1	0	.000	13	27
Philadelphia	0	1	0	.000	0	17
North Division	**W**	**L**	**T**	**Pct.**	**Pts.**	**OP**
Detroit	1	0	0	1.000	42	24
Minnesota	1	0	0	1.000	30	25
Chicago	0	1	0	.000	7	49
Green Bay	0	1	0	.000	25	30
South Division	**W**	**L**	**T**	**Pct.**	**Pts.**	**OP**
Atlanta	1	0	0	1.000	27	13
Carolina	1	0	0	1.000	24	23
Tampa Bay	1	0	0	1.000	17	0
New Orleans	0	1	0	.000	10	27
West Division	**W**	**L**	**T**	**Pct.**	**Pts.**	**OP**
San Francisco	1	0	0	1.000	49	7
Seattle	1	0	0	1.000	27	10
Arizona	0	1	0	.000	24	42
St. Louis	0	1	0	.000	13	23

THURSDAY NIGHT, SEPTEMBER 4

WASHINGTON 16, N.Y. JETS 13—at FedExField, attendance 85,420. John Hall kicked a 50-yard field goal with five seconds remaining to lift the Redskins past his former team. The Jets drove 72 yards for a touchdown on their initial drive to take a 7-3 lead, but failed to gain more than 1 first down on any of their remaining eight drives. The Redskins scored on their first three possessions to take a 13-7 halftime lead. Donnie Abraham's interception and 12-yard return to the Redskins' 26 set up Doug Brien's third-quarter field goal, and Jason Ferguson's recovery of Patrick Ramsey's fumble at the Redskins' 43 following John Abraham's sack led to Brien's game-tying field goal with 8:25 remaining in the game. After an exchange of possessions, starting from the Redskins' 39, and keyed by Ramsey's 24-yard scramble and Ladell Betts' 11-yard run, Hall booted the game-winning field goal. The Redskins' defense limited the Jets to 158 total yards. Ramsey was 17 of 23 for 185 yards and 1 touchdown, with 1 interception. Thirty-nine-year old Vinny Testaverde, starting because of a hand injury suffered in the preseason by Chad Pennington, was 15 of 24 for 105 yards.

N.Y. Jets	7	0	3	3	—	13
Washington	3	10	0	3	—	16

Wash — FG Hall 50
NYJ — Jordan 1 run (Brien kick)
Wash — McCants 4 pass from Ramsey (Hall kick)
Wash — FG Hall 22
NYJ — FG Brien 30
NYJ — FG Brien 41
Wash — FG Hall 33

SUNDAY, SEPTEMBER 7

BUFFALO 31, NEW ENGLAND 0—at Ralph Wilson Stadium, attendance 73,262. Travis Henry scored 2 touchdowns and the Bills' defense intercepted 4 passes, 2 by newcomer Takeo Spikes, to record their largest margin of victory since 1992. Buffalo put together a 9-play, 80-yard drive and 15-play, 90-yard drive on its first two possessions, consuming 14 minutes and 30 seconds, to take a 14-0 lead. Sam Adams' 37-yard interception return for a touchdown with 10:14 left in the half gave Buffalo a 21-0 lead. The Patriots reached the Bills' 2 in the third quarter, but a false start penalty and fourth-down incomplete pass stifled the drive. In the fourth quarter, a pass interference penalty placed the ball at the Bills' 1 with 18 seconds left, but an incomplete pass was followed by Antowain Smith being stopped at the goal line as time ran out to preserve the shutout. Drew Bledsoe was 17 of 28 for 230 yards and 1 touchdown, with 1 interception. Tom Brady was 14 of 29 for 123 yards, with 4 interceptions.

New England	0	0	0	0	—	0
Buffalo	7	14	0	10	—	31

Buff — Henry 1 run (Lindell kick)
Buff — Moore 7 pass from Bledsoe (Lindell kick)
Buff — Adams 37 interception return (Lindell kick)
Buff — Henry 9 run (Lindell kick)
Buff — FG Lindell 44

CAROLINA 24, JACKSONVILLE 23—at Ericsson Stadium, attendance 72,134. Jake Delhomme came off the bench in the third quarter to help the Panthers overcome a 17-0 deficit, capped by his 12-yard touchdown pass to Ricky Proehl with 16 seconds left, to lift the Panthers. The comeback spoiled the coaching debut of Jaguars' head coach Jack Del Rio, who had been the Panthers' defensive coordinator in 2002. Mark Brunell's 33-yard touchdown pass to Matthew Hatchette as the first half expired gave Jacksonville a 14-0 lead. Jake Delhomme entered the game with 8:52 left in the third quarter and completed a 13-yard touchdown pass to Muhsin Muhammad four plays later. A field goal on the next possession was followed by Rod Smart's blocked punt, which resulted in a safety, to cut the deficit to 17-12 with 12:56 left. Steve Smith's 24-yard touchdown catch gave Carolina the lead, but two plays later Jermaine Lewis scored on a 65-yard touchdown catch to give Jacksonville a 23-18 lead with 5:14 left. After an exchange of possessions, Smith's 36-yard punt return to the Panthers' 46 led to Delhomme's 12-yard touchdown pass to Proehl, on fourth-and-11, with 16 seconds left. Seth Marler's 55-yard field-goal attempt was blocked by Mike Minter as time expired. Rodney Peete was 4 for 10 for 19 yards and Delhomme was 12 of 20 for 122 yards and 3 touchdowns, with 2 interceptions. Stephen Davis rushed for 111 yards. Brunell was 23 of 27 for 272 yards and 2 touchdowns.

Jacksonville	0	14	3	6	—	23
Carolina	0	0	7	17	—	24

Jax — Edwards 2 run (Marler kick)
Jax — Hatchette 33 pass from Brunell (Marler kick)
Jax — FG Marler 40
Car — Muhammad 13 pass from Delhomme (Kasay kick)
Car — FG Kasay 49
Car — Safety, Smart blocks punt and Jaguars recover in own end zone
Car — Smith 24 pass from Delhomme (pass failed)
Jax — Lewis 65 pass from Brunell (run failed)
Car — Proehl 12 pass from Delhomme (run failed)

DENVER 30, CINCINNATI 10—at Paul Brown Stadium, attendance 63,820. Clinton Portis rushed for 120 yards and scored 2 touchdowns, and the Broncos' defense recorded 4 sacks and forced 4 turnovers, to defeat the Bengals. Denver drove into Bengals territory on all six of its first half possessions to take a 20-3 lead, and Ian Gold's 12-yard interception return for a touchdown of a desperation shovel pass staked the Broncos to a 27-3 lead with 10:18 left in the third quarter. The Bengals only drove inside the Broncos' 30 once, and had to settle for Shayne Graham's 26-yard field goal. Jake Plummer was 12 of 25 for 115 yards, with 3 interceptions, in his Denver debut. Jon Kitna was 20 of 37 for 264 yards and 1 touchdown, with 2 interceptions.

Denver	3	17	7	3	—	30
Cincinnati	0	3	0	7	—	10

Den — FG Elam 51
Den — Portis 2 run (Elam kick)
Cin — FG Graham 26
Den — Portis 8 run (Elam kick)
Den — FG Elam 27
Den — Gold 12 interception return (Elam kick)
Den — FG Elam 39
Cin — C. Johnson 41 pass from Kitna (Graham kick)

INDIANAPOLIS 9, CLEVELAND 6—at Cleveland Browns Stadium, attendance 73,358. Mike Vanderjagt kicked 3 field goals, including the game-winning 45-yarder as time expired, to give the Colts a victory. The Browns put together two drives in excess of eight minutes, and reached the Colts' 1 and 2-yard line, but settled for field goals both times. The Colts twice drove inside the Browns' 5, but Kevin Bentley's interception in the end zone stopped one drive and Vanderjagt's 22-yard field goal came on the last play of the first half. With the score tied 6-6, the Colts forced a punt and, beginning at their own 8-yard line with 2:39 remaining, drove 65 yards, highlighted by Peyton Manning's 15-yard pass to Reggie Wayne on third-and-10, to set up Vanderjagt's winning kick. Manning was 27 of 43 for 211 yards, with 2 interceptions. Kelly Holcomb was 20 of 29 for 182 yards, with 2 interceptions.

Indianapolis	0	3	3	3	—	9
Cleveland	3	0	0	3	—	6

Cle — FG Dawson 19
Ind — FG Vanderjagt 22
Ind — FG Vanderjagt 46
Cle — FG Dawson 20
Ind — FG Vanderjagt 45

ATLANTA 27, DALLAS 13—at Texas Stadium, attendance 64,104. Doug Johnson, playing in place of injured Michael Vick, passed for 2 touchdowns and ran for another, all in the second half, as the Falcons rallied from a halftime deficit to defeat Dallas in Bill Parcells' debut as the Cowboys' head coach. The Cowboys outgained Atlanta 403-318, but committed 2 turnovers, missed a 33-yard field-goal attempt, and had an extra-point attempt blocked. Atlanta scored on four of its five second half possessions, highlighted by Johnson's 41-yard touchdown pass to Alge Crumpler, who was wide open on the weak side of the field and outran the Cowboys to the end zone. Quincy Carter's 49-yard touchdown pass to Joey Galloway trimmed the deficit to 20-13 with 11:37 to play, but the Falcons responded with a 13-play, 75-yard drive that consumed 8:26, capped by Johnson's 1-yard run, to finish the scoring. Johnson was 16 of 27 for 228 yards and 2 touchdowns, with 1 interception. Carter was 15 of 32 for 268 yards and 1 touchdown, with 1 interception.

Atlanta	3	0	14	10	—	27
Dallas	7	0	0	6	—	13

Atl — FG Feely 37
Dall — Cason 63 run (Cundiff kick)
Atl — Dunn 7 pass from D.Johnson (Feely kick)
Atl — Crumpler 41 pass from D.Johnson (Feely kick)
Atl — FG Feely 31
Dall — Galloway 49 pass from Carter (kick blocked)
Atl — D.Johnson 1 run (Feely kick)

DETROIT 42, ARIZONA 24—at Ford Field, attendance 60,691. Joey Harrington passed for a career-high 4 touchdowns as the Lions prevailed in Steve Mariucci's first game as Detroit's head coach. The victory overshadowed Arizona wide receiver Anquan Boldin's 10 receptions for a first-game-rookie-record 217 receiving yards. Rookie Charles Rogers caught 2 touchdown passes six minutes apart to give Detroit a 14-7 lead. Boldin's 71-yard touchdown pass on a crossing pattern gave the Cardinals a 21-14 lead early in the third quarter, but Eddie Drummond's 57-yard punt return tied the game midway through the third quarter. The Cardinals outgained the Lions 439-261, but committed 3 turnovers that led directly to Detroit's final three touchdowns: a muffed punt by Boldin that set up Harrington's go-ahead touchdown pass to Cory Schlesinger; James Hall's sack, forced fumble, and fumble recovery led to Harrington's fourth touchdown pass and a 35-24 lead; and an interception returned 48 yards for a touchdown by Dre' Bly to cap the scoring. Jeff Blake was 28 of 46 for 363 yards and 3 touchdowns, with 1 interception. Harrington was 17 of 30 for 195 yards and 4 touchdowns.

Arizona	7	7	10	0	—	24
Detroit	7	7	14	14	—	42

Ariz — Boldin 7 pass from Blake (Gramatica kick)
Det — Rogers 4 pass from Harrington (Hanson kick)
Det — Rogers 13 pass from Harrington (Hanson kick)
Ariz — Jones 12 pass from Blake (Gramatica kick)
Ariz — Boldin 71 pass from Blake (Gramatica kick)
Det — Drummond 57 punt return (Hanson kick)
Det — Schlesinger 8 pass from Harrington (Hanson kick)
Ariz — FG Gramatica 38
Det — Schroeder 5 pass from Harrington (Hanson kick)
Det — Bly 48 interception return (Hanson kick)

MINNESOTA 30, GREEN BAY 25—at Lambeau Field, attendance 70,505. Daunte Culpepper passed for 3 touchdowns and the Vikings' defense forced 5 turnovers as Minnesota took a 27-3 lead and held on to defeat Green Bay. The Packers fell behind 10-0 before gaining their initial first down. Green Bay drove into Vikings' territory in each of their final four possessions of the first half, but only kicked 1 field goal and committed 3 turnovers, capped by Brian Williams' 77-yard interception return to set up Aaron Elling's 46-yard field goal as the half expired for a 20-3 lead. Trailing 27-3, the Packers scored on three of their final four drives to cut the deficit to 30-25 with 1:55 left, but Ryan Longwell's onside-kick attempt went out of bounds and the Vikings ran out the clock. Culpepper was 15 of 30 for 195 yards and 3 touchdowns, and Randy Moss had 9 receptions for 150 yards and 1 touchdown. Brett Favre was 25 of 41 for 248 yards and 1 touchdown, with 4 interceptions.

Minnesota	10	10	7	3	—	30
Green Bay	0	3	8	14	—	25

Minn — Avery 11 pass from Culpepper (Elling kick)
Minn — FG Elling 22
GB — FG Longwell 27
Minn — Bates 2 pass from Culpepper (Elling kick)
Minn — FG Elling 46
Minn — Moss 13 pass from Culpepper (Elling kick)
GB — Green 8 run (Franks pass from Favre)
Minn — FG Elling 34
GB — Green 1 run (Longwell kick)
GB — Walker 24 pass from Favre (Longwell kick)

KANSAS CITY 27, SAN DIEGO 14—at Arrowhead Stadium, attendance 78,048. Priest Holmes scored 2 first quarter touchdowns and the Chiefs jumped out to a 24-0 halftime lead en route to a divisional victory. Kansas City scored on 4 of its first 5 possessions, including touchdown drives of 68, 59, and 72 yards, as the Chiefs outgained San Diego 281-49 in the first half. In the middle of the fourth quarter leading 27-7, the Chiefs' defense stopped LaDainian Tomlinson for no gain on third- and fourth-and-1 at the Chiefs' 14 to quell any hope of a comeback. Trent Green was 21 of 32 for 282 yards and 1 touchdown, with 1 interception. Holmes had 183 all-purpose yards. Drew Brees was 18 of 33 for 202 yards and 2 touchdowns, with 2 interceptions.

San Diego	0	0	7	7	—	14
Kansas City	14	10	3	0	—	27

KC — Holmes 24 run (Andersen kick)
KC — Holmes 5 run (Andersen kick)
KC — Morton 20 pass from Green (Andersen kick)
KC — FG Andersen 42
SD — Norman 21 pass from Brees (Christie kick)
KC — FG Andersen 46
SD — Parker 20 pass from Brees (Christie kick)

HOUSTON 21, MIAMI 20—at Pro Player Stadium, attendance 73,010. Kris Brown kicked 5 field goals, including a 35-yard boot with 25 seconds remaining, as the Texans snapped the Dolphins' 11-game opening day winning streak. Chris Chambers caught 2 first-half touchdown passes to give the Dolphins a 14-6 halftime lead. The Texans scored on their last four possessions, sparked by Corey Bradford's 78-yard touchdown catch and capped by 3 field goals by Brown. The final field goal was set up by Marcus Coleman's interception at the Dolphins' 36 with 3:53 remaining. Coleman also intercepted Jay Fiedler's Hail Mary pass at the Texans' 5 as time expired to preserve the victory. David Carr was 17 of 31 for 266 yards and 1 touchdown. Fiedler was 17 of 32 for 227 yards and 3 touchdowns, with 2 interceptions. Chambers had 7 catches for 118 yards.

Houston	3	3	9	6	—	21
Miami	0	14	0	6	—	20

Hous — FG Brown 36
Mia — Chambers 57 pass from Fiedler (Mare kick)
Hous — FG Brown 50
Mia — Chambers 21 pass from Fiedler (Mare kick)
Hous — Bradford 78 pass from Carr (run failed)
Hous — FG Brown 23
Mia — Williams 35 pass from Fiedler (pass failed)
Hous — FG Brown 24
Hous — FG Brown 35

N.Y. GIANTS 23, ST. LOUIS 13—at Giants Stadium, attendance 68,804. The Giants' defense recorded 6 sacks and forced 4 turnovers, including a fumble recovery for a touchdown, as New York stifled the Rams. St. Louis led 3-0 when William Joseph fumbled in his own end zone and Kenny Holmes recovered for a touchdown. On St. Louis' next possession, the Rams drove to the Giants' 5, but Mike Barrow forced Kurt Warner to fumble, and Holmes recovered. Kerry Collins' 77-yard pass to Amani Toomer on the next play led to the first of Matt Bryant's 3 field goals. Leading 13-6 in the third quarter, Tiki Barber had consecutive runs of 15 and 22 yards to reach the Rams' 1 and lead to Brian Mitchell's 1-yard scoring run. Omar Stoutmire intercepted Warner's pass two plays later to set up Bryant's final field goal and an insurmountable 23-6 lead. Collins was 14 of 26 for 202 yards. Barber had 24 carries for 146 yards. Warner was 34 of 54 for 342 yards and 1 touchdown, with 1 interception and 6 fumbles, 3 of which the Giants' recovered.

St. Louis	3	3	0	7	—	13
N.Y. Giants	7	3	13	0	—	23

StL — FG Wilkins 39
NYG — Holmes fumble recovery in end zone (Bryant kick)
NYG — FG Bryant 24
StL — FG Wilkins 28
NYG — FG Bryant 47
NYG — Mitchell 1 run (Bryant kick)
NYG — FG Bryant 44
StL — Holt 37 pass from Warner (Wilkins kick)

PITTSBURGH 34, BALTIMORE 15—at Heinz Field, attendance 63,157. Tommy Maddox passed for 260 yards and 3 touchdowns as the Steelers won a divisional game against the Ravens. The Steelers outgained Baltimore 339-231 and forced 2 turnovers, which led directly to 10 points. Maddox fired touchdown passes to Jay Riemersma and Hines Ward in an eight-minute span bracketing halftime to take a 20-0 lead. Jason Gildon recovered a fumble by Jamal Lewis late in the third quarter, and Maddox completed a 28-yard touchdown pass to Ward on the next play to give Pittsburgh a 27-0 lead. Maddox was 21 of 29 for 260 yards and 3 touchdowns. Plaxico Burress had 6 receptions for 116 yards. Rookie Kyle Boller was 22 of 43 for 152 yards and 1 touchdown, with 1 interception.

Baltimore	0	0	7	8	—	15
Pittsburgh	6	7	14	7	—	34

Pitt — FG Reed 29
Pitt — FG Reed 31
Pitt — Ward 4 pass from Maddox (Reed kick)
Pitt — Riemersma 20 pass from Maddox (Reed kick)
Pitt — Ward 28 pass from Maddox (Reed kick)
Balt — J. Lewis 14 run (Stover kick)
Pitt — Zereoue 8 run (Reed kick)
Balt — Taylor 5 pass from Boller (Heap pass from Boller)

SAN FRANCISCO 49, CHICAGO 7—at 3Com Park, attendance 67,554. The 49ers outgained the Bears 391-127 total yards, had a 23-8 advantage in first downs, forced 5 turnovers, and maintained possession for more than 38 minutes to defeat the Bears. Mike Brown's interception at the 49ers' 16 led to Kordell Stewart's 3-yard touchdown pass to Desmond Clark early in the second quarter, and then forced the 49ers to punt. But Bobby Wade fumbled the ensuing punt return, Jimmy Williams recovered, and the 49ers proceeded to score 23 points in the final 6:01 of the first half, keyed by 2 interceptions and a blocked punt, to take a 33-7 halftime lead. The

49ers scored 27 points off the 5 Bears turnovers. Jeff Garcia was 19 of 35 for 229 yards and 2 touchdowns, with 1 interception. Terrell Owens had 7 receptions for 112 yards. Stewart was 14 of 34 for 95 yards and 1 touchdown, with 3 interceptions, in his first game for the Bears.

Chicago	0	7	0	0	—	7
San Francisco	10	23	6	10	—	49

SF — FG Chandler 22
SF — Hearst 12 pass from Garcia (Chandler kick)
Chi — Clark 3 pass from Stewart (Edinger kick)
SF — Garcia 3 run (Chandler kick)
SF — Streets 16 pass from Garcia (kick failed)
SF — Plummer 68 interception return (Chandler kick)
SF — FG Chandler 29
SF — FG Chandler 28
SF — FG Chandler 24
SF — FG Chandler 26
SF — Hearst 1 run (Chandler kick)

SEATTLE 27, NEW ORLEANS 10—at Seahawks Stadium, attendance 52.250. Shaun Alexander rushed for 108 yards and scored 2 touchdowns as the Seahawks stifled the Saints. The Seahawks' defense forced 4 turnovers, which resulted in 13 points for Seattle. Trailing 3-0, Alexander's 1-yard touchdown run began a string of 3 touchdowns in the final seven minutes of the first half. Two plays after Alexander's touchdown, Antonio Cochran recovered Michael Lewis' fumble and Matt Hasselbeck fired a 35-yard touchdown pass to Koren Robinson for a 14-3 lead. After forcing a punt, Seattle drove 77 yards for another touchdown by Alexander, with 17 seconds left in the half, for a 21-3 halftime lead. Chike Okeafor forced a fumble and intercepted a pass in the second half to stop the Saints. Hasselbeck was 12 of 23 for 137 yards and 2 touchdowns. Aaron Brooks was 29 of 47 for 274 yards and 1 touchdown, with 1 interception.

New Orleans	3	0	0	7	—	10
Seattle	0	21	3	3	—	27

NO — FG Carney 33
Sea — Alexander 1 run (J. Brown kick)
Sea — Robinson 35 pass from Hasselbeck (J. Brown kick)
Sea — Alexander 10 pass from Hasselbeck (J. Brown kick)
Sea — FG J. Brown 37
NO — Horn 2 pass from Brooks (Carney kick)
Sea — FG J. Brown 25

SUNDAY NIGHT, SEPTEMBER 7
TENNESSEE 25, OAKLAND 20—at The Coliseum, attendance 68.809. Steve McNair passed for 269 yards and 2 touchdowns and punter Craig Hentrich kicked 3 field goals as the Titans won a rematch of the 2002 AFC Championship Game. Joe Nedney kicked a 50-yard field goal to give the Titans a 9-3 second quarter lead, but Nedney injured his knee on the ensuing kickoff return. Rich Gannon's 46-yard touchdown pass to Charlie Garner gave Oakland a 10-9 lead with 1:06 left in the first half, but McNair completed passes of 12, 18, and 11 yards to set up Hentrich's 49-yard field goal. Hentrich entered the game with 3 field goals in his 10-year career. Derrick Mason's 3-yard touchdown catch midway through the fourth quarter gave Tennessee a 22-13 lead, but the Raiders pulled within two points on Gannon's 25-yard strike to Tim Brown with 3:30 left. Hentrich's 33-yard field goal with 32 seconds remaining iced the game. McNair was 25 of 38 for 269 yards and 2 touchdowns, with 1 interception. Mason had 10 receptions for 99 yards and 1 touchdown. Gannon was 24 of 38 for 264 yards and 2 touchdowns. Garner had 8 receptions for 112 yards.

Oakland	3	7	0	10	—	20
Tennessee	6	6	3	10	—	25

Tenn — Calico 11 pass from McNair (kick failed)
Oak — FG Janikowski 47
Tenn — FG Nedney 50
Oak — Garner 46 pass from Gannon (Janikowski kick)
Tenn — FG Hentrich 49
Tenn — FG Hentrich 34
Oak — FG Janikowski 47
Tenn — Mason 3 pass from McNair (Hentrich kick)
Oak — Brown 25 pass from Gannon (Janikowski kick)
Tenn — FG Hentrich 33

MONDAY NIGHT, SEPTEMBER 8
TAMPA BAY 17, PHILADELPHIA 0—at Lincoln Financial Field, attendance 67,772. Joe Jurevicius caught 2 touchdown passes as the defending Super Bowl champions shut out the Eagles in the first game at Lincoln Financial Field. The Buccaneers' defense permitted the Eagles to convert just 2 of 11 third-down situations and the offense maintained possession for more than 37 minutes. The Eagles only drove inside the Buccaneers' 20 one time, and failed to score when L.J. Smith dropped a potential touchdown pass in the end zone on a fake field-goal attempt five minutes into the game. Jurevicius made 2 spectacular touchdown catches in the second half, one in which he leaped and landed both tiptoes in the corner of the end zone, and the second in which he tipped a pass behind himself, spun around 270 degrees, dove and caught the ball before it could be intercepted. Brad Johnson was 27 of 36 for 238 yards and 2 touchdowns, with 1 interception. Donovan McNabb was 19 of 36 for 148 yards, with 1 interception.

Tampa Bay	0	3	7	7	—	17
Philadelphia	0	0	0	0	—	0

TB — FG Gramatica 23
TB — Jurevicius 13 pass from B. Johnson (Gramatica kick)
TB — Jurevicius 7 pass from B. Johnson (Gramatica kick)

SECOND WEEK SUMMARIES
American Football Conference

East Division	**W**	**L**	**T**	**Pct.**	**Pts.**	**OP**
Buffalo	2	0	0	1.000	69	17
Miami	1	1	0	.500	41	31
New England	1	1	0	.500	31	41
N.Y. Jets	0	2	0	.000	23	37
North Division	**W**	**L**	**T**	**Pct.**	**Pts.**	**OP**
Baltimore	1	1	0	.500	48	47
Pittsburgh	1	1	0	.500	54	56
Cincinnati	0	2	0	.000	30	53
Cleveland	0	2	0	.000	19	42
South Division	**W**	**L**	**T**	**Pct.**	**Pts.**	**OP**
Indianapolis	2	0	0	1.000	42	13
Houston	1	1	0	.500	31	51
Tennessee	1	1	0	.500	32	53
Jacksonville	0	2	0	.000	40	62
West Division	**W**	**L**	**T**	**Pct.**	**Pts.**	**OP**
Denver	2	0	0	1.000	67	23
Kansas City	2	0	0	1.000	68	34
Oakland	1	1	0	.500	43	45
San Diego	0	2	0	.000	27	64

National Football Conference

East Division	**W**	**L**	**T**	**Pct.**	**Pts.**	**OP**
Washington	2	0	0	1.000	49	44
Dallas	1	1	0	.500	48	59
N.Y. Giants	1	1	0	.500	55	48
Philadelphia	0	2	0	.000	10	48
North Division	**W**	**L**	**T**	**Pct.**	**Pts.**	**OP**
Minnesota	2	0	0	1.000	54	38
Detroit	1	1	0	.500	48	55
Green Bay	1	1	0	.500	56	36
Chicago	0	2	0	.000	20	73
South Division	**W**	**L**	**T**	**Pct.**	**Pts.**	**OP**
Carolina	2	0	0	1.000	36	32
Atlanta	1	1	0	.500	58	46
New Orleans	1	1	0	.500	41	37
Tampa Bay	1	1	0	.500	26	12
West Division	**W**	**L**	**T**	**Pct.**	**Pts.**	**OP**
Seattle	2	0	0	1.000	65	10
St. Louis	1	1	0	.500	40	47
San Francisco	1	1	0	.500	73	34
Arizona	0	2	0	.000	24	80

SUNDAY, SEPTEMBER 14
SEATTLE 38, ARIZONA 0—at Sun Devil Stadium, attendance 23,127. Darrell Jackson caught 2 long touchdown passes and the Seahawks' defense forced 6 turnovers en route to Seattle's first shutout since 1998. The Cardinals committed turnovers on their first four possessions, leading to 17 Seahawks points. Bill Gramatica missed a 53-yard field goal late in the first half, and the Seahawks responded three plays later with Matt Hasselbeck's 55-yard touchdown pass to Jackson with 1:16 left in the half for a 24-0 lead. The pair hooked up again 1:01 into the second half for a 66-yard touchdown and 31-0 lead. Hasselbeck was 8 of 19 for 175 yards and 2 touchdowns. Jackson had 3 receptions for 133 yards and 2 touchdowns. Jeff Blake was 7 of 14 for 55 yards, with 2 interceptions, before leaving with a heel injury. His replacement, Josh McCown, was 18 of 32 for 150 yards, with 2 interceptions.

Seattle	7	17	7	7	—	38
Arizona	0	0	0	0	—	0

Sea — Hasselbeck 2 run (Brown kick)
Sea — Godfrey 55 fumble return (Brown kick)
Sea — FG Brown 37
Sea — Jackson 55 pass from Hasselbeck (Brown kick)
Sea — Jackson 66 pass from Hasselbeck (Brown kick)
Sea — Alexander 2 run (Brown kick)

WASHINGTON 33, ATLANTA 31—at Georgia Dome, attendance 70,241. The Redskins began the season 2-0 for the first time since their Super Bowl XXVI-winning 1991 season as Patrick Ramsey passed for 2 touchdowns to rally Washington from a 17-0 deficit to defeat the Falcons. Leading 10-0 early in the second quarter, Ed Jasper recovered Ramsey's fumble at the Redskins' 1 to set up T.J. Duckett's second touchdown in just over a minute to give Atlanta a 17-0 lead. Ramsey fumbled again on the next possession, but Jay Feely missed a 45-yard field goal, and Washington outscored Atlanta 33-7 in the next 27 minutes, 31 seconds. John Hall's 54-yard field goal at the end of the half, and Ramsey's 21-yard touchdown pass to Rod Gardner to begin the third quarter tied the game 24-24, and Jessie Armstead sacked Doug Johnson for a safety with 26 seconds left in the third quarter for a 26-24 lead. Johnson's 42-yard touchdown pass to Jimmy Farris cut the deficit to 33-31 with 2:22 left, but Atlanta did not regain possession until the final 19 seconds deep in its own territory. The Redskins outgained Atlanta 435-283 in total yards. Ramsey was 25 of 39 for 356 yards and 2 touchdowns. Johnson was 16 of 36 for 197 yards and 2 touchdowns, with 2 interceptions.

Washington	0	17	9	7	—	33
Atlanta	3	21	0	7	—	31

Atl — FG Feely 37
Atl — Duckett 13 run (Feely kick)
Atl — Duckett 1 run (Feely kick)

Wash — Betts 13 run (Hall kick)
Wash — Cartwright 1 run (Hall kick)
Atl — Crumpler 1 pass from D. Johnson (Feely kick)
Wash — FG Hall 54
Wash — Gardner 21 pass from Ramsey (Hall kick)
Wash — Safety, Armstead sacked D. Johnson in end zone
Wash — Coles 19 pass from Ramsey (Hall kick)
Atl — Farris 42 pass from D. Johnson (Feely kick)

BALTIMORE 33, CLEVELAND 13—at M&T Bank Stadium, attendance 69,473. Jamal Lewis rushed for an NFL record 295 yards as the Ravens evened their record. Lewis carried 30 times, breaking Corey Dillon's record of 278 yards on his twenty-sixth carry, a 3-yard run, with 7:40 remaining in the game. Lewis scored on an 82-yard run two plays into the game to set the tone. Lewis had a 60-yard run nullified by a holding penalty in the second quarter, making it a 48-yard run and setting up Matt Stover's 40-yard field goal for a 13-3 Ravens lead. Lewis had 180 yards on 16 carries at halftime, but Gerard Warren's recovery of Chris Redman's fumble at the Ravens' 22 late in the third quarter pulled the Browns within 16-13 on Kelly Holcomb's 4-yard touchdown pass to Kevin Johnson. Lewis responded two plays later with a 63-yard touchdown run. Ed Reed's 54-yard interception return as time expired made the final score deceivingly one-sided. The Ravens outgained Cleveland 393-175, including 343-60 on the ground. Kyle Boller was 7 of 17 for 78 yards, with 1 interception before leaving with an injury, and Redman was 0 for 1. Holcomb was 17 of 37 for 147 yards and 1 touchdown, with 2 interceptions.

Cleveland	0	3	10	0	—	13
Baltimore	10	6	0	17	—	33

Balt — J. Lewis 82 run (Stover kick)
Balt — FG Stover 20
Cle — FG Dawson 44
Balt — FG Stover 40
Balt — FG Richey 56
Cle — FG Dawson 35
Cle — Johnson 4 pass from Holcomb (Dawson kick)
Balt — J. Lewis 63 run (Stover kick)
Balt — FG Stover 21
Balt — Reed 54 interception return (Stover kick)

GREEN BAY 31, DETROIT 6—at Lambeau Field, attendance 70,244. Ahman Green rushed for 160 yards and Brett Favre passed for 2 touchdowns as the Packers downed the Lions. Green raced 65 yards for a touchdown on the second play of the game to give the Packers all the points they would need. Favre's 5-yard touchdown pass to Tony Fisher capped their next possession, and the Packers led 17-6 at halftime. Green Bay intercepted Joey Harrington twice in the first five minutes of the second half, with the second pick leading to Robert Ferguson's 14-yard scoring catch. Al Harris' 56-yard interception return early in the fourth quarter capped the scoring, as the Lions never got inside the Packers' 30 in the second half. Favre was 15 of 28 for 132 yards and 2 touchdowns, with 1 interception. Harrington was 26 of 55 for 241 yards, with 3 interceptions.

Detroit	0	6	0	0	—	6
Green Bay	14	3	7	7	—	31

GB — Green 65 run (Longwell kick)
GB — Fisher 5 pass from Favre (Longwell kick)
Det — FG Hanson 22
GB — FG Longwell 46
Det — FG Hanson 52
GB — Ferguson 14 pass from Favre (Longwell kick)
GB — Harris 56 interception return (Longwell kick)

INDIANAPOLIS 33, TENNESSEE 7—at RCA Dome, attendance 56,999. Mike Vanderjagt kicked 4 field goals and Steve McNair suffered an injury and missed the second half as the Colts defeated their division rival. The Titans led 7-3 in the second quarter when Peyton Manning's 42-yard pass to Dallas Clark set up Edgerrin James' 2-yard touchdown run. Manning's 35-yard touchdown pass to Marvin Harrison on the Colts' next possession gave Indianapolis a 17-7 lead with 56 seconds left in the half, and McNair dislocated his right ring finger two plays later while completing a 5-yard pass to Derrick Mason. Billy Volek replaced McNair, and in 6 second-half possessions, the Titans failed to drive inside the Colts' 30 and Indianapolis maintained control of the ball for more than 19 minutes after intermission. Nick Harper's 75-yard interception return with 22 seconds remaining completed the scoring. Manning was 14 of 21 for 173 yards and 1 touchdown. McNair was 15 of 24 for 138 yards and 1 touchdown, and Volek was 6 of 9 for 61 yards, with 1 interception. Mason had 10 catches for 98 yards.

Tennessee	0	7	0	0	—	7
Indianapolis	3	14	3	13	—	33

Ind — FG Vanderjagt 29
Tenn — Calico 7 pass from McNair (Anderson kick)
Ind — James 2 run (Vanderjagt kick)
Ind — Harrison 35 pass from Manning (Vanderjagt kick)
Ind — FG Vanderjagt 41
Ind — FG Vanderjagt 23
Ind — FG Vanderjagt 48
Ind — Harper 75 interception return (Vanderjagt kick)

BUFFALO 38, JACKSONVILLE 17—at ALLTEL Stadium, attendance 58,613. Travis Henry rushed for 3 touchdowns and Drew Bledsoe passed for 314 yards and 2 touchdowns as the Bills improved their record to 2-0. Buffalo scored touchdowns on five of its first seven possessions with drives of 49, 68, 62, 78, and 99 yards, capped by Henry's 4-yard run with 59 seconds left in the third quarter, for a 35-10 lead. Rookie Byron Leftwich played the final series for Jacksonville, and guided the Jaguars on a 9-play, 90-yard touchdown drive. Leftwich completed the drive with a 5-yard scoring pass to George Wrighster. Bledsoe was 19 of 25 for 314 yards and 2 touchdowns. Eric Moulds had 7 receptions for 133 yards and 1 touchdown. Henry scored 3 touchdowns despite gaining just 26 yards on 21 carries. Mark Brunell was 19 of 32 for 122 yards, and Leftwich was 7 of 8 for 92 yards and 1 touchdown.

Buffalo	14	7	14	3	—	38
Jacksonville	0	7	3	7	—	17

Buff — Henry 1 run (Lindell kick)
Buff — Henry 6 run (Lindell kick)
Jax — Brunell 1 run (Marler kick)
Buff — Shaw 54 pass from Bledsoe (Lindell kick)
Jax — FG Marler 44
Buff — Moulds 36 pass from Bledsoe (Lindell kick)
Buff — Henry 4 run (Lindell kick)
Buff — FG Lindell 27
Jax — Wrighster 5 pass from Leftwich (Marler kick)

KANSAS CITY 41, PITTSBURGH 20—at Arrowhead Stadium, attendance 78,416. Priest Holmes scored 3 touchdowns and the Chiefs' defense forced 4 turnovers and recorded 4 sacks as Kansas City defeated Pittsburgh. Chad Scott's 26-yard interception return for a touchdown in the opening minute began the scoring, and James Farrior's interception late in the first quarter was followed on the next play by a 33-yard touchdown pass from Tommy Maddox to Plaxico Burress to give Pittsburgh a 17-7 lead. Dante Hall's 100-yard kickoff return got the Chiefs on the board, and the offense scored touchdowns on its next two possessions on drives of 72 and 86 yards, and Jerome Woods scored on a 46-yard interception return to give Kansas City a 27-17 lead with 2:25 left in the half. Hall's 45-yard punt return set up Holmes' second touchdown early in the second half, and on the Steelers' next possession, Shawn Barber intercepted Maddox in the end zone to help the Chiefs retain a 34-20 lead. Woods' fumble recovery in the fourth quarter led to Holmes' 31-yard scoring scamper with 5:06 remaining to ice the game. Trent Green was 15 of 21 for 125 yards and 1 touchdown, with 2 interceptions. Holmes rushed for 122 yards and 3 touchdowns. Maddox was 27 of 48 for 336 yards and 1 touchdown, with 3 interceptions. Hines Ward had 9 receptions for 146 yards, and Burress added 7 catches for 115 yards and 1 touchdown.

Pittsburgh	17	3	0	0	—	20
Kansas City	7	20	7	7	—	41

Pitt — Scott 26 interception return (Reed kick)
Pitt — FG Reed 20
KC — Hall 100 kickoff return (Andersen kick)
Pitt — Burress 33 pass from Maddox (Reed kick)
KC — Holmes 3 run (Andersen kick)
KC — Dunn 3 pass from Green (Andersen kick)
KC — Woods 46 interception return (kick failed)
Pitt — FG Reed 51
KC — Holmes 4 run (Andersen kick)
KC — Holmes 31 run (Andersen kick)

NEW ORLEANS 31, HOUSTON 10—at Louisiana Superdome, attendance 68,390. Aaron Brooks passed for 2 second-half touchdowns as the Saints rallied to defeat the Texans. Kris Brown's 30-yard field goal with one second left in the half gave Houston a 10-7 lead and the possibility of a second consecutive road upset. The Saints answered by scoring on their first three possessions of the second half, on drives of 64, 57, and 72 yards, and Derrick Rodgers' 40-yard interception return for a touchdown with 2:43 remaining dashed any comeback hopes for the Texans. New Orleans outgained Houston 219-97 in the second half, and did not allow Houston to run a play inside the Saints' 40. Brooks was 18 of 27 for 189 yards and 2 touchdowns. Joe Horn had 10 receptions for 111 yards. David Carr was 17 of 36 for 213 yards, with 2 interceptions.

Houston	0	10	0	0	—	10
New Orleans	7	0	10	14	—	31

NO — McAllister 24 run (Carney kick)
Hou — Carr 2 run (Brown kick)
Hou — FG Brown 30
NO — Stallworth 35 pass from Brooks (Carney kick)
NO — FG Carney 39
NO — Conwell 2 pass from Brooks (Carney kick)
NO — Rodgers 40 interception return (Carney kick)

MIAMI 21, N.Y. JETS 10—at The Meadowlands, attendance 77,461. Jay Fiedler passed for 1 touchdown and ran for another as the Dolphins defeated the Jets. Trailing 3-0, Miami scored on three consecutive possessions, on drives of 71, 79, and 84 yards, capped by Ricky Williams' 2-yard touchdown run with 17 seconds left in the half for a 21-3 lead. Chester McGlockton's fumble recovery on the first play of the fourth quarter set up Vinny Testaverde's 32-yard touchdown pass to Santana Moss with 12:42 remaining, but Patrick Surtain's interception with 2:37 left quelled the Jets' comeback attempt. Fiedler was 14 of 19 for 190 yards and 1 touchdown. Testaverde was 29 of 45 for 373 yards and 1 touchdown, with 1 interception. Moss had 5 receptions for 142 yards and 1 touchdown.

Miami	7	14	0	0	—	21
N.Y. Jets	3	0	0	7	—	10

NYJ — FG Brien 30
Mia — Fiedler 9 run (Mare kick)
Mia — McMichael 8 pass from Fiedler (Mare kick)
Mia — Williams 2 run (Mare kick)
NYJ — Moss 32 pass from Testaverde (Brien kick)

OAKLAND 23, CINCINNATI 20—at Network Associates Coliseum, attendance 50,135. Sebastian Janikowski's 39-yard field goal with nine seconds remaining lifted the Raiders past Cincinnati. The Bengals had a 27-12 advantage in first downs, led in total yards 416-237, 39:24-20:36 in time of possession, and 82-48 in total plays, with seven drives of at least 35 yards. But the biggest play of the game was turned in by Phillip Buchanon, who intercepted a pass and returned it 83 yards for an Oakland touchdown with 3:46 remaining to give the Raiders a 20-13 lead. Undaunted, the Bengals tied the game on Jon Kitna's 8-yard touchdown pass to Peter Warrick with 1:18 left. Charlie Garner turned a short pass into a 24-yard gain, and on third-and-10 three plays later, the Raiders picked up the blitz and Artrell Hawkins held Jerry Rice and was flagged for pass interference at the Bengals' 22 to set up Janikowski's winning kick. Gannon was 13 of 28 for 103 yards. Kitna was 25 of 41 for 303 yards and 1 touchdown, with 2 interceptions. Chad Johnson had 8 receptions for 131 yards, and Warrick added 8 catches for 109 yards.

Cincinnati	3	7	3	7	—	20
Oakland	10	0	3	10	—	23

Oak — FG Janikowski 40
Oak — Wheatley 2 run (Janikowski kick)
Cin — FG Graham 31
Cin — Dillon 1 run (Graham kick)
Oak — FG Janikowski 26
Cin — FG Graham 22
Oak — Buchanon 83 interception return (Janikowski kick)
Cin — Warrick 8 pass from Kitna (Graham kick)
Oak — FG Janikowski 39

NEW ENGLAND 31, PHILADELPHIA 10—at Lincoln Financial Field, attendance 67,624. Tom Brady passed for 3 touchdowns and the Patriots' defense recorded 7 sacks and forced 6 turnovers to defeat the Eagles. The Eagles led 7-3 in the second quarter, and the Patriots had a bad snap on a field-goal attempt to turn the ball over. But on the next play, Ted Washington sacked Donovan McNabb and forced him to fumble, and Roman Phifer recovered. Four plays later, Brady fired an 8-yard touchdown pass to Christian Fauria. Later in the quarter, Brian Westbrook muffed a punt and Bethel Johnson recovered at the Eagles' 14. Fauria caught a 5-yard touchdown pass two plays later for a 17-7 lead, A 16-yard punt return in the third quarter led to Brady's 26-yard touchdown pass to Deion Branch. The Eagles failed to cross the Patriots' 30 in the second half. Brady was 30 of 44 for 255 yards and 3 touchdowns. McNabb was 18 of 46 for 186 yards, with 2 interceptions.

New England	3	14	7	7	—	31
Philadelphia	0	7	0	3	—	10

NE — FG Vinatieri 27
Phil — Staley 2 run (Akers kick)
NE — Fauria 8 pass from Brady (Vinatieri kick)
NE — Fauria 5 pass from Brady (Vinatieri kick)
NE — Branch 26 pass from Brady (Vinatieri kick)
Phil — FG Akers 57
NE — Bruschi 18 interception return (Vinatieri kick)

ST. LOUIS 27, SAN FRANCISCO 24 (OT)—at Edward Jones Dome, attendance 65,990. Jeff Wilkins kicked a 28-yard field goal in overtime as the Rams withstood a 49ers rally to win a key divisional game. Trailing 10-7 at halftime, the Rams, who ran just 7 times in the first half, carried 8 times on their initial drive of the second half, capped by Marshall Faulk's 2-yard scoring run. The Rams scored on their next two possessions as well, with the benefit of a 37-yard pass interference penalty on third-and-19, and Wilkins' 29-yard field goal with 3:24 remaining for a 24-17 lead. The 49ers drove to the Rams' 13, and on fourth-and-8, Jeff Garcia fired a 13-yard touchdown pass to Terrell Owens with 19 seconds left to tie the game. In a bizarre play, Jeff Chandler's ensuing kickoff inadvertently hit one of the Rams' front five blockers, and Arnaz Battle recovered at midfield for San Francisco. The 49ers had a chance for a winning field goal at the end of regulation, but Cedric Wilson failed to fall to the ground and call timeout after catching a pass at the Rams' 30 with time running out. He was tackled at the Rams' 26 after time expired. In overtime, Marc Bulger's 22-yard pass to Faulk, set up Wilkins' winning kick. Bulger, named the starter the previous Monday, was 25 of 36 for 236 yards and 2 touchdowns. Garcia was 19 of 35 for 222 yards and 2 touchdowns, with 1 interception.

San Francisco	7	3	7	7	0	—	24
St. Louis	7	0	7	10	3	—	27

SF — Streets 16 pass from Garcia (Chandler kick)
StL — Holt 11 pass from Bulger (Wilkins kick)
SF — FG Chandler 35
StL — Faulk 2 run (Wilkins kick)
SF — Barlow 19 run (Chandler kick)
StL — Looker 19 pass from Bulger (Wilkins kick)
StL — FG Wilkins 29
SF — Owens 13 pass from Garcia (Chandler kick)
StL — FG Wilkins 28

DENVER 37, SAN DIEGO 13—at Qualcomm Stadium, attendance 65,445. Clinton Portis rushed for 129 yards and Jake Plummer passed for 3 touchdowns as the Broncos improved their record to 2-0. All three of Plummer's first-half touchdown passes came on play-action passes. Plummer threw the final one, a 6-yard touchdown pass to tackle eligible Cooper Carlisle, with a separated shoulder suffered two plays earlier when Plummer dove for a first down on fourth-and-1. The Chargers, trailing 21-3, scored on their next two drives to cut the deficit to 24-13. Even with Plummer and Portis both injured and out of the game, Denver scored on its next three possessions to pull away. Plummer was 9 of 13 for 94 yards and 3 touchdowns, and Steve Beuerlein was 7 of 16 for 98 yards. Drew Brees was 20 of 41 for 182 yards and 1 touchdown, with 1 interception.

Denver	14	10	10	3	—	37
San Diego	3	7	3	0	—	13

Den — Droughns 12 pass from Plummer (Elam kick)
SD — FG Christie 19
Den — Sharpe 1 pass from Plummer (Elam kick)
Den — Carlisle 6 pass from Plummer (Elam kick)
SD — Parker 23 pass from Brees (Christie kick)
Den — FG Elam 30
SD — FG Christie 25
Den — Anderson 1 run (Elam kick)
Den — FG Elam 45
Den — FG Elam 34

CAROLINA 12, TAMPA BAY 9 (OT)—at Raymond James Stadium, attendance 65,621. John Kasay kicked 4 field goals, including the game-winner in overtime, and the Panthers blocked 2 field goals and an extra point at the end of regulation, to defeat the defending Super Bowl champions. A 53-yard interception return by Al Wallace set up Kasay's second field goal just before halftime, and the Panthers drove nearly five minutes to begin the second half, capped by Kasay's third field goal, for a 9-0 lead. Martín Gramatica, who had a 38-yard attempt in the first half blocked by Kris Jenkins, made a 41-yard field goal following Brian Kelly's interception late in the third quarter to cut the deficit to 9-3. Julius Peppers blocked Gramatica's 47-yard attempt with 8:18 remaining to thwart another scoring effort. The Buccaneers had one last chance, starting from their own 18 with no timeouts and 1:49 left. Brad Johnson completed a 43-yard pass to Karl Williams and a key third-and-15 pass to Keyshawn Johnson to set up Keenan McCardell's 6-yard touchdown catch as time expired. However, the potential game-winning extra point was blocked by Jenkins, his second block of the game. Steve Smith's 52-yard punt return and a 10-yard run by Stephen Davis set up Kasay's game-winning 47-yard kick with 3:34 left in overtime. Jake Delhomme was 9 of 23 for 96 yards, with 2 interceptions. Davis had 33 carries for 142 yards. Brad Johnson was 34 of 61 for 339 yards and 1 touchdown, with 1 interception. Keyshawn Johnson had 9 catches for 102 yards.

Carolina	3	3	3	0	3	—	12
Tampa Bay	0	0	3	6	0	—	9

Car — FG Kasay 28
Car — FG Kasay 35
Car — FG Kasay 20
TB — FG Gramatica 41
TB — McCardell 6 pass from B. Johnson (kick blocked)
Car — FG Kasay 47

SUNDAY NIGHT, SEPTEMBER 14

MINNESOTA 24, CHICAGO 13—at Metrodome, attendance 64,144. Daunte Culpepper passed for 214 yards and 2 touchdowns, both to Jim Kleinsasser, as the Vikings held off the Bears. The Vikings dominated in first downs (25-10), total yards (400-208), and time of possession (38:42-21:18), but led just 17-13 going into the fourth quarter. But Minnesota manufactured a 16-play, 93-yard drive that consumed nine minutes, 42 seconds, capped by Kleinsasser's 11-yard touchdown catch with 3:02 remaining, for a 24-13 lead. Brian Russell's interception four plays later sealed the Vikings' victory. Culpepper was 20 of 26 for 214 yards and 2 touchdowns. Moe Williams rushed for 108 yards. Stewart was 13 of 21 for 137 yards before being injured in the final moments. Chris Chandler was 1 of 2 for 8 yards, with 1 interception.

Chicago	3	7	3	0	—	13
Minnesota	7	10	0	7	—	24

Minn — Williams 1 run (Elling kick)
Chi — FG Edinger 42
Minn — FG Elling 23
Minn — Kleinsasser 3 pass from Culpepper (Elling kick)
Chi — Terrell 14 pass from Stewart (Edinger kick)
Chi — FG Edinger 43
Minn — Kleinsasser 11 pass from Culpepper (Elling kick)

MONDAY NIGHT, SEPTEMBER 15
DALLAS 35, N.Y. GIANTS 32 (OT)—at Giants Stadium, attendance 78,907. Billy Cundiff tied an NFL record with 7 field goals, including the game-tying kick as regulation expired and the game-winner in overtime. The victory was Bill Parcells' first with Dallas. The Cowboys scored 10 points off turnovers in the first half and led 20-7. Cundiff kicked field goals on each of the Cowboys' first three drives of the second half for a 29-14 lead with 12:43 remaining. Kerry Collins completed 7 consecutive passes on the Giants' next two drives, capped by Amani Toomer's 20-yard touchdown catch with 6:31 left. The Giants went for a two-point conversion, and following two defensive pass interference penalties, Tiki Barber scored on the third chance to tie the game 29-29. Matt Bryant kicked a 30-yard field goal with 11 seconds left to give the Giants a 32-29 lead, but Bryant's ensuing kickoff dribbled out of bounds. Quincy Carter completed a 26-yard pass to Antonio Bryant, and Cundiff made a 52-yard field goal as time expired to force overtime. After an exchange of punts, Carter completed an 8-yard pass to Terry Glenn on third-and-4 and a 23-yard misdirection pass to Dan Campbell on third-and-1 to set up Cundiff's game winner. Carter was 25 of 40 for 321 yards, with 1 interception. Glenn had 8 catches for 113 yards. Collins was 21 of 51 for 265 yards and 3 touchdowns, with 2 interceptions. Toomer had 7 catches for 126 yards and 1 touchdown.

Dallas	7	13	6	6	3	—	35
N.Y. Giants	7	0	7	18	0	—	32

NYG — Brown 29 interception return (Bryant kick)
Dall — Carter 8 run (Cundiff kick)
Dall — FG Cundiff 37
Dall — FG Cundiff 49
Dall — Singleton 41 interception return (Cundiff kick)
Dall — FG Cundiff 42
NYG — Hilliard 5 pass from Collins (Bryant kick)
Dall — FG Cundiff 21
Dall — FG Cundiff 36
NYG — Shockey 1 pass from Collins (Bryant kick)
NYG — Toomer 20 pass from Collins (Barber run)
NYG — FG Bryant 30
Dall — FG Cundiff 52
Dall — FG Cundiff 25

THIRD WEEK SUMMARIES
American Football Conference

East Division	**W**	**L**	**T**	**Pct.**	**Pts.**	**OP**
Buffalo	2	1	0	.667	76	34
Miami	2	1	0	.667	58	38
New England	2	1	0	.667	54	57
N.Y. Jets	0	3	0	.000	39	60
North Division	**W**	**L**	**T**	**Pct.**	**Pts.**	**OP**
Baltimore	2	1	0	.667	72	57
Pittsburgh	2	1	0	.667	71	66
Cleveland	1	2	0	.333	32	54
Cincinnati	0	3	0	.000	40	70
South Division	**W**	**L**	**T**	**Pct.**	**Pts.**	**OP**
Indianapolis	3	0	0	1.000	65	26
Tennessee	2	1	0	.667	59	65
Houston	1	2	0	.333	45	93
Jacksonville	0	3	0	.000	53	85
West Division	**W**	**L**	**T**	**Pct.**	**Pts.**	**OP**
Denver	3	0	0	1.000	98	33
Kansas City	3	0	0	1.000	110	48
Oakland	1	2	0	.333	53	76
San Diego	0	3	0	.000	37	88

National Football Conference

East Division	**W**	**L**	**T**	**Pct.**	**Pts.**	**OP**
N.Y. Giants	2	1	0	.667	79	69
Washington	2	1	0	.667	70	68
Dallas	1	1	0	.500	48	59
Philadelphia	0	2	0	.000	10	48
North Division	**W**	**L**	**T**	**Pct.**	**Pts.**	**OP**
Minnesota	3	0	0	1.000	77	51
Detroit	1	2	0	.333	61	78
Green Bay	1	2	0	.333	69	56
Chicago	0	2	0	.000	20	73
South Division	**W**	**L**	**T**	**Pct.**	**Pts.**	**OP**
Carolina	2	0	0	1.000	36	32
Tampa Bay	2	1	0	.667	57	22
Atlanta	1	2	0	.333	68	77
New Orleans	1	2	0	.333	53	64
West Division	**W**	**L**	**T**	**Pct.**	**Pts.**	**OP**
Seattle	3	0	0	1.000	89	33
Arizona	1	2	0	.333	44	93
St. Louis	1	2	0	.333	63	71
San Francisco	1	2	0	.333	85	47

SUNDAY, SEPTEMBER 21
ARIZONA 20, GREEN BAY 13—at Sun Devil Stadium, attendance 58,784. Dexter Jackson intercepted a pass in the end zone with two seconds remaining as the Cardinals outlasted the Packers in 102 degree heat. In the first quarter, Ray Thompson's recovery of Ahman Green's fumble and Jeff Blake's 38-yard pass to Anquan Boldin moments later set up Blake's 1-yard touchdown run. The Packers scored on consecutive second-quarter drives to take a 10-7 lead, but Blake engineered a 77-yard drive in the final 1:17 of the first half, capped by Bill Gramatica's 21-yard field goal, to tie the game 10-10. With the score tied 13-13 in the fourth quarter, the Cardinals drove 68 yards in 11 plays and took a 20-13 lead on Blake's 1-yard touchdown pass to James Hodgins with 4:03 left. The Packers drove to the Cardinals' 7, but Brett Favre's third-and-goal pass was intercepted in the end zone by Jackson with two seconds remaining. Blake was 20 of 31 for 273 yards and 1 touchdown, with 1 interception. Favre was 23 of 33 for 245 yards and 1 touchdown, with 1 interception.

Green Bay	0	10	0	3	—	13
Arizona	7	3	3	7	—	20

Ariz — Blake 1 run (Gramatica kick)
GB — Martin 4 pass from Favre (Longwell kick)
GB — FG Longwell 40
Ariz — FG Gramatica 21
Ariz — FG Gramatica 37
GB — FG Longwell 40
Ariz — Hodgins 1 pass from Blake (Gramatica kick)

TAMPA BAY 31, ATLANTA 10—at Georgia Dome, attendance 70,871. Mike Alstott scored 2 touchdowns and Warren Sapp had his first touchdown reception as Tampa Bay defeated the Falcons. The Buccaneers had advantages in yards (316-136) and time of possession (35:04-24:56). On third-and-2 early in the second quarter, Michael Pittman caught a pass deep down the left sideline for a 68-yard touchdown. The first of Dwight Smith's 2 interceptions set up Brad Johnson's 6-yard touchdown pass to Sapp, who had lined up as a tight end, with 1:55 left in the half for a 17-3 lead. Sam Rogers returned Thomas Jones' fumble 37 yards to the Buccaneers' 2 to set up Woody Dantzler's 1-yard touchdown run, the first touchdown allowed by the Buccaneers' defense in 2003. Alstott touchdown runs capped the Buccaneers' next two possessions, in between John Howell's fumble recovery of Brian Kozlowski's kickoff return, to provide the final margin. Brad Johnson was 16 of 24 for 192 yards and 2 touchdowns. Doug Johnson was 13 of 19 for 95 yards, with 3 interceptions, and Kurt Kittner was 5 of 12 for 32 yards, with 1 interception.

Tampa Bay	3	14	14	0	—	31
Atlanta	0	3	7	0	—	10

TB — FG Gramatica 24
Atl — FG Feely 29
TB — Pittman 68 pass from B. Johnson (Gramatica kick)
TB — Sapp 6 pass from B. Johnson (Gramatica kick)
Atl — Dantzler 1 run (Feely kick)
TB — Alstott 2 run (Gramatica kick)
TB — Alstott 1 run (Gramatica kick)

PITTSBURGH 17, CINCINNATI 10—at Paul Brown Stadium, attendance 64,596. Jerome Bettis carried 16 times for 59 yards and 1 touchdown, all in the second half, as the Steelers defeated the Bengals. Rogers Beckett's interception set up Shayne Graham's 44-yard field goal early in the second half to trim the Bengals' deficit to 7-3. The Steelers reached the Bengals' 23 on the ensuing drive and then handed the ball to Bettis 6 consecutive times, who scored on a 1-yard run for a 14-3 lead. Trailing 17-3, Peter Warrick returned a punt 31 yards to set up his 5-yard touchdown reception from Jon Kitna with 5:54 left. But Bettis carried 6 times on the next drive, including a 2-yard run on third-and-2 with 1:21 remaining, as Pittsburgh never relinquished possession as time expired. The Steelers had more first downs (22-11), yards (376-182), and controlled the ball for more than 37 minutes. Tommy Maddox was 21 of 34 for 240 yards and 1 touchdown, with 1 interception. Kitna was 16 of 24 for 157 yards and 1 touchdown, with 1 interception.

Pittsburgh	0	7	7	3	—	17
Cincinnati	0	0	3	7	—	10

Pitt — Ward 7 pass from Maddox (Reed kick)
Cin — FG Graham 44
Pitt — Bettis 1 run (Reed kick)
Pitt — FG Reed 33
Cin — Warrick 5 pass from Kitna (Graham kick)

MINNESOTA 23, DETROIT 13—at Ford Field, attendance 60,865. Daunte Culpepper rushed for 2 touchdowns and the Vikings' defense intercepted 3 passes to improve to 3-0. Eddie Drummond's 26-yard punt return midway through the first quarter set up Jason Hanson's 27-yard field goal to give Detroit a 10-0 lead. Culpepper had scoring runs to cap consecutive second-quarter possessions, but injured his hip on the second touchdown. Gus Frerotte replaced Culpepper, and on his second pass fired a 72-yard pass to Randy Moss to set up Aaron Elling's 21-yard field goal just before halftime for a 16-10 lead. After Hanson's second field goal cut the lead to 16-13, Frerotte responded with another 72-yard pass, this time to Kelly Campbell for a touchdown. In the final five minutes, Corey Chavous and Denard Walker had interceptions in the end zone, and the Vikings stopped the Lions at the 1-yard line on a third possession to maintain their lead. Culpepper was 8 of 19 for 184 yards and 1 touchdown, with 1 interception, and had 2 touchdown runs, and Frerotte was 8 of 19 for 184 yards and 1 touchdown, with 1 interception. Joey Harrington was 24 of 42 for 235 yards, with 3 interceptions.

Minnesota	0	16	7	0	—	23
Detroit	10	0	3	0	—	13

Det — Bryson 5 run (Hanson kick)

Det — FG Hanson 27
Minn — Culpepper 14 run (snap bobbled)
Minn — Culpepper 2 run (Elling kick)
Minn — FG Elling 21
Det — FG Hanson 37
Minn — Campbell 72 pass from Frerotte (Elling kick)

KANSAS CITY 42, HOUSTON 14—at Reliant Stadium, attendance 70,487. Priest Holmes scored 2 touchdowns as the Chiefs remained undefeated by pulling away from the Texans. Houston trailed just 14-7 and had the ball with 4:38 left in the third quarter, but Tony Hollings fumbled and Dexter McCleon recovered at the Texans' 32. Trent Green threw a 15-yard touchdown pass to Eddie Kennison three plays later. Following a three-and-out, the Texans punted and Dante Hall returned the punt 73 yards for a touchdown and a 28-7 lead with 1:50 left in the third quarter. It was Hall's fifth kick/punt return for a touchdown in his last eight games. Derrick Blaylock's 20-yard touchdown run on the Chiefs' next possession and Shaunard Harts' 39-yard interception return for a touchdown capped a 28-point scoring spree in 11 minutes, 14 seconds. Green was 16 of 28 for 262 yards and 1 touchdown, with 2 interceptions. David Carr was 17 of 27 for 167 yards and 1 touchdown, with 2 interceptions, and Tony Banks was 7 of 11 for 51 yards and 1 touchdown. Rookie Andre Johnson had 7 receptions for 102 yards and 2 touchdowns.

Kansas City	7	7	14	14	— 42
Houston	0	7	0	7	— 14

KC — Holmes 6 run (Andersen kick)
Hous — A. Johnson 43 pass from Carr (Brown kick)
KC — Holmes 5 run (Andersen kick)
KC — Kennison 15 pass from Green (Andersen kick)
KC — Hall 73 punt return (Andersen kick)
KC — Blaylock 20 run (Andersen kick)
KC — Harts 39 interception return (Andersen kick)
Hous — A. Johnson 4 pass from Banks (Brown kick)

INDIANAPOLIS 23, JACKSONVILLE 13—at RCA Dome, attendance 55,770. Reggie Wayne had 10 receptions for 141 yards and 2 touchdowns as the Colts rallied to defeat the Jaguars. The Jaguars drove into Colts' territory on all four first-half possessions, but Seth Marler made just 1 of 3 field-goal attempts, and the Jaguars led 3-0. The Colts scored on 5 of their first 6 possessions of the second half, with Wayne's touchdown catches capping the first two drives, as the Colts scored 20 consecutive points. Peyton Manning was 21 of 33 for 216 yards and 2 touchdowns, with 1 interception. Mark Brunell was 12 of 23 for 90 yards, and Byron Leftwich entered for the final drive and was 4 of 5 for 32 yards and 1 touchdown.

Jacksonville	0	3	0	10	— 13
Indianapolis	0	0	17	6	— 23

Jax — FG Marler 49
Ind — Wayne 28 pass from Manning (Vanderjagt kick)
Ind — Wayne 4 pass from Manning (Vanderjagt kick)
Ind — FG Vanderjagt 46
Ind — FG Vanderjagt 36
Jax — FG Marler 37
Ind — FG Vanderjagt 29
Jax — Hatchette 8 pass from Leftwich (Marler kick)

NEW ENGLAND 23, N.Y. JETS 16—at Gillette Stadium, attendance 68,436. Asante Samuel returned an interception for a touchdown as the Patriots held off the Jets. The Jets trailed 6-3 early in the second quarter when Herman Edwards eschewed a 26-yard field-goal attempt and instead attempted a pass by holder Dan Stryzinski. But the punter's pass was dropped by center Kevin Mawae. In the third quarter, Chester McGlockton forced Tom Brady to fumble, and James Reed recovered to set up Doug Brien's third field goal to tie the game 9-9. The Patriots responded with a 7-play, 73-yard drive and took a 16-9 lead on Brady's 1-yard scramble. Five plays later, Samuel intercepted Vinny Testaverde's pass and raced untouched 55 yards for a touchdown and 23-9 lead. Testaverde's 29-yard touchdown pass to Wayne Chrebet four plays later trimmed the deficit to 23-16 with 12:53 remaining. On the Jets' next possession, Brien missed a 42-yard field-goal attempt, and the Jets failed to cross midfield on their final possession. Brady was 15 of 25 for 181 yards. Testaverde was 25 of 43 for 264 yards and 1 touchdown, with 1 interception.

N.Y. Jets	3	3	3	7	— 16
New England	3	3	10	7	— 23

NYJ — FG Brien 41
NE — FG Vinatieri 24
NE — FG Vinatieri 22
NYJ — FG Brien 39
NE — FG Vinatieri 47
NYJ — FG Brien 30
NE — Brady 1 run (Vinatieri kick)
NE — Samuel 55 interception return (Vinatieri kick)
NYJ — Chrebet 29 pass from Testaverde (Brien kick)

BALTIMORE 24, SAN DIEGO 10—at Qualcomm Stadium, attendance 52,028. Jamal Lewis rushed for 132 yards and 1 touchdown as the Ravens won on the road in San Diego. Lewis fumbled in the first quarter, but Alan Ricard picked up the bouncing ball and raced 50 yards for a Ravens touchdown. Steve Christie missed a 50-yard field goal with 46 seconds left in the half, and Matt Stover answered with a 49-yard field goal as the half expired for a 10-3 lead. Kyle Boller's 25-yard touchdown pass to Todd Heap with 3:00 left in the third quarter increased the lead to 17-3, and Terrell Suggs' interception three plays later led to Lewis' touchdown and a 24-3 lead. The Chargers cut the deficit to 24-10, and had two scoring chances late in the game, but Ed Reed and Gary Baxter each quashed drives with interceptions deep in Ravens' territory. Boller was 12 of 21 for 98 yards and 1 touchdown, with 1 interception. Lewis rushed for 132 yards and 1 touchdown. Drew Brees was 28 of 45 for 270 yards, with 3 interceptions. LaDainian Tomlinson rushed 23 times for 105 yards and 1 touchdown.

Baltimore	7	3	14	0	— 24
San Diego	3	0	0	7	— 10

SD — FG Christie 24
Balt — Ricard 50 fumble recovery (Stover kick)
Balt — FG Stover 49
Balt — Heap 25 pass from Boller (Stover kick)
Balt — J. Lewis 7 run (Stover kick)
SD — Tomlinson 2 run (Christie kick)

CLEVELAND 13, SAN FRANCISCO 12—at 3Com Park, attendance 67,412. Kelly Holcomb completed 2 fourth-quarter touchdown passes to Andre' Davis as the Browns rallied to stun the 49ers. The Browns stuffed Fred Beasley on fourth-and-1 in the first quarter, but the 49ers drove inside the Browns' 30 four more times and Owen Pochman, just signed during the week, made all 4 field-goal attempts for a 12-0 lead. The Browns drove 75 yards, aided by a roughing-the-passer penalty and a 21-yard pass interference penalty, and cut the deficit to 12-7 on Holcomb's 2-yard pass to Davis with 10:42 left. Later in the quarter, the Browns put together a 17-play, 91-yard drive, with 5 third-down conversions, capped by Davis' 11-yard touchdown catch on third-and-10 with 29 seconds remaining. Anthony Henry's interception near midfield clinched the victory. Holcomb was 25 of 38 for 222 yards and 2 touchdowns, with 1 interception. Jeff Garcia was 21 of 35 for 198 yards, with 1 interception.

Cleveland	0	0	0	13	— 13
San Francisco	0	6	3	3	— 12

SF — FG Pochman 38
SF — FG Pochman 44
SF — FG Pochman 46
SF — FG Pochman 36
Cle — Andre' Davis 2 pass from Holcomb (Dawson kick)
Cle — Andre' Davis 11 pass from Holcomb (pass failed)

SEATTLE 24, ST. LOUIS 23—at Seahawks Stadium, attendance 65,841. Matt Hasselbeck passed for 2 fourth-quarter touchdown passes as the Seahawks rallied to defeat the Rams and take control of the NFC West. The Rams' defense stopped Seattle on its opening possession and forced them to punt, but Arlen Harris fumbled at the 4-yard-line and Orlando Huff recovered in the end zone for a Seahawks touchdown. Tommy Polley's interception later in the quarter set up Marc Bulger's 3-yard run, and St. Louis scored on its next two possessions for a 17-7 lead. Jeff Wilkins kicked field goals on the Rams' first two possessions of the second half for a 23-10 lead. Hasselbeck's 15-yard touchdown pass to Darrell Jackson cut the deficit to 23-17, but Josh Brown missed a 35-yard field-goal attempt and the Seahawks were stopped on downs at their 41 with 4:12 remaining. Anthony Simmons gave the Seahawks one more chance as he intercepted Bulger's pass at the Seahawks' 26 with 3:15 left, and Seattle went on a 10-play, 74-yard drive, capped by Koren Robinson's 3-yard touchdown catch with 1:00 left, for a 24-23 lead. The Rams failed to gain a first down on their final possession. Hasselbeck was 22 of 39 for 256 yards and 2 touchdowns, with 1 interception. Shaun Alexander had 14 carries for 58 yards despite missing the Seahawks' first three possessions to be at the hospital with his wife for the birth of their child. Bulger was 21 of 34 for 226 yards, with 2 interceptions. Marshall Faulk had 15 carries for 31 yards before leaving the game with a broken hand.

St. Louis	7	10	6	0	— 23
Seattle	7	3	0	14	— 24

Sea — Huff fumble recovery in end zone (Brown kick)
StL — Bulger 3 run (Wilkins kick)
StL — Bruce 7 pass from Bulger (Wilkins kick)
StL — FG Wilkins 28
Sea — FG Brown 36
StL — FG Wilkins 33
StL — FG Wilkins 33
Sea — Jackson 15 pass from Hasselbeck (Brown kick)
Sea — Robinson 3 pass from Hasselbeck (Brown kick)

TENNESSEE 27, NEW ORLEANS 12—at The Coliseum, attendance 68,809. Steve McNair passed for 2 touchdowns as Tennessee defeated the Saints. The Titans' defense throttled Deuce McAllister, limiting him to 8 yards on 11 carries, and Tennessee had advantages in first downs (28-11), yards (385-188), and time of possession (39:11-20:49). The Titans led 3-0 when Justin McCareins fumbled during a punt return. Tony Beckham retrieved the ball in the end zone, but as he was about to get tackled, he was penalized for tossing a forward lateral, giving the Saints a safety and 2 points. But the Saints muffed the ensuing free kick and Tyrone Calico recovered. McNair completed a 2-yard touchdown pass to McCareins seven plays later for a 10-2 lead. Donte' Stallworth fumbled on the second play of the second half, and Peter Sirmon recovered to set up McNair's 5-yard touchdown pass to Drew Bennett to give the Titans a 20-5 lead early in the third quarter. The Saints pulled within 20-12 early in the fourth quarter, but the Titans responded with a 14-play, 76-yard drive that consumed more than seven minutes and was culminated by Eddie George's 6-yard scoring run with 6:13 remaining to finish the scoring. McNair was 22 of 33 for 252 yards and 2 touchdowns. Bennett had 8 receptions for 105 yards and 1 touchdown. George had 29 carries for 100 yards and 1 score. Aaron Brooks was 15 of 23 for 185 yards and 1 touchdown.

New Orleans	2	3	0	7 —	12
Tennessee	10	3	7	7 —	27

Tenn — FG Anderson 22
NO — Safety, penalty for illegal forward pass by Beckham in end zone
Tenn — McCareins 2 pass from McNair (Anderson kick)
Tenn — FG Anderson 43
NO — FG Carney 31
Tenn — Bennett 5 pass from McNair (Anderson kick)
NO — Pathon 10 pass from Brooks (Carney kick)
Tenn — George 6 run (Anderson kick)

N.Y. GIANTS 24, WASHINGTON 21 (OT)—at FedExField, attendance 84,856. Matt Bryant kicked a 29-yard field goal in overtime as the Giants withstood a late rally by the Redskins. The Giants scored touchdowns on 3 of their 5 first-half possessions, capped by Kerry Collins' 5-yard scoring pass to Ike Hilliard with 19 seconds left in the half, for a 21-3 lead. The Giants led 21-10, but Bryant missed a 37-yard field goal with 4:10 remaining. Patrick Ramsey engineered a 9-play, 73-yard drive and cut the deficit to three points on his 6-yard touchdown pass to Rod Gardner and 2-point conversion completion to Darnerien McCants with 2:27 left. The Redskins' defense forced a three-and-out, and Ramsey connected on a 32-yard pass to McCants to set up John Hall's game-tying 33-yard field goal with 13 seconds left. In overtime, Collins completed a 27-yard pass to Jim Finn to set up Bryant's game-winning kick. Collins was 24 of 39 for 276 yards and 3 touchdowns. Tiki Barber had 28 carries for 126 yards. Ramsey was 23 of 45 for 348 yards and 2 touchdowns, with 1 interception. Laveranues Coles had 7 receptions for 105 yards.

N.Y. Giants	7	14	0	0	3 —	24
Washington	3	0	7	11	0 —	21

Wash — FG Hall 42
NYG — Hilliard 5 pass from Collins (Bryant kick)
NYG — Toomer 54 pass from Collins (Bryant kick)
NYG — Hilliard 5 pass from Collins (Bryant kick)
Wash — McCants 4 pass from Ramsey (Hall kick)
Wash — Gardner 6 pass from Ramsey (McCants pass from Ramsey)
Wash — FG Hall 33
NYG — FG Bryant 29

SUNDAY NIGHT, SEPTEMBER 21
MIAMI 17, BUFFALO 7—at Pro Player Stadium, attendance 73,458. Ricky Williams carried a club-record 42 times for 153 yards and the game-clinching touchdown as the Dolphins defeated the Bills. Miami's defense limited the Bills to just 118 total yards and 8 first downs, while the offense maintained possession for 40:50 of the game's 60 minutes. Buffalo twice drove into the red zone in the first half, but Travis Henry and Drew Bledsoe each threw an interception to thwart the drives. Chris Chambers' 12-yard touchdown catch with 25 seconds left in the half capped a 76-yard drive to give Miami a 7-0 lead. The Dolphins forced a punt to begin the second half, and the offense held the ball for more than seven minutes and drove 85 yards to Olindo Mare's field goal. Nate Clements intercepted a pass from Jay Fiedler and returned it 54 yards for a touchdown with 13:51 remaining to cut the deficit to 10-7, and Mare missed a 44-yard field goal with 6:43 left to give the Bills a chance, but Buffalo once again went three-and-out, and Williams carried on all eight plays of the ensuing drive, capped by his 1-yard touchdown run with 1:52 left, to clinch the victory. Fiedler was 16 of 28 for 154 yards and 1 touchdown, with 2 interceptions. Bledsoe was 10 of 25 for 98 yards, with 2 interceptions.

Buffalo	0	0	0	7 —	7
Miami	0	7	3	7 —	17

Mia — Chambers 12 pass from Fiedler (Mare kick)
Mia — FG Mare 26
Buff — Clements 54 interception return (Lindell kick)
Mia — Williams 1 run (Mare kick)

MONDAY NIGHT, SEPTEMBER 22
DENVER 31, OAKLAND 10—at INVESCO Field at Mile High, attendance 76,753. Jake Plummer passed for 2 touchdowns and ran for another, all in the first quarter, as the Broncos took a 31-0 lead en route to improving their perfect record. The Broncos had distinct advantages in first downs (20-11) and total yards (383-195), including a 257-74 edge in yards in the first half as the Broncos took a 24-0 lead. The Broncos scored on their first three possessions, capped by Plummer's 6-yard bootleg. The Raiders were forced to punt on all six of their first-half possessions. Denver scored on its initial drive of the second half, a 1-yard run by Mike Anderson, to take a 31-0 lead with 12:11 left in the third quarter. The Raiders trimmed the deficit to 31-10, and O.J. Santiago blocked Micah Knorr's punt early in the fourth quarter to give Oakland the ball at the Broncos' 10. But Lenny Walls tipped away Rich Gannon's fourth-down pass in the end zone to maintain the lead. Plummer was 14 of 21 for 197 yards and 2 touchdowns. Ashley Lelie had 3 receptions for 108 yards. Gannon was 14 of 29 for 149 yards.

Oakland	0	0	7	3 —	10
Denver	21	3	7	0 —	31

Den — Sharpe 18 pass from Plummer (Elam kick)
Den — Lelie 44 pass from Plummer (Elam kick)
Den — Plummer 6 run (Elam kick)
Den — FG Elam 20
Den — Anderson 1 run (Elam kick)
Oak — Crockett 4 run (Janikowski kick)
Oak — FG Janikowski 41

FOURTH WEEK SUMMARIES
American Football Conference

East Division	**W**	**L**	**T**	**Pct.**	**Pts.**	**OP**
Miami	2	1	0	.667	58	38
Buffalo	2	2	0	.500	89	57
New England	2	2	0	.500	71	77
N.Y. Jets	0	4	0	.000	45	77
North Division	**W**	**L**	**T**	**Pct.**	**Pts.**	**OP**
Baltimore	2	2	0	.500	82	74
Pittsburgh	2	2	0	.500	84	96
Cincinnati	1	3	0	.250	61	84
Cleveland	1	3	0	.250	46	75
South Division	**W**	**L**	**T**	**Pct.**	**Pts.**	**OP**
Indianapolis	4	0	0	1.000	120	47
Tennessee	3	1	0	.750	89	78
Houston	2	2	0	.500	69	113
Jacksonville	0	4	0	.000	73	109
West Division	**W**	**L**	**T**	**Pct.**	**Pts.**	**OP**
Denver	4	0	0	1.000	118	49
Kansas City	4	0	0	1.000	127	58
Oakland	2	2	0	.500	87	107
San Diego	0	4	0	.000	68	122

National Football Conference

East Division	**W**	**L**	**T**	**Pct.**	**Pts.**	**OP**
Washington	3	1	0	.750	90	85
Dallas	2	1	0	.667	65	65
N.Y. Giants	2	1	0	.667	79	69
Philadelphia	1	2	0	.333	33	61
North Division	**W**	**L**	**T**	**Pct.**	**Pts.**	**OP**
Minnesota	4	0	0	1.000	112	58
Green Bay	2	2	0	.500	107	79
Detroit	1	3	0	.250	77	98
Chicago	0	3	0	.000	43	111
South Division	**W**	**L**	**T**	**Pct.**	**Pts.**	**OP**
Carolina	3	0	0	1.000	59	35
Tampa Bay	2	1	0	.667	57	22
Atlanta	1	3	0	.250	71	100
New Orleans	1	3	0	.250	74	119
West Division	**W**	**L**	**T**	**Pct.**	**Pts.**	**OP**
Seattle	3	0	0	1.000	89	33
St. Louis	2	2	0	.500	100	84
Arizona	1	3	0	.250	57	130
San Francisco	1	3	0	.250	92	82

SUNDAY, SEPTEMBER 28
KANSAS CITY 17, BALTIMORE 10—at M&T Bank Stadium, attendance 69,459. Dante Hall set an NFL record by becoming the first player to return a kick for a touchdown in three consecutive games, helping the Chiefs to remain undefeated. Early in the fourth quarter, the Ravens drove into Chiefs' territory, but Dexter McCleon stopped the drive with an interception in the end zone. After forcing a punt, the Ravens marched into the red zone and tied the game with Jamal Lewis' 1-yard touchdown run with 5:27 remaining. Hall returned the ensuing kickoff just 12 yards, to the Chiefs' 17, but Adalius Thomas was offside for the Ravens. Baltimore kicked off again, and Hall scooted 97 yards for the go-ahead touchdown with 5:08 left. Ed Reed muffed a punt for the Ravens with 2:21 left, and McCleon posted his second interception of the quarter with 29 seconds remaining to clinch the victory. Trent Green was 17 of 28 for 159 yards and 1 touchdown. Kyle Boller was 15 of 26 for 140 yards, with 3 interceptions. Lewis rushed 26 times for 115 yards.

Kansas City	0	3	7	7 —	17
Baltimore	0	0	3	7 —	10

KC — FG Andersen 46
Balt — FG Stover 29
KC — Gonzalez 1 pass from Green (Andersen kick)
Balt — J. Lewis 1 run (Stover kick)
KC — Hall 97 kickoff return (Andersen kick)

PHILADELPHIA 23, BUFFALO 13—at Ralph Wilson Stadium, attendance 73,305. Brian Westbrook capped the scoring with a 62-yard touchdown run with 2:10 remaining as the Eagles posted their first victory. The Eagles converted 9 of 16 third-down situations to help propel themselves to a 16-0 lead after three quarters. The Eagles' defense did not allow the Bills to penetrate their 30-yard line until the final quarter, when Drew Bledsoe engineered an 11-play, 67-yard drive capped by his 3-yard scoring pass to Bobby Shaw with 9:12 left, but Bledsoe's 2-point conversion pass fell incomplete. After forcing a punt, the Bills drove 69 yards and scored on Bledsoe's 1-yard sneak on fourth-and-goal with 2:40 left to cut the deficit to 16-13. On second-and-9 with 2:19 left, Westbrook took a handoff and raced 62 yards for the game-clinching touchdown. Donovan McNabb was 18 of 29 for 172 yards. Bledsoe was 27 of 43 for 296 yards and 1 touchdowns. Eric Moulds had 8 receptions for 114 yards.

Philadelphia	10	3	3	7	— 23
Buffalo	0	0	0	13	— 13

Phil — Buckhalter 2 run (Akers kick)
Phil — FG Akers 26
Phil — FG Akers 34
Phil — FG Akers 22
Buff — Shaw 3 pass from Bledsoe (pass failed)
Buff — Bledsoe 1 run (Lindell kick)
Phil — Westbrook 62 run (Akers kick)

CAROLINA 23, ATLANTA 3—at Ericsson Stadium, attendance 23,127. Stephen Davis rushed for 153 yards, becoming the first running back in franchise history with 3 consecutive 100-yard games to start a season, and scored a touchdown for the undefeated Panthers. Carolina's defense forced the Falcons to punt on all five of their first-half possessions, and John Kasay's 53-yard field goal with 21 seconds left in the half staked the Panthers to a 17-0 lead. Atlanta's lone drive into the red zone produced their only points, a 28-yard field goal by Jay Feely with 3:46 left. Jake Delhomme passed for 168 yards and 1 touchdown. Doug Johnson was 14 of 23 for 152 yards, with 1 interception.

Atlanta	0	0	0	3	— 3
Carolina	7	10	0	6	— 23

Car — Davis 1 run (Kasay kick)
Car — Proehl 5 pass from Delhomme (Kasay kick)
Car — FG Kasay 53
Car — FG Kasay 23
Atl — FG Feely 28
Car — FG Kasay 38

CINCINNATI 21, CLEVELAND 14—at Cleveland Browns Stadium, attendance 73,428. Jon Kitna passed for 3 touchdowns, including 2 to Chad Johnson, as the Bengals won their first game under the tutelage of Marvin Lewis. The Browns scored 54 seconds into the game on Quincy Morgan's 71-yard touchdown catch from Tim Couch, who was starting his first game of the season. The Bengals did not flinch, responding with a 14-play, 76-yard touchdown drive to tie the game. Trailing 14-7 just before halftime, the Bengals drove 80 yards in four plays, with Kitna's 55-yard touchdown pass to Chad Johnson tying the game. Cincinnati opened the second half with the ball and moved 80 yards in 10 plays, with Reggie Kelly's 1-yard touchdown grab giving the Bengals a 21-14 lead. The Browns twice drove into Bengals' territory in the fourth quarter, but Couch's fourth-and-4 pass from the 28 fell incomplete with 14:06 left, and Jeff Burris iced the game with an interception at the Bengals' 28 with 51 seconds remaining. Kitna was 23 of 31 for 215 yards and 3 touchdowns. Couch was 23 of 36 for 280 yards and 2 touchdowns, with 1 interception.

Cincinnati	7	7	7	0	— 21
Cleveland	7	7	0	0	— 14

Cle — Morgan 71 pass from Couch (Dawson kick)
Cin — C. Johnson 3 pass from Kitna (Graham kick)
Cle — White 4 pass from Couch (Dawson kick)
Cin — C. Johnson 55 pass from Kitna (Graham kick)
Cin — Kelly 1 pass from Kitna (Graham kick)

DENVER 20, DETROIT 16—at INVESCO Field at Mile High, attendance 75,719. Jake Plummer passed for 2 touchdowns as the Broncos held off the Lions. Rookie Charles Rogers caught a 33-yard touchdown pass from Joey Harrington midway through the first quarter, but the Broncos answered with two consecutive touchdown drives, of 80 and 56 yards, both capped by Plummer scoring tosses, to give Denver a 14-7 lead. Detriot's defense toughened, and the Broncos led just 17-10 in the fourth quarter when the Lions engineered a 70-yard drive that culminated with Scotty Anderson's 43-yard touchdown catch with 13:36 remaining. However, Bradford Banta's snap on the extra point was low, and by the time holder John Jett got the ball down, kicker Jason Hanson pushed the kick, allowing Denver to maintain a 17-16 lead. Jason Elam kicked a 41-yard field goal with 3:13 left, and Detroit failed to cross midfield on its final possession. Plummer was 25 of 34 for 277 yards and 2 touchdowns. Harrington was 15 of 33 for 149 yards and 2 touchdowns.

Detroit	7	3	0	6	— 16
Denver	7	7	3	3	— 20

Det — Rogers 33 pass from Harrington (Hanson kick)
Den — Lelie 29 pass from Plummer (Elam kick)
Den — Sharpe 1 pass from Plummer (Elam kick)
Det — FG Hanson 53
Den — FG Elam 37
Det — Anderson 43 pass from Harrington (kick failed)
Den — FG Elam 41

HOUSTON 24, JACKSONVILLE 20—at Reliant Stadium, attendance 70,041. David Carr scored on a 1-yard quarterback sneak with no time remaining as the Texans defeated Jacksonville. Byron Leftwich guided the Jaguars to a field goal on the opening possession of his first start, which included a 14-yard pass to Jimmy Redmond on fourth-and-10, but Houston drove for touchdowns between Seth Marler's field goal and the Texans jumped to a 14-3 lead. Leftwich's 84-yard touchdown pass to Troy Edwards early in the third quarter tied the game at 17-17. Kris Brown missed a 50-yard field goal and the Jaguars responded with Marler's 20-yard field goal for a 20-17 lead with 4:04 left in the third quarter. The Texans drove to the Jaguars' 21 in the fourth quarter and Stacey Mack attempted a halfback pass, but Jason Craft intercepted it for Houston's fourth turnover of the game with 4:24 left. Four plays later, the Texans forced the Jaguars' fifth turnover, as Matt Stevens recovered Leftwich's fumble at the Jaguars' 41. The Texans drove to the Jaguars' 2, and two pass interference penalties in the final 20 seconds placed the ball at the 1-yard line with two seconds left. Carr dove over the top of the line for the winning score. Carr was 23 of 36 for 234 yards and 1 touchdown, with 1 interception. Kenny Wright had 2 interceptions. Leftwich was 17 of 36 for 231 yards and 1 touchdown, with 3 interceptions. Edwards had 3 receptions for 111 yards.

Jacksonville	3	7	10	0	— 20
Houston	7	7	3	7	— 24

Hous — Mack 5 run (Brown kick)
Jax — FG Marler 29
Hous — Gaffney 24 pass from Carr (Brown kick)
Jax — Taylor 1 run (Marler kick)
Hous — FG Brown 48
Jax — Edwards 84 pass from Leftwich (Marler kick)
Jax — FG Marler 20
Hous — Carr 1 run (Brown kick)

MINNESOTA 35, SAN FRANCISCO 7—at Metrodome, attendance 64,111. Gus Frerotte, in his first start in place of injured Daunte Culpepper, passed for 4 touchdowns, including 3 to Randy Moss, as the Vikings rolled to another victory. The Vikings scored on four of their five first-half possessions, including two drives set up on interceptions by Corey Chavous and Brian Williams, to jump to a 28-0 halftime lead. The 49ers drove to the Vikings' 4 to open the second half, but Jeff Garcia's fourth-down pass fell incomplete, and Frerotte's 59-yard touchdown pass to Moss on the first play of the fourth quarter stretched the lead to 35-0. Frerotte was 16 of 21 for 267 yards and 4 touchdowns, and Moss had 8 receptions for 172 yards. Garcia was 11 of 23 for 108 yards, with 3 interceptions, and Tim Rattay was 12 of 18 for 146 yards and 1 touchdown.

San Francisco	0	0	0	7	— 7
Minnesota	14	14	0	7	— 35

Minn — Moss 15 pass from Frerotte (Elling kick)
Minn — Smith 5 run (Elling kick)
Minn — Moss 35 pass from Frerotte (Elling kick)
Minn — Burleson 22 pass from Frerotte (Elling kick)
Minn — Moss 59 pass from Frerotte (Elling kick)
SF — Streets 37 pass from Rattay (Pochman kick)

DALLAS 17, N.Y. JETS 6—at The Meadowlands, attendance 58,613. Troy Hambrick rushed for 127 yards and 1 touchdown as the Cowboys won their second consecutive game in East Rutherford. Coming off a come-from-behind win against the Giants in Week 2, and following the bye in Week 3, the Cowboys allowed a Doug Brien field goal on the Jets' opening drive. Second-quarter fumbles by Santana Moss and Curtis Martin led to Dallas touchdowns, the second of which, a 13-yard pass from Quincy Carter to Antonio Bryant, came with just 11 seconds left in the half, to give the Cowboys a 14-3 halftime lead. Sam Garnes' third-quarter interception led to Brien's second field goal, but Carter engineered an 11-play fourth-quarter drive capped by Billy Cundiff's 26-yard field goal with 4:56 remaining. Vinny Testaverde's fourth-and-3 pass to Wayne Chrebet netted just 2 yards, thanks to Patrick Hunter's tackle, with 2:29 remaining to clinch the victory. Carter was 11 of 23 for 165 yards and 1 touchdown, with 1 interception. Joey Galloway had 5 catches for 100 yards. Testaverde was 21 of 29 for 219 yards.

Dallas	0	14	0	3	— 17
N.Y. Jets	3	0	3	0	— 6

NYJ — FG Brien 34
Dall — Hambrick 31 run (Cundiff kick)
Dall — Bryant 13 pass from Carter (Cundiff kick)
NYJ — FG Brien 38
Dall — FG Cundiff 26

OAKLAND 34, SAN DIEGO 31 (OT)—at Network Associates Coliseum, attendance 54,078. Sebastian Janikowski booted a 46-yard field goal with 5:01 left in overtime to give the Raiders a comeback victory. LaDainian Tomlinson's 55-yard touchdown run broke a 14-14 tie and gave the Chargers the lead with 6:44 left in the first half, and Lorenzo Neal's 3-yard plunge with 5:59 left in the game extended the lead to 31-17. Rich Gannon, on three successive plays, completed passes of 16 yards to Jerry Rice, 18 yards to Doug Jolley, and 36 yards for a touchdown to Alvis Whitted, to cut the deficit to 31-24 with 4:38 left. The Raiders forced a three-and-out, and Charlie Garner tied the game with a 24-yard run five plays later with 1:24 remaining. In overtime, each team had the ball twice, and on its second possession, Oakland drove from its own 8, on the strength of a 29-yard pass to Rice, to set up Janikowski's winning kick. Gannon was 26 of 43 for 348 yards and 3 touchdowns, with 1 interception. Rice had 7 catches for 118 yards and Tim Brown added 6 receptions for 110 yards. Drew Brees was 21 of 31 for 187 yards and 1 touchdown, with 1 interception. Tomlinson had 28 carries for 187 yards, and completed a 21-yard scoring pass to Brees.

San Diego	7	14	3	7	0	— 31
Oakland	7	7	0	17	3	— 34

Oak — Brown 36 pass from Gannon (Janikowski kick)
SD — Brees 21 pass from Tomlinson (Christie kick)
SD — Peelle 7 pass from Brees (Christie kick)
Oak — Jolley 2 pass from Gannon (Janikowski kick)
SD — Tomlinson 55 run (Christie kick)
SD — FG Christie 32
Oak — FG Janikowski 23
SD — Neal 3 run (Christie kick)
Oak — Whitted 36 pass from Gannon (Janikowski kick)
Oak — Garner 24 run (Janikowski kick)
Oak — FG Janikowski 46

TENNESSEE 30, PITTSBURGH 13—at Heinz Field, attendance 63,244. Steve McNair completed 15 of 16 passes for 161 yards and 3 touchdowns as the Titans handled the Steelers. Pittsburgh completely dominated the stats, with more first downs (25-9), yards (376-198), and time of possession (35:50-24:10), but the Titans scored 14 points off 2 turnovers, and added a safety. The Steelers scored on their first two possessions for a 10-0 lead, and forced another Titans punt. However, Rocky Boiman sacked Tommy Maddox for a safety. Three plays later, McNair hit Drew Bennett with a 10-yard scoring pass, set up by the pair's 42-yard connection two plays earlier, to cut the deficit to 10-9. Pittsburgh responded with a field goal, and the defense forced another punt, but Samari Rolle intercepted Maddox's pass near midfield and returned it to the 1-yard line to set up McNair's short toss to Erron Kinney with 26 seconds left in the half for a 16-13 lead. Jeff Reed missed a potential game-tying 30-yard field goal in the third quarter, and McNair responded with an 80-yard drive, capped by Justin McCareins' 29-yard grab, for a 23-13 lead. Boiman iced the victory with a 60-yard interception return with 12:46 left. McNair was 15 of 16 for 161 yards and 3 touchdowns. Maddox was 31 of 47 for 332 yards, with 2 interceptions.

Tennessee	0	16	7	7	— 30
Pittsburgh	3	10	0	0	— 13

Pitt — FG Reed 26
Pitt — Zereoue 5 run (Reed kick)
Tenn — Safety, Maddox sacked by Boiman in end zone
Tenn — Bennett 10 pass from McNair (Anderson kick)
Pitt — FG Reed 23
Tenn — Kinney 1 pass from McNair (Anderson kick)
Tenn — McCareins 29 pass from McNair (Anderson kick)
Tenn — Boiman 60 interception return (Anderson kick)

ST. LOUIS 37, ARIZONA 13—at Edward Jones Dome, attendance 65,758. Marc Bulger passed for 2 touchdowns and the Rams' defense allowed just 7 first downs and 161 yards to defeat the Cardinals. The Rams offense tallied 34 first downs and 401 total yards and maintained possession for 42:27. Emmitt Smith scored his first touchdown for the Cardinals on a 1-yard run with 36 seconds left in the half, and Dexter Jackson intercepted a pass at the Cardinals' 5. But Arlen Harris forced Jackson to fumble during his interception return, and Dave Wohlabaugh recovered at the Cardinals' 35 with three seconds left. Jeff Wilkins made a 53-yard field goal, and capped a 13-play drive to begin the second half with a field goal for a 23-7 lead. Josh Scobey returned the ensuing kickoff 100 yards for a touchdown, and the Cardinals had the ball near midfield early in the fourth quarter, but Leonard Little forced Jeff Blake to fumble and Brian Young recovered. Four plays later, Bulger hit Torry Holt with a 7-yard touchdown to help the Rams pull away. Bulger was 28 of 42 for 272 yards and 2 touchdowns, with 1 interception. Holt had 12 catches for 133 yards. Blake was 10 of 17 for 88 yards, and Josh McCown was 3 of 4 for 47 yards.

Arizona	0	7	6	0	— 13
St. Louis	14	6	3	14	— 37

StL — Gordon 3 run (Wilkins kick)
StL — Looker 6 pass from Bulger (Wilkins kick)
StL — FG Wilkins 24
Ariz — Smith 1 run (Gramatica kick)
StL — FG Wilkins 53
StL — FG Wilkins 31
Ariz — Scobey 100 kickoff return (pass failed)
StL — Holt 7 pass from Bulger (Wilkins kick)
StL — Bulger 2 run (Wilkins kick)

WASHINGTON 20, NEW ENGLAND 17—at FedExField, attendance 83,632. The Redskins' defense forced 4 turnovers as Washington held off a late rally to defeat the Patriots. The Redskins intercepted two passes in their own territory in the first half en route to a 6-3 halftime lead. Kevin Faulk fumbled on the third play of the second half, and Matt Bowen returned the ball to the 1-yard line to set up Ladell Betts' touchdown run. Adam Vinatieri missed a 46-yard field goal on New England's ensuing possession, and the Redskins responded with a 64-yard drive, which featured a 20-yard run by Trung Canidate and a fumble which Rod Gardner recovered 26 yards upfield, capped by Rock Cartwright's 3-yard run for a 20-3 lead. Tom Brady completed 2 touchdown passes, the second to Larry Centers with 2:10 remaining, and the Patriots got the ball back at the Redskins' 45 trailing by three points with 1:39 left, but Brady's fourth-and-3 pass fell incomplete. Patrick Ramsey was 10 of 22 for 147 yards. Brady was 25 of 38 for 289 yards and 2 touchdowns, with 3 interceptions.

New England	3	0	7	7	— 17
Washington	3	3	14	0	— 20

Wash — FG Hall 38
NE — FG Vinatieri 23
Wash — FG Hall 29
Wash — Betts 1 run (Hall kick)
Wash — Cartwright 3 run (Hall kick)
NE — Givens 29 pass from Brady (Vinatieri kick)
NE — Centers 7 pass from Brady (Vinatieri kick)

SUNDAY NIGHT, SEPTEMBER 28

INDIANAPOLIS 55, NEW ORLEANS 21—at Louisiana Superdome, attendance 70,020. Peyton Manning passed for a club-record 6 touchdowns as the Colts defeated the Saints. Jim Nelson intercepted Aaron Brooks' pass on the game's second play, and three plays later Manning fired a 17-yard touchdown pass to Ricky Williams for a 7-0 lead. Two touchdown passes to Marvin Harrison extended the lead to 21-0, but Brooks engineered an 8-play, 71-yard drive, capped by Deuce McAllister's 1-yard scoring run with 42 seconds left in the half to cut the deficit to 24-10 at halftime. Mike Vanderjagt's 42-yard field goal began the scoring in the third quarter. Marcus Washington forced Brooks to fumble on the next play and Washington recovered. Two plays later, Manning's fourth touchdown pass was caught by Dominic Rhodes. After a Saints field goal, Manning connected with Harrison for the third time. Two plays later, Nelson recorded his second interception, and Manning completed his club-record sixth touchdown pass, to Dallas Clark, as the third quarter ended for a 48-13 lead. Three plays later, Dwight Freeney sacked Brooks, forced him to fumble, and recovered the ball and returned it 19 yards for the Colts' final points. Indianapolis scored 28 points off the Saints' 4 turnovers, and scored their final 4 touchdowns in a 9:05 span. Manning was 20 of 25 for 314 yards and 6 touchdowns. Harrison had 6 receptions for 158 yards. Brooks was 16 of 28 for 166 yards, with 2 interceptions. McAllister had 17 carries for 101 yards.

Indianapolis	14	10	24	7	— 55
New Orleans	0	10	3	8	— 21

Ind — Williams 17 pass from Manning (Vanderjagt kick)
Ind — Harrison 14 pass from Manning (Vanderjagt kick)
Ind — Harrison 79 pass from Manning (Vanderjagt kick)
NO — FG Carney 38
Ind — FG Vanderjagt 41
NO — McAllister 1 run (Carney kick)
Ind — FG Vanderjagt 42
Ind — Rhodes 12 pass from Manning (Vanderjagt kick)
NO — FG Carney 43
Ind — Harrison 32 pass from Manning (Vanderjagt kick)
Ind — Clark 11 pass from Manning (Vanderjagt kick)
Ind — Freeney 19 fumble return (Vanderjagt kick)
NO — Pathon 11 pass from Bouman (Fenderson pass from Bouman)

MONDAY NIGHT, SEPTEMBER 29

GREEN BAY 38, CHICAGO 23—at Soldier Field, attendance 61,500. Brett Favre passed for 3 touchdowns, and Ahman Green rushed for 2 scores, as the Packers held off the Bears in the first game at the remodeled Soldier Field. Green's 60-yard touchdown run three minutes into the game began the scoring, and Marcus Wilkins' blocked punt later in the quarter set up Green's second touchdown as the Packers jumped to a 17-0 lead. Green Bay led 24-9 after three quarters, but Anthony Thomas got the Bears back into the game with a 67-yard scoring run with 12:36 left to pull within eight points. But the Packers drove 64 yards for a touchdown, highlighted by Green's 32-yard run on third-and-1, and then forced a punt and drove 54 yards for Favre's third touchdown pass, to Bubba Franks with 4:21 remaining, to quickly extend the lead to 38-16. Favre was 21 of 30 for 179 yards and 3 touchdowns, with 1 interception. Green rushed 19 times for 176 yards. Kordell Stewart was 25 of 44 for 201 yards, with 2 interceptions. Thomas rushed 13 times for 110 yards.

Green Bay	17	7	0	14	— 38
Chicago	0	6	3	14	— 23

GB — Green 60 run (Longwell kick)
GB — FG Longwell 34
GB — Green 6 run (Longwell kick)
Chi — FG Edinger 31
GB — Henderson 14 pass from Favre (Longwell kick)

Chi — FG Edinger 38
Chi — FG Edinger 41
Chi — Thomas 67 run (Edinger kick)
GB — Walker 9 pass from Favre (Longwell kick)
GB — Franks 1 pass from Favre (Longwell kick)
Chi — Stewart 1 run (Edinger kick)

FIFTH WEEK SUMMARIES
American Football Conference

East Division	**W**	**L**	**T**	**Pct.**	**Pts.**	**OP**
Miami	3	1	0	.750	81	48
Buffalo	3	2	0	.600	111	73
New England	3	2	0	.600	109	107
N.Y. Jets	0	4	0	.000	45	77
North Division	**W**	**L**	**T**	**Pct.**	**Pts.**	**OP**
Baltimore	2	2	0	.500	82	74
Cleveland	2	3	0	.400	79	88
Pittsburgh	2	3	0	.400	97	129
Cincinnati	1	4	0	.200	77	106
South Division	**W**	**L**	**T**	**Pct.**	**Pts.**	**OP**
Indianapolis	5	0	0	1.000	158	82
Tennessee	3	2	0	.600	119	116
Houston	2	2	0	.500	69	113
Jacksonville	1	4	0	.200	100	130
West Division	**W**	**L**	**T**	**Pct.**	**Pts.**	**OP**
Kansas City	5	0	0	1.000	151	81
Denver	4	1	0	.800	141	73
Oakland	2	3	0	.400	108	131
San Diego	0	5	0	.000	89	149

National Football Conference

East Division	**W**	**L**	**T**	**Pct.**	**Pts.**	**OP**
Dallas	3	1	0	.750	89	72
Washington	3	2	0	.600	115	112
N.Y. Giants	2	2	0	.500	89	92
Philadelphia	2	2	0	.500	60	86
North Division	**W**	**L**	**T**	**Pct.**	**Pts.**	**OP**
Minnesota	5	0	0	1.000	151	84
Green Bay	3	2	0	.600	142	92
Chicago	1	3	0	.250	67	132
Detroit	1	4	0	.200	94	122
South Division	**W**	**L**	**T**	**Pct.**	**Pts.**	**OP**
Carolina	4	0	0	1.000	78	48
Tampa Bay	2	2	0	.500	92	60
Atlanta	1	4	0	.200	97	139
New Orleans	1	4	0	.200	87	138
West Division	**W**	**L**	**T**	**Pct.**	**Pts.**	**OP**
Seattle	3	1	0	.750	102	68
St. Louis	2	2	0	.500	100	84
San Francisco	2	3	0	.400	116	99
Arizona	1	4	0	.200	64	154

SUNDAY, OCTOBER 5

MINNESOTA 39, ATLANTA 26—at Georgia Dome, attendance 70,427. Randy Moss caught 2 scoring passes and the Vikings scored 27 unanswered points in a less-than-20-minute stretch of the second half to remain undefeated. The Falcons outgained Minnesota 440-399, but the Vikings' defense forced 3 turnovers and 2 safeties. The Vikings scored three times in a five-minute, 29-second stretch of the second quarter to erase a 6-0 deficit and take a 12-6 lead. But Atlanta scored on its last two possessions of the half, capped by Doug Johnson's 6-yard touchdown pass to Peerless Price with 10 seconds remaining, for a 20-12 halftime lead. The Vikings' defense forced three consecutive punts to begin the second half, and the offense responded with touchdown drives of 45, 77, and 59 yards for a 34-20 lead with 13:05 to play. On Atlanta's next four possessions, the Vikings' defense forced 3 turnovers and their second safety of the game for a 39-20 lead with 2:52 left. Gus Frerotte was 14 of 24 for 239 yards and 2 touchdowns. Johnson was 28 of 40 for 352 yards and 2 touchdowns, with 2 interceptions. Price had 12 catches for 168 yards.

Minnesota	0	12	15	12	—	39
Atlanta	6	14	0	6	—	26

Atl — FG Feely 34
Atl — FG Feely 33
Minn — Moss 32 pass from Frerotte (Elling kick)
Minn — Safety, D. Johnson penalized for intentional grounding in end zone
Minn — FG Elling 32
Atl — Dunn 8 run (Feely kick)
Atl — Price 6 pass from D. Johnson (Feely kick)
Minn — Moss 17 pass from Frerotte (Smith pass from Frerotte)
Minn — M. Williams 11 run (Elling kick)
Minn — M. Williams 5 run (Elling kick)
Minn — Safety, Whitfield penalized for holding in end zone
Minn — FG Elling 24
Atl — Farris 8 pass from D. Johnson (pass failed)

BUFFALO 22, CINCINNATI 16 (OT)—at Ralph Wilson Stadium, attendance 72,615. Travis Henry scored 2 touchdowns, including the game-winning 2-yard run in overtime, as the Bills fought off the Bengals. The Bills tied the game 6-6 on Rian Lindell's 38-yard field goal to culminate the second half. Late in the third quarter, Aaron Schobel intercepted a pass at the Bengals' 35 to set up Drew Bledsoe's 9-yard touchdown pass to Henry for a 13-6 lead. The Bengals responded with a 13-play, 74-yard drive capped by Rudi Johnson's 16-yard scoring run with 9:14 left. After a punt and 30-yard return by Peter Warrick, Shayne Graham kicked a 30-yard field goal with 5:33 left to give Cincinnati a 16-13 lead. Buffalo answered with a 13-play drive of its own, highlighted by a 19-yard pass to Eric Moulds on fourth-and-3, and capped by Lindell's 29-yard field goal to tie the game with 28 seconds left. In overtime, the Bills forced a three-and-out and Nick Harris' 29-yard punt gave Buffalo the ball at their own 43. Bledsoe completed a 20-yard pass to Mark Campbell and 28-yard pass to Moulds to set up Henry's winning run 3:48 into overtime. Bledsoe was 19 of 35 for 211 yards and 1 touchdown. Jon Kitna was 26 of 44 for 225 yards, with 1 interception.

Cincinnati	0	6	0	10	0	—	16
Buffalo	3	0	10	3	6	—	22

Buff — FG Lindell 27
Cin — FG Graham 39
Cin — FG Graham 37
Buff — FG Lindell 38
Buff — Henry 9 pass from Bledsoe (Lindell kick)
Cin — Ru. Johnson 16 run (Graham kick)
Cin — FG Graham 30
Buff — FG Lindell 29
Buff — Henry 2 run (no attempt)

CAROLINA 19, NEW ORLEANS 13—at Ericsson Stadium, attendance 72,496. Stephen Davis rushed for 159 yards and 1 touchdown as the Panthers remained undefeated. Rod Smart's 100-yard kickoff return for a touchdown early in the second quarter and Davis' touchdown run to begin the second half gave Carolina a 16-3 lead. Aaron Brooks fired a 21-yard touchdown pass to Joe Horn on the ensuing drive to cut the deficit to 16-10. Carolina used an eight-minute drive to extend the lead to nine points on John Kasay's field goal, and after an exchange of punts, John Carney kicked a 26-yard field goal with 1:43 left. On third-and-3 with 1:29 remaining, Davis gained 4 yards to secure the victory. Jake Delhomme was 15 of 23 for 124 yards, and Stephen Davis rushed 30 times for 159 yards. Brooks was 16 of 31 for 189 yards, with 1 interception.

New Orleans	0	3	7	3	—	13
Carolina	3	7	6	3	—	19

Car — FG Kasay 49
NO — FG Carney 38
Car — Smart 100 kickoff return (Kasay kick)
Car — S. Davis 1 run (pass failed)
NO — Horn 21 pass from Brooks (Carney kick)
Car — FG Kasay 23
NO — FG Carney 26

CHICAGO 24, OAKLAND 18—at Soldier Field, attendance 61,500. Paul Edinger kicked a 48-yard field goal as time expired to cap an 18-point fourth-quarter by the Bears to post their first victory at remodeled Soldier Field. The Raiders scored on five of their first six possessions, including four drives into the red zone, but led just 18-3 because of 4 field goals and a missed extra point by Sebastian Janikowski. Alex Brown's interception in the third quarter set up Edinger's 50-yard field goal and sparked the comeback. Kordell Stewart fired a 14-yard touchdown pass to Marty Booker on the first play of the fourth quarter to cut the deficit to 18-13, and R.W. McQuarters' interception at the Bears' 12 stifled the Raiders and led to Stanley Pritchett's go-ahead touchdown run and Stewart's 2-point conversion for a three-point lead with 6:58 remaining. The Raiders answered with Janikowski's 49-yard field goal, which clanked off the left upright before gonig through, to tie the game with 3:30 left. With 15 seconds remaining, the Bears were on their own 40, but Dez White got open down the left sideline for 29 yards to set up Edinger's winning kick. Stewart was 13 of 24 for 160 yards and 1 touchdown, with 2 interceptions. Anthony Thomas rushed for 123 yards. Rich Gannon was 16 of 34 for 183 yards, with 2 interceptions.

Oakland	6	12	0	3	—	21
Chicago	0	3	3	18	—	24

Oak — Crockett 1 run (kick failed)
Chi — FG Edinger 35
Oak — FG Janikowski 36
Oak — FG Janikowski 39
Oak — FG Janikowski 32
Oak — FG Janikowski 33
Chi — FG Edinger 50
Chi — Booker 14 pass from Stewart (Edinger kick)
Chi — Pritchett 8 run (Stewart run)
Oak — FG Janikowski 49
Chi — FG Edinger 48

DALLAS 24, ARIZONA 7—at Texas Stadium, attendance 63,601. Quincy Carter passed for 277 yards and 2 touchdowns and the Cowboys' defense registered 2 safeties to defeat the Cardinals. The Cowboys had advantages in first downs (18-9), total yards (365-151), and time of possession (36:28-23:32). A flea-flicker produced a 51-yard touchdown pass from Carter to Terry Glenn to get Dallas on the board, but Josh Scobey returned the ensuing kickoff 63 yards and Jeff Blake hit Bryan Gilmore with a 24-yard scoring pass to tie the game. Arizona did not cross the Cowboys' 40 on any of its final nine possessions. Dallas led 20-7 in the third quarter when a punt pinned the Cardinals on their own 5-yard-line. Three plays later, La'Roi Glover sacked Blake in the end zone for a safety. Toby Gowin's next punt was downed by Pete Hunter at the Cardinals' 1, and after two rushing plays for no gain, Blake was sacked by Kenyon Coleman for another safety just 3:22 after the first one. Carter was 20 of 31 for 277 yards and 2 touchdowns, with 1 interception. Glenn had 4 catches for 104 yards. Blake was 14 of 28 for 121 yards and 1 touchdown, with 2 interceptions, and Emmitt Smith was limited to minus-1 yard on 6 carries before leaving with a fractured shoulder blade.

Arizona	7	0	0	0	— 7
Dallas	7	10	7	0	— 24

Dall — Glenn 51 pass from Carter (Cundiff kick)
Ariz — Gilmore 24 pass from Blake (Duncan kick)
Dall — Anderson 18 pass from Carter (Cundiff kick)
Dall — FG Cundiff 33
Dall — FG Cundiff 36
Dall — Safety, Blake sacked by Glover in end zone
Dall — Safety, Blake sacked by Coleman in end zone

GREEN BAY 35, SEATTLE 13—at Lambeau Field, attendance 70,365. Brett Favre passed for 2 touchdowns and Ahman Green rushed for 2 scores as the Packers knocked Seattle from the ranks of the unbeaten. The Packers and Seahawks each scored on their final three possessions of the first half, but the difference was Green Bay scored 3 touchdowns and Seattle settled for 2 field goals, albeit one was a 58-yard boot by rookie Josh Brown as the half expired to cut the lead to 21-13. The Packers added touchdowns on their initial two possessions of the second half as well, giving Green Bay five consecutive touchdown drives, with Darren Sharper's inteception setting up Favre's second scoring pass for a 35-13 lead with 39 seconds left in the third quarter. Favre was 19 of 25 for 185 yards and 2 touchdowns. Green rushed 27 times for 118 yards. Matt Hasselbeck was 23 of 39 for 225 yards, with 1 interception. Shaun Alexander rushed for 102 yards.

Seattle	7	6	0	0	— 13
Green Bay	7	14	14	0	— 35

GB — Driver 34 pass from Favre (Longwell kick)
Sea — Alexander 1 run (J. Brown kick)
GB — Green 1 run (Longwell kick)
Sea — FG J. Brown 27
GB — Green 3 run (Longwell kick)
Sea — FG J. Brown 58
GB — Fisher 11 run (Longwell kick)
GB — Henderson 2 pass from Favre (Longwell kick)

JACKSONVILLE 27, SAN DIEGO 21—at ALLTEL Stadium, attendance 48,954. Byron Leftwich passed for 336 yards and 2 touchdowns as the Jaguars won their first game under coach Jack Del Rio. The Jaguars led 10-7 in the third quarter when Tony Brackens forced Antonio Gates to fumble and Mike Peterson recovered at the Jaguars' 10. Leftwich engineered an 11-play, 90-yard drive, capped by Troy Edwards' touchdown catch. Following a Chargers punt, Seth Marler booted a 27-yard field goal to give Jacksonville a 20-7 lead with 2:38 left in the third quarter. Drew Brees lofted a 33-yard scoring pass to Eric Parker with 4:19 remaining in the game, but on third-and-7 with 2:00 left, Leftwich completed a screen pass to Fred Taylor, who raced 60 yards for a touchdown. David Boston caught a 13-yard touchdown with 20 seconds left, but Nick Sorensen recovered the onside kick to secure the victory. Leftwich was 19 of 28 for 336 yards and 2 touchdowns. Jimmy Smith, in his first game of the season, had 8 catches for 137 yards. Brees was 24 of 41 for 296 yards and 3 touchdowns. Boston had 14 receptions for 181 yards and 2 touchdowns.

San Diego	0	7	0	14	— 21
Jacksonville	7	3	10	7	— 27

Jax — Taylor 1 run (Marler kick)
SD — Boston 46 pass from Brees (Christie kick)
Jax — FG Marler 53
Jax — Edwards 18 pass from Leftwich (Marler kick)
Jax — FG Marler 27
SD — Parker 33 pass from Brees (Christie kick)
Jax — Taylor 60 pass from Leftwich (Marler kick)
SD — Boston 13 pass from Brees (Christie kick)

KANSAS CITY 24, DENVER 23—at Arrowhead Stadium, attendance 78,903. Dante Hall tied an NFL record with his fourth kick return touchdown of the season as the Chiefs remained undefeated. Hall's 93-yard touchdown return with 8:20 remaining not only tied an NFL record, it gave the Chiefs the lead and, dating back to last season, was his seventh return touchdown in the past 10 games. Wide receiver Rod Smith completed a 72-yard pass to Clinton Portis to set up Denver's first touchdown, but Deltha O'Neal's fumbled punt moments later set up Trent Green's touchdown pass to Tony Gonzalez to tie the score. O'Neal intercepted a pass and had a punt return for a touchdown nullified later in the half, but both plays set up Jason Elam field goals, as the Broncos took a 13-10 halftime lead. Portis' 65-yard touchdown run on the third play of the second half extended Denver's lead, but the Chiefs responded with a 77-yard scoring drive. Trailing 23-17 in the fourth quarter, Hall fielded a punt on his own 7, dodged a few Broncos, went to his right, then cut back to his left, veering toward his own goal line before turning the corner and scampering untouched for a 24-23 lead. Elam missed a 53-yard field-goal attempt on the ensuing possession and the Chiefs held on. The Broncos outgained the Chiefs 469-231, but Hall was the difference. Green was 15 of 28 for 128 yards and 2 touchdowns, with 1 interception. Jake Plummer was 20 of 38 for 221 yards and 1 touchdown. Portis had 23 carries for 141 yards and 1 touchdown.

Denver	7	6	7	3	— 23
Kansas City	7	3	7	7	— 24

Den — Carswell 6 pass from Plummer (Elam kick)
KC — Gonzalez 20 pass from Green (Andersen kick)
Den — FG Elam 48
KC — FG Andersen 23
Den — FG Elam 29
Den — Portis 65 run (Elam kick)
KC — Morton 28 pass from Green (Andersen kick)
Den — FG Elam 21
KC — Hall 93 punt return (Andersen kick)

NEW ENGLAND 38, TENNESSEE 30—at Gillette Stadium, attendance 68,436. Mike Cloud rushed for 2 touchdowns as the Patriots scored 31 second-half points to defeat the Titans. Tennessee drove inside the red zone five times, but managed just 2 touchdowns and 3 field goals. Troy Brown caught a 58-yard touchdown pass in the first half, and had an 89-yard punt return nullified by a penalty, as the Titans took a 13-7 halftime lead. Neither team could stop the other in the second half, as the Patriots scored 3 touchdowns and a field goal to take a 31-27 lead with 3:14 left. The Titans drove across midfield, but Ty Law stepped in front of Steve McNair's out-pattern pass and returned it untouched 65 yards for a 38-27 lead with 1:49 remaining. Gary Anderson's 41-yard field goal with 36 seconds left trimmed the deficit to within one possession, but Christian Fauria recovered the onside kick for the Patriots. Tom Brady was 17 of 31 for 219 yards and 1 touchdown. McNair was 23 of 45 for 391 yards, with 1 interception, and 2 touchdown runs.

Tennessee	6	7	3	14	— 30
New England	7	0	14	17	— 38

Tenn — FG Hentrich 48
Tenn — FG Anderson 43
NE — Brown 58 pass from Brady (Vinatieri kick)
Tenn — McNair 1 run (Anderson kick)
NE — A. Smith 1 run (Vinatieri kick)
Tenn — FG Anderson 33
NE — Cloud 1 run (Vinatieri kick)
Tenn — FG Anderson 37
NE — FG Vinatieri 48
Tenn — McNair 1 run (Calico pass from McNair)
NE — Cloud 15 run (Vinatieri kick)
NE — Law 65 interception return (Vinatieri kick)
Tenn — FG Anderson 41

MIAMI 23, N.Y. GIANTS 10—at Giants Stadium, attendance 78,863. James McKnight scored on a 68-yard reverse as the Dolphins won in New Jersey for the second time in four weeks. Michael Strahan's sack and Cournelius Griffin's fumble recovery at the Dolphins' 16 set up Tiki Barber's 1-yard touchdown run to give the Giants a 7-3 lead. Three plays later, McKnight raced 68 yards for a touchdown down the right sideline for a 10-7 Dolphins lead. Matt Bryant kicked a 43-yard field goal as the half expired to cut the deficit to 13-10, but injured his leg on the kick and left the game. Sixteen-year punter Jeff Feagles attempted his first career field-goal attempt in the third quarter, but his 29-yard kick sailed wide right. The Dolphins responded with a 6:30-drive for Olindo Mare's third field goal, and on their next possession maintained control for almost seven minutes, and capped the scoring with Ricky Williams' 1-yard run with 4:16 left. Patrick Surtain's second interception of the game, in the end zone with 2:22 left, stopped the Giants' final threat. Jay Fiedler was 14 of 26 for 167 yards. Kerry Collins was 31 of 43 for 276 yards, with 3 interceptions. Jeremy Shockey had 11 receptions for 110 yards.

Miami	0	13	0	10	— 23
N.Y. Giants	0	10	0	0	— 10

Mia — FG Mare 43
NYG — Barber 2 run (Bryant kick)
Mia — McKnight 68 run (Mare kick)
Mia — FG Mare 23
NYG — FG Bryant 43
Mia — FG Mare 48
Mia — Williams 1 run (Mare kick)

PHILADELPHIA 27, WASHINGTON 25—at Lincoln Financial Field, attendance 67,792. The Eagles recorded their first victory at Lincoln Financial Field, but needed a 2-point conversion stop in the final minute to defeat the Redskins. Philadelphia led 10-0 in the second quarter when Jeremiah Trotter's 21-yard interception return to the Eagles' 1 set up Patrick Ramsey's touchdown run. The Eagles' defense supplied points in the third quarter when N.D. Kalu intercepted a tipped pass and returned it 15 yards for a touchdown and 20-13 lead late in the third quarter. The Eagles responded to a field goal with a 70-yard, 5:46 drive capped by Brian Westbrook's 19-yard run with 3:15 remaining for a 27-16 lead. John Hall kicked a 53-yard field goal with 1:14 left to cut the deficit to 27-19, and Bryan Johnson recovered the Redskins' onside kick. Five plays later, Ramsey fired a 32-yard touchdown pass to Darnerien McCants with 13 seconds left, but his 2-point conversion attempt pass to Laveraneus Coles was overthrown. Freddie Mitchell's onside-kick recovery iced the victory. Donovan McNabb was 16 of 30 for 157 yards and 1 touchdown, with 2 interceptions. Ramsey was 25 of 50 for 271 yards and 1 touchdown, with 2 interceptions.

Washington	0	10	3	12	—	25
Philadelphia	3	10	7	7	—	27

Phil — FG Akers 52
Phil — Ritchie 4 pass from McNabb (Akers kick)
Wash — Ramsey 1 run (Hall kick)
Phil — FG Akers 36
Wash — FG Hall 48
Wash — FG Hall 45
Phil — Kalu 15 interception return (Akers kick)
Wash — FG Hall 37
Phil — Westbrook 19 run (Akers kick)
Wash — FG Hall 53
Wash — McCants 32 pass from Ramsey (pass failed)

SAN FRANCISCO 24, DETROIT 17—at 3Com Park, attendance 67,365. Jeff Garcia passed for 2 touchdowns and ran for another as the 49ers held off the Lions. The 49ers scored on their first three possessions, sparked by Ahmed Plummer's interception on the game's second play, to take a 17-0 lead with 12:18 left in the first half. The Lions scored twice in three minutes late in the first half, with Dre' Bly's interception setting up Mikhael Ricks' touchdown catch, to trim the deficit to 17-10. An interception by Tony Parrish late in the third quarter was followed three plays later by Garcia's 1-yard run for a 24-10 lead. Olandis Gary scored on a 2-yard run on the ensuing possession, and the Lions got the ball back twice but failed to gain a first down either time. Garcia was 15 of 27 for 192 yards and 2 touchdowns, with 1 interception. Joey Harrington was 19 of 35 for 200 yards, with 2 interceptions.

Detroit	0	10	0	7	—	17
San Francisco	10	7	7	0	—	24

SF — Owens 6 pass from Garcia (Pochman kick)
SF — FG Pochman 48
SF — Walker 14 pass from Garcia (Pochman kick)
Det — FG Hanson 28
Det — Ricks 6 pass from Harrington (Hanson kick)
SF — Garcia 1 run (Pochman kick)
Det — Gary 2 run (Hanson kick)

SUNDAY NIGHT, OCTOBER 5
CLEVELAND 33, PITTSBURGH 13—at Heinz Field, attendance 64,595. Tim Couch passed for 2 touchdowns as the Browns downed the Steelers. Cleveland scored on its first three possessions, with help from Courtney Brown's fumble recovery and Andre' Davis' 69-yard kickoff return, to take a 16-3 lead. The Steelers cut the deficit to six points, but Couch scored on a 9-yard run with six seconds left in the half for a 23-10 lead. Daylon McCutcheon's 75-yard interception return for a touchdown early in the third quarter increased the advantage to 30-10. Couch was 20 of 25 for 208 yards and 2 touchdowns, with 1 interception. William Green rushed for 115 yards. Tommy Maddox was 11 of 24 for 136 yards, with 2 interceptions.

Cleveland	10	13	7	3	—	33
Pittsburgh	0	10	3	0	—	13

Cle — Andre' Davis 6 pass from Couch (Dawson kick)
Cle — FG Dawson 19
Pitt — FG Reed 30
Cle — Johnson 9 pass from Couch (kick blocked)
Pitt — Bettis 1 run (Reed kick)
Cle — Couch 9 run (Dawson kick)
Cle — McCutcheon 75 interception return (Dawson kick)
Pitt — FG Reed 37
Cle — FG Dawson 22

MONDAY NIGHT, OCTOBER 6
INDIANAPOLIS 38, TAMPA BAY 35 (OT)—at Raymond James Stadium, attendance 65,647. Peyton Manning passed for 386 yards and 2 touchdowns as the Colts became the first team in NFL history to win a game in which they trailed by 21 points with less than four minutes left. Keenan McCardell caught a 74-yard touchdown pass, picked up a fumble by Mike Doss, who had just intercepted a pass for the Colts, and raced 57 yards untouched for a second touchdown, and caught a 15-yard scoring pass to give Tampa Bay a 28-7 lead with 1:14 left in the third quarter. The Colts drove 75 yards on their next drive to score, and then forced a punt, but Ronde Barber intercepted Manning's pass and returned it 29 yards for a touchdown and a seemingly insurmountable 35-14 lead with 5:09 remaining in the fourth quarter. However, Brad Pyatt returned the ensuing kickoff 90 yards to set up James Mungro's 3-yard run with 3:37 left, and Idrees Bashir recovered the onside kick for the Colts. Manning engineered a 6-play, 58-yard drive, capped by his fourth-and-6 28-yard touchdown pass to Marvin Harrison, to cut the deficit to 35-28 with 2:29 left. Aaron Stecker recovered the next onside kick, but the Colts forced a three-and-out and benefited from a personal foul penalty by Kenyatta Walker that stopped the clock to get the ball back at their 15 with no timeouts and 1:41 remaining. A roughing-the-passer penalty on Warren Sapp following a completion moved the ball to the Colts' 42, and Manning hit Harrison with a 52-yard pass to the Buccaneers' 6 to set up Ricky Williams' game-tying touchdown with 35 secodns left. Martín Gramatica attempted a 62-yard field goal as time expired, but it was tipped at the line of scrimmage. In overtime, the Colts forced a punt and Manning converted 3 third-down passes, to Harrison, Reggie Wayne, and Troy Walters, to set up Mike Vanderjagt's game-winning field-goal attempt. Vanderjagt initially missed wide right from 40 yards, but an unsportsmanlike conduct penalty on the Buccaneers gave him a second chance, and his 29-yard game-winner was partially tipped at the line by Ellis Wyms and deflected off the right goalpost before going through. Manning was 34 of 47 for 386 yards and 2 touchdowns, with 1 interception. Harrison had 11 catcheds for 176 yards. Brad Johnson was 26 of 39 for 318 yards and 3 touchdowns, with 1 interception. Michael Pittman rushed for 106 yards, and McCardell had 4 catches for 106 yards.

Indianapolis	0	0	7	28	3	—	38
Tampa Bay	14	7	7	7	0	—	35

TB — McCardell 74 pass from B. Johnson (Gramatica kick)
TB — McCardell 57 fumble return (Gramatica kick)
TB — Barlow 3 pass from B. Johnson (Gramatica kick)
Ind — Harrison 37 pass from Manning (Vanderjagt kick)
TB — McCardell 15 pass from B. Johnson (Gramatica kick)
Ind — Williams 1 run (Vanderjagt kick)
TB — Barber 29 interception return (Gramatica kick)
Ind — Mungro 3 run (Vanderjagt kick)
Ind — Harrison 28 pass from Manning (Vanderjagt kick)
Ind — Williams 1 run (Vanderjagt kick)
Ind — FG Vanderjagt 29

SIXTH WEEK SUMMARIES
American Football Conference

East Division	**W**	**L**	**T**	**Pct.**	**Pts.**	**OP**
Miami	4	1	0	.800	105	58
New England	4	2	0	.667	126	113
Buffalo	3	3	0	.500	114	103
N.Y. Jets	1	4	0	.200	75	80
North Division	**W**	**L**	**T**	**Pct.**	**Pts.**	**OP**
Baltimore	3	2	0	.600	108	92
Cleveland	3	3	0	.500	92	95
Pittsburgh	2	4	0	.333	111	146
Cincinnati	1	4	0	.200	77	106
South Division	**W**	**L**	**T**	**Pct.**	**Pts.**	**OP**
Indianapolis	5	1	0	.833	178	105
Tennessee	4	2	0	.667	157	133
Houston	2	3	0	.400	86	151
Jacksonville	1	5	0	.167	110	154
West Division	**W**	**L**	**T**	**Pct.**	**Pts.**	**OP**
Kansas City	6	0	0	1.000	191	115
Denver	5	1	0	.833	158	87
Oakland	2	4	0	.333	115	144
San Diego	0	5	0	.000	89	149

National Football Conference

East Division	**W**	**L**	**T**	**Pct.**	**Pts.**	**OP**
Dallas	4	1	0	.800	112	93
Washington	3	3	0	.500	128	147
N.Y. Giants	2	3	0	.400	95	109
Philadelphia	2	3	0	.400	81	109
North Division	**W**	**L**	**T**	**Pct.**	**Pts.**	**OP**
Minnesota	5	0	0	1.000	151	84
Green Bay	3	3	0	.500	176	132
Chicago	1	4	0	.200	80	152
Detroit	1	4	0	.200	94	122
South Division	**W**	**L**	**T**	**Pct.**	**Pts.**	**OP**
Carolina	5	0	0	1.000	101	68
Tampa Bay	3	2	0	.600	127	73
New Orleans	2	4	0	.333	107	151
Atlanta	1	5	0	.167	97	175
West Division	**W**	**L**	**T**	**Pct.**	**Pts.**	**OP**
Seattle	4	1	0	.800	122	87
St. Louis	3	2	0	.600	136	84
San Francisco	2	4	0	.333	135	119
Arizona	1	5	0	.167	82	180

SUNDAY, OCTOBER 12
BALTIMORE 26, ARIZONA 18—at Sun Devil Stadium, attendance 24,193. Ed Reed blocked a punt and returned it for a touchdown and Chris McAlister returned an interception for a score for the Ravens. The Cardinals scored on their first drive, but then allowed the Ravens to drive into their red zone on three of their next four possessions. However, the Ravens settled for field goals each time and led just 9-7 late in the first half. Reed then blocked Scott Player's punt and returned the ball 17 yards for a touchdown and 16-7 lead. The Cardinals cut the deficit to six points and drove to the Ravens' 22 late in the third quarter when McAlister stepped in front of a pass in the right flat and went 83 yards for a score and a 23-10 lead. Reed intercepted a pass at the Ravens' 7 to stop a drive late in the game, but the Cardinals scored on Jeff Blake's 12-yard pass to Freddie Jones with 15 seconds left. On the ensuing onside kick, the Cardinals were penalized for illegal touching and Baltimore was awarded possession and ran out the clock. Kyle Boller was 9 of 18 for 75 yards. Lewis had 21 carries for 131 yards. Blake was 22 of 36 for 247 yards and 2 touchdowns, with 3 interceptions.

Baltimore	3	13	7	3	—	26
Arizona	7	3	0	8	—	18

Ariz — Gilmore 14 pass from Blake (Duncan kick)
Balt — FG Stover 31
Balt — FG Stover 22
Balt — FG Stover 29
Balt — Reed 22 blocked punt return (Stover kick)
Ariz — FG Duncan 46
Balt — McAlister 83 interception return (Stover kick)
Balt — FG Stover 37
Ariz — Jones 12 pass from Blake (Blake run)

CLEVELAND 13, OAKLAND 7—at Cleveland Browns Stadium, attendance 73,318. William Green rushed for 165 yards and a touchdown as the Browns held off the Raiders. Green fumbled four plays into the game, and Anthony Dorsett recovered to set up Rich Gannon's 10-yard touchdown pass to Teyo Johnson for a 7-0 lead 5:12 into the game. The Raiders failed to cross the Browns' 40 on their next seven possessions. Cleveland didn't take the lead until Green's 5-yard run with 14 seconds left in the third quarter, and the Browns drove 80 yards on their next drive, including 7 carries by Green, to extend the lead to 13-7 on Phil Dawson's 32-yard field goal with 2:29 left. The Raiders had a fourth- and third-down conversion on their final drive to reach the Browns' 24 with 28 seconds remaining. But on fourth-and-1, Jerry Rice caught Gannon's short pass out of bounds to end the threat. Tim Couch was 16 of 26 for 127 yards. Green rushed 26 times for 145 yards. Gannon was 21 of 33 for 165 yards and 1 touchdown.

Oakland	7	0	0	0	—	7
Cleveland	0	3	7	3	—	13

Oak — Johnson 10 pass from Gannon (Janikowski kick)
Cle — FG Dawson 52
Cle — Green 5 run (Dawson kick)
Cle — FG Dawson 32

DALLAS 23, PHILADELPHIA 21—at Texas Stadium, attendance 73,318. A trick play to open the game backfired for the Eagles and the Cowboys posted their fourth consecutive victory. On the opening kickoff, the Eagles attempted an onside kick, but Randal Williams grabbed the bouncing ball and raced 37 yards for a touchdown three seconds into the game, the quickest score in NFL history. Dallas led 17-7 lead and took a 20-14 lead with 14:12 remaining on Billy Cundiff's 22-yard field goal. Donovan McNabb engineered the Eagles' best drive, a 14-play, 61-yard possession spanning nearly seven minutes, and took a 21-20 lead on Correll Buckhalter's 20-yard scamper with 4:14 left. Zuriel Smith returned the ensuing kickoff 54 yards, and Cundiff made a 28-yard field goal with 1:11 remaining for a 23-21 lead. Three plays later, Dexter Coakley and Roy Williams sacked McNabb and forced him to fumble. La'Roi Glover recovered to clinch the victory. Quincy Carter was 14 of 25 for 146 yards, with 1 interception. McNabb was 11 of 26 for 126 yards and 1 touchdown.

Philadelphia	0	7	7	7	—	21
Dallas	7	3	7	6	—	23

Dall — Ra. Williams 37 kickoff return (Cundiff kick)
Phil — Westbrook 5 run (Akers kick)
Dall — FG Cundiff 51
Dall — Hambrick 1 run (Cundiff kick)
Phil — Staley 52 pass from McNabb (Akers kick)
Dall — FG Cundiff 22
Phil — Buckhalter 20 run (Akers kick)
Dall — FG Cundiff 28

DENVER 17, PITTSBURGH 14—at INVESCO Field at Mile High, attendance 75,974. Jason Elam kicked a 47-yard field goal as time expired to lift the Broncos to victory. Neither defense allowed 250 yards, and the Broncos led 7-6 early in the fourth quarter. Pittsburgh had the ball near midfield when Jerome Bettis fumbled and Bertrand Berry recovered. Steve Beuerlein, starting for the injured Jake Plummer, completed a 38-yard pass to Rod Smith and two plays later hit Smith with an 11-yard fade pass in the corner of the end zone for a 14-6 lead. The Steelers responded with a 13-play, 74-yard drive, capped by Bettis' 1-yard touchdown and 2-point conversion runs to tie the game with 2:41 remaining. Beuerlein completed 3 passes to Shannon Sharpe on the ensuing drive to set up Elam's winning kick. Beuerlein was 17 of 28 for 172 yards and 2 touchdowns, with 2 interceptions. Tommy Maddox was 19 of 30 for 182 yards.

Pittsburgh	3	3	0	8	—	14
Denver	0	7	0	10	—	17

Pitt — FG Reed 24
Den — Sharpe 10 pass from Beuerlein (Elam kick)
Pitt — FG Reed 26
Den — R. Smith 11 pass from Beuerlein (Elam kick)
Pitt — Bettis 1 run (Bettis run)
Den — FG Elam 47

KANSAS CITY 40, GREEN BAY 34 (OT)—at Lambeau Field, attendance 70,407. Trent Green completed a 51-yard touchdown pass to Eddie Kennison in overtime as the Chiefs rallied from a 17-point fourth-quarter deficit to remain undefeated. The Packers scored touchdowns on their first two possessions, driving 80 and 74 yards, to take a 14-0 lead. After the Chiefs tied the game, the Packers scored on an 80-yard drive just before halftime, and then scored on their first two possessions of the second half for a 31-14 lead with 6:01 left in the third quarter. Dante Hall's 32-yard punt return in the fourth quarter led to Priest Holmes' 1-yard touchdown run with 12:20 left in regulation. The Packers drove to the Chiefs' 32, but Jerome Woods intercepted Brett Favre's pass and returned it 79 yards for a touchdown to cut the deficit to 31-28 with 8:46 left. After a three-and-out, Trent Green completed a 67-yard pass to Tony Gonzalez to set up Morten Andersen's game-tying field goal with 5:41 left. Ryan Longwell's 41-yard field goal with 2:43 remaining gave the Packers the lead, but Green completed third-down passes to Johnnie Morton and Holmes on the ensuing possession to keep the drive alive to set up Andersen's 31-yard field goal as time expired to force overtime. The Chiefs won the coin toss and drove to the Packers' 30, but Andersen's 48-yard field goal was tipped by Rod Walker. However, Woods forced Ahman Green to fumble on the next play, and Mike Maslowski recovered. On the ensuing play, Trent Green completed a 51-yard touchdown pass to Kennison with 8:50 left for the victory. Trent Green was 27 of 45 for 400 yards and 3 touchdowns. Morton had 6 receptions for 109 yards and Gonzalez had 4 catches for 121 yards. Favre was 25 of 36 for 272 yards and 2 touchdowns, with 1 interception. Ahman Green had 26 carries for 139 yards.

Kansas City	7	7	0	20	6	—	40
Green Bay	14	7	10	3	0	—	34

GB — Franks 1 pass from Favre (Longwell kick)
GB — A. Green 4 run (Longwell kick)
KC — Gonzalez 26 pass from T. Green (Andersen kick)
KC — Morton 10 pass from T. Green (Andersen kick)
GB — A. Green 11 pass from Favre (Longwell kick)
GB — Davenport 18 run (Longwell kick)
GB — FG Longwell 50
KC — Holmes 1 run (Andersen kick)
KC — Woods 79 interception return (Andersen kick)
KC — FG Andersen 34
GB — FG Longwell 41
KC — FG Andersen 31
KC — Kennison 51 pass from T. Green

CAROLINA 23, INDIANAPOLIS 20 (OT)—at RCA Dome, attendance 57,082. In a battle of undefeated teams, John Kasay's 47-yard field goal in overtime allowed the Panthers to triumph. The Colts outgained the Panthers, but Carolina had a 10-minute advantage in time of possession, and seemingly wore down the Colts' defense. The Colts scored on their final three possessions of the first half to take a 13-3 halftime lead and had the ball to begin the second half. But Ricky Manning Jr. intercepted Peyton Manning on the third play of the half, and Stephen Davis ran 28 yards for a touchdown on the next play to cut the deficit to 13-10. Following a Colts' punt, Jake Delhomme fired a 52-yard touchdown pass to Steve Smith for a 17-13 Carolina lead with 10:22 left in the third quarter. Smith's 36-yard punt return early in the fourth quarter set up Kasay's 23-yard field goal for a 20-13 lead. With 3:08 remaining, Manning engineered a 9-play, 91-yard drive, highlighted by a 6-yard pass to Marcus Pollard on fourth-and-4, and capped by his 25-yard touchdown pass to Reggie Wayne with 45 seconds left to tie the game. The Panthers held the ball for 10 plays, with 2 third-down conversions, and DeShaun Foster's 12-yard run led to Kasay's winning kick with 9:21 left in overtime. Delhomme was 12 of 20 for 181 yards and 1 touchdown, with 1 interception. Smith had 6 catches for 103 yards. Manning was 23 of 34 for 293 yards and 1 touchdown, and 1 interception. Marvin Harrison had 8 catches for 119 yards.

Carolina	3	0	14	3	3	—	23
Indianapolis	0	13	0	7	0	—	20

Car — FG Kasay 29
Ind — Mungro 1 run (Vanderjagt kick)
Ind — FG Vanderjagt 39
Ind — FG Vanderjagt 22
Car — Davis 28 run (Kasay kick)
Car — Smith 52 pass from Delhomme (Kasay kick)
Car — FG Kasay 23
Ind — Wayne 25 pass from Manning (Vanderjagt kick)
Car — FG Kasay 47

MIAMI 24, JACKSONVILLE 10—at ALLTEL Stadium, attendance 66,437. The Dolphins' defense forced 5 turnovers and recorded 4 sacks, and Sam Madison's 29-yard interception return with 1:28 left clinched Miami's victory. Miami scored on its first two possessions, but Jason Craft intercepted Jay Fiedler at the Jaguars' 16 to stall the Dolphins' third drive and change the game's momentum. Late in the third quarter, a 45-yard pass interference penalty on the Dolphins set up Byron Leftwich's 8-yard touchdown scramble to tie the game. Fiedler responded with a 33-yard pass to James McKnight on third-and-10 to jumpstart the Dolphins and drive to the Jaguars' 6. On third-and-goal, Fiedler completed a short pass to Obafemi Ayanbadejo, who fumbled at the 3-yard line. The ball flew into the air and was caught by Randy McMichael, who fell into the end zone for a touchdown and 17-10 Miami lead with 11:29 left. Jacksonville drove into Dolphins' territory on its next two possessions, but Seth Marler missed a 31-yard field goal and Leftwich's fourth-and-4 pass was incomplete from the 44-yard line with 3:23 left. With one final chance, Madison intercepted his second pass of the day and scored with 1:28 left to clinch the victory. Fiedler was 14 of 27 for 147 yards, with 1 interception. Leftwich was 24 of 42 for 256 yards, with 3 interceptions.

Miami	10	0	0	14	—	24
Jacksonville	0	3	7	0	—	10

Mia — Williams 14 run (Mare kick)
Mia — FG Mare 51
Jax — FG Marler 20
Jax — Leftwich 8 run (Marler kick)
Mia — McMichael 2 fumble recovery (Mare kick)
Mia — Madison 29 interception return (Mare kick)

NEW ENGLAND 17, N.Y. GIANTS 6—at Gillette Stadium, attendance 61,500. The Patriots' defense forced 5 turnovers as New England won in the rain. The Giants outgained the Patriots 381-220, and drove into New England territory on 9 of their 13 possessions. In those 9 drives, the Giants made 2 field goals, missed 2 field goals, were intercepted 3 times, stopped on downs once, and punted once. Matt Chatham's 38-yard fumble return 2:36 into the game began the scoring, and the Patriots had scoring drives of 63 and 85 yards to begin the second half to take a 17-3 lead. Tom Brady was 8 of 21 for 112 yards. Kerry Collins was 35 of 59 for 314 yards, with 4 interceptions.

N.Y. Giants	3	0	0	3 —	6
New England	7	0	10	0 —	17

NE — Chatham 38 fumble return (Vinatieri kick)
NYG — FG Conway 22
NE — FG Vinatieri 28
NE — Cloud 1 run (Vinatieri kick)
NYG — FG Conway 34

NEW ORLEANS 20, CHICAGO 13—at Louisiana Superdome, attendance 68,390. Aaron Brooks passed for 2 touchdowns and the Saints' defense forced 2 fumbles that led to 10 points en route to victory. With the score tied 3-3 late in the first half, Charles Grant forced Kordell Stewart to fumble, and Willie Whitehead recovered at the Bears' 23 to set up John Carney's 30-yard field goal as the half expired for a 6-3 lead. Three plays into the second half, Fred Thomas forced Stewart to fumble. Melvin Williams recovered at the Bears' 12, and Brooks completed a 9-yard touchdown pass to Ernie Conwell three plays later for a 13-3 lead. Brooks extended the Saints' lead to 20-6 with a 6-yard touchdown pass to Joe Horn to cap a 13-play drive with 7:18 left in the game. Stewart engineered a 12-play touchdown drive to cut the deficit to 20-13 with 2:10 left, but Paul Edinger's onside kick went out of bounds, and Deuce McAllister gained 8 yards on third-and-6 with 1:59 left to clinch the victory. Brooks was 14 of 29 for 153 yards and 2 touchdowns. McAllister had 29 carries for 116 yards. Stewart was 10 of 21 for 152 yards and 1 touchdown.

Chicago	0	3	0	10 —	13
New Orleans	3	3	7	7 —	20

NO — FG Carney 50
Chi — FG Edinger 28
NO — FG Carney 30
NO — Conwell 9 pass from Brooks (Carney kick)
Chi — FG Edinger 31
NO — Horn 6 pass from Brooks (Carney kick)
Chi — White 4 pass from Stewart (Edinger kick)

N.Y. JETS 30, BUFFALO 3—at The Meadowlands, attendance 77,740. Vinny Testaverde passed for 3 touchdowns as the Jets broke into the win column. The Jets' defense forced 4 turnovers and recorded 7 sacks. The Bills took an early 3-0 lead and drove to the Jets' 34 with their second possession, but Travis Henry was stopped for no gain on fourth down. Testaverde responded with a 9-play touchdown drive for a 7-3 lead. A poor Shotgun snap on Buffalo's next possession was recovered by Bryan Thomas at the Bills' 17 to set up Doug Brien's 27-yard field goal. After a Bills punt, Brien made a 33-yard field goal with 45 seconds left in the half for a 13-3 halftime lead. Santana Moss' 47-yard punt return early in the second half was immediately followed by Testaverde's 18-yard touchdown pass to Anthony Becht for a 20-3 lead with 13:09 left in the third quarter. Drew Bledsoe's fourth-and-11 pass from the Jets' 38 fell incomplete on the next possession, and the Jets answered with a 10-play, 62-yard drive, capped by Moss' 4-yard touchdown catch to take a 27-3 lead late in the third quarter. Testaverde was 11 of 17 for 130 yards and 3 touchdowns. Bledsoe was 24 of 40 for 202 yards, with 1 interception.

Buffalo	3	0	0	0 —	3
N.Y. Jets	0	13	14	3 —	30

Buff — FG Lindell 44
NYJ — Becht 1 pass from Testaverde (Brien kick)
NYJ — FG Brien 27
NYJ — FG Brien 33
NYJ — Becht 18 pass from Testaverde (Brien kick)
NYJ — Moss 4 pass from Testaverde (Brien kick)
NYJ — FG Brien 43

TENNESSEE 38, HOUSTON 17—at The Coliseum, attendance 68,809. Steve McNair completed 3 long touchdown passes to Derrick Mason as the Titans rolled up 535 yards. McNair completed 32- and 46-yard touchdown passes to Mason to cap 74- and 69-yard drives on the Titans' first two possessions for a 14-0 lead less than nine minutes into the game. The Texans' Kris Brown kicked a 29-yard field goal just before halftime, and David Carr hit Corey Bradford with a 65-yard touchdown to cut the deficit to 21-10 early in the third quarter. The Titans added a field goal and put the game away with a 98-yard drive, capped by Mason's 50-yard touchdown catch with 14:46 remaining for a 31-10 lead. McNair was 18 of 27 for 421 yards and 3 touchdowns. Mason had 6 catches for 177 yards. Carr was 25 of 42 for 371 yards and 2 touchdowns, with 3 interceptions. Bradford had 5 catches for 127 yards.

Houston	0	3	7	7 —	17
Tennessee	14	7	3	14 —	38

Tenn — Mason 32 pass from McNair (Anderson kick)
Tenn — Mason 46 pass from McNair (Anderson kick)
Tenn — Holcombe 5 run (Anderson kick)
Hous — FG Brown 29
Hous — Bradford 65 pass from Carr (Brown kick)
Tenn — FG Anderson 33
Tenn — Mason 50 pass from McNair (Anderson kick)
Tenn — Dyson 51 interception return (Anderson kick)
Hous — Armstrong 13 pass from Carr (Brown kick)

TAMPA BAY 35, WASHINGTON 13—at FedExField, attendance 85,490. Brad Johnson passed for 4 touchdowns and the Buccaneers' defense forced 4 turnovers and registered 6 sacks to defeat the Redskins. Patrick Ramsey's 2-yard touchdown pass to Darnerien McCants with 14 seconds left in the half gave Washington a 10-7 lead. The Redskins added a John Hall 51-yard field goal on their first drive of the third quarter for a 13-7 lead. The Buccaneers scored touchdowns on their next three possessions. Dwight Smith intercepted Ramsey two plays after Todd Yoder's 11-yard touchdown catch. Twelve plays later, Will Heller caught a 4-yard touchdown pass for a 21-13 lead with 13:31 left. After a Redskins punt, Brad Johnson connected on a 39-yard touchdown pass to Keyshawn Johnson for a 28-13 lead, and Derrick Brooks returned an interception for a touchdown five plays later for a 35-13 lead with 6:55 left. Brad Johnson was 22 of 30 for 268 yards and 4 touchdowns. Ramsey was 21 of 32 for 211 yards and 1 touchdown, with 2 interceptions.

Tampa Bay	0	7	7	21 —	35
Washington	3	7	3	0 —	13

Wash — FG Hall 33
TB — Yoder 1 pass from B. Johnson (Gramatica kick)
Wash — McCants 2 pass from Ramsey (Hall kick)
Wash — FG Hall 51
TB — Yoder 11 pass from B. Johnson (Gramatica kick)
TB — Heller 4 pass from B. Johnson (Gramatica kick)
TB — K. Johnson 39 pass from B. Johnson (Gramatica kick)
TB — Brooks 44 interception return (Gramatica kick)

SUNDAY NIGHT, OCTOBER 12
SEATTLE 20, SAN FRANCISCO 19—at Seahawks Stadium, attendance 66,437. Josh Brown kicked a 37-yard field goal with 3:04 remaining as the Seahawks rebounded from losing a 17-0 lead to defeat the 49ers. The Seahawks had scoring drives of 72, 57, and 62 yards to take a 17-0 lead. Owen Pochman kicked a 42-yard field goal three seconds before halftime, and Garrison Hearst had a 6-yard scoring run to cap the 49ers' first possession of the second half to cut the deficit to 17-10. Tony Parrish intercepted Matt Hasselbeck's pass late in the third quarter to set up Jeff Garcia's 2-yard touchdown run. However, Bill LaFleur bobbled the extra-point attempt, and Pochman's kick went wide right. But the 49ers' defense forced a punt and Pochman made a 33-yard field goal with 8:09 left to give San Francisco a 19-17 lead. The Seahawks responded with a 10-play drive, capped by Brown's 37-yard field goal. The 49ers drove to almost midfield, but Chad Brown forced Hearst to fumble and Ken Hamlin recovered. Hasselbeck then completed an 18-yard pass to Koren Robinson on third-and-9 with 1:47 remaining to clinch the victory. Hasselbeck was 17 of 27 for 207 yards and 1 touchdown, with 1 interception. Garcia was 16 of 27 for 168 yards.

San Francisco	0	3	13	3 —	19
Seattle	7	10	0	3 —	20

Sea — Mili 15 pass from Hasselbeck (J. Brown kick)
Sea — FG J. Brown 27
Sea — Strong 21 run (J. Brown kick)
SF — FG Pochman 42
SF — Hearst 6 run (Pochman kick)
SF — Garcia 2 run (kick failed)
SF — FG Pochman 33
Sea — FG J. Brown 37

MONDAY NIGHT, OCTOBER 12
ST. LOUIS 36, ATLANTA 0—at Edward Jones Dome, attendance 66,075. Marc Bulger passed for 2 touchdowns and the Rams posted their first shutout in 10 years. The Rams had advantages in first downs (26-9), yards (496-209), and time of possession (37:20-22:40). Aeneas Williams intercepted Doug Johnson's pass in the end zone to stop the Falcons' second possession, and Atlanta never drove inside the Rams' 40 the remainder of the game. The Rams led just 10-0 at halftime, but Bulger's 21-yard touchdown pass to Torry Holt increased the lead to 17-0 with 12:16 left in the third quarter, and the defense added to the scoring with Grant Wistrom's safety and Travis Fisher's 74-yard interception return with 1:33 left to cap the scoring. Bulger was 23 of 34 for 352 yards and 2 touchdowns, with 2 interceptions. Holt had 11 catches for 161 yards. Johnson was 10 of 23 for 134 yards, with 1 interception.

Atlanta	0	0	0	0 —	0
St. Louis	3	7	9	17 —	36

StL — FG Wilkins 28
StL — Bulger 3 run (Wilkins kick)
StL — Holt 21 pass from Bulger (Wilkins kick)

StL — Safety, Wistrom tackled Duckett in end zone
StL — Holt 14 pass from Bulger (Wilkins kick)
StL — FG Wilkins 38
StL — Fisher 74 interception return (Wilkins kick)

SEVENTH WEEK SUMMARIES
American Football Conference

East Division	**W**	**L**	**T**	**Pct.**	**Pts.**	**OP**
New England	5	2	0	.714	145	126
Miami	4	2	0	.667	118	77
Buffalo	4	3	0	.571	138	110
N.Y. Jets	2	4	0	.333	94	94
North Division	**W**	**L**	**T**	**Pct.**	**Pts.**	**OP**
Baltimore	3	3	0	.500	134	126
Cleveland	3	4	0	.429	112	121
Cincinnati	2	4	0	.333	111	132
Pittsburgh	2	4	0	.333	111	146
South Division	**W**	**L**	**T**	**Pct.**	**Pts.**	**OP**
Indianapolis	5	1	0	.833	178	105
Tennessee	5	2	0	.714	194	150
Houston	2	4	0	.333	100	170
Jacksonville	1	5	0	.167	110	154
West Division	**W**	**L**	**T**	**Pct.**	**Pts.**	**OP**
Kansas City	7	0	0	1.000	208	125
Denver	5	2	0	.714	178	115
Oakland	2	5	0	.286	125	161
San Diego	1	5	0	.167	115	169

National Football Conference

East Division	**W**	**L**	**T**	**Pct.**	**Pts.**	**OP**
Dallas	5	1	0	.833	150	100
Philadelphia	3	3	0	.500	95	119
Washington	3	4	0	.429	135	171
N.Y. Giants	2	4	0	.333	105	123
North Division	**W**	**L**	**T**	**Pct.**	**Pts.**	**OP**
Minnesota	6	0	0	1.000	179	104
Green Bay	3	4	0	.429	200	166
Chicago	1	5	0	.167	97	176
Detroit	1	5	0	.167	101	160
South Division	**W**	**L**	**T**	**Pct.**	**Pts.**	**OP**
Carolina	5	1	0	.833	118	105
Tampa Bay	3	3	0	.500	134	97
New Orleans	3	4	0	.429	152	168
Atlanta	1	6	0	.143	114	220
West Division	**W**	**L**	**T**	**Pct.**	**Pts.**	**OP**
Seattle	5	1	0	.833	146	104
St. Louis	4	2	0	.667	170	108
San Francisco	3	4	0	.429	159	126
Arizona	1	5	0	.167	82	180

SUNDAY, OCTOBER 19
NEW ORLEANS 45, ATLANTA 17—at Georgia Dome, attendance 70,837. Aaron Brooks passed for 3 touchdowns as the Saints scored 35 first-half points to defeat the Falcons. The Saints had advantages in first downs (27-11), total yards (507-238), and time of possession (38:10-21:50). Warrick Dunn raced 69 yards for a touchdown on the game's second play. But the Saints scored on their first three, and five of their six first-half possessions on drives of 80, 87, 78, 52, and 68 yards. Deuce McAllister's 10-yard run with 30 seconds left in the half gave the Saints a 35-14 lead. The Saints' defense allowed the Falcons to cross midfield just once in the second half. Brooks was 23 of 30 for 352 yards and 3 touchdowns. McAllister had 21 carries for 116 yards and 2 touchdowns, and Joe Horn had 8 catches for 133 yards. Kurt Kittner, in his first start of the season, was 9 of 29 for 115 yards and 1 touchdown, with 1 interception.

New Orleans	14	21	3	7	—	45
Atlanta	14	0	3	0	—	17

Atl — Dunn 69 run (Feely kick)
NO — Stallworth 69 pass from Brooks (Carney kick)
NO — Horn 32 pass from Brooks (Carney kick)
Atl — Finneran 18 pass from Kittner (Feely kick)
NO — McAllister 4 run (Carney kick)
NO — B. Williams 12 pass from Brooks (Carney kick)
NO — McAllister 10 run (Carney kick)
Atl — FG Feely 28
NO — FG Carney 42
NO — Carter 1 run (Carney kick)

BUFFALO 24, WASHINGTON 7—at Ralph Wilson Stadium, attendance 73,149. Travis Henry rushed for 167 yards and 2 touchdowns as the Bills pulled away from the Redskins. Buffalo outgained the Redskins (432-169), had more first downs (25-8), and led in time of possession (36:55-23:05). The Bills outgained Washington 240-76 in the first half, and Patrick Ramsey fumbled at the Bills' 1 yard-line to ruin Washington's only first-half scoring threat, but Buffalo led just 10-0 at halftime. The Redskins began the second half with a 12-play, 76-yard drive, which included a 5-yard run on fourth-and-1 by Rock Cartwright, and was capped by Ramsey's 25-yard touchdown pass to Rod Gardner. But Henry had runs of 21 and 13 yards on the ensuing drive for Buffalo, and Drew Bledsoe hit Josh Reed with a 10-yard touchdown pass to extend Buffalo's lead to 17-7. Henry had 6 carries on an eight-play drive that culminated with his 14-yard run for a 24-7 lead with 10:24 left in the game. Bledsoe was 19 of 26 for 244 yards and 1 touchdown, with 1 interception. Henry had 31 carries for 167 yards, and Reed had 8 catches for 109 yards. Ramsey was 9 of 26 for 115 yards and 1 touchdown.

Washington	0	0	7	0	—	7
Buffalo	3	7	7	7	—	24

Buff — FG Lindell 20
Buff — Henry 4 run (Lindell kick)
Wash — Gardner 25 pass from Ramsey (Hall kick)
Buff — Reed 10 pass from Bledsoe (Lindell kick)
Buff — Henry 14 run (Lindell kick)

TENNESSEE 37, CAROLINA 17—at Ericsson Stadium, attendance 72,851. The Titans' defense forced 4 turnovers and the offense surpassed 30 points for the fourth consecutive game to hand the Panthers their first defeat. The Titans led 7-0 midway through the first quarter and had the ball at midfield and lined up to punt on fourth-and-2. The Titans went into a Swinging Gate formation, with most of the offense lined up to the left of the field, and backup quarterback Billy Volek took a Shotgun snap and completed a short pass to Eddie Berlin, who streaked 50 yards down the right sideline for a touchdown and 14-0 lead. The Titans led 20-0 before John Kasay put the Panthers on the board with a field goal, and Steve McNair answered with a 6-play, 71-yard drive capped by Drew Bennett's 22-yard touchdown catch with 11 seconds left in the half for a 27-3 lead. Carolina trailed 30-10 and got the ball with 8:44 remaining, but DeShaun Foster fumbled and Keith Bulluck returned the ball 32 yards for a touchdown to put the game away. McNair was 12 of 22 for 190 yards and 1 touchdown. Delhomme was 31 of 49 for 362 yards and 2 touchdowns. Smith had 10 catches for 151 yards.

Tennessee	17	10	0	10	—	37
Carolina	0	3	0	14	—	17

Tenn — McNair 7 run (Anderson kick)
Tenn — Berlin 50 pass from Volek (Anderson kick)
Tenn — FG Anderson 40
Tenn — FG Anderson 32
Car — FG Kasay 53
Tenn — Bennett 22 pass from McNair (Anderson kick)
Tenn — FG Anderson 34
Car — Smith 67 pass from Delhomme (Kasay kick)
Tenn — Bulluck 32 fumble return (Anderson kick)
Car — Goings 8 pass from Delhomme (Kasay kick)

CINCINNATI 34, BALTIMORE 26—at Paul Brown Stadium, attendance 53,553. Jon Kitna passed for 274 yards and 3 touchdowns as the Bengals won a key AFC North game. The Bengals ran off 27 unanswered points to take a 27-7 lead in the third quarter. The Bengals scored 17 of those points off of Baltimore's 3 turnovers. Kyle Boller fumbled twice within two minutes, both times setting up Cincinnati touchdowns in the first quarter, and Kitna hit Chad Johnson with an 82-yard touchdown pass early in the second quarter for a 21-7 lead. The Bengals scored on their first two second-half possessions to lead 34-10 with 14:53 left. Boller connected with Travis Taylor on a 73-yard touchdown two plays later, and Chester Taylor scored with 1:16 left, both scores culminating with Todd Heap 2-point conversion catches, to pull within eight points. But Baltimore's onside-kick attempt went out of bounds and Cincinnati ran out the clock. Kitna was 16 of 27 for 274 yards and 3 touchdowns. Johnson had 5 catches for 130 yards. Boller was 15 of 27 for 302 yards and 2 touchdowns, with 1 interception. Heap had 7 catches for 129 yards, and Taylor had 4 catches for 138 yards. Jamal Lewis had 19 carries for 101 yards.

Baltimore	7	0	3	16	—	26
Cincinnati	14	10	3	7	—	34

Balt — T. Taylor 19 pass from Boller (Stover kick)
Cin — Schobel 45 pass from Kitna (Graham kick)
Cin — Dillon 2 run (Graham kick)
Cin — C. Johnson 82 pass from Kitna (Graham kick)
Cin — FG Graham 44
Cin — FG Graham 37
Balt — FG Stover 25
Cin — Warrick 21 pass from Kitna (Graham kick)
Balt — T. Taylor 73 pass from Boller (Heap pass from Boller)
Balt — C. Taylor 2 run (Heap pass from Boller)

SAN DIEGO 26, CLEVELAND 20—at Cleveland Browns Stadium, attendance 73,238. LaDainian Tomlinson rushed for 200 yards and 1 touchdown as the Chargers held on to win their first game. Kwamie Lassiter's 38-yard interception return in the second quarter gave the Chargers a 13-0 lead. Phil Dawson kicked 2 field goals within four minutes bracketed around halftime to cut the deficit to 13-6. But Tomlinson scored on a 70-yard run on the next play from scrimmage and Terrence Kiel's interception set up Steve Christie's third field goal for a 23-6 lead with 2:57 left in the third quarter. Kelly Holcomb replaced Tim Couch and promptly engineered a 74-yard touchdown drive. Tim Dwight fumbled the ensuing kickoff return, and Jamel White recovered to set up Holcomb's 1-yard scoring pass to Darnell Sanders to cut the deficit to 23-20 with 11:40 left. The Chargers responded with a 13-play drive that consumed almost eight minutes, and included a 5-yard run by Tomlinson on fourth-and-1, but had to settle for Christie's fourth field goal for a 26-20 lead with 3:44 left. Holcomb was unable to guide the Browns across midfield and only had 25 seconds left for their final possession. Drew Brees was 9 of

18 for 74 yards, with 1 interception. Tomlinson had 26 carries for 200 yards. Couch was 13 of 24 for 102 yards, with 2 interceptions, and Holcomb was 11 of 19 for 90 yards and 2 touchdowns.

San Diego	6	7	10	3	—	26
Cleveland	0	3	3	14	—	20

SD — FG Christie 44
SD — FG Christie 50
SD — Lassiter 38 interception return (Christie kick)
Cle — FG Dawson 46
Cle — FG Dawson 42
SD — Tomlinson 70 run (Christie kick)
SD — FG Christie 42
Cle — Northcutt 6 pass from Holcomb (Dawson kick)
Cle — Sanders 1 pass from Holcomb (Dawson kick)
SD — FG Christie 32

DALLAS 38, DETROIT 7—at Ford Field, attendance 61,160. Quincy Carter and Terry Glenn hooked up for 3 touchdowns as the Cowboys won their fifth consecutive game. Dallas had advantages in yards (331-157), first downs (25-9), and time of possession (37:21-22:39). Dre' Bly recovered a Troy Hambrick fumble and returned it 67 yards for a touchdown in the middle of the first quarter. Dallas responded with three consecutive drives that finished with Carter finding Glenn in the end zone, the last of which was set up by Dexter Coakley's 24-yard interception return. Mario Edwards intercepted a Joey Harrington pass and returned it 27 yards for a touchdown and 28-7 lead with 4:20 left in the half. Carter was 18 of 25 for 190 yards and 3 touchdowns. Harrington was 5 of 13 for 30 yards, with 2 interceptions, and Mike McMahon was 5 of 20 for 51 yards, with 1 interception.

Dallas	7	21	7	3	—	38
Detroit	7	0	0	0	—	7

Det — Bly 67 fumble return (Hanson kick)
Dall — Glenn 20 pass from Carter (Cundiff kick)
Dall — Glenn 19 pass from Carter (Cundiff kick)
Dall — Glenn 8 pass from Carter (Cundiff kick)
Dall — Edwards 27 interception return (Cundiff kick)
Dall — FG Cundiff 23

N.Y. JETS 19, HOUSTON 14—at Reliant Stadium, attendance 70,623. LaMont Jordan scored on an 8-yard touchdown run with 1:21 left as the Jets rallied to defeat Houston. The Jets trailed 14-0 before they gained their initial first down. Trailing 14-7 at halftime, the Jets' defense did not allow the Texans to gain more than 29 yards on any of their six second-half possessions. The Jets trailed 14-13 when they started on their own 14 with 2:48 left, but Vinny Testaverde connected on a 25-yard pass to Santana Moss, and Curtis Martin had carries of 14 and 20 yards to set up Jordan's scoring run. J.J. Moses returned the ensuing kickoff 63 yards to the Texans' 27, but faced with fourth-and-4 from the Jets' 9, Andre Johnson dropped David Carr's pass at the 5-yard line with 21 seconds left to seal the Jets' victory. Testaverde was 15 of 29 for 182 yards and 1 touchdown, and Moss had 6 catches for 111 yards. Carr was 15 of 23 for 170 yards, and Domanick Davis had the Texans' first-ever 100-yard rushing game with 27 carries for 129 yards in his first start.

N.Y. Jets	0	7	3	9	—	19
Houston	7	7	0	0	—	14

Hous — Mack 10 run (Brown kick)
Hous — Mack 1 run (Brown kick)
NYJ — Moss 18 pass from Testaverde (Brien kick)
NYJ — FG Brien 39
NYJ — FG Brien 40
NYJ — Jordan 8 run (pass failed)

NEW ENGLAND 19, MIAMI 13 (OT)—at Pro Player Stadium, attendance 73,650. Tom Brady completed an 82-yard touchdown pass to Troy Brown in overtime to move into first place in the AFC East. Fumbles in Patriots' territory by Tom Brady and Kevin Faulk in the second quarter led to 10 Dolphins points and a 10-3 lead. The Dolphins led 13-6, but Brady engineered a 14-play, 76-yard, 7:57 drive to tie the game on David Givens' 24-yard touchdown catch late in the third quarter. The Dolphins drove 73 yards and took more than nine minutes off the clock in the fourth quarter, but Olindo Mare's 35-yard field-goal attempt was blocked by Richard Seymour with 2:00 left. The Dolphins got the ball first in overtime, and again drove into field-goal range. With the Florida Marlins in the World Series, the field still contained the infield dirt, and Mare once again was forced to attempt a field goal from the dirt. The kick sailed wide right. After a Patriots' punt, Tyrone Poole intercepted Jay Fiedler's long pass at the Patriots' 18. New England went for it all on the next play, and Brady connected with Brown on an 82-yard touchdown pass with 5:57 left in overtime. Brady was 24 of 34 for 283 yards and 2 touchdowns. Brown had 6 catches for 131 yards. Fiedler was 20 of 35 for 230 yards and 1 touchdown, with 2 interceptions. Randy McMichael had 8 catches for 102 yards.

New England	3	3	7	0	6	—	19
Miami	0	10	3	0	0	—	13

NE — FG Vinatieri 25
Mia — Chambers 6 pass from Fiedler (Mare kick)
Mia — FG Mare 23
NE — FG Vinatieri 30
Mia — FG Mare 34
NE — Givens 24 pass from Brady (Vinatieri kick)
NE — Brown 82 pass from Brady

MINNESOTA 28, DENVER 20—at Metrodome, attendance 68,390. Randy Moss made an acrobatic lateral for a touchdown as the first half expired to spark the Vikings. With the score tied and on Minnesota's 41 with nine seconds left in the first half, Daunte Culpepper rolled right and lofted the ball downfield. Moss caught the ball at the 12-yard line as time expired and as he was being tackled, he flipped the ball backwards to an oncoming Moe Williams, who caught the ball in stride at the 15-yard line and ran untouched into the end zone for a 14-7 halftime lead. The Vikings drove 71 yards to begin the second half, capped by Onterrio Smith's 5-yard scoring run, and scored just over a minute later on Lance Johnstone's 33-yard interception return for a 28-7 lead with 7:57 left in the third quarter. Trailing 28-10, Steve Beuerlein injured his finger and was replaced by Danny Kanell, who guided Denver to 2 consecutive scoring drives, cutting the deficit to 28-20 on Mike Anderson's 1-yard run with 6:45 left. The Broncos drove to the Vikings' 25, but Kanell's fourth-and-10 pass fell incomplete with 27 seconds left. Culpepper was 19 of 26 for 277 yards and 2 touchdowns. Moss had 10 catches for 151 yards. Beuerlein was 9 of 19 for 119 yards, with 3 interceptions, and Kanell was 12 of 18 for 104 yards and 1 touchdown.

Denver	0	7	3	10	—	20
Minnesota	7	7	14	0	—	28

Minn — Campbell 47 pass from Culpepper (Elling kick)
Den — Portis 4 run (Elam kick)
Minn — Williams 15 lateral from Moss on 59 pass from Culpepper (Elling kick)
Minn — Smith 5 run (Elling kick)
Minn — Johnstone 33 interception return (Elling kick)
Den — FG Elam 46
Den — FG Elam 46
Den — Anderson 1 pass from Kanell (Elam kick)

PHILADELPHIA 14, N.Y. GIANTS 10—at Giants Stadium, attendance 78,883. Brian Westbrook returned a punt 84 yards for a touchdown with 1:16 remaining as the Eagles shocked the Giants. The Giants had advantages in first downs (25-9), total yards (339-134), and time of possession (35:42-24:18), but trailed 7-3 at halftime. Kerry Collins completed a 1-yard touchdown pass to Jeremy Shockey to cap a 62-yard third-quarter drive to give the Giants a 10-7 lead. The Giants had a chance to extend the lead midway through the fourth quarter, but Mark Simoneau forced Collins to fumble and Corey Simon recovered at the Eagles' 10. The Eagles forced a punt with 1:34 left, but with the Giants' defense having allowed just 1 first down in the Eagles' previous seven possessions, the odds were stacked against Philadelphia. But Westbrook returned the punt 84 yards for a touchdown, and Collins' fourth-and-4 pass from the Eagles' 38 fell incomplete with 44 seconds left. Donovan McNabb was 9 of 23 for 64 yards, with 1 interception. Collins was 22 of 36 for 174 yards and 1 touchdown.

Philadelphia	7	0	0	7	—	14
N.Y. Giants	0	3	7	0	—	10

Phil — Westbrook 6 run (Akers kick)
NYG — FG Conway 39
NYG — Shockey 1 pass from Collins (Conway kick)
Phil — Westbrook 84 punt return (Akers kick)

ST. LOUIS 34, GREEN BAY 24—at Edward Jones Dome, attendance 66,201. Marc Bulger passed for 3 touchdowns, 2 to Torry Holt, as the Rams won their third consecutive game. The Rams turned 4 Packers turnovers into 17 points. Al Harris muffed a punt at the Packers' 40 to set up Bulger's 39-yard touchdown pass to Holt for a 7-3 Rams lead. Harris atoned for his error with an interception early in the second quarter to set up Brett Favre's 21-yard touchdown pass to Ahman Green to cut the deficit to 14-10. Green fumbled at the Rams' 31 late in the first half, and Bulger took advantage with a 9-yard scoring strike to Holt for a 21-10 lead with 57 seconds left in the half. The Packers trailed 31-17 with 4:52 left, but drove to midfield only to have Leonard Little intercept Favre's pass to set up Jeff Wilkins' 43-yard field goal with 2:56 remaining for a 34-17 lead. Bulger was 22 of 34 for 247 yards and 3 touchdowns, with 2 interceptions. Isaac Bruce had 9 catches for 129 yards. Favre was 23 of 32 for 268 yards and 2 touchdowns, with 1 interception.

Green Bay	3	7	7	7	—	24
St. Louis	14	7	7	6	—	34

GB — FG Longwell 33
StL — Holt 39 pass from Bulger (Wilkins kick)
StL — Harris 3 run (Wilkins kick)
GB — Green 21 pass from Favre (Longwell kick)
StL — Holt 9 pass from Bulger (Wilkins kick)
GB — Henderson 1 pass from Favre (Longwell kick)
StL — Looker 20 pass from Bulger (Wilkins kick)
StL — FG Wilkins 39

StL — FG Wilkins 43
GB — Davenport 76 run (Longwell kick)

SAN FRANCISCO 24, TAMPA BAY 7—at 3Com Park, attendance 67,809. Garrison Hearst had 117 of the 49ers' 212 rushing yards, and the defense forced 4 turnovers, as San Francisco defeated the defending Super Bowl champions. Ahmed Plummer's interception on the second play of the game led to Hearst's 7-yard scoring run for a 7-0 lead just 3:22 into the game. The Buccaneers tied the game on Brad Johnson's 75-yard touchdown pass to Keenan McCardell later in the quarter, but the 49ers answered immediately with Jeff Garcia's 14-yard touchdown pass to Tai Streets in the second quarter. Two possessions later, Terrell Owens took a short pass from Garcia and accelerated 75 yards down the left sideline for a touchdown and 21-7 lead. Owen Pochman's third missed field goal of the game, blocked by Ronde Barber in the middle of the third quarter, gave Tampa Bay hope. The Buccaneers drove to the 49ers' 26, but Thomas Jones fumbled and Jamie Winborn recovered. Tampa Bay drove to the 49ers' 25 in the fourth quarter, but Julian Peterson intercepted Johnson's pass, and Pochman made a 27-yard field goal 12 plays later to make it a three-possession game with 2:05 remaining. Garcia was 15 of 29 for 253 yards and 2 touchdowns, with 1 interception. Owens had 6 catches for 152 yards. Johnson was 21 of 34 for 241 yards and 1 touchdown, with 3 interceptions. Michael Pittman had 10 catches for 60 yards, and McCardell had 3 catches for 119 yards.

Tampa Bay	7	0	0	0	—	7
San Francisco	7	14	0	3	—	24

SF — Hearst 7 run (Pochman kick)
TB — McCardell 75 pass from B. Johnson (Gramatica kick)
SF — Streets 14 pass from Garcia (Pochman kick)
SF — Owens 75 pass from Garcia (Pochman kick)
SF — FG Pochman 27

SEATTLE 24, CHICAGO 17—at Seahawks Stadium, attendance 65,671. Shaun Alexander's 25-yard touchdown run with 58 seconds left allowed the Seahawks to hold off a Bears rally and remain in first place in the NFC West. Trailing 3-0, the Seahawks scored on consecutive possessions, the second set up by Anthony Simmons' 33-yard interception return, to take a 14-3 lead. Mike Brown's interception in the end zone just before halftime allowed Chicago to stay within eight points. Paul Edinger's third field goal cut the deficit to 17-9 early in the fourth quarter, and Koren Robinson fumbled and Bobby Gray recovered at the Bears' 33. Thirteen plays later, following 2 third-down conversions and a successful fourth-and-1 sneak by Chris Chandler, Stanley Pritchett scored on a 1-yard run with 4:12 left. The Bears went for the 2-point conversion, and Chandler, after rolling right and not finding an open receiver, dove headlong into the end zone to tie the game. But Alexander had carries of 9 and 14 yards to set up his 25-yard scoring jaunt. Rookie Marcus Trufant's interception with 37 seconds left sealed the victory. Hasselbeck was 19 of 27 for 215 yards and 1 touchdown, with 1 interception. Alexander had 21 carries for 101 yards. Chandler, making his first start of the season, was 19 of 34 for 149 yards, with 2 interceptions.

Chicago	3	3	0	11	—	17
Seattle	0	14	3	7	—	24

Chi — FG Edinger 50
Sea — Alexander 1 run (Brown kick)
Sea — Engram 25 pass from Hasselbeck (Brown kick)
Chi — FG Edinger 35
Sea — FG Brown 45
Chi — FG Edinger 40
Chi — Pritchett 1 run (Chandler run)
Sea — Alexander 25 run (Brown kick)

MONDAY NIGHT, OCTOBER 20
KANSAS CITY 17, OAKLAND 10—at Network Associates Coliseum, attendance 62,391. Greg Wesley and Jerome Woods tackled Tim Brown at the 1-yard line as time expired as the Chiefs remained undefeated. The Chiefs led 10-0 at halftime and Oakland's Rich Gannon did not play in the second half after suffering a shoulder injury. In the fourth quarter, Marques Tuiasosopo drove the Raiders into the red zone for the first time, and Sebastian Janikowski's 27-yard field goal cut the deficit to 10-3. The Raiders' defense then forced a punt, but Phillip Buchanon muffed it and Marc Boerigter recovered at the Raiders' 11 to set up Priest Holmes' 2-yard run with 4:57 left for a 17-3 lead. Tuiasosopo completed 5 of 6 passes on the ensuing drive, and Zack Crockett scored from the 1-yard line with 2:25 left. After another punt, and starting from Oakland's 6, Tuiasosopo completed passes of 23 yards to Jerry Rice and 35 yards to Jerry Porter to reach the Chiefs' 29. On fourth-and-10 with 29 seconds left, Tuiasosopo hit Rice with a 15-yard pass. With seven seconds left, Tuiasosopo rolled right and fired a pass to Brown, who stepped up to catch the pass at the 1-yard line and was tackled immediately by Woods and Wesley. Green was 11 of 22 for 206 yards, with 1 interception. Holmes had 27 carries for 123 yards. Gannon was 10 of 19 for 58 yards, with 1 interception, and Tuiasosopo was 16 of 28 for 224 yards, with 1 interception.

Kansas City	7	3	0	7	—	17
Oakland	0	0	0	10	—	10

KC — Green 2 run (Andersen kick)
KC — FG Andersen 37
Oak — FG Janikowski 27
KC — Holmes 2 run (Andersen kick)
Oak — Crockett 1 run (Janikowski kick)

EIGHTH WEEK SUMMARIES
American Football Conference

East Division	**W**	**L**	**T**	**Pct.**	**Pts.**	**OP**
New England	6	2	0	.750	154	129
Miami	5	2	0	.714	144	87
Buffalo	4	4	0	.500	143	148
N.Y. Jets	2	5	0	.286	111	118
North Division	**W**	**L**	**T**	**Pct.**	**Pts.**	**OP**
Baltimore	4	3	0	.571	160	132
Cincinnati	3	4	0	.429	138	156
Cleveland	3	5	0	.375	115	130
Pittsburgh	2	5	0	.286	132	179
South Division	**W**	**L**	**T**	**Pct.**	**Pts.**	**OP**
Indianapolis	6	1	0	.857	208	126
Tennessee	6	2	0	.750	224	167
Houston	2	5	0	.286	121	200
Jacksonville	1	6	0	.143	127	184
West Division	**W**	**L**	**T**	**Pct.**	**Pts.**	**OP**
Kansas City	8	0	0	1.000	246	130
Denver	5	3	0	.625	184	141
Oakland	2	5	0	.286	125	161
San Diego	1	6	0	.143	125	195

National Football Conference

East Division	**W**	**L**	**T**	**Pct.**	**Pts.**	**OP**
Dallas	5	2	0	.714	150	116
Philadelphia	4	3	0	.571	119	136
N.Y. Giants	3	4	0	.429	134	140
Washington	3	4	0	.429	135	171
North Division	**W**	**L**	**T**	**Pct.**	**Pts.**	**OP**
Minnesota	6	1	0	.857	196	133
Green Bay	3	4	0	.429	200	166
Chicago	2	5	0	.286	121	192
Detroit	1	6	0	.143	117	184
South Division	**W**	**L**	**T**	**Pct.**	**Pts.**	**OP**
Carolina	6	1	0	.857	141	125
Tampa Bay	4	3	0	.571	150	97
New Orleans	3	5	0	.375	172	191
Atlanta	1	6	0	.143	114	220
West Division	**W**	**L**	**T**	**Pct.**	**Pts.**	**OP**
St. Louis	5	2	0	.714	203	129
Seattle	5	2	0	.714	170	131
San Francisco	3	5	0	.375	172	142
Arizona	2	5	0	.286	98	193

SUNDAY, OCTOBER 26
ARIZONA 16, SAN FRANCISCO 13 (OT)—at Sun Devil Stadium, attendance 40,824. Tim Duncan made a 39-yard field goal in overtime to lift the Cardinals to victory in an NFC West matchup. Duncan made a 53-yard field goal just before halftime to give Arizona a 10-7 halftime lead. Adrian Wilson blocked Bill LaFleur's punt in the third quarter to set up Duncan's 20-yard field goal. But Duncan missed a 37-yard field goal early in the fourth quarter and the 49ers responded with an 11-play, 73-yard drive capped by a wild game-tying play. Jeff Garcia scrambled to the Cardinals' 1 but fumbled. The ball popped into the air and was caught by tackle Kwame Harris, who ran 1-yard for a touchdown to make the score 13-13 with 7:12 left. Owen Pochman, who in the first half had a bad snap ruin his first extra-point attempt and missed a 45-yard field goal, missed wide right from 35 yards with 2:25 remaining. Arizona had a chance to win, but Duncan's 50-yard field-goal attempt fell short as time expired. In overtime, Blake completed a 9-yard pass to Bryant Johnson to the 49ers' 22 to set up Duncan's winning kick with 10:01 left. Blake was 14 of 24 for 97 yards. Marcel Shipp had 35 carries for 165 yards. Garcia was 13 of 24 for 153 yards.

San Francisco	6	0	0	7	0	—	13
Arizona	7	3	3	0	3	—	16

SF — Garcia 21 run (pass failed)
Ariz — Blake 1 run (Duncan kick)
Ariz — FG Duncan 53
Ariz — FG Duncan 20
SF — Harris 1 fumble recovery (Pochman kick)
Ariz — FG Duncan 39

BALTIMORE 26, DENVER 6—at M&T Bank Stadium, attendance 69,721. Matt Stover kicked 4 field goals and the defense intercepted 2 passes that both led to touchdowns as the Ravens continued a trend of winning every other game. Stover missed a 45-yard field goal on the Ravens' first possession, and the Broncos responded with a 55-yard drive capped by Jason Elam's 28-yard boot. The Ravens ended the half with 3 successive drives that culminated with field goals, capped by Stover's 22-yard kick as the half expired. Trailing 9-6 in the fourth quarter, Denver had the ball near midfield, but Ray Lewis intercepted Danny Kanell's pass and returned it 37 yards to the Broncos' 20 to set up Kyle Boller's 5-yard touchdown pass to Terry Jones with 7:35 left. The Ravens stopped the Broncos on downs with 4:03 left, leading to Stover's fourth field goal, and Gary Baxter's interception set up Jamal Lewis' 28-yard jaunt with 1:56 left to finish the scoring. Boller was 15 of 27 for 137 yards and 1 touchdown. Jamal Lewis had 32 carries for 134 yards. Kanell was 16 of 31 for 114 yards, with 2 interceptions.

Denver	3	0	3	0	—	6
Baltimore	0	9	0	17	—	26

Den — FG Elam 28
Balt — FG Stover 25
Balt — FG Stover 39
Balt — FG Stover 22
Den — FG Elam 22
Balt — Jones 5 pass from Boller (Stover kick)
Balt — FG Stover 29
Balt — J. Lewis 28 run (Stover kick)

CHICAGO 24, DETROIT 16—at Soldier Field, attendance 61,428. Making his second start of the season, Chris Chandler passed for 207 yards and a touchdown as the Bears jumped to a 24-0 lead and held off the Lions. The Bears led 7-0 late in the first half when Chandler engineered a 7-play, 64-yard drive capped by Paul Edinger's 37-yard field goal as the half expired. Jerry Azumah returned the second half's opening kickoff 89 yards in traffic down the left sideline for a touchdown, and Brock Forsey's 8-yard scoring run gave Chicago a 24-0 lead with 5:23 left in the third quarter. Reggie Swinton's kickoff return got the Lions on the board, and Detroit drove to the Bears' 3 before Joey Harrington's fourth-and-2 pass fell incomplete with 2:05 left in the game. The Lions got the ball back and scored with 53 seconds left, but Bill Schroeder illegally recovered the onside kick just before the 10-yard marker and Chicago ran out the clock. Chandler was 20 of 31 for 207 yards and 1 touchdown. Harrington was 23 of 40 for 180 yards and 1 touchdown, with 2 interceptions.

Detroit	0	0	8	8	— 16
Chicago	0	10	14	0	— 24

Chi — Gage 21 pass from Chandler (Edinger kick)
Chi — FG Edinger 37
Chi — Azumah 89 kickoff return (Edinger kick)
Chi — Forsey 8 run (Edinger kick)
Det — Swinton 96 kickoff return (Hakim pass from Harrington)
Det — Ricks 3 pass from Harrington (Anderson pass from Harrington)

CINCINNATI 27, SEATTLE 24—at Paul Brown Stadium, attendance 52,131. Jon Kitna passed for 2 touchdowns, and the Bengals' defense forced 5 turnovers to defeat the NFC West-leading Seahawks. With the score tied 14-14, Tory James intercepted Matt Hasselbeck's pass at the Seahawks' 39 to set up Shayne Graham's field goal with 59 seconds left in the half, but Hasselbeck completed 3 passes in the final minute to lead to Josh Brown's 27-yard field goal to tie the score as the half expired. Itula Mili's second touchdown catch gave Seattle a 24-17 lead, and the Bengals responded with a 17-play drive but had to settle for Graham's 25-yard field goal late in the third quarter. Seattle had a chance to extend its lead, but John Thornton blocked Brown's 49-yard field-goal attempt with 9:00 left, and three plays later, Kitna hit Chad Johnson on a slant pattern for a 53-yard touchdown for a 27-24 lead. Seattle drove to the Bengals' 31 and 35, but interceptions by Jason Simmons and Jeff Burris quelled the threats, with Burris' pick at the Bengals' 24 with 1:46 left ending Seattle's comeback hopes. Kitna was 19 of 31 for 240 yards and 2 touchdowns. Rudi Johnson had 27 carries for 101 yards. Hasselbeck was 26 of 43 for 347 yards and 3 touchdowns, with 3 interceptions.

Seattle	7	10	7	0	— 24
Cincinnati	7	10	3	7	— 27

Sea — Mili 46 pass from Hasselbeck (Brown kick)
Cin — R. Johnson 18 run (Graham kick)
Cin — Washington 8 pass from Kitna (Graham kick)
Sea — Alexander 2 pass from Hasselbeck (Brown kick)
Cin — FG Graham 30
Sea — FG Brown 27
Sea — Mili 6 pass from Hasselbeck (Brown kick)
Cin — FG Graham 25
Cin — C. Johnson 53 pass from Kitna (Graham kick)

INDIANAPOLIS 30, HOUSTON 21—at RCA Dome, attendance 56,132. Peyton Manning passed for 269 yards and 3 touchdowns as the Colts rallied from a 14-3 deficit to remain in first place in the AFC South. The Texans took a 14-3 lead on David Carr's 1-yard touchdown pass to Billy Miller with 4:55 left in the second quarter, but Carr injured his ankle on the play and was forced to leave the game. The Colts responded by scoring on their next five possessions. Manning's 2-yard touchdown pass to Reggie Wayne with 15 seconds left in the half put the Colts ahead 17-14, and his 57-yard pass two plays into the second half extended the advantage to 24-14. Domanick Davis' 2-yard scoring run capped a 12-play drive early in the fourth quarter to cut the deficit to six points, but the Colts answered with a 13-play drive that ended with Mike Vanderjagt's 22-yard field goal with 5:16 remaining. The Texans failed to cross midfield on their final two possessions. Manning was 22 of 30 for 269 yards and 3 touchdowns. Edgerrin James had 23 carries for 104 yards, and Marvin Harrison had 8 catches for 100 yards. Carr was 8 of 9 for 62 yards and 1 touchdown, and Tony Banks was 12 of 17 for 88 yards, with 1 interception. Davis had 25 carries for 109 yards.

Houston	0	14	0	7	— 21
Indianapolis	3	14	10	3	— 30

Ind — FG Vanderjagt 31
Hous — Davis 15 run (Brown kick)
Hous — Miller 1 pass from Carr (Brown kick)
Ind — Pollard 1 pass from Manning (Vanderjagt kick)
Ind — Wayne 2 pass from Manning (Vanderjagt kick)
Ind — Wayne 57 pass from Manning (Vanderjagt kick)
Ind — FG Vanderjagt 29
Hous — Davis 2 run (Brown kick)
Ind — FG Vanderjagt 22

TENNESSEE 30, JACKSONVILLE 17—at ALLTEL Stadium, attendance 55,918. Steve McNair passed for 187 yards and Eddie George rushed for 2 touchdowns as the Titans scored at least 30 points for the fifth consecutive game. The Titans rushed 38 times and completed 78 percent of their passes to maintain possession for 39:14. The Titans scored on their first two possessions to take a 10-0 lead, but Byron Leftwich completed a 49-yard scoring pass to Jimmy Smith to pull within 17-10 with 3:38 left in the half. But Gary Anderson kicked a 43-yard field goal just before halftime, and Robaire Smith's 43-yard interception return to the Jaguars' 7 set up George's second 1-yard touchdown run for a 27-10 lead with 8:36 left in the third quarter. Tony Beckham intercepted Leftwich's pass in the end zone for a touchback early in the fourth quarter to spark the Titans' 17-play, 11:14 drive, which included 13 carries by George, and was capped by Anderson's third field goal with 1:47 left. McNair was 21 of 27 for 187 yards and 1 touchdown, with 1 interception. Leftwich was 15 of 28 for 158 yards and 1 touchdown, with 3 interceptions, and David Garrard was 9 of 12 for 86 yards and 1 touchdown.

Tennessee	10	10	7	3	— 30
Jacksonville	0	10	0	7	— 17

Tenn — FG Anderson 43
Tenn — George 1 run (Anderson kick)
Jax — FG Marler 49
Tenn — Calico 7 pass from McNair (Anderson kick)
Jax — Smith 49 pass from Leftwich (Marler kick)
Tenn — FG Anderson 43
Tenn — George 1 run (Anderson kick)
Tenn — FG Anderson 33
Jax — Wrighster 5 pass from Garrard (Marler kick)

N.Y. GIANTS 29, MINNESOTA 17—at Metrodome, attendance 64,114. Kerry Collins completed 2 touchdown passes to Ike Hilliard as the Giants knocked the Vikings from the ranks of the unbeaten. The Giants drove deep into Vikings' territory on their initial five possessions, but had to settle for 3 field goals by Brett Conway and led just 16-10 early in the third quarter. Daunte Culpepper's 1-yard touchdown pass to Randy Moss, set up by his 32-yard strike to Nate Burleson, gave Minnesota a 17-16 lead with 6:22 left in the third quarter. In the middle of the fourth quarter, Collins engineered a 6-play, 80-yard drive, highlighted by 46- and 19-yard passes to Jeremy Shockey, to take a 22-17 lead on Tiki Barber's 2-yard run with 5:29 left. Frank Walker intercepted Culpepper's pass on the next play, and Collins connected with Hilliard on a 14-yard touchdown on third-and-7 with 3:39 remaining to clinch the victory. Collins was 23 of 39 for 375 yards and 2 touchdowns, with 1 interception. Hilliard had 9 catches for 100 yards. Culpepper was 18 of 31 for 241 yards and 2 touchdowns, with 2 interceptions, and Moss had 7 catches for 125 yards.

N.Y. Giants	7	6	3	13	— 29
Minnesota	3	7	7	0	— 17

Minn — FG Elling 51
NYG — Hilliard 19 pass from Collins (Conway kick)
NYG — FG Conway 20
Minn — Moss 33 pass from Culpepper (Elling kick)
NYG — FG Conway 44
NYG — FG Conway 37
Minn — Moss 1 pass from Culpepper (Elling kick)
NYG — Barber 2 run (pass failed)
NYG — Hilliard 14 pass from Collins (Conway kick)

NEW ENGLAND 9, CLEVELAND 3—at Gillette Stadium, attendance 64,114. Adam Vinatieri kicked 3 field goals and the Patriots' defense only allowed the Browns to cross midfield once en route to victory. Vinatieri missed a 48-yard field goal in the second quarter and the Browns responded with their longest drive, 12 plays for 51 yards, and capped by Phil Dawson's 29-yard field goal just before halftime to tie the score. Brady engineered 8- and 11-play drives in the second half that both culminated with Vinatieri kicks, the last with 2:05 remaining. Cleveland drove to the Browns' 45, but Ty Law intercepted Kelly Holcomb's pass to preserve the win. Brady was 20 of 33 for 259 yards. Daniel Graham had 7 catches for 110 yards. Tim Couch started and was 7 of 11 for 40 yards before leaving with a sprained thumb and was replaced by Holcomb, who led the team to its lone scoring drive and was 15 of 25 for 115 yards, with 1 interception.

Cleveland	0	3	0	0	— 3
New England	3	0	3	3	— 9

NE — FG Vinatieri 27
Cle — FG Dawson 29
NE — FG Vinatieri 28
NE — FG Vinatieri 38

CAROLINA 23, NEW ORLEANS 20 (OT)—at Louisiana Superdome, attendance 68,370. John Kasay kicked his third overtime game-winning field goal in the Panthers' first seven games. The Panthers forced 3 turnovers, while committing none, and turned them into 10 points. A fumble by Aaron Brooks was recovered by Dan Morgan and set up Stephen Davis' 1-yard touchdown run early in the second quarter for a 10-0 lead. New Orleans responded by scoring on its next three possessions, capped by Steve Gleason's blocked punt with four seconds left in the half to set up John Carney's 46-yard field goal for a 17-10 lead. The Saints still led 17-13 in the fourth quarter when Steve Smith's 19-yard punt return and 16-yard reception led to Davis' second touchdown for a 20-17 advantage with 3:46 left. The Saints responded with a 10-play drive, highlighted by Brooks' 16-yard pass to Jerome Pathon on fourth-and-10, to set up Carney's tying kick with 36 seconds left. The Saints won the overtime coin toss and Michael Lewis returned the kick 53 yards, but on fourth-and-1 Deuce McAllister was stopped behind the line and fumbled. Kris Jenkins recovered at the Panthers' 38, and Davis' 34-yard run set up Kasay's 31-yard field goal with 10:24 left in overtime. Delhomme, in his return to New Orleans, was 12 of 27 for 148 yards. Davis rushed 31 times for 178 yards, and Smith had 9 catches for 100 yards. Brooks was 20 of 33 for 187 yards and 2 touchdowns, with 1 interception. McAllister had 26 carries for 101 yards.

Carolina	3	7	3	7	3	—	23
New Orleans	0	17	0	3	0	—	20

Car — FG Kasay 24
Car — Davis 1 run (Kasay kick)
NO — Horn 14 pass from Brooks (Carney kick)
NO — Horn 23 pass from Brooks (Carney kick)
NO — FG Carney 46
Car — FG Kasay 29
Car — Davis 1 run (Kasay kick)
NO — FG Carney 42
Car — FG Kasay 31

PHILADELPHIA 24, N.Y. JETS 17—at Lincoln Financial Field, attendance 67,853. Correll Buckhalter rushed for 2 touchdowns as the Eagles rallied to defeat the Jets. Both teams scored on their first two possessions, and the Eagles led 14-10. The Jets drove to the Eagles' 20 late in the first half, but Santana Moss fumbled and Ike Reese recovered. Aaron Beasley's interception and 25-yard return to beyond midfield set up LaMont Jordan's 4-yard touchdown run for a 17-14 Jets lead with four seconds left in the third quarter. David Akers attempted to tie the game with a 55-yard field goal, but it fell short. However, two plays later, Michael Lewis intercepted Chad Pennington's pass and returned it 23 yards to the Eagles' 43 to set up Donovan McNabb's 4-yard touchdown toss to Jon Ritchie with 6:42 to play. The Eagles' defense forced a three-and-out, and Akers added a 30-yard field goal with 1:12 left. The Jets drove to the Eagles' 42, but Pennington's Hail Mary fell incomplete in the end zone as time expired. McNabb was 17 of 23 for 141 yards and 1 touchdown, with 1 interception. Buckhalter had 15 carries for 100 yards. Vinny Testaverde started and was 7 of 11 for 112 yards and 1 touchdown before being replaced, as scheduled, by Pennington, who was 14 of 24 for 154 yards, with 1 interception. Curtis Martin had 20 carries for 110 yards.

N.Y. Jets	10	0	7	0	—	17
Philadelphia	7	7	0	10	—	24

NYJ — FG Brien 30
Phil — Buckhalter 6 run (Akers kick)
NYJ — Moss 60 pass from Testaverde (Brien kick)
Phil — Buckhalter 7 run (Akers kick)
NYJ — Jordan 4 run (Brien kick)
Phil — Ritchie 4 pass from McNabb (Akers kick)
Phil — FG Akers 30

ST. LOUIS 33, PITTSBURGH 21—at Heinz Field, attendance 62,665. Marc Bulger, who passed for 375 yards, and rookie Arlen Harris, who scored 3 touchdowns, led the Rams to their fourth consecutive victory. The Rams had advantages in first downs (26-11), yards (448-245), and time of possession (40:00-20:00). Antwaan Randle El lined up at quarterback and ran 32 yards to set up Maddox's 22-yard scoring pass to Hines Ward to allow the Steelers to take a 21-20 lead with 6:51 left in the third quarter. The Rams responded with a 70-yard drive, highlighted by Bulger's 30-yard pass to Brandon Manumaleuna to set up Harris' second touchdown. Harris capped an 11-play fourth-quarter drive with another 9-yard run to give the Rams a 33-21 lead with 7:54 left. Interceptions by Aeneas Williams and DeJuan Groce ended the Steelers' final two drives. Bulger was 22 of 37 for 375 yards and 1 touchdown. Torry Holt had 7 catches for 174 yards. Maddox was 12 of 28 for 159 yards and 2 touchdowns, with 3 interceptions.

St. Louis	7	10	10	6	—	33
Pittsburgh	7	7	7	0	—	21

StL — Holt 36 pass from Bulger (Wilkins kick)
Pitt — Randle El 84 punt return (Reed kick)
StL — Harris 1 run (Wilkins kick)
Pitt — Ward 9 pass from Maddox (Reed kick)
StL — FG Wilkins 20
StL — FG Wilkins 22
Pitt — Ward 22 pass from Maddox (Reed kick)
StL — Harris 9 run (Wilkins kick)
StL — Harris 9 run (run failed)

TAMPA BAY 16, DALLAS 0—at Raymond James Stadium, attendance 65,602. The Buccaneers' defense allowed just 178 yards and 9 first downs to snap the Cowboys' five-game winning streak. Billy Cundiff missed a 41-yard field-goal attempt late in the first quarter and fumbled the ball away at the Buccaneers' 27 with 4:09 left in the game. In between, Tampa Bay scored 16 points, 10 of which were set up by Ronde Barber's and Jermaine Phillips' interceptions, to take a 16-0 lead with 2:03 left in the third quarter. Shelton Quarles recovered Quincy Carter's fumble late in the fourth quarter, and Tampa Bay ran out the clock. Brad Johnson was 13 of 26 for 151 yards and 1 touchdown. Michael Pittman had 30 carries for 113 yards. Carter was 15 of 25 for 140 yards, with 2 interceptions.

Dallas	0	0	0	0	—	0
Tampa Bay	0	10	6	0	—	16

TB — FG Gramatica 24
TB — K. Johnson 7 pass from B. Johnson (Gramatica kick)
TB — FG Gramatica 26
TB — FG Gramatica 50

SUNDAY NIGHT, OCTOBER 26

KANSAS CITY 38, BUFFALO 5—at Arrowhead Stadium, attendance 65,671. Priest Holmes scored 3 touchdowns and the Chiefs' defense forced 7 turnovers to remain the lone undefeated team. Pierson Prioleau blocked Jason Baker's punt out of the end zone for a safety to give Buffalo a 2-0 lead less than five minutes into the game. Kansas City scored touchdowns on four of its next five possessions, capped by Trent Green's 1-yard scoring pass to Tony Gonzalez with 10 seconds left in the first half for a 28-5 halftime lead. Ryan Sims intercepted Drew Bledsoe's pass at the Chiefs' 1 late in the third quarter, and John Browning recovered Bledsoe's fourth-quarter fumble to set up Holmes' 15-yard touchdown run with 7:16 to play. Green was 20 of 35 for 273 yards and 2 touchdowns. Dante Hall had 4 catches for 107 yards. Bledsoe was 23 of 34 for 153 yards, with 3 interceptions, and Alex Van Pelt was 2 for 4 for 12 yards, with 2 interceptions. Travis Henry rushed 22 times for 124 yards.

Buffalo	2	3	0	0	—	5
Kansas City	7	21	0	10	—	38

Buff — Safety, Prioleau blocked punt out of end zone
KC — Hall 67 pass from Green (Andersen kick)
KC — Holmes 4 run (Andersen kick)
KC — Holmes 13 run (Andersen kick)
Buff — FG Lindell 20
KC — Gonzalez 1 pass from Green (Andersen kick)
KC — Holmes 15 run (Andersen kick)
KC — FG Andersen 49

MONDAY NIGHT, OCTOBER 27

MIAMI 26, SAN DIEGO 10—at Sun Devil Stadium, attendance 62,391. Brian Griese, in his first game with the Dolphins, passed for 3 touchdowns as Miami defeated the Chargers in a game that was moved to Tempe 24 hours prior to kickoff because of the wildfires in the San Diego area. Miami took advantage of 3 interceptions to score on four of its first five possessions en route to a 24-3 halftime lead. San Diego drove inside the Dolphins' 10 three times, once in the first half and twice after halftime, without scoring. An interception by Patrick Surtain allowed Miami to maintain a 17-3 lead, and the Dolphins' defense twice stopped the Chargers on downs, once at the 9-yard line and another time at the Dolphins' 5, in the second half. The Dolphins registered 6 sacks, highlighted by Rob Burnett's sack in the fourth quarter that forced Drew Brees to fumble at the Chargers' 10. The ball was recovered in the end zone by tackle Damion McIntosh, who was tackled by Jason Taylor for a safety with 8:06 left. Griese was 20 of 29 for 192 yards and 3 touchdowns. Brees was 19 of 30 for 190 yards, with 3 interceptions.

Miami	10	14	0	2	—	26
San Diego	3	0	0	7	—	10

Mia — Chambers 5 pass from Griese (Mare kick)
Mia — FG Mare 44
SD — FG Christie 51
Mia — McKnight 2 pass from Griese (Mare kick)
Mia — McMichael 7 pass from Griese (Mare kick)
SD — Tomlinson 1 run (Christie kick)
Mia — Safety, Taylor tackled McIntosh in end zone

NINTH WEEK SUMMARIES

American Football Conference

East Division	**W**	**L**	**T**	**Pct.**	**Pts.**	**OP**
New England	7	2	0	.778	184	155
Miami	5	3	0	.625	161	110
Buffalo	4	4	0	.500	143	148
N.Y. Jets	2	6	0	.250	139	149
North Division	**W**	**L**	**T**	**Pct.**	**Pts.**	**OP**
Baltimore	5	3	0	.625	184	149
Cincinnati	3	5	0	.375	152	173
Cleveland	3	5	0	.375	115	130
Pittsburgh	2	6	0	.250	148	202
South Division	**W**	**L**	**T**	**Pct.**	**Pts.**	**OP**
Indianapolis	7	1	0	.875	231	143
Tennessee	6	2	0	.750	224	167
Houston	3	5	0	.375	135	210
Jacksonville	1	7	0	.125	144	208
West Division	**W**	**L**	**T**	**Pct.**	**Pts.**	**OP**
Kansas City	8	0	0	1.000	246	130
Denver	5	4	0	.556	210	171
Oakland	2	6	0	.250	138	184
San Diego	1	7	0	.125	132	215

National Football Conference

East Division	**W**	**L**	**T**	**Pct.**	**Pts.**	**OP**
Dallas	6	2	0	.750	171	130
Philadelphia	5	3	0	.625	142	152

	W	L	T	Pct.	Pts.	OP
N.Y. Giants	4	4	0	.500	165	168
Washington	3	5	0	.375	149	192
North Division	**W**	**L**	**T**	**Pct.**	**Pts.**	**OP**
Minnesota	6	2	0	.750	223	163
Green Bay	4	4	0	.500	230	193
Chicago	3	5	0	.375	141	199
Detroit	2	6	0	.250	140	197
South Division	**W**	**L**	**T**	**Pct.**	**Pts.**	**OP**
Carolina	6	2	0	.750	151	139
Tampa Bay	4	4	0	.500	164	114
New Orleans	4	5	0	.444	189	205
Atlanta	1	7	0	.125	130	243
West Division	**W**	**L**	**T**	**Pct.**	**Pts.**	**OP**
Seattle	6	2	0	.750	193	147
St. Louis	5	3	0	.625	213	159
San Francisco	4	5	0	.444	202	152
Arizona	3	5	0	.375	115	207

SUNDAY, NOVEMBER 2

ARIZONA 17, CINCINNATI 14—at Sun Devil Stadium, attendance 23,531. Jeff Blake passed for 166 yards and 2 touchdowns as Arizona won its second consecutive game. The Cardinals scored on their first possession, but Tyrone Williams recovered Marcel Shipp's fumble near midfield to set up consecutive touchdown drives by Cincinnati for a 14-7 lead. Arizona drove 13 plays for 80 yards to begin the second half, capped by Blake's 7-yard touchdown pass to Anquan Boldin, for a 17-14 lead. The Cardinals' defense did not allow the Bengals to cross midfield on any of their remaining eight possessions, with Dexter Jackson's interception near midfield with 1:49 left damaging Cincinnati's best scoring opportunity. Blake was 18 of 28 for 166 yards and 2 touchdowns. Shipp had 29 carries for 141 yards. Jon Kitna was 21 of 38 for 218 yards and 1 touchdown, with 2 interceptions.

Cincinnati	7	7	0	0	—	14
Arizona	7	3	7	0	—	17

Ariz — F. Jones 1 pass from Blake (Duncan kick)
Cin — Ru. Johnson 2 run (Graham kick)
Cin — Warrick 15 pass from Kitna (Graham kick)
Ariz — FG Duncan 31
Ariz — Boldin 7 pass from Blake (Duncan kick)

PHILADELPHIA 23, ATLANTA 16—at Georgia Dome, attendance 70,064. Donovan McNabb passed for 312 yards and 1 touchdown as the Eagles rallied to defeat the Falcons. The Eagles scored on their first two possessions, including a 37-yard touchdown pass to Freddie Mitchell, to give the Eagles a 10-0 lead. The Falcons scored on their next three possessions, the third score set up by Allen Rossum's 72-yard punt return, to give Atlanta a 13-10 halftime lead. David Akers kicked a 25-yard field goal to conclude the Eagles' first drive of the second half to tie the game, but Ed Jasper blocked Akers' 41-yard attempt on the next possession. The Eagles' defense forced another punt, and McNabb completed passes of 36 and 28 yards to L.J. Smith to set up Duce Staley's 4-yard touchdown run with 14:09 left. Doug Johnson entered the game and guided the Falcons to a field goal to cut the deficit to 23-16. Atlanta got the ball back with 3:28 left, but was forced to punt with 2:49 remaining. Correll Buckhalter ran for a first down, so the Falcons didn't get the ball back until there were 14 seconds left. McNabb was 21 of 33 for 312 yards and 1 touchdown. Kurt Kittner was 11 of 18 for 78 yards, with 1 interception, and Johnson was 5 of 10 for 86 yards.

Philadelphia	10	0	3	10	—	23
Atlanta	0	13	0	3	—	16

Phil — FG Akers 21
Phil — F. Mitchell 37 pass from McNabb (Akers kick)
Atl — Duckett 1 run (Feely kick)
Atl — FG Feely 40
Atl — FG Feely 25
Phil — FG Akers 25
Phil — Staley 4 run (Akers kick)
Phil — FG Akers 40
Atl — FG Feely 46

BALTIMORE 24, JACKSONVILLE 17—at M&T Bank Stadium, attendance 69,486. Kyle Boller passed for 1 touchdown and the Ravens' defense forced 3 second-half turnovers to lead the Ravens to victory. The Ravens won despite recording just 9 first downs. Baltimore scored a touchdown 1:26 into the game, but Akin Ayodele's 15-yard fumble return in the third quarter tied the game. Lamont Brightful returned the ensuing kickoff 58 yards to set up Matt Stover's second field goal for a 13-10 Ravens' lead. Anthony Weaver sacked Byron Leftwich, forced him to fumble, and recovered the ball at the Jaguars' 24 on the first play of the fourth quarter to set up Stover's third field goal. Three plays later, Peter Boulware forced Leftwich to fumble. Tom Knight recovered, and three plays later Chester Taylor scored on a 29-yard run with 7:33 remaining for a 24-10 lead. Leftwich completed a 5-yard touchdown pass to David Allen with 3:11 left, and the Jaguars got the ball back on their own 20 with 1:49 remaining. Jacksonville drove to the Ravens' 31 with 1:00 left, but Ray Lewis made a leaping interception to clinch the victory. Boller was 10 of 23 for 156 yards and 1 touchdown, with 1 interception. Leftwich was 22 of 34 for 208 yards and 1 touchdown, with 1 interception.

Jacksonville	0	3	7	7	—	17
Baltimore	7	0	6	11	—	24

Balt — Heap 33 pass from Boller (Stover kick)
Jax — FG Marler 24
Balt — FG Stover 23
Jax — Ayodele 15 fumble return (Marler kick)
Balt — FG Stover 32
Balt — FG Stover 23
Balt — C. Taylor 29 run (Heap pass from Boller)
Jax — Allen 5 pass from Leftwich (Marler kick)

CHICAGO 20, SAN DIEGO 7—at Soldier Field, attendance 61,500. Anthony Thomas rushed for 111 yards and 2 touchdowns as the Bears won their second consecutive game. The Bears' defense permitted just 199 yards, 114 of which came when Doug Flutie replaced Drew Brees in the fourth quarter. Chicago drove 56 and 74 yards on its first two possessions, sandwiched around a missed Steve Christie 46-yard field goal, to take a 10-0 lead. The Chargers went five consecutive possessions without a first down, but trailed just 13-0 when Sammy Davis intercepted Chris Chandler's pass at the Chargers' 26 with 13:17 remaining. Flutie entered the game and guided the club on a 74-yard drive, including a 17-yard scramble, to cut the deficit to 13-7 on LaDainian Tomlinson's 3-yard run with 9:13 left. San Diego forced a punt, but Charles Tillman saved Brad Maynard's punt from going into the end zone and the ball was downed at the Chargers' 1. The Chargers punted from their own 17 moments later, and R.W. McQuarters' 36-yard return set up Thomas' 1-yard run with 21 seconds left. Chandler was 21 of 30 for 224 yards, with 1 interception. Brees was 7 of 15 for 49 yards, with 1 interception, and Flutie was 8 of 11 for 70 yards.

San Diego	0	0	0	7	—	7
Chicago	3	7	3	7	—	20

Chi — FG Edinger 38
Chi — Thomas 1 run (Edinger kick)
Chi — FG Edinger 22
SD — Tomlinson 3 run (Christie kick)
Chi — Thomas 1 run (Edinger kick)

DALLAS 21, WASHINGTON 14—at Texas Stadium, attendance 64,002. Troy Hambrick rushed for 100 yards and 2 touchdowns for the Cowboys. Dallas outgained the Redskins 400-213 and the Cowboys' defense recorded 4 sacks. The Redskins' defense forced 4 turnovers, including one on each of Dallas' first three possessions, but Washington only managed 6 points from the trio of miscues. Dallas led 7-6 at halftime and scored on its first two possessions of the second half to take a 21-6 lead with 11:21 remaining. Patrick Ramsey engineered an 81-yard drive to cut the deficit to 21-14 with 2:30 left. Washington kicked deep, but two plays later, Terry Glenn raced 47 yards down the right sideline on a reverse, and Jamar Martin got another first down with 1:46 remaining to allow Dallas to run out the clock. Quincy Carter was 17 of 33 for 196 yards and 1 touchdown, with 2 interceptions. Ramsey was 16 of 30 for 147 yards and 2 touchdowns.

Washington	6	0	0	8	—	14
Dallas	0	7	7	7	—	21

Wash — Coles 7 pass from Ramsey (kick blocked)
Dall — Hambrick 2 run (Cundiff kick)
Dall — Hambrick 1 run (Cundiff kick)
Dall — Glenn 19 pass from Carter (Cundiff kick)
Wash — Jacobs 19 pass from Ramsey (McCants pass from Ramsey)

DETROIT 23, OAKLAND 13—at Ford Field, attendance 61,561. Jason Hanson kicked 3 field goals and the Lions' defense forced 4 turnovers as Detroit snapped a six-game losing streak. Marques Tuiasosopo, making his first career start in place of injured Rich Gannon, was intercepted by Otis Smith on his opening possession to set up Hanson's 54-yard field goal. On Oakland's second possession, Sebastian Janikowski missed a 55-yard field goal, and on its third possession, Jerry Rice fumbled and Barrett Green returned it 38 yards to the Raiders' 12 to set up Olandis Gary's 2-yard touchdown run. Tuiasosopo left with a season-ending knee injury in the second quarter and was replaced by Rick Mirer. Joey Harrington completed a 33-yard touchdown pass to Cory Schlesinger on the opening possession of the third quarter to extend the Lions' lead to 17-3. Detroit added field goals on its next two drives to take a 23-13 lead with 5:52 left, but Mirer was intercepted on each of the Raiders' final two possessions. Harrington was 13 of 21 for 117 yards and 1 touchdown, with 1 interception. Tuiasosopo was 6 of 11 for 65 yards, with 1 interception, and Mirer was 15 of 28 for 125 yards, with 2 interceptions.

Oakland	0	3	7	3	—	13
Detroit	10	0	7	6	—	23

Det — FG Hanson 54
Det — Gary 2 run (Hanson kick)
Oak — FG Janikowski 55
Det — Schlesinger 33 pass from Harrington (Hanson kick)
Oak — Garner 7 run (Janikowski kick)
Det — FG Hanson 42
Oak — FG Janikowski 24
Det — FG Hanson 39

HOUSTON 14, CAROLINA 10—at Reliant Stadium, attendance 70,052. Tony Banks, starting for the injured David Carr, passed for 154 yards and a fourth-quarter touchdown as the Texans defeated the first-place Panthers. Each team had just seven possessions in the game, and the Panthers' lone touchdown came on their first drive. Houston drove 88 yards for a touchdown to begin the second half, and following John Kasay's field goal, drove 72 yards, highlighted by Banks' 35-yard pass to Andre Johnson on third-and-18, and capped by Billy Miller's 20-yard touchdown catch with 9:30 left. Carolina punted with 6:04 remaining, but allowed 2 key third-down conversions and did not get the ball back until there was just one second left. Banks was 13 of 19 for 154 yards and 1 touchdown. Jake Delhomme was 13 of 23 for 193 yards and 1 touchdown, with 1 interception, and Stephen Davis rushed 30 times for 153 yards.

Carolina	7	0	3	0	— 10
Houston	0	0	7	7	— 14

Car — Smith 24 pass from Delhomme (Kasay kick)
Hous — Mack 1 run (Brown kick)
Car — FG Kasay 23
Hous — Miller 20 pass from Banks (Brown kick)

INDIANAPOLIS 23, MIAMI 17—at Pro Player Stadium, attendance 73,258. Peyton Manning passed for 266 yards and 1 touchdown as the Colts won in Miami. The Colts maintained possession for 37:40 and scored on five of their six possessions during the middle of the game, the last four on drives of 65, 72, 74, and 91 yards, to take a 23-14 lead with 9:40 remaining. A fumble by Marvin Harrison set up Olindo Mare's 23-yard field goal with 3:10 remaining, and Terrell Buckley intercepted Manning's pass at the Colts' 15 with 2:45 left. But Brian Griese was sacked by Dwight Freeney two plays later and fumbled. Raheem Brock recovered to allow the Colts to run out the clock. Manning was 23 of 37 for 266 yards and 1 touchdown, with 1 interception. Griese was 18 of 29 for 231 yards and 1 touchdown.

Indianapolis	0	9	7	7	— 23
Miami	7	0	7	3	— 17

Mia — Williams 3 run (Mare kick)
Ind — FG Vanderjagt 50
Ind — FG Vanderjagt 44
Ind — FG Vanderjagt 25
Ind — James 1 run (Vanderjagt kick)
Mia — Chambers 28 pass from Griese (Mare kick)
Ind — Walters 3 pass from Manning (Vanderjagt kick)
Mia — FG Mare 23

N.Y. GIANTS 31, N.Y. JETS 28 (OT)—at The Meadowlands, attendance 78,132. Brett Conway kicked a 29-yard field goal with four seconds left in overtime as the Giants withstood a Jets rally. The Giants' defense forced 4 turnovers, which led to 13 points, the last of which was a 3-yard scoring run by Dorsey Levens set up by Shaun Williams' interception to give the Giants a 28-13 lead with 9:58 remaining in the game. Chad Pennington, making his first start of the season following a preseason injury, engineered a 9-play, 67-yard drive, capped by Santana Moss' third touchdown catch, to cut the deficit to 28-21 with 5:59 left. The Jets got the ball back on their own 14 with 3:07 remaining, and Pennington completed 6 passes, including a 15-yard pass to Moss on fourth-and-1 and capped by his 9-yard strike to Anthony Becht with 29 seconds left to tie the game. The Giants won the overtime coin toss and drove to the Jets' 21, but Conway missed a 39-yard field-goal attempt wide left. After an exchange of punts, the Jets drove to the Giants' 32, but Doug Brien's 51-yard attempt was blocked by Will Allen. Kerry Collins connected on a 19-yard pass to Amani Toomer and 12-yard toss to Tiki Barber, and Barber had a 10-yard carry, setting up Conway's winning kick. Collins was 24 of 40 for 303 yards and 2 touchdowns, and Toomer had 6 catches for 127 yards. Pennington was 27 of 45 for 281 yards and 4 touchdowns, with 2 interceptions, and Moss had 10 catches for 121 yards and 3 touchdowns. Curtis Martin had 28 carries for 108 yards.

N.Y. Giants	0	13	7	8	3	— 31
N.Y. Jets	7	0	7	14	0	— 28

NYJ — Moss 8 pass from Pennington (Brien kick)
NYG — FG Conway 39
NYG — Toomer 39 pass from Collins (Conway kick)
NYG — FG Conway 36
NYJ — Moss 25 pass from Pennington (Brien kick)
NYG — Hilliard 6 pass from Collins (Conway kick)
NYG — Levens 3 run (Collins run)
NYJ — Moss 11 pass from Pennington (Brien kick)
NYJ — Becht 9 pass from Pennington (Brien kick)
NYG — FG Conway 29

SAN FRANCISCO 30, ST. LOUIS 10—at 3Com Park, attendance 67,812. Tim Rattay, making his first career start in place of injured Jeff Garcia, passed for 3 touchdowns to snap the Rams' four-game winning streak. The 49ers' defense forced 3 turnovers and registered 5 sacks. Cedric Wilson jump-started the 49ers by returning the opening kickoff 95 yards for a touchdown. The Rams responded with a field goal, but the 49ers scored on three of their next four possessions for a 24-3 lead with 4:15 left in the first half. Two plays into the second half, Bryant Young forced Marc Bulger to fumble, and Derek Smith recovered to set up Tai Streets' 5-yard touchdown catch for a 30-3 lead just over two minutes into the second half. Rattay was 19 of 29 for 236 yards and 3 touchdowns, with 1 interception. Bulger was 26 of 42 for 378 yards and 1 touchdown, with 2 interceptions. Torry Holt had 11 receptions for 200 yards.

St. Louis	3	0	0	7	— 10
San Francisco	14	10	6	0	— 30

SF — Wilson 95 kickoff return (Peterson kick)
StL — FG Wilkins 39
SF — Owens 5 pass from Rattay (Peterson kick)
SF — FG Peterson 44
SF — Lloyd 7 pass from Rattay (Peterson kick)
SF — Streets 5 pass from Rattay (kick blocked)
StL — Holt 41 pass from Bulger (Wilkins kick)

SEATTLE 23, PITTSBURGH 16—at Seahawks Stadium, attendance 66,507. Matt Hasselbeck passed for 215 yards and 1 touchdown as the Seahawks moved back into sole possession of first place in the NFC West. In a game that had no turnovers, the Seahawks led 6-3 at halftime and extended the advantage to 9-3 following D.D. Lewis' blocked punt early in the third quarter. Both teams scored on their next two possessions, with Jeff Reed's 21-yard field goal with 3:24 left cutting the deficit to 23-16. The Steelers forced a punt and got the ball back with 1:05 remaining, but gained just one first down before being stopped on downs. Hasselbeck was 18 of 31 for 215 yards and 1 touchdown. Tommy Maddox was 21 of 35 for 226 yards and 1 touchdown.

Pittsburgh	0	3	3	10	— 16
Seattle	3	3	3	14	— 23

Sea — FG Brown 36
Pitt — FG Reed 49
Sea — FG Brown 46
Sea — FG Brown 34
Pitt — FG Reed 33
Sea — Jackson 14 pass from Hasselbeck (Brown kick)
Pitt — Ward 2 pass from Maddox (Reed kick)
Sea — Alexander 1 run (Brown kick)
Pitt — FG Reed 21

NEW ORLEANS 17, TAMPA BAY 14—at Raymond James Stadium, attendance 65,524. Ashley Ambrose intercepted 2 passes and John Carney kicked a game-winning 47-yard field goal with eight seconds left for the Saints. The Saints were limited to 10 first downs on offense, and only had first downs on two of their final nine drives, but the defense forced 6 turnovers. Ambrose intercepted a pass at the Buccaneers' 38 early in the second quarter, and Aaron Brooks fired a touchdown pass to Michael Lewis on the next play for a 7-0 lead. In the third quarter, the Buccaneers drove to the Saints' 17, but Willie Whitehead forced Brad Johnson to fumble, and Roger Knight recovered. On Tampa Bay's next possession, Ambrose intercepted a pass and raced untouched 73 yards down the left sideline for a touchdown and 14-0 lead after three quarters. Johnson engineered a 97-yard scoring drive midway through the fourth quarter, and when Carney missed a 39-yard field goal attempt with 3:53 left, Tampa Bay had a chance to tie. The Buccaneers drove to the Saints' 30, and on fourth-and-10, Johnson completed a 30-yard touchdown pass to Keenan McCardell to tie the game with 2:08 remaining. But Brooks completed a 17-yard pass to Lewis and 13-yard pass to Boo Williams to set up Carney's winning kick. Brooks was 13 of 29 for 142 yards and 1 touchdown, with 1 interception. Deuce McAllister had 26 carries for 110 yards. Brad Johnson was 27 of 46 for 333 yards and 2 touchdowns, with 2 interceptions, and Keyshawn Johnson had 10 receptions for 124 yards.

New Orleans	0	7	7	3	— 17
Tampa Bay	0	0	0	14	— 14

NO — Lewis 38 pass from Brooks (Carney kick)
NO — Ambrose 73 interception return (Carney kick)
TB — Pittman 26 pass from B. Johnson (Gramatica kick)
TB — McCardell 30 pass from B. Johnson (Gramatica kick)
NO — FG Carney 47

SUNDAY NIGHT, NOVEMBER 2
GREEN BAY 30, MINNESOTA 27—at Metrodome, attendance 64,482. Brett Favre passed for 194 yards and 3 touchdowns, 2 caught by Javon Walker, as the Packers pulled within two games of the Vikings. Corey Chavous' interception at the Vikings' 30 in the second quarter stopped a Packers' drive and set up Daunte Culpepper's 4-yard touchdown pass to Jimmy Kleinsasser for a 14-13 lead with 2:07 left in the half. But Favre engineered a 7-play, 73-yard drive capped by Walker's 12-yard touchdown catch with 21 seconds left in the half for a 20-14 lead. Aaron Elling kicked field goals to culminate the Vikings' first two drives of the second half to tie the game, but Favre responded with another 73-yard drive, capped again by Walker's 12-yard touchdown catch, for a 27-20 lead. The Packers forced a punt and then took nearly seven minutes off the clock before Ryan Longwell's 27-yard field goal extended the lead with 2:37 remaining. Culpepper scored with 33 seconds left, but Darren Sharper recovered the onside kick to preserve the victory. Favre was 18 of 28 for 194 yards and 3 touchdowns, with 1 interception. Ahman Green had 21 carries for 137 yards. Culpepper was 21 of 34 for 202 yards and 2 touchdowns.

Green Bay	6	14	0	10	—	30
Minnesota	7	7	6	7	—	27

GB — FG Longwell 21
Minn — Moss 43 pass from Culpepper (Elling kick)
GB — FG Longwell 43
GB — Green 5 pass from Favre (Longwell kick)
Minn — Kleinsasser 4 pass from Culpepper (Elling kick)
GB — Walker 12 pass from Favre (Longwell kick)
Minn — FG Elling 47
Minn — FG Elling 37
GB — Walker 12 pass from Favre (Longwell kick)
GB — FG Longwell 27
Minn — Culpepper 1 run (Elling kick)

MONDAY NIGHT, NOVEMBER 3
NEW ENGLAND 30, DENVER 26—at INVESCO Field at Mile High, attendance 76,203. Tom Brady's 18-yard touchdown pass to David Givens with 30 seconds remaining, which was set up by a daring coaching decision, gave the Patriots a victory. Jason Elam made a 43-yard field goal in the second quarter to give Denver a 10-7 lead, but injured his hamstring and did not return. Danny Kanell's 1-yard touchdown pass to Mike Anderson with 28 seconds left in the half capped a 14-play drive and gave Denver a 17-10 lead, but Bethel Johnson's 63-yard kickoff return set up Adam Vinatieri's 46-yard field goal with one second left in the half. Late in the third quarter, Deltha O'Neal returned a punt 57 yards for a touchdown to give Denver a 24-20 lead. New England trailed 24-23 and faced fourth down from their own 1-yard line with 2:51 remaining. With three timeouts still at his disposal, Patriots coach Bill Belichick intentionally took a safety by having snapper Lonie Paxton snap the ball over punter Ken Walter's head and out of the end zone, hoping to enhance the Patriots' field possession. The plan worked perfectly, as O'Neal lost a yard returning the free kick, giving Denver the ball on its 15-yard line. The Patriots forced a three-and-out, got the ball back at their own 42 with 2:15 left, and Brady completed 4 of 5 passes, including 19- and 16-yard tosses to Kevin Faulk, to set up Givens' winning catch. Brady was 20 of 35 for 350 yards and 3 touchdowns, with 1 interception. Deion Branch had 3 receptions for 107 yards. Kanell was 16 of 35 for 163 yards and 1 touchdown, with 1 interception. Clinton Portis had 26 carries for 111 yards.

New England	7	6	7	10	—	30
Denver	7	10	7	2	—	26

Den — Portis 15 run (Elam kick)
NE — Branch 66 pass from Brady (Vinatieri kick)
Den — FG Elam 43
NE — FG Vinatieri 40
Den — Anderson 1 pass from Kanell (Knorr kick)
NE — FG Vinatieri 46
NE — Graham 6 pass from Brady (Vinatieri kick)
Den — O'Neal 57 punt return (Knorr kick)
NE — FG Vinatieri 28
Den — Safety, Paxton snap hit goal post
NE — Givens 18 pass from Brady (Vinatieri kick)

TENTH WEEK SUMMARIES
American Football Conference

East Division	**W**	**L**	**T**	**Pct.**	**Pts.**	**OP**
New England	7	2	0	.778	184	155
Miami	5	4	0	.556	168	141
Buffalo	4	5	0	.444	149	158
N.Y. Jets	3	6	0	.333	166	173
North Division	**W**	**L**	**T**	**Pct.**	**Pts.**	**OP**
Baltimore	5	4	0	.556	206	182
Cincinnati	4	5	0	.444	186	200
Cleveland	3	6	0	.333	135	171
Pittsburgh	3	6	0	.333	176	217
South Division	**W**	**L**	**T**	**Pct.**	**Pts.**	**OP**
Indianapolis	7	2	0	.778	254	171
Tennessee	7	2	0	.778	255	174
Houston	3	6	0	.333	162	244
Jacksonville	2	7	0	.222	172	231
West Division	**W**	**L**	**T**	**Pct.**	**Pts.**	**OP**
Kansas City	9	0	0	1.000	287	150
Denver	5	4	0	.556	210	171
Oakland	2	7	0	.222	162	211
San Diego	2	7	0	.222	174	243

National Football Conference

East Division	**W**	**L**	**T**	**Pct.**	**Pts.**	**OP**
Dallas	7	2	0	.778	181	136
Philadelphia	6	3	0	.667	159	166
N.Y. Giants	4	5	0	.444	172	195
Washington	4	5	0	.444	176	212
North Division	**W**	**L**	**T**	**Pct.**	**Pts.**	**OP**
Minnesota	6	3	0	.667	251	205
Green Bay	4	5	0	.444	244	210
Chicago	3	6	0	.333	151	211
Detroit	3	6	0	.333	152	207
South Division	**W**	**L**	**T**	**Pct.**	**Pts.**	**OP**
Carolina	7	2	0	.778	178	163
New Orleans	4	5	0	.444	189	205
Tampa Bay	4	5	0	.444	188	141
Atlanta	2	7	0	.222	157	250
West Division	**W**	**L**	**T**	**Pct.**	**Pts.**	**OP**
St. Louis	6	3	0	.667	246	181
Seattle	6	3	0	.667	213	174
San Francisco	4	5	0	.444	202	152
Arizona	3	6	0	.333	130	235

SUNDAY, NOVEMBER 9
CAROLINA 27, TAMPA BAY 24—at Ericsson Stadium, attendance 73,245. Jake Delhomme completed a 5-yard touchdown pass to Steve Smith with 1:06 remaining as the Panthers defeated the Buccaneers for the second time this season. Each team scored a defensive touchdown in the first half, but the Panthers' defense did not allow the Buccaneers to cross midfield until late in the third quarter en route to a 20-7 lead. A 31-yard punt set up a 5-play, 63-yard drive for Tampa Bay, capped by Brad Johnson's 23-yard touchdown pass to Keyshawn Johnson, to cut the deficit to 20-14 with 10:19 left. The Buccaneers' defense then forced a three-and-out, and Tampa Bay drove 65 yards, capped by Keenan McCardell's spinning one-handed 36-yard touchdown catch, to take a 21-20 lead with 4:44 remaining. Tim Wansley's second interception of the game two plays later set up Martín Gramatica's 39-yard field goal with 2:41 left. Delhomme connected on a 29-yard pass to Ricky Proehl and 22-yard blitz-beating pass to Muhsin Muhammad to set up Smith's game-winning catch. The Buccaneers reached no further than their own 41 before being stopped on downs. Delhomme was 20 of 32 for 277 yards and 2 touchdowns, with 2 interceptions. Proehl had 3 catches for 133 yards. Brad Johnson was 24 of 43 for 275 yards and 2 touchdowns, with 1 interception. McCardell had 9 catches for 118 yards.

Tampa Bay	0	7	0	17	—	24
Carolina	10	0	10	7	—	27

Car — Minter 29 interception return (Kasay kick)
Car — FG Kasay 47
TB — Wansley 23 interception return (Gramatica kick)
Car — FG Kasay 45
Car — Proehl 66 pass from Delhomme (Kasay kick)
TB — K. Johnson 23 pass from B. Johnson (Gramatica kick)
TB — McCardell 36 pass from B. Johnson (Gramatica kick)
TB — FG Gramatica 39
Car — Smith 5 pass from Delhomme (Kasay kick)

CINCINNATI 34, HOUSTON 27—at Paul Brown Stadium, attendance 50,437. Rudi Johnson tied the NFL record for most carries in a non-overtime game with 43, and rushed for 182 yards and 2 touchdowns for the winning Bengals. Cincinnati dominated the numbers with more first downs (27-13), yards (422-269), and time of possession (41:15-18:45). The Bengals led 17-10 and had the ball near midfield when Kenny Wright intercepted Jon Kitna's pass with 1:12 left in the first half. Six plays later, David Carr hit Jabar Gaffney with an 8-yard touchdown pass to tie the game, and Houston needed just six plays to drive 83 yards to begin the second half, highlighted by Domanick Davis' 53-yard run, and capped by his 2-yard touchdown for a 24-17 lead. The Bengals responded with touchdown drives of 73 and 65 yards, sandwiched between a Kris Brown field goal, to take a 31-27 lead with 10:56 left. The Bengals forced a three-and-out, and then held the ball for a 15-play, 56-yard, 7:07 drive, capped by Shayne Graham's 40-yard field goal with 2:32 remaining, for a 34-27 lead. On the next play, Duane Clemons tipped Carr's pass and Terrell Roberts intercepted it to ice the victory. Kitna was 18 of 26 for 182 yards and 1 touchdown, with 1 interception. Johnson rushed 43 times for 182 yards. Carr was 11 of 25 for 146 yards and 2 touchdowns, with 1 interception.

Houston	3	14	10	0	—	27
Cincinnati	7	10	7	10	—	34

Cin — Bennett 6 pass from Kitna (Graham kick)
Hous — FG Brown 45
Hous — Bradford 73 pass from Carr (Brown kick)
Cin — J. Johnson 1 run (Graham kick)
Cin — FG Graham 40
Hous — Gaffney 8 pass from Carr (Brown kick)
Hous — Davis 2 run (Brown kick)
Cin — Ru. Johnson 17 run (Graham kick)
Hous — FG Brown 33
Cin — Ru. Johnson 1 run (Graham kick)
Cin — FG Graham 40

DALLAS 10, BUFFALO 6—at Texas Stadium, attendance 63,770. The Cowboys' defense allowed just 185 yards, and did not allow a first down on 4 Bills' fourth-quarter possessions, as Dallas held off Buffalo. Late in the first quarter, Eric Ogbogu sacked Drew Bledsoe and forced him to fumble. La'Roi Glover recovered at the Bills' 24, and Quincy Carter connected on a 2-yard touchdown pass to Dan Campbell five plays later for a 7-0 lead. Dallas held a 7-6 halftime lead and used a 33-yard kickoff return by Derek Ross to open the second half to set up Billy Cundiff's 51-yard field goal. The Bills drove to the Cowboys' 25 late in the third quarter, but Greg Ellis forced Bledsoe to fumble and Dat Nguyen recovered at the Cowboys' 30. The Bills had one last chance to get the ball back with 1:09 remaining, but Adrian Murrell had a 17-yard run on third-and-8 to wrap up the victory. Carter was 15 of 32 for 116 yards and 1 touchdown. Bledsoe was 17 of 34 for 104 yards, with 2 fumbles.

Buffalo	0	6	0	0	—	6
Dallas	7	0	3	0	—	10

Dall — Campbell 2 pass from Carter (Cundiff kick)
Buff — FG Lindell 41
Buff — FG Lindell 29
Dall — FG Cundiff 51

DETROIT 12, CHICAGO 10—at Ford Field, attendance 61,492. Jason Hanson kicked a field goal each quarter, including the game-winner from 48 yards with 39 seconds left, to give the Lions consecutive victories for the first time since 2000. Trailing 6-3 in the third quarter, Chris Chandler completed a 23-yard pass to Marty Booker to set up Desmond Clark's 12-yard touchdown catch for a 10-6 lead. The Lions answered with Hanson's third field goal, and the Bears responded by driving to the Lions' 23, but Paul Edinger missed a 41-yard attempt, after missing from 48 yards earlier, to keep the score 10-9 with 12:03 left. The Lions had the ball on their own 35 with 2:27 left when Joey Harrington completed 5 consecutive passes, including an 18-yard pass to Az-Zahir Hakim, to set up Hanson's winning kick. Corey Harris intercepted Chandler's pass at the Lions' 37 with 27 seconds left to clinch the victory. Harrington was 24 of 38 for 238 yards. Chandler was 16 of 28 for 149 yards and 1 touchdown, with 1 interception.

Chicago	0	3	7	0	—	10
Detroit	3	3	3	3	—	12

Det — FG Hanson 24
Chi — FG Edinger 43
Det — FG Hanson 25
Chi — Clark 12 pass from Chandler (Edinger kick)
Det — FG Hanson 30
Det — FG Hanson 48

JACKSONVILLE 28, INDIANAPOLIS 23—at ALLTEL Stadium, attendance 45,037. Fred Taylor raced 32 yards for a touchdown with 1:08 remaining as the Jaguars shocked the Colts. In a game played in a steady rain, the Colts scored on four of their six first-half possessions, including each of the last three, to take a 20-7 halftime lead. The Jaguars opened the second half with an 80-yard drive, capped by Byron Leftwich's 4-yard run, and took the lead two possessions later when Leftwich fired a 43-yard strike to Jimmy Smith with 11:32 left. Peyton Manning's 70-yard pass to Marcus Pollard put the ball at the Jaguars' 9, and Manning completed a 4-yard touchdown pass to Troy Walters only to have the score nullified because Walters had stepped out of bounds prior to coming back and catching the pass. The Colts settled for Mike Vanderjagt's 27-yard field goal. The Jaguars then drove to the Colts' 11 and lined up for a field goal, but Mark Royals had trouble with the snap, and his pass attempt was intercepted by David Thornton with 2:09 left. However, the Colts were unable to get a first down and David Allen returned the ensuing punt 27 yards to the Colts' 31. Two plays later, Taylor broke three tackles en route to his game-winning 32-yard run. The Colts reached the Jaguars' 38 but Deke Cooper intercepted Manning's pass with 11 seconds left to preserve the victory. Leftwich was 12 of 22 for 179 yards and 1 touchdown. Taylor had 28 carries for 152 yards. Manning was 28 of 45 for 347 yards and 2 touchdowns, with 2 interceptions.

Indianapolis	7	13	0	3	—	23
Jacksonville	7	0	7	14	—	28

Ind — Harrison 30 pass from Manning (Vanderjagt kick)
Jax — Taylor 5 run (Marler kick)
Ind — FG Vanderjagt 27
Ind — FG Vanderjagt 26
Ind — Pollard 13 pass from Manning (Vanderjagt kick)
Jax — Leftwich 4 run (Marler kick)
Jax — Smith 43 pass from Leftwich (Marler kick)
Ind — FG Vanderjagt 27
Jax — Taylor 32 run (Marler kick)

KANSAS CITY 41, CLEVELAND 20—at Arrowhead Stadium, attendance 78,560. Trent Green passed for 368 yards and 3 touchdowns, and Priest Holmes scored twice, as the Chiefs improved to 9-0. Kansas City had more first downs (30-16) and total yards (438-199). Trailing 3-0, the Chiefs scored on six consecutive possessions, capped by Green's 28-yard touchdown pass to Johnnie Morton with 7:16 left in the third quarter, for a 34-17 lead. The Browns responded with a field goal, and had two more possessions but failed to cross midfield before Green iced the game with a 27-yard scoring pass to Eddie Kennison on fourth-and-3 with 2:19 left. Green was 29 of 42 for 368 yards and 3 touchdowns. Kennison had 7 catches for 115 yards. Kelly Holcomb was 19 of 27 for 149 yards and 1 touchdown, with 1 interception.

Cleveland	3	14	3	0	—	20
Kansas City	14	13	7	7	—	41

Cle — FG Dawson 50
KC — Holmes 1 run (Andersen kick)
KC — Holmes 9 run (Andersen kick)
Cle — Jackson 1 run (Dawson kick)
KC — Gonzalez 14 pass from Green (Andersen kick)
Cle — Bowers 2 pass from Holcomb (Dawson kick)
KC — FG Andersen 29
KC — FG Andersen 27
KC — Morton 28 pass from Green (Andersen kick)
Cle — FG Dawson 22
KC — Kennison 27 pass from Green (Andersen kick)

ATLANTA 27, N.Y. GIANTS 7—at Giants Stadium, attendance 78,813. Warrick Dunn rushed for 178 yards and 1 touchdown, and T.J. Duckett scored twice, as the Falcons' defense forced 4 turnovers to defeat the Giants. Dunn scored on a 45-yard touchdown run on the game's opening possession. The Giants tied the score in the second quarter, but were unable to take the lead because of 2 turnovers committed inside the Falcons' 25. Atlanta scored on its first drive of the second half, and Tod McBride intercepted Kerry Collins' pass three plays later and returned it to the Giants' 8 to set up Duckett's first touchdown. Bryan Scott recovered Tiki Barber's fumble at the Falcons' 5 early in the fourth quarter to thwart a scoring chance, and the Falcons' defense stopped New York on downs at the Giants' 40 later in the quarter to set up Duckett's second touchdown with 2:16 left. Kurt Kittner was 9 of 23 for 65 yards and 1 touchdown. Dunn rushed 25 times for 178 yards. Collins was 25 of 40 for 202 yards, with 2 interceptions. Barber rushed 16 times for 120 yards, and had 10 catches for 38 yards, but lost 2 fumbles.

Atlanta	7	0	13	7	—	27
N.Y. Giants	0	7	0	0	—	7

Atl — Dunn 45 run (Feely kick)
NYG — Levens 2 run (Conway kick)
Atl — Griffith 4 pass from Kittner (Feely kick)
Atl — Duckett 1 run (kick blocked)
Atl — Duckett 12 run (Feely kick)

N.Y. JETS 27, OAKLAND 24 (OT)—at Network Associates Coliseum, attendance 51,909. Doug Brien kicked a 38-yard field goal in overtime to cap the Jets' fourth-quarter comeback. Oakland used a 19-play, 80-yard drive that featured zero passes, and culminated with Zack Crockett's 1-yard plunge on fourth-and-goal, to take a 14-7 lead. The Raiders led 21-10 in the third quarter and drove into the Jets' red zone, but Tyrone Wheatley fumbled and Marvin Jones recovered at the Raiders' 7. Sebastian Janikowski kicked a field goal with 3:27 remaining for a 24-16 lead but Pennington, who in his first start of the season the previous week guided the Jets to a fourth-quarter comeback only to lose in overtime, once again worked his magic, engineering a 5-play, 73-yard drive, keyed by his 44-yard pass to Jerald Sowell, and capped by Sowell's 2-yard touchdown catch with 1:09 left. Pennington then completed a 2-point conversion pass to Anthony Becht to tie the game. In overtime, the Jets converted 2 third downs on a 12-play drive to set up Brien's winning kick. Pennington was 18 of 27 for 269 yards and 2 touchdowns. Moss had 6 catches for 146 yards. Rick Mirer, in his first start since 1999, was 18 of 25 for 186 yards and 1 touchdown.

N.Y. Jets	7	3	0	14	3	—	27
Oakland	7	14	0	3	0	—	24

Oak — Buchanon 78 punt return (Janikowski kick)
NYJ — Moss 65 pass from Pennington (Brien kick)
Oak — Crockett 1 run (Janikowski kick)
NYJ — FG Brien 48
Oak — Porter 2 pass from Mirer (Janikowski kick)
NYJ — Jordan 2 run (pass failed)
Oak — FG Janikowski 22
NYJ — Sowell 3 pass from Pennington (Becht pass from Pennington)
NYJ — FG Brien 38

PITTSBURGH 28, ARIZONA 15—at Heinz Field, attendance 59,520. Tommy Maddox passed for 3 touchdowns and Pittsburgh scored 3 touchdowns in a span of six minutes, 43 seconds to snap a five-game losing streak. The Steelers led 3-0 late in the first half when Jerome Bettis fumbled. Ronald McKinnon recovered at the Steelers' 17, but Arizona had to settle for Tim Duncan's 20-yard field goal just before halftime. A 24-yard punt by Scott Player on the opening possession of the second half set up Maddox's 5-yard touchdown pass to Hines Ward. Two plays later, Deshea Townsend sacked Jeff Blake and forced him to fumble. Kimo von Oelhoffen recovered and, on the ensuing play, Maddox fired a 22-yard scoring strike to Ward for his second touchdown in 1:07. Less than six minutes later, Antwaan Randle El returned a punt 52 yards for a touchdown, givng Pittsburgh a 28-3 lead with 6:33 left in the third quarter. Maddox was 12 of 24 for 159 yards and 3 touchdowns. Blake was 23 of 43 for 307 yards and 2 touchdowns. Anquan Boldin had 8 receptions for 118 yards.

Arizona	0	3	6	6	—	15
Pittsburgh	0	7	21	0	—	28

Pitt — Doering 9 pass from Maddox (Reed kick)
Ariz — FG Duncan 20
Pitt — Ward 5 pass from Maddox (Reed kick)
Pitt — Ward 22 pass from Maddox (Reed kick)
Pitt — Randle El 52 punt return (Reed kick)
Ariz — Boldin 11 pass from Blake (kick failed)
Ariz — B. Johnson 54 pass from Blake (pass failed)

SAN DIEGO 42, MINNESOTA 28—at Qualcomm Stadium, attendance 64,738. Forty-one-year-old Doug Flutie, making his first start in two years, passed for 248 yards and 2 touchdowns, and ran for 2 touchdowns for the first time in his career, to lead the Chargers to victory. The teams combined for 918 yards and 53 first downs. San Diego scored on all four of its first-half possessions, on drives of 63, 85, 68, and 66 yards, and Flutie's 4-yard touchdown pass to Antonio Gates with 25 seconds left in the half gave the Chargers a 28-14 lead. With the score

35-21, Flutie hit Tim Dwight with a 32-yard pass and, two plays later, picked up a fumbled snap and ran up the middle 13 yards for his second rushing touchdown for a 42-21 lead with 8:11 remaining. The Vikings cut the deficit to 42-28, recovered the onside kick, and drove to the Chargers' 7, but Terrence Kiel intercepted Daunte Culpepper's pass in the end zone for a touchback with 2:32 left to clinch the victory. Flutie was 21 of 29 for 248 yards and 2 touchdowns. LaDainian Tomlinson had 16 carries for 162 yards. Culpepper was 32 of 44 for 370 yards and 4 touchdowns, with 1 interception. Moe Williams had 11 catches for 126 yards, and Randy Moss added 11 receptions for 120 yards.

Minnesota	7	7	0	14	— 28
San Diego	14	14	7	7	— 42

SD — Boston 3 pass from Flutie (Christie kick)
SD — Tomlinson 73 run (Christie kick)
Minn — Moss 4 pass from Culpepper (Elling kick)
SD — Flutie 3 run (Christie kick)
Minn — Burleson 19 pass from Culpepper (Elling kick)
SD — Gates 4 pass from Flutie (Christie kick)
SD — Tomlinson 1 run (Christie kick)
Minn — Williams 31 pass from Culpepper (Elling kick)
SD — Flutie 13 run (Christie kick)
Minn — Williams 2 pass from Culpepper (Elling kick)

TENNESSEE 31, MIAMI 7—at The Coliseum, attendance 68,809. Steve McNair passed for 2 touchdowns and the Titans' defense forced 5 turnovers to defeat the Dolphins. Tennessee drove 69 and 82 yards on its first two possessions to take a 14-0 lead, and then scored its remaining 17 points off of turnovers. Miami never ran a play inside the Titans' 20, and needed a touchdown pass from Sage Rosenfels to Donald Lee with 20 seconds left to avoid being shut out. McNair was 17 of 23 for 201 yards and 2 touchdowns. Brian Griese was 15 of 27 for 131 yards, with 3 interceptions and 2 lost fumbles. Rosenfels, who played the final two drives, was 4 of 6 for 50 yards and 1 touchdown.

Miami	0	0	0	7	— 7
Tennessee	14	7	7	3	— 31

Tenn — Calico 12 pass from McNair (Anderson kick)
Tenn — George 2 run (Anderson kick)
Tenn — McCareins 24 pass from McNair (Anderson kick)
Tenn — Dyson 11 interception return (Anderson kick)
Tenn — FG Anderson 35
Mia — Lee 21 pass from Rosenfels (Mare kick)

WASHINGTON 27, SEATTLE 20—at FedExField, attendance 80,728. Wide receiver Rod Gardner completed a 10-yard touchdown pass to Trung Canidate with 1:57 remaining as the Redskins snapped a four-game losing streak. The Seahawks' Maurice Morris muffed the opening kickoff to set up John Hall's 20-yard field goal, but Seattle scored on its next two possessions, including a 14-play, 90-yard drive capped by Shaun Alexander's 1-yard run, to take a 14-3 lead. The Redskins drove into the Seahawks' red zone on four consecutive possessions to take a 20-17 third-quarter lead. Josh Brown then missed a 49-yard field-goal attempt before connecting from 48 yards on the next possession to tie the game with 9:59 left. Following an exchange of punts, the Redskins had the ball in their own territory, facing fourth-and-1 on their own 25 with 6:13 remaining. Coach Steve Spurrier decided to go for the first down, and Rock Cartwright gained 2 yards to maintain possession. Seven plays later, faced with third-and-5 from the Seahawks' 10, Spurrier had Patrick Ramsey throw a lateral to Gardner, who then threw across the field into the end zone to a wide open Canidate. The Seahawks drove to the Redskins' 30 with 44 seconds left, but Fred Smoot intercepted Matt Hasselbeck's pass, after it bounced off of Darrell Jackson's hands, to thwart the rally. Ramsey was 17 of 32 for 232 yards and 2 touchdowns, with 2 interceptions. Lavernaues Coles had 5 catches for 125 yards. Hasselbeck was 19 of 29 for 241 yards and 1 touchdown, with 1 interception.

Seattle	14	3	0	3	— 20
Washington	3	14	3	7	— 27

Wash — FG Hall 20
Sea — Engram 5 pass from Hasselbeck (Brown kick)
Sea — Alexander 1 run (Brown kick)
Wash — Coles 15 pass from Ramsey (Hall kick)
Sea — FG Brown 27
Wash — Gardner 14 pass from Ramsey (Hall kick)
Wash — FG Hall 34
Sea — FG Brown 48
Wash — Canidate 10 pass from Gardner (Hall kick)

SUNDAY NIGHT, NOVEMBER 9
ST. LOUIS 33, BALTIMORE 22—at Arrowhead Stadium, attendance 66,085. Jeff Wilkins kicked 4 fourth-quarter field goals as the Rams won despite getting just 7 first downs. The Rams set a record for the fewest yards (121) by a team that scored at least 30 points. The Ravens had more first downs (16-7), yards (267-121), and time of possession (37:21-22:39), but the Rams benefited from a few big plays and forced 7 turnovers, which they turned into 20 points. Jerametrius Butler's interception five plays into the game set up a 36-yard touchdown drive, and Dane Looker's 44-yard punt return to the Ravens' 1 led to Marshall Faulk's second touchdown run in the game's first 5:29. The Ravens cut the deficit to 14-12, but Kyle Boller fumbled and a blitzing Adam Archuleta grabbed the ball and raced 45 yards untouched for a 21-12 lead. Six-time Pro Bowl tackle Jonathan Ogden made his first NFL catch, on a 1-yard touchdown pass, just before halftime to cap an 80-yard drive to cut the deficit to 21-19. Chad Williams recovered DeJuan Groce's muffed punt in the third quarter to set up Matt Stover's go-ahead field goal, but Wilkins kicked field goals on four consecutive possessions, the last three starting at the Ravens' 36-, 35-, and 35-yard line, to put the game away. Marc Bulger was 13 of 26 for 110 yards, with 2 interceptions. Boller was 10 of 21 for 112 yards and 1 touchdown, with 1 interception. Chris Redman replaced the injured Boller for the second half and was 7 of 12 for 58 yards, with 2 interceptions, 1 lost fumble, and was sacked 5 times. Jamal Lewis rushed 27 times for 111 yards.

Baltimore	3	16	3	0	— 22
St. Louis	14	7	0	12	— 33

StL — Faulk 5 run (Wilkins kick)
StL — Faulk 1 run (Wilkins kick)
Balt — FG Stover 41
Balt — FG Stover 25
Balt — J. Lewis 2 run (pass failed)
StL — Archuleta 45 fumble return (Wilkins kick)
Balt — Ogden 1 pass from Boller (Stover kick)
Balt — FG Stover 41
StL — FG Wilkins 49
StL — FG Wilkins 46
StL — FG Wilkins 48
StL — FG Wilkins 27

MONDAY NIGHT, NOVEMBER 10
PHILADELPHIA 17, GREEN BAY 14—at Lambeau Field, attendance 70,291. Donovan McNabb completed a 6-yard touchdown pass to Todd Pinkston with 27 seconds remaining to cap a 65-yard drive and give the Eagles a road victory in the rain. With wet conditions, both defenses excelled in the first half, with the Packers breaking the ice with Brett Favre's screen pass to Ahman Green for a 24-yard touchdown with 40 seconds left in the half. The Eagles opened the third quarter with a field goal and took the lead early in the fourth quarter when McNabb hit James Thrash for 51 yards to set up McNabb's 1-yard scramble for a 10-7 lead. Faced with fourth-and-1 on the ensuing possession, Green streaked 45 yards for a touchdown. The Eagles were stopped at the 32-yard line with 4:35 left, but forced a punt with 2:43 remaining. McNabb engineered an 8-play, 65-yard drive, highlighted by McNabb's 20-yard pass to Chad Lewis, to set up his winning pass to Pinkston. The Packers reached the Eagles' 42 with eight seconds left, but Favre had the ball slip out of his hand and Darwin Walker recovered with one second remaining to ice the victory. McNabb was 15 of 31 for 198 yards and 1 touchdown. Favre was 14 of 22 for 109 yards and 1 touchdown, with 1 interception. Green rushed 29 times for 192 yards.

Philadelphia	0	0	3	14	— 17
Green Bay	0	7	0	7	— 14

GB — Green 24 pass from Favre (Longwell kick)
Phil — FG Akers 21
Phil — McNabb 1 run (Akers kick)
GB — Green 45 run (Longwell kick)
Phil — Pinkston 6 pass from McNabb (Akers kick)

ELEVENTH WEEK SUMMARIES
American Football Conference

East Division	**W**	**L**	**T**	**Pct.**	**Pts.**	**OP**
New England	8	2	0	.800	196	155
Miami	6	4	0	.600	177	147
Buffalo	4	6	0	.400	159	170
N.Y. Jets	3	7	0	.300	197	211
North Division	**W**	**L**	**T**	**Pct.**	**Pts.**	**OP**
Baltimore	5	5	0	.500	212	191
Cincinnati	5	5	0	.500	210	219
Cleveland	4	6	0	.400	179	177
Pittsburgh	3	7	0	.300	190	247
South Division	**W**	**L**	**T**	**Pct.**	**Pts.**	**OP**
Indianapolis	8	2	0	.800	292	202
Tennessee	8	2	0	.800	265	177
Houston	4	6	0	.400	174	254
Jacksonville	2	8	0	.200	175	241
West Division	**W**	**L**	**T**	**Pct.**	**Pts.**	**OP**
Kansas City	9	1	0	.900	306	174
Denver	6	4	0	.600	247	179
Oakland	3	7	0	.300	190	229
San Diego	2	8	0	.200	182	280

National Football Conference

East Division	**W**	**L**	**T**	**Pct.**	**Pts.**	**OP**
Dallas	7	3	0	.700	181	148
Philadelphia	7	3	0	.700	187	176
N.Y. Giants	4	6	0	.400	182	223
Washington	4	6	0	.400	193	232
North Division	**W**	**L**	**T**	**Pct.**	**Pts.**	**OP**
Minnesota	6	4	0	.600	269	233
Green Bay	5	5	0	.500	264	223
Chicago	3	7	0	.300	172	234
Detroit	3	7	0	.300	166	242
South Division	**W**	**L**	**T**	**Pct.**	**Pts.**	**OP**
Carolina	8	2	0	.800	198	180
New Orleans	5	5	0	.500	212	225
Tampa Bay	4	6	0	.400	201	161
Atlanta	2	8	0	.200	177	273
West Division	**W**	**L**	**T**	**Pct.**	**Pts.**	**OP**
St. Louis	7	3	0	.700	269	202
Seattle	7	3	0	.700	248	188

San Francisco	5	5	0	.500	232	166
Arizona	3	7	0	.300	136	279

SUNDAY, NOVEMBER 16

HOUSTON 12, BUFFALO 10—at Ralph Wilson Stadium, attendance 72,677. Andre Johnson caught a 46-yard touchdown pass from reserve Tony Banks to propel the Texans to victory. The Bills failed to score a touchdown for the third consecutive game. The Bills completely dominated the first 28 minutes, outgaining the Texans 139-50, but led just 5-0 because Rian Lindell was just 1-for-3 on field-goal attempts. Banks connected with Johnson for a touchdown with 1:12 left in the half, and Houston added a field goal to begin the second half for a 9-5 lead. An exchange of field goals gave the Texans a 12-8 lead with 3:23 left, and Jamie Sharper forced Drew Bledsoe to fumble and Shantee Orr recovered with 1:51 remaining. Johnson took the snap in punt formation with three seconds left and ran out of the end zone for a game-ending safety. Carr was 2 of 4 for 12 yards before suffering an injured shoulder and being replaced by Banks, who was 11 of 16 for 207 yards and 1 touchdown, with 1 interception. Johnson had 4 receptions for 122 yards. Bledsoe was 15 of 26 for 184 yards, and Travis Henry rushed 23 times for 149 yards.

Houston	0	6	3	3	—	12
Buffalo	2	3	3	2	—	10

Buff — Safety, Posey forced Carr fumble out of bounds in end zone
Buff — FG Lindell 23
Hous — Johnson 46 pass from Banks (run failed)
Hous — FG Brown 41
Buff — FG Lindell 20
Hous — FG Brown 34
Buff — Safety, Johnson ran out of end zone

CAROLINA 20, WASHINGTON 17—at Ericsson Stadium, attendance 73,263. Stephen Davis scored on a 3-yard touchdown run with 1:09 remaining to lift the Panthers past his former team. The Panthers outgained the Redskins 427-181, but committed 4 turnovers to allow the Redskins to stay close. The Redskins had just 2 first downs and 41 yards in the first half, but John Hall's 23-yard field goal following Matt Bowen's interception enabled the score to be 3-3 at halftime. With the score tied 10-10, John Kasay gave Carolina the lead on a 26-yard field goal with 5:24 left in the game, but a 29-yard pass interference penalty led to Patrick Ramsey's 10-yard touchdown pass to Patrick Johnson for the Redskins' first lead, 17-13, with 4:19 left. Delhomme completed a 25-yard pass to Davis and 30-yard toss to Steve Smith, to set up Davis' scoring run with 1:09 left. The Panthers' defense forced 4 consecutive incompletions to secure the victory. Delhomme was 20 of 30 for 317 yards, with 2 interceptions. Muhsin Muhammad had 9 catches for 189 yards. Ramsey was 16 of 3 for 150 yards and 2 touchdowns, with 1 interception.

Washington	0	3	0	14	—	17
Carolina	0	3	7	10	—	20

Car — FG Kasay 25
Wash — FG Hall 23
Car — Delhomme 1 run (Kasay kick)
Wash — McCants 4 pass from Ramsey (Hall kick)
Car — FG Kasay 26
Wash — Johnson 10 pass from Ramsey (Hall kick)
Car — Davis 3 run (Kasay kick)

ST. LOUIS 23, CHICAGO 21—at Soldier Field, attendance 61,820. Jeff Wilkins kicked a 31-yard field goal with 38 seconds left as the Rams fought off the Bears. Late in the third quarter, the Bears led 14-3, highlighted by R.W. McQuarters' 60-yard punt return for a touchdown, and the Rams had the ball fourth-and-1 on their own 40. The Rams went for it, and Marshall Faulk gained 52 yards to set up Marc Bulger's 4-yard touchdown pass to Torry Holt. Rams coach Mike Martz then called for an onside kick, and Arlen Harris recovered to spark a 13-play touchdown drive. The Rams added a field goal on their next possession for a 20-14 lead with 7:21 left. Chris Chandler calmly completed 3 consecutive passes, capped by an 11-yard toss to Dez White, for a 21-20 lead with 5:58 remaining. With 2:41 left, the Rams started at their own 20 and Bulger engineered a 13-play drive, with key third-down catches by Holt and Isaac Bruce, to set up Wilkins' winning kick. Bulger was 29 of 46 for 240 yards and 2 touchdowns, with 2 interceptions. Holt had 9 catches for 124 yards, and Faulk rushed 20 times for 103 yards. Chandler was 16 of 32 for 153 yards and 1 touchdown, with 2 interceptions.

St. Louis	3	0	7	13	—	23
Chicago	0	14	0	7	—	21

StL — FG Wilkins 41
Chi — McQuarters 60 punt return (Edinger kick)
Chi — Thomas 1 run (Edinger kick)
StL — Holt 4 pass from Bulger (Wilkins kick)
StL — Manumaleuna 4 pass from Bulger (Wilkins kick)
StL — FG Wilkins 44
Chi — White 11 pass from Chandler (Edinger kick)
StL — FG Wilkins 31

CINCINNATI 24, KANSAS CITY 19—at Paul Brown Stadium, attendance 64,923. Peter Warrick scored 2 long fourth-quarter touchdowns to help hand the Chiefs their first loss. The vaunted Chiefs offense gained just 1 first down on its first five possessions, but Morten Andersen kicked a 37-yard field goal as the half expired and a 39-yard kick to begin the second half for a 6-3 lead. The Bengals responded with a 63-yard touchdown drive, and Warrick returned a punt 68 yards for a touchdown early in the fourth quarter for a 17-6 lead. The Chiefs trimmed the deficit to 17-12 with 6:24 left, but on the next play, Jon Kitna hit Warrick with a 77-yard touchdown pass. The Chiefs used the no huddle to drive 71 yards for a touchdown with 3:19 left, but Rudi Johnson rushed for 2 first downs in the final minutes to preserve the victory. Kitna was 19 of 32 for 233 yards and 2 touchdowns. Warrick had 6 catches for 114 yards, an 11-yard rush, and returned 4 punts for 87 yards. Johnson had 22 carries for 165 yards. Trent Green was 28 of 42 for 313 yards and 2 touchdowns.

Kansas City	0	3	3	13	—	19
Cincinnati	0	3	7	14	—	24

Cin — FG Graham 27
KC — FG Andersen 37
KC — FG Andersen 39
Cin — J. Johnson 13 pass from Kitna (Graham kick)
Cin — Warrick 68 punt return (Graham kick)
KC — Gonzalez 12 pass from Green (pass failed)
Cin — Warrick 77 pass from Kitna (Graham kick)
KC — Dunn 3 pass from Green (Andersen kick)

CLEVELAND 44, ARIZONA 6—at Cleveland Browns Stadium, attendance 72,908. Kelly Holcomb passed for 392 yards and 3 touchdowns and the Browns' defense forced 4 turnovers to defeat Arizona. The Browns outgained the Cardinals 481-187 and maintained possession for 39:33, but led just 20-6 early in the third quarter. The Browns, who jumped to a 20-0 lead by scoring on their first four drives, responded by again scoring on four consecutive possessions, including touchdown drives of 47, 86, and 45 yards, for a 44-6 lead with 8:57 left. Holcomb was 29 of 35 for 392 yards and 3 touchdowns. Andre' Davis had 7 catches for 117 yards, and Quincy Morgan added 5 receptions for 116 yards. Jeff Blake was 9 of 21 for 121 yards, with 1 interception, and Josh McCown was 4 for 11, with 2 interceptions.

Arizona	0	3	3	0	—	6
Cleveland	10	10	14	10	—	44

Cle — FG Dawson 34
Cle — Andre' Davis 4 pass from Holcomb (Dawson kick)
Cle — FG Dawson 24
Cle — Northcutt 1 pass from Holcomb (Dawson kick)
Ariz — FG Rackers 42
Ariz — FG Rackers 26
Cle — Jackson 4 run (Dawson kick)
Cle — Morgan 68 pass from Holcomb (Dawson kick)
Cle — Jackson 4 run (Dawson kick)
Cle — FG Dawson 29

DENVER 37, SAN DIEGO 8—at INVESCO Field at Mile High, attendance 75,217. Jake Plummer passed for 3 touchdowns as the Broncos' defense stifled the Chargers. Denver had sizeable advantages in first downs (26-5), total yards (448-96), and time of possession (44:11-15:49). Four of the Chargers' 5 first downs came on a 67-yard touchdown drive early in the fourth quarter to cut the deficit to 34-8. Prior to that drive, the Broncos had outgained San Diego 406-21. The Broncos had five drives of at least 9 plays, and converted on just 3 of their 5 red zone possessions. Plummer was 23 of 34 for 253 yards and 3 touchdowns, with 1 interception. Rod Smith had 10 catches for 84 yards, and Shannon Sharpe added 7 for 101 yards and 3 touchdowns. Clinton Portis had 25 carries for 106 yards. Flutie was 9 of 25 for 70 yards and 1 touchdown, with 1 interception.

San Diego	0	0	0	8	—	8
Denver	10	17	7	3	—	37

Den — Sharpe 11 pass from Plummer (Elam kick)
Den — FG Elam 42
Den — FG Elam 22
Den — R. Smith 65 punt return (Elam kick)
Den — Sharpe 26 pass from Plummer (Elam kick)
Den — Sharpe 26 pass from Plummer (Elam kick)
Den — FG Knorr 27
SD — Osgood 19 pass from Flutie (Alexander pass from Flutie)

INDIANAPOLIS 38, N.Y. JETS 31—at RCA Dome, attendance 56,801. Edgerrin James rushed for 127 yards and 3 touchdowns, and Peyton Manning passed for 401 yards, as the Colts held off the Jets. The Colts had advantages in yards (538-324), plays (77-34), first downs (30-12), and time of possession (38:52-21:08), but the Jets made some big plays, including 6 kickoff returns for 242 yards by Jonathan Carter. Trailing 24-10 at halftime, the Jets scored 3 touchdowns in the first 8:10 of the third quarter, including returns of 39 and a 90-yard score by Carter, to tie the game 31-31. The Colts responded by driving to the Jets' 21, and on fourth-and-3 perfectly executed a fake field-goal attempt as holder Hunter Smith ran untouched 21 yards for a touchdown. Manning's 35-yard pass to Reggie Wayne on third-and-7 with 1:46 left clinched the victory. Manning was 27 of 36 for 401 yards and 1 touchdown. Marvin Harrison missed the game with a hamstring injury, but Wayne had 9 receptions for 141 yards and Dallas Clark added 5 catches for 100 yards. James had 36 carries for 127 yards. Chad Pennington was 11 of 14 for 219 yards and 3 touchdowns. Curtis Martin rushed 13 times for 105 yards.

N.Y. Jets	7	3	21	0 —	31
Indianapolis	10	14	14	0 —	38

Ind — FG Vanderjagt 31
NYJ — Carter 62 pass from Pennington (Brien kick)
Ind — Walters 46 pass from Manning (Vanderjagt kick)
Ind — James 1 run (Vanderjagt kick)
NYJ — FG Brien 43
Ind — James 4 run (Vanderjagt kick)
NYJ — Conway 28 pass from Pennington (Brien kick)
Ind — James 1 run (Vanderjagt kick)
NYJ — Carter 90 kickoff return (Brien kick)
NYJ — Moss 48 pass from Pennington (Brien kick)
Ind — Smith 21 run (Vanderjagt kick)

MIAMI 9, BALTIMORE 6 (OT)—at Pro Player Stadium, attendance 73,333. Olindo Mare kicked 3 field goals, including a 43-yard boot in overtime, to give the Dolphins a tough victory. An interception by Sammy Knight gave the Dolphins the ball at their 47 with 5:00 left in regulation, but Mare missed a 48-yard attempt with 2:29 remaining. In overtime, the Ravens forced a punt, but four plays later, Jamal Lewis fumbled and Zach Thomas recovered at the Ravens' 33. Four plays later, Mare rectified his earlier miss by converting 6:12 into overtime. Brian Griese was 13 of 32 for 126 yards, with 1 interception. Ricky Williams rushed 36 times for 105 yards. Anthony Wright was 14 of 25 for 112 yards, with 2 interceptions.

Baltimore	0	3	0	3	0 —	6
Miami	0	3	3	0	3 —	9

Mia — FG Mare 23
Balt — FG Stover 39
Mia — FG Mare 52
Balt — FG Stover 45
Mia — FG Mare 43

NEW ORLEANS 23, ATLANTA 20 (OT)—at Louisiana Superdome, attendance 68,432. Deuce McAllister rushed for 173 yards and 2 touchdowns and John Carney kicked the game-tying and winning field goals as the Saints rallied from a 17-point halftime deficit. The Saints outgained Atlanta 403-244, but Atlanta led 20-3 at halftime thanks to Tod McBride's interception return, two drives of less than 50 yards that resulted in field goals, and a 5-yard touchdown drive set up by Juran Bolden's interception. In the third quarter, Fred Thomas intercepted Kurt Kittner's pass to set up McAllister's first touchdown. Trailing by three points, McAllister fumbled at the Falcons' 13 with 2:00 left and nose tackle Ellis Johnson recovered and attempted to return the ball but fumbled, too. Boo Williams recovered at the Falcons' 17, and Carney drilled a 26-yard field goal with five seconds left to force overtime. In overtime, Jay Feely's 54-yard field-goal attempt was short, and a 23-yard run by McAllister two plays later set up Carney's winning kick 3:59 into overtime. Aaron Brooks was 21 of 37 for 228 yards, with 2 interceptions. McAllister had 28 carries for 173 yards. Kittner was 8 of 27 for 80 yards, with 2 interceptions. Warrick Dunn had 23 carries for 162 yards.

Atlanta	10	10	0	0	0 —	20
New Orleans	0	3	7	10	3 —	23

Atl — McBride 15 interception return (Feely kick)
Atl — FG Feely 38
Atl — Duckett 4 run (Feely kick)
NO — FG Carney 28
Atl — FG Feely 27
NO — McAllister 5 run (Carney kick)
NO — McAllister 7 run (Carney kick)
NO — FG Carney 26
NO — FG Carney 36

OAKLAND 28, MINNESOTA 18—at Network Associates Coliseum, attendance 56,653. The Raiders' defense forced 6 turnovers, which resulted in 21 points, to defeat the Vikings. Napoleon Harris forced Daunte Culpepper to fumble in the second quarter, and Rod Coleman recovered at the Vikings' 1 to set up Zack Crockett's touchdown run for a 14-3 lead. The Vikings trailed 21-10 early in the fourth quarter and drove to the Raiders' 12, but Culpepper fumbled again and Chris Cooper recovered. With the score 21-18, Rod Woodson intercepted Culpepper's pass and returned it 13 yards to the Vikings' 11 to set up Crockett's second touchdown with 2:16 left. The Vikings reached the Raiders' 14 in the final minute before the Raiders stopped them on downs. Rick Mirer was 9 of 13 for 195 yards. Tyrone Wheatley had 32 carries for 109 yards. Culpepper was 27 of 49 for 396 yards and 1 touchdown, with 3 interceptions and 3 lost fumbles. Kelly Campbell had 4 catches for 115 yards.

Minnesota	0	3	7	8 —	18
Oakland	7	7	7	7 —	28

Oak — Buchanon 64 interception return (Janikowski kick)
Minn — FG Elling 35
Oak — Crockett 1 run (Janikowski kick)
Oak — Wheatley 2 run (Janikowski kick)
Minn — Culpepper 11 run (Elling kick)
Minn — Campbell 29 pass from Culpepper (Elling kick)
Oak — Crockett 2 run (Janikowski kick)

PHILADELPHIA 28, N.Y. GIANTS 10—at Lincoln Financial Field, attendance 67,867. Brian Westbrook scored 3 touchdowns for the Eagles. Leading 7-3 in the second quarter, Donovan McNabb completed a 38-yard pass to Duce Staley to set up a 29-yard scoring pass to Westbrook. On the ensuing possession, the Giants reached the Eagles' 1, but Philadelphia's defense stopped Dorsey Levens twice, with an incomplete Kerry Collins pass in between, and dropped Tiki Barber for a 2-yard loss on fourth down to maintain a 14-3 lead. The Eagles led 21-10 in the fourth quarter, and Westbrook enticed a 23-yard pass interference penalty three plays before his third touchdown, a 5-yard catch, for a 28-10 lead with 5:26 left. McNabb was 24 of 30 for 314 yards and 2 touchdowns. Collins was 25 of 33 for 268 yards and 1 touchdown, with 1 interception. David Tyree had 5 catches for 106 yards, and Barber rushed 19 times for 111 yards.

N.Y. Giants	3	0	0	7 —	10
Philadelphia	7	7	7	7 —	28

NYG — FG Bryant 30
Phil — Buckhalter 1 run (Akers kick)
Phil — Westbrook 29 pass from McNabb (Akers kick)
Phil — Westbrook 4 run (Akers kick)
NYG — Barber 10 pass from Collins (Bryant kick)
Phil — Westbrook 5 pass from McNabb (Akers kick)

SEATTLE 35, DETROIT 14—at Seahawks Stadium, attendance 65,865. Bobby Engram caught a touchdown pass and returned a punt for a score within a three-minute span of the second quarter to propel the Seahawks. Seattle scored on its first three possessions, capped by Koren Robinson's recovery of Matt Hasselbeck's fumble in the end zone, to take a 21-7 lead. Engram caught a 34-yard touchdown pass with 6:38 left in the second quarter for a 28-7 lead, and an 83-yard punt return with 3:51 left following the ensuing Lions possession. Neither team scored in the second half, with the Lions twice stopped inside the Seahawks' 10, once on downs and the other on Shawn Springs' interception. Hasselbeck was 21 of 28 for 207 yards and 1 touchdown. Alexander had 20 carries for 110 yards. Joey Harrington was 26 of 48 for 285 yards and 2 touchdowns, with 2 interceptions.

Detroit	7	7	0	0 —	14
Seattle	14	21	0	0 —	35

Sea — Hasselbeck 4 run (Brown kick)
Sea — Alexander 1 run (Brown kick)
Det — Anderson 72 pass from Harrington (Hanson kick)
Sea — Robinson fumble recovery in end zone (Brown kick)
Sea — Engram 34 pass from Hasselbeck (Brown kick)
Sea — Engram 83 punt return (Brown kick)
Det — Hakim 15 pass from Harrington (Hanson kick)

GREEN BAY 20, TAMPA BAY 13—at Raymond James Stadium, attendance 65,614. Ahman Green rushed for 109 yards and the game-winning touchdown as the Packers snapped a five-game losing streak at Raymond James Stadium. The Packers' Ryan Longwell kicked field goal following a fumble by Brad Johnson at the Packers' 22 and a 56-yard kickoff return by Najeh Davenport to take a 13-6 halftime lead. A 51-yard run by Thomas Jones set up Johnson's 3-yard touchdown pass to Keenan McCardell four plays into the second half to tie the game. Pinned against Green Bay's 3-yard line late in the third quarter, Brett Favre completed a 23-yard pass to Robert Ferguson on third-and-9. The Packers posted two more third-down conversions, along with a 5-yard run by Davenport on fourth-and-1, and capped the 17-play, 98-yard drive with Green's 1-yard run with 8:54 left. Darren Sharper intercepted Johnson's Hail Mary pass at the Packers' 6 as time expired. Favre was 13 of 28 for 92 yards and 1 touchdown, with 1 interception. Green had 21 carries for 109 yards. Johnson was 17 of 28 for 149 yards and 1 touchdown, with 2 interceptions. Jones had 9 carries for 134 yards.

Green Bay	7	6	0	7 —	20
Tampa Bay	0	6	7	0 —	13

GB — Fisher 5 pass from Favre (Longwell kick)
GB — FG Longwell 31
TB — FG Gramatica 24
GB — FG Longwell 33
TB — FG Gramatica 47
TB — McCardell 3 pass from B. Johnson (Gramatica kick)
GB — Green 1 run (Longwell kick)

TENNESSEE 10, JACKSONVILLE 3—at The Coliseum, attendance 68,809. A goal-line stand by the Titans' defense in the final minute enabled Tennessee to post its fifth consecutive victory. The Jaguars snapped the Titans' 6-game streak of scoring at least 30 points. The Titans jumped to a 10-0 lead early in the second quarter, but then committed 2 turnovers deep in Jaguars' territory and missed a 48-yard field-goal attempt to allow Jacksonville to stay close. Seth Marler trimmed the deficit to 10-3 with 7:51 left, and on the ensuing possession, the

Jaguars drove to the Titans' 3 with 2:34 left. Chris Fuamatu-Ma'afala was dropped for a 1-yard loss on consecutive plays, and a delay of game penalty moved the ball to the Titans' 10. An 8-yard pass to Carl Hankton placed the ball at the Titans' 2 with 48 seconds left, but Byron Leftwich's fourth-down pass fell incomplete. McNair completed 13 of 25 passes for 166 yards and 1 touchdown, with 1 interception. Leftwich was 15 of 31 for 151 yards, with 2 interceptions.

Jacksonville	0	0	0	3 —	3
Tennessee	3	7	0	0 —	10

Tenn — FG Anderson 33
Tenn — McCareins 5 pass from McNair (Anderson kick)
Jax — FG Marler 39

SUNDAY NIGHT, NOVEMBER 16
NEW ENGLAND 12, DALLAS 0—at Gillette Stadium, attendance 68,436. The Patriots' defense intercepted 3 passes, 2 by Ty Law, in the second half as the Patriots won a game between division leaders coached by former colleagues Bill Belichick and Bill Parcells. Tom Brady's 57-yard pass to David Givens set up Antowain Smith's 2-yard touchdown run for a 9-0 Patriots lead just before halftime. The Cowboys had chances in the second half, but Law intercepted a Quincy Carter pass at the Patriots' 17 late in the third quarter, Troy Hambrick was stopped on fourth-and-1 at midfield with 9:17 left, and Tyrone Poole's interception set up Adam Vinatieri's 26-yard field goal with 1:56 left. Law intercepted Carter's pass in the end zone as time expired to preserve the shutout. Brady was 15 of 34 for 212 yards. Carter was 20 of 36 for 210 yards, with 3 interceptions.

Dallas	0	0	0	0 —	0
New England	3	6	0	3 —	12

NE — FG Vinatieri 23
NE — Smith 2 run (kick blocked)
NE — FG Vinatieri 26

MONDAY NIGHT, NOVEMBER 17
SAN FRANCISCO 30, PITTSBURGH 14—at 3Com Park, attendance 67,877. The 49ers scored 14 points in a 14-second span of the third quarter to stifle the Steelers. A 61-yard touchdown pass from Tim Rattay, starting for an injured Jeff Garcia, to Terrell Owens helped the 49ers take a 10-0 halftime lead. Leading 10-7, Kevan Barlow broke free for a 78-yard touchdown run. Antwaan Randle El fumbled the ensuing kickoff, and Sean Moran recovered at the Steelers' 28. On the next play, Rattay lofted a pass to Fred Beasley for a touchdown and 24-7 lead with 4:19 left in the third quarter. Randle El caught a touchdown pass with 7:55 left in the game, but the 49ers pounded Pittsburgh with a 5:55 drive to run out most of the clock. Rattay was 21 of 27 for 254 yards and 2 touchdowns. Owens had 8 catches for 155 yards. Tommy Maddox was 25 of 44 for 327 yards and 1 touchdown, with 1 interception.

Pittsburgh	0	0	7	7 —	14
San Francisco	7	3	14	6 —	30

SF — Owens 61 pass from Rattay (Peterson kick)
SF — FG Peterson 32
Pitt — Bettis 1 run (Reed kick)
SF — Barlow 78 run (Peterson kick)
SF — Beasley 28 pass from Rattay (Peterson kick)
SF — FG Peterson 22
SF — FG Peterson 44
Pitt — Randle El 32 pass from Maddox (Reed kick)

TWELFTH WEEK SUMMARIES

American Football Conference						
East Division	**W**	**L**	**T**	**Pct.**	**Pts.**	**OP**
New England	9	2	0	.818	219	175
Miami	7	4	0	.636	201	170
Buffalo	4	7	0	.364	173	187
N.Y. Jets	4	7	0	.364	210	221
North Division	**W**	**L**	**T**	**Pct.**	**Pts.**	**OP**
Baltimore	6	5	0	.545	256	232
Cincinnati	6	5	0	.545	244	246
Cleveland	4	7	0	.364	185	190
Pittsburgh	4	7	0	.364	203	253
South Division	**W**	**L**	**T**	**Pct.**	**Pts.**	**OP**
Indianapolis	9	2	0	.818	309	216
Tennessee	9	2	0	.818	303	208
Houston	4	7	0	.364	194	277
Jacksonville	2	9	0	.182	185	254
West Division	**W**	**L**	**T**	**Pct.**	**Pts.**	**OP**
Kansas City	10	1	0	.909	333	198
Denver	6	5	0	.545	257	198
Oakland	3	8	0	.273	214	256
San Diego	2	9	0	.182	209	314
National Football Conference						
East Division	**W**	**L**	**T**	**Pct.**	**Pts.**	**OP**
Dallas	8	3	0	.727	205	168
Philadelphia	8	3	0	.727	220	196
N.Y. Giants	4	7	0	.364	195	242
Washington	4	7	0	.364	216	256
North Division	**W**	**L**	**T**	**Pct.**	**Pts.**	**OP**
Minnesota	7	4	0	.636	293	247
Green Bay	6	5	0	.545	284	233
Chicago	4	7	0	.364	191	244
Detroit	3	8	0	.273	180	266
South Division	**W**	**L**	**T**	**Pct.**	**Pts.**	**OP**
Carolina	8	3	0	.727	218	204
New Orleans	5	6	0	.455	232	258
Tampa Bay	5	6	0	.455	220	174
Atlanta	2	9	0	.182	208	311
West Division	**W**	**L**	**T**	**Pct.**	**Pts.**	**OP**
St. Louis	8	3	0	.727	299	229
Seattle	7	4	0	.636	289	232
San Francisco	5	6	0	.455	242	186
Arizona	3	8	0	.273	163	309

SUNDAY, NOVEMBER 23
ST. LOUIS 30, ARIZONA 27 (OT)—at Sun Devil Stadium, attendance 42,089. Jeff Wilkins kicked 3 field goals, including one with no time remaining to force overtime and the game-winner in overtime, as the Rams moved into first place. The Cardinals' defense forced 5 turnovers to stay in the game. The Rams led 14-0, but David Barrett's interception set up Neil Rackers' first field goal, and Renaldo Hill's interception just before halftime was returned 70 yards for a touchdown. The Rams took a 24-0 lead on Travis Fisher's interception return, and then stopped the Cardinals on downs at the Rams' 2. But Jeff Blake completed a 54-yard touchdown pass to Anquan Boldin on the last play of the third quarter, and Hill corralled his second interception on the next play to set up Boldin's game-tying 3-yard catch with 11:59 left. After a pair of punts, Ronald McKinnon forced Bulger to fumble, and Kenny King recovered at the Rams' 19 to set up Rackers' field goal for a 27-24 lead with 6:05 left. The Rams got the ball back with 3:23 remaining and drove 82 yards in 16 plays, including a 23-yard pass to Torry Holt on fourth-and-7, and capped by Wilkins' 24-yard field goal as regulation ended. In overtime, Bulger's 18-yard scramble set up Wilkins' 49-yard kick at 10:22. Bulger was 28 of 44 for 329 yards and 1 touchdown, with 4 interceptions. Torry Holt had 9 catches for 145 yards, and Marshall Faulk rushed 24 times for 100 yards. Blake was 15 of 28 for 192 yards and 2 touchdowns, with 2 interceptions. Boldin had 6 receptions for 123 yards.

St. Louis	14	3	7	3	3 —	30
Arizona	0	10	7	10	0 —	27

StL — Faulk 1 run (Wilkins kick)
StL — Bruce 14 pass from Bulger (Wilkins kick)
Ariz — FG Rackers 22
Ariz — Hill 70 interception return (Rackers kick)
StL — FG Wilkins 29
StL — Fisher 57 interception return (Wilkins kick)
Ariz — Boldin 54 pass from Blake (Rackers kick)
Ariz — Boldin 3 pass from Blake (Rackers kick)
Ariz — FG Rackers 27
StL — FG Wilkins 24
StL — FG Wilkins 49

TENNESSEE 38, ATLANTA 31—at Georgia Dome, attendance 70,891. Eddie George rushed for 115 yards as the Titans rallied from a 21-0 deficit to defeat the Falcons. Warrick Dunn took a short pass from Doug Johnson and raced 86 yards for a touchdown for a 21-0 lead with 41 seconds left in the first quarter. The Titans answered immediately with 2 touchdown catches by Frank Wycheck within 49 seconds of each other, sandwiched between a fumbled kickoff by Travis Jervey. Trailing 24-14, the Titans scored four times in less than 13 minutes, highlighted by Justin McCareins' 58-yard punt return for a touchdown and capped by his 14-yard touchdown catch following Rocky Calmus' interception, to take a 38-24 lead with 7:03 left. Peerless Price caught a 41-yard touchdown pass with 5:05 left, but the Falcons only got the ball back one more time and were stopped on downs. Steve McNair was 9 of 11 for 95 yards and 2 touchdowns before leaving with an injured calf just before halftime. Billy Volek was 9 of 15 for 117 yards and 1 touchdown. George rushed 26 times for 115 yards. Johnson was 19 of 32 for 276 yards and 2 touchdowns, with 1 interception. Dunn had 9 catches for 129 yards.

Tennessee	0	14	14	10 —	38
Atlanta	21	0	3	7 —	31

Atl — Rossum 59 punt return (Feely kick)
Atl — Duckett 2 run (Feely kick)
Atl — Dunn 86 pass from Johnson (Feely kick)
Tenn — Wycheck 6 pass from McNair (Anderson kick)
Tenn — Wycheck 5 pass from McNair (Anderson kick)
Atl — FG Feely 40
Tenn — George 2 run (Anderson kick)
Tenn — McCareins 58 punt return (Anderson kick)
Tenn — FG Anderson 22
Tenn — McCareins 14 pass from Volek (Anderson kick)
Atl — Price 41 pass from Johnson (Feely kick)

BALTIMORE 44, SEATTLE 41 (OT)—at M&T Bank Stadium, attendance 69,477. In a game that featured 10 touchdowns in a span of 29 minutes, 11 seconds, Anthony Wright completed 4 second-half touchdown passes to Marcus Robinson as the Ravens rallied from a 17-point fourth-quarter deficit to knock the Seahawks out of first place. The score was tied 3-3 with 23 seconds left in the first half before Seattle scored twice before halftime, the second set up by Chester Taylor's fumble as the Ravens attempted to run out the clock. The Seahawks scored on their first four possessions of the second half, needing less than 1:30 on three of the drives, but couldn't stop the Ravens, who scored on three times in that span. Seattle led 41-24 with 6:41 left when Ed Reed blocked Jeff Feagles' punt and returned it 16 yards for a touchdown. Ray Lewis recovered a fumble at the Ravens' 29 with 4:16 left and Wright engineered a 12-play, 71-yard drive, capped by Robinson's fourth touchdown, to cut the deficit to 41-38 with 1:12 remaining. The Seahawks recovered the onside kick, but Matt Hasselbeck was stopped for no gain on fourth-and-1 at the Ravens' 33 with 39 seconds left. A 44-yard pass interference penalty on a pass intended for Robinson set up Matt Stover's 40-yard field goal to force overtime. In overtime, the Ravens forced a punt and the offense moved the ball, including a 19-yard pass to Robinson on third-and-15, that led to Stover's game-winning kick with 6:32 left in overtime. Wright was 20 of 37 for 319 yards and 4 touchdowns. Robinson had 7 catches for 131 yards, and Jamal Lewis had 26 carries for 117 yards. Hasselbeck was 23 of 41 for 333 yards and 5 touchdowns. Jackson had 7 catches for 146 yards.

Seattle	0	17	17	7	0	—	41
Baltimore	0	3	21	17	3	—	44

Sea — FG Brown 45
Balt — FG Stover 21
Sea — Jackson 2 pass from Hasselbeck (Brown kick)
Sea — Engram 10 pass from Hasselbeck (Brown kick)
Balt — M. Robinson 13 pass from Wright (Stover kick)
Sea — K. Robinson 38 pass from Hasselbeck (Brown kick)
Sea — FG Brown 46
Balt — M. Robinson 50 pas from Wright (Stover kick)
Sea — Jackson 80 pass from Hasselbeck (Brown kick)
Balt — M. Robinson 25 pass from Wright (Stover kick)
Sea — Engram 5 pass from Hasselbeck (Brown kick)
Balt — Reed 16 blocked punt return (Stover kick)
Balt — M. Robinson 9 pass from Wright (Stover kick)
Balt — FG Stover 40
Balt — FG Stover 42

INDIANAPOLIS 17, BUFFALO 14—at Ralph Wilson Stadium, attendance 73,004. Edgerrin James scored 2 touchdowns, including the game-winner on fourth-and-goal with 1:38 left, to rally the Colts. Drew Bledsoe's 1-yard scoring run in the second quarter was the Bills' first touchdown in 14 quarters, and Sammy Morris extended the lead to 14-3 with a 7-yard run early in the fourth quarter. But the Colts drove 9 plays for 61 yards and 16 plays for 83 yards on their next two possessions to take the lead, capped by James' 1-yard plunge after having been stopped for no gain on the previous two plays. On the ensuing possession, David Thornton intercepted Bledsoe's pass near midfield to secure the victory. Peyton Manning was 26 of 42 for 229 yards. James had 28 carries for 108 yards. Bledsoe was 15 of 28 for 135 yards, with 1 interception.

Indianapolis	0	3	0	14	—	17
Buffalo	0	7	0	7	—	14

Ind — FG Vanderjagt 24
Buff — Bledsoe 1 run (Lindell kick)
Buff — Morris 7 run (Lindell kick)
Ind — James 14 run (run failed)
Ind — James 1 run (Mungro pass from Manning)

PITTSBURGH 13, CLEVELAND 6—at Cleveland Browns Stadium, attendance 73,658. The Steelers' defense forced 5 turnovers, which resulted in all 13 points, to propel the Steelers to victory. Cleveland drove into the Steelers' red zone twice early, but settled for field goals. The Browns' defense limited Pittsburgh to just 168 yards, but the Steelers only needed to drive 17 yards for their touchdown following James Farrior's fumble recovery in the second quarter. Two minutes later, Brent Alexander recovered a fumble at the Browns' 22 to set up Jeff Reed's first field goal just before halftime for a 10-6 lead. Cleveland drove to the Steelers' 1 on the first possession of the second half, but James Jackson was stopped for no gain on second and third down, and Dennis Northcutt was stopped on a reverse on fourth down. On the next possession, Cleveland drove to the Steelers' 7, but Alexander intercepted Kelly Holcomb's pass in the end zone. Jackson's second fumble of the game on the next drive was recovered at the Steelers' 28 by Kendrick Clancy to set up Reed's second field goal, following a game-long 47-yard Steelers' drive. Chad Scott intercepted Holcomb's pass at the Steelers' 39 with 1:41 left to stop the last scoring chance. Tommy Maddox was 9 of 24 for 73 yards and 1 touchdown. Holcomb was 25 of 44 for 234 yards, with 2 interceptions.

Pittsburgh	0	10	0	3	—	13
Cleveland	3	3	0	0	—	6

Cle — FG Dawson 27
Cle — FG Dawson 31
Pitt — Bruener 1 pass from Maddox (Reed kick)
Pitt — FG Reed 23
Pitt — FG Reed 46

DALLAS 24, CAROLINA 20—at Texas Stadium, attendance 63,871. Quincy Carter passed for 254 yards and 2 touchdowns as the Cowboys defeated Carolina in a battle of two first-place teams. The game was tied at 3-3, 10-10, and 17-17, before the Cowboys took the lead for good on a 16-yard wishbone option play, in which Carter handed off to Richie Anderson, who ran left and then pitched the ball to Aveion Cason, who flew around left end and cut back inside for the touchdown. Carolina, who had both of its touchdowns set up by defensive pass interference penalties that placed the ball on the 1-yard line, reached the Cowboys' 6 with four minutes left, but a false start and two incompletions forced the Panthers to set up for John Kasay's field goal with 3:47 left. Carolina stopped a scrambling Carter five yards shy of a first down on third-and-9, but Deon Grant committed a 15-yard penalty while corralling Carter. Three plays later, on third-and-8, Carter completed a 13-yard pass to Jason Witten to secure the victory. Carter was 29 of 44 for 254 yards and 2 touchdowns, with 1 interception. Jake Delhomme was 9 of 24 for 175 yards and 1 touchdown, with 1 interception.

Carolina	3	7	7	3	—	20
Dallas	10	0	14	0	—	24

Dall — FG Cundiff 24
Car — FG Kasay 44
Dall — Galloway 24 pass from Carter (Cundiff kick)
Car — Davis 1 run (Kasay kick)
Dall — Robinson 5 pass from Carter (Cundiff kick)
Car — Hoover 1 pass from Delhomme (Kasay kick)
Dall — Cason 16 run (Cundiff kick)
Car — FG Kasay 34

CHICAGO 19, DENVER 10—at INVESCO Field at Mile High, attendance 75,540. Paul Edinger kicked 4 field goals and reserve Kordell Stewart scored on a 1-yard run early in the fourth quarter to help the Bears snap a 12-game road losing streak. In the second coldest home game in Broncos history, 18 degrees, Denver drove 78 yards on its initial drive for a touchdown, but Edinger kicked 3 first-half field goals, capped by a 54-yard boot just before halftime, for a 9-7 Chicago lead. Chris Chandler injured his shoulder and was replaced in the third quarter by Stewart, who on his second drive guided the Bears on a 15-play, 55-yard, 8:38 drive, capped by his own sneak on fourth-and-goal from the 1-yard line. The last five plays of the drive were runs by Stewart. Edinger added his fourth field goal on the ensuing possession, and the Broncos fumbled away their last scoring chance, as holder Micah Knorr fumbled the snap for a potential 40-yard field-goal attempt with 3:45 remaining. Chandler was 8 of 18 for 79 yards, and Stewart was 7 of 15 for 47 yards. Plummer was 19 of 35 for 176 yards and 1 touchdown. Clinton Portis had 14 carries for 165 yards, setting a team record with 11.9 yards per carry.

Chicago	3	6	0	10	—	19
Denver	7	0	3	0	—	10

Den — Smith 1 pass from Plummer (Elam kick)
Chi — FG Edinger 33
Chi — FG Edinger 23
Chi — FG Edinger 54
Den — FG Elam 25
Chi — Stewart 1 run (Edinger kick)
Chi — FG Edinger 47

GREEN BAY 20, SAN FRANCISCO 10—at Lambeau Field, attendance 70,250. The Packers rushed for 243 yards, 154 by Ahman Green, on 48 carries to defeat the 49ers. Brett Favre completed a 66-yard touchdown pass to Javon Walker on the Packers' third play from scrimmage for a 7-0 lead. Another touchdown pass and Ryan Longwell's 38-yard field goal as the half expired lengthened the lead to 17-3. Mike Rumph intercepted a pass by Favre late in the third quarter, and on fourth-and-3, Rattay completed a 24-yard touchdown pass to Terrell Owens. Following Longwell's second field goal, Antuan Edwards intercepted Rattay's pass at the Packers' 48 with 6:08 left, and Green Bay converted three third-down situations, capped by Favre's 5-yard scramble on third-and-4 with 2:23 left, to run out the clock. Favre was 10 of 15 for 138 yards and 2 touchdowns, with 3 interceptions. Rattay was 14 of 30 for 142 yards and 1 touchdown, with 1 interception.

San Francisco	0	3	7	0	—	10
Green Bay	7	10	0	3	—	20

GB — Walker 66 pass from Favre (Longwell kick)
GB — Ferguson 16 pass from Favre (Longwell kick)
SF — FG Peterson 24
GB — FG Longwell 38
SF — Owens 24 pass from Rattay (Peterson kick)
GB — FG Longwell 37

NEW ENGLAND 23, HOUSTON 20 (OT)—at Reliant Stadium, attendance 70,719. Adam Vinatieri's 28-yard field goal with 41 seconds left in overtime gave New England its seventh consecutive victory. The Patriots had huge advantages in first downs (29-11) and total yards (472-169), but committed 3 turnovers, 2 of which set up 31- and 11-yard touchdown drives for Houston. New England led 7-3 in the second quarter and drove to the Texans' 10, but Eric Brown intercepted Tom Brady's pass. However, Brown fumbled during the return and Bethel Johnson recovered at the Texans' 7 to set up Vinatieri's first field goal. A third-quarter interception by Marcus Coleman along with Jay Foreman's 33-yard fumble return, on a fumble by Brady caused by Kailee Wong, led to Houston's touchdowns and a 17-13 lead. Moments later, Ramon Walker blocked Ken Walter's punt to set up Kris Brown's 31-yard field goal with 3:11 left. New England drove to the Texans' 4, thanks to a 33-yard pass by Brady to Daniel Graham on third-and-10, and on fourth-and-1 Brady lofted a pass into the end zone that was caught by Graham to tie the score with 40 seconds left. In overtime, Mike Vrabel intercepted Banks' pass on the first play, but Walker blocked Vinatieri's

37-yard game-winning field-goal attempt. After three punts, New England got the ball on its own 14 with 4:20 left and Brady completed 5 of 7 passes to set up Vinatieri's winning kick. Brady was 29 of 47 for 368 yards and 2 touchdowns, with 2 interceptions. Kevin Faulk had 8 catches for 108 yards. Banks was 10 of 25 for 93 yards and 2 touchdowns, with 1 interception.

New England	0	10	0	10	3	—	23
Houston	3	0	7	10	0	—	20

Hous — FG Brown 19
NE — Johnson 27 pass from Brady (Vinatieri kick)
NE — FG Vinatieri 21
Hous — Johnson 10 pass from Banks (Brown kick)
NE — FG Vinatieri 32
Hous — Miller 16 pass from Banks (Brown kick)
Hous — FG Brown 31
NE — Graham 4 pass from Brady (Vinatieri kick)
NE — FG Vinatieri 28

KANSAS CITY 27, OAKLAND 24—at Arrowhead Stadium, attendance 78,889. Morten Andersen kicked a 35-yard field goal with four seconds left as the Chiefs held off the Raiders. Trent Green's 2-yard touchdown pass to Jason Dunn with 22 seconds left in the half capped a perfectly run two-minute drill and gave the Chiefs a 21-7 lead. Oakland scored on two of its first three second-half possessions, capped by Rick Mirer's 47-yard touchdown pass to Jerry Rice, the career touchdown leader's first of the season, to cut the deficit to 24-21. Later in the quarter, Phillip Buchanon returned a punt to the Chiefs' 26. But he was penalized 15 yards for unsportsmanlike conduct, forcing the Raiders to settle for Sebastian Janikowski's game-tying field goal with 2:18 left. On fourth-and-14 at the Chiefs' 33 with 19 seconds left, Green completed a 16-yard pass to Marc Boerigter to set up Andersen's thirty-first career game-winning kick. Green was 23 of 33 for 244 yards and 1 touchdown. Holmes had 6 catches for 100 yards. Mirer was 19 of 31 for 19 yards and 1 touchdown.

Oakland	0	7	7	10	—	24
Kansas City	14	7	3	3	—	27

KC — Blaylock 25 run (Andersen kick)
KC — Holmes 2 run (Andersen kick)
Oak — Mirer 13 run (Janikowski kick)
KC — Dunn 2 pass from Green (Andersen kick)
Oak — Wheatley 15 run (Janikowski kick)
KC — FG Andersen 43
Oak — Rice 47 pass from Mirer (Janikowski kick)
Oak — FG Janikowski 41
KC — FG Andersen 35

MINNESOTA 24, DETROIT 14—at Metrodome, attendance 63,946. The Vikings scored 17 points in a 39-second span of the game's final three minutes to snap a four-game losing streak. The Vikings' defense intercepted 4 passes, 3 by Brian Williams. Minnesota led 7-0 at halftime thanks to a missed 43-yard field-goal attempt by Jason Hanson and 2 interceptions by Williams, one at the Vikings' 3-yard line. Early in the third quarter, Moe Williams fumbled and Dre' Bly recovered at the Lions' 21. Bly returned the ball 44 yards before lateralling the ball to Corey Harris, who went the remaining 35 yards to tie the game. The game remained tied until Aaron Elling capped a 14-play drive with a 24-yard field goal with 2:45 left. Three plays later, Corey Chavous intercepted Joey Harrington's pass and returned it 32 yards for a touchdown and 17-7 lead. On the next play from scrimmage, Williams hoisted his third interception and returned it 42 yards for a score with 2:06 left. Culpepper was 20 of 30 for 196 yards, with 1 interception. Harrington was 21 of 41 for 167 yards and 1 touchdown, with 4 interceptions.

Detroit	0	0	7	7	—	14
Minnesota	7	0	0	17	—	24

Minn — Bennett 25 run (Elling kick)
Det — Harris 35 fumble return (Hanson kick)
Minn — FG Elling 24
Minn — Chavous 32 interception return (Elling kick)
Minn — B. Williams 42 interception return (Elling kick)
Det — Hakim 5 pass from Harrington (Hanson kick)

N.Y. JETS 13, JACKSONVILLE 10—at The Meadowlands, attendance 77,614. Chad Pennington capped a 94-yard drive with a 3-yard touchdown pass to Santana Moss with 26 seconds left to lift the Jets to another comeback victory. Jacksonville drove inside the Jets' red zone three times in the first half, but an interception by Aaron Beasley and a missed 36-yard field goal by Seth Marler kept the Jaguars from taking control. The Jets took a 6-3 lead early in the fourth quarter, but the Jaguars responded with a 13-play, 74-yard drive capped by Chris Fuamatu-Ma'afala's 1-yard run on fourth-and-goal with 4:24 left. Following an exchange of punts, the Jets started from the Jaguars' 6 with 3:00 left. Pennington completed 9 of 11 passes, to five different receivers, including a 14-yard pass to Curtis Martin on third-and-6 and a 14-yard pass to Jerald Sowell on third-and-3, before finding Moss on the left side of the end zone with 26 seconds left. Pennington was 25 of 39 for 236 yards and 1 touchdown, with 1 interception. Byron Leftwich was 17 of 33 for 172 yards, with 1 interception. Fred Taylor had 32 carries for 119 yards.

Jacksonville	0	3	0	7	—	10
N.Y. Jets	3	0	0	10	—	13

NYJ — FG Brien 36
Jax — FG Marler 23
NYJ — FG Brien 35
Jax — Fuamatu-Ma'afala 1 run (Marler kick)
NYJ — Moss 3 pass from Pennington (Brien kick)

PHILADELPHIA 33, NEW ORLEANS 20—at Lincoln Financial Field, attendance 67,802. Donovan McNabb passed for 259 yards and 1 touchdown as the Eagles won their sixth consecutive game. The Saints drove into Eagles' territory on all four of their first-half possessions but scored just once, with 2 fumbles, including one at the 1-yard line by Aaron Brooks, and a fourth-down stop by the Eagles' defense allowing Philadelphia to take a 20-7 lead. A career-long 76-yard touchdown run by Deuce McAllister cut the deficit to 23-14 in the third quarter, and the Saints had a chance to get closer but Michael Lewis blocked John Carney's 45-yard field-goal attempt. The Eagles responded on the ensuing possession with David Akers' fourth field goal, and following a punt, McNabb dumped a 2-yard touchdown pass to Jon Ritchie with 5:28 left. McNabb was 16 of 25 for 259 yards and 1 touchdown, completing passes to 10 different receivers. Brooks was 24 of 39 for 287 yards and 1 touchdown. McAllister had 19 carries for 184 yards, his eighth consecutive 100-yard game. Boo Williams had 9 catches for 110 yards.

New Orleans	0	7	7	6	—	20
Philadelphia	10	10	3	10	—	33

Phil — FG Akers 36
Phil — Westbrook 15 run (Akers kick)
Phil — Buckhalter 1 run (Akers kick)
NO — Williams 6 pass from Brooks (Carney kick)
Phil — FG Akers 41
Phil — FG Akers 42
NO — McAllister 76 run (Carney kick)
Phil — FG Akers 33
Phil — Ritchie 2 pass from McNabb (Akers kick)
NO — McAllister 22 run (pass failed)

CINCINNATI 34, SAN DIEGO 27—at Qualcomm Stadium, attendance 52,069. Jon Kitna passed for 243 yards and 4 touchdowns, 3 to Chad Johnson, as the Bengals won their third consecutive game. The Bengals rolled up 454 yards, including 305 yards in the first half as they scored twice in the final 1:25 of the half as Cincinnati stretched a 14-13 lead to 28-13. The Bengals gained at least 1 first down on all 11 of their possessions, and had at least 8 plays in each of their final four drives, but settled for 2 field goals in the second half. LaDainian Tomlinson's 6-yard touchdown run with 3:04 left cut the deficit to 34-27, but Kitna twice completed passes on third down to maintain possession and run out the clock. Kitna was 24 of 38 for 243 yards and 4 touchdowns. Johnson had 10 catches for 107 yards, and Corey Dillon rushed 18 times for 108 yards. Doug Flutie was 15 of 33 for 210 yards and 2 touchdowns. David Boston had 9 receptions for 139 yards.

Cincinnati	14	14	3	3	—	34
San Diego	7	6	0	14	—	27

Cin — C. Johnson 5 pass from Kitna (Graham kick)
Cin — C. Johnson 4 pass from Kitna (Graham kick)
SD — Boston 37 pass from Flutie (Christie kick)
SD — FG Christie 48
SD — FG Christie 26
Cin — C. Johnson 12 pass from Kitna (Graham kick)
Cin — Washington 4 pass from Kitna (Graham kick)
Cin — FG Graham 37
SD — Boston 26 pass from Flutie (Christie kick)
Cin — FG Graham 47
SD — Tomlinson 6 run (Christie kick)

SUNDAY NIGHT, NOVEMBER 23

MIAMI 24, WASHINGTON 23—at Pro Player Stadium, attendance 73,578. Jay Fiedler entered the game in the second half and guided the Dolphins to a comeback victory behind Ricky Williams' 107 yards and 2 touchdowns. Brian Griese completed an 80-yard touchdown pass to James McKnight three plays into the game, but the Redskins responded by scoring the next 20 points. Tim Hasselbeck, who replaced an injured Patrick Ramsey trailing 7-3, completed 10 of 14 first-half passes. In the third quarter, Rashad Bauman intercepted a pass by Griese at the Redskins' 2. Fiedler entered the game with the score 23-10, and promptly engineered 71- and 69-yard scoring drives, capped by Williams' 24-yard run with 4:19 left. On the ensuing possession, Brock Marion intercepted a pass at the Dolphins' 9. Washington forced a punt with 2:23 left, but Patrick Johnson muffed the punt and McKnight recovered at the Redskins' 16 to secure the victory. Griese was 8 of 13 for 133 yards and 1 touchdown, with 2 interceptions, before being replaced by Fiedler, who was 5 of 10 for 59 yards. Hasselbeck was 15 of 30 for 150 yards and 1 touchdown, with 1 interception.

Washington	6	14	3	0	—	23
Miami	7	3	0	14	—	24

Mia — McKnight 80 pass from Griese (Mare kick)

Wash — FG Hall 28
Wash — FG Hall 31
Wash — Coles 37 pass from Hasselbeck (Hall kick)
Wash — Canidate 2 run (Hall kick)
Mia — FG Mare 51
Wash — FG Hall 22
Mia — Williams 1 run (Mare kick)
Mia — Williams 24 run (Mare kick)

MONDAY NIGHT, NOVEMBER 24
TAMPA BAY 19, N.Y. GIANTS 13—at Raymond James Stadium, attendance 65,648. Brad Johnson passed for 269 yards and 1 touchdown as the Buccaneers defeated the Giants. The Tampa Bay defense allowed just 212 yards and forced 4 turnovers, as the offense held the ball for 37:31. Johnson's 53-yard touchdown pass to Charles Lee gave Tampa Bay a 14-3 lead. The Giants had a chance to cut into the advantage just before halftime, but Simeon Rice forced Kerry Collins to fumble at the Buccaneers' 29 and Chartric Darby recovered as time expired. Late in the third quarter, Dwight Smith intercepted a long pass in the end zone for a touchback to thwart another Giants' threat, but the Giants pulled within 17-13 on Frank Walker's 56-yard interception return with 12:42 left. Pinned against their own 3-yard line with 1:59 left, Carson Dach purposely snapped the ball out of the end zone for a safety. However, Ken Dilger recovered the ensuing onside kick for Tampa Bay to preserve the victory. Johnson was 22 of 32 for 269 yards and 1 touchdown, with 1 interception. Collins was 18 of 34 for 160 yards, with 2 interceptions.

N.Y. Giants	0	3	3	7	—	13
Tampa Bay	0	14	3	2	—	19

TB — Jones 1 run (Gramatica kick)
NYG — FG Bryant 30
TB — Lee 53 pass from Johnson (Gramatica kick)
NYG — FG Bryant 30
TB — FG Gramatica 21
NYG — Walker 56 interception return (Bryant kick)
TB — Safety, Dach snapped ball out of end zone

THIRTEENTH WEEK SUMMARIES
American Football Conference

East Division	**W**	**L**	**T**	**Pct.**	**Pts.**	**OP**
New England	10	2	0	.833	257	209
Miami	8	4	0	.667	241	191
Buffalo	5	7	0	.417	197	194
N.Y. Jets	5	7	0	.417	234	238
North Division	**W**	**L**	**T**	**Pct.**	**Pts.**	**OP**
Baltimore	7	5	0	.583	300	238
Cincinnati	7	5	0	.583	268	266
Cleveland	4	8	0	.333	192	224
Pittsburgh	4	8	0	.333	223	277
South Division	**W**	**L**	**T**	**Pct.**	**Pts.**	**OP**
Indianapolis	9	3	0	.750	343	254
Tennessee	9	3	0	.750	320	232
Houston	5	7	0	.417	211	290
Jacksonville	3	9	0	.250	202	264
West Division	**W**	**L**	**T**	**Pct.**	**Pts.**	**OP**
Kansas City	11	1	0	.917	361	222
Denver	7	5	0	.583	279	206
Oakland	3	9	0	.250	222	278
San Diego	2	10	0	.167	233	342

National Football Conference

East Division	**W**	**L**	**T**	**Pct.**	**Pts.**	**OP**
Philadelphia	9	3	0	.750	245	212
Dallas	8	4	0	.667	226	208
N.Y. Giants	4	8	0	.333	202	266
Washington	4	8	0	.333	236	280
North Division	**W**	**L**	**T**	**Pct.**	**Pts.**	**OP**
Minnesota	7	5	0	.583	310	295
Green Bay	6	6	0	.500	298	255
Chicago	5	7	0	.417	219	247
Detroit	4	8	0	.333	202	280
South Division	**W**	**L**	**T**	**Pct.**	**Pts.**	**OP**
Carolina	8	4	0	.667	234	229
New Orleans	6	6	0	.500	256	278
Tampa Bay	5	7	0	.417	230	191
Atlanta	2	10	0	.167	221	328
West Division	**W**	**L**	**T**	**Pct.**	**Pts.**	**OP**
St. Louis	9	3	0	.750	347	246
Seattle	8	4	0	.667	323	239
San Francisco	5	7	0	.417	248	230
Arizona	3	9	0	.250	166	337

THURSDAY, NOVEMBER 27
DETROIT 22, GREEN BAY 14—at Ford Field, attendance 62,123. The Lions' defense forced 5 turnovers, 3 of which resulted in fourth-quarter field goals, to win their third consecutive home game. Detroit scored on its first three possessions, on drives of 56, 64, and 62 yards, to take a 13-7 lead. Brett Favre's second scoring pass of the game, a 45-yard strike to Javon Walker late in the third quarter, gave Green Bay a 14-13 lead. But Walker fumbled on the first play of the fourth quarter, and despite not gaining a yard on the next three plays, the Lions took the lead on Jason Hanson's 49-yard field goal. Favre fumbled two possessions later, and without getting a first down Detroit extended the lead to 19-14 with Hanson's 46-yard field goal. Dre' Bly's interception three plays later led to Hanson's fifth field goal with 3:34 left. Doug Evans intercepted Favre's pass at the Lions' 30 with 1:03 left to clinch the victory. Joey Harrington was 21 of 32 for 183 yards, with 1 interception. Favre was 23 of 37 for 296 yards and 2 touchdowns, with 3 interceptions.

Green Bay	0	7	7	0	—	14
Detroit	10	3	0	9	—	22

Det — Bryson 6 run (Hanson kick)
Det — FG Hanson 42
GB — Franks 5 pass from Favre (Longwell kick)
Det — FG Hanson 28
GB — Walker 45 pass from Favre (Longwell kick)
Det — FG Hanson 49
Det — FG Hanson 46
Det — FG Hanson 32

MIAMI 40, DALLAS 21—at Texas Stadium, attendance 64,110. Jay Fiedler passed for 239 yards and 3 touchdowns, all to Chris Chambers, and the Dolphins' defense forced 5 turnovers to defeat the Cowboys. Miami drove into Dallas territory on all six first half possessions, but led just 16-14 before Chambers' 6-yard scoring catch with 10 seconds left in the half. On the third play of the second half, Adewale Ogunleye sacked Quincy Carter and forced him to fumble. Jason Taylor recovered the ball and raced 34 yards for a touchdown, and Chambers' 35-yard touchdown catch with 7:42 left in the quarter gave the Dolphins 21 points in less than eight minutes and a 37-14 lead. Carter was intercepted three times in Cowboys' territory in the final 17 minutes. Fiedler was 16 of 20 for 239 yards and 3 touchdowns. Ricky Williams rushed 31 times for 104 yards. Carter was 24 of 40 for 288 yards and 2 touchdowns, with 3 interceptions.

Miami	7	16	14	3	—	40
Dallas	0	14	0	7	—	21

Mia — Fiedler 1 run (Mare kick)
Mia — FG Mare 33
Dall — Anderson 4 run (Cundiff kick)
Mia — Chambers 39 pass from Fiedler (Mare kick)
Dall — Anderson 27 pass from Carter (Cundiff kick)
Mia — Chambers 6 pass from Fiedler (kick blocked)
Mia — Taylor 34 fumble return (Mare kick)
Mia — Chambers 35 pass from Fiedler (Mare kick)
Mia — FG Mare 42
Dall — Bryant 18 pass from Carter (Cundiff kick)

SUNDAY, NOVEMBER 30
BALTIMORE 44, SAN FRANCISCO 6—at M&T Bank Stadium, attendance 69,549. The Ravens outgained the 49ers by just 18 yards (282-264), but Baltimore forced 4 turnovers which resulted in 24 points to remain in first place in the AFC North. Edgerton Hartwell's interception four plays into the game led to Jamal Lewis' 6-yard touchdown run. The Ravens led just 7-6 with two minutes left in the first half. Following Matt Stover's field goal, the Ravens' defense forced a punt, and Anthony Wright completed a 38-yard touchdown pass to Marcus Robinson with 46 seconds left in the half for a 17-6 lead. Two plays later, Ray Lewis intercepted Jeff Garcia's pass and returned it 29 yards for a touchdown, giving the Ravens 17 points in 1:25. Gary Baxter's interception at the 49ers' 21 early in the fourth quarter set up Terry Jones' touchdown catch, and Will Demps' interception midway through the final quarter set up Stover's third field goal. Wright was 14 of 25 for 177 yards and 2 touchdowns, with 1 interception. Garcia was 14 of 29 for 112 yards, with 4 interceptions.

San Francisco	3	3	0	0	—	6
Baltimore	7	17	0	20	—	44

Balt — J. Lewis 6 run (Stover kick)
SF — FG Peterson 48
SF — FG Peterson 40
Balt — FG Stover 28
Balt — Robinson 38 pass from Wright (Stover kick)
Balt — R. Lewis 29 interception return (Stover kick)
Balt — FG Stover 47
Balt — Jones 6 pass from Wright (Stover kick)
Balt — FG Stover 41
Balt — M. Smith 2 run (Stover kick)

PHILADELPHIA 25, CAROLINA 16—at Ericsson Stadium, attendance 72,977. Donovan McNabb passed for 182 yards and 1 touchdown as the Eagles won their sixth consecutive game. The Panthers drove into Eagles' territory on six of their first seven possessions, but trailed 13-10 after three quarters. John Kasay missed 3 field goals, and Carolina was stopped on downs at the Eagles' 8. David Akers' third field goal gave the Eagles a 16-10 lead early in the fourth quarter, and on the next play from scrimmage, Jake Delhomme fumbled and Darwin Walker recovered at the Eagles' 11. Two plays later, McNabb fired a 10-yard touchdown pass to James Thrash for a 22-10 lead with 11:56 left. Delhomme's 23-yard scoring pass to Muhsin Muhammad cut the deficit to 22-16 with 6:42 left, but, following a false start penalty that nullified his extra point, Kasay missed the 25-yard conversion. Following an exchange of possessions, the Panthers punted with 5:41 left, but didn't get the ball back until after Akers' fourth field goal with 25 seconds remaining. McNabb was 18 of 26 for 182 yards and 1 touchdown, with 1 interception. Delhomme was 18 of 29 for 216 yards and 2 touchdowns.

Philadelphia	7	3	3	12	—	25
Carolina	3	0	7	6	—	16

Car — FG Kasay 20
Phil — Staley 2 run (Akers kick)
Phil — FG Akers 35
Phil — FG Akers 48

Car — Smith 24 pass from Delhomme (Kasay kick)
Phil — FG Akers 38
Phil — Thrash 10 pass from McNabb (pass failed)
Car — Muhammad 23 pass from Delhomme (kick failed)
Phil — FG Akers 29

CHICAGO 28, ARIZONA 3—at Soldier Field, attendance 61,550. Kordell Stewart passed for 2 touchdowns and ran for another and the Bears' defense allowed just 9 first downs to defeat the Cardinals. Arizona punted on seven of its first eight possessions, but trailed just 7-3 early and had the ball following a missed 43-yard field-goal attempt by Paul Edinger early in the fourth quarter. But R.W. McQuarters intercepted Jeff Blake's pass on the next play from scrimmage and returned it to the Cardinals' 12. Two plays later, Stewart completed a 10-yard touchdown pass to Dez White. Following another punt, Stewart capped a 65-yard drive with an 8-yard run, and following Blake's fumble at the Cardinals' 34 on the ensuing possession, Brock Forsey scored with 3:33 left to finish the scoring. Stewart was 22 of 37 for 284 yards and 2 touchdowns. Forsey, playing for the injured Anthony Thomas, had 27 carries for 134 yards, and Justin Gage had 4 catches for 100 yards. Blake was 20 of 32 for 163 yards, with 2 interceptions.

Arizona	3	0	0	0 —	3
Chicago	7	0	0	21 —	28

Chi — Booker 2 pass from Stewart (Edinger kick)
Ariz — FG Rackers 32
Chi — White 10 pass from Stewart (Edinger kick)
Chi — Stewart 8 run (Edinger kick)
Chi — Forsey 9 run (Edinger kick)

HOUSTON 17, ATLANTA 13—at Reliant Stadium, attendance 70,388. Domanick Davis rushed for 101 yards and 2 touchdowns as the Texans held off the Falcons in Michael Vick's 2003 debut. Vick, who missed the first 11 games with a fractured right leg, entered the game with 6:24 left in the third quarter after Davis had scored 2 touchdowns in a span of 2:20, the second set up by Marcus Coleman's interception of Doug Johnson's pass. Chris Draft's interception at the Texans' 33 late in the third quarter set up Jay Feely's 35-yard field goal to cut the deficit to 17-10. The Falcons forced a punt and started at their own 20 with 7:09 left. Vick drove the club to the Texans' 11, but a 14-yard intentional grounding penalty forced Atlanta to settle for another Feely field goal with 1:24 left. Coleman recovered the ensuing onside kick to preserve the victory. Tony Banks was 8 of 14 for 100 yards before leaving with a broken right hand. David Carr, who didn't start with an injured shoulder, was 2 of 5 for 25 yards, with 1 interception. Johnson was 12 of 27 for 116 yards, with 1 interception. Vick was 8 of 11 for 60 yards.

Atlanta	0	7	0	6 —	13
Houston	0	3	14	0 —	17

Atl — Duckett 1 run (Feely kick)
Hous — FG Brown 40
Hous — Davis 7 run (Brown kick)
Hous — Davis 2 run (Brown kick)
Atl — FG Feely 35
Atl — FG Feely 42

NEW ENGLAND 38, INDIANAPOLIS 34—at RCA Dome, attendance 57,102. The Patriots' defense stopped the Colts three times from the 1-yard line in the final seconds to stifle an Indianapolis comeback attempt. Peyton Manning had guided the Colts 81 yards, capped by his 8-yard touchdown pass to Marcus Pollard with 12 seconds left in the half to cut the deficit to 17-10. But Bethel Johnson returned the ensuing kickoff 92 yards as the half ended, and Mike Cloud's second touchdown on their first possession of the second half stretched the lead to 31-10. At the time, New England had scored on five of its six possessions, and the Colts had only been in Patriots' territory twice. Donald Strickland's interception set up Manning's 13-yard touchdown pass to Reggie Wayne with 1:20 left in the quarter. Three plays later, Nick Harper intercepted Tom Brady's pass at the Patriots' 26, and Manning fired a scoring strike to Harrison on the next play for 14 points in exactly one minute to cut the deficit to 31-24. Following a three-and-out, the Colts drove 69 yards, capped by Troy Walters' 6-yard catch with 10:21 left to tie the game. But Johnson returned the ensuing kickoff 67 yards and Brady completed a 13-yard touchdown pass to Deion Branch four plays later. Trailing 38-34, the Colts got the ball at the Patriots' 48 with 2:57 left and drove to the Patriots' 2 with 40 seconds remaining. Edgerrin James gained 1 yard on the first play and no yards on second down. On third down, with 18 seconds left, Manning threw an incompletion. On fourth-and-goal, Willie McGinest tackled James for a loss of a yard to save the game. Brady was 26 of 35 for 236 yards and 2 touchdowns, with 2 interceptions. Manning was 29 of 48 for 278 yards and 4 touchdowns, with 1 interception.

New England	10	14	7	7 —	38
Indianapolis	0	10	14	10 —	34

NE — FG Vinatieri 43
NE — Cloud 4 run (Vinatieri kick)
NE — Ward 31 pass from Brady (Vinatieri kick)
Ind — FG Vanderjagt 40
Ind — Pollard 8 pass from Manning (Vanderjagt kick)
NE — B. Johnson 92 kickoff return (Vinatieri kick)
NE — Cloud 1 run (Vinatieri kick)
Ind — Wayne 13 pass from Manning (Vanderjagt kick)
Ind — Harrison 26 pass from Manning (Vanderjagt kick)
Ind — Walters 6 pass from Manning (Vanderjagt kick)
NE — Branch 13 pass from Brady (Vinatieri kick)
Ind — FG Vanderjagt 29

BUFFALO 24, N.Y. GIANTS 7—at Giants Stadium, attendance 78,481. Travis Henry rushed for 113 yards and 1 touchdown, and Drew Bledsoe passed for 252 yards and 2 scores, as the Bills snapped a four-game road losing streak. Buffalo hadn't scored a touchdown in its last three road games, but posted advantages in first downs (23-10), total yards (403-222), and time of possession (39:07-20:53). Buffalo scored on three consecutive possessions in the second quarter for a 17-7 lead. In the second half, the Bills' defense forced four three-and-out's in five possessions, as Buffalo held the ball 22:30 of the third and fourth quarters. Bledsoe was 19 of 29 for 252 yards and 2 touchdowns. Henry carried 26 times for 113 yards. Kerry Collins was 17 of 35 for 233 yards and 1 touchdown. Amani Toomer had 3 catches for 110 yards.

Buffalo	0	17	7	0 —	24
N.Y. Giants	0	7	0	0 —	7

Buff — Moore 24 pass from Bledsoe (Lindell kick)
NYG — Toomer 77 pass from Collins (Bryant kick)
Buff — FG Lindell 26
Buff — Shaw 22 pass from Bledsoe (Lindell kick)
Buff — Henry 13 run (Lindell kick)

DENVER 22, OAKLAND 8—at Network Associates Coliseum, attendance 57,201. Clinton Portis rushed 34 times for 170 yards and 2 touchdowns for the Broncos. Oakland led 5-0 in the second quarter, and stopped Jake Plummer shy of a first down on third-and-14, but Eric Barton hit Plummer out of bounds for an unnecessary roughness penalty, which led to Plummer's 4-yard touchdown pass to Shannon Sharpe. Oakland took an 8-7 lead, and then forced a punt, but O.J. Santiago, who in the first quarter had blocked a punt out of the end zone for a safety, jumped offside for an automatic first down. Portis scored six plays later for a 14-8 halftime lead. Kelly Herndon recovered Jerry Porter's fumble at the Broncos' 32 with 9:19 left. Denver then drove 68 yards in 10 plays, including 8 carries by Portis capped by his 1-yard scoring plunge with 3:15 left. Plummer was 11 of 20 for 105 yards and 1 touchdown, with 1 interception. Rick Mirer was 13 of 30 for 153 yards.

Denver	0	14	0	8 —	22
Oakland	5	3	0	0 —	8

Oak — Safety, Santiago blocked punt out of end zone
Oak — FG Janikowski 46
Den — Sharpe 4 pass from Plummer (Elam kick)
Oak — FG Janikowski 48
Den — Portis 1 run (Elam kick)
Den — Portis 1 run (Portis run)

CINCINNATI 24, PITTSBURGH 20—at Heinz Field, attendance 58,797. Jon Kitna completed an 18-yard touchdown pass to Matt Schobel with 13 seconds remaining to cap a 52-second drive and shock the Steelers. The Bengals led 14-3 just before halftime, but the Steelers drove to the Bengals' 10. However, Charlie Batch, who played the last 30 seconds of the half after Tommy Maddox had been shaken up, fumbled and John Thornton recovered at the Bengals' 12 to allow Cincinnati to maintain its lead. The Bengals led 17-13 with 4:20 when the Steelers forced a punt and started at their own 20. Maddox engineered an 11-play drive, capped by his 16-yard touchdown pass to Hines Ward with 1:05 left for a 20-17 lead. Brandon Bennett returned the ensuing kickoff 27 yards to the Bengals' 48, Kitna completed an 18-yard pass to Peter Warrick and Bennett raced 16 yards up the middle to get to the Steelers' 18. Following an incompletion, Kitna fired a pass to Schobel in the end zone with 13 seconds left. Kitna was 18 of 32 for 271 yards and 3 touchdowns. Chad Johnson had 6 receptions for 117 yards. Maddox was 28 of 42 for 313 yards and 1 touchdown, with 1 interception. Ward had 13 catches for 149 yards, and Plaxico Burress had 8 receptions for 112 yards.

Cincinnati	7	7	0	10 —	24
Pittsburgh	0	3	7	10 —	20

Cin — Washington 51 pass from Kitna (Graham kick)
Pitt — FG Reed 23
Cin — C. Johnson 4 pass from Kitna (Graham kick)
Pitt — Bettis 1 run (Reed kick)
Pitt — FG Reed 39
Cin — FG Graham 44
Pitt — Ward 16 pass from Maddox (Reed kick)
Cin — Schobel 18 pass from Kitna (Graham kick)

ST. LOUIS 48, MINNESOTA 17—at Edward Jones Dome, attendance 66,134. Marshall Faulk rushed for 108 yards and 3 touchdowns as the Rams scored the final 31 points. The Rams scored on their first three possessions, the first set up by Jamie Duncan's blocked punt, for a 17-7 lead. But Brian

Russell's interception late in the first half led to Moe Williams' 1-yard run to tie the game with 51 seconds left in the half. Marc Bulger completed a 30-yard pass to Faulk and 18-yard pass to Torry Holt to set up Jeff Wilkins' 51-yard field goal as the half expired for a 20-17 lead. The Vikings eschewed a 42-yard field-goal attempt in the third quarter, instead faking the kick on fourth-and-4, but holder Gus Frerotte's shovel pass fell incomplete. A 41-yard pass from wide receiver Isaac Bruce to Dane Looker set up Faulk's 5-yard scoring run, and Tyoka Jackson's interception three plays later was followed by Bulger's 12-yard run for a 34-17 lead. On the ensuing possession, the Vikings drove to the Rams' 5, but Leonard Little forced Daunte Culpepper to fumble and Aeneas Williams raced 90 yards for a touchdown. Bulger was 15 of 20 for 222 yards and 1 touchdown, with 1 interception. Holt had 8 catches for 102 yards. Culpepper was 33 of 47 for 330 yards and 1 touchdown, with 1 interception. Randy Moss had 10 catches for 160 yards, and Jim Kleinsasser added 10 receptions for 79 yards.

Minnesota	7	10	0	0	— 17
St. Louis	10	10	14	14	— 48

StL — Faulk 18 run (Wilkins kick)
StL — FG Wilkins 28
Minn — Moss 15 pass from Culpepper (Elling kick)
StL — Bruce 4 pass from Bulger (Wilkins kick)
Minn — FG Elling 28
Minn — M. Williams 1 run (Elling kick)
StL — FG Wilkins 51
StL — Faulk 5 run (Wilkins kick)
StL — Bulger 12 run (Wilkins kick)
StL — A. Williams 90 fumble return (Wilkins kick)
StL — Faulk 7 run (Wilkins kick)

KANSAS CITY 28, SAN DIEGO 24—at Qualcomm Stadium, attendance 57,671. Priest Holmes rushed for 162 yards and 2 touchdowns, and Tony Gonzalez caught 2 scoring passes for the Chiefs. The Chargers had four scoring chances in the first half, but Steve Christie missed 40- and 48-yard field goals and Dexter McCleon intercepted Doug Flutie's pass at the Chiefs' 19 to thwart another rally. In the second half, San Diego scored on its first two possessions to cut the lead to 21-17, and Quentin Jammer's second interception, in the end zone, allowed San Diego to regain possession. But Flutie fumbled and Gary Stills recovered at the Chargers' 27 and Gonzalez caught a 3-yard touchdown pass with 6:28 left. Greg Wesley intercepted Flutie in the end zone with 4:07 remaining, and the Chargers got the ball back with 1:08 left and scored as time expired. Green was 17 of 30 for 155 yards and 2 touchdowns, with 2 interceptions. Holmes had 31 carries for 162 yards. Flutie was 16 of 34 for 213 yards and 2 touchdowns, with 2 interceptions. LaDainian Tomlinson had 19 carries for 106 yards.

Kansas City	7	14	0	7	— 28
San Diego	0	7	10	7	— 24

KC — Holmes 7 run (Andersen kick)
KC — Holmes 2 run (Andersen kick)
SD — Tomlinson 6 run (Christie kick)
KC — Gonzalez 7 pass from Green (Andersen kick)
SD — FG Christie 21
SD — Boston 20 pass from Flutie (Christie kick)
KC — Gonzalez 3 pass from Green (Andersen kick)
SD — Gates 18 pass from Flutie (Christie kick)

SEATTLE 34, CLEVELAND 7—at Seahawks Stadium, attendance 64,680. Matt Hasselbeck passed for 3 touchdowns as the Seahawks improved to 7-0 at home. The Seahawks had sizeable advantages in first downs (26-11), total yards (463-214), and time of possession (38:39-21:21). The Seahawks were inside the Browns' 30 five times in the first half, but a missed field goal and interception limited their lead to 17-0. The Seahawks scored on their first two possessions of the second half before the Browns finally drove inside Seattle's red zone, only to have Ken Lucas intercept Kelly Holcomb's pass. Cleveland's only score came when Tom Rouen's punt was blocked, and Andre King picked up the ball and rambled 28 yards for a score with 3:23 left. Hasselbeck was 26 of 35 for 328 yards and 3 touchdowns, with 1 interception. Darrell Jackson had 8 receptions for 102 yards and Koren Robinson added 6 catches for 122 yards. Shaun Alexander rushed 27 times for 127 yards. Holcomb was 22 of 31 for 186 yards, with 1 interception.

Cleveland	0	0	0	7	— 7
Seattle	7	10	10	7	— 34

Sea — Mili 2 pass from Hasselbeck (Brown kick)
Sea — FG Brown 36
Sea — Jackson 3 pass from Hasselbeck (Brown kick)
Sea — Jackson 26 pass from Hasselbeck (Brown kick)
Sea — FG Brown 41
Sea — Alexander 3 run (Brown kick)
Cle — King 28 blocked punt return (Dawson kick)

NEW ORLEANS 24, WASHINGTON 20—at FedExField attendance 76,821. Aaron Brooks ran for 2 touchdowns and passed for another as the Saints rallied to defeat the Redskins. Chad Morton's 94-yard kickoff return gave the Redskins a 14-10 halftime lead. Brooks scrambled 3 yards for a touchdown late in the third quarter to tie the game. John Hall gave Washington a 20-17 lead early in the fourth quarter, but Keyuo Craver returned the ensuing kickoff 52 yards to set up Brooks' go-ahead touchdown pass to Boo Williams with 9:38 left. The Redskins failed to cross midfield on their final three possessions. Brooks was 14 of 30 for 121 yards and 1 touchdown. Deuce McAllister had 30 carries for 165 yards. Tim Hasselbeck, making his first start, was 22 of 42 for 231 yards, with 1 interception. Trung Canidate rushed 16 times for 115 yards.

New Orleans	0	10	7	7	— 24
Washington	0	14	3	3	— 20

NO — Brooks 7 run (Carney kick)
Wash — Cartwright 2 run (Hall kick)
NO — FG Carney 25
Wash — Morton 94 kickoff return (Hall kick)
Wash — FG Hall 45
NO — Brooks 3 run (Carney kick)
Wash — FG Hall 49
NO — B. Williams 15 pass from Brooks (Carney kick)

SUNDAY NIGHT, NOVEMBER 30
JACKSONVILLE 17, TAMPA BAY 10—at ALLTEL Stadium, attendance 60,543. Byron Leftwich completed a 48-yard touchdown pass to Jimmy Smith early in the fourth quarter to snap a 10-10 tie and defeat the Buccaneers. Mike Peterson's interception at the Buccaneers' 40 set up Leftwich's first touchdown pass, to Kyle Brady, for a 7-0 lead. But the Jaguars missed a field goal and were stopped on downs in the red zone on another first-half possession, and Tampa Bay briefly led 10-7 before Seth Marler capped a 60-yard drive with a 28-yard field goal just before halftime. Each team missed a field goal in the third quarter, prior to Leftwich lofting a 48-yard pass to Smith for a touchdown and 17-10 lead with 10:23 to play. Tampa Bay was stopped on downs near midfield with 3:11 left, and Fred Taylor gained 2 first downs to run out the clock. Leftwich was 20 of 34 for 224 yards and 2 touchdowns. Smith had 10 catches for 136 yards, and Taylor rushed 29 times for 118 yards. Brad Johnson was 21 of 38 for 156 yards, with 1 interception.

Tampa Bay	0	10	0	0	— 10
Jacksonville	0	10	0	7	— 17

Jax — Brady 10 pass from Leftwich (Marler kick)
TB — Jones 5 run (Gramatica kick)
TB — FG Gramatica 47
Jax — FG Marler 28
Jax — J. Smith 48 pass from Leftwich (Marler kick)

MONDAY NIGHT, DECEMBER 1
N.Y. JETS 24, TENNESSEE 17—at The Meadowlands, attendance 77,710. Chad Pennington passed for 2 touchdowns as the Jets held off the Titans. The Titans scored five plays into the game, but the Jets promptly drove 61 yards to tie the game and then added a 49-yard drive just before halftime to take a 10-7 lead. Tennessee's first drive of the second half ended with a tying field goal, but the Jets responded with touchdown drives of 67 and 80 yards, with Pennington completing all 5 of his pass attempts, including 2 touchdowns, to take a 24-10 lead with 10:45 left. The Jets' defense stopped the Titans on downs at the 3-yard line with 5:21 left, but Steve McNair completed an 8-yard touchdown pass to Derrick Mason with 1:52 to play. Chris Baker recovered the onside kick to secure the victory. Pennington was 18 of 23 for 231 yards and 2 touchdowns, with 2 interceptions. McNair was 21 of 35 for 272 yards and 2 touchdowns, with 2 interceptions. Mason had 11 catches for 133 yards.

Tennessee	7	0	3	7	— 17
N.Y. Jets	7	3	7	7	— 24

Tenn — McCareins 59 pass from McNair (Anderson kick)
NYJ — Martin 6 run (Brien kick)
NYJ — FG Brien 27
Tenn — FG Anderson 35
NYJ — Swayne 27 pass from Pennington (Brien kick)
NYJ — Conway 8 pass from Pennington (Brien kick)
Tenn — Mason 8 pass from McNair (Anderson kick)

FOURTEENTH WEEK SUMMARIES
American Football Conference

East Division	**W**	**L**	**T**	**Pct.**	**Pts.**	**OP**
New England*	11	2	0	.846	269	209
Miami	8	5	0	.615	241	203
Buffalo	6	7	0	.462	214	200
N.Y. Jets	5	8	0	.385	240	255
North Division	**W**	**L**	**T**	**Pct.**	**Pts.**	**OP**
Baltimore	8	5	0	.615	331	251
Cincinnati	7	6	0	.538	281	297
Pittsburgh	5	8	0	.385	250	284
Cleveland	4	9	0	.308	212	250
South Division	**W**	**L**	**T**	**Pct.**	**Pts.**	**OP**
Indianapolis	10	3	0	.769	372	281
Tennessee	9	4	0	.692	347	261
Houston	5	8	0	.385	211	317
Jacksonville	4	9	0	.308	229	264
West Division	**W**	**L**	**T**	**Pct.**	**Pts.**	**OP**
Kansas City#	11	2	0	.846	388	267
Denver	8	5	0	.615	324	233
Oakland	3	10	0	.231	229	305
San Diego	3	10	0	.231	247	349

National Football Conference

East Division	**W**	**L**	**T**	**Pct.**	**Pts.**	**OP**
Philadelphia#	10	3	0	.769	281	222
Dallas	8	5	0	.615	236	244

	W	L	T	Pct.	Pts.	OP
Washington	5	8	0	.385	256	287
N.Y. Giants	4	9	0	.308	209	286
North Division	**W**	**L**	**T**	**Pct.**	**Pts.**	**OP**
Minnesota	8	5	0	.615	344	302
Green Bay	7	6	0	.538	332	276
Chicago	5	8	0	.385	240	281
Detroit	4	9	0	.308	209	294
South Division	**W**	**L**	**T**	**Pct.**	**Pts.**	**OP**
Carolina	8	5	0	.615	248	249
New Orleans	6	7	0	.462	263	292
Tampa Bay	6	7	0	.462	244	198
Atlanta	3	10	0	.231	241	342
West Division	**W**	**L**	**T**	**Pct.**	**Pts.**	**OP**
St. Louis#	10	3	0	.769	373	266
Seattle	8	5	0	.615	330	273
San Francisco	6	7	0	.462	298	244
Arizona	3	10	0	.231	180	387

**Clinched division title*
#Clinched playoff berth

SUNDAY, DECEMBER 7

BALTIMORE 31, CINCINNATI 13—at M & T Bank Stadium, attendance 69,468. Jamal Lewis rushed for 180 yards and 3 touchdowns as the Ravens moved into first place in the AFC North. The Ravens forced 5 turnovers, which resulted in 21 points. Chad Williams recovered Peter Warrick's muffed punt at the Bengals' 27 late in the first quarter to set up Lewis' first touchdown run. The Bengals' defense helped the cause in the second quarter when Rogers Beckett intercepted Anthony Wright's pass to set up Jon Kitna's 4-yard scoring pass to Warrick to cut the deficit to 14-10. The Ravens led 17-13 in the third quarter when Terrell Suggs sacked Kitna, forced him to fumble, and recovered the ball at the Ravens' 17 to set up Lewis' second touchdown. Will Demps' 54-yard interception return early in the fourth quarter led to Lewis' 13-yard touchdown run for a 31-13 lead with 11:48 to play. Wright was 8 of 19 for 145 yards and 1 touchdown, with 2 interceptions. Lewis had 30 carries for 180 yards. Kitna was 23 of 31 for 214 yards and 1 touchdown, with 2 interceptions. Warrick had 11 receptions for 90 yards.

Cincinnati	3	7	3	0	—	13
Baltimore	7	10	7	7	—	31

Cin — FG Graham 25
Balt — J. Lewis 1 run (Stover kick)
Balt — Robinson 8 pass from Wright (Stover kick)
Cin — Warrick 4 pass from Kitna (Graham kick)
Balt — FG Stover 22
Cin — FG Graham 38
Balt — J. Lewis 3 run (Stover kick)
Balt — J. Lewis 13 run (Stover kick)

BUFFALO 17, N.Y. JETS 6—at Ralph Wilson Stadium, attendance 72,791. Travis Henry rushed for 169 yards and 1 touchdown as the Bills won back-to-back games for the first time since the first and second weeks of the season. The Jets opened the game with a 17-play, 67-yard, 9:37 drive, but settled for Doug Brien's 38-yard field goal. It was the Jets' only drive into the Bills' red zone all day. The Bills responded with a 13-play, 71-yard touchdown drive. The Bills extended their lead to 14-3 in the third quarter when Henry capped an 11-play, 85-yard drive, highlighted by runs of 9, 11, and 12 yards, with a 4-yard scoring run. Drew Bledsoe was 9 of 15 for 72 yards and 1 touchdown, with 1 interception. Henry rushed 32 times for 169 yards. Chad Pennington was 15 of 29 for 155 yards, with 1 interception.

N.Y. Jets	3	0	3	0	—	6
Buffalo	0	7	7	3	—	17

NYJ — FG Brien 38
Buff — Reed 6 pass from Bledsoe (Lindell kick)
Buff — Henry 4 run (Lindell kick)
NYJ — FG Brien 40
Buff — FG Lindell 32

DENVER 45, KANSAS CITY 27—at INVESCO Field at Mile High, attendance 76,403. Clinton Portis rushed for 218 yards and a club record 5 touchdowns as the Broncos handed the Chiefs just their second defeat. The teams combined for 952 yards, 508 gained by the Broncos, and each scored on their first three possessions as the Chiefs took a 21-17 halftime lead. The Broncos scored touchdowns on their first four possessions of the second half, on drives of 78, 79, 74, and 53 yards. Portis, who scored twice in the first half, scored on a 59-yard run with 2:42 left in the third quarter for a 31-21 lead. Portis' 28-yard scoring run early in the fourth quarter extended the lead to 38-21, and after the Chiefs were stopped on downs, Portis raced 53 yards for a touchdown on the next play for a 45-21 lead with 7:58 to play. Jake Plummer was 20 of 29 for 238 yards and 1 touchdown. Portis rushed 22 times for 218 yards. Trent Green was 34 of 47 for 397 yards and 1 touchdown. Dante Hall had 11 receptions for 124 yards.

Kansas City	7	14	0	6	—	27
Denver	7	10	14	14	—	45

Den — Portis 11 run (Elam kick)
KC — Holmes 2 run (Andersen kick)
Den — Portis 1 run (Elam kick)
KC — Holmes 1 run (Andersen kick)
Den — FG Elam 47
KC — Kennison 42 pass from Green (Andersen kick)
Den — Droughns 3 pass from Plummer (Elam kick)
Den — Portis 59 run (Elam kick)
Den — Portis 28 run (Elam kick)
Den — Portis 53 run (Elam kick)
KC — Green 1 run (pass failed)

SAN DIEGO 14, DETROIT 7—at Ford Field, attendance 61,544. LaDainian Tomlinson had 236 total yards and scored 2 touchdowns for the Chargers. Doug Flutie's 16-yard touchdown pass to Tomlinson capped a 70-yard drive in the first quarter, and his 73-yard scoring catch came on a short pass over the middle in which he raced untouched for a 14-0 lead. The Lions punted on eight of their nine possessions, with the lone productive drive stalling at the Chargers' 25 when Joey Harrington completed a 5-yard pass to Bill Schroeder with 12 seconds left in the half but Detroit was unable to stop the clock for a field-goal attempt. Harrington did complete a 4-yard touchdown pass to Casey Fitzsimmons with 7:22 remaining to cut the deficit to 14-7. The Lions drove to the Chargers' 33 with 23 seconds left, but a spike and three more incomplete passes ended the scoring threat. Flutie was 17 of 25 for 244 yards, with 1 interception. Tomlinson rushed 25 times for 88 yards and had 9 receptions for 148 yards. Harrington was 26 of 46 for 208 yards and 1 touchdown.

San Diego	7	7	0	0	—	14
Detroit	0	0	0	7	—	7

SD — Tomlinson 16 pass from Flutie (Christie kick)
SD — Tomlinson 73 pass from Flutie (Christie kick)
Det — Fitzsimmons 4 pass from Harrington (Hanson kick)

GREEN BAY 34, CHICAGO 21—at Lambeau Field, attendance 70,458. The Packers' defense forced 5 turnovers, including a key 90-yard interception return by Mike McKenzie, to stay within one game of first place. The Bears scored twice in a 56-second span late in the first quarter, capped by Lance Briggs' 45-yard interception return, for a 14-0 lead. The Packers then scored on five of their next six possessions, but since four were field goals by Ryan Longwell, Green Bay led just 19-14. Early in the fourth quarter, the Bears drove to the Packers' 16, but on third-and-8 Kordell Stewart attempted a pass to Dez White in the flat. McKenzie jumped the route and stepped in front of the pass and outran Stewart and a host of Bears 90 yards down the left sideline for a touchdown. Brett Favre completed a 2-point conversion pass to Bubba Franks for a 27-14 lead with 9:16 to play. Favre was 22 of 33 for 210 yards and 1 touchdown, with 1 interception. Stewart was 17 of 40 for 256 yards and 1 touchdown, with 3 interceptions. Marty Booker had 5 receptions for 115 yards.

Chicago	14	0	0	7	—	21
Green Bay	0	13	6	15	—	34

Chi — Booker 61 pass from Stewart (Edinger kick)
Chi — Briggs 45 interception return (Edinger kick)
GB — FG Longwell 24
GB — FG Longwell 38
GB — Walker 22 pass from Favre (Longwell kick)
GB — FG Longwell 35
GB — FG Longwell 45
GB — McKenzie 90 interception return (Franks pass from Favre)
GB — Green 2 run (Longwell kick)
Chi — Azumah 88 kickoff return (Edinger kick)

JACKSONVILLE 27, HOUSTON 0—at ALLTEL Stadium, attendance 43,363. The Jaguars' defense permitted just 7 first downs and 124 total yards to post the club's first shutout since 2000. The Texans, who started rookie Dave Ragone because of injuries to David Carr and Tony Banks and were also without leading rusher Domanick Davis, punted 6 times in the first half but trailed just 10-0 with 1:49 left in the half. However, Byron Leftwich engineered a 9-play, 84-yard drive, capped by Fred Taylor's 2-yard run with 15 seconds left in the half for a 17-0 lead. A 62-yard run by Taylor in the fourth quarter led to LaBrandon Toefield's first career touchdown run with 10:21 to play. Leftwich was 18 of 29 for 194 yards and 1 touchdown. Taylor rushed 24 times for 163 yards. Ragone was 11 of 23 for 71 yards, with 1 interception.

Houston	0	0	0	0	—	0
Jacksonville	7	10	0	10	—	27

Jax — J. Smith 32 pass from Leftwich (Marler kick)
Jax — FG Marler 35
Jax — Taylor 2 run (Marler kick)
Jax — Toefield 1 run (Marler kick)
Jax — FG Marler 28

MINNESOTA 34, SEATTLE 7—at Metrodome, attendance 63,968. Daunte Culpepper threw for 274 yards and completed 3 touchdown passes in excess of 40 yards to defeat the Seahawks. The Vikings, who had 465 yards and maintained possession for 38:51, took a 7-0 lead early in the second quarter as Culpepper hit Randy Moss in stride in the end zone with a 47-yard scoring pass. Minnesota scored on its next three possessions as well, capped by another long pass, 45 yards, to Moss, for a 20-7 lead with 9:24 left in the third quarter. Culpepper found Kelly Campbell deep down the right side for a 43-yard touchdown early in the fourth quarter, and Mike Nattiel returned an interception 80 yards for a touchdown with 1:34 left to finish the scoring. Culpepper was 21 of 33 for 274 yards and 3 touchdowns. Moss had 8 catches for 133 yards, and Michael Bennett rushed 25 times for 103 yards. Matt Hasselbeck was 17 of 34 for 218 yards, with 2 interceptions.

Seattle	0	0	7	0	—	7
Minnesota	0	13	7	14	—	34

Minn — Moss 47 pass from Culpepper (Elling kick)
Minn — FG Elling 36
Minn — FG Elling 35
Sea — Alexander 1 run (Brown kick)
Minn — Moss 45 pass from Culpepper (Elling kick)
Minn — Campbell 43 pass from Culpepper (Elling kick)
Minn — Nattiel 80 interception return (Elling kick)

NEW ENGLAND 12, MIAMI 0—at Gillette Stadium, attendance 68,436. Tedy Bruschi returned an interception for a touchdown as the Patriots won in the snow and 28 degree temperature. The Patriots' defense, which didn't allow a touchdown at home for the fourth consecutive game, permitted just 7 first downs and 134 yards. Adam Vinatieri's 29-yard field goal capped a 41-yard first quarter drive. The Dolphins punted 10 times in their first 11 possessions. In their lone productive drive, the Dolphins drove to the Patriots' 10, but on third down Rodney Harrison blitzed, sacked Jay Fiedler, forced him to fumble and Mike Vrabel recovered late in the third quarter. Patriots punter Brooks Barnard, signed during the week, pinned four punts inside the Dolphins' 20, including a punt that went out of bounds at the 4-yard-line with 8:59 to play. On the next play, Bruschi leaped into the air and intercepted Fiedler's pass and went 5 yards into the end zone for a 10-0 lead. Jarvis Green sacked Fiedler for a safety with 1:13 remaining to finish the scoring. Tom Brady was 16 of 31 for 163 yards. Fiedler was 13 of 31 for 111 yards, with 2 interceptions.

Miami	0	0	0	0	—	0
New England	3	0	0	9	—	12

NE — FG Vinatieri 29
NE — Bruschi 5 interception return (Vinatieri kick)
NE — Safety, Green sacked Fiedler in end zone

TAMPA BAY 14, NEW ORLEANS 7—at Louisiana Superdome, attendance 68,442. Defense and special teams set up 2 Tampa Bay touchdowns in the final two minutes of the first half as the defending Super Bowl champions kept alive their slim playoff hopes. Trailing 7-0, Jermaine Phillips recovered an Aaron Brooks fumble and Brad Johnson completed a 14-yard touchdown pass to Ken Dilger two plays later to tie the game with 1:25 left in the half. Three plays later, David Gibson blocked Mitch Berger's punt and Ronde Barber returned it 20 yards to the Saints' 1. Johnson completed a 1-yard scoring pass to Warren Sapp, his second touchdown of the season, on the next play for a 14-7 lead with 17 seconds left in the half. The Saints drove to the Buccaneers' 6 in the middle of the fourth quarter, but Greg Spires sacked Brooks and forced him to fumble. Chartric Darby recovered with 8:11 left, and the Saints never threatened again. Johnson was 20 of 34 for 213 yards and 2 touchdowns, with 1 interception. Brooks was 20 of 30 for 238 yards and 1 touchdown. Joe Horn had 9 catches for 118 yards.

Tampa Bay	0	14	0	0	—	14
New Orleans	7	0	0	0	—	7

NO — B. Williams 31 pass from Brooks (Carney kick)
TB — Dilger 14 pass from Johnson (Gramatica kick)
TB — Sapp 1 pass from Johnson (Gramatica kick)

WASHINGTON 20, N.Y. GIANTS 7—at Giants Stadium, attendance 78,217. Tim Hasselbeck passed for 154 yards and 2 touchdowns as the Giants lost their fifth consecutive game. Bruce Smith set the all-time NFL sack record with a 7-yard sack of Jesse Palmer with 8:33 left in the fourth quarter. His 199th sack surpassed Reggie White. The Giants had two scoring chances in the first quarter. Matt Bryant missed a 26-yard field-goal attempt to quell the first threat, but Dorsey Levens scored on a 5-yard run for a 7-3 lead. Patrick Johnson returned the ensuing kickoff 50 yards and Hasselbeck completed a 6-yard touchdown pass to Darnerien McCants for a 10-7 lead. Champ Bailey intercepted Kerry Collins' pass at the Redskins' 19 just before halftime to stop another scoring chance. Hasselbeck engineered an 80-yard scoring drive to begin the third quarter, highlighted by McCants' 22-yard catch on third-and-7, and capped by Rod Gardner's 7-yard touchdown catch. The Giants drove to the Redskins' 12 but were stopped on downs with 5:53 left, and Rock Cartwright and Chad Morton allowed the Redskins to maintain possession for the remainder of the game. Hasselbeck was 13 of 19 for 154 yards and 2 touchdowns. Collins was 5 of 14 for 62 yards, with 1 interception, before leaving early in the second half with a sprained ankle. Palmer was 7 of 11 for 83 yards.

Washington	3	7	7	3	—	20
N.Y. Giants	7	0	0	0	—	7

Wash — FG Hall 28
NYG — Levens 5 run (Bryant kick)
Wash — McCants 6 pass from Hasselbeck (Hall kick)
Wash — Gardner 7 pass from Hasselbeck (Hall kick)
Wash — FG Hall 41

PHILADELPHIA 36, DALLAS 10—at Lincoln Financial Field, attendance 69,773. Donovan McNabb passed for 3 touchdowns as the Eagles won their eighth consecutive game. Quincy Carter's 3-yard touchdown pass to Jeff Robinson with 26 seconds left in the half tied the game 10-10. Sheldon Brown intercepted Carter three plays into the second half, and McNabb's 5-yard scoring shovel pass to Duce Staley five plays later gave the Eagles the lead for good. Matt Lehr's Shotgun snap from the 13-yard line went out of the end zone for a safety late in the third quarter, and McNabb's' 6-yard touchdown pass to L.J. Smith on the ensuing possession gave Philadelphia a 26-10 lead with 12:52 left. The Cowboys didn't cross midfield on their final five possessions. McNabb was 19 of 35 for 248 yards and 3 touchdowns. Correll Buckhalter rushed 13 times for 115 yards. Carter was 15 of 24 for 93 yards and 1 touchdown, with 2 interceptions.

Dallas	3	7	0	0	—	10
Philadelphia	0	10	9	17	—	36

Dall — FG Cundiff 29
Phil — FG Akers 22
Phil — Westbrook 16 pass from McNabb (Akers kick)
Dall — Robinson 3 pass from Carter (Cundiff kick)
Phil — Staley 5 pass from McNabb (Akers kick)
Phil — Safety, Lehr Shotgun snap went out of end zone
Phil — Smith 6 pass from McNabb (Akers kick)
Phil — FG Akers 21
Phil — Buckhalter 64 run (Akers kick)

PITTSBURGH 27, OAKLAND 7—at Heinz Field, attendance 53,079. The Steelers' defense permitted just 161 yards, including only 53 in the second half, as Pittsburgh defeated the Raiders. Tyrone Wheatley's 22-yard touchdown run capped a 63-yard drive and gave Oakland a 7-0 lead. The Steelers scored on three of their next four possessions, capped by Tommy Maddox's 14-yard touchdown pass to Plaxico Burress with 2:06 left in the half, for a 17-7 lead. Burress' catch was set up by Dewayne Washington's interception of a Rick Mirer pass. A 51-yard punt return by Antwaan Randle El set up Dan Kreider's 1-yard touchdown run in the third quarter for a 24-7 lead. Maddox was 19 of 28 for 266 yards and 1 touchdown, with 1 interception. Jerome Bettis rushed 27 times for 106 yards, and moved past Thurman Thomas into ninth place on the all-time rushing list with 12,116 yards. Mirer was 10 of 25 for 68 yards, with 2 interceptions.

Oakland	7	0	0	0	—	7
Pittsburgh	0	17	7	3	—	27

Oak — Wheatley 22 run (Janikowski kick)
Pitt — FG Reed 44
Pitt — Bettis 11 run (Reed kick)
Pitt — Burress 14 pass from Maddox (Reed kick)
Pitt — Kreider 1 run (Reed kick)
Pitt — FG Reed 40

SAN FRANCISCO 50, ARIZONA 14—at 3Com Park, attendance 66,975. Jeff Garcia passed for 4 touchdowns and rushed for 2 more scores as the 49ers throttled the Cardinals. The 49ers outgained Arizona 496-217 and scored touchdowns on five of their seven first-half possessions. The last two scores were set up by Tony Parrish, who recovered a fumble and had an interception, to help stake the 49ers to a 34-0 halftime lead. In the first half, Garcia was 16 of 19 for 221 yards and 4 touchdowns, and rushed for a score. For the game, Garcia was 19 of 28 for 252 yards and 4 touchdowns, and rushed 5 times for 32 yards. Kevan Barlow rushed 18 times for 154 yards. Jeff Blake started and was 8 of 20 for 59 yards, with 1 interception, and Josh McCown was 11 of 20 for 120 yards and 2 touchdowns. Anquan Boldin had 9 receptions for 123 yards.

Arizona	0	0	7	7	—	14
San Francisco	14	20	9	7	—	50

SF — Garcia 3 run (Peterson kick)
SF — Owens 1 pass from Garcia (Peterson kick)
SF — Streets 18 pass from Garcia (Peterson kick)
SF — Wilson 27 pass from Garcia (mishandled snap)
SF — Owens 2 pass from Garcia (Peterson kick)
SF — Safety, Ulbrich tackled Shipp in end zone
Ariz — Hodgins 3 pass from McCown (Rackers kick)
SF — Garcia 4 run (Peterson kick)
SF — Barlow 46 run (Peterson kick)
Ariz — Boldin 16 pass from McCown (Rackers kick)

INDIANAPOLIS 29, TENNESSEE 27—at The Coliseum, attendance 68,809. Edgerrin James rushed for 2 touchdowns and the Colts took advantage of four Tennessee fumbles to defeat the Titans. Tennessee led 10-6 when the Colts forced a punt with 7:17 left in the second quarter. The ensuing 67-yard drive resulted in Mike Vanderjagt's second field goal with 1:48 left in the half. Eddie Berlin fumbled during the kickoff return and Robert Mathis recovered to set up Vanderjagt's third field goal with two seconds left in the half. The Colts took the opening kickoff of the second half and scored on James' 2-yard run. Berlin fumbled the ensuing kickoff, and Ricky Williams recovered which resulted in Vanderjagt's fourth field goal for a 22-10 lead with 7:16 left in the third quarter. The Colts scored 16 points in a span of 15:01 without the Titans running a play from scrimmage.

James' 5-yard run on their next possession increased the lead to 29-13 with 37 seconds left in the third quarter. Steve McNair engineered a 12-play, 69-yard drive which ended with Robert Holcombe's 1-yard touchdown catch and McNair's 2-point conversion run. Trailing 29-21, McNair completed a 29-yard pass to Justin McCareins to the Colts' 19 with 2:34 left, and an 18-yard pass to McCareins to the 1-yard line to set up McNair's 2-yard touchdown pass to Derrick Mason with 1:52 left. However, McNair's 2-point pass attempt fell incomplete. The Titans forced a punt with 50 seconds left, but McCareins fumbled during the punt return and Anthony Floyd recovered to preserve the victory. Peyton Manning was 22 of 34 for 228 yards. Marvin Harrison had 10 receptions for 124 yards. McNair was 22 of 38 for 235 yards and 2 touchdowns.

Indianapolis	3	9	17	0	—	29
Tennessee	10	0	3	14	—	27

Tenn — FG Anderson 40
Ind — FG Vanderjagt 21
Tenn — McNair 2 run (Anderson kick)
Ind — FG Vanderjagt 35
Ind — FG Vanderjagt 36
Ind — FG Vanderjagt 23
Ind — James 2 run (Vanderjagt kick)
Ind — FG Vanderjagt 26
Tenn — FG Anderson 40
Ind — James 5 run (Vanderjagt kick)
Tenn — Holcombe 1 pass from McNair (McNair run)
Tenn — Mason 2 pass from McNair (pass failed)

SUNDAY NIGHT, DECEMBER 7
ATLANTA 20, CAROLINA 14 (OT)—at Georgia Dome, attendance 70,079. In his first start of the season, Michael Vick passed for 179 yards and rushed for 141 yards and a touchdown as the Falcons defeated the first-place Panthers. The Falcons drove into the Panthers' red zone four times in the first half, but were stopped on downs and missed 2 field goals resulting in a 7-7 halftime score. Ricky Manning Jr. recovered T.J. Duckett's fumble in the third quarter to set up Stephen's Davis go-ahead 1-yard touchdown run, but Atlanta tied the score on Vick's 1-yard run with 8:17 remaining, a play that began with a 43-yard run by Vick. The Falcons drove to the Panthers' 31 with 14 seconds left, but Deon Grant intercepted Vick's pass to force overtime. Carolina won the coin toss, but on the third play Kevin Mathis intercepted Jake Delhomme's pass and returned it 32 yards for a touchdown. Vick was 16 of 33 for 179 yards, with 1 interception, and rushed 14 times for 141 yards. Delhomme was 13 of 25 for 153 yards and 1 touchdown, with 2 interceptions.

Carolina	0	7	7	0	0	—	14
Atlanta	0	7	0	7	6	—	20

Atl — Duckett 9 run (Feely kick)
Car — Wiggins 16 pass from Delhomme (Kasay kick)
Car — Davis 1 run (Kasay kick)
Atl — Vick 1 run (Feely kick)
Atl — Mathis 32 interception return

MONDAY NIGHT, DECEMBER 8
ST. LOUIS 26, CLEVELAND 20—at Cleveland Browns Stadium, attendance 73,108. Aeneas Williams had 2 interceptions to help the Rams score 17 points in the final two minutes of the first half to defeat the Browns. Jeff Wilkins' 29-yard field goal with 1:52 left in the half gave the Rams a 9-7 lead. Three plays later Williams intercepted Kelly Holcomb's pass and returned it 46 yards for a touchdown with 1:04 left in the second quarter. Two plays later, Williams again intercepted Holcomb's pass attempt and returned it 27 yards to the Browns' 20. Marc Bulger completed a 16-yard touchdown pass to Isaac Bruce two plays later with 22 second left in the half to give St. Louis 17 points in a span of 1:30 and a 23-7 lead. Tim Couch entered the game and completed a 28-yard touchdown pass to Quincy Morgan on the Browns' first possession of the second half, and a 2-yard touchdown run by Jamel White with 10:17 left cut the deficit to 26-20. Wilkins missed a 39-yard field-goal attempt with 4:48 left, but Cleveland failed to threaten on its final two possessions. Bulger was 22 of 36 for 223 yards and 1 touchdown, with 1 interception. Marshall Faulk rushed 24 times for 102 yards. Holcomb was 10 of 17 for 80 yards and 1 touchdown, with 2 interceptions, and Couch was 6 of 9 for 98 yards and 1 touchdown. White rushed 16 times for 101 yards.

St. Louis	3	20	3	0	—	26
Cleveland	7	0	6	7	—	20

StL — FG Wilkins 28
Cle — Heinrich 2 pass from Holcomb (Dawson kick)
StL — FG Wilkins 26
StL — FG Wilkins 29
StL — A. Williams 46 interception return (Wilkins kick)
StL — Bruce 16 pass from Bulger (Wilkins kick)
Cle — Morgan 28 pass from Couch (pass failed)
StL — FG Wilkins 37
Cle — White 2 run (Dawson kick)

FIFTEENTH WEEK SUMMARIES

American Football Conference						
East Division	**W**	**L**	**T**	**Pct.**	**Pts.**	**OP**
New England*	12	2	0	.857	296	222
Miami	8	6	0	.571	268	237
Buffalo	6	8	0	.429	240	228
N.Y. Jets	6	8	0	.429	246	255
North Division	**W**	**L**	**T**	**Pct.**	**Pts.**	**OP**
Baltimore	8	6	0	.571	343	271
Cincinnati	8	6	0	.571	322	335
Pittsburgh	5	9	0	.357	250	290
Cleveland	4	10	0	.286	232	273
South Division	**W**	**L**	**T**	**Pct.**	**Pts.**	**OP**
Indianapolis#	11	3	0	.786	410	288
Tennessee	10	4	0	.714	375	287
Houston	5	9	0	.357	214	333
Jacksonville	4	10	0	.286	242	291
West Division	**W**	**L**	**T**	**Pct.**	**Pts.**	**OP**
Kansas City*	12	2	0	.857	433	284
Denver	9	5	0	.643	347	253
Oakland	4	10	0	.286	249	317
San Diego	3	11	0	.214	268	387
National Football Conference						
East Division	**W**	**L**	**T**	**Pct.**	**Pts.**	**OP**
Philadelphia#	11	3	0	.786	315	249
Dallas	9	5	0	.643	263	244
Washington	5	9	0	.357	256	314
N.Y. Giants	4	10	0	.286	216	331
North Division	**W**	**L**	**T**	**Pct.**	**Pts.**	**OP**
Minnesota	8	6	0	.571	354	315
Green Bay	8	6	0	.571	370	297
Chicago	6	8	0	.429	253	291
Detroit	4	10	0	.286	226	339
South Division	**W**	**L**	**T**	**Pct.**	**Pts.**	**OP**
Carolina*	9	5	0	.643	268	266
New Orleans	7	7	0	.500	308	299
Tampa Bay	7	7	0	.500	260	201
Atlanta	3	11	0	.214	248	380
West Division	**W**	**L**	**T**	**Pct.**	**Pts.**	**OP**
St. Louis*	11	3	0	.786	400	288
Seattle	8	6	0	.571	352	300
San Francisco	6	8	0	.429	336	285
Arizona	3	11	0	.214	197	407

**Clinched division title*
#Clinched playoff berth

SUNDAY, DECEMBER 14
CAROLINA 20, ARIZONA 17—at Sun Devil Stadium, attendance 23,217. John Kasay kicked a 49-yard field goal with four seconds left as the Panthers rallied to victory and clinched their first division title since 1996. Emmitt Smith's 4-yard touchdown run with 6:04 left in the second quarter capped consecutive scoring drives for Arizona and gave the Cardinals a 14-7 lead. The Panthers took a 17-14 lead early in the fourth quarter on DeShaun Foster's 31-yard touchdown catch. The play capped a 9-play, 93-yard drive in which Jake Delhomme completed 5 of 6 passes for 75 yards. Neil Rackers missed a 35-yard field goal on the ensuing possession, but Rackers converted a 44-yard field goal with 1:09 remaining to tie the game. Delhomme then completed 6 of 8 passes, including 5 to Steve Smith, on the next possession to set up Kasay's game-winning kick. Delhomme was 20 of 32 for 236 yards and 1 touchdown, with 1 interception. Josh McCown, making his first NFL start, was 14 of 25 for 172 yards, with 1 interception.

Carolina	7	0	3	10	—	20
Arizona	7	7	0	3	—	17

Car — Minter 35 interception return (Kasay kick)
Ariz — McCown 16 run (Rackers kick)
Ariz — Smith 4 run (Rackers kick)
Car — FG Kasay 21
Car — Foster 31 pass from Delhomme (Kasay kick)
Ariz — FG Rackers 44
Car — FG Kasay 49

CHICAGO 13, MINNESOTA 10—at Soldier Field, attendance 61,804. Rookie cornerback Charles Tillman out-muscled Randy Moss for a pass in the end zone with 1:02 remaining which resulted in a game-winning interception for the Bears. Playing in his first NFL game, let alone his first start, Rex Grossman's first pass, a fly pattern attempt to Justin Gage, resulted in a 33-yard penalty and set up Paul Edinger's 38-yard field goal. A fumbled snap by Vikings punter Eddie Johnson in the third quarter set up Edinger's second field goal and a 13-3 lead. Edinger missed from 46 yards early in the fourth quarter, and Daunte Culpepper completed 5 of 6 passes on the ensuing drive, capped by a 16-yard scoring pass to Moss, to cut the deficit to 13-10 with 10:23 left. The Vikings drove to the Bears' 10 with 1:11 left, and on second down Culpepper lofted a pass into the end zone. Moss had one-on-one coverage with Tillman, and both players got their hands on the ball, with the Bears rookie ripping it away from Moss. Grossman was 13 of 30 for 157 yards. Culpepper was 24 of 34 for 222 yards and 1 touchdown, with 1 interception. Onterrio Smith had 27 carries for 148 yards.

Minnesota	0	3	0	7	—	10
Chicago	3	7	3	0	—	13

Chi — FG Edinger 38
Chi — Thomas 1 run (Edinger kick)
Minn — FG Elling 22
Chi — FG Edinger 22
Minn — Moss 16 pass from Culpepper (Elling kick)

CINCINNATI 41, SAN FRANCISCO 38—at Paul Brown Stadium, attendance 64,666. Rudi Johnson rushed for 174 yards and 2 touchdowns, and Jon Kitna passed for 2 scores, as the Bengals remained in the playoff hunt. The 49ers rolled up 31 first downs and 502 total yards, but were playing from behind nearly the entire game. Trailing 14-0 early in the second quarter, Jeff Garcia completed long touchdown passes to Terrell Owens and Tai Streets on the next two possessions to tie the game, but the 49ers would never get closer as the Bengals scored on their next five possessions. Peter Warrick's 31-yard touchdown catch on the ensuing possession gave Cincinnati a 21-14 lead, and Rudi Johnson's 49-yard touchdown run on fourth-and-1 early in the third quarter increased the lead to 28-17. The 49ers trailed 31-17 with 13 minutes left, but cut the deficit to 34-31 with 3:49 remaining. A 47-yard run by Johnson set up his 3-yard scoring run with 2:18 left. Kevan Barlow scored on a 3-yard run with 1:13 remaining, but Johnson recovered the ensuing onside kick to preserve the victory. Kitna was 18 of 25 for 189 yards and 2 touchdowns. Johnson rushed 21 times for 174 yards. Garcia was 26 of 33 for 344 yards and 2 touchdowns. Owens had 8 receptions for 127 yards.

San Francisco	0	17	0	21	—	38
Cincinnati	7	14	10	10	—	41

Cin — C. Johnson 10 pass from Kitna (Graham kick)
Cin — Hardy 10 fumble return (Graham kick)
SF — Owens 58 pass from Garcia (Peterson kick)
SF — Streets 41 pass from Garcia (Peterson kick)
Cin — Warrick 31 pass from Kitna (Graham kick)
SF — FG Peterson 23
Cin — Ru. Johnson 49 run (Graham kick)
Cin — FG Graham 34
SF — Garcia 6 run (Peterson kick)
Cin — FG Graham 30
SF — Barlow 1 run (Peterson kick)
Cin — Ru. Johnson 3 run (Graham kick)
SF — Barlow 3 run (Peterson kick)

DENVER 23, CLEVELAND 20 (OT)—at INVESCO Field at Mile High, attendance 75,358. Jason Elam kicked a game-tying field goal with six seconds left and game-winning field goal in overtime as the Broncos stayed in the playoff chase. The Broncos had advantages in first downs (28-12), total yards (417-275), and time of possession (44:35-20:35), but could not pull away. The score was 10-10 at halftime, and Robert Griffith intercepted Jake Plummer's pass in the end zone for a touchback early in the third quarter. Clinton Portis scored on a 1-yard run with 10:43 to play, but a 38-yard punt return by Dennis Northcutt a few minutes later set up Tim Couch's game-tying 35-yard touchdown pass to Andre' Davis. The Browns forced a punt, and a 33-yard pass interference penalty set up Brett Conway's go-ahead 48-yard field goal with 1:11 to play. Plummer responded with three consecutive passes to Ashley Lelie, the last being a 46-yard play to the Browns' 17 with 12 seconds left, to set up Elam's 36-yard field goal. In overtime, the Browns won the toss but went three-and-out, and a 23-yard bootleg by Plummer followed by six consecutive carries by Portis set up Elam's winning kick 5:10 into overtime. Plummer was 22 of 36 for 269 yards, with 1 interception. Portis rushed 38 times for 139 yards, but was injured on the last play from scrimmage in overtime, a 3-yard run to the Browns' 7, and missed the season's final two game. Couch was 8 of 18 for 181 yards and 2 touchdowns, with 1 interception. Northcutt had 3 receptions for 115 yards.

Cleveland	0	10	0	10	0	—	20
Denver	10	0	0	10	3	—	23

Den — Portis 1 run (Elam kick)
Den — FG Elam 51
Cle — FG Conway 39
Cle — Heinrich 1 pass from Couch (Conway kick)
Den — Portis 13 run (Elam kick)
Cle — Andre' Davis 35 pass from Couch (Conway kick)
Cle — FG Conway 48
Den — FG Elam 36
Den — FG Elam 25

INDIANAPOLIS 38, ATLANTA 7—at RCA Dome, attendance 57,103. Peyton Manning passed for 5 touchdowns and the Colts' defense allowed just 154 yards to defeat the Falcons in Wade Phillips' first game as head coach. Phillips, who had been the defensive coordinator, replaced Dan Reeves. Michael Vick, making his second start, was sacked by Ron Mathis and fumbled on the first series, and Dwight Freeney recovered at the Falcons' 14. Manning fired a touchdown pass to Reggie Wayne on the next play. The Colts led 17-0 in the second quarter when a Colts fumble gave Atlanta the ball at the Colts' 26. But David Macklin intercepted a pass in the end zone, and seven plays later Manning found Harrison open for a 17-yard touchdown and 24-0 lead. The Colts outgained the Falcons 303-28 in the first half. Manning was 25 of 30 for 290 yards and 5 touchdowns. Harrison had 7 receptions for 117 yards. Edgerrin James rushed 20 times for 126 yards. Vick was 6 of 19 for 47 yards, with 1 interception.

Atlanta	0	0	7	0	—	7
Indianapolis	14	10	14	0	—	38

Ind — Wayne 14 pass from Manning (Vanderjagt kick)
Ind — Stokley 4 pass from Manning (Vanderjagt kick)
Ind — FG Vanderjagt 43
Ind — Harrison 17 pass from Manning (Vanderjagt kick)
Ind — Stokley 37 pass from Manning (Vanderjagt kick)
Atl — Duckett 17 run (Feely kick)
Ind — Harrison 16 pass from Manning (Vanderjagt kick)

KANSAS CITY 45, DETROIT 17—at Arrowhead Stadium, attendance 77,922. Trent Green passed for 341 yards and 3 touchdowns and Priest Holmes rushed for 3 scores as the Chiefs rolled up 521 yards in victory. The Chiefs scored touchdowns on their first four possessions, and scored on seven of their first eight drives, with the lone setback coming when Morten Andersen's 48-yard field-goal attempt landed short as the first half ended. Four of the six touchdown drives were in excess of 65 yards. Green was 20 of 25 for 341 yards and 3 touchdowns. Derrick Blaylock had 5 receptions for 106 yards. Joey Harrington was 20 of 36 for 197 yards and 1 touchdown, with 1 interception. Shawn Bryson rushed 18 times for 105 yards.

Detroit	0	10	7	0	—	17
Kansas City	14	14	17	0	—	45

KC — Gonzalez 27 pass from Green (Andersen kick)
KC — Holmes 14 run (Andersen kick)
KC — Holmes 9 run (Andersen kick)
Det — FG Hanson 29
KC — Blaylock 63 pass from Green (Andersen kick)
Det — Hakim 8 pass from Harrington (Hanson kick)
KC — Holmes 3 run (Andersen kick)
KC — FG Andersen 35
Det — Bryson 1 run (Hanson kick)
KC — Gonzalez 9 pass from Green (Andersen kick)

NEW ENGLAND 27, JACKSONVILLE 13—at Gillette Stadium, attendance 68,436. Tom Brady passed for 228 yards and 2 touchdowns as the Patriots extended their club-record winning streak to 10 games. The Jaguars reached the Patriots' 5 on each of their first two possessions, but settled for field goals both times and trailed 10-6. Seth Marler had a chance to cut the deficit to 13-9 just before halftime, but he missed a 34-yard attempt. With snow falling in the second half, Tyrone Poole intercepted a pass early in the fourth quarter to spark a 35-yard drive capped by Brady's 10-yard touchdown pass to Troy Brown on third-and-8 for a 20-6 lead. Poole's second interception of the quarter, and return to the Jaguars' 3, set up Antowain Smith's 1-yard run with 4:18 left. Byron Leftwich's 27-yard scoring pass to Kevin Johnson with 3:22 left was the first touchdown allowed by the Patriots at home in five games. The last team to play four consecutive home games without allowing a touchdown was the 1938 Giants, and the last team to post five consecutive home games without a touchdown was the 1932 Bears. Brady was 22 of 34 for 228 yards and 2 touchdowns. Leftwich was 21 of 40 for 288 yards and 1 touchdown, with 2 interceptions.

Jacksonville	3	3	0	7	—	13
New England	7	6	0	14	—	27

NE — Graham 27 pass from Brady (Vinatieri kick)
Jax — FG Marler 24
NE — FG Vinatieri 22
Jax — FG Marler 23
NE — FG Vinatieri 31
NE — Brown 10 pass from Brady (Vinatieri kick)
NE — Smith 1 run (Vinatieri kick)
Jax — Johnson 27 pass from Leftwich (Marler kick)

N.Y. JETS 6, PITTSBURGH 0—at The Meadowlands, attendance 77.900. In a game played in a snow storm, Curtis Martin rushed for 174 yards and Doug Brien made 2 field goals while Jeff Reed missed 2 field-goal attempts as the Jets prevailed. Brien's 28-yard field goal capped a game-opening 12-play, 56-yard drive. The Steelers responded with a 41-yard drive, but Reed's 43-yard attempt sailed wide left. Brien knuckled a 41-yard attempt through the uprights with three seconds left in the half for a 6-0 lead. The Steelers reached the Jets' 3 early in the fourth quarter, but Amos Zereoue was held to no gain and two incompletions by Tommy Maddox sent Reed onto the field. But his 20-yard attempt went wide left. A 56-yard run by Martin got the Jets to the Steelers' 10, but Chad Pennington fumbled on the next play and Mike Logan recovered. The Steelers drove to the Jets' 16 with 3:04 left, but Maddox threw four consecutive incomplete passes. The Steelers forced a punt and got the ball back on their 45 with 2:13 left, but Maddox again misfired four consecutive times and the Jets held on. Pennington was 15 of 25 for 144 yards. Martin rushed 30 times for 174 yards. Maddox was 16 of 38 for 137 yards.

Pittsburgh	0	0	0	0	—	0
N.Y. Jets	3	3	0	0	—	6

NYJ — FG Brien 28
NYJ — FG Brien 41

OAKLAND 20, BALTIMORE 12—at Network Associates Coliseum, attendance 45,398. Rick Mirer passed for 186 yards and 1 touchdown as the Raiders defeated the Ravens. Phillip Buchanon's interception and 29-yard return to the Raiders' 1 three plays into the game set up Zack Crockett's touchdown. The Ravens answered with a field goal, but Doug Gabriel returned the ensuing kickoff 71 yards to set up Sebastian Janikowski's 37-yard field goal. Mirer's 21-yard touchdown pass to Jerry Rice on third-and-7 with 1:20 left in the half gave Oakland a 17-6 lead. A 28-yard punt return by Lamont Brightful set up Anthony Wright's 13-yard touchdown pass to Todd Heap late in the third quarter to cut the deficit to 17-12, but Chester Taylor was stopped short on a 2-point conversion attempt. The Ravens drove to the Raiders' 27 on their next possession, but Napoleon Harris sacked Wright and forced him to fumble. Tyler Brayton recovered the ball and sparked a 10-play, 64-yard drive capped by Janikowski's 23-yard field goal for a 20-12 lead with 5:58 to play. The Ravens failed to cross midfield on their final two possessions. Mirer was 16 of 35 for 186 yards and 1 touchdown. Wright was 12 of 27 for 193 yards and 1 touchdown, with 1 interception. Jamal Lewis rushed 24 times for 125 yards.

Baltimore	3	3	6	0 —	12
Oakland	10	7	0	3 —	20

Oak — Crockett 1 run (Janikowski kick)
Balt — FG Stover 32
Oak — FG Janikowski 37
Balt — FG Stover 28
Oak — Rice 21 pass from Mirer (Janikowski kick)
Balt — Heap 13 pass from Wright (run failed)
Oak — FG Janikowski 23

ST. LOUIS 27, SEATTLE 22—at Edward Jones Dome, attendance 66,152. Marc Bulger passed for 2 touchdowns and the Rams held off a late rally to clinch the NFC West. Orlando Huff sacked Bulger for a safety on the Rams' second play from scrimmage, following a punt by Tom Rouen, to take a 2-0 lead. The Rams responded by scoring touchdowns on three of their next four possessions, capped by Bulger's 40-yard touchdown pass to Torry Holt for a 21-9 lead with 5:06 left in the half. Randall Godfrey's interception at the Rams' 36 with 2:07 left in the half changed the momentum, as Seattle capitalized with Josh Brown's 31-yard field goal. The Seahawks scored on their first two second-half possessions, sandwiched between Jeff Wilkins' 33-yard field goal, to cut the deficit to 24-22 with 10:18 remaining. Following an exchange of punts, the Rams got the ball on their own 15-yard line with 5:57 left. Marshall Faulk then carried eight times in nine plays, including a 28-yard run to begin the drive, to set up Wilkins' 46-yard field goal with 1:37 left. The Seahawks reached the Rams' 34 in the final seconds, but Matt Hasselbeck's Hail Mary pass to Koren Robinson fell incomplete. Bulger was 20 of 32 for 236 yards and 2 touchdowns, with 1 interception. Holt had 6 receptions for 100 yards. Hasselbeck was 21 of 37 for 246 yards and 1 touchdown, with 1 interception. Shaun Alexander had 25 carries for 126 yards.

Seattle	2	10	3	7 —	22
St. Louis	14	7	0	6 —	27

Sea — Safety, Huff sacked Bulger in end zone
StL — Faulk 5 run (Wilkins kick)
StL — Bruce 18 pass from Bulger (Wilkins kick)
Sea — Jackson 9 pass from Hasselbeck (Brown kick)
StL — Holt 40 pass from Bulger (Wilkins kick)
Sea — FG Brown 31
Sea — FG Brown 38
StL — FG Wilkins 33
Sea — Alexander 2 run (Brown kick)
StL — FG Wilkins 46

GREEN BAY 38, SAN DIEGO 21—at Qualcomm Stadium, attendance 64,978. Brett Favre passed for 278 yards and 4 touchdowns as the Packers had to rally to pull even in the win column with the Vikings. The Chargers trailed 10-3 and drove to the Packers' 14 just before halftime, but Darren Sharper intercepted Drew Brees' pass with 1:17 left in the half, and seven plays later Favre completed a 7-yard touchdown pass to Donald Driver for a 17-3 halftime lead. The Chargers were trailing 17-6 late in the third quarter when Stephen Cooper intercepted Favre's pass to set up Brees' 7-yard touchdown pass to LaDainian Tomlinson. Following a punt, Brees connected with Tomlinson on a 68-yard touchdown pass. The two touchdowns within 2:46 of each other gave San Diego its first lead, 21-17, with 12:10 to play. But Najeh Davenport returned the ensuing kickoff 45 yards, and two plays later Favre hit Robert Ferguson with a 40-yard touchdown pass. Two possessions later, Grady Jackson forced Brees to fumble, and Hannibal Navies recovered at the Chargers' 1. Favre lofted a touchdown pass to Ahman Green on the next play for a 31-21 lead with 8:37 remaining, and Ferguson's touchdown catch on the next drive, with 3:58 to play, finished the scoring. Favre was 23 of 33 for 278 yards and 4 touchdowns, with 1 interception. Driver had 8 receptions for 112 yards. Brees, making his first start since week nine, was 28 of 48 for 363 yard and 2 touchdowns, with 1 interception. Tomlinson had 11 receptions for 144 yards, and Antonio Gates had 5 catches for 117 yards.

Green Bay	7	10	0	21 —	38
San Diego	3	0	3	15 —	21

GB — Green 4 run (Longwell kick)
SD — FG Christie 20
GB — FG Longwell 32
GB — Driver 7 pass from Favre (Longwell kick)
SD — FG Christie 26
SD — Tomlinson 7 pass from Brees (Boston pass from Brees)
SD — Tomlinson 68 pass from Brees (Christie kick)
GB — Ferguson 40 pass from Favre (Longwell kick)
GB — Green 1 pass from Favre (Longwell kick)
GB — Ferguson 16 pass from Favre (Longwell kick)

TAMPA BAY 16, HOUSTON 3—at Raymond James Stadium, attendance 65,124. The Buccaneers' defense permitted just 7 first downs and 107 total yards and Thomas Jones rushed for 134 yards and the game's lone touchdown for Tampa Bay. Tampa Bay drove inside the Texans' 22 six times, but settled for just 1 touchdown and 3 field goals, with the two non-scoring drives ending in a missed field goal and the game's conclusion. But Houston's only venture into Buccaneers' territory was on its first possession of the second half, which resulted in Kris Brown's 38-yard field goal to cut the deficit to 13-3. Brad Johnson was 17 of 28 for 237 yards. Jones rushed 34 times for 134 yards. Dave Ragone was 9 of 17 for 64 yards.

Houston	0	0	3	0 —	3
Tampa Bay	7	6	3	0 —	16

TB — Jones 18 run (Gramatica kick)
TB — FG Gramatica 36
TB — FG Gramatica 23
Hous — FG Brown 38
TB — FG Gramatica 26

TENNESSEE 28, BUFFALO 26—at The Coliseum, attendance 68,809. Billy Volek, starting in place of injured Steve McNair, passed for 2 touchdowns and ran for another score, all in the second half, as the Titans rallied and then held off the Bills. The Bills led 10-6 at halftime, and three plays into the second half James Posey sacked Volek and forced him to fumble. Pat Williams recovered the ball and rumbled 28 yards for a touchdown. Later in the quarter, Keith Bulluck returned the favor, as he forced Drew Bledsoe to fumble. Bulluck recovered the ball at the Bills' 18, and Erron Kinney caught a 14-yard touchdown pass three plays later. In the fourth quarter, Rian Lindell's 32-yard field goal trimmed the deficit to 21-20, but Volek was 3-for-3 on the ensuing drive, including a 37-yard perfectly placed pass to Derrick Mason, and scored on a 1-yard run with 4:23 to play. After an exchange of punts, the Bills began on their own 19-yard line with 2:24 left. Bledsoe completed 6 of 7 passes, capped by a 6-yard toss to Mark Campbell, to cut the deficit to 28-26 with 24 seconds left. On the 2-point conversion attempt, Bledsoe's pass to Bobby Shaw fell incomplete. Kinney recovered the ensuing onside kick to preserve the victory. Volek was 26 of 41 for 295 yards and 2 touchdowns. Mason had 9 receptions for 137 yards. Bledsoe was 17 of 30 for 168 yards and 2 touchdowns.

Buffalo	0	10	7	9 —	26
Tennessee	3	3	8	14 —	28

Tenn — FG Anderson 29
Tenn — FG Anderson 39
Buff — FG Lindell 27
Buff — Shaw 6 pass from Bledsoe (Lindell kick)
Buff — P. Williams 28 fumble return (Lindell kick)
Tenn — Kinney 14 pass from Volek (Holcombe run)
Tenn — McCareins 2 pass from Volek (Anderson kick)
Buff — FG Lindell 32
Tenn — Volek 1 run (Anderson kick)
Buff — Campbell 6 pass from Bledsoe (pass failed)

DALLAS 27, WASHINGTON 0—at FedExField, attendance 70,284. Troy Hambrick rushed for 189 yards and the Cowboys' defense forced 6 turnovers and allowed just 8 first downs to defeat the Redskins. The Cowboys drove 74 yards with their first possession, capped by Quincy Carter's touchdown pass to Richie Anderson. Of the remaining 20 points, 17 were set up by turnovers, including Terence Newman's 25-yard interception return to the Redskins' 9 just before halftime that resulted in Carter's 3-yard touchdown run for a 14-0 halftime lead. Newman, a rookie, had 3 interceptions. Carter was 10 of 24 for 108 yards and 1 touchdown. Hambrick rushed 33 times for 189 yards. Tim Hasselbeck was 6 of 26 for 56 yards, with 4 interceptions.

Dallas	7	7	3	10 —	27
Washington	0	0	0	0 —	0

Dall — Anderson 21 pass from Carter (Cundiff kick)
Dall — Carter 3 run (Cundiff kick)
Dall — FG Cundiff 34
Dall — FG Cundiff 20
Dall — Bickerstaff 2 run (Cundiff kick)

SUNDAY NIGHT, DECEMBER 14

NEW ORLEANS 45, N.Y. GIANTS 7—at Louisiana Superdome, attendance 68,399. Aaron Brooks passed for 5 touchdowns, including 4 to Joe Horn, as the Saints rolled past the Giants. A fumble recovery by Dhani Jones at the Saints' 39 set up Jesse Palmer's 4-yard touchdown pass to Visanthe Shiancoe to cut the deficit to 10-7. Horn caught his second touchdown on the next drive and then Fred Thomas returned Kenny Smith's blocked field goal for a touchdown late in the first half for a 24-7 lead. The Saints scored touchdowns on their first three possessions of the second half, capped by Horn's fourth touchdown with 14:55 to play, for a 45-7 lead. Brooks was 26 of 35 for 296 yards and 5 touchdowns. Horn had 9 receptions for 133 yards. Palmer, making his first NFL start in place of injured Kerry Collins, was 15 of 26 for 140 yards and 1 touchdown.

N.Y. Giants	0	7	0	0 —	7
New Orleans	10	14	14	7 —	45

NO — Horn 50 pass from Brooks (Carney kick)

NO — FG Carney 35
NYG — Shiancoe 4 pass from Palmer (Bryant kick)
NO — Horn 13 pass from Brooks (Carney kick)
NO — Thomas 64 blocked field goal return (Carney kick)
NO — Horn 7 pass from Brooks (Carney kick)
NO — Pathon 26 pass from Brooks (Carney kick)
NO — Horn 18 pass from Brooks (Carney kick)

MONDAY NIGHT, DECEMBER 15
PHILADELPHIA 34, MIAMI 27—at Pro Player Stadium, attendance 73,780. Brian Westbrook scored 2 touchdowns as the Eagles matched the franchise record with their ninth consecutive victory, joining the 1960 club, which won the NFL title that season. The Eagles had touchdown drives of 80, 80, and 75 yards in the first half, but Olindo Mare's 27-yard field goal just before halftime trimmed Philadelphia's lead to just 24-17. Ricky Williams' 3-yard touchdown run capped the opening drive of the second half to tie the game, but after an exchange of punts, Correll Buckhalter scored on an acrobatic dive into the end zone, contorting the ball around the pylon while in midair, to give the Eagles a 31-24 lead with 14:53 remaining. An interception by Michael Lewis at the Dolphins' 32 set up David Akers' 42-yard field goal with 2:00 left for a 34-24 lead. Mare kicked a 50-yard field goal with 14 seconds to play, but his onside kick attempt went out of bounds. McNabb was 15 of 27 for 236 yards, with 1 interception. Jay Fiedler was 21 of 40 for 240 yards, with 2 interceptions. Williams rushed 18 times for 107 yards.

Philadelphia	14	10	0	10	—	34
Miami	7	10	7	3	—	27

Phil — Westbrook 21 run (Akers kick)
Mia — Fiedler 1 run (Mare kick)
Phil — McNabb 1 run (Akers kick)
Mia — Minor 2 run (Mare kick)
Phil — Westbrook 25 pass from Mitchell (Akers kick)
Phil — FG Akers 46
Mia — FG Mare 27
Mia — Williams 3 run (Mare kick)
Phil — Buckhalter 2 run (Akers kick)
Phil — FG Akers 42
Mia — FG Mare 50

SIXTEENTH WEEK SUMMARIES
American Football Conference

East Division	**W**	**L**	**T**	**Pct.**	**Pts.**	**OP**
New England*	13	2	0	.867	317	238
Miami	9	6	0	.600	288	240
Buffalo	6	9	0	.400	243	248
N.Y. Jets	6	9	0	.400	262	276
North Division	**W**	**L**	**T**	**Pct.**	**Pts.**	**OP**
Baltimore	9	6	0	.600	378	271
Cincinnati	8	7	0	.533	332	362
Pittsburgh	6	9	0	.400	290	314
Cleveland	4	11	0	.267	232	308
South Division	**W**	**L**	**T**	**Pct.**	**Pts.**	**OP**
Indianapolis#	11	4	0	.733	427	319
Tennessee#	11	4	0	.733	402	311
Jacksonville	5	10	0	.333	262	310
Houston	5	10	0	.333	238	360
West Division	**W**	**L**	**T**	**Pct.**	**Pts.**	**OP**
Kansas City*	12	3	0	.800	453	329
Denver#	10	5	0	.667	378	270
Oakland	4	11	0	.267	256	358
San Diego	3	12	0	.200	292	427

National Football Conference

East Division	**W**	**L**	**T**	**Pct.**	**Pts.**	**OP**
Philadelphia#	11	4	0	.733	343	280
Dallas#	10	5	0	.667	282	247
Washington	5	10	0	.333	280	341
N.Y. Giants	4	11	0	.267	219	350
North Division	**W**	**L**	**T**	**Pct.**	**Pts.**	**OP**
Minnesota	9	6	0	.600	399	335
Green Bay	9	6	0	.600	411	304
Chicago	7	8	0	.467	280	315
Detroit	4	11	0	.267	240	359
South Division	**W**	**L**	**T**	**Pct.**	**Pts.**	**OP**
Carolina*	10	5	0	.667	288	280
New Orleans	7	8	0	.467	327	319
Tampa Bay	7	8	0	.467	288	231
Atlanta	4	11	0	.267	278	408
West Division	**W**	**L**	**T**	**Pct.**	**Pts.**	**OP**
St. Louis*	12	3	0	.800	427	298
Seattle	9	6	0	.600	380	310
San Francisco	7	8	0	.467	367	313
Arizona	3	12	0	.200	207	435

**Clinched division title*
#Clinched playoff berth

SATURDAY, DECEMBER 20
ATLANTA 30, TAMPA BAY 28—at Raymond James Stadium, attendance 65,572. Michael Vick passed for 2 touchdowns as the Falcons held off a late rally to eliminate the defending Super Bowl champions' postseason aspirations. The Buccaneers outgained Atlanta 440-267 in total yards, but committed 4 turnovers, all interceptions in the first half, which resulted in a 27-7 halftime deficit. Atlanta led just 10-7 with two minutes left in the first half. Vick then completed a 13-yard touchdown pass to Brian Finnernan, a drive set up by Keion Carpenter's interception. Four plays later, Juran Bolden intercepted Johnson's pass and returned it 41 yards for a touchdown and 24-7 lead. Two plays later, Bryan Scott's interception set up Jay Feely's 38-yard field goal as the half expired. Atlanta led 30-7 entering the fourth quarter, and was up 30-14 when T.J. Duckett fumbled at the goal line with 3:45 left. Greg Spires recovered at the Buccaneers' 4, and four plays later Brad Johnson connected with Keenan McCardell on a 76-yard touchdown with 2:20 to play. Johnson completed a 2-point conversion pass to Karl Williams to make the score 30-22, and Martín Gramatica's line-drive onside kick bounced off a Falcons player and was recovered by Dwight Smith. Johnson tossed an 11-yard touchdown to Jameel Cook with 27 seconds left to cut the deficit to 30-28, but on the 2-point conversion attempt the Falcons blitzed and Travis Hall knocked down Johnson's pass in the backfield. Allen Rossum recovered the onside kick to preserve the victory. Vick was 8 of 15 for 119 yards and 2 touchdowns. Johnson was 34 of 48 for 346 yards and 4 touchdowns, with 4 interceptions. Charles Lee had 10 receptions for 88 yards, and McCardell had 6 catches for 122 yards.

Atlanta	10	17	3	0	—	30
Tampa Bay	0	7	0	21	—	28

Atl — FG Feely 26
Atl — Crumpler 6 pass from Vick (Feely kick)
TB — Dudley 3 pass from Johnson (Gramatica kick)
Atl — Finneran 13 pass from Vick (Feely kick)
Atl — Bolden 41 interception return (Feely kick)
Atl — FG Feely 38
Atl — FG Feely 37
TB — Lee 3 pass from Johnson (Gramatica kick)
TB — McCardell 76 pass from Johnson (Williams pass from Johnson)
TB — Cook 11 pass from Johnson (pass failed)

MINNESOTA 45, KANSAS CITY 20—at Metrodome, attendance 64,291. Daunte Culpepper passed for 3 first-half touchdowns, and Onterrio Smith rushed for 3 second-half scores, as the Vikings remained in control of their own destiny. The Chiefs already trailed 7-0 when they got the ball for the first time, but they drove to the Vikings' 46 and Eddie Kennison caught a long pass, but Brian Williams stripped Kennison of the ball and Brian Russell recovered at the Vikings' 3. Kansas City failed to cross midfield the rest of the half, while the Vikings engineered three more scoring drives, capped by Aaron Elling's 46-yard field goal as the half expired. It was 31-0 before Priest Holmes scored 3 touchdowns in a span of 8:11 to cut the deficit to 31-20 with 10:05 remaining. But Onterrio Smith scored on an 11-yard run five plays later, and LaShaun Ward fumbled the ensuing kickoff and E.J. Henderson recovered to set up Smith's second touchdown in a 1:00 span to give the Vikings a 45-20 lead with 6:00 to play. Culpepper was 20 of 29 for 260 yards and 3 touchdowns, with 1 interception. Moss had 7 receptions for 111 yards, and Smith rushed 21 times for 146 yards. Trent Green was 18 of 38 for 224 yards, with 2 interceptions.

Kansas City	0	0	7	13	—	20
Minnesota	7	17	7	14	—	45

Minn — Moss 30 pass from Culpepper (Elling kick)
Minn — Moss 21 pass from Culpepper (Elling kick)
Minn — Kleinsasser 4 pass from Culpepper (Elling kick)
Minn — FG Elling 46
Minn — Smith 1 run (Elling kick)
KC — Holmes 2 run (Andersen kick)
KC — Holmes 4 run (pass failed)
KC — Holmes 1 run (Andersen kick)
Minn — Smith 11 run (Elling kick)
Minn — Smith 10 run (Elling kick)

SATURDAY NIGHT, DECEMBER 20
NEW ENGLAND 21, N.Y. JETS 16—at The Meadowlands, attendance 77,835. Tom Brady passed for 2 touchdowns and the Patriots' defense registered 4 sacks and forced 5 turnovers to extend their winning streak to 11 games. Tedy Bruschi intercepted Chad Pennington's second pass of the game, and Brady connected with David Givens on a 35-yard touchdown pass on the next play for a 7-0 lead 48 seconds into the game. Willie McGinest intercepted a pass and returned it 15 yards for a touchdown and 14-7 lead early in the second quarter. The Jets countered with a field goal just before halftime, but the Patriots drove 60 yards to begin the second half, capped by Brady's second scoring pass to Givens for a 21-10 lead. Pennington capped a 12-play drive with his second touchdown run of the game early in the fourth quarter, but his 2-point conversion pass attempt to Kevin Lockett fell incomplete with 12:11 to play. Eugene Wilson preserved the win with an interception near midfield with 35 seconds left. Brady was 15 of 25 for 138 yards and 2 touchdowns. Smith had 18 carries for 121 yards. Pennington was 24 of 43 for 229 yards, with 5 interceptions.

New England	7	7	7	0	—	21
N.Y. Jets	7	3	0	6	—	16

NE — Givens 35 pass from Brady (Vinatieri kick)
NYJ — Pennington 1 run (Brien kick)
NE — McGinest 15 interception return (Vinatieri kick)
NYJ — FG Brien 29
NE — Givens 5 pass from Brady (Vinatieri kick)
NYJ — Pennington 10 run (pass failed)

SUNDAY, DECEMBER 20

MIAMI 20, BUFFALO 3—at Ralph Wilson Stadium, attendance 73,319. The Dolphins' defense forced 4 turnovers and recorded 6 sacks to defeat the Bills. In a game played in 35-degree weather with 20 mile-per-hour winds, both teams gained just 11 first downs and neither team gained 180 yards. A 27-yard punt into the wind gave the Dolphins the ball at the Bills' 36 on their first drive, and Jay Fiedler completed a 23-yard touchdown pass to Chris Chambers four plays later. Later in the first quarter, Nate Clements muffed a punt at the Bills' 24 and Arturo Freeman recovered to set up Olindo Mare's first field goal. In the second quarter, Tim Bowens sacked Drew Bledsoe and forced him to fumble. Zach Thomas recovered at the Bills' 33 to set up Mare's second field goal. The Bills trailed 13-3 in the third quarter and drove to the Dolphins' 29, but Terrell Buckley intercepted Bledsoe's pass and returned 74 yards for a game-clinching touchdown. Fiedler was 8 of 17 for 46 yards and 1 touchdown, with 1 interception. Ricky Williams rushed 29 times for 111 yards. Bledsoe was 12 of 24 for 114 yards, with 1 interception.

Miami	10	3	7	0	—	20
Buffalo	0	0	3	0	—	3

Mia — Chambers 23 pass from Fiedler (Mare kick)
Mia — FG Mare 28
Mia — FG Mare 30
Buff — FG Lindell 23
Mia — Buckley 74 interception return (Mare kick)

CAROLINA 20, DETROIT 14—at Ericsson Stadium, attendance 72,835. Jake Delhomme passed for 260 yards and 2 touchdowns, with 1 interception, as the Panthers handed the Lions their NFL record 24th consecutive road defeat. Carolina had more first downs (22-8), total yards (384-106), and time of possession (38:14-21:46), and only allowed one drive into Panthers' territory, which was thwarted by Mike Minter's interception that led to John Kasay's 42-yard field goal just before halftime for a 17-0 lead. Reggie Swinton cut the deficit to 20-7 with an 89-yard punt return with 12:02 left, and Boss Bailey's 62-yard fumble recovery with 3:44 remaining trimmed the lead to 20-14. The Lions twice stopped the Panthers on third down in the final moments, only to have defensive penalties give Carolina an automatic first down. Delhomme was 29 of 35 for 260 yards and 2 touchdowns, with 1 interception. Joey Harrington was 3 of 8 for 17 yards before being replaced by Mike McMahon, who was 4 of 11 for 36 yards, with 1 interception.

Detroit	0	0	0	14	—	14
Carolina	7	10	3	0	—	20

Car — Smith 20 pass from Delhomme (Kasay kick)
Car — Foster 10 pass from Delhomme (Kasay kick)
Car — FG Kasay 42
Car — FG Kasay 44
Det — Swinton 89 punt return (Hanson kick)
Det — Bailey 62 fumble return (Hanson kick)

CHICAGO 27, WASHINGTON 24—at Soldier Field, attendance 61,719. Rex Grossman improved to 2-0 as a starter by passing for 249 yards and 2 touchdowns as the Bears rallied in the second half to defeat the Redskins. A wide-receiver option 36-yard touchdown pass from Rod Gardner to Chad Morton tied the game 10-10 after the first quarter. Laveranues Coles' 14-yard touchdown catch just before halftime gave Washington a 17-10 lead, but the Bears scored touchdowns on their first two drives of the second half, traveling 73 and 76 yards, to take a 24-17 lead. Tim Hasselbeck's second touchdown pass to Coles tied the game with 12:52 left, and Paul Edinger missed a 33-yard field goal with 8:09 left before drilling a 45-yard attempt with five seconds remaining to cap a 13-play, 51-yard drive. The Bears maintained possession for 23:08 of the 30 second-half minutes. Grossman was 19 of 32 for 249 yards and 2 touchdowns, with 1 interception. Anthony Thomas rushed 32 times for 141 yards. Hasselbeck was 16 of 25 for 209 yards and 2 touchdowns.

Washington	10	7	0	7	—	24
Chicago	10	0	14	3	—	27

Wash — FG Hall 27
Chi — Booker 59 pass from Grossman (Edinger kick)
Chi — FG Edinger 19
Wash — Morton 36 pass from Gardner (Hall kick)
Wash — Coles 14 pass from Hasselbeck (Hall kick)
Chi — Gage 11 pass from Grossman (Edinger kick)
Chi — Thomas 3 run (Edinger kick)
Wash — Coles 19 pass from Hasselbeck (Hall kick)
Chi — FG Edinger 45

BALTIMORE 35, CLEVELAND 0—at Cleveland Browns Stadium, attendance 72,548. Jamal Lewis rushed for 205 yards and 2 touchdowns as the Ravens regained control of the AFC North. Lewis rushed for 500 yards in the two games this season against the Browns, an NFL single-season record for a player against an opponent. The Ravens' defense permitted Cleveland to drive inside the Ravens' 30 just once, and Brett Conway missed a 37-yard field goal as the first half expired, allowing Baltimore to maintain a 7-0 lead. Lewis rushed 8 times for 164 yards in the second half, highlighted by his 72-yard touchdown run in the third quarter and capped by his 24-yard scoring scamper with 11:55 to play. Four plays later, Chad Williams intercepted a pass and returned it 52 yards for a touchdown and 28-0 lead. Anthony Wright was 10 of 18 for 90 yards and 1 touchdown, with 1 interception. Lewis rushed 22 times for 205 yards. Tim Couch was 17 of 33 for 163 yards, with 1 interception.

Baltimore	0	7	7	21	—	35
Cleveland	0	0	0	0	—	0

Balt — Jones 1 pass from Wright (Stover kick)
Balt — J. Lewis 72 run (Stover kick)
Balt — J. Lewis 24 run (Stover kick)
Balt — C. Williams 52 interception return (Stover kick)
Balt — M. Smith 11 run (Stover kick)

DALLAS 19, N.Y. GIANTS 3—at Texas Stadium, attendance 64,118. The Cowboys' defense allowed just 213 yards and Billy Cundiff kicked 4 field goals as the Cowboys clinched their first postseason appearance since 1999. A 64-yard pass from Quincy Carter to Joey Galloway on the game's first play set up Cundiff's initial field goal. The Giants responded with a field goal, but New York did not cross midfield on its next six possessions. The Cowboys led 16-3, thanks to rookie Jason Witten's first career touchdown catch and 2 more Cundiff field goals, by the time the Giants drove to the Cowboys' 12 late in the third quarter, but Roy Williams sacked Jesse Palmer on fourth down to quell the threat. Carter engineered a 13-play drive on the ensuing possession to set up Cundiff's fourth field goal. Carter was 17 of 25 for 240 yards and 1 touchdown. Palmer was 18 of 32 for 190 yards.

N.Y. Giants	3	0	0	0	—	3
Dallas	10	3	3	3	—	19

Dall — FG Cundiff 24
NYG — FG Bryant 45
Dall — Witten 36 pass from Carter (Cundiff kick)
Dall — FG Cundiff 42
Dall — FG Cundiff 21
Dall — FG Cundiff 49

TENNESSEE 27, HOUSTON 24—at Reliant Stadium, attendance 70,758. Steve McNair completed a 23-yard touchdown pass to Drew Bennett with 17 seconds left to cap a 75-yard drive for the Titans. Tennessee scored twice in the final 3:16 of the first half to take a 10-3 lead, and was driving for another score to begin the second half when Marlon McCree intercepted McNair's pass and returned it 95 yards for a touchdown. Just over three minutes later, the Titans' Samari Rolle picked up a Domanick Davis fumble and returned it 61 yards for a touchdown and 17-10 lead. The Texans trailed 20-17 when they forced a punt and started at their own 20 with 2:50 left. David Carr completed a 42-yard pass to Andre Johnson to set up Davis' 5-yard touchdown run for a 24-20 lead with 1:48 remaining. After an incompletion, McNair completed 3 consecutive passes, including 20- and 24-yard tosses to Bennett, to get to the Texans' 23 with 37 seconds left. After a spike and two incomplete passes, McNair lofted a fourth-and-10 pass to Bennett, who caught the ball in the corner of the end zone. Rolle intercepted Carr's desperation pass with four seconds left to preserve the win. McNair was 17 of 26 for 268 yards and 2 touchdowns, with 1 interception. Carr was 17 of 34 for 242 yards and 1 touchdown, with 2 interceptions. Johnson had 5 receptions for 108 yards.

Tennessee	0	10	7	10	—	27
Houston	0	3	14	7	—	24

Hous — FG Brown 49
Tenn — Kinney 2 pass from McNair (Anderson kick)
Tenn — FG Anderson 41
Hous — McCree 95 interception return (Brown kick)
Tenn — Rolle 61 fumble return (Anderson kick)
Hous — Bradford 20 pass from Carr (Brown kick)
Tenn — FG Anderson 26
Hous — Davis 5 run (Brown kick)
Tenn — Bennett 23 pass from McNair (Anderson kick)

JACKSONVILLE 20, NEW ORLEANS 19—at ALLTEL Stadium, attendance 49,207. The Jaguars defeated the Saints when John Carney missed an extra-point attempt following a three-lateral, 75-yard touchdown on the game's final play to eliminate New Orleans from playoff contention. The Jaguars took a 17-10 lead with 21 seconds left in the first half on Fred Taylor's 1-yard run to cap a 65-yard drive. Seth Marler kicked a 35-yard field goal just before the end of the third quarter for a 20-13 lead, but Marler's 21-yard attempt with 9:24 remaining was blocked by Fakhir Brown. Two possessions later, the Saints drove to the Jaguars' 9, but Brooks' fourth-and-goal pass fell incomplete with 2:07 to play. The Saints got the ball back on their own 25 with 11 seconds left. Brooks completed a 30-yard pass to Donte' Stallworth, who broke a few tackles and cut across field before lateraling to Michael Lewis at the Jaguars' 33. Lewis ran 7 yards before shoveling the ball to Deuce McAllister, who ran 5 yards before drawing a crowd. McAllister turned and threw an overhand lateral to Jerome Pathon, who caught the ball in stride and raced the final 21 yards for a touchdown. However, Carney's extra-point attempt sailed wide right. Byron Leftwich was 9 of 17 for 131 yards and 1 touchdown, with 2 interceptions. Taylor rushed 34 times for 194 yards. Brooks was 22 of 38 for 296 yards and 2 touchdowns.

New Orleans	3	7	3	6	—	19
Jacksonville	0	17	3	0	—	20

NO — FG Carney 33
Jax — FG Marler 43
Jax — Toefield 14 pass from Leftwich (Marler kick)
NO — B. Williams 2 pass from Brooks (Carney kick)
Jax — Taylor 1 run (Marler kick)
NO — FG Carney 38
Jax — FG Marler 35
NO — Pathon 21 lateral from McAllister on 75 pass from Brooks (kick failed)

SAN FRANCISCO 31, PHILADELPHIA 28 (OT)—at Lincoln Financial Field, attendance 67,866. Tony Parrish intercepted 2 passes, including one in overtime to set up Todd Peterson's game-winning field goal to snap the Eagles' nine-game winning streak. Brian Westbrook's 81-yard punt return early in the third quarter gave the Eagles a 21-14 lead. The 49ers responded by scoring on their next three possessions, two of which came after missed field goals of 42 and 47 yards by David Akers, and took a 28-21 lead with 5:03 remaining on Kevan Barlow's 1-yard run and Jeff Garcia's 2-point conversion pass to Brandon Lloyd. Donovan McNabb responded with a 10-play, 65-yard drive, capped by his 19-yard touchdown pass to Todd Pinkston on third-and-15 with 1:02 to play. The Eagles won the overtime coin toss, but on the first play Parrish intercepted McNabb's pass and returned it 29 yards to the Eagles' 4 to set up Peterson's winning kick 1:05 into overtime. Garcia was 15 of 29 for 225 yards and 2 touchdowns. Barlow rushed 30 times for 154 yards. McNabb was 17 of 27 for 238 yards and 1 touchdown, with 2 interceptions. Pinkston had 5 receptions for 121 yards.

San Francisco	7	7	3	11	3	—	31
Philadelphia	0	14	7	7	0	—	28

SF — Barlow 15 pass from Garcia (Peterson kick)
Phil — Staley 7 run (Akers kick)
Phil — Staley 1 run (Akers kick)
SF — Lloyd 33 pass from Garcia (Peterson kick)
Phil — Westbrook 81 punt return (Akers kick)
SF — FG Peterson 33
SF — FG Peterson 25
SF — Barlow 1 run (Lloyd pass from Garcia)
Phil — Pinkston 19 pass from McNabb (Akers kick)
SF — FG Peterson 22

PITTSBURGH 40, SAN DIEGO 24—at Heinz Field, attendance 52,527. Tommy Maddox passed for 3 touchdowns as the Steelers defeated the Chargers. Jerome Bettis rushed for 115 yards, and moved past Marcus Allen into seventh place on the NFL's all-time rushing list, finishing the game with 12,299 yards. The Steelers scored touchdowns on their first three possessions for a 21-0 lead. The Chargers trimmed the deficit to 21-17 in the third quarter, but the Steelers scored on their next three drives again to take a 34-24 lead with 5:04 left. Deshea Townsend intercepted Drew Brees' pass two plays later and returned it 25 yards for the game's final points. Maddox was 11 of 18 for 160 yards and 3 touchdowns. Bettis rushed 32 times for 115 yards. Drew Brees was 16 of 26 for 198 yards and 1 touchdown, with 2 interceptions, and Flutie replaced him and was 5 of 10 for 42 yards. Kassim Osgood had 4 receptions for 102 yards.

San Diego	0	10	7	7	—	24
Pittsburgh	14	7	7	12	—	40

Pitt — Burress 25 pass from Maddox (Reed kick)
Pitt — Bettis 1 run (Reed kick)
Pitt — Burress 16 pass from Maddox (Reed kick)
SD — Tomlinson 5 run (Christie kick)
SD — FG Christie 31
SD — Osgood 57 pass from Brees (Christie kick)
Pitt — Ward 20 pass from Maddox (Reed kick)
Pitt — FG Reed 47
SD — Tomlinson 2 run (Christie kick)
Pitt — FG Reed 40
Pitt — Townsend 25 interception return (kick failed)

ST. LOUIS 27, CINCINNATI 10—at Edward Jones Dome, attendance 66,061. Marc Bulger passed for 2 touchdowns and Marshall Faulk scored twice as the Rams knocked the Bengals out of first place in the AFC North. Jon Kitna's 2-yard touchdown pass to Kelley Washington tied the game early in the second quarter, but the Rams responded by scoring on their next two possessions. Shayne Graham's 47-yard field goal as the half expired cut the deficit to 17-10 at halftime. Faulk's 9-yard touchdown catch early in the fourth quarter stretched the Rams' lead to 27-10. The Bengals drove to the Rams' 2, but Jerametrius Butler intercepted Kitna's pass in the end zone with 8:26 left, and the Rams ran out the clock. Bulger was 24 of 38 for 229 yards and 2 touchdowns, with 1 interception. Torry Holt had 10 receptions for 124 yards. Faulk rushed 22 times for 121 yards. Kitna was 16 of 29 for 202 yards and 1 touchdown, with 3 interceptions. Chad Johnson had 7 receptions for 115 yards.

Cincinnati	0	10	0	0	—	10
St. Louis	7	10	3	7	—	27

StL — Faulk 1 run (Wilkins kick)
Cin — Washington 2 pass from Kitna (Graham kick)
StL — FG Wilkins 26
StL — Holt 28 pass from Bulger (Wilkins kick)
Cin — FG Graham 48
StL — FG Wilkins 50
StL — Faulk 9 pass from Bulger (Wilkins kick)

SEATTLE 28, ARIZONA 10—at Seahawks Stadium, attendance 64,899. Shaun Alexander scored 2 touchdowns and rushed for 135 yards as the Seahawks remained in the playoff hunt. The Seahawks scored touchdowns on three of their first four drives, with their lone non-scoring drive ending with a lost fumble at the Cardinals' 1 yard-line, to take a 21-3 lead. Neil Rackers missed 2 field goals inside 40 yards just before halftime, but the Cardinals trimmed the lead to 21-10 on Anquan Boldin's 60-yard touchdown catch with 12:49 to play. The Cardinals forced a punt, but from their own 41 Josh McCown was stopped for no gain on third-and-1 and fourth-and-1 with 8:07 to play. Bobby Engram's 3-yard touchdown catch, on a drive engineered by Trent Dilfer, who was in for an injured Matt Hasselbeck, capped the scoring with 3:12 remaining. Hasselbeck was 17 of 24 for 179 yards and 1 touchdown, with 1 interception, but left the game with an ankle injury. Dilfer was 2 of 3 for 11 yards and 1 touchdown, with 1 interception. McCown was 25 of 40 for 274 yards and 1 touchdown. Boldin had 10 receptions for 122 yards.

Arizona	0	3	0	7	—	10
Seattle	14	7	0	7	—	28

Sea — Alexander 9 run (Brown kick)
Sea — Morris 4 pass from Hasselbeck (Brown kick)
Ariz — FG Rackers 49
Sea — Alexander 44 run (Brown kick)
Ariz — Boldin 60 pass from McCown (Rackers kick)
Sea — Engram 3 pass from Dilfer (Brown kick)

SUNDAY NIGHT, DECEMBER 21

DENVER 31, INDIANAPOLIS 17—at RCA Dome, attendance 57,149. Jake Plummer passed for 1 touchdown and ran for 2 scores and rookie Quentin Griffin rushed for 136 yards in his first NFL start as the Broncos clinched a playoff berth. The Broncos had advantages in first downs (26-11), total yards (465-183), and time of possession (44:58-15:02). Gary Brackett returned an interception 31 yards for a touchdown 2:01 into the game to give the Colts a 7-0 lead, but the Broncos responded by scoring touchdowns on their next four possessions, on drives of 75, 72, 91, and 52 yards, to take a 28-14 lead. Mike Vanderjagt kicked a field goal just before halftime, but the Colts ran just 11 plays in the game's final 24 minutes, as the Broncos drove inside the Colts' 10 three times, resulting in a field goal, stopped on downs, and the end of the game. Plummer was 14 of 17 for 238 yards and 1 touchdown, with 1 interception, and rushed 6 times for 22 yards and 2 touchdowns. Griffin rushed 28 times for 136 yards. Ashley Lelie had 5 receptions for 115 yards. Peyton Manning was 12 of 23 for 146 yards.

Denver	14	14	0	3	—	31
Indianapolis	7	10	0	0	—	17

Ind — Brackett 31 interception return (Vanderjagt kick)
Den — Anderson 2 run (Elam kick)
Den — Plummer 6 run (Elam kick)
Ind — James 16 run (Vanderjagt kick)
Den — Plummer 1 run (Elam kick)
Den — R. Smith 15 pass from Plummer (Elam kick)
Ind — FG Vanderjagt 40
Den — FG Elam 24

MONDAY NIGHT, DECEMBER 22

GREEN BAY 41, OAKLAND 7—at Network Associates Coliseum, attendance 62,298. One day after his father passed away from a heart attack, Brett Favre passed for 399 yards and 4 touchdowns to keep the Packers in playoff contention. The Packers gained 548 yards, including 362 in the first half when Favre completed 15 of 18 passes for 311 yards and 4 touchdowns. His second touchdown, a 23-yard toss to Javon Walker, moved him past Fran Tarkenton into second place on the NFL's all-time passing touchdown list. He finished with 345, 75 behind Dan Marino. The Packers scored on their first four, and five of their initial six, possessions, capped by Favre's 6-yard touchdown pass to David Martin 54 seconds before halftime, for a 31-7 lead. The Packers' defense forced 3 second-half turnovers, including two in their red zone, to keep the Raiders from scoring again. Favre was 22 of 30 for 399 yards and 4 touchdowns. Walker had 4 catches for 124 yards, and Ahman Green rushed 24 times for 127 yards. Rick Mirer was 12 of 23 for 114 yards, with 1 interception. Rob Johnson was 6 of 13 for 54 yards, with 1 interception, and Tee Martin was 4 of 5 for 55 yards. Jerry Rice had 10 receptions for 159 yards.

Green Bay	14	17	3	7	—	41
Oakland	7	0	0	0	—	7

GB — Walls 22 pass from Favre (Longwell kick)
GB — Walker 23 pass from Favre (Longwell kick)
Oak — Garner 25 run (Janikowski kick)
GB — FG Longwell 31

GB — Walker 43 pass from Favre (Longwell kick)
GB — Martin 6 pass from Favre (Longwell kick)
GB — FG Longwell 27
GB — Green 7 run (Longwell kick)

SEVENTEENTH WEEK SUMMARIES

American Football Conference

East Division	**W**	**L**	**T**	**Pct.**	**Pts.**	**OP**
New England*	14	2	0	.875	348	238
Miami	10	6	0	.625	311	261
Buffalo	6	10	0	.375	243	279
N.Y. Jets	6	10	0	.375	283	299
North Division	**W**	**L**	**T**	**Pct.**	**Pts.**	**OP**
Baltimore*	10	6	0	.625	391	281
Cincinnati	8	8	0	.500	346	384
Pittsburgh	6	10	0	.375	300	327
Cleveland	5	11	0	.312	254	322
South Division	**W**	**L**	**T**	**Pct.**	**Pts.**	**OP**
Indianapolis*	12	4	0	.750	447	336
Tennessee#	12	4	0	.750	435	324
Jacksonville	5	11	0	.312	276	331
Houston	5	11	0	.312	255	380
West Division	**W**	**L**	**T**	**Pct.**	**Pts.**	**OP**
Kansas City*	13	3	0	.812	484	332
Denver#	10	6	0	.625	381	301
Oakland	4	12	0	.250	270	379
San Diego	4	12	0	.250	313	441

National Football Conference

East Division	**W**	**L**	**T**	**Pct.**	**Pts.**	**OP**
Philadelphia*	12	4	0	.750	374	287
Dallas#	10	6	0	.625	289	260
Washington	5	11	0	.312	287	372
N.Y. Giants	4	12	0	.250	243	387
North Division	**W**	**L**	**T**	**Pct.**	**Pts.**	**OP**
Green Bay*	10	6	0	.625	442	307
Minnesota	9	7	0	.562	416	353
Chicago	7	9	0	.438	283	346
Detroit	5	11	0	.312	270	379
South Division	**W**	**L**	**T**	**Pct.**	**Pts.**	**OP**
Carolina*	11	5	0	.688	325	304
New Orleans	8	8	0	.500	340	326
Tampa Bay	7	9	0	.438	301	264
Atlanta	5	11	0	.312	299	422
West Division	**W**	**L**	**T**	**Pct.**	**Pts.**	**OP**
St. Louis*	12	4	0	.750	447	328
Seattle#	10	6	0	.625	404	327
San Francisco	7	9	0	.438	384	337
Arizona	4	12	0	.250	225	452

**Clinched division title*
#Clinched playoff berth

Buffalo finished ahead of New York Jets based on better division record (2-4 to 1-5). Indianapolis finished ahead of Tennessee based on head-to-head sweep (2-0). Jacksonville finished ahead of Houston based on better division record (2-4 to 1-5). Denver finished ahead of Miami based on better conference record (9-3 to 7-5). Oakland finished ahead of San Diego based on better conference record (3-9 to 2-10). Philadelphia finished ahead of St. Louis based on better conference record (9-3 to 8-4). Seattle finished ahead of Dallas based on better strength of victory (65-95 to 62-98).

SATURDAY, DECEMBER 27

NEW ENGLAND 31, BUFFALO 0—at Gillette Stadium, attendance 68,436. Tom Brady passed for 4 first-half touchdowns and the Patriots' defense recorded its third shutout at home this season to clinch home-field advantage throughout the playoffs. The Patriots held the opponent without a touchdown in five of their last six home games, and became just the third team to win their final 12 regular-season games, joining the 1934 Bears and 1972 Dolphins. New England scored on its first two possessions to take a 14-0 lead less than 10 minutes into the game, and all four touchdown drives were at least eight plays long. At halftime, the Patriots had advantages in first downs (20-5), total yards (201-82), and time of possession (19:36-10:24). The Patriots reached the red zone three times, but Rian Lindell missed a 40-yard field goal in the first half, Drew Bledsoe's fourth-and-21 pass fell incomplete early in the third quarter, and Travis Brown's pass was intercepted in the end zone by Larry Izzo with 13 seconds left to preserve the shutout. Brady was 21 of 32 for 204 yards and 4 touchdowns. Bledsoe was 12 of 29 for 83 yards, with 1 interception, and Brown was 11 of 14 for 119 yards, with 1 interception.

Buffalo	0	0	0	0	—	0
New England	14	14	0	3	—	31

NE — Graham 1 pass from Brady (Vinatieri kick)
NE — Johnson 9 pass from Brady (Vinatieri kick)
NE — Brown 19 pass from Brady (Vinatieri kick)
NE — Givens 10 pass from Brady (Vinatieri kick)
NE — FG Vinatieri 24

SEATTLE 24, SAN FRANCISCO 17—at 3Com Park, attendance 67,840. Matt Hasselbeck passed for 315 yards and 2 touchdowns as the Seahawks kept their playoff hopes alive. The next day, Dallas' loss at New Orleans vaulted Seattle into the post-season for the first time since 1999. A missed 49-yard field goal and an interception by Jeff Ulbrich set up San Francisco's first two touchdowns for a 14-0 lead. The Seahawks responded with touchdown drives of 68 and 63 yards, in the final six minutes of the first half to tie the score. Todd Peterson hit the right upright with a 29-yard field goal just before halftime, but made a 38-yard field goal in the third quarter. Hasselbeck's 30-yard touchdown pass with 3:28 left in the third quarter gave the Seahawks a 21-17 lead, and the 49ers never crossed the Seahawks' 49 on their final four possessions. Hasselbeck was 24 of 37 for 315 yards and 2 touchdowns, with 2 interceptions. Garcia was 22 of 38 for 248 yards and 2 touchdowns, with 1 interception.

Seattle	0	14	7	3	—	24
San Francisco	0	14	3	0	—	17

SF — Weaver 18 pass from Garcia (Peterson kick)
SF — Wilson 14 pass from Garcia (Peterson kick)
Sea — Bannister 31 pass from Hasselbeck (Brown kick)
Sea — Alexander 3 run (Brown kick)
SF — FG Peterson 38
Sea — Robinson 30 pass from Hasselbeck (Brown kick)
Sea — FG Brown 33

SATURDAY NIGHT, DECEMBER 27

PHILADELPHIA 31, WASHINGTON 7—at FedExField, attendance 76,766. Donovan McNabb passed for 242 yards and 2 touchdowns, and ran for another score, as the Eagles clinched the NFC East for the third consecutive season. Following a missed 52-yard field goal by John Hall to begin the game, the Eagles scored on their first three possessions to take a 21-0 lead with 9:29 left in the half. The third touchdown was set up by Corey Simon's sack of Tim Hasselbeck that forced a fumble that was recovered by N.D. Kalu at the Redskins' 19. The Redskins responded with Rock Cartwright's 1-yard touchdown run, but McNabb engineered a 12-play, 74-yard drive to begin the second half, capped by Correll Buckhalter's 11-yard touchdown reception, for a 28-7 lead. The Redskins failed to cross the Eagles' 39 on their final four drives. McNabb was 23 of 32 for 242 yards and 3 touchdowns. Hasselbeck was 21 of 32 for 192 yards, with 1 interception.

Philadelphia	7	14	7	3	—	31
Washington	0	7	0	0	—	7

Phil — Lewis 3 pass from McNabb (Akers kick)
Phil — McNabb 1 run (Akers kick)
Phil — Mitchell 8 pass from McNabb (Akers kick)
Wash — Cartwright 1 run (Hall kick)
Phil — Buckhalter 11 pass from McNabb (Akers kick)
Phil — FG Akers 26

SUNDAY, DECEMBER 28

ARIZONA 18, MINNESOTA 17—at Sun Devil Stadium, attendance 52,734. Nate Poole caught a 28-yard touchdown pass from Josh McCown as time expired, the Cardinals' second touchdown in the final 1:54, to knock the Vikings out of playoff contention. The Vikings drove deep into Cardinals' territory twice in the first half, but Daunte Culpepper's fourth-and-goal pass from the Cardinals' 1 was incomplete on their opening possession, and Aaron Elling missed a 44-yard field goal early in the second quarter. Dexter Jackson's interception and 30-yard return to the Vikings' 13 with 42 seconds left in the first half set up Neil Rackers' second field goal and gave Arizona a 6-0 halftime lead. The Vikings put together touchdown drives of 67 and 57 yards to take a 14-6 lead, and Kevin Williams' interception set up Elling's 46-yard field goal with 6:48 to play. McCown's 2-yard touchdown pass to Steve Bush on fourth-and-1 with 1:54 to play cut the deficit to 17-12. Damien Anderson recovered the ensuing onside kick, and the Cardinals reached the Vikings' 9 with 39 seconds left. Consecutive sacks pushed the ball back to the Vikings' 28 and, with no time-outs, the Cardinals regrouped and McCown rolled right and fired a pass that a leaping Poole caught along the far sideline of the end zone. McCown was 20 of 33 for 224 yards and 2 touchdowns, with 1 interception. Culpepper was 18 of 28 for 197 yards and 1 touchdown, with 1 interception.

Minnesota	0	0	7	10	—	17
Arizona	3	3	0	12	—	18

Ariz — FG Rackers 22
Ariz — FG Rackers 26
Minn — Williams 1 run (Elling kick)
Minn — Moss 7 pass from Culpepper (Elling kick)
Minn — FG Elling 46
Ariz — Bush 2 pass from McCown (pass failed)
Ariz — Poole 28 pass from McCown (run failed)

ATLANTA 21, JACKSONVILLE 14—at Georgia Dome, attendance 70,266. Michael Vick passed for 2 touchdowns as the Falcons finished 3-1 with Vick as a starter. The Falcons scored touchdowns on three of their first four possessions on drives of 50, 80, and 77 yards for a 21-7 lead. LaBrandon Toefield's 4-yard touchdown run late in the third quarter cut the deficit to 21-14, and Atlanta's lone productive drive of the second half was quelled by Akin Ayodele's interception at the Jaguars' 38 with 12:17 to play. The Jaguars responded by driving to the Falcons' 12, but Juran Bolden blocked Seth Marler's 30-yard field-goal attempt with 7:36 remaining. Starting at their own 12 with 4:16 to play, the Jaguars reached the Falcons' 14 with 32 seconds left, but Byron Leftwich's fourth-and-2 pass fell incomplete. Vick was 12 of 22 for 180 yards and 2 touchdowns, with 1 interception. Leftwich was 19 of 32 for 167 yards and 1 touchdown. Fred Taylor rushed 22 times for 121 yards.

Jacksonville	7	0	7	0	—	14
Atlanta	14	7	0	0	—	21

Atl	—	Duckett 2 run (Feely kick)
Jax	—	Edwards 15 pass from Leftwich (Marler kick)
Atl	—	Price 44 pass from Vick (Feely kick)
Atl	—	Griffith 1 pass from Vick (Feely kick)
Jax	—	Toefield 4 run (Marler kick)

CLEVELAND 22, CINCINNATI 14—at Paul Brown Stadium, attendance 65,362. Rookie Lee Suggs rushed for 186 yards and 2 touchdowns as the Browns ended Cincinnati's playoff aspirations. The Bengals needed to win and for the Ravens to lose on Sunday night. The Bengals drove 56 yards for a touchdown to begin the game, but Suggs' 78-yard touchdown run with 2:06 left in the first half gave Cleveland a 13-7 lead. The Bengals drove to the Browns' 6 with 10 seconds left in the half, but Jon Kitna was sacked by Tyrone Rogers, instead of throwing the ball away to set up a field goal, and the half expired. Shayne Graham's 52-yard field-goal attempt to begin the third quarter hit the left upright, but Rudi Johnson scored his second touchdown two possessions later to give Cincinnati a 14-13 lead with 12:15 remaining. Suggs rushed 6 times on the ensuing 8-play drive, capped by a 25-yard scoring scamper, for a 19-14 lead with 7:54 to play. The Browns' defense forced a punt, and Suggs carried nine times in 10 plays, but was stopped at the Bengals' 1 and Brett Conway kicked an 18-yard field goal with 1:13 to play. With their final possession, Kitna was intercepted by Robert Griffith at the Browns' 39 with 41 seconds left to end Cincinnati's season. Tim Couch was 9 of 18 for 115 yards. Suggs rushed 26 times for 186 yards. Kitna was 23 of 35 for 175 yards, with 1 interception.

Cleveland	3	10	0	9	—	22
Cincinnati	7	0	0	7	—	14

Cin	—	Ru. Johnson 5 run (Graham kick)
Cle	—	FG Conway 42
Cle	—	FG Conway 42
Cle	—	Suggs 78 run (Conway kick)
Cin	—	Ru. Johnson 2 run (Graham kick)
Cle	—	Suggs 25 run (pass failed)
Cle	—	FG Conway 18

DETROIT 30, ST. LOUIS 20—at Ford Field, attendance 61,006. Joey Harrington passed for 238 yards and 3 touchdowns as the Lions ruined the Rams' chances of having home-field advantage throughout the playoffs. The Lions' defense held the Rams to just 194 yards, most of which came in the second quarter when the Rams scored on four consecutive possessions, the last two set up by a blocked punt and fumble recovery, for a 20-10 halftime lead. But the Lions answered by scoring on their first four possessions of the second half. The first score was set up by Shaun Rogers' sack of Marc Bulger, which resulted in a fumble recovered by Barrett Green at the Rams' 24. With the Lions leading 24-20, Green tipped a pass that was intercepted by Boss Bailey to set up the first of two second-half field goals by Jason Hanson. Kurt Warner replaced Bulger, who suffered a bruised forearm, with 9:35 left, but was unable to guide the team across midfield on either possession. Harrington was 26 of 36 for 238 yards and 3 touchdowns, with 1 interception. Bulger was 18 of 31 for 170 yards and 1 touchdown, with 1 interception, and Warner was 4 of 11 for 23 yards.

St. Louis	0	20	0	0	—	20
Detroit	3	7	17	3	—	30

Det	—	FG Hanson 39
StL	—	Manumaleuna 8 pass from Bulger (Wilkins kick)
Det	—	Schroeder 13 pass from Harrington (Hanson kick)
StL	—	FG Wilkins 51
StL	—	Faulk 2 run (Wilkins kick)
StL	—	FG Wilkins 36
Det	—	Hakim 13 pass from Harrington (Hanson kick)
Det	—	Fitzsimmons 2 pass from Harrington (Hanson kick)
Det	—	FG Hanson 38
Det	—	FG Hanson 50

GREEN BAY 31, DENVER 3—at Lambeau Field, attendance 70,299. Ahman Green rushed for 218 yards and 2 touchdowns, including a 98-yard scoring run, to win the NFC North. The Packers led 31-3 with less than four minutes remaining when the Vikings lost to Arizona, catapulting the Packers into the postseason. Ensured of a wild-card berth, the Broncos did not have Jake Plummer, Clinton Portis, Shannon Sharpe, or Rod Smith active, but trailed just 10-3 following Jason Elam's field goal with 4:00 left in the third quarter. Two plays later, Green rushed 47 yards to the Broncos' 7 to set up his 2-yard touchdown run for a 17-3 lead. An 83-yard kickoff return by Adrian Madise put the Broncos in scoring position. Quentin Griffin was stopped for no gain on second-and-goal from the Broncos' 1, and two incomplete passes by Danny Kanell gave the ball back to Green Bay. With the ball officially on the Packers' 2 following the change of possession, Green burst through the right side of the line and raced 98 yards untouched for the second-longest touchdown run in NFL history. Madise then fumbled the ensuing kickoff and Marcus Wilkins recovered in the end zone for the Packers' second touchdown in eight seconds and a 31-3 lead with 13:10 to play. Favre was 12 of 21 for 116 yards and 1 touchdown, with 1 interception. Green rushed 20 times for 218 yards. Kanell was 9 of 18 for 61 yards, with 1 interception, and Jarious Jackson was 4 of 9 for 41 yards, with 1 interception.

Denver	0	0	3	0	—	3
Green Bay	7	3	7	14	—	31

GB	—	Franks 2 pass from Favre (Longwell kick)
GB	—	FG Longwell 33
Den	—	FG Elam 31
GB	—	Green 2 run (Longwell kick)
GB	—	Green 98 run (Longwell kick)
GB	—	Wilkins fumble recovery in end zone (Longwell kick)

INDIANAPOLIS 20, HOUSTON 17—at Reliant Stadium, attendance 70,680. Mike Vanderjagt kicked a 43-yard field goal as time expired as the Colts won the AFC South title. With the kick, Vanderjagt also set an NFL record by making his forty-first consecutive field goal, surpassing the mark previously held by Gary Anderson. The Colts had more first downs (27-10) and yards (418-204), and allowed just 3 of the Texans' 12 drives to compile more than 10 yards. But Indianapolis fell behind 17-3 on a 78-yard drive by Houston, capped by Domanick Davis' 11-yard run, an interception by Marcus Coleman just before halftime to set up a field goal, and Davis' 13-yard scamper to culminate a 63-yard drive to begin the second half. Edgerrin James capped an 11-play, 67-yard drive with a 6-yard touchdown to begin the fourth quarter. With 5:22 remaining, Colts coach Tony Dungy eschewed a 51-yard field goal, and had Vanderjagt pooch punt from field-goal formation. Justin Snow downed the ball at the Texans' 4, and three plays later Donald Strickland intercepted David Carr's pass. Peyton Manning's 5-yard touchdown pass to Brandon Stokley on the next play tied the game with 3:50 to play. The Colts' defense forced another three-and-out, and a 16-yard pass by Manning to Marvin Harrison on third-and-10 kept the drive alive and set up Vanderjagt's winning kick. Manning was 26 of 38 for 220 yards and 1 touchdown, with 1 interception. James rushed 27 times for 171 yards. Carr was 13 of 23 for 105 yards, with 1 interception.

Indianapolis	0	3	0	17	—	20
Houston	0	10	7	0	—	17

Ind	—	FG Vanderjagt 39
Hous	—	Davis 11 run (Brown kick)
Hous	—	FG Brown 36
Hous	—	Davis 13 run (Brown kick)
Ind	—	James 6 run (Vanderjagt kick)
Ind	—	Stokley 5 pass from Manning (Vanderjagt kick)
Ind	—	FG Vanderjagt 43

KANSAS CITY 31, CHICAGO 3—at Arrowhead Stadium, attendance 78,413. Priest Holmes scored 2 touchdowns to set the NFL record with 27 touchdowns in a season as the Chiefs downed the Bears. Holmes scored his record-tying twenty-sixth touchdown on a 1-yard run with 13:40 left in the first half. His second touchdown, in which he leaped over the top of the linemen, came with 58 seconds left in the third quarter to give the Chiefs a 21-3 lead. The second touchdown was set up by Greg Wesley's interception at the Bears' 28. The Chiefs scored on their next two possessions as well to pull away. Trent Green was 19 of 27 for 162 yards and 1 touchdown, with 1 interception. Rex Grossman was 6 of 10 for 31 yards, before leaving in the second quarter with an injured hand. Kordell Stewart was 5 of 15 for 86 yards, with 2 interceptions, and Chris Chandler was 6 of 17 for 81 yards.

Chicago	0	0	3	0	—	3
Kansas City	0	14	7	10	—	31

KC	—	Holmes 1 run (Andersen kick)
KC	—	Kennison 6 pass from Green (Andersen kick)
Chi	—	FG Edinger 48
KC	—	Holmes 2 run (Andersen kick)
KC	—	FG Andersen 38
KC	—	L. Johnson 5 run (Andersen kick)

MIAMI 23, N.Y. JETS 21—at Pro Player Stadium, attendance 73,720. Olindo Mare kicked a 22-yard field goal with three seconds remaining as the Dolphins defeated the Jets. The Dolphins scored on their first four possessions to take a 20-7 lead. Doug Brien kicked field goals on consecutive drives sandwiched around halftime to trim the Jets' deficit to 20-13, and Jeff Grau's punt formation snap sailed out of the end zone for a safety to make the score 20-15. The Jets took the ensuing free kick and drove 57 yards in over six minutes to take a 21-20 lead on Chad Pennington's 1-yard touchdown pass to Anthony Becht. The duo's 2-point conversion attempt was unsuccessful, and the Dolphins drove to the Jets' 1. But Victor Hobson intercepted Jay Fiedler's pass with 4:06 to go. The Dolphins' defense forced a punt and Fiedler completed passes of 11, 11, and 14 yards to Chris Chambers to set up Mare's winning kick. Fiedler was 21 of 29 for 328 yards and 1 touchdown, with 1 interception. Chambers had 9 receptions for 153 yards. Pennington was 22 of 28 for 221 yards and 1 touchdown.

N.Y. Jets	0	10	5	6	—	21
Miami	3	17	0	3	—	23

Mia	—	FG Mare 23
Mia	—	FG Mare 43
Mia	—	Williams 16 run (Mare kick)
NYJ	—	Martin 8 run (Brien kick)
Mia	—	Chambers 20 pass from Fiedler (Mare kick)
NYJ	—	FG Brien 36
NYJ	—	FG Brien 22
NYJ	—	Safety, Grau snap went out of end zone

NYJ — Becht 1 pass from Pennington (pass failed)
Mia — FG Mare 22

NEW ORLEANS 13, DALLAS 7—at Louisiana Superdome, attendance 68,451. Donte' Stallworth caught a 76-yard touchdown pass in the second quarter and John Carney added 2 field goals for the Saints. Dallas drove 93 yards in 16 plays to take a 7-3 lead in the second quarter, but Aaron Brooks hit Stallworth with a pass on the next play. Stallworth broke a tackle at midfield and raced into the end zone for a 10-7 lead. The Cowboys answered by driving to the Saints' 14, but Tebucky Jones intercepted Quincy Carter's pass for a touchback. Jay Bellamy's interception two plays into the second half set up Carney's second field goal. The Cowboys' only other scoring threat came when they reached the Saints' 27 with 1:33 left, but Bellamy's second interception preserved the victory. Brooks was 15 of 32 for 243 yards and 1 touchdown. Stallworth had 3 receptions for 114 yards. Carter was 27 of 47 for 290 yards and 1 touchdown, with 3 interceptions.

Dallas	0	7	0	0	—	7
New Orleans	3	7	3	0	—	13

NO — FG Carney 24
Dall — Anderson 3 pass from Carter (Cundiff kick)
NO — Stallworth 76 pass from Brooks (Carney kick)
NO — FG Carney 27

CAROLINA 37, N.Y. GIANTS 24—at Giants Stadium, attendance 78,130. Jake Delhomme passed for 2 touchdowns and Carolina's defense forced 5 turnovers as the Panthers defeated the Giants in Jim Fassel's final game as New York's coach. The Panthers gained just 251 yards, but scored on a punt return and interception in the first quarter, and had a field goal set up by a second interception, to take a 20-0 lead less than 17 minutes into the game. A blocked punt by Osi Umenyiora set up Jesse Palmer's 7-yard touchdown pass to Amani Toomer to cut the deficit to 20-10, and Johnnie Harris intercepted a pass by Delhomme on the next possession. But Harris fumbled during the return and Kris Mangum recovered. Four plays later Delhomme dumped a 1-yard scoring pass to Muhsin Muhammad, and John Kasay added his third field goal of the half as time expired for a 30-10 lead. Umenyiora's second blocked punt of the game set up Palmer's second touchdown pass, but Carolina responded with a 12-play, 73-yard touchdown drive for a 37-17 lead. Umenyiora sacked Delhomme and forced him to fumble early in the fourth quarter. Keith Washington recovered for a touchdown, but the Giants were stopped on downs at the Panthers' 13 with 3:06 left to preserve the victory. Umenyiora, a second-round rookie from Troy State, blocked 2 punts that set up 1-play touchdown drives, and forced a sack that was recovered in the end zone for a defensive touchdown. Delhomme was 16 of 30 for 191 yards and 2 touchdowns, with 1 interception. Palmer was 18 of 43 for 110 yards and 2 touchdowns, with 4 interceptions.

Carolina	17	13	7	0	—	37
N.Y. Giants	0	10	7	7	—	24

Car — Smith 53 punt return (Kasay kick)
Car — FG Kasay 42
Car — Manning 27 interception return (Kasay kick)
Car — FG Kasay 33
NYG — FG Bryant 28
NYG — Toomer 7 pass from Palmer (Bryant kick)
Car — Muhammad 1 pass from Delhomme (Kasay kick)
Car — FG Kasay 34
NYG — Shiancoe 1 pass from Palmer (Bryant kick)
Car — Proehl 5 pass from Delhomme (Kasay kick)
NYG — Washington fumble recovery in end zone

SAN DIEGO 21, OAKLAND 14—at Qualcomm Stadium, attendance 62,222. LaDainian Tomlinson rushed for 243 yards and 2 touchdowns as the Chargers limited the Raiders to 141 yards to defeat Oakland. With 8 receptions, Tomlinson became the first player in NFL history with 1,000 rushing yards and 100 receptions in a season, his 243 rushing yards tied for tenth-best all-time, and he tied Jim Brown, Earl Campbell, and Barry Sanders for the second-most career 200-yard rushing games (four). Tomlinson's first touchdown capped a game-opening 10-play, 62-yard drive. The Raiders tied the score 7-7 on Phillip Buchanon's 80-yard punt return, and following David Boston's 18-yard touchdown catch, Oakland tied the score again on Doug Gabriel's 85-yard kickoff return for a touchdown with 24 seconds left in the half. A 35-yard run by Tomlinson early in the fourth quarter set up his second touchdown, with 11:42 to play, and the Raiders failed to cross the Chargers' 46 on their final four possessions. Drew Brees was 15 of 28 for 97 yards and 1 touchdown. Rick Mirer was 4 of 11 for 21 yards, and Tee Martin was 2 of 11 for 14 yards, with 1 interception.

Oakland	0	14	0	0	—	14
San Diego	7	7	0	7	—	21

SD — Tomlinson 2 run (Christie kick)
Oak — Buchanon 80 punt return (Janikowski kick)
SD — Boston 18 pass from Brees (Christie kick)
Oak — Gabriel 85 kickoff return (Janikowski kick)
SD — Tomlinson 2 run (Christie kick)

TENNESSEE 33, TAMPA BAY 13—at The Coliseum, attendance 68,809. Neil O'Donnell, playing for the injured Steve McNair, passed for 232 yards and 2 touchdowns for the Titans. The Titans' defense intercepted 4 passes, 2 by Tank Williams, to set up 13 points. The score was 3-3 in the second quarter when O'Donnell, who was out of football until being signed just 10 days earlier and making his first start since September 23, 2001, completed a 23-yard touchdown pass to Derrick Mason. The Titans scored on their next four possessions as well, capped by Mason's 34-yard touchdown catch with 2:18 left in the third quarter, for a 26-6 lead. O'Donnell was 18 of 27 for 232 yards and 2 touchdowns, with 1 interception. Brad Johnson was 13 of 23 for 96 yards, with 3 interceptions. Shaun King was 11 of 15 for 106 yards and 1 touchdown, with 1 interception.

Tampa Bay	3	0	3	7	—	13
Tennessee	3	13	10	7	—	33

Tenn — FG Anderson 37
TB — FG Gramatica 27
Tenn — Mason 23 pass from O'Donnell (Anderson kick)
Tenn — FG Anderson 33
Tenn — FG Anderson 43
Tenn — FG Anderson 23
TB — FG Gramatica 33
Tenn — Mason 34 pass from O'Donnell (Anderson kick)
TB — Stecker 14 pass from King (Gramatica kick)
Tenn — Kinney fumble recovery in end zone (Anderson kick)

SUNDAY NIGHT, DECEMBER 28
BALTIMORE 13, PITTSBURGH 10 (OT)—at M & T Bank Stadium, attendance 70,001. Jamal Lewis rushed for 114 yards and 1 touchdown and Matt Stover kicked a 47-yard field goal in overtime for the Ravens, who clinched the AFC North title earlier in the day when the Bengals lost to the Browns. Lewis finished the game with 2,066 rushing yards, the second-most in a single season and just 39 yards shy of tying Eric Dickerson's 1984 record of 2,105. Lewis' 25-yard touchdown run in the first quarter gave him 2,025 yards, becoming just the fifth player to rush for 2,000 yards in a season. The Steelers had just 88 yards of offense when they lined up to punt on fourth-and-1 in the middle of the third quarter. Punter Josh Miller tossed a short pass to Chris Hope, who weaved his way 81 yards for a touchdown. The Steelers then forced a punt and reserve quarterback Kyle Boller, in for the injured Dave Zastudil, punted just 29 yards to set up Jeff Reed's 42-yard field goal for a 10-7 lead. The Ravens responded with Stover's 46-yard field goal early in the fourth quarter to tie the game. Stover's 52-yard attempt with 41 seconds left was short. Chris McAlister intercepted a pass by Tommy Maddox two plays later, and the Ravens drove to the Steelers' 33 with five seconds left. Kickoff specialist Wade Richey attempted a 51-yard field goal that was also short. In overtime, the Steelers won the toss but the Ravens' defense forced a three-and-out, and a 22-yard pass from Anthony Wright to Marcus Robinson, along with a roughing-the-passer penalty, set up Stover's winning kick. Wright was 16 of 27 for 163 yards, with 1 interception. Robinson had 6 catches for 102 yards. Lewis rushed 27 times for 114 yards, but had just 9 yards after the third quarter, including just 3 yards on 2 carries in overtime. Maddox was 14 of 27 for 108 yards, with 3 interceptions.

Pittsburgh	0	0	10	0	0	—	10
Baltimore	7	0	0	3	3	—	13

Balt — J. Lewis 25 run (Stover kick)
Pitt — Hope 81 pass from Miller (Reed kick)
Pitt — FG Reed 42
Balt — FG Stover 46
Balt — FG Stover 47

AFC WILD CARD PLAYOFF GAME
SATURDAY, JANUARY 3, 2004
TENNESSEE 20, BALTIMORE 17—at M & T Bank Stadium, attendance 69,452. Gary Anderson kicked a 46-yard field goal with 29 seconds left as the Titans snapped a five-game losing streak to the Ravens. Chris Brown's first professional touchdown, on a 6-yard run, capped a 10-play, 67-yard opening drive for the Titans. Tennessee then forced a punt, but two plays later Steve McNair's pass was tipped by Ed Reed and intercepted by Will Demps, who returned it 56 yards for his first-ever NFL touchdown. The Titans drove to the Ravens' 17 early in the second quarter, but Reed intercepted his third-down pass. Baltimore led 10-7 in the middle of the third quarter when McNair lofted a pass down the left sideline. Justin McCareins adjusted to the underthrown ball, caught it near the 15-yard line before racing untouched into the end zone. Samari Rolle intercepted Anthony Wright's pass at the Ravens' 31 with 11:33 left to set up a 45-yard field goal by Anderson for a 17-10 lead with 9:13 to play. The 44-year-old Anderson had not made a field goal longer than 43 yards all season, but surpassed that feat twice in the final 10 minutes of the game. Wright engineered a 9-play, 71-yard drive after Anderson's first field goal and hit Todd Heap with a 35-yard scoring pass with 4:30 left. The Titans got the ball at their own 37 with 2:44 left and drove 35 yards in 8 plays, highlighted by a 13-yard pass to Derrick

Mason and an 8-yard run by Eddie George on third-and-1, to set up Anderson's winning kick. The Ravens reached their own 40 before Wright's final pass fell incomplete. McNair was 14 of 23 for 159 yards and 1 touchdown, with 3 interceptions. Wright was 20 of 37 for 214 yards and 1 touchdown, with 2 interceptions.

Tennessee	7	0	7	6	—	20
Baltimore	7	3	0	7	—	17

Tenn — Brown 6 run (Anderson kick)
Balt — Demps 56 interception return (Stover kick)
Balt — FG Stover 43
Tenn — McCareins 49 pass from McNair (Anderson kick)
Tenn — FG Anderson 45
Balt — Heap 35 pass from Wright (Stover kick)
Tenn — FG Anderson 46

NFC WILD CARD PLAYOFF GAME
SATURDAY, JANUARY 3, 2004
CAROLINA 29, DALLAS 10—at Ericsson Stadium, attendance 73,014. Stephen Davis rushed for 104 yards and 1 touchdown, Jake Delhomme passed for 273 yards and a score, and John Kasay kicked 5 field goals as the Panthers won their first playoff game in seven seasons. The Panthers' defense limited Dallas to 204 yards and 10 first downs and forced 2 turnovers. On Carolina's first possession, Steve Smith turned a short pass into a 70-yard gain to the Cowboys' 1, where only tremendous hustle by Pete Hunter, who raced across the field to knock down Smith, prevented a touchdown. Two runs by Davis and an incompletion forced the Panthers to settle for Kasay's first field goal. Later in the quarter, a 32-yard punt by Toby Gowin gave Carolina the ball at the Cowboys' 41, setting up Kasay's second field goal. A 17-yard punt by Gowin gave the Panthers the ball at their 49 in the second quarter to set up Davis' 23-yard touchdown run on third-and-10 with 6:10 left in the half. Billy Cundiff made a 37-yard field goal for Dallas with 1:12 left in the half, but any momentum shift was nullified when Delhomme completed a 49-yard pass to Muhsin Muhammad, who fumbled at the 10-yard line but recovered the ball at the Cowboys' 2 to set up Kasay's third field goal and a 16-3 halftime lead. Delhomme's 32-yard touchdown pass to Smith capped a 4-play, 63-yard drive early in the third quarter and gave Carolina a commanding 23-3 lead. It took a 41-yard kickoff return by Michael Bates with the Cowboys trailing 26-3 to set up a 47-yard touchdown drive, capped by Quincy Carter's 9-yard run with 7:36 to play. An interception by Julius Peppers with 4:59 to play set up Kasay's final field goal. Delhomme was 18 of 29 for 273 yards and 1 touchdown. Smith had 5 receptions for 135 yards. Muhammad had 4 catches for 103 yards. Davis rushed 26 times for 104 yards. Carter was 21 of 36 for 154 yards, with 1 interception.

Dallas	0	3	0	7	—	10
Carolina	6	10	7	6	—	29

Car — FG Kasay 18
Car — FG Kasay 38
Car — Davis 23 run (Kasay kick)
Dall — FG Cundiff 37
Car — FG Kasay 19
Car — Smith 32 pass from Delhomme (Kasay kick)
Car — FG Kasay 32
Dall — Carter 9 run (Cundiff kick)
Car — FG Kasay 34

NFC WILD CARD PLAYOFF GAME
SUNDAY, JANUARY 4, 2004
GREEN BAY 33, SEATTLE 27 (OT)—at Lambeau Field, attendance 71,457. Al Harris returned an interception 52 yards for a touchdown 4:25 into overtime as the Packers improved their home postseason record to 14-1. With the score 3-3 in the second quarter, Koren Robinson dropped a touchdown pass on third down, forcing the Seahawks to settle for Josh Brown's second field goal with 6:50 left in the half. Brett Favre responded with a 44-yard pass to Javon Walker on the next play to set up his 23-yard touchdown pass to Bubba Franks. Favre set a postseason record with a touchdown pass in 14 consecutive postseason games. The Packers' defense forced a punt and Ryan Longwell booted a 27-yard field goal just before halftime for a 13-6 lead. Seattle came out of the locker room and put together touchdown drives of 10-plays, 74-yards and 11-plays, 77-yards, both culminated by 1-yard runs by Shaun Alexander, for a 20-13 lead with 1:57 left in the third quarter. Alexander's second touchdown came on fourth-and-goal, and was set up by tackle Steve Hutchinson's 4-yard reception of a deflected third-down pass. Seattle ran just three plays in the next 14:13, as Green Bay countered with consecutive 12-play touchdown drives of 60 and 51 yards. Both featured successful fourth-and-1 carries by Ahman Green and were capped by 1-yard scoring runs by Green, giving Green Bay a 27-20 lead with 2:44 to play. Matt Hasselbeck completed a 34-yard pass to Bobby Engram to the Packers' 8, and a pass interference penalty in the end zone gave Seattle the ball at the 1-yard line to set up Alexander's third touchdown with just 51 seconds left. A 27-yard pass by Favre to Walker got the Packers to the Seahawks' 30, but Longwell's 47-yard field-goal attempt in the 20 degree weather fell short. The Seahawks won the coin toss, and after an exchange of punts, faced third-and-11 from their own 45. The Packers blitzed, and Harris stepped in front of Alex Bannister to intercept Hasselbeck's pass and outrun the pair down the right sideline to the end zone. Favre was 26 of 38 for 319 yards and 1 touchdown. Walker had 5 receptions for 111 yards. Hasselbeck was 25 of 45 for 305 yards, with 1 interception.

Seattle	3	3	14	7	0	—	27
Green Bay	0	13	0	14	6	—	33

Sea — FG Brown 30
GB — FG Longwell 31
Sea — FG Brown 35
GB — Franks 23 pass from Favre (Longwell kick)
GB — FG Longwell 27
Sea — Alexander 1 run (Brown kick)
Sea — Alexander 1 run (Brown kick)
GB — Green 1 run (Longwell kick)
GB — Green 1 run (Longwell kick)
Sea — Alexander 1 run (Brown kick)
GB — Harris 52 interception return

AFC WILD CARD PLAYOFF GAME
SUNDAY, JANUARY 4, 2004
INDIANAPOLIS 41, DENVER 10—at RCA Dome, attendance 56,586. Peyton Manning passed for 5 touchdowns as the Colts scored on their first seven possessions and avenged a 31-17 home loss to the Broncos two weeks earlier. The Colts took the opening kickoff and drove 70 yards in 6 plays, capped by Brandon Stokley's 31-yard touchdown catch. The Broncos responded with a 8:14 drive that culminated with Jason Elam's 49-yard field goal. The Colts answered with another touchdown, which came when Marvin Harrison made a diving catch at the 30-yard line, and when nobody touched him he got up and ran into the end zone. The Colts scored on all three of their second quarter possessions, highlighted by Manning's 87-yard touchdown pass to Stokley with 1:51 left in the half, and capped by Mike Vanderjagt's 27-yard field goal, which was set up by David Macklin's interception, as the half expired for a 31-3 lead. At halftime Manning was 16 of 18 for 327 yards and 4 touchdowns. Raheem Brock blocked Elam's 46-yard field-goal attempt to begin the second half, and Manning engineered a 12-play, 64-yard drive that ended with Reggie Wayne's 7-yard touchdown catch for a 38-3 lead with 5:19 left in the third quarter. Dwight Freeney forced a fumble by Jake Plummer and Rob Morris recovered to set up Vanderjagt's second field goal with 55 seconds left in the third quarter. Plummer's 7-yard touchdown pass to Rod Smith with 7:04 remaining ended the scoring. The Colts outgained Denver 479-322. Manning was 22 of 26 for 377 yards and 5 touchdowns, for a perfect 158.3 passer rating. Harrison had 7 receptions for 133 yards, and Stokley had 4 catches for 144 yards. Plummer was 23 of 30 for 181 yards and 1 touchdown, with 2 interceptions.

Denver	3	0	0	7	—	10
Indianapolis	14	17	10	0	—	41

Ind — Stokley 31 pass from Manning (Vanderjagt kick)
Den — FG Elam 49
Ind — Harrison 46 pass from Manning (Vanderjagt kick)
Ind — Harrison 23 pass from Manning (Vanderjagt kick)
Ind — Stokley 87 pass from Manning (Vanderjagt kick)
Ind — FG Vanderjagt 27
Ind — Wayne 7 pass from Manning (Vanderjagt kick)
Ind — FG Vanderjagt 20
Den — Smith 7 pass from Plummer (Elam kick)

NFC DIVISIONAL PLAYOFF GAME
SATURDAY, JANUARY 10, 2004
CAROLINA 29, ST. LOUIS 23 (2OT)—at Edward Jones Dome, attendance 66,165. Steve Smith caught a 69-yard touchdown pass from Jake Delhomme on the first play of the second overtime as Carolina advanced to the NFC Championship Game. The Rams drove inside the Panthers' 10 on each of their three first-half possessions, but settled for a field goal each time. After struggling on its first two possessions, Carolina scored on five consecutive drives, capped by Brad Hoover's 7-yard touchdown run following Mike Minter's interception, to give Carolina a 23-12 lead with 8:50 to play. Deon Grant intercepted Marc Bulger's pass on the next play from scrimmage, giving the Panthers a chance to put the game away. But Tyoka Jackson dropped Delhomme for an 11-yard loss on third-and-6, and John Kasay's 53-yard field-goal attempt hit the left upright with 6:29 remaining. The Rams converted four third downs and a fourth down, on a 16-yard pass from Bulger to Marshall Faulk, and scored on Faulk's 1-yard run with 2:39 left. Bulger's 2-point conversion pass to Dane Looker pulled the Rams within three points, and Jeff Wilkins recovered his own onside kick to give the Rams a chance to tie or win. St. Louis reached the Panthers' 19 with 42 seconds left, but the Rams opted to let the clock run down, and Wilkins tied the game with a 33-yard attempt as regulation expired. In overtime, the Panthers won the toss and reached the Rams' 22 to set up Kasay for an opportunity to win the game. Kasay made a 40-yard attempt, but the play was nullified by a delay of game penalty. After a few unsuccessful runs, Kasay attempted a 45-yard field goal, but pulled it wide right. The Rams responded by driving to the Panthers' 35, but Wilkins' 53-yard field-goal attempt landed short. The Rams' defense stiffened to force a punt, but Ricky Manning Jr. intercepted Bulger at the Panthers' 35 with 1:01 left in overtime. On third-and-14, Delhomme completed a pass to Smith near midfield. Smith split the seam and outran the secondary for the game-winning touchdown 10 seconds into the second overtime. Delhomme was 16 of 26 for 290 yards and 1 touchdown, with 1

interception. Smith had 6 receptions for 163 yards and 1 touchdown. Bulger was 27 of 46 for 332 yards, with 3 interceptions. Isaac Bruce had 7 receptions for 116 yards.

Carolina	0	10	6	7	0	6	—	29
St. Louis	3	6	3	11	0	0	—	23

StL — FG Wilkins 20
StL — FG Wilkins 26
Car — Muhammad fumble recovery in end zone (Kasay kick)
StL — FG Wilkins 24
Car — FG Kasay 45
StL — FG Wilkins 51
Car — FG Kasay 52
Car — FG Kasay 34
Car — Hoover 7 run (Kasay kick)
StL — Faulk 1 run (Looker pass from Bulger)
StL — FG Wilkins 33
Car — Smith 69 pass from Delhomme

AFC DIVISIONAL PLAYOFF GAME
SATURDAY, JANUARY 10, 2004
NEW ENGLAND 17, TENNESSEE 14—at Gillette Stadium, attendance 68,436. Adam Vinatieri's 46-yard field goal with 4:06 remaining lifted the Patriots past the Titans in four-degree weather. Tom Brady's 41-yard touchdown pass to Bethel Johnson on the Patriots' sixth offensive play staked New England to a 7-0 lead. The Titans needed just six plays to answer, as Chris Brown scored from 5 yards to tie the game. Vinatieri missed a 44-yard field goal on the Patriots' next possession, but Rodney Harrison intercepted a pass by Steve McNair on the next play to set up Antowain Smith's 1-yard touchdown run. The Titans reached the Patriots' 13 just before halftime, but Richard Seymour blocked Gary Anderson's 31-yard field-goal attempt. Tennessee had success moving the ball on its first possession of the second half, too, driving 11 plays and 70 yards, highlighted by third-down conversion passes to Tyrone Calico and Justin McCareins, to set up McNair's game-tying 11-yard scoring pass to Derrick Mason with 4:14 left in the third quarter. A 32-yard punt by Craig Hentrich and 9-yard return by Troy Brown gave New England the ball at the Titans' 40 with 6:40 remaining. Brady completed a 4-yard pass to Brown on fourth-and-3 with 5:14 left and Vinatieri's 46-yard field goal three plays later gave the Patriots a 17-14 lead. McNair's fourth-and-12 desperation heave intended for Drew Bennett fell incomplete with 1:45 remaining, and New England ran out the clock. Brady was 21 of 41 for 201 yards and 1 touchdown, as he completed passes to 10 different receivers. McNair was 18 of 26 for 210 yards and 1 touchdown, with 1 interception.

Tennessee	7	0	7	0	—	14
New England	7	7	0	3	—	17

NE — Be. Johnson 41 pass from Brady (Vinatieri kick)
Tenn — Brown 5 run (Anderson kick)
NE — Smith 1 run (Vinatieri kick)
Tenn — Mason 11 pass from McNair (Anderson kick)
NE — FG Vinatieri 46

AFC DIVISIONAL PLAYOFF GAME
SUNDAY, JANUARY 11, 2004
INDIANAPOLIS 38, KANSAS CITY 31—at Arrowhead Stadium, attendance 79,159. Peyton Manning passed for 304 yards and 3 touchdowns, and Edgerrin James rushed for 125 yards and 2 scores, as the Colts advanced to their first AFC Championship Game since 1995. The teams combined for 842 yards, 434 by the Colts, and it was the first postseason game in history without a punt. The Colts scored on six of their first seven possessions, with the lone non-scoring drive coming on a three-play series in their own territory as the half expired. The Colts' five touchdown drives were 70, 76, 71, 64, and 76 yards. The Chiefs attempted to keep pace, scoring on five of their first seven possessions. But Morten Andersen missed a 31-yard field goal just before halftime, allowing the Colts to maintain a 21-10 lead, and Kansas City fumbled two plays into the second half, with David Macklin recovering Priest Holmes' fumble at the Colts' 22 at the end of a 48-yard run. Holmes' 1-yard scoring run with 4:22 left cut the deficit to 38-31, but the Colts got two first downs on their ensuing possession, and by the time the Chiefs stopped the Colts on downs, Kansas City was at its own 27 with eight seconds left. Trent Green completed a screen pass to Holmes, who was tackled immediately by Gary Brackett to clinch the victory. Manning was 22 of 30 for 304 yards and 3 touchdowns. James rushed 26 times for 125 yards and 2 touchdowns. Green was 18 of 30 for 212 yards and 1 touchdown. Holmes rushed 24 times for 176 yards.

Indianapolis	14	7	10	7	—	38
Kansas City	3	7	14	7	—	31

Ind — Stokley 29 pass from Manning (Vanderjagt kick)
KC — FG Andersen 22
Ind — James 11 run (Vanderjagt kick)
KC — Hall 9 pass from Green (Andersen kick)
Ind — Lopienski 2 pass from Manning (Vanderjagt kick)
Ind — FG Vanderjagt 45
KC — Holmes 1 run (Andersen kick)
Ind — Wayne 19 pass from Manning (Vanderjagt kick)
KC — Hall 92 kickoff return (Andersen kick)
Ind — James 1 run (Vanderjagt kick)
KC — Holmes 1 run (Andersen kick)

NFC DIVISIONAL PLAYOFF GAME
SUNDAY, JANUARY 11, 2004
PHILADELPHIA 20, GREEN BAY 17 (OT)—at Lincoln Financial Field, attendance 67,707. The Eagles used an improbable 28-yard pass on fourth-and-26 to set up David Akers' game-tying field goal in the final seconds en route to an overtime victory and a berth in the NFC Championship Game for the third consecutive season. In the middle of the first quarter, Brett Favre's 40-yard touchdown pass to Robert Ferguson came one play after Mike McKenzie's cornerback blitz forced Donovan McNabb to fumble the ball away. Akers missed a 33-yard field-goal attempt on the Eagles' next possession, and Green Bay responded with an eight-play, 77-yard drive, capped by Favre's 17-yard touchdown pass to Ferguson, for a 14-0 lead with 1:22 left in the first quarter. A 45-yard pass from McNabb to Todd Pinkston set up Duce Staley's 7-yard touchdown on a shovel pass. The Packers once again drove right down field, but on fourth-and-goal from the Eagles' 1 with 2:00 left in the half, Ahman Green was stopped short of the goal line. A 24-yard scramble by McNabb set up his 12-yard touchdown pass to Pinkston on the first play of the fourth quarter to tie the score. Two possessions later, Favre's 44-yard pass to Javon Walker set up Ryan Longwell's go-ahead field goal with 10:22 left. After an exchange of punts, the Eagles started on their own 20 with 2:21 left. With 1:12 left, McNabb was sacked for a 16-yard loss by Bhawoh Jue, setting up fourth-and-26. McNabb fired a pass down the middle to Freddie Mitchell, who caught the ball beyond the marker for a 28-yard gain. Akers' 37-yard field goal with five seconds left forced overtime. The Eagles won the toss, but were forced to punt. But on the Packers' first play, Favre lofted a pass downfield which was intercepted by Brian Dawkins, who returned it 35 yards to the Packers' 34. Six plays later, Akers kicked a 31-yard field goal with 10:12 left on the clock for the victory. McNabb was 21 of 39 for 248 yards and 2 touchdowns, and rushed for 107 yards on 11 carries. Favre was 15 of 28 for 180 yards and 2 touchdowns, with 1 interception. Green rushed 25 times for 156 yards.

Green Bay	14	0	0	3	0	—	17
Philadelphia	0	7	0	10	3	—	20

GB — Ferguson 40 pass from Favre (Longwell kick)
GB — Ferguson 17 pass from Favre (Longwell kick)
Phil — Staley 7 pass from McNabb (Akers kick)
Phil — Pinkston 12 pass from McNabb (Akers kick)
GB — FG Longwell 21
Phil — FG Akers 37
Phil — FG Akers 31

AFC CHAMPIONSHIP GAME
SUNDAY, JANUARY 18, 2004
NEW ENGLAND 24, INDIANAPOLIS 14—at Gillette Stadium, attendance 68,436. Adam Vinatieri kicked 5 field goals and the Patriots' defense forced 6 turnovers en route to New England's second Super Bowl appearance in three years. The Colts had 4 first-half possessions, and turned the ball over all four times. The Patriots began the game with a 65-yard touchdown drive. Peyton Manning was intercepted on the Colts' first two possessions, including the first one in the end zone by Rodney Harrison, to set up 2 field goals for a 13-0 lead. The Colts were then forced to punt for the first time in two and a half postseason games, and Justin Snow's snap sailed over Hunter Smith's head. Smith intentionally kicked the ball out of the end zone for a safety. A New England fumble gave Indianapolis life, but Marvin Harrison fumbled at the Patriots' 16 just before halftime, and Tyrone Poole recovered. The Colts scored on Edgerrin James' 2-yard run to open the second half, a drive that featured James' 3-yard run on fourth-and-1. The Patriots drove inside the Colts' 10 on each of their next two possessions, but settled for field goals by Vinatieri for a 21-7 lead. An interception by Ty Law gave New England a chance to put the game away, but Walt Harris intercepted Tom Brady in the end zone for a touchback with 13:28 to play. The Colts took five minutes off the clock on the ensuing drive, but Law intercepted Manning's fourth-and-13 pass with 8:17 left. The Colts forced a punt, but it took them nearly four minutes to drive 67 yards to cut the deficit to 21-14 on Marcus Pollard's 7-yard catch with 2:27 to play. Christian Fauria recovered the onside kick, but the Patriots failed to gain a first down and the Colts got the ball back with 2:01 left, but Manning threw four consecutive incompletions. Vinatieri's 34-yard field goal with 50 seconds left iced the game. Brady was 22 of 37 for 237 yards and 1 touchdown, with 1 interception. Antowain Smith had 22 carries for 100 yards. Law had 3 interceptions. Manning was 23 of 47 for 237 yards and 1 touchdown, with 4 interceptions.

Indianapolis	0	0	7	7	—	14
New England	7	8	6	3	—	24

NE — Givens 7 pass from Brady (Vinatieri kick)
NE — FG Vinatieri 31
NE — FG Vinatieri 25
NE — Safety, Snow's snap sailed over punter's head and was kicked through end zone
Ind — James 2 run (Vanderjagt kick)
NE — FG Vinatieri 27
NE — FG Vinatieri 21
Ind — Pollard 7 pas from Manning (Vanderjagt kick)
NE — FG Vinatieri 34

NFC CHAMPIONSHIP GAME
SUNDAY, JANUARY 18, 2004
CAROLINA 14, PHILADELPHIA 3—at Lincoln Financial Field, attendance 67,862 Jake Delhomme passed for a touchdown and the Panthers forced 4 turnovers to advance to their first Super Bowl appearance. After a scoreless first quarter, Delhomme engineered an 8-play, 79-yard drive with 2 third-down conversions and capped by Muhsin Muhammad's 24-yard touchdown catch. The Eagles responded with a 41-yard field goal by David Akers. Two plays before the field goal, Donovan McNabb injured his ribs when, after tripping, he was hit by Mike Rucker. In the third quarter, Ricky Manning Jr. twice intercepted McNabb's passes. The first came at the Panthers' 14 to stop a drive, and the latter came at the Eagles' 37 to setup DeShaun Foster's 1-yard run with 4:11 left in the third quarter. Koy Detmer replaced the injured McNabb with 9:31 left, and drove the Eagles 81 yards to the Panthers' 11, but Dan Morgan intercepted his third-and-3 pass with 5:16 left. The Eagles got the ball back one last time, but Detmer's fourth-and-18 pass from midfield fell incomplete with 1:58 left. Delhomme was 9 of 14 for 101 yards and 1 touchdown. McNabb was 10 of 22 for 100 yards, with 3 interceptions, and Detmer was 7 of 14 for 88 yards, with 1 interception.

Carolina	0	7	7	0 —	14
Philadelphia	0	3	0	0 —	3

Car — Muhammad 24 pass from Delhomme (Kasay kick)
Phil — FG Akers 41
Car — Foster 1 run (Kasay kick)

SUPER BOWL XXXVIII
SUNDAY, FEBRUARY 1, 2004
NEW ENGLAND 32, CAROLINA 29—at Reliant Stadium, attendance 71,525. Adam Vinatieri kicked a 41-yard field goal with four seconds remaining as the Patriots won their second Super Bowl in three seasons. While it took a Super Bowl-record 26 minutes and 55 seconds for the first points to be scored, the teams combined for 868 yards (481 by New England) and the game also featured the highest scoring quarter (combined 37 points in the fourth). Vinatieri missed a 31-yard field goal on the Patriots' first possession, and had a 36-yard attempt blocked by Shane Burton with 6:00 left in the second quarter. But three plays later, Mike Vrabel sacked Jake Delhomme and forced him to fumble. Richard Seymour recovered at the Panthers' 20, and a 12-yard scramble by Tom Brady on third-and-7 set up his 5-yard touchdown pass to Deion Branch with 3:05 left in the first half. The Panthers responded with an 8-play, 95-yard drive capped by Delhomme's 39-yard perfectly placed touchdown pass to Steve Smith with 1:07 left in the half. Delhomme beat the blitz by lofting the pass deep down the left sideline. Brady's 52-yard pass to Branch with 37 seconds left in the half set up David Givens' 5-yard touchdown catch with 18 seconds left. New England squibbed the ensuing kickoff and Kris Mangum returned it 12 yards to the Panthers' 47. A 21-yard run by Stephen Davis set up John Kasay's 50-yard field goal as the half expired for a 14-10 New England lead. Neither team scored in the third quarter, but Antowain Smith's 2-yard touchdown run two plays into the final quarter capped a 71-yard drive and gave the Patriots a 21-10 lead. Undaunted, Carolina scored on its next two possessions. First, Delhomme completed passes of 18 and 22 yards to Smith to set up DeShaun Foster's 33-yard touchdown run to cut the deficit to 21-16 with 12:39 to play. Carolina went for the 2-point conversion, but Delhomme's pass was incomplete. New England marched to the Panthers' 9 with the ensuing kickoff, but Reggie Howard intercepted Brady's third-and-goal pass in the end zone. Two plays later, Delhomme rolled left and fired a Super Bowl-record 85-yard touchdown pass to Muhammad for a 22-21 lead with 6:53 left. Once again, the Panthers went for 2 points and Delhomme's pass was incomplete. New England drove 68 yards on its next possession, with Givens catching a 25-yard pass and 18-yard pass on third-and-9, to set up Brady's 1-yard touchdown pass to Vrabel, who was lined up as a tight end. A direct snap to Kevin Faulk resulted in a 2-point conversion for a 29-22 lead with 2:51 left. Delhomme completed passes of 19 yards to Muhammad and 31 yards to Ricky Proehl before finding Proehl from 12 yards with the tying touchdown with 1:08 remaining. Kasay's ensuing kickoff went out of bounds, giving New England the ball at their own 40. Five plays later, faced with third-and-3 from the Panthers' 40 with 14 seconds left, Brady fired a 17-yard pass to Branch to set up Vinatieri's Super Bowl-winning 41-yard field goal. Brady, who was named the Super Bowl most valuable player for the second time in his career, was 32 of 48 for 354 yards and 3 touchdowns, with 1 interception. Branch had 10 receptions for 143 yards. Delhomme was 16 of 33 for 323 yards and 3 touchdowns, and Muhammad had 4 catches for 140 yards.

Carolina	0	10	0	19 —	29
New England	0	14	0	18 —	32

NE — Branch 5 pass from Brady (Vinatieri kick)
Car — Smith 39 pass from Delhomme (Kasay kick)
NE — Givens 5 pass from Brady (Vinatieri kick)
Car — FG Kasay 50
NE — Smith 2 run (Vinatieri kick)
Car — Foster 33 run (pass failed)
Car — Muhammad 85 pass from Delhomme (pass failed)
NE — Vrabel 1 pass from Brady (Faulk run)
Car — Proehl 12 pass from Delhomme (Kasay kick)
NE — FG Vinatieri 41

2004 PRO BOWL
SUNDAY, FEBRUARY 8, 2004
NFC 55, AFC 52—at Aloha Stadium, attendance 50,127. Marc Bulger passed for a Pro Bowl-record 4 touchdowns as the NFC rallied from a 25-point deficit to win the highest scoring game in Pro Bowl history. The AFC set a record with 626 yards, but committed 6 turnovers which led to 35 points. Steve McNair fired a 90-yard touchdown pass to Chad Johnson on the AFC's first play, and Ed Reed blocked Todd Sauerbrun's punt and returned it 23 yards for a touchdown for a 14-0 lead 3:58 into the game. The AFC led 17-13 in the second quarter when Peyton Manning fired a 50-yard touchdown pass to Marvin Harrison, and his 9-yard scoring pass to Tony Gonzalez on the next possession gave the AFC a 31-13 lead. Jamal Lewis' 22-yard touchdown run gave the AFC a 38-13 lead with 11:08 left in the third quarter. The comeback started when Trent Green fumbled and Leonard Little recovered. Bulger completed a 12-yard touchdown pass to Torry Holt two plays later with 8:08 left in the third quarter. Two plays later, Derrick Mason fumbled and Jerry Azumah returned it 36 yards to the AFC's 7 to set up Bulger's 2-yard touchdown toss to Keenan McCardell. But following an exchange of punts, Green completed a 23-yard touchdown pass to Clinton Portis to give the AFC a 45-27 lead with 13:14 left. The NFC scored 28 points in the next 9:42, set up by Azumah's 60-yard kickoff return, Champ Bailey's interception of a pass by Harrison, and interception returns by Dre' Bly, 32 yards for a touchdown, and Corey Chavous, 39 yards to set up Shaun Alexander's 2-yard touchdown run with 3:32 left, for a 55-45 NFC lead. Manning's 10-yard touchdown pass to Hines Ward with 1:54 left pulled the AFC within three points, and Bulger was intercepted by Brock Marion on fourth-and-10 from the AFC's 28-yard line with 1:15 left. The AFC drove to the NFC 21, but Kris Jenkins sacked Manning for a 12-yard loss, forcing Vanderjagt, who was 37-for-37 on the season but missed from 52 yards just before halftime, to attempt a 51-yard field goal as time expired. But the kick sailed wide right and the NFC prevailed. Bulger was 12 of 21 for 152 yards and 4 touchdowns, with 1 interception, and was selected as the player of the game. Holt had 7 receptions for 128 yards. Manning was 22 of 41 for 342 yards and 3 touchdowns, with 2 interceptions. Mason had 6 catches for 113 yards, and Johnson had 5 receptions for 156 yards.

AFC	17	14	7	14 —	52
NFC	10	3	14	28 —	55

AFC — C. Johnson 90 pass from McNair (Vanderjagt kick)
AFC — Reed 23 return of blocked punt (Vanderjagt kick)
NFC — Alexander 12 run (Wilkins kick)
NFC — FG Wilkins 28
AFC — FG Vanderjagt 27
NFC — FG Wilkins 38
AFC — Harrison 50 pass from Manning (Vanderjagt kick)
AFC — Gonzalez 9 pass from Manning (Vanderjagt kick)
AFC — Lewis 22 run (Vanderjagt kick)
NFC — Holt 12 pass from Bulger (Wilkins kick)
NFC — McCardell 2 pass from Bulger (Wilkins kick)
AFC — Portis 23 pass from Green (Vanderjagt kick)
NFC — Crumpler 33 pass from Bulger (Wilkins kick)
NFC — Alexander 5 pass from Bulger (pass failed)
NFC — Bly 32 interception return (Green run)
NFC — Alexander 2 run (Wilkins kick)
AFC — Ward 10 pass from Manning (Vanderjagt kick)

2003 PRO FOOTBALL AWARDS/ALL-PRO TEAMS

2003 PRO FOOTBALL AWARDS

ASSOCIATED PRESS

Most Valuable Player	Peyton Manning and Steve McNair
Offensive Player of the Year	Jamal Lewis
Defensive Player of the Year	Ray Lewis
Offensive Rookie of the Year	Anquan Boldin
Defensive Rookie of the Year	Terrell Suggs
Coach of the Year	Bill Belichick
Comeback Player of the Year	Jon Kitna

THE SPORTING NEWS

Player of the Year	Peyton Manning
Rookie of the Year	Anquan Boldin
Coach of the Year	Bill Belichick

PRO FOOTBALL WEEKLY/PFWA

Executive of the Year	Scott Pioli
Most Valuable Player	Jamal Lewis
Defensive Most Valuable Player	Ray Lewis
Offensive Rookie of the Year	Anquan Boldin
Defensive Rookie of the Year	Terrell Suggs
Coach of the Year	Bill Belichick
Assistant Coach of the Year	Romeo Crennel
Golden Toe	Mike Vanderjagt
Comeback Player of the Year	Jon Kitna
Most Improved Player of the Year	Jon Kitna

FOOTBALL DIGEST

Offensive Player of the Year	Peyton Manning
Defensive Player of the Year	Ray Lewis
Offensive Rookie of the Year	Anquan Boldin
Defensive Rookie of the Year	Charles Tillman
Comeback Player of the Year	Aeneas Williams
Coach of the Year	Bill Belichick
Most Improved Player	Jon Kitna
Executive of the Year	Jerry Jones
Assistant Coach of the Year	Mike Nolan
Rookie Coach of the Year	Marvin Lewis

SPORTS ILLUSTRATED

Player of the Year	Steve McNair
Rookie of the Year	Anquan Boldin
Coach of the Year	Bill Belichick

MAXWELL CLUB PLAYER OF THE YEAR

(Bert Bell Trophy)	Peyton Manning

MAXWELL CLUB COACH OF THE YEAR

(Earle "Greasy" Neale Trophy)	Dick Vermeil

PEPSI ROOKIE OF THE YEAR

Rookie of the Year	Domanick Davis

WALTER PAYTON/ NFL MAN OF THE YEAR

Man of the Year	Will Shields

SUPER BOWL MOST VALUABLE PLAYER

Pete Rozelle Trophy	Tom Brady

AFC-NFC PRO BOWL PLAYER OF THE GAME

Dan McGuire Award	Marc Bulger

2003 ALL-PRO TEAMS

2003 PFW/PFWA ALL-PRO TEAM

Selected by *Pro Football Weekly* and the Professional Football Writers of America

Offense:	
Peyton Manning, Indianapolis	Quarterback
Priest Holmes, Kansas City	Running Back
Jamal Lewis, Baltimore	Running Back
Torry Holt, St. Louis	Wide Receiver
Randy Moss, Minnesota	Wide Receiver
Tony Gonzalez, Kansas City	Tight End
Jonathan Ogden, Baltimore	Tackle
Willie Roaf, Kansas City	Tackle
Steve Hutchinson, Seattle	Guard
Will Shields, Kansas City	Guard
Tom Nalen, Denver	Center
Defense:	
Leonard Little, St. Louis	End
Michael Strahan, New York Giants	End
Kris Jenkins, Carolina	Tackle
Richard Seymour, New England	Tackle
Keith Bulluck, Tennessee	Linebacker
Ray Lewis, Baltimore	Linebacker
Julian Peterson, San Francisco	Linebacker
Ty Law, New England	Cornerback
Chris McAlister, Baltimore	Cornerback
Ed Reed, Baltimore	Safety
Roy Williams, Dallas	Safety
Special Teams:	
Mike Vanderjagt, Indianapolis	Kicker
Shane Lechler, Oakland	Punter
Dante Hall, Kansas City	Kick Returner
Dante Hall, Kansas City	Punt Returner
Alex Bannister, Seattle	Special Teams Player

2003 ASSOCIATED PRESS ALL-PRO TEAM

Selected by the *Associated Press*

Offense:	
Peyton Manning, Indianapolis	Quarterback
Jamal Lewis, Baltimore	Running Back
Priest Holmes, Kansas City	Running Back
Torry Holt, St. Louis	Wide Receiver
Randy Moss, Minnesota	Wide Receiver
Tony Gonzalez, Kansas City	Tight End
Jonathan Ogden, Baltimore	Tackle
Willie Roaf, Kansas City	Tackle
Orlando Pace, St. Louis	Tackle
Steve Hutchinson, Seattle	Guard
Will Shields, Kansas City	Guard
Tom Nalen, Denver	Center
Defense:	
Leonard Little, St. Louis	End
Michael Strahan, New York Giants	End
Kris Jenkins, Carolina	Tackle
Richard Seymour, New England	Tackle
Keith Bulluck, Tennessee	Linebacker
Ray Lewis, Baltimore	Linebacker
Julian Peterson, San Francisco	Linebacker
Zach Thomas, Miami	Linebacker
Ty Law, New England	Cornerback
Chris McAlister, Baltimore	Cornerback
Rodney Harrison, New England	Safety
Roy Williams, Dallas	Safety
Specialists:	
Mike Vanderjagt, Indianapolis	Kicker
Dante Hall, Kansas City	Kick Returner
Shane Lechler, Oakland	Punter

2003 ALL-NFL TEAM

Selected by the *Associated Press, Pro Football Weekly,* and the Professional Football Writers of America

Offense:

Peyton Manning, Indianapolis (AP, PFW)	Quarterback
Priest Holmes, Kansas City (AP, PFW)	Running Back
Jamal Lewis, Baltimore (AP, PFW)	Running Back
Torry Holt, St. Louis (AP, PFW)	Wide Receiver
Randy Moss, Minnesota (AP, PFW)	Wide Receiver
Tony Gonzalez, Kansas City (AP, PFW)	Tight End
Jonathan Ogden, Baltimore (AP, PFW)	Tackle
Willie Roaf, Kansas City (AP, PFW)	Tackle
Orlando Pace, St. Louis (AP)	Tackle
Steve Hutchinson, Seattle (AP, PFW)	Guard
Will Shields, Kansas City (AP, PFW)	Guard
Tom Nalen, Denver (AP, PFW)	Center

Defense:

Leonard Little, St. Louis (AP, PFW)	End
Michael Strahan, N.Y. Giants (AP, PFW)	End
Kris Jenkins, Carolina (AP, PFW)	Tackle
Richard Seymour, New England (AP, PFW)	Tackle
Keith Bulluck, Tennessee (AP, PFW)	Linebacker
Ray Lewis, Baltimore (AP, PFW)	Linebacker
Julian Peterson, San Francisco (AP, PFW)	Linebacker
Zach Thomas, Miami (AP)	Linebacker
Ty Law, New England (AP, PFW)	Cornerback
Chris McAlister, Baltimore (AP, PFW)	Cornerback
Roy Williams, Dallas (AP, PFW)	Safety
Rodney Harrison, New England (AP)	Safety
Ed Reed, Baltimore (PFW)	Safety

Special Teams:

Mike Vanderjagt, Indianapolis (AP, PFW)	Kicker
Shane Lechler, Oakland (AP, PFW)	Punter
Dante Hall, Kansas City (AP, PFW)	Kick Returner
Dante Hall, Kansas City (PFW)	Punt Returner
Alex Bannister, Seattle (PFW)	Special Teams Player

2003 PFW/PFWA ALL-ROOKIE TEAM

Selected by *Pro Football Weekly* and the Professional Football Writers of America

Offense:

Byron Leftwich, Jacksonville	Quarterback
Domanick Davis, Houston	Running Back
Onterrio Smith, Minnesota	Running Back
Anquan Boldin, Arizona	Wide Receiver
Andre Johnson, Houston	Wide Receiver
Jason Witten, Dallas	Tight End
Jordan Gross, Carolina	Tackle
Wade Smith, Miami	Tackle
Vince Manuwai, Jacksonville	Guard
Eric Steinbach, Cincinnati	Guard
Dan Koppen, New England	Center

Defense:

Tyler Brayton, Oakland	Lineman
Dewayne Robertson, New York Jets	Lineman
Jonathan Sullivan, New Orleans	Lineman
Kevin Williams, Minnesota	Lineman
Nick Barnett, Green Bay	Linebacker
Terrell Suggs, Baltimore	Linebacker
Pisa Tinoisamoa, St. Louis	Linebacker
Terence Newman, Dallas	Cornerback
Marcus Trufant, Seattle	Cornerback
Ken Hamlin, Seattle	Safety
Eugene Wilson, New England	Safety

Special Teams:

Josh Brown, Seattle	Kicker
Eddie Johnson, Minnesota	Punter
Bethel Johnson, New England	Kick Returner
Zuriel Smith, Dallas	Punt Returner
David Tyree, New York Giants	Special Teams Player

2003 PLAYERS OF THE WEEK/MONTH

2003 AFC PLAYERS OF THE WEEK

	Offense		Defense		Special Teams	
Week 1	QB	Tommy Maddox, Pittsburgh	LB	Takeo Spikes, Buffalo	P-K	Craig Hentrich, Tennessee
Week 2	RB	Jamal Lewis, Baltimore	LB	Tedy Bruschi, New England	KR-PR	Dante Hall, Kansas City
Week 3	QB	Jake Plummer, Denver	DE	Adewale Ogunleye, Miami	KR-PR	Dante Hall, Kansas City
Week 4	QB	Peyton Manning, Indianapolis	LB	Rocky Boiman, Tennessee	KR-PR	Dante Hall, Kansas City
Week 5	WR	Marvin Harrison, Indianapolis	DE	Courtney Brown, Cleveland	KR-PR	Dante Hall, Kansas City
Week 6	QB	Trent Green, Kansas City	DT	Jason Ferguson, New York Jets	S	Ed Reed, Baltimore
Week 7	RB	LaDainian Tomlinson, San Diego	DE	Jevon Kearse, Tennessee	DE	Richard Seymour, New England
Week 8	TE	Daniel Graham, New England	LB	Brian Simmons, Cincinnati	KR-PR	Antwaan Randle El, Pittsburgh
Week 9	QB	Tom Brady, New England	DE	Dwight Freeney, Indianapolis	P	Chad Stanley, Houston
Week 10	QB	Doug Flutie, San Diego	LB	Jason Gildon, Pittsburgh	K	Doug Brien, New York Jets
Week 11	TE	Shannon Sharpe, Denver	CB	Phillip Buchanon, Oakland	PR	Peter Warrick, Cincinnati
Week 12	QB	Anthony Wright, Baltimore	DE	Jason Taylor, Miami	PR	Justin McCareins, Tennessee
Week 13	QB	Jay Fiedler, Miami	DE	Aaron Schobel, Buffalo	KR	Bethel Johnson, New England
Week 14	RB	Clinton Portis, Denver	LB	Tedy Bruschi, New England	K	Mike Vanderjagt, Indianapolis
Week 15	QB	Peyton Manning, Indianapolis	DT	Rod Coleman, Oakland	K	Jason Elam, Denver
Week 16	RB	Jamal Lewis, Baltimore	LB	Willie McGinest, New England	P	Craig Hentrich, Tennessee
Week 17	QB	Tom Brady, New England	LB	Ray Lewis, Baltimore	K	Gary Anderson, Tennessee

2003 AFC PLAYERS OF THE MONTH

	Offense		Defense		Special Teams	
September	QB	Peyton Manning, Indianapolis	CB	Marcus Coleman, Houston	KR-PR	Dante Hall, Kansas City
October	QB	Steve McNair, Tennessee	CB	Patrick Surtain, Miami	K	Mike Vanderjagt, Indianapolis
November	QB	Jon Kitna, Cincinnati	LB	Ray Lewis, Baltimore	K	Mike Vanderjagt, Indianapolis
December	RB	Jamal Lewis, Baltimore	LB	Mike Vrabel, New England	K	Mike Vanderjagt, Indianapolis

2003 NFC PLAYERS OF THE WEEK

	Offense		Defense		Special Teams	
Week 1	QB	Joey Harrington, Detroit	S	Corey Chavous, Minnesota	RB	Terry Jackson, San Francisco
Week 2	RB	Stephen Davis, Carolina	S	Ken Hamlin, Seattle	K	Billy Cundiff, Dallas
Week 3	QB	Kerry Collins, New York Giants	S	Dexter Jackson, Arizona	P	Tom Tupa, Tampa Bay
Week 4	RB	Ahman Green, Green Bay	CB	Champ Bailey, Washington	K	David Akers, Philadelphia
Week 5	RB	Stephen Davis, Carolina	CB	Ahmed Plummer, San Francisco	K	Paul Edinger, Chicago
Week 6	QB	Brad Johnson, Tampa Bay	DE	Simeon Rice, Tampa Bay	WR	Randal Williams, Dallas
Week 7	QB	Aaron Brooks, New Orleans	DE	Lance Johnstone, Minnesota	PR	Brian Westbrook, Philadelphia
Week 8	RB	Stephen Davis, Carolina	DE	Michael Strahan, New York Giants	KR	Jerry Azumah, Chicago
Week 9	WR	Amani Toomer, New York Giants	DE	Willie Whitehead, New Orleans	KR	Cedrick Wilson, San Francisco
Week 10	RB	Warrick Dunn, Atlanta	DT	Brian Young, St. Louis	K	Jason Hanson, Detroit
Week 11	QB	Donovan McNabb, Philadelphia	LB	Nick Barnett, Green Bay	PR	Bobby Engram, Seattle
Week 12	RB	Ahman Green, Green Bay	CB	Brian Williams, Minnesota	K	Paul Edinger, Chicago
Week 13	RB	Deuce McAllister, New Orleans	DE	Leonard Little, St. Louis	K	David Akers, Philadelphia
Week 14	QB	Jeff Garcia, San Francisco	S	Aeneas Williams, St. Louis	K	Ryan Longwell, Green Bay
Week 15	QB	Aaron Brooks, New Orleans	CB	Terence Newman, Dallas	K	John Kasay, Carolina
Week 16	QB	Brett Favre, Green Bay	S	Tony Parrish, San Francisco	K	Billy Cundiff, Dallas
Week 17	RB	Ahman Green, Green Bay	LB	Chad Brown, Seattle	DE	Osi Umenyiora, New York Giants

2003 NFC PLAYERS OF THE MONTH

	Offense		Defense		Special Teams	
September	QB	Daunte Culpepper, Minnesota	DE	Mike Rucker, Carolina	K	Jeff Wilkins, St. Louis
October	WR	Torry Holt, St. Louis	LB	Mark Simoneau, Philadelphia	K	John Kasay, Carolina
November	QB	Donovan McNabb, Philadelphia	S	Adam Archuleta, St. Louis	K	Jason Hanson, Detroit
December	QB	Brett Favre, Green Bay	DE	Grant Wistrom, St. Louis	K	Jeff Wilkins, St. Louis

2003 NFL PLAYOFF PLAYERS OF THE WEEK

	Offense		Defense		Special Teams	
Wild Card	QB	Peyton Manning, Indianapolis	CB	Al Harris, Green Bay	K	Gary Anderson, Tennessee
Divisional	QB	Donovan McNabb, Philadelphia	CB	Ricky Manning Jr., Carolina	DT	Richard Seymour, New England
Championship	RB	Antowain Smith, New England	CB	Ricky Manning Jr., Carolina	K	Adam Vinatieri, New England

2003 NFL ROOKIES OF THE MONTH

	Offense (College)		Defense (College)	
September	WR	Anquan Boldin, Arizona (Florida State)	LB	Terrell Suggs, Baltimore (Arizona State)
October	RB	Domanick Davis, Houston (LSU)	LB	Nick Barnett, Green Bay (Oregon State)
November	WR	Anquan Boldin, Arizona (Florida State)	CB	Rashean Mathis, Jacksonville (Bethune-Cookman)
December	QB	Byron Leftwich, Jacksonville (Marshall)	DE	Kevin Williams, Minnesota (Oklahoma State)

TEN BEST RUSHING PERFORMANCES, 2003

		Att.	Yards	TD
1.	Jamal Lewis Baltimore vs. Cleveland, Sept. 14	30	295	2
2.	LaDainian Tomlinson San Diego vs. Oakland, Dec. 28	31	243	2
3.	Clinton Portis Denver vs. Kansas City, Dec. 7	22	218	5
	Ahman Green Green Bay vs. Denver, Dec. 28	20	218	2
5.	Jamal Lewis Baltimore vs. Cleveland, Dec. 21	22	205	2
6.	LaDainian Tomlinson San Diego vs. Cleveland, Oct. 19	26	200	1
7.	Fred Taylor Jacksonville vs. New Orleans, Dec. 21	34	194	1
8.	Ahman Green Green Bay vs. Philadelphia, Nov. 10	29	192	1
9.	Troy Hambrick Dallas vs. Washington, Dec. 14	33	189	0
10.	LaDainian Tomlinson San Diego vs. Oakland, Sept. 28	28	187	1

100-YARD RUSHING PERFORMANCES, 2003

First Week

Tiki Barber, New York Giants — 146 yards vs. St. Louis
Clinton Portis, Denver — 120 yards vs. Cincinnati
Stephen Davis, Carolina — 111 yards vs. Jacksonville
Shaun Alexander, Seattle — 108 yards vs. New Orleans

Second Week

Jamal Lewis, Baltimore — 295 yards vs. Cleveland
Ahman Green, Green Bay — 160 yards vs. Detroit
Stephen Davis, Carolina — 142 yards vs. Tampa Bay
Clinton Portis, Denver — 129 yards vs. San Diego
Ricky Williams, Miami — 125 yards vs. New York Jets
Priest Holmes, Kansas City — 122 yards vs. Pittsburgh
Edgerrin James, Indianapolis — 120 yards vs. Tennessee
Moe Williams, Minnesota — 108 yards vs. Chicago

Third Week

Ricky Williams, Miami — 153 yards vs. Buffalo
Jamal Lewis, Baltimore — 132 yards vs. San Diego
Tiki Barber, New York Giants — 126 yards vs. Washington
Fred Taylor, Jacksonville — 126 yards vs. Indianapolis
LaDainian Tomlinson, San Diego — 105 yards vs. Baltimore
Eddie George, Tennessee — 100 yards vs. New Orleans

Fourth Week

LaDainian Tomlinson, San Diego — 187 yards vs. Oakland
Ahman Green, Green Bay — 176 yards vs. Chicago
Stephen Davis, Carolina — 153 yards vs. Atlanta
Troy Hambrick, Dallas — 127 yards vs. New York Jets
Jamal Lewis, Baltimore — 115 yards vs. Kansas City
Anthony Thomas, Chicago — 110 yards vs. Green Bay
Deuce McAllister, New Orleans — 101 yards vs. Indianapolis
T.J. Duckett, Atlanta — 100 yards vs. Carolina

Fifth Week

Stephen Davis, Carolina — 159 yards vs. New Orleans
Clinton Portis, Denver — 141 yards vs. Kansas City
Deuce McAllister, New Orleans — 124 yards vs. Carolina
Anthony Thomas, Chicago — 123 yards vs. Oakland
Ahman Green, Green Bay — 118 yards vs. Seattle
William Green, Cleveland — 115 yards vs. Pittsburgh
Michael Pittman, Tampa Bay — 106 yards vs. Indianapolis
Shaun Alexander, Seattle — 102 yards vs. Green Bay

Sixth Week

William Green, Cleveland — 145 yards vs. Oakland
Ahman Green, Green Bay — 139 yards vs. Kansas City
Jamal Lewis, Baltimore — 131 yards vs. Arizona
Deuce McAllister, New Orleans — 116 yards vs. Chicago

Seventh Week

LaDainian Tomlinson, San Diego — 200 yards vs. Cleveland
Travis Henry, Buffalo — 167 yards vs. Washington
Domanick Davis, Houston — 129 yards vs. New York Jets
Priest Holmes, Kansas City — 123 yards vs. Oakland
Garrison Hearst, San Francisco — 117 yards vs. Tampa Bay
Clinton Portis, Denver — 117 yards vs. Minnesota
Deuce McAllister, New Orleans — 116 yards vs. Atlanta
Shaun Alexander, Seattle — 101 yards vs. Chicago
Jamal Lewis, Baltimore — 101 yards vs. Cincinnati

Eighth Week

Stephen Davis, Carolina — 178 yards vs. New Orleans
Marcel Shipp, Arizona — 165 yards vs. San Francisco
Jamal Lewis, Baltimore — 134 yards vs. Denver
Travis Henry, Buffalo — 124 yards vs. Kansas City
Michael Pittman, Tampa Bay — 113 yards vs. Dallas
Curtis Martin, New York Jets — 110 yards vs. Philadelphia
Domanick Davis, Houston — 109 yards vs. Indianapolis
Edgerrin James, Indianapolis — 104 yards vs. Houston
Rudi Johnson, Cincinnati — 101 yards vs. Seattle
Deuce McAllister, New Orleans — 101 yards vs. Carolina
Correll Buckhalter, Philadelphia — 100 yards vs. New York Jets

Ninth Week

Stephen Davis, Carolina — 153 yards vs. Houston
Marcel Shipp, Arizona — 141 yards vs. Cincinnati
Ahman Green, Green Bay — 137 yards vs. Minnesota
Clinton Portis, Denver — 111 yards vs. New England
Anthony Thomas, Chicago — 111 yards vs. San Diego
Deuce McAllister, New Orleans — 110 yards vs. Tampa Bay
Curtis Martin, New York Jets — 108 yards vs. New York Giants
Troy Hambrick, Dallas — 100 yards vs. Washington

Tenth Week

Ahman Green, Green Bay — 192 yards vs. Philadelphia
Rudi Johnson, Cincinnati — 182 yards vs. Houston
Warrick Dunn, Atlanta — 178 yards vs. New York Giants
LaDainian Tomlinson, San Diego — 162 yards vs. Minnesota
Fred Taylor, Jacksonville — 152 yards vs. Indianapolis
Tiki Barber, New York Giants — 120 yards vs. Atlanta
Jamal Lewis, Baltimore — 111 yards vs. St. Louis
Domanick Davis, Houston — 104 yards vs. Cincinnati

Eleventh Week

Deuce McAllister, New Orleans — 173 yards vs. Atlanta
Rudi Johnson, Cincinnati — 165 yards vs. Kansas City
Warrick Dunn, Atlanta — 162 yards vs. New Orleans
Travis Henry, Buffalo — 149 yards vs. Houston
Thomas Jones, Tampa Bay — 134 yards vs. Green Bay
Edgerrin James, Indianapolis — 127 yards vs. New York Jets
Tiki Barber, New York Giants — 111 yards vs. Philadelphia
Shaun Alexander, Seattle — 110 yards vs. Detroit
Ahman Green, Green Bay — 109 yards vs. Tampa Bay
Tyrone Wheatley, Oakland — 109 yards vs. Minnesota
Clinton Portis, Denver — 106 yards vs. San Diego
Curtis Martin, New York Jets — 105 yards vs. Indianapolis
Ricky Williams, Miami — 105 yards vs. Baltimore
Marshall Faulk, St. Louis — 103 yards vs. Chicago

Twelfth Week

Deuce McAllister, New Orleans — 184 yards vs. Philadelphia
Clinton Portis, Denver — 165 yards vs. Chicago
Ahman Green, Green Bay — 154 yards vs. San Francisco
Fred Taylor, Jacksonville — 119 yards vs. New York Jets
Jamal Lewis, Baltimore — 117 yards vs. Seattle
Eddie George, Tennessee — 115 yards vs. Atlanta
Corey Dillon, Cincinnati — 108 yards vs. San Diego
Edgerrin James, Indianapolis — 108 yards vs. Buffalo
Ricky Williams, Miami — 107 yards vs. Washington
Marshall Faulk, St. Louis — 100 yards vs. Arizona

2003 BEST PERFORMANCES

Thirteenth Week

Clinton Portis, Denver 170 yards vs. Oakland
Deuce McAllister, New Orleans 165 yards vs. Washington
Priest Holmes, Kansas City 162 yards vs. San Diego
Brock Forsey, Chicago 134 yards vs. Arizona
Shaun Alexander, Seattle 127 yards vs. Cleveland
Fred Taylor, Jacksonville 118 yards vs. Tampa Bay
Trung Canidate, Washington 115 yards vs. New Orleans
Domanick Davis, Houston 115 yards vs. Philadelphia
Travis Henry, Buffalo 113 yards vs. New York Giants
Marshall Faulk, St. Louis 108 yards vs. Minnesota
LaDainian Tomlinson, San Diego 106 yards vs. Kansas City
Ricky Williams, Miami 104 yards vs. Dallas
Domanick Davis, Houston 101 yards vs. Atlanta

Fourteenth Week

Clinton Portis, Denver 218 yards vs. Kansas City
Jamal Lewis, Baltimore 180 yards vs. Cincinnati
Travis Henry, Buffalo 169 yards vs. New York Jets
Fred Taylor, Jacksonville 163 yards vs. Houston
Kevan Barlow, San Francisco 154 yards vs. Arizona
Michael Vick, Atlanta 141 yards vs. Carolina
Correll Buckhalter, Philadelphia 115 yards vs. Dallas
Jerome Bettis, Pittsburgh 106 yards vs. Oakland
Michael Bennett, Minnesota 103 yards vs. Seattle
Marshall Faulk, St. Louis 102 yards vs. Cleveland
Jamel White, Cleveland 101 yards vs. St. Louis

Fifteenth Week

Troy Hambrick, Dallas 189 yards vs. Washington
Rudi Johnson, Cincinnati 174 yards vs. San Francisco
Curtis Martin, New York Jets 174 yards vs. Pittsburgh
Onterrio Smith, Minnesota 148 yards vs. Chicago
Clinton Portis, Denver 139 yards vs. Cleveland
Thomas Jones, Tampa Bay 134 yards vs. Houston
Shaun Alexander, Seattle 126 yards vs. St. Louis
Edgerrin James, Indianapolis 126 yards vs. Atlanta
Jamal Lewis, Baltimore 125 yards vs. Oakland
Ricky Williams, Miami 107 yards vs. Philadelphia
Shawn Bryson, Detroit 105 yards vs. Kansas City

Sixteenth Week

Jamal Lewis, Baltimore 205 yards vs. Cleveland
Fred Taylor, Jacksonville 194 yards vs. New Orleans
Kevan Barlow, San Francisco 154 yards vs. Philadelphia
Onterrio Smith, Minnesota 146 yards vs. Kansas City
Anthony Thomas, Chicago 141 yards vs. Washington
Quentin Griffin, Denver 136 yards vs. Indianapolis
Shaun Alexander, Seattle 135 yards vs. Arizona
Ahman Green, Green Bay 127 yards vs. Oakland
Marshall Faulk, St. Louis 121 yards vs. Cincinnati
Antowain Smith, New England 121 yards vs. New York Jets
Jerome Bettis, Pittsburgh 115 yards vs. San Diego
Ricky Williams, Miami 111 yards vs. Buffalo

Seventeenth Week

LaDainian Tomlinson, San Diego 243 yards vs. Oakland
Ahman Green, Green Bay 218 yards vs. Denver
Lee Suggs, Cleveland 186 yards vs. Cincinnati
Edgerrin James, Indianapolis 171 yards vs. Houston
Fred Taylor, Jacksonville 121 yards vs. Atlanta
Jamal Lewis, Baltimore 114 yards vs. Pittsburgh

Times 100 or More (151)

Lewis, 12; Portis, 10; A. Green, McAllister, 9; Alexander, Taylor, R. Williams, 7; S. Davis, James, Tomlinson, 6; D. Davis, Faulk, Henry, 5; Barber, Johnson, Martin, Thomas, 4; Hambrick, Holmes, 3; Barlow, Bettis, Buckhalter, Dunn, George, W. Green, Jones, Pittman, Shipp, O. Smith, 2.

TEN BEST PASSING PERFORMANCES, 2003

		Att.	Comp.	Yards	TD
1.	Steve McNair Tennessee vs. Houston, Oct. 12	27	18	421	3
2.	Peyton Manning Indianapolis vs. New York Jets, Nov. 16	36	27	401	1
3.	Trent Green Kansas City vs. Green Bay, Oct. 12	45	27	400	3
4.	Brett Favre Green Bay vs. Oakland, Dec. 22	30	22	399	4
5.	Trent Green Kansas City vs. Denver, Dec. 7	47	34	397	1
6.	Daunte Culpepper Minnesota vs. Oakland, Nov. 16	49	27	396	1
7.	Kelly Holcomb Cleveland vs. Arizona, Nov. 16	35	29	392	1
8.	Peyton Manning Indianapolis vs. Tampa Bay, Oct. 6	47	34	386	2
9.	Marc Bulger St. Louis vs. San Francisco, Nov. 2	42	26	378	1
10.	Marc Bulger St. Louis vs. Pittsburgh, Oct. 26	37	22	375	1
	Kerry Collins New York Giants vs. Minnesota, Oct. 26	39	23	375	2

300-YARD PASSING PERFORMANCES, 2003

First Week

Jeff Blake, Arizona 358 yards vs. Detroit
Kurt Warner, St. Louis 342 yards vs. New York Giants

Second Week

Vinny Testaverde, New York Jets 373 yards vs. Miami
Patrick Ramsey, Washington 356 yards vs. Atlanta
Brad Johnson, Tampa Bay 339 yards vs. Carolina
Tommy Maddox, Pittsburgh 336 yards vs. Kansas City
Quincy Carter, Dallas 321 yards vs. New York Giants
Drew Bledsoe, Buffalo 314 yards vs. Jacksonville
Jon Kitna, Cincinnati 303 yards vs. Oakland

Third Week

Patrick Ramsey, Washington 348 yards vs. New York Giants

Fourth Week

Rich Gannon, Oakland 348 yards vs. San Diego
Tommy Maddox, Pittsburgh 332 yards vs. Tennessee
Peyton Manning, Indianapolis 314 yards vs. New Orleans

Fifth Week

Peyton Manning, Indianapolis 386 yards vs. Tampa Bay
Steve McNair, Tennessee 360 yards vs. New England
Doug Johnson, Atlanta 352 yards vs. Minnesota
Byron Leftwich, Jacksonville 336 yards vs. San Diego
Brad Johnson, Tampa Bay 318 yards vs. Indianapolis

Sixth Week

Steve McNair, Tennessee 421 yards vs. Houston
Trent Green, Kansas City 400 yards vs. Green Bay
David Carr, Houston 371 yards vs. Tennessee
Marc Bulger, St. Louis 352 yards vs. Atlanta
Kerry Collins, New York Giants 314 yards vs. New England

Seventh Week

Jake Delhomme, Carolina 362 yards vs. Tennessee
Aaron Brooks, New Orleans 352 yards vs. Atlanta
Kyle Boller, Baltimore 302 yards vs. Cincinnati

Eighth Week

Marc Bulger, St. Louis 375 yards vs. Pittsburgh
Kerry Collins, New York Giants 375 yards vs. Minnesota
Matt Hasselbeck, Seattle 344 yards vs. Cincinnati

Ninth Week

Marc Bulger, St. Louis 378 yards vs. San Francisco
Tom Brady, New England 350 yards vs. Denver
Brad Johnson, Tampa Bay 323 yards vs. New Orleans
Donovan McNabb, Philadelphia 312 yards vs. Atlanta
Kerry Collins, New York Giants 303 yards vs. New York Jets

Tenth Week

Daunte Culpepper, Minnesota	370 yards vs. San Diego
Trent Green, Kansas City	368 yards vs. Cleveland
Peyton Manning, Indianapolis	347 yards vs. Jacksonville
Jeff Blake, Arizona	307 yards vs. Pittsburgh
Eleventh Week	
Peyton Manning, Indianapolis	401 yards vs. New York Jets
Daunte Culpepper, Minnesota	396 yards vs. Oakland
Kelly Holcomb, Cleveland	392 yards vs. Arizona
Tommy Maddox, Pittsburgh	327 yards vs. San Francisco
Jake Delhomme, Carolina	317 yards vs. Washington
Donovan McNabb, Philadelphia	314 yards vs. New York Giants
Trent Green, Kansas City	313 yards vs. Cincinnati
Twelfth Week	
Tom Brady, New England	368 yards vs. Houston
Matt Hasselbeck, Seattle	333 yards vs. Baltimore
Marc Bulger, St. Louis	329 yards vs. Arizona
Anthony Wright, Baltimore	319 yards vs. Seattle
Thirteenth Week	
Daunte Culpepper, Minnesota	330 yards vs. St. Louis
Matt Hasselbeck, Seattle	328 yards vs. Cleveland
Tommy Maddox, Pittsburgh	313 yards vs. Cincinnati
Fourteenth Week	
Trent Green, Kansas City	397 yards vs. Denver
Fifteenth Week	
Drew Brees, San Diego	363 yards vs. Green Bay
Jeff Garcia, San Francisco	344 yards vs. Cincinnati
Trent Green, Kansas City	341 yards vs. Detroit
Sixteenth Week	
Brett Favre, Green Bay	399 yards vs. Oakland
Brad Johnson, Tampa Bay	346 yards vs. Atlanta
Seventeenth Week	
Jay Fiedler, Miami	328 yards vs. New York Jets
Matt Hasselbeck, Seattle	315 yards vs. San Francisco

Times 300 or more (60)
Green, 5; Bulger, Hasselbeck, B. Johnson, Maddox, Manning, 4; Collins, Culpepper, 3; Blake, Brady, Delhomme, McNabb, McNair, Ramsey, 2.

TEN BEST RECEIVING PERFORMANCES, 2003

	No.	Yards	TD
1. Anquan Boldin Arizona vs. Detroit, Sept. 7	10	217	2
2. Torry Holt St. Louis vs. San Francisco, Nov. 2	11	200	1
3. Muhsin Muhammad Carolina vs. Washington, Nov. 16	9	189	0
4. David Boston San Diego vs. Jacksonville, Oct. 5	14	181	2
5. Laveranues Coles Washington vs. Atlanta, Sept. 14	11	180	1
6. Derrick Mason Tennessee vs. Houston, Oct. 12	6	177	3
7. Marvin Harrison Indianapolis vs. Tampa Bay, Oct. 6	11	176	2
8. Torry Holt St. Louis vs. Pittsburgh, Oct. 26	7	174	1
9. Randy Moss Minnesota vs. San Francisco, Sept. 28	8	172	3
10. Peerless Price Atlanta vs. Minnesota, Oct. 5	12	168	1

100-YARD RECEIVING PERFORMANCES, 2003

First Week

Anquan Boldin, Arizona	217 yards vs. Detroit
Randy Moss, Minnesota	150 yards vs. Green Bay
Joey Galloway, Dallas	139 yards vs. Atlanta
Isaac Bruce, St. Louis	120 yards vs. New York Giants
Chris Chambers, Miami	118 yards vs. Houston
Plaxico Burress, Pittsburgh	116 yards vs. Baltimore
Charlie Garner, Oakland	112 yards vs. Tennessee
Terrell Owens, San Francisco	112 yards vs. Chicago
Torry Holt, St. Louis	111 yards vs. New York Giants
Laveranues Coles, Washington	106 yards vs. New York Jets
Donte' Stallworth, New Orleans	101 yards vs. Seattle
Second Week	
Laveranues Coles, Washington	180 yards vs. Atlanta
Hines Ward, Pittsburgh	146 yards vs. Kansas City
Santana Moss, New York Jets	142 yards vs. Miami
Darrell Jackson, Seattle	133 yards vs. Arizona
Eric Moulds, Buffalo	133 yards vs. Jacksonville
Chad Johnson, Cincinnati	131 yards vs. Oakland
Amani Toomer, New York Giants	126 yards vs. Dallas
Rod Gardner, Washington	118 yards vs. Atlanta
Plaxico Burress, Pittsburgh	115 yards vs. Kansas City
Terry Glenn, Dallas	113 yards vs. New York Giants
Joe Horn, New Orleans	111 yards vs. Houston
Peter Warrick, Cincinnati	109 yards vs. Oakland
Keyshawn Johnson, Tampa Bay	102 yards vs. Carolina
Third Week	
Reggie Wayne, Indianapolis	141 yards vs. Jacksonville
Kevin Johnson, Cleveland	109 yards vs. San Francisco
Ashley Lelie, Denver	108 yards vs. Oakland
Drew Bennett, Tennessee	105 yards vs. New Orleans
Laveranues Coles, Washington	105 yards vs. New York Giants
Andre Johnson, Houston	102 yards vs. Kansas City
Fourth Week	
Randy Moss, Minnesota	172 yards vs. San Francisco
Marvin Harrison, Indianapolis	158 yards vs. New Orleans
Torry Holt, St. Louis	133 yards vs. Arizona
Jerry Rice, Oakland	126 yards vs. San Diego
Eric Moulds, Buffalo	114 yards vs. Philadelphia
Troy Edwards, Jacksonville	111 yards vs. Houston
Tim Brown, Oakland	110 yards vs. San Diego
Joey Galloway, Dallas	100 yards vs. New York Jets

2003 BEST PERFORMANCES

Fifth Week

David Boston, San Diego	181 yards vs. Jacksonville
Marvin Harrison, Indianapolis	176 yards vs. Tampa Bay
Peerless Price, Atlanta	168 yards vs. Minnesota
Jimmy Smith, Jacksonville	137 yards vs. San Diego
Rod Smith, Denver	130 yards vs. Kansas City
Jeremy Shockey, New York Giants	110 yards vs. Miami
Keenan McCardell, Tampa Bay	106 yards vs. Indianapolis
Terry Glenn, Dallas	104 yards vs. Arizona

Sixth Week

Derrick Mason, Tennessee	177 yards vs. Houston
Torry Holt, St. Louis	161 yards vs. Atlanta
Corey Bradford, Houston	127 yards vs. Tennessee
Tony Gonzalez, Kansas City	121 yards vs. Green Bay
Marvin Harrison, Indianapolis	119 yards vs. Carolina
Johnnie Morton, Kansas City	109 yards vs. Green Bay
Steve Smith, Carolina	103 yards vs. Indianapolis

Seventh Week

Terrell Owens, San Francisco	152 yards vs. Tampa Bay
Randy Moss, Minnesota	151 yards vs. Denver
Steve Smith, Carolina	151 yards vs. Tennessee
Travis Taylor, Baltimore	138 yards vs. Cincinnati
Joe Horn, New Orleans	133 yards vs. Atlanta
Troy Brown, New England	131 yards vs. Miami
Chad Johnson, Cincinnati	130 yards vs. Baltimore
Isaac Bruce, St. Louis	129 yards vs. Green Bay
Todd Heap, Baltimore	129 yards vs. Cincinnati
Keenan McCardell, Tampa Bay	119 yards vs. San Francisco
Santana Moss, New York Jets	111 yards vs. Houston
Josh Reed, Buffalo	109 yards vs. Washington
Randy McMichael, Miami	102 yards vs. New England

Eighth Week

Torry Holt, St. Louis	174 yards vs. Pittsburgh
Randy Moss, Minnesota	125 yards vs. New York Giants
Daniel Graham, New England	110 yards vs. Cleveland
Dante Hall, Kansas City	107 yards vs. Buffalo
Marvin Harrison, Indianapolis	100 yards vs. Houston
Ike Hilliard, New York Giants	100 yards vs. Minnesota
Steve Smith, Carolina	100 yards vs. New Orleans

Ninth Week

Torry Holt, St. Louis	200 yards vs. San Francisco
Amani Toomer, New York Giants	127 yards vs. New York Jets
Keyshawn Johnson, Tampa Bay	123 yards vs. New Orleans
Santana Moss, New York Jets	121 yards vs. New York Giants
Deion Branch, New England	107 yards vs. Denver

Tenth Week

Santana Moss, New York Jets	146 yards vs. Oakland
Ricky Proehl, Carolina	133 yards vs. Tampa Bay
Moe Williams, Minnesota	126 yards vs. San Diego
Laveranues Coles, Washington	125 yards vs. Seattle
Randy Moss, Minnesota	120 yards vs. San Diego
Anquan Boldin, Arizona	118 yards vs. Pittsburgh
Keenan McCardell, Tampa Bay	118 yards vs. Carolina
Eddie Kennison, Kansas City	115 yards vs. Cleveland

Eleventh Week

Muhsin Muhammad, Carolina	189 yards vs. Washington
Terrell Owens, San Francisco	155 yards vs. Pittsburgh
Reggie Wayne, Indianapolis	141 yards vs. New York Jets
Torry Holt, St. Louis	124 yards vs. Chicago
Andre Johnson, Houston	122 yards vs. Buffalo
Andre Davis, Cleveland	117 yards vs. Arizona
Quincy Morgan, Cleveland	116 yards vs. Arizona
Kelly Campbell, Minnesota	115 yards vs. Oakland
Peter Warrick, Cincinnati	114 yards vs. Kansas City
David Tyree, New York Giants	106 yards vs. Philadelphia
Shannon Sharpe, Denver	101 yards vs. San Diego
Dallas Clark, Indianapolis	100 yards vs. New York Jets

Twelfth Week

Darrell Jackson, Seattle	146 yards vs. Baltimore
Torry Holt, St. Louis	145 yards vs. Arizona
David Boston, San Diego	139 yards vs. Cincinnati
Marcus Robinson, Baltimore	131 yards vs. Seattle
Warrick Dunn, Atlanta	129 yards vs. Tennessee
Anquan Boldin, Arizona	123 yards vs. St. Louis
Boo Williams, New Orleans	110 yards vs. Philadelphia
Kevin Faulk, New England	108 yards vs. Houston
Chad Johnson, Cincinnati	107 yards vs. San Diego
Priest Holmes, Kansas City	100 yards vs. Oakland

Thirteenth Week

Randy Moss, Minnesota	160 yards vs. St. Louis
Hines Ward, Pittsburgh	149 yards vs. Cincinnati
Jimmy Smith, Jacksonville	136 yards vs. Tampa Bay
Derrick Mason, Tennessee	133 yards vs. New York Jets
Koren Robinson, Seattle	122 yards vs. Cleveland
Chad Johnson, Cincinnati	117 yards vs. Pittsburgh
Plaxico Burress, Pittsburgh	112 yards vs. Cincinnati
Amani Toomer, New York Giants	110 yards vs. Buffalo
Torry Holt, St. Louis	102 yards vs. Minnesota
Darrell Jackson, Seattle	102 yards vs. Cleveland
Justin Gage, Chicago	100 yards vs. Arizona

Fourteenth Week

LaDainian Tomlinson, San Diego	148 yards vs. Detroit
Randy Moss, Minnesota	133 yards vs. Seattle
Dante Hall, Kansas City	124 yards vs. Denver
Marvin Harrison, Indianapolis	124 yards vs. Tennessee
Anquan Boldin, Arizona	123 yards vs. San Francisco
Joe Horn, New Orleans	118 yards vs. Tampa Bay
Marty Booker, Chicago	115 yards vs. Green Bay

Fifteenth Week

LaDainian Tomlinson, San Diego	144 yards vs. Green Bay
Derrick Mason, Tennessee	137 yards vs. Buffalo
Joe Horn, New Orleans	133 yards vs. New York Giants
Terrell Owens, San Francisco	127 yards vs. Cincinnati
Antonio Gates, San Diego	117 yards vs. Green Bay
Marvin Harrison, Indianapolis	117 yards vs. Atlanta
Dennis Northcutt, Cleveland	115 yards vs. Denver
Donald Driver, Green Bay	112 yards vs. San Diego
Derrick Blaylock, Kansas City	106 yards vs. Detroit
Torry Holt, St. Louis	100 yards vs. Seattle

Sixteenth Week

Jerry Rice, Oakland	159 yards vs. Green Bay
Torry Holt, St. Louis	124 yards vs. Cincinnati
Javon Walker, Green Bay	124 yards vs. Oakland
Anquan Boldin, Arizona	122 yards vs. Seattle
Keenan McCardell, Tampa Bay	122 yards vs. Atlanta
Todd Pinkston, Philadelphia	121 yards vs. San Francisco
Chad Johnson, Cincinnati	115 yards vs. St. Louis
Ashley Lelie, Denver	115 yards vs. Indianapolis
Randy Moss, Minnesota	111 yards vs. Kansas City
Andre Johnson, Houston	108 yards vs. Tennessee
Kassim Osgood, San Diego	102 yards vs. Pittsburgh

Seventeenth Week

Chris Chambers, Miami	153 yards vs. New York Jets
Donte' Stallworth, New Orleans	114 yards vs. Dallas
Marcus Robinson, Baltimore	102 yards vs. Pittsburgh

Times 100 or more (150)

Holt, 10; R. Moss, 8; Harrison, 6; Boldin, C. Johnson, 5; Coles, Horn, McCardell, S. Moss, Owens, 4; Burress, Jackson, A. Johnson, Mason, S. Smith, Toomer, 3; Boston, Bruce, Chambers, Galloway, Glenn, Hall, Key. Johnson, Lelie, Moulds, Rice, M. Robinson, J. Smith, Stallworth, Tomlinson, Ward, Warrick, Wayne, 2.

TOP QUARTERBACK SACK PERFORMANCES, 2003

(2.5 or More Sacks Per Game Needed to Qualify)

First Week

Vonnie Holliday, Kansas City	3.0 vs. San Diego
Mike Rucker, Carolina	3.0 vs. Jacksonville

Second Week

None

Third Week

Bertrand Berry, Denver	2.5 vs. Oakland
Reggie Hayward, Denver	2.5 vs. Oakland

Fourth Week

None

Fifth Week

Duane Clemons, Cincinnati	3.0 vs. Buffalo

Sixth Week

Simeon Rice, Tampa Bay	4.0 vs. Washington
Adewale Ogunleye, Miami	3.0 vs. Jacksonville

Seventh Week

None

Eighth Week

John Abraham, New York Jets	3.5 vs. Philadelphia
Mike Vrabel, New England	3.0 vs. Cleveland

Ninth Week

Dwight Freeney, Indianapolis	3.0 vs. Miami
Willie Whitehead, New Orleans	3.0 vs. Tampa Bay

Tenth Week

Andra Davis, Cleveland	4.0 vs. Kansas City
Jason Gildon, Pittsburgh	3.0 vs. Arizona

Eleventh Week

None

Twelfth Week

None

Thirteenth Week

Leonard Little, St. Louis	4.0 vs. Minnesota
Aaron Schobel, Buffalo	3.0 vs. New York Giants

Fourteenth Week

Bertrand Berry, Denver	3.0 vs. Kansas City
Simeon Rice, Tampa Bay	3.0 vs. New Orleans
Kimo von Oelhoffen, Pittsburgh	3.0 vs. Oakland

Fifteenth Week

Greg Spires, Tampa Bay	2.5 vs. Houston

Sixteenth Week

Kabeer Gbaja-Biamila, Green Bay	3.0 vs. Oakland
Michael Strahan, New York Giants	3.0 vs. Dallas
Jason Taylor, Miami	3.0 vs. Buffalo
Grant Wistrom, St. Louis	2.5 vs. Cincinnati

Seventeenth Week

Kevin Williams, Minnesota	3.0 vs. Arizona
Marques Douglas, Baltimore	2.5 vs. Pittsburgh

2003 TEAM STATISTICS

AMERICAN FOOTBALL CONFERENCE OFFENSE

	Balt.	Buff.	Cin.	Cle.	Den.	Hou.	Ind.	Jax.	KC	Mia.	NE	NYJ	Oak.	Pitt.	SD	Tenn.
First Downs	259	268	313	276	334	237	348	305	348	266	294	274	258	275	290	310
Rushing	115	96	101	91	133	86	104	118	120	99	91	78	98	77	117	84
Passing	121	150	181	153	162	127	212	163	201	145	177	181	140	174	146	211
Penalty	23	22	31	32	39	24	32	24	27	22	26	15	20	24	27	15
Rushes	552	427	461	412	543	421	453	481	446	487	473	409	423	446	417	486
Net Yds. Gained	2674	1664	1987	1670	2629	1651	1695	2073	1929	1817	1607	1635	1822	1488	2146	1623
Avg. Gain	4.8	3.9	4.1	4.1	4.8	3.9	3.7	4.3	4.3	3.7	3.4	4.0	4.3	3.3	5.1	3.3
Avg. Yds. per Game	167.1	104.0	124.2	104.4	164.3	103.2	105.9	129.6	120.6	113.6	100.4	102.2	113.9	93.0	134.1	101.4
Passes Attempted	415	502	520	509	479	439	569	515	536	450	537	496	521	532	525	502
Completed	217	293	324	313	280	248	381	303	339	257	320	312	278	306	297	315
% Completed	52.3	58.4	62.3	61.5	58.5	56.5	67.0	58.8	63.2	57.1	59.6	62.9	53.4	57.5	56.6	62.7
Total Yds. Gained	2517	3069	3591	3116	3126	2841	4289	3421	4113	3001	3651	3524	2988	3548	3226	4031
Times Sacked	42	51	37	40	25	36	19	28	21	31	32	31	43	42	29	25
Yds. Lost	262	385	249	282	157	186	110	136	132	209	219	208	237	244	205	153
Net Yds. Gained	2255	2684	3342	2834	2969	2655	4179	3285	3981	2792	3432	3316	2751	3304	3021	3878
Avg. Yds. per Game	140.9	167.8	208.9	177.1	185.6	165.9	261.2	205.3	248.8	174.5	214.5	207.3	171.9	206.5	188.8	242.4
Net Yds. per Pass Play	4.93	4.85	6.00	5.16	5.89	5.59	7.11	6.05	7.15	5.80	6.03	6.29	4.88	5.76	5.45	7.36
Yds. Gained per Comp.	11.60	10.47	11.08	9.96	11.16	11.46	11.26	11.29	12.13	11.68	11.41	11.29	10.75	11.59	10.86	12.80
Combined Net Yds. Gained	4929	4348	5329	4504	5598	4306	5874	5358	5910	4609	5039	4951	4573	4792	5167	5501
% Total Yds. Rushing	54.3	38.3	37.3	37.1	47.0	38.3	28.9	38.7	32.6	39.4	31.9	33.0	39.8	31.1	41.5	29.5
% Total Yds. Passing	45.7	61.7	62.7	62.9	53.0	61.7	71.1	61.3	67.4	60.6	68.1	67.0	60.2	68.9	58.5	70.5
Avg. Yds. per Game	308.1	271.8	333.1	281.5	349.9	269.1	367.1	334.9	369.4	288.1	314.9	309.4	285.8	299.5	322.9	343.8
Ball Control Plays	1009	980	1038	961	1047	896	1041	1024	1003	968	1042	936	987	1020	971	1013
Avg. Yds. per Play	4.9	4.4	5.1	4.7	5.3	4.8	5.6	5.2	5.9	4.8	4.8	5.3	4.6	4.7	5.3	5.4
Avg. Time of Poss.	30:14	29:40	30:52	29:21	33:53	27:39	30:54	30:09	29:23	29:49	30:50	27:50	27:41	30:42	27:52	32:52
Third Down Efficiency	31.9	31.6	44.7	36.6	38.9	30.9	41.9	37.0	41.8	32.7	37.0	39.8	30.4	36.1	31.5	40.8
Had Intercepted	19	17	15	18	18	18	10	17	12	19	13	14	14	17	19	9
Yds. Opp Returned	269	186	225	391	319	207	125	198	150	194	122	164	132	386	196	264
Ret. by Opp. for TD	0	1	2	4	2	3	1	1	1	3	1	2	0	3	1	3
Punts	91	85	77	73	70	97	64	69	81	84	88	72	96	85	83	71
Yds. Punted	3712	3788	3045	3048	2937	4028	2646	2853	3156	3274	3266	2655	4503	3521	3456	3117
Avg. Yds. per Punt	40.8	44.6	39.5	41.8	42.0	41.5	41.3	41.3	39.0	39.0	37.1	36.9	46.9	41.4	41.6	43.9
Punt Returns	53	41	30	37	39	40	31	34	33	31	50	30	38	45	49	37
Yds. Returned	410	248	331	302	442	266	240	376	542	288	462	332	492	551	391	429
Avg. Yds. per Return	7.7	6.0	11.0	8.2	11.3	6.7	7.7	11.1	16.4	9.3	9.2	11.1	12.9	12.2	8.0	11.6
Returned for TD	0	0	1	0	2	0	0	0	2	0	0	0	2	2	0	1
Kickoff Returns	57	63	74	71	59	80	64	67	62	57	60	60	77	68	84	68
Yds. Returned	1222	1369	1474	1501	1302	1700	1510	1316	1577	1202	1428	1461	1596	1405	1804	1299
Avg. Yds. per Return	21.4	21.7	19.9	21.1	22.1	21.3	23.6	19.6	25.4	21.1	23.8	24.4	20.7	20.7	21.5	19.1
Returned for TD	0	0	0	0	0	0	0	0	2	0	1	1	1	0	0	0
Fumbles	37	36	16	32	24	18	25	27	13	26	25	18	25	24	20	24
Lost	19	17	7	15	6	9	10	14	6	15	11	6	12	11	12	12
Out of Bounds	2	1	4	0	1	1	4	4	1	3	3	1	1	1	1	0
Own Rec. for TD	1	0	0	0	0	0	0	0	0	1	0	0	0	0	0	1
Opp. Rec. by	17	8	10	7	11	8	15	12	12	14	12	9	11	11	7	13
Opp. Rec. for TD	0	1	1	0	0	0	1	1	0	1	1	0	0	0	0	2
Penalties	126	106	107	98	107	121	92	108	79	103	111	69	134	111	126	110
Yds. Penalized	970	891	846	767	922	961	662	895	698	913	998	550	1120	1005	1016	887
Total Points Scored	391	243	346	254	381	255	447	276	484	311	348	283	270	300	313	435
Total TDs	41	27	40	27	42	29	48	31	63	35	39	29	29	33	38	48
TDs Rushing	18	13	12	8	20	14	16	13	32	14	9	8	15	10	16	11
TDs Passing	16	11	26	17	19	14	29	17	24	17	23	20	9	19	21	30
TDs on Ret. and Rec.	7	3	2	2	3	1	3	1	7	4	7	1	5	4	1	7
Extra Point Kicks	35	24	40	23	41	27	46	30	58	33	37	24	28	31	36	43
Extra Point Kicks Att.	35	24	40	24	41	27	46	30	59	34	38	24	29	32	36	44
2Pt Conversions	4	0	0	0	1	0	1	0	0	0	0	1	0	1	2	3
2Pt Conversions Att.	6	2	0	3	1	2	2	1	3	1	0	5	0	1	2	4
Safeties	0	3	0	0	1	0	0	0	0	1	1	1	1	0	0	1
Field Goals Made	34	17	22	23	28	18	37	20	16	22	25	27	22	23	15	32
Field Goals Attempted	40	24	25	28	32	22	37	33	20	29	34	32	25	32	20	37
% Successful	85.0	70.8	88.0	82.1	87.5	81.8	100.0	60.6	80.0	75.9	73.5	84.4	88.0	71.9	75.0	86.5

AMERICAN FOOTBALL CONFERENCE DEFENSE

	Balt.	Buff.	Cin.	Cle.	Den.	Hou.	Ind.	Jax.	KC	Mia.	NE	NYJ	Oak.	Pitt.	SD	Tenn.
First Downs	248	270	320	283	241	336	279	276	322	283	293	316	317	270	326	275
Rushing	78	92	119	100	77	130	117	84	120	82	91	134	127	89	124	79
Passing	144	153	177	160	141	179	138	172	184	171	177	168	159	155	178	167
Penalty	26	25	24	23	23	27	24	20	18	30	25	14	31	26	24	29
Rushes	448	464	461	457	379	533	437	442	453	441	401	542	544	449	518	342
Net Yds. Gained	1536	1606	2218	2113	1605	2370	1980	1406	2344	1452	1434	2294	2510	1741	2218	1295
Avg. Gain	3.4	3.5	4.8	4.6	4.2	4.4	4.5	3.2	5.2	3.3	3.6	4.2	4.6	3.9	4.3	3.8
Avg. Yds. per Game	96.0	100.4	138.6	132.1	100.3	148.1	123.8	87.9	146.5	90.8	89.6	143.4	156.9	108.8	138.6	80.9
Passes Attempted	531	508	508	502	495	502	445	510	565	529	618	455	467	484	524	546
Completed	296	285	297	297	265	297	277	303	332	319	328	281	286	294	322	332
% Completed	55.7	56.1	58.5	59.2	53.5	59.2	62.2	59.4	58.8	60.3	53.1	61.8	61.2	60.7	61.5	60.8
Total Yds. Gained	3158	2938	3598	3049	3049	3835	3034	3385	3614	3588	3485	3243	3556	3245	3575	3829
Times Sacked	47	38	30	35	36	19	31	24	36	44	41	35	25	35	30	38
Yds. Lost	353	231	196	203	221	123	225	134	251	253	253	218	162	203	200	223
Net Yds. Gained	2805	2707	3402	2846	2828	3712	2809	3251	3363	3335	3232	3025	3394	3042	3375	3606
Avg. Yds. per Game	175.3	169.2	212.6	177.9	176.8	232.0	175.6	203.2	210.2	208.4	202.0	189.1	212.1	190.1	210.9	225.4
Net Yds. per Pass Play	4.85	4.96	6.32	5.30	5.33	7.12	5.90	6.09	5.60	5.82	4.90	6.17	6.90	5.86	6.09	6.17
Yds. Gained per Comp.	10.67	10.31	12.11	10.27	11.51	12.91	10.95	11.17	10.89	11.25	10.63	11.54	12.43	11.04	11.10	11.53
Combined Net Yds. Gained	4341	4313	5620	4959	4433	6082	4789	4657	5707	4787	4666	5319	5904	4783	5593	4901
% Total Yds. Rushing	35.4	37.2	39.5	42.6	36.2	39.0	41.3	30.2	41.1	30.3	30.7	43.1	42.5	36.4	39.7	26.4
% Total Yds. Passing	64.6	62.8	60.5	57.4	63.8	61.0	58.7	69.8	58.9	69.7	69.3	56.9	57.5	63.6	60.3	73.6
Avg. Yds. per Game	271.3	269.6	351.3	309.9	277.1	380.1	299.3	291.1	356.7	299.2	291.6	332.4	369.0	298.9	349.6	306.3
Ball Control Plays	1026	1010	999	994	910	1054	913	976	1054	1014	1060	1032	1036	968	1072	926
Avg. Yds. per Play	4.2	4.3	5.6	5.0	4.9	5.8	5.2	4.8	5.4	4.7	4.4	5.2	5.7	4.9	5.2	5.3
Avg. Time of Poss.	29:46	30:20	29:08	30:39	26:07	32:21	29:06	29:51	30:37	30:11	29:10	32:10	32:19	29:18	32:08	27:08
Third Down Efficiency	29.4	38.2	41.3	39.2	29.5	40.1	38.3	42.2	36.6	36.5	34.5	40.6	37.2	34.0	42.0	27.7
Intercepted By	24	10	14	15	9	14	15	15	25	22	29	11	14	14	13	21
Yds. Returned By	511	114	123	168	39	205	244	78	310	338	358	155	280	215	157	312
Returned for TD	4	2	0	1	1	1	2	0	3	2	5	0	2	2	1	3
Punts	105	93	67	76	85	75	74	75	73	80	90	66	82	91	74	78
Yds. Punted	4211	3553	2845	3146	3663	3130	3115	3077	2974	3294	3658	2518	3271	3694	3162	3290
Avg. Yds. per Punt	40.1	38.2	42.5	41.4	43.1	41.7	42.1	41.0	40.7	41.2	40.6	38.2	39.9	40.6	42.7	42.2
Punt Returns	42	52	47	33	46	43	32	40	38	29	38	22	52	47	38	30
Yds. Returned	354	577	403	316	560	407	319	420	327	185	240	322	669	299	409	276
Avg. Yds. per Return	8.4	11.1	8.6	9.6	12.2	9.5	10.0	10.5	8.6	6.4	6.3	14.6	12.9	6.4	10.8	9.2
Returned for TD	0	0	0	0	1	1	0	0	1	0	1	1	0	0	2	1
Kickoff Returns	70	55	71	60	73	53	93	58	87	47	77	71	57	66	67	81
Yds. Returned	1495	1080	1470	1231	1679	1149	1999	1227	2043	1010	1623	1496	1474	1359	1437	1521
Avg. Yds. per Return	21.4	19.6	20.7	20.5	23.0	21.7	21.5	21.2	23.5	21.5	21.1	21.1	25.9	20.6	21.4	18.8
Returned for TD	1	0	0	0	0	0	2	0	0	0	0	0	0	1	1	0
Fumbles	29	22	26	24	27	18	30	26	21	26	31	17	24	24	22	21
Lost	17	8	10	7	11	8	15	12	12	14	12	9	11	11	7	13
Out of Bounds	1	2	2	5	3	2	2	0	0	1	3	1	0	4	0	0
Own Rec. for TD	0	0	0	0	0	0	0	1	0	0	0	0	0	0	1	0
Opp. Rec. by	19	17	7	15	6	9	10	14	6	15	11	6	12	11	12	12
Opp. Rec. for TD	2	0	0	0	1	1	1	0	0	0	0	0	0	0	0	1
Penalties	106	110	108	141	137	96	123	103	95	98	107	79	115	96	110	96
Yds. Penalized	935	996	921	1095	1031	767	1005	881	781	766	845	620	981	709	1006	793
Total Points Scored	281	279	384	322	301	380	336	331	332	261	238	299	379	327	441	324
Total TDs	28	30	43	31	32	42	41	37	39	26	23	34	42	38	53	35
TDs Rushing	6	11	18	14	11	15	19	12	18	11	10	17	21	14	12	10
TDs Passing	19	18	23	13	17	22	18	23	19	12	11	14	21	20	36	20
TDs on Ret. and Rec.	3	1	2	4	4	5	4	2	2	3	2	3	0	4	5	5
Extra Point Kicks	27	26	38	31	28	40	38	33	39	23	21	33	35	32	52	34
Extra Point Kicks Att.	27	26	38	31	29	40	38	34	39	23	21	33	36	35	53	34
2Pt Conversions	1	2	2	0	2	0	2	1	0	0	1	1	4	1	0	0
2Pt Conversions Att.	1	4	4	0	3	2	3	3	0	2	2	1	6	3	0	1
Safeties	0	0	0	0	1	2	0	1	1	2	1	0	0	1	1	1
Field Goals Made	28	23	28	35	25	28	16	24	19	26	25	20	28	21	23	26
Field Goals Attempted	31	31	33	43	28	35	21	27	25	31	35	27	34	24	26	30
% Successful	90.3	74.2	84.8	81.4	89.3	80.0	76.2	88.9	76.0	83.9	71.4	74.1	82.4	87.5	88.5	86.7

2003 TEAM STATISTICS

NATIONAL FOOTBALL CONFERENCE OFFENSE

	Ariz.	Atl.	Car.	Chi.	Dall.	Det.	GB	Minn.	NO	NYG	Phil.	StL	SF	Sea.	TB	Wash.
First Downs	256	252	284	264	286	250	315	336	302	300	302	335	313	338	307	272
Rushing	80	99	114	104	115	69	127	124	100	90	105	97	118	121	86	95
Passing	147	127	146	143	149	152	166	194	177	184	156	211	172	190	190	156
Penalty	29	26	24	17	22	29	22	18	25	26	41	27	23	27	31	21
Rushes	403	435	522	443	515	376	507	493	448	387	417	411	499	453	421	421
Net Yds. Gained	1531	1949	2091	1763	1999	1338	2558	2343	2000	1559	2015	1496	2279	2009	1648	1653
Avg. Gain	3.8	4.5	4.0	4.0	3.9	3.6	5.0	4.8	4.5	4.0	4.8	3.6	4.6	4.4	3.9	3.9
Avg. Yds. per Game	95.7	121.8	130.7	110.2	124.9	83.6	159.9	146.4	125.0	97.4	125.9	93.5	142.4	125.6	103.0	103.3
Passes Attempted	534	460	460	515	510	588	473	520	535	616	484	600	511	521	592	527
Completed	303	230	270	271	294	319	310	333	314	344	279	377	299	317	369	283
% Completed	56.7	50.0	58.7	52.6	57.6	54.3	65.5	64.0	58.7	55.8	57.6	62.8	58.5	60.8	62.3	53.7
Total Yds. Gained	3265	2631	3238	2905	3347	2988	3377	4169	3641	3642	3273	4287	3566	3872	3941	3273
Times Sacked	44	35	26	43	37	11	19	42	36	44	43	43	28	43	23	43
Yds. Lost	306	223	188	288	185	64	137	218	203	259	253	326	158	254	136	267
Net Yds. Gained	2959	2408	3050	2617	3162	2924	3240	3951	3438	3383	3020	3961	3408	3618	3805	3006
Avg. Yds. per Game	184.9	150.5	190.6	163.6	197.6	182.8	202.5	246.9	214.9	211.4	188.8	247.6	213.0	226.1	237.8	187.9
Net Yds. per Pass Play	5.12	4.86	6.28	4.69	5.78	4.88	6.59	7.03	6.02	5.13	5.73	6.16	6.32	6.41	6.19	5.27
Yds. Gained per Comp.	10.78	11.44	11.99	10.72	11.38	9.37	10.89	12.52	11.60	10.59	11.73	11.37	11.93	12.21	10.68	11.57
Combined Net Yds. Gained	4490	4357	5141	4380	5161	4262	5798	6294	5438	4942	5035	5457	5687	5627	5453	4659
% Total Yds. Rushing	34.1	44.7	40.7	40.3	38.7	31.4	44.1	37.2	36.8	31.5	40.0	27.4	40.1	35.7	30.2	35.5
% Total Yds. Passing	65.9	55.3	59.3	59.7	61.3	68.6	55.9	62.8	63.2	68.5	60.0	72.6	59.9	64.3	69.8	64.5
Avg. Yds. per Game	280.6	272.3	321.3	273.8	322.6	266.4	362.4	393.4	339.9	308.9	314.7	341.1	355.4	351.7	340.8	291.2
Ball Control Plays	981	930	1008	1001	1062	975	999	1055	1019	1047	944	1054	1038	1017	1036	991
Avg. Yds. per Play	4.6	4.7	5.1	4.4	4.9	4.4	5.8	6.0	5.3	4.7	5.3	5.2	5.5	5.5	5.3	4.7
Avg. Time of Poss.	29:41	27:38	30:27	29:39	32:34	28:21	30:52	32:52	30:18	28:04	28:17	31:53	30:54	28:33	31:36	28:45
Third Down Efficiency	37.4	29.9	35.6	33.8	36.5	35.1	41.1	46.6	46.3	33.5	36.3	42.6	40.0	46.8	35.5	34.0
Had Intercepted	22	21	16	20	21	24	21	13	8	20	11	23	15	16	22	16
Yds. Opp Returned	418	310	225	390	285	377	429	149	104	169	161	300	291	164	394	178
Ret. by Opp. for TD	4	1	2	2	1	4	2	1	1	2	1	1	1	1	4	2
Punts	83	87	81	81	95	96	71	64	72	91	79	59	69	69	83	84
Yds. Punted	3511	3473	3466	3258	3697	3790	2933	2462	3144	3641	3207	2525	2629	2762	3590	3377
Avg. Yds. per Punt	42.3	39.9	42.8	40.2	38.9	39.5	41.3	38.5	43.7	40.0	40.6	42.8	38.1	40.0	43.3	40.2
Punt Returns	22	43	45	39	51	47	35	36	40	32	31	39	40	34	35	22
Yds. Returned	140	613	453	461	390	576	277	247	360	163	378	337	276	320	242	205
Avg. Yds. per Return	6.4	14.3	10.1	11.8	7.6	12.3	7.9	6.9	9.0	5.1	12.2	8.6	6.9	9.4	6.9	9.3
Returned for TD	0	1	1	1	0	2	0	0	0	0	2	0	0	1	0	0
Kickoff Returns	82	79	60	73	60	70	64	71	72	75	65	70	64	64	55	66
Yds. Returned	1881	1572	1345	1738	1292	1584	1511	1428	1524	1492	1387	1488	1327	1336	1042	1482
Avg. Yds. per Return	22.9	19.9	22.4	23.8	21.5	22.6	23.6	20.1	21.2	19.9	21.3	21.3	20.7	20.9	18.9	22.5
Returned for TD	1	0	1	2	1	1	0	0	0	0	0	0	1	0	0	1
Fumbles	29	22	33	25	26	18	19	31	33	35	21	33	24	23	23	21
Lost	14	10	15	9	8	4	11	11	20	18	11	16	10	13	9	12
Out of Bounds	1	1	2	1	5	1	1	2	4	2	1	3	3	2	0	1
Own Rec. for TD	0	0	0	0	0	0	0	0	0	0	0	0	1	1	0	0
Opp. Rec. by	10	16	10	5	12	13	11	7	13	12	13	22	13	12	13	13
Opp. Rec. for TD	0	0	0	0	0	3	1	0	0	2	0	2	0	2	1	0
Penalties	98	90	116	92	98	107	88	127	103	127	96	92	104	91	117	124
Yds. Penalized	761	790	966	806	837	859	699	1029	878	1090	817	667	807	777	1104	1038
Total Points Scored	225	299	325	283	289	270	442	416	340	243	374	447	384	404	301	287
Total TDs	25	35	33	29	31	29	53	51	39	26	43	47	44	48	36	30
TDs Rushing	5	17	9	13	11	5	18	15	11	6	23	19	16	17	5	8
TDs Passing	18	14	19	12	17	17	32	32	25	16	17	23	25	27	27	21
TDs on Ret. and Rec.	2	4	5	4	3	7	3	4	3	4	3	5	3	4	4	1
Extra Point Kicks	19	32	29	27	30	26	51	48	36	23	42	46	38	48	33	26
Extra Point Kicks Att.	20	33	30	27	31	27	51	48	37	23	42	46	41	48	34	27
2Pt Conversions	1	0	0	2	0	2	2	2	1	2	0	0	1	0	1	2
2Pt Conversions Att.	5	1	3	2	0	2	2	3	2	3	1	1	3	0	2	3
Safeties	0	0	1	0	2	0	0	2	1	0	1	1	1	1	1	1
Field Goals Made	18	19	32	26	23	22	23	18	22	20	24	39	26	22	16	25
Field Goals Attempted	26	27	38	36	29	23	26	25	30	27	29	42	37	30	26	33
% Successful	69.2	70.4	84.2	72.2	79.3	95.7	88.5	72.0	73.3	74.1	82.8	92.9	70.3	73.3	61.5	75.8

NATIONAL FOOTBALL CONFERENCE DEFENSE

	Ariz.	Atl.	Car.	Chi.	Dall.	Det.	GB	Minn.	NO	NYG	Phil.	StL	SF	Sea.	TB	Wash.
First Downs	326	333	274	289	228	298	288	316	298	314	306	272	292	304	249	325
Rushing	120	122	83	104	68	105	91	94	109	102	116	92	99	93	89	122
Passing	184	187	161	156	127	166	172	186	165	178	171	164	165	183	140	176
Penalty	22	24	30	29	33	27	25	36	24	34	19	16	28	28	20	27
Rushes	475	499	434	449	413	447	413	387	480	496	461	412	420	456	451	504
Net Yds. Gained	1915	2308	1722	1865	1425	1782	1701	1879	2241	1908	2071	1980	1690	1759	1756	2217
Avg. Gain	4.0	4.6	4.0	4.2	3.5	4.0	4.1	4.9	4.7	3.8	4.5	4.8	4.0	3.9	3.9	4.4
Avg. Yds. per Game	119.7	144.3	107.6	116.6	89.1	111.4	106.3	117.4	140.1	119.3	129.4	123.8	105.6	109.9	109.8	138.6
Passes Attempted	497	508	522	525	492	522	589	531	485	519	559	510	514	573	475	483
Completed	311	323	299	326	239	331	326	311	264	309	337	296	310	343	274	285
% Completed	62.6	63.6	57.3	62.1	48.6	63.4	55.3	58.6	54.4	59.5	60.3	58.0	60.3	59.9	57.7	59.0
Total Yds. Gained	3686	4005	3215	3187	2820	3760	3600	3722	3164	3710	3484	3363	3544	3728	2944	3354
Times Sacked	21	36	40	18	32	28	34	37	32	45	38	42	42	40	36	27
Yds. Lost	97	205	212	105	189	182	200	245	171	298	248	291	306	248	234	159
Net Yds. Gained	3589	3800	3003	3082	2631	3578	3400	3477	2993	3412	3236	3072	3238	3480	2710	3195
Avg. Yds. per Game	224.3	237.5	187.7	192.6	164.4	223.6	212.5	217.3	187.1	213.3	202.3	192.0	202.4	217.5	169.4	199.7
Net Yds. per Pass Play	6.93	6.99	5.34	5.68	5.02	6.51	5.46	6.12	5.79	6.05	5.42	5.57	5.82	5.68	5.30	6.26
Yds. Gained per Comp.	11.85	12.40	10.75	9.78	11.80	11.36	11.04	11.97	11.98	12.01	10.34	11.36	11.43	10.87	10.74	11.77
Combined Net Yds. Gained	5504	6108	4725	4947	4056	5360	5101	5356	5234	5320	5307	5052	4928	5239	4466	5412
% Total Yds. Rushing	34.8	37.8	36.4	37.7	35.1	33.2	33.3	35.1	42.8	35.9	39.0	39.2	34.3	33.6	39.3	41.0
% Total Yds. Passing	65.2	62.2	63.6	62.3	64.9	66.8	66.7	64.9	57.2	64.1	61.0	60.8	65.7	66.4	60.7	59.0
Avg. Yds. per Game	344.0	381.8	295.3	309.2	253.5	335.0	318.8	334.8	327.1	332.5	331.7	315.8	308.0	327.4	279.1	338.3
Ball Control Plays	993	1043	996	992	937	997	1036	955	997	1060	1058	964	976	1069	962	1014
Avg. Yds. per Play	5.5	5.9	4.7	5.0	4.3	5.4	4.9	5.6	5.2	5.0	5.0	5.2	5.0	4.9	4.6	5.3
Avg. Time of Poss.	30:19	32:22	29:33	30:21	27:26	31:39	29:08	27:08	29:42	31:56	31:43	28:07	29:06	31:27	28:24	31:15
Third Down Efficiency	46.2	39.8	34.7	39.4	30.4	40.7	37.3	38.5	38.0	37.8	35.3	35.9	40.7	42.1	31.8	40.2
Intercepted By	13	15	16	15	13	15	21	28	14	10	13	24	23	16	20	17
Yds. Returned By	271	197	238	191	183	130	315	693	226	199	158	505	389	157	229	184
Returned for TD	1	3	3	1	2	1	2	4	2	2	1	3	1	0	3	0
Punts	67	82	90	76	105	84	83	64	76	82	78	74	76	76	82	71
Yds. Punted	2679	3557	3778	3073	4471	3574	3399	2576	3183	2922	3037	3061	2975	3028	3559	2997
Avg. Yds. per Punt	40.0	43.4	42.0	40.4	42.6	42.5	41.0	40.3	41.9	35.6	38.9	41.4	39.1	39.8	43.4	42.2
Punt Returns	41	35	35	36	34	59	32	29	36	40	35	32	28	29	39	40
Yds. Returned	472	301	402	277	227	390	316	310	294	432	272	484	258	140	489	393
Avg. Yds. per Return	11.5	8.6	11.5	7.7	6.7	6.6	9.9	10.7	8.2	10.8	7.8	15.1	9.2	4.8	12.5	9.8
Returned for TD	2	1	1	0	0	1	0	0	0	2	0	2	1	0	0	0
Kickoff Returns	48	62	70	64	66	53	82	75	67	56	74	83	77	79	59	60
Yds. Returned	1042	1204	1425	1367	1448	1313	1707	1608	1587	1128	1590	1985	1641	1626	1393	1238
Avg. Yds. per Return	21.7	19.4	20.4	21.4	21.9	24.8	20.8	21.4	23.7	20.1	21.5	23.9	21.3	20.6	23.6	20.6
Returned for TD	0	0	0	1	0	1	1	0	2	0	1	2	0	0	0	0
Fumbles	21	33	20	19	24	32	21	28	29	31	26	31	23	25	29	26
Lost	10	16	10	5	12	13	11	7	13	12	13	22	14	12	13	13
Out of Bounds	3	2	1	1	0	2	1	4	3	3	2	2	1	2	5	0
Own Rec. for TD	1	0	0	0	0	1	0	0	0	0	0	0	0	0	1	0
Opp. Rec. by	14	10	15	9	8	4	11	11	20	18	10	16	10	13	9	12
Opp. Rec. for TD	1	0	3	0	2	0	0	2	1	1	0	2	1	0	0	0
Penalties	86	130	111	93	88	119	97	90	101	118	129	114	78	105	104	95
Yds. Penalized	754	1001	1011	746	763	953	767	720	1012	983	1105	882	720	825	817	835
Total Points Scored	452	422	304	346	260	379	307	353	326	387	287	328	337	327	264	372
Total TDs	55	51	35	36	28	47	31	42	36	43	32	39	41	36	27	45
TDs Rushing	17	21	10	13	7	14	10	22	12	12	13	9	13	9	6	20
TDs Passing	29	28	19	20	18	26	18	17	20	25	17	23	25	24	16	23
TDs on Ret. and Rec.	9	2	6	3	3	7	3	3	4	6	2	7	3	3	5	2
Extra Point Kicks	53	47	31	31	23	46	29	36	35	41	27	35	40	34	27	45
Extra Point Kicks Att.	53	48	32	33	26	46	29	36	35	42	28	36	40	35	27	45
2Pt Conversions	0	2	0	3	2	0	1	1	0	1	1	0	0	1	0	0
2Pt Conversions Att.	2	3	2	3	2	1	1	6	1	1	4	3	1	1	0	0
Safeties	3	4	0	0	1	0	0	0	0	1	0	1	0	0	0	0
Field Goals Made	21	19	21	31	21	17	30	21	25	28	22	19	17	25	25	19
Field Goals Attempted	28	25	32	38	23	24	33	26	31	37	30	24	26	31	34	31
% Successful	75.0	76.0	65.6	81.6	91.3	70.8	90.9	80.8	80.6	75.7	73.3	79.2	65.4	80.6	73.5	61.3

2003 TEAM STATISTICS

AFC, NFC, AND NFL SUMMARY

	AFC Offense Total	AFC Offense Average	AFC Defense Total	AFC Defense Average	NFC Offense Total	NFC Offense Average	NFC Defense Total	NFC Defense Average	NFL Total	NFL Average
First Downs	4655	290.9	4655	290.9	4712	294.5	4712	294.5	9367	292.7
Rushing	1608	100.5	1643	102.7	1644	102.8	1609	100.6	3252	101.6
Passing	2644	165.3	2623	163.9	2660	166.3	2681	167.6	5304	165.8
Penalty	403	25.2	389	24.3	408	25.5	422	26.4	811	25.3
Rushes	7357	459.8	7311	456.9	7151	446.9	7197	449.8	14508	453.4
Net Yds. Gained	30110	1881.9	30122	1882.6	30231	1889.4	30219	1888.7	60341	1885.7
Avg. Gain	—	4.1	—	4.1	—	4.2	—	4.2	—	4.2
Avg. Yds. per Game	—	117.6	—	117.7	—	118.1	—	118.0	—	117.9
Passes Attempted	8047	502.9	8189	511.8	8446	527.9	8304	519.0	16493	515.4
Completed	4783	298.9	4811	300.7	4912	307.0	4884	305.3	9695	303.0
% Completed	—	59.4	—	58.7	—	58.2	—	58.8	—	58.8
Total Yds. Gained	54052	3378.3	54181	3386.3	55415	3463.4	55286	3455.4	109467	3420.8
Times Sacked	532	33.3	544	34.0	560	35.0	548	34.3	1092	34.1
Yds. Lost	3374	210.9	3449	215.6	3465	216.6	3390	211.9	6839	213.7
Net Yds. Gained	50678	3167.4	50732	3170.8	51950	3246.9	51896	3243.5	102628	3207.1
Avg. Yds. per Game	—	198.0	—	198.2	—	202.9	—	202.7	—	200.4
Net Yds. per Pass Play	—	5.91	—	5.81	—	5.77	—	5.86	—	5.84
Yds. Gained per Comp.	—	11.30	—	11.26	—	11.28	—	11.32	—	11.29
Combined Net Yds. Gained	80788	5049.3	80854	5053.4	82181	5136.3	82115	5132.2	162969	5092.8
% Total Yds. Rushing	—	37.3	—	37.3	—	36.8	—	36.8	—	37.0
% Total Yds. Passing	—	62.7	—	62.7	—	63.2	—	63.2	—	63.0
Avg. Yds. per Game	—	315.6	—	315.8	—	321.0	—	320.8	—	318.3
Ball Control Plays	15936	996.0	16044	1002.8	16157	1009.8	16049	1003.1	32093	1002.9
Avg. Yds. per Play	—	5.1	—	5.0	—	5.1	—	5.1	—	5.1
Third Down Efficiency	—	36.5	—	36.8	—	38.2	—	38.0	—	37.4
Interceptions	249	15.6	265	16.6	289	18.1	273	17.1	538	16.8
Yds. Returned	3528	220.5	3607	225.4	4344	271.5	4265	266.6	7872	246.0
Returned for TD	28	1.8	29	1.8	30	1.9	29	1.8	58	1.8
Punts	1286	80.4	1284	80.3	1264	79.0	1266	79.1	2550	79.7
Yds. Punted	53005	3312.8	52601	3287.6	51465	3216.6	51869	3241.8	104470	3264.7
Avg. Yds. per Punt	—	41.2	—	41.0	—	40.7	—	41.0	—	41.0
Punt Returns	618	38.6	629	39.3	591	36.9	580	36.3	1209	37.8
Yds. Returned	6102	381.4	6083	380.2	5438	339.9	5457	341.1	11540	360.6
Avg. Yds. per Return	—	9.9	—	9.7	—	9.2	—	9.4	—	9.5
Returned for TD	10	0.6	8	0.5	8	0.5	10	0.6	18	0.6
Kickoff Returns	1071	66.9	1086	67.9	1090	68.1	1075	67.2	2161	67.5
Yds. Returned	23166	1447.9	23293	1455.8	23429	1464.3	23302	1456.4	46595	1456.1
Avg. Yds. per Return	—	21.6	—	21.4	—	21.5	—	21.7	—	21.6
Returned for TD	5	0.3	5	0.3	8	0.5	8	0.5	13	0.4
Fumbles	390	24.4	388	24.3	416	26.0	418	26.1	806	25.2
Lost	182	11.4	177	11.1	191	11.9	196	12.3	373	11.7
Out of Bounds	28	1.8	26	1.6	30	1.9	32	2.0	58	1.8
Own Rec. for TD	3	0.2	2	0.1	2	0.1	3	0.2	5	0.2
Opp. Rec.	177	11.1	182	11.4	195	12.2	190	11.9	372	11.6
Opp. Rec. for TD	8	0.5	6	0.4	11	0.7	13	0.8	19	0.6
Penalties	1708	106.8	1720	107.5	1670	104.4	1658	103.6	3378	105.6
Yds. Penalized	14101	881.3	14132	883.3	13925	870.3	13894	868.4	28026	875.8
Total Points Scored	5337	333.6	5215	325.9	5329	333.1	5451	340.7	10666	333.3
Total TDs	599	37.4	574	35.9	599	37.4	624	39.0	1198	37.4
TDs Rushing	229	14.3	219	13.7	198	12.4	208	13.0	427	13.3
TDs Passing	312	19.5	306	19.1	342	21.4	348	21.8	654	20.4
TDs on Ret. and Rec.	58	3.6	49	3.1	59	3.7	68	4.3	117	3.7
Extra Point Kicks	556	34.8	530	33.1	554	34.6	580	36.3	1110	34.7
Extra Point Kicks Att.	563	35.2	537	33.6	565	35.3	591	36.9	1128	35.3
2Pt Conversions	13	0.8	17	1.1	16	1.0	12	0.8	29	0.9
2Pt Conversions Att.	33	2.1	35	2.2	33	2.1	31	1.9	66	2.1
Safeties	9	0.6	11	0.7	12	0.8	10	0.6	21	0.7
Field Goals Made	381	23.8	395	24.7	375	23.4	361	22.6	756	23.6
Field Goals Attempted	470	29.4	481	30.1	484	30.3	473	29.6	954	29.8
% Successful	—	81.1	—	82.1	—	77.5	—	76.3	—	79.2

CLUB LEADERS

	Offense	Defense
First Downs	Indianapolis & Kansas City 348	Dallas 228
Rushing	Denver 133	Dallas 68
Passing	Indianapolis 212	Dallas 127
Penalty	Philadelphia 41	N.Y. Jets 14
Rushes	Baltimore 552	Tennessee 342
Net Yds. Gained	Baltimore 2674	Tennessee 1295
Avg. Gain	San Diego 5.1	Jacksonville 3.2
Passes Attempted	N.Y. Giants 616	Indianapolis 445
Completed	Indianapolis 381	Dallas 239
% Completed	Indianapolis 67.0	Dallas 48.6
Total Yds. Gained	Indianapolis 4289	Dallas 2820
Times Sacked	Detroit 11	Baltimore 47
Yds. Lost	Detroit 64	Baltimore 353
Net Yds. Gained	Indianapolis 4179	Dallas 2631
Net Yds. per Pass Play	Tennessee 7.4	Baltimore 4.9
Yds. Gained per Comp.	Tennessee 12.8	Chicago 9.8
Combined Net Yds. Gained	Minnesota 6294	Dallas 4056
% Total Yds. Rushing	Baltimore 54.3	Tennessee 26.4
% Total Yds. Passing	St. Louis 72.6	N.Y. Jets 56.9
Ball Control Plays	Dallas 1062	Denver 910
Avg. Yds. per Play	Minnesota 6.0	Baltimore 4.2
Avg. Time of Poss.	Denver 33:53	—
Third Down Efficiency	Seattle 46.8	Tennessee 27.7
Interceptions	—	New England 29
Yds. Returned	—	Minnesota 693
Returned for TD	—	New England 5
Punts	Houston 97	—
Yds. Punted	Oakland 4503	—
Avg. Yds. per Punt	Oakland 46.9	—
Punt Returns	Baltimore 53	N.Y. Jets 22
Yds. Returned	Atlanta 613	Seattle 140
Avg. Yds. per Return	Kansas City 16.4	Seattle 4.8
Returned for TD	Denver & Detroit & Kansas City & Oakland & Philadelphia & Pittsburgh 2	—
Kickoff Returns	San Diego 84	Miami 47
Yds. Returned	Arizona 1881	Miami 1010
Avg. Yds. per Return	Kansas City 25.4	Tennessee 18.8
Returned for TD	Chicago & Kansas City 2	—
Total Points Scored	Kansas City 484	New England 238
Total TDs	Kansas City 63	New England 23
TDs Rushing	Kansas City 32	Baltimore & Tampa Bay 6
TDs Passing	Green Bay & Minnesota 32	New England 11
TDs on Ret. and Rec.	Baltimore & Detroit & Kansas City & New England & Tennessee 7	Oakland 0
Extra Point Kicks	Kansas City 58	New England 21
2-Point Conversions	Baltimore 4	—
Safeties	Buffalo 3	—
Field Goals Made	St. Louis 39	Indianapolis 16
Field Goals Attempted	St. Louis 42	Indianapolis 21
% Successful	Indianapolis 100.0	Washington 61.3

NFL CLUB RANKINGS BY YARDS

	Offense			Defense		
	Total	Rush	Pass	Total	Rush	Pass
Arizona	27	29	23	26	19	29
Atlanta	29	14	31	32	29	32
Baltimore	21	*1	32	3	6	4
Buffalo	30	21	28	2	8	2
Carolina	16	7	18	8	11	9
Chicago	28	18	30	14	16	13
Cincinnati	13	13	12	28	25T	24
Cleveland	26	20	25	15	23	7
Dallas	15	12	17	*1	3	*1
Denver	7	2	22	4	7	6
Detroit	32	32	24	24	15	28
Green Bay	4	3	16	17	10	23
Houston	31	23	29	31	31	31
Indianapolis	3	19	*1	11	20T	5
Jacksonville	12	8	15	6	2	18
Kansas City	2	15	2	29	30	20
Miami	24	17	26	10	5	19
Minnesota	*1	4	4	23	17	26
New England	17	27	9	7	4	15
New Orleans	11	11	8	18	27	8
New York Giants	20	28	11	22	18	25
New York Jets	19	25	13	21	28	10
Oakland	25	16	27	30	32	22
Philadelphia	18	9	20	20	22	16
Pittsburgh	22	31	14	9	12	11
St. Louis	9	30	3	16	20T	12
San Diego	14	6	19	27	25T	21
San Francisco	5	5	10	13	9	17
Seattle	6	10	7	19	14	27
Tampa Bay	10	24	6	5	13	3
Tennessee	8	26	5	12	*1	30
Washington	23	22	21	25	24	14

T = Tied for position * = League Leader

AFC TAKEAWAYS/GIVEAWAYS

	Takeaways			Giveaways			Net
	Int	Fum	Total	Int	Fum	Total	Diff.
Kansas City	25	12	37	12	6	18	+19
New England	29	12	41	13	11	24	+17
Tennessee	21	13	34	9	12	21	+13
Indianapolis	15	15	30	10	10	20	+10
Baltimore	24	17	41	19	19	38	+3
Cincinnati	14	10	24	15	7	22	+2
Miami	22	14	36	19	15	34	+2
New York Jets	11	9	20	14	6	20	0
Oakland	14	11	25	14	12	26	-1
Pittsburgh	14	11	25	17	11	28	-3
Denver	9	11	20	18	6	24	-4
Jacksonville	15	12	27	17	14	31	-4
Houston	14	8	22	18	9	27	-5
Cleveland	15	7	22	18	15	33	-11
San Diego	13	7	20	19	12	31	-11
Buffalo	10	8	18	17	17	34	-16
AFC Totals	265	177	442	249	182	431	+11

NFC TAKEAWAYS/GIVEAWAYS

	Takeaways			Giveaways			Net
	Int	Fum	Total	Int	Fum	Total	Diff.
San Francisco	23	14	37	15	10	25	+12
Minnesota	28	7	35	13	11	24	+11
St. Louis	24	22	46	23	16	39	+7
Philadelphia	13	13	26	11	11	22	+4
Tampa Bay	20	13	33	22	9	31	+2
Washington	17	13	30	16	12	28	+2
Atlanta	15	16	31	21	10	31	0
Detroit	15	13	28	24	4	28	0
Green Bay	21	11	32	21	11	32	0
New Orleans	14	13	27	8	20	28	-1
Seattle	16	12	28	16	13	29	-1
Dallas	13	12	25	21	8	29	-4
Carolina	16	10	26	16	15	31	-5
Chicago	15	5	20	20	9	29	-9
Arizona	13	10	23	22	14	36	-13
New York Giants	10	12	22	20	18	38	-16
NFC Totals	273	196	469	289	191	480	-11

2003 INDIVIDUAL STATISTICS—SCORING

SCORING

POINTS

NFC: 163 Jeff Wilkins, St. Louis
AFC: 162 Priest Holmes, Kansas City

TOUCHDOWNS

AFC: 27 Priest Holmes, Kansas City
NFC: 20 Ahman Green, Green Bay

EXTRA POINT KICKS

AFC: 58 Morten Andersen, Kansas City
NFC: 51 Ryan Longwell, Green Bay

TWO-POINT EXTRA POINT PLAYS

AFC: 4 Todd Heap, Baltimore
NFC: 2 Bubba Franks, Green Bay
2 Darnerien McCants, Washington

FIELD GOALS

NFC: 39 Jeff Wilkins, St. Louis
AFC: 37 Mike Vanderjagt, Indianapolis

FIELD GOAL ATTEMPTS

NFC: 42 Jeff Wilkins, St. Louis
AFC: 38 Matt Stover, Baltimore

LONGEST FIELD GOAL

NFC: 58 Josh Brown, Seattle at Green Bay, October 5
AFC: 56 Wade Richey, Baltimore vs. Cleveland, September 14

MOST POINTS, GAME

AFC: 30 Clinton Portis, Denver vs. Kansas City, December 7 (5 TD)
NFC: 24 Joe Horn, New Orleans vs. N.Y. Giants, December 14 (4 TD)

TEAM LEADERS, POINTS

AFC: BALTIMORE, 134, Matt Stover; BUFFALO, 75, Rian Lindell; CINCINNATI, 106, Shayne Graham; CLEVELAND, 74, Phil Dawson; DENVER, 120, Jason Elam; HOUSTON, 81, Kris Brown; INDIANAPOLIS, 157, Mike Vanderjagt; JACKSONVILLE, 90, Seth Marler; KANSAS CITY, 162, Priest Holmes; MIAMI, 99, Olindo Mare; NEW ENGLAND, 112, Adam Vinatieri; N.Y. JETS, 105, Doug Brien; OAKLAND, 94, Sebastian Janikowski; PITTSBURGH, 100, Jeff Reed; SAN DIEGO, 102, LaDainian Tomlinson; TENNESSEE, 123, Gary Anderson

NFC: ARIZONA, 48, Anquan Boldin; ATLANTA, 89, Jay Feely; CAROLINA, 125, John Kasay; CHICAGO, 105, Paul Edinger; DALLAS, 99, Billy Cundiff; DETROIT, 92, Jason Hanson; GREEN BAY, 120, Ahman Green, Ryan Longwell; MINNESOTA, 102, Aaron Elling, Randy Moss; NEW ORLEANS, 102, John Carney; N.Y. GIANTS, 50, Matt Bryant; PHILADELPHIA, 114, David Akers; ST. LOUIS, 163, Jeff Wilkins; SAN FRANCISCO, 58, Todd Peterson; SEATTLE, 114, Josh Brown; TAMPA BAY, 81, Martín Gramatica; WASHINGTON, 101, John Hall

TEAM CHAMPION

AFC: 484 Kansas City
NFC: 447 St. Louis

NFL TOP TEN SCORERS—KICKERS

	XP	XPA	FG	FGA	PTS
Wilkins, Jeff, St.L	46	46	39	42	163
Vanderjagt, Mike, Ind.	46	46	37	37	157
Stover, Matt, Bal.	35	35	33	38	134
Kasay, John, Car.	29	30	32	38	125
Anderson, Gary, Ten.	42	42	27	31	123
Elam, Jason, Den.	39	39	27	31	120
Longwell, Ryan, G.B.	51	51	23	26	120
Akers, David, Phi.	42	42	24	29	114
Brown, Josh, Sea.	48	48	22	30	114
Vinatieri, Adam, N.E.	37	38	25	34	112

NFL TOP TEN SCORERS—NONKICKERS

	TD	TDR	TDP	TDM	2-PT.	PTS
Holmes, Priest, K.C.	27	27	0	0	0	162
Green, Ahman, G.B.	20	15	5	0	0	120
Moss, Randy, Min.	17	0	17	0	0	102
Tomlinson, LaDainian, S.D.	17	13	4	0	0	102
Alexander, Shaun, Sea.	16	14	2	0	0	96
Portis, Clinton, Den.	14	14	0	0	1	86
Lewis, Jamal, Bal.	14	14	0	0	0	84
Westbrook, Brian, Phi.	13	7	4	2	0	78
Holt, Torry, St.L	12	0	12	0	0	72
Chambers, Chris, Mia.	11	0	11	0	0	66
Duckett, T.J., Atl.	11	11	0	0	0	66
Faulk, Marshall, St.L	11	10	1	0	0	66
Henry, Travis, Buf.	11	10	1	0	0	66
James, Edgerrin, Ind.	11	11	0	0	0	66

AFC—INDIVIDUAL SCORERS

KICKERS

	XP	XPA	FG	FGA	PTS
Vanderjagt, Mike, Ind.	46	46	37	37	157
Stover, Matt, Bal.	35	35	33	38	134
Anderson, Gary, Ten.	42	42	27	31	123
Elam, Jason, Den.	39	39	27	31	120
Vinatieri, Adam, N.E.	37	38	25	34	112
Andersen, Morten, K.C.	58	59	16	20	106
Graham, Shayne, Cin.	40	40	22	25	106
Brien, Doug, NYJ	24	24	27	32	105
Reed, Jeff, Pit.	31	32	23	32	100
Mare, Olindo, Mia.	33	34	22	29	99
Janikowski, Sebastian, Oak.	28	29	22	25	94
Marler, Seth, Jac.	30	30	20	33	90
Brown, Kris, Hou.	27	27	18	22	81
Christie, Steve, S.D.	36	36	15	20	81
Lindell, Rian, Buf.	24	24	17	24	75
Dawson, Phil, Cle.	20	21	18	21	74
Conway, Brett, NYG-Cle.	9	9	14	19	51
Hentrich, Craig, Ten.	1	1	4	5	13
Knorr, Micah, Den.	2	2	1	1	5
Nedney, Joe, Ten.	0	1	1	1	3
Richey, Wade, Bal.	0	0	1	2	3

NONKICKERS

	TD	TDR	TDP	TDM	2-PT.	PTS
Holmes, Priest, K.C.	27	27	0	0	0	162
Tomlinson, LaDainian, S.D.	17	13	4	0	0	102
Portis, Clinton, Den.	14	14	0	0	1	86
Lewis, Jamal, Bal.	14	14	0	0	0	84
Chambers, Chris, Mia.	11	0	11	0	0	66
Henry, Travis, Buf.	11	10	1	0	0	66
James, Edgerrin, Ind.	11	11	0	0	0	66
Gonzalez, Tony, K.C.	10	0	10	0	0	60
Harrison, Marvin, Ind.	10	0	10	0	0	60
Johnson, Chad, Cin.	10	0	10	0	0	60
Moss, Santana, NYJ	10	0	10	0	0	60
Ward, Hines, Pit.	10	0	10	0	0	60
Williams, Ricky, Mia.	10	9	1	0	0	60
Johnson, Rudi, Cin.	9	9	0	0	0	54
Davis, Domanick, Hou.	8	8	0	0	0	48
Mason, Derrick, Ten.	8	0	8	0	0	48

	TD	TDR	TDP	TDM	2-PT.	PTS
Law, Ty, N.E.	1	0	0	1	0	6
Lee, Donald, Mia.	1	0	1	0	0	6
Lewis, Jermaine, Jac.	1	0	1	0	0	6
Lewis, Ray, Bal.	1	0	0	1	0	6
Madison, Sam, Mia.	1	0	0	1	0	6
McAlister, Chris, Bal.	1	0	0	1	0	6
McCree, Marlon, Hou.	1	0	0	1	0	6
McCutcheon, Daylon, Cle.	1	0	0	1	0	6
McGinest, Willie, N.E.	1	0	0	1	0	6
Minor, Travis, Mia.	1	1	0	0	0	6
Mirer, Rick, Oak.	1	1	0	0	0	6
Morris, Sammy, Buf.	1	1	0	0	0	6
Moulds, Eric, Buf.	1	0	1	0	0	6
Neal, Lorenzo, S.D.	1	1	0	0	0	6
Norman, Josh, S.D.	1	0	1	0	0	6
Ogden, Jonathan, Bal.	1	0	1	0	0	6
O'Neal, Deltha, Den.	1	0	0	1	0	6
Peelle, Justin, S.D.	1	0	1	0	0	6
Porter, Jerry, Oak.	1	0	1	0	0	6
Rhodes, Dominic, Ind.	1	0	1	0	0	6
Ricard, Alan, Bal.	1	0	0	1	0	6
Riemersma, Jay, Pit.	1	0	1	0	0	6
Rolle, Samari, Ten.	1	0	0	1	0	6
Samuel, Asante, N.E.	1	0	0	1	0	6
Sanders, Darnell, Cle.	1	0	1	0	0	6
Scott, Chad, Pit.	1	0	0	1	0	6
Smith, Hunter, Ind.	1	1	0	0	0	6
Sowell, Jerald, NYJ	1	0	1	0	0	6
Swayne, Kevin, NYJ	1	0	1	0	0	6
Townsend, Deshea, Pit.	1	0	0	1	0	6
Volek, Billy, Ten.	1	1	0	0	0	6
Ward, Dedric, N.E.	1	0	1	0	0	6
Whitted, Alvis, Oak.	1	0	1	0	0	6
Williams, Chad, Bal.	1	0	0	1	0	6
Williams, Pat, Buf.	1	0	0	1	0	6
Alexander, Stephen, S.D.	0	0	0	0	1	2
Prioleau, Pierson, Buf.	0	0	0	0	0	*2

* Safety
Team safety credited to Buffalo (2), Denver, Oakland, New England, and N.Y. Jets.

NFC—INDIVIDUAL SCORERS

KICKERS

	XP	XPA	FG	FGA	PTS
Wilkins, Jeff, St.L	46	46	39	42	163
Kasay, John, Car.	29	30	32	38	125
Longwell, Ryan, G.B.	51	51	23	26	120
Akers, David, Phi.	42	42	24	29	114
Brown, Josh, Sea.	48	48	22	30	114
Edinger, Paul, Chi.	27	27	26	36	105
Carney, John, N.O.	36	37	22	30	102
Elling, Aaron, Min.	48	48	18	25	102
Hall, John, Was.	26	27	25	33	101
Cundiff, Billy, Dal.	30	31	23	29	99
Hanson, Jason, Det.	26	27	22	23	92
Feely, Jay, Atl.	32	33	19	27	89
Gramatica, Martín, T.B.	33	34	16	26	81
Peterson, Todd, S.F.	22	23	12	15	58
Bryant, Matt, NYG	17	17	11	14	50
Rackers, Neil, Ariz	8	8	9	12	35
Pochman, Owen, S.F.	9	10	8	15	33
Chandler, Jeff, S.F.	7	8	6	7	25
Duncan, Tim, Ariz	5	6	6	10	23
Gramatica, Bill, Ariz	6	6	3	4	15
Feagles, Jeff, NYG	0	0	0	1	0

NONKICKERS

	TD	TDR	TDP	TDM	2-PT.	PTS
Green, Ahman, G.B.	20	15	5	0	0	120
Moss, Randy, Min.	17	0	17	0	0	102

		XP	XPA	FG	FGA	PTS
Alexander, Shaun, Sea.	16	14	2	0	0	96
Westbrook, Brian, Phi.	13	7	4	2	0	78
Holt, Torry, St.L	12	0	12	0	0	72
Duckett, T.J., Atl.	11	11	0	0	0	66
Faulk, Marshall, St.L	11	10	1	0	0	66
Horn, Joe, N.O.	10	0	10	0	0	60
Buckhalter, Correll, Phi.	9	8	1	0	0	54
Jackson, Darrell, Sea.	9	0	9	0	0	54
McCardell, Keenan, T.B.	9	0	8	1	0	54
Owens, Terrell, S.F.	9	0	9	0	0	54
Walker, Javon, G.B.	9	0	9	0	0	54
Boldin, Anquan, Ariz	8	0	8	0	0	48
Davis, Stephen, Car.	8	8	0	0	0	48
McAllister, Deuce, N.O.	8	8	0	0	0	48
Smith, Steve, Car.	8	0	7	1	0	48
Williams, Moe, Min.	8	5	3	0	0	48
Barlow, Kevan, S.F.	7	6	1	0	0	42
Engram, Bobby, Sea.	7	0	6	1	0	42
Garcia, Jeff, S.F.	7	7	0	0	0	42
Staley, Duce, Phi.	7	5	2	0	0	42
Streets, Tai, S.F.	7	0	7	0	0	42
McCants, Darnerien, Was.	6	0	6	0	2	40
Coles, Laveranues, Was.	6	0	6	0	0	36
Hilliard, Ike, NYG	6	0	6	0	0	36
Thomas, Anthony, Chi.	6	6	0	0	0	36
Smith, Onterrio, Min.	5	5	0	0	1	32
Anderson, Richie, Dal.	5	1	4	0	0	30
Bruce, Isaac, St.L	5	0	5	0	0	30
Dunn, Warrick, Atl.	5	3	2	0	0	30
Gardner, Rod, Was.	5	0	5	0	0	30
Glenn, Terry, Dal.	5	0	5	0	0	30
Hambrick, Troy, Dal.	5	5	0	0	0	30
Robinson, Koren, Sea.	5	0	4	1	0	30
Toomer, Amani, NYG	5	0	5	0	0	30
Williams, Boo, N.O.	5	0	5	0	0	30
Franks, Bubba, G.B.	4	0	4	0	2	28
Hakim, Az-Zahir, Det.	4	0	4	0	1	26
Booker, Marty, Chi.	4	0	4	0	0	24
Bulger, Marc, St.L	4	4	0	0	0	24
Campbell, Kelly, Min.	4	0	4	0	0	24
Cartwright, Rock, Was.	4	4	0	0	0	24
Culpepper, Daunte, Min.	4	4	0	0	0	24
Ferguson, Robert, G.B.	4	0	4	0	0	24
Harris, Arlen, St.L	4	4	0	0	0	24
Hearst, Garrison, S.F.	4	3	1	0	0	24
Kleinsasser, Jimmy, Min.	4	0	4	0	0	24
Mili, Itula, Sea.	4	0	4	0	0	24
Pathon, Jerome, N.O.	4	0	4	0	0	24
Proehl, Ricky, Car.	4	0	4	0	0	24
Barber, Tiki, NYG	3	2	1	0	1	20
Stewart, Kordell, Chi.	3	3	0	0	1	20
Bryson, Shawn, Det.	3	3	0	0	0	18
Crumpler, Alge, Atl.	3	0	3	0	0	18
Fisher, Tony, G.B.	3	1	2	0	0	18
Henderson, William, G.B.	3	0	3	0	0	18
Johnson, Keyshawn, T.B.	3	0	3	0	0	18
Jones, Freddie, Ariz	3	0	3	0	0	18
Jones, Thomas, T.B.	3	3	0	0	0	18
Levens, Dorsey, NYG	3	3	0	0	0	18
Looker, Dane, St.L	3	0	3	0	0	18
McNabb, Donovan, Phi.	3	3	0	0	0	18
Muhammad, Muhsin, Car.	3	0	3	0	0	18
Price, Peerless, Atl.	3	0	3	0	0	18
Ritchie, Jon, Phi.	3	0	3	0	0	18
Rogers, Charles, Det.	3	0	3	0	0	18
Stallworth, Donte', N.O.	3	0	3	0	0	18
White, Dez, Chi.	3	0	3	0	0	18
Wilson, Cedrick, S.F.	3	0	2	1	0	18
Anderson, Scotty, Det.	2	0	2	0	1	14
Blake, Jeff, Ariz	2	2	0	0	1	14
Lloyd, Brandon, S.F.	2	0	2	0	1	14

2003 INDIVIDUAL STATISTICS—SCORING

	TD	TDR	TDP	TDM	2-PT.	PTS
McCareins, Justin, Ten.	8	0	7	1	0	48
Sharpe, Shannon, Den.	8	0	8	0	0	48
Warrick, Peter, Cin.	8	0	7	1	0	48
Bettis, Jerome, Pit.	7	7	0	0	1	44
Boston, David, S.D.	7	0	7	0	1	44
Crockett, Zack, Oak.	7	7	0	0	0	42
Taylor, Fred, Jac.	7	6	1	0	0	42
Wayne, Reggie, Ind.	7	0	7	0	0	42
Givens, David, N.E.	6	0	6	0	0	36
Robinson, Marcus, Bal.	6	0	6	0	0	36
Anderson, Mike, Den.	5	3	2	0	0	30
Cloud, Mike, N.E.	5	5	0	0	0	30
Davis, Andre', Cle.	5	0	5	0	0	30
George, Eddie, Ten.	5	5	0	0	0	30
Hall, Dante, K.C.	5	0	1	4	0	30
Kennison, Eddie, K.C.	5	0	5	0	0	30
Becht, Anthony, NYJ	4	0	4	0	1	26
Calico, Tyrone, Ten.	4	0	4	0	1	26
Heap, Todd, Bal.	3	0	3	0	4	26
McNair, Steve, Ten.	4	4	0	0	1	26
Bennett, Drew, Ten.	4	0	4	0	0	24
Bradford, Corey, Hou.	4	0	4	0	0	24
Brown, Troy, N.E.	4	0	4	0	0	24
Buchanon, Phillip, Oak.	4	0	0	4	0	24
Burress, Plaxico, Pit.	4	0	4	0	0	24
Garner, Charlie, Oak.	4	3	1	0	0	24
Graham, Daniel, N.E.	4	0	4	0	0	24
Johnson, Andre, Hou.	4	0	4	0	0	24
Jordan, LaMont, NYJ	4	4	0	0	0	24
Kinney, Erron, Ten.	4	0	3	1	0	24
Mack, Stacey, Hou.	4	4	0	0	0	24
Morton, Johnnie, K.C.	4	0	4	0	0	24
Shaw, Bobby, Buf.	4	0	4	0	0	24
Smith, Jimmy, Jac.	4	0	4	0	0	24
Smith, Rod, Den.	4	0	3	1	0	24
Washington, Kelley, Cin.	4	0	4	0	0	24
Wheatley, Tyrone, Oak.	4	4	0	0	0	24
Blaylock, Derrick, K.C.	3	2	1	0	0	18
Branch, Deion, N.E.	3	0	3	0	0	18
Dunn, Jason, K.C.	3	0	3	0	0	18
Edwards, Troy, Jac.	3	0	3	0	0	18
Fiedler, Jay, Mia.	3	3	0	0	0	18
Jackson, James, Cle.	3	3	0	0	0	18
Johnson, Bethel, N.E.	3	0	2	1	0	18
Johnson, Kevin, Cle.-Jac.	3	0	3	0	0	18
Jones, Terry, Bal.	3	0	3	0	0	18
McKnight, James, Mia.	3	1	2	0	0	18
McMichael, Randy, Mia.	3	0	2	1	0	18
Miller, Billy, Hou.	3	0	3	0	0	18
Morgan, Quincy, Cle.	3	0	3	0	0	18
Parker, Eric, S.D.	3	0	3	0	0	18
Plummer, Jake, Den.	3	3	0	0	0	18
Pollard, Marcus, Ind.	3	0	3	0	0	18
Randle El, Antwaan, Pit.	3	0	1	2	0	18
Reed, Ed, Bal.	3	0	0	3	0	18
Smith, Antowain, N.E.	3	3	0	0	0	18
Stokley, Brandon, Ind.	3	0	3	0	0	18
Taylor, Travis, Bal.	3	0	3	0	0	18
Toefield, LaBrandon, Jac.	3	2	1	0	0	18
Walters, Troy, Ind.	3	0	3	0	0	18
Williams, Ricky, Ind.	3	2	1	0	0	18
Holcombe, Robert, Ten.	2	1	1	0	1	14
Mungro, James, Ind.	2	2	0	0	1	14
Bledsoe, Drew, Buf.	2	2	0	0	0	12
Brown, Tim, Oak.	2	0	2	0	0	12
Bruschi, Tedy, N.E.	2	0	0	2	0	12
Carr, David, Hou.	2	2	0	0	0	12
Carter, Jonathan, NYJ	2	0	1	1	0	12
Conway, Curtis, NYJ	2	0	2	0	0	12
Dillon, Corey, Cin.	2	2	0	0	0	12
Droughns, Reuben, Den.	2	0	2	0	0	12
Dyson, Andre, Ten.	2	0	0	2	0	12
Fauria, Christian, N.E.	2	0	2	0	0	12
Flutie, Doug, S.D.	2	2	0	0	0	12
Gaffney, Jabar, Hou.	2	0	2	0	0	12
Gates, Antonio, S.D.	2	0	2	0	0	12
Green, Trent, K.C.	2	2	0	0	0	12
Hatchette, Matt, Jac.	2	0	2	0	0	12
Heinrich, Keith, Cle.	2	0	2	0	0	12
Johnson, Jeremi, Cin.	2	1	1	0	0	12
Leftwich, Byron, Jac.	2	2	0	0	0	12
Lelie, Ashley, Den.	2	0	2	0	0	12
Martin, Curtis, NYJ	2	2	0	0	0	12
Moore, Dave, Buf.	2	0	2	0	0	12
Northcutt, Dennis, Cle.	2	0	2	0	0	12
Osgood, Kassim, S.D.	2	0	2	0	0	12
Pennington, Chad, NYJ	2	2	0	0	0	12
Reed, Josh, Buf.	2	0	2	0	0	12
Rice, Jerry, Oak.	2	0	2	0	0	12
Schobel, Matt, Cin.	2	0	2	0	0	12
Smith, Musa, Bal.	2	2	0	0	0	12
Suggs, Lee, Cle.	2	2	0	0	0	12
Taylor, Chester, Bal.	2	2	0	0	0	12
White, Jamel, Cle.	2	1	1	0	0	12
Woods, Jerome, K.C.	2	0	0	2	0	12
Wrighster, George, Jac.	2	0	2	0	0	12
Wycheck, Frank, Ten.	2	0	2	0	0	12
Zereoue, Amos, Pit.	2	2	0	0	0	12
Boiman, Rocky, Ten.	1	0	0	1	0	*8
Taylor, Jason, Mia.	1	0	0	1	0	*8
Adams, Sam, Buf.	1	0	0	1	0	6
Allen, David, Jac.	1	0	1	0	0	6
Armstrong, Derick, Hou.	1	0	1	0	0	6
Ayodele, Akin, Jac.	1	0	0	1	0	6
Bennett, Brandon, Cin.	1	0	1	0	0	6
Berlin, Eddie, Ten.	1	0	1	0	0	6
Bowers, R.J., Cle.	1	0	1	0	0	6
Brackett, Gary, Ind.	1	0	0	1	0	6
Brady, Kyle, Jac.	1	0	1	0	0	6
Brady, Tom, N.E.	1	1	0	0	0	6
Brees, Drew, S.D.	1	0	1	0	0	6
Bruener, Mark, Pit.	1	0	1	0	0	6
Brunell, Mark, Jac.	1	1	0	0	0	6
Buckley, Terrell, Mia.	1	0	0	1	0	6
Bulluck, Keith, Ten.	1	0	0	1	0	6
Campbell, Mark, Buf.	1	0	1	0	0	6
Carlisle, Cooper, Den.	1	0	1	0	0	6
Carswell, Dwayne, Den.	1	0	1	0	0	6
Centers, Larry, N.E.	1	0	1	0	0	6
Chatham, Matt, N.E.	1	0	0	1	0	6
Chrebet, Wayne, NYJ	1	0	1	0	0	6
Clark, Dallas, Ind.	1	0	1	0	0	6
Clements, Nate, Buf.	1	0	0	1	0	6
Couch, Tim, Cle.	1	1	0	0	0	6
Doering, Chris, Pit.	1	0	1	0	0	6
Edwards, Marc, Jac.	1	1	0	0	0	6
Freeney, Dwight, Ind.	1	0	0	1	0	6
Fuamatu-Ma'afala, Chris, Jac.	1	1	0	0	0	6
Gabriel, Doug, Oak.	1	0	0	1	0	6
Gold, Ian, Den.	1	0	0	1	0	6
Green, William, Cle.	1	1	0	0	0	6
Hardy, Kevin, Cin.	1	0	0	1	0	6
Harper, Nick, Ind.	1	0	0	1	0	6
Harts, Shaunard, K.C.	1	0	0	1	0	6
Hope, Chris, Pit.	1	0	1	0	0	6
Johnson, Larry, K.C.	1	1	0	0	0	6
Johnson, Teyo, Oak.	1	0	1	0	0	6
Jolley, Doug, Oak.	1	0	1	0	0	6
Kelly, Reggie, Cin.	1	0	1	0	0	6
King, Andre, Cle.	1	0	0	1	0	6
Kreider, Dan, Pit.	1	1	0	0	0	6
Lassiter, Kwamie, S.D.	1	0	0	1	0	6

	TD	TDR	TDP	TDM	2-PT.	PTS
Alstott, Mike, T.B.	2	2	0	0	0	12
Azumah, Jerry, Chi.	2	0	0	2	0	12
Betts, Ladell, Was.	2	2	0	0	0	12
Bly, Dre', Det.	2	0	0	2	0	12
Brooks, Aaron, N.O.	2	2	0	0	0	12
Bryant, Antonio, Dal.	2	0	2	0	0	12
Burleson, Nate, Min.	2	0	2	0	0	12
Canidate, Trung, Was.	2	1	1	0	0	12
Carter, Quincy, Dal.	2	2	0	0	0	12
Cason, Aveion, Dal.	2	2	0	0	0	12
Clark, Desmond, Chi.	2	0	2	0	0	12
Conwell, Ernie, N.O.	2	0	2	0	0	12
Davenport, Najeh, G.B.	2	2	0	0	0	12
Driver, Donald, G.B.	2	0	2	0	0	12
Farris, Jimmy, Atl.	2	0	2	0	0	12
Finneran, Brian, Atl.	2	0	2	0	0	12
Fisher, Travis, St.L	2	0	0	2	0	12
Fitzsimmons, Casey, Det.	2	0	2	0	0	12
Forsey, Brock, Chi.	2	2	0	0	0	12
Foster, DeShaun, Car.	2	0	2	0	0	12
Gage, Justin, Chi.	2	0	2	0	0	12
Galloway, Joey, Dal.	2	0	2	0	0	12
Gary, Olandis, Det.	2	2	0	0	0	12
Gilmore, Bryan, Ariz	2	0	2	0	0	12
Griffith, Justin, Atl.	2	0	2	0	0	12
Hasselbeck, Matt, Sea.	2	2	0	0	0	12
Hodgins, James, Ariz	2	0	2	0	0	12
Jurevicius, Joe, T.B.	2	0	2	0	0	12
Lee, Charles, T.B.	2	0	2	0	0	12
Manumaleuna, Brandon, St.L	2	0	2	0	0	12
Martin, David, G.B.	2	0	2	0	0	12
Minter, Mike, Car.	2	0	0	2	0	12
Mitchell, Freddie, Phi.	2	0	2	0	0	12
Morton, Chad, Was.	2	0	1	1	0	12
Pinkston, Todd, Phi.	2	0	2	0	0	12
Pittman, Michael, T.B.	2	0	2	0	0	12
Pritchett, Stanley, Chi.	2	2	0	0	0	12
Ricks, Mikhael, Det.	2	0	2	0	0	12
Robinson, Jeff, Dal.	2	0	2	0	0	12
Sapp, Warren, T.B.	2	0	2	0	0	12
Schlesinger, Cory, Det.	2	0	2	0	0	12
Schroeder, Bill, Det.	2	0	2	0	0	12
Shiancoe, Visanthe, NYG	2	0	2	0	0	12
Shockey, Jeremy, NYG	2	0	2	0	0	12
Smith, Emmitt, Ariz	2	2	0	0	0	12
Swinton, Reggie, Det.	2	0	0	2	0	12
Williams, Aeneas, St.L	2	0	0	2	0	12
Yoder, Todd, T.B.	2	0	2	0	0	12
Huff, Orlando, Sea.	1	0	0	1	0	*8
Ambrose, Ashley, N.O.	1	0	0	1	0	6
Archuleta, Adam, St.L	1	0	0	1	0	6
Avery, John, Min.	1	0	1	0	0	6
Bailey, Boss, Det.	1	0	0	1	0	6
Bannister, Alex, Sea.	1	0	1	0	0	6
Barber, Ronde, T.B.	1	0	0	1	0	6
Barlow, Reggie, T.B.	1	0	1	0	0	6
Bates, D'Wayne, Min.	1	0	1	0	0	6
Beasley, Fred, S.F.	1	0	1	0	0	6
Bennett, Michael, Min.	1	1	0	0	0	6
Bickerstaff, Erik, Dal.	1	1	0	0	0	6
Bolden, Juran, Atl.	1	0	0	1	0	6
Briggs, Lance, Chi.	1	0	0	1	0	6
Brooks, Derrick, T.B.	1	0	0	1	0	6
Brown, Ralph, NYG	1	0	0	1	0	6
Bush, Steve, Ariz	1	0	1	0	0	6
Campbell, Dan, Dal.	1	0	1	0	0	6
Carter, Ki-Jana, N.O.	1	1	0	0	0	6
Chavous, Corey, Min.	1	0	0	1	0	6
Cook, Jameel, T.B.	1	0	1	0	0	6
Dantzler, Woody, Atl.	1	1	0	0	0	6
Delhomme, Jake, Car.	1	1	0	0	0	6
Dilger, Ken, T.B.	1	0	1	0	0	6
Drummond, Eddie, Det.	1	0	0	1	0	6
Dudley, Rickey, T.B.	1	0	1	0	0	6
Edwards, Mario, Dal.	1	0	0	1	0	6
Godfrey, Randall, Sea.	1	0	0	1	0	6
Goings, Nick, Car.	1	0	1	0	0	6
Gordon, Lamar, St.L	1	1	0	0	0	6
Harris, Al, G.B.	1	0	0	1	0	6
Harris, Corey, Det.	1	0	0	1	0	6
Harris, Kwame, S.F.	1	0	0	1	0	6
Heller, Will, T.B.	1	0	1	0	0	6
Hill, Renaldo, Ariz	1	0	0	1	0	6
Holmes, Kenny, NYG	1	0	0	1	0	6
Hoover, Brad, Car.	1	0	1	0	0	6
Jacobs, Taylor, Was.	1	0	1	0	0	6
Johnson, Bryant, Ariz	1	0	1	0	0	6
Johnson, Doug, Atl.	1	1	0	0	0	6
Johnson, Patrick, Was.	1	0	1	0	0	6
Johnstone, Lance, Min.	1	0	0	1	0	6
Kalu, N. D., Phi.	1	0	0	1	0	6
Lewis, Chad, Phi.	1	0	1	0	0	6
Lewis, Michael, N.O.	1	0	1	0	0	6
Manning, Ricky, Car.	1	0	0	1	0	6
Mathis, Kevin, Atl.	1	0	0	1	0	6
McBride, Tod, Atl.	1	0	0	1	0	6
McCown, Josh, Ariz	1	1	0	0	0	6
McKenzie, Mike, G.B.	1	0	0	1	0	6
McQuarters, R.W., Chi.	1	0	0	1	0	6
Mitchell, Brian, NYG	1	1	0	0	0	6
Morris, Maurice, Sea.	1	0	1	0	0	6
Nattiel, Michael, Min.	1	0	0	1	0	6
Plummer, Ahmed, S.F.	1	0	0	1	0	6
Poole, Nate, Ariz	1	0	1	0	0	6
Ramsey, Patrick, Was.	1	1	0	0	0	6
Rodgers, Derrick, N.O.	1	0	0	1	0	6
Rossum, Allen, Atl.	1	0	0	1	0	6
Scobey, Josh, Ariz	1	0	0	1	0	6
Singleton, Alshermond, Dal.	1	0	0	1	0	6
Smart, Rod, Car.	1	0	0	1	0	6
Smith, L.J., Phi.	1	0	1	0	0	6
Stecker, Aaron, T.B.	1	0	1	0	0	6
Strong, Mack, Sea.	1	1	0	0	0	6
Terrell, David, Chi.	1	0	1	0	0	6
Thomas, Fred, N.O.	1	0	0	1	0	6
Thrash, James, Phi.	1	0	1	0	0	6
Vick, Michael, Atl.	1	1	0	0	0	6
Walker, Aaron, S.F.	1	0	1	0	0	6
Walker, Frank, NYG	1	0	0	1	0	6
Walls, Wesley, G.B.	1	0	1	0	0	6
Wansley, Tim, T.B.	1	0	0	1	0	6
Washington, Keith, NYG	1	0	0	1	0	6
Weaver, Jed, S.F.	1	0	1	0	0	6
Wiggins, Jermaine, Car.	1	0	1	0	0	6
Wilkins, Marcus, G.B.	1	0	0	1	0	6
Williams, Brian, Min.	1	0	0	1	0	6
Williams, Randal, Dal.	1	0	0	1	0	6
Witten, Jason, Dal.	1	0	1	0	0	6
Allen, James, N.O.	0	0	0	0	0	*2
Armstead, Jessie, Was.	0	0	0	0	0	*2
Chandler, Chris, Chi.	0	0	0	0	1	2
Coleman, Kenyon, Dal.	0	0	0	0	0	*2
Collins, Kerry, NYG	0	0	0	0	1	2
Fenderson, James, N.O.	0	0	0	0	1	2
Glover, La'Roi, Dal.	0	0	0	0	0	*2
Goodwin, Hunter, Min.	0	0	0	0	1	2
Ulbrich, Jeff, S.F.	0	0	0	0	0	*2
Williams, Karl, T.B.	0	0	0	0	1	2
Wistrom, Grant, St.L	0	0	0	0	0	*2

Team safety credited to Carolina, Minnesota, Philadelphia, and Tampa Bay.

2003 INDIVIDUAL STATISTICS—SCORING

AMERICAN FOOTBALL CONFERENCE—SCORING

	TD	TDR	TDP	TDM	XKG	XKAtt	X2G	X2Att	FG	FGA	SAF	POINTS
Kansas City	63	32	24	7	58	59	0	3	16	20	0	484
Indianapolis	48	16	29	3	46	46	1	2	37	37	0	447
Tennessee	48	11	30	7	43	44	3	4	32	37	1	435
Baltimore	41	18	16	7	35	35	4	6	34	40	0	391
Denver	42	20	19	3	41	41	1	1	28	32	1	381
New England	39	9	23	7	37	38	0	0	25	34	1	348
Cincinnati	40	12	26	2	40	40	0	0	22	25	0	346
San Diego	38	16	21	1	36	36	2	2	15	20	0	313
Miami	35	14	17	4	33	34	0	1	22	29	1	311
Pittsburgh	33	10	19	4	31	32	1	1	23	32	0	300
N.Y. Jets	29	8	20	1	24	24	1	5	27	32	1	283
Jacksonville	31	13	17	1	30	30	0	1	20	33	0	276
Oakland	29	15	9	5	28	29	0	0	22	25	1	270
Houston	29	14	14	1	27	27	0	2	18	22	0	255
Cleveland	27	8	17	2	23	24	0	3	23	28	0	254
Buffalo	27	13	11	3	24	24	0	2	17	24	3	243
AFC Total	599	229	312	58	556	563	13	33	381	470	9	5337
AFC Average	37.4	14.3	19.5	3.6	34.8	35.2	0.8	2.1	23.8	29.4	0.6	333.6

NATIONAL FOOTBALL CONFERENCE—SCORING

	TD	TDR	TDP	TDM	XKG	XKAtt	X2G	X2Att	FG	FGA	SAF	POINTS
St. Louis	47	19	23	5	46	46	0	1	39	42	1	447
Green Bay	53	18	32	3	51	51	2	2	23	26	0	442
Minnesota	51	15	32	4	48	48	2	3	18	25	2	416
Seattle	48	17	27	4	48	48	0	0	22	30	1	404
San Francisco	44	16	25	3	38	41	1	3	26	37	1	384
Philadelphia	43	23	17	3	42	42	0	1	24	29	1	374
New Orleans	39	11	25	3	36	37	1	2	22	30	1	340
Carolina	33	9	19	5	29	30	0	3	32	38	1	325
Tampa Bay	36	5	27	4	33	34	1	2	16	26	1	301
Atlanta	35	17	14	4	32	33	0	1	19	27	0	299
Dallas	31	11	17	3	30	31	0	0	23	29	2	289
Washington	30	8	21	1	26	27	2	3	25	33	1	287
Chicago	29	13	12	4	27	27	2	2	26	36	0	283
Detroit	29	5	17	7	26	27	2	2	22	23	0	270
N.Y. Giants	26	6	16	4	23	23	2	3	20	27	0	243
Arizona	25	5	18	2	19	20	1	5	18	26	0	225
NFC Total	599	198	342	59	554	565	16	33	375	484	12	5329
NFC Average	37.4	12.4	21.4	3.7	34.6	35.3	1.0	2.1	23.4	30.3	0.8	333.1
NFL Total	1198	427	654	117	1110	1128	29	66	756	954	21	10666
NFL Average	37.4	13.3	20.4	3.7	34.7	35.3	0.9	2.1	23.6	29.8	0.7	333.3

FIELD GOALS

FIELD GOAL PERCENTAGE

AFC: 1.000 Mike Vanderjagt, Indianapolis
NFC: .957 Jason Hanson, Detroit

FIELD GOALS

NFC: 39 Jeff Wilkins, St. Louis
AFC: 37 Mike Vanderjagt, Indianapolis

FIELD GOAL ATTEMPTS

NFC: 42 Jeff Wilkins, St. Louis
AFC: 38 Matt Stover, Baltimore

FIELD GOALS, GAME

NFC: 7 Billy Cundiff, Dallas at N.Y. Giants, September 15 (8 attempts) - (OT)
AFC: 5 Kris Brown, Houston at Miami, September 7 (7 attempts)
5 Sebastian Janikowski, Oakland at Chicago, October 5 (6 attempts)
5 Mike Vanderjagt, Indianapolis at Tennessee, December 7 (5 attempts)

LONGEST FIELD GOAL

NFC: 58 Josh Brown, Seattle at Green Bay, October 5
AFC: 56 Wade Richey, Baltimore vs. Cleveland, September 14

AVERAGE YARDS MADE

NFC: 37.9 Jason Hanson, Detroit
AFC: 37.3 Sebastian Janikowski, Oakland

AMERICAN FOOTBALL CONFERENCE—FIELD GOALS

	FG	FGA	Pct	Long
Indianapolis	37	37	1.000	50
Cincinnati	22	25	.880	48
Oakland	22	25	.880	55
Denver	28	32	.875	51
Tennessee	32	37	.865	50
Baltimore	34	40	.850	56
N.Y. Jets	27	32	.844	48
Cleveland	23	28	.821	52
Houston	18	22	.818	50
Kansas City	16	20	.800	49
Miami	22	29	.759	52
San Diego	15	20	.750	51
New England	25	34	.735	48
Pittsburgh	23	32	.719	51
Buffalo	17	24	.708	44
Jacksonville	20	33	.606	53
AFC Total	381	470	—	56
AFC Average	23.8	29.4	.811	—

NATIONAL FOOTBALL CONFERENCE—FIELD GOALS

	FG	FGA	Pct	Long
Detroit	22	23	.957	54
St. Louis	39	42	.929	53
Green Bay	23	26	.885	50
Carolina	32	38	.842	53
Philadelphia	24	29	.828	57
Dallas	23	29	.793	52
Washington	25	33	.758	54
N.Y. Giants	20	27	.741	47
New Orleans	22	30	.733	50
Seattle	22	30	.733	58
Chicago	26	36	.722	54
Minnesota	18	25	.720	51
Atlanta	19	27	.704	46
San Francisco	26	37	.703	48
Arizona	18	26	.692	53
Tampa Bay	16	26	.615	50
NFC Total	375	484	—	58
NFC Average	23.4	30.3	.775	—
League Total	756	954	—	58
League Average	23.6	29.8	.792	—

2003 INDIVIDUAL STATISTICS—FIELD GOALS

AFC—INDIVIDUAL FIELD GOALS

	1-19 Yards	20-29 Yards	30-39 Yards	40-49 Yards	50 or Longer	Totals	Avg Yds Att	Avg Yds Made	Avg Yds Miss	Long
Vanderjagt, Mike, Ind.	0-0 —	17-17 1.000	7-7 1.000	12-12 1.000	1-1 1.000	37-37 1.000	33.8	33.8	—	50
Graham, Shayne, Cin.	0-0 —	5-5 1.000	10-10 1.000	7-8 .875	0-2 .000	22-25 .880	37.2	35.2	51.3	48
Janikowski, Sebastian, Oak.	0-0 —	6-6 1.000	6-6 1.000	9-10 .900	1-3 .333	22-25 .880	39.0	37.3	51.3	55
Anderson, Gary, Ten.	0-0 —	5-5 1.000	12-12 1.000	10-14 .714	0-0 —	27-31 .871	36.5	35.3	44.8	43
Elam, Jason, Den.	0-0 —	10-11 .909	6-6 1.000	9-11 .818	2-3 .667	27-31 .871	36.2	35.4	41.5	51
Stover, Matt, Bal.	0-0 —	16-16 1.000	6-6 1.000	11-14 .786	0-2 .000	33-38 .868	34.7	32.8	47.6	49
Dawson, Phil, Cle.	2-2 1.000	7-7 1.000	4-5 .800	3-5 .600	2-2 1.000	18-21 .857	33.6	32.1	43.0	52
Brien, Doug, NYJ	0-0 —	5-5 1.000	15-15 1.000	7-8 .875	0-4 .000	27-32 .844	37.3	35.0	49.6	48
Brown, Kris, Hou.	1-1 1.000	3-3 1.000	8-8 1.000	5-6 .833	1-4 .250	18-22 .818	38.2	35.6	49.8	50
Andersen, Morten, K.C.	0-0 —	3-3 1.000	8-8 1.000	5-8 .625	0-1 .000	16-20 .800	39.1	36.9	47.5	49
Mare, Olindo, Mia.	0-0 —	9-9 1.000	3-6 .500	6-8 .750	4-6 .667	22-29 .759	37.4	35.5	43.1	52
Christie, Steve, S.D.	1-1 1.000	6-6 1.000	3-3 1.000	3-7 .429	2-3 .667	15-20 .750	35.9	32.7	45.4	51
Conway, Brett, NYG-Cle.	1-1 1.000	3-3 1.000	6-9 .667	4-6 .667	0-0 —	14-19 .737	36.8	34.9	42.0	48
Vinatieri, Adam, N.E.	0-0 —	16-17 .941	4-8 .500	5-8 .625	0-1 .000	25-34 .735	33.0	30.4	40.2	48
Reed, Jeff, Pit.	0-0 —	9-12 .750	6-7 .857	7-12 .583	1-1 1.000	23-32 .719	34.4	33.8	36.1	51
Lindell, Rian, Buf.	0-0 —	11-12 .917	3-3 1.000	3-7 .429	0-2 .000	17-24 .708	33.9	29.5	44.4	44
Marler, Seth, Jac.	0-0 —	10-11 .909	4-8 .500	5-12 .417	1-2 .500	20-33 .606	35.9	33.5	39.5	53
(Nonqualifiers)										
Hentrich, Craig, Ten.	0-0 —	0-0 —	2-2 1.000	2-2 1.000	0-1 .000	4-5 .800	43.2	41.0	52.0	49
Richey, Wade, Bal.	0-0 —	0-0 —	0-0 —	0-0 —	1-2 .500	1-2 .500	53.5	56.0	51.0	56
Knorr, Micah, Den.	0-0 —	1-1 1.000	0-0 —	0-0 —	0-0 —	1-1 1.000	27.0	27.0	—	27
Nedney, Joe, Ten.	0-0 —	0-0 —	0-0 —	0-0 —	1-1 1.000	1-1 1.000	50.0	50.0	—	50
AFC Totals	5-5 1.000	139-146 .952	108-123 .878	112-155 .723	17-41 .415	381-470 .811	36.0	34.3	43.6	56
NFL Totals	6-6 1.000	270-281 .961	229-277 .827	206-297 .694	45-93 .484	756-954 .792	36.5	34.7	43.6	58

Leader based on overall percentage, minimum 16 field goals.

NFC—INDIVIDUAL FIELD GOALS

	1-19 Yards	20-29 Yards	30-39 Yards	40-49 Yards	50 or Longer	Totals	Avg Yds Att	Avg Yds Made	Avg Yds Miss	Long
Hanson, Jason, Det.	0-0 —	7-7 1.000	6-6 1.000	5-6 .833	4-4 1.000	22-23 .957	38.1	37.9	43.0	54
Wilkins, Jeff, St.L	0-0 —	16-16 1.000	11-13 .846	8-9 .889	4-4 1.000	39-42 .929	35.9	35.5	41.7	53
Longwell, Ryan, G.B.	0-0 —	5-5 1.000	11-11 1.000	6-9 .667	1-1 1.000	23-26 .885	36.2	35.0	44.7	50
Kasay, John, Car.	0-0 —	13-13 1.000	6-8 .750	11-13 .846	2-4 .500	32-38 .842	36.9	35.3	45.3	53
Akers, David, Phi.	0-0 —	9-9 1.000	7-7 1.000	6-10 .600	2-3 .667	24-29 .828	36.4	34.3	46.4	57
Cundiff, Billy, Dal.	0-0 —	11-11 1.000	5-6 .833	4-7 .571	3-5 .600	23-29 .793	36.0	33.7	45.0	52
Hall, John, Was.	0-0 —	8-8 1.000	7-9 .778	6-9 .667	4-7 .571	25-33 .758	38.8	36.6	45.5	54
Brown, Josh, Sea.	0-0 —	5-5 1.000	10-11 .909	6-11 .545	1-3 .333	22-30 .733	39.7	37.1	46.8	58
Carney, John, N.O.	0-0 —	6-6 1.000	10-12 .833	5-9 .556	1-3 .333	22-30 .733	38.4	35.3	47.0	50
Edinger, Paul, Chi.	1-1 1.000	4-4 1.000	9-13 .692	9-14 .643	3-4 .750	26-36 .722	38.4	37.7	40.3	54
Elling, Aaron, Min.	0-0 —	7-7 1.000	6-8 .750	4-7 .571	1-3 .333	18-25 .720	36.8	33.8	44.4	51
Feely, Jay, Atl.	0-0 —	6-6 1.000	9-11 .818	4-7 .571	0-3 .000	19-27 .704	38.1	34.3	47.1	46
Gramatica, Martín, T.B.	0-0 —	9-9 1.000	3-6 .500	3-8 .375	1-3 .333	16-26 .615	37.2	31.9	45.6	50
(Nonqualifiers)										
Peterson, Todd, S.F.	0-0 —	5-7 .714	3-3 1.000	4-4 1.000	0-1 .000	12-15 .800	33.7	32.9	36.7	48
Pochman, Owen, S.F.	0-0 —	1-1 1.000	3-8 .375	4-5 .800	0-1 .000	8-15 .533	39.3	39.3	39.3	48
Bryant, Matt, NYG	0-0 —	3-4 .750	4-5 .800	4-5 .800	0-0 —	11-14 .786	34.7	34.5	35.3	47
Rackers, Neil, Ariz	0-0 —	5-5 1.000	1-4 .250	3-3 1.000	0-0 —	9-12 .750	33.0	32.2	35.3	49
Duncan, Tim, Ariz	0-0 —	2-2 1.000	2-4 .500	1-2 .500	1-2 .500	6-10 .600	37.1	34.8	40.5	53
Chandler, Jeff, S.F.	0-0 —	5-5 1.000	1-1 1.000	0-1 .000	0-0 —	6-7 .857	29.6	27.3	43.0	35
Gramatica, Bill, Ariz	0-0 —	1-1 1.000	2-2 1.000	0-0 —	0-1 .000	3-4 .750	37.3	32.0	53.0	38
Feagles, Jeff, NYG	0-0 —	0-1 .000	0-0 —	0-0 —	0-0 —	0-1 .000	29.0	—	29.0	—
NFC Totals	1-1 1.000	131-135 .970	121-154 .786	94-142 .662	28-52 .538	375-484 .775	37.0	35.1	43.6	58
NFL Totals	6-6 1.000	270-281 .961	229-277 .827	206-297 .694	45-93 .484	756-954 .792	36.5	34.7	43.6	58

Leader based on overall percentage, minimum 16 field goals

RUSHING

YARDS

AFC: 2066 Jamal Lewis, Baltimore
NFC: 1883 Ahman Green, Green Bay

YARDS, GAME

AFC: 295 Jamal Lewis, Baltimore vs. Cleveland, September 14 (30 attempts, 2 TD)
NFC: 218 Ahman Green, Green Bay vs. Denver, December 28 (20 attempts, 2 TD)

LONGEST

NFC: 98 Ahman Green, Green Bay vs. Denver, December 28 - TD
AFC: 82 Jamal Lewis, Baltimore vs. Cleveland, September 14 - TD

ATTEMPTS

AFC: 392 Ricky Williams, Miami
NFC: 355 Ahman Green, Green Bay

ATTEMPTS, GAME

AFC: 43 Rudi Johnson, Cincinnati vs. Houston, November 9 (182 yards, 2 TD)
NFC: 35 Marcel Shipp, Arizona vs. San Francisco, October 26 (165 yards, 0 TD) - (OT)

YARDS PER ATTEMPT

AFC: 5.5 Clinton Portis, Denver
NFC: 5.4 Onterrio Smith, Minnesota

TOUCHDOWNS

AFC: 27 Priest Holmes, Kansas City
NFC: 15 Ahman Green, Green Bay

TEAM LEADERS, YARDS

AFC: BALTIMORE, 2066, Jamal Lewis; BUFFALO, 1356, Travis Henry; CINCINNATI, 957, Rudi Johnson; CLEVELAND, 559, William Green; DENVER, 1591, Clinton Portis; HOUSTON, 1031, Domanick Davis; INDIANAPOLIS, 1259, Edgerrin James; JACKSONVILLE, 1572, Fred Taylor; KANSAS CITY, 1420, Priest Holmes; MIAMI, 1372, Ricky Williams; NEW ENGLAND, 642, Antowain Smith; N.Y. JETS, 1308, Curtis Martin; OAKLAND, 678, Tyrone Wheatley; PITTSBURGH, 811, Jerome Bettis; SAN DIEGO, 1645, LaDainian Tomlinson; TENNESSEE, 1031, Eddie George

NFC: ARIZONA, 830, Marcel Shipp; ATLANTA, 779, T.J. Duckett; CAROLINA, 1444, Stephen Davis; CHICAGO, 1024, Anthony Thomas; DALLAS, 972, Troy Hambrick; DETROIT, 606, Shawn Bryson; GREEN BAY, 1883, Ahman Green; MINNESOTA, 745, Moe Williams; NEW ORLEANS, 1641, Deuce McAllister; N.Y. GIANTS, 1216, Tiki Barber; PHILADELPHIA, 613, Brian Westbrook; ST. LOUIS, 818, Marshall Faulk; SAN FRANCISCO, 1024, Kevan Barlow; SEATTLE, 1435, Shaun Alexander; TAMPA BAY, 751, Michael Pittman; WASHINGTON, 600, Trung Canidate

TEAM CHAMPION

AFC: 2674 Baltimore
NFC: 2558 Green Bay

NFL TOP TEN RUSHERS

	Att	Yards	Avg	Long	TD
Lewis, Jamal, Bal.	387	2066	5.3	82t	14
Green, Ahman, G.B.	355	1883	5.3	98t	15
Tomlinson, LaDainian, S.D.	313	1645	5.3	73t	13
McAllister, Deuce, N.O.	351	1641	4.7	76t	8
Portis, Clinton, Den.	290	1591	5.5	65t	14
Taylor, Fred, Jac.	345	1572	4.6	62	6
Davis, Stephen, Car.	318	1444	4.5	40	8
Alexander, Shaun, Sea.	326	1435	4.4	55	14
Holmes, Priest, K.C.	320	1420	4.4	31t	27
Williams, Ricky, Mia.	392	1372	3.5	45	9

AFC—INDIVIDUAL RUSHERS

	Att	Yards	Avg	Long	TD
Lewis, Jamal, Bal.	387	2066	5.3	82t	14
Tomlinson, LaDainian, S.D.	313	1645	5.3	73t	13
Portis, Clinton, Den.	290	1591	5.5	65t	14
Taylor, Fred, Jac.	345	1572	4.6	62	6
Holmes, Priest, K.C.	320	1420	4.4	31t	27
Williams, Ricky, Mia.	392	1372	3.5	45	9
Henry, Travis, Buf.	331	1356	4.1	64	10
Martin, Curtis, NYJ	323	1308	4.0	56	2
James, Edgerrin, Ind.	310	1259	4.1	43	11
Davis, Domanick, Hou.	238	1031	4.3	51	8
George, Eddie, Ten.	312	1031	3.3	27	5
Johnson, Rudi, Cin.	215	957	4.5	54	9
Bettis, Jerome, Pit.	246	811	3.3	21	7
Wheatley, Tyrone, Oak.	159	678	4.3	41	4
Smith, Antowain, N.E.	182	642	3.5	30	3
Faulk, Kevin, N.E.	178	638	3.6	23	0
Green, William, Cle.	142	559	3.9	26	1
Garner, Charlie, Oak.	120	553	4.6	33	3
Dillon, Corey, Cin.	138	541	3.9	39	2
Zereoue, Amos, Pit.	132	433	3.3	22	2
Jackson, James, Cle.	102	382	3.7	18	3
Griffin, Quentin, Den.	94	345	3.7	23	0
Suggs, Lee, Cle.	56	289	5.2	78t	2
Taylor, Chester, Bal.	63	276	4.4	32	2
White, Jamel, Cle.	70	266	3.8	23	1
Anderson, Mike, Den.	70	257	3.7	44	3
Mack, Stacey, Hou.	93	253	2.7	13	4
Brown, Chris, Ten.	56	221	3.9	28	0
Toefield, LaBrandon, Jac.	53	212	4.0	30	2
Plummer, Jake, Den.	37	205	5.5	40	3
Fargas, Justin, Oak.	40	203	5.1	53	0
Holcombe, Robert, Ten.	63	201	3.2	21	1
Minor, Travis, Mia.	41	193	4.7	26	1
Jordan, LaMont, NYJ	46	190	4.1	39	4
Bennett, Brandon, Cin.	56	173	3.1	19	0
Flutie, Doug, S.D.	33	168	5.1	17	2
Rhodes, Dominic, Ind.	37	157	4.2	25	0
Warrick, Peter, Cin.	18	157	8.7	50	0
Williams, Ricky, Ind.	48	155	3.2	19	2
Carr, David, Hou.	27	151	5.6	36	2
Crockett, Zack, Oak.	48	145	3.0	44	7
Fuamatu-Ma'afala, Chris, Jac.	35	144	4.1	18	1
McNair, Steve, Ten.	38	138	3.6	23	4
Cloud, Mike, N.E.	27	118	4.4	42	5
Burns, Joe, Buf.	39	113	2.9	12	0
Kitna, Jon, Cin.	38	113	3.0	15	0
Blaylock, Derrick, K.C.	22	112	5.1	25t	2
Leftwich, Byron, Jac.	25	108	4.3	18	2
Hollings, Tony, Hou.	38	102	2.7	17	0
Smith, Rod, Den.	10	98	9.8	26	0
Morton, Johnnie, K.C.	8	94	11.8	39	0
Dwight, Tim, S.D.	9	88	9.8	20	0
Fiedler, Jay, Mia.	34	88	2.6	14	3
Johnson, Larry, K.C.	20	85	4.3	15	1
Brees, Drew, S.D.	21	84	4.0	18	0

	Att	Yards	Avg	Long	TD
Green, Trent, K.C.	26	83	3.2	14	2
Mirer, Rick, Oak.	20	83	4.2	20	1
Northcutt, Dennis, Cle.	12	83	6.9	23	0
Centers, Larry, N.E.	21	82	3.9	13	0
Ricard, Alan, Bal.	19	79	4.2	30	0
McKnight, James, Mia.	2	75	37.5	68t	1
Randle El, Antwaan, Pit.	15	75	5.0	32	0
Hall, Dante, K.C.	16	73	4.6	16	0
Wright, Anthony, Bal.	28	73	2.6	17	0
Morris, Sammy, Buf.	19	70	3.7	12	1
Moss, Santana, NYJ	10	67	6.7	25	0
Brady, Tom, N.E.	42	63	1.5	11	1
Haynes, Verron, Pit.	20	63	3.2	15	0
Boller, Kyle, Bal.	30	62	2.1	15	0
Taylor, Travis, Bal.	11	62	5.6	16	0
Ward, Hines, Pit.	11	61	5.5	25	0
Mungro, James, Ind.	24	60	2.5	9	2
Richardson, Tony, K.C.	24	60	2.5	8	0
Ragone, Dave, Hou.	6	51	8.5	14	0
Lelie, Ashley, Den.	8	43	5.4	13	0
Pennington, Chad, NYJ	21	42	2.0	10t	2
Johnson, Jeremi, Cin.	15	41	2.7	12	1
Neal, Lorenzo, S.D.	18	40	2.2	7	1
Caldwell, Reche, S.D.	5	39	7.8	14	0
Couch, Tim, Cle.	11	39	3.5	17	1
Reed, Josh, Buf.	3	38	12.7	16	0
Whitted, Alvis, Oak.	6	37	6.2	16	0
Sapp, Cecil, Den.	12	31	2.6	5	0
Smith, Musa, Bal.	9	31	3.4	11t	2
Chambers, Chris, Mia.	4	30	7.5	12	0
Redmond, J.R., Oak.	9	30	3.3	9	0
Turk, Matt, Mia.	3	30	10.0	23	0
Bledsoe, Drew, Buf.	24	29	1.2	11	2
Kreider, Dan, Pit.	7	29	4.1	9	1
Davis, Andre', Cle.	5	28	5.6	7	0
Martin, Tee, Oak.	5	28	5.6	8	0
Banks, Tony, Hou.	6	27	4.5	13	0
Brown, Troy, N.E.	6	27	4.5	11	0
Pass, Patrick, N.E.	6	27	4.5	11	0
Johnson, Leon, S.D.	4	26	6.5	18	0
Manning, Peyton, Ind.	28	26	0.9	10	0
Tuiasosopo, Marques, Oak.	6	22	3.7	8	0
Heap, Todd, Bal.	3	21	7.0	9	0
Johnson, Rob, Was.-Oak.	3	21	7.0	14	0
Moorman, Brian, Buf.	1	21	21.0	21	0
Parker, Eric, S.D.	3	21	7.0	13	0
Smith, Hunter, Ind.	1	21	21.0	21t	1
Brunell, Mark, Jac.	8	19	2.4	12	1
Boston, David, S.D.	3	18	6.0	13	0
Gannon, Rich, Oak.	6	18	3.0	6	0
Brown, Antonio, Buf.	1	17	17.0	17	0
Chatman, Jesse, S.D.	8	17	2.1	6	0
Konrad, Rob, Mia.	4	17	4.3	11	0
Testaverde, Vinny, NYJ	6	17	2.8	13	0
Griese, Brian, Mia.	5	15	3.0	9	0
Dawson, Phil, Cle.	1	14	14.0	14	0
Droughns, Reuben, Den.	6	14	2.3	12	0
Neufeld, Ryan, Buf.	1	14	14.0	14	0
Wells, Jonathan, Hou.	5	14	2.8	10	0
Beuerlein, Steve, Den.	5	13	2.6	7	0
Edwards, Marc, Jac.	7	13	1.9	3	1
Gaffney, Jabar, Hou.	1	13	13.0	13	0
McCareins, Justin, Ten.	1	13	13.0	13	0
Maddox, Tommy, Pit.	13	12	0.9	6	0
Stanley, Chad, Hou.	1	12	12.0	12	0
Batch, Charlie, Pit.	1	11	11.0	11	0
Branch, Deion, N.E.	1	11	11.0	11	0
Mason, Derrick, Ten.	3	11	3.7	7	0
Madise, Adrian, Den.	1	10	10.0	10	0
Porter, Jerry, Oak.	1	10	10.0	10	0
Askew, B.J., NYJ	2	9	4.5	6	0
Jackson, Jarious, Den.	1	9	9.0	9	0
Kennison, Eddie, K.C.	2	9	4.5	5	0
Allen, David, Jac.	4	8	2.0	6	0
Cole, Chris, Den.	2	8	4.0	8	0
Huard, Brock, Ind.	3	8	2.7	9	0
Boyer, Brant, Cle.	1	7	7.0	7	0
Holcomb, Kelly, Cle.	8	7	0.9	6	0
Simmons, Jason, Hou.	1	7	7.0	7	0
Lewis, Jermaine, Jac.	1	6	6.0	6	0
Walters, Troy, Ind.	1	6	6.0	6	0
Brown, Travis, Buf.	1	5	5.0	5	0
Calico, Tyrone, Ten.	1	5	5.0	5	0
Kanell, Danny, Den.	6	5	0.8	9	0
Klecko, Dan, N.E.	2	5	2.5	5	0
Washington, Kelley, Cin.	1	5	5.0	5	0
Patten, David, N.E.	1	4	4.0	4	0
Redman, Chris, Bal.	2	4	2.0	4	0
Simonton, Ken, Buf.	2	4	2.0	2	0
Volek, Billy, Ten.	11	4	0.4	5	1
Gash, Sam, Buf.	1	3	3.0	3	0
Harrison, Marvin, Ind.	1	3	3.0	3	0
McCrary, Fred, N.E.	3	3	1.0	4	0
Sowell, Jerald, NYJ	1	2	2.0	2	0
Curry, Ronald, Oak.	1	0	0.0	0	0
Faine, Jeff, Cle.	1	0	0.0	0	0
O'Neal, Deltha, Den.	1	0	0.0	0	0
Walter, Ken, N.E.	2	0	0.0	0	0
Huard, Damon, N.E.	1	-1	-1.0	-1	0
O'Donnell, Neil, Ten.	1	-1	-1.0	-1	0
Rosenfels, Sage, Mia.	1	-1	-1.0	-1	0
Ayanbadejo, Obafemi, Mia.	1	-2	-2.0	-2	0
Morgan, Quincy, Cle.	3	-4	-1.3	2	0
Van Pelt, Alex, Buf.	4	-6	-1.5	-1	0
Burress, Plaxico, Pit.	1	-7	-7.0	-7	0
Collins, Todd, K.C.	8	-7	-0.9	0	0
Edwards, Troy, Jac.	3	-9	-3.0	4	0
Johnson, Andre, Hou.	5	-10	-2.0	11	0
Johnson, Bethel, N.E.	1	-12	-12.0	-12	0

t = Touchdown
Leader based on most yards gained

NFC—INDIVIDUAL RUSHERS

	Att	Yards	Avg	Long	TD
Green, Ahman, G.B.	355	1883	5.3	98t	15
McAllister, Deuce, N.O.	351	1641	4.7	76t	8
Davis, Stephen, Car.	318	1444	4.5	40	8
Alexander, Shaun, Sea.	326	1435	4.4	55	14
Barber, Tiki, NYG	278	1216	4.4	27	2
Barlow, Kevan, S.F.	201	1024	5.1	78t	6
Thomas, Anthony, Chi.	244	1024	4.2	67t	6
Hambrick, Troy, Dal.	275	972	3.5	42	5
Shipp, Marcel, Ariz	228	830	3.6	36	0
Faulk, Marshall, St.L	209	818	3.9	52	10
Duckett, T.J., Atl.	197	779	4.0	55	11
Hearst, Garrison, S.F.	178	768	4.3	36	3
Pittman, Michael, T.B.	187	751	4.0	17	0
Williams, Moe, Min.	174	745	4.3	61	5
Dunn, Warrick, Atl.	125	672	5.4	69t	3
Jones, Thomas, T.B.	137	627	4.6	61	3
Westbrook, Brian, Phi.	117	613	5.2	62t	7
Bryson, Shawn, Det.	158	606	3.8	39	3
Canidate, Trung, Was.	142	600	4.2	38	1
Smith, Onterrio, Min.	107	579	5.4	47	5
Buckhalter, Correll, Phi.	126	542	4.3	64t	8

2003 INDIVIDUAL STATISTICS—RUSHING

	Att	Yards	Avg	Long	TD
Staley, Duce, Phi.	96	463	4.8	22	5
Bennett, Michael, Min.	90	447	5.0	28	1
Foster, DeShaun, Car.	113	429	3.8	21	0
Culpepper, Daunte, Min.	73	422	5.8	42	4
Davenport, Najeh, G.B.	77	420	5.5	76t	2
Cartwright, Rock, Was.	107	411	3.8	22	4
Gary, Olandis, Det.	113	384	3.4	27	2
McNabb, Donovan, Phi.	71	355	5.0	34	3
Garcia, Jeff, S.F.	56	319	5.7	21t	7
Anderson, Richie, Dal.	70	306	4.4	19	1
Gordon, Lamar, St.L	71	298	4.2	20	1
Stewart, Kordell, Chi.	59	290	4.9	25	3
Carter, Quincy, Dal.	68	257	3.8	19	2
Smith, Emmitt, Ariz	90	256	2.8	22	2
Betts, Ladell, Was.	77	255	3.3	13t	2
Harris, Arlen, St.L	85	255	3.0	18	4
Vick, Michael, Atl.	40	255	6.4	43	1
Morris, Maurice, Sea.	38	239	6.3	43	0
Cason, Aveion, Dal.	40	220	5.5	63t	2
Morton, Chad, Was.	48	216	4.5	27	0
Fisher, Tony, G.B.	40	200	5.0	19	1
Levens, Dorsey, NYG	68	197	2.9	17	3
Forsey, Brock, Chi.	50	191	3.8	17	2
Blake, Jeff, Ariz	30	177	5.9	19	2
Brooks, Aaron, N.O.	54	175	3.2	15	2
Strong, Mack, Sea.	37	174	4.7	21t	1
Griffith, Justin, Atl.	38	168	4.4	15	0
McCown, Josh, Ariz	28	158	5.6	16t	1
Robertson, Jamal, S.F.	32	136	4.3	23	0
Hasselbeck, Matt, Sea.	36	125	3.5	18	2
Stecker, Aaron, T.B.	37	125	3.4	15	0
Murrell, Adrian, Dal.	28	107	3.8	17	0
Pinner, Artose, Det.	39	99	2.5	12	0
Pritchett, Stanley, Chi.	21	93	4.4	18	2
Harrington, Joey, Det.	30	86	2.9	26	0
Alstott, Mike, T.B.	27	77	2.9	29	2
Bulger, Marc, St.L	29	75	2.6	28	4
Carter, Ki-Jana, N.O.	19	72	3.8	31	1
Campbell, Kelly, Min.	10	71	7.1	19	0
Peterson, Adrian, Chi.	22	70	3.2	10	0
Goings, Nick, Car.	10	69	6.9	17	0
Anderson, Damien, Ariz	18	68	3.8	17	0
Ramsey, Patrick, Was.	15	62	4.1	24	1
Smith, Lamar, N.O.	11	61	5.5	17	0
Bickerstaff, Erik, Dal.	19	56	2.9	9	1
Glenn, Terry, Dal.	3	55	18.3	47	0
Thrash, James, Phi.	5	52	10.4	47	0
Driver, Donald, G.B.	5	51	10.2	45	0
Hakim, Az-Zahir, Det.	3	51	17.0	35	0
Collins, Kerry, NYG	17	49	2.9	22	0
Smart, Rod, Car.	20	49	2.5	6	0
Smith, Steve, Car.	11	42	3.8	14	0
Hasselbeck, Tim, Was.	15	41	2.7	11	0
Boldin, Anquan, Ariz	5	40	8.0	23	0
Coles, Laveranues, Was.	10	39	3.9	23	0
Delhomme, Jake, Car.	42	39	0.9	9	1
Joyce, Delvin, NYG	11	39	3.5	8	0
Abdullah, Rabih, Chi.	18	37	2.1	10	0
Chandler, Chris, Chi.	14	35	2.5	11	0
Chapman, Doug, Min.	15	33	2.2	6	0
Johnson, Brad, T.B.	25	33	1.3	13	0
McMahon, Mike, Det.	5	32	6.4	12	0
Cobourne, Avon, Det.	10	27	2.7	19	0
Beasley, Fred, S.F.	17	24	1.4	5	0
Evans, Heath, Sea.	7	24	3.4	8	0
Palmer, Jesse, NYG	4	23	5.8	26	0
Galloway, Joey, Dal.	4	22	5.5	10	0
Dantzler, Woody, Atl.	8	21	2.6	12	1
Hoover, Brad, Car.	6	21	3.5	5	0
Johnson, Doug, Atl.	14	21	1.5	13	1
King, Shaun, T.B.	4	20	5.0	12	0
Mitchell, Brian, NYG	4	20	5.0	18	1
Hilliard, Ike, NYG	2	19	9.5	13	0
Moss, Randy, Min.	6	18	3.0	11	0
Bruce, Isaac, St.L	2	17	8.5	14	0
Rogers, Charles, Det.	2	17	8.5	12	0
Schlesinger, Cory, Det.	9	16	1.8	4	0
Favre, Brett, G.B.	18	15	0.8	7	0
Horn, Joe, N.O.	2	15	7.5	13	0
Johnson, Eddie, Min.	2	15	7.5	15	0
Kleinsasser, Jimmy, Min.	2	15	7.5	12	0
Layne, George, Atl.	1	15	15.0	15	0
Manumaleuna, Brandon, St.L	4	15	3.8	8	0
Robinson, Koren, Sea.	4	15	3.8	16	0
Battle, Arnaz, S.F.	2	14	7.0	9	0
Fenderson, James, N.O.	4	14	3.5	6	0
Lee, Charles, T.B.	2	14	7.0	8	0
Wade, Bobby, Chi.	5	14	2.8	6	0
Kittner, Kurt, Atl.	8	13	1.6	7	0
McAfee, Fred, N.O.	1	13	13.0	13	0
White, Dez, Chi.	2	13	6.5	12	0
Swinton, Reggie, Det.	3	11	3.7	9	0
McCullough, Sultan, Was.	1	9	9.0	9	0
Simon, John, Was.	3	9	3.0	6	0
Martin, Jamar, Dal.	4	7	1.8	3	0
McDonald, Shaun, St.L	2	7	3.5	5	0
Wilkins, Jeff, St.L	1	7	7.0	7	0
Hodgins, James, Ariz	2	6	3.0	3	0
Furrey, Mike, St.L	3	5	1.7	2	0
Holt, Torry, St.L	1	5	5.0	5	0
Johnson, Bryan, Was.	2	5	2.5	4	0
Smith, Paul, Det.	2	5	2.5	3	0
Toomer, Amani, NYG	1	5	5.0	5	0
Terrell, David, Chi.	1	4	4.0	4	0
Carney, John, N.O.	1	3	3.0	3	0
Jefferson, Shawn, Det.	1	3	3.0	3	0
Luchey, Nicolas, G.B.	1	3	3.0	3	0
Price, Peerless, Atl.	2	3	1.5	5	0
Stallworth, Donte', N.O.	1	3	3.0	3	0
Lewis, Michael, N.O.	1	2	2.0	2	0
McCord, Quentin, Atl.	2	2	1.0	1	0
Williams, Karl, T.B.	1	2	2.0	2	0
Bouman, Todd, N.O.	3	1	0.3	2	0
Drummond, Eddie, Det.	1	1	1.0	1	0
Ritchie, Jon, Phi.	1	1	1.0	1	0
Walker, Javon, G.B.	2	1	0.5	1	0
Avery, John, Min.	1	0	0.0	0	0
Bryant, Antonio, Dal.	2	0	0.0	2	0
Feagles, Jeff, NYG	1	0	0.0	0	0
Gilmore, Bryan, Ariz	1	0	0.0	0	0
Lafleur, Bill, S.F.	1	0	0.0	0	0
Maynard, Brad, Chi.	1	0	0.0	0	0
Rattay, Tim, S.F.	8	0	0.0	6	0
Stackhouse, Charles, Min.	1	0	0.0	0	0
Warner, Kurt, St.L	1	0	0.0	0	0
Cook, Jameel, T.B.	1	-1	-1.0	-1	0
Dilfer, Trent, Sea.	2	-1	-0.5	0	0
Grossman, Rex, Chi.	3	-1	-0.3	0	0
Massey, Chris, St.L	1	-1	-1.0	-1	0
Carter, Kerry, Sea.	3	-2	-0.7	1	0
Frerotte, Gus, Min.	12	-2	-0.2	4	0
Muhammad, Muhsin, Car.	2	-2	-1.0	0	0
Nall, Craig, G.B.	2	-2	-1.0	-1	0
Owens, Terrell, S.F.	3	-2	-0.7	3	0
Hutchinson, Chad, Dal.	2	-3	-1.5	-1	0
Kasper, Kevin, Ariz	1	-4	-4.0	-4	0

	Att	Yards	Avg	Long	TD
Wilson, Cedrick, S.F.	1	-4	-4.0	-4	0
Cleeland, Cameron, St.L	2	-5	-2.5	0	0
Pederson, Doug, G.B.	6	-5	-0.8	0	0
Booker, Marty, Chi.	3	-7	-2.3	1	0
Ferguson, Robert, G.B.	1	-8	-8.0	-8	0
Tyree, David, NYG	1	-9	-9.0	-9	0
Pinkston, Todd, Phi.	1	-11	-11.0	-11	0

t = Touchdown
Leader based on most yards gained

AMERICAN FOOTBALL CONFERENCE—RUSHING

	Att	Yards	Avg	Long	TD
Baltimore	552	2674	4.8	82t	18
Denver	543	2629	4.8	65t	20
San Diego	417	2146	5.1	73t	16
Jacksonville	481	2073	4.3	62	13
Cincinnati	481	1987	4.1	54	12
Kansas City	446	1929	4.3	39	32
Oakland	423	1822	4.3	53	15
Miami	487	1817	3.7	68t	14
Indianapolis	453	1695	3.7	43	16
Cleveland	412	1670	4.1	78t	8
Buffalo	427	1664	3.9	64	13
Houston	421	1651	3.9	51	14
N.Y. Jets	409	1635	4.0	56	8
Tennessee	486	1623	3.3	28	11
New England	473	1607	3.4	42	9
Pittsburgh	446	1488	3.3	32	10
AFC Total	7357	30110	4.1	82t	229
AFC Average	459.8	1881.9	4.1	—	14.3

NATIONAL FOOTBALL CONFERENCE—RUSHING

	Att	Yards	Avg	Long	TD
Green Bay	507	2558	5.0	98t	18
Minnesota	493	2343	4.8	61	15
San Francisco	499	2279	4.6	78t	16
Carolina	522	2091	4.0	40	9
Philadelphia	417	2015	4.8	64t	23
Seattle	453	2009	4.4	55	17
New Orleans	448	2000	4.5	76t	11
Dallas	515	1999	3.9	63t	11
Atlanta	435	1949	4.5	69t	17
Chicago	443	1763	4.0	67t	13
Washington	421	1653	3.9	38	8
Tampa Bay	421	1648	3.9	61	5
N.Y. Giants	387	1559	4.0	27	6
Arizona	403	1531	3.8	36	5
St. Louis	411	1496	3.6	52	19
Detroit	376	1338	3.6	39	5
NFC Total	7151	30231	4.2	98t	198
NFC Average	446.9	1889.4	4.2	—	12.4
League Total	14508	60341	—	98t	427
League Average	453.4	1885.7	4.2	—	13.3

2003 INDIVIDUAL STATISTICS—PASSING

PASSING

HIGHEST RATING
AFC: 100.4 Steve McNair, Tennessee
NFC: 96.4 Daunte Culpepper, Minnesota

COMPLETION PERCENTAGE
AFC: 67.0 Peyton Manning, Indianapolis
NFC: 65.4 Brett Favre, Green Bay

ATTEMPTS
NFC: 570 Brad Johnson, Tampa Bay
AFC: 566 Peyton Manning, Indianapolis

COMPLETIONS
AFC: 379 Peyton Manning, Indianapolis
NFC: 354 Brad Johnson, Tampa Bay

YARDS
AFC: 4267 Peyton Manning, Indianapolis
NFC: 3845 Marc Bulger, St. Louis

YARDS, GAME
AFC: 421 Steve McNair, Tennessee vs. Houston, October 12 (18-27, 3 TD)
NFC: 399 Brett Favre, Green Bay at Oakland, December 22 (22-30, 4 TD)

LONGEST
NFC: 86 Doug Johnson (to Warrick Dunn) Atlanta vs. Tennessee, November 23 - TD
AFC: 84 Byron Leftwich (to Troy Edwards) Jacksonville at Houston, September 28 - TD

YARDS PER ATTEMPT
AFC: 8.04 Steve McNair, Tennessee
NFC: 7.66 Daunte Culpepper, Minnesota

TOUCHDOWN PASSES
NFC: 32 Brett Favre, Green Bay
AFC: 29 Peyton Manning, Indianapolis

TOUCHDOWN PASSES, GAME
AFC: 6 Peyton Manning, Indianapolis at New Orleans, September 28 (20-25, 314 yards)
NFC: 5 Matt Hasselbeck, Seattle at Baltimore, November 23 (23-41, 333 yards) - (OT)
5 Aaron Brooks, New Orleans vs. N.Y. Giants, December 14 (26-35, 296 yards)

LOWEST INTERCEPTION PERCENTAGE
AFC: 1.8 Steve McNair, Tennessee
NFC: 1.5 Aaron Brooks, New Orleans

TEAM CHAMPION (MOST NET YARDS)
AFC: 4179 Indianapolis
NFC: 3961 St. Louis

NFL TOP TEN PASSERS

	Att	Comp	Pct Comp	Yds	Avg Gain	TD	Pct TD	Long	Int	Pct Int	Sack	Yds Lost	Rating Points
McNair, Steve, Ten.	400	250	62.5	3215	8.04	24	6.0	73	7	1.8	19	108	100.4
Manning, Peyton, Ind.	566	379	67.0	4267	7.54	29	5.1	79t	10	1.8	18	107	99.0
Culpepper, Daunte, Min.	454	295	65.0	3479	7.66	25	5.5	59t	11	2.4	37	196	96.4
Green, Trent, K.C.	523	330	63.1	4039	7.72	24	4.6	67t	12	2.3	20	130	92.6
Plummer, Jake, Den.	302	189	62.6	2182	7.23	15	5.0	60	7	2.3	14	73	91.2
Favre, Brett, G.B.	471	308	65.4	3361	7.14	32	6.8	66t	21	4.5	19	137	90.4
Brooks, Aaron, N.O.	518	306	59.1	3546	6.85	24	4.6	76t	8	1.5	34	195	88.8
Hasselbeck, Matt, Sea.	513	313	61.0	3841	7.49	26	5.1	80t	15	2.9	42	246	88.8
Kitna, Jon, Cin.	520	324	62.3	3591	6.91	26	5.0	82t	15	2.9	37	249	87.4
Brady, Tom, N.E.	527	317	60.2	3620	6.87	23	4.4	82t	12	2.3	32	219	85.9

AMERICAN FOOTBALL CONFERENCE—PASSING

	Att	Comp	Pct Comp	Gross Yards	Sacked	Yds Lost	Net Yards	Yds/ Att	Yards/ Comp	TD	Pct TD	Long	Int	Pct Int
Indianapolis	569	381	67.0	4289	19	110	4179	7.54	11.26	29	5.10	79t	10	1.8
Kansas City	536	339	63.2	4113	21	132	3981	7.67	12.13	24	4.48	67t	12	2.2
Tennessee	502	315	62.7	4031	25	153	3878	8.03	12.80	30	5.98	73	9	1.8
New England	537	320	59.6	3651	32	219	3432	6.80	11.41	23	4.28	82t	13	2.4
Cincinnati	520	324	62.3	3591	37	249	3342	6.91	11.08	26	5.00	82t	15	2.9
Pittsburgh	532	306	57.5	3548	42	244	3304	6.67	11.59	19	3.57	81t	17	3.2
N.Y. Jets	496	312	62.9	3524	31	208	3316	7.10	11.29	20	4.03	65t	14	2.8
Jacksonville	515	303	58.8	3421	28	136	3285	6.64	11.29	17	3.30	84t	17	3.3
San Diego	525	297	56.6	3226	29	205	3021	6.14	10.86	21	4.00	73t	19	3.6
Denver	479	280	58.5	3126	25	157	2969	6.53	11.16	19	3.97	72	18	3.8
Cleveland	509	313	61.5	3116	40	282	2834	6.12	9.96	17	3.34	71t	18	3.5
Buffalo	502	293	58.4	3069	51	385	2684	6.11	10.47	11	2.19	54t	17	3.4
Miami	450	257	57.1	3001	31	209	2792	6.67	11.68	17	3.78	80t	19	4.2
Oakland	521	278	53.4	2988	43	237	2751	5.74	10.75	9	1.73	47t	14	2.7
Houston	439	248	56.5	2841	36	186	2655	6.47	11.46	14	3.19	78t	18	4.1
Baltimore	415	217	52.3	2517	42	262	2255	6.07	11.60	16	3.86	73t	19	4.6
AFC Total	8047	4783	—	54052	532	3374	50678	—	—	312	—	84t	249	—
AFC Average	502.9	298.9	59.4	3378.3	33.3	210.9	3167.4	6.72	11.30	19.5	3.9	—	15.6	3.1

NATIONAL FOOTBALL CONFERENCE—PASSING

	Att	Comp	Pct Comp	Gross Yards	Sacked	Yds Lost	Net Yards	Yds/ Att	Yards/ Comp	TD	Pct TD	Long	Int	Pct Int
St. Louis	600	377	62.8	4287	43	326	3961	7.15	11.37	23	3.83	48	23	3.8
Minnesota	520	333	64.0	4169	42	218	3951	8.02	12.52	32	6.15	72t	13	2.5
Tampa Bay	592	369	62.3	3941	23	136	3805	6.66	10.68	27	4.56	76t	22	3.7
Seattle	521	317	60.8	3872	43	254	3618	7.43	12.21	27	5.18	80t	16	3.1
N.Y. Giants	616	344	55.8	3642	44	259	3383	5.91	10.59	16	2.60	77t	20	3.2
New Orleans	535	314	58.7	3641	36	203	3438	6.81	11.60	25	4.67	76t	8	1.5
San Francisco	511	299	58.5	3566	28	158	3408	6.98	11.93	25	4.89	75t	15	2.9
Green Bay	473	310	65.5	3377	19	137	3240	7.14	10.89	32	6.77	66t	21	4.4
Dallas	510	294	57.6	3347	37	185	3162	6.56	11.38	17	3.33	64	21	4.1
Philadelphia	484	279	57.6	3273	43	253	3020	6.76	11.73	17	3.51	59	11	2.3
Washington	527	283	53.7	3273	43	267	3006	6.21	11.57	21	3.98	64	16	3.0
Arizona	534	303	56.7	3265	44	306	2959	6.11	10.78	18	3.37	71t	22	4.1
Carolina	460	270	58.7	3238	26	188	3050	7.04	11.99	19	4.13	67t	16	3.5
Detroit	588	319	54.3	2988	11	64	2924	5.08	9.37	17	2.89	72t	24	4.1
Chicago	515	271	52.6	2905	43	288	2617	5.64	10.72	12	2.33	61t	20	3.9
Atlanta	460	230	50.0	2631	35	223	2408	5.72	11.44	14	3.04	86t	21	4.6
NFC Total	8446	4912	—	55415	560	3465	51950	—	—	342	—	86t	289	—
NFC Average	527.9	307.0	58.2	3463.4	35.0	216.6	3246.9	6.56	11.28	21.4	4.0	—	18.1	3.4
League Total	16493	9695	—	109467	1092	6839	102628	—	—	654	—	86t	538	—
League Average	515.4	303.0	58.8	3420.8	34.1	213.7	3207.1	6.64	11.29	20.4	4.0	—	16.8	3.3

2003 INDIVIDUAL STATISTICS—PASSING

AFC—INDIVIDUAL PASSERS

	Att	Comp	Pct Comp	Yds	Avg Gain	TD	Pct TD	Long	Int	Pct Int	Sack	Yds Lost	Rating Points
McNair, Steve, Ten.	400	250	62.5	3215	8.04	24	6.0	73	7	1.8	19	108	100.4
Manning, Peyton, Ind.	566	379	67.0	4267	7.54	29	5.1	79t	10	1.8	18	107	99.0
Green, Trent, K.C.	523	330	63.1	4039	7.72	24	4.6	67t	12	2.3	20	130	92.6
Plummer, Jake, Den.	302	189	62.6	2182	7.23	15	5.0	60	7	2.3	14	73	91.2
Kitna, Jon, Cin.	520	324	62.3	3591	6.91	26	5.0	82t	15	2.9	37	249	87.4
Brady, Tom, N.E.	527	317	60.2	3620	6.87	23	4.4	82t	12	2.3	32	219	85.9
Pennington, Chad, NYJ	297	189	63.6	2139	7.20	13	4.4	65t	12	4.0	25	160	82.9
Maddox, Tommy, Pit.	519	298	57.4	3414	6.58	18	3.5	53	17	3.3	41	242	75.3
Holcomb, Kelly, Cle.	302	193	63.9	1797	5.95	10	3.3	68t	12	4.0	21	166	74.6
Gannon, Rich, Oak.	225	125	55.6	1274	5.66	6	2.7	46t	4	1.8	17	90	73.5
Leftwich, Byron, Jac.	418	239	57.2	2819	6.74	14	3.3	84t	16	3.8	19	90	73.0
Bledsoe, Drew, Buf.	471	274	58.2	2860	6.07	11	2.3	54t	12	2.5	49	371	73.0
Fiedler, Jay, Mia.	314	179	57.0	2138	6.81	11	3.5	59	13	4.1	19	126	72.4
Carr, David, Hou.	295	167	56.6	2013	6.82	9	3.1	78t	13	4.4	15	90	69.5
Brees, Drew, S.D.	356	205	57.6	2108	5.92	11	3.1	68t	15	4.2	21	178	67.5
Boller, Kyle, Bal.	224	116	51.8	1260	5.63	7	3.1	73t	9	4.0	17	92	62.4
(Nonqualifiers)													
Garrard, David, Jac.	12	9	75.0	86	7.17	1	8.3	28	0	0.0	0	0	122.2
O'Donnell, Neil, Ten.	27	18	66.7	232	8.59	2	7.4	34t	1	3.7	0	0	102.7
Volek, Billy, Ten.	69	44	63.8	545	7.90	4	5.8	50t	1	1.4	6	45	101.4
Testaverde, Vinny, NYJ	198	123	62.1	1385	6.99	7	3.5	61	2	1.0	6	48	90.6
Collins, Todd, K.C.	12	9	75.0	74	6.17	0	0.0	20	0	0.0	0	0	90.3
Brunell, Mark, Jac.	82	54	65.9	484	5.90	2	2.4	65t	0	0.0	9	46	89.7
Banks, Tony, Hou.	102	61	59.8	693	6.79	5	4.9	46t	3	2.9	13	57	84.3
Flutie, Doug, S.D.	167	91	54.5	1097	6.57	9	5.4	73t	4	2.4	8	27	82.8
Brown, Travis, Buf.	18	14	77.8	160	8.89	0	0.0	28	1	5.6	1	7	80.6
Couch, Tim, Cle.	203	120	59.1	1319	6.50	7	3.4	71t	6	3.0	19	116	77.6
Wright, Anthony, Bal.	178	94	52.8	1199	6.74	9	5.1	64	8	4.5	19	125	72.3
Griese, Brian, Mia.	130	74	56.9	813	6.25	5	3.8	80t	6	4.6	12	83	69.2
Mirer, Rick, Oak.	221	116	52.5	1267	5.73	3	1.4	47t	5	2.3	22	122	64.8
Tuiasosopo, Marques, Oak.	45	25	55.6	324	7.20	0	0.0	35	3	6.7	2	14	50.6
Kanell, Danny, Den.	103	53	51.5	442	4.29	2	1.9	26	5	4.9	2	24	49.1
Beuerlein, Steve, Den.	63	33	52.4	389	6.17	2	3.2	38	5	7.9	9	60	49.0
Ragone, Dave, Hou.	40	20	50.0	135	3.38	0	0.0	24	1	2.5	8	39	47.4
Johnson, Rob, Was.-Oak.	20	11	55.0	93	4.65	0	0.0	15	1	5.0	4	21	46.5
Redman, Chris, Bal.	13	7	53.8	58	4.46	0	0.0	16	2	15.4	6	45	26.0
Martin, Tee, Oak.	16	6	37.5	69	4.31	0	0.0	17	1	6.3	1	5	25.3
Van Pelt, Alex, Buf.	12	5	41.7	49	4.08	0	0.0	14	3	25.0	1	7	14.2
(Fewer than 10 attempts)													
Batch, Charlie, Pit.	8	4	50.0	47	5.88	0	0.0	22	0	0.0	1	2	68.2
Bennett, Drew, Ten.	1	1	100.0	14	14.00	0	0.0	14	0	0.0	0	0	118.8
Bennett, Darren, S.D.	1	0	0.0	0	0.00	0	0.0	0	0	0.0	0	0	39.6
Boyer, Brant, Cle.	1	0	0.0	0	0.00	0	0.0	0	0	0.0	0	0	39.6
Davey, Rohan, N.E.	7	3	42.9	31	4.43	0	0.0	16	0	0.0	0	0	56.3
Faulk, Kevin, N.E.	1	0	0.0	0	0.00	0	0.0	0	0	0.0	0	0	39.6
Gaffney, Jabar, Hou.	1	0	0.0	0	0.00	0	0.0	0	0	0.0	0	0	39.6
Givens, David, N.E.	1	0	0.0	0	0.00	0	0.0	0	1	100.0	0	0	0.0
Hall, Dante, K.C.	0	0	—	0	—	0	—	—	0	—	1	2	—
Henry, Travis, Buf.	1	0	0.0	0	0.00	0	0.0	0	1	100.0	0	0	0.0
Hentrich, Craig, Ten.	5	2	40.0	25	5.00	0	0.0	15	0	0.0	0	0	56.3
Holmes, Priest, K.C.	1	0	0.0	0	0.00	0	0.0	0	0	0.0	0	0	39.6
Huard, Brock, Ind.	3	2	66.7	22	7.33	0	0.0	13	0	0.0	1	3	88.2
Huard, Damon, N.E.	1	0	0.0	0	0.00	0	0.0	0	0	0.0	0	0	39.6
Jackson, Frisman, Cle.	1	0	0.0	0	0.00	0	0.0	0	0	0.0	0	0	39.6
Jackson, Jarious, Den.	9	4	44.4	41	4.56	0	0.0	16	1	11.1	0	0	18.5
Johnson, Kevin, Cle.	1	0	0.0	0	0.00	0	0.0	0	0	0.0	0	0	39.6
Knorr, Micah, Den.	1	0	0.0	0	0.00	0	0.0	0	0	0.0	0	0	39.6
Mack, Stacey, Hou.	1	0	0.0	0	0.00	0	0.0	0	1	100.0	0	0	0.0
Miller, Josh, Pit.	1	1	100.0	81	81.00	1	100.0	81t	0	0.0	0	0	158.3
Northcutt, Dennis, Cle.	1	0	0.0	0	0.00	0	0.0	0	0	0.0	0	0	39.6
Randle El, Antwaan, Pit.	4	3	75.0	6	1.50	0	0.0	9	0	0.0	0	0	77.1
Rice, Jerry, Oak.	1	0	0.0	0	0.00	0	0.0	0	0	0.0	0	0	39.6
Rosenfels, Sage, Mia.	6	4	66.7	50	8.33	1	16.7	21t	0	0.0	0	0	131.9
Royals, Mark, Jac.	1	0	0.0	0	0.00	0	0.0	0	1	100.0	0	0	0.0
Smith, Rod, Den.	1	1	100.0	72	72.00	0	0.0	72	0	0.0	0	0	118.8
Stryzinski, Dan, NYJ	1	0	0.0	0	0.00	0	0.0	0	0	0.0	0	0	39.6
Toefield, LaBrandon, Jac.	2	1	50.0	32	16.00	0	0.0	32	0	0.0	0	0	95.8
Tomlinson, LaDainian, S.D.	1	1	100.0	21	21.00	1	100.0	21t	0	0.0	0	0	158.3

t = Touchdown

Leader based on rating points, minimum 224 attempts

NFC—INDIVIDUAL PASSERS

	Att	Comp	Pct Comp	Yds	Avg Gain	TD	Pct TD	Long	Int	Pct Int	Sack	Yds Lost	Rating Points
Culpepper, Daunte, Min.	454	295	65.0	3479	7.66	25	5.5	59t	11	2.4	37	196	96.4
Favre, Brett, G.B.	471	308	65.4	3361	7.14	32	6.8	66t	21	4.5	19	137	90.4
Brooks, Aaron, N.O.	518	306	59.1	3546	6.85	24	4.6	76t	8	1.5	34	195	88.8
Hasselbeck, Matt, Sea.	513	313	61.0	3841	7.49	26	5.1	80t	15	2.9	42	246	88.8
Johnson, Brad, T.B.	570	354	62.1	3811	6.69	26	4.6	76t	21	3.7	20	111	81.5
Bulger, Marc, St.L	532	336	63.2	3845	7.23	22	4.1	48	22	4.1	37	288	81.4
Delhomme, Jake, Car.	449	266	59.2	3219	7.17	19	4.2	67t	16	3.6	23	168	80.6
Garcia, Jeff, S.F.	392	225	57.4	2704	6.90	18	4.6	75t	13	3.3	21	104	80.1
McNabb, Donovan, Phi.	478	275	57.5	3216	6.73	16	3.3	59	11	2.3	43	253	79.6
Ramsey, Patrick, Was.	337	179	53.1	2166	6.43	14	4.2	64	9	2.7	30	206	75.8
Carter, Quincy, Dal.	505	292	57.8	3302	6.54	17	3.4	64	21	4.2	37	185	71.4
Collins, Kerry, NYG	500	284	56.8	3110	6.22	13	2.6	77t	16	3.2	28	164	70.7
Blake, Jeff, Ariz	367	208	56.7	2247	6.12	13	3.5	71t	15	4.1	19	132	69.6
Johnson, Doug, Atl.	243	136	56.0	1655	6.81	8	3.3	86t	12	4.9	19	121	67.5
Harrington, Joey, Det.	554	309	55.8	2880	5.20	17	3.1	72t	22	4.0	9	55	63.9
Stewart, Kordell, Chi.	251	126	50.2	1418	5.65	7	2.8	61t	12	4.8	25	146	56.8
(Nonqualifiers)													
Frerotte, Gus, Min.	65	38	58.5	690	10.62	7	10.8	72t	2	3.1	5	22	118.1
Bouman, Todd, N.O.	13	7	53.8	81	6.23	1	7.7	19	0	0.0	2	8	98.6
Rattay, Tim, S.F.	118	73	61.9	856	7.25	7	5.9	61t	2	1.7	7	54	96.6
King, Shaun, T.B.	22	15	68.2	130	5.91	1	4.5	20	1	4.5	3	25	79.7
Grossman, Rex, Chi.	72	38	52.8	437	6.07	2	2.8	59t	1	1.4	4	41	74.8
Warner, Kurt, St.L	65	38	58.5	365	5.62	1	1.5	37t	1	1.5	6	38	72.9
McCown, Josh, Ariz	166	95	57.2	1018	6.13	5	3.0	60t	6	3.6	25	174	70.3
Vick, Michael, Atl.	100	50	50.0	585	5.85	4	4.0	49	3	3.0	9	64	69.0
Hasselbeck, Tim, Was.	177	95	53.7	1012	5.72	5	2.8	40	7	4.0	9	44	63.6
Chandler, Chris, Chi.	192	107	55.7	1050	5.47	3	1.6	37	7	3.6	14	101	61.3
Palmer, Jesse, NYG	116	60	51.7	532	4.59	3	2.6	40	4	3.4	16	95	58.5
Peete, Rodney, Car.	10	4	40.0	19	1.90	0	0.0	8	0	0.0	3	20	47.9
Kittner, Kurt, Atl.	114	44	38.6	391	3.43	2	1.8	31	6	5.3	5	30	32.5
McMahon, Mike, Det.	31	9	29.0	87	2.81	0	0.0	26	2	6.5	2	9	12.7
(Fewer than 10 attempts)													
Anderson, Richie, Dal.	1	0	0.0	0	0.00	0	0.0	0	0	0.0	0	0	39.6
Barker, Bryan, Was.	1	1	100.0	3	3.00	0	0.0	3	0	0.0	0	0	79.2
Berger, Mitch, N.O.	1	0	0.0	0	0.00	0	0.0	0	0	0.0	0	0	39.6
Boldin, Anquan, Ariz	1	0	0.0	0	0.00	0	0.0	0	1	100.0	0	0	0.0
Bruce, Isaac, St.L	2	2	100.0	66	33.00	0	0.0	41	0	0.0	0	0	118.8
Cason, Aveion, Dal.	1	1	100.0	37	37.00	0	0.0	37	0	0.0	0	0	118.8
Dantzler, Woody, Atl.	1	0	0.0	0	0.00	0	0.0	0	0	0.0	1	5	39.6
Detmer, Koy, Phi.	5	3	60.0	32	6.40	0	0.0	15	0	0.0	0	0	78.8
Dilfer, Trent, Sea.	8	4	50.0	31	3.88	1	12.5	14	1	12.5	1	8	59.9
Duckett, T.J., Atl.	1	0	0.0	0	0.00	0	0.0	0	0	0.0	0	0	39.6
Dunn, Warrick, Atl.	0	0	—	0	—	0	—	—	0	—	1	3	—
Gardner, Rod, Was.	3	2	66.7	46	15.33	2	66.7	36t	0	0.0	0	0	149.3
Glenn, Terry, Dal.	1	0	0.0	0	0.00	0	0.0	0	0	0.0	0	0	39.6
Hakim, Az-Zahir, Det.	1	1	100.0	21	21.00	0	0.0	21	0	0.0	0	0	118.8
Hamdan, Gibran, Was.	2	1	50.0	7	3.50	0	0.0	7	0	0.0	1	2	58.3
Harris, Nick, Det.	1	0	0.0	0	0.00	0	0.0	0	0	0.0	0	0	39.6
Horn, Joe, N.O.	1	1	100.0	14	14.00	0	0.0	14	0	0.0	0	0	118.8
Hutchinson, Chad, Dal.	2	1	50.0	8	4.00	0	0.0	8	0	0.0	0	0	60.4
Looker, Dane, St.L	1	1	100.0	11	11.00	0	0.0	11	0	0.0	0	0	112.5
McAllister, Deuce, N.O.	2	0	0.0	0	0.00	0	0.0	0	0	0.0	0	0	39.6
Mitchell, Freddie, Phi.	1	1	100.0	25	25.00	1	100.0	25t	0	0.0	0	0	158.3
Mohr, Chris, Atl.	1	0	0.0	0	0.00	0	0.0	0	0	0.0	0	0	39.6
Moss, Randy, Min.	1	0	0.0	0	0.00	0	0.0	0	0	0.0	0	0	39.6
Pederson, Doug, G.B.	2	2	100.0	16	8.00	0	0.0	14	0	0.0	0	0	100.0
Sauerbrun, Todd, Car.	1	0	0.0	0	0.00	0	0.0	0	0	0.0	0	0	39.6
Schroeder, Bill, Det.	1	0	0.0	0	0.00	0	0.0	0	0	0.0	0	0	39.6
Wilson, Cedrick, S.F.	1	1	100.0	6	6.00	0	0.0	6	0	0.0	0	0	91.7

t = Touchdown
Leader based on rating points, minimum 224 attempts

2003 INDIVIDUAL STATISTICS—PASS RECEIVING

PASS RECEIVING

RECEPTIONS

NFC: 117 Torry Holt, St. Louis
AFC: 100 LaDainian Tomlinson, San Diego

RECEPTIONS, GAME

AFC: 14 David Boston, San Diego at Jacksonville, October 5 (181 yards, 2 TD)
NFC: 12 Torry Holt, St. Louis vs. Arizona, September 28 (133 yards, 1 TD)
12 Peerless Price, Atlanta vs. Minnesota, October 5 (168 yards, 1 TD)

YARDS

NFC: 1696 Torry Holt, St. Louis
AFC: 1355 Chad Johnson, Cincinnati

YARDS, GAME

NFC: 217 Anquan Boldin, Arizona at Detroit, September 7 (10 receptions, 2 TD)
AFC: 181 David Boston, San Diego at Jacksonville, October 5 (14 receptions, 2 TD)

LONGEST

NFC: 86 Warrick Dunn (from Doug Johnson) Atlanta vs. Tennessee, November 23 - TD
AFC: 84 Troy Edwards (from Byron Leftwich) Jacksonville at Houston, September 28 - TD

YARDS PER RECEPTION

NFC: 19.8 Joey Galloway, Dallas
AFC: 17.3 Justin McCareins, Tennessee

TOUCHDOWNS

NFC: 17 Randy Moss, Minnesota
AFC: 11 Chris Chambers, Miami

TEAM LEADERS, RECEPTIONS

AFC: BALTIMORE, 57, Todd Heap; BUFFALO, 64, Eric Moulds; CINCINNATI, 90, Chad Johnson; CLEVELAND, 62, Dennis Northcutt; DENVER, 74, Rod Smith; HOUSTON, 66, Andre Johnson; INDIANAPOLIS, 94, Marvin Harrison; JACKSONVILLE, 54, Jimmy Smith; KANSAS CITY, 74, Priest Holmes; MIAMI, 64, Chris Chambers; NEW ENGLAND, 57, Deion Branch; N.Y. JETS, 74, Santana Moss; OAKLAND, 63, Jerry Rice; PITTSBURGH, 95, Hines Ward; SAN DIEGO, 100, LaDainian Tomlinson; TENNESSEE, 95, Derrick Mason

NFC: ARIZONA, 101, Anquan Boldin; ATLANTA, 64, Peerless Price; CAROLINA, 88, Steve Smith; CHICAGO, 52, Marty Booker; DALLAS, 69, Richie Anderson; DETROIT, 54, Shawn Bryson; GREEN BAY, 52, Donald Driver; MINNESOTA, 111, Randy Moss; NEW ORLEANS, 78, Joe Horn; N.Y. GIANTS, 69, Tiki Barber; PHILADELPHIA, 49, James Thrash; ST. LOUIS, 117, Torry Holt; SAN FRANCISCO, 80, Terrell Owens; SEATTLE, 68, Darrell Jackson; TAMPA BAY, 84, Keenan McCardell; WASHINGTON, 82, Laveranues Coles

NFL TOP TEN PASS RECEIVERS

	No	Yards	Avg	Long	TD
Holt, Torry, St.L	117	1696	14.5	48	12
Moss, Randy, Min.	111	1632	14.7	72	17
Boldin, Anquan, Ariz	101	1377	13.6	71t	8
Tomlinson, LaDainian, S.D.	100	725	7.3	73t	4
Mason, Derrick, Ten.	95	1303	13.7	50t	8
Ward, Hines, Pit.	95	1163	12.2	50	10
Harrison, Marvin, Ind.	94	1272	13.5	79t	10
Johnson, Chad, Cin.	90	1355	15.1	82t	10
Smith, Steve, Car.	88	1110	12.6	67t	7
McCardell, Keenan, T.B.	84	1174	14.0	76t	8

NFL TOP TEN RECEIVERS BY YARDS

	Yards	No	Avg	Long	TD
Holt, Torry, St.L	1696	117	14.5	48	12
Moss, Randy, Min.	1632	111	14.7	72	17
Boldin, Anquan, Ariz	1377	101	13.6	71t	8
Johnson, Chad, Cin.	1355	90	15.1	82t	10
Mason, Derrick, Ten.	1303	95	13.7	50t	8
Harrison, Marvin, Ind.	1272	94	13.5	79t	10
Coles, Laveranues, Was.	1204	82	14.7	64	6
McCardell, Keenan, T.B.	1174	84	14.0	76t	8
Ward, Hines, Pit.	1163	95	12.2	50	10
Jackson, Darrell, Sea.	1137	68	16.7	80t	9

AFC—INDIVIDUAL RECEIVERS

	No	Yards	Avg	Long	TD
Tomlinson, LaDainian, S.D.	100	725	7.3	73t	4
Mason, Derrick, Ten.	95	1303	13.7	50t	8
Ward, Hines, Pit.	95	1163	12.2	50	10
Harrison, Marvin, Ind.	94	1272	13.5	79t	10
Johnson, Chad, Cin.	90	1355	15.1	82t	10
Warrick, Peter, Cin.	79	819	10.4	77t	7
Moss, Santana, NYJ	74	1105	14.9	65t	10
Smith, Rod, Den.	74	845	11.4	38	3
Holmes, Priest, K.C.	74	690	9.3	36	0
Gonzalez, Tony, K.C.	71	916	12.9	67	10
Boston, David, S.D.	70	880	12.6	46t	7
Wayne, Reggie, Ind.	68	838	12.3	57t	7
Johnson, Andre, Hou.	66	976	14.8	46t	4
Chambers, Chris, Mia.	64	963	15.0	57t	11
Moulds, Eric, Buf.	64	780	12.2	49	1
Rice, Jerry, Oak.	63	869	13.8	47t	2
Sharpe, Shannon, Den.	62	770	12.4	28	8
Northcutt, Dennis, Cle.	62	729	11.8	44	2
Burress, Plaxico, Pit.	60	860	14.3	47	4
Johnson, Kevin, Cle.-Jac.	58	634	10.9	41	3
Reed, Josh, Buf.	58	588	10.1	26	2
Branch, Deion, N.E.	57	803	14.1	66t	3
Heap, Todd, Bal.	57	693	12.2	33t	3
Kennison, Eddie, K.C.	56	853	15.2	51t	5
Shaw, Bobby, Buf.	56	732	13.1	54t	4
Smith, Jimmy, Jac.	54	805	14.9	67	4
Brown, Tim, Oak.	52	567	10.9	36t	2
James, Edgerrin, Ind.	51	292	5.7	17	0
Morton, Johnnie, K.C.	50	740	14.8	50	4
Williams, Ricky, Mia.	50	351	7.0	59	1
McMichael, Randy, Mia.	49	598	12.2	46	2
Faulk, Kevin, N.E.	48	440	9.2	27	0
Garner, Charlie, Oak.	48	386	8.0	46t	1
Taylor, Fred, Jac.	48	370	7.7	60t	1
McCareins, Justin, Ten.	47	813	17.3	73	7
Sowell, Jerald, NYJ	47	436	9.3	44	1
Davis, Domanick, Hou.	47	351	7.5	17	0
Conway, Curtis, NYJ	46	640	13.9	45	2
White, Jamel, Cle.	46	303	6.6	22	1
Martin, Curtis, NYJ	42	262	6.2	29	0
Kinney, Erron, Ten.	41	381	9.3	28	3
Davis, Andre', Cle.	40	576	14.4	49	5

	No	Yards	Avg	Long	TD
Pollard, Marcus, Ind.	40	541	13.5	70	3
Brown, Troy, N.E.	40	472	11.8	82t	4
Hall, Dante, K.C.	40	423	10.6	67t	1
Becht, Anthony, NYJ	40	356	8.9	29	4
Miller, Billy, Hou.	40	355	8.9	25	3
Zereoue, Amos, Pit.	40	310	7.8	29	0
Taylor, Travis, Bal.	39	632	16.2	73t	3
Morgan, Quincy, Cle.	38	516	13.6	71t	3
Graham, Daniel, N.E.	38	409	10.8	38	4
Portis, Clinton, Den.	38	314	8.3	72	0
Lelie, Ashley, Den.	37	628	17.0	60	2
Randle El, Antwaan, Pit.	37	364	9.8	32t	1
Walters, Troy, Ind.	36	456	12.7	46t	3
Edwards, Troy, Jac.	35	487	13.9	84t	3
Givens, David, N.E.	34	510	15.0	57	6
Gaffney, Jabar, Hou.	34	402	11.8	33	2
Campbell, Mark, Buf.	34	339	10.0	31	1
Bennett, Drew, Ten.	32	504	15.8	48	4
Robinson, Marcus, Bal.	31	451	14.5	50t	6
Jolley, Doug, Oak.	31	250	8.1	26	1
Edwards, Marc, Jac.	31	226	7.3	32	0
Clark, Dallas, Ind.	29	340	11.7	42	1
Brady, Kyle, Jac.	29	281	9.7	26	1
Porter, Jerry, Oak.	28	361	12.9	35	1
Fauria, Christian, N.E.	28	285	10.2	28	2
Henry, Travis, Buf.	28	158	5.6	18	1
Chrebet, Wayne, NYJ	27	289	10.7	29t	1
Thompson, Derrius, Mia.	26	359	13.8	31	0
Lewis, Jamal, Bal.	26	205	7.9	26	0
Bennett, Brandon, Cin.	25	176	7.0	16	1
Bradford, Corey, Hou.	24	460	19.2	78t	4
Gates, Antonio, S.D.	24	389	16.2	48	2
Schobel, Matt, Cin.	24	332	13.8	45t	2
McKnight, James, Mia.	23	285	12.4	80t	2
Washington, Kelley, Cin.	22	299	13.6	51t	4
Stokley, Brandon, Ind.	22	211	9.6	37t	3
George, Eddie, Ten.	22	163	7.4	22	0
Williams, Ricky, Ind.	22	157	7.1	17t	1
Stewart, Tony, Cin.	21	212	10.1	21	0
Johnson, Rudi, Cin.	21	146	7.0	17	0
Taylor, Chester, Bal.	20	132	6.6	23	0
McCaffrey, Ed, Den.	19	195	10.3	23	0
Jones, Terry, Bal.	19	159	8.4	25	3
Holcombe, Robert, Ten.	19	121	6.4	11	1
Centers, Larry, N.E.	19	106	5.6	14	1
Calico, Tyrone, Ten.	18	297	16.5	45	4
Parker, Eric, S.D.	18	244	13.6	33t	3
Doering, Chris, Pit.	18	240	13.3	53	1
Heiden, Steve, Cle.	18	134	7.4	17	0
Hankton, Cortez, Jac.	17	166	9.8	22	0
Wycheck, Frank, Ten.	17	165	9.7	25	2
Johnson, Bethel, N.E.	16	209	13.1	45	2
Konrad, Rob, Mia.	16	166	10.4	25	0
Peelle, Justin, S.D.	16	133	8.3	24	1
Neal, Lorenzo, S.D.	16	62	3.9	11	0
Hatchette, Matt, Jac.	15	203	13.5	45	2
Blaylock, Derrick, K.C.	15	181	12.1	63t	1
Stokes, J.J., Jac.-N.E.	15	154	10.3	31	0
Sanders, Darnell, Cle.	15	95	6.3	12	1
Johnson, Jeremi, Cin.	15	82	5.5	16	1
Dwight, Tim, S.D.	14	193	13.8	32	0
Sanders, Frank, Bal.	14	170	12.1	44	0
Baker, Chris, NYJ	14	137	9.8	24	0
Johnson, Teyo, Oak.	14	128	9.1	21	1
Jackson, James, Cle.	14	114	8.1	18	0
Toefield, LaBrandon, Jac.	14	105	7.5	16	1
Morris, Sammy, Buf.	14	100	7.1	24	0
Smith, Antowain, N.E.	14	92	6.6	16	0
Osgood, Kassim, S.D.	13	278	21.4	57t	2
Meier, Shad, Ten.	13	159	12.2	27	0
Wrighster, George, Jac.	13	150	11.5	30	2
Bettis, Jerome, Pit.	13	86	6.6	16	0
Kelly, Reggie, Cin.	13	81	6.2	13	1
Wheatley, Tyrone, Oak.	12	120	10.0	25	0
Tuman, Jerame, Pit.	12	113	9.4	23	0
Richardson, Tony, K.C.	12	76	6.3	14	0
Anderson, Mike, Den.	12	53	4.4	18	2
Ayanbadejo, Obafemi, Mia.	12	53	4.4	12	0
Boerigter, Marc, K.C.	11	158	14.4	30	0
Jordan, LaMont, NYJ	11	101	9.2	25	0
Gash, Sam, Buf.	11	83	7.5	18	0
Dillon, Corey, Cin.	11	71	6.5	14	0
Riemersma, Jay, Pit.	10	138	13.8	24	1
Green, William, Cle.	10	50	5.0	12	0
Patten, David, N.E.	9	140	15.6	42	0
Kreider, Dan, Pit.	9	107	11.9	26	0
King, Andre, Cle.	9	88	9.8	28	0
Droughns, Reuben, Den.	9	87	9.7	15	2
Ricard, Alan, Bal.	9	62	6.9	15	0
Mack, Stacey, Hou.	9	55	6.1	10	0
Holloway, Jabari, Hou.	8	84	10.5	33	0
Caldwell, Reche, S.D.	8	80	10.0	15	0
Coleman, Clarence, Buf.	8	69	8.6	12	0
Heinrich, Keith, Cle.	8	64	8.0	17	2
Brown, Chris, Ten.	8	61	7.6	11	0
Griffin, Quentin, Den.	8	61	7.6	24	0
Lee, Donald, Mia.	7	110	15.7	25	1
Ward, Dedric, N.E.	7	106	15.1	31t	1
Whitted, Alvis, Oak.	7	106	15.1	36t	1
Moorehead, Aaron, Ind.	7	101	14.4	35	0
Moore, Dave, Buf.	7	82	11.7	28	2
Armstrong, Derick, Hou.	7	75	10.7	18	1
Burns, Joe, Buf.	7	62	8.9	14	0
Haynes, Verron, Pit.	7	57	8.1	13	0
Crockett, Zack, Oak.	7	53	7.6	16	0
Norris, Moran, Hou.	7	40	5.7	11	0
Gilliam, Dondre, S.D.	6	95	15.8	37	0
Norman, Josh, S.D.	6	72	12.0	21t	1
Rhodes, Dominic, Ind.	6	62	10.3	27	1
Allen, David, Jac.	6	60	10.0	31	1
Carswell, Dwayne, Den.	6	53	8.8	19	1
Lockett, Kevin, NYJ	5	76	15.2	23	0
Santiago, O.J., Oak.	5	69	13.8	36	0
Chatman, Jesse, S.D.	5	54	10.8	23	0
Dunn, Jason, K.C.	5	35	7.0	15	3
Curry, Ronald, Oak.	5	31	6.2	16	0
Lewis, Jermaine, Jac.	4	100	25.0	65t	1
Carter, Jonathan, NYJ	4	93	23.3	62t	1
Gadsden, Oronde, Mia.	4	48	12.0	23	0
Putzier, Jeb, Den.	4	34	8.5	13	0
Mustard, Chad, Cle.	4	29	7.3	12	0
Pass, Patrick, N.E.	4	21	5.3	11	0
Minor, Travis, Mia.	4	13	3.3	12	0
Redmond, Jimmy, Jac.	3	67	22.3	29	0
Neufeld, Ryan, Buf.	3	41	13.7	25	0
Cole, Chris, Den.	3	36	12.0	18	0
Aiken, Sam, Buf.	3	35	11.7	19	0
Hape, Patrick, Den.	3	30	10.0	12	0
Luzar, Chris, Jac.	3	30	10.0	21	0
Davenport, Joe Dean, Ind.	3	23	7.7	9	0
Easy, Omar, K.C.	3	19	6.3	8	0
Walter, Kevin, Cin.	3	18	6.0	9	0
Newson, Kendall, Mia.	2	55	27.5	37	0
Jackson, Frisman, Cle.	2	29	14.5	19	0
Swayne, Kevin, NYJ	2	29	14.5	27t	1
Hollings, Tony, Hou.	2	25	12.5	19	0

2003 INDIVIDUAL STATISTICS—PASS RECEIVING

	No	Yards	Avg	Long	TD
Hetherington, Chris, Oak.	2	23	11.5	17	0
Mays, Lee, Pit.	2	17	8.5	9	0
Wells, Jonathan, Hou.	2	17	8.5	12	0
Bruener, Mark, Pit.	2	12	6.0	11	1
McCrary, Fred, N.E.	2	12	6.0	9	0
Madise, Adrian, Den.	2	10	5.0	5	0
Shea, Aaron, Cle.	2	9	4.5	7	0
O'Neal, Deltha, Den.	2	4	2.0	3	0
Fargas, Justin, Oak.	2	2	1.0	6	0
Suggs, Lee, Cle.	2	0	0.0	1	0
Hope, Chris, Pit.	1	81	81.0	81t	1
Berlin, Eddie, Ten.	1	50	50.0	50t	1
Brees, Drew, S.D.	1	21	21.0	21t	1
Baber, Billy, K.C.	1	20	20.0	20	0
Gabriel, Doug, Oak.	1	17	17.0	17	0
Johnson, Ron, Bal.	1	12	12.0	12	0
McGarrahan, Scott, Ten.	1	10	10.0	10	0
Cloud, Mike, N.E.	1	8	8.0	8	0
Carlisle, Cooper, Den.	1	6	6.0	6t	1
Coleman, Marcus, Hou.	1	6	6.0	6	0
Redmond, J.R., Oak.	1	6	6.0	6	0
McNair, Steve, Ten.	1	4	4.0	4	0
Bowers, R.J., Cle.	1	2	2.0	2t	1
Fuamatu-Ma'afala, Chris, Jac.	1	2	2.0	2	0
Johnson, Larry, K.C.	1	2	2.0	2	0
Pyatt, Brad, Ind.	1	2	2.0	2	0
Ogden, Jonathan, Bal.	1	1	1.0	1t	1
Andruzzi, Joe, N.E.	1	0	0.0	0	0
Manning, Peyton, Ind.	1	-2	-2.0	-2	0
Couch, Tim, Cle.	1	-3	-3.0	-3	0
Mungro, James, Ind.	1	-4	-4.0	-4	0
Ragone, Dave, Hou.	1	-5	-5.0	-5	0

t = Touchdown
Leader based on receptions

NFC—INDIVIDUAL RECEIVERS

	No	Yards	Avg	Long	TD
Holt, Torry, St.L	117	1696	14.5	48	12
Moss, Randy, Min.	111	1632	14.7	72	17
Boldin, Anquan, Ariz	101	1377	13.6	71t	8
Smith, Steve, Car.	88	1110	12.6	67t	7
McCardell, Keenan, T.B.	84	1174	14.0	76t	8
Coles, Laveranues, Was.	82	1204	14.7	64	6
Owens, Terrell, S.F.	80	1102	13.8	75t	9
Horn, Joe, N.O.	78	973	12.5	50t	10
Pittman, Michael, T.B.	75	597	8.0	68t	2
Bruce, Isaac, St.L	69	981	14.2	41	5
McAllister, Deuce, N.O.	69	516	7.5	39	0
Anderson, Richie, Dal.	69	493	7.1	37	4
Barber, Tiki, NYG	69	461	6.7	36	1
Jackson, Darrell, Sea.	68	1137	16.7	80t	9
Robinson, Koren, Sea.	65	896	13.8	38t	4
Williams, Moe, Min.	65	644	9.9	42	3
Price, Peerless, Atl.	64	838	13.1	49	3
Toomer, Amani, NYG	63	1057	16.8	77t	5
Hilliard, Ike, NYG	60	608	10.1	38	6
Gardner, Rod, Was.	59	600	10.2	35	5
Jones, Freddie, Ariz	55	517	9.4	34	3
Muhammad, Muhsin, Car.	54	837	15.5	60	3
Bryson, Shawn, Det.	54	340	6.3	26	0
Glenn, Terry, Dal.	52	754	14.5	51t	5
Booker, Marty, Chi.	52	715	13.8	61t	4
Engram, Bobby, Sea.	52	637	12.3	34t	6
Driver, Donald, G.B.	52	621	11.9	41	2
Green, Ahman, G.B.	50	367	7.3	27	5
White, Dez, Chi.	49	583	11.9	49	3
Thrash, James, Phi.	49	558	11.4	51	1
Hakim, Az-Zahir, Det.	49	449	9.2	28	4
Shockey, Jeremy, NYG	48	535	11.1	46	2
Streets, Tai, S.F.	47	595	12.7	41t	7
Looker, Dane, St.L	47	495	10.5	41	3
Mili, Itula, Sea.	46	492	10.7	46t	4
Kleinsasser, Jimmy, Min.	46	401	8.7	19	4
Johnson, Keyshawn, T.B.	45	600	13.3	39t	3
Faulk, Marshall, St.L	45	290	6.4	30	1
Pathon, Jerome, N.O.	44	578	13.1	40	4
Crumpler, Alge, Atl.	44	552	12.5	63	3
Clark, Desmond, Chi.	44	433	9.8	31	2
Terrell, David, Chi.	43	361	8.4	35	1
Alexander, Shaun, Sea.	42	295	7.0	22	2
Walker, Javon, G.B.	41	716	17.5	66t	9
Williams, Boo, N.O.	41	436	10.6	31t	5
Bryant, Antonio, Dal.	39	550	14.1	54	2
Ferguson, Robert, G.B.	38	520	13.7	47	4
Ricks, Mikhael, Det.	37	434	11.7	38	2
Dunn, Warrick, Atl.	37	336	9.1	86t	2
Westbrook, Brian, Phi.	37	332	9.0	38	4
Pinkston, Todd, Phi.	36	575	16.0	59	2
Schroeder, Bill, Det.	36	397	11.0	26	2
Staley, Duce, Phi.	36	382	10.6	52t	2
Mitchell, Freddie, Phi.	35	498	14.2	39	2
Johnson, Bryant, Ariz	35	438	12.5	54t	1
Weaver, Jed, S.F.	35	437	12.5	30	1
Wilson, Cedrick, S.F.	35	396	11.3	29	2
Witten, Jason, Dal.	35	347	9.9	36t	1
Barlow, Kevan, S.F.	35	307	8.8	48	1
Galloway, Joey, Dal.	34	672	19.8	64	2
Schlesinger, Cory, Det.	34	247	7.3	33t	2
Lee, Charles, T.B.	33	432	13.1	72	2
Franks, Bubba, G.B.	30	241	8.0	24	4
Shipp, Marcel, Ariz	30	184	6.1	34	0
Burleson, Nate, Min.	29	455	15.7	52	2
Manumaleuna, Brandon, St.L	29	238	8.2	39	2
Strong, Mack, Sea.	29	216	7.4	32	0
Proehl, Ricky, Car.	27	389	14.4	66t	4
McCants, Darnerien, Was.	27	360	13.3	32t	6
Smith, L.J., Phi.	27	321	11.9	36	1
Finneran, Brian, Atl.	26	368	14.2	38	2
Carter, Tim, NYG	26	309	11.9	30	0
Conwell, Ernie, N.O.	26	290	11.2	32	2
Foster, DeShaun, Car.	26	207	8.0	47	2
Campbell, Kelly, Min.	25	522	20.9	72t	4
Stallworth, Donte', N.O.	25	485	19.4	76t	3
Hearst, Garrison, S.F.	25	211	8.4	26	1
Henderson, William, G.B.	24	214	8.9	22	3
Jones, Thomas, T.B.	24	180	7.5	29	0
Lewis, Chad, Phi.	23	293	12.7	29	1
Fitzsimmons, Casey, Det.	23	160	7.0	22	2
Dilger, Ken, T.B.	22	244	11.1	48	1
Rogers, Charles, Det.	22	243	11.0	33t	3
Fisher, Tony, G.B.	21	206	9.8	32	2
Griffith, Justin, Atl.	21	122	5.8	24	2
Walls, Wesley, G.B.	20	222	11.1	36	1
Campbell, Dan, Dal.	20	195	9.8	23	1
Furrey, Mike, St.L	20	189	9.5	24	0
Cook, Jameel, T.B.	20	120	6.0	19	1
Beasley, Fred, S.F.	19	184	9.7	32	1
Cartwright, Rock, Was.	18	176	9.8	40	0
Pritchett, Stanley, Chi.	18	83	4.6	20	0
Gage, Justin, Chi.	17	338	19.9	57	2
Anderson, Scotty, Det.	17	325	19.1	72t	2
Gilmore, Bryan, Ariz	17	208	12.2	32	2
Mangum, Kris, Car.	17	199	11.7	34	0
Rivers, Marcellus, NYG	17	155	9.1	27	0
Cason, Aveion, Dal.	17	142	8.4	28	0

2003 INDIVIDUAL STATISTICS—PASS RECEIVING

	No	Yards	Avg	Long	TD
Hambrick, Troy, Dal.	17	99	5.8	13	0
Ritchie, Jon, Phi.	17	86	5.1	12	3
Tyree, David, NYG	16	211	13.2	48	0
Morton, Chad, Was.	15	187	12.5	36t	1
Johnson, Patrick, Was.	15	170	11.3	31	1
Betts, Ladell, Was.	15	167	11.1	34	0
Bates, D'Wayne, Min.	15	151	10.1	18	1
Smith, Onterrio, Min.	15	129	8.6	20	0
Harris, Arlen, St.L	15	102	6.8	26	0
Lloyd, Brandon, S.F.	14	212	15.1	44	2
Davis, Stephen, Car.	14	159	11.4	25	0
Freeman, Antonio, G.B.	14	141	10.1	15	0
Finn, Jim, NYG	14	115	8.2	27	0
Smith, Emmitt, Ariz	14	107	7.6	36	0
Hodgins, James, Ariz	14	58	4.1	9	2
Poole, Nate, Ariz	13	177	13.6	37	1
Martin, David, G.B.	13	79	6.1	14	2
Gary, Olandis, Det.	13	69	5.3	13	0
Lewis, Michael, N.O.	12	226	18.8	39	1
Wade, Bobby, Chi.	12	137	11.4	24	0
Bennett, Michael, Min.	12	132	11.0	40	0
Jurevicius, Joe, T.B.	12	118	9.8	22	2
Goings, Nick, Car.	12	97	8.1	14	1
Hoover, Brad, Car.	12	72	6.0	17	1
Duckett, T.J., Atl.	11	94	8.5	21	0
Lyman, Dustin, Chi.	11	80	7.3	12	0
Bush, Steve, Ariz	11	71	6.5	14	1
Cleeland, Cameron, St.L	10	145	14.5	29	0
Buckhalter, Correll, Phi.	10	133	13.3	27	1
Kozlowski, Brian, Atl.	10	87	8.7	19	0
Alstott, Mike, T.B.	10	83	8.3	17	0
Canidate, Trung, Was.	10	71	7.1	25	1
McDonald, Shaun, St.L	10	62	6.2	13	0
Shiancoe, Visanthe, NYG	10	56	5.6	10	2
McCord, Quentin, Atl.	9	121	13.4	33	0
Swinton, Reggie, Det.	9	100	11.1	25	0
Flemister, Zeron, Was.	9	89	9.9	18	0
Johnson, Bryan, Was.	9	71	7.9	19	0
Stecker, Aaron, T.B.	9	48	5.3	14t	1
Thomas, Anthony, Chi.	9	36	4.0	9	0
Walker, Aaron, S.F.	8	116	14.5	26	1
Wiggins, Jermaine, Car.	8	80	10.0	23	1
Gordon, Lamar, St.L	8	59	7.4	21	0
Abdullah, Rabih, Chi.	8	55	6.9	17	0
Williams, Karl, T.B.	7	114	16.3	43	0
Yoder, Todd, T.B.	7	68	9.7	20	2
Dudley, Rickey, T.B.	7	42	6.0	9	1
Ponder, Willie, NYG	7	35	5.0	16	0
Farris, Jimmy, Atl.	6	100	16.7	42t	2
Lewis, Greg, Phi.	6	95	15.8	25	0
Stevens, Jerramy, Sea.	6	72	12.0	26	0
Rasby, Walter, N.O.	6	55	9.2	17	0
Jefferson, Shawn, Det.	6	46	7.7	13	0
Davenport, Najeh, G.B.	6	38	6.3	12	0
Anderson, Damien, Ariz	6	36	6.0	11	0
Stackhouse, Charles, Min.	6	30	5.0	10	0
Smith, Terrelle, N.O.	6	28	4.7	8	0
Royal, Robert, Was.	5	48	9.6	20	0
Smith, Paul, Det.	5	45	9.0	12	0
Pinner, Artose, Det.	5	40	8.0	21	0
Levens, Dorsey, NYG	5	39	7.8	11	0
Seidman, Mike, Car.	5	35	7.0	14	0
McAddley, Jason, Ariz	4	53	13.3	25	0
Sapp, Warren, T.B.	4	39	9.8	18	2
Mitchell, Brian, NYG	4	38	9.5	11	0
Shepherd, Edell, T.B.	4	38	9.5	14	0
Morris, Maurice, Sea.	4	32	8.0	13	1
Murrell, Adrian, Dal.	4	32	8.0	14	0
Cobourne, Avon, Det.	4	30	7.5	13	0
Chamberlain, Byron, Was.	4	29	7.3	15	0
Goodwin, Hunter, Min.	4	26	6.5	12	0
Curtis, Kevin, St.L	4	13	3.3	8	0
Bannister, Alex, Sea.	3	61	20.3	31t	1
Kircus, David, Det.	3	53	17.7	19	0
Merritt, Ahmad, Chi.	3	50	16.7	25	0
Smith, Zuriel, Dal.	3	46	15.3	32	0
Forsey, Brock, Chi.	3	37	12.3	22	0
Jacobs, Taylor, Was.	3	37	12.3	19t	1
Gardner, Talman, N.O.	3	29	9.7	11	0
Barlow, Reggie, T.B.	3	27	9.0	13	1
Simon, John, Was.	3	21	7.0	12	0
Ware, Kevin, Was.	3	17	5.7	7	0
McCullough, Sultan, Was.	3	13	4.3	8	0
Smart, Rod, Car.	3	11	3.7	5	0
Joyce, Delvin, NYG	3	7	2.3	5	0
Evans, Heath, Sea.	2	34	17.0	20	0
Hankton, Karl, Car.	2	27	13.5	15	0
Avery, John, Min.	2	24	12.0	13	1
Dinkins, Darnell, NYG	2	16	8.0	10	0
Dyson, Kevin, Car.	2	15	7.5	9	0
Heller, Will, T.B.	2	15	7.5	11	1
Howry, Keenan, Min.	2	15	7.5	8	0
Russell, Cliff, Was.	2	10	5.0	7	0
Martin, Jamar, Dal.	2	9	4.5	6	0
Robinson, Jeff, Dal.	2	8	4.0	5t	2
Kasper, Kevin, Ariz	1	23	23.0	23	0
St. Clair, John, St.L	1	18	18.0	18	0
Luchey, Nicolas, G.B.	1	12	12.0	12	0
Carter, Ki-Jana, N.O.	1	11	11.0	11	0
Edwards, Terrence, Atl.	1	10	10.0	10	0
Scobey, Josh, Ariz	1	9	9.0	9	0
Chapman, Doug, Min.	1	8	8.0	8	0
Harrington, Joey, Det.	1	8	8.0	8	0
Foster, Larry, Ariz	1	7	7.0	7	0
Lewis, Derrick, N.O.	1	7	7.0	7	0
Barnes, Darian, T.B.	1	6	6.0	6	0
Garcia, Jeff, S.F.	1	6	6.0	6	0
Nead, Spencer, St.L	1	6	6.0	6	0
Fenderson, James, N.O.	1	5	5.0	5	0
Mahe, Reno, Phi.	1	5	5.0	5	0
Peterson, Adrian, Chi.	1	5	5.0	5	0
Layne, George, Atl.	1	3	3.0	3	0
Ohalete, Ifeanyi, Was.	1	3	3.0	3	0
McMullen, Billy, Phi.	1	2	2.0	2	0
Smith, Lamar, N.O.	1	2	2.0	2	0
Trejo, Stephen, Det.	1	2	2.0	2	0
McNabb, Donovan, Phi.	1	-7	-7.0	-7	0
Timmerman, Adam, St.L	1	-7	-7.0	-7	0
Kreutz, Olin, Chi.	1	-8	-8.0	-8	0
Coleman, Cosey, T.B.	0	1	—	1	0
Johnson, Brad, T.B.	0	-2	—	-2	0
Green, Cornell, T.B.	0	-3	—	-3	0

t = Touchdown
Leader based on receptions

2003 INDIVIDUAL STATISTICS—INTERCEPTIONS

INTERCEPTIONS

INTERCEPTIONS

NFC:	9	Tony Parrish, San Francisco
	9	Brian Russell, Minnesota
AFC:	7	Marcus Coleman, Houston
	7	Ed Reed, Baltimore
	7	Patrick Surtain, Miami

INTERCEPTIONS, GAME

NFC:	3	Brian Williams, Minnesota vs. Detroit, November 23 (71 yards, 1 TD)
	3	Terence Newman, Dallas at Washington, December 14 (23 yards, 0 TD)
AFC:	2	Nick Harper, Indianapolis at Cleveland, September 7 (43 yards, 0 TD)
	2	Marcus Coleman, Houston at Miami, September 7 (3 yards, 0 TD)
	2	Takeo Spikes, Buffalo vs. New England, September 7 (1 yard, 0 TD)
	2	Ed Reed, Baltimore vs. Cleveland, September 14 (55 yards, 1 TD)
	2	Nate Clements, Buffalo at Miami, September 21 (54 yards, 1 TD)
	2	Dexter McCleon, Kansas City at Baltimore, September 28 (0 yards, 0 TD)
	2	Jim Nelson, Indianapolis at New Orleans, September 28 (22 yards, 0 TD)
	2	Kenny Wright, Houston vs. Jacksonville, September 28 (-2 yards, 0 TD)
	2	Charles Woodson, Oakland at Chicago, October 5 (67 yards, 0 TD)
	2	Patrick Surtain, Miami at N.Y. Giants, October 5 (2 yards, 0 TD)
	2	Sam Madison, Miami at Jacksonville, October 12 (46 yards, 1 TD)
	2	Rodney Harrison, New England vs. N.Y. Giants, October 12 (0 yards, 0 TD)
	2	Chris McAlister, Baltimore at Arizona, October 12 (87 yards, 1 TD)
	2	Eric Warfield, Kansas City vs. Buffalo, October 26 (20 yards, 0 TD)
	2	Patrick Surtain, Miami at San Diego, October 27 (32 yards, 0 TD)
	2	Ty Law, New England vs. Dallas, November 16 (47 yards, 0 TD)
	2	Phillip Buchanon, Oakland vs. Minnesota, November 16 (64 yards, 1 TD)
	2	Quentin Jammer, San Diego vs. Kansas City, November 30 (0 yards, 0 TD)
	2	Tyrone Poole, New England vs. Jacksonville, December 14 (61 yards, 0 TD)
	2	Samari Rolle, Tennessee at Houston, December 21 (0 yards, 0 TD)
	2	Deshea Townsend, Pittsburgh vs. San Diego, December 21 (24 yards, 1 TD)
	2	Tank Williams, Tennessee vs. Tampa Bay, December 28 (0 yards, 0 TD)

YARDS

NFC:	205	Travis Fisher, St. Louis
	205	Brian Williams, Minnesota
AFC:	176	Phillip Buchanon, Oakland

LONGEST

AFC:	95	Marlon McCree, Houston vs. Tennessee, December 21 - TD
NFC:	90	Mike McKenzie, Green Bay vs. Chicago, December 7 - TD

TOUCHDOWNS

AFC:	2	Tedy Bruschi, New England
	2	Phillip Buchanon, Oakland
	2	Andre Dyson, Tennessee
	2	Jerome Woods, Kansas City
NFC:	2	Travis Fisher, St. Louis
	2	Mike Minter, Carolina

TEAM LEADERS, INTERCEPTIONS

AFC: BALTIMORE, 7, Ed Reed; BUFFALO, 3, Nate Clements; CINCINNATI, 4, Tory James; CLEVELAND, 6, Earl Little; DENVER, 3, Kelly Herndon; HOUSTON, 7, Marcus Coleman; INDIANAPOLIS, 4, Nick Harper; JACKSONVILLE, 3, Mike Peterson; KANSAS CITY, 6, Dexter McCleon, Greg Wesley; MIAMI, 7, Patrick Surtain; NEW ENGLAND, 6, Ty Law, Tyrone Poole; N.Y. JETS, 3, Aaron Beasley; OAKLAND, 6, Phillip Buchanon; PITTSBURGH, 4, Brent Alexander; SAN DIEGO, 4, Quentin Jammer; TENNESSEE, 6, Samari Rolle

NFC: ARIZONA, 6, Dexter Jackson; ATLANTA, 3, Juran Bolden, Keion Carpenter, Tod McBride; CAROLINA, 3, Deon Grant, Ricky Manning, Mike Minter; CHICAGO, 4, Jerry Azumah, Charles Tillman; DALLAS, 4, Terence Newman; DETROIT, 6, Dre' Bly; GREEN BAY, 5, Darren Sharper; MINNESOTA, 9, Brian Russell; NEW ORLEANS, 4, Fred Thomas; N.Y. GIANTS, 2, Will Allen, Ralph Brown, Johnnie Harris, Frank Walker; PHILADELPHIA, 3, Michael Lewis, Troy Vincent; ST. LOUIS, 4, Jerametrius Butler, Travis Fisher, Tommy Polley, Aeneas Williams; SAN FRANCISCO, 9, Tony Parrish; SEATTLE, 4, Reggie Tongue; TAMPA BAY, 5, Dwight Smith; WASHINGTON, 4, Fred Smoot

TEAM CHAMPION

AFC:	29	New England
NFC:	28	Minnesota

NFL TOP TEN INTERCEPTORS

	No	Yards	Avg	Long	TD
Parrish, Tony, S.F.	9	202	22.4	49	0
Russell, Brian, Min.	9	185	20.6	50	0
Chavous, Corey, Min.	8	143	17.9	39	1
Coleman, Marcus, Hou.	7	95	13.6	41	0
Reed, Ed, Bal.	7	132	18.9	54t	1
Surtain, Patrick, Mia.	7	59	8.4	32	0
Bly, Dre', Det.	6	89	14.8	48t	1
Buchanon, Phillip, Oak.	6	176	29.3	83t	2
Jackson, Dexter, Ariz	6	122	20.3	30	0
Law, Ty, N.E.	6	112	18.7	65t	1
Lewis, Ray, Bal.	6	99	16.5	37	1
Little, Earl, Cle.	6	41	6.8	21	0
McCleon, Dexter, K.C.	6	-3	-0.5	0	0
Poole, Tyrone, N.E.	6	81	13.5	44	0
Rolle, Samari, Ten.	6	141	23.5	52	0
Wesley, Greg, K.C.	6	63	10.5	27	0

AFC—INDIVIDUAL INTERCEPTORS

	No	Yards	Avg	Long	TD
Reed, Ed, Bal.	7	132	18.9	54t	1
Coleman, Marcus, Hou.	7	95	13.6	41	0
Surtain, Patrick, Mia.	7	59	8.4	32	0
Buchanon, Phillip, Oak.	6	176	29.3	83t	2
Rolle, Samari, Ten.	6	141	23.5	52	0
Law, Ty, N.E.	6	112	18.7	65t	1
Lewis, Ray, Bal.	6	99	16.5	37	1
Poole, Tyrone, N.E.	6	81	13.5	44	0
Wesley, Greg, K.C.	6	63	10.5	27	0
Little, Earl, Cle.	6	41	6.8	21	0
McCleon, Dexter, K.C.	6	-3	-0.5	0	0
Harper, Nick, Ind.	4	121	30.3	75t	1
Alexander, Brent, Pit.	4	63	15.8	34	0
Dyson, Andre, Ten.	4	62	15.5	51t	2
James, Tory, Cin.	4	56	14.0	31	0
Warfield, Eric, K.C.	4	39	9.8	20	0
Wilson, Eugene, N.E.	4	18	4.5	10	0
Jammer, Quentin, S.D.	4	6	1.5	6	0
Woods, Jerome, K.C.	3	125	41.7	79t	2
Knight, Sammy, Mia.	3	98	32.7	70	0
McAlister, Chris, Bal.	3	93	31.0	83t	1
Madison, Sam, Mia.	3	82	27.3	36	1
Woodson, Charles, Oak.	3	67	22.3	51	0
Beasley, Aaron, NYJ	3	64	21.3	39	0
Clements, Nate, Buf.	3	54	18.0	54t	1
Scott, Chad, Pit.	3	50	16.7	26t	1
Baxter, Gary, Bal.	3	41	13.7	34	0
Bruschi, Tedy, N.E.	3	26	8.7	18t	2
Townsend, Deshea, Pit.	3	24	8.0	25t	1
Thomas, Zach, Mia.	3	21	7.0	19	0
Herndon, Kelly, Den.	3	19	6.3	16	0
Peterson, Mike, Jac.	3	8	2.7	7	0
Marion, Brock, Mia.	3	3	1.0	3	0
Harrison, Rodney, N.E.	3	0	0.0	2	0
Wright, Kenny, Hou.	3	-2	-0.7	0	0
Buckley, Terrell, Mia.	2	75	37.5	74t	1
Boiman, Rocky, Ten.	2	70	35.0	60t	1
Demps, Will, Bal.	2	57	28.5	54	0
Samuel, Asante, N.E.	2	55	27.5	55t	1
Davis, Sammy, S.D.	2	48	24.0	41	0
Strickland, Donald, Ind.	2	43	21.5	24	0
Harts, Shaunard, K.C.	2	39	19.5	39t	1
Carter, Tyrone, NYJ	2	37	18.5	23	0
Craft, Jason, Jac.	2	29	14.5	21	0
Edwards, Donnie, S.D.	2	27	13.5	15	0
Calmus, Rocky, Ten.	2	26	13.0	15	0
Nelson, Jim, Ind.	2	22	11.0	12	0
Vrabel, Mike, N.E.	2	18	9.0	14	0
Woodson, Rod, Oak.	2	18	9.0	13	0
Burris, Jeff, Cin.	2	17	8.5	17	0
Gibson, Derrick, Oak.	2	16	8.0	11	0
Mickens, Ray, NYJ	2	16	8.0	16	0
Ayodele, Akin, Jac.	2	15	7.5	13	0
Kiel, Terrence, S.D.	2	15	7.5	15	0
Gold, Ian, Den.	2	14	7.0	12t	1
Simmons, Brian, Cin.	2	14	7.0	13	0
Beckett, Rogers, Cin.	2	11	5.5	11	0
Bashir, Idrees, Ind.	2	9	4.5	9	0
Bulluck, Keith, Ten.	2	9	4.5	9	0
McGee, Terrence, Buf.	2	5	2.5	3	0
Griffith, Robert, Cle.	2	3	1.5	3	0
Thornton, David, Ind.	2	3	1.5	2	0
Spikes, Takeo, Buf.	2	1	0.5	1	0
Garnes, Sam, NYJ	2	0	0.0	0	0
Mathis, Rashean, Jac.	2	0	0.0	0	0
Williams, Tank, Ten.	2	0	0.0	0	0
McCree, Marlon, Hou.	1	95	95.0	95t	1
McCutcheon, Daylon, Cle.	1	75	75.0	75t	1
Bell, Kendrell, Pit.	1	61	61.0	42	0
Williams, Chad, Bal.	1	52	52.0	52t	1
Lassiter, Kwamie, S.D.	1	38	38.0	38t	1
Adams, Sam, Buf.	1	37	37.0	37t	1
Morris, Aric, N.E.	1	33	33.0	33	0
Brackett, Gary, Ind.	1	31	31.0	31t	1
Barber, Shawn, K.C.	1	28	28.0	28	0
Hartwell, Edgerton, Bal.	1	26	26.0	26	0
Hobson, Victor, NYJ	1	26	26.0	26	0
Bentley, Kevin, Cle.	1	25	25.0	25	0
Cooper, Stephen, S.D.	1	25	25.0	25	0
Henry, Anthony, Cle.	1	19	19.0	19	0
Doss, Mike, Ind.	1	15	15.0	15	0
McGinest, Willie, N.E.	1	15	15.0	15t	1
Abraham, Donnie, NYJ	1	12	12.0	12	0
Cooper, Deke, Jac.	1	12	12.0	12	0
Stevens, Matt, Hou.	1	12	12.0	12	0
Suggs, Terrell, Bal.	1	11	11.0	11	0
Winfield, Antoine, Buf.	1	11	11.0	11	0
Kaesviharn, Kevin, Cin.	1	10	10.0	10	0
Farrior, James, Pit.	1	9	9.0	9	0
Fujita, Scott, K.C.	1	8	8.0	8	0
Hawkins, Artrell, Cin.	1	8	8.0	8	0
Sims, Ryan, K.C.	1	8	8.0	8	0
Washington, Dewayne, Pit.	1	7	7.0	7	0
O'Neal, Deltha, Den.	1	6	6.0	6	0
Roberts, Terrell, Cin.	1	6	6.0	6	0
Schobel, Aaron, Buf.	1	6	6.0	6	0
Brown, Eric, Hou.	1	5	5.0	5	0
Boyer, Brant, Cle.	1	4	4.0	4	0
Brackens, Tony, Jac.	1	4	4.0	4	0
Darius, Donovin, Jac.	1	4	4.0	4	0
Trapp, James, Jac.	1	4	4.0	4	0
Woolfolk, Andre, Ten.	1	4	4.0	4	0
Johnson, Eric, Oak.	1	3	3.0	3	0
Mitchell, Kawika, K.C.	1	3	3.0	3	0
Spicer, Paul, Jac.	1	2	2.0	2	0
Bodden, Leigh, Cle.	1	1	1.0	1	0
Gildon, Jason, Pit.	1	1	1.0	1	0
Roman, Mark, Cin.	1	1	1.0	1	0
Beckham, Tony, Ten.	1	0	0.0	0	0
Brandon, Sam, Den.	1	0	0.0	0	0
Bryant, Fernando, Jac.	1	0	0.0	0	0
Glenn, Aaron, Hou.	1	0	0.0	0	0
Izzo, Larry, N.E.	1	0	0.0	0	0
Kearse, Jevon, Ten.	1	0	0.0	0	0
Kennedy, Kenoy, Den.	1	0	0.0	0	0
Lang, Kenard, Cle.	1	0	0.0	0	0
Macklin, David, Ind.	1	0	0.0	0	0
Taylor, Ben, Cle.	1	0	0.0	0	0

2003 INDIVIDUAL STATISTICS—INTERCEPTIONS

	No	Yards	Avg	Long	TD
Walls, Lenny, Den.	1	0	0.0	0	0
Zgonina, Jeff, Mia.	1	0	0.0	0	0
Wilson, Jerry, S.D.	1	-2	-2.0	-2	0

t = Touchdown Leader based on interceptions

NFC—INDIVIDUAL INTERCEPTORS

	No	Yards	Avg	Long	TD
Parrish, Tony, S.F.	9	202	22.4	49	0
Russell, Brian, Min.	9	185	20.6	50	0
Chavous, Corey, Min.	8	143	17.9	39	1
Jackson, Dexter, Ariz	6	122	20.3	30	0
Bly, Dre', Det.	6	89	14.8	48t	1
Williams, Brian, Min.	5	205	41.0	77	1
Hill, Renaldo, Ariz	5	119	23.8	70t	1
Sharper, Darren, G.B.	5	78	15.6	50	0
Smith, Dwight, T.B.	5	3	0.6	3	0
Fisher, Travis, St.L	4	205	51.3	74t	2
McKenzie, Mike, G.B.	4	98	24.5	90t	1
Plummer, Ahmed, S.F.	4	85	21.3	68t	1
Williams, Aeneas, St.L	4	82	20.5	46t	1
Butler, Jerametrius, St.L	4	72	18.0	45	0
Thomas, Fred, N.O.	4	47	11.8	20	0
Azumah, Jerry, Chi.	4	44	11.0	25	0
Smoot, Fred, Was.	4	35	8.8	35	0
Polley, Tommy, St.L	4	32	8.0	22	0
Tillman, Charles, Chi.	4	27	6.8	32	0
Newman, Terence, Dal.	4	23	5.8	25	0
Tongue, Reggie, Sea.	4	11	2.8	10	0
Minter, Mike, Car.	3	100	33.3	35t	2
Harris, Al, G.B.	3	89	29.7	56t	1
Ambrose, Ashley, N.O.	3	78	26.0	73t	1
Bolden, Juran, Atl.	3	61	20.3	41t	1
Ohalete, Ifeanyi, Was.	3	60	20.0	30	0
Tinoisamoa, Pisa, St.L	3	46	15.3	29	0
Bowen, Matt, Was.	3	44	14.7	44	0
McBride, Tod, Atl.	3	44	14.7	25	1
Holt, Terrence, Det.	3	42	14.0	30	0
Simmons, Anthony, Sea.	3	38	12.7	33	0
Manning, Ricky, Car.	3	33	11.0	27t	1
Lewis, Michael, Phi.	3	31	10.3	23	0
Vincent, Troy, Phi.	3	28	9.3	28	0
Grant, Deon, Car.	3	25	8.3	25	0
Carpenter, Keion, Atl.	3	22	7.3	14	0
Barnett, Nick, G.B.	3	21	7.0	14	0
Bellamy, Jay, N.O.	3	19	6.3	10	0
Rumph, Mike, S.F.	3	19	6.3	12	0
Walker, Frank, NYG	2	74	37.0	56t	1
McQuarters, R.W., Chi.	2	72	36.0	43	0
Williams, Roy, Dal.	2	69	34.5	39	0
Wallace, Al, Car.	2	58	29.0	53	0
Brooks, Derrick, T.B.	2	56	28.0	44t	1
Barber, Ronde, T.B.	2	53	26.5	29t	1
Brown, Ralph, NYG	2	51	25.5	29t	1
Singleton, Alshermond, Dal.	2	42	21.0	41t	1
Wansley, Tim, T.B.	2	38	19.0	23t	1
Peterson, Julian, S.F.	2	31	15.5	31	0
Allen, Will, NYG	2	23	11.5	22	0
Terrell, David, Was.	2	21	10.5	20	0
Trufant, Marcus, Sea.	2	21	10.5	15	0
Lynch, John, T.B.	2	18	9.0	18	0
Diggs, Na'il, G.B.	2	13	6.5	13	0
Rice, Simeon, T.B.	2	12	6.0	12	0
Hawthorne, Michael, G.B.	2	8	4.0	8	0
Harris, Johnnie, NYG	2	3	1.5	3	0
Scott, Bryan, Atl.	2	3	1.5	3	0
Bailey, Champ, Was.	2	2	1.0	2	0
Howard, Reggie, Car.	2	2	1.0	2	0
Bauman, Rashad, Was.	2	1	0.5	1	0
Brown, Mike, Chi.	2	0	0.0	0	0
Walker, Brian, Det.	2	0	0.0	0	0
Nattiel, Michael, Min.	1	80	80.0	80t	1
Briggs, Lance, Chi.	1	45	45.0	45t	1
Phillips, Jermaine, T.B.	1	41	41.0	41	0
Rodgers, Derrick, N.O.	1	40	40.0	40t	1
Sheppard, Lito, Phi.	1	34	34.0	34	0
Stoutmire, Omar, NYG	1	34	34.0	34	0
Johnstone, Lance, Min.	1	33	33.0	33t	1
Wayne, Nate, Phi.	1	33	33.0	33	0
Mathis, Kevin, Atl.	1	32	32.0	32t	1
Newman, Keith, Atl.	1	29	29.0	29	0
Little, Leonard, St.L	1	28	28.0	28	0
Edwards, Mario, Dal.	1	27	27.0	27t	1
Lucas, Ken, Sea.	1	27	27.0	27	0
Robinson, Damien, Sea.	1	26	26.0	26	0
Barrett, David, Ariz	1	25	25.0	25	0
Coakley, Dexter, Dal.	1	24	24.0	24	0
Archuleta, Adam, St.L	1	22	22.0	22	0
Bronson, Zack, S.F.	1	22	22.0	22	0
Trotter, Jeremiah, Was.	1	21	21.0	21	0
Okeafor, Chike, Sea.	1	18	18.0	18	0
Webster, Jason, S.F.	1	17	17.0	17	0
Kalu, N. D., Phi.	1	15	15.0	15t	1
Williams, Shaun, NYG	1	14	14.0	14	0
Jackson, Tyoka, St.L	1	11	11.0	11	0
Brown, Sheldon, Phi.	1	10	10.0	10	0
Burton, Shane, Car.	1	10	10.0	10	0
Witherspoon, Will, Car.	1	10	10.0	10	0
Smith, Darrin, N.O.	1	9	9.0	9	0
Springs, Shawn, Sea.	1	8	8.0	8	0
Godfrey, Randall, Sea.	1	7	7.0	7	0
Groce, DeJuan, St.L	1	7	7.0	7	0
Ruff, Orlando, N.O.	1	7	7.0	7	0
Ulbrich, Jeff, S.F.	1	7	7.0	7	0
Robinson, Travaris, T.B.	1	6	6.0	6	0
Williams, Jimmy, S.F.	1	6	6.0	6	0
Edwards, Antuan, G.B.	1	5	5.0	5	0
Hood, Roderick, Phi.	1	5	5.0	5	0
Rhinehart, Coby, Ariz	1	5	5.0	5	0
Draft, Chris, Atl.	1	4	4.0	4	0
Anderson, Marques, G.B.	1	3	3.0	3	0
Claiborne, Chris, Min.	1	3	3.0	3	0
Green, Michael, Chi.	1	3	3.0	3	0
Williams, Kevin, Min.	1	3	3.0	3	0
Buchanan, Ray, Atl.	1	2	2.0	2	0
Evans, Doug, Det.	1	2	2.0	2	0
Hamlin, Ken, Sea.	1	2	2.0	2	0
Jones, Tebucky, N.O.	1	2	2.0	2	0
Nece, Ryan, T.B.	1	2	2.0	2	0
Taylor, Bobby, Phi.	1	2	2.0	2	0
Irvin, Ken, Min.	1	1	1.0	1	0
Brown, Alex, Chi.	1	0	0.0	0	0
Dawkins, Brian, Phi.	1	0	0.0	0	0
Duncan, Jamie, St.L	1	0	0.0	0	0
Heard, Ronnie, S.F.	1	0	0.0	0	0
Hunter, Pete, Dal.	1	0	0.0	0	0
Kelly, Brian, T.B.	1	0	0.0	0	0
McFarland, Anthony, T.B.	1	0	0.0	0	0
Ross, Derek, Dal.	1	0	0.0	0	0
Rucker, Mike, Car.	1	0	0.0	0	0
Smith, Otis, Det.	1	0	0.0	0	0
Walker, Denard, Min.	1	0	0.0	0	0
Brown, Chad, Sea.	1	-1	-1.0	-1	0
Harris, Corey, Det.	1	-1	-1.0	-1	0
Bailey, Boss, Det.	1	-2	-2.0	-2	0
Woodson, Darren, Dal.	1	-2	-2.0	-2	0
Kelly, Eric, Min.	0	40	—	40	0
Green, Victor, N.O.	0	24	—	24	0

t = Touchdown; Leader based on interceptions

AMERICAN FOOTBALL CONFERENCE—INTERCEPTIONS

	No	Yards	Avg	Long	TD
New England	29	358	12.3	65t	5
Kansas City	25	310	12.4	79t	3
Baltimore	24	511	21.3	83t	4
Miami	22	338	15.4	74t	2
Tennessee	21	312	14.9	60t	3
Cleveland	15	168	11.2	75t	1
Indianapolis	15	244	16.3	75t	2
Jacksonville	15	78	5.2	21	0
Cincinnati	14	123	8.8	31	0
Houston	14	205	14.6	95t	1
Oakland	14	280	20.0	83t	2
Pittsburgh	14	215	15.4	42	2
San Diego	13	157	12.1	41	1
N.Y. Jets	11	155	14.1	39	0
Buffalo	10	114	11.4	54t	2
Denver	9	39	4.3	16	1
AFC Total	265	3607	13.6	95t	29
AFC Average	16.6	225.4	13.6	—	1.8

NATIONAL FOOTBALL CONFERENCE—INTERCEPTIONS

	No	Yards	Avg	Long	TD
Minnesota	28	693	24.8	80t	4
St. Louis	24	505	21.0	74t	3
San Francisco	23	389	16.9	68t	1
Green Bay	21	315	15.0	90t	2
Tampa Bay	20	229	11.5	44t	3
Washington	17	184	10.8	44	0
Carolina	16	238	14.9	53	3
Seattle	16	157	9.8	33	0
Atlanta	15	197	13.1	41t	3
Chicago	15	191	12.7	45t	1
Detroit	15	130	8.7	48t	1
New Orleans	14	226	16.1	73t	2
Arizona	13	271	20.8	70t	1
Dallas	13	183	14.1	41t	2
Philadelphia	13	158	12.2	34	1
N.Y. Giants	10	199	19.9	56t	2
NFC Total	273	4265	15.6	90t	29
NFC Average	17.1	266.6	15.6	—	1.8
League Total	538	7872	—	95t	58
League Average	16.8	246.0	14.6	—	1.8

KICKOFF RETURNS

YARDS PER RETURN
NFC: 29.0 Jerry Azumah, Chicago
AFC: 28.2 Bethel Johnson, New England

YARDS
NFC: 1684 Josh Scobey, Arizona
AFC: 1478 Dante Hall, Kansas City

YARDS, GAME
NFC: 252 Josh Scobey, Arizona at St. Louis, September 28 (7 returns, 1 TD)
AFC: 242 Jonathan Carter, N.Y. Jets at Indianapolis, November 16 (6 returns, 1 TD)

LONGEST
AFC: 100 Dante Hall, Kansas City vs. Pittsburgh, September 14 - TD
NFC: 100 Josh Scobey, Arizona at St. Louis, September 28 - TD
100 Rod Smart, Carolina vs. New Orleans, October 5 - TD

RETURNS
NFC: 73 Josh Scobey, Arizona
AFC: 58 J.J. Moses, Houston

RETURNS, GAME
NFC: 9 Ahmad Merritt, Chicago at San Francisco, September 7 (170 yards, 0 TD)
9 Josh Scobey, Arizona at Cleveland, November 16 (165 yards, 0 TD)
AFC: 8 Leon Johnson, San Diego at Pittsburgh, December 21 (141 yards, 0 TD)

TOUCHDOWNS
AFC: 2 Dante Hall, Kansas City
NFC: 2 Jerry Azumah, Chicago

TEAM CHAMPION
AFC: 25.4 Kansas City
NFC: 23.8 Chicago

NFL TOP TEN KICKOFF RETURNERS

	No	Yards	Avg	Long	TD
Azumah, Jerry, Chi.	41	1191	29.0	89t	2
Johnson, Bethel, N.E.	30	847	28.2	92t	1
Bates, Michael, NYJ-Dal.	26	686	26.4	48	0
Hall, Dante, K.C.	57	1478	25.9	100t	2
Brightful, Lamont, Bal.	29	716	24.7	75	0
Thrash, James, Phi.	34	815	24.0	54	0
Swinton, Reggie, Dal.-Det.	43	1029	23.9	96t	1
Cole, Chris, Den.	30	714	23.8	34	0
Lewis, Michael, N.O.	45	1068	23.7	53	0
Morton, Chad, Was.	44	1029	23.4	94t	1

AFC—INDIVIDUAL KICKOFF RETURNERS

	No	Yards	Avg	Long	TD
Johnson, Bethel, N.E.	30f	847	28.2	92t	1
Hall, Dante, K.C.	57	1478	25.9	100t	2
Brightful, Lamont, Bal.	29	716	24.7	75	0
Cole, Chris, Den.	30	714	23.8	34	0
Moses, J.J., Hou.	58	1355	23.4	70	0
Johnson, Leon, S.D.	50	1151	23.0	60	0
Taylor, Ike, Pit.	37	831	22.5	53	0
Gabriel, Doug, Oak.	29	646	22.3	85t	1
Dwight, Tim, S.D.	22	488	22.2	32	0
Jenkins, Ronney, Oak.	25	553	22.1	33	0
Brown, Antonio, Buf.	48	1046	21.8	75	0
Bennett, Brandon, Cin.	53	1146	21.6	46	0

2003 INDIVIDUAL STATISTICS—KICKOFF RETURNS

	No	Yards	Avg	Long	TD
Minor, Travis, Mia.	34	727	21.4	49	0
Davis, Andre', Cle.	38	803	21.1	69	0
Allen, David, Jac.	41	831	20.3	61	0
Schifino, Jake, Ten.	35	703	20.1	39	0
Taylor, Chester, Bal.	23	448	19.5	29	0
Randle El, Antwaan, Pit.	24	466	19.4	34	0
(Nonqualifiers)					
Pyatt, Brad, Ind.	19	544	28.6	90	0
Rogers, Charlie, Mia.	19	383	20.2	33	0
Carter, Jonathan, NYJ	18	517	28.7	90t	1
Rhodes, Dominic, Ind.	16	411	25.7	49	0
Fargas, Justin, Oak.	16	315	19.7	32	0
Wilkins, Terrence, Ind.	14	325	23.2	42	0
Suggs, Lee, Cle.	14	318	22.7	42	0
Toefield, LaBrandon, Jac.	14	272	19.4	35	0
McCareins, Justin, Ten.	13	256	19.7	25	0
Droughns, Reuben, Den.	12	293	24.4	36	0
Pass, Patrick, N.E.	11	254	23.1	36	0
Jordan, LaMont, NYJ	11	209	19.0	25	0
Faulk, Kevin, N.E.	10	207	20.7	30	0
King, Andre, Cle.	9	172	19.1	30	0
McGee, Terrence, Buf.	8	160	20.0	26	0
Hollings, Tony, Hou.	8	142	17.8	30	0
O'Neal, Deltha, Den.	8	128	16.0	24	0
Roberts, Terrell, Cin.	7	128	18.3	23	0
Watson, Kenny, Cin.	7	113	16.1	27	0
Morris, Sammy, Buf.	6	146	24.3	52	0
Walters, Troy, Ind.	6	126	21.0	34	0
Lewis, Jermaine, Jac.	6	111	18.5	26	0
Madise, Adrian, Den.	5	137	27.4	83	0
Mason, Derrick, Ten.	5	106	21.2	34	0
Norris, Moran, Hou.	5	71	14.2	19	0
Mays, Lee, Pit.	4	79	19.8	27	0
Berlin, Eddie, Ten.	4	73	18.3	25	0
Williams, Ricky, Ind.	4	67	16.8	23	0
Whitted, Alvis, Oak.	4	48	12.0	18	0
Florence, Drayton, S.D.	4	47	11.8	24	0
Holcombe, Robert, Ten.	4	38	9.5	20	0
Jackson, Ray, Ten.	3	77	25.7	31	0
Simmons, Sam, Mia.	3	64	21.3	34	0
Davis, Domanick, Hou.	3	61	20.3	28	0
Maddox, Nick, Cle.	3	58	19.3	26	0
Swayne, Kevin, NYJ	3	48	16.0	23	0
Vaughn, Darrick, Hou.	3	47	15.7	22	0
Kinney, Erron, Ten.	3	37	12.3	17	0
Kreider, Dan, Pit.	3	29	9.7	15	0
Morgan, Quincy, Cle.	2	67	33.5	47	0
Johnson, Albert, NYJ	2	50	25.0	29	0
Pinnock, Andrew, S.D.	2	50	25.0	41	0
Edwards, Marc, Jac.	2	44	22.0	24	0
Cloud, Mike, N.E.	2	38	19.0	19	0
Powell, Carl, Cin.	2	33	16.5	20	0
Chatman, Jesse, S.D.	2	31	15.5	23	0
Givens, David, N.E.	2	31	15.5	20	0
Buchanon, Phillip, Oak.	2	25	12.5	17	0
Wells, Jonathan, Hou.	2	24	12.0	14	0
Johnson, Rudi, Cin.	2	23	11.5	15	0
Vrabel, Mike, N.E.	2	22	11.0	14	0
Klecko, Dan, N.E.	2	20	10.0	10	0
Smith, Musa, Bal.	2	17	8.5	15	0
Anderson, Mike, Den.	2	14	7.0	14	0
Mungro, James, Ind.	2	7	3.5	5	0
Baker, Chris, NYJ	2f	6	3.0	4	0
White, Jamel, Cle.	2	2	1.0	2	0
Jackson, James, Cle.	1	68	68.0	39	0
Boerigter, Marc, K.C.	1	44	44.0	44	0
Blaylock, Derrick, K.C.	1	32	32.0	32	0
Askew, B.J., NYJ	1	27	27.0	27	0
Redmond, Jimmy, Jac.	1	21	21.0	21	0
Thomas, Adalius, Bal.	1	21	21.0	21	0
Edwards, Troy, Jac.	1	20	20.0	20	0
Ward, Dedric, Bal.	1	20	20.0	20	0
Burns, Joe, Buf.	1	17	17.0	17	0
Johnson, Jeremi, Cin.	1	16	16.0	16	0
Putzier, Jeb, Den.	1	16	16.0	16	0
Smith, Detron, Ind.	1	15	15.0	15	0
Peelle, Justin, S.D.	1	14	14.0	14	0
Carson, Leonardo, S.D.	1	13	13.0	13	0
Stewart, Tony, Cin.	1	13	13.0	13	0
Johnson, Darrius, K.C.	1	12	12.0	12	0
Ward, LaShaun, K.C.	1	11	11.0	11	0
Brady, Kyle, Jac.	1	10	10.0	10	0
Bruschi, Tedy, N.E.	1	9	9.0	9	0
Meier, Shad, Ten.	1	9	9.0	9	0
Pollard, Marcus, Ind.	1	9	9.0	9	0
Santiago, O.J., Oak.	1	9	9.0	9	0
Scott, DeQuincy, S.D.	1	9	9.0	9	0
Machado, J.P., NYJ	1	8	8.0	8	0
Mathis, Rashean, Jac.	1	7	7.0	7	0
Stokes, Barry, Cle.	1	7	7.0	7	0
Allen, Brian, Ind.	1	6	6.0	6	0
Mustard, Chad, Cle.	1	6	6.0	6	0
Steele, Glen, Cin.	1	2	2.0	2	0
Neal, Lorenzo, S.D.	1	1	1.0	1	0
Fatafehi, Mario, Den.	1	0	0.0	0	0
Lee, Donald, Mia.	1	0	0.0	0	0
Martin, Terrance, Hou.	1	0	0.0	0	0
Walls, Raymond, Bal.	1	0	0.0	0	0
Wilkerson, Jimmy, K.C.	1	0	0.0	0	0
McKnight, James, Mia.	0	28	—	28	0

t = Touchdown
f = Fair Catch
Leader based on average return, minimum 20 returns

NFC—INDIVIDUAL KICKOFF RETURNERS

	No	Yards	Avg	Long	TD
Azumah, Jerry, Chi.	41	1191	29.0	89t	2
Bates, Michael, NYJ-Dal.	26	686	26.4	48	0
Thrash, James, Phi.	34	815	24.0	54	0
Swinton, Reggie, Dal.-Det.	43	1029	23.9	96t	1
Lewis, Michael, N.O.	45	1068	23.7	53	0
Morton, Chad, Was.	44	1029	23.4	94t	1
Smart, Rod, Car.	41	947	23.1	100t	1
Scobey, Josh, Ariz	73	1684	23.1	100t	1
Harris, Arlen, St.L	51	1175	23.0	42	0
Wilson, Cedrick, S.F.	37	836	22.6	95t	1
Chatman, Antonio, G.B.	36	804	22.3	46	0
Drummond, Eddie, Det.	21	469	22.3	38	0
Smith, Onterrio, Min.	27	588	21.8	46	0
Smith, Zuriel, Dal.	23	495	21.5	54	0
Morris, Maurice, Sea.	47	1007	21.4	56	0
Westbrook, Brian, Phi.	23	487	21.2	47	0
Rossum, Allen, Atl.	62	1291	20.8	52	0
Stecker, Aaron, T.B.	25	520	20.8	44	0
Mitchell, Brian, NYG	55	1117	20.3	29	0
Merritt, Ahmad, Chi.	20	405	20.3	35	0
(Nonqualifiers)					
Ross, Derek, Dal.	18	434	24.1	37	0
Jones, Thomas, T.B.	17	271	15.9	25	0
Davenport, Najeh, G.B.	16	505	31.6	60	0
Avery, John, Min.	16	346	21.6	48	0
Joyce, Delvin, NYG	15	309	20.6	36	0
Johnson, Patrick, Was.	13f	310	23.8	50	0
Howry, Keenan, Min.	12	271	22.6	42	0
Smith, Steve, Car.	11	309	28.1	42	0
Williams, Jimmy, S.F.	11	207	18.8	41	0
Barlow, Reggie, T.B.	10	221	22.1	32	0

	No	Yards	Avg	Long	TD
McAfee, Fred, N.O.	9	140	15.6	23	0
Carter, Kerry, Sea.	8	185	23.1	33	0
Stallworth, Donte', N.O.	8	171	21.4	28	0
Ferguson, Robert, G.B.	7	148	21.1	31	0
Furrey, Mike, St.L	7	140	20.0	27	0
Dantzler, Woody, Atl.	7	136	19.4	29	0
Cobourne, Avon, Det.	7	123	17.6	22	0
Jervey, Travis, Atl.	7	118	16.9	25	0
Morey, Sean, Phi.	7	93	13.3	24	0
Bruce, Arland, S.F.	6	125	20.8	29	0
Reynolds, Joffrey, St.L	6	109	18.2	25	0
Kasper, Kevin, Ariz	5	136	27.2	37	0
Craver, Keyuo, N.O.	5	128	25.6	52	0
Campbell, Kelly, Min.	5	101	20.2	23	0
Battle, Arnaz, S.F.	5	88	17.6	21	0
Cason, Aveion, Dal.	5	81	16.2	19	0
Abdullah, Rabih, Chi.	5	62	12.4	17	0
Tafoya, Joe, Chi.	4	55	13.8	19	0
Chapman, Doug, Min.	4	51	12.8	20	0
Strong, Mack, Sea.	3	60	20.0	27	0
Betts, Ladell, Was.	3	59	19.7	26	0
Henderson, William, G.B.	3	33	11.0	15	0
Kozlowski, Brian, Atl.	3	27	9.0	12	0
Gilmore, John, Chi.	3	25	8.3	11	0
Williams, Randal, Dal.	2	60	30.0	37t	1
Galloway, Joey, Dal.	2	38	19.0	22	0
Moran, Sean, S.F.	2	35	17.5	19	0
Proehl, Ricky, Car.	2	34	17.0	19	0
Clark, Kenny, Min.	2	33	16.5	21	0
Lloyd, Brandon, S.F.	2	32	16.0	21	0
Anderson, Damien, Ariz	2	31	15.5	16	0
Nead, Spencer, St.L	2	27	13.5	20	0
Cartwright, Rock, Was.	2	26	13.0	13	0
Greisen, Nick, NYG	2	26	13.0	13	0
Bickerstaff, Erik, Dal.	2	24	12.0	15	0
Seidman, Mike, Car.	2	24	12.0	17	0
Flemister, Zeron, Was.	2	22	11.0	11	0
Luchey, Nicolas, G.B.	2	21	10.5	12	0
Rasby, Walter, N.O.	2	9	4.5	6	0
Williams, Melvin, N.O.	2	0	0.0	0	0
Groce, DeJuan, St.L	1	33	33.0	25	0
Schlesinger, Cory, Det.	1	23	23.0	23	0
Moss, Randy, Min.	1	22	22.0	22	0
Simon, John, Was.	1	21	21.0	21	0
Finn, Jim, NYG	1	19	19.0	19	0
Engram, Bobby, Sea.	1	18	18.0	18	0
Garcia, Frank, Ariz	1	17	17.0	17	0
Hannam, Ryan, Sea.	1	17	17.0	17	0
Rasmussen, Kemp, Car.	1	16	16.0	16	0
Johnson, Bryan, Was.	1	15	15.0	15	0
Williams, Karl, T.B.	1	15	15.0	15	0
Evans, Heath, Sea.	1	14	14.0	14	0
Palepoi, Anton, Sea.	1	14	14.0	14	0
Hodgins, James, Ariz	1	13	13.0	13	0
Wallace, Al, Car.	1	13	13.0	13	0
Rivers, Marcellus, NYG	1	12	12.0	12	0
Womack, Floyd, Sea.	1	11	11.0	11	0
Wunsch, Jerry, Sea.	1	10	10.0	10	0
Carter, Tim, NYG	1	9	9.0	9	0
Allen, James, N.O.	1	8	8.0	8	0
Withrow, Cory, Min.	1	8	8.0	8	0
Yoder, Todd, T.B.	1	8	8.0	8	0
Berton, Sean, Min.	1	7	7.0	7	0
White, Dewayne, T.B.	1	7	7.0	7	0
Ogbogu, Eric, Dal.	1	5	5.0	5	0
Redding, Cory, Det.	1	5	5.0	5	0
Gutierrez, Brock, S.F.	1	4	4.0	4	0
St. Clair, John, St.L	1	3	3.0	3	0
Muhammad, Muhsin, Car.	1	2	2.0	2	0
Goodspeed, Joey, St.L	1	1	1.0	1	0
Rogers, Nick, Min.	1	1	1.0	1	0
Coady, Rich, St.L	1	0	0.0	0	0
Henderson, E.J., Min.	1	0	0.0	0	0
Hoover, Brad, Car.	1	0	0.0	0	0
Mitchell, Freddie, Phi.	1	-8	-8.0	-8	0
Barnes, Darian, T.B.	0f	0	—	—	0
Wiggins, Jermaine, Car.	0f	0	—	—	0

t = Touchdown
f = Fair Catch
Leader based on average return, minimum 20 returns

AMERICAN FOOTBALL CONFERENCE—KICKOFF RETURNS

	No	Yards	Avg	Long	TD
Kansas City	62	1577	25.4	100t	2
N.Y. Jets	60	1461	24.4	90t	1
New England	60	1428	23.8	92t	1
Indianapolis	64	1510	23.6	90	0
Denver	59	1302	22.1	83	0
Buffalo	63	1369	21.7	75	0
San Diego	84	1804	21.5	60	0
Baltimore	57	1222	21.4	75	0
Houston	80	1700	21.3	70	0
Cleveland	71	1501	21.1	69	0
Miami	57	1202	21.1	49	0
Oakland	77	1596	20.7	85t	1
Pittsburgh	68	1405	20.7	53	0
Cincinnati	74	1474	19.9	46	0
Jacksonville	67	1316	19.6	61	0
Tennessee	68	1299	19.1	39	0
AFC Total	1071	23166	21.6	100t	5
AFC Average	66.9	1447.9	21.6	—	0.3

NATIONAL FOOTBALL CONFERENCE—KICKOFF RETURNS

	No	Yards	Avg	Long	TD
Chicago	73	1738	23.8	89t	2
Green Bay	64	1511	23.6	60	0
Arizona	82	1881	22.9	100t	1
Detroit	70	1584	22.6	96t	1
Washington	66	1482	22.5	94t	1
Carolina	60	1345	22.4	100t	1
Dallas	60	1292	21.5	54	1
Philadelphia	65	1387	21.3	54	0
St. Louis	70	1488	21.3	42	0
New Orleans	72	1524	21.2	53	0
Seattle	64	1336	20.9	56	0
San Francisco	64	1327	20.7	95t	1
Minnesota	71	1428	20.1	48	0
Atlanta	79	1572	19.9	52	0
N.Y. Giants	75	1492	19.9	36	0
Tampa Bay	55	1042	18.9	44	0
NFC Total	1090	23429	21.5	100t	8
NFC Average	68.1	1464.3	21.5	—	0.5
League Total	2161	46595	—	100t	13
League Average	67.5	1456.1	21.6	—	0.4

2003 INDIVIDUAL STATISTICS—PUNTING

PUNTING

AVERAGE YARDS PER PUNT
AFC: 46.9 Shane Lechler, Oakland
NFC: 44.6 Todd Sauerbrun, Carolina

NET AVERAGE YARDS PER PUNT
NFC: 38.2 Mitch Berger, New Orleans
AFC: 37.8 Craig Hentrich, Tennessee

LONGEST
AFC: 73 Shane Lechler, Oakland vs. San Diego, September 28 - (OT)
NFC: 69 Bryan Barker, Washington vs. Philadelphia, December 27

PUNTS
AFC: 97 Chad Stanley, Houston
NFC: 94 Toby Gowin, Dallas

PUNTS, GAME
AFC: 11 Matt Turk, Miami at New England, December 7 (406 yards)
NFC: 10 Bryan Barker, Washington at Buffalo, October 19 (417 yards)

TEAM CHAMPION
AFC: 46.9 Oakland
NFC: 43.7 New Orleans

AMERICAN FOOTBALL CONFERENCE—PUNTING

	Total Punts	Yards	Long	Avg	TB	Blk	Opp Ret	Return Yards	In 20	Net Avg
Oakland	96	4503	73	46.9	13	0	52	669	27	37.2
Buffalo	85	3788	71	44.6	3	0	52	577	20	37.1
Tennessee	71	3117	58	43.9	8	0	30	276	26	37.8
Denver	70	2937	62	42.0	6	2	46	560	14	32.2
Cleveland	73	3048	60	41.8	10	0	33	316	19	34.7
San Diego	83	3456	56	41.6	3	0	38	409	29	36.0
Houston	97	4028	58	41.5	3	0	43	407	36	36.7
Pittsburgh	85	3521	72	41.4	8	1	47	299	27	36.0
Jacksonville	69	2853	58	41.3	6	1	40	420	13	33.5
Indianapolis	64	2646	55	41.3	3	1	32	319	21	35.4
Baltimore	91	3712	67	40.8	9	0	42	354	21	34.9
Cincinnati	77	3045	58	39.5	8	0	47	403	14	32.2
Miami	84	3274	57	39.0	8	0	29	185	28	34.9
Kansas City	81	3156	68	39.0	7	1	38	327	21	33.2
New England	88	3266	52	37.1	4	1	38	240	30	33.5
N.Y. Jets	72	2655	55	36.9	4	1	22	322	22	31.3
AFC Total	1286	53005	73	—	103	8	629	6083	368	—
AFC Average	80.4	3312.8	—	41.2	6.4	0.5	39.3	380.2	23.0	34.9

NATIONAL FOOTBALL CONFERENCE—PUNTING

	Total Punts	Yards	Long	Avg	TB	Blk	Opp Ret	Return Yards	In 20	Net Avg
	Punts	Yards	Long	Avg	TB	Blk	Ret	Yards	20	Avg
New Orleans	72	3144	59	43.7	5	1	36	294	28	38.2
Tampa Bay	83	3590	60	43.3	6	0	39	489	26	35.9
St. Louis	59	2525	57	42.8	5	0	32	484	14	32.9
Carolina	81	3466	64	42.8	9	3	35	402	23	35.6
Arizona	83	3511	64	42.3	9	1	41	472	19	34.4
Green Bay	71	2933	60	41.3	8	0	32	316	17	34.6
Philadelphia	79	3207	60	40.6	10	0	35	272	27	34.6
Chicago	81	3258	53	40.2	9	2	36	277	23	34.6
Washington	84	3377	69	40.2	5	0	40	393	24	34.3
Seattle	69	2762	61	40.0	3	2	29	140	29	37.1
N.Y. Giants	91	3641	59	40.0	6	1	40	432	31	33.9
Atlanta	87	3473	54	39.9	2	0	35	301	19	36.0
Detroit	96	3790	58	39.5	8	1	59	390	20	33.8
Dallas	95	3697	59	38.9	9	0	34	227	25	34.6
Minnesota	64	2462	55	38.5	5	1	29	310	13	32.1
San Francisco	69	2629	56	38.1	3	1	28	258	17	33.5
NFC Total	1264	51465	69	—	102	13	580	5457	355	—
NFC Average	79.0	3216.6	—	40.7	6.4	0.8	36.3	341.1	22.2	34.8
NFL Total	2550	104470	73	—	205	21	1209	11540	723	—
NFL Average	79.7	3264.7	—	41.0	6.4	0.7	37.8	360.6	22.6	34.8

2003 INDIVIDUAL STATISTICS—PUNTING

NFL TOP TEN PUNTERS

	No	Yards	Long	Avg	Total Punts	TB	Blk	Opp Ret	Return Yards	In 20	Net Avg
Lechler, Shane, Oak.	96	4503	73	46.9	96	13	0	52	669	27	37.2
Sauerbrun, Todd, Car.	77	3433	64	44.6	80	9	3	35	402	22	35.6
Moorman, Brian, Buf.	85	3788	71	44.6	85	3	0	52	577	20	37.1
Berger, Mitch, N.O.	71	3144	59	44.3	72	5	1	36	294	28	38.2
Hentrich, Craig, Ten.	71	3117	58	43.9	71	8	0	30	276	26	37.8
Tupa, Tom, T.B.	83	3590	60	43.3	83	6	0	39	489	26	35.9
Knorr, Micah, Den.	68	2937	62	43.2	70	6	2	46	560	14	32.2
Player, Scott, Ariz	82	3511	64	42.8	83	9	1	41	472	19	34.4
Landeta, Sean, St.L	59	2525	57	42.8	59	5	0	32	484	14	32.9
Smith, Hunter, Ind.	62	2617	55	42.2	63	3	1	32	319	20	35.5

AFC—INDIVIDUAL PUNTERS

	No	Yards	Long	Avg	Total Punts	TB	Blk	Opp Ret	Return Yards	In 20	Net Avg
Lechler, Shane, Oak.	96	4503	73	46.9	96	13	0	52	669	27	37.2
Moorman, Brian, Buf.	85	3788	71	44.6	85	3	0	52	577	20	37.1
Hentrich, Craig, Ten.	71	3117	58	43.9	71	8	0	30	276	26	37.8
Knorr, Micah, Den.	68	2937	62	43.2	70	6	2	46	560	14	32.2
Smith, Hunter, Ind.	62	2617	55	42.2	63	3	1	32	319	20	35.5
Gardocki, Chris, Cle.	72	3019	60	41.9	72	10	0	33	316	18	34.8
Miller, Josh, Pit.	84	3521	72	41.9	85	8	1	47	299	27	36.0
Bennett, Darren, S.D.	82	3436	56	41.9	82	3	0	38	409	28	36.2
Stanley, Chad, Hou.	97	4028	58	41.5	97	3	0	43	407	36	36.7
Zastudil, Dave, Bal.	89	3649	67	41.0	89	8	0	41	354	21	35.2
Royals, Mark, Mia.-Jac.	61	2495	51	40.9	61	6	0	33	227	14	35.2
Richardson, Kyle, Cin.	49	1961	58	40.0	49	5	0	28	220	9	33.5
Baker, Jason, K.C.	80	3156	68	39.5	81	7	1	38	327	21	33.2
Turk, Matt, Mia.	68	2631	57	38.7	68	7	0	20	143	23	34.5
Walter, Ken, N.E.	76	2865	52	37.7	77	3	1	33	220	25	33.6
Stryzinski, Dan, NYJ	71	2655	55	37.4	72	4	1	22	322	22	31.3
(Nonqualifiers)											
Hanson, Chris, Jac.	23	1001	58	43.5	24	1	1	16	235	4	31.1
Barnard, Brooks, N.E.	10	365	49	36.5	10	1	0	5	20	4	32.5
Brady, Tom, N.E.	1	36	36	36.0	1	0	0	0	0	1	36.0
Stover, Matt, Bal.	1	34	34	34.0	1	1	0	0	0	0	14.0
Boller, Kyle, Bal.	1	29	29	29.0	1	0	0	1	0	0	29.0
Dawson, Phil, Cle.	1	29	29	29.0	1	0	0	0	0	1	29.0
Vanderjagt, Mike, Ind.	1	29	29	29.0	1	0	0	0	0	1	29.0
Christie, Steve, S.D.	1	20	20	20.0	1	0	0	0	0	1	20.0

NFC—INDIVIDUAL PUNTERS

	No	Yards	Long	Avg	Total Punts	TB	Blk	Opp Ret	Return Yards	In 20	Net Avg
Sauerbrun, Todd, Car.	77	3433	64	44.6	80	9	3	35	402	22	35.6
Berger, Mitch, N.O.	71	3144	59	44.3	72	5	1	36	294	28	38.2
Tupa, Tom, T.B.	83	3590	60	43.3	83	6	0	39	489	26	35.9
Player, Scott, Ariz	82	3511	64	42.8	83	9	1	41	472	19	34.4
Landeta, Sean, St.L	59	2525	57	42.8	59	5	0	32	484	14	32.9
Bidwell, Josh, G.B.	69	2875	60	41.7	69	7	0	32	316	16	35.1
Maynard, Brad, Chi.	79	3258	53	41.2	81	9	2	36	277	23	34.6
Rouen, Tom, Sea.	67	2762	61	41.2	69	3	2	29	140	29	37.1
Johnson, Dirk, Phi.	79	3207	60	40.6	79	10	0	35	272	27	34.6
Feagles, Jeff, NYG	90	3641	59	40.5	91	6	1	40	432	31	33.9
Barker, Bryan, Was.	84	3377	69	40.2	84	5	0	40	393	24	34.3
Mohr, Chris, Atl.	87	3473	54	39.9	87	2	0	35	301	19	36.0
Harris, Nick, Cin.-Det.	91	3615	53	39.7	92	8	1	63	498	16	32.1
Johnson, Eddie, Min.	56	2191	55	39.1	57	5	1	25	233	12	32.6
Gowin, Toby, Dal.	94	3665	59	39.0	94	8	0	34	227	25	34.9
Lafleur, Bill, S.F.	68	2629	56	38.7	69	3	1	28	258	17	33.5
(Nonqualifiers)											
Jett, John, Det.	25	995	58	39.8	25	3	0	11	45	8	35.6
Araguz, Leo, Min.	7	271	44	38.7	7	0	0	4	77	1	27.7
Hanson, Jason, Det.	7	264	50	37.7	7	0	0	4	30	1	33.4
Longwell, Ryan, G.B.	2	58	30	29.0	2	1	0	0	0	1	19.0
Kasay, John, Car.	1	33	33	33.0	1	0	0	0	0	1	33.0
Cundiff, Billy, Dal.	1	32	32	32.0	1	1	0	0	0	0	12.0

Leader based on average, minimum 40 punts

2003 INDIVIDUAL STATISTICS—PUNT RETURNS

PUNT RETURNS

YARDS PER RETURN

AFC: 16.3 Dante Hall, Kansas City
NFC: 15.3 Brian Westbrook, Philadelphia

YARDS

NFC: 545 Allen Rossum, Atlanta
AFC: 542 Antwaan Randle El, Pittsburgh

YARDS, GAME

AFC: 132 Antwaan Randle El, Pittsburgh vs. Oakland, December 7 (5 returns, 0 TD)
NFC: 102 Steve Smith, Carolina vs. Jacksonville, September 7 (6 returns, 0 TD)

LONGEST

AFC: 93 Dante Hall, Kansas City vs. Denver, October 5 - TD
NFC: 89 Reggie Swinton, Detroit at Carolina, December 21 - TD

RETURNS

AFC: 45 Lamont Brightful, Baltimore
45 Antwaan Randle El, Pittsburgh
NFC: 44 Steve Smith, Carolina

RETURNS, GAME

AFC: 8 Leon Johnson, San Diego at Detroit, December 7 (40 yards, 0 TD)
NFC: 6 Steve Smith, Carolina vs. Jacksonville, September 7 (102 yards, 0 TD)
6 Brian Mitchell, N.Y. Giants at New England, October 12 (28 yards, 0 TD)
6 Zuriel Smith, Dallas at Detroit, October 19 (19 yards, 0 TD)
6 Joey Galloway, Dallas vs. Buffalo, November 9 (64 yards, 0 TD)
6 Zuriel Smith, Dallas vs. N.Y. Giants, December 21 (61 yards, 0 TD)

FAIR CATCHES

NFC: 22 Bobby Engram, Seattle
AFC: 20 Lamont Brightful, Baltimore

TOUCHDOWNS

AFC: 2 Phillip Buchanon, Oakland
2 Dante Hall, Kansas City
2 Antwaan Randle El, Pittsburgh
NFC: 2 Brian Westbrook, Philadelphia

TEAM CHAMPION

AFC: 16.4 Kansas City
NFC: 14.3 Atlanta

NFL TOP TEN PUNT RETURNERS

	No	FC	Yards	Avg	Long	TD
Hall, Dante, K.C.	29	14	472	16.3	93t	2
Westbrook, Brian, Phi.	20	16	306	15.3	84t	2
Rossum, Allen, Atl.	39	11	545	14.0	72	1
Buchanon, Phillip, Oak.	36	14	491	13.6	80t	2
Swinton, Reggie, Dal.-G.B.-Det.	24	12	318	13.3	89t	1
McQuarters, R.W., Chi.	37	12	452	12.2	60t	1
Randle El, Antwaan, Pit.	45	12	542	12.0	84t	2
Allen, David, Jac.	27	15	324	12.0	52	0
McCareins, Justin, Ten.	29	17	330	11.4	58t	1
Moss, Santana, NYJ	30	18	332	11.1	47	0

AFC—INDIVIDUAL PUNT RETURNERS

	No	FC	Yards	Avg	Long	TD
Hall, Dante, K.C.	29	14	472	16.3	93t	2
Buchanon, Phillip, Oak.	36	14	491	13.6	80t	2
Randle El, Antwaan, Pit.	45	12	542	12.0	84t	2
Allen, David, Jac.	27	15	324	12.0	52	0
McCareins, Justin, Ten.	29	17	330	11.4	58t	1
Moss, Santana, NYJ	30	18	332	11.1	47	0
Warrick, Peter, Cin.	25	8	273	10.9	68t	1
Brown, Troy, N.E.	29	13	293	10.1	23	0
O'Neal, Deltha, Den.	33	10	315	9.5	57t	1
Parker, Eric, S.D.	23	2	207	9.0	49	0
Rogers, Charlie, Mia.	21	13	186	8.9	48	0
Northcutt, Dennis, Cle.	36	10	295	8.2	38	0
Brightful, Lamont, Bal.	45	20	351	7.8	44	0
Johnson, Leon, S.D.	24	5	184	7.7	21	0
Moses, J.J., Hou.	36	7	244	6.8	40	0
Brown, Antonio, Buf.	25	10	111	4.4	18	0
(Nonqualifiers)						
Clements, Nate, Buf.	14	11	137	9.8	35	0
Pyatt, Brad, Ind.	12	8	110	9.2	21	0
Walters, Troy, Ind.	11	7	105	9.5	26	0
Poole, Tyrone, N.E.	11	3	75	6.8	18	0
Simmons, Sam, Mia.	8	6	100	12.5	32	0
Mason, Derrick, Ten.	8	5	99	12.4	21	0
Wilkins, Terrence, Ind.	7	0	25	3.6	16	0
Smith, Rod, Den.	6	8	127	21.2	65t	1
Faulk, Kevin, N.E.	5	6	66	13.2	19	0
Burris, Jeff, Cin.	5	0	58	11.6	34	0
Lewis, Jermaine, Jac.	5	0	45	9.0	14	0
Reed, Ed, Bal.	5	3	33	6.6	19	0
Branch, Deion, N.E.	4	1	26	6.5	11	0
Gaffney, Jabar, Hou.	4	1	22	5.5	15	0
Kennison, Eddie, K.C.	3	0	70	23.3	46	0
Ward, Dedric, Bal.	3	2	26	8.7	16	0
Mathis, Rashean, Jac.	2	3	7	3.5	6	0
Dwight, Tim, S.D.	2	2	0	0.0	2	0
Davis, Andre', Cle.	1	1	7	7.0	7	0
Buckley, Terrell, Mia.	1	0	2	2.0	2	0
Johnson, Bethel, N.E.	1	0	2	2.0	2	0
Johnson, Eric, Oak.	1	0	1	1.0	1	0
Bartee, William, K.C.	1	0	0	0.0	0	0
Dorsett, Anthony, Oak.	1	0	0	0.0	0	0
Macklin, David, Ind.	1	0	0	0.0	0	0
Newson, Kendall, Mia.	1	0	0	0.0	0	0
Prioleau, Pierson, Buf.	1	0	0	0.0	0	0
Winfield, Antoine, Buf.	1	0	0	0.0	0	0
Doering, Chris, Pit.	0	0	9	—	9	0
Harrison, Marvin, Ind.	0	1	0	—	—	0

t = Touchdown
Leader based on average return, minimum 20 returns

NFC—INDIVIDUAL PUNT RETURNERS

	No	FC	Yards	Avg	Long	TD
Westbrook, Brian, Phi.	20	16	306	15.3	84t	2
Rossum, Allen, Atl.	39	11	545	14.0	72	1
Swinton, Reggie, Dal.-Det.	24	12	318	13.3	89t	1
McQuarters, R.W., Chi.	37	12	452	12.2	60t	1
Engram, Bobby, Sea.	31	22	320	10.3	83t	1
Smith, Steve, Car.	44	14	439	10.0	53t	1
Lewis, Michael, N.O.	30	10	275	9.2	27	0
Galloway, Joey, Dal.	20	8	178	8.9	36	0
Chatman, Antonio, G.B.	33	18	277	8.4	33	0
Smith, Zuriel, Dal.	30	13	212	7.1	46	0
Howry, Keenan, Min.	35	16	247	7.1	52	0
Williams, Jimmy, S.F.	35	10	240	6.9	20	0
Boldin, Anquan, Ariz	20	12	130	6.5	19	0
Mitchell, Brian, NYG	29	14	154	5.3	15	0
(Nonqualifiers)						
Morton, Chad, Was.	19	16	188	9.9	28	0
Groce, DeJuan, St.L	19	3	135	7.1	19	0
Williams, Karl, T.B.	15	10	110	7.3	19	0
Drummond, Eddie, Det.	12	4	151	12.6	57t	1
Barlow, Reggie, T.B.	12	6	58	4.8	17	0
Furrey, Mike, St.L	11	7	119	10.8	28	0
Hakim, Az-Zahir, Det.	9	0	85	9.4	20	0
Wansley, Tim, T.B.	8	2	74	9.3	12	0
Harris, Arlen, St.L	7	0	36	5.1	13	0
Mahe, Reno, Phi.	6	6	55	9.2	17	0
Stallworth, Donte', N.O.	5	1	44	8.8	18	0
Bruce, Arland, S.F.	4	2	24	6.0	18	0
Sheppard, Lito, Phi.	4	1	15	3.8	5	0
Bly, Dre', Det.	3	0	22	7.3	14	0
Johnson, Patrick, Was.	3	3	17	5.7	11	0
Looker, Dane, St.L	2	1	47	23.5	44	0
Craver, Keyuo, N.O.	2	1	22	11.0	19	0
Green, Victor, N.O.	2	0	15	7.5	9	0
Joyce, Delvin, NYG	2	1	9	4.5	8	0
Wade, Bobby, Chi.	2	1	9	4.5	10	0
McCord, Quentin, Atl.	1	0	46	46.0	46	0
Bolden, Juran, Atl.	1	0	14	14.0	14	0
Dyson, Kevin, Car.	1	1	14	14.0	14	0
Wilson, Cedrick, S.F.	1	3	12	12.0	12	0
Goss, Jason, Ariz	1	0	7	7.0	7	0
Dantzler, Woody, Atl.	1	0	6	6.0	6	0
Thomas, Fred, N.O.	1	0	4	4.0	4	0
Johnson, Bryant, Ariz	1	3	3	3.0	3	0
Edwards, Terrence, Atl.	1	0	2	2.0	2	0
Thrash, James, Phi.	1	1	2	2.0	2	0
Burleson, Nate, Min.	1	0	0	0.0	0	0
Harris, Al, G.B.	1	0	0	0.0	0	0
Lucas, Ken, Sea.	1	0	0	0.0	0	0
Richard, Kris, Sea.	1	0	0	0.0	0	0
Robinson, Damien, Sea.	1	0	0	0.0	0	0
Stoutmire, Omar, NYG	1	0	0	0.0	0	0
Wilkins, Marcus, G.B.	1	0	0	0.0	0	0

t = Touchdown
Leader based on average return, minimum 20 returns

AMERICAN FOOTBALL CONFERENCE—PUNT RETURNS

	No	FC	Yards	Avg	Long	TD
Kansas City	33	14	542	16.4	93t	2
Oakland	38	14	492	12.9	80t	2
Pittsburgh	45	12	551	12.2	84t	2
Tennessee	37	22	429	11.6	58t	1
Denver	39	18	442	11.3	65t	2
N.Y. Jets	30	18	332	11.1	47	0
Jacksonville	34	18	376	11.1	52	0
Cincinnati	30	8	331	11.0	68t	1
Miami	31	19	288	9.3	48	0
New England	50	25	462	9.2	23	0
Cleveland	37	11	302	8.2	38	0
San Diego	49	9	391	8.0	49	0
Indianapolis	31	16	240	7.7	26	0
Baltimore	53	23	410	7.7	44	0
Houston	40	8	266	6.7	40	0
Buffalo	41	21	248	6.0	35	0
AFC Total	618	256	6102	9.9	93t	10
AFC Average	38.6	16.0	381.4	9.9	—	0.6

NATIONAL FOOTBALL CONFERENCE—PUNT RETURNS

	No	FC	Yards	Avg	Long	TD
Atlanta	43	11	613	14.3	72	1
Detroit	47	13	576	12.3	89t	2
Philadelphia	31	24	378	12.2	84t	2
Chicago	39	13	461	11.8	60t	1
Carolina	45	15	453	10.1	53t	1
Seattle	34	22	320	9.4	83t	1
Washington	22	19	205	9.3	28	0
New Orleans	40	12	360	9.0	27	0
St. Louis	39	11	337	8.6	44	0
Green Bay	35	18	277	7.9	33	0
Dallas	51	24	390	7.6	46	0
Tampa Bay	35	18	242	6.9	19	0
San Francisco	40	15	276	6.9	20	0
Minnesota	36	16	247	6.9	52	0
Arizona	22	15	140	6.4	19	0
N.Y. Giants	32	15	163	5.1	15	0
NFC Total	591	261	5438	9.2	89t	8
NFC Average	36.9	16.3	339.9	9.2	—	0.5
League Total	1209	517	11540	—	93t	18
League Average	37.8	16.2	360.6	9.5	—	0.6

FUMBLES

MOST FUMBLES

NFC: 16 Daunte Culpepper, Minnesota
AFC: 15 Drew Bledsoe, Buffalo

MOST FUMBLES, GAME

NFC: 6 Kurt Warner, St. Louis at N.Y. Giants, September 7
AFC: 3 Tom Brady, New England vs. N.Y. Jets, September 21
3 Kyle Boller, Baltimore at Cincinnati, October 19
3 Byron Leftwich, Jacksonville at Baltimore, November 2
3 Doug Flutie, San Diego at Denver, November 16
3 Jon Kitna, Cincinnati at Baltimore, December 7
3 Peyton Manning, Indianapolis vs. Denver, December 21

OWN FUMBLES RECOVERED

AFC: 6 Chad Pennington, N.Y. Jets
NFC: 6 Daunte Culpepper, Minnesota

OWN FUMBLES RECOVERED, GAME

AFC: 3 Chad Pennington, N.Y. Jets at Oakland, November 9 (0 yards, 0 TD) - (OT)
NFC: 2 Josh McCown, Arizona vs. Seattle, September 14 (0 yards, 0 TD)
2 Daunte Culpepper, Minnesota vs. Chicago, September 14 (0 yards, 0 TD)
2 Tiki Barber, N.Y. Giants at Washington, September 21 (0 yards, 0 TD) - (OT)
2 Quincy Carter, Dallas at Washington, December 14 (0 yards, 0 TD)
2 Daunte Culpepper, Minnesota vs. Kansas City, December 20 (0 yards, 0 TD)

OPPONENTS' FUMBLES RECOVERED

NFC: 5 Brian Young, St. Louis
AFC: 4 Brian Simmons, Cincinnati
4 Terrell Suggs, Baltimore

OPPONENTS' FUMBLES RECOVERED, GAME

NFC: 3 Brian Young, St. Louis vs. Baltimore, November 9 (0 yards, 0 TD)
AFC: 2 Albert Haynesworth, Tennessee vs. Miami, November 9 (12 yards, 0 TD)
2 Brian Simmons, Cincinnati vs. San Francisco, December 14 (13 yards, 0 TD)

YARDS

NFC: 113 Dre' Bly, Detroit
AFC: 64 Samari Rolle, Tennessee

LONGEST

NFC: 90 Aeneas Williams, St. Louis vs. Minnesota, November 30 - TD
AFC: 61 Samari Rolle, Tennessee at Houston, December 21 - TD

AFC—TOUCHDOWNS ON FUMBLE RECOVERIES

Ayodele, Akin, Jac.	1
Bulluck, Keith, Ten.	1
Chatham, Matt, N.E.	1
Freeney, Dwight, Ind.	1
Hardy, Kevin, Cin.	1
Kinney, Erron, Ten.	1
McMichael, Randy, Mia.	1
Ricard, Alan, Bal.	1
Rolle, Samari, Ten.	1
Taylor, Jason, Mia.	1
Williams, Pat, Buf.	1

NFC—TOUCHDOWNS ON FUMBLE RECOVERIES

Archuleta, Adam, St.L	1
Bailey, Boss, Det.	1
Bly, Dre', Det.	1
Godfrey, Randall, Sea.	1
Harris, Corey, Det.	1
Harris, Kwame, S.F.	1
Holmes, Kenny, NYG	1
Huff, Orlando, Sea.	1
McCardell, Keenan, T.B.	1
Robinson, Koren, Sea.	1
Washington, Keith, NYG	1
Wilkins, Marcus, G.B.	1
Williams, Aeneas, St.L	1

AFC FUMBLES—INDIVIDUAL

	Fum	Own Rec	Opp Rec	Yards	Tot Rec
Adams, Sam, Buf.	0	0	1	0	1
Alexander, Brent, Pit.	0	1	1	2	2
Allen, David, Jac.	2	1	0	0	1
Anderson, Mike, Den.	2	1	0	0	1
Andruzzi, Joe, N.E.	1	1	0	0	1
Asomugha, Nnamdi, Oak.	0	0	1	0	1
Atkins, James, Ten.	0	0	1	0	1
Ayanbadejo, Obafemi, Mia.	1	0	0	0	0
Ayodele, Akin, Jac.	0	0	3	15	3
Badger, Brad, Oak.	0	1	0	0	1
Banks, Tony, Hou.	1	1	0	0	1
Barnes, Lionel, Jac.	0	0	1	0	1
Bartee, William, K.C.	1	0	1	0	1
Bashir, Idrees, Ind.	0	0	1	0	1
Batch, Charlie, Pit.	1	0	0	0	0
Beasley, Aaron, NYJ	0	0	1	0	1
Becht, Anthony, NYJ	1	0	0	0	0
Beckham, Tony, Ten.	0	1	0	-2	1
Bell, Kendrell, Pit.	0	0	1	0	1
Bennett, Drew, Ten.	0	1	0	0	1
Bennett, Brandon, Cin.	2	2	0	1	2
Berlin, Eddie, Ten.	2	0	0	0	0
Berry, Bert, Den.	0	0	1	3	1
Bettis, Jerome, Pit.	5	1	0	0	1
Beuerlein, Steve, Den.	3	0	0	0	0
Blaylock, Derrick, K.C.	1	0	0	0	0
Bledsoe, Drew, Buf.	15	4	0	-18	4
Boerigter, Marc, K.C.	0	0	2	0	2
Boller, Kyle, Bal.	9	3	0	-25	3
Boston, David, S.D.	2	1	0	0	1
Boulware, Peter, Bal.	0	0	1	0	1
Brady, Kyle, Jac.	3	2	0	0	2
Brady, Tom, N.E.	13	3	0	-5	3
Brayton, Tyler, Oak.	0	0	1	0	1
Brees, Drew, S.D.	5	0	0	-1	0
Brightful, Lamont, Bal.	2	1	0	0	1
Brock, Raheem, Ind.	0	0	3	8	3
Brown, Antonio, Buf.	1	1	0	0	1
Brown, Chris, Ten.	1	0	0	0	0
Brown, Courtney, Cle.	0	0	1	0	1
Brown, Eric, Hou.	1	0	0	0	0
Brown, Orlando, Bal.	0	1	0	0	1
Brown, Troy, N.E.	2	1	0	0	1
Browning, John, K.C.	0	0	1	7	1
Brunell, Mark, Jac.	1	0	0	-5	0
Bruschi, Tedy, N.E.	0	0	1	13	1
Buchanon, Phillip, Oak.	3	2	0	0	2

	Fum	Own Rec	Opp Rec	Yards	Tot Rec
Buckley, Terrell, Mia.	1	2	2	8	4
Bulluck, Keith, Ten.	0	0	2	32	2
Burns, Joe, Buf.	1	0	0	0	0
Burress, Plaxico, Pit.	1	0	0	0	0
Calico, Tyrone, Ten.	0	0	1	0	1
Campbell, Mark, Buf.	0	1	0	0	1
Carlisle, Cooper, Den.	0	1	0	0	1
Carr, David, Hou.	4	1	0	-1	1
Carswell, Dwayne, Den.	0	1	0	0	1
Caver, Quinton, K.C.	0	1	0	0	1
Centers, Larry, N.E.	0	1	0	0	1
Chambers, Chris, Mia.	1	0	0	0	0
Chatham, Matt, N.E.	0	0	2	38	2
Chatman, Jesse, S.D.	0	0	1	0	1
Chester, Larry, Mia.	0	0	1	0	1
Clancy, Kendrick, Pit.	0	0	1	0	1
Clements, Nate, Buf.	3	1	0	0	1
Clemons, Charlie, Hou.	0	0	2	0	2
Clemons, Duane, Cin.	0	0	1	0	1
Cole, Chris, Den.	1	1	0	0	1
Coleman, Rod, Oak.	0	0	1	0	1
Colvin, Rosevelt, N.E.	0	0	1	1	1
Cooper, Chris, Oak.	0	0	3	0	3
Cooper, Deke, Jac.	0	0	1	10	1
Couch, Tim, Cle.	6	2	0	-3	2
Cowart, Sam, NYJ	0	0	1	0	1
Crockett, Zack, Oak.	1	0	0	0	0
Curry, Ronald, Oak.	1	0	0	-12	0
Darius, Donovin, Jac.	1	0	1	0	1
Davis, Andre', Cle.	2	0	0	0	0
Davis, Domanick, Hou.	4	1	0	0	1
DeMar, Enoch, Cle.	0	1	0	0	1
DeMulling, Rick, Ind.	0	3	0	16	3
Dingle, Adrian, S.D.	0	0	1	0	1
Dorsett, Anthony, Oak.	1	0	1	7	1
Doss, Mike, Ind.	1	0	0	0	0
Droughns, Reuben, Den.	0	1	0	0	1
Dunn, Jason, K.C.	0	1	0	0	1
Dwight, Tim, S.D.	1	0	0	0	0
Faine, Jeff, Cle.	3	1	0	-18	1
Fargas, Justin, Oak.	1	0	0	0	0
Farrior, James, Pit.	1	0	1	0	1
Faulk, Kevin, N.E.	4	1	0	0	1
Ferguson, Jason, NYJ	0	0	1	0	1
Fiedler, Jay, Mia.	7	2	0	-5	2
Fisk, Jason, S.D.	0	0	1	0	1
Fletcher, London, Buf.	0	0	1	3	1
Floyd, Anthony, Ind.	0	0	1	0	1
Flutie, Doug, S.D.	7	1	0	-16	1
Foote, Larry, Pit.	0	1	0	0	1
Foreman, Jay, Hou.	0	0	2	33	2
Fowler, Melvin, Cle.	1	0	0	0	0
Freeman, Arturo, Mia.	0	0	1	0	1
Freeney, Dwight, Ind.	0	0	2	23	2
Gannon, Rich, Oak.	2	0	0	0	0
Garner, Charlie, Oak.	1	1	0	0	1
Garnes, Sam, NYJ	0	0	1	0	1
Gash, Sam, Buf.	1	1	0	0	1
Gates, Antonio, S.D.	1	0	0	0	0
George, Eddie, Ten.	1	1	0	1	1
Gibson, Derrick, Oak.	1	0	0	0	0
Gildon, Jason, Pit.	1	0	1	0	1
Grau, Jeff, Mia.	1	0	0	-15	0
Green, Trent, K.C.	5	0	0	-19	0
Green, William, Cle.	5	1	0	0	1
Gregg, Kelly, Bal.	0	0	1	0	1
Griese, Brian, Mia.	4	0	0	0	0
Griffin, Quentin, Den.	3	1	0	0	1
Hall, Dante, K.C.	3	0	0	0	0
Hardy, Kevin, Cin.	0	0	1	10	1
Harris, Walt, Ind.	0	0	1	0	1
Harrison, Marvin, Ind.	2	0	0	0	0
Harrison, Rodney, N.E.	0	0	1	16	1
Harts, Shaunard, K.C.	0	1	1	8	2
Hartwig, Justin, Ten.	1	1	0	-2	1
Haynes, Verron, Pit.	2	1	0	0	1
Haynesworth, Albert, Ten.	0	0	2	12	2
Hayward, Reggie, Den.	0	0	2	0	2
Heap, Todd, Bal.	1	0	0	0	0
Heiden, Steve, Cle.	0	1	0	0	1
Henderson, John, Jac.	0	0	1	0	1
Henry, Travis, Buf.	7	2	0	0	2
Herndon, Kelly, Den.	0	0	1	0	1
Holcomb, Kelly, Cle.	5	4	0	-3	4
Holcombe, Robert, Ten.	2	1	0	29	1
Hollings, Tony, Hou.	2	1	0	0	1
Holmes, Priest, K.C.	1	0	0	0	0
Huard, Brock, Ind.	1	0	0	-3	0
Iwuoma, Chidi, Pit.	0	1	0	0	1
Jackson, James, Cle.	3	0	0	0	0
James, Edgerrin, Ind.	5	0	0	0	0
Jammer, Quentin, S.D.	0	0	1	2	1
Johnson, Bethel, N.E.	0	0	2	0	2
Johnson, Leon, S.D.	1	0	0	0	0
Jones, Marvin, NYJ	0	0	1	0	1
Jones, Terry, Bal.	0	0	1	0	1
Kanell, Danny, Den.	3	1	0	-2	1
Kennedy, Kenoy, Den.	0	0	1	0	1
Kennedy, Lincoln, Oak.	0	1	0	0	1
Kennison, Eddie, K.C.	1	0	0	0	0
Kinney, Erron, Ten.	1	1	0	0	1
Kitna, Jon, Cin.	9	1	0	0	1
Klecko, Dan, N.E.	0	0	1	4	1
Knight, Tom, Bal.	0	0	1	0	1
Knorr, Micah, Den.	1	1	0	0	1
Koppen, Dan, N.E.	0	1	0	0	1
Kriewaldt, Clint, Pit.	0	0	1	0	1
Lang, Kenard, Cle.	0	0	1	8	1
Law, Ty, N.E.	1	0	0	0	0
Leftwich, Byron, Jac.	11	2	0	0	2
Lehan, Michael, Cle.	0	0	1	0	1
Lepsis, Matt, Den.	0	1	0	0	1
Lewis, Jamal, Bal.	8	1	0	0	1
Lewis, Ray, Bal.	0	0	2	1	2
Logan, Mike, Pit.	0	0	3	14	3
Mack, Stacey, Hou.	2	1	0	0	1
Macklin, David, Ind.	1	0	1	0	1
Maddox, Nick, Cle.	1	0	0	0	0
Maddox, Tommy, Pit.	5	1	0	-6	1
Madise, Adrian, Den.	1	0	0	0	0
Madison, Sam, Mia.	0	1	1	0	2
Maese, Joe, Bal.	0	0	1	0	1
Manning, Peyton, Ind.	6	4	0	-9	4
Manuwai, Vince, Jac.	0	1	0	0	1
Martin, Curtis, NYJ	2	0	0	0	0
Martin, Tee, Oak.	3	2	0	0	2
Maslowski, Mike, K.C.	0	0	1	0	1
Mason, Derrick, Ten.	0	1	0	0	1
Mathis, Rashean, Jac.	0	0	1	0	1
Mathis, Robert, Ind.	0	0	1	0	1
Mawae, Kevin, NYJ	2	0	0	-2	0
McCareins, Justin, Ten.	2	1	0	0	1
McCleon, Dexter, K.C.	0	0	2	10	2
McGinest, Willie, N.E.	0	0	2	20	2
McGlockton, Chester, NYJ	0	0	1	0	1
McIntosh, Damion, S.D.	0	1	0	0	1

2003 INDIVIDUAL STATISTICS—FUMBLES

	Fum	Own Rec	Opp Rec	Yards	Tot Rec
McKenzie, Kareem, NYJ	0	1	0	0	1
McKinney, Steve, Hou.	0	1	0	0	1
McKnight, James, Mia.	1	0	1	0	1
McMichael, Randy, Mia.	0	1	0	2	1
McNair, Steve, Ten.	12	3	0	-5	3
Meester, Brad, Jac.	2	2	0	-17	2
Meier, Rob, Jac.	0	0	1	0	1
Meier, Shad, Ten.	1	0	0	0	0
Miller, Fred, Ten.	0	1	0	0	1
Miller, Josh, Pit.	1	1	0	0	1
Milloy, Lawyer, Buf.	0	0	1	2	1
Mirer, Rick, Oak.	4	0	0	0	0
Moore, Dave, Buf.	1	1	0	0	1
Moorehead, Aaron, Ind.	1	0	0	0	0
Moorman, Brian, Buf.	1	1	0	0	1
Moreno, Zeke, S.D.	0	0	2	0	2
Moss, Santana, NYJ	4	3	0	0	3
Moulds, Eric, Buf.	0	1	0	4	1
Mulitalo, Edwin, Bal.	0	1	0	0	1
Mungro, James, Ind.	0	1	0	0	1
Mustard, Chad, Cle.	0	1	0	0	1
Neal, Lorenzo, S.D.	0	1	0	0	1
Nelson, Jim, Ind.	1	1	0	0	1
Newson, Kendall, Mia.	1	0	0	0	0
Northcutt, Dennis, Cle.	2	2	0	0	2
Ogden, Jonathan, Bal.	0	1	0	0	1
Ogunleye, Adewale, Mia.	0	0	1	0	1
Olson, Benji, Ten.	0	0	1	0	1
O'Neal, Deltha, Den.	2	0	0	0	0
Orr, Shantee, Hou.	0	0	1	-1	1
Parker, Eric, S.D.	1	1	0	0	1
Pass, Patrick, N.E.	0	1	0	0	1
Paxton, Lonie, N.E.	2	0	0	-20	0
Pennington, Chad, NYJ	8	6	0	-17	6
Peterson, Mike, Jac.	0	0	2	0	2
Pittman, Bryan, Hou.	0	0	1	0	1
Pitts, Chester, Hou.	0	1	0	0	1
Pleasant, Anthony, N.E.	0	0	1	6	1
Pittman, Bryan, Hou.	0	0	1	0	1
Pitts, Chester, Hou.	0	1	0	0	1
Pleasant, Anthony, N.E.	0	0	1	6	1
Plummer, Jake, Den.	4	3	0	0	3
Pollard, Marcus, Ind.	1	0	0	0	0
Poole, Tyrone, N.E.	1	0	0	0	0
Porter, Jerry, Oak.	1	0	0	0	0
Porter, Joey, Pit.	0	1	0	0	1
Portis, Clinton, Den.	3	1	0	0	1
Powell, Carl, Cin.	0	0	1	0	1
Pryce, Trevor, Den.	1	0	1	0	1
Pyatt, Brad, Ind.	2	1	0	0	1
Ragone, Dave, Hou.	4	1	0	0	1
Randle El, Antwaan, Pit.	5	2	0	-7	2
Reagor, Montae, Ind.	0	0	1	0	1
Redman, Chris, Bal.	3	1	0	-5	1
Reed, Ed, Bal.	1	0	0	0	0
Reed, James, NYJ	0	0	1	16	1
Reed, Josh, Buf.	1	1	0	0	1
Ricard, Alan, Bal.	0	1	0	50	1
Rice, Jerry, Oak.	2	1	0	0	1
Richardson, Tony, K.C.	0	1	0	0	1
Robbins, Barret, Oak.	0	1	0	0	1
Rogers, Charlie, Mia.	2	0	0	0	0
Rolle, Samari, Ten.	0	0	2	64	2
Roye, Orpheus, Cle.	0	0	1	0	1
Salaam, Ephraim, Den.	0	1	0	0	1
Sanders, Darnell, Cle.	1	1	0	0	1
Santiago, O.J., Oak.	0	0	1	0	1
Sapp, Gerome, Bal.	0	0	1	0	1
Saturday, Jeff, Ind.	1	0	1	-3	1
Schifino, Jake, Ten.	0	0	1	0	1
Schobel, Aaron, Buf.	0	0	1	0	1
Schobel, Matt, Cin.	2	1	0	0	1
Scioli, Brad, Ind.	0	0	1	0	1
Scott, Bart, Bal.	0	0	1	0	1
Sears, Corey, Hou.	0	0	1	0	1
Sharpe, Shannon, Den.	0	1	0	0	1
Shaw, Bobby, Buf.	1	1	0	0	1
Shields, Will, K.C.	0	1	0	0	1
Simmons, Brian, Cin.	0	0	4	13	4
Simmons, Kendall, Pit.	0	1	0	0	1
Sims, Ryan, K.C.	0	0	1	0	1
Smith, Antowain, N.E.	1	0	0	0	0
Smith, Brent, NYJ	0	1	0	0	1
Smith, Jimmy, Jac.	1	0	0	0	0
Smith, Musa, Bal.	1	0	0	0	0
Smith, Robaire, Ten.	0	0	2	43	2
Spicer, Paul, Jac.	0	0	1	0	1
Spikes, Takeo, Buf.	0	0	2	29	2
Spragan, Donnie, Den.	0	2	1	9	3
Steinbach, Eric, Cin.	0	1	0	0	1
Stevens, Matt, Hou.	0	0	1	0	1
Stills, Gary, K.C.	0	0	2	0	2
Stubblefield, Dana, Oak.	0	0	1	0	1
Suggs, Lee, Cle.	2	1	0	0	1
Suggs, Terrell, Bal.	0	0	4	7	4
Sykes, Jashon, Den.	0	0	1	0	1
Taylor, Chester, Bal.	3	1	0	0	1
Taylor, Fred, Jac.	6	1	0	0	1
Taylor, Ike, Pit.	1	0	0	0	0
Taylor, Jason, Mia.	0	0	2	34	2
Taylor, Travis, Bal.	0	1	0	-2	1
Teague, Trey, Buf.	4	2	0	-35	2
Testaverde, Vinny, NYJ	1	0	0	-6	0
Thomas, Bryan, NYJ	0	0	1	0	1
Thomas, Kevin, Buf.	0	0	1	0	1
Thomas, Zach, Mia.	0	0	2	0	2
Thornton, John, Cin.	0	0	2	2	2
Tomlinson, LaDainian, S.D.	2	2	0	0	2
Townsend, Deshea, Pit.	0	0	1	0	1
Treu, Adam, Oak.	0	1	0	0	1
Tucker, Ryan, Cle.	0	1	0	0	1
Tuiasosopo, Marques, Oak.	2	1	0	0	1
Volek, Billy, Ten.	1	0	0	0	0
von Oelhoffen, Kimo, Pit.	0	0	1	0	1
Vrabel, Mike, N.E.	0	0	1	0	1
Wade, Todd, Mia.	0	1	0	0	1
Walker, Langston, Oak.	0	1	0	0	1
Walls, Lenny, Den.	0	0	1	0	1
Walter, Ken, N.E.	0	1	0	0	1
Walters, Matt, NYJ	0	0	1	0	1
Walters, Troy, Ind.	0	1	0	0	1
Ward, Hines, Pit.	0	1	0	0	1
Ward, LaShaun, K.C.	1	0	0	0	0
Warren, Gerard, Cle.	0	0	2	0	2
Warrick, Peter, Cin.	2	0	0	0	0
Washington, Dewayne, Pit.	1	0	0	0	0
Washington, Marcus, Ind.	0	0	1	0	1
Watson, Kenny, Cin.	1	0	0	0	0
Weaver, Tony, Bal.	0	0	2	0	2
Wells, Ray, Ten.	0	0	1	0	1
Wheatley, Tyrone, Oak.	2	0	0	0	0
White, Jamel, Cle.	1	1	1	0	2
Wiley, Marcellus, S.D.	0	0	1	0	1
Wilkins, Terrence, Ind.	1	0	0	0	0
Williams, Chad, Bal.	0	1	2	1	3
Williams, Ricky, Mia.	7	1	0	0	1

	Fum	Own Rec	Opp Rec	Yards	Tot Rec
Williams, Jay, Mia.	0	0	2	0	2
Williams, Mike, Buf.	0	1	0	0	1
Williams, Pat, Buf.	0	0	1	28	1
Williams, Ricky, Ind.	2	0	1	0	1
Williams, Tony, Cin.	0	0	1	-1	1
Willis, Donald, K.C.	0	1	0	0	1
Wilson, Al, Den.	0	0	2	0	2
Wooden, Shawn, Mia.	0	0	1	0	1
Woods, Jerome, K.C.	0	0	1	0	1
Woodson, Charles, Oak.	0	0	1	3	1
Woodson, Rod, Oak.	0	0	1	0	1
Woody, Damien, N.E.	0	1	0	0	1
Wright, Anthony, Bal.	9	3	0	-22	3

Yards includes aborted plays, own recoveries, and opponents' recoveries.

NFC FUMBLES—INDIVIDUAL

	Fum	Own Rec	Opp Rec	Yards	Tot Rec
Abdullah, Rabih, Chi.	0	1	0	0	1
Adams, Flozell, Dal.	0	1	0	0	1
Ahanotu, Chidi, S.F.	0	0	1	1	1
Alexander, Shaun, Sea.	4	2	0	0	2
Allen, Brian, Car.	0	1	0	0	1
Allen, Will, NYG	0	0	1	0	1
Alstott, Mike, T.B.	0	1	0	0	1
Ambrose, Ashley, N.O.	0	0	1	25	1
Anderson, Marques, G.B.	0	0	2	1	2
Anderson, Richie, Dal.	1	0	0	0	0
Archuleta, Adam, St.L	0	0	1	45	1
Armstead, Jessie, Was.	0	0	1	3	1
Arrington, LaVar, Was.	0	0	2	-7	2
Avery, John, Min.	1	0	0	0	0
Azumah, Jerry, Chi.	1	0	0	0	0
Backus, Jeff, Det.	0	1	0	0	1
Bailey, Boss, Det.	0	0	1	62	1
Bailey, Champ, Was.	0	0	2	1	2
Barber, Tiki, NYG	9	4	0	0	4
Barber, Ronde, T.B.	0	0	1	0	1
Barlow, Kevan, S.F.	5	1	0	0	1
Barlow, Reggie, T.B.	1	0	0	0	0
Barnett, Nick, G.B.	0	0	1	0	1
Battle, Arnaz, S.F.	0	0	2	0	2
Bennett, Michael, Min.	2	1	0	0	1
Beverly, Eric, Det.	0	1	0	0	1
Birk, Matt, Min.	0	1	0	0	1
Blake, Jeff, Ariz	8	4	0	-1	4
Bly, Dre', Det.	0	1	2	113	3
Bober, Chris, NYG	0	1	0	0	1
Boldin, Anquan, Ariz	3	1	0	0	1
Booker, Marty, Chi.	1	0	0	0	0
Bouman, Todd, N.O.	1	0	0	0	0
Bowen, Matt, Was.	0	0	2	5	2
Brooking, Keith, Atl.	0	0	2	0	2
Brooks, Aaron, N.O.	14	0	0	-21	0
Brown, Alex, Chi.	0	0	1	0	1
Brown, Chad, Sea.	0	0	2	0	2
Brown, Gilbert, G.B.	0	0	1	0	1
Bruce, Arland, S.F.	1	0	0	0	0
Bryson, Shawn, Det.	2	2	0	0	2
Buckhalter, Correll, Phi.	3	0	0	0	0
Bulger, Marc, St.L	8	2	0	0	2
Burleson, Nate, Min.	1	0	0	0	0
Burton, Shane, Car.	0	0	1	0	1
Butler, Jerametrius, St.L	0	0	2	0	2
Caldwell, Mike, Car.	0	0	1	0	1
Campbell, Kelly, Min.	2	1	0	0	1
Canidate, Trung, Was.	1	1	0	0	1
Carpenter, Dwaine, S.F.	0	0	1	0	1
Carson, Leonardo, Dal.	0	1	0	0	1
Carter, Quincy, Dal.	10	4	0	-16	4
Cartwright, Rock, Was.	2	0	0	0	0
Cason, Aveion, Dal.	2	0	0	0	0
Chandler, Chris, Chi.	4	2	0	-4	2
Chavous, Corey, Min.	1	0	0	0	0
Claiborne, Chris, Min.	0	0	2	0	2
Clark, Desmond, Chi.	2	0	0	0	0
Cleeland, Cameron, St.L	1	1	0	0	1
Clifton, Chad, G.B.	0	1	0	0	1
Coady, Rich, St.L	1	0	1	0	1
Cochran, Antonio, Sea.	0	0	1	0	1
Coleman, Kenyon, Dal.	0	0	1	0	1
Coles, Laveranues, Was.	0	1	0	0	1
Collins, Kerry, NYG	12	3	0	-24	3
Conwell, Ernie, N.O.	1	1	0	0	1
Crumpler, Alge, Atl.	1	0	0	0	0
Culpepper, Daunte, Min.	16	6	0	0	6
Curry, Donte, Det.	0	0	1	0	1
Dach, Carson, NYG	1	0	0	-3	0
Dantzler, Woody, Atl.	0	1	0	0	1
Darby, Chartric, T.B.	0	0	2	0	2
Davenport, Najeh, G.B.	4	0	0	-8	0
Davis, Russell, Ariz	0	0	1	0	1
Davis, Stephen, Car.	3	0	0	0	0
Delhomme, Jake, Car.	15	3	0	-21	3
Dilfer, Trent, Sea.	2	0	0	0	0
Dilger, Ken, T.B.	1	3	0	0	3
Dinkins, Darnell, NYG	0	0	1	0	1
Dishman, Chris, Ariz	0	1	0	0	1
Dixon, David, Min.	0	1	0	0	1
Donnalley, Kevin, Car.	0	1	0	0	1
Draft, Chris, Atl.	0	0	1	0	1
Driver, Donald, G.B.	0	1	0	0	1
Drummond, Eddie, Det.	1	1	0	0	1
Duckett, T.J., Atl.	3	0	0	0	0
Dunn, Warrick, Atl.	2	1	0	0	1
Edwards, Steve, Chi.	0	1	0	0	1
Emmons, Carlos, Phi.	0	0	1	0	1
Engelberger, John, S.F.	0	0	2	0	2
Engram, Bobby, Sea.	5	1	0	0	1
Faulk, Marshall, St.L	0	1	0	0	1
Favre, Brett, G.B.	5	0	0	0	0
Ferguson, Robert, G.B.	0	1	0	0	1
Fisher, Levar, Ariz	0	0	1	0	1
Fisher, Travis, St.L	0	0	1	0	1
Flanagan, Mike, G.B.	0	1	0	0	1
Flemister, Zeron, Was.	1	0	1	0	1
Fontenot, Jerry, N.O.	0	2	0	0	2
Foster, DeShaun, Car.	3	1	0	0	1
Fraley, Hank, Phi.	0	1	0	0	1
Frerotte, Gus, Min.	2	2	0	-2	2
Furrey, Mike, St.L	3	2	0	0	2
Gage, Justin, Chi.	1	0	0	0	0
Galloway, Joey, Dal.	1	1	0	0	1
Garcia, Frank, Ariz	0	1	0	0	1
Garcia, Jeff, S.F.	9	3	0	-3	3
Gardner, Rod, Was.	1	1	0	0	1
Gary, Olandis, Det.	1	1	0	0	1
Gbaja-Biamila, Kabeer, G.B.	0	0	2	0	2
Gleason, Steve, N.O.	0	0	1	0	1
Glenn, Terry, Dal.	2	0	0	0	0
Glover, La'Roi, Dal.	0	0	2	0	2
Godfrey, Randall, Sea.	0	0	1	55	1
Gooch, Jeff, Det.	0	0	1	10	1
Gordon, Lamar, St.L	1	1	0	0	1

2003 INDIVIDUAL STATISTICS—FUMBLES

	Fum	Own Rec	Opp Rec	Yards	Tot Rec
Gragg, Scott, S.F.	0	2	0	1	2
Grant, Deon, Car.	0	0	1	0	1
Gray, Bobby, Chi.	0	0	1	2	1
Green, Ahman, G.B.	7	2	0	0	2
Green, Barrett, Det.	0	0	2	38	2
Green, Cornell, T.B.	1	1	0	0	1
Green, Victor, N.O.	0	1	0	0	1
Griffin, Cornelius, NYG	0	0	1	0	1
Griffith, Justin, Atl.	0	1	0	0	1
Groce, DeJuan, St.L	5	1	0	0	1
Grossman, Rex, Chi.	3	1	0	-1	1
Hakim, Az-Zahir, Det.	2	0	0	0	0
Hall, James, Det.	0	0	1	0	1
Hambrick, Troy, Dal.	4	2	0	0	2
Hamlin, Ken, Sea.	0	0	1	0	1
Hankton, Karl, Car.	0	1	0	0	1
Harper, Deveron, N.O.	0	0	1	0	1
Harrington, Joey, Det.	6	3	0	-7	3
Harris, Al, G.B.	1	0	0	0	0
Harris, Arlen, St.L	3	1	1	0	2
Harris, Corey, Det.	0	0	0	35	0
Harris, Johnnie, NYG	1	0	0	0	0
Harris, Kwame, S.F.	0	1	0	1	1
Hart, Clinton, Phi.	0	1	0	0	1
Hasselbeck, Matt, Sea.	4	0	0	-7	0
Hasselbeck, Tim, Was.	3	1	0	0	1
Heard, Ronnie, S.F.	0	0	1	0	1
Hearst, Garrison, S.F.	2	1	0	0	1
Henderson, E.J., Min.	0	0	1	0	1
Hill, Matt, Sea.	0	1	0	0	1
Hilliard, Ike, NYG	2	1	0	-2	1
Hodgins, James, Ariz	1	1	0	0	1
Holmes, Kenny, NYG	0	0	2	0	2
Holsey, Bernard, Was.	0	0	1	0	1
Holt, Terrence, Det.	1	1	1	0	2
Holt, Torry, St.L	1	1	0	0	1
Hood, Roderick, Phi.	1	0	1	27	1
Hoover, Brad, Car.	1	0	0	0	0
Horn, Joe, N.O.	2	0	0	0	0
Howard, Darren, N.O.	0	0	1	2	1
Howell, John, T.B.	0	0	1	0	1
Huff, Orlando, Sea.	0	0	1	0	1
Hunt, Cletidus, G.B.	0	0	1	0	1
Hunter, Pete, Dal.	0	1	1	0	2
Jackson, Darrell, Sea.	1	0	0	0	0
Jackson, Dexter, Ariz	1	0	0	0	0
Jackson, Terry, S.F.	0	1	0	0	1
Jackson, Tyoka, St.L	0	0	1	0	1
James, Bradie, Dal.	0	1	0	0	1
Jasper, Ed, Atl.	0	0	1	0	1
Jenkins, Kris, Car.	0	0	1	0	1
Jervey, Travis, Atl.	1	0	0	0	0
Johnson, Bryant, Ariz	1	0	0	0	0
Johnson, Doug, Atl.	3	2	0	0	2
Johnson, Eddie, Min.	2	2	0	-5	2
Johnson, Ellis, Atl.	1	0	1	4	1
Johnson, Brad, T.B.	6	4	0	0	4
Johnson, Patrick, Was.	2	1	0	0	1
Johnstone, Lance, Min.	0	1	0	0	1
Jones, Dhani, NYG	0	0	1	0	1
Jones, Thomas, T.B.	4	1	0	0	1
Joyce, Delvin, NYG	1	0	0	0	0
Kalu, N. D., Phi.	0	0	3	0	3
Kampman, Aaron, G.B.	0	0	1	0	1
Kerney, Patrick, Atl.	0	0	3	0	3
King, Kenny, Ariz	0	0	1	0	1
Kleinsasser, Jimmy, Min.	0	1	0	0	1
Knight, Bryan, Chi.	0	0	1	0	1

	Fum	Own Rec	Opp Rec	Yards	Tot Rec
Knight, Roger, N.O.	0	0	1	0	1
Kozlowski, Brian, Atl.	1	0	0	0	0
Lafleur, Bill, S.F.	1	0	0	-11	0
Legree, Lance, NYG	0	0	1	0	1
Lehr, Matt, Dal.	1	0	0	-13	0
Lewis, Michael, N.O.	2	1	0	0	1
Lewis, Michael, Phi.	0	0	1	0	1
Little, Leonard, St.L	0	0	1	0	1
Lloyd, Brandon, S.F.	0	1	0	0	1
Looker, Dane, St.L	1	0	0	0	0
Lucas, Ken, Sea.	1	0	1	24	1
Lynch, John, T.B.	1	1	0	0	1
Mangum, Kris, Car.	0	0	1	0	1
Mannelly, Patrick, Chi.	0	0	1	0	1
Manning, Ricky, Car.	0	0	1	0	1
Marshall, Torrance, G.B.	0	0	1	0	1
Mathis, Kevin, Atl.	0	0	2	6	2
Maynard, Brad, Chi.	1	0	0	-5	0
McAfee, Fred, N.O.	1	0	0	0	0
McAllister, Deuce, N.O.	6	3	0	-3	3
McBride, Tod, Atl.	2	0	0	0	0
McBurrows, Gerald, Atl.	0	1	0	0	1
McCardell, Keenan, T.B.	1	0	1	57	1
McClure, Todd, Atl.	1	3	0	-7	3
McCown, Josh, Ariz	10	4	0	-12	4
McDonald, Shaun, St.L	1	0	0	0	0
McDougle, Stockar, Det.	0	1	0	0	1
McFarland, Anthony, T.B.	0	0	1	0	1
McKinnon, Ronald, Ariz	0	0	1	0	1
McMahon, Mike, Det.	1	0	0	0	0
McNabb, Donovan, Phi.	9	2	0	-6	2
McQuarters, R.W., Chi.	1	0	0	0	0
Merritt, Ahmad, Chi.	1	1	0	0	1
Mitchell, Brian, NYG	5	4	0	0	4
Moore, Rashad, Sea.	0	0	1	0	1
Moran, Sean, S.F.	0	0	1	0	1
Morey, Sean, Phi.	1	0	1	0	1
Morgan, Dan, Car.	0	0	2	0	2
Morris, Maurice, Sea.	2	1	0	0	1
Morton, Chad, Was.	1	0	0	0	0
Moss, Randy, Min.	1	0	0	0	0
Muhammad, Muhsin, Car.	3	2	0	0	2
Navies, Hannibal, G.B.	0	0	1	0	1
Nead, Spencer, St.L	1	0	0	0	0
Newberry, Jeremy, S.F.	1	0	0	0	0
Newman, Terence, Dal.	0	0	1	0	1
Nguyen, Dat, Dal.	0	0	2	0	2
Odom, Joe, Chi.	0	0	1	0	1
Ohalete, Ifeanyi, Was.	0	0	1	0	1
Pace, Calvin, Ariz	0	0	1	0	1
Pace, Orlando, St.L	0	1	0	0	1
Palmer, Jesse, NYG	2	1	0	0	1
Parrish, Tony, S.F.	0	0	1	0	1
Pathon, Jerome, N.O.	1	0	0	0	0
Peterson, Adrian, Chi.	0	1	0	0	1
Peterson, Todd, S.F.	0	1	0	0	1
Phillips, Jermaine, T.B.	0	0	1	20	1
Pinkston, Todd, Phi.	1	0	0	0	0
Pittman, Michael, T.B.	4	0	0	0	0
Polley, Tommy, St.L	0	0	1	0	1
Pritchett, Stanley, Chi.	0	1	0	0	1
Quarles, Shelton, T.B.	0	0	2	0	2
Raiola, Dominic, Det.	0	1	0	0	1
Ramsey, Patrick, Was.	8	1	0	-11	1
Randle, John, Sea.	0	0	1	0	1
Reese, Ike, Phi.	0	0	1	0	1
Rice, Simeon, T.B.	0	0	1	0	1
Richard, Kris, Sea.	1	0	0	0	0

	Fum	Own Rec	Opp Rec	Yards	Tot Rec
Riley, Karon, Atl.	0	1	0	0	1
Robbins, Fred, Min.	0	0	1	0	1
Robinson, Damien, Sea.	1	0	1	3	1
Robinson, Koren, Sea.	1	1	0	0	1
Rodgers, Derrick, N.O.	0	0	2	3	2
Rogers, Sam, Atl.	0	0	1	37	1
Ross, Derek, Dal.	2	0	0	0	0
Rossum, Allen, Atl.	3	0	0	0	0
Royal, Robert, Was.	1	1	0	0	1
Ruff, Orlando, N.O.	0	0	1	0	1
Runyan, Jon, Phi.	0	2	0	0	2
Russell, Brian, Min.	0	0	1	0	1
Scott, Bryan, Atl.	0	0	1	0	1
Shabazz, Siddeeq, Atl.	0	0	1	0	1
Shiancoe, Visanthe, NYG	0	1	0	0	1
Shipp, Marcel, Ariz	3	1	0	0	1
Shockey, Jeremy, NYG	1	0	0	0	0
Short, Brandon, NYG	0	0	1	-3	1
Simmons, Anthony, Sea.	0	0	1	4	1
Simon, Corey, Phi.	0	0	1	0	1
Simon, John, Was.	1	1	0	0	1
Singleton, Alshermond, Dal.	0	0	1	0	1
Smart, Rod, Car.	2	1	0	0	1
Smith, Derek M., S.F.	0	0	1	7	1
Smith, Emmitt, Ariz	2	0	0	-19	0
Smith, L.J., Phi.	1	0	0	0	0
Smith, Kenny, N.O.	0	0	1	0	1
Smith, Onterrio, Min.	1	0	0	0	0
Smith, Otis, Det.	0	0	1	0	1
Smith, Raonall, Min.	0	1	0	0	1
Smith, Steve, Car.	5	4	0	0	4
Smith, Zuriel, Dal.	3	1	0	0	1
Spires, Greg, T.B.	0	0	1	0	1
Staley, Duce, Phi.	2	1	0	0	1
Stallworth, Donte', N.O.	3	1	0	0	1
Stecker, Aaron, T.B.	1	0	0	0	0
Steussie, Todd, Car.	0	2	0	0	2
Stewart, Kordell, Chi.	7	3	0	-23	3
Stewart, Matt, Atl.	0	0	3	3	3
Stoutmire, Omar, NYG	1	0	0	0	0
Strahan, Michael, NYG	0	0	1	0	1
Strong, Mack, Sea.	1	0	0	0	0
Swinton, Reggie, Det.	4	0	0	0	0
Tauscher, Mark, G.B.	0	1	0	0	1
Terrell, David, Chi.	1	1	0	0	1
Terrell, David, Was.	0	0	1	0	1
Thomas, Anthony, Chi.	1	1	0	0	1
Thomas, Fred, N.O.	0	0	1	0	1
Thomas, Randy, Was.	0	0	1	0	1
Thomas, Robert, St.L	0	0	1	0	1
Thompson, Raynoch, Ariz	0	0	1	0	1
Timmerman, Adam, St.L	0	1	0	0	1
Tinoisamoa, Pisa, St.L	0	0	1	5	1
Tongue, Reggie, Sea.	0	1	0	0	1
Trotter, Jeremiah, Was.	0	0	1	0	1
Trufant, Marcus, Sea.	0	0	1	31	1
Turley, Kyle, St.L	0	1	0	0	1
Ulbrich, Jeff, S.F.	0	0	1	0	1
Vick, Michael, Atl.	4	1	0	0	1
Vincent, Troy, Phi.	0	0	1	0	1
Wade, John, T.B.	2	2	0	-6	2
Wade, Bobby, Chi.	1	0	0	0	0
Wakefield, Fred, Ariz	0	0	1	0	1
Walker, Bracy, Det.	0	0	1	0	1
Walker, Darwin, Phi.	0	0	2	0	2
Walker, Javon, G.B.	1	0	0	0	0
Wallace, Al, Car.	1	0	1	0	1
Wansley, Tim, T.B.	1	0	1	0	1
Warner, Kurt, St.L	6	1	0	-9	1
Washington, Keith, NYG	0	0	2	0	2
Weaver, Jed, S.F.	1	0	0	0	0
Webster, Nate, T.B.	0	0	1	0	1
Welbourn, John, Phi.	0	2	0	0	2
Wells, Reggie, Ariz	0	1	0	0	1
Wesley, Dante, Car.	0	0	1	0	1
Westbrook, Brian, Phi.	3	1	0	0	1
White, Dez, Chi.	0	1	0	0	1
Whitehead, Willie, N.O.	0	0	1	0	1
Whiting, Brandon, Phi.	0	0	1	0	1
Wiley, Chuck, Min.	0	0	1	0	1
Wilkins, Marcus, G.B.	1	0	1	0	1
Wilkinson, Dan, Det.	0	0	1	0	1
Williams, Aeneas, St.L	0	0	4	93	4
Williams, Boo, N.O.	0	0	1	0	1
Williams, Jimmy, S.F.	3	0	1	0	1
Williams, Kevin, Min.	0	0	1	0	1
Williams, Moe, Min.	2	1	0	0	1
Williams, Melvin, N.O.	2	0	1	2	1
Williams, Randal, Dal.	0	1	1	0	2
Williams, Roy, Dal.	0	0	1	0	1
Williams, Shaun, NYG	0	0	1	2	1
Williams, Willie, Sea.	0	1	0	0	1
Wilson, Cedrick, S.F.	1	0	0	0	0
Winborn, Jamie, S.F.	0	0	1	13	1
Wistrom, Grant, St.L	0	0	1	0	1
Wohlabaugh, Dave, St.L	1	0	1	-5	1
Woods, LeVar, Ariz	0	0	3	0	3
Woodson, Darren, Dal.	0	0	2	0	2
Worrell, Cameron, Chi.	0	1	0	0	1
Wyrick, Jimmy, Det.	0	0	1	7	1
Yoder, Todd, T.B.	0	1	0	0	1
Young, Brian, St.L	0	0	5	21	5

Yards includes aborted plays, own recoveries, and opponents' recoveries.

2003 INDIVIDUAL STATISTICS—FUMBLES/SACKS

AMERICAN FOOTBALL CONFERENCE—FUMBLES

	Fum	Own Rec	Fum OB	TD	Opp Rec	TD	Fum Yards	Tot Rec
Kansas City	13	6	1	0	12	0	6	18
Cincinnati	16	5	4	0	10	1	25	15
Houston	18	8	1	0	8	0	31	16
N.Y. Jets	18	11	1	0	9	0	-9	20
San Diego	20	7	1	0	7	0	-15	14
Denver	24	17	1	0	11	0	10	28
Pittsburgh	24	12	1	0	11	0	3	23
Tennessee	24	12	0	1	13	2	172	25
Indianapolis	25	11	4	0	15	1	32	26
New England	25	11	3	0	12	1	73	23
Oakland	25	12	1	0	11	0	-2	23
Miami	26	8	3	1	14	1	24	22
Jacksonville	27	9	4	0	12	1	3	21
Cleveland	32	17	0	0	7	0	-16	24
Buffalo	36	18	1	0	8	1	13	26
Baltimore	37	16	2	1	17	0	5	33
AFC Total	390	180	28	3	177	8	355	357
AFC Average	24.4	11.3	1.8	0.2	11.1	0.5	22.2	22.3

NATIONAL FOOTBALL CONFERENCE—FUMBLES

	Fum	Own Rec	Fum OB	TD	Opp Rec	TD	Fum Yards	Tot Rec
Detroit	18	13	1	0	13	3	258	26
Green Bay	19	7	1	0	11	1	-7	18
Philadelphia	21	10	1	0	13	0	21	23
Washington	21	8	1	0	13	0	-9	21
Atlanta	22	11	1	0	16	0	43	27
Seattle	23	8	2	1	12	2	110	20
Tampa Bay	23	14	0	0	13	1	71	27
San Francisco	24	11	3	1	13	0	9	24
Chicago	25	15	1	0	5	0	-31	20
Dallas	26	13	5	0	12	0	-29	25
Arizona	29	14	1	0	10	0	-32	24
Minnesota	31	18	2	0	7	0	-7	25
Carolina	33	16	2	0	10	0	-21	26
New Orleans	33	9	4	0	13	0	8	22
St. Louis	33	14	3	0	22	2	150	36
N.Y. Giants	35	15	2	0	12	2	-30	27
NFC Total	416	196	30	2	195	11	504	391
NFC Average	26.0	12.3	1.9	0.1	12.2	0.7	31.5	24.4
NFL Total	806	376	58	5	372	19	859	748
NFL Average	25.2	11.8	1.8	0.2	11.6	0.6	26.8	23.4

SACKS

MOST SACKS

NFC: 18.5 Michael Strahan, N.Y. Giants
AFC: 15.0 Adewale Ogunleye, Miami

MOST SACKS, GAME

AFC: 4.0 Andra Davis, Cleveland at Kansas City, November 9
NFC: 4.0 Simeon Rice, Tampa Bay at Washington, October 12
4.0 Leonard Little, St. Louis vs. Minnesota, November 30

AFC: BALTIMORE, 12.0, Terrell Suggs; BUFFALO, 11.5, Aaron Schobel; CINCINNATI, 6.0, Duane Clemons, John Thornton; CLEVELAND, 8.0, Kenard Lang; DENVER, 11.5, Bert Berry; HOUSTON, 4.0, Jamie Sharper; INDIANAPOLIS, 11.0, Dwight Freeney; JACKSONVILLE, 6.0, Tony Brackens; KANSAS CITY, 5.5, Vonnie Holliday; MIAMI, 15.0, Adewale Ogunleye; NEW ENGLAND, 9.5, Mike Vrabel; N.Y. JETS, 12.5, Shaun Ellis; OAKLAND, 5.5, Rod Coleman; PITTSBURGH, 8.0, Kimo von Oelhoffen; SAN DIEGO, 6.5, DeQuincy Scott; TENNESSEE, 9.5, Jevon Kearse

NFC: ARIZONA, 3.0, Dennis Johnson, Raynoch Thompson; ATLANTA, 8.0, Ellis Johnson; CAROLINA, 12.0, Mike Rucker; CHICAGO, 5.5, Alex Brown; DALLAS, 8.0, Greg Ellis; DETROIT, 4.5, James Hall, Robert Porcher; GREEN BAY, 10.0, Kabeer Gbaja-Biamila; MINNESOTA, 10.5, Kevin Williams; NEW ORLEANS, 10.0, Charles Grant; N.Y. GIANTS, 18.5, Michael Strahan; PHILADELPHIA, 7.5, Corey Simon; ST. LOUIS, 12.5, Leonard Little; SAN FRANCISCO, 7.0, Julian Peterson; SEATTLE, 8.0, Chike Okeafor; TAMPA BAY, 15.0, Simeon Rice; WASHINGTON, 6.5, Jessie Armstead

TEAM CHAMPION

AFC: 47 Baltimore
NFC: 45 N.Y. Giants

NFL TOP TEN LEADERS—SACKS

Strahan, Michael, NYG	18.5
Ogunleye, Adewale, Mia.	15.0
Rice, Simeon, T.B.	15.0
Taylor, Jason, Mia.	13.0
Ellis, Shaun, NYJ	12.5
Little, Leonard, St.L	12.5
Rucker, Mike, Car.	12.0
Suggs, Terrell, Bal.	12.0
Berry, Bert, Den.	11.5
Schobel, Aaron, Buf.	11.5

AMERICAN FOOTBALL CONFERENCE—SACKS

	Sacks	Yards
Baltimore	47	353
Miami	44	253
New England	41	253
Buffalo	38	231
Tennessee	38	223
Denver	36	221
Kansas City	36	251
Cleveland	35	203
N.Y. Jets	35	218
Pittsburgh	35	203
Indianapolis	31	225
Cincinnati	30	196
San Diego	30	200
Oakland	25	162
Jacksonville	24	134
Houston	19	123
AFC Total	544	3449
AFC Average	34.0	215.6

NATIONAL FOOTBALL CONFERENCE—SACKS

	Sacks	Yards
N.Y. Giants	45	298
St. Louis	42	291
San Francisco	42	306
Carolina	40	212

Seattle	40	248
Philadelphia	38	248
Minnesota	37	245
Atlanta	36	205
Tampa Bay	36	234
Green Bay	34	200
Dallas	32	189
New Orleans	32	171
Detroit	28	182
Washington	27	159
Arizona	21	97
Chicago	18	105
NFC Total	548	3390
NFC Average	34.3	211.9
League Total	1092	6839
League Average	34.1	213.7

AFC—INDIVIDUAL SACKS

Ogunleye, Adewale, Mia.	15.0
Taylor, Jason, Mia.	13.0
Ellis, Shaun, NYJ	12.5
Suggs, Terrell, Bal.	12.0
Berry, Bert, Den.	11.5
Schobel, Aaron, Buf.	11.5
Freeney, Dwight, Ind.	11.0
Kearse, Jevon, Ten.	9.5
Vrabel, Mike, N.E.	9.5
Boulware, Peter, Bal.	8.5
Hayward, Reggie, Den.	8.5
Pryce, Trevor, Den.	8.5
Lang, Kenard, Cle.	8.0
Seymour, Richard, N.E.	8.0
von Oelhoffen, Kimo, Pit.	8.0
Scott, DeQuincy, S.D.	6.5
Abraham, John, NYJ	6.0
Brackens, Tony, Jac.	6.0
Brown, Courtney, Cle.	6.0
Clemons, Duane, Cin.	6.0
Dingle, Adrian, S.D.	6.0
Gildon, Jason, Pit.	6.0
Thornton, John, Cin.	6.0
Washington, Marcus, Ind.	6.0
Carter, Kevin, Ten.	5.5
Coleman, Rod, Oak.	5.5
Holliday, Vonnie, K.C.	5.5
McGinest, Willie, N.E.	5.5
Posey, Jeff, Buf.	5.5
Warren, Gerard, Cle.	5.5
Adams, Sam, Buf.	5.0
Barber, Shawn, K.C.	5.0
Bell, Kendrell, Pit.	5.0
Davis, Andra, Cle.	5.0
Hicks, Eric, K.C.	5.0
Porter, Joey, Pit.	5.0
Smith, Justin, Cin.	5.0
Truluck, R-Kal, K.C.	5.0
Weaver, Tony, Bal.	5.0
Douglas, Marques, Bal.	4.5
Ferguson, Jason, NYJ	4.5
Smith, Robaire, Ten.	4.5
Stroud, Marcus, Jac.	4.5
Fujita, Scott, K.C.	4.0
Johnson, Raylee, S.D.	4.0
Sharper, Jamie, Hou.	4.0
Thomas, Adalius, Bal.	4.0
Thomas, Juqua, Ten.	4.0
Word, Mark, Cle.	4.0
Denney, Ryan, Buf.	3.5
Douglas, Hugh, Jac.	3.5
Henderson, John, Jac.	3.5
Mathis, Robert, Ind.	3.5
Armstrong, Trace, Oak.	3.0
Beckett, Rogers, Cin.	3.0
Bratzke, Chad, Ind.	3.0
Bulluck, Keith, Ten.	3.0
Gregg, Kelly, Bal.	3.0
Hall, Carlos, Ten.	3.0
Harrison, Rodney, N.E.	3.0
Hartwell, Edgerton, Bal.	3.0
Leber, Ben, S.D.	3.0
Milloy, Lawyer, Buf.	3.0
Myers, Michael, Cle.	3.0
Seau, Junior, Mia.	3.0
Sims, Ryan, K.C.	3.0
Stills, Gary, K.C.	3.0
Wiley, Marcellus, S.D.	3.0
Wong, Kailee, Hou.	3.0
Zgonina, Jeff, Mia.	3.0
Brayton, Tyler, Oak.	2.5
Cooper, Chris, Oak.	2.5
Fatafehi, Mario, Den.	2.5
Haynesworth, Albert, Ten.	2.5
Williams, Jay, Mia.	2.5
Bailey, Rodney, Pit.	2.0
Bowens, Tim, Mia.	2.0
Brock, Raheem, Ind.	2.0
Bromell, Lorenzo, Oak.	2.0
Bruschi, Tedy, N.E.	2.0
Burnett, Rob, Mia.	2.0
Colvin, Rosevelt, N.E.	2.0
Cowart, Sam, NYJ	2.0
Fletcher, London, Buf.	2.0
Foreman, Jay, Hou.	2.0
Green, Jarvis, N.E.	2.0
Harris, Napoleon, Oak.	2.0
Hobson, Victor, NYJ	2.0
Moreno, Zeke, S.D.	2.0
Orr, Shantee, Hou.	2.0
Polamalu, Troy, Pit.	2.0
Romanowski, Bill, Oak.	2.0
Smith, Aaron, Pit.	2.0
Spikes, Takeo, Buf.	2.0
Washington, Ted, N.E.	2.0
Wesley, Greg, K.C.	2.0
Williams, Tony, Cin.	2.0
Boiman, Rocky, Ten.	1.5
Chatham, Matt, N.E.	1.5
Hardy, Kevin, Cin.	1.5
Klecko, Dan, N.E.	1.5
Lewis, Ray, Bal.	1.5
Meier, Rob, Jac.	1.5
Robertson, Dewayne, NYJ	1.5
Roye, Orpheus, Cle.	1.5
Simmons, Brian, Cin.	1.5
Alexander, Brent, Pit.	1.0
Ayodele, Akin, Jac.	1.0
Banta-Cain, Tully, N.E.	1.0
Barnes, Lionel, Jac.	1.0
Baxter, Gary, Bal.	1.0
Beisel, Monty, K.C.	1.0
Bowens, David, Mia.	1.0
Brackett, Gary, Ind.	1.0
Brown, Cornell, Bal.	1.0
Calmus, Rocky, Ten.	1.0
Cherry, Je'Rod, N.E.	1.0
Clemons, Charlie, Hou.	1.0

2003 INDIVIDUAL STATISTICS—SACKS

Cooper, Stephen, S.D.	1.0
Evans, Josh, NYJ	1.0
Ferguson, Nick, Den.	1.0
Fisk, Jason, S.D.	1.0
Foley, Steve, Hou.	1.0
Freeman, Arturo, Mia.	1.0
Gbaja-Biamila, Akbar, Oak.	1.0
Gibson, Derrick, Oak.	1.0
Grant, DeLawrence, Oak.	1.0
Haggans, Clark, Pit.	1.0
Hampton, Casey, Pit.	1.0
James, Tory, Cin.	1.0
Kaesviharn, Kevin, Cin.	1.0
Kemoeatu, Maake, Bal.	1.0
Kennedy, Kenoy, Den.	1.0
Leverette, Otis, S.D.	1.0
Logan, Mike, Pit.	1.0
Long, Rien, Ten.	1.0
Martin, Steve, Hou.	1.0
McGarrahan, Scott, Ten.	1.0
McGee, Terrence, Buf.	1.0
McGlockton, Chester, NYJ	1.0
Payne, Seth, Hou.	1.0
Peek, Antwan, Hou.	1.0
Peterson, Mike, Jac.	1.0
Pleasant, Anthony, N.E.	1.0
Pope, Monsanto, Den.	1.0
Reed, Ed, Bal.	1.0
Reed, James, NYJ	1.0
Roberts, Terrell, Cin.	1.0
Rogers, Tyrone, Cle.	1.0
Schulters, Lance, Ten.	1.0
Sears, Corey, Hou.	1.0
Sharpe, Montique, K.C.	1.0
Slaughter, T.J., Jac.	1.0
Smith, Travian, Oak.	1.0
Thomas, Bryan, NYJ	1.0
Thomas, Kiwaukee, Jac.	1.0
Thomas, Zach, Mia.	1.0
Thornton, David, Ind.	1.0
Townsend, Deshea, Pit.	1.0
Tripplett, Larry, Ind.	1.0
Warfield, Eric, K.C.	1.0
Warren, Ty, N.E.	1.0
Williams, Chad, Bal.	1.0
Williams, Jamal, S.D.	1.0
Williams, Josh, Ind.	1.0
Wilson, Al, Den.	1.0
Wilson, Jerry, S.D.	1.0
Winfield, Antoine, Buf.	1.0
Wire, Coy, Buf.	1.0
Woodson, Charles, Oak.	1.0
Wright, Kenny, Hou.	1.0
Barton, Eric, Oak.	0.5
Brown, Eric, Hou.	0.5
Browning, John, K.C.	0.5
Edwards, Donnie, S.D.	0.5
Edwards, Ron, Buf.	0.5
Garnes, Sam, NYJ	0.5
Gibson, Oliver, Cin.	0.5
Greenwood, Morlon, Mia.	0.5
Ioane, Junior, Hou.	0.5
Knight, Tom, Bal.	0.5
Powell, Carl, Cin.	0.5
Prioleau, Pierson, Buf.	0.5
Reagor, Montae, Ind.	0.5
Roman, Mark, Cin.	0.5
Steele, Glen, Cin.	0.5
Thomas, Kevin, Buf.	0.5
Williams, Tank, Ten.	0.5

NFC—INDIVIDUAL SACKS

Strahan, Michael, NYG	18.5
Rice, Simeon, T.B.	15.0
Little, Leonard, St.L	12.5
Rucker, Mike, Car.	12.0
Williams, Kevin, Min.	10.5
Gbaja-Biamila, Kabeer, G.B.	10.0
Grant, Charles, N.O.	10.0
Johnstone, Lance, Min.	10.0
Ellis, Greg, Dal.	8.0
Johnson, Ellis, Atl.	8.0
Okeafor, Chike, Sea.	8.0
Simon, Corey, Phi.	7.5
Wistrom, Grant, St.L	7.5
Brown, Chad, Sea.	7.0
Peppers, Julius, Car.	7.0
Peterson, Julian, S.F.	7.0
Armstead, Jessie, Was.	6.5
Carter, Andre, S.F.	6.5
Kerney, Patrick, Atl.	6.5
Arrington, LaVar, Was.	6.0
Jackson, Grady, N.O.-G.B.	6.0
Walker, Darwin, Phi.	6.0
Brown, Alex, Chi.	5.5
Holmes, Kenny, NYG	5.5
Jackson, Tyoka, St.L	5.5
Kalu, N. D., Phi.	5.5
Randle, John, Sea.	5.5
Whitehead, Willie, N.O.	5.5
Archuleta, Adam, St.L	5.0
Glover, La'Roi, Dal.	5.0
Hall, Travis, Atl.	5.0
Howard, Darren, N.O.	5.0
Jenkins, Kris, Car.	5.0
Mixon, Kenny, Min.	5.0
Sapp, Warren, T.B.	5.0
Smith, Bruce, Was.	5.0
Wallace, Al, Car.	5.0
Engelberger, John, S.F.	4.5
Hall, James, Det.	4.5
Porcher, Robert, Det.	4.5
Ahanotu, Chidi, S.F.	4.0
Hunt, Cletidus, G.B.	4.0
Rogers, Shaun, Det.	4.0
Smith, Brady, Atl.	4.0
Ogbogu, Eric, Dal.	3.5
Smith, Derek M., S.F.	3.5
Spires, Greg, T.B.	3.5
Young, Bryant, S.F.	3.5
Claiborne, Chris, Min.	3.0
Green, Barrett, Det.	3.0
Jasper, Ed, Atl.	3.0
Johnson, Dennis, Ariz	3.0
Jones, Dhani, NYG	3.0
King, Lamar, Sea.	3.0
Mitchell, Brandon, Sea.	3.0
Short, Brandon, NYG	3.0
Simmons, Anthony, Sea.	3.0
Thompson, Raynoch, Ariz	3.0
Wayne, Nate, Phi.	3.0
Williams, Brian, Min.	3.0
Winborn, Jamie, S.F.	3.0
Daniels, Phillip, Chi.	2.5
Ekuban, Ebenezer, Dal.	2.5
Holsey, Bernard, Was.	2.5
McFarland, Anthony, T.B.	2.5
Nwokorie, Chukie, G.B.	2.5
Stewart, Matt, Atl.	2.5
Ulbrich, Jeff, S.F.	2.5
Urlacher, Brian, Chi.	2.5

2003 INDIVIDUAL STATISTICS—SACKS

Player	Sacks
Barnett, Nick, G.B.	2.0
Barrow, Micheal, NYG	2.0
Bernard, Rocky, Sea.	2.0
Burton, Shane, Car.	2.0
Cousin, Terry, Car.	2.0
Darby, Chartric, T.B.	2.0
Darling, James, Ariz	2.0
Draft, Chris, Atl.	2.0
Edwards, Kalimba, Det.	2.0
Fisher, Bryce, St.L	2.0
Haynes, Michael, Chi.	2.0
Hill, Renaldo, Ariz	2.0
Holmes, Earl, Det.	2.0
Hovan, Chris, Min.	2.0
Kampman, Aaron, G.B.	2.0
King, Kenny, Ariz	2.0
Legree, Lance, NYG	2.0
Lewis, Michael, Phi.	2.0
McKinnon, Ronald, Ariz	2.0
Newman, Keith, Atl.	2.0
Nguyen, Dat, Dal.	2.0
Rayburn, Sam, Phi.	2.0
Rumph, Mike, S.F.	2.0
Sharper, Darren, G.B.	2.0
Simoneau, Mark, Phi.	2.0
Thomas, Robert, St.L	2.0
Tinoisamoa, Pisa, St.L	2.0
Tongue, Reggie, Sea.	2.0
Whiting, Brandon, Phi.	2.0
Wilkinson, Dan, Det.	2.0
Williams, Roy, Dal.	2.0
Wyms, Ellis, T.B.	2.0
Wynn, Renaldo, Was.	2.0
Young, Brian, St.L	2.0
Adams, Anthony, S.F.	1.5
Bailey, Boss, Det.	1.5
Barber, Ronde, T.B.	1.5
Carson, Leonardo, Dal.	1.5
Hamilton, Keith, NYG	1.5
Jue, Bhawoh, G.B.	1.5
Kirschke, Travis, S.F.	1.5
Moran, Sean, S.F.	1.5
Smith, Larry, G.B.	1.5
Smith, Otis, Det.	1.5
Springs, Shawn, Sea.	1.5
Stewart, Daleroy, Dal.	1.5
Trotter, Jeremiah, Was.	1.5
Williams, Shaun, NYG	1.5
Allen, Brian, Car.	1.0
Azumah, Jerry, Chi.	1.0
Bell, Marcus, Ariz	1.0
Bellamy, Jay, N.O.	1.0
Biekert, Greg, Min.	1.0
Blade, Willie, Dal.	1.0
Bly, Dre', Det.	1.0
Boone, Alfonso, Chi.	1.0
Brooks, Derrick, T.B.	1.0
Brown, Ralph, NYG	1.0
Brown, Sheldon, Phi.	1.0
Carter, Dale, N.O.	1.0
Clark, Ryan, NYG	1.0
Coakley, Dexter, Dal.	1.0
Cochran, Antonio, Sea.	1.0
Coleman, Kenyon, Dal.	1.0
Dalton, Lional, Was.	1.0
Davis, Russell, Ariz	1.0
DeVries, Jared, Det.	1.0
Diggs, Na'il, G.B.	1.0
Duncan, Jamie, St.L	1.0
Edwards, Antuan, G.B.	1.0
Fisher, Levar, Ariz	1.0
Grant, Deon, Car.	1.0
Grasmanis, Paul, Phi.	1.0
Gray, Bobby, Chi.	1.0
Griffin, Cornelius, NYG	1.0
Hand, Norman, Sea.	1.0
Harris, Corey, Det.	1.0
Hart, Clinton, Phi.	1.0
Hawthorne, Michael, G.B.	1.0
Hodge, Sedrick, N.O.	1.0
Huff, Orlando, Sea.	1.0
Joseph, William, NYG	1.0
Marshall, Torrance, G.B.	1.0
Mathis, Kevin, Atl.	1.0
McCadam, Kevin, Atl.	1.0
Moore, Rashad, Sea.	1.0
Navies, Hannibal, G.B.	1.0
Newman, Terence, Dal.	1.0
Pace, Calvin, Ariz	1.0
Pickett, Ryan, St.L	1.0
Pinkney, Cleveland, T.B.	1.0
Rasmussen, Kemp, Car.	1.0
Reese, Ike, Phi.	1.0
Richard, Kris, Sea.	1.0
Robinson, Bryan, Chi.	1.0
Rogers, Sam, Atl.	1.0
Russell, Brian, Min.	1.0
Singleton, Alshermond, Dal.	1.0
Smith, Darrin, N.O.	1.0
Smith, Kenny, N.O.	1.0
Stoutmire, Omar, NYG	1.0
Sullivan, Johnathan, N.O.	1.0
Tanner, Barron, Ariz	1.0
Thomas, Fred, N.O.	1.0
Tillman, Charles, Chi.	1.0
Umenyiora, Osi, NYG	1.0
Upshaw, Regan, Was.	1.0
Wakefield, Fred, Ariz	1.0
Washington, Keith, NYG	1.0
Webster, Nate, T.B.	1.0
Wesley, Dante, Car.	1.0
Wiley, Chuck, Min.	1.0
Williams, Aeneas, St.L	1.0
Witherspoon, Will, Car.	1.0
Woods, LeVar, Ariz	1.0
Woodson, Darren, Dal.	1.0
Zellner, Peppi, Was.	1.0
Buckner, Brentson, Car.	0.5
Coleman, Marco, Phi.	0.5
Dawkins, Brian, Phi.	0.5
Green, Michael, Chi.	0.5
Heard, Ronnie, S.F.	0.5
Howard, Reggie, Car.	0.5
Lewis, Damione, St.L	0.5
Lynch, John, T.B.	0.5
Marshall, Lemar, Was.	0.5
Parrish, Tony, S.F.	0.5
Robbins, Fred, Min.	0.5

2003 NFL PAID ATTENDANCE BREAKDOWN

	Games	Attendance	Average
NFL Preseason Total	66	3,919,910	59,393
NFL Regular-Season Total	*255	16,913,584	66,328
NFL Postseason Total	12	805,546	67,129
NFL All Games	*333	21,639,040	64,982

**The Week 8 Miami at San Diego game is not included. The game was moved to Arizona due to the San Diego wildfires and tickets were distributed at no charge.*

1.1-MILLION CLUB

During the 2003 season, nine teams drew more than 1.1 million paid attendance home and away during the regular season. The Washington Redskins led the league for the fourth consecutive season by drawing 1,220,724 fans in 2003, and set an NFL home attendance record for the fourth year in a row with 667,033 fans.

Team	Total Paid Home Attendance	Total Paid Visiting Attendance	Total Paid Attendance
Washington	667,033	553,691	1,220,724
New York Giants	628,962	550,195	1,179,157
Kansas City	627,981	536,840	1,164,821
New York Jets	622,781	535,953	1,158,734
Buffalo	572,887	568,457	1,141,344
Denver	593,770	521,329	1,115,099
Cleveland	567,731	545,709	1,113,440
Philadelphia	532,888	580,492	1,113,380
New England	538,707	571,984	1,110,691

For complete year-by-year attendance records, see pages 608-609.

Inside the Numbers

GREATEST COMEBACKS IN NFL HISTORY (Most Points Overcome To Win Game)

REGULAR SEASON GAMES

FROM 28 POINTS BEHIND TO WIN: December 7, 1980, at San Francisco

New Orleans	14	21	0	0	0	— 35
San Francisco	0	7	14	14	3	— 38

NO — Harris 33 pass from Manning (Ricardo kick)
NO — Childs 21 pass from Manning (Ricardo kick)
NO — Holmes 1 run (Ricardo kick)
SF — Solomon 57 punt return (Wersching kick)
NO — Holmes 1 run (Ricardo kick)
NO — Harris 41 pass from Manning (Ricardo kick)
SF — Montana 1 run (Wersching kick)
SF — Clark 71 pass from Montana (Wersching kick)
SF — Solomon 14 pass from Montana (Wersching kick)
SF — Elliott 7 run (Wersching kick)
SF — FG Wersching 36

FROM 26 POINTS BEHIND TO WIN: September 21, 1997, at Buffalo

Indianapolis	14	12	0	9	— 35
Buffalo	0	10	6	21	— 37

Ind — Bailey 10 pass from Harbaugh (Blanchard kick)
Ind — Faulk 10 run (Blanchard kick)
Ind — FG Blanchard 39
Ind — FG Blanchard 36
Ind — FG Blanchard 49
Ind — FG Blanchard 22
Buff — Johnson 16 pass from Collins (Christie kick)
Buff — FG Christie 27
Buff — A. Smith 15 run (2-pt attempt failed)
Ind — FG Blanchard 25
Buff — Early 4 pass from Collins (Christie kick)
Buff — A. Smith 1 run (Christie kick)
Buff — A. Smith 54 run (Christie kick)
Ind — Harrison 2 pass from Justin (2-pt attempt failed)

FROM 25 POINTS BEHIND TO WIN: November 8, 1987, at St. Louis

Tampa Bay	7	7	14	0	— 28
St. Louis	0	3	0	28	— 31

TB — Carrier 5 pass from DeBerg (Igwebuike kick)
TB — Carter 3 pass from DeBerg (Igwebuike kick)
StL — FG Gallery 31
TB — Smith 34 pass from DeBerg (Igwebuike kick)
TB — Smith 3 run (Igwebuike kick)
StL — Awalt 4 pass from Lomax (Gallery kick)
StL — Noga 23 fumble recovery (Gallery kick)
StL — J. Smith 11 pass from Lomax (Gallery kick)
StL — J. Smith 17 pass from Lomax (Gallery kick)

FROM 24 POINTS BEHIND TO WIN: October 27, 1946, at Washington

Philadelphia	0	0	14	14	— 28
Washington	10	14	0	0	— 24

Wash— Rosato 2 run (Poillon kick)
Wash— FG Poillon 28
Wash— Rosato 4 run (Poillon kick)
Wash— Lapka recovered fumble in end zone (Poillon kick)
Phil — Steele 1 run (Lio kick)
Phil — Pritchard 45 pass from Thompson (Lio kick)
Phil — Steinke 7 pass from Thompson (Lio kick)
Phil — Ferrante 30 pass from Thompson (Lio kick)

FROM 24 POINTS BEHIND TO WIN: October 20, 1957, at Detroit

Baltimore	7	14	6	0	— 27
Detroit	0	3	7	21	— 31

Balt — Mutscheller 15 pass from Unitas (Rechichar kick)
Det — FG Martin 47
Balt — Moore 72 pass from Unitas (Rechichar kick)
Balt — Mutscheller 52 pass from Unitas (Rechichar kick)
Balt — Moore 4 pass from Unitas (kick failed)
Det — Junker 14 pass from Rote (Layne kick)
Det — Cassady 26 pass from Layne (Layne kick)
Det — Johnson 1 run (Layne kick)
Det — Cassady 29 pass from Layne (Layne kick)

FROM 24 POINTS BEHIND TO WIN: October 25, 1959, at Minneapolis

Philadelphia	0	0	21	7	— 28
Chicago Cardinals	7	10	7	0	— 24

Cardinals— Crow 10 pass from Roach (Conrad kick)
Cardinals— J. Hill 77 blocked field goal return (Conrad kick)
Cardinals— FG Conrad 15
Cardinals— Lane 37 interception return (Conrad kick)
Phil — Barnes 1 run (Walston kick)
Phil — McDonald 29 pass from Van Brocklin (Walston kick)
Phil — Barnes 2 run (Walston kick)
Phil — McDonald 22 pass from Van Brocklin (Walston kick)

FROM 24 POINTS BEHIND TO WIN: October 23, 1960, at Denver

Boston	10	7	7	0	— 24
Denver	0	0	14	17	— 31

Bos — FG Cappelletti 12
Bos — Colclough 10 pass from Songin (Cappelletti kick)
Bos — Wells 6 pass from Songin (Cappelletti kick)
Bos — Miller 47 pass from Songin (Cappelletti kick)
Den — Carmichael 21 pass from Tripucka (Mingo kick)
Den — Jessup 19 pass from Tripucka (Mingo kick)
Den — Carmichael 35 lateral from Taylor, pass from Tripucka (Mingo kick)
Den — Taylor 8 pass from Tripucka (Mingo kick)
Den — FG Mingo 9

FROM 24 POINTS BEHIND TO WIN: December 15, 1974, at Miami

New England	21	3	0	3	— 27
Miami	0	17	7	10	— 34

NE — Hannah recovered fumble in end zone (J. Smith kick)
NE — Sanders 23 interception return (J. Smith kick)
NE — Herron 4 pass from Plunkett (J. Smith kick)
NE — FG J. Smith 46
Mia — Nottingham 1 run (Yepremian kick)
Mia — Baker 37 pass from Morrall (Yepremian kick)
Mia — FG Yepremian 28
Mia — Baker 46 pass from Morrall (Yepremian kick)
NE — FG J. Smith 34
Mia — Nottingham 2 run (Yepremian kick)
Mia — FG Yepremian 40

FROM 24 POINTS BEHIND TO WIN: December 4, 1977, at Minnesota

San Francisco	0	10	14	3	— 27
Minnesota	0	0	7	21	— 28

SF — Delvin Williams 2 run (Wersching kick)
SF — FG Wersching 31
SF — Dave Williams 80 kickoff return (Wersching kick)
SF — Delvin Williams 5 run (Wersching kick)
Minn — McClanahan 15 pass from Lee (Cox kick)
Minn — Rashad 8 pass from Kramer (Cox kick)
Minn — Tucker 9 pass from Kramer (Cox kick)
SF — FG Wersching 31
Minn — S. White 69 pass from Kramer (Cox kick)

FROM 24 POINTS BEHIND TO WIN: September 23, 1979, at Denver

Seattle	10	10	14	0	— 34
Denver	0	10	21	6	— 37

Sea — FG Herrera 28
Sea — Doornink 5 run (Herrera kick)
Den — FG Turner 27

Sea — Doornink 5 run (Herrera kick)
Den — Armstrong 2 run (Turner kick)
Sea — FG Herrera 22
Sea — McCullum 13 pass from Zorn (Herrera kick)
Sea — Smith 1 run (Herrera kick)
Den — Studdard 2 pass from Morton (Turner kick)
Den — Moses 11 pass from Morton (Turner kick)
Den — Upchurch 35 pass from Morton (Turner kick)
Den — Lytle 1 run (kick failed)

FROM 24 POINTS BEHIND TO WIN:
September 23, 1979, at Cincinnati

Houston	0	10	17	0	3	—	30
Cincinnati	14	10	0	3	0	—	27

Cin — Johnson 1 run (Bahr kick)
Cin — Alexander 2 run (Bahr kick)
Cin — Johnson 1 run (Bahr kick)
Cin — FG Bahr 52
Hou — Burrough 35 pass from Pastorini (Fritsch kick)
Hou — FG Fritsch 33
Hou — Campbell 8 run (Fritsch kick)
Hou — Caster 22 pass from Pastorini (Fritsch kick)
Hou — FG Fritsch 47
Cin — FG Bahr 55
Hou — FG Fritsch 29

FROM 24 POINTS BEHIND TO WIN:
November 22, 1982, at Los Angeles

San Diego	10	14	0	0	—	24
L.A. Raiders	0	7	14	7	—	28

SD — FG Benirschke 19
SD — Scales 29 pass from Fouts (Benirschke kick)
SD — Muncie 2 run (Benirschke kick)
SD — Muncie 1 run (Benirschke kick)
Raiders — Christensen 1 pass from Plunkett (Bahr kick)
Raiders — Allen 3 run (Bahr kick)
Raiders — Allen 6 run (Bahr kick)
Raiders — Hawkins 1 run (Bahr kick)

FROM 24 POINTS BEHIND TO WIN:
September 26, 1988, at Denver

L.A. Raiders	0	0	14	13	3	—	30
Denver	7	17	0	3	0	—	27

Den — Dorsett 1 run (Karlis kick)
Den — Dorsett 1 run (Karlis kick)
Den — Sewell 7 pass from Elway (Karlis kick)
Den — FG Karlis 39
Raiders — Smith 40 pass from Schroeder (Bahr kick)
Raiders — Smith 42 pass from Schroeder (Bahr kick)
Raiders — FG Bahr 28
Raiders — Allen 4 run (Bahr kick)
Den — FG Karlis 25
Raiders — FG Bahr 44
Raiders — FG Bahr 35

FROM 24 POINTS BEHIND TO WIN:
December 6, 1992, at Tampa

L.A. Rams	0	3	21	7	—	31
Tampa Bay	6	21	0	0	—	27

TB — FG Murray 34
TB — FG Murray 47
TB — Armstrong 81 pass from Testaverde (Murray kick)
TB — Jones 26 fumble recovery (Murray kick)
Rams— FG Zendejas 18
TB — Carrier 10 pass from Testaverde (Murray kick)
Rams— Anderson 40 pass from Everett (Zendejas kick)
Rams— Chadwick 27 pass from Everett (Zendejas kick)
Rams— Lang 1 run (Zendejas kick)
Rams— Carter 8 pass from Everett (Zendejas kick)

POSTSEASON GAMES

FROM 32 POINTS BEHIND TO WIN:
AFC First-Round Playoff Game
January 3, 1993, at Buffalo

Houston	7	21	7	3	0	—	38
Buffalo	3	0	28	7	3	—	41

Hou — Jeffires 3 pass from Moon (Del Greco kick)
Buff — FG Christie 36
Hou — Slaughter 7 pass from Moon (Del Greco kick)
Hou — Duncan 26 pass from Moon (Del Greco kick)
Hou — Jeffires 27 pass from Moon (Del Greco kick)
Hou — McDowell 58 interception return (Del Greco kick)
Buff — Davis 1 run (Christie kick)
Buff — Beebe 38 pass from Reich (Christie kick)
Buff — Reed 26 pass from Reich (Christie kick)
Buff — Reed 18 pass from Reich (Christie kick)
Buff — Reed 17 pass from Reich (Christie kick)
Hou — FG Del Greco 26
Buff — FG Christie 32

FROM 24 POINTS BEHIND TO WIN:
NFC First-Round Playoff Game
January 5, 2003, at San Francisco

N.Y. Giants	7	21	10	0	—	38
San Francisco	7	7	8	17	—	39

SF — Owens 76 pass from Garcia (Chandler kick)
NYG — Toomer 12 pass from Collins (Bryant kick)
NYG — Shockey 2 pass from Collins (Bryant kick)
SF — Barlow 1 run (Chandler kick)
NYG — Toomer 8 pass from Collins (Bryant kick)
NYG — Toomer 24 pass from Collins (Bryant kick)
NYG — Barber 6 run (Bryant kick)
NYG — FG Bryant 21
SF — Owens 26 pass from Garcia (Owens from Garcia)
SF — Garcia 14 run (Owens from Garcia)
SF — Garcia 14 run (Owens from Garcia)
SF — FG Chandler 25
SF — Streets 13 pass from Garcia (2-pt attempt failed)

FROM 20 POINTS BEHIND TO WIN:
Western Conference Playoff Game
December 22, 1957, at San Francisco

Detroit	0	7	14	10	—	31
San Francisco	14	10	3	0	—	27

SF — Owens 34 pass from Tittle (Soltau kick)
SF — McElhenny 47 pass from Tittle (Soltau kick)
Det — Junker 4 pass from Rote (Martin kick)
SF — Wilson 12 pass from Tittle (Soltau kick)
SF — FG Soltau 25
SF — FG Soltau 10
Det — Tracy 2 run (Martin kick)
Det — Tracy 58 run (Martin kick)
Det — Gedman 3 run (Martin kick)
Det — FG Martin 14

FROM 18 POINTS BEHIND TO WIN:
NFC Divisional Playoff Game
December 23, 1972, at San Francisco

Dallas	3	10	0	17	—	30
San Francisco	7	14	7	0	—	28

SF — Washington 97 kickoff return (Gossett kick)
Dall — FG Fritsch 37
SF — Schreiber 1 run (Gossett kick)
SF — Schreiber 1 run (Gossett kick)
Dall — FG Fritsch 45
Dall — Alworth 28 pass from Morton (Fritsch kick)
SF — Schreiber 1 run (Gossett kick)
Dall — FG Fritsch 27
Dall — Parks 20 pass from Staubach (Fritsch kick)
Dall — Sellers 10 pass from Staubach (Fritsch kick)

FROM 18 POINTS BEHIND TO WIN:
AFC Divisional Playoff Game
January 4, 1986, at Miami

Cleveland	7	7	7	0	—	21
Miami	3	0	14	7	—	24

Mia — FG Reveiz 51
Cle — Newsome 16 pass from Kosar (Bahr kick)
Cle — Byner 21 run (Bahr kick)
Cle — Byner 66 run (Bahr kick)
Mia — Moore 6 pass from Marino (Reveiz kick)
Mia — Davenport 31 run (Reveiz kick)
Mia — Davenport 1 run (Reveiz kick)

RECORDS FOR NFL TEAMS FOR MOST POINTS IN A GAME (REGULAR SEASON ONLY)

Note: *When the record has been achieved more than once, only the most recent game is shown; summaries are listed in alphabetical order by conference. Bold face indicates team holding record.*

BALTIMORE RAVENS
November 30, 2003, at Baltimore

	1	2	3	4	Final
San Francisco	3	3	0	0	6
Baltimore	7	17	0	20	44

TD: Balt—Terry Jones, Jamal Lewis, Ray Lewis, Marcus Robinson, Musa Smith. TD Passes: Balt—Anthony Wright 2. FG: Balt—Matt Stover 3; SF—Todd Peterson 2.

BUFFALO BILLS
September 18, 1966, at Buffalo

	1	2	3	4	Final
Miami	3	7	0	14	24
Buffalo	21	27	3	7	58

TD: Buff—Bobby Burnett 2, Butch Byrd 2, Jack Spikes 2, Bobby Crockett, Jack Kemp; Mia—Dave Kocourek, Bo Roberson, John Roderick. TD Passes: Buff—Jack Kemp, Daryle Lamonica; Mia—George Wilson 3. FG: Buff—Booth Lusteg; Mia—Gene Mingo.

CINCINNATI BENGALS
December 17, 1989, at Cincinnati

	1	2	3	4	Final
Houston	0	0	0	7	7
Cincinnati	21	10	21	9	61

TD: Cin—Eddie Brown 2, Eric Ball, James Brooks, Ira Hillary, Rodney Holman, Tim McGee, Craig Taylor; Hou—Lorenzo White. TD Passes: Cin—Boomer Esiason 4, Erik Wilhelm. FG: Cin—Jim Breech 2.

CLEVELAND BROWNS
November 7, 1954, at Cleveland

	1	2	3	4	Final
Washington	0	3	0	0	3
Cleveland	13	14	21	14	62

TD: Cle—Darrell Brewster 2, Mo Bassett, Ken Gorgal, Otto Graham, Dub Jones, Dante Lavelli, Curley Morrison. TD Passes: Cle—George Ratterman 3, Otto Graham. FG: Cle—Lou Groza 2; Wash—Vic Janowicz.

DENVER BRONCOS
October 6, 1963, at Denver

	1	2	3	4	Final
San Diego	13	7	0	14	34
Denver	3	14	9	24	50

TD: Den—Lionel Taylor 2, Goose Gonsoulin, Gene Prebola, Donnie Stone; SD—Keith Lincoln 2, Lance Alworth, Paul Lowe, Jacque MacKinnon. TD Passes: Den—John McCormick 3; SD—Tobin Rote 3, John Hadl 2. FG: Den—Gene Mingo 5.

HOUSTON TEXANS
November 9, 2003 at Cincinnati

	1	2	3	4	Final
Houston	3	14	10	0	27
Cincinnati	7	10	7	10	34

TD: Hou—Corey Bradford, Domanick Davis, Jabar Gaffney; Cin—Rudi Johnson 2, Brandon Bennett, Jeremi Johnson. TD Passes: Hou—David Carr 2; Cin—Jon Kitna. FG: Hou—Kris Brown 2; Cin—Shayne Graham 2.

INDIANAPOLIS COLTS
December 12, 1976, at Baltimore

	1	2	3	4	Final
Buffalo	3	3	7	7	20
Baltimore Colts	7	13	28	10	58

TD: Balt—Roger Carr, Raymond Chester, Glenn Doughty, Roosevelt Leaks, Derrel Luce, Lydell Mitchell, Howard Stevens; Buff—Bob Chandler, O.J. Simpson. TD Passes: Balt—Bert Jones 3; Buff—Gary Marangi. FG: Balt—Toni Linhart 3; Buff—George Jakowenko 2.

JACKSONVILLE JAGUARS
December 3, 2000, at Jacksonville

	1	2	3	4	Final
Cleveland	0	0	0	0	0
Jacksonville	3	17	21	7	48

TD: Jax—Fred Taylor 3, Keenan McCardell, Mark Brunell, Shyrone Stith. TD Passes: Jax—Mark Brunell. FG: Jax—Mike Hollis 2.

KANSAS CITY CHIEFS
September 7, 1963, at Denver

	1	2	3	4	Final
Kansas City	14	14	21	10	59
Denver	0	7	0	0	7

TD: KC—Chris Burford 2, Frank Jackson 2, Dave Grayson, Abner Haynes, Sherrill Headrick, Curtis McClinton; Den—Lionel Taylor. TD Passes: KC—Len Dawson 4, Curtis McClinton; Den—Mickey Slaughter. FG: KC—Tommy Brooker.

MIAMI DOLPHINS
November 24, 1977, at St. Louis

	1	2	3	4	Final
Miami	14	14	20	7	55
St. Louis Cardinals	7	0	0	7	14

TD: Mia—Nat Moore 3, Gary Davis, Duriel Harris, Leroy Harris, Benny Malone, Andre Tillman; StL—Ike Harris, Terry Metcalf. TD Passes: Mia—Bob Griese 6; StL—Jim Hart.

NEW ENGLAND PATRIOTS
September 9, 1979, at New England

	1	2	3	4	Final
New York Jets	3	0	0	0	3
New England	14	21	7	14	56

TD: NE—Harold Jackson 3, Stanley Morgan 2, Allan Clark, Andy Johnson, Don Westbrook. TD Passes: NE—Steve Grogan 5, Tom Owen. FG: NYJ—Pat Leahy.

NEW YORK JETS
November 17, 1985, at New York

	1	2	3	4	Final
Tampa Bay	14	7	7	0	28
New York Jets	17	24	14	7	62

TD: NYJ—Mickey Shuler 3, Johnny Hector 2, Tony Paige, Al Toon, Wesley Walker; TB—James Wilder 2, Kevin House, Calvin Magee. TD Passes: NYJ—Ken O'Brien 5; TB—Steve DeBerg 2. FG: NYJ—Pat Leahy 2.

OAKLAND RAIDERS
September 29, 2002 at Oakland

	1	2	3	4	Final
Tennessee	7	0	12	6	25
Oakland	21	10	7	14	52

TD: Oak—Tim Brown, Phillip Buchanon, Charlie Garner, Terry Kirby, Jerry Porter, Jim Rice, Rod Woodson; Tenn—Drew Bennett, Eddie George, Justin McCareins, John Simon. TD Passes: Oak—Rich Gannon 4; Tenn—Steve McNair 2. FG: Oak—Sebastian Janikowski.

PITTSBURGH STEELERS
November 30, 1952, at Pittsburgh

	1	2	3	4	Final
New York Giants	0	0	7	0	7
Pittsburgh	14	14	7	28	63

TD: Pitt—Lynn Chandnois 2, Dick Hensley 2, Jack Butler, George Hays, Ray Mathews, Ed Modzelewski, Elbie Nickel; NYG—Bill Stribling. TD Passes: Pitt—Jim Finks 4, Gary Kerkorian; NYG—Tom Landry.

SAN DIEGO CHARGERS
December 22, 1963, at San Diego

	1	2	3	4	Final
Denver	7	10	3	0	20
San Diego	10	16	10	22	58

TD: SD—Paul Lowe 2, Chuck Allen, Bobby Jackson, Dave Kocourek, Keith Lincoln, Jacque MacKinnon; Den—Billy Joe, Donnie Stone. TD Passes: SD—John Hadl, Tobin Rote; Den—Don Breaux. FG: SD—George Blair 3; Den—Gene Mingo 2.

TENNESSEE TITANS
December 9, 1990, at Houston

	1	2	3	4	Final
Cleveland	0	7	7	0	14
Houston Oilers	14	31	7	6	58

TD: Hou—Lorenzo White 4, Ernest Givins, Leonard Harris, Tony Jones, Terry Kinard; Cle—Eric Metcalf 2. TD Passes: Hou—Warren Moon 2, Cody Carlson; Cle—Bernie Kosar. FG: Hou—Teddy Garcia.

ARIZONA CARDINALS
November 13, 1949, at New York

Chicago Cardinals	7	31	14	13	— 65
New York Bulldogs	7	0	6	7	— 20

TD: Chi—Red Cochran 2, Pat Harder 2, Bill Dewell, Mel Kutner, Bob Ravensburg, Vic Schwall, Charlie Trippi; NY—Joe Golding, Frank Muehlheuser, Johnny Rauch. TD Passes: Chi—Paul Christman 3, Jim Hardy 3; NY—Bobby Layne. FG: Chi—Pat Harder.

ATLANTA FALCONS
September 16, 1973, at New Orleans

Atlanta	0	24	21	17	— 62
New Orleans	0	0	7	0	— 7

TD: Atl—Ken Burrow 2, Eddie Ray 2, Wes Chesson, Tom Hayes, Art Malone, Joe Profit; NO—Bill Butler. TD Passes: Atl—Dick Shiner 3, Bob Lee; NO—Archie Manning. FG: Atl—Nick Mike-Mayer 2.

CAROLINA PANTHERS
December 8, 2002, at Carolina

Cincinnati	7	10	14	0	— 31
Carolina	9	7	21	15	— 52

TD: Car—Steve Smith 3, Dee Brown, Muhsin Muhammad, Al Wallace, Wesley Walls; Cin—Peter Warrick 2, Jon Kitna, Takeo Spikes. TD Passes: Car—Rodney Peete 3; Cin—Jon Kitna 2. FG: Cin—Neil Rackers.

CHICAGO BEARS
December 7, 1980, at Chicago

Green Bay	0	7	0	0	— 7
Chicago	0	28	13	20	— 61

TD: Chi—Walter Payton 3, Brian Baschnagel, Robin Earl, Roland Harper, Willie McClendon, Len Walterscheid, Rickey Watts; GB—James Lofton. TD Passes: Chi—Vince Evans 3; GB—Lynn Dickey.

DALLAS COWBOYS
October 12, 1980, at Dallas

San Francisco	0	7	0	7	— 14
Dallas	14	24	14	7	— 59

TD: Dall—Drew Pearson 3, Ron Springs 2, Tony Dorsett, Billy Joe DuPree, Robert Newhouse; SF—Dwight Clark 2. TD Passes: Dall—Danny White 4; SF—Steve DeBerg 2. FG: Dall—Rafael Septien.

DETROIT LIONS
November 27, 1997, at Detroit

Chicago	14	6	0	0	— 20
Detroit	3	14	17	21	— 55

TD: Det—Herman Moore, Johnnie Morton, Ron Rivers, Barry Sanders 3, Tracy Scroggins; Chi—Raymont Harris, Ricky Proehl. TD Passes: Det—Scott Mitchell 2; Chi—Erik Kramer. FG: Det—Jason Hanson 2; Chi—Jeff Jaeger 2.

GREEN BAY PACKERS
October 7, 1945, at Milwaukee

Detroit	0	7	7	7	— 21
Green Bay	0	41	9	7	— 57

TD: GB—Don Hutson 4, Charley Brock, Irv Comp, Ted Fritsch, Clyde Goodnight; Det—Chuck Fenenbock, John Greene, Bob Westfall. TD Passes: GB—Tex McKay 4, Lou Brock, Irv Comp; Det—Dave Ryan.

MINNESOTA VIKINGS
October 18, 1970, at Minnesota

Dallas	3	3	0	7	— 13
Minnesota	14	20	17	3	— 54

TD: Minn—Clint Jones 2, Ed Sharockman 2, John Beasley, Dave Osborn; Dall—Calvin Hill. TD Pass: Minn—Gary Cuozzo. FG: Minn—Fred Cox 4; Dall—Mike Clark 2.

NEW ORLEANS SAINTS
November 21, 1976, at Seattle

New Orleans	3	17	28	3	— 51
Seattle	6	0	7	14	— 27

TD: NO—Bobby Douglass 2, Tony Galbreath, Chuck Muncie, Tom Myers, Elex Price; Sea—Sherman Smith 2, Steve Largent, Jim Zorn. TD Pass: Sea—Bill Munson. FG: NO—Rich Szaro 3.

NEW YORK GIANTS
November 26, 1972, at New York

Philadelphia	3	7	0	0	— 10
New York Giants	14	24	10	14	— 62

TD: NYG—Don Herrmann 2, Ron Johnson 2, Bob Tucker 2, Randy Johnson; Phil—Harold Jackson. TD Passes: NYG—Norm Snead 3, Randy Johnson 2; Phil—John Reaves. FG: NYG—Pete Gogolak 2; Phil—Tom Dempsey.

PHILADELPHIA EAGLES
November 6, 1934, at Philadelphia

Cincinnati Reds	0	0	0	0	— 0
Philadelphia	26	6	12	20	— 64

TD: Phil—Joe Carter 3, Swede Hanson 3, Marvin Ellstrom, Roger Kirkman, Ed Matesic, Ed Storm. TD Passes: Phil—Ed Matesic 2, Albert Weiner 2, Marvin Elstrom.

ST. LOUIS RAMS
October 22, 1950, at Los Angeles

Baltimore	13	0	7	7	— 27
Los Angeles Rams	21	14	14	21	— 70

TD: LA—Bob Boyd 2, Vitamin T. Smith 2, Tom Fears, Elroy (Crazylegs) Hirsch, Dick Hoerner, Ralph Pasquariello, Dan Towler, Bob Waterfield; Balt—Chet Mutryn 2, Adrian Burk, Billy Stone. TD Passes: LA—Norm Van Brocklin 2, Bob Waterfield 2, Glenn Davis; Balt—Adrian Burk 3.

SAN FRANCISCO 49ERS
October 18, 1992, at San Francisco

Atlanta	7	3	0	7	— 17
San Francisco	21	21	14	0	— 56

TD: SF—Jerry Rice 3, Ricky Watters 3, Brent Jones, Tom Rathman; Atl—Michael Haynes, Jason Phillips. TD Passes: SF—Steve Young 3; Atl—Chris Miller, Wade Wilson. FG: Atl—Norm Johnson.

SEATTLE SEAHAWKS
October 30, 1977, at Seattle

Buffalo	3	0	7	7	— 17
Seattle	14	28	7	7	— 56

TD: Sea—Steve Largent 2, Duke Fergerson, Al Hunter, David Sims, Sherman Smith, Don Testerman, Jim Zorn; Buff—Joe Ferguson, John Kimbrough. TD Passes: Sea—Jim Zorn 4; Buff—Joe Ferguson. FG: Buff—Carson Long.

TAMPA BAY BUCCANEERS
December 23, 2001, at Tampa Bay

New Orleans	0	0	7	14	— 21
Tampa Bay	17	13	3	15	— 48

TD: TB—Mike Alstott, Ronde Barber, Warrick Dunn, Dave Moore, Karl Williams; NO—Joe Horn 2, Eddie Williams. TD Passes: TB—Brad Johnson 3; NO—Aaron Brooks 3. FG: TB—Martin Gramatica 4.

WASHINGTON REDSKINS
November 27, 1966, at Washington

New York Giants	0	14	14	13	— 41
Washington	13	21	14	24	— 72

TD: Wash—A.D. Whitfield 3, Brig Owens 2, Charley Taylor 2, Rickie Harris, Joe Don Looney, Bobby Mitchell; NYG—Allen Jacobs, Homer Jones, Dan Lewis, Joe Morrison, Aaron Thomas, Gary Wood. TD Passes: Wash—Sonny Jurgensen 3; NYG—Gary Wood 2, Tom Kennedy. FG: Wash—Charlie Gogolak.

INSIDE THE NUMBERS

RECORDS OF NFL TEAMS SINCE 1970 AFL-NFL MERGER

AFC	W	L	T	Pct.	Division Titles	Playoff Berths	Postseason Record	Super Bowl Record
Miami	334	184	2	.645	12	21	20-19	2-3
Oakland	308	206	6	.599	12	18	22-15	3-1
Pittsburgh	307	211	2	.592	16	20	23-16	4-1
Denver	300	214	6	.583	9	15	16-13	2-4
Kansas City	262	251	7	.511	5	10	3-10	0-0
Jacksonville**	73	71	0	.507	2	4	4-4	0-0
Baltimore***	63	64	1	.496	1	3	5-2	1-0
Tennessee	253	265	2	.488	4	14	12-14	0-1
New England	251	269	0	.483	6	11	12-9	2-2
Buffalo	248	270	2	.479	7	13	12-13	0-4
Cleveland+	220	249	3	.469	6	11	4-11	0-0
Indianapolis	231	287	2	.446	7	12	8-11	1-0
Cincinnati	227	293	0	.437	5	7	5-7	0-2
N.Y. Jets	225	293	2	.435	2	8	5-8	0-0
San Diego	222	293	5	.431	5	7	6-7	0-1
Houston****	9	23	0	.281	0	0	0-0	0-0

NFC	W	L	T	Pct.	Division Titles	Playoff Berths	Postseason Record	Super Bowl Record
San Francisco	312	205	3	.603	17	21	25-16	5-0
Dallas	310	210	0	.596	15	23	31-18	5-3
Minnesota	302	216	2	.583	14	21	15-21	0-3
Washington	295	223	2	.569	6	14	19-11	3-2
St. Louis	285	231	4	.552	11	18	15-17	1-2
Green Bay	258	254	8	.504	6	11	12-10	1-1
Philadelphia	258	255	7	.503	5	14	10-14	0-1
Chicago	254	265	1	.489	7	11	7-10	1-0
N.Y. Giants	247	270	3	.478	5	10	12-8	2-1
Seattle*	205	231	0	.470	2	6	3-6	0-0
Carolina**	64	80	0	.444	2	2	4-2	0-1
Detroit	225	291	4	.436	3	9	1-9	0-0
Atlanta	214	301	5	.416	2	7	5-7	0-1
New Orleans	214	302	4	.415	2	5	1-5	0-0
Arizona	208	306	6	.405	2	4	1-4	0-0
Tampa Bay*	167	268	1	.384	4	8	6-7	1-0

**Entered NFL in 1976.*
***Entered NFL in 1995.*
****Entered NFL in 1996.*
*****Entered NFL in 2002.*
+Did not play 1996-98.
Oakland totals include L.A. Raiders, 1982-1994.
Tennessee totals include Houston, 1970-1996.
Indianapolis totals include Baltimore, 1970-1983.
St. Louis totals include L.A. Rams, 1970-1994.
Arizona totals include St. Louis, 1970-1987, and Phoenix, 1988-1993.
Tie games before 1972 are not calculated in won-lost percentage.

HOME RECORDS OF NFL TEAMS SINCE 1970 AFL-NFL MERGER

AFC	W	L	T	Pct.
Miami	191	67	1	.739
Denver	184	73	4	.714
Pittsburgh	185	74	1	.713
Oakland	171	87	2	.662
Jacksonville**	45	27	0	.625
Kansas City	159	97	3	.621
Baltimore***	38	25	1	.602
New England	147	113	0	.565
Tennessee	146	113	1	.564
Buffalo	146	114	1	.561
Cincinnati	141	119	0	.542
Cleveland+	120	113	2	.515
San Diego	128	129	2	.498
Indianapolis	122	136	2	.473
N.Y. Jets	119	139	1	.461
Houston****	5	11	0	.313

NFC	W	L	T	Pct.
Dallas	179	81	0	.688
Minnesota	177	83	1	.680
Washington	168	89	2	.653
San Francisco	167	91	2	.647
Green Bay	158	97	5	.618
St. Louis	157	101	2	.609
Chicago	152	107	1	.587
Detroit	147	112	1	.567
Philadelphia	145	113	3	.562
Seattle*	122	97	0	.557
N.Y. Giants	138	122	1	.531
Carolina**	37	35	0	.514
Atlanta	129	131	1	.496
Arizona	122	134	3	.477
Tampa Bay*	103	114	1	.475
New Orleans	117	142	1	.452

**Entered NFL in 1976.*
***Entered NFL in 1995.*
****Entered NFL in 1996.*
*****Entered NFL in 2002.*
+Did not play 1996-98.
Oakland totals include L.A. Raiders, 1982-1994.
Tennessee totals include Houston, 1970-1996.
Indianapolis totals include Baltimore, 1970-1983.
St. Louis totals include L.A. Rams, 1970-1994.
Arizona totals include St. Louis, 1970-1987, and Phoenix, 1988-1993.
Tie games before 1972 are not calculated in won-lost percentage.

ROAD RECORDS OF NFL TEAMS SINCE 1970 AFL-NFL MERGER

AFC	W	L	T	Pct.
Miami	143	117	1	.550
Oakland	137	119	4	.535
Pittsburgh	122	137	1	.471
Denver	116	141	2	.452
Cleveland+	100	136	1	.424
Indianapolis	109	151	0	.419
Tennessee	107	152	1	.413
N.Y. Jets	106	154	1	.408
Kansas City	103	154	4	.402
New England	104	156	0	.400
Buffalo	102	156	1	.395
Baltimore***	25	39	0	.391
Jacksonville**	28	44	0	.389
San Diego	94	164	3	.365
Cincinnati	86	174	0	.331
Houston****	4	12	0	.250

NFC	W	L	T	Pct.
San Francisco	145	114	1	.560
Dallas	131	129	0	.504
St. Louis	128	130	2	.496
Washington	127	134	0	.487
Minnesota	125	133	1	.485
Philadelphia	113	142	4	.444
N.Y. Giants	109	148	2	.425
Chicago	102	158	0	.392
Green Bay	100	157	3	.390
Seattle*	83	134	0	.382
New Orleans	97	160	3	.378
Carolina**	27	45	0	.375
Arizona	86	172	3	.335
Atlanta	85	170	4	.334
Detroit	78	179	3	.305
Tampa Bay*	64	154	0	.294

**Entered NFL in 1976.*
***Entered NFL in 1995.*
****Entered NFL in 1996.*
*****Entered NFL in 2002.*
+Did not play 1996-98.
Oakland totals include L.A. Raiders, 1982-1994.
Tennessee totals include Houston, 1970-1996.
Indianapolis totals include Baltimore, 1970-1983.
St. Louis totals include L.A. Rams, 1970-1994.
Arizona totals include St. Louis, 1970-1987, and Phoenix, 1988-1993.
Tie games before 1972 are not calculated in won-lost percentage.

RECORDS OF TEAMS ON OPENING DAY, 1933-2003

AFC	W	L	T	Pct.	Longest W Strk.	Longest L Strk.	Current Streak
Houston	2	0	0	1.000	2	0	W-2
Jacksonville	6	3	0	.667	6	2	L-2
Denver	28	15	1	.651	4	4	W-3
Miami	22	15	1	.595	11	5	L-1
Kansas City	25	19	0	.568	7	4	W-2
San Diego	25	19	0	.568	6	6	L-1
Oakland	24	20	0	.545	5	5	L-1
Tennessee	23	21	0	.523	4	3	W-2
Cleveland	26	25	0	.510	5	6	L-6
Indianapolis	30	29	1	.508	8	8	W-5
Pittsburgh	33	32	4	.508	4	3	W-1
New England	20	24	0	.455	6	3	L-1
Cincinnati	16	20	0	.444	4	4	L-2
Buffalo	18	26	0	.409	6	5	W-1
N.Y. Jets	18	26	0	.409	3	5	L-1
Baltimore	3	5	0	.375	2	3	L-2

NFC	W	L	T	Pct.	Longest W Strk.	Longest L Strk.	Current Streak
Dallas	30	13	1	.698	17	4	L-4
N.Y. Giants	40	27	4	.597	4	3	W-1
Chicago	40	30	1	.571	9	6	L-1
Minnesota	24	18	1	.571	5	3	W-1
St. Louis	36	30	0	.545	5	6	L-2
Green Bay	37	31	3	.544	5	6	L-1
San Francisco	28	25	1	.528	5	3	W-3
Detroit	36	33	2	.522	7	4	W-1
Washington	34	33	4	.507	6	5	W-2
Atlanta	19	19	0	500	5	3	W-1
Carolina	4	5	0	.444	3	4	W-3
Tampa Bay	12	16	0	.429	3	5	W-1
Arizona	27	42	1	.391	6	7	L-4
Philadelphia	27	42	1	.391	5	9	L-3
New Orleans	11	26	0	.297	2	6	L-1
Seattle	8	20	0	.286	3	8	W-1

Kansas City totals include Dallas Texans, 1960-62.
Oakland totals include L.A. Raiders, 1982-1994.
San Diego totals include L.A. Chargers, 1960.
Indianapolis totals include Baltimore, 1953-1983.
Tennessee totals include Houston, 1960-1996.
New England totals include Boston, 1960-1970.
St. Louis totals include Cleveland, 1937-1942 and 1944-45, and L.A. Rams, 1946-1994.
Detroit totals include Portsmouth, 1933.
Arizona totals include Chi. Cardinals, 1933-1959, St. Louis, 1960-1987, and Phoenix, 1988-1993.
NOTE: All tied games occurred prior to 1972, when calculation of ties in percentages as half-win, half-loss was begun.

RECORDS OF NFL TEAMS, 1994-2003

AFC	W	L	T	Pct.	Division Titles	Playoff Berths	Postseason Record	Super Bowl Record
Denver	98	62	0	.613	2	5	7-3	2-0
Miami	96	64	0	.600	2	7	4-7	0-0
Pittsburgh	95	64	1	.597	6	6	7-6	0-1
Kansas City	94	66	0	.588	3	4	0-4	0-0
New England	93	67	0	.581	4	6	9-4	2-1
Tennessee	89	71	0	.556	2	4	5-4	0-1
Indianapolis	83	77	0	.519	2	6	4-6	0-0
Jacksonville	73	71	0	.507	2	4	4-4	0-0
Oakland	81	79	0	.506	3	3	4-3	0-1
Baltimore	63	64	1	.496	1	3	5-2	1-0
Buffalo	79	81	0	.494	1	4	1-4	0-0
N.Y. Jets	73	87	0	.456	2	3	2-3	0-0
San Diego	63	97	0	.394	1	2	2-2	0-1
Cleveland	42	70	0	.375	0	2	1-2	0-0
Cincinnati	52	108	0	.325	0	0	0-0	0-0
Houston	9	23	0	.281	0	0	0-0	0-0

Oakland totals include L.A. Raiders, 1994
Tennessee totals include Houston, 1994-96

NFC	W	L	T	Pct.	Division Titles	Playoff Berths	Postseason Record	Super Bowl Record
Green Bay	108	52	0	.675	5	8	10-7	1-1
San Francisco	100	60	0	.625	4	7	7-6	1-0
Minnesota	92	68	0	.575	3	6	4-6	0-0
Philadelphia	87	72	1	.547	3	6	6-6	0-0
Tampa Bay	86	74	0	.538	2	5	5-4	1-0
Dallas	83	77	0	.519	4	6	5-5	1-0
St. Louis	82	78	0	.513	3	4	5-3	1-1
N.Y. Giants	78	81	1	.491	2	3	2-3	0-1
Seattle	78	82	0	.488	1	2	0-2	0-0
Carolina	64	80	0	.444	2	2	4-2	0-1
Atlanta	70	89	1	.441	1	3	3-3	0-1
Washington	70	89	1	.441	1	1	1-1	0-0
Chicago	68	92	0	.425	1	2	1-2	0-0
New Orleans	66	94	0	.413	1	1	1-1	0-0
Detroit	65	95	0	.406	0	4	0-4	0-0
Arizona	57	103	0	.356	0	1	1-1	0-0

St. Louis totals include L.A. Rams, 1994
Seattle was in the AFC from 1994-2001

HOME RECORDS, 1994-2003

AFC	W-L-T	Pct.
Denver	60-20-0	.750
Kansas City	59-21-0	.738
Miami	56-24-0	.700
Pittsburgh	54-25-1	.681
New England	53-27-0	.663
Jacksonville	45-27-0	.625
Baltimore	38-25-1	.602
Buffalo	48-32-0	.600
Indianapolis	47-33-0	.588
Tennessee	47-33-0	.588
Oakland	45-35-0	.563
N.Y. Jets	39-41-0	.488
San Diego	37-43-0	.463
Cincinnati	33-47-0	.413
Cleveland	20-36-0	.357
Houston	5-11-0	.313

NFC	W-L-T	Pct.
Green Bay	68-12-0	.850
San Francisco	60-20-0	.750
Minnesota	58-22-0	.725
Dallas	53-27-0	.663
Tampa Bay	52-28-0	.650
Philadelphia	50-30-0	.625
St. Louis	48-32-0	.600
Detroit	47-33-0	.588
Seattle	47-33-0	.588
Chicago	43-37-0	.538
Atlanta	42-38-0	.525
Carolina	37-35-0	.514
N.Y. Giants	41-39-0	.513
Washington	40-39-1	.506
Arizona	38-42-0	.475
New Orleans	34-46-0	.425

Oakland totals include L.A. Raiders, 1994
St. Louis totals include L.A. Rams, 1994
Tennessee totals include Houston, 1994-96
Seattle was in the AFC from 1994-2001

ROAD RECORDS, 1994-2003

AFC	W-L-T	Pct.
Tennessee	42-38-0	.525
Pittsburgh	41-39-0	.513
Miami	40-40-0	.500
New England	40-40-0	.500
Denver	38-42-0	.475
Indianapolis	36-44-0	.450
Oakland	36-44-0	.450
Kansas City	35-45-0	.438
N.Y. Jets	34-46-0	.425
Cleveland	22-34-0	.393
Baltimore	25-39-0	.391
Jacksonville	28-44-0	.389
Buffalo	31-49-0	.388
San Diego	26-54-0	.325
Houston	4-12-0	.250
Cincinnati	19-61-0	.238

NFC	W-L-T	Pct.
Green Bay	40-40-0	.500
San Francisco	40-40-0	.500
N.Y. Giants	37-42-1	.469
Philadelphia	37-42-1	.469
Minnesota	34-46-0	.425
St. Louis	34-46-0	.425
Tampa Bay	34-46-0	.425
New Orleans	32-48-0	.400
Seattle	31-49-0	.388
Carolina	27-45-0	.375
Dallas	30-50-0	.375
Washington	30-50-0	.375
Atlanta	28-51-1	.356
Chicago	25-55-0	.313
Arizona	19-61-0	.238
Detroit	18-62-0	.225

Oakland totals include L.A. Raiders, 1994
St. Louis totals include L.A. Rams, 1994
Tennessee totals include Houston, 1994-96
Seattle was in the AFC from 1994-2001

RECORDS BY MONTHS, 1994-2003

AFC	Sept. W-L-T	Oct. W-L-T	Nov. W-L-T	Dec. W-L-T	Total W-L-T	Pct.
Denver	26-14-0	23-15-0	29-11-0	20-22-0	98-62-0	.613
Miami	26-8-0	25-15-0	24-19-0	21-22-0	96-64-0	.600
Pittsburgh	18-17-0	28-11-0	25-17-1	24-19-0	95-64-1	.597
Kansas City	28-12-0	22-15-0	21-21-0	23-18-0	94-66-0	.588
New England	20-16-0	19-22-0	27-15-0	27-14-0	93-67-0	.581
Tennessee	16-20-0	24-15-0	22-19-0	27-17-0	89-71-0	.556
Indianapolis	18-17-0	21-19-0	18-24-0	26-17-0	83-77-0	.519
Jacksonville	17-17-0	14-21-0	21-15-0	21-18-0	73-71-0	.507
Oakland	21-18-0	23-13-0	19-23-0	18-25-0	81-79-0	.506
Baltimore	16-14-0	11-19-0	17-17-1	19-14-0	63-64-1	.496
Buffalo	18-17-0	24-18-0	20-21-0	17-25-0	79-81-0	.494
N.Y. Jets	13-25-0	18-21-0	24-15-0	18-26-0	73-87-0	.456
San Diego	23-16-0	15-22-0	11-31-0	14-28-0	63-97-0	.394
Cleveland	13-13-0	11-18-0	10-17-0	8-22-0	42-70-0	.375
Cincinnati	8-29-0	10-29-0	16-26-0	18-24-0	52-108-0	.325
Houston	3-5-0	1-5-0	4-5-0	1-8-0	9-23-0	.281

Oakland totals include L.A. Raiders, 1994
Tennessee totals include Houston, 1994-96
September totals include August; December totals include January

NFC	Sept. W-L-T	Oct. W-L-T	Nov. W-L-T	Dec. W-L-T	Total W-L-T	Pct.
Green Bay	28-12-0	19-14-0	25-18-0	36-8-0	108-52-0	.675
San Francisco	23-13-0	24-16-0	27-14-0	26-17-0	100-60-0	.625
Minnesota	25-14-0	24-13-0	21-20-0	22-21-0	92-68-0	.575
Philadelphia	15-22-0	26-13-0	25-18-1	21-19-0	87-72-1	.547
Tampa Bay	20-18-0	16-22-0	24-17-0	26-17-0	86-74-0	.538
Dallas	20-16-0	24-15-0	23-21-0	16-25-0	83-77-0	.519
St. Louis	21-17-0	19-18-0	18-24-0	24-19-0	82-78-0	.513
N.Y. Giants	20-18-0	18-21-0	15-26-1	25-16-0	78-81-1	.491
Seattle	19-19-0	14-22-0	23-20-0	22-21-0	78-82-0	.488
Carolina	14-17-0	13-24-0	16-22-0	21-17-0	64-80-0	.444
Atlanta	13-24-0	15-24-0	22-19-1	20-22-0	70-89-1	.441
Washington	17-21-0	18-22-0	15-25-1	20-21-0	70-89-1	.441
Chicago	10-28-0	20-18-0	19-23-0	19-23-0	68-92-0	.425
New Orleans	12-25-0	20-20-0	17-23-0	17-26-0	66-94-0	.413
Detroit	17-22-0	13-22-0	21-25-0	14-26-0	65-95-0	.406
Arizona	11-25-0	14-24-0	18-26-0	14-28-0	57-103-0	.356

St. Louis totals include L.A. Rams, 1994
Seattle was in the AFC from 1994-2001
September totals include August; December totals include January

TAKEAWAYS/GIVEAWAYS, 1994-2003

AFC	Takeaways Int.	Fum.	Total	Giveaways Int.	Fum.	Total	Net.Diff.
Kansas City	175	158	333	145	94	239	94
New England	198	127	325	168	113	281	44
Pittsburgh	178	142	320	167	113	280	40
Jacksonville	125	123	248	122	96	218	30
Miami	202	122	324	168	130	298	26
Denver	162	127	289	156	109	265	24
N.Y. Jets	175	130	305	178	106	284	21
Tennessee	158	140	298	143	138	281	17
Oakland	164	127	291	149	132	281	10
Baltimore	158	95	253	143	116	259	-6
Houston	24	19	43	33	23	56	-13
Cleveland	120	73	193	136	86	222	-29
Indianapolis	128	120	248	165	120	285	-37
Cincinnati	139	110	249	169	134	303	-54
Buffalo	139	104	243	176	131	307	-64
San Diego	171	104	275	215	125	340	-65

Oakland totals include L.A. Raiders, 1994
Tennessee totals include Houston, 1994-96

NFC	Takeaways Int.	Fum.	Total	Giveaways Int.	Fum.	Total	Net.Diff.
San Francisco	207	109	316	135	103	238	78
Green Bay	206	122	328	172	117	289	39
Tampa Bay	190	124	314	159	119	278	36
Philadelphia	171	150	321	154	136	290	31
N.Y. Giants	173	125	298	162	118	280	18
Seattle	182	126	308	169	135	304	4
Atlanta	167	134	301	182	119	301	0
Dallas	162	110	272	149	124	273	-1
Washington	178	121	299	178	122	300	-1
Detroit	156	115	271	183	95	278	-7
Minnesota	168	126	294	185	124	309	-15
Carolina	162	130	292	172	143	315	-23
New Orleans	171	138	309	191	149	340	-31
Chicago	141	134	275	171	137	308	-33
St. Louis	208	116	324	207	164	371	-47
Arizona	162	119	281	218	149	367	-86

St. Louis totals include L.A. Rams, 1994
Seattle was in the AFC from 1994-2001

BEST TAKEAWAY/GIVEAWAY DIFFERENTIAL, SEASON

+43 Washington, 1983
+26 Kansas City, 1990
+25 N.Y. Giants, 1997

HIGH AND LOW SINGLE-GAME YARDAGE TOTALS, 1994-2003

Most Total Yards, Game

645 Pittsburgh vs. Atlanta, Nov. 10, 2002 (OT)
615 Arizona at Washington, Nov. 10, 1996 (OT)
614 St. Louis vs. San Diego, Oct. 1, 2000
591 Seattle at San Diego, Dec. 29, 2002 (OT)
579 Buffalo at Seattle, Dec. 23, 2000

Fewest Total Yards, Game

40 Cleveland vs. Pittsburgh, Sept. 12, 1999
47 Houston at Pittsburgh, Dec. 8, 2002
53 Cleveland at Jacksonville, Dec. 3, 2000
89 Seattle at Kansas City, Dec. 24, 1995
93 Oakland at Kansas City, Dec. 7, 1997

Most Yards Rushing, Game

407 Cincinnati vs. Denver, Oct. 22, 2000
343 Baltimore vs. Cleveland, Sept. 14, 2003
337 St. Louis vs. Carolina, Nov. 11, 2001
328 San Francisco vs. Detroit, Dec. 14, 1998
319 Seattle vs. Oakland, Nov. 11, 2001

Fewest Yards Rushing, Game

4 Buffalo at Tennessee, Nov. 23, 1997
Cincinnati at Baltimore, Sept. 24, 2000
8 Oakland vs. Kansas City, Dec. 3, 1995
Dallas at New Orleans, Dec. 6, 1998
9 Cleveland vs. Pittsburgh, Sept. 12, 1999
St. Louis at San Francisco, Nov. 2, 2003

Most Yards Passing, Game

507 Arizona at Washington, Nov. 10, 1996 (OT)
474 Kansas City at Oakland, Nov. 5, 2000
473 N.Y. Jets at Baltimore, Dec. 24, 2000
463 Pittsburgh vs. Atlanta, Nov. 10, 2002 (OT)
456 Miami vs. New England, Sept. 4, 1994

Fewest Yards Passing, Game

-19 San Diego at Kansas City, Sept. 20, 1998
-9 Cleveland at Jacksonville, Dec. 3, 2000
0 Oakland at San Diego, Dec. 28, 2003
9 Dallas at Tennessee, Dec. 25, 2000
10 Houston at Pittsburgh, Dec. 8, 2002

NFL INDIVIDUAL LEADERS, 1994-2003

Points	
Jason Elam	1,194
Gary Anderson	1,107
Matt Stover	1,107
Morten Andersen	1,057
Jason Hanson	1,013

Touchdowns	
Marshall Faulk	131
Emmitt Smith	113
Cris Carter	88
Marvin Harrison	83
Terrell Owens	83

Field Goals	
Matt Stover	268
Jason Elam	262
John Carney	246
Gary Anderson	236
Two tied	229

Rushes	
Curtis Martin	2,927
Emmitt Smith	2,880
Jerome Bettis	2,825
Eddie George	2,733
Marshall Faulk	2,576

Rushing Yards	
Emmitt Smith	11,719
Curtis Martin	11,669
Marshall Faulk	11,213
Jerome Bettis	10,924
Eddie George	10,009

Rushing TDs	
Emmitt Smith	105
Marshall Faulk	97
Curtis Martin	73
Priest Holmes	66
Eddie George	64

Pass Attempts	
Brett Favre	5,466
Drew Bledsoe	5,170
Kerry Collins	4,004
Mark Brunell	3,643
Vinny Testaverde	3,535

Completions	
Brett Favre	3,340
Drew Bledsoe	2,979
Kerry Collins	2,235
Mark Brunell	2,196
Peyton Manning	2,128

Passing Yards	
Brett Favre	39,116
Drew Bledsoe	34,382
Kerry Collins	26,383
Mark Brunell	25,793
Peyton Manning	24,885

TD Passes	
Brett Favre	309
Drew Bledsoe	186
Peyton Manning	167
Vinny Testaverde	160
Mark Brunell	144

Receptions	
Tim Brown	843
Jerry Rice	811
Cris Carter	774
Marvin Harrison	759
Jimmy Smith	718

Reception Yards	
Tim Brown	11,309
Jerry Rice	10,690
Isaac Bruce	10,461
Jimmy Smith	10,092
Marvin Harrison	10,072

Receiving TDs	
Cris Carter	88
Marvin Harrison	83
Terrell Owens	81
Randy Moss	77
Jerry Rice	76

Interceptions	
Aeneas Williams	44
Rod Woodson	43
Terrell Buckley	42
Ray Buchanan	42
Ashley Ambrose	39

Sacks	
Michael Strahan	113.0
John Randle	103.0
Bruce Smith	94.0
Simeon Rice	93.0
Robert Porcher	86.0

NFL GAMES IN WHICH A TEAM HAS SCORED 60 OR MORE POINTS

(Home team in capitals)

Regular Season

WASHINGTON 72, New York Giants 41	November 27, 1966
LOS ANGELES RAMS 70, Baltimore 27	October 22, 1950
Chicago Cardinals 65, NEW YORK BULLDOGS 20	November 13, 1949
LOS ANGELES RAMS 65, Detroit 24	October 29, 1950
PHILADELPHIA 64, Cincinnati 0	November 6, 1934
CHICAGO CARDINALS 63, New York Giants 35	October 17, 1948
AKRON 62, Oorang 0	October 29, 1922
PITTSBURGH 62, New York Giants 7	November 30, 1952
CLEVELAND 62, New York Giants 14	December 6, 1953
CLEVELAND 62, Washington 3	November 7, 1954
NEW YORK GIANTS 62, Philadelphia 10	November 26, 1972
Atlanta 62, NEW ORLEANS 7	September 16, 1973
NEW YORK JETS 62, Tampa Bay 28	November 17, 1985
CHICAGO 61, San Francisco 20	December 12, 1965
Cincinnati 61, HOUSTON 17	December 17, 1972
CHICAGO 61, Green Bay 7	December 7, 1980
CINCINNATI 61, Houston 7	December 17, 1989
ROCK ISLAND 60, Evansville 0	October 15, 1922
CHICAGO CARDINALS 60, Rochester 0	October 7, 1923

Postseason

Chicago Bears 73, WASHINGTON 0	December 8, 1940
JACKSONVILLE 62, Miami 7	January 15, 2000

YOUNGEST AND OLDEST PLAYERS IN NFL IN 2003

10 Youngest Players	Birthdate	Games	Starts	Position
Terrell Suggs, Baltimore	10/11/1982	16	1	LB
Shurron Pierson, Oakland	5/31/1982	6	0	DE
Musa Smith, Baltimore	5/31/1982	11	0	RB
Jason Witten, Dallas	5/6/1982	15	7	TE
Solomon Bates, Seattle	4/18/1982	7	0	LB
Kwame Harris, San Francisco	3/15/1982	14	5	T
Tony Hollings, Houston	12/1/1981	14	1	RB
Teyo Johnson, Oakland	11/29/1981	16	5	TE
Alonzo Ephraim, Philadelphia	11/8/1981	16	0	C
Ian Scott, Chicago	11/8/1981	6	0	DT

10 Oldest Players	Birthdate	Games	Starts	Position
Gary Anderson, Tennessee	7/16/1959	15	0	K
Morten Andersen, Kansas City	8/19/1960	16	0	K
Sean Landeta, St. Louis	1/6/1962	16	0	P
Jerry Rice, Oakland	10/13/1962	16	15	WR
Doug Flutie, San Diego	10/23/1962	7	5	QB
Ray Brown, Detroit	12/12/1962	16	16	G
Bruce Smith, Washington	6/18/1963	16	8	DE
Vinny Testaverde, N.Y. Jets	11/13/1963	7	7	QB
John Carney, New Orleans	4/20/1964	16	0	K
Bryan Barker, Washington	6/28/1964	16	0	P

YOUNGEST AND OLDEST REGULAR STARTERS BY POSITION IN 2003

Minimum: 8 Games Started

	Youngest		Oldest	
QB	6/17/1981	Kyle Boller, Balt.	9/13/1968	Brad Johnson, TB
RB	9/1/1981	Clinton Portis, Den.	3/7/1969	Sam Gash, Buff.
WR	8/19/1981	Nate Burleson, Minn.	10/13/1962	Jerry Rice, Oak.
TE	10/10/1980	Casey Fitzsimmons, Det.	6/26/1968	Shannon Sharpe, Den.
T	4/26/1981	Wade Smith, Mia.	4/18/1970	Willie Roaf, KC
G	9/15/1980	David Diehl, NYG	12/12/1962	Ray Brown, Det.
C	4/6/1981	Jeff Faine, Cle.	11/21/1966	Jerry Fontenot, NO
DE	10/28/1980	Calvin Pace, Ariz.	6/18/1963	Bruce Smith, Wash.
DT	10/16/1981	Dewayne Robertson, NYJ	12/12/1967	John Randle, Sea.
LB	7/15/1981	Pisa Tinoisamoa, St.L.	3/5/1968	Roman Phifer, NE
CB	4/8/1981	Lito Sheppard, Phil.	10/22/1965	Otis Smith, NE
S	3/24/1981	Mike Doss, Ind.	3/10/1965	Rod Woodson, Oak.

OLDEST INDIVIDUAL SINGLE-SEASON OR SINGLE-GAME RECORDS IN NFL RECORD & FACT BOOK

Most Points, Game—40, Ernie Nevers, Chi. Cardinals vs. Chi. Bears, Nov. 28, 1929 (6-td, 4-pat)

Most Touchdowns Rushing, Game—6, Ernie Nevers, Chi. Cardinals vs. Chi. Bears, Nov. 28, 1929

Highest Rushing Average Gain, Season (Qualifiers)—8.44, Beattie Feathers, Chi. Bears, 1934 (119-1,004)

Highest Punting Average, Season (Qualifiers)—51.40, Sammy Baugh, Washington, 1940 (35-1,799)

Highest Punting Average, Rookie, Season (Qualifiers)—45.92, Frank Sinkwich, Detroit, 1943 (12-551)

Highest Punting Average, Game (minimum: 4 punts)—61.75, Bob Cifers, Detroit vs. Chi. Bears, Nov. 24, 1946 (4-247)

Highest Average Gain, Pass Receptions, Season (minimum: 24 receptions)—32.58, Don Currivan, Boston, 1947 (24-782)

Highest Average Gain, Passing, Game (minimum: 20 passes)—18.58, Sammy Baugh, Washington vs. Boston, Oct. 31, 1948 (24-446)

Most Touchdowns, Fumble Recoveries, Game—2, Fred (Dippy) Evans, Chi. Bears vs. Washington, Nov. 28, 1948

Most Yards Gained, Intercepted Passes, Rookie, Season—301, Don Doll, Detroit, 1949

Most Passes Had Intercepted, Game—8, Jim Hardy, Chi. Cardinals vs. Philadelphia, Sept. 24, 1950

Highest Kickoff Return Average, Game (minimum: 3 returns)—73.50, Wally Triplett, Detroit vs. Los Angeles, Oct. 29, 1950 (4-294)

Highest Punt Return Average, Season (Qualifiers)—23.00, Herb Rich, Baltimore, 1950 (12-276)

Highest Punt Return Average, Rookie, Season (Qualifiers)—23.00, Herb Rich, Baltimore, 1950 (12-276)

Most Yards Passing, Game—554, Norm Van Brocklin, Los Angeles vs. N.Y. Yanks, Sept. 28, 1951

Most Touchdowns, Punt Returns, Rookie, Season—4, Jack Christiansen, Detroit, 1951

Most Interceptions By, Season—14, Dick (Night Train) Lane, Los Angeles, 1952

Most Interceptions By, Rookie, Season—14, Dick (Night Train) Lane, Los Angeles, 1952

Highest Average Gain, Passing, Season (Qualifiers)—11.17, Tommy O'Connell, Cleveland, 1957 (110-1,229)

Most Points, Season—176, Paul Hornung, Green Bay, 1960 (15-td, 41-pat,15-fg)

Most Yards Gained, Pass Receptions, Rookie, Season—1,473, Bill Groman, Houston, 1960

NFL INDIVIDUAL LEADERS OVER RECENT SEASONS

Points

Last 2 Seasons		Last 3 Seasons		Last 4 Seasons	
306	Priest Holmes	385	Mike Vanderjagt	506	Mike Vanderjagt
260	Mike Vanderjagt	384	Jeff Wilkins	483	David Akers
257	Jeff Wilkins	366	Priest Holmes	483	Ryan Longwell
248	Ryan Longwell	364	Jason Elam	480	Matt Stover
247	David Akers	362	David Akers	473	Jeff Wilkins

Touchdowns

Last 2 Seasons		Last 3 Seasons		Last 4 Seasons	
51	Priest Holmes	61	Priest Holmes	68	Marshall Faulk
34	Shaun Alexander	50	Shaun Alexander	63	Priest Holmes
32	LaDainian Tomlinson	42	Marshall Faulk	53	Ahman Green
31	Clinton Portis	42	LaDainian Tomlinson	52	Shaun Alexander
29	Ahman Green	40	Ahman Green	52	Terrell Owens

Field Goals

Last 2 Seasons		Last 3 Seasons		Last 4 Seasons	
60	Mike Vanderjagt	88	Mike Vanderjagt	119	Matt Stover
58	Jeff Wilkins	84	Jason Elam	113	Mike Vanderjagt
54	David Akers	84	Matt Stover	109	David Akers
54	Matt Stover	81	Jeff Wilkins	104	Ryan Longwell
53	Two tied	80	Three tied	103	Adam Vinatieri

Rushes

Last 2 Seasons		Last 3 Seasons		Last 4 Seasons	
775	Ricky Williams	1,088	Ricky Williams	1,373	Eddie George
695	Jamal Lewis	1,024	LaDainian Tomlinson	1,336	Ricky Williams
685	LaDainian Tomlinson	970	Eddie George	1,233	Curtis Martin
676	Deuce McAllister	960	Priest Holmes	1,213	Stephen Davis
656	Travis Henry	945	Ahman Green	1,208	Ahman Green

Rushing Yards

Last 2 Seasons		Last 3 Seasons		Last 4 Seasons	
3,393	Jamal Lewis	4,590	Priest Holmes	5,685	Ahman Green
3,328	LaDainian Tomlinson	4,564	LaDainian Tomlinson	5,470	Ricky Williams
3,225	Ricky Williams	4,510	Ahman Green	5,178	Priest Holmes
3,123	Ahman Green	4,470	Ricky Williams	5,119	Curtis Martin
3,099	Clinton Portis	3,928	Shaun Alexander	5,014	Stephen Davis

Rushing Touchdowns

Last 2 Seasons		Last 3 Seasons		Last 4 Seasons	
48	Priest Holmes	56	Priest Holmes	58	Priest Holmes
30	Shaun Alexander	44	Shaun Alexander	48	Marshall Faulk
29	Clinton Portis	37	LaDainian Tomlinson	46	Shaun Alexander
27	LaDainian Tomlinson	31	Ahman Green	41	Ahman Green
25	Ricky Williams	31	Ricky Williams	39	Ricky Williams

Passes

Last 2 Seasons		Last 3 Seasons		Last 4 Seasons	
1,157	Peyton Manning	1,704	Peyton Manning	2,275	Peyton Manning
1,128	Tom Brady	1,613	Kerry Collins	2,142	Kerry Collins
1,081	Drew Bledsoe	1,604	Aaron Brooks	2,112	Brett Favre
1,046	Aaron Brooks	1,580	Brad Johnson	1,992	Jon Kitna
1,045	Kerry Collins	1,574	Jon Kitna	1,985	Jeff Garcia

Completions

Last 2 Seasons		Last 3 Seasons		Last 4 Seasons	
771	Peyton Manning	1,114	Peyton Manning	1,471	Peyton Manning
690	Tom Brady	975	Brad Johnson	1,301	Brett Favre
649	Drew Bledsoe	963	Brett Favre	1,257	Kerry Collins
649	Brett Favre	954	Tom Brady	1,224	Jeff Garcia
635	Brad Johnson	946	Kerry Collins	1,203	Brad Johnson

Passing Yards

Last 2 Seasons		Last 3 Seasons		Last 4 Seasons	
8,467	Peyton Manning	12,598	Peyton Manning	17,011	Peyton Manning
7,729	Trent Green	11,512	Trent Green	14,752	Brett Favre
7,384	Tom Brady	10,950	Aaron Brooks	14,557	Kerry Collins
7,332	Daunte Culpepper	10,947	Kerry Collins	13,881	Daunte Culpepper
7,219	Drew Bledsoe	10,940	Brett Favre	13,864	Jeff Garcia

Last 2 Seasons	Last 3 Seasons	Last 4 Seasons
Touchdown Passes		
59 Brett Favre	91 Brett Favre	115 Peyton Manning
56 Peyton Manning	82 Peyton Manning	111 Brett Favre
51 Tom Brady	77 Aaron Brooks	102 Jeff Garcia
51 Aaron Brooks	71 Jeff Garcia	90 Daunte Culpepper
50 Trent Green	69 Tom Brady	87 Rich Gannon
Receptions		
237 Marvin Harrison	346 Marvin Harrison	448 Marvin Harrison
217 Randy Moss	301 Hines Ward	376 Randy Moss
208 Torry Holt	299 Randy Moss	376 Rod Smith
207 Hines Ward	289 Torry Holt	371 Torry Holt
180 Terrell Owens	276 Rod Smith	370 Terrell Owens
Reception Yards		
2,998 Torry Holt	4,518 Marvin Harrison	5,996 Torry Holt
2,994 Marvin Harrison	4,361 Torry Holt	5,931 Marvin Harrison
2,979 Randy Moss	4,212 Randy Moss	5,649 Randy Moss
2,521 Chad Johnson	3,814 Terrell Owens	5,265 Terrell Owens
2,492 Hines Ward	3,550 Joe Horn	4,890 Joe Horn
Receiving Touchdowns		
24 Randy Moss	38 Terrell Owens	51 Terrell Owens
22 Terrell Owens	36 Marvin Harrison	50 Marvin Harrison
22 Hines Ward	34 Randy Moss	49 Randy Moss
21 Marvin Harrison	26 Joe Horn	34 Joe Horn
17 Two tied	26 Hines Ward	32 Tony Gonzalez
Interceptions		
16 Tony Parrish	19 Tony Parrish	27 Darren Sharper
13 Patrick Surtain	18 Darren Sharper	22 Tony Parrish
12 Ed Reed	16 Patrick Surtain	21 Patrick Surtain
12 Darren Sharper	15 Earl Little	19 Sammy Knight
12 Greg Wesley	15 Deltha O'Neal	19 Dexter McCleon
Sacks		
31.5 Jason Taylor	52.0 Michael Strahan	61.5 Michael Strahan
30.5 Simeon Rice	41.5 Simeon Rice	54.5 Jason Taylor
29.5 Michael Strahan	40.0 Jason Taylor	49.0 Simeon Rice
24.5 Leonard Little	39.0 Leonard Little	44.0 Leonard Little
24.5 Adewale Ogunleye	35.5 Kabeer Gbaja-Biamila	40.5 Two tied

NFL TEAM LEADERS OVER RECENT SEASONS

Last 2 Seasons	Last 3 Seasons	Last 4 Seasons
Highest Won-Lost Percentage		
.750 Philadelphia	.729 Philadelphia	.719 Philadelphia
.719 New England	.708 Green Bay	.672 Green Bay
.719 Tennessee	.708 New England	.672 St. Louis
.688 Green Bay	.688 St. Louis	.672 Tennessee
.688 Indianapolis	.625 Two tied	.641 Miami
Most Points		
951 Kansas City	1,271 Kansas City	1,806 St. Louis
840 Green Bay	1,266 St. Louis	1,638 Indianapolis
806 Minnesota	1,230 Green Bay	1,626 Kansas City
802 Tennessee	1,209 Indianapolis	1,598 Denver
796 Indianapolis	1,160 San Francisco	1,598 Oakland
Most Total Yards		
12,486 Minnesota	17,706 St. Louis	24,781 St. Louis
11,910 Kansas City	17,671 Minnesota	23,632 Minnesota
11,688 Denver	17,583 Kansas City	23,586 Indianapolis
11,490 Indianapolis	17,445 Indianapolis	23,197 Kansas City
11,445 Seattle	17,077 San Francisco	23,117 San Francisco

INSIDE THE NUMBERS

Most Rushing Yards

Last 2 Seasons		Last 3 Seasons		Last 4 Seasons	
4,895	Denver	6,772	Denver	9,083	Denver
4,850	Minnesota	6,767	San Francisco	8,630	Pittsburgh
4,523	San Francisco	6,459	Minnesota	8,588	Minnesota
4,491	Green Bay	6,382	Pittsburgh	8,568	San Francisco
4,466	Baltimore	6,315	Kansas City	8,475	Baltimore

Most Passing Yards

Last 2 Seasons		Last 3 Seasons		Last 4 Seasons	
8,234	Indianapolis	12,778	St. Louis	18,010	St. Louis
8,115	St. Louis	12,223	Indianapolis	16,505	Indianapolis
7,696	Seattle	11,268	Kansas City	15,417	Kansas City
7,636	Minnesota	11,212	Minnesota	15,044	Minnesota
7,603	Kansas City	10,933	Oakland	14,549	San Francisco

*Fewest Turnovers

Last 2 Seasons		Last 3 Seasons		Last 4 Seasons	
33	Kansas City	60	N.Y. Jets	80	San Francisco
39	N.Y. Jets	61	San Francisco	90	Oakland
42	San Francisco	66	Kansas City	92	Kansas City
45	Oakland	70	Oakland	98	Tampa Bay
46	Three tied	70	Philadelphia	99	Philadelphia

*Fewest Points Allowed

Last 2 Seasons		Last 3 Seasons		Last 4 Seasons	
460	Tampa Bay	736	Philadelphia	981	Philadelphia
528	Philadelphia	740	Tampa Bay	1,009	Tampa Bay
562	Miami	852	Miami	1,065	Baltimore
584	New England	856	New England	1,078	Miami
589	Dallas	884	Pittsburgh	1,139	Pittsburgh

*Fewest Total Yards Allowed

Last 2 Seasons		Last 3 Seasons		Last 4 Seasons	
8,510	Tampa Bay	13,163	Tampa Bay	17,963	Tampa Bay
9,259	Denver	13,755	Pittsburgh	18,107	Baltimore
9,323	Dallas	13,922	Dallas	18,468	Pittsburgh
9,371	Carolina	14,033	Denver	18,687	Miami
9,443	Miami	14,051	Miami	19,193	Tennessee

*Fewest Rushing Yards Allowed

Last 2 Seasons		Last 3 Seasons		Last 4 Seasons	
2,719	Tennessee	4,150	Tennessee	5,540	Tennessee
3,006	Miami	4,311	Pittsburgh	5,679	Baltimore
3,094	Denver	4,586	Denver	6,004	Pittsburgh
3,116	Pittsburgh	4,709	Baltimore	6,184	Denver
3,243	Dallas	4,785	Miami	6,439	N.Y. Giants

*Fewest Passing Yards Allowed

Last 2 Seasons		Last 3 Seasons		Last 4 Seasons	
5,200	Tampa Bay	8,151	Tampa Bay	11,303	Tampa Bay
5,726	Indianapolis	8,933	Buffalo	11,662	Dallas
5,774	Buffalo	8,969	Dallas	11,800	Buffalo
5,996	Carolina	9,194	Philadelphia	11,826	Washington
6,080	Dallas	9,204	Cleveland	12,166	Miami

Most Opponents' Turnovers

Last 2 Seasons		Last 3 Seasons		Last 4 Seasons	
77	Green Bay	116	Green Bay	151	Tampa Bay
72	Baltimore	110	Tampa Bay	149	Baltimore
72	St. Louis	106	St. Louis	144	Green Bay
71	Tampa Bay	105	New England	135	Miami
70	Two tied	100	Two tied	133	Carolina

**Houston excluded from last three and four seasons list.*

EMMITT SMITH'S CAREER RUSHING VS. EACH OPPONENT

Opponent	Games	Rushes	Yards	Yards Per Rush	Yards Per Game	TD
Arizona	25	534	2,286	4.3	91.4	25
Atlanta	7	143	695	4.9	99.3	9
Baltimore	1	11	48	4.4	48.0	0
Buffalo	1	15	25	1.7	25.0	1
Carolina	5	69	329	4.8	65.8	3
Chicago	5	68	319	4.7	63.8	1
Cincinnati	4	73	238	3.3	59.5	1
Cleveland	2	58	224	3.9	112.0	1
Dallas	1	6	1	0.2	1.0	0
Denver	4	81	278	3.4	69.5	3
Detroit	6	111	456	4.1	76.0	5
Green Bay	7	159	617	3.9	88.1	6
Houston	1	17	67	3.9	67.0	0
Indianapolis	4	81	320	4.0	80.0	4
Jacksonville	3	68	250	3.7	83.3	2
Kansas City	3	56	193	3.4	64.3	2
Miami	3	69	228	3.3	76.0	0
Minnesota	6	89	558	6.3	93.0	8
New England	2	46	160	3.5	80.0	0
New Orleans	5	104	387	3.7	77.4	3
N.Y. Giants	24	465	1,960	4.2	81.7	19
N.Y. Jets	3	54	256	4.7	85.3	0
Oakland	4	95	346	3.6	86.5	7
Philadelphia	26	533	2,466	4.6	94.8	13
Pittsburgh	3	89	349	3.9	116.3	2
St. Louis	4	65	217	3.3	54.3	2
San Diego	3	41	155	3.8	51.7	2
San Francisco	10	170	660	3.9	66.0	7
Seattle	6	93	363	3.9	60.5	3
Tampa Bay	4	72	289	4.0	72.3	2
Tennessee	5	79	240	3.0	48.0	1
Washington	24	528	2,440	4.6	101.7	23
Totals	211	4,142	17,418	4.2	82.5	155

Arizona totals include eight games vs. Phoenix
Oakland totals include one game vs. L.A. Raiders
St. Louis totals include two games vs. L.A. Rams
Tennessee totals include two games vs. Houston

JEROME BETTIS' CAREER RUSHING VS. EACH OPPONENT

Opponent	Games	Rushes	Yards	Yards Per Rush	Yards Per Game	TD
Arizona	4	91	363	4.0	90.8	4
Atlanta	9	160	686	4.3	76.2	2
Baltimore	12	226	830	3.7	69.2	2
Buffalo	4	56	274	4.9	68.5	3
Carolina	5	99	378	3.8	75.6	5
Chicago	4	90	358	4.0	89.5	2
Cincinnati	16	366	1,587	4.3	99.2	14
Cleveland	9	187	770	4.1	85.6	4
Dallas	1	15	63	4.2	63.0	0
Denver	3	71	250	3.5	83.3	2
Detroit	2	49	180	3.7	90.0	0
Green Bay	4	68	193	2.8	48.3	0
Houston	1	14	30	2.1	30.0	0
Indianapolis	3	52	228	4.4	76.0	3
Jacksonville	13	261	940	3.6	72.3	3
Kansas City	7	154	639	4.1	91.3	1
Miami	3	46	188	4.1	62.7	0
Minnesota	1	19	81	4.3	81.0	1
New England	3	48	163	3.4	54.3	0
New Orleans	6	122	597	4.9	99.5	2
N.Y. Giants	3	56	160	2.9	53.3	0
N.Y. Jets	3	49	187	3.8	62.3	1
Oakland	4	71	288	4.1	72.0	1
Philadelphia	3	60	241	4.0	80.3	1
Pittsburgh	1	16	76	4.8	76.0	1
St. Louis	2	31	171	5.5	85.5	2
San Diego	4	84	275	3.3	68.8	1
San Francisco	9	129	493	3.8	54.8	6
Seattle	3	56	227	4.1	75.7	0
Tampa Bay	4	73	295	4.0	73.8	1
Tennessee	14	209	749	3.6	53.5	5
Washington	5	91	393	4.3	78.6	2
Totals	165	3,119	12,353	4.0	74.9	69

Arizona totals include one game vs. Phoenix
Oakland totals include one game vs. L.A. Raiders
Tennessee totals include three games vs. Houston

MARSHALL FAULK'S CAREER RUSHING VS. EACH OPPONENT

Opponent	Games	Rushes	Yards	Yards Per Rush	Yards Per Game	TD
Arizona	4	72	363	5.0	90.8	2
Atlanta	7	131	886	6.8	126.6	4
Baltimore	4	75	338	4.5	84.5	4
Buffalo	10	194	690	3.6	69.0	5
Carolina	7	136	795	5.8	113.6	5
Chicago	2	30	157	5.2	78.5	0
Cincinnati	7	125	471	3.8	67.3	4
Cleveland	3	62	296	4.8	98.7	2
Dallas	1	18	73	4.1	73.0	0
Denver	2	24	97	4.0	48.5	2
Detroit	4	49	159	3.2	39.8	2
Green Bay	1	17	116	6.8	116.0	0
Indianapolis	1	25	118	4.7	118.0	3
Jacksonville	1	22	54	2.5	54.0	1
Kansas City	3	47	151	3.2	50.3	1
Miami	10	181	676	3.7	67.6	4
Minnesota	3	65	345	5.3	115.0	9
New England	10	154	537	3.5	53.7	1
New Orleans	7	153	716	4.7	102.3	6
N.Y. Giants	4	47	208	4.4	52.0	2
N.Y. Jets	10	186	710	3.8	71.0	5
Oakland	2	40	199	5.0	99.5	2
Philadelphia	4	51	281	5.5	70.3	4
Pittsburgh	2	35	116	3.3	58.0	0
St. Louis	1	19	177	9.3	177.0	3
San Diego	6	82	237	2.9	39.5	1
San Francisco	11	199	879	4.4	79.9	8
Seattle	9	182	676	3.7	75.1	8
Tampa Bay	5	72	287	4.0	57.4	5
Tennessee	2	39	233	6.0	116.5	3
Washington	3	44	172	3.9	57.3	1
Totals	146	2,576	11,213	4.4	76.8	97

Tennessee totals include one game vs. Houston

CURTIS MARTIN'S CAREER RUSHING VS. EACH OPPONENT

Opponent	Games	Rushes	Yards	Yards Per Rush	Yards Per Game	TD
Arizona	2	65	223	3.4	111.5	1
Atlanta	2	39	145	3.7	72.5	2
Baltimore	3	61	157	2.6	52.3	0
Buffalo	18	396	1,487	3.8	82.6	9
Carolina	3	72	354	4.9	118.0	4
Chicago	3	52	235	4.5	78.3	1
Cincinnati	1	24	78	3.3	78.0	0
Cleveland	2	37	167	4.5	83.5	1
Dallas	3	67	268	4.0	89.3	0
Denver	6	91	310	3.4	51.7	4
Detroit	2	38	164	4.3	82.0	1
Green Bay	3	66	258	3.9	86.0	2
Houston	1	17	88	5.2	88.0	0
Indianapolis	15	345	1,645	4.8	109.7	7
Jacksonville	4	70	254	3.6	63.5	1
Kansas City	4	84	305	3.6	76.3	4
Miami	17	335	1,210	3.6	71.2	11

Opponent	Games	Rushes	Yards	Yards Per Rush	Yards Per Game	TD
Minnesota	2	42	174	4.1	87.0	1
New England	12	263	1,086	4.1	90.5	5
New Orleans	2	52	178	3.4	89.0	2
N.Y. Giants	3	42	121	2.9	40.3	0
N.Y. Jets	6	163	737	4.5	122.8	7
Oakland	5	89	271	3.0	54.2	0
Philadelphia	1	20	110	5.5	110.0	0
Pittsburgh	4	83	411	5.0	102.8	0
St. Louis	1	14	63	4.5	63.0	0
San Diego	3	54	175	3.2	58.3	1
San Francisco	3	66	197	3.0	65.7	2
Seattle	2	51	195	3.8	97.5	2
Tampa Bay	2	26	116	4.5	58.0	0
Tennessee	2	51	190	3.7	95.0	2
Washington	3	52	297	5.7	99.0	3
Totals	140	2,927	11,669	4.0	83.4	73

EDDIE GEORGE'S CAREER RUSHING VS. EACH OPPONENT

Opponent	Games	Rushes	Yards	Yards Per Rush	Yards Per Game	TD
Arizona	1	17	71	4.2	71.0	0
Atlanta	3	68	279	4.1	93.0	1
Baltimore	13	223	789	3.5	60.7	3
Buffalo	3	65	197	3.0	65.7	1
Carolina	2	37	113	3.1	56.5	0
Chicago	1	21	137	6.5	137.0	0
Cincinnati	13	301	1,182	3.9	90.9	6
Cleveland	7	199	760	3.8	108.6	14
Dallas	3	72	258	3.6	86.0	1
Detroit	1	26	51	2.0	51.0	0
Green Bay	2	30	56	1.9	28.0	0
Houston	4	88	327	3.7	81.8	1
Indianapolis	4	70	243	3.5	60.8	2
Jacksonville	16	334	1,266	3.8	79.1	10
Kansas City	2	42	130	3.1	65.0	0
Miami	5	85	323	3.8	64.6	2
Minnesota	2	35	150	4.3	75.0	2
New England	3	69	236	3.4	78.7	0
New Orleans	3	82	346	4.2	115.3	2
N.Y. Giants	3	87	311	3.6	103.7	3
N.Y. Jets	3	66	286	4.3	95.3	2
Oakland	5	105	506	4.8	101.2	4
Philadelphia	2	50	143	2.9	71.5	1
Pittsburgh	14	277	856	3.1	61.1	5
St. Louis	1	17	68	4.0	68.0	0
San Diego	1	15	11	0.7	11.0	0
San Francisco	2	37	103	2.8	51.5	0
Seattle	3	70	283	4.0	94.3	0
Tampa Bay	3	82	306	3.7	102.0	2
Washington	3	63	222	3.5	74.0	2
Totals	128	2,733	10,009	3.7	78.2	64

JERRY RICE'S CAREER RECEIVING VS. EACH OPPONENT

Opponent	Games	Rec.	Yards	Yards/ Rec.	Yards/ Game	TD
Arizona	9	49	766	15.6	85.1	9
Atlanta	29	175	2,731	15.6	94.2	25
Baltimore	2	9	106	11.8	53.0	2
Buffalo	5	18	235	13.1	47.0	2
Carolina	10	58	783	13.5	78.3	4
Chicago	7	34	551	16.2	78.7	7
Cincinnati	6	36	548	15.2	91.3	4
Cleveland	4	21	294	14.0	73.5	4
Dallas	9	54	795	14.7	88.3	7
Denver	11	55	738	13.4	67.1	4
Detroit	10	50	630	12.6	63.0	2
Green Bay	9	57	875	15.4	97.2	7
Indianapolis	5	26	458	17.6	91.6	5
Jacksonville	1	2	17	8.5	17.0	0
Kansas City	10	44	541	12.3	54.1	4
Miami	5	22	341	15.5	68.2	5
Minnesota	11	56	939	16.8	85.4	10
New England	6	30	474	15.8	79.0	6
New Orleans	30	147	2,025	13.8	67.5	14
N.Y. Giants	9	40	615	15.4	68.3	5
N.Y. Jets	7	32	516	16.1	73.7	4
Oakland	5	23	408	17.7	81.6	3
Philadelphia	7	33	524	15.9	74.9	5
Pittsburgh	7	42	401	9.5	57.3	4
St. Louis	31	165	2,542	15.4	82.0	20
San Diego	10	69	1,069	15.5	106.9	11
San Francisco	1	6	74	12.3	74.0	0
Seattle	6	27	473	17.5	78.8	6
Tampa Bay	8	47	710	15.1	88.8	10
Tennessee	8	51	601	11.8	75.1	3
Washington	8	41	686	16.7	85.8	2
Totals	286	1,519	22,466	14.8	78.6	194

Arizona totals include one game vs. St. Louis, four games vs. Phoenix
Oakland totals include four games vs. L.A. Raiders
St. Louis totals include 20 games vs. L.A. Rams
Tennessee totals include four games vs. Houston

TIM BROWN'S CAREER RECEIVING VS. EACH OPPONENT

Opponent	Games	Rec.	Yards	Yards/ Rec.	Yards/ Game	TD
Arizona	3	11	108	9.8	36.0	2
Atlanta	5	24	393	16.4	78.6	3
Baltimore	3	13	140	10.8	46.7	2
Buffalo	8	28	591	21.1	73.9	5
Carolina	2	13	181	13.9	90.5	1
Chicago	5	20	235	11.8	47.0	2
Cincinnati	8	25	441	17.6	55.1	6
Cleveland	4	7	97	13.9	24.3	0
Dallas	4	25	338	13.5	84.5	1
Denver	30	142	1,823	12.8	60.8	13
Detroit	3	12	97	8.1	32.3	1
Green Bay	4	17	191	11.2	47.8	0
Indianapolis	4	20	329	16.5	82.3	0
Jacksonville	2	19	224	11.8	112.0	1
Kansas City	29	148	2,021	13.7	69.7	6
Miami	10	49	613	12.5	61.3	5
Minnesota	5	17	200	11.8	40.0	1
New England	2	7	117	16.7	58.5	0
New Orleans	5	20	268	13.4	53.6	3
N.Y. Giants	4	17	371	21.8	92.8	4
N.Y. Jets	9	59	831	14.1	92.3	5
Philadelphia	3	12	158	13.2	52.7	1
Pittsburgh	6	26	264	10.2	44.0	0
St. Louis	5	14	243	17.4	48.6	1
San Diego	31	131	1,697	13.0	54.7	9
San Francisco	5	18	294	16.3	58.8	3
Seattle	27	107	1,637	15.3	60.6	14
Tampa Bay	3	13	180	13.8	60.0	1
Tennessee	8	37	476	12.9	59.5	7
Washington	3	19	176	9.3	58.7	2
Totals	240	1,070	14,734	13.8	61.4	99

St. Louis totals include three games vs. L.A. Rams
Tennessee totals include three games vs. Houston

SHANNON SHARPE'S CAREER RECEIVING VS. EACH OPPONENT

Opponent	Games	Rec.	Yards	Yards/ Rec.	Yards/ Game	TD
Arizona	4	12	144	12.0	36.0	1
Atlanta	2	10	163	16.3	81.5	1
Baltimore	3	20	251	12.6	83.7	0

Opponent	Games	Rec.	Yards	Yards/ Rec.	Yards/ Game	TD
Buffalo	6	25	414	16.6	69.0	1
Carolina	1	8	174	21.8	174.0	0
Chicago	5	14	196	14.0	39.2	1
Cincinnati	10	40	430	10.8	43.0	4
Cleveland	10	48	596	12.4	59.6	1
Dallas	4	19	281	14.8	70.3	3
Denver	1	5	50	10.0	50.0	0
Detroit	2	8	107	13.4	53.5	1
Green Bay	4	16	130	8.1	32.5	0
Indianapolis	4	9	121	13.4	30.3	1
Jacksonville	6	23	293	12.7	48.8	3
Kansas City	22	112	1,386	12.4	63.0	12
Miami	4	19	164	8.6	41.0	0
Minnesota	6	21	327	15.6	54.5	0
New England	8	19	218	11.5	27.3	3
New Orleans	1	5	39	7.8	39.0	1
N.Y. Giants	2	8	59	7.4	29.5	0
N.Y. Jets	6	31	375	12.1	62.5	1
Oakland	22	66	842	12.8	38.3	6
Philadelphia	3	15	91	6.1	30.3	1
Pittsburgh	9	23	281	12.2	31.2	2
St. Louis	3	12	120	10.0	40.0	0
San Diego	21	87	1,224	14.1	58.3	13
San Francisco	3	17	186	10.9	62.0	0
Seattle	17	51	661	13.0	38.9	6
Tampa Bay	4	20	172	8.6	43.0	0
Tennessee	7	32	373	11.7	53.3	0
Washington	4	20	192	9.6	48.0	0
Totals	204	815	10,060	12.3	49.3	62

Arizona totals include one game vs. Phoenix
Oakland totals include 10 games vs. L.A. Raiders
St. Louis totals include one game vs. L.A. Rams
Tennessee totals include three games vs. Houston

MARVIN HARRISON'S CAREER RECEIVING VS. EACH OPPONENT

Opponent	Games	Rec.	Yards	Yards/ Rec.	Yards/ Game	TD
Arizona	1	6	85	14.2	85.0	1
Atlanta	2	12	183	15.3	91.5	2
Baltimore	4	20	294	14.7	73.5	1
Buffalo	13	59	810	13.7	62.3	9
Carolina	1	8	119	14.9	119.0	0
Chicago	1	6	42	7.0	42.0	0
Cincinnati	4	31	469	15.1	117.3	3
Cleveland	3	32	354	11.1	118.0	2
Dallas	3	23	239	10.4	79.7	3
Denver	3	26	320	12.3	106.7	2
Detroit	2	12	139	11.6	69.5	2
Green Bay	2	10	126	12.6	63.0	1
Houston	4	27	345	12.8	86.3	0
Jacksonville	5	17	226	13.3	45.2	3
Kansas City	4	30	409	13.6	102.3	4
Miami	14	79	1,059	13.4	75.6	8
Minnesota	2	19	174	9.2	87.0	4
New England	13	78	1,141	14.6	87.8	9
New Orleans	3	19	308	16.2	102.7	3
N.Y. Giants	2	16	237	14.8	118.5	3
N.Y. Jets	12	66	747	11.3	62.3	5
Oakland	2	18	201	11.2	100.5	3
Philadelphia	3	17	303	17.8	101.0	4
Pittsburgh	2	11	128	11.6	64.0	1
St. Louis	1	5	96	19.2	96.0	0
San Diego	4	23	317	13.8	79.3	2
San Francisco	2	14	226	16.1	113.0	4
Seattle	2	11	172	15.6	86.0	0
Tampa Bay	2	14	233	16.6	116.5	2
Tennessee	4	33	358	10.8	89.5	2
Washington	3	17	212	12.5	70.7	0
Totals	123	759	10,072	13.3	81.9	83

GARY ANDERSON'S CAREER KICKING VS. EACH OPPONENT

Opponent	Games	FG	FGA	FG%	Long FG	XP	XPA	Pts.
Arizona	8	14	19	73.7	44	22	22	64
Atlanta	9	10	14	71.4	39	34	34	64
Baltimore	2	7	7	100.0	46	2	2	23
Buffalo	11	19	23	82.6	49	23	23	80
Carolina	7	10	12	83.3	48	20	21	50
Chicago	13	22	26	84.6	50	27	27	93
Cincinnati	26	39	48	81.3	52	60	60	177
Cleveland	26	35	52	67.3	49	47	47	152
Dallas	13	22	28	78.6	49	27	27	93
Denver	11	19	23	82.6	42	24	24	81
Detroit	15	21	29	72.4	44	44	44	107
Green Bay	14	22	27	81.5	48	32	34	98
Houston	2	3	3	100.0	41	8	8	17
Indianapolis	10	13	15	86.7	53	24	24	63
Jacksonville	4	8	9	88.9	53	9	9	33
Kansas City	10	23	29	79.3	49	24	24	93
Miami	12	19	24	79.2	53	30	30	87
Minnesota	5	3	7	42.9	44	10	10	19
New England	10	15	18	83.3	49	23	23	68
New Orleans	11	23	25	92.0	51	25	25	94
N.Y. Giants	10	12	14	85.7	46	24	24	60
N.Y. Jets	10	14	20	70.0	45	27	27	69
Oakland	5	5	12	41.7	37	8	8	23
Philadelphia	5	6	8	75.0	52	11	11	29
Pittsburgh	2	1	2	50.0	25	5	5	8
St. Louis	8	9	11	81.8	46	22	22	49
San Diego	14	25	27	92.6	55	41	42	116
San Francisco	5	8	11	72.7	50	12	12	36
Seattle	11	14	17	82.4	43	12	12	54
Tampa Bay	14	21	25	84.0	44	30	30	93
Tennessee	27	47	52	90.4	54	56	58	197
Washington	8	12	13	92.3	49	20	21	56
Totals	338	521	650	80.2	55	783	790	2,346

Arizona totals include one game vs. St. Louis, one game vs. Phoenix
Indianapolis totals include one game vs. Baltimore
Oakland totals include three games vs. L.A. Raiders
Tennessee totals include 25 games vs. Houston
St. Louis totals include three games vs. L.A. Rams

MORTEN ANDERSEN'S CAREER KICKING VS. EACH OPPONENT

Opponent	Games	FG	FGA	FG%	Long FG	XP	XPA	Pts.
Arizona	15	23	25	92.0	52	43	44	112
Atlanta	25	40	51	78.4	49	56	58	176
Baltimore	2	3	4	75.0	46	3	3	12
Buffalo	6	9	14	64.3	50	14	14	41
Carolina	12	22	28	78.6	51	23	23	89
Chicago	7	6	9	66.7	60	18	18	36
Cincinnati	6	7	11	63.6	49	18	18	39
Cleveland	6	11	12	91.7	53	16	16	49
Dallas	13	22	30	73.3	54	22	22	88
Denver	10	8	14	57.1	55	31	33	55
Detroit	11	12	19	63.2	50	25	25	61
Green Bay	8	13	15	86.7	52	21	21	60
Houston	1	0	0	—	0	6	6	6
Indianapolis	3	3	5	60.0	46	11	11	20
Jacksonville	3	4	5	80.0	46	4	4	16
Kansas City	6	11	12	91.7	50	10	10	43
Miami	6	7	9	77.8	50	21	21	42
Minnesota	12	18	23	78.3	51	20	20	74
New England	7	11	13	84.6	54	21	21	54
New Orleans	13	22	28	78.6	55	31	31	97
N.Y. Giants	9	17	20	85.0	45	15	15	66
N.Y. Jets	7	13	14	92.9	53	14	14	53
Oakland	10	13	16	81.3	51	21	21	60
Philadelphia	13	24	29	82.8	56	21	21	93

Opponent	Games	FG	FGA	FG%	Long FG	XP	XPA	Pts.
Pittsburgh	7	7	10	70.0	50	15	16	36
St. Louis	37	53	62	85.5	51	94	96	253
San Diego	7	7	11	63.6	46	20	20	41
San Francisco	38	62	74	83.8	59	60	62	246
Seattle	7	10	11	90.9	47	15	15	45
Tampa Bay	16	24	32	75.0	50	35	35	107
Tennessee	6	9	13	69.2	47	13	13	40
Washington	9	11	17	64.7	50	16	16	49
Totals	338	502	636	78.9	60	753	763	2,259

Arizona totals include five games vs. St. Louis, four games vs. Phoenix
Oakland totals include four games vs. L.A. Raiders
St. Louis totals include 23 games vs. L.A. Rams
Tennessee totals include five games vs. Houston

BRETT FAVRE'S CAREER PASSING VS. EACH OPPONENT

Opponent	Games	Att.	Cmp.	Pct.	Yards	Avg. Gain	TD	Int.	Sacked
Arizona	3	98	61	62.2	833	8.50	4	2	3/21
Atlanta	4	152	103	67.8	1,143	7.52	7	5	8/56
Baltimore	2	75	49	65.3	597	7.96	5	2	3/14
Buffalo	4	126	74	58.7	753	5.98	8	3	7/54
Carolina	6	239	145	60.7	1,721	7.20	15	11	14/105
Chicago	24	769	488	63.5	5,688	7.40	48	23	38/245
Cincinnati	3	117	76	65.0	902	7.71	6	2	9/68
Cleveland	3	89	61	68.5	572	6.43	6	0	4/22
Dallas	6	240	138	57.5	1,383	5.76	11	4	12/91
Denver	4	114	59	51.8	751	6.59	6	9	4/26
Detroit	24	853	532	62.4	6,444	7.55	43	31	46/294
Indianapolis	2	61	41	67.2	664	10.89	5	3	5/43
Jacksonville	2	72	44	61.1	564	7.83	5	1	3/19
Kansas City	3	119	72	60.5	799	6.71	5	5	11/65
Miami	4	147	92	62.6	996	6.78	5	3	9/42
Minnesota	23	750	453	60.4	4,909	6.55	36	28	45/298
New England	3	108	65	60.2	680	6.30	7	2	6/46
New Orleans	3	106	68	64.2	728	6.87	7	1	9/48
N.Y. Giants	4	132	77	58.3	1,002	7.59	6	3	7/44
N.Y. Jets	3	95	50	52.6	507	5.34	4	2	3/21
Oakland	3	105	64	61.0	922	8.78	9	3	6/31
Philadelphia	8	262	147	56.1	1,825	6.97	11	13	20/134
Pittsburgh	3	90	59	65.6	745	8.28	4	1	7/44
St. Louis	8	251	153	61.0	1,739	6.93	12	11	16/136
San Diego	4	111	70	63.1	828	7.46	10	4	5/56
San Francisco	6	199	122	61.3	1,515	7.61	10	8	9/54
Seattle	3	94	53	56.4	574	6.11	7	4	6/36
Tampa Bay	22	750	460	61.3	4,930	6.57	35	20	42/235
Tennessee	3	90	53	58.9	607	6.74	6	2	7/18
Washington	3	50	31	62.0	325	6.50	3	3	3/33
Totals	193	6,464	3,960	61.3	45,646	7.06	346	209	367/2,398

Oakland totals include one game vs. L.A. Raiders
St. Louis totals include four games vs. L.A. Rams
Tennessee totals include one game vs. Houston

DREW BLEDSOE'S CAREER PASSING VS. EACH OPPONENT

Opponent	Games	Att.	Cmp.	Pct.	Yards	Avg. Gain	TD	Int.	Sacked
Arizona	3	74	43	58.1	582	7.86	8	0	9/55
Atlanta	1	34	19	55.9	229	6.74	1	1	5/48
Baltimore	2	64	40	62.5	418	6.53	5	1	2/6
Buffalo	16	504	280	55.6	3,327	6.60	22	10	37/261
Carolina	1	44	22	50.0	228	5.18	0	0	0/0
Chicago	4	157	100	63.7	1,131	7.20	9	2	9/72
Cincinnati	6	212	127	59.9	1,412	6.66	6	3	11/63
Cleveland	5	215	119	55.3	1,283	5.97	3	6	11/74
Dallas	3	99	51	51.5	458	4.63	0	5	4/19
Denver	7	260	144	55.4	1,751	6.73	9	3	21/152
Detroit	4	150	87	58.0	940	6.27	3	3	9/52
Green Bay	3	125	67	53.6	781	6.25	3	6	10/72
Houston	2	59	34	57.6	438	7.42	2	0	7/55
Indianapolis	16	518	315	60.8	3,622	6.99	25	11	25/185
Jacksonville	3	104	72	69.2	803	7.72	5	1	6/32
Kansas City	6	236	145	61.4	1,457	6.17	10	7	14/107
Miami	20	707	378	53.5	4,908	6.94	25	29	46/296
Minnesota	4	196	128	65.3	1,392	7.10	9	2	9/72
New England	4	153	89	58.2	943	6.16	4	7	11/88

Opponent	Games	Att.	Cmp.	Pct.	Yards	Avg. Gain	TD	Int.	Sacked
New Orleans	2	66	39	59.1	514	7.79	1	5	5/32
N.Y. Giants	3	104	70	67.3	786	7.56	4	2	6/45
N.Y. Jets	20	675	375	55.6	4,163	6.17	18	28	52/379
Oakland	2	108	55	50.9	738	6.83	4	6	8/34
Philadelphia	2	92	50	54.3	627	.82	1	4	8/52
Pittsburgh	4	178	99	55.6	1,170	6.57	8	11	4/37
St. Louis	1	35	11	31.4	176	5.03	1	1	4/30
San Diego	4	137	77	56.2	903	6.59	9	2	5/16
San Francisco	1	51	21	41.2	241	4.73	0	3	4/22
Seattle	1	44	20	45.5	238	5.41	1	2	2/15
Tampa Bay	2	64	39	60.9	333	5.20	1	2	11/84
Tennessee	2	60	35	58.3	418	6.97	3	0	7/38
Washington	2	74	42	56.8	466	6.30	1	2	3/25
Totals	156	5,599	3,193	57.0	36,876	6.59	201	165	365/2,518

Arizona totals include one game vs. Phoenix
Oakland totals include one game vs. L.A. Raiders

PEYTON MANNING'S CAREER PASSING VS. EACH OPPONENT

Opponent	Games	Att.	Cmp.	Pct.	Yards	Avg. Gain	TD	Int.	Sacked
Atlanta	3	92	67	72.8	774	8.41	10	3	1/9
Baltimore	3	130	84	64.6	951	7.32	6	3	10/87
Buffalo	9	281	168	59.8	2,014	7.17	12	9	9/66
Carolina	2	68	40	58.8	518	7.62	2	3	5/18
Chicago	1	39	26	66.7	302	7.74	2	1	2/21
Cincinnati	3	93	55	59.1	718	7.72	7	2	1/6
Cleveland	3	120	74	61.7	764	6.37	2	3	2/910
Dallas	2	72	51	70.8	565	7.85	3	1	1/13
Denver	3	97	55	56.7	566	5.84	2	2	5/30
Detroit	1	33	22	66.7	288	8.73	3	2	1/7
Green Bay	1	44	25	56.8	294	6.68	3	1	4/27
Houston	4	124	84	67.7	951	7.67	7	1	4/30
Jacksonville	5	173	111	64.2	1,360	7.86	12	3	1/8
Kansas City	3	95	62	65.3	764	8.04	4	2	7/62
Miami	10	341	208	61.0	2,372	6.96	14	18	17/126
Minnesota	1	36	25	69.4	283	7.86	4	1	0/0
New England	9	332	202	60.8	2,286	6.89	18	14	13/76
New Orleans	3	85	57	67.1	885	10.41	8	4	5/26
N.Y. Giants	2	81	50	61.7	602	7.43	5	3	2/16
N.Y. Jets	9	343	212	61.8	2,286	6.66	12	11	11/60
Oakland	2	89	59	66.3	608	6.83	5	4	3/23
Philadelphia	2	49	34	69.4	554	11.31	6	0	1/8
Pittsburgh	1	48	32	66.7	304	6.33	1	3	2/9
St. Louis	1	28	15	53.6	195	6.96	0	1	2/17
San Diego	2	77	41	53.2	541	7.03	3	2	0/0
San Francisco	2	81	49	60.5	601	7.42	4	4	2/6
Seattle	2	69	43	62.3	616	8.93	2	1	3/3
Tampa Bay	1	47	34	72.3	186	8.21	2	1	1/5
Tennessee	4	147	99	67.3	1,025	6.97	4	4	7/42
Washington	2	69	44	63.8	512	7.42	4	3	4/26
Totals	96	3,383	2,128	62.9	24,885	7.36	167	110	126/84

INSIDE THE NUMBERS

The NFL rates its passers for statistical purposes against a fixed performance standard based on statistical achievements of all qualified pro passers since 1960. The current system replaced one that rated passers in relation to their position in a total group based on various criteria. The current system, which was adopted in 1973, removes inequities that existed in the former method and, at the same time, provides a means of comparing passing performances from one season to the next.

It is important to remember that the system is used to rate passers, not quarterbacks. Statistics do not reflect leadership, play-calling, and other intangible factors that go into making a successful professional quarterback. Four categories are used as a basis for compiling a rating:

—Percentage of completions per attempt
—Average yards gained per attempt
—Percentage of touchdown passes per attempt
—Percentage of interceptions per attempt

The average standard is 1.000. The bottom is .000. To earn a 2.000 rating, a passer must perform at exceptional levels, i.e., 70 percent in completions, 10 percent in touchdowns, 1.5 percent in interceptions, and 11 yards average gain per pass attempt. The maximum a passer can receive in any category is 2.375.

For example, to gain a 2.375 in completion percentage, a passer would have to complete 77.5 percent of his passes. The NFL record is 70.55 by Ken Anderson (Cincinnati, 1982). To earn a 2.375 in percentage of touchdowns, a passer would have to achieve a percentage of 11.9. The record is 13.9 by Sid Luckman (Chicago, 1943). To gain 2.375 in percentage of interceptions, a passer would have to go the entire season without an interception. The 2.375 figure in average yards is 12.50, compared with the NFL record of 11.17 by Tommy O'Connell (Cleveland, 1957).

In order to make the rating more understandable, the point rating is then converted into a scale of 100, with 158.3 being the highest rating a passer can achieve. In cases where statistical performance has been superior, it is possible for a passer to surpass a 100 rating. For example, take Steve Young's record-setting season in 1994 when he completed 324 of 461 passes for 3,969 yards, 35 touchdowns, and 10 interceptions. The four calculations would be:

—Percentage of Completions—324 of 461 is 70.28 percent. Subtract 30 from the completion percentage (40.28) and multiply the result by 0.05. The result is a point rating of 2.014.
Note: If the result is less than zero (Comp. Pct. less than 30.0), award zero points. If the results are greater than 2.375 (Comp. Pct. greater than 77.5), award 2.375.

—Average Yards Gained Per Attempt—3,969 yards divided by 461 attempts is 8.61. Subtract three yards from yards-per-attempt (5.61) and multiply the result by 0.25. The result is 1.403.
Note: If the result is less than zero (yards per attempt less than 3.0), award zero points. If the result is greater than 2.375 (yards per attempt greater than 12.5), award 2.375 points.

—Percentage of Touchdown Passes—35 touchdowns in 461 attempts is 7.59 percent. Multiply the touchdown percentage by 0.2. The result is 1.518.
Note: If the result is greater than 2.375 (touchdown percentage greater than 11.875), award 2.375.

—Percentage of Interceptions—10 interceptions in 461 attempts is 2.17 percent. Multiply the interception percentage by 0.25 (0.542) and subtract the number from 2.375. The result is 1.833.
Note: If the result is less than zero (interception percentage greater than 9.5), award zero points.

The sum of the four steps is (2.014 + 1.403 + 1.518 + 1.833) 6.768. The sum is then divided by six (1.128) and multiplied by 100. In this case, the result is 112.8. This same formula can be used to determine a passer rating for any player who attempts at least one pass.

The following is a list of qualifying passers who had a single-season passer rating of 100 or higher:

Player, Team	Season	Rating	Att.	Comp.	Pct.	Yds.	Avg.	TD	TD Pct.	Int.	Int. Pct.
Steve Young, San Francisco	1994	112.8	461	324	70.2	3,969	8.61	35	7.6	10	2.2
Joe Montana, San Francisco	1989	112.4	386	271	70.2	3,521	9.12	26	6.7	8	2.1
Milt Plum, Cleveland	1960	110.4	250	151	60.4	2,297	9.19	21	8.4	5	2.0
Sammy Baugh, Washington	1945	109.9	182	128	70.3	1,669	9.17	11	6.0	4	2.2
Kurt Warner, St. Louis	1999	109.2	499	325	65.1	4,353	8.72	41	8.2	13	2.6
Dan Marino, Miami	1984	108.9	564	362	64.2	5,084	9.01	48	8.5	17	3.0
Sid Luckman, Chicago Bears	1943	107.5	202	110	54.5	2,194	10.86	28	13.9	12	5.9
Steve Young, San Francisco	1992	107.0	402	268	66.7	3,465	8.62	25	6.2	7	1.7
Randall Cunningham, Minnesota	1998	106.0	425	259	60.9	3,704	8.72	34	8.0	10	2.4
Bart Starr, Green Bay	1966	105.0	251	156	62.2	2,257	8.99	14	5.6	3	1.2
Roger Staubach, Dallas	1971	104.8	211	126	59.7	1,882	8.92	15	7.1	4	1.9
Y.A. Tittle, N.Y. Giants	1963	104.8	367	221	60.2	3,145	8.57	36	9.8	14	3.8
Steve Young, San Francisco	1997	104.7	356	241	67.7	3,029	8.51	19	5.3	6	1.7
Bart Starr, Green Bay	1968	104.3	171	109	63.7	1,617	9.46	15	8.8	8	4.7
Chad Pennington, N.Y. Jets	2002	104.2	399	275	68.9	3,120	7.82	22	5.5	6	1.5
Ken Stabler, Oakland	1976	103.4	291	194	66.7	2,737	9.41	27	9.3	17	5.8
Brian Griese, Denver	2000	102.9	336	216	64.3	2,688	8.00	19	5.7	4	1.2
Joe Montana, San Francisco	1984	102.9	432	279	64.6	3,630	8.40	28	6.5	10	2.3
Charlie Conerly, N.Y. Giants	1959	102.7	194	113	58.2	1,706	8.79	14	7.2	4	2.1
Bert Jones, Baltimore	1976	102.5	343	207	60.3	3,104	9.05	24	7.0	9	2.6
Joe Montana, San Francisco	1987	102.1	398	266	66.8	3,054	7.67	31	7.8	13	3.3
Trent Green, St. Louis	2000	101.8	240	145	60.4	2,063	8.60	16	6.7	5	2.1
Steve Young, San Francisco	1991	101.8	279	180	64.5	2,517	9.02	17	6.1	8	2.9
Len Dawson, Kansas City	1966	101.7	284	159	56.0	2,527	8.90	26	9.2	10	3.5
Vinny Testaverde, N.Y. Jets	1998	101.6	421	259	61.5	3,256	7.73	29	6.9	7	1.7
Steve Young, San Francisco	1993	101.5	462	314	68.0	4,023	8.71	29	6.3	16	3.5
Kurt Warner, St. Louis	2001	101.4	546	375	68.7	4,830	8.85	36	6.6	22	4.0
Jim Kelly, Buffalo	1990	101.2	346	219	63.3	2,829	8.18	24	6.9	9	2.6
Steve Young, San Francisco	1998	101.1	517	322	62.3	4,170	8.07	36	7.0	12	2.3
Chris Chandler, Atlanta	1998	100.9	327	190	58.1	3,154	9.65	25	7.6	12	3.7
Jim Harbaugh, Indianapolis	1995	100.7	314	200	63.7	2,575	8.20	17	5.4	5	1.6
Steve McNair, Tennessee	2003	100.4	400	250	62.5	3,215	8.04	24	6.0	7	1.8

HIGHEST NFL POSTSEASON PASSER RATINGS (MINIMUM: 150 ATTEMPTS)

Player	Games	Att.	Cmp.	Pct.	Yards	Avg. Gain	TD	Int.	Rating
Bart Starr	10	213	130	61.0	1,753	8.23	15	3	104.8
Joe Montana	23	734	460	62.7	5,772	7.86	45	21	95.6
Ken Anderson	6	166	110	66.3	1,321	7.96	9	6	93.5
Kurt Warner	7	268	169	63.1	2,221	8.29	15	10	92.3
Joe Theismann	10	211	128	60.7	1,782	8.45	11	7	91.4
Troy Aikman	16	502	320	63.7	3,849	7.67	23	17	88.3
Brett Favre	19	630	379	60.2	4,686	7.44	33	22	86.1
Steve Young	22	471	292	62.0	3,326	7.06	20	13	85.8
Warren Moon	10	403	259	64.3	2,870	7.12	17	14	84.9
Rich Gannon	10	240	154	64.2	1,691	7.05	11	9	84.6

HIGHEST NFL POSTSEASON PASSER RATINGS, ACTIVE PLAYERS (MINIMUM: 150 ATTEMPTS)

Player	Games	Att.	Cmp.	Pct.	Yards	Avg. Gain	TD	Int.	Rating
Kurt Warner	7	268	169	63.1	2,221	8.29	15	10	92.3
Brett Favre	19	630	379	60.2	4,686	7.44	33	22	86.1
Rich Gannon	10	240	154	64.2	1,691	7.05	11	9	84.6
Peyton Manning	6	208	117	56.3	1,476	7.10	10	6	82.5
Tom Brady	6	223	135	60.5	1,364	6.12	6	3	81.4
Vinny Testaverde	5	189	114	60.3	1,320	6.98	6	5	81.0
Kerry Collins	6	199	115	57.8	1,275	6.41	12	10	76.1
Donovan McNabb	9	309	181	58.6	1,807	5.85	11	9	75.0
Neil O'Donnell	9	275	159	57.8	1,709	6.21	9	8	74.9
Steve McNair	9	282	166	58.9	1,591	5.64	6	9	68.4

ALL-TIME RANKINGS OF PLAYERS IN FOUR CATEGORIES THAT DETERMINE NFL PASSER RATING

Minimum: 1,500 Attempts

COMPLETION PERCENTAGE	Pct.	Att.	Comp.
Kurt Warner	66.41	1,688	1,121
Steve Young	64.28	4,149	2,667
Joe Montana	63.24	5,391	3,409
Daunte Culpepper	62.94	1,843	1,160
Peyton Manning	62.90	3,383	2,128
Tom Brady	61.85	1,544	955
Briane Griese	61.84	1,808	1,118
Brad Johnson	61.78	3,401	2,101
Troy Aikman	61.46	4,715	2,898
Jeff Garcia	61.40	2,360	1,449

AVERAGE YARDS PER PASS	Avg.	Att.	Yards
Otto Graham	8.63	1,565	13,499
Kurt Waner	8.56	1,688	14,447
Sid Luckman	8.42	1,744	14,686
Norm Van Brocklin	8.16	2,895	23,611
Steve Young	7.98	4,149	33,124
Ed Brown	7.85	1,987	15,600
Bart Starr	7.85	3,149	24,718
Johnny Unitas	7.76	5,186	40,239
Earl Morrall	7.74	2,689	20,809
Dan Fouts	7.68	5,604	43,040

TOUCHDOWN PERCENTAGE	Pct.	Att.	TD
Sid Luckman	7.86	1,744	137
Frank Ryan	6.99	2,133	149
Len Dawson	6.39	3,741	239
Daryle Lamonica	6.31	2,601	164
Sammy Baugh	6.24	2,995	187
Charley Conerly	6.11	2,833	173
Kurt Warner	6.04	1,688	102
Bob Waterfield	6.00	1,617	97
Earl Morrall	5.99	2,689	161
Sonny Jurgensen	5.98	4,262	255

INTERCEPTION PERCENTAGE	Pct.	Att.	Int.
Neil O'Donnell	2.11	3,229	68
Donovan McNabb	2.31	2,117	49
Mark Brunell	2.36	3,643	86
Jeff Garcia	2.37	2,360	56
Tom Brady	2.46	1,544	38
Rich Gannon	2.46	4,138	102
Steve Bono	2.47	1,701	42
Joe Montana	2.58	5,391	139
Steve Young	2.58	4,149	107
Bernie Kosar	2.59	3,365	87

STARTING RECORDS OF ACTIVE NFL QUARTERBACKS

Minimum: 10 starts

	W - L - T	Pct.
Marc Bulger	18-4-0	.818
Tom Brady	34-12-0	.739
Kurt Warner	35-15-0	.700
Jay Fiedler	36-17-0	.679
Donovan McNabb	43-21-0	.672
Brett Favre	125-64-0	.661
Jake Delhomme	11-6-0	.647
Shaun King	14-8-0	.636
Steve McNair	69-40-0	.633
Brad Johnson	58-37-0	.611
Michael Vick	12-8-1	.595
Kordell Stewart	48-34-0	.585
Rich Gannon	74-55-0	.574
Chad Pennington	12-9-0	.571
Doug Flutie	37-28-0	.569
Peyton Manning	54-42-0	.563
Jim Miller	15-12-0	.556
Neil O'Donnell	55-45-0	.550
Trent Dilfer	51-43-0	.543
Mark Brunell	63-54-0	.538
Brian Griese	30-26-0	.536
Ray Lucas	8-7-0	.533
Matt Hasselbeck	20-18-0	.526
Trent Green	35-32-0	.522
Rodney Peete	45-42-0	.517
Quincy Carter	16-15-0	.516
Aaron Brooks	27-26-0	.509
Kerry Collins	59-58-0	.504
Shane Matthews	11-11-0	.500
Anthony Wright	6-6-0	.500
Drew Bledsoe	77-78-0	.497
Jeff Garcia	35-36-0	.493
Daunte Culpepper	28-29-0	.491
Steve Beuerlein	47-55-0	.461
Tony Banks	35-43-0	.449
Jon Kitna	34-42-0	.447
Chris Chandler	67-83-0	.447
Ty Detmer	11-14-0	.440
Danny Kanell	10-13-1	.438
Vinny Testaverde	82-106-1	.437
Tommy Maddox	13-17-1	.435
Gus Frerotte	27-36-1	.430
Jake Plummer	39-54-0	.419
Rob Johnson	12-17-0	.414
Charlie Batch	19-27-0	.413
Todd Collins	7-10-0	.412
Jeff Blake	39-61-0	.390
Byron Leftwich	5-8-0	.385
Patrick Ramsey	6-10-0	.375
Tim Couch	22-37-0	.373
Drew Brees	10-17-0	.370
Rick Mirer	24-44-0	.353
Joey Harrington	8-20-0	.286
Kelly Holcomb	3-8-0	.273
Alex Van Pelt	3-8-0	.273
David Carr	7-20-0	.259
Doug Johnson	2-9-0	.182
Doug Pederson	3-14-0	.176
Chris Weinke	1-15-0	.063

TEAMS THAT FINISHED IN FIRST PLACE IN THEIR DIVISION THE SEASON AFTER FINISHING IN LAST PLACE

Season	Team	Record	Prior Season
1967	Houston	9-4-1	*3-11-0
1968	Minnesota	8-6-0	3- 8-3
1970	Cincinnati	8-6-0	4- 9-1
1970	San Francisco	10-3-1	4- 8-2
1972	Green Bay	10-4-0	4- 8-2
1975	Baltimore	10-4-0	2-12-0
1979	Tampa Bay	10-6-0	5-11-0
1981	Cincinnati	12-4-0	6-10-0
1987	Indianapolis	9-6-0	3-13-0
1988	Cincinnati	12-4-0	4-11-0
1990	Cincinnati	9-7-0	8- 8-0
1991	Denver	12-4-0	5-11-0
1992	San Diego	11-5-0	4-12-0
1993	Detroit	10-6-0	5-11-0
1997	N.Y. Giants	10-5-1	6-10-0
1999	Indianapolis	13-3-0	3-13-0
1999	St. Louis	13-3-0	4-12-0
2000	New Orleans	10-6-0	3-13-0
2001	Chicago	13-3-0	5-11-0
2001	New England	11-5-0	5-11-0
2003	Carolina	11-5-0	7- 9-0
2003	Kansas City	13-3-0	*8- 8-0

*tied for last place

LONGEST WINNING STREAKS SINCE 1970

16	Miami, 1971-73	(1 in 1971, 14 in 1972, 1 in 1973)
16	Miami, 1983-84	(5 in 1983, 11 in 1984)
15	San Francisco, 1989-90	(5 in 1989, 10 in 1990)
14	Oakland, 1976-77	(10 in 1976, 4 in 1977)
14	Denver, 1997-98	(1 in 1997, 13 in 1998)
13	Minnesota, 1974-75	(3 in 1974, 10 in 1975)
13	Chicago, 1984-85	(1 in 1984, 12 in 1985)
13	N.Y. Giants, 1989-90	(3 in 1989, 10 in 1990)
12	Washington, 1990-91	(1 in 1990, 11 in 1991)
12	New England, 2003	
11	Pittsburgh, 1975	
11	Baltimore, 1975-76	(9 in 1975, 2 in 1976)
11	Chicago, 1986-87	(7 in 1986, 4 in 1987)
11	Houston, 1993	
11	San Francisco, 1997	
11	Jacksonville, 1999	
11	Indianapolis, 1999	
10	Miami, 1973	
10	Pittsburgh, 1976-77	(9 in 1976, 1 in 1977)
10	Denver, 1984	
10	San Francisco, 1994	
10	Minnesota, 1999-00	(3 in 1999, 7 in 2000)

NFL PLAYOFF APPEARANCES BY SEASONS

Team	Number of Seasons in Playoffs
Dallas	27
N.Y. Giants	26
St. Louis	26
Cleveland	24
Minnesota	23
Chicago	22
Green Bay	22
San Francisco	22
Miami	21
Oakland	21
Pittsburgh	21
Washington	20
Tennessee	19
Philadelphia	18
Buffalo	17
Indianapolis	17
Denver	15
Detroit	14
Kansas City	14
New England	12
San Diego	12
N.Y. Jets	10
Tampa Bay	8
Cincinnati	7
Atlanta	7
Arizona	6
Seattle	6
New Orleans	5

Jacksonville	4
Baltimore	3
Carolina	2

TEAMS IN SUPER BOWL CONTENTION (1978-2003)

	With 3 Weeks to Play	With 2 Weeks to Play	With 1 Week to Play
2003	22	17	14
2002	21	21	*19
2001	23	16	13
2000	19	17	16
1999	23	20	16
1998	22	19	14
1997	22	18	14
1996	23	21	13
1995	*27	21	18
1994	25	*22	15
1993	20	18	16
1992	20	16	14
1991	20	18	13
1990	23	20	15
1989	21	18	17
1988	21	18	15
1987	19	19	15
1986	19	17	14
1985	21	18	13
1984	18	14	13
1983	24	19	15
1982	20	17	16
1981	21	20	16
1980	20	14	12
1979	19	15	13
1978	20	17	12

RECORD OF TEAMS ON THE ROAD (1970-2003)

Year	W	L	T	Pct
1970	72	101	9	.420
1971	74	100	8	.429
1972	87	90	5	.492
1973	66	109	7	.382
1974	82	99	1	.453
1975	81	101	0	.445
1976	83	112	1	.426
1977	83	113	0	.423
1978	93	130	1	.417
1979	92	132	0	.411
1980	101	122	1	.453
1981	84	139	1	.377
1982	57	68	1	.456
1983	104	119	1	.467
1984	94	129	1	.422
1985	80	144	0	.357
1986	104	118	2	.469
1987	95	114	1	.455
1988	92	131	1	.413
1989	95	128	1	.426
1990	93	131	0	.415
1991	92	132	0	.411
1992	88	136	0	.393
1993	101	123	0	.451
1994	96	128	0	.429
1995	96	144	0	.400
1996	91	149	0	.379
1997	93	145	2	.392
1998	89	151	0	.371
1999	100	148	0	.403
2000	110	138	0	.444
2001	112	136	0	.452
2002	107	148	1	.420
2003	99	157	0	.387

GAMES DECIDED BY 7 POINTS OR LESS AND 3 POINTS OR LESS (1970-2003)

	Games Decided by 7 Points or Less	Games Decided by 3 Points or Less
1970	59 of 182 (32.4%)	34 of 182 (18.7%)
1971	76 of 182 (41.8%)	35 of 182 (19.2%)
1972	71 of 182 (39.0%)	38 of 182 (20.9%)
1973	60 of 182 (32.9%)	28 of 182 (15.4%)
1974	91 of 182 (50.0%)	37 of 182 (20.3%)
1975	62 of 182 (34.1%)	35 of 182 (19.2%)
1976	73 of 196 (37.2%)	38 of 196 (19.4%)
1977	85 of 196 (43.4%)	36 of 196 (18.4%)
1978	108 of 224 (48.2%)	49 of 224 (21.9%)
1979	104 of 224 (46.4%)	51 of 224 (22.8%)
1980	108 of 224 (48.2%)	58 of 224 (25.9%)
1981	91 of 224 (40.6%)	60 of 224 (26.8%)
1982	61 of 126 (48.4%)	33 of 126 (26.2%)
1983	106 of 224 (47.3%)	54 of 224 (24.1%)
1984	95 of 224 (42.4%)	58 of 224 (25.9%)
1985	87 of 224 (38.8%)	38 of 224 (17.0%)
1986	106 of 224 (47.3%)	48 of 224 (21.4%)
1987	99 of 210 (47.1%)	40 of 210 (19.0%)
1988	113 of 224 (50.4%)	62 of 224 (27.7%)
1989	107 of 224 (47.8%)	55 of 224 (24.6%)
1990	97 of 224 (43.3%)	54 of 224 (24.1%)
1991	112 of 224 (50.0%)	57 of 224 (25.4%)
1992	88 of 224 (39.3%)	48 of 224 (21.4%)
1993	*105 of 224 (46.9%)	53 of 224 (23.7%)
1994	115 of 224 (51.3%)	60 of 224 (26.8%)
1995	115 of 240 (47.9%)	61 of 240 (25.4%)
1996	109 of 240 (45.4%)	47 of 240 (19.6%)
1997	111 of 240 (46.3%)	67 of 240 (27.9%)
1998	113 of 240 (47.1%)	50 of 240 (20.8%)
1999	115 of 248 (46.4%)	**64 of 248 (25.8%)
2000	109 of 248 (44.0%)	61 of 248 (24.6%)
2001	121 of 248 (48.8%)	62 of 248 (25.0%)
2002	126 of 256 (49.2%)	63 of 256 (24.6%)
2003	124 of 256 (48.4%)	60 of 256 (23.4%)

*Week record: Dec. 11-13, 1993 (Week 15), 12 of 14 games (86%) decided by 7 points or less.
**Week record: Oct. 10-11, 1999 (Week 5), 10 of 14 games (71%) decided by 3 points or less.

GAMES DECIDED BY 8 PTS. OR LESS (1994-2003)

1994	121 of 224 (54.0%)	1999	124 of 248 (50.0%)
1995	123 of 240 (51.3%)	2000	119 of 248 (48.0%)
1996	115 of 240 (47.9%)	2001	128 of 248 (51.6%)
1997	120 of 240 (50.0%)	2002	137 of 256 (53.5%)
1998	120 of 240 (50.0%)	2003	132 of 256 (51.6%)

RECORDS AFTER BYE WEEKS (1990-2003)

AFC		NFC	
Baltimore	4-4	Arizona	7-8
Buffalo	10-5	Atlanta	7-8
Cincinnati	4-11	Carolina	3-6
Cleveland	3-7	Chicago	10-5
Denver	11-4	Dallas	11-4
Houston	0-2	Detroit	6-9
Indianapolis	7-8	Green Bay	8-7
Jacksonville	5-4	Minnesota	12-3
Kansas City	10-5	New Orleans	8-7
Miami	10-5	N.Y. Giants	3-12
New England	6-9	Philadelphia	11-4
N.Y. Jets	7-8	St. Louis	9-6
Oakland	9-6	San Francisco	8-7
Pittsburgh	8-7	Seattle	3-12
San Diego	6-8	Tampa Bay	5-10
Tennessee	9-6	Washington	8-7

INSIDE THE NUMBERS

2003 RECORDS OF TEAMS IN CLOSE GAMES

AFC	Overall Record	Decided by 8 Pts. or Less	Decided By 3 Pts. or Less
Baltimore	10-6	4-4	2-1
Buffalo	6-10	1-4	0-3
Cincinnati	8-8	8-5	2-2
Cleveland	5-11	3-7	1-2
Denver	10-6	3-3	2-1
Houston	5-11	5-5	2-3
Indianapolis	12-4	7-3	5-1
Jacksonville	5-11	4-6	1-2
Kansas City	13-3	6-1	2-0
Miami	10-6	3-4	3-1
New England	14-2	8-1	1-1
N.Y. Jets	6-10	5-7	2-3
Oakland	4-12	3-7	2-3
Pittsburgh	6-10	2-5	0-2
San Diego	4-12	3-4	0-1
Tennessee	12-4	5-3	2-1

NFC	Overall Record	Decided by 8 Pts. or Less	Decided By 3 Pts. or Less
Arizona	4-12	4-3	3-2
Atlanta	5-11	3-5	1-2
Carolina	11-5	9-3	7-0
Chicago	7-9	4-4	3-2
Dallas	10-6	5-1	2-0
Detroit	5-11	2-5	1-0
Green Bay	10-6	2-5	1-1
Minnesota	9-7	2-3	0-3
New Orleans	8-8	5-4	2-2
N.Y. Giants	4-12	2-3	2-1
Philadelphia	12-4	6-2	2-2
St. Louis	12-4	5-1	3-1
San Francisco	7-9	2-6	1-5
Seattle	10-6	5-4	2-2
Tampa Bay	7-9	2-7	0-5
Washington	5-11	4-7	3-5

SUPER BOWL CHAMPIONS THAT DID NOT MAKE PLAYOFFS THE FOLLOWING YEAR

Tampa Bay—Super Bowl XXXVII champions did not make playoffs in 2003 season.

New England—Super Bowl XXXVI champions did not make playoffs in the 2002 season.

Denver—Super Bowl XXXIII champions did not make playoffs in the 1999 season.

N.Y. Giants—Super Bowl XXV champions did not make playoffs in the 1991 season.

Washington—Super Bowl XXII champions did not make playoffs in the 1988 season.

N.Y. Giants—Super Bowl XXI champions did not make playoffs in the 1987 season.

San Francisco—Super Bowl XVI champions did not make playoffs in the 1982 season.

Oakland—Super Bowl XV champions did not make playoffs in the 1981 season.

Pittsburgh—Super Bowl XIV champions did not make playoffs in the 1980 season.

Kansas City—Super Bowl IV champions did not make playoffs in the 1970 season.

Green Bay—Super Bowl II champions did not make playoffs in the 1968 season.

NON-DIVISION WINNERS THAT PLAYED IN SUPER BOWL

2000 Baltimore Ravens .... Super Bowl XXXV
(Defeated N.Y. Giants, 34-7)

1999 Tennessee Titans .... Super Bowl XXXIV
(Lost to St. Louis, 23-16)

1997 Denver Broncos .... Super Bowl XXXII
(Defeated Green Bay, 31-24)

1992 Buffalo Bills .... Super Bowl XXVII
(Lost to Dallas, 52-17)

1985 New England Patriots .... Super Bowl XX
(Lost to Chicago, 46-10)

1980 Oakland Raiders .... Super Bowl XV
(Defeated Philadelphia, 27-10)

1975 Dallas Cowboys .... Super Bowl X
(Lost to Pittsburgh, 21-17)

1969 Kansas City Chiefs .... Super Bowl IV
(Defeated Minnesota, 23-7)

TEAMS AT OR UNDER .500 IN POSTSEASON PLAY

1999 Dallas Cowboys 8-8
1999 Detroit Lions 8-8
1991 New York Jets 8-8
1990 New Orleans Saints 8-8
1985 Cleveland Browns 8-8
1982 Cleveland Browns 4-5
1982 Detroit Lions 4-5
1969 Houston Oilers 6-6-2

COLDEST NFL GAMES ON RECORD

-13 degrees (-48 degree wind chill)—December 31, 1967, Lambeau Field, Green Bay, Wisconsin, NFL Championship (Green Bay 21, Dallas 17)

-9 degrees (-59 degree wind chill)—January 10, 1982, Riverfront Stadium, Cincinnati, Ohio, AFC Championship (Cincinnati 27, San Diego 7)

0 degrees (-32 degree wind chill)—January 15, 1994, Rich Stadium, Orchard Park, New York, AFC Divisional Playoff (Buffalo 29, Los Angeles Raiders 23)

TEAM LEADERS

Offense	Most Scored		Fewest Scored	
1st Quarter	123	St. Louis	23	Houston
2nd Quarter	166	Seattle	48	NY Jets
3rd Quarter	130	Indianapolis	31	Oakland
4th Quarter	150	Baltimore	51	Dallas

Defense	Most Allowed		Fewest Allowed	
1st Quarter	121	San Diego	41	Carolina
2nd Quarter	156	Detroit	64	Green Bay
3rd Quarter	116	Atlanta	44	Carolina
4th Quarter	125	Houston	33	Detroit

2003 NFL SCORE BY QUARTERS

AFC Offense	1	2	3	4	OT	PTS
Kansas City	112	153	82	131	6	484
Indianapolis	61	135	130	118	3	447
Tennessee	103	120	82	130	0	435
Baltimore	61	90	84	150	6	391
Denver	110	122	74	72	3	381
New England	80	83	79	97	9	348
Cincinnati	83	115	49	99	0	346
San Diego	60	86	50	117	0	313
Miami	68	124	44	72	3	311
Pittsburgh	50	94	93	63	0	300
N.Y. Jets	70	48	76	86	3	283
Jacksonville	34	93	57	92	0	276
Oakland	76	81	31	79	3	270
Houston	23	87	84	61	0	255
Cleveland	46	79	50	79	0	254
Buffalo	34	81	58	64	6	243

NFC Offense	1	2	3	4	OT	PTS
St. Louis	123	120	76	122	6	447
Green Bay	103	138	69	132	0	442
Minnesota	76	136	84	120	0	416
Seattle	89	166	67	82	0	404
San Francisco	85	133	78	85	3	384
Philadelphia	82	102	59	131	0	374
New Orleans	52	112	78	95	3	340
Carolina	73	70	87	86	9	325
Tampa Bay	34	105	60	102	0	301
Atlanta	88	99	50	56	6	299
Dallas	72	106	57	51	3	289
Washington	40	113	59	75	0	287
Chicago	46	76	53	108	0	283
Detroit	64	56	66	84	0	270
N.Y. Giants	44	83	47	63	6	243
Arizona	55	55	52	60	3	225

AFC Defense	1	2	3	4	OT	PTS
New England	42	73	51	72	0	238
Miami	49	86	48	72	6	261
Buffalo	54	93	54	78	0	279
Baltimore	63	73	77	65	3	281
N.Y. Jets	64	130	48	54	3	299
Denver	63	87	45	106	0	301
Cleveland	74	102	59	84	3	322
Tennessee	52	75	75	122	0	324
Pittsburgh	61	98	71	94	3	327
Jacksonville	85	81	57	108	0	331
Kansas City	57	94	85	96	0	332
Indianapolis	75	89	83	86	3	336
Oakland	99	110	59	108	3	379
Houston	64	115	73	125	3	380
Cincinnati	71	117	74	116	6	384
San Diego	121	140	60	117	3	441

NFC Defense	1	2	3	4	OT	PTS
Dallas	52	69	70	69	0	260
Tampa Bay	50	83	56	69	6	264
Philadelphia	43	91	62	88	3	287
Carolina	41	94	44	119	6	304
Green Bay	86	64	49	102	6	307
New Orleans	64	140	55	64	3	326
Seattle	51	104	73	96	3	327
St. Louis	67	117	82	62	0	328
San Francisco	66	113	48	104	6	337
Chicago	69	109	50	118	0	346
Minnesota	69	92	72	120	0	353
Washington	78	106	76	109	6	372
Detroit	94	156	96	33	0	379
N.Y. Giants	91	111	98	84	3	387
Atlanta	65	132	116	106	3	422
Arizona	117	117	99	116	3	452
NFL Totals	**2,197**	**3,261**	**2,165**	**2,962**	**81**	**10,666**

LARGEST TRADES IN NFL HISTORY

(Based on number of players or draft choices involved)

18—October 13, 1989—RB Herschel Walker from the Dallas Cowboys to Minnesota. Dallas also traded its third-round choice in 1990, its tenth-round choice in 1990, and its third-round choice in 1991 to Minnesota. Minnesota traded LB Jesse Solomon, LB David Howard, CB Issiac Holt, and DE Alex Stewart along with its first-round choice in 1990, its second-round choice in 1990, its sixth-round choice in 1990, its first-round choice in 1991, its second-round choice in 1991, its first-round choice in 1992, its second-round choice in 1992, and its third-round choice in 1992 to Dallas. Minnesota traded RB Darrin Nelson to Dallas, which traded Nelson to San Diego for the Chargers' fifth-round choice in 1990, which Dallas then sent to Minnesota.

15—March 26, 1953—T Mike McCormack, DT Don Colo, LB Tom Catlin, DB John Petitbon, and G Herschell Forester from Baltimore to Cleveland for DB Don Shula, DB Bert Rechichar, DB Carl Taseff, LB Ed Sharkey, E Gern Nagler, QB Harry Agganis, T Dick Batten, T Stu Sheets, G Art Spinney, and G Elmer Willhoite.

15—January 28, 1971—LB Marlin McKeever, first- and third-round choices in 1971, and third-, fourth-, fifth-, sixth-, and seventh-round choices in 1972 from Washington to the Los Angeles Rams for LB Maxie Baughan, LB Jack Pardee, LB Myron Pottios, RB Jeff Jordan, G John Wilbur, DT Diron Talbert, and a fifth-round choice in 1971.

12—June 13, 1952—Selection rights to Les Richter from the Dallas Texans to the Los Angeles Rams for RB Dick Hoerner, DB Tom Keane, DB George Sims, C Joe Reid, HB Billy Baggett, T Jack Halliday, FB Dick McKissack, LB Vic Vasicek, E Richard Wilkins, C Aubrey Phillips, and RB Dave Anderson.

10—March 23, 1959—HB Ollie Matson from the Chicago Cardinals to the Los Angeles Rams for T Frank Fuller, DE Glenn Holtzman, T Ken Panfil, DT Art Hauser, E John Tracey, FB Larry Hickman, HB Don Brown, the Rams second-round choice in 1960, and a player to be delivered during the 1959 training camp.

10—October 31, 1987—RB Eric Dickerson from the Los Angeles Rams to Indianapolis. The rights to LB Cornelius Bennett from Indianapolis to Buffalo. Indianapolis running back Owen Gill and the Colts' first- and second-round choices in 1988 and second-round choice in 1989, plus Bills running back Greg Bell and Buffalo's first-round choice in 1988 and first- and second-round choices in 1989 to the Rams.

INSIDE THE NUMBERS

2004 TOP 100 TELEVISION MARKETS
(NFL TEAM MARKETS IN BOLD)

RANK	DMA	TV HHLDS	Cable TV HHLD'S	% of Cable Penetration
1	**New York**	**7,542,800**	**7,376,330**	**6.804**
2	Los Angeles	5,520,800	5,402,260	4.983
3	**Chicago**	**3,449,500**	**3,399,460**	**3.136**
4	**Philadelphia**	**2,908,000**	**2,874,330**	**2.651**
5	**San Francisco-Oakland-San Jose**	**2,533,800**	**2,440,920**	**2.252**
6	**Boston (Manchester, NH)**	**2,424,800**	**2,391,830**	**2.206**
7	**Dallas-Ft. Worth**	**2,287,700**	**2,255,970**	**2.081**
8	**Washington, DC (Hagerstown)**	**2,260,300**	**2,224,070**	**2.052**
9	**Atlanta**	**2,065,500**	**2,035,060**	**1.877**
10	**Detroit**	**1,942,400**	**1,923,230**	**1.774**
11	**Houston**	**1,882,700**	**1,848,770**	**1.705**
12	**Seattle-Tacoma**	**1,746,900**	**1,685,480**	**1.555**
13	**Tampa-St. Petersburg (Sarasota)**	**1,667,100**	**1,644,270**	**1.517**
14	**Minneapolis-St. Paul**	**1,657,300**	**1,635,650**	**1.509**
15	**Phoenix**	**1,599,500**	**1,561,760**	**1.441**
16	**Cleveland**	**1,563,300**	**1,542,970**	**1.423**
17	**Miami-Ft. Lauderdale**	**1,536,900**	**1,510,740**	**1.394**
18	**Denver**	**1,437,000**	**1,399,100**	**1.291**
19	Sacramnto-Stockton-Modesto	1,308,100	1,278,430	1.179
20	Orlando-Daytona Beach-Melbourne	1,281,000	1,263,900	1.166
21	**St. Louis**	**1,217,300**	**1,202,170**	**1.109**
22	**Pittsburgh**	**1,189,000**	**1,175,410**	**1.084**
23	**Baltimore**	**1,095,800**	**1,083,030**	**0.999**
24	Portland, OR	1,111,500	1,073,210	0.990
25	**Indianapolis**	**1,052,000**	**1,038,370**	**0.958**
26	**San Diego**	**1,055,600**	**1,029,210**	**0.949**
27	Hartford & New Haven	1,014,900	1,001,320	0.924
28	**Charlotte**	**1,000,500**	**986,830**	**0.910**
29	Raleigh-Durham (Fayeteville)	961,600	947,750	0.874
30	**Nashville**	**919,000**	**904,380**	**0.834**
31	**Kansas City**	**886,700**	**875,090**	**0.807**
32	**Cincinnati**	**882,100**	**872,330**	**0.805**
33	Milwaukee	878,400	871,490	0.804
34	Columbus, OH	863,500	854,040	0.788
35	Greenville-Spartanburg-Asheville-Anderson	820,600	806,930	0.744
36	Salt Lake City	804,100	786,030	0.725
37	San Antonio	751,600	736,240	0.679
38	Grand Rapids-Kalamazoo-Battle Creek	733,500	724,290	0.668
39	West Palm Beach-Ft. Pierce	721,600	709,290	0.654
40	Birmingham (Anniston,Tuscaloosa)	707,000	697,570	0.643
41	Norfolk-Portsmouth-Newport News	702,400	693,660	0.640
42	**New Orleans**	**674,500**	**665,190**	**0.614**
43	Memphis	672,800	662,280	0.611
44	**Buffalo**	**655,500**	**647,920**	**0.598**
45	Oklahoma City	656,400	647,390	0.597
46	Greensboro-High Point-Winston-Salem	653,500	645,430	0.595
47	Harrisburg-Lancaster-Lebanon-York	654,100	637,240	0.588
48	Providence-New Bedford	641,700	635,610	0.586
49	Albuquerque-Santa Fe	662,100	633,500	0.584
50	Louisville	632,600	624,470	0.576

2004 TOP 100 TELEVISION MARKETS
(NFL TEAM MARKETS IN BOLD)

RANK	DMA	TV HHLDS	Cable TV HHLD'S	% of Cable Penetration
51	Las Vegas	611,400	601,700	0.555
52	**Jacksonville, Brunswick**	**608,100**	**598,070**	**0.552**
53	Wilkes Barre-Scranton	599,300	590,100	0.544
54	Austin	591,200	577,740	0.533
55	Albany-Schenectady-Troy	550,400	542,670	0.501
56	Little Rock-Pine Bluff	533,400	524,090	0.483
57	Fresno-Visalia	531,500	521,160	0.481
58	Richmond-Petersburg	519,000	512,310	0.473
59	Dayton	517,100	511,770	0.472
60	Tulsa	513,400	505,000	0.466
61	Knoxville	507,300	499,040	0.460
62	Mobile-Pensacola (Ft. Walton Beach)	505,200	497,570	0.459
63	Charleston-Huntington	503,900	495,190	0.457
64	Flint-Saginaw-Bay City	478,100	473,910	0.437
65	Lexington	478,100	466,980	0.431
66	Roanoke-Lynchburg	458,100	450,090	0.415
67	Wichita-Hutchinson Plus	455,600	447,710	0.413
68	**Green Bay-Appleton**	**429,600**	**426,820**	**0.394**
69	Toledo	429,700	425,770	0.393
70	Ft. Myers-Naples	426,500	421,130	0.388
71	Tucson (Sierra Vista)	424,300	413,460	0.381
72	Honolulu	427,700	412,190	0.380
73	Des Moines-Ames	409,000	404,580	0.373
74	Portland-Auburn	405,200	398,500	0.368
75	Rochester, NY	399,200	395,350	0.365
76	Paducah, KY-Cape Girardeau, MO-Harrisburg-Mount Vernon, IL	397,000	391,080	0.361
77	Omaha	393,600	389,270	0.359
78	Springfield, MO	397,900	389,150	0.359
79	Syracuse	390,800	384,290	0.354
80	Spokane	396,100	381,820	0.352
81	Shreveport	386,800	379,880	0.350
82	Champaign & Sprngfld-Decatur	384,100	378,560	0.349
83	Huntsville-Decatur (Florence)	368,900	364,340	0.336
84	Columbia, SC	369,200	363,750	0.336
85	Madison	360,700	355,010	0.327
86	Chattanooga	354,300	349,260	0.322
87	South Bend-Elkhart	335,200	330,200	0.305
88	Cedar Rapids-Waterloo & Dubuque	332,300	328,060	0.303
89	Burlington-Plattsburgh	332,200	323,070	0.298
90	Jackson, MS	328,800	322,480	0.297
91	Tri-Cities, TN-VA	327,200	322,130	0.297
92	Waco-Temple-Bryan	315,700	310,280	0.286
93	Colorado Springs-Pueblo	315,900	309,960	0.286
94	Davenport-Rock Island-Moline	311,600	308,460	0.285
95	Baton Rouge	304,100	299,980	0.277
96	Johnstown-Altoona	302,400	297,460	0.274
97	Harlingen-Weslaco-Brownsville-McAllen	305,100	297,390	0.274
98	Savannah	294,200	288,830	0.266
99	Evansville	286,900	284,000	0.262
100	El Paso	288,200	283,870	0.262
TOTAL NFL MARKETS		**52,171,200**	**51,254,760**	**47.279**
TOTAL TOP 100 MARKETS		**94,778,800**	**93,107,680**	**85.885**
TOTAL		**110,395,700**	**108,410,160**	**100.000**

RETIRED UNIFORM NUMBERS IN NFL

AFC

Baltimore	None	
Buffalo	Jim Kelly	12
Cincinnati	Bob Johnson	54
Cleveland	Otto Graham	14
	Jim Brown	32
	Ernie Davis	45
	Don Fleming	46
	Lou Groza	76
Denver	John Elway	7
	Frank Tripucka	18
	Floyd Little	44
Houston	None	
Indianapolis	Johnny Unitas	19
	Buddy Young	22
	Lenny Moore	24
	Art Donovan	70
	Jim Parker	77
	Raymond Berry	82
	Gino Marchetti	89
Jacksonville	None	
Kansas City	Jan Stenerud	3
	Len Dawson	16
	Abner Haynes	28
	Stone Johnson	33
	Mack Lee Hill	36
	Willie Lanier	63
	Bobby Bell	78
	Buck Buchanan	86
Miami	Bob Griese	12
	Dan Marino	13
	Larry Csonka	39
New England	Gino Cappelletti	20
	Mike Haynes	40
	Steve Nelson	57
	John Hannah	73
	Jim Hunt	79
	Bob Dee	89
New York Jets	Joe Namath	12
	Don Maynard	13
Oakland	None	
Pittsburgh	Ernie Stautner	70
San Diego	Dan Fouts	14
Tennessee	Earl Campbell	34
	Jim Norton	43
	Mike Munchak	63
	Elvin Bethea	65
	Bruce Matthews	74

NFC

Arizona	Larry Wilson	8
	Stan Mauldin	77
	J.V. Cain	88
	Marshall Goldberg	99
Atlanta	Steve Bartowski	10
	William Andrews	31
	Jeff Van Note	57
	Tommy Nobis	60
Carolina	None	
Chicago	Bronko Nagurski	3
	George McAfee	5
	George Halas	7
	Willie Galimore	28
	Walter Payton	34
	Gale Sayers	40
	Brian Piccolo	41
	Sid Luckman	42
	Dick Butkus	51
	Bill Hewitt	56
	Bill George	61
	Bulldog Turner	66
	Red Grange	77
Dallas	None	
Detroit	Dutch Clark	7
	Bobby Layne	22
	Doak Walker	37
	Joe Schmidt	56
	Chuck Hughes	85
Green Bay	Tony Canadeo	3
	Don Hutson	14
	Bart Starr	15
	Ray Nitschke	66
Minnesota	Fran Tarkenton	10
	Mick Tingelhoff	53
	Jim Marshall	70
	Korey Stringer	77
	Cris Carter	80
	Alan Page	88
New Orleans	Jim Taylor	31
	Doug Atkins	81
New York Giants	Ray Flaherty	1
	Tuffy Leemans	4
	Mel Hein	7
	Phil Simms	11
	Y.A. Tittle	14
	Frank Gifford	16
	Al Blozis	32
	Joe Morrison	40
	Charlie Conerly	42
	Ken Strong	50
	Lawrence Taylor	56
Philadelphia	Steve Van Buren	15
	Tom Brookshier	40
	Pete Retzlaff	44
	Chuck Bednarik	60
	Al Wistert	70
	Jerome Brown	99
St. Louis	Bob Waterfield	7
	Eric Dickerson	29
	Merlin Olsen	74
	Jackie Slater	78
	Jack Youngblood	85
San Francisco	John Brodie	12
	Joe Montana	16
	Joe Perry	34
	Jimmy Johnson	37
	Hugh McElhenny	39
	Ronnie Lott	42
	Charlie Krueger	70
	Leo Nomellini	73
	Bob St. Clair	79
	Dwight Clark	87
Seattle	"Fans/the twelfth man"	12
	Steve Largent	80
Tampa Bay	Lee Roy Selmon	63
Washington	Sammy Baugh	33

ALL-TIME REGULAR-SEASON RECORDS OF CURRENT NFL TEAMS

AFC

BALTIMORE RAVENS

	All Games			Home Games			Road Games		
Season	W	L	T	W	L	T	W	L	T
1996	4	12		4	4		0	8	
1997	6	9	1	3	4	1	3	5	
1998	6	10		4	4		2	6	
1999	8	8		4	4		4	4	
2000	12	4		6	2		6	2	
2001	10	6		6	2		4	4	
2002	7	9		4	4		3	5	
2003	10	6		7	1		3	5	
	63	64	1	38	25	1	25	39	

BUFFALO BILLS

	All Games			Home Games			Road Games		
Season	W	L	T	W	L	T	W	L	T
1960	5	8	1	3	4		2	4	1
1961	6	8		2	5		4	3	
1962	7	6	1	3	3	1	4	3	
1963	7	6	1	4	2	1	3	4	
1964	12	2		6	1		6	1	
1965	10	3	1	5	2		5	1	1
1966	9	4	1	4	2	1	5	2	
1967	4	10		2	5		2	5	
1968	1	12	1	1	6		0	6	1
1969	4	10		4	3		0	7	
1970	3	10	1	1	6		2	4	1
1971	1	13		1	6		0	7	
1972	4	9	1	2	4	1	2	5	
1973	9	5		5	2		4	3	
1974	9	5		5	2		4	3	
1975	8	6		3	4		5	2	
1976	2	12		1	6		1	6	
1977	3	11		1	6		2	5	
1978	5	11		4	4		1	7	
1979	7	9		3	5		4	4	
1980	11	5		6	2		5	3	
1981	10	6		7	1		3	5	
1982	4	5		4	1		0	4	
1983	8	8		3	5		5	3	
1984	2	14		2	6		0	8	
1985	2	14		2	6		0	8	
1986	4	12		3	5		1	7	
1987	7	8		4	4		3	4	
1988	12	4		8	0		4	4	
1989	9	7		6	2		3	5	
1990	13	3		8	0		5	3	
1991	13	3		7	1		6	2	
1992	11	5		6	2		5	3	
1993	12	4		6	2		6	2	
1994	7	9		4	4		3	5	
1995	10	6		6	2		4	4	
1996	10	6		7	1		3	5	
1997	6	10		4	4		2	6	
1998	10	6		6	2		4	4	
1999	11	5		6	2		5	3	
2000	8	8		5	3		3	5	
2001	3	13		1	7		2	6	
2002	8	8		5	3		3	5	
2003	6	10		4	4		2	6	
	313	339	8	180	147	4	133	192	4

CINCINNATI BENGALS

	All Games			Home Games			Road Games		
Season	W	L	T	W	L	T	W	L	T
1968	3	11		2	5		1	6	
1969	4	9	1	4	3		0	6	1
1970	8	6		5	2		3	4	
1971	4	10		3	4		1	6	
1972	8	6		4	3		4	3	
1973	10	4		7	0		3	4	
1974	7	7		4	3		3	4	
1975	11	3		6	1		5	2	
1976	10	4		6	1		4	3	
1977	8	6		5	2		3	4	
1978	4	12		3	5		1	7	
1979	4	12		4	4		0	8	
1980	6	10		3	5		3	5	
1981	12	4		6	2		6	2	
1982	7	2		4	0		3	2	
1983	7	9		4	4		3	5	
1984	8	8		5	3		3	5	
1985	7	9		5	3		2	6	
1986	10	6		6	2		4	4	
1987	4	11		1	7		3	4	
1988	12	4		8	0		4	4	
1989	8	8		5	3		3	5	
1990	9	7		5	3		4	4	
1991	3	13		3	5		0	8	
1992	5	11		3	5		2	6	
1993	3	13		3	5		0	8	
1994	3	13		2	6		1	7	
1995	7	9		3	5		4	4	
1996	8	8		6	2		2	6	
1997	7	9		6	2		1	7	
1998	3	13		1	7		2	6	
1999	4	12		2	6		2	6	
2000	4	12		3	5		1	7	
2001	6	10		4	4		2	6	
2002	2	14		1	7		1	7	
2003	8	8		5	3		3	5	
	234	313	1	147	127		87	186	1

CLEVELAND BROWNS*

	All Games			Home Games			Road Games		
Season	W	L	T	W	L	T	W	L	T
1950	10	2		5	1		5	1	
1951	11	1		6	0		5	1	
1952	8	4		4	2		4	2	
1953	11	1		6	0		5	1	
1954	9	3		5	1		4	2	
1955	9	2	1	5	1		4	1	1
1956	5	7		1	5		4	2	
1957	9	2	1	6	0		3	2	1
1958	9	3		4	2		5	1	
1959	7	5		3	3		4	2	
1960	8	3	1	4	2		4	1	1
1961	8	5	1	4	3		4	2	1
1962	7	6	1	4	2	1	3	4	
1963	10	4		5	2		5	2	
1964	10	3	1	5	1	1	5	2	
1965	11	3		5	2		6	1	
1966	9	5		5	2		4	3	
1967	9	5		6	1		3	4	
1968	10	4		5	2		5	2	
1969	10	3	1	5	1	1	5	2	
1970	7	7		4	3		3	4	
1971	9	5		4	3		5	2	
1972	10	4		4	3		6	1	
1973	7	5	2	5	1	1	2	4	1
1974	4	10		3	4		1	6	
1975	3	11		3	4		0	7	
1976	9	5		6	1		3	4	
1977	6	8		2	5		4	3	
1978	8	8		5	3		3	5	
1979	9	7		5	3		4	4	
1980	11	5		6	2		5	3	

Season	W	L	T	W	L	T	W	L	T
1981	5	11		3	5		2	6	
1982	4	5		2	2		2	3	
1983	9	7		6	2		3	5	
1984	5	11		2	6		3	5	
1985	8	8		5	3		3	5	
1986	12	4		6	2		6	2	
1987	10	5		5	2		5	3	
1988	10	6		6	2		4	4	
1989	9	6	1	5	2	1	4	4	
1990	3	13		2	6		1	7	
1991	6	10		3	5		3	5	
1992	7	9		4	4		3	5	
1993	7	9		4	4		3	5	
1994	11	5		6	2		5	3	
1995	5	11		3	5		2	6	
1999	2	14		0	8		2	6	
2000	3	13		2	6		1	7	
2001	7	9		4	4		3	5	
2002	9	7		3	5		6	2	
2003	5	11		2	6		3	5	
	400	320	10	213	146	5	187	174	5

Did not play from 1996-98.

DENVER BRONCOS

	All Games			Home Games			Road Games		
Season	W	L	T	W	L	T	W	L	T
1960	4	9	1	2	4	1	2	5	
1961	3	11		2	5		1	6	
1962	7	7		3	4		4	3	
1963	2	11	1	2	5		0	6	1
1964	2	11	1	2	4	1	0	7	
1965	4	10		2	5		2	5	
1966	4	10		3	4		1	6	
1967	3	11		1	6		2	5	
1968	5	9		3	4		2	5	
1969	5	8	1	4	2	1	1	6	
1970	5	8	1	3	3	1	2	5	
1971	4	9	1	2	4	1	2	5	
1972	5	9		3	4		2	5	
1973	7	5	2	3	3	1	4	2	1
1974	7	6	1	3	3	1	4	3	
1975	6	8		5	2		1	6	
1976	9	5		6	1		3	4	
1977	12	2		6	1		6	1	
1978	10	6		6	2		4	4	
1979	10	6		6	2		4	4	
1980	8	8		4	4		4	4	
1981	10	6		8	0		2	6	
1982	2	7		1	4		1	3	
1983	9	7		6	2		3	5	
1984	13	3		7	1		6	2	
1985	11	5		6	2		5	3	
1986	11	5		7	1		4	4	
1987	10	4	1	7	1		3	3	1
1988	8	8		6	2		2	6	
1989	11	5		6	2		5	3	
1990	5	11		4	4		1	7	
1991	12	4		7	1		5	3	
1992	8	8		7	1		1	7	
1993	9	7		5	3		4	4	
1994	7	9		4	4		3	5	
1995	8	8		6	2		2	6	
1996	13	3		8	0		5	3	
1997	12	4		8	0		4	4	
1998	14	2		8	0		6	2	
1999	6	10		3	5		3	5	
2000	11	5		6	2		5	3	
2001	8	8		6	2		2	6	
2002	9	7		5	3		4	4	
2003	10	6		6	2		4	4	
	339	311	10	208	116	7	131	195	3

HOUSTON TEXANS

	All Games			Home Games			Road Games		
Season	W	L	T	W	L	T	W	L	T
2002	4	12		2	6		2	6	
2003	5	11		3	5		2	6	
	9	23		5	11		4	12	

INDIANAPOLIS COLTS*

	All Games			Home Games			Road Games		
Season	W	L	T	W	L	T	W	L	T
1953	3	9		2	4		1	5	
1954	3	9		2	4		1	5	
1955	5	6	1	4	1	1	1	5	
1956	5	7		4	2		1	5	
1957	7	5		4	2		3	3	
1958	9	3		6	0		3	3	
1959	9	3		4	2		5	1	
1960	6	6		4	2		2	4	
1961	8	6		5	2		3	4	
1962	7	7		3	4		4	3	
1963	8	6		4	3		4	3	
1964	12	2		7	1		5	1	
1965	10	3	1	5	2		5	1	1
1966	9	5		5	2		4	3	
1967	11	1	2	6	0	1	5	1	1
1968	13	1		6	1		7	0	
1969	8	5	1	4	2	1	4	3	
1970	11	2	1	5	1	1	6	1	
1971	10	4		5	2		5	2	
1972	5	9		2	5		3	4	
1973	4	10		3	4		1	6	
1974	2	12		0	7		2	5	
1975	10	4		5	2		5	2	
1976	11	3		6	1		5	2	
1977	10	4		6	1		4	3	
1978	5	11		2	6		3	5	
1979	5	11		3	5		2	6	
1980	7	9		2	6		5	3	
1981	2	14		1	7		1	7	
1982	0	8	1	0	3	1	0	5	
1983	7	9		3	5		4	4	
1984	4	12		2	6		2	6	
1985	5	11		4	4		1	7	
1986	3	13		1	7		2	6	
1987	9	6		4	4		5	2	
1988	9	7		6	2		3	5	
1989	8	8		6	2		2	6	
1990	7	9		3	5		4	4	
1991	1	15		0	8		1	7	
1992	9	7		4	4		5	3	
1993	4	12		2	6		2	6	
1994	8	8		5	3		3	5	
1995	9	7		5	3		4	4	
1996	9	7		6	2		3	5	
1997	3	13		2	6		1	7	
1998	3	13		3	5		0	8	
1999	13	3		7	1		6	2	
2000	10	6		6	2		4	4	
2001	6	10		3	5		3	5	
2002	10	6		5	3		5	3	
2003	12	4		5	3		7	1	
	364	371	7	197	170	5	167	201	2

includes Baltimore Colts (1953-1983).

JACKSONVILLE JAGUARS

Season	All Games W	L	T	Home Games W	L	T	Road Games W	L	T
1995	4	12		2	6		2	6	
1996	9	7		7	1		2	6	
1997	11	5		7	1		4	4	
1998	11	5		7	1		4	4	
1999	14	2		7	1		7	1	
2000	7	9		4	4		3	5	
2001	6	10		3	5		3	5	
2002	6	10		3	5		3	5	
2003	5	11		5	3		0	8	
	73	71		45	27		28	44	

KANSAS CITY CHIEFS*

Season	All Games W	L	T	Home Games W	L	T	Road Games W	L	T
1960	8	6		5	2		3	4	
1961	6	8		4	3		2	5	
1962	11	3		6	1		5	2	
1963	5	7	2	4	3		1	4	2
1964	7	7		4	3		3	4	
1965	7	5	2	5	2		2	3	2
1966	11	2	1	4	2	1	7	0	
1967	9	5		4	3		5	2	
1968	12	2		6	1		6	1	
1969	11	3		6	1		5	2	
1970	7	5	2	4	1	2	3	4	
1971	10	3	1	7	0		3	3	1
1972	8	6		3	4		5	2	
1973	7	5	2	5	1	1	2	4	1
1974	5	9		1	6		4	3	
1975	5	9		3	4		2	5	
1976	5	9		1	6		4	3	
1977	2	12		1	6		1	6	
1978	4	12		3	5		1	7	
1979	7	9		3	5		4	4	
1980	8	8		3	5		5	3	
1981	9	7		5	3		4	4	
1982	3	6		2	2		1	4	
1983	6	10		5	3		1	7	
1984	8	8		5	3		3	5	
1985	6	10		5	3		1	7	
1986	10	6		6	2		4	4	
1987	4	11		3	4		1	7	
1988	4	11	1	4	4		0	7	1
1989	8	7	1	5	3		3	4	1
1990	11	5		6	2		5	3	
1991	10	6		6	2		4	4	
1992	10	6		7	1		3	5	
1993	11	5		7	1		4	4	
1994	9	7		5	3		4	4	
1995	13	3		8	0		5	3	
1996	9	7		5	3		4	4	
1997	13	3		8	0		5	3	
1998	7	9		5	3		2	6	
1999	9	7		6	2		3	5	
2000	7	9		5	3		2	6	
2001	6	10		3	5		3	5	
2002	8	8		6	2		2	6	
2003	13	3		8	0		5	3	
	349	299	12	207	118	4	142	181	8

**includes Dallas Texans (1960-62).*

MIAMI DOLPHINS

Season	All Games W	L	T	Home Games W	L	T	Road Games W	L	T
1966	3	11		2	5		1	6	
1967	4	10		4	3		0	7	
1968	5	8	1	1	5	1	4	3	
1969	3	10	1	2	4	1	1	6	
1970	10	4		6	1		4	3	
1971	10	3	1	6	1		4	2	1
1972	14	0		7	0		7	0	
1973	12	2		7	0		5	2	
1974	11	3		7	0		4	3	
1975	10	4		5	2		5	2	
1976	6	8		3	4		3	4	
1977	10	4		6	1		4	3	
1978	11	5		7	1		4	4	
1979	10	6		6	2		4	4	
1980	8	8		5	3		3	5	
1981	11	4	1	6	1	1	5	3	
1982	7	2		4	0		3	2	
1983	12	4		7	1		5	3	
1984	14	2		7	1		7	1	
1985	12	4		8	0		4	4	
1986	8	8		4	4		4	4	
1987	8	7		4	3		4	4	
1988	6	10		4	4		2	6	
1989	8	8		4	4		4	4	
1990	12	4		7	1		5	3	
1991	8	8		5	3		3	5	
1992	11	5		6	2		5	3	
1993	9	7		4	4		5	3	
1994	10	6		6	2		4	4	
1995	9	7		5	3		4	4	
1996	8	8		4	4		4	4	
1997	9	7		6	2		3	5	
1998	10	6		7	1		3	5	
1999	9	7		5	3		4	4	
2000	11	5		5	3		6	2	
2001	11	5		7	1		4	4	
2002	9	7		7	1		2	6	
2003	10	6		4	4		6	2	
	349	223	4	200	84	3	149	139	1

NEW ENGLAND PATRIOTS*

Season	All Games W	L	T	Home Games W	L	T	Road Games W	L	T
1960	5	9		3	4		2	5	
1961	9	4	1	4	2	1	5	2	
1962	9	4	1	6	1		3	3	1
1963	7	6	1	5	1	1	2	5	
1964	10	3	1	4	2	1	6	1	
1965	4	8	2	1	4	2	3	4	
1966	8	4	2	4	2	1	4	2	1
1967	3	10	1	2	4		1	6	1
1968	4	10		2	5		2	5	
1969	4	10		2	5		2	5	
1970	2	12		1	6		1	6	
1971	6	8		5	2		1	6	
1972	3	11		2	5		1	6	
1973	5	9		3	4		2	5	
1974	7	7		3	4		4	3	
1975	3	11		2	5		1	6	
1976	11	3		6	1		5	2	
1977	9	5		6	1		3	4	
1978	11	5		5	3		6	2	
1979	9	7		6	2		3	5	
1980	10	6		6	2		4	4	
1981	2	14		2	6		0	8	
1982	5	4		3	1		2	3	
1983	8	8		5	3		3	5	
1984	9	7		5	3		4	4	
1985	11	5		7	1		4	4	
1986	11	5		4	4		7	1	
1987	8	7		5	3		3	4	
1988	9	7		7	1		2	6	
1989	5	11		3	5		2	6	

Season	W	L	T	W	L	T	W	L	T
1990	1	15		0	8		1	7	
1991	6	10		4	4		2	6	
1992	2	14		1	7		1	7	
1993	5	11		3	5		2	6	
1994	10	6		5	3		5	3	
1995	6	10		3	5		3	5	
1996	11	5		6	2		5	3	
1997	10	6		6	2		4	4	
1998	9	7		6	2		3	5	
1999	8	8		5	3		3	5	
2000	5	11		3	5		2	6	
2001	11	5		6	2		5	3	
2002	9	7		5	3		4	4	
2003	14	2		8	0		6	2	
	314	337	9	180	143	6	134	194	3

**includes Boston Patriots (1960-1970).*

NEW YORK JETS*

	All Games			Home Games			Road Games		
Season	W	L	T	W	L	T	W	L	T
1960	7	7		3	4		4	3	
1961	7	7		5	2		2	5	
1962	5	9		2	5		3	4	
1963	5	8	1	4	2	1	1	6	
1964	5	8	1	5	1	1	0	7	
1965	5	8	1	3	3	1	2	5	
1966	6	6	2	4	3		2	3	2
1967	8	5	1	4	2	1	4	3	
1968	11	3		6	1		5	2	
1969	10	4		5	2		5	2	
1970	4	10		2	5		2	5	
1971	6	8		4	3		2	5	
1972	7	7		4	3		3	4	
1973	4	10		2	4		2	6	
1974	7	7		3	4		4	3	
1975	3	11		1	6		2	5	
1976	3	11		2	5		1	6	
1977	3	11		1	6		2	5	
1978	8	8		4	4		4	4	
1979	8	8		6	2		2	6	
1980	4	12		2	6		2	6	
1981	10	5	1	6	2		4	3	1
1982	6	3		3	1		3	2	
1983	7	9		2	6		5	3	
1984	7	9		3	5		4	4	
1985	11	5		7	1		4	4	
1986	10	6		5	3		5	3	
1987	6	9		4	4		2	5	
1988	8	7	1	5	2	1	3	5	
1989	4	12		1	7		3	5	
1990	6	10		3	5		3	5	
1991	8	8		4	4		4	4	
1992	4	12		3	5		1	7	
1993	8	8		3	5		5	3	
1994	6	10		4	4		2	6	
1995	3	13		2	6		1	7	
1996	1	15		0	8		1	7	
1997	9	7		5	3		4	4	
1998	12	4		7	1		5	3	
1999	8	8		4	4		4	4	
2000	9	7		5	3		4	4	
2001	10	6		3	5		7	1	
2002	9	7		5	3		4	4	
2003	6	10		4	4		2	6	
	294	358	8	160	164	5	134	194	3

**includes New York Titans (1960-62).*

OAKLAND RAIDERS*

	All Games			Home Games			Road Games		
Season	W	L	T	W	L	T	W	L	T
1960	6	8		3	4		3	4	
1961	2	12		1	6		1	6	
1962	1	13		1	6		0	7	
1963	10	4		6	1		4	3	
1964	5	7	2	5	2		0	5	2
1965	8	5	1	5	2		3	3	1
1966	8	5	1	3	3	1	5	2	
1967	13	1		7	0		6	1	
1968	12	2		6	1		6	1	
1969	12	1	1	7	0		5	1	1
1970	8	4	2	6	1		2	3	2
1971	8	4	2	5	1	1	3	3	1
1972	10	3	1	5	1	1	5	2	
1973	9	4	1	5	2		4	2	1
1974	12	2		6	1		6	1	
1975	11	3		6	1		5	2	
1976	13	1		7	0		6	1	
1977	11	3		6	1		5	2	
1978	9	7		4	4		5	3	
1979	9	7		6	2		3	5	
1980	11	5		6	2		5	3	
1981	7	9		4	4		3	5	
1982	8	1		4	0		4	1	
1983	12	4		6	2		6	2	
1984	11	5		6	2		5	3	
1985	12	4		7	1		5	3	
1986	8	8		3	5		5	3	
1987	5	10		3	5		2	5	
1988	7	9		3	5		4	4	
1989	8	8		7	1		1	7	
1990	12	4		6	2		6	2	
1991	9	7		5	3		4	4	
1992	7	9		5	3		2	6	
1993	10	6		5	3		5	3	
1994	9	7		4	4		5	3	
1995	8	8		4	4		4	4	
1996	7	9		4	4		3	5	
1997	4	12		2	6		2	6	
1998	8	8		4	4		4	4	
1999	8	8		5	3		3	5	
2000	12	4		7	1		5	3	
2001	10	6		5	3		5	3	
2002	11	5		6	2		5	3	
2003	4	12		4	4		0	8	
	385	264	11	215	112	3	170	152	8

**includes Los Angeles Raiders (1982-1994).*

PITTSBURGH STEELERS*

	All Games			Home Games			Road Games		
Season	W	L	T	W	L	T	W	L	T
1933	3	6	2	2	3		1	3	2
1934	2	10		1	5		1	5	
1935	4	8		2	5		2	3	
1936	6	6		4	1		2	5	
1937	4	7		2	4		2	3	
1938	2	9		0	5		2	4	
1939	1	9	1	1	4		0	5	1
1940	2	7	2	1	2	2	1	5	
1941	1	9	1	1	4		0	5	1
1942	7	4		3	2		4	2	
1945	2	8		1	4		1	4	
1946	5	5	1	4	1		1	4	1
1947	8	4		5	1		3	3	
1948	4	8		4	2		0	6	
1949	6	5	1	3	2	1	3	3	
1950	6	6		2	4		4	2	
1951	4	7	1	1	4	1	3	3	

Season	W	L	T	W	L	T	W	L	T
1952	5	7		2	4		3	3	
1953	6	6		3	3		3	3	
1954	5	7		4	2		1	5	
1955	4	8		3	2		1	6	
1956	5	7		3	3		2	4	
1957	6	6		4	2		2	4	
1958	7	4	1	5	1		2	3	1
1959	6	5	1	3	2	1	3	3	
1960	5	6	1	4	2		1	4	1
1961	6	8		4	3		2	5	
1962	9	5		4	3		5	2	
1963	7	4	3	5	0	2	2	4	1
1964	5	9		2	5		3	4	
1965	2	12		1	6		1	6	
1966	5	8	1	3	3	1	2	5	
1967	4	9	1	1	6		3	3	1
1968	2	11	1	1	6		1	5	1
1969	1	13		1	6		0	7	
1970	5	9		4	3		1	6	
1971	6	8		5	2		1	6	
1972	11	3		7	0		4	3	
1973	10	4		7	1		3	3	
1974	10	3	1	5	2		5	1	1
1975	12	2		6	1		6	1	
1976	10	4		6	1		4	3	
1977	9	5		6	1		3	4	
1978	14	2		7	1		7	1	
1979	12	4		8	0		4	4	
1980	9	7		6	2		3	5	
1981	8	8		5	3		3	5	
1982	6	3		4	0		2	3	
1983	10	6		4	4		6	2	
1984	9	7		6	2		3	5	
1985	7	9		5	3		2	6	
1986	6	10		4	4		2	6	
1987	8	7		4	3		4	4	
1988	5	11		4	4		1	7	
1989	9	7		4	4		5	3	
1990	9	7		6	2		3	5	
1991	7	9		5	3		2	6	
1992	11	5		7	1		4	4	
1993	9	7		6	2		3	5	
1994	12	4		7	1		5	3	
1995	11	5		6	2		5	3	
1996	10	6		7	1		3	5	
1997	11	5		7	1		4	4	
1998	7	9		5	3		2	6	
1999	6	10		2	6		4	4	
2000	9	7		4	4		5	3	
2001	13	3		7	1		6	2	
2002	10	5	1	5	2	1	5	3	
2003	6	10		4	4		2	6	
	464	464	20	275	186	9	189	278	11

**includes Pittsburgh Pirates (1933-1940).*

SAN DIEGO CHARGERS*

	All Games			Home Games			Road Games		
Season	W	L	T	W	L	T	W	L	T
1960	10	4		5	2		5	2	
1961	12	2		6	1		6	1	
1962	4	10		3	4		1	6	
1963	11	3		6	1		5	2	
1964	8	5	1	4	3		4	2	1
1965	9	2	3	4	1	2	5	1	1
1966	7	6	1	5	2		2	4	1
1967	8	5	1	5	2	1	3	3	
1968	9	5		4	3		5	2	
1969	8	6		5	2		3	4	
1970	5	6	3	2	3	2	3	3	1
1971	6	8		6	1		0	7	
1972	4	9	1	2	5		2	4	1
1973	2	11	1	2	5		0	6	1
1974	5	9		3	4		2	5	
1975	2	12		1	6		1	6	
1976	6	8		3	4		3	4	
1977	7	7		3	4		4	3	
1978	9	7		5	3		4	4	
1979	12	4		7	1		5	3	
1980	11	5		6	2		5	3	
1981	10	6		5	3		5	3	
1982	6	3		3	1		3	2	
1983	6	10		4	4		2	6	
1984	7	9		4	4		3	5	
1985	8	8		6	2		2	6	
1986	4	12		2	6		2	6	
1987	8	7		4	3		4	4	
1988	6	10		3	5		3	5	
1989	6	10		4	4		2	6	
1990	6	10		3	5		3	5	
1991	4	12		3	5		1	7	
1992	11	5		6	2		5	3	
1993	8	8		4	4		4	4	
1994	11	5		5	3		6	2	
1995	9	7		5	3		4	4	
1996	8	8		5	3		3	5	
1997	4	12		2	6		2	6	
1998	5	11		4	4		1	7	
1999	8	8		4	4		4	4	
2000	1	15		1	7		0	8	
2001	5	11		4	4		1	7	
2002	8	8		5	3		3	5	
2003	4	12		2	6		2	6	
	308	341	11	175	150	5	133	191	6

**includes Los Angeles Chargers (1960).*

TENNESSEE TITANS*

	All Games			Home Games			Road Games		
Season	W	L	T	W	L	T	W	L	T
1960	10	4		6	1		4	3	
1961	10	3	1	6	1		4	2	1
1962	11	3		6	1		5	2	
1963	6	8		4	3		2	5	
1964	4	10		3	4		1	6	
1965	4	10		3	4		1	6	
1966	3	11		3	4		0	7	
1967	9	4	1	5	2		4	2	1
1968	7	7		3	4		4	3	
1969	6	6	2	4	2	1	2	4	1
1970	3	10	1	1	6		2	4	1
1971	4	9	1	3	3	1	1	6	
1972	1	13		1	6		0	7	
1973	1	13		0	7		1	6	
1974	7	7		3	4		4	3	
1975	10	4		5	2		5	2	
1976	5	9		3	4		2	5	
1977	8	6		5	2		3	4	
1978	10	6		5	3		5	3	
1979	11	5		6	2		5	3	
1980	11	5		6	2		5	3	
1981	7	9		5	3		2	6	
1982	1	8		1	4		0	4	
1983	2	14		2	6		0	8	
1984	3	13		2	6		1	7	
1985	5	11		4	4		1	7	
1986	5	11		4	4		1	7	
1987	9	6		5	2		4	4	
1988	10	6		7	1		3	5	
1989	9	7		6	2		3	5	
1990	9	7		6	2		3	5	
1991	11	5		7	1		4	4	

Season	W	L	T	W	L	T	W	L	T
1992	10	6		5	3		5	3	
1993	12	4		7	1		5	3	
1994	2	14		2	6		0	8	
1995	7	9		3	5		4	4	
1996	8	8		2	6		6	2	
1997	8	8		6	2		2	6	
1998	8	8		3	5		5	3	
1999	13	3		8	0		5	3	
2000	13	3		7	1		6	2	
2001	7	9		3	5		4	4	
2002	11	5		6	2		5	3	
2003	12	4		7	1		5	3	
	323	331	6	189	139	2	134	192	4

includes Houston Oilers (1960-1996) and Tennessee Oilers (1997-98).

NFC

ARIZONA CARDINALS*

	All Games			Home Games			Road Games		
Season	W	L	T	W	L	T	W	L	T
1920	6	2	2	5	1	1	1	1	1
1921	3	3	2	3	3	1	0	0	1
1922	8	3		8	3		0	0	
1923	8	4		8	3		0	1	
1924	5	4	1	5	3	1	0	1	
1925	11	2	1	11	2		0	0	1
1926	5	6	1	3	3		2	3	1
1927	3	7	1	2	3	1	1	4	
1928	1	5		1	1		0	4	
1929	6	6	1	3	2		3	4	1
1930	5	6	2	3	2		2	4	2
1931	5	4		3	0		2	4	
1932	2	6	2	1	2	1	1	4	1
1933	1	9	1	0	4	1	1	5	
1934	5	6		2	2		3	4	
1935	6	4	2	2	2		4	2	2
1936	3	8	1	3	1	1	0	7	
1937	5	5	1	1	3		4	2	1
1938	2	9		1	4		1	5	
1939	1	10		0	4		1	6	
1940	2	7	2	2	1	1	0	6	1
1941	3	7	1	0	3	1	3	4	
1942	3	8		2	2		1	6	
1943	0	10		0	3		0	7	
1945	1	9		0	3		1	6	
1946	6	5		2	2		4	3	
1947	9	3		5	0		4	3	
1948	11	1		5	1		6	0	
1949	6	5	1	2	3	1	4	2	
1950	5	7		3	3		2	4	
1951	3	9		1	5		2	4	
1952	4	8		2	4		2	4	
1953	1	10	1	0	5	1	1	5	
1954	2	10		2	4		0	6	
1955	4	7	1	3	2	1	1	5	
1956	7	5		4	2		3	3	
1957	3	9		0	6		3	3	
1958	2	9	1	1	4	1	1	5	
1959	2	10		2	4		0	6	
1960	6	5	1	3	2	1	3	3	
1961	7	7		3	4		4	3	
1962	4	9	1	2	4	1	2	5	
1963	9	5		3	4		6	1	
1964	9	3	2	4	1	1	5	2	1
1965	5	9		2	5		3	4	
1966	8	5	1	5	1	1	3	4	
1967	6	7	1	3	3	1	3	4	
1968	9	4	1	4	2	1	5	2	
1969	4	9	1	3	4		1	5	1
1970	8	5	1	6	1		2	4	1
1971	4	9	1	1	5	1	3	4	
1972	4	9	1	2	5		2	4	1
1973	4	9	1	2	4	1	2	5	
1974	10	4		5	2		5	2	
1975	11	3		6	1		5	2	
1976	10	4		6	1		4	3	
1977	7	7		4	3		3	4	
1978	6	10		3	5		3	5	
1979	5	11		3	5		2	6	
1980	5	11		2	6		3	5	
1981	7	9		5	3		2	6	
1982	5	4		1	3		4	1	
1983	8	7	1	4	3	1	4	4	
1984	9	7		5	3		4	4	
1985	5	11		4	4		1	7	
1986	4	11	1	3	5		1	6	1
1987	7	8		4	3		3	5	
1988	7	9		4	4		3	5	
1989	5	11		2	6		3	5	
1990	5	11		3	5		2	6	
1991	4	12		2	6		2	6	
1992	4	12		3	5		1	7	
1993	7	9		4	4		3	5	
1994	8	8		5	3		3	5	
1995	4	12		3	5		1	7	
1996	7	9		5	3		2	6	
1997	4	12		3	5		1	7	
1998	9	7		5	3		4	4	
1999	6	10		4	4		2	6	
2000	3	13		3	5		0	8	
2001	7	9		3	5		4	4	
2002	5	11		3	5		2	6	
2003	4	12		4	4		0	8	
	440	617	39	255	269	22	185	348	17

includes Chicago Cardinals (1920-1959), St. Louis Cardinals (1960-1987), and Phoenix Cardinals (1988-1993).

ATLANTA FALCONS

	All Games			Home Games			Road Games		
Season	W	L	T	W	L	T	W	L	T
1966	3	11		1	6		2	5	
1967	1	12	1	1	5	1	0	7	
1968	2	12		1	6		1	6	
1969	6	8		4	3		2	5	
1970	4	8	2	3	4		1	4	2
1971	7	6	1	4	3		3	3	1
1972	7	7		4	3		3	4	
1973	9	5		4	3		5	2	
1974	3	11		2	5		1	6	
1975	4	10		3	4		1	6	
1976	4	10		3	4		1	6	
1977	7	7		4	3		3	4	
1978	9	7		7	1		2	6	
1979	6	10		3	5		3	5	
1980	12	4		6	2		6	2	
1981	7	9		4	4		3	5	
1982	5	4		2	3		3	1	
1983	7	9		4	4		3	5	
1984	4	12		2	6		2	6	
1985	4	12		3	5		1	7	
1986	7	8	1	2	5	1	5	3	
1987	3	12		2	6		1	6	
1988	5	11		2	6		3	5	
1989	3	13		3	5		0	8	
1990	5	11		5	3		0	8	
1991	10	6		6	2		4	4	
1992	6	10		5	3		1	7	
1993	6	10		4	4		2	6	
1994	7	9		5	3		2	6	
1995	9	7		7	1		2	6	

Season	W	L	T	W	L	T	W	L	T
1996	3	13		2	6		1	7	
1997	7	9		3	5		4	4	
1998	14	2		8	0		6	2	
1999	5	11		4	4		1	7	
2000	4	12		3	5		1	7	
2001	7	9		3	5		4	4	
2002	9	6	1	5	3		4	3	1
2003	5	11		2	6		3	5	
	226	344	6	136	151	2	90	193	4

CAROLINA PANTHERS

	All Games			Home Games			Road Games		
Season	W	L	T	W	L	T	W	L	T
1995	7	9		5	3		2	6	
1996	12	4		8	0		4	4	
1997	7	9		2	6		5	3	
1998	4	12		2	6		2	6	
1999	8	8		5	3		3	5	
2000	7	9		5	3		2	6	
2001	1	15		0	8		1	7	
2002	7	9		4	4		3	5	
2003	11	5		6	2		5	3	
	64	80		37	35		27	45	

CHICAGO BEARS*

	All Games			Home Games			Road Games		
Season	W	L	T	W	L	T	W	L	T
1920	10	1	2	6	0	1	4	1	1
1921	9	1	1	9	1	1	0	0	
1922	9	3		7	1		2	2	
1923	9	2	1	7	1	1	2	1	
1924	6	1	4	5	0	3	1	1	1
1925	9	5	3	7	1	1	2	4	2
1926	12	1	3	10	0	2	2	1	1
1927	9	3	2	7	1	1	2	2	1
1928	7	5	1	6	3		1	2	1
1929	4	9	2	1	5	2	3	4	
1930	9	4	1	5	2	1	4	2	
1931	8	5		6	3		2	2	
1932	7	1	6	6	1	1	1	0	5
1933	10	2	1	6	0		4	2	1
1934	13	0		5	0		8	0	
1935	6	4	2	1	2	2	5	2	
1936	9	3		3	1		6	2	
1937	9	1	1	4	1		5	0	1
1938	6	5		2	3		4	2	
1939	8	3		4	1		4	2	
1940	8	3		5	0		3	3	
1941	10	1		5	1		5	0	
1942	11	0		6	0		5	0	
1943	8	1	1	5	0		3	1	1
1944	6	3	1	4	0	1	2	3	
1945	3	7		2	3		1	4	
1946	8	2	1	4	1	1	4	1	
1947	8	4		4	2		4	2	
1948	10	2		5	1		5	1	
1949	9	3		5	1		4	2	
1950	9	3		6	0		3	3	
1951	7	5		3	3		4	2	
1952	5	7		3	3		2	4	
1953	3	8	1	1	4	1	2	4	
1954	8	4		4	2		4	2	
1955	8	4		5	1		3	3	
1956	9	2	1	6	0		3	2	1
1957	5	7		2	4		3	3	
1958	8	4		5	1		3	3	
1959	8	4		4	2		4	2	
1960	5	6	1	4	2		1	4	1
1961	8	6		5	2		3	4	
1962	9	5		4	3		5	2	
1963	11	1	2	6	0	1	5	1	1
1964	5	9		2	5		3	4	
1965	9	5		5	2		4	3	
1966	5	7	2	4	1	2	1	6	
1967	7	6	1	3	3	1	4	3	
1968	7	7		2	5		5	2	
1969	1	13		1	6		0	7	
1970	6	8		3	4		3	4	
1971	6	8		4	3		2	5	
1972	4	9	1	1	5	1	3	4	
1973	3	11		1	6		2	5	
1974	4	10		4	3		0	7	
1975	4	10		3	4		1	6	
1976	7	7		4	3		3	4	
1977	9	5		5	2		4	3	
1978	7	9		4	4		3	5	
1979	10	6		6	2		4	4	
1980	7	9		5	3		2	6	
1981	6	10		4	4		2	6	
1982	3	6		2	2		1	4	
1983	8	8		5	3		3	5	
1984	10	6		6	2		4	4	
1985	15	1		8	0		7	1	
1986	14	2		7	1		7	1	
1987	11	4		6	2		5	2	
1988	12	4		7	1		5	3	
1989	6	10		4	4		2	6	
1990	11	5		7	1		4	4	
1991	11	5		6	2		5	3	
1992	5	11		4	4		1	7	
1993	7	9		3	5		4	4	
1994	9	7		5	3		4	4	
1995	9	7		5	3		4	4	
1996	7	9		6	2		1	7	
1997	4	12		2	6		2	6	
1998	4	12		3	5		1	7	
1999	6	10		3	5		3	5	
2000	5	11		3	5		2	6	
2001	13	3		7	1		6	2	
2002	4	12		3	5		1	7	
2003	7	9		6	2		1	7	
	641	463	42	379	192	24	262	271	18

includes Decatur Staleys (1920) and Chicago Staleys (1921).

DALLAS COWBOYS

	All Games			Home Games			Road Games		
Season	W	L	T	W	L	T	W	L	T
1960	0	11	1	0	6		0	5	1
1961	4	9	1	2	4	1	2	5	
1962	5	8	1	2	4	1	3	4	
1963	4	10		3	4		1	6	
1964	5	8	1	2	4	1	3	4	
1965	7	7		5	2		2	5	
1966	10	3	1	6	1		4	2	1
1967	9	5		5	2		4	3	
1968	12	2		5	2		7	0	
1969	11	2	1	6	0	1	5	2	
1970	10	4		6	1		4	3	
1971	11	3		6	1		5	2	
1972	10	4		5	2		5	2	
1973	10	4		6	1		4	3	
1974	8	6		5	2		3	4	
1975	10	4		5	2		5	2	
1976	11	3		6	1		5	2	
1977	12	2		6	1		6	1	
1978	12	4		7	1		5	3	
1979	11	5		6	2		5	3	
1980	12	4		8	0		4	4	
1981	12	4		8	0		4	4	
1982	6	3		3	2		3	1	

Season	W	L	T	W	L	T	W	L	T
1983	12	4		6	2		6	2	
1984	9	7		5	3		4	4	
1985	10	6		7	1		3	5	
1986	7	9		3	5		4	4	
1987	7	8		3	4		4	4	
1988	3	13		1	7		2	6	
1989	1	15		0	8		1	7	
1990	7	9		5	3		2	6	
1991	11	5		6	2		5	3	
1992	13	3		7	1		6	2	
1993	12	4		6	2		6	2	
1994	12	4		6	2		6	2	
1995	12	4		6	2		6	2	
1996	10	6		6	2		4	4	
1997	6	10		5	3		1	7	
1998	10	6		6	2		4	4	
1999	8	8		7	1		1	7	
2000	5	11		3	5		2	6	
2001	5	11		4	4		1	7	
2002	5	11		4	4		1	7	
2003	10	6		6	2		4	4	
	377	275	6	215	110	4	162	165	2

DETROIT LIONS*

	All Games			Home Games			Road Games		
Season	**W**	**L**	**T**	**W**	**L**	**T**	**W**	**L**	**T**
1930	5	6	3	5	1	2	0	5	1
1931	11	3		8	0		3	3	
1932	6	2	4	3	0	2	3	2	2
1933	6	5		4	1		2	4	
1934	10	3		6	2		4	1	
1935	7	3	2	5	0	1	2	3	1
1936	8	4		5	1		3	3	
1937	7	4		4	2		3	2	
1938	7	4		4	3		3	1	
1939	6	5		4	2		2	3	
1940	5	5	1	3	3		2	2	1
1941	4	6	1	3	2		1	4	1
1942	0	11		0	7		0	4	
1943	3	6	1	2	2	1	1	4	
1944	6	3	1	4	2		2	1	1
1945	7	3		4	1		3	2	
1946	1	10		1	5		0	5	
1947	3	9		2	4		1	5	
1948	2	10		2	4		0	6	
1949	4	8		2	4		2	4	
1950	6	6		4	2		2	4	
1951	7	4	1	3	3	1	4	1	
1952	9	3		6	1		3	2	
1953	10	2		5	1		5	1	
1954	9	2	1	5	0	1	4	2	
1955	3	9		3	4		0	5	
1956	9	3		5	1		4	2	
1957	8	4		5	1		3	3	
1958	4	7	1	2	4		2	3	1
1959	3	8	1	2	4		1	4	1
1960	7	5		5	1		2	4	
1961	8	5	1	2	5		6	0	1
1962	11	3		7	0		4	3	
1963	5	8	1	3	3	1	2	5	
1964	7	5	2	3	3	1	4	2	1
1965	6	7	1	2	4	1	4	3	
1966	4	9	1	3	4		1	5	1
1967	5	7	2	3	4		2	3	2
1968	4	8	2	1	4	2	3	4	
1969	9	4	1	5	2		4	2	1
1970	10	4		6	1		4	3	
1971	7	6	1	3	4		4	2	1
1972	8	5	1	5	2		3	3	1
1973	6	7	1	4	3		2	4	1
1974	7	7		5	2		2	5	
1975	7	7		4	3		3	4	
1976	6	8		5	2		1	6	
1977	6	8		5	2		1	6	
1978	7	9		5	3		2	6	
1979	2	14		2	6		0	8	
1980	9	7		6	2		3	5	
1981	8	8		7	1		1	7	
1982	4	5		2	3		2	2	
1983	9	7		6	2		3	5	
1984	4	11	1	2	5	1	2	6	
1985	7	9		6	2		1	7	
1986	5	11		1	7		4	4	
1987	4	11		1	6		3	5	
1988	4	12		2	6		2	6	
1989	7	9		4	4		3	5	
1990	6	10		3	5		3	5	
1991	12	4		8	0		4	4	
1992	5	11		3	5		2	6	
1993	10	6		5	3		5	3	
1994	9	7		6	2		3	5	
1995	10	6		7	1		3	5	
1996	5	11		4	4		1	7	
1997	9	7		6	2		3	5	
1998	5	11		4	4		1	7	
1999	8	8		6	2		2	6	
2000	9	7		4	4		5	3	
2001	2	14		2	6		0	8	
2002	3	13		3	5		0	8	
2003	5	11		5	3		0	8	
	467	510	32	292	209	14	175	301	18

**includes Portsmouth Spartans (1930-33).*

GREEN BAY PACKERS

	All Games			Home Games			Road Games		
Season	**W**	**L**	**T**	**W**	**L**	**T**	**W**	**L**	**T**
1921	3	2	1	2	1		1	1	1
1922	4	3	3	4	1	1	0	2	2
1923	7	2	1	4	2	1	3	0	
1924	7	4		5	0		2	4	
1925	8	5		6	0		2	5	
1926	7	3	3	4	1	2	3	2	1
1927	7	2	1	6	1		1	1	1
1928	6	4	3	2	2	2	4	2	1
1929	12	0	1	5	0		7	0	1
1930	10	3	1	6	0		4	3	1
1931	12	2		8	0		4	2	
1932	10	3	1	5	0	1	5	3	
1933	5	7	1	3	2	1	2	5	
1934	7	6		4	2		3	4	
1935	8	4		5	2		3	2	
1936	10	1	1	5	1		5	0	1
1937	7	4		3	2		4	2	
1938	8	3		4	2		4	1	
1939	9	2		4	1		5	1	
1940	6	4	1	4	2		2	2	1
1941	10	1		4	1		6	0	
1942	8	2	1	4	1		4	1	1
1943	7	2	1	2	1	1	5	1	
1944	8	2		5	0		3	2	
1945	6	4		4	1		2	3	
1946	6	5		2	3		4	2	
1947	6	5	1	4	2		2	3	1
1948	3	9		2	4		1	5	
1949	2	10		1	5		1	5	
1950	3	9		3	3		0	6	
1951	3	9		2	4		1	5	
1952	6	6		3	3		3	3	
1953	2	9	1	1	5		1	4	1
1954	4	8		2	4		2	4	

Season	W	L	T	W	L	T	W	L	T
1955	6	6		5	1		1	5	
1956	4	8		2	4		2	4	
1957	3	9		1	5		2	4	
1958	1	10	1	1	4	1	0	6	
1959	7	5		4	2		3	3	
1960	8	4		4	2		4	2	
1961	11	3		6	1		5	2	
1962	13	1		7	0		6	1	
1963	11	2	1	6	1		5	1	1
1964	8	5	1	4	3		4	2	1
1965	10	3	1	6	1		4	2	1
1966	12	2		6	1		6	1	
1967	9	4	1	4	2	1	5	2	
1968	6	7	1	2	5		4	2	1
1969	8	6		5	2		3	4	
1970	6	8		4	3		2	5	
1971	4	8	2	3	3	1	1	5	1
1972	10	4		4	3		6	1	
1973	5	7	2	3	2	2	2	5	
1974	6	8		4	3		2	5	
1975	4	10		3	4		1	6	
1976	5	9		4	3		1	6	
1977	4	10		2	5		2	5	
1978	8	7	1	5	2	1	3	5	
1979	5	11		4	4		1	7	
1980	5	10	1	4	4		1	6	1
1981	8	8		4	4		4	4	
1982	5	3	1	3	1		2	2	1
1983	8	8		5	3		3	5	
1984	8	8		5	3		3	5	
1985	8	8		5	3		3	5	
1986	4	12		1	7		3	5	
1987	5	9	1	2	5	1	3	4	
1988	4	12		2	6		2	6	
1989	10	6		6	2		4	4	
1990	6	10		3	5		3	5	
1991	4	12		2	6		2	6	
1992	9	7		6	2		3	5	
1993	9	7		6	2		3	5	
1994	9	7		7	1		2	6	
1995	11	5		7	1		4	4	
1996	13	3		8	0		5	3	
1997	13	3		8	0		5	3	
1998	11	5		7	1		4	4	
1999	8	8		5	3		3	5	
2000	9	7		6	2		3	5	
2001	12	4		7	1		5	3	
2002	12	4		8	0		4	4	
2003	10	6		5	3		5	3	
	602	474	36	349	190	16	253	284	20

MINNESOTA VIKINGS

	All Games			Home Games			Road Games		
Season	**W**	**L**	**T**	**W**	**L**	**T**	**W**	**L**	**T**
1961	3	11		3	4		0	7	
1962	2	11	1	1	5	1	1	6	
1963	5	8	1	3	4		2	4	1
1964	8	5	1	4	3		4	2	1
1965	7	7		2	5		5	2	
1966	4	9	1	2	5		2	4	1
1967	3	8	3	1	4	2	2	4	1
1968	8	6		4	3		4	3	
1969	12	2		7	0		5	2	
1970	12	2		7	0		5	2	
1971	11	3		5	2		6	1	
1972	7	7		3	4		4	3	
1973	12	2		7	0		5	2	
1974	10	4		4	3		6	1	
1975	12	2		7	0		5	2	
1976	11	2	1	6	0	1	5	2	
1977	9	5		5	2		4	3	
1978	8	7	1	5	3		3	4	1
1979	7	9		5	3		2	6	
1980	9	7		5	3		4	4	
1981	7	9		5	3		2	6	
1982	5	4		4	1		1	3	
1983	8	8		3	5		5	3	
1984	3	13		2	6		1	7	
1985	7	9		4	4		3	5	
1986	9	7		5	3		4	4	
1987	8	7		5	3		3	4	
1988	11	5		7	1		4	4	
1989	10	6		8	0		2	6	
1990	6	10		4	4		2	6	
1991	8	8		4	4		4	4	
1992	11	5		5	3		6	2	
1993	9	7		4	4		5	3	
1994	10	6		6	2		4	4	
1995	8	8		6	2		2	6	
1996	9	7		5	3		4	4	
1997	9	7		5	3		4	4	
1998	15	1		8	0		7	1	
1999	10	6		6	2		4	4	
2000	11	5		7	1		4	4	
2001	5	11		5	3		0	8	
2002	6	10		4	4		2	6	
2003	9	7		6	2		3	5	
	354	283	9	204	116	4	150	167	5

NEW ORLEANS SAINTS

	All Games			Home Games			Road Games		
Season	**W**	**L**	**T**	**W**	**L**	**T**	**W**	**L**	**T**
1967	3	11		2	5		1	6	
1968	4	9	1	3	4		1	5	1
1969	5	9		3	4		2	5	
1970	2	11	1	2	5		0	6	1
1971	4	8	2	2	4	1	2	4	1
1972	2	11	1	2	5		0	6	1
1973	5	9		5	2		0	7	
1974	5	9		4	3		1	6	
1975	2	12		2	5		0	7	
1976	4	10		2	5		2	5	
1977	3	11		2	5		1	6	
1978	7	9		3	5		4	4	
1979	8	8		3	5		5	3	
1980	1	15		0	8		1	7	
1981	4	12		2	6		2	6	
1982	4	5		2	3		2	2	
1983	8	8		5	3		3	5	
1984	7	9		3	5		4	4	
1985	5	11		3	5		2	6	
1986	7	9		4	4		3	5	
1987	12	3		6	1		6	2	
1988	10	6		5	3		5	3	
1989	9	7		5	3		4	4	
1990	8	8		5	3		3	5	
1991	11	5		6	2		5	3	
1992	12	4		6	2		6	2	
1993	8	8		4	4		4	4	
1994	7	9		3	5		4	4	
1995	7	9		4	4		3	5	
1996	3	13		2	6		1	7	
1997	6	10		3	5		3	5	
1998	6	10		4	4		2	6	
1999	3	13		3	5		0	8	
2000	10	6		3	5		7	1	
2001	7	9		3	5		4	4	
2002	9	7		4	4		5	3	
2003	8	8		5	3		3	5	
	226	331	5	125	155	1	101	176	4

NEW YORK GIANTS

	All Games			Home Games			Road Games		
Season	W	L	T	W	L	T	W	L	T
1925	8	4		7	2		1	2	
1926	8	4	1	5	2	1	3	2	
1927	11	1	1	7	1		4	0	1
1928	4	7	2	1	2	2	3	5	
1929	13	1	1	7	1		6	0	1
1930	13	4		6	2		7	2	
1931	7	6	1	4	2	1	3	4	
1932	4	6	2	3	2	1	1	4	1
1933	11	3		7	0		4	3	
1934	8	5		5	1		3	4	
1935	9	3		4	2		5	1	
1936	5	6	1	3	3	1	2	3	
1937	6	3	2	4	2	1	2	1	1
1938	8	2	1	6	1		2	1	1
1939	9	1	1	6	0		3	1	1
1940	6	4	1	4	3		2	1	1
1941	8	3		5	2		3	1	
1942	5	5	1	3	2	1	2	3	
1943	6	3	1	4	2		2	1	1
1944	8	1	1	5	1		3	0	1
1945	3	6	1	2	4		1	2	1
1946	7	3	1	5	1	1	2	2	
1947	2	8	2	2	3	1	0	5	1
1948	4	8		2	4		2	4	
1949	6	6		2	4		4	2	
1950	10	2		5	1		5	1	
1951	9	2	1	5	1		4	1	1
1952	7	5		2	4		5	1	
1953	3	9		2	4		1	5	
1954	7	5		4	2		3	3	
1955	6	5	1	4	1	1	2	4	
1956	8	3	1	4	1	1	4	2	
1957	7	5		3	3		4	2	
1958	9	3		5	1		4	2	
1959	10	2		5	1		5	1	
1960	6	4	2	1	3	2	5	1	
1961	10	3	1	4	2	1	6	1	
1962	12	2		6	1		6	1	
1963	11	3		5	2		6	1	
1964	2	10	2	2	5		0	5	2
1965	7	7		3	4		4	3	
1966	1	12	1	1	6		0	6	1
1967	7	7		5	2		2	5	
1968	7	7		3	4		4	3	
1969	6	8		5	2		1	6	
1970	9	5		5	2		4	3	
1971	4	10		1	6		3	4	
1972	8	6		4	3		4	3	
1973	2	11	1	2	4	1	0	7	
1974	2	12		0	7		2	5	
1975	5	9		2	5		3	4	
1976	3	11		3	4		0	7	
1977	5	9		3	4		2	5	
1978	6	10		5	3		1	7	
1979	6	10		4	4		2	6	
1980	4	12		2	6		2	6	
1981	9	7		4	4		5	3	
1982	4	5		2	3		2	2	
1983	3	12	1	1	7		2	5	1
1984	9	7		6	2		3	5	
1985	10	6		6	2		4	4	
1986	14	2		8	0		6	2	
1987	6	9		5	3		1	6	
1988	10	6		5	3		5	3	
1989	12	4		7	1		5	3	
1990	13	3		7	1		6	2	
1991	8	8		5	3		3	5	
1992	6	10		4	4		2	6	
1993	11	5		6	2		5	3	
1994	9	7		4	4		5	3	
1995	5	11		3	5		2	6	
1996	6	10		3	5		3	5	
1997	10	5	1	6	2		4	3	1
1998	8	8		5	3		3	5	
1999	7	9		4	4		3	5	
2000	12	4		5	3		7	1	
2001	7	9		5	3		2	6	
2002	10	6		5	3		5	3	
2003	4	12		1	7		3	5	
	571	477	33	321	221	16	250	256	17

PHILADELPHIA EAGLES

	All Games			Home Games			Road Games		
Season	W	L	T	W	L	T	W	L	T
1933	3	5	1	2	3	1	1	2	
1934	4	7		2	4		2	3	
1935	2	9		0	5		2	4	
1936	1	11		1	6		0	5	
1937	2	8	1	0	5	1	2	3	
1938	5	6		2	3		3	3	
1939	1	9	1	1	3	1	0	6	
1940	1	10		1	4		0	6	
1941	2	8	1	1	4	1	1	4	
1942	2	9		0	5		2	4	
1944	7	1	2	3	1	2	4	0	
1945	7	3		6	0		1	3	
1946	6	5		3	2		3	3	
1947	8	4		6	1		2	3	
1948	9	2	1	6	0		3	2	1
1949	11	1		6	0		5	1	
1950	6	6		2	4		4	2	
1951	4	8		1	5		3	3	
1952	7	5		4	2		3	3	
1953	7	4	1	5	0	1	2	4	
1954	7	4	1	5	1		2	3	1
1955	4	7	1	4	2		0	5	1
1956	3	8	1	2	3	1	1	5	
1957	4	8		3	3		1	5	
1958	2	9	1	2	4		0	5	1
1959	7	5		5	1		2	4	
1960	10	2		5	1		5	1	
1961	10	4		5	2		5	2	
1962	3	10	1	2	5		1	5	1
1963	2	10	2	1	5	1	1	5	1
1964	6	8		3	4		3	4	
1965	5	9		2	5		3	4	
1966	9	5		5	2		4	3	
1967	6	7	1	5	2		1	5	1
1968	2	12		1	6		1	6	
1969	4	9	1	2	5		2	4	1
1970	3	10	1	3	3	1	0	7	
1971	6	7	1	3	4		3	3	1
1972	2	11	1	0	6	1	2	5	
1973	5	8	1	4	3		1	5	1
1974	7	7		5	2		2	5	
1975	4	10		2	5		2	5	
1976	4	10		2	5		2	5	
1977	5	9		4	3		1	6	
1978	9	7		5	3		4	4	
1979	11	5		5	3		6	2	
1980	12	4		7	1		5	3	
1981	10	6		6	2		4	4	
1982	3	6		1	4		2	2	
1983	5	11		1	7		4	4	
1984	6	9	1	5	3		1	6	1
1985	7	9		4	4		3	5	
1986	5	10	1	2	5	1	3	5	

1987	7	8		4	4		3	4	
1988	10	6		5	3		5	3	
1989	11	5		6	2		5	3	
1990	10	6		6	2		4	4	
1991	10	6		4	4		6	2	
1992	11	5		8	0		3	5	
1993	8	8		3	5		5	3	
1994	7	9		5	3		2	6	
1995	10	6		6	2		4	4	
1996	10	6		5	3		5	3	
1997	6	9	1	6	2		0	7	1
1998	3	13		3	5		0	8	
1999	5	11		4	4		1	7	
2000	11	5		5	3		6	2	
2001	11	5		4	4		7	1	
2002	12	4		7	1		5	3	
2003	12	4		5	3		7	1	
	437	493	24	249	221	12	188	272	12

ST. LOUIS RAMS*

	All Games			Home Games			Road Games		
Season	W	L	T	W	L	T	W	L	T
1937	1	10		0	5		1	5	
1938	4	7		2	2		2	5	
1939	5	5	1	3	2	1	2	3	
1940	4	6	1	3	1	1	1	5	
1941	2	9		1	4		1	5	
1942	5	6		3	2		2	4	
1944	4	6		1	2		3	4	
1945	9	1		4	0		5	1	
1946	6	4	1	3	2		3	2	1
1947	6	6		3	3		3	3	
1948	6	5	1	3	2	1	3	3	
1949	8	2	2	5	1		3	1	2
1950	9	3		5	1		4	2	
1951	8	4		5	2		3	2	
1952	9	3		5	1		4	2	
1953	8	3	1	5	1		3	2	1
1954	6	5	1	3	2	1	3	3	
1955	8	3	1	5	1		3	2	1
1956	4	8		4	2		0	6	
1957	6	6		5	1		1	5	
1958	8	4		4	2		4	2	
1959	2	10		0	6		2	4	
1960	4	7	1	2	3	1	2	4	
1961	4	10		4	3		0	7	
1962	1	12	1	0	7		1	5	1
1963	5	9		3	4		2	5	
1964	5	7	2	3	2	2	2	5	
1965	4	10		3	4		1	6	
1966	8	6		5	2		3	4	
1967	11	1	2	5	1	1	6	0	1
1968	10	3	1	5	2		5	1	1
1969	11	3		5	2		6	1	
1970	9	4	1	3	3	1	6	1	
1971	8	5	1	4	2	1	4	3	
1972	6	7	1	4	3		2	4	1
1973	12	2		7	0		5	2	
1974	10	4		6	1		4	3	
1975	12	2		6	1		6	1	
1976	10	3	1	5	2		5	1	1
1977	10	4		7	0		3	4	
1978	12	4		6	2		6	2	
1979	9	7		4	4		5	3	
1980	11	5		6	2		5	3	
1981	6	10		4	4		2	6	
1982	2	7		1	4		1	3	
1983	9	7		5	3		4	4	
1984	10	6		5	3		5	3	
1985	11	5		6	2		5	3	
1986	10	6		6	2		4	4	
1987	6	9		3	4		3	5	
1988	10	6		4	4		6	2	
1989	11	5		6	2		5	3	
1990	5	11		2	6		3	5	
1991	3	13		2	6		1	7	
1992	6	10		4	4		2	6	
1993	5	11		3	5		2	6	
1994	4	12		3	5		1	7	
1995	7	9		4	4		3	5	
1996	6	10		4	4		2	6	
1997	5	11		2	6		3	5	
1998	4	12		2	6		2	6	
1999	13	3		8	0		5	3	
2000	10	6		5	3		5	3	
2001	14	2		6	2		8	0	
2002	7	9		6	2		1	7	
2003	12	4		8	0		4	4	
	476	415	20	264	176	10	212	239	10

**includes Cleveland Rams (1937-1942, 1944-45) and Los Angeles Rams (1946-1994).*

SAN FRANCISCO 49ERS

	All Games			Home Games			Road Games		
Season	W	L	T	W	L	T	W	L	T
1950	3	9		3	3		0	6	
1951	7	4	1	5	1		2	3	1
1952	7	5		3	3		4	2	
1953	9	3		5	1		4	2	
1954	7	4	1	4	2		3	2	1
1955	4	8		2	4		2	4	
1956	5	6	1	3	3		2	3	1
1957	8	4		5	1		3	3	
1958	6	6		4	2		2	4	
1959	7	5		4	2		3	3	
1960	7	5		3	3		4	2	
1961	7	6	1	5	1	1	2	5	
1962	6	8		1	6		5	2	
1963	2	12		2	5		0	7	
1964	4	10		3	4		1	6	
1965	7	6	1	4	2	1	3	4	
1966	6	6	2	4	2	1	2	4	1
1967	7	7		3	4		4	3	
1968	7	6	1	3	3	1	4	3	
1969	4	8	2	3	3	1	1	5	1
1970	10	3	1	5	1	1	5	2	
1971	9	5		4	3		5	2	
1972	8	5	1	4	2	1	4	3	
1973	5	9		3	4		2	5	
1974	6	8		3	4		3	4	
1975	5	9		2	5		3	4	
1976	8	6		4	3		4	3	
1977	5	9		3	4		2	5	
1978	2	14		2	6		0	8	
1979	2	14		2	6		0	8	
1980	6	10		4	4		2	6	
1981	13	3		7	1		6	2	
1982	3	6		0	5		3	1	
1983	10	6		4	4		6	2	
1984	15	1		7	1		8	0	
1985	10	6		5	3		5	3	
1986	10	5	1	6	2		4	3	1
1987	13	2		6	1		7	1	
1988	10	6		4	4		6	2	
1989	14	2		6	2		8	0	
1990	14	2		6	2		8	0	
1991	10	6		7	1		3	5	
1992	14	2		7	1		7	1	
1993	10	6		6	2		4	4	
1994	13	3		7	1		6	2	

Season	W	L	T	W	L	T	W	L	T
1995	11	5		6	2		5	3	
1996	12	4		6	2		6	2	
1997	13	3		8	0		5	3	
1998	12	4		8	0		4	4	
1999	4	12		3	5		1	7	
2000	6	10		4	4		2	6	
2001	12	4		7	1		5	3	
2002	10	6		5	3		5	3	
2003	7	9		6	2		1	7	
	432	333	13	236	146	7	196	187	6

SEATTLE SEAHAWKS

	All Games			Home Games			Road Games		
Season	W	L	T	W	L	T	W	L	T
1976	2	12		1	6		1	6	
1977	5	9		3	4		2	5	
1978	9	7		5	3		4	4	
1979	9	7		5	3		4	4	
1980	4	12		0	8		4	4	
1981	6	10		5	3		1	7	
1982	4	5		3	2		1	3	
1983	9	7		5	3		4	4	
1984	12	4		7	1		5	3	
1985	8	8		5	3		3	5	
1986	10	6		7	1		3	5	
1987	9	6		6	2		3	4	
1988	9	7		5	3		4	4	
1989	7	9		3	5		4	4	
1990	9	7		5	3		4	4	
1991	7	9		5	3		2	6	
1992	2	14		1	7		1	7	
1993	6	10		4	4		2	6	
1994	6	10		3	5		3	5	
1995	8	8		5	3		3	5	
1996	7	9		4	4		3	5	
1997	8	8		4	4		4	4	
1998	8	8		6	2		2	6	
1999	9	7		5	3		4	4	
2000	6	10		3	5		3	5	
2001	9	7		6	2		3	5	
2002	7	9		3	5		4	4	
2003	10	6		8	0		2	6	
	205	231		122	97		83	134	

TAMPA BAY BUCCANEERS

	All Games			Home Games			Road Games		
Season	W	L	T	W	L	T	W	L	T
1976	0	14		0	7		0	7	
1977	2	12		1	6		1	6	
1978	5	11		3	5		2	6	
1979	10	6		5	3		5	3	
1980	5	10	1	2	5	1	3	5	
1981	9	7		6	2		3	5	
1982	5	4		4	1		1	3	
1983	2	14		1	7		1	7	
1984	6	10		6	2		0	8	
1985	2	14		2	6		0	8	
1986	2	14		1	7		1	7	
1987	4	11		2	5		2	6	
1988	5	11		3	5		2	6	
1989	5	11		2	6		3	5	
1990	6	10		4	4		2	6	
1991	3	13		3	5		0	8	
1992	5	11		3	5		2	6	
1993	5	11		3	5		2	6	
1994	6	10		4	4		2	6	
1995	7	9		5	3		2	6	
1996	6	10		5	3		1	7	
1997	10	6		5	3		5	3	
1998	8	8		6	2		2	6	
1999	11	5		7	1		4	4	
2000	10	6		6	2		4	4	
2001	9	7		5	3		4	4	
2002	12	4		6	2		6	2	
2003	7	9		3	5		4	4	
	167	268	1	103	114	1	64	154	

WASHINGTON REDSKINS*

	All Games			Home Games			Road Games		
Season	W	L	T	W	L	T	W	L	T
1932	4	4	2	2	3	1	2	1	1
1933	5	5	2	4	2		1	3	2
1934	6	6		4	3		2	3	
1935	2	8	1	2	5		0	3	1
1936	7	5		4	3		3	2	
1937	8	3		4	2		4	1	
1938	6	3	2	3	1	1	3	2	1
1939	8	2	1	5	0	1	3	2	
1940	9	2		6	0		3	2	
1941	6	5		4	2		2	3	
1942	10	1		5	1		5	0	
1943	6	3	1	4	2		2	1	1
1944	6	3	1	4	2		2	1	1
1945	8	2		6	0		2	2	
1946	5	5	1	3	2	1	2	3	
1947	4	8		4	2		0	6	
1948	7	5		4	2		3	3	
1949	4	7	1	3	3		1	4	1
1950	3	9		1	5		2	4	
1951	5	7		2	4		3	3	
1952	4	8		1	5		3	3	
1953	6	5	1	3	3		3	2	1
1954	3	9		3	3		0	6	
1955	8	4		3	3		5	1	
1956	6	6		4	2		2	4	
1957	5	6	1	2	3	1	3	3	
1958	4	7	1	3	2	1	1	5	
1959	3	9		2	4		1	5	
1960	1	9	2	1	4	1	0	5	1
1961	1	12	1	1	6		0	6	1
1962	5	7	2	3	4		2	3	2
1963	3	11		1	6		2	5	
1964	6	8		4	3		2	5	
1965	6	8		3	4		3	4	
1966	7	7		4	3		3	4	
1967	5	6	3	2	4	1	3	2	2
1968	5	9		3	4		2	5	
1969	7	5	2	4	2	1	3	3	1
1970	6	8		4	3		2	5	
1971	9	4	1	4	2	1	5	2	
1972	11	3		6	1		5	2	
1973	10	4		7	0		3	4	
1974	10	4		6	1		4	3	
1975	8	6		5	2		3	4	
1976	10	4		5	2		5	2	
1977	9	5		5	2		4	3	
1978	8	8		5	3		3	5	
1979	10	6		6	2		4	4	
1980	6	10		4	4		2	6	
1981	8	8		5	3		3	5	
1982	8	1		3	1		5	0	
1983	14	2		7	1		7	1	
1984	11	5		7	1		4	4	
1985	10	6		5	3		5	3	
1986	12	4		7	1		5	3	
1987	11	4		6	1		5	3	
1988	7	9		4	4		3	5	
1989	10	6		4	4		6	2	
1990	10	6		7	1		3	5	
1991	14	2		7	1		7	1	

1992	9	7		6	2		3	5	
1993	4	12		3	5		1	7	
1994	3	13		0	8		3	5	
1995	6	10		4	4		2	6	
1996	9	7		5	3		4	4	
1997	8	7	1	5	2	1	3	5	
1998	6	10		4	4		2	6	
1999	10	6		6	2		4	4	
2000	8	8		4	4		4	4	
2001	8	8		4	4		4	4	
2002	7	9		5	3		2	6	
2003	5	11		3	5		2	6	
	499	452	27	289	198	11	210	254	16

**includes Boston Braves (1932) and Boston Redskins (1933-36).*

ALL-TIME RECORDS OF NFL TEAMS

AFC	W	L	T	Pct.
Miami	349	223	4	.610
Oakland	385	264	11	.593
Cleveland	400	320	10	.555
Kansas City	349	299	12	.538
Denver	339	311	10	.521
Jacksonville	73	71	0	.507
Pittsburgh	464	464	20	.500
Baltimore	63	64	1	.496
Indianapolis	364	371	7	.495
Tennessee	323	331	6	.494
New England	314	337	9	.482
Buffalo	313	339	8	.480
San Diego	308	341	11	.475
N.Y. Jets	294	358	8	.450
Cincinnati	234	313	1	.427
Houston	9	23	0	.281

NFC	W	L	T	Pct.
Chicago	641	463	42	.581
Dallas	377	275	6	.578
San Francisco	432	333	13	.565
Green Bay	602	474	36	.559
Minnesota	354	283	9	.556
N.Y. Giants	571	477	33	.545
St. Louis	476	415	20	.534
Washington	499	452	27	.525
Detroit	467	510	32	.478
Philadelphia	437	493	24	.470
Seattle	205	231	0	.470
Carolina	64	80	0	.444
Arizona	440	617	39	.417
New Orleans	226	331	5	.406
Atlanta	226	344	6	.397
Tampa Bay	167	268	1	.384

History

The Professional Football Hall of Fame is located in Canton, Ohio, site of the organizational meeting on September 17, 1920, from which the National Football League evolved. The NFL recognized Canton as the Hall of Fame site on April 27, 1961. Canton area individuals, foundations, and companies donated almost $400,000 in cash and services to provide funds for the construction of the original two-building complex, which was dedicated on September 7, 1963. Since that time, the Hall added three buildings with major expansion projects in 1971, 1978, and 1995. The Hall's largest-ever expansion, a $9.2 million project, was completed in early fall 1995. With the new fifth building, the Hall's size is now 82,307 square feet, more than four times its original size.

The expanded Hall represents the sport of pro football in many ways—through (1) GameDay Stadium, a dynamic two-part turntable theater featuring NFL action in Cinemascope for the first time, (2) a standard theater showing NFL films hourly, (3) six large exhibition areas where the history of pro football is detailed in memento, picture, and story form, (4) an extensive archive and information center, and (5) a new and enlarged museum store.

Throughout the years, the Pro Football Hall of Fame has become an extremely popular tourist attraction. At the end of 2003, a total of 7,412,349 fans had visited the Hall of Fame.

New members of the Pro Football Hall of Fame are elected annually by a 39-member National Board of Selectors, made up of media representatives from every league city, six at-large representatives, and a representative of the Pro Football Writers of America. Between three and six new members are elected each year. An affirmative vote of approximately 80 percent is needed for election.

Any fan may nominate any eligible player or contributor simply by writing to the Pro Football Hall of Fame. Players must be retired five years to be eligible, while a coach needs only to be retired with no time limit specified. Contributors (administrators, owners, *et al.*) may be elected while they are still active.

The charter class of 17 enshrinees was elected in 1963 and the honor roll now stands at 225 (145 living as of June 1, 2004) with the election of a four-man class in 2004. That class consists of Bob Brown, Carl Eller, John Elway, and Barry Sanders.

ROSTER OF MEMBERS

HERB ADDERLEY
Cornerback. 6-0, 205. Born in Philadelphia, Pennsylvania, June 8, 1939. Michigan State. Inducted in 1980. 1961-69 Green Bay Packers, 1970-72 Dallas Cowboys. **Highlights:** 48 interceptions, 7 touchdowns. Played in four Super Bowls, five Pro Bowls.

GEORGE ALLEN
Coach. Born in Detroit, Michigan, April 29, 1918. Died December 31, 1990. Alma College, Eastern Michigan, Marquette, Michigan. Inducted in 2002. 1966-1970 Los Angeles Rams, 1971-77 Washington Redskins. **Highlights:** 118-54-5 overall record. Never suffered a losing season, and ranked tenth in coaching victories at time of retirement.

MARCUS ALLEN
Running back. 6-2, 210. Born in San Diego, California, March 26, 1960. Southern California. Inducted in 2003. 1982-1992 Los Angeles Raiders, 1993-1997 Kansas City Chiefs. **Highlights:** First player in NFL history to tally 10,000 rushing yards and 5,000 receiving yards. MVP, Super Bowl XVIII.

LANCE ALWORTH
Wide receiver. 6-0, 184. Born in Houston, Texas, August 3, 1940. Arkansas. Inducted in 1978. 1962-1970 San Diego Chargers, 1971-72 Dallas Cowboys. **Highlights:** 542 receptions for 10,266 yards, 85 touchdowns. All-AFL seven times, seven All-Star games.

DOUG ATKINS
Defensive end. 6-8, 275. Born in Humboldt, Tennessee, May 8, 1930. Tennessee. Inducted in 1982. 1953-54 Cleveland Browns, 1955-1966 Chicago Bears, 1967-69 New Orleans Saints. **Highlights:** Eight Pro Bowls, All-NFL four times. Played for 17 years, 205 games.

MORRIS (RED) BADGRO
End. 6-0, 190. Born in Orillia, Washington, December 1, 1902. Died July 13, 1998. Southern California. Inducted in 1981. 1927-28 New York Yankees, 1930-35 New York Giants, 1936 Brooklyn Dodgers. **Highlights:** First- or second-team All-NFL four times. Scored first touchdown in NFL Championship Game series.

LEM BARNEY
Cornerback. 6-0, 190. Born in Gulfport, Mississippi, September 8, 1945. Jackson State. Inducted in 1992. 1967-1977 Detroit Lions. **Highlights:** 56 interceptions for 1,077 yards, 11 touchdowns (7 defensive, 4 special teams). Seven Pro Bowls, All-NFL/NFC four times.

CLIFF BATTLES
Halfback. 6-1, 195. Born in Akron, Ohio, May 1, 1910. Died April 28, 1981. West Virginia Wesleyan. Inducted in 1968. 1932 Boston Braves, 1933-36 Boston Redskins, 1937 Washington Redskins. **Highlights:** NFL rushing champion 1932, 1937. First to gain more than 200 yards in a game, 1933.

SAMMY BAUGH
Quarterback. 6-2, 180. Born in Temple, Texas, March 17, 1914. Texas Christian. Inducted in 1963. 1937-1952 Washington Redskins. **Highlights:** Charter enshrinee. Six-time NFL passing leader. NFL passing, punting, interception champ, 1943.

CHUCK BEDNARIK
Center-linebacker. 6-3, 230. Born in Bethlehem, Pennsylvania, May 1, 1925. Pennsylvania. Inducted in 1967. 1949-1962 Philadelphia Eagles. **Highlights:** Eight Pro Bowls. Missed three games in 14 years. Named NFL all-time center, 1969.

BERT BELL
Team owner. Commissioner. Born in Philadelphia, Pennsylvania, February 25, 1895. Died October 11, 1959. Pennsylvania. Inducted in 1963. 1933-1940 Philadelphia Eagles, 1941-42 Pittsburgh Steelers, 1943 Phil-Pitt, 1944 Card-Pitt, 1945-46 Pittsburgh Steelers. Commissioner, 1946-1959. **Highlights:** Charter enshrinee. Built NFL image as commissioner, 1946-1959. Set up long-term television policies.

BOBBY BELL
Linebacker. 6-4, 225. Born in Shelby, North Carolina, June 17, 1940. Minnesota. Inducted in 1983. 1963-1974 Kansas City Chiefs. **Highlights:** 26 interceptions. All-AFL/AFC eight times. Nine career touchdowns, 1 on onside kick return.

RAYMOND BERRY
End. 6-2, 187. Born in Corpus Christi, Texas, February 27, 1933. Southern Methodist. Inducted in 1973. 1955-1967 Baltimore Colts. **Highlights:** 631 receptions for 9,275 yards, 68 touchdowns. Set NFL title game mark with 12 catches for 178 yards, 1958.

ELVIN BETHEA
Defensive end. 6-2, 260. Born in Trenton, New Jersey, March 1, 1946. North Carolina A&T. Inducted in 2003. 1968-1983 Houston Oilers. **Highlights:** Led team in sacks six times. Elected to eight Pro Bowls. Played for 16 years, 210 games.

CHARLES W. BIDWILL SR.
Team owner. Born in Chicago, Illinois, September 16, 1895. Died April 19, 1947. Loyola of Chicago. Inducted in 1967. 1933-1943 Chicago Cardinals, 1944 Card-Pitt, 1945-47 Chicago Cardinals. **Highlights:** Guiding light for NFL during depression years. Built famous "Dream Backfield."

FRED BILETNIKOFF
Wide receiver. 6-1, 190. Born in Erie, Pennsylvania, February 23, 1943. Florida State. Inducted in 1988. 1965-1978 Oakland Raiders. **Highlights:** 589 receptions for 8,974 yards, 76 touchdowns. 40 catches 10 straight years. MVP, Super Bowl XI.

GEORGE BLANDA
Quarterback-kicker. 6-2, 215. Born in Youngwood, Pennsylvania, September 17, 1927. Kentucky. Inducted in 1981. 1949-1958 Chicago Bears, 1950 Baltimore Colts, 1960-66 Houston Oilers, 1967-1975 Oakland Raiders. **Highlights:** 2,002 career points. 26-season, 340-game career longest in NFL history.

MEL BLOUNT
Cornerback. 6-3, 205. Born in Vidalia, Georgia, April 10, 1948. Southern University. Inducted in 1989. 1970-1983 Pittsburgh Steelers. **Highlights:** 57 interceptions for 736 yards. NFL defensive MVP, 1975. Played in five Pro Bowls.

TERRY BRADSHAW
Quarterback. 6-3, 210. Born in Shreveport, Louisiana, September 2, 1948. Louisiana Tech. Inducted in 1989. 1970-1983 Pittsburgh Steelers. **Highlights:** 27,989 yards passing, 212 touchdowns. MVP in Super Bowls XIII, XIV.

BOB (BOOMER) BROWN
Tackle. 6-4, 280. Born in Cleveland, Ohio, December 8, 1941. Nebraska. Inducted in 2004. 1964-68 Philadelphia Eagles, 1969-1970 Los Angeles Rams, 1971-73 Oakland Raiders. **Highlights:** All-NFL seven of 10 seasons, six Pro Bowls. Named to 1960s All-Decade Team.

JIM BROWN
Fullback. 6-2, 228. Born in St. Simons, Georgia, February 17, 1936. Syracuse. Inducted in 1971. 1957-1965 Cleveland Browns. **Highlights:** 12,312 yards rushing, 756 points. Led NFL rushers eight years. Nine consecutive Pro Bowls.

PAUL BROWN
Coach. Born in Norwalk, Ohio, September 7, 1908. Died August 5, 1991. Miami (Ohio). Inducted in 1967. 1946-49 Cleveland Browns (AAFC), 1950-1962 Cleveland Browns. **Highlights:** Built Cleveland dynasty with 167-53-8 record, four AAFC titles, three NFL crowns. Returned to coaching with Cincinnati Bengals after induction, 1968-1975.

ROOSEVELT BROWN
Tackle. 6-3, 255. Born in Charlottesville, Virginia, October 20, 1932. Morgan State. Inducted in 1975. 1953-1965 New York Giants. **Highlights:** All-NFL eight consecutive years, nine Pro Bowls. NFL's lineman of year, 1956.

WILLIE BROWN
Cornerback. 6-1, 210. Born in Yazoo City, Mississippi, December 2, 1940. Grambling. Inducted in 1984. 1963-66 Denver Broncos, 1967-1978 Oakland Raiders. **Highlights:** 54 interceptions for 472 yards. Scored on 75-yard interception in Super Bowl XI.

BUCK BUCHANAN
Defensive tackle. 6-7, 274. Born in Gainesville, Alabama, September 10, 1940. Died July 16, 1992. Grambling. Inducted in 1990. 1963-1975 Kansas City Chiefs. **Highlights:** Led Chiefs defensive efforts in Super Bowl I, IV. Did not miss a game in 13 years.

NICK BUONICONTI
Linebacker. 5-11, 220. Born in Springfield, Massachusetts, December 15, 1940. Notre Dame. Inducted in 2001. 1962-68 Boston Patriots, 1969-1974, 1976 Miami Dolphins. **Highlights:** All-AFL/AFC eight times. Named to AFL's All-Time Team.

DICK BUTKUS
Linebacker. 6-3, 245. Born in Chicago, Illinois, December 9, 1942. Illinois. Inducted in 1979. 1965-1973 Chicago Bears. **Highlights:** All-NFL six years, eight consecutive Pro Bowls. 27 fumble recoveries.

EARL CAMPBELL
Running back. 5-11, 233. Born in Tyler, Texas, March 29, 1955. Texas. Inducted in 1991. 1978-1984 Houston Oilers, 1984-85 New Orleans Saints. **Highlights:** 9,407 yards rushing, 74 touchdowns. 1,934 yards rushing in 1980, including four games with at least 200 yards.

TONY CANADEO
Halfback. 5-11, 195. Born in Chicago, Illinois, May 5, 1919. Died November 29, 2003. Gonzaga. Inducted in 1974. 1941-44, 1946-1952 Green Bay Packers. **Highlights:** Two-way player. Third player to rush for 1,000 yards in single season, 1949.

JOE CARR
NFL president. Born in Columbus, Ohio, October 22, 1880. Died May 20, 1939. Did not attend college. Inducted in 1963. President, 1921-1939 National Football League. **Highlights:** Charter enshrinee. NFL co-organizer, 1920. Introduced standard player contract.

DAVE CASPER
Tight end. 6-4, 240. Born in Bemidji, Minnesota, February 2, 1952. Notre Dame. Inducted in 2002. 1974-1980 Oakland Raiders, 1980-83 Houston Oilers, 1983 Minnesota Vikings, 1984 Los Angeles Raiders. **Highlights:** 378 receptions for 5,216 yards, 52 touchdowns. Five consecutive Pro Bowls.

GUY CHAMBERLIN
End. Coach. 6-2, 196. Born in Blue Springs, Nebraska, January 16, 1894. Died April 4, 1967. Nebraska. Inducted in 1965. 1919 Canton Bulldogs, 1920 Decatur Staleys, 1921 Chicago Staleys, player-coach 1922-23 Canton Bulldogs, 1924 Cleveland Bulldogs, 1925-26 Frankford Yellowjackets, 1927-28 Chicago Cardinals. **Highlights:** Player-coach of four NFL championship teams. Six-year coaching record of 58-16-7.

JACK CHRISTIANSEN
Safety. 6-1, 185. Born in Sublette, Kansas, December 20, 1928. Died June 29, 1986. Colorado State. Inducted in 1970. 1951-58 Detroit Lions. **Highlights:** 46 interceptions. NFL interception leader, 1953, 1957. Eight punt returns for touchdowns.

EARL (DUTCH) CLARK
Quarterback. 6-0, 185. Born in Fowler, Colorado, October 11, 1906. Died August 5, 1978. Colorado College. Inducted in 1963. 1931-32 Portsmouth Spartans, 1934-38 Detroit Lions. **Highlights:** Charter enshrinee. NFL scoring champion three years. Led Lions to 1935 NFL title.

GEORGE CONNOR
Tackle-linebacker. 6-3, 240. Born in Chicago, Illinois, January 21, 1925. Died March 31, 2003. Holy Cross, Notre Dame. Inducted in 1975. 1948-1955 Chicago Bears. **Highlights:** All-NFL at three positions—T, DT, LB. All-NFL five years. Played in first four Pro Bowls.

JIMMY CONZELMAN
Quarterback. Coach. Team owner. 6-0, 180. Born in St. Louis, Missouri, March 6, 1898. Died July 31, 1970. Washington of St. Louis. Inducted in 1964. 1920 Decatur Staleys, 1921-22 Rock Island Independents, 1922-24 Milwaukee Badgers; owner-coach 1925-26 Detroit Panthers; player-coach 1927-29, coach 1930 Providence Steam Roller; coach 1940-42, 1946-48 Chicago Cardinals. **Highlights:** Player-coach of four NFL teams in 1920's. Coached Cardinals to 1947 NFL crown.

LOU CREEKMUR
Tackle-guard. 6-4, 255. Born in Hopelawn, New Jersey. January 22, 1927. William & Mary. Inducted in 1996. 1950-59 Detroit Lions. **Highlights:** All-NFL six times, twice at guard and four times at tackle. Selected to eight Pro Bowls and played on three NFL championship teams.

LARRY CSONKA
Running back. 6-3, 235. Born in Stow, Ohio, December 25, 1946. Syracuse. Inducted in 1987. 1968-1974, 1979 Miami Dolphins, 1976-78 New York Giants. **Highlights:** 8,081 yards rushing, 68 touchdowns. MVP Super Bowl VIII. Only 21 fumbles in 1,891 carries and 106 receptions.

AL DAVIS
Team, League Administrator. Born in Brockton, Massachusetts, July 4, 1929. Wittenberg, Syracuse. Inducted in 1992. 1963-1981, 1995-present Oakland Raiders, 1982-1994 Los Angeles Raiders, 1966 American Football League. **Highlights:** Only person to serve in pros as personnel assistant, scout, assistant coach, head coach, general manager, commissioner, team owner/CEO.

WILLIE DAVIS
Defensive end. 6-3, 245. Born in Lisbon, Louisiana, July 24, 1934. Grambling. Inducted in 1981. 1958-59 Cleveland Browns, 1960-69 Green Bay Packers. **Highlights:** All-NFL five seasons, five Pro Bowls. Did not miss game in 12-year career.

LEN DAWSON
Quarterback. 6-0, 190. Born in Alliance, Ohio, June 20, 1935. Purdue. Inducted in 1987. 1957-59 Pittsburgh Steelers, 1960-61 Cleveland Browns, 1962 Dallas Texans, 1963-1975 Kansas City Chiefs. **Highlights:** 28,711 yards passing, 239 touchdowns. Four AFL passing crowns. MVP, Super Bowl IV.

JOE DeLAMIELLEURE
Guard. 6-3, 254. Born in Detroit, Michigan, March 16, 1951. Michigan State. Inducted in 2003. 1973-1979, 1985 Buffalo Bills, 1980-1984 Cleveland Browns. **Highlights:** Selected All-Pro and All-AFC six consecutive times, 1975-1980. Named to six Pro Bowls. Played 13 years, 185 games.

ERIC DICKERSON
Running back. 6-3, 220. Born in Sealy, Texas, September 2, 1960. Southern Methodist. Inducted in 1999. 1983-87 Los Angeles Rams, 1987-1991 Indianapolis Colts, 1992 Los Angeles Raiders, 1993 Atlanta Falcons. **Highlights:** Rushed for 13,259 career yards, including an NFL record 2,105 yards in 1984. All-Pro five times, six Pro Bowls.

DAN DIERDORF
Tackle. 6-3, 290. Born in Canton, Ohio, June 29, 1949. Michigan. Inducted in 1996. 1971-1983 St. Louis Cardinals. **Highlights:** All-Pro five times, played in six Pro Bowls, named NFL's best blocker three times.

MIKE DITKA
Tight end. 6-3, 225. Born in Carnegie, Pennsylvania, October 18, 1939. Pittsburgh. Inducted in 1988. 1961-66 Chicago Bears, 1967-68 Philadelphia Eagles, 1969-1972 Dallas Cowboys. **Highlights:** 427 receptions for 5,812 yards, 43 touchdowns. First tight end selected to Hall of Fame. Five consecutive Pro Bowls.

ART DONOVAN
Defensive tackle. 6-3, 265. Born in Bronx, New York, June 5, 1925. Boston College. Inducted in 1968. 1950 Baltimore Colts, 1951 New York Yanks, 1952 Dallas Texans, 1953-1961 Baltimore Colts. **Highlights:** Five Pro Bowls. Vital part of Baltimore's climb to powerhouse status in 1950s.

TONY DORSETT
Running back. 5-11, 184. Born in Rochester, Pennsylvania, April 7, 1954. Pittsburgh. Inducted in 1994. 1977-1987 Dallas Cowboys, 1988 Denver Broncos. **Highlights:** 12,739 yards rushing, 398 receptions, 91 touchdowns. Ran record 99 yards for touchdown vs. Minnesota, January, 1983.

JOHN (PADDY) DRISCOLL
Quarterback. 5-11, 160. Born in Evanston, Illinois, January 11, 1896. Died June 29, 1968. Northwestern. Inducted in 1965. 1919 Hammond Pros, 1920 Decatur Staleys, 1920-25 Chicago Cardinals, 1926-29 Chicago Bears. **Highlights:** All-NFL seven times. Dropkicked record 4 field goals in one game, 1925.

BILL DUDLEY
Halfback. 5-10, 182. Born in Bluefield, Virginia, December 24, 1921. Virginia. Inducted in 1966. 1942, 1945-46 Pittsburgh Steelers, 1947-49 Detroit Lions, 1950-51, 1953 Washington Redskins. **Highlights:** Won NFL rushing, interception, punt return titles, 1946. All-NFL 1942, 1946, and 1947.

ALBERT GLEN (TURK) EDWARDS
Tackle. 6-2, 260. Born in Mold, Washington, September 28, 1907. Died January 12, 1973. Washington State. Inducted in 1969. 1932 Boston Braves, 1933-36 Boston Redskins, 1937-1940 Washington Redskins. **Highlights:** All-NFL 1932-34, 1936, 1937. Steamrolling blocker, smothering tackler.

CARL ELLER
Defensive end. 6-6, 247. Born in Winston-Salem, North Carolina, January 25, 1942. Minnesota. Inducted in 2004. 1964-1978 Minnesota Vikings, 1979 Seattle Seahawks. **Highlights:** Fixture on Vikings' "Purple People Eaters" defensive line, All-Pro five time, elected to six Pro Bowls.

JOHN ELWAY
Quarterback. 6-3, 215. Born in Port Angeles, Washington, June 28, 1960. Stanford. Inducted in 2004. 1983-1998 Denver Broncos. **Highlights:** Passed for 51,475 yards, 300 touchdowns. Named to nine Pro Bowls. NFL MVP, 1987; MVP, Super Bowl XXXIII.

WEEB EWBANK
Coach. Born in Richmond, Indiana, May 6, 1907. Died November 17, 1998. Miami (Ohio). Inducted in 1978. 1954-1962 Baltimore Colts, 1963-1973 New York Jets. **Highlights:** Only coach to win championships in both NFL, AFL. Led both Colts (1958 and 1959) and Jets (1968) to championships.

TOM FEARS
End. 6-2, 215. Born in Guadalajara, Mexico, December 3, 1923. Died January 4, 2000. Santa Clara, UCLA. Inducted in 1970. 1948-1956 Los Angeles Rams. **Highlights:** 400 receptions for 5,397 yards, 38 touchdowns. Led NFL receivers first three seasons. Had then-record 18 receptions in single game.

JIM FINKS
Administrator. Born in St. Louis, Missouri, August 31, 1927. Died May 8, 1994. Tulsa. Inducted 1995. 1964-1973 Minnesota Vikings, 1974-1982 Chicago Bears, 1986-1993 New Orleans Saints. **Highlights:** Developed Vikings, Bears, Saints—all teams with losing records—into winners.

RAY FLAHERTY
Coach. Born in Spokane, Washington, September 1, 1903. Died July 19, 1994. Gonzaga. Inducted in 1976. 1936-1942 Boston/Washington Redskins, 1946-48 New York Yankees (AAFC), 1949 Chicago Hornets (AAFC). **Highlights:** 82-41-5 coaching record. Introduced screen pass in 1937 title game and platoon system.

LEN FORD
Defensive end. 6-4, 260. Born in Washington, D.C., February 18, 1926. Died March 14, 1972. Morgan State, Michigan. Inducted in 1976. 1948-49 Los Angeles Dons (AAFC), 1950-57 Cleveland Browns, 1958 Green Bay Packers. **Highlights:** All-NFL five times, four Pro Bowls. Recovered 20 opponents' fumbles.

DAN FORTMANN
Guard. 6-0, 210. Born in Pearl River, New York, April 11, 1916. Died May 23, 1995. Colgate. Inducted in 1965. 1936-1943 Chicago Bears. **Highlights:** At 20, became youngest starter in NFL. First- or second-team All-NFL every season of career.

DAN FOUTS
Quarterback. 6-3, 210. Born in San Francisco, California, June 10, 1951. Oregon. Inducted in 1993. 1973-1987 San Diego Chargers. **Highlights:** 43,040 passing yards, 254 touchdowns. Six Pro Bowls, NFL MVP, 1982.

FRANK GATSKI
Center. 6-3, 240. Born in Farmington, West Virginia, March 18, 1922. Marshall, Auburn. Inducted in 1985. 1946-49 Cleveland Browns (AAFC), 1950-56 Cleveland Browns, 1957 Detroit Lions. **Highlights:** Never missed game in high school, college, or pro football. Played 11 championship games, winning eight.

BILL GEORGE
Linebacker. 6-2, 230. Born in Waynesburg, Pennsylvania, October 27, 1930. Died September 30, 1982. Wake Forest. Inducted in 1974. 1952-1965 Chicago Bears, 1966 Los Angeles Rams. **Highlights:** All-NFL eight years, eight consecutive Pro Bowls. 14 years of service, longest of any Bears player.

JOE GIBBS
Coach. Born in Mocksville, North Carolina, November 25, 1940. Cerritos (Calif.) J.C., San Diego State. Inducted in 1996. 1981-1992 Washington Redskins. **Highlights:** 124-60-0 record in regular season, 16-5 in postseason, including four Super Bowl appearances—winning three. Won 10 or more games eight times.

FRANK GIFFORD
Halfback. 6-1, 195. Born in Santa Monica, California, August 16, 1930. Southern California. Inducted in 1977. 1952-1960, 1962-64 New York Giants. **Highlights:** Starred on both offense and defense. Seven Pro Bowls, 1956 NFL player of the year.

SID GILLMAN
Coach. Born in Minneapolis, Minnesota, October 26, 1911. Died January 3, 2003. Ohio State. Inducted in 1983. 1955-59 Los Angeles Rams, 1960-1969, 1971 Los Angeles/San Diego Chargers, 1973-74 Houston Oilers. **Highlights:** 123-104-7 coaching record. First to win division titles in both NFL, AFL.

OTTO GRAHAM
Quarterback. 6-1, 195. Born in Waukegan, Illinois, December 6, 1921. Died December 17, 2003. Northwestern. Inducted in 1965. 1946-49 Cleveland Browns (AAFC), 1950-55 Cleveland Browns. **Highlights:** 23,584 passing yards, 174 touchdowns. Guided Browns to 10 division or league crowns in 10 years.

HAROLD (RED) GRANGE
Halfback. 6-0, 185. Born in Forksville, Pennsylvania, June 13, 1903. Died January 28, 1991. Illinois. Inducted in 1963. 1925 Chicago Bears, 1926 New York Yankees (AFL), 1927 New York Yankees, 1929-1934 Chicago Bears. **Highlights:** Charter enshrinee. Nicknamed "Galloping Ghost." Name produced first huge pro football crowds.

BUD GRANT
Coach. Born in Superior, Wisconsin, May 20, 1927. Minnesota. Inducted in 1994. 1967-1983, 1985 Minnesota Vikings. **Highlights:** 168-108-5 coaching record. Led Vikings to 11 division championships, four Super Bowls.

JOE GREENE
Defensive tackle. 6-4, 260. Born in Temple, Texas, September 24, 1946. North Texas State. Inducted in 1987. 1969-1981 Pittsburgh Steelers. **Highlights:** NFL defensive player of the year, 1972, 1974. Four-time Super Bowl champion, 10 Pro Bowls.

FORREST GREGG
Tackle. 6-4, 250. Born in Birthright, Texas, October 18, 1933. Southern Methodist. Inducted in 1977. 1956, 1958-1970 Green Bay Packers, 1971 Dallas Cowboys. **Highlights:** Played 188 consecutive games. Nine Pro Bowls. Played on six NFL championship teams, three Super Bowl winners.

BOB GRIESE
Quarterback. 6-1, 190. Born in Evansville, Indiana, February 3, 1945. Purdue. Inducted in 1990. 1967-1980 Miami Dolphins. **Highlights:** 25,092 passing yards, 192 touchdowns. Led Miami to three AFC titles, Super Bowl VII, VIII wins.

LOU GROZA
Tackle-kicker. 6-3, 250. Born in Martins Ferry, Ohio, January 25, 1924. Died November 29, 2000. Ohio State. Inducted in 1974. 1946-49 Cleveland Browns (AAFC), 1950-59, 1961-67 Cleveland Browns. **Highlights:** 1,608 points in 21 years. Nine Pro Bowls, All-NFL six years. NFL player of the year, 1954.

JOE GUYON
Halfback. 6-1, 180. Born on White Earth Indian Reservation, Minnesota, November 26, 1892. Died November 27, 1971. Carlisle, Georgia Tech. Inducted in 1966. 1919-1920 Canton Bulldogs, 1921 Cleveland Indians, 1922-23 Oorang Indians, 1924 Rock Island Independents, 1924-25 Kansas City Cowboys, 1927 New York Giants. **Highlights:** Touchdown pass gave Giants victory over Bears to win 1927 championship.

GEORGE HALAS
End. Coach. Team owner. Born in Chicago, Illinois, February 2, 1895. Died October 31, 1983. Illinois. Inducted in 1963. Player-coach 1920 Decatur Staleys, 1921 Chicago Staleys, 1922-29 Chicago Bears; coach 1933-1942, 1946-1955, 1958-1967 Chicago Bears. **Highlights:** Charter enshrinee. 324 coaching wins. Only person associated with NFL throughout first 50 years. Coached Bears 40 seasons, won six NFL titles.

JACK HAM
Linebacker. 6-1, 225. Born in Johnstown, Pennsylvania, December 23, 1948. Penn State. Inducted in 1988. 1971-1982 Pittsburgh Steelers. **Highlights:** Won four Super Bowls, 21 opponents' fumbles recovered, 32 interceptions. Eight consecutive Pro Bowls.

DAN HAMPTON
Defensive tackle-defensive end. 6-5, 264. Born in Oklahoma City, Oklahoma, September 19, 1957. Arkansas. Inducted in 2002. 1979-1990 Chicago Bears. **Highlights:** A versatile player, he earned all-pro honors at both defensive tackle and defensive end. Named to four Pro Bowls.

JOHN HANNAH
Guard. 6-3, 265. Born in Canton, Georgia, April 4, 1951. Alabama. Inducted in 1991. 1973-1985 New England Patriots. **Highlights:** Renowned as premier guard of era. All-Pro 10 years, nine Pro Bowls.

FRANCO HARRIS
Running back. 6-2, 225. Born in Fort Dix, New Jersey, March 7, 1950. Penn State. Inducted in 1990. 1972-1983 Pittsburgh Steelers, 1984 Seattle Seahawks. **Highlights:** 12,120 rushing yards, 100 total touchdowns. 1,556 rushing yards in 19 postseason games. MVP in Super Bowl IX.

MIKE HAYNES
Cornerback. 6-2, 195. Born in Denison, Texas, July 1, 1953. Arizona State. Inducted in 1997. 1976-1982 New England Patriots, 1983-89 Los Angeles Raiders. **Highlights:** Defensive rookie of the year. Selected to nine Pro Bowls and intercepted 46 passes, plus one pick in Super Bowl XVIII.

ED HEALEY
Tackle. 6-3, 220. Born in Indian Orchard, Massachusetts, December 28, 1894. Died December 9, 1978. Dartmouth. Inducted in 1964. 1920-22 Rock Island Independents, 1922-27 Chicago Bears. **Highlights:** Two-way star. Perennial all-pro with Bears.

MEL HEIN
Center. 6-2, 225. Born in Redding, California, August 22, 1909. Died January 31, 1992. Washington State. Inducted in 1963. 1931-1945 New York Giants. **Highlights:** Charter enshrinee. 60-minute regular for 15 years. All-NFL eight consecutive years.

TED HENDRICKS
Linebacker. 6-7, 235. Born in Guatemala City, Guatemala, November 1, 1947. Miami. Inducted in 1990. 1969-1973 Baltimore Colts, 1974 Green Bay Packers, 1975-1981 Oakland Raiders, 1982-83 Los Angeles Raiders. **Highlights:** 25 blocked field goals, extra points, and punts, 26 interceptions. Played in 215 consecutive games.

WILBUR (PETE) HENRY
Tackle. 6-0, 250. Born in Mansfield, Ohio, October 31, 1897. Died February 7, 1952. Washington & Jefferson. Inducted in 1963. 1920-23, 1925-26 Canton Bulldogs, 1927 New York Giants, 1927-28 Pottsville Maroons. **Highlights:** Charter enshrinee. Largest player of his time at 250 pounds. Bulwark of Canton's championship lines.

ARNIE HERBER
Quarterback. 6-0, 200. Born in Green Bay, Wisconsin, April 2, 1910. Died October 14, 1969. Wisconsin, Regis College. Inducted in 1966. 1930-1940 Green Bay Packers, 1944-45 New York Giants. **Highlights:** NFL passing leader 1932, 1934, 1936. Came out of retirement to lead 1944 Giants to NFL Eastern crown.

BILL HEWITT
End. 5-11, 191. Born in Bay City, Michigan, October 8, 1909. Died January 14, 1947. Michigan. Inducted in 1971. 1932-36 Chicago Bears, 1937-39 Philadelphia Eagles, 1943 Phil-Pitt. **Highlights:** First to be named all-NFL with two teams—1933, 1934, 1936 Bears; 1937 Eagles.

CLARKE HINKLE
Fullback. 5-11, 201. Born in Toronto, Ohio, April 10, 1909. Died November 9, 1988. Bucknell. Inducted in 1964. 1932-1941 Green Bay Packers. **Highlights:** 3,860 yards rushing, 379 points. Fullback on offense, linebacker on defense.

ELROY (CRAZYLEGS) HIRSCH
Halfback-end. 6-2, 190. Born in Wausau, Wisconsin, June 17, 1923. Died January 28, 2004. Wisconsin, Michigan. Inducted in 1968. 1946-48 Chicago Rockets (AAFC), 1949-1957 Los Angeles Rams. **Highlights:** 387 receptions for 7,029 yards, 60 touchdowns. Key part of Rams' revolutionary "three end" offense, 1949.

PAUL HORNUNG
Halfback. 6-2, 220. Born in Louisville, Kentucky, December 23, 1935. Notre Dame. Inducted in 1986. 1957-1962, 1964-66 Green Bay Packers. **Highlights:** 760 points. Led NFL scorers three years, including record 176 points, 1960. Record 19 points scored in 1961 NFL title game.

KEN HOUSTON
Safety. 6-3, 198. Born in Lufkin, Texas, November 12, 1944. Prairie View A&M. Inducted in 1986. 1967-1972 Houston Oilers, 1973-1980 Washington Redskins. **Highlights:** 49 interceptions, 898 yards, 9 touchdowns. NFL's premier strong safety of 1970s. 12 Pro Bowls.

ROBERT (CAL) HUBBARD
Tackle. 6-5, 250. Born in Keytesville, Missouri, October 31, 1900. Died October 17, 1977. Centenary, Geneva. Inducted in 1963. 1927-28 New York Giants, 1929-1933, 1935 Green Bay Packers, 1936 New York Giants, 1936 Pittsburgh Pirates. **Highlights:** Charter enshrinee. Most feared lineman of his time. All-NFL six years, 1927-29, 1931-33.

SAM HUFF
Linebacker. 6-1, 230. Born in Morgantown, West Virginia, October 4, 1934. West Virginia. Inducted in 1982. 1956-1963 New York Giants, 1964-67, 1969 Washington Redskins. **Highlights:** 30 interceptions. Played in six NFL title games, five Pro Bowls. Redskins player-coach, 1969.

LAMAR HUNT
Team owner. Born in El Dorado, Arkansas, August 2, 1932. Southern Methodist. Inducted in 1972. 1959-present Dallas Texans/Kansas City Chiefs. **Highlights:** Driving force behind organization of AFL. Spearheaded merger negotiations with NFL, 1966.

DON HUTSON
End. 6-1, 180. Born in Pine Bluff, Arkansas, January 31, 1913. Died June 26, 1997. Alabama. Inducted in 1963. 1935-1945 Green Bay Packers. **Highlights:** Charter enshrinee. 488 receptions for 7,991 yards, 99 touchdowns. NFL receiving champion eight years. NFL MVP, 1941, 1942.

JIMMY JOHNSON
Cornerback. 6-2, 187. Born in Dallas, Texas, March 31, 1938. UCLA. Inducted in 1994. 1961-1976 San Francisco 49ers. **Highlights:** 47 interceptions for 615 yards. Five Pro Bowls. Opposing passers avoided throwing in his area.

JOHN HENRY JOHNSON
Fullback. 6-2, 225. Born in Waterproof, Louisiana, November 24, 1929. St. Mary's, Arizona State. Inducted in 1987. 1954-56 San Francisco 49ers, 1957-59 Detroit Lions, 1960-65 Pittsburgh Steelers, 1966 Houston Oilers. **Highlights:** 6,803 yards rushing, 55 total touchdowns. Member of San Francisco's "Million-Dollar" backfield.

CHARLIE JOINER
Wide receiver. 5-11, 180. Born in Many, Louisiana, October 14, 1947. Grambling. Inducted in 1996. 1969-1972 Houston Oilers, 1972-75 Cincinnati Bengals, 1976-1986 San Diego Chargers. **Highlights:** 750 receptions for 12,146 yards and 65 touchdowns. Played 18 seasons, 239 games, most ever for wide receiver at time of retirement.

DAVID (DEACON) JONES
Defensive end. 6-5, 260. Born in Eatonville, Florida, December 9, 1938. South Carolina State, Mississippi Vocational. Inducted in 1980. 1961-1971 Los Angeles Rams, 1972-73 San Diego Chargers, 1974 Washington Redskins. **Highlights:** Specialized in quarterback "sacks," a term he invented. Unanimous all-league five consecutive years.

STAN JONES
Guard-defensive tackle. 6-1, 250. Born in Altoona, Pennsylvania, November 24, 1931. Maryland. Inducted in 1991. 1954-1965 Chicago Bears, 1966 Washington Redskins. **Highlights:** Seven consecutive Pro Bowls. First to rely on weightlifting for football preparation.

HENRY JORDAN
Defensive tackle, 6-3, 240. Born in Emporia, Virginia, January 26, 1935. Died February 21, 1977. Virginia. Inducted in 1995. 1957-58 Cleveland Browns, 1959-1969 Green Bay Packers. **Highlights:** Fixture at DT during Packers' dynasty. Played in four Pro Bowls, seven NFL title games, Super Bowls I, II.

SONNY JURGENSEN
Quarterback. 6-0, 203. Born in Wilmington, North Carolina, August 23, 1934. Duke. Inducted in 1983. 1957-1963 Philadelphia Eagles, 1964-1974 Washington Redskins. **Highlights:** 32,224 yards passing, 255 touchdowns, 82.63 passer rating. Surpassed 3,000 yards passing in five seasons.

JIM KELLY
Quarterback. 6-3, 225. Born in Pittsburgh, Pennsylvania, February 14, 1960. Miami. Inducted in 2002. 1986-1996 Buffalo Bills. **Highlights:** Passed for more than 3,000 yards eight times. Mastered the no-huddle offense that propelled Bills to four consecutive Super Bowls.

LEROY KELLY
Running back. 6-0, 205. Born in Philadelphia, Pennsylvania, May 20, 1942. Morgan State. Inducted in 1994. 1964-1973 Cleveland Browns. **Highlights:** 7,274 yards rushing, 90 total touchdowns, 1,000-yard rusher first three years as starter. Punt return champion, 1965.

WALT KIESLING
Guard. Coach. 6-2, 245. Born in St. Paul, Minnesota, March 27, 1903. Died March 2, 1962. St. Thomas (Minnesota). Inducted in 1966. 1926-27 Duluth Eskimos, 1928 Pottsville Maroons, 1929-1933 Chicago Cardinals, 1934 Chicago Bears, 1935-36 Green Bay Packers, 1937-38 Pittsburgh Pirates; coach, 1939 Pittsburgh Pirates, 1940-42 Pittsburgh Steelers; co-coach, 1943 Phil-Pitt, 1944 Card-Pitt; coach, 1954-56 Pittsburgh Steelers. **Highlights:** 34-year career as pro player, assistant coach, head coach. Led Steelers to first winning season, 1942.

FRANK (BRUISER) KINARD
Tackle. 6-1, 210. Born in Pelahatchie, Mississippi, October 23, 1914. Died September 7, 1985. Mississippi. Inducted in 1971. 1938-1943 Brooklyn Dodgers, 1944 Brooklyn Tigers, 1946-47 New York Yankees (AAFC). **Highlights:** First man to earn both All-NFL, All-AAFC honors. Out because of injury only once.

PAUL KRAUSE
Safety. 6-3, 200. Born in Flint, Michigan, February 19, 1942. Iowa. Inducted in 1998. 1964-67 Washington Redskins, 1968-1979 Minnesota Vikings. **Highlights:** NFL all-time leader with 81 interceptions. Played in eight Pro Bowls. Starting safety in four Super Bowls.

EARL (CURLY) LAMBEAU
Coach. Born in Green Bay, Wisconsin, April 9, 1898. Died June 1, 1965. Notre Dame. Inducted in 1963. 1919-1949 Green Bay Packers, 1950-51 Chicago Cardinals, 1952-53 Washington Redskins. **Highlights:** Charter enshrinee. 229-134-22 coaching record with six NFL championships. Founded pre-NFL Packers, 1919.

JACK LAMBERT
Linebacker. 6-4, 220. Born in Mantua, Ohio, July 8, 1952. Kent State. Inducted in 1990. 1974-1984 Pittsburgh Steelers. **Highlights:** Leader of 'Steel Curtain.' NFL defensive player of year in 1976, nine Pro Bowls.

TOM LANDRY
Coach. Born in Mission, Texas, September 11, 1924. Died February 12, 2000. Texas. Inducted in 1990. 1960-1988 Dallas Cowboys. **Highlights:** 270-178-6 coaching record. 20 consecutive winning seasons. Innovator on offense and defense.

DICK (NIGHT TRAIN) LANE
Cornerback. 6-2, 210. Born in Austin, Texas, April 16, 1928. Died January 29, 2002. Scottsbluff Junior College. Inducted in 1974. 1952-53 Los Angeles Rams, 1954-59 Chicago Cardinals, 1960-65 Detroit Lions. **Highlights:** 68 interceptions for 1,207 yards, 5 touchdowns. Record 14 interceptions as rookie. Seven Pro Bowls.

JIM LANGER
Center. 6-2, 255. Born in Little Falls, Minnesota, May 16, 1948. South Dakota State. Inducted in 1987. 1970-79 Miami Dolphins, 1980-81 Minnesota Vikings. **Highlights:** Played every offensive down in Dolphins' perfect 1972 season. Six Pro Bowls.

WILLIE LANIER
Linebacker. 6-1, 245. Born in Clover, Virginia, August 21, 1945. Morgan State. Inducted in 1986. 1967-1977 Kansas City Chiefs. **Highlights:** 27 interceptions. Defensive star in Super Bowl IV upset. Nicknamed 'Contact' for ferocious tackling.

STEVE LARGENT
Wide receiver. 5-11, 191. Born in Tulsa, Oklahoma, September 28, 1954, Tulsa. Inducted in 1995. 1976-1989 Seattle Seahawks. **Highlights:** 819 receptions for 13,089 yards, 100 touchdowns. Receptions in 177 consecutive games.

YALE LARY
Defensive back-punter. 5-11, 189. Born in Fort Worth, Texas, November 24, 1930. Texas A&M. Inducted in 1979. 1952-53, 1956-1964 Detroit Lions. **Highlights:** 50 interceptions. Three NFL punting crowns, three touchdowns on punt returns. Nine Pro Bowls.

DANTE LAVELLI
End. 6-0, 199. Born in Hudson, Ohio, February 23, 1923. Ohio State. Inducted in 1975. 1946-49 Cleveland Browns (AAFC), 1950-56 Cleveland Browns. **Highlights:** 386 receptions for 6,488 yards, 62 touchdowns. 24 catches in six NFL title games.

BOBBY LAYNE
Quarterback. 6-2, 190. Born in Santa Anna, Texas, December 19, 1926. Died December 1, 1986. Texas. Inducted in 1967. 1948 Chicago Bears, 1949 New York Bulldogs, 1950-58 Detroit Lions, 1958-1962 Pittsburgh Steelers. **Highlights:** 26,768 yards passing, 196 touchdowns, 2,451 yards rushing. Late touchdown pass won 1953 NFL title game.

ALPHONSE (TUFFY) LEEMANS
Fullback. 6-0, 200. Born in Superior, Wisconsin, November 12, 1912. Died January 19, 1979. Oregon, George Washington. Inducted in 1978. 1936-1943 New York Giants. **Highlights:** 3,132 yards rushing, 2,318 yards passing, 422 yards receiving. Led NFL rushers as rookie, 1936.

MARV LEVY
Coach. Born in Chicago, Illinois, August 3, 1925. Coe College, Harvard. Inducted in 2001. 1978-1982 Kansas City Chiefs, 1986-1997 Buffalo Bills. **Highlights:** Led Bills to unprecedented four consecutive Super Bowls. Had 154-120 record. Coaching victories ranked 10th when retired.

BOB LILLY
Defensive tackle. 6-5, 260. Born in Olney, Texas, July 26, 1939. Texas Christian. Inducted in 1980. 1961-1974 Dallas Cowboys. **Highlights:** Eleven Pro Bowls. Played 196 consecutive games. Foundation of great Dallas defensive units.

LARRY LITTLE
Guard. 6-1, 265. Born in Groveland, Georgia, November 2, 1945. Bethune-Cookman. Inducted in 1993. 1967-68 San Diego Chargers, 1969-1980 Miami Dolphins. **Highlights:** Five Pro Bowls, started in three Super Bowls. Epitome of powerful Dolphins rushing game of 1970s.

JAMES LOFTON
Wide receiver. 6-3, 192. Born in Fort Ord, California, July 5, 1956. Stanford. Inducted in 2003. 1978-1986 Green Bay Packers, 1987-88 Los Angeles Raiders, 1989-1992 Buffalo Bills, 1993 Los Angeles Rams, 1993 Philadelphia Eagles. **Highlights:** Played 16 seasons, 233 games. Caught 764 passes for 75 touchdowns and a then-record 14,004 yards. All-Pro four times, eight Pro Bowls.

VINCE LOMBARDI
Coach. Born in Brooklyn, New York, June 11, 1913. Died September 3, 1970. Fordham. Inducted in 1971. 1959-1967 Green Bay Packers, 1969 Washington Redskins. **Highlights:** 105-35-6 coaching record in 10 years, including five NFL titles and victories in Super Bowls I and II.

HOWIE LONG
Defensive end. 6-5, 268. Born in Somerville, Massachusetts, January 6, 1960. Villanova. Inducted in 2000. 1981-1993 Oakland/Los Angeles Raiders. **Highlights:** All-Pro 1983, 1984, 1985. Named All-AFC four times, 1983-1986. Eight Pro Bowls.

RONNIE LOTT
Cornerback-safety. 6-0, 203. Born in Albuquerque, New Mexico, May 8, 1959. Southern California. Inducted in 2000. 1981-1990 San Francisco 49ers, 1991-92 Los Angeles Raiders, 1993-94 New York Jets. **Highlights:** Ten Pro Bowls, 63 career interceptions, and was named to the NFL's 75th Anniversary Team.

SID LUCKMAN
Quarterback. 6-0, 195. Born in Brooklyn, New York, November 21, 1916. Died July 5, 1998. Columbia. Inducted in 1965. 1939-1950 Chicago Bears. **Highlights:** 137 touchdown passes. All-NFL five times. League MVP in 1943.

WILLIAM ROY (LINK) LYMAN
Tackle. 6-2, 252. Born in Table Rock, Nebraska, November 30, 1898. Died December 28, 1972. Nebraska. Inducted in 1964. 1922-23, 1925 Canton Bulldogs, 1924 Cleveland Bulldogs, 1925 Frankford Yellowjackets, 1926-28, 1930-31, 1933-34 Chicago Bears. **Highlights:** Played for four NFL champions. In 16 seasons of college and pro football, played on one losing team.

TOM MACK
Guard. 6-3, 250. Born in Cleveland, Ohio, November 1, 1943. Michigan. Inducted in 1999. 1966-1978 Los Angeles Rams. **Highlights:** Never missed a game in entire 184-game career. Elected to 11 Pro Bowls.

JOHN MACKEY
Tight end. 6-2, 224. Born in New York, New York, September 24, 1941. Syracuse. Inducted in 1992. 1963-1971 Baltimore Colts, 1972 San Diego Chargers. **Highlights:** 331 receptions for 5,236 yards, 38 touchdowns. Second tight end to enter Hall of Fame.

TIM MARA
Team owner. Born in New York, New York, July 29, 1887. Died February 16, 1959. Did not attend college. Inducted in 1963. 1925-1959 New York Giants. **Highlights:** Charter enshrinee. Founder of New York Giants. Built team into powerhouse winning four NFL titles, 10 division titles.

WELLINGTON MARA
Team owner. Born in New York, New York, August 14, 1916. Fordham. Inducted in 1997. 1937-present New York Giants. **Highlights:** Lifetime contributor to NFL and New York Giants. Worked as Giants' ballboy, secretary, vice-president, president and co-CEO. NFC president 1984-present.

GINO MARCHETTI
Defensive end. 6-4, 245. Born in Smithers, West Virginia, January 2, 1927. San Francisco. Inducted in 1972. 1952 Dallas Texans, 1953-1964, 1966 Baltimore Colts. **Highlights:** Named top defensive end of NFL's first 50 years. 10 consecutive Pro Bowls. All-NFL seven times.

GEORGE PRESTON MARSHALL
Team owner. Born in Grafton, West Virginia, October 11, 1896. Died August 9, 1969. Randolph-Macon. Inducted in 1963. 1932 Boston Braves, 1933-36 Boston Redskins, 1937-1969 Washington Redskins. **Highlights:** Charter enshrinee. Sponsored progressive rules changes. Organized first team band, pioneered halftime shows.

OLLIE MATSON
Halfback. 6-2, 220. Born in Trinity, Texas, May 1, 1930. San Francisco. Inducted in 1972. 1952, 1954-58 Chicago Cardinals, 1959-1962 Los Angeles Rams, 1963 Detroit Lions, 1964-66 Philadelphia Eagles. **Highlights:** Nine touchdowns on kickoff, punt returns. Traded for nine players in 1959.

DON MAYNARD
Wide receiver. 6-1, 185. Born in Crosbyton, Texas, January 25, 1935. Texas Western. Inducted in 1987. 1958 New York Giants, 1960-62 New York Titans, 1963-1972 New York Jets, 1973 St. Louis Cardinals. **Highlights:** 633 receptions for 11,834 yards, 88 touchdowns. At least 50 catches and 1,000 yards in five different seasons.

GEORGE McAFEE
Halfback. 6-0, 177. Born in Corbin, Kentucky, March 13, 1918. Duke. Inducted in 1966. 1940-41, 1945-1950 Chicago Bears. **Highlights:** Two-way star. 25 interceptions, 234 points. Career punt-return average of 12.78 yards per return.

MIKE McCORMACK
Tackle. 6-4, 250. Born in Chicago, Illinois, June 21, 1930. Kansas. Inducted in 1984. 1951 New York Yanks, 1954-1962 Cleveland Browns. **Highlights:** Excelled as offensive right tackle for eight years. Six Pro Bowls.

TOMMY McDONALD
Wide receiver. 5-9, 175. Born in Roy, New Mexico, July 26, 1934. Oklahoma. Inducted in 1998. 1957-1963 Philadelphia Eagles, 1964 Dallas Cowboys, 1965-66 Los Angeles Rams, 1967 Atlanta Falcons, 1968 Cleveland Browns. **Highlights:** Recorded 495 receptions for 8,410 yards, 84 touchdowns.

HUGH McELHENNY
Halfback. 6-1, 198. Born in Los Angeles, California, December 31, 1928. Washington. Inducted in 1970. 1952-1960 San Francisco 49ers, 1961-62 Minnesota Vikings, 1963 New York Giants, 1964 Detroit Lions. **Highlights:** 5,281 rushing yards, 360 points. Totaled 11,369 yards rushing, receiving, and returning kicks.

JOHNNY (BLOOD) McNALLY
Halfback. 6-0, 185. Born in New Richmond, Wisconsin, November 27, 1903. Died November 28, 1985. Notre Dame, St. John's (Minnesota). Inducted in 1963. 1925-26 Milwaukee Badgers, 1926-27 Duluth Eskimos, 1928 Pottsville Maroons, 1929-1933, 1935-36 Green Bay Packers, 1934 Pittsburgh Pirates; player-coach, 1937-38 Pittsburgh Pirates. **Highlights:** Charter enshrinee. 49 touchdowns, 297 points in 14 seasons with five teams.

MIKE MICHALSKE
Guard. 6-0, 209. Born in Cleveland, Ohio, April 24, 1903. Died October 26, 1983. Penn State. Inducted in 1964. 1926 New York Yankees (AFL), 1927-28 New York Yankees, 1929-1935, 1937 Green Bay Packers. **Highlights:** Anchored Packers' championship lines, 1929-1931. First guard enshrined in Canton.

WAYNE MILLNER
End. 6-0, 191. Born in Roxbury, Massachusetts, January 31, 1913. Died November 19, 1976. Notre Dame. Inducted in 1968. 1936 Boston Redskins, 1937-1941, 1945 Washington Redskins. **Highlights:** Redskins' all-time leader with 124 catches when retired. 55- and 78-yard touchdown receptions in 1937 NFL Championship Game.

BOBBY MITCHELL
Running back-wide receiver. 6-0, 195. Born in Hot Springs, Arkansas, June 6, 1935. Illinois. Inducted in 1983. 1958-1961 Cleveland Browns, 1962-68 Washington Redskins. **Highlights:** 91 touchdowns, including 8 on kickoff and punt returns. 14,078 combined yards.

RON MIX
Tackle. 6-4, 255. Born in Los Angeles, California, March 10, 1938. Southern California. Inducted in 1979. 1960 Los Angeles Chargers, 1961-69 San Diego Chargers, 1971 Oakland Raiders. **Highlights:** All-AFL nine times. Only two holding penalties in 10 years with the Chargers.

JOE MONTANA
Quarterback. 6-2, 200. Born in New Eagle, Pennsylvania, June, 11, 1956. Notre Dame. Inducted in 2000. 1979-1992 San Francisco 49ers, 1993-94 Kansas City Chiefs. **Highlights:** MVP in Super Bowl's XVI, XIX, and XXIV. Eight Pro Bowls and All-NFL three times.

LENNY MOORE
Flanker-running back. 6-1, 198. Born in Reading, Pennsylvania, November 25, 1933. Penn State. Inducted in 1975. 1956-1967 Baltimore Colts. **Highlights:** From 1963-65, scored touchdowns in record 18 consecutive games. 113 career touchdowns, 12,451 combined net yards.

MARION MOTLEY
Fullback. 6-1, 238. Born in Leesburg, Georgia, June 5, 1920. Died June 27, 1999. South Carolina State, Nevada. Inducted in 1968. 1946-49 Cleveland Browns (AAFC), 1950-53 Cleveland Browns, 1955 Pittsburgh Steelers. **Highlights:** AAFC's all-time rushing champion. Led league in rushing in first NFL season.

MIKE MUNCHAK
Guard. 6-3, 281. Born in Scranton, Pennsylvania, March 5, 1960. Penn State. Inducted in 2001. 1982-1993 Houston Oilers. **Highlights:** Devastating blocker, All-AFC seven times, elected to nine Pro Bowls.

ANTHONY MUÑOZ
Tackle. 6-6, 278. Born in Ontario, California, August 19, 1958. Southern California. Inducted in 1998. 1980-1992 Cincinnati Bengals. **Highlights:** All-Pro choice 11 consecutive years, 1981-1991. Selected to 11 straight Pro Bowls.

GEORGE MUSSO
Guard-tackle. 6-2, 270. Born in Collinsville, Illinois. April 8, 1910. Died September 5, 2000. Millikin. Inducted in 1982. 1933-1944 Chicago Bears. **Highlights:** First player to achieve All-NFL status at two positions—tackle in 1935 and guard in 1937.

BRONKO NAGURSKI
Fullback. 6-2, 225. Born in Rainy River, Ontario, Canada, November 3, 1908. Died January 7, 1990. Minnesota. Inducted in 1963. 1930-37, 1943 Chicago Bears. **Highlights:** Charter enshrinee. 2,778 rushing yards in nine seasons. All-NFL five times.

JOE NAMATH
Quarterback. 6-2, 200. Born in Beaver Falls, Pennsylvania, May 31, 1943. Alabama. Inducted in 1985. 1965-1976 New York Jets, 1977 Los Angeles Rams. **Highlights:** First quarterback to pass for more than 4,000 yards in season, 1967. Guaranteed, delivered victory over Colts in Super Bowl III.

EARLE (GREASY) NEALE
Coach. Born in Parkersburg, West Virginia, November 5, 1891. Died November 2, 1973. West Virginia Wesleyan. Inducted in 1969. 1941-42, 1944-1950 Philadelphia Eagles; co-coach, 1943 Phil-Pitt. **Highlights:** Turned Eagles into winners with three consecutive division crowns, NFL championships in 1948 and 1949.

ERNIE NEVERS
Fullback. 6-1, 205. Born in Willow River, Minnesota, June 11, 1903. Died May 3, 1976. Stanford. Inducted in 1963. 1926-27 Duluth Eskimos, 1929-1931 Chicago Cardinals. **Highlights:** Charter enshrinee. Holds NFL's longest-standing record, 40 points in one game in 1929.

OZZIE NEWSOME
Tight end. 6-2, 232. Born in Muscle Shoals, Alabama, March 16, 1956. Alabama. Inducted in 1999. 1978-1990 Cleveland Browns. **Highlights:** Finished career as all-time leader among tight ends with 662 receptions for 7,980 yards.

RAY NITSCHKE
Linebacker. 6-3, 235. Born in Elmwood Park, Illinois, December 29, 1936. Died March 8, 1998. Illinois. Inducted in 1978. 1958-1972 Green Bay Packers. **Highlights:** MVP of 1962 title game. Named NFL's all-time linebacker in 1969.

CHUCK NOLL
Coach. Born in Cleveland, Ohio, January 5, 1932. Dayton. Inducted in 1993. 1969-1991 Pittsburgh Steelers. **Highlights:** Coached for 23 years. Only coach to win four Super Bowl titles (IX, X, XIII, XIV).

LEO NOMELLINI
Defensive tackle. 6-3, 264. Born in Lucca, Italy, June 19, 1924. Died October 17, 2000. Minnesota. Inducted in 1969. 1950-1963 San Francisco 49ers. **Highlights:** Played every 49ers game for 14 seasons. 10 Pro Bowls.

MERLIN OLSEN
Defensive tackle. 6-5, 270. Born in Logan, Utah, September 15, 1940. Utah State. Inducted in 1982. 1962-1976 Los Angeles Rams. **Highlights:** Member of the Fearsome "Foursome. Named" to 14 consecutive Pro Bowls, Rams' all-time team.

JIM OTTO
Center. 6-2, 255. Born in Wausau, Wisconsin, January 5, 1938. Miami. Inducted in 1980. 1960-1974 Oakland Raiders. **Highlights:** Named AFL's all-time center. Played in 210 games, 12 AFL All-Star Games or Pro Bowls, six AFL/AFC title games.

STEVE OWEN
Tackle. Coach. 6-2, 235. Born in Cleo Springs, Oklahoma, April 21, 1898. Died May 17, 1964. Phillips. Inducted in 1966. 1924-25 Kansas City Cowboys, 1925 Cleveland Bulldogs, 1926-1931, 1933 New York Giants; coach, 1930-1953 New York Giants. **Highlights:** Both player and coach. Coached Giants to record of 155-108-17, eight divisional titles, two NFL championships.

ALAN PAGE
Defensive tackle. 6-4, 225. Born in Canton, Ohio, August 7, 1945. Notre Dame. Inducted in 1988. 1967-1978 Minnesota Vikings, 1978-1981 Chicago Bears. **Highlights:** Dominating defensive tackle played in 218 consecutive games, four Super Bowls. Won league MVP honors in 1971.

PRO FOOTBALL HALL OF FAME

CLARENCE (ACE) PARKER
Quarterback. 5-11, 168. Born in Portsmouth, Virginia, May 17, 1912. Duke. Inducted in 1972. 1937-1941 Brooklyn Dodgers, 1945 Boston Yanks, 1946 New York Yankees (AAFC). **Highlights:** Two-way threat. Two-time All-NFL performer, league MVP in 1940.

JIM PARKER
Guard-tackle. 6-3, 273. Born in Macon, Georgia, April 3, 1934. Ohio State. Inducted in 1973. 1957-1967 Baltimore Colts. **Highlights:** First full-time offensive lineman elected to Hall of Fame. All-NFL eight consecutive years, eight Pro Bowls.

WALTER PAYTON
Running back. 5-10, 202. Born in Columbia, Mississippi, July 25, 1954. Died November 1, 1999. Jackson State. Inducted in 1993. 1975-1987 Chicago Bears. **Highlights:** NFL's all-time leading rusher with 16,726 yards and combined net yardage with 21,803 at time of retirement.

JOE PERRY
Fullback. 6-0, 200. Born in Stevens, Arkansas, January 22, 1927. Compton Junior College. Inducted in 1969. 1948-49 San Francisco 49ers (AAFC), 1950-1960, 1963 San Francisco 49ers, 1961-62 Baltimore Colts. **Highlights:** First player in NFL history to gain 1,000 yards two consecutive seasons. 12,532 combined yards.

PETE PIHOS
End. 6-1, 210. Born in Orlando, Florida, October 22, 1923. Indiana. Inducted in 1970. 1947-1955 Philadelphia Eagles. **Highlights:** Three-time NFL receiving champion. Caught winning touchdown in 1949 NFL Championship Game.

HUGH (SHORTY) RAY
Supervisor of officials 1938-1952. Born in Highland Park, Illinois, September 21, 1884. Died September 16, 1956. Illinois. Inducted in 1966. **Highlights:** Supervisor of Officials, 1938-1952. Streamlined rules to improve game tempo, player safety.

DAN REEVES
Team owner. Born in New York, New York, June 30, 1912. Died April 15, 1971. Georgetown. Inducted in 1967. 1941-45 Cleveland Rams, 1946-1971 Los Angeles Rams. **Highlights:** Moved Rams to Los Angeles in 1946 and opened up West Coast to pro football. First postwar owner to sign African-American player.

MEL RENFRO
Cornerback-safety. 6-0, 192. Born in Houston, Texas, December 30, 1941. Oregon. Inducted in 1996. 1964-1977 Dallas Cowboys. **Highlights:** 52 interceptions for 626 yards and 3 touchdowns. Also added 842 yards on punt returns, 2,246 yards on kickoff returns. Elected to Pro Bowl first 10 seasons.

JOHN RIGGINS
Running back. 6-2, 240. Born in Seneca, Kansas, August 4, 1949. Kansas. Inducted in 1992. 1971-75 New York Jets, 1976-79, 1981-85 Washington Redskins. **Highlights:** 11,352 rushing yards, 116 total touchdowns. MVP of Super Bowl XVII with 166 rushing yards including game-winning 43-yard touchdown.

JIM RINGO
Center. 6-2, 230. Born in Orange, New Jersey, November 21, 1931. Syracuse. Inducted in 1981. 1953-1963 Green Bay Packers, 1964-67 Philadelphia Eagles. **Highlights:** Ten-time Pro Bowl selection, seven-time All-NFL selection. Started in then-record 182 consecutive games.

ANDY ROBUSTELLI
Defensive end. 6-0, 230. Born in Stamford, Connecticut, December 6, 1925. Arnold College. Inducted in 1971. 1951-55 Los Angeles Rams, 1956-1964 New York Giants. **Highlights:** Anchored defense in eight championship games. Named NFL's top player in 1962.

ART ROONEY
Team owner. Born in Coulterville, Pennsylvania, January 27, 1901. Died August 25, 1988. Georgetown, Duquesne. Inducted in 1964. 1933-39 Pittsburgh Pirates, 1940-42, 1945-1988 Pittsburgh Steelers, 1943 Phil-Pitt, 1944 Card-Pitt. **Highlights:** Founded Pittsburgh Pirates in 1933 and renamed them Steelers in 1940. Team won four Super Bowls in 1970s.

DAN ROONEY
Team owner. Born in Pittsburgh, Pennsylvania, July, 20, 1932. Duquesne. Inducted in 2000. 1955-present Pittsburgh Steelers. **Highlights:** Has been on the board of directors for the NFL Trust Fund, NFL Films, and Scheduling Committee. Played a key role in the labor agreement reached in 1993 between the NFL owners and players.

PETE ROZELLE
Commissioner. Born in South Gate, California, March 1, 1926. Died December 6, 1996. Compton Junior College, San Francisco. Inducted in 1985. Commissioner, 1960-1989. **Highlights:** Negotiated first league-wide television contract in 1962. Generally recognized as premiere commissioner in all of sports. Credited with making NFL the nation's most popular sport.

BOB ST. CLAIR
Tackle. 6-9, 265. Born in San Francisco, California, February 18, 1931. San Francisco, Tulsa. Inducted in 1990. 1953-1963 San Francisco 49ers. **Highlights:** Exceptional offensive lineman. Also played goal-line defense and had 10 blocked field goals, 1956.

BARRY SANDERS
Running back. 5-8, 203. Born in Wichita, Kansas, July 16, 1968. Oklahoma State. Inducted in 2004. 1989-1998 Detroit Lions. **Highlights:** 15,269 rushing yards, 99 touchdowns. Rushed for 1,000 yards in each of 10 seasons. NFL co-MVP, 1997. Selected to 10 Pro Bowls.

GALE SAYERS
Running back. 6-0, 200. Born in Wichita, Kansas, May 30, 1943. Kansas. Inducted in 1977. 1965-1971 Chicago Bears. **Highlights:** Broke into league by scoring rookie-record 22 touchdowns. Led league in rushing in 1966, 1969. MVP of three Pro Bowls.

JOE SCHMIDT
Linebacker. 6-0, 222. Born in Pittsburgh, Pennsylvania, January 18, 1932. Pittsburgh. Inducted in 1973. 1953-1965 Detroit Lions. **Highlights:** 24 interceptions. Lions' team captain for nine years. Mastered middle linebacker position that evolved in 1950s.

TEX SCHRAMM
Team president-general manager. Born in San Gabriel, California, June 2, 1920. Died July 15, 2003. Texas. Inducted in 1991. 1947-1956 Los Angeles Rams. 1960-1989 Dallas Cowboys. **Highlights:** Played prominent role in AFL-NFL merger. Chairman of Competition Committee from 1966-1988.

LEE ROY SELMON
Defensive end. 6-3, 250. Born in Eufaula, Oklahoma, October 20, 1954. Oklahoma. Inducted in 1995. 1976-1984 Tampa Bay Buccaneers. **Highlights:** 78½ sacks, 380 quarterback pressures, forced 28 fumbles. Six consecutive Pro Bowl selections.

BILLY SHAW
Guard. 6-2, 258. Born in Natchez, Mississippi, December 15, 1938. Georgia Tech. Inducted in 1999. 1961-69 Buffalo Bills. **Highlights:** First player who played entire career in AFL to be elected to Hall of Fame. Named to AFL's all-time team.

ART SHELL
Tackle. 6-5, 285. Born in Charleston, South Carolina, November 26, 1946. Maryland State-Eastern Shore. Inducted in 1989. 1968-82 Oakland/Los Angeles Raiders. **Highlights:** Cornerstone of Raiders' offensive line in 1970s. 207 regular-season games, 23 postseason games, eight Pro Bowls.

DON SHULA
Coach. Born in Grand River, Ohio, January 4, 1930. John Carroll. Inducted in 1997. 1963-69 Baltimore Colts, 1970-1995 Miami Dolphins. **Highlights:** Won more games (347) than any coach in NFL history. Won two Super Bowl titles, including Super Bowl VII when Dolphins recorded NFL's only perfect season (17-0).

O.J. SIMPSON
Running back. 6-1, 212. Born in San Francisco, California, July 9, 1947. City College (San Francisco), Southern California. Inducted in 1985. 1969-1977 Buffalo Bills, 1978-79 San Francisco 49ers. **Highlights:** In 1973, became first player to rush for 2,000 yards in season. Finished career with four rushing titles, 11,236 yards.

MIKE SINGLETARY
Linebacker. 6-0, 230. Born in Houston, Texas, October 9, 1958. Baylor. Inducted in 1998. 1981-1992 Chicago Bears. **Highlights:** All-Pro choice eight times and All-NFC nine consecutive seasons. Selected to 10 Pro Bowls.

JACKIE SLATER
Tackle. 6-4, 277. Born in Jackson, Mississippi, May 27, 1954. Jackson State. Inducted in 2001. 1976-1995 Los Angeles/St. Louis Rams. **Highlights:** Played 20 seasons, 259 games. Blocked for seven different 1,000-yard rushers. Seven Pro Bowls.

JACKIE SMITH
Tight end. 6-4, 232. Born in Columbia, Mississippi, February 23, 1940. Northwestern State (Louisiana). Inducted in 1994. 1963-1977 St. Louis Cardinals, 1978 Dallas Cowboys. **Highlights:** 480 receptions for 7,918 yards, 40 touchdowns. Third tight end to be elected to Hall of Fame.

JOHN STALLWORTH
Wide receiver. 6-2, 191. Born in Tuscaloosa, Alabama, July 15, 1952. Alabama A&M. Inducted in 2002. 1974-1987 Pittsburgh Steelers. **Highlights:** 537 receptions for 8,723 yards, 63 touchdowns. Scored go-ahead touchdown in Super Bowl XIV on 73-yard reception.

BART STARR
Quarterback. 6-1, 200. Born in Montgomery, Alabama, January 9, 1934. Alabama. Inducted in 1977. 1956-1971 Green Bay Packers. **Highlights:** Quarterbacked Packers to six division titles, five NFL titles, and first two Super Bowls in which he was MVP.

ROGER STAUBACH
Quarterback. 6-3, 202. Born in Cincinnati, Ohio, February 5, 1942. New Mexico Military Institute, Navy. Inducted in 1985. 1969-1979 Dallas Cowboys. **Highlights:** Led Cowboys to four NFC titles and victories in Super Bowls VI, XII. When retired, 83.4 career passer rating was best of all time.

ERNIE STAUTNER
Defensive tackle. 6-2, 235. Born in Prinzing-by-Cham, Bavaria, April 20, 1925. Boston College. Inducted in 1969. 1950-1963 Pittsburgh Steelers. **Highlights:** Played in nine Pro Bowls and won the best lineman award in 1957. Recorded 3 safeties.

JAN STENERUD
Kicker. 6-2, 190. Born in Fetsund, Norway, November 26, 1942. Montana State. Inducted in 1991. 1967-1979 Kansas City Chiefs, 1980-83 Green Bay Packers, 1984-85 Minnesota Vikings. **Highlights:** 1,699 points on 580 extra points, 373 field goals. First pure placekicker to enter Hall of Fame.

DWIGHT STEPHENSON
Center. 6-2, 255. Born in Murfreesboro, North Carolina, November 20, 1957. Alabama. Inducted in 1998. 1980-87 Miami Dolphins. **Highlights:** Recognized as premier center of his time. All-Pro, All-AFC five straight years. Selected to five Pro Bowls.

HANK STRAM
Coach. Born in Chicago, Illinois, January 3, 1923. Purdue. Inducted in 2003. 1960-1974 Dallas Texans/Kansas City Chiefs, 1976-1977 New Orleans Saints. **Highlights:** Overall record of 136-100-10. Recorded most wins in AFL history. Guided teams to titles in 1962, 1966, and 1969. Led Chiefs to AFL win in Super Bowl IV.

KEN STRONG
Halfback. 5-11, 210. Born in West Haven, Connecticut, April 21, 1906. Died October 5, 1979. New York University. Inducted in 1967. 1929-1932 Staten Island Stapletons, 1933-35, 1939, 1944-47 New York Giants, 1936-37 New York Yanks (AFL). **Highlights:** Scored 17 points to lead Giants to victory in 1934 'Sneakers' game, led NFL with 64 points, 1933.

JOE STYDAHAR
Tackle. 6-4, 230. Born in Kaylor, Pennsylvania, March 17, 1912. Died March 23, 1977. West Virginia. Inducted in 1967. 1936-1942, 1945-46 Chicago Bears. **Highlights:** One of stalwarts of Bears' 'Monsters of the Midway.' Played on five divisional, three NFL championship teams.

LYNN SWANN
Wide receiver. 5-11, 180. Born in Alcoa, Tennessee, March 7, 1952. Southern California. Inducted in 2001. 1974-1982 Pittsburgh Steelers. **Highlights:** All-AFC three times. Selected to three Pro Bowls. MVP, Super Bowl X.

FRAN TARKENTON
Quarterback. 6-0, 185. Born in Richmond, Virginia, February 3, 1940. Georgia. Inducted in 1986. 1961-66, 1972-78 Minnesota Vikings, 1967-1971 New York Giants. **Highlights:** At retirement, held NFL records for attempts (6,467), completions (3,686), yards (47,003), and touchdowns (342). Four touchdown passes in first NFL game.

CHARLEY TAYLOR
Running back-wide receiver. 6-3, 210. Born in Grand Prairie, Texas, September 28, 1941. Arizona State. Inducted in 1984. 1964-1975, 1977 Washington Redskins. **Highlights:** Won rookie of year honors as running back. Switched to wide receiver and won receiving titles in 1966, 1967.

JIM TAYLOR
Fullback. 6-0, 216. Born in Baton Rouge, Louisiana, September 20, 1935. Louisiana State. Inducted in 1976. 1958-1966 Green Bay Packers, 1967 New Orleans Saints. **Highlights:** 8,597 rushing yards, 558 points. In 1962, led league in rushing and scoring with 19 touchdowns.

LAWRENCE TAYLOR
Linebacker. 6-3, 237. Born in Williamsburg, Virginia, February 4, 1959. North Carolina. Inducted in 1999. 1981-1993 New York Giants. **Highlights:** Redefined the position of outside linebacker. All-Pro nine times, 10 Pro Bowls. NFL MVP in 1986.

JIM THORPE
Halfback. 6-1, 190. Born in Prague, Oklahoma, May 28, 1888. Died March 28, 1953. Carlisle. Inducted in 1963. 1915-17, 1919-1920, 1926 Canton Bulldogs, 1921 Cleveland Indians, 1922-23 Oorang Indians, 1924 Rock Island Independents, 1925 New York Giants, 1928 Chicago Cardinals. **Highlights:** Charter enshrinee. First president of American Professional Football Association, 1920. Played for 12 seasons.

Y.A. TITTLE
Quarterback. 6-0, 200. Born in Marshall, Texas, October 24, 1926. Louisiana State. Inducted in 1971. 1948-49 Baltimore Colts (AAFC), 1950 Baltimore Colts, 1951-1960 San Francisco 49ers, 1961-64 New York Giants. **Highlights:** 33,070 yards, 242 touchdowns. 33 touchdown passes in 1962 and 36 in 1963. Two-time league MVP.

GEORGE TRAFTON
Center. 6-2, 235. Born in Chicago, Illinois, December 6, 1896. Died September 5, 1971. Notre Dame. Inducted in 1964. 1920-1932 Decatur Staleys/Chicago Staleys/ Chicago Bears. **Highlights:** First center to snap with one hand. Named top NFL center of 1920s.

CHARLEY TRIPPI
Halfback-quarterback. 6-0, 185. Born in Pittston, Pennsylvania, December 14, 1922. Georgia. Inducted in 1968. 1947-1955 Chicago Cardinals. **Highlights:** One of football's most versatile performers. Played halfback five years, quarterback for two, defense for two.

EMLEN TUNNELL
Safety. 6-1, 200. Born in Bryn Mawr, Pennsylvania, March 29, 1925. Died July 22, 1975. Toledo, Iowa. Inducted in 1967. 1948-1958 New York Giants, 1959-1961 Green Bay Packers. **Highlights:** 79 interceptions. Gained more yards on kickoff, punt, and interception returns (924) in 1952 than that season's NFL rushing leader.

CLYDE (BULLDOG) TURNER
Center. 6-2, 235. Born in Plains, Texas, March 10, 1919. Died October 30, 1998. Hardin-Simmons. Inducted in 1966. 1940-1952 Chicago Bears. **Highlights:** Anchored defense for four NFL championship teams, including 4 interceptions in five title games.

JOHNNY UNITAS
Quarterback. 6-1, 195. Born in Pittsburgh, Pennsylvania, May 7, 1933. Died September 11, 2002. Louisville. Inducted in 1979. 1956-1972 Baltimore Colts, 1973 San Diego Chargers. **Highlights:** 40,239 passing yards, 290 touchdowns. Led Colts to two NFL championships. Passed for at least one touchdown in 47 consecutive games.

GENE UPSHAW
Guard. 6-5, 255. Born in Robstown, Texas, August 15, 1945. Texas A & I. Inducted in 1987. 1967-1981 Oakland Raiders. **Highlights:** Premier guard of his era played in 10 AFL/AFC Championship Games, three Super Bowls, seven Pro Bowls.

NORM VAN BROCKLIN
Quarterback. 6-1, 190. Born in Eagle Butte, South Dakota, March 15, 1926. Died May 2, 1983. Oregon. Inducted in 1971. 1949-1957 Los Angeles Rams, 1958-1960 Philadelphia Eagles. **Highlights:** NFL-record 554 yards passing in 1951 season opener. Guided Eagles to NFL crown as league MVP in 1960.

STEVE VAN BUREN
Halfback. 6-1, 200. Born in La Ceiba, Honduras, December 28, 1920. Louisiana State. Inducted in 1965. 1944-1951 Philadelphia Eagles. **Highlights:** Four-time rushing champion. Won 1944 punt-return title and was 1945 kick-off-return champion.

DOAK WALKER
Halfback. 5-11, 173. Born in Dallas, Texas, January 1, 1927. Died September 27, 1998. Southern Methodist. Inducted in 1986. 1950-55 Detroit Lions. **Highlights:** 534 points. Won two NFL scoring titles. Had winning 67-yard scoring run in 1952 title game.

BILL WALSH
Coach. Born in Los Angeles, California, November 30, 1931. San Jose State. Inducted in 1993. 1979-1988 San Francisco 49ers. **Highlights:** 102-63-1 coaching record. Guided 49ers to three Super Bowl titles (XVI, XIX, XXIII) in 10 years.

PAUL WARFIELD
Wide receiver. 6-0, 188. Born in Warren, Ohio, November 28, 1942. Ohio State. Inducted in 1983. 1964-69, 1976-77 Cleveland Browns, 1970-74 Miami Dolphins. **Highlights:** 8,565 yards receiving, 85 touchdowns. Eight-time Pro Bowl player. Key to both Cleveland and Miami offenses.

BOB WATERFIELD
Quarterback. 6-2, 200. Born in Elmira, New York, July 26, 1920. Died March 25, 1983. UCLA. Inducted in 1965. 1945 Cleveland Rams, 1946-1952 Los Angeles Rams. **Highlights:** NFL MVP as rookie in 1945 and led Rams to NFL title. Grabbed 20 interceptions in limited defensive duties.

MIKE WEBSTER
Center. 6-2, 260. Born in Tomahawk, Wisconsin, March 18, 1952. Died September 24, 2002. Wisconsin. Inducted in 1997. 1974-1988 Pittsburgh Steelers, 1989-1990 Kansas City Chiefs. **Highlights:** Played in 245 games, nine Pro Bowls, and won four Super Bowls during 17-year career.

ARNIE WEINMEISTER
Defensive tackle. 6-4, 235. Born in Rhein, Saskatchewan, Canada, March 23, 1923. Died June 29, 2000. Washington. Inducted in 1984. 1948-49 New York Yankees (AAFC), 1950-53 New York Giants. **Highlights:** Dominant defensive tackle of his time. Four-time All-NFL selection, four Pro Bowls.

RANDY WHITE
Defensive tackle. 6-4, 265. Born in Pittsburgh, Pennsylvania, January 15, 1953. Maryland. Inducted in 1994. 1975-1988 Dallas Cowboys. **Highlights:** Missed only one game in 14 seasons. Co-MVP of Super Bowl XII. Nine-time Pro Bowl selection.

DAVE WILCOX
Linebacker. 6-3, 241. Born in Ontario, Oregon, September, 29, 1942. Boise State, Oregon. Inducted in 2000. 1964-1974 San Francisco 49ers. **Highlights:** Seven Pro Bowls, All-NFL five times. Missed only one game because of injury.

BILL WILLIS
Guard. 6-2, 215. Born in Columbus, Ohio, October 5, 1921. Ohio State. Inducted in 1977. 1946-1953 Cleveland Browns (AAFC/NFL). **Highlights:** Two-way player who excelled on defense. Four-time All-NFL player, played in three Pro Bowls.

LARRY WILSON
Safety. 6-0, 190. Born in Rigby, Idaho, March 24, 1938. Utah. Inducted in 1978. 1960-1972 St. Louis Cardinals. **Highlights:** 52 interceptions. Had interception in seven consecutive games in 1966. Made "safety blitz" famous.

KELLEN WINSLOW
Tight end. 6-5, 250. Born in St. Louis, Missouri, November 5, 1957. Missouri. Inducted in 1995. 1979-1987 San Diego Chargers **Highlights:** 541 receptions for 6,741 yards, 45 touchdowns. 13 catches, blocked field goal in 1981 playoff win over Miami.

ALEX WOJCIECHOWICZ
Center. 6-0, 235. Born in South River, New Jersey, August 12, 1915. Died July 13, 1992. Fordham. Inducted in 1968. 1938-1946 Detroit Lions, 1946-1950 Philadelphia Eagles. **Highlights:** One of league's first iron men. Played both ways for eight years with Lions.

WILLIE WOOD
Safety. 5-10, 190. Born in Washington, D.C., December 23, 1936. Southern California. Inducted in 1989. 1960-1971 Green Bay Packers. **Highlights:** 48 interceptions. Competed in six NFL Championship Games and Super Bowls I and II.

RON YARY
Tackle. 6-5, 255. Born in Chicago, Illinois, July 16, 1946. Cerritos (Calif.) J.C., Southern California. Inducted in 2001. 1968-1981 Minnesota Vikings, 1982 Los Angeles Rams. **Highlights:** All-Pro six consecutive seasons, All-NFC eight consecutive years. Named to seven Pro Bowls. Started in four Super Bowls and five NFL/NFC Championship Games.

JACK YOUNGBLOOD
Defensive end. 6-4, 247. Born in Jacksonville, Florida, January 26, 1950. Florida. Inducted in 2001. 1971-1984 Los Angeles Rams. **Highlights:** Played in club-record 201 consecutive games. Played in five NFC Championship Games, one Super Bowl. Named All-Pro five times, All-NFC seven times. Elected to seven consecutive Pro Bowls.

ENSHRINEES BY YEAR OF INDUCTION

**Deceased*
(Date of enshrinement in parentheses)

1963 CHARTER CLASS
(September 7, 1963)
Sammy Baugh
Bert Bell*
Joe Carr*
Earl (Dutch) Clark*
Harold (Red) Grange*
George Halas*
Mel Hein*
Wilbur (Pete) Henry*
Robert (Cal) Hubbard*
Don Hutson*
Earl (Curly) Lambeau*
Tim Mara*
George Preston Marshall*
John (Blood) McNally*
Bronko Nagurski*
Ernie Nevers*
Jim Thorpe*

CLASS OF 1964
(September 6, 1964)
Jimmy Conzelman*
Ed Healey*
Clarke Hinkle*
William Roy (Link) Lyman*
Mike Michalske*
Art Rooney*
George Trafton*

CLASS OF 1965
(September 12, 1965)
Guy Chamberlin*
John (Paddy) Driscoll*
Dan Fortmann*
Otto Graham*
Sid Luckman*
Steve Van Buren
Bob Waterfield*

CLASS OF 1966
(September 17, 1966)
Bill Dudley
Joe Guyon*
Arnie Herber*
Walt Kiesling*
George McAfee
Steve Owen*
Hugh (Shorty) Ray*
Clyde (Bulldog) Turner*

CLASS OF 1967
(August 5, 1967)
Chuck Bednarik
Charles W. Bidwill Sr.*
Paul Brown*
Bobby Layne*
Dan Reeves*
Ken Strong*
Joe Stydahar*
Emlen Tunnell*

CLASS OF 1968
(August 3, 1968)
Cliff Battles*
Art Donovan
Elroy (Crazylegs) Hirsch*
Wayne Millner*
Marion Motley*
Charley Trippi
Alex Wojciechowicz*

CLASS OF 1969
(September 13, 1969)
Albert Glen (Turk) Edwards*
Earle (Greasy) Neale*
Leo Nomellini*
Joe Perry
Ernie Stautner

CLASS OF 1970
(August 8, 1970)
Jack Christiansen*
Tom Fears*
Hugh McElhenny
Pete Pihos

CLASS OF 1971
(July 31, 1971)
Jim Brown
Bill Hewitt*
Frank (Bruiser) Kinard*
Vince Lombardi*
Andy Robustelli
Y. A. Tittle
Norm Van Brocklin*

CLASS OF 1972
(July 29, 1972)
Lamar Hunt
Gino Marchetti
Ollie Matson
Clarence (Ace) Parker

CLASS OF 1973
(July 28, 1973)
Raymond Berry
Jim Parker
Joe Schmidt

CLASS OF 1974
(July 27, 1974)
Tony Canadeo*
Bill George*
Lou Groza*
Dick (Night Train) Lane*

CLASS OF 1975
(August 2, 1975)
Roosevelt Brown
George Connor*
Dante Lavelli
Lenny Moore

CLASS OF 1976
(July 24, 1976)
Ray Flaherty*
Len Ford*
Jim Taylor

CLASS OF 1977
(July 30, 1977)
Frank Gifford
Forrest Gregg
Gale Sayers
Bart Starr
Bill Willis

CLASS OF 1978
(July 29, 1978)
Lance Alworth
Weeb Ewbank*
Alphonse (Tuffy) Leemans*
Ray Nitschke*
Larry Wilson

CLASS OF 1979
(July 28, 1979)
Dick Butkus
Yale Lary
Ron Mix
Johnny Unitas*

CLASS OF 1980
(August 2, 1980)
Herb Adderley
David (Deacon) Jones
Bob Lilly
Jim Otto

CLASS OF 1981
(August 1, 1981)
Morris (Red) Badgro*
George Blanda
Willie Davis
Jim Ringo

CLASS OF 1982
(August 7, 1982)
Doug Atkins
Sam Huff
George Musso*
Merlin Olsen

CLASS OF 1983
(July 30, 1983)
Bobby Bell
Sid Gillman*
Sonny Jurgensen
Bobby Mitchell
Paul Warfield

CLASS OF 1984
(July 28, 1984)
Willie Brown
Mike McCormack
Charley Taylor
Arnie Weinmeister*

CLASS OF 1985
(August 3, 1985)
Frank Gatski
Joe Namath
Pete Rozelle*
O. J. Simpson
Roger Staubach

PRO FOOTBALL HALL OF FAME

CLASS OF 1986
(August 2, 1986)
Paul Hornung
Ken Houston
Willie Lanier
Fran Tarkenton
Doak Walker*

CLASS OF 1987
(August 8, 1987)
Larry Csonka
Len Dawson
Joe Greene
John Henry Johnson
Jim Langer
Don Maynard
Gene Upshaw

CLASS OF 1988
(July 30, 1988)
Fred Biletnikoff
Mike Ditka
Jack Ham
Alan Page

CLASS OF 1989
(August 5, 1989)
Mel Blount
Terry Bradshaw
Art Shell
Willie Wood

CLASS OF 1990
(August 4, 1990)
Buck Buchanan*
Bob Griese
Franco Harris
Ted Hendricks
Jack Lambert
Tom Landry*
Bob St. Clair

CLASS OF 1991
(July 27, 1991)
Earl Campbell
John Hannah
Stan Jones
Tex Schramm*
Jan Stenerud

CLASS OF 1992
(August 1, 1992)
Lem Barney
Al Davis
John Mackey
John Riggins

CLASS OF 1993
(July 31, 1993)
Dan Fouts
Larry Little
Chuck Noll
Walter Payton*
Bill Walsh

CLASS OF 1994
(July 30, 1994)
Tony Dorsett
Bud Grant
Jimmy Johnson
Leroy Kelly
Jackie Smith
Randy White

CLASS OF 1995
(July 29, 1995)
Jim Finks*
Henry Jordan*
Steve Largent
Lee Roy Selmon
Kellen Winslow

CLASS OF 1996
(July 27, 1996)
Lou Creekmur
Dan Dierdorf
Joe Gibbs
Charlie Joiner
Mel Renfro

CLASS OF 1997
(July 26, 1997)
Mike Haynes
Wellington Mara
Don Shula
Mike Webster*

CLASS OF 1998
(August 1, 1998)
Paul Krause
Tommy McDonald
Anthony Muñoz
Mike Singletary
Dwight Stephenson

CLASS OF 1999
(August 7, 1999)
Eric Dickerson
Tom Mack
Ozzie Newsome
Billy Shaw
Lawrence Taylor

CLASS OF 2000
(July 29, 2000)
Howie Long
Ronnie Lott
Joe Montana
Dan Rooney
Dave Wilcox

CLASS OF 2001
(August 4, 2001)
Nick Buoniconti
Marv Levy
Mike Munchak
Jackie Slater
Lynn Swann
Ron Yary
Jack Youngblood

CLASS OF 2002
(August 3, 2002)
George Allen*
Dave Casper
Dan Hampton
Jim Kelly
John Stallworth

CLASS OF 2003
(August 3, 2003)
Marcus Allen
Elvin Bethea
Joe DeLamielleure
James Lofton
Hank Stram

CLASS OF 2004
(August 8, 2004)
Bob (Boomer) Brown
Carl Eller
John Elway
Barry Sanders

1869
Rutgers and Princeton played a college soccer football game, the first ever, November 6. The game used modified London Football Association rules. During the next seven years, rugby gained favor with the major eastern schools over soccer, and modern football began to develop from rugby.

1876
At the Massasoit convention, the first rules for American football were written. Walter Camp, who would become known as the father of American football, first became involved with the game.

1892
In an era in which football was a major attraction of local athletic clubs, an intense competition between two Pittsburgh-area clubs, the Allegheny Athletic Association (AAA) and the Pittsburgh Athletic Club (PAC), led to the making of the first professional football player. Former Yale All-America guard William (Pudge) Heffelfinger was paid $500 by the AAA to play in a game against the PAC, becoming the first person to be paid to play football, November 12. The AAA won the game 4-0 when Heffelfinger picked up a PAC fumble and ran 35 yards for a touchdown.

1893
The Pittsburgh Athletic Club signed one of its players, probably halfback Grant Dibert, to the first known pro football contract, which covered all of the PAC's games for the year.

1895
John Brallier became the first football player to openly turn pro, accepting $10 and expenses to play for the Latrobe YMCA against the Jeannette Athletic Club.

1896
The Allegheny Athletic Association team fielded the first completely professional team for its abbreviated two-game season.

1897
The Latrobe Athletic Association football team went entirely professional, becoming the first team to play a full season with only professionals.

1898
A touchdown was changed from four points to five.

1899
Chris O'Brien formed a neighborhood team, which played under the name the Morgan Athletic Club, on the south side of Chicago. The team later became known as the Normals, then the Racine (for a street in Chicago) Cardinals, the Chicago Cardinals, the St. Louis Cardinals, the Phoenix Cardinals, and, in 1994, the Arizona Cardinals. The team remains the oldest continuing operation in pro football.

1900
William C. Temple took over the team payments for the Duquesne Country and Athletic Club, becoming the first known individual club owner.

1902
Baseball's Philadelphia Athletics, managed by Connie Mack, and the Philadelphia Phillies formed professional football teams, joining the Pittsburgh Stars in the first attempt at a pro football league, named the National Football League. The Athletics won the first night football game ever played, 39-0 over Kanaweola AC at Elmira, New York, November 21.

All three teams claimed the pro championship for the year, but the league president, Dave Berry, named the Stars the champions. Pitcher Rube Waddell was with the Athletics, and pitcher Christy Mathewson a fullback for Pittsburgh.

The first World Series of pro football, actually a five-team tournament, was played among a team made up of players from both the Athletics and the Phillies, but simply named New York; the New York Knickerbockers; the Syracuse AC; the Warlow AC; and the Orange (New Jersey) AC at New York's original Madison Square Garden. New York and Syracuse played the first indoor football game before 3,000, December 28. Syracuse, with Glen (Pop) Warner at guard, won 6-0 and went on to win the tournament.

1903
The Franklin (Pa.) Athletic Club won the second and last World Series of pro football over the Oreos AC of Asbury Park, New Jersey; the Watertown Red and Blacks; and the Orange AC.

Pro football was popularized in Ohio when the Massillon Tigers, a strong amateur team, hired four Pittsburgh pros to play in the season-ending game against Akron. At the same time, pro football declined in the Pittsburgh area, and the emphasis on the pro game moved west from Pennsylvania to Ohio.

1904
A field goal was changed from five points to four.

Ohio had at least seven pro teams, with Massillon winning the Ohio Independent Championship, that is, the pro title. Talk surfaced about forming a state-wide league to end spiraling salaries brought about by constant bidding for players and to write universal rules for the game. The feeble attempt to start the league failed.

Halfback Charles Follis signed a contract with the Shelby (Ohio) AC, making him the first known black pro football player.

1905
The Canton AC, later to become known as the Bulldogs, became a professional team. Massillon again won the Ohio League championship.

1906
The forward pass was legalized. The first authenticated pass completion in a pro game came on October 27, when George (Peggy) Parratt of Massillon threw a completion to Dan (Bullet) Riley in a victory over a combined Benwood-Moundsville team.

Arch-rivals Canton and Massillon, the two best pro teams in America, played twice, with Canton winning the first game but Massillon winning the second and the Ohio League championship. A betting scandal and the financial disaster wrought upon the two clubs by paying huge salaries caused a temporary decline in interest in pro football in the two cities and, somewhat, throughout Ohio.

1909
A field goal dropped from four points to three.

1912
A touchdown was increased from five points to six.

Jack Cusack revived a strong pro team in Canton.

1913
Jim Thorpe, a former football and track star at the Carlisle Indian School (Pa.) and a double gold medal winner at the 1912 Olympics in Stockholm, played for the Pine Village Pros in Indiana.

1915
Massillon again fielded a major team, reviving the old rivalry with Canton. Cusack signed Thorpe to play for Canton for $250 a game.

1916
With Thorpe and former Carlisle teammate Pete Calac starring, Canton went 9-0-1, won the Ohio League championship, and was acclaimed the pro football champion.

1917
Despite an upset by Massillon, Canton again won the Ohio League championship.

1919
Canton again won the Ohio League championship, despite the team having been turned over from Cusack to Ralph Hay. Thorpe and Calac were joined in the backfield by Joe Guyon.

Earl (Curly) Lambeau and George Calhoun organized the Green Bay Packers. Lambeau's employer at the Indian Packing Company provided $500 for equipment and allowed the team to use the company field for practices. The Packers went 10-1.

1920
Pro football was in a state of confusion due to three major problems: dramatically rising salaries; players continually

jumping from one team to another following the highest offer; and the use of college players still enrolled in school. A league in which all the members would follow the same rules seemed the answer. An organizational meeting, at which the Akron Pros, Canton Bulldogs, Cleveland Indians, and Dayton Triangles were represented, was held at the Jordan and Hupmobile auto showroom in Canton, Ohio, August 20. This meeting resulted in the formation of the American Professional Football Conference.

A second organizational meeting was held in Canton, September 17. The teams were from four states—Akron, Canton, Cleveland, and Dayton from Ohio; the Hammond Pros and Muncie Flyers from Indiana; the Rochester Jeffersons from New York; and the Rock Island Independents, Decatur Staleys, and Racine Cardinals from Illinois. The name of the league was changed to the American Professional Football Association. Hoping to capitalize on his fame, the members elected Thorpe president; Stanley Cofall of Cleveland was elected vice president. A membership fee of $100 per team was charged to give an appearance of respectability, but no team ever paid it. Scheduling was left up to the teams, and there were wide variations, both in the overall number of games played and in the number played against APFA member teams.

Four other teams—the Buffalo All-Americans, Chicago Tigers, Columbus Panhandles, and Detroit Heralds—joined the league sometime during the year. On September 26, the first game featuring an APFA team was played at Rock Island's Douglas Park. A crowd of 800 watched the Independents defeat the St. Paul Ideals 48-0. A week later, October 3, the first game matching two APFA teams was held. At Triangle Park, Dayton defeated Columbus 14-0, with Lou Partlow of Dayton scoring the first touchdown in a game between Association teams. The same day, Rock Island defeated Muncie 45-0.

By the beginning of December, most of the teams in the APFA had abandoned their hopes for a championship, and some of them, including the Chicago Tigers and the Detroit Heralds, had finished their seasons, disbanded, and had their franchises canceled by the Association. Four teams—Akron, Buffalo, Canton, and Decatur—still had championship as-pirations, but a series of late-season games among them left Akron as the only undefeated team in the Association. At one of these games, Akron sold tackle Bob Nash to Buffalo for $300 and five percent of the gate receipts—the first APFA player deal.

1921

At the league meeting in Akron, April 30, the championship of the 1920 season was awarded to the Akron Pros. The APFA was reorganized, with Joe Carr of the Columbus Panhandles named president and Carl Storck of Dayton secretary-treasurer. Carr moved the Association's headquarters to Columbus, drafted a league constitution and by-laws, gave teams territorial rights, restricted player movements, developed membership criteria for the franchises, and issued standings for the first time, so that the APFA would have a clear champion.

The Association's membership increased to 22 teams, including the Green Bay Packers, who were awarded to John Clair of the Acme Packing Company.

Thorpe moved from Canton to the Cleveland Indians, but he was hurt early in the season and played very little.

A.E. Staley turned the Decatur Staleys over to player-coach George Halas, who moved the team to Cubs Park in Chicago. Staley paid Halas $5,000 to keep the name Staleys for one more year. Halas made halfback Ed (Dutch) Sternaman his partner.

Player-coach Fritz Pollard of the Akron Pros became the first black head coach.

The Staleys claimed the APFA championship with a 9-1-1 record, as did Buffalo at 9-1-2. Carr ruled in favor of the Staleys, giving Halas his first championship.

1922

After admitting the use of players who had college eligibility remaining during the 1921 season, Clair and the Green Bay management withdrew from the APFA, January 28. Curly Lambeau promised to obey league rules and then used $50 of his own money to buy back the franchise. Bad weather and low attendance plagued the Packers, and Lambeau went broke, but local merchants arranged a $2,500 loan for the club. A public nonprofit corporation was set up to operate the team, with Lambeau as head coach and manager.

The American Professional Football Association changed its name to the National Football League, June 24. The Chicago Staleys became the Chicago Bears.

The NFL fielded 18 teams, including the new Oorang Indians of Marion, Ohio, an all-Indian team featuring Thorpe, Joe Guyon, and Pete Calac, and sponsored by the Oorang dog kennels.

Canton, led by player-coach Guy Chamberlin and tackles Link Lyman and Wilbur (Pete) Henry, emerged as the league's first true powerhouse, going 10-0-2.

1923

For the first time, all of the franchises considered to be part of the NFL fielded teams. Thorpe played his second and final season for the Oorang Indians. Against the Bears, Thorpe fumbled, and Halas picked up the ball and returned it 98 yards for a touchdown, a record that would last until 1972.

Canton had its second consecutive undefeated season, going 11-0-1 for the NFL title.

1924

The league had 18 franchises, including new ones in Kansas City, Kenosha, and Frankford, a section of Philadelphia. League champion Canton, successful on the field but not at the box office, was purchased by the owner of the Cleveland franchise, who kept the Canton franchise inactive, while using the best players for his Cleveland team, which he renamed the Bulldogs. Cleveland won the title with a 7-1-1 record.

1925

Five new franchises were admitted to the NFL—the New York Giants, who were awarded to Tim Mara and Billy Gibson for $500; the Detroit Panthers, featuring Jimmy Conzelman as owner, coach, and tailback; the Providence Steam Roller; a new Canton Bulldogs team; and the Pottsville Maroons, who had been perhaps the most successful independent pro team. The NFL established its first player limit, at 16 players.

Late in the season, the NFL made its greatest coup in gaining national recognition. Shortly after the University of Illinois season ended in November, All-America halfback Harold (Red) Grange signed a contract to play with the Chicago Bears. On Thanksgiving Day, a crowd of 36,000—the largest in pro football history—watched Grange and the Bears play the Chicago Cardinals to a scoreless tie at Wrigley Field. At the beginning of December, the Bears left on a barnstorming tour that saw them play eight games in 12 days, in St. Louis, Philadelphia, New York City, Washington, Boston, Pittsburgh, Detroit, and Chicago. A crowd of 73,000 watched the game against the Giants at the Polo Grounds, helping assure the future of the troubled NFL franchise in New York. The Bears then played nine more games in the South and West, including a game in Los Angeles, in which 75,000 fans watched them defeat the Los Angeles Tigers in the Los Angeles Memorial Coliseum.

Pottsville and the Chicago Cardinals were the top contenders for the league title, with Pottsville winning a late-season meeting 21-7. Pottsville scheduled a game against a team of former Notre Dame players for Shibe Park in Philadelphia. Frankford lodged a protest not only because the game was in Frankford's protected territory, but because it was being played the same day as a Yellow Jackets home game. Carr gave three different notices forbidding Pottsville to play the game, but Pottsville played anyway, December 12. That day, Carr fined the club, suspended it from all rights and privileges (including the right to play for the NFL championship), and re-turned its franchise to the league. The Cardinals, who ended the season with the best record in the league, were named the 1925 champions.

1926
Grange's manager, C.C. Pyle, told the Bears that Grange wouldn't play for them unless he was paid a five-figure salary and given one-third ownership of the team. The Bears refused. Pyle leased Yankee Stadium in New York City, then petitioned for an NFL franchise. After he was refused, he started the first American Football League. It lasted one season and included Grange's New York Yankees and eight other teams. The AFL champion Philadelphia Quakers played a December game against the New York Giants, seventh in the NFL, and the Giants won 31-0. At the end of the season, the AFL folded.

Halas pushed through a rule that prohibited any team from signing a player whose college class had not graduated.

The NFL grew to 22 teams, including the Duluth Eskimos, who signed All-America fullback Ernie Nevers of Stanford, giving the league a gate attraction to rival Grange. The 15-member Eskimos, dubbed the Iron Men of the North, played 29 exhibition and league games, 28 on the road, and Nevers played in all but 29 minutes of them.

Frankford edged the Bears for the championship, despite Halas having obtained John (Paddy) Driscoll from the Cardinals. On December 4, the Yellow Jackets scored in the final two minutes to defeat the Bears 7-6 and move ahead of them in the standings.

1927
At a special meeting in Cleveland, April 23, Carr decided to secure the NFL's future by eliminating the financially weaker teams and consolidating the quality players onto a limited number of more successful teams. The new-look NFL dropped to 12 teams, and the center of gravity of the league left the Midwest, where the NFL had started, and began to emerge in the large cities of the East. One of the new teams was Grange's New York Yankees, but Grange suffered a knee injury and the Yankees finished in the middle of the pack. The NFL championship was won by the cross-town rival New York Giants, who posted 10 shutouts in 13 games.

1928
Grange and Nevers both retired from pro football, and Duluth disbanded, as the NFL was reduced to only 10 teams. The Providence Steam Roller of Jimmy Conzelman and Pearce Johnson won the championship, playing in the Cycledrome, a 10,000-seat oval that had been built for bicycle races.

1929
Chris O'Brien sold the Chicago Cardinals to David Jones, July 27.

The NFL added a fourth official, the field judge, July 28.

Grange and Nevers returned to the NFL. Nevers scored six rushing touchdowns and four extra points as the Cardinals beat Grange's Bears 40-6, November 28. The 40 points set a record that remains the NFL's oldest.

Providence became the first NFL team to host a game at night under floodlights, against the Cardinals, November 3.

The Packers added back Johnny Blood (McNally), tackle Cal Hubbard, and guard Mike Michalske, and won their first NFL championship, edging the Giants, who featured quarterback Benny Friedman.

1930
Dayton, the last of the NFL's original franchises, was purchased by William B. Dwyer and John C. Depler, moved to Brooklyn, and renamed the Dodgers. The Portsmouth, Ohio, Spartans entered the league.

The Packers edged the Giants for the title, but the most improved team was the Bears. Halas retired as a player and replaced himself as coach of the Bears with Ralph Jones, who refined the T-formation by introducing wide ends and a halfback in motion. Jones also introduced rookie All-America fullback-tackle Bronko Nagurski.

The Giants defeated a team of former Notre Dame players coached by Knute Rockne 22-0 before 55,000 at the Polo Grounds, December 14. The proceeds went to the New York Unemployment Fund to help those suffering because of the Great Depression, and the easy victory helped give the NFL credibility with the press and the public.

1931
The NFL decreased to 10 teams, and halfway through the season the Frankford franchise folded. Carr fined the Bears, Packers, and Portsmouth $1,000 each for using players whose college classes had not graduated.

The Packers won an unprecedented third consecutive title, beating out the Spartans, who were led by rookie backs Earl (Dutch) Clark and Glenn Presnell.

1932
George Preston Marshall, Vincent Bendix, Jay O'Brien, and M. Dorland Doyle were awarded a franchise for Boston, July 9. Despite the presence of two rookies—halfback Cliff Battles and tackle Glen (Turk) Edwards—the new team, named the Braves, lost money and Marshall was left as the sole owner at the end of the year.

NFL membership dropped to eight teams, the lowest in history. Official statistics were kept for the first time. The Bears and the Spartans finished the season in the first-ever tie for first place. After the season finale, the league office arranged for an additional regular-season game to determine the league champion. The game was moved indoors to Chicago Stadium because of bitter cold and heavy snow. The arena allowed only an 80-yard field that came right to the walls. The goal posts were moved from the end lines to the goal lines and, for safety, inbounds lines or hashmarks where the ball would be put in play were drawn 10 yards from the walls that butted against the sidelines. The Bears won 9-0, December 18, scoring the winning touchdown on a two-yard pass from Nagurski to Grange. The Spartans claimed Nagurski's pass was thrown from less than five yards behind the line of scrimmage, violating the existing passing rule, but the play stood.

1933
The NFL, which long had followed the rules of college football, made a number of significant changes from the college game for the first time and began to develop rules serving its needs and the style of play it preferred. The innovations from the 1932 championship game—inbounds line or hashmarks and goal posts on the goal lines—were adopted. Also the forward pass was legalized from anywhere behind the line of scrimmage, February 25.

Marshall and Halas pushed through a proposal that divided the NFL into two divisions, with the winners to meet in an annual championship game, July 8.

Three new franchises joined the league—the Pittsburgh Pirates of Art Rooney, the Philadelphia Eagles of Bert Bell and Lud Wray, and the Cincinnati Reds. The Staten Island Stapletons suspended operations for a year, but never returned to the league.

Halas bought out Sternaman, became sole owner of the Bears, and reinstated himself as head coach. Marshall changed the name of the Boston Braves to the Redskins. David Jones sold the Chicago Cardinals to Charles W. Bidwill.

In the first NFL Championship Game scheduled before the season, the Western Division champion Bears defeated the Eastern Division champion Giants 23-21 at Wrigley Field, December 17.

1934
G.A. (Dick) Richards pur-

chased the Portsmouth Spartans, moved them to Detroit, and renamed them the Lions.

Professional football gained new prestige when the Bears were matched against the best college football players in the first Chicago College All-Star Game, August 31. The game ended in a scoreless tie before 79,432 at Soldier Field.

The Cincinnati Reds lost their first eight games, then were suspended from the league for defaulting on payments. The St. Louis Gunners, an independent team, joined the NFL by buying the Cincinnati franchise and went 1-2 the last three weeks.

Rookie Beattie Feathers of the Bears became the NFL's first 1,000-yard rusher, gaining 1,004 on 101 carries. The Thanksgiving Day game between the Bears and the Lions became the first NFL game broadcast nationally, with Graham McNamee the announcer for NBC radio.

In the championship game, on an extremely cold and icy day at the Polo Grounds, the Giants trailed the Bears 13-3 in the third quarter before changing to basketball shoes for better footing. The Giants won 30-13 in what has come to be known as the Sneakers Game, December 9.

The player waiver rule was adopted, December 10.

1935

The NFL adopted Bert Bell's proposal to hold an annual draft of college players, to begin in 1936, with teams selecting in an inverse order of finish, May 19. The inbounds line or hashmarks were moved nearer the center of the field, 15 yards from the sidelines.

All-America end Don Hutson of Alabama joined Green Bay. The Lions defeated the Giants 26-7 in the NFL Championship Game, December 15.

1936

There were no franchise transactions for the first year since the formation of the NFL. It also was the first year in which all member teams played the same number of games.

The Eagles made University of Chicago halfback and Heisman Trophy winner Jay Berwanger the first player ever selected in the NFL draft, February 8. The Eagles traded his rights to the Bears, but Berwanger never played pro football. The first player selected to actually sign was the number-two pick, Riley Smith of Alabama, who was selected by Boston.

A rival league was formed, and it became the second to call itself the American Football League. The Boston Shamrocks were its champions.

Because of poor attendance, Marshall, the owner of the host team, moved the Championship Game from Boston to the Polo Grounds in New York. Green Bay defeated the Redskins 21-6, December 13.

1937

Homer Marshman was granted a Cleveland franchise, named the Rams, February 12. Marshall moved the Redskins to Washington, D.C., February 13. The Redskins signed TCU All-America tailback Sammy Baugh, who led them to a 28-21 victory over the Bears in the NFL Championship Game, December 12.

The Los Angeles Bulldogs had an 8-0 record to win the AFL title, but then the 2-year-old league folded.

1938

At the suggestion of Halas, Hugh (Shorty) Ray became a technical advisor on rules and officiating to the NFL. A new rule called for a 15-yard penalty for roughing the passer.

Rookie Byron (Whizzer) White of the Pittsburgh Pirates led the NFL in rushing. The Giants defeated the Packers 23-17 for the NFL title, December 11.

Marshall, *Los Angeles Times* sports editor Bill Henry, and promoter Tom Gallery established the Pro Bowl game between the NFL champion and a team of pro all-stars.

1939

The New York Giants defeated the Pro All-Stars 13-10 in the first Pro Bowl, at Wrigley Field, Los Angeles, January 15.

Carr, NFL president since 1921, died in Columbus, May 20. Carl Storck was named acting president, May 25.

An NFL game was televised for the first time when NBC broadcast the Brooklyn Dodgers-Philadelphia Eagles game from Ebbets Field to the approximately 1,000 sets then in New York, October 22.

Green Bay defeated New York 27-0 in the NFL Championship Game, December 10 at Milwaukee. NFL attendance exceeded 1 million in a season for the first time, reaching 1,071,200.

1940

A six-team rival league, the third to call itself the American Football League, was formed, and the Columbus Bullies won its championship.

Halas' Bears, with additional coaching by Clark Shaughnessy of Stanford, defeated the Redskins 73-0 in the NFL Championship Game, December 8. The game, which was the most decisive victory in NFL history, popularized the Bears' T-formation with a man-in-motion. It was the first championship carried on network radio, broadcast by Red Barber to 120 stations of the Mutual Broadcasting System, which paid $2,500 for the rights.

Art Rooney sold the Pittsburgh franchise to Alexis Thompson, December 9, then bought part interest in the Philadelphia Eagles.

1941

Elmer Layden was named the first Commissioner of the NFL, March 1; Storck, the acting president, resigned, April 5. NFL headquarters were moved to Chicago.

Bell and Rooney traded the Eagles to Thompson for the Pirates, then re-named their new team the Steelers. Homer Marshman sold the Rams to Daniel F. Reeves and Fred Levy, Jr.

The league by-laws were revised to provide for playoffs in case there were ties in division races, and sudden-death overtimes in case a playoff game was tied after four quarters. An official *NFL Record Manual* was published for the first time.

Columbus again won the championship of the AFL, but the two-year-old league then folded.

The Bears and the Packers finished in a tie for the Western Division championship, setting up the first divisional playoff game in league history. The Bears won 33-14, then defeated the Giants 37-9 for the NFL championship, December 21.

1942

Players departing for service in World War II depleted the rosters of NFL teams. Halas left the Bears in midseason to join the Navy, and Luke Johnsos and Heartley (Hunk) Anderson served as co-coaches as the Bears went 11-0 in the regular season. The Redskins defeated the Bears 14-6 in the NFL Championship Game, December 13.

1943

The Cleveland Rams, with co-owners Reeves and Levy in the service, were granted permission to suspend operations for one season, April 6. Levy transferred his stock in the team to Reeves, April 16.

The NFL adopted free substitution, April 7. The league also made the wearing of helmets mandatory and approved a 10-game schedule for all teams.

Philadelphia and Pittsburgh were granted permission to merge for one season, June 19. The team, known as Phil-Pitt (and called the Steagles by fans), divided home games between the two cities, and Earle (Greasy) Neale of Philadelphia and Walt Kiesling of Pittsburgh served as co-coaches. The merger automatically dissolved the last day of the season, December 5.

Ted Collins was granted a franchise for Boston, to become active in 1944.

Sammy Baugh led the league in passing, punting, and interceptions. He led the Redskins to a tie with the Giants for the Eastern Division title, and then to a 28-0 victory in a divisional playoff game. The Bears beat the Redskins 41-21 in the NFL Championship Game, December 26.

1944

Collins, who had wanted a

franchise in Yankee Stadium in New York, named his new team in Boston the Yanks. Cleveland resumed operations. The Brooklyn Dodgers changed their name to the Tigers.

Coaching from the bench was legalized, April 20.

The Cardinals and the Steelers were granted permission to merge for one year under the name Card-Pitt, April 21. Phil Handler of the Cardinals and Walt Kiesling of the Steelers served as co-coaches. The merger automatically dissolved the last day of the season, December 3.

In the NFL Championship Game, Green Bay defeated the New York Giants 14-7, December 17.

1945
The inbounds lines or hashmarks were moved from 15 yards away from the sidelines to nearer the center of the field—20 yards from the sidelines.

Brooklyn and Boston merged into a team that played home games in both cities and was known simply as The Yanks. The team was coached by former Boston head coach Herb Kopf. In December, the Brooklyn franchise withdrew from the NFL to join the new All-America Football Conference; all the players on its active and reserve lists were assigned to The Yanks, who once again became the Boston Yanks.

Halas rejoined the Bears late in the season after service with the U.S. Navy. Although Halas took over much of the coaching duties, Anderson and Johnsos remained the coaches of record throughout the season.

Steve Van Buren of Philadelphia led the NFL in rushing, kickoff returns, and scoring.

After the Japanese surrendered ending World War II, a count showed that the NFL service roster, limited to men who had played in league games, totaled 638, 21 of whom had died in action.

Rookie quarterback Bob Waterfield led Cleveland to a 15-14 victory over Washington in the NFL Championship Game, December 16.

1946
The contract of Commissioner Layden was not renewed, and Bert Bell, the co-owner of the Steelers, replaced him, January 11. Bell moved the league headquarters from Chicago to the Philadelphia suburb of Bala-Cynwyd.

Free substitution was withdrawn and substitutions were limited to no more than three men at a time. Forward passes were made automatically incomplete upon striking the goal posts, January 11.

The NFL took on a truly national appearance for the first time when Reeves was granted permission by the league to move his NFL champion Rams to Los Angeles.

Halfback Kenny Washington (March 21) and end Woody Strode (May 7) signed with the Los Angeles Rams to become the first African-Americans to play in the NFL in the modern era. Guard Bill Willis (August 6) and running back Marion Motley (August 9) joined the AAFC with the Cleveland Browns.

The rival All-America Football Conference began play with eight teams. The Cleveland Browns, coached by Paul Brown, won the AAFC's first championship, defeating the New York Yankees 14-9.

Bill Dudley of the Steelers led the NFL in rushing, interceptions, and punt returns, and won the league's most valuable player award.

Backs Frank Filchock and Merle Hapes of the Giants were questioned about an attempt by a New York man to fix the championship game with the Bears. Bell suspended Hapes but allowed Filchock to play; he played well, but Chicago won 24-14, December 15.

1947
The NFL added a fifth official, the back judge.

A bonus choice was made for the first time in the NFL draft. One team each year would select the special choice before the first round began. The Chicago Bears won a lottery and the rights to the first choice and drafted back Bob Fenimore of Oklahoma A&M.

The Cleveland Browns again won the AAFC title, defeating the New York Yankees 14-3.

Charles Bidwill, Sr., owner of the Cardinals, died April 19, but his wife and sons retained ownership of the team. On December 28, the Cardinals won the NFL Championship Game 28-21 over the Philadelphia Eagles, who had beaten Pittsburgh 21-0 in a playoff.

1948
Plastic helmets were prohibited. A flexible artificial tee was permitted at the kickoff. Officials other than the referee were equipped with whistles, not horns, January 14.

Fred Mandel sold the Detroit Lions to a syndicate headed by D. Lyle Fife, January 15.

Halfback Fred Gehrke of the Los Angeles Rams painted horns on the Rams' helmets, the first modern helmet emblems in pro football.

The Cleveland Browns won their third straight championship in the AAFC, going 14-0 and then defeating the Buffalo Bills 49-7.

In a blizzard, the Eagles defeated the Cardinals 7-0 in the NFL Championship Game, December 19.

1949
Alexis Thompson sold the champion Eagles to a syndicate headed by James P. Clark, January 15. The Boston Yanks became the New York Bulldogs, sharing the Polo Grounds with the Giants.

Free substitution was adopted for one year, January 20.

The NFL had two 1,000-yard rushers in the same season for the first time—Steve Van Buren of Philadelphia and Tony Canadeo of Green Bay.

The AAFC played its season with a one-division, seven-team format. On December 9, Bell announced a merger agreement in which three AAFC franchises—Cleveland, San Francisco, and Baltimore—would join the NFL in 1950. The Browns won their fourth consecutive AAFC title, defeating the 49ers 21-7, December 11.

In a heavy rain, the Eagles defeated the Rams 14-0 in the NFL Championship Game, December 18.

1950
Unlimited free substitution was restored, opening the way for the era of two platoons and specialization in pro football, January 20.

Curly Lambeau, founder of the franchise and Green Bay's head coach since 1921, resigned under fire, February 1.

The name National Football League was restored after about three months as the National-American Football League. The American and National conferences were created to replace the Eastern and Western divisions, March 3.

The New York Bulldogs became the Yanks and divided the players of the former AAFC Yankees with the Giants. A special allocation draft was held in which the 13 teams drafted the remaining AAFC players, with special consideration for Baltimore, which received 15 choices compared to 10 for other teams.

The Los Angeles Rams became the first NFL team to have all of its games—both home and away—televised. The Washington Redskins followed the Rams in arranging to televise their games; other teams made deals to put selected games on television.

In the first game of the season, former AAFC champion Cleveland defeated NFL champion Philadelphia 35-10. For the first time, deadlocks occurred in both conferences and playoffs were necessary. The Browns defeated the Giants in the American and the Rams defeated the Bears in the National. Cleveland defeated Los Angeles 30-28 in the NFL Championship Game, December 24.

1951
The Pro Bowl game, dormant since 1942, was revived under a new format matching the all-stars of each conference at the Los Angeles Memorial Coliseum. The American Conference defeated the National Conference 28-27, January 14.

Abraham Watner returned the Baltimore franchise and its player contracts back to the NFL for $50,000. Baltimore's former players were made available for drafting at the same time as college players, January 18.

A rule was passed that no tackle, guard, or center would be eligible to catch a forward pass, January 18.

The Rams reversed their television policy and televised only road games.

The NFL Championship Game was televised coast-to-coast for the first time, December 23. The DuMont Network paid $75,000 for the rights to the game, in which the Rams defeated the Browns 24-17.

1952
Ted Collins sold the New York Yanks' franchise back to the NFL, January 19. A new franchise was awarded to a group in Dallas after it purchased the assets of the Yanks, January 24. The new Texans went 1-11, with the owners turning the franchise back to the league in midseason. For the last five games of the season, the commissioner's office operated the Texans as a road team, using Hershey, Pennsylvania, as a home base. At the end of the season the franchise was canceled, the last time an NFL team failed.

The Pittsburgh Steelers abandoned the Single-Wing for the T-formation, the last pro team to do so.

The Detroit Lions won their first NFL championship in 17 years, defeating the Browns 17-7 in the title game, December 28.

1953
A Baltimore group headed by Carroll Rosenbloom was granted a franchise and was awarded the holdings of the defunct Dallas organization, January 23. The team, named the Colts, put together the largest trade in league history, acquiring 10 players from Cleveland in exchange for five.

The names of the American and National conferences were changed to the Eastern and Western conferences, January 24.

Jim Thorpe died, March 28.

Mickey McBride, founder of the Cleveland Browns, sold the franchise to a syndicate headed by Dave R. Jones, June 10.

The NFL policy of blacking out home games was upheld by Judge Allan K. Grim of the U.S. District Court in Philadelphia, November 12.

The Lions again defeated the Browns in the NFL Championship Game, winning 17-16, December 27.

1954
The Canadian Football League began a series of raids on NFL teams, signing quarterback Eddie LeBaron and defensive end Gene Brito of Washington and defensive tackle Arnie Weinmeister of the Giants, among others.

Fullback Joe Perry of the 49ers became the first player in league history to gain 1,000 yards rushing in consecutive seasons.

Cleveland defeated Detroit 56-10 in the NFL Championship Game, December 26.

1955
The sudden-death overtime rule was used for the first time in a preseason game between the Rams and Giants at Portland, Oregon, August 28. The Rams won 23-17 three minutes into overtime.

A rule change declared the ball dead immediately if the ball carrier touched the ground with any part of his body except his hands or feet while in the grasp of an opponent.

The Baltimore Colts made an 80-cent phone call to Johnny Unitas and signed him as a free agent. Another quarterback, Otto Graham, played his last game as the Browns defeated the Rams 38-14 in the NFL Championship Game, December 26. Graham had quarterbacked the Browns to 10 championship-game appearances in 10 years.

NBC replaced DuMont as the network for the title game, paying a rights fee of $100,000.

1956
The NFL Players Association was founded.

Grabbing an opponent's facemask (other than the ball carrier) was made illegal. Using radio receivers to communicate with players on the field was prohibited. A natural leather ball with white end stripes replaced the white ball with black stripes for night games.

The Giants moved from the Polo Grounds to Yankee Stadium.

Halas retired as coach of the Bears, and was replaced by Paddy Driscoll.

CBS became the first network to broadcast some NFL regular-season games to selected television markets across the nation.

The Giants routed the Bears 47-7 in the NFL Championship Game, December 30.

1957
Pete Rozelle was named general manager of the Rams. Anthony J. Morabito, founder and co-owner of the 49ers, died of a heart attack during a game against the Bears at Kezar Stadium, October 28. An NFL-record crowd of 102,368 saw the 49ers-Rams game at the Los Angeles Memorial Coliseum, November 10.

The Lions came from 20 points down to post a 31-27 playoff victory over the 49ers, December 22. Detroit defeated Cleveland 59-14 in the NFL Championship Game, December 29.

1958
The bonus selection in the draft was eliminated, January 29. The last selection was quarterback King Hill of Rice by the Chicago Cardinals.

Halas reinstated himself as coach of the Bears.

Jim Brown of Cleveland gained an NFL-record 1,527 yards rushing. In a divisional playoff game, the Giants held Brown to eight yards and defeated Cleveland 10-0.

Baltimore, coached by Weeb Ewbank, defeated the Giants 23-17 in the first sudden-death overtime in an NFL Championship Game, December 28. The game ended when Colts fullback Alan Ameche scored on a one-yard touchdown run after 8:15 of overtime.

1959
Vince Lombardi was named head coach of the Green Bay Packers, January 28. Tim Mara, the co-founder of the Giants, died, February 17.

Lamar Hunt of Dallas announced his intentions to form a second pro football league. The first meeting was held in Chicago, August 14, and consisted of Hunt representing Dallas; Bob Howsam, Denver; K.S. (Bud) Adams, Houston; Barron Hilton, Los Angeles; Max Winter and Bill Boyer, Minneapolis; and Harry Wismer, New York City. They made plans to begin play in 1960.

The new league was named the American Football League, August 22. Buffalo, owned by Ralph Wilson, became the seventh franchise, October 28. Boston, owned by William H. Sullivan, became the eighth team, November 22. The first AFL draft, lasting 33 rounds, was held, November 22. Joe Foss was named AFL Commissioner, November 30. An additional draft of 20 rounds was held by the AFL, December 2.

NFL Commissioner Bert Bell died of a heart attack suffered at Franklin Field, Philadelphia, during the last two minutes of a game between the Eagles and the Steelers, October 11. Treasurer Austin Gunsel was named president in the office of the commissioner, October 14.

The Colts again defeated the Giants in the NFL Championship Game, 31-16, December 27.

1960
Pete Rozelle was elected NFL Commissioner as a compromise choice on the twenty-third ballot, January 26. Rozelle moved the league offices to New York City.

Hunt was elected AFL president for 1960, January 26. Minneapolis withdrew from the AFL, January 27, and the same ownership was given an NFL franchise for Minnesota (to start in 1961), January 28. Dallas received an NFL franchise for 1960, January 28. Oakland received an AFL franchise, January 30.

The AFL adopted the two-point option on points after touchdown, January 28. A no-tampering verbal pact, relative to players' contracts, was agreed to between the NFL and AFL, February 9.

The NFL owners voted to allow the transfer of the Chicago Cardinals to St. Louis, March 13.

The AFL signed a five-year television contract with ABC, June 9.

The Boston Patriots defeated the Buffalo Bills 28-7 before 16,000 at Buffalo in the first AFL preseason game, July 30. The Denver Broncos defeated the Patriots 13-10 before 21,597 at Boston in the first AFL regular-season game, September 9.

Philadelphia defeated Green Bay 17-13 in the NFL Championship Game, December 26.

1961

The Houston Oilers defeated the Los Angeles Chargers 24-16 before 32,183 in the first AFL Championship Game, January 1.

Detroit defeated Cleveland 17-16 in the first Playoff Bowl, or Bert Bell Benefit Bowl, between second-place teams in each conference in Miami, January 7.

End Willard Dewveall of the Bears played out his option and joined the Oilers, becoming the first player to play out his contract and jump from the NFL to the AFL, January 14.

Ed McGah, Wayne Valley, and Robert Osborne bought out their partners in the ownership of the Raiders, January 17. The Chargers were transferred to San Diego, February 10. Dave R. Jones sold the Browns to a group headed by Arthur B. Modell, March 22. The Howsam brothers sold the Broncos to a group headed by Calvin Kunz and Gerry Phipps, May 26.

NBC was awarded a two-year contract for radio and television rights to the NFL Championship Game for $615,000 annually, $300,000 of which was to go directly into the NFL Player Benefit Plan, April 5.

Canton, Ohio, where the league that became the NFL was formed in 1920, was chosen as the site of the Pro Football Hall of Fame, April 27. Dick McCann, a former Redskins executive, was named executive director.

A bill legalizing single-network television contracts by professional sports leagues was introduced in Congress by Representative Emanuel Celler. It passed the House and Senate and was signed into law by President John F. Kennedy, September 30.

Houston defeated San Diego 10-3 for the AFL championship, December 24. Green Bay won its first NFL championship since 1944, defeating the New York Giants 37-0, December 31.

1962

The Western Division defeated the Eastern Division 47-27 in the first AFL All-Star Game, played before 20,973 in San Diego, January 7.

Both leagues prohibited grabbing any player's facemask. The AFL voted to make the scoreboard clock the official timer of the game.

The NFL entered into a single-network agreement with CBS for telecasting all regular-season games for $4.65 million annually, January 10.

Judge Roszel Thompson of the U.S. District Court in Baltimore ruled against the AFL in its antitrust suit against the NFL, May 21. The AFL had charged the NFL with monopoly and conspiracy in areas of expansion, television, and player signings. The case lasted two and a half years, the trial two months.

McGah and Valley acquired controlling interest in the Raiders, May 24. The AFL assumed financial responsibility for the New York Titans, November 8. With Commissioner Rozelle as referee, Daniel F. Reeves regained the ownership of the Rams, outbidding his partners in sealed-envelope bidding for the team, November 27.

The Dallas Texans defeated the Oilers 20-17 for the AFL championship at Houston after 17 minutes, 54 seconds of overtime on a 25-yard field goal by Tommy Brooker, December 23. The game lasted a record 77 minutes, 54 seconds.

Judge Edward Weinfeld of the U.S. District Court in New York City upheld the legality of the NFL's television blackout within a 75-mile radius of home games and denied an injunction that would have forced the championship game between the Giants and the Packers to be televised in the New York City area, December 28. The Packers beat the Giants 16-7 for the NFL title, December 30.

1963

The Dallas Texans transferred to Kansas City, becoming the Chiefs, February 8. The New York Titans were sold to a five-man syndicate headed by David (Sonny) Werblin, March 28. Weeb Ewbank became the Titans' new head coach and the team's name was changed to the Jets, April 15. They began play in Shea Stadium.

NFL Properties, Inc., was founded to serve as the licensing arm of the NFL.

Rozelle indefinitely suspended Green Bay halfback Paul Hornung and Detroit defensive tackle Alex Karras for placing bets on their own teams and on other NFL games; he also fined five other Detroit players $2,000 each for betting on one game in which they did not participate, and the Detroit Lions Football Company $2,000 on each of two counts for failure to report information promptly and for lack of sideline supervision.

Paul Brown, head coach of the Browns since their inception, was fired and replaced by Blanton Collier. Don Shula replaced Weeb Ewbank as head coach of the Colts.

The AFL allowed the Jets and Raiders to select players from other franchises in hopes of giving the league more competitive balance, May 11.

NBC was awarded exclusive network broadcasting rights for the 1963 AFL Championship Game for $926,000, May 23.

The Pro Football Hall of Fame was dedicated at Canton, Ohio, September 7.

The U.S. Fourth Circuit Court of Appeals reaffirmed the lower court's finding for the NFL in the $10-million suit brought by the AFL, ending three and a half years of litigation, November 21.

Jim Brown of Cleveland rushed for an NFL single-season record 1,863 yards.

Boston defeated Buffalo 26-8 in the first divisional playoff game in AFL history, December 28.

The Bears defeated the Giants 14-10 in the NFL Championship Game, a record sixth and last title for Halas in his thirty-sixth season as the Bears' coach, December 29.

1964

The Chargers defeated the Patriots 51-10 in the AFL Championship Game, January 5.

William Clay Ford, the Lions' president since 1961, purchased the team, January 10. A group representing the late James P. Clark sold the Eagles to a group headed by Jerry Wolman, January 21. Carroll Rosenbloom, the majority owner of the Colts since 1953, acquired complete ownership of the team, January 23.

The AFL signed a five-year, $36-million television contract with NBC to begin with the 1965 season, January 29.

Commissioner Rozelle negotiated an agreement on behalf of the NFL clubs to purchase Ed Sabol's Blair Motion Pictures, which was renamed NFL Films, March 5.

Hornung and Karras were reinstated by Rozelle, March 16.

CBS submitted the winning bid of $14.1 million per year for the NFL regular-season television rights for 1964 and 1965, January 24. CBS acquired the rights to the championship games for 1964 and 1965 for $1.8 million per game, April 17.

Pete Gogolak of Cornell signed a contract with Buffalo, becoming the first soccer-style kicker in pro football.

Buffalo defeated San Diego 20-7 in the AFL Championship Game, December 26. Cleveland defeated Baltimore 27-0 in the NFL Championship Game, December 27.

1965

The NFL teams pledged not to sign college seniors until completion of all their games, including bowl games, and empowered the Commissioner to discipline the clubs up to as much as the loss of an entire draft list for a violation of the pledge, February 15.

The NFL added a sixth official, the line judge, February 19. The color of the officials' penalty flags was changed from white to bright gold, April 5.

Atlanta was awarded an NFL franchise for 1966, with Rankin Smith, Sr., as owner, June 30. Miami was awarded an AFL franchise for 1966, with Joe Robbie and Danny Thomas as owners, August 16.

Field Judge Burl Toler became the first black official in NFL history, September 19.

According to a Harris survey, sports fans chose professional football (41 percent) as their favorite sport, overtaking baseball (38 percent) for the first time, October.

Green Bay defeated Baltimore 13-10 in sudden-death overtime in a Western Conference playoff game. Don Chandler kicked a 25-yard field goal for the Packers after 13 minutes, 39 seconds of overtime, December 26. The Packers then defeated the Browns 23-12 in the NFL Championship Game, January 2.

In the AFL Championship Game, the Bills again defeated the Chargers, 23-0, December 26.

CBS acquired the rights to the NFL regular-season games in 1966 and 1967, with an option for 1968, for $18.8 million per year, December 29.

1966

The AFL-NFL war reached its peak, as the leagues spent a combined $7 million to sign their 1966 draft choices. The NFL signed 75 percent of its 232 draftees, the AFL 46 percent of its 181. Of the 111 common draft choices, 79 signed with the NFL, 28 with the AFL, and 4 went unsigned.

Buddy Young became the first African-American to work in the league office when Commissioner Rozelle named him director of player relations, February 1.

The rights to the 1966 and 1967 NFL Championship Games were sold to CBS for $2 million per game, February 14.

Foss resigned as AFL Commissioner, April 7. Al Davis, the head coach and general manager of the Raiders, was named to replace him, April 8.

Goal posts offset from the goal line, painted bright yellow, and with uprights 20 feet above the cross-bar were made standard in the NFL, May 16.

A series of secret meetings regarding a possible AFL-NFL merger were held in the spring between Hunt of Kansas City and Tex Schramm of Dallas. Rozelle announced the merger, June 8. Under the agreement, the two leagues would combine to form an expanded league with 24 teams, to be increased to 26 in 1968 and to 28 by 1970 or soon thereafter. All existing franchises would be retained, and no franchises would be transferred outside their metropolitan areas. While maintaining separate schedules through 1969, the leagues agreed to play an annual AFL-NFL World Championship Game beginning in January, 1967, and to hold a combined draft, also beginning in 1967. Preseason games would be held between teams of each league starting in 1967. Official regular-season play would start in 1970 when the two leagues would officially merge to form one league with two conferences. Rozelle was named Commissioner of the expanded league setup.

Davis rejoined the Raiders, and Milt Woodard was named president of the AFL, July 25.

The St. Louis Cardinals moved into newly constructed Busch Memorial Stadium.

Barron Hilton sold the Chargers to a group headed by Eugene Klein and Sam Schulman, August 25.

Congress approved the AFL-NFL merger, passing legislation exempting the agreement itself from antitrust action, October 21.

New Orleans was awarded an NFL franchise to begin play in 1967, November 1. John Mecom, Jr., of Houston was designated majority stockholder and president of the franchise, December 15.

The NFL was realigned for the 1967-69 seasons into the Capitol and Century Divisions in the Eastern Conference and the Central and Coastal Divisions in the Western Conference, December 2. New Orleans and the New York Giants agreed to switch divisions in 1968 and return to the 1967 alignment in 1969.

The rights to the Super Bowl for four years were sold to CBS and NBC for $9.5 million, December 13.

1967

Green Bay earned the right to represent the NFL in the first AFL-NFL World Championship Game by defeating Dallas 34-27, January 1. The same day, Kansas City defeated Buffalo 31-7 to represent the AFL. The Packers defeated the Chiefs 35-10 before 61,946 fans at the Los Angeles Memorial Coliseum in the first game between AFL and NFL teams, January 15. The winning players' share for the Packers was $15,000 each, and the losing players' share for the Chiefs was $7,500 each. The game was televised by both CBS and NBC.

The "sling-shot" goal post and a six-foot-wide border around the field were made standard in the NFL, February 22.

Baltimore made Bubba Smith, a Michigan State defensive lineman, the first choice in the first combined AFL-NFL draft, March 14.

The AFL awarded a franchise to begin play in 1968 to Cincinnati, May 24. A group with Paul Brown as part owner, general manager, and head coach, was awarded the Cincinnati franchise, September 27.

Arthur B. Modell, the president of the Cleveland Browns, was elected president of the NFL, May 28.

Defensive back Emlen Tunnell of the New York Giants became the first black player to enter the Pro Football Hall of Fame, August 5.

An AFL team defeated an NFL team for the first time, when Denver beat Detroit 13-7 in a preseason game, August 5.

Green Bay defeated Dallas 21-17 for the NFL championship on a last-minute 1-yard quarterback sneak by Bart Starr in 13-below-zero temperature at Green Bay, December 31. The same day, Oakland defeated Houston 40-7 for the AFL championship.

1968

Green Bay defeated Oakland 33-14 in Super Bowl II at Miami, January 14. The game had the first $3-million gate in pro football history.

Vince Lombardi resigned as head coach of the Packers, but remained as general manager, January 28.

Art McNally, a nine-year NFL game official, was named Supervisor of Officials, April 8.

Werblin sold his shares in the Jets to his partners Don Lillis, Leon Hess, Townsend Martin, and Phil Iselin, May 21. Lillis assumed the presidency of the club, but then died July 23. Iselin was appointed president, August 6.

Halas retired for the fourth and last time as head coach of the Bears, May 27.

The Oilers left Rice Stadium for the Astrodome and became the first NFL team to play its home games in a domed stadium.

The movie *Heidi* became a footnote in sports history when NBC didn't show the last 50 seconds of the Jets-Raiders game in order to permit the children's special to begin on time. The Raiders scored two touchdowns in the last 42 seconds to win 43-32, November 17.

Ewbank became the first coach to win titles in both the NFL and AFL when his Jets defeated the Raiders 27-23 for the AFL championship, December 29. The same day, Baltimore defeated Cleveland 34-0.

1969

The AFL established a playoff format for the 1969 season, with the winner in one division playing the runner-up in the other, January 11.

An AFL team won the Super Bowl for the first time, as the Jets defeated the Colts 16-7 at Miami, January 12 in Super Bowl III. The title Super Bowl was recognized by the NFL for the first time.

Vince Lombardi became part owner, executive vice-president, and head coach of the Washington Redskins, February 7.

Wolman sold the Eagles to Leonard Tose, May 1.

Baltimore, Cleveland, and Pittsburgh agreed to join the AFL teams to form the 13-team American Football Conference of the NFL in 1970, May 17. The NFL also agreed on a playoff format that would include one "wild-card" team per conference—the second-place team with the best record.

The NFL announced a three-year agreement with ABC to televise *Monday Night Football*. The new series makes the NFL the first league with a regular series of national telecasts in prime time, May 26.

George Preston Marshall, president emeritus of the Redskins, died at 72, August 9.

The NFL marked its fiftieth year by the wearing of a special patch by each of the 16 teams.

1970

Kansas City defeated Minnesota 23-7 in Super Bowl IV at New Orleans, January 11. The gross receipts of approximately $3.8 million were the largest ever for a one-day sports event.

Four-year television contracts, under which CBS would televise all NFC games and NBC all AFC games (except Monday night games) and the two would divide televising the Super Bowl and AFC-NFC Pro Bowl games, were announced, January 26.

Art Modell resigned as president of the NFL, March 12. Milt Woodard resigned as president of the AFL, March 13. Lamar Hunt was elected president of the AFC and George Halas was elected president of the NFC, March 19.

The merged 26-team league adopted rules changes putting names on the backs of players' jerseys, making a point after touchdown worth only one point, and making the scoreboard clock the official timing device of the game, March 18.

The Players Negotiating Committee and the NFL Players Association announced a four-year agreement guaranteeing approximately $4,535,000 annually to player pension and insurance benefits, August 3. The owners also agreed to contribute $250,000 annually to improve or implement items such as disability payments, widows' benefits, maternity benefits, and dental benefits. The agreement also provided for increased preseason game and per diem payments, averaging approximately $2.6 million annually.

The Pittsburgh Steelers moved into Three Rivers Stadium. The Cincinnati Bengals moved to Riverfront Stadium.

Vince Lombardi died of cancer at 57, September 3.

The Super Bowl trophy was renamed the Vince Lombardi trophy, September 10.

Tom Dempsey of New Orleans kicked a game-winning NFL-record 63-yard field goal against Detroit, November 8.

1971

Baltimore defeated Dallas 16-13 on Jim O'Brien's 32-yard field goal with five seconds to go in Super Bowl V at Miami, January 17. The NBC telecast was viewed in an estimated 23,980,000 homes, the largest audience ever for a one-day sports event.

The NFC defeated the AFC 27-6 in the first AFC-NFC Pro Bowl at Los Angeles, January 24.

The Boston Patriots changed their name to the New England Patriots, March 25. Their new stadium, Schaefer Stadium, was dedicated in a 20-14 preseason victory over the Giants.

The Philadelphia Eagles left Franklin Field and played their games at the new Veterans Stadium.

The San Francisco 49ers left Kezar Stadium and moved their games to Candlestick Park.

Daniel F. Reeves, the president and general manager of the Rams, died at 58, April 15.

The Dallas Cowboys moved from the Cotton Bowl into their new home, Texas Stadium, October 24.

Miami defeated Kansas City 27-24 in sudden-death overtime in an AFC Divisional Playoff Game, December 25. Garo Yepremian kicked a 37-yard field goal for the Dolphins after 22 minutes, 40 seconds of overtime, as the game lasted 82 minutes, 40 seconds overall, making it the longest game in history.

1972

Dallas defeated Miami 24-3 in Super Bowl VI at New Orleans, January 16. The CBS telecast was viewed in an estimated 27,450,000 homes, the top-rated one-day telecast ever.

The inbounds lines or hashmarks were moved nearer the center of the field, 23 yards, 1 foot, 9 inches from the sidelines, March 23. The method of determining won-lost percentage in standings changed. Tie games, previously not counted in the standings, were made equal to a half-game won and a half-game lost, May 24.

Robert Irsay purchased the Los Angeles Rams and transferred ownership of the club to Carroll Rosenbloom in exchange for the Baltimore Colts, July 13.

William V. Bidwill purchased the stock of his brother Charles (Stormy) Bidwill to become the sole owner of the St. Louis Cardinals, September 2.

The National District Attorneys Association endorsed the position of professional leagues in opposing proposed legalization of gambling on professional team sports, September 28.

Franco Harris' "Immaculate Reception" gave the Steelers their first postseason win ever, 13-7 over the Raiders, December 23.

1973

Rozelle announced that all Super Bowl VII tickets were sold and that the game would be telecast in Los Angeles, the site of the game, on an experimental basis, January 3.

Miami defeated Washington 14-7 in Super Bowl VII at Los Angeles, completing a 17-0 season, the first perfect-record regular-season and postseason mark in NFL history, January 14. The NBC telecast was viewed by approximately 75 million people.

The AFC defeated the NFC 33-28 in the Pro Bowl in Dallas, the first time since 1942 that the game was played outside Los Angeles, January 21.

A jersey numbering system was adopted, April 5: 1-19 for quarterbacks and specialists, 20-49 for running backs and defensive backs, 50-59 for centers and linebackers, 60-79 for defensive linemen and interior offensive linemen other than centers, and 80-89 for wide receivers and tight ends. Players who had been in the NFL in 1972 could continue to use old numbers.

NFL Charities, a nonprofit organization, was created to derive an income from monies generated from NFL Properties' licensing of NFL trademarks and team names, June 26. NFL Charities was set up to support education and charitable activities and to supply economic support to persons formerly associated with professional football who were no longer able to support themselves.

Congress adopted experimental legislation (for three years) requiring any NFL game that had been declared a sellout 72 hours prior to kickoff to be made available for local televising, September 14. The legislation provided for an annual review to be made by the Federal Communications Commission.

The Buffalo Bills moved their home games from War Memorial Stadium to Rich Stadium in nearby Orchard Park. The Giants tied the Eagles 23-23 in the final game in Yankee Stadium, September 23. The Giants played the rest of their home games at the Yale Bowl in New Haven, Connecticut.

A rival league, the World Football League, was formed and was reported in operation, October 2. It had plans to start play in 1974.

O.J. Simpson of Buffalo became the first player to rush for more than 2,000 yards in a season, gaining 2,003.

1974

Miami defeated Minnesota 24-7 in Super Bowl VIII at Houston, the second consecutive Super Bowl championship for the Dolphins, January 13. The CBS telecast was viewed by approximately 75 million people.

Rozelle was given a 10-year contract effective January 1, 1973, February 27.

Tampa Bay was awarded a franchise to begin operation in 1976, April 24.

Sweeping rules changes were adopted to add action and tempo to games: one sudden-death overtime period was added for preseason and regular-season games; the goal posts were moved from the goal line to the end lines; kickoffs were moved from the 40- to the 35-yard line; after missed field goals from beyond the 20, the ball was to be returned to the line of scrimmage; restrictions were placed on members of the punting team to open up return possibilities; roll-blocking and cutting of wide receivers was eliminated; the extent of downfield contact a defender could have with an eligible receiver was restricted; the penalties for offensive holding, illegal use of the hands, and tripping were reduced from 15 to 10 yards; wide receivers blocking back toward the ball within three yards of the line of scrimmage were prevented from blocking below the waist, April 25.

Seattle was awarded an NFL franchise to begin play in 1976, June 4. Lloyd W. Nordstrom, president of the Seattle Seahawks, and Hugh Culverhouse, president of the Tampa Bay Buccaneers, signed franchise agreements, December 5.

The Birmingham Americans defeated the Florida Blazers 22-21 in the WFL World Bowl, winning the league championship, December 5.

1975

Pittsburgh defeated Minnesota 16-6 in Super Bowl IX at New Orleans, the Steelers' first championship since entering the NFL in 1933. The NBC telecast was viewed by approximately 78 million people.

The Memphis Southmen of the WFL signed Larry Csonka, Jim Kiick, and Paul Warfield of Miami, March 31.

The divisional winners with the highest won-loss percentage were made the home team for the divisional playoffs, and the surviving winners with the highest percentage made home teams for the championship games, June 26.

Referees were equipped with wireless microphones for all preseason, regular-season, and playoff games.

The Lions moved to the new Pontiac Silverdome. The Giants played their home games in Shea Stadium. The Saints moved into the Louisiana Superdome.

The World Football League folded, October 22.

1976

Pittsburgh defeated Dallas 21-17 in Super Bowl X in Miami. The Steelers joined Green Bay and Miami as the only teams to win two Super Bowls; the Cowboys became the first wild-card team to play in the Super Bowl. The CBS telecast was viewed by an estimated 80 million people, the largest television audience in history.

Lloyd Nordstrom, the president of the Seahawks, died at 66, January 20. His brother Elmer succeeded him as majority representative of the team.

The owners awarded Super Bowl XII, to be played on January 15, 1978, to New Orleans. They also adopted the use of two 30-second clocks for all games, visible to both players and fans to note the official time between the ready-for-play signal and snap of the ball, March 16.

A veteran player allocation was held to stock the Seattle and Tampa Bay franchises with 39 players each, March 30-31. In the college draft, Seattle and Tampa Bay each received eight extra choices, April 8-9.

The Giants moved into new Giants Stadium in East Rutherford, New Jersey.

The Steelers defeated the College All-Stars in a storm-shortened Chicago College All-Star Game, the last of the series, July 23. St. Louis defeated San Diego 20-10 in a preseason game before 38,000 in Korakuen Stadium, Tokyo, in the first NFL game outside of North America, August 16.

1977

Oakland defeated Minnesota 32-14 in Super Bowl XI at Pasadena, January 9. The paid attendance was a pro record 103,438. The NBC telecast was viewed by 81.9 million people, the largest ever to view a sports event. The victory was the fifth consecutive for the AFC in the Super Bowl.

The NFL Players Association and the NFL Management Council ratified a collective bargaining agreement extending until 1982, covering five football seasons while continuing the pension plan—including years 1974, 1975, and 1976—with contributions totaling more than $55 million. The total cost of the agreement was estimated at $107 million. The agreement called for a college draft at least through 1986; contained a no-strike, no-suit clause; established a 43-man active player limit; reduced pension vesting to four years; provided for increases in minimum salaries and preseason and postseason pay; improved insurance, medical, and dental benefits; modified previous practices in player movement and control; and reaffirmed the NFL Commissioner's disciplinary authority. Additionally, the agreement called for the NFL member clubs to make payments totaling $16 million the next 10 years to settle various legal disputes, February 25.

The San Francisco 49ers were sold to Edward J. DeBartolo, Jr., March 28.

A 16-game regular season, 4-game preseason was adopted to begin in 1978, March 29. A second wild-card team was adopted for the playoffs beginning in 1978, with the wild-card teams to play each other and the winners advancing to a round of eight postseason series.

The Seahawks were permanently aligned in the AFC Western Division and the Buccaneers in the NFC Central Division, March 31.

The owners awarded Super Bowl XIII, to be played on January 21, 1979, to Miami, to be played in the Orange Bowl; Super Bowl XIV, to be played January 20, 1980, was awarded to Pasadena, to be played in the Rose Bowl, June 14.

Rules changes were adopted to open up the passing game and to cut down on injuries. Defenders were permitted to make contact with eligible receivers only once; the head slap was outlawed; offensive linemen were prohibited from thrusting their hands to an opponent's neck, face, or head; and wide receivers were prohibited from clipping, even in the legal clipping zone.

Rozelle negotiated contracts with the three television networks to televise all NFL regular-season and postseason games, plus selected preseason games, for four years beginning with the 1978 season. ABC was awarded yearly rights to 16 Monday night games, four prime-time games, the AFC-NFC Pro Bowl, and the Hall of Fame games. CBS received the rights to all NFC regular-season and postseason games (except those in the ABC package) and to Super Bowls XIV and XVI. NBC received the rights to all AFC regular-season and postseason games (except those in the ABC package) and to Super Bowls XIII and XV. Industry sources considered it the largest single television package ever negotiated, October 12.

Chicago's Walter Payton set a single-game rushing record with 275 yards (40 carries) against Minnesota, November 20.

1978

Dallas defeated Denver 27-10 in Super Bowl XII, held indoors for the first time, at the Louisiana Superdome in New Orleans, January 15. The CBS telecast was viewed by more than 102 million people, meaning the game was watched by more viewers than any other show of any kind in the history of television. Dallas' victory was the first for the NFC in six years.

According to a Louis Harris Sports Survey, 70 percent of the nation's sports fans said they followed football, compared to 54 percent who followed baseball. Football increased its lead as the country's favorite, 26 percent to 16 percent for baseball, January 19.

A seventh official, the side judge, was added to the officiating crew, March 14.

The NFL continued a trend toward opening up the game. Rules changes permitted a defender to maintain contact with a receiver within five yards of the line of scrimmage, but restricted contact beyond that point. The pass-blocking rule was interpreted to permit the extending of arms and open hands, March 17.

A study on the use of instant replay as an officiating aid was made during seven nationally televised preseason games.

The NFL played for the first time in Mexico City, with the Saints defeating the Eagles 14-7 in a preseason game, August 5.

Bolstered by the expansion of the regular-season schedule from 14 to 16 weeks, NFL paid attendance exceeded 12 million (12,771,800) for the first time. The per-game average of 57,017 was the third-highest in league history and the most since 1973.

1979
Pittsburgh defeated Dallas 35-31 in Super Bowl XIII at Miami to become the first team ever to win three Super Bowls, January 21. The NBC telecast was viewed in 35,090,000 homes, by an estimated 96.6 million fans.

The owners awarded three future Super Bowl sites: Super Bowl XV to the Louisiana Superdome in New Orleans, to be played on January 25, 1981; Super Bowl XVI to the Pontiac Silverdome in Pontiac, Michigan, to be played on January 24, 1982; and Super Bowl XVII to Pasadena's Rose Bowl, to be played on January 30, 1983, March 13.

NFL rules changes emphasized additional player safety. The changes prohibited players on the receiving team from blocking below the waist during kickoffs, punts, and field-goal attempts; prohibited the wearing of torn or altered equipment and exposed pads that could be hazardous; extended the zone in which there could be no crackback blocks; and instructed officials to quickly whistle a play dead when a quarterback was clearly in the grasp of a tackler, March 16.

Carroll Rosenbloom, the president of the Rams, drowned at 72, April 2. His widow, Georgia, assumed control of the club.

1980
Pittsburgh defeated the Los Angeles Rams 31-19 in Super Bowl XIV at Pasadena to become the first team to win four Super Bowls, January 20. The game was viewed in a record 35,330,000 homes.

The AFC-NFC Pro Bowl, won 37-27 by the NFC, was played before 48,060 fans at Aloha Stadium in Honolulu, Hawaii. It was the first time in the 30-year history of the Pro Bowl that the game was played in a non-NFL city.

Rules changes placed greater restrictions on contact in the area of the head, neck, and face. Under the heading of "personal foul," players were prohibited from directly striking, swinging, or clubbing on the head, neck, or face. Starting in 1980, a penalty could be called for such contact whether or not the initial contact was made below the neck area.

CBS, with a record bid of $12 million, won the national radio rights to 26 NFL regular-season games, including Monday Night Football, and all 10 postseason games for the 1980-83 seasons.

The Los Angeles Rams moved their home games to Anaheim Stadium in nearby Orange County, California.

The Oakland Raiders joined the Los Angeles Coliseum Commission's antitrust suit against the NFL. The suit contended the league violated antitrust laws in declining to approve a proposed move by the Raiders from Oakland to Los Angeles.

NFL regular-season attendance of nearly 13.4 million set a record for the third year in a row. The average paid attendance for the 224-game 1980 regular season was 59,787, the highest in the league's 61-year history. NFL games in 1980 were played before 92.4 percent of total stadium capacity.

Television ratings in 1980 were the second-best in NFL history, trailing only the combined ratings of the 1976 season. All three networks posted gains, and NBC's 15.0 rating was its best ever. CBS and ABC had their best ratings since 1977, with 15.3 and 20.8 ratings, respectively. CBS Radio reported a record audience of 7 million for Monday night and special games.

1981
Oakland defeated Philadelphia 27-10 in Super Bowl XV at the Louisiana Superdome in New Orleans, to become the first wild-card team to win a Super Bowl, January 25.

Edgar F. Kaiser, Jr., purchased the Denver Broncos from Gerald and Allan Phipps, February 26.

The owners adopted a disaster plan for re-stocking a team should the club be involved in a fatal accident, March 20.

The owners awarded Super Bowl XVIII to Tampa, to be played in Tampa Stadium on January 22, 1984, June 3.

A CBS-New York Times poll showed that 48 percent of sports fans preferred football to 31 percent for baseball.

The NFL teams hosted 167 representatives from 44 predominantly black colleges during training camps for a total of 289 days. The program was adopted for renewal during each training camp period.

NFL regular-season attendance—13.6 million for an average of 60,745—set a record for the fourth year in a row. It also was the first time the per-game average exceeded 60,000. NFL games in 1981 were played before 93.8 percent of total stadium capacity.

ABC and CBS set all-time rating highs. ABC finished with a 21.7 rating and CBS with a 17.5 rating. NBC was down slightly to 13.9.

1982
San Francisco defeated Cincinnati 26-21 in Super Bowl XVI at the Pontiac Silverdome, in the first Super Bowl held in the North, January 24. The CBS telecast achieved the highest rating of any televised sports event ever, 49.1 with a 73.0 share. The game was viewed by a record 110.2 million fans. CBS Radio reported a record 14 million listeners for the game.

The NFL signed a five-year contract with the three television networks (ABC, CBS, and NBC) to televise all NFL regular-season and postseason games starting with the 1982 season.

The owners awarded the 1983, 1984, and 1985 AFC-NFC Pro Bowls to Honolulu's Aloha Stadium.

A jury ruled against the NFL in the antitrust trial brought by the Los Angeles Coliseum Commission and the Oakland Raiders, May 7. The verdict cleared the way for the Raiders to move to Los Angeles, where they defeated Green Bay 24-3 in their first preseason game, August 29.

The 1982 season was reduced from a 16-game schedule to nine as the result of a 57-day players' strike. The strike was called by the NFLPA at midnight on Monday, September 20, following the Green Bay at New York Giants game. Play resumed November 21-22 following ratification of the Collective Bargaining Agreement by NFL owners, November 17 in New York.

Under the Collective Bargaining Agreement, which was to run through the 1986 season, the NFL draft was extended through 1992 and the veteran free-agent system was left basically unchanged. A minimum salary schedule for years of experience was established; training camp and postseason pay were increased; players' medical, insurance, and retirement benefits were increased; and a severance-pay system was introduced to aid in career transition, a first in professional sports.

Despite the players' strike, the average paid attendance in 1982 was 58,472, the fifth-highest in league history.

The owners awarded the sites of two Super Bowls, December 14: Super Bowl XIX, to be played on January 20, 1985, to Stanford University Stadium in Stanford, California, with San Francisco as host team; and Super Bowl XX, to be played on January 26, 1986, to the Louisiana Superdome in New Orleans.

1983
Because of the shortened season, the NFL adopted a format of 16 teams competing in a Super Bowl Tournament for the 1982 playoffs. The NFC's number-one seed, Washington, defeated the AFC's num-

ber-two seed, Miami, 27-17 in Super Bowl XVII at the Rose Bowl in Pasadena, January 30.

Super Bowl XVII was the second-highest rated live television program of all time, giving the NFL a sweep of the top 10 live programs in television history. The game was viewed in more than 40 million homes, the largest ever for a live telecast.

George Halas, the owner of the Bears and the last surviving member of the NFL's second organizational meeting, died at 88, October 31.

1984
The Los Angeles Raiders defeated Washington 38-9 in Super Bowl XVIII at Tampa Stadium, January 22. The game achieved a 46.4 rating and 71.0 share.

An 11-man group headed by H.R. (Bum) Bright purchased the Dallas Cowboys from Clint Murchison, Jr., March 20. Club president Tex Schramm was designated as managing general partner.

Wellington Mara was named president of the NFC, March 20.

Patrick Bowlen purchased a majority interest in the Denver Broncos from Edgar Kaiser, Jr., March 21.

The Colts relocated to Indianapolis, March 28. Their new home became the Hoosier Dome.

The owners awarded two Super Bowl sites at their May 23-25 meetings: Super Bowl XXI, to be played on January 25, 1987, to the Rose Bowl in Pasadena; and Super Bowl XXII, to be played on January 31, 1988, to San Diego Jack Murphy Stadium.

The New York Jets moved their home games to Giants Stadium in East Rutherford, New Jersey.

Alex G. Spanos purchased a majority interest in the San Diego Chargers from Eugene V. Klein, August 28.

Houston defeated Pittsburgh 23-20 to mark the one-hundredth overtime game in regular-season play since overtime was adopted in 1974, December 2.

On the field, many all-time records were set: Dan Marino of Miami passed for 5,084 yards and 48 touchdowns; Eric Dickerson of the Los Angeles Rams rushed for 2,105 yards; Art Monk of Washington caught 106 passes; and Walter Payton of Chicago broke Jim Brown's career rushing mark, finishing the season with 13,309 yards.

According to a CBS Sports/*New York Times* survey, 53 percent of the nation's sports fans said they most enjoyed watching football, compared to 18 percent for baseball, December 2-4.

NFL paid attendance exceeded 13 million for the fifth consecutive complete regular season when 13,398,112, an average of 59,813, attended games. The figure was the second-highest in league history. Teams averaged 42.4 points per game, the second-highest total since the 1970 merger.

1985
San Francisco defeated Miami 38-16 in Super Bowl XIX at Stanford Stadium in Stanford, California, January 20. The game was viewed on television by more people than any other live event in history. President Ronald Reagan, who took his second oath of office before tossing the coin for the game, was one of 115,936,000 viewers. The game drew a 46.4 rating and a 63.0 share. In addition, 6 million people watched the Super Bowl in the United Kingdom and a similar number in Italy. Super Bowl XIX had a direct economic impact of $113.5 million on the San Francisco Bay area.

NBC Radio and the NFL entered into a two-year agreement granting NBC the radio rights to a 37-game package in each of the 1985-86 seasons, March 6. The package included 27 regular-season games and 10 postseason games.

The owners awarded two Super Bowl sites at their annual meeting, March 10-15: Super Bowl XXIII, to be played on January 22, 1989, to the proposed Dolphins Stadium in Miami; and Super Bowl XXIV, to be played on January 28, 1990, to the Louisiana Superdome in New Orleans.

Norman Braman, in partnership with Edward Leibowitz, bought the Philadelphia Eagles from Leonard Tose, April 29.

A group headed by Tom Benson, Jr., was approved to purchase the New Orleans Saints from John W. Mecom, Jr., June 3.

The NFL owners adopted a resolution calling for a series of overseas preseason games, beginning in 1986, with one game to be played in England/Europe and/or one game in Japan each year. The game would be a fifth preseason game for the clubs involved and all arrangements and selection of the clubs would be under the control of the Commissioner, May 23.

The league-wide conversion to videotape from movie film for coaching study was approved.

Commissioner Rozelle was authorized to extend the commitment to Honolulu's Aloha Stadium for the AFC-NFC Pro Bowl for 1988, 1989, and 1990, October 15.

The NFL set a single-weekend paid attendance record when 902,657 tickets were sold for the weekend of October 27-28.

A Louis Harris poll in December revealed that pro football remained the sport most followed by Americans. Fifty-nine percent of those surveyed followed pro football, compared with 54 percent who followed baseball.

The Chicago-Miami Monday game had the highest rating, 29.6, and share, 46.0, of any prime-time game in NFL history, December 2. The game was viewed in more than 25 million homes.

The NFL showed a ratings increase on all three networks for the season, gaining 4 percent on NBC, 10 on CBS, and 16 on ABC.

1986
Chicago defeated New England 46-10 in Super Bowl XX at the Louisiana Superdome, January 26. The Patriots had earned the right to play the Bears by becoming the first wild-card team to win three consecutive games on the road. The NBC telecast replaced the final episode of *M*A*S*H* as the most-viewed television program in history, with an audience of 127 million viewers, according to A.C. Nielsen figures. In addition to drawing a 48.3 rating and a 70 percent share in the United States, Super Bowl XX was televised to 59 foreign countries and beamed via satellite to the QE II. An estimated 300 million Chinese viewed a tape delay of the game in March. CBS Radio figures indicated an audience of 10 million for the game.

The owners adopted limited use of instant replay as an officiating aid, prohibited players from wearing or otherwise displaying equipment, apparel, or other items that carry commercial names, names of organizations, or personal messages of any type, March 11.

After an 11-week trial, a jury in U.S. District Court in New York awarded the United States Football League one dollar in its $1.7 billion antitrust suit against the NFL. The jury rejected all of the USFL's television-related claims, which were the self-proclaimed heart of the USFL's case. The jury deliberated five days, July 29.

Chicago defeated Dallas 17-6 at Wembley Stadium in London in the first American Bowl. The game drew a sellout crowd of 82,699 and the NBC national telecast in this country produced a 12.4 rating and 36 percent share, making it the highest daytime preseason television audience ever with 10.65-million viewers, August 3.

ABC's *NFL Monday Night Football,* in its seventeenth season, became the longest-running prime-time series in the history of the network.

1987
The New York Giants defeated Denver 39-20 in Super Bowl XXI and captured their first NFL title since 1956. The game, played in Pasadena's Rose Bowl, drew a sellout crowd of 101,063. According to A.C. Nielsen figures, the CBS broadcast of the game was viewed in the U.S. on television by 122.64-million people, making the telecast the second most-watched television show of all-time behind

Super Bowl XX. The game was watched live or on tape in 55 foreign countries and NBC Radio's broadcast of the game was heard by a record 10.1 million people.

New three-year TV contracts with ABC, CBS, and NBC were announced for 1987-89 at the NFL annual meeting in Maui, Hawaii, March 15. Commissioner Rozelle and Broadcast Committee Chairman Art Modell also announced a three-year contract with ESPN to televise 13 prime-time games each season. The ESPN contract was the first with a cable network. However, NFL games on ESPN also were scheduled for regular television in the city of the visiting team and in the home city if the game was sold out 72 hours in advance.

A special payment program was adopted to benefit nearly 1,000 former NFL players who participated in the League before the current Bert Bell NFL Pension Plan was created and made retroactive to the 1959 season. Players covered by the new program spent at least five years in the League and played all or part of their career prior to 1959. Each vested player would receive $60 per month for each year of service in the League for life.

NFL and CBS Radio jointly announced agreement granting CBS the radio rights to a 40-game package in each of the next three NFL seasons, 1987-89, April 7.

NFL owners awarded Super Bowl XXV, to be played on January 27, 1991, to Tampa Stadium, May 20.

Over 400 former NFL players from the pre-1959 era received first payments from NFL owners, July 1.

The NFL's debut on ESPN produced the two highest-rated and most-watched sports programs in basic cable history. The Chicago at Miami game on August 16 drew an 8.9 rating in 3.81 million homes. Those records fell two weeks later when the Los Angeles Raiders at Dallas game achieved a 10.2 cable rating in 4.36 million homes.

The 1987 season was reduced from a 16-game season to 15 as the result of a 24-day players' strike. The strike was called by the NFLPA on Tuesday, September 22, following the New England at New York Jets game. Games scheduled for the third weekend were canceled but the games of weeks four, five, and six were played with replacement teams. Striking players returned for the seventh week of the season, October 25.

In a three-team deal involving 10 players and/or draft choices, the Los Angeles Rams traded running back Eric Dickerson to the Indianapolis Colts for six draft choices and two players. Buffalo obtained the rights to linebacker Cornelius Bennett from Indianapolis, sending Greg Bell and three draft choices to the Rams. The Colts added Owen Gill and three draft choices of their own to complete the deal with the Rams, October 31.

The Chicago at Minnesota game became the highest-rated and most-watched sports program in basic cable history when it drew a 14.4 cable rating in 6.5 million homes, December 6.

1988

Washington defeated Denver 42-10 in Super Bowl XXII to earn its second victory this decade in the NFL Championship Game. The game, played for the first time in San Diego Jack Murphy Stadium, drew a sellout crowd of 73,302. According to A.C. Nielsen figures, the ABC broadcast of the game was viewed in the U.S. on television by 115,000,000 people. The game was seen live or on tape in 60 foreign countries, including the People's Republic of China, and CBS's radio broadcast of the game was heard by 13.7 million people.

In a unanimous 3-0 decision, the 2nd Circuit Court of Appeals in New York upheld the verdict of the jury that in July, 1986, had awarded the United States Football League one dollar in its $1.7 billion antitrust suit against the NFL. In a 91-page opinion, Judge Ralph K. Winter said the USFL sought through court decree the success it failed to gain among football fans, March 10.

By a 23-5 margin, owners voted to continue the instant replay system for the third consecutive season with the Instant Replay Official to be assigned to a regular seven-man, on-the-field crew. At the NFL annual meeting in Phoenix, Arizona, a 45-second clock was also approved to replace the 30-second clock. For a normal sequence of plays, the interval between plays was changed to 45 seconds from the time the ball is signaled dead until it is snapped on the succeeding play.

NFL owners approved the transfer of the Cardinals' franchise from St. Louis to Phoenix; approved two supplemental drafts each year—one prior to training camp and one prior to the regular season; and voted to initiate an annual series of games in Japan/Asia as early as the 1989 preseason, March 14-18.

The NFL Annual Selection Meeting returned to a separate two-day format and for the first time originated on a Sunday. ESPN drew a 3.6 rating during their seven-hour coverage of the draft, which was viewed in 1.6 million homes, April 24-25.

Art Rooney, founder and owner of the Steelers, died at 87, August 25.

Johnny Grier became the first African-American referee in NFL history, September 4.

Commissioner Rozelle announced that two teams would play a preseason game as part of the American Bowl series on August 6, 1989, in the Korakuen Tokyo Dome in Japan, December 16.

1989

San Francisco defeated Cincinnati 20-16 in Super Bowl XXIII. The game, played for the first time at Joe Robbie Stadium in Miami, was attended by a sellout crowd of 75,129. NBC's telecast of the game was watched by an estimated 110,780,000 viewers, according to A.C. Nielsen, making it the sixth most-watched program in television history. The game was seen live or on tape in 60 foreign countries, including an estimated 300 million in China. The CBS Radio broadcast of the game was heard by 11.2 million people.

Commissioner Rozelle announced his retirement, pending the naming of a successor, March 22 at the NFL annual meeting in Palm Desert, California.

Following the announcement, AFC president Lamar Hunt and NFC president Wellington Mara announced the formation of a six-man search committee composed of Art Modell, Robert Parins, Dan Rooney, and Ralph Wilson. Hunt and Mara served as co-chairmen.

By a 24-4 margin, owners voted to continue the instant replay system for the fourth straight season. A strengthened policy regarding anabolic steroids and masking agents was announced by Commissioner Rozelle. NFL clubs called for strong disciplinary measures in cases of feigned injuries and adopted a joint proposal by the Long-Range Planning and Finance committees regarding player personnel rules, March 19-23.

Two hundred twenty-nine unconditional free agents signed with new teams under management's Plan B system, April 1.

Jerry Jones purchased a majority interest in the Dallas Cowboys from H.R. (Bum) Bright, April 18.

Tex Schramm was named president of the new World League of American Football to work with a six-man committee of Dan Rooney, chairman; Norman Braman, Lamar Hunt, Victor Kiam, Mike Lynn, and Bill Walsh, April 18.

NFL and CBS Radio jointly announced agreement extending CBS's radio rights to an annual 40-game package through the 1994 season, April 18.

NFL owners awarded Super Bowl XXVI, to be played on January 26, 1992, to Minneapolis, May 24.

As of opening day, September 10, of the 229 Plan B free agents, 111 were active and 23 others were on teams' reserve lists. Ninety-two others were waived and three retired.

Art Shell was named head coach of the Los Angeles Raiders making him the NFL's first black head coach since Fritz Pollard coached the Akron Pros in 1921, October 3.

The site of the New England Patriots at San Francisco 49ers game scheduled for Candlestick Park on October 22 was switched to Stanford Stadium in the aftermath of the Bay Area Earthquake of October 17. The change was announced on October 19.

Paul Tagliabue became the seventh chief executive of the NFL on October 26 when he was chosen to succeed Commissioner Pete Rozelle on the sixth ballot of a three-day meeting in Cleveland, Ohio.

In all, 12 ballots were required to select Tagliabue. Two were conducted at a meeting in Chicago on July 6, and four at a meeting in Dallas on October 10-11. On the twelfth ballot, with Seattle absent, Tagliabue received more than the 19 affirmative votes required for election from among the 27 clubs present.

The transfer from Commissioner Rozelle to Commissioner Tagliabue took place at 12:01 A.M. on Sunday, November 5.

NFL Charities donated $1 million through United Way to benefit Bay Area earthquake victims, November 6.

NFL paid attendance of 17,399,538 was the highest total in league history. This included a total of 13,625,662 for an average of 60,829—both NFL records—for the 224-game regular season.

1990

San Francisco defeated Denver 55-10 in Super Bowl XXIV at the Louisiana Superdome, January 28. San Francisco joined Pittsburgh as the NFL's only teams to win four Super Bowls.

The NFL announced revisions in its 1990 draft eligibility rules. College juniors became eligible but must renounce their collegiate football eligibility before applying for the NFL Draft, February 16.

Commissioner Tagliabue announced NFL teams will play their 16-game schedule over 17 weeks in 1990 and 1991 and 16 games over 18 weeks in 1992 and 1993, February 27.

The NFL revised its playoff format to include two additional wild-card teams (one per conference), which raised the total to six wild-card teams.

Commissioner Tagliabue and Broadcast Committee Chairman Art Modell announced a four-year contract with Turner Broadcasting to televise nine Sunday-night games.

New four-year TV agreements were ratified for 1990-93 for ABC, CBS, NBC, ESPN, and TNT at the NFL annual meeting in Orlando, Florida, March 12. The contracts totaled $3.6 billion, the largest in TV history.

The NFL announced plans to expand its American Bowl series of preseason games. In addition to games in London and Tokyo, American Bowl games were scheduled for Berlin, Germany, and Montreal, Canada, in 1990.

For the fifth straight year, NFL owners voted to continue a limited system of Instant Replay. Beginning in 1990, the replay official will have a two-minute time limit to make a decision. The vote was 21-7, March 12.

Commissioner Tagliabue announced the formation of a Committee on Expansion and Realignment, March 13. He also named a Player Advisory Council, comprised of 12 former NFL players, March 14.

One-hundred eighty-four Plan B unconditional free agents signed with new teams, April 2.

Commissioner Tagliabue appointed Dr. John Lombardo as the League's Drug Advisor for Anabolic Steroids, April 25 and named Dr. Lawrence Brown as the League's Advisor for Drugs of Abuse, May 17.

NFL owners awarded Super Bowl XXVIII, to be played in 1994, to the proposed Georgia Dome, May 23.

Commissioner Tagliabue named NFL referee Jerry Seeman as NFL Director of Officiating, replacing Art McNally, who announced his retirement after 31 years on the field and at the league office, July 12.

NFL International Week was celebrated with four preseason games in seven days in Tokyo, London, Berlin, and Montreal. More than 200,000 fans on three continents attended the four games, August 4-11.

Commissioner Tagliabue announced the NFL Teacher of the Month program in which the League furnishes grants and scholarships in recognition of teachers who provided a positive influence upon NFL players in elementary and secondary schools, September 20.

For the first time since 1957, every NFL club won at least one of its first four games, October 1.

The Super Bowl Most Valuable Player trophy was renamed the Pete Rozelle trophy, October 8.

NFL total paid attendance of 17,665,671 was the highest total in League history. The regular-season total paid attendance of 13,959,896 and average of 62,321 for 224 games were the highest ever, surpassing the previous records set in the 1989 season.

1991

The New York Giants defeated Buffalo 20-19 in Super Bowl XXV to capture their second title in five years. The game was played before a sellout crowd of 73,813 at Tampa Stadium and became the first Super Bowl decided by one point, January 26. The ABC broadcast of the game was seen by more than 112-million people in the United States and was seen live or taped in 60 other countries.

NFL playoff games earned the top television rating spot of the week for each week of the month-long playoffs, January 29.

New York businessman Robert Tisch purchased a 50 percent interest in the New York Giants from Mrs. Helen Mara Nugent and her children, Tim Mara and Maura Mara Concannon, February 2.

NFL owners awarded Super Bowl XXVII, to be played on January 31, 1993, to Pasadena, March 19.

NFL clubs voted to continue a limited system of Instant Replay for the sixth consecutive year. The vote was 21-7, March 19.

The NFL launched the World League of American Football, the first sports league to operate on a weekly basis on two separate continents, March 23.

NFL Charities presented a $250,000 donation to the United Service Organization. The donation was the second largest single grant ever by NFL Charities, April 5.

Commissioner Tagliabue named Harold Henderson as Executive Vice President for Labor Relations and Chairman of the NFL Management Council Executive Committee, April 8.

NFL clubs approved a recommendation by the Expansion and Realignment Committee to add two teams for the 1994 season, resulting in six divisions of five teams each, May 22.

NFL clubs awarded Super Bowl XXIX, to be played on January 29, 1995, to Miami, May 23.

"NFL International Week" featured six 1990 playoff teams playing nationally televised games in London, Berlin, and Tokyo on July 28 and August 3-4. The games drew more than 150,000 fans.

Paul Brown, founder of the Cleveland Browns and Cincinnati Bengals, died at age 82, August 5.

NFL clubs approved a resolution establishing an international division. A three-year financial plan for the World League was approved by NFL clubs at a meeting in Dallas, October 23.

1992

The NFL agreed to provide a minimum of $2.5 million in financial support to the NFL Alumni Association and assistance to NFL Alumni-related programs. The agreement included contributions from NFL Charities to the Pre-59ers and Dire Need Programs for former players, January 25.

The Washington Redskins defeated the Buffalo Bills 37-24 in Super Bowl XXVI to capture their third world championship in 10 years, January 26. The game was played before a sellout crowd of 63,130 at the Hubert H. Humphrey Metrodome in Minneapolis and attracted the second largest television audience in Super Bowl history. The CBS broadcast was seen by more than 123 million people nationally, second only to the 127 million who viewed Super Bowl XX.

The use in officiating of a limited system of Instant Replay was not approved. The vote was 17-11 in favor of approval (21 votes were required). Instant Replay had been used for six consecutive years (1986-1991), March 18.

St. Louis businessman James Orthwein purchased controlling interest in the New England Patriots from Victor Kiam, May 11.

In a Harris Poll taken during the NFL offseason, professional football again was declared the nation's most popular sport. Professional football finished atop similar surveys conducted by Harris in 1985 and 1989, May 23.

NFL clubs accepted the report of the Expansion Committee at a league meeting in Pasadena. The report names five cities as finalists for the two expansion teams—Baltimore, Charlotte, Jacksonville, Memphis, and St. Louis, May 19.

At a league meeting in Dallas, NFL clubs approved a proposal by the World League Board of Directors to restructure the World League and place future emphasis on its international success, September 17.

NFL teams played their 16-game regular-season schedule over 18 weeks for the only time in league history.

1993

The NFL and lawyers for the players announced a settlement of various lawsuits and an agreement on the terms of a seven-year deal that included a new player system to be in place through the 1999 season, January 6.

Commissioner Tagliabue announced the establishment of the "NFL World Partnership Program" to develop amateur football internationally through a series of clinics conducted by former NFL players and coaches, January 14.

As part of Super Bowl XXVII, the NFL announced the creation of the first NFL Youth Education Town, a facility located in south central Los Angeles for inner city youth. January 25.

The Dallas Cowboys defeated the Buffalo Bills 52-17 in Super Bowl XXVII to capture their first NFL title since 1978. The game was played before a crowd of 98,374 at the Rose Bowl in Pasadena, California. The NBC broadcast of the game was the most watched program in television history and was seen by 133,400,000 people in the United States. The rating for the game was 45.1, the tenth highest for any televised sports event. The game also was seen live or taped in 101 other countries, January 31.

NFL clubs awarded Super Bowl XXX to the city of Phoenix, to be played on January 28, 1996, at Sun Devil Stadium, March 23.

The NFL and the NFL Players Association officially signed a 7-year Collective Bargaining Agreement in Washington, D.C., which guarantees more than $1 billion in pension, health, and post-career benefits for current and retired players—the most extensive benefits plan in pro sports. It was the NFL's first CBA since the 1982 agreement expired in 1987, June 29.

NFL Enterprises, a newly formed division of the NFL responsible for NFL Films, home video, and special domestic and international television programming was announced, August 19.

NFL announced plans to allow fans, for the first time ever, to join players and coaches in selecting the annual AFC and NFC Pro Bowl teams, October 12.

NFL clubs unanimously awarded the league's twenty-ninth franchise to the Carolina Panthers and owner Jerry Richardson at a meeting in Chicago. NFL clubs also awarded Super Bowl XXXI to New Orleans and Super Bowl XXXII to San Diego, October 26.

At the same meeting in Chicago, NFL clubs approved a plan to form a European league with joint venture partners, October 27.

Don Shula became the winningest coach in NFL history when Miami beat Philadelphia to give Shula his 325th victory, one more than George Halas, November 14.

NFL clubs awarded the league's thirtieth franchise to the Jacksonville Jaguars and owner Wayne Weaver at a meeting in Chicago, November 30.

The NFL announced new 4-year television agreements with NBC, ABC, ESPN, TNT, and NFL newcomer FOX, which took over the NFC package from CBS, December 18.

The NFL completed its new TV agreements by announcing that NBC would retain the rights to the AFC package, December 20.

1994

The Dallas Cowboys defeated the Buffalo Bills 30-13 in Super Bowl XXVIII to become the fifth team to win back-to-back Super Bowl titles. The game was viewed by the largest U.S. audience in television history—134.8 million people. The game's 45.5 rating was the highest for a Super Bowl since 1987 and the tenth highest-rated Super Bowl ever, January 30.

NFL clubs unanimously approved the transfer of the New England Patriots from James Orthwein to Robert Kraft at a meeting in Orlando, February 22.

In a move to increase offensive production, NFL clubs at the league's annual meeting in Orlando adopted a package of changes, including modifications in line play, chucking rules, and the roughing-the-passer rule, plus the adoption of the two-point conversion and moving the spot of the kickoff back to the 30-yard line, March 22.

NFL clubs approved the transfer of the majority interest in the Miami Dolphins from the Robbie family to H. Wayne Huizenga, March 23.

The NFL and FOX announced the formation of a joint venture to create a six-team World League to begin play in Europe in April, 1995, March 23.

The Carolina Panthers earned the right to select first in the 1995 NFL draft by winning a coin toss with the Jacksonville Jaguars. The Jaguars received the second selection in the 1995 draft, April 24.

NFL clubs approved the transfer of the Philadelphia Eagles from Norman Braman to Jeffrey Lurie, May 6.

The NFL launched "NFL Sunday Ticket," a new season subscription service for satellite television dish owners, June 1.

An all-time NFL record crowd of 112,376 attended the American Bowl game between Dallas and Houston in Mexico City. It concluded the biggest American Bowl series in NFL history with four games attracting a record 256,666 fans, August 15.

The NFL reached agreement on a new seven-year contract with its game officials, September 22.

The NFL Management Council and the NFL Players Association announced an agreement on the formulation and implementation of the most comprehensive drug and alcohol policy in sports, October 28.

At an NFL meeting in Chicago, Commissioner Tagliabue slotted the two new expansion teams into the AFC Central (Jacksonville Jaguars) and NFC West (Carolina Panthers) for the 1995 season only. He also appointed a special committee on realignment to make recommendations on the 1996 season and beyond, November 2.

1995

The San Francisco 49ers became the first team to win five Super Bowls when they defeated the San Diego Chargers 49-26 in Super Bowl XXIX at Joe Robbie Stadium in Miami, January 29.

Carolina and Jacksonville stocked their expansion rosters with a total of 66 players from other NFL teams in a veteran player allocation draft in New York, February 16.

CBS Radio and the NFL agreed to a new four-year contract for an annual 53-game package of games, continuing a relationship that spanned 15 of the past 17 years, February 22.

NFL clubs approved the transfer of the Tampa Bay Buccaneers from the estate of the late Hugh Culverhouse to South Florida businessman Malcolm Glazer, March 13.

A series of safety-related rules changes were adopted at a league meeting in Phoenix, primarily related to the use of the helmet against defenseless players, March 14.

After a two-year hiatus, the World League of American Football returned to action with six teams in Europe, April 8.

The NFL became the first major sports league to establish a site on the Internet system of on-line computer communication, April 10.

The transfer of the Rams from Los Angeles to St. Louis was approved by a vote of the NFL clubs at a meeting in Dallas, April 12.

ABC's *NFL Monday Night Football* finished the 1994-95 television season as the fifth highest-rated show out of 146 with a 17.8 average rating, the highest finish in the 25-year history of the series, April 18.

In an ABC News Poll taken during the NFL offseason, America's sports fans chose football as their favorite spectator sport by more than a 2-to-1 margin over basketball and baseball (35%-16%-12%), April 26.

The Frankfurt Galaxy defeated the Amsterdam Admirals 26-22 to win the 1995 World Bowl before a crowd of 23,847 in Amsterdam's Olympic Stadium, June 23.

Former NFL quarterback and Rhein Fire general manager Oliver Luck was named President of the World League, July 13.

The transfer of the Raiders from Los Angeles to Oakland was approved by a vote of the NFL clubs at a meeting in Chicago, July 22.

Jacksonville Municipal Stadium opened in Jacksonville, Florida before a sold-out crowd of more than 70,000 as the St. Louis Rams defeated the Jacksonville Jaguars 27-10 in their first preseason game, August 18.

NFL Charities and 50 NFL players donated $1 million to the United Negro College Fund in honor of the fiftieth anniversity of the UNCF and the integration of the modern NFL, September 15.

The Pro Football Hall of Fame in Canton, Ohio, completed an $8.9 million expansion including a $4 million contribution by the NFL clubs, October 14.

The Trans World Dome opened in St. Louis with a sold-out crowd of 65,598 as the Rams defeated the Carolina Panthers 28-17, November 12.

NFL paid attendance totaled 963,521 for 15 games in Week 12, the highest weekend total in the league's 76-year history, November 19-20.

On the field, many significant records and milestones were achieved: Miami's Dan Marino surpassed Pro Football Hall of Famer Fran Tarkenton in four major passing categories—attempts, completions, yards, and touchdowns—to become the NFL's all-time career leader. San Francisco's Jerry Rice became the all-time reception and receiving-yardage leader with career totals of 942 catches and 15,123 yards. Dallas' Emmitt Smith scored 25 touchdowns, breaking the season record of 24 set by Washington's John Riggins in 1983.

1996

The Dallas Cowboys won their third Super Bowl title in four years when they defeated the Pittsburgh Steelers 27-17 in Super Bowl XXX at Sun Devil Stadium in Tempe, Arizona. The game was viewed by the largest audience in U.S. television history—138.5 million people, January 28.

An agreement between the NFL and the city of Cleveland regarding the Cleveland Browns' relocation was approved by a vote of the NFL clubs, February 9. According to the agreement, the city of Cleveland retained the Browns' heritage and records, including the name, logo, colors, history, playing records, trophies, and memorabilia, and committed to building a new 72,000-seat stadium for a reactivated Browns' franchise to begin play there no later than 1999. Art Modell received approval to move his franchise to Baltimore and rename it.

NFL total paid attendance for all 1995 games reached a record level for the seventh consecutive year, exceeding 19 million for the first time (19,202,757), March 7.

The transfer of the Oilers from Houston to Nashville for the 1998 season was approved by a vote of the NFL clubs at a meeting in Atlanta, April 30.

The Scottish Claymores defeated the Frankfurt Galaxy 32-27 to win the 1996 World Bowl in front of 38,982 at Murrayfield Stadium in Edinburgh, Scotland, June 23.

The NFL returned to Baltimore when the new Baltimore Ravens defeated the Philadelphia Eagles 17-9 in a preseason game before a crowd of 63,804 at Memorial Stadium, August 3.

Ericsson Stadium opened in Charlotte, North Carolina with a crowd of 65,350 as the Carolina Panthers defeated the Chicago Bears 30-12 in a preseason game, August 3.

NFL owners awarded Super Bowl XXXIII, to be played on January 31, 1999, to South Florida; Super Bowl XXXIV, to be played on January, 30, 2000, to Atlanta; and Super Bowl XXXV, to be played on January 28, 2001, to Tampa, October 31.

Points scored totaled 762 and NFL paid attendance totaled 964,079 for 15 games in Week 11, the highest weekend totals in either category in the league's 77-year history, November 10-11.

Former NFL Commissioner Pete Rozelle died at his home in Rancho Santa Fe, California. Rozelle, regarded as the premiere commissioner in sports history, led the NFL for 29 years, from 1960-1989, December 6.

1997

Indianapolis Colts owner Robert Irsay died from complications related to a stroke he suffered in 1995. Irsay acquired the club in 1972 when he traded his Los Angeles Rams to Carrol Rosenbloom for the Colts. He later moved the Colts from Baltimore to Indianapolis in 1984, January 14.

The Green Bay Packers won their first NFL title in 29 years by defeating the New England Patriots 35-21 in Super Bowl XXXI at the Louisiana Superdome in New Orleans. The game was viewed by the fourth-largest audience in U.S. television history—128 million people, January 26.

The rules governing cross-ownership were modified, permitting NFL club owners to also own teams in other sports in their home market or markets without NFL teams. The vote was 24-5 (one abstention) in favor of approval, March 11.

Washington Redskins owner Jack Kent Cooke died at his home in Washington, D.C. Cooke became majority owner in 1974 and the Redskins won three Super Bowls under his leadership, April 6.

The Barcelona Dragons defeated the Rhein Fire 38-24 to win the 1997 World Bowl in front of 31,100 fans at Estadi Olimpic de Montjuic in Barcelona, Spain, June 22.

NFL clubs approved the transfer of the Seattle Seahawks from Ken Behring to Paul Allen, August 19.

Jack Kent Cooke Stadium opened in Raljon, Maryland with a crowd of 78,270 as the Washington Redskins defeated the Arizona Cardinals 19-13 in overtime, September 14.

The 10,000th regular-season game in NFL history was played when the Seattle Seahawks defeated the Tennessee Oilers 16-13 at the Kingdome in Seattle, October 5.

Atlanta Falcons owner Rankin Smith died of heart failure three days prior to his seventy-third birthday. Smith was the founder of the Falcons and was instrumental in bringing Super Bowls XXVIII and XXXIV to Atlanta, October 26.

NFL paid attendance totaled 999,778 for 15 games in Week 12, the highest weekend total in league history, November 16-17.

1998

The NFL reached agreement on record eight-year television contracts with four networks. ABC (*NFL Monday Night Football*) and FOX (NFC) retained their previous rights, CBS took over the AFC package from NBC, and ESPN won the right to broadcast the entire Sunday night cable package, January 13.

The World League was

renamed the NFL Europe League, January 22.

The Denver Broncos won their first Super Bowl by defeating the defending champion Green Bay Packers 31-24 in Super Bowl XXXII at Qualcomm Stadium in San Diego. The game tied Super Bowl XXVII for the third-largest audience in U.S. television history with 133.4 million viewers, January 25.

The NFL clubs approved an extension of the Collective Bargaining Agreement through 2003. The extended CBA also created a $100 million fund for youth football, March 22.

The NFL clubs unanimously approved an expansion team for Cleveland to fulfill the commitment to return the Browns to the field in 1999, March 23.

A total of $25.1 million, the largest NFL postseason pool ever, was divided among 737 players who participated in the 1997 playoffs, March 24.

The Rhein Fire defeated the Frankfurt Galaxy 34-10 to win the 1998 World Bowl in front of 47,846 fans in Frankfurt's Waldstadion—the biggest crowd to witness a World Bowl since 1991, June 14.

NFL clubs approved the transfer of the Minnesota Vikings from a 10-man ownership group to Red McCombs, July 28.

The NFL Stadium at Camden Yards opened in Baltimore, Maryland before a crowd of 65,938 as the Baltimore Ravens defeated the Chicago Bears 19-14 in a preseason game, August 8.

NFL paid attendance totaled 997,835 for 15 games in Week 1, the highest opening weekend total in league history and the second-highest total ever. In 1997, paid attendance totaled 999,778 for 15 games in Week 12, September 6-7.

Raymond James Stadium opened in Tampa, Florida before a crowd of 62,410 as the Tampa Bay Buccaneers defeated the Chicago Bears 27-15, September 20.

A Harris Poll says 55 percent of adults follow professional football, up 4 percent from 1997 and 6 percent from 1992, October 15.

NFL owners awarded Super Bowl XXXVI, to be played on January 27, 2002, to New Orleans, October 28.

Tennessee Oilers owner Bud Adams announced the team will change its name to the Tennessee Titans following the 1998 season. The NFL announced that the name Oilers will be retired—a first in league history, November 14.

1999

The Denver Broncos won their second consecutive Super Bowl title by defeating the NFC champion Atlanta Falcons 34-19 in Super Bowl XXXIII at Pro Player Stadium in Miami. The game was viewed by 127.5 million viewers, the sixth most-watched program in U.S. television history, January 31.

Jim Pyne, a center allocated by the Detroit Lions, was the first selection of the Cleveland Browns in the 1999 NFL Expansion Draft. The Browns eventually selected 37 players, February 9.

CBS Radio/Westwood One agreed to a 3-year extension of their exclusive national radio rights to NFL games, March 11.

NFL paid attendance of 19,741,493 for all games played during the 1998 season was the highest in league history, topping the 19,202,757 fans who paid to attend games in 1995. The 1998 regular-season total paid attendance of 15,364,873 for an average of 64,020 were also records, March 15.

By a vote of 28-3, the owners adopted an instant replay system as an officiating aid for the 1999 season, March 17.

New York Jets owner Leon Hess died from complications of a blood disease. Hess had been involved in the ownership of the Jets since 1963 and was sole owner of the club since 1984, May 9.

A group led by Washington area businessman Daniel Snyder is approved by NFL clubs as the new owner of the Washington Redskins at a league meeting in Atlanta, May 25.

NFL owners awarded Super Bowl XXXVII, to be played on January 26, 2003, to San Diego, May 26.

The Frankfurt Galaxy became the first team in NFL Europe League history to win a second World Bowl by defeating the Barcelona Dragons 38-24 at Rheinstadion, in Düsseldorf, Germany, June 27.

The Cleveland Browns returned to the field for the first time since 1995 and defeated the Dallas Cowboys 20-17 in overtime in the annual Hall of Fame Game at Canton, Ohio, August 9.

Cleveland Browns Stadium opened in Cleveland, Ohio before a crowd of 71,398 as the Minnesota Vikings defeated the Browns in a preseason game, 24-17, August 21.

Adelphia Coliseum opened in Nashville, Tennessee before a crowd of 65,729 with the Tennessee Titans defeating the Atlanta Falcons 17-3 in a preseason game, August 26.

Houston, Texas and owner Robert McNair were awarded the NFL's thirty-second franchise in a vote of the NFL clubs at a league meeting in Atlanta. The team will begin play in 2002. The NFL clubs also voted to realign into eight divisions of four teams each for the 2002 season, October 6.

Walter Payton, the NFL's all-time leading rusher, died of liver cancer at the age of 45. Payton played for the Chicago Bears from 1975-1987 and rushed for an NFL-record 16,726 yards, November 1.

Former NFL Commissioner Pete Rozelle, who guided a still-developing league to its position today as America's most popular sport, was named by *The Sporting News* as the most powerful person in sports in the 20th Century, December 15.

2000

New York businessman Robert Wood Johnson IV was approved by NFL clubs as the new owner of the New York Jets at a league meeting, January 18.

The St. Louis Rams won their first Super Bowl by defeating the AFC champion Tennessee Titans 23-16 in Super Bowl XXXIV at the Georgia Dome in Atlanta. The game was viewed by 130.7 million viewers, the fifth most-watched program in U.S. television history, January 30.

For the first time in league history, paid attendance topped 16 million for the regular season and more than 65,000 per game, an increase of 1,300 per game over 1998. Paid attendance for all NFL games increased in 1999 for the third year in a row and was the highest ever in the 80-year history of the league. It marked the first time in league history that the 20-million paid attendance mark was reached for all games in a season, March 27.

The Rhein Fire won their second World Bowl in three years, defeating the Scottish Claymores 13-10 to win World Bowl 2000 in front of 35,680 at Frankfurt's Waldstadion, June 25.

More than 100 of the 136 living members of the Pro Football Hall of Fame gathered to celebrate Pro Football's Greatest Reunion in Canton, Ohio, July 28-31.

Paul Brown Stadium opened in Cincinnati, Ohio with a crowd of 56,180 as the Cincinnati Bengals defeated the Chicago Bears 24-20 in a preseason game, August 19.

Cincinnati's Corey Dillon set a single-game rushing record with 278 yards (22 carries) against Denver, breaking the previous record of 275 yards by Chicago's Walter Payton in 1977, October 22.

Minnesota's Gary Anderson converted a 21-yard field goal against Buffalo to pass George Blanda as the NFL's all-time scoring leader with 2,004 points, October 22.

NFL owners awarded Super Bowl XXXVIII, to be played on February 1, 2004, to Houston; Super Bowl XXXIX, to be played on February 6, 2005, to Jacksonville; and Super Bowl XL, to be played on February 5, 2006, to Detroit, November 1.

The NFL named Mike Pereira as Director of Officiating and Larry Upson as Director of Officiating Operations to replace retiring Senior Director of Officiating Jerry Seeman, December 1.

San Francisco's Terrell Owens set a single-game receiving record with 20 receptions (283 yards) against Chicago, surpassing the previous mark of 18 by

Tom Fears of the Los Angeles Rams in 1950, December 17.

2001

NFL clubs approved additional league-wide revenue sharing at a special league meeting in Dallas. The teams agreed to pool the visiting team share of gate receipts for all preseason and regular-season games and divide the pool equally starting in 2002, January 17.

The Baltimore Ravens won their first Super Bowl by defeating the NFC champion New York Giants 34-7 in Super Bowl XXXV at Raymond James Stadium in Tampa. The game was witnessed by 131.2 million viewers, the fifth most-watched program in U.S. television history, January 28.

The *Sports Business Daily* named NFL Commissioner Paul Tagliabue the 2000 Sports Industrialist of the Year, February 28.

The NFL set an all-time paid attendance record in 2000 for the third consecutive year, reaching the 20-million paid attendance mark for only the second time in league history. Regular-season paid attendance of 16,387,289 for an average of 66,078 per game also was an all-time record for the third consecutive season. The Washington Redskins set an all-time NFL regular-season home paid attendance record with a total of 656,599 for eight games, breaking the record of 634,204 held by the 1980 Detroit Lions, March 26.

NFL owners unanimously approved a realignment plan for the league starting in 2002. With the addition of the Houston Texans, the league's 32 teams will be divided into eight four-team divisions. Seven clubs change divisions, and the Seattle Seahawks change conferences, moving from the AFC to the NFC. A new scheduling format ensures that every team meets every other team in the league at least once every four years, May 22.

The Berlin Thunder won their first World Bowl, defeating the Barcelona Dragons 24-17 to win World Bowl IX in front of 32,116 at Amsterdam ArenA, June 30.

Heinz Field opened in Pittsburgh, Pennsylvania before a crowd of 57,829 with the Pittsburgh Steelers defeating the Detroit Lions 20-7 in a preseason game; and INVESCO Field at Mile High opened in Denver, Colorado before a crowd of 74,063 with the Denver Broncos defeating the New Orleans Saints 31-24 in a preseason game, August 25.

President George W. Bush became the first United States President to be involved in an NFL regular-season pregame coin toss as he helped kick off the 2001 season from the White House. Via satellite, President Bush tossed the coin for the 10 regular-season games that started at 1:00 P.M. ET, September 9.

In the wake of the September 11 terrorist attacks, Commissioner Paul Tagliabue postponed the games scheduled for September 16-17, September 13.

The league's 16-game regular season was retained when the postponed Week 2 games were rescheduled for the weekend of January 6-7, September 18.

The NFL and its game officials agreed to a new six-year Collective Bargaining Agreement, ending a two-week lockout of the regular officials, who returned to work on September 23, September 19.

The NFL announced that the league's prohibition of anabolic steroids and related substances had been strengthened to include supplements containing ephedrine and other high-risk supplements, September 27.

The NFL announced that the Super Bowl would be rescheduled from January 27 to February 3 in order to retain the full playoff format for the 2002 season. It will be the first Super Bowl played in February, October 3.

President Bush designated Super Bowl XXXVI as a "National Special Security Event," allowing all security for the game to be coordinated by the Secret Service, November 26.

George Young, the NFL's senior vice president of football operations and former general manager of the New York Giants, died at the age of 71, December 8.

2002

The NFL and the NFL Players Association agreed to a fourth extension of the 1993 Collective Bargaining Agreement through 2007, January 7.

In an AFC Wild Card matchup, the Oakland Raiders defeated the New York Jets 38-24 in the NFL's first-ever prime-time playoff game, January 12.

In a special meeting in New Orleans, NFL owners voted unanimously to approve the purchase of the Atlanta Falcons to Home Depot co-founder Arthur Blank, February 2.

The New England Patriots won their first Super Bowl by defeating the NFC champion St. Louis Rams 20-17 in Super Bowl XXXVI at the Louisiana Superdome in New Orleans. The game marked the first time in Super Bowl history that the winning points came on the final play, a 48-yard field goal by Patriots kicker Adam Vinatieri. Super Bowl XXXVI was viewed by 131.7 million viewers, the fifth-most watched program in U.S. television history, February 3.

Tennessee Titans head coach Jeff Fisher was named co-chairman of the NFL Competition Committee, February 6.

Tony Boselli, a five-time Pro Bowl tackle allocated by the Jacksonville Jaguars, was the first selection of the Houston Texans in the 2002 NFL Expansion Draft. The Texans selected 19 players, February 18.

The NFL and Westwood One/CBS Radio Sports announced the renewal of a multiyear agreement for Westwood One/CBS Radio Sports to continue as the exclusive network radio home of the NFL, April 9.

NFL Europe kicked off its tenth season with a record 254 players allocated by NFL clubs, April 13-14.

The Berlin Thunder became the first team to win consecutive World Bowls, defeating the Rhein Fire 26-20 to win World Bowl X in front of 53,109 fans at Rheinstadion, June 22.

Seahawks Stadium opened in Seattle, Washington with an attendance of 52,902 fans as the Indianapolis Colts defeated the Seattle Seahawks 28-10 in a preseason game, August 10.

Gillette Stadium opened in Foxboro, Massachusetts with a crowd of 68,436 fans as the New England Patriots defeated the Philadelphia Eagles 16-15 in a preseason game, August 17.

Reliant Stadium opened in Houston, Texas with 69,432 fans in attendance, the largest non-Super Bowl crowd to ever watch an NFL game in Houston as the Miami Dolphins defeated the Houston Texans 24-3 in a preseason game, August 24.

For the first time, the NFL season kicked off on a Thursday night in prime time as the San Francisco 49ers defeated the New York Giants 16-13 at Giants Stadium. The game was preceded by "NFL Kickoff Live From Times Square," presented by New York City and the NFL, a football and music festival honoring the resilient spirit of New York and America, September 5.

Week 1 of the 2002 season produced the highest-scoring and most competitive Kickoff Weekend in NFL history. The 16 games averaged 49.3 points per game. A total of 788 points and 89 touchdowns were scored, the most in league history for an opening weekend. Eleven of the 16 games were decided by one score (eight points or less), a Kickoff Weekend record, September 5-9.

Johnny Unitas, the legendary quarterback for the Baltimore Colts and a Pro Football Hall of Fame member, died of a heart attack at the age of 69, September 11.

Oakland Raiders wide receiver Jerry Rice became the all-time leader in yards from scrimmage, surpassing Pro Football Hall of Fame running back Walter Payton (21,281 yards), September 29.

Baltimore Ravens cornerback Chris McAlister set an NFL record for the longest scoring play with a 107-yard touchdown return of an errant 57-yard field goal attempt by Denver Broncos kicker Jason Elam, September 30.

Cleveland Browns owner Al Lerner, the NFL Finance Committee Chairman and Chairman and CEO of MBNA Corporation, died at the age of 69, October 23.

Dallas Cowboys running back Emmitt Smith became the NFL's all-time rushing leader, surpassing Pro Football Hall of Fame running back Walter Payton (16,726 yards), October 27.

The NFL and NFLPA announced the creation of USA Football, the first national advocacy organization representing all levels of amateur football, December 5.

Indianapolis Colts wide receiver Marvin Harrison set the NFL single-season record for pass receptions with 143, surpassing Herman Moore (123), December 29.

The 2002 season concluded with 25 overtime games, the most in NFL history, December 30.

2003

The NFL announced the appointment of Steve Bornstein as executive vice president-media and president and chief executive officer of the NFL Network, to be launched in 2003. The NFL Network will be the first television programming service fully dedicated to the NFL and the sport of football, January 16.

The Tampa Bay Buccaneers won their first Super Bowl by defeating the AFC champion Oakland Raiders 48-21 in Super Bowl XXXVII at Qualcomm Stadium in San Diego. The game was witnessed by 138.9 million viewers, making Super Bowl XXXVII the most-watched program in U.S. television history, January 26.

The NFL set an all-time paid attendance record in 2002 with 21,505,138, the first time paid attendance topped 21-million. Regular-season paid attendance of 16,833,310 was also an all-time record, March 26.

Chicago Bears chairman emeritus Edward W. McCaskey died at the age of 83, April 8.

The Frankfurt Galaxy became the first team to win three World Bowls, defeating the Rhein Fire 35-16 to win World Bowl XI in front of 28,138 fans at Hampden Park, June 14.

Tex Schramm, the legendary team president and general manager of the Dallas Cowboys and a member of the Pro Football Hall of Fame, died at the age of 83, July 15.

Lincoln Financial Field opened in Philadelphia, Pennsylvania with an attendance of 66,279 fans as the New England Patriots defeated the Philadelphia Eagles 24-12 in a preseason game, August 22.

A renovated Lambeau Field opened in Green Bay, Wisconsin with a crowd of 69,831 fans as the Carolina Panthers defeated the Green Bay Packers 20-7 in a preseason game, August 23.

NFL owners awarded Super Bowl XLI, to be played on February 4, 2007 to Miami, September 17.

A renovated Soldier Field opened in Chicago, Illinois with an attendance of 61,500 fans as the Green Bay Packers defeated the Chicago Bears 38-23 in a regular season game on ABC's *NFL Monday Night Football*, September 29.

NFL owners awarded Super Bowl XLII, to be played on February 3, 2008 to Glendale, Arizona, October 30.

NFL Network, the first 24-hour, year-round television channel dedicated to the NFL and the sport of football, launched on DirecTV, November 4.

Otto Graham, the legendary quarterback of the Cleveland Browns and a member of the Pro Football Hall of Fame, died at the age of 82, December 17.

NFL paid attendance totaled 1,106,818 for 16 games in Week 17, the highest weekend total in league history, December 27-28.

2004

The NFL set an all-time paid attendance record in 2003 for the second consecutive year with a mark of 21,639,040. Regular-season paid attendance of 16,913,584 for an average of 66,328 per game were both all-time records, March 29.

By a vote of 29-3, NFL owners extended the instant replay system for another five seasons through 2008, March 30.

Steve Bisciotti took over as the controlling owner of the Baltimore Ravens, succeeding Art Modell, who operated the franchise for 43 years, April 8.

Former Arizona Cardinals safety Pat Tillman was killed in a firefight while on combat patrol with the U.S. Army Rangers in Afghanistan, April 22.

NFL COMMISSIONERS AND PRESIDENTS*

1920....Jim Thorpe, President
1921-39...Joe Carr, President
1939-41.Carl Storck, President
1941-46..........Elmer Layden, Commissioner
1946-59..................Bert Bell, Commissioner
1960-89............Pete Rozelle, Commissioner
1989-present..Paul Tagliabue, Commissioner

**NFL treasurer Austin Gunsel served as president in the office of the commissioner following the death of Bert Bell (Oct. 11, 1959) until the election of Pete Rozelle (Jan. 26, 1960).*

PAST STANDINGS

2003

AMERICAN CONFERENCE

East Division

	W	L	T	Pct.	Pts.	OP
New England#	14	2	0	.875	348	238
Miami	10	6	0	.625	311	261
Buffalo	6	10	0	.375	243	279
N.Y. Jets	6	10	0	.375	283	299

North Division

	W	L	T	Pct.	Pts.	OP
Baltimore	10	6	0	.625	391	281
Cincinnati	8	8	0	.500	346	384
Pittsburgh	6	10	0	.375	300	327
Cleveland	5	11	0	.313	254	322

South Division

	W	L	T	Pct.	Pts.	OP
Indianapolis	12	4	0	.750	447	336
Tennessee*	12	4	0	.750	435	324
Houston	5	11	0	.313	255	380
Jacksonville	5	11	0	.313	276	331

West Division

	W	L	T	Pct.	Pts.	OP
Kansas City	13	3	0	.813	484	332
Denver*	10	6	0	.625	381	301
Oakland	4	12	0	.250	270	379
San Diego	4	12	0	.250	313	441

NATIONAL CONFERENCE

East Division

	W	L	T	Pct.	Pts.	OP
Philadelphia#	12	4	0	.750	374	287
Dallas*	10	6	0	.625	289	260
Washington	5	11	0	.313	287	372
N.Y. Giants	4	12	0	.250	243	387

North Division

	W	L	T	Pct.	Pts.	OP
Green Bay	10	6	0	.625	442	307
Minnesota	9	7	0	.563	416	353
Chicago	7	9	0	.438	283	346
Detroit	5	11	0	.313	270	379

South Division

	W	L	T	Pct.	Pts.	OP
Carolina	11	5	0	.688	325	304
New Orleans	8	8	0	.500	340	326
Tampa Bay	7	9	0	.438	301	264
Atlanta	5	11	0	.313	299	422

West Division

	W	L	T	Pct.	Pts.	OP
St. Louis	12	4	0	.750	447	328
Seattle*	10	6	0	.625	404	327
San Francisco	7	9	0	.438	384	337
Arizona	4	12	0	.250	225	452

**Wild-Card qualifier for playoffs; #Top playoff seed in conference*

Buffalo finished ahead of New York Jets based on better division record (2-4 to Jets' 1-5). Indianapolis finished ahead of Tennessee based on head-to-head sweep (2-0). Jacksonville finished ahead of Houston based on better division record (2-4 to Texans' 1-5). Denver finished ahead of Miami based on better conference record (9-3 to Dolphins' 7-5). Oakland finished ahead of San Diego based on better conference record (3-9 to Chargers' 2-10). Philadelphia finished ahead of St. Louis based on better conference record (9-3 to Rams' 8-4). Seattle finished ahead of Dallas based on better strength of victory (65-95 to Cowboys' 62-98).

Wild-Card playoffs: Tennessee 20, BALTIMORE 17; INDIANAPOLIS 41, Denver 10

Divisional playoffs: NEW ENGLAND 17, Tennessee 14; Indianapolis 38, KANSAS CITY 31

AFC Championship: NEW ENGLAND 24, Indianapolis 14

Wild-Card playoffs: CAROLINA 29, Dallas 10; GREEN BAY 33, Seattle 27 (OT)

Divisional playoffs: Carolina 29, ST. LOUIS 23 (2OT); PHILADELPHIA 20, Green Bay 17 (OT)

NFC Championship: Carolina 14, PHILADELPHIA 3

Super Bowl XXXVIII: New England (AFC) 32, Carolina (NFC) 29 at Reliant Stadium, Houston, Texas

In Past Standings section, home teams in playoff games are indicated by capital letters.

Playoff Seeds

AFC

1. New England
2. Kansas City
3. Indianapolis
4. Baltimore
5. Tennessee
6. Denver

NFC

1. Philadelphia
2. St. Louis
3. Carolina
4. Green Bay
5. Seattle
6. Dallas

2002

AMERICAN CONFERENCE

East Division

	W	L	T	Pct.	Pts.	OP
N.Y. Jets	9	7	0	.563	359	336
New England	9	7	0	.563	381	346
Miami	9	7	0	.563	378	301
Buffalo	8	8	0	.500	379	397

North Division

	W	L	T	Pct.	Pts.	OP
Pittsburgh	10	5	1	.656	390	345
Cleveland*	9	7	0	.563	344	320
Baltimore	7	9	0	.438	316	354
Cincinnati	2	14	0	.125	279	456

South Division

	W	L	T	Pct.	Pts.	OP
Tennessee	11	5	0	.688	367	324
Indianapolis*	10	6	0	.625	349	313
Jacksonville	6	10	0	.375	328	315
Houston	4	12	0	.250	213	356

West Division

	W	L	T	Pct.	Pts.	OP
Oakland#	11	5	0	.688	450	304
Denver	9	7	0	.563	392	344
San Diego	8	8	0	.500	333	367
Kansas City	8	8	0	.500	467	399

NATIONAL CONFERENCE

East Division

	W	L	T	Pct.	Pts.	OP
Philadelphia#	12	4	0	.750	415	241
N.Y. Giants*	10	6	0	.625	320	279
Washington	7	9	0	.438	307	365
Dallas	5	11	0	.313	217	329

North Division

	W	L	T	Pct.	Pts.	OP
Green Bay	12	4	0	.750	398	328
Minnesota	6	10	0	.375	390	442
Chicago	4	12	0	.250	281	379
Detroit	3	13	0	.188	306	451

South Division

	W	L	T	Pct.	Pts.	OP
Tampa Bay	12	4	0	.750	346	196
Atlanta*	9	6	1	.594	402	314
New Orleans	9	7	0	.563	432	388
Carolina	7	9	0	.438	258	302

West Division

	W	L	T	Pct.	Pts.	OP
San Francisco	10	6	0	.625	367	351
St. Louis	7	9	0	.438	316	369
Seattle	7	9	0	.438	355	369
Arizona	5	11	0	.313	262	417

**Wild-Card qualifier for playoffs; #Top playoff seed in conference*

New York Jets finished ahead of New England based on better record in common games (8-4 to Patriots' 7-5) and Miami based on better division record (4-2 to Dolphins' 2-4). New England finished ahead of Miami based on better division record (4-2 to Dolphins' 2-4). Cleveland finished ahead of Denver and New England based on better conference record (7-5 to Broncos' 5-7 and Patriots' 6-6). Oakland finished ahead of Tennessee based on better head-to-head record (1-0). San Diego finished ahead of Kansas City based on better division record (3-3 to Chiefs' 2-4). Philadelphia finished ahead of Green Bay and Tampa Bay based on better conference record (11-1 to Packers' 9-3 and Buccaneers' 9-3). Tampa Bay finished ahead of Green Bay based on better head-to-head record (1-0). St. Louis finished ahead of Seattle based on better division record (4-2 to Seahawks' 2-4).

Wild-Card playoffs: NEW YORK JETS 41, Indianapolis 0; PITTSBURGH 36, Cleveland 33

Divisional playoffs: TENNESSEE 34, Pittsburgh 31 (OT); OAKLAND 30, New York Jets 10

AFC Championship: OAKLAND 41, Tennessee 24

Wild-Card playoffs: Atlanta 27, GREEN BAY 7; SAN FRANCISCO 39, New York Giants 38

Divisional playoffs: PHILADELPHIA 20, Atlanta 6; TAMPA BAY 31, San Francisco 6

NFC Championship: Tampa Bay 27, PHILADELPHIA 10

Super Bowl XXXVII: Tampa Bay (NFC) 48, Oakland (AFC) 21 at Qualcomm Stadium, San Diego, California

Playoff Seeds

AFC

1. Oakland
2. Tennessee
3. Pittsburgh
4. N.Y. Jets
5. Indianapolis
6. Cleveland

NFC

1. Philadelphia
2. Tampa Bay
3. Green Bay
4. San Francisco
5. N.Y. Giants
6. Atlanta

2001

AMERICAN CONFERENCE

Eastern Division

	W	L	T	Pct.	Pts.	OP
New England	11	5	0	.688	371	272
Miami*	11	5	0	.688	344	290
N.Y. Jets*	10	6	0	.625	308	295
Indianapolis	6	10	0	.375	413	486
Buffalo	3	13	0	.188	265	420

Central Division

	W	L	T	Pct.	Pts.	OP
Pittsburgh#	13	3	0	.813	352	212
Baltimore*	10	6	0	.625	303	265
Cleveland	7	9	0	.438	285	319
Tennessee	7	9	0	.438	336	388
Jacksonville	6	10	0	.375	294	286
Cincinnati	6	10	0	.375	226	309

Western Division

	W	L	T	Pct.	Pts.	OP
Oakland	10	6	0	.625	399	327
Seattle	9	7	0	.563	301	324
Denver	8	8	0	.500	340	339
Kansas City	6	10	0	.375	320	344
San Diego	5	11	0	.313	332	321

NATIONAL CONFERENCE

Eastern Division

	W	L	T	Pct.	Pts.	OP
Philadelphia	11	5	0	.688	343	208
Washington	8	8	0	.500	256	303
N.Y. Giants	7	9	0	.438	294	321
Arizona	7	9	0	.438	295	343
Dallas	5	11	0	.313	246	338

Central Division

	W	L	T	Pct.	Pts.	OP
Chicago	13	3	0	.813	338	203
Green Bay*	12	4	0	.750	390	266
Tampa Bay*	9	7	0	.563	324	280
Minnesota	5	11	0	.313	290	390
Detroit	2	14	0	.125	270	424

Western Division

	W	L	T	Pct.	Pts.	OP
St. Louis#	14	2	0	.875	503	273
San Francisco*	12	4	0	.750	409	282
New Orleans	7	9	0	.438	333	409
Atlanta	7	9	0	.438	291	377
Carolina	1	15	0	.063	253	410

**Wild-Card qualifier for playoffs; #Top playoff seed in conference*

New England finished ahead of Miami based on better division record (6-2 to Dolphins' 5-3). Baltimore was second Wild Card ahead of N.Y. Jets based on better record against common opponents (3-2 to Jets' 2-2). Cleveland finished ahead of Tennessee based on better division record (5-5 to Titans' 3-7). Jacksonville finished ahead of Cincinnati based on head-to-head record (2-0). N.Y. Giants finished ahead of Arizona based on head-to-head record (2-0). Green Bay was first Wild Card ahead of San Francisco based on better conference record (9-3 to 49ers' 8-4). New Orleans finished ahead of Atlanta based on better division record (4-4 to Falcons' 3-5).

Wild-Card playoffs: OAKLAND 38, New York Jets 24; Baltimore 20, MIAMI 3

Divisional playoffs: NEW ENGLAND 16, Oakland 13 (OT); PITTSBURGH 27, Baltimore 10

AFC Championship: New England 24, PITTSBURGH 17

Wild-Card playoffs: PHILADELPHIA 31, Tampa Bay 9; GREEN BAY 25, San Francisco 15

Divisional playoffs: Philadelphia 33, CHICAGO 19; ST. LOUIS 45, Green Bay 17

NFC Championship: ST. LOUIS 29, Philadelphia 24

Super Bowl XXXVI: New England (AFC) 20, St. Louis (NFC) 17 at Louisiana Superdome, New Orleans, Louisiana

Playoff Seeds

AFC

1. Pittsburgh
2. **New England**
3. Oakland
4. Miami
5. Baltimore
6. N.Y. Jets

NFC

1. **St. Louis**
2. Chicago
3. Philadelphia
4. Green Bay
5. San Francisco
6. Tampa Bay

2000

AMERICAN CONFERENCE

Eastern Division

	W	L	T	Pct.	Pts.	OP
Miami	11	5	0	.688	323	226
Indianapolis*	10	6	0	.625	429	326
N.Y. Jets	9	7	0	.563	321	321
Buffalo	8	8	0	.500	315	350
New England	5	11	0	.313	276	338

Central Division

	W	L	T	Pct.	Pts.	OP
Tennessee#	13	3	0	.813	346	191
Baltimore*	12	4	0	.750	333	165
Pittsburgh	9	7	0	.563	321	255
Jacksonville	7	9	0	.438	367	327
Cincinnati	4	12	0	.250	185	359
Cleveland	3	13	0	.188	161	419

Western Division

	W	L	T	Pct.	Pts.	OP
Oakland	12	4	0	.750	479	299
Denver*	11	5	0	.688	485	369
Kansas City	7	9	0	.438	355	354
Seattle	6	10	0	.375	320	405
San Diego	1	15	0	.063	269	440

NATIONAL CONFERENCE

Eastern Division

	W	L	T	Pct.	Pts.	OP
N.Y. Giants#	12	4	0	.750	328	246
Philadelphia*	11	5	0	.688	351	245
Washington	8	8	0	.500	281	269
Dallas	5	11	0	.313	294	361
Arizona	3	13	0	.188	210	443

Central Division

	W	L	T	Pct.	Pts.	OP
Minnesota	11	5	0	.688	397	371
Tampa Bay*	10	6	0	.625	388	269
Green Bay	9	7	0	.563	353	323
Detroit	9	7	0	.563	307	307
Chicago	5	11	0	.313	216	355

Western Division

	W	L	T	Pct.	Pts.	OP
New Orleans	10	6	0	.625	354	305
St. Louis*	10	6	0	.625	540	471
Carolina	7	9	0	.438	310	310
San Francisco	6	10	0	.375	388	422
Atlanta	4	12	0	.250	252	413

**Wild-Card qualifier for playoffs; #Top playoff seed in conference*

Green Bay finished ahead of Detroit based on better division record (5-3 to Lions' 3-5). New Orleans finished ahead of St. Louis based on better division record (7-1 to Rams' 5-3). Tampa Bay was second Wild Card based on head-to-head victory over St. Louis (1-0).

Wild-Card playoffs: MIAMI 23, Indianapolis 17 (OT); BALTIMORE 21, Denver 3

Divisional playoffs: OAKLAND 27, Miami 0; Baltimore 24, TENNESSEE 10

AFC Championship: Baltimore 16, OAKLAND 3

Wild-Card playoffs: NEW ORLEANS 31, St. Louis 28; PHILADELPHIA 21, Tampa Bay 3

Divisional playoffs: MINNESOTA 34, New Orleans 16; N.Y. GIANTS 20, Philadelphia 10

NFC Championship: N.Y. GIANTS 41, Minnesota 0

Super Bowl XXXV: Baltimore (AFC) 34, N.Y. Giants (NFC) 7 at Raymond James Stadium, Tampa, Florida

Playoff Seeds

AFC

1. Tennessee
2. Oakland
3. Miami
4. **Baltimore**
5. Denver
6. Indianapolis

NFC

1. **N.Y. Giants**
2. Minnesota
3. New Orleans
4. Philadelphia
5. Tampa Bay
6. St. Louis

1999

AMERICAN CONFERENCE

Eastern Division

	W	L	T	Pct.	Pts.	OP
Indianapolis	13	3	0	.813	423	333
Buffalo*	11	5	0	.688	320	229
Miami*	9	7	0	.563	326	336
N.Y. Jets	8	8	0	.500	308	309
New England	8	8	0	.500	299	284

Central Division

	W	L	T	Pct.	Pts.	OP
Jacksonville#	14	2	0	.875	396	217
Tennessee*	13	3	0	.813	392	324
Baltimore	8	8	0	.500	324	277
Pittsburgh	6	10	0	.375	317	320
Cincinnati	4	12	0	.250	283	460
Cleveland	2	14	0	.125	217	437

Western Division

	W	L	T	Pct.	Pts.	OP
Seattle	9	7	0	.563	338	298
Kansas City	9	7	0	.563	390	322
San Diego	8	8	0	.500	269	316
Oakland	8	8	0	.500	390	329
Denver	6	10	0	.375	314	318

NATIONAL CONFERENCE

Eastern Division

	W	L	T	Pct.	Pts.	OP
Washington	10	6	0	.625	443	377
Dallas*	8	8	0	.500	352	276
N.Y. Giants	7	9	0	.438	299	358
Arizona	6	10	0	.375	245	382
Philadelphia	5	11	0	.313	272	357

Central Division

	W	L	T	Pct.	Pts.	OP
Tampa Bay	11	5	0	.688	270	235
Minnesota*	10	6	0	.625	399	335
Detroit*	8	8	0	.500	322	323
Green Bay	8	8	0	.500	357	341
Chicago	6	10	0	.375	272	341

Western Division

	W	L	T	Pct.	Pts.	OP
St. Louis#	13	3	0	.813	526	242
Carolina	8	8	0	.500	421	381
Atlanta	5	11	0	.313	285	380
San Francisco	4	12	0	.250	295	453
New Orleans	3	13	0	.188	260	434

**Wild-Card qualifier for playoffs; #Top playoff seed in conference*

Miami was third Wild Card ahead of Kansas City based on better record against common opponents (6-1 to Chiefs' 5-3). N.Y. Jets finished ahead of New England based on better division record (4-4 to Patriots' 2-6). Seattle finished ahead of Kansas City based on head-to-head sweep (2-0). San Diego finished ahead of Oakland based on better division record (5-3 to Raiders' 3-5). Dallas was second Wild Card based on better record against common opponents (3-2 to Lions' 3-3) and better conference record than Carolina (7-5 to Panthers' 6-6). Detroit was third Wild Card based on better conference record than Green Bay (7-5 to Packers' 6-6) and better conference record than Carolina (7-5 to Panthers' 6-6).

Wild-Card playoffs: TENNESSEE 22, Buffalo 16; Miami 20, SEATTLE 17

Divisional playoffs: JACKSONVILLE 62, Miami 7; Tennessee 19, INDIANAPOLIS 16

AFC Championship: Tennessee 33, JACKSONVILLE 14

Wild-Card playoffs: WASHINGTON 27, Detroit 13; MINNESOTA 27, Dallas 10

Divisional playoffs: TAMPA BAY 14, Washington 13; ST. LOUIS 49, Minnesota 37

NFC Championship: ST. LOUIS 11, Tampa Bay 6

Super Bowl XXXIV: St. Louis (NFC) 23, Tennessee (AFC) 16 at Georgia Dome, Atlanta, Georgia

Playoff Seeds

AFC	NFC
1. Jacksonville	**1. St. Louis**
2. Indianapolis	2. Tampa Bay
3. Seattle	3. Washington
4. Tennessee	4. Minnesota
5. Buffalo	5. Dallas
6. Miami	6. Detroit

1998

AMERICAN CONFERENCE

Eastern Division

	W	L	T	Pct.	Pts.	OP
N.Y. Jets	12	4	0	.750	416	266
Miami*	10	6	0	.625	321	265
Buffalo*	10	6	0	.625	400	333
New England*	9	7	0	.563	337	329
Indianapolis	3	13	0	.188	310	444

Central Division

	W	L	T	Pct.	Pts.	OP
Jacksonville	11	5	0	.688	392	338
Tennessee	8	8	0	.500	330	320
Pittsburgh	7	9	0	.438	263	303
Baltimore	6	10	0	.375	269	335
Cincinnati	3	13	0	.188	268	452

Western Division

	W	L	T	Pct.	Pts.	OP
Denver#	14	2	0	.875	501	309
Oakland	8	8	0	.500	288	356
Seattle	8	8	0	.500	372	310
Kansas City	7	9	0	.438	327	363
San Diego	5	11	0	.313	241	342

NATIONAL CONFERENCE

Eastern Division

	W	L	T	Pct.	Pts.	OP
Dallas	10	6	0	.625	381	275
Arizona*	9	7	0	.563	325	378
N.Y. Giants	8	8	0	.500	287	309
Washington	6	10	0	.375	319	421
Philadelphia	3	13	0	.188	161	344

Central Division

	W	L	T	Pct.	Pts.	OP
Minnesota#	15	1	0	.938	556	296
Green Bay*	11	5	0	.688	408	319
Tampa Bay	8	8	0	.500	314	295
Detroit	5	11	0	.313	306	378
Chicago	4	12	0	.250	276	368

Western Division

	W	L	T	Pct.	Pts.	OP
Atlanta	14	2	0	.875	442	289
San Francisco*	12	4	0	.750	479	328
New Orleans	6	10	0	.375	305	359
Carolina	4	12	0	.250	336	413
St. Louis	4	12	0	.250	285	378

**Wild-Card qualifier for playoffs; #Top playoff seed in conference*

Miami finished ahead of Buffalo based on better net division points (6 to Bills' 0). Oakland finished ahead of Seattle based on head-to-head sweep (2-0). Carolina finished ahead of St. Louis based on head-to-head sweep (2-0).

Wild-Card playoffs: MIAMI 24, Buffalo 17; JACKSONVILLE 25, New England 10

Divisional playoffs: DENVER 38, Miami 3; N.Y. JETS 34, Jacksonville 24

AFC Championship: DENVER 23, N.Y. Jets 10

Wild-Card playoffs: Arizona 20, DALLAS 7; SAN FRANCISCO 30, Green Bay 27

Divisional playoffs: ATLANTA 20, San Francisco 18; MINNESOTA 41, Arizona 21

NFC Championship: Atlanta 30, MINNESOTA 27 (OT)

Super Bowl XXXIII: Denver (AFC) 34, Atlanta (NFC) 19, at Pro Player Stadium, Miami, Florida

Playoff Seeds

AFC	NFC
1. Denver	1. Minnesota
2. N.Y. Jets	**2. Atlanta**
3. Jacksonville	3. Dallas
4. Miami	4. San Francisco
5. Buffalo	5. Green Bay
6. New England	6. Arizona

1997

AMERICAN CONFERENCE

Eastern Division

	W	L	T	Pct.	Pts.	OP
New England	10	6	0	.625	369	289
Miami*	9	7	0	.563	339	327
N.Y. Jets	9	7	0	.563	348	287
Buffalo	6	10	0	.375	255	367
Indianapolis	3	13	0	.188	313	401

Central Division

	W	L	T	Pct.	Pts.	OP
Pittsburgh	11	5	0	.688	372	307
Jacksonville*	11	5	0	.688	394	318
Tennessee	8	8	0	.500	333	310
Cincinnati	7	9	0	.438	355	405
Baltimore	6	9	1	.406	326	345

Western Division

	W	L	T	Pct.	Pts.	OP
Kansas City#	13	3	0	.813	375	232
Denver*	12	4	0	.750	472	287
Seattle	8	8	0	.500	365	362
Oakland	4	12	0	.250	324	419
San Diego	4	12	0	.250	266	425

NATIONAL CONFERENCE

Eastern Division

	W	L	T	Pct.	Pts.	OP
N.Y. Giants	10	5	1	.656	307	265
Washington	8	7	1	.531	327	289
Philadelphia	6	9	1	.406	317	372
Dallas	6	10	0	.375	304	314
Arizona	4	12	0	.250	283	379

Central Division

	W	L	T	Pct.	Pts.	OP
Green Bay	13	3	0	.813	422	282
Tampa Bay*	10	6	0	.625	299	263
Detroit*	9	7	0	.563	379	306
Minnesota*	9	7	0	.563	354	359
Chicago	4	12	0	.250	263	421

Western Division

	W	L	T	Pct.	Pts.	OP
San Francisco#	13	3	0	.813	375	265
Carolina	7	9	0	.438	265	314
Atlanta	7	9	0	.438	320	361
New Orleans	6	10	0	.375	237	327
St. Louis	5	11	0	.313	299	359

**Wild-Card qualifier for playoffs; #Top playoff seed in conference*

Miami finished ahead of N.Y. Jets based on head-to-head sweep (2-0). Pittsburgh finished ahead of Jacksonville based on better net division points (78 to Jaguars' 23). Oakland finished ahead of San Diego based on better division record (2-6 to Chargers' 1-7). San Francisco was top playoff seed based on better conference record than Green Bay (11-1 to Packers' 10-2). Detroit finished ahead of Minnesota based on head-to-head sweep (2-0). Carolina finished ahead of Atlanta based on head-to-head sweep (2-0).

Wild-Card playoffs: DENVER 42, Jacksonville 17; NEW ENGLAND 17, Miami 3

Divisional playoffs: PITTSBURGH 7, New England 6; Denver 14, KANSAS CITY 10

AFC Championship: Denver 24, PITTSBURGH 21

Wild-Card playoffs: Minnesota 23, N.Y. GIANTS 22; TAMPA BAY 20, Detroit 10

Divisional playoffs: SAN FRANCISCO 38, Minnesota 22; GREEN BAY 21, Tampa Bay 7

NFC Championship: Green Bay 23, SAN FRANCISCO 10

Super Bowl XXXII: Denver (AFC) 31, Green Bay (NFC) 24, at Qualcomm Stadium, San Diego, California

Playoff Seeds

AFC	NFC
1. Kansas City	1. San Francisco
2. Pittsburgh	**2. Green Bay**
3. New England	3. N.Y. Giants
4. Denver	4. Tampa Bay
5. Jacksonville	5. Detroit
6. Miami	6. Minnesota

1996

AMERICAN CONFERENCE

Eastern Division

	W	L	T	Pct.	Pts.	OP
New England	11	5	0	.688	418	313
Buffalo*	10	6	0	.625	319	266
Indianapolis*	9	7	0	.563	317	334
Miami	8	8	0	.500	339	325
N.Y. Jets	1	15	0	.063	279	454

Central Division

	W	L	T	Pct.	Pts.	OP
Pittsburgh	10	6	0	.625	344	257
Jacksonville*	9	7	0	.563	325	335
Cincinnati	8	8	0	.500	372	369
Houston	8	8	0	.500	345	319
Baltimore	4	12	0	.250	371	441

Western Division

	W	L	T	Pct.	Pts.	OP
Denver#	13	3	0	.813	391	275
Kansas City	9	7	0	.563	297	300
San Diego	8	8	0	.500	310	376
Oakland	7	9	0	.438	340	293
Seattle	7	9	0	.438	317	376

NATIONAL CONFERENCE

Eastern Division

	W	L	T	Pct.	Pts.	OP
Dallas	10	6	0	.625	286	250
Philadelphia*	10	6	0	.625	363	341
Washington	9	7	0	.563	364	312
Arizona	7	9	0	.438	300	397
N.Y. Giants	6	10	0	.375	242	297

Central Division

	W	L	T	Pct.	Pts.	OP
Green Bay#	13	3	0	.813	456	210
Minnesota*	9	7	0	.563	298	315
Chicago	7	9	0	.438	283	305
Tampa Bay	6	10	0	.375	221	293
Detroit	5	11	0	.313	302	368

Western Division

	W	L	T	Pct.	Pts.	OP
Carolina	12	4	0	.750	367	218
San Francisco*	12	4	0	.750	398	257
St. Louis	6	10	0	.375	303	409
Atlanta	3	13	0	.188	309	461
New Orleans	3	13	0	.188	229	339

**Wild-Card qualifier for playoffs; #Top playoff seed in conference*

Jacksonville was second Wild Card ahead of Indianapolis and Kansas City based on better conference record (7-5 to Colts' 6-6 and Chiefs' 5-7). Indianapolis was third Wild Card based on head-to-head victory over Kansas City (1-0). Cincinnati finished ahead of Houston based on better net division points (19 to Oilers' 11). Oakland finished ahead of Seattle based on better division record (3-5 to Seahawks' 2-6). Dallas finished ahead of Philadelphia based on better record against common opponents (8-5 to Eagles' 7-6). Minnesota was third Wild Card based on better conference record than Washington (8-4 to Redskins' 6-6). Carolina finished ahead of San Francisco based on head-to-head sweep (2-0). Atlanta finished ahead of New Orleans based on head-to-head sweep (2-0).

Wild-Card playoffs: Jacksonville 30, BUFFALO 27; PITTSBURGH 42, Indianapolis 14

Divisional playoffs: Jacksonville 30, DENVER 27; NEW ENGLAND 28, Pittsburgh 3

AFC Championship: NEW ENGLAND 20, Jacksonville 6

Wild-Card playoffs: DALLAS 40, Minnesota 15; SAN FRANCISCO 14, Philadelphia 0

Divisional playoffs: GREEN BAY 35, San Francisco 14; CAROLINA 26, Dallas 17

NFC Championship: GREEN BAY 30, Carolina 13

Super Bowl XXXI: Green Bay (NFC) 35, New England (AFC) 21, at Louisiana Superdome, New Orleans, Louisiana

Playoff Seeds

AFC	NFC
1. Denver	**1. Green Bay**
2. New England	2. Carolina
3. Pittsburgh	3. Dallas
4. Buffalo	4. San Francisco
5. Jacksonville	5. Philadelphia
6. Indianapolis	6. Minnesota

PAST STANDINGS

1995

AMERICAN CONFERENCE

Eastern Division

	W	L	T	Pct.	Pts.	OP
Buffalo	10	6	0	.625	350	335
Indianapolis*	9	7	0	.563	331	316
Miami*	9	7	0	.563	398	332
New England	6	10	0	.375	294	377
N.Y. Jets	3	13	0	.188	233	384

Central Division

	W	L	T	Pct.	Pts.	OP
Pittsburgh	11	5	0	.688	407	327
Cincinnati	7	9	0	.438	349	374
Houston	7	9	0	.438	348	324
Cleveland	5	11	0	.313	289	356
Jacksonville	4	12	0	.250	275	404

Western Division

	W	L	T	Pct.	Pts.	OP
Kansas City#	13	3	0	.813	358	241
San Diego*	9	7	0	.563	321	323
Seattle	8	8	0	.500	363	366
Denver	8	8	0	.500	388	345
Oakland	8	8	0	.500	348	332

NATIONAL CONFERENCE

Eastern Division

	W	L	T	Pct.	Pts.	OP
Dallas#	12	4	0	.750	435	291
Philadelphia*	10	6	0	.625	318	338
Washington	6	10	0	.375	326	359
N.Y. Giants	5	11	0	.313	290	340
Arizona	4	12	0	.250	275	422

Central Division

	W	L	T	Pct.	Pts.	OP
Green Bay	11	5	0	.688	404	314
Detroit*	10	6	0	.625	436	336
Chicago	9	7	0	.563	392	360
Minnesota	8	8	0	.500	412	385
Tampa Bay	7	9	0	.438	238	335

Western Division

	W	L	T	Pct.	Pts.	OP
San Francisco	11	5	0	.688	457	258
Atlanta*	9	7	0	.563	362	349
St. Louis	7	9	0	.438	309	418
Carolina	7	9	0	.438	289	325
New Orleans	7	9	0	.438	319	348

**Wild-Card qualifier for playoffs; #Top playoff seed in conference*

Indianapolis finished ahead of Miami based on head-to-head sweep (2-0). San Diego was first Wild Card based on head-to-head victory over Indianapolis (1-0). Cincinnati finished ahead of Houston based on better division record (4-4 to Oilers' 3-5). Seattle finished ahead of Denver and Oakland based on best head-to-head record (3-1 to Broncos' 2-2 and Raiders' 1-3). Denver finished ahead of Oakland based on head-to-head sweep (2-0). Philadelphia was first Wild Card ahead of Detroit based on better conference record (9-3 to Lions' 7-5). San Francisco was second playoff seed ahead of Green Bay based on better conference record (8-4 to Packers' 7-5). Atlanta was third Wild Card ahead of Chicago based on better record against common opponents (4-2 to Bears' 3-3). St. Louis finished ahead of Carolina and New Orleans based on best head-to-head record (3-1 to Panthers' 1-3 and Saints' 2-2). Carolina finished ahead of New Orleans based on better conference record (4-8 to 3-9).

Wild-Card playoffs: BUFFALO 37, Miami 22; Indianapolis 35, SAN DIEGO 20

Divisional playoffs: PITTSBURGH 40, Buffalo 21; Indianapolis 10, KANSAS CITY 7

AFC Championship: PITTSBURGH 20, Indianapolis 16

Wild-Card playoffs: PHILADELPHIA 58, Detroit 37; GREEN BAY 37, Atlanta 20

Divisional playoffs: Green Bay 27, SAN FRANCISCO 17; DALLAS 30, Philadelphia 11

NFC Championship: DALLAS 38, Green Bay 27

Super Bowl XXX: Dallas (NFC) 27, Pittsburgh (AFC)17, at Sun Devil Stadium, Tempe, Arizona

Playoff Seeds

AFC
1. Kansas City
2. **Pittsburgh**
3. Buffalo
4. San Diego
5. Indianapolis
6. Miami

NFC
1. **Dallas**
2. San Francisco
3. Green Bay
4. Philadelphia
5. Detroit
6. Atlanta

1994

AMERICAN CONFERENCE

Eastern Division

	W	L	T	Pct.	Pts.	OP
Miami	10	6	0	.625	389	327
New England*	10	6	0	.625	351	312
Indianapolis	8	8	0	.500	307	320
Buffalo	7	9	0	.438	340	356
N.Y. Jets	6	10	0	.375	264	320

Central Division

	W	L	T	Pct.	Pts.	OP
Pittsburgh#	12	4	0	.750	316	234
Cleveland*	11	5	0	.688	340	204
Cincinnati	3	13	0	.188	276	406
Houston	2	14	0	.125	226	352

Western Division

	W	L	T	Pct.	Pts.	OP
San Diego	11	5	0	.688	381	306
Kansas City*	9	7	0	.563	319	298
L.A. Raiders	9	7	0	.563	303	327
Denver	7	9	0	.438	347	396
Seattle	6	10	0	.375	287	323

NATIONAL CONFERENCE

Eastern Division

	W	L	T	Pct.	Pts.	OP
Dallas	12	4	0	.750	414	248
N.Y. Giants	9	7	0	.563	279	305
Arizona	8	8	0	.500	235	267
Philadelphia	7	9	0	.438	308	308
Washington	3	13	0	.188	320	412

Central Division

	W	L	T	Pct.	Pts.	OP
Minnesota	10	6	0	.625	356	314
Green Bay*	9	7	0	.563	382	287
Detroit*	9	7	0	.563	357	342
Chicago*	9	7	0	.563	271	307
Tampa Bay	6	10	0	.375	251	351

Western Division

	W	L	T	Pct.	Pts.	OP
San Francisco#	13	3	0	.813	505	296
New Orleans	7	9	0	.438	348	407
Atlanta	7	9	0	.438	317	385
L.A. Rams	4	12	0	.250	286	365

**Wild-Card qualifier for playoffs; #Top playoff seed in conference*

Miami finished ahead of New England based on head-to-head sweep (2-0). Kansas City finished ahead of L.A. Raiders based on head-to-head sweep (2-0). Green Bay was first Wild Card based on best head-to-head record (3-1) vs. Detroit (2-2) and Chicago (1-3) and better conference record (8-4) than N.Y. Giants (6-6). Detroit was second Wild Card based on better division record (4-4) than Chicago (3-5) and head-to-head victory over N.Y. Giants (1-0). Chicago was third Wild Card based on better record against common opponents (4-4) than N.Y. Giants (3-5). New Orleans finished ahead of Atlanta based on head-to-head sweep (2-0).

Wild-Card playoffs: MIAMI 27, Kansas City 17; CLEVELAND 20, New England 13

Divisional playoffs: PITTSBURGH 29, Cleveland 9; SAN DIEGO 22, Miami 21

AFC Championship: San Diego 17, PITTSBURGH 13

Wild-Card playoffs: GREEN BAY 16, Detroit 12; Chicago 35, MINNESOTA 18

Divisional playoffs: SAN FRANCISCO 44, Chicago 15; DALLAS 35, Green Bay 9

NFC Championship: SAN FRANCISCO 38, Dallas 28

Super Bowl XXIX: San Francisco (NFC) 49, San Diego (AFC) 26, at Joe Robbie Stadium, Miami, Florida

Playoff Seeds

AFC
1. Pittsburgh
2. **San Diego**
3. Miami
4. Cleveland
5. New England
6. Kansas City

NFC
1. **San Francisco**
2. Dallas
3. Minnesota
4. Green Bay
5. Detroit
6. Chicago

1993

AMERICAN CONFERENCE

Eastern Division

	W	L	T	Pct.	Pts.	OP
Buffalo#	12	4	0	.750	329	242
Miami	9	7	0	.563	349	351
N.Y. Jets	8	8	0	.500	270	247
New England	5	11	0	.313	238	286
Indianapolis	4	12	0	.250	189	378

Central Division

	W	L	T	Pct.	Pts.	OP
Houston	12	4	0	.750	368	238
Pittsburgh*	9	7	0	.563	308	281
Cleveland	7	9	0	.438	304	307
Cincinnati	3	13	0	.188	187	319

Western Division

	W	L	T	Pct.	Pts.	OP
Kansas City	11	5	0	.688	328	291
L.A. Raiders*	10	6	0	.625	306	326
Denver*	9	7	0	.563	373	284
San Diego	8	8	0	.500	322	290
Seattle	6	10	0	.375	280	314

NATIONAL CONFERENCE

Eastern Division

	W	L	T	Pct.	Pts.	OP
Dallas#	12	4	0	.750	376	229
N.Y. Giants*	11	5	0	.688	288	205
Philadelphia	8	8	0	.500	293	315
Phoenix	7	9	0	.438	326	269
Washington	4	12	0	.250	230	345

Central Division

	W	L	T	Pct.	Pts.	OP
Detroit	10	6	0	.625	298	292
Minnesota*	9	7	0	.563	277	290
Green Bay*	9	7	0	.563	340	282
Chicago	7	9	0	.438	234	230
Tampa Bay	5	11	0	.313	237	376

Western Division

	W	L	T	Pct.	Pts.	OP
San Francisco	10	6	0	.625	473	295
New Orleans	8	8	0	.500	317	343
Atlanta	6	10	0	.375	316	385
L.A. Rams	5	11	0	.313	221	367

**Wild-Card qualifier for playoffs; #Top playoff seed in conference*

Buffalo was top playoff seed based on head-to-head victory over Houston (1-0). Denver was second Wild Card, and Pittsburgh was third Wild Card ahead of Miami, based on better conference record (8-4 to Steelers' 7-5 to Dolphins' 6-6). San Francisco was second playoff seed based on head-to-head victory over Detroit (1-0). Minnesota finished ahead of Green Bay based on head-to-head sweep (2-0).

Wild-Card playoffs: KANSAS CITY 27, Pittsburgh 24 (OT); L.A. RAIDERS 42, Denver 24

Divisional playoffs: BUFFALO 29, L.A. Raiders 23; Kansas City 28, HOUSTON 20

AFC Championship: BUFFALO 30, Kansas City 13

Wild-Card playoffs: Green Bay 28, DETROIT 24; N.Y. GIANTS 17, Minnesota 10

Divisional playoffs: SAN FRANCISCO 44, N.Y. Giants 3; DALLAS 27, Green Bay 17

NFC Championship: DALLAS 38, San Francisco 21

Super Bowl XXVIII: Dallas (NFC) 30, Buffalo (AFC) 13, at Georgia Dome, Atlanta, Georgia

Playoff Seeds

AFC	NFC
1. Buffalo	**1. Dallas**
2. Houston	2. San Francisco
3. Kansas City	3. Detroit
4. L.A. Raiders	4. N.Y. Giants
5. Denver	5. Minnesota
6. Pittsburgh	6. Green Bay

1992

AMERICAN CONFERENCE

Eastern Division

	W	L	T	Pct.	Pts.	OP
Miami	11	5	0	.688	340	281
Buffalo*	11	5	0	.688	381	283
Indianapolis	9	7	0	.563	216	302
N.Y. Jets	4	12	0	.250	220	315
New England	2	14	0	.125	205	363

Central Division

	W	L	T	Pct.	Pts.	OP
Pittsburgh#	11	5	0	.688	299	225
Houston*	10	6	0	.625	352	258
Cleveland	7	9	0	.438	272	275
Cincinnati	5	11	0	.313	274	364

Western Division

	W	L	T	Pct.	Pts.	OP
San Diego	11	5	0	.688	335	241
Kansas City*	10	6	0	.625	348	282
Denver	8	8	0	.500	262	329
L.A. Raiders	7	9	0	.438	249	281
Seattle	2	14	0	.125	140	312

NATIONAL CONFERENCE

Eastern Division

	W	L	T	Pct.	Pts.	OP
Dallas	13	3	0	.813	409	243
Philadelphia*	11	5	0	.688	354	245
Washington*	9	7	0	.563	300	255
N.Y. Giants	6	10	0	.375	306	367
Phoenix	4	12	0	.250	243	332

Central Division

	W	L	T	Pct.	Pts.	OP
Minnesota	11	5	0	.688	374	249
Green Bay	9	7	0	.563	276	296
Tampa Bay	5	11	0	.313	267	365
Chicago	5	11	0	.313	295	361
Detroit	5	11	0	.313	273	332

Western Division

	W	L	T	Pct.	Pts.	OP
San Francisco#	14	2	0	.875	431	236
New Orleans*	12	4	0	.750	330	202
Atlanta	6	10	0	.375	327	414
L.A. Rams	6	10	0	.375	313	383

**Wild-Card qualifier for playoffs; #Top playoff seed in conference*

Pittsburgh was top playoff seed, and Miami was second playoff seed ahead of San Diego, based on conference record (10-2 to Dolphins' 9-3 to Chargers' 9-5). Miami finished ahead of Buffalo based on better conference record (9-3 to Bills' 7-5). Houston was second Wild Card based on head-to-head victory over Kansas City (1-0). Washington was third Wild Card based on better conference record than Green Bay (7-5 to Packers' 6-6). Tampa Bay finished ahead of Chicago and Detroit based on better conference record (5-9 to Bears' 4-8 and Lions' 3-9). Atlanta finished ahead of L.A. Rams based on better record against common opponents (5-7 to Rams' 4-8).

Wild-Card playoffs: SAN DIEGO 17, Kansas City 0; BUFFALO 41, Houston 38 (OT)

Divisional playoffs: Buffalo 24, PITTSBURGH 3; MIAMI 31, San Diego 0

AFC Championship: Buffalo 29, MIAMI 10

Wild-Card playoffs: Washington 24, MINNESOTA 7; Philadelphia 36, NEW ORLEANS 20

Divisional playoffs: SAN FRANCISCO 20, Washington 13; DALLAS 34, Philadelphia 10

NFC Championship: Dallas 30, SAN FRANCISCO 20

Super Bowl XXVII: Dallas (NFC) 52, Buffalo (AFC) 17, at Rose Bowl, Pasadena, California

Playoff Seeds

AFC	NFC
1. Pittsburgh	1. San Francisco
2. Miami	**2. Dallas**
3. San Diego	3. Minnesota
4. Buffalo	4. New Orleans
5. Houston	5. Philadelphia
6. Kansas City	6. Washington

PAST STANDINGS

1991

AMERICAN CONFERENCE

Eastern Division

	W	L	T	Pct.	Pts.	OP
Buffalo#	13	3	0	.813	458	318
N.Y. Jets*	8	8	0	.500	314	293
Miami	8	8	0	.500	343	349
New England	6	10	0	.375	211	305
Indianapolis	1	15	0	.063	143	381

Central Division

	W	L	T	Pct.	Pts.	OP
Houston	11	5	0	.688	386	251
Pittsburgh	7	9	0	.438	292	344
Cleveland	6	10	0	.375	293	298
Cincinnati	3	13	0	.188	263	435

Western Division

	W	L	T	Pct.	Pts.	OP
Denver	12	4	0	.750	304	235
Kansas City*	10	6	0	.625	322	252
L.A. Raiders*	9	7	0	.563	298	297
Seattle	7	9	0	.438	276	261
San Diego	4	12	0	.250	274	342

NATIONAL CONFERENCE

Eastern Division

	W	L	T	Pct.	Pts.	OP
Washington#	14	2	0	.875	485	224
Dallas*	11	5	0	.688	342	310
Philadelphia	10	6	0	.625	285	244
N.Y. Giants	8	8	0	.500	281	297
Phoenix	4	12	0	.250	196	344

Central Division

	W	L	T	Pct.	Pts.	OP
Detroit	12	4	0	.750	339	295
Chicago*	11	5	0	.688	299	269
Minnesota	8	8	0	.500	301	306
Green Bay	4	12	0	.250	273	313
Tampa Bay	3	13	0	.188	199	365

Western Division

	W	L	T	Pct.	Pts.	OP
New Orleans	11	5	0	.688	341	211
Atlanta*	10	6	0	.625	361	338
San Francisco	10	6	0	.625	393	239
L.A. Rams	3	13	0	.188	234	390

**Wild-Card qualifier for playoffs; #Top playoff seed in conference*

N.Y. Jets finished ahead of Miami based on head-to-head sweep (2-0). Chicago was first Wild Card based on better conference record than Dallas (9-3 to Cowboys' 8-4). Atlanta finished ahead of San Francisco based on head-to-head sweep (2-0), and was third Wild Card ahead of Philadelphia based on better conference record (7-5 to Eagles' 6-6).

Wild-Card playoffs: KANSAS CITY 10, L.A. Raiders 6; HOUSTON 17, N.Y. Jets 10

Divisional playoffs: DENVER 26, Houston 24; BUFFALO 37, Kansas City 14

AFC Championship: BUFFALO 10, Denver 7

Wild-Card playoffs: Atlanta 27, NEW ORLEANS 20; Dallas 17, CHICAGO 13

Divisional playoffs: WASHINGTON 24, Atlanta 7; DETROIT 38, Dallas 6

NFC Championship: WASHINGTON 41, Detroit 10

Super Bowl XXVI: Washington (NFC) 37, Buffalo (AFC) 24, at Hubert H. Humphrey Metrodome, Minneapolis, Minnesota

Playoff Seeds

AFC

1. Buffalo
2. Denver
3. Houston
4. Kansas City
5. L.A. Raiders
6. N.Y. Jets

NFC

1. Washington
2. Detroit
3. New Orleans
4. Chicago
5. Dallas
6. Atlanta

1990

AMERICAN CONFERENCE

Eastern Division

	W	L	T	Pct.	Pts.	OP
Buffalo#	13	3	0	.813	428	263
Miami*	12	4	0	.750	336	242
Indianapolis	7	9	0	.438	281	353
N.Y. Jets	6	10	0	.375	295	345
New England	1	15	0	.063	181	446

Central Division

	W	L	T	Pct.	Pts.	OP
Cincinnati	9	7	0	.563	360	352
Houston*	9	7	0	.563	405	307
Pittsburgh	9	7	0	.563	292	240
Cleveland	3	13	0	.188	228	462

Western Division

	W	L	T	Pct.	Pts.	OP
L.A. Raiders	12	4	0	.750	337	268
Kansas City*	11	5	0	.688	369	257
Seattle	9	7	0	.563	306	286
San Diego	6	10	0	.375	315	281
Denver	5	11	0	.313	331	374

NATIONAL CONFERENCE

Eastern Division

	W	L	T	Pct.	Pts.	OP
N.Y. Giants	13	3	0	.813	335	211
Philadelphia*	10	6	0	.625	396	299
Washington*	10	6	0	.625	381	301
Dallas	7	9	0	.438	244	308
Phoenix	5	11	0	.313	268	396

Central Division

	W	L	T	Pct.	Pts.	OP
Chicago	11	5	0	.688	348	280
Tampa Bay	6	10	0	.375	264	367
Detroit	6	10	0	.375	373	413
Green Bay	6	10	0	.375	271	347
Minnesota	6	10	0	.375	351	326

Western Division

	W	L	T	Pct.	Pts.	OP
San Francisco#	14	2	0	.875	353	239
New Orleans*	8	8	0	.500	274	275
L.A. Rams	5	11	0	.313	345	412
Atlanta	5	11	0	.313	348	365

**Wild-Card qualifier for playoffs; #Top playoff seed in conference*

Cincinnati finished ahead of Houston and Pittsburgh based on best head-to-head record (3-1 to Oilers' 2-2 to Steelers' 1-3). Houston was Wild Card based on better conference record (8-4) than Seattle (7-5) and Pittsburgh (6-6). Philadelphia finished ahead of Washington based on better division record (5-3 to Redskins' 4-4). Tampa Bay was second in NFC Central based on best head-to-head record (5-1) against Detroit (2-4), Green Bay (3-3), and Minnesota (2-4). Detroit finished third based on best net division points (minus 8) against Green Bay (minus 40). Green Bay finished ahead of Minnesota based on better conference record (5-7 to Vikings' 4-8). The L.A. Rams finished ahead of Atlanta based on net points in division (plus 1 to Falcons' minus 31).

Wild-Card playoffs: MIAMI 17, Kansas City 16; CINCINNATI 41, Houston 14

Divisional playoffs: BUFFALO 44, Miami 34; L.A. RAIDERS 20, Cincinnati 10

AFC Championship: BUFFALO 51, L.A. Raiders 3

Wild-Card playoffs: Washington 20, PHILADELPHIA 6; CHICAGO 16, New Orleans 6

Divisional playoffs: SAN FRANCISCO 28, Washington 10; N.Y. GIANTS 31, Chicago 3

NFC Championship: N.Y. Giants 15, SAN FRANCISCO 13

Super Bowl XXV: N.Y. Giants (NFC) 20, Buffalo (AFC) 19, at Tampa Stadium, Tampa, Florida

Playoff Seeds

AFC

1. Buffalo
2. L.A. Raiders
3. Cincinnati
4. Miami
5. Kansas City
6. Houston

NFC

1. San Francisco
2. N.Y. Giants
3. Chicago
4. Philadelphia
5. Washington
6. New Orleans

1989

AMERICAN CONFERENCE

Eastern Division

	W	L	T	Pct.	Pts.	OP
Buffalo	9	7	0	.563	409	317
Indianapolis	8	8	0	.500	298	301
Miami	8	8	0	.500	331	379
New England	5	11	0	.313	297	391
N.Y. Jets	4	12	0	.250	253	411

Central Division

	W	L	T	Pct.	Pts.	OP
Cleveland	9	6	1	.594	334	254
Houston*	9	7	0	.563	365	412
Pittsburgh*	9	7	0	.563	265	326
Cincinnati	8	8	0	.500	404	285

Western Division

	W	L	T	Pct.	Pts.	OP
Denver#	11	5	0	.688	362	226
Kansas City	8	7	1	.531	318	286
L.A. Raiders	8	8	0	.500	315	297
Seattle	7	9	0	.438	241	327
San Diego	6	10	0	.375	266	290

NATIONAL CONFERENCE

Eastern Division

	W	L	T	Pct.	Pts.	OP
N.Y. Giants	12	4	0	.750	348	252
Philadelphia*	11	5	0	.688	342	274
Washington	10	6	0	.625	386	308
Phoenix	5	11	0	.313	258	377
Dallas	1	15	0	.063	204	393

Central Division

	W	L	T	Pct.	Pts.	OP
Minnesota	10	6	0	.625	351	275
Green Bay	10	6	0	.625	362	356
Detroit	7	9	0	.438	312	364
Chicago	6	10	0	.375	358	377
Tampa Bay	5	11	0	.313	320	419

Western Division

	W	L	T	Pct.	Pts.	OP
San Francisco#	14	2	0	.875	442	253
L.A. Rams*	11	5	0	.688	426	344
New Orleans	9	7	0	.563	386	301
Atlanta	3	13	0	.188	279	437

**Wild-Card qualifier for playoffs; #Top playoff seed in conference*

Indianapolis finished ahead of Miami based on better conference record (7-5 vs. Dolphins' 6-8). Houston finished ahead of Pittsburgh based on head-to-head sweep (2-0). The L.A. Rams did not play San Francisco in the divisional playoffs because, from 1970-1989, two teams from the same division could not meet prior to the conference championship game. Philadelphia was first Wild Card ahead of L.A. Rams based on better record against common opponents (6-3 to Rams' 5-4). Minnesota finished ahead of Green Bay based on better division record (6-2 vs. Packers' 5-3).

Wild-Card playoff: Pittsburgh 26, HOUSTON 23 (OT)
Divisional playoffs: CLEVELAND 34, Buffalo 30; DENVER 24, Pittsburgh 23
AFC Championship: DENVER 37, Cleveland 21
Wild-Card playoff: L.A. Rams 21, PHILADELPHIA 7
Divisional playoffs: L.A. Rams 19, N.Y. GIANTS 13 (OT); SAN FRANCISCO 41, Minnesota 13
NFC Championship: SAN FRANCISCO 30, L.A. Rams 3
Super Bowl XXIV: San Francisco (NFC) 55, Denver (AFC) 10, at Louisiana Superdome, New Orleans, Louisiana

1988

AMERICAN CONFERENCE

Eastern Division

	W	L	T	Pct.	Pts.	OP
Buffalo	12	4	0	.750	329	237
Indianapolis	9	7	0	.563	354	315
New England	9	7	0	.563	250	284
N.Y. Jets	8	7	1	.531	372	354
Miami	6	10	0	.375	319	380

Central Division

	W	L	T	Pct.	Pts.	OP
Cincinnati#	12	4	0	.750	448	329
Cleveland*	10	6	0	.625	304	288
Houston*	10	6	0	.625	424	365
Pittsburgh	5	11	0	.313	336	421

Western Division

	W	L	T	Pct.	Pts.	OP
Seattle	9	7	0	.563	339	329
Denver	8	8	0	.500	327	352
L.A. Raiders	7	9	0	.438	325	369
San Diego	6	10	0	.375	231	332
Kansas City	4	11	1	.281	254	320

NATIONAL CONFERENCE

Eastern Division

	W	L	T	Pct.	Pts.	OP
Philadelphia	10	6	0	.625	379	319
N.Y. Giants	10	6	0	.625	359	304
Washington	7	9	0	.438	345	387
Phoenix	7	9	0	.438	344	398
Dallas	3	13	0	.188	265	381

Central Division

	W	L	T	Pct.	Pts.	OP
Chicago#	12	4	0	.750	312	215
Minnesota*	11	5	0	.688	406	233
Tampa Bay	5	11	0	.313	261	350
Detroit	4	12	0	.250	220	313
Green Bay	4	12	0	.250	240	315

Western Division

	W	L	T	Pct.	Pts.	OP
San Francisco	10	6	0	.625	369	294
L.A. Rams*	10	6	0	.625	407	293
New Orleans	10	6	0	.625	312	283
Atlanta	5	11	0	.313	244	315

**Wild-Card qualifier for playoffs; #Top playoff seed in conference*

Cincinnati was top playoff seed ahead of Buffalo based on head-to-head victory (1-0). Indianapolis finished ahead of New England based on better record against common opponents (7-5 to Patriots' 6-6). Cleveland finished ahead of Houston based on better division record (4-2 to Oilers' 3-3). Houston did not play Cincinnati, and Minnesota did not play Chicago in the divisional playoffs because, from 1970-1989, two teams from the same division could not meet prior to the conference championship game. Philadelphia finished first in NFC East based on head-to-head sweep of N.Y. Giants (2-0). Washington finished third in NFC East based on better division record (4-4) than Phoenix (3-5). Detroit finished fourth in NFC Central based on head-to-head sweep of Green Bay (2-0). San Francisco finished first in NFC West based on better head-to-head record (3-1) against L.A. Rams (2-2) and New Orleans (1-3). L.A. Rams finished second in NFC West based on better division record (4-2) than New Orleans (3-3) and earned Wild-Card position based on better conference record (8-4) than N.Y. Giants (9-5) and New Orleans (6-6).

Wild-Card playoff: Houston 24, CLEVELAND 23
Divisional playoffs: CINCINNATI 21, Seattle 13; BUFFALO 17, Houston 10
AFC Championship: CINCINNATI 21, Buffalo 10
Wild-Card playoff: MINNESOTA 28, L.A. Rams 17
Divisional playoffs: CHICAGO 20, Philadelphia 12; SAN FRANCISCO 34, Minnesota 9
NFC Championship: San Francisco 28, CHICAGO 3
Super Bowl XXIII: San Francisco (NFC) 20, Cincinnati (AFC) 16, at Joe Robbie Stadium, Miami, Florida

PAST STANDINGS

1987

AMERICAN CONFERENCE

Eastern Division

	W	L	T	Pct.	Pts.	OP
Indianapolis	9	6	0	.600	300	238
New England	8	7	0	.533	320	293
Miami	8	7	0	.533	362	335
Buffalo	7	8	0	.467	270	305
N.Y. Jets	6	9	0	.400	334	360

Central Division

	W	L	T	Pct.	Pts.	OP
Cleveland	10	5	0	.667	390	239
Houston*	9	6	0	.600	345	349
Pittsburgh	8	7	0	.533	285	299
Cincinnati	4	11	0	.267	285	370

Western Division

	W	L	T	Pct.	Pts.	OP
Denver#	10	4	1	.700	379	288
Seattle*	9	6	0	.600	371	314
San Diego	8	7	0	.533	253	317
L.A. Raiders	5	10	0	.333	301	289
Kansas City	4	11	0	.267	273	388

NATIONAL CONFERENCE

Eastern Division

	W	L	T	Pct.	Pts.	OP
Washington	11	4	0	.733	379	285
Dallas	7	8	0	.467	340	348
St. Louis	7	8	0	.467	362	368
Philadelphia	7	8	0	.467	337	380
N.Y. Giants	6	9	0	.400	280	312

Central Division

	W	L	T	Pct.	Pts.	OP
Chicago	11	4	0	.733	356	282
Minnesota*	8	7	0	.533	336	335
Green Bay	5	9	1	.367	255	300
Tampa Bay	4	11	0	.267	286	360
Detroit	4	11	0	.267	269	384

Western Division

	W	L	T	Pct.	Pts.	OP
San Francisco#	13	2	0	.867	459	253
New Orleans*	12	3	0	.800	422	283
L.A. Rams	6	9	0	.400	317	361
Atlanta	3	12	0	.200	205	436

**Wild-Card qualifier for playoffs; #Top playoff seed in conference*

New England finished ahead of Miami based on head-to-head sweep (2-0). Houston was first Wild Card ahead of Seattle based on better conference record (7-4 to Seahawks' 5-6). Chicago was second playoff seed ahead of Washington based on better conference record (9-2 to Redskins' 9-3). Dallas finished ahead of St. Louis and Philadelphia based on better division record (4-4 to Cardinals' 3-5 and Eagles' 3-5). St. Louis finished ahead of Philadelphia based on better conference record (7-7 to Eagles' 4-7). Tampa Bay finished ahead of Detroit based on better division record (3-4 to Lions' 2-5).

Wild-Card playoff: HOUSTON 23, Seattle 20 (OT)

Divisional playoffs: CLEVELAND 38, Indianapolis 21; DENVER 34, Houston 10

AFC Championship: DENVER 38, Cleveland 33

Wild-Card playoff: Minnesota 44, NEW ORLEANS 10

Divisional playoffs: Minnesota 36, SAN FRANCISCO 24; Washington 21, CHICAGO 17

NFC Championship: WASHINGTON 17, Minnesota 10

Super Bowl XXII: Washington (NFC) 42, Denver (AFC) 10, at San Diego Jack Murphy Stadium, San Diego, California

Note: 1987 regular season was reduced from 16 to 15 games for each team due to players' strike.

1986

AMERICAN CONFERENCE

Eastern Division

	W	L	T	Pct.	Pts.	OP
New England	11	5	0	.688	412	307
N.Y. Jets*	10	6	0	.625	364	386
Miami	8	8	0	.500	430	405
Buffalo	4	12	0	.250	287	348
Indianapolis	3	13	0	.188	229	400

Central Division

	W	L	T	Pct.	Pts.	OP
Cleveland#	12	4	0	.750	391	310
Cincinnati	10	6	0	.625	409	394
Pittsburgh	6	10	0	.375	307	336
Houston	5	11	0	.313	274	329

Western Division

	W	L	T	Pct.	Pts.	OP
Denver	11	5	0	.688	378	327
Kansas City*	10	6	0	.625	358	326
Seattle	10	6	0	.625	366	293
L.A. Raiders	8	8	0	.500	323	346
San Diego	4	12	0	.250	335	396

NATIONAL CONFERENCE

Eastern Division

	W	L	T	Pct.	Pts.	OP
N.Y. Giants#	14	2	0	.875	371	236
Washington*	12	4	0	.750	368	296
Dallas	7	9	0	.438	346	337
Philadelphia	5	10	1	.344	256	312
St. Louis	4	11	1	.281	218	351

Central Division

	W	L	T	Pct.	Pts.	OP
Chicago	14	2	0	.875	352	187
Minnesota	9	7	0	.563	398	273
Detroit	5	11	0	.313	277	326
Green Bay	4	12	0	.250	254	418
Tampa Bay	2	14	0	.125	239	473

Western Division

	W	L	T	Pct.	Pts.	OP
San Francisco	10	5	1	.656	374	247
L.A. Rams*	10	6	0	.625	309	267
Atlanta	7	8	1	.469	280	280
New Orleans	7	9	0	.438	288	287

**Wild-Card qualifier for playoffs; #Top playoff seed in conference*

Denver was second playoff seed ahead of New England based on head-to-head victory (1-0). N.Y. Jets were first Wild Card based on better conference record (8-4) than Kansas City (9-5), Seattle (7-5), and Cincinnati (7-5). Kansas City was second Wild Card based on better conference record (9-5) than Seattle (7-5) and Cincinnati (7-5). N.Y. Giants were top playoff seed based on better conference record than Chicago (11-1 to Bears' 10-2). Washington did not play the N.Y. Giants in the divisional playoffs because, from 1970-1989, two teams from the same division could not meet prior to the conference championship game.

Wild-Card playoff: N.Y. JETS 35, Kansas City 15

Divisional playoffs: CLEVELAND 23, N.Y. Jets 20 (OT); DENVER 22, New England 17

AFC Championship: Denver 23, CLEVELAND 20 (OT)

Wild-Card playoff: WASHINGTON 19, L.A. Rams 7

Divisional playoffs: Washington 27, CHICAGO 13 N.Y. GIANTS 49, San Francisco 3

NFC Championship: N.Y. GIANTS 17, Washington 0

Super Bowl XXI: N.Y. Giants (NFC) 39, Denver (AFC) 20, at Rose Bowl, Pasadena, California

1985

AMERICAN CONFERENCE

Eastern Division

	W	L	T	Pct.	Pts.	OP
Miami	12	4	0	.750	428	320
N.Y. Jets*	11	5	0	.688	393	264
New England*	11	5	0	.688	362	290
Indianapolis	5	11	0	.313	320	386
Buffalo	2	14	0	.125	200	381

Central Division

	W	L	T	Pct.	Pts.	OP
Cleveland	8	8	0	.500	287	294
Cincinnati	7	9	0	.438	441	437
Pittsburgh	7	9	0	.438	379	355
Houston	5	11	0	.313	284	412

Western Division

	W	L	T	Pct.	Pts.	OP
L.A. Raiders#	12	4	0	.750	354	308
Denver	11	5	0	.688	380	329
Seattle	8	8	0	.500	349	303
San Diego	8	8	0	.500	467	435
Kansas City	6	10	0	.375	317	360

NATIONAL CONFERENCE

Eastern Division

	W	L	T	Pct.	Pts.	OP
Dallas	10	6	0	.625	357	333
N.Y. Giants*	10	6	0	.625	399	283
Washington	10	6	0	.625	297	312
Philadelphia	7	9	0	.438	286	310
St. Louis	5	11	0	.313	278	414

Central Division

	W	L	T	Pct.	Pts.	OP
Chicago#	15	1	0	.938	456	198
Green Bay	8	8	0	.500	337	355
Minnesota	7	9	0	.438	346	359
Detroit	7	9	0	.438	307	366
Tampa Bay	2	14	0	.125	294	448

Western Division

	W	L	T	Pct.	Pts.	OP
L.A. Rams	11	5	0	.688	340	277
San Francisco*	10	6	0	.625	411	263
New Orleans	5	11	0	.313	294	401
Atlanta	4	12	0	.250	282	452

**Wild-Card qualifier for playoffs; #Top playoff seed in conference*

L.A. Raiders were top playoff seed ahead of Miami based on better record against common opponents (5-1 to 4-2). N.Y. Jets were first Wild Card based on better conference record (9-3) than New England (8-4) and Denver (8-4). New England was second Wild Card ahead of Denver based on better record against common opponents (4-2 to Broncos' 3-3). Cincinnati finished ahead of Pittsburgh based on head-to-head sweep (2-0). Seattle finished ahead of San Diego based on head-to-head sweep (2-0). Dallas finished ahead of N.Y. Giants and Washington based on better head-to-head record (4-0 to Giants' 1-3 and Redskins' 1-3). N.Y. Giants were first Wild Card based on better conference record (8-4) than San Francisco (7-5) and Washington (6-6). San Francisco was second Wild Card based on head-to-head victory over Washington (1-0). Minnesota finished ahead of Detroit based on better division record (3-5 to Lions' 2-6).

Wild-Card playoff: New England 26, N.Y. JETS 14
Divisional playoffs: MIAMI 24, Cleveland 21;
New England 27, L.A. RAIDERS 20
AFC Championship: New England 31, MIAMI 14
Wild-Card playoff: N.Y. GIANTS 17, San Francisco 3
Divisional playoffs: L.A. RAMS 20, Dallas 0;
CHICAGO 21, N.Y. Giants 0
NFC Championship: CHICAGO 24, L.A. Rams 0
Super Bowl XX: Chicago (NFC) 46, New England (AFC) 10,
at Louisiana Superdome, New Orleans, Louisiana

1984

AMERICAN CONFERENCE

Eastern Division

	W	L	T	Pct.	Pts.	OP
Miami#	14	2	0	.875	513	298
New England	9	7	0	.563	362	352
N.Y. Jets	7	9	0	.438	332	364
Indianapolis	4	12	0	.250	239	414
Buffalo	2	14	0	.125	250	454

Central Division

	W	L	T	Pct.	Pts.	OP
Pittsburgh	9	7	0	.563	387	310
Cincinnati	8	8	0	.500	339	339
Cleveland	5	11	0	.313	250	297
Houston	3	13	0	.188	240	437

Western Division

	W	L	T	Pct.	Pts.	OP
Denver	13	3	0	.813	353	241
Seattle*	12	4	0	.750	418	282
L.A. Raiders*	11	5	0	.688	368	278
Kansas City	8	8	0	.500	314	324
San Diego	7	9	0	.438	394	413

NATIONAL CONFERENCE

Eastern Division

	W	L	T	Pct.	Pts.	OP
Washington	11	5	0	.688	426	310
N.Y. Giants*	9	7	0	.563	299	301
St. Louis	9	7	0	.563	423	345
Dallas	9	7	0	.563	308	308
Philadelphia	6	9	1	.406	278	320

Central Division

	W	L	T	Pct.	Pts.	OP
Chicago	10	6	0	.625	325	248
Green Bay	8	8	0	.500	390	309
Tampa Bay	6	10	0	.375	335	380
Detroit	4	11	1	.281	283	408
Minnesota	3	13	0	.188	276	484

Western Division

	W	L	T	Pct.	Pts.	OP
San Francisco#	15	1	0	.938	475	227
L.A. Rams*	10	6	0	.625	346	316
New Orleans	7	9	0	.438	298	361
Atlanta	4	12	0	.250	281	382

**Wild-Card qualifier for playoffs; #Top playoff seed in conference*

N.Y. Giants finished ahead of St. Louis and Dallas based on best head-to-head record (3-1 to Cardinals' 2-2 and Cowboys' 1-3). St. Louis finished ahead of Dallas based on better division record (5-3 to Cowboys' 3-5).

Wild-Card playoff: SEATTLE 13, L.A. Raiders 7
Divisional playoffs: MIAMI 31, Seattle 10;
Pittsburgh 24, DENVER 17
AFC Championship: MIAMI 45, Pittsburgh 28
Wild-Card playoff: N.Y. Giants 16, L.A. RAMS 13
Divisional playoffs: SAN FRANCISCO 21, N.Y. Giants 10;
Chicago 23, WASHINGTON 19
NFC Championship: SAN FRANCISCO 23, Chicago 0
Super Bowl XIX: San Francisco (NFC) 38, Miami (AFC) 16,
at Stanford Stadium, Stanford, California

1983

AMERICAN CONFERENCE

Eastern Division

	W	L	T	Pct.	Pts.	OP
Miami	12	4	0	.750	389	250
New England	8	8	0	.500	274	289
Buffalo	8	8	0	.500	283	351
Baltimore	7	9	0	.438	264	354
N.Y. Jets	7	9	0	.438	313	331

Central Division

	W	L	T	Pct.	Pts.	OP
Pittsburgh	10	6	0	.625	355	303
Cleveland	9	7	0	.563	356	342
Cincinnati	7	9	0	.438	346	302
Houston	2	14	0	.125	288	460

Western Division

	W	L	T	Pct.	Pts.	OP
L.A. Raiders#	12	4	0	.750	442	338
Seattle*	9	7	0	.563	403	397
Denver*	9	7	0	.563	302	327
San Diego	6	10	0	.375	358	462
Kansas City	6	10	0	.375	386	367

NATIONAL CONFERENCE

Eastern Division

	W	L	T	Pct.	Pts.	OP
Washington#	14	2	0	.875	541	332
Dallas*	12	4	0	.750	479	360
St. Louis	8	7	1	.531	374	428
Philadelphia	5	11	0	.313	233	322
N.Y. Giants	3	12	1	.219	267	347

Central Division

	W	L	T	Pct.	Pts.	OP
Detroit	9	7	0	.563	347	286
Green Bay	8	8	0	.500	429	439
Chicago	8	8	0	.500	311	301
Minnesota	8	8	0	.500	316	348
Tampa Bay	2	14	0	.125	241	380

Western Division

	W	L	T	Pct.	Pts.	OP
San Francisco	10	6	0	.625	432	293
L.A. Rams*	9	7	0	.563	361	344
New Orleans	8	8	0	.500	319	337
Atlanta	7	9	0	.438	370	389

**Wild-Card qualifier for playoffs; #Top playoff seed in conference*

L.A. Raiders were top playoff seed ahead of Miami based on head-to-head victory (1-0). Seattle was second Wild Card ahead of Denver based on better division record (5-3 to Broncos' 3-5) after Cleveland was eliminated from three-way tie based on head-to-head record (Seattle and Denver 2-1 to Browns' 0-2). Seattle did not play the L.A. Raiders in the divisional playoffs because, from 1970-1989, two teams from the same division could not meet prior to the conference championship game. New England finished ahead of Buffalo based on head-to-head sweep (2-0). Baltimore finished ahead of N.Y. Jets based on better conference record (5-9 to Jets' 4-8). San Diego finished ahead of Kansas City based on head-to-head sweep (2-0). Green Bay finished ahead of Chicago based on better record against common opponents (5-5 to Bears' 4-6) after Minnesota was eliminated from three-way tie based on conference record (Chicago 7-7 and Green Bay 6-6 to Vikings' 4-8).

Wild-Card playoff: SEATTLE 31, Denver 7
Divisional playoffs: Seattle 27, MIAMI 20;
L.A. RAIDERS 38, Pittsburgh 10
AFC Championship: L.A. RAIDERS 30, Seattle 14
Wild-Card playoff: L.A. Rams 24, DALLAS 17
Divisional playoffs: SAN FRANCISCO 24, Detroit 23;
WASHINGTON 51, L.A. Rams 7
NFC Championship: WASHINGTON 24, San Francisco 21
Super Bowl XVIII: L.A. Raiders (AFC) 38, Washington (NFC) 9, at Tampa Stadium, Tampa, Florida

1982

AMERICAN CONFERENCE

	W	L	T	Pct.	Pts.	OP
L.A. Raiders#	8	1	0	.889	260	200
Miami	7	2	0	.778	198	131
Cincinnati	7	2	0	.778	232	177
Pittsburgh	6	3	0	.667	204	146
San Diego	6	3	0	.667	288	221
N.Y. Jets	6	3	0	.667	245	166
New England	5	4	0	.556	143	157
Cleveland	4	5	0	.444	140	182
Buffalo	4	5	0	.444	150	154
Seattle	4	5	0	.444	127	147
Kansas City	3	6	0	.333	176	184
Denver	2	7	0	.222	148	226
Houston	1	8	0	.111	136	245
Baltimore	0	8	1	.056	113	236

NATIONAL CONFERENCE

	W	L	T	Pct.	Pts.	OP
Washington#	8	1	0	.889	190	128
Dallas	6	3	0	.667	226	145
Green Bay	5	3	1	.611	226	169
Minnesota	5	4	0	.556	187	198
Atlanta	5	4	0	.556	183	199
St. Louis	5	4	0	.556	135	170
Tampa Bay	5	4	0	.556	158	178
Detroit	4	5	0	.444	181	176
New Orleans	4	5	0	.444	129	160
N.Y. Giants	4	5	0	.444	164	160
San Francisco	3	6	0	.333	209	206
Chicago	3	6	0	.333	141	174
Philadelphia	3	6	0	.333	191	195
L.A. Rams	2	7	0	.222	200	250

As the result of a 57-day players' strike, the 1982 NFL regular season schedule was reduced from 16 weeks to 9. At the conclusion of the regular season, the NFL conducted a 16-team postseason Super Bowl Tournament. Eight teams from each conference were seeded 1-8 based on their records during the season.

#Top playoff seed in conference

Miami finished ahead of Cincinnati based on better conference record (6-1 to Bengals' 6-2). Pittsburgh finished ahead of San Diego based on better record against common opponents (3-1 to Chargers' 2-1) after N.Y. Jets were eliminated from three-way tie based on conference record (Pittsburgh and San Diego 5-3 to Jets' 2-3). Cleveland finished ahead of Buffalo and Seattle based on better conference record (4-3 to Bills' 3-3 to Seahawks' 3-5). Buffalo finished ahead of Seattle based on better conference record (3-3 to Seahawks' 3-5). Minnesota (4-1), Atlanta (4-3), St. Louis (5-4), Tampa Bay (3-3) seeds were determined by best won-lost record in conference games. Detroit finished ahead of New Orleans and the N.Y. Giants based on best conference record (4-4 to Saints' 3-5 to Giants' 3-5). San Francisco finished ahead of Chicago, and Chicago finished ahead of Philadelphia, based on conference record (49ers' 2-3 to Bears' 2-5 to Eagles' 1-5).

First round playoff: MIAMI 28, New England 13;
L.A. RAIDERS 27, Cleveland 10;
N.Y. Jets 44, CINCINNATI 17;
San Diego 31, PITTSBURGH 28
Second round playoff: N.Y. Jets 17, L.A. RAIDERS 14;
MIAMI 34, San Diego 13
AFC Championship: MIAMI 14, N.Y. Jets 0
First round playoff: WASHINGTON 31, Detroit 7;
GREEN BAY 41, St. Louis 16;
MINNESOTA 30, Atlanta 24;
DALLAS 30, Tampa Bay 17
Second round playoff: WASHINGTON 21, Minnesota 7;
DALLAS 37, Green Bay 26
NFC Championship: WASHINGTON 31, Dallas 17
Super Bowl XVII: Washington (NFC) 27, Miami (AFC) 17, at Rose Bowl, Pasadena, California

1981

AMERICAN CONFERENCE

Eastern Division

	W	L	T	Pct.	Pts.	OP
Miami	11	4	1	.719	345	275
N.Y. Jets*	10	5	1	.656	355	287
Buffalo*	10	6	0	.625	311	276
Baltimore	2	14	0	.125	259	533
New England	2	14	0	.125	322	370

Central Division

	W	L	T	Pct.	Pts.	OP
Cincinnati#	12	4	0	.750	421	304
Pittsburgh	8	8	0	.500	356	297
Houston	7	9	0	.438	281	355
Cleveland	5	11	0	.313	276	375

Western Division

	W	L	T	Pct.	Pts.	OP
San Diego	10	6	0	.625	478	390
Denver	10	6	0	.625	321	289
Kansas City	9	7	0	.563	343	290
Oakland	7	9	0	.438	273	343
Seattle	6	10	0	.375	322	388

NATIONAL CONFERENCE

Eastern Division

	W	L	T	Pct.	Pts.	OP
Dallas	12	4	0	.750	367	277
Philadelphia*	10	6	0	.625	368	221
N.Y. Giants*	9	7	0	.563	295	257
Washington	8	8	0	.500	347	349
St. Louis	7	9	0	.438	315	408

Central Division

	W	L	T	Pct.	Pts.	OP
Tampa Bay	9	7	0	.563	315	268
Detroit	8	8	0	.500	397	322
Green Bay	8	8	0	.500	324	361
Minnesota	7	9	0	.438	325	369
Chicago	6	10	0	.375	253	324

Western Division

	W	L	T	Pct.	Pts.	OP
San Francisco#	13	3	0	.813	357	250
Atlanta	7	9	0	.438	426	355
Los Angeles	6	10	0	.375	303	351
New Orleans	4	12	0	.250	207	378

**Wild-Card qualifier for playoffs; #Top playoff seed in conference*

Baltimore finished ahead of New England based on head-to-head sweep (2-0). San Diego finished ahead of Denver based on better division record (6-2 to Broncos' 5-3). Buffalo was second Wild Card based on head-to-head victory over Denver (1-0). Detroit finished ahead of Green Bay based on better record against common opponents (5-5 to Packers' 4-6).

Wild-Card playoff: Buffalo 31, N.Y. JETS 27

Divisional playoffs: San Diego 41, MIAMI 38 (OT); CINCINNATI 28, Buffalo 21

AFC Championship: CINCINNATI 27, San Diego 7

Wild-Card playoff: N.Y. Giants 27, PHILADELPHIA 21

Divisional playoffs: DALLAS 38, Tampa Bay 0; SAN FRANCISCO 38, N.Y. Giants 24

NFC Championship: SAN FRANCISCO 28, Dallas 27

Super Bowl XVI: San Francisco (NFC) 26, Cincinnati (AFC) 21, at Silverdome, Pontiac, Michigan

1980

AMERICAN CONFERENCE

Eastern Division

	W	L	T	Pct.	Pts.	OP
Buffalo	11	5	0	.688	320	260
New England	10	6	0	.625	441	325
Miami	8	8	0	.500	266	305
Baltimore	7	9	0	.438	355	387
N.Y. Jets	4	12	0	.250	302	395

Central Division

	W	L	T	Pct.	Pts.	OP
Cleveland	11	5	0	.688	357	310
Houston*	11	5	0	.688	295	251
Pittsburgh	9	7	0	.563	352	313
Cincinnati	6	10	0	.375	244	312

Western Division

	W	L	T	Pct.	Pts.	OP
San Diego#	11	5	0	.688	418	327
Oakland*	11	5	0	.688	364	306
Kansas City	8	8	0	.500	319	336
Denver	8	8	0	.500	310	323
Seattle	4	12	0	.250	291	408

NATIONAL CONFERENCE

Eastern Division

	W	L	T	Pct.	Pts.	OP
Philadelphia	12	4	0	.750	384	222
Dallas*	12	4	0	.750	454	311
Washington	6	10	0	.375	261	293
St. Louis	5	11	0	.313	299	350
N.Y. Giants	4	12	0	.250	249	425

Central Division

	W	L	T	Pct.	Pts.	OP
Minnesota	9	7	0	.563	317	308
Detroit	9	7	0	.563	334	272
Chicago	7	9	0	.438	304	264
Tampa Bay	5	10	1	.344	271	341
Green Bay	5	10	1	.344	231	371

Western Division

	W	L	T	Pct.	Pts.	OP
Atlanta#	12	4	0	.750	405	272
Los Angeles*	11	5	0	.688	424	289
San Francisco	6	10	0	.375	320	415
New Orleans	1	15	0	.063	291	487

**Wild-Card qualifier for playoffs; #Top playoff seed in conference*

San Diego was top playoff seed based on better conference record than Cleveland and Buffalo (9-3 to Browns' 8-4 and Bills' 8-4). Cleveland was second playoff seed based on better record against common opponents (5-2 to Bills' 5-3). Cleveland finished ahead of Houston based on better conference record (8-4 to Oilers' 7-5). Oakland was first Wild Card based on better conference record than Houston (9-3 to Oilers' 7-5). San Diego finished ahead of Oakland based on better net points in division games (plus 60 net points to Raiders' plus 37). Oakland did not play San Diego in the divisional playoffs because, from 1970-1989, two teams from the same division could not meet prior to the conference championship game. Kansas City finished ahead of Denver based on head-to-head sweep (2-0). Atlanta was top playoff seed based on head-to-head victory over Philadelphia (1-0). Philadelphia finished ahead of Dallas based on better net points in division games (plus 84 net points to Cowboys' plus 50). Minnesota finished ahead of Detroit based on better conference record (8-4 to Lions' 9-5). Tampa Bay finished ahead of Green Bay based on better head-to-head record (1-0-1 to Packers' 0-1-1).

Wild-Card playoff: OAKLAND 27, Houston 7

Divisional playoffs: SAN DIEGO 20, Buffalo 14; Oakland 14, CLEVELAND 12

AFC Championship: Oakland 34, SAN DIEGO 27

Wild-Card playoff: DALLAS 34, Los Angeles 13

Divisional playoffs: PHILADELPHIA 31, Minnesota 16; Dallas 30, ATLANTA 27

NFC Championship: PHILADELPHIA 20, Dallas 7

Super Bowl XV: Oakland (AFC) 27, Philadelphia (NFC) 10, at Louisiana Superdome, New Orleans, Louisiana

1979

AMERICAN CONFERENCE

Eastern Division

	W	L	T	Pct.	Pts.	OP
Miami	10	6	0	.625	341	257
New England	9	7	0	.563	411	326
N.Y. Jets	8	8	0	.500	337	383
Buffalo	7	9	0	.438	268	279
Baltimore	5	11	0	.313	271	351

Central Division

	W	L	T	Pct.	Pts.	OP
Pittsburgh	12	4	0	.750	416	262
Houston*	11	5	0	.688	362	331
Cleveland	9	7	0	.563	359	352
Cincinnati	4	12	0	.250	337	421

Western Division

	W	L	T	Pct.	Pts.	OP
San Diego#	12	4	0	.750	411	246
Denver*	10	6	0	.625	289	262
Seattle	9	7	0	.563	378	372
Oakland	9	7	0	.563	365	337
Kansas City	7	9	0	.438	238	262

NATIONAL CONFERENCE

Eastern Division

	W	L	T	Pct.	Pts.	OP
Dallas#	11	5	0	.688	371	313
Philadelphia*	11	5	0	.688	339	282
Washington	10	6	0	.625	348	295
N.Y. Giants	6	10	0	.375	237	323
St. Louis	5	11	0	.313	307	358

Central Division

	W	L	T	Pct.	Pts.	OP
Tampa Bay	10	6	0	.625	273	237
Chicago*	10	6	0	.625	306	249
Minnesota	7	9	0	.438	259	337
Green Bay	5	11	0	.313	246	316
Detroit	2	14	0	.125	219	365

Western Division

	W	L	T	Pct.	Pts.	OP
Los Angeles	9	7	0	.563	323	309
New Orleans	8	8	0	.500	370	360
Atlanta	6	10	0	.375	300	388
San Francisco	2	14	0	.125	308	416

**Wild-Card qualifier for playoffs; #Top playoff seed in conference*

San Diego was top playoff seed based on head-to-head victory over Pittsburgh (1-0). Seattle finished ahead of Oakland based on head-to-head sweep (2-0). Dallas finished ahead of Philadelphia based on better conference record (10-2 to Eagles' 9-3). Philadelphia did not play Dallas in the divisional playoffs because, from 1970-1989, two teams from the same division could not meet prior to the conference championship game. Tampa Bay finished ahead of Chicago based on a better division record (6-2 to Bears' 5-3). Chicago was second Wild Card ahead of Washington based on better net points in all games (57 to Redskins' 53).

Wild-Card playoff: HOUSTON 13, Denver 7

Divisional playoffs: Houston 17, SAN DIEGO 14; PITTSBURGH 34, Miami 14

AFC Championship: PITTSBURGH 27, Houston 13

Wild-Card playoff: PHILADELPHIA 27, Chicago 17

Divisional playoffs: TAMPA BAY 24, Philadelphia 17; Los Angeles 21, DALLAS 19

NFC Championship: Los Angeles 9, TAMPA BAY 0

Super Bowl XIV: Pittsburgh (AFC) 31, Los Angeles (NFC) 19, at Rose Bowl, Pasadena, California

1978

AMERICAN CONFERENCE

Eastern Division

	W	L	T	Pct.	Pts.	OP
New England	11	5	0	.688	358	286
Miami*	11	5	0	.688	372	254
N.Y. Jets	8	8	0	.500	359	364
Buffalo	5	11	0	.313	302	354
Baltimore	5	11	0	.313	239	421

Central Division

	W	L	T	Pct.	Pts.	OP
Pittsburgh#	14	2	0	.875	356	195
Houston*	10	6	0	.625	283	298
Cleveland	8	8	0	.500	334	356
Cincinnati	4	12	0	.250	252	284

Western Division

	W	L	T	Pct.	Pts.	OP
Denver	10	6	0	.625	282	198
Oakland	9	7	0	.563	311	283
Seattle	9	7	0	.563	345	358
San Diego	9	7	0	.563	355	309
Kansas City	4	12	0	.250	243	327

NATIONAL CONFERENCE

Eastern Division

	W	L	T	Pct.	Pts.	OP
Dallas	12	4	0	.750	384	208
Philadelphia*	9	7	0	.563	270	250
Washington	8	8	0	.500	273	283
St. Louis	6	10	0	.375	248	296
N.Y. Giants	6	10	0	.375	264	298

Central Division

	W	L	T	Pct.	Pts.	OP
Minnesota	8	7	1	.531	294	306
Green Bay	8	7	1	.531	249	269
Detroit	7	9	0	.438	290	300
Chicago	7	9	0	.438	253	274
Tampa Bay	5	11	0	.313	241	259

Western Division

	W	L	T	Pct.	Pts.	OP
Los Angeles#	12	4	0	.750	316	245
Atlanta*	9	7	0	.563	240	290
New Orleans	7	9	0	.438	281	298
San Francisco	2	14	0	.125	219	350

**Wild-Card qualifier for playoffs; #Top playoff seed in conference*

New England finished ahead of Miami based on better division record (6-2 to Dolphins' 5-3). Buffalo finished ahead of Baltimore based on head-to-head sweep (2-0). Oakland finished ahead of Seattle and San Diego based on better record against common opponents (6-2 to Seahawks' 5-3 and Chargers' 4-4). Atlanta was first WIld Card based on better conference record than Philadelphia (8-4 to Eagles' 6-6). Houston did not play Pittsburgh, and Atlanta did not play Los Angeles in the divisional playoffs because, from 1970-1989, two teams from the same division could not meet prior to the conference championship game. St. Louis finished ahead of N.Y. Giants based on better division record (3-5 to Giants' 2-6). Minnesota finished ahead of Green Bay based on better head-to-head record (1-0-1). Detroit finished ahead of Chicago based on better division record (4-4 to Bears' 3-5).

Wild-Card playoff: Houston 17, MIAMI 9

Divisional playoffs: Houston 31, NEW ENGLAND 14; PITTSBURGH 33, Denver 10

AFC Championship: PITTSBURGH 34, Houston 5

Wild-Card playoff: ATLANTA 14, Philadelphia 13

Divisional playoffs: DALLAS 27, Atlanta 20; LOS ANGELES 34, Minnesota 10

NFC Championship: Dallas 28, LOS ANGELES 0

Super Bowl XIII: Pittsburgh (AFC) 35, Dallas (NFC) 31, at Orange Bowl, Miami, Florida

1977

AMERICAN CONFERENCE

Eastern Division

	W	L	T	Pct.	Pts.	OP
Baltimore	10	4	0	.714	295	221
Miami	10	4	0	.714	313	197
New England	9	5	0	.643	278	217
Buffalo	3	11	0	.214	160	313
N.Y. Jets	3	11	0	.214	191	300

Central Division

	W	L	T	Pct.	Pts.	OP
Pittsburgh	9	5	0	.643	283	243
Cincinnati	8	6	0	.571	238	235
Houston	8	6	0	.571	299	230
Cleveland	6	8	0	.429	269	267

Western Division

	W	L	T	Pct.	Pts.	OP
Denver#	12	2	0	.857	274	148
Oakland*	11	3	0	.786	351	230
San Diego	7	7	0	.500	222	205
Seattle	5	9	0	.357	282	373
Kansas City	2	12	0	.143	225	349

NATIONAL CONFERENCE

Eastern Division

	W	L	T	Pct.	Pts.	OP
Dallas#	12	2	0	.857	345	212
Washington	9	5	0	.643	196	189
St. Louis	7	7	0	.500	272	287
Philadelphia	5	9	0	.357	220	207
N.Y. Giants	5	9	0	.357	181	265

Central Division

	W	L	T	Pct.	Pts.	OP
Minnesota	9	5	0	.643	231	227
Chicago*	9	5	0	.643	255	253
Detroit	6	8	0	.429	183	252
Green Bay	4	10	0	.286	134	219
Tampa Bay	2	12	0	.143	103	223

Western Division

	W	L	T	Pct.	Pts.	OP
Los Angeles	10	4	0	.714	302	146
Atlanta	7	7	0	.500	179	129
San Francisco	5	9	0	.357	220	260
New Orleans	3	11	0	.214	232	336

**Wild-Card qualifier for playoffs; #Top playoff seed in conference*

Baltimore finished ahead of Miami based on better conference record (9-3 to Dolphins' 8-4). Buffalo finished ahead of N.Y. Jets based on better strength of schedule (.582 to Jets' .536). Cincinnati finished ahead of Houston based on better division record (6-3 to Oilers' 5-4). Oakland did not play Denver in the divisional playoffs because, from 1970-1989, two teams from the same division could not meet prior to the conference championship game. Minnesota finished ahead of Chicago based on fewer losses by common opponents (11 losses to 14 losses by the Bears' opponents). Chicago won Wild Card ahead of Washington based on better net points in conference games (48 to Redskins' 4). Philadelphia finished ahead of N.Y. Giants based on head-to-head sweep (2-0).

Divisional playoffs: DENVER 34, Pittsburgh 21; Oakland 37, BALTIMORE 31 (OT)

AFC Championship: DENVER 20, Oakland 17

Divisional playoffs: DALLAS 37, Chicago 7; Minnesota 14, LOS ANGELES 7

NFC Championship: DALLAS 23, Minnesota 6

Super Bowl XII: Dallas (NFC) 27, Denver (AFC) 10, at Louisiana Superdome, New Orleans, Louisiana

1976

AMERICAN CONFERENCE

Eastern Division

	W	L	T	Pct.	Pts.	OP
Baltimore	11	3	0	.786	417	246
New England*	11	3	0	.786	376	236
Miami	6	8	0	.429	263	264
N.Y. Jets	3	11	0	.214	169	383
Buffalo	2	12	0	.143	245	363

Central Division

	W	L	T	Pct.	Pts.	OP
Pittsburgh	10	4	0	.714	342	138
Cincinnati	10	4	0	.714	335	210
Cleveland	9	5	0	.643	267	287
Houston	5	9	0	.357	222	273

Western Division

	W	L	T	Pct.	Pts.	OP
Oakland#	13	1	0	.929	350	237
Denver	9	5	0	.643	315	206
San Diego	6	8	0	.429	248	285
Kansas City	5	9	0	.357	290	376
Tampa Bay	0	14	0	.000	125	412

NATIONAL CONFERENCE

Eastern Division

	W	L	T	Pct.	Pts.	OP
Dallas	11	3	0	.786	296	194
Washington*	10	4	0	.714	291	217
St. Louis	10	4	0	.714	309	267
Philadelphia	4	10	0	.286	165	286
N.Y. Giants	3	11	0	.214	170	250

Central Division

	W	L	T	Pct.	Pts.	OP
Minnesota#	11	2	1	.821	305	176
Chicago	7	7	0	.500	253	216
Detroit	6	8	0	.429	262	220
Green Bay	5	9	0	.357	218	299

Western Division

	W	L	T	Pct.	Pts.	OP
Los Angeles	10	3	1	.750	351	190
San Francisco	8	6	0	.571	270	190
Atlanta	4	10	0	.286	172	312
New Orleans	4	10	0	.286	253	346
Seattle	2	12	0	.143	229	429

**Wild-Card qualifier for playoffs; #Top playoff seed in conference*

Baltimore finished ahead of New England based on better division record (7-1 to Patriots' 6-2). Pittsburgh finished ahead of Cincinnati based on head-to-head sweep (2-0). Washington finished ahead of St. Louis based on head-to-head sweep (2-0). Atlanta finished ahead of New Orleans based on better division record (2-4 to Saints' 1-5).

Divisional playoffs: OAKLAND 24, New England 21; Pittsburgh 40, BALTIMORE 14

AFC Championship: OAKLAND 24, Pittsburgh 7

Divisional playoffs: MINNESOTA 35, Washington 20; Los Angeles 14, DALLAS 12

NFC Championship: MINNESOTA 24, Los Angeles 13

Super Bowl XI: Oakland (AFC) 32, Minnesota (NFC) 14, at Rose Bowl, Pasadena, California

1975

AMERICAN CONFERENCE

Eastern Division

	W	L	T	Pct.	Pts.	OP
Baltimore	10	4	0	.714	395	269
Miami	10	4	0	.714	357	222
Buffalo	8	6	0	.571	420	355
N.Y. Jets	3	11	0	.214	258	433
New England	3	11	0	.214	258	358

Central Division

	W	L	T	Pct.	Pts.	OP
Pittsburgh#	12	2	0	.857	373	162
Cincinnati*	11	3	0	.786	340	246
Houston	10	4	0	.714	293	226
Cleveland	3	11	0	.214	218	372

Western Division

	W	L	T	Pct.	Pts.	OP
Oakland	11	3	0	.786	375	255
Denver	6	8	0	.429	254	307
Kansas City	5	9	0	.357	282	341
San Diego	2	12	0	.143	189	345

NATIONAL CONFERENCE

Eastern Division

	W	L	T	Pct.	Pts.	OP
St. Louis	11	3	0	.786	356	276
Dallas*	10	4	0	.714	350	268
Washington	8	6	0	.571	325	276
N.Y. Giants	5	9	0	.357	216	306
Philadelphia	4	10	0	.286	225	302

Central Division

	W	L	T	Pct.	Pts.	OP
Minnesota#	12	2	0	.857	377	180
Detroit	7	7	0	.500	245	262
Chicago	4	10	0	.286	191	379
Green Bay	4	10	0	.286	226	285

Western Division

	W	L	T	Pct.	Pts.	OP
Los Angeles	12	2	0	.857	312	135
San Francisco	5	9	0	.357	255	286
Atlanta	4	10	0	.286	240	289
New Orleans	2	12	0	.143	165	360

**Wild-Card qualifier for playoffs; #Top playoff seed in conference*

Baltimore finished ahead of Miami based on head-to-head sweep (2-0). Cincinnati did not play Pittsburgh in the divisional playoffs because, from 1970-1989, two teams from the same division could not meet prior to the conference championship game. N.Y. Jets finished ahead of New England based on head-to-head sweep (2-0). Minnesota was top playoff seed based on better Point Rating system than Los Angeles (3 to 6). Chicago finished ahead of Green Bay based on better division record (2-4 to Bears' 1-5).

Divisional playoffs: PITTSBURGH 28, Baltimore 10; OAKLAND 31, Cincinnati 28

AFC Championship: PITTSBURGH 16, Oakland 10

Divisional playoffs: LOS ANGELES 35, St. Louis 23; Dallas 17, MINNESOTA 14

NFC Championship: Dallas 37, LOS ANGELES 7

Super Bowl X: Pittsburgh (AFC) 21, Dallas (NFC) 17, at Orange Bowl, Miami, Florida

1974

AMERICAN CONFERENCE

Eastern Division

	W	L	T	Pct.	Pts.	OP
Miami	11	3	0	.786	327	216
Buffalo*	9	5	0	.643	264	244
New England	7	7	0	.500	348	289
N.Y. Jets	7	7	0	.500	279	300
Baltimore	2	12	0	.143	190	329

Central Division

	W	L	T	Pct.	Pts.	OP
Pittsburgh	10	3	1	.750	305	189
Houston	7	7	0	.500	236	282
Cincinnati	7	7	0	.500	283	259
Cleveland	4	10	0	.286	251	344

Western Division

	W	L	T	Pct.	Pts.	OP
Oakland	12	2	0	.857	355	228
Denver	7	6	1	.536	302	294
Kansas City	5	9	0	.357	233	293
San Diego	5	9	0	.357	212	285

NATIONAL CONFERENCE

Eastern Division

	W	L	T	Pct.	Pts.	OP
St. Louis	10	4	0	.714	285	218
Washington*	10	4	0	.714	320	196
Dallas	8	6	0	.571	297	235
Philadelphia	7	7	0	.500	242	217
N.Y. Giants	2	12	0	.143	195	299

Central Division

	W	L	T	Pct.	Pts.	OP
Minnesota	10	4	0	.714	310	195
Detroit	7	7	0	.500	256	270
Green Bay	6	8	0	.429	210	206
Chicago	4	10	0	.286	152	279

Western Division

	W	L	T	Pct.	Pts.	OP
Los Angeles	10	4	0	.714	263	181
San Francisco	6	8	0	.429	226	236
New Orleans	5	9	0	.357	166	263
Atlanta	3	11	0	.214	111	271

**Wild-Card qualifier for playoffs*

New England finished ahead of N.Y. Jets based on better record against common opponents (5-4 to Jets' 4-5). Houston finished ahead of Cincinnati based on head-to-head sweep (2-0). Kansas City finished ahead of San Diego based on better record against common opponents (4-6 to Chargers' 3-7). St. Louis finished ahead of Washington based on head-to-head sweep (2-0).

Divisional playoffs: OAKLAND 28, Miami 26; PITTSBURGH 32, Buffalo 14

AFC Championship: Pittsburgh 24, OAKLAND 13

Divisional playoffs: MINNESOTA 30, St. Louis 14; LOS ANGELES 19, Washington 10

NFC Championship: MINNESOTA 14, Los Angeles 10

Super Bowl IX: Pittsburgh (AFC) 16, Minnesota (NFC) 6, at Tulane Stadium, New Orleans, Louisiana

From 1933-1974, sites for league/conference championship games alternated by division.

1973

AMERICAN CONFERENCE

Eastern Division

	W	L	T	Pct.	Pts.	OP
Miami	12	2	0	.857	343	150
Buffalo	9	5	0	.643	259	230
New England	5	9	0	.357	258	300
N.Y. Jets	4	10	0	.286	240	306
Baltimore	4	10	0	.286	226	341

Central Division

	W	L	T	Pct.	Pts.	OP
Cincinnati	10	4	0	.714	286	231
Pittsburgh*	10	4	0	.714	347	210
Cleveland	7	5	2	.571	234	255
Houston	1	13	0	.071	199	447

Western Division

	W	L	T	Pct.	Pts.	OP
Oakland	9	4	1	.679	292	175
Kansas City	7	5	2	.571	231	192
Denver	7	5	2	.571	354	296
San Diego	2	11	1	.179	188	386

NATIONAL CONFERENCE

Eastern Division

	W	L	T	Pct.	Pts.	OP
Dallas	10	4	0	.714	382	203
Washington*	10	4	0	.714	325	198
Philadelphia	5	8	1	.393	310	393
St. Louis	4	9	1	.321	286	365
N.Y. Giants	2	11	1	.179	226	362

Central Division

	W	L	T	Pct.	Pts.	OP
Minnesota	12	2	0	.857	296	168
Detroit	6	7	1	.464	271	247
Green Bay	5	7	2	.429	202	259
Chicago	3	11	0	.214	195	334

Western Division

	W	L	T	Pct.	Pts.	OP
Los Angeles	12	2	0	.857	388	178
Atlanta	9	5	0	.643	318	224
San Francisco	5	9	0	.357	262	319
New Orleans	5	9	0	.357	163	312

**Wild-Card qualifier for playoffs*

Cincinnati finished ahead of Pittsburgh based on better conference record (8-3 to Steelers' 7-4). N.Y. Jets finished ahead of Baltimore based on head-to-head sweep (2-0). Kansas City finished ahead of Denver based on better division record (4-2 to Broncos' 3-2-1). Dallas finished ahead of Washington based on better point differential in head-to-head games (13 points). San Francisco finished ahead of New Orleans based on better division record (2-4 to Saints' 1-5).

Divisional playoffs: OAKLAND 33, Pittsburgh 14; MIAMI 34, Cincinnati 16

AFC Championship: MIAMI 27, Oakland 10

Divisional playoffs: MINNESOTA 27, Washington 20; DALLAS 27, Los Angeles 16

NFC Championship: Minnesota 27, DALLAS 10

Super Bowl VIII: Miami (AFC) 24, Minnesota (NFC) 7, at Rice Stadium, Houston, Texas

1972

AMERICAN CONFERENCE

Eastern Division

	W	L	T	Pct.	Pts.	OP
Miami	14	0	0	1.000	385	171
N.Y. Jets	7	7	0	.500	367	324
Baltimore	5	9	0	.357	235	252
Buffalo	4	9	1	.321	257	377
New England	3	11	0	.214	192	446

Central Division

	W	L	T	Pct.	Pts.	OP
Pittsburgh	11	3	0	.786	343	175
Cleveland*	10	4	0	.714	268	249
Cincinnati	8	6	0	.571	299	229
Houston	1	13	0	.071	164	380

Western Division

	W	L	T	Pct.	Pts.	OP
Oakland	10	3	1	.750	365	248
Kansas City	8	6	0	.571	287	254
Denver	5	9	0	.357	325	350
San Diego	4	9	1	.321	264	344

NATIONAL CONFERENCE

Eastern Division

	W	L	T	Pct.	Pts.	OP
Washington	11	3	0	.786	336	218
Dallas*	10	4	0	.714	319	240
N.Y. Giants	8	6	0	.571	331	247
St. Louis	4	9	1	.321	193	303
Philadelphia	2	11	1	.179	145	352

Central Division

	W	L	T	Pct.	Pts.	OP
Green Bay	10	4	0	.714	304	226
Detroit	8	5	1	.607	339	290
Minnesota	7	7	0	.500	301	252
Chicago	4	9	1	.321	225	275

Western Division

	W	L	T	Pct.	Pts.	OP
San Francisco	8	5	1	.607	353	249
Atlanta	7	7	0	.500	269	274
Los Angeles	6	7	1	.464	291	286
New Orleans	2	11	1	.179	215	361

**Wild-Card qualifier for playoffs*

Dallas did not play Washington in the divisional playoffs because, from 1970-1989, two teams from the same division could not meet prior to the conference championship game.

Divisional playoffs: PITTSBURGH 13, Oakland 7; MIAMI 20, Cleveland 14

AFC Championship: Miami 21, PITTSBURGH 17

Divisional playoffs: Dallas 30, SAN FRANCISCO 28; WASHINGTON 16, Green Bay 3

NFC Championship: WASHINGTON 26, Dallas 3

Super Bowl VII: Miami (AFC) 14, Washington (NFC) 7, at Memorial Coliseum, Los Angeles, California

PAST STANDINGS

1971

AMERICAN CONFERENCE

Eastern Division

	W	L	T	Pct.	Pts.	OP
Miami	10	3	1	.769	315	174
Baltimore*	10	4	0	.714	313	140
New England	6	8	0	.429	238	325
N.Y. Jets	6	8	0	.429	212	299
Buffalo	1	13	0	.071	184	394

Central Division

	W	L	T	Pct.	Pts.	OP
Cleveland	9	5	0	.643	285	273
Pittsburgh	6	8	0	.429	246	292
Houston	4	9	1	.308	251	330
Cincinnati	4	10	0	.286	284	265

Western Division

	W	L	T	Pct.	Pts.	OP
Kansas City	10	3	1	.769	302	208
Oakland	8	4	2	.667	344	278
San Diego	6	8	0	.429	311	341
Denver	4	9	1	.308	203	275

NATIONAL CONFERENCE

Eastern Division

	W	L	T	Pct.	Pts.	OP
Dallas	11	3	0	.786	406	222
Washington*	9	4	1	.692	276	190
Philadelphia	6	7	1	.462	221	302
St. Louis	4	9	1	.308	231	279
N.Y. Giants	4	10	0	.286	228	362

Central Division

	W	L	T	Pct.	Pts.	OP
Minnesota	11	3	0	.786	245	139
Detroit	7	6	1	.538	341	286
Chicago	6	8	0	.429	185	276
Green Bay	4	8	2	.333	274	298

Western Division

	W	L	T	Pct.	Pts.	OP
San Francisco	9	5	0	.643	300	216
Los Angeles	8	5	1	.615	313	260
Atlanta	7	6	1	.538	274	277
New Orleans	4	8	2	.333	266	347

**Wild-Card qualifier for playoffs*

New England finished ahead of N.Y. Jets based on better strength of schedule (.537 to Jets' .510).

Divisional playoffs: Miami 27, KANSAS CITY 24 (OT); Baltimore 20, CLEVELAND 3

AFC Championship: MIAMI 21, Baltimore 0

Divisional playoffs: Dallas 20, MINNESOTA 12; SAN FRANCISCO 24, Washington 20

NFC Championship: DALLAS 14, San Francisco 3

Super Bowl VI: Dallas (NFC) 24, Miami (AFC) 3, at Tulane Stadium, New Orleans, Louisiana

From 1920-1971, tie games were not included in winning percentage.

1970

AMERICAN CONFERENCE

Eastern Division

	W	L	T	Pct.	Pts.	OP
Baltimore	11	2	1	.846	321	234
Miami*	10	4	0	.714	297	228
N.Y. Jets	4	10	0	.286	255	286
Buffalo	3	10	1	.231	204	337
Boston Patriots	2	12	0	.143	149	361

Central Division

	W	L	T	Pct.	Pts.	OP
Cincinnati	8	6	0	.571	312	255
Cleveland	7	7	0	.500	286	265
Pittsburgh	5	9	0	.357	210	272
Houston	3	10	1	.231	217	352

Western Division

	W	L	T	Pct.	Pts.	OP
Oakland	8	4	2	.667	300	293
Kansas City	7	5	2	.583	272	244
San Diego	5	6	3	.455	282	278
Denver	5	8	1	.385	253	264

NATIONAL CONFERENCE

Eastern Division

	W	L	T	Pct.	Pts.	OP
Dallas	10	4	0	.714	299	221
N.Y. Giants	9	5	0	.643	301	270
St. Louis	8	5	1	.615	325	228
Washington	6	8	0	.429	297	314
Philadelphia	3	10	1	.231	241	332

Central Division

	W	L	T	Pct.	Pts.	OP
Minnesota	12	2	0	.857	335	143
Detroit*	10	4	0	.714	347	202
Green Bay	6	8	0	.429	196	293
Chicago	6	8	0	.429	256	261

Western Division

	W	L	T	Pct.	Pts.	OP
San Francisco	10	3	1	.769	352	267
Los Angeles	9	4	1	.692	325	202
Atlanta	4	8	2	.333	206	261
New Orleans	2	11	1	.154	172	347

**Wild-Card qualifier for playoffs*

Miami did not play Baltimore, and Detroit did not play Minnesota, in the divisional playoffs because, from 1970-1989, two teams from the same division could not meet prior to the conference championship game. Green Bay finished ahead of Chicago based on better division record (2-4 to Bears' 1-5).

Divisional playoffs: BALTIMORE 17, Cincinnati 0; OAKLAND 21, Miami 14

AFC Championship: BALTIMORE 27, Oakland 17

Divisional playoffs: DALLAS 5, Detroit 0; San Francisco 17, MINNESOTA 14

NFC Championship: Dallas 17, SAN FRANCISCO 10

Super Bowl V: Baltimore (AFC) 16, Dallas (NFC) 13, at Orange Bowl, Miami, Florida

1969 NFL

EASTERN CONFERENCE

Capitol Division

	W	L	T	Pct.	Pts.	OP
Dallas	11	2	1	.846	369	223
Washington	7	5	2	.583	307	319
New Orleans	5	9	0	.357	311	393
Philadelphia	4	9	1	.308	279	377

Century Division

	W	L	T	Pct.	Pts.	OP
Cleveland	10	3	1	.769	351	300
N.Y. Giants	6	8	0	.429	264	298
St. Louis	4	9	1	.308	314	389
Pittsburgh	1	13	0	.071	218	404

WESTERN CONFERENCE

Coastal Division

	W	L	T	Pct.	Pts.	OP
Los Angeles	11	3	0	.786	320	243
Baltimore	8	5	1	.615	279	268
Atlanta	6	8	0	.429	276	268
San Francisco	4	8	2	.333	277	319

Central Division

	W	L	T	Pct.	Pts.	OP
Minnesota	12	2	0	.857	379	133
Detroit	9	4	1	.692	259	188
Green Bay	8	6	0	.571	269	221
Chicago	1	13	0	.071	210	339

Conference championships: Cleveland 38, DALLAS 14; MINNESOTA 23, Los Angeles 20
NFL championship: MINNESOTA 27, Cleveland 7
Super Bowl IV: Kansas City (AFL) 23, Minnesota (NFL) 7, at Tulane Stadium, New Orleans, Louisiana

1969 AFL

EASTERN DIVISION

	W	L	T	Pct.	Pts.	OP
N.Y. Jets	10	4	0	.714	353	269
Houston	6	6	2	.500	278	279
Boston Patriots	4	10	0	.286	266	316
Buffalo	4	10	0	.286	230	359
Miami	3	10	1	.231	233	332

WESTERN DIVISION

	W	L	T	Pct.	Pts.	OP
Oakland	12	1	1	.923	377	242
Kansas City	11	3	0	.786	359	177
San Diego	8	6	0	.571	288	276
Denver	5	8	1	.385	297	344
Cincinnati	4	9	1	.308	280	367

Divisional playoffs: Kansas City 13, N.Y. JETS 6; OAKLAND 56, Houston 7
AFL championship: Kansas City 17, OAKLAND 7

1968 NFL

EASTERN CONFERENCE

Capitol Division

	W	L	T	Pct.	Pts.	OP
Dallas	12	2	0	.857	431	186
N.Y. Giants	7	7	0	.500	294	325
Washington	5	9	0	.357	249	358
Philadelphia	2	12	0	.143	202	351

Century Division

	W	L	T	Pct.	Pts.	OP
Cleveland	10	4	0	.714	394	273
St. Louis	9	4	1	.692	325	289
New Orleans	4	9	1	.308	246	327
Pittsburgh	2	11	1	.154	244	397

WESTERN CONFERENCE

Coastal Division

	W	L	T	Pct.	Pts.	OP
Baltimore	13	1	0	.929	402	144
Los Angeles	10	3	1	.769	312	200
San Francisco	7	6	1	.538	303	310
Atlanta	2	12	0	.143	170	389

Central Division

	W	L	T	Pct.	Pts.	OP
Minnesota	8	6	0	.571	282	242
Chicago	7	7	0	.500	250	333
Green Bay	6	7	1	.462	281	227
Detroit	4	8	2	.333	207	241

Conference championships: CLEVELAND 31, Dallas 20; BALTIMORE 24, Minnesota 14
NFL championship: Baltimore 34, CLEVELAND 0
Super Bowl III: N.Y. Jets (AFL) 16, Baltimore (NFL) 7, at Orange Bowl, Miami, Florida

1968 AFL

EASTERN DIVISION

	W	L	T	Pct.	Pts.	OP
N.Y. Jets	11	3	0	.786	419	280
Houston	7	7	0	.500	303	248
Miami	5	8	1	.385	276	355
Boston Patriots	4	10	0	.286	229	406
Buffalo	1	12	1	.077	199	367

WESTERN DIVISION

	W	L	T	Pct.	Pts.	OP
Oakland	12	2	0	.857	453	233
Kansas City	12	2	0	.857	371	170
San Diego	9	5	0	.643	382	310
Denver	5	9	0	.357	255	404
Cincinnati	3	11	0	.214	215	329

Western Division playoff: OAKLAND 41, Kansas City 6
AFL championship: N.Y. JETS 27, Oakland 23

1967 NFL

EASTERN CONFERENCE

Capitol Division

	W	L	T	Pct.	Pts.	OP
Dallas	9	5	0	.643	342	268
Philadelphia	6	7	1	.462	351	409
Washington	5	6	3	.455	347	353
New Orleans	3	11	0	.214	233	379

Century Division

	W	L	T	Pct.	Pts.	OP
Cleveland	9	5	0	.643	334	297
N.Y. Giants	7	7	0	.500	369	379
St. Louis	6	7	1	.462	333	356
Pittsburgh	4	9	1	.308	281	320

WESTERN CONFERENCE

Coastal Division

	W	L	T	Pct.	Pts.	OP
Los Angeles	11	1	2	.917	398	196
Baltimore	11	1	2	.917	394	198
San Francisco	7	7	0	.500	273	337
Atlanta	1	12	1	.077	175	422

Central Division

	W	L	T	Pct.	Pts.	OP
Green Bay	9	4	1	.692	332	209
Chicago	7	6	1	.538	239	218
Detroit	5	7	2	.417	260	259
Minnesota	3	8	3	.273	233	294

Los Angeles finished ahead of Baltimore based on better point differential in head-to-head games (net 24 points).
Conference championships: DALLAS 52, Cleveland 14; GREEN BAY 28, Los Angeles 7
NFL championship: GREEN BAY 21, Dallas 17
Super Bowl II: Green Bay (NFL) 33, Oakland (AFL) 14, at Orange Bowl, Miami, Florida

1967 AFL

EASTERN DIVISION

	W	L	T	Pct.	Pts.	OP
Houston	9	4	1	.692	258	199
N.Y. Jets	8	5	1	.615	371	329
Buffalo	4	10	0	.286	237	285
Miami	4	10	0	.286	219	407
Boston Patriots	3	10	1	.231	280	389

WESTERN DIVISION

	W	L	T	Pct.	Pts.	OP
Oakland	13	1	0	.929	468	233
Kansas City	9	5	0	.643	408	254
San Diego	8	5	1	.615	360	352
Denver	3	11	0	.214	256	409

AFL championship: OAKLAND 40, Houston 7

1966 NFL

EASTERN CONFERENCE

	W	L	T	Pct.	Pts.	OP
Dallas	10	3	1	.769	445	239
Cleveland	9	5	0	.643	403	259
Philadelphia	9	5	0	.643	326	340
St. Louis	8	5	1	.615	264	265
Washington	7	7	0	.500	351	355
Pittsburgh	5	8	1	.385	316	347
Atlanta	3	11	0	.214	204	437
N.Y. Giants	1	12	1	.077	263	501

WESTERN CONFERENCE

	W	L	T	Pct.	Pts.	OP
Green Bay	12	2	0	.857	335	163
Baltimore	9	5	0	.643	314	226
Los Angeles	8	6	0	.571	289	212
San Francisco	6	6	2	.500	320	325
Chicago	5	7	2	.417	234	272
Detroit	4	9	1	.308	206	317
Minnesota	4	9	1	.308	292	304

NFL championship: Green Bay 34, DALLAS 27
Super Bowl I: Green Bay (NFL) 35, Kansas City (AFL) 10, at Memorial Coliseum, Los Angeles, California

1966 AFL

EASTERN DIVISION

	W	L	T	Pct.	Pts.	OP
Buffalo	9	4	1	.692	358	255
Boston Patriots	8	4	2	.677	315	283
N.Y. Jets	6	6	2	.500	322	312
Houston	3	11	0	.214	335	396
Miami	3	11	0	.214	213	362

WESTERN DIVISION

	W	L	T	Pct.	Pts.	OP
Kansas City	11	2	1	.846	448	276
Oakland	8	5	1	.615	315	288
San Diego	7	6	1	.538	335	284
Denver	4	10	0	.286	196	381

AFL championship: Kansas City 31, BUFFALO 7

PAST STANDINGS

1965 NFL

EASTERN CONFERENCE	W	L	T	Pct.	Pts.	OP	WESTERN CONFERENCE	W	L	T	Pct.	Pts.	OP
Cleveland	11	3	0	.786	363	325	Green Bay	10	3	1	.769	316	224
Dallas	7	7	0	.500	325	280	Baltimore	10	3	1	.769	389	284
N.Y. Giants	7	7	0	.500	270	338	Chicago	9	5	0	.643	409	275
Washington	6	8	0	.429	257	301	San Francisco	7	6	1	.538	421	402
Philadelphia	5	9	0	.357	363	359	Minnesota	7	7	0	.500	383	403
St. Louis	5	9	0	.357	296	309	Detroit	6	7	1	.462	257	295
Pittsburgh	2	12	0	.143	202	397	Los Angeles	4	10	0	.286	269	328

Western Conference playoff: GREEN BAY 13, Baltimore 10 (OT)
NFL championship: GREEN BAY 23, Cleveland 12

1965 AFL

EASTERN DIVISION	W	L	T	Pct.	Pts.	OP	WESTERN DIVISION	W	L	T	Pct.	Pts.	OP
Buffalo	10	3	1	.769	313	226	San Diego	9	2	3	.818	340	227
N.Y. Jets	5	8	1	.385	285	303	Oakland	8	5	1	.615	298	239
Boston Patriots	4	8	2	.333	244	302	Kansas City	7	5	2	.583	322	285
Houston	4	10	0	.286	298	429	Denver	4	10	0	.286	303	392

AFL championship: Buffalo 23, SAN DIEGO 0

1964 NFL

EASTERN CONFERENCE	W	L	T	Pct.	Pts.	OP	WESTERN CONFERENCE	W	L	T	Pct.	Pts.	OP
Cleveland	10	3	1	.769	415	293	Baltimore	12	2	0	.857	428	225
St. Louis	9	3	2	.750	357	331	Green Bay	8	5	1	.615	342	245
Philadelphia	6	8	0	.429	312	313	Minnesota	8	5	1	.615	355	296
Washington	6	8	0	.429	307	305	Detroit	7	5	2	.583	280	260
Dallas	5	8	1	.385	250	289	Los Angeles	5	7	2	.417	283	339
Pittsburgh	5	9	0	.357	253	315	Chicago	5	9	0	.357	260	379
N.Y. Giants	2	10	2	.167	241	399	San Francisco	4	10	0	.286	236	330

NFL championship: CLEVELAND 27, Baltimore 0

1964 AFL

EASTERN DIVISION	W	L	T	Pct.	Pts.	OP	WESTERN DIVISION	W	L	T	Pct.	Pts.	OP
Buffalo	12	2	0	.857	400	242	San Diego	8	5	1	.615	341	300
Boston Patriots	10	3	1	.769	365	297	Kansas City	7	7	0	.500	366	306
N.Y. Jets	5	8	1	.385	278	315	Oakland	5	7	2	.417	303	350
Houston	4	10	0	.286	310	355	Denver	2	11	1	.154	240	438

AFL championship: BUFFALO 20, San Diego 7

1963 NFL

EASTERN CONFERENCE	W	L	T	Pct.	Pts.	OP	WESTERN CONFERENCE	W	L	T	Pct.	Pts.	OP
N.Y. Giants	11	3	0	.786	448	280	Chicago	11	1	2	.917	301	144
Cleveland	10	4	0	.714	343	262	Green Bay	11	2	1	.846	369	206
St. Louis	9	5	0	.643	341	283	Baltimore	8	6	0	.571	316	285
Pittsburgh	7	4	3	.636	321	295	Detroit	5	8	1	.385	326	265
Dallas	4	10	0	.286	305	378	Minnesota	5	8	1	.385	309	390
Washington	3	11	0	.214	279	398	Los Angeles	5	9	0	.357	210	350
Philadelphia	2	10	2	.167	242	381	San Francisco	2	12	0	.143	198	391

NFL championship: CHICAGO 14, N.Y. Giants 10

1963 AFL

EASTERN DIVISION	W	L	T	Pct.	Pts.	OP	WESTERN DIVISION	W	L	T	Pct.	Pts.	OP
Boston Patriots	7	6	1	.538	327	257	San Diego	11	3	0	.786	399	255
Buffalo	7	6	1	.538	304	291	Oakland	10	4	0	.714	363	282
Houston	6	8	0	.429	302	372	Kansas City	5	7	2	.417	347	263
N.Y. Jets	5	8	1	.385	249	399	Denver	2	11	1	.154	301	473

Eastern Division playoff: Boston 26, BUFFALO 8
AFL championship: SAN DIEGO 51, Boston 10

1962 NFL

EASTERN CONFERENCE	W	L	T	Pct.	Pts.	OP	WESTERN CONFERENCE	W	L	T	Pct.	Pts.	OP
N.Y. Giants	12	2	0	.857	398	283	Green Bay	13	1	0	.929	415	148
Pittsburgh	9	5	0	.643	312	363	Detroit	11	3	0	.786	315	177
Cleveland	7	6	1	.538	291	257	Chicago	9	5	0	.643	321	287
Washington	5	7	2	.417	305	376	Baltimore	7	7	0	.500	293	288
Dallas Cowboys	5	8	1	.385	398	402	San Francisco	6	8	0	.429	282	331
St. Louis	4	9	1	.308	287	361	Minnesota	2	11	1	.154	254	410
Philadelphia	3	10	1	.231	282	356	Los Angeles	1	12	1	.077	220	334

NFL championship: Green Bay 16, N.Y. GIANTS 7

1962 AFL

EASTERN DIVISION	W	L	T	Pct.	Pts.	OP	WESTERN DIVISION	W	L	T	Pct.	Pts.	OP
Houston	11	3	0	.786	387	270	Dallas Texans	11	3	0	.786	389	233
Boston Patriots	9	4	1	.692	346	295	Denver	7	7	0	.500	353	334
Buffalo	7	6	1	.538	309	272	San Diego	4	10	0	.286	314	392
N.Y. Titans	5	9	0	.357	278	423	Oakland	1	13	0	.071	213	370

AFL championship: Dallas Texans 20, HOUSTON 17 (OT)

1961 NFL

EASTERN CONFERENCE	W	L	T	Pct.	Pts.	OP	WESTERN CONFERENCE	W	L	T	Pct.	Pts.	OP
N.Y. Giants	10	3	1	.769	368	220	Green Bay	11	3	0	.786	391	223
Philadelphia	10	4	0	.714	361	297	Detroit	8	5	1	.615	270	258
Cleveland	8	5	1	.615	319	270	Baltimore	8	6	0	.571	302	307
St. Louis	7	7	0	.500	279	267	Chicago	8	6	0	.571	326	302
Pittsburgh	6	8	0	.429	295	287	San Francisco	7	6	1	.538	346	272
Dallas Cowboys	4	9	1	.308	236	380	Los Angeles	4	10	0	.286	263	333
Washington	1	12	1	.077	174	392	Minnesota	3	11	0	.214	285	407

NFL championship: GREEN BAY 37, N.Y. Giants 0

1961 AFL

EASTERN DIVISION	W	L	T	Pct.	Pts.	OP	WESTERN DIVISION	W	L	T	Pct.	Pts.	OP
Houston	10	3	1	.769	513	242	San Diego	12	2	0	.857	396	219
Boston Patriots	9	4	1	.692	413	313	Dallas Texans	6	8	0	.429	334	343
N.Y. Titans	7	7	0	.500	301	390	Denver	3	11	0	.214	251	432
Buffalo	6	8	0	.429	294	342	Oakland	2	12	0	.143	237	458

AFL championship: Houston 10, SAN DIEGO 3

1960 NFL

EASTERN CONFERENCE	W	L	T	Pct.	Pts.	OP	WESTERN CONFERENCE	W	L	T	Pct.	Pts.	OP
Philadelphia	10	2	0	.833	321	246	Green Bay	8	4	0	.667	332	209
Cleveland	8	3	1	.727	362	217	Detroit	7	5	0	.583	239	212
N.Y. Giants	6	4	2	.600	271	261	San Francisco	7	5	0	.583	208	205
St. Louis	6	5	1	.545	288	230	Baltimore	6	6	0	.500	288	234
Pittsburgh	5	6	1	.455	240	275	Chicago	5	6	1	.455	194	299
Washington	1	9	2	.100	178	309	L.A. Rams	4	7	1	.364	265	297
							Dallas Cowboys	0	11	1	.000	177	369

NFL championship: PHILADELPHIA 17, Green Bay 13

1960 AFL

EASTERN CONFERENCE	W	L	T	Pct.	Pts.	OP	WESTERN CONFERENCE	W	L	T	Pct.	Pts.	OP
Houston	10	4	0	.714	379	285	L.A. Chargers	10	4	0	.714	373	336
N.Y. Titans	7	7	0	.500	382	399	Dallas Texans	8	6	0	.571	362	253
Buffalo	5	8	1	.385	296	303	Oakland	6	8	0	.429	319	388
Boston	5	9	0	.357	286	349	Denver	4	9	1	.308	309	393

AFL championship: HOUSTON 24, L.A. Chargers 16

1959

EASTERN CONFERENCE	W	L	T	Pct.	Pts.	OP
N.Y. Giants	10	2	0	.833	284	170
Cleveland	7	5	0	.583	270	214
Philadelphia	7	5	0	.583	268	278
Pittsburgh	6	5	1	.545	257	216
Washington	3	9	0	.250	185	350
Chi. Cardinals	2	10	0	.167	234	324

WESTERN CONFERENCE	W	L	T	Pct.	Pts.	OP
Baltimore	9	3	0	.750	374	251
Chi. Bears	8	4	0	.667	252	196
Green Bay	7	5	0	.583	248	246
San Francisco	7	5	0	.583	255	237
Detroit	3	8	1	.273	203	275
Los Angeles	2	10	0	.167	242	315

NFL championship: BALTIMORE 31, N.Y. Giants 16

1958

EASTERN CONFERENCE	W	L	T	Pct.	Pts.	OP
N.Y. Giants	9	3	0	.750	246	183
Cleveland	9	3	0	.750	302	217
Pittsburgh	7	4	1	.636	261	230
Washington	4	7	1	.364	214	268
Chi. Cardinals	2	9	1	.182	261	356
Philadelphia	2	9	1	.182	235	306

WESTERN CONFERENCE	W	L	T	Pct.	Pts.	OP
Baltimore	9	3	0	.750	381	203
Chi. Bears	8	4	0	.667	298	230
Los Angeles	8	4	0	.667	344	278
San Francisco	6	6	0	.500	257	324
Detroit	4	7	1	.364	261	276
Green Bay	1	10	1	.091	193	382

Eastern Conference playoff: N.Y. GIANTS 10, Cleveland 0
NFL championship: Baltimore 23, N.Y. GIANTS 17 (OT)

1957

EASTERN CONFERENCE	W	L	T	Pct.	Pts.	OP
Cleveland	9	2	1	.818	269	172
N.Y. Giants	7	5	0	.583	254	211
Pittsburgh	6	6	0	.500	161	178
Washington	5	6	1	.455	251	230
Philadelphia	4	8	0	.333	173	230
Chi. Cardinals	3	9	0	.250	200	299

WESTERN CONFERENCE	W	L	T	Pct.	Pts.	OP
Detroit	8	4	0	.667	251	231
San Francisco	8	4	0	.667	260	264
Baltimore	7	5	0	.583	303	235
Los Angeles	6	6	0	.500	307	278
Chi. Bears	5	7	0	.417	203	211
Green Bay	3	9	0	.250	218	311

Western Conference playoff: Detroit 31, SAN FRANCISCO 27
NFL championship: DETROIT 59, Cleveland 14

1956

EASTERN CONFERENCE	W	L	T	Pct.	Pts.	OP
N.Y. Giants	8	3	1	.727	264	197
Chi. Cardinals	7	5	0	.583	240	182
Washington	6	6	0	.500	183	225
Cleveland	5	7	0	.417	167	177
Pittsburgh	5	7	0	.417	217	250
Philadelphia	3	8	1	.273	143	215

WESTERN CONFERENCE	W	L	T	Pct.	Pts.	OP
Chi. Bears	9	2	1	.818	363	246
Detroit	9	3	0	.750	300	188
San Francisco	5	6	1	.455	233	284
Baltimore	5	7	0	.417	270	322
Green Bay	4	8	0	.333	264	342
Los Angeles	4	8	0	.333	291	307

NFL championship: N.Y. GIANTS 47, Chi. Bears 7

1955

EASTERN CONFERENCE	W	L	T	Pct.	Pts.	OP
Cleveland	9	2	1	.818	349	218
Washington	8	4	0	.667	246	222
N.Y. Giants	6	5	1	.545	267	223
Chi. Cardinals	4	7	1	.364	224	252
Philadelphia	4	7	1	.364	248	231
Pittsburgh	4	8	0	.333	195	285

WESTERN CONFERENCE	W	L	T	Pct.	Pts.	OP
Los Angeles	8	3	1	.727	260	231
Chi. Bears	8	4	0	.667	294	251
Green Bay	6	6	0	.500	258	276
Baltimore	5	6	1	.455	214	239
San Francisco	4	8	0	.333	216	298
Detroit	3	9	0	.250	230	275

NFL championship: Cleveland 38, LOS ANGELES 14

1954

EASTERN CONFERENCE	W	L	T	Pct.	Pts.	OP
Cleveland	9	3	0	.750	336	162
Philadelphia	7	4	1	.636	284	230
N.Y. Giants	7	5	0	.583	293	184
Pittsburgh	5	7	0	.417	219	263
Washington	3	9	0	.250	207	432
Chi. Cardinals	2	10	0	.167	183	347

WESTERN CONFERENCE	W	L	T	Pct.	Pts.	OP
Detroit	9	2	1	.818	337	189
Chi. Bears	8	4	0	.667	301	279
San Francisco	7	4	1	.636	313	251
Los Angeles	6	5	1	.545	314	285
Green Bay	4	8	0	.333	234	251
Baltimore	3	9	0	.250	131	279

NFL championship: CLEVELAND 56, Detroit 10

1953

EASTERN CONFERENCE	W	L	T	Pct.	Pts.	OP
Cleveland	11	1	0	.917	348	162
Philadelphia	7	4	1	.636	352	215
Washington	6	5	1	.545	208	215
Pittsburgh	6	6	0	.500	211	263
N.Y. Giants	3	9	0	.250	179	277
Chi. Cardinals	1	10	1	.091	190	337

WESTERN CONFERENCE	W	L	T	Pct.	Pts.	OP
Detroit	10	2	0	.833	271	205
San Francisco	9	3	0	.750	372	237
Los Angeles	8	3	1	.727	366	236
Chi. Bears	3	8	1	.273	218	262
Baltimore	3	9	0	.250	182	350
Green Bay	2	9	1	.182	200	338

NFL championship: DETROIT 17, Cleveland 16

1952

AMERICAN CONFERENCE	W	L	T	Pct.	Pts.	OP
Cleveland	8	4	0	.667	310	213
N.Y. Giants	7	5	0	.583	234	231
Philadelphia	7	5	0	.583	252	271
Pittsburgh	5	7	0	.417	300	273
Chi. Cardinals	4	8	0	.333	172	221
Washington	4	8	0	.333	240	287

NATIONAL CONFERENCE	W	L	T	Pct.	Pts.	OP
Detroit	9	3	0	.750	344	192
Los Angeles	9	3	0	.750	349	234
San Francisco	7	5	0	.583	285	221
Green Bay	6	6	0	.500	295	312
Chi. Bears	5	7	0	.417	245	326
Dallas Texans	1	11	0	.083	182	427

National Conference playoff: DETROIT 31, Los Angeles 21
NFL championship: Detroit 17, CLEVELAND 7

1951

AMERICAN CONFERENCE	W	L	T	Pct.	Pts.	OP
Cleveland	11	1	0	.917	331	152
N.Y. Giants	9	2	1	.818	254	161
Washington	5	7	0	.417	183	296
Pittsburgh	4	7	1	.364	183	235
Philadelphia	4	8	0	.333	234	264
Chi. Cardinals	3	9	0	.250	210	287

NATIONAL CONFERENCE	W	L	T	Pct.	Pts.	OP
Los Angeles	8	4	0	.667	392	261
Detroit	7	4	1	.636	336	259
San Francisco	7	4	1	.636	255	205
Chi. Bears	7	5	0	.583	286	282
Green Bay	3	9	0	.250	254	375
N.Y. Yanks	1	9	2	.100	241	382

NFL championship: LOS ANGELES 24, Cleveland 17

1950

AMERICAN CONFERENCE	W	L	T	Pct.	Pts.	OP
Cleveland	10	2	0	.833	310	144
N.Y. Giants	10	2	0	.833	268	150
Philadelphia	6	6	0	.500	254	141
Pittsburgh	6	6	0	.500	180	195
Chi. Cardinals	5	7	0	.417	233	287
Washington	3	9	0	.250	232	326

NATIONAL CONFERENCE	W	L	T	Pct.	Pts.	OP
Los Angeles	9	3	0	.750	466	309
Chi. Bears	9	3	0	.750	279	207
N.Y. Yanks	7	5	0	.583	366	367
Detroit	6	6	0	.500	321	285
Green Bay	3	9	0	.250	244	406
San Francisco	3	9	0	.250	213	300
Baltimore	1	11	0	.083	213	462

American Conference playoff: CLEVELAND 8, N.Y. Giants 3
National Conference playoff: LOS ANGELES 24, Chi. Bears 14
NFL championship: CLEVELAND 30, Los Angeles 28

PAST STANDINGS

1949

EASTERN DIVISION	W	L	T	Pct.	Pts.	OP	WESTERN DIVISION	W	L	T	Pct.	Pts.	OP
Philadelphia	11	1	0	.917	364	134	Los Angeles	8	2	2	.800	360	239
Pittsburgh	6	5	1	.545	224	214	Chi. Bears	9	3	0	.750	332	218
N.Y. Giants	6	6	0	.500	287	298	Chi. Cardinals	6	5	1	.545	360	301
Washington	4	7	1	.364	268	339	Detroit	4	8	0	.333	237	259
N.Y. Bulldogs	1	10	1	.091	153	368	Green Bay	2	10	0	.167	114	329

NFL championship: Philadelphia 14, LOS ANGELES 0

1948

EASTERN DIVISION	W	L	T	Pct.	Pts.	OP	WESTERN DIVISION	W	L	T	Pct.	Pts.	OP
Philadelphia	9	2	1	.818	376	156	Chi. Cardinals	11	1	0	.917	395	226
Washington	7	5	0	.583	291	287	Chi. Bears	10	2	0	.833	375	151
N.Y. Giants	4	8	0	.333	297	388	Los Angeles	6	5	1	.545	327	269
Pittsburgh	4	8	0	.333	200	243	Green Bay	3	9	0	.250	154	290
Boston	3	9	0	.250	174	372	Detroit	2	10	0	.167	200	407

NFL championship: PHILADELPHIA 7, Chi. Cardinals 0

1947

EASTERN DIVISION	W	L	T	Pct.	Pts.	OP	WESTERN DIVISION	W	L	T	Pct.	Pts.	OP
Philadelphia	8	4	0	.667	308	242	Chi. Cardinals	9	3	0	.750	306	231
Pittsburgh	8	4	0	.667	240	259	Chi. Bears	8	4	0	.667	363	241
Boston	4	7	1	.364	168	256	Green Bay	6	5	1	.545	274	210
Washington	4	8	0	.333	295	367	Los Angeles	6	6	0	.500	259	214
N.Y. Giants	2	8	2	.200	190	309	Detroit	3	9	0	.250	231	305

Eastern Division playoff: Philadelphia 21, PITTSBURGH 0
NFL championship: CHI. CARDINALS 28, Philadelphia 21

1946

EASTERN DIVISION	W	L	T	Pct.	Pts.	OP	WESTERN DIVISION	W	L	T	Pct.	Pts.	OP
N.Y. Giants	7	3	1	.700	236	162	Chi. Bears	8	2	1	.800	289	193
Philadelphia	6	5	0	.545	231	220	Los Angeles	6	4	1	.600	277	257
Washington	5	5	1	.500	171	191	Green Bay	6	5	0	.545	148	158
Pittsburgh	5	5	1	.500	136	117	Chi. Cardinals	6	5	0	.545	260	198
Boston	2	8	1	.200	189	273	Detroit	1	10	0	.091	142	310

NFL championship: Chi. Bears 24, N.Y. GIANTS 14

1945

EASTERN DIVISION	W	L	T	Pct.	Pts.	OP	WESTERN DIVISION	W	L	T	Pct.	Pts.	OP
Washington	8	2	0	.800	209	121	Cleveland	9	1	0	.900	244	136
Philadelphia	7	3	0	.700	272	133	Detroit	7	3	0	.700	195	194
N.Y. Giants	3	6	1	.333	179	198	Green Bay	6	4	0	.600	258	173
Boston	3	6	1	.333	123	211	Chi. Bears	3	7	0	.300	192	235
Pittsburgh	2	8	0	.200	79	220	Chi. Cardinals	1	9	0	.100	98	228

NFL championship: CLEVELAND 15, Washington 14

1944

EASTERN DIVISION	W	L	T	Pct.	Pts.	OP	WESTERN DIVISION	W	L	T	Pct.	Pts.	OP
N.Y. Giants	8	1	1	.889	206	75	Green Bay	8	2	0	.800	238	141
Philadelphia	7	1	2	.875	267	131	Chi. Bears	6	3	1	.667	258	172
Washington	6	3	1	.667	169	180	Detroit	6	3	1	.667	216	151
Boston	2	8	0	.200	82	233	Cleveland	4	6	0	.400	188	224
Brooklyn	0	10	0	.000	69	166	Card-Pitt	0	10	0	.000	108	328

NFL championship: Green Bay 14, N.Y. GIANTS 7

1943

EASTERN DIVISION	W	L	T	Pct.	Pts.	OP	WESTERN DIVISION	W	L	T	Pct.	Pts.	OP
Washington	6	3	1	.667	229	137	Chi. Bears	8	1	1	.889	303	157
N.Y. Giants	6	3	1	.667	197	170	Green Bay	7	2	1	.778	264	172
Phil-Pitt	5	4	1	.556	225	230	Detroit	3	6	1	.333	178	218
Brooklyn	2	8	0	.200	65	234	Chi. Cardinals	0	10	0	.000	95	238

Eastern Division playoff: Washington 28, N.Y. GIANTS 0
NFL championship: CHI. BEARS 41, Washington 21

1942

EASTERN DIVISION	W	L	T	Pct.	Pts.	OP	WESTERN DIVISION	W	L	T	Pct.	Pts.	OP
Washington	10	1	0	.909	227	102	Chi. Bears	11	0	0	1.000	376	84
Pittsburgh	7	4	0	.636	167	119	Green Bay	8	2	1	.800	300	215
N.Y. Giants	5	5	1	.500	155	139	Cleveland	5	6	0	.455	150	207
Brooklyn	3	8	0	.273	100	168	Chi. Cardinals	3	8	0	.273	98	209
Philadelphia	2	9	0	.182	134	239	Detroit	0	11	0	.000	38	263

NFL championship: WASHINGTON 14, Chi. Bears 6

1941

EASTERN DIVISION	W	L	T	Pct.	Pts.	OP	WESTERN DIVISION	W	L	T	Pct.	Pts.	OP
N.Y. Giants	8	3	0	.727	238	114	Chi. Bears	10	1	0	.909	396	147
Brooklyn	7	4	0	.636	158	127	Green Bay	10	1	0	.909	258	120
Washington	6	5	0	.545	176	174	Detroit	4	6	1	.400	121	195
Philadelphia	2	8	1	.200	119	218	Chi. Cardinals	3	7	1	.300	127	197
Pittsburgh	1	9	1	.100	103	276	Cleveland	2	9	0	.182	116	244

Western Division playoff: CHI. BEARS 33, Green Bay 14
NFL championship: CHI. BEARS 37, N.Y. Giants 9

1940

EASTERN DIVISION	W	L	T	Pct.	Pts.	OP	WESTERN DIVISION	W	L	T	Pct.	Pts.	OP
Washington	9	2	0	.818	245	142	Chi. Bears	8	3	0	.727	238	152
Brooklyn	8	3	0	.727	186	120	Green Bay	6	4	1	.600	238	155
N.Y. Giants	6	4	1	.600	131	133	Detroit	5	5	1	.500	138	153
Pittsburgh	2	7	2	.222	60	178	Cleveland	4	6	1	.400	171	191
Philadelphia	1	10	0	.091	111	211	Chi. Cardinals	2	7	2	.222	139	222

NFL championship: Chi. Bears 73, WASHINGTON 0

1939

EASTERN DIVISION	W	L	T	Pct.	Pts.	OP	WESTERN DIVISION	W	L	T	Pct.	Pts.	OP
N.Y. Giants	9	1	1	.900	168	85	Green Bay	9	2	0	.818	233	153
Washington	8	2	1	.800	242	94	Chi. Bears	8	3	0	.727	298	157
Brooklyn	4	6	1	.400	108	219	Detroit	6	5	0	.545	145	150
Philadelphia	1	9	1	.100	105	200	Cleveland	5	5	1	.500	195	164
Pittsburgh	1	9	1	.100	114	216	Chi. Cardinals	1	10	0	.091	84	254

NFL championship: GREEN BAY 27, N.Y. Giants 0

1938

EASTERN DIVISION	W	L	T	Pct.	Pts.	OP	WESTERN DIVISION	W	L	T	Pct.	Pts.	OP
N.Y. Giants	8	2	1	.800	194	79	Green Bay	8	3	0	.727	223	118
Washington	6	3	2	.667	148	154	Detroit	7	4	0	.636	119	108
Brooklyn	4	4	3	.500	131	161	Chi. Bears	6	5	0	.545	194	148
Philadelphia	5	6	0	.455	154	164	Cleveland	4	7	0	.364	131	215
Pittsburgh	2	9	0	.182	79	169	Chi. Cardinals	2	9	0	.182	111	168

NFL championship: N.Y. GIANTS 23, Green Bay 17

1937

EASTERN DIVISION

	W	L	T	Pct.	Pts.	OP
Washington	8	3	0	.727	195	120
N.Y. Giants	6	3	2	.667	128	109
Pittsburgh	4	7	0	.364	122	145
Brooklyn	3	7	1	.300	82	174
Philadelphia	2	8	1	.200	86	177

WESTERN DIVISION

	W	L	T	Pct.	Pts.	OP
Chi. Bears	9	1	1	.900	201	100
Green Bay	7	4	0	.636	220	122
Detroit	7	4	0	.636	180	105
Chi. Cardinals	5	5	1	.500	135	165
Cleveland	1	10	0	.091	75	207

NFL championship: Washington 28, CHI. BEARS 21

1936

EASTERN DIVISION

	W	L	T	Pct.	Pts.	OP
Boston	7	5	0	.583	149	110
Pittsburgh	6	6	0	.500	98	187
N.Y. Giants	5	6	1	.455	115	163
Brooklyn	3	8	1	.273	92	161
Philadelphia	1	11	0	.083	51	206

WESTERN DIVISION

	W	L	T	Pct.	Pts.	OP
Green Bay	10	1	1	.909	248	118
Chi. Bears	9	3	0	.750	222	94
Detroit	8	4	0	.667	235	102
Chi. Cardinals	3	8	1	.273	74	143

NFL championship: Green Bay 21, Boston 6, at Polo Grounds, N.Y.

1935

EASTERN DIVISION

	W	L	T	Pct.	Pts.	OP
N.Y. Giants	9	3	0	.750	180	96
Brooklyn	5	6	1	.455	90	141
Pittsburgh	4	8	0	.333	100	209
Boston	2	8	1	.200	65	123
Philadelphia	2	9	0	.182	60	179

WESTERN DIVISION

	W	L	T	Pct.	Pts.	OP
Detroit	7	3	2	.700	191	111
Green Bay	8	4	0	.667	181	96
Chi. Bears	6	4	2	.600	192	106
Chi. Cardinals	6	4	2	.600	99	97

NFL championship: DETROIT 26, N.Y. Giants 7

One game between Boston and Philadelphia was canceled.

1934

EASTERN DIVISION

	W	L	T	Pct.	Pts.	OP
N.Y. Giants	8	5	0	.615	147	107
Boston	6	6	0	.500	107	94
Brooklyn	4	7	0	.364	61	153
Philadelphia	4	7	0	.364	127	85
Pittsburgh	2	10	0	.167	51	206

WESTERN DIVISION

	W	L	T	Pct.	Pts.	OP
Chi. Bears	13	0	0	1.000	286	86
Detroit	10	3	0	.769	238	59
Green Bay	7	6	0	.538	156	112
Chi. Cardinals	5	6	0	.455	80	84
St. Louis	1	2	0	.333	27	61
Cincinnati	0	8	0	.000	10	243

NFL championship: N.Y. GIANTS 30, Chi. Bears 13

1933

EASTERN DIVISION

	W	L	T	Pct.	Pts.	OP
N.Y. Giants	11	3	0	.786	244	101
Brooklyn	5	4	1	.556	93	54
Boston	5	5	2	.500	103	97
Philadelphia	3	5	1	.375	77	158
Pittsburgh	3	6	2	.333	67	208

WESTERN DIVISION

	W	L	T	Pct.	Pts.	OP
Chi. Bears	10	2	1	.833	133	82
Portsmouth	6	5	0	.545	128	87
Green Bay	5	7	1	.417	170	107
Cincinnati	3	6	1	.333	38	110
Chi. Cardinals	1	9	1	.100	52	101

NFL championship: CHI. BEARS 23, N.Y. Giants 21

1932

	W	L	T	Pct.
Chicago Bears	7	1	6	.875
Green Bay Packers	10	3	1	.769
Portsmouth Spartans	6	2	4	.750
Boston Braves	4	4	2	.500
New York Giants	4	6	2	.400
Brooklyn Dodgers	3	9	0	.250
Chicago Cardinals	2	6	2	.250
Staten Island Stapletons	2	7	3	.222

Chicago Bears and Portsmouth finished regularly scheduled games tied for first place. Bears won playoff game, which counted in standings, 9-0.

1931

	W	L	T	Pct.
Green Bay Packers	12	2	0	.857
Portsmouth Spartans	11	3	0	.786
Chicago Bears	8	5	0	.615
Chicago Cardinals	5	4	0	.556
New York Giants	7	6	1	.538
Providence Steam Roller	4	4	3	.500
Staten Island Stapletons	4	6	1	.400
Cleveland Indians	2	8	0	.200
Brooklyn Dodgers	2	12	0	.143
Frankford Yellow Jackets	1	6	1	.143

1930

	W	L	T	Pct.
Green Bay Packers	10	3	1	.769
New York Giants	13	4	0	.765
Chicago Bears	9	4	1	.692
Brooklyn Dodgers	7	4	1	.636
Providence Steam Roller	6	4	1	.600
Staten Island Stapletons	5	5	2	.500
Chicago Cardinals	5	6	2	.455
Portsmouth Spartans	5	6	3	.455
Frankford Yellow Jackets	4	13	1	.222
Minneapolis Red Jackets	1	7	1	.125
Newark Tornadoes	1	10	1	.091

1929

	W	L	T	Pct.
Green Bay Packers	12	0	1	1.000
New York Giants	13	1	1	.929
Frankford Yellow Jackets	10	4	5	.714
Chicago Cardinals	6	6	1	.500
Boston Bulldogs	4	4	0	.500
Staten Island Stapletons	3	4	3	.429
Providence Steam Roller	4	6	2	.400
Orange Tornadoes	3	5	4	.375
Chicago Bears	4	9	2	.308
Buffalo Bisons	1	7	1	.125
Minneapolis Red Jackets	1	9	0	.100
Dayton Triangles	0	6	0	.000

1928

	W	L	T	Pct.
Providence Steam Roller	8	1	2	.889
Frankford Yellow Jackets	11	3	2	.786
Detroit Wolverines	7	2	1	.778
Green Bay Packers	6	4	3	.600
Chicago Bears	7	5	1	.583
New York Giants	4	7	2	.364
New York Yankees	4	8	1	.333
Pottsville Maroons	2	8	0	.200
Chicago Cardinals	1	5	0	.167
Dayton Triangles	0	7	0	.000

1927

	W	L	T	Pct.
New York Giants	11	1	1	.917
Green Bay Packers	7	2	1	.778
Chicago Bears	9	3	2	.750
Cleveland Bulldogs	8	4	1	.667
Providence Steam Roller	8	5	1	.615
New York Yankees	7	8	1	.467
Frankford Yellow Jackets	6	9	3	.400
Pottsville Maroons	5	8	0	.385
Chicago Cardinals	3	7	1	.300
Dayton Triangles	1	6	1	.143
Duluth Eskimos	1	8	0	.111
Buffalo Bisons	0	5	0	.000

1926

	W	L	T	Pct.
Frankford Yellow Jackets	14	1	2	.933
Chicago Bears	12	1	3	.923
Pottsville Maroons	10	2	2	.833
Kansas City Cowboys	8	3	0	.727
Green Bay Packers	7	3	3	.700
Los Angeles Buccaneers	6	3	1	.667
New York Giants	8	4	1	.667
Duluth Eskimos	6	5	3	.545
Buffalo Rangers	4	4	2	.500
Chicago Cardinals	5	6	1	.455
Providence Steam Roller	5	7	1	.417
Detroit Panthers	4	6	2	.400
Hartford Blues	3	7	0	.300
Brooklyn Lions	3	8	0	.273
Milwaukee Badgers	2	7	0	.222
Akron Pros	1	4	3	.200
Dayton Triangles	1	4	1	.200
Racine Tornadoes	1	4	0	.200
Columbus Tigers	1	6	0	.143
Canton Bulldogs	1	9	3	.100
Hammond Pros	0	4	0	.000
Louisville Colonels	0	4	0	.000

1925

	W	L	T	Pct.
Chicago Cardinals	11	2	1	.846
Pottsville Maroons	10	2	0	.833
Detroit Panthers	8	2	2	.800
New York Giants	8	4	0	.667
Akron Indians	4	2	2	.667
Frankford Yellow Jackets	13	7	0	.650
Chicago Bears	9	5	3	.643
Rock Island Independents	5	3	3	.625
Green Bay Packers	8	5	0	.615
Providence Steam Roller	6	5	1	.545
Canton Bulldogs	4	4	0	.500
Cleveland Bulldogs	5	8	1	.385
Kansas City Cowboys	2	5	1	.286
Hammond Pros	1	4	0	.200
Buffalo Bisons	1	6	2	.143
Duluth Kelleys	0	3	0	.000
Rochester Jeffersons	0	6	1	.000
Milwaukee Badgers	0	6	0	.000
Dayton Triangles	0	7	1	.000
Columbus Tigers	0	9	0	.000

PAST STANDINGS

1924

	W	L	T	Pct.
Cleveland Bulldogs	7	1	1	.875
Chicago Bears	6	1	4	.857
Frankford Yellow Jackets	11	2	1	.846
Duluth Kelleys	5	1	0	.833
Rock Island Independents	5	2	2	.714
Green Bay Packers	7	4	0	.636
Racine Legion	4	3	3	.571
Chicago Cardinals	5	4	1	.556
Buffalo Bisons	6	5	0	.545
Columbus Tigers	4	4	0	.500
Hammond Pros	2	2	1	.500
Milwaukee Badgers	5	8	0	.385
Akron Indians	2	6	0	.250
Dayton Triangles	2	6	0	.250
Kansas City Blues	2	7	0	.222
Kenosha Maroons	0	4	1	.000
Minneapolis Marines	0	6	0	.000
Rochester Jeffersons	0	7	0	.000

1923

	W	L	T	Pct.
Canton Bulldogs	11	0	1	1.000
Chicago Bears	9	2	1	.818
Green Bay Packers	7	2	1	.778
Milwaukee Badgers	7	2	3	.778
Cleveland Indians	3	1	3	.750
Chicago Cardinals	8	4	0	.667
Duluth Kelleys	4	3	0	.571
Buffalo All-Americans	5	4	3	.556
Columbus Tigers	5	4	1	.556
Racine Legion	4	4	2	.500
Toledo Maroons	3	3	2	.500
Rock Island Independents	2	3	3	.400
Minneapolis Marines	2	5	2	.286
St. Louis All-Stars	1	4	2	.200
Hammond Pros	1	5	1	.167
Dayton Triangles	1	6	1	.143
Akron Indians	1	6	0	.143
Oorang Indians	1	10	0	.091
Louisville Brecks	0	3	0	.000
Rochester Jeffersons	0	4	0	.000

1922

	W	L	T	Pct.
Canton Bulldogs	10	0	2	1.000
Chicago Bears	9	3	0	.750
Chicago Cardinals	8	3	0	.727
Toledo Maroons	5	2	2	.714
Rock Island Independents	4	2	1	.667
Racine Legion	6	4	1	.600
Dayton Triangles	4	3	1	.571
Green Bay Packers	4	3	3	.571
Buffalo All-Americans	5	4	1	.556
Akron Pros	3	5	2	.375
Milwaukee Badgers	2	4	3	.333
Oorang Indians	3	6	0	.333
Minneapolis Marines	1	3	0	.250
Louisville Brecks	1	3	0	.250
Evansville Crimson Giants	0	3	0	.000
Rochester Jeffersons	0	4	1	.000
Hammond Pros	0	5	1	.000
Columbus Panhandles	0	8	0	.000

1921

	W	L	T	Pct.
Chicago Staleys	9	1	1	.900
Buffalo All-Americans	9	1	2	.900
Akron Pros	8	3	1	.727
Canton Bulldogs	5	2	3	.714
Rock Island Independents	4	2	1	.667
Evansville Crimson Giants	3	2	0	.600
Green Bay Packers	3	2	1	.600
Dayton Triangles	4	4	1	.500
Chicago Cardinals	3	3	2	.500
Rochester Jeffersons	2	3	0	.400
Cleveland Indians	3	5	0	.375
Washington Senators	1	2	0	.333
Cincinnati Celts	1	3	0	.250
Hammond Pros	1	3	1	.250
Minneapolis Marines	1	3	0	.250
Detroit Heralds	1	5	1	.167
Columbus Panhandles	1	8	0	.111
Tonawanda Kardex	0	1	0	.000
Muncie Flyers	0	2	0	.000
Louisville Brecks	0	2	0	.000
New York Giants	0	2	0	.000

1920*

	W	L	T	Pct.
Akron Pros	8	0	3	1.000
Decatur Staleys	10	1	2	.909
Buffalo All-Americans	9	1	1	.900
Chicago Cardinals	6	2	2	.750
Rock Island Independents	6	2	2	.750
Dayton Triangles	5	2	2	.714
Rochester Jeffersons	6	3	2	.667
Canton Bulldogs	7	4	2	.636
Detroit Heralds	2	3	3	.400
Cleveland Tigers	2	4	2	.333
Chicago Tigers	2	5	1	.286
Hammond Pros	2	5	0	.286
Columbus Panhandles	2	6	2	.250
Muncie Flyers	0	1	0	.000

**No official standings were maintained for the 1920 season, and the championship was awarded to the Akron Pros in a League meeting on April 30, 1921. Clubs played schedules that included games against nonleague opponents.*

RS=REGULAR SEASON
PS=POSTSEASON

***ARIZONA vs. ATLANTA**
RS: Cardinals lead series, 13-8
1966—Falcons, 16-10 (A)
1968—Cardinals, 17-12 (StL)
1971—Cardinals, 26-9 (A)
1973—Cardinals, 32-10 (A)
1975—Cardinals, 23-20 (StL)
1978—Cardinals, 42-21 (StL)
1980—Falcons, 33-27 (StL) OT
1981—Falcons, 41-20 (A)
1982—Cardinals, 23-20 (A)
1986—Falcons, 33-13 (A)
1987—Cardinals, 34-21 (A)
1989—Cardinals, 34-20 (P)
1990—Cardinals, 24-13 (A)
1991—Cardinals, 16-10 (P)
1992—Falcons, 20-17 (A)
1993—Cardinals, 27-10 (A)
1994—Falcons, 10-6 (Atl)
1995—Cardinals, 40-37 (Ariz) OT
1997—Cardinals, 29-26 (Ariz)
1999—Falcons, 37-14 (Atl)
2001—Falcons, 34-14 (Ariz)
(RS Pts.—Cardinals 488, Falcons 453)
**Franchise known as Phoenix prior to 1994 and in St. Louis prior to 1988*

***ARIZONA vs. BALTIMORE**
RS: Ravens lead series, 2-1
1997—Cardinals, 16-13 (B)
2000—Ravens, 13-7 (B)
2003—Ravens, 26-18 (B)
(RS Pts.—Ravens 52, Cardinals 41)

***ARIZONA vs. BUFFALO**
RS: Bills lead series, 4-3
1971—Cardinals, 28-23 (B)
1975—Bills, 32-14 (StL)
1981—Cardinals, 24-0 (StL)
1984—Cardinals, 37-7 (StL)
1986—Bills, 17-10 (B)
1990—Bills, 45-14 (B)
1999—Bills, 31-21 (A)
(RS Pts.—Bills 155, Cardinals 148)
**Franchise known as Phoenix prior to 1994 and in St. Louis prior to 1988*

ARIZONA vs. CAROLINA
RS: Series tied, 2-2
1995—Panthers, 27-7 (C)
2001—Cardinals, 30-7 (C)
2002—Cardinals, 16-13 (C)
2003—Panthers, 20-17 (A)
(RS Pts.—Cardinals 70, Panthers 67)

***ARIZONA vs. **CHICAGO**
RS: Bears lead series, 54-26-6
(NP denotes Normal Park;
Wr denotes Wrigley Field;
Co denotes Comiskey Park;
So denotes Soldier Field;
all Chicago)
1920—Cardinals, 7-6 (NP)
Staleys, 10-0 (Wr)
1921—Tie, 0-0 (Wr)
1922—Cardinals, 6-0 (Co)
Cardinals, 9-0 (Co)
1923—Bears, 3-0 (Wr)
1924—Bears, 6-0 (Wr)
Bears, 21-0 (Co)
1925—Cardinals, 9-0 (Co)
Tie, 0-0 (Wr)
1926—Bears, 16-0 (Wr)
Bears, 10-0 (So)
Tie, 0-0 (Wr)
1927—Bears, 9-0 (NP)
Cardinals, 3-0 (Wr)
1928—Bears, 15-0 (NP)
Bears, 34-0 (Wr)
1929—Tie, 0-0 (Wr)
Cardinals, 40-6 (Co)
1930—Bears, 32-6 (Co)
Bears, 6-0 (Wr)
1931—Bears, 26-13 (Wr)
Bears, 18-7 (Wr)
1932—Tie, 0-0 (Wr)
Bears, 34-0 (Wr)
1933—Bears, 12-9 (Wr)
Bears, 22-6 (Wr)
1934—Bears, 20-0 (Wr)
Bears, 17-6 (Wr)
1935—Tie, 7-7 (Wr)
Bears, 13-0 (Wr)
1936—Bears, 7-3 (Wr)
Cardinals, 14-7 (Wr)
1937—Bears, 16-7 (Wr)
Bears, 42-28 (Wr)
1938—Bears, 16-13 (So)
Bears, 34-28 (Wr)
1939—Bears, 44-7 (Wr)
Bears, 48-7 (Co)
1940—Cardinals, 21-7 (Co)
Bears, 31-23 (Wr)
1941—Bears, 53-7 (Wr)
Bears, 34-24 (Co)
1942—Bears, 41-14 (Wr)
Bears, 21-7 (Co)
1943—Bears, 20-0 (Wr)
Bears, 35-24 (Co)
1945—Cardinals, 16-7 (Wr)
Bears, 28-20 (Co)
1946—Bears, 34-17 (Co)
Cardinals, 35-28 (Wr)
1947—Cardinals, 31-7 (Co)
Cardinals, 30-21 (Wr)
1948—Bears, 28-17 (Co)
Cardinals, 24-21 (Wr)
1949—Bears, 17-7 (Co)
Bears, 52-21 (Wr)
1950—Bears, 27-6 (Wr)
Cardinals, 20-10 (Co)
1951—Cardinals, 28-14 (Co)
Cardinals, 24-14 (Wr)
1952—Cardinals, 21-10 (Co)
Bears, 10-7 (Wr)
1953—Cardinals, 24-17 (Wr)
1954—Bears, 29-7 (Co)
1955—Cardinals, 53-14 (Co)
1956—Bears, 10-3 (Wr)
1957—Bears, 14-6 (Co)
1958—Bears, 30-14 (Wr)
1959—Bears, 31-7 (So)
1965—Bears, 34-13 (Wr)
1966—Cardinals, 24-17 (StL)
1967—Bears, 30-3 (Wr)
1969—Cardinals, 20-17 (StL)
1972—Bears, 27-10 (StL)
1975—Cardinals, 34-20 (So)
1977—Cardinals, 16-13 (StL)
1978—Bears, 17-10 (So)
1979—Bears, 42-6 (So)
1982—Cardinals, 10-7 (So)
1984—Cardinals, 38-21 (StL)
1990—Bears, 31-21 (P)
1994—Bears, 19-16 (A) OT
1998—Cardinals, 20-7 (A)
2001—Bears, 20-13 (A)
2003—Bears, 28-3 (C)
(RS Pts.—Bears 1,622, Cardinals 1,050)
**Franchise known as Phoenix prior to 1994, in St. Louis prior to 1988, and in Chicago prior to 1960*
***Franchise in Decatur prior to 1921 and known as Staleys prior to 1922*

***ARIZONA vs. CINCINNATI**
RS: Bengals lead series, 5-3
1973—Bengals, 42-24 (C)
1979—Bengals, 34-28 (C)
1985—Cardinals, 41-27 (StL)
1988—Bengals, 21-14 (C)
1994—Cardinals, 28-7 (A)
1997—Bengals, 24-21 (C)
2000—Bengals, 24-13 (C)
2003—Cardinals, 17-14 (A)
(RS Pts.—Bengals 193, Cardinals 186)
**Franchise known as Phoenix prior to 1994 and in St. Louis prior to 1988*

***ARIZONA vs. CLEVELAND**
RS: Browns lead series, 33-11-3
1950—Browns, 34-24 (Cle)
Browns, 10-7 (Chi)
1951—Browns, 34-17 (Chi)
Browns, 49-28 (Cle)
1952—Browns, 28-13 (Cle)
Browns, 10-0 (Chi)
1953—Browns, 27-7 (Chi)
Browns, 27-16 (Cle)
1954—Browns, 31-7 (Cle)
Browns, 35-3 (Chi)
1955—Browns, 26-20 (Chi)
Browns, 35-24 (Cle)
1956—Cardinals, 9-7 (Chi)
Cardinals, 24-7 (Cle)
1957—Browns, 17-7 (Chi)
Browns, 31-0 (Cle)
1958—Browns, 35-28 (Cle)
Browns, 38-24 (Chi)
1959—Browns, 34-7 (Chi)
Browns, 17-7 (Cle)
1960—Browns, 28-27 (Cle)
Tie, 17-17 (StL)
1961—Browns, 20-17 (Cle)
Browns, 21-10 (StL)
1962—Browns, 34-7 (StL)
Browns, 38-14 (Cle)
1963—Cardinals, 20-14 (Cle)
Browns, 24-10 (StL)
1964—Tie, 33-33 (Cle)
Cardinals, 28-19 (StL)
1965—Cardinals, 49-13 (Cle)
Browns, 27-24 (StL)
1966—Cardinals, 34-28 (Cle)
Browns, 38-10 (StL)
1967—Browns, 20-16 (Cle)
Browns, 20-16 (StL)
1968—Cardinals, 27-21 (Cle)
Cardinals, 27-16 (StL)
1969—Tie, 21-21 (Cle)
Browns, 27-21 (StL)
1974—Cardinals, 29-7 (StL)
1979—Browns, 38-20 (StL)
1985—Cardinals, 27-24 (Cle) OT

1988—Browns, 29-21 (P)
1994—Browns, 32-0 (Cle)
2000—Cardinals, 29-21 (A)
2003—Browns, 44-6 (Cle)
(RS Pts.—Browns 1,206, Cardinals 832)
Franchise known as Phoenix prior to 1994, in St. Louis prior to 1988, and in Chicago prior to 1960

***ARIZONA vs. DALLAS**
RS: Cowboys lead series, 53-27-1
PS: Cardinals lead series, 1-0
1960—Cardinals, 12-10 (StL)
1961—Cardinals, 31-17 (D)
Cardinals, 31-13 (StL)
1962—Cardinals, 28-24 (D)
Cardinals, 52-20 (StL)
1963—Cardinals, 34-7 (D)
Cowboys, 28-24 (StL)
1964—Cardinals, 16-6 (D)
Cowboys, 31-13 (StL)
1965—Cardinals, 20-13 (StL)
Cowboys, 27-13 (D)
1966—Tie, 10-10 (StL)
Cowboys, 31-17 (D)
1967—Cowboys, 46-21 (D)
1968—Cowboys, 27-10 (StL)
1969—Cowboys, 24-3 (D)
1970—Cardinals, 20-7 (StL)
Cardinals, 38-0 (D)
1971—Cowboys, 16-13 (StL)
Cowboys, 31-12 (D)
1972—Cowboys, 33-24 (D)
Cowboys, 27-6 (StL)
1973—Cowboys, 45-10 (D)
Cowboys, 30-3 (StL)
1974—Cardinals, 31-28 (StL)
Cowboys, 17-14 (D)
1975—Cowboys, 37-31 (D) OT
Cardinals, 31-17 (StL)
1976—Cardinals, 21-17 (StL)
Cowboys, 19-14 (D)
1977—Cowboys, 30-24 (StL)
Cardinals, 24-17 (D)
1978—Cowboys, 21-12 (D)
Cowboys, 24-21 (StL) OT
1979—Cowboys, 22-21 (StL)
Cowboys, 22-13 (D)
1980—Cowboys, 27-24 (StL)
Cowboys, 31-21 (D)
1981—Cowboys, 30-17 (D)
Cardinals, 20-17 (StL)
1982—Cowboys, 24-7 (StL)
1983—Cowboys, 34-17 (StL)
Cowboys, 35-17 (D)
1984—Cardinals, 31-20 (D)
Cowboys, 24-17 (StL)
1985—Cardinals, 21-10 (StL)
Cowboys, 35-17 (D)
1986—Cowboys, 31-7 (StL)
Cowboys, 37-6 (D)
1987—Cardinals, 24-13 (StL)
Cowboys, 21-16 (D)
1988—Cowboys, 17-14 (P)
Cardinals, 16-10 (D)
1989—Cardinals, 19-10 (D)
Cardinals, 24-20 (P)
1990—Cardinals, 20-3 (P)
Cowboys, 41-10 (D)
1991—Cowboys, 17-9 (P)
Cowboys, 27-7 (D)
1992—Cowboys, 31-20 (D)
Cowboys, 16-10 (P)
1993—Cowboys, 17-10 (P)
Cowboys, 20-15 (D)
1994—Cowboys, 38-3 (D)
Cowboys, 28-21 (A)
1995—Cowboys, 34-20 (D)
Cowboys, 37-13 (A)
1996—Cowboys, 17-3 (D)
Cowboys, 10-6 (A)
1997—Cardinals, 25-22 (A) OT
Cowboys, 24-6 (D)
1998—Cowboys, 38-10 (D)
Cowboys, 35-28 (A)
**Cardinals, 20-7 (D)
1999—Cowboys, 35-7 (D)
Cardinals, 13-9 (A)
2000—Cardinals, 32-31 (A)
Cowboys, 48-7 (D)
2001—Cowboys, 17-3 (D)
Cardinals, 17-10 (A)
2002—Cardinals, 9-6 (A) OT
2003—Cowboys, 24-7 (D)
(RS Pts.—Cowboys 1,875, Cardinals 1,384)
(PS Pts.—Cardinals 20, Cowboys 7)
Franchise known as Phoenix prior to 1994 and in St. Louis prior to 1988
***NFC First-Round Playoff*

***ARIZONA vs. DENVER**
RS: Broncos lead series, 6-0-1
1973—Tie, 17-17 (StL)
1977—Broncos, 7-0 (D)
1989—Broncos, 37-0 (P)
1991—Broncos, 24-19 (D)
1995—Broncos, 38-6 (D)
2001—Broncos, 38-17 (A)
2002—Broncos, 37-7 (D)
(RS Pts.—Broncos 198, Cardinals 66)
Franchise known as Phoenix prior to 1994 and in St. Louis prior to 1988

***ARIZONA vs. **DETROIT**
RS: Lions lead series, 29-21-5
1930—Tie, 0-0 (Port)
Cardinals, 23-0 (C)
1931—Spartans, 13-3 (Port)
Cardinals, 20-19 (C)
1932—Tie, 7-7 (Port)
1933—Spartans, 7-6 (Port)
1934—Lions, 6-0 (D)
Lions, 17-13 (C)
1935—Tie, 10-10 (D)
Lions, 7-6 (C)
1936—Lions, 39-0 (D)
Lions, 14-7 (C)
1937—Lions, 16-7 (C)
Lions, 16-7 (D)
1938—Lions, 10-0 (D)
Lions, 7-3 (C)
1939—Lions, 21-3 (D)
Lions, 17-3 (C)
1940—Tie, 0-0 (Buffalo)
Lions, 43-14 (C)
1941—Tie, 14-14 (C)
Lions, 21-3 (D)
1942—Cardinals, 13-0 (C)
Cardinals, 7-0 (D)
1943—Lions, 35-17 (D)
Lions, 7-0 (Buffalo)
1945—Lions, 10-0 (Milwaukee)
Lions, 26-0 (D)
1946—Cardinals, 34-14 (C)
Cardinals, 36-14 (D)
1947—Cardinals, 45-21 (C)
Cardinals, 17-7 (D)
1948—Cardinals, 56-20 (C)
Cardinals, 28-14 (D)
1949—Lions, 24-7 (C)
Cardinals, 42-19 (D)
1959—Lions, 45-21 (D)
1961—Lions, 45-14 (StL)
1967—Cardinals, 38-28 (StL)
1969—Lions, 20-0 (D)
1970—Lions, 16-3 (D)
1973—Lions, 20-16 (StL)
1975—Cardinals, 24-13 (D)
1978—Cardinals, 21-14 (StL)
1980—Lions, 20-7 (D)
Cardinals, 24-23 (StL)
1989—Cardinals, 16-13 (D)
1993—Lions, 26-20 (D)
Lions, 21-14 (Phx)
1995—Cardinals, 20-17 (D)
1998—Cardinals, 17-15 (D)
1999—Cardinals, 23-19 (A)
2001—Cardinals, 45-38 (A)
2002—Cardinals, 23-20 (A) OT
2003—Lions, 42-24 (D)
(RS Pts.—Lions 970, Cardinals 831)
Franchise known as Phoenix prior to 1994, in St. Louis prior to 1988, and in Chicago prior to 1960
***Franchise in Portsmouth prior to 1934 and known as the Spartans*

***ARIZONA vs. GREEN BAY**
RS: Packers lead series, 41-22-4
PS: Packers lead series, 1-0
1921—Tie, 3-3 (C)
1922—Cardinals, 16-3 (C)
1924—Cardinals, 3-0 (C)
1925—Cardinals, 9-6 (C)
1926—Cardinals, 13-7 (GB)
Packers, 3-0 (C)
1927—Packers, 13-0 (GB)
Tie, 6-6 (C)
1928—Packers, 20-0 (GB)
1929—Packers, 9-2 (GB)
Packers, 7-6 (C)
Packers, 12-0 (C)
1930—Packers, 14-0 (GB)
Cardinals, 13-6 (C)
1931—Packers, 26-7 (GB)
Cardinals, 21-13 (C)
1932—Packers, 15-7 (GB)
Packers, 19-9 (C)
1933—Packers, 14-6 (C)
1934—Packers, 15-0 (GB)
Cardinals, 9-0 (Mil)
Cardinals, 6-0 (C)
1935—Cardinals, 7-6 (GB)
Cardinals, 3-0 (Mil)
Cardinals, 9-7 (C)
1936—Packers, 10-7 (GB)
Packers, 24-0 (Mil)
Tie, 0-0 (C)
1937—Cardinals, 14-7 (GB)
Packers, 34-13 (Mil)
1938—Packers, 28-7 (Mil)
Packers, 24-22 (Buffalo)
1939—Packers, 14-10 (GB)
Packers, 27-20 (Mil)

1940—Packers, 31-6 (Mil)
Packers, 28-7 (C)
1941—Packers, 14-13 (Mil)
Packers, 17-9 (GB)
1942—Packers, 17-13 (C)
Packers, 55-24 (GB)
1943—Packers, 28-7 (C)
Packers, 35-14 (Mil)
1945—Packers, 33-14 (GB)
1946—Packers, 19-7 (C)
Cardinals, 24-6 (GB)
1947—Cardinals, 14-10 (GB)
Cardinals, 21-20 (C)
1948—Cardinals, 17-7 (Mil)
Cardinals, 42-7 (C)
1949—Cardinals, 39-17 (Mil)
Cardinals, 41-21 (C)
1955—Packers, 31-14 (GB)
1956—Packers, 24-21 (C)
1962—Packers, 17-0 (Mil)
1963—Packers, 30-7 (StL)
1967—Packers, 31-23 (StL)
1969—Packers, 45-28 (GB)
1971—Tie, 16-16 (StL)
1973—Packers, 25-21 (GB)
1976—Cardinals, 29-0 (StL)
1982—**Packers, 41-16 (GB)
1984—Packers, 24-23 (GB)
1985—Cardinals, 43-28 (StL)
1988—Packers, 26-17 (P)
1990—Packers, 24-21 (P)
1999—Packers, 49-24 (GB)
2000—Packers, 29-3 (A)
2003—Cardinals, 20-13 (A)
(RS Pts.—Packers 1,169, Cardinals 870)
(PS Pts.—Packers 41, Cardinals 16)
Franchise known as Phoenix prior to 1994, in St. Louis prior to 1988, and in Chicago prior to 1960
***NFC First-Round Playoff*

***ARIZONA vs. **INDIANAPOLIS**
RS: Series tied, 6-6
1961—Colts, 16-0 (B)
1964—Colts, 47-27 (B)
1968—Colts, 27-0 (B)
1972—Cardinals, 10-3 (B)
1976—Cardinals, 24-17 (StL)
1978—Colts, 30-17 (StL)
1980—Cardinals, 17-10 (B)
1981—Cardinals, 35-24 (B)
1984—Cardinals, 34-33 (I)
1990—Cardinals, 20-17 (P)
1992—Colts, 16-13 (I)
1996—Colts, 20-13 (I)
(RS Pts.—Colts 260, Cardinals 210)
Franchise known as Phoenix prior to 1994 and in St. Louis prior to 1988
***Franchise in Baltimore prior to 1984*

ARIZONA vs. JACKSONVILLE
RS: Jaguars lead series, 1-0
2000—Jaguars, 44-10 (J)
(RS Pts.—Jaguars 44, Cardinals 10)

***ARIZONA vs. KANSAS CITY**
RS: Chiefs lead series, 6-2-1
1970—Tie, 6-6 (KC)
1974—Chiefs, 17-13 (StL)
1980—Chiefs, 21-13 (StL)
1983—Chiefs, 38-14 (KC)
1986—Cardinals, 23-14 (StL)
1995—Chiefs, 24-3 (A)
1998—Chiefs, 34-24 (KC)
2001—Cardinals, 24-16 (A)
2002—Chiefs, 49-0 (KC)
(RS Pts.—Chiefs 219, Cardinals 120)
Franchise known as Phoenix prior to 1994 and in St. Louis prior to 1988

***ARIZONA vs. MIAMI**
RS: Dolphins lead series, 8-0
1972—Dolphins, 31-10 (M)
1977—Dolphins, 55-14 (StL)
1978—Dolphins, 24-10 (M)
1981—Dolphins, 20-7 (StL)
1984—Dolphins, 36-28 (StL)
1990—Dolphins, 23-3 (M)
1996—Dolphins, 38-10 (A)
1999—Dolphins, 19-16 (M)
(RS Pts.—Dolphins 246, Cardinals 98)
Franchise known as Phoenix prior to 1994 and in St. Louis prior to 1988

***ARIZONA vs. MINNESOTA**
RS: Cardinals lead series, 9-8
PS: Vikings lead series, 2-0
1963—Cardinals, 56-14 (M)
1967—Cardinals, 34-24 (M)
1969—Vikings, 27-10 (StL)
1972—Cardinals, 19-17 (M)
1974—Vikings, 28-24 (StL)
**Vikings, 30-14 (M)
1977—Cardinals, 27-7 (M)
1979—Cardinals, 37-7 (StL)
1981—Cardinals, 30-17 (StL)
1983—Cardinals, 41-31 (StL)
1991—Vikings, 34-7 (M)
Vikings, 28-0 (P)
1994—Cardinals, 17-7 (A)
1995—Vikings, 30-24 (A) OT
1996—Vikings, 41-17 (M)
1997—Vikings, 20-19 (A)
1998—**Vikings, 41-21 (M)
2000—Vikings, 31-14 (M)
2003—Cardinals, 18-17 (A)
(RS Pts.—Cardinals 394, Vikings 380)
(PS Pts.—Vikings 71, Cardinals 35)
Franchise known as Phoenix prior to 1994 and in St. Louis prior to 1988
***NFC Divisional Playoff*

***ARIZONA vs. **NEW ENGLAND**
RS: Cardinals lead series, 6-4
1970—Cardinals, 31-0 (StL)
1975—Cardinals, 24-17 (StL)
1978—Patriots, 16-6 (StL)
1981—Cardinals, 27-20 (NE)
1984—Cardinals, 33-10 (NE)
1990—Cardinals, 34-14 (P)
1991—Cardinals, 24-10 (P)
1993—Patriots, 23-21 (P)
1996—Patriots, 31-0 (NE)
1999—Patriots, 27-3 (A)
(RS Pts.—Cardinals 203, Patriots 168)
Franchise known as Phoenix prior to 1994 and in St. Louis prior to 1988
***Franchise in Boston prior to 1971*

***ARIZONA vs. NEW ORLEANS**
RS: Cardinals lead series, 12-11
1967—Cardinals, 31-20 (StL)
1968—Cardinals, 21-20 (NO)
Cardinals, 31-17 (StL)
1969—Saints, 51-42 (StL)
1970—Cardinals, 24-17 (StL)
1974—Saints, 14-0 (NO)
1977—Cardinals, 49-31 (StL)
1980—Cardinals, 40-7 (NO)
1981—Cardinals, 30-3 (StL)
1982—Cardinals, 21-7 (NO)
1983—Saints, 28-17 (NO)
1984—Saints, 34-24 (NO)
1985—Cardinals, 28-16 (StL)
1986—Saints, 16-7 (StL)
1987—Cardinals, 24-19 (StL)
1990—Saints, 28-7 (NO)
1991—Saints, 27-3 (P)
1992—Saints, 30-21 (P)
1993—Saints, 20-17 (P)
1996—Cardinals, 28-14 (NO)
1997—Saints, 27-10 (NO)
1998—Cardinals, 19-17 (A)
2000—Saints, 21-10 (A)
(RS Pts.—Cardinals 504, Saints 484)
Franchise known as Phoenix prior to 1994 and in St. Louis prior to 1988

***ARIZONA vs. N.Y. GIANTS**
RS: Giants lead series, 77-40-2
1926—Giants, 20-0 (NY)
1927—Giants, 28-7 (NY)
1929—Giants, 24-21 (NY)
1930—Giants, 25-12 (NY)
Giants, 13-7 (C)
1935—Cardinals, 14-13 (NY)
1936—Giants, 14-6 (NY)
1938—Giants, 6-0 (NY)
1939—Giants, 17-7 (NY)
1941—Cardinals, 10-7 (NY)
1942—Giants, 21-7 (NY)
1943—Giants, 24-13 (NY)
1946—Giants, 28-24 (NY)
1947—Giants, 35-31 (NY)
1948—Cardinals, 63-35 (NY)
1949—Giants, 41-38 (C)
1950—Cardinals, 17-3 (C)
Giants, 51-21 (NY)
1951—Giants, 28-17 (NY)
Giants, 10-0 (C)
1952—Cardinals, 24-23 (NY)
Giants, 28-6 (C)
1953—Giants, 21-7 (NY)
Giants, 23-20 (C)
1954—Giants, 41-10 (C)
Giants, 31-17 (NY)
1955—Cardinals, 28-17 (C)
Giants, 10-0 (NY)
1956—Cardinals, 35-27 (C)
Giants, 23-10 (NY)
1957—Giants, 27-14 (NY)
Giants, 28-21 (C)
1958—Giants, 37-7 (Buffalo)
Cardinals, 23-6 (NY)
1959—Giants, 9-3 (NY)
Giants, 30-20 (Minn)
1960—Giants, 35-14 (StL)
Cardinals, 20-13 (NY)
1961—Cardinals, 21-10 (NY)
Giants, 24-9 (StL)
1962—Giants, 31-14 (StL)
Giants, 31-28 (NY)
1963—Giants, 38-21 (StL)
Cardinals, 24-17 (NY)
1964—Giants, 34-17 (NY)
Tie, 10-10 (StL)
1965—Giants, 14-10 (NY)
Giants, 28-15 (StL)

1966—Cardinals, 24-19 (StL)
Cardinals, 20-17 (NY)
1967—Giants, 37-20 (StL)
Giants, 37-14 (NY)
1968—Cardinals, 28-21 (NY)
1969—Cardinals, 42-17 (StL)
Giants, 49-6 (NY)
1970—Giants, 35-17 (NY)
Giants, 34-17 (StL)
1971—Giants, 21-20 (StL)
Cardinals, 24-7 (NY)
1972—Giants, 27-21 (NY)
Giants, 13-7 (StL)
1973—Cardinals, 35-27 (StL)
Giants, 24-13 (New Haven)
1974—Cardinals, 23-21 (New Haven)
Cardinals, 26-14 (StL)
1975—Cardinals, 26-14 (StL)
Cardinals, 20-13 (NY)
1976—Cardinals, 27-21 (StL)
Cardinals, 17-14 (NY)
1977—Cardinals, 28-0 (StL)
Giants, 27-7 (NY)
1978—Cardinals, 20-10 (StL)
Giants, 17-0 (NY)
1979—Cardinals, 27-14 (NY)
Cardinals, 29-20 (StL)
1980—Giants, 41-35 (StL)
Cardinals, 23-7 (NY)
1981—Giants, 34-14 (NY)
Giants, 20-10 (StL)
1982—Cardinals, 24-21 (StL)
1983—Tie, 20-20 (StL) OT
Cardinals, 10-6 (NY)
1984—Giants, 16-10 (NY)
Cardinals, 31-21 (StL)
1985—Giants, 27-17 (NY)
Giants, 34-3 (StL)
1986—Giants, 13-6 (StL)
Giants, 27-7 (NY)
1987—Giants, 30-7 (NY)
Cardinals, 27-24 (StL)
1988—Cardinals, 24-17 (P)
Giants, 44-7 (NY)
1989—Giants, 35-7 (NY)
Giants, 20-13 (P)
1990—Giants, 20-19 (NY)
Giants, 24-21 (P)
1991—Giants, 20-9 (NY)
Giants, 21-14 (P)
1992—Giants, 31-21 (NY)
Cardinals, 19-0 (P)
1993—Giants, 19-17 (NY)
Cardinals, 17-6 (P)
1994—Giants, 20-17 (A)
Cardinals, 10-9 (NY)
1995—Giants, 27-21 (NY) OT
Giants, 10-6 (A)
1996—Giants, 16-8 (NY)
Cardinals, 31-23 (A)
1997—Giants, 27-13 (A)
Giants, 19-10 (NY)
1998—Giants, 34-7 (NY)
Giants, 23-19 (A)
1999—Cardinals, 14-3 (A)
Cardinals, 34-24 (NY)
2000—Giants, 21-16 (NY)
Giants, 31-7 (A)
2001—Giants, 17-10 (A)
Giants, 17-13 (NY)
2002—Cardinals, 21-7 (A)
(RS Pts.—Giants 2,605, Cardinals 2,010)
Franchise known as Phoenix prior to 1994, in St. Louis prior to 1988, and in Chicago prior to 1960

***ARIZONA vs. N.Y. JETS**
RS: Jets lead series, 3-2
1971—Cardinals, 17-10 (StL)
1975—Cardinals, 37-6 (NY)
1978—Jets, 23-10 (NY)
1996—Jets, 31-21 (A)
1999—Jets, 12-7 (NY)
(RS Pts.—Cardinals 92, Jets 82)
**Franchise known as Phoenix prior to 1994 and in St. Louis prior to 1988*

***ARIZONA vs. **OAKLAND**
RS: Raiders lead series, 4-2
1973—Raiders, 17-10 (StL)
1983—Cardinals, 34-24 (LA)
1989—Raiders, 16-14 (LA)
1998—Raiders, 23-20 (A)
2001—Cardinals, 34-31 (O) OT
2002—Raiders, 41-20 (A)
(RS Pts.— Raiders 152, Cardinals 132)
**Franchise known as Phoenix prior to 1994 and in St. Louis prior to 1988*
***Franchise in Los Angeles from 1982-1994*

***ARIZONA vs. PHILADELPHIA**
RS: Series tied, 52-52-5
PS: Series tied, 1-1
1935—Cardinals, 12-3 (C)
1936—Cardinals, 13-0 (C)
1937—Tie, 6-6 (P)
1938—Eagles, 7-0 (Erie, Pa.)
1941—Eagles, 21-14 (P)
1945—Eagles, 21-6 (P)
1947—Cardinals, 45-21 (P)
**Cardinals, 28-21 (C)
1948—Cardinals, 21-14 (C)
**Eagles, 7-0 (P)
1949—Eagles, 28-3 (P)
1950—Eagles, 45-7 (C)
Cardinals, 14-10 (P)
1951—Eagles, 17-14 (C)
1952—Eagles, 10-7 (P)
Cardinals, 28-22 (C)
1953—Eagles, 56-17 (C)
Eagles, 38-0 (P)
1954—Eagles, 35-16 (C)
Eagles, 30-14 (P)
1955—Tie, 24-24 (C)
Eagles, 27-3 (P)
1956—Cardinals, 20-6 (P)
Cardinals, 28-17 (C)
1957—Eagles, 38-21 (C)
Cardinals, 31-27 (P)
1958—Tie, 21-21 (C)
Eagles, 49-21 (P)
1959—Eagles, 28-24 (Minn)
Eagles, 27-17 (P)
1960—Eagles, 31-27 (P)
Eagles, 20-6 (StL)
1961—Cardinals, 30-27 (P)
Eagles, 20-7 (StL)
1962—Cardinals, 27-21 (P)
Cardinals, 45-35 (StL)
1963—Cardinals, 28-24 (P)
Cardinals, 38-14 (StL)
1964—Cardinals, 38-13 (P)
Cardinals, 36-34 (StL)
1965—Eagles, 34-27 (P)
Eagles, 28-24 (StL)
1966—Cardinals, 16-13 (StL)
Cardinals, 41-10 (P)
1967—Cardinals, 48-14 (StL)
1968—Cardinals, 45-17 (P)
1969—Eagles, 34-30 (StL)
1970—Cardinals, 35-20 (P)
Cardinals, 23-14 (StL)
1971—Eagles, 37-20 (StL)
Eagles, 19-7 (P)
1972—Tie, 6-6 (P)
Cardinals, 24-23 (StL)
1973—Cardinals, 34-23 (P)
Eagles, 27-24 (StL)
1974—Cardinals, 7-3 (StL)
Cardinals, 13-3 (P)
1975—Cardinals, 31-20 (StL)
Cardinals, 24-23 (P)
1976—Cardinals, 33-14 (StL)
Cardinals, 17-14 (P)
1977—Cardinals, 21-17 (P)
Cardinals, 21-16 (StL)
1978—Cardinals, 16-10 (P)
Eagles, 14-10 (StL)
1979—Eagles, 24-20 (StL)
Eagles, 16-13 (P)
1980—Cardinals, 24-14 (StL)
Eagles, 17-3 (P)
1981—Eagles, 52-10 (StL)
Eagles, 38-0 (P)
1982—Cardinals, 23-20 (P)
1983—Cardinals, 14-11 (P)
Cardinals, 31-7 (StL)
1984—Cardinals, 34-14 (P)
Cardinals, 17-16 (StL)
1985—Eagles, 30-7 (P)
Eagles, 24-14 (StL)
1986—Cardinals, 13-10 (StL)
Tie, 10-10 (P) OT
1987—Eagles, 28-23 (StL)
Cardinals, 31-19 (P)
1988—Eagles, 31-21 (P)
Eagles, 23-17 (Phx)
1989—Eagles, 17-5 (Phx)
Eagles, 31-14 (P)
1990—Cardinals, 23-21 (P)
Eagles, 23-21 (Phx)
1991—Cardinals, 26-10 (P)
Eagles, 34-14 (Phx)
1992—Eagles, 31-14 (Phx)
Eagles, 7-3 (P)
1993—Eagles, 23-17 (P)
Cardinals, 16-3 (Phx)
1994—Eagles, 17-7 (P)
Cardinals, 12-6 (A)
1995—Eagles, 31-19 (A)
Eagles, 21-20 (P)
1996—Cardinals, 36-30 (A)
Eagles, 29-19 (P)
1997—Eagles, 13-10 (P) OT
Cardinals, 31-21 (A)
1998—Cardinals, 17-3 (A)
Cardinals, 20-17 (P) OT
1999—Cardinals, 25-24 (P)
Cardinals, 21-17 (A)
2000—Eagles, 33-14 (A)
Eagles, 34-9 (P)
2001—Cardinals, 21-20 (P)

Eagles, 21-7 (A)
2002—Eagles, 38-14 (P)
(RS Pts.—Eagles 2,319, Cardinals 2,106)
(PS Pts.—Eagles 28, Cardinals 28)
Franchise known as Phoenix prior to 1994, in St. Louis prior to 1988, and in Chicago prior to 1960
***NFL Championship*

***ARIZONA vs. **PITTSBURGH**
RS: Steelers lead series, 31-22-3
1933—Pirates, 14-13 (C)
1935—Pirates, 17-13 (P)
1936—Cardinals, 14-6 (C)
1937—Cardinals, 13-7 (P)
1939—Cardinals, 10-0 (P)
1940—Tie, 7-7 (P)
1942—Steelers, 19-3 (P)
1945—Steelers, 23-0 (P)
1946—Steelers, 14-7 (P)
1948—Cardinals, 24-7 (P)
1950—Steelers, 28-17 (C)
Steelers, 28-7 (P)
1951—Steelers, 28-14 (C)
1952—Steelers, 34-28 (C)
Steelers, 17-14 (P)
1953—Steelers, 31-28 (P)
Steelers, 21-17 (C)
1954—Cardinals, 17-14 (C)
Steelers, 20-17 (P)
1955—Steelers, 14-7 (P)
Cardinals, 27-13 (C)
1956—Steelers, 14-7 (P)
Cardinals, 38-27 (C)
1957—Steelers, 29-20 (P)
Steelers, 27-2 (C)
1958—Steelers, 27-20 (C)
Steelers, 38-21 (P)
1959—Cardinals, 45-24 (C)
Steelers, 35-20 (P)
1960—Steelers, 27-14 (P)
Cardinals, 38-7 (StL)
1961—Steelers, 30-27 (P)
Cardinals, 20-0 (StL)
1962—Steelers, 26-17 (StL)
Steelers, 19-7 (P)
1963—Steelers, 23-10 (P)
Cardinals, 24-23 (StL)
1964—Cardinals, 34-30 (StL)
Cardinals, 21-20 (P)
1965—Cardinals, 20-7 (P)
Cardinals, 21-17 (StL)
1966—Steelers, 30-9 (P)
Cardinals, 6-3 (StL)
1967—Cardinals, 28-14 (P)
Tie, 14-14 (StL)
1968—Tie, 28-28 (StL)
Cardinals, 20-10 (P)
1969—Cardinals, 27-14 (P)
Cardinals, 47-10 (StL)
1972—Steelers, 25-19 (StL)
1979—Steelers, 24-21 (StL)
1985—Steelers, 23-10 (P)
1988—Cardinals, 31-14 (Phx)
1994—Cardinals, 20-17 (A) OT
1997—Steelers, 26-20 (A) OT
2003—Steelers, 28-15 (P)
(RS Pts.—Steelers 1,092, Cardinals 1,038)
Franchise known as Phoenix prior to 1994, in St. Louis prior to 1988, and in Chicago prior to 1960
***Steelers known as Pirates prior to 1941*

***ARIZONA vs. **ST. LOUIS**
RS: Rams lead series, 27-21-2
PS: Rams lead series, 1-0
1937—Cardinals, 6-0 (Clev)
Cardinals, 13-7 (Chi)
1938—Cardinals, 7-6 (Clev)
Cardinals, 31-17 (Chi)
1939—Rams, 24-0 (Chi)
Rams, 14-0 (Clev)
1940—Rams, 26-14 (Clev)
Cardinals, 17-7 (Chi)
1941—Rams, 10-6 (Clev)
Cardinals, 7-0 (Chi)
1942—Cardinals, 7-0 (Buffalo)
Rams, 7-3 (Clev)
1945—Rams, 21-0 (Clev)
Rams, 35-21 (Chi)
1946—Cardinals, 34-10 (Chi)
Rams, 17-14 (LA)
1947—Rams, 27-7 (LA)
Cardinals, 17-10 (Chi)
1948—Cardinals, 27-22 (LA)
Cardinals, 27-24 (Chi)
1949—Tie, 28-28 (Chi)
Cardinals, 31-27 (LA)
1951—Rams, 45-21 (LA)
1953—Tie, 24-24 (Chi)
1954—Rams, 28-17 (LA)
1958—Rams, 20-14 (Chi)
1960—Cardinals, 43-21 (LA)
1965—Rams, 27-3 (StL)
1968—Rams, 24-13 (StL)
1970—Rams, 34-13 (LA)
1972—Cardinals, 24-14 (StL)
1975—***Rams, 35-23 (LA)
1976—Cardinals, 30-28 (LA)
1979—Rams, 21-0 (LA)
1980—Rams, 21-13 (StL)
1984—Rams, 16-13 (StL)
1985—Rams, 46-14 (LA)
1986—Rams, 16-10 (StL)
1987—Rams, 27-24 (StL)
1988—Cardinals, 41-27 (LA)
1989—Rams, 37-14 (LA)
1991—Cardinals, 24-14 (LA)
1992—Cardinals, 20-14 (LA)
1993—Cardinals, 38-10 (P)
1994—Rams, 14-12 (LA)
1996—Cardinals, 31-28 (A) OT
1998—Cardinals, 20-17 (StL)
2002—Rams, 27-14 (A)
Rams, 30-28 (StL)
2003—Rams, 37-13 (StL)
Rams, 30-27 (A) OT
(RS Pts.—Rams 1,036, Cardinals 875)
(PS Pts.—Rams 35, Cardinals 23)
Franchise known as Phoenix prior to 1994, in St. Louis prior to 1988, and in Chicago prior to 1960
***Franchise in Los Angeles prior to 1995 and in Cleveland prior to 1946*
****NFC Divisional Playoff*

***ARIZONA vs. SAN DIEGO**
RS: Chargers lead series, 7-3
1971—Chargers, 20-17 (SD)
1976—Chargers, 43-24 (SD)
1983—Cardinals, 44-14 (StL)
1987—Chargers, 28-24 (SD)
1989—Chargers, 24-13 (P)
1992—Chargers, 27-21 (P)
1995—Chargers, 28-25 (SD)
1998—Cardinals, 16-13 (A)
2001—Cardinals, 20-17 (SD)
2002—Chargers, 23-15 (A)
(RS Pts.—Chargers 237, Cardinals 219)
Franchise known as Phoenix prior to 1994, in St. Louis prior to 1988,

***ARIZONA vs. SAN FRANCISCO**
RS: 49ers lead series, 15-10
1951—Cardinals, 27-21 (SF)
1957—Cardinals, 20-10 (SF)
1962—49ers, 24-17 (StL)
1964—Cardinals, 23-13 (SF)
1968—49ers, 35-17 (SF)
1971—49ers, 26-14 (StL)
1974—Cardinals, 34-9 (SF)
1976—Cardinals, 23-20 (StL) OT
1978—Cardinals, 16-10 (SF)
1979—Cardinals, 13-10 (StL)
1980—49ers, 24-21 (SF) OT
1982—49ers, 31-20 (StL)
1983—49ers, 42-27 (StL)
1986—49ers, 43-17 (SF)
1987—49ers, 34-28 (SF)
1988—Cardinals, 24-23 (P)
1991—49ers, 14-10 (SF)
1992—Cardinals, 24-14 (P)
1993—49ers, 28-14 (SF)
1999—49ers, 24-10 (A)
2000—49ers, 27-20 (SF)
2002—49ers, 38-28 (SF)
49ers, 17-14 (A)
2003—Cardinals, 16-13 (A) OT
49ers, 50-14 (SF)
(RS Pts.—49ers 600, Cardinals 491)
Franchise known as Phoenix prior to 1994, in St. Louis prior to 1988, and in Chicago prior to 1960

***ARIZONA vs. SEATTLE**
RS: Cardinals lead series, 6-4
1976—Cardinals, 30-24 (S)
1983—Cardinals, 33-28 (StL)
1989—Cardinals, 34-24 (S)
1993—Cardinals, 30-27 (S) OT
1995—Cardinals, 20-14 (A) OT
1998—Seahawks, 33-14 (S)
2002—Cardinals, 24-13 (S)
Seahawks, 27-6 (A)
2003—Seahawks, 38-0 (A)
Seahawks, 28-10 (S)
(RS Pts.—Seahawks 256, Cardinals 201)
Franchise known as Phoenix prior to 1994 and in St. Louis prior to 1988

***ARIZONA vs. TAMPA BAY**
RS: Series tied, 7-7
1977—Buccaneers, 17-7 (TB)
1981—Buccaneers, 20-10 (TB)
1983—Cardinals, 34-27 (TB)
1985—Buccaneers, 16-0 (TB)
1986—Cardinals, 30-19 (TB)
Cardinals, 21-17 (StL)
1987—Cardinals, 31-28 (StL)
Cardinals, 31-14 (TB)
1988—Cardinals, 30-24 (TB)
1989—Buccaneers, 14-13 (P)
1992—Buccaneers, 23-7 (TB)
Buccaneers, 7-3 (P)
1996—Cardinals, 13-9 (A)
1997—Buccaneers, 19-18 (TB)

(RS Pts.—Buccaneers 254, Cardinals 248)
**Franchise known as Phoenix prior to 1994 and in St. Louis prior to 1988*

***ARIZONA vs. **TENNESSEE**
RS: Cardinals lead series, 4-3
1970—Cardinals, 44-0 (StL)
1974—Cardinals, 31-27 (H)
1979—Cardinals, 24-17 (H)
1985—Oilers, 20-10 (StL)
1988—Oilers, 38-20 (H)
1994—Cardinals, 30-12 (H)
1997—Oilers, 41-14 (A)
(RS Pts.—Cardinals 173, Titans 155)
**Franchise known as Phoenix prior to 1994 and in St. Louis prior to 1988*
***Franchise in Houston prior to 1997; known as Oilers prior to 1999*

***ARIZONA vs. **WASHINGTON**
RS: Redskins lead series, 70-44-2
1932—Cardinals, 9-0 (B)
Braves, 8-6 (C)
1933—Redskins, 10-0 (C)
Tie, 0-0 (B)
1934—Redskins, 9-0 (B)
1935—Cardinals, 6-0 (B)
1936—Redskins, 13-10 (B)
1937—Cardinals, 21-14 (W)
1939—Redskins, 28-7 (W)
1940—Redskins, 28-21 (W)
1942—Redskins, 28-0 (W)
1943—Redskins, 13-7 (W)
1945—Redskins, 24-21 (W)
1947—Redskins, 45-21 (W)
1949—Cardinals, 38-7 (C)
1950—Cardinals, 38-28 (W)
1951—Redskins, 7-3 (C)
Redskins, 20-17 (W)
1952—Redskins, 23-7 (C)
Cardinals, 17-6 (W)
1953—Redskins, 24-13 (C)
Redskins, 28-17 (W)
1954—Cardinals, 38-16 (C)
Redskins, 37-20 (W)
1955—Cardinals, 24-10 (W)
Redskins, 31-0 (C)
1956—Cardinals, 31-3 (W)
Redskins, 17-14 (C)
1957—Redskins, 37-14 (C)
Cardinals, 44-14 (W)
1958—Cardinals, 37-10 (C)
Redskins, 45-31 (W)
1959—Cardinals, 49-21 (C)
Redskins, 23-14 (W)
1960—Cardinals, 44-7 (StL)
Cardinals, 26-14 (W)
1961—Cardinals, 24-0 (W)
Cardinals, 38-24 (StL)
1962—Redskins, 24-14 (W)
Tie, 17-17 (StL)
1963—Cardinals, 21-7 (W)
Cardinals, 24-20 (StL)
1964—Cardinals, 23-17 (W)
Cardinals, 38-24 (StL)
1965—Cardinals, 37-16 (W)
Redskins, 24-20 (StL)
1966—Cardinals, 23-7 (StL)
Redskins, 26-20 (W)
1967—Cardinals, 27-21 (W)
1968—Cardinals, 41-14 (StL)
1969—Redskins, 33-17 (W)
1970—Cardinals, 27-17 (StL)
Redskins, 28-27 (W)
1971—Redskins, 24-17 (StL)
Redskins, 20-0 (W)
1972—Redskins, 24-10 (W)
Redskins, 33-3 (StL)
1973—Cardinals, 34-27 (StL)
Redskins, 31-13 (W)
1974—Cardinals, 17-10 (W)
Cardinals, 23-20 (StL)
1975—Redskins, 27-17 (W)
Cardinals, 20-17 (StL) OT
1976—Redskins, 20-10 (W)
Redskins, 16-10 (StL)
1977—Redskins, 24-14 (W)
Redskins, 26-20 (StL)
1978—Redskins, 28-10 (StL)
Cardinals, 27-17 (W)
1979—Redskins, 17-7 (StL)
Redskins, 30-28 (W)
1980—Redskins, 23-0 (W)
Redskins, 31-7 (StL)
1981—Cardinals, 40-30 (StL)
Redskins, 42-21 (W)
1982—Redskins, 12-7 (StL)
Redskins, 28-0 (W)
1983—Redskins, 38-14 (StL)
Redskins, 45-7 (W)
1984—Cardinals, 26-24 (StL)
Redskins, 29-27 (W)
1985—Redskins, 27-10 (W)
Redskins, 27-16 (StL)
1986—Redskins, 28-21 (W)
Redskins, 20-17 (StL)
1987—Redskins, 28-21 (W)
Redskins, 34-17 (StL)
1988—Cardinals, 30-21 (P)
Redskins, 33-17 (W)
1989—Redskins, 30-28 (W)
Redskins, 29-10 (P)
1990—Redskins, 31-0 (W)
Redskins, 38-10 (P)
1991—Redskins, 34-0 (W)
Redskins, 20-14 (P)
1992—Cardinals, 27-24 (P)
Redskins, 41-3 (W)
1993—Cardinals, 17-10 (W)
Cardinals, 36-6 (P)
1994—Cardinals, 19-16 (W) OT
Cardinals, 17-15 (A)
1995—Redskins, 27-7 (W)
Cardinals, 24-20 (A)
1996—Cardinals, 37-34 (W) OT
Cardinals, 27-26 (A)
1997—Redskins, 19-13 (W) OT
Redskins, 38-28 (A)
1998—Cardinals, 29-27 (A)
Cardinals, 45-42 (W)
1999—Redskins, 24-10 (A)
Redskins, 28-3 (W)
2000—Cardinals, 16-15 (A)
Redskins, 20-3 (W)
2001—Redskins, 20-10 (A)
Redskins, 20-17 (W)
2002—Redskins, 31-23 (W)
(RS Pts.—Redskins 2,583, Cardinals 2,154)
**Franchise known as Phoenix prior to 1994, in St. Louis prior to 1988, and in Chicago prior to 1960*
***Franchise in Boston prior to 1937 and known as Braves prior to 1933*

ATLANTA vs. ARIZONA
RS: Cardinals lead series, 13-8;
See Arizona vs. Atlanta

ATLANTA vs. BALTIMORE
RS: Series tied, 1-1
1999—Ravens, 19-13 (A) OT
2002—Falcons, 20-17 (A)
(RS Pts.—Ravens 36, Falcons 33)

ATLANTA vs. BUFFALO
RS: Series tied, 4-4
1973—Bills, 17-6 (A)
1977—Bills, 3-0 (B)
1980—Falcons, 30-14 (B)
1983—Falcons, 31-14 (A)
1989—Falcons, 30-28 (A)
1992—Bills, 41-14 (B)
1995—Bills, 23-17 (B)
2001—Falcons, 33-30 (A)
(RS Pts.—Bills 170, Falcons 161)

ATLANTA vs. CAROLINA
RS: Falcons lead series, 12-6
1995—Falcons, 23-20 (A) OT
Panthers, 21-17 (C)
1996—Panthers, 29-6 (C)
Falcons, 20-17 (A)
1997—Panthers, 9-6 (A)
Panthers, 21-12 (C)
1998—Falcons, 19-14 (C)
Falcons, 51-23 (A)
1999—Falcons, 27-20 (A)
Panthers, 34-28 (C)
2000—Falcons, 15-10 (C)
Falcons, 13-12 (A)
2001—Falcons, 24-16 (A)
Falcons, 10-7 (C)
2002—Falcons, 30-0 (A)
Falcons, 41-0 (C)
2003—Panthers, 23-3 (C)
Falcons, 20-14 (A) OT
(RS Pts.—Falcons 365, Panthers 290)

ATLANTA vs. CHICAGO
RS: Bears lead series, 11-10
1966—Bears, 23-6 (C)
1967—Bears, 23-14 (A)
1968—Falcons, 16-13 (C)
1969—Falcons, 48-31 (A)
1970—Bears, 23-14 (A)
1972—Falcons, 37-21 (C)
1973—Falcons, 46-6 (A)
1974—Falcons, 13-10 (A)
1976—Falcons, 10-0 (C)
1977—Falcons, 16-10 (C)
1978—Bears, 13-7 (C)
1980—Falcons, 28-17 (A)
1983—Falcons, 20-17 (C)
1985—Bears, 36-0 (C)
1986—Bears, 13-10 (A)
1990—Bears, 30-24 (C)
1992—Bears, 41-31 (C)
1993—Bears, 6-0 (C)
1998—Falcons, 20-13 (A)
2001—Bears, 31-3 (A)
2002—Bears, 14-13 (A)
(RS Pts.—Bears 391, Falcons 376)

ATLANTA vs. CINCINNATI
RS: Bengals lead series, 7-3
1971—Falcons, 9-6 (C)
1975—Bengals, 21-14 (A)

1978—Bengals, 37-7 (C)
1981—Bengals, 30-28 (A)
1984—Bengals, 35-14 (C)
1987—Bengals, 16-10 (A)
1990—Falcons, 38-17 (A)
1993—Bengals, 21-17 (C)
1996—Bengals, 41-31 (C)
2002—Falcons, 30-3 (A)
(RS Pts.—Bengals 227, Falcons 198)

ATLANTA vs. CLEVELAND
RS: Browns lead series, 9-2
1966—Browns, 49-17 (A)
1968—Browns, 30-7 (C)
1971—Falcons, 31-14 (C)
1976—Browns, 20-17 (A)
1978—Browns, 24-16 (A)
1981—Browns, 28-17 (C)
1984—Browns, 23-7 (A)
1987—Browns, 38-3 (C)
1990—Browns, 13-10 (C)
1993—Falcons, 17-14 (A)
2002—Browns, 24-16 (C)
(RS Pts.—Browns 277, Falcons 158)

ATLANTA vs. DALLAS
RS: Cowboys lead series, 12-8
PS: Cowboys lead series, 2-0
1966—Cowboys, 47-14 (A)
1967—Cowboys, 37-7 (D)
1969—Cowboys, 24-17 (A)
1970—Cowboys, 13-0 (D)
1974—Cowboys, 24-0 (A)
1976—Falcons, 17-10 (A)
1978—*Cowboys, 27-20 (D)
1980—*Cowboys, 30-27 (A)
1985—Cowboys, 24-10 (D)
1986—Falcons, 37-35 (D)
1987—Falcons, 21-10 (D)
1988—Cowboys, 26-20 (D)
1989—Falcons 27-21 (A)
1990—Falcons, 26-7 (A)
1991—Cowboys, 31-27 (D)
1992—Cowboys, 41-17 (A)
1993—Falcons, 27-14 (A)
1995—Cowboys, 28-13 (A)
1996—Cowboys, 32-28 (D)
1999—Cowboys, 24-7 (D)
2001—Falcons, 20-13 (A)
2003—Falcons, 27-13 (D)
(RS Pts.—Cowboys 474, Falcons 362)
(PS Pts.—Cowboys 57, Falcons 47)
NFC Divisional Playoff

ATLANTA vs. DENVER
RS: Broncos lead series, 7-3
PS: Broncos lead series, 1-0
1970—Broncos, 24-10 (D)
1972—Falcons, 23-20 (A)
1975—Falcons, 35-21 (A)
1979—Broncos, 20-17 (A) OT
1982—Falcons, 34-27 (D)
1985—Broncos, 44-28 (A)
1988—Broncos, 30-14 (D)
1994—Broncos, 32-28 (D)
1997—Broncos, 29-21 (A)
1998—*Broncos, 34-19 (Miami)
2000—Broncos, 42-14 (D)
(RS Pts.—Broncos 289, Falcons 224)
(PS Pts.—Broncos 34, Falcons 19)
Super Bowl XXXIII

ATLANTA vs. DETROIT
RS: Lions lead series, 21-8
1966—Lions, 28-10 (D)
1967—Lions, 24-3 (D)
1968—Lions, 24-7 (A)
1969—Lions, 27-21 (D)
1971—Lions, 41-38 (D)
1972—Lions, 26-23 (A)
1973—Lions, 31-6 (D)
1975—Lions, 17-14 (A)
1976—Lions, 24-10 (D)
1977—Falcons, 17-6 (A)
1978—Falcons, 14-0 (A)
1979—Lions, 24-23 (D)
1980—Falcons, 43-28 (A)
1983—Falcons, 30-14 (D)
1984—Lions, 27-24 (A) OT
1985—Lions, 28-27 (A)
1986—Falcons, 20-6 (D)
1987—Lions, 30-13 (A)
1988—Lions, 31-17 (D)
1989—Lions, 31-24 (A)
1990—Lions, 21-14 (D)
1993—Lions, 30-13 (D)
1994—Lions, 31-28 (D) OT
1995—Falcons, 34-22 (A)
1996—Lions, 28-24 (D)
1997—Lions, 28-17 (D)
1998—Falcons, 24-17 (D)
2000—Lions, 13-10 (D)
2002—Falcons, 36-15 (A)
(RS Pts.—Lions 672, Falcons 584)

ATLANTA vs. GREEN BAY
RS: Packers lead series, 11-10
PS: Series tied, 1-1
1966—Packers, 56-3 (Mil)
1967—Packers, 23-0 (Mil)
1968—Packers, 38-7 (A)
1969—Packers, 28-10 (GB)
1970—Packers, 27-24 (GB)
1971—Falcons, 28-21 (A)
1972—Falcons, 10-9 (Mil)
1974—Falcons, 10-3 (A)
1975—Packers, 22-13 (GB)
1976—Packers, 24-20 (A)
1979—Falcons, 25-7 (A)
1981—Falcons, 31-17 (GB)
1982—Packers, 38-7 (A)
1983—Falcons, 47-41 (A) OT
1988—Falcons, 20-0 (A)
1989—Packers, 23-21 (Mil)
1991—Falcons, 35-31 (A)
1992—Falcons, 24-10 (A)
1994—Packers, 21-17 (Mil)
1995—*Packers, 37-20 (GB)
2001—Falcons, 23-20 (GB)
2002—Packers, 37-34 (GB) OT
*Falcons, 27-7 (GB)
(RS Pts.—Packers 496, Falcons 409)
(PS Pts.—Falcons 47, Packers 44)
NFC First-Round Playoff

ATLANTA vs. HOUSTON
RS: Texans lead series, 1-0
2003—Texans, 17-13 (H)
(RS Pts.—Texans 17, Falcons 13)

ATLANTA vs. *INDIANAPOLIS
RS: Colts lead series, 12-1
1966—Colts, 19-7 (A)
1967—Colts, 38-31 (B)
Colts, 49-7 (A)
1968—Colts, 28-20 (A)
Colts, 44-0 (B)
1969—Colts, 21-14 (A)
Colts, 13-6 (B)
1974—Colts, 17-7 (A)
1986—Colts, 28-23 (A)
1989—Colts, 13-9 (I)
1998—Falcons, 28-21 (A)
2001—Colts, 41-27 (I)
2003—Colts, 38-7 (I)
(RS Pts.—Colts 370, Falcons 186)
Franchise in Baltimore prior to 1984

ATLANTA vs. JACKSONVILLE
RS: Jaguars lead series, 2-1
1996—Jaguars, 19-17 (J)
1999—Jaguars, 30-7 (A)
2003—Falcons, 21-14 (A)
(RS Pts.—Jaguars 63, Falcons 45)

ATLANTA vs. KANSAS CITY
RS: Chiefs lead series, 4-1
1972—Chiefs, 17-14 (A)
1985—Chiefs, 38-10 (KC)
1991—Chiefs, 14-3 (KC)
1994—Chiefs, 30-10 (A)
2000—Falcons, 29-13 (A)
(RS Pts.—Chiefs 112, Falcons 66)

ATLANTA vs. MIAMI
RS: Dolphins lead series, 7-2
1970—Dolphins, 20-7 (A)
1974—Dolphins, 42-7 (M)
1980—Dolphins, 20-17 (A)
1983—Dolphins, 31-24 (M)
1986—Falcons, 20-14 (M)
1992—Dolphins, 21-17 (M)
1995—Dolphins, 21-20 (M)
1998—Falcons, 38-16 (A)
2001—Dolphins, 21-14 (M)
(RS Pts.—Dolphins 206, Falcons 164)

ATLANTA vs. MINNESOTA
RS: Vikings lead series, 14-7
PS: Series tied, 1-1
1966—Falcons, 20-13 (M)
1967—Falcons, 21-20 (A)
1968—Vikings, 47-7 (M)
1969—Falcons, 10-3 (A)
1970—Vikings, 37-7 (A)
1971—Vikings, 24-7 (M)
1973—Falcons, 20-14 (A)
1974—Vikings, 23-10 (M)
1975—Vikings, 38-0 (M)
1977—Vikings, 14-7 (A)
1980—Vikings, 24-23 (M)
1981—Falcons, 31-30 (A)
1982—*Vikings, 30-24 (M)
1984—Vikings, 27-20 (M)
1985—Falcons, 14-13 (A)
1987—Vikings, 24-13 (M)
1989—Vikings, 43-17 (M)
1991—Vikings, 20-19 (A)
1996—Vikings, 23-17 (A)
1998—**Falcons, 30-27 (M) OT
1999—Vikings, 17-14 (A)
2002—Falcons, 30-24 (M) OT
2003—Vikings, 39-26 (A)
(RS Pts.—Vikings 517, Falcons 333)
(PS Pts.—Vikings 57, Falcons 54)
NFC First-Round Playoff
**NFC Championship*

ATLANTA vs. NEW ENGLAND
RS: Falcons lead series, 6-4
1972—Patriots, 21-20 (NE)
1977—Patriots, 16-10 (A)

ALL-TIME TEAM VS. TEAM RESULTS

1980—Falcons, 37-21 (NE)
1983—Falcons, 24-13 (A)
1986—Patriots, 25-17 (NE)
1989—Falcons, 16-15 (A)
1992—Falcons, 34-0 (A)
1995—Falcons, 30-17 (A)
1998—Falcons, 41-10 (NE)
2001—Patriots, 24-10 (A)
(RS Pts.—Falcons 239, Patriots 162)

ATLANTA vs. NEW ORLEANS
RS: Falcons lead series, 40-29
PS: Falcons lead series, 1-0
1967—Saints, 27-24 (NO)
1969—Falcons, 45-17 (A)
1970—Falcons, 14-3 (NO)
Falcons, 32-14 (A)
1971—Falcons, 28-6 (A)
Falcons, 24-20 (NO)
1972—Falcons, 21-14 (NO)
Falcons, 36-20 (A)
1973—Falcons, 62-7 (NO)
Falcons, 14-10 (A)
1974—Saints, 14-13 (NO)
Saints, 13-3 (A)
1975—Falcons, 14-7 (A)
Saints, 23-7 (NO)
1976—Saints, 30-0 (NO)
Falcons, 23-20 (A)
1977—Saints, 21-20 (NO)
Falcons, 35-7 (A)
1978—Falcons, 20-17 (NO)
Falcons, 20-17 (A)
1979—Falcons, 40-34 (NO) OT
Saints, 37-6 (A)
1980—Falcons, 41-14 (NO)
Falcons, 31-13 (A)
1981—Falcons, 27-0 (A)
Falcons, 41-10 (NO)
1982—Falcons, 35-0 (A)
Saints, 35-6 (NO)
1983—Saints, 19-17 (A)
Saints, 27-10 (NO)
1984—Falcons, 36-28 (NO)
Saints, 17-13 (A)
1985—Falcons, 31-24 (A)
Falcons, 16-10 (NO)
1986—Falcons, 31-10 (NO)
Saints, 14-9 (A)
1987—Saints, 38-0 (A)
1988—Saints, 29-21 (A)
Saints, 10-9 (NO)
1989—Saints, 20-13 (NO)
Saints, 26-17 (A)
1990—Falcons, 28-27 (A)
Saints, 10-7 (NO)
1991—Saints, 27-6 (A)
Falcons, 23-20 (NO) OT
*Falcons, 27-20 (NO)
1992—Saints, 10-7 (A)
Saints, 22-14 (NO)
1993—Saints, 34-31 (A)
Falcons, 26-15 (NO)
1994—Saints, 33-32 (NO)
Saints, 29-20 (A)
1995—Falcons, 27-24 (NO) OT
Falcons, 19-14 (A)
1996—Falcons, 17-15 (A)
Falcons, 31-15 (NO)
1997—Falcons, 23-17 (NO)
Falcons, 20-3 (A)
1998—Falcons, 31-23 (A)
Falcons, 27-17 (NO)
1999—Falcons, 20-17 (NO)
Falcons, 35-12 (A)
2000—Saints, 21-19 (A)
Saints, 23-7 (NO)
2001—Falcons, 20-13 (NO)
Saints, 28-10 (A)
2002—Falcons, 37-35 (NO)
Falcons, 24-17 (A)
2003—Saints, 45-17 (A)
Saints, 23-20 (NO)
(RS Pts.—Falcons 1,503, Saints 1,311)
(PS Pts.—Falcons 27, Saints 20)
NFC First-Round Playoff

ATLANTA vs. N.Y. GIANTS
RS: Falcons lead series, 9-7
1966—Falcons, 27-16 (NY)
1968—Falcons, 24-21 (A)
1971—Giants, 21-17 (A)
1974—Falcons, 14-7 (New Haven)
1977—Falcons, 17-3 (A)
1978—Falcons, 23-20 (A)
1979—Giants, 24-3 (NY)
1981—Giants, 27-24 (A) OT
1982—Falcons, 16-14 (NY)
1983—Giants, 16-13 (A) OT
1984—Giants, 19-7 (A)
1988—Giants, 23-16 (A)
1998—Falcons, 34-20 (NY)
2000—Giants, 13-6 (A)
2002—Falcons, 17-10 (NY)
2003—Falcons, 27-7 (NY)
(RS Pts.—Falcons 285, Giants 261)

ATLANTA vs. N.Y. JETS
RS: Series tied, 4-4
1973—Falcons, 28-20 (NY)
1980—Jets, 14-7 (A)
1983—Falcons, 27-21 (NY)
1986—Jets, 28-14 (A)
1989—Jets, 27-7 (NY)
1992—Falcons, 20-17 (A)
1995—Falcons, 13-3 (A)
1998—Jets, 28-3 (NY)
(RS Pts.—Jets 158, Falcons 119)

ATLANTA vs. *OAKLAND
RS: Raiders lead series, 7-3
1971—Falcons, 24-13 (A)
1975—Raiders, 37-34 (O) OT
1979—Raiders, 50-19 (O)
1982—Raiders, 38-14 (A)
1985—Raiders, 34-24 (A)
1988—Falcons, 12-6 (LA)
1991—Falcons, 21-17 (A)
1994—Raiders, 30-17 (LA)
1997—Raiders, 36-31 (A)
2000—Raiders, 41-14 (O)
(RS Pts.—Raiders 302, Falcons 210)
Franchise in Los Angeles from 1982-1994

ATLANTA vs. PHILADELPHIA
RS: Eagles lead series, 11-9-1
PS: Series tied, 1-1
1966—Eagles, 23-10 (P)
1967—Eagles, 38-7 (A)
1969—Falcons, 27-3 (P)
1970—Tie, 13-13 (P)
1973—Falcons, 44-27 (P)
1976—Eagles, 14-13 (A)
1978—*Falcons, 14-13 (A)
1979—Falcons, 14-10 (P)
1980—Falcons, 20-17 (P)
1981—Eagles, 16-13 (P)
1983—Eagles, 28-24 (A)
1984—Falcons, 26-10 (A)
1985—Eagles, 23-17 (P) OT
1986—Eagles, 16-0 (A)
1988—Falcons, 27-24 (P)
1990—Eagles, 24-23 (A)
1994—Falcons, 28-21 (A)
1996—Eagles, 33-18 (A)
1997—Falcons, 20-17 (A)
1998—Falcons, 17-12 (A)
2000—Eagles, 38-10 (P)
2002—**Eagles, 20-6 (P)
2003—Eagles, 23-16 (A)
(RS Pts.—Eagles 430, Falcons 387)
(PS Pts.—Eagles 33, Falcons 20)
NFC First-Round Playoff
***NFC Divisional Playoff*

ATLANTA vs. PITTSBURGH
RS: Steelers lead series, 11-1-1
1966—Steelers, 57-33 (A)
1968—Steelers, 41-21 (A)
1970—Falcons, 27-16 (A)
1974—Steelers, 24-17 (P)
1978—Steelers, 31-7 (P)
1981—Steelers, 34-20 (A)
1984—Steelers, 35-10 (P)
1987—Steelers, 28-12 (A)
1990—Steelers, 21-9 (P)
1993—Steelers, 45-17 (A)
1996—Steelers, 20-17 (A)
1999—Steelers, 13-9 (P)
2002—Tie, 34-34 (P) OT
(RS Pts.—Steelers 399, Falcons 233)

ATLANTA vs. *ST. LOUIS
RS: Rams lead series, 46-23-2
1966—Rams, 19-14 (A)
1967—Rams, 31-3 (A)
Rams, 20-3 (LA)
1968—Rams, 27-14 (LA)
Rams, 17-10 (A)
1969—Rams, 17-7 (LA)
Rams, 38-6 (A)
1970—Tie, 10-10 (LA)
Rams, 17-7 (A)
1971—Tie, 20-20 (LA)
Rams, 24-16 (A)
1972—Falcons, 31-3 (A)
Rams, 20-7 (LA)
1973—Rams, 31-0 (LA)
Falcons, 15-13 (A)
1974—Rams, 21-0 (LA)
Rams, 30-7 (A)
1975—Rams, 22-7 (LA)
Rams, 16-7 (A)
1976—Rams, 30-14 (A)
Rams, 59-0 (LA)
1977—Falcons, 17-6 (A)
Rams, 23-7 (LA)
1978—Rams, 10-0 (LA)
Falcons, 15-7 (A)
1979—Rams, 20-14 (LA)
Rams, 34-13 (A)
1980—Falcons, 13-10 (A)
Rams, 20-17 (LA) OT
1981—Rams, 37-35 (A)
Rams, 21-16 (LA)
1982—Falcons, 34-17 (A)
1983—Rams, 27-21 (LA)

Rams, 36-13 (A)
1984—Falcons, 30-28 (LA)
Rams, 24-10 (A)
1985—Rams, 17-6 (LA)
Falcons, 30-14 (A)
1986—Falcons, 26-14 (A)
Rams, 14-7 (LA)
1987—Falcons, 24-20 (A)
Rams, 33-0 (LA)
1988—Rams, 33-0 (A)
Rams, 22-7 (LA)
1989—Rams, 31-21 (A)
Rams, 26-14 (LA)
1990—Rams, 44-24 (LA)
Falcons, 20-13 (A)
1991—Falcons, 31-14 (A)
Falcons, 31-14 (LA)
1992—Falcons, 30-28 (A)
Rams, 38-27 (LA)
1993—Falcons, 30-24 (A)
Falcons, 13-0 (LA)
1994—Falcons, 31-13 (A)
Falcons, 8-5 (LA)
1995—Rams, 21-19 (StL)
Falcons, 31-6 (A)
1996—Rams, 59-16 (StL)
Rams, 34-27 (A)
1997—Falcons, 34-31 (A)
Falcons, 27-21 (StL)
1998—Falcons, 37-15 (A)
Falcons, 21-10 (StL)
1999—Rams, 35-7 (StL)
Rams, 41-13 (A)
2000—Rams, 41-20 (A)
Rams, 45-29 (StL)
2001—Rams, 35-6 (A)
Rams, 31-13 (StL)
2003—Rams, 36-0 (StL)
(RS Pts.—Rams 1,683, Falcons 1,133)
Franchise in Los Angeles prior to 1995

ATLANTA vs. SAN DIEGO
RS: Falcons lead series, 5-1
1973—Falcons, 41-0 (SD)
1979—Falcons, 28-26 (SD)
1988—Chargers, 10-7 (A)
1991—Falcons, 13-10 (SD)
1994—Falcons, 10-9 (A)
1997—Falcons, 14-3 (SD)
(RS Pts.—Falcons 113, Chargers 58)

ATLANTA vs. SAN FRANCISCO
RS: 49ers lead series, 44-25-1
PS: Falcons lead series, 1-0
1966—49ers, 44-7 (A)
1967—49ers, 38-7 (SF)
49ers, 34-28 (A)
1968—49ers, 28-13 (SF)
49ers, 14-12 (A)
1969—Falcons, 24-12 (A)
Falcons, 21-7 (SF)
1970—Falcons, 21-20 (A)
49ers, 24-20 (SF)
1971—Falcons, 20-17 (A)
49ers, 24-3 (SF)
1972—49ers, 49-14 (A)
49ers, 20-0 (SF)
1973—49ers, 13-9 (A)
Falcons, 17-3 (SF)
1974—49ers, 16-10 (A)
49ers, 27-0 (SF)
1975—Falcons, 17-3 (SF)
Falcons, 31-9 (A)
1976—49ers, 15-0 (SF)
Falcons, 21-16 (A)
1977—Falcons, 7-0 (SF)
49ers, 10-3 (A)
1978—Falcons, 20-17 (SF)
Falcons, 21-10 (A)
1979—49ers, 20-15 (SF)
Falcons, 31-21 (A)
1980—Falcons, 20-17 (SF)
Falcons, 35-10 (A)
1981—Falcons, 34-17 (A)
49ers, 17-14 (SF)
1982—Falcons, 17-7 (SF)
1983—49ers, 24-20 (SF)
Falcons, 28-24 (A)
1984—49ers, 14-5 (SF)
49ers, 35-17 (A)
1985—49ers, 35-16 (SF)
49ers, 38-17 (A)
1986—Tie, 10-10 (A) OT
49ers, 20-0 (SF)
1987—49ers, 25-17 (A)
49ers, 35-7 (SF)
1988—Falcons, 34-17 (SF)
49ers, 13-3 (A)
1989—49ers, 45-3 (SF)
49ers, 23-10 (A)
1990—49ers, 19-13 (SF)
49ers, 45-35 (A)
1991—Falcons, 39-34 (SF)
Falcons, 17-14 (A)
1992—49ers, 56-17 (SF)
49ers, 41-3 (A)
1993—49ers, 37-30 (SF)
Falcons, 27-24 (A)
1994—49ers, 42-3 (A)
49ers, 50-14 (SF)
1995—49ers, 41-10 (SF)
Falcons, 28-27 (A)
1996—49ers, 39-17 (SF)
49ers, 34-10 (A)
1997—49ers, 34-7 (SF)
49ers, 35-28 (A)
1998—49ers, 31-20 (SF)
Falcons, 31-19 (A)
*Falcons, 20-18 (A)
1999—49ers, 26-7 (SF)
Falcons, 34-29 (A)
2000—Falcons, 36-28 (A)
49ers, 16-6 (SF)
2001—49ers, 16-13 (SF) OT
49ers, 37-31 (A) OT
(RS Pts.—49ers 1,711, Falcons 1,175)
(PS Pts.—Falcons 20, 49ers 18)
NFC Divisional Playoff

ATLANTA vs. SEATTLE
RS: Seahawks lead series, 6-2
1976—Seahawks, 30-13 (S)
1979—Seahawks, 31-28 (A)
1985—Seahawks, 30-26 (S)
1988—Seahawks, 31-20 (A)
1991—Falcons, 26-13 (A)
1997—Falcons, 24-17 (S)
2000—Seahawks, 30-10 (A)
2002—Seahawks, 30-24 (A) OT
(RS Pts.—Seahawks 212, Falcons 171)

ATLANTA vs. TAMPA BAY
RS: Buccaneers lead series, 12-9
1977—Falcons, 17-0 (TB)
1978—Buccaneers, 14-9 (TB)
1979—Falcons, 17-14 (A)
1981—Buccaneers, 24-23 (TB)
1984—Buccaneers, 23-6 (TB)
1986—Falcons, 23-20 (TB) OT
1987—Buccaneers, 48-10 (TB)
1988—Falcons, 17-10 (A)
1990—Buccaneers, 23-17 (TB)
1991—Falcons, 43-7 (A)
1992—Falcons, 35-7 (TB)
1993—Buccaneers, 31-24 (A)
1994—Falcons, 34-13 (A)
1995—Falcons, 24-21 (TB)
1997—Buccaneers, 31-10 (A)
1999—Buccaneers, 19-10 (TB)
2000—Buccaneers, 27-14 (A)
2002—Buccaneers, 20-6 (A)
Buccaneers, 34-10 (TB)
2003—Buccaneers, 31-10 (A)
Falcons, 30-28 (TB)
(RS Pts.—Buccaneers 445, Falcons 389)

ATLANTA vs. *TENNESSEE
RS: Titans lead series, 6-5
1972—Falcons, 20-10 (A)
1976—Oilers, 20-14 (H)
1978—Falcons, 20-14 (A)
1981—Falcons, 31-27 (H)
1984—Falcons, 42-10 (A)
1987—Oilers, 37-33 (H)
1990—Falcons, 47-27 (A)
1993—Oilers, 33-17 (H)
1996—Oilers, 23-13 (A)
1999—Titans, 30-17 (T)
2003—Titans, 38-31 (A)
(RS Pts.—Falcons 285, Titans 269)
Franchise in Houston prior to 1997; known as Oilers prior to 1999

ATLANTA vs. WASHINGTON
RS: Redskins lead series, 14-4-1
PS: Redskins lead series, 1-0
1966—Redskins, 33-20 (W)
1967—Tie, 20-20 (A)
1969—Redskins, 27-20 (W)
1972—Redskins, 24-13 (W)
1975—Redskins, 30-27 (A)
1977—Redskins, 10-6 (W)
1978—Falcons, 20-17 (A)
1979—Redskins, 16-7 (A)
1980—Falcons, 10-6 (A)
1983—Redskins, 37-21 (W)
1984—Redskins, 27-14 (W)
1985—Redskins, 44-10 (A)
1987—Falcons, 21-20 (A)
1989—Redskins, 31-30 (A)
1991—Redskins, 56-17 (W)
*Redskins, 24-7 (W)
1992—Redskins, 24-17 (W)
1993—Redskins, 30-17 (W)
1994—Falcons, 27-20 (W)
2003—Redskins, 33-31 (A)
(RS Pts.—Redskins 505, Falcons 348)
(PS Pts.—Redskins 24, Falcons 7)
NFC Divisional Playoff

BALTIMORE vs. ARIZONA
RS: Ravens lead series, 2-1;
See Arizona vs. Baltimore

BALTIMORE vs. ATLANTA
RS: Series tied, 1-1;
See Atlanta vs. Baltimore

ALL-TIME TEAM VS. TEAM RESULTS

BALTIMORE vs. BUFFALO
RS: Bills lead series, 1-0
1999—Bills, 13-10 (Balt)
(RS Pts.—Bills 13, Ravens 10)
BALTIMORE vs. CAROLINA
RS: Panthers lead series, 2-0
1996—Panthers, 27-16 (C)
2002—Panthers, 10-7 (C)
(RS Pts.—Panthers 37, Ravens 23)
BALTIMORE vs. CHICAGO
RS: Series tied, 1-1
1998—Bears, 24-3 (C)
2001—Ravens, 17-6 (B)
(RS Pts.—Bears 30, Ravens 20)
BALTIMORE vs. CINCINNATI
RS: Ravens lead series, 11-5
1996—Bengals, 24-21 (B)
Bengals, 21-14 (C)
1997—Ravens, 23-10 (B)
Bengals, 16-14 (C)
1998—Ravens, 31-24 (B)
Ravens, 20-13 (C)
1999—Ravens, 34-31 (C)
Ravens, 22-0 (B)
2000—Ravens, 37-0 (B)
Ravens, 27-7 (C)
2001—Bengals, 21-10 (C)
Ravens, 16-0 (B)
2002—Ravens, 38-27 (B)
Ravens, 27-23 (C)
2003—Bengals, 34-26 (C)
Ravens, 31-13 (B)
(RS Pts.—Ravens 391, Bengals 264)
BALTIMORE vs. CLEVELAND
RS: Ravens lead series, 7-3
1999—Ravens, 17-10 (B)
Ravens, 41-9 (C)
2000—Ravens, 12-0 (C)
Ravens, 44-7 (B)
2001—Browns, 24-14 (C)
Browns, 27-17 (B)
2002—Ravens, 26-21 (C)
Browns, 14-13 (B)
2003—Ravens, 33-13 (B)
Ravens, 35-0 (C)
(RS Pts.—Ravens 252, Browns 125)
BALTIMORE vs. DALLAS
RS: Ravens lead series, 1-0
2000—Ravens, 27-0 (B)
(RS Pts.—Ravens 27, Cowboys 0)
BALTIMORE vs. DENVER
RS: Ravens lead series, 3-1
PS: Ravens lead series, 1-0
1996—Broncos, 45-34 (D)
2000—*Ravens, 21-3 (B)
2001—Ravens, 20-13 (D)
2002—Ravens, 34-23 (B)
2003—Ravens, 26-6 (B)
(RS Pts.—Ravens 114, Broncos 87)
(PS Pts.—Ravens 21, Broncos 3)
**AFC First-Round Playoff*
BALTIMORE vs. DETROIT
RS: Ravens lead series, 1-0
1998—Ravens, 19-10 (B)
(RS Pts.—Ravens 19, Lions 10)
BALTIMORE vs. GREEN BAY
RS: Packers lead series, 2-0
1998—Packers, 28-10 (GB)
2001—Packers, 31-23 (GB)
(RS Pts.—Packers 59, Ravens 33)
BALTIMORE vs. HOUSTON
RS: Ravens lead series, 1-0
2002—Ravens, 23-19 (H)
(RS Pts.—Ravens 23, Texans 19)
BALTIMORE vs. INDIANAPOLIS
RS: Series tied, 2-2
1996—Colts, 26-21 (I)
1998—Ravens, 38-31 (B)
2001—Ravens, 39-27 (B)
2002—Colts, 22-20 (I)
(RS Pts.—Ravens 118, Colts 106)
BALTIMORE vs. JACKSONVILLE
RS: Jaguars lead series, 8-6
1996—Jaguars, 30-27 (J)
Jaguars, 28-25 (B) OT
1997—Jaguars, 28-27 (B)
Jaguars, 29-27 (J)
1998—Jaguars, 24-10 (J)
Jaguars, 45-19 (B)
1999—Jaguars, 6-3 (J)
Jaguars, 30-23 (B)
2000—Ravens, 39-36 (B)
Ravens, 15-10 (J)
2001—Ravens, 18-17 (B)
Ravens, 24-21 (J)
2002—Ravens, 17-10 (B)
2003—Ravens, 24-17 (B)
(RS Pts.—Jaguars 331, Ravens 298)
BALTIMORE vs. KANSAS CITY
RS: Chiefs lead series, 2-0
1999—Chiefs, 35-8 (B)
2003—Chiefs, 17-10 (B)
(RS Pts.—Chiefs 52, Ravens 18)
BALTIMORE vs. MIAMI
RS: Dolphins lead series, 4-0
PS: Ravens lead series, 1-0
1997—Dolphins, 24-13 (B)
2000—Dolphins, 19-6 (M)
2001—*Ravens, 20-3 (M)
2002—Dolphins, 26-7 (M)
2003—Dolphins, 9-6 (M) OT
(RS Pts.—Dolphins 78, Ravens 32)
(PS Pts.—Ravens 20, Dolphins 3)
**AFC First-Round Playoff*
BALTIMORE vs. MINNESOTA
RS: Series tied, 1-1
1998—Vikings, 38-28 (B)
2001—Ravens, 19-3 (B)
(RS Pts.—Ravens 47, Vikings 41)
BALTIMORE vs. NEW ENGLAND
RS: Patriots lead series, 2-0
1996—Patriots, 46-38 (B)
1999—Patriots, 20-3 (NE)
(RS Pts.—Patriots 66, Ravens 41)
BALTIMORE vs. NEW ORLEANS
RS: Ravens lead series, 2-1
1996—Ravens, 17-10 (B)
1999—Ravens, 31-8 (B)
2002—Saints, 37-25 (B)
(RS Pts.—Ravens 73, Saints 55)
BALTIMORE vs. N.Y. GIANTS
RS: Ravens lead series, 1-0
PS: Ravens lead series, 1-0
1997—Ravens, 24-23 (NY)
2000—*Ravens, 34-7 (Tampa)
(RS Pts.—Ravens 24, Giants 23)
(PS Pts.—Ravens 34, Giants 7)
**Super Bowl XXXV*
BALTIMORE vs. N.Y. JETS
RS: Ravens lead series, 2-1
1997—Jets, 19-16 (NY) OT
1998—Ravens, 24-10 (NY)
2000—Ravens, 34-20 (B)
(RS Pts.—Ravens 74, Jets 49)
BALTIMORE vs. OAKLAND
RS: Ravens lead series, 2-1
PS: Ravens lead series, 1-0
1996—Ravens, 19-14 (B)
1998—Ravens, 13-10 (B)
2000—*Ravens, 16-3 (O)
2003—Raiders, 20-12 (O)
(RS Pts.—Ravens 44, Raiders 44)
(PS Pts.—Ravens 16, Raiders 3)
**AFC Championship*
BALTIMORE vs. PHILADELPHIA
RS: Series tied, 0-0-1
1997—Tie, 10-10 (B) OT
(RS Pts.—Ravens 10, Eagles 10)
BALTIMORE vs. PITTSBURGH
RS: Steelers lead series, 11-5
PS: Steelers lead series, 1-0
1996—Steelers, 31-17 (P)
Ravens, 31-17 (B)
1997—Steelers, 42-34 (B)
Steelers, 37-0 (P)
1998—Steelers, 20-13 (B)
Steelers, 16-6 (P)
1999—Steelers, 23-20 (B)
Ravens, 31-24 (P)
2000—Ravens, 16-0 (P)
Steelers, 9-6 (B)
2001—Ravens, 13-10 (P)
Steelers, 26-21 (B)
*Steelers, 27-10 (P)
2002—Steelers, 31-18 (B)
Steelers, 34-31 (P)
2003—Steelers, 34-15 (P)
Ravens, 13-10 (B) OT
(RS Pts.—Steelers 364, Ravens 285)
(PS Pts.—Steelers 27, Ravens 10)
**AFC Divisional Playoff*
BALTIMORE vs. ST. LOUIS
RS: Rams lead series, 2-1
1996—Ravens, 37-31 (B) OT
1999—Rams, 27-10 (StL)
2003—Rams, 33-22 (StL)
(RS Pts.—Rams 91, Ravens 69)
BALTIMORE vs. SAN DIEGO
RS: Series tied, 2-2
1997—Chargers, 21-17 (SD)
1998—Chargers, 14-13 (SD)
2000—Ravens, 24-3 (B)
2003—Ravens, 24-10 (SD)
(RS Pts.—Ravens 78, Chargers 48)
BALTIMORE vs. SAN FRANCISCO
RS: Series tied, 1-1
1996—49ers, 38-20 (SF)
2003—Ravens, 44-6 (B)
(RS Pts.—Ravens 64, 49ers 44)
BALTIMORE vs. SEATTLE
RS: Ravens lead series, 2-0
1997—Ravens, 31-24 (B)
2003—Ravens, 44-41 (B) OT
(RS Pts.—Ravens 75, Seahawks 65)
BALTIMORE vs. TAMPA BAY
RS: Buccaneers lead series, 2-0
2001—Buccaneers, 22-10 (TB)
2002—Buccaneers, 25-0 (B)
(RS Pts.—Buccaneers 47, Ravens 10)

BALTIMORE vs. *TENNESSEE
RS: Ravens lead series, 7-6
PS: Series tied, 1-1
1996—Oilers, 29-13 (H)
Oilers, 24-21 (B)
1997—Ravens, 36-10 (T)
Ravens, 21-19 (B)
1998—Oilers, 12-8 (B)
Oilers, 16-14 (T)
1999—Titans, 14-11 (T)
Ravens, 41-14 (B)
2000—Titans, 14-6 (B)
Ravens, 24-23 (T)
**Ravens, 24-10 (T)
2001—Ravens, 26-7 (B)
Ravens, 16-10 (T)
2002—Ravens, 13-12 (B)
2003—***Titans, 20-17 (B)
(RS Pts.—Ravens 250, Titans 204)
(PS Pts.—Ravens 41, Titans 30)
Franchise in Houston prior to 1997; known as Oilers prior to 1999
***AFC Divisional Playoff*
****AFC First-Round Playoff*

BALTIMORE vs. WASHINGTON
RS: Series tied, 1-1
1997—Ravens, 20-17 (W)
2000—Redskins, 10-3 (W)
(RS Pts.—Redskins 27, Ravens 23)

BUFFALO vs. ARIZONA
RS: Bills lead series, 4-3;
See Arizona vs. Buffalo

BUFFALO vs. ATLANTA
RS: Series tied, 4-4;
See Atlanta vs. Buffalo

BUFFALO vs. BALTIMORE
RS: Bills lead series, 1-0;
See Baltimore vs. Buffalo

BUFFALO vs. CAROLINA
RS: Bills lead series, 3-0
1995—Bills, 31-9 (B)
1998—Bills, 30-14 (C)
2001—Bills, 25-24 (B)
(RS Pts.—Bills 86, Panthers 47)

BUFFALO vs. CHICAGO
RS: Bears lead series, 5-4
1970—Bears, 31-13 (C)
1974—Bills, 16-6 (B)
1979—Bears, 7-0 (B)
1988—Bears, 24-3 (C)
1991—Bills, 35-20 (B)
1994—Bears, 20-13 (C)
1997—Bears, 20-3 (C)
2000—Bills, 20-3 (B)
2002—Bills, 33-27 (B) OT
(RS Pts.—Bears 158, Bills 136)

BUFFALO vs. CINCINNATI
RS: Bills lead series, 11-9
PS: Bengals lead series, 2-0
1968—Bengals, 34-23 (C)
1969—Bills, 16-13 (B)
1970—Bengals, 43-14 (B)
1973—Bengals, 16-13 (B)
1975—Bengals, 33-24 (C)
1978—Bills, 5-0 (B)
1979—Bills, 51-24 (B)
1980—Bills, 14-0 (C)
1981—Bengals, 27-24 (C) OT
*Bengals, 28-21 (C)
1983—Bills, 10-6 (C)
1984—Bengals, 52-21 (C)
1985—Bengals, 23-17 (B)
1986—Bengals, 36-33 (C) OT
1988—Bengals, 35-21 (C)
**Bengals, 21-10 (C)
1989—Bills, 24-7 (B)
1991—Bills, 35-16 (B)
1996—Bills, 31-17 (B)
1998—Bills, 33-20 (C)
2002—Bills, 27-9 (B)
2003—Bills, 22-16 (B) OT
(RS Pts.—Bills 458, Bengals 427)
(PS Pts.—Bengals 49, Bills 31)
**AFC Divisional Playoff*
***AFC Championship*

BUFFALO vs. CLEVELAND
RS: Browns lead series, 7-4
PS: Browns lead series, 1-0
1972—Browns, 27-10 (C)
1974—Bills, 15-10 (C)
1977—Browns, 27-16 (B)
1978—Browns, 41-20 (C)
1981—Bills, 22-13 (B)
1984—Browns, 13-10 (B)
1985—Browns, 17-7 (C)
1986—Browns, 21-17 (B)
1987—Browns, 27-21 (C)
1989—*Browns, 34-30 (C)
1990—Bills, 42-0 (C)
1995—Bills, 22-19 (C)
(RS Pts.—Browns 215, Bills 202)
(PS Pts.—Browns 34, Bills 30)
**AFC Divisional Playoff*

BUFFALO vs. DALLAS
RS: Cowboys lead series, 4-3
PS: Cowboys lead series, 2-0
1971—Cowboys, 49-37 (B)
1976—Cowboys, 17-10 (D)
1981—Cowboys, 27-14 (D)
1984—Bills, 14-3 (B)
1992—*Cowboys, 52-17 (Pasadena)
1993—Bills, 13-10 (D)
**Cowboys, 30-13 (Atlanta)
1996—Bills, 10-7 (B)
2003—Cowboys, 10-6 (D)
(RS Pts.—Cowboys 123, Bills 104)
(PS Pts.—Cowboys 82, Bills 30)
**Super Bowl XXVII*
***Super Bowl XXVIII*

BUFFALO vs. DENVER
RS: Bills lead series, 17-13-1
PS: Bills lead series, 1-0
1960—Broncos, 27-21 (B)
Tie, 38-38 (D)
1961—Broncos, 22-10 (B)
Bills, 23-10 (D)
1962—Broncos, 23-20 (B)
Bills, 45-38 (D)
1963—Bills, 30-28 (D)
Bills, 27-17 (B)
1964—Bills, 30-13 (B)
Bills, 30-19 (D)
1965—Bills, 30-15 (D)
Bills, 31-13 (B)
1966—Bills, 38-21 (B)
1967—Bills, 17-16 (D)
Broncos, 21-20 (B)
1968—Broncos, 34-32 (D)
1969—Bills, 41-28 (B)
1970—Broncos, 25-10 (B)
1975—Bills, 38-14 (B)
1977—Broncos, 26-6 (D)
1979—Broncos, 19-16 (B)
1981—Bills, 9-7 (B)
1984—Broncos, 37-7 (B)
1987—Bills, 21-14 (B)
1989—Broncos, 28-14 (B)
1990—Bills, 29-28 (B)
1991—*Bills, 10-7 (B)
1992—Bills, 27-17 (B)
1994—Bills, 27-20 (B)
1995—Broncos, 22-7 (D)
1997—Broncos, 23-20 (B) OT
2002—Broncos, 28-23 (D)
(RS Pts.—Bills 737, Broncos 691)
(PS Pts.—Bills 10, Broncos 7)
**AFC Championship*

BUFFALO vs. DETROIT
RS: Series tied, 3-3-1
1972—Tie, 21-21 (B)
1976—Lions, 27-14 (D)
1979—Bills, 20-17 (D)
1991—Lions, 17-14 (B) OT
1994—Lions, 35-21 (D)
1997—Bills, 22-13 (B)
2002—Bills, 24-17 (B)
(RS Pts.—Lions 147, Bills 136)

BUFFALO vs. GREEN BAY
RS: Bills lead series, 6-3
1974—Bills, 27-7 (GB)
1979—Bills, 19-12 (B)
1982—Packers, 33-21 (Mil)
1988—Bills, 28-0 (B)
1991—Bills, 34-24 (Mil)
1994—Bills 29-20 (B)
1997—Packers, 31-21 (GB)
2000—Bills 27-18 (B)
2002—Packers, 10-0 (GB)
(RS Pts.—Bills 206, Packers 155)

BUFFALO vs. HOUSTON
RS: Series tied, 1-1
2002—Bills, 31-24 (H)
2003—Texans, 12-10 (B)
(RS Pts.—Bills 41, Texans 36)

BUFFALO vs. *INDIANAPOLIS
RS: Bills lead series, 34-29-1
1970—Tie, 17-17 (Balt)
Colts, 20-14 (Buff)
1971—Colts, 43-0 (Buff)
Colts, 24-0 (Balt)
1972—Colts, 17-0 (Buff)
Colts, 35-7 (Balt)
1973—Bills, 31-13 (Buff)
Bills, 24-17 (Balt)
1974—Bills, 27-14 (Balt)
Bills, 6-0 (Buff)
1975—Bills, 38-31 (Balt)
Colts, 42-35 (Buff)
1976—Colts, 31-13 (Buff)
Colts, 58-20 (Balt)
1977—Colts, 17-14 (Balt)
Colts, 31-13 (Buff)
1978—Bills, 24-17 (Buff)
Bills, 21-14 (Balt)
1979—Bills, 31-13 (Balt)
Colts, 14-13 (Buff)
1980—Colts, 17-12 (Buff)
Colts, 28-24 (Balt)
1981—Bills, 35-3 (Balt)

Bills, 23-17 (Buff)
1982—Bills, 20-0 (Buff)
1983—Bills, 28-23 (Buff)
Bills, 30-7 (Balt)
1984—Colts, 31-17 (I)
Bills, 21-15 (Buff)
1985—Colts, 49-17 (I)
Bills, 21-9 (Buff)
1986—Bills, 24-13 (Buff)
Colts, 24-14 (I)
1987—Colts, 47-6 (Buff)
Bills, 27-3 (I)
1988—Bills, 34-23 (Buff)
Colts, 17-14 (I)
1989—Colts, 37-14 (I)
Bills, 30-7 (Buff)
1990—Bills, 26-10 (Buff)
Bills, 31-7 (I)
1991—Bills, 42-6 (Buff)
Bills, 35-7 (I)
1992—Bills, 38-0 (Buff)
Colts, 16-13 (I) OT
1993—Bills, 23-9 (Buff)
Bills, 30-10 (I)
1994—Colts, 27-17 (Buff)
Colts, 10-9 (I)
1995—Bills, 20-14 (Buff)
Bills, 16-10 (I)
1996—Bills, 16-13 (Buff) OT
Colts, 13-10 (I) OT
1997—Bills, 37-35 (B)
Bills, 9-6 (I)
1998—Bills, 31-24 (I)
Bills, 34-11 (B)
1999—Colts, 31-14 (I)
Bills, 31-6 (B)
2000—Colts, 18-16 (B)
Colts, 44-20 (I)
2001—Colts, 42-26 (I)
Colts, 30-14 (B)
2003—Colts, 17-14 (B)
(RS Pts.—Bills 1,331, Colts 1,254)
Franchise in Baltimore prior to 1984

BUFFALO vs. JACKSONVILLE
RS: Bills lead series, 3-1
PS: Jaguars lead series, 1-0
1996—*Jaguars, 30-27 (B)
1997—Jaguars, 20-14 (B)
1998—Bills, 17-16 (B)
2001—Bills, 13-10 (J)
2003—Bills, 38-17 (J)
(RS Pts.—Bills 82, Jaguars 63)
(PS Pts.—Jaguars 30, Bills 27)
**AFC First-Round Playoff*

BUFFALO vs. *KANSAS CITY
RS: Bills lead series, 18-16-1
PS: Bills lead series, 2-1
1960—Texans, 45-28 (B)
Texans, 24-7 (D)
1961—Bills, 27-24 (B)
Bills, 30-20 (D)
1962—Texans, 41-21 (D)
Bills, 23-14 (B)
1963—Tie, 27-27 (B)
Bills, 35-26 (KC)
1964—Bills, 34-17 (B)
Bills, 35-22 (KC)
1965—Bills, 23-7 (KC)
Bills, 34-25 (B)
1966—Chiefs, 42-20 (B)
Bills, 29-14 (KC)
**Chiefs, 31-7 (B)
1967—Chiefs, 23-13 (KC)
1968—Chiefs, 18-7 (B)
1969—Chiefs, 29-7 (B)
Chiefs, 22-19 (KC)
1971—Chiefs, 22-9 (KC)
1973—Bills, 23-14 (B)
1976—Bills, 50-17 (B)
1978—Bills, 28-13 (B)
Chiefs, 14-10 (KC)
1982—Bills, 14-9 (B)
1983—Bills, 14-9 (KC)
1986—Chiefs, 20-17 (B)
Bills, 17-14 (KC)
1991—Chiefs, 33-6 (KC)
***Bills, 37-14 (B)
1993—Chiefs, 23-7 (KC)
****Bills, 30-13 (B)
1994—Bills, 44-10 (B)
1996—Bills, 20-9 (B)
1997—Chiefs, 22-16 (KC)
2000—Bills, 21-17 (KC)
2002—Chiefs, 17-16 (KC)
2003—Chiefs, 38-5 (KC)
(RS Pts.—Chiefs 741, Bills 736)
(PS Pts.—Bills 74, Chiefs 58)
**Franchise in Dallas prior to 1963 and known as Texans*
***AFL Championship*
****AFC Divisional Playoff*
*****AFC Championship*

BUFFALO vs. MIAMI
RS: Dolphins lead series, 48-27-1
PS: Bills lead series, 3-1
1966—Bills, 58-24 (B)
Bills, 29-0 (M)
1967—Bills, 35-13 (B)
Dolphins, 17-14 (M)
1968—Tie, 14-14 (M)
Dolphins, 21-17 (B)
1969—Dolphins, 24-6 (M)
Bills, 28-3 (B)
1970—Dolphins, 33-14 (B)
Dolphins, 45-7 (M)
1971—Dolphins, 29-14 (B)
Dolphins, 34-0 (M)
1972—Dolphins, 24-23 (M)
Dolphins, 30-16 (B)
1973—Dolphins, 27-6 (M)
Dolphins, 17-0 (B)
1974—Dolphins, 24-16 (B)
Dolphins, 35-28 (M)
1975—Dolphins, 35-30 (B)
Dolphins, 31-21 (M)
1976—Dolphins, 30-21 (B)
Dolphins, 45-27 (M)
1977—Dolphins, 13-0 (B)
Dolphins, 31-14 (M)
1978—Dolphins, 31-24 (M)
Dolphins, 25-24 (B)
1979—Dolphins, 9-7 (B)
Dolphins, 17-7 (M)
1980—Bills, 17-7 (B)
Dolphins, 17-14 (M)
1981—Bills, 31-21 (B)
Dolphins, 16-6 (M)
1982—Dolphins, 9-7 (B)
Dolphins, 27-10 (M)
1983—Dolphins, 12-0 (B)
Bills, 38-35 (M) OT
1984—Dolphins, 21-17 (B)
Dolphins, 38-7 (M)
1985—Dolphins, 23-14 (B)
Dolphins, 28-0 (M)
1986—Dolphins, 27-14 (M)
Dolphins, 34-24 (B)
1987—Bills, 34-31 (M) OT
Bills, 27-0 (B)
1988—Bills, 9-6 (B)
Bills, 31-6 (M)
1989—Bills, 27-24 (M)
Bills, 31-17 (B)
1990—Dolphins, 30-7 (M)
Bills, 24-14 (B)
*Bills, 44-34 (B)
1991—Bills, 35-31 (B)
Bills, 41-27 (M)
1992—Dolphins, 37-10 (B)
Bills, 26-20 (M)
**Bills, 29-10 (M)
1993—Dolphins, 22-13 (B)
Bills, 47-34 (M)
1994—Bills, 21-11 (B)
Bills, 42-31 (M)
1995—Dolphins, 23-6 (M)
Bills, 23-20 (B)
***Bills, 37-22 (B)
1996—Dolphins, 21-7 (B)
Dolphins, 16-14 (M)
1997—Bills, 9-6 (B)
Dolphins, 30-13 (M)
1998—Dolphins, 13-7 (M)
Bills, 30-24 (B)
***Dolphins, 24-17 (M)
1999—Bills, 23-18 (M)
Bills, 23-3 (B)
2000—Dolphins, 22-13 (M)
Dolphins, 33-6 (B)
2001—Dolphins, 34-27 (B)
Dolphins, 34-7 (M)
2002—Bills, 23-10 (M)
Bills, 38-21 (B)
2003—Dolphins, 17-7 (M)
Dolphins, 20-3 (B)
(RS Pts.—Dolphins 1,702, Bills 1,403)
(PS Pts.—Bills 127, Dolphins 90)
**AFC Divisional Playoff*
***AFC Championship*
****AFC First-Round Playoff*

BUFFALO vs. MINNESOTA
RS: Vikings lead series, 7-3
1971—Vikings, 19-0 (M)
1975—Vikings, 35-13 (B)
1979—Vikings, 10-3 (M)
1982—Bills, 23-22 (B)
1985—Vikings, 27-20 (B)
1988—Bills, 13-10 (B)
1994—Vikings, 21-17 (B)
1997—Vikings, 34-13 (B)
2000—Vikings, 31-27 (M)
2002—Bills, 45-39 (M) OT
(RS Pts.—Vikings 248, Bills 174)

BUFFALO vs. *NEW ENGLAND
RS: Patriots lead series, 46-40-1
PS: Patriots lead series, 1-0
1960—Bills, 13-0 (Bos)
Bills, 38-14 (Buff)
1961—Patriots, 23-21 (Buff)
Patriots, 52-21 (Bos)

1962—Tie, 28-28 (Buff)
Patriots, 21-10 (Bos)
1963—Bills, 28-21 (Buff)
Patriots, 17-7 (Bos)
**Patriots, 26-8 (Buff)
1964—Patriots, 36-28 (Buff)
Bills, 24-14 (Bos)
1965—Bills, 24-7 (Buff)
Bills, 23-7 (Bos)
1966—Patriots, 20-10 (Buff)
Patriots, 14-3 (Bos)
1967—Patriots, 23-0 (Buff)
Bills, 44-16 (Bos)
1968—Patriots, 16-7 (Buff)
Patriots, 23-6 (Bos)
1969—Bills, 23-16 (Buff)
Patriots, 35-21 (Bos)
1970—Bills, 45-10 (Bos)
Patriots, 14-10 (Buff)
1971—Patriots, 38-33 (NE)
Bills, 27-20 (Buff)
1972—Bills, 38-14 (Buff)
Bills, 27-24 (NE)
1973—Bills, 31-13 (NE)
Bills, 37-13 (Buff)
1974—Bills, 30-28 (Buff)
Bills, 29-28 (NE)
1975—Bills, 45-31 (Buff)
Bills, 34-14 (NE)
1976—Patriots, 26-22 (Buff)
Patriots, 20-10 (NE)
1977—Bills, 24-14 (NE)
Patriots, 20-7 (Buff)
1978—Patriots, 14-10 (Buff)
Patriots, 26-24 (NE)
1979—Patriots, 26-6 (Buff)
Bills, 16-13 (NE) OT
1980—Bills, 31-13 (Buff)
Patriots, 24-2 (NE)
1981—Bills, 20-17 (Buff)
Bills, 19-10 (NE)
1982—Patriots, 30-19 (NE)
1983—Patriots, 31-0 (Buff)
Patriots, 21-7 (NE)
1984—Patriots, 21-17 (Buff)
Patriots, 38-10 (NE)
1985—Patriots, 17-14 (Buff)
Patriots, 14-3 (NE)
1986—Patriots, 23-3 (Buff)
Patriots, 22-19 (NE)
1987—Patriots, 14-7 (NE)
Patriots, 13-7 (Buff)
1988—Bills, 16-14 (NE)
Bills, 23-20 (Buff)
1989—Bills, 31-10 (Buff)
Patriots, 33-24 (NE)
1990—Bills, 27-10 (NE)
Bills, 14-0 (Buff)
1991—Bills, 22-17 (Buff)
Patriots, 16-13 (NE)
1992—Bills, 41-7 (NE)
Bills, 16-7 (Buff)
1993—Bills, 38-14 (Buff)
Bills, 13-10 (NE) OT
1994—Bills, 38-35 (NE)
Patriots, 41-17 (Buff)
1995—Patriots, 27-14 (NE)
Patriots, 35-25 (Buff)
1996—Bills, 17-10 (Buff)
Patriots, 28-25 (NE)
1997—Patriots, 33-6 (NE)
Patriots, 31-10 (Buff)
1998—Bills, 13-10 (Buff)
Patriots, 25-21 (NE)
1999—Bills, 17-7 (Buff)
Bills, 13-10 (NE) OT
2000—Bills, 16-13 (NE) OT
Patriots, 13-10 (Buff) OT
2001—Patriots, 21-11 (NE)
Patriots, 12-9 (Buff) OT
2002—Patriots, 38-7 (Buff)
Patriots, 27-17 (NE)
2003—Bills, 31-0 (B)
Patriots, 31-0 (NE)
(RS Pts.—Patriots 1,722, Bills 1,657)
(PS Pts.—Patriots 26, Bills 8)
Franchise in Boston prior to 1971
***Division Playoff*

BUFFALO vs. NEW ORLEANS
RS: Bills lead series, 4-3
1973—Saints, 13-0 (NO)
1980—Bills, 35-26 (NO)
1983—Bills, 27-21 (B)
1989—Saints, 22-19 (B)
1992—Bills, 20-16 (NO)
1998—Bills, 45-33 (NO)
2001—Saints, 24-6 (B)
(RS Pts.—Saints 155, Bills 152)

BUFFALO vs. N.Y. GIANTS
RS: Bills lead series, 6-3
PS: Giants lead series, 1-0
1970—Giants, 20-6 (NY)
1975—Giants, 17-14 (B)
1978—Bills, 41-17 (B)
1987—Bills, 6-3 (B) OT
1990—Bills, 17-13 (NY)
*Giants, 20-19 (Tampa)
1993—Bills, 17-14 (B)
1996—Bills, 23-20 (NY) OT
1999—Giants, 19-17 (B)
2003—Bills, 24-7 (NY)
(RS Pts.—Bills 165, Giants 130)
(PS Pts.—Giants 20, Bills 19)
**Super Bowl XXV*

BUFFALO vs. *N.Y. JETS
RS: Bills lead series, 47-39
PS: Bills lead series, 1-0
1960—Titans, 27-3 (NY)
Titans, 17-13 (B)
1961—Bills, 41-31 (B)
Titans, 21-14 (NY)
1962—Titans, 17-6 (B)
Bills, 20-3 (NY)
1963—Bills, 45-14 (B)
Bills, 19-10 (NY)
1964—Bills, 34-24 (B)
Bills, 20-7 (NY)
1965—Bills, 33-21 (B)
Jets, 14-12 (NY)
1966—Bills, 33-23 (NY)
Bills, 14-3 (B)
1967—Bills, 20-17 (B)
Jets, 20-10 (NY)
1968—Bills, 37-35 (B)
Jets, 25-21 (NY)
1969—Jets, 33-19 (B)
Jets, 16-6 (NY)
1970—Bills, 34-31 (B)
Bills, 10-6 (NY)
1971—Jets, 28-17 (NY)
Jets, 20-7 (B)
1972—Jets, 41-24 (B)
Jets, 41-3 (NY)
1973—Bills, 9-7 (B)
Bills, 34-14 (NY)
1974—Bills, 16-12 (B)
Jets, 20-10 (NY)
1975—Bills, 42-14 (B)
Bills, 24-23 (NY)
1976—Jets, 17-14 (NY)
Jets, 19-14 (B)
1977—Jets, 24-19 (B)
Bills, 14-10 (NY)
1978—Jets, 21-20 (B)
Jets, 45-14 (NY)
1979—Bills, 46-31 (B)
Bills, 14-12 (NY)
1980—Bills, 20-10 (B)
Bills, 31-24 (NY)
1981—Bills, 31-0 (B)
Jets, 33-14 (NY)
**Bills, 31-27 (NY)
1983—Jets, 34-10 (B)
Bills, 24-17 (NY)
1984—Jets, 28-26 (B)
Jets, 21-17 (NY)
1985—Jets, 42-3 (NY)
Jets, 27-7 (B)
1986—Jets, 28-24 (B)
Jets, 14-13 (NY)
1987—Jets, 31-28 (B)
Bills, 17-14 (NY)
1988—Bills, 37-14 (NY)
Bills, 9-6 (B) OT
1989—Bills, 34-3 (B)
Bills, 37-0 (NY)
1990—Bills, 30-7 (NY)
Bills, 30-27 (B)
1991—Bills, 23-20 (NY)
Bills, 24-13 (B)
1992—Bills, 24-20 (NY)
Jets, 24-17 (B)
1993—Bills, 19-10 (NY)
Bills, 16-14 (B)
1994—Jets, 23-3 (B)
Jets, 22-17 (NY)
1995—Bills, 29-10 (B)
Bills, 28-26 (NY)
1996—Bills, 25-22 (NY)
Bills, 35-10 (B)
1997—Bills, 28-22 (NY)
Bills, 20-10 (B)
1998—Jets, 34-12 (NY)
Jets, 17-10 (B)
1999—Bills, 17-3 (B)
Jets, 17-7 (NY)
2000—Jets, 27-14 (NY)
Bills, 23-20 (B)
2001—Jets, 42-36 (B)
Bills, 14-9 (NY)
2002—Jets, 37-31 (B) OT
Jets, 31-13 (NY)
2003—Jets, 30-3 (NY)
Bills, 17-6 (B)
(RS Pts.—Bills 1,752, Jets 1,713)
(PS Pts.—Bills 31, Jets 27)
**Jets known as Titans prior to 1963*
***AFC First-Round Playoff*

BUFFALO vs. *OAKLAND
RS: Raiders lead series, 17-15

PS: Bills lead series, 2-0
1960—Bills, 38-9 (B)
Raiders, 20-7 (O)
1961—Raiders, 31-22 (B)
Bills, 26-21 (O)
1962—Bills, 14-6 (B)
Bills, 10-6 (O)
1963—Raiders, 35-17 (O)
Bills, 12-0 (B)
1964—Bills, 23-20 (B)
Raiders, 16-13 (O)
1965—Bills, 17-12 (B)
Bills, 17-14 (O)
1966—Bills, 31-10 (O)
1967—Raiders, 24-20 (B)
Raiders, 28-21 (O)
1968—Raiders, 48-6 (B)
Raiders, 13-10 (O)
1969—Raiders, 50-21 (O)
1972—Raiders, 28-16 (O)
1974—Bills, 21-20 (B)
1977—Raiders, 34-13 (O)
1980—Bills, 24-7 (B)
1983—Raiders, 27-24 (B)
1987—Raiders, 34-21 (LA)
1988—Bills, 37-21 (B)
1990—Bills, 38-24 (B)
**Bills, 51-3 (B)
1991—Bills, 30-27 (LA) OT
1992—Raiders, 20-3 (LA)
1993—Raiders, 25-24 (B)
***Bills, 29-23 (B)
1998—Bills, 44-21 (B)
1999—Raiders, 20-14 (B)
2002—Raiders, 49-31 (B)
(RS Pts.—Raiders 720, Bills 665)
(PS Pts.—Bills 80, Raiders 26)
Franchise in Los Angeles from 1982-1994
**AFC Championship*
***AFC Divisional Playoff*

BUFFALO vs. PHILADELPHIA
RS: Bills lead series, 5-5
1973—Bills, 27-26 (B)
1981—Eagles, 20-14 (B)
1984—Eagles, 27-17 (B)
1985—Eagles, 21-17 (P)
1987—Eagles, 17-7 (P)
1990—Bills, 30-23 (B)
1993—Bills, 10-7 (P)
1996—Bills, 24-17 (P)
1999—Bills, 26-0 (B)
2003—Eagles, 23-13 (B)
(RS Pts.—Bills 185, Eagles 181)

BUFFALO vs. PITTSBURGH
RS: Steelers lead series, 9-8
PS: Steelers lead series, 2-1
1970—Steelers, 23-10 (P)
1972—Steelers, 38-21 (B)
1974—*Steelers, 32-14 (P)
1975—Bills, 30-21 (P)
1978—Steelers, 28-17 (B)
1979—Steelers, 28-0 (P)
1980—Bills, 28-13 (B)
1982—Bills, 13-0 (B)
1985—Steelers, 30-24 (P)
1986—Bills, 16-12 (B)
1988—Bills, 36-28 (B)
1991—Bills, 52-34 (B)
1992—Bills, 28-20 (B)
*Bills, 24-3 (P)
1993—Steelers, 23-0 (P)
1994—Steelers, 23-10 (P)
1995—*Steelers, 40-21 (P)
1996—Steelers, 24-6 (P)
1999—Bills, 24-21 (B)
2001—Steelers, 20-3 (B)
(RS Pts.—Steelers 386, Bills 318)
(PS Pts.—Steelers 75, Bills 59)
AFC Divisional Playoff

BUFFALO vs. *ST. LOUIS
RS: Series tied, 4-4
1970—Rams, 19-0 (B)
1974—Rams, 19-14 (LA)
1980—Bills, 10-7 (B) OT
1983—Rams, 41-17 (LA)
1989—Bills, 23-20 (B)
1992—Bills, 40-7 (B)
1995—Bills, 45-27 (StL)
1998—Rams, 34-33 (B)
(RS Pts.—Bills 182, Rams 174)
Franchise in Los Angeles prior to 1995

BUFFALO vs. *SAN DIEGO
RS: Chargers lead series, 18-9-2
PS: Bills lead series, 2-1
1960—Chargers, 24-10 (B)
Bills, 32-3 (LA)
1961—Chargers, 19-11 (B)
Chargers, 28-10 (SD)
1962—Bills, 35-10 (B)
Bills, 40-20 (SD)
1963—Chargers, 14-10 (SD)
Chargers, 23-13 (B)
1964—Bills, 30-3 (B)
Bills, 27-24 (SD)
**Bills, 20-7 (B)
1965—Chargers, 34-3 (B)
Tie, 20-20 (SD)
**Bills, 23-0 (SD)
1966—Chargers, 27-7 (SD)
Tie, 17-17 (B)
1967—Chargers, 37-17 (B)
1968—Chargers, 21-6 (B)
1969—Chargers, 45-6 (SD)
1971—Chargers, 20-3 (SD)
1973—Chargers, 34-7 (SD)
1976—Chargers, 34-13 (B)
1979—Chargers, 27-19 (SD)
1980—Bills, 26-24 (SD)
***Chargers, 20-14 (SD)
1981—Bills, 28-27 (SD)
1985—Chargers, 14-9 (B)
Chargers, 40-7 (SD)
1998—Chargers, 16-14 (SD)
2000—Bills, 27-24 (B) OT
2001—Chargers, 27-24 (SD)
2002—Bills, 20-13 (B)
(RS Pts.—Chargers 669, Bills 491)
(PS Pts.—Bills 57, Chargers 27)
Franchise in Los Angeles prior to 1961
**AFL Championship*
***AFC Divisional Playoff*

BUFFALO vs. SAN FRANCISCO
RS: Series tied, 4-4
1972—Bills, 27-20 (B)
1980—Bills, 18-13 (SF)
1983—49ers, 23-10 (B)
1989—49ers, 21-10 (SF)
1992—Bills, 34-31 (SF)
1995—49ers, 27-17 (SF)
1998—Bills, 26-21 (B)
2001—49ers, 35-0 (SF)
(RS Pts.—49ers 191, Bills 142)

BUFFALO vs. SEATTLE
RS: Seahawks lead series, 6-3
1977—Seahawks, 56-17 (S)
1984—Seahawks, 31-28 (S)
1988—Bills, 13-3 (S)
1989—Seahawks, 17-16 (S)
1995—Bills, 27-21 (B)
1996—Seahawks, 26-18 (S)
1999—Seahawks, 26-16 (S)
2000—Bills, 42-23 (S)
2001—Seahawks, 23-20 (B)
(RS Pts.—Seahawks 226, Bills 197)

BUFFALO vs. TAMPA BAY
RS: Buccaneers lead series, 5-2
1976—Bills, 14-9 (TB)
1978—Buccaneers, 31-10 (TB)
1982—Buccaneers, 24-23 (TB)
1986—Buccaneers, 34-28 (TB)
1988—Buccaneers, 10-5 (TB)
1991—Bills, 17-10 (TB)
2000—Buccaneers, 31-17 (TB)
(RS Pts.—Buccaneers 149, Bills 114)

BUFFALO vs. *TENNESSEE
RS: Titans lead series, 23-14
PS: Bills lead series, 2-1
1960—Bills, 25-24 (B)
Oilers, 31-23 (H)
1961—Bills, 22-12 (H)
Oilers, 28-16 (B)
1962—Oilers, 28-23 (B)
Oilers, 17-14 (H)
1963—Oilers, 31-20 (B)
Oilers, 28-14 (H)
1964—Bills, 48-17 (H)
Bills, 24-10 (B)
1965—Oilers, 19-17 (B)
Bills, 29-18 (H)
1966—Bills, 27-20 (B)
Bills, 42-20 (H)
1967—Oilers, 20-3 (B)
Oilers, 10-3 (H)
1968—Oilers, 30-7 (B)
Oilers, 35-6 (H)
1969—Oilers, 17-3 (B)
Oilers, 28-14 (H)
1971—Oilers, 20-14 (B)
1974—Oilers, 21-9 (B)
1976—Oilers, 13-3 (B)
1978—Oilers, 17-10 (H)
1983—Bills, 30-13 (B)
1985—Bills, 20-0 (B)
1986—Oilers, 16-7 (H)
1987—Bills, 34-30 (B)
1988—**Bills, 17-10 (B)
1989—Bills, 47-41 (H) OT
1990—Oilers, 27-24 (H)
1992—Oilers, 27-3 (H)
***Bills, 41-38 (B) OT
1993—Bills, 35-7 (B)
1994—Bills, 15-7 (H)
1995—Oilers, 28-17 (B)
1997—Oilers, 31-14 (T)
1999—***Titans, 22-16 (T)
2000—Bills, 16-13 (B)
2003—Titans, 28-26 (T)
(RS Pts.—Titans 782, Bills 704)
(PS Pts.—Bills 74, Titans 70)
Franchise in Houston prior to 1997;

known as Oilers prior to 1999
***AFC Divisional Playoff*
****AFC First-Round Playoff*

BUFFALO vs. WASHINGTON
RS: Bills lead series, 6-4
PS: Redskins lead series, 1-0
1972—Bills, 24-17 (W)
1977—Redskins, 10-0 (B)
1981—Bills, 21-14 (B)
1984—Redskins, 41-14 (W)
1987—Redskins, 27-7 (B)
1990—Redskins, 29-14 (W)
1991—*Redskins, 37-24 (Minneapolis)
1993—Bills, 24-10 (B)
1996—Bills, 38-13 (B)
1999—Bills, 34-17 (W)
2003—Bills, 24-7 (B)
(RS Pts.—Bills 200, Redskins 185)
(PS Pts.—Redskins 37, Bills 24)
**Super Bowl XXVI*

CAROLINA vs. ARIZONA
RS: Series tied, 2-2;
See Arizona vs. Carolina

CAROLINA vs. ATLANTA
RS: Falcons lead series, 12-6;
See Atlanta vs. Carolina

CAROLINA vs. BALTIMORE
RS: Panthers lead series, 2-0;
See Baltimore vs. Carolina

CAROLINA vs. BUFFALO
RS: Bills lead series, 3-0;
See Buffalo vs. Carolina

CAROLINA vs. CHICAGO
RS: Series tied, 1-1
1995—Bears, 31-27 (Chi)
2002—Panthers, 24-14 (Car)
(RS Pts.—Panthers 51, Bears 45)

CAROLINA vs. CINCINNATI
RS: Panthers lead series, 2-0
1999—Panthers, 27-3 (Car)
2002—Panthers, 52-31 (Car)
(RS Pts.—Panthers 79, Bengals 34)

CAROLINA vs. CLEVELAND
RS: Panthers lead series, 2-0
1999—Panthers, 31-17 (Cle)
2002—Panthers, 13-6 (Cle)
(RS Pts.—Panthers 44, Browns 23)

CAROLINA vs. DALLAS
RS: Cowboys lead series, 4-1
PS: Panthers lead series, 2-0
1996—*Panthers, 26-17 (C)
1997—Panthers, 23-13 (D)
1998—Cowboys, 27-20 (D)
2000—Cowboys, 16-13 (C) OT
2002—Cowboys, 14-13 (D)
2003—Cowboys, 24-20 (D)
        **Panthers, 29-10 (C)
(RS Pts.—Cowboys 94, Panthers 89)
(PS Pts.—Panthers 55, Cowboys 27)
**NFC Divisional Playoff*
**NFC First-Round Playoff*

CAROLINA vs. DENVER
RS: Broncos lead series, 1-0
1997—Broncos, 34-0 (D)
(RS Pts.—Broncos 34, Panthers 0)

CAROLINA vs. DETROIT
RS: Panthers lead series, 2-1
1999—Lions, 24-9 (C)
2002—Panthers, 31-7 (C)
2003—Panthers, 20-14 (C)
(RS Pts.—Panthers 60, Lions 45)

CAROLINA vs. GREEN BAY
RS: Packers lead series, 4-2
PS: Packers lead series, 1-0
1996—*Packers, 30-13 (GB)
1997—Packers, 31-10 (C)
1998—Packers, 37-30 (C)
1999—Panthers, 33-31 (GB)
2000—Panthers, 31-14 (C)
2001—Packers, 28-7 (C)
2002—Packers, 17-14 (GB)
(RS Pts.—Packers 158, Panthers 125)
(PS Pts.—Packers 30, Panthers 13)
**NFC Championship*

CAROLINA vs. HOUSTON
RS: Texans lead series, 1-0
2003—Texans, 14-10 (H)
(RS Pts.—Texans 14, Panthers 10)

CAROLINA vs. INDIANAPOLIS
RS: Panthers lead series, 3-0
1995—Panthers, 13-10 (C)
1998—Panthers, 27-19 (I)
2003—Panthers, 23-20 (I) OT
(RS Pts.—Panthers 63, Colts 49)

CAROLINA vs. JACKSONVILLE
RS: Jaguars lead series, 2-1
1996—Jaguars, 24-14 (J)
1999—Jaguars, 22-20 (C)
2003—Panthers, 24-23 (C)
(RS Pts.—Jaguars 69, Panthers 58)

CAROLINA vs. KANSAS CITY
RS: Chiefs lead series, 2-0
1997—Chiefs, 35-14 (C)
2000—Chiefs, 15-14 (KC)
(RS Pts.—Chiefs 50, Panthers 28)

CAROLINA vs. MIAMI
RS: Dolphins lead series, 2-0
1998—Dolphins, 13-9 (C)
2001—Dolphins, 23-6 (M)
(RS Pts.—Dolphins 36, Panthers 15)

CAROLINA vs. MINNESOTA
RS: Vikings lead series, 3-2
1996—Vikings, 14-12 (M)
1997—Vikings, 21-14 (M)
2000—Vikings, 31-17 (M)
2001—Panthers, 24-13 (M)
2002—Panthers, 21-14 (M)
(RS Pts.—Vikings 93, Panthers 88)

CAROLINA vs. NEW ENGLAND
RS: Series tied, 1-1
PS: Patriots lead series, 1-0
1995—Panthers, 20-17 (NE) OT
2001—Patriots, 38-6 (C)
2003—*Patriots, 32-29 (Houston)
(RS Pts.—Patriots 55, Panthers 26)
(PS Pts.—Patriots 32, Panthers 29)
**Super Bowl XXXVIII*

CAROLINA vs. NEW ORLEANS
RS: Series tied, 9-9
1995—Panthers, 20-3 (C)
        Saints, 34-26 (NO)
1996—Panthers, 22-20 (NO)
        Panthers, 19-7 (C)
1997—Panthers, 13-0 (NO)
        Saints, 16-13 (C)
1998—Saints, 19-14 (NO)
        Panthers, 31-17 (C)
1999—Saints, 19-10 (NO)
        Panthers, 45-13 (C)
2000—Saints, 24-6 (NO)
        Saints, 20-10 (C)
2001—Saints, 27-25 (C)
        Saints, 27-23 (NO)
2002—Saints, 34-24 (C)
        Panthers, 10-6 (NO)
2003—Panthers, 19-13 (C)
        Panthers, 23-20 (NO) OT
(RS Pts.—Panthers 353, Saints 319)

CAROLINA vs. N.Y. GIANTS
RS: Panthers lead series, 2-0
1996—Panthers, 27-17 (C)
2003—Panthers, 37-24 (NY)
(RS Pts.—Panthers 64, Giants 41)

CAROLINA vs. N.Y. JETS
RS: Jets lead series, 2-1
1995—Panthers, 26-15 (C)
1998—Jets, 48-21 (NY)
2001—Jets, 13-12 (C)
(RS Pts.—Jets 76, Panthers 59)

CAROLINA vs. OAKLAND
RS: Series tied, 1-1
1997—Panthers, 38-14 (C)
2000—Raiders, 52-9 (O)
(RS Pts.— Raiders 66, Panthers 47)

CAROLINA vs. PHILADELPHIA
RS: Eagles lead series, 2-1
PS: Panthers lead series, 1-0
1996—Eagles, 20-9 (P)
1999—Panthers, 33-7 (C)
2003—Eagles, 25-16 (C)
        *Panthers, 14-3 (P)
(RS Pts.—Panthers 58, Eagles 52)
(PS Pts.—Panthers 14, Eagles 3)
**NFC Championship*

CAROLINA vs. PITTSBURGH
RS: Steelers lead series, 2-1
1996—Panthers, 18-14 (C)
1999—Steelers, 30-20 (P)
2002—Steelers, 30-14 (P)
(RS Pts.—Steelers 74, Panthers 52)

CAROLINA vs. ST. LOUIS
RS: Series tied, 7-7
PS: Panthers lead series, 1-0
1995—Rams, 31-10 (C)
        Rams, 28-17 (StL)
1996—Panthers, 45-13 (C)
        Panthers, 20-10 (StL)
1997—Panthers, 16-10 (StL)
        Rams, 30-18 (C)
1998—Panthers, 24-20 (StL)
        Panthers, 20-13 (C)
1999—Rams, 35-10 (StL)
        Rams, 34-21 (C)
2000—Panthers, 27-24 (StL)
        Panthers, 16-3 (C)
2001—Rams, 48-14 (StL)
        Rams, 38-32 (C)
2003—*Panthers, 29-23 (StL) 2OT
(RS Pts.—Rams 337, Panthers 290)
(PS Pts.—Panthers 29, Rams 23)
**NFC Divisional Playoff*

CAROLINA vs. SAN DIEGO
RS: Panthers lead series, 2-0
1997—Panthers, 26-7 (SD)
2000—Panthers, 30-22 (C)
(RS Pts.—Panthers 56, Chargers 29)

CAROLINA vs. SAN FRANCISCO
RS: Series tied, 7-7
1995—Panthers, 13-7 (SF)

49ers, 31-10 (C)
1996—Panthers, 23-7 (C)
Panthers, 30-24 (SF)
1997—49ers, 34-21 (C)
49ers, 27-19 (SF)
1998—49ers, 25-23 (SF)
49ers, 31-28 (C) OT
1999—Panthers, 31-29 (SF)
Panthers, 41-24 (C)
2000—Panthers, 38-22 (SF)
Panthers, 34-16 (C)
2001—49ers, 24-14 (SF)
49ers, 25-22 (C) OT
(RS Pts.—Panthers 347, 49ers 326)

CAROLINA vs. SEATTLE
RS: Panthers lead series, 1-0
2000—Panthers, 26-3 (C)
(RS Pts.—Panthers 26, Seahawks 3)

CAROLINA vs. TAMPA BAY
RS: Buccaneers lead series, 4-3
1995—Buccaneers, 20-13 (C)
1996—Panthers, 24-0 (C)
1998—Buccaneers, 16-13 (TB)
2002—Buccaneers, 12-9 (C)
Buccaneers, 23-10 (TB)
2003—Panthers, 12-9 (TB) OT
Panthers, 27-24 (C)
(RS Pts.—Panthers 108, Buccaneers 104)

CAROLINA vs. *TENNESSEE
RS: Series tied, 1-1
1996—Panthers, 31-6 (H)
2003—Titans, 37-17 (C)
(RS Pts.—Panthers 48, Titans 43)
**Franchise in Houston prior to 1997; known as Oilers prior to 1999*

CAROLINA vs. WASHINGTON
RS: Redskins lead series, 6-1
1995—Redskins, 20-17 (W)
1997—Redskins, 24-10 (C)
1998—Redskins, 28-25 (C)
1999—Redskins, 38-36 (W)
2000—Redskins, 20-17 (W)
2001—Redskins, 17-14 (W) OT
2003—Panthers, 20-17 (C)
(RS Pts.—Redskins 164, Panthers 139)

CHICAGO vs. ARIZONA
RS: Bears lead series, 54-26-6;
See Arizona vs. Chicago

CHICAGO vs. ATLANTA
RS: Bears lead series, 11-10;
See Atlanta vs. Chicago

CHICAGO vs. BALTIMORE
RS: Series tied, 1-1;
See Baltimore vs. Chicago

CHICAGO vs. BUFFALO
RS: Bears lead series, 5-4;
See Buffalo vs. Chicago

CHICAGO vs. CAROLINA
RS: Series tied, 1-1;
See Carolina vs. Chicago

CHICAGO vs. CINCINNATI
RS: Bengals lead series, 4-3
1972—Bengals, 13-3 (Chi)
1980—Bengals, 17-14 (Chi) OT
1986—Bears, 44-7 (Cin)
1989—Bears, 17-14 (Chi)
1992—Bengals, 31-28 (Chi) OT
1995—Bengals, 16-10 (Cin)
2001—Bears, 24-0 (Cin)
(RS Pts.—Bears 140, Bengals 98)

CHICAGO vs. CLEVELAND
RS: Browns lead series, 8-4
1951—Browns, 42-21 (Cle)
1954—Browns, 39-10 (Chi)
1960—Browns, 42-0 (Cle)
1961—Bears, 17-14 (Chi)
1967—Browns, 24-0 (Cle)
1969—Browns, 28-24 (Chi)
1972—Bears, 17-0 (Cle)
1980—Browns, 27-21 (Cle)
1986—Bears, 41-31 (Chi)
1989—Browns, 27-7 (Cle)
1992—Browns, 27-14 (Cle)
2001—Bears, 27-21 (Chi) OT
(RS Pts.—Browns 322, Bears 199)

CHICAGO vs. DALLAS
RS: Cowboys lead series, 9-8
PS: Cowboys lead series, 2-0
1960—Bears, 17-7 (C)
1962—Bears, 34-33 (D)
1964—Cowboys, 24-10 (C)
1968—Cowboys, 34-3 (C)
1971—Bears, 23-19 (C)
1973—Cowboys, 20-17 (C)
1976—Cowboys, 31-21 (D)
1977—*Cowboys, 37-7 (D)
1979—Cowboys, 24-20 (D)
1981—Cowboys, 10-9 (D)
1984—Cowboys, 23-14 (C)
1985—Bears, 44-0 (D)
1986—Bears, 24-10 (D)
1988—Bears, 17-7 (C)
1991—**Cowboys, 17-13 (C)
1992—Cowboys, 27-14 (D)
1996—Bears, 22-6 (C)
1997—Cowboys, 27-3 (D)
1998—Bears, 13-12 (C)
(RS Pts.—Cowboys 314, Bears 305)
(PS Pts.—Cowboys 54, Bears 20)
**NFC Divisional Playoff*
***NFC First-Round Playoff*

CHICAGO vs. DENVER
RS: Series tied, 6-6
1971—Broncos, 6-3 (D)
1973—Bears, 33-14 (D)
1976—Broncos, 28-14 (C)
1978—Broncos, 16-7 (D)
1981—Bears, 35-24 (C)
1983—Bears, 31-14 (C)
1984—Bears, 27-0 (C)
1987—Broncos, 31-29 (D)
1990—Bears, 16-13 (D) OT
1993—Broncos, 13-3 (C)
1996—Broncos, 17-12 (D)
2003—Bears, 19-10 (D)
(RS Pts.—Bears 229, Broncos 186)

CHICAGO vs. *DETROIT
RS: Bears lead series, 83-60-5
1930—Spartans, 7-6 (P)
Bears, 14-6 (C)
1931—Bears, 9-6 (C)
Spartans, 3-0 (P)
1932—Tie, 13-13 (C)
Tie, 7-7 (P)
Bears, 9-0 (C)
1933—Bears, 17-14 (C)
Bears, 17-7 (P)
1934—Bears, 19-16 (D)
Bears, 10-7 (C)
1935—Tie, 20-20 (C)
Lions, 14-2 (D)
1936—Bears, 12-10 (C)
Lions, 13-7 (D)
1937—Bears, 28-20 (C)
Bears, 13-0 (D)
1938—Lions, 13-7 (C)
Lions, 14-7 (D)
1939—Lions, 10-0 (C)
Bears, 23-13 (D)
1940—Bears, 7-0 (C)
Lions, 17-14 (D)
1941—Bears, 49-0 (C)
Bears, 24-7 (D)
1942—Bears, 16-0 (C)
Bears, 42-0 (D)
1943—Bears, 27-21 (D)
Bears, 35-14 (C)
1944—Tie, 21-21 (C)
Lions, 41-21 (D)
1945—Lions, 16-10 (D)
Lions, 35-28 (C)
1946—Bears, 42-6 (C)
Bears, 45-24 (D)
1947—Bears, 33-24 (C)
Bears, 34-14 (D)
1948—Bears, 28-0 (C)
Bears, 42-14 (D)
1949—Bears, 27-24 (C)
Bears, 28-7 (D)
1950—Bears, 35-21 (D)
Bears, 6-3 (C)
1951—Bears, 28-23 (D)
Lions, 41-28 (C)
1952—Bears, 24-23 (C)
Lions, 45-21 (D)
1953—Lions, 20-16 (C)
Lions, 13-7 (D)
1954—Lions, 48-23 (D)
Bears, 28-24 (C)
1955—Bears, 24-14 (D)
Bears, 21-20 (C)
1956—Lions, 42-10 (D)
Bears, 38-21 (C)
1957—Bears, 27-7 (D)
Lions, 21-13 (C)
1958—Bears, 20-7 (D)
Bears, 21-16 (C)
1959—Bears, 24-14 (D)
Bears, 25-14 (C)
1960—Bears, 28-7 (C)
Lions, 36-0 (D)
1961—Bears, 31-17 (D)
Lions, 16-15 (C)
1962—Lions, 11-3 (D)
Bears, 3-0 (C)
1963—Bears, 37-21 (D)
Bears, 24-14 (C)
1964—Lions, 10-0 (C)
Bears, 27-24 (D)
1965—Bears, 38-10 (C)
Bears, 17-10 (D)
1966—Lions, 14-3 (D)
Tie, 10-10 (C)
1967—Bears, 14-3 (C)
Bears, 27-13 (D)
1968—Lions, 42-0 (D)
Lions, 28-10 (C)
1969—Lions, 13-7 (D)
Lions, 20-3 (C)

1970—Lions, 28-14 (D)
Lions, 16-10 (C)
1971—Bears, 28-23 (D)
Lions, 28-3 (C)
1972—Lions, 38-24 (C)
Lions, 14-0 (D)
1973—Lions, 30-7 (C)
Lions, 40-7 (D)
1974—Bears, 17-9 (C)
Lions, 34-17 (D)
1975—Lions, 27-7 (D)
Bears, 25-21 (C)
1976—Bears, 10-3 (C)
Lions, 14-10 (D)
1977—Bears, 30-20 (C)
Bears, 31-14 (D)
1978—Bears, 19-0 (D)
Lions, 21-17 (C)
1979—Bears, 35-7 (C)
Lions, 20-0 (D)
1980—Bears, 24-7 (C)
Bears, 23-17 (D) OT
1981—Lions, 48-17 (D)
Lions, 23-7 (C)
1982—Lions, 17-10 (D)
Bears, 20-17 (C)
1983—Lions, 31-17 (D)
Lions, 38-17 (C)
1984—Bears, 16-14 (C)
Bears, 30-13 (D)
1985—Bears, 24-3 (C)
Bears, 37-17 (D)
1986—Bears, 13-7 (C)
Bears, 16-13 (D)
1987—Bears, 30-10 (C)
1988—Bears, 24-7 (D)
Bears, 13-12 (C)
1989—Bears, 47-27 (D)
Lions, 27-17 (C)
1990—Bears, 23-17 (C) OT
Lions, 38-21 (D)
1991—Bears, 20-10 (C)
Lions, 16-6 (D)
1992—Bears, 27-24 (C)
Lions, 16-3 (D)
1993—Bears, 10-6 (D)
Lions, 20-14 (C)
1994—Lions, 21-16 (D)
Bears, 20-10 (C)
1995—Lions, 24-17 (C)
Lions, 27-7 (D)
1996—Lions, 35-16 (D)
Bears, 31-14 (C)
1997—Lions, 32-7 (C)
Lions, 55-20 (D)
1998—Bears, 31-27 (C)
Lions, 26-3 (D)
1999—Lions, 21-17 (D)
Bears, 28-10 (C)
2000—Lions, 21-14 (C)
Bears, 23-20 (D)
2001—Bears, 13-10 (C)
Bears, 24-0 (D)
2002—Lions, 23-20 (D) OT
Bears, 20-17 (C) OT
2003—Bears, 24-16 (C)
Lions, 12-10 (D)
(RS Pts.—Bears 2,747, Lions 2,577)
Franchise in Portsmouth prior to 1934 and known as the Spartans

***CHICAGO vs. GREEN BAY**
RS: Bears lead series, 83-77-6
PS: Bears lead series, 1-0
1921—Staleys, 20-0 (C)
1923—Bears, 3-0 (GB)
1924—Bears, 3-0 (C)
1925—Packers, 14-10 (GB)
Bears, 21-0 (C)
1926—Tie, 6-6 (GB)
Bears, 19-13 (C)
Tie, 3-3 (C)
1927—Bears, 7-6 (GB)
Bears, 14-6 (C)
1928—Tie, 12-12 (GB)
Packers, 16-6 (C)
Packers, 6-0 (C)
1929—Packers, 23-0 (GB)
Packers, 14-0 (C)
Packers, 25-0 (C)
1930—Packers, 7-0 (GB)
Packers, 13-12 (C)
Bears, 21-0 (C)
1931—Packers, 7-0 (GB)
Packers, 6-2 (C)
Bears, 7-6 (C)
1932—Tie, 0-0 (GB)
Packers, 2-0 (C)
Bears, 9-0 (C)
1933—Bears, 14-7 (GB)
Bears, 10-7 (C)
Bears, 7-6 (C)
1934—Bears, 24-10 (GB)
Bears, 27-14 (C)
1935—Packers, 7-0 (GB)
Packers, 17-14 (C)
1936—Bears, 30-3 (GB)
Packers, 21-10 (C)
1937—Bears, 14-2 (GB)
Packers, 24-14 (C)
1938—Bears, 2-0 (GB)
Packers, 24-17 (C)
1939—Packers, 21-16 (GB)
Bears, 30-27 (C)
1940—Bears, 41-10 (GB)
Bears, 14-7 (C)
1941—Bears, 25-17 (GB)
Packers, 16-14 (C)
**Bears, 33-14 (C)
1942—Bears, 44-28 (GB)
Bears, 38-7 (C)
1943—Tie, 21-21 (GB)
Bears, 21-7 (C)
1944—Packers, 42-28 (GB)
Bears, 21-0 (C)
1945—Packers, 31-21 (GB)
Bears, 28-24 (C)
1946—Bears, 30-7 (GB)
Bears, 10-7 (C)
1947—Packers, 29-20 (GB)
Bears, 20-17 (C)
1948—Bears, 45-7 (GB)
Bears, 7-6 (C)
1949—Bears, 17-0 (GB)
Bears, 24-3 (C)
1950—Packers, 31-21 (GB)
Bears, 28-14 (C)
1951—Bears, 31-20 (GB)
Bears, 24-13 (C)
1952—Bears, 24-14 (GB)
Packers, 41-28 (C)
1953—Bears, 17-13 (GB)
Tie, 21-21 (C)
1954—Bears, 10-3 (GB)
Bears, 28-23 (C)
1955—Packers, 24-3 (GB)
Bears, 52-31 (C)
1956—Bears, 37-21 (GB)
Bears, 38-14 (C)
1957—Packers, 21-17 (GB)
Bears, 21-14 (C)
1958—Bears, 34-20 (GB)
Bears, 24-10 (C)
1959—Packers, 9-6 (GB)
Bears, 28-17 (C)
1960—Bears, 17-14 (GB)
Packers, 41-13 (C)
1961—Packers, 24-0 (GB)
Packers, 31-28 (C)
1962—Packers, 49-0 (GB)
Packers, 38-7 (C)
1963—Bears, 10-3 (GB)
Bears, 26-7 (C)
1964—Packers, 23-12 (GB)
Packers, 17-3 (C)
1965—Packers, 23-14 (GB)
Bears, 31-10 (C)
1966—Packers, 17-0 (C)
Packers, 13-6 (GB)
1967—Packers, 13-10 (GB)
Packers, 17-13 (C)
1968—Bears, 13-10 (GB)
Packers, 28-27 (C)
1969—Packers, 17-0 (GB)
Packers, 21-3 (C)
1970—Packers, 20-19 (GB)
Bears, 35-17 (C)
1971—Packers, 17-14 (C)
Packers, 31-10 (GB)
1972—Packers, 20-17 (GB)
Packers, 23-17 (C)
1973—Bears, 31-17 (GB)
Packers, 21-0 (C)
1974—Bears, 10-9 (C)
Packers, 20-3 (Mil)
1975—Bears, 27-14 (C)
Packers, 28-7 (GB)
1976—Bears, 24-13 (C)
Bears, 16-10 (GB)
1977—Bears, 26-0 (GB)
Bears, 21-10 (C)
1978—Packers, 24-14 (GB)
Bears, 14-0 (C)
1979—Bears, 6-3 (C)
Bears, 15-14 (GB)
1980—Packers, 12-6 (GB) OT
Bears, 61-7 (C)
1981—Packers, 16-9 (C)
Packers, 21-17 (GB)
1983—Packers, 31-28 (GB)
Bears, 23-21 (C)
1984—Bears, 9-7 (GB)
Packers, 20-14 (C)
1985—Bears, 23-7 (C)
Bears, 16-10 (GB)
1986—Bears, 25-12 (GB)
Bears, 12-10 (C)
1987—Bears, 26-24 (GB)
Bears, 23-10 (C)
1988—Bears, 24-6 (GB)
Bears, 16-0 (C)

1989—Packers, 14-13 (GB)
Packers, 40-28 (C)
1990—Bears, 31-13 (GB)
Bears, 27-13 (C)
1991—Bears, 10-0 (GB)
Bears, 27-13 (C)
1992—Bears, 30-10 (GB)
Packers, 17-3 (C)
1993—Packers, 17-3 (GB)
Bears, 30-17 (C)
1994—Packers, 33-6 (C)
Packers, 40-3 (GB)
1995—Packers, 27-24 (C)
Packers, 35-28 (GB)
1996—Packers, 37-6 (C)
Packers, 28-17 (GB)
1997—Packers, 38-24 (GB)
Packers, 24-23 (C)
1998—Packers, 26-20 (GB)
Packers, 16-13 (C)
1999—Bears, 14-13 (GB)
Packers, 35-19 (C)
2000—Bears, 27-24 (GB)
Packers, 28-6 (C)
2001—Packers, 20-12 (C)
Packers, 17-7 (GB)
2002—Packers, 34-21 (C)
Packers, 30-20 (GB)
2003—Packers, 38-23 (C)
Packers, 34-21 (GB)
(RS Pts.—Bears 2,812, Packers 2,707)
(PS Pts.—Bears 33, Packers 14)
Bears known as Staleys prior to 1922
***Division Playoff*

CHICAGO vs. *INDIANAPOLIS
RS: Colts lead series, 21-17
1953—Colts, 13-9 (B)
Colts, 16-14 (C)
1954—Bears, 28-9 (C)
Bears, 28-13 (B)
1955—Colts, 23-17 (B)
Bears, 38-10 (C)
1956—Colts, 28-21 (B)
Bears, 58-27 (C)
1957—Colts, 21-10 (B)
Colts, 29-14 (C)
1958—Colts, 51-38 (B)
Colts, 17-0 (C)
1959—Bears, 26-21 (B)
Colts, 21-7 (C)
1960—Colts, 42-7 (B)
Colts, 24-20 (C)
1961—Bears, 24-10 (C)
Bears, 21-20 (B)
1962—Bears, 35-15 (C)
Bears, 57-0 (B)
1963—Bears, 10-3 (C)
Bears, 17-7 (B)
1964—Colts, 52-0 (B)
Colts, 40-24 (C)
1965—Colts, 26-21 (C)
Bears, 13-0 (B)
1966—Bears, 27-17 (C)
Colts, 21-16 (B)
1967—Colts, 24-3 (C)
1968—Colts, 28-7 (B)
1969—Colts, 24-21 (C)
1970—Colts, 21-20 (B)
1975—Colts, 35-7 (C)
1983—Colts, 22-19 (B) OT
1985—Bears, 17-10 (C)
1988—Bears, 17-13 (I)
1991—Bears, 31-17 (I)
2000—Bears, 27-24 (C)
(RS Pts.—Colts 794, Bears 769)
Franchise in Baltimore prior to 1984

CHICAGO vs. JACKSONVILLE
RS: Bears lead series, 2-1
1995—Bears, 30-27 (J)
1998—Jaguars, 24-23 (C)
2001—Bears, 33-13 (C)
(RS Pts.—Bears 86, Jaguars 64)

CHICAGO vs. KANSAS CITY
RS: Bears lead series, 5-4
1973—Chiefs, 19-7 (KC)
1977—Bears, 28-27 (C)
1981—Bears, 16-13 (KC) OT
1987—Bears, 31-28 (C)
1990—Chiefs, 21-10 (C)
1993—Bears, 19-17 (KC)
1996—Chiefs, 14-10 (KC)
1999—Bears, 20-17 (C)
2003—Chiefs, 31-3 (KC)
(RS Pts.—Chiefs 187, Bears 144)

CHICAGO vs. MIAMI
RS: Dolphins lead series, 6-3
1971—Dolphins, 34-3 (M)
1975—Dolphins, 46-13 (C)
1979—Dolphins, 31-16 (M)
1985—Dolphins, 38-24 (M)
1988—Bears, 34-7 (C)
1991—Dolphins, 16-13 (C) OT
1994—Bears, 17-14 (M)
1997—Bears, 36-33 (M) OT
2002—Dolphins, 27-9 (M)
(RS Pts.—Dolphins 246, Bears 165)

CHICAGO vs. MINNESOTA
RS: Vikings lead series, 46-37-2
PS: Bears lead series, 1-0
1961—Vikings, 37-13 (M)
Bears, 52-35 (C)
1962—Bears, 13-0 (M)
Bears, 31-30 (C)
1963—Bears, 28-7 (M)
Tie, 17-17 (C)
1964—Bears, 34-28 (M)
Vikings, 41-14 (C)
1965—Bears, 45-37 (M)
Vikings, 24-17 (C)
1966—Bears, 13-10 (M)
Bears, 41-28 (C)
1967—Bears, 17-7 (M)
Tie, 10-10 (C)
1968—Bears, 27-17 (M)
Bears, 26-24 (C)
1969—Vikings, 31-0 (C)
Vikings, 31-14 (M)
1970—Vikings, 24-0 (C)
Vikings, 16-13 (M)
1971—Bears, 20-17 (M)
Vikings, 27-10 (C)
1972—Bears, 13-10 (C)
Vikings, 23-10 (M)
1973—Vikings, 22-13 (C)
Vikings, 31-13 (M)
1974—Vikings, 11-7 (M)
Vikings, 17-0 (C)
1975—Vikings, 28-3 (M)
Vikings, 13-9 (C)
1976—Vikings, 20-19 (M)
Bears, 14-13 (C)
1977—Vikings, 22-16 (M) OT
Bears, 10-7 (C)
1978—Vikings, 24-20 (C)
Vikings, 17-14 (M)
1979—Bears, 26-7 (C)
Vikings, 30-27 (M)
1980—Vikings, 34-14 (C)
Vikings, 13-7 (M)
1981—Vikings, 24-21 (M)
Bears, 10-9 (C)
1982—Vikings, 35-7 (M)
1983—Vikings, 23-14 (C)
Bears, 19-13 (M)
1984—Bears, 16-7 (C)
Bears, 34-3 (M)
1985—Bears, 33-24 (M)
Bears, 27-9 (C)
1986—Bears, 23-0 (C)
Vikings, 23-7 (M)
1987—Bears, 27-7 (C)
Bears, 30-24 (M)
1988—Vikings, 31-7 (C)
Vikings, 28-27 (M)
1989—Bears, 38-7 (C)
Vikings, 27-16 (M)
1990—Bears, 19-16 (C)
Vikings, 41-13 (M)
1991—Bears, 10-6 (C)
Bears, 34-17 (M)
1992—Vikings, 21-20 (M)
Vikings, 38-10 (C)
1993—Vikings, 10-7 (M)
Vikings, 19-12 (C)
1994—Vikings, 42-14 (C)
Vikings, 33-27 (M) OT
*Bears, 35-18 (M)
1995—Bears, 31-14 (C)
Bears, 14-6 (M)
1996—Vikings, 20-14 (C)
Bears, 15-13 (M)
1997—Vikings, 27-24 (C)
Vikings, 29-22 (M)
1998—Vikings, 31-28 (C)
Vikings, 48-22 (M)
1999—Bears, 24-22 (M)
Vikings, 27-24 (C) OT
2000—Vikings, 30-27 (M)
Vikings, 28-16 (C)
2001—Bears, 17-10 (C)
Bears, 13-6 (M)
2002—Bears, 27-23 (C)
Vikings, 25-7 (M)
2003—Vikings, 24-13 (M)
Bears, 13-10 (C)
RS Pts.—Vikings 1,770, Bears 1,563)
(PS Pts.—Bears 35, Vikings 18)
**NFC First-Round Playoff*

CHICAGO vs. NEW ENGLAND
RS: Patriots lead series, 6-3
PS: Bears lead series, 1-0
1973—Patriots, 13-10 (C)
1979—Patriots, 27-7 (C)
1982—Bears, 26-13 (C)
1985—Bears, 20-7 (C)
*Bears, 46-10 (New Orleans)
1988—Patriots, 30-7 (NE)
1994—Patriots, 13-3 (C)
1997—Patriots, 31-3 (NE)
2000—Bears, 24-17 (C)

2002—Patriots, 33-30 (C)
(RS Pts.—Patriots 184, Bears 130)
(PS Pts.—Bears 46, Patriots 10)
*Super Bowl XX

CHICAGO vs. NEW ORLEANS
RS: Saints lead series, 11-10
PS: Bears lead series, 1-0
1968—Bears, 23-17 (NO)
1970—Bears, 24-3 (NO)
1971—Bears, 35-14 (C)
1973—Saints, 21-16 (NO)
1974—Bears, 24-10 (C)
1975—Bears, 42-17 (NO)
1977—Saints, 42-24 (C)
1980—Bears, 22-3 (C)
1982—Saints, 10-0 (C)
1983—Saints, 34-31 (NO) OT
1984—Bears, 20-7 (C)
1987—Saints, 19-17 (C)
1990—*Bears, 16-6 (C)
1991—Bears, 20-17 (NO)
1992—Saints, 28-6 (NO)
1994—Bears, 17-7 (C)
1996—Saints, 27-24 (NO)
1997—Saints, 20-17 (C)
1999—Bears, 14-10 (C)
2000—Saints, 31-10 (C)
2002—Saints, 29-23 (C)
2003—Saints, 20-13 (NO)
(RS Pts.—Bears 422, Saints 386)
(PS Pts.—Bears 16, Saints 6)
*NFC First-Round Playoff

CHICAGO vs. N.Y. GIANTS
RS: Bears lead series, 25-17-2
PS: Bears lead series, 5-3
1925—Bears, 19-7 (NY)
Giants, 9-0 (C)
1926—Bears, 7-0 (C)
1927—Giants, 13-7 (NY)
1928—Bears, 13-0 (C)
1929—Giants, 26-14 (C)
Giants, 34-0 (NY)
Giants, 14-9 (C)
1930—Giants, 12-0 (C)
Bears, 12-0 (NY)
1931—Bears, 6-0 (C)
Bears, 12-6 (NY)
Giants, 25-6 (C)
1932—Bears, 28-8 (NY)
Bears, 6-0 (C)
1933—Bears, 14-10 (C)
Giants, 3-0 (NY)
*Bears, 23-21 (C)
1934—Bears, 27-7 (C)
Bears, 10-9 (NY)
*Giants, 30-13 (NY)
1935—Bears, 20-3 (NY)
Giants, 3-0 (C)
1936—Bears, 25-7 (NY)
1937—Tie, 3-3 (NY)
1939—Giants, 16-13 (NY)
1940—Bears, 37-21 (NY)
1941—*Bears, 37-9 (C)
1942—Bears, 26-7 (NY)
1943—Bears, 56-7 (NY)
1946—Giants, 14-0 (NY)
*Bears, 24-14 (NY)
1948—Bears, 35-14 (C)
1949—Giants, 35-28 (NY)
1956—Tie, 17-17 (NY)
*Giants, 47-7 (NY)
1962—Giants, 26-24 (C)
1963—*Bears, 14-10 (C)
1965—Bears, 35-14 (NY)
1967—Bears, 34-7 (C)
1969—Giants, 28-24 (NY)
1970—Bears, 24-16 (NY)
1974—Bears, 16-13 (C)
1977—Bears, 12-9 (NY) OT
1985—**Bears, 21-0 (C)
1987—Bears, 34-19 (C)
1990—**Giants, 31-3 (NY)
1991—Bears, 20-17 (C)
1992—Giants, 27-14 (C)
1993—Giants, 26-20 (C)
1995—Bears, 27-24 (NY)
2000—Giants, 14-7 (C)
(RS Pts.—Bears 741, Giants 570)
(PS Pts.—Giants 162, Bears 142)
*NFL Championship
**NFC Divisional Playoff

CHICAGO vs. N.Y. JETS
RS: Bears lead series, 5-3
1974—Jets, 23-21 (C)
1979—Bears, 23-13 (C)
1985—Bears, 19-6 (NY)
1991—Bears, 19-13 (C) OT
1994—Bears, 19-7 (NY)
1997—Jets, 23-15 (C)
2000—Jets, 17-10 (NY)
2002—Bears, 20-13 (C)
(RS Pts.—Bears 146, Jets 115)

CHICAGO vs. *OAKLAND
RS: Raiders lead series, 6-5
1972—Raiders, 28-21 (O)
1976—Raiders, 28-27 (C)
1978—Raiders, 25-19 (C) OT
1981—Bears, 23-6 (O)
1984—Bears, 17-6 (C)
1987—Bears, 6-3 (LA)
1990—Raiders, 24-10 (LA)
1993—Raiders, 16-14 (C)
1996—Bears, 19-17 (C)
1999—Raiders, 24-17 (O)
2003—Bears, 24-21 (C)
(RS Pts.—Raiders 198, Bears 197)
*Franchise in Los Angeles from 1982-1994

CHICAGO vs. PHILADELPHIA
RS: Bears lead series, 24-7-1
PS: Eagles lead series, 2-1
1933—Tie, 3-3 (P)
1935—Bears, 39-0 (P)
1936—Bears, 17-0 (P)
Bears, 28-7 (P)
1938—Bears, 28-6 (P)
1939—Bears, 27-14 (C)
1941—Bears, 49-14 (P)
1942—Bears, 45-14 (C)
1944—Bears, 28-7 (P)
1946—Bears, 21-14 (C)
1947—Bears, 40-7 (C)
1948—Eagles, 12-7 (P)
1949—Bears, 38-21 (C)
1955—Bears, 17-10 (C)
1961—Eagles, 16-14 (P)
1963—Bears, 16-7 (C)
1968—Bears, 29-16 (P)
1970—Bears, 20-16 (C)
1972—Bears, 21-12 (P)
1975—Bears, 15-13 (C)
1979—*Eagles, 27-17 (P)
1980—Eagles, 17-14 (P)
1983—Bears, 7-6 (P)
Bears, 17-14 (C)
1986—Bears, 13-10 (C) OT
1987—Bears, 35-3 (P)
1988—**Bears, 20-12 (C)
1989—Bears, 27-13 (C)
1993—Bears, 17-6 (P)
1994—Eagles, 30-22 (P)
1995—Bears, 20-14 (C)
1999—Eagles, 20-16 (C)
2000—Eagles, 13-9 (P)
2001—**Eagles, 33-19 (C)
2002—Eagles, 19-13 (C)
(RS Pts.—Bears 712, Eagles 374)
(PS Pts.—Eagles 72, Bears 56)
*NFC First-Round Playoff
**NFC Divisional Playoff

CHICAGO vs. *PITTSBURGH
RS: Bears lead series, 16-6-1
1934—Bears, 28-0 (P)
1935—Bears, 23-7 (P)
1936—Bears, 27-9 (P)
Bears, 26-6 (C)
1937—Bears, 7-0 (P)
1939—Bears, 32-0 (P)
1941—Bears, 34-7 (C)
1945—Bears, 28-7 (C)
1947—Bears, 49-7 (C)
1949—Bears, 30-21 (C)
1958—Steelers, 24-10 (P)
1959—Bears, 27-21 (C)
1963—Tie, 17-17 (P)
1967—Steelers, 41-13 (P)
1969—Bears, 38-7 (C)
1971—Bears, 17-15 (C)
1975—Steelers, 34-3 (P)
1980—Steelers, 38-3 (P)
1986—Bears, 13-10 (C) OT
1989—Bears, 20-0 (P)
1992—Bears, 30-6 (C)
1995—Steelers, 37-34 (C) OT
1998—Steelers, 17-12 (P)
(RS Pts.—Bears 521, Steelers 331)
*Steelers known as Pirates prior to 1941

CHICAGO vs. *ST. LOUIS
RS: Bears lead series, 47-34-3
PS: Series tied, 1-1
1937—Bears, 20-2 (Clev)
Bears, 15-7 (C)
1938—Rams, 14-7 (C)
Rams, 23-21 (Clev)
1939—Bears, 30-21 (Clev)
Bears, 35-21 (C)
1940—Bears, 21-14 (Clev)
Bears, 47-25 (C)
1941—Bears, 48-21 (Clev)
Bears, 31-13 (C)
1942—Bears, 21-7 (Clev)
Bears, 47-0 (C)
1944—Rams, 19-7 (Clev)
Bears, 28-21 (C)
1945—Rams, 17-0 (Clev)
Rams, 41-21 (C)
1946—Tie, 28-28 (C)
Bears, 27-21 (LA)
1947—Bears, 41-21 (LA)
Rams, 17-14 (C)
1948—Bears, 42-21 (C)

Bears, 21-6 (LA)
1949—Rams, 31-16 (C)
Rams, 27-24 (LA)
1950—Bears, 24-20 (LA)
Bears, 24-14 (C)
**Rams, 24-14 (LA)
1951—Rams, 42-17 (C)
1952—Rams, 31-7 (LA)
Rams, 40-24 (C)
1953—Rams, 38-24 (LA)
Bears, 24-21 (C)
1954—Rams, 42-38 (LA)
Bears, 24-13 (C)
1955—Bears, 31-20 (LA)
Bears, 24-3 (C)
1956—Bears, 35-24 (LA)
Bears, 30-21 (C)
1957—Bears, 34-26 (C)
Bears, 16-10 (LA)
1958—Bears, 31-10 (C)
Rams, 41-35 (LA)
1959—Rams, 28-21 (C)
Bears, 26-21 (LA)
1960—Bears, 34-27 (C)
Tie, 24-24 (LA)
1961—Bears, 21-17 (LA)
Bears, 28-24 (C)
1962—Bears, 27-23 (LA)
Bears, 30-14 (C)
1963—Bears, 52-14 (LA)
Bears, 6-0 (C)
1964—Bears, 38-17 (C)
Bears, 34-24 (LA)
1965—Rams, 30-28 (LA)
Bears, 31-6 (C)
1966—Rams, 31-17 (LA)
Bears, 17-10 (C)
1967—Rams, 28-17 (C)
1968—Bears, 17-16 (LA)
1969—Rams, 9-7 (C)
1971—Rams, 17-3 (LA)
1972—Tie, 13-13 (C)
1973—Rams, 26-0 (C)
1975—Rams, 38-10 (LA)
1976—Rams, 20-12 (LA)
1977—Bears, 24-23 (C)
1979—Bears, 27-23 (C)
1981—Rams, 24-7 (C)
1982—Bears, 34-26 (LA)
1983—Rams, 21-14 (LA)
1984—Rams, 29-13 (LA)
1985—***Bears, 24-0 (C)
1986—Rams, 20-17 (C)
1988—Rams, 23-3 (LA)
1989—Bears, 20-10 (C)
1990—Bears, 38-9 (C)
1993—Rams, 20-6 (LA)
1994—Bears, 27-13 (C)
1995—Rams, 34-28 (StL)
1996—Bears, 35-9 (C)
1997—Bears, 13-10 (StL)
1998—Rams, 20-12 (C)
1999—Rams, 34-12 (StL)
2002—Rams, 21-16 (StL)
2003—Rams, 23-21 (C)
(RS Pts.—Bears 1,934, Rams 1,723)
(PS Pts.—Bears 38, Rams 24)
Franchise in Los Angeles prior to 1995 and in Cleveland prior to 1946
***Conference Playoff*
****NFC Championship*

CHICAGO vs. SAN DIEGO
RS: Bears lead series, 5-4
1970—Chargers, 20-7 (C)
1974—Chargers, 28-21 (SD)
1978—Chargers, 40-7 (SD)
1981—Bears, 20-17 (C) OT
1984—Chargers, 20-7 (SD)
1993—Bears, 16-13 (SD)
1996—Bears, 27-14 (C)
1999—Bears, 23-20 (SD) OT
2003—Bears, 20-7 (C)
(RS Pts.—Chargers 179, Bears 148)

CHICAGO vs. SAN FRANCISCO
RS: 49ers lead series, 27-26-1
PS: 49ers lead series, 3-0
1950—Bears, 32-20 (SF)
Bears, 17-0 (C)
1951—Bears, 13-7 (C)
1952—49ers, 40-16 (C)
Bears, 20-17 (SF)
1953—49ers, 35-28 (C)
49ers, 24-14 (SF)
1954—49ers, 31-24 (C)
Bears, 31-27 (SF)
1955—49ers, 20-19 (C)
Bears, 34-23 (SF)
1956—Bears, 31-7 (C)
Bears, 38-21 (SF)
1957—49ers, 21-17 (C)
49ers, 21-17 (SF)
1958—Bears, 28-6 (C)
Bears, 27-14 (SF)
1959—49ers, 20-17 (SF)
Bears, 14-3 (C)
1960—Bears, 27-10 (C)
49ers, 25-7 (SF)
1961—Bears, 31-0 (C)
49ers, 41-31 (SF)
1962—Bears, 30-14 (SF)
49ers, 34-27 (C)
1963—49ers, 20-14 (SF)
Bears, 27-7 (C)
1964—49ers, 31-21 (SF)
Bears, 23-21 (C)
1965—49ers, 52-24 (SF)
Bears, 61-20 (C)
1966—Tie, 30-30 (C)
49ers, 41-14 (SF)
1967—Bears, 28-14 (SF)
1968—Bears, 27-19 (C)
1969—49ers, 42-21 (SF)
1970—49ers, 37-16 (C)
1971—49ers, 13-0 (SF)
1972—49ers, 34-21 (C)
1974—49ers, 34-0 (C)
1975—49ers, 31-3 (SF)
1976—Bears, 19-12 (SF)
1978—Bears, 16-13 (SF)
1979—Bears, 28-27 (SF)
1981—49ers, 28-17 (SF)
1983—Bears, 13-3 (C)
1984—*49ers, 23-0 (SF)
1985—Bears, 26-10 (SF)
1987—49ers, 41-0 (SF)
1988—Bears, 10-9 (C)
*49ers, 28-3 (C)
1989—49ers, 26-0 (SF)
1991—49ers, 52-14 (SF)
1994—**49ers, 44-15 (SF)
2000—49ers, 17-0 (SF)
2001—Bears, 37-31 (C) OT
2003—49ers, 49-7 (SF)
(RS Pts.—49ers 1,245, Bears 1,107)
(PS Pts.—49ers 95, Bears 18)
**NFC Championship*
***NFC Divisional Playoff*

CHICAGO vs. SEATTLE
RS: Seahawks lead series, 6-2
1976—Bears, 34-7 (S)
1978—Seahawks, 31-29 (C)
1982—Seahawks, 20-14 (S)
1984—Seahawks, 38-9 (S)
1987—Seahawks, 34-21 (C)
1990—Bears, 17-0 (C)
1999—Seahawks, 14-13 (C)
2003—Seahawks, 24-17 (S)
(RS Pts.—Seahawks 168, Bears 154)

CHICAGO vs. TAMPA BAY
RS: Bears lead series, 33-16
1977—Bears, 10-0 (TB)
1978—Buccaneers, 33-19 (TB)
Bears, 14-3 (C)
1979—Buccaneers, 17-13 (C)
Bears, 14-0 (TB)
1980—Bears, 23-0 (C)
Bears, 14-13 (TB)
1981—Bears, 28-17 (C)
Buccaneers, 20-10 (TB)
1982—Buccaneers, 26-23 (TB) OT
1983—Bears, 17-10 (C)
Bears, 27-0 (TB)
1984—Bears, 34-14 (C)
Bears, 44-9 (TB)
1985—Bears, 38-28 (C)
Bears, 27-19 (TB)
1986—Bears, 23-3 (TB)
Bears, 48-14 (C)
1987—Bears, 20-3 (C)
Bears, 27-26 (TB)
1988—Bears, 28-10 (C)
Bears, 27-15 (TB)
1989—Buccaneers, 42-35 (TB)
Buccaneers, 32-31 (C)
1990—Bears, 26-6 (TB)
Bears, 27-14 (C)
1991—Bears, 21-20 (TB)
Bears, 27-0 (C)
1992—Bears, 31-14 (C)
Buccaneers, 20-17 (TB)
1993—Bears, 47-17 (C)
Buccaneers, 13-10 (TB)
1994—Bears, 21-9 (C)
Bears, 20-6 (TB)
1995—Bears, 25-6 (TB)
Bears, 31-10 (C)
1996—Bears, 13-10 (C)
Buccaneers, 34-19 (TB)
1997—Bears, 13-7 (C)
Buccaneers, 31-15 (TB)
1998—Buccaneers, 27-15 (TB)
Buccaneers, 31-17 (C)
1999—Buccaneers, 6-3 (TB)
Buccaneers, 20-6 (C)
2000—Buccaneers, 41-0 (TB)
Bears, 13-10 (C)
2001—Bears, 27-24 (TB)
Bears, 27-3 (C)
2002—Buccaneers, 15-0 (C)
(RS Pts.—Bears 1,065, Buccaneers 748)

CHICAGO vs. *TENNESSEE
RS: Series tied, 4-4
1973—Bears, 35-14 (C)
1977—Oilers, 47-0 (H)
1980—Oilers, 10-6 (C)
1986—Bears, 20-7 (H)
1989—Oilers, 33-28 (C)
1992—Oilers, 24-7 (H)
1995—Bears, 35-32 (C)
1998—Bears, 23-20 (T)
(RS Pts.—Titans 187, Bears 154)
Franchise in Houston prior to 1997; known as Oilers prior to 1999

CHICAGO vs. *WASHINGTON
RS: Bears lead series, 20-15-1
PS: Redskins lead series, 4-3
1932—Tie, 7-7 (B)
1933—Bears, 7-0 (C)
Redskins, 10-0 (B)
1934—Bears, 21-0 (B)
1935—Bears, 30-14 (B)
1936—Bears, 26-0 (B)
1937—**Redskins, 28-21 (C)
1938—Bears, 31-7 (C)
1940—Redskins, 7-3 (W)
**Bears, 73-0 (W)
1941—Bears, 35-21 (C)
1942—**Redskins, 14-6 (W)
1943—Redskins, 21-7 (W)
**Bears, 41-21 (C)
1945—Redskins, 28-21 (W)
1946—Bears, 24-20 (C)
1947—Bears, 56-20 (W)
1948—Bears, 48-13 (C)
1949—Bears, 31-21 (W)
1951—Bears, 27-0 (W)
1953—Bears, 27-24 (W)
1957—Redskins, 14-3 (C)
1964—Redskins, 27-20 (W)
1968—Redskins, 38-28 (C)
1971—Bears, 16-15 (C)
1974—Redskins, 42-0 (W)
1976—Bears, 33-7 (C)
1978—Bears, 14-10 (W)
1980—Bears, 35-21 (C)
1981—Redskins, 24-7 (C)
1984—***Bears, 23-19 (W)
1985—Bears, 45-10 (C)
1986—***Redskins, 27-13 (C)
1987—***Redskins, 21-17 (C)
1988—Bears, 34-14 (W)
1989—Redskins, 38-14 (W)
1990—Redskins, 10-9 (W)
1991—Redskins, 20-7 (C)
1996—Redskins, 10-3 (W)
1997—Redskins, 31-8 (C)
1999—Redskins, 48-22 (W)
2001—Bears, 20-15 (W)
2003—Bears, 27-24 (C)
(RS Pts.—Bears 746, Redskins 631)
(PS Pts.—Bears 194, Redskins 130)
Franchise in Boston prior to 1937 and known as Braves prior to 1933
***NFL Championship*
****NFC Divisional Playoff*

CINCINNATI vs. ARIZONA
RS: Bengals lead series, 5-3;
See Arizona vs. Cincinnati

CINCINNATI vs. ATLANTA
RS: Bengals lead series, 7-3;
See Atlanta vs. Cincinnati

CINCINNATI vs. BALTIMORE
RS: Ravens lead series, 11-5;
See Baltimore vs. Cincinnati

CINCINNATI vs. BUFFALO
RS: Bills lead series, 11-9
PS: Bengals lead series, 2-0;
See Buffalo vs. Cincinnati

CINCINNATI vs. CAROLINA
RS: Panthers lead series, 2-0;
See Carolina vs. Cincinnati

CINCINNATI vs. CHICAGO
RS: Bengals lead series, 4-3;
See Chicago vs. Cincinnati

CINCINNATI vs. CLEVELAND
RS: Browns lead series, 32-29
1970—Browns, 30-27 (Cle)
Bengals, 14-10 (Cin)
1971—Browns, 27-24 (Cin)
Browns, 31-27 (Cle)
1972—Browns, 27-6 (Cle)
Browns, 27-24 (Cin)
1973—Browns, 17-10 (Cle)
Bengals, 34-17 (Cin)
1974—Bengals, 33-7 (Cin)
Bengals, 34-24 (Cle)
1975—Bengals, 24-17 (Cin)
Browns, 35-23 (Cle)
1976—Bengals, 45-24 (Cle)
Bengals, 21-6 (Cin)
1977—Browns, 13-3 (Cin)
Bengals, 10-7 (Cle)
1978—Browns, 13-10 (Cle) OT
Bengals, 48-16 (Cin)
1979—Browns, 28-27 (Cle)
Bengals, 16-12 (Cin)
1980—Browns, 31-7 (Cle)
Browns, 27-24 (Cin)
1981—Browns, 20-17 (Cin)
Bengals, 41-21 (Cle)
1982—Bengals, 23-10 (Cin)
1983—Browns, 17-7 (Cle)
Bengals, 28-21 (Cin)
1984—Bengals, 12-9 (Cin)
Bengals, 20-17 (Cle) OT
1985—Bengals, 27-10 (Cin)
Browns, 24-6 (Cle)
1986—Bengals, 30-13 (Cle)
Browns, 34-3 (Cin)
1987—Browns, 34-0 (Cin)
Browns, 38-24 (Cle)
1988—Bengals, 24-17 (Cin)
Browns, 23-16 (Cle)
1989—Bengals, 21-14 (Cin)
Bengals, 21-0 (Cle)
1990—Bengals, 34-13 (Cle)
Bengals, 21-14 (Cin)
1991—Browns, 14-13 (Cle)
Bengals, 23-21 (Cin)
1992—Bengals, 30-10 (Cin)
Browns, 37-21 (Cle)
1993—Browns, 27-14 (Cle)
Browns, 28-17 (Cin)
1994—Browns, 28-20 (Cin)
Browns, 37-13 (Cle)
1995—Browns, 29-26 (Cin) OT
Browns, 26-10 (Cle)
1999—Bengals, 18-17 (Cle)
Bengals, 44-28 (Cin)
2000—Browns, 24-7 (Cin)
Bengals, 12-3 (Cle)
2001—Bengals, 24-14 (Cin)
Browns, 18-0 (Cle)
2002—Browns, 20-7 (Cle)
Browns, 27-20 (Cin)
2003—Bengals, 21-14 (Cle)
Browns, 22-14 (Cin)
(RS Pts.—Browns 1,239, Bengals 1,220)

CINCINNATI vs. DALLAS
RS: Cowboys lead series, 5-3
1973—Cowboys, 38-10 (D)
1979—Cowboys, 38-13 (D)
1985—Bengals, 50-24 (C)
1988—Bengals, 38-24 (D)
1991—Cowboys, 35-23 (D)
1994—Cowboys, 23-20 (C)
1997—Bengals, 31-24 (C)
2000—Cowboys, 23-6 (D)
(RS Pts.—Cowboys 229, Bengals 191)

CINCINNATI vs. DENVER
RS: Broncos lead series, 15-7
1968—Bengals, 24-10 (C)
Broncos, 10-7 (D)
1969—Broncos, 30-23 (C)
Broncos, 27-16 (D)
1971—Bengals, 24-10 (D)
1972—Bengals, 21-10 (C)
1973—Broncos, 28-10 (D)
1975—Bengals, 17-16 (D)
1976—Bengals, 17-7 (C)
1977—Broncos, 24-13 (C)
1979—Broncos, 10-0 (D)
1981—Bengals, 38-21 (C)
1983—Broncos, 24-17 (D)
1984—Broncos, 20-17 (D)
1986—Broncos, 34-28 (D)
1991—Broncos, 45-14 (D)
1994—Broncos, 15-13 (D)
1996—Broncos, 14-10 (C)
1997—Broncos, 38-20 (D)
1998—Broncos, 33-26 (C)
2000—Bengals, 31-21 (C)
2003—Broncos, 30-10 (C)
(RS Pts.—Broncos 477, Bengals 396)

CINCINNATI vs. DETROIT
RS: Bengals lead series, 5-3
1970—Lions, 38-3 (D)
1974—Lions, 23-19 (C)
1983—Bengals, 17-9 (C)
1986—Bengals, 24-17 (D)
1989—Bengals, 42-7 (C)
1992—Lions, 19-13 (C)
1998—Bengals, 34-28 (D) OT
2001—Bengals, 31-27 (D)
(RS Pts.—Bengals 183, Lions 168)

CINCINNATI vs. GREEN BAY
RS: Packers lead series, 5-4
1971—Packers, 20-17 (GB)
1976—Bengals, 28-7 (C)
1977—Bengals, 17-7 (Mil)
1980—Packers, 14-9 (GB)
1983—Bengals, 34-14 (C)
1986—Bengals, 34-28 (Mil)
1992—Packers, 24-23 (GB)
1995—Packers, 24-10 (GB)
1998—Packers, 13-6 (C)
(RS Pts.—Bengals 178, Packers 151)

CINCINNATI vs. HOUSTON
RS: Bengals lead series, 2-0

2002—Bengals, 38-3 (H)
2003—Bengals, 34-27 (C)
(RS Pts.—Bengals 72, Texans 30)

CINCINNATI vs. *INDIANAPOLIS
RS: Colts lead series, 12-8
PS: Colts lead series, 1-0
1970—**Colts, 17-0 (B)
1972—Colts, 20-19 (C)
1974—Bengals, 24-14 (B)
1976—Colts, 28-27 (B)
1979—Colts, 38-28 (B)
1980—Bengals, 34-33 (C)
1981—Bengals, 41-19 (B)
1982—Bengals, 20-17 (B)
1983—Colts, 34-31 (C)
1987—Bengals, 23-21 (I)
1989—Colts, 23-12 (C)
1990—Colts, 34-20 (C)
1992—Colts, 21-17 (C)
1993—Colts, 9-6 (C)
1994—Colts, 17-13 (C)
1995—Bengals, 24-21 (I) OT
1996—Bengals, 31-24 (C)
1997—Bengals, 28-13 (I)
1998—Colts, 39-26 (I)
1999—Colts, 31-10 (I)
2002—Colts, 28-21 (I)
(RS Pts.—Colts 484, Bengals 455)
(PS Pts.—Colts 17, Bengals 0)
Franchise in Baltimore prior to 1984
***AFC Divisional Playoff*

CINCINNATI vs. JACKSONVILLE
RS: Jaguars lead series, 10-5
1995—Bengals, 24-17 (C)
Bengals, 17-13 (J)
1996—Bengals, 28-21 (C)
Jaguars, 30-27 (J)
1997—Jaguars, 21-13 (J)
Bengals, 31-26 (C)
1998—Jaguars, 24-11 (J)
Jaguars, 34-17 (C)
1999—Jaguars, 41-10 (C)
Jaguars, 24-7 (J)
2000—Jaguars, 13-0 (J)
Bengals, 17-14 (C)
2001—Jaguars, 30-13 (J)
Jaguars, 14-10 (C)
2002—Jaguars, 29-15 (C)
(RS Pts.—Jaguars 351, Bengals 240)

CINCINNATI vs. KANSAS CITY
RS: Chiefs lead series, 11-10
1968—Chiefs, 13-3 (KC)
Chiefs, 16-9 (C)
1969—Bengals, 24-19 (C)
Chiefs, 42-22 (KC)
1970—Chiefs, 27-19 (C)
1972—Bengals, 23-16 (KC)
1973—Bengals, 14-6 (C)
1974—Bengals, 33-6 (C)
1976—Bengals, 27-24 (KC)
1977—Bengals, 27-7 (KC)
1978—Chiefs, 24-23 (C)
1979—Chiefs, 10-7 (C)
1980—Bengals, 20-6 (KC)
1983—Chiefs, 20-15 (KC)
1984—Chiefs, 27-22 (C)
1986—Chiefs, 24-14 (KC)
1987—Bengals, 30-27 (C) OT
1988—Chiefs, 31-28 (KC)
1989—Bengals, 21-17 (KC)
1993—Chiefs, 17-15 (KC)
2003—Bengals, 24-19 (C)
(RS Pts.—Bengals 420, Chiefs 398)

CINCINNATI vs. MIAMI
RS: Dolphins lead series, 12-3
PS: Dolphins lead series, 1-0
1968—Dolphins, 24-22 (C)
Bengals, 38-21 (M)
1969—Bengals, 27-21 (C)
1971—Dolphins, 23-13 (C)
1973—*Dolphins, 34-16 (M)
1974—Dolphins, 24-3 (M)
1977—Bengals, 23-17 (C)
1978—Dolphins, 21-0 (M)
1980—Dolphins, 17-16 (M)
1983—Dolphins, 38-14 (M)
1987—Dolphins, 20-14 (C)
1989—Dolphins, 20-13 (C)
1991—Dolphins, 37-13 (M)
1994—Dolphins, 23-7 (C)
1995—Dolphins, 26-23 (C)
2000—Dolphins, 31-16 (C)
(RS Pts.—Dolphins 363, Bengals 242)
(PS Pts.—Dolphins 34, Bengals 16)
**AFC Divisional Playoff*

CINCINNATI vs. MINNESOTA
RS: Vikings lead series, 5-4
1973—Bengals, 27-0 (C)
1977—Vikings, 42-10 (M)
1980—Bengals, 14-0 (C)
1983—Vikings, 20-14 (M)
1986—Bengals, 24-20 (C)
1989—Vikings, 29-21 (M)
1992—Vikings, 42-7 (C)
1995—Bengals, 27-24 (C)
1998—Vikings, 24-3 (M)
(RS Pts.—Vikings 201, Bengals 147)

CINCINNATI vs. *NEW ENGLAND
RS: Patriots lead series, 10-8
1968—Patriots, 33-14 (B)
1969—Patriots, 25-14 (C)
1970—Bengals, 45-7 (C)
1972—Bengals, 31-7 (NE)
1975—Bengals, 27-10 (C)
1978—Patriots, 10-3 (C)
1979—Patriots, 20-14 (C)
1984—Patriots, 20-14 (NE)
1985—Patriots, 34-23 (NE)
1986—Bengals, 31-7 (NE)
1988—Patriots, 27-21 (NE)
1990—Bengals, 41-7 (C)
1991—Bengals, 29-7 (C)
1992—Bengals, 20-10 (C)
1993—Patriots, 7-2 (NE)
1994—Patriots, 31-28 (C)
2000—Patriots, 16-13 (NE)
2001—Bengals, 23-17 (C)
(RS Pts.—Bengals 393, Patriots 295)
**Franchise in Boston prior to 1971*

CINCINNATI vs. NEW ORLEANS
RS: Series tied, 5-5
1970—Bengals, 26-6 (C)
1975—Bengals, 21-0 (NO)
1978—Saints, 20-18 (C)
1981—Saints, 17-7 (NO)
1984—Bengals, 24-21 (NO)
1987—Saints, 41-24 (C)
1990—Saints, 21-7 (C)
1993—Saints, 20-13 (NO)
1996—Bengals, 30-15 (C)
2002—Bengals, 20-13 (C)
(RS Pts.—Bengals 190, Saints 174)

CINCINNATI vs. N.Y. GIANTS
RS: Bengals lead series, 4-2
1972—Bengals, 13-10 (C)
1977—Bengals, 30-13 (C)
1985—Bengals, 35-30 (C)
1991—Bengals, 27-24 (C)
1994—Giants, 27-20 (NY)
1997—Giants, 29-27 (NY)
(RS Pts.—Bengals 152, Giants 133)

CINCINNATI vs. N.Y. JETS
RS: Jets lead series, 11-6
PS: Jets lead series, 1-0
1968—Jets, 27-14 (NY)
1969—Jets, 21-7 (C)
Jets, 40-7 (NY)
1971—Jets, 35-21 (NY)
1973—Bengals, 20-14 (C)
1976—Bengals, 42-3 (NY)
1981—Bengals, 31-30 (NY)
1982—*Jets, 44-17 (C)
1984—Jets, 43-23 (NY)
1985—Jets, 29-20 (C)
1986—Bengals, 52-21 (C)
1987—Jets, 27-20 (NY)
1988—Bengals, 36-19 (C)
1990—Bengals, 25-20 (C)
1992—Jets, 17-14 (NY)
1993—Jets, 17-12 (NY)
1997—Jets, 31-14 (C)
2001—Jets, 15-14 (NY)
(RS Pts.—Jets 409, Bengals 372)
(PS Pts.—Jets 44, Bengals 17)
**AFC First-Round Playoff*

CINCINNATI vs. *OAKLAND
RS: Raiders lead series, 17-7
PS: Raiders lead series, 2-0
1968—Raiders, 31-10 (O)
Raiders, 34-0 (C)
1969—Bengals, 31-17 (C)
Raiders, 37-17 (O)
1970—Bengals, 31-21 (C)
1971—Raiders, 31-27 (O)
1972—Raiders, 20-14 (C)
1974—Raiders, 30-27 (O)
1975—Bengals, 14-10 (C)
**Raiders, 31-28 (O)
1976—Raiders, 35-20 (O)
1978—Raiders, 34-21 (C)
1980—Raiders, 28-17 (O)
1982—Bengals, 31-17 (C)
1983—Raiders, 20-10 (C)
1985—Raiders, 13-6 (LA)
1988—Bengals, 45-21 (LA)
1989—Raiders, 28-7 (LA)
1990—Raiders, 24-7 (LA)
**Raiders, 20-10 (LA)
1991—Raiders, 38-14 (C)
1992—Bengals, 24-21 (C) OT
1993—Bengals, 16-10 (C)
1995—Raiders, 20-17 (C)
1998—Raiders, 27-10 (O)
2003—Raiders, 23-20 (O)
(RS Pts.—Raiders 590, Bengals 436)
(PS Pts.—Raiders 51, Bengals 38)
**Franchise in Los Angeles from 1982-1994*
***AFC Divisional Playoff*

CINCINNATI vs. PHILADELPHIA
RS: Bengals lead series, 6-3

1971—Bengals, 37-14 (C)
1975—Bengals, 31-0 (P)
1979—Bengals, 37-13 (C)
1982—Bengals, 18-14 (P)
1988—Bengals, 28-24 (P)
1991—Eagles, 17-10 (P)
1994—Bengals, 33-30 (C)
1997—Eagles, 44-42 (P)
2000—Eagles, 16-7 (P)
(RS Pts.—Bengals 243, Eagles 172)

CINCINNATI vs. PITTSBURGH
RS: Steelers lead series, 39-28
1970—Steelers, 21-10 (P)
Bengals, 34-7 (C)
1971—Steelers, 21-10 (P)
Steelers, 21-13 (C)
1972—Bengals, 15-10 (C)
Steelers, 40-17 (P)
1973—Bengals, 19-7 (C)
Steelers, 20-13 (P)
1974—Bengals, 17-10 (C)
Steelers, 27-3 (P)
1975—Steelers, 30-24 (C)
Steelers, 35-14 (P)
1976—Steelers, 23-6 (P)
Steelers, 7-3 (C)
1977—Steelers, 20-14 (P)
Bengals, 17-10 (C)
1978—Steelers, 28-3 (C)
Steelers, 7-6 (P)
1979—Bengals, 34-10 (C)
Steelers, 37-17 (P)
1980—Bengals, 30-28 (C)
Bengals, 17-16 (P)
1981—Bengals, 34-7 (C)
Bengals, 17-10 (P)
1982—Steelers, 26-20 (P) OT
1983—Steelers, 24-14 (C)
Bengals, 23-10 (P)
1984—Steelers, 38-17 (P)
Bengals, 22-20 (C)
1985—Bengals, 37-24 (P)
Bengals, 26-21 (C)
1986—Bengals, 24-22 (C)
Steelers, 30-9 (P)
1987—Steelers, 23-20 (P)
Steelers, 30-16 (C)
1988—Bengals, 17-12 (P)
Bengals, 42-7 (C)
1989—Bengals, 41-10 (C)
Bengals, 26-16 (P)
1990—Bengals, 27-3 (C)
Bengals, 16-12 (P)
1991—Steelers, 33-27 (C) OT
Steelers, 17-10 (P)
1992—Steelers, 20-0 (P)
Steelers, 21-9 (C)
1993—Steelers, 34-7 (P)
Steelers, 24-16 (C)
1994—Steelers, 14-10 (P)
Steelers, 38-15 (C)
1995—Bengals, 27-9 (P)
Steelers, 49-31 (C)
1996—Steelers, 20-10 (P)
Bengals, 34-24 (C)
1997—Steelers, 26-10 (C)
Steelers, 20-3 (P)
1998—Bengals, 25-20 (C)
Bengals, 25-24 (P)
1999—Steelers, 17-3 (C)
Bengals, 27-20 (P)
2000—Steelers, 15-0 (P)
Steelers, 48-28 (C)
2001—Steelers, 16-7 (P)
Bengals, 26-23 (C) OT
2002—Steelers, 34-7 (C)
Steelers, 29-21 (P)
2003—Steelers, 17-10 (C)
Bengals, 24-20 (P)
(RS Pts.—Steelers 1,412, Bengals 1,196)

CINCINNATI vs. *ST. LOUIS
RS: Series tied, 5-5
1972—Rams, 15-12 (LA)
1976—Bengals, 20-12 (C)
1978—Bengals, 20-19 (LA)
1981—Bengals, 24-10 (C)
1984—Rams, 24-14 (C)
1990—Bengals, 34-31 (LA) OT
1993—Bengals, 15-3 (C)
1996—Rams, 26-16 (StL)
1999—Rams, 38-10 (C)
2003—Rams, 27-10 (StL)
(RS Pts.—Rams 205, Bengals 175)
**Franchise in Los Angeles prior to 1995*

CINCINNATI vs. SAN DIEGO
RS: Chargers lead series, 17-10
PS: Bengals lead series, 1-0
1968—Chargers, 29-13 (SD)
Chargers, 31-10 (C)
1969—Bengals, 34-20 (C)
Chargers, 21-14 (SD)
1970—Bengals, 17-14 (SD)
1971—Bengals, 31-0 (C)
1973—Bengals, 20-13 (SD)
1974—Chargers, 20-17 (C)
1975—Bengals, 47-17 (C)
1977—Chargers, 24-3 (SD)
1978—Chargers, 22-13 (SD)
1979—Chargers, 26-24 (C)
1980—Chargers, 31-14 (C)
1981—Bengals, 40-17 (SD)
*Bengals, 27-7 (C)
1982—Chargers, 50-34 (SD)
1985—Chargers, 44-41 (C)
1987—Chargers, 10-9 (C)
1988—Bengals, 27-10 (C)
1990—Bengals, 21-16 (SD)
1992—Chargers, 27-10 (SD)
1994—Chargers, 27-10 (SD)
1996—Chargers, 27-14 (SD)
1997—Bengals, 38-31 (C)
1999—Chargers, 34-7 (C)
2001—Chargers, 28-14 (SD)
2002—Chargers, 34-6 (C)
2003—Bengals, 34-27 (SD)
(RS Pts.—Chargers 650, Bengals 562)
(PS Pts.—Bengals 27, Chargers 7)
**AFC Championship*

CINCINNATI vs. SAN FRANCISCO
RS: 49ers lead series, 7-3
PS: 49ers lead series, 2-0
1974—Bengals, 21-3 (SF)
1978—49ers, 28-12 (SF)
1981—49ers, 21-3 (C)
*49ers, 26-21 (Detroit)
1984—49ers, 23-17 (SF)
1987—49ers, 27-26 (C)
1988—**49ers, 20-16 (Miami)
1990—49ers, 20-17 (C) OT
1993—49ers, 21-8 (SF)
1996—49ers, 28-21 (SF)
1999—Bengals, 44-30 (C)
2003—Bengals, 41-38 (C)
(RS Pts.—49ers 239, Bengals 210)
(PS Pts.—49ers 46, Bengals 37)
**Super Bowl XVI*
***Super Bowl XXIII*

CINCINNATI vs. SEATTLE
RS: Series tied, 8-8
PS: Bengals lead series, 1-0
1977—Bengals, 42-20 (C)
1981—Bengals, 27-21 (C)
1982—Bengals, 24-10 (C)
1984—Seahawks, 26-6 (C)
1985—Seahawks, 28-24 (C)
1986—Bengals, 34-7 (C)
1987—Bengals, 17-10 (S)
1988—*Bengals, 21-13 (C)
1989—Seahawks, 24-17 (C)
1990—Seahawks, 31-16 (S)
1991—Seahawks, 13-7 (C)
1992—Bengals, 21-3 (S)
1993—Seahawks, 19-10 (C)
1994—Bengals, 20-17 (S) OT
1995—Seahawks, 24-21 (S)
1999—Seahawks, 37-20 (S)
2003—Bengals, 27-24 (C)
(RS Pts.—Bengals 333, Seahawks 314)
(PS Pts.—Bengals 21, Seahawks 13)
**AFC Divisional Playoff*

CINCINNATI vs. TAMPA BAY
RS: Buccaneers lead series, 5-3
1976—Bengals, 21-0 (C)
1980—Buccaneers, 17-12 (C)
1983—Bengals, 23-17 (TB)
1989—Bengals, 56-23 (C)
1995—Buccaneers, 19-16 (TB)
1998—Buccaneers, 35-0 (C)
2001—Buccaneers, 16-13 (C) OT
2002—Buccaneers, 35-7 (C)
(RS Pts.— Buccaneers 162, Bengals 148)

CINCINNATI vs. *TENNESSEE
RS: Titans lead series, 37-29-1
PS: Bengals lead series, 1-0
1968—Oilers, 27-17 (C)
1969—Tie, 31-31 (H)
1970—Oilers, 20-13 (C)
Bengals, 30-20 (H)
1971—Oilers, 10-6 (H)
Bengals, 28-13 (C)
1972—Bengals, 30-7 (C)
Bengals, 61-17 (H)
1973—Bengals, 24-10 (C)
Bengals, 27-24 (H)
1974—Oilers, 34-21 (C)
Oilers, 20-3 (H)
1975—Bengals, 21-19 (H)
Bengals, 23-19 (C)
1976—Bengals, 27-7 (H)
Bengals, 31-27 (C)
1977—Bengals, 13-10 (C) OT
Oilers, 21-16 (H)
1978—Bengals, 28-13 (C)
Oilers, 17-10 (H)
1979—Oilers, 30-27 (C) OT
Oilers, 42-21 (H)
1980—Oilers, 13-10 (C)
Oilers, 23-3 (H)
1981—Oilers, 17-10 (H)
Bengals, 34-21 (C)

1982—Bengals, 27-6 (C)
Bengals, 35-27 (H)
1983—Bengals, 55-14 (H)
Bengals, 38-10 (C)
1984—Bengals, 13-3 (C)
Bengals, 31-13 (H)
1985—Oilers, 44-27 (H)
Bengals, 45-27 (C)
1986—Bengals, 31-28 (C)
Oilers, 32-28 (H)
1987—Oilers, 31-29 (C)
Oilers, 21-17 (H)
1988—Bengals, 44-21 (C)
Oilers, 41-6 (H)
1989—Oilers, 26-24 (H)
Bengals, 61-7 (C)
1990—Oilers, 48-17 (H)
Bengals, 40-20 (C)
**Bengals, 41-14 (C)
1991—Oilers, 30-7 (C)
Oilers, 35-3 (H)
1992—Oilers, 38-24 (C)
Oilers, 26-10 (H)
1993—Oilers, 28-12 (H)
Oilers, 38-3 (C)
1994—Oilers, 20-13 (H)
Bengals, 34-31 (C)
1995—Oilers, 38-28 (C)
Bengals, 32-25 (H)
1996—Oilers, 30-27 (C) OT
Bengals, 21-13 (H)
1997—Oilers, 30-7 (T)
Bengals, 41-14 (C)
1998—Oilers, 23-14 (C)
Oilers, 44-14 (T)
1999—Titans, 36-35 (T)
Titans, 24-14 (C)
2000—Titans, 23-14 (C)
Titans, 35-3 (T)
2001—Titans, 20-7 (C)
Bengals, 23-21 (T)
2002—Titans, 30-24 (C)
(RS Pts.—Titans 1,583, Bengals 1,543)
(PS Pts.—Bengals 41, Titans 14)
Franchise in Houston prior to 1997; known as Oilers prior to 1999
***AFC First-Round Playoff*

CINCINNATI vs. WASHINGTON
RS: Redskins lead series, 4-2
1970—Redskins, 20-0 (W)
1974—Bengals, 28-17 (C)
1979—Redskins, 28-14 (W)
1985—Redskins, 27-24 (W)
1988—Bengals, 20-17 (C) OT
1991—Redskins, 34-27 (C)
(RS Pts.—Redskins 143, Bengals 113)

CLEVELAND vs. ARIZONA
RS: Browns lead series, 33-11-3;
See Arizona vs. Cleveland

CLEVELAND vs. ATLANTA
RS: Browns lead series, 9-2;
See Atlanta vs. Cleveland

CLEVELAND vs. BALTIMORE
RS: Ravens lead series, 7-3;
See Baltimore vs. Cleveland

CLEVELAND vs. BUFFALO
RS: Browns lead series, 7-4
PS: Browns lead series, 1-0;
See Buffalo vs. Cleveland

CLEVELAND vs. CAROLINA
RS: Panthers lead series, 2-0;
See Carolina vs. Cleveland

CLEVELAND vs. CHICAGO
RS: Browns lead series, 8-4;
See Chicago vs. Cleveland

CLEVELAND vs. CINCINNATI
RS: Browns lead series, 32-29;
See Cincinnati vs. Cleveland

CLEVELAND vs. DALLAS
RS: Browns lead series, 15-9
PS: Browns lead series, 2-1
1960—Browns, 48-7 (D)
1961—Browns, 25-7 (C)
Browns, 38-17 (D)
1962—Browns, 19-10 (C)
Cowboys, 45-21 (D)
1963—Browns, 41-24 (D)
Browns, 27-17 (C)
1964—Browns, 27-6 (C)
Browns, 20-16 (D)
1965—Browns, 23-17 (C)
Browns, 24-17 (D)
1966—Browns, 30-21 (C)
Cowboys, 26-14 (D)
1967—Cowboys, 21-14 (C)
*Cowboys, 52-14 (D)
1968—Cowboys, 28-7 (C)
*Browns, 31-20 (C)
1969—Browns, 42-10 (C)
*Browns, 38-14 (D)
1970—Cowboys, 6-2 (C)
1974—Cowboys, 41-17 (D)
1979—Browns, 26-7 (C)
1982—Cowboys, 31-14 (D)
1985—Cowboys, 20-7 (D)
1988—Browns, 24-21 (C)
1991—Cowboys, 26-14 (C)
1994—Browns, 19-14 (D)
(RS Pts.—Browns 543, Cowboys 455)
(PS Pts.—Cowboys 86, Browns 83)
**Conference Championship*

CLEVELAND vs. DENVER
RS: Broncos lead series, 15-5
PS: Broncos lead series, 3-0
1970—Browns, 27-13 (D)
1971—Broncos, 27-0 (C)
1972—Browns, 27-20 (D)
1974—Browns, 23-21 (C)
1975—Broncos, 16-15 (D)
1976—Broncos, 44-13 (D)
1978—Broncos, 19-7 (C)
1980—Broncos, 19-16 (C)
1981—Broncos, 23-20 (D) OT
1983—Broncos, 27-6 (D)
1984—Broncos, 24-14 (C)
1986—*Broncos, 23-20 (C) OT
1987—*Broncos, 38-33 (D)
1988—Broncos, 30-7 (D)
1989—Browns, 16-13 (C)
*Broncos, 37-21 (D)
1990—Browns, 30-29 (D)
1991—Broncos, 17-7 (C)
1992—Broncos, 12-0 (C)
1993—Broncos, 29-14 (C)
1994—Broncos, 26-14 (D)
2000—Broncos, 44-10 (D)
2003—Broncos, 23-20 (D) OT
(RS Pts.—Broncos 476, Browns 286)
(PS Pts.—Broncos 98, Browns 74)
**AFC Championship*

CLEVELAND vs. DETROIT
RS: Lions lead series, 12-4
PS: Lions lead series, 3-1
1952—Lions, 17-6 (D)
*Lions, 17-7 (C)
1953—*Lions, 17-16 (D)
1954—Lions, 14-10 (C)
*Browns, 56-10 (C)
1957—Lions, 20-7 (D)
*Lions, 59-14 (D)
1958—Lions, 30-10 (C)
1963—Lions, 38-10 (D)
1964—Browns, 37-21 (C)
1967—Lions, 31-14 (D)
1969—Lions, 28-21 (C)
1970—Lions, 41-24 (C)
1975—Lions, 21-10 (D)
1983—Browns, 31-26 (D)
1986—Browns, 24-21 (C)
1989—Lions, 13-10 (D)
1992—Lions, 24-14 (D)
1995—Lions, 38-20 (D)
2001—Browns, 24-14 (C)
(RS Pts.—Lions 397, Browns 272)
(PS Pts.—Lions 103, Browns 93)
**NFL Championship*

CLEVELAND vs. GREEN BAY
RS: Packers lead series, 9-6
PS: Packers lead series, 1-0
1953—Browns, 27-0 (Mil)
1955—Browns, 41-10 (C)
1956—Browns, 24-7 (Mil)
1961—Packers, 49-17 (C)
1964—Packers, 28-21 (Mil)
1965—*Packers, 23-12 (GB)
1966—Packers, 21-20 (C)
1967—Packers, 55-7 (Mil)
1969—Browns, 20-7 (C)
1972—Packers, 26-10 (C)
1980—Browns, 26-21 (C)
1983—Packers, 35-21 (Mil)
1986—Packers, 17-14 (C)
1992—Browns, 17-6 (C)
1995—Packers, 31-20 (C)
2001—Packers, 30-7 (GB)
(RS Pts.—Packers 343, Browns 292)
(PS Pts.—Packers 23, Browns 12)
**NFL Championship*

CLEVELAND vs. HOUSTON
RS: Browns lead series, 1-0
2002—Browns, 34-17 (C)
(RS Pts.—Browns 34, Texans 17)

CLEVELAND vs. *INDIANAPOLIS
RS: Browns lead series, 13-10
PS: Series tied, 2-2
1956—Colts, 21-7 (C)
1959—Browns, 38-31 (B)
1962—Colts, 36-14 (C)
1964—**Browns, 27-0 (C)
1968—Browns, 30-20 (B)
**Colts, 34-0 (C)
1971—Browns, 14-13 (B)
***Colts, 20-3 (C)
1973—Browns, 24-14 (C)
1975—Colts, 21-7 (B)
1978—Browns, 45-24 (B)
1979—Browns, 13-10 (C)
1980—Browns, 28-27 (B)
1981—Browns, 42-28 (C)

1983—Browns, 41-23 (C)
1986—Browns, 24-9 (I)
1987—Colts, 9-7 (C)
***Browns, 38-21 (C)
1988—Browns, 23-17 (C)
1989—Colts, 23-17 (I) OT
1991—Browns, 31-0 (I)
1992—Colts, 14-3 (I)
1993—Colts, 23-10 (I)
1994—Browns, 21-14 (I)
1999—Colts, 29-28 (C)
2002—Colts, 28-23 (C)
2003—Colts, 9-6 (C)
(RS Pts.—Browns 496, Colts 443)
(PS Pts.—Colts 75, Browns 68)
Franchise in Baltimore prior to 1984
***NFL Championship*
****AFC Divisional Playoff*

CLEVELAND vs. JACKSONVILLE
RS: Jaguars lead series, 7-2
1995—Jaguars, 23-15 (C)
Jaguars, 24-21 (J)
1999—Jaguars, 24-7 (J)
Jaguars, 24-14 (C)
2000—Jaguars, 27-7 (C)
Jaguars, 48-0 (J)
2001—Browns, 23-14 (J)
Jaguars, 15-10 (C)
2002—Browns, 21-20 (J)
(RS Pts.—Jaguars 219, Browns 118)

CLEVELAND vs. KANSAS CITY
RS: Chiefs lead series, 9-8-2
1971—Chiefs, 13-7 (KC)
1972—Chiefs, 31-7 (C)
1973—Tie, 20-20 (KC)
1975—Browns, 40-14 (C)
1976—Chiefs, 39-14 (KC)
1977—Browns, 44-7 (C)
1978—Chiefs, 17-3 (KC)
1979—Browns, 27-24 (KC)
1980—Browns, 20-13 (C)
1984—Chiefs, 10-6 (KC)
1986—Browns, 20-7 (C)
1988—Browns, 6-3 (KC)
1989—Tie, 10-10 (C) OT
1990—Chiefs, 34-0 (KC)
1991—Browns, 20-15 (C)
1994—Chiefs, 20-13 (KC)
1995—Browns, 35-17 (C)
2002—Chiefs, 40-39 (C)
2003—Chiefs, 41-20 (KC)
(RS Pts.—Chiefs 375, Browns 351)

CLEVELAND vs. MIAMI
RS: Dolphins lead series, 6-4
PS: Dolphins lead series, 2-0
1970—Browns, 28-0 (M)
1972—*Dolphins, 20-14 (M)
1973—Dolphins, 17-9 (C)
1976—Browns, 17-13 (C)
1979—Browns, 30-24 (C) OT
1985—*Dolphins, 24-21 (M)
1986—Browns, 26-16 (C)
1988—Dolphins, 38-31 (M)
1989—Dolphins, 13-10 (M) OT
1990—Dolphins, 30-13 (C)
1992—Dolphins, 27-23 (C)
1993—Dolphins, 24-14 (C)
(RS Pts.—Dolphins 202, Browns 201)
(PS Pts.—Dolphins 44, Browns 35)
**AFC Divisional Playoff*

CLEVELAND vs. MINNESOTA
RS: Vikings lead series, 8-3
PS: Vikings lead series, 1-0
1965—Vikings, 27-17 (C)
1967—Browns, 14-10 (C)
1969—Vikings, 51-3 (M)
*Vikings, 27-7 (M)
1973—Vikings, 26-3 (M)
1975—Vikings, 42-10 (C)
1980—Vikings, 28-23 (M)
1983—Vikings, 27-21 (C)
1986—Browns, 23-20 (M)
1989—Browns, 23-17 (C) OT
1992—Vikings, 17-13 (M)
1995—Vikings, 27-11 (M)
(RS Pts.—Vikings 292, Browns 161)
(PS Pts.—Vikings 27, Browns 7)
**NFL Championship*

CLEVELAND vs. NEW ENGLAND
RS: Browns lead series, 11-7
PS: Browns lead series, 1-0
1971—Browns, 27-7 (C)
1974—Browns, 21-14 (NE)
1977—Browns, 30-27 (C) OT
1980—Patriots, 34-17 (NE)
1982—Browns, 10-7 (C)
1983—Browns, 30-0 (NE)
1984—Patriots, 17-16 (C)
1985—Browns, 24-20 (C)
1987—Browns, 20-10 (NE)
1991—Browns, 20-0 (NE)
1992—Browns, 19-17 (NE)
1993—Patriots, 20-17 (C)
1994—Browns, 13-6 (C)
*Browns, 20-13 (C)
1995—Patriots, 17-14 (NE)
1999—Patriots, 19-7 (C)
2000—Browns, 19-11 (C)
2001—Patriots, 27-16 (NE)
2003—Patriots, 9-3 (NE)
(RS Pts.—Browns 323, Patriots 262)
(PS Pts.—Browns 20, Patriots 13)
**AFC First-Round Playoff*

CLEVELAND vs. NEW ORLEANS
RS: Browns lead series, 11-3
1967—Browns, 42-7 (NO)
1968—Browns, 24-10 (NO)
Browns, 35-17 (C)
1969—Browns, 27-17 (NO)
1971—Browns, 21-17 (NO)
1975—Browns, 17-16 (C)
1978—Browns, 24-16 (NO)
1981—Browns, 20-17 (C)
1984—Saints, 16-14 (C)
1987—Saints, 28-21 (NO)
1990—Saints, 25-20 (NO)
1993—Browns, 17-13 (C)
1999—Browns, 21-16 (NO)
2002—Browns, 24-15 (NO)
(RS Pts.—Browns 327, Saints 230)

CLEVELAND vs. N.Y. GIANTS
RS: Browns lead series, 25-18-2
PS: Series tied, 1-1
1950—Giants, 6-0 (C)
Giants, 17-13 (NY)
*Browns, 8-3 (C)
1951—Browns, 14-13 (C)
Browns, 10-0 (NY)
1952—Giants, 17-9 (C)
Giants, 37-34 (NY)
1953—Browns, 7-0 (NY)
Browns, 62-14 (C)
1954—Browns, 24-14 (C)
Browns, 16-7 (NY)
1955—Browns, 24-14 (C)
Tie, 35-35 (NY)
1956—Giants, 21-9 (C)
Browns, 24-7 (NY)
1957—Browns, 6-3 (C)
Browns, 34-28 (NY)
1958—Giants, 21-17 (C)
Giants, 13-10 (NY)
*Giants, 10-0 (NY)
1959—Giants, 10-6 (C)
Giants, 48-7 (NY)
1960—Giants, 17-13 (C)
Browns, 48-34 (NY)
1961—Giants, 37-21 (C)
Tie, 7-7 (NY)
1962—Browns, 17-7 (C)
Giants, 17-13 (NY)
1963—Browns, 35-24 (NY)
Giants, 33-6 (C)
1964—Browns, 42-20 (C)
Browns, 52-20 (NY)
1965—Browns, 38-14 (NY)
Browns, 34-21 (C)
1966—Browns, 28-7 (NY)
Browns, 49-40 (C)
1967—Giants, 38-34 (NY)
Browns, 24-14 (C)
1968—Browns, 45-10 (C)
1969—Browns, 28-17 (C)
Giants, 27-14 (NY)
1973—Browns, 12-10 (C)
1977—Browns, 21-7 (NY)
1985—Browns, 35-33 (NY)
1991—Giants, 13-10 (NY)
1994—Giants, 16-13 (C)
2000—Giants, 24-3 (C)
(RS Pts.—Browns 1,003, Giants 832)
(PS Pts.—Giants 13, Browns 8)
**Conference Playoff*

CLEVELAND vs. N.Y. JETS
RS: Browns lead series, 10-6
PS: Browns lead series, 1-0
1970—Browns, 31-21 (C)
1972—Browns, 26-10 (NY)
1976—Browns, 38-17 (C)
1978—Browns, 37-34 (C) OT
1979—Browns, 25-22 (NY) OT
1980—Browns, 17-14 (C)
1981—Jets, 14-13 (C)
1983—Browns, 10-7 (C)
1984—Jets, 24-20 (C)
1985—Jets, 37-10 (NY)
1986—*Browns, 23-20 (C) OT
1988—Jets, 23-3 (C)
1989—Browns, 38-24 (C)
1990—Jets, 24-21 (NY)
1991—Jets, 17-14 (C)
1994—Browns, 27-7 (C)
2002—Browns, 24-21 (NY)
(RS Pts.—Browns 354, Jets 316)
(PS Pts.—Browns 23, Jets 20)
**AFC Divisional Playoff*

CLEVELAND vs. *OAKLAND
RS: Raiders lead series, 9-5
PS: Raiders lead series, 2-0
1970—Raiders, 23-20 (O)

1971—Raiders, 34-20 (C)
1973—Browns, 7-3 (O)
1974—Raiders, 40-24 (C)
1975—Raiders, 38-17 (O)
1977—Raiders, 26-10 (C)
1979—Raiders, 19-14 (O)
1980—**Raiders, 14-12 (C)
1982—***Raiders, 27-10 (LA)
1985—Raiders, 21-20 (C)
1986—Raiders, 27-14 (LA)
1987—Browns, 24-17 (LA)
1992—Browns, 28-16 (LA)
1993—Browns, 19-16 (LA)
2000—Raiders, 36-10 (O)
2003—Browns, 13-7 (C)
(RS Pts.—Raiders 323, Browns 240)
(PS Pts.—Raiders 41, Browns 22)
Franchise in Los Angeles from 1982-1994
***AFC Divisional Playoff*
****AFC First-Round Playoff*

CLEVELAND vs. PHILADELPHIA
RS: Browns lead series, 31-13-1
1950—Browns, 35-10 (P)
Browns, 13-7 (C)
1951—Browns, 20-17 (C)
Browns, 24-9 (P)
1952—Browns, 49-7 (P)
Eagles, 28-20 (C)
1953—Browns, 37-13 (C)
Eagles, 42-27 (P)
1954—Eagles, 28-10 (P)
Browns, 6-0 (C)
1955—Browns, 21-17 (C)
Eagles, 33-17 (P)
1956—Browns, 16-0 (P)
Browns, 17-14 (C)
1957—Browns, 24-7 (C)
Eagles, 17-7 (P)
1958—Browns, 28-14 (C)
Browns, 21-14 (P)
1959—Browns, 28-7 (C)
Browns, 28-21 (P)
1960—Browns, 41-24 (P)
Eagles, 31-29 (C)
1961—Eagles, 27-20 (P)
Browns, 45-24 (C)
1962—Eagles, 35-7 (P)
Tie, 14-14 (C)
1963—Browns, 37-7 (C)
Browns, 23-17 (P)
1964—Browns, 28-20 (P)
Browns, 38-24 (C)
1965—Browns, 35-17 (P)
Browns, 38-34 (C)
1966—Browns, 27-7 (C)
Eagles, 33-21 (P)
1967—Eagles, 28-24 (P)
1968—Browns, 47-13 (C)
1969—Browns, 27-20 (P)
1972—Browns, 27-17 (P)
1976—Browns, 24-3 (C)
1979—Browns, 24-19 (P)
1982—Eagles, 24-21 (C)
1988—Browns, 19-3 (C)
1991—Eagles, 32-30 (C)
1994—Browns, 26-7 (P)
2000—Eagles, 35-24 (C)
(RS Pts.—Browns 1,144, Eagles 820)

CLEVELAND vs. PITTSBURGH
RS: Browns lead series, 55-47
PS: Steelers lead series, 2-0
1950—Browns, 30-17 (P)
Browns, 45-7 (C)
1951—Browns, 17-0 (C)
Browns, 28-0 (P)
1952—Browns, 21-20 (P)
Browns, 29-28 (C)
1953—Browns, 34-16 (C)
Browns, 20-16 (P)
1954—Steelers, 55-27 (P)
Browns, 42-7 (C)
1955—Browns, 41-14 (C)
Browns, 30-7 (P)
1956—Browns, 14-10 (P)
Steelers, 24-16 (C)
1957—Browns, 23-12 (P)
Browns, 24-0 (C)
1958—Browns, 45-12 (P)
Browns, 27-10 (C)
1959—Steelers, 17-7 (P)
Steelers, 21-20 (C)
1960—Browns, 28-20 (C)
Steelers, 14-10 (P)
1961—Browns, 30-28 (P)
Steelers, 17-13 (C)
1962—Browns, 41-14 (P)
Browns, 35-14 (C)
1963—Browns, 35-23 (C)
Steelers, 9-7 (P)
1964—Steelers, 23-7 (C)
Browns, 30-17 (P)
1965—Browns, 24-19 (C)
Browns, 42-21 (P)
1966—Browns, 41-10 (C)
Steelers, 16-6 (P)
1967—Browns, 21-10 (C)
Browns, 34-14 (P)
1968—Browns, 31-24 (C)
Browns, 45-24 (P)
1969—Browns, 42-31 (C)
Browns, 24-3 (P)
1970—Browns, 15-7 (C)
Steelers, 28-9 (P)
1971—Browns, 27-17 (C)
Steelers, 26-9 (P)
1972—Browns, 26-24 (C)
Steelers, 30-0 (P)
1973—Steelers, 33-6 (P)
Browns, 21-16 (C)
1974—Steelers, 20-16 (P)
Steelers, 26-16 (C)
1975—Steelers, 42-6 (C)
Steelers, 31-17 (P)
1976—Steelers, 31-14 (P)
Browns, 18-16 (C)
1977—Steelers, 28-14 (C)
Steelers, 35-31 (P)
1978—Steelers, 15-9 (P) OT
Steelers, 34-14 (C)
1979—Steelers, 51-35 (C)
Steelers, 33-30 (P) OT
1980—Browns, 27-26 (C)
Steelers, 16-13 (P)
1981—Steelers, 13-7 (P)
Steelers, 32-10 (C)
1982—Browns, 10-9 (C)
Steelers, 37-21 (P)
1983—Steelers, 44-17 (P)
Browns, 30-17 (C)
1984—Browns, 20-10 (C)
Steelers, 23-20 (P)
1985—Browns, 17-7 (C)
Steelers, 10-9 (P)
1986—Browns, 27-24 (P)
Browns, 37-31 (C) OT
1987—Browns, 34-10 (C)
Browns, 19-13 (P)
1988—Browns, 23-9 (P)
Browns, 27-7 (C)
1989—Browns, 51-0 (P)
Steelers, 17-7 (C)
1990—Browns, 13-3 (C)
Steelers, 35-0 (P)
1991—Browns, 17-14 (C)
Steelers, 17-10 (P)
1992—Browns, 17-9 (C)
Steelers, 23-13 (P)
1993—Browns, 28-23 (C)
Steelers, 16-9 (P)
1994—Steelers, 17-10 (C)
Steelers, 17-7 (P)
*Steelers, 29-9 (P)
1995—Steelers, 20-3 (P)
Steelers, 20-17 (C)
1999—Steelers, 43-0 (C)
Browns, 16-15 (P)
2000—Browns, 23-20 (C)
Steelers, 22-0 (P)
2001—Steelers, 15-12 (C) OT
Steelers, 28-7 (P)
2002—Steelers, 16-13 (P) OT
Steelers, 23-20 (C)
**Steelers, 36-33 (P)
2003—Browns, 33-13 (P)
Steelers, 13-6 (C)
(RS Pts.—Browns 2,119, Steelers 1,964)
(PS Pts.—Steelers 65, Browns 42)
**AFC Divisional Playoff*
***AFC First-Round Playoff*

CLEVELAND vs. *ST. LOUIS
RS: Rams lead series, 9-8
PS: Browns lead series, 2-1
1950—**Browns, 30-28 (C)
1951—Browns, 38-23 (LA)
**Rams, 24-17 (LA)
1952—Browns, 37-7 (C)
1955—**Browns, 38-14 (LA)
1957—Browns, 45-31 (C)
1958—Browns, 30-27 (LA)
1963—Browns, 20-6 (C)
1965—Rams, 42-7 (LA)
1968—Rams, 24-6 (C)
1973—Rams, 30-17 (LA)
1977—Rams, 9-0 (C)
1978—Browns, 30-19 (C)
1981—Rams, 27-16 (LA)
1984—Rams, 20-17 (LA)
1987—Browns, 30-17 (C)
1990—Rams, 38-23 (C)
1993—Browns, 42-14 (LA)
1999—Rams, 34-3 (StL)
2003—Rams, 26-20 (C)
(RS Pts.—Rams 394, Browns 381)
(PS Pts.—Browns 85, Rams 66)
**Franchise in Los Angeles prior to 1995*
***NFL Championship*

CLEVELAND vs. SAN DIEGO
RS: Chargers lead series, 11-7-1
1970—Chargers, 27-10 (C)
1972—Browns, 21-17 (SD)

1973—Tie, 16-16 (C)
1974—Chargers, 36-35 (SD)
1976—Browns, 21-17 (C)
1977—Chargers, 37-14 (SD)
1981—Chargers, 44-14 (C)
1982—Chargers, 30-13 (C)
1983—Browns, 30-24 (SD) OT
1985—Browns, 21-7 (SD)
1986—Browns, 47-17 (C)
1987—Chargers, 27-24 (SD) OT
1990—Chargers, 24-14 (C)
1991—Browns, 30-24 (SD) OT
1992—Chargers, 14-13 (C)
1995—Chargers, 31-13 (SD)
1999—Chargers, 23-10 (SD)
2001—Browns, 20-16 (C)
2003—Chargers, 26-20 (C)
(RS Pts.—Chargers 457, Browns 386)

CLEVELAND vs. SAN FRANCISCO
RS: Browns lead series, 10-6
1950—Browns, 34-14 (C)
1951—49ers, 24-10 (SF)
1953—Browns, 23-21 (C)
1955—Browns, 38-3 (SF)
1959—49ers, 21-20 (C)
1962—Browns, 13-10 (SF)
1968—Browns, 33-21 (SF)
1970—49ers, 34-31 (SF)
1974—Browns, 7-0 (C)
1978—Browns, 24-7 (C)
1981—Browns, 15-12 (SF)
1984—49ers, 41-7 (C)
1987—49ers, 38-24 (SF)
1990—49ers, 20-17 (SF)
1993—Browns, 23-13 (C)
2003—Browns, 13-12 (SF)
(RS Pts.—Browns 332, 49ers 291)

CLEVELAND vs. SEATTLE
RS: Seahawks lead series, 11-4
1977—Seahawks, 20-19 (S)
1978—Seahawks, 47-24 (S)
1979—Seahawks, 29-24 (C)
1980—Browns, 27-3 (S)
1981—Seahawks, 42-21 (S)
1982—Browns, 21-7 (S)
1983—Seahawks, 24-9 (C)
1984—Seahawks, 33-0 (S)
1985—Seahawks, 31-13 (S)
1988—Seahawks, 16-10 (C)
1989—Browns, 17-7 (S)
1993—Seahawks, 22-5 (S)
1994—Browns, 35-9 (C)
2001—Seahawks, 9-6 (C)
2003—Seahawks, 34-7 (S)
(RS Pts.—Seahawks 333, Browns 238)

CLEVELAND vs. TAMPA BAY
RS: Browns lead series, 5-1
1976—Browns, 24-7 (TB)
1980—Browns, 34-27 (TB)
1983—Browns, 20-0 (C)
1989—Browns, 42-31 (TB)
1995—Browns, 22-6 (C)
2002—Buccaneers 17-3 (TB)
(RS Pts.—Browns 145, Buccaneers 88)

CLEVELAND vs. *TENNESSEE
RS: Browns lead series, 32-26
PS: Titans lead series, 1-0
1970—Browns, 28-14 (C)
Browns, 21-10 (H)
1971—Browns, 31-0 (C)
Browns, 37-24 (H)
1972—Browns, 23-17 (H)
Browns, 20-0 (C)
1973—Browns, 42-13 (C)
Browns, 23-13 (H)
1974—Browns, 20-7 (C)
Oilers, 28-24 (H)
1975—Oilers, 40-10 (C)
Oilers, 21-10 (H)
1976—Browns, 21-7 (H)
Browns, 13-10 (C)
1977—Browns, 24-23 (H)
Oilers, 19-15 (C)
1978—Oilers, 16-13 (C)
Oilers, 14-10 (H)
1979—Oilers, 31-10 (H)
Browns, 14-7 (C)
1980—Oilers, 16-7 (C)
Browns, 17-14 (H)
1981—Oilers, 9-3 (C)
Oilers, 17-13 (H)
1982—Browns, 20-14 (H)
1983—Browns, 25-19 (C) OT
Oilers, 34-27 (H)
1984—Browns, 27-10 (C)
Browns, 27-20 (H)
1985—Browns, 21-6 (H)
Browns, 28-21 (C)
1986—Browns, 23-20 (H)
Browns, 13-10 (C) OT
1987—Oilers, 15-10 (C)
Browns, 40-7 (H)
1988—Oilers, 24-17 (H)
Browns, 28-23 (C)
**Oilers, 24-23 (C)
1989—Browns, 28-17 (C)
Browns, 24-20 (H)
1990—Oilers, 35-23 (C)
Oilers, 58-14 (H)
1991—Oilers, 28-24 (H)
Oilers, 17-14 (C)
1992—Browns, 24-14 (H)
Oilers, 17-14 (C)
1993—Oilers, 27-20 (C)
Oilers, 19-17 (H)
1994—Browns, 11-8 (H)
Browns, 34-10 (C)
1995—Browns, 14-7 (H)
Oilers, 37-10 (C)
1999—Titans, 26-9 (T)
Titans, 33-21 (C)
2000—Titans, 24-10 (T)
Titans, 24-0 (C)
2001—Titans, 31-15 (C)
Browns, 41-38 (T)
2002—Browns, 31-28 (T) OT
(RS Pts.—Browns 1,153, Titans 1,111)
(PS Pts.—Titans 24, Browns 23)
Franchise in Houston prior to 1997; known as Oilers prior to 1999
***AFC First-Round Playoff*

CLEVELAND vs. WASHINGTON
RS: Browns lead series, 32-9-1
1950—Browns, 20-14 (C)
Browns, 45-21 (W)
1951—Browns, 45-0 (C)
1952—Browns, 19-15 (C)
Browns, 48-24 (W)
1953—Browns, 30-14 (W)
Browns, 27-3 (C)
1954—Browns, 62-3 (C)
Browns, 34-14 (W)
1955—Redskins, 27-17 (C)
Browns, 24-14 (W)
1956—Redskins, 20-9 (W)
Redskins, 20-17 (C)
1957—Browns, 21-17 (C)
Tie, 30-30 (W)
1958—Browns, 20-10 (W)
Browns, 21-14 (C)
1959—Browns, 34-7 (C)
Browns, 31-17 (W)
1960—Browns, 31-10 (W)
Browns, 27-16 (C)
1961—Browns, 31-7 (C)
Browns, 17-6 (W)
1962—Redskins, 17-16 (C)
Redskins, 17-9 (W)
1963—Browns, 37-14 (C)
Browns, 27-20 (W)
1964—Browns, 27-13 (W)
Browns, 34-24 (C)
1965—Browns, 17-7 (W)
Browns, 24-16 (C)
1966—Browns, 38-14 (W)
Browns, 14-3 (C)
1967—Browns, 42-37 (C)
1968—Browns, 24-21 (W)
1969—Browns, 27-23 (C)
1971—Browns, 20-13 (W)
1975—Redskins, 23-7 (C)
1979—Redskins, 13-9 (C)
1985—Redskins, 14-7 (C)
1988—Browns, 17-13 (W)
1991—Redskins, 42-17 (W)
(RS Pts.—Browns 1,073, Redskins 667)

DALLAS vs. ARIZONA
RS: Cowboys lead series, 53-27-1
PS: Cardinals lead series, 1-0;
See Arizona vs. Dallas

DALLAS vs. ATLANTA
RS: Cowboys lead series, 12-8
PS: Cowboys lead series, 2-0;
See Atlanta vs. Dallas

DALLAS vs. BALTIMORE
RS: Ravens lead series, 1-0;
See Baltimore vs. Dallas

DALLAS vs. BUFFALO
RS: Cowboys lead series, 4-3
PS: Cowboys lead series, 2-0;
See Buffalo vs. Dallas

DALLAS vs. CAROLINA
RS: Cowboys lead series, 4-1
PS: Panthers lead series, 2-0;
See Carolina vs. Dallas

DALLAS vs. CHICAGO
RS: Cowboys lead series, 9-8
PS: Cowboys lead series, 2-0;
See Chicago vs. Dallas

DALLAS vs. CINCINNATI
RS: Cowboys lead series, 5-3;
See Cincinnati vs. Dallas

DALLAS vs. CLEVELAND
RS: Browns lead series, 15-9
PS: Browns lead series, 2-1;
See Cleveland vs. Dallas

DALLAS vs. DENVER
RS: Series tied, 4-4
PS: Cowboys lead series, 1-0

1973—Cowboys, 22-10 (Den)
1977—Cowboys, 14-6 (Dall)
*Cowboys, 27-10 (New Orleans)
1980—Broncos, 41-20 (Den)
1986—Broncos, 29-14 (Den)
1992—Cowboys, 31-27 (Den)
1995—Cowboys, 31-21 (Dall)
1998—Broncos, 42-23 (Den)
2001—Broncos, 26-24 (Dall)
(RS Pts.—Broncos 202, Cowboys 179)
(PS Pts.—Cowboys 27, Broncos 10)
Super Bowl XII

DALLAS vs. DETROIT
RS: Series tied, 8-8
PS: Series tied, 1-1
1960—Lions, 23-14 (Det)
1963—Cowboys, 17-14 (Dal)
1968—Cowboys, 59-13 (Dal)
1970—*Cowboys, 5-0 (Dal)
1972—Cowboys, 28-24 (Dal)
1975—Cowboys, 36-10 (Det)
1977—Cowboys, 37-0 (Dal)
1981—Lions, 27-24 (Det)
1985—Lions, 26-21 (Det)
1986—Cowboys, 31-7 (Det)
1987—Lions, 27-17 (Det)
1991—Lions, 34-10 (Det)
*Lions, 38-6 (Det)
1992—Cowboys, 37-3 (Det)
1994—Lions, 20-17 (Dal) OT
2001—Lions, 15-10 (Det)
2002—Lions, 9-7 (Det)
2003—Cowboys, 38-7 (Det)
(RS Pts.—Cowboys 403, Lions 259)
(PS Pts.—Lions 38, Cowboys 11)
NFC Divisional Playoff

DALLAS vs. GREEN BAY
RS: Cowboys lead series, 10-9
PS: Cowboys lead series, 4-2
1960—Packers, 41-7 (GB)
1964—Packers, 45-21 (D)
1965—Packers, 13-3 (Mil)
1966—*Packers, 34-27 (D)
1967—*Packers, 21-17 (GB)
1968—Packers, 28-17 (D)
1970—Cowboys, 16-3 (D)
1972—Packers, 16-13 (Mil)
1975—Packers, 19-17 (D)
1978—Cowboys, 42-14 (Mil)
1980—Cowboys, 28-7 (Mil)
1982—**Cowboys, 37-26 (D)
1984—Cowboys, 20-6 (D)
1989—Packers, 31-13 (GB)
Packers, 20-10 (D)
1991—Cowboys, 20-17 (Mil)
1993—Cowboys, 36-14 (D)
***Cowboys, 27-17 (D)
1994—Cowboys, 42-31 (D)
***Cowboys, 35-9 (D)
1995—Cowboys, 34-24 (D)
****Cowboys, 38-27 (D)
1996—Cowboys, 21-6 (D)
1997—Packers, 45-17 (GB)
1999—Cowboys, 27-13 (D)
(RS Pts.—Cowboys 404, Packers 393)
(PS Pts.—Cowboys 181, Packers 134)
NFL Championship
**NFC Second-Round Playoff*
***NFC Divisional Playoff*
****NFC Championship*

DALLAS vs. HOUSTON
RS: Texans lead series, 1-0
2002—Texans, 19-10 (H)
(RS Pts.—Texans 19, Cowboys 10)

DALLAS vs. *INDIANAPOLIS
RS: Cowboys lead series, 7-5
PS: Colts lead series, 1-0
1960—Colts, 45-7 (D)
1967—Colts, 23-17 (B)
1969—Cowboys, 27-10 (D)
1970—**Colts, 16-13 (Miami)
1972—Cowboys, 21-0 (B)
1976—Cowboys, 30-27 (D)
1978—Cowboys, 38-0 (D)
1981—Cowboys, 37-13 (B)
1984—Cowboys, 22-3 (D)
1993—Cowboys, 27-3 (I)
1996—Colts, 25-24 (D)
1999—Colts, 34-24 (I)
2002—Colts, 20-3 (I)
(RS Pts.—Cowboys 277, Colts 203)
(PS Pts.—Colts 16, Cowboys 13)
Franchise in Baltimore prior to 1984
**Super Bowl V*

DALLAS VS. JACKSONVILLE
RS: Cowboys lead series, 2-1
1997—Cowboys, 26-22 (D)
2000—Jaguars, 23-17 (D) OT
2002—Cowboys, 21-19 (D)
(RS Pts.—Cowboys 64, Jaguars 64)

DALLAS vs. KANSAS CITY
RS: Cowboys lead series, 4-3
1970—Cowboys, 27-16 (KC)
1975—Chiefs, 34-31 (D)
1983—Cowboys, 41-21 (D)
1989—Chiefs, 36-28 (KC)
1992—Cowboys, 17-10 (D)
1995—Cowboys, 24-12 (D)
1998—Chiefs, 20-17 (KC)
(RS Pts.—Cowboys 185, Chiefs 149)

DALLAS vs. MIAMI
RS: Dolphins lead series, 7-3
PS: Cowboys lead series, 1-0
1971—*Cowboys, 24-3 (New Orleans)
1973—Dolphins, 14-7 (D)
1978—Dolphins, 23-16 (M)
1981—Cowboys, 28-27 (D)
1984—Dolphins, 28-21 (M)
1987—Dolphins, 20-14 (D)
1989—Dolphins, 17-14 (D)
1993—Dolphins, 16-14 (D)
1996—Cowboys, 29-10 (M)
1999—Cowboys, 20-0 (D)
2003—Dolphins, 40-21 (D)
(RS Pts.—Dolphins 195, Cowboys 184)
(PS Pts.—Cowboys 24, Dolphins 3)
Super Bowl VI

DALLAS vs. MINNESOTA
RS: Series tied, 9-9
PS: Cowboys lead series, 4-2
1961—Cowboys, 21-7 (D)
Cowboys, 28-0 (M)
1966—Cowboys, 28-17 (D)
1968—Cowboys, 20-7 (M)
1970—Vikings, 54-13 (M)
1971—*Cowboys, 20-12 (M)
1973—**Vikings, 27-10 (D)
1974—Vikings, 23-21 (D)
1975—*Cowboys, 17-14 (M)
1977—Cowboys, 16-10 (M) OT
**Cowboys, 23-6 (D)
1978—Vikings, 21-10 (D)
1979—Cowboys, 36-20 (M)
1982—Vikings, 31-27 (M)
1983—Cowboys, 37-24 (M)
1987—Vikings, 44-38 (D) OT
1988—Vikings, 43-3 (D)
1993—Cowboys, 37-20 (M)
1995—Cowboys, 23-17 (M) OT
1996—***Cowboys, 40-15 (D)
1998—Vikings, 46-36 (D)
1999—Vikings, 27-17 (M)
***Vikings, 27-10 (M)
2000—Vikings, 27-15 (D)
(RS Pts.—Vikings 438, Cowboys 426)
(PS Pts.—Cowboys 120, Vikings 101)
NFC Divisional Playoff
**NFC Championship*
***NFC First-Round Playoff*

DALLAS vs. NEW ENGLAND
RS: Cowboys lead series, 7-2
1971—Cowboys, 44-21 (D)
1975—Cowboys, 34-31 (NE)
1978—Cowboys, 17-10 (D)
1981—Cowboys, 35-21 (NE)
1984—Cowboys, 20-17 (D)
1987—Cowboys, 23-17 (NE) OT
1996—Cowboys, 12-6 (D)
1999—Patriots, 13-6 (NE)
2003—Patriots, 12-0 (NE)
(RS Pts.—Cowboys 191, Patriots 148)

DALLAS vs. NEW ORLEANS
RS: Cowboys lead series, 14-6
1967—Cowboys, 14-10 (D)
Cowboys, 27-10 (NO)
1968—Cowboys, 17-3 (NO)
1969—Cowboys, 21-17 (NO)
Cowboys, 33-17 (D)
1971—Saints, 24-14 (NO)
1973—Cowboys, 40-3 (D)
1976—Cowboys, 24-6 (NO)
1978—Cowboys, 27-7 (D)
1982—Cowboys, 21-7 (D)
1983—Cowboys, 21-20 (D)
1984—Cowboys, 30-27 (D) OT
1988—Saints, 20-17 (NO)
1989—Saints, 28-0 (NO)
1990—Cowboys, 17-13 (D)
1991—Cowboys, 23-14 (D)
1994—Cowboys, 24-16 (NO)
1998—Saints, 22-3 (NO)
1999—Saints, 31-24 (NO)
2003—Saints, 13-7 (NO)
(RS Pts.—Cowboys 404, Saints 308)

DALLAS vs. N.Y. GIANTS
RS: Cowboys lead series, 50-31-2
1960—Tie, 31-31 (NY)
1961—Giants, 31-10 (D)
Cowboys, 17-16 (NY)
1962—Giants, 41-10 (D)
Giants, 41-31 (NY)
1963—Giants, 37-21 (NY)
Giants, 34-27 (D)
1964—Tie, 13-13 (D)
Cowboys, 31-21 (NY)
1965—Cowboys, 31-2 (D)
Cowboys, 38-20 (NY)
1966—Cowboys, 52-7 (D)
Cowboys, 17-7 (NY)
1967—Cowboys, 38-24 (D)

1968—Giants, 27-21 (D)
Cowboys, 28-10 (NY)
1969—Cowboys, 25-3 (D)
1970—Cowboys, 28-10 (D)
Giants, 23-20 (NY)
1971—Cowboys, 20-13 (D)
Cowboys, 42-14 (NY)
1972—Cowboys, 23-14 (NY)
Giants, 23-3 (D)
1973—Cowboys, 45-28 (D)
Cowboys, 23-10 (New Haven)
1974—Giants, 14-6 (D)
Cowboys, 21-7 (New Haven)
1975—Cowboys, 13-7 (NY)
Cowboys, 14-3 (D)
1976—Cowboys, 24-14 (NY)
Cowboys, 9-3 (D)
1977—Cowboys, 41-21 (D)
Cowboys, 24-10 (NY)
1978—Cowboys, 34-24 (NY)
Cowboys, 24-3 (D)
1979—Cowboys, 16-14 (NY)
Cowboys, 28-7 (D)
1980—Cowboys, 24-3 (D)
Giants, 38-35 (NY)
1981—Cowboys, 18-10 (D)
Giants, 13-10 (NY) OT
1983—Cowboys, 28-13 (D)
Cowboys, 38-20 (NY)
1984—Giants, 28-7 (NY)
Giants, 19-7 (D)
1985—Cowboys, 30-29 (NY)
Cowboys, 28-21 (D)
1986—Cowboys, 31-28 (D)
Giants, 17-14 (NY)
1987—Cowboys, 16-14 (NY)
Cowboys, 33-24 (D)
1988—Giants, 12-10 (D)
Giants, 29-21 (NY)
1989—Giants, 30-13 (D)
Giants, 15-0 (NY)
1990—Giants, 28-7 (D)
Giants, 31-17 (NY)
1991—Cowboys, 21-16 (D)
Giants, 22-9 (NY)
1992—Cowboys, 34-28 (NY)
Cowboys, 30-3 (D)
1993—Cowboys, 31-9 (D)
Cowboys, 16-13 (NY) OT
1994—Cowboys, 38-10 (D)
Giants, 15-10 (NY)
1995—Cowboys, 35-0 (NY)
Cowboys, 21-20 (D)
1996—Cowboys, 27-0 (D)
Giants, 20-6 (NY)
1997—Giants, 20-17 (NY)
Giants, 20-7 (D)
1998—Cowboys, 31-7 (NY)
Cowboys, 16-6 (D)
1999—Giants, 13-10 (NY)
Cowboys, 26-18 (D)
2000—Giants, 19-14 (NY)
Giants, 17-13 (D)
2001—Giants, 27-24 (NY) OT
Cowboys, 20-13 (D)
2002—Giants, 21-17 (D)
Giants, 37-7 (NY)
2003—Cowboys, 35-32 (NY)
Cowboys, 19-3 (D)
(RS Pts.—Cowboys 1,820, Giants 1,458)

DALLAS vs. N.Y. JETS
RS: Cowboys lead series, 6-2
1971—Cowboys, 52-10 (D)
1975—Cowboys, 31-21 (NY)
1978—Cowboys, 30-7 (NY)
1987—Cowboys, 38-24 (NY)
1990—Jets, 24-9 (NY)
1993—Cowboys, 28-7 (NY)
1999—Jets, 22-21 (D)
2003—Cowboys, 17-6 (NY)
(RS Pts.—Cowboys 226, Jets 121)

DALLAS vs. *OAKLAND
RS: Raiders lead series, 5-3
1974—Raiders, 27-23 (O)
1980—Cowboys, 19-13 (O)
1983—Raiders, 40-38 (D)
1986—Raiders, 17-13 (D)
1992—Cowboys, 28-13 (LA)
1995—Cowboys, 34-21 (O)
1998—Raiders, 13-12 (D)
2001—Raiders, 28-21 (O)
(RS Pts.—Cowboys 188, Raiders 172)
Franchise in Los Angeles from 1982-1994

DALLAS vs. PHILADELPHIA
RS: Cowboys lead series, 49-37
PS: Cowboys lead series, 2-1
1960—Eagles, 27-25 (D)
1961—Eagles, 43-7 (D)
Eagles, 35-13 (P)
1962—Cowboys, 41-19 (D)
Eagles, 28-14 (P)
1963—Eagles, 24-21 (P)
Cowboys, 27-20 (D)
1964—Eagles, 17-14 (D)
Eagles, 24-14 (P)
1965—Eagles, 35-24 (D)
Cowboys, 21-19 (P)
1966—Cowboys, 56-7 (D)
Eagles, 24-23 (P)
1967—Eagles, 21-14 (P)
Cowboys, 38-17 (D)
1968—Cowboys, 45-13 (P)
Cowboys, 34-14 (D)
1969—Cowboys, 38-7 (P)
Cowboys, 49-14 (D)
1970—Cowboys, 17-7 (P)
Cowboys, 21-17 (D)
1971—Cowboys, 42-7 (P)
Cowboys, 20-7 (D)
1972—Cowboys, 28-6 (D)
Cowboys, 28-7 (P)
1973—Eagles, 30-16 (P)
Cowboys, 31-10 (D)
1974—Eagles, 13-10 (P)
Cowboys, 31-24 (D)
1975—Cowboys, 20-17 (P)
Cowboys, 27-17 (D)
1976—Cowboys, 27-7 (D)
Cowboys, 26-7 (P)
1977—Cowboys, 16-10 (P)
Cowboys, 24-14 (D)
1978—Cowboys, 14-7 (D)
Cowboys, 31-13 (P)
1979—Eagles, 31-21 (D)
Cowboys, 24-17 (P)
1980—Eagles, 17-10 (P)
Cowboys, 35-27 (D)
*Eagles, 20-7 (P)
1981—Cowboys, 17-14 (P)
Cowboys, 21-10 (D)
1982—Eagles, 24-20 (D)
1983—Cowboys, 37-7 (D)
Cowboys, 27-20 (P)
1984—Cowboys, 23-17 (D)
Cowboys, 26-10 (P)
1985—Eagles, 16-14 (P)
Cowboys, 34-17 (D)
1986—Cowboys, 17-14 (P)
Eagles, 23-21 (D)
1987—Cowboys, 41-22 (D)
Eagles, 37-20 (P)
1988—Eagles, 24-23 (P)
Eagles, 23-7 (D)
1989—Eagles, 27-0 (D)
Eagles, 20-10 (P)
1990—Eagles, 21-20 (D)
Eagles, 17-3 (P)
1991—Eagles, 24-0 (D)
Cowboys, 25-13 (P)
1992—Eagles, 31-7 (P)
Cowboys, 20-10 (D)
**Cowboys, 34-10 (D)
1993—Cowboys, 23-10 (P)
Cowboys, 23-17 (D)
1994—Cowboys, 24-13 (D)
Cowboys, 31-19 (P)
1995—Cowboys, 34-12 (D)
Eagles, 20-17 (P)
**Cowboys, 30-11 (D)
1996—Cowboys, 23-19 (P)
Eagles, 31-21 (D)
1997—Cowboys, 21-20 (D)
Eagles, 13-12 (P)
1998—Cowboys, 34-0 (P)
Cowboys, 13-9 (D)
1999—Eagles, 13-10 (P)
Cowboys, 20-10 (D)
2000—Eagles, 41-14 (D)
Eagles, 16-13 (P) OT
2001—Eagles, 40-18 (P)
Eagles, 36-3 (D)
2002—Eagles, 44-13 (P)
Eagles, 27-3 (D)
2003—Cowboys, 23-21 (D)
Eagles, 36-10 (P)
(RS Pts.—Cowboys 1,873, Eagles 1,628)
(PS Pts.—Cowboys 71, Eagles 41)
NFC Championship
***NFC Divisional Playoff*

DALLAS vs. PITTSBURGH
RS: Cowboys lead series, 14-11
PS: Steelers lead series, 2-1
1960—Steelers, 35-28 (D)
1961—Cowboys, 27-24 (D)
Steelers, 37-7 (P)
1962—Steelers, 30-28 (D)
Cowboys, 42-27 (P)
1963—Steelers, 27-21 (P)
Steelers, 24-19 (D)
1964—Steelers, 23-17 (P)
Cowboys, 17-14 (D)
1965—Steelers, 22-13 (P)
Cowboys, 24-17 (D)
1966—Cowboys, 52-21 (D)
Cowboys, 20-7 (P)
1967—Cowboys, 24-21 (P)
1968—Cowboys, 28-7 (D)
1969—Cowboys, 10-7 (P)
1972—Cowboys, 17-13 (D)
1975—*Steelers, 21-17 (Miami)

1977—Steelers, 28-13 (P)
1978—**Steelers, 35-31 (Miami)
1979—Steelers, 14-3 (P)
1982—Steelers, 36-28 (D)
1985—Cowboys, 27-13 (D)
1988—Steelers, 24-21 (P)
1991—Cowboys, 20-10 (D)
1994—Cowboys, 26-9 (P)
1995—***Cowboys, 27-17 (Tempe)
1997—Cowboys, 37-7 (P)
(RS Pts.—Cowboys 569, Steelers 497)
(PS Pts.—Cowboys 75, Steelers 73)
Super Bowl X
***Super Bowl XIII*
****Super Bowl XXX*

DALLAS vs. *ST. LOUIS
RS: Series tied, 9-9
PS: Series tied, 4-4
1960—Rams, 38-13 (D)
1962—Cowboys, 27-17 (LA)
1967—Rams, 35-13 (D)
1969—Rams, 24-23 (LA)
1971—Cowboys, 28-21 (D)
1973—Rams, 37-31 (LA)
**Cowboys, 27-16 (D)
1975—Cowboys, 18-7 (D)
***Cowboys, 37-7 (LA)
1976—**Rams, 14-12 (D)
1978—Rams, 27-14 (LA)
***Cowboys, 28-0 (LA)
1979—Cowboys, 30-6 (D)
**Rams, 21-19 (D)
1980—Rams, 38-14 (LA)
****Cowboys, 34-13 (D)
1981—Cowboys, 29-17 (D)
1983—****Rams, 24-17 (D)
1984—Cowboys, 20-13 (LA)
1985—**Rams, 20-0 (LA)
1986—Rams, 29-10 (LA)
1987—Cowboys, 29-21 (LA)
1989—Rams, 35-31 (D)
1990—Cowboys, 24-21 (LA)
1992—Rams, 27-23 (D)
2002—Cowboys, 13-10 (StL)
(RS Pts.—Rams 423, Cowboys 390)
(PS Pts.—Cowboys 174, Rams 115)
**Franchise in Los Angeles prior to 1995*
***NFC Divisional Playoff*
****NFC Championship*
*****NFC First-Round Playoff*

DALLAS vs. SAN DIEGO
RS: Cowboys lead series, 5-2
1972—Cowboys, 34-28 (SD)
1980—Cowboys, 42-31 (D)
1983—Chargers, 24-23 (SD)
1986—Cowboys, 24-21 (SD)
1990—Cowboys, 17-14 (D)
1995—Cowboys, 23-9 (SD)
2001—Chargers, 32-21 (D)
(RS Pts.—Cowboys 184, Chargers 159)

DALLAS vs. SAN FRANCISCO
RS: 49ers lead series, 14-8-1
PS: Cowboys lead series, 5-2
1960—49ers, 26-14 (D)
1963—49ers, 31-24 (SF)
1965—Cowboys, 39-31 (D)
1967—49ers, 24-16 (SF)
1969—Tie, 24-24 (D)
1970—*Cowboys, 17-10 (SF)
1971—*Cowboys, 14-3 (D)
1972—49ers, 31-10 (D)
**Cowboys, 30-28 (SF)
1974—Cowboys, 20-14 (D)
1977—Cowboys, 42-35 (SF)
1979—Cowboys, 21-13 (SF)
1980—Cowboys, 59-14 (D)
1981—49ers, 45-14 (SF)
*49ers, 28-27 (SF)
1983—49ers, 42-17 (SF)
1985—49ers, 31-16 (SF)
1989—49ers, 31-14 (D)
1990—49ers, 24-6 (D)
1992—*Cowboys, 30-20 (SF)
1993—Cowboys, 26-17 (D)
*Cowboys, 38-21 (D)
1994—49ers, 21-14 (SF)
*49ers, 38-28 (SF)
1995—49ers, 38-20 (D)
1996—Cowboys, 20-17 (SF) OT
1997—49ers, 17-10 (SF)
2000—49ers, 41-24 (D)
2001—Cowboys, 27-21 (D)
2002—49ers, 31-27 (D)
(RS Pts.—49ers 619, Cowboys 504)
(PS Pts.—Cowboys 184, 49ers 148)
**NFC Championship*
***NFC Divisional Playoff*

DALLAS vs. SEATTLE
RS: Cowboys lead series, 5-3
1976—Cowboys, 28-13 (S)
1980—Cowboys, 51-7 (D)
1983—Cowboys, 35-10 (S)
1986—Seahawks, 31-14 (D)
1992—Cowboys, 27-0 (D)
1998—Cowboys, 30-22 (D)
2001—Seahawks, 29-3 (S)
2002—Seahawks, 17-14 (D)
(RS Pts.—Cowboys 202, Seahawks 129)

DALLAS vs. TAMPA BAY
RS: Cowboys lead series, 6-3
PS: Cowboys lead series, 2-0
1977—Cowboys, 23-7 (D)
1980—Cowboys, 28-17 (D)
1981—*Cowboys, 38-0 (D)
1982—Cowboys, 14-9 (D)
**Cowboys, 30-17 (D)
1983—Cowboys, 27-24 (D) OT
1990—Cowboys, 14-10 (D)
Cowboys, 17-13 (TB)
2000—Buccaneers, 27-7 (TB)
2001—Buccaneers, 10-6 (D)
2003—Buccaneers, 16-0 (TB)
(RS Pts.—Cowboys 136, Buccaneers 133)
(PS Pts.—Cowboys 68, Buccaneers 17)
**NFC Divisional Playoff*
***NFC First-Round Playoff*

DALLAS vs. *TENNESSEE
RS: Cowboys lead series, 6-5
1970—Cowboys, 52-10 (D)
1974—Cowboys, 10-0 (H)
1979—Oilers, 30-24 (D)
1982—Cowboys, 37-7 (H)
1985—Cowboys, 17-10 (H)
1988—Oilers, 25-17 (D)
1991—Oilers, 26-23 (H) OT
1994—Cowboys, 20-17 (D)
1997—Oilers, 27-14 (D)
2000—Titans, 31-0 (T)
2002—Cowboys, 21-13 (D)
(RS Pts.—Cowboys 235, Titans 196)
**Franchise in Houston prior to 1997; known as Oilers prior to 1999*

DALLAS vs. WASHINGTON
RS: Cowboys lead series, 52-32-2
PS: Redskins lead series, 2-0
1960—Redskins, 26-14 (W)
1961—Tie, 28-28 (D)
Redskins, 34-24 (W)
1962—Tie, 35-35 (D)
Cowboys, 38-10 (W)
1963—Redskins, 21-17 (W)
Cowboys, 35-20 (D)
1964—Cowboys, 24-18 (D)
Redskins, 28-16 (W)
1965—Cowboys, 27-7 (D)
Redskins, 34-31 (W)
1966—Cowboys, 31-30 (W)
Redskins, 34-31 (D)
1967—Cowboys, 17-14 (W)
Redskins, 27-20 (D)
1968—Cowboys, 44-24 (W)
Cowboys, 29-20 (D)
1969—Cowboys, 41-28 (W)
Cowboys, 20-10 (D)
1970—Cowboys, 45-21 (W)
Cowboys, 34-0 (D)
1971—Redskins, 20-16 (D)
Cowboys, 13-0 (W)
1972—Redskins, 24-20 (W)
Cowboys, 34-24 (D)
*Redskins, 26-3 (W)
1973—Redskins, 14-7 (W)
Cowboys, 27-7 (D)
1974—Redskins, 28-21 (W)
Cowboys, 24-23 (D)
1975—Redskins, 30-24 (W) OT
Cowboys, 31-10 (D)
1976—Cowboys, 20-7 (W)
Redskins, 27-14 (D)
1977—Cowboys, 34-16 (D)
Cowboys, 14-7 (W)
1978—Redskins, 9-5 (W)
Cowboys, 37-10 (D)
1979—Redskins, 34-20 (W)
Cowboys, 35-34 (D)
1980—Cowboys, 17-3 (W)
Cowboys, 14-10 (D)
1981—Cowboys, 26-10 (W)
Cowboys, 24-10 (D)
1982—Cowboys, 24-10 (W)
*Redskins, 31-17 (W)
1983—Cowboys, 31-30 (W)
Redskins, 31-10 (D)
1984—Redskins, 34-14 (W)
Redskins, 30-28 (D)
1985—Cowboys, 44-14 (D)
Cowboys, 13-7 (W)
1986—Cowboys, 30-6 (D)
Redskins, 41-14 (W)
1987—Redskins, 13-7 (D)
Redskins, 24-20 (W)
1988—Redskins, 35-17 (D)
Cowboys, 24-17 (W)
1989—Redskins, 30-7 (D)
Cowboys, 13-3 (W)
1990—Redskins, 19-15 (W)
Cowboys, 27-17 (D)
1991—Redskins, 33-31 (D)
Cowboys, 24-21 (W)
1992—Cowboys, 23-10 (D)

Redskins, 20-17 (W)
1993—Redskins, 35-16 (W)
Cowboys, 38-3 (D)
1994—Cowboys, 34-7 (W)
Cowboys, 31-7 (D)
1995—Redskins, 27-23 (W)
Redskins, 24-17 (D)
1996—Cowboys, 21-10 (D)
Redskins, 37-10 (W)
1997—Redskins, 21-16 (W)
Cowboys, 17-14 (D)
1998—Cowboys, 31-10 (W)
Cowboys, 23-7 (D)
1999—Cowboys, 41-35 (W) OT
Cowboys, 38-20 (D)
2000—Cowboys, 27-21 (W)
Cowboys, 32-13 (D)
2001—Cowboys, 9-7 (D)
Cowboys, 20-14 (W)
2002—Cowboys, 27-20 (D)
Redskins, 20-14 (W)
2003—Cowboys, 21-14 (D)
Cowboys, 27-0 (W)
(RS Pts.—Cowboys 2,044, Redskins 1,637)
(PS Pts.—Redskins 57, Cowboys 20)
NFC Championship

DENVER vs. ARIZONA
RS: Broncos lead series, 6-0-1;
See Arizona vs. Denver
DENVER vs. ATLANTA
RS: Broncos lead series, 7-3
PS: Broncos lead series, 1-0;
See Atlanta vs. Denver
DENVER vs. BALTIMORE
RS: Ravens lead series, 3-1
PS: Ravens lead series, 1-0;
See Baltimore vs. Denver
DENVER vs. BUFFALO
RS: Bills lead series, 17-13-1
PS: Bills lead series, 1-0;
See Buffalo vs. Denver
DENVER vs. CAROLINA
RS: Broncos lead series, 1-0;
See Carolina vs. Denver
DENVER vs. CHICAGO
RS: Series tied, 6-6;
See Chicago vs. Denver
DENVER vs. CINCINNATI
RS: Broncos lead series, 15-7;
See Cincinnati vs. Denver
DENVER vs. CLEVELAND
RS: Broncos lead series, 15-5
PS: Broncos lead series, 3-0;
See Cleveland vs. Denver
DENVER vs. DALLAS
RS: Series tied, 4-4
PS: Cowboys lead series, 1-0;
See Dallas vs. Denver
DENVER vs. DETROIT
RS: Broncos lead series, 6-3
1971—Lions, 24-20 (Den)
1974—Broncos, 31-27 (Det)
1978—Lions, 17-14 (Det)
1981—Broncos, 27-21 (Den)
1984—Broncos, 28-7 (Det)
1987—Broncos, 34-0 (Den)
1990—Lions, 40-27 (Det)
1999—Broncos, 17-7 (Det)
2003—Broncos, 20-16 (Den)
(RS Pts.—Broncos 218, Lions 159)
DENVER vs. GREEN BAY
RS: Broncos lead series, 5-4-1
PS: Broncos lead series, 1-0
1971—Packers, 34-13 (Mil)
1975—Broncos, 23-13 (D)
1978—Broncos, 16-3 (D)
1984—Broncos, 17-14 (D)
1987—Tie, 17-17 (Mil) OT
1990—Broncos, 22-13 (D)
1993—Packers, 30-27 (GB)
1996—Packers, 41-6 (GB)
1997—*Broncos, 31-24 (San Diego)
1999—Broncos, 31-10 (D)
2003—Packers, 31-3 (GB)
(RS Pts.—Packers 206, Broncos 175)
(PS Pts.—Broncos 31, Packers 24)
Super Bowl XXXII
DENVER vs. *INDIANAPOLIS
RS: Broncos lead series, 10-4
PS: Colts lead series, 1-0
1974—Broncos, 17-6 (B)
1977—Broncos, 27-13 (D)
1978—Colts, 7-6 (B)
1981—Broncos, 28-10 (D)
1983—Broncos, 17-10 (B)
Broncos, 21-19 (D)
1985—Broncos, 15-10 (I)
1988—Colts, 55-23 (I)
1989—Broncos, 14-3 (D)
1990—Broncos, 27-17 (I)
1993—Broncos, 35-13 (D)
2001—Colts, 29-10 (I)
2002—Colts, 23-20 (D) OT
2003—Broncos, 31-17 (I)
**Colts, 41-10 (I)
(RS Pts.—Broncos 291, Colts 232)
(PS Pts.—Colts 41, Broncos 10)
**Franchise in Baltimore prior to 1984*
***AFC First-Round Playoff*
DENVER vs. JACKSONVILLE
RS: Broncos lead series, 2-1
PS: Series tied, 1-1
1995—Broncos, 31-23 (D)
1996—*Jaguars, 30-27 (D)
1997—**Broncos, 42-17 (D)
1998—Broncos, 37-24 (D)
1999—Jaguars, 27-24 (J)
(RS Pts.—Broncos 92, Jaguars 74)
(PS Pts.—Broncos 69, Jaguars 47)
**AFC Divisional Playoff*
***AFC First-Round Playoff*
DENVER vs. *KANSAS CITY
RS: Chiefs lead series, 49-38
PS: Broncos lead series, 1-0
1960—Texans, 17-14 (D)
Texans, 34-7 (Dal)
1961—Texans, 19-12 (D)
Texans, 49-21 (Dal)
1962—Texans, 24-3 (D)
Texans, 17-10 (Dal)
1963—Chiefs, 59-7 (D)
Chiefs, 52-21 (KC)
1964—Broncos, 33-27 (D)
Chiefs, 49-39 (KC)
1965—Chiefs, 31-23 (D)
Chiefs, 45-35 (KC)
1966—Chiefs, 37-10 (KC)
Chiefs, 56-10 (D)
1967—Chiefs, 52-9 (KC)
Chiefs, 38-24 (D)
1968—Chiefs, 34-2 (KC)
Chiefs, 30-7 (D)
1969—Chiefs, 26-13 (D)
Chiefs, 31-17 (KC)
1970—Broncos, 26-13 (D)
Chiefs, 16-0 (KC)
1971—Chiefs, 16-3 (D)
Chiefs, 28-10 (KC)
1972—Chiefs, 45-24 (D)
Chiefs, 24-21 (KC)
1973—Chiefs, 16-14 (KC)
Broncos, 14-10 (D)
1974—Broncos, 17-14 (KC)
Chiefs, 42-34 (D)
1975—Broncos, 37-33 (D)
Chiefs, 26-13 (KC)
1976—Broncos, 35-26 (KC)
Broncos, 17-16 (D)
1977—Broncos, 23-7 (D)
Broncos, 14-7 (KC)
1978—Broncos, 23-17 (KC) OT
Broncos, 24-3 (D)
1979—Broncos, 24-10 (KC)
Broncos, 20-3 (D)
1980—Chiefs, 23-17 (D)
Chiefs, 31-14 (KC)
1981—Chiefs, 28-14 (KC)
Broncos, 16-13 (D)
1982—Chiefs, 37-16 (D)
1983—Broncos, 27-24 (D)
Chiefs, 48-17 (KC)
1984—Broncos, 21-0 (D)
Chiefs, 16-13 (KC)
1985—Broncos, 30-10 (KC)
Broncos, 14-13 (D)
1986—Broncos, 38-17 (D)
Chiefs, 37-10 (KC)
1987—Broncos, 26-17 (KC)
Broncos, 20-17 (D)
1988—Chiefs, 20-13 (KC)
Broncos, 17-11 (D)
1989—Broncos, 34-20 (D)
Broncos, 16-13 (KC)
1990—Broncos, 24-23 (D)
Chiefs, 31-20 (KC)
1991—Broncos, 19-16 (D)
Broncos, 24-20 (KC)
1992—Broncos, 20-19 (D)
Chiefs, 42-20 (KC)
1993—Chiefs, 15-7 (KC)
Broncos, 27-21 (D)
1994—Chiefs, 31-28 (D)
Broncos, 20-17 (KC) OT
1995—Chiefs, 21-7 (D)
Chiefs, 20-17 (KC)
1996—Chiefs, 17-14 (KC)
Broncos, 34-7 (D)
1997—Broncos, 19-3 (D)
Chiefs, 24-22 (KC)
**Broncos, 14-10 (KC)
1998—Broncos, 30-7 (KC)
Broncos, 35-31 (D)
1999—Chiefs, 26-10 (KC)
Chiefs, 16-10 (D)
2000—Chiefs, 23-22 (D)
Chiefs, 20-7 (KC)
2001—Broncos, 20-6 (D)
Chiefs, 26-23 (KC) OT
2002—Broncos, 37-34 (KC) OT

Broncos, 31-24 (D)
2003—Chiefs, 24-23 (KC)
Broncos, 45-27 (D)
(RS Pts.—Chiefs 2,085, Broncos 1,698)
(PS Pts.—Broncos 14, Chiefs 10)
Franchise in Dallas prior to 1963 and known as Texans
***AFC Divisional Playoff*

DENVER vs. MIAMI
RS: Dolphins lead series, 9-2-1
PS: Broncos lead series, 1-0
1966—Dolphins, 24-7 (M)
Broncos, 17-7 (D)
1967—Dolphins, 35-21 (M)
1968—Broncos, 21-14 (D)
1969—Dolphins, 27-24 (M)
1971—Tie, 10-10 (D)
1975—Dolphins, 14-13 (M)
1985—Dolphins, 30-26 (D)
1998—Dolphins, 31-21 (M)
*Broncos, 38-3 (D)
1999—Dolphins, 38-21 (D)
2001—Dolphins, 21-10 (M)
2002—Dolphins, 24-22 (D)
(RS Pts.—Dolphins 275, Broncos 213)
(PS Pts.—Broncos 38, Dolphins 3)
**AFC Divisonal Playoff*

DENVER vs. MINNESOTA
RS: Vikings lead series, 7-4
1972—Vikings, 23-20 (D)
1978—Vikings, 12-9 (M) OT
1981—Broncos, 19-17 (D)
1984—Broncos, 42-21 (D)
1987—Vikings, 34-27 (M)
1990—Vikings, 27-22 (M)
1991—Broncos, 13-6 (M)
1993—Vikings, 26-23 (D)
1996—Broncos, 21-17 (M)
1999—Vikings, 23-20 (D)
2003—Vikings, 28-20 (M)
(RS Pts.—Broncos 236, Vikings 234)

DENVER vs. *NEW ENGLAND
RS: Broncos lead series, 22-15
PS: Broncos lead series, 1-0
1960—Broncos, 13-10 (B)
Broncos, 31-24 (D)
1961—Patriots, 45-17 (B)
Patriots, 28-24 (D)
1962—Patriots, 41-16 (B)
Patriots, 33-29 (D)
1963—Broncos, 14-10 (D)
Patriots, 40-21 (B)
1964—Patriots, 39-10 (D)
Patriots, 12-7 (B)
1965—Broncos, 27-10 (B)
Patriots, 28-20 (D)
1966—Patriots, 24-10 (D)
Broncos, 17-10 (B)
1967—Broncos, 26-21 (D)
1968—Patriots, 20-17 (D)
Broncos, 35-14 (B)
1969—Broncos, 35-7 (D)
1972—Broncos, 45-21 (D)
1976—Patriots, 38-14 (NE)
1979—Broncos, 45-10 (D)
1980—Patriots, 23-14 (NE)
1984—Broncos, 26-19 (D)
1986—Broncos, 27-20 (D)
**Broncos, 22-17 (D)
1987—Broncos, 31-20 (D)
1988—Broncos, 21-10 (D)
1991—Broncos, 9-6 (NE)
Broncos, 20-3 (D)
1995—Broncos, 37-3 (NE)
1996—Broncos, 34-8 (NE)
1997—Broncos, 34-13 (D)
1998—Broncos, 27-21 (D)
1999—Patriots, 24-23 (NE)
2000—Patriots, 28-19 (D)
2001—Broncos, 31-20 (D)
2002—Broncos, 24-16 (NE)
2003—Patriots, 30-26 (D)
(RS Pts.—Broncos 876, Patriots 749)
(PS Pts.—Broncos 22, Patriots 17)
**Franchise in Boston prior to 1971*
***AFC Divisional Playoff*

DENVER vs. NEW ORLEANS
RS: Broncos lead series, 5-2
1970—Broncos, 31-6 (NO)
1974—Broncos, 33-17 (D)
1979—Broncos, 10-3 (D)
1985—Broncos, 34-23 (D)
1988—Saints, 42-0 (NO)
1994—Saints, 30-28 (D)
2000—Broncos, 38-23 (NO)
(RS Pts.—Broncos 174, Saints 144)

DENVER vs. N.Y. GIANTS
RS: Series tied, 4-4
PS: Giants lead series, 1-0
1972—Giants, 29-17 (NY)
1976—Broncos, 14-13 (D)
1980—Broncos, 14-9 (NY)
1986—Giants, 19-16 (NY)
*Giants, 39-20 (Pasadena)
1989—Giants, 14-7 (D)
1992—Broncos, 27-13 (D)
1998—Giants, 20-16 (NY)
2001—Broncos, 31-20 (D)
(RS Pts.—Broncos 142, Giants 137)
(PS Pts.—Giants 39, Broncos 20)
**Super Bowl XXI*

DENVER vs. *N.Y. JETS
RS: Series tied, 14-14-1
PS: Broncos lead series, 1-0
1960—Titans, 28-24 (NY)
Titans, 30-27 (D)
1961—Titans, 35-28 (NY)
Broncos, 27-10 (D)
1962—Broncos, 32-10 (NY)
Titans, 46-45 (D)
1963—Tie, 35-35 (NY)
Jets, 14-9 (D)
1964—Jets, 30-6 (NY)
Broncos, 20-16 (D)
1965—Broncos, 16-13 (D)
Jets, 45-10 (NY)
1966—Jets, 16-7 (D)
1967—Jets, 38-24 (D)
Broncos, 33-24 (NY)
1968—Broncos, 21-13 (NY)
1969—Broncos, 21-19 (D)
1973—Broncos, 40-28 (NY)
1976—Broncos, 46-3 (D)
1978—Jets, 31-28 (D)
1980—Broncos, 31-24 (D)
1986—Jets, 22-10 (NY)
1992—Broncos, 27-16 (D)
1993—Broncos, 26-20 (NY)
1994—Jets, 25-22 (NY) OT
1996—Broncos, 31-6 (D)
1998—**Broncos, 23-10 (D)
1999—Jets, 21-13 (D)
2000—Broncos, 30-23 (NY)
2002—Jets, 19-13 (NY)
(RS Pts.—Broncos 702, Jets 660)
(PS Pts.—Broncos 23, Jets 10)
**Jets known as Titans prior to 1963*
***AFC Championship*

DENVER vs. *OAKLAND
RS: Raiders lead series, 52-33-2
PS: Series tied, 1-1
1960—Broncos, 31-14 (D)
Raiders, 48-10 (O)
1961—Raiders, 33-19 (O)
Broncos, 27-24 (D)
1962—Broncos, 44-7 (D)
Broncos, 23-6 (O)
1963—Raiders, 26-10 (D)
Raiders, 35-31 (O)
1964—Raiders, 40-7 (O)
Tie, 20-20 (D)
1965—Raiders, 28-20 (D)
Raiders, 24-13 (O)
1966—Raiders, 17-3 (D)
Raiders, 28-10 (O)
1967—Raiders, 51-0 (O)
Raiders, 21-17 (D)
1968—Raiders, 43-7 (D)
Raiders, 33-27 (O)
1969—Raiders, 24-14 (D)
Raiders, 41-10 (O)
1970—Raiders, 35-23 (O)
Raiders, 24-19 (D)
1971—Raiders, 27-16 (D)
Raiders, 21-13 (O)
1972—Broncos, 30-23 (O)
Raiders, 37-20 (D)
1973—Tie, 23-23 (D)
Raiders, 21-17 (O)
1974—Raiders, 28-17 (D)
Broncos, 20-17 (O)
1975—Raiders, 42-17 (D)
Raiders, 17-10 (O)
1976—Raiders, 17-10 (D)
Raiders, 19-6 (O)
1977—Broncos, 30-7 (O)
Raiders, 24-14 (D)
**Broncos, 20-17 (D)
1978—Broncos, 14-6 (D)
Broncos, 21-6 (O)
1979—Raiders, 27-3 (O)
Raiders, 14-10 (D)
1980—Raiders, 9-3 (O)
Raiders, 24-21 (D)
1981—Broncos, 9-7 (D)
Broncos, 17-0 (O)
1982—Raiders, 27-10 (LA)
1983—Raiders, 22-7 (D)
Raiders, 22-20 (LA)
1984—Broncos, 16-13 (D)
Broncos, 22-19 (LA) OT
1985—Raiders, 31-28 (LA) OT
Raiders, 17-14 (D) OT
1986—Broncos, 38-36 (D)
Broncos, 21-10 (LA)
1987—Broncos, 30-14 (D)
Broncos, 23-17 (LA)
1988—Raiders, 30-27 (D) OT
Raiders, 21-20 (LA)
1989—Broncos, 31-21 (D)

Raiders, 16-13 (LA) OT
1990—Raiders, 14-9 (LA)
Raiders, 23-20 (D)
1991—Raiders, 16-13 (LA)
Raiders, 17-16 (D)
1992—Broncos, 17-13 (D)
Raiders, 24-0 (LA)
1993—Raiders, 23-20 (D)
Raiders, 33-30 (LA) OT
***Raiders, 42-24 (LA)
1994—Raiders, 48-16 (D)
Raiders, 23-13 (LA)
1995—Broncos, 27-0 (D)
Broncos, 31-28 (O)
1996—Broncos, 22-21 (O)
Broncos, 24-19 (D)
1997—Raiders, 28-25 (O)
Broncos, 31-3 (D)
1998—Broncos, 34-17 (O)
Broncos, 40-14 (D)
1999—Broncos, 16-13 (O)
Broncos, 27-21 (D) OT
2000—Broncos, 33-24 (O)
Broncos, 27-24 (D)
2001—Raiders, 38-28 (O)
Broncos, 23-17 (D)
2002—Raiders, 34-10 (D)
Raiders, 28-16 (O)
2003—Broncos, 31-10 (D)
Broncos, 22-8 (O)
(RS Pts.—Raiders 1,935, Broncos 1,667)
(PS Pts.—Raiders 59, Broncos 44)
Franchise in Los Angeles from 1982-1994
***AFC Championship*
****AFC First-Round Playoff*

DENVER vs. PHILADELPHIA
RS: Eagles lead series, 6-3
1971—Eagles, 17-16 (P)
1975—Broncos, 25-10 (D)
1980—Eagles, 27-6 (P)
1983—Eagles, 13-10 (D)
1986—Broncos, 33-7 (P)
1989—Eagles, 28-24 (D)
1992—Eagles, 30-0 (P)
1995—Eagles, 31-13 (P)
1998—Broncos, 41-16 (D)
(RS Pts.—Eagles 179, Broncos 168)

DENVER vs. PITTSBURGH
RS: Broncos lead series, 11-6-1
PS: Broncos lead series, 3-2
1970—Broncos, 16-13 (D)
1971—Broncos, 22-10 (P)
1973—Broncos, 23-13 (P)
1974—Tie, 35-35 (D) OT
1975—Steelers, 20-9 (P)
1977—Broncos, 21-7 (D)
*Broncos, 34-21 (D)
1978—Steelers, 21-17 (D)
*Steelers, 33-10 (P)
1979—Steelers, 42-7 (P)
1983—Broncos, 14-10 (P)
1984—*Steelers, 24-17 (D)
1985—Broncos, 31-23 (P)
1986—Broncos, 21-10 (P)
1988—Steelers, 39-21 (P)
1989—Broncos, 34-7 (D)
*Broncos, 24-23 (D)
1990—Steelers, 34-17 (D)
1991—Broncos, 20-13 (D)
1993—Broncos, 37-13 (D)
1997—Steelers, 35-24 (P)
**Broncos, 24-21 (P)
2003—Broncos, 17-14 (D)
(RS Pts.—Broncos 386, Steelers 359)
(PS Pts.—Steelers 122, Broncos 109)
**AFC Divisional Playoff*
***AFC Championship*

DENVER vs. *ST. LOUIS
RS: Series tied, 5-5
1972—Broncos, 16-10 (LA)
1974—Rams, 17-10 (D)
1979—Rams, 13-9 (D)
1982—Broncos, 27-24 (LA)
1985—Rams, 20-16 (LA)
1988—Broncos, 35-24 (D)
1994—Rams, 27-21 (LA)
1997—Broncos, 35-14 (D)
2000—Rams, 41-36 (StL)
2002—Broncos, 23-16 (D)
(RS Pts.—Broncos 228, Rams 206)
**Franchise in Los Angeles prior to 1995*

DENVER vs. *SAN DIEGO
RS: Broncos lead series, 49-38-1
1960—Chargers, 23-19 (D)
Chargers, 41-33 (LA)
1961—Chargers, 37-0 (SD)
Chargers, 19-16 (D)
1962—Broncos, 30-21 (D)
Broncos, 23-20 (SD)
1963—Broncos, 50-34 (D)
Chargers, 58-20 (SD)
1964—Chargers, 42-14 (SD)
Chargers, 31-20 (D)
1965—Chargers, 34-31 (SD)
Chargers, 33-21 (D)
1966—Chargers, 24-17 (SD)
Broncos, 20-17 (D)
1967—Chargers, 38-21 (D)
Chargers, 24-20 (SD)
1968—Chargers, 55-24 (SD)
Chargers, 47-23 (D)
1969—Broncos, 13-0 (D)
Chargers, 45-24 (SD)
1970—Chargers, 24-21 (SD)
Tie, 17-17 (D)
1971—Broncos, 20-16 (D)
Chargers, 45-17 (SD)
1972—Chargers, 37-14 (SD)
Broncos, 38-13 (D)
1973—Broncos, 30-19 (D)
Broncos, 42-28 (SD)
1974—Broncos, 27-7 (D)
Chargers, 17-0 (SD)
1975—Broncos, 27-17 (SD)
Broncos, 13-10 (D) OT
1976—Broncos, 26-0 (D)
Broncos, 17-0 (SD)
1977—Broncos, 17-14 (SD)
Broncos, 17-9 (D)
1978—Broncos, 27-14 (D)
Chargers, 23-0 (SD)
1979—Broncos, 7-0 (D)
Chargers, 17-7 (SD)
1980—Chargers, 30-13 (D)
Broncos, 20-13 (SD)
1981—Broncos, 42-24 (D)
Chargers, 34-17 (SD)
1982—Chargers, 23-3 (D)
Chargers, 30-20 (SD)
1983—Broncos, 14-6 (D)
Chargers, 31-7 (SD)
1984—Broncos, 16-13 (SD)
Broncos, 16-13 (D)
1985—Chargers, 30-10 (SD)
Broncos, 30-24 (D) OT
1986—Broncos, 31-14 (SD)
Chargers, 9-3 (D)
1987—Broncos, 31-17 (SD)
Broncos, 24-0 (D)
1988—Broncos, 34-3 (D)
Broncos, 12-0 (SD)
1989—Broncos, 16-10 (D)
Chargers, 19-16 (SD)
1990—Chargers, 19-7 (SD)
Broncos, 20-10 (D)
1991—Broncos, 27-19 (D)
Broncos, 17-14 (SD)
1992—Broncos, 21-13 (D)
Chargers, 24-21 (SD)
1993—Broncos, 34-17 (D)
Chargers, 13-10 (SD)
1994—Chargers, 37-34 (D)
Broncos, 20-15 (SD)
1995—Chargers, 17-6 (SD)
Broncos, 30-27 (D)
1996—Broncos, 28-17 (D)
Chargers, 16-10 (SD)
1997—Broncos, 38-28 (SD)
Broncos, 38-3 (D)
1998—Broncos, 27-10 (D)
Broncos, 31-16 (SD)
1999—Broncos, 33-17 (SD)
Chargers, 12-6 (D)
2000—Broncos, 21-7 (SD)
Broncos, 38-37 (D)
2001—Chargers, 27-10 (SD)
Broncos, 26-16 (D)
2002—Broncos, 26-9 (D)
Chargers, 30-27 (SD) OT
2003—Broncos, 37-13 (SD)
Broncos, 37-8 (D)
(RS Pts.—Broncos 1,878, Chargers 1,806)
**Franchise in Los Angeles prior to 1961*

DENVER vs. SAN FRANCISCO
RS: Broncos lead series, 6-4
PS: 49ers lead series, 1-0
1970—49ers, 19-14 (SF)
1973—49ers, 36-34 (D)
1979—Broncos, 38-28 (SF)
1982—Broncos, 24-21 (D)
1985—Broncos, 17-16 (D)
1988—Broncos, 16-13 (SF) OT
1989—*49ers, 55-10 (New Orleans)
1994—49ers, 42-19 (SF)
1997—49ers, 34-17 (SF)
2000—Broncos, 38-9 (D)
2002—Broncos, 24-14 (SF)
(RS Pts.—Broncos 241, 49ers 232)
(PS Pts.—49ers 55, Broncos 10)
**Super Bowl XXIV*

DENVER vs. SEATTLE
RS: Broncos lead series, 33-17
PS: Seahawks lead series, 1-0
1977—Broncos, 24-13 (S)
1978—Broncos, 28-7 (D)
Broncos, 20-17 (S) OT
1979—Broncos, 37-34 (D)
Seahawks, 28-23 (S)
1980—Broncos, 36-20 (D)
Broncos, 25-17 (S)

1981—Seahawks, 13-10 (S)
Broncos, 23-13 (D)
1982—Seahawks, 17-10 (D)
Seahawks, 13-11 (S)
1983—Seahawks, 27-19 (S)
Broncos, 38-27 (D)
*Seahawks, 31-7 (S)
1984—Seahawks, 27-24 (D)
Broncos, 31-14 (S)
1985—Broncos, 13-10 (D) OT
Broncos, 27-24 (S)
1986—Broncos, 20-13 (D)
Seahawks, 41-16 (S)
1987—Broncos, 40-17 (D)
Seahawks, 28-21 (S)
1988—Seahawks, 21-14 (D)
Seahawks, 42-14 (S)
1989—Broncos, 24-21 (S) OT
Broncos, 41-14 (D)
1990—Broncos, 34-31 (D) OT
Seahawks, 17-12 (S)
1991—Broncos, 16-10 (D)
Seahawks, 13-10 (S)
1992—Seahawks, 16-13 (S) OT
Broncos, 10-6 (D)
1993—Broncos, 28-17 (D)
Broncos, 17-9 (S)
1994—Broncos, 16-9 (S)
Broncos, 17-10 (D)
1995—Seahawks, 27-10 (S)
Seahawks, 31-27 (D)
1996—Broncos, 30-20 (S)
Broncos, 34-7 (D)
1997—Broncos, 35-14 (S)
Broncos, 30-27 (D)
1998—Broncos, 21-16 (S)
Broncos, 28-21 (D)
1999—Seahawks, 20-17 (S)
Broncos, 36-30 (D) OT
2000—Broncos, 38-31 (S)
Broncos, 31-24 (D)
2001—Seahawks, 34-21 (S)
Broncos, 20-7 (D)
2002—Broncos, 31-9 (S)
(RS Pts.—Broncos 1,171, Seahawks 974)
(PS Pts.—Seahawks 31, Broncos 7)
AFC First-Round Playoff

DENVER vs. TAMPA BAY
RS: Broncos lead series, 3-2
1976—Broncos, 48-13 (D)
1981—Broncos, 24-7 (TB)
1993—Buccaneers, 17-10 (D)
1996—Broncos, 27-23 (D)
1999—Buccaneers, 13-10 (TB)
(RS Pts.—Broncos 119, Buccaneers 73)

DENVER vs. *TENNESSEE
RS: Titans lead series, 20-11-1
PS: Broncos lead series, 2-1
1960—Oilers, 45-25 (D)
Oilers, 20-10 (H)
1961—Oilers, 55-14 (D)
Oilers, 45-14 (H)
1962—Broncos, 20-10 (D)
Oilers, 34-17 (H)
1963—Oilers, 20-14 (H)
Oilers, 33-24 (D)
1964—Oilers, 38-17 (D)
Oilers, 34-15 (H)
1965—Broncos, 28-17 (D)
Broncos, 31-21 (H)
1966—Oilers, 45-7 (H)
Broncos, 40-38 (D)
1967—Oilers, 10-6 (H)
Oilers, 20-18 (D)
1968—Oilers, 38-17 (H)
1969—Oilers, 24-21 (H)
Tie, 20-20 (D)
1970—Oilers, 31-21 (H)
1972—Broncos, 30-17 (D)
1973—Broncos, 48-20 (H)
1974—Broncos, 37-14 (D)
1976—Oilers, 17-3 (H)
1977—Broncos, 24-14 (H)
1979—**Oilers, 13-7 (H)
1980—Oilers, 20-16 (D)
1983—Broncos, 26-14 (H)
1985—Broncos, 31-20 (D)
1987—Oilers, 40-10 (D)
***Broncos, 34-10 (D)
1991—Oilers, 42-14 (H)
***Broncos, 26-24 (D)
1992—Broncos, 27-21 (D)
1995—Oilers, 42-33 (H)
(RS Pts.—Titans 879, Broncos 678)
(PS Pts.—Broncos 67, Titans 47)
Franchise in Houston prior to 1997; known as the Oilers prior to 1999
***AFC First-Round Playoff*
****AFC Divisional Playoff*

DENVER vs. WASHINGTON
RS: Broncos lead series, 5-4
PS: Redskins lead series, 1-0
1970—Redskins, 19-3 (D)
1974—Redskins, 30-3 (W)
1980—Broncos, 20-17 (D)
1986—Broncos, 31-30 (D)
1987—*Redskins, 42-10 (San Diego)
1989—Broncos, 14-10 (W)
1992—Redskins, 34-3 (W)
1995—Broncos, 38-31 (D)
1998—Broncos, 38-16 (W)
2001—Redskins, 17-10 (D)
(RS Pts.—Redskins 204, Broncos 160)
(PS Pts.—Redskins 42, Broncos 10)
Super Bowl XXII

DETROIT vs. ARIZONA
RS: Lions lead series, 29-21-5;
See Arizona vs. Detroit

DETROIT vs. ATLANTA
RS: Lions lead series, 21-8;
See Atlanta vs. Detroit

DETROIT vs. BALTIMORE
RS: Ravens lead series, 1-0;
See Baltimore vs. Detroit

DETROIT vs. BUFFALO
RS: Series tied, 3-3-1;
See Buffalo vs. Detroit

DETROIT vs. CAROLINA
RS: Panthers lead series, 2-1;
See Carolina vs. Detroit

DETROIT vs. CHICAGO
RS: Bears lead series, 83-60-5;
See Chicago vs. Detroit

DETROIT vs. CINCINNATI
RS: Bengals lead series, 5-3;
See Cincinnati vs. Detroit

DETROIT vs. CLEVELAND
RS: Lions lead series, 12-4
PS: Lions lead series, 3-1;
See Cleveland vs. Detroit

DETROIT vs. DALLAS
RS: Series tied, 8-8
PS: Series tied, 1-1;
See Dallas vs. Detroit

DETROIT vs. DENVER
RS: Broncos lead series, 6-3;
See Denver vs. Detroit

***DETROIT vs. GREEN BAY**
RS: Packers lead series, 77-63-7
PS: Packers lead series, 2-0
1930—Packers, 47-13 (GB)
Tie, 6-6 (P)
1932—Packers, 15-10 (GB)
Spartans, 19-0 (P)
1933—Packers, 17-0 (GB)
Spartans, 7-0 (P)
1934—Lions, 3-0 (GB)
Packers, 3-0 (D)
1935—Packers, 13-9 (Mil)
Packers, 31-7 (GB)
Lions, 20-10 (D)
1936—Packers, 20-18 (GB)
Packers, 26-17 (D)
1937—Packers, 26-6 (GB)
Packers, 14-13 (D)
1938—Lions, 17-7 (GB)
Packers, 28-7 (D)
1939—Packers, 26-7 (GB)
Packers, 12-7 (D)
1940—Lions, 23-14 (GB)
Packers, 50-7 (D)
1941—Packers, 23-0 (GB)
Packers, 24-7 (D)
1942—Packers, 38-7 (Mil)
Packers, 28-7 (D)
1943—Packers, 35-14 (GB)
Packers, 27-6 (D)
1944—Packers, 27-6 (Mil)
Packers, 14-0 (D)
1945—Packers, 57-21 (Mil)
Lions, 14-3 (D)
1946—Packers, 10-7 (Mil)
Packers, 9-0 (D)
1947—Packers, 34-17 (GB)
Packers, 35-14 (D)
1948—Packers, 33-21 (GB)
Lions, 24-20 (D)
1949—Packers, 16-14 (Mil)
Lions, 21-7 (D)
1950—Lions, 45-7 (GB)
Lions, 24-21 (D)
1951—Lions, 24-17 (GB)
Lions, 52-35 (D)
1952—Lions, 52-17 (GB)
Lions, 48-24 (D)
1953—Lions, 14-7 (GB)
Lions, 34-15 (D)
1954—Lions, 21-17 (GB)
Lions, 28-24 (D)
1955—Packers, 20-17 (GB)
Lions, 24-10 (D)
1956—Lions, 20-16 (GB)
Packers, 24-20 (D)
1957—Lions, 24-14 (GB)
Lions, 18-6 (D)
1958—Tie, 13-13 (GB)
Lions, 24-14 (D)
1959—Packers, 28-10 (GB)
Packers, 24-17 (D)

1960—Packers, 28-9 (GB)
Lions, 23-10 (D)
1961—Lions, 17-13 (Mil)
Packers, 17-9 (D)
1962—Packers, 9-7 (GB)
Lions, 26-14 (D)
1963—Packers, 31-10 (Mil)
Tie, 13-13 (D)
1964—Packers, 14-10 (D)
Packers, 30-7 (GB)
1965—Packers, 31-21 (D)
Lions, 12-7 (GB)
1966—Packers, 23-14 (GB)
Packers, 31-7 (D)
1967—Tie, 17-17 (GB)
Packers, 27-17 (D)
1968—Lions, 23-17 (GB)
Tie, 14-14 (D)
1969—Packers, 28-17 (D)
Lions, 16-10 (GB)
1970—Lions, 40-0 (GB)
Lions, 20-0 (D)
1971—Lions, 31-28 (D)
Tie, 14-14 (Mil)
1972—Packers, 24-23 (D)
Packers, 33-7 (GB)
1973—Tie, 13-13 (GB)
Lions, 34-0 (D)
1974—Packers, 21-19 (Mil)
Lions, 19-17 (D)
1975—Lions, 30-16 (Mil)
Lions, 13-10 (D)
1976—Packers, 24-14 (GB)
Lions, 27-6 (D)
1977—Lions, 10-6 (D)
Packers, 10-9 (GB)
1978—Packers, 13-7 (D)
Packers, 35-14 (Mil)
1979—Packers, 24-16 (Mil)
Packers, 18-13 (D)
1980—Lions, 29-7 (Mil)
Lions, 24-3 (D)
1981—Lions, 31-27 (D)
Packers, 31-17 (GB)
1982—Lions, 30-10 (GB)
Lions, 27-24 (D)
1983—Lions, 38-14 (D)
Lions, 23-20 (Mil) OT
1984—Packers, 41-9 (GB)
Lions, 31-28 (D)
1985—Packers, 43-10 (GB)
Packers, 26-23 (D)
1986—Lions, 21-14 (GB)
Packers, 44-40 (D)
1987—Lions, 19-16 (GB) OT
Packers, 34-33 (D)
1988—Lions, 19-9 (Mil)
Lions, 30-14 (D)
1989—Packers, 23-20 (Mil) OT
Lions, 31-22 (D)
1990—Packers, 24-21 (D)
Lions, 24-17 (GB)
1991—Lions, 23-14 (D)
Lions, 21-17 (GB)
1992—Packers, 27-13 (D)
Packers, 38-10 (Mil)
1993—Packers, 26-17 (Mil)
Lions, 30-20 (D)
**Packers, 28-24 (D)
1994—Packers, 38-30 (Mil)
Lions, 34-31 (D)
**Packers, 16-12 (GB)
1995—Packers, 30-21 (GB)
Lions, 24-16 (D)
1996—Packers, 28-18 (GB)
Packers, 31-3 (D)
1997—Lions, 26-15 (D)
Packers, 20-10 (GB)
1998—Packers, 38-19 (GB)
Lions, 27-20 (D)
1999—Lions, 23-15 (D)
Packers, 26-17 (GB)
2000—Lions, 31-24 (D)
Packers, 26-13 (GB)
2001—Packers, 28-6 (GB)
Packers, 29-27 (D)
2002—Packers, 37-31 (D)
Packers, 40-14 (GB)
2003—Packers, 31-6 (GB)
Lions, 22-14 (D)
(RS Pts.—Packers 3,024, Lions 2,673)
(PS Pts.—Packers 44, Lions 36)
Franchise in Portsmouth prior to 1934 and known as the Spartans
***NFC First-Round Playoff*

DETROIT vs. *INDIANAPOLIS
RS: Series tied, 18-18-2
1953—Lions, 27-17 (B)
Lions, 17-7 (D)
1954—Lions, 35-0 (D)
Lions, 27-3 (B)
1955—Colts, 28-13 (B)
Lions, 24-14 (D)
1956—Lions, 31-14 (B)
Lions, 27-3 (D)
1957—Colts, 34-14 (B)
Lions, 31-27 (D)
1958—Colts, 28-15 (B)
Colts, 40-14 (D)
1959—Colts, 21-9 (B)
Colts, 31-24 (D)
1960—Lions, 30-17 (D)
Lions, 20-15 (B)
1961—Lions, 16-15 (B)
Colts, 17-14 (D)
1962—Lions, 29-20 (B)
Lions, 21-14 (D)
1963—Colts, 25-21 (D)
Colts, 24-21 (B)
1964—Colts, 34-0 (D)
Lions, 31-14 (B)
1965—Colts, 31-7 (B)
Tie, 24-24 (D)
1966—Colts, 45-14 (B)
Lions, 20-14 (D)
1967—Colts, 41-7 (B)
1968—Colts, 27-10 (D)
1969—Tie, 17-17 (B)
1973—Colts, 29-27 (D)
1977—Lions, 13-10 (B)
1980—Colts, 10-9 (D)
1985—Colts, 14-6 (I)
1991—Lions, 33-24 (I)
1997—Lions, 32-10 (D)
2000—Colts, 30-18 (I)
(RS Pts.—Colts 788, Lions 748)
Franchise in Baltimore prior to 1984

DETROIT vs. JACKSONVILLE
RS: Series tied, 1-1
1995—Lions, 44-0 (D)
1998—Jaguars, 37-22 (J)
(RS Pts.—Lions 66, Jaguars 37)

DETROIT vs. KANSAS CITY
RS: Chiefs lead series, 7-3
1971—Lions, 32-21 (D)
1975—Chiefs, 24-21 (KC) OT
1980—Chiefs, 20-17 (KC)
1981—Lions, 27-10 (D)
1987—Chiefs, 27-20 (D)
1988—Lions, 7-6 (KC)
1990—Chiefs, 43-24 (KC)
1996—Chiefs, 28-24 (D)
1999—Chiefs, 31-21 (KC)
2003—Chiefs, 45-17 (KC)
(RS Pts.—Chiefs 255, Lions 210)

DETROIT vs. MIAMI
RS: Dolphins lead series, 6-2
1973—Dolphins, 34-7 (M)
1979—Dolphins, 28-10 (D)
1985—Lions, 31-21 (D)
1991—Lions, 17-13 (D)
1994—Dolphins, 27-20 (M)
1997—Dolphins, 33-30 (M)
2000—Dolphins, 23-8 (D)
2002—Dolphins, 49-21 (M)
(RS Pts.—Dolphins 228, Lions 144)

DETROIT vs. MINNESOTA
RS: Vikings lead series, 54-29-2
1961—Lions, 37-10 (M)
Lions, 13-7 (D)
1962—Lions, 17-6 (M)
Lions, 37-23 (D)
1963—Lions, 28-10 (D)
Vikings, 34-31 (M)
1964—Lions, 24-20 (M)
Tie, 23-23 (D)
1965—Lions, 31-29 (M)
Vikings, 29-7 (D)
1966—Lions, 32-31 (M)
Vikings, 28-16 (D)
1967—Tie, 10-10 (M)
Lions, 14-3 (D)
1968—Vikings, 24-10 (M)
Vikings, 13-6 (D)
1969—Vikings, 24-10 (M)
Vikings, 27-0 (D)
1970—Vikings, 30-17 (D)
Vikings, 24-20 (M)
1971—Vikings, 16-13 (D)
Vikings, 29-10 (M)
1972—Vikings, 34-10 (D)
Vikings, 16-14 (M)
1973—Vikings, 23-9 (D)
Vikings, 28-7 (M)
1974—Vikings, 7-6 (D)
Lions, 20-16 (M)
1975—Vikings, 25-19 (M)
Lions, 17-10 (D)
1976—Vikings, 10-9 (D)
Vikings, 31-23 (M)
1977—Vikings, 14-7 (M)
Vikings, 30-21 (D)
1978—Vikings, 17-7 (M)
Lions, 45-14 (D)
1979—Vikings, 13-10 (D)
Vikings, 14-7 (M)
1980—Lions, 27-7 (D)
Vikings, 34-0 (M)
1981—Vikings, 26-24 (M)
Lions, 45-7 (D)

1982—Vikings, 34-31 (D)
1983—Vikings, 20-17 (M)
Lions, 13-2 (D)
1984—Vikings, 29-28 (D)
Lions, 16-14 (M)
1985—Vikings, 16-13 (M)
Lions, 41-21 (D)
1986—Lions, 13-10 (M)
Vikings, 24-10 (D)
1987—Vikings, 34-19 (M)
Vikings, 17-14 (D)
1988—Vikings, 44-17 (M)
Vikings, 23-0 (D)
1989—Vikings, 24-17 (M)
Vikings, 20-7 (D)
1990—Lions, 34-27 (M)
Vikings, 17-7 (D)
1991—Lions, 24-20 (D)
Lions, 34-14 (M)
1992—Lions, 31-17 (D)
Vikings, 31-14 (M)
1993—Lions, 30-27 (M)
Vikings, 13-0 (D)
1994—Vikings, 10-3 (M)
Lions, 41-19 (D)
1995—Vikings, 20-10 (M)
Lions, 44-38 (D)
1996—Vikings, 17-13 (M)
Vikings, 24-22 (D)
1997—Lions, 38-15 (D)
Lions, 14-13 (M)
1998—Vikings, 29-6 (M)
Vikings, 34-13 (D)
1999—Lions, 25-23 (D)
Vikings, 24-17 (M)
2000—Vikings, 31-24 (D)
Vikings, 24-17 (M)
2001—Vikings, 31-26 (M)
Lions, 27-24 (D)
2002—Vikings, 31-24 (M)
Vikings, 38-36 (D)
2003—Vikings, 23-13 (D)
Vikings, 24-14 (M)
(RS Pts.—Vikings 1,816, Lions 1,590)

DETROIT vs. NEW ENGLAND
RS: Series tied, 4-4
1971—Lions, 34-7 (NE)
1976—Lions, 30-10 (D)
1979—Patriots, 24-17 (NE)
1985—Patriots, 23-6 (NE)
1993—Lions, 19-16 (NE) OT
1994—Patriots, 23-17 (D)
2000—Lions, 34-9 (D)
2002—Patriots, 20-12 (D)
(RS Pts.—Lions 169, Patriots 132)

DETROIT vs. NEW ORLEANS
RS: Series tied, 8-8-1
1968—Tie, 20-20 (D)
1970—Saints, 19-17 (NO)
1972—Lions, 27-14 (D)
1973—Saints, 20-13 (NO)
1974—Lions, 19-14 (D)
1976—Saints, 17-16 (NO)
1977—Lions, 23-19 (D)
1979—Saints, 17-7 (NO)
1980—Lions, 24-13 (D)
1988—Saints, 22-14 (D)
1989—Lions, 21-14 (D)
1990—Lions, 27-10 (NO)
1992—Saints, 13-7 (D)
1993—Saints, 14-3 (NO)
1997—Saints, 35-17 (NO)
2000—Lions, 14-10 (NO)
2002—Lions, 26-21 (D)
(RS Pts.—Lions 295, Saints 292)

***DETROIT vs. N.Y. GIANTS**
RS: Lions lead series, 19-17-1
PS: Lions lead series, 1-0
1930—Giants, 19-6 (P)
1931—Spartans, 14-6 (P)
Giants, 14-0 (NY)
1932—Spartans, 7-0 (P)
Spartans, 6-0 (NY)
1933—Spartans, 17-7 (P)
Giants, 13-10 (NY)
1934—Lions, 9-0 (D)
1935—**Lions, 26-7 (D)
1936—Giants, 14-7 (NY)
Lions, 38-0 (D)
1937—Lions, 17-0 (NY)
1939—Lions, 18-14 (D)
1941—Giants, 20-13 (NY)
1943—Tie, 0-0 (D)
1945—Giants, 35-14 (NY)
1947—Lions, 35-7 (D)
1949—Lions, 45-21 (NY)
1953—Lions, 27-16 (NY)
1955—Giants, 24-19 (D)
1958—Giants, 19-17 (D)
1962—Giants, 17-14 (NY)
1964—Lions, 26-3 (D)
1967—Lions, 30-7 (NY)
1969—Lions, 24-0 (D)
1972—Lions, 30-16 (D)
1974—Lions, 20-19 (D)
1976—Giants, 24-10 (NY)
1982—Giants, 13-6 (D)
1983—Lions, 15-9 (D)
1988—Giants, 30-10 (NY)
Giants, 13-10 (D) OT
1989—Giants, 24-14 (NY)
1990—Giants, 20-0 (NY)
1994—Lions, 28-25 (NY) OT
1996—Giants, 35-7 (D)
1997—Giants, 26-20 (D) OT
2000—Lions, 31-21 (NY)
(RS Pts.—Lions 614, Giants 531)
(PS Pts.—Lions 26, Giants 7)
**Franchise in Portsmouth prior to 1934 and known as the Spartans*
***NFL Championship*

DETROIT vs. N.Y. JETS
RS: Lions lead series, 6-4
1972—Lions, 37-20 (D)
1979—Jets, 31-10 (NY)
1982—Jets, 28-13 (D)
1985—Lions, 31-20 (D)
1988—Jets, 17-10 (D)
1991—Lions, 34-20 (D)
1994—Lions, 18-7 (NY)
1997—Lions, 13-10 (D)
2000—Lions, 10-7 (NY)
2002—Jets, 31-14 (D)
(RS Pts.—Jets 191, Lions 190)

DETROIT vs. *OAKLAND
RS: Raiders lead series, 6-3
1970—Lions, 28-14 (D)
1974—Raiders, 35-13 (O)
1978—Raiders, 29-17 (O)
1981—Lions, 16-0 (D)
1984—Raiders, 24-3 (D)
1987—Raiders, 27-7 (LA)
1990—Raiders, 38-31 (D)
1996—Raiders, 37-21 (O)
2003—Lions, 23-13 (D)
(RS Pts.—Raiders 217, Lions 159)
**Franchise in Los Angeles from 1982-1994*

***DETROIT vs. PHILADELPHIA**
RS: Lions lead series, 12-11-2
PS: Eagles lead series, 1-0
1933—Spartans, 25-0 (P)
1934—Lions, 10-0 (P)
1935—Lions, 35-0 (D)
1936—Lions, 23-0 (P)
1938—Eagles, 21-7 (D)
1940—Lions, 21-0 (P)
1941—Lions, 21-17 (D)
1945—Lions, 28-24 (D)
1948—Eagles, 45-21 (P)
1949—Eagles, 22-14 (D)
1951—Lions, 28-10 (P)
1954—Tie, 13-13 (D)
1957—Lions, 27-16 (P)
1960—Eagles, 28-10 (P)
1961—Eagles, 27-24 (D)
1965—Lions, 35-28 (P)
1968—Eagles, 12-0 (D)
1971—Eagles, 23-20 (D)
1974—Eagles, 28-17 (P)
1977—Lions, 17-13 (D)
1979—Eagles, 44-7 (P)
1984—Tie, 23-23 (D) OT
1986—Lions, 13-11 (P)
1995—**Eagles, 58-37 (P)
1996—Eagles, 24-17 (P)
1998—Eagles, 10-9 (P)
(RS Pts.—Lions 465, Eagles 439)
(PS Pts.—Eagles 58, Lions 37)
**Franchise in Portsmouth prior to 1934 and known as the Spartans*
***NFC First-Round Playoff*

DETROIT vs. *PITTSBURGH
RS: Lions lead series, 14-13-1
1934—Lions, 40-7 (D)
1936—Lions, 28-3 (D)
1937—Lions, 7-3 (D)
1938—Lions, 16-7 (D)
1940—Pirates, 10-7 (D)
1942—Steelers, 35-7 (D)
1946—Lions, 17-7 (D)
1947—Steelers, 17-10 (P)
1948—Lions, 17-14 (D)
1949—Steelers, 14-7 (P)
1950—Lions, 10-7 (D)
1952—Lions, 31-6 (P)
1953—Lions, 38-21 (D)
1955—Lions, 31-28 (P)
1956—Lions, 45-7 (D)
1959—Tie, 10-10 (P)
1962—Lions, 45-7 (D)
1966—Steelers, 17-3 (P)
1967—Steelers, 24-14 (D)
1969—Steelers, 16-13 (P)
1973—Steelers, 24-10 (P)
1983—Lions, 45-3 (D)
1986—Steelers, 27-17 (P)
1989—Steelers, 23-3 (D)
1992—Steelers, 17-14 (P)
1995—Steelers, 23-20 (P)
1998—Lions, 19-16 (D) OT

2001—Steelers, 47-14 (P)
(RS Pts.—Lions 538, Steelers 440)
Steelers known as Pirates prior to 1941

DETROIT vs. *ST. LOUIS
RS: Rams lead series, 40-37-1
PS: Lions lead series, 1-0
1937—Lions, 28-0 (C)
Lions, 27-7 (D)
1938—Rams, 21-17 (C)
Lions, 6-0 (D)
1939—Lions, 15-7 (D)
Rams, 14-3 (C)
1940—Lions, 6-0 (D)
Rams, 24-0 (C)
1941—Lions, 17-7 (D)
Lions, 14-0 (C)
1942—Rams, 14-0 (D)
Rams, 27-7 (C)
1944—Rams, 20-17 (D)
Lions, 26-14 (C)
1945—Rams, 28-21 (D)
1946—Rams, 35-14 (LA)
Rams, 41-20 (D)
1947—Rams, 27-13 (D)
Rams, 28-17 (LA)
1948—Rams, 44-7 (LA)
Rams, 34-27 (D)
1949—Rams, 27-24 (LA)
Rams, 21-10 (D)
1950—Rams, 30-28 (D)
Rams, 65-24 (LA)
1951—Rams, 27-21 (D)
Lions, 24-22 (LA)
1952—Lions, 17-14 (LA)
Lions, 24-16 (D)
**Lions, 31-21 (D)
1953—Rams, 31-19 (D)
Rams, 37-24 (LA)
1954—Lions, 21-3 (D)
Lions, 27-24 (LA)
1955—Rams, 17-10 (D)
Rams, 24-13 (LA)
1956—Lions, 24-21 (D)
Lions, 16-7 (LA)
1957—Lions, 10-7 (D)
Rams, 35-17 (LA)
1958—Rams, 42-28 (D)
Lions, 41-24 (LA)
1959—Lions, 17-7 (LA)
Lions, 23-17 (D)
1960—Rams, 48-35 (LA)
Lions, 12-10 (D)
1961—Lions, 14-13 (D)
Lions, 28-10 (LA)
1962—Lions, 13-10 (D)
Lions, 12-3 (LA)
1963—Lions, 23-2 (LA)
Rams, 28-21 (D)
1964—Tie, 17-17 (LA)
Lions, 37-17 (D)
1965—Lions, 20-0 (D)
Lions, 31-7 (LA)
1966—Rams, 14-7 (D)
Rams, 23-3 (LA)
1967—Rams, 31-7 (D)
1968—Rams, 10-7 (LA)
1969—Lions, 28-0 (D)
1970—Lions, 28-23 (LA)
1971—Rams, 21-13 (D)
1972—Lions, 34-17 (LA)
1974—Rams, 16-13 (LA)
1975—Rams, 20-0 (D)
1976—Rams, 20-17 (D)
1980—Lions, 41-20 (LA)
1981—Rams, 20-13 (LA)
1982—Lions, 19-14 (LA)
1983—Rams, 21-10 (LA)
1986—Rams, 14-10 (LA)
1987—Rams, 37-16 (D)
1988—Rams, 17-10 (LA)
1991—Lions, 21-10 (D)
1993—Lions, 16-13 (LA)
1999—Lions, 31-27 (D)
2001—Rams, 35-0 (D)
2003—Lions, 30-20 (D)
(RS Pts.—Rams 1,518, Lions 1,401)
(PS Pts.—Lions 31, Rams 21)
Franchise in Los Angeles prior to 1995 and in Cleveland prior to 1946
***Conference Playoff*

DETROIT vs. SAN DIEGO
RS: Chargers lead series, 5-3
1972—Lions, 34-20 (D)
1977—Lions, 20-0 (D)
1978—Lions, 31-14 (D)
1981—Chargers, 28-23 (SD)
1984—Chargers, 27-24 (SD)
1996—Chargers, 27-21 (SD)
1999—Chargers, 20-10 (D)
2003—Chargers, 14-7 (D)
(RS Pts.—Lions 170, Chargers 150)

DETROIT vs. SAN FRANCISCO
RS: 49ers lead series, 31-26-1
PS: Series tied, 1-1
1950—Lions, 24-7 (D)
49ers, 28-27 (SF)
1951—49ers, 20-10 (D)
49ers, 21-17 (SF)
1952—49ers, 17-3 (SF)
49ers, 28-0 (D)
1953—Lions, 24-21 (D)
Lions, 14-10 (SF)
1954—49ers, 37-31 (SF)
Lions, 48-7 (D)
1955—49ers, 27-24 (D)
49ers, 38-21 (SF)
1956—Lions, 20-17 (D)
Lions, 17-13 (SF)
1957—49ers, 35-31 (SF)
Lions, 31-10 (D)
*Lions, 31-27 (SF)
1958—49ers, 24-21 (SF)
Lions, 35-21 (D)
1959—49ers, 34-13 (D)
49ers, 33-7 (SF)
1960—49ers, 14-10 (D)
Lions, 24-0 (SF)
1961—49ers, 49-0 (D)
Tie, 20-20 (SF)
1962—Lions, 45-24 (D)
Lions, 38-24 (SF)
1963—Lions, 26-3 (D)
Lions, 45-7 (SF)
1964—Lions, 26-17 (SF)
Lions, 24-7 (D)
1965—49ers, 27-21 (D)
49ers, 17-14 (SF)
1966—49ers, 27-24 (SF)
49ers, 41-14 (D)
1967—Lions, 45-3 (SF)
1968—49ers, 14-7 (D)
1969—Lions, 26-14 (SF)
1970—Lions, 28-7 (D)
1971—49ers, 31-27 (SF)
1973—Lions, 30-20 (D)
1974—Lions, 17-13 (D)
1975—Lions, 28-17 (SF)
1977—49ers, 28-7 (SF)
1978—Lions, 33-14 (D)
1980—Lions, 17-13 (D)
1981—Lions, 24-17 (D)
1983—**49ers, 24-23 (SF)
1984—49ers, 30-27 (D)
1985—Lions, 23-21 (D)
1988—49ers, 20-13 (SF)
1991—49ers, 35-3 (SF)
1992—49ers, 24-6 (SF)
1993—49ers, 55-17 (D)
1994—49ers, 27-21 (D)
1995—Lions, 27-24 (D)
1996—49ers, 24-14 (SF)
1998—49ers, 35-13 (SF)
2001—49ers, 21-13 (SF)
2003—49ers, 24-17 (SF)
(RS Pts.—49ers 1,256, Lions 1,232)
(PS Pts.—Lions 54, 49ers 51)
**Conference Playoff*
***NFC Divisional Playoff*

DETROIT vs. SEATTLE
RS: Seahawks lead series, 5-4
1976—Lions, 41-14 (S)
1978—Seahawks, 28-16 (S)
1984—Seahawks, 38-17 (S)
1987—Seahawks, 37-14 (D)
1990—Seahawks, 30-10 (S)
1993—Lions, 30-10 (D)
1996—Lions, 17-16 (D)
1999—Lions, 28-20 (S)
2003—Seahawks, 35-14 (S)
(RS Pts.—Seahawks 228, Lions 187)

DETROIT vs. TAMPA BAY
RS: Lions lead series, 26-23
PS: Buccaneers lead series, 1-0
1977—Lions, 16-7 (D)
1978—Lions, 15-7 (TB)
Lions, 34-23 (D)
1979—Buccaneers, 31-16 (TB)
Buccaneers, 16-14 (D)
1980—Lions, 24-10 (TB)
Lions, 27-14 (D)
1981—Buccaneers, 28-10 (TB)
Buccaneers, 20-17 (D)
1982—Buccaneers, 23-21 (TB)
1983—Lions, 11-0 (TB)
Lions, 23-20 (D)
1984—Buccaneers, 21-17 (TB)
Lions, 13-7 (D) OT
1985—Lions, 30-9 (D)
Buccaneers, 19-16 (TB) OT
1986—Buccaneers, 24-20 (D)
Lions, 38-17 (TB)
1987—Buccaneers, 31-27 (D)
Lions, 20-10 (TB)
1988—Buccaneers, 23-20 (D)
Buccaneers, 21-10 (TB)
1989—Lions, 17-16 (TB)
Lions, 33-7 (D)
1990—Buccaneers, 38-21 (D)
Buccaneers, 23-20 (TB)
1991—Lions, 31-3 (D)

Buccaneers, 30-21 (TB)
1992—Buccaneers, 27-23 (D)
Lions, 38-7 (TB)
1993—Buccaneers, 27-10 (TB)
Lions, 23-0 (D)
1994—Buccaneers, 24-14 (TB)
Lions, 14-9 (D)
1995—Lions, 27-24 (D)
Lions, 37-10 (TB)
1996—Lions, 21-6 (D)
Lions, 27-0 (TB)
1997—Buccaneers, 24-17 (D)
Lions, 27-9 (TB)
*Buccaneers, 20-10 (TB)
1998—Lions, 27-6 (D)
Lions, 28-25 (TB)
1999—Lions, 20-3 (D)
Buccaneers, 23-16 (TB)
2000—Buccaneers, 31-10 (D)
Lions, 28-14 (TB)
2001—Buccaneers, 20-17 (D)
Buccaneers, 15-12 (TB)
2002—Buccaneers, 23-20 (D)
(RS Pts—Lions 1,038, Buccaneers 825)
(PS Pts.—Buccaneers 20, Lions 10)
NFC First-Round Playoff

DETROIT vs. *TENNESSEE
RS: Titans lead series, 5-3
1971—Lions, 31-7 (H)
1975—Oilers, 24-8 (H)
1983—Oilers, 27-17 (H)
1986—Lions, 24-13 (D)
1989—Oilers, 35-31 (H)
1992—Oilers, 24-21 (D)
1995—Lions, 24-17 (H)
2001—Titans, 27-24 (D)
(RS Pts.—Lions 180, Titans 174)
**Franchise in Houston prior to 1997; known as Oilers prior to 1999*

***DETROIT vs. **WASHINGTON**
RS: Redskins lead series, 24-10
PS: Redskins lead series, 3-0
1932—Spartans, 10-0 (P)
1933—Spartans, 13-0 (B)
1934—Lions, 24-0 (D)
1935—Lions, 17-7 (B)
Lions, 14-0 (D)
1938—Redskins, 7-5 (D)
1939—Redskins, 31-7 (W)
1940—Redskins, 20-14 (D)
1942—Redskins, 15-3 (D)
1943—Redskins, 42-20 (W)
1946—Redskins, 17-16 (W)
1947—Lions, 38-21 (D)
1948—Redskins, 46-21 (W)
1951—Lions, 35-17 (D)
1956—Redskins, 18-17 (W)
1965—Lions, 14-10 (D)
1968—Redskins, 14-3 (W)
1970—Redskins, 31-10 (W)
1973—Redskins, 20-0 (D)
1976—Redskins, 20-7 (W)
1978—Redskins, 21-19 (D)
1979—Redskins, 27-24 (D)
1981—Redskins, 33-31 (W)
1982—***Redskins, 31-7 (W)
1983—Redskins, 38-17 (W)
1984—Redskins, 28-14 (W)
1985—Redskins, 24-3 (W)
1987—Redskins, 20-13 (W)
1990—Redskins, 41-38 (D) OT
1991—Redskins, 45-0 (W)
****Redskins, 41-10 (W)
1992—Redskins, 13-10 (W)
1995—Redskins, 36-30 (W) OT
1997—Redskins, 30-7 (W)
1999—Lions, 33-17 (D)
***Redskins, 27-13 (W)
2000—Lions, 15-10 (D)
(RS Pts.—Redskins 719, Lions 542)
(PS Pts.—Redskins 99, Lions 30)
**Franchise in Portsmouth prior to 1934 and known as the Spartans.*
***Franchise in Boston prior to 1937*
****NFC First-Round Playoff*
*****NFC Championship*

GREEN BAY vs. ARIZONA
RS: Packers lead series, 41-22-4
PS: Packers lead series, 1-0;
See Arizona vs. Green Bay

GREEN BAY vs. ATLANTA
RS: Packers lead series, 11-10
PS: Series tied, 1-1;
See Atlanta vs. Green Bay

GREEN BAY vs. BALTIMORE
RS: Packers lead series, 2-0;
See Baltimore vs. Green Bay

GREEN BAY vs. BUFFALO
RS: Bills lead series, 6-3;
See Buffalo vs. Green Bay

GREEN BAY vs. CAROLINA
RS: Packers lead series, 4-2
PS: Packers lead series, 1-0;
See Carolina vs. Green Bay

GREEN BAY vs. CHICAGO
RS: Bears lead series, 83-77-6
PS: Bears lead series, 1-0;
See Chicago vs. Green Bay

GREEN BAY vs. CINCINNATI
RS: Packers lead series, 5-4;
See Cincinnati vs. Green Bay

GREEN BAY vs. CLEVELAND
RS: Packers lead series, 9-6
PS: Packers lead series, 1-0;
See Cleveland vs. Green Bay

GREEN BAY vs. DALLAS
RS: Cowboys lead series, 10-9
PS: Cowboys lead series, 4-2;
See Dallas vs. Green Bay

GREEN BAY vs. DENVER
RS: Broncos lead series, 5-4-1
PS: Broncos lead series, 1-0;
See Denver vs. Green Bay

GREEN BAY vs. DETROIT
RS: Packers lead series, 77-63-7
PS: Packers lead series, 2-0;
See Detroit vs. Green Bay

GREEN BAY vs. *INDIANAPOLIS
RS: Series tied, 19-19-1
PS: Packers lead series, 1-0
1953—Packers, 37-14 (GB)
Packers, 35-24 (B)
1954—Packers, 7-6 (B)
Packers, 24-13 (Mil)
1955—Colts, 24-20 (Mil)
Colts, 14-10 (B)
1956—Packers, 38-33 (Mil)
Colts, 28-21 (B)
1957—Colts, 45-17 (Mil)
Packers, 24-21 (B)
1958—Colts, 24-17 (Mil)
Colts, 56-0 (B)
1959—Colts, 38-21 (B)
Colts, 28-24 (Mil)
1960—Packers, 35-21 (GB)
Colts, 38-24 (B)
1961—Packers, 45-7 (GB)
Colts, 45-21 (B)
1962—Packers, 17-6 (B)
Packers, 17-13 (GB)
1963—Packers, 31-20 (GB)
Packers, 34-20 (B)
1964—Colts, 21-20 (GB)
Colts, 24-21 (B)
1965—Packers, 20-17 (Mil)
Packers, 42-27 (B)
**Packers, 13-10 (GB) OT
1966—Packers, 24-3 (Mil)
Packers, 14-10 (B)
1967—Colts, 13-10 (B)
1968—Colts, 16-3 (GB)
1969—Colts, 14-6 (B)
1970—Colts, 13-10 (Mil)
1974—Packers, 20-13 (B)
1982—Tie, 20-20 (B) OT
1985—Colts, 37-10 (I)
1988—Colts, 20-13 (GB)
1991—Packers, 14-10 (Mil)
1997—Colts, 41-38 (I)
2000—Packers, 26-24 (GB)
(RS Pts.—Colts 861, Packers 830)
(PS Pts.—Packers 13, Colts 10)
**Franchise in Baltimore prior to 1984*
***Conference Playoff*

GREEN BAY vs. JACKSONVILLE
RS: Packers lead series, 2-0
1995—Packers, 24-14 (J)
2001—Packers, 28-21 (J)
(RS Pts.—Packers 52, Jaguars 35)

GREEN BAY vs. KANSAS CITY
RS: Chiefs lead series, 6-1-1
PS: Packers lead series, 1-0
1966—*Packers, 35-10 (Los Angeles)
1973—Tie, 10-10 (Mil)
1977—Chiefs, 20-10 (KC)
1987—Packers, 23-3 (KC)
1989—Chiefs, 21-3 (GB)
1990—Chiefs, 17-3 (GB)
1993—Chiefs, 23-16 (KC)
1996—Chiefs, 27-20 (KC)
2003—Chiefs, 40-34 (GB) OT
(RS Pts.—Chiefs 161, Packers 119)
(PS Pts.—Packers 35, Chiefs 10)
**Super Bowl I*

GREEN BAY vs. MIAMI
RS: Dolphins lead series, 9-2
1971—Dolphins, 27-6 (Mia)
1975—Dolphins, 31-7 (GB)
1979—Dolphins, 27-7 (Mia)
1985—Dolphins, 34-24 (GB)
1988—Dolphins, 24-17 (Mia)
1989—Dolphins, 23-20 (Mia)
1991—Dolphins, 16-13 (Mia)
1994—Dolphins, 24-14 (Mil)
1997—Packers, 23-18 (GB)
2000—Dolphins, 28-20 (Mia)
2002—Packers, 24-10 (GB)
(RS Pts.—Dolphins 262, Packers 175)

GREEN BAY vs. MINNESOTA
RS: Series tied, 42-42-1
1961—Packers, 33-7 (Minn)
Packers, 28-10 (Mil)
1962—Packers, 34-7 (GB)
Packers, 48-21 (Minn)
1963—Packers, 37-28 (Minn)
Packers, 28-7 (GB)
1964—Vikings, 24-23 (GB)
Packers, 42-13 (Minn)
1965—Packers, 38-13 (Minn)
Packers, 24-19 (GB)
1966—Vikings, 20-17 (GB)
Packers, 28-16 (Minn)
1967—Vikings, 10-7 (Mil)
Packers, 30-27 (Minn)
1968—Vikings, 26-13 (Mil)
Vikings, 14-10 (Minn)
1969—Vikings, 19-7 (Minn)
Vikings, 9-7 (Mil)
1970—Packers, 13-10 (Mil)
Vikings, 10-3 (Minn)
1971—Vikings, 24-13 (GB)
Vikings, 3-0 (Minn)
1972—Vikings, 27-13 (GB)
Packers, 23-7 (Minn)
1973—Vikings, 11-3 (Minn)
Vikings, 31-7 (GB)
1974—Vikings, 32-17 (GB)
Packers, 19-7 (Minn)
1975—Vikings, 28-17 (GB)
Vikings, 24-3 (Minn)
1976—Vikings, 17-10 (Mil)
Vikings, 20-9 (Minn)
1977—Vikings, 19-7 (Minn)
Vikings, 13-6 (GB)
1978—Vikings, 21-7 (Minn)
Tie, 10-10 (GB) OT
1979—Vikings, 27-21 (Minn) OT
Packers, 19-7 (Mil)
1980—Packers, 16-3 (GB)
Packers, 25-13 (Minn)
1981—Vikings, 30-13 (Mil)
Packers, 35-23 (Minn)
1982—Packers, 26-7 (Mil)
1983—Vikings, 20-17 (GB) OT
Packers, 29-21 (Minn)
1984—Packers, 45-17 (Mil)
Packers, 38-14 (Minn)
1985—Packers, 20-17 (Mil)
Packers, 27-17 (Minn)
1986—Vikings, 42-7 (Minn)
Vikings, 32-6 (GB)
1987—Packers, 23-16 (Minn)
Packers, 16-10 (Mil)
1988—Packers, 34-14 (Minn)
Packers, 18-6 (GB)
1989—Vikings, 26-14 (Minn)
Packers, 20-19 (Mil)
1990—Packers, 24-10 (Mil)
Vikings, 23-7 (Minn)
1991—Vikings, 35-21 (GB)
Packers, 27-7 (Minn)
1992—Vikings, 23-20 (GB) OT
Vikings, 27-7 (Minn)
1993—Vikings, 15-13 (Minn)
Vikings, 21-17 (Mil)
1994—Packers, 16-10 (GB)
Vikings, 13-10 (Minn) OT
1995—Packers, 38-21 (GB)
Vikings, 27-24 (Minn)
1996—Vikings, 30-21 (Minn)
Packers, 38-10 (GB)
1997—Packers, 38-32 (GB)
Packers, 27-11 (Minn)
1998—Vikings, 37-24 (GB)
Vikings, 28-14 (Minn)
1999—Packers, 23-20 (GB)
Vikings, 24-20 (Minn)
2000—Packers, 26-20 (GB) OT
Packers, 33-28 (Minn)
2001—Vikings, 35-13 (Minn)
Packers, 24-13 (GB)
2002—Vikings, 31-21 (Minn)
Packers, 26-22 (GB)
2003—Vikings, 30-25 (GB)
Packers, 30-27 (M)
(RS Pts.—Packers 1,730, Vikings 1,615)

GREEN BAY vs. NEW ENGLAND
RS: Packers lead series, 4-3
PS: Packers lead series, 1-0
1973—Patriots, 33-24 (NE)
1979—Packers, 27-14 (GB)
1985—Patriots, 26-20 (NE)
1988—Packers, 45-3 (Mil)
1994—Patriots, 17-16 (NE)
1996—*Packers, 35-21 (New Orleans)
1997—Packers, 28-10 (NE)
2002—Packers, 28-10 (NE)
(RS Pts.—Packers 188, Patriots 113)
(PS Pts.—Packers 35, Patriots 21)
**Super Bowl XXXI*

GREEN BAY vs. NEW ORLEANS
RS: Packers lead series, 13-5
1968—Packers, 29-7 (Mil)
1971—Saints, 29-21 (Mil)
1972—Packers, 30-20 (NO)
1973—Packers, 30-10 (Mil)
1975—Saints, 20-19 (NO)
1976—Packers, 32-27 (Mil)
1977—Packers, 24-20 (NO)
1978—Packers, 28-17 (Mil)
1979—Packers, 28-19 (Mil)
1981—Packers, 35-7 (NO)
1984—Packers, 23-13 (NO)
1985—Packers, 38-14 (Mil)
1986—Saints, 24-10 (NO)
1987—Saints, 33-24 (NO)
1989—Packers, 35-34 (GB)
1993—Packers, 19-17 (NO)
1995—Packers, 34-23 (NO)
2002—Saints, 35-20 (NO)
(RS Pts.—Packers 479, Saints 369)

GREEN BAY vs. N.Y. GIANTS
RS: Packers lead series, 24-20-2
PS: Packers lead series, 4-1
1928—Giants, 6-0 (GB)
Packers, 7-0 (NY)
1929—Packers, 20-6 (NY)
1930—Packers, 14-7 (GB)
Giants, 13-6 (NY)
1931—Packers, 27-7 (GB)
Packers, 14-10 (NY)
1932—Packers, 13-0 (GB)
Giants, 6-0 (NY)
1933—Giants, 10-7 (Mil)
Giants, 17-6 (NY)
1934—Packers, 20-6 (Mil)
Giants, 17-3 (NY)
1935—Packers, 16-7 (GB)
1936—Packers, 26-14 (NY)
1937—Giants, 10-0 (NY)
1938—Giants, 15-3 (NY)
*Giants, 23-17 (NY)
1939—*Packers, 27-0 (Mil)
1940—Giants, 7-3 (NY)
1942—Tie, 21-21 (NY)
1943—Packers, 35-21 (NY)
1944—Giants, 24-0 (NY)
*Packers, 14-7 (NY)
1945—Packers, 23-14 (NY)
1947—Tie, 24-24 (NY)
1948—Giants, 49-3 (Mil)
1949—Giants, 30-10 (GB)
1952—Packers, 17-3 (NY)
1957—Giants, 31-17 (GB)
1959—Giants, 20-3 (NY)
1961—Packers, 20-17 (Mil)
*Packers, 37-0 (GB)
1962—*Packers, 16-7 (NY)
1967—Packers, 48-21 (NY)
1969—Packers, 20-10 (Mil)
1971—Giants, 42-40 (GB)
1973—Packers, 16-14 (New Haven)
1975—Packers, 40-14 (Mil)
1980—Giants, 27-21 (NY)
1981—Packers, 27-14 (NY)
Packers, 26-24 (Mil)
1982—Packers, 27-19 (NY)
1983—Giants, 27-3 (NY)
1985—Packers, 23-20 (GB)
1986—Giants, 55-24 (NY)
1987—Giants, 20-10 (NY)
1992—Giants, 27-7 (NY)
1995—Packers, 14-6 (GB)
1998—Packers, 37-3 (NY)
2001—Packers, 34-25 (NY)
(RS Pts.—Giants 780, Packers 775)
(PS Pts.—Packers 111, Giants 37)
**NFL Championship*

GREEN BAY vs. N.Y. JETS
RS: Jets lead series, 7-2
1973—Packers, 23-7 (Mil)
1979—Jets, 27-22 (GB)
1981—Jets, 28-3 (NY)
1982—Jets, 15-13 (NY)
1985—Jets, 24-3 (Mil)
1991—Jets, 19-16 (NY) OT
1994—Packers, 17-10 (GB)
2000—Jets, 20-16 (GB)
2002—Jets, 42-17 (NY)
(RS Pts.—Jets 192, Packers 130)

GREEN BAY vs. *OAKLAND
RS: Raiders lead series, 5-4
PS: Packers lead series, 1-0
1967—**Packers, 33-14 (Miami)
1972—Raiders, 20-14 (GB)
1976—Raiders, 18-14 (O)
1978—Raiders, 28-3 (GB)
1984—Raiders, 28-7 (LA)
1987—Raiders, 20-0 (GB)
1990—Packers, 29-16 (LA)
1993—Packers, 28-0 (GB)
1999—Packers, 28-24 (GB)
2003—Packers, 41-7 (O)
(RS Pts.—Packers 164, Raiders 161)
(PS Pts.—Packers 33, Raiders 14)
**Franchise in Los Angeles from 1982-1994*
***Super Bowl II*

GREEN BAY vs. PHILADELPHIA
RS: Packers lead series, 22-10
PS: Eagles lead series, 2-0
1933—Packers, 35-9 (GB)
Packers, 10-0 (P)
1934—Packers, 19-6 (GB)
1935—Packers, 13-6 (P)
1937—Packers, 37-7 (Mil)
1939—Packers, 23-16 (P)
1940—Packers, 27-20 (GB)
1942—Packers, 7-0 (P)
1946—Packers, 19-7 (P)
1947—Eagles, 28-14 (P)
1951—Packers, 37-24 (GB)
1952—Packers, 12-10 (Mil)
1954—Packers, 37-14 (P)
1958—Packers, 38-35 (GB)
1960—*Eagles, 17-13 (P)
1962—Packers, 49-0 (P)
1968—Packers, 30-13 (GB)
1970—Packers, 30-17 (Mil)
1974—Eagles, 36-14 (P)
1976—Packers, 28-13 (GB)
1978—Eagles, 10-3 (P)
1979—Eagles, 21-10 (GB)
1987—Packers, 16-10 (GB) OT
1990—Eagles, 31-0 (P)
1991—Eagles, 20-3 (GB)
1992—Packers, 27-24 (Mil)
1993—Eagles, 20-17 (GB)
1994—Eagles, 13-7 (P)
1996—Packers, 39-13 (GB)
1997—Eagles, 10-9 (P)
1998—Packers, 24-16 (GB)
2000—Packers, 6-3 (GB)
2003—Eagles, 17-14 (GB)
**Eagles, 20-17 (P) OT
(RS Pts.—Packers 654, Eagles 469)
(PS Pts.—Eagles 37, Packers 30)
**NFL Championship*
***NFC Divisional Playoff*

GREEN BAY vs. *PITTSBURGH
RS: Packers lead series, 18-12
1933—Packers, 47-0 (GB)
1935—Packers, 27-0 (GB)
Packers, 34-14 (P)
1936—Packers, 42-10 (Mil)
1938—Packers, 20-0 (GB)
1940—Packers, 24-3 (Mil)
1941—Packers, 54-7 (P)
1942—Packers, 24-21 (Mil)
1946—Packers, 17-7 (GB)
1947—Steelers, 18-17 (Mil)
1948—Steelers, 38-7 (P)
1949—Steelers, 30-7 (Mil)
1951—Packers, 35-33 (Mil)
Steelers, 28-7 (P)
1953—Steelers, 31-14 (P)
1954—Steelers, 21-20 (GB)
1957—Packers, 27-10 (P)
1960—Packers, 19-13 (P)
1963—Packers, 33-14 (Mil)
1965—Packers, 41-9 (P)
1967—Steelers, 24-17 (GB)
1969—Packers, 38-34 (P)
1970—Packers, 20-12 (P)
1975—Steelers, 16-13 (Mil)
1980—Steelers, 22-20 (P)
1983—Steelers, 25-21 (GB)
1986—Steelers, 27-3 (P)
1992—Packers, 17-3 (GB)
1995—Packers, 24-19 (GB)
1998—Steelers, 27-20 (P)
(RS Pts.—Packers 709, Steelers 516)
**Steelers known as Pirates prior to 1941*

GREEN BAY vs. *ST. LOUIS
RS: Rams lead series, 44-39-2
PS: Series tied, 1-1
1937—Packers, 35-10 (C)
Packers, 35-7 (GB)
1938—Packers, 26-17 (GB)
Packers, 28-7 (C)
1939—Rams, 27-24 (GB)
Packers, 7-6 (C)
1940—Packers, 31-14 (GB)
Tie, 13-13 (C)
1941—Packers, 24-7 (Mil)
Packers, 17-14 (C)
1942—Packers, 45-28 (GB)
Packers, 30-12 (C)
1944—Packers, 30-21 (GB)
Packers, 42-7 (C)
1945—Rams, 27-14 (GB)
Rams, 20-7 (C)
1946—Rams, 21-17 (Mil)
Rams, 38-17 (LA)
1947—Packers, 17-14 (Mil)
Packers, 30-10 (LA)
1948—Packers, 16-0 (GB)
Rams, 24-10 (LA)
1949—Rams, 48-7 (GB)
Rams, 35-7 (LA)
1950—Rams, 45-14 (Mil)
Rams, 51-14 (LA)
1951—Rams, 28-0 (Mil)
Rams, 42-14 (LA)
1952—Rams, 30-28 (Mil)
Rams, 45-27 (LA)
1953—Rams, 38-20 (Mil)
Rams, 33-17 (LA)
1954—Packers, 35-17 (Mil)
Rams, 35-27 (LA)
1955—Packers, 30-28 (Mil)
Rams, 31-17 (LA)
1956—Packers, 42-17 (Mil)
Rams, 49-21 (LA)
1957—Rams, 31-27 (Mil)
Rams, 42-17 (LA)
1958—Rams, 20-7 (GB)
Rams, 34-20 (LA)
1959—Rams, 45-6 (Mil)
Packers, 38-20 (LA)
1960—Rams, 33-31 (Mil)
Packers, 35-21 (LA)
1961—Packers, 35-17 (GB)
Packers, 24-17 (LA)
1962—Packers, 41-10 (Mil)
Packers, 20-17 (LA)
1963—Packers, 42-10 (GB)
Packers, 31-14 (LA)
1964—Rams, 27-17 (Mil)
Tie, 24-24 (LA)
1965—Packers, 6-3 (Mil)
Rams, 21-10 (LA)
1966—Packers, 24-13 (GB)
Packers, 27-23 (LA)
1967—Rams, 27-24 (LA)
**Packers, 28-7 (Mil)
1968—Rams, 16-14 (Mil)
1969—Rams, 34-21 (LA)
1970—Rams, 31-21 (GB)
1971—Rams, 30-13 (LA)
1973—Rams, 24-7 (LA)
1974—Packers, 17-6 (Mil)
1975—Rams, 22-5 (LA)
1977—Rams, 24-6 (Mil)
1978—Rams, 31-14 (LA)
1980—Rams, 51-21 (LA)
1981—Rams, 35-23 (LA)
1982—Packers, 35-23 (Mil)
1983—Packers, 27-24 (Mil)
1984—Packers, 31-6 (Mil)
1985—Rams, 34-17 (LA)
1988—Rams, 34-7 (GB)
1989—Rams, 41-38 (LA)
1990—Packers, 36-24 (GB)
1991—Rams, 23-21 (LA)
1992—Packers, 28-13 (GB)
1993—Packers, 36-6 (Mil)
1994—Packers, 24-17 (GB)
1995—Rams, 17-14 (GB)
1996—Packers, 24-9 (StL)
1997—Packers, 17-7 (GB)
2001—***Rams, 45-17 (StL)
2003—Rams, 34-24 (StL)
(RS Pts.—Rams 2,001, Packers 1,882)
(PS Pts.—Rams 52, Packers 45)
**Franchise in Los Angeles prior to 1995 and in Cleveland prior to 1946*
***Conference Championship*
****NFC Divisional Playoff*

GREEN BAY vs. SAN DIEGO
RS: Packers lead series, 7-1
1970—Packers, 22-20 (SD)
1974—Packers, 34-0 (GB)
1978—Packers, 24-3 (SD)
1984—Chargers, 34-28 (GB)
1993—Packers, 20-13 (SD)
1996—Packers, 42-10 (GB)
1999—Packers, 31-3 (SD)
2003—Packers, 38-21 (SD)
(RS Pts.—Packers 239, Chargers 104)

GREEN BAY vs. SAN FRANCISCO
RS: Packers lead series, 27-25-1
PS: Packers lead series, 4-1
1950—Packers, 25-21 (GB)
49ers, 30-14 (SF)
1951—49ers, 31-19 (SF)
1952—49ers, 24-14 (SF)
1953—49ers, 37-7 (Mil)
49ers, 48-14 (SF)
1954—49ers, 23-17 (Mil)
49ers, 35-0 (SF)
1955—Packers, 27-21 (Mil)
Packers, 28-7 (SF)
1956—49ers, 17-16 (GB)
49ers, 38-20 (SF)
1957—49ers, 24-14 (Mil)
49ers, 27-20 (SF)
1958—49ers, 33-12 (Mil)
49ers, 48-21 (SF)
1959—Packers, 21-20 (GB)
Packers, 36-14 (SF)
1960—Packers, 41-14 (Mil)
Packers, 13-0 (SF)
1961—Packers, 30-10 (GB)
49ers, 22-21 (SF)
1962—Packers, 31-13 (Mil)
Packers, 31-21 (SF)
1963—Packers, 28-10 (Mil)

Packers, 21-17 (SF)
1964—Packers, 24-14 (Mil)
49ers, 24-14 (SF)
1965—Packers, 27-10 (GB)
Tie, 24-24 (SF)
1966—49ers, 21-20 (SF)
Packers, 20-7 (Mil)
1967—Packers, 13-0 (GB)
1968—49ers, 27-20 (SF)
1969—Packers, 14-7 (Mil)
1970—49ers, 26-10 (SF)
1972—Packers, 34-24 (Mil)
1973—49ers, 20-6 (SF)
1974—49ers, 7-6 (SF)
1976—49ers, 26-14 (GB)
1977—Packers, 16-14 (Mil)
1980—Packers, 23-16 (Mil)
1981—49ers, 13-3 (Mil)
1986—49ers, 31-17 (Mil)
1987—49ers, 23-12 (GB)
1989—Packers, 21-17 (SF)
1990—49ers, 24-20 (GB)
1995—*Packers, 27-17 (SF)
1996—Packers, 23-20 (GB) OT
*Packers, 35-14 (GB)
1997—**Packers, 23-10 (SF)
1998—Packers, 36-22 (GB)
***49ers, 30-27 (SF)
1999—Packers, 20-3 (SF)
2000—Packers, 31-28 (GB)
2001—***Packers, 25-15 (GB)
2002—Packers, 20-14 (SF)
2003—Packers, 20-10 (GB)
(RS Pts.—49ers 1,077, Packers 1,049)
(PS Pts.—Packers 137, 49ers 86)
NFC Divisional Playoff
***NFC Championship*
****NFC First-Round Playoff*

GREEN BAY vs. SEATTLE
RS: Packers lead series, 5-4
PS: Packers lead series, 1-0
1976—Packers, 27-20 (Mil)
1978—Packers, 45-28 (Mil)
1981—Packers, 34-24 (GB)
1984—Seahawks, 30-24 (Mil)
1987—Seahawks, 24-13 (S)
1990—Seahawks, 20-14 (Mil)
1996—Packers, 31-10 (S)
1999—Seahawks, 27-7 (GB)
2003—Packers, 35-13 (GB)
*Packers, 33-27 (GB) OT
(RS Pts.—Packers 230, Seahawks 196)
(PS Pts.—Packers 33, Seahawks 27)
NFC First-Round Playoff

GREEN BAY vs. TAMPA BAY
RS: Packers lead series, 29-18-1
PS: Packers lead series, 1-0
1977—Packers, 13-0 (TB)
1978—Packers, 9-7 (GB)
Packers, 17-7 (TB)
1979—Buccaneers, 21-10 (GB)
Buccaneers, 21-3 (TB)
1980—Tie, 14-14 (TB) OT
Buccaneers, 20-17 (Mil)
1981—Buccaneers, 21-10 (GB)
Buccaneers, 37-3 (TB)
1983—Packers, 55-14 (GB)
Packers, 12-9 (TB) OT
1984—Buccaneers, 30-27 (TB) OT
Packers, 27-14 (GB)
1985—Packers, 21-0 (GB)
Packers, 20-17 (TB)
1986—Packers, 31-7 (Mil)
Packers, 21-7 (TB)
1987—Buccaneers, 23-17 (Mil)
1988—Buccaneers, 13-10 (GB)
Buccaneers, 27-24 (TB)
1989—Buccaneers, 23-21 (GB)
Packers, 17-16 (TB)
1990—Buccaneers, 26-14 (TB)
Packers, 20-10 (Mil)
1991—Packers, 15-13 (GB)
Packers, 27-0 (TB)
1992—Buccaneers, 31-3 (TB)
Packers, 19-14 (Mil)
1993—Packers, 37-14 (TB)
Packers, 13-10 (GB)
1994—Packers, 30-3 (GB)
Packers, 34-19 (TB)
1995—Packers, 35-13 (GB)
Buccaneers, 13-10 (TB) OT
1996—Packers, 34-3 (TB)
Packers, 13-7 (GB)
1997—Packers, 21-16 (GB)
Packers, 17-6 (TB)
*Packers, 21-7 (GB)
1998—Packers, 23-15 (GB)
Buccaneers, 24-22 (TB)
1999—Packers, 26-23 (GB)
Buccaneers, 29-10 (TB)
2000—Buccaneers, 20-15 (TB)
Packers, 17-14 (GB) OT
2001—Buccaneers, 14-10 (TB)
Packers, 21-20 (GB)
2002—Buccaneers, 21-7 (TB)
2003—Packers, 20-13 (TB)
(RS Pts.—Packers 912, Buccaneers 739)
(PS Pts.—Packers 21, Buccaneers 7)
NFC Divisional Playoff

GREEN BAY vs. *TENNESSEE
RS: Series tied, 4-4
1972—Packers, 23-10 (H)
1977—Oilers, 16-10 (GB)
1980—Oilers, 22-3 (GB)
1983—Packers, 41-38 (H) OT
1986—Oilers, 31-3 (GB)
1992—Packers, 16-14 (H)
1998—Packers, 30-22 (GB)
2001—Titans, 26-20 (T)
(RS Pts.—Titans 179, Packers 146)
Franchise in Houston prior to 1997; known as Oilers prior to 1999

GREEN BAY vs. *WASHINGTON
RS: Packers lead series, 15-12-1
PS: Series tied, 1-1
1932—Packers, 21-0 (B)
1933—Tie, 7-7 (GB)
Redskins, 20-7 (B)
1934—Packers, 10-0 (B)
1936—Packers, 31-2 (GB)
Packers, 7-3 (B)
**Packers, 21-6 (New York)
1937—Redskins, 14-6 (W)
1939—Packers, 24-14 (Mil)
1941—Packers, 22-17 (W)
1943—Redskins, 33-7 (Mil)
1946—Packers, 20-7 (W)
1947—Packers, 27-10 (Mil)
1948—Redskins, 23-7 (Mil)
1949—Redskins, 30-0 (W)
1950—Packers, 35-21 (Mil)
1952—Packers, 35-20 (Mil)
1958—Redskins, 37-21 (W)
1959—Packers, 21-0 (GB)
1968—Packers, 27-7 (W)
1972—Redskins, 21-16 (W)
***Redskins, 16-3 (W)
1974—Redskins, 17-6 (GB)
1977—Redskins, 10-9 (W)
1979—Redskins, 38-21 (W)
1983—Packers, 48-47 (GB)
1986—Redskins, 16-7 (GB)
1988—Redskins, 20-17 (Mil)
2001—Packers, 37-0 (GB)
2002—Packers, 30-9 (GB)
(RS Pts.—Packers 526, Redskins 443)
(PS Pts.—Packers 24, Redskins 22)
**Franchise in Boston prior to 1937 and known as Braves prior to 1933*
***NFL Championship*
****NFC Divisional Playoff*

HOUSTON vs. ATLANTA
RS: Texans lead series, 1-0;
See Atlanta vs. Houston

HOUSTON vs. BALTIMORE
RS: Ravens lead series, 1-0;
See Baltimore vs. Houston

HOUSTON vs. BUFFALO
RS: Series tied, 1-1;
See Buffalo vs. Houston

HOUSTON vs. CAROLINA
RS: Texans lead series, 1-0;
See Carolina vs. Houston

HOUSTON vs. CINCINNATI
RS: Bengals lead series, 2-0;
See Cincinnati vs. Houston

HOUSTON vs. CLEVELAND
RS: Browns lead series, 1-0;
See Cleveland vs. Houston

HOUSTON vs. DALLAS
RS: Texans lead series, 1-0;
See Dallas vs. Houston

HOUSTON vs. INDIANAPOLIS
RS: Colts lead series, 4-0
2002—Colts, 23-3 (H)
Colts, 19-3 (I)
2003—Colts, 30-21 (I)
Colts, 20-17 (H)
(RS Pts.—Colts 92, Texans 44)

HOUSTON vs. JACKSONVILLE
RS: Series tied, 2-2
2002—Texans, 21-19 (J)
Jaguars, 24-21 (H)
2003—Texans, 24-20 (H)
Jaguars, 27-0 (J)
(RS Pts.—Jaguars 90, Texans 66)

HOUSTON vs. KANSAS CITY
RS: Chiefs lead series, 1-0
2003—Chiefs, 42-14 (H)
(RS Pts.—Chiefs 42, Texans 14)

HOUSTON vs. MIAMI
RS: Texans lead series, 1-0
2003—Texans, 21-20 (M)
(RS Pts.—Texans 21, Dolphins 20)

HOUSTON vs. NEW ENGLAND
RS: Patriots lead series, 1-0
2003—Patriots, 23-20 (H) OT
(RS Pts.—Patriots 23, Texans 20)

HOUSTON vs. NEW ORLEANS
RS: Saints lead series, 1-0
2003—Saints, 31-10 (NO)
(RS Pts.—Saints 31, Texans 10)

HOUSTON vs. N.Y. GIANTS
RS: Texans lead series, 1-0
2002—Texans, 16-14 (H)
(RS Pts.—Texans 16, Giants 14)

HOUSTON vs. N.Y. JETS
RS: Jets lead series, 1-0
2003—Jets, 19-14 (H)
(RS Pts.—Jets 19, Texans 14)

HOUSTON vs. PHILADELPHIA
RS: Eagles lead series, 1-0
2002—Eagles, 35-17 (P)
(RS Pts.—Eagles 35, Texans 17)

HOUSTON vs. PITTSBURGH
RS: Texans lead series, 1-0
2002—Texans, 24-6 (P)
(RS Pts.—Texans 24, Steelers 6)

HOUSTON vs. SAN DIEGO
RS: Chargers lead series, 1-0
2002—Chargers, 24-3 (SD)
(RS Pts.—Chargers 24, Texans 3)

HOUSTON vs. TAMPA BAY
RS: Buccaneers lead series, 1-0
2003—Buccaneers, 16-3 (TB)
(RS Pts.—Buccaneers 16, Texans 3)

HOUSTON vs. TENNESSEE
RS: Titans lead series, 4-0
2002—Titans, 17-10 (T)
Titans, 13-3 (H)
2003—Titans, 38-17 (T)
Titans, 27-24 (H)
(RS Pts.—Titans 95, Texans 54)

HOUSTON vs. WASHINGTON
RS: Redskins lead series, 1-0
2002—Redskins, 26-10 (W)
(RS Pts.—Redskins 26, Texans 10)

INDIANAPOLIS vs. ARIZONA
RS: Series tied, 6-6;
See Arizona vs. Indianapolis

INDIANAPOLIS vs. ATLANTA
RS: Colts lead series, 12-1;
See Atlanta vs. Indianapolis

INDIANAPOLIS vs. BALTIMORE
RS: Series tied, 2-2;
See Baltimore vs. Indianapolis

INDIANAPOLIS vs. BUFFALO
RS: Bills lead series, 34-29-1;
See Buffalo vs. Indianapolis

INDIANAPOLIS vs. CAROLINA
RS: Panthers lead series, 3-0;
See Carolina vs. Indianapolis

INDIANAPOLIS vs. CHICAGO
RS: Colts lead series, 21-17;
See Chicago vs. Indianapolis

INDIANAPOLIS vs. CINCINNATI
RS: Colts lead series, 12-8
PS: Colts lead series, 1-0;
See Cincinnati vs. Indianapolis

INDIANAPOLIS vs. CLEVELAND
RS: Browns lead series, 13-10
PS: Series tied, 2-2;
See Cleveland vs. Indianapolis

INDIANAPOLIS vs. DALLAS
RS: Cowboys lead series, 7-5
PS: Colts lead series, 1-0;
See Dallas vs. Indianapolis

INDIANAPOLIS vs. DENVER
RS: Broncos lead series, 10-4
PS: Colts lead series, 1-0;
See Denver vs. Indianapolis

INDIANAPOLIS vs. DETROIT
RS: Series tied, 18-18-2;
See Detroit vs. Indianapolis

INDIANAPOLIS vs. GREEN BAY
RS: Series tied, 19-19-1
PS: Packers lead series, 1-0;
See Green Bay vs. Indianapolis

INDIANAPOLIS vs. HOUSTON
RS: Colts lead series, 4-0;
See Houston vs. Indianapolis

INDIANAPOLIS vs. JACKSONVILLE
RS: Colts lead series, 5-1
1995—Colts, 41-31 (J)
2000—Colts, 43-14 (I)
2002—Colts, 28-25 (J)
Colts, 20-13 (I)
2003—Colts, 23-13 (I)
Jaguars, 28-23 (J)
(RS Pts.—Colts 178, Jaguars 124)

***INDIANAPOLIS vs. KANSAS CITY**
RS: Colts lead series, 8-6
PS: Colts lead series, 2-0
1970—Chiefs, 44-24 (B)
1972—Chiefs, 24-10 (KC)
1975—Colts, 28-14 (B)
1977—Colts, 17-6 (KC)
1979—Chiefs, 14-0 (KC)
Chiefs, 10-7 (B)
1980—Colts, 31-24 (KC)
Chiefs, 38-28 (B)
1985—Chiefs, 20-7 (KC)
1990—Colts, 23-19 (I)
1995—**Colts, 10-7 (KC)
1996—Colts, 24-19 (KC)
1999—Colts, 25-17 (I)
2000—Colts, 27-14 (KC)
2001—Colts, 35-28 (KC)
2003—**Colts, 38-31 (KC)
(RS Pts.—Chiefs 291, Colts 286)
(PS Pts.—Colts 48, Chiefs 38)
**Franchise in Baltimore prior to 1984*
***AFC Divisional Playoff*

***INDIANAPOLIS vs. MIAMI**
RS: Dolphins lead series, 44-22
PS: Dolphins lead series, 2-0
1970—Colts, 35-0 (B)
Dolphins, 34-17 (M)
1971—Dolphins, 17-14 (M)
Colts, 14-3 (B)
**Dolphins, 21-0 (M)
1972—Dolphins, 23-0 (B)
Dolphins, 16-0 (M)
1973—Dolphins, 44-0 (M)
Colts, 16-3 (B)
1974—Dolphins, 17-7 (M)
Dolphins, 17-16 (B)
1975—Colts, 33-17 (M)
Colts, 10-7 (B) OT
1976—Colts, 28-14 (B)
Colts, 17-16 (M)
1977—Colts, 45-28 (B)
Dolphins, 17-6 (M)
1978—Dolphins, 42-0 (B)
Dolphins, 26-8 (M)
1979—Dolphins, 19-0 (M)
Dolphins, 28-24 (B)
1980—Colts, 30-17 (M)
Dolphins, 24-14 (B)
1981—Dolphins, 31-28 (B)
Dolphins, 27-10 (M)
1982—Dolphins, 24-20 (M)
Dolphins, 34-7 (B)
1983—Dolphins, 21-7 (B)
Dolphins, 37-0 (M)
1984—Dolphins, 44-7 (M)
Dolphins, 35-17 (I)
1985—Dolphins, 30-13 (M)
Dolphins, 34-20 (I)
1986—Dolphins, 30-10 (M)
Dolphins, 17-13 (I)
1987—Dolphins, 23-10 (I)
Colts, 40-21 (M)
1988—Colts, 15-13 (I)
Colts, 31-28 (M)
1989—Dolphins, 19-13 (M)
Colts, 42-13 (I)
1990—Dolphins, 27-7 (I)
Dolphins, 23-17 (M)
1991—Dolphins, 17-6 (M)
Dolphins, 10-6 (I)
1992—Colts, 31-20 (M)
Dolphins, 28-0 (I)
1993—Dolphins, 24-20 (I)
Dolphins, 41-27 (M)
1994—Dolphins, 22-21 (M)
Colts, 10-6 (I)
1995—Colts, 27-24 (M) OT
Colts, 36-28 (I)
1996—Colts, 10-6 (I)
Dolphins, 37-13 (M)
1997—Dolphins, 16-10 (M)
Colts, 41-0 (I)
1998—Dolphins, 24-15 (I)
Dolphins, 27-14 (M)
1999—Dolphins, 34-31 (I)
Colts, 37-34 (M)
2000—Dolphins, 17-14 (I)
Colts, 20-13 (M)
***Dolphins 23-17 (M) OT
2001—Dolphins, 27-24 (I)
Dolphins, 41-6 (M)
2002—Dolphins, 21-13 (I)
2003—Colts, 23-17 (M)
(RS Pts.—Dolphins 1,494, Colts 1,116)
(PS Pts.—Dolphins 44, Colts 17)
**Franchise in Baltimore prior to 1984*
***AFC Championship*
****AFC First-Round Playoff*

***INDIANAPOLIS vs. MINNESOTA**
RS: Colts lead series, 12-7-1
PS: Colts lead series, 1-0
1961—Colts, 34-33 (B)
Vikings, 28-20 (M)
1962—Colts, 34-7 (M)
Colts, 42-17 (B)
1963—Colts, 37-34 (M)
Colts, 41-10 (B)
1964—Vikings, 34-24 (M)
Colts, 17-14 (B)
1965—Colts, 35-16 (B)
Colts, 41-21 (M)
1966—Colts, 38-23 (M)
Colts, 20-17 (B)
1967—Tie, 20-20 (M)
1968—Colts, 21-9 (B)
**Colts, 24-14 (B)

1969—Vikings, 52-14 (M)
1971—Vikings, 10-3 (M)
1982—Vikings, 13-10 (M)
1988—Vikings, 12-3 (M)
1997—Vikings, 39-28 (M)
2000—Colts, 31-10 (I)
(RS Pts.—Colts 513, Vikings 419)
(PS Pts.—Colts 24, Vikings 14)
Franchise in Baltimore prior to 1984
***Conference Championship*

***INDIANAPOLIS vs. **NEW ENGLAND**
RS: Patriots lead series, 40-24
PS: Patriots lead series, 1-0
1970—Colts, 14-6 (Bos)
Colts, 27-3 (Balt)
1971—Colts, 23-3 (NE)
Patriots, 21-17 (Balt)
1972—Colts, 24-17 (NE)
Colts, 31-0 (Balt)
1973—Patriots, 24-16 (NE)
Colts, 18-13 (Balt)
1974—Patriots, 42-3 (NE)
Patriots, 27-17 (Balt)
1975—Patriots, 21-10 (NE)
Colts, 34-21 (Balt)
1976—Colts, 27-13 (NE)
Patriots, 21-14 (Balt)
1977—Patriots, 17-3 (NE)
Colts, 30-24 (Balt)
1978—Colts, 34-27 (NE)
Patriots, 35-14 (Balt)
1979—Colts, 31-26 (Balt)
Patriots, 50-21 (NE)
1980—Patriots, 37-21 (Balt)
Patriots, 47-21 (NE)
1981—Colts, 29-28 (NE)
Colts, 23-21 (Balt)
1982—Patriots, 24-13 (Balt)
1983—Colts, 29-23 (NE) OT
Colts, 12-7 (Balt)
1984—Patriots, 50-17 (I)
Patriots, 16-10 (NE)
1985—Patriots, 34-15 (NE)
Patriots, 38-31 (I)
1986—Patriots, 33-3 (NE)
Patriots, 30-21 (I)
1987—Colts, 30-16 (I)
Patriots, 24-0 (NE)
1988—Patriots, 21-17 (NE)
Colts, 24-21 (I)
1989—Patriots, 23-20 (I) OT
Patriots, 22-16 (NE)
1990—Patriots, 16-14 (I)
Colts, 13-10 (NE)
1991—Patriots, 16-7 (I)
Patriots, 23-17 (NE) OT
1992—Patriots, 37-34 (I) OT
Colts, 6-0 (NE)
1993—Colts, 9-6 (I)
Patriots, 38-0 (NE)
1994—Patriots, 12-10 (I)
Patriots, 28-13 (NE)
1995—Colts, 24-10 (NE)
Colts, 10-7 (I)
1996—Patriots, 27-9 (I)
Patriots, 27-13 (NE)
1997—Patriots, 31-6 (I)
Patriots, 20-17 (NE)
1998—Patriots, 29-6 (NE)
Patriots, 21-16 (I)
1999—Patriots, 31-28 (NE)
Colts, 20-15 (I)
2000—Patriots, 24-16 (NE)
Colts, 30-23 (I)
2001—Patriots, 44-13 (NE)
Patriots, 38-17 (I)
2003—Patriots, 38-34 (I)
***Patriots, 24-14 (NE)
(RS Pts.—Patriots 1,497, Colts 1,142)
(PS Pts.—Patriots 24, Colts 14)
**Franchise in Baltimore prior to 1984*
***Franchise in Boston prior to 1971*
****AFC Championship*

***INDIANAPOLIS vs. NEW ORLEANS**
RS: Saints lead series, 5-4
1967—Colts, 30-10 (B)
1969—Colts, 30-10 (NO)
1973—Colts, 14-10 (B)
1986—Saints, 17-14 (I)
1989—Saints, 41-6 (NO)
1995—Saints, 17-14 (NO)
1998—Saints, 19-13 (I) OT
2001—Saints, 34-20 (NO)
2003—Colts, 55-21 (NO)
(RS Pts.—Colts 196, Saints 179)
**Franchise in Baltimore prior to 1984*

***INDIANAPOLIS vs. N.Y. GIANTS**
RS: Series tied, 6-6
PS: Colts lead series, 2-0
1954—Colts, 20-14 (B)
1955—Giants, 17-7 (NY)
1958—Giants, 24-21 (NY)
**Colts, 23-17 (NY) OT
1959—**Colts, 31-16 (B)
1963—Giants, 37-28 (B)
1968—Colts, 26-0 (NY)
1971—Colts, 31-7 (NY)
1975—Colts, 21-0 (NY)
1979—Colts, 31-7 (NY)
1990—Giants, 24-7 (I)
1993—Giants, 20-6 (NY)
1999—Colts, 27-19 (NY)
2002—Giants, 44-27 (I)
(RS Pts.—Colts 252, Giants 213)
(PS Pts.—Colts 54, Giants 33)
**Franchise in Baltimore prior to 1984*
***NFL Championship*

***INDIANAPOLIS vs. N.Y. JETS**
RS: Colts lead series, 39-25
PS: Jets lead series, 2-0
1968—**Jets 16-7 (Miami)
1970—Colts, 29-22 (NY)
Colts, 35-20 (B)
1971—Colts, 22-0 (B)
Colts, 14-13 (NY)
1972—Jets, 44-34 (B)
Jets, 24-20 (NY)
1973—Jets, 34-10 (B)
Jets, 20-17 (NY)
1974—Colts, 35-20 (NY)
Jets, 45-38 (B)
1975—Colts, 45-28 (NY)
Colts, 52-19 (B)
1976—Colts, 20-0 (NY)
Colts, 33-16 (B)
1977—Colts, 20-12 (NY)
Colts, 33-12 (B)
1978—Jets, 33-10 (B)
Jets, 24-16 (NY)
1979—Colts, 10-8 (B)
Jets, 30-17 (NY)
1980—Colts, 17-14 (NY)
Colts, 35-21 (B)
1981—Jets, 41-14 (B)
Jets, 25-0 (NY)
1982—Jets, 37-0 (NY)
1983—Colts, 17-14 (NY)
Jets, 10-6 (B)
1984—Jets, 23-14 (I)
Colts, 9-5 (NY)
1985—Jets, 25-20 (NY)
Jets, 35-17 (I)
1986—Jets, 26-7 (I)
Jets, 31-16 (NY)
1987—Colts, 6-0 (I)
Colts, 19-14 (NY)
1988—Colts, 38-14 (I)
Jets, 34-16 (NY)
1989—Colts, 17-10 (NY)
Colts, 27-10 (I)
1990—Colts, 17-14 (I)
Colts, 29-21 (NY)
1991—Jets, 17-6 (I)
Colts, 28-27 (NY)
1992—Colts, 6-3 (I) OT
Colts, 10-6 (NY)
1993—Jets, 31-17 (I)
Colts, 9-6 (NY)
1994—Jets, 16-6 (NY)
Colts, 28-25 (I)
1995—Colts, 27-24 (NY) OT
Colts, 17-10 (I)
1996—Colts, 21-7 (NY)
Colts, 34-29 (I)
1997—Jets, 16-12 (I)
Colts, 22-14 (NY)
1998—Jets, 44-6 (NY)
Colts, 24-23 (I)
1999—Colts, 16-13 (NY)
Colts, 13-6 (I)
2000—Colts, 23-15 (I)
Jets, 27-17 (NY)
2001—Colts, 45-24 (NY)
Jets, 29-28 (I)
2002—***Jets, 41-0 (NY)
2003—Colts, 38-31 (I)
(RS Pts.—Colts 1,304, Jets 1,291)
(PS Pts.—Jets 57, Colts 7)
**Franchise in Baltimore prior to 1984*
***Super Bowl III*
****AFC First-Round Playoff*

***INDIANAPOLIS vs **OAKLAND**
RS: Raiders lead series, 7-2
PS: Series tied, 1-1
1970—***Colts, 27-17 (B)
1971—Colts, 37-14 (O)
1973—Raiders, 34-21 (B)
1975—Raiders, 31-20 (B)
1977—****Raiders, 37-31 (B) OT
1984—Raiders, 21-7 (LA)
1986—Colts, 30-24 (LA)
1991—Raiders, 16-0 (LA)
1995—Raiders, 30-17 (O)
2000—Raiders, 38-31 (I)
2001—Raiders, 23-18 (I)
(RS Pts.—Raiders 231, Colts 181)
(PS Pts.—Colts 58, Raiders 54)
**Franchise in Baltimore prior to 1984*
***Franchise in Los Angeles from 1982-1994*

****AFC Championship*
*****AFC Divisional Playoff*

***INDIANAPOLIS vs. PHILADELPHIA**
RS: Colts lead series, 9-6
1953—Eagles, 45-14 (P)
1965—Colts, 34-24 (B)
1967—Colts, 38-6 (P)
1969—Colts, 24-20 (B)
1970—Colts, 29-10 (B)
1974—Eagles, 30-10 (P)
1978—Eagles, 17-14 (B)
1981—Eagles, 38-13 (P)
1983—Colts, 22-21 (P)
1984—Eagles, 16-7 (P)
1990—Colts, 24-23 (P)
1993—Eagles, 20-10 (I)
1996—Colts, 37-10 (I)
1999—Colts, 44-17 (P)
2002—Colts, 35-13 (P)
(RS Pts.—Colts 355, Eagles 310)
**Franchise in Baltimore prior to 1984*

***INDIANAPOLIS vs. PITTSBURGH**
RS: Steelers lead series, 13-4
PS: Steelers lead series, 4-0
1957—Steelers, 19-13 (B)
1968—Colts, 41-7 (P)
1971—Colts, 34-21 (B)
1974—Steelers, 30-0 (P)
1975—**Steelers, 28-10 (P)
1976—**Steelers, 40-14 (B)
1977—Colts, 31-21 (B)
1978—Steelers, 35-13 (P)
1979—Steelers, 17-13 (P)
1980—Steelers, 20-17 (B)
1983—Steelers, 24-13 (B)
1984—Colts, 17-16 (I)
1985—Steelers, 45-3 (P)
1987—Steelers, 21-7 (P)
1991—Steelers, 21-3 (I)
1992—Steelers, 30-14 (P)
1994—Steelers, 31-21 (P)
1995—***Steelers, 20-16 (P)
1996—****Steelers, 42-14 (P)
1997—Steelers, 24-22 (P)
2002—Steelers, 28-10 (P)
(RS Pts.—Steelers 410, Colts 272)
(PS Pts.—Steelers 130, Colts 54)
**Franchise in Baltimore prior to 1984*
***AFC Divisional Playoff*
****AFC Championship*
*****AFC First-Round Playoff*

***INDIANAPOLIS vs. **ST. LOUIS**
RS: Colts lead series, 21-17-2
1953—Rams, 21-13 (B)
Rams, 45-2 (LA)
1954—Rams, 48-0 (B)
Colts, 22-21 (LA)
1955—Tie, 17-17 (B)
Rams, 20-14 (LA)
1956—Colts, 56-21 (B)
Rams, 31-7 (LA)
1957—Colts, 31-14 (B)
Rams, 37-21 (LA)
1958—Colts, 34-7 (B)
Rams, 30-28 (LA)
1959—Colts, 35-21 (B)
Colts, 45-26 (LA)
1960—Colts, 31-17 (B)
Rams, 10-3 (LA)
1961—Colts, 27-24 (B)
Rams, 34-17 (LA)
1962—Colts, 30-27 (B)
Colts, 14-2 (LA)
1963—Rams, 17-16 (LA)
Colts, 19-16 (B)
1964—Colts, 35-20 (B)
Colts, 24-7 (LA)
1965—Colts, 35-20 (B)
Colts, 20-17 (LA)
1966—Colts, 17-3 (LA)
Rams, 23-7 (B)
1967—Tie, 24-24 (B)
Rams, 34-10 (LA)
1968—Colts, 27-10 (B)
Colts, 28-24 (LA)
1969—Rams, 27-20 (B)
Colts, 13-7 (LA)
1971—Colts, 24-17 (B)
1975—Rams, 24-13 (LA)
1986—Rams, 24-7 (I)
1989—Rams, 31-17 (LA)
1995—Colts, 21-18 (I)
2001—Rams, 42-17 (StL)
(RS Pts.—Rams 878, Colts 841)
**Franchise in Baltimore prior to 1984*
***Franchise in Los Angeles prior to 1995*

***INDIANAPOLIS vs. SAN DIEGO**
RS: Chargers lead series, 12-7
PS: Colts lead series, 1-0
1970—Colts, 16-14 (SD)
1972—Chargers, 23-20 (B)
1976—Colts, 37-21 (SD)
1981—Chargers, 43-14 (B)
1982—Chargers, 44-26 (SD)
1984—Chargers, 38-10 (I)
1986—Chargers, 17-3 (I)
1987—Chargers, 16-13 (I)
Colts, 20-7 (SD)
1988—Colts, 16-0 (SD)
1989—Colts, 10-6 (I)
1992—Chargers, 34-14 (I)
Chargers, 26-0 (SD)
1993—Chargers, 31-0 (I)
1995—Chargers, 27-24 (I)
**Colts, 35-20 (SD)
1996—Chargers, 26-19 (I)
1997—Chargers, 35-19 (SD)
1998—Colts, 17-12 (I)
1999—Colts, 27-19 (SD)
(RS Pts.—Chargers 439, Colts 305)
(PS Pts.—Colts 35, Chargers 20)
**Franchise in Baltimore prior to 1984*
***AFC First-Round Playoff*

***INDIANAPOLIS vs. SAN FRANCISCO**
RS: Colts lead series, 22-18
1953—49ers, 38-21 (B)
49ers, 45-14 (SF)
1954—Colts, 17-13 (B)
49ers, 10-7 (SF)
1955—Colts, 26-14 (B)
49ers, 35-24 (SF)
1956—49ers, 20-17 (B)
49ers, 30-17 (SF)
1957—Colts, 27-21 (B)
49ers, 17-13 (SF)
1958—Colts, 35-27 (B)
49ers, 21-12 (SF)
1959—Colts, 45-14 (B)
Colts, 34-14 (SF)
1960—49ers, 30-22 (B)
49ers, 34-10 (SF)
1961—Colts, 20-17 (B)
Colts, 27-24 (SF)
1962—49ers, 21-13 (B)
Colts, 22-3 (SF)
1963—Colts, 20-14 (SF)
Colts, 20-3 (B)
1964—Colts, 37-7 (B)
Colts, 14-3 (SF)
1965—Colts, 27-24 (B)
Colts, 34-28 (SF)
1966—Colts, 36-14 (B)
Colts, 30-14 (SF)
1967—Colts, 41-7 (B)
Colts, 26-9 (SF)
1968—Colts, 27-10 (B)
Colts, 42-14 (SF)
1969—49ers, 24-21 (B)
49ers, 20-17 (SF)
1972—49ers, 24-21 (SF)
1986—49ers, 35-14 (SF)
1989—49ers, 30-24 (I)
1995—Colts, 18-17 (I)
1998—49ers, 34-31 (SF)
2001—49ers, 40-21 (I)
(RS Pts.—Colts 944, 49ers 819)
**Franchise in Baltimore prior to 1984*

***INDIANAPOLIS vs. SEATTLE**
RS: Colts lead series, 5-3
1977—Colts, 29-14 (S)
1978—Colts, 17-14 (S)
1991—Seahawks, 31-3 (S)
1994—Colts, 17-15 (I)
Colts, 31-19 (S)
1997—Seahawks, 31-3 (I)
1998—Seahawks, 27-23 (S)
2000—Colts, 37-24 (S)
(RS Pts.—Seahawks 175, Colts 160)
**Franchise in Baltimore prior to 1984*

***INDIANAPOLIS vs. TAMPA BAY**
RS: Colts lead series, 6-4
1976—Colts, 42-17 (B)
1979—Buccaneers, 29-26 (B) OT
1985—Colts, 31-23 (TB)
1987—Colts, 24-6 (I)
1988—Colts, 35-31 (I)
1991—Buccaneers, 17-3 (TB)
1992—Colts, 24-14 (TB)
1994—Buccaneers, 24-10 (TB)
1997—Buccaneers, 31-28 (I)
2003—Colts, 38-35 (TB) OT
(RS Pts.—Colts 261, Buccaneers 227)
**Franchise in Baltimore prior to 1984*

***INDIANAPOLIS vs. **TENNESSEE**
RS: Series tied, 9-9
PS: Titans lead series, 1-0
1970—Colts, 24-20 (H)
1973—Oilers, 31-27 (B)
1976—Colts, 38-14 (B)
1979—Oilers, 28-16 (B)
1980—Oilers, 21-16 (H)
1983—Colts, 20-10 (B)
1984—Colts, 35-21 (H)
1985—Colts, 34-16 (I)
1986—Oilers, 31-17 (H)
1987—Colts, 51-27 (I)
1988—Oilers, 17-14 (I) OT
1990—Oilers, 24-10 (H)
1992—Oilers, 20-10 (I)
1994—Colts, 45-21 (I)

1999—***Titans, 19-16 (I)
2002—Titans, 23-15 (I)
Titans, 27-17 (T)
2003—Colts, 33-7 (I)
Colts, 29-27 (T)
(RS Pts.—Colts 451, Titans 385)
(PS Pts.—Titans 19, Colts 16)
Franchise in Baltimore prior to 1984
***Franchise in Houston prior to 1997; known as Oilers prior to 1999*
****AFC Divisional Playoff*

***INDIANAPOLIS vs. WASHINGTON**
RS: Colts lead series, 17-10
1953—Colts, 27-17 (B)
1954—Redskins, 24-21 (W)
1955—Redskins, 14-13 (B)
1956—Colts, 19-17 (B)
1957—Colts, 21-17 (W)
1958—Colts, 35-10 (B)
1959—Redskins, 27-24 (W)
1960—Colts, 20-0 (B)
1961—Colts, 27-6 (W)
1962—Colts, 34-21 (B)
1963—Colts, 36-20 (W)
1964—Colts, 45-17 (B)
1965—Colts, 38-7 (W)
1966—Colts, 37-10 (B)
1967—Colts, 17-13 (W)
1969—Colts, 41-17 (B)
1973—Redskins, 22-14 (W)
1977—Colts, 10-3 (B)
1978—Colts, 21-17 (B)
1981—Redskins, 38-14 (W)
1984—Redskins, 35-7 (I)
1990—Colts, 35-28 (I)
1993—Redskins, 30-24 (W)
1994—Redskins, 41-27 (I)
1996—Redskins, 31-16 (W)
1999—Colts, 24-21 (I)
2002—Redskins, 26-21 (W)
(RS Pts.—Colts 668, Redskins 529)
**Franchise in Baltimore prior to 1984*

JACKSONVILLE vs. ARIZONA
RS: Jaguars lead series, 1-0;
See Arizona vs. Jacksonville

JACKSONVILLE vs. ATLANTA
RS: Jaguars lead series, 2-1;
See Atlanta vs. Jacksonville

JACKSONVILLE vs. BALTIMORE
RS: Jaguars lead series, 8-6;
See Baltimore vs. Jacksonville

JACKSONVILLE vs. BUFFALO
RS: Bills lead series, 3-1
PS: Jaguars lead series, 1-0;
See Buffalo vs. Jacksonville

JACKSONVILLE vs. CAROLINA
RS: Jaguars lead series, 2-1;
See Carolina vs. Jacksonville

JACKSONVILLE vs. CHICAGO
RS: Bears lead series, 2-1;
See Chicago vs. Jacksonville

JACKSONVILLE vs. CINCINNATI
RS: Jaguars lead series, 10-5;
See Cincinnati vs. Jacksonville

JACKSONVILLE vs. CLEVELAND
RS: Jaguars lead series, 7-2;
See Cleveland vs. Jacksonville

JACKSONVILLE vs. DALLAS
RS: Cowboys lead series, 2-1;
See Dallas vs. Jacksonville

JACKSONVILLE vs. DENVER
RS: Broncos lead series, 2-1
PS: Series tied, 1-1;
See Denver vs. Jacksonville

JACKSONVILLE vs. DETROIT
RS: Series tied, 1-1;
See Detroit vs. Jacksonville

JACKSONVILLE vs. GREEN BAY
RS: Packers lead series, 2-0;
See Green Bay vs. Jacksonville

JACKSONVILLE vs. HOUSTON
RS: Series tied, 2-2;
See Houston vs. Jacksonville

JACKSONVILLE vs. INDIANAPOLIS
RS: Colts lead series, 5-1;
See Indianapolis vs. Jacksonville

JACKSONVILLE vs. KANSAS CITY
RS: Jaguars lead series, 3-1
1997—Jaguars, 24-10 (J)
1998—Jaguars, 21-16 (J)
2001—Chiefs, 30-26 (J)
2002—Jaguars, 23-16 (KC)
(RS Pts.—Jaguars 94, Chiefs 72)

JACKSONVILLE vs. MIAMI
RS: Series tied, 1-1
PS: Jaguars lead series, 1-0
1998—Jaguars, 28-21 (J)
1999—*Jaguars, 62-7 (J)
2003—Dolphins, 24-10 (J)
(RS Pts.—Dolphins 45, Jaguars 38)
(PS Pts.—Jaguars 62, Dolphins 7)
**AFC Divisional Playoff*

JACKSONVILLE vs. MINNESOTA
RS: Series tied, 1-1
1998—Vikings, 50-10 (M)
2001—Jaguars, 33-3 (M)
(RS Pts.—Vikings 53, Jaguars 43)

JACKSONVILLE vs. NEW ENGLAND
RS: Patriots lead series, 3-0
PS: Series tied, 1-1
1996—Patriots, 28-25 (NE) OT
*Patriots, 20-6 (NE)
1997—Patriots, 26-20 (J)
1998—**Jaguars, 25-10 (J)
2003—Patriots, 27-13 (NE)
(RS Pts.—Patriots 81, Jaguars 58)
(PS Pts.—Jaguars 31, Patriots 30)
**AFC Championship*
***AFC First-Round Playoff*

JACKSONVILLE vs. NEW ORLEANS
RS: Jaguars lead series, 2-1
1996—Saints, 17-13 (NO)
1999—Jaguars, 41-23 (J)
2003—Jaguars, 20-19 (J)
(RS Pts.—Jaguars 74, Saints 59)

JACKSONVILLE vs. N.Y. GIANTS
RS: Giants lead series, 2-1
1997—Jaguars, 40-13 (J)
2000—Giants, 28-25 (NY)
2002—Giants, 24-17 (NY)
(RS Pts.—Jaguars 82, Giants 65)

JACKSONVILLE vs. N.Y. JETS
RS: Jaguars lead series, 3-2
PS: Jets lead series, 1-0
1995—Jets, 27-10 (NY)
1996—Jaguars, 21-17 (J)
1998—*Jets, 34-24 (NY)
1999—Jaguars, 16-6 (NY)
2002—Jaguars, 28-3 (J)
2003—Jets, 13-10 (NY)
(RS Pts.—Jaguars 85, Jets 66)
(PS Pts.—Jets 34, Jaguars 24
**AFC Divisional Playoff*

JACKSONVILLE vs. OAKLAND
RS: Series tied, 1-1
1996—Raiders, 17-3 (O)
1997—Jaguars, 20-9 (O)
(RS Pts.—Raiders 26, Jaguars 23)

JACKSONVILLE vs. PHILADELPHIA
RS: Jaguars lead series, 2-0
1997—Jaguars, 38-21 (J)
2002—Jaguars, 28-25 (J)
(RS Pts.—Jaguars 66, Eagles 46)

JACKSONVILLE vs. PITTSBURGH
RS: Jaguars lead series, 8-7
1995—Jaguars, 20-16 (J)
Steelers, 24-7 (P)
1996—Jaguars, 24-9 (J)
Steelers, 28-3 (P)
1997—Jaguars, 30-21 (J)
Steelers, 23-17 (P) OT
1998—Steelers, 30-15 (P)
Jaguars, 21-3 (J)
1999—Jaguars, 17-3 (P)
Jaguars, 20-6 (J)
2000—Steelers, 24-13 (J)
Jaguars, 34-24 (P)
2001—Jaguars, 21-3 (J)
Steelers, 20-7 (P)
2002—Steelers, 25-23 (J)
(RS Pts.—Jaguars 272, Steelers 259)

JACKSONVILLE vs. ST. LOUIS
RS: Rams lead series, 1-0
1996—Rams, 17-14 (StL)
(RS Pts.—Rams 17, Jaguars 14)

JACKSONVILLE vs. SAN DIEGO
RS: Jaguars lead series, 1-0
2003—Jaguars, 27-21 (J)
(RS Pts.—Jaguars 27, Chargers 21)

JACKSONVILLE vs. SAN FRANCISCO
RS: Jaguars lead series, 1-0
1999—Jaguars, 41-3 (J)
(RS Pts.—Jaguars 41, 49ers 3)

JACKSONVILLE vs. SEATTLE
RS: Seahawks lead series, 3-1
1995—Seahawks, 47-30 (J)
1996—Jaguars, 20-13 (J)
2000—Seahawks, 28-21 (J)
2001—Seahawks, 24-15 (S)
(RS Pts.—Seahawks 112, Jaguars 86)

JACKSONVILLE vs. TAMPA BAY
RS: Jaguars lead series, 2-1
1995—Buccaneers, 17-16 (TB)
1998—Jaguars, 29-24 (J)
2003—Jaguars, 17-10 (J)
(RS Pts.—Jaguars 62, Buccaneers 51)

JACKSONVILLE vs. *TENNESSEE
RS: Titans lead series, 11-7
PS: Titans lead, 1-0
1995—Oilers, 10-3 (J)
Jaguars, 17-16 (H)
1996—Oilers, 34-27 (J)
Jaguars, 23-17 (H)
1997—Jaguars, 30-24 (T)
Jaguars, 17-9 (J)
1998—Jaguars, 27-22 (T)
Oilers, 16-13 (J)
1999—Titans, 20-19 (J)
Titans, 41-14 (T)

**Titans, 33-14 (J)
2000—Titans, 27-13 (T)
Jaguars, 16-13 (J)
2001—Jaguars, 13-6 (J)
Titans, 28-24 (T)
2002—Titans, 23-14 (T)
Titans, 28-10 (J)
2003—Titans, 30-17 (J)
Titans, 10-3 (T)
(RS Pts.—Titans 374, Jaguars 300)
(PS Pts.—Titans 33, Jaguars 14)
Franchise in Houston prior to 1997; known as Oilers prior to 1999
***AFC Championship*

JACKSONVILLE vs. WASHINGTON
RS: Redskins lead series, 2-1
1997—Redskins, 24-12 (W)
2000—Redskins, 35-16 (J)
2002—Jaguars, 26-7 (J)
(RS Pts.—Redskins 66, Jaguars 54)

KANSAS CITY vs. ARIZONA
RS: Chiefs lead series, 6-2-1;
See Arizona vs. Kansas City

KANSAS CITY vs. ATLANTA
RS: Chiefs lead series, 4-1;
See Atlanta vs. Kansas City

KANSAS CITY vs. BALTIMORE
RS: Chiefs lead series, 2-0;
See Baltimore vs. Kansas City

KANSAS CITY vs. BUFFALO
RS: Bills lead series, 18-16-1
PS: Bills lead series, 2-1;
See Buffalo vs. Kansas City

KANSAS CITY vs. CAROLINA
RS: Chiefs lead series, 2-0;
See Carolina vs. Kansas City

KANSAS CITY vs. CHICAGO
RS: Bears lead series, 5-4;
See Chicago vs. Kansas City

KANSAS CITY vs. CINCINNATI
RS: Chiefs lead series, 11-10;
See Cincinnati vs. Kansas City

KANSAS CITY vs. CLEVELAND
RS: Chiefs lead series, 9-8-2;
See Cleveland vs. Kansas City

KANSAS CITY vs. DALLAS
RS: Cowboys lead series, 4-3;
See Dallas vs. Kansas City

KANSAS CITY vs. DENVER
RS: Chiefs lead series, 49-38
PS: Broncos lead series, 1-0;
See Denver vs. Kansas City

KANSAS CITY vs. DETROIT
RS: Chiefs lead series, 7-3;
See Detroit vs. Kansas City

KANSAS CITY vs. GREEN BAY
RS: Chiefs lead series, 6-1-1
PS: Packers lead series, 1-0;
See Green Bay vs. Kansas City

KANSAS CITY vs. HOUSTON
RS: Chiefs lead series, 1-0;
See Houston vs. Kansas City

KANSAS CITY vs. INDIANAPOLIS
RS: Colts lead series, 8-6
PS: Colts lead series, 2-0;
See Indianapolis vs. Kansas City

KANSAS CITY vs. JACKSONVILLE
RS: Jaguars lead series, 3-1;
See Jacksonville vs. Kansas City

KANSAS CITY vs. MIAMI
RS: Chiefs lead series, 11-10
PS: Dolphins lead series, 3-0
1966—Chiefs, 34-16 (KC)
Chiefs, 19-18 (M)
1967—Chiefs, 24-0 (M)
Chiefs, 41-0 (KC)
1968—Chiefs, 48-3 (M)
1969—Chiefs, 17-10 (KC)
1971—*Dolphins, 27-24 (KC) OT
1972—Dolphins, 20-10 (KC)
1974—Dolphins, 9-3 (M)
1976—Chiefs, 20-17 (M) OT
1981—Dolphins, 17-7 (KC)
1983—Dolphins, 14-6 (M)
1985—Dolphins, 31-0 (M)
1987—Dolphins, 42-0 (M)
1989—Chiefs, 26-21 (KC)
Chiefs, 27-24 (M)
1990—**Dolphins, 17-16 (M)
1991—Chiefs, 42-7 (KC)
1993—Dolphins, 30-10 (M)
1994—Dolphins, 45-28 (M)
**Dolphins, 27-17 (M)
1995—Dolphins, 13-6 (M)
1997—Dolphins, 17-14 (M)
2002—Chiefs, 48-30 (KC)
(RS Pts.—Chiefs 430, Dolphins 384)
(PS Pts.—Dolphins 71, Chiefs 57)
**AFC Divisional Playoff*
***AFC First-Round Playoff*

KANSAS CITY vs. MINNESOTA
RS: Series tied, 4-4
PS: Chiefs lead series, 1-0
1969—*Chiefs, 23-7 (New Orleans)
1970—Vikings, 27-10 (M)
1974—Vikings, 35-15 (KC)
1981—Chiefs, 10-6 (M)
1990—Chiefs, 24-21 (KC)
1993—Vikings, 30-10 (M)
1996—Chiefs, 21-6 (M)
1999—Chiefs, 31-28 (KC)
2003—Vikings, 45-20 (M)
(RS Pts.—Vikings 198, Chiefs 141)
(PS Pts.—Chiefs 23, Vikings 7)
**Super Bowl IV*

***KANSAS CITY vs. **NEW ENGLAND**
RS: Chiefs lead series, 15-10-3
1960—Patriots, 42-14 (B)
Texans, 34-0 (D)
1961—Patriots, 18-17 (D)
Patriots, 28-21 (B)
1962—Texans, 42-28 (D)
Texans, 27-7 (B)
1963—Tie, 24-24 (B)
Chiefs, 35-3 (KC)
1964—Patriots, 24-7 (B)
Patriots, 31-24 (KC)
1965—Chiefs, 27-17 (KC)
Tie, 10-10 (B)
1966—Chiefs, 43-24 (B)
Tie, 27-27 (KC)
1967—Chiefs, 33-10 (B)
1968—Chiefs, 31-17 (KC)
1969—Chiefs, 31-0 (B)
1970—Chiefs, 23-10 (KC)
1973—Chiefs, 10-7 (NE)
1977—Patriots, 21-17 (NE)
1981—Patriots, 33-17 (NE)
1990—Chiefs, 37-7 (NE)
1992—Chiefs, 27-20 (KC)
1995—Chiefs, 31-26 (KC)
1998—Patriots, 40-10 (NE)
1999—Chiefs, 16-14 (KC)
2000—Patriots, 30-24 (NE)
2002—Patriots, 41-38 (NE) OT
(RS Pts.—Chiefs 697, Patriots 559)
**Franchise located in Dallas prior to 1963 and known as Texans*
***Franchise in Boston prior to 1971*

KANSAS CITY vs. NEW ORLEANS
RS: Chiefs lead series, 4-3
1972—Chiefs, 20-17 (NO)
1976—Saints, 27-17 (KC)
1982—Saints, 27-17 (NO)
1985—Chiefs, 47-27 (NO)
1991—Saints, 17-10 (KC)
1994—Chiefs, 30-17 (NO)
1997—Chiefs, 25-13 (KC)
(RS Pts.—Chiefs 166, Saints 145)

KANSAS CITY vs. N.Y. GIANTS
RS: Giants lead series, 8-2
1974—Giants, 33-27 (KC)
1978—Giants, 26-10 (NY)
1979—Giants, 21-17 (KC)
1983—Chiefs, 38-17 (KC)
1984—Giants, 28-27 (NY)
1988—Giants, 28-12 (NY)
1992—Giants, 35-21 (NY)
1995—Chiefs, 20-17 (KC) OT
1998—Giants, 28-7 (NY)
2001—Giants, 13-3 (KC)
(RS Pts.—Giants 246, Chiefs 182)

***KANSAS CITY vs. **N.Y. JETS**
RS: Chiefs lead series, 15-14-1
PS: Series tied, 1-1
1960—Titans, 37-35 (D)
Titans, 41-35 (NY)
1961—Titans, 28-7 (NY)
Texans, 35-24 (D)
1962—Texans, 20-17 (D)
Texans, 52-31 (NY)
1963—Jets, 17-0 (NY)
Chiefs, 48-0 (KC)
1964—Jets, 27-14 (NY)
Chiefs, 24-7 (KC)
1965—Chiefs, 14-10 (NY)
Jets, 13-10 (KC)
1966—Chiefs, 32-24 (NY)
1967—Chiefs, 42-18 (KC)
Chiefs, 21-7 (NY)
1968—Jets, 20-19 (KC)
1969—Chiefs, 34-16 (NY)
***Chiefs, 13-6 (NY)
1971—Jets, 13-10 (NY)
1974—Chiefs, 24-16 (KC)
1975—Jets, 30-24 (KC)
1982—Chiefs, 37-13 (KC)
1984—Jets, 17-16 (KC)
Jets, 28-7 (NY)
1986—****Jets, 35-15 (NY)
1987—Jets, 16-9 (KC)
1988—Tie, 17-17 (NY)
Chiefs, 38-34 (KC)
1992—Chiefs, 23-7 (NY)
1998—Jets, 20-17 (KC)
2001—Jets, 27-7 (NY)
2002—Chiefs, 29-25 (NY)
(RS Pts.—Chiefs 700, Jets 600)
(PS Pts.—Jets 41, Chiefs 28)

**Franchise in Dallas prior to 1963 and known as Texans*
***Jets known as Titans prior to 1963*
****Inter-Divisional Playoff*
*****AFC First-Round Playoff*

***KANSAS CITY vs. **OAKLAND**
RS: Chiefs lead series, 43-42-2
PS: Chiefs lead series, 2-1
1960—Texans, 34-16 (O)
Raiders, 20-19 (D)
1961—Texans, 42-35 (O)
Texans, 43-11 (D)
1962—Texans, 26-16 (O)
Texans, 35-7 (D)
1963—Raiders, 10-7 (O)
Raiders, 22-7 (KC)
1964—Chiefs, 21-9 (O)
Chiefs, 42-7 (KC)
1965—Raiders, 37-10 (O)
Chiefs, 14-7 (KC)
1966—Chiefs, 32-10 (O)
Raiders, 34-13 (KC)
1967—Raiders, 23-21 (O)
Raiders, 44-22 (KC)
1968—Chiefs, 24-10 (KC)
Raiders, 38-21 (O)
***Raiders, 41-6 (O)
1969—Raiders, 27-24 (KC)
Raiders, 10-6 (O)
****Chiefs, 17-7 (O)
1970—Tie, 17-17 (KC)
Raiders, 20-6 (O)
1971—Tie, 20-20 (O)
Chiefs, 16-14 (KC)
1972—Chiefs, 27-14 (KC)
Raiders, 26-3 (O)
1973—Chiefs, 16-3 (KC)
Raiders, 37-7 (O)
1974—Raiders, 27-7 (O)
Raiders, 7-6 (KC)
1975—Chiefs, 42-10 (KC)
Raiders, 28-20 (O)
1976—Raiders, 24-21 (KC)
Raiders, 21-10 (O)
1977—Raiders, 37-28 (KC)
Raiders, 21-20 (O)
1978—Raiders, 28-6 (O)
Raiders, 20-10 (KC)
1979—Chiefs, 35-7 (KC)
Chiefs, 24-21 (O)
1980—Raiders, 27-14 (KC)
Chiefs, 31-17 (O)
1981—Chiefs, 27-0 (KC)
Chiefs, 28-17 (O)
1982—Raiders, 21-16 (KC)
1983—Raiders, 21-20 (LA)
Raiders, 28-20 (KC)
1984—Raiders, 22-20 (KC)
Raiders, 17-7 (LA)
1985—Chiefs, 36-20 (KC)
Raiders, 19-10 (LA)
1986—Raiders, 24-17 (KC)
Chiefs, 20-17 (LA)
1987—Raiders, 35-17 (LA)
Chiefs, 16-10 (KC)
1988—Raiders, 27-17 (KC)
Raiders, 17-10 (LA)
1989—Chiefs, 24-19 (KC)
Raiders, 20-14 (LA)
1990—Chiefs, 9-7 (KC)
Chiefs, 27-24 (LA)
1991—Chiefs, 24-21 (KC)
Chiefs, 27-21 (LA)
*****Chiefs, 10-6 (KC)
1992—Chiefs, 27-7 (KC)
Raiders, 28-7 (LA)
1993—Chiefs, 24-9 (KC)
Chiefs, 31-20 (LA)
1994—Chiefs, 13-3 (KC)
Chiefs, 19-9 (LA)
1995—Chiefs, 23-17 (KC) OT
Chiefs, 29-23 (O)
1996—Chiefs, 19-3 (KC)
Raiders, 26-7 (O)
1997—Chiefs, 28-27 (O)
Chiefs, 30-0 (KC)
1998—Chiefs, 28-8 (KC)
Chiefs, 31-24 (O)
1999—Chiefs, 37-34 (O)
Raiders, 41-38 (KC) OT
2000—Raiders, 20-17 (KC)
Raiders, 49-31 (O)
2001—Raiders, 27-24 (KC)
Raiders, 28-26 (O)
2002—Chiefs, 20-10 (KC)
Raiders, 24-0 (O)
2003—Chiefs, 17-10 (O)
Chiefs, 27-24 (KC)
(RS Pts.—Chiefs 1,808, Raiders 1,717)
(PS Pts.—Raiders 54, Chiefs 33)
**Franchise in Dallas prior to 1963 and known as Texans*
***Franchise in Los Angeles from 1982-1994*
****Division Playoff*
*****AFL Championship*
******AFC First-Round Playoff*

KANSAS CITY vs. PHILADELPHIA
RS: Series tied, 2-2
1972—Eagles, 21-20 (KC)
1992—Chiefs, 24-17 (KC)
1998—Chiefs, 24-21 (P)
2001—Eagles, 23-10 (KC)
(RS Pts.—Eagles 82, Chiefs 78)

KANSAS CITY vs. PITTSBURGH
RS: Steelers lead series, 16-8
PS: Chiefs lead series, 1-0
1970—Chiefs, 31-14 (P)
1971—Chiefs, 38-16 (KC)
1972—Steelers, 16-7 (P)
1974—Steelers, 34-24 (KC)
1975—Steelers, 28-3 (P)
1976—Steelers, 45-0 (KC)
1978—Steelers, 27-24 (P)
1979—Steelers, 30-3 (KC)
1980—Steelers, 21-16 (P)
1981—Chiefs, 37-33 (P)
1982—Steelers, 35-14 (P)
1984—Chiefs, 37-27 (P)
1985—Steelers, 36-28 (KC)
1986—Chiefs, 24-19 (P)
1987—Steelers, 17-16 (KC)
1988—Steelers, 16-10 (P)
1989—Steelers, 23-17 (P)
1992—Steelers, 27-3 (KC)
1993—*Chiefs, 27-24 (KC) OT
1996—Steelers, 17-7 (KC)
1997—Chiefs, 13-10 (KC)
1998—Steelers, 20-13 (KC)
1999—Chiefs, 35-19 (KC)
2001—Steelers, 20-17 (KC)
2003—Chiefs, 41-20 (KC)
(RS Pts.—Steelers 570, Chiefs 458)
(PS Pts.—Chiefs 27, Steelers 24)
**AFC First-Round Playoff*

KANSAS CITY vs. *ST. LOUIS
RS: Series tied, 4-4
1973—Rams, 23-13 (KC)
1982—Rams, 20-14 (LA)
1985—Rams, 16-0 (KC)
1991—Chiefs, 27-20 (LA)
1994—Rams, 16-0 (KC)
1997—Chiefs, 28-20 (StL)
2000—Chiefs, 54-34 (KC)
2002—Chiefs, 49-10 (KC)
(RS Pts.—Chiefs 185, Rams 159)
**Franchise in Los Angeles prior to 1995*

***KANSAS CITY vs. **SAN DIEGO**
RS: Chiefs lead series, 47-39-1
PS: Chargers lead series, 1-0
1960—Chargers, 21-20 (LA)
Texans, 17-0 (D)
1961—Chargers, 26-10 (D)
Chargers, 24-14 (SD)
1962—Chargers, 32-28 (SD)
Texans, 26-17 (D)
1963—Chargers, 24-10 (SD)
Chargers, 38-17 (KC)
1964—Chargers, 28-14 (KC)
Chiefs, 49-6 (SD)
1965—Tie, 10-10 (SD)
Chiefs, 31-7 (KC)
1966—Chiefs, 24-14 (KC)
Chiefs, 27-17 (SD)
1967—Chargers, 45-31 (SD)
Chargers, 17-16 (KC)
1968—Chiefs, 27-20 (KC)
Chiefs, 40-3 (SD)
1969—Chiefs, 27-9 (SD)
Chiefs, 27-3 (KC)
1970—Chiefs, 26-14 (KC)
Chargers, 31-13 (SD)
1971—Chargers, 21-14 (SD)
Chiefs, 31-10 (KC)
1972—Chiefs, 26-14 (SD)
Chargers, 27-17 (KC)
1973—Chiefs, 19-0 (SD)
Chiefs, 33-6 (KC)
1974—Chiefs, 24-14 (SD)
Chargers, 14-7 (KC)
1975—Chiefs, 12-10 (SD)
Chargers, 28-20 (KC)
1976—Chargers, 30-16 (KC)
Chiefs, 23-20 (SD)
1977—Chargers, 23-7 (KC)
Chiefs, 21-16 (SD)
1978—Chargers, 29-23 (SD) OT
Chiefs, 23-0 (KC)
1979—Chargers, 20-14 (KC)
Chargers, 28-7 (SD)
1980—Chargers, 24-7 (KC)
Chargers, 20-7 (SD)
1981—Chargers, 42-31 (KC)
Chargers, 22-20 (SD)
1982—Chiefs, 19-12 (KC)
1983—Chargers, 17-14 (KC)
Chargers, 41-38 (SD)
1984—Chiefs, 31-13 (KC)
Chiefs, 42-21 (SD)
1985—Chargers, 31-20 (SD)

Chiefs, 38-34 (KC)
1986—Chiefs, 42-41 (KC)
Chiefs, 24-23 (SD)
1987—Chiefs, 20-13 (KC)
Chargers, 42-21 (SD)
1988—Chargers, 24-23 (KC)
Chargers, 24-13 (SD)
1989—Chargers, 21-6 (SD)
Chargers, 20-13 (KC)
1990—Chiefs, 27-10 (KC)
Chiefs, 24-21 (SD)
1991—Chiefs, 14-13 (SD)
Chiefs, 20-17 (KC) OT
1992—Chiefs, 24-10 (SD)
Chiefs, 16-14 (KC)
***Chargers, 17-0 (SD)
1993—Chiefs, 17-14 (SD)
Chiefs, 28-24 (KC)
1994—Chargers, 20-6 (SD)
Chargers, 14-13 (KC)
1995—Chiefs, 29-23 (KC) OT
Chiefs, 22-7 (SD)
1996—Chargers, 22-19 (SD)
Chargers, 28-14 (KC)
1997—Chiefs, 31-3 (KC)
Chiefs, 29-7 (SD)
1998—Chiefs, 23-7 (KC)
Chargers, 38-37 (SD)
1999—Chargers, 21-14 (SD)
Chiefs, 34-0 (KC)
2000—Chiefs, 42-10 (KC)
Chargers, 17-16 (SD)
2001—Chiefs, 25-20 (SD)
Chiefs, 20-17 (KC)
2002—Chargers, 35-34 (SD)
Chiefs, 24-22 (KC)
2003—Chiefs, 27-14 (KC)
Chiefs, 28-24 (SD)
(RS Pts.—Chiefs 1,972, Chargers 1,673)
(PS Pts.—Chargers 17, Chiefs 0)
Franchise in Dallas prior to 1963 and known as Texans
***Franchise in Los Angeles prior to 1961*
****AFC First-Round Playoff*

KANSAS CITY vs. SAN FRANCISCO
RS: 49ers lead series, 6-3
1971—Chiefs, 26-17 (SF)
1975—49ers, 20-3 (KC)
1982—49ers, 26-13 (KC)
1985—49ers, 31-3 (SF)
1991—49ers, 28-14 (SF)
1994—Chiefs, 24-17 (KC)
1997—Chiefs, 44-9 (KC)
2000—49ers, 21-7 (SF)
2002—49ers, 17-13 (SF)
(PS Pts.—49ers 186, Chiefs 147)

KANSAS CITY vs. SEATTLE
RS: Chiefs lead series, 30-18
1977—Seahawks, 34-31 (KC)
1978—Seahawks, 13-10 (KC)
Seahawks, 23-19 (S)
1979—Chiefs, 24-6 (S)
Chiefs, 37-21 (KC)
1980—Seahawks, 17-16 (KC)
Chiefs, 31-30 (S)
1981—Chiefs, 20-14 (S)
Chiefs, 40-13 (KC)
1983—Chiefs, 17-13 (KC)
Seahawks, 51-48 (S) OT
1984—Seahawks, 45-0 (S)
Chiefs, 34-7 (KC)
1985—Chiefs, 28-7 (KC)
Seahawks, 24-6 (S)
1986—Seahawks, 23-17 (S)
Chiefs, 27-7 (KC)
1987—Seahawks, 43-14 (S)
Chiefs, 41-20 (KC)
1988—Seahawks, 31-10 (S)
Chiefs, 27-24 (KC)
1989—Chiefs, 20-16 (S)
Chiefs, 20-10 (KC)
1990—Seahawks, 19-7 (S)
Seahawks, 17-16 (KC)
1991—Chiefs, 20-13 (KC)
Chiefs, 19-6 (S)
1992—Chiefs, 26-7 (KC)
Chiefs, 24-14 (S)
1993—Chiefs, 31-16 (S)
Chiefs, 34-24 (KC)
1994—Chiefs, 38-23 (KC)
Seahawks, 10-9 (S)
1995—Chiefs, 34-10 (S)
Chiefs, 26-3 (KC)
1996—Chiefs, 35-17 (S)
Chiefs, 34-16 (KC)
1997—Chiefs, 20-17 (KC) OT
Chiefs, 19-14 (S)
1998—Chiefs, 17-6 (KC)
Seahawks, 24-12 (S)
1999—Seahawks, 31-19 (KC)
Seahawks, 23-14 (S)
2000—Chiefs, 24-17 (KC)
Chiefs, 24-19 (S)
2001—Chiefs, 19-7 (KC)
Seahawks, 21-18 (S)
2002—Seahawks, 39-32 (S)
(RS Pts.—Chiefs 1,108, Seahawks 905)

KANSAS CITY vs. TAMPA BAY
RS: Chiefs lead series, 5-3
1976—Chiefs, 28-19 (TB)
1978—Buccaneers, 30-13 (KC)
1979—Buccaneers, 3-0 (TB)
1981—Chiefs, 19-10 (KC)
1984—Chiefs, 24-20 (KC)
1986—Chiefs, 27-20 (KC)
1993—Chiefs, 27-3 (TB)
1999—Buccaneers, 17-10 (TB)
(RS Pts.—Chiefs 148, Buccaneers 122)

***KANSAS CITY vs. **TENNESSEE**
RS: Chiefs lead series, 24-18
PS: Chiefs lead series, 2-0
1960—Oilers, 20-10 (H)
Texans, 24-0 (D)
1961—Texans, 26-21 (D)
Oilers, 38-7 (H)
1962—Texans, 31-7 (H)
Oilers, 14-6 (D)
***Texans, 20-17 (H) OT
1963—Chiefs, 28-7 (KC)
Oilers, 28-7 (H)
1964—Chiefs, 28-7 (KC)
Chiefs, 28-19 (H)
1965—Chiefs, 52-21 (KC)
Oilers, 38-36 (H)
1966—Chiefs, 48-23 (KC)
1967—Chiefs, 25-20 (H)
Oilers, 24-19 (KC)
1968—Chiefs, 26-21 (H)
Chiefs, 24-10 (KC)
1969—Chiefs, 24-0 (KC)
1970—Chiefs, 24-9 (KC)
1971—Chiefs, 20-16 (H)
1973—Chiefs, 38-14 (KC)
1974—Chiefs, 17-7 (H)
1975—Oilers, 17-13 (KC)
1977—Oilers, 34-20 (H)
1978—Oilers, 20-17 (KC)
1979—Oilers, 20-6 (H)
1980—Chiefs, 21-20 (KC)
1981—Chiefs, 23-10 (KC)
1983—Chiefs, 13-10 (H) OT
1984—Oilers, 17-16 (KC)
1985—Oilers, 23-20 (H)
1986—Chiefs, 27-13 (KC)
1988—Oilers, 7-6 (H)
1989—Chiefs, 34-0 (KC)
1990—Oilers, 27-10 (KC)
1991—Oilers, 17-7 (H)
1992—Oilers, 23-20 (H) OT
1993—Oilers, 30-0 (H)
****Chiefs, 28-20 (H)
1994—Chiefs, 31-9 (KC)
1995—Chiefs, 20-13 (KC)
1996—Chiefs, 20-19 (H)
2000—Titans, 17-14 (T) OT
(RS Pts.—Chiefs 886, Titans 710)
(PS Pts.—Chiefs 48, Titans 37)
Franchise in Dallas prior to 1963 and known as Texans
***Franchise in Houston prior to 1997; known as Oilers prior to 1999*
****AFL Championship*
*****AFC Divisional Playoff*

KANSAS CITY vs. WASHINGTON
RS: Chiefs lead series, 5-1
1971—Chiefs, 27-20 (KC)
1976—Chiefs, 33-30 (W)
1983—Redskins, 27-12 (W)
1992—Chiefs, 35-16 (KC)
1995—Chiefs, 24-3 (KC)
2001—Chiefs, 45-13 (W)
(RS Pts.—Chiefs 176, Redskins 109)

MIAMI vs. ARIZONA
RS: Dolphins lead series, 8-0;
See Arizona vs. Miami

MIAMI vs. ATLANTA
RS: Dolphins lead series, 7-2;
See Atlanta vs. Miami

MIAMI vs. BALTIMORE
RS: Dolphins lead series, 4-0
PS: Ravens lead series, 1-0;
See Baltimore vs. Miami

MIAMI vs. BUFFALO
RS: Dolphins lead series, 48-27-1
PS: Bills lead series, 3-1;
See Buffalo vs. Miami

MIAMI vs. CAROLINA
RS: Dolphins lead series, 2-0;
See Carolina vs. Miami

MIAMI vs. CHICAGO
RS: Dolphins lead series, 6-3;
See Chicago vs. Miami

MIAMI vs. CINCINNATI
RS: Dolphins lead series, 12-3
PS: Dolphins lead series, 1-0;
See Cincinnati vs. Miami

MIAMI vs. CLEVELAND
RS: Dolphins lead series, 6-4
PS: Dolphins lead series, 2-0;

See Cleveland vs. Miami
MIAMI vs. DALLAS
RS: Dolphins lead series, 7-3
PS: Cowboys lead series, 1-0;
See Dallas vs. Miami
MIAMI vs. DENVER
RS: Dolphins lead series, 9-2-1
PS: Broncos lead series, 1-0;
See Denver vs. Miami
MIAMI vs. DETROIT
RS: Dolphins lead series, 6-2;
See Detroit vs. Miami
MIAMI vs. GREEN BAY
RS: Dolphins lead series, 9-2;
See Green Bay vs. Miami
MIAMI vs. HOUSTON
RS: Texans lead series, 1-0;
See Houston vs. Miami
MIAMI vs. INDIANAPOLIS
RS: Dolphins lead series, 44-22
PS: Dolphins lead series, 2-0;
See Indianapolis vs. Miami
MIAMI vs. JACKSONVILLE
RS: Series tied, 1-1
PS: Jaguars lead series, 1-0;
See Jacksonville vs. Miami
MIAMI vs. KANSAS CITY
RS: Chiefs lead series, 11-10
PS: Dolphins lead series, 3-0;
See Kansas City vs. Miami
MIAMI vs. MINNESOTA
RS: Series tied, 4-4
PS: Dolphins lead series, 1-0
1972—Dolphins, 16-14 (Minn)
1973—*Dolphins, 24-7 (Houston)
1976—Vikings, 29-7 (Mia)
1979—Dolphins, 27-12 (Minn)
1982—Dolphins, 22-14 (Mia)
1988—Dolphins, 24-7 (Mia)
1994—Vikings, 38-35 (Minn)
2000—Vikings, 13-7 (Minn)
2002—Vikings, 20-17 (Minn)
(RS Pts.—Dolphins 155, Vikings 147)
(PS Pts.—Dolphins 24, Vikings 7)
**Super Bowl VIII*
MIAMI vs. *NEW ENGLAND
RS: Dolphins lead series, 44-30
PS: Patriots lead series, 2-1
1966—Patriots, 20-14 (M)
1967—Patriots, 41-10 (B)
Dolphins, 41-32 (M)
1968—Dolphins, 34-10 (B)
Dolphins, 38-7 (M)
1969—Dolphins, 17-16 (B)
Patriots, 38-23 (Tampa)
1970—Patriots, 27-14 (B)
Dolphins, 37-20 (M)
1971—Dolphins, 41-3 (M)
Patriots, 34-13 (NE)
1972—Dolphins, 52-0 (M)
Dolphins, 37-21 (NE)
1973—Dolphins, 44-23 (M)
Dolphins, 30-14 (NE)
1974—Patriots, 34-24 (NE)
Dolphins, 34-27 (M)
1975—Dolphins, 22-14 (NE)
Dolphins, 20-7 (M)
1976—Patriots, 30-14 (NE)
Dolphins, 10-3 (M)
1977—Dolphins, 17-5 (M)
Patriots, 14-10 (NE)
1978—Patriots, 33-24 (NE)
Dolphins, 23-3 (M)
1979—Patriots, 28-13 (NE)
Dolphins, 39-24 (M)
1980—Patriots, 34-0 (NE)
Dolphins, 16-13 (M) OT
1981—Dolphins, 30-27 (NE) OT
Dolphins, 24-14 (M)
1982—Patriots, 3-0 (NE)
**Dolphins, 28-13 (M)
1983—Dolphins, 34-24 (M)
Patriots, 17-6 (NE)
1984—Dolphins, 28-7 (M)
Dolphins, 44-24 (NE)
1985—Patriots, 17-13 (NE)
Dolphins, 30-27 (M)
***Patriots, 31-14 (M)
1986—Patriots, 34-7 (NE)
Patriots, 34-27 (M)
1987—Patriots, 28-21 (NE)
Patriots, 24-10 (M)
1988—Patriots, 21-10 (NE)
Patriots, 6-3 (M)
1989—Dolphins, 24-10 (NE)
Dolphins, 31-10 (M)
1990—Dolphins, 27-24 (NE)
Dolphins, 17-10 (M)
1991—Dolphins, 20-10 (NE)
Dolphins, 30-20 (M)
1992—Dolphins, 38-17 (M)
Dolphins, 16-13 (NE) OT
1993—Dolphins, 17-13 (M)
Patriots, 33-27 (NE) OT
1994—Dolphins, 39-35 (M)
Dolphins, 23-3 (NE)
1995—Dolphins, 20-3 (NE)
Patriots, 34-17 (M)
1996—Dolphins, 24-10 (M)
Patriots, 42-23 (NE)
1997—Patriots, 27-24 (NE)
Patriots, 14-12 (M)
**Patriots, 17-3 (NE)
1998—Dolphins, 12-9 (M) OT
Patriots, 26-23 (NE)
1999—Dolphins, 31-30 (NE)
Dolphins, 27-17 (M)
2000—Dolphins, 10-3 (M)
Dolphins, 27-24 (NE)
2001—Dolphins, 30-10 (M)
Patriots, 20-13 (NE)
2002—Dolphins, 26-13 (M)
Patriots, 27-24 (NE) OT
2003—Patriots, 19-13 (M) OT
Patriots, 12-0 (NE)
(RS Pts.—Dolphins 1,663, Patriots 1,420)
(PS Pts.—Patriots 61, Dolphins 45)
**Franchise in Boston prior to 1971*
***AFC First-Round Playoff*
****AFC Championship*
MIAMI vs. NEW ORLEANS
RS: Dolphins lead series, 5-3
1970—Dolphins, 21-10 (M)
1974—Dolphins, 21-0 (NO)
1980—Dolphins, 21-16 (M)
1983—Saints, 17-7 (NO)
1986—Dolphins, 31-27 (NO)
1992—Saints, 24-13 (NO)
1995—Saints, 33-30 (NO)
1998—Dolphins, 30-10 (M)
(RS Pts.—Dolphins 174, Saints 137)
MIAMI vs. N.Y. GIANTS
RS: Giants lead series, 3-2
1972—Dolphins, 23-13 (NY)
1990—Giants, 20-3 (NY)
1993—Giants, 19-14 (M)
1996—Giants, 17-7 (M)
2003—Dolphins, 23-10 (NY)
(RS Pts.—Giants 79, Dolphins 70)
MIAMI vs. N.Y. JETS
RS: Jets lead series, 38-37-1
PS: Dolphins lead series, 1-0
1966—Jets, 19-14 (M)
Jets, 30-13 (NY)
1967—Jets, 29-7 (NY)
Jets, 33-14 (M)
1968—Jets, 35-17 (NY)
Jets, 31-7 (M)
1969—Jets, 34-31 (NY)
Jets, 27-9 (M)
1970—Dolphins, 20-6 (NY)
Dolphins, 16-10 (M)
1971—Jets, 14-10 (M)
Dolphins, 30-14 (NY)
1972—Dolphins, 27-17 (NY)
Dolphins, 28-24 (M)
1973—Dolphins, 31-3 (M)
Dolphins, 24-14 (NY)
1974—Dolphins, 21-17 (M)
Jets, 17-14 (NY)
1975—Dolphins, 43-0 (NY)
Dolphins, 27-7 (M)
1976—Dolphins, 16-0 (M)
Dolphins, 27-7 (NY)
1977—Dolphins, 21-17 (M)
Dolphins, 14-10 (NY)
1978—Jets, 33-20 (NY)
Jets, 24-13 (M)
1979—Jets, 33-27 (NY)
Jets, 27-24 (M)
1980—Jets, 17-14 (NY)
Jets, 24-17 (M)
1981—Tie, 28-28 (M) OT
Jets, 16-15 (NY)
1982—Dolphins, 45-28 (NY)
Dolphins, 20-19 (M)
*Dolphins, 14-0 (M)
1983—Dolphins, 32-14 (NY)
Dolphins, 34-14 (M)
1984—Dolphins, 31-17 (NY)
Dolphins, 28-17 (M)
1985—Jets, 23-7 (NY)
Dolphins, 21-17 (M)
1986—Jets, 51-45 (NY) OT
Dolphins, 45-3 (M)
1987—Jets, 37-31 (NY) OT
Dolphins, 37-28 (M)
1988—Jets, 44-30 (M)
Jets, 38-34 (NY)
1989—Jets, 40-33 (M)
Dolphins, 31-23 (NY)
1990—Dolphins, 20-16 (M)
Dolphins, 17-3 (NY)
1991—Jets, 41-23 (NY)
Jets, 23-20 (M) OT
1992—Jets, 26-14 (NY)
Dolphins, 19-17 (M)
1993—Jets, 24-14 (M)
Jets, 27-10 (NY)
1994—Dolphins, 28-14 (M)

Dolphins, 28-24 (NY)
1995—Dolphins, 52-14 (M)
Jets, 17-16 (NY)
1996—Dolphins, 36-27 (M)
Dolphins, 31-28 (NY)
1997—Dolphins, 31-20 (NY)
Dolphins, 24-17 (M)
1998—Jets, 20-9 (NY)
Jets, 21-16 (M)
1999—Jets, 28-20 (NY)
Jets, 38-31 (M)
2000—Jets, 40-37 (NY) OT
Jets, 20-3 (M)
2001—Jets, 21-17 (NY)
Jets, 24-0 (M)
2002—Dolphins, 30-3 (M)
Jets, 13-10 (NY)
2003—Dolphins, 21-10 (NY)
Dolphins, 23-21 (M)
(RS Pts.—Dolphins 1,743, Jets 1,627)
(PS Pts.—Dolphins 14, Jets 0)
AFC Championship

MIAMI vs. *OAKLAND
RS: Raiders lead series, 15-10-1
PS: Raiders lead series, 3-1
1966—Raiders, 23-14 (M)
Raiders, 21-10 (O)
1967—Raiders, 31-17 (O)
1968—Raiders, 47-21 (M)
1969—Raiders, 20-17 (O)
Tie, 20-20 (M)
1970—Dolphins, 20-13 (M)
**Raiders, 21-14 (O)
1973—Raiders, 12-7 (O)
***Dolphins, 27-10 (M)
1974—**Raiders, 28-26 (O)
1975—Raiders, 31-21 (M)
1978—Dolphins, 23-6 (M)
1979—Raiders, 13-3 (O)
1980—Raiders, 16-10 (O)
1981—Raiders, 33-17 (M)
1983—Raiders, 27-14 (LA)
1984—Raiders, 45-34 (M)
1986—Raiders, 30-28 (M)
1988—Dolphins, 24-14 (LA)
1990—Raiders, 13-10 (M)
1992—Dolphins, 20-7 (M)
1994—Dolphins, 20-17 (M) OT
1996—Raiders, 17-7 (O)
1997—Dolphins, 34-16 (O)
1998—Dolphins, 27-17 (O)
1999—Dolphins, 16-9 (O)
2000—**Raiders, 27-0 (O)
2001—Dolphins, 18-15 (M)
2002—Dolphins, 23-17 (M)
(RS Pts.—Raiders 530, Dolphins 475)
(PS Pts.—Raiders 86, Dolphins 67)
Franchise in Los Angeles from 1982-1994
***AFC Divisional Playoff*
****AFC Championship*

MIAMI vs. PHILADELPHIA
RS: Dolphins lead series, 7-4
1970—Eagles, 24-17 (P)
1975—Dolphins, 24-16 (M)
1978—Eagles, 17-3 (P)
1981—Dolphins, 13-10 (M)
1984—Dolphins, 24-23 (M)
1987—Dolphins, 28-10 (P)
1990—Dolphins, 23-20 (M) OT
1993—Dolphins, 19-14 (P)
1996—Eagles, 35-28 (P)
1999—Dolphins, 16-13 (M)
2003—Eagles, 34-27 (M)
(RS Pts.—Dolphins 222, Eagles 216)

MIAMI vs. PITTSBURGH
RS: Dolphins lead series, 9-7
PS: Dolphins lead series, 2-1
1971—Dolphins, 24-21 (M)
1972—*Dolphins, 21-17 (P)
1973—Dolphins, 30-26 (M)
1976—Steelers, 14-3 (P)
1979—**Steelers, 34-14 (P)
1980—Steelers, 23-10 (P)
1981—Dolphins, 30-10 (M)
1984—Dolphins, 31-7 (P)
*Dolphins, 45-28 (M)
1985—Dolphins, 24-20 (M)
1987—Dolphins, 35-24 (M)
1988—Steelers, 40-24 (P)
1989—Steelers, 34-14 (M)
1990—Dolphins, 28-6 (P)
1993—Steelers, 21-20 (M)
1994—Steelers, 16-13 (P) OT
1995—Dolphins, 23-10 (M)
1996—Steelers, 24-17 (M)
1998—Dolphins, 21-0 (M)
(RS Pts.—Dolphins 347, Steelers 296)
(PS Pts.—Dolphins 80, Steelers 79)
AFC Championship
***AFC Divisional Playoff*

MIAMI vs. *ST. LOUIS
RS: Dolphins lead series, 7-2
1971—Dolphins, 20-14 (LA)
1976—Rams, 31-28 (M)
1980—Dolphins, 35-14 (LA)
1983—Dolphins, 30-14 (M)
1986—Dolphins, 37-31 (LA) OT
1992—Dolphins, 26-10 (M)
1995—Dolphins, 41-22 (StL)
1998—Dolphins, 14-0 (M)
2001—Rams, 42-10 (StL)
(RS Pts.—Dolphins 241, Rams 178)
Franchise in Los Angeles prior to 1995

MIAMI vs. SAN DIEGO
RS: Series tied, 10-10
PS: Series tied, 2-2
1966—Chargers, 44-10 (SD)
1967—Chargers, 24-0 (SD)
Dolphins, 41-24 (M)
1968—Chargers, 34-28 (SD)
1969—Chargers, 21-14 (M)
1972—Dolphins, 24-10 (M)
1974—Dolphins, 28-21 (SD)
1977—Chargers, 14-13 (M)
1978—Dolphins, 28-21 (SD)
1980—Chargers, 27-24 (M) OT
1981—*Chargers, 41-38 (M) OT
1982—**Dolphins, 34-13 (M)
1984—Chargers, 34-28 (SD) OT
1986—Chargers, 50-28 (SD)
1988—Dolphins, 31-28 (M)
1991—Chargers, 38-30 (SD)
1992—*Dolphins, 31-0 (M)
1993—Chargers, 45-20 (SD)
1994—*Chargers, 22-21 (SD)
1995—Dolphins, 24-14 (SD)
1999—Dolphins, 12-9 (M)
2000—Dolphins, 17-7 (SD)
2002—Dolphins, 30-3 (M)
2003—Dolphins, 26-10 (Ariz)
(RS Pts.—Chargers 478, Dolphins 456)
(PS Pts.—Dolphins 124, Chargers 76)
AFC Divisional Playoff
***AFC Second-Round Playoff*

MIAMI vs. SAN FRANCISCO
RS: Series tied, 4-4
PS: 49ers lead series, 1-0
1973—Dolphins, 21-13 (M)
1977—Dolphins, 19-15 (SF)
1980—Dolphins, 17-13 (M)
1983—Dolphins, 20-17 (SF)
1984—*49ers, 38-16 (Stanford)
1986—49ers, 31-16 (M)
1992—49ers, 27-3 (SF)
1995—49ers, 44-20 (M)
2001—49ers, 21-0 (SF)
(RS Pts.—49ers 181, Dolphins 116)
(PS Pts.—49ers 38, Dolphins 16)
Super Bowl XIX

MIAMI vs. SEATTLE
RS: Dolphins lead series, 6-2
PS: Dolphins lead series, 2-1
1977—Dolphins, 31-13 (M)
1979—Dolphins, 19-10 (M)
1983—*Seahawks, 27-20 (M)
1984—*Dolphins, 31-10 (M)
1987—Seahawks, 24-20 (S)
1990—Dolphins, 24-17 (M)
1992—Dolphins, 19-17 (S)
1996—Seahawks, 22-15 (M)
1999—**Dolphins, 20-17 (S)
2000—Dolphins, 23-0 (M)
2001—Dolphins, 24-20 (S)
(RS Pts.—Dolphins 175, Seahawks 123)
(PS Pts.—Dolphins 71, Seahawks 54)
AFC Divisional Playoff
***AFC First-Round Playoff*

MIAMI vs. TAMPA BAY
RS: Dolphins lead series, 4-3
1976—Dolphins, 23-20 (TB)
1982—Buccaneers, 23-17 (TB)
1985—Dolphins, 41-38 (M)
1988—Dolphins, 17-14 (TB)
1991—Dolphins, 33-14 (M)
1997—Buccaneers, 31-21 (TB)
2000—Buccaneers, 16-13 (M)
(RS Pts.—Dolphins 165, Buccaneers 156)

MIAMI vs. *TENNESSEE
RS: Dolphins lead series, 15-12
PS: Titans lead series, 1-0
1966—Dolphins, 20-13 (H)
Dolphins, 29-28 (M)
1967—Oilers, 17-14 (H)
Oilers, 41-10 (M)
1968—Oilers, 24-10 (M)
Dolphins, 24-7 (H)
1969—Oilers, 22-10 (H)
Oilers, 32-7 (M)
1970—Dolphins, 20-10 (H)
1972—Dolphins, 34-13 (M)
1975—Oilers, 20-19 (H)
1977—Dolphins, 27-7 (M)
1978—Oilers, 35-30 (H)
**Oilers, 17-9 (M)
1979—Oilers, 9-6 (M)
1981—Dolphins, 16-10 (H)
1983—Dolphins, 24-17 (H)
1984—Dolphins, 28-10 (M)
1985—Oilers, 26-23 (H)
1986—Dolphins, 28-7 (M)

1989—Oilers, 39-7 (H)
1991—Oilers, 17-13 (M)
1992—Dolphins, 19-16 (M)
1996—Dolphins, 23-20 (H)
1997—Dolphins, 16-13 (M) OT
1999—Dolphins, 17-0 (M)
2001—Dolphins, 31-23 (T)
2003—Titans, 31-7 (T)
(RS Pts.—Dolphins 512, Titans 507)
(PS Pts.—Titans 17, Dolphins 9)
Franchise in Houston prior to 1997; known as Oilers prior to 1999
**AFC First-Round Playoff*

MIAMI vs. WASHINGTON
RS: Dolphins lead series, 6-3
PS: Series tied, 1-1
1972—*Dolphins, 14-7 (Los Angeles)
1974—Redskins, 20-17 (W)
1978—Dolphins, 16-0 (W)
1981—Dolphins, 13-10 (M)
1982—**Redskins, 27-17 (Pasadena)
1984—Dolphins, 35-17 (W)
1987—Dolphins, 23-21 (M)
1990—Redskins, 42-20 (W)
1993—Dolphins, 17-10 (M)
1999—Redskins, 21-10 (W)
2003—Dolphins, 24-23 (M)
(RS Pts.—Dolphins 175, Redskins 164)
(PS Pts.—Redskins 34, Dolphins 31)
Super Bowl VII
**Super Bowl XVII*

MINNESOTA vs. ARIZONA
RS: Cardinals lead series, 9-8
PS: Vikings lead series, 2-0;
See Arizona vs. Minnesota

MINNESOTA vs. ATLANTA
RS: Vikings lead series, 14-7
PS: Series tied, 1-1;
See Atlanta vs. Minnesota

MINNESOTA vs. BALTIMORE
RS: Series tied, 1-1;
See Baltimore vs. Minnesota

MINNESOTA vs. BUFFALO
RS: Vikings lead series, 7-3;
See Buffalo vs. Minnesota

MINNESOTA vs. CAROLINA
RS: Vikings lead series, 3-2;
See Carolina vs. Minnesota

MINNESOTA vs. CHICAGO
RS: Vikings lead series, 46-37-2
PS: Bears lead series, 1-0;
See Chicago vs. Minnesota

MINNESOTA vs. CINCINNATI
RS: Vikings lead series, 5-4;
See Cincinnati vs. Minnesota

MINNESOTA vs. CLEVELAND
RS: Vikings lead series, 8-3
PS: Vikings lead series, 1-0;
See Cleveland vs. Minnesota

MINNESOTA vs. DALLAS
RS: Series tied, 9-9
PS: Cowboys lead series, 4-2;
See Dallas vs. Minnesota

MINNESOTA vs. DENVER
RS: Vikings lead series, 7-4;
See Denver vs. Minnesota

MINNESOTA vs. DETROIT
RS: Vikings lead series, 54-29-2;
See Detroit vs. Minnesota

MINNESOTA vs. GREEN BAY
RS: Series tied, 42-42-1;
See Green Bay vs. Minnesota

MINNESOTA vs. INDIANAPOLIS
RS: Colts lead series, 12-7-1
PS: Colts lead series, 1-0;
See Indianapolis vs. Minnesota

MINNESOTA vs. JACKSONVILLE
RS: Series tied, 1-1;
See Jacksonville vs. Minnesota

MINNESOTA vs. KANSAS CITY
RS: Series tied, 4-4
PS: Chiefs lead series, 1-0;
See Kansas City vs. Minnesota

MINNESOTA vs. MIAMI
RS: Series tied, 4-4
PS: Dolphins lead series, 1-0;
See Miami vs. Minnesota

MINNESOTA vs. *NEW ENGLAND
RS: Patriots lead series, 5-4
1970—Vikings, 35-14 (B)
1974—Patriots, 17-14 (M)
1979—Patriots, 27-23 (NE)
1988—Vikings, 36-6 (M)
1991—Patriots, 26-23 (NE) OT
1994—Patriots, 26-20 (NE) OT
1997—Vikings, 23-18 (M)
2000—Vikings, 21-13 (NE)
2002—Patriots, 24-17 (NE)
(RS Pts.—Vikings 212, Patriots 171)
Franchise in Boston prior to 1971

MINNESOTA vs. NEW ORLEANS
RS: Vikings lead series, 15-7
PS: Vikings lead series, 2-0
1968—Saints, 20-17 (NO)
1970—Vikings, 26-0 (M)
1971—Vikings, 23-10 (NO)
1972—Vikings, 37-6 (M)
1974—Vikings, 29-9 (M)
1975—Vikings, 20-7 (NO)
1976—Vikings, 40-9 (NO)
1978—Saints, 31-24 (NO)
1980—Vikings, 23-20 (NO)
1981—Vikings, 20-10 (M)
1983—Saints, 17-16 (NO)
1985—Saints, 30-23 (M)
1986—Vikings, 33-17 (M)
1987—*Vikings, 44-10 (NO)
1988—Vikings, 45-3 (M)
1990—Vikings, 32-3 (M)
1991—Saints, 26-0 (NO)
1993—Saints, 17-14 (M)
1994—Vikings, 21-20 (M)
1995—Vikings, 43-24 (M)
1998—Vikings, 31-24 (M)
2000—**Vikings, 34-16 (M)
2001—Saints, 28-15 (NO)
2002—Vikings, 32-31 (NO)
(RS Pts.—Vikings 564, Saints 362)
(PS Pts.—Vikings 78, Saints 26)
NFC First-Round Playoff
**NFC Divisional Playoff*

MINNESOTA vs. N.Y. GIANTS
RS: Vikings lead series, 9-7
PS: Giants lead series, 2-1
1964—Vikings, 30-21 (NY)
1965—Vikings, 40-14 (M)
1967—Vikings, 27-24 (M)
1969—Giants, 24-23 (NY)
1971—Vikings, 17-10 (NY)
1973—Vikings, 31-7 (New Haven)
1976—Vikings, 24-7 (M)
1986—Giants, 22-20 (M)
1989—Giants, 24-14 (NY)
1990—Giants, 23-15 (NY)
1993—*Giants, 17-10 (NY)
1994—Vikings, 27-10 (NY)
1996—Giants, 15-10 (NY)
1997—*Vikings, 23-22 (NY)
1999—Vikings, 34-17 (NY)
2000—**Giants, 41-0 (NY)
2001—Vikings, 28-16 (M)
2002—Giants, 27-20 (M)
2003—Giants, 29-17 (M)
(RS Pts.—Vikings 377, Giants 290)
(PS Pts.—Giants 80, Vikings 33)
NFC First-Round Playoff
**NFC Championship*

MINNESOTA vs. N.Y. JETS
RS: Jets lead series, 6-1
1970—Jets, 20-10 (NY)
1975—Vikings, 29-21 (M)
1979—Jets, 14-7 (NY)
1982—Jets, 42-14 (M)
1994—Jets, 31-21 (M)
1997—Jets, 23-21 (NY)
2002—Jets, 20-7 (NY)
(RS Pts.—Jets 171, Vikings 109)

MINNESOTA vs. *OAKLAND
RS: Raiders lead series, 8-3
PS: Raiders lead series, 1-0
1973—Vikings, 24-16 (M)
1976—**Raiders, 32-14 (Pasadena)
1977—Raiders, 35-13 (O)
1978—Raiders, 27-20 (O)
1981—Raiders, 36-10 (M)
1984—Raiders, 23-20 (LA)
1987—Vikings, 31-20 (M)
1990—Raiders, 28-24 (M)
1993—Raiders, 24-7 (LA)
1996—Vikings, 16-13 (O) OT
1999—Raiders, 22-17 (M)
2003—Raiders, 28-18 (O)
(RS Pts.—Raiders 272, Vikings 200)
(PS Pts.—Raiders 32, Vikings 14)
Franchise in Los Angeles from 1982-1994
**Super Bowl XI*

MINNESOTA vs. PHILADELPHIA
RS: Vikings lead series, 11-7
PS: Eagles lead series, 1-0
1962—Vikings, 31-21 (M)
1963—Vikings, 34-13 (P)
1968—Vikings, 24-17 (P)
1971—Vikings, 13-0 (P)
1973—Vikings, 28-21 (M)
1976—Vikings, 31-12 (P)
1978—Vikings, 28-27 (M)
1980—Eagles, 42-7 (M)
*Eagles, 31-16 (P)
1981—Vikings, 35-23 (M)
1984—Eagles, 19-17 (P)
1985—Vikings, 28-23 (P)
Eagles, 37-35 (M)
1988—Vikings, 23-21 (M)
1989—Eagles, 10-9 (P)
1990—Eagles, 32-24 (P)
1992—Eagles, 28-17 (P)
1997—Vikings, 28-19 (M)
2001—Eagles, 48-17 (P)
(RS Pts.—Vikings 429, Eagles 413)

(PS Pts.—Eagles 31, Vikings 16)
NFC Divisional Playoff

MINNESOTA vs. PITTSBURGH
RS: Vikings lead series, 8-5
PS: Steelers lead series, 1-0
1962—Steelers, 39-31 (P)
1964—Vikings, 30-10 (M)
1967—Vikings, 41-27 (P)
1969—Vikings, 52-14 (M)
1972—Steelers, 23-10 (P)
1974—*Steelers, 16-6 (New Orleans)
1976—Vikings, 17-6 (M)
1980—Steelers, 23-17 (M)
1983—Vikings, 17-14 (P)
1986—Vikings, 31-7 (M)
1989—Steelers, 27-14 (P)
1992—Vikings, 6-3 (P)
1995—Vikings, 44-24 (P)
2001—Steelers, 21-16 (P)
(RS Pts.—Vikings 326, Steelers 238)
(PS Pts.—Steelers 16, Vikings 6)
**Super Bowl IX*

MINNESOTA vs. *ST. LOUIS
RS: Vikings lead series, 16-13-2
PS: Vikings lead series, 5-2
1961—Rams, 31-17 (LA)
Vikings, 42-21 (M)
1962—Vikings, 38-14 (LA)
Tie, 24-24 (M)
1963—Rams, 27-24 (LA)
Vikings, 21-13 (M)
1964—Rams, 22-13 (LA)
Vikings, 34-13 (M)
1965—Vikings, 38-35 (LA)
Vikings, 24-13 (M)
1966—Vikings, 35-7 (M)
Rams, 21-6 (LA)
1967—Rams, 39-3 (LA)
1968—Rams, 31-3 (M)
1969—Vikings, 20-13 (LA)
**Vikings, 23-20 (M)
1970—Vikings, 13-3 (M)
1972—Vikings, 45-41 (LA)
1973—Vikings, 10-9 (M)
1974—Rams, 20-17 (LA)
***Vikings, 14-10 (M)
1976—Tie, 10-10 (M) OT
***Vikings, 24-13 (M)
1977—Rams, 35-3 (LA)
****Vikings, 14-7 (LA)
1978—Rams, 34-17 (M)
****Rams, 34-10 (LA)
1979—Rams, 27-21 (LA) OT
1985—Rams, 13-10 (LA)
1987—Vikings, 21-16 (LA)
1988—*****Vikings, 28-17 (M)
1989—Vikings, 23-21 (M) OT
1991—Vikings, 20-14 (M)
1992—Vikings, 31-17 (LA)
1998—Vikings, 38-31 (StL)
1999—****Rams, 49-37 (StL)
2000—Rams, 40-29 (StL)
2003—Rams, 48-17 (StL)
(RS Pts.—Rams 703, Vikings 667)
(PS Pts.—Rams 150, Vikings 150)
**Franchise in Los Angeles prior to 1995*
***Conference Championship*
****NFC Championship*
*****NFC Divisional Playoff*
******NFC First-Round Playoff*

MINNESOTA vs. SAN DIEGO
RS: Chargers lead series, 5-4
1971—Chargers, 30-14 (SD)
1975—Vikings, 28-13 (M)
1978—Chargers, 13-7 (M)
1981—Vikings, 33-31 (SD)
1984—Chargers, 42-13 (M)
1985—Vikings, 21-17 (M)
1993—Chargers, 30-17 (M)
1999—Vikings, 35-27 (M)
2003—Chargers, 42-28 (SD)
(RS Pts.—Chargers 245, Vikings 196)

MINNESOTA vs. SAN FRANCISCO
RS: Vikings lead series, 18-17-1
PS: 49ers lead series, 4-1
1961—49ers, 38-24 (M)
49ers, 38-28 (SF)
1962—49ers, 21-7 (SF)
49ers, 35-12 (M)
1963—Vikings, 24-20 (SF)
Vikings, 45-14 (M)
1964—Vikings, 27-22 (SF)
Vikings, 24-7 (M)
1965—Vikings, 42-41 (SF)
49ers, 45-24 (M)
1966—Tie, 20-20 (SF)
Vikings, 28-3 (SF)
1967—49ers, 27-21 (M)
1968—Vikings, 30-20 (SF)
1969—Vikings, 10-7 (M)
1970—*49ers, 17-14 (M)
1971—49ers, 13-9 (M)
1972—49ers, 20-17 (SF)
1973—Vikings, 17-13 (SF)
1975—Vikings, 27-17 (M)
1976—49ers, 20-16 (SF)
1977—Vikings, 28-27 (M)
1979—Vikings, 28-22 (M)
1983—49ers, 48-17 (M)
1984—49ers, 51-7 (SF)
1985—Vikings, 28-21 (M)
1986—Vikings, 27-24 (SF) OT
1987—*Vikings, 36-24 (SF)
1988—49ers, 24-21 (SF)
*49ers, 34-9 (SF)
1989—*49ers, 41-13 (SF)
1990—49ers, 20-17 (M)
1991—Vikings, 17-14 (M)
1992—49ers, 20-17 (M)
1993—49ers, 38-19 (SF)
1994—Vikings, 21-14 (M)
1995—49ers, 37-30 (SF)
1997—49ers, 28-17 (SF)
*49ers, 38-22 (SF)
1999—Vikings, 40-16 (M)
2003—Vikings, 35-7 (M)
(RS Pts.—49ers 852, Vikings 821)
(PS Pts.—49ers 154, Vikings 94)
**NFC Divisional Playoff*

MINNESOTA vs. SEATTLE
RS: Seahawks lead series, 5-3
1976—Vikings, 27-21 (M)
1978—Seahawks, 29-28 (S)
1984—Seahawks, 20-12 (M)
1987—Seahawks, 28-17 (S)
1990—Vikings, 24-21 (S)
1996—Seahawks, 42-23 (S)
2002—Seahawks, 48-23 (S)
2003—Vikings, 34-7 (M)
(RS Pts.—Seahawks 216, Vikings 188)

MINNESOTA vs. TAMPA BAY
RS: Vikings lead series, 31-18
1977—Vikings, 9-3 (TB)
1978—Buccaneers, 16-10 (M)
Vikings, 24-7 (TB)
1979—Buccaneers, 12-10 (M)
Vikings, 23-22 (TB)
1980—Vikings, 38-30 (M)
Vikings, 21-10 (TB)
1981—Buccaneers, 21-13 (TB)
Vikings, 25-10 (M)
1982—Vikings, 17-10 (M)
1983—Vikings, 19-16 (TB) OT
Buccaneers, 17-12 (M)
1984—Buccaneers, 35-31 (TB)
Vikings, 27-24 (M)
1985—Vikings, 31-16 (TB)
Vikings, 26-7 (M)
1986—Vikings, 23-10 (TB)
Vikings, 45-13 (M)
1987—Buccaneers, 20-10 (TB)
Vikings, 23-17 (M)
1988—Vikings, 14-13 (M)
Vikings, 49-20 (TB)
1989—Vikings, 17-3 (M)
Vikings, 24-10 (TB)
1990—Buccaneers, 23-20 (M) OT
Buccaneers, 26-13 (TB)
1991—Vikings, 28-13 (M)
Vikings, 26-24 (TB)
1992—Vikings, 26-20 (M)
Vikings, 35-7 (TB)
1993—Vikings, 15-0 (M)
Buccaneers, 23-10 (TB)
1994—Vikings, 36-13 (TB)
Buccaneers, 20-17 (M) OT
1995—Buccaneers, 20-17 (TB) OT
Vikings, 31-17 (M)
1996—Buccaneers, 24-13 (TB)
Vikings, 21-10 (M)
1997—Buccaneers, 28-14 (M)
Vikings, 10-6 (TB)
1998—Vikings, 31-7 (M)
Buccaneers, 27-24 (TB)
1999—Vikings, 21-14 (M)
Buccaneers, 24-17 (TB)
2000—Vikings, 30-23 (M)
Buccaneers, 41-13 (TB)
2001—Vikings, 20-16 (M)
Buccaneers, 41-14 (TB)
2002—Buccaneers, 38-24 (TB)
(RS Pts.—Vikings 1,067, Buccaneers 867)

MINNESOTA vs. *TENNESSEE
RS: Vikings lead series, 6-3
1974—Vikings, 51-10 (M)
1980—Oilers, 20-16 (H)
1983—Vikings, 34-14 (M)
1986—Oilers, 23-10 (H)
1989—Vikings, 38-7 (M)
1992—Oilers, 17-13 (M)
1995—Vikings, 23-17 (M) OT
1998—Vikings, 26-16 (T)
2001—Vikings, 42-24 (M)
(RS Pts.—Vikings 253, Titans 148)
**Franchise in Houston prior to 1997; known as Oilers prior to 1999*

MINNESOTA vs. WASHINGTON
RS: Redskins lead series, 6-5
PS: Redskins lead series, 3-2
1968—Vikings, 27-14 (M)

1970—Vikings, 19-10 (W)
1972—Redskins, 24-21 (M)
1973—*Vikings, 27-20 (M)
1975—Redskins, 31-30 (W)
1976—*Vikings, 35-20 (M)
1980—Vikings, 39-14 (W)
1982—**Redskins, 21-7 (W)
1984—Redskins, 31-17 (M)
1986—Redskins, 44-38 (W) OT
1987—Redskins, 27-24 (M) OT
***Redskins, 17-10 (W)
1992—Redskins, 15-13 (M)
****Redskins, 24-7 (M)
1993—Vikings, 14-9 (W)
1998—Vikings, 41-7 (M)
(RS Pts.—Vikings 283, Redskins 226)
(PS Pts.—Redskins 102, Vikings 86)
NFC Divisional Playoff
***NFC Second-Round Playoff*
****NFC Championship*
*****NFC First-Round Playoff*

NEW ENGLAND vs. ARIZONA
RS: Cardinals lead series, 6-4;
See Arizona vs. New England
NEW ENGLAND vs. ATLANTA
RS: Falcons lead series, 6-4;
See Atlanta vs. New England
NEW ENGLAND vs. BALTIMORE
RS: Patriots lead series, 2-0;
See Baltimore vs. New England
NEW ENGLAND vs. BUFFALO
RS: Patriots lead series, 46-40-1
PS: Patriots lead series, 1-0;
See Buffalo vs. New England
NEW ENGLAND vs. CAROLINA
RS: Series tied, 1-1
PS: Patriots lead series, 1-0;
See Carolina vs. New England
NEW ENGLAND vs. CHICAGO
RS: Patriots lead series, 6-3
PS: Bears lead series, 1-0;
See Chicago vs. New England
NEW ENGLAND vs. CINCINNATI
RS: Patriots lead series, 10-8;
See Cincinnati vs. New England
NEW ENGLAND vs. CLEVELAND
RS: Browns lead series, 11-7
PS: Browns lead series, 1-0;
See Cleveland vs. New England
NEW ENGLAND vs. DALLAS
RS: Cowboys lead series, 7-2;
See Dallas vs. New England
NEW ENGLAND vs. DENVER
RS: Broncos lead series, 22-15
PS: Broncos lead series, 1-0;
See Denver vs. New England
NEW ENGLAND vs. DETROIT
RS: Series tied, 4-4;
See Detroit vs. New England
NEW ENGLAND vs. GREEN BAY
RS: Packers lead series, 4-3
PS: Packers lead series, 1-0;
See Green Bay vs. New England
NEW ENGLAND vs. HOUSTON
RS: Patriots lead series, 1-0;
See Houston vs. New England
NEW ENGLAND vs. INDIANAPOLIS
RS: Patriots lead series, 40-24
PS: Patriots lead series, 1-0;
See Indianapolis vs. New England
NEW ENGLAND vs. JACKSONVILLE
RS: Patriots lead series, 3-0
PS: Series tied, 1-1;
See Jacksonville vs. New England
NEW ENGLAND vs. KANSAS CITY
RS: Chiefs lead series, 15-10-3;
See Kansas City vs. New England
NEW ENGLAND vs. MIAMI
RS: Dolphins lead series, 44-30
PS: Patriots lead series, 2-1;
See Miami vs. New England
NEW ENGLAND vs. MINNESOTA
RS: Patriots lead series, 5-4;
See Minnesota vs. New England
NEW ENGLAND vs. NEW ORLEANS
RS: Patriots lead series, 7-3
1972—Patriots, 17-10 (NO)
1976—Patriots, 27-6 (NE)
1980—Patriots, 38-27 (NO)
1983—Patriots, 7-0 (NE)
1986—Patriots, 21-20 (NO)
1989—Saints, 28-24 (NE)
1992—Saints, 31-14 (NE)
1995—Saints, 31-17 (NE)
1998—Patriots, 30-27 (NO)
2001—Patriots, 34-17 (NE)
(RS Pts.—Patriots 229, Saints 197)
***NEW ENGLAND vs. N.Y. GIANTS**
RS: Patriots lead series, 4-3
1970—Giants, 16-0 (B)
1974—Patriots, 28-20 (New Haven)
1987—Giants, 17-10 (NY)
1990—Giants, 13-10 (NE)
1996—Patriots, 23-22 (NY)
1999—Patriots, 16-14 (NE)
2003—Patriots, 17-6 (NE)
(RS Pts.—Giants 108, Patriots 104)
**Franchise in Boston prior to 1971*
***NEW ENGLAND vs. **N.Y. JETS**
RS: Jets lead series, 47-39-1
PS: Patriots lead series, 1-0
1960—Patriots, 28-24 (NY)
Patriots, 38-21 (B)
1961—Titans, 21-20 (B)
Titans, 37-30 (NY)
1962—Patriots, 43-14 (NY)
Patriots, 24-17 (B)
1963—Patriots, 38-14 (B)
Jets, 31-24 (NY)
1964—Patriots, 26-10 (B)
Jets, 35-14 (NY)
1965—Jets, 30-20 (B)
Patriots, 27-23 (NY)
1966—Tie, 24-24 (B)
Jets, 38-28 (NY)
1967—Jets, 30-23 (NY)
Jets, 29-24 (B)
1968—Jets, 47-31 (Birmingham)
Jets, 48-14 (NY)
1969—Jets, 23-14 (B)
Jets, 23-17 (NY)
1970—Jets, 31-21 (B)
Jets, 17-3 (NY)
1971—Patriots, 20-0 (NE)
Jets, 13-6 (NY)
1972—Jets, 41-13 (NE)
Jets, 34-10 (NY)
1973—Jets, 9-7 (NE)
Jets, 33-13 (NY)
1974—Patriots, 24-0 (NY)
Jets, 21-16 (NE)
1975—Jets, 36-7 (NY)
Jets, 30-28 (NE)
1976—Patriots, 41-7 (NE)
Patriots, 38-24 (NY)
1977—Jets, 30-27 (NY)
Patriots, 24-13 (NE)
1978—Patriots, 55-21 (NE)
Patriots, 19-17 (NY)
1979—Patriots, 56-3 (NE)
Jets, 27-26 (NY)
1980—Patriots, 21-11 (NY)
Patriots, 34-21 (NE)
1981—Jets, 28-24 (NY)
Jets, 17-6 (NE)
1982—Jets, 31-7 (NE)
1983—Patriots, 23-13 (NE)
Jets, 26-3 (NY)
1984—Patriots, 28-21 (NY)
Patriots, 30-20 (NE)
1985—Patriots, 20-13 (NE)
Jets, 16-13 (NY) OT
***Patriots, 26-14 (NY)
1986—Patriots, 20-6 (NY)
Jets, 31-24 (NE)
1987—Jets, 43-24 (NY)
Patriots, 42-20 (NE)
1988—Patriots, 28-3 (NE)
Patriots, 14-13 (NY)
1989—Patriots, 27-24 (NY)
Jets, 27-26 (NE)
1990—Jets, 37-13 (NE)
Jets, 42-7 (NY)
1991—Jets, 28-21 (NE)
Patriots, 6-3 (NY)
1992—Jets, 30-21 (NY)
Patriots, 24-3 (NE)
1993—Jets, 45-7 (NY)
Jets, 6-0 (NE)
1994—Jets, 24-17 (NY)
Patriots, 24-13 (NE)
1995—Patriots, 20-7 (NY)
Patriots, 31-28 (NE)
1996—Patriots, 31-27 (NY)
Patriots, 34-10 (NE)
1997—Patriots, 27-24 (NE) OT
Jets, 24-19 (NY)
1998—Jets, 24-14 (NE)
Jets, 31-10 (NY)
1999—Patriots, 30-28 (NY)
Jets, 24-17 (NE)
2000—Jets, 20-19 (NY)
Jets, 34-17 (NE)
2001—Jets, 10-3 (NE)
Patriots, 17-16 (NY)
2002—Patriots, 44-7 (NY)
Jets, 30-17 (NE)
2003—Patriots, 23-16 (NE)
Patriots, 21-16 (NY)
(RS Pts.—Jets 1,937, Patriots 1,909)
(PS Pts.—Patriots 26, Jets 14)
**Franchise in Boston prior to 1971*
***Jets known as Titans prior to 1963*
****AFC First-Round Playoff*
***NEW ENGLAND vs. **OAKLAND**
RS: Raiders lead series, 14-12-1
PS: Patriots lead series, 2-1
1960—Raiders, 27-14 (O)
Patriots, 34-28 (B)

1961—Patriots, 20-17 (B)
Patriots, 35-21 (O)
1962—Patriots, 26-16 (B)
Raiders, 20-0 (O)
1963—Patriots, 20-14 (O)
Patriots, 20-14 (B)
1964—Patriots, 17-14 (O)
Tie, 43-43 (B)
1965—Raiders, 24-10 (B)
Raiders, 30-21 (O)
1966—Patriots, 24-21 (B)
1967—Raiders, 35-7 (O)
Raiders, 48-14 (B)
1968—Raiders, 41-10 (O)
1969—Raiders, 38-23 (B)
1971—Patriots, 20-6 (NE)
1974—Raiders, 41-26 (O)
1976—Patriots, 48-17 (NE)
***Raiders, 24-21 (O)
1978—Patriots, 21-14 (O)
1981—Raiders, 27-17 (O)
1985—Raiders, 35-20 (NE)
***Patriots, 27-20 (LA)
1987—Patriots, 26-23 (NE)
1989—Raiders, 24-21 (LA)
1994—Raiders, 21-17 (NE)
2001—***Patriots, 16-13 (NE) OT
2002—Raiders, 27-20 (O)
(RS Pts.—Raiders 686, Patriots 574)
(PS Pts.—Patriots 64, Raiders 57)
Franchise in Boston prior to 1971
***Franchise in Los Angeles from 1982-1994*
****AFC Divisional Playoff*

NEW ENGLAND vs. PHILADELPHIA
RS: Eagles lead series, 6-3
1973—Eagles, 24-23 (P)
1977—Patriots, 14-6 (NE)
1978—Patriots, 24-14 (NE)
1981—Eagles, 13-3 (P)
1984—Eagles, 27-17 (P)
1987—Eagles, 34-31 (NE) OT
1990—Eagles, 48-20 (P)
1999—Eagles, 24-9 (P)
2003—Patriots, 31-10 (P)
(RS Pts.—Eagles 200, Patriots 172)

NEW ENGLAND vs. PITTSBURGH
RS: Steelers lead series, 11-5
PS: Patriots lead series, 2-1
1972—Steelers, 33-3 (P)
1974—Steelers, 21-17 (NE)
1976—Patriots, 30-27 (P)
1979—Steelers, 16-13 (NE) OT
1981—Steelers, 27-21 (P) OT
1982—Steelers, 37-14 (P)
1983—Patriots, 28-23 (P)
1986—Patriots, 34-0 (P)
1989—Steelers, 28-10 (P)
1990—Steelers, 24-3 (P)
1991—Steelers, 20-6 (P)
1993—Steelers, 17-14 (P)
1995—Steelers, 41-27 (P)
1996—*Patriots, 28-3 (NE)
1997—Steelers, 24-21 (NE) OT
*Steelers, 7-6 (P)
1998—Patriots, 23-9 (P)
2001—**Patriots, 24-17 (P)
2002—Patriots, 30-14 (NE)
(RS Pts.—Steelers 361, Patriots 294)
(PS Pts.—Patriots 58, Steelers 27)
**AFC Divisional Playoff*
***AFC Championship*

NEW ENGLAND vs. *ST. LOUIS
RS: Rams lead series, 5-3
PS: Patriots lead series, 1-0
1974—Patriots, 20-14 (NE)
1980—Rams, 17-14 (NE)
1983—Patriots, 21-7 (LA)
1986—Patriots, 30-28 (LA)
1989—Rams, 24-20 (NE)
1992—Rams, 14-0 (LA)
1998—Rams, 32-18 (StL)
2001—Rams, 24-17 (NE)
**Patriots, 20-17 (New Orleans)
(RS Pts.—Rams 160, Patriots 140)
(PS Pts.—Patriots 20, Rams 17)
**Franchise in Los Angeles prior to 1995*
***Super Bowl XXXVI*

***NEW ENGLAND vs. **SAN DIEGO**
RS: Patriots lead series, 17-12-2
PS: Chargers lead series, 1-0
1960—Patriots, 35-0 (LA)
Chargers, 45-16 (B)
1961—Chargers, 38-27 (B)
Patriots, 41-0 (SD)
1962—Patriots, 24-20 (B)
Patriots, 20-14 (SD)
1963—Chargers, 17-13 (SD)
Chargers, 7-6 (B)
***Chargers, 51-10 (SD)
1964—Patriots, 33-28 (SD)
Chargers, 26-17 (B)
1965—Tie, 10-10 (B)
Patriots, 22-6 (SD)
1966—Chargers, 24-0 (SD)
Patriots, 35-17 (B)
1967—Chargers, 28-14 (SD)
Tie, 31-31 (SD)
1968—Chargers, 27-17 (B)
1969—Chargers, 13-10 (B)
Chargers, 28-18 (SD)
1970—Chargers, 16-14 (B)
1973—Patriots, 30-14 (NE)
1975—Patriots, 33-19 (SD)
1977—Patriots, 24-20 (SD)
1978—Patriots, 28-23 (NE)
1979—Patriots, 27-21 (NE)
1983—Patriots, 37-21 (NE)
1994—Patriots, 23-17 (NE)
1996—Patriots, 45-7 (SD)
1997—Patriots, 41-7 (NE)
2001—Patriots, 29-26 (NE) OT
2002—Chargers, 21-14 (SD)
(RS Pts.—Patriots 734, Chargers 591)
(PS Pts.—Chargers 51, Patriots 10)
**Franchise in Boston prior to 1971*
***Franchise in Los Angeles prior to 1961*
****AFL Championship*

NEW ENGLAND vs. SAN FRANCISCO
RS: 49ers lead series, 7-2
1971—49ers, 27-10 (SF)
1975—Patriots, 24-16 (NE)
1980—49ers, 21-17 (SF)
1983—49ers, 33-13 (NE)
1986—49ers, 29-24 (NE)
1989—49ers, 37-20 (SF)
1992—49ers, 24-12 (NE)
1995—49ers, 28-3 (SF)
1998—Patriots, 24-21 (NE)
(RS Pts.—49ers 236, Patriots 147)

NEW ENGLAND vs. SEATTLE
RS: Seahawks lead series, 7-6
1977—Patriots, 31-0 (NE)
1980—Patriots, 37-31 (S)
1982—Patriots, 16-0 (S)
1983—Seahawks, 24-6 (S)
1984—Patriots, 38-23 (NE)
1985—Patriots, 20-13 (S)
1986—Seahawks, 38-31 (NE)
1988—Patriots, 13-7 (NE)
1989—Seahawks, 24-3 (NE)
1990—Seahawks, 33-20 (NE)
1992—Seahawks, 10-6 (NE)
1993—Seahawks, 17-14 (NE)
Seahawks, 10-9 (S)
(RS Pts.—Patriots 244, Seahawks 230)

NEW ENGLAND vs. TAMPA BAY
RS: Patriots lead series, 3-2
1976—Patriots, 31-14 (TB)
1985—Patriots, 32-14 (TB)
1988—Patriots, 10-7 (NE) OT
1997—Buccaneers, 27-7 (TB)
2000—Buccaneers, 21-16 (NE)
(RS Pts.—Patriots 96, Buccaneers 83)

***NEW ENGLAND vs. **TENNESSEE**
RS: Patriots lead series, 19-15-1
PS: Series tied, 1-1
1960—Oilers, 24-10 (B)
Oilers, 37-21 (H)
1961—Tie, 31-31 (B)
Oilers, 27-15 (H)
1962—Patriots, 34-21 (B)
Oilers, 21-17 (H)
1963—Patriots, 45-3 (B)
Patriots, 46-28 (H)
1964—Patriots, 25-24 (B)
Patriots, 34-17 (H)
1965—Oilers, 31-10 (H)
Patriots, 42-14 (B)
1966—Patriots, 27-21 (B)
Patriots, 38-14 (H)
1967—Patriots, 18-7 (B)
Oilers, 27-6 (H)
1968—Oilers, 16-0 (B)
Oilers, 45-17 (H)
1969—Patriots, 24-0 (B)
Oilers, 27-23 (H)
1971—Patriots, 28-20 (NE)
1973—Patriots, 32-0 (H)
1975—Oilers, 7-0 (NE)
1978—Oilers, 26-23 (NE)
***Oilers, 31-14 (NE)
1980—Oilers, 38-34 (H)
1981—Patriots, 38-10 (NE)
1982—Patriots, 29-21 (NE)
1987—Patriots, 21-7 (H)
1988—Oilers, 31-6 (H)
1989—Patriots, 23-13 (NE)
1991—Patriots, 24-20 (NE)
1993—Oilers, 28-14 (NE)
1998—Patriots, 27-16 (NE)
2002—Titans, 24-7 (T)
2003—Patriots, 38-30 (NE)
***Patriots, 17-14 (NE)
(RS Pts.—Patriots 827, Titans 726)
(PS Pts.—Titans 45, Patriots 31)
**Franchise in Boston prior to 1971*
***Franchise in Houston prior to 1997; known as Oilers prior to 1999*
****AFC Divisional Playoff*

NEW ENGLAND vs. WASHINGTON
RS: Redskins lead series, 6-1
1972—Patriots, 24-23 (NE)
1978—Redskins, 16-14 (NE)
1981—Redskins, 24-22 (W)
1984—Redskins, 26-10 (NE)
1990—Redskins, 25-10 (NE)
1996—Redskins, 27-22 (NE)
2003—Redskins, 20-17 (W)
(RS Pts.—Redskins 161, Patriots 119)

NEW ORLEANS vs. ARIZONA
RS: Cardinals lead series, 12-11;
See Arizona vs. New Orleans
NEW ORLEANS vs. ATLANTA
RS: Falcons lead series, 40-29
PS: Falcons lead series, 1-0;
See Atlanta vs. New Orleans
NEW ORLEANS vs. BALTIMORE
RS: Ravens lead series, 2-1;
See Baltimore vs. New Orleans
NEW ORLEANS vs. BUFFALO
RS: Bills lead series, 4-3;
See Buffalo vs. New Orleans
NEW ORLEANS vs. CAROLINA
RS: Series tied, 9-9;
See Carolina vs. New Orleans
NEW ORLEANS vs. CHICAGO
RS: Saints lead series, 11-10
PS: Bears lead series, 1-0;
See Chicago vs. New Orleans
NEW ORLEANS vs. CINCINNATI
RS: Series tied, 5-5;
See Cincinnati vs. New Orleans
NEW ORLEANS vs. CLEVELAND
RS: Browns lead series, 11-3;
See Cleveland vs. New Orleans
NEW ORLEANS vs. DALLAS
RS: Cowboys lead series, 14-6;
See Dallas vs. New Orleans
NEW ORLEANS vs. DENVER
RS: Broncos lead series, 5-2;
See Denver vs. New Orleans
NEW ORLEANS vs. DETROIT
RS: Series tied, 8-8-1;
See Detroit vs. New Orleans
NEW ORLEANS vs. GREEN BAY
RS: Packers lead series, 13-5;
See Green Bay vs. New Orleans
NEW ORLEANS vs. HOUSTON
RS: Saints lead series, 1-0;
See Houston vs. New Orleans
NEW ORLEANS vs. INDIANAPOLIS
RS: Saints lead series, 5-4;
See Indianapolis vs. New Orleans
NEW ORLEANS vs. JACKSONVILLE
RS: Jaguars lead series, 2-1;
See Jacksonville vs. New Orleans
NEW ORLEANS vs. KANSAS CITY
RS: Chiefs lead series, 4-3;
See Kansas City vs. New Orleans
NEW ORLEANS vs. MIAMI
RS: Dolphins lead series, 5-3;
See Miami vs. New Orleans
NEW ORLEANS vs. MINNESOTA
RS: Vikings lead series, 15-7
PS: Vikings lead series, 2-0;
See Minnesota vs. New Orleans
NEW ORLEANS vs. NEW ENGLAND
RS: Patriots lead series, 7-3;
See New England vs. New Orleans
NEW ORLEANS vs. N.Y. GIANTS
RS: Giants lead series, 13-9
1967—Giants, 27-21 (NY)
1968—Giants, 38-21 (NY)
1969—Saints, 25-24 (NY)
1970—Saints, 14-10 (NO)
1972—Giants, 45-21 (NY)
1975—Giants, 28-14 (NY)
1978—Saints, 28-17 (NO)
1979—Saints, 24-14 (NO)
1981—Giants, 20-7 (NY)
1984—Saints, 10-3 (NY)
1985—Giants, 21-13 (NO)
1986—Giants, 20-17 (NY)
1987—Saints, 23-14 (NO)
1988—Giants, 13-12 (NO)
1993—Giants, 24-14 (NO)
1994—Saints, 27-22 (NO)
1995—Giants, 45-29 (NY)
1996—Saints 17-3 (NY)
1997—Giants, 14-9 (NY)
1999—Giants, 31-3 (NY)
2001—Giants, 21-13 (NY)
2003—Saints, 45-7 (NO)
(RS Pts.—Giants 461, Saints 407)
NEW ORLEANS vs. N.Y. JETS
RS: Jets lead series, 5-4
1972—Jets, 18-17 (NY)
1977—Jets, 16-13 (NO)
1980—Saints, 21-20 (NY)
1983—Jets, 31-28 (NO)
1986—Jets, 28-23 (NY)
1989—Saints, 29-14 (NO)
1992—Saints, 20-0 (NY)
1995—Saints, 12-0 (NY)
2001—Jets, 16-9 (NO)
(RS Pts.—Saints 172, Jets 143)
NEW ORLEANS vs. *OAKLAND
RS: Raiders lead series, 5-3-1
1971—Tie, 21-21 (NO)
1975—Raiders, 48-10 (O)
1979—Raiders, 42-35 (NO)
1985—Raiders, 23-13 (LA)
1988—Saints, 20-6 (NO)
1991—Saints, 27-0 (NO)
1994—Raiders, 24-19 (LA)
1997—Saints, 13-10 (O)
2000—Raiders, 31-22 (NO)
(RS Pts.—Raiders 205, Saints 180)
Franchise in Los Angeles from 1982-1994
NEW ORLEANS vs. PHILADELPHIA
RS: Eagles lead series, 14-8
PS: Eagles lead series, 1-0
1967—Saints, 31-24 (NO)
Eagles, 48-21 (P)
1968—Eagles, 29-17 (P)
1969—Eagles, 13-10 (P)
Saints, 26-17 (NO)
1972—Saints, 21-3 (NO)
1974—Saints, 14-10 (NO)
1977—Eagles, 28-7 (P)
1978—Eagles, 24-17 (NO)
1979—Eagles, 26-14 (NO)
1980—Eagles, 34-21 (NO)
1981—Eagles, 31-14 (NO)
1983—Saints, 20-17 (P) OT
1985—Saints, 23-21 (NO)
1987—Eagles, 27-17 (P)
1989—Saints, 30-20 (NO)
1991—Saints, 13-6 (P)
1992—Eagles, 15-13 (P)
*Eagles, 36-20 (NO)
1993—Eagles, 37-26 (P)
1995—Eagles, 15-10 (NO)
2000—Eagles, 21-7 (NO)
2003—Eagles, 33-20 (P)
(RS Pts.—Eagles 499, Saints 392)
(PS Pts.—Eagles 36, Saints 20)
NFC First-Round Playoff
NEW ORLEANS vs. PITTSBURGH
RS: Series tied, 6-6
1967—Steelers, 14-10 (NO)
1968—Saints, 16-12 (P)
Saints, 24-14 (NO)
1969—Saints, 27-24 (NO)
1974—Steelers, 28-7 (NO)
1978—Steelers, 20-14 (P)
1981—Steelers, 20-6 (NO)
1984—Saints, 27-24 (NO)
1987—Saints, 20-16 (P)
1990—Steelers, 9-6 (NO)
1993—Steelers, 37-14 (P)
2002—Saints, 32-29 (NO)
(RS Pts.—Steelers 247, Saints 203)
NEW ORLEANS vs. *ST. LOUIS
RS: Rams lead series, 36-28
PS: Saints lead series, 1-0
1967—Rams, 27-13 (NO)
1969—Rams, 36-17 (LA)
1970—Rams, 30-17 (NO)
Rams, 34-16 (LA)
1971—Saints, 24-20 (NO)
Rams, 45-28 (LA)
1972—Rams, 34-14 (LA)
Saints, 19-16 (NO)
1973—Rams, 29-7 (LA)
Rams, 24-13 (NO)
1974—Rams, 24-0 (LA)
Saints, 20-7 (NO)
1975—Rams, 38-14 (LA)
Rams, 14-7 (NO)
1976—Rams, 16-10 (NO)
Rams, 33-14 (LA)
1977—Rams, 14-7 (LA)
Saints, 27-26 (NO)
1978—Rams, 26-20 (NO)
Saints, 10-3 (LA)
1979—Rams, 35-17 (NO)
Saints, 29-14 (LA)
1980—Rams, 45-31 (LA)
Rams, 27-7 (NO)
1981—Saints, 23-17 (NO)
Saints, 21-13 (LA)
1983—Rams, 30-27 (LA)
Rams, 26-24 (NO)
1984—Rams, 28-10 (NO)
Rams, 34-21 (LA)
1985—Rams, 28-10 (LA)
Saints, 29-3 (NO)
1986—Saints, 6-0 (NO)
Rams, 26-13 (LA)
1987—Saints, 37-10 (NO)
Saints, 31-14 (LA)
1988—Rams, 12-10 (NO)
Saints, 14-10 (LA)
1989—Saints, 40-21 (LA)
Rams, 20-17 (NO) OT
1990—Saints, 24-20 (LA)
Saints, 20-17 (NO)

1991—Saints, 24-7 (NO)
Saints, 24-17 (LA)
1992—Saints, 13-10 (NO)
Saints, 37-14 (LA)
1993—Saints, 37-6 (LA)
Rams, 23-20 (NO)
1994—Saints, 37-34 (NO)
Saints, 31-15 (LA)
1995—Rams, 17-13 (StL)
Saints, 19-10 (NO)
1996—Rams, 26-10 (NO)
Rams, 14-13 (StL)
1997—Rams, 38-24 (StL)
Rams, 34-27 (NO)
1998—Saints, 24-17 (StL)
Saints, 24-3 (NO)
1999—Rams, 43-12 (StL)
Rams, 30-14 (NO)
2000—Saints, 31-24 (StL)
Rams, 26-21 (NO)
**Saints, 31-28 (NO)
2001—Saints, 34-31 (StL)
Rams, 34-21 (NO)
(RS Pts.—Rams 1,419, Saints 1,268)
(PS Pts.—Saints 31, Rams 28)
Franchise in Los Angeles prior to 1995
***NFC First-Round Playoff*

NEW ORLEANS vs. SAN DIEGO
RS: Chargers lead series, 6-2
1973—Chargers, 17-14 (SD)
1977—Chargers, 14-0 (NO)
1979—Chargers, 35-0 (NO)
1988—Saints, 23-17 (SD)
1991—Chargers, 24-21 (SD)
1994—Chargers, 36-22 (NO)
1997—Chargers, 20-6 (NO)
2000—Saints, 28-27 (SD)
(RS Pts.—Chargers 190, Saints 114)

NEW ORLEANS vs. SAN FRANCISCO
RS: 49ers lead series, 45-19-2
1967—49ers, 27-13 (SF)
1969—Saints, 43-38 (NO)
1970—Tie, 20-20 (SF)
49ers, 38-27 (NO)
1971—49ers, 38-20 (NO)
Saints, 26-20 (SF)
1972—49ers, 37-2 (NO)
Tie, 20-20 (SF)
1973—49ers, 40-0 (SF)
Saints, 16-10 (NO)
1974—49ers, 17-13 (NO)
49ers, 35-21 (SF)
1975—49ers, 35-21 (SF)
49ers, 16-6 (NO)
1976—49ers, 33-3 (SF)
49ers, 27-7 (NO)
1977—49ers, 10-7 (NO) OT
49ers, 20-17 (SF)
1978—Saints, 14-7 (SF)
Saints, 24-13 (NO)
1979—Saints, 30-21 (SF)
Saints, 31-20 (NO)
1980—49ers, 26-23 (NO)
49ers, 38-35 (SF) OT
1981—49ers, 21-14 (SF)
49ers, 21-17 (NO)
1982—Saints, 23-20 (SF)
1983—49ers, 32-13 (NO)
49ers, 27-0 (SF)
1984—49ers, 30-20 (SF)
49ers, 35-3 (NO)
1985—Saints, 20-17 (SF)
49ers, 31-19 (NO)
1986—49ers, 26-17 (SF)
Saints, 23-10 (NO)
1987—49ers, 24-22 (NO)
Saints, 26-24 (SF)
1988—49ers, 34-33 (NO)
49ers, 30-17 (SF)
1989—49ers, 24-20 (NO)
49ers, 31-13 (SF)
1990—49ers, 13-12 (NO)
Saints, 13-10 (SF)
1991—Saints, 10-3 (NO)
49ers, 38-24 (SF)
1992—49ers, 16-10 (NO)
49ers, 21-20 (SF)
1993—Saints, 16-13 (NO)
49ers, 42-7 (SF)
1994—49ers, 24-13 (SF)
49ers, 35-14 (NO)
1995—49ers, 24-22 (NO)
Saints, 11-7 (SF)
1996—49ers, 27-11 (SF)
49ers, 24-17 (NO)
1997—49ers, 33-7 (SF)
49ers, 23-0 (NO)
1998—49ers, 31-0 (NO)
49ers, 31-20 (SF)
1999—49ers, 28-21 (SF)
Saints, 24-6 (NO)
2000—Saints, 31-15 (NO)
Saints, 31-27 (SF)
2001—49ers, 28-27 (SF)
49ers, 38-0 (NO)
2002—Saints, 35-27 (NO)
(RS Pts.—49ers 1,627, Saints 1,135)

NEW ORLEANS vs. SEATTLE
RS: Series tied, 4-4
1976—Saints, 51-27 (S)
1979—Seahawks, 38-24 (S)
1985—Seahawks, 27-3 (NO)
1988—Saints, 20-19 (S)
1991—Saints, 27-24 (NO)
1997—Saints, 20-17 (NO) OT
2000—Seahawks, 20-10 (S)
2003—Seahawks, 27-10 (S)
(RS Pts.—Seahawks 199, Saints 165)

NEW ORLEANS vs. TAMPA BAY
RS: Saints lead series, 16-8
1977—Buccaneers, 33-14 (NO)
1978—Saints, 17-10 (TB)
1979—Saints, 42-14 (TB)
1981—Buccaneers, 31-14 (NO)
1982—Buccaneers, 13-10 (NO)
1983—Saints, 24-21 (TB)
1984—Saints, 17-13 (NO)
1985—Saints, 20-13 (NO)
1986—Saints, 38-7 (NO)
1987—Saints, 44-34 (NO)
1988—Saints, 13-9 (NO)
1989—Buccaneers, 20-10 (TB)
1990—Saints, 35-7 (NO)
1991—Saints, 23-7 (NO)
1992—Saints, 23-21 (NO)
1994—Saints, 9-7 (TB)
1996—Buccaneers, 13-7 (TB)
1998—Saints, 9-3 (NO)
1999—Buccaneers, 31-16 (NO)
2001—Buccaneers, 48-21 (TB)
2002—Saints, 26-20 (TB) OT
Saints, 23-20 (NO)
2003—Saints, 17-14 (TB)
Buccaneers, 14-7 (NO)
(RS Pts.—Saints 479, Buccaneers 423)

NEW ORLEANS vs. *TENNESSEE
RS: Titans lead series, 6-4-1
1971—Tie, 13-13 (H)
1976—Oilers, 31-26 (NO)
1978—Oilers, 17-12 (NO)
1981—Saints, 27-24 (H)
1984—Saints, 27-10 (H)
1987—Saints, 24-10 (NO)
1990—Oilers, 23-10 (H)
1993—Saints, 33-21 (NO)
1996—Oilers, 31-14 (NO)
1999—Titans, 24-21 (NO)
2003—Titans, 27-12 (T)
(RS Pts.—Titans 231, Saints 219)
**Franchise in Houston prior to 1997; known as Oilers prior to 1999*

NEW ORLEANS vs. WASHINGTON
RS: Redskins lead series, 13-7
1967—Redskins, 30-10 (NO)
Saints, 30-14 (W)
1968—Saints, 37-17 (NO)
1969—Redskins, 26-20 (NO)
Redskins, 17-14 (W)
1971—Redskins, 24-14 (W)
1973—Saints, 19-3 (NO)
1975—Redskins, 41-3 (W)
1979—Saints, 14-10 (W)
1980—Redskins, 22-14 (W)
1982—Redskins, 27-10 (NO)
1986—Redskins, 14-6 (NO)
1988—Redskins, 27-24 (W)
1989—Redskins, 16-14 (NO)
1990—Redskins, 31-17 (W)
1992—Saints, 20-3 (NO)
1994—Redskins, 38-24 (NO)
2001—Redskins, 40-10 (NO)
2002—Saints, 43-27 (W)
2003—Saints, 24-20 (W)
(RS Pts.—Redskins 447, Saints 367)

N.Y. GIANTS vs. ARIZONA
RS: Giants lead series, 77-40-2;
See Arizona vs. N.Y. Giants

N.Y. GIANTS vs. ATLANTA
RS: Falcons lead series, 9-7;
See Atlanta vs. N.Y. Giants

N.Y. GIANTS vs. BALTIMORE
RS: Ravens lead series, 1-0
PS: Ravens lead series, 1-0;
See Baltimore vs. N.Y. Giants

N.Y. GIANTS vs. BUFFALO
RS: Bills lead series, 6-3
PS: Giants lead series, 1-0;
See Buffalo vs. N.Y. Giants

N.Y. GIANTS vs. CAROLINA
RS: Panthers lead series, 2-0;
See Carolina vs. N.Y. Giants

N.Y. GIANTS vs. CHICAGO
RS: Bears lead series, 25-17-2
PS: Bears lead series, 5-3;
See Chicago vs. N.Y. Giants

N.Y. GIANTS vs. CINCINNATI
RS: Bengals lead series, 4-2;
See Cincinnati vs. N.Y. Giants

N.Y. GIANTS vs. CLEVELAND
RS: Browns lead series, 25-18-2
PS: Series tied, 1-1;
See Cleveland vs. N.Y. Giants

N.Y. GIANTS vs. DALLAS
RS: Cowboys lead series, 50-31-2;
See Dallas vs. N.Y. Giants

N.Y. GIANTS vs. DENVER
RS: Series tied, 4-4
PS: Giants lead series, 1-0;
See Denver vs. N.Y. Giants

N.Y. GIANTS vs. DETROIT
RS: Lions lead series, 19-17-1
PS: Lions lead series, 1-0;
See Detroit vs. N.Y. Giants

N.Y. GIANTS vs. GREEN BAY
RS: Packers lead series, 24-20-2
PS: Packers lead series, 4-1;
See Green Bay vs. N.Y. Giants

N.Y. GIANTS vs. HOUSTON
RS: Texans lead series, 1-0;
See Houston vs. N.Y. Giants

N.Y. GIANTS vs. INDIANAPOLIS
RS: Series tied, 6-6
PS: Colts lead series, 2-0;
See Indianapolis vs. N.Y. Giants

N.Y. GIANTS vs. JACKSONVILLE
RS: Giants lead series, 2-1;
See Jacksonville vs. N.Y. Giants

N.Y. GIANTS vs. KANSAS CITY
RS: Giants lead series, 8-2;
See Kansas City vs. N.Y. Giants

N.Y. GIANTS vs. MIAMI
RS: Giants lead series, 3-2;
See Miami vs. N.Y. Giants

N.Y. GIANTS vs. MINNESOTA
RS: Vikings lead series, 9-7
PS: Giants lead series, 2-1;
See Minnesota vs. N.Y. Giants

N.Y. GIANTS vs. NEW ENGLAND
RS: Patriots lead series, 4-3;
See New England vs. N.Y. Giants

N.Y. GIANTS vs. NEW ORLEANS
RS: Giants lead series, 13-9;
See New Orleans vs. N.Y. Giants

N.Y. GIANTS vs. N.Y. JETS
RS: Giants lead series, 6-4
1970—Giants, 22-10 (NYJ)
1974—Jets, 26-20 (New Haven) OT
1981—Jets, 26-7 (NYG)
1984—Giants, 20-10 (NYJ)
1987—Giants, 20-7 (NYG)
1988—Jets, 27-21 (NYJ)
1993—Jets, 10-6 (NYG)
1996—Giants, 13-6 (NYJ)
1999—Giants, 41-28 (NYG)
2003—Giants, 31-28 (NYG) OT
(RS Pts.—Giants 201, Jets 178)

N.Y. GIANTS vs. *OAKLAND
RS: Raiders lead series, 7-2
1973—Raiders, 42-0 (O)
1980—Raiders, 33-17 (NY)
1983—Raiders, 27-12 (LA)
1986—Giants, 14-9 (LA)
1989—Giants, 34-17 (NY)
1992—Raiders, 13-10 (LA)
1995—Raiders, 17-13 (NY)
1998—Raiders, 20-17 (O)
2001—Raiders, 28-10 (NY)
(RS Pts.—Raiders 206, Giants 127)
Franchise in Los Angeles from 1982-1994

N.Y. GIANTS vs. PHILADELPHIA
RS: Giants lead series, 73-63-2
PS: Giants lead series, 2-0
1933—Giants, 56-0 (NY)
Giants, 20-14 (P)
1934—Giants, 17-0 (NY)
Eagles, 6-0 (P)
1935—Giants, 10-0 (NY)
Giants, 21-14 (P)
1936—Eagles, 10-7 (P)
Giants, 21-17 (NY)
1937—Giants, 16-7 (P)
Giants, 21-0 (NY)
1938—Eagles, 14-10 (P)
Giants, 17-7 (NY)
1939—Giants, 13-3 (P)
Giants, 27-10 (NY)
1940—Giants, 20-14 (P)
Giants, 17-7 (NY)
1941—Giants, 24-0 (P)
Giants, 16-0 (NY)
1942—Giants, 35-17 (NY)
Giants, 14-0 (P)
1944—Eagles, 24-17 (NY)
Tie, 21-21 (P)
1945—Eagles, 38-17 (P)
Giants, 28-21 (NY)
1946—Eagles, 24-14 (P)
Giants, 45-17 (NY)
1947—Eagles, 23-0 (P)
Eagles, 41-24 (NY)
1948—Eagles, 45-0 (P)
Eagles, 35-14 (NY)
1949—Eagles, 24-3 (NY)
Eagles, 17-3 (P)
1950—Giants, 7-3 (NY)
Giants, 9-7 (P)
1951—Giants, 26-24 (NY)
Giants, 23-7 (P)
1952—Giants, 31-7 (P)
Eagles, 14-10 (NY)
1953—Eagles, 30-7 (P)
Giants, 37-28 (NY)
1954—Giants, 27-14 (NY)
Eagles, 29-14 (P)
1955—Eagles, 27-17 (P)
Giants, 31-7 (NY)
1956—Giants, 20-3 (NY)
Giants, 21-7 (P)
1957—Giants, 24-20 (P)
Giants, 13-0 (NY)
1958—Eagles, 27-24 (P)
Giants, 24-10 (NY)
1959—Eagles, 49-21 (P)
Giants, 24-7 (NY)
1960—Eagles, 17-10 (NY)
Eagles, 31-23 (P)
1961—Giants, 38-21 (NY)
Giants, 28-24 (P)
1962—Giants, 29-13 (P)
Giants, 19-14 (NY)
1963—Giants, 37-14 (P)
Giants, 42-14 (NY)
1964—Eagles, 38-7 (P)
Eagles, 23-17 (NY)
1965—Giants, 16-14 (P)
Giants, 35-27 (NY)
1966—Eagles, 35-17 (P)
Eagles, 31-3 (NY)
1967—Giants, 44-7 (NY)
1968—Giants, 34-25 (P)
Giants, 7-6 (NY)
1969—Eagles, 23-20 (NY)
1970—Giants, 30-23 (NY)
Eagles, 23-20 (P)
1971—Eagles, 23-7 (P)
Eagles, 41-28 (NY)
1972—Giants, 27-12 (P)
Giants, 62-10 (NY)
1973—Tie, 23-23 (NY)
Eagles, 20-16 (P)
1974—Eagles, 35-7 (P)
Eagles, 20-7 (New Haven)
1975—Giants, 23-14 (P)
Eagles, 13-10 (NY)
1976—Eagles, 20-7 (P)
Eagles, 10-0 (NY)
1977—Eagles, 28-10 (NY)
Eagles, 17-14 (P)
1978—Eagles, 19-17 (NY)
Eagles, 20-3 (P)
1979—Eagles, 23-17 (P)
Eagles, 17-13 (NY)
1980—Eagles, 35-3 (P)
Eagles, 31-16 (NY)
1981—Eagles, 24-10 (NY)
Giants, 20-10 (P)
*Giants, 27-21 (P)
1982—Giants, 23-7 (NY)
Giants, 26-24 (P)
1983—Eagles, 17-13 (NY)
Giants, 23-0 (P)
1984—Giants, 28-27 (NY)
Eagles, 24-10 (P)
1985—Giants, 21-0 (NY)
Giants, 16-10 (P) OT
1986—Giants, 35-3 (NY)
Giants, 17-14 (P)
1987—Giants, 20-17 (P)
Giants, 23-20 (NY) OT
1988—Eagles, 24-13 (P)
Eagles, 23-17 (NY) OT
1989—Eagles, 21-19 (P)
Eagles, 24-17 (NY)
1990—Giants, 27-20 (NY)
Eagles, 31-13 (P)
1991—Eagles, 30-7 (P)
Eagles, 19-14 (NY)
1992—Eagles, 47-34 (NY)
Eagles, 20-10 (P)
1993—Giants, 21-10 (NY)
Giants, 7-3 (P)
1994—Giants, 28-23 (NY)
Giants, 16-13 (P)
1995—Eagles, 17-14 (NY)
Eagles, 28-19 (P)
1996—Eagles, 19-10 (NY)
Eagles, 24-0 (P)
1997—Giants, 31-17 (NY)
Giants, 31-21 (P)
1998—Giants, 20-0 (NY)
Giants, 20-10 (P)
1999—Giants, 16-15 (NY)
Giants, 23-17 (P) OT
2000—Giants, 33-18 (P)
Giants, 24-7 (NY)
**Giants, 20-10 (NY)
2001—Eagles, 10-9 (NY)
Eagles, 24-21 (P)

2002—Eagles, 17-3 (P)
Giants, 10-7 (NY) OT
2003—Eagles, 14-10 (NY)
Eagles, 28-10 (P)
(RS Pts.—Giants 2,596, Eagles 2,442)
(PS Pts.—Giants 47, Eagles 31)
NFC First-Round Playoff
**NFC Divisional Playoff*

N.Y. GIANTS vs. *PITTSBURGH
RS: Giants lead series, 43-27-3
1933—Giants, 23-2 (P)
Giants, 27-3 (NY)
1934—Giants, 14-12 (P)
Giants, 17-7 (NY)
1935—Giants, 42-7 (P)
Giants, 13-0 (NY)
1936—Pirates, 10-7 (P)
1937—Giants, 10-7 (P)
Giants, 17-0 (NY)
1938—Giants, 27-14 (P)
Pirates, 13-10 (NY)
1939—Giants, 14-7 (P)
Giants, 23-7 (NY)
1940—Tie, 10-10 (P)
Giants, 12-0 (NY)
1941—Giants, 37-10 (P)
Giants, 28-7 (NY)
1942—Steelers, 13-10 (P)
Steelers, 17-9 (NY)
1945—Giants, 34-6 (P)
Steelers, 21-7 (NY)
1946—Giants, 17-14 (P)
Giants, 7-0 (NY)
1947—Steelers, 38-21 (NY)
Steelers, 24-7 (P)
1948—Giants, 34-27 (NY)
Steelers, 38-28 (P)
1949—Steelers, 28-7 (P)
Steelers, 21-17 (NY)
1950—Giants, 18-7 (P)
Steelers, 17-6 (NY)
1951—Tie, 13-13 (P)
Giants, 14-0 (NY)
1952—Steelers, 63-7 (P)
1953—Steelers, 24-14 (P)
Steelers, 14-10 (NY)
1954—Giants, 30-6 (P)
Giants, 24-3 (NY)
1955—Steelers, 30-23 (P)
Steelers, 19-17 (NY)
1956—Giants, 38-10 (NY)
Giants, 17-14 (P)
1957—Giants, 35-0 (NY)
Steelers, 21-10 (P)
1958—Giants, 17-6 (NY)
Steelers, 31-10 (P)
1959—Giants, 21-16 (P)
Steelers, 14-9 (NY)
1960—Giants, 19-17 (P)
Giants, 27-24 (NY)
1961—Giants, 17-14 (P)
Giants, 42-21 (NY)
1962—Giants, 31-27 (P)
Steelers, 20-17 (NY)
1963—Steelers, 31-0 (P)
Giants, 33-17 (NY)
1964—Steelers, 27-24 (P)
Steelers, 44-17 (NY)
1965—Giants, 23-13 (P)
Giants, 35-10 (NY)
1966—Tie, 34-34 (P)
Steelers, 47-28 (NY)
1967—Giants, 27-24 (P)
Giants, 28-20 (NY)
1968—Giants, 34-20 (P)
1969—Giants, 10-7 (NY)
Giants, 21-17 (P)
1971—Steelers, 17-13 (P)
1976—Steelers, 27-0 (NY)
1985—Giants, 28-10 (NY)
1991—Giants, 23-20 (P)
1994—Steelers, 10-6 (NY)
2000—Giants, 30-10 (NY)
(RS Pts.—Giants 1,429, Steelers 1,199)
Steelers known as Pirates prior to 1941

N.Y. GIANTS vs. *ST. LOUIS
RS: Rams lead series, 25-11
PS: Series tied, 1-1
1938—Giants, 28-0 (NY)
1940—Rams, 13-0 (NY)
1941—Giants, 49-14 (NY)
1945—Rams, 21-17 (NY)
1946—Rams, 31-21 (NY)
1947—Rams, 34-10 (LA)
1948—Rams, 52-37 (NY)
1953—Rams, 21-7 (LA)
1954—Rams, 17-16 (NY)
1959—Giants, 23-21 (LA)
1961—Giants, 24-14 (NY)
1966—Rams, 55-14 (LA)
1968—Rams, 24-21 (LA)
1970—Rams, 31-3 (NY)
1973—Rams, 40-6 (LA)
1976—Rams, 24-10 (LA)
1978—Rams, 20-17 (NY)
1979—Giants, 20-14 (LA)
1980—Rams, 28-7 (NY)
1981—Giants, 10-7 (NY)
1983—Rams, 16-6 (NY)
1984—Rams, 33-12 (LA)
**Giants, 16-13 (LA)
1985—Giants, 24-19 (NY)
1988—Rams, 45-31 (NY)
1989—Rams, 31-10 (LA)
***Rams, 19-13 (NY) OT
1990—Giants, 31-7 (LA)
1991—Rams, 19-13 (NY)
1992—Rams, 38-17 (LA)
1993—Giants, 20-10 (NY)
1994—Rams, 17-10 (LA)
1997—Rams, 13-3 (StL)
1999—Rams, 31-10 (StL)
2000—Rams, 38-24 (NY)
2001—Rams, 15-14 (StL)
2002—Giants, 26-21 (StL)
2003—Giants, 23-13 (NY)
(RS Pts.—Rams 847, Giants 614)
(PS Pts.—Rams 32, Giants 29)
Franchise in Los Angeles prior to 1995 and in Cleveland prior to 1946
**NFC First-Round Playoff*
***NFC Divisional Playoff*

N.Y. GIANTS vs. SAN DIEGO
RS: Giants lead series, 5-3
1971—Giants, 35-17 (NY)
1975—Giants, 35-24 (NY)
1980—Chargers, 44-7 (SD)
1983—Chargers, 41-34 (NY)
1986—Giants, 20-7 (NY)
1989—Giants, 20-13 (SD)
1995—Chargers, 27-17 (NY)
1998—Giants, 34-16 (SD)
(RS Pts.—Giants 202, Chargers 189)

N.Y. GIANTS vs. SAN FRANCISCO
RS: 49ers lead series, 13-11
PS: 49ers lead series, 4-3
1952—Giants, 23-14 (NY)
1956—Giants, 38-21 (SF)
1957—49ers, 27-17 (NY)
1960—Giants, 21-19 (SF)
1963—Giants, 48-14 (NY)
1968—49ers, 26-10 (NY)
1972—Giants, 23-17 (SF)
1975—Giants, 26-23 (SF)
1977—Giants, 20-17 (NY)
1978—Giants, 27-10 (NY)
1979—Giants, 32-16 (NY)
1980—49ers, 12-0 (SF)
1981—49ers, 17-10 (SF)
*49ers, 38-24 (SF)
1984—49ers, 31-10 (NY)
*49ers, 21-10 (SF)
1985—**Giants, 17-3 (NY)
1986—Giants, 21-17 (SF)
*Giants, 49-3 (NY)
1987—49ers, 41-21 (NY)
1988—49ers, 20-17 (NY)
1989—49ers, 34-24 (SF)
1990—49ers, 7-3 (SF)
***Giants, 15-13 (SF)
1991—Giants, 16-14 (NY)
1992—49ers, 31-14 (NY)
1993—*49ers, 44-3 (SF)
1995—49ers, 20-6 (SF)
1998—49ers, 31-7 (SF)
2002—49ers, 16-13 (NY)
**49ers, 39-38 (SF)
(RS Pts.—49ers 495, Giants 447)
(PS Pts.—49ers 161, Giants 156)
NFC Divisional Playoff
**NFC First-Round Playoff*
***NFC Championship*

N.Y. GIANTS vs. SEATTLE
RS: Giants lead series, 7-3
1976—Giants, 28-16 (NY)
1980—Giants, 27-21 (S)
1981—Giants, 32-0 (S)
1983—Seahawks, 17-12 (NY)
1986—Seahawks, 17-12 (S)
1989—Giants, 15-3 (NY)
1992—Giants, 23-10 (NY)
1995—Seahawks, 30-28 (S)
2001—Giants, 27-24 (NY)
2002—Giants, 9-6 (NY)
(RS Pts.—Giants 213, Seahawks 144)

N.Y. GIANTS vs. TAMPA BAY
RS: Giants lead series, 9-6
1977—Giants, 10-0 (TB)
1978—Giants, 19-13 (TB)
Giants, 17-14 (NY)
1979—Giants, 17-14 (NY)
Buccaneers, 31-3 (TB)
1980—Buccaneers, 30-13 (TB)
1984—Giants, 17-14 (NY)
Buccaneers, 20-17 (TB)
1985—Giants, 22-20 (NY)
1991—Giants, 21-14 (TB)
1993—Giants, 23-7 (NY)
1997—Buccaneers, 20-8 (NY)
1998—Buccaneers, 20-3 (TB)

1999—Giants, 17-13 (TB)
2003—Buccaneers, 19-13 (TB)
(RS Pts.—Buccaneers 249, Giants 220)

N.Y. GIANTS vs. *TENNESSEE
RS: Giants lead series, 5-3
1973—Giants, 34-14 (NY)
1982—Giants, 17-14 (NY)
1985—Giants, 35-14 (H)
1991—Giants, 24-20 (NY)
1994—Giants, 13-10 (H)
1997—Oilers, 10-6 (T)
2000—Titans, 28-14 (T)
2002—Titans, 32-29 (NY) OT
(RS Pts.—Giants 172, Titans 142)
Franchise in Houston prior to 1997; known as Oilers prior to 1999

N.Y. GIANTS vs. *WASHINGTON
RS: Giants lead series, 80-58-4
PS: Series tied, 1-1
1932—Braves, 14-6 (B)
Tie, 0-0 (NY)
1933—Redskins, 21-20 (B)
Giants, 7-0 (NY)
1934—Giants, 16-13 (B)
Giants, 3-0 (NY)
1935—Giants, 20-12 (B)
Giants, 17-6 (NY)
1936—Giants, 7-0 (B)
Redskins, 14-0 (NY)
1937—Redskins, 13-3 (W)
Redskins, 49-14 (NY)
1938—Giants, 10-7 (W)
Giants, 36-0 (NY)
1939—Tie, 0-0 (W)
Giants, 9-7 (NY)
1940—Redskins, 21-7 (W)
Giants, 21-7 (NY)
1941—Giants, 17-10 (W)
Giants, 20-13 (NY)
1942—Giants, 14-7 (W)
Redskins, 14-7 (NY)
1943—Giants, 14-10 (NY)
Giants, 31-7 (W)
**Redskins, 28-0 (NY)
1944—Giants, 16-13 (NY)
Giants, 31-0 (W)
1945—Redskins, 24-14 (NY)
Redskins, 17-0 (W)
1946—Redskins, 24-14 (W)
Giants, 31-0 (NY)
1947—Redskins, 28-20 (W)
Giants, 35-10 (NY)
1948—Redskins, 41-10 (W)
Redskins, 28-21 (NY)
1949—Giants, 45-35 (W)
Giants, 23-7 (NY)
1950—Giants, 21-17 (W)
Giants, 24-21 (NY)
1951—Giants, 35-14 (W)
Giants, 28-14 (NY)
1952—Giants, 14-10 (W)
Redskins, 27-17 (NY)
1953—Redskins, 13-9 (W)
Redskins, 24-21 (NY)
1954—Giants, 51-21 (W)
Giants, 24-7 (NY)
1955—Giants, 35-7 (NY)
Giants, 27-20 (W)
1956—Redskins, 33-7 (W)
Giants, 28-14 (NY)
1957—Giants, 24-20 (W)
Redskins, 31-14 (NY)
1958—Giants, 21-14 (W)
Giants, 30-0 (NY)
1959—Giants, 45-14 (NY)
Giants, 24-10 (W)
1960—Tie, 24-24 (NY)
Giants, 17-3 (W)
1961—Giants, 24-21 (W)
Giants, 53-0 (NY)
1962—Giants, 49-34 (NY)
Giants, 42-24 (W)
1963—Giants, 24-14 (W)
Giants, 44-14 (NY)
1964—Giants, 13-10 (NY)
Redskins, 36-21 (W)
1965—Redskins, 23-7 (NY)
Giants, 27-10 (W)
1966—Giants, 13-10 (NY)
Redskins, 72-41 (W)
1967—Redskins, 38-34 (W)
1968—Giants, 48-21 (NY)
Giants, 13-10 (W)
1969—Redskins, 20-14 (W)
1970—Giants, 35-33 (NY)
Giants, 27-24 (W)
1971—Redskins, 30-3 (NY)
Redskins, 23-7 (W)
1972—Redskins, 23-16 (NY)
Redskins, 27-13 (W)
1973—Redskins, 21-3 (New Haven)
Redskins, 27-24 (W)
1974—Redskins, 13-10 (New Haven)
Redskins, 24-3 (W)
1975—Redskins, 49-13 (W)
Redskins, 21-13 (NY)
1976—Redskins, 19-17 (W)
Giants, 12-9 (NY)
1977—Giants, 20-17 (NY)
Giants, 17-6 (W)
1978—Giants, 17-6 (NY)
Redskins, 16-13 (W) OT
1979—Redskins, 27-0 (W)
Giants, 14-6 (NY)
1980—Redskins, 23-21 (NY)
Redskins, 16-13 (W)
1981—Giants, 17-7 (W)
Redskins, 30-27 (NY) OT
1982—Redskins, 27-17 (NY)
Redskins, 15-14 (W)
1983—Redskins, 33-17 (NY)
Redskins, 31-22 (W)
1984—Redskins, 30-14 (W)
Giants, 37-13 (NY)
1985—Giants, 17-3 (NY)
Redskins, 23-21 (W)
1986—Giants, 27-20 (NY)
Giants, 24-14 (W)
***Giants, 17-0 (NY)
1987—Redskins, 38-12 (NY)
Redskins, 23-19 (W)
1988—Giants, 27-20 (NY)
Giants, 24-23 (W)
1989—Giants, 27-24 (W)
Giants, 20-17 (NY)
1990—Giants, 24-20 (W)
Giants, 21-10 (NY)
1991—Redskins, 17-13 (NY)
Redskins, 34-17 (W)
1992—Giants, 24-7 (W)
Redskins, 28-10 (NY)
1993—Giants, 41-7 (W)
Giants, 20-6 (NY)
1994—Giants, 31-23 (NY)
Giants, 21-19 (W)
1995—Giants, 24-15 (W)
Giants, 20-13 (NY)
1996—Redskins, 31-10 (NY)
Redskins, 31-21 (W)
1997—Tie, 7-7 (W) OT
Giants, 30-10 (NY)
1998—Giants, 31-24 (NY)
Redskins, 21-14 (W)
1999—Redskins, 50-21 (NY)
Redskins, 23-13 (W)
2000—Redskins, 16-6 (NY)
Giants, 9-7 (W)
2001—Giants, 23-9 (NY)
Redskins, 35-21 (W)
2002—Giants, 19-17 (NY)
Giants, 27-21 (W)
2003—Giants, 24-21 (W) OT
Redskins, 20-7 (NY)
(RS Pts.—Giants 2,809, Redskins 2,580)
(PS Pts.—Redskins 28, Giants 17)
**Franchise in Boston prior to 1937 and known as Braves prior to 1933*
***Division Playoff*
****NFC Championship*

N.Y. JETS vs. ARIZONA
RS: Jets lead series, 3-2;
See Arizona vs. N.Y. Jets

N.Y. JETS vs. ATLANTA
RS: Series tied, 4-4;
See Atlanta vs. N.Y. Jets

N.Y. JETS vs BALTIMORE
RS: Ravens lead series, 2-1;
See Baltimore vs. N.Y. Jets

N.Y. JETS vs. BUFFALO
RS: Bills lead series, 47-39
PS: Bills lead series, 1-0;
See Buffalo vs. N.Y. Jets

N.Y. JETS vs. CAROLINA
RS: Jets lead series, 2-1;
See Carolina vs. N.Y. Jets

N.Y. JETS vs. CHICAGO
RS: Bears lead series, 5-3;
See Chicago vs. N.Y. Jets

N.Y. JETS vs. CINCINNATI
RS: Jets lead series, 11-6
PS: Jets lead series, 1-0;
See Cincinnati vs. N.Y. Jets

N.Y. JETS vs. CLEVELAND
RS: Browns lead series, 10-6
PS: Browns lead series, 1-0;
See Cleveland vs. N.Y. Jets

N.Y. JETS vs. DALLAS
RS: Cowboys lead series, 6-2;
See Dallas vs. N.Y. Jets

N.Y. JETS vs. DENVER
RS: Series tied, 14-14-1
PS: Broncos lead series, 1-0;
See Denver vs. N.Y. Jets

N.Y. JETS vs. DETROIT
RS: Lions lead series, 6-4;
See Detroit vs. N.Y. Jets

N.Y. JETS vs. GREEN BAY
RS: Jets lead series, 7-2;
See Green Bay vs. N.Y. Jets

N.Y. JETS vs. HOUSTON
RS: Jets lead series, 1-0;
See Houston vs. N.Y. Jets

N.Y. JETS vs. INDIANAPOLIS
RS: Colts lead series, 39-25
PS: Jets lead series, 2-0;
See Indianapolis vs. N.Y. Jets

N.Y. JETS vs. JACKSONVILLE
RS: Jaguars lead series, 3-2
PS: Jets lead series, 1-0;
See Jacksonville vs. N.Y. Jets

N.Y. JETS vs. KANSAS CITY
RS: Chiefs lead series, 15-14-1
PS: Series tied, 1-1;
See Kansas City vs. N.Y. Jets

N.Y. JETS vs. MIAMI
RS: Jets lead series, 38-37-1
PS: Dolphins lead series, 1-0;
See Miami vs. N.Y. Jets

N.Y. JETS vs. MINNESOTA
RS: Jets lead series, 6-1;
See Minnesota vs. N.Y. Jets

N.Y. JETS vs. NEW ENGLAND
RS: Jets lead series, 47-39-1
PS: Patriots lead series, 1-0;
See New England vs. N.Y. Jets

N.Y. JETS vs. NEW ORLEANS
RS: Jets lead series, 5-4;
See New Orleans vs. N.Y. Jets

N.Y. JETS vs. N.Y. GIANTS
RS: Giants lead series, 6-4;
See N.Y. Giants vs. N.Y. Jets

***N.Y. JETS vs. **OAKLAND**
RS: Raiders lead series, 19-12-2
PS: Series tied, 2-2
1960—Raiders, 28-27 (NY)
Titans, 31-28 (O)
1961—Titans, 14-6 (O)
Titans, 23-12 (NY)
1962—Titans, 28-17 (O)
Titans, 31-21 (NY)
1963—Jets, 10-7 (NY)
Raiders, 49-26 (O)
1964—Jets, 35-13 (NY)
Raiders, 35-26 (O)
1965—Tie, 24-24 (NY)
Raiders, 24-14 (O)
1966—Raiders, 24-21 (NY)
Tie, 28-28 (O)
1967—Jets, 27-14 (NY)
Raiders, 38-29 (O)
1968—Raiders, 43-32 (O)
***Jets, 27-23 (NY)
1969—Raiders, 27-14 (NY)
1970—Raiders, 14-13 (NY)
1972—Raiders, 24-16 (O)
1977—Raiders, 28-27 (NY)
1979—Jets, 28-19 (NY)
1982—****Jets, 17-14 (LA)
1985—Raiders, 31-0 (LA)
1989—Raiders, 14-7 (NY)
1993—Raiders, 24-20 (LA)
1995—Raiders, 47-10 (NY)
1996—Raiders, 34-13 (NY)
1997—Jets 23-22 (NY)
1999—Raiders, 24-23 (O)
2000—Raiders, 31-7 (O)
2001—Jets, 24-22 (O)
*****Raiders, 38-24 (O)
2002—Raiders, 26-20 (O)
****Raiders, 30-10 (O)
2003—Jets, 27-24 (O) OT
(RS Pts.—Raiders 822, Jets 698)
(PS Pts.—Raiders 105, Jets 78)
Jets known as Titans prior to 1963
***Franchise in Los Angeles from 1982-1994*
****AFL Championship*
*****AFC Second-Round Playoff*
******AFC First-Round Playoff*

N.Y. JETS vs. PHILADELPHIA
RS: Eagles lead series, 7-0
1973—Eagles, 24-23 (P)
1977—Eagles, 27-0 (P)
1978—Eagles, 17-9 (P)
1987—Eagles, 38-27 (NY)
1993—Eagles, 35-30 (NY)
1996—Eagles, 21-20 (NY)
2003—Eagles, 24-17 (P)
(RS Pts.—Eagles 186, Jets 126)

N.Y. JETS vs. PITTSBURGH
RS: Steelers lead series, 14-2
1970—Steelers, 21-17 (P)
1973—Steelers, 26-14 (P)
1975—Steelers, 20-7 (NY)
1977—Steelers, 23-20 (NY)
1978—Steelers, 28-17 (NY)
1981—Steelers, 38-10 (P)
1983—Steelers, 34-7 (NY)
1984—Steelers, 23-17 (NY)
1986—Steelers, 45-24 (NY)
1988—Jets, 24-20 (NY)
1989—Steelers, 13-0 (NY)
1990—Steelers, 24-7 (NY)
1992—Steelers, 27-10 (P)
2000—Steelers, 20-3 (NY)
2001—Steelers, 18-7 (P)
2003—Jets, 6-0 (NY)
(RS Pts.—Steelers 380, Jets 190)

N.Y. JETS vs. *ST. LOUIS
RS: Rams lead series, 8-2
1970—Jets, 31-20 (LA)
1974—Rams, 20-13 (NY)
1980—Rams, 38-13 (LA)
1983—Jets, 27-24 (NY) OT
1986—Rams, 17-3 (NY)
1989—Rams, 38-14 (LA)
1992—Rams, 18-10 (LA)
1995—Rams, 23-20 (NY)
1998—Rams, 30-10 (StL)
2001—Rams, 34-14 (NY)
(RS Pts.—Rams 262, Jets 155)
**Franchise in Los Angeles prior to 1995*

***N.Y. JETS vs. **SAN DIEGO**
RS: Chargers lead series, 17-10-1
1960—Chargers, 21-7 (NY)
Chargers, 50-43 (LA)
1961—Chargers, 25-10 (NY)
Chargers, 48-13 (SD)
1962—Chargers, 40-14 (SD)
Titans, 23-3 (NY)
1963—Chargers, 24-20 (SD)
Chargers, 53-7 (NY)
1964—Tie, 17-17 (NY)
Chargers, 38-3 (SD)
1965—Chargers, 34-9 (NY)
Chargers, 38-7 (SD)
1966—Jets, 17-16 (NY)
Chargers, 42-27 (SD)
1967—Jets, 42-31 (SD)
1968—Jets, 23-20 (NY)
Jets, 37-15 (SD)
1969—Chargers, 34-27 (SD)
1971—Chargers, 49-21 (SD)
1974—Jets, 27-14 (NY)
1975—Chargers, 24-16 (SD)
1983—Jets, 41-29 (SD)
1989—Jets, 20-17 (SD)
1990—Chargers, 39-3 (NY)
Chargers, 38-17 (SD)
1991—Jets, 24-3 (NY)
1994—Chargers, 21-6 (NY)
2002—Jets, 44-13 (SD)
(RS Pts.—Chargers 796, Jets 565)
**Jets known as Titans prior to 1963*
***Franchise in Los Angeles prior to 1961*

N.Y. JETS vs. SAN FRANCISCO
RS: 49ers lead series, 8-1
1971—49ers, 24-21 (NY)
1976—49ers, 17-6 (SF)
1980—49ers, 37-27 (NY)
1983—Jets, 27-13 (SF)
1986—49ers, 24-10 (SF)
1989—49ers, 23-10 (NY)
1992—49ers, 31-14 (NY)
1998—49ers, 36-30 (SF) OT
2001—49ers, 19-17 (NY)
(RS Pts.—49ers 224, Jets 162)

N.Y. JETS vs. SEATTLE
RS: Seahawks lead series, 8-7
1977—Seahawks, 17-0 (NY)
1978—Seahawks, 24-17 (NY)
1979—Seahawks, 30-7 (S)
1980—Seahawks, 27-17 (NY)
1981—Seahawks, 19-3 (NY)
Seahawks, 27-23 (S)
1983—Seahawks, 17-10 (NY)
1985—Jets, 17-14 (NY)
1986—Jets, 38-7 (S)
1987—Jets, 30-14 (NY)
1991—Seahawks, 20-13 (S)
1995—Jets, 16-10 (S)
1997—Jets, 41-3 (S)
1998—Jets, 32-31 (NY)
1999—Jets, 19-9 (NY)
(RS Pts.—Jets 283, Seahawks 269)

N.Y. JETS vs. TAMPA BAY
RS: Jets lead series, 7-1
1976—Jets, 34-0 (NY)
1982—Jets, 32-17 (NY)
1984—Buccaneers, 41-21 (TB)
1985—Jets, 62-28 (NY)
1990—Jets, 16-14 (TB)
1991—Jets, 16-13 (NY)
1997—Jets, 31-0 (NY)
2000—Jets, 21-17 (TB)
(RS Pts.—Jets 233, Buccaneers 130)

***N.Y. JETS vs. **TENNESSEE**
RS: Titans lead series, 20-14-1
PS: Titans lead series, 1-0
1960—Oilers, 27-21 (H)
Oilers, 42-28 (NY)
1961—Oilers, 49-13 (H)
Oilers, 48-21 (NY)
1962—Oilers, 56-17 (H)
Oilers, 44-10 (NY)
1963—Jets, 24-17 (NY)
Oilers, 31-27 (H)
1964—Jets, 24-21 (NY)
Oilers, 33-17 (H)

1965—Oilers, 27-21 (H)
Jets, 41-14 (NY)
1966—Jets, 52-13 (NY)
Oilers, 24-0 (H)
1967—Tie, 28-28 (NY)
1968—Jets, 20-14 (H)
Jets, 26-7 (NY)
1969—Jets, 26-17 (NY)
Jets, 34-26 (H)
1972—Oilers, 26-20 (H)
1974—Oilers, 27-22 (NY)
1977—Oilers, 20-0 (H)
1979—Oilers, 27-24 (H) OT
1980—Jets, 31-28 (NY) OT
1981—Jets, 33-17 (NY)
1984—Oilers, 31-20 (H)
1988—Jets, 45-3 (NY)
1990—Jets, 17-12 (H)
1991—Oilers, 23-20 (NY)
***Oilers, 17-10 (H)
1993—Oilers, 24-0 (H)
1994—Oilers, 24-10 (H)
1995—Oilers, 23-6 (H)
1996—Oilers, 35-10 (NY)
1998—Jets, 24-3 (T)
2003—Jets, 24-17 (NY)
(RS Pts.—Titans 878, Jets 756)
(PS Pts.—Titans 17, Jets 10)
Jets known as Titans prior to 1963
***Franchise in Houston prior to 1997; known as Oilers prior to 1999*
****AFC First-Round Playoff*

N.Y. JETS vs. WASHINGTON
RS: Redskins lead series, 7-1
1972—Redskins, 35-17 (NY)
1976—Redskins, 37-16 (NY)
1978—Redskins, 23-3 (W)
1987—Redskins, 17-16 (W)
1993—Jets, 3-0 (W)
1996—Redskins, 31-16 (W)
1999—Redskins, 27-20 (NY)
2003—Redskins, 16-13 (W)
(RS Pts.—Redskins 186, Jets 104)

OAKLAND vs. ARIZONA
RS: Raiders lead series, 4-2;
See Arizona vs. Oakland

OAKLAND vs. ATLANTA
RS: Raiders lead series, 7-3;
See Atlanta vs. Oakland

OAKLAND vs. BALTIMORE
RS: Ravens lead series, 2-1
PS: Ravens lead series, 1-0;
See Baltimore vs. Oakland

OAKLAND vs. BUFFALO
RS: Raiders lead series, 17-15
PS: Bills lead series, 2-0;
See Buffalo vs. Oakland

OAKLAND vs CAROLINA
RS: Series tied, 1-1;
See Carolina vs Oakland

OAKLAND vs. CHICAGO
RS: Raiders lead series, 6-5;
See Chicago vs. Oakland

OAKLAND vs. CINCINNATI
RS: Raiders lead series, 17-7
PS: Raiders lead series, 2-0;
See Cincinnati vs. Oakland

OAKLAND vs. CLEVELAND
RS: Raiders lead series, 9-5
PS: Raiders lead series, 2-0;
See Cleveland vs. Oakland

OAKLAND vs. DALLAS
RS: Raiders lead series, 5-3;
See Dallas vs. Oakland

OAKLAND vs. DENVER
RS: Raiders lead series, 52-33-2
PS: Series tied, 1-1;
See Denver vs. Oakland

OAKLAND vs. DETROIT
RS: Raiders lead series, 6-3;
See Detroit vs. Oakland

OAKLAND vs. GREEN BAY
RS: Raiders lead series, 5-4
PS: Packers lead series, 1-0;
See Green Bay vs. Oakland

OAKLAND vs. INDIANAPOLIS
RS: Raiders lead series, 7-2
PS: Series tied, 1-1;
See Indianapolis vs. Oakland

OAKLAND vs. JACKSONVILLE
RS: Series tied, 1-1;
See Jacksonville vs. Oakland

OAKLAND vs. KANSAS CITY
RS: Chiefs lead series, 43-42-2
PS: Chiefs lead series, 2-1;
See Kansas City vs. Oakland

OAKLAND vs. MIAMI
RS: Raiders lead series, 15-10-1
PS: Raiders lead series, 3-1;
See Miami vs. Oakland

OAKLAND vs. MINNESOTA
RS: Raiders lead series, 8-3
PS: Raiders lead series, 1-0;
See Minnesota vs. Oakland

OAKLAND vs. NEW ENGLAND
RS: Raiders lead series, 14-12-1
PS: Patriots lead series, 2-1;
See New England vs. Oakland

OAKLAND vs. NEW ORLEANS
RS: Raiders lead series, 5-3-1;
See New Orleans vs. Oakland

OAKLAND vs. N.Y. GIANTS
RS: Raiders lead series, 7-2;
See N.Y. Giants vs. Oakland

OAKLAND vs. N.Y. JETS
RS: Raiders lead series, 19-12-2
PS: Series tied, 2-2;
See N.Y. Jets vs. Oakland

***OAKLAND vs. PHILADELPHIA**
RS: Series tied, 4-4
PS: Raiders lead series, 1-0
1971—Raiders, 34-10 (O)
1976—Raiders, 26-7 (P)
1980—Eagles, 10-7 (P)
**Raiders, 27-10 (New Orleans)
1986—Eagles, 33-27 (LA) OT
1989—Eagles, 10-7 (P)
1992—Eagles, 31-10 (P)
1995—Raiders, 48-17 (O)
2001—Raiders, 20-10 (P)
(RS Pts.—Raiders 179, Eagles 128)
(PS Pts.—Raiders 27, Eagles 10)
**Franchise in Los Angeles from 1982-1994*
***Super Bowl XV*

***OAKLAND vs. PITTSBURGH**
RS: Raiders lead series, 8-7
PS: Series tied, 3-3
1970—Raiders, 31-14 (O)
1972—Steelers, 34-28 (P)
**Steelers, 13-7 (P)
1973—Steelers, 17-9 (O)
**Raiders, 33-14 (O)
1974—Raiders, 17-0 (P)
***Steelers, 24-13 (O)
1975—***Steelers, 16-10 (P)
1976—Raiders, 31-28 (O)
***Raiders, 24-7 (O)
1977—Raiders, 16-7 (P)
1980—Raiders, 45-34 (P)
1981—Raiders, 30-27 (O)
1983—**Raiders, 38-10 (LA)
1984—Steelers, 13-7 (LA)
1990—Raiders, 20-3 (LA)
1994—Steelers, 21-3 (LA)
1995—Steelers, 29-10 (O)
2000—Steelers, 21-20 (P)
2002—Raiders, 30-17 (P)
2003—Steelers, 27-7 (P)
(RS Pts.—Raiders 304, Steelers 292)
(PS Pts.—Raiders 125, Steelers 84)
**Franchise in Los Angeles from 1982-1994*
***AFC Divisional Playoff*
****AFC Championship*

***OAKLAND vs. **ST. LOUIS**
RS: Raiders lead series, 7-3
1972—Raiders, 45-17 (O)
1977—Rams, 20-14 (LA)
1979—Raiders, 24-17 (LA)
1982—Raiders, 37-31 (LA Raiders)
1985—Raiders, 16-6 (LA Rams)
1988—Rams, 22-17 (LA Raiders)
1991—Raiders, 20-17 (LA Raiders)
1994—Raiders, 20-17 (LA Rams)
1997—Raiders, 35-17 (O)
2002—Rams, 28-13 (StL)
(RS Pts.—Raiders 241, Rams 192)
**Franchise in Los Angeles from 1982-1994*
***Franchise in Los Angeles prior to 1995*

***OAKLAND vs. **SAN DIEGO**
RS: Raiders lead series, 54-32-2
PS: Raiders lead series, 1-0
1960—Chargers, 52-28 (LA)
Chargers, 41-17 (O)
1961—Chargers, 44-0 (SD)
Chargers, 41-10 (O)
1962—Chargers, 42-33 (O)
Chargers, 31-21 (SD)
1963—Raiders, 34-33 (SD)
Raiders, 41-27 (O)
1964—Chargers, 31-17 (SD)
Raiders, 21-20 (O)
1965—Chargers, 17-6 (O)
Chargers, 24-14 (SD)
1966—Chargers, 29-20 (O)
Raiders, 41-19 (SD)
1967—Raiders, 51-10 (O)
Raiders, 41-21 (SD)
1968—Chargers, 23-14 (O)
Raiders, 34-27 (SD)
1969—Raiders, 24-12 (SD)
Raiders, 21-16 (O)
1970—Tie, 27-27 (SD)
Raiders, 20-17 (O)
1971—Raiders, 34-0 (SD)
Raiders, 34-33 (O)
1972—Tie, 17-17 (O)
Raiders, 21-19 (SD)
1973—Raiders, 27-17 (SD)
Raiders, 31-3 (O)

1974—Raiders, 14-10 (SD)
Raiders, 17-10 (O)
1975—Raiders, 6-0 (SD)
Raiders, 25-0 (O)
1976—Raiders, 27-17 (SD)
Raiders, 24-0 (O)
1977—Raiders, 24-0 (O)
Chargers, 12-7 (SD)
1978—Raiders, 21-20 (SD)
Chargers, 27-23 (O)
1979—Chargers, 30-10 (SD)
Raiders, 45-22 (O)
1980—Chargers, 30-24 (SD) OT
Raiders, 38-24 (O)
***Raiders, 34-27 (SD)
1981—Chargers, 55-21 (O)
Chargers, 23-10 (SD)
1982—Raiders, 28-24 (LA)
Raiders, 41-34 (SD)
1983—Raiders, 42-10 (SD)
Raiders, 30-14 (LA)
1984—Raiders, 33-30 (LA)
Raiders, 44-37 (SD)
1985—Raiders, 34-21 (LA)
Chargers, 40-34 (SD) OT
1986—Raiders, 17-13 (LA)
Raiders, 37-31 (SD) OT
1987—Chargers, 23-17 (LA)
Chargers, 16-14 (SD)
1988—Raiders, 24-13 (LA)
Raiders, 13-3 (SD)
1989—Raiders, 40-14 (LA)
Chargers, 14-12 (SD)
1990—Raiders, 24-9 (SD)
Raiders, 17-12 (LA)
1991—Chargers, 21-13 (LA)
Raiders, 9-7 (SD)
1992—Chargers, 27-3 (SD)
Chargers, 36-14 (LA)
1993—Chargers, 30-23 (LA)
Raiders, 12-7 (SD)
1994—Chargers, 26-24 (LA)
Raiders, 24-17 (SD)
1995—Raiders, 17-7 (O)
Chargers, 12-6 (SD)
1996—Chargers, 40-34 (O)
Raiders, 23-14 (SD)
1997—Chargers, 25-10 (O)
Raiders, 38-13 (SD)
1998—Raiders, 7-6 (O)
Raiders, 17-10 (SD)
1999—Raiders, 28-9 (O)
Chargers, 23-20 (SD)
2000—Raiders, 9-6 (O)
Raiders, 15-13 (SD)
2001—Raiders, 34-24 (O)
Raiders, 13-6 (SD)
2002—Chargers, 27-21 (O) OT
Raiders, 27-7 (SD)
2003—Raiders, 34-31 (O) OT
Chargers, 21-14 (SD)
(RS Pts.—Raiders 2,025, Chargers 1,796)
(PS Pts.—Raiders 34, Chargers 27)
Franchise in Los Angeles from 1982-1994
***Franchise in Los Angeles prior to 1961*
****AFC Championship*

***OAKLAND vs. SAN FRANCISCO**
RS: Raiders lead series, 6-4
1970—49ers, 38-7 (O)
1974—Raiders, 35-24 (SF)
1979—Raiders, 23-10 (O)
1982—Raiders, 23-17 (SF)
1985—49ers, 34-10 (LA)
1988—Raiders, 9-3 (SF)
1991—Raiders, 12-6 (LA)
1994—49ers, 44-14 (SF)
2000—Raiders, 34-28 (SF) OT
2002—49ers, 23-20 (O) OT
(RS Pts.—49ers 227, Raiders 187)
**Franchise in Los Angeles from 1982-1994*

***OAKLAND vs. SEATTLE**
RS: Raiders lead series, 27-22
PS: Series tied, 1-1
1977—Raiders, 44-7 (O)
1978—Seahawks, 27-7 (S)
Seahawks, 17-16 (O)
1979—Seahawks, 27-10 (S)
Seahawks, 29-24 (O)
1980—Raiders, 33-14 (O)
Raiders, 19-17 (S)
1981—Raiders, 20-10 (O)
Raiders, 32-31 (S)
1982—Raiders, 28-23 (LA)
1983—Seahawks, 38-36 (S)
Seahawks, 34-21 (LA)
**Raiders, 30-14 (LA)
1984—Raiders, 28-14 (LA)
Seahawks, 17-14 (S)
***Seahawks, 13-7 (S)
1985—Seahawks, 33-3 (S)
Raiders, 13-3 (LA)
1986—Raiders, 14-10 (LA)
Seahawks, 37-0 (S)
1987—Seahawks, 35-13 (LA)
Raiders, 37-14 (S)
1988—Seahawks, 35-27 (S)
Seahawks, 43-37 (LA)
1989—Seahawks, 24-20 (LA)
Seahawks, 23-17 (S)
1990—Raiders, 17-13 (S)
Raiders, 24-17 (LA)
1991—Raiders, 23-20 (S) OT
Raiders, 31-7 (LA)
1992—Raiders, 19-0 (S)
Raiders, 20-3 (LA)
1993—Raiders, 17-13 (S)
Raiders, 27-23 (LA)
1994—Seahawks, 38-9 (LA)
Raiders, 17-16 (S)
1995—Raiders, 34-14 (O)
Seahawks, 44-10 (S)
1996—Raiders, 27-21 (S)
Seahawks, 28-21 (O)
1997—Seahawks, 45-34 (S)
Seahawks, 22-21 (O)
1998—Raiders, 31-18 (S)
Raiders, 20-17 (O)
1999—Seahawks, 22-21 (S)
Raiders, 30-21 (O)
2000—Raiders, 31-3 (O)
Seahawks, 27-24 (S)
2001—Raiders, 38-14 (O)
Seahawks, 34-27 (S)
2002—Raiders, 31-17 (O)
(RS Pts.—Raiders 1,117, Seahawks 1,059)
(PS Pts.—Raiders 37, Seahawks 27)
**Franchise in Los Angeles from 1982-1994*
***AFC Championship*
****AFC First-Round Playoff*

***OAKLAND vs. TAMPA BAY**
RS: Raiders lead series, 4-1
PS: Buccaneers lead series, 1-0
1976—Raiders, 49-16 (O)
1981—Raiders, 18-16 (O)
1993—Raiders, 27-20 (LA)
1996—Buccaneers, 20-17 (TB) OT
1999—Raiders, 45-0 (O)
2002—**Buccaneers, 48-21 (San Diego)
(RS Pts.—Raiders 156, Buccaneers 72)
(PS Pts.—Buccaneers 48, Raiders 21)
**Franchise in Los Angeles from 1982-1994*
***Super Bowl XXXVII*

***OAKLAND vs. **TENNESSEE**
RS: Raiders lead series, 21-17
PS: Raiders lead series, 4-0
1960—Oilers, 37-22 (O)
Raiders, 14-13 (H)
1961—Oilers, 55-0 (H)
Oilers, 47-16 (O)
1962—Oilers, 28-20 (O)
Oilers, 32-17 (H)
1963—Raiders, 24-13 (H)
Raiders, 52-49 (O)
1964—Oilers, 42-28 (H)
Raiders, 20-10 (O)
1965—Raiders, 21-17 (O)
Raiders, 33-21 (H)
1966—Oilers, 31-0 (H)
Raiders, 38-23 (O)
1967—Raiders, 19-7 (H)
***Raiders, 40-7 (O)
1968—Raiders, 24-15 (H)
1969—Raiders, 21-17 (O)
****Raiders, 56-7 (O)
1971—Raiders, 41-21 (O)
1972—Raiders, 34-0 (H)
1973—Raiders, 17-6 (H)
1975—Oilers, 27-26 (O)
1976—Raiders, 14-13 (H)
1977—Raiders, 34-29 (O)
1978—Raiders, 21-17 (O)
1979—Oilers, 31-17 (H)
1980—*****Raiders, 27-7 (O)
1981—Oilers, 17-16 (H)
1983—Raiders, 20-6 (LA)
1984—Raiders, 24-14 (H)
1986—Raiders, 28-17 (H)
1988—Oilers, 38-35 (H)
1989—Oilers, 23-7 (H)
1991—Oilers, 47-17 (H)
1994—Raiders, 17-14 (LA)
1997—Oilers, 24-21 (T) OT
1999—Titans, 21-14 (T)
2001—Titans, 13-10 (O)
2002—Raiders, 52-25 (O)
******Raiders, 41-24 (O)
2003—Titans, 25-20 (T)
(RS Pts.—Titans 885, Raiders 854)
(PS Pts.—Raiders 164, Titans 45)
**Franchise in Los Angeles from 1982-1994*
***Franchise in Houston prior to 1997; known as Oilers prior to 1999*
****AFL Championship*
*****Inter-Divisional Playoff*
******AFC First-Round Playoff*
*******AFC Championship*

***OAKLAND vs. WASHINGTON**
RS: Raiders lead series, 6-3
PS: Raiders lead series, 1-0

1970—Raiders, 34-20 (O)
1975—Raiders, 26-23 (W) OT
1980—Raiders, 24-21 (O)
1983—Redskins, 37-35 (W)
**Raiders, 38-9 (Tampa)
1986—Redskins, 10-6 (W)
1989—Raiders, 37-24 (LA)
1992—Raiders, 21-20 (W)
1995—Raiders, 20-8 (W)
1998—Redskins, 29-19 (O)
(RS Pts.—Raiders 222, Redskins 192)
(PS Pts.—Raiders 38, Redskins 9)
Franchise in Los Angeles from 1982-1994
***Super Bowl XVIII*

PHILADELPHIA vs. ARIZONA
RS: Series tied, 52-52-5
PS: Series tied, 1-1;
See Arizona vs. Philadelphia
PHILADELPHIA vs. ATLANTA
RS: Eagles lead series, 11-9-1
PS: Series tied, 1-1;
See Atlanta vs. Philadelphia
PHILADELPHIA vs. BALTIMORE
RS: Series tied, 0-0-1;
See Baltimore vs. Philadelphia
PHILADELPHIA vs. BUFFALO
RS: Series tied, 5-5;
See Buffalo vs. Philadelphia
PHILADELPHIA vs. CAROLINA
RS: Eagles lead series, 2-1
PS: Panthers lead series, 1-0;
See Carolina vs. Philadelphia
PHILADELPHIA vs. CHICAGO
RS: Bears lead series, 24-7-1
PS: Eagles lead series, 2-1;
See Chicago vs. Philadelphia
PHILADELPHIA vs. CINCINNATI
RS: Bengals lead series, 6-3;
See Cincinnati vs. Philadelphia
PHILADELPHIA vs. CLEVELAND
RS: Browns lead series, 31-13-1;
See Cleveland vs. Philadelphia
PHILADELPHIA vs. DALLAS
RS: Cowboys lead series, 49-37
PS: Cowboys lead series, 2-1;
See Dallas vs. Philadelphia
PHILADELPHIA vs. DENVER
RS: Eagles lead series, 6-3;
See Denver vs. Philadelphia
PHILADELPHIA vs. DETROIT
RS: Lions lead series, 12-11-2
PS: Eagles lead series, 1-0;
See Detroit vs. Philadelphia
PHILADELPHIA vs. GREEN BAY
RS: Packers lead series, 22-10
PS: Eagles lead series, 2-0;
See Green Bay vs. Philadelphia
PHILADELPHIA vs. HOUSTON
RS: Eagles lead series, 1-0;
See Houston vs. Philadelphia
PHILADELPHIA vs. INDIANAPOLIS
RS: Colts lead series, 9-6;
See Indianapolis vs. Philadelphia
PHILADELPHIA vs. JACKSONVILLE
RS: Jaguars lead series, 2-0;
See Jacksonville vs. Philadelphia
PHILADELPHIA vs. KANSAS CITY
RS: Series tied, 2-2;
See Kansas City vs. Philadelphia
PHILADELPHIA vs. MIAMI
RS: Dolphins lead series, 7-4;
See Miami vs. Philadelphia
PHILADELPHIA vs. MINNESOTA
RS: Vikings lead series, 11-7
PS: Eagles lead series, 1-0;
See Minnesota vs. Philadelphia
PHILADELPHIA vs. NEW ENGLAND
RS: Eagles lead series, 6-3;
See New England vs. Philadelphia
PHILADELPHIA vs. NEW ORLEANS
RS: Eagles lead series, 14-8
PS; Eagles lead series, 1-0;
See New Orleans vs. Philadelphia
PHILADELPHIA vs. N.Y. GIANTS
RS: Giants lead series, 73-63-2
PS: Giants lead series, 2-0;
See N.Y. Giants vs. Philadelphia
PHILADELPHIA vs. N.Y. JETS
RS: Eagles lead series, 7-0;
See N.Y. Jets vs. Philadelphia
PHILADELPHIA vs. OAKLAND
RS: Series tied, 4-4
PS: Raiders lead series, 1-0;
See Oakland vs. Philadelphia
PHILADELPHIA vs. *PITTSBURGH
RS: Eagles lead series, 45-26-3
PS: Eagles lead series, 1-0
1933—Eagles, 25-6 (Phila)
1934—Eagles, 17-0 (Pitt)
Pirates, 9-7 (Phila)
1935—Pirates, 17-7 (Phila)
Eagles, 17-6 (Pitt)
1936—Pirates, 17-0 (Pitt)
Pirates, 6-0 (Johnstown, Pa.)
1937—Pirates, 27-14 (Pitt)
Pirates, 16-7 (Pitt)
1938—Eagles, 27-7 (Buffalo)
Eagles, 14-7 (Charleston, W. Va.)
1939—Eagles, 17-14 (Phila)
Pirates, 24-12 (Pitt)
1940—Pirates, 7-3 (Pitt)
Eagles, 7-0 (Phila)
1941—Eagles, 10-7 (Pitt)
Tie, 7-7 (Phila)
1942—Eagles, 24-14 (Pitt)
Steelers, 14-0 (Phila)
1945—Eagles, 45-3 (Pitt)
Eagles, 30-6 (Phila)
1946—Steelers, 10-7 (Pitt)
Eagles, 10-7 (Phila)
1947—Steelers, 35-24 (Pitt)
Eagles, 21-0 (Phila)
**Eagles, 21-0 (Pitt)
1948—Eagles, 34-7 (Pitt)
Eagles, 17-0 (Phila)
1949—Eagles, 38-7 (Pitt)
Eagles, 34-17 (Phila)
1950—Eagles, 17-10 (Pitt)
Steelers, 9-7 (Phila)
1951—Eagles, 34-13 (Pitt)
Steelers, 17-13 (Phila)
1952—Eagles, 31-25 (Pitt)
Eagles, 26-21 (Phila)
1953—Eagles, 23-17 (Phila)
Eagles, 35-7 (Pitt)
1954—Eagles, 24-22 (Phila)
Steelers, 17-7 (Pitt)
1955—Steelers, 13-7 (Pitt)
Eagles, 24-0 (Phila)
1956—Eagles, 35-21 (Pitt)
Eagles, 14-7 (Phila)
1957—Steelers, 6-0 (Pitt)
Eagles, 7-6 (Phila)
1958—Steelers, 24-3 (Pitt)
Steelers, 31-24 (Phila)
1959—Eagles, 28-24 (Phila)
Steelers, 31-0 (Pitt)
1960—Eagles, 34-7 (Phila)
Steelers, 27-21 (Pitt)
1961—Eagles, 21-16 (Phila)
Eagles, 35-24 (Pitt)
1962—Steelers, 13-7 (Pitt)
Steelers, 26-17 (Phila)
1963—Tie, 21-21 (Phila)
Tie, 20-20 (Pitt)
1964—Eagles, 21-7 (Phila)
Eagles, 34-10 (Pitt)
1965—Steelers, 20-14 (Phila)
Eagles, 47-13 (Pitt)
1966—Eagles, 31-14 (Pitt)
Eagles, 27-23 (Phila)
1967—Eagles, 34-24 (Phila)
1968—Steelers, 6-3 (Pitt)
1969—Eagles, 41-27 (Phila)
1970—Eagles, 30-20 (Phila)
1974—Steelers, 27-0 (Pitt)
1979—Eagles, 17-14 (Phila)
1988—Eagles, 27-26 (Pitt)
1991—Eagles, 23-14 (Phila)
1994—Steelers, 14-3 (Pitt)
1997—Eagles, 23-20 (Phila)
2000—Eagles, 26-23 (Pitt) OT
(RS Pts.—Eagles 1,411, Steelers 1,064)
(PS Pts.—Eagles 21, Steelers 0)
**Steelers known as Pirates prior to 1941*
***Division Playoff*
PHILADELPHIA vs. *ST. LOUIS
RS: Rams lead series, 16-15-1
PS: Rams lead series, 2-1
1937—Rams, 21-3 (P)
1939—Rams, 35-13 (Colorado Springs)
1940—Rams, 21-13 (C)
1942—Rams, 24-14 (Akron)
1944—Eagles, 26-13 (P)
1945—Eagles, 28-14 (P)
1946—Eagles, 25-14 (LA)
1947—Eagles, 14-7 (P)
1948—Tie, 28-28 (LA)
1949—Eagles, 38-14 (P)
**Eagles, 14-0 (LA)
1950—Eagles, 56-20 (P)
1955—Rams, 23-21 (P)
1956—Rams, 27-7 (LA)
1957—Rams, 17-13 (LA)
1959—Eagles, 23-20 (P)
1964—Rams, 20-10 (LA)
1967—Rams, 33-17 (LA)
1969—Rams, 23-17 (P)
1972—Rams, 34-3 (P)
1975—Rams, 42-3 (P)
1977—Rams, 20-0 (LA)
1978—Rams, 16-14 (P)
1983—Eagles, 13-9 (P)
1985—Rams, 17-6 (P)
1986—Eagles, 34-20 (P)
1988—Eagles, 30-24 (P)
1989—***Rams, 21-7 (P)
1990—Eagles, 27-21 (LA)

1995—Eagles, 20-9 (P)
1998—Eagles, 17-14 (P)
1999—Eagles, 38-31 (P)
2001—Rams, 20-17 (P) OT
****Rams, 29-24 (StL)
2002—Eagles, 10-3 (P)
(RS Pts.—Rams 654, Eagles 598)
(PS Pts.—Rams 50, Eagles 45)
Franchise in Los Angeles prior to 1995 and in Cleveland prior to 1946
***NFL Championship*
****NFC First-Round Playoff*
*****NFC Championship*

PHILADELPHIA vs. SAN DIEGO
RS: Chargers lead series, 5-3
1974—Eagles, 13-7 (SD)
1980—Chargers, 22-21 (SD)
1985—Chargers, 20-14 (SD)
1986—Eagles, 23-7 (P)
1989—Chargers, 20-17 (SD)
1995—Chargers, 27-21 (P)
1998—Chargers, 13-10 (SD)
2001—Eagles, 24-14 (P)
(RS Pts.—Eagles 143, Chargers 130)

PHILADELPHIA vs. SAN FRANCISCO
RS: 49ers lead series, 16-7-1
PS: 49ers lead series, 1-0
1951—Eagles, 21-14 (P)
1953—49ers, 31-21 (SF)
1956—Tie, 10-10 (P)
1958—49ers, 30-24 (P)
1959—49ers, 24-14 (SF)
1964—49ers, 28-24 (P)
1966—Eagles, 35-34 (SF)
1967—49ers, 28-27 (P)
1969—49ers, 14-13 (SF)
1971—49ers, 31-3 (P)
1973—49ers, 38-28 (SF)
1975—Eagles, 27-17 (P)
1983—Eagles, 22-17 (SF)
1984—49ers, 21-9 (P)
1985—49ers, 24-13 (SF)
1989—49ers, 38-28 (P)
1991—49ers, 23-7 (P)
1992—49ers, 20-14 (SF)
1993—Eagles, 37-34 (SF) OT
1994—Eagles, 40-8 (SF)
1996—*49ers, 14-0 (SF)
1997—49ers, 24-12 (P)
2001—49ers, 13-3 (SF)
2002—Eagles, 38-17 (SF)
2003—49ers, 31-28 (P) OT
(RS Pts.—49ers 569, Eagles 498)
(PS Pts.—49ers 14, Eagles 0)
**NFC First-Round Playoff*

PHILADELPHIA vs. SEATTLE
RS: Eagles lead series, 6-3
1976—Eagles, 27-10 (P)
1980—Eagles, 27-20 (S)
1986—Seahawks, 24-20 (S)
1989—Eagles, 31-7 (P)
1992—Eagles, 20-17 (S) OT
1995—Seahawks, 26-14 (S)
1998—Seahawks, 38-0 (P)
2001—Eagles, 27-3 (S)
2002—Eagles, 27-20 (S)
(RS Pts.—Eagles 193, Seahawks 165)

PHILADELPHIA vs. TAMPA BAY
RS: Eagles lead series, 5-4
PS: Series tied, 2-2
1977—Eagles, 13-3 (P)
1979—*Buccaneers, 24-17 (TB)
1981—Eagles, 20-10 (P)
1988—Eagles, 41-14 (TB)
1991—Buccaneers, 14-13 (TB)
1995—Buccaneers, 21-6 (P)
1999—Buccaneers, 19-5 (P)
2000—**Eagles, 21-3 (P)
2001—Eagles, 17-13 (TB)
**Eagles, 31-9 (P)
2002—Eagles, 20-10 (P)
***Buccaneers, 27-10 (P)
2003—Buccaneers, 17-0 (P)
(RS Pts.—Eagles 135, Buccaneers 121)
(PS Pts.—Eagles 79, Buccaneers 63)
**NFC Divisional Playoff*
***NFC First-Round Playoff*
****NFC Championship*

PHILADELPHIA vs. *TENNESSEE
RS: Eagles lead series, 6-2
1972—Eagles, 18-17 (H)
1979—Eagles, 26-20 (H)
1982—Eagles, 35-14 (P)
1988—Eagles, 32-23 (P)
1991—Eagles, 13-6 (H)
1994—Eagles, 21-6 (P)
2000—Titans, 15-13 (P)
2002—Titans, 27-24 (T)
(RS Pts.—Eagles 182, Titans 128)
**Franchise in Houston prior to 1997; known as Oilers prior to 1999*

PHILADELPHIA vs. *WASHINGTON
RS: Redskins lead series, 72-60-5
PS: Redskins lead series, 1-0
1934—Redskins, 6-0 (B)
Redskins, 14-7 (P)
1935—Eagles, 7-6 (B)
1936—Redskins, 26-3 (P)
Redskins, 17-7 (B)
1937—Eagles, 14-0 (W)
Redskins, 10-7 (P)
1938—Redskins, 26-23 (P)
Redskins, 20-14 (W)
1939—Redskins, 7-0 (P)
Redskins, 7-6 (W)
1940—Redskins, 34-17 (P)
Redskins, 13-6 (W)
1941—Redskins, 21-17 (P)
Redskins, 20-14 (W)
1942—Redskins, 14-10 (P)
Redskins, 30-27 (W)
1944—Tie, 31-31 (P)
Eagles, 37-7 (W)
1945—Redskins, 24-14 (W)
Eagles, 16-0 (P)
1946—Eagles, 28-24 (W)
Redskins, 27-10 (P)
1947—Eagles, 45-42 (P)
Eagles, 38-14 (W)
1948—Eagles, 45-0 (W)
Eagles, 42-21 (P)
1949—Eagles, 49-14 (P)
Eagles, 44-21 (W)
1950—Eagles, 35-3 (P)
Eagles, 33-0 (W)
1951—Redskins, 27-23 (P)
Eagles, 35-21 (W)
1952—Eagles, 38-20 (P)
Redskins, 27-21 (W)
1953—Tie, 21-21 (P)
Redskins, 10-0 (W)
1954—Eagles, 49-21 (W)
Eagles, 41-33 (P)
1955—Redskins, 31-30 (P)
Redskins, 34-21 (W)
1956—Eagles, 13-9 (P)
Redskins, 19-17 (W)
1957—Eagles, 21-12 (P)
Redskins, 42-7 (W)
1958—Redskins, 24-14 (P)
Redskins, 20-0 (W)
1959—Eagles, 30-23 (P)
Eagles, 34-14 (W)
1960—Eagles, 19-13 (P)
Eagles, 38-28 (W)
1961—Eagles, 14-7 (P)
Eagles, 27-24 (W)
1962—Redskins, 27-21 (P)
Eagles, 37-14 (W)
1963—Eagles, 37-24 (W)
Redskins, 13-10 (P)
1964—Redskins, 35-20 (W)
Redskins, 21-10 (P)
1965—Redskins, 23-21 (W)
Eagles, 21-14 (P)
1966—Redskins, 27-13 (P)
Eagles, 37-28 (W)
1967—Eagles, 35-24 (P)
Tie, 35-35 (W)
1968—Redskins, 17-14 (W)
Redskins, 16-10 (P)
1969—Tie, 28-28 (W)
Redskins, 34-29 (P)
1970—Redskins, 33-21 (P)
Redskins, 24-6 (W)
1971—Tie, 7-7 (W)
Redskins, 20-13 (P)
1972—Redskins, 14-0 (W)
Redskins, 23-7 (P)
1973—Redskins, 28-7 (P)
Redskins, 38-20 (W)
1974—Redskins, 27-20 (P)
Redskins, 26-7 (W)
1975—Eagles, 26-10 (P)
Eagles, 26-3 (W)
1976—Redskins, 20-17 (P) OT
Redskins, 24-0 (W)
1977—Redskins, 23-17 (W)
Redskins, 17-14 (P)
1978—Redskins, 35-30 (W)
Eagles, 17-10 (P)
1979—Eagles, 28-17 (P)
Redskins, 17-7 (W)
1980—Eagles, 24-14 (P)
Eagles, 24-0 (W)
1981—Eagles, 36-13 (P)
Redskins, 15-13 (W)
1982—Redskins, 37-34 (P) OT
Redskins, 13-9 (W)
1983—Redskins, 23-13 (P)
Redskins, 28-24 (W)
1984—Redskins, 20-0 (W)
Eagles, 16-10 (P)
1985—Eagles, 19-6 (W)
Redskins, 17-12 (P)
1986—Redskins, 41-14 (W)
Redskins, 21-14 (P)
1987—Redskins, 34-24 (W)
Eagles, 31-27 (P)
1988—Redskins, 17-10 (W)

Redskins, 20-19 (P)
1989—Eagles, 42-37 (W)
Redskins, 10-3 (P)
1990—Redskins, 13-7 (W)
Eagles, 28-14 (P)
**Redskins, 20-6 (P)
1991—Redskins, 23-0 (W)
Eagles, 24-22 (P)
1992—Redskins, 16-12 (W)
Eagles, 17-13 (P)
1993—Eagles, 34-31 (P)
Eagles, 17-14 (W)
1994—Eagles, 21-17 (P)
Eagles, 31-29 (W)
1995—Eagles, 37-34 (P) (OT)
Eagles, 14-7 (W)
1996—Eagles, 17-14 (W)
Redskins, 26-21 (P)
1997—Eagles, 24-10 (P)
Redskins, 35-32 (W)
1998—Eagles, 17-12 (P)
Redskins, 28-3 (W)
1999—Eagles, 35-28 (P)
Redskins, 20-17 (W) OT
2000—Redskins, 17-14 (P)
Eagles, 23-20 (W)
2001—Redskins, 13-3 (P)
Eagles, 20-6 (W)
2002—Eagles, 37-7 (W)
Eagles, 34-21 (P)
2003—Eagles, 27-25 (P)
Eagles, 31-7 (W)
(RS Pts.—Eagles 2,805, Redskins 2,700)
(PS Pts.—Redskins 20, Eagles 6)
Franchise in Boston prior to 1937
**NFC First-Round Playoff*

PITTSBURGH vs. ARIZONA
RS: Steelers lead series, 31-22-3;
See Arizona vs. Pittsburgh
PITTSBURGH vs. ATLANTA
RS: Steelers lead series, 11-1-1;
See Atlanta vs. Pittsburgh
PITTSBURGH vs. BALTIMORE
RS: Steelers lead series, 11-5
PS: Steelers lead series, 1-0;
See Baltimore vs. Pittsburgh
PITTSBURGH vs. BUFFALO
RS: Steelers lead series, 9-8
PS: Steelers lead series, 2-1;
See Buffalo vs. Pittsburgh
PITTSBURGH vs. CAROLINA
RS: Steelers lead series, 2-1;
See Carolina vs. Pittsburgh
PITTSBURGH vs. CHICAGO
RS: Bears lead series, 16-6-1;
See Chicago vs. Pittsburgh
PITTSBURGH vs. CINCINNATI
RS: Steelers lead series, 39-28;
See Cincinnati vs. Pittsburgh
PITTSBURGH vs. CLEVELAND
RS: Browns lead series, 55-47
PS: Steelers lead series, 2-0;
See Cleveland vs. Pittsburgh
PITTSBURGH vs. DALLAS
RS: Cowboys lead series, 14-11
PS: Steelers lead series, 2-1;
See Dallas vs. Pittsburgh
PITTSBURGH vs. DENVER
RS: Broncos lead series, 11-6-1
PS: Broncos lead series, 3-2;
See Denver vs. Pittsburgh
PITTSBURGH vs. DETROIT
RS: Lions lead series, 14-13-1;
See Detroit vs. Pittsburgh
PITTSBURGH vs. GREEN BAY
RS: Packers lead series, 18-12;
See Green Bay vs. Pittsburgh
PITTSBURGH vs. HOUSTON
RS: Texans lead series, 1-0;
See Houston vs. Pittsburgh
PITTSBURGH vs. INDIANAPOLIS
RS: Steelers lead series, 13-4
PS: Steelers lead series, 4-0;
See Indianapolis vs. Pittsburgh
PITTSBURGH vs. JACKSONVILLE
RS: Jaguars lead series, 8-7;
See Jacksonville vs. Pittsburgh
PITTSBURGH vs. KANSAS CITY
RS: Steelers lead series, 16-8
PS: Chiefs lead series, 1-0;
See Kansas City vs. Pittsburgh
PITTSBURGH vs. MIAMI
RS: Dolphins lead series, 9-7
PS: Dolphins lead series, 2-1;
See Miami vs. Pittsburgh
PITTSBURGH vs. MINNESOTA
RS: Vikings lead series, 8-5
PS: Steelers lead series, 1-0;
See Minnesota vs. Pittsburgh
PITTSBURGH vs. NEW ENGLAND
RS: Steelers lead series, 11-5
PS: Patriots lead series, 2-1;
See New England vs. Pittsburgh
PITTSBURGH vs. NEW ORLEANS
RS: Series tied, 6-6;
See New Orleans vs. Pittsburgh
PITTSBURGH vs. N.Y. GIANTS
RS: Giants lead series, 43-27-3;
See N.Y. Giants vs. Pittsburgh
PITTSBURGH vs. N.Y. JETS
RS: Steelers lead series, 14-2;
See N.Y. Jets vs. Pittsburgh
PITTSBURGH vs. OAKLAND
RS: Raiders lead series, 8-7
PS: Series tied, 3-3;
See Oakland vs. Pittsburgh
PITTSBURGH vs. PHILADELPHIA
RS: Eagles lead series, 45-26-3
PS: Eagles lead series, 1-0;
See Philadelphia vs. Pittsburgh
***PITTSBURGH vs. **ST. LOUIS**
RS: Rams lead series, 15-5-2
PS: Steelers lead series, 1-0
1938—Rams, 13-7 (New Orleans)
1939—Tie, 14-14 (C)
1941—Rams, 17-14 (Akron)
1947—Rams, 48-7 (P)
1948—Rams, 31-14 (LA)
1949—Tie, 7-7 (P)
1952—Rams, 28-14 (LA)
1955—Rams, 27-26 (LA)
1956—Steelers, 30-13 (P)
1961—Rams, 24-14 (LA)
1964—Rams, 26-14 (P)
1968—Rams, 45-10 (LA)
1971—Rams, 23-14 (P)
1975—Rams, 10-3 (LA)
1978—Rams, 10-7 (LA)
1979—***Steelers, 31-19 (Pasadena)
1981—Steelers, 24-0 (P)
1984—Steelers, 24-14 (P)
1987—Rams, 31-21 (LA)
1990—Steelers, 41-10 (P)
1993—Rams, 27-0 (LA)
1996—Steelers, 42-6 (P)
2003—Rams, 33-21 (P)
(RS Pts.—Rams 457, Steelers 368)
(PS Pts.—Steelers 31, Rams 19)
Steelers known as Pirates prior to 1941
**Franchise in Los Angeles prior to 1995 and in Cleveland prior to 1946*
***Super Bowl XIV*
PITTSBURGH vs. SAN DIEGO
RS: Steelers lead series, 18-5
PS: Chargers lead series, 2-0
1971—Steelers, 21-17 (P)
1972—Steelers, 24-2 (SD)
1973—Steelers, 38-21 (P)
1975—Steelers, 37-0 (SD)
1976—Steelers, 23-0 (P)
1977—Steelers, 10-9 (SD)
1979—Chargers, 35-7 (SD)
1980—Chargers, 26-17 (SD)
1982—*Chargers, 31-28 (P)
1983—Steelers, 26-3 (P)
1984—Steelers, 52-24 (P)
1985—Chargers, 54-44 (SD)
1987—Steelers, 20-16 (SD)
1988—Chargers, 20-14 (SD)
1989—Steelers, 20-17 (P)
1990—Steelers, 36-14 (P)
1991—Steelers, 26-20 (P)
1992—Steelers, 23-6 (SD)
1993—Steelers,.16-3 (P)
1994—Chargers, 37-34 (SD)
**Chargers, 17-13 (P)
1995—Steelers, 31-16 (P)
1996—Steelers, 16-3 (P)
2000—Steelers, 34-21 (SD)
2003—Steelers, 40-24 (P)
(RS Pts.—Steelers 609, Chargers 388)
(PS Pts.—Chargers 48, Steelers 41)
AFC First-Round Playoff
**AFC Championship*
PITTSBURGH vs. SAN FRANCISCO
RS: 49ers lead series, 10-8
1951—49ers, 28-24 (P)
1952—Steelers, 24-7 (SF)
1954—49ers, 31-3 (SF)
1958—49ers, 23-20 (SF)
1961—Steelers, 20-10 (P)
1965—49ers, 27-17 (SF)
1968—49ers, 45-28 (P)
1973—Steelers, 37-14 (SF)
1977—Steelers, 27-0 (P)
1978—Steelers, 24-7 (SF)
1981—49ers, 17-14 (P)
1984—Steelers, 20-17 (SF)
1987—Steelers, 30-17 (P)
1990—49ers, 27-7 (SF)
1993—49ers, 24-13 (P)
1996—49ers, 25-15 (P)
1999—Steelers, 27-6 (SF)
2003—49ers, 30-14 (SF)
(RS Pts.—Steelers 364, 49ers 355)
PITTSBURGH vs. SEATTLE
RS: Seahawks lead series, 8-6
1977—Steelers, 30-20 (P)
1978—Steelers, 21-10 (P)

1981—Seahawks, 24-21 (S)
1982—Seahawks, 16-0 (S)
1983—Steelers, 27-21 (S)
1986—Seahawks, 30-0 (S)
1987—Steelers, 13-9 (P)
1991—Seahawks, 27-7 (P)
1992—Steelers, 20-14 (P)
1993—Seahawks, 16-6 (S)
1994—Seahawks, 30-13 (S)
1998—Steelers, 13-10 (P)
1999—Seahawks, 29-10 (P)
2003—Seahawks, 23-16 (S)
(RS Pts.—Seahawks 279, Steelers 197)

PITTSBURGH vs. TAMPA BAY
RS: Steelers lead series, 6-1
1976—Steelers, 42-0 (P)
1980—Steelers, 24-21 (TB)
1983—Steelers, 17-12 (P)
1989—Steelers, 31-22 (TB)
1998—Buccaneers, 16-3 (TB)
2001—Steelers, 17-10 (TB)
2002—Steelers, 17-7 (TB)
(RS Pts.—Steelers 151, Buccaneers 88)

PITTSBURGH vs. *TENNESSEE
RS: Steelers lead series, 37-28
PS: Steelers lead series, 3-1
1970—Oilers, 19-7 (P)
Steelers, 7-3 (H)
1971—Steelers, 23-16 (P)
Oilers, 29-3 (H)
1972—Steelers, 24-7 (P)
Steelers, 9-3 (H)
1973—Steelers, 36-7 (H)
Steelers, 33-7 (P)
1974—Steelers, 13-7 (H)
Oilers, 13-10 (P)
1975—Steelers, 24-17 (P)
Steelers, 32-9 (H)
1976—Steelers, 32-16 (P)
Steelers, 21-0 (H)
1977—Oilers, 27-10 (H)
Steelers, 27-10 (P)
1978—Oilers, 24-17 (P)
Steelers, 13-3 (H)
**Steelers, 34-5 (P)
1979—Steelers, 38-7 (P)
Oilers, 20-17 (H)
**Steelers, 27-13 (P)
1980—Steelers, 31-17 (P)
Oilers, 6-0 (H)
1981—Steelers, 26-13 (P)
Oilers, 21-20 (H)
1982—Steelers, 24-10 (H)
1983—Steelers, 40-28 (H)
Steelers, 17-10 (P)
1984—Steelers, 35-7 (P)
Oilers, 23-20 (H) OT
1985—Steelers, 20-0 (P)
Steelers, 30-7 (H)
1986—Steelers, 22-16 (H) OT
Steelers, 21-10 (P)
1987—Oilers, 23-3 (P)
Oilers, 24-16 (H)
1988—Oilers, 34-14 (P)
Steelers, 37-34 (H)
1989—Oilers, 27-0 (H)
Oilers, 23-16 (P)
***Steelers, 26-23 (H) OT
1990—Steelers, 20-9 (P)
Oilers, 34-14 (H)
1991—Steelers, 26-14 (P)
Oilers, 31-6 (H)
1992—Steelers, 29-24 (H)
Steelers, 21-20 (P)
1993—Oilers, 23-3 (H)
Oilers, 26-17 (P)
1994—Steelers, 30-14 (P)
Steelers, 12-9 (H) OT
1995—Steelers, 34-17 (H)
Steelers, 21-7 (P)
1996—Steelers, 30-16 (P)
Oilers, 23-13 (H)
1997—Steelers, 37-24 (P)
Oilers, 16-6 (T)
1998—Oilers, 41-31 (P)
Oilers, 23-14 (T)
1999—Titans, 16-10 (T)
Titans, 47-36 (P)
2000—Titans, 23-20 (P)
Titans, 9-7 (T)
2001—Steelers, 34-7 (P)
Steelers, 34-24 (T)
2002—Titans, 31-23 (T)
****Titans, 34-31 (T) OT
2003—Titans, 30-13 (P)
(RS Pts.—Steelers 1,329, Titans 1,135)
(PS Pts.—Steelers 118, Titans 75)
**Franchise in Houston prior to 1997; known as Oilers prior to 1999*
***AFC Championship*
****AFC First-Round Playoff*
*****AFC Divisional Playoff*

***PITTSBURGH vs. **WASHINGTON**
RS: Redskins lead series, 42-29-3
1933—Redskins, 21-6 (P)
Pirates, 16-14 (B)
1934—Redskins, 7-0 (P)
Redskins, 39-0 (B)
1935—Pirates, 6-0 (P)
Redskins, 13-3 (B)
1936—Pirates, 10-0 (P)
Redskins, 30-0 (B)
1937—Redskins, 34-20 (W)
Pirates, 21-13 (P)
1938—Redskins, 7-0 (P)
Redskins, 15-0 (W)
1939—Redskins, 44-14 (W)
Redskins, 21-14 (P)
1940—Redskins, 40-10 (P)
Redskins, 37-10 (W)
1941—Redskins, 24-20 (P)
Redskins, 23-3 (W)
1942—Redskins, 28-14 (W)
Redskins, 14-0 (P)
1945—Redskins, 14-0 (P)
Redskins, 24-0 (W)
1946—Tie, 14-14 (W)
Steelers, 14-7 (P)
1947—Redskins, 27-26 (W)
Steelers, 21-14 (P)
1948—Redskins, 17-14 (W)
Steelers, 10-7 (P)
1949—Redskins, 27-14 (P)
Redskins, 27-14 (W)
1950—Steelers, 26-7 (W)
Redskins, 24-7 (P)
1951—Redskins, 22-7 (P)
Steelers, 20-10 (W)
1952—Redskins, 28-24 (P)
Steelers, 24-23 (W)
1953—Redskins, 17-9 (P)
Steelers, 14-13 (W)
1954—Steelers, 37-7 (P)
Redskins, 17-14 (W)
1955—Redskins, 23-14 (P)
Redskins, 28-17 (W)
1956—Steelers, 30-13 (P)
Steelers, 23-0 (W)
1957—Steelers, 28-7 (P)
Redskins, 10-3 (W)
1958—Steelers, 24-16 (P)
Tie, 14-14 (W)
1959—Redskins, 23-17 (P)
Steelers, 27-6 (W)
1960—Tie, 27-27 (W)
Steelers, 22-10 (P)
1961—Steelers, 20-0 (P)
Steelers, 30-14 (W)
1962—Steelers, 23-21 (P)
Steelers, 27-24 (W)
1963—Steelers, 38-27 (P)
Steelers, 34-28 (W)
1964—Redskins, 30-0 (P)
Steelers, 14-7 (W)
1965—Redskins, 31-3 (P)
Redskins, 35-14 (W)
1966—Redskins, 33-27 (P)
Redskins, 24-10 (W)
1967—Redskins, 15-10 (P)
1968—Redskins, 16-13 (W)
1969—Redskins, 14-7 (P)
1973—Steelers, 21-16 (P)
1979—Steelers, 38-7 (P)
1985—Redskins, 30-23 (P)
1988—Redskins, 30-29 (W)
1991—Redskins, 41-14 (P)
1997—Steelers, 14-13 (P)
2000—Steelers, 24-3 (P)
(RS Pts.—Redskins 1,406, Steelers 1,155)
**Steelers known as Pirates prior to 1941*
***Franchise in Boston prior to 1937*

ST. LOUIS vs. ARIZONA
RS: Rams lead series, 27-21-2
PS: Rams lead series, 1-0;
See Arizona vs. St. Louis

ST. LOUIS vs. ATLANTA
RS: Rams lead series, 46-23-2;
See Atlanta vs. St. Louis

ST. LOUIS vs. BALTIMORE
RS: Rams lead series, 2-1;
See Baltimore vs. St. Louis

ST. LOUIS vs. BUFFALO
RS: Series tied, 4-4;
See Buffalo vs. St. Louis

ST. LOUIS vs. CAROLINA
RS: Series tied, 7-7
PS: Panthers lead series, 1-0;
See Carolina vs. St. Louis

ST. LOUIS vs. CHICAGO
RS: Bears lead series, 47-34-3
PS: Series tied, 1-1;
See Chicago vs. St. Louis

ST. LOUIS vs. CINCINNATI
RS: Series tied, 5-5;
See Cincinnati vs. St. Louis

ST. LOUIS vs. CLEVELAND
RS: Rams lead series, 9-8
PS: Browns lead series, 2-1;
See Cleveland vs. St. Louis

ST. LOUIS vs. DALLAS
RS: Series tied, 9-9
PS: Series tied, 4-4;
See Dallas vs. St. Louis
ST. LOUIS vs. DENVER
RS: Series tied, 5-5;
See Denver vs. St. Louis
ST. LOUIS vs. DETROIT
RS: Rams lead series, 40-37-1
PS: Lions lead series, 1-0;
See Detroit vs. St. Louis
ST. LOUIS vs. GREEN BAY
RS: Rams lead series, 44-39-2
PS: Series tied, 1-1;
See Green Bay vs. St. Louis
ST. LOUIS vs. INDIANAPOLIS
RS: Colts lead series, 21-17-2;
See Indianapolis vs. St. Louis
ST. LOUIS vs. JACKSONVILLE
RS: Rams lead series, 1-0;
See Jacksonville vs. St. Louis
ST. LOUIS vs. KANSAS CITY
RS: Series tied, 4-4;
See Kansas City vs. St. Louis
ST. LOUIS vs. MIAMI
RS: Dolphins lead series, 7-2;
See Miami vs. St. Louis
ST. LOUIS vs. MINNESOTA
RS: Vikings lead series, 16-13-2
PS: Vikings lead series, 5-2;
See Minnesota vs. St. Louis
ST. LOUIS vs. NEW ENGLAND
RS: Rams lead series, 5-3
PS: Patriots lead series, 1-0;
See New England vs. St. Louis
ST. LOUIS vs. NEW ORLEANS
RS: Rams lead series, 36-28
PS: Saints lead series, 1-0;
See New Orleans vs. St. Louis
ST. LOUIS vs. N.Y. GIANTS
RS: Rams lead series, 25-11
PS: Series tied, 1-1;
See N.Y. Giants vs. St. Louis
ST. LOUIS vs. N.Y. JETS
RS: Rams lead series, 8-2;
See N.Y. Jets vs. St. Louis
ST. LOUIS vs. OAKLAND
RS: Raiders lead series, 7-3;
See Oakland vs. St. Louis
ST. LOUIS vs. PHILADELPHIA
RS: Rams lead series, 16-15-1
PS: Rams lead series, 2-1;
See Philadelphia vs. St. Louis
ST. LOUIS vs. PITTSBURGH
RS: Rams lead series, 15-5-2
PS: Steelers lead series, 1-0;
See Pittsburgh vs. St. Louis
***ST. LOUIS vs. SAN DIEGO**
RS: Rams lead series, 5-3
1970—Rams, 37-10 (LA)
1975—Rams, 13-10 (SD) OT
1979—Chargers, 40-16 (LA)
1988—Chargers, 38-24 (LA)
1991—Rams, 30-24 (LA)
1994—Chargers, 31-17 (SD)
2000—Rams, 57-31 (StL)
2002—Rams, 28-24 (StL)
(RS Pts.—Rams 222, Chargers 208)
Franchise in Los Angeles prior to 1995

***ST. LOUIS vs. SAN FRANCISCO**
RS: Rams lead series, 56-50-2
PS: 49ers lead series, 1-0
1950—Rams, 35-14 (SF)
Rams, 28-21 (LA)
1951—49ers, 44-17 (SF)
Rams, 23-16 (LA)
1952—Rams, 35-9 (LA)
Rams, 34-21 (SF)
1953—49ers, 31-30 (SF)
49ers, 31-27 (LA)
1954—Tie, 24-24 (LA)
Rams, 42-34 (SF)
1955—Rams, 23-14 (SF)
Rams, 27-14 (LA)
1956—49ers, 33-30 (SF)
Rams, 30-6 (LA)
1957—49ers, 23-20 (SF)
Rams, 37-24 (LA)
1958—Rams, 33-3 (SF)
Rams, 56-7 (LA)
1959—49ers, 34-0 (SF)
49ers, 24-16 (LA)
1960—49ers, 13-9 (SF)
49ers, 23-7 (LA)
1961—49ers, 35-0 (SF)
Rams, 17-7 (LA)
1962—Rams, 28-14 (SF)
49ers, 24-17 (LA)
1963—Rams, 28-21 (LA)
Rams, 21-17 (SF)
1964—Rams, 42-14 (LA)
49ers, 28-7 (SF)
1965—49ers, 45-21 (LA)
49ers, 30-27 (SF)
1966—Rams, 34-3 (LA)
49ers, 21-13 (SF)
1967—49ers, 27-24 (LA)
Rams, 17-7 (SF)
1968—Rams, 24-10 (LA)
Tie, 20-20 (SF)
1969—Rams, 27-21 (SF)
Rams, 41-30 (LA)
1970—49ers, 20-6 (LA)
Rams, 30-13 (SF)
1971—Rams, 20-13 (SF)
Rams, 17-6 (LA)
1972—Rams, 31-7 (LA)
Rams, 26-16 (SF)
1973—Rams, 40-20 (SF)
Rams, 31-13 (LA)
1974—Rams, 37-14 (LA)
Rams, 15-13 (SF)
1975—Rams, 23-14 (SF)
49ers, 24-23 (LA)
1976—49ers, 16-0 (LA)
Rams, 23-3 (SF)
1977—Rams, 34-14 (LA)
Rams, 23-10 (SF)
1978—Rams, 27-10 (LA)
Rams, 31-28 (SF)
1979—Rams, 27-24 (LA)
Rams, 26-20 (SF)
1980—Rams, 48-26 (LA)
Rams, 31-17 (SF)
1981—49ers, 20-17 (SF)
49ers, 33-31 (LA)
1982—49ers, 30-24 (LA)
Rams, 21-20 (SF)
1983—Rams, 10-7 (SF)
49ers, 45-35 (LA)
1984—49ers, 33-0 (LA)
49ers, 19-16 (SF)
1985—49ers, 28-14 (LA)
Rams, 27-20 (SF)
1986—Rams, 16-13 (LA)
49ers, 24-14 (SF)
1987—49ers, 31-10 (LA)
49ers, 48-0 (SF)
1988—49ers, 24-21 (LA)
Rams, 38-16 (SF)
1989—Rams, 13-12 (SF)
49ers, 30-27 (LA)
**49ers, 30-3 (SF)
1990—Rams, 28-17 (SF)
49ers, 26-10 (LA)
1991—49ers, 27-10 (SF)
49ers, 33-10 (LA)
1992—49ers, 27-24 (SF)
49ers, 27-10 (LA)
1993—49ers, 40-17 (SF)
49ers, 35-10 (LA)
1994—49ers, 34-19 (LA)
49ers, 31-27 (SF)
1995—49ers, 44-10 (StL)
49ers, 41-13 (SF)
1996—49ers, 34-0 (SF)
49ers, 28-11 (StL)
1997—49ers, 15-12 (StL)
49ers, 30-10 (SF)
1998—49ers, 28-10 (StL)
49ers, 38-19 (SF)
1999—Rams, 42-20 (StL)
Rams, 23-7 (SF)
2000—Rams, 41-24 (StL)
Rams, 34-24 (SF)
2001—Rams, 30-26 (SF)
Rams, 27-14 (StL)
2002—49ers, 37-13 (SF)
Rams, 31-20 (StL)
2003—Rams, 27-24 (StL) OT
49ers, 30-10 (SF)
(RS Pts.—Rams 2,422, 49ers 2,412)
(PS Pts.—49ers 30, Rams 3)
Franchise in Los Angeles prior to 1995
***NFC Championship*
***ST. LOUIS vs. SEATTLE**
RS: Rams lead series, 7-4
1976—Rams, 45-6 (LA)
1979—Rams, 24-0 (S)
1985—Rams, 35-24 (S)
1988—Rams, 31-10 (LA)
1991—Seahawks, 23-9 (S)
1997—Seahawks, 17-9 (StL)
2000—Rams, 37-34 (Sea)
2002—Rams, 37-20 (StL)
Seahawks, 30-10 (Sea)
2003—Seahawks, 24-23 (Sea)
Rams, 27-22 (StL)
(RS Pts.—Rams 287, Seahawks 210)
Franchise in Los Angeles prior to 1995
***ST. LOUIS vs. TAMPA BAY**
RS: Rams lead series, 8-6
PS: Rams lead series, 2-0
1977—Rams, 31-0 (LA)
1978—Rams, 26-23 (LA)
1979—Buccaneers, 21-6 (TB)
**Rams, 9-0 (TB)
1980—Buccaneers, 10-9 (TB)
1984—Rams, 34-33 (TB)

1985—Rams, 31-27 (TB)
1986—Rams, 26-20 (LA) OT
1987—Rams, 35-3 (LA)
1990—Rams, 35-14 (TB)
1992—Rams, 31-27 (TB)
1994—Buccaneers, 24-14 (TB)
1999—**Rams, 11-6 (StL)
2000—Buccaneers, 38-35 (TB)
2001—Buccaneers, 24-17 (StL)
2002—Buccaneers, 26-14 (TB)
(RS Pts.—Rams 344, Buccaneers 290)
(PS Pts.—Rams 20, Buccaneers 6)
Franchise in Los Angeles prior to 1995
***NFC Championship*

***ST. LOUIS vs. **TENNESSEE**
RS: Rams lead series, 5-3
PS: Rams lead series, 1-0
1973—Rams, 31-26 (H)
1978—Rams, 10-6 (H)
1981—Oilers, 27-20 (LA)
1984—Rams, 27-16 (LA)
1987—Oilers, 20-16 (H)
1990—Rams, 17-13 (LA)
1993—Rams, 28-13 (H)
1999—Titans, 24-21 (T)
***Rams, 23-16 (Atlanta)
(RS Pts.—Rams 170, Titans 145)
(PS Pts.—Rams 23, Titans 16)
Franchise in Los Angeles prior to 1995
***Franchise in Houston prior to 1997; known as Oilers prior to 1999*
****Super Bowl XXXIV*

***ST. LOUIS vs. WASHINGTON**
RS: Redskins lead series, 19-6-1
PS: Series tied, 2-2
1937—Redskins, 16-7 (C)
1938—Redskins, 37-13 (W)
1941—Redskins, 17-13 (W)
1942—Redskins, 33-14 (W)
1944—Redskins, 14-10 (W)
1945—**Rams, 15-14 (C)
1948—Rams, 41-13 (W)
1949—Rams, 53-27 (LA)
1951—Redskins, 31-21 (W)
1962—Redskins, 20-14 (W)
1963—Redskins, 37-14 (LA)
1967—Tie, 28-28 (LA)
1969—Rams, 24-13 (W)
1971—Redskins, 38-24 (LA)
1974—Redskins, 23-17 (LA)
***Rams, 19-10 (LA)
1977—Redskins, 17-14 (W)
1981—Redskins, 30-7 (LA)
1983—Redskins, 42-20 (LA)
***Redskins, 51-7 (W)
1986—****Redskins, 19-7 (W)
1987—Rams, 30-26 (W)
1991—Redskins, 27-6 (LA)
1993—Rams, 10-6 (LA)
1994—Redskins, 24-21 (LA)
1995—Redskins, 35-23 (StL)
1996—Redskins, 17-10 (StL)
1997—Rams, 23-20 (W)
2000—Redskins, 33-20 (StL)
2002—Redskins, 20-17 (W)
(RS Pts.—Redskins 644, Rams 494)
(PS Pts.—Redskins 94, Rams 48)
Franchise in Los Angeles prior to 1995 and in Cleveland prior to 1946
***NFL Championship*
****NFC Divisional Playoff*
*****NFC First-Round Playoff*

SAN DIEGO vs. ARIZONA
RS: Chargers lead series, 7-3;
See Arizona vs. San Diego

SAN DIEGO vs. ATLANTA
RS: Falcons lead series, 5-1;
See Atlanta vs. San Diego

SAN DIEGO vs BALTIMORE
RS: Series tied, 2-2;
See Baltimore vs. San Diego

SAN DIEGO vs. BUFFALO
RS: Chargers lead series, 18-9-2
PS: Bills lead series, 2-1;
See Buffalo vs. San Diego

SAN DIEGO vs. CAROLINA
RS: Panthers lead series, 2-0;
See Carolina vs. San Diego

SAN DIEGO vs. CHICAGO
RS: Bears lead series, 5-4;
See Chicago vs. San Diego

SAN DIEGO vs. CINCINNATI
RS: Chargers lead series, 17-10
PS: Bengals lead series, 1-0;
See Cincinnati vs. San Diego

SAN DIEGO vs. CLEVELAND
RS: Chargers lead series, 11-7-1;
See Cleveland vs. San Diego

SAN DIEGO vs. DALLAS
RS: Cowboys lead series, 5-2;
See Dallas vs. San Diego

SAN DIEGO vs. DENVER
RS: Broncos lead series, 49-38-1;
See Denver vs. San Diego

SAN DIEGO vs. DETROIT
RS: Chargers lead series, 5-3;
See Detroit vs. San Diego

SAN DIEGO vs. GREEN BAY
RS: Packers lead series, 7-1;
See Green Bay vs. San Diego

SAN DIEGO vs. HOUSTON
RS: Chargers lead series, 1-0;
See Houston vs. San Diego

SAN DIEGO vs. INDIANAPOLIS
RS: Chargers lead series, 12-7
PS: Colts lead series, 1-0;
See Indianapolis vs. San Diego

SAN DIEGO vs. JACKSONVILLE
RS: Jaguars lead series, 1-0;
See Jacksonville vs. San Diego

SAN DIEGO vs. KANSAS CITY
RS: Chiefs lead series, 47-39-1
PS: Chargers lead series, 1-0;
See Kansas City vs. San Diego

SAN DIEGO vs. MIAMI
RS: Series tied, 10-10
PS: Series tied, 2-2;
See Miami vs. San Diego

SAN DIEGO vs. MINNESOTA
RS: Chargers lead series, 5-4;
See Minnesota vs. San Diego

SAN DIEGO vs. NEW ENGLAND
RS: Patriots lead series, 17-12-2
PS: Chargers lead series, 1-0;
See New England vs. San Diego

SAN DIEGO vs. NEW ORLEANS
RS: Chargers lead series, 6-2;
See New Orleans vs. San Diego

SAN DIEGO vs. N.Y. GIANTS
RS: Giants lead series, 5-3;
See N.Y. Giants vs. San Diego

SAN DIEGO vs. N.Y. JETS
RS: Chargers lead series, 17-10-1;
See N.Y. Jets vs. San Diego

SAN DIEGO vs. OAKLAND
RS: Raiders lead series, 54-32-2
PS: Raiders lead series, 1-0;
See Oakland vs. San Diego

SAN DIEGO vs. PHILADELPHIA
RS: Chargers lead series, 5-3;
See Philadelphia vs. San Diego

SAN DIEGO vs. PITTSBURGH
RS: Steelers lead series, 18-5
PS: Chargers lead series, 2-0;
See Pittsburgh vs. San Diego

SAN DIEGO vs. ST. LOUIS
RS: Rams lead series, 5-3;
See St. Louis vs. San Diego

SAN DIEGO vs. SAN FRANCISCO
RS: 49ers lead series, 6-4
PS: 49ers lead series, 1-0
1972—49ers, 34-3 (SF)
1976—Chargers, 13-7 (SD) OT
1979—Chargers, 31-9 (SD)
1982—Chargers, 41-37 (SF)
1988—49ers, 48-10 (SD)
1991—49ers, 34-14 (SF)
1994—49ers, 38-15 (SD)
*49ers, 49-26 (Miami)
1997—49ers, 17-10 (SF)
2000—49ers, 45-17 (SD)
2002—Chargers, 20-17 (SD) OT
(RS Pts.—49ers 286, Chargers 174)
(PS Pts.—49ers 49, Chargers 26)
Super Bowl XXIX

SAN DIEGO vs. SEATTLE
RS: Seahawks lead series, 25-22
1977—Chargers, 30-28 (S)
1978—Chargers, 24-20 (S)
Chargers, 37-10 (SD)
1979—Chargers, 33-16 (S)
Chargers, 20-10 (SD)
1980—Chargers, 34-13 (S)
Chargers, 21-14 (SD)
1981—Chargers, 24-10 (SD)
Seahawks, 44-23 (S)
1983—Seahawks, 34-31 (S)
Chargers, 28-21 (SD)
1984—Seahawks, 31-17 (S)
Seahawks, 24-0 (SD)
1985—Seahawks, 49-35 (SD)
Seahawks, 26-21 (S)
1986—Seahawks, 33-7 (S)
Seahawks, 34-24 (SD)
1987—Seahawks, 34-3 (S)
1988—Chargers, 17-6 (SD)
Seahawks, 17-14 (S)
1989—Seahawks, 17-16 (SD)
Seahawks, 10-7 (S)
1990—Chargers, 31-14 (S)
Seahawks, 13-10 (SD) OT
1991—Seahawks, 20-9 (S)
Chargers, 17-14 (SD)
1992—Chargers, 17-6 (SD)
Chargers, 31-14 (S)
1993—Chargers, 18-12 (SD)
Seahawks, 31-14 (S)
1994—Chargers, 24-10 (S)

Chargers, 35-15 (SD)
1995—Chargers, 14-10 (SD)
Chargers, 35-25 (S)
1996—Chargers, 29-7 (SD)
Seahawks, 32-13 (S)
1997—Seahawks, 26-22 (S)
Seahawks, 37-31 (SD)
1998—Seahawks, 27-20 (SD)
Seahawks, 38-17 (S)
1999—Chargers, 13-10 (SD)
Chargers, 19-16 (S)
2000—Seahawks, 20-12 (SD)
Seahawks, 17-15 (S)
2001—Seahawks, 13-10 (S) OT
Seahawks, 25-22 (SD)
2002—Seahawks, 31-28 (SD) OT
(RS Pts.—Seahawks 984, Chargers 972)

SAN DIEGO vs. TAMPA BAY
RS: Chargers lead series, 6-1
1976—Chargers, 23-0 (TB)
1981—Chargers, 24-23 (TB)
1987—Chargers, 17-13 (TB)
1990—Chargers, 41-10 (SD)
1992—Chargers, 29-14 (SD)
1993—Chargers, 32-17 (TB)
1996—Buccaneers, 25-17 (SD)
(RS Pts.—Chargers 183, Buccaneers 102)

***SAN DIEGO vs. **TENNESSEE**
RS: Chargers lead series, 19-13-1
PS: Titans lead series, 3-0
1960—Oilers, 38-28 (H)
Chargers, 24-21 (LA)
***Oilers, 24-16 (H)
1961—Chargers, 34-24 (SD)
Oilers, 33-13 (H)
***Oilers, 10-3 (SD)
1962—Oilers, 42-17 (SD)
Oilers, 33-27 (H)
1963—Chargers, 27-0 (SD)
Chargers 20-14 (H)
1964—Chargers, 27-21 (SD)
Chargers, 20-17 (H)
1965—Chargers, 31-14 (SD)
Chargers, 37-26 (H)
1966—Chargers, 28-22 (H)
1967—Chargers, 13-3 (SD)
Oilers, 24-17 (H)
1968—Chargers, 30-14 (SD)
1969—Chargers, 21-17 (H)
1970—Tie, 31-31 (SD)
1971—Oilers, 49-33 (H)
1972—Chargers, 34-20 (SD)
1974—Oilers, 21-14 (H)
1975—Oilers, 33-17 (H)
1976—Chargers, 30-27 (SD)
1978—Chargers, 45-24 (H)
1979—****Oilers, 17-14 (SD)
1984—Chargers, 31-14 (SD)
1985—Oilers, 37-35 (H)
1986—Chargers, 27-0 (SD)
1987—Oilers, 33-18 (H)
1989—Oilers, 34-27 (SD)
1990—Oilers, 17-7 (SD)
1992—Oilers, 27-0 (H)
1993—Chargers, 18-17 (SD)
1998—Chargers, 13-7 (T)
(RS Pts.—Chargers 794, Titans 754)
(PS Pts.—Titans 51, Chargers 33)
**Franchise in Los Angeles prior to 1961*
***Franchise in Houston prior to 1997; known as Oilers prior to 1999*
****AFL Championship*
*****AFC Divisional Playoff*

SAN DIEGO vs. WASHINGTON
RS: Redskins lead series, 6-1
1973—Redskins, 38-0 (W)
1980—Redskins, 40-17 (W)
1983—Redskins, 27-24 (SD)
1986—Redskins, 30-27 (SD)
1989—Redskins, 26-21 (W)
1998—Redskins, 24-20 (W)
2001—Chargers, 30-3 (SD)
(RS Pts.—Redskins 188, Chargers 139)

SAN FRANCISCO vs. ARIZONA
RS: 49ers lead series, 15-10;
See Arizona vs. San Francisco

SAN FRANCISCO vs. ATLANTA
RS: 49ers lead series, 44-25-1
PS: Falcons lead series, 1-0;
See Atlanta vs. San Francisco

SAN FRANCISCO vs. BALTIMORE
RS: Series tied, 1-1;
See Baltimore vs. San Francisco

SAN FRANCISCO vs. BUFFALO
RS: Series tied, 4-4;
See Buffalo vs. San Francisco

SAN FRANCISCO vs. CAROLINA
RS: Series tied, 7-7;
See Carolina vs. San Francisco

SAN FRANCISCO vs. CHICAGO
RS: 49ers lead series, 27-26-1
PS: 49ers lead series, 3-0;
See Chicago vs. San Francisco

SAN FRANCISCO vs. CINCINNATI
RS: 49ers lead series, 7-3
PS: 49ers lead series, 2-0;
See Cincinnati vs. San Francisco

SAN FRANCISCO vs. CLEVELAND
RS: Browns lead series, 10-6;
See Cleveland vs. San Francisco

SAN FRANCISCO vs. DALLAS
RS: 49ers lead series, 14-8-1
PS: Cowboys lead series, 5-2;
See Dallas vs. San Francisco

SAN FRANCISCO vs. DENVER
RS: Broncos lead series, 6-4
PS: 49ers lead series, 1-0;
See Denver vs. San Francisco

SAN FRANCISCO vs. DETROIT
RS: 49ers lead series, 31-26-1
PS: Series tied, 1-1;
See Detroit vs. San Francisco

SAN FRANCISCO vs. GREEN BAY
RS: Packers lead series, 27-25-1
PS: Packers lead series, 4-1;
See Green Bay vs. San Francisco

SAN FRANCISCO vs. INDIANAPOLIS
RS: Colts lead series, 22-18;
See Indianapolis vs. San Francisco

SAN FRANCISCO vs. JACKSONVILLE
RS: Jaguars lead series, 1-0;
See Jacksonville vs. San Francisco

SAN FRANCISCO vs. KANSAS CITY
RS: 49ers lead series, 6-3;
See Kansas City vs. San Francisco

SAN FRANCISCO vs. MIAMI
RS: Series tied, 4-4
PS: 49ers lead series, 1-0;
See Miami vs. San Francisco

SAN FRANCISCO vs. MINNESOTA
RS: Vikings lead series, 18-17-1
PS: 49ers lead series, 4-1;
See Minnesota vs. San Francisco

SAN FRANCISCO vs. NEW ENGLAND
RS: 49ers lead series, 7-2;
See New England vs. San Francisco

SAN FRANCISCO vs. NEW ORLEANS
RS: 49ers lead series, 45-19-2;
See New Orleans vs. San Francisco

SAN FRANCISCO vs. N.Y. GIANTS
RS: 49ers lead series, 13-11
PS: 49ers lead series, 4-3;
See N.Y. Giants vs. San Francisco

SAN FRANCISCO vs. N.Y. JETS
RS: 49ers lead series, 8-1;
See N.Y. Jets vs. San Francisco

SAN FRANCISCO vs. OAKLAND
RS: Raiders lead series, 6-4;
See Oakland vs. San Francisco

SAN FRANCISCO vs. PHILADELPHIA
RS: 49ers lead series, 16-7-1
PS: 49ers lead series, 1-0;
See Philadelphia vs. San Francisco

SAN FRANCISCO vs. PITTSBURGH
RS: 49ers lead series, 10-8;
See Pittsburgh vs. San Francisco

SAN FRANCISCO vs. ST. LOUIS
RS: Rams lead series, 56-50-2
PS: 49ers lead series, 1-0;
See St. Louis vs. San Francisco

SAN FRANCISCO vs. SAN DIEGO
RS: 49ers lead series, 6-4
PS: 49ers lead series, 1-0;
See San Diego vs. San Francisco

SAN FRANCISCO vs. SEATTLE
RS: 49ers lead series, 6-4
1976—49ers, 37-21 (Sea)
1979—Seahawks, 35-24 (SF)
1985—49ers, 19-6 (SF)
1988—49ers, 38-7 (Sea)
1991—49ers, 24-22 (Sea)
1997—Seahawks, 38-9 (Sea)
2002—49ers, 28-21 (Sea)
49ers, 31-24 (SF)
2003—Seahawks, 20-19 (Sea)
Seahawks, 24-17 (SF)
(RS Pts.—49ers 246, Seahawks 218)

SAN FRANCISCO vs. TAMPA BAY
RS: 49ers lead series, 13-2
PS: Buccaneers lead series, 1-0
1977—49ers, 20-10 (SF)
1978—49ers, 6-3 (SF)
1979—49ers, 23-7 (SF)
1980—Buccaneers, 24-23 (SF)
1983—49ers, 35-21 (SF)
1984—49ers, 24-17 (SF)
1986—49ers, 31-7 (TB)
1987—49ers, 24-10 (TB)
1989—49ers, 20-16 (TB)
1990—49ers, 31-7 (SF)
1992—49ers, 21-14 (SF)
1993—49ers, 45-21 (TB)
1994—49ers, 41-16 (SF)
1997—Buccaneers, 13-6 (TB)
2002—*Buccaneers, 31-6 (TB)
2003—49ers, 24-7 (SF)
(RS Pts.—49ers 374, Buccaneers 193)
(PS Pts.—Buccaneers 31, 49ers 6)
**NFC Divisional Playoff*

SAN FRANCISCO vs. *TENNESSEE
RS: 49ers lead series, 7-3
1970—49ers, 30-20 (H)
1975—Oilers, 27-13 (SF)
1978—Oilers, 20-19 (H)
1981—49ers, 28-6 (SF)
1984—49ers, 34-21 (H)
1987—49ers, 27-20 (SF)
1990—49ers, 24-21 (H)
1993—Oilers, 10-7 (SF)
1996—49ers, 10-9 (H)
1999—49ers, 24-22 (SF)
(RS Pts.—49ers 216, Titans 176)
**Franchise in Houston prior to 1997; known as Oilers prior to 1999*

SAN FRANCISCO vs. WASHINGTON
RS: 49ers lead series, 13-7-1
PS: 49ers lead series, 3-1
1952—49ers, 23-17 (W)
1954—49ers, 41-7 (SF)
1955—Redskins, 7-0 (W)
1961—49ers, 35-3 (SF)
1967—Redskins, 31-28 (W)
1969—Tie, 17-17 (SF)
1970—49ers, 26-17 (SF)
1971—*49ers, 24-20 (SF)
1973—Redskins, 33-9 (W)
1976—Redskins, 24-21 (SF)
1978—Redskins, 38-20 (W)
1981—49ers, 30-17 (W)
1983—**Redskins, 24-21 (W)
1984—49ers, 37-31 (SF)
1985—49ers, 35-8 (W)
1986—Redskins, 14-6 (W)
1988—49ers, 37-21 (SF)
1990—49ers, 26-13 (SF)
*49ers, 28-10 (SF)
1992—*49ers, 20-13 (SF)
1994—49ers, 37-22 (W)
1996—49ers, 19-16 (W) OT
1998—49ers, 45-10 (W)
1999—Redskins, 26-20 (SF) OT
2002—49ers, 20-10 (SF)
(RS Pts.—49ers 532, Redskins 382)
(PS Pts.—49ers 93, Redskins 67)
**NFC Divisional Playoff*
***NFC Championship*

SEATTLE vs. ARIZONA
RS: Cardinals lead series, 6-4;
See Arizona vs. Seattle

SEATTLE vs. ATLANTA
RS: Seahawks lead series, 6-2;
See Atlanta vs. Seattle

SEATTLE vs. BALTIMORE
RS: Ravens lead series, 2-0;
See Baltimore vs. Seattle

SEATTLE vs. BUFFALO
RS: Seahawks lead series, 6-3;
See Buffalo vs. Seattle

SEATTLE vs. CAROLINA
RS: Panthers lead series, 1-0;
See Carolina vs. Seattle

SEATTLE vs. CHICAGO
RS: Seahawks lead series, 6-2;
See Chicago vs. Seattle

SEATTLE vs. CINCINNATI
RS: Series tied, 8-8
PS: Bengals lead series, 1-0;
See Cincinnati vs. Seattle

SEATTLE vs. CLEVELAND
RS: Seahawks lead series, 11-4;
See Cleveland vs. Seattle

SEATTLE vs. DALLAS
RS: Cowboys lead series, 5-3;
See Dallas vs. Seattle

SEATTLE vs. DENVER
RS: Broncos lead series, 33-17
PS: Seahawks lead series, 1-0;
See Denver vs. Seattle

SEATTLE vs. DETROIT
RS: Seahawks lead series, 5-4;
See Detroit vs. Seattle

SEATTLE vs. GREEN BAY
RS: Packers lead series, 5-4
PS: Packers lead series, 1-0;
See Green Bay vs. Seattle

SEATTLE vs. INDIANAPOLIS
RS: Colts lead series, 5-3;
See Indianapolis vs. Seattle

SEATTLE vs. JACKSONVILLE
RS: Seahawks lead series, 3-1;
See Jacksonville vs. Seattle

SEATTLE vs. KANSAS CITY
RS: Chiefs lead series, 30-18;
See Kansas City vs. Seattle

SEATTLE vs. MIAMI
RS: Dolphins lead series, 6-2
PS: Dolphins lead series, 2-1;
See Miami vs. Seattle

SEATTLE vs. MINNESOTA
RS: Seahawks lead series, 5-3;
See Minnesota vs. Seattle

SEATTLE vs. NEW ENGLAND
RS: Seahawks lead series, 7-6;
See New England vs. Seattle

SEATTLE vs. NEW ORLEANS
RS: Series tied, 4-4;
See New Orleans vs. Seattle

SEATTLE vs. N.Y. GIANTS
RS: Giants lead series, 7-3;
See N.Y. Giants vs. Seattle

SEATTLE vs. N.Y. JETS
RS: Seahawks lead series, 8-7;
See N.Y. Jets vs. Seattle

SEATTLE vs. OAKLAND
RS: Raiders lead series, 27-22
PS: Series tied, 1-1;
See Oakland vs. Seattle

SEATTLE vs. PHILADELPHIA
RS: Eagles lead series, 6-3;
See Philadelphia vs. Seattle

SEATTLE vs. PITTSBURGH
RS: Seahawks lead series, 8-6;
See Pittsburgh vs. Seattle

SEATTLE vs. ST. LOUIS
RS: Rams lead series, 7-4;
See St. Louis vs. Seattle

SEATTLE vs. SAN DIEGO
RS: Seahawks lead series, 25-22;
See San Diego vs. Seattle

SEATTLE vs. SAN FRANCISCO
RS: 49ers lead series, 6-4;
See San Francisco vs. Seattle

SEATTLE vs. TAMPA BAY
RS: Seahawks lead series, 4-1
1976—Seahawks, 13-10 (TB)
1977—Seahawks, 30-23 (S)
1994—Seahawks, 22-21 (S)
1996—Seahawks, 17-13 (TB)
1999—Buccaneers, 16-3 (S)
(RS Pts.—Seahawks 85, Buccaneers 83)

SEATTLE vs. *TENNESSEE
RS: Seahawks lead series, 8-4
PS: Titans lead series, 1-0
1977—Oilers, 22-10 (S)
1979—Seahawks, 34-14 (S)
1980—Seahawks, 26-7 (H)
1981—Oilers, 35-17 (H)
1982—Oilers, 23-21 (H)
1987—**Oilers, 23-20 (H) OT
1988—Seahawks, 27-24 (S)
1990—Seahawks, 13-10 (S) OT
1993—Oilers, 24-14 (H)
1994—Seahawks, 16-14 (H)
1996—Seahawks, 23-16 (S)
1997—Seahawks, 16-13 (S)
1998—Seahawks, 20-18 (S)
(RS Pts.—Seahawks 237, Titans 220)
(PS Pts.—Titans 23, Seahawks 20)
**Franchise in Houston prior to 1997; known as Oilers prior to 1999*
***AFC First-Round Playoff*

SEATTLE vs. WASHINGTON
RS: Redskins lead series, 8-4
1976—Redskins, 31-7 (W)
1980—Seahawks, 14-0 (W)
1983—Redskins, 27-17 (S)
1986—Redskins, 19-14 (W)
1989—Redskins, 29-0 (S)
1992—Redskins, 16-3 (S)
1994—Seahawks, 28-7 (W)
1995—Seahawks, 27-20 (W)
1998—Seahawks, 24-14 (S)
2001—Redskins, 27-14 (W)
2002—Redskins, 14-3 (S)
2003—Redskins, 27-20 (W)
(RS Pts.—Redskins 231, Seahawks 171)

TAMPA BAY vs. ARIZONA
RS: Series tied, 7-7;
See Arizona vs. Tampa Bay

TAMPA BAY vs. ATLANTA
RS: Buccaneers lead series, 12-9;
See Atlanta vs. Tampa Bay

TAMPA BAY vs. BALTIMORE
RS: Buccaneers lead series, 2-0;
See Baltimore vs. Tampa Bay

TAMPA BAY vs. BUFFALO
RS: Buccaneers lead series, 5-2;
See Buffalo vs. Tampa Bay

TAMPA BAY vs. CAROLINA
RS: Buccaneers lead series, 4-3;
See Carolina vs. Tampa Bay

TAMPA BAY vs. CHICAGO
RS: Bears lead series, 33-16;
See Chicago vs. Tampa Bay

TAMPA BAY vs. CINCINNATI
RS: Buccaneers lead series, 5-3;
See Cincinnati vs. Tampa Bay

TAMPA BAY vs. CLEVELAND
RS: Browns lead series, 5-1;
See Cleveland vs. Tampa Bay

TAMPA BAY vs. DALLAS
RS: Cowboys lead series, 6-3
PS: Cowboys lead series, 2-0;
See Dallas vs. Tampa Bay

TAMPA BAY vs. DENVER
RS: Broncos lead series, 3-2;
See Denver vs. Tampa Bay

TAMPA BAY vs. DETROIT
RS: Lions lead series, 26-23
PS: Buccaneers lead series, 1-0;
See Detroit vs. Tampa Bay
TAMPA BAY vs. GREEN BAY
RS: Packers lead series, 29-18-1
PS: Packers lead series, 1-0;
See Green Bay vs. Tampa Bay
TAMPA BAY vs. HOUSTON
RS: Buccaneers lead series, 1-0;
See Houston vs. Tampa Bay
TAMPA BAY vs. INDIANAPOLIS
RS: Colts lead series, 6-4;
See Indianapolis vs. Tampa Bay
TAMPA BAY vs. JACKSONVILLE
RS: Jaguars lead series, 2-1;
See Jacksonville vs. Tampa Bay
TAMPA BAY vs. KANSAS CITY
RS: Chiefs lead series, 5-3;
See Kansas City vs. Tampa Bay
TAMPA BAY vs. MIAMI
RS: Dolphins lead series, 4-3;
See Miami vs. Tampa Bay
TAMPA BAY vs. MINNESOTA
RS: Vikings lead series, 31-18;
See Minnesota vs. Tampa Bay
TAMPA BAY vs. NEW ENGLAND
RS: Patriots lead series, 3-2;
See New England vs. Tampa Bay
TAMPA BAY vs. NEW ORLEANS
RS: Saints lead series, 16-8;
See New Orleans vs. Tampa Bay
TAMPA BAY vs. N.Y. GIANTS
RS: Giants lead series, 9-6;
See N.Y. Giants vs. Tampa Bay
TAMPA BAY vs. N.Y. JETS
RS: Jets lead series, 7-1;
See N.Y. Jets vs. Tampa Bay
TAMPA BAY vs. OAKLAND
RS: Raiders lead series, 4-1
PS: Buccaneers lead series, 1-0;
See Oakland vs. Tampa Bay
TAMPA BAY vs. PHILADELPHIA
RS: Eagles lead series, 5-4
PS: Series tied, 2-2;
See Philadelphia vs. Tampa Bay
TAMPA BAY vs. PITTSBURGH
RS: Steelers lead series, 6-1;
See Pittsburgh vs. Tampa Bay
TAMPA BAY vs. ST. LOUIS
RS: Rams lead series, 8-6
PS: Rams lead series, 2-0;
See St. Louis vs. Tampa Bay
TAMPA BAY vs. SAN DIEGO
RS: Chargers lead series, 6-1;
See San Diego vs. Tampa Bay
TAMPA BAY vs. SAN FRANCISCO
RS: 49ers lead series, 13-2
PS: Buccaneers lead series, 1-0;
See San Francisco vs. Tampa Bay
TAMPA BAY vs. SEATTLE
RS: Seahawks lead series, 4-1;
See Seattle vs. Tampa Bay
TAMPA BAY vs. *TENNESSEE
RS: Titans lead series, 7-1
1976—Oilers, 20-0 (H)
1980—Oilers, 20-14 (H)
1983—Buccaneers, 33-24 (TB)
1989—Oilers, 20-17 (H)
1995—Oilers, 19-7 (H)
1998—Oilers, 31-22 (TB)
2001—Titans, 31-28 (Tenn) OT
2003—Titans, 33-13 (T)
(RS Pts.—Titans 198, Buccaneers 134)
**Franchise in Houston prior to 1997; known as Oilers prior to 1999*
TAMPA BAY vs. WASHINGTON
RS: Redskins lead series, 6-5
PS: Buccaneers lead series, 1-0;
1977—Redskins, 10-0 (TB)
1982—Redskins, 21-13 (TB)
1989—Redskins, 32-28 (W)
1993—Redskins, 23-17 (TB)
1994—Buccaneers, 26-21 (TB)
Buccaneers, 17-14 (W)
1995—Buccaneers, 14-6 (TB)
1996—Buccaneers, 24-10 (TB)
1998—Redskins, 20-16 (W)
1999—*Buccaneers, 14-13 (TB)
2000—Redskins, 20-17 (W) OT
2003—Buccaneers, 35-13 (W)
(RS Pts.—Buccaneers 207, Redskins 190)
(PS Pts.—Buccaneers 14, Redskins 13)
**NFC Divisional Playoff*

TENNESSEE VS. ARIZONA
RS: Cardinals lead series, 4-3;
See Arizona vs. Tennessee
TENNESSEE vs. ATLANTA
RS: Titans lead series, 6-5;
See Atlanta vs. Tennessee
TENNESSEE vs. BALTIMORE
RS: Ravens lead series, 7-6
PS: Series tied, 1-1;
See Baltimore vs. Tennessee
TENNESSEE vs. BUFFALO
RS: Titans lead series, 23-14
PS: Bills lead series, 2-1;
See Buffalo vs. Tennessee
TENNESSEE vs. CAROLINA
RS: Series tied, 1-1;
See Carolina vs. Tennessee
TENNESSEE vs. CHICAGO
RS: Series tied, 4-4;
See Chicago vs. Tennessee
TENNESSEE vs. CINCINNATI
RS: Titans lead series, 37-29-1
PS: Bengals lead series, 1-0;
See Cincinnati vs. Tennessee
TENNESSEE vs. CLEVELAND
RS: Browns lead series, 32-26
PS: Titans lead series, 1-0;
See Cleveland vs. Tennessee
TENNESSEE vs. DALLAS
RS: Cowboys lead series, 6-5;
See Dallas vs. Tennessee
TENNESSEE vs. DENVER
RS: Titans lead series, 20-11-1
PS: Broncos lead series, 2-1;
See Denver vs. Tennessee
TENNESSEE vs. DETROIT
RS: Titans lead series, 5-3;
See Detroit vs. Tennessee
TENNESSEE vs. GREEN BAY
RS: Series tied, 4-4;
See Green Bay vs. Tennessee
TENNESSEE vs. HOUSTON
RS: Titans lead series, 4-0;
See Houston vs. Tennessee
TENNESSEE vs. INDIANAPOLIS
RS: Series tied, 9-9
PS: Titans lead series, 1-0;
See Indianapolis vs. Tennessee
TENNESSEE vs. JACKSONVILLE
RS: Titans lead series, 11-7
PS: Titans lead series, 1-0;
See Jacksonville vs. Tennessee
TENNESSEE vs. KANSAS CITY
RS: Chiefs lead series, 24-18
PS: Chiefs lead series, 2-0;
See Kansas City vs. Tennessee
TENNESSEE vs. MIAMI
RS: Dolphins lead series, 15-12
PS: Titans lead series, 1-0;
See Miami vs. Tennessee
TENNESSEE vs. MINNESOTA
RS: Vikings lead series, 6-3;
See Minnesota vs. Tennessee
TENNESSEE vs. NEW ENGLAND
RS: Patriots lead series, 19-15-1
PS: Series tied, 1-1;
See New England vs. Tennessee
TENNESSEE vs. NEW ORLEANS
RS: Titans lead series, 6-4-1;
See New Orleans vs. Tennessee
TENNESSEE vs. N.Y. GIANTS
RS: Giants lead series, 5-3;
See N.Y. Giants vs. Tennessee
TENNESSEE vs. N.Y. JETS
RS: Titans lead series, 20-14-1
PS: Titans lead series, 1-0;
See N.Y. Jets vs. Tennessee
TENNESSEE vs. OAKLAND
RS: Raiders lead series, 21-17
PS: Raiders lead series, 4-0;
See Oakland vs. Tennessee
TENNESSEE vs. PHILADELPHIA
RS: Eagles lead series, 6-2;
See Philadelphia vs. Tennessee
TENNESSEE vs. PITTSBURGH
RS: Steelers lead series, 37-28
PS: Steelers lead series, 3-1;
See Pittsburgh vs. Tennessee
TENNESSEE vs. ST. LOUIS
RS: Rams lead series, 5-3
PS: Rams lead series, 1-0;
See St. Louis vs. Tennessee
TENNESSEE vs. SAN DIEGO
RS: Chargers lead series, 19-13-1
PS: Titans lead series, 3-0;
See San Diego vs. Tennessee
TENNESSEE vs. SAN FRANCISCO
RS: 49ers lead series, 7-3;
See San Francisco vs. Tennessee
TENNESSEE vs. SEATTLE
RS: Seahawks lead series, 8-4
PS: Titans lead series, 1-0;
See Seattle vs. Tennessee
TENNESSEE vs. TAMPA BAY
RS: Titans lead series, 7-1;
See Tampa Bay vs. Tennessee
***TENNESSEE vs. WASHINGTON**
RS: Titans lead series, 5-4
1971—Redskins, 22-13 (W)
1975—Oilers, 13-10 (H)
1979—Oilers, 29-27 (W)
1985—Redskins, 16-13 (W)
1988—Oilers, 41-17 (H)
1991—Redskins, 16-13 (W) OT

1997—Oilers, 28-14 (T)
2000—Titans, 27-21 (W)
2002—Redskins, 31-14 (T)
(RS—Titans 191, Redskins 174)
**Franchise in Houston prior to 1997; known as Oilers prior to 1999*

WASHINGTON vs. ARIZONA
RS: Redskins lead series, 70-44-2;
See Arizona vs. Washington
WASHINGTON vs. ATLANTA
RS: Redskins lead series, 14-4-1
PS: Redskins lead series, 1-0;
See Atlanta vs. Washington
WASHINGTON vs BALTIMORE
RS: Series tied, 1-1;
See Baltimore vs. Washington
WASHINGTON vs. BUFFALO
RS: Bills lead series, 6-4
PS: Redskins lead series, 1-0;
See Buffalo vs. Washington
WASHINGTON vs. CAROLINA
RS: Redskins lead series, 6-1;
See Carolina vs. Washington
WASHINGTON vs. CHICAGO
RS: Bears lead series, 20-15-1
PS: Redskins lead series, 4-3;
See Chicago vs. Washington
WASHINGTON vs. CINCINNATI
RS: Redskins lead series, 4-2;
See Cincinnati vs. Washington
WASHINGTON vs. CLEVELAND
RS: Browns lead series, 32-9-1;
See Cleveland vs. Washington
WASHINGTON vs. DALLAS
RS: Cowboys lead series, 52-32-2
PS: Redskins lead series, 2-0;
See Dallas vs. Washington
WASHINGTON vs. DENVER
RS: Broncos lead series, 5-4
PS: Redskins lead series, 1-0;
See Denver vs. Washington
WASHINGTON vs. DETROIT
RS: Redskins lead series, 24-10
PS: Redskins lead series, 3-0;
See Detroit vs. Washington
WASHINGTON vs. GREEN BAY
RS: Packers lead series, 15-12-1
PS: Series tied, 1-1;
See Green Bay vs. Washington
WASHINGTON vs. HOUSTON
RS: Redskins lead series, 1-0;
See Houston vs. Washington
WASHINGTON vs. INDIANAPOLIS
RS: Colts lead series, 17-10;
See Indianapolis vs. Washington
WASHINGTON vs. JACKSONVILLE
RS: Redskins lead series, 2-1;
See Jacksonville vs. Washington
WASHINGTON vs. KANSAS CITY
RS: Chiefs lead series, 5-1;
See Kansas City vs. Washington
WASHINGTON vs. MIAMI
RS: Dolphins lead series, 6-3
PS: Series tied, 1-1;
See Miami vs. Washington
WASHINGTON vs. MINNESOTA
RS: Redskins lead series, 6-5
PS: Redskins lead series, 3-2;
See Minnesota vs. Washington
WASHINGTON vs. NEW ENGLAND
RS: Redskins lead series, 6-1;
See New England vs. Washington
WASHINGTON vs. NEW ORLEANS
RS: Redskins lead series, 13-7;
See New Orleans vs. Washington
WASHINGTON vs. N.Y. GIANTS
RS: Giants lead series, 80-58-4
PS: Series tied, 1-1;
See N.Y. Giants vs. Washington
WASHINGTON vs. N.Y. JETS
RS: Redskins lead series, 7-1;
See N.Y. Jets vs. Washington
WASHINGTON vs. OAKLAND
RS: Raiders lead series, 6-3
PS: Raiders lead series, 1-0;
See Oakland vs. Washington
WASHINGTON vs. PHILADELPHIA
RS: Redskins lead series, 72-60-5
PS: Redskins lead series, 1-0;
See Philadelphia vs. Washington
WASHINGTON vs. PITTSBURGH
RS: Redskins lead series, 42-29-3;
See Pittsburgh vs. Washington
WASHINGTON vs. ST. LOUIS
RS: Redskins lead series, 19-6-1
PS: Series tied, 2-2;
See St. Louis vs. Washington
WASHINGTON vs. SAN DIEGO
RS: Redskins lead series, 6-1;
See San Diego vs. Washington
WASHINGTON vs. SAN FRANCISCO
RS: 49ers lead series, 13-7-1
PS: 49ers lead series, 3-1;
See San Francisco vs. Washington
WASHINGTON vs. SEATTLE
RS: Redskins lead series, 8-4;
See Seattle vs. Washington
WASHINGTON vs. TAMPA BAY
RS: Redskins lead series, 6-5
PS: Buccaneers lead series, 1-0;
See Tampa Bay vs. Washington
WASHINGTON vs. TENNESSEE
RS: Titans lead series, 5-4;
See Tennessee vs. Washington

SUPER BOWL COMPOSITE STANDINGS

	W	L	Pct.	Pts.	OP
San Francisco 49ers	5	0	1.000	188	89
Baltimore Ravens	1	0	1.000	34	7
Chicago Bears	1	0	1.000	46	10
New York Jets	1	0	1.000	16	7
Tampa Bay Buccaneers	1	0	1.000	48	21
Pittsburgh Steelers	4	1	.800	120	100
Green Bay Packers	3	1	.750	127	76
New York Giants	2	1	.667	66	73
Dallas Cowboys	5	3	.625	221	132
Oakland/L.A. Raiders	3	2	.600	132	114
Washington Redskins	3	2	.600	122	103
New England Patriots	2	2	.500	83	127
Baltimore Colts	1	1	.500	23	29
Kansas City Chiefs	1	1	.500	33	42
Miami Dolphins	2	3	.400	74	103
Denver Broncos	2	4	.333	115	206
St. Louis/L.A. Rams	1	2	.333	59	67
Atlanta Falcons	0	1	.000	19	34
Carolina Panthers	0	1	.000	29	32
Philadelphia Eagles	0	1	.000	10	27
San Diego Chargers	0	1	.000	26	49
Tennessee Titans	0	1	.000	16	23
Cincinnati Bengals	0	2	.000	37	46
Buffalo Bills	0	4	.000	73	139
Minnesota Vikings	0	4	.000	34	95

SUPER BOWL HOST CITIES

New Orleans	9	
Miami	8	
Los Angeles	7	(LA Coliseum 2, Rose Bowl 5)
San Diego	3	
Tampa	3	
Atlanta	2	
Houston	2	
Detroit	1	
Minneapolis	1	
Tempe	1	
Stanford	1	

FUTURE SUPER BOWL SITES

Super Bowl XXXIX	February 6, 2005	ALLTEL Stadium, Jacksonville, Florida
Super Bowl XL	February 5, 2006	Ford Field, Detroit, Michigan
Super Bowl XLI	February 4, 2007	Pro Player Stadium, Miami, Florida
Super Bowl XLII	February 3, 2008	Cardinals Stadium, Glendale, Arizona

SUPER BOWL MOST VALUABLE PLAYERS*

Super Bowl I	— QB Bart Starr, Green Bay
Super Bowl II	— QB Bart Starr, Green Bay
Super Bowl III	— QB Joe Namath, N.Y. Jets
Super Bowl IV	— QB Len Dawson, Kansas City
Super Bowl V	— LB Chuck Howley, Dallas
Super Bowl VI	— QB Roger Staubach, Dallas
Super Bowl VII	— S Jake Scott, Miami
Super Bowl VIII	— RB Larry Csonka, Miami
Super Bowl IX	— RB Franco Harris, Pittsburgh
Super Bowl X	— WR Lynn Swann, Pittsburgh
Super Bowl XI	— WR Fred Biletnikoff, Oakland
Super Bowl XII	— DT Randy White and DE Harvey Martin, Dallas
Super Bowl XIII	— QB Terry Bradshaw, Pittsburgh
Super Bowl XIV	— QB Terry Bradshaw, Pittsburgh
Super Bowl XV	— QB Jim Plunkett, Oakland
Super Bowl XVI	— QB Joe Montana, San Francisco
Super Bowl XVII	— RB John Riggins, Washington
Super Bowl XVIII	— RB Marcus Allen, L.A. Raiders
Super Bowl XIX	— QB Joe Montana, San Francisco
Super Bowl XX	— DE Richard Dent, Chicago
Super Bowl XXI	— QB Phil Simms, N.Y. Giants
Super Bowl XXII	— QB Doug Williams, Washington
Super Bowl XXIII	— WR Jerry Rice, San Francisco
Super Bowl XXIV	— QB Joe Montana, San Francisco
Super Bowl XXV	— RB Ottis Anderson, N.Y. Giants
Super Bowl XXVI	— QB Mark Rypien, Washington
Super Bowl XXVII	— QB Troy Aikman, Dallas
Super Bowl XXVIII	— RB Emmitt Smith, Dallas
Super Bowl XXIX	— QB Steve Young, San Francisco
Super Bowl XXX	— CB Larry Brown, Dallas
Super Bowl XXXI	— KR-PR Desmond Howard, Green Bay
Super Bowl XXXII	— RB Terrell Davis, Denver
Super Bowl XXXIII	— QB John Elway, Denver
Super Bowl XXXIV	— QB Kurt Warner, St. Louis
Super Bowl XXXV	— LB Ray Lewis, Baltimore
Super Bowl XXXVI	— QB Tom Brady, New England
Super Bowl XXXVII	— S Dexter Jackson, Tampa Bay
Super Bowl XXXVIII	— QB Tom Brady, New England

** Award named Pete Rozelle Trophy since Super Bowl XXV.*

SUPER BOWL MVP BY POSITION

Quarterback	20
Running Back	7
Wide Receiver	3
Defensive End	2
Linebacker	2
Safety	2
Cornerback	1
Defensive Tackle	1
Kick Returner-Punt Returner	1

A defensive end and defensive tackle shared the Super Bowl XII MVP award.

RESULTS

NFC leads AFC, 21-17

Super Bowl	Date	Winner (Share)	Loser (Share)	Score	Site	Attendance
XXXVIII	2-1-04	New England ($68,000)	Carolina ($36,500)	32-29	Houston	71,525
* XXXVII	1-26-03	Tampa Bay ($63,000)	Oakland ($35,000)	48-21	San Diego	67,603
* XXXVI	2-3-02	New England ($63,000)	St. Louis ($34,500)	20-17	New Orleans	72,922
XXXV	1-28-01	Baltimore ($58,000)	N.Y. Giants ($34,500)	34-7	Tampa	71,921
* XXXIV	1-30-00	St. Louis ($58,000)	Tennessee ($33,000)	23-16	Atlanta	72,625
XXXIII	1-31-99	Denver ($53,000)	Atlanta ($32,500)	34-19	Miami	74,803
XXXII	1-25-98	Denver ($48,000)	Green Bay ($29,000)	31-24	San Diego	68,912
XXXI	1-26-97	Green Bay ($48,000)	New England ($29,000)	35-21	New Orleans	72,301
XXX	1-28-96	Dallas ($42,000)	Pittsburgh ($27,000)	27-17	Tempe	76,347
XXIX	1-29-95	San Francisco ($42,000)	San Diego ($26,000)	49-26	Miami	74,107
* XXVIII	1-30-94	Dallas ($38,000)	Buffalo ($23,500)	30-13	Atlanta	72,817
XXVII	1-31-93	Dallas ($36,000)	Buffalo ($18,000)	52-17	Pasadena	98,374
XXVI	1-26-92	Washington ($36,000)	Buffalo ($18,000)	37-24	Minneapolis	63,130
* XXV	1-27-91	N.Y. Giants ($36,000)	Buffalo ($18,000)	20-19	Tampa	73,813
XXIV	1-28-90	San Francisco ($36,000)	Denver ($18,000)	55-10	New Orleans	72,919
XXIII	1-22-89	San Francisco ($36,000)	Cincinnati ($18,000)	20-16	Miami	75,129
XXII	1-31-88	Washington ($36,000)	Denver ($18,000)	42-10	San Diego	73,302
XXI	1-25-87	N.Y. Giants ($36,000)	Denver ($18,000)	39-20	Pasadena	101,063
XX	1-26-86	Chicago ($36,000)	New England ($18,000)	46-10	New Orleans	73,818
XIX	1-20-85	San Francisco ($36,000)	Miami ($18,000)	38-16	Stanford	84,059
XVIII	1-22-84	L.A. Raiders ($36,000)	Washington ($18,000)	38-9	Tampa	72,920
* XVII	1-30-83	Washington ($36,000)	Miami ($18,000)	27-17	Pasadena	103,667
XVI	1-24-82	San Francisco ($18,000)	Cincinnati ($9,000)	26-21	Pontiac	81,270
XV	1-25-81	Oakland ($18,000)	Philadelphia ($9,000)	27-10	New Orleans	76,135
XIV	1-20-80	Pittsburgh ($18,000)	Los Angeles ($9,000)	31-19	Pasadena	103,985
XIII	1-21-79	Pittsburgh ($18,000)	Dallas ($9,000)	35-31	Miami	79,484
XII	1-15-78	Dallas ($18,000)	Denver ($9,000)	27-10	New Orleans	75,583
XI	1-9-77	Oakland ($15,000)	Minnesota ($7,500)	32-14	Pasadena	103,438
X	1-18-76	Pittsburgh ($15,000)	Dallas ($7,500)	21-17	Miami	80,187
IX	1-12-75	Pittsburgh ($15,000)	Minnesota ($7,500)	16-6	New Orleans	80,997
VIII	1-13-74	Miami ($15,000)	Minnesota ($7,500)	24-7	Houston	71,882
VII	1-14-73	Miami ($15,000)	Washington ($7,500)	14-7	Los Angeles	90,182
VI	1-16-72	Dallas ($15,000)	Miami ($7,500)	24-3	New Orleans	81,023
V	1-17-71	Baltimore ($15,000)	Dallas ($7,500)	16-13	Miami	79,204
* IV	1-11-70	Kansas City ($15,000)	Minnesota ($7,500)	23-7	New Orleans	80,562
III	1-12-69	N.Y. Jets ($15,000)	Baltimore ($7,500)	16-7	Miami	75,389
II	1-14-68	Green Bay ($15,000)	Oakland ($7,500)	33-14	Miami	75,546
I	1-15-67	Green Bay ($15,000)	Kansas City ($7,500)	35-10	Los Angeles	61,946

** One week between conference championship games and Super Bowl; all others had two weeks between conference championship games and Super Bowl.*

SUPER BOWL XXXVIII

Reliant Stadium, Houston, Texas

February 1, 2004, Attendance: 71,525

NEW ENGLAND 32, CAROLINA 29—Adam Vinatieri kicked a 41-yard field goal with four seconds remaining as the Patriots won their second Super Bowl in three seasons. While it took a Super Bowl-record 26 minutes and 55 seconds for the first points to be scored, the teams combined for 868 yards (481 by New England) and the game also featured the highest scoring quarter (combined 37 points in the fourth). Vinatieri missed a 31-yard field goal on the Patriots' first possession, and had a 36-yard attempt blocked by Shane Burton with 6:00 left in the second quarter. But three plays later, Mike Vrabel sacked Jake Delhomme and forced him to fumble. Richard Seymour recovered at the Panthers' 20, and a 12-yard scramble by Tom Brady on third-and-7 set up his 5-yard touchdown pass to Deion Branch with 3:05 left in the first half. The Panthers responded with an 8-play, 95-yard drive capped by Delhomme's 39-yard perfectly placed touchdown pass to Steve Smith with 1:07 left in the half. Delhomme beat the blitz by lofting the pass deep down the left sideline. Brady's 52-yard pass to Branch with 37 seconds left in the half set up David Givens' 5-yard touchdown catch with 18 seconds left. New England squibbed the ensuing kickoff and Kris Mangum returned it 12 yards to the Panthers' 47. A 21-yard run by Stephen Davis set up John Kasay's 50-yard field goal as the half expired for a 14-10 New England lead. Neither team scored in the third quarter, but Antowain Smith's 2-yard touchdown run two plays into the final quarter capped a 71-yard drive and gave the Patriots a 21-10 lead. Undaunted, Carolina scored on its next two possessions. First, Delhomme completed passes of 18 and 22 yards to Smith to set up DeShaun Foster's 33-yard touchdown run to cut the deficit to 21-16 with 12:39 to play. Carolina went for the 2-point conversion, but Delhomme's pass was incomplete. New England marched to the Panthers' 9 with the ensuing kickoff, but Reggie Howard intercepted Brady's third-and-goal pass in the end zone. Two plays later, Delhomme rolled left and fired a Super Bowl-record 85-yard touchdown pass to Muhammad for a 22-21 lead with 6:53 left. Once again, the Panthers went for 2 points and Delhomme's pass was incomplete. New England drove 68 yards on its next possession, with Givens catching a 25-yard pass and 18-yard pass on third-and-9, to set up Brady's 1-yard touchdown pass to Vrabel, who was lined up as a tight end. A direct snap to Kevin Faulk resulted in a 2-point conversion for a 29-22 lead with

2:51 left. Delhomme completed passes of 19 yards to Muhammad and 31 yards to Ricky Proehl before finding Proehl from 12 yards with the tying touchdown with 1:08 remaining. Kasay's ensuing kickoff went out of bounds, giving New England the ball at their own 40. Five plays later, faced with third-and-3 from the Panthers' 40 with 14 seconds left, Brady fired a 17-yard pass to Branch to set up Vinatieri's Super Bowl-winning 41-yard field goal. Brady, who was named the Super Bowl most valuable player for the second time in his career, was 32 of 48 for 354 yards and 3 touchdowns, with 1 interception. Branch had 10 receptions for 143 yards. Delhomme was 16 of 33 for 323 yards and 3 touchdowns, and Muhammad had 4 catches for 140 yards.

Carolina (29)	Offense	New England (32)
Muhsin Muhammad	WR	Deion Branch
Todd Steussie	LT	Matt Light
Jeno James	LG	Russ Hochstein
Jeff Mitchell	C	Dan Koppen
Kevin Donnalley	RG	Joe Andruzzi
Jordan Gross	RT	Tom Ashworth
Jermaine Wiggins	TE	Daniel Graham
Steve Smith	WR	Troy Brown
Jake Delhomme	QB	Tom Brady
Brad Hoover	FB	Larry Centers
Stephen Davis	RB	Antowain Smith
	Defense	
Julius Peppers	LE	Bobby Hamilton
Brentson Buckner	LT-NT	Ted Washington
Kris Jenkins	RT-RE	Richard Seymour
Mike Rucker	RE-OLB	Willie McGinest
Greg Favors	SLB-ILB	Tedy Bruschi
Dan Morgan	MLB-ILB	Roman Phifer
Will Witherspoon	WLB-OLB	Mike Vrabel
Ricky Manning Jr.	LCB	Ty Law
Reggie Howard	RCB	Tyrone Poole
Mike Minter	SS	Eugene Wilson
Deon Grant	FS	Rodney Harrison

SUBSTITUTIONS

CAROLINA—Specialists: K—John Kasay. P—Todd Sauerbrun. Offense: RB—DeShaun Foster, Rod Smart, Nick Goings. WR—Ricky Proehl, Kevin Dyson, Karl Hankton. TE—Kris Mangum. G—Bruce Nelson. T—Matt Willig. Defense: DE—Kemp Rasmussen, Al Wallace. DT—Shane Burton. LB—Brian Allen, Vinny Ciurciu, Jason Kyle, Lester Towns. CB—Jarrod Cooper, Terry Cousin, Dante Wesley. S—Colin Branch. DNP: QB—Rodney Peete. Inactive: QB—Chris Weinke. WR—Eugene Baker. TE—Marco Battaglia. G—Doug Brzezinski. G-T—Tutan Reyes. DT—Kindal Moorehead. CB—William Hampton. S—Traveres Tillman.

NEW ENGLAND—Specialists: K—Adam Vinatieri. P—Ken Walter. LS—Brian Kinchen. Offense: RB—Kevin Faulk. FB—Patrick Pass. WR—David Givens, Bethel Johnson, Dedric Ward. TE—Christian Fauria. G—Wilbert Brown. Defense: DE-DT—Jarvis Green, Ty Warren. LB—Tully Banta-Cain, Matt Chatham, Don Davis, Larry Izzo, Ted Johnson. CB—Asante Samuel. S—Chris Akins, Je'Rod Cherry, Shawn Mayer. DNP: QB—Damon Huard. T—Brandon Gorin. Inactive: QB—Rohan Davey. RB—Mike Cloud. WR—J.J. Stokes. TE—Fred Baxter. DE—Anthony Pleasant. DT—Dan Klecko. DE-DT—Rick Lyle. CB—Antwan Harris.

OFFICIALS

Referee—Ed Hochuli. Umpire—Jeff Rice. Line Judge—Ben Montgomery. Side Judge—Laird Hayes. Head Linesman—Mark Hittner. Back Judge—Scott Green. Field Judge—Tom Sifferman. Replay Official—Larry Hill. Video Operator—Gene Cunningham.

SCORING

Carolina (NFC)	0	10	0	19	—29
New England (AFC)	0	14	0	18	—32

NE — Branch 5 pass from Brady (Vinatieri kick) (3:05)
Car— Smith 39 pass from Delhomme (Kasay kick) (1:07)
NE — Givens 5 pass from Brady (Vinatieri kick) (0:18)
Car— FG Kasay 50 (0:00)
NE — Smith 2 run (Vinatieri kick) (14:49)
Car— Foster 33 run (pass failed) (12:39)
Car— Muhammad 85 pass from Delhomme (pass failed) (6:53)
NE — Vrabel 1 pass from Brady (Faulk run) (2:51)
Car— Proehl 12 pass from Delhomme (Kasay kick) (1:08)
NE — FG Vinatieri 41 (0:04)

TEAM STATISTICS	CAR	NE
Total First Downs	17	29
Rushing	3	7
Passing	12	19
Penalty	2	3
Total Net Yardage	387	481
Total Offensive Plays	53	83
Avg. Gain Per Offensive Play	7.3	5.8
Rushes	16	35
Yards Gained Rushing (Net)	92	127
Avg. Yards per Rush	5.8	3.6
Passes Attempted	33	48
Passes Completed	16	32
Had Intercepted	0	1
Tackled Attempting to Pass	4	0
Yards Lost Attempting to Pass	28	0
Yards Gained Passing (Net)	295	354
Punts	7	5
Avg. Distance	44.3	34.6
Punt Returns	1	5
Punt Return Yardage	2	42
Kickoff Returns	6	4
Kickoff Return Yardage	116	78
Interception Return Yardage	12	0
Total Return Yardage	130	120
Fumbles	1	1
Fumbles Lost	1	0
Own Fumbles Recovered	0	1
Opponent Fumbles Recovered	0	1
Penalties	12	8
Yards Penalized	73	60
Field Goals	1	1
Field Goals Attempted	1	3
Third-Down Efficiency	4/12	8/17
Fourth-Down Efficiency	0/0	1/1
Time of Possession	21:02	38:58

INDIVIDUAL STATISTICS

RUSHING: CAR: Davis 13-49-0. Foster 3-43-1. NE: Smith 26-83-1, Faulk 6-42-0, Brady 2-12-0, Brown 1-(-10)-0.
PASSING: CAR: Delhomme 33-16-323-3-0. NE: Brady 48-32-354-3-1.
RECEIVING: CAR: Muhammad 4-140-1, Smith 4-80-1, Proehl 4-71-1, Wiggins 2-21-0, Foster 1-9-0, Mangum 1-2-0. NE: Branch 10-143-1, Brown 8-76-0, Givens 5-69-1, Graham 4-46-0, Faulk 4-19-0, Vrabel 1-1-1.
KICKOFF RETURNS: CAR: Smart 4-74-0, Smith 1-30-0, Mangum 1-12-0. NE: B. Johnson 4-78-0.
PUNT RETURNS: CAR: Smith 1-2-0. NE: Brown 4-40-0, Branch 1-2-0.
PUNTING: CAR: Sauerbrun 7-310-44.3. NE: Walter 5-173-34.6.
INTERCEPTIONS: CAR: Howard 1-12-0. NE: None.
SACKS: CAR: None. NE: Vrabel 2, Harrison, McGinest.

SUPER BOWL XXXVII

Qualcomm Stadium, San Diego, CA
January 26, 2003, Attendance: 67,603

TAMPA BAY 48, OAKLAND 21—The Buccaneers' defense intercepted 5 passes, 3 of which were returned for touchdowns, and recorded 5 sacks as Tampa Bay scored 34 unanswered points en route to its first Super Bowl victory. Charles Woodson intercepted Brad Johnson three plays into the game to give Oakland the ball at the Buccaneers' 36. But Simeon Rice sacked Rich Gannon on third down to force the Raiders to settle for Sebastian Janikowski's 40-yard field goal. On their next nine possessions, the Raiders registered just 2 first downs and did not run a play inside the Buccaneers' 40 as Tampa Bay scored the next 34 points. The Buccaneers answered Janikowski's field goal with Martín Gramatica's 31-yard boot to tie the game. An interception by Dexter Jackson set up Gramatica's go-ahead field goal early in the second quarter. Midway through the second quarter, a 25-yard punt return by Karl Williams and a 19-yard run by Michael Pittman led to Mike Alstott's 2-yard touchdown run. Late in the half, the Buccaneers drove 77 yards, aided by 3 defensive penalties and pass receptions of 16 and 12 yards by Alstott, to set up Brad Johnson's 5-yard touchdown pass to Keenan McCardell with 30 seconds left in the half, which gave Tampa Bay a 20-3 lead. With their first possession of the second half, the Buccaneers put together a 14-play, 89-yard drive that consumed 7:52 and was culminated by Johnson's 8-yard scoring toss to McCardell. Two plays later, Dwight

Smith intercepted Gannon's pass and returned it 44 yards for a touchdown and a 34-3 lead with 4:47 left in the third quarter. Tampa Bay scored 4 touchdowns in a span of 16:37. Jerry Porter's 39-yard touchdown catch in the back of the end zone made it 34-9. Less than three minutes later, Tim Johnson blocked Tom Tupa's punt. Eric Johnson caught the ball and dove into the end zone for a touchdown to cut the deficit to 34-15 with 14:16 remaining. The Buccaneers drove deep downfield again, but Tupa mishandled the snap for a field-goal attempt, allowing the Raiders to regain possession. Gannon hit Jerry Rice with a 48-yard touchdown pass with 6:06 left to trim the lead to 34-21. A 9-yard pass by Johnson to Alstott on third-and-7 allowed Tampa Bay to take another two minutes off the clock before Tupa punted with 2:44 remaining. On third-and-18 from the Raiders' 29, Derrick Brooks intercepted Gannon's pass and raced 44 yards down the left sideline for a touchdown with 1:18 remaining to give Tampa Bay a commanding 41-21 lead. Smith intercepted a tipped pass and returned it 50 yards for a touchdown with two seconds left to finish the scoring. Johnson was 18 of 34 for 215 yards and 2 touchdowns, with 1 interception. Pittman had 29 carries for 124 yards. Gannon was 24 of 44 for 272 yards and 2 touchdowns, with a Super Bowl record 5 interceptions. Jackson, who had the first 2 interceptions, 1 of which led to the go-ahead field goal, was named the game's most valuable player.

Oakland (AFC)	3	0	6	12	— 21
Tampa Bay (NFC)	3	17	14	14	— 48

Oak — FG Janikowski 40 (10:40)
TB — FG Gramatica 31 (7:51)
TB — FG Gramatica 43 (11:16)
TB — Alstott 2 run (Gramatica kick) (6:24)
TB — McCardell 5 pass from B. Johnson (Gramatica kick) (0:30)
TB — McCardell 8 pass from B. Johnson (Gramatica kick) (5:30)
TB — D. Smith 44 interception return (Gramatica kick) (4:47)
Oak — Porter 39 pass from Gannon (pass failed) (2:14)
Oak — E. Johnson 13 return of blocked punt (pass failed) (14:16)
Oak — Rice 48 pass from Gannon (pass failed) (6:06)
TB — Brooks 44 interception return (Gramatica kick) (1:18)
TB — D. Smith 50 interception return (Gramatica kick) (0:02)

SUPER BOWL XXXVI
Louisiana Superdome, New Orleans, LA
February 3, 2002, Attendance: 72,922
NEW ENGLAND 20, ST. LOUIS 17—Adam Vinatieri's 48-yard field goal as time expired gave the New England Patriots their first Super Bowl title. The Rams outgained the Patriots 427-267 in total yards, but the Patriots forced 3 turnovers, which resulted in 17 points, while committing no turnovers. Jeff Wilkins' 50-yard field goal capped a 10-play, 48-yard drive midway through the first quarter to give the Rams a 3-0 lead. The first turnover came with 8:49 left in the second quarter, when Ty Law stepped in front of an out-pattern pass intended for Isaac Bruce and raced 47 yards untouched down the left sideline into the end zone. Late in the first half, Kurt Warner completed a 15-yard pass to Ricky Proehl to the Patriots' 40, but Antwan Harris forced Proehl to fumble and Terrell Buckley recovered. Five plays later, Tom Brady's 8-yard touchdown pass to David Patten with 31 seconds left in the quarter gave New England a 14-3 halftime lead. Late in the third quarter, Torry Holt slipped coming off the line of scrimmage, and Otis Smith intercepted Warner's pass and returned it 30 yards to the Rams' 33 to set up Vinatieri's 37-yard field goal and a 17-3 lead. The Rams responded by driving to the Patriots' 3. On fourth-and-goal, Warner scrambled, was tackled by Roman Phifer, and fumbled. Tebucky Jones picked up the ball and raced the length of the field for an apparent touchdown, but the play was negated by Willie McGinest's holding penalty. Warner scored two plays later to trim the deficit to 17-10 with 9:31 left. The Patriots went three and out on their next two possessions, giving the Rams the ball on their 45-yard-line with 1:51 left. Warner completed an 18-yard pass to Az-Zahir Hakim and an 11-yard pass to Yo Murphy before connecting on a 26-yard touchdown pass to Proehl with 1:30 left to tie the game. Operating without any time outs, Brady completed 3 short passes to J.R. Redmond to reach the Patriots' 41 with 33 seconds left. After an incompletion, Brady completed 23- and 16-yard passes to Troy Brown and Jermaine Wiggins, respectively, to reach the Rams' 30, and then spiked the ball with 7 seconds remaining. Vinatieri drilled the 48-yard field-goal attempt, marking the first time in Super Bowl history the game had been won on the final play. Brady, who earned most valuable player honors, was 16 of 27 for 145 yards and 1 touchdown. Warner was 28 of 44 for 365 yards and 1 touchdown, with 2 interceptions.

St. Louis (NFC)	3	0	0	14	— 17
New England (AFC)	0	14	3	3	— 20

StL — FG Wilkins 50 (11:50)
NE — Law 47 interception return (Vinatieri kick) (6:11)
NE — Patten 8 pass from Brady (Vinatieri kick) (14:29)
NE — FG Vinatieri 37 (13:42)
StL — Warner 2 run (Wilkins kick) (5:29)
StL — Proehl 26 pass from Warner (Wilkins kick) (13:30)
NE — FG Vinatieri 48 (15:00)

SUPER BOWL XXXV
Raymond James Stadium, Tampa, Florida
January 28, 2001, Attendance: 71,921
BALTIMORE 34, N.Y. GIANTS 7—The Ravens' defense completed a dominating season by permitting just 152 yards, forcing 5 turnovers, recording 4 sacks, and not allowing an offensive touchdown en route to the franchise's first Super Bowl victory. Jermaine Lewis' punt return into Giants' territory midway through the first quarter was followed two plays later by Trent Dilfer's 38-yard touchdown pass to Brandon Stokley, which gave the Ravens a 7-0 lead. Early in the second quarter, Jessie Armstead intercepted a short pass by Dilfer and returned it 43 yards for a touchdown, but the play was nullified by a penalty. Dilfer's 36-yard pass to Qadry Ismail in the second quarter set up Matt Stover's 47-yard field goal with 1:48 left in the half. Tiki Barber's 27-yard run gave the Giants their deepest penetration of the game, to the Ravens' 29, but Chris McAlister intercepted Kerry Collins' pass on the next play to preserve a 10-0 lead. In the third quarter, Duane Starks stepped in front of Amani Toomer and intercepted Collins' pass. Starks returned it 49 yards untouched for a 17-0 lead. The Giants immediately cut the lead to 10 points when Ron Dixon returned the ensuing kickoff 97 yards for a touchdown. However, Jermaine Lewis then matched Dixon's kickoff return as he cut across the field and raced 84 yards for a 24-7 lead with 3:13 left in the third quarter. The 3 touchdowns in 36 seconds were a Super Bowl record. The Giants gained just 1 first down on their final four possessions. Jamal Lewis' 3-yard touchdown run midway through the fourth quarter gave Baltimore a 31-7 lead, and Robert Bailey recovered Dixon's fumble on the ensuing kickoff return to set up Stover's 34-yard field goal with 5:27 remaining to finish the scoring. Dilfer completed 12 of 25 passes for 153 yards and 1 touchdown. Jamal Lewis had 27 carries for 102 yards. Collins was 15 of 39 for 112 yards, with 4 interceptions. Ray Lewis was named Super Bowl most valuable player.

Baltimore (AFC)	7	3	14	10	— 34
N.Y. Giants (NFC)	0	0	7	0	— 7

Balt — Stokley 38 pass from Dilfer (Stover kick) (8:10)
Balt — FG Stover 47 (13:19)
Balt — Starks 49 interception return (Stover kick) (11:11)
NYG — Dixon 97 kickoff return (Daluiso kick) (11:29)
Balt — Je. Lewis 84 kickoff return (Stover kick) (11:47)

Balt — Ja. Lewis 3 run (Stover kick) (6:15)
Balt — FG Stover 34 (9:33)

SUPER BOWL XXXIV
Georgia Dome, Atlanta, Georgia
January 30, 2000, Attendance: 72,625

ST. LOUIS 23, TENNESSEE 16—Mike Jones tackled Kevin Dyson at the 1-yard line as time expired, preserving the Rams' first-ever Super Bowl title. The Rams drove inside the Titans' 20 with each of their first six possessions, but compiled just 3 field goals and 1 touchdown to take a 16-0 lead. Holder Mike Horan's bobbled snap averted a 35-yard field-goal attempt to conclude the Rams' first drive. The Titans responded with a 42-yard drive, their longest of the half, but Al Del Greco missed a 47-yard attempt. Jeff Wilkins added 3 field goals and missed a 34-yard attempt while the Titans did not threaten the rest of the half, giving the Rams a 9-0 lead at intermission despite outgaining the Titans in total yards (294-89). Tennessee drove 43 yards with the second half's opening kickoff, but Todd Lyght blocked Del Greco's 47-yard attempt to keep the Titans off the board. Kurt Warner's 31-yard pass to Isaac Bruce keyed the ensuing drive that was capped by Warner's 9-yard touchdown pass to Torry Holt with 7:20 left in the third quarter to give the Rams a 16-0 lead. The Titans responded with touchdown drives in excess of seven minutes on each of their next two possessions. Steve McNair's 23-yard scramble set up Eddie George's 1-yard run in the final minute of the third quarter. McNair's 2-point conversion pass to Frank Wycheck was incomplete, but the Titans' defense forced a punt and the offense drove 79 yards in 13 plays, highlighted by 21-yard passes from McNair to Isaac Byrd and Jackie Harris, and capped by George's 2-yard run to cut the deficit to 16-13 with 7:21 remaining. The Rams once again failed to get a first down, and following a punt, the Titans needed just 28 yards to set up Del Greco's game-tying 43-yard kick with 2:12 left. On the next play from scrimmage, Warner fired a deep pass down the right sideline to Bruce, who caught the ball at the Titans' 38, cut toward the inside, and outran the defense to the end zone to give the Rams a 23-16 lead with 1:54 left. The Titans drove downfield, and McNair avoided a sack and completed a 16-yard pass to Kevin Dyson at the Rams' 10 with six seconds remaining. With no timeouts, McNair attempted a quick pass to a slanting Dyson, who caught the ball in stride at the Rams' 3. However, Jones reacted quickly and stepped up to tackle Dyson at the 1-yard line as time expired. Warner, who was named the game's most valuable player, was 24 of 45 for a Super Bowl-record 414 yards and 2 touchdowns. Bruce had 6 catches for 162 yards, and Holt had 7 for 109 yards. McNair was 22 of 36 for 214 yards. The Titans were the first team in Super Bowl history to come back from a 16-point deficit.

St. Louis (NFC)	3	6	7	7	— 23
Tennessee (AFC)	0	0	6	10	— 16

StL — FG Wilkins 27 (12:00)
StL — FG Wilkins 29 (10:44)
StL — FG Wilkins 28 (14:45)
StL — Holt 9 pass from Warner (Wilkins kick) (11:01)
Tenn — George 1 run (pass failed) (14:46)
Tenn — George 2 run (Del Greco kick) (7:39)
Tenn — FG Del Greco 43 (12:48)
StL — Bruce 73 pass from Warner (Wilkins kick) (13:06)

SUPER BOWL XXXIII
Pro Player Stadium, Miami, Florida
January 31, 1999, Attendance: 74,803

DENVER 34, ATLANTA 19—John Elway, in his last game, passed for 336 yards and ran for a touchdown to earn most valuable player honors as the Broncos became the first AFC team to win consecutive Super Bowls since the Steelers won XIII and XIV. A 25-yard pass interference penalty on Ray Crockett assisted the Falcons' nine-play, 48-yard game-opening drive that was capped by Morten Andersen's 32-yard field goal. Elway's 41-yard pass to Rod Smith kept alive Denver's ensuing drive and led to Howard Griffith's 1-yard touchdown run. Ronnie Bradford's interception and return to the Broncos' 35 late in the first quarter gave Atlanta excellent field position. However, Jamal Anderson was stopped for no gain on third-and-1 and thrown for a 2-yard loss on fourth down. Denver capitalized on its defensive effort with Jason Elam's 26-yard field goal. The Falcons responded by driving to the Broncos' 8, but Andersen's 26-yard field-goal attempt sailed wide right and on the next play, Elway fired an 80-yard touchdown pass to Smith to turn a possible 10-6 game into a 17-3 Broncos lead. Andersen's 28-yard field goal and 2 misses by Elam on the Broncos' first two second-half possessions gave Atlanta an opportunity to climb back into the game. However, Darrien Gordon dashed the Falcons' hopes with interceptions on consecutive possessions inside the Broncos' 20 to stop drives and set up Broncos touchdowns. Gordon returned the first interception, on a tipped pass, 58 yards to the Falcons' 24 to set up Griffith's second touchdown five plays later, and picked the second pass off at the Broncos' 2 and returned it 50 yards. Terrell Davis turned a short pass into a 39-yard gain, and Elway scored two plays later to give Denver a 31-6 lead. Tim Dwight returned the ensuing kickoff for a touchdown, and, after a field goal by Elam, the Falcons' offense scored with 2:04 remaining on Chandler's 3-yard pass to Tony Martin. Byron Chamberlain recovered the ensuing onside kick, but Tyrone Braxton recovered Anderson's fumble at the Falcons' 33 with 1:30 remaining to ice the game. The Falcons drove inside the Broncos' 30 seven times, but tallied just 1 touchdown and 2 field goals, throwing 2 interceptions, missing 1 field goal, and turning the ball over 1 time on downs during the other possessions. Elway was 18 of 29 for 336 yards and 1 touchdown, with 1 interception. Davis had 25 carries for 102 yards. Smith had 5 receptions for 152 yards. Chandler was 19 of 35 for 219 yards and 1 touchdown, with 3 interceptions.

Denver (AFC)	7	10	0	17	— 34
Atlanta (NFC)	3	3	0	13	— 19

Atl — FG Andersen 32 (5:25)
Den — Griffith 1 run (Elam kick) (11:05)
Den — FG Elam 26 (5:43)
Den — R. Smith 80 pass from Elway (Elam kick) (10:06)
Atl — FG Andersen 28 (12:35)
Den — Griffith 1 run (Elam kick) (:04)
Den — Elway 3 run (Elam kick) (3:40)
Atl — Dwight 94 kickoff return (Andersen kick) (3:59)
Den — FG Elam 37 (7:52)
Atl — Mathis 3 pass from Chandler (pass failed) (12:56)

SUPER BOWL XXXII
Qualcomm Stadium, San Diego, California
January 25, 1998, Attendance: 68,912

DENVER 31, GREEN BAY 24—Terrell Davis rushed for 157 yards and a Super Bowl-record 3 touchdowns to lead the Broncos to their first NFL championship and break the NFC's streak of Super Bowl victories at 13. The defending Super Bowl champion Packers took the opening kickoff and marched 76 yards in just over four minutes, scoring the first points on Brett Favre's 22-yard touchdown pass to Antonio Freeman. The Broncos responded with a 10-play, 58-yard drive capped by Davis' 1-yard run to tie the game. Tyrone Braxton intercepted Favre two plays later, and John Elway scored on a third-and-goal play to begin the second quarter. Steve Atwater forced Favre to fumble three plays later, and Neil Smith recovered at the Packers' 33. Jason Elam converted a 51-yard field goal, the second longest in Super Bowl history, to give the Broncos a 17-7 lead with 12:21 left in the half. After an exchange of punts, the Packers produced a 17-play, 95-yard drive that consumed 7:26 and finished with Favre's 6-yard touchdown pass to Mark Chmura on third-and-5 with 12 seconds left in the half. Tyrone Williams forced and recovered Davis' fumble at the Broncos' 26 on the first play from scrimmage in the second half. However, the Broncos' defense kept the Packers out of the end zone as Ryan Longwell's 27-yard field goal tied the game with 11:59 left in the third quarter. After another exchange of punts, Elway's 36-yard pass to Ed McCaffrey keyed a 13-play, 92-yard drive capped by Davis' 1-yard touchdown run with 34 seconds left in the third quarter. Tim McKyer recovered Freeman's fumble at the Packers' 22 on the ensuing kickoff return, giving the Broncos a golden opportunity, but Eugene Robinson intercepted Elway's pass in the end zone on the next play. Sparked by Robinson's play, the Packers took just four plays, three on passes to Freeman, to score the tying touchdown with 13:32 remaining. Each defense stiffened, forcing two punts, but the Broncos got great field position following Craig Hentrich's 39-yard punt to the Packers' 49 with 3:27 left and the score tied 24-24. Davis rushed for 2 yards on the first play, but Darrius Holland's 15-yard facemask penalty moved the ball to the Packers' 32. Elway threw a 23-yard pass to Howard Griffith two plays later, and after a holding penalty, Davis rushed 17 yards to the Packers' 1 with 1:47 left. After a timeout, Davis waltzed into the end zone to give Denver a 31-24 lead with 1:45 remaining. Freeman returned the kickoff 22 yards to the Broncos' 30, and Favre completed 22- and 13-yard screen passes to Dorsey Levens to reach the Broncos' 35 with 1:04 left. But after a 4-yard pass to Levens and incompletions to Freeman and Brooks, John Mobley knocked away Favre's pass to Chmura with 32 seconds left to give the Broncos the Vince Lombardi Trophy. Elway was 12 of 22 for 123 yards, with 1 interception. Favre was 25 of 42 for 256 yards and 1 touchdown, with 1 interception. Freeman had 9 receptions for 126 yards. Davis was named the game's most valuable player.

Green Bay (NFC)	7	7	3	7	— 24
Denver (AFC)	7	10	7	7	— 31

GB — Freeman 22 pass from Favre (Longwell kick) (4:02)
Den — Davis 1 run (Elam kick) (9:21)
Den — Elway 1 run (Elam kick) (:05)
Den — FG Elam 51 (2:39)
GB — Chmura 6 pass from Favre (Longwell kick) (14:48)
GB — FG Longwell 27 (3:01)
Den — Davis 1 run (Elam kick) (14:26)
GB — Freeman 13 pass from Favre (Longwell kick) (1:28)
Den — Davis 1 run (Elam kick) (13:15)

SUPER BOWL XXXI

Louisiana Superdome, New Orleans, LA
January 26, 1997, Attendance: 72,301

GREEN BAY 35, NEW ENGLAND 21—Desmond Howard returned a kickoff 99 yards for a touchdown and Brett Favre passed for 2 touchdowns and ran for a score as the Packers won their first Super Bowl in twenty-nine years. Howard, en route to garnering the MVP trophy, equaled a Super Bowl record with 244 total return yards. It was Favre's arm that struck first, as he hit Andre Rison for a 54-yard touchdown pass on the Packers' second play from scrimmage to take a 7-0 lead. Two plays later Doug Evans made a diving interception of Drew Bledsoe's pass at the 28-yard line, setting up Chris Jacke's field goal and giving the Packers a 10-0 lead just 6:18 into the Super Bowl. The Patriots answered with touchdowns on their next two possessions. Craig Newsome's pass interference penalty set up the first touchdown and a 44-yard completion from Bledsoe to Terry Glenn preceeding Ben Coates' touchdown gave New England its first and only lead. The 24 combined first quarter points were the most in Super Bowl history. Green Bay struck again 56 seconds into the second quarter as Favre hit Antonio Freeman with a Super Bowl-record 81-yard touchdown bomb. Jacke booted his second field goal on Green Bay's next possession. After a Mike Prior interception, Favre orchestrated a 74-yard, nearly 6-minute drive that concluded with a diving Favre touching the ball against the pylon to give Green Bay a 27-14 halftime lead. Curtis Martin brought the Patriots to within a score by running in from 18 yards out with 3:27 left in the third quarter. But Howard broke the Patriots' spirit by returning the ensuing kickoff a Super Bowl-record 99 yards. Favre found Mark Chmura for the 2-point conversion to finish the scoring. Bledsoe was intercepted twice in the fourth quarter as the Patriots never crossed midfield in 4 fourth-quarter possessions. Reggie White set a Super Bowl record with 3 sacks. Favre completed 14 of 27 passes for 246 yards, with no interceptions. Bledsoe completed 11 more passes than Favre, but for just 7 more yards, and threw 4 interceptions.

New England (AFC)	14	0	7	0	— 21
Green Bay (NFC)	10	17	8	0	— 35

GB — Rison 54 pass from Favre (Jacke kick) (3:32)
GB — FG Jacke 37 (6:18)
NE — Byars 1 pass from Bledsoe (Vinatieri kick) (8:25)
NE — Coates 4 pass from Bledsoe (Vinatieri kick) (12:27)
GB — Freeman 81 pass from Favre (Jacke kick) (0:56)
GB — FG Jacke 31 (6:45)
GB — Favre 2 run (Jacke kick) (13:49)
NE — Martin 18 run (Vinatieri kick) (11:33)
GB — Howard 99 kickoff return (Chmura pass from Favre) (11:50)

SUPER BOWL XXX

Sun Devil Stadium, Tempe, Arizona
January 28, 1996, Attendance: 76,347

DALLAS 27, PITTSBURGH 17—Cornerback Larry Brown's 2 interceptions led to 14 second-half points and helped lift the Cowboys to their third Super Bowl victory in the last four seasons and their record-tying fifth title overall. Brown's interceptions foiled the comeback efforts of the Steelers, and earned him the Pete Rozelle Trophy as the game's most valuable player. Dallas scored on each of its first three possessions, taking a 13-0 lead on Troy Aikman's 3-yard touchdown pass to Jay Novacek and a pair of field goals by Chris Boniol. Neil O'Donnell's 6-yard touchdown pass to Yancey Thigpen 13 seconds before halftime pulled Pittsburgh within 6 points, and the Steelers had the ball near midfield midway through the third quarter. But O'Donnell's third-down pass was intercepted by Brown at the Cowboys' 38-yard line, and his 44-yard return carried to Pittsburgh's 18. After Aikman's 17-yard completion to Michael Irvin, Emmitt Smith ran 1 yard for the touchdown that put Dallas ahead again by 13 points. The Steelers rallied, though, behind Norm Johnson's 46-yard field goal, a successful surprise onside kick, and Byron (Bam) Morris' 1-yard touchdown run with 6:36 to play in the game. And when they forced a punt and took possession at their own 32-yard line trailing only 20-17 with 4:15 remaining, it appeared they might have a chance to break the NFC's recent domination in the Super Bowl. But on second down, Brown struck again, intercepting O'Donnell's pass at the 39 and returning it 33 yards to the 6. Two plays later, Smith barreled over from 4 yards out for the clinching touchdown with 3:43 to go. Pittsburgh limited the Cowboys' powerful running game to only 56 yards and enjoyed a whopping 201-61 advantage in total yards in the second half, but could not overcome the 3 interceptions (another came on the game's final play) thrown by O'Donnell, the NFL's career leader for fewest interceptions per pass attempt. In all, O'Donnell completed 28 of 49 passes for 239 yards. Morris rushed for a game-high 73 yards on 19 carries. For Dallas, Aikman completed 15 of 23 pass attempts for 209 yards. The Cowboys' victory was the twelfth in a row for NFC teams over AFC teams in the Super Bowl.

Dallas (NFC)	10	3	7	7	— 27
Pittsburgh (AFC)	0	7	0	10	— 17

Dall — FG Boniol 42 (2:55)
Dall — Novacek 3 pass from Aikman (Boniol kick) (9:37)
Dall — FG Boniol 35 (8:57)
Pitt — Thigpen 6 pass from O'Donnell (N. Johnson kick) (14:47)
Dall — E. Smith 1 run (Boniol kick) (8:18)
Pitt — FG N. Johnson 46 (3:40)
Pitt — Morris 1 run (N. Johnson kick) (8:24)
Dall — E. Smith 4 run (Boniol kick) (11:17)

SUPER BOWL XXIX
Joe Robbie Stadium, Miami, Florida
January 29, 1995, Attendance: 74,107
SAN FRANCISCO 49, SAN DIEGO 26—Steve Young passed for a record 6 touchdowns, and the 49ers became the first team to win five Super Bowls when they routed the Chargers. Young, the game's most valuable player, directed an explosive offense that generated 7 touchdowns, 28 first downs, and 455 total yards. He completed 24 of 36 passes for 325 yards, and broke the record of 5 touchdown passes set by fromer 49ers quarterback Joe Montana in Super Bowl XXIV. San Francisco wasted little time scoring, taking the lead for good on Young's 44-yard touchdown pass to Jerry Rice only three plays and 1:24 into the game. The next time they had the ball, the 49ers marched 79 yards in four plays, taking a 14-0 lead when Young teamed with running back Ricky Watters on a 51-yard touchdown pass with 10:05 still to play in the opening period. San Diego then put together its most impressive possession of the game, a 13-play, 78-yard drive that consumed more than 7 minutes and was capped by Natrone Means' 1-yard touchdown run, to cut its deficit to 14-7 late in the quarter. But San Francisco countered with a 70-yard drive of its own, and Young's 5-yard touchdown pass to fullback William Floyd made it 21-7. Young's fourth touchdown pass of the half, 8 yards to Watters 4:44 before halftime, increased the advantage to 28-7, and the Chargers could get no closer than 18 points after that. Watters, who ran 9 yards for a touchdown in the third quarter, equaled the Super Bowl record with 3 touchdowns. Rice also scored 3 touchdowns (the second time in his career he'd done that in a Super Bowl) while catching 10 passes for 149 yards. He established career records for receptions, yards, and touchdowns in a Super Bowl. Young, who scrambled 21 yards and 15 yards to set up touchdowns in the first half, was the game's leading rusher with 49 yards on 5 carries. San Diego's Means, who rushed for 1,350 yards during the regular season, was limited to 33 yards on 13 attempts. Chargers quarterback Stan Humphries completed 24 of 49 passes for 275 yards. Rookie Andre Coleman became only the third player in Super Bowl history to return a kickoff for a touchdown, going 98 yards in the third quarter. The 75 points scored by the two teams established another record, breaking the previous mark of 69 set in Dallas' 52-17 victory over Buffalo in XXVII. The 49ers' victory was the eleventh straight for NFC teams over AFC teams in the Super Bowl.

San Diego (AFC)	7	3	8	8	— 26
San Francisco (NFC)	14	14	14	7	— 49

SF — Rice 44 pass from S. Young (Brien kick) (1:24)
SF — Watters 51 pass from S. Young (Brien kick) (4:55)
SD — Means 1 run (Carney kick) (12:16)
SF — Floyd 5 pass from S. Young (Brien kick) (1:58)
SF — Watters 8 pass from S. Young (Brien kick) (10:16)
SD — FG Carney 31 (13:16)
SF — Watters 9 run (Brien kick) (5:25)
SF — Rice 15 pass from S. Young (Brien kick) (11:42)
SD — Coleman 98 kickoff return (Seay pass from Humphries) (11:59)
SF — Rice 7 pass from S. Young (Brien kick) (1:11)
SD — Martin 30 pass from Humphries (Pupunu pass from Humphries) (12:35)

SUPER BOWL XXVIII
Georgia Dome, Atlanta, Georgia
January 30, 1994, Attendance: 72,817
DALLAS 30, BUFFALO 13—Emmitt Smith rushed for 132 yards and 2 second-half touchdowns to power the Cowboys to their second consecutive NFL title. By winning, Dallas joined San Francisco and Pittsburgh as the only franchises with four Super Bowl victories. The Bills, meanwhile, extended a dubious string by losing in the Super Bowl for the fourth consecutive year. To win, the Cowboys had to rally from a 13-6 halftime deficit. Buffalo had forged its lead on Thurman Thomas' 4-yard touchdown run and a pair of field goals by Steve Christie, including a 54-yard kick, the longest in Super Bowl history. But just 55 seconds into the second half, Thomas was stripped of the ball by Dallas defensive tackle Leon Lett. Safety James Washington recovered and weaved his way 46 yards for a touchdown to tie the game at 13-13. After forcing the Bills to punt, the Cowboys began their next possession on their 36-yard line and Smith, the game's most valuable player, took over. He carried 7 times for 61 yards on the ensuing 8-play, 64-yard drive, capping the march with a 15-yard touchdown run to give Dallas the lead for good with 8:42 remaining in the third quarter. Early in the fourth quarter, Washington intercepted Jim Kelly's pass and returned it 12 yards to Buffalo's 34. A penalty moved the ball back to the 39, but Smith carried twice for 10 yards and caught a screen pass for 9, and quarterback Troy Aikman completed a 16-yard pass to Alvin Harper to give the Cowboys a first-and-goal at the 6. Smith took it from there, cracking the end zone on fourth-and-goal from the 1 to put Dallas ahead 27-13 with 9:50 remaining. Eddie Murray's third field goal, from 20 yards with 2:50 left, ended any doubt about the game's outcome. Smith had 30 carries in all, with 19 of his attempts and 92 yards coming after intermission. Washington, normally a reserve who played most of the game because the Cowboys used five defensive backs to combat the Bills' No-Huddle offense, had 11 tackles and forced another fumble by Thomas in the first quarter. Aikman completed 19 of 27 passes for 207 yards. Buffalo's Kelly completed a Super Bowl-record 31 passes in 50 attempts for 260 yards. Dallas, the first team in NFL history to begin the regular season 0-2 and go on to win the Super Bowl, also became the fifth to win back-to-back titles, following Green Bay, Miami, Pittsburgh (the Steelers did it twice), and San Francisco. Buffalo became the third team, along with Minnesota and Denver, to lose four Super Bowls. The Cowboys' victory was the tenth in succession for the NFC over the AFC.

Dallas (NFC)	6	0	14	10	— 30
Buffalo (AFC)	3	10	0	0	— 13

Dall — FG Murray 41 (2:19)
Buff — FG Christie 54 (4:41)
Dall — FG Murray 24 (11:05)
Buff — Thomas 4 run (Christie kick) (2:34)
Buff — FG Christie 28 (15:00)
Dall — Washington 46 fumble return (Murray kick) (0:55)
Dall — E. Smith 15 run (Murray kick) (6:18)
Dall — E. Smith 1 run (Murray kick) (5:10)
Dall — FG Murray 20 (12:10)

SUPER BOWL XXVII
Rose Bowl, Pasadena, California
January 31, 1993, Attendance: 98,374
DALLAS 52, BUFFALO 17—Troy Aikman passed for 4 touchdowns, Emmitt Smith rushed for 108 yards, and the Cowboys converted 9 turnovers into 35 points while coasting to the victory. Dallas' win was its third in its record sixth Super Bowl appearance; the Bills became the first team to drop three in succession. Buffalo led 7-0 until the first 2 of its record number of turnovers helped the Cowboys take the lead for good late in the opening quarter. First, Dallas safety James Washington intercepted Jim Kelly's pass and returned it 13 yards to the Bills' 47, setting up Aikman's 23-yard touchdown pass to tight end Jay Novacek with 1:36 remaining in the period. On the next play from scrimmage, Kelly was sacked by Charles Haley and fumbled at the Bills' 2-yard line where the Cowboys' Jimmie Jones picked up the loose ball and ran 2 yards for a touchdown. Dallas, which recovered 5 fumbles and intercepted 4 passes, struck just as quickly late in the first half, when Aikman tossed 19- and 18-yard touchdown passes to Michael Irvin 18 seconds apart to give the Cowboys a 28-10 lead at intermission. The second score was set up when Bills running back Thurman Thomas lost a fumble at his 19-yard line. Buffalo scored for the last time when backup

quarterback Frank Reich, playing because Kelly was injured while attempting to pass midway through the second quarter, threw a 40-yard touchdown pass to Don Beebe on the final play of the third period to trim the deficit to 31-17. But Dallas put the game out of reach by scoring three times in a span of 2:33 of the fourth quarter. Aikman, the game's most valuable player, completed 22 of 30 passes for 273 yards. The victory was the ninth in succession for the NFC over the AFC.

Buffalo (AFC)	7	3	7	0	— 17
Dallas (NFC)	14	14	3	21	— 52

Buff — Thomas 2 run (Christie kick) (5:00)
Dall — Novacek 23 pass from Aikman (Elliott kick) (13:24)
Dall — J. Jones 2 fumble recovery return (Elliott kick) (13:39)
Buff — FG Christie 21 (11:36)
Dall — Irvin 19 pass from Aikman (Elliott kick) (13:06)
Dall — Irvin 18 pass from Aikman (Elliott kick) (13:24)
Dall — FG Elliott 20 (6:39)
Buff — Beebe 40 pass from Reich (Christie kick) (15:00)
Dall — Harper 45 pass from Aikman (Elliott kick) (4:56)
Dall — E. Smith 10 run (Elliott kick) (6:48)
Dall — Norton 9 fumble recovery return (Elliott kick) (7:29)

SUPER BOWL XXVI

Metrodome, Minneapolis, Minnesota
January 26, 1992, Attendance: 63,130

WASHINGTON 37, BUFFALO 24—Mark Rypien passed for 292 yards and 2 touchdowns as the Redskins overwhelmed the Bills to win their third Super Bowl in the past 10 years. Rypien, the game's most valuable player, completed 18 of 33 passes, including a 10-yard scoring strike to Earnest Byner and a 30-yard touchdown to Gary Clark. The latter came late in the third quarter after Buffalo had trimmed a 24-0 deficit to 24-10, and effectively put the game out of reach. Washington went on to lead by as much as 37-10 before the Bills made it close wih a pair of touchdowns in the final six minutes. Though the Redskins struggled early, converting their first three drives inside the Bills' 20-yard line into only 3 points, they built a 17-0 halftime lead. And they made it 24-0 just 16 seconds into the second half, after Kurt Gouveia intercepted Buffalo quarterback Jim Kelly's pass on the first play of the third quarter and returned it 23 yards to the Bills' 2. One play later, Gerald Riggs scored his second touchdown of the game to make it 24-0. Kelly, forced to bring Buffalo from behind, completed 28 of a Super Bowl-record 58 passes for 275 yards and 2 touchdowns, but was intercepted 4 tlmes. Bills running back Thurman Thomas, who had an AFC-high 1,407 yards rushing and an NFL-best 2,038 total yards from scrimmage during the regular season, ran for only 13 yards on 10 carries and was limited to 27 yards on 4 receptions. Clark had 7 catches for 114 yards and Art Monk added 7 for 113 for the Redskins, who amassed 417 yards of total offense while limiting the explosive Bills to 283. Washington's Joe Gibbs became only the third head coach to win three Super Bowls.

Washington (NFC)	0	17	14	6	— 37
Buffalo (AFC)	0	0	10	14	— 24

Wash — FG Lohmiller 34 (1:58)
Wash — Byner 10 pass from Rypien (Lohmiller kick) (5:06)
Wash — Riggs 1 run (Lohmiller kick) (7:43)
Wash — Riggs 2 run (Lohmiller kick) (0:16)
Buff — FG Norwood 21 (3:01)
Buff — Thomas 1 run (Norwood kick) (9:02)
Wash — Clark 30 pass from Rypien (Lohmiller kick) (13:36)
Wash — FG Lohmiller 25 (0:06)
Wash — FG Lohmiller 39 (3:24)
Buff — Metzelaars 2 pass from Kelly (Norwood kick) (9:01)
Buff — Beebe 4 pass from Kelly (Norwood kick) (11:05)

SUPER BOWL XXV

Tampa Stadium, Tampa, Florida
January 27, 1991, Attendance: 73,813

NEW YORK GIANTS 20, BUFFALO 19—The NFC champion New York Giants won their second Super Bowl in five years with a 20-19 victory over AFC titlist Buffalo. New York, employing its ball-control offense, had possession for 40 minutes, 33 seconds, a Super Bowl record. The Bills, who scored 95 points in their previous two playoff games leading to Super Bowl XXV, had the ball for less than eight minutes in the second half and just 19:27 for the game. Fourteen of New York's 73 plays came on its initial drive of the third quarter, which covered 75 yards and consumed a Super Bowl-record 9:29 before running back Ottis Anderson ran 1 yard for a touchdown. Giants quarterback Jeff Hostetler kept the long drive going by converting three third-down plays—an 11-yard pass to running back David Meggett on third-and-eight, a 14-yard toss to wide receiver Mark Ingram on third-and-13, and a 9-yard pass to Howard Cross on third-and-four—to give New York a 17-12 lead in the third quarter. Buffalo jumped to a 12-3 lead midway through the second quarter before Hostetler completed a 14-yard scoring strike to wide receiver Stephen Baker to close the score to 12-10 at halftime. Buffalo's Thurman Thomas ran 31 yards for a touchdown on the opening play of the fourth quarter to help Buffalo recapture the lead 19-17. Matt Bahr's 21-yard field goal gave the Giants a 20-19 lead, but Buffalo's Scott Norwood had a chance to win the game with seconds remaining before his 47-yard field-goal attempt sailed wide right. Hostetler completed 20 of 32 passes for 222 yards and 1 touchdown. Anderson rushed 21 times for 102 yards and 1 touchdown to capture most-valuable-player honors. Thomas totaled 190 scrimmage yards, rushing 15 times for 135 yards and catching 5 passes for 55 yards.

Buffalo (AFC)	3	9	0	7	— 19
N.Y. Giants (NFC)	3	7	7	3	— 20

NYG — FG Bahr 28 (7:46)
Buff — FG Norwood 23 (9:09)
Buff — D. Smith 1 run (Norwood kick) (2:30)
Buff — Safety, B. Smith tackled Hostetler in end zone (6:33)
NYG — Baker 14 pass from Hostetler (Bahr kick) (14:35)
NYG — Anderson 1 run (Bahr kick) (9:29)
Buff — Thomas 31 run (Norwood kick) (0:08)
NYG — FG Bahr 21 (7:40)

SUPER BOWL XXIV

Louisiana Superdome, New Orleans, LA
January 28, 1990, Attendance: 72,919

SAN FRANCISCO 55, DENVER 10—NFC titlist San Francisco won its fourth Super Bowl championship with a 55-10 victory over AFC champion Denver. The 49ers, who also won Super Bowls XVI, XIX, and XXIII, tied the Pittsburgh Steelers for most Super Bowl victories. The Steelers captured Super Bowls IX, X, XIII, and XIV. San Francisco's 55 points broke the previous Super Bowl scoring mark of 46 points by Chicago in Super Bowl XX. San Francisco scored touchdowns on four of its six first-half possessions to hold a 27-3 lead at halftime. Interceptions by Michael Walter and Chet Brooks ended the Broncos' first two possessions of the second half. San Francisco quarterback Joe Montana was named the Super Bowl most valuable player for a record third time. Montana completed 22 of 29 passes for 297 yards and a Super Bowl-record 5 touchdowns. Jerry Rice, Super Bowl XXIII most valuable player, caught 7 passes for 148 yards and 3 touchdowns. The 49ers' domination included first downs (28 to 12), net yards (461 to 167), and time of possession (39:31 to 20:29).

San Francisco (NFC)	13	14	14	14	— 55
Denver (AFC)	3	0	7	0	— 10

SF — Rice 20 pass from Montana (Cofer kick) (4:54)
Den — FG Treadwell 42 (8:13)
SF — Jones 7 pass from Montana (kick failed) (14:57)
SF — Rathman 1 run (Cofer kick) (7:45)
SF — Rice 38 pass from Montana (Cofer kick) (14:26)
SF — Rice 28 pass from Montana (Cofer kick) (2:12)
SF — Taylor 35 pass from Montana (Cofer kick) (5:16)

Den — Elway 3 run (Treadwell kick) (8:07)
SF — Rathman 3 run (Cofer kick) (0:03)
SF — Craig 1 run (Cofer kick) (1:13)

SUPER BOWL XXIII
Joe Robbie Stadium, Miami, Florida
January 22, 1989, Attendance: 75,129
SAN FRANCISCO 20, CINCINNATI 16—NFC champion San Francisco captured its third Super Bowl of the 1980s by defeating AFC champion Cincinnati 20-16. The 49ers, who also won Super Bowls XVI and XIX, became the first NFC team to win three Super Bowls. Pittsburgh, with four Super Bowl titles (IX, X, XIII, and XIV), and the Oakland/Los Angeles Raiders, with three (XI, XV, and XVIII), lead AFC franchises. Even though San Francisco held an advantage in total net yards (453 to 229), the 49ers found themselves trailing the Bengals late in the game. With the score 13-13, Cincinnati took a 16-13 lead on Jim Breech's 40-yard field goal with 3:20 remaining. It was Breech's third field goal of the day, following earlier successes from 34 and 43 yards. The 49ers started their winning drive at their 8-yard line. Over the next 11 plays, San Francisco covered 92 yards with the decisive score coming on a 10-yard pass from quarterback Joe Montana to wide receiver John Taylor with 34 seconds remaining. At halftime, the score was 3-3, the first time in Super Bowl history the game was tied at intermission. After the teams traded third-period field goals, the Bengals jumped ahead 13-6 on Stanford Jennings' 93-yard kickoff return for a touchdown with 34 seconds remaining in the quarter. The 49ers didn't waste any time coming back as they covered 85 yards in four plays, concluding with Montana's 14-yard scoring pass to Jerry Rice 57 seconds into the final stanza. Rice was named the game's most valuable player after compiling 11 catches for a Super Bowl-record 215 yards. Montana completed 23 of 36 passes for a Super Bowl-record 357 yards and 2 touchdowns.

Cincinnati (AFC)	0	3	10	3	— 16
San Francisco (NFC)	3	0	3	14	— 20

SF — FG Cofer 41 (11:46)
Cin — FG Breech 34 (13:45)
Cin — FG Breech 43 (9:21)
SF — FG Cofer 32 (14:10)
Cin — Jennings 93 kickoff return (Breech kick) (14:26)
SF — Rice 14 pass from Montana (Cofer kick) (0:57)
Cin — FG Breech 40 (11:40)
SF — Taylor 10 pass from Montana (Cofer kick) (14:26)

SUPER BOWL XXII
San Diego Jack Murphy Stadium, San Diego, CA
January 31, 1988, Attendance: 73,302
WASHINGTON 42, DENVER 10—NFC champion Washington won Super Bowl XXII and its second NFL championship of the 1980s with a 42-10 decision over AFC champion Denver. The Redskins, who also won Super Bowl XVII, enjoyed a record-setting second quarter en route to the victory. The Broncos broke in front 10-0 when quarterback John Elway threw a 56-yard touchdown pass to wide receiver Ricky Nattiel on the Broncos' first play from scrimmage. Following a Washington punt, Denver's Rich Karlis kicked a 24-yard field goal to cap a seven-play, 61-yard scoring drive. The Redskins then erupted for 35 points on five straight possessions in the second period and coasted thereafter. The 35 points established an NFL postseason mark for most points in a period. Redskins quarterback Doug Williams led the second-period explosion by passing for a Super Bowl record-tying 4 touchdowns, including 80- and 50-yard passes to wide receiver Ricky Sanders, a 27-yard toss to wide receiver Gary Clark, and an 8-yard pass to tight end Clint Didier. Washington scored 5 touchdowns in 18 plays with total time of possession of only 5:47. Overall, Williams completed 18 of 29 passes for 340 yards and was named the game's most valuable player. His pass-yardage total eclipsed the Super Bowl record of 331 yards by Joe Montana of San Francisco in Super Bowl XIX. Sanders ended with 193 yards on 8 catches, breaking the previous Super Bowl yardage record of 161 yards by Lynn Swann of Pittsburgh in Game X. Rookie running back Timmy Smith was the game's leading rusher with 22 carries for a Super Bowl-record 204 yards, breaking the previous mark of 191 yards by Marcus Allen of the Raiders in Game XVIII. Smith also scored twice on runs of 58 and 4 yards. Washington's 6 touchdowns and 602 total yards gained also set Super Bowl records. Redskins cornerback Barry Wilburn had 2 of the team's 3 interceptions, and strong safety Alvin Walton had 2 of Washington's 5 sacks.

Washington (NFC)	0	35	0	7	— 42
Denver (AFC)	10	0	0	0	— 10

Den — Nattiel 56 pass from Elway (Karlis kick) (1:57)
Den — FG Karlis 24 (5:51)
Wash — Sanders 80 pass from Williams (Haji-Sheikh kick) (0:53)
Wash — Clark 27 pass from Williams (Haji-Sheikh kick) (4:45)
Wash — Smith 58 run (Haji-Sheikh kick) (8:33)
Wash — Sanders 50 pass from Williams (Haji-Sheikh kick) (11:18)
Wash — Didier 8 pass from Williams (Haji-Sheikh kick) (13:56)
Wash — Smith 4 run (Haji-Sheikh kick) (1:51)

SUPER BOWL XXI
Rose Bowl, Pasadena, California
January 25, 1987, Attendance: 101,063
NEW YORK GIANTS 39, DENVER 20—The NFC champion New York Giants captured their first NFL title since 1956 when they downed the AFC champion Denver Broncos 39-20 in Super Bowl XXI. The victory marked the NFC's fifth NFL title in the past six seasons. The Broncos, behind the passing of quarterback John Elway, who was 13 of 20 for 187 yards in the first half, held a 10-9 lead at intermission, the narrowest halftime margin in Super Bowl history. Denver's Rich Karlis opened the scoring with a Super Bowl record-tying 48-yard field goal. New York drove 78 yards in nine plays on the next series to take a 7-3 lead on quarterback Phil Simms' 6-yard touchdown pass to tight end Zeke Mowatt. The Broncos came right back with a 58-yard scoring drive on six plays capped by Elway's 4-yard touchdown run. The only scoring in the second period was the sack of Elway in the end zone by defensive end George Martin for a New York safety. The Giants produced a key defensive stand early in the second quarter when the Broncos had a first down at the New York 1-yard line, but failed to score on three running plays and Karlis' 23-yard missed field-goal attempt. The Giants took command of the game in the third period en route to a 30-point second half, the most ever scored in one half of Super Bowl play. New York took the lead for good on tight end Mark Bavaro's 13-yard touchdown catch 4:52 into the third period. The nine-play, 63-yard scoring drive included the successful conversion of a fourth-and-1 play on the New York 46-yard line. Denver was limited to only 2 net yards on 10 offensive plays in the third period. Simms set Super Bowl records for most consecutive completions (10) and highest completion percentage (88 percent on 22 completions in 25 attempts). He also passed for 268 yards and 3 touchdowns and was named the game's most valuable player. New York running back Joe Morris was the game's leading rusher with 20 carries for 67 yards. Denver wide receiver Vance Johnson led all receivers with 5 catches for 121 yards.

Denver (AFC)	10	0	0	10	— 20
N.Y. Giants (NFC)	7	2	17	13	— 39

Den — FG Karlis 48 (4:09)
NYG — Mowatt 6 pass from Simms (Allegre kick) (9:33)
Den — Elway 4 run (Karlis kick) (12:54)
NYG — Safety, Martin tackled Elway in end zone (12:14)
NYG — Bavaro 13 pass from Simms (Allegre kick) (4:52)
NYG — FG Allegre 21 (11:06)
NYG — Morris 1 run (Allegre kick) (14:36)

NYG — McConkey 6 pass from Simms (Allegre kick) (4:04)
Den — FG Karlis 28 (8:59)
NYG — Anderson 2 run (kick failed) (10:42)
Den — V. Johnson 47 pass from Elway (Karlis kick) (12:54)

SUPER BOWL XX
Louisiana Superdome, New Orleans, LA
January 26, 1986, Attendance: 73,818

CHICAGO 46, NEW ENGLAND 10—The NFC champion Chicago Bears, seeking their first NFL title since 1963, scored a Super Bowl-record 46 points in downing AFC champion New England 46-10 in Super Bowl XX. The previous record for most points in a Super Bowl was 38, shared by San Francisco in XIX and the Los Angeles Raiders in XVIII. The Bears' league-leading defense tied the Super Bowl record for sacks (7) and limited the Patriots to a record-low 7 rushing yards. New England took the quickest lead in Super Bowl history when Tony Franklin kicked a 36-yard field goal with 1:19 elapsed in the first period. The score came about because of Larry McGrew's fumble recovery at the Chicago 19-yard line. However, the Bears rebounded for a 23-3 first-half lead, while building a yardage advantage of 236 total yards to New England's minus 19. Running back Matt Suhey rushed 8 times for 37 yards, including an 11-yard touchdown run, and caught 1 pass for 24 yards in the first half. After the Patriot's first drive of the second half ended with a punt to the Bears' 4-yard line, Chicago marched 96 yards in nine plays with quarterback Jim McMahon's 1-yard scoring run capping the drive. McMahon became the first quarterback in Super Bowl history to rush for a pair of touchdowns. The Bears completed their scoring via a 28-yard interception return by reserve cornerback Reggie Phillips, a 1-yard run by defensive tackle/fullback William Perry, and a safety when defensive end Henry Waechter tackled Patriots quarterback Steve Grogan in the end zone. Bears defensive end Richard Dent became the fourth defender to be named the game's most valuable player after contributing 1 1/2 sacks. The Bears' victory margin of 36 points was the largest in Super Bowl history, bettering the previous mark of 29 by the Los Angeles Raiders when they topped Washington 38-9 in Game XVIII. McMahon completed 12 of 20 passes for 256 yards before leaving the game in the fourth period with a wrist injury. The NFL's all-time leading rusher, Bears running back Walter Payton, carried 22 times for 61 yards. Wide receiver Willie Gault caught 4 passes for 129 yards, the fourth-most receiving yards in a Super Bowl. Chicago coach Mike Ditka became the second man (Tom Flores of Raiders was the other) to win a Super Bowl ring as a player and as a coach.

Chicago (NFC)	13	10	21	2	— 46
New England (AFC)	3	0	0	7	— 10

NE — FG Franklin 36 (1:19)
Chi — FG Butler 28 (5:40)
Chi — FG Butler 24 (13:34)
Chi — Suhey 11 run (Butler kick) (14:37)
Chi — McMahon 2 run (Butler kick) (7:36)
Chi — FG Butler 24 (15:00)
Chi — McMahon 1 run (Butler kick) (7:38)
Chi — Phillips 28 interception return (Butler kick) (8:44)
Chi — Perry 1 run (Butler kick) (11:38)
NE — Fryar 8 pass from Grogan (Franklin kick) (1:46)
Chi — Safety, Waechter tackled Grogan in end zone (9:24)

SUPER BOWL XIX
Stanford Stadium, Stanford, California
January 20, 1985, Attendance: 84,059

SAN FRANCISCO 38, MIAMI 16—The San Francisco 49ers captured their second Super Bowl title with a dominating offense and a defense that tamed Miami's explosive passing attack. The Dolphins held a 10-7 lead at the end of the first period, which represented the most points scored by two teams in an opening quarter of a Super Bowl. However, the 49ers used excellent field position in the second period to build a 28-16 halftime lead. Running back Roger Craig set a Super Bowl record by scoring 3 touchdowns on pass receptions of 8 and 16 yards and a run of 2 yards. San Francisco's Joe Montana was voted the game's most valuable player. He joined Green Bay's Bart Starr and Pittsburgh's Terry Bradshaw as the only two-time Super Bowl most valuable players. Montana completed 24 of 35 passes for a Super Bowl-record 331 yards and 3 touchdowns, and rushed 5 times for 59 yards, including a 6-yard touchdown. Craig had 58 yards on 15 carries and caught 7 passes for 77 yards. Wendell Tyler rushed 13 times for 65 yards and had 4 catches for 70 yards. Dwight Clark had 6 receptions for 77 yards, while Russ Francis had 5 for 60. San Francisco's 537 total net yards bettered the previous Super Bowl record of 429 yards by Oakland in Super Bowl XI. The 49ers also held a time of possession advantage over the Dolphins of 37:11 to 22:49.

Miami (AFC)	10	6	0	0	— 16
San Francisco (NFC)	7	21	10	0	— 38

Mia — FG von Schamann 37 (7:36)
SF — Monroe 33 pass from Montana (Wersching kick) (11:48)
Mia — D. Johnson 2 pass from Marino (von Schamann kick) (14:15)
SF — Craig 8 pass from Montana (Wersching kick) (3:26)
SF — Montana 6 run (Wersching kick) (8:02)
SF — Craig 2 run (Wersching kick) (12:55)
Mia — FG von Schamann 31 (14:48)
Mia — FG von Schamann 30 (15:00)
SF — FG Wersching 27 (4:48)
SF — Craig 16 pass from Montana (Wersching kick) (8:42)

SUPER BOWL XVIII
Tampa Stadium, Tampa, Florida
January 22, 1984, Attendance: 72,920

LOS ANGELES RAIDERS 38, WASHINGTON 9—The Los Angeles Raiders dominated the Washington Redskins from the beginning in Super Bowl XVIII and achieved the most lopsided victory in Super Bowl history, surpassing Green Bay's 35-10 win over Kansas City in Super Bowl I. The Raiders took a 7-0 lead 4:52 into the game when Derrick Jensen blocked Jeff Hayes' punt and recovered it in the end zone for a touchdown. With 9:14 remaining in the first half, Raiders quarterback Jim Plunkett fired a 12-yard touchdown pass to wide receiver Cliff Branch to complete a three-play, 65-yard drive. Washington cut the Raiders' lead to 14-3 on a 24-yard field goal by Mark Moseley. With seven seconds left in the first half, Raiders linebacker Jack Squirek intercepted Joe Theismann's pass at the Redskins' 5-yard line and ran it in for a touchdown to give Los Angeles a 21-3 halftime lead. In the third period, running back Marcus Allen, who rushed for a Super Bowl-record 191 yards on 20 carries, increased the Raiders' lead to 35-9 on touchdown runs of 5 and 74 yards, the latter erasing the Super Bowl record of 58 yards set by Baltimore's Tom Matte in Game III. Allen was named the game's most valuable player. The victory over Washington raised Raiders coach Tom Flores' playoff record to 8-1, including a 27-10 win against Philadelphia in Super Bowl XV. The 38 points scored by the Raiders were the highest total by a Super Bowl team. The previous high was 35 points by Green Bay in Game I.

Washington (NFC)	0	3	6	0	— 9
L.A. Raiders (AFC)	7	14	14	3	— 38

Raiders — Jensen recovered blocked punt in end zone (Bahr kick) (4:52)
Raiders — Branch 12 pass from Plunkett (Bahr kick) (5:46)
Wash — FG Moseley 24 (11:55)
Raiders — Squirek 5 interception return (Bahr kick) (14:53)
Wash — Riggins 1 run (kick blocked) (4:08)
Raiders — Allen 5 run (Bahr kick) (7:54)
Raiders — Allen 74 run (Bahr kick) (15:00)
Raiders — FG Bahr 21 (12:36)

SUPER BOWL XVII

Rose Bowl, Pasadena, California
January 30, 1983, Attendance: 103,667

WASHINGTON 27, MIAMI 17—Fullback John Riggins ran for a Super Bowl-record 166 yards on 38 carries to spark Washington to a 27-17 victory over AFC champion Miami. It was Riggins' fourth straight 100-yard rushing game during the playoffs, also a record. The win marked Washington's first NFL title since 1942, and was only the second time in Super Bowl history NFL/NFC teams scored consecutive victories (Green Bay did it in Super Bowls I and II and San Francisco won Super Bowl XVI). The Redskins, under second-year head coach Joe Gibbs, used a balanced offense that accounted for 400 total yards (a Super Bowl-record 276 yards rushing and 124 passing), second in Super Bowl history to 429 yards by Oakland in Super Bowl XI. The Dolphins built a 17-10 halftime lead on a 76-yard touchdown pass from quarterback David Woodley to wide receiver Jimmy Cefalo 6:49 into the first period, a 20-yard field goal by Uwe von Schamann with 6:00 left in the half, and a Super Bowl-record 98-yard kickoff return by Fulton Walker with 1:38 remaining. Washington had tied the score at 10-10 with 1:51 left on a 4-yard touchdown pass from Joe Theismann to wide receiver Alvin Garrett. Mark Moseley started the Redskins' scoring with a 31-yard field goal late in the first period, and added a 20-yard kick midway through the third period to cut the Dolphins' lead to 17-13. Riggins, who was voted the game's most valuable player, gave Washington its first lead of the game with 10:01 left when he ran 43 yards off left tackle for a touchdown in a fourth-and-1 situation. Wide receiver Charlie Brown caught a 6-yard scoring pass from Theismann with 1:55 left to complete the scoring. The Dolphins managed only 176 yards (142 in first half). Theismann completed 15 of 23 passes for 143 yards, with 2 touchdowns and 2 interceptions. For Miami, Woodley was 4 of 14 for 97 yards, with 1 touchdown, and 1 interception. Don Strock was 0 for 3 in relief.

Miami (AFC)	7	10	0	0	— 17
Washington (NFC)	0	10	3	14	— 27

Mia — Cefalo 76 pass from Woodley (von Schamann kick) (6:49)
Wash — FG Moseley 31 (0:21)
Mia — FG von Schamann 20 (9:00)
Wash — Garrett 4 pass from Theismann (Moseley kick) (13:09)
Mia — Walker 98 kickoff return (von Schamann kick) (13:22)
Wash — FG Moseley 20 (6:51)
Wash — Riggins 43 run (Moseley kick) (4:59)
Wash — Brown 6 pass from Theismann (Moseley kick) (13:05)

SUPER BOWL XVI

Pontiac Silverdome, Pontiac, Michigan
January 24, 1982, Attendance: 81,270

SAN FRANCISCO 26, CINCINNATI 21—Ray Wersching's Super Bowl record-tying 4 field goals and Joe Montana's controlled passing helped lift the San Francisco 49ers to their first NFL championship with a 26-21 victory over Cincinnati. The 49ers built a game-record 20-0 halftime lead via Montana's 1-yard touchdown run, which capped an 11-play, 68-yard drive; fullback Earl Cooper's 11-yard scoring pass from Montana, which climaxed a Super Bowl record 92-yard drive on 12 plays; and Wersching's 22- and 26-yard field goals. The Bengals rebounded in the second half, closing the gap to 20-14 on quarterback Ken Anderson's 5-yard run and Dan Ross' 4-yard reception from Anderson, who established Super Bowl passing records for completions (25) and completion percentage (73.5 percent on 25 of 34). Wersching added early fourth-period field goals of 40 and 23 yards to increase the 49ers' lead to 26-14. The Bengals managed to score on an Anderson-to-Ross 3-yard pass with only 16 seconds remaining. Ross set a Super Bowl record with 11 receptions for 104 yards. Montana, the game's most valuable player, completed 14 of 22 passes for 157 yards. Cincinnati compiled 356 yards to San Francisco's 275, which marked the first time in Super Bowl history that the team that gained the most yards from scrimmage lost the game.

San Francisco (NFC)	7	13	0	6	— 26
Cincinnati (AFC)	0	0	7	14	— 21

SF — Montana 1 run (Wersching kick) (9:08)
SF — Cooper 11 pass from Montana (Wersching kick) (8:07)
SF — FG Wersching 22 (14:45)
SF — FG Wersching 26 (14:58)
Cin — Anderson 5 run (Breech kick) (3:35)
Cin — Ross 4 pass from Anderson (Breech kick) (4:54)
SF — FG Wersching 40 (9:35)
SF — FG Wersching 23 (13:03)
Cin — Ross 3 pass from Anderson (Breech kick) (14:44)

SUPER BOWL XV

Louisiana Superdome, New Orleans, LA
January 25, 1981, Attendance: 76,135

OAKLAND 27, PHILADELPHIA 10—Jim Plunkett passed for 3 touchdowns, including an 80-yard strike to Kenny King, as the Raiders became the first wild-card team to win the Super Bowl. Plunkett's touchdown bomb to King—the longest play in Super Bowl history—gave Oakland a decisive 14-0 lead with nine seconds left in the first period. Linebacker Rod Martin had set up Oakland's first touchdown, a 2-yard reception by Cliff Branch, with a 17-yard interception return to the Eagles' 30-yard line. The Eagles never recovered from that early deficit, managing only Tony Franklin's field goal (30 yards) and an 8-yard touchdown pass from Ron Jaworski to Keith Krepfle. Plunkett, who became a starter in the sixth game of the season, completed 13 of 21 for 261 yards and was named the game's most valuable player. Oakland won 9 of 11 games with Plunkett starting, but that was good enough only for second place in the AFC West, although they tied division winner San Diego with an 11-5 record. The Raiders, who had previously won Super Bowl XI over Minnesota, had to win three playoff games to get to the championship game. Oakland defeated Houston 27-7 at home followed by road victories over Cleveland (14-12) and San Diego (34-27). Oakland's Mark van Eeghen was the game's leading rusher with 75 yards on 18 carries. Philadelphia's Wilbert Montgomery led all receivers with 6 receptions for 91 yards. Branch had 5 for 67 and Harold Carmichael of Philadelphia 5 for 83. Martin finished the game with 3 interceptions, a Super Bowl record.

Oakland (AFC)	14	0	10	3	— 27
Philadelphia (NFC)	0	3	0	7	— 10

Oak — Branch 2 pass from Plunkett (Bahr kick) (6:04)
Oak — King 80 pass from Plunkett (Bahr kick) (14:51)
Phil — FG Franklin 30 (4:32)
Oak — Branch 29 pass from Plunkett (Bahr kick) (2:36)
Oak — FG Bahr 46 (10:25)
Phil — Krepfle 8 pass from Jaworski (Franklin kick) (1:01)
Oak — FG Bahr 35 (6:31)

SUPER BOWL XIV

Rose Bowl, Pasadena, California
January 20, 1980, Attendance: 103,985

PITTSBURGH 31, LOS ANGELES 19—Terry Bradshaw completed 14 of 21 passes for 309 yards and set two passing records as the Steelers became the first team to win four Super Bowls. Despite 3 interceptions by the Rams, Bradshaw kept his poise and brought the Steelers from behind twice in the second half. Trailing 13-10 at halftime, Pittsburgh went ahead 17-13 when Bradshaw hit Lynn Swann with a 47-yard touchdown pass after 2:48 of the third quarter. On the Rams' next possession Vince Ferragamo, who was 15 of 25 for 212 yards, responded with a 50-yard pass to Billy Waddy that moved Los Angeles from its 26 to the Steelers' 24. On the following play, Lawrence McCutcheon connected with Ron Smith on a halfback option pass that gave the Rams a 19-17 lead. On Pittsburgh's initial possession of the final period, Bradshaw lofted a 73-yard scoring pass to John Stallworth to put the Steelers in front to stay 24-19. Franco Harris scored on a 1-yard run later in the quarter to seal the verdict. A 45-yard pass from Bradshaw to Stallworth was the key play in the drive to

Harris' score. Bradshaw, the game's most valuable player for the second straight year, set career Super Bowl records for most touchdown passes (9) and most passing yards (932). Larry Anderson gave the Steelers excellent field position throughout the game with 5 kickoff returns for a record 162 yards.

Los Angeles (NFC)	7	6	6	0	— 19
Pittsburgh (AFC)	3	7	7	14	— 31

Pitt — FG Bahr 41 (7:29)
LA — Bryant 1 run (Corral kick) (12:16)
Pitt — Harris 1 run (Bahr kick) (2:08)
LA — FG Corral 31 (7:39)
LA — FG Corral 45 (14:46)
Pitt — Swann 47 pass from Bradshaw (Bahr kick) (2:48)
LA — Smith 24 pass from McCutcheon (kick failed) (4:45)
Pitt — Stallworth 73 pass from Bradshaw (Bahr kick) (2:56)
Pitt — Harris 1 run (Bahr kick) (13:11)

SUPER BOWL XIII

Orange Bowl, Miami, Florida
January 21, 1979, Attendance: 79,484

PITTSBURGH 35, DALLAS 31—Terry Bradshaw passed for a record 4 touchdowns to lead the Steelers to victory. The Steelers became the first team to win three Super Bowls, mostly because of Bradshaw's accurate arm. Bradshaw, voted the game's most valuable player, completed 17 of 30 passes for 318 yards, a personal high. Four of those passes went for touchdowns—2 to John Stallworth and the third, with 26 seconds remaining in the second period, to Rocky Bleier for a 21-14 halftime lead. The Cowboys scored twice before intermission on Roger Staubach's 39-yard pass to Tony Hill and a 37-yard fumble return by linebacker Mike Hegman, who stole the ball from Bradshaw. The Steelers broke open the contest with 2 touchdowns in a span of 19 seconds midway through the final period. Franco Harris rambled 22 yards up the middle to give the Steelers a 28-17 lead with 7:10 left. Pittsburgh got the ball right back when Randy White fumbled the kickoff and Dennis Winston recovered for the Steelers. On first down, Bradshaw fired his fourth touchdown pass, an 18-yard pass to Lynn Swann to boost the Steelers' lead to 35-17 with 6:51 to play. The Cowboys refused to let the Steelers run away with the contest. Staubach connected with Billy Joe DuPree on a 7-yard scoring pass with 2:23 left. Then the Cowboys recovered an onside kick and Staubach took them in for another score, passing 4 yards to Butch Johnson with 22 seconds remaining. Bleier recovered another onside kick with 17 seconds left to seal the victory for the Steelers.

Pittsburgh (AFC)	7	14	0	14	— 35
Dallas (NFC)	7	7	3	14	— 31

Pitt — Stallworth 28 pass from Bradshaw (Gerela kick) (5:13)
Dall — Hill 39 pass from Staubach (Septien kick) (15:00)
Dall — Hegman 37 fumble recovery return (Septien kick) (2:52)
Pitt — Stallworth 75 pass from Bradshaw (Gerela kick) (4:35)
Pitt — Bleier 7 pass from Bradshaw (Gerela kick) (14:34)
Dall — FG Septien 27 (12:24)
Pitt — Harris 22 run (Gerela kick) (7:50)
Pitt — Swann 18 pass from Bradshaw (Gerela kick) (8:09)
Dall — DuPree 7 pass from Staubach (Septien kick) (12:37)
Dall — B. Johnson 4 pass from Staubach (Septien kick) (14:38)

SUPER BOWL XII

Louisiana Superdome, New Orleans, LA
January 15, 1978, Attendance: 75,583

DALLAS 27, DENVER 10—The Cowboys evened their Super Bowl record at 2-2 by defeating Denver before a sellout crowd plus 102,010,000 television viewers, the largest audience ever to watch a sporting event. Dallas converted 2 interceptions into 10 points and Efren Herrera added a 35-yard field goal for a 13-0 halftime advantage. In the third period Craig Morton engineered a drive to the Cowboys' 30 and Jim Turner's 47-yard field goal made the score 13-3. After an exchange of punts, Butch Johnson made a spectacular diving catch in the end zone to complete a 45-yard pass from Roger Staubach and put the Cowboys ahead 20-3. Following Rick Upchurch's 67-yard kickoff return, Norris Weese guided the Broncos to a touchdown to cut the deficit to 20-10. Dallas clinched the victory when running back Robert Newhouse tossed a 29-yard touchdown pass to Golden Richards with 7:04 left in the game. It was the first pass thrown by Newhouse since 1975. Harvey Martin and Randy White, who were named co-most valuable players, led the Cowboys' defense, which recovered 4 fumbles and intercepted 4 passes.

Dallas (NFC)	10	3	7	7	— 27
Denver (AFC)	0	0	10	0	— 10

Dall — Dorsett 3 run (Herrera kick) (10:31)
Dall — FG Herrera 35 (13:29)
Dall — FG Herrera 43 (3:44)
Den — FG Turner 47 (2:28)
Dall — Johnson 45 pass from Staubach (Herrera kick) (8:01)
Den — Lytle 1 run (Turner kick) (9:21)
Dall — Richards 29 pass from Newhouse (Herrera kick) (7:56)

SUPER BOWL XI

Rose Bowl, Pasadena, California
January 9, 1977, Attendance: 103,438

OAKLAND 32, MINNESOTA 14—The Raiders won their first NFL championship before a record Super Bowl crowd plus 81 million television viewers, the largest audience ever to watch a sporting event. The Raiders gained a record-breaking 429 yards, including running back Clarence Davis' 137 rushing yards. Wide receiver Fred Biletnikoff made 4 key receptions, which earned him the game's most valuable player trophy. Oakland scored on three successive possessions in the second quarter to build a 16-0 halftime lead. Errol Mann's 24-yard field goal opened the scoring, then the AFC champions put together drives of 64 and 35 yards, scoring on a 1-yard pass from Ken Stabler to Dave Casper and a 1-yard run by Pete Banaszak. The Raiders increased their lead to 19-0 on a 40-yard field goal in the third quarter, but Minnesota responded with a 12-play, 58-yard drive late in the period, with Fran Tarkenton passing 8 yards to wide receiver Sammy White to cut the deficit to 19-7. Two fourth-quarter interceptions clinched the title for the Raiders. One set up Banaszak's second touchdown run, the other resulted in cornerback Willie Brown's Super Bowl-record 75-yard interception return.

Oakland (AFC)	0	16	3	13	— 32
Minnesota (NFC)	0	0	7	7	— 14

Oak — FG Mann 24 (0:48)
Oak — Casper 1 pass from Stabler (Mann kick) (7:50)
Oak — Banaszak 1 run (kick failed) (11:27)
Oak — FG Mann 40 (9:44)
Minn — S. White 8 pass from Tarkenton (Cox kick) (14:13)
Oak — Banaszak 2 run (Mann kick) (7:21)
Oak — Brown 75 interception return (kick failed) (9:17)
Minn — Voigt 13 pass from Lee (Cox kick) (14:35)

SUPER BOWL X

Orange Bowl, Miami, Florida
January 18, 1976, Attendance: 80,187

PITTSBURGH 21, DALLAS 17—The Steelers won the Super Bowl for the second year in a row on Terry Bradshaw's 64-yard touchdown pass to Lynn Swann and an aggressive defense that snuffed out a late rally by the Cowboys with an end-zone interception on the final play of the game. In the fourth quarter, Pittsburgh ran on fourth down and gave up the ball on the Cowboys' 39 with 1:22 to play. Roger Staubach ran and passed for 2 first downs but his last desperation pass was picked off by Glen Edwards. Dallas' scoring was the result of 2 touchdown passes by Staubach, one to Drew Pearson for 29 yards and the other to Percy Howard for 34 yards. Howard's reception was the only catch of his NFL career. Toni Fritsch had a 36-yard field goal. The Steelers scored on 2 touchdown passes by Bradshaw, 1 to Randy Grossman for 7 yards and the long bomb to Swann. Roy Gerela had 36- and 18-yard field goals. Reggie Harrison blocked a punt through the end zone for a safety. Swann set a Super Bowl record by gaining 161 yards on his 4 receptions.

Dallas (NFC)	7	3	0	7	—17
Pittsburgh (AFC)	7	0	0	14	—21

Dall — D. Pearson 29 pass from Staubach (Fritsch kick) (4:36)
Pitt — Grossman 7 pass from Bradshaw (Gerela kick) (9:03)
Dall — FG Fritsch 36 (0:15)
Pitt — Safety, Harrison blocked Hoopes' punt through end zone (3:32)
Pitt — FG Gerela 36 (6:19)
Pitt — FG Gerela 18 (8:23)
Pitt — Swann 64 pass from Bradshaw (kick failed) (11:58)
Dall — P. Howard 34 pass from Staubach (Fritsch kick) (13:12)

SUPER BOWL IX

Tulane Stadium, New Orleans, Louisiana
January 12, 1975, Attendance: 80,997

PITTSBURGH 16, MINNESOTA 6—AFC champion Pittsburgh, in its initial Super Bowl appearance, and NFC champion Minnesota, making a third bid for its first Super Bowl title, struggled through a first half in which the only score was produced by the Steelers' defense when Dwight White downed Vikings' quarterback Fran Tarkenton in the end zone for a safety 7:49 into the second period. The Steelers forced another break and took advantage on the second-half kickoff when Minnesota's Bill Brown fumbled and Marv Kellum recovered for Pittsburgh on the Vikings' 30. After Rocky Bleier failed to gain on first down, Franco Harris carried 3 consecutive times for 24 yards, a loss of 3, and a 9-yard touchdown and a 9-0 lead. Though its offense was completely stymied by Pittsburgh's defense, Minnesota managed to move into a threatening position after 4:27 of the final period when Matt Blair blocked Bobby Walden's punt and Terry Brown recovered the ball in the end zone for a touchdown. Fred Cox's kick failed and the Steelers led 9-6. Pittsburgh wasted no time putting the victory away. The Steelers took the ensuing kickoff and marched 66 yards in 11 plays, climaxed by Terry Bradshaw's 4-yard scoring pass to Larry Brown with 3:31 left. Pittsburgh's defense permitted Minnesota only 119 yards total offense, including a Super Bowl low of 17 rushing yards. The Steelers, meanwhile, gained 333 yards, including Harris' record 158 yards on 34 carries.

Pittsburgh (AFC)	0	2	7	7	—16
Minnesota (NFC)	0	0	0	6	— 6

Pitt — Safety, White downed Tarkenton in end zone (7:49)
Pitt — Harris 9 run (Gerela kick) (1:35)
Minn — T. Brown recovered blocked punt in end zone (kick failed) (4:27)
Pitt — L. Brown 4 pass from Bradshaw (Gerela kick) (11:29)

SUPER BOWL VIII

Rice Stadium, Houston, Texas
January 13, 1974, Attendance: 71,882

MIAMI 24, MINNESOTA 7—The defending NFL champion Dolphins, representing the AFC for the third straight year, scored the first two times they had possession on marches of 62 and 56 yards while the Miami defense limited the Vikings to only seven plays in the first period. Larry Csonka climaxed the initial 10-play drive with a 5-yard touchdown bolt through right guard after 5:27 had elapsed. Four plays later, Miami began another 10-play scoring drive, which ended with Jim Kiick bursting 1 yard through the middle for another touchdown after 13:38 of the period. Garo Yepremian added a 28-yard field goal midway in the second period for a 17-0 Miami lead. Minnesota then drove from its 20 to a second-and-2 situation on the Miami 7 yard line with 1:18 left in the half. But on two plays, Miami limited Oscar Reed to 1 yard. On fourth-and-1 from the 6, Reed went over right tackle, but Dolphins middle linebacker Nick Buoniconti jarred the ball loose and Jake Scott recovered for Miami to halt the Minnesota threat. The Vikings were unable to muster enough offense in the second half to threaten the Dolphins. Csonka rushed 33 times for a Super Bowl-record 145 yards. Bob Griese of Miami completed 6 of 7 passes for 73 yards.

Minnesota (NFC)	0	0	0	7	— 7
Miami (AFC)	14	3	7	0	—24

Mia — Csonka 5 run (Yepremian kick) (9:33)
Mia — Kiick 1 run (Yepremian kick) (13:38)
Mia — FG Yepremian 28 (8:58)
Mia — Csonka 2 run (Yepremian kick) (6:16)
Minn — Tarkenton 4 run (Cox kick) (1:35)

SUPER BOWL VII

Memorial Coliseum, Los Angeles, CA
January 14, 1973, Attendance: 90,182

MIAMI 14, WASHINGTON 7—The Dolphins played virtually perfect football in the first half as their defense permitted the Redskins to cross midfield only once and their offense turned good field position into 2 touchdowns. On its third possession, Miami opened its first scoring drive from the Dolphins' 37 yard line. An 18-yard pass from Bob Griese to Paul Warfield preceded by three plays Griese's 28-yard touchdown pass to Howard Twilley. After Washington moved from its 17 to the Miami 48 with two minutes remaining in the first half, Dolphins linebacker Nick Buoniconti intercepted Billy Kilmer's pass at the Miami 41 and returned it to the Washington 27. Jim Kiick ran for 3 yards, Larry Csonka for 3, Griese passed to Jim Mandich for 19, and Kiick gained 1 to the 1-yard line. With 18 seconds left until intermission, Kiick scored from the 1. Washington's only touchdown came with 2:07 left in the game and resulted from a misplayed field-goal attempt and fumble by Garo Yepremian, with the Redskins' Mike Bass picking the ball out of the air and running 49 yards for the score. Dolphins safety Jake Scott, who had 2 interceptions, including 1 in the end zone to kill a Redskins' drive, was voted the game's most valuable player.

Miami (AFC)	7	7	0	0	—14
Washington (NFC)	0	0	0	7	— 7

Mia — Twilley 28 pass from Griese (Yepremian kick) (14:59)
Mia — Kiick 1 run (Yepremian kick) (14:42)
Wash — Bass 49 fumble recovery return (Knight kick) (12:53)

SUPER BOWL VI

Tulane Stadium, New Orleans, Louisiana
January 16, 1972, Attendance: 81,023

DALLAS 24, MIAMI 3—The Cowboys rushed for a record 252 yards and their defense limited the Dolphins to a low of 185 yards while not permitting a touchdown for the first time in Super Bowl history. Dallas converted Chuck Howley's recovery of Larry Csonka's first fumble of the season into a 3-0 advantage and led at halftime 10-3. After Dallas received the second-half kickoff, Duane Thomas led a 71-yard march in eight plays for a 17-3 margin. Howley intercepted Bob Griese's pass at the 50 and returned it to the Miami 9 early in the fourth period, and three plays later Roger Staubach passed 7 yards to Mike Ditka for the final touchdown. Thomas rushed for 95 yards and Walt Garrison gained 74. Staubach, voted the game's most valuable player, completed 12 of 19 passes for 119 yards and 2 touchdowns.

Dallas (NFC)	3	7	7	7	—24
Miami (AFC)	0	3	0	0	— 3

Dall — FG Clark 9 (13:37)
Dall — Alworth 7 pass from Staubach (Clark kick) (13:45)
Mia — FG Yepremian 31 (14:56)
Dall — D. Thomas 3 run (Clark kick) (5:17)
Dall — Ditka 7 pass from Staubach (Clark kick) (3:18)

SUPER BOWL V
Orange Bowl, Miami, Florida
January 17, 1971, Attendance: 79,204
BALTIMORE 16, DALLAS 13—A 32-yard field goal by rookie kicker Jim O'Brien brought the Baltimore Colts a victory over the Dallas Cowboys in the final five seconds of Super Bowl V. The game between the champions of the AFC and NFC was played on artificial turf for the first time. Dallas led 13-6 at the half but interceptions by Rick Volk and Mike Curtis set up a Baltimore touchdown and O'Brien's decisive kick in the fourth period. Earl Morrall relieved an injured Johnny Unitas late in the first half, although Unitas completed the Colts' only scoring pass. It caromed off receiver Eddie Hinton's fingertips, off Dallas defensive back Mel Renfro, and finally settled into the grasp of John Mackey, who went 45 yards to score on a 75-yard play.

Baltimore (AFC)	0	6	0	10	— 16
Dallas (NFC)	3	10	0	0	— 13

Dall — FG Clark 14 (9:28)
Dall — FG Clark 30 (0:08)
Balt — Mackey 75 pass from Unitas (kick blocked) (0:05)
Dall — Thomas 7 pass from Morton (Clark kick) (7:07)
Balt — Nowatzke 2 run (O'Brien kick) (7:25)
Balt — FG O'Brien 32 (14:55)

SUPER BOWL IV
Tulane Stadium, New Orleans, Louisiana
January 11, 1970, Attendance: 80,562
KANSAS CITY 23, MINNESOTA 7—The AFL squared the Super Bowl at two games apiece with the NFL, building a 16-0 halftime lead behind Len Dawson's superb quarterbacking and a powerful defense. Dawson, the fourth consecutive quarterback to be chosen the Super Bowl's top player, called an almost flawless game, completing 12 of 17 passes and hitting Otis Taylor on a 46-yard play for the final Chiefs touchdown. The Kansas City defense limited Minnesota's strong rushing game to 67 yards and had 3 interceptions and 2 fumble recoveries. The crowd of 80,562 set a Super Bowl record, as did the gross receipts of $3,817,872.69.

Minnesota (NFL)	0	0	7	0	— 7
Kansas City (AFL)	3	13	7	0	— 23

KC — FG Stenerud 48 (8:08)
KC — FG Stenerud 32 (1:40)
KC — FG Stenerud 25 (7:08)
KC — Garrett 5 run (Stenerud kick) (9:26)
Minn — Osborn 4 run (Cox kick) (10:28)
KC — Taylor 46 pass from Dawson (Stenerud kick) (13:38)

SUPER BOWL III
Orange Bowl, Miami, Florida
January 12, 1969, Attendance: 75,389
NEW YORK JETS 16, BALTIMORE 7—Jets quarterback Joe Namath "guaranteed" victory on the Thursday before the game, then went out and led the AFL to its first Super Bowl victory over a Baltimore team that had lost only once in 16 games all season. Namath, chosen the outstanding player, completed 17 of 28 passes for 206 yards and directed a steady attack that dominated the NFL champions after the Jets' defense had intercepted Colts quarterback Earl Morrall 3 times in the first half. The Jets had 337 total yards, including 121 rushing yards by Matt Snell. Johnny Unitas, who had missed most of the season with a sore elbow, came off the bench and led Baltimore to its only touchdown late in the fourth quarter after New York led 16-0.

New York Jets (AFL)	0	7	6	3	— 16
Baltimore (NFL)	0	0	0	7	— 7

NYJ — Snell 4 run (Turner kick) (5:57)
NYJ — FG Turner 32 (4:52)
NYJ — FG Turner 30 (11:02)
NYJ — FG Turner 9 (1:34)
Balt — Hill 1 run (Michaels kick) (11:41)

SUPER BOWL II
Orange Bowl, Miami, Florida
January 14, 1968, Attendance: 75,546
GREEN BAY 33, OAKLAND 14—Green Bay, after winning its third consecutive NFL championship, won the Super Bowl title for the second straight year, defeating the AFL champion Raiders in a game that drew the first $3-million gate in football history. Bart Starr again was chosen the game's most valuable player as he completed 13 of 24 passes for 202 yards and 1 touchdown and directed a Packers' attack that was in control all the way after building a 16-7 halftime lead. Don Chandler kicked 4 field goals and all-pro cornerback Herb Adderley capped the Green Bay scoring with a 60-yard interception return. The game marked the last for Vince Lombardi as Packers coach, ending nine years at Green Bay in which he won six Western Conference championships, five NFL championships, and two Super Bowls.

Green Bay (NFL)	3	13	10	7	— 33
Oakland (AFL)	0	7	0	7	— 14

GB — FG Chandler 39 (5:07)
GB — FG Chandler 20 (3:08)
GB — Dowler 62 pass from Starr (Chandler kick) (4:10)
Oak — Miller 23 pass from Lamonica (Blanda kick) (8:45)
GB — FG Chandler 43 (14:59)
GB — Anderson 2 run (Chandler kick) (9:06)
GB — FG Chandler 31 (14:58)
GB — Adderley 60 interception return (Chandler kick) (3:57)
Oak — Miller 23 pass from Lamonica (Blanda kick) (5:47)

SUPER BOWL I
Memorial Coliseum, Los Angeles, CA
January 15, 1967, Attendance: 61,946
GREEN BAY 35, KANSAS CITY 10—The Green Bay Packers opened the Super Bowl series by defeating the AFL champion Chiefs behind the passing of Bart Starr, the receiving of Max McGee, and a key interception by all-pro safety Willie Wood. Green Bay broke open the game with 3 second-half touchdowns, the first of which was set up by Wood's 50-yard return of an interception. McGee, filling in for ailing Boyd Dowler after having caught only 4 passes all season, caught 7 from Starr for 138 yards and 2 touchdowns. Elijah Pitts ran for 2 other scores. The Chiefs' 10 points came in the second quarter, the only touchdown on a 7-yard pass from Len Dawson to Curtis McClinton. Starr completed 16 of 23 passes for 250 yards and 2 touchdowns and was chosen the most valuable player. The Packers collected $15,000 per man and the Chiefs $7,500—the largest single-game shares in the history of team sports.

Kansas City (AFL)	0	10	0	0	— 10
Green Bay (NFL)	7	7	14	7	— 35

GB — McGee 37 pass from Starr (Chandler kick) (8:56)
KC — McClinton 7 pass from Dawson (Mercer kick) (4:20)
GB — Taylor 14 run (Chandler kick) (10:23)
KC — FG Mercer 31 (14:06)
GB — Pitts 5 run (Chandler kick) (2:27)
GB — McGee 13 pass from Starr (Chandler kick) (14:09)
GB — Pitts 1 run (Chandler kick) (8:25)

AFC CHAMPIONSHIP GAME RESULTS

Includes AFL Championship Games (1960-69)

Season	Date	Winner (Share)	Loser (Share)	Score	Site	Attendance
2003	Jan. 18	New England ($36,500)	Indianapolis ($36,500)	24-14	Foxborough	68,436
2002	Jan. 19	Oakland ($35,000)	Tennessee ($35,000)	41-24	Oakland	62,544
2001	Jan. 27	New England ($34,500)	Pittsburgh ($34,500)	24-17	Pittsburgh	64,704
2000	Jan. 14	Baltimore ($34,500)	Oakland ($34,500)	16-3	Oakland	62,784
1999	Jan. 23	Tennessee ($33,000)	Jacksonville ($33,000)	33-14	Jacksonville	75,206
1998	Jan. 17	Denver ($32,500)	N.Y. Jets ($32,500)	23-10	Denver	75,482
1997	Jan. 11	Denver ($30,000)	Pittsburgh ($30,000)	24-21	Pittsburgh	61,382
1996	Jan. 12	New England ($29,000)	Jacksonville ($29,000)	20-6	Foxborough	60,190
1995	Jan. 14	Pittsburgh ($27,000)	Indianapolis ($27,000)	20-16	Pittsburgh	61,062
1994	Jan. 15	San Diego ($26,000)	Pittsburgh ($26,000)	17-13	Pittsburgh	61,545
1993	Jan. 23	Buffalo ($23,500)	Kansas City ($23,500)	30-13	Buffalo	76,642
1992	Jan. 17	Buffalo ($18,000)	Miami ($18,000)	29-10	Miami	72,703
1991	Jan. 12	Buffalo ($18,000)	Denver ($18,000)	10-7	Buffalo	80,272
1990	Jan. 20	Buffalo ($18,000)	L.A. Raiders ($18,000)	51-3	Buffalo	80,325
1989	Jan. 14	Denver ($18,000)	Cleveland ($18,000)	37-21	Denver	76,046
1988	Jan. 8	Cincinnati ($18,000)	Buffalo ($18,000)	21-10	Cincinnati	59,747
1987	Jan. 17	Denver ($18,000)	Cleveland ($18,000)	38-33	Denver	76,197
1986	Jan. 11	Denver ($18,000)	Cleveland ($18,000)	23-20*	Cleveland	79,973
1985	Jan. 12	New England ($18,000)	Miami ($18,000)	31-14	Miami	75,662
1984	Jan. 6	Miami ($18,000)	Pittsburgh ($18,000)	45-28	Miami	76,029
1983	Jan. 8	L.A. Raiders ($18,000)	Seattle ($18,000)	30-14	Los Angeles	91,445
1982	Jan. 23	Miami ($18,000)	N.Y. Jets ($18,000)	14-0	Miami	67,396
1981	Jan. 10	Cincinnati ($9,000)	San Diego ($9,000)	27-7	Cincinnati	46,302
1980	Jan. 11	Oakland ($9,000)	San Diego ($9,000)	34-27	San Diego	52,675
1979	Jan. 6	Pittsburgh ($9,000)	Houston ($9,000)	27-13	Pittsburgh	50,475
1978	Jan. 7	Pittsburgh ($9,000)	Houston ($9,000)	34-5	Pittsburgh	50,725
1977	Jan. 1	Denver ($9,000)	Oakland ($9,000)	20-17	Denver	75,044
1976	Dec. 26	Oakland ($8,500)	Pittsburgh ($5,500)	24-7	Oakland	53,821
1975	Jan. 4	Pittsburgh ($8,500)	Oakland ($5,500)	16-10	Pittsburgh	50,609
1974	Dec. 29	Pittsburgh ($8,500)	Oakland ($5,500)	24-13	Oakland	53,800
1973	Dec. 30	Miami ($8,500)	Oakland ($5,500)	27-10	Miami	79,325
1972	Dec. 31	Miami ($8,500)	Pittsburgh ($5,500)	21-17	Pittsburgh	50,845
1971	Jan. 2	Miami ($8,500)	Baltimore ($5,500)	21-0	Miami	76,622
1970	Jan. 3	Baltimore ($8,500)	Oakland ($5,500)	27-17	Baltimore	54,799
1969	Jan. 4	Kansas City ($7,755)	Oakland ($6,252)	17-7	Oakland	53,564
1968	Dec. 29	N.Y. Jets ($7,007)	Oakland ($5,349)	27-23	New York	62,627
1967	Dec. 31	Oakland ($6,321)	Houston ($4,996)	40-7	Oakland	53,330
1966	Jan. 1	Kansas City ($5,309)	Buffalo ($3,799)	31-7	Buffalo	42,080
1965	Dec. 26	Buffalo ($5,189)	San Diego ($3,447)	23-0	San Diego	30,361
1964	Dec. 26	Buffalo ($2,668)	San Diego ($1,738)	20-7	Buffalo	40,242
1963	Jan. 5	San Diego ($2,498)	Boston ($1,596)	51-10	San Diego	30,127
1962	Dec. 23	Dallas ($2,206)	Houston ($1,471)	20-17*	Houston	37,981
1961	Dec. 24	Houston ($1,792)	San Diego ($1,111)	10-3	San Diego	29,556
1960	Jan. 1	Houston ($1,025)	L.A. Chargers ($718)	24-16	Houston	32,183

**Sudden death overtime*

AFC CHAMPIONSHIP GAME COMPOSITE STANDINGS

	W	L	Pct.	Pts.	OP
Cincinnati Bengals	2	0	1.000	48	17
Baltimore Ravens	1	0	1.000	16	3
Denver Broncos	6	1	.857	172	132
New England Patriots**	4	1	.800	109	102
Buffalo Bills	6	2	.750	180	92
Kansas City Chiefs*	3	1	.750	81	61
Miami Dolphins	5	2	.714	152	115
Pittsburgh Steelers	5	6	.455	224	212
Tennessee Titans##	3	5	.375	133	195
Oakland Raiders###	5	9	.357	272	304
New York Jets	1	2	.333	37	60
San Diego Chargers***	2	6	.250	128	161
Indianapolis Colts#	1	3	.250	57	82
Seattle Seahawks	0	1	.000	14	30
Jacksonville Jaguars	0	2	.000	20	53
Cleveland Browns	0	3	.000	74	98

* *One game played when franchise was in Dallas (Texans) (Won 20-17)*
** *One game played when franchise was in Boston (Lost 51-10)*
*** *One game played when franchise was in Los Angeles (Lost 24-16)*
\# *Two games played when franchise was in Baltimore (Won 27-17, lost 21-0)*
\#\# *Six games played when franchise was in Houston and known as Oilers (Won 2, lost 4)*
\#\#\# *Two games played when franchise was in Los Angeles (Won 30-14, lost 51-3)*

2003 AFC CHAMPIONSHIP GAME

Gillette Stadium, Foxborough, Massachusetts
January 18, 2004, Attendance: 68,436

NEW ENGLAND 24, INDIANAPOLIS 14—Adam Vinatieri kicked 5 field goals and the Patriots' defense forced 6 turnovers en route to New England's second Super Bowl appearance in three years.

The Colts had 4 first-half possessions, and turned the ball over all four times. The Patriots began the game with a 65-yard touchdown drive. Peyton Manning was intercepted on the Colts' first two possessions, including the first one in the end zone by Rodney Harrison, to set up 2 field goals for a 13-0 lead. The Colts were then forced to punt for the first time in two and a half postseason games, and Justin Snow's snap sailed over Hunter Smith's head. Smith intentionally kicked the ball out of the end zone for a safety. A New England fumble gave Indianapolis life, but Marvin Harrison fumbled at the Patriots' 16 just before halftime, and Tyrone Poole recovered. The Colts scored on Edgerrin James' 2-yard run to open the second half, a drive that featured James' 3-yard run on fourth-and-1. The Patriots drove inside the Colts' 10 on each of their next two possessions, but settled for field goals by Vinatieri for a 21-7 lead. An interception by Ty Law gave New England a chance to put the game away, but Walt Harris intercepted Tom Brady in the end zone for a touchback with 13:28 to play. The Colts took five minutes off the clock on the ensuing drive, but Law intercepted Manning's fourth-and-13 pass with 8:17 left. The Colts forced a punt, but it took them nearly four minutes to drive 67 yards to cut the deficit to 21-14 on Marcus Pollard's 7-yard catch with 2:27 to play. Christian Fauria recovered the onside kick, but the Patriots failed to gain a first down and the Colts got the ball back with 2:01 left, but Manning threw four consecutive incompletions. Vinatieri's 34-yard field goal with 50 seconds left iced the game. Brady was 22 of 37 for 237 yards and 1 touchdown, with 1 interception. Antowain Smith had 22 carries for 100 yards. Law had 3 interceptions. Manning was 23 of 47 for 237 yards and 1 touchdown, with 4 interceptions.

Indianapolis (14)	Offense	New England (24)
Reggie Wayne	WR	Deion Branch
Tarik Glenn	LT	Matt Light
Rick DeMulling	LG	Russ Hochstein
Jeff Saturday	C	Daniel Koppen
Tupe Peko	RG	Joe Andruzzi
Ryan Diem	RT	Tom Ashworth
Marcus Pollard	TE	Christian Fauria
Marvin Harrison	WR	David Givens
Peyton Manning	QB	Tom Brady
Edgerrin James	RB	Antowain Smith
Joe Dean Davenport	TE-FB	Larry Centers
	Defense	
Raheem Brock	LE	Bobby Hamilton
Larry Tripplett	LT-NT	Ted Washington
Montae Reagor	RT-RE	Richard Seymour
Dwight Freeney	RE-OLB	Willie McGinest
Marcus Washington	LLB-ILB	Tedy Bruschi
Rob Morris	MLB-ILB	Roman Phifer
David Thornton	RLB-OLB	Mike Vrabel
Walt Harris	LCB	Ty Law
David Macklin	RCB	Tyrone Poole
Mike Doss	SS	Rodney Harrison
Donald Strickland	FS	Eugene Wilson

SUBSTITUTIONS

Indianapolis—Specialists: K—Mike Vanderjagt. P—Hunter Smith. Offense: RB—Tom Lopienski, Dominic Rhodes, Ricky Williams. WR—Brandon Stokley, Troy Walters. TE—Justin Snow. G—Steve Sciullo. Defense: DT—Josh Williams. DE—Chad Bratzke, Robert Mathis, Brad Scioli. LB—Gary Brackett, Jim Nelson, Keyon Whiteside. DB—Cory Bird, Cliff Crosby, Jason Doering, Anthony Floyd, Nick Harper. DNP: QB—Brock Huard. T—Makoa Freitas

New England—Specialists: K—Adam Vinatieri. P—Ken Walter. LS—Brian Kinchen. Offense: FB—Patrick Pass. RB—Kevin Faulk. WR—Troy Brown, Bethel Johnson, Dedric Ward. TE—Daniel Graham. T—Brandon Gorin. G—Wilbert Brown. Defense: DT-DE—Jarvis Green, Ty Warren. LB—Tully Banta-Cain, Matt Chatham, Don Davis, Larry Izzo, Ted Johnson. CB—Asante Samuel. S—Chris Akins, Je'Rod Cherry, Shawn Mayer. DNP: QB— Damon Huard.

OFFICIALS

Referee—Walt Coleman. Umpire—Butch Hannah. Line Judge—Ron Phares. Side Judge—Dave Wyant. Head Linesman—Paul Weidner. Back Judge—Bill Schmitz. Field Judge—Scott Steenson.

SCORING

Indianapolis	0	0	7	7	—	14
New England	7	8	6	3	—	24

NE — Givens 7 pass from Brady (Vinatieri kick)
NE — FG Vinatieri 31
NE — FG Vinatieri 25
NE — Safety, Snow's snap sailed over punter's head and was kicked through end zone
Ind — James 2 run (Vanderjagt kick)
NE — FG Vinatieri 27
NE — FG Vinatieri 21
Ind — Pollard 7 pas from Manning (Vanderjagt kick)
NE — FG Vinatieri 34

TEAM STATISTICS	IND	NE
Total First Downs	21	20
Rushing	8	5
Passing	13	15
Penalty	0	0
Total Net Yardage	306	349
Total Offensive Plays	76	69
Average Gain Per Offensive Play	4.0	5.1
Rushes	25	32
Yards Gained Rushing (Net)	98	112
Average Yards per Rush	3.9	3.5
Passes Attempted	47	37
Passes Completed	23	22
Had Intercepted	4	1
Tackled Attempting to Pass	4	0
Yards Lost Attempting to Pass	29	0
Yards Gained Passing (Net)	208	237
Punts	1	2
Average Distance	55.0	37.0
Punt Returns	0	1
Punt Return Yardage	0	16
Kickoff Returns	7	3
Kickoff Return Yardage	145	53
Interception Return Yardage	0	26
Total Return Yardage	152	95
Fumbles	2	1
Fumbles Lost	1	1
Own Fumbles Recovered	1	0
Opponent Fumbles Recovered	1	1
Penalties	4	3
Yards Penalized	20	15
Field Goals	0	5
Field Goals Attempted	0	5
Third-Down Efficiency	5/14	5/15
Fourth-Down Efficiency	3/7	2/2
Time of Possession	27:46	32:14

INDIVIDUAL STATISTICS

RUSHING: IND: James 19-78-1, Rhodes 3-16-0, Manning 2-4-0, H. Smith 1-0-0. NE: Smith 22-100-0, Faulk 3-8-0, B. Johnson 1-3-0, Brady 5-1-0, Centers 1-0-0.

PASSING: IND: Manning 47-23-237-1-4. NE: Brady 37-22-237-1-1.

RECEIVING: IND: Pollard 6-90-1, Wayne 4-46-0, Walters 3-30-0, Stokley 3-22-0, Harrison 3-19-0, Rhodes 2-17-0, James 2-13-0. NE: Givens 8-68-1, Brown 7-88-0, Branch 2-23-0, Centers 1-28-0, Smith 1-8-0, Fauria 1-8-0, Faulk 1-8-0, B. Johnson 1-6-0.

KICKOFF RETURNS: IND: Rhodes 5-121-0, Williams 1-13-0, Peko 1-11-0. NE: Pass 1-21-0, Faulk 1-16-0, Brown 1-16-0.

PUNT RETURNS: IND: Walters 0-0-0. NE: Brown 1-16-0.

PUNTING: IND: H. Smith 1-55-0. NE: Walter 2-74-0.

INTERCEPTIONS: IND: Harris 1-0-0. NE: Law 3-26, Harrison 1-0.

SACKS: IND: None. NE: Green 2.5, McGinest 1.0, Phifer 0.5.

NFC CHAMPIONSHIP GAME RESULTS

Includes NFL Championship Games (1933-1969)

Season	Date	Winner (Share)	Loser (Share)	Score	Site	Attendance
2003	Jan. 18	Carolina ($36,500)	Philadelphia ($36,500)	14-3	Philadelphia	67,862
2002	Jan. 19	Tampa Bay ($35,000)	Philadelphia ($35,000)	27-10	Philadelphia	66,713
2001	Jan. 27	St. Louis ($34,500)	Philadelphia ($34,500)	29-24	St. Louis	66,502
2000	Jan. 14	N.Y. Giants ($34,500)	Minnesota ($34,500)	41-0	East Rutherford	79,310
1999	Jan. 23	St. Louis ($33,000)	Tampa Bay ($33,000)	11-6	St. Louis	66,396
1998	Jan. 17	Atlanta ($32,500)	Minnesota ($32,500)	30-27*	Minneapolis	64,060
1997	Jan. 11	Green Bay ($30,000)	San Francisco ($30,000)	23-10	San Francisco	68,987
1996	Jan. 12	Green Bay ($29,000)	Carolina ($29,000)	30-13	Green Bay	60,216
1995	Jan. 14	Dallas ($27,000)	Green Bay ($27,000)	38-27	Dallas	65,135
1994	Jan. 15	San Francisco ($26,000)	Dallas ($26,000)	38-28	San Francisco	69,125
1993	Jan. 23	Dallas ($23,500)	San Francisco ($23,500)	38-21	Dallas	64,902
1992	Jan. 17	Dallas ($18,000)	San Francisco ($18,000)	30-20	San Francisco	64,920
1991	Jan. 12	Washington ($18,000)	Detroit ($18,000)	41-10	Washington	55,585
1990	Jan. 20	N.Y. Giants ($18,000)	San Francisco ($18,000)	15-13	San Francisco	65,750
1989	Jan. 14	San Francisco ($18,000)	L.A. Rams ($18,000)	30-3	San Francisco	65,634
1988	Jan. 8	San Francisco ($18,000)	Chicago ($18,000)	28-3	Chicago	66,946
1987	Jan. 17	Washington ($18,000)	Minnesota ($18,000)	17-10	Washington	55,212
1986	Jan. 11	New York Giants ($18,000)	Washington ($18,000)	17-0	East Rutherford	76,891
1985	Jan. 12	Chicago ($18,000)	L.A. Rams ($18,000)	24-0	Chicago	66,030
1984	Jan. 6	San Francisco ($18,000)	Chicago ($18,000)	23-0	San Francisco	61,336
1983	Jan. 8	Washington ($18,000)	San Francisco ($18,000)	24-21	Washington	55,363
1982	Jan. 22	Washington ($18,000)	Dallas ($18,000)	31-17	Washington	55,045
1981	Jan. 10	San Francisco ($9,000)	Dallas ($9,000)	28-27	San Francisco	60,525
1980	Jan. 11	Philadelphia ($9,000)	Dallas ($9,000)	20-7	Philadelphia	71,522
1979	Jan. 6	Los Angeles ($9,000)	Tampa Bay ($9,000)	9-0	Tampa	72,033
1978	Jan. 7	Dallas ($9,000)	Los Angeles ($9,000)	28-0	Los Angeles	71,086
1977	Jan. 1	Dallas ($9,000)	Minnesota ($9,000)	23-6	Dallas	64,293
1976	Dec. 26	Minnesota ($8,500)	Los Angeles ($5,500)	24-13	Minneapolis	48,379
1975	Jan. 4	Dallas ($8,500)	Los Angeles ($5,500)	37-7	Los Angeles	88,919
1974	Dec. 29	Minnesota ($8,500)	Los Angeles ($5,500)	14-10	Minneapolis	48,444
1973	Dec. 30	Minnesota ($8,500)	Dallas ($5,500)	27-10	Dallas	64,422
1972	Dec. 31	Washington ($8,500)	Dallas ($5,500)	26-3	Washington	53,129
1971	Jan. 2	Dallas ($8,500)	San Francisco ($5,500)	14-3	Dallas	63,409
1970	Jan. 3	Dallas ($8,500)	San Francisco ($5,500)	17-10	San Francisco	59,364
1969	Jan. 4	Minnesota ($7,930)	Cleveland ($5,118)	27-7	Minneapolis	46,503
1968	Dec. 29	Baltimore ($9,306)	Cleveland ($5,963)	34-0	Cleveland	78,410
1967	Dec. 31	Green Bay ($7,950)	Dallas ($5,299)	21-17	Green Bay	50,861
1966	Jan. 1	Green Bay ($9,813)	Dallas ($6,527)	34-27	Dallas	74,152
1965	Jan. 2	Green Bay ($7,819)	Cleveland ($5,288)	23-12	Green Bay	50,777
1964	Dec. 27	Cleveland ($8,052)	Baltimore ($5,571)	27-0	Cleveland	79,544
1963	Dec. 29	Chicago ($5,899)	New York ($4,218)	14-10	Chicago	45,801
1962	Dec. 30	Green Bay ($5,888)	New York ($4,166)	16-7	New York	64,892
1961	Dec. 31	Green Bay ($5,195)	New York ($3,339)	37-0	Green Bay	39,029
1960	Dec. 26	Philadelphia ($5,116)	Green Bay ($3,105)	17-13	Philadelphia	67,325
1959	Dec. 27	Baltimore ($4,674)	New York ($3,083)	31-16	Baltimore	57,545
1958	Dec. 28	Baltimore ($4,718)	New York ($3,111)	23-17*	New York	64,185
1957	Dec. 29	Detroit ($4,295)	Cleveland ($2,750)	59-14	Detroit	55,263
1956	Dec. 30	New York ($3,779)	Chi. Bears ($2,485)	47-7	New York	56,836
1955	Dec. 26	Cleveland ($3,508)	Los Angeles ($2,316)	38-14	Los Angeles	85,693
1954	Dec. 26	Cleveland ($2,478)	Detroit ($1,585)	56-10	Cleveland	43,827
1953	Dec. 27	Detroit ($2,424)	Cleveland ($1,654)	17-16	Detroit	54,577
1952	Dec. 28	Detroit ($2,274)	Cleveland ($1,712)	17-7	Cleveland	50,934
1951	Dec. 23	Los Angeles ($2,108)	Cleveland ($1,483)	24-17	Los Angeles	57,522
1950	Dec. 24	Cleveland ($1,113)	Los Angeles ($686)	30-28	Cleveland	29,751
1949	Dec. 18	Philadelphia ($1,094)	Los Angeles ($739)	14-0	Los Angeles	27,980
1948	Dec. 19	Philadelphia ($1,540)	Chi. Cardinals ($874)	7-0	Philadelphia	36,309
1947	Dec. 28	Chi. Cardinals ($1,132)	Philadelphia ($754)	28-21	Chicago	30,759
1946	Dec. 15	Chi. Bears ($1,975)	New York ($1,295)	24-14	New York	58,346
1945	Dec. 16	Cleveland ($1,469)	Washington ($902)	15-14	Cleveland	32,178
1944	Dec. 17	Green Bay ($1,449)	New York ($814)	14-7	New York	46,016
1943	Dec. 26	Chi. Bears ($1,146)	Washington ($765)	41-21	Chicago	34,320
1942	Dec. 13	Washington ($965)	Chi. Bears ($637)	14-6	Washington	36,006
1941	Dec. 21	Chi. Bears ($430)	New York ($288)	37-9	Chicago	13,341
1940	Dec. 8	Chi. Bears ($873)	Washington ($606)	73-0	Washington	36,034
1939	Dec. 10	Green Bay ($703.97)	New York ($455.57)	27-0	Milwaukee	32,279

Season	Date	Winner (Share)	Loser (Share)	Score	Site	Attendance
1938	Dec. 11	New York ($504.45)	Green Bay ($368.81)	23-17	New York	48,120
1937	Dec. 12	Washington ($225.90)	Chi. Bears ($127.78)	28-21	Chicago	15,870
1936	Dec. 13	Green Bay ($250)	Boston ($180)	21-6	New York	29,545
1935	Dec. 15	Detroit ($313.35)	New York ($200.20)	26-7	Detroit	15,000
1934	Dec. 9	New York ($621)	Chi. Bears ($414.02)	30-13	New York	35,059
1933	Dec. 17	Chi. Bears ($210.34)	New York ($140.22)	23-21	Chicago	26,000

**Sudden death overtime*

NFC CHAMPIONSHIP GAME COMPOSITE STANDINGS

	W	L	Pct.	Pts.	OP
Atlanta Falcons	1	0	1.000	30	27
Green Bay Packers	10	3	.769	303	177
Baltimore Colts	3	1	.750	88	60
Detroit Lions	4	2	.667	139	141
Washington Redskins*	7	5	.583	222	255
Chicago Bears	7	6	.538	286	245
Dallas Cowboys	8	8	.500	361	319
Minnesota Vikings	4	4	.500	135	151
Philadelphia Eagles	4	4	.500	116	118
Arizona Cardinals**	1	1	.500	28	28
Carolina Panthers	1	1	.500	27	33
San Francisco 49ers	5	7	.417	245	222
Cleveland Browns	4	7	.364	224	253
St. Louis Rams***	5	9	.357	163	300
New York Giants	6	11	.353	281	322
Tampa Bay Buccaneers	1	2	.333	33	30

**One game played when franchise was in Boston (Lost 21-6)*

***Both games played when franchise was in Chicago (Won 28-21, lost 7-0)*

****One game played when franchise was in Cleveland (Won 15-14), and 11 games when franchise was in Los Angeles (Won 2, lost 9, scored 108 points, allowed 256 points).*

2003 NFC CHAMPIONSHIP GAME

Lincoln Financial Field, Philadelphia, Pennsylvania
January 18, 2004, Attendance: 67,862

CAROLINA 14, PHILADELPHIA 3—Jake Delhomme passed for a touchdown and the Panthers forced 4 turnovers to advance to their first Super Bowl appearance. After a scoreless first quarter, Delhomme engineered an 8-play, 79-yard drive with 2 third-down conversions and capped by Muhsin Muhammad's 24-yard touchdown catch. The Eagles responded with a 41-yard field goal by David Akers. Two plays before the field goal, Donovan McNabb injured his ribs when, after tripping, he was hit by Mike Rucker. In the third quarter, Ricky Manning Jr. twice intercepted McNabb's passes. The first came at the Panthers' 14 to stop a drive, and the latter came at the Eagles' 37 to setup DeShaun Foster's 1-yard run with 4:11 left in the third quarter. Koy Detmer replaced the injured McNabb with 9:31 left, and drove the Eagles 81 yards to the Panthers' 11, but Dan Morgan intercepted his third-and-3 pass with 5:16 left. The Eagles got the ball back one last time, but Detmer's fourth-and-18 pass from midfield fell incomplete with 1:58 left. Delhomme was 9 of 14 for 101 yards and 1 touchdown. McNabb was 10 of 22 for 100 yards, with 3 interceptions, and Detmer was 7 of 14 for 88 yards, with 1 interception.

Carolina (14)	Offense	Philadelphia (3)
Muhsin Muhammad	WR	Todd Pinkston
Todd Steussie	LT	Tra Thomas
Jeno James	LG	John Welbourn
Jeff Mitchell	C	Hank Fraley
Kevin Donnalley	RG	Brandon Williams
Jordan Gross	RT	Jon Runyan
Kris Mangum	TE	Chad Lewis
Steve Smith	WR	James Thrash
Jake Delhomme	QB	Donovan McNabb
Stephen Davis	RB	Duce Staley
Jermaine Wiggins	TE-RB	Reno Mahe
	Defense	
Julius Peppers	LE	Brandon Whiting
Brentson Buckner	LT	Corey Simon
Kris Jenkins	RT	Darwin Walker
Mike Rucker	RE	N.D. Kalu
Terry Cousin	CB-WLB	Nate Wayne
Dan Morgan	MLB	Mark Simoneau
Will Witherspoon	SLB	Ike Reese
Ricky Manning Jr.	LCB	Troy Vincent
Reggie Howard	RCB	Bobby Taylor
Mike Minter	SS	Michael Lewis
Deon Grant	FS	Brian Dawkins

SUBSTITUTIONS

Carolina—Specialists: K—John Kasay. P—Todd Sauerbrun. Offense: FB—Brad Hoover. RB—DeShaun Foster, Nick Goings, Rod Smart. WR—Kevin Dyson, Karl Hankton, Ricky Proehl. G—Bruce Nelson. T—Matt Willig. Defense: DT—Shane Burton. DE—Kemp Rasmussen, Al Wallace. LB—Brian Allen, Vinny Ciurciu, Greg Favors, Jason Kyle, Lester Towns. CB—Dante Wesley. S—Colin Branch, Jarrod Cooper. DNP: QB—Rodney Peete.

Philadelphia—Specialists: K—David Akers. P—Dirk Johnson. Offense: QB—Koy Detmer. FB—Jon Ritchie. RB—Correll Buckhalter. WR—Greg Lewis, Freddie Mitchell, Sean Morey. TE—L.J. Smith. TE-LS—Mike Bartrum. C—Alonzo Ephraim. T—Artis Hicks. Defense: DT—Sam Rayburn. DE—Marco Coleman, Jerome McDougle. LB—Keith Adams, Justin Ena, Tyreo Harrison. CB—Sheldon Brown, Roderick Hood, Lito Sheppard. S—Clinton Hart, Quintin Mikell.

OFFICIALS

Referee—Bernie Kukar. Umpire—Bill Schuster. Line Judge—Tom Barnes. Side Judge—Tom Hill. Head Linesman—Mike Baltz. Back Judge—Jim Howey. Field Judge—Steve Zimmer.

SCORING

Carolina	0	7	7	0	—	14
Philadelphia	0	3	0	0	—	3

Car — Muhammad 24 pass from Delhomme (Kasay kick)
Phil — FG Akers 41
Car — Foster 1 run (Kasay kick)

TEAM STATISTICS	CAR	PHIL
Total First Downs	14	18
Rushing	8	8
Passing	5	7
Penalty	1	3
Total Net Yardage	256	289
Total Offensive Plays	54	67
Average Gain Per Offensive Play	4.7	4.3
Rushes	40	26
Yards Gained Rushing (Net)	155	137
Average Yards per Rush	3.9	5.3
Passes Attempted	14	36
Passes Completed	9	17
Had Intercepted	0	4
Tackled Attempting to Pass	0	5
Yards Lost Attempting to Pass	0	36
Yards Gained Passing (Net)	101	152
Punts	8	4
Average Distance	38.3	36.8
Punt Returns	0	2
Punt Return Yardage	0	14
Kickoff Returns	2	3
Kickoff Return Yardage	57	62
Interception Return Yardage	13	0
Total Return Yardage	70	76
Fumbles	1	1
Fumbles Lost	0	0
Own Fumbles Recovered	1	1
Opponent Fumbles Recovered	0	0
Penalties	5	4
Yards Penalized	35	34
Field Goals	0	1
Field Goals Attempted	0	1
Third-Down Efficiency	4/13	2/13
Fourth-Down Efficiency	0/0	1/2
Time of Possession	30:11	29:49

INDIVIDUAL STATISTICS

RUSHING: CAR: Davis 19-76-0, Foster 14-60-1, Delhomme 4-7-0, Muhammad 1-5-0, Smart 1-5-0, Hoover 1-2-0. PHIL: Staley 13-79-0, Buckhalter 11-48-0, McNabb 2-10-0.

PASSING: CAR: Delhomme 14-9-101-1-0. PHIL: McNabb 22-10-100-0-3, Detmer 14-7-88-0-1.

RECEIVING: CAR: Smith 3-26-0, Muhammad 2-39-1, Davis 1-21-0, Hoover 1-6-0, Foster 1-6-0, Goings 1-3-0. PHIL: Lewis 4-69-0, Mithcell 4-38-0, Staley 4-33-0, Buckhalter 2-26-0, Smith 1-12-0, Thrash 1-9-0, Ritchie 1-1-0.

KICKOFF RETURNS: CAR: Smart 1-40-0, Dyson 1-17-0. PHIL: Thrash 3-62-0.

PUNT RETURNS: CAR: Smith 0-0-0. PHIL: Sheppard 1-11-0, Mahe 1-3-0.

PUNTING: CAR: Sauerbrun 7-285-40.7, Kasay 1-21-0. PHIL: Johnson 4-147-36.8.

INTERCEPTIONS: CAR: Manning 3-15-0, Morgan 1-(-2)-0. PHIL: None.

SACKS: CAR: Buckner 1.5, Rucker 1.0, Witherspoon 1.0, Burton 0.5, Minter 0.5, Wallace 0.5. PHIL: None.

AFC DIVISIONAL PLAYOFFS RESULTS

Includes Second-Round Playoff Games (1982), AFC Inter-Divisional Games (1969), and special playoff games to break ties for AFL Division Championships (1963, 1968)

Season	Date	Winner (Share)	Loser (Share)	Score	Site	Attendance
2003	Jan. 11	Indianapolis ($18,000)	Kansas City ($18,000)	38-31	Kansas City	79,159
	Jan. 10	New England ($18,000)	Tennessee ($18,000)	17-14	Foxborough	68,436
2002	Jan. 12	Oakland ($17,000)	N.Y. Jets ($17,000)	30-10	Oakland	62,207
	Jan. 11	Tennessee ($17,000)	Pittsburgh ($17,000)	34-31*	Nashville	68,809
2001	Jan. 20	Pittsburgh ($17,000)	Baltimore ($17,000)	27-10	Pittsburgh	63,976
	Jan. 19	New England ($17,000)	Oakland ($17,000)	16-13*	Foxborough	60,292
2000	Jan. 7	Baltimore ($16,000)	Tennessee ($16,000)	24-10	Nashville	68,527
	Jan. 6	Oakland ($16,000)	Miami ($16,000)	27-0	Oakland	61,998
1999	Jan. 16	Tennessee ($16,000)	Indianapolis ($16,000)	19-16	Indianapolis	57,097
	Jan. 15	Jacksonville ($16,000)	Miami ($16,000)	62-7	Jacksonville	75,173
1998	Jan. 10	N.Y. Jets ($15,000)	Jacksonville ($15,000)	34-24	East Rutherford	78,817
	Jan. 9	Denver ($15,000)	Miami ($15,000)	38-3	Denver	75,729
1997	Jan. 4	Denver ($15,000)	Kansas City ($15,000)	14-10	Kansas City	76,965
	Jan. 3	Pittsburgh ($15,000)	New England ($15,000)	7-6	Pittsburgh	61,228
1996	Jan. 5	New England ($14,000)	Pittsburgh ($14,000)	28-3	Foxborough	60,188
	Jan. 4	Jacksonville ($14,000)	Denver ($14,000)	30-27	Denver	75,678
1995	Jan. 7	Indianapolis ($13,000)	Kansas City ($13,000)	10-7	Kansas City	77,594
	Jan. 6	Pittsburgh ($13,000)	Buffalo ($13,000)	40-21	Pittsburgh	59,072
1994	Jan. 8	San Diego ($12,000)	Miami ($12,000)	22-21	San Diego	63,381
	Jan. 7	Pittsburgh ($12,000)	Cleveland ($12,000)	29-9	Pittsburgh	58,185
1993	Jan. 16	Kansas City ($12,000)	Houston ($12,000)	28-20	Houston	64,011
	Jan. 15	Buffalo ($12,000)	L.A. Raiders ($12,000)	29-23	Buffalo	61,923
1992	Jan. 10	Miami ($10,000)	San Diego ($10,000)	31-0	Miami	71,224
	Jan. 9	Buffalo ($10,000)	Pittsburgh ($10,000)	24-3	Pittsburgh	60,407
1991	Jan. 5	Buffalo ($10,000)	Kansas City ($10,000)	37-14	Buffalo	80,182
	Jan. 4	Denver ($10,000)	Houston ($10,000)	26-24	Denver	75,301
1990	Jan. 13	L.A. Raiders ($10,000)	Cincinnati ($10,000)	20-10	Los Angeles	92,045
	Jan. 12	Buffalo ($10,000)	Miami ($10,000)	44-34	Buffalo	77,087
1989	Jan. 7	Denver ($10,000)	Pittsburgh ($10,000)	24-23	Denver	75,477
	Jan. 6	Cleveland ($10,000)	Buffalo ($10,000)	34-30	Cleveland	78,921
1988	Jan. 1	Buffalo ($10,000)	Houston ($10,000)	17-10	Buffalo	79,532
	Dec. 31	Cincinnati ($10,000)	Seattle ($10,000)	21-13	Cincinnati	58,560
1987	Jan. 10	Denver ($10,000)	Houston ($10,000)	34-10	Denver	75,440
	Jan. 9	Cleveland ($10,000)	Indianapolis ($10,000)	38-21	Cleveland	79,372

PLAYOFF GAME SUMMARIES

Season	Date	Winner (Share)	Loser (Share)	Score	Site	Attendance
1986	Jan. 4	Denver ($10,000)	New England ($10,000)	22-17	Denver	75,262
	Jan. 3	Cleveland ($10,000)	N.Y. Jets ($10,000)	23-20*	Cleveland	79,720
1985	Jan. 5	New England ($10,000)	L.A. Raiders ($10,000)	27-20	Los Angeles	87,163
	Jan. 4	Miami ($10,000)	Cleveland ($10,000)	24-21	Miami	74,667
1984	Dec. 30	Pittsburgh ($10,000)	Denver ($10,000)	24-17	Denver	74,981
	Dec. 29	Miami ($10,000)	Seattle ($10,000)	31-10	Miami	73,469
1983	Jan. 1	L.A. Raiders ($10,000)	Pittsburgh ($10,000)	38-10	Los Angeles	90,380
	Dec. 31	Seattle ($10,000)	Miami ($10,000)	27-20	Miami	74,136
1982	Jan. 16	Miami ($10,000)	San Diego ($10,000)	34-13	Miami	71,383
	Jan. 15	N.Y. Jets ($10,000)	L.A. Raiders ($10,000)	17-14	Los Angeles	90,038
1981	Jan. 3	Cincinnati ($5,000)	Buffalo ($5,000)	28-21	Cincinnati	55,420
	Jan. 2	San Diego ($5,000)	Miami ($5,000)	41-38*	Miami	73,735
1980	Jan. 4	Oakland ($5,000)	Cleveland ($5,000)	14-12	Cleveland	78,245
	Jan. 3	San Diego ($5,000)	Buffalo ($5,000)	20-14	San Diego	52,253
1979	Dec. 30	Pittsburgh ($5,000)	Miami ($5,000)	34-14	Pittsburgh	50,214
	Dec. 29	Houston ($5,000)	San Diego ($5,000)	17-14	San Diego	51,192
1978	Dec. 31	Houston ($5,000)	New England ($5,000)	31-14	Foxborough	60,735
	Dec. 30	Pittsburgh ($5,000)	Denver ($5,000)	33-10	Pittsburgh	50,230
1977	Dec. 24	Oakland ($5,000)	Baltimore ($5,000)	37-31*	Baltimore	59,925
	Dec. 24	Denver ($5,000)	Pittsburgh ($5,000)	34-21	Denver	75,059
1976	Dec. 19	Pittsburgh [$]	Baltimore [$]	40-14	Baltimore	59,296
	Dec. 18	Oakland [$]	New England [$]	24-21	Oakland	53,050
1975	Dec. 28	Oakland [$]	Cincinnati [$]	31-28	Oakland	53,030
	Dec. 27	Pittsburgh [$]	Baltimore [$]	28-10	Pittsburgh	49,557
1974	Dec. 22	Pittsburgh [$]	Buffalo [$]	32-14	Pittsburgh	49,841
	Dec. 21	Oakland [$]	Miami [$]	28-26	Oakland	53,023
1973	Dec. 23	Miami [$]	Cincinnati [$]	34-16	Miami	78,928
	Dec. 22	Oakland [$]	Pittsburgh [$]	33-14	Oakland	52,646
1972	Dec. 24	Miami [$]	Cleveland [$]	20-14	Miami	78,916
	Dec. 23	Pittsburgh [$]	Oakland [$]	13-7	Pittsburgh	50,327
1971	Dec. 26	Baltimore [$]	Cleveland [$]	20-3	Cleveland	70,734
	Dec. 25	Miami [$]	Kansas City [$]	27-24*	Kansas City	50,374
1970	Dec. 27	Oakland [$]	Miami [$]	21-14	Oakland	52,594
	Dec. 26	Baltimore [$]	Cincinnati [$]	17-0	Baltimore	49,694
1969	Dec. 21	Oakland [$]	Houston [$]	56-7	Oakland	53,539
	Dec. 20	Kansas City [$]	N.Y. Jets [$]	13-6	New York	62,977
1968	Dec. 22	Oakland [$]	Kansas City [$]	41-6	Oakland	53,605
1963	Dec. 28	Boston [$]	Buffalo [$]	26-8	Buffalo	33,044

**Sudden death overtime*

$ Players received 1/14 of annual salary for playoff appearances.

2003 AFC DIVISIONAL PLAYOFF GAMES

Arrowhead Stadium, Kansas City, Missouri
January 11, 2004, Attendance: 79,159

INDIANAPOLIS 38, KANSAS CITY 31—Peyton Manning passed for 304 yards and 3 touchdowns, and Edgerrin James rushed for 125 yards and 2 scores, as the Colts advanced to their first AFC Championship Game since 1995. The teams combined for 842 yards, 434 by the Colts, and it was the first postseason game in history without a punt. The Colts scored on six of their first seven possessions, with the lone non-scoring drive coming on a three-play series in their own territory as the half expired. The Colts' five touchdown drives were 70, 76, 71, 64, and 76 yards. The Chiefs attempted to keep pace, scoring on five of their first seven possessions. But Morten Andersen missed a 31-yard field goal just before halftime, allowing the Colts to maintain a 21-10 lead, and Kansas City fumbled two plays into the second half, with David Macklin recovering Priest Holmes' fumble at the Colts' 22 at the end of a 48-yard run. Holmes' 1-yard scoring run with 4:22 left cut the deficit to 38-31, but the Colts got two first downs on their ensuing possession, and by the time the Chiefs stopped the Colts on downs, Kansas City was at its own 27 with eight seconds left. Trent Green completed a screen pass to Holmes, who was tackled immediately by Gary Brackett to clinch the victory. Manning was 22 of 30 for 304 yards and 3 touchdowns. James rushed 26 times for 125 yards and 2 touchdowns. Green was 18 of 30 for 212 yards and 1 touchdown. Holmes rushed 24 times for 176 yards.

Indianapolis	14	7	10	7	—	38
Kansas City	3	7	14	7	—	31

Ind — Stokley 29 pass from Manning (Vanderjagt kick)
KC — FG Andersen 22
Ind — James 11 run (Vanderjagt kick)
KC — Hall 9 pass from Green (Andersen kick)
Ind — Lopienski 2 pass from Manning (Vanderjagt kick)
Ind — FG Vanderjagt 45
KC — Holmes 1 run (Andersen kick)
Ind — Wayne 19 pass from Manning (Vanderjagt kick)
KC — Hall 92 kickoff return (Andersen kick)
Ind — James 1 run (Vanderjagt kick)
KC — Holmes 1 run (Andersen kick)

Gillette Stadium, Foxborough, Massachusetts
January 10, 2004, Attendance: 68,436

NEW ENGLAND 17, TENNESSEE 14—Adam Vinatieri's 46-yard field goal with 4:06 remaining lifted the Patriots past the Titans in four-degree weather. Tom Brady's 41-yard touchdown pass to Bethel Johnson on the Patriots' sixth offensive play staked New England to a 7-0 lead. The Titans needed just six plays to answer, as Chris Brown scored from 5 yards to tie the game. Vinatieri missed a 44-yard field goal on the Patriots' next possession, but

Rodney Harrison intercepted a pass by Steve McNair on the next play to set up Antowain Smith's 1-yard touchdown run. The Titans reached the Patriots' 13 just before halftime, but Richard Seymour blocked Gary Anderson's 31-yard field-goal attempt. Tennessee had success moving the ball on its first possession of the second half, too, driving 11 plays and 70 yards, highlighted by third-down conversion passes to Tyrone Calico and Justin McCareins, to set up McNair's game-tying 11-yard scoring pass to Derrick Mason with 4:14 left in the third quarter. A 32-yard punt by Craig Hentrich and 9-yard return by Troy Brown gave New England the ball at the Titans' 40 with 6:40 remaining. Brady completed a 4-yard pass to Brown on fourth-and-3 with 5:14 left and Vinatieri's 46-yard field goal three plays later gave the Patriots a 17-14 lead. McNair's fourth-and-12 desperation heave intended for Drew Bennett fell incomplete with 1:45 remaining, and New England ran out the clock. Brady was 21 of 41 for 201 yards and 1 touchdown, as he completed passes to 10 different receivers. McNair was 18 of 26 for 210 yards and 1 touchdown, with 1 interception.

Tennessee	7	0	7	0	—	14
New England	7	7	0	3	—	17

NE — B. Johnson 41 pass from Brady (Vinatieri kick)
Tenn — Brown 5 run (Anderson kick)
NE — Smith 1 run (Vinatieri kick)
Tenn — Mason 11 pass from McNair (Anderson kick)
NE — FG Vinatieri 46

NFC DIVISIONAL PLAYOFFS RESULTS

Includes Second-Round Playoff Games (1982), NFL Conference Championship Games (1967-69), and special playoff games to break ties for NFL Division or Conference Championships (1941, 1943, 1947, 1950, 1952, 1957, 1958, 1965)

Season	Date	Winner (Share)	Loser (Share)	Score	Site	Attendance
2003	Jan. 11	Philadelphia ($18,000)	Green Bay ($18,000)	20-17*	Philadelphia	67,707
	Jan. 10	Carolina ($18,000)	St. Louis ($18,000)	29-23*	St. Louis	66,165
2002	Jan. 12	Tampa Bay ($17,000)	San Francisco ($17,000)	31-6	Tampa	65,599
	Jan. 11	Philadelphia ($17,000)	Atlanta ($17,000)	20-6	Philadelphia	66,452
2001	Jan. 20	St. Louis ($17,000)	Green Bay ($17,000)	45-17	St. Louis	66,338
	Jan. 19	Philadelphia ($17,000)	Chicago ($17,000)	33-19	Chicago	66,944
2000	Jan. 7	N.Y. Giants ($16,000)	Philadelphia ($16,000)	20-10	East Rutherford	78,765
	Jan. 6	Minnesota ($16,000)	New Orleans ($16,000)	34-16	Minneapolis	63,881
1999	Jan. 16	St. Louis ($16,000)	Minnesota ($16,000)	49-37	St. Louis	66,194
	Jan. 15	Tampa Bay ($16,000)	Washington ($16,000)	14-13	Tampa	65,835
1998	Jan. 10	Minnesota ($15,000)	Arizona ($15,000)	41-21	Minneapolis	63,760
	Jan. 9	Atlanta ($15,000)	San Francisco ($15,000)	20-18	Atlanta	70,262
1997	Jan. 4	Green Bay ($15,000)	Tampa Bay ($15,000)	21-7	Green Bay	60,327
	Jan. 3	San Francisco ($15,000)	Minnesota ($15,000)	38-22	San Francisco	65,018
1996	Jan. 5	Carolina ($14,000)	Dallas ($14,000)	26-17	Charlotte	72,808
	Jan. 4	Green Bay ($14,000)	San Francisco ($14,000)	35-14	Green Bay	60,787
1995	Jan. 7	Dallas ($13,000)	Philadelphia ($13,000)	30-11	Dallas	64,371
	Jan. 6	Green Bay ($13,000)	San Francisco ($13,000)	27-17	San Francisco	69,311
1994	Jan. 8	Dallas ($12,000)	Green Bay ($12,000)	35-9	Dallas	64,745
	Jan. 7	San Francisco ($12,000)	Chicago ($12,000)	44-15	San Francisco	64,644
1993	Jan. 16	Dallas ($12,000)	Green Bay ($12,000)	27-17	Dallas	64,790
	Jan. 15	San Francisco ($12,000)	N.Y. Giants ($12,000)	44-3	San Francisco	67,143
1992	Jan. 10	Dallas ($10,000)	Philadelphia ($10,000)	34-10	Dallas	63,721
	Jan. 9	San Francisco ($10,000)	Washington ($10,000)	20-13	San Francisco	64,991
1991	Jan. 5	Detroit ($10,000)	Dallas ($10,000)	38-6	Detroit	78,290
	Jan. 4	Washington ($10,000)	Atlanta ($10,000)	24-7	Washington	55,181
1990	Jan. 13	N.Y. Giants ($10,000)	Chicago ($10,000)	31-3	East Rutherford	77,025
	Jan. 12	San Francisco ($10,000)	Washington ($10,000)	28-10	San Francisco	65,292
1989	Jan. 7	L.A. Rams ($10,000)	N.Y. Giants ($10,000)	19-13*	East Rutherford	76,526
	Jan. 6	San Francisco ($10,000)	Minnesota ($10,000)	41-13	San Francisco	64,918
1988	Jan. 1	San Francisco ($10,000)	Minnesota ($10,000)	34-9	San Francisco	61,848
	Dec. 31	Chicago ($10,000)	Philadelphia ($10,000)	20-12	Chicago	65,534
1987	Jan. 10	Washington ($10,000)	Chicago ($10,000)	21-17	Chicago	65,268
	Jan. 9	Minnesota ($10,000)	San Francisco ($10,000)	36-24	San Francisco	63,008
1986	Jan. 4	N.Y. Giants ($10,000)	San Francisco ($10,000)	49-3	East Rutherford	75,691
	Jan. 3	Washington ($10,000)	Chicago ($10,000)	27-13	Chicago	65,524
1985	Jan. 5	Chicago ($10,000)	N.Y. Giants ($10,000)	21-0	Chicago	65,670
	Jan. 4	L.A. Rams ($10,000)	Dallas ($10,000)	20-0	Anaheim	66,581
1984	Dec. 30	Chicago ($10,000)	Washington ($10,000)	23-19	Washington	55,431
	Dec. 29	San Francisco ($10,000)	N.Y. Giants ($10,000)	21-10	San Francisco	60,303
1983	Jan. 1	Washington ($10,000)	L.A. Rams ($10,000)	51-7	Washington	54,440
	Dec. 31	San Francisco ($10,000)	Detroit ($10,000)	24-23	San Francisco	59,979
1982	Jan. 16	Dallas ($10,000)	Green Bay ($10,000)	37-26	Dallas	63,972
	Jan. 15	Washington ($10,000)	Minnesota ($10,000)	21-7	Washington	54,593
1981	Jan. 3	San Francisco ($5,000)	N.Y. Giants ($5,000)	38-24	San Francisco	58,360
	Jan. 2	Dallas ($5,000)	Tampa Bay ($5,000)	38-0	Dallas	64,848
1980	Jan. 4	Dallas ($5,000)	Atlanta ($5,000)	30-27	Atlanta	59,793
	Jan. 3	Philadelphia ($5,000)	Minnesota ($5,000)	31-16	Philadelphia	70,178

Season	Date	Winner (Share)	Loser (Share)	Score	Site	Attendance
1979	Dec. 30	Los Angeles ($5,000)	Dallas ($5,000)	21-19	Dallas	64,792
	Dec. 29	Tampa Bay ($5,000)	Philadelphia ($5,000)	24-17	Tampa	71,402
1978	Dec. 31	Los Angeles ($5,000)	Minnesota ($5,000)	34-10	Los Angeles	70,436
	Dec. 30	Dallas ($5,000)	Atlanta ($5,000)	27-20	Dallas	63,406
1977	Dec. 26	Dallas ($5,000)	Chicago ($5,000)	37-7	Dallas	63,260
	Dec. 26	Minnesota ($5,000)	Los Angeles ($5,000)	14-7	Los Angeles	70,203
1976	Dec. 19	Los Angeles [$]	Dallas [$]	14-12	Dallas	63,283
	Dec. 18	Minnesota [$]	Washington [$]	35-20	Minneapolis	47,466
1975	Dec. 28	Dallas [$]	Minnesota [$]	17-14	Minneapolis	48,050
	Dec. 27	Los Angeles [$]	St. Louis [$]	35-23	Los Angeles	73,459
1974	Dec. 22	Los Angeles [$]	Washington [$]	19-10	Los Angeles	77,925
	Dec. 21	Minnesota [$]	St. Louis [$]	30-14	Minneapolis	48,150
1973	Dec. 23	Dallas [$]	Los Angeles [$]	27-16	Dallas	63,272
	Dec. 22	Minnesota [$]	Washington [$]	27-20	Minneapolis	48,040
1972	Dec. 24	Washington [$]	Green Bay [$]	16-3	Washington	52,321
	Dec. 23	Dallas [$]	San Francisco [$]	30-28	San Francisco	59,746
1971	Dec. 26	San Francisco [$]	Washington [$]	24-20	San Francisco	45,327
	Dec. 25	Dallas [$]	Minnesota [$]	20-12	Minneapolis	47,307
1970	Dec. 27	San Francisco [$]	Minnesota [$]	17-14	Minneapolis	45,103
	Dec. 26	Dallas [$]	Detroit [$]	5-0	Dallas	69,613
1969	Dec. 28	Cleveland [$]	Dallas [$]	38-14	Dallas	69,321
	Dec. 27	Minnesota [$]	Los Angeles [$]	23-20	Minneapolis	47,900
1968	Dec. 22	Baltimore [$]	Minnesota [$]	24-14	Baltimore	60,238
	Dec. 21	Cleveland [$]	Dallas [$]	31-20	Cleveland	81,497
1967	Dec. 24	Dallas [$]	Cleveland [$]	52-14	Dallas	70,786
	Dec. 23	Green Bay [$]	Los Angeles [$]	28-7	Milwaukee	49,861
1965	Dec. 26	Green Bay [$]	Baltimore [$]	13-10*	Green Bay	50,484
1958	Dec. 21	N.Y. Giants (#)	Cleveland (#)	10-0	New York	61,274
1957	Dec. 22	Detroit (#)	San Francisco (#)	31-27	San Francisco	60,118
1952	Dec. 21	Detroit (#)	Los Angeles (#)	31-21	Detroit	47,645
1950	Dec. 17	Los Angeles (#)	Chicago Bears (#)	24-14	Los Angeles	83,501
	Dec. 17	Cleveland (#)	N.Y. Giants (#)	8-3	Cleveland	33,054
1947	Dec. 21	Philadelphia (#)	Pittsburgh (#)	21-0	Pittsburgh	35,729
1943	Dec. 19	Washington (¢)	N.Y. Giants (¢)	28-0	New York	42,800
1941	Dec. 14	Chicago Bears (¢)	Green Bay (¢)	33-14	Chicago	43,425

**Sudden death overtime*
 # Players received 1/12 of annual salary for playoff appearances.
$ Players received 1/14 of annual salary for playoff appearances.
¢ Players received 1/10 of annual salary for playoff appearances.

2003 NFC DIVISIONAL PLAYOFF GAMES

Lincoln Financial Field, Philadelphia, Pennsylvania
January 11, 2004, Attendance: 67,707

PHILADELPHIA 20, GREEN BAY 17 (OT)—The Eagles used an improbable 28-yard pass on fourth-and-26 to set up David Akers' game-tying field goal in the final seconds en route to an overtime victory and a berth in the NFC Championship Game for the third consecutive season. In the middle of the first quarter, Brett Favre's 40-yard touchdown pass to Robert Ferguson came one play after Mike McKenzie's cornerback blitz forced Donovan McNabb to fumble the ball away. Akers missed a 33-yard field-goal attempt on the Eagles' next possession, and Green Bay responded with an eight-play, 77-yard drive, capped by Favre's 17-yard touchdown pass to Ferguson, for a 14-0 lead with 1:22 left in the first quarter. A 45-yard pass from McNabb to Todd Pinkston set up Duce Staley's 7-yard touchdown on a shovel pass. The Packers once again drove right down field, but on fourth-and-goal from the Eagles' 1 with 2:00 left in the half, Ahman Green was stopped short of the goal line. A 24-yard scramble by McNabb set up his 12-yard touchdown pass to Pinkston on the first play of the fourth quarter to tie the score. Two possessions later, Favre's 44-yard pass to Javon Walker set up Ryan Longwell's go-ahead field goal with 10:22 left. After an exchange of punts, the Eagles started on their own 20 with 2:21 left. With 1:12 left, McNabb was sacked for a 16-yard loss by Bhawoh Jue, setting up fourth-and-26. McNabb fired a pass down the middle to Freddie Mitchell, who caught the ball beyond the marker for a 28-yard gain. Akers' 37-yard field goal with five seconds left forced overtime. The Eagles won the toss, but were forced to punt. But on the Packers' first play, Favre lofted a pass downfield which was intercepted by Brian Dawkins, who returned it 35 yards to the Packers' 34. Six plays later, Akers kicked a 31-yard field goal with 10:12 left on the clock for the victory. McNabb was 21 of 39 for 248 yards and 2 touchdowns, and rushed for 107 yards on 11 carries. Favre was 15 of 28 for 180 yards and 2 touchdowns, with 1 interception. Green rushed 25 times for 156 yards.

Green Bay	14	0	0	3	0	—	17
Philadelphia	0	7	0	10	3	—	20

GB — Ferguson 40 pass from Favre (Longwell kick)
GB — Ferguson 17 pass from Favre (Longwell kick)
Phil — Staley 7 pass from McNabb (Akers kick)
Phil — Pinkston 12 pass from McNabb (Akers kick)
GB — FG Longwell 21
Phil — FG Akers 37
Phil — FG Akers 31

Edward Jones Dome, St. Louis, Missouri
January 10, 2004, Attendance: 66,165

CAROLINA 29, ST. LOUIS 23 (2OT)—Steve Smith caught a 69-yard touchdown pass from Jake Delhomme on the first play of the second overtime as Carolina advanced to the NFC Championship Game. The Rams drove inside the Panthers' 10 on each of their three first-half possessions, but settled for a field goal each time. After struggling on its first two possessions, Carolina scored on five consecutive drives, capped by Brad Hoover's 7-

yard touchdown run following Mike Minter's interception, to give Carolina a 23-12 lead with 8:50 to play. Deon Grant intercepted Marc Bulger's pass on the next play from scrimmage, giving the Panthers a chance to put the game away. But Tyoka Jackson dropped Delhomme for an 11-yard loss on third-and-6, and John Kasay's 53-yard field-goal attempt hit the left upright with 6:29 remaining. The Rams converted four third downs and a fourth down, on a 16-yard pass from Bulger to Marshall Faulk, and scored on Faulk's 1-yard run with 2:39 left. Bulger's 2-point conversion pass to Dane Looker pulled the Rams within three points, and Jeff Wilkins recovered his own onside kick to give the Rams a chance to tie or win. St. Louis reached the Panthers' 19 with 42 seconds left, but the Rams opted to let the clock run down, and Wilkins tied the game with a 33-yard attempt as regulation expired. In overtime, the Panthers won the toss and reached the Rams' 22 to set up Kasay for an opportunity to win the game. Kasay made a 40-yard attempt, but the play was nullified by a delay of game penalty. After a few unsuccessful runs, Kasay attempted a 45-yard field goal, but pulled it wide right. The Rams responded by driving to the Panthers' 35, but Wilkins' 53-yard field-goal attempt landed short. The Rams' defense stiffened to force a punt, but Ricky Manning Jr. intercepted Bulger at the Panthers' 35 with 1:01 left in overtime. On third-and-14, Delhomme completed a pass to Smith near midfield. Smith split the seam and outran the secondary for the game-winning touchdown 10 seconds into the second overtime. Delhomme was 16 of 26 for 290 yards and 1 touchdown, with 1 interception. Smith had 6 receptions for 163 yards and 1 touchdown. Bulger was 27 of 46 for 332 yards, with 3 interceptions. Isaac Bruce had 7 receptions for 116 yards.

Carolina	0	10	6	7	0	6	—	29
St. Louis	3	6	3	11	0	0	—	23

StL— FG Wilkins 20
StL— FG Wilkins 26
Car— Muhammad fumble recovery in end zone (Kasay kick)
StL— FG Wilkins 24
Car— FG Kasay 45
StL— FG Wilkins 51
Car— FG Kasay 52
Car— FG Kasay 34
Car— Hoover 7 run (Kasay kick)
StL— Faulk 1 run (Looker pass from Bulger)
StL— FG Wilkins 33
Car— Smith 69 pass from Delhomme

AFC WILD CARD PLAYOFF GAMES RESULTS

Season	Date	Winner (Share)	Loser (Share)	Score	Site	Attendance
2003	Jan. 4	Indianapolis ($18,000)	Denver ($15,000)	41-10	Indianapolis	56,586
	Jan. 3	Tennessee ($15,000)	Baltimore ($18,000)	20-17	Baltimore	69,452
2002	Jan. 5	Pittsburgh ($17,000)	Cleveland ($12,500)	36-33	Pittsburgh	62,595
	Jan. 4	N.Y. Jets ($17,000)	Indianapolis ($12,500)	41-0	East Rutherford	78,524
2001	Jan. 13	Baltimore ($12,500)	Miami ($12,500)	20-3	Miami	72,251
	Jan. 12	Oakland ($17,000)	N.Y. Jets ($12,500)	38-24	Oakland	61,503
2000	Dec. 31	Baltimore (12,500)	Denver ($12,500)	21-3	Baltimore	69,638
	Dec. 30	Miami ($16,000)	Indianapolis ($12,500)	23-17*	Miami	73,193
1999	Jan. 9	Miami ($10,000)	Seattle ($16,000)	20-17	Seattle	66,170
	Jan. 8	Tennessee ($10,000)	Buffalo ($10,000)	22-16	Nashville	66,672
1998	Jan. 3	Jacksonville ($15,000)	New England ($10,000)	25-10	Jacksonville	71,139
	Jan. 2	Miami ($10,000)	Buffalo ($10,000)	24-17	Miami	72,698
1997	Dec. 28	New England ($15,000)	Miami ($10,000)	17-3	Foxboro	60,041
	Dec. 27	Denver ($10,000)	Jacksonville ($10,000)	42-17	Denver	74,481
1996	Dec. 29	Pittsburgh ($14,000)	Indianapolis ($10,000)	42-14	Pittsburgh	58,078
	Dec. 28	Jacksonville ($10,000)	Buffalo ($10,000)	30-27	Buffalo	70,213
1995	Dec. 31	Indianapolis ($7,500)	San Diego ($7,500)	35-20	San Diego	61,182
	Dec. 30	Buffalo ($13,000)	Miami ($7,500)	37-22	Buffalo	73,103
1994	Jan. 1	Cleveland ($7,500)	New England ($7,500)	20-13	Cleveland	77,452
	Dec. 31	Miami ($12,000)	Kansas City ($7,500)	27-17	Miami	67,487
1993	Jan. 9	L.A. Raiders ($7,500)	Denver ($7,500)	42-24	Los Angeles	65,314
	Jan. 8	Kansas City ($12,000)	Pittsburgh ($7,500)	27-24*	Kansas City	74,515
1992	Jan. 3	Buffalo ($6,000)	Houston ($6,000)	41-38*	Buffalo	75,141
	Jan. 2	San Diego ($10,000)	Kansas City ($6,000)	17-0	San Diego	58,278
1991	Dec. 29	Houston ($10,000)	N.Y. Jets ($6,000)	17-10	Houston	61,485
	Dec. 28	Kansas City ($6,000)	L.A. Raiders ($6,000)	10-6	Kansas City	75,827
1990	Jan. 6	Cincinnati ($10,000)	Houston ($6,000)	41-14	Cincinnati	60,012
	Jan. 5	Miami ($6,000)	Kansas City ($6,000)	17-16	Miami	67,276
1989	Dec. 31	Pittsburgh ($6,000)	Houston ($6,000)	26-23*	Houston	59,406
1988	Dec. 26	Houston ($6,000)	Cleveland ($6,000)	24-23	Cleveland	75,896
1987	Jan. 3	Houston ($6,000)	Seattle ($6,000)	23-20*	Houston	50,519
1986	Dec. 28	N.Y. Jets ($6,000)	Kansas City ($6,000)	35-15	East Rutherford	75,210
1985	Dec. 28	New England ($6,000)	N.Y. Jets ($6,000)	26-14	East Rutherford	75,945
1984	Dec. 22	Seattle ($6,000)	L.A. Raiders ($6,000)	13-7	Seattle	62,049
1983	Dec. 24	Seattle ($6,000)	Denver ($6,000)	31-7	Seattle	64,275
1982	Jan. 9	N.Y. Jets ($6,000)	Cincinnati ($6,000)	44-17	Cincinnati	57,560
	Jan. 9	San Diego ($6,000)	Pittsburgh ($6,000)	31-28	Pittsburgh	53,546
	Jan. 8	L.A. Raiders ($6,000)	Cleveland ($6,000)	27-10	Los Angeles	56,555
	Jan. 8	Miami ($6,000)	New England ($6,000)	28-13	Miami	68,842
1981	Dec. 27	Buffalo ($3,000)	N.Y. Jets ($3,000)	31-27	New York	57,050
1980	Dec. 28	Oakland ($3,000)	Houston ($3,000)	27-7	Oakland	53,333
1979	Dec. 23	Houston ($3,000)	Denver ($3,000)	13-7	Houston	48,776
1978	Dec. 24	Houston ($3,000)	Miami ($3,000)	17-9	Miami	72,445

**Sudden death overtime*

PLAYOFF GAME SUMMARIES

2003 AFC WILD CARD PLAYOFF GAMES

RCA Dome, Indianapolis, Indiana
January 4, 2004, Attendance: 56,586

INDIANAPOLIS 41, DENVER 10—Peyton Manning passed for 5 touchdowns as the Colts scored on their first seven possessions and avenged a 31-17 home loss to the Broncos two weeks earlier. The Colts took the opening kickoff and drove 70 yards in 6 plays, capped by Brandon Stokley's 31-yard touchdown catch. The Broncos responded with a 8:14 drive that culminated with Jason Elam's 49-yard field goal. The Colts answered with another touchdown, which came when Marvin Harrison made a diving catch at the 30-yard line, and when nobody touched him he got up and ran into the end zone. The Colts scored on all three of their second quarter possessions, highlighted by Manning's 87-yard touchdown pass to Stokley with 1:51 left in the half, and capped by Mike Vanderjagt's 27-yard field goal, which was set up by David Macklin's interception, as the half expired for a 31-3 lead. At halftime Manning was 16 of 18 for 327 yards and 4 touchdowns. Raheem Brock blocked Elam's 46-yard field-goal attempt to begin the second half, and Manning engineered a 12-play, 64-yard drive that ended with Reggie Wayne's 7-yard touchdown catch for a 38-3 lead with 5:19 left in the third quarter. Dwight Freeney forced a fumble by Jake Plummer and Rob Morris recovered to set up Vanderjagt's second field goal with 55 seconds left in the third quarter. Plummer's 7-yard touchdown pass to Rod Smith with 7:04 remaining ended the scoring. The Colts outgained Denver 479-322. Manning was 22 of 26 for 377 yards and 5 touchdowns, for a perfect 158.3 passer rating. Harrison had 7 receptions for 133 yards, and Stokley had 4 catches for 144 yards. Plummer was 23 of 30 for 181 yards and 1 touchdown, with 2 interceptions.

Denver	3	0	0	7	—	10
Indianapolis	14	17	10	0	—	41

Ind— Stokley 31 pass from Manning (Vanderjagt kick)
Den— FG Elam 49
Ind— Harrison 46 pass from Manning (Vanderjagt kick)
Ind— Harrison 23 pass from Manning (Vanderjagt kick)
Ind— Stokley 87 pass from Manning (Vanderjagt kick)
Ind— FG Vanderjagt 27
Ind— Wayne 7 pass from Manning (Vanderjagt kick)
Ind— FG Vanderjagt 20
Den— Smith 7 pass from Plummer (Elam kick)

M&T Bank Stadium, Baltimore, Maryland
January 3, 2004, Attendance: 69,452

TENNESSEE 20, BALTIMORE 17—Gary Anderson kicked a 46-yard field goal with 29 seconds left as the Titans snapped a five-game losing streak to the Ravens. Chris Brown's first professional touchdown, on a 6-yard run, capped a 10-play, 67-yard opening drive for the Titans. Tennessee then forced a punt, but two plays later Steve McNair's pass was tipped by Ed Reed and intercepted by Will Demps, who returned it 56 yards for his first-ever NFL touchdown. The Titans drove to the Ravens' 17 early in the second quarter, but Reed intercepted his third-down pass. Baltimore led 10-7 in the middle of the third quarter when McNair lofted a pass down the left sideline. Justin McCareins adjusted to the underthrown ball, caught it near the 15-yard line before racing untouched into the end zone. Samari Rolle intercepted Anthony Wright's pass at the Ravens' 31 with 11:33 left to set up a 45-yard field goal by Anderson for a 17-10 lead with 9:13 to play. The 44-year-old Anderson had not made a field goal longer than 43 yards all season, but surpassed that feat twice in the final 10 minutes of the game. Wright engineered a 9-play, 71-yard drive after Anderson's first field goal and hit Todd Heap with a 35-yard scoring pass with 4:30 left. The Titans got the ball at their own 37 with 2:44 left and drove 35 yards in 8 plays, highlighted by a 13-yard pass to Derrick Mason and an 8-yard run by Eddie George on third-and-1, to set up Anderson's winning kick. The Ravens reached their own 40 before Wright's final pass fell incomplete. McNair was 14 of 23 for 159 yards and 1 touchdown, with 3 interceptions. Wright was 20 of 37 for 214 yards and 1 touchdown, with 2 interceptions.

Tennessee	7	0	7	6	—	20
Baltimore	7	3	0	7	—	17

Tenn— Brown 6 run (Anderson kick)
Balt— Demps 56 interception return (Stover kick)
Balt— FG Stover 43
Tenn— McCareins 49 pass from McNair (Anderson kick)
Tenn— FG Anderson 45
Balt— Heap 35 pass from Wright (Stover kick)
Tenn— FG Anderson 46

NFC WILD CARD PLAYOFF GAMES RESULTS

Season	Date	Winner (Share)	Loser (Share)	Score	Site	Attendance
2003	Jan. 4	Green Bay ($18,000)	Seattle ($15,000)	33-27*	Green Bay	71,457
	Jan. 3	Carolina ($18,000)	Dallas ($15,000)	29-10	Charlotte	73,014
2002	Jan. 5	San Francisco ($17,000)	N.Y. Giants ($12,500)	39-38	San Francisco	66,318
	Jan. 4	Atlanta ($12,500)	Green Bay ($17,000)	27-7	Green Bay	65,358
2001	Jan. 13	Green Bay ($12,500)	San Francisco ($12,500)	25-15	Green Bay	59,825
	Jan. 12	Philadelphia ($17,000)	Tampa Bay ($12,500)	31-9	Philadelphia	65,847
2000	Dec. 31	Philadelphia ($12,500)	Tampa Bay ($12,500)	21-3	Philadelphia	65,813
	Dec. 30	New Orleans ($16,000)	St. Louis ($12,500)	31-28	New Orleans	64,900
1999	Jan. 9	Minnesota ($10,000)	Dallas ($10,000)	27-10	Minneapolis	64,056
	Jan. 8	Washington ($16,000)	Detroit ($10,000)	27-13	Washington	79,411
1998	Jan. 3	San Francisco ($10,000)	Green Bay ($10,000)	30-27	San Francisco	66,506
	Jan. 2	Arizona ($10,000)	Dallas ($15,000)	20-7	Dallas	62,969
1997	Dec. 28	Tampa Bay ($10,000)	Detroit ($10,000)	20-10	Tampa	73,361
	Dec. 27	Minnesota ($10,000)	N.Y. Giants ($15,000)	23-22	East Rutherford	77,497
1996	Dec. 29	San Francisco ($10,000)	Philadelphia ($10,000)	14-0	San Francisco	56,460
	Dec. 28	Dallas ($14,000)	Minnesota ($10,000)	40-15	Dallas	64,682
1995	Dec. 31	Green Bay ($13,000)	Atlanta ($7,500)	37-20	Green Bay	60,453
	Dec. 30	Philadelphia ($7,500)	Detroit ($7,500)	58-37	Philadelphia	66,099
1994	Jan. 1	Chicago ($7,500)	Minnesota ($12,000)	35-18	Minnesota	60,347
	Dec. 31	Green Bay ($7,500)	Detroit ($7,500)	16-12	Green Bay	58,125
1993	Jan. 9	N.Y. Giants ($7,500)	Minnesota ($7,500)	17-10	East Rutherford	75,089
	Jan. 8	Green Bay ($7,500)	Detroit ($12,000)	28-24	Detroit	68,479

Season	Date	Winner (Share)	Loser (Share)	Score	Site	Attendance
1992	Jan. 3	Philadelphia ($6,000)	New Orleans ($6,000)	36-20	New Orleans	68,893
	Jan. 2	Washington ($6,000)	Minnesota ($10,000)	24-7	Minnesota	57,353
1991	Dec. 29	Dallas ($6,000)	Chicago ($6,000)	17-13	Chicago	62,594
	Dec. 28	Atlanta ($6,000)	New Orleans ($10,000)	27-20	New Orleans	68,794
1990	Jan. 6	Chicago ($10,000)	New Orleans ($6,000)	16-6	Chicago	60,767
	Jan. 5	Washington ($6,000)	Philadelphia ($6,000)	20-6	Philadelphia	65,287
1989	Dec. 31	L.A. Rams ($6,000)	Philadelphia ($6,000)	21-7	Philadelphia	65,479
1988	Dec. 26	Minnesota ($6,000)	L.A. Rams ($6,000)	28-17	Minnesota	61,204
1987	Jan. 3	Minnesota ($6,000)	New Orleans ($6,000)	44-10	New Orleans	68,546
1986	Dec. 28	Washington ($6,000)	L.A. Rams ($6,000)	19-7	Washington	54,567
1985	Dec. 29	N.Y. Giants ($6,000)	San Francisco ($6,000)	17-3	East Rutherford	75,131
1984	Dec. 23	N.Y. Giants ($6,000)	L.A. Rams ($6,000)	16-13	Anaheim	67,037
1983	Dec. 26	L.A. Rams ($6,000)	Dallas ($6,000)	24-17	Dallas	62,118
1982	Jan. 9	Dallas ($6,000)	Tampa Bay ($6,000)	30-17	Dallas	65,042
	Jan. 9	Minnesota ($6,000)	Atlanta ($6,000)	30-24	Minnesota	60,560
	Jan. 8	Green Bay ($6,000)	St. Louis ($6,000)	41-16	Green Bay	54,282
	Jan. 8	Washington ($6,000)	Detroit ($6,000)	31-7	Washington	55,045
1981	Dec. 27	N.Y. Giants ($3,000)	Philadelphia ($3,000)	27-21	Philadelphia	71,611
1980	Dec. 28	Dallas ($3,000)	Los Angeles ($3,000)	34-13	Dallas	63,052
1979	Dec. 23	Philadelphia ($3,000)	Chicago ($3,000)	27-17	Philadelphia	69,397
1978	Dec. 24	Atlanta ($3,000)	Philadelphia ($3,000)	14-13	Atlanta	59,403

**Sudden death overtime*

2003 NFC WILD CARD PLAYOFF GAMES

Lambeau Field, Green Bay, Wisconsin
January 4, 2004, Attendance: 71,457

GREEN BAY 33, SEATTLE 27 (OT)—Al Harris returned an interception 52 yards for a touchdown 4:25 into overtime as the Packers improved their home postseason record to 14-1. With the score 3-3 in the second quarter, Koren Robinson dropped a touchdown pass on third down, forcing the Seahawks to settle for Josh Brown's second field goal with 6:50 left in the half. Brett Favre responded with a 44-yard pass to Javon Walker on the next play to set up his 23-yard touchdown pass to Bubba Franks. Favre set a postseason record with a touchdown pass in 14 consecutive postseason games. The Packers' defense forced a punt and Ryan Longwell booted a 27-yard field goal just before halftime for a 13-6 lead. Seattle came out of the locker room and put together touchdown drives of 10-plays, 74-yards and 11-plays, 77-yards, both culminated by 1-yard runs by Shaun Alexander, for a 20-13 lead with 1:57 left in the third quarter. Alexander's second touchdown came on fourth-and-goal, and was set up by tackle Steve Hutchinson's 4-yard reception of a deflected third-down pass. Seattle ran just three plays in the next 14:13, as Green Bay countered with consecutive 12-play touchdown drives of 60 and 51 yards. Both featured successful fourth-and-1 carries by Ahman Green and were capped by 1-yard scoring runs by Green, giving Green Bay a 27-20 lead with 2:44 to play. Matt Hasselbeck completed a 34-yard pass to Bobby Engram to the Packers' 8, and a pass interference penalty in the end zone gave Seattle the ball at the 1-yard line to set up Alexander's third touchdown with just 51 seconds left. A 27-yard pass by Favre to Walker got the Packers to the Seahawks' 30, but Longwell's 47-yard field-goal attempt in the 20 degree weather fell short. The Seahawks won the coin toss, and after an exchange of punts, faced third-and-11 from their own 45. The Packers blitzed, and Harris stepped in front of Alex Bannister to intercept Hasselbeck's pass and outrun the pair down the right sideline to the end zone. Favre was 26 of 38 for 319 yards and 1 touchdown. Walker had 5 receptions for 111 yards. Hasselbeck was 25 of 45 for 305 yards, with 1 interception.

Seattle	3	3	14	7	0	—	27
Green Bay	0	13	0	14	6	—	33

Sea— FG Brown 30
GB— FG Longwell 31
Sea— FG Brown 35
GB— Franks 23 pass from Favre (Longwell kick)
GB— FG Longwell 27
Sea— Alexander 1 run (Brown kick)
Sea— Alexander 1 run (Brown kick)
GB— Green 1 run (Longwell kick)
GB— Green 1 run (Longwell kick)
Sea— Alexander 1 run (Brown kick)
GB— Harris 52 interception return

Ericsson Stadium, Charlotte, North Carolina
January 3, 2004, Attendance: 73,014

CAROLINA 29, DALLAS 10—Stephen Davis rushed for 104 yards and 1 touchdown, Jake Delhomme passed for 273 yards and a score, and John Kasay kicked 5 field goals as the Panthers won their first playoff game in seven seasons. The Panthers' defense limited Dallas to 204 yards and 10 first downs and forced 2 turnovers. On Carolina's first possession, Steve Smith turned a short pass into a 70-yard gain to the Cowboys' 1, where only tremendous hustle by Pete Hunter, who raced across the field to knock down Smith, prevented a touchdown. Two runs by Davis and an incompletion forced the Panthers to settle for Kasay's first field goal. Later in the quarter, a 32-yard punt by Toby Gowin gave Carolina the ball at the Cowboys' 41, setting up Kasay's second field goal. A 17-yard punt by Gowin gave the Panthers the ball at their 49 in the second quarter to set up Davis' 23-yard touchdown run on third-and-10 with 6:10 left in the half. Billy Cundiff made a 37-yard field goal for Dallas with 1:12 left in the half, but any momentum shift was nullified when Delhomme completed a 49-yard pass to Muhsin Muhammad, who fumbled at the 10-yard line but recovered the ball at the Cowboys' 2 to set up Kasay's third field goal and a 16-3 halftime lead. Delhomme's 32-yard touchdown pass to Smith capped a 4-play, 63-yard drive early in the third quarter and gave Carolina a commanding 23-3 lead. It took a 41-yard kickoff return by Michael Bates with the Cowboys trailing 26-3 to set up a 47-yard touchdown drive, capped by Quincy Carter's 9-yard run with 7:36 to play. An interception by Julius Peppers with 4:59 to play set up Kasay's final field goal. Delhomme was 18 of 29 for 273 yards and 1 touchdown. Smith had 5 receptions for 135 yards. Muhammad had 4 catches for 103 yards. Davis rushed 26 times for 104 yards. Carter was 21 of 36 for 154 yards, with 1 interception.

Dallas	0	3	0	7	—	10
Caolina	6	10	7	6	—	29

Car— FG Kasay 18
Car— FG Kasay 38
Car— Davis 23 run (Kasay kick)
Dall— FG Cundiff 37
Car— FG Kasay 19
Car— Smith 32 pass from Delhomme (Kasay kick)
Car— FG Kasay 32
Dall— Carter 9 run (Cundiff kick)
Car— FG Kasay 34

AFC-NFC PRO BOWL RESULTS (1971-2004)

Series tied, 17-17

Year	Date	Winner (Share)	Loser (Share)	Score	Site	Attendance
2004	Feb. 8	NFC ($35,000)	AFC ($17,500)	55-52	Honolulu	50,127
2003	Feb. 2	AFC ($30,000)	NFC ($15,000)	45-20	Honolulu	50,125
2002	Feb. 9	AFC ($30,000)	NFC ($15,000)	38-30	Honolulu	50,301
2001	Feb. 4	AFC ($30,000)	NFC ($15,000)	38-17	Honolulu	50,128
2000	Feb. 6	NFC ($25,000)	AFC ($12,500)	51-31	Honolulu	50,112
1999	Feb. 7	AFC ($25,000)	NFC ($12,500)	23-10	Honolulu	50,075
1998	Feb. 1	AFC ($25,000)	NFC ($12,500)	29-24	Honolulu	49,995
1997	Feb. 2	AFC ($20,000)	NFC ($10,000)	26-23 (OT)	Honolulu	50,031
1996	Feb. 4	NFC ($20,000)	AFC ($10,000)	20-13	Honolulu	50,034
1995	Feb. 5	AFC ($20,000)	NFC ($10,000)	41-13	Honolulu	50,529
1994	Feb. 6	NFC ($20,000)	AFC ($10,000)	17-3	Honolulu	50,026
1993	Feb. 7	AFC ($10,000)	NFC ($5,000)	23-20 (OT)	Honolulu	50,007
1992	Feb. 2	NFC ($10,000)	AFC ($5,000)	21-15	Honolulu	50,209
1991	Feb. 3	AFC ($10,000)	NFC ($5,000)	23-21	Honolulu	50,345
1990	Feb. 4	NFC ($10,000)	AFC ($5,000)	27-21	Honolulu	50,445
1989	Jan. 29	NFC ($10,000)	AFC ($5,000)	34-3	Honolulu	50,113
1988	Feb. 7	AFC ($10,000)	NFC ($5,000)	15-6	Honolulu	50,113
1987	Feb. 1	AFC ($10,000)	NFC ($5,000)	10-6	Honolulu	50,101
1986	Feb. 2	NFC ($10,000)	AFC ($5,000)	28-24	Honolulu	50,101
1985	Jan. 27	AFC ($10,000)	NFC ($5,000)	22-14	Honolulu	50,385
1984	Jan. 29	NFC ($10,000)	AFC ($5,000)	45-3	Honolulu	50,445
1983	Feb. 6	NFC ($10,000)	AFC ($5,000)	20-19	Honolulu	49,883
1982	Jan. 31	AFC ($5,000)	NFC ($2,500)	16-13	Honolulu	50,402
1981	Feb. 1	NFC ($5,000)	AFC ($2,500)	21-7	Honolulu	50,360
1980	Jan. 27	NFC ($5,000)	AFC ($2,500)	37-27	Honolulu	49,800
1979	Jan. 29	NFC ($5,000)	AFC ($2,500)	13-7	Los Angeles	46,281
1978	Jan. 23	NFC ($5,000)	AFC ($2,500)	14-13	Tampa	51,337
1977	Jan. 17	AFC ($2,000)	NFC ($1,500)	24-14	Seattle	64,752
1976	Jan. 26	NFC ($2,000)	AFC ($1,500)	23-20	New Orleans	30,546
1975	Jan. 20	NFC ($2,000)	AFC ($1,500)	17-10	Miami	26,484
1974	Jan. 20	AFC ($2,000)	NFC ($1,500)	15-13	Kansas City	66,918
1973	Jan. 21	AFC ($2,000)	NFC ($1,500)	33-28	Dallas	37,091
1972	Jan. 23	AFC ($2,000)	NFC ($1,500)	26-13	Los Angeles	53,647
1971	Jan. 24	NFC ($2,000)	AFC ($1,500)	27-6	Los Angeles	48,222

2004 AFC-NFC PRO BOWL

Aloha Stadium, Honolulu, Hawaii
February 8, 2004, Attendance: 50,127

NFC 55, AFC 52—Marc Bulger passed for a Pro Bowl-record 4 touchdowns as the NFC rallied from a 25-point deficit to win the highest scoring game in Pro Bowl history. The AFC set a record with 626 yards, but committed 6 turnovers which led to 35 points. Steve McNair fired a 90-yard touchdown pass to Chad Johnson on the AFC's first play, and Ed Reed blocked Todd Sauerbrun's punt and returned it 23 yards for a touchdown for a 14-0 lead 3:58 into the game. The AFC led 17-13 in the second quarter when Peyton Manning fired a 50-yard touchdown pass to Marvin Harrison, and his 9-yard scoring pass to Tony Gonzalez on the next possession gave the AFC a 31-13 lead. Jamal Lewis' 22-yard touchdown run gave the AFC a 38-13 lead with 11:08 left in the third quarter. The comeback started when Trent Green fumbled and Leonard Little recovered. Bulger completed a 12-yard touchdown pass to Torry Holt two plays later with 8:08 left in the third quarter. Two plays later, Derrick Mason fumbled and Jerry Azumah returned it 36 yards to the AFC's 7 to set up Bulger's 2-yard touchdown toss to Keenan McCardell. But following an exchange of punts, Green completed a 23-yard touchdown pass to Clinton Portis to give the AFC a 45-27 lead with 13:14 left. The NFC scored 28 points in the next 9:42, set up by Azumah's 60-yard kickoff return, Champ Bailey's interception of a pass by Harrison, and interception returns by Dre' Bly, 32 yards for a touchdown, and Corey Chavous, 39 yards to set up Shaun Alexander's 2-yard touchdown run with 3:32 left, for a 55-45 NFC lead. Manning's 10-yard touchdown pass to Hines Ward with 1:54 left pulled the AFC within three points, and Bulger was intercepted by Brock Marion on fourth-and-10 from the AFC's 28-yard line with 1:15 left. The AFC drove to the NFC 21, but Kris Jenkins sacked Manning for a 12-yard loss, forcing Vanderjagt, who was 37-for-37 on the season but missed from 52 yards just before halftime, to attempt a 51-yard field goal as time expired. But the kick sailed wide right and the NFC prevailed. Bulger was 12 of 21 for 152 yards and 4 touchdowns, with 1 interception, and was selected as the player of the game. Holt had 7 receptions for 128 yards. Manning was 22 of 41 for 342 yards and 3 touchdowns, with 2 interceptions. Mason had 6 catches for 113 yards, and Johnson had 5 receptions for 156 yards.

AFC (52)	Offense	NFC (55)
Marvin Harrison (Indianapolis)	WR	Torry Holt (St. Louis)
Jonathan Ogden (Baltimore)	LT	Orlando Pace (St. Louis)
Alan Faneca (Pittsburgh)	LG	Larry Allen (Dallas)
Kevin Mawae (N.Y. Jets)	C	Matt Birk (Minnesota)
Will Shields (Kansas City)	RG	Marco Rivera (Green Bay)
Willie Anderson (Cincinnati)	RT	Flozell Adams (Dallas)
Tony Gonzalez (Kansas City)	TE	Alge Crumpler (Atlanta)
Chad Johnson (Cincinnati)	WR	Anquan Boldin (Arizona)
Steve McNair (Tennessee)	QB	Daunte Culpepper (Minnesota)
Tony Richardson (Kansas City)	FB	Fred Beasley (San Francisco)
Jamal Lewis (Baltimore)	RB	Ahman Green (Green Bay)

Defense

AFC		NFC
Adewale Ogunleye (Miami)	LE	Leonard Little (St. Louis)
Marcus Stroud (Jacksonville)	LT	Kris Jenkins (Carolina)
Richard Seymour (New England)	RT	La'Roi Glover (Dallas)
Dwight Freeney (Indianapolis)	RE	Michael Strahan (N.Y. Giants)
Takeo Spikes (Buffalo)	LOLB	LaVar Arrington (Washington)
Ray Lewis (Baltimore)	MLB	Brian Urlacher (Chicago)
Keith Bulluck (Tennessee)	ROLB	Julian Peterson (San Francisco)
Patrick Surtain (Miami)	LCB	Dre' Bly (Detroit)
Ty Law (New England)	RCB	Champ Bailey (Washington)
Ed Reed (Baltimore)	SS	Corey Chavous (Minnesota)
Brock Marion (Miami)	FS	Roy Williams (Dallas)

SUBSTITUTIONS

NFC—Specialists: K—Jeff Wilkins (St. Louis). P—Todd Sauerbrun (Carolina). KR—Jerry Azumah (Chicago). ST—Alex Bannister (Seattle). Offense: QB—Marc Bulger (St. Louis), Matt Hasselbeck (Seattle). RB—Shaun Alexander (Seattle), Stephen Davis (Carolina). WR—Laveranues Coles (Washington), Keenan McCardell (Tampa Bay), Terrell Owens (San Francisco). TE—Bubba Franks (Green Bay). G—Steve Hutchinson (Seattle). T—Walter Jones (Seattle). C—Mike Flanagan (Green Bay). Defense: DT—Corey Simon (Philadelphia). DE—Kabeer Gbaja-Biamila (Green Bay), Mike Rucker (Carolina). LB—Keith Brooking (Atlanta), Dexter Coakley (Dallas). DB—Troy Vincent (Philadelphia), Aeneas Williams (St. Louis). Not Active: QB—Brett Favre (Green Bay), Donovan McNabb (Philadelphia). RB—Deuce McAllister (New Orleans). WR—Randy Moss (Minnesota). TE—Jeremy Shockey (N.Y. Giants). G—LeCharles Bentley (New Orleans). C—Olin Kreutz (Chicago). DT—Warren Sapp (Tampa Bay). DE—Simeon Rice (Tampa Bay). LB—Derrick Brooks (Tampa Bay).

AFC—Specialists: K—Mike Vanderjagt (Indianapolis). P—Craig Hentrich (Tennessee). KR—Dante Hall (Kansas City). ST—Gary Stills (Kansas City). Offense: QB—Trent Green (Kansas City), Peyton Manning (Indianapolis). RB—Priest Holmes (Kansas City), Clinton Portis (Denver). WR—Derrick Mason (Tennessee), Hines Ward (Pittsburgh). TE—Todd Heap (Baltimore). G—Ruben Brown (Buffalo). T—Brad Hopkins (Tennessee). C—Tom Nalen (Denver). Defense: DT—Casey Hampton (Pittsburgh). DE—Shaun Ellis (N.Y. Jets), Willie McGinest (New England). LB—Zack Thomas (Miami), Al Wilson (Denver). DB—Chris McAlister (Baltimore), Jerome Woods (Kansas City). Not Active: ST—Adalius Thomas (Baltimore). T—William Roaf (Kansas City). LB—Peter Boulware (Baltimore).

HEAD COACHES

AFC—Tony Dungy (Indianapolis)
NFC—Andy Reid (Philadelphia)

OFFICIALS

Referee—Peter Morelli. Umpire—Jim Quirk. Side Judge—Carl Cheffers. Head Linesman—Aaron Pointer. Back Judge—Kirk Dornan. Field Judge—Ron Spitler. Line Judge—Mark Steinkerchner.

AFC	17	14	7	14	—	52
NFC	10	3	14	28	—	55

AFC — C. Johnson 90 pass from McNair (Vanderjagt kick)
AFC — Reed 23 return of blocked punt (Vanderjagt kick)
NFC — Alexander 12 run (Wilkins kick)
NFC — FG Wilkins 28
AFC — FG Vanderjagt 27
NFC — FG Wilkins 38
AFC — Harrison 50 pass from Manning (Vanderjagt kick)
AFC — Gonzalez 9 pass from Manning (Vanderjagt kick)
AFC — J. Lewis 22 run (Vanderjagt kick)
NFC — Holt 12 pass from Bulger (Wilkins kick)
NFC — McCardell 2 pass from Bulger (Wilkins kick)
AFC — Portis 23 pass from Green (Vanderjagt kick)
NFC — Crumpler 33 pass from Bulger (Wilkins kick)
NFC — Alexander 5 pass from Bulger (pass failed)
NFC — Bly 32 interception return (Green run)
NFC — Alexander 2 run (Wilkins kick)
AFC — Ward 10 pass from Manning (Vanderjagt kick)

TEAM STATISTICS	AFC	NFC
Total First Downs	34	22
Rushing	6	7
Passing	24	12
Penalty	4	3
Total Net Yardage	626	396
Total Offensive Plays	86	64
Avg. Gain Per Offensive Play	7.3	6.2
Rushes	26	26
Yards Gained Rushing (Net)	111	136
Avg. Yards per Rush	4.3	5.2
Passes Attempted	57	37
Passes Completed	30	18
Had Intercepted	3	2
Tackled Attempting to Pass	3	1
Yards Lost Attempting to Pass	27	0
Yards Gained Passing (Net)	515	260
Punts	3	5
Avg. Distance	52.7	37.6
Punt Returns	3	2
Punt Return Yardage	18	20
Kickoff Returns	10	8
Kickoff Return Yardage	214	247
Interception Return Yardage	27	71
Total Return Yardage	259	338
Fumbles	6	1
Fumbles Lost	3	0
Own Fumbles Recovered	3	1
Opponent Fumbles Recovered	0	3
Penalties	5	7
Yards Penalized	52	61
Field Goals	1	2
Field Goals Attempted	3	4
Third-Down Efficiency	6/11	2/12
Fourth-Down Efficiency	0/1	0/1
Time of Possession	32:09	27:51

INDIVIDUAL STATISTICS

RUSHING: AFC: J. Lewis 8-58-1, Portis 5-27-0, Holmes 6-9-0, Ward 1-9-0, Richardson 3-8-0, Green 2-0-0, Manning 1-0-0. NFC: Alexander 13-66-2, Green 7-40-0, Davis 4-21-0, Culpepper 1-9-0, Bulger 1-0-0.

PASSING: AFC: Manning 41-22-342-3-2, Green 12-7-110-1-0, McNair 3-1-90-1-0, Harrison 1-0-0-0-1. NFC: Bulger 21-12-152-4-1, Hasselbeck 9-4-51-0-1, Culpepper 7-2-57-0-0.

RECEIVING: AFC: Mason 6-113-0, C. Johnson 5-156-1, Harrison 5-94-1, Gonzalez 5-56-1, Heap 3-43-0, Ward 3-36-1, Portis 1-23-1, J. Lewis 1-14-0, Holmes 1-7-0. NFC: Holt 7-128-1, Coles 4-55-0, Alexander 2-6-1, Crumpler 1-33-1, Franks 1-19-0, Davis 1-9-0, Beasley 1-8-0, McCardell 1-2-1.

KICKOFF RETURNS: AFC: Mason 8-186-0, Hall 2-28-0. NFC: Azumah 7-228-0, Beasley 1-19-0, Bannister 0-0-0.

PUNT RETURNS: AFC: Mason 3-18-0, Hall 0-0-0. NFC: Boldin 1-7-0, McCardell 1-1-0, Coles 0-12-0.

PUNTING: AFC: Hentrich 3-158-52.7. NFC: Sauerbrun 4-188-47.0.

INTERCEPTIONS: AFC: Marion 1-27-0, Surtain 1-0-0. NFC: Chavous 1-39-0, Bly 1-32-1, Bailey 1-0-0.

SACKS: AFC: Hampton 1.0. NFC: Gbaja-Biamila 2.0, Jenkins 1.0.

2003 AFC-NFC PRO BOWL

Aloha Stadium, Honolulu, Hawaii
February 2, 2003, Attendance: 50,125

AFC 45, NFC 20—Ricky Williams rushed for a game-high 56 yards, scored 2 touchdowns, and forced a fumble on special teams to earn player of the game honors. The AFC, which led by as many as 39 points, won for the third consecutive time. Jason Taylor's interception three plays into the game set up Williams' first touchdown run, and Rich Gannon's 11-yard touchdown pass to Tony Gonzalez capped a 71-yard drive on the AFC's next possession to take a 14-3 lead. Rod Woodson's interception early in the second quarter led to Gannon's 13-yard touchdown pass to Travis Henry, and Williams capped another 71-yard drive with a 1-yard run with 47 seconds left in the half to give the AFC a 28-6 lead. Brad Johnson entered the game in the fourth quarter, and Ty Law intercepted a pass and returned it 43 yards for a touchdown on his first possession, and Sam Madison intercepted Johnson during his second drive to set up Peyton Manning's 32-yard touchdown pass to Hines Ward, which gave the AFC a 45-6 lead with 7:31 left. Johnson guided the NFC to touchdowns on its next two possessions, with the help of Julian Peterson's onside kick recovery, for the game's final points. All three AFC quarterbacks passed for at least 100 yards, led by Drew Bledsoe's 9 of 18 for 122-yard performance. Gonzalez had 5 receptions for 98 yards to lead all receivers. The AFC's defense had 6 interceptions, 3 of which were thrown by NFC starter Jeff Garcia.

NFC	3	3	0	14	—	20
AFC	14	14	3	14	—	45

AFC — R. Williams 1 run (Vinatieri kick)
NFC — FG Akers 45
AFC — Gonzalez 11 pass from Gannon (Vinatieri kick)
AFC — Henry 13 pass from Gannon (Vinatieri kick)
NFC — FG Akers 53
AFC — R. Williams 1 run (Vinatieri kick)
AFC — FG Vinatieri 20
AFC — Law 43 interception return (Vinatieri kick)
AFC — Ward 32 pass from Manning (Vinatieri kick)
NFC — Horn 12 pass from B. Johnson (Akers kick)
NFC — Alstott 4 pass from B. Johnson (Akers kick)

2002 AFC-NFC PRO BOWL

Aloha Stadium, Honolulu, Hawaii
February 9, 2002, Attendance: 50,301

AFC 38, NFC 30—Rich Gannon passed for 137 yards and 2 touchdowns to become the first player to earn back-to-back Pro Bowl player of the game honors. The game had an inauspicious beginning for Gannon, who fumbled the game's first snap. Hugh Doulgas recovered the fumble and returned the ball to the AFC's 2-yard line to set up Ahman Green's touchdown 27 seconds into the game. After a three-and-out series, Kurt Warner's 23-yard pass to David Boston set up David Akers' 29-yard field goal to give the NFC a 10-0 lead. Gannon responded two plays later with a 55-yard touchdown pass to Marvin Harrison. Deltha O'Neal's 24-yard interception return to the NFC's 6-yard line moments later set up Curtis Martin's 4-yard touchdown run and gave the AFC a 14-10 lead. After the NFC went three-and-out, the AFC needed just five plays, keyed by Gannon's 30-yard pass to Troy Brown, and capped by Priest Holmes' 39-yard touchdown run to give the AFC its third touchdown in less than six minutes and a 21-10 lead. A 10-play NFC drive led to Akers' second field goal, but Jermaine Lewis' 54-yard kickoff return set up Gannon's 18-yard touchdown pass to Ken Dilger and gave the AFC a 28-10 lead with 12:03 left in the first half. The NFC overcame Shane Lechler's Pro Bowl-record 73-yard punt with Akers' 49-yard field goal just before halftime to cut the deficit to 28-16. Junior Seau's interception at the AFC's 5-yard line early in the fourth quarter thrwarted one NFC rally, but Champ Bailey's interception led to Donovan McNabb's 8-yard touchdown pass to Terrell Owens to cut the deficit to 28-23 with 8:12 left. Runs of 29 and 16 yards by Corey Dillon led to Jason Elam's 38-yard field goal and, two plays later, Ty Law intercepted McNabb at the NFC 44-yard line, returned the ball to the NFC 13 before lateralling to Ray Lewis, who dragged three players into the end zone for a 38-23 lead with 2:49 remaining. McNabb's 15-yard touchdown pass to Garrison Hearst with 1:32 left cut the deficit to 38-30, but Rod Woodson recovered the ensuing onside kick to clinch the victory. Gannon was 8 of 10 for 137 yards and 2 touchdowns. McNabb was 12 of 25 for 149 yards and 2 touchdowns, with 2 interceptions, to lead the NFC. Owens had 8 receptions for 122 yards and 1 touchdown.

AFC	21	7	0	10	—	38
NFC	13	3	0	14	—	30

NFC — Green 2 run (Akers kick)
NFC — FG Akers 29
AFC — Harrison 55 pass from Gannon (Elam kick)
AFC — Martin 4 run (Elam kick)
AFC — Holmes 39 run (Elam kick)
NFC — FG Akers 41
AFC — Dilger 18 pass from Gannon (Elam kick)
NFC — FG Akers 49
NFC — Owens 8 pass from McNabb (Akers kick)
AFC — FG Elam 38
AFC — R. Lewis 13 lateral from Law (Elam kick)
NFC — Hearst 15 pass from McNabb (Akers kick)

2001 AFC-NFC PRO BOWL

Aloha Stadium, Honolulu, Hawaii
February 4, 2001, Attendance: 50,128

AFC 38, NFC 17—Rich Gannon completed 12 of 14 passes for 160 yards during the game's first two possessions to win player of the game honors and lead the AFC to victory. Gannon's touchdown passes capped 87- and 90-yard drives and staked the AFC to a 14-0 lead. Gannon, who was still recovering from a separated non-throwing shoulder suffered in the AFC Championship Game, was replaced by Peyton Manning. The Colts' quarterback engineered a scoring drive, capped by Matt Stover's field goal, to give the AFC a 17-0 lead early in the second quarter. At that point, the AFC had 14 first downs and 231 yards of offense while limiting the NFC to no first downs and 6 yards. Jimmy Smith caught a 2-yard touchdown pass 54 seconds before halftime to give the AFC a 24-3 lead. Third-quarter touchdown passes by Donovan McNabb and Daunte Culpepper trimmed the AFC's lead to 31-17, but Jason Taylor batted down Culpepper's fourth-and-1 pass early in the fourth quarter, and Edgerrin James' 20-yard touchdown run a few plays later iced the game. The NFC attempted a Pro Bowl record 56 pass attempts, and the two teams combined for a Pro Bowl record 98 pass attempts. Tony Gonzalez had 6 receptions for 108 yards, all in the first half, for the AFC. Torry Holt had 7 receptions for 103 yards. Smith's touchdown reception gives him 5 for his career, an AFC-NFC Pro Bowl record.

NFC	0	3	14	0	—	17
AFC	14	10	7	7	—	38

AFC — Gonzalez 8 pass from Gannon (Stover kick)
AFC — Harrison 16 pass from Gannon (Stover kick)
AFC — FG Stover 29
NFC — FG Gramatica 48
AFC — J. Smith 2 pass from Manning (Stover kick)
NFC — Owens 17 pass from McNabb (Gramatica kick)
AFC — Harrison 24 pass from Manning (Stover kick)
NFC — Holt 20 pass from Culpepper (Gramatica kick)
AFC — James 20 run (Stover kick)

2000 AFC-NFC PRO BOWL

Aloha Stadium, Honolulu, Hawaii
February 6, 2000, Attendance: 50,112

NFC 51, AFC 31—Randy Moss earned player of the game honors by setting records with 9 receptions for 212 yards as the NFC defeated the AFC in the highest-scoring Pro Bowl ever. Aeneas Williams intercepted Peyton Manning's pass and raced 62 yards down the left sideline to give the NFC an early 7-0 lead. Kurt Warner's 48-yard pass to Moss on the NFC's first possession set up Jason Hanson's first field goal. Mike Alstott and Jimmy Smith each scored twice in the first half, and Michael Bates' 66-yard kickoff return led to Hanson's Pro Bowl-record tying 51-yard field goal as the half expired to give the NFC a 27-21 lead. Alstott's third touchdown increased the NFC's lead to 37-21, and Derrick Brooks' interception of Mark Brunell and 20-yard return staked the NFC to a 44-24 lead with 11:12 left. The AFC responded with Manning's 52-yard touchdown pass to Smith with 6:30 remaining, but Steve Beuerlein found Moss with a 25-yard scoring pass with 1:05 left to finish the scoring. Warner led the three NFC quarterbacks by completing 8 of 11 passes for 123 yards. Alstott led all rushers with 13 carries for 67 yards. The NFC forced 6 turnovers. Manning was 17 of 23 for 270 yards and 2 touchdowns, with 2 interceptions. Smith had 8 receptions for 119 yards. The previous record, 64 points, was set in 1980.

AFC	7	14	0	10	—	31
NFC	10	17	10	14	—	51

NFC — A. Williams 62 interception return (Hanson kick)
NFC — FG Hanson 21
AFC — J. Smith 5 pass from Brunell (Mare kick)
NFC — Alstott 1 run (Hanson kick)
AFC — Gonzalez 10 pass from Gannon (Mare kick)
NFC — Alstott 3 run (Hanson kick)
AFC — J. Smith 21 pass from Manning (Mare kick)
NFC — FG Hanson 51
NFC — Alstott 1 run (Hanson kick)
NFC — FG Hanson 23
AFC — FG Mare 33
NFC — Brooks 20 interception return (Hanson kick)
AFC — J. Smith 52 pass from Manning (Mare kick)
NFC — Moss 25 pass from Beuerlein (Hanson kick)

1999 AFC-NFC PRO BOWL

Aloha Stadium, Honolulu, Hawaii
February 7, 1999, Attendance: 50,075
AFC 23, NFC 10—John Elway, appearing in uniform on a football field for the final time, drove the AFC to its initial touchdown and then watched a strong defensive effort as the AFC won the Pro Bowl for the third consecutive season. Elway capped a game-opening 61-yard drive with a touchdown pass to Sam Gash. The AFC led 10-3 late in the first half when Deion Sanders intercepted a Vinny Testaverde pass at the NFC's 10 and raced downfield, only to be caught by Ed McCaffrey at the AFC 3-yard line as the half expired. The NFC drove into AFC territory early in the second half, but Ty Law thwarted the NFC's spirits with a 67-yard interception return for a touchdown to give the AFC a 17-3 lead with 9:42 left in the third quarter. The NFC reached the end zone three minutes later as Emmitt Smith scored, but the AFC responded with a field goal on its ensuing possession. Jason Elam's third field goal with 1:02 remaining finished the scoring. Elway played just one drive and was 4 of 5 for 55 yards and 1 touchdown. Keyshawn Johnson had 7 catches for 87 yards and shared player of the game honors with Law. Chandler completed 9 of 25 passes for 133 yards en route to leading the NFC to its only touchdown. Randy Moss had 7 catches for 108 yards.

NFC	3	0	7	0	—	10
AFC	7	3	10	3	—	23

AFC — Gash 3 pass from Elway (Elam kick)
NFC — FG Anderson 23
AFC — FG Elam 23
AFC — Law 67 interception return (Elam kick)
NFC — E. Smith 3 run (Anderson kick)
AFC — FG Elam 46
AFC — FG Elam 26

1998 AFC-NFC PRO BOWL

Aloha Stadium, Honolulu, Hawaii
February 1, 1998, Attendance: 49,995
AFC 29, NFC 24—Warren Moon guided the AFC to points on all three of his drives, including the winning touchdown from 1 yard with 1:49 left as the AFC scored the game's final 15 points to beat the NFC. Steve Young threw a 22-yard touchdown pass to Herman Moore to cap the game's opening drive and give the NFC a 7-0 lead. Late in the first quarter, Mark Brunell threw a 17-yard touchdown pass to Andre Rison to tie the game. Both touchdown passes came on third-and-8 plays. The NFC responded with a 7-play, 71-yard drive capped by Young's 36-yard touchdown pass to Rob Moore. Trent Dilfer guided the NFC to its third touchdown, keyed by a 21-yard pass to Irving Fryar and 23-yard pass to Mike Alstott, and capped by Dorsey Levens' 12-yard touchdown run with 1:36 left in the half to give the NFC a 21-7 lead. The NFC had a chance to pad its lead on its first possession of the second half, but Jason Hanson missed a 44-yard field goal. The AFC bounced back with a 10-play, 65-yard drive that culminated with Drew Bledsoe's 14-yard touchdown pass to Jimmy Smith late in the third quarter. After Hanson's 35-yard field goal gave the NFC a 24-14 lead with 13:42 left, Moon entered the game and drove the AFC into field-goal range, where Mike Hollis drilled a 48-yard attempt with 8:51 left. Attempting to grind out the clock, Warrick Dunn fumbled, and Darryl Williams recovered at the AFC's 49 with 3:03 remaining. After a holding penalty moved the AFC back 10 yards, Moon fired a 57-yard pass to Tim Brown to set up Eddie George's 4-yard run with 2:31 left. The AFC went for the lead instead of a tie, but Moon's pass to Rison fell incomplete. However, the AFC got the ball back when Chris Chandler fumbled the snap on the NFC's first play, and Michael Sinclair recovered at the NFC's 16 with 2:19 left. Three runs by George set up Moon's winning sneak with 1:49 remaining. Moon's 2-point conversion pass to Brown was incomplete, keeping the AFC's lead at 29-24. The NFC was unable to move beyond its own 31-yard line in the final moments, and the AFC prevailed. Tim Brown had 5 receptions for 129 yards. Moon, who was 4 of 8 for 89 yards, earned player of the game honors.

AFC	7	0	7	15	—	29
NFC	7	14	0	3	—	24

NFC — H. Moore 22 pass from Young (Hanson kick)
AFC — Rison 17 pass from Brunell (Hollis kick)
NFC — R. Moore 36 pass from Young (Hanson kick)
NFC — Levens 12 run (Hanson kick)
AFC — J. Smith 14 pass from Bledsoe (Hollis kick)
NFC — FG Hanson 35
AFC — FG Hollis 48
AFC — George 4 run (pass failed)
AFC — Moon 1 run (pass failed)

1997 AFC-NFC PRO BOWL

Aloha Stadium, Honolulu, Hawaii
February 2, 1997, Attendance: 50,031
AFC 26, NFC 23 (OT)—Cary Blanchard's 37-yard field goal 8:16 into overtime gave the AFC a 26-23 victory. The field goal was an ironic ending to a game that saw Blanchard and NFC kicker John Kasay, who each broke the previous single-season record of 35 field goals, combine to miss 5 of 8 field-goal attempts. The NFC scored on its first two possessions, with Vikings guard Randall McDaniel, who lined up as a fullback, scoring his first professional touchdown to give the NFC a 9-0 lead. However, the follies of the kicking unit began as holder Matt Turk muffed the snap on the extra point attempt. Blanchard booted a 28-yard field goal with 27 seconds left in the half to cut the NFC's lead to 9-3. In the third quarter, Barry Sanders scored from 6 yards out, but Kerry Collins was sacked on the 2-point attempt. A 41-yard pass from Drew Bledsoe to Tony Martin led to Curtis Martin's 3-yard run, and after Ashley Ambrose ran an interception back 54 yards for a touchdown 11 seconds into the fourth quarter, the AFC found itself with a 16-15 lead. The NFC drove for more than six minutes, only to have Kasay miss a 40-yard field goal attempt. After an AFC punt, Cris Carter caught a 47-yard touchdown bomb from Gus Frerotte to put the NFC ahead 23-16. After each team punted, the AFC got the ball on its own 20-yard line with 55 seconds left. Mark Brunell hit Tim Brown with an 80-yard bomb down the right sideline to tie the game with 44 seconds left. Wesley Walls caught a 33-yard pass to give the NFC a chance to win in regulation, but Kasay missed a 39-yard attempt and the game went to overtime. The AFC won the overtime toss, but Blanchard missed a 41-yard field goal attempt. The NFC had to punt after three plays, and Brunell hit Ben Coates with a 43-yard pass on the AFC's first play. After three running plays failed to gain a first down, Blanchard trotted onto the field and made the game-winning kick. The teams combined for a Pro Bowl record 962 total yards. Brunell, who completed 12 of 22 pass attempts for 236 yards, was selected as the player of the game.

AFC	0	3	7	13	3	—	26
NFC	9	0	6	8	0	—	23

NFC — FG Kasay 20
NFC — R. McDaniel 5 pass from Favre (muffed snap)
AFC — FG Blanchard 28
NFC — Sanders 6 run (pass failed)
AFC — Martin 3 run (Blanchard kick)

AFC — Ambrose 54 interception return (pass failed)
NFC — Carter 53 pass from Frerotte (Walls pass from Frerotte)
AFC — T. Brown 80 pass from Brunell (Blanchard kick)
AFC — FG Blanchard 37

1996 AFC-NFC PRO BOWL
Aloha Stadium, Honolulu, Hawaii
February 4, 1996, Attendance: 50,034

NFC 20, AFC 13—Jerry Rice had 6 receptions for 82 yards and 1 touchdown to earn player of the game honors in the NFC's victory. The 49ers' wide receiver, who was named to the Pro Bowl for the tenth consecutive year, caught a 1-yard touchdown pass from Packers quarterback Brett Favre 1:41 into the second quarter to cap an 80-yard drive and give the NFC the lead for good at 10-7. The AFC had taken a 7-0 lead 2:26 into the game when Bengals quarterback Jeff Blake connected with Steelers wide receiver Yancey Thigpen on a Pro Bowl-record 93-yard touchdown pass. The NFC increased its advantage to 20-7 at halftime on Redskins linebacker Ken Harvey's 36-yard interception return for a touchdown and Falcons kicker Morten Andersen's 24-yard field goal. The AFC trimmed its deficit to 20-13 when Colts quarterback Jim Harbaugh teamed with Patriots running back Curtis Martin on a 17-yard touchdown pass in the final minute of the third quarter, but its bid to win or tie was rebuffed twice in the final minutes of the fourth quarter. First, 49ers safety Tim McDonald intercepted Harbaugh's pass in the end zone with 1:50 remaining. Then, after the AFC forced a punt and got the ball back near midfield, Harbaugh drove his team to the NFC's 9-yard line in the closing seconds. But he spiked the ball once to stop the clock and threw 3 consecutive incompletions as time ran out. The AFC outgained the NFC 390 total yards to 287, but its quarterbacks suffered 4 interceptions, including 3 off Harbaugh, the NFL's leading passer during the regular season. The NFC raised its edge to 15-11 in Pro Bowl games since the AFL-NFL merger in 1970.

NFC	3	17	0	0	—	20
AFC	7	0	6	0	—	13

AFC — Thigpen 93 pass from Blake (Elam kick)
NFC — FG Andersen 36
NFC — Rice 1 pass from Favre (Andersen kick)
NFC — Harvey 36 interception return (Andersen kick)
NFC — FG Andersen 24
AFC — Martin 17 pass from Harbaugh (kick failed)

1995 AFC-NFC PRO BOWL
Aloha Stadium, Honolulu, Hawaii
February 5, 1995, Attendance: 50,529

AFC 41, NFC 13—Colts rookie Marshal Faulk rushed for a Pro Bowl-record 180 yards to key the AFC's rout of the NFC. Faulk, who earned the Dan McGuire Trophy as the player of the game, averaged nearly 14 yards on his 13 carries and shattered the previous rushing mark of 112 yards set by O.J. Simpson in the 1973 game. Faulk's 49-yard touchdown run from punt formation in the fourth quarter was the longest in Pro Bowl history. The Seahawks' Chris Warren added 127 yards on 14 carries as the AFC amassed records for rushing yards (400) and total yards (552). Steelers tight end Eric Green caught 2 touchdown passes for the victors. The NFC managed only 196 total yards, a large chunk coming when 49ers quarterback Steve Young and Vikings wide receiver Cris Carter teamed on a 51-yard touchdown pass in the first quarter. That gave the NFC a 10-0 advantage, but the AFC rallied in the second quarter and took the lead for good when the Browns' Leroy Hoard scored on a 4-yard touchdown run 2:07 before halftime.

AFC	0	17	3	21	—	41
NFC	10	0	3	0	—	13

NFC — FG Reveiz 28
NFC — Carter 51 pass from Young (Reveiz kick)
AFC — Green 22 pass from Elway (Carney kick)
AFC — FG Carney 22
AFC — Hoard 4 run (Carney kick)
NFC — FG Reveiz 49
AFC — FG Carney 23
AFC — Warren 11 run (Carney kick)
AFC — Green 16 pass from Hostetler (Carney kick)
AFC — Faulk 49 run (Carney kick)

1994 AFC-NFC PRO BOWL
Aloha Stadium, Honolulu, Hawaii
February 6, 1994, Attendance: 50,026

NFC 17, AFC 3—The NFC converted a blocked punt and a fumble recovery into touchdowns just 2:20 apart in the second half of its victory over the AFC. With the score tied 3-3 late in the third quarter, Saints linebacker Renaldo Turnbull deflected a punt by the Oilers' Greg Montgomery, and the NFC took possession at the AFC's 48-yard line. A 32-yard pass from Bobby Hebert to Falcons teammate Andre Rison positioned Rams running back Jerome Bettis for a 4-yard touchdown run with 1:27 left in the third quarter. Moments later, Rams defensive tackle Sean Gilbert recovered a fumble by Oilers quarterback Warren Moon at the AFC's 19. Hebert then teamed with the Vikings' Cris Carter on a 15-yard touchdown pass 53 seconds into the fourth period. The NFC kept the AFC out of the end zone by maintaining possession for more than 38 minutes and forcing 6 turnovers. Rison earned the Dan McGuire Trophy as the player of the game by catching 6 passes for 86 yards. The victory was the fourth in the last six years for the NFC, which leads the series 14-10.

NFC	3	0	7	7	—	17
AFC	0	3	0	0	—	3

NFC — FG Johnson 35
AFC — FG Anderson 25
NFC — Bettis 4 run (Johnson kick)
NFC — Carter 15 pass from Hebert (Johnson kick)

1993 AFC-NFC PRO BOWL
Aloha Stadium, Honolulu, Hawaii
February 7, 1993, Attendance: 50,007

AFC 23, NFC 20—Nick Lowery's 33-yard field goal 4:09 into overtime gave the American Conference all-stars an unlikely 23-20 victory over the National Conference. Despite being overwhelmed by the NFC in first downs (30-9), and total yards (471-114), the AFC won because it forced 6 turnovers, blocked a pair of field goals (1 of which was returned for a touchdown), and returned an interception for a score. Special-teams star Steve Tasker of the Bills earned the Dan McGuire Trophy as the player of the game for making 4 tackles, forcing a fumble, and blocking a field goal. The block came with eight minutes left in regulation and the game tied at 13-13. The Raiders' Terry McDaniel picked up the loose ball and ran 28 yards for a touchdown and a 20-13 AFC lead. The NFC rallied behind 49ers quarterback Steve Young, whose fourth-down, 23-yard touchdown pass to Giants running back Rodney Hampton tied the game at 20-20 with 10 seconds left in regulation. Young completed 18 of 32 passes for 196 yards but was intercepted 3 times and lost a fumble when sacked in overtime. Raiders defensive end Howie Long fell on that fumble at the NFC 28-yard line, and five plays later, Lowery converted the winning field goal.

AFC	0	10	3	7	3	—	23
NFC	3	10	0	7	0	—	20

NFC — FG Andersen 27
AFC — Seau 31 interception return (Lowery kick)
NFC — FG Andersen 37
NFC — Irvin 9 pass from Aikman (Andersen kick)
AFC — FG Lowery 42
AFC — FG Lowery 29
AFC — McDaniel 28 blocked field goal return (Lowery kick)
NFC — Hampton 23 pass from Young (Andersen kick)
AFC — FG Lowery 33

1992 AFC-NFC PRO BOWL
Aloha Stadium, Honolulu, Hawaii
February 2, 1992, Attendance: 50,209

NFC 21, AFC 15—Atlanta's Chris Miller threw an 11-yard touchdown pass to San Francisco's Jerry Rice with 4:04 remaining in the game to lift the NFC over the AFC. It was the NFC's thirteenth win in the 22-game series. The AFC had taken a 15-14 lead when the Raiders' Jeff Jaeger kicked a 27-yard field goal 1:49 into the fourth quarter. But the NFC, aided by a key roughing-the-passer penalty on a third-down incompletion from the AFC 24-yard line, drove 85 yards to the winning score. The Cowboys' Michael Irvin, playing in his first Pro Bowl, caught 8 passes for 125 yards, including a 13-yard touchdown in the first quarter, and was named the player of the game. Rice had 7 catches for 77 yards. Mark Rypien of Washington, the Super Bowl most valuable player one week earlier, completed 11 of 18 passes for 165 yards and 2 touchdowns for the NFC, including a 35-yard pass to Redskins teammate Gary Clark just 26 seconds before halftime. Miller completed 7 of his 10 attempts for 85 yards.

NFC	7	7	0	7	—	21
AFC	7	5	0	3	—	15

AFC — Clayton 4 pass from Kelly (Jaeger kick)
NFC — Irvin 13 pass from Rypien (Lohmiller kick)
AFC — Safety, Townsend tackled Byner in end zone
AFC — FG Jaeger 48
NFC — Clark 35 pass from Rypien (Lohmiller kick)
AFC — FG Jaeger 27
NFC — Rice 11 pass from Miller (Lohmiller kick)

1991 AFC-NFC PRO BOWL

Aloha Stadium, Honolulu, Hawaii
February 3, 1991, Attendance: 50,345

AFC 23, NFC 21—Buffalo's Jim Kelly and Houston's Ernest Givins combined for a 13-yard scoring pass late in the fourth quarter to rally the AFC over the NFC. Phoenix rookie Johnny Johnson scored on runs of 1 and 9 yards to put the NFC ahead 14-3 in the third quarter. Buffalo's Andre Reed, who led all receivers with 4 catches for 80 yards, caught a 20-yard scoring reception from Kelly early in the fourth quarter to move the AFC to within 1 point. Barry Sanders ran 22 yards for a touchdown to increase the NFC's lead to 21-13. Miami's Jeff Cross blocked a 46-yard field-goal attempt by New Orleans' Morten Andersen with seven seconds remaining to preserve the win. Buffalo's Bruce Smith recorded 3 sacks and also had a blocked field goal. Kelly, who completed 13 of 19 passes for 210 yards and 2 touchdowns, was presented the Dan McGuire Award as player of the game. The AFC's victory narrowed the NFC's Pro Bowl series lead to 12-9.

AFC	3	0	3	17	—	23
NFC	0	7	7	7	—	21

AFC — FG Lowery 26
NFC — J. Johnson 1 run (Andersen kick)
AFC — FG Lowery 43
NFC — J. Johnson 9 run (Andersen kick)
AFC — Reed 20 pass from Kelly (Lowery kick)
NFC — Sanders 22 run (Andersen kick)
AFC — FG Lowery 34
AFC — Givins 13 pass from Kelly (Lowery kick)

1990 AFC-NFC PRO BOWL

Aloha Stadium, Honolulu, Hawaii
February 4, 1990, Attendance: 50,445

NFC 27, AFC 21—The NFC captured its second straight Pro Bowl as the defense accounted for a pair of touchdowns and forced 5 turnovers before the eleventh consecutive sellout crowd at Aloha Stadium. The AFC held a 7-6 halftime edge on a 1-yard scoring run by Christian Okoye of the Chiefs. The NFC then rallied with 21 unanswered points in the third quarter. David Meggett of the Giants began the comeback with an 11-yard touchdown reception from Philadelphia's Randall Cunningham. The Rams' Jerry Gray followed with a 51-yard interception return for a score and the Vikings' Keith Millard added an 8-yard fumble return for a touchdown four minutes later to give the NFC a commanding 27-7 lead. Seattle's Dave Krieg rallied the AFC with a 5-yard touchdown pass to Miami's Ferrell Edmunds. Cleveland's Mike Johnson then returned an interception 22 yards for a score to pull the AFC to within 27-21. Gray, who was credited with 7 tackles, was given the Dan McGuire Award as player of the game. Krieg led all quarterbacks by completing 15 of 23 for 148 yards and 1 touchdown. Buffalo's Thurman Thomas topped all receivers with 5 catches for 47 yards, while Indianapolis' Eric Dickerson led all rushers with 46 yards on 15 carries. The win gave the NFC a 12-8 advantage in Pro Bowl games since 1971.

NFC	3	3	21	0	—	27
AFC	0	7	0	14	—	21

NFC — FG Murray 23
NFC — FG Murray 41
AFC — Okoye 1 run (Treadwell kick)
NFC — Meggett 11 pass from Cunningham (Murray kick)
NFC — Gray 51 interception return (Murray kick)
NFC — Millard 8 fumble recovery return (Murray kick)
AFC — Edmunds 5 pass from Krieg (Treadwell kick)
AFC — M. Johnson 22 interception return (Treadwell kick)

1989 AFC-NFC PRO BOWL

Aloha Stadium, Honolulu, Hawaii
January 29, 1989, Attendance: 50,113

NFC 34, AFC 3—The NFC scored 34 unanswered points to snap a two-game losing streak to the AFC before the tenth straight sellout crowd in Honolulu's Aloha Stadium. Bills kicker Scott Norwood provided the AFC's only points on a 38-yard field goal 6:23 into the game. Touchdown runs by Dallas' Herschel Walker (4 yards) and Atlanta's John Settle (1) brought the NFC a 14-3 halftime lead. Walker added a 7-yard scoring run, the Saints' Morten Andersen kicked field goals of 27 and 51 yards, and Los Angeles Rams' wide receiver Henry Ellard caught an 8-yard scoring pass from Minnesota quarterback Wade Wilson in the second half to complete the scoring. Chicago running back Neal Anderson and Philadelphia quarterback Randall Cunningham, who were both appearing in their first Pro Bowl, also played major roles in the NFC's victory. Anderson rushed 13 times for 85 yards and had 2 receptions for 17. Cunningham, who was voted the game's outstanding player, completed 10 of 14 passes for 63 yards and rushed for 49 yards. The NFC, which had 5 takeaways, outgained the AFC 355 yards to 167 and held a time-of-possession advantage of 35:18 to 24:42. Houston quarterback Warren Moon completed 13 of 20 passes for 134 yards for the AFC. The win gave the NFC an 11-8 advantage in Pro Bowl games.

AFC	3	0	0	0	—	3
NFC	7	7	10	10	—	34

AFC — FG Norwood 38
NFC — Walker 4 run (Andersen kick)
NFC — Settle 1 run (Andersen kick)
NFC — FG Andersen 27
NFC — Walker 7 run (Andersen kick)
NFC — FG Andersen 51
NFC — Ellard 8 pass from Wilson (Andersen kick)

1988 AFC-NFC PRO BOWL

Aloha Stadium, Honolulu, Hawaii
February 7, 1988, Attendance: 50,113

AFC 15, NFC 6—Led by a tenacious pass rush, the AFC defeated the NFC for the second consecutive year before the ninth straight sellout crowd in Honolulu's Aloha Stadium. Buffalo quarterback Jim Kelly scored the game's lone touchdown on a 1-yard run for a 7-6 halftime lead. Colts kicker Dean Biasucci added field goals from 37 and 30 yards to complete the AFC's scoring. Saints kicker Morten Andersen had 25- and 36-yard field goals to account for the NFC's points. AFC defenders held the NFC to 213 yards and recorded 8 sacks. Bills defensive end Bruce Smith, who had 2 sacks among his 5 tackles, was voted the game's outstanding player. Oilers running back Mike Rozier led all rushers with 49 yards on 9 carries. Jets wide receiver Al Toon had 5 receptions for 75 yards. The AFC generated 341 yards total offense and held a time-of-possession advantage of 34:14 to 25:46. By winning, the AFC cut the NFC's lead in the Pro Bowl series to 10-8.

NFC	0	6	0	0	—	6
AFC	0	7	6	2	—	15

NFC — FG Andersen 25
AFC — Kelly 1 run (Biasucci kick)
NFC — FG Andersen 36
AFC — FG Biasucci 37
AFC — FG Biasucci 30

AFC — Safety, Montana forced out of end zone

1987 AFC-NFC PRO BOWL
Aloha Stadium, Honolulu, Hawaii
February 1, 1987, Attendance: 50,101
AFC 10, NFC 6—The AFC defeated the NFC in the lowest-scoring game in AFC-NFC Pro Bowl history. The AFC took a 10-0 halftime lead on Broncos quarterback John Elway's 10-yard touchdown pass to Raiders tight end Todd Christensen and Patriots kicker Tony Franklin's 26-yard field goal. The AFC defense made the lead stand by forcing the NFC to settle for a pair of field goals from 38 and 19 yards by Saints kicker Morten Andersen after the NFC had first downs at the AFC 31-, 7-, 16-, 15-, 5-, and 7-yard lines. Both AFC scores were set up by fumble recoveries by Seahawks linebacker Fredd Young and Dolphins linebacker John Offerdahl, respectively. Eagles defensive end Reggie White, who tied a Pro Bowl record with 4 sacks among his 7 solo tackles, was voted the game's outstanding player. The AFC victory cut the NFC's lead in the Pro Bowl series to 10-7.

AFC	7	3	0	0	—	10
NFC	0	0	3	3	—	6

AFC — Christensen 10 pass from Elway (Franklin kick)
AFC — FG Franklin 26
NFC — FG Andersen 38
NFC — FG Andersen 19

1986 AFC-NFC PRO BOWL
Aloha Stadium, Honolulu, Hawaii
February 2, 1986, Attendance: 50,101
NFC 28, AFC 24—New York Giants quarterback Phil Simms brought the NFC back from a 24-7 halftime deficit to defeat the AFC. Simms, who completed 15 of 27 passes for 212 yards and 3 touchdowns, was named the most valuable player of the game. The AFC had taken its first-half lead behind a 2-yard run by Los Angeles Raiders running back Marcus Allen, who also threw a 51-yard scoring pass to San Diego wide receiver Wes Chandler, an 11-yard touchdown catch by Pittsburgh wide receiver Louis Lipps, and a 34-yard field goal by Steelers kicker Gary Anderson. Minnesota's Joey Browner accounted for the NFC's only score before halftime with a 48-yard interception return. After intermission, the NFC blanked the AFC while scoring 3 touchdowns via a 15-yard catch by Washington wide receiver Art Monk, a 2-yard reception by Dallas tight end Doug Cosbie, and a 15-yard catch by Tampa Bay tight end Jimmie Giles with 2:47 remaining in the game. The victory gave the NFC a 10-6 Pro Bowl record against the AFC.

NFC	0	7	7	14	—	28
AFC	7	17	0	0	—	24

AFC — Allen 2 run (Anderson kick)
NFC — Browner 48 interception return (Andersen kick)
AFC — Chandler 51 pass from Allen (Anderson kick)
AFC — FG Anderson 34
AFC — Lipps 11 pass from O'Brien (Anderson kick)
NFC — Monk 15 pass from Simms (Andersen kick)
NFC — Cosbie 2 pass from Simms (Andersen kick)
NFC — Giles 15 pass from Simms (Andersen kick)

1985 AFC-NFC PRO BOWL
Aloha Stadium, Honolulu, Hawaii
January 27, 1985, Attendance: 50,385
AFC 22, NFC 14—Defensive end Art Still of the Kansas City Chiefs recovered a fumble and returned it 83 yards for a touchdown to clinch the AFC's victory over the NFC. Still's touchdown came in the fourth period with the AFC trailing 14-12 and was one of several outstanding defensive plays in a Pro Bowl dominated by two record-breaking defenses. The teams combined for a Pro Bowl-record 17 sacks, including 4 by New York Jets defensive end Mark Gastineau, who was named the game's outstanding player. The AFC's first score came on a safety when Gastineau tackled running back Eric Dickerson of the Los Angeles Rams in the end zone. The AFC's second score, a 6-yard pass from Miami's Dan Marino to Los Angeles Raiders running back Marcus Allen, was set up by a partial block of a punt by Seahawks linebacker Fredd Young. The NFC leads the series 9-6.

AFC	0	9	0	13	—	22
NFC	0	0	7	7	—	14

AFC — Safety, Gastineau tackled Dickerson in end zone
AFC — Allen 6 pass from Marino (Johnson kick)
NFC — Lofton 13 pass from Montana (Stenerud kick)
NFC — Payton 1 run (Stenerud kick)
AFC — FG Johnson 33
AFC — Still 83 fumble recovery return (Johnson kick)
AFC — FG Johnson 22

1984 AFC-NFC PRO BOWL
Aloha Stadium, Honolulu, Hawaii
January 29, 1984, Attendance: 50,445
NFC 45, AFC 3—The NFC won its sixth Pro Bowl in the last seven seasons by routing the AFC. The NFC was led by the passing of most valuable player Joe Theismann of Washington, who completed 21 of 27 passes for 242 yards and 3 touchdowns. Theismann set Pro Bowl records for completions and touchdown passes. The NFC established Pro Bowl marks for most points scored and fewest points allowed. Running back William Andrews of Atlanta had 6 carries for 43 yards and caught 4 passes for 49 yards, including scoring receptions of 16 and 2 yards. Los Angeles Rams rookie Eric Dickerson gained 46 yards on 11 carries, including a 14-yard touchdown run, and had 45 yards on 5 catches. Rams safety Nolan Cromwell had a 44-yard interception return for a touchdown early in the third period to give the NFC a commanding 24-3 lead. Green Bay wide receiver James Lofton caught an 8-yard touchdown pass, while tight end teammate Paul Coffman had a 6-yard scoring catch.

NFC	3	14	14	14	—	45
AFC	0	3	0	0	—	3

NFC — FG Haji-Sheikh 23
NFC — Andrews 16 pass from Theismann (Haji-Sheikh kick)
NFC — Andrews 2 pass from Montana (Haji-Sheikh kick)
AFC — FG Anderson 43
NFC — Cromwell 44 interception return (Haji-Sheikh kick)
NFC — Lofton 8 pass from Theismann (Haji-Sheikh kick)
NFC — Coffman 6 pass from Theismann (Haji-Sheikh kick)
NFC — Dickerson 14 run (Haji-Sheikh kick)

1983 AFC-NFC PRO BOWL
Aloha Stadium, Honolulu, Hawaii
February 6, 1983, Attendance: 49,883
NFC 20, AFC 19—Dallas' Danny White threw an 11-yard touchdown pass to the Packers' John Jefferson with 35 seconds remaining to rally the NFC over the AFC. White, who completed 14 of 26 passes for 162 yards, kept the winning 65-yard drive alive with a 14-yard completion to Jefferson on a fourth-and-7 play at the AFC 25. The AFC was ahead 12-10 at halftime and increased the lead to 19-10 in the third period, when Marcus Allen scored on a 1-yard run. San Diego's Dan Fouts, who attempted 30 passes, set Pro Bowl records for most completions (17) and yards (274). Pittsburgh's John Stallworth was the AFC's leading receiver with 7 catches for 67 yards. William Andrews topped the NFC with 5 receptions for 48 yards. Fouts and Jefferson were co-winners of the player of the game award.

AFC	9	3	7	0	—	19
NFC	0	10	0	10	—	20

AFC — Walker 34 pass from Fouts (Benirschke kick)
AFC — Safety, Still tackled Theismann in end zone
NFC — Andrews 3 run (Moseley kick)
NFC — FG Moseley 35
AFC — FG Benirschke 29
AFC — Allen 1 run (Benirschke kick)
NFC — FG Moseley 41
NFC — Jefferson 11 pass from D. White (Moseley kick)

1982 AFC-NFC PRO BOWL
Aloha Stadium, Honolulu, Hawaii
January 31, 1982, Attendance: 50,402
AFC 16, NFC 13—Nick Lowery of Kansas City kicked a 23-yard field goal with three seconds remaining to give the AFC a last-second victory over the NFC. Lowery's

kick climaxed a 69-yard drive directed by quarterback Dan Fouts. The NFC gained a 13-13 tie with 2:43 to go when Dallas' Tony Dorsett ran 4 yards for a touchdown. In the drive to the winning field goal, Fouts completed 3 passes, including a 23-yard toss to San Diego teammate Kellen Winslow that put the ball on the NFC's 5-yard line. Two plays later, Lowery kicked the field goal. Winslow, who caught 6 passes for 86 yards, was named co-player of the game along with Tampa Bay defensive end Lee Roy Selmon.

NFC	0	6	0	7	—	13
AFC	0	0	13	3	—	16

NFC — Giles 4 pass from Montana (kick blocked)
AFC — Muncie 2 run (kick failed)
AFC — Campbell 1 run (Lowery kick)
NFC — Dorsett 4 run (Septien kick)
AFC — FG Lowery 23

1981 AFC-NFC PRO BOWL
Aloha Stadium, Honolulu, Hawaii
February 1, 1981, Attendance: 50,360
NFC 21, AFC 7—Eddie Murray kicked 4 field goals and Steve Bartkowski fired a 55-yard scoring pass to Alfred Jenkins to lead the NFC to its fourth straight victory over the AFC and a 7-4 edge in the series. Murray was named the game's most valuable player and missed tying Garo Yepremian's Pro Bowl record of 5 field goals when a 37-yard attempt hit the crossbar with 22 seconds left. The AFC's only score came on a 9-yard pass from Brian Sipe to Stanley Morgan. Bartkowski completed 9 of 21 passes for 173 yards, while Sipe connected on 10 of 15 for 142 yards. Ottis Anderson led all rushers with 70 yards on 10 carries. Earl Campbell, the NFL's leading rusher in 1980, was limited to 24 yards on 8 attempts.

AFC	0	7	0	0	—	7
NFC	3	6	0	12	—	21

NFC — FG Murray 31
AFC — Morgan 9 pass from Sipe (J. Smith kick)
NFC — FG Murray 31
NFC — FG Murray 34
NFC — Jenkins 55 pass from Bartkowski (Murray kick)
NFC — FG Murray 36
NFC — Safety, Shell called for holding in end zone

1980 AFC-NFC PRO BOWL
Aloha Stadium, Honolulu, Hawaii
January 27, 1980, Attendance: 49,800
NFC 37, AFC 27—Chuck Muncie ran for 2 touchdowns and threw a 25-yard option pass for another score to give the NFC its third consecutive victory over the AFC. The Saints' Muncie, who was selected the game's most valuable player, snapped a 3-3 tie on a 1-yard touchdown run at 1:41 of the second quarter, then scored on an 11-yard run in the fourth quarter for the NFC's final touchdown. Two scoring records were set in the game—37 points by the NFC, eclipsing the 33 by the AFC in 1973, and the 64 points by both teams, surpassing the 61 scored in 1973.

NFC	3	20	7	7	—	37
AFC	3	7	10	7	—	27

NFC — FG Moseley 37
AFC — FG Fritsch 19
NFC — Muncie 1 run (Moseley kick)
AFC — Pruitt 1 pass from Bradshaw (Fritsch kick)
NFC — D. Hill 13 pass from Manning (kick failed)
NFC — T. Hill 25 pass from Muncie (Moseley kick)
NFC — Henry 86 punt return (Moseley kick)
AFC — Campbell 2 run (Fritsch kick)
AFC — FG Fritsch 29
NFC — Muncie 11 run (Moseley kick)
AFC — Campbell 1 run (Fritsch kick)

1979 AFC-NFC PRO BOWL
Memorial Coliseum, Los Angeles, CA
January 29, 1979, Attendance: 46,281
NFC 13, AFC 7—Roger Staubach completed 9 of 15 passes for 125 yards, including the winning touchdown on a 19-yard strike to Dallas Cowboys teammate Tony Hill in the third period. The winning drive began at the AFC's 45-yard line after a shanked punt. Staubach hit Ahmad Rashad with passes of 15 and 17 yards to set up Hill's decisive catch. The victory gave the NFC a 5-4 advantage in Pro Bowl games. Rashad, who accounted for 89 yards on 5 receptions, was named the player of the game. The AFC led 7-6 at halftime on Bob Griese's 8-yard scoring toss to Steve Largent late in the second quarter. Largent had 5 receptions for 75 yards. The NFC scored first as Archie Manning marched his team 70 yards in 11 plays, capped by Wilbert Montgomery's 2-yard touchdown run. The AFC's Earl Campbell was the game's leading rusher with 66 yards on 12 carries.

AFC	0	7	0	0	—	7
NFC	0	6	7	0	—	13

NFC — Montgomery 2 run (kick failed)
AFC — Largent 8 pass from Griese (Yepremian kick)
NFC — T. Hill 19 pass from Staubach (Corral kick)

1978 AFC-NFC PRO BOWL
Tampa Stadium, Tampa, Florida
January 23, 1978, Attendance: 51,337
NFC 14, AFC 13—Walter Payton, the NFL's leading rusher in 1977, sparked a second-half comeback to give the NFC the win and tie the series between the two conferences at four victories each. Payton, who was the game's most valuable player, gained 77 yards on 13 carries and scored the tying touchdown on a 1-yard burst with 7:37 left in the game. Efren Herrera kicked the winning extra point. The AFC dominated the first half of the game, taking a 13-0 lead on field goals of 21 and 39 yards by Toni Linhart and a 10-yard touchdown pass from Ken Stabler to Oakland teammate Cliff Branch. On the NFC's first possession of the second half, Pat Haden put together the first touchdown drive after Eddie Brown returned a punt to the AFC 46-yard line. Haden connected on all 4 of his passes on that drive, finally hitting Terry Metcalf with a 4-yard scoring toss. The NFC continued to rally and, with Jim Hart at quarterback, moved 63 yards in 12 plays for the go-ahead score. During the winning drive, Hart completed 5 of 6 passes for 38 yards and Payton picked up 20 more on the ground.

AFC	3	10	0	0	—	13
NFC	0	0	7	7	—	14

AFC — FG Linhart 21
AFC — Branch 10 pass from Stabler (Linhart kick)
AFC — FG Linhart 39
NFC — Metcalf 4 pass from Haden (Herrera kick)
NFC — Payton 1 run (Herrera kick)

1977 AFC-NFC PRO BOWL
Kingdome, Seattle, Washington
January 17, 1977, Attendance: 64,752
AFC 24, NFC 14—O.J. Simpson's 3-yard touchdown burst at 7:03 of the first quarter gave the AFC a lead it would not surrender, breaking a two-game NFC win streak and giving the AFC stars a 4-3 series lead. The AFC took a 17-7 lead midway through the second period on the first of 2 Ken Anderson touchdown passes, a 12-yard toss to Charlie Joiner. But the NFC mounted a 73-yard drive capped by Lawrence McCutcheon's 1-yard touchdown plunge to pull within 17-14 at the half. Following a scoreless third quarter, player of the game Mel Blount thwarted a possible NFC score when he intercepted Jim Hart's pass in the end zone. Less than three minutes later, Blount again picked off a Hart pass. That set up Anderson's 27-yard touchdown strike to Cliff Branch for the final score.

NFC	0	14	0	0	—	14
AFC	10	7	0	7	—	24

AFC — Simpson 3 run (Linhart kick)
AFC — FG Linhart 31
NFC — Thomas 15 run (Bakken kick)
AFC — Joiner 12 pass from Anderson (Linhart kick)
NFC — McCutcheon 1 run (Bakken kick)
AFC — Branch 27 pass from Anderson (Linhart kick)

1976 AFC-NFC PRO BOWL
Superdome, New Orleans, Louisiana
January 26, 1976, Attendance: 30,546
NFC 23, AFC 20—Mike Boryla, a late substitute who did not enter the game until 5:39 remained, lifted the National Football Conference to the victory over the American Football Conference with 2 touchdown passes in the final minutes. It was the second straight NFC win, squaring the

series at 3-3. Until Boryla started firing the ball the AFC was in control, leading 13-0 at the half. Boryla entered the game after Billy Johnson had raced 90 yards with a punt to give the AFC a 20-9 lead. He floated a 14-yard touchdown pass to Terry Metcalf and later fired an 8-yard scoring pass to Mel Gray for the winner.

AFC	0	13	0	7	—	20
NFC	0	0	9	14	—	23

AFC — FG Stenerud 20
AFC — FG Stenerud 35
AFC — Burrough 64 pass from Pastorini (Stenerud kick)
NFC — FG Bakken 42
NFC — Foreman 4 pass from Hart (kick blocked)
AFC — Johnson 90 punt return (Stenerud kick)
NFC — Metcalf 14 pass from Boryla (Bakken kick)
NFC — Gray 8 pass from Boryla (Bakken kick)

1975 AFC-NFC PRO BOWL

Orange Bowl, Miami, Florida
January 20, 1975, Attendance: 26,484

NFC 17, AFC 10—Los Angeles quarterback James Harris, who took over the NFC offense after Jim Hart of St. Louis suffered a laceration above his right eye in the second period, threw 2 touchdown passes early in the fourth period to pace the NFC to its second victory in the five-game Pro Bowl series. The NFC win snapped a three-game AFC victory string. Harris, who was named the player of the game, connected with St. Louis' Mel Gray for an 8-yard touchdown 2:03 into the final period. One minute and 24 seconds later, following a fumble recovery by Washington's Ken Houston, Harris tossed another 8-yard scoring pass to Washington's Charley Taylor for the decisive points.

NFC	0	3	0	14	—	17
AFC	0	0	10	0	—	10

NFC — FG Marcol 33
AFC — Warfield 32 pass from Griese (Gerela kick)
AFC — FG Gerela 33
NFC — Gray 8 pass from J. Harris (Marcol kick)
NFC — Taylor 8 pass from J. Harris (Marcol kick)

1974 AFC-NFC PRO BOWL

Arrowhead Stadium, Kansas City, MO
January 20, 1974, Attendance: 66,918

AFC 15, NFC 13—Miami's Garo Yepremian's fifth field goal—a 42-yard kick with 21 seconds remaining—gave the AFC its third straight victory since the NFC won the inaugural game following the 1970 season. The field goal by Yepremian, who was voted the game's outstanding player, offset a 21-yard field goal by Atlanta's Nick Mike-Mayer that had given the NFC a 13-12 advantage with 1:41 remaining. The only touchdown in the game was scored by the NFC on a 14-yard pass from Philadelphia's Roman Gabriel to the Rams' Lawrence McCutcheon.

NFC	0	10	0	3	—	13
AFC	3	3	3	6	—	15

AFC — FG Yepremian 16
NFC — FG Mike-Mayer 27
NFC — McCutcheon 14 pass from Gabriel (Mike-Mayer kick)
AFC — FG Yepremian 37
AFC — FG Yepremian 27
AFC — FG Yepremian 41
NFC — FG Mike-Mayer 21
AFC — FG Yepremian 42

1973 AFC-NFC PRO BOWL

Texas Stadium, Irving, Texas
January 21, 1973, Attendance: 37,091

AFC 33, NFC 28—Paced by the rushing and receiving of player of the game O.J. Simpson, the AFC erased a 14-0 first period deficit and built a commanding 33-14 lead midway through the fourth period before the NFC managed 2 touchdowns in the final minute of play. Simpson rushed for 112 yards and caught 3 passes for 58 more to gain unanimous recognition in the balloting for player of the game. Green Bay Packers running back John Brockington scored 3 touchdowns for the NFC.

AFC	0	10	10	13	—	33
NFC	14	0	0	14	—	28

NFC — Brockington 1 run (Marcol kick)
NFC — Brockington 3 pass from Kilmer (Marcol kick)
AFC — Simpson 7 run (Gerela kick)
AFC — FG Gerela 18
AFC — FG Gerela 22
AFC — Hubbard 11 run (Gerela kick)
AFC — O. Taylor 5 pass from Lamonica (kick failed)
AFC — Bell 12 interception return (Gerela kick)
NFC — Brockington 1 run (Marcol kick)
NFC — Kwalick 12 pass from Snead (Marcol kick)

1972 AFC-NFC PRO BOWL

Memorial Coliseum, Los Angeles, CA
January 23, 1972, Attendance: 53,647

AFC 26, NFC 13—Kansas City's Jan Stenerud kicked 4 field goals to lead the AFC from a 6-0 deficit to victory. The AFC defense picked off 3 passes. Stenerud was selected as the outstanding offensive player and his Kansas City teammate, linebacker Willie Lanier, was the game's outstanding defensive player.

AFC	0	3	13	10	—	26
NFC	0	6	0	7	—	13

NFC — Grim 50 pass from Landry (kick failed)
AFC — FG Stenerud 25
AFC — FG Stenerud 23
AFC — FG Stenerud 48
AFC — Morin 5 pass from Dawson (Stenerud kick)
AFC — FG Stenerud 42
NFC — V. Washington 2 run (Knight kick)
AFC — F. Little 6 run (Stenerud kick)

1971 AFC-NFC PRO BOWL

Memorial Coliseum, Los Angeles, CA
January 24, 1971, Attendance: 48,222

NFC 27, AFC 6—Mel Renfro of Dallas broke open the first meeting between the American Football Conference and National Football Conference all-star teams as he returned a pair of punts 82 and 56 yards for touchdowns in the final period to clinch the NFC victory over the AFC. Renfro was voted the game's outstanding back and linebacker Fred Carr of Green Bay the outstanding lineman.

AFC	0	3	3	0	—	6
NFC	0	3	10	14	—	27

AFC — FG Stenerud 37
NFC — FG Cox 13
NFC — Osborn 23 pass from Brodie (Cox kick)
NFC — FG Cox 35
AFC — FG Stenerud 16
NFC — Renfro 82 punt return (Cox kick)
NFC — Renfro 56 punt return (Cox kick)

Includes AFL All-Star Game played after the 1961-69 seasons.

Date	Result/Honored players	Site (attendance)
Jan. 15, 1939	New York Giants 13, Pro All-Stars 10	Wrigley Field, Los Angeles (20,000)
Jan. 14, 1940	Green Bay 16, NFL All-Stars 7	Gilmore Stadium, Los Angeles (18,000)
Dec. 29, 1940	Chicago Bears 28, NFL All-Stars 14	Gilmore Stadium, Los Angeles (21,624)
Jan. 4, 1942	Chicago Bears 35, NFL All-Stars 24	Polo Grounds, New York (17,725)
Dec. 27, 1942	NFL All-Stars 17, Washington 14	Shibe Park, Philadelphia (18,671)
Jan. 14, 1951	American Conf. 28, National Conf. 27 Otto Graham, Cleveland, player of the game	Los Angeles Memorial Coliseum (53,676)
Jan. 12, 1952	National Conf. 30, American Conf. 13 Dan Towler, Los Angeles, player of the game	Los Angeles Memorial Coliseum (19,400)
Jan. 10, 1953	National Conf. 27, American Conf. 7 Don Doll, Detroit, player of the game	Los Angeles Memorial Coliseum (34,208)
Jan. 17, 1954	East 20, West 9 Chuck Bednarik, Philadelphia, player of the game	Los Angeles Memorial Coliseum (44,214)
Jan. 16, 1955	West 26, East 19 Billy Wilson, San Francisco, player of the game	Los Angeles Memorial Coliseum (43,972)
Jan. 15, 1956	East 31, West 30 Ollie Matson, Chi. Cardinals, player of the game	Los Angeles Memorial Coliseum (37,867)
Jan. 13, 1957	West 19, East 10 Bert Rechichar, Baltimore, outstanding back Ernie Stautner, Pittsburgh, outstanding lineman	Los Angeles Memorial Coliseum (44,177)
Jan. 12, 1958	West 26, East 7 Hugh McElhenny, San Francisco, outstanding back Gene Brito, Washington, outstanding lineman	Los Angeles Memorial Coliseum (66,634)
Jan. 11, 1959	East 28, West 21 Frank Gifford, N.Y. Giants, outstanding back Doug Atkins, Chi. Bears, outstanding lineman	Los Angeles Memorial Coliseum (72,250)
Jan. 17, 1960	West 38, East 21 Johnny Unitas, Baltimore, outstanding back Gene (Big Daddy) Lipscomb, Baltimore, outstanding lineman	Los Angeles Memorial Coliseum (56,876)
Jan. 15, 1961	West 35, East 31 Johnny Unitas, Baltimore, outstanding back Sam Huff, N.Y. Giants, outstanding lineman	Los Angeles Memorial Coliseum (62,971)
Jan. 7, 1962	AFL West 47, East 27 Cotton Davidson, Dallas Texans, player of the game	Balboa Stadium, San Diego (20,973)
Jan. 14, 1962	NFL West 31, East 30 Jim Brown, Cleveland, outstanding back Henry Jordan, Green Bay, outstanding lineman	Los Angeles Memorial Coliseum (57,409)
Jan. 13, 1963	AFL West 21, East 14 Curtis McClinton, Dallas Texans, outstanding offensive player Earl Faison, San Diego, outstanding defensive player	Balboa Stadium, San Diego (27,641)
Jan. 13, 1963	NFL East 30, West 20 Jim Brown, Cleveland, outstanding back Gene (Big Daddy) Lipscomb, Pittsburgh, outstanding lineman	Los Angeles Memorial Coliseum (61,374)
Jan. 12, 1964	NFL West 31, East 17 Johnny Unitas, Baltimore, player of the game Gino Marchetti, Baltimore, outstanding lineman	Los Angeles Memorial Coliseum (67,242)
Jan. 19, 1964	AFL West 27, East 24 Keith Lincoln, San Diego, outstanding offensive player Archie Matsos, Oakland, outstanding defensive player	Balboa Stadium, San Diego (20,016)
Jan. 10, 1965	NFL West 34, East 14 Fran Tarkenton, Minnesota, outstanding back Terry Barr, Detroit, outstanding lineman	Los Angeles Memorial Coliseum (60,598)
Jan. 16, 1965	AFL West 38, East 14 Keith Lincoln, San Diego, outstanding offensive player Willie Brown, Denver, outstanding defensive player	Jeppesen Stadium, Houston (15,446)
Jan. 15, 1966	AFL All-Stars 30, Buffalo 19 Joe Namath, N.Y. Jets, most valuable player, offense Frank Buncom, San Diego, most valuable player, defense	Rice Stadium, Houston (35,572)
Jan. 15, 1966	NFL East 36, West 7 Jim Brown, Cleveland, outstanding back Dale Meinert, St. Louis, outstanding lineman	Los Angeles Memorial Coliseum (60,124)
Jan. 21, 1967	AFL East 30, West 23 Babe Parilli, Boston, outstanding offensive player Verlon Biggs, N.Y. Jets, outstanding defensive player	Oakland-Alameda County Coliseum (18,876)
Jan. 22, 1967	NFL East 20, West 10 Gale Sayers, Chicago, outstanding back Floyd Peters, Philadelphia, outstanding lineman	Los Angeles Memorial Coliseum (15,062)

PRO BOWL ALL-TIME RESULTS

Jan. 21, 1968 AFL East 25, West 24 ..... Gator Bowl, Jacksonville, Fla. (40,103)
Joe Namath and Don Maynard, N.Y. Jets, out. off. players
Leslie (Speedy) Duncan, San Diego, out. def. player

Jan. 21, 1968 NFL West 38, East 20 ..... Los Angeles Memorial Coliseum (53,289)
Gale Sayers, Chicago, outstanding back
Dave Robinson, Green Bay, outstanding lineman

Jan. 19, 1969 AFL West 38, East 25 ..... Gator Bowl, Jacksonville, Fla. (41,058)
Len Dawson, Kansas City, outstanding offensive player
George Webster, Houston, outstanding defensive player

Jan. 19, 1969 NFL West 10, East 7 ..... Los Angeles Memorial Coliseum (32,050)
Roman Gabriel, Los Angeles, outstanding back
Merlin Olsen, Los Angeles, outstanding lineman

Jan. 17, 1970 AFL West 26, East 3 ..... Astrodome, Houston (30,170)
John Hadl, San Diego, player of the game

Jan. 18, 1970 NFL West 16, East 13 ..... Los Angeles Memorial Coliseum (57,786)
Gale Sayers, Chicago, outstanding back
George Andrie, Dallas, outstanding lineman

Jan. 24, 1971 NFC 27, AFC 6 ..... Los Angeles Memorial Coliseum (48,222)
Mel Renfro, Dallas, outstanding back
Fred Carr, Green Bay, outstanding lineman

Jan. 23, 1972 AFC 26, NFC 13 ..... Los Angeles Memorial Coliseum (53,647)
Jan Stenerud, Kansas City, outstanding offensive player
Willie Lanier, Kansas City, outstanding defensive player

Jan. 21, 1973 AFC 33, NFC 28 ..... Texas Stadium, Irving (37,091)
O.J. Simpson, Buffalo, player of the game

Jan. 20, 1974 AFC 15, NFC 13 ..... Arrowhead Stadium, Kansas City (66,918)
Garo Yepremian, Miami, player of the game

Jan. 20, 1975 NFC 17, AFC 10 ..... Orange Bowl, Miami (26,484)
James Harris, Los Angeles, player of the game

Jan. 26, 1976 NFC 23, AFC 20 ..... Louisiana Superdome, New Orleans (30,546)
Billy Johnson, Houston, player of the game

Jan. 17, 1977 AFC 24, NFC 14 ..... Kingdome, Seattle (64,752)
Mel Blount, Pittsburgh, player of the game

Jan. 23, 1978 NFC 14, AFC 13 ..... Tampa Stadium (51,337)
Walter Payton, Chicago, player of the game

Jan. 29, 1979 NFC 13, AFC 7 ..... Los Angeles Memorial Coliseum (46,281)
Ahmad Rashad, Minnesota, player of the game

Jan. 27, 1980 NFC 37, AFC 27 ..... Aloha Stadium, Honolulu (49,800)
Chuck Muncie, New Orleans, player of the game

Feb. 1, 1981 NFC 21, AFC 7 ..... Aloha Stadium, Honolulu (50,360)
Eddie Murray, Detroit, player of the game

Jan. 31, 1982 AFC 16, NFC 13 ..... Aloha Stadium, Honolulu (50,402)
Kellen Winslow, San Diego, and Lee Roy Selmon, Tampa Bay, players of the game

Feb. 6, 1983 NFC 20, AFC 19 ..... Aloha Stadium, Honolulu (49,883)
Dan Fouts, San Diego, and John Jefferson, Green Bay, players of the game

Jan. 29, 1984 NFC 45, AFC 3 ..... Aloha Stadium, Honolulu (50,445)
Joe Theismann, Washington, player of the game

Jan. 27, 1985 AFC 22, NFC 14 ..... Aloha Stadium, Honolulu (50,385)
Mark Gastineau, N.Y. Jets, player of the game

Feb. 2, 1986 NFC 28, AFC 24 ..... Aloha Stadium, Honolulu (50,101)
Phil Simms, N.Y. Giants, player of the game

Feb. 1, 1987 AFC 10, NFC 6 ..... Aloha Stadium, Honolulu (50,101)
Reggie White, Philadelphia, player of the game

Feb. 7, 1988 AFC 15, NFC 6 ..... Aloha Stadium, Honolulu (50,113)
Bruce Smith, Buffalo, player of the game

Jan. 29, 1989 NFC 34, AFC 3 ..... Aloha Stadium, Honolulu (50,113)
Randall Cunningham, Philadelphia, player of the game

Feb. 4, 1990 NFC 27, AFC 21 ..... Aloha Stadium, Honolulu (50,445)
Jerry Gray, L.A. Rams, player of the game

Feb. 3, 1991 AFC 23, NFC 21 ..... Aloha Stadium, Honolulu (50,345)
Jim Kelly, Buffalo, player of the game

Feb. 2, 1992 NFC 21, AFC 15 ..... Aloha Stadium, Honolulu (50,209)
Michael Irvin, Dallas, player of the game

Feb. 7, 1993 AFC 23, NFC 20 (OT) ..... Aloha Stadium, Honolulu (50,007)
Steve Tasker, Buffalo, player of the game

Feb. 6, 1994 NFC 17, AFC 3 ..... Aloha Stadium, Honolulu (50,026)
Andre Rison, Atlanta, player of the game

Feb. 5, 1995 AFC 41, NFC 13 ..... Aloha Stadium, Honolulu (50,529)
Marshall Faulk, Indianapolis, player of the game

Feb. 4, 1996 NFC 20, AFC 13 .... Aloha Stadium, Honolulu (50,034)
Jerry Rice, San Francisco, player of the game
Feb. 2, 1997 AFC 26, NFC 23 (OT) .... Aloha Stadium, Honolulu (50,031)
Mark Brunell, Jacksonville, player of the game
Feb. 1, 1998 AFC 29, NFC 24 .... Aloha Stadium, Honolulu (49,995)
Warren Moon, Seattle, player of the game
Feb. 7, 1999 AFC 23, NFC 10 .... Aloha Stadium, Honolulu (50,075)
Keyshawn Johnson, N.Y. Jets and Ty Law, New England, co-players of the game
Feb. 6, 2000 NFC 51, AFC 31 .... Aloha Stadium, Honolulu (50,112)
Randy Moss, Minnesota, player of the game
Feb. 4, 2001 AFC 38, NFC 17 .... Aloha Stadium, Honolulu (50,128)
Rich Gannon, Oakland, player of the game
Feb. 9, 2002 AFC 38, NFC 30 .... Aloha Stadium, Honolulu (50,301)
Rich Gannon, Oakland, player of the game
Feb. 2, 2003 AFC 45, NFC 20 .... Aloha Stadium, Honolulu (50,125)
Ricky Williams, Miami, player of the game
Feb. 8, 2004 NFC 55, AFC 52 .... Aloha Stadium, Honolulu (50,127)
Marc Bulger, St. Louis, player of the game

INTERCONFERENCE GAMES

AFC VS. NFC (REGULAR SEASON), 1970-2003

	Balt	Buff	Cin	Cle	Den	Hou	Ind	Jax	KC	Mia
1970		0-3	1-2	0-3	2-2		3-0		0-2-1	2-1
1971		0-3	1-2	2-1	1-3		2-1		2-1	3-0
1972		2-0-1	2-1	1-2	1-3		0-3		2-1	3-0
1973		2-1	2-1	1-2	0-3-1		2-1		1-1-1	3-0
1974		2-1	2-1	1-2	2-2		1-2		1-2	2-1
1975		1-2	3-0	1-3	2-1		2-1		2-1	3-0
1976		0-2	2-0	2-0	2-0		0-2		1-1	0-2
1977		1-1	2-1	1-1	1-1		1-1		1-1	2-0
1978		1-1	2-2	4-0	2-2		2-2		0-2	3-1
1979		2-2	2-2	3-1	3-1		1-1		0-2	4-0
1980		3-1	2-2	3-1	3-1		1-1		2-0	4-0
1981		1-3	2-2	3-1	3-1		0-4		2-2	3-1
1982		1-2	1-0	0-2	2-1		0-1-1		0-3	1-1
1983		1-3	3-1	2-2	0-2		2-0		2-2	3-1
1984		1-3	2-2	1-3	3-1		0-4		1-1	4-0
1985		0-2	2-2	1-3	3-1		3-1		2-2	3-1
1986		1-1	3-1	2-2	3-1		1-3		1-1	2-2
1987		1-2	1-2	2-2	2-1-1		1-0		1-2	3-0
1988		2-2	4-0	4-0	3-1		2-2		0-2	3-1
1989		1-3	2-2	3-1	2-2		1-3		2-0	2-0
1990		3-1	1-3	1-3	1-3		2-2		4-0	2-2
1991		3-1	1-3	0-4	2-0		0-4		2-2	3-1
1992		4-0	1-3	2-2	1-3		2-0		2-2	2-2
1993		4-0	2-2	3-1	1-3		0-4		2-2	3-1
1994		1-3	1-3	3-1	1-3		0-2		3-1	2-2
1995		3-1	2-2	1-3	2-2		2-2	0-4	3-1	2-2
1996	2-2	4-0	2-2		3-1		3-1	2-2	4-0	1-3
1997	2-1-1	1-3	2-2		3-1		1-3	2-2	4-0	1-3
1998	1-3	3-1	1-3		3-1		0-4	3-1	3-1	3-1
1999	2-1	3-1	1-2	1-2	2-2		4-0	4-0	2-2	2-2
2000	2-1	2-2	1-2	0-3	3-1		2-2	2-2	2-2	2-2
2001	2-2	1-3	1-2	1-2	3-1		1-3	1-2	1-3	2-2
2002	0-4	3-1	1-3	2-2	4-0	2-2	2-2	2-2	2-2	2-2
2003	3-1	2-2	2-2	2-2	1-3	2-2	3-1	2-2	3-1	3-1
Total	**14-15-1**	**60-57-1**	**60-60**	**53-57**	**70-54-2**	**4-4**	**47-63-1**	**18-17**	**60-48-2**	**83-38**

	NE	NYJ	Oak	Pitt	SD	Sea	TB	Tenn	TOTALS
1970	0-3	2-1	1-2	0-3	1-2			0-3	12-27-1
1971	0-3	0-3	1-1-1	1-2	2-1			0-2-1	15-23-2
1972	3-0	1-2	3-0	2-1	0-3			0-3	20-19-1
1973	2-1	0-3	2-1	3-0	1-2			0-3	19-19-2
1974	3-0	2-1	3-0	3-0	1-2			0-3	23-17
1975	1-2	0-3	3-0	2-1	0-3			3-0	23-17
1976	1-1	0-2	3-0	1-1	2-0		0-1	2-0	16-12
1977	2-0	1-1	1-1	2-0	1-1	1-0		2-0	19-9
1978	2-2	1-3	4-0	3-1	2-2	3-1		2-2	31-21
1979	3-1	3-1	4-0	3-1	3-1	3-1		2-2	36-16
1980	1-3	1-3	2-2	4-0	2-2	1-3		4-0	33-19
1981	0-4	2-0	2-2	3-1	2-2	0-2		1-3	24-28
1982	0-1	4-0	3-0	1-0	1-0	1-0		0-3	15-14-1
1983	2-2	3-1	2-2	2-2	2-2	1-3		1-3	26-26
1984	0-4	0-2	3-1	3-1	4-0	4-0		0-4	26-26
1985	3-1	2-2	3-1	1-3	1-1	2-2		1-3	27-25
1986	3-1	2-2	1-3	2-2	0-4	3-1		2-2	26-26
1987	0-3	0-4	2-2	2-2	2-0	4-0		2-2	23-22-1
1988	2-2	2-0	1-3	1-3	2-2	1-3		3-1	30-22
1989	0-4	1-3	2-2	3-1	2-2	0-4		3-1	24-28
1990	0-4	2-0	3-1	3-1	1-1	2-2		1-3	26-26
1991	1-1	2-2	2-2	0-4	1-3	1-3		1-3	19-33
1992	0-4	0-4	2-2	1-3	2-0	0-4		3-1	22-30
1993	1-1	2-2	3-1	2-2	2-2	0-2		2-2	27-25
1994	4-0	1-3	3-1	2-2	2-2	2-0		0-4	25-27
1995	0-4	0-4	3-1	2-2	3-1	3-1		1-3	27-33
1996	2-2	1-3	1-3	2-2	1-3	2-2		2-2	32-28
1997	1-3	3-1	2-2	2-2	1-3	2-2		4-0	31-28-1
1998	2-2	2-2	3-1	2-2	1-3	3-1		1-3	31-29
1999	3-1	2-2	3-1	3-0	1-3	2-2		3-1	38-22
2000	0-4	3-1	4-0	1-2	0-4	2-2		4-0	30-30
2001	3-1	2-2	3-1	3-0	2-2	1-3		3-1	30-30
2002	3-1	3-1	2-2	2-1-1	2-2			2-2	34-29-1
2003	3-1	0-4	1-3	1-3	2-2			4-0	34-30
Total	**51-67**	**50-68**	**81-44-1**	**68-51-1**	**52-63**	**44-44**	**0-1**	**59-65-1**	**874-816-10**

NFC VS. AFC (REGULAR SEASON), 1970-2003

	Ariz	Atl	Car	Chi	Dall	Det	GB	Minn	NO
1970	2-0-1	1-2		1-2	3-0	3-0	2-1	2-1	0-3
1971	2-1	3-0		1-2	3-0	4-0	2-1	2-1	0-1-2
1972	1-2	2-2		1-2	3-0	2-0-1	2-1	1-2	0-3
1973	0-2-1	2-1		2-2	2-1	0-3	1-1-1	2-1	1-2
1974	2-1	0-3		0-3	2-1	1-2	2-1	2-1	0-3
1975	2-1	1-2		0-3	2-1	1-2	0-3	4-0	0-3
1976	1-1	0-2		0-2	2-0	2-0	0-2	2-0	1-2
1977	0-2	0-2		1-1	1-1	2-0	0-3	1-1	0-2
1978	0-4	1-3		0-4	3-1	2-2	2-2	1-3	1-3
1979	1-3	1-3		2-2	1-3	0-4	1-3	1-3	0-4
1980	1-1	2-2		0-4	3-1	0-2	1-3	1-3	1-3
1981	3-1	1-3		4-0	4-0	2-2	1-1	1-3	2-2
1982		1-1		1-1	2-1	0-1	1-1-1	1-3	1-0
1983	3-1	3-1		1-1	2-2	1-3	2-2	4-0	1-3
1984	3-1	1-3		2-2	2-2	0-4	0-4	0-4	3-1
1985	2-2	0-4		3-1	3-1	2-2	0-4	2-0	0-4
1986	1-1	1-3		4-0	1-3	1-3	1-3	1-3	1-3
1987	0-1	0-4		2-2	2-1	0-4	1-2-1	2-1	4-0
1988	1-3	1-3		3-1	0-4	1-1	1-3	2-2	4-0
1989	1-3	2-2		2-2	0-2	1-3	0-2	2-2	4-0
1990	2-2	2-2		2-2	1-1	1-3	1-3	2-2	2-2
1991	1-1	3-1		2-2	3-1	4-0	1-3	0-2	3-1
1992	0-2	2-2		1-3	4-0	2-2	3-1	3-1	3-1
1993	1-1	1-3		2-2	2-2	2-0	3-1	2-2	2-2
1994	3-1	1-3		3-1	3-1	2-2	1-3	2-2	1-3
1995	1-3	2-2	3-1	2-2	4-0	3-1	4-0	3-1	4-0
1996	0-4	0-4	3-1	2-2	2-2	1-3	3-1	1-3	1-3
1997	1-3	2-2	2-2	2-2	2-2	2-2	3-1	3-1	2-2
1998	1-3	3-1	1-3	2-2	1-3	1-3	3-1	4-0	1-3
1999	0-4	0-4	2-2	2-2	1-3	1-3	2-2	2-2	0-4
2000	1-3	1-3	2-2	2-2	1-3	2-2	1-3	3-1	1-3
2001	3-1	1-3	0-4	3-1	0-4	0-4	3-1	1-3	2-2
2002	0-4	2-1-1	3-1	1-3	2-2	0-4	3-1	1-3	2-2
2003	1-3	1-3	2-2	3-1	2-2	1-3	3-1	2-2	1-3
Total	**41-66-2**	**44-80-1**	**18-18**	**59-64**	**69-51**	**47-70-1**	**54-65-3**	**63-59**	**49-73-2**

	NYG	Phil	StL	SF	Sea	TB	Wash	TOTALS
1970	3-0	2-1	2-1	4-0			2-1	27-12-1
1971	1-2	1-2	1-2	2-1			1-2	23-15-2
1972	1-2	2-1	1-2	2-1			1-2	19-20-1
1973	1-2	2-1	3-0	1-2			2-1	19-19-2
1974	1-2	2-1	3-1	0-3			2-1	17-23
1975	2-1	0-3	3-0	1-2			1-2	17-23
1976	0-2	0-2	1-1	1-1	1-0		1-1	12-16
1977	0-2	1-1	2-0	0-2		0-1	1-1	9-19
1978	1-1	3-1	2-2	1-3		2-0	2-2	21-31
1979	1-1	2-2	2-2	0-4		2-0	2-2	16-36
1980	1-3	3-1	2-2	2-2		1-3	1-3	19-33
1981	1-1	3-1	1-3	3-1		0-4	2-2	28-24
1982	1-0	2-1	1-2	1-3		2-1		14-15-1
1983	0-4	1-1	1-3	2-2		1-3	4-0	26-26
1984	2-0	3-1	3-1	3-1		1-1	3-1	26-26
1985	2-2	1-1	3-1	3-1		0-4	4-0	25-27
1986	3-1	2-2	2-2	4-0		1-1	3-1	26-26
1987	2-1	3-1	1-2	3-1		0-2	2-1	22-23-1
1988	1-1	2-2	2-2	2-2		1-3	1-3	22-30
1989	4-0	3-1	3-1	4-0		0-4	2-2	28-24
1990	3-1	1-3	2-2	4-0		0-2	3-1	26-26
1991	3-1	4-0	1-3	3-1		1-3	4-0	33-19
1992	2-2	3-1	2-2	3-1		0-2	2-2	30-22
1993	2-2	2-2	2-2	2-2		1-3	1-3	25-27
1994	3-1	1-3	2-2	3-1		1-1	1-1	27-25
1995	0-4	1-3	1-3	3-1		2-2	0-4	33-27
1996	2-2	2-2	2-2	4-0		2-2	3-1	28-32
1997	1-3	2-1-1	0-4	2-2		3-1	1-3	28-31-1
1998	3-1	0-4	3-1	2-2		2-2	2-2	29-31
1999	2-2	1-3	3-1	1-3		3-1	2-2	22-38
2000	3-1	3-1	3-1	2-2		3-1	2-2	30-30
2001	2-2	3-1	4-0	4-0		2-2	2-2	30-30
2002	2-2	1-3	2-2	2-2	2-2	3-1	3-1	29-34-1
2003	1-3	3-1	4-0	1-3	2-2	1-3	2-2	30-34
Total	**57-55**	**65-55-1**	**70-55**	**75-52**	**5-4**	**35-53**	**65-54**	**816-874-10**

INTERCONFERENCE GAMES

2003 INTERCONFERENCE GAMES

(Home Team in capital letters)

AFC 34, NFC 30

AFC Victories

New England 31, PHILADELPHIA 10
TENNESSEE 27, New Orleans 12
Cleveland 13, SAN FRANCISCO 12
DENVER 20, Detroit 16
Indianapolis 55, NEW ORLEANS 21
Miami 23, NEW YORK GIANTS 10
Indianapolis 38, TAMPA BAY 35 (OT)
Kansas City 40, GREEN BAY 34 (OT)
NEW ENGLAND 17, New York Giants 6
Baltimore 26, ARIZONA 18
Tennessee 37, CAROLINA 17
BUFFALO 24, Washington 7
CINCINNATI 27, Seattle 24
HOUSTON 14, Carolina 10
PITTSBURGH 28, Arizona 15
SAN DIEGO 42, Minnesota 28
CLEVELAND 44, Arizona 6
OAKLAND 28, Minnesota 18
NEW ENGLAND 12, Dallas 0
BALTIMORE 44, Seattle 41 (OT)
Tennessee 38, ATLANTA 31
MIAMI 24, Washington 23
Miami 40, DALLAS 21
BALTIMORE 44, San Francisco 6
Buffalo 24, NEW YORK GIANTS 7
HOUSTON 17, Atlanta 13
JACKSONVILLE 17, Tampa Bay 10
San Diego 14, DETROIT 7
CINCINNATI 41, San Francisco 38
INDIANAPOLIS 38, Atlanta 7
KANSAS CITY 45, Detroit 17
JACKSONVILLE 20, New Orleans 19
KANSAS CITY 31, Chicago 3
TENNESSEE 33, Tampa Bay 13

NFC Victories

WASHINGTON 16, New York Jets 13
CAROLINA 24, Jacksonville 23
NEW ORLEANS 31, Houston 10
Philadelphia 23, BUFFALO 13
WASHINGTON 20, New England 17
Dallas 17, NEW YORK JETS 6
CHICAGO 24, Oakland 21
Carolina 23, INDIANAPOLIS 20 (OT)
MINNESOTA 28, Denver 20
St. Louis 33, PITTSBURGH 21
PHILADELPHIA 24, New York Jets 17
CHICAGO 20, San Diego 7
DETROIT 23, Oakland 13
New York Giants 31, NEW YORK JETS 28 (OT)
ARIZONA 17, Cincinnati 14
SEATTLE 23, Pittsburgh 16
DALLAS 10, Buffalo 6
ST. LOUIS 33, Baltimore 22
SAN FRANCISCO 30, Pittsburgh 14
Chicago 19, DENVER 10
SEATTLE 34, Cleveland 7
St. Louis 26, CLEVELAND 20
TAMPA BAY 16, Houston 3
Green Bay 38, SAN DIEGO 21
Philadelphia 34, MIAMI 27
MINNESOTA 45, Kansas City 20
ST. LOUIS 27, Cincinnati 10
Green Bay 41, OAKLAND 7
ATLANTA 21, Jacksonville 14
GREEN BAY 31, Denver 3

REGULAR SEASON INTERCONFERENCE RECORDS, 1970-2003

AMERICAN FOOTBALL CONFERENCE

East	W	L	T	Pct.
Miami	83	38	0	.686
Buffalo	60	57	1	.513
New England	51	67	0	.432
New York Jets	50	68	0	.424
North	**W**	**L**	**T**	**Pct.**
Pittsburgh	68	51	1	.571
Cincinnati	60	60	0	.500
Baltimore	14	15	1	.483
Cleveland	53	57	0	.482
South	**W**	**L**	**T**	**Pct.**
Jacksonville	18	17	0	.514
Houston	4	4	0	.500
Tennessee	59	65	1	.476
Indianapolis	47	63	1	.428
West	**W**	**L**	**T**	**Pct.**
Oakland	81	44	1	.648
Denver	70	54	2	.563
Kansas City	60	48	2	.555
San Diego	52	63	0	.452

NATIONAL FOOTBALL CONFERENCE

East	W	L	T	Pct.
Dallas	69	51	0	.575
Washington	65	54	0	.546
Philadelphia	65	55	1	.541
New York Giants	57	55	0	.509
North	**W**	**L**	**T**	**Pct.**
Minnesota	63	59	0	.516
Chicago	59	64	0	.480
Green Bay	54	65	3	.455
Detroit	47	70	1	.403
South	**W**	**L**	**T**	**Pct.**
Carolina	18	18	0	.500
New Orleans	49	73	2	.402
Tampa Bay*	35	53	0	.398
Atlanta	44	80	1	.356
West	**W**	**L**	**T**	**Pct.**
San Francisco	75	52	0	.591
St. Louis	70	55	0	.560
Seattle* #	49	48	0	.505
Arizona	41	66	2	.384

* Records include one game played between Seattle and Tampa Bay, won by the Seahawks 13-10, in their inaugural season (1976) when Seattle competed in the NFC and Tampa Bay in the AFC.

Seattle was a member of the AFC from 1977-2001.

INTERCONFERENCE VICTORIES, 1970-2003

REGULAR SEASON

	AFC	NFC	Tie
1970	12	27	1
1971	15	23	2
1972	20	19	1
1973	19	19	2
1974	23	17	0
1975	23	17	0
1976	16	12	0
1977	19	9	0
1978	31	21	0
1979	36	16	0
1980	33	19	0
1981	24	28	0
1982	15	14	1
1983	26	26	0
1984	26	26	0
1985	27	25	0
1986	26	26	0
1987	23	22	1
1988	30	22	0
1989	24	28	0
1990	26	26	0
1991	19	33	0
1992	22	30	0
1993	27	25	0
1994	25	27	0
1995	27	33	0
1996	32	28	0
1997	31	28	1
1998	31	29	0
1999	38	22	0
2000	30	30	0
2001	30	30	0
2002	34	29	1
2003	34	30	0
Total	874	816	10

PRESEASON

	AFC	NFC	Tie
1970	21	28	1
1971	28	28	3
1972	27	25	4
1973	23	35	2
1974	35	25	0
1975	30	26	1
1976	30	31	0
1977	38	25	0
1978	20	19	0
1979	25	18	0
1980	22	20	1
1981	18	19	0
1982	25	16	0
1983	15	24	0
1984	16	19	0
1985	10	22	1
1986	22	17	0
1987	22	22	0
1988	23	16	1
1989	16	27	0
1990	15	29	0
1991	19	27	0
1992	30	22	0
1993	17	22	0
1994	22	16	0
1995	19	26	0
1996	27	19	0
1997	26	17	0
1998	34	16	0
1999	22	25	0
2000	34	17	0
2001	28	23	0
2002	25	24	0
2003	25	21	0
Total	809	766	14

PRO FOOTBALL HALL OF FAME GAME (41)

Date	Winner	Loser	Attendance
August 11, 1962	New York Giants 21	St. Louis Cardinals 21	14,000
September 8, 1963	Pittsburgh Steelers 16	Cleveland Browns 7	18,462
September 6, 1964	Baltimore Colts 48	Pittsburgh Steelers 17	11,479
September 12, 1965	Washington Redskins 20	Detroit Lions 3	14,416
1966	No game was played		
August 5, 1967	Philadelphia Eagles 28	Cleveland Browns 13	17,304
August 3, 1968	Chicago Bears 30	Dallas Cowboys 24	14,578
September 13, 1969	Green Bay Packers 38	Atlanta Falcons 24	17,411
August 8, 1970	New Orleans Saints 14	Minnesota Vikings 13	17,932
July 31, 1971	Los Angeles Rams (NFC) 17	Houston Oilers (AFC) 6	19,384
July 29, 1972	Kansas City Chiefs (AFC) 23	New York Giants (NFC) 17	19,304
July 28, 1973	San Francisco 49ers (NFC) 20	New England Patriots (AFC) 7	19,685
July 27, 1974	St. Louis Cardinals (NFC) 21	Buffalo Bills (AFC) 13	17,286
August 2, 1975	Washington Redskins (NFC) 17	Cincinnati Bengals (AFC) 9	19,360
July 24, 1976	Denver Broncos (AFC) 10	Detroit Lions (NFC) 7	17,639
July 30, 1977	Chicago Bears (NFC) 20	New York Jets (AFC) 6	19,057
July 29, 1978	Philadelphia Eagles (NFC) 17	Miami Dolphins (AFC) 3	19,255
July 28, 1979	Oakland Raiders (AFC) 20	Dallas Cowboys (NFC) 13	20,648
August 2, 1980*	San Diego Chargers (AFC) 0	Green Bay Packers (NFC) 0	19,972
August 1, 1981	Cleveland Browns (AFC) 24	Atlanta Falcons (NFC) 10	23,921
August 7, 1982	Minnesota Vikings (NFC) 30	Baltimore Colts (AFC) 14	23,379
July 30, 1983	Pittsburgh Steelers (AFC) 27	New Orleans Saints (NFC) 14	23,909
July 28, 1984	Seattle Seahawks (AFC) 38	Tampa Bay Buccaneers (NFC) 0	22,250
August 3, 1985	New York Giants (NFC) 21	Houston Oilers (AFC) 20	23,940
August 2, 1986	New England Patriots (AFC) 21	St. Louis Cardinals (NFC) 16	22,739
August 8, 1987	San Francisco 49ers (NFC) 20	Kansas City Chiefs (AFC) 7	23,826
July 30, 1988	Cincinnati Bengals (AFC) 14	Los Angeles Rams (NFC) 7	23,801
August 5, 1989	Washington Redskins (NFC) 31	Buffalo Bills (AFC) 6	23,948
August 4, 1990	Chicago Bears (NFC) 13	Cleveland Browns (AFC) 0	23,952
July 27, 1991	Detroit Lions (NFC) 14	Denver Broncos (AFC) 3	23,815
August 1, 1992	New York Jets (AFC) 41	Philadelphia Eagles (NFC) 14	23,853
July 31, 1993	Los Angeles Raiders (AFC) 19	Green Bay Packers (NFC) 3	23,863
July 30, 1994	Atlanta Falcons (NFC) 21	San Diego Chargers (AFC) 17	23,185
July 29, 1995	Carolina Panthers (NFC) 20	Jacksonville Jaguars (AFC) 14	24,625
July 27, 1996	Indianapolis Colts (AFC) 10	New Orleans Saints (NFC) 3	23,376
July 26, 1997	Minnesota Vikings (NFC) 28	Seattle Seahawks (AFC) 26	23,846
August 1, 1998	Tampa Bay Buccaneers (NFC) 30	Pittsburgh Steelers (AFC) 6	23,875
August 9, 1999	Cleveland Browns (AFC) 20	Dallas Cowboys (NFC) 17 (OT)	25,156
July 31, 2000	New England Patriots (AFC) 20	San Francisco 49ers (NFC) 0	22,840
August 6, 2001	St. Louis Rams (NFC) 17	Miami Dolphins (AFC) 10	22,736
August 5, 2002	New York Giants (NFC) 34	Houston Texans (AFC) 17	22,461
August 4, 2003**	Kansas City Chiefs (AFC) 9	Green Bay Packers (NFC) 0	22,385

**Game called with 5:29 remaining because of severe thunder and lightning.*
***Game called with 5:49 remaining in the third quarter because of lightning and torrential rain.*

INTERNATIONAL GAMES

NFL INTERNATIONAL GAMES (55)

Date	Site	Teams
August 12, 1950	Ottawa, Canada	N.Y. Giants 27, Ottawa Rough Riders 6
August 11, 1951	Ottawa, Canada	N.Y. Giants 41, Ottawa Rough Riders 18
August 5, 1959	Toronto, Canada	Chi. Cardinals 55, Tor. Argonauts 26
August 3, 1960	Toronto, Canada	Pittsburgh 43, Toronto Argonauts 16
August 15, 1960	Toronto, Canada	Chicago 16, N.Y. Giants 7
August 2, 1961	Toronto, Canada	St. Louis 36, Toronto Argonauts 7
August 5, 1961	Montreal, Canada	Chicago 34, Montreal Allouettes 16
August 8, 1961	Hamilton, Canada	Hamilton Tiger-Cats 38, Buffalo 21
Sept. 11, 1969	Montreal, Canada	Pittsburgh 17, N.Y. Giants 13
August 25, 1969	Montreal, Canada	Detroit 22, Boston 9
August 16, 1976	Tokyo, Japan	St. Louis 20, San Diego 10
August 5, 1978	Mexico City, Mexico	New Orleans 14, Philadelphia 7
August 6, 1983	London, England	Minnesota 28, St. Louis 10
* August 3, 1986	London, England	Chicago 17, Dallas 6
* August 9, 1987	London, England	L.A. Rams 28, Denver 27
* July 31, 1988	London, England	Miami 27, San Francisco 21
August 14, 1988	Goteborg, Sweden	Minnesota 28, Chicago 21
August 18, 1988	Montreal, Canada	N.Y. Jets 11, Cleveland 7
* August 5, 1989	Tokyo, Japan	L.A. Rams 16, San Francisco 13 (OT)
* August 6, 1989	London, England	Philadelphia 17, Cleveland 13
* August 4, 1990	Tokyo, Japan	Denver 10, Seattle 7
* August 5, 1990	London, England	New Orleans 17, L.A. Raiders 10
* August 9, 1990	Montreal, Canada	Pittsburgh 30, New England 14
* August 11, 1990	Berlin, Germany	L.A. Rams 19, Kansas City 3
* July 28, 1991	London, England	Buffalo 17, Philadelphia 13
* August 3, 1991	Berlin, Germany	San Francisco 21, Chicago 7
* August 3, 1991	Tokyo, Japan	Miami 19, L.A. Raiders 17
* August 1, 1992	Tokyo, Japan	Houston 34, Dallas 23
* August 15, 1992	Berlin, Germany	Miami 31, Denver 27
* August 16, 1992	London, England	San Francisco 17, Washington 15
* July 31, 1993	Tokyo, Japan	New Orleans 28, Philadelphia 16
* August 1, 1993	Barcelona, Spain	San Francisco 21, Pittsburgh 14
* August 7, 1993	Berlin, Germany	Minnesota 20, Buffalo 6
* August 8, 1993	London, England	Dallas 13, Detroit 13 (OT)
August 14, 1993	Toronto, Canada	Cleveland 12, New England 9
* July 31, 1994	Barcelona, Spain	L.A. Raiders 25, Denver 22
* August 6, 1994	Tokyo, Japan	Minnesota 17, Kansas City 9
* August 13, 1994	Berlin, Germany	N.Y. Giants 28, San Diego 20
* August 15, 1994	Mexico City, Mexico	Houston 6, Dallas 0
* August 5, 1995	Tokyo, Japan	Denver 24, San Francisco 10
* August 12, 1995	Toronto, Canada	Buffalo 9, Dallas 7
* July 27, 1996	Tokyo, Japan	San Diego 20, Pittsburgh 10
* August 5, 1996	Monterrey, Mexico	Kansas City 32, Dallas 6
* July 27, 1997	Dublin, Ireland	Pittsburgh 30, Chicago 17
* August 4, 1997	Mexico City, Mexico	Miami 38, Denver 19
* August 16, 1997	Toronto, Canada	Green Bay 35, Buffalo 3
* August 1, 1998	Tokyo, Japan	Green Bay 27, Kansas City 24 (OT)
* August 15, 1998	Vancouver, Canada	San Francisco 24, Seattle 21
* August 17, 1998	Mexico City, Mexico	New England 21, Dallas 3
* August 7, 1999	Sydney, Australia	Denver 20, San Diego 17
* August 5, 2000	Tokyo, Japan	Atlanta 20, Dallas 9
* August 19, 2000	Mexico City, Mexico	Indianapolis 24, Pittsburgh 23
* August 27, 2001	Mexico City, Mexico	Dallas 21, Oakland 6
* August 3, 2002	Osaka, Japan	Washington 38, San Francisco 7
* August 2, 2003	Tokyo, Japan	Tampa Bay 30, N.Y. Jets 14

**American Bowl Game*

CHICAGO ALL-STAR GAME

Pro teams won 31, lost 9, and tied 2. The game was discontinued after 1976.

Date	Winner	Loser	Attendance
August 31, 1934	Chicago Bears 0	All-Stars 0 (tie)	79,432
August 29, 1935	Chicago Bears 5	All-Stars 0	77,450
September 3, 1936	Detroit Lions 7	All-Stars 7 (tie)	76,000
September 1, 1937	All-Stars 6	Green Bay Packers 0	84,560
August 31, 1938	All-Stars 28	Washington Redskins 16	74,250
August 30, 1939	N.Y. Giants 9	All-Stars 0	81,456
August 29, 1940	Green Bay Packers 45	All-Stars 28	84,567
August 28, 1941	Chicago Bears 37	All-Stars 13	98,203
August 28, 1942	Chicago Bears 21	All-Stars 0	101,100
August 25, 1943	All-Stars 27	Washington Redskins 7	48,471
August 30, 1944	Chicago Bears 24	All-Stars 21	48,769
August 30, 1945	Green Bay Packers 19	All-Stars 7	92,753
August 23, 1946	All-Stars 16	Los Angeles Rams 0	97,380
August 22, 1947	All-Stars 16	Chicago Bears 0	105,840
August 20, 1948	Chicago Cardinals 28	All-Stars 0	101,220
August 12, 1949	Philadelphia Eagles 38	All-Stars 0	93,780
August 11, 1950	All-Stars 17	Philadelphia Eagles 7	88,885
August 17, 1951	Cleveland Browns 33	All-Stars 0	92,180
August 15, 1952	Los Angeles Rams 10	All-Stars 7	88,316
August 14, 1953	Detroit Lions 24	All-Stars 10	93,818
August 13, 1954	Detroit Lions 31	All-Stars 6	93,470
August 12, 1955	All-Stars 30	Cleveland Browns 27	75,000
August 10, 1956	Cleveland Browns 26	All-Stars 0	75,000
August 9, 1957	N.Y. Giants 22	All-Stars 12	75,000
August 15, 1958	All-Stars 35	Detroit Lions 19	70,000
August 14, 1959	Baltimore Colts 29	All-Stars 0	70,000
August 12, 1960	Baltimore Colts 32	All-Stars 7	70,000
August 4, 1961	Philadelphia Eagles 28	All-Stars 14	66,000
August 3, 1962	Green Bay Packers 42	All-Stars 20	65,000
August 2, 1963	All-Stars 20	Green Bay Packers 17	65,000
August 7, 1964	Chicago Bears 28	All-Stars 17	65,000
August 6, 1965	Cleveland Browns 24	All-Stars 16	68,000
August 5, 1966	Green Bay Packers 38	All-Stars 0	72,000
August 4, 1967	Green Bay Packers 27	All-Stars 0	70,934
August 2, 1968	Green Bay Packers 34	All-Stars 17	69,917
August 1, 1969	N.Y. Jets 26	All-Stars 24	74,208
July 31, 1970	Kansas City Chiefs 24	All-Stars 3	69,940
July 30, 1971	Baltimore Colts 24	All-Stars 17	52,289
July 28, 1972	Dallas Cowboys 20	All-Stars 7	54,162
July 27, 1973	Miami Dolphins 14	All-Stars 3	54,103
1974	No game was played		
August 1, 1975	Pittsburgh Steelers 21	All-Stars 14	54,103
July 23, 1976*	Pittsburgh Steelers 24	All-Stars 0	52,895

*Game shortened because of thunderstorms.

NFL PLAYOFF BOWL

Consolation game that matched conference runners-up.
Western Conference won 8, Eastern Conference won 2.
All games played at Miami's Orange Bowl.

January 7, 1961	Detroit Lions 17, Cleveland Browns 16
January 6, 1962	Detroit Lions 38, Philadelphia Eagles 10
January 6, 1963	Detroit Lions 17, Pittsburgh Steelers 10
January 5, 1964	Green Bay Packers 40, Cleveland Browns 23
January 3, 1965	St. Louis Cardinals 24, Green Bay Packers 17
January 9, 1966	Baltimore Colts 35, Dallas Cowboys 3
January 8, 1967	Baltimore Colts 20, Philadelphia Eagles 14
January 7, 1968	Los Angeles Rams 30, Cleveland Browns 6
January 5, 1969	Dallas Cowboys 17, Minnesota Vikings 13
January 3, 1970	Los Angeles Rams 31, Dallas Cowboys 0

MONDAY NIGHT RECORDS

Compiled by Elias Sports Bureau
*NFL record.

MONDAY NIGHT RECORDS

SCORING
TOUCHDOWNS
Most Touchdowns, Career
- 35 Jerry Rice, San Francisco, 1985-2000; Oakland, 2001-03
- 24 Emmitt Smith, Dallas, 1990-2002; Arizona 2003
- 19 Marcus Allen, L.A. Raiders, 1982-1992; Kansas City, 1993-97

Most Touchdowns, Game
- 4 Ron Johnson, N.Y. Giants at Philadelphia, Oct. 2, 1972
  - Earl Campbell, Houston vs. Miami, Nov. 20, 1978
  - Marcus Allen, L.A. Raiders vs. San Diego, Sept. 24, 1984
  - Eric Dickerson, Indianapolis vs. Denver, Oct. 31, 1988
  - Emmitt Smith, Dallas at N.Y. Giants, Sept. 4, 1995
  - Marshall Faulk, St. Louis at Tampa Bay, Dec. 18, 2000

FIELD GOALS
Most Field Goals, Career
- 48 Gary Anderson, Pittsburgh, 1982-1994; Philadelphia, 1995-96; San Francisco, 1997; Minnesota, 1998-2002; Tennessee, 2003
- 37 Jason Elam, Denver, 1993-2003
- 33 Mark Moseley, Philadelphia, 1970; Houston, 1971-72; Washington, 1974-1986; Cleveland, 1986

Most Field Goals, Game
- 7 Chris Boniol, Dallas vs. Green Bay, Nov. 18, 1996*
  - Billy Cundiff, Dallas at N.Y. Giants, Sept. 15, 2003 (OT)*
- 5 Tim Mazzetti, Atlanta vs. Los Angeles, Oct. 30, 1978
  - Roger Ruzek, Dallas at L.A. Rams, Dec. 21, 1987
  - Rich Karlis, Minnesota vs. Cincinnati, Dec. 25, 1989
  - Nick Lowery, Kansas City vs. Denver, Sept. 20, 1993
  - Chris Jacke, Green Bay vs. San Francisco, Oct. 14, 1996 (OT)
  - Richie Cunningham, Dallas vs. Philadelphia, Sept. 15, 1997

RUSHING
YARDS GAINED
Most Yards Gained, Career
- 2,434 Emmitt Smith, Dallas, 1990-2002; Arizona, 2003
- 1,897 Tony Dorsett, Dallas, 1977-1987; Denver, 1988
- 1,769 Thurman Thomas, Buffalo, 1988-1999; Miami, 2000

Most Yards Gained, Game
- 221 Bo Jackson, L.A. Raiders at Seattle, Nov. 30, 1987
- 216 Ricky Williams, Miami vs. Chicago, Dec. 9, 2002
- 214 Thurman Thomas, Buffalo at N.Y. Jets, Sept. 24, 1990

Longest Run From Scrimage, Game
- 99 Tony Dorsett, Dallas at Minnesota, Jan. 3, 1983 (TD)*
- 91 Bo Jackson, L.A. Raiders at Seattle, Nov. 30, 1987 (TD)
- 83 James Lofton, Green Bay at N.Y. Giants, Sept. 20, 1982 (TD)

TOUCHDOWNS
Most Rushing Touchdowns, Career
- 23 Emmitt Smith, Dallas, 1990-2002; Arizona, 2003
- 17 Marcus Allen, L.A. Raiders, 1982-1992; Kansas City, 1993-97
- 14 Eric Dickerson, L.A. Rams, 1983-87; Indianapolis, 1987-1991; L.A. Raiders, 1992; Atlanta, 1993

Most Rushing Touchdowns, Game
- 4 Earl Campbell, Houston vs. Miami, Nov. 20, 1978
  - Eric Dickerson, Indianapolis vs. Denver, Oct. 31, 1988
  - Emmitt Smith, Dallas at N.Y. Giants, Sept. 4, 1995

PASSING
YARDS GAINED
Most Yards Gained, Career
- 9,654 Dan Marino, Miami, 1983-1999
- 5,706 Brett Favre, Atlanta, 1991; Green Bay, 1992-2003
- 5,148 Joe Montana, San Francisco, 1979-1992; Kansas City, 1993-94

Most Yards Gained, Game
- 458 Joe Montana, San Francisco at L.A. Rams, Dec. 11, 1989
- 447 Ken Anderson, Cincinnati vs. Buffalo, Nov. 17, 1975
- 445 Charley Johnson, Denver vs. Kansas City, Nov. 18, 1974

Longest Pass Play
- 99 Brett Favre to Robert Brooks, Green Bay at Chicago, Sept. 11, 1995 (TD)*
- 97 Bernie Kosar to Webster Slaughter, Cleveland vs. Chicago, Oct. 23, 1989 (TD)
- 95 Joe Montana to John Taylor, San Francisco at L.A. Rams, Dec. 11, 1989 (TD)

TOUCHDOWNS
Most Touchdown Passes, Career
- 74 Dan Marino, Miami, 1983-1999
- 42 Steve Young, Tampa Bay, 1985-86; San Francisco, 1987-1999
  - Brett Favre, Atlanta, 1991; Green Bay, 1992-2003
- 36 Joe Montana, San Francisco, 1979-1992; Kansas City, 1993-94

Most Touchdown Passes, Game
- 5 Dave Krieg, Seattle vs. L.A. Raiders, Nov. 28, 1988
  - Jim Kelly, Buffalo vs. Cincinnati, Oct. 21, 1991
  - Vinny Testaverde, N.Y. Jets vs. Miami, Oct. 23, 2000 (OT)

RECEIVING
PASS RECEPTIONS
Most Pass Receptions, Career
- 246 Jerry Rice, San Francisco, 1985-2000; Oakland, 2001-03
- 124 Andre Reed, Buffalo, 1985-1999; Washington, 2000
- 123 Cris Carter, Philadelphia, 1987-89; Minnesota, 1990-2001; Miami, 2002

Most Pass Receptions, Game
- 14 Herman Moore, Detroit vs. Chicago, Dec. 4, 1995
  - Jerry Rice, San Francisco vs. Minnesota, Dec. 18, 1995
- 13 Andre Reed, Buffalo vs. Denver, Sept. 18, 1989
  - Terrell Owens, San Francisco vs. Philadelphia, Nov. 25, 2002

YARDS GAINED
Most Yards Gained, Career
- 3,884 Jerry Rice, San Francisco, 1985-2000; Oakland, 2001-03
- 1,783 Andre Reed, Buffalo, 1985-1999; Washington, 2000
- 1,537 Art Monk, Washington, 1980-1993; N.Y. Jets, 1994; Philadelphia, 1995

Most Yards Gained, Game
- 289 Jerry Rice, San Francisco vs. Minnesota, Dec. 18, 1995
- 286 John Taylor, San Francisco at L.A. Rams, Dec. 11, 1989
- 260 Wes Chandler, San Diego vs. Cincinnati, Dec. 20, 1982

TOUCHDOWNS

Most Receiving Touchdowns, Career

33 Jerry Rice, San Francisco, 1985-2000; Oakland, 2001-03
15 Mark Clayton, Miami, 1983-1992; Green Bay, 1993
13 Andre Reed, Buffalo, 1985-1999; Washington, 2000

Most Receiving Touchdowns, Game

3 Ron Johnson, N.Y. Giants at Philadelphia, Oct. 2, 1972
Wesley Walker, N.Y. Jets at Detroit, Dec. 6, 1982
Steve Largent, Seattle at San Diego, Oct. 29, 1984
Mark Clayton, Miami vs. Dallas, Dec. 17, 1984
Jerry Rice, San Francisco vs. Chicago, Dec. 14, 1987
Jerry Rice, San Francisco vs. Minnesota, Dec. 18, 1995
Lamar Thomas, Miami vs. Denver, Dec. 21, 1998
Ed McCaffrey, Denver vs. Miami, Sept. 13, 1999
Randy Moss, Minnesota vs. N.Y. Giants, Nov. 19, 2001
Isaac Bruce, St. Louis at New Orleans, Dec. 17, 2001

YARDS FROM SCRIMMAGE

Most Scrimmage Yards, Career

3,971 Jerry Rice, San Francisco, 1985-2000; Oakland, 2001-03
2,836 Emmitt Smith, Dallas, 1990-2002; Arizona, 2003
2,567 Tony Dorsett, Dallas, 1977-1987; Denver, 1988

INTERCEPTIONS BY

Most Interceptions, Career

11 Everson Walls, Dallas, 1981-89; N.Y. Giants, 1990-92; Cleveland, 1992-93
9 Merton Hanks, San Francisco, 1991-98; Seattle, 1999
8 Emmitt Thomas, Kansas City, 1966-1978

Most Interceptions, Game

4 Dick Anderson, Miami vs. Pittsburgh, Dec. 3, 1973*
3 Johnny Robinson, Kansas City at Baltimore, Sept. 28, 1970
Charlie Babb, Miami vs. Oakland, Sept. 22, 1975
Charles Phillips, Oakland vs. Denver, Dec. 8, 1975
Mark Murphy, Washington at San Diego, Oct. 31, 1983
Ken Easley, Seattle at San Diego, Oct. 29, 1984
Dwayne Harper, San Diego vs. Oakland, Nov. 27, 1995
Marcus Coleman, N.Y. Jets vs. Miami, Oct. 23, 2000 (OT)

Longest Interception Return

102 Eddie Anderson, L.A. Raiders at Miami, Dec. 14, 1992 (TD)
98 Marcus Coleman, N.Y. Jets vs. Miami, Dec. 27, 1999 (TD)
Rod Woodson, Oakland at Denver, Nov. 11, 2002 (TD)
94 Nolan Cromwell, L.A. Rams vs. Atlanta, Dec. 14, 1981
Walker Lee Ashley, Minnesota vs. Chicago, Dec. 19, 1988 (TD)

SACKS

Most Sacks, Career

24.5 Bruce Smith, Buffalo, 1985-1999; Washington, 2000-03
20.0 Richard Dent, Chicago, 1983-1993, 1995; San Francisco, 1994; Indianapolis, 1996; Philadelphia, 1997
18.0 Kevin Greene, L.A. Rams, 1985-1992; Pittsburgh, 1993-95; Carolina, 1996, 1998-99; San Francisco, 1997

PUNTING

Highest Punt Average, Career (Minimum: 25 Punts)

47.3 Shane Lechler, Oakland, 2000-03
44.5 Tom Tupa, Phoenix, 1988-1991; Indianapolis, 1992; Cleveland, 1994-95; New England, 1996-98; N.Y. Jets, 1999-2001; Tampa Bay, 2002-03
44.3 Tom Rouen, Denver, 1993-2002; N.Y. Giants, 2002; Pittsburgh, 2002; Seattle, 2003

Longest Punt

90 Rodney Williams, N.Y. Giants at Denver, Sept. 10, 2001
83 Bryan Barker, Jacksonville vs. N.Y. Jets, Oct. 11, 1999
74 Craig Colquitt, Pittsburgh vs. Oakland, Dec. 7, 1981

PUNT RETURNS

Longest Punt Return

95 John Taylor, San Francisco vs. Washington, Nov. 21, 1988 (TD)
94 Dennis McKinnon, Chicago vs. N.Y. Giants, Sept. 14, 1987 (TD)
91 JoJo Townsell, N.Y. Jets vs. Seattle, Nov. 9, 1987 (TD)

KICKOFF RETURNS

Longest Kickoff Return

105 Terry Fair, Detroit vs. Tampa Bay, Sept. 28, 1998 (TD)
102 Harold Hart, Oakland at Miami, Sept. 22, 1975 (TD)
101 Roell Preston, Green Bay vs. Minnesota, Oct. 5, 1998 (TD)

FUMBLES

Longest Fumble Return

99 Don Griffin, San Francisco vs. Chicago, Dec. 23, 1991 (TD)
96 Joe Lavender, Philadelphia vs. Dallas, Sept. 23, 1974 (TD)
88 Keith McKenzie, Green Bay at Pittsburgh, Nov. 9, 1998

MONDAY NIGHT FOOTBALL, 1970-2003

(Home Team in capitals, games listed in chronological order.)

2003
Tampa Bay 17, PHILADELPHIA 0
Dallas 35, NEW YORK GIANTS 32 (OT)
DENVER 31, Oakland 10
Green Bay 38, CHICAGO 23
Indianapolis 38, TAMPA BAY 35 (OT)
ST. LOUIS 36, Atlanta 0
Kansas City 17, OAKLAND 10
Miami 26, SAN DIEGO 10
New England 30, DENVER 26
Philadelphia 17, GREEN BAY 14
SAN FRANCISCO 30, Pittsburgh 14
TAMPA BAY 19, New York Giants 13
NEW YORK JETS 24, Tennessee 17
St. Louis 26, CLEVELAND 20
Philadelphia 34, MIAMI 27
Green Bay 41, OAKLAND 7

2002
NEW ENGLAND 30, Pittsburgh 14
Philadelphia 37, WASHINGTON 7
TAMPA BAY 26, St. Louis 14
BALTIMORE 34, Denver 23
Green Bay 34, CHICAGO 21
San Francisco 28, SEATTLE 21
PITTSBURGH 28, Indianapolis 10
PHILADELPHIA 17, New York Giants 3
GREEN BAY 24, Miami 10
Oakland 34, DENVER 10
ST. LOUIS 21, Chicago 16
Philadelphia 38, SAN FRANCISCO 17
OAKLAND 26, New York Jets 20
MIAMI 27, Chicago 9
TENNESSEE 24, New England 7
Pittsburgh 17, TAMPA BAY 7
ST. LOUIS 31, San Francisco 20

2001
DENVER 31, N.Y. Giants 20
GREEN BAY 37, Washington 0
San Francisco 19, N.Y. JETS 17
St. Louis 35, DETROIT 0
DALLAS 9, Washington 7
Philadelphia 10, N.Y. GIANTS 9
PITTSBURGH 34, Tennessee 7
OAKLAND 38, Denver 28
Baltimore 16, TENNESSEE 10
MINNESOTA 28, N.Y. Giants 16
Tampa Bay 24, ST. LOUIS 17
Green Bay 28, JACKSONVILLE 21
MIAMI 41, Indianapolis 6
St. Louis 34, NEW ORLEANS 21
BALTIMORE 19, Minnesota 3

2000
ST. LOUIS 41, Denver 36
N.Y. JETS 20, New England 19
Dallas 27, WASHINGTON 21
INDIANAPOLIS 43, Jacksonville 14
KANSAS CITY 24, Seattle 17
MINNESOTA 30, Tampa Bay 23
TENNESSEE 27, Jacksonville 13
N.Y. JETS 40, Miami 37 (OT)
Tennessee 27, WASHINGTON 21
GREEN BAY 26, Minnesota 20 (OT)
DENVER 27, Oakland 24
Washington 33, ST. LOUIS 20
CAROLINA 31, Green Bay 14
NEW ENGLAND 30, Kansas City 24
INDIANAPOLIS 44, Buffalo 20
TAMPA BAY 38, St. Louis 35
TENNESSEE 31, Dallas 0

1999
Miami 38, DENVER 21
DALLAS 24, Atlanta 7
San Francisco 24, ARIZONA 10
Buffalo 23, MIAMI 18
Jacksonville 16, N.Y. JETS 6
N.Y. GIANTS 13, Dallas 10
PITTSBURGH 13, Atlanta 9
Seattle 27, GREEN BAY 7
MINNESOTA 27, Dallas 17
N.Y. Jets 24, NEW ENGLAND 17
DENVER 27, Oakland 21 (OT)
Green Bay 20, SAN FRANCISCO 3
TAMPA BAY 24, Minnesota 17
JACKSONVILLE 27, Denver 24
MINNESOTA 24, Green Bay 20
N.Y. Jets 38, MIAMI 31
ATLANTA 34, San Francisco 29

1998
DENVER 27, New England 21
San Francisco 45, WASHINGTON 10
Dallas 31, N.Y. GIANTS 7
DETROIT 27, Tampa Bay 6
Minnesota 37, GREEN BAY 24
JACKSONVILLE 28, Miami 21
N.Y. Jets 24, NEW ENGLAND 14
Pittsburgh 20, KANSAS CITY 13
Dallas 34, PHILADELPHIA 0
PITTSBURGH 27, Green Bay 20
Denver 30, KANSAS CITY 7
NEW ENGLAND 26, Miami 23
SAN FRANCISCO 31, N.Y. Giants 7
TAMPA BAY 24, Green Bay 22
SAN FRANCISCO 35, Detroit 13
MIAMI 31, Denver 21
JACKSONVILLE 21, Pittsburgh 3

1997
GREEN BAY 38, Chicago 24
Kansas City 28, OAKLAND 27
DALLAS 21, Philadelphia 20
JACKSONVILLE 30, Pittsburgh 21
San Francisco 34, CAROLINA 21
DENVER 34, New England 13
WASHINGTON 21, Dallas 16
Buffalo 9, INDIANAPOLIS 6
Green Bay 28, NEW ENGLAND 10
Chicago 36, MIAMI 33 (OT)
KANSAS CITY 13, Pittsburgh 10
San Francisco 24, PHILADELPHIA 12
MIAMI 30, Buffalo 13
DENVER 31, Oakland 3
Green Bay 27, MINNESOTA 11
Carolina 23, DALLAS 13
SAN FRANCISCO 34, Denver 17
New England 14, MIAMI 12

1996
CHICAGO 22, Dallas 6
GREEN BAY 39, Philadelphia 13
PITTSBURGH 24, Buffalo 6
INDIANAPOLIS 10, Miami 6
Dallas 23, PHILADELPHIA 19
Pittsburgh 17, KANSAS CITY 7
GREEN BAY 23, San Francisco 20 (OT)
Oakland 23, SAN DIEGO 14
Chicago 15, MINNESOTA 13
Denver 22, OAKLAND 21
SAN DIEGO 27, Detroit 21
DALLAS 21, Green Bay 6
Pittsburgh 24, MIAMI 17
San Francisco 34, ATLANTA 10
OAKLAND 26, Kansas City 7
MIAMI 16, Buffalo 14
SAN FRANCISCO 24, Detroit 14

1995
Dallas 35, N.Y. GIANTS 0
Green Bay 27, CHICAGO 24
MIAMI 23, Pittsburgh 10
DETROIT 27, San Francisco 24
Buffalo 22, CLEVELAND 19
KANSAS CITY 29, San Diego 23 (OT)
DENVER 27, Oakland 0
NEW ENGLAND 27, Buffalo 14
Chicago 14, MINNESOTA 6
DALLAS 34, Philadelphia 12
PITTSBURGH 20, Cleveland 3
San Francisco 44, MIAMI 20
SAN DIEGO 12, Oakland 6
DETROIT 27, Chicago 7
MIAMI 13, Kansas City 6
SAN FRANCISCO 37, Minnesota 30
Dallas 37, ARIZONA 13

1994
SAN FRANCISCO 44, L.A. Raiders 14
PHILADELPHIA 30, Chicago 22
Detroit 20, DALLAS 17 (OT)
BUFFALO 27, Denver 20
PITTSBURGH 30, Houston 14
Minnesota 27, N.Y. GIANTS 10
Kansas City 31, DENVER 28
PHILADELPHIA 21, Houston 6
Green Bay 33, CHICAGO 6
DALLAS 38, N.Y. Giants 10
PITTSBURGH 23, Buffalo 10
N.Y. Giants 13, HOUSTON 10
San Francisco 35, NEW ORLEANS 14
L.A. Raiders 24, SAN DIEGO 17
MIAMI 45, Kansas City 28
Dallas 24, NEW ORLEANS 16
MINNESOTA 21, San Francisco 14

1993
WASHINGTON 35, Dallas 16
CLEVELAND 23, San Francisco 13
KANSAS CITY 15, Denver 7
Pittsburgh 45, ATLANTA 17
MIAMI 17, Washington 10
BUFFALO 35, Houston 7
L.A. Raiders 23, DENVER 20
Minnesota 19, CHICAGO 12
BUFFALO 24, Washington 10
KANSAS CITY 23, Green Bay 16
PITTSBURGH 23, Buffalo 0
SAN FRANCISCO 42, New Orleans 7
San Diego 31, INDIANAPOLIS 0
DALLAS 23, Philadelphia 17
Pittsburgh 21, MIAMI 20
N.Y. Giants 24, NEW ORLEANS 14
SAN DIEGO 45, Miami 20
Philadelphia 37, SAN FRANCISCO 34 (OT)

1992
DALLAS 23, Washington 10
Miami 27, CLEVELAND 23
N.Y. Giants 27, CHICAGO 14
KANSAS CITY 27, L.A. Raiders 7
PHILADELPHIA 31, Dallas 7
WASHINGTON 34, Denver 3
PITTSBURGH 20, Cincinnati 0
Buffalo 24, N.Y. JETS 20
Minnesota 38, CHICAGO 10
San Francisco 41, ATLANTA 3
Buffalo 26, MIAMI 20
NEW ORLEANS 20, Washington 3
SEATTLE 16, Denver 13 (OT)
HOUSTON 24, Chicago 7
MIAMI 20, L.A. Raiders 7
Dallas 41, ATLANTA 17
SAN FRANCISCO 24, Detroit 6

1991
N.Y. GIANTS 16, San Francisco 14
Washington 33, DALLAS 31
HOUSTON 17, Kansas City 7
CHICAGO 19, N.Y. Jets 13 (OT)
WASHINGTON 23, Philadelphia 0
KANSAS CITY 33, Buffalo 6
N.Y. Giants 23, PITTSBURGH 20
BUFFALO 35, Cincinnati 16
KANSAS CITY 24, L.A. Raiders 21
PHILADELPHIA 30, N.Y. Giants 7
Chicago 34, MINNESOTA 17
Buffalo 41, MIAMI 27
San Francisco 33, L.A. RAMS 10
Philadelphia 13, HOUSTON 6
MIAMI 37, Cincinnati 13
NEW ORLEANS 27, L.A. Raiders 0
SAN FRANCISCO 52, Chicago 14

1990
San Francisco 13, NEW ORLEANS 12
DENVER 24, Kansas City 23
Buffalo 30, N.Y. JETS 7
SEATTLE 31, Cincinnati 16
Cleveland 30, DENVER 29
PHILADELPHIA 32, Minnesota 24
Cincinnati 34, CLEVELAND 13
PITTSBURGH 41, L.A. Rams 10
N.Y. Giants 24, INDIANAPOLIS 7
PHILADELPHIA 28, Washington 14
L.A. Raiders 13, MIAMI 10
HOUSTON 27, Buffalo 24
SAN FRANCISCO 7, N.Y. Giants 3
L.A. Raiders 38, DETROIT 31
San Francisco 26, L.A. RAMS 10
NEW ORLEANS 20, L.A. Rams 17

1989
N.Y. Giants 27, WASHINGTON 24
Denver 28, BUFFALO 14
CINCINNATI 21, Cleveland 14
CHICAGO 27, Philadelphia 13
L.A. Raiders 14, N.Y. JETS 7
BUFFALO 23, L.A. Rams 20
CLEVELAND 27, Chicago 7
N.Y. GIANTS 24, Minnesota 14
SAN FRANCISCO 31, New Orleans 13
HOUSTON 26, Cincinnati 24
Denver 14, WASHINGTON 10
SAN FRANCISCO 34, N.Y. Giants 24
SEATTLE 17, Buffalo 16
San Francisco 30, L.A. RAMS 27
NEW ORLEANS 30, Philadelphia 20
MINNESOTA 29, Cincinnati 21

1988
N.Y. GIANTS 27, Washington 20
Dallas 17, PHOENIX 14
CLEVELAND 23, Indianapolis 17
L.A. Raiders 30, DENVER 27 (OT)
NEW ORLEANS 20, Dallas 17
PHILADELPHIA 24, N.Y. Giants 13
Buffalo 37, N.Y. JETS 14
CHICAGO 10, San Francisco 9
INDIANAPOLIS 55, Denver 23
HOUSTON 24, Cleveland 17
Buffalo 31, MIAMI 6
SAN FRANCISCO 37, Washington 21
SEATTLE 35, L.A. Raiders 27
L.A. RAMS 23, Chicago 3
MIAMI 38, Cleveland 31
MINNESOTA 28, Chicago 27

1987
CHICAGO 34, N.Y. Giants 19
N.Y. JETS 43, New England 24
San Francisco 41, N.Y. GIANTS 21
DENVER 30, L.A. Raiders 14
Washington 13, DALLAS 7
CLEVELAND 30, L.A. Rams 17
MINNESOTA 34, Denver 27
DALLAS 33, N.Y. Giants 24
N.Y. JETS 30, Seattle 14
DENVER 31, Chicago 29
L.A. Rams 30, WASHINGTON 26
L.A. Raiders 37, SEATTLE 14
MIAMI 37, N.Y. Jets 28
SAN FRANCISCO 41, Chicago 0
Dallas 29, L.A. RAMS 21
New England 24, MIAMI 10

1986
DALLAS 31, N.Y. Giants 28
Denver 21, PITTSBURGH 10
Chicago 25, GREEN BAY 12
Dallas 31, ST. LOUIS 7
SEATTLE 33, San Diego 7
CINCINNATI 24, Pittsburgh 22
N.Y. JETS 22, Denver 10
N.Y. GIANTS 27, Washington 20
L.A. Rams 20, CHICAGO 17
CLEVELAND 26, Miami 16
WASHINGTON 14, San Francisco 6
MIAMI 45, N.Y. Jets 3
N.Y. Giants 21, SAN FRANCISCO 17
SEATTLE 37, L.A. Raiders 0
Chicago 16, DETROIT 13
New England 34, MIAMI 27

MONDAY NIGHT FOOTBALL

1985
DALLAS 44, Washington 14
CLEVELAND 17, Pittsburgh 7
L.A. Rams 35, SEATTLE 24
Cincinnati 37, PITTSBURGH 24
WASHINGTON 27, St. Louis 10
N.Y. JETS 23, Miami 7
CHICAGO 23, Green Bay 7
L.A. RAIDERS 34, San Diego 21
ST. LOUIS 21, Dallas 10
DENVER 17, San Francisco 16
WASHINGTON 23, N.Y. Giants 21
SAN FRANCISCO 19, Seattle 6
MIAMI 38, Chicago 24
L.A. Rams 27, SAN FRANCISCO 20
MIAMI 30, New England 27
L.A. Raiders 16, L.A. RAMS 6

1984
Dallas 20, L.A. RAMS 13
SAN FRANCISCO 37, Washington 31
Miami 21, BUFFALO 17
L.A. RAIDERS 33, San Diego 30
PITTSBURGH 38, Cincinnati 17
San Francisco 31, N.Y. GIANTS 10
DENVER 17, Green Bay 14
L.A. Rams 24, ATLANTA 10
Seattle 24, SAN DIEGO 0
WASHINGTON 27, Atlanta 14
SEATTLE 17, L.A. Raiders 14
NEW ORLEANS 27, Pittsburgh 24
MIAMI 28, N.Y. Jets 17
SAN DIEGO 20, Chicago 7
L.A. Raiders 24, DETROIT 3
MIAMI 28, Dallas 21

1983
Dallas 31, WASHINGTON 30
San Diego 17, KANSAS CITY 14
L.A. RAIDERS 27, Miami 14
N.Y. GIANTS 27, Green Bay 3
N.Y. Jets 34, BUFFALO 10
Pittsburgh 24, CINCINNATI 14
GREEN BAY 48, Washington 47
ST. LOUIS 20, N.Y. Giants 20 (OT)
Washington 27, SAN DIEGO 24
DETROIT 15, N.Y. Giants 9
L.A. Rams 36, ATLANTA 13
N.Y. Jets 31, NEW ORLEANS 28
MIAMI 38, Cincinnati 14
DETROIT 13, Minnesota 2
Green Bay 12, TAMPA BAY 9 (OT)
SAN FRANCISCO 42, Dallas 17

1982
Pittsburgh 36, DALLAS 28
Green Bay 27, N.Y. GIANTS 19
L.A. RAIDERS 28, San Diego 24
TAMPA BAY 23, Miami 17
N.Y. Jets 28, DETROIT 13
Dallas 37, HOUSTON 7
SAN DIEGO 50, Cincinnati 34
MIAMI 27, Buffalo 10
MINNESOTA 31, Dallas 27

1981
San Diego 44, CLEVELAND 14
Oakland 36, MINNESOTA 10
Dallas 35, NEW ENGLAND 21
Los Angeles 24, CHICAGO 7
PHILADELPHIA 16, Atlanta 13
BUFFALO 31, Miami 21
DETROIT 48, Chicago 17
PITTSBURGH 26, Houston 13
DENVER 19, Minnesota 17
DALLAS 27, Buffalo 14
SEATTLE 44, San Diego 23
ATLANTA 31, Minnesota 30
MIAMI 13, Philadelphia 10
OAKLAND 30, Pittsburgh 27
LOS ANGELES 21, Atlanta 16
SAN DIEGO 23, Oakland 10

1980
Dallas 17, WASHINGTON 3
Houston 16, CLEVELAND 7
PHILADELPHIA 35, N.Y. Giants 3
NEW ENGLAND 23, Denver 14
CHICAGO 23, Tampa Bay 0
DENVER 20, Washington 17
Oakland 45, PITTSBURGH 34
N.Y. JETS 17, Miami 14
CLEVELAND 27, Chicago 21
HOUSTON 38, New England 34
Oakland 19, SEATTLE 17
Los Angeles 27, NEW ORLEANS 7
OAKLAND 9, Denver 3
MIAMI 16, New England 13 (OT)
LOS ANGELES 38, Dallas 14
SAN DIEGO 26, Pittsburgh 17

1979
Pittsburgh 16, NEW ENGLAND 13 (OT)
Atlanta 14, PHILADELPHIA 10
WASHINGTON 27, N.Y. Giants 0
CLEVELAND 26, Dallas 7
GREEN BAY 27, New England 14
OAKLAND 13, Miami 3
N.Y. JETS 14, Minnesota 7
PITTSBURGH 42, Denver 7
Seattle 31, ATLANTA 28
Houston 9, MIAMI 6
Philadelphia 31, DALLAS 21
LOS ANGELES 20, Atlanta 14
SEATTLE 30, N.Y. Jets 7
Oakland 42, NEW ORLEANS 35
HOUSTON 20, Pittsburgh 17
SAN DIEGO 17, Denver 7

1978
DALLAS 38, Baltimore 0
MINNESOTA 12, Denver 9 (OT)
Baltimore 34, NEW ENGLAND 27
Minnesota 24, CHICAGO 20
WASHINGTON 9, Dallas 5
MIAMI 21, Cincinnati 0
DENVER 16, Chicago 7
Houston 24, PITTSBURGH 17
ATLANTA 15, Los Angeles 7
BALTIMORE 21, Washington 17
Oakland 34, CINCINNATI 21
HOUSTON 35, Miami 30
Pittsburgh 24, SAN FRANCISCO 7
SAN DIEGO 40, Chicago 7
Cincinnati 20, LOS ANGELES 19
MIAMI 23, New England 3

1977
PITTSBURGH 27, San Francisco 0
CLEVELAND 30, New England 27 (OT)
Oakland 37, KANSAS CITY 28
CHICAGO 24, Los Angeles 23
PITTSBURGH 20, Cincinnati 14
LOS ANGELES 35, Minnesota 3
ST. LOUIS 28, N.Y. Giants 0
BALTIMORE 10, Washington 3
St. Louis 24, DALLAS 17
WASHINGTON 10, Green Bay 9
OAKLAND 34, Buffalo 13
MIAMI 17, Baltimore 6
Dallas 42, SAN FRANCISCO 35

1976
Miami 30, BUFFALO 21
Oakland 24, KANSAS CITY 21
Washington 20, PHILADELPHIA 17 (OT)
MINNESOTA 17, Pittsburgh 6
San Francisco 16, LOS ANGELES 0
NEW ENGLAND 41, N.Y. Jets 7
WASHINGTON 20, St. Louis 10
BALTIMORE 38, Houston 14
CINCINNATI 20, Los Angeles 12
DALLAS 17, Buffalo 10
Baltimore 17, MIAMI 16
SAN FRANCISCO 20, Minnesota 16
OAKLAND 35, Cincinnati 20

1975
Oakland 31, MIAMI 21
DENVER 23, Green Bay 13
Dallas 36, DETROIT 10
WASHINGTON 27, St. Louis 17
N.Y. Giants 17, BUFFALO 14
Minnesota 13, CHICAGO 9
Los Angeles 42, PHILADELPHIA 3
Kansas City 34, DALLAS 31
CINCINNATI 33, Buffalo 24
Pittsburgh 32, HOUSTON 9
MIAMI 20, New England 7
OAKLAND 17, Denver 10
SAN DIEGO 24, N.Y. Jets 16

1974
BUFFALO 21, Oakland 20
PHILADELPHIA 13, Dallas 10
WASHINGTON 30, Denver 3
MIAMI 21, N.Y. Jets 17
DETROIT 17, San Francisco 13
CHICAGO 10, Green Bay 9
PITTSBURGH 24, Atlanta 17
Los Angeles 15, SAN FRANCISCO 13
Minnesota 28, ST. LOUIS 24
Kansas City 42, DENVER 34
Pittsburgh 28, NEW ORLEANS 7
MIAMI 24, Cincinnati 3
Washington 23, LOS ANGELES 17

1973
GREEN BAY 23, N.Y. Jets 7
DALLAS 40, New Orleans 3
DETROIT 31, Atlanta 6
WASHINGTON 14, Dallas 7
Miami 17, CLEVELAND 9
DENVER 23, Oakland 23
BUFFALO 23, Kansas City 14
PITTSBURGH 21, Washington 16
KANSAS CITY 19, Chicago 7
ATLANTA 20, Minnesota 14
SAN FRANCISCO 20, Green Bay 6
MIAMI 30, Pittsburgh 26
LOS ANGELES 40, N.Y. Giants 6

1972
Washington 24, MINNESOTA 21
Kansas City 20, NEW ORLEANS 17
N.Y. Giants 27, PHILADELPHIA 12
Oakland 34, HOUSTON 0
Green Bay 24, DETROIT 23
CHICAGO 13, Minnesota 10
DALLAS 28, Detroit 24
Baltimore 24, NEW ENGLAND 17
Cleveland 21, SAN DIEGO 17
WASHINGTON 24, Atlanta 13
MIAMI 31, St. Louis 10
Los Angeles 26, SAN FRANCISCO 16
OAKLAND 24, N.Y. Jets 16

1971
Minnesota 16, DETROIT 13
ST. LOUIS 17, N.Y. Jets 10
Oakland 34, CLEVELAND 20
DALLAS 20, N.Y. Giants 13
KANSAS CITY 38, Pittsburgh 16
MINNESOTA 10, Baltimore 3
GREEN BAY 14, Detroit 14
BALTIMORE 24, Los Angeles 17
SAN DIEGO 20, St. Louis 17
ATLANTA 28, Green Bay 21
MIAMI 34, Chicago 3
Kansas City 26, SAN FRANCISCO 17
Washington 38, LOS ANGELES 24

1970
CLEVELAND 31, N.Y. Jets 21
Kansas City 44, BALTIMORE 24
DETROIT 28, Chicago 14
Green Bay 22, SAN DIEGO 20
OAKLAND 34, Washington 20
MINNESOTA 13, Los Angeles 3
PITTSBURGH 21, Cincinnati 10
Baltimore 13, GREEN BAY 10
St. Louis 38, DALLAS 0
PHILADELPHIA 23, N.Y. Giants 20
Miami 20, ATLANTA 7
Cleveland 21, HOUSTON 10
Detroit 28, LOS ANGELES 23

MONDAY NIGHT FOOTBALL

MONDAY NIGHT WON-LOST RECORDS, 1970-2003

AMERICAN FOOTBALL CONFERENCE

	Balt.	Buff.	Cin.	Cle.	Den.	Hou.	Ind.	Jax.	K.C.	Mia.	N.E.	N.Y.J.	Oak.	Pitt.	S.D.	Tenn.
Total	3-0	17-20	7-16	13-12	22-28-1	0-0	13-10	5-3	18-13	38-31	10-19	15-19	36-21-1	31-20	14-13	15-14
2003				0-1	1-1		1-0		1-0	1-1	1-0	1-0	0-3	0-1	0-1	0-1
2002	1-0				0-2		0-1			1-1	1-1	0-1	2-0	2-1		1-0
2001	2-0				1-1		0-1	0-1		1-0		0-1	1-0	1-0		0-2
2000		0-1			1-1		2-0	0-2	1-1	0-1	1-1	2-0	0-1			3-0
1999		1-0			1-2			2-0		1-2	0-1	2-1	0-1	1-0		
1998					2-1			2-0	0-2	1-2	1-2	1-0		2-1		
1997		1-1			2-1		0-1	1-0	2-0	1-2	1-2		0-2	0-2		
1996		0-2			1-0		1-0		0-2	1-2			2-1	3-0	1-1	
1995		1-1		0-2	1-0				1-1	2-1	1-0		0-2	1-1	1-1	
1994		1-1			0-2				1-1	1-0			1-1	2-0	0-1	0-3
1993		2-1		1-0	0-2		0-1		2-0	1-2			1-0	3-0	2-0	0-1
1992		2-0	0-1	0-1	0-2				1-0	2-1		0-1	0-2	1-0		1-0
1991		2-1	0-2						2-1	1-1		0-1	0-2	0-1		1-1
1990		1-1	1-1	1-1	1-1		0-1		0-1	0-1		0-1	2-0	1-0		1-0
1989		1-2	1-2	1-1	2-0							0-1	1-0			1-0
1988		2-0		1-2	0-2		1-1			1-1		0-1	1-1			1-0
1987				1-0	2-1					1-1	1-1	2-1	1-1			
1986			1-0	1-0	1-1					1-2	1-0	1-1	0-1	0-2	0-1	
1985			1-0	1-0	1-0					2-1	0-1	1-0	2-0	0-2	0-1	
1984		0-1	0-1		1-0					3-0		0-1	2-1	1-1	1-2	
1983		0-1	0-2						0-1	1-1		2-0	1-0	1-0	1-1	
1982		0-1	0-1							1-1		1-0	1-0	1-0	1-1	0-1
1981		1-1		0-1	1-0					1-1	0-1		2-1	1-1	2-1	0-1
1980				1-1	1-2					1-1	1-2	1-0	3-0	0-2	1-0	2-0
1979				1-0	0-2					0-2	0-2	1-1	2-0	2-1	1-0	2-0
1978			1-2		1-1		2-1			2-1	0-2		1-0	1-1	1-0	2-0
1977		0-1	0-1	1-0			1-1		0-1	1-0	0-1		2-0	2-0		
1976		0-2	1-1				2-0		0-1	1-1	1-0	0-1	2-0	0-1		0-1
1975		0-2	1-0		1-1				1-0	1-1	0-1	0-1	2-0	1-0	1-0	0-1
1974		1-0	0-1		0-2				1-0	2-0		0-1	0-1	2-0		
1973		1-0		0-1	0-0-1				1-1	2-0		0-1	0-0-1	1-1		
1972				1-0			1-0		1-0	1-0	0-1	0-1	2-0		0-1	0-1
1971				0-1			1-1		2-0	1-0		0-1	1-0	0-1	1-0	
1970			0-1	2-0			1-1		1-0	1-0		0-1	1-0	1-0	0-1	0-1

MONDAY NIGHT FOOTBALL ALL-TIME STANDINGS

AMERICAN FOOTBALL CONFERENCE

East	W	L	T	Pct.
Miami	38	31	0	.551
Buffalo	17	20	0	.459
New York Jets	15	19	0	.441
New England	10	19	0	.345

North	W	L	T	Pct.
Baltimore	3	0	0	1.000
Pittsburgh	31	20	0	.608
Cleveland	13	12	0	.520
Cincinnati	7	16	0	.304

South	W	L	T	Pct.
Jacksonville	5	3	0	.625
Indianapolis	13	10	0	.565
Tennessee	15	14	0	.517
Houston	0	0	0	.000

West	W	L	T	Pct.
Oakland	36	21	1	.629
Kansas City	18	13	0	.581
San Diego	14	13	0	.519
Denver	22	28	1	.441

MONDAY NIGHT WON-LOST RECORDS, 1970-2003

NATIONAL FOOTBALL CONFERENCE

	Ariz.	Atl.	Car.	Chi.	Dall.	Det.	G.B.	Minn.	N.O.	N.Y.G.	Phil.	St.L.	S.F.	Sea.	T.B.	Wash.
Total	5-10-1	6-18	2-1	16-32	36-26	11-13-1	22-19-1	21-20	6-13	15-29-1	20-16	24-24	37-22	12-7	8-6	24-27
2003		0-1		0-1	1-0		2-1			0-2	2-1	2-0	1-0		2-1	
2002				0-3			2-0			0-1	3-0	2-1	1-2	0-1	1-1	0-1
2001					1-0	0-1	2-0	1-1	0-1	0-3	1-0	2-1	1-0		1-0	0-2
2000			1-0		1-1		1-1	1-1				1-2		0-1	1-1	1-2
1999	0-1	1-2			1-2		1-2	2-1		1-0			1-2	1-0	1-0	
1998					2-0	1-1	0-3	1-0		0-2	0-1		3-0		1-1	0-1
1997			1-1	1-1	1-2		3-0	0-1			0-2		3-0			1-0
1996		0-1		2-0	2-1	0-2	2-1	0-1			0-2		2-1			
1995	0-1			1-2	3-0	2-0	1-0	0-2		0-1	0-1		2-1			
1994				0-2	2-1	1-0	1-0	2-0	0-2	1-2	2-0		2-1			
1993		0-1		0-1	1-1		0-1	1-0	0-2	1-0	1-1		1-2			1-2
1992		0-2		0-3	2-1	0-1		1-0	1-0	1-0	1-0		2-0	1-0		1-2
1991				2-1	0-1			0-1	1-0	2-1	2-1	0-1	2-1			2-0
1990						0-1		0-1	1-1	1-1	2-0	0-3	3-0	1-0		0-1
1989				1-1				1-1	1-1	2-1	0-2	0-2	3-0	1-0		0-2
1988	0-1			1-2	1-1			1-0	1-0	1-1	1-0	1-0	1-1	1-0		0-2
1987				1-2	2-1			1-0		0-3		1-2	2-0	0-2		1-1
1986	0-1			2-1	2-0	0-1	0-1			2-1		1-0	0-2	2-0		1-1
1985	1-1			1-1	1-1		0-1			0-1		2-1	1-2	0-2		2-1
1984		0-2		0-1	1-1	0-1	0-1		1-0	0-1		1-1	2-0	2-0		1-1
1983	0-0-1	0-1			1-1	2-0	2-1	0-1	0-1	1-1-1		1-0	1-0		0-1	1-2
1982					1-2	0-1	1-0	1-0		0-1					1-0	
1981		1-2		0-2	2-0	1-0		0-3			1-1	2-0		1-0		
1980				1-1	1-1				0-1	0-1	1-0	2-0		0-1	0-1	0-2
1979		1-2			0-2		1-0	0-1	0-1	0-1	1-1	1-0		2-0		1-0
1978		1-0		0-3	1-1			2-0				0-2	0-1			1-1
1977	2-0			1-0	1-1		0-1	0-1		0-1		1-1	0-2			1-1
1976	0-1				1-0			1-1			0-1	0-2	2-0			2-0
1975	0-1			0-1	1-1	0-1	0-1	1-0		1-0	0-1	1-0				1-0
1974	0-1	0-1		1-0	0-1	1-0	0-1	1-0	0-1		1-0	1-1	0-2			2-0
1973		1-1		0-1	1-1	1-0	1-1	0-1	0-1	0-1		1-0	1-0			1-1
1972	0-1	0-1		1-0	1-0	0-2	1-0	0-2	0-1	1-0	0-1	1-0	0-1			2-0
1971	1-1	1-0		0-1	1-0	0-1-1	0-1-1	2-0		0-1		0-2	0-1			1-0
1970	1-0	0-1		0-1	0-1	2-0	1-1	1-0		0-1	1-0	0-2				0-1

MONDAY NIGHT FOOTBALL ALL-TIME STANDINGS

NATIONAL FOOTBALL CONFERENCE

East	W	L	T	Pct.
Dallas	36	26	0	.581
Philadelphia	20	16	0	.556
Washington	24	27	0	.471
New York Giants	15	29	1	.344

North	W	L	T	Pct.
Green Bay	22	19	1	.537
Minnesota	21	20	0	.512
Detroit	11	13	1	.458
Chicago	16	32	0	.333

South	W	L	T	Pct.
Carolina	2	1	0	.667
Tampa Bay	8	6	0	.571
New Orleans	6	13	0	.316
Atlanta	6	18	0	.250

West	W	L	T	Pct.
Seattle	12	7	0	.632
San Francisco	37	22	0	.627
St. Louis	24	24	0	.500
Arizona	5	10	1	.344

THURSDAY-SUNDAY NIGHT FOOTBALL

THURSDAY-SUNDAY NIGHT FOOTBALL, 1974-2003
(Home Team in capitals, games listed in chronological order.)

2003
WASHINGTON 16, New York Jets 13 (Thurs.)
TENNESSEE 25, Oakland 20 (Sun.)
MINNESOTA 24, Chicago 13 (Sun.)
MIAMI 17, Buffalo 7 (Sun.)
Indianapolis 55, NEW ORLEANS 21 (Sun.)
Cleveland 33, PITTSBURGH 13 (Sun.)
SEATTLE 20, San Francisco 19 (Sun.)
KANSAS CITY 38, Buffalo 5 (Sun.)
Green Bay 30, MINNESOTA 27 (Sun.)
ST. LOUIS 33, Baltimore 22 (Sun.)
NEW ENGLAND 12, Dallas 0 (Sun.)
MIAMI 24, Washington 23 (Sun.)
JACKSONVILLE 17, Tampa Bay 10 (Sun.)
ATLANTA 20, Carolina 14 (OT) (Sun.)
NEW ORLEANS 45, New York Giants 7 (Sun.)
New England 21, NEW YORK JETS 16 (Sat.)
Denver 31, INDIANAPOLIS 17 (Sun.)
Philadelphia 31, WASHINGTON 7 (Sat.)
BALTIMORE 13, Pittsburgh 10 (OT) (Sun.)

2002
San Francisco 16, NEW YORK GIANTS 13 (Thurs.)
HOUSTON 19, Dallas 10 (Sun.)
Oakland 30, PITTSBURGH 17 (Sun.)
ATLANTA 30, Cincinnati 3 (Sun.)
SEATTLE 48, Minnesota 23 (Sun.)
Baltimore 26, CLEVELAND 21 (Sun.)
Miami 24, DENVER 22 (Sun.)
WASHINGTON 26, Indianapolis 21 (Sun.)
NEW YORK GIANTS 24, Jacksonville 17 (Sun.)
NEW YORK JETS 13, Miami 10 (Sun.)
OAKLAND 27, New England 20 (Sun.)
Indianapolis 23, DENVER 20 (OT) (Sun.)
NEW ORLEANS 23, Tampa Bay 20 (Sun.)
GREEN BAY 26, Minnesota 22 (Sun.)
ST. LOUIS 30, Arizona 28 (Sun.)
Philadelphia 27, DALLAS 3 (Sat.)
New York Jets 30, NEW ENGLAND 17 (Sun.)
Tampa Bay 15, CHICAGO 0 (Sun.)

2001
Miami 31, TENNESSEE 23 (Sun.)
Denver 38, ARIZONA 17 (Sun.)
PHILADELPHIA 40, Dallas 18 (Sun.)
SAN FRANCISCO 24, Carolina 14 (Sun.)
Oakland 23, INDIANAPOLIS 18 (Sun.)
Buffalo 13, JACKSONVILLE 10 (Thurs.)
Indianapolis 35, KANSAS CITY 28 (Thurs.)
New York Jets 16, NEW ORLEANS 9 (Sun.)
SEATTLE 34, Oakland 27 (Sun.)
St. Louis 24, NEW ENGLAND 17 (Sun.)
Chicago 13, MINNESOTA 6 (Sun.)
SAN FRANCISCO 35, Buffalo 0 (Sun.)
DENVER 20, Seattle 7 (Sun.)
Pittsburgh 26, BALTIMORE 21 (Sun.)
Tennessee 13, OAKLAND 10 (Sat.)
New York Jets 29, INDIANAPOLIS 28 (Sun.)
TAMPA BAY 22, Baltimore 10 (Sat.)
Washington 40, NEW ORLEANS 10 (Sun.)
Philadelphia 17, TAMPA BAY 13 (Sun.)

2000
BUFFALO 16, Tennessee 13 (Sun.)
ARIZONA 32, Dallas 31 (Sun.)
MIAMI 19, Baltimore 6 (Sun.)
Washington 16, NEW YORK GIANTS 6 (Sun.)
PHILADELPHIA 38, Atlanta 10 (Sun.)
Baltimore 15, JACKSONVILLE 10 (Sun.)
Minnesota 28, CHICAGO 16 (Sun.)
Detroit 28, TAMPA BAY 14 (Thurs.)
Oakland 15, SAN DIEGO 13 (Sun.)
Carolina 27, ST. LOUIS 24 (Sun.)
INDIANAPOLIS 23, New York Jets 15 (Sun.)
Jacksonville 34, PITTSBURGH 24 (Sun.)
New York Giants 31, ARIZONA 7 (Sun.)
MINNESOTA 24, Detroit 17 (Thurs.)
Green Bay 28, CHICAGO 6 (Sun.)
OAKLAND 31, New York Jets 7 (Sun.)
New York Giants 17, DALLAS 13 (Sun.)
Buffalo 42, SEATTLE 23 (Sat.)

1999
Pittsburgh 43, CLEVELAND 0 (Sun.)
BUFFALO 17, N.Y. Jets 3 (Sun.)
NEW ENGLAND 16, N.Y. Giants 14 (Sun.)
SEATTLE 22, Oakland 21 (Sun.)
GREEN BAY 26, Tampa Bay 23 (Sun.)
Washington 24, ARIZONA 10 (Sun.)
Kansas City 35, BALTIMORE 8 (Thurs.)
DETROIT 20, Tampa Bay 3 (Sun.)
MIAMI 17, Tennessee 0 (Sun.)
SEATTLE 20, Denver 17 (Sun.)
JACKSONVILLE 41, New Orleans 23 (Sun.)
CAROLINA 34, Atlanta 28 (Sun.)
JACKSONVILLE 20, Pittsburgh 6 (Thurs.)
NEW ENGLAND 13, Dallas 6 (Sun.)
TENNESSEE 21, Oakland 14 (Thurs.)
KANSAS CITY 31, Minnesota 28 (Sun.)
Buffalo 31, ARIZONA 21 (Sun.)
Washington 26, SAN FRANCISCO 20 (OT) (Sun.)

1998
KANSAS CITY 28, Oakland 8 (Sun.)
NEW ENGLAND 29, Indianapolis 6 (Sun.)
ARIZONA 17, Philadelphia 3 (Sun.)
BALTIMORE 31, Cincinnati 24 (Sun.)
KANSAS CITY 17, Seattle 6 (Sun.)
Atlanta 34, NEW YORK GIANTS 20 (Sun.)
DETROIT 27, Green Bay 20 (Thurs.)
Buffalo 30, CAROLINA 14 (Sun.)
Oakland 31, SEATTLE 18 (Sun.)
Tennessee 31, TAMPA BAY 22 (Sun.)
DETROIT 26, Chicago 3 (Sun.)
SAN FRANCISCO 31, New Orleans 20 (Sun.)
Denver 31, SAN DIEGO 16 (Sun.)
PHILADELPHIA 17, St. Louis 14 (Thurs.)
MINNESOTA 48, Chicago 22 (Sun.)
New York Jets 21, MIAMI 16 (Sun.)
MINNESOTA 50, Jacksonville 10 (Sun.)
DALLAS 23, Washington 7 (Sun.)

1997
Washington 24, CAROLINA 10 (Sun.)
ARIZONA 25, Dallas 22 (OT) (Sun.)
NEW ENGLAND 27, New York Jets 24 (OT) (Sun.)
TAMPA BAY 31, Miami 21 (Sun.)
MINNESOTA 28, Philadelphia 19 (Sun.)
New Orleans 20, CHICAGO 17 (Sun.)
PITTSBURGH 24, Indianapolis 22 (Sun.)
KANSAS CITY 31, San Diego 3 (Thurs.)
CAROLINA 21, Atlanta 12 (Sun.)
GREEN BAY 20, Detroit 10 (Sun.)
PITTSBURGH 37, Baltimore 0 (Sun.)
Oakland 38, SAN DIEGO 13 (Sun.)
WASHINGTON 7, New York Giants 7 (OT) (Sun.)
Denver 38, SAN DIEGO 28 (Sun.)
CINCINNATI 41, Tennessee 14 (Thurs.)
MIAMI 33, Detroit 30 (Sun.)
Chicago 13, ST. LOUIS 10 (Sun.)
SEATTLE 38, San Francisco 9 (Sun.)

1996
Buffalo 23, NEW YORK GIANTS 20 (OT) (Sun.)
Miami 38, ARIZONA 10 (Sun.)
DENVER 27, Tampa Bay 23 (Sun.)
Philadelphia 33, ATLANTA 18 (Sun.)
WASHINGTON 31, New York Jets 16 (Sun.)
Houston 30, CINCINNATI 27 (OT) (Sun.)
INDIANAPOLIS 26, Baltimore 21 (Sun.)
KANSAS CITY 34, Seattle 16 (Thurs.)
NEW ENGLAND 28, Buffalo 25 (Sun.)
San Francisco 24, NEW ORLEANS 17 (Sun.)
CAROLINA 27, New York Giants 17 (Sun.)
Minnesota 16, OAKLAND 13 (OT) (Sun.)
Green Bay 24, ST. LOUIS 9 (Sun.)
New England 45, SAN DIEGO 7 (Sun.)
INDIANAPOLIS 37, Philadelphia 10 (Thurs.)
Minnesota 24, DETROIT 22 (Sun.)
JACKSONVILLE 20, Seattle 13 (Sun.)
SAN DIEGO 16, Denver 10 (Sun.)

1995
DENVER 22, Buffalo 7 (Sun.)
Philadelphia 31, ARIZONA 19 (Sun.)
Dallas 23, MINNESOTA 17 (OT) (Sun.)
Green Bay 24, JACKSONVILLE 14 (Sun.)
Oakland 47, NEW YORK JETS 10 (Sun.)
Denver 37, NEW ENGLAND 3 (Sun.)
ST. LOUIS 21, Atlanta 19 (Thurs.)
Cincinnati 27, PITTSBURGH 9 (Thurs.)
New York Giants 24, WASHINGTON 15 (Sun.)
Miami 24, SAN DIEGO 14 (Sun.)
PHILADELPHIA 31, Denver 13 (Sun.)
KANSAS CITY 20, Houston 13 (Sun.)
NEW ORLEANS 34, Carolina 26 (Sun.)
New York Giants 10, ARIZONA 6 (Thurs.)
SAN FRANCISCO 27, Buffalo 17 (Sun.)
TAMPA BAY 13, Green Bay 10 (OT) (Sun.)
SEATTLE 44, Oakland 10 (Sun.)
INDIANAPOLIS 10, New England 7 (Sat.)

1994
San Diego 17, DENVER 34 (Sun.)
New York Giants 20, ARIZONA 17 (Sun.)
Kansas City 30, ATLANTA 10 (Sun.)
Chicago 19, NEW YORK JETS 7 (Sun.)
Miami 23, CINCINNATI 7 (Sun.)
PHILADELPHIA 21, Washington 17 (Sun.)
Cleveland 11, HOUSTON 8 (Thurs.)
MINNESOTA 13, Green Bay 10 (OT) (Thurs.)
ARIZONA 20, Pittsburgh 17 (OT) (Sun.)
KANSAS CITY 13, Los Angeles Raiders 3 (Sun.)
DETROIT 14, Tampa Bay 9 (Sun.)
SAN FRANCISCO 31, Los Angeles Rams 27 (Sun.)
New England 12, INDIANAPOLIS 10 (Sun.)
MINNESOTA 33, Chicago 27 (OT) (Thurs.)
Buffalo 42, MIAMI 31 (Sun.)
New Orleans 29, ATLANTA 20 (Sun.)
Los Angeles Raiders 17, SEATTLE 16 (Sun.)
MIAMI 27, Detroit 20 (Sun.)

1993
NEW ORLEANS 33, Houston 21 (Sun.)
Los Angeles Raiders 17, SEATTLE 13 (Sun.)
Dallas 17, PHOENIX 10 (Sun.)
NEW YORK JETS 45, New England 7 (Sun.)
BUFFALO 17, New York Giants 14 (Sun.)
GREEN BAY 30, Denver 27 (Sun.)
ATLANTA 30, Los Angeles Rams 24 (Thurs.)
MIAMI 41, Indianapolis 27 (Sun.)
Detroit 30, MINNESOTA 27 (Sun.)
WASHINGTON 30, Indianapolis 24 (Sun.)
Chicago 16, SAN DIEGO 13 (Sun.)
TAMPA BAY 23, Minnesota 10 (Sun.)
HOUSTON 23, Pittsburgh 3 (Sun.)
SAN FRANCISCO 21, Cincinnati 8 (Sun.)
Green Bay 20, SAN DIEGO 13 (Sun.)
Philadelphia 20, INDIANAPOLIS 10 (Sun.)
MINNESOTA 30, Kansas City 10 (Sun.)
HOUSTON 24, New York Jets 0 (Sun.)

1992
DENVER 17, Los Angeles Raiders 13 (Sun.)
Philadelphia 31, PHOENIX 14 (Sun.)
BUFFALO 38, Indianapolis 0 (Sun.)
San Francisco 16, NEW ORLEANS 10 (Sun.)
NEW YORK JETS 30, New England 21 (Sun.)
NEW ORLEANS 13, Los Angeles Rams 10 (Sun.)
MINNESOTA 31, Detroit 14 (Thurs.)
Pittsburgh 27, KANSAS CITY 3 (Sun.)
New York Giants 24, WASHINGTON 7 (Sun.)
Cincinnati 31, CHICAGO 28 (OT) (Sun.)
DENVER 27, New York Giants 13 (Sun.)
Kansas City 24, SEATTLE 14 (Sun.)
SAN DIEGO 27, Los Angeles Raiders 3 (Sun.)
NEW ORLEANS 22, Atlanta 14 (Thurs.)
Los Angeles Rams 31, TAMPA BAY 27 (Sun.)
Green Bay 16, HOUSTON 14 (Sun.)
MIAMI 19, New York Jets 17 (Sun.)
HOUSTON 27, Buffalo 3 (Sun.)

THURSDAY-SUNDAY NIGHT FOOTBALL

1991
WASHINGTON 45, Detroit 0 (Sun.)
Houston 30, CINCINNATI 7 (Sun.)
NEW ORLEANS 24, Los Angeles Rams 7 (Sun.)
Dallas 17, PHOENIX 9 (Sun.)
Denver 13, MINNESOTA 6 (Sun.)
Pittsburgh 21, INDIANAPOLIS 3 (Sun.)
Los Angeles Raiders 23, SEATTLE 20 (Sun.)
Chicago 10, GREEN BAY 0 (Thurs.)
Washington 17, NEW YORK GIANTS 13 (Sun.)
DENVER 20, Pittsburgh 13 (Sun.)
MIAMI 30, New England 20 (Sun.)
HOUSTON 28, Cleveland 24 (Sun.)
Atlanta 23, NEW ORLEANS 20 (OT) (Sun.)
Los Angeles Raiders 9, SAN DIEGO 7 (Sun.)
Minnesota 26, TAMPA BAY 24 (Sun.)
Buffalo 35, INDIANAPOLIS 7 (Sun.)
SEATTLE 23, Los Angeles Rams 9 (Sun.)

1990
NEW YORK GIANTS 27, Philadelphia 20 (Sun.)
PITTSBURGH 20, Houston 9 (Sun.)
TAMPA BAY 23, Detroit 20 (Sun.)
Washington 38, PHOENIX 10 (Sun.)
BUFFALO 38, Los Angeles Raiders 24 (Sun.)
CHICAGO 38, Los Angeles Rams 9 (Sun.)
MIAMI 17, New England 10 (Thurs.)
ATLANTA 38, Cincinnati 17 (Sun.)
MINNESOTA 27, Denver 22 (Sun.)
San Francisco 24, DALLAS 6 (Sun.)
CINCINNATI 27, Pittsburgh 3 (Sun.)
Seattle 13, SAN DIEGO 10 (Sun.)
MINNESOTA 23, Green Bay 7 (Sun.)
MIAMI 23, Philadelphia 20 (Sun.)
DETROIT 38, Chicago 21 (Sun.)
INDIANAPOLIS 35, Washington 28 (Sat.)
SEATTLE 17, Denver 12 (Sun.)
HOUSTON 34, Pittsburgh 14 (Sun.)

1989
Dallas 13, WASHINGTON 3 (Sun.)
SAN DIEGO 14, Los Angeles Raiders 12 (Sun.)
INDIANAPOLIS 27, New York Jets 10 (Sun.)
Los Angeles Rams 20, NEW ORLEANS 17 (Sun.)
MINNESOTA 27, Chicago 16 (Sun.)
MIAMI 31, New England 10 (Sun.)
SEATTLE 23, Los Angeles Raiders 17 (Sun.)
Cleveland 24, HOUSTON 20 (Sat.)

1988
HOUSTON 41, Washington 17 (Sun.)
Los Angeles Raiders 13, SAN DIEGO 3 (Sun.)
Minnesota 43, DALLAS 3 (Sun.)
New England 6, MIAMI 3 (Sun.)
New York Giants 13, NEW ORLEANS 12 (Sun.)
Pittsburgh 37, HOUSTON 34 (Sun.)
SEATTLE 42, Denver 14 (Sun.)
Los Angeles Rams 38, SAN FRANCISCO 16 (Sun.)

1987
NEW YORK GIANTS 17, New England 10 (Sun.)
SAN DIEGO 16, Los Angeles Raiders 14 (Sun.)
Miami 20, DALLAS 14 (Sun.)
SAN FRANCISCO 38, Cleveland 24 (Sun.)
Chicago 30, MINNESOTA 24 (Sun.)
SEATTLE 28, Denver 21 (Sun.)
MIAMI 23, Washington 21 (Sun.)
SAN FRANCISCO 48, Los Angeles Rams 0 (Sun.)

1986
New England 20, NEW YORK JETS 6 (Thurs.)
Cincinnati 30, CLEVELAND 13 (Thurs.)
Los Angeles Raiders 37, SAN DIEGO 31 (OT) (Thurs.)
LOS ANGELES RAMS 29, Dallas 10 (Sun.)
SAN FRANCISCO 24, Los Angeles Rams 14 (Fri.)

1985
KANSAS CITY 36, Los Angeles Raiders 20 (Thurs.)
Chicago 33, MINNESOTA 24 (Thurs.)
Dallas 30, NEW YORK GIANTS 29 (Sun.)
SAN DIEGO 54, Pittsburgh 44 (Sun.)
Denver 27, SEATTLE 24 (Fri.)

1984
Pittsburgh 23, NEW YORK JETS 17 (Thurs.)
Denver 24, CLEVELAND 14 (Sun.)
DALLAS 30, New Orleans 27 (Sun.)
Washington 31, MINNESOTA 17 (Thurs.)
SAN FRANCISCO 19, Los Angeles Rams 16 (Fri.)

1983
San Francisco 48, MINNESOTA 17 (Thurs.)
CLEVELAND 17, Cincinnati 7 (Thurs.)
Los Angeles Raiders 40, DALLAS 38 (Sun.)
Los Angeles Raiders 42, SAN DIEGO 10 (Thurs.)
MIAMI 34, New York Jets 14 (Fri.)

1982
BUFFALO 23, Minnesota 22 (Thurs.)
SAN FRANCISCO 30, Los Angeles Rams 24 (Thurs.)
ATLANTA 17, San Francisco 7 (Sun.)

1981
MIAMI 30, Pittsburgh 10 (Thurs.)
Philadelphia 20, BUFFALO 14 (Thurs.)
DALLAS 29, Los Angeles 17 (Sun.)
HOUSTON 17, Cleveland 13 (Thurs.)

1980
TAMPA BAY 10, Los Angeles 9 (Thurs.)
DALLAS 42, San Diego 31 (Sun.)
San Diego 27, MIAMI 24 (OT) (Thurs.)
HOUSTON 6, Pittsburgh 0 (Thurs.)

1979
Los Angeles 13, DENVER 9 (Thurs.)
DALLAS 30, Los Angeles 6 (Sun.)
OAKLAND 45, San Diego 22 (Thurs.)
MIAMI 39, New England 24 (Thurs.)

1978
New England 21, OAKLAND 14 (Sun.)
Minnesota 21, DALLAS 10 (Thurs.)
LOS ANGELES 10, Pittsburgh 7 (Sun.)
Denver 21, OAKLAND 6 (Sun.)

1977
Minnesota 30, DETROIT 21 (Sat.)

1976
Los Angeles 20, DETROIT 17 (Sat.)

1975
LOS ANGELES 10, Pittsburgh 3 (Sat.)

1974
OAKLAND 27, Dallas 23 (Sat.)

THANKSGIVING DAY FOOTBALL, 1920-2003

(Home Team in capitals, games listed in chronological order.)

(AFL)-American Football League, 1960-69.

Nov. 25, 1920	AKRON PROS 7, Canton Bulldogs 0 Decatur Staleys 6, CHICAGO TIGERS 0 ELYRIA (OH) ATHLETICS* 0, Columbus Panhandles 0 DAYTON TRIANGLES 28, Detroit Heralds 0 CHICAGO BOOSTERS* 27, Hammond Pros 0 All-Tonawanda (NY) 14, ROCHESTER JEFFERSONS 3 * Non league team. Games between league teams and non league teams counted in standings in 1920.
Nov. 24, 1921	Canton Bulldogs 14, AKRON PROS 0 Buffalo All-Americans 7, CHICAGO STALEYS 6
Nov. 30, 1922	Buffalo All-Americans 21, ROCHESTER JEFFERSONS 0 CHICAGO CARDINALS 6, Chicago Bears 0 RACINE LEGION 3, Milwaukee Badgers 0 Oorang Indians 18, COLUMBUS PANHANDLES 6 CANTON BULLDOGS 14, Akron Pros 0
Nov. 29, 1923	CANTON BULLDOGS 28, Toledo Maroons 0 CHICAGO BEARS 3, Chicago Cardinals 0 GREEN BAY PACKERS 19, Hammond Pros 0 Milwaukee Badgers 16, RACINE LEGION 0 AKRON PROS 2, Buffalo All-Americans 0
Nov. 27, 1924	AKRON PROS 22, Buffalo Bisons 0 Chicago Bears 21, CHICAGO CARDINALS 0 FRANKFORD YELLOWJACKETS 32, Dayton Triangles 7 CLEVELAND BULLDOGS 53, Milwaukee Badgers 10 (at Canton, Ohio) Green Bay Packers 17, KANSAS CITY BLUES 6
Nov. 26, 1925	CHICAGO BEARS 0, Chicago Cardinals 0 Kansas City Cowboys 17, CLEVELAND BULLDOGS 0 (at Hartford, Connecticut) Rock Island Independents 6, DETROIT PANTHERS 3 POTTSVILLE MAROONS 31, Green Bay Packers 0
Nov. 25, 1926	New York Giants 17, BROOKLYN LIONS 0 Los Angeles Buccaneers 9, DETROIT PANTHERS 6 CHICAGO BEARS 0, Chicago Cardinals 0 FRANKFORD YELLOWJACKETS 20, Green Bay Packers 14 POTTSVILLE MAROONS 8, Providence Steam Roller 0 CANTON BULLDOGS 0, Akron Pros 0
Nov. 24, 1927	Chicago Cardinals 3, CHICAGO BEARS 0 POTTSVILLE MAROONS 6, Providence Steam Roller 0 Green Bay Packers 17, FRANKFORD YELLOWJACKETS 9 Cleveland Bulldogs 30, NEW YORK YANKEES 19
Nov. 29, 1928	Providence Steam Roller 7, POTTSVILLE MAROONS 0 DETROIT WOLVERINES 33, Dayton Triangles 0 FRANKFORD YELLOWJACKETS 2, Green Bay Packers 0 CHICAGO BEARS 34, Chicago Cardinals 0
Nov. 28, 1929	New York Giants 21, STATEN ISLAND STAPLETONS 7 FRANKFORD YELLOWJACKETS 0, Green Bay Packers 0 Chicago Cardinals 40, CHICAGO BEARS 6
Nov. 27, 1930	STATEN ISLAND STAPLETONS 7, New York Giants 6 BROOKLYN DODGERS 33, Providence Steam Roller 12 Green Bay Packers 25, FRANKFORD YELLOWJACKETS 7 CHICAGO BEARS 6, Chicago Cardinals 0
Nov. 26, 1931	Green Bay Packers 38, PROVIDENCE STEAM ROLLER 7 STATEN ISLAND STAPLETONS 9, New York Giants 6 CHICAGO BEARS 18, Chicago Cardinals 7
Nov. 24, 1932	CHICAGO BEARS 24, Chicago Cardinals 0 Green Bay Packers 7, BROOKLYN DODGERS 0 STATEN ISLAND STAPLETONS 13, New York Giants 13

THANKSGIVING DAY FOOTBALL

Nov. 30, 1933	Chicago Bears 22, CHICAGO CARDINALS 6 New York Giants 10, BROOKLYN DODGERS 0
Nov. 29, 1934	CHICAGO CARDINALS 6, Green Bay Packers 0 Chicago Bears 19, DETROIT LIONS 16 New York Giants 27, BROOKLYN DODGERS 0
Nov. 28, 1935	New York Giants 21, BROOKLYN DODGERS 0 CHICAGO CARDINALS 9, Green Bay Packers 7 DETROIT LIONS 14, Chicago Bears 2
Nov. 26, 1936	DETROIT LIONS 13, Chicago Bears 7 New York Giants 14, BROOKLYN DODGERS 0
Nov. 25, 1937	Chicago Bears 13, DETROIT LIONS 0 BROOKLYN DODGERS 13, New York Giants 13
Nov. 24, 1938	DETROIT LIONS 14, Chicago Bears 7 BROOKLYN DODGERS 7, New York Giants 7
Nov. 23, 1939#	PHILADELPHIA EAGLES 17, Pittsburgh Steelers 14
Nov. 28, 1940#	Pittsburgh Steelers 7, PHILADELPHIA EAGLES 0

In 1939 and 1940, President Roosevelt moved Thanksgiving one week earlier. Various states celebrated on the date declared by the President, while other states recognized the traditional fourth Thursday of the month. In 1941, Thanksgiving was sanctioned by Congress to be celebrated on the fourth Thursday of November, which it has been ever since.

Nov. 22, 1945	Cleveland Rams 28, DETROIT LIONS 21
Nov. 28, 1946	Boston Yanks 34, DETROIT LIONS 10
Nov. 27, 1947	Chicago Bears 34, DETROIT LIONS 14
Nov. 25, 1948	Chicago Cardinals 28, DETROIT LIONS 14
Nov. 24, 1949	Chicago Bears 28, DETROIT LIONS 7
Nov. 23, 1950	DETROIT LIONS 49, New York Yanks 14 Pittsburgh Steelers 28, CHICAGO CARDINALS 17
Nov. 22, 1951	DETROIT LIONS 52, Green Bay Packers 35
Nov. 27, 1952	DETROIT LIONS 48, Green Bay Packers 24 DALLAS TEXANS 27, Chicago Bears 23 (at Akron, Ohio)
Nov. 26, 1953	DETROIT LIONS 34, Green Bay Packers 15
Nov. 25, 1954	DETROIT LIONS 28, Green Bay Packers 24
Nov. 24, 1955	DETROIT LIONS 24, Green Bay Packers 10
Nov. 22, 1956	Green Bay Packers 24, DETROIT LIONS 20
Nov. 28, 1957	DETROIT LIONS 18, Green Bay Packers 6
Nov. 27, 1958	DETROIT LIONS 24, Green Bay Packers 14
Nov. 26, 1959	Green Bay Packers 24, DETROIT LIONS 17
Nov. 24, 1960	DETROIT LIONS 23, Green Bay Packers 10 (AFL) - NEW YORK TITANS 41, Dallas Texans 35
Nov. 23, 1961	Green Bay Packers 17, DETROIT LIONS 9 (AFL) - NEW YORK TITANS 21, Buffalo Bills 14
Nov. 22, 1962	DETROIT LIONS 26, Green Bay Packers 14 (AFL) - New York Titans 46, DENVER BRONCOS 45
Nov. 28, 1963	DETROIT LIONS 13, Green Bay Packers 13 (AFL) - Oakland Raiders 26, DENVER BRONCOS 10
Nov. 26, 1964	Chicago Bears 27, DETROIT LIONS 24 (AFL) - Buffalo Bills 27, SAN DIEGO CHARGERS 24
Nov. 25, 1965	DETROIT LIONS 24, Baltimore Colts 24 (AFL) - SAN DIEGO CHARGERS 20, Buffalo Bills 20

Nov. 24, 1966	San Francisco 49ers 41, DETROIT LIONS 14 DALLAS COWBOYS 26, Cleveland Browns 14 (AFL) - Buffalo Bills 31, OAKLAND RAIDERS 10
Nov. 23, 1967	Los Angeles Rams 31, DETROIT LIONS 7 DALLAS COWBOYS 46, St. Louis Cardinals 21 (AFL) - Oakland Raiders 44, KANSAS CITY CHIEFS 22 (AFL) - SAN DIEGO CHARGERS 24, Denver Broncos 20
Nov. 28, 1968	Philadelphia Eagles 12, DETROIT LIONS 0 DALLAS COWBOYS 29, Washington Redskins 20 (AFL) - OAKLAND RAIDERS 13, Buffalo Bills 10 (AFL) - KANSAS CITY CHIEFS 24, Houston Oilers 10
Nov. 27, 1969	Minnesota Vikings 27, DETROIT LIONS 0 DALLAS COWBOYS 24, San Francisco 49ers 24 (AFL) - KANSAS CITY CHIEFS 31, Denver Broncos 17 (AFL) - San Diego Chargers 21, HOUSTON OILERS 17
Nov. 26, 1970	DETROIT LIONS 28, Oakland Raiders 14 DALLAS COWBOYS 16, Green Bay Packers 3
Nov. 25, 1971	DETROIT LIONS 32, Kansas City Chiefs 21 DALLAS COWBOYS 28, Los Angeles Rams 21
Nov. 23, 1972	DETROIT LIONS 37, New York Jets 20 San Francisco 49ers 31, DALLAS COWBOYS 10
Nov. 22, 1973	Washington Redskins 20, DETROIT LIONS 0 Miami Dolphins 14, DALLAS COWBOYS 7
Nov. 28, 1974	Denver Broncos 31, DETROIT LIONS 27 DALLAS COWBOYS 24, Washington Redskins 23
Nov. 27, 1975	Los Angeles Rams 20, DETROIT LIONS 0 Buffalo Bills 32, ST. LOUIS CARDINALS 14
Nov. 25, 1976	DETROIT LIONS 27, Buffalo Bills 14 DALLAS COWBOYS 19, St. Louis Cardinals 14
Nov. 24, 1977	Chicago Bears 31, DETROIT LIONS 14 Miami Dolphins 55, ST. LOUIS CARDINALS 14
Nov. 23, 1978	DETROIT LIONS 17, Denver Broncos 14 DALLAS COWBOYS 37, Washington Redskins 10
Nov. 22, 1979	DETROIT LIONS 20, Chicago Bears 0 Houston Oilers 30, DALLAS COWBOYS 24
Nov. 27, 1980	Chicago Bears 23, DETROIT LIONS 17 (OT) DALLAS COWBOYS 51, Seattle Seahawks 7
Nov. 26, 1981	DETROIT LIONS 27, Kansas City Chiefs 10 DALLAS COWBOYS 10, Chicago Bears 9
Nov. 25, 1982	New York Giants 13, DETROIT LIONS 6 DALLAS COWBOYS 31, Cleveland Browns 14
Nov. 24, 1983	DETROIT LIONS 45, Pittsburgh Steelers 3 DALLAS COWBOYS 35, St. Louis Cardinals 17
Nov. 22, 1984	DETROIT LIONS 31, Green Bay Packers 28 DALLAS COWBOYS 20, New England Patriots 17
Nov. 28, 1985	DETROIT LIONS 31, New York Jets 20 DALLAS COWBOYS 35, St. Louis Cardinals 17
Nov. 27, 1986	Green Bay Packers 44, DETROIT LIONS 40 Seattle Seahawks 31, DALLAS COWBOYS 14
Nov. 26, 1987	Kansas City Chiefs 27, DETROIT LIONS 20 Minnesota Vikings 44, DALLAS COWBOYS 38 (OT)
Nov. 24, 1988	Minnesota Vikings 23, DETROIT LIONS 0 Houston Oilers 25, DALLAS COWBOYS 17

Nov. 23, 1989	DETROIT LIONS 13, Cleveland Browns 10 Philadelphia Eagles 27, DALLAS COWBOYS 0
Nov. 22, 1990	DETROIT LIONS 40, Denver Broncos 27 DALLAS COWBOYS 27, Washington Redskins 17
Nov. 28, 1991	DETROIT LIONS 16, Chicago Bears 6 DALLAS COWBOYS 20, Pittsburgh Steelers 10
Nov. 26, 1992	Houston Oilers 24, DETROIT LIONS 21 DALLAS COWBOYS 30, New York Giants 3
Nov. 25, 1993	Chicago Bears 10, DETROIT LIONS 6 Miami Dolphins 16, DALLAS COWBOYS 14
Nov. 24, 1994	DETROIT LIONS 35, Buffalo Bills 21 DALLAS COWBOYS 42, Green Bay Packers 31
Nov. 23, 1995	DETROIT LIONS 44, Minnesota Vikings 38 DALLAS COWBOYS 24, Kansas City Chiefs 12
Nov. 28, 1996	Kansas City Chiefs 28, DETROIT LIONS 24 DALLAS COWBOYS 21, Washington Redskins 10
Nov. 27, 1997	DETROIT LIONS 55, Chicago Bears 20 Tennessee Titans 27, DALLAS COWBOYS 14
Nov. 26, 1998	DETROIT LIONS 19, Pittsburgh Steelers 16 (OT) Minnesota Vikings 46, DALLAS COWBOYS 36
Nov. 25, 1999	DETROIT LIONS 21, Chicago Bears 17 DALLAS COWBOYS 20, Miami Dolphins 0
Nov. 23, 2000	DETROIT LIONS 34, New England Patriots 9 Minnesota Vikings 27, DALLAS COWBOYS 15
Nov. 22, 2001	Green Bay Packers 29, DETROIT LIONS 27 Denver Broncos 26, DALLAS COWBOYS 24
Nov. 28, 2002	New England Patriots 20, DETROIT LIONS 12 DALLAS COWBOYS 27, Washington Redskins 20
Nov. 27, 2003	DETROIT LIONS 22, Green Bay Packers 14 Miami Dolphins 40, DALLAS COWBOYS 21

THANKSGIVING DAY RECORDS

*NFL record; stats compiled by Elias Sports Bureau.

SCORING / Most Touchdowns, Game

6 Ernie Nevers, Chi. Cardinals vs. Chi. Bears, Nov. 28, 1929*
4 Sterling Sharpe, Green Bay at Dallas, Nov. 24, 1994
3 By many players

RUSHING / Most Yards Rushing, Game

273 O.J. Simpson, Buffalo at Detroit, Nov. 25, 1976
198 Bob Hoernschemeyer, Detroit vs. N.Y. Yankees, Nov. 23, 1950
195 Earl Campbell, Houston at Dallas, Nov. 22, 1979

PASSING / Most Yards Passing, Game

455 Troy Aikman, Dallas vs. Minnesota, Nov. 26, 1998
410 Scott Mitchell, Detroit vs. Minnesota, Nov. 23, 1995
384 Warren Moon, Minnesota at Detroit, Nov. 23, 1995

PASS RECEIVING

RECEPTIONS / Most Pass Receptions, Game

12 Brett Perriman, Detroit vs. Minnesota, Nov. 23, 1995
11 Daryl Johnston, Dallas vs. Miami, Nov. 25, 1993
Michael Irvin, Dallas vs Kansas City, Nov. 23, 1995

YARDS GAINED / Most Yards on Pass Receptions, Game

303 Jim Benton, Cleveland at Detroit, Nov. 22, 1945
185 Lance Alworth, San Diego vs. Buffalo, Nov. 26, 1964
184 Anthony Carter, Minnesota at Dallas, Nov. 26, 1987 (OT)

HISTORY OF OVERTIME GAMES

PRESEASON

Aug. 28, 1955 Los Angeles 23, New York Giants 17, at Portland, Oregon
Aug. 24, 1962 Denver 27, Dallas Texans 24, at Fort Worth, Texas
Aug. 10, 1974 San Diego 20, New York Jets 14, at San Diego
Aug. 17, 1974 Pittsburgh 33, Philadelphia 30, at Philadelphia
Aug. 17, 1974 Dallas 19, Houston 13, at Dallas
Aug. 17, 1974 Cincinnati 13, Atlanta 7, at Atlanta
Sept. 6, 1974 Buffalo 23, New York Giants 17, at Buffalo
Aug. 9, 1975 Baltimore 23, Denver 20, at Denver
Aug. 30, 1975 New England 20, Green Bay 17, at Milwaukee
Sept. 13, 1975 Minnesota 14, San Diego 14, at San Diego
Aug. 1, 1976 New England 13, New York Giants 7, at New England
Aug. 2, 1976 Kansas City 9, Houston 3, at Kansas City
Aug. 20, 1976 New Orleans 26, Baltimore 20, at Baltimore
Sept. 4, 1976 Dallas 26, Houston 20, at Dallas
Aug. 13, 1977 Seattle 23, Dallas 17, at Seattle
Aug. 28, 1977 New England 13, Pittsburgh 10, at New England
Aug. 28, 1977 New York Giants 24, Buffalo 21, at East Rutherford, N.J.
Aug. 2, 1979 Seattle 12, Minnesota 9, at Minnesota
Aug. 4, 1979 Los Angeles 20, Oakland 14, at Los Angeles
Aug. 24, 1979 Denver 20, New England 17, at Denver
Aug. 23, 1980 Tampa Bay 20, Cincinnati 14, at Tampa Bay
Aug. 5, 1981 San Francisco 27, Seattle 24, at Seattle
Aug. 29, 1981 New Orleans 20, Detroit 17, at New Orleans
Aug. 28, 1982 Miami 17, Kansas City 17, at Kansas City
Sept. 3, 1982 Miami 16, New York Giants 13, at Miami
Aug. 6, 1983 L.A. Raiders 26, San Francisco 23, at Los Angeles
Aug. 6, 1983 Atlanta 13, Washington 10, at Atlanta
Aug. 13, 1983 St. Louis 27, Chicago 24, at St. Louis
Aug. 18, 1983 New York Jets 20, Cincinnati 17, at Cincinnati
Aug. 27, 1983 Chicago 20, Kansas City 17, at Chicago
Aug. 11, 1984 Pittsburgh 20, Philadelphia 17, at Pittsburgh
Aug. 9, 1985 Buffalo 10, Detroit 10, at Pontiac, Mich.
Aug. 10, 1985 Minnesota 16, Miami 13, at Miami
Aug. 17, 1985 Dallas 27, San Diego 24, at San Diego
Aug. 24, 1985 N.Y. Giants 34, N.Y. Jets 31, at East Rutherford, N.J.
Aug. 15, 1986 Washington 27, Pittsburgh 24, at Washington
Aug. 15, 1986 Detroit 30, Seattle 27, at Detroit
Aug. 23, 1986 Los Angeles Rams 20, San Diego 17, at Anaheim
Aug. 30, 1986 Minnesota 23, Indianapolis 20, at Indianapolis
Aug. 23, 1987 Philadelphia 19, New England 13, at New England
Sept. 5, 1987 Cleveland 30, Green Bay 24, at Milwaukee
Sept. 6, 1987 Kansas City 13, St. Louis 10, at Memphis, Tenn.
Aug. 11, 1988 Seattle 16, Detroit 13, at Detroit
Aug. 19, 1988 Miami 16, Denver 13, at Miami
Aug. 19, 1988 Green Bay 21, Kansas City 21, at Milwaukee
Aug. 20, 1988 Houston 20, Los Angeles Rams 17, at Anaheim
Aug. 21, 1988 Minnesota 19, Phoenix 16, at Phoenix
Aug. 5, 1989 Los Angeles Rams 16, San Francisco 13, at Tokyo, Japan
Aug. 26, 1989 Denver 24, Dallas 21, at Denver
Sept. 1, 1989 N.Y. Jets 15, Kansas City 13, at Kansas City
Aug. 24, 1990 Cincinnati 13, New England 10, at New England
Aug. 16, 1991 Cleveland 24, Washington 21, at Washington
Aug. 17, 1991 Cincinnati 27, Minnesota 24, at Cincinnati
Aug. 23, 1991 Dallas 20, Atlanta 17, at Dallas
Aug. 24, 1991 Cincinnati 19, Green Bay 16, at Green Bay
Aug. 22, 1992 Los Angeles Rams 16, Green Bay 13, at Anaheim
Aug. 8, 1993 Dallas 13, Detroit 13, at London, England
Aug. 12, 1995 Washington 16, Houston 13, at Knoxville, Tenn.
Aug. 19, 1995 Indianapolis 20, Green Bay 17, at Green Bay
Aug. 3, 1996 Minnesota 23, San Diego 20, at Minnesota
Aug. 10, 1996 San Francisco 16, San Diego 13, at San Francisco
Aug. 1, 1998 Green Bay 27, Kansas City 24, at Tokyo, Japan
Aug. 7, 1998 Detroit 13, Arizona 10, at Pontiac, Mich.
Aug. 22, 1998 Minnesota 25, Carolina 22, at Charlotte, N.C.
Aug. 9, 1999 Cleveland 20, Dallas 17, at Canton, Ohio
Aug. 4, 2001 Chicago 16, Cincinnati 13, at Chicago
Aug. 18, 2001 San Diego 23, Miami 20, at Miami
Aug. 18, 2001 Arizona 16, Seattle 13, at Seattle
Aug. 25, 2001 San Diego 13, St. Louis 10, at San Diego
Aug. 10, 2002 Kansas City 17, San Francisco 14, at San Francisco

OVERTIME GAMES

** indicates Monday-night game*
 # indicates Thursday/Sunday-night game
+ indicates Thanksgiving Day game

REGULAR SEASON

Sept. 22, 1974—Pittsburgh 35, Denver 35, at Denver; Steelers win toss. Gilliam's pass intercepted and returned by Rowser to Denver's 42. Turner misses 41-yard field goal. Walden punts and Greer returns to Broncos' 39. Van Heusen punts and Edwards returns to Steelers' 16. Game ends with Steelers on own 26.

Nov. 10, 1974—New York Jets 26, New York Giants 20, at New Haven, Conn.; Giants win toss. Gogolak misses 42-yard field goal. Namath passes to Boozer for five yards and touchdown at 6:53.

Sept. 28, 1975—Dallas 37, St. Louis 31, at Dallas; Cardinals win toss. Hart's pass intercepted and returned by Jordan to Cardinals' 37. Staubach passes to DuPree for three yards and touchdown at 7:53.

Oct. 12, 1975—Los Angeles 13, San Diego 10, at San Diego; Chargers win toss. Partee punts to Rams' 14. Dempsey kicks 22-yard field goal at 9:27.

Nov. 2, 1975—Washington 30, Dallas 24, at Washington; Cowboys win toss. Staubach's pass intercepted and returned by Houston to Cowboys' 35. Kilmer runs one yard for touchdown at 6:34.

Nov. 16, 1975—St. Louis 20, Washington 17, at St. Louis; Cardinals win toss. Bakken kicks 37-yard field goal at 7:00.

Nov. 23, 1975—Kansas City 24, Detroit 21, at Kansas City; Lions win toss. Chiefs take over on downs at own 38. Stenerud kicks 26-yard field goal at 6:44.

Nov. 23, 1975—Oakland 26, Washington 23, at Washington; Redskins win toss. Bragg punts to Raiders' 42. Blanda kicks 27-yard field goal at 7:13.

Nov. 30, 1975—Denver 13, San Diego 10, at Denver; Broncos win toss. Turner kicks 25-yard field goal at 4:13.

Nov. 30, 1975—Oakland 37, Atlanta 34, at Oakland; Falcons win toss. James punts to Raiders' 16. Guy punts and Herron returns to Falcons' 41. Nick Mike-Mayer misses 45-yard field goal. Guy punts into Falcons' end zone. James punts to Raiders' 39. Blanda kicks 36-yard field goal at 15:00.

Dec. 14, 1975—Baltimore 10, Miami 7, at Baltimore; Dolphins win toss. Seiple punts to Colts' 4. Linhart kicks 31-yard field goal at 12:44.

Sept. 19, 1976—Minnesota 10, Los Angeles 10, at Minnesota; Vikings win toss. Tarkenton's pass intercepted by Monte Jackson and returned to Minnesota 16. Allen blocks Dempsey's 30-yard field goal attempt, ball rolls into end zone for touchback. Clabo punts and Scribner returns to Rams' 20. Rusty Jackson punts to Vikings' 35. Tarkenton's pass intercepted by Kay at Rams' 1, no return. Game ends with Rams on own 3.

* **Sept. 27, 1976—Washington 20, Philadelphia 17,** at Philadelphia; Eagles win toss. Jones punts and E. Brown loses one yard on return to Redskins' 40. Bragg punts 51 yards into end zone for touchback. Jones punts and E. Brown returns to Redskins' 42. Bragg punts and Marshall returns to Eagles' 41. Boryla's pass intercepted by Dusek at Redskins' 37, no return. Bragg punts and Bradley returns. Philadelphia holding penalty moves ball back to Eagles' 8. Boryla pass intercepted by E. Brown and returned to Eagles' 22. Moseley kicks 29-yard field goal at 12:49.

Oct. 17, 1976—Kansas City 20, Miami 17, at Miami; Chiefs win toss. Wilson punts into end zone for touchback. Bulaich fumbles into Kansas City end zone, Collier recovers for touchback. Stenerud kicks 34-yard field goal at 14:48.

Oct. 31, 1976—St. Louis 23, San Francisco 20, at St. Louis; Cardinals win toss. Joyce punts and Leonard fumbles on return, Jones recovers at 49ers' 43. Bakken kicks 21-yard field goal at 6:42.

Dec. 5, 1976—San Diego 13, San Francisco 7, at San Diego; Chargers win toss. Morris runs 13 yards for touchdown at 5:12.

Sept. 18, 1977—Dallas 16, Minnesota 10, at Minnesota; Vikings win toss. Dallas starts on Vikings' 47 after a punt early in the overtime period. Staubach scores seven plays later on a four-yard run at 6:14.

* **Sept. 26, 1977—Cleveland 30, New England 27,** at Cleveland; Browns win toss. Sipe throws a 22-yard pass to Logan at Patriots' 19. Cockroft kicks 35-yard field goal at 4:45.

Oct. 16, 1977—Minnesota 22, Chicago 16, at Minnesota; Bears win toss. Parsons punts 53 yards to Vikings' 18. Minnesota drives to Bears' 11. On a first-and-10, Vikings fake a field goal and holder Krause hits Voigt with a touchdown pass at 6:45.

Oct. 30, 1977—Cincinnati 13, Houston 10, at Cincinnati; Bengals win toss. Bahr kicks a 22-yard field goal at 5:51.

Nov. 13, 1977—San Francisco 10, New Orleans 7, at New Orleans; Saints win toss. Saints fail to move ball and Blanchard punts to 49ers' 41. Wersching kicks a 33-yard field goal at 6:33.

Dec. 18, 1977—Chicago 12, New York Giants 9, at East Rutherford, N.J.; Giants win toss. The ball changes hands eight times before Thomas kicks a 28-yard field goal at 14:51.

Sept. 10, 1978—Cleveland 13, Cincinnati 10, at Cleveland; Browns win toss. Collins returns kickoff 41 yards to Browns' 47. Cockroft kicks 27-yard field goal at 4:30.

* **Sept. 11, 1978—Minnesota 12, Denver 9,** at Minnesota; Vikings win toss. Danmeier kicks 44-yard field goal at 2:56.

Sept. 24, 1978—Pittsburgh 15, Cleveland 9, at Pittsburgh; Steelers win toss. Cunningham scores on a 37-yard "gadget" pass from Bradshaw at 3:43. Steelers start winning drive on their 21.

Sept. 24, 1978—Denver 23, Kansas City 17, at Kansas City; Broncos win toss. Dilts punts to Kansas City. Chiefs advance to Broncos' 40 where Reed fails to make first down on fourth-and-one situation. Broncos march downfield. Preston scores two-yard touchdown at 10:28.

Oct. 1, 1978—Oakland 25, Chicago 19, at Chicago; Bears win toss. Both teams punt on first possession. On Chicago's second offensive series, Colzie intercepts Avellini's pass and returns it to Bears' 3. Three plays later, Whittington runs two yards for a touchdown at 5:19.

Oct. 15, 1978—Dallas 24, St. Louis 21, at St. Louis; Cowboys win toss. Dallas drives from its 23 into field goal range. Septien kicks 27-yard field goal at 3:28.

Oct. 29, 1978—Denver 20, Seattle 17, at Seattle; Broncos win toss. Ball changes hands four times before Turner kicks 18-yard field goal at 12:59.

Nov. 12, 1978—San Diego 29, Kansas City 23, at San Diego; Chiefs win toss. Fouts hits Jefferson for decisive 14-yard touchdown pass on the last play (15:00) of overtime period.

Nov. 12, 1978—Washington 16, New York Giants 13, at Washington; Redskins win toss. Moseley kicks winning 45-yard field goal at 8:32 after missing first down field goal attempt of 35 yards at 4:50.

Nov. 26, 1978—Green Bay 10, Minnesota 10, at Green Bay; Packers win toss. Both teams have possession of the ball four times.

Dec. 9, 1978—Cleveland 37, New York Jets 34, at Cleveland; Browns win toss. Cockroft kicks 22-yard field goal at 3:07.

Sept. 2, 1979—Atlanta 40, New Orleans 34, at New Orleans; Falcons win toss. Bartkowski's pass intercepted by Myers and returned to Falcons' 46. Erxleben punts to Falcons' 4. James punts to Chandler on Saints' 43. Erxleben punts and Ryckman returns to Falcons' 28. James punts and Chandler returns to Saints' 36. Erxleben retrieves punt snap on Saints' 1 and attempts pass. Mayberry intercepts and returns six yards for touchdown at 8:22.

Sept. 2, 1979—Cleveland 25, New York Jets 22, at New York;

Jets win toss. Leahy's 43-yard field goal attempt goes wide right at 4:41. Evans's punt blocked by Dykes is recovered by Newton. Ramsey punts into end zone for touchback. Evans punts and Harper returns to Jets' 24. Robinson's pass intercepted by Davis and returned 33 yards to Jets' 31. Cockroft kicks 27-yard field goal at 14:45.

* **Sept. 3, 1979—Pittsburgh 16, New England 13,** at Foxboro; Patriots win toss. Hare punts to Swann at Steelers' 31. Bahr kicks 41-yard field goal at 5:10.

Sept. 9, 1979—Tampa Bay 29, Baltimore 26, at Baltimore; Colts win toss. Landry fumbles, recovered by Kollar at Colts' 14. O'Donoghue kicks 31-yard, first-down field goal at 1:41.

Sept. 16, 1979—Denver 20, Atlanta 17, at Atlanta; Broncos win toss. Broncos march 65 yards to Falcons' 7. Turner kicks 24-yard field goal at 6:15.

Sept. 23, 1979—Houston 30, Cincinnati 27, at Cincinnati; Oilers win toss. Parsley punts and Lusby returns to Bengals' 33. Bahr's 32-yard field goal attempt is wide right at 8:05. Parsley's punt downed on Bengals' 5. McInally punts and Ellender returns to Bengals' 42. Fritsch's third down, 29-yard field goal attempt hits left upright and bounces through at 14:28.

Sept. 23, 1979—Minnesota 27, Green Bay 21, at Minnesota; Vikings win toss. Kramer throws 50-yard touchdown pass to Rashad at 3:18.

Oct. 28, 1979—Houston 27, New York Jets 24, at Houston; Oilers win toss. Oilers march 58 yards to Jets' 18. Fritsch kicks 35-yard field goal at 5:10.

Nov. 18, 1979—Cleveland 30, Miami 24, at Cleveland; Browns win toss. Sipe passes 39 yards to Rucker for touchdown at 1:59.

Nov. 25, 1979—Pittsburgh 33, Cleveland 30, at Pittsburgh; Browns win toss. Sipe's pass intercepted by Blount on Steelers' 4. Bradshaw pass intercepted by Bolton on Browns' 12. Evans punts and Bell returns to Steelers' 17. Bahr kicks 37-yard field goal at 14:51.

Nov. 25, 1979—Buffalo 16, New England 13, at Foxboro; Patriots win toss. Hare's punt downed on Bills' 38. Jackson punts and Morgan returns to Patriots' 20. Grogan's pass intercepted by Haslett and returned to Bills' 42. Ferguson's 51-yard pass to Butler sets up N. Mike-Mayer's 29-yard field goal at 9:15.

Dec. 2, 1979—Los Angeles 27, Minnesota 21, at Los Angeles; Rams win toss. Clark punts and Miller returns to Vikings' 25. Kramer's pass intercepted by Brown and returned to Rams' 40. Cromwell, holding for 22-yard field goal attempt, runs around left end untouched for winning score at 6:53.

Sept. 7, 1980—Green Bay 12, Chicago 6, at Green Bay; Bears win toss. Parsons punts and Nixon returns 16 yards. Five plays later, Marcol returns own blocked field goal attempt 24 yards for touchdown at 6:00.

Sept. 14, 1980—San Diego 30, Oakland 24, at San Diego; Raiders win toss. Pastorini's first-down pass intercepted by Edwards. Millen intercepts Fouts' first-down pass and returns to San Diego 46. Bahr's 50-yard field goal attempt partially blocked by Williams and recovered on Chargers' 32. Eight plays later, Fouts throws 24-yard touchdown pass to Jefferson at 8:09.

Sept. 14, 1980—San Francisco 24, St. Louis 21, at San Francisco; Cardinals win toss. Swider punts and Robinson returns to 49ers' 32. San Francisco drives 52 yards to St. Louis 16, where Wersching kicks 33-yard field goal at 4:12.

Oct. 12, 1980—Green Bay 14, Tampa Bay 14, at Tampa Bay; Packers win toss. Teams trade punts twice. Lee returns second Tampa Bay punt to Green Bay 42. Dickey completes three passes to Buccaneers' 18, where Birney's 36-yard field goal attempt is wide right as time expires.

Nov. 9, 1980—Atlanta 33, St. Louis 27, at St. Louis; Falcons win toss. Strong runs 21 yards for touchdown at 4:20.

\# **Nov. 20, 1980—San Diego 27, Miami 24,** at Miami; Chargers win toss. Partridge punts into end zone, Dolphins take over on their own 20. Woodley's pass for Nathan intercepted by Lowe and returned 28 yards to Dolphins' 12. Benirschke kicks 28-yard field goal at 7:14.

Nov. 23, 1980—New York Jets 31, Houston 28, at New York; Jets win toss. Leahy kicks 38-yard field goal at 3:58.

\+ **Nov. 27, 1980—Chicago 23, Detroit 17,** at Detroit; Bears win toss. Williams returns kickoff 95 yards for touchdown at 0:21.

Dec. 7, 1980—Buffalo 10, Los Angeles 7, at Buffalo; Rams win toss. Corral punts and Hooks returns to Bills' 34. Ferguson's 30-yard pass to Lewis sets up N. Mike-Mayer's 30-yard field goal at 5:14.

Dec. 7, 1980—San Francisco 38, New Orleans 35, at San Francisco; Saints win toss. Erxleben's punt downed by Hardy on 49ers' 27. Wersching kicks 36-yard field goal at 7:40.

* **Dec. 8, 1980—Miami 16, New England 13,** at Miami; Dolphins win toss. Von Schamann kicks 23-yard field goal at 3:20.

Dec. 14, 1980—Cincinnati 17, Chicago 14, at Chicago; Bengals win toss. Breech kicks 28-yard field goal at 4:23.

Dec. 21, 1980—Los Angeles 20, Atlanta 17, at Los Angeles; Rams win toss. Corral's punt downed at Rams' 37. James punts into end zone for touchback. Corral's punt downed on Falcons' 17. Bartkowski fumbles when hit by Harris, recovered by Delaney. Corral kicks 23-yard field goal on first play of possession at 7:00.

Sept. 27, 1981—Cincinnati 27, Buffalo 24, at Cincinnati; Bills win toss. Cater punts into end zone for touchback. Bengals drive to the Bills' 10 where Breech kicks 28-yard field goal at 9:33.

Sept. 27, 1981—Pittsburgh 27, New England 21, at Pittsburgh; Patriots win toss. Hubach punts and Smith returns five yards to midfield. Four plays later Bradshaw throws 24-yard touchdown pass to Swann at 3:19.

Oct. 4, 1981—Miami 28, New York Jets 28, at Miami; Jets win toss. Teams trade punts twice. Leahy's 48-yard field goal attempt is wide right as time expires.

Oct. 25, 1981—New York Giants 27, Atlanta 24, at Atlanta; Giants win toss. Jennings' punt goes out of bounds at New York 47. Bright returns Atlanta punt to Giants' 14. Woerner fair catches punt at own 28. Andrews fumbles on first play, recovered by Van Pelt. Danelo kicks 40-yard field goal four plays later at 9:20.

Oct. 25, 1981—Chicago 20, San Diego 17, at Chicago; Bears win toss. Teams trade punts. Bears' second punt returned by Brooks to Chargers' 33. Fouts pass intercepted by Fencik and returned 32 yards to San Diego 27. Roveto kicks 27-yard field goal seven plays later at 9:30.

Nov. 8, 1981—Chicago 16, Kansas City 13, at Kansas City; Bears win toss. Teams trade punts. Kansas City takes over on downs on its own 38. Fuller's fumble recovered by Harris on Chicago 36. Roveto's 37-yard field goal wide, but Chiefs penalized for leverage. Roveto's 22-yard field goal attempt three plays later is good at 13:07.

Nov. 8, 1981—Denver 23, Cleveland 20, at Denver; Browns win toss. D. Smith recovers Hill's fumble at Denver 48. Morton's 33-yard pass to Upchurch and 6-yard run by Preston set up Steinfort's 30-yard field goal at 4:10.

Nov. 8, 1981—Miami 30, New England 27, at New England; Dolphins win toss. Orosz punts and Morgan returns six yards to New England 26. Grogan's pass intercepted by Brudzinski who returns 19 yards to Patriots' 26. Von Schamann kicks 30-yard field goal on first down at 7:09.

Nov. 15, 1981—Washington 30, New York Giants 27, at New York; Giants win toss. Nelms returns Giants' punt 26 yards to New York 47. Five plays later Moseley kicks 48-yard field goal at 3:44.

Dec. 20, 1981—New York Giants 13, Dallas 10, at New York; Cowboys win toss and kick off. Jennings punts to Dallas 40. Taylor recovers Dorsett's fumble on second down. Danelo's 33-yard field goal attempt hits right upright and bounces back. White's pass for Pearson intercepted by Hunt and returned seven yards to Dallas 24. Four plays later Danelo kicks 35-yard field goal at 6:19.

Sept. 12, 1982—Washington 37, Philadelphia 34, at Philadelphia; Redskins win toss. Theismann completes five passes for 63 yards to set up Moseley's 26-yard field goal at 4:47.

Sept. 19, 1982—Pittsburgh 26, Cincinnati 20, at Pittsburgh; Bengals win toss. Anderson's pass intended for Kreider intercepted by Woodruff and returned 30 yards to Cincinnati 2. Bradshaw completes two-yard touchdown pass to Stallworth on first down at 1:08.

Dec. 19, 1982—Baltimore 20, Green Bay 20, at Baltimore; Packers win toss. K. Anderson intercepts Dickey's first-down pass and returns to Packers' 42. Miller's 44-yard field goal attempt blocked by G. Lewis. Teams trade punts before Stenerud's 47-yard field goal attempt is wide right. Teams trade punts again before time expires in Colts possession.

Jan. 2, 1983—Tampa Bay 26, Chicago 23, at Tampa; Bears win toss. Parsons punts to T. Bell at Buccaneers' 40. Capece kicks 33-yard field goal at 3:14.

Sept. 4, 1983—Baltimore 29, New England 23, at New England; Patriots win toss. Cooks runs 52 yards with fumble recovery three plays into overtime at 0:30.

Sept. 4, 1983—Green Bay 41, Houston 38, at Houston; Packers win toss. Stenerud kicks 42-yard field goal at 5:55.

Sept. 11, 1983—New York Giants 16, Atlanta 13, at Atlanta; Giants win toss. Dennis returns kickoff 54 yards to Atlanta 41. Haji-Sheikh kicks 30-yard field goal at 3:38.

Sept. 18, 1983—New Orleans 34, Chicago 31, at New Orleans; Bears win toss. Parsons punts and Groth returns five yards to New Orleans 34. Stabler pass intercepted by Schmidt at Chicago 47. Parsons punt downed by Gentry at New Orleans 2. Stabler gains 36 yards in four passes; Wilson 38 on six carries. Andersen kicks 41-yard field goal at 10:57.

Sept. 18, 1983—Minnesota 19, Tampa Bay 16, at Tampa; Vikings win toss. Coleman punts and Bell returns eight yards to Tampa Bay 47. Capece's 33-yard field goal attempt sails wide at 7:26. Dils and Young combine for 48-yard gain to Tampa Bay 27. Ricardo kicks 42-yard field goal at 9:27.

Sept. 25, 1983—Baltimore 22, Chicago 19, at Baltimore; Colts win toss. Allegre kicks 33-yard field goal nine plays later at 4:51.

Sept. 25, 1983—Cleveland 30, San Diego 24, at San Diego; Browns win toss. Walker returns kickoff 33 yards to Cleveland 37. Sipe completes 48-yard touchdown pass to Holt four plays later at 1:53.

Sept. 25, 1983—New York Jets 27, Los Angeles Rams 24, at New York; Jets win toss. Ramsey punts to Irvin who returns to 25 but penalty puts Rams on own 13. Holmes 30-yard interception return sets up Leahy's 26-yard field goal at 3:22.

Oct. 9, 1983—Buffalo 38, Miami 35, at Miami; Dolphins win toss. Von Schamann's 52-yard field goal attempt goes wide at 12:36. Cater punts to Clayton who loses 11 to own 13. Von Schamann's 43-yard field goal attempt sails wide at 5:15. Danelo kicks 36-yard field goal nine plays later at 13:58.

Oct. 9, 1983—Dallas 27, Tampa Bay 24, at Dallas; Cowboys win toss. Septien's 51-yard field-goal attempt goes wide but Buccaneers penalized for roughing kicker. Septien kicks 42-yard field goal at 4:38.

Oct. 23, 1983—Kansas City 13, Houston 10, at Houston; Chiefs win toss. Lowery kicks 41-yard field goal 13 plays later at 7:41.

Oct. 23, 1983—Minnesota 20, Green Bay 17, at Green Bay; Packers win toss. Scribner's punt downed on Vikings' 42. Ricardo kicks 32-yard field goal eight plays later at 5:05.

* **Oct. 24, 1983—New York Giants 20, St. Louis 20,** at St. Louis; Cardinals win toss. Teams trade punts before O'Donoghue's 44-yard field goal attempt is wide left. Jennings' punt returned by Bird to St. Louis 21. Lomax pass intercepted by Haynes who loses six yards to New York 33. Jennings' punt downed on St. Louis 17. O'Donoghue's 19-yard field goal attempt is wide right. Rutledge's pass intercepted by L. Washington who returns 25 yards to New York 25. O'Donoghue's 42-yard field goal attempt is wide right. Rutledge's pass intercepted by W. Smith at St. Louis 33 to end game.

Oct. 30, 1983—Cleveland 25, Houston 19, at Cleveland; Oilers win toss. Teams trade punts. Nielsen's pass intercepted by Whitwell who returns to Houston 20. Green runs 20 yards for touchdown on first down at 6:34.

Nov. 20, 1983—Detroit 23, Green Bay 20, at Milwaukee; Packers win toss. Scribner punts and Jenkins returns 14 yards to Green Bay 45. Murray's 33-yard field goal attempt is wide left at 9:32. Whitehurst's pass intercepted by Watkins and returned to Green Bay 27. Murray kicks 37-yard field goal four plays later at 8:30.

Nov. 27, 1983—Atlanta 47, Green Bay 41, at Atlanta; Packers win toss. K. Johnson returns interception 31 yards for touchdown at 2:13.

Nov. 27, 1983—Seattle 51, Kansas City 48, at Seattle; Seahawks win toss. Dixon's 47-yard kickoff return sets up N. Johnson's 42-yard field goal at 1:36.

Dec. 11, 1983—New Orleans 20, Philadelphia 17, at Philadelphia; Eagles win toss. Runager punts to Groth who fair catches on New Orleans 32. Stabler completes two passes for 36 yards to Goodlow to set up Andersen's 50-yard field goal at 5:30.

* **Dec. 12, 1983—Green Bay 12, Tampa Bay 9,** at Tampa; Packers win toss. Stenerud kicks 23-yard field goal 11 plays later at 4:07.

Sept. 9, 1984—Detroit 27, Atlanta 24, at Atlanta; Lions win toss. Murray kicks 48-yard field goal nine plays later at 5:06.

Sept. 30, 1984—Tampa Bay 30, Green Bay 27, at Tampa; Packers win toss. Scribner punts 44 yards to Tampa Bay 2. Epps returns Garcia's punt three yards to Green Bay 27. Scribner's punt downed on Buccaneers' 33. Ariri kicks 46-yard field goal 11 plays later at 10:32.

Oct. 14, 1984—Detroit 13, Tampa Bay 7, at Detroit; Buccaneers win toss. Tampa Bay drives to Lions' 39 before Wilder fumbles. Five plays later Danielson hits Thompson with 37-yard touchdown pass at 4:34.

Oct. 21, 1984—Dallas 30, New Orleans 27, at Dallas; Cowboys win toss. Septien kicks 41-yard field goal eight plays later at 3:42.

Oct. 28, 1984—Denver 22, Los Angeles Raiders 19, at Los Angeles; Raiders win toss. Hawkins fumble recovered by Foley at Denver 7. Teams trade punts. Karlis's 42-yard field goal attempt is wide left. Teams trade punts. Wilson pass intercepted by R. Jackson at Los Angeles 45, returned 23 yards to Los Angeles 22. Karlis kicks 35-yard field goal two plays later at 15:00.

Nov. 4, 1984—Philadelphia 23, Detroit 23, at Detroit; Lions win toss. Lions drive to Eagles' 3 in eight plays. Murray's 21-yard field goal attempt hits right upright and bounces back. Jaworski's pass intercepted by Watkins at Detroit 5. Teams trade punts. Cooper returns Black's punt five yards to Eagles' 14. Time expires four plays later with Eagles on own 21.

Nov. 18, 1984—San Diego 34, Miami 28, at San Diego; Chargers win toss. McGee scores eight plays later on a 25-yard run at 3:17.

Dec. 2, 1984—Cincinnati 20, Cleveland 17, at Cleveland; Browns win toss. Simmons returns Cox's punt 30 yards to Cleveland 35. Breech kicks 35-yard field goal seven plays later at 4:34.

Dec. 2, 1984—Houston 23, Pittsburgh 20, at Houston; Oilers win toss. Cooper kicks 30-yard field goal 16 plays later at 5:53.

Sept. 8, 1985—St. Louis 27, Cleveland 24, at Cleveland; Cardinals win toss. O'Donoghue kicks 35-yard field goal nine plays later at 5:27.

Sept. 29, 1985—New York Giants 16, Philadelphia 10, at Philadelphia; Eagles win toss. Jaworski's pass tipped by Quick and intercepted by Patterson who returns 29 yards for touchdown at 0:55.

Oct. 20, 1985—Denver 13, Seattle 10, at Denver; Seahawks win toss. Teams trade punts twice. Krieg's pass intercepted by Hunter and returned to Seahawks' 15. Karlis kicks 24-yard field goal four plays later at 9:19.

Nov. 10, 1985—Philadelphia 23, Atlanta 17, at Philadelphia; Falcons win toss. Donnelly's 62-yard punt goes out of bounds at Eagles' 1. Jaworski completes 99-yard touchdown pass to Quick two plays later at 1:49.

Nov. 10, 1985—San Diego 40, Los Angeles Raiders 34, at San Diego; Chargers win toss. James scores on 17-yard run seven plays later at 3:44.

Nov. 17, 1985—Denver 30, San Diego 24, at Denver; Chargers win toss. Thomas' 40-yard field goal attempt blocked by Smith and returned 60 yards by Wright for touchdown at 4:45.

Nov. 24, 1985—New York Jets 16, New England 13, at New York; Jets win toss. Teams trade punts twice. Patriots' second punt returned 46 yards by Sohn to Patriots' 15. Leahy kicks 32-yard field goal one play later at 10:05.

Nov. 24, 1985—Tampa Bay 19, Detroit 16, at Tampa; Lions win toss. Teams trade punts. Lions' punt downed on Buccaneers' 38. Igwebuike kicks 24-yard field goal 11 plays later at 12:31.

Nov. 24, 1985—Los Angeles Raiders 31, Denver 28, at Los Angeles; Raiders win toss. Bahr kicks 32-yard field goal six plays later at 2:42.

Dec. 8, 1985—Los Angeles Raiders 17, Denver 14, at Denver; Broncos win toss. Teams trade punts twice. Elway's fumble recovered by Townsend at Broncos' 8. Bahr kicks 26-yard field goal one play later at 4:55.

Sept. 14, 1986—Chicago 13, Philadelphia 10, at Chicago; Eagles win toss. Crawford's fumble of kickoff recovered by Jackson at Eagles' 35. Butler kicks 23-yard field goal 10 plays later at 5:56.

Sept. 14, 1986—Cincinnati 36, Buffalo 33, at Cincinnati; Bills win toss. Zander intercepts Kelly's first-down pass and returns it to Bills' 17. Breech kicks 20-yard field goal two plays later at 0:56.

Sept. 21, 1986—New York Jets 51, Miami 45, at New York; Jets win toss. O'Brien completes 43-yard touchdown pass to Walker five plays later at 2:35.

Sept. 28, 1986—Pittsburgh 22, Houston 16, at Houston; Oilers win toss. Johnson's punt returned 41 yards by Woods to Oilers' 15. Abercrombie scores on three-yard run three plays later at 2:35.

Sept. 28, 1986—Atlanta 23, Tampa Bay 20, at Tampa; Falcons win toss. Teams trade punts. Luckhurst kicks 34-yard field goal 10 plays later at 12:35.

Oct. 5, 1986—Los Angeles Rams 26, Tampa Bay 20, at Anaheim; Rams win toss. Dickerson scores four plays later on 42-yard run at 2:16.

Oct. 12, 1986—Minnesota 27, San Francisco 24, at San Francisco; Vikings win toss. C. Nelson kicks 28-yard field goal nine plays later at 4:27.

Oct. 19, 1986—San Francisco 10, Atlanta 10, at Atlanta; Falcons win toss. Teams trade punts twice. Donnelly punts to 49ers' 27. The following play Wilson recovers Rice's fumble at 49ers' 46 as time expires.

Nov. 2, 1986—Washington 44, Minnesota 38, at Washington; Redskins win toss. Schroeder completes 38-yard touchdown pass to Clark four plays later at 1:46.

#**Nov. 20, 1986—Los Angeles Raiders 37, San Diego 31,** at San Diego; Raiders win toss. Teams trade punts. Allen scores five plays later on 28-yard run at 8:33.

Nov. 23, 1986—Cleveland 37, Pittsburgh 31, at Cleveland; Browns win toss. Teams trade punts. Six plays later Kosar hits Slaughter with 36-yard touchdown pass at 6:37.

Nov. 30, 1986—Chicago 13, Pittsburgh 10, at Chicago; Bears win toss and kick off. Newsome's punt returned by Barnes to Chicago 49. Butler kicks 42-yard field goal five plays later at 3:55.

Nov. 30, 1986—Philadelphia 33, Los Angeles Raiders 27, at Los Angeles; Eagles win toss. Teams trade punts. Long recovers Cunningham's fumble at Philadelphia 42. Waters returns Allen's fumble 81 yards to Los Angeles 4. Cunningham scores on one-yard run two plays later at 6:53.

Nov. 30, 1986—Cleveland 13, Houston 10, at Cleveland; Oilers win toss and kick off. Gossett punts to Houston 39. Luck's pass intercepted by Minnifield at Cleveland 21. Gossett punts to Houston 34. Luck's pass intercepted by Minnifield at Cleveland 43 who returns 20 yards to Houston 37. Moseley kicks 29-yard field goal nine plays later at 14:44.

Dec. 7, 1986—St. Louis 10, Philadelphia 10, at Philadelphia; Cardinals win toss. White blocks Schubert's 40-yard field goal attempt. Teams trade punts. McFadden's 43-yard field goal attempt is wide left. Schubert's 37-yard field goal attempt is wide right. Cavanaugh's pass intercepted by Carter and returned to Eagles' 48 to end game.

Dec. 14, 1986—Miami 37, Los Angeles Rams 31, at Anaheim; Dolphins win toss. Marino completes 20-yard touchdown pass to Duper six plays later at 3:04.

Sept. 20, 1987—Denver 17, Green Bay 17, at Milwaukee; Packers win toss. Del Greco's 47-yard field goal attempt is short. Teams trade punts. Elway intercepted by Noble who returns 10 yards to Green Bay 34. Davis fumbles on next play and Smith recovers. Two plays later, Karlis's 40-yard field goal attempt is wide left. Time expires two plays later with Packers on own 23.

Oct. 11, 1987—Detroit 19, Green Bay 16, at Green Bay; Lions win toss. Prindle's 42-yard field goal attempt is wide left. Packers punt downed on Detroit 17. Prindle kicks 31-yard field goal 16 plays later at 12:26.

Oct. 18, 1987—New York Jets 37, Miami 31, at New York; Jets win toss. Teams trade punts. Ryan intercepted by Hooper at Jets' 47 who returns 11 yards. Mackey intercepted by Haslett at Jets' 37 who returns 9 yards. Jets punt. Mackey intercepted by Radachowsky who returns 45 yards to Miami 24. Ryan completes eight-yard touchdown pass to Hunter five plays later at 14:26.

Oct. 18, 1987—Green Bay 16, Philadelphia 10, at Green Bay; Packers win toss. Hargrove scores on seven-yard run 10 plays later at 5:04.

Oct. 18, 1987—Buffalo 6, New York Giants 3, at Buffalo; Bills win toss. Schlopy's 28-yard field goal attempt is wide left. Teams trade punts. Rutledge intercepted by Clark who returns 23 yards to Buffalo 40. Schlopy kicks 27-yard field goal nine plays later at 14:41.

Oct. 25, 1987—Buffalo 34, Miami 31, at Miami; Bills win toss. Norwood kicks 27-yard field goal seven plays later at 4:12.

Nov. 1, 1987—San Diego 27, Cleveland 24, at San Diego; Browns win toss. Kosar intercepted by Glenn who returns 20 yards to Browns' 25. Abbott kicks 33-yard field goal three plays later at 2:16.

Nov. 15, 1987—Dallas 23, New England 17, at New England; Cowboys win toss. Walker scores on 60-yard run four plays later at 1:50.

+**Nov. 26, 1987—Minnesota 44, Dallas 38,** at Dallas; Vikings win toss. Coleman's punt downed by Hilton at Cowboys' 37. White intercepted by Studwell who returns 12 yards to Vikings' 37. D. Nelson scores on 24-yard run seven plays later at 7:51.

Nov. 29, 1987—Philadelphia 34, New England 31, at New England; Patriots win toss. Ramsey intercepted by Joyner who returns 29 yards to Eagles' 32. Fryar fair catches Teltschik's punt at Patriots' 13. Franklin's 46-yard field-goal attempt is short. McFadden's 39-yard field goal attempt is wide left. Tatupu fumbles on next play and Cobb recovers. McFadden kicks 38-yard field goal four plays later at 12:16.

Dec. 6, 1987—New York Giants 23, Philadelphia 20, at New York; Giants win toss and kick off. Teams trade punts twice.

Teltschik's punt is returned 16 yards by McConkey to Eagles' 33. Three plays later, Allegre's 50-yard field goal attempt is blocked by Joyner and returned 25 yards by Hoage to Eagles' 30. McConkey returns Teltschik's punt four yards to Giants' 44. Allegre kicks 28-yard field goal four plays later at 10:42.

Dec. 6, 1987—Cincinnati 30, Kansas City 27, at Cincinnati; Bengals win toss. Teams trade punts. Breech kicks 32-yard field goal 16 plays later at 9:44.

Dec. 26, 1987—Washington 27, Minnesota 24, at Minnesota; Redskins win toss. Haji-Sheikh kicks 26-yard field goal six plays later at 2:09.

Sept. 4, 1988—Houston 17, Indianapolis 14, at Indianapolis; Colts win toss. Dickerson fumble recovered by Lyles who returns six yards to Colts' 42. Zendejas kicks 35-yard field goal six plays later at 3:51.

* **Sept. 26, 1988—Los Angeles Raiders 30, Denver 27,** at Denver; Broncos win toss. Teams trade punts twice. Elway intercepted by Lee who returns 20 yards to Broncos' 31. Bahr kicks 35-yard field goal four plays later at 12:35.

Oct. 2, 1988—New York Jets 17, Kansas City 17, at New York; Chiefs win toss. Chiefs punt goes into end zone for touchback. Leahy's 44-yard field goal attempt is wide right. Chiefs punt is returned by Townsell to Jets' 26. Burruss recovers McNeil's fumble at Chiefs' 11. DeBerg intercepted by Humphery at Jets' 49. Three plays later, time expires.

Oct. 9, 1988—Denver 16, San Francisco 13, at San Francisco; Broncos win toss and kick off. Young intercepted by Haynes at Broncos' 32. Denver punt downed at 49ers' 5. Young intercepted by Wilson who returns seven yards to 49ers' 5. Karlis kicks 22-yard field goal two plays later at 8:11.

Oct. 30, 1988—New York Giants 13, Detroit 10, at Detroit; Lions win toss. James's fumble recovered by Taylor at Lions' 22. Three plays later, McFadden kicks 33-yard field goal at 1:13.

Nov. 20, 1988—Buffalo 9, New York Jets 6, at Buffalo; Jets win toss. Vick's fumble recovered by Bennett at Bills' 32. Norwood kicks 30-yard field goal five plays later at 3:47.

Nov. 20, 1988—Philadelphia 23, New York Giants 17, at New York; Eagles win toss. Philadelphia's punt goes into end zone for touchback. Hostetler intercepted by Hoage who returns 11 yards to Giants' 41. Six plays later, Zendejas's 30-yard field-goal attempt is blocked and ball is recovered behind line of scrimmage by Eagles' Simmons, who runs 15 yards for touchdown at 3:09.

Dec. 11, 1988—New England 10, Tampa Bay 7, at New England; Buccaneers win toss and kick off. Staurovsky kicks 27-yard field goal six plays later at 3:08.

Dec. 17, 1988—Cincinnati 20, Washington 17, at Cincinnati; Bengals win toss. Cincinnati's punt returned by Oliphant to Redskins' 16. Grant recovers Williams's fumble at Redskins' 17. Breech kicks 20-yard field goal three plays later at 7:01.

Sept. 24, 1989—Buffalo 47, Houston 41, at Houston; Oilers win toss. Johnson returns Brady's kickoff 17 yards to Oilers' 19. Oilers drive to Buffalo 25, Zendejas's 37-yard field goal blocked, but Bills offsides and Zendejas's second attempt is wide left. Bills' ball and Kelly completes series of passes, including 28-yard game-winner to Andre Reed, at 8:42.

Oct. 8, 1989—Miami 13, Cleveland 10, at Miami; Browns win toss. Metcalf returns Stoyanovich's kickoff 20 yards to Browns' 28. Browns drive ball 46 yards in eight plays; Bahr wide left on 44-yard field goal attempt. Dolphins ball. Browns called for pass interference on Marino pass to Banks at Cleveland 47. Two plays later, Banks's 20-yard reception at Browns' 23 sets up winning 35-yard field goal by Stoyanovich at 6:23.

Oct. 22, 1989—Denver 24, Seattle 21, at Seattle; Seahawks win toss. Treadwell's 56-yard kickoff returned 18 yards by Jefferson to Seahawks' 27. Seahawks drive to Broncos' 22 in 10 plays, but Johnson's 40-yard field goal attempt wide left. Smith intercepts a Krieg pass and returns it 28 yards to Seahawks' 10. Treadwell kicks winning 27-yard field goal at 7:46.

Oct. 29, 1989—New England 23, Indianapolis 20, at Indianapolis; Patriots win toss. Biasucci kickoff returned 13 yards to Patriots' 23 by Martin. Holding penalty brings ball back to Patriots' 13. After six plays, Feagles punt returned 11 yards by Verdin to Colts' 28. Six plays later, Colts punt to Martin at Patriots' 12. Grogan completes three straight passes to Patriots' 44. Five consecutive runs put New England on Colts' 33. Davis kicks a 51-yard winning field goal for Patriots at 9:46.

Oct. 29, 1989—Green Bay 23, Detroit 20, at Milwaukee; Lions win toss. Sanders touchback on Jacke kickoff. On first play, Murphy intercepts Lions' Peete and returns it three yards to Lions' 26. Fullwood gains five yards on three plays to set up Jacke's 38-yard field goal at 2:14.

Nov. 5, 1989—Minnesota 23, Los Angeles Rams 21, at Minneapolis; Rams win toss. Karlis's kick returned 18 yards by Delpino to Rams' 19. Drive stops at Rams' 28. Merriweather blocks Hatcher's punt at 12. Ball rolls out of end zone for safety.

Nov. 19, 1989—Cleveland 10, Kansas City 10, at Cleveland; Browns win toss. Browns punt three times; Chiefs twice; before Kansas City's Lowery misses 47-yard field goal with 17 seconds remaining in overtime. Kosar's pass intercepted as time expired.

Nov. 26, 1989—Los Angeles Rams 20, New Orleans 17, at New Orleans; Saints win toss. Lansford's kickoff returned 27 yards to Saints' 30. After four plays, Barnhardt punts to Rams' 15. Saints penalized 35 yards for interference to Rams' 43. Three plays later, Everett hits Anderson with 14-yard pass to Saints' 40, then 26-yarder to put Rams in field goal position. Lansford kicks 31-yard field goal at 6:38.

Dec. 3, 1989—Los Angeles Raiders 16, Denver 13, at Los Angeles; Broncos win toss. Bell returns Jaeger kickoff 14 yards to Broncos' 18. Broncos' penalized for illegal block to Broncos' 9. Elway completes three passes for two first downs. On third and eight Elway sacked for 10-yard loss. Horan punts, Adams calls for fair catch at Raiders' 29. Dyal's 26-yard reception moves Raiders to Denver 43. Raiders move ball 34 yards in three plays to set up Jaeger's 26-yard field goal at 7:02.

Dec. 10, 1989—Indianapolis 23, Cleveland 17, at Indianapolis; Browns win toss. Teams trade punts. McNeil returns Colts' punt 42 yards to 42. Seven plays later, Bahr misses 35-yard field goal attempt. Three plays later, Stark punts and McNeil returns ball to 50-yard line. Two plays later, Prior intercepts Kosar's pass at Colts' 42 and returns it 58 yards for touchdown at 10:54.

Dec. 17, 1989—Cleveland 23, Minnesota 17, at Cleveland; Browns win toss. Browns punt to Vikings' 18. Six plays later, Vikings punt to Browns' 22. Nine plays later, Bahr lines up to attempt 31-yard field goal. Holder Pagel takes snap and passes 14 yards to Waiters for touchdown at 9:30.

Sept. 23, 1990—Denver 34, Seattle 31, at Denver; Seahawks win toss. Loville returns kickoff 19 yards to Seahawks' 27. Seahawks drive to Broncos' 26, where Johnson misses 44-yard field goal wide right. Broncos take over and Elway completes series of passes to set up Treadwell's 25-yard field goal at 9:14.

Sept. 30, 1990—Tampa Bay 23, Minnesota 20, at Minnesota; Vikings win toss. Vikings drive to Buccaneers' 31; Igwebuike's 48-yard field goal attempt wide left. Buccaneers drive to Vikings' 43 and punt. Gannon's pass is intercepted at Vikings' 26 by Wayne Haddix. Buccaneers drive to Vikings' 19 to set up Christie's 36-yard field goal at 9:11.

Oct. 7, 1990—Cincinnati 34, Los Angeles Rams 31, at Anaheim; Rams win toss. Berry returns kickoff to Rams' 21. After 3 plays, English punts and Green downs ball at Bengals' 25. After 3 plays, Johnson punts and Sutton downs ball at Rams' 29-yard line. After 3 plays, English punts and Price signals fair catch at Bengals' 47. Esiason completes series of passes to 26-yard line to set up Breech's 44-yard field goal at 11:56.

Nov. 4, 1990—Washington 41, Detroit 38, at Detroit; Redskins win toss. Howard downs kickoff on Redskins' 15. After 3 plays, Mojsiejenko punts to Redskins' 45. After 3 plays, Arnold punts to Redskins' 10. Rutledge completes series of passes to set up

Lohmiller's 34-yard field goal at 9:10.

Nov. 18, 1990—Chicago 16, Denver 13, at Denver; Broncos win toss. Ezor returns kickoff to Broncos' 12. Both teams have ball twice and have to punt after each possession. Broncos punt after third possession of overtime and Bailey returns 20 yards to Broncos' 34. Harbaugh completes 10-yard pass to Thornton to set up Butler's 44-yard field goal at 13:14.

Nov. 25, 1990—Seattle 13, San Diego 10, at San Diego; Chargers win toss. Lewis returns kickoff to Chargers' 22. After 2 plays, Cox fumbles and ball is recovered by Porter at Chargers' 23. After two plays, Johnson kicks 40-yard field goal at 3:01.

Dec. 2, 1990—Chicago 23, Detroit 17, at Chicago; Lions win toss. Gray returns kickoff to Lions' 35. After 10 plays, Murray misses 35-yard field goal. Bears take possession at Chicago 20. Harbaugh completes 50-yard game-winning pass to Anderson at 10:57.

Dec. 2, 1990—Seattle 13, Houston 10, at Seattle; Seahawks win toss. Warren returns kickoff to Seahawks' 13. After 5 plays, Donnelly punts to Oilers' 23-yard line. Ford's fumble recovered by Wyman. Seahawks take possession at Oilers' 27. After 2 plays, Johnson kicks 42-yard field goal at 4:25.

Dec. 9, 1990—Miami 23, Philadelphia 20, at Miami; Eagles win toss. After 11 plays, Feagles punts to Dolphins' 26. After 6 plays, Roby punts to Eagles' 14 and Harris returns to 25. After 3 plays, Feagles punts to Dolphins' 43. Marino completes series of passes to Eagles' 22. Stoyanovich kicks 39-yard field goal at 12:32.

Dec. 9, 1990—San Francisco 20, Cincinnati 17, at Cincinnati; 49ers win toss. Carter returns kickoff to 49ers' 19. After 10 plays, Cofer kicks 23-yard field goal at 6:12.

* **Sept. 23, 1991—Chicago 19, New York Jets 13,** at Chicago; Jets win toss. Mathis returns kickoff seven yards to New York's 12. Jets drive to New York 26; Bailey returns punt to Chicago 39. Bears drive to Jets' 44-yard line and punt into the end zone. Jets drive to Bears' 11 where Leahy's 28-yard field goal attempt is wide left. Bears drive from 20 to Jets' 1 where Harbaugh runs for touchdown at 14:42.

Oct. 13, 1991—Los Angeles Raiders 23, Seattle 20, at Seattle; Seahawks win toss. Seahawks begin on 20. After 5 plays, Tuten punts and Brown signals fair catch at Raiders' 24. After 3 plays, Gossett punts and Land downs ball at Seattle 9. After 1 play, Lott intercepts at Seahawks' 19 to set up Jaeger's game-winning 37-yard field goal at 6:37.

Oct. 20, 1991—Cleveland 30, San Diego 24, at San Diego; Chargers win toss. After kickoff, Chargers drive to Browns' 45 and punt to Browns' 6 where Hendrickson downs ball. Browns drive to 38 and punt; Taylor fair catches on Chargers' 14. After 3 plays, Brandon intercepts at Chargers' 30 and scores at 5:58.

Oct. 20, 1991—New England 26, Minnesota 23, at New England; Patriots win toss. Martin returns kickoff 18 yards to New England 22. Patriots drive to Minnesota 19. Staurovsky's 36-yard field goal attempt is wide left. Minnesota drives to the 50 where Newsome punts into end zone. On first play, McMillian intercepts at the 40 for Minnesota. After 2 plays, Marion causes Jordan fumble and Pool recovers at New England 20. New England drives to Minnesota 24 where Staurovsky kicks 42-yard field goal as time expires.

Nov. 3, 1991—New York Jets 19, Green Bay 16, at New York; Packers win toss. Thompson returns kickoff 30 yards to Packers' 39. Green Bay drives to New York 24 where Jacke's 42-yard field-goal attempt is wide right. Jets drive to 50. Aguiar's punt is fumbled by Sikahema and recovered by New York at Packers' 23. After 2 plays, Leahy kicks 37-yard field goal at 9:40.

Nov. 3, 1991—Washington 16, Houston 13, at Washington; Redskins win toss. Mitchell returns kickoff 9 yards to Washington 14. After 4 plays, Goodburn punts and Givins returns to Houston 31. After 1 play, Moon's pass is intercepted by Green at Oilers' 35. After 3 plays, Lohmiller kicks 41-yard field goal at 4:01.

Nov. 10, 1991—Houston 26, Dallas 23, at Houston; Oilers win toss. Pinkett returns kickoff 20 yards to Houston 24. After 6 plays, Montgomery punts and Martin returns to Dallas 24. Cowboys drive to Oilers' 24 where Smith fumbles and McDowell recovers at Oilers' 15. Houston drives to Dallas 5 where Del Greco kicks 23-yard field goal at 14:31.

Nov. 10, 1991—Pittsburgh 33, Cincinnati 27, at Cincinnati; Steelers wins toss. Woodson downs kickoff for touchback. After 3 plays, Stryzinski punts and Barber returns 7 yards to Cincinnati 38. Bengals drive to Pittsburgh 37 where Woods fumbles and Lloyd returns recovery to Cincinnati 44. After 2 plays, O'Donnell passes to Green for 26-yard touchdown at 6:32.

#**Nov. 24, 1991—Atlanta 23, New Orleans 20,** at New Orleans; Falcons wins toss. Falcons begin at 20. After 3 plays, Fulhage punts and Fenerty signals fair catch at New Orleans 43. After 3 plays, Barnhardt punts and Thompson downs ball at Atlanta 23. After 3 plays, Fulhage punts and Fenerty fair catches at New Orleans 25. Saints drive to Atlanta 38 where Andersen misses 55-yard field-goal attempt. After 1 play, Rozier fumbles and Martin recovers on 50. Saints drive to Atlanta 38 where Barnhardt punts to Falcons' 2. Atlanta drives to New Orleans 33 where Johnson kicks 50-yard field goal at 13:03.

Nov. 24, 1991—Miami 16, Chicago 13, at Chicago; Dolphins wins toss. Butler kicks to Miami 20 where Paige returns kickoff 15 yards to 35. Miami drives to Chicago 9 where Stoyanovich kicks 27-yard field goal at 4:11.

Dec. 8, 1991—Buffalo 30, Los Angeles Raiders 27, at Los Angeles; Raiders win toss. Daluiso kicks into end zone for touchback. On third play, Kelso intercepts for Buffalo and returns ball to Bills' 36. Bills drive to Los Angeles 24 where Norwood kicks 42-yard field goal at 2:34.

Dec. 8, 1991—Kansas City 20, San Diego 17, at Kansas City; Chiefs win toss. Carney kicks to Kansas City 10 where Stradford returns 23 yards to 33. After 3 plays, Barker punts to San Diego 4. Chargers drive to 40 where Kidd punts 60 yards into end zone for touchback. Kansas City drives to San Diego 39 where Barker punts 38 yards to 1. After 3 plays, Kidd punts 41 yards to San Diego 42 where Stradford returns 12 yards to 30. Chiefs drive to San Diego 1 where Lowery kicks 18-yard field goal at 11:26.

Dec. 8, 1991—New England 23, Indianapolis 17, at New England; Colts wins toss. Baumann kicks off to Indianapolis 2 where Martin returns 23 yards to 25. After 3 downs, Stark punts to New England 17 where Henderson returns 8 yards to 25. New England drives to 50 where McCarthy punts and Prior signals fair catch at Indianapolis 15. After 3 plays, Stark punts to New England 40 where Henderson returns 7 yards to 47. After 2 plays, Millen passes to Timpson for 45-yard touchdown at 8:55.

Dec. 22, 1991—Detroit 17, Buffalo 14, at Buffalo; Lions wins toss. Daluiso kicks off to Detroit 20 where Dozier returns 15 yards to Lions 35. Lions drive to Bills' 3 where Murray kicks 21-yard field goal at 4:23.

Dec. 22, 1991—New York Jets 23, Miami 20, at Miami; Jets win toss. Aguiar kicks to Miami's 30 where Logan returns 3 yards to the 33. After 4 downs, Stoyanovich punts to Jets' 15 where Baty returns 8 yards to 23. Jets drive to Miami 12 where Allegre kicks 30-yard field goal at 6:33.

Sept. 6, 1992—Minnesota 23, Green Bay 20, at Green Bay; Vikings win toss. Nelson returns kickoff 14 yards to the Minnesota 23. After 5 plays, Newsome punts 49 yards to Green Bay 21 where Brooks returns 12 yards to the 33. After 2 plays, Glenn intercepts pass at the Vikings' 48. On first play, Allen fumbles and Billups recovers at Green Bay 35. After 3 plays, McJulien punts 33 yards to Vikings' 35. Vikings drive to Minnesota 48; Newsome punts 52 yards for touchback. After 3 plays, McJulien punts and Parker returns 10 yards to Green Bay 48. Vikings drive to Packers' 9 where Reveiz kicks 26-yard field goal at 10:20.

Sept. 13, 1992—Cincinnati 24, Los Angeles Raiders 21, at Cincinnati; Raiders win toss. Land returns kickoff 13 yards but fumbles at Los Angeles's 20; ball recovered by Bengals' Bennett at Raiders' 21. After 1 play, Breech kicks 34-yard field goal at

1:01.

Sept. 20, 1992—Houston 23, Kansas City 20, at Houston; Chiefs win toss. Carter returns kickoff 25 yards to Kansas City 28. On third play of drive, Birden fumbles at Kansas City 34; ball recovered by Houston's D. Smith at Chiefs' 23. After one play, Del Greco kicks 39-yard field goal at 1:55.

Oct. 11, 1992—Indianapolis 6, New York Jets 3, at Indianapolis; Colts win toss. Verdin returns kickoff 33 yards to Colts' 36. Colts drive to Jets' 30 where Biasucci kicks 47-yard field goal at 3:01.

#**Nov. 8, 1992—Cincinnati 31, Chicago 28,** at Chicago; Bears win toss. Lewis returns kickoff 22 yards to Chicago's 29. Bears drive to Chicago's 46 where Gardocki punts; fair catch by Wright at the Cincinnati 17. Bengals drive to Bears' 18 where Breech kicks 36-yard field goal at 8:39.

Nov. 15, 1992—New England 37, Indianapolis 34, at Indianapolis; Colts win toss. Verdin returns kickoff 10 yards to Colts' 20; holding penalty brings ball back to Colts' 10. After two plays, Henderson intercepts pass at Colts' 38 and returns it 9 yards to the 29. In three plays, Patriots drive to 1 where Baumann kicks 18-yard field goal at 3:25.

Nov. 29, 1992—Indianapolis 16, Buffalo 13, at Indianapolis; Colts win toss. Verdin returns kickoff 24 yards to Colts' 22. Colts drive to Buffalo 22 where Biasucci kicks 40-yard field goal at 3:51.

* **Nov. 30, 1992—Seattle 16, Denver 13,** at Seattle; Seahawks win toss. Daluiso kicks through end zone for touchback. After three plays, Tuten punts 53 yards to Denver 18 where Marshall returns for no gain. After three plays, Rodriguez punts 29 yards to Seattle 45 where Warren signals fair catch. Seahawks drive to Denver 15 where Kasay's 33-yard field goal attempt misses. Broncos take over at Denver 20. After three plays, Rodriguez punts 43 yards to Seattle 38 where Warren signals for fair catch. After four plays, Tuten punts 39 yards to Denver 4 where Daniels downs punt. After three plays, Rodriguez punts 46 yards to Denver 48 where Warren returns 10 yards to the 38. Seahawks drive to Denver 14 where Kasay kicks 32-yard field goal at 11:10.

Dec. 13, 1992—Philadelphia 20, Seattle 17, at Seattle; Eagles win toss. Sydner returns kick 12 yards to Eagles' 16; illegal block penalty brings ball back to 8. Eagles drive to Philadelphia 45 where Feagles punts for a touchback. After 6 plays, Tuten punts 45 yards to Philadelphia 22 where Sydner returns 7 yards to 29. After 6 plays, Feagles punts 44 yards to Seattle 26 where Warren returns 5 yards to 31. After 5 plays, Tuten punts 32 yards to Philadelphia 20 where Sydner signals for fair catch. Eagles drive to Seattle 27 where Ruzek kicks 44-yard field goal with no time remaining.

Dec. 27, 1992—Miami 16, New England 13, at New England; Patriots win toss. Lockwood returns kickoff 15 yards to Patriots' 21. After three plays, McCarthy punts 39 yards to Miami 33 where Miller returns 2 yards to the 35. Miami drives to New England 18 where Stoyanovich kicks 35-yard field goal at 8:17.

Sept. 12, 1993—Detroit 19, New England 16, at New England; Patriots win toss. Patriots begin at 20. After 3 plays, Saxon punts 42 yards to Detroit 29 where Gray returns 12 yards to the 41. After 3 plays, Arnold punts 41 yards to New England 12 where Brown returns 16 yards to the 28. Patriots drive to Detroit 44 where Saxon punts into the end zone for a touchback. Detroit drives to New England 20 where Hanson kicks 38-yard field goal at 11:04.

Nov. 7, 1993—Buffalo 13, New England 10, at New England; Patriots win toss. T. Brown returns kickoff 27 yards to Patriots 30. Patriots drive to Buffalo 48 where Bills take over on downs. Bills drive to New England 25 where Metzelaars fumbles, and C. Brown recovers. After 3 plays, Saxon punts 46 yards to Buffalo 24 where Copeland returns 11 yards to the 35. Bills drive to New England 14 where Christie kicks 32-yard field goal at 9:22.

Dec. 19, 1993—Phoenix 30, Seattle 27, at Seattle; Cardinals win toss. Bailey returns kickoff 14 yards to Cardinals 20. Cardinals drive to Seattle 23 where Davis kicks 41-yard field goal at 6:45.

Jan. 2, 1994—Dallas 16, New York Giants 13, at New York; Giants win toss. Meggett returns kickoff 19 yards to Giants 19. After 6 plays, Horan punts 45 yards to Cowboys 25 where Widmer downs punt. Cowboys drive to Giants' 23 where Murray kicks 41-yard field goal at 10:44.

Jan. 2, 1994—New England 33, Miami 27, at New England; Dolphins win toss. McDuffie returns kickoff 21 yards to Miami 27. After 3 plays, Hatcher punts 43 yards to New England 29 where Harris returns 6 yards to the 35. After 2 plays, Brown intercepts pass from Bledsoe and returns 3 yards to Miami 49. After 3 plays, Hatcher punts 37 yards to New England 14 where Harris returns 18 yards to the 32. After 2 plays, Bledsoe passes 36 yards to Timpson for touchdown at 4:44.

Jan. 2, 1994—Los Angeles Raiders 33, Denver 30, at Los Angeles; Broncos win toss. Delpino returns kickoff 12 yards to Denver 25. Broncos drive to Los Angeles 22 where Elam's 40-yard field goal attempt is wide left. Raiders drive to Denver 29 where Jaeger kicks 47-yard field goal at 7:10.

* **Jan. 3, 1994—Philadelphia 37, San Francisco 34,** at San Francisco; 49ers win toss. Walker returns kickoff, 19 yards to San Francisco 27. 49ers drive to Philadelphia 14 where Cofer misses 32-yard field goal. Eagles start at their 20-yard line, and, after 3 plays, Feagles punts 48 yards to San Francisco 36 where Carter fumbles and 49ers recover. After 7 plays, Wilmsmeyer punts 57 yards to Philadelphia 6 where Sikahema returns 16 yards to the 22. Eagles drive to San Francisco 10 where Ruzek kicks 28-yard field goal with no time remaining.

Sept. 4, 1994—Detroit 31, Atlanta 28, at Detroit; Falcons win toss. Falcons start at their own 16 after holding penalty on kickoff. After 3 plays, Alexander punts 41 yards to Detroit 39 where Clay returns 12 yards to Atlanta 49. Detroit drives to Atlanta 20 where Hanson kicks 37-yard field goal at 5:14.

Sept. 11, 1994—New York Jets 25, Denver 22, at New York; Jets win toss. Murrell returns kickoff 24 yards to New York 33. Jets drive to Denver 22 where Lowery kicks 39-yard field goal at 3:57.

* **Sept. 19, 1994—Detroit 20, Dallas 17,** at Dallas; Lions win toss. Gray returns kickoff 24 yards to Detroit 32. Lions drive to Dallas 34 where Hanson's 51-yard field-goal attempt is blocked by Lett. Cowboys take possession at Dallas 42. Cowboys drive to Detroit 37 where Kennard fumbles and Swilling recovers. Lions take possession at Detroit 45. After 6 plays, Montgomery punts 31 yards to Dallas 16. Cowboys drive to Dallas 49 where Aikman fumbles and Thomas recovers at Dallas 43. Lions drive to Dallas 26 where Hanson kicks 44-yard field goal at 14:33.

Oct. 16, 1994—Arizona 19, Washington 16, at Washington; Redskins win toss. Mitchell returns kickoff 27 yards to Washington 41. Redskins drive to Arizona 34 where Lohmiller's 51-yard field-goal attempt is blocked by Joyner and recovered by Williams who returns it to the Washington 37. After 5 plays, Peterson's 45-yard field-goal attempt is wide right. Redskins take possession at the Washington 36. After 3 plays, Roby punts 36 yards to the Arizona 37 where Robinson returns 3 yards to the 40. After 3 plays, Feagles punts 51 yards for a touchback. After 1 play, Shuler's pass is intercepted by Hoage who returns it to the Washington 12. Peterson kicks 29-yard field goal at 10:00.

Oct. 16, 1994—Miami 20, Los Angeles Raiders 17, at Miami; Dolphins win toss. McDuffie returns kickoff 19 yards to Miami 23. Dolphins drive to Los Angeles 12 where Stoyanovich kicks 29-yard field goal at 5:46.

#**Oct. 20, 1994—Minnesota 13, Green Bay 10,** at Minnesota; Vikings win toss. Ismail returns kickoff 22 yards to Minnesota 29. Vikings drive to Green Bay 9 where Fuad Reveiz kicks 27-yard field goal at 4:26.

Oct. 30, 1994—Detroit 28, New York Giants 25, at New York; Giants win toss. Lewis returns kickoff 16 yards to New York 27. After 3 plays, Horan punts 42 yards to Detroit 24 where Gray calls for fair catch. Detroit drives to New York 6 where Hanson kicks 24-yard field goal at 6:43.

#**Oct. 30, 1994—Arizona 20, Pittsburgh 17,** at Arizona; Steelers win toss. Johnson returns kickoff 24 yards to Pittsburgh 30 where he fumbles and Arizona's Merritt recovers at Pittsburgh 32. After 3 plays, Davis kicks 51-yard field goal at 1:40.

Nov. 6, 1994—Cincinnati 20, Seattle 17, at Seattle; Seahawks win toss. Warren returns kickoff 32 yards to Seattle 33. After 3 plays, Tuten punts 37 yards to Cincinnati 28 where Sawyer calls for fair catch. After 3 plays, Johnson punts 64 yards to Seattle 2 where Truitt downs ball. Seahawks drive to Seattle 38 where Tuten punts 50 yards to Cincinnati 12 and Sawyer returns 5 yards to 17. Blake passes to Scott for 76 yards to Seattle 7. Pelfrey kicks 26-yard field goal at 8:14.

Nov. 6, 1994—Pittsburgh 12, Houston 9, at Houston; Steelers win toss. Stone returns kickoff 15 yards to Pittsburgh 28. After 3 plays, Royals punts 53 yards to Houston 13 where Givins downs ball. After 3 plays, Camarillo punts 57 yards to Pittsburgh 31 where Woodson returns 20 yards to Houston 49. After 3 plays, Royals punts 43 yards to Houston 15 where Coleman returns 3 yards to 18. After 5 plays, Camarillo punts 57 yards to Pittsburgh 12 where Hastings returns 12 yards to 24. Steelers drive to Houston 41 where Royals punts 29 yards to Houston 12, and Coleman calls for fair catch. Brown fumbles on first play and Jones recovers at Houston 22. After 1 play, Anderson kicks 40-yard field goal at 11:24.

Nov. 13, 1994—New England 26, Minnesota 20, at New England; Patriots win toss. Thompson returns kickoff 27 yards to New England 33. Patriots drive to Minnesota 14 where Bledsoe passes 14 yards to Turner for touchdown at 4:10.

Nov. 20, 1994—Pittsburgh 16, Miami 13, at Pittsburgh; Steelers win toss. Stone returns kickoff 15 yards to Pittsburgh 16. Steelers drive to Miami 39 where they lose possession on downs. Dolphins drive to Pittsburgh 47 where Arnold punts 35 yards to Pittsburgh 12 and Oliver downs ball. Steelers drive to Miami 21 where Anderson kicks 39-yard field goal at 10:19.

Nov. 27, 1994—Chicago 19, Arizona 16, at Arizona; Cardinals win toss. Levy returns kickoff 31 yards to Arizona 45. After 5 plays, Feagles punts 38 yards to the end zone for a touchback. Bears drive to Arizona 10 where Butler kicks 27-yard field goal at 8:11.

Nov. 27, 1994—Tampa Bay 20, Minnesota 17, at Minnesota; Buccaneers win toss. Harris returns kickoff 12 yards to Tampa Bay 38. After 6 plays, Stryzinski punts 40 yards to Minnesota 4 where Guliford muffs punt and Buccaneers' Brady recovers. Husted kicks 22-yard field goal at 2:08.

Dec. 1, 1994—Minnesota 33, Chicago 27, at Minnesota; Bears win toss. Lewis returns kickoff 23 yards to Chicago 33. Bears drive to Minnesota 22 where Butler's 40-yard field goal attempt is wide left. After 1 play, Moon passes 65 yards to Carter for touchdown at 5:46.

Dec. 4, 1994—Denver 20, Kansas City 17, at Kansas City; Broncos win toss. Milburn returns kickoff 24 yards to Denver 29. After 3 plays, Millen fumbles and Phillips recovers at Denver 35. After 4 plays, Allen fumbles and Smith recovers at Denver 27. After 6 plays, Rouen punts 45 yards to Kansas City 25 where Hughes calls for fair catch. After 3 plays, Aguiar punts 33 yards to Denver 42 where Chiefs down ball. Broncos drive to Kansas City 17 where Elam kicks 34-yard field goal at 12:12.

Sept. 3, 1995—Cincinnati 24, Indianapolis 21, at Indianapolis; Bengals win toss. Dunn returns kickoff 15 yards to Bengals' 17. Cincinnati drives to Indianapolis 29 where Pelfrey kicks 47-yard field goal at 2:36.

Sept. 3, 1995—Atlanta 23, Carolina 20, at Atlanta; Panthers win toss. Baldwin downs kickoff for touchback. Panthers drive to Carolina 42 where Reich fumbles and ball is recovered by Archambeau at Carolina 31. Falcons drive to Panthers' 16 where Andersen kicks 35-yard field goal at 6:17.

Sept. 10, 1995—Indianapolis 27, New York Jets 24, at New York; Jets win toss. Carter downs kickoff for touchback. Jets punt downed at Colts' 37. Colts drive to Jets' 35 where Cofer kicks 52-yard field goal at 4:27.

Sept. 10, 1995—Kansas City 20, New York Giants 17, at Kansas City; Chiefs win toss. Vanover returns kickoff 30 yards to Chiefs' 28. Aguiar punts to Giants' 3. Horan punts to Chiefs' 49. Chiefs drive to Giants' 6 where Elliott kicks 23-yard field goal at 7:49.

Sept. 17, 1995—Kansas City 23, Oakland 17, at Kansas City; Chiefs win toss. Vanover returns kickoff 28 yards to Chiefs' 41. M. Allen fumbles, ball recovered by Robbins at Raiders' 38. Hasty intercepts pass at Chiefs' 36 and returns it 64 yards for touchdown at 4:27.

Sept. 17, 1995—Atlanta 27, New Orleans 24, at Atlanta; Saints win toss. Hughes returns kickoff 21 yards to Saints' 17. Metcalf returns Wilmsmeyer's punt 18 yards to Saints' 39. Stryzinski punts, fair catch by Hughes at Saints' 14. Wilmsmeyer punt downed at Falcons' 6. Falcons drive to Saints' 3 where Andersen kicks 21-yard field goal at 7:58.

#**Sept. 17, 1995—Dallas 23, Minnesota 17,** at Minnesota; Cowboys win toss. K. Williams returns kickoff 23 yards to Cowboys' 27. E. Smith scores on 31-yard run at 2:26.

Oct. 8, 1995—Indianapolis 27, Miami 24, at Miami; Colts win toss. Warren returns kickoff 25 yards to Colts' 33. Colts drive to Dolphins' 10 where Blanchard kicks 27-yard field goal at 4:58.

Oct. 8, 1995—New York Giants 27, Arizona 21, at New York; Cardinals win toss. Terry returns kickoff 20 yards to Cardinals' 23. Hamilton recovers Krieg's fumble at Cardinals' 36. Lynch recovers Brown's fumble at Cardinals' 38. Armstead intercepts pass at Giants' 42 and returns it 58 yards for touchdown at 4:05.

Oct. 8, 1995—Minnesota 23, Houston 17, at Minnesota; Vikings win toss. Palmer returns kickoff 10 yards to Vikings' 15. Saxon's punt downed at Oilers' 8. Washington intercepts pass at Vikings' 47 and returns it 25 yards to Oilers' 28. R. Smith scores on 20-yard run at 7:10.

Oct. 8, 1995—Philadelphia 37, Washington 34, at Philadelphia; Redskins win toss. Redskins take possession at their 20 after touchback. Turk punt out of bounds at Eagles' 9. Eagles drive to Redskins' 18 where Anderson kicks 35-yard field goal at 10:06.

* **Oct. 9, 1995—Kansas City 29, San Diego 23,** at Kansas City; Chargers win toss. Coleman returns kickoff 24 yards to Chargers' 28. Vanover makes fair catch of Bennett's punt at Chiefs' 15. Coleman makes fair catch of Aguiar's punt at Chargers' 43. Vanover returns Bennett's punt 86 yards for a touchdown at 7:27.

Oct. 15, 1995—Tampa Bay 20, Minnesota 17, at Tampa Bay; Buccaneers win toss. Edmonds returns kickoff 19 yards to Buccaneers' 22. A. Lee returns Roby's punt to Vikings' 48. Vikings drive to Tampa Bays' 35 where Reveiz's 53-yard field-goal attempt is wide right. Buccaneers take over at own 43 and drive to Vikings' 33 where Husted kicks 51-yard field goal at 6:23.

Oct. 22, 1995—Washington 36, Detroit 30, at Washington; Redskins win toss. B. Mitchell returns kickoff 16 yards to Redskins' 27. Turk's punt downed at Lions' 4. D. Green intercepts S. Mitchell's pass and returns it 7 yards for touchdown at 3:41.

Oct. 29, 1995—Carolina 20, New England 17, at New England; Panthers win toss. Baldwin returns kickoff 22 yards to Panthers' 25. Meggett makes fair catch of Barnhardt's punt at Patriots' 9. Guliford returns O'Neill's punt 9 yards to Patriots' 32. Panthers drive to Patriots' 12 where Kasay kicks 29-yard field goal at 7:08.

Oct. 29, 1995—Cleveland 29, Cincinnati 26, at Cincinnati; Browns win toss. Hunter returns kickoff 31 yards to Browns' 31. Bieniemy returns Tupa's punt 9 yards to Bengals' 37. McCardell makes fair catch of Johnson's punt at Browns' 12. Bieniemy returns Tupa's punt 0 yards to Bengals' 38. Hall intercepts Blake's pass and returns it 5 yards to Bengals' 45. Browns drive to Bengals' 11 where Stover kicks 28-yard field goal at 6:30.

Oct. 29, 1995—Arizona 20, Seattle 14, at Arizona; Cardinals win toss. Dowdell returns kickoff 16 yards to Cardinals' 25. Cardinals drive to Seahawks' 10 where G. Davis' 27-yard field goal attempt is blocked. L. Lynch intercepts Friesz's pass at Cardinals' 28 and returns it 72 yards for a touchdown at 11:16.

Nov. 5, 1995—Pittsburgh 37, Chicago 34, at Chicago; Bears win toss. Timpson returns kickoff 23 yards to Bears' 33. Hastings returns Sauerbrun's punt 2 yards to Steelers' 31. Steelers drive to Bears' 6 where N. Johnson kicks 24-yard field goal at 8:19.

Nov. 12, 1995—Minnesota 30, Arizona 24, at Arizona; Vikings win toss. A. Lee returns kickoff 20 yards to Vikings' 25. Moon throws 50-yard touchdown pass to Ismail at 2:16.

Nov. 26, 1995—Arizona 40, Atlanta 37, at Arizona; Falcons win toss. J. Anderson returns kickoff 20 yards to Falcons' 20. Stryzinski fumbles punt snap. Recovered by England at Falcons' 10 where G. Davis kicks 28-yard field goal at 1:43.

#**Dec. 10, 1995—Tampa Bay 13, Green Bay 10,** at Tampa Bay; Buccaneers win toss. Edmonds returns kickoff 24 yards to Buccaneers' 23. Tampa Bay drives to Packers' 29 where Husted kicks 47-yard field goal at 3:46.

#**Sept. 1, 1996—Buffalo 23, New York Giants 20,** at New York; Bills win toss. Daluiso kick is a touchback. Bills drive to Buffalo 46. Toomer returns Mohr's punt to Giants' 16. Dave Brown's fumble recovered by Spielman at Giants' 33. Bills drive to Giants' 16 where Christie kicks 34-yard field goal at 9:08.

Sept. 22, 1996—New England 28, Jacksonville 25, at New England; Patriots win toss. T. Brown returns kickoff 18 yards to Patriots' 29. Patriots drive to Jaguars' 22 where Vinatieri kicks 40-yard field goal at 2:36.

Sept. 29, 1996—Arizona 31, St. Louis 28, at Arizona; Cardinals win toss. Lohmiller kick is a touchback. Cardinals drive to Rams' 7 where G. Davis kicks 24-yard field goal at 1:54.

Oct. 6, 1996—Buffalo 16, Indianapolis 13, at Buffalo; Colts win toss. Christie kick is a touchback. Colts drive to Indianapolis 32. Burris returns Gardocki's punt to Bills' 35. Bills drive to Colts' 48. Mohr punts out of bounds at Colts' 14. Colts drive to Indianapolis 9. Burris returns Gardocki's punt to Colts' 48. Bills drive to Colts' 22 where Christie kicks 39-yard field goal at 9:22.

#**Oct. 6, 1996—Houston 30, Cincinnati 27,** at Cincinnati; Bengals win toss. Dunn returns kickoff 23 yards to Bengals' 34. Bengals drive to Cincinnati 36. Floyd returns L. Johnson's punt to Oilers' 18. Oilers drive to Bengals' 31 where Del Greco kicks 49-yard field goal at 7:07.

* **Oct. 14, 1996—Green Bay 23, San Francisco 20,** at Green Bay; 49ers win toss. D. Carter returns kickoff 23 yards to 49ers' 22. 49ers' drive to San Francisco 25. Howard makes fair catch of Thompson's punt at Packers' 44. Packers drive to 49ers' 35 where Jacke kicks 53-yard field goal at 3:41.

Oct. 27, 1996—Baltimore 37, St. Louis 31, at Baltimore; Rams win toss. J. Thomas returns kickoff 17 yard to Rams' 17. Rams drive to Ravens' 15. F. Miller fumble in field goal formation recovered by S. Moore at Ravens' 17. Ravens drive to Baltimore 49 and turn ball over on downs. Rams drive to Ravens' 40 and turn ball over on downs. Testaverde throws 22-yard scoring pass to M. Jackson at 14:50.

Nov. 10, 1996—Dallas 20, San Francisco 17, at San Francisco; Cowboys win toss. H. Walker returns kickoff 10 yards to Cowboys' 23. Cowboys drive to 49ers' 11 where Boniol kicks 29-yard field goal at 6:17.

Nov. 10, 1996—Arizona 37, Washington 34, at Washington; Cardinals win toss. Blanton's kickoff is a touchback. Cardinals drive to Redskins' 15 where Butler misses 32-yard field goal. Redskins drive to Cardinals' 43 where Turk punts for touchback. L. Johnson fumble returned by Morrison to Cardinals' 27. Redskins drive to Cardinals' 31 where Blanton misses 48-yard field goal. Cardinals drive to Redskins' 15 where Butler kicks 32-yard field goal at 14:27.

Nov. 10, 1996—Tampa Bay 20, Oakland 17, at Tampa Bay; Buccaneers win toss. M. Marshall returns kickoff 15 yards to Bucs' 17. Bucs drive to Tampa Bay 36. T. Brown returns Barnhardt's punt four yards to Raiders' 22. Raiders drive to Oakland 25. M. Marshall returns Gossett's punt nine yards to Bucs' 39. Bucs drive to Raiders' 4 where Husted kicks 23-yard field goal at 11:56.

#**Nov. 17, 1996—Minnesota 16, Oakland 13,** at Oakland; Raiders win toss. Kaufman returns kickoff 32 yards to Raiders' 27. Raiders drive to Oakland 46 where Gossett punts to Vikings' 17. Vikings drive to Raiders' 12 where Sisson kicks 31-yard field goal at 11:53.

Nov. 24, 1996—Jacksonville 28, Baltimore 25, at Baltimore; Jaguars win toss. Jordon returns kickoff 16 yards to Jaguars' 30. Jaguars drive to Jacksonville 37. Barker's punt is downed at Ravens' 6. Ravens drive to Jaguars' 37 where Pritchett recovers Byner's fumble. Jaguars drive to Ravens' 15 where Hollis kicks 34-yard field goal at 9:06.

Nov. 24, 1996—San Francisco 19, Washington 16, at Washington; 49ers win toss. D. Carter returns kickoff 20 yards to 49ers' 32. 49ers drive to Redskins' 20 where Wilkins kicks 38-yard field goal at 3:24.

Dec. 1, 1996—Indianapolis 13, Buffalo 10, at Indianapolis; Bills win toss. Moulds returns kickoff 26 yards to Bills' 25. Bills drive to Buffalo 49. Stock returns Mohr's punt one yard to Colts' 16. Colts drive to Bills' 32 where Blanchard kicks 49-yard field goal at 10:46.

Aug. 31, 1997—Tennessee 24, Oakland 21, at Tennessee; Oilers win toss. Gray returns kickoff 32 yards to Tennessee 33. Oilers drive to Tennessee 38. Roby's punt is downed at the Oakland 33. Raiders drive to Oakland 32. Gray returns Araguz punt to Tennessee 35. Oilers drive to Oakland 15 where Del Greco kicks 33-yard field goal at 6:57.

Sept. 7, 1997—Miami 16, Tennessee 13, at Miami; Dolphins win toss. Spikes returns kickoff 48 yards to Tennessee 45. Dolphins drive to Tennessee 11 where Mare kicks 29-yard field goal at 2:15.

#**Sept. 7, 1997— Arizona 25, Dallas 22**, at Arizona; Cowboys win toss. Walker returns kickoff 21 yards to Dallas 25. Cowboys drive to Arizona 43. Gowin punts 43 yards for a touchback. Cardinals drive to Dallas 44. Graham fumbles. Cowboys drive to Arizona 42. Williams fumbles. Cardinals drive to Dallas 3 where Butler kicks 20-yard field goal at 8:30.

Sept. 14, 1997—Washington 19, Arizona 13, at Washington; Cardinals win toss. K. Williams returns kickoff 27 yards to Arizona 34. Cardinals drive to Arizona 40. McElroy fumbles. Redskins drive to Arizona 40. Westbrook catches 40-yard touchdown pass from Frerotte at 1:36.

#**Sept. 14, 1997—New England 27, New York Jets 24**, at New England; Patriots win toss. Hall's kickoff is a touchback. Patriots drive to New England 15. Bledsoe pass intercepted by O. Smith. Jets drive to New York 46. Hansen punts 47 yards. Meggett returns to New England 21. Patriots drive to New York 17 where Vinatieri kicks 34-yard field goal at 8:03.

Sept. 28, 1997—Kansas City 20, Seattle 17, at Kansas City; Seahawks win toss. Broussard returns kickoff 12 yards to Seattle 14. Seahawks drive to Seattle 17. Vanover returns Tuten punt 8 yards to Kansas City 26. Chiefs drive to Seattle 44. Aguiar punt downed at Seattle 11. Seahawks drive to Seattle 26. Moon pass intercepted by Woods and returned 13 yards to 50. Chiefs drive to Seattle 23 where Stoyanovich kicks 41-yard field goal at 13:04.

Oct. 19, 1997—Philadelphia 13, Arizona 10, at Philadelphia; Cardinals win toss. K. Williams returns kickoff 28 yards to Arizona 42. Cardinals drive to Philadelphia 48. Feagles punts 48 yards for touchback. Eagles drive to Arizona 7 where Boniol kicks 24-yard field goal at 4:02.

Oct. 19, 1997—New York Giants 26, Detroit 20, at Detroit; Giants win toss. Pegram returns kickoff 16 yards to New York 18. Giants drive to New York 32. Calloway catches 68-yard touchdown pass from Kanell at 1:40.

Oct. 26, 1997—Denver 23, Buffalo 20, at Buffalo; Broncos win toss and elects to kickoff. Holmes returns kickoff 20 yards to Buffalo 25. Bills drive to Buffalo 23. Mohr punt downed at

Denver 40. Broncos drive to Buffalo 48. Rouen punt downed at Buffalo 1. Bills drive to Buffalo 20. Gordon returns Mohr punt to Denver 42. Broncos drive to Buffalo 15 where Elam kicks 33-yard field goal at 13:04.

Oct. 26, 1997—Pittsburgh 23, Jacksonville 17, at Pittsburgh; Steelers win toss. Coleman returns kickoff 23 yards to Pittsburgh 23. Steelers drive to Jacksonville 17. Bettis catches 17-yard touchdown pass from Stewart at 3:47.

* **Oct. 27, 1997—Chicago 36, Miami 33**, at Miami; Dolphins win toss. McPhail returns kickoff 23 yards to Miami 27. Dolphins drive to Miami 36. Kidd punts out of bounds at Chicago 10. Bears drive to the Chicago 39. Sauerbrun punt out of bounds at Miami 27. Reeves recovers Marino fumble at Miami 17. Bears drive to Miami 17 where Jaeger kicks 35-yard field goal at 9:25.

Nov. 2, 1997—New York Jets 19, Baltimore 16, at New York; Jets win toss. Stover's kickoff is a touchback. Jets drive to Baltimore 20 where Hall kicks 37-yard field goal at 4:58.

Nov. 16, 1997—Philadelphia 10, Baltimore 10, at Baltimore; Eagles win toss. Stover's kickoff is a touchback. Eagles drive to Philadelphia 19. Hutton punts 36 yards to Baltimore 45. Ravens drive to Baltimore 36 where Eagles take over on downs. Eagles drive to Baltimore 33 where Ravens take over on downs. Ravens drive to Baltimore 37. Montgomery punts 55 yards, and Solomon returns to Philadelphia 22. Eagles drive to Philadelphia 16. Hutton punts 41 yards, and Roe returns to Baltimore 46. Ravens drive to Philadelphia 35 where Stover's 53-yard field-goal attempt is no good. Eagles drive to Baltimore 22 where Boniol's 40-yard field-goal is no good as time expires.

Nov. 16, 1997—New Orleans 20, Seattle 17, at New Orleans; Seahawks win toss. Brien's kickoff is a touchback. Seahawks start at Seattle 20 where Moon's pass intercepted by Tubbs who returns 15 yards to Seattle 20. Saints Brien kicks 38-yard field goal at 17 seconds.

#**Nov. 23, 1997—New York Giants 7, Washington 7**, at Washington; Redskins win toss. Davis returns kickoff 28 yards to Washington 39. Redskins drive to Washington 36 where Hostetler's pass intercepted by Sehorn who returns minus–2 yards before lateralling to Wooten who returns 5 yards to New York 41. Giants drive to New York 26 where Maynard punts 37 yards to Washington 37. Redskins drive to New York 39 where Hostetler fumble is recovered by Harris at New York 40. Giants drive to New York 43 where Maynard punts 57 yards for a touchback. Washington drives to New York 41. Giants take over on downs at New York 40. Giants drive to Washington 36 where Daluiso's 54-yard field-goal attempt is no good. Redskins drive to Washington 45 where Hostetler's pass intercepted by Sparks at New York 49. Giants drive to Washington 36 where Maynard punts 36 yards for a touchback. Redskins drive to New York 36 where Blanton's 54-yard field-goal attempt is no good. Giants drive to New York 45 where Kanell's pass intercepted by Patton who laterals to Pounds who returns 11 yards to Washington 24 as time expires.

Nov. 30, 1997—Pittsburgh 26, Arizona 20, at Arizona; Cardinals win toss. K. Williams returns kickoff 11 yards to Arizona 23. Cardinals drive to Arizona 18 where Feagles punts 43 yards. Hawkins returns punt 9 yards to Pittsburgh 48. Steelers drive to Arizona 10 where Bettis scores on a 10-yard touchdown run at 5:34.

Dec. 13, 1997—Pittsburgh 24, New England 21, at New England; Steelers win toss. Coleman returns kickoff 19 yards to Pittsburgh 26. Steelers drive to New England 13 where Johnson kicks a 31-yard field goal at 4:43.

Sept. 6, 1998—San Francisco 36, New York Jets 30, at San Francisco; Jets win toss. Richey's kickoff is a touchback. Jets drive to New York 11. Gallery punts 48 yards. McQuarters returns to New York 43. 49ers drive to New York 44. Howard punts 23 yards to New York 21. Johnson calls fair catch. Jets drive to New York 47. Gallery's 49-yard punt downed at San Francisco 4. Hearst runs for a 96-yard touchdown at 4:08.

Sept. 13, 1998—Cincinnati 34, Detroit 28, at Detroit; Lions win toss. Johnson's kickoff is a touchback. Lions drive to Detroit 47 where Mitchell's pass is intercepted by Sawyer and returned for a 58-yard touchdown at 2:06.

Sept. 27, 1998—New Orleans 19, Indianapolis 13, at Indianapolis; Saints win toss. Gardocki's kickoff is returned by Ismail to New Orleans 28. Saints drive to New Orleans 30. Royals punts 64 yards. Poole returns to Indianapolis 12. Colts drive to Indianapolis 20. Gardocki punts 58 yards. Hastings returns to New Orleans 29. Saints drive to New Orleans 32. Royals punts 59 yards. Punt downed at Indianapolis 9. Colts drive to Indianapolis 44 where Manning's pass is intercepted by Drakeford and returned to Indianapolis 36. Saints drive to Indianapolis 33. Wuerffel throws 33-yard touchdown pass to Cleeland at 6:10.

Oct. 25, 1998—Miami 12, New England 9, at Miami; Dolphins win toss. Vinatieri's kickoff is returned by Avery to Miami 15. Dolphins drive to New England 26 where Mare kicks 43-yard field goal at 4:36.

+**Nov. 26, 1998—Detroit 19, Pittsburgh 16,** at Detroit; Lions win toss. Johnson's kickoff is returned by Fair to Detroit 35. Lions drive to Pittsburgh 24 where Hanson kicks 42-yard field goal at 2:52.

Dec. 6, 1998—San Francisco 31, Carolina 28, at Carolina; Panthers win toss. Richey's kickoff is returned by Floyd to Carolina 36. Panthers drive to Carolina 38 where Beuerlein's fumble is recovered by Doleman at Carolina 30. 49ers drive to Carolina 5 where Richey kicks 23-yard field goal at 4:16.

Dec. 13, 1998—Arizona 20, Philadelphia 17, at Philadelphia; Cardinals win toss. Boniol's kickoff is returned by Metcalf to Arizona 28. Cardinals drive to Philadelphia 15 where Jacke kicks 32-yard field goal at 4:30.

Sept. 12, 1999—Dallas 41, Washington 35, at Washington; Redskins win toss. Gowin's kickoff is returned by B. Mitchell to Washington 24. Redskins drive to Washington 47. M. Turk punts 48 yards. Punt downed at Dallas 5. Cowboys drive to Dallas 24. Aikman passes 76-yard touchdown to R. Ismail at 4:09.

Oct. 3, 1999—Baltimore 19, Atlanta 13, at Atlanta; Falcons win toss. Stover's kickoff is returned by Oliver to Atlanta 18. Falcons drive to Atlanta 23. Stryzinski punts 41 yards, out of bounds at Baltimore 36. Baltimore drives to Baltimore 46. Case passes 54-yard touchdown to Armour at 2:29.

Oct. 31, 1999—New York Giants 23, Philadelphia 17, at Philadelphia; Giants win toss. Akers' kickoff is returned by Levingston to New York 27. New York drives to Giants 31. Maynard punts 43 yards to Philadelphia 26. Rossum returns to Eagles 28. Pederson drives to New York 45. Pederson's pass is intercepted by Strahan at Philadelphia 44. Giants' Peter batted ball up in the air as Pederson backpedaled. Strahan for 44 yards and touchdown at 4:24.

Nov. 14, 1999—Minnesota 27, Chicago 24, at Chicago; Vikings win toss. Boniol kicks to Minnesota 2, Williams touchback. Minnesota starts from own 20. George's pass is intercepted by Harris at Minnesota 29 for -1 yard. Chicago starts at Minnesota 29 and moves to Minnesota 23. Boniol's 41-yard field goal is no good. Minnesota starts from own 31 and drives to Chicago 20. Anderson kicks 38-yard field goal at 9:02.

Nov. 21, 1999—Chicago 23, San Diego 20, at San Diego; Bears win toss. Chicago starts from own 22. Miller completes four consecutive passes and Bears drive to San Diego 22. Enis rushes twice to San Diego 19. Boniol kicks 36-yard field goal at 4:58.

* **Nov. 22, 1999—Denver 27, Oakland 21,** at Denver; Broncos win toss. Denver starts from own 33 and drives to Broncos' 35. Rouen punts 46 yards to Oakland 19. Oakland starts at own 19 and drives to Raiders' 25. Gannon fumbles and Broncos' Pryce recovers at Oakland 25. Denver running back Gary scores on 24-yard run at 2:40.

OVERTIME GAMES

Nov. 28, 1999—Washington 20, Philadelphia 17, at Washington; Redskins win toss. Akers' kickoff is returned by Thrash for 48 yards to Philadelphia 46. Johnson completes 20-yard pass to Connell to Philadelphia 26. Johnson completes 9-yard pass to Mitchell to Philadelphia 9. Mitchell runs for seven yards to Philadelphia 2. On third down, Washington attempts field goal from Philadelphia 2. Johnson fumbles and recovers at Philadelphia 9. Conway kicks 27-yard field goal at 4:34.

Dec. 19, 1999—Denver 36, Seattle 30, at Denver; Broncos win toss. Peterson kicks to Denver 8. Watson returns kick to Denver 27 for 19 yards. Broncos do not convert a first down. Rouen punts 46 yards, out of bounds at Seattle 25. Kitna passes to Dawkins for 17 yards at Seattle 47. Watters runs for 6 yards to Denver 47. Kitna sacked for 11-yard loss by Crockett. Kitna fumbles, forced by Crockett, recovered by Cadrez at Seattle 37. Cadrez for 37 yards and touchdown at 2:34.

Dec. 26, 1999—Buffalo 13, New England 10, at New England; Patriots win toss. New England's Vinatieri misses 44-yard field goal from Buffalo 26. Buffalo takes over at Bills 34. Flutie passes to Moulds to New England 21 for 17 yards. Moulds fumbles, recovered by Bruschi at Patriots 21. New England drives to own 34. Johnson punts from New England 34 to Buffalo 42. Flutie passes to Price for 7 yards to New England 44. Flutie passes to Moulds for 11 yards to New England 27. Thomas runs for 9 yards to New England 6. Christie kicks 23-yard field goal at 13:12.

#**Dec. 26, 1999—Washington 26, San Francisco 20,** at San Francisco; Redskins win toss. Richey kicks to Washington 9, Thrash returns 13 yards to Washington 22. Johnson passes to Hicks for 25 yards to Washington 47. Centers runs for 12 yards to San Francisco 33. Johnson passes to Centers for 33 yards and touchdown at 2:00.

Jan. 2, 2000—Oakland 41, Kansas City 38, at Kansas City; Raiders win toss. Baker kicks 69 yards from Kansas City 30 to Oakland 1 and out of bounds. Oakland starts at Raiders 40. Gannon passes to Dudley for 21 yards to Kansas City 40. Gannon passes to Brown at Kansas City 16 for 24 yards. Crockett runs to Kansas City 15 for 1 yard. Nedney kicks 33-yard field goal at 3:13.

Sept. 10, 2000—Tennessee 17, Kansas City 14, at Tennessee; Titans win toss. Mason returns kickoff 28 yards to Tennesse 29. Face-mask penalty on Kansas City, 5 yards, enforced at 29. Titans drive to Kansas City 18 where Del Greco kicks 36-yard field goal at 2:58.

Oct. 1, 2000—Dallas 16, Carolina 13, at Carolina; Cowboys win toss. Tucker returns kickoff 20 yards to Dallas 26. Dallas drives to Carolina 6 where Seder kicks 24-yard field goal at 3:52.

Oct. 1, 2000—Washington 20, Tampa Bay 17, at Washington; Redskins win toss. Thrash returns kickoff 32 yards to Washington 30. Washington gains five yards where Barnhardt punts 52 yards to Tampa Bay 13. Green returns for one yard to Tampa Bay 14. Buccaneers gain one yard to Tampa Bay 15 where Royals punts 50 yards to Washington 35. Sanders returns punt 57 yards to Tampa Bay 8. Davis rushes three times and gets to Tampa Bay 2 where Husted kicks 20-yard field goal at 4:09.

Oct. 8, 2000—Oakland 34, San Francisco 28, at San Francisco; Raiders win toss. Dunn returns kickoff 20 yards to Oakland 19. Raiders drive to San Francisco 17 where Janikowski misses 35-yard field-goal attempt wide right. San Francisco drives to Oakland 11 where Richey's 29-yard field-goal attempt is blocked by Dorsett. Raiders recover at Oakland 16. Oakland drives to San Francisco 31 where Gannon passes to Brown for 31-yard touchdown at 10:15.

Oct. 15, 2000—Buffalo 27, San Diego 24, at Buffalo; Bills win toss. Bills drive to Buffalo 47. Mohr punts 42 yards to San Diego 11. Chargers drive to San Diego 38 where Harbaugh is intercepted at Buffalo 41. Flutie in for injured Johnson. Bills drive to San Diego 28. Christie kicks 46-yard field goal at 8:26.

* **Oct. 23, 2000—New York Jets 40, Miami 37,** at New York; Dolphins win toss. Marion returns kickoff 31 yards to Miami 37. Fielder is intercepted at Miami 46 by Coleman, who returns ball to 39 where he fumbles. Gadsden recovers ball for Dolphins and runs out of bounds at Miami 34. Dolphins drive to New York 43 where Fiedler is intercepted again by Coleman at the Jets 34. Jets drive to Miami 23 where Hall kicks 40-yard field goal at 6:47.

Oct. 29, 2000—Jacksonville 23, Dallas 17, at Dallas; Jaguars win toss. Stith returns kickoff 24 yards to Jacksonville 34. Jaguars drive to Dallas 37 where Brunell passes to Whitted for a 37-yard touchdown at 3:02.

Nov. 5, 2000—Buffalo 16, New England 13, at New England; Patriots win toss. Faulk returns kickoff 38 yards to New England 43. Penalty on New England for offensive holding, 10 yards, enforced at New England 33. Patriots lose one yard on three plays. Johnson punts 43 yards to Buffalo 35. Bills drive to New England 13 where Christie kicks 32-yard field goal at 4:21.

Nov. 5, 2000—Philadelphia 16, Dallas 13, at Philadelphia; Eagles win toss. Mitchell returns kickoff 30 yards to Philadelphia 34. Eagles drive to Dallas 36 where McNabb is intercepted by Wortham at Dallas 30. Wortham returns interception to Dallas 31. Cowboys drive to Dallas 48 where Thomas fumbles. Recovered by Hauck at Dallas 48. Eagles drive to Dallas 13 where Akers kicks 32-yard field goal at 7:52.

* **Nov. 6, 2000—Green Bay 26, Minnesota 20,** at Green Bay; Packers win toss. Rossum returns kickoff 13 yards to Green Bay 18. Packers drive to Minnesota 43 where Favre passes to Freeman for a 43-yard touchdown at 3:27.

Nov. 12, 2000—Philadelphia 26, Pittsburgh 23, at Pittsburgh; Eagles win toss. Mitchell returns kickoff 24 yards to Philadelphia 37. Eagles drive to Pittsburgh 24 where Akers kicks 42-yard field goal at 4:09.

Dec. 17, 2000—New England 13, Buffalo 10, at Buffalo; Bills win toss and elect to defend the South goal. Patriots elect to receive. Jackson returns kickoff 38 yards to New England 48. Patriots drive to Buffalo 31 where they turn the ball over on downs. Bills drive to New England 12 where Christie's 30-yard field goal attempt is blocked by Eaton. Patriots recover at New England 11. Patriots drive to Buffalo 6 where Vinatieri kicks 24-yard field goal at 14:37.

Dec. 24, 2000—Green Bay 17, Tampa Bay 14, at Green Bay; Packers win toss. Rossum returns kickoff 29 yards to Green Bay 38. Packers drive to Tampa Bay 4 where Longwell kicks 22-yard field goal at 6:28.

Sept. 9, 2001—St. Louis 20, Philadelphia 17, at Philadelphia; Eagles win toss. Wilkins' kickoff is a touchback. Eagles drive to Philadelphia 30. Landeta punts 34 yards to St. Louis 36. Rams drive to Philadelphia 8. Wilkins kicks 26-yard field goal at 7:56.

Sept. 9, 2001—San Francisco 16, Atlanta 13, at San Francisco; 49ers win toss. Feely's kickoff is a touchback. 49ers drive to Atlanta 6. Cortez kicks 24-yard field goal at 4:04.

Oct. 14, 2001—New England 29, San Diego 26, at New England; Chargers win toss. Jenkins returns kickoff 39 yards to San Diego 40. Chargers drive to San Diego 45. Bennett punts 32 yards to New England 23. Patriots drive to San Diego 26. Vinatieri kicks 44-yard field goal at 4:00.

Oct. 14, 2001—San Francisco 37, Atlanta 31, at Atlanta; 49ers win toss. Sutherland returns kickoff 24 yards to San Francisco 24. 49ers drive to Atlanta 14. Garcia fumbles, Hall recovers at Atlanta 16. Falcons drive to Atlanta 23. Mohr punts 44 yards to San Francisco 33. Garcia throws 52-yard touchdown to Owens at 8:34.

Oct. 14, 2001—Tennessee 31, Tampa Bay 28, at Tennessee; Buccaneers win toss. D. Smith returns kickoff 17 yards to Tampa Bay 18. Buccaneers forced back to Tampa Bay 9. Royals punts 45 yards to Tennessee 46. Titans drive to Tampa Bay 32. Nedney kicks 49-yard field goal at 1:52.

Oct. 21, 2001—Washington 17, Carolina 14, at Washington; Redskins win toss. Bates returns kickoff 17 yards to Washington 14. Redskins drive to Carolina 5. Conway kicks 23-yard field goal at 1:47.

Oct. 28, 2001—Chicago 37, San Francisco 31, at Chicago; 49ers win toss. Edinger's kickoff is a touchback. M. Brown intercepts Garcia pass and returns it 33 yards for touchdown at 16 seconds.

Nov. 4, 2001—Chicago 27, Cleveland 21, at Chicago; Bears win toss. L. Johnson returns kickoff 31 yards to Chicago 32. Bears drive to Chicago 40. Maynard punts 52 yards to Cleveland 8. M. Brown intercepts Couch pass and returns it 16 yards for touchdown at 2:50.

Nov. 4, 2001—New York Giants 27, Dallas 24, at New York; Cowboys win toss. Swinton returns kickoff 21 yards to Dallas 29. Cowboys drive to New York 48. Knorr punts 33 yards to New York 15. Giants drive to Dallas 24. Andersen kicks 42-yard field goal at 7:12.

Nov. 11, 2001—Pittsburgh 15, Cleveland 12, at Cleveland; Steelers win toss. T. Edwards returns kickoff 21 yards to Pittsburgh 28. Steelers drive to Cleveland 14. Brown kicks 32-yard field goal at 5:22.

Nov. 18, 2001—San Francisco 25, Carolina 22, at Carolina; 49ers win toss. Sutherland returns kickoff 24 yards to San Francisco 26. 49ers drive to Carolina 8. Cortez kicks 26-yard field goal at 4:41.

Dec. 2, 2001—Arizona 34, Oakland 31, at Oakland; Raiders win toss. Gramatica's kickoff is a touchback. Raiders drive to Oakland 40. Lechler punts 37 yards to Arizona 23. Cardinals drive to Arizona 48. Stanley punts 29 yards to Oakland 23. Woods recovers Dunn fumble on Oakland 25. Arizona drives to Oakland 18. Gramatica kicks 36-yard field goal at 7:29.

Dec. 2, 2001—Seattle 13, San Diego 10, at Seattle; Seahawks win toss. Rogers returns kickoff 33 yards to Seattle 32. Seahawks drive to San Diego 6. Lindell kicks 24-yard field goal at 6:23.

Dec. 2, 2001—Tampa Bay 16, Cincinnati 13, at Cincinnati; Buccaneers win toss. F. Murphy returns kickoff 20 yards to Tampa Bay 38. Buccaneers drive to Cincinnati 35. Royals punts 31 yards to Cincinnati 4. Lynch recovers Dillon fumble on Cincinnati 3. Gramatica kicks 21-yard field goal at 5:06.

Dec. 16, 2001—Kansas City 26, Denver 23, at Kansas City; Broncos win toss. Carter returns kickoff 24 yards to Denver 41. Broncos drive to Denver 35. Rouen punts 35 yards to Kansas City 30. Chiefs drive to Denver 23. T. Peterson misses 41-yard field-goal attempt. Broncos drive to Denver 32. Rouen punts 38 yards to Kansas City 30. Chiefs drive to Denver 14. T. Peterson kicks 32-yard field goal at 9:04.

Dec. 16, 2001—New England 12, Buffalo 9, at Buffalo; Bills win toss. Bryson returns kickoff 23 yards to Buffalo 28. Bills drive to Buffalo 48. Moorman punts 52 yards to end zone. Patriots drive to Buffalo 5. Vinatieri kicks 23-yard field goal at 5:45.

Dec. 30, 2001—Cincinnati 26, Pittsburgh 23, at Cincinnati; Steelers win toss. Geason returns kickoff and laterals to Logan who carries ball 9 yards to Pittsburgh 38. Steelers drive to Cincinnati 39. Miller punts 38 yards to Cincinnati 1. Bengals drive to Pittsburgh 13. Rackers kicks 31-yard field goal at 10:52.

Sept. 8, 2002—New York Jets 37, Buffalo 31, at Buffalo; Jets win toss. Morton returns kickoff 96 yards for touchdown at 14 seconds.

Sept. 8, 2002—Green Bay 37, Atlanta 34, at Green Bay; Packers win toss. J. Walker returns kickoff 26 yards to Green Bay 34. Packers drive to Atlanta 39. Bidwell punts 27 yards to Atlanta 12. Falcons drive to Atlanta 14. Mohr punts 46 yards to Green Bay 40. Packers drive to Atlanta 19. Longwell kicks 34-yard field goal at 9:40.

Sept. 8, 2002—New Orleans 26, Tampa Bay 20, at Tampa Bay; Tampa Bay wins toss. Stecker returns kickoff 31 yards to Tampa Bay 42. Buccaneers drive to New Orleans 39. Tupa punts 39 yards into end zone. Saints drive to New Orleans 20. Williams returns Johnson's punt 4 yards to Tampa Bay 46. Buccaneers drive to Tampa Bay 48. Tupa punts 52 yards into end zone. Saints drive to New Orleans 41. Williams returns Johnson's punt -4 yards to Tampa Bay 6. Buccaneers drive to Tampa Bay 5. Tupa pass intercepted by Allen in Tampa Bay end zone at 12:01.

Sept. 15, 2002—Buffalo 45, Minnesota 39, at Minnesota; Buffalo wins toss. Rodgers returns kickoff 22 yards to Buffalo 22. Bills drive to Buffalo 48. Moorman punts 27 yards, downed at Minnesota 25. Vikings drive to Minnesota 32. Richardson punts 45 yards. Downed at Buffalo 23. Bills drive to Minnesota 26. Hollis' 44-yard field-goal attempt is no good. Vikings take over on Minnesota 35. Drive to Minnesota 41. Richardson punts 52 yards. Returned by Rogers 16 yards to Buffalo 24. Bills drive to Minnesota 48. Bledsoe throws 48-yard pass to Price for touchdown at 10:12.

Sept. 22, 2002—Cleveland 31, Tennessee 28, at Tennessee; Cleveland wins toss. White returns kickoff 6 yards to Cleveland 26. Browns drive to Tennessee 15. Dawson kicks 33-yard field goal at 4:09.

Sept. 22, 2002—New England 41, Kansas City 38, at New England; New England wins toss. Branch returns kickoff 30 yards to New England 30. Patriots drive to Kansas City 17. Vinatieri kicks 35-yard field goal at 4:36.

Sept. 29, 2002—Buffalo 33, Chicago 27, at Buffalo; Chicago wins toss. Johnson returns kickoff 19 yards to Chicago 20. Bears drive to Chicago 25. Maynard punts 31 yards to Buffalo 44. Fair catch by Mannelly. Buffalo drives to Chicago 26. Bledsoe throws 26-yard pass to Henry for touchdown at 2:48.

Sept. 29, 2002—Pittsburgh 16, Cleveland 13, at Pittsburgh; Pittsburgh wins toss. Mays returns kickoff 32 yards to Pittsburgh 32. Maddox's pass intercepted by Davis at Pittsburgh 34, returned for no gain. Cleveland drives to Pittsburgh 27. Dawson's 45-yard field-goal attempt no good, tipped at line of scrimmage by Flowers. Steelers take over at Pittsburgh 35. Steelers drive to Cleveland 6, and 24-yard field-goal attempt by Peterson blocked by McKinley, recovered by Peterson, fumbles, recovered by Fiala. Peterson's 31-yard field goal is good at 6:58.

Oct. 20, 2002—Denver 37, Kansas City 34, at Denver; Denver wins toss. Kasper returns kickoff 15 yards to Denver 24. Broncos drive to Denver 33. Rouen punts 43 yards to Kansas City 24. Hall returns punt 13 yards to Kansas City 37. Chiefs drive to Kansas City 43. Stryzinski's punt is blocked and recovered by Burns at Kansas City 32. Denver drives to Kansas City 7. Elam's 25-yard field goal is good at 2:52.

Oct. 20, 2002—Detroit 23, Chicago 20, at Detroit; Detroit wins toss. Edinger's kickoff goes out of bounds at Detroit 2. Lions take over at Detroit 40. Lions drive to Chicago 30. Hanson's 48-yard field goal is good at 4:42.

Oct. 20, 2002—San Diego 27, Oakland 21, at Oakland; San Diego wins toss. Chargers start at San Diego 20 after touchback. Chargers drive to Oakland 19. Tomlinson runs 19 yards for touchdown at 3:33.

Oct. 20, 2002—Arizona 9, Dallas 6, at Arizona; Dallas wins toss. Swinton returns kickoff 26 yards to Dallas 24. Cowboys drive to Dallas 29. Knorr punts 45 yards to Arizona 26. Jackson returns 5 yards to Arizona 31. Cardinals drive to Dallas 38. Player punts 38 yards into end zone. Cowboys take over at Dallas 20. Cowboys drive to Arizona 49. Knorr punts 31 yards to Arizona 18. Fair catch by Jackson. Cardinals drive to Dallas 22. Gramatica's 40-yard field goal is good at 11:45.

Nov. 3, 2002—San Francisco 23, Oakland 20, at Oakland; San Francisco wins toss. Janikowski's kickoff returned to SF 22 by J. Williams. 49ers drive to Oakland 5. Cortez's 23-yard field goal at 8:41.

Nov. 10, 2002—Atlanta 34, Pittsburgh 34, at Pittsburgh; Pittsburgh wins toss. Touchback on Feely kickoff. Pittsburgh starts at own 20, drives to Atlanta 30. Peterson's 48-yard field-goal attempt blocked by Finneran. Atlanta takes over at own 47, drives to Atlanta 33. Mohr punts 47 yards to Randle El, who returns to Pittsburgh 18. Steelers drive to Atlanta 33. Miller punts 22 yards to Atlanta 12, no return. Falcons drive to Atlanta 23. Mohr punts 52 yards. Randle El returns 1 yard to Pittsburgh 26. Steelers drive to Pittsburgh 44. Maddox intercepted by Mathis at Atlanta 43. Mathis returns to Pittsburgh 44. Atlanta drives to Pittsburgh 37. Feely's 56-yard field-goal attempt blocked by Farrior. Pittsburgh takes over on own 49. Maddox pass to Burress downed at Atlanta 1 as time expires.

Nov. 17, 2002—San Diego 20, San Francisco 17, at San Diego; San Diego wins toss. Jenkins returns Cortez kickoff 39 yards to San Diego 38. Chargers drive to San Diego 38. Bennett punts 47 yards to San Francisco 15. Williams returns 9 yards to San Francisco 24. 49ers drive to San Diego 23. Cortez's 41-yard field-goal attempt is no good. San Diego takes over on San Diego 31. Chargers drive to San Francisco 22. Christie's 40-yard field goal is good at 10:49.

Nov. 24, 2002—Chicago 20, Detroit 17, at Chicago; Detroit wins toss. Elects to defend the north goal. Hanson kicks 72 yards. Kick returned 37 yards to Chicago 35. Chicago drives to Detroit 22. Edinger's 40-yard field-goal attempt is good at 6:02.

#**Nov. 24, 2002—Indianapolis 23, Denver 20,** at Denver; Indianapolis wins toss. Knorr kicks 66 yards. Returned by Walters 28 yards to Indianapolis 32. Colts drive to Denver 33. Vanderjagt's 51-yard field-goal attempt is good at 5:38.

Dec. 1, 2002—Atlanta 30, Minnesota 24, at Minnesota; Minnesota wins toss. Feely kicks 60 yards. Returned by Carter 10 yards to Minnesota 20. Vikings drive to Minnesota 11. Richardson punts 47 yards to Atlanta 42. Returned by Rossum 10 yards to Minnesota 48. Falcons drive to Minnesota 46. Vick runs 46 yards for touchdown at 2:25.

Dec. 1, 2002—Tennessee 32, New York Giants 29, at New York; New York wins toss. Nedney kicks 68 yards. Returned by Joyce 38 yards to New York 40. Giants drive to New York 46. Allen punts 34 yards to Tennessee 20. Fair catch by O'Leary. Titans drive to New York 20. Nedney's 38-yard field goal good at 5:00.

Dec. 1, 2002—San Diego 30, Denver 27, at San Diego; Denver wins toss. Christie kicks 65 yards. Droughns returns 27 yards to Denver 32. Broncos drive to Denver 23. Knorr punts 36 yards to San Diego 41. Fair catch by Dwight. Chargers drive to Denver 19. Christie's 38-yard field-goal attempt blocked. Denver takes over on own 27. Broncos drive to San Diego 34. Elam's 53-yard field-goal attempt is no good. San Diego takes over on own 43. Chargers drive to Denver 9. Christie's field goal is good from 27 yards at 11:59.

Dec. 8, 2002—Arizona 23, Detroit 20, at Arizona; Arizona wins toss. Hanson kicks 64 yards. Kasper returns 19 yards to Arizona 30. Cardinals drive to Detroit 24. Gramatica's 42-yard field-goal attempt is good at 4:12.

Dec. 15, 2002—Seattle 30, Atlanta 24, at Atlanta; Atlanta wins toss. Lindell kicks 69 yards. Returned 17 yards to Atlanta 18 by Rossum. Atlanta drives to Seattle 18. Feely's 36-yard field-goal attempt wide right. Seattle takes over at own 26. Seahawks drive to Atlanta 27. Alexander runs 27 yards for a touchdown at 10:36.

Dec. 29, 2002—New York Giants 10, Philadelphia 7, at N.Y. Giants; Philadelphia wins toss. Bryant kicks 57 yards. Returned by Mitchell 32 yards to Philadelphia 45. Eagles drive to mid-field. Feeley's pass intercepted by Williams at New York 37, returned for no gain. Giants drive to Philadelphia 22. Bryant's 39-yard field-goal attempt is good at 5:10.

Dec. 29, 2002—New England 27, Miami 24, at New England; New England wins toss. Mare kicks 68 yards out of bounds. Patriots begin at own 40. New England drives to Miami 17. Vinatieri's 35-yard field goal is good at 2:03.

Dec. 29, 2002—Seattle 31, San Diego 28, at San Diego; Seattle wins toss. Christie kicks 64 yards. Returned by Williams 26 yards to Seattle 32. Seahawks drive to San Diego 28. Hasselbeck's pass is intercepted by Molden at San Diego 20 and returned 1 yard to the 21. Chargers drive to San Diego 12. Bennett punts 48 yards to Seattle 40. Returned by Engram 8 yards to Seattle 48. Seahawks drive to San Diego 6. Lindell's 24-yard field goal is good at 9:58.

Sept. 14, 2003—St. Louis 27, San Francisco 24, at St. Louis; Rams win the toss. Harris returns kick 42 yards to St. Louis 48. Rams drive to San Francisco 10. Wilkins kicks 28-yard field goal at 1:56.

Sept. 14, 2003—Carolina 12, Tampa Bay 9, at Tampa Bay; Panthers win toss. Touchback. Carolina starts at own 20, drives to own 37. Sauerbrun punts 45 yards to Tampa Bay 18. Buccaneers drive to Carolina 42. Tupa punts 34 yards to Carolina 8. Smith returns punt 52 yards to Tampa Bay 40. Panthers drive to Tampa Bay 29. Kasay kicks 47-yard field goal at 11:26.

* **Sept. 15, 2003—Dallas 35, New York Giants 32**, at New York; Cowboys win toss. Smith returns kickoff 21 yards to Dallas 29. Cowboys drive to Dallas 48. Gowin punts 32 yards to Giants 20. Giants drive to New York 15. Feagles punts 42 yards to Dallas 43. Cowboys drive to New York 6. Cundiff kicks 25-yard field goal at 9:04.

Sept. 21, 2003—New York Giants 24, Washington 21, at Washington; Giants win toss. Begin drive on New York 6 due to penalty on kickoff return. Giants drive to Washington 11. Bryant kicks 29-yard field goal at 4:15.

Sept. 28, 2003—Oakland 34, San Diego 31, at Oakland; Chargers win toss. Johnson returns kickoff to San Diego 24. Chargers drive to San Diego 36. Bennett punts 46 yards to Oakland 18. Raiders drive to Oakland 8. Lechler punts 49 yards to San Diego 43. Chargers drive to San Diego 39. Bennett punts to Oakland 8. Raiders drive to San Diego 28. Janikowski kicks 46-yard field goal at 9:59.

Oct. 5, 2003—Buffalo 22, Cincinnati 16, at Buffalo; Bengals win toss. Begin drive on Cincinnati 20 after touchback. Bengals drive to Cincinnati 28. Harris punts 29 yards to Buffalo 43. Bills drive to Cincinnati 2. Henry scores on 2-yard touchdown run at 3:53.

* **Oct. 6, 2003—Indianapolis 38, Tampa Bay 35**, at Tampa Bay; Buccaneers win toss. Barlow returns kickoff 30 yards to Tampa Bay 30. Buccaneers drive to Indianapolis 41. Tupa punts to Indianapolis 13. Colts drive to Tampa Bay 11. Vanderjagt kicks 29-yard field goal at 11:13.

Oct. 12, 2003—Carolina 23, Indianapolis 20, at Indianapolis; Panthers win toss. Smart returns kickoff to Carolina 27. Panthers drive to Indianapolis 30. Kasay kicks 47-yard field goal at 5:39.

Oct. 12, 2003—Kansas City 40, Green Bay 34, at Green Bay; Chiefs win toss. Hall returns kick to Kansas City 29. Chiefs drive to Green Bay 30. Andersen misses 48-yard field goal (ball tipped at line). Packers take over possession at Green Bay 39. A. Green fumbles after eight-yard run. Chiefs recover at Kansas City 49. T. Green throws 51-yard touchdown pass to Kennison at 6:18.

Oct. 19, 2003—New England 19, Miami 13, at Miami; Dolphins win toss. Rogers returns kickoff 24 yards to Miami 26. Dolphins drive to New England 17. Mare's 35-yard field-goal attempt no good. Patriots take over on New England 26. Patriots drive to New England 40. Walter punts to Miami 21. Returned by Rogers to Miami 30. Dolphins drive to Miami 45. Fiedler pass intercepted by Poole at New England 18. Brady passes 82 yards to Brown for touchdown at 9:15.

Oct. 26, 2003—Carolina 23, New Orleans 20, at New Orleans; Saints win toss. Lewis returns kickoff 53 yards to Carolina 46. Saints drive to Carolina 37. McAllister fumbles on fourth-and-one. Panthers take over at Carolina 38 and drive to New Orleans 12. Kasay kicks 31-yard field goal at 4:36.

Oct. 26, 2003—Arizona 16, San Francisco 13, at Arizona; Cardinals win toss. 49ers' Pochman kicks out of bounds. Cardinals take possession at Arizona 40 and drive to San Francisco 22. Duncan kicks 39-yard field goal at 4:59.

Nov. 2, 2003—New York Giants 31, New York Jets 28, at New York Jets; Giants win toss. Mitchell returns kick 26 yards to Giants 34. Giants drive to Jets 21. Conway misses 39-yard field-goal attempt. Jets take over on own 30. Drive to Giants 49. Stryzinski's punt returned by Mitchell two yards to Giants 18. Giants drive to own 35. Feagles' punt returned six yards by Moss to Jets 29. Jets drive to Giants 32. Brien's 51-yard field goal attempt is blocked by Allen. Giants take over on own 36, drive to Jets 11. Conway kicks 29-yard field goal at 14:56.

Nov. 9, 2003—New York Jets 27, Oakland 24, at Oakland; Jets win toss. Jordan returns kick 12 yards to New York 25. Jets drive to Oakland 21. Brien kicks 38-yard field goal at 5:56.

Nov. 16, 2003—Miami 9, Baltimore 6, at Miami; Dolphins win toss. Dolphins start at Miami 20 after touchback, drive to Baltimore 45. Turk punts 36 yards to Baltimore 9. Ravens drive to Baltimore 36. Lewis fumbles, recovered by Dolphins' Thomas. Dolphins drive to Baltimore 25. Mare kicks 43-yard field goal at 6:12.

Nov. 16, 2003—New Orleans 23, Atlanta 20, at New Orleans; Saints win toss. Lewis returns kick 39 yards to New Orleans 38. Saints drive to New Orleans 40. McAllister fumbles on Atlanta 2 after 58-yard run. Ball recovered by Falcons' Stewart for touchback. Falcons drive to New Orleans 37. Feely's 54-yard field-goal attempt no good. Saints take over on New Orleans 45. Drive to Atlanta 18. Carney kicks 36-yard field goal at 3:59.

Nov. 23, 2003—New England 23, Houston 20, at Houston; Texans win toss, take over possession at own 13 after penalty on Hollings' return. Patriots intercept Texans at Houston 23. Patriots drive to Houston 19. Vinatieri's 37-yard field-goal attempt blocked. Texans take over at own 27, drive to New England 40. Stanley punts 31 yards to New England 9. Patriots drive to New England 4. Walter punts 31 yards to New England 35. Texans drive to New England 40. Stanley punts 26 yards to New England 14. Patriots drive to Houston 10. Vinatieri kicks 28-yard field goal at 14:19.

Nov. 23, 2003—Baltimore 44, Seattle 41, at Baltimore; Seahawks win toss. Morris returns kick to Seattle 27. Seahawks drive to Seattle 30. Rouen punts 50 yards to Baltimore 20, returned 1 yard by Brightful to Baltimore 21. Ravens drive to Seattle 24. Stover kicks 42-yard field goal at 8:28.

Nov. 23, 2003—St. Louis 30, Arizona 27, at Arizona; Rams win toss. Harris returns kick to St. Louis 14. Rams drive to Arizona 31. Wilkins kicks 49-yard field goal at 3:38.

#Dec. 7, 2003—Atlanta 20, Carolina 14, at Atlanta; Panthers win toss. Smart returns kickoff 19 yards to Carolina 22. Panthers drive to Carolina 29. Delhomme's pass intercepted by Mathis at Carolina 32 and returned for touchdown at 1:19.

Dec. 14, 2003—Denver 23, Cleveland 20, at Cleveland; Browns win toss, start on Cleveland 20 after touchback. Browns drive to Cleveland 17. Gardocki punts 42 yards, returned by O'Neal 6 yards to Denver 47. Broncos drive to Cleveland 7. Elam kicks 25-yard field goal at 5:10.

Dec. 21, 2003—San Francisco 31, Philadelphia 28, at Philadelphia; Eagles win toss, start on Philadelphia 21 after penalty on Thrash's return. McNabb's pass intercepted by 49ers' Parrish and returned 29 yards to Philadelphia 4. On second down, Peterson kicks 22-yard field goal at 1:05.

#Dec. 28, 2003—Baltimore 13, Pittsburgh 10, at Baltimore; Steelers win toss. Mays returns kick to Pittsburgh 20. Steelers drive to Pittsburgh 27. Miller punts 43 yards, returned 6 yards by Brightful to Baltimore 36. Ravens drive to Pittsburgh 29. Stover kicks 47-yard field goal at 3:28.

POSTSEASON

Dec. 28, 1958—Baltimore 23, New York Giants 17, at New York in NFL Championship Game; Giants win toss. Maynard returns kickoff to Giants' 20. Chandler punts and Taseff returns one yard to Colts' 20. Ameche scores on 1-yard run at 8:15.

Dec. 23, 1962—Dallas Texans 20, Houston Oilers 17, at Houston in AFL Championship Game; Texans win toss and kick off. Jancik returns kickoff to Oilers' 33. Norton punts and Jackson makes fair catch on Texans' 22. Wilson punts and Jancik makes fair catch on Oilers' 45. Robinson intercepts Blanda's pass and returns 13 yards to Oilers' 47. Wilson's punt rolls dead at Oilers' 12. Hull intercepts Blanda's pass and returns 23 yards to midfield. Brooker kicks 25-yard field goal at 17:54.

Dec. 26, 1965—Green Bay 13, Baltimore 10, at Green Bay in NFL Divisional Playoff Game; Packers win toss. Moore returns kickoff to Packers' 22. Chandler punts and Haymond returns nine yards to Colts' 41. Gilburg punts and Wood makes fair catch at Packers' 21. Chandler punts and Haymond returns one yard to Colts' 41. Michaels misses 47-yard field goal. Chandler kicks 25-yard field goal at 13:39.

Dec. 25, 1971—Miami 27, Kansas City 24, at Kansas City in AFC Divisional Playoff Game; Chiefs win toss. Podolak, after a lateral from Buchanan, returns kickoff to Chiefs' 46. Stenerud's 42-yard field goal is blocked. Seiple punts and Podolak makes fair catch at Chiefs' 17. Wilson punts and Scott returns 18 yards to Dolphins' 39. Yepremian misses 62-yard field goal. Scott intercepts Dawson's pass and returns 13 yards to Dolphins' 46. Seiple punts and Podolak loses one yard to Chiefs' 15. Wilson punts and Scott makes fair catch on Dolphins' 30. Yepremian kick 37-yard field goal at 22:40.

Dec. 24, 1977—Oakland 37, Baltimore 31, at Baltimore in AFC Divisional Playoff Game; Colts win toss. Raiders start on own 42 following a punt late in the first overtime. Oakland works way into field-goal range on Stabler's 19-yard pass to Branch at Colts' 26. Four plays later, on the second play of the second overtime, Stabler hits Casper with a 10-yard touchdown pass at 15:43.

Jan. 2, 1982—San Diego 41, Miami 38, at Miami in AFC Divisional Playoff Game; Chargers win toss. San Diego drives from its 13 to Miami 8. On second-and-goal, Benirschke misses 27-yard field goal attempt wide left at 9:15. Miami has the ball twice and San Diego twice more before the Dolphins get their third possession. Miami drives from the San Diego 46 to Chargers' 17 and on fourth-and-two, von Schamann's 34-yard field goal attempt is blocked by San Diego's Winslow after 11:27. Fouts then completes four of five passes, including a 39-yarder to Joiner that puts the ball on Dolphins' 10. On first down, Benirschke kicks a 29-yard field goal at 13:52.

Jan. 3, 1987—Cleveland 23, New York Jets 20, at Cleveland in AFC Divisional Playoff Game; Jets win toss. Jets' punt downed at Browns' 26. Moseley's 23-yard field goal attempt is wide right. Teams trade punts. Jets' second punt downed at Browns' 31. First overtime period expires eight plays later with Browns in possession at Jets' 42. Moseley kicks 27-yard field goal four plays into second overtime at 17:02.

Jan. 11, 1987—Denver 23, Cleveland 20, at Cleveland in AFC Championship Game; Browns win toss. Broncos hold Browns on four downs. Browns' punt returned four yards to Denver's 25. Elway completes 22- and 28-yard passes to set up Karlis's 33-yard field goal nine plays into drive at 5:38.

Jan. 3, 1988—Houston 23, Seattle 20, at Houston in AFC Wild Card Game; Seahawks win toss. Rodriguez punts to K. Johnson who returns one yard to Houston 15. Zendejas kicks 32-yard field goal 12 plays later at 8:05.

Dec. 31, 1989—Pittsburgh 26, Houston 23, at Houston in AFC Wild Card Playoff Game; Steelers win toss. Steelers punt to Oilers. Oilers' fumble recovered by Woodson and returned three yards. Four plays and 13 yards later, Anderson kicks a 50-yard field goal at 3:26.

Jan. 7, 1990—Los Angeles Rams 19, New York Giants 13, at New York in NFC Divisional Game; Rams win toss. Everett completes two passes to move ball to Giants' 48. White called for pass interference; ball spotted on Giants' 25. Everett hits Anderson with a 30-yard touchdown pass at 1:06.

OVERTIME GAMES

Jan. 3, 1993—Buffalo 41, Houston 38, at Buffalo in AFC Wild Card Game; Oilers win toss. Oilers begin at 20. After 2 plays, Moon's pass is intercepted by Odomes who returns ball 2 yards to Houston 35. After 2 plays, Christie kicks 32-yard field goal at 3:06.

Jan. 8, 1994—Kansas City 27, Pittsburgh 24, at Kansas City in AFC Wild Card Game; Cheifs win toss. Hughes returns kickoff 20 yards to Kansas City 25. After 3 plays, Barker punts 48 yards to Pittsburgh 18 where Woodson returns 8 yards to the 26. After 6 plays, Royals punts 30 yards to Kansas City 20. Kansas City drives to Pittsburgh 14 where Lowery kicks 32-yard field goal at 11:03.

Jan. 17, 1999—Atlanta 30, Minnesota 27, at Minnesota in NFC Championship Game; Vikings win toss. Palmer returns kickoff 30 yards to Minnesota 29. After four plays, Berger punts 51 yards to Atlanta 7 where Dwight returns 8 yards to Atlanta 15. Falcons drive to Atlanta 36. Stryzinski punts 37 yards to Vikings' 27. Palmer calls fair catch. Vikings drive to Minnesota 39. Berger punts 52 yards to Atlanta 9. Downed by Vikings. Atlanta drives to Minnesota 21 where Andersen kicks 38-yard field goal at 11:52.

Dec. 30, 2000—Miami 23, Indianapolis 17, at Miami in AFC Wild Card Game; Dolphins win toss. Williams returns kickoff 18 yards to Miami 20. Offensive holding penalty on Freeman, 10 yards, ball spotted on Miami 10. Dolphins drive to Miami 29 where Turk punts 53 yards to Indianapolis 18. Colts drive to Miami 31 where Vanderjagt misses 49-yard field-goal attempt wide right. Dolphins drive to Indianapolis 17 where Smith rushes for a 17-yard touchdown at 11:16.

Jan. 19, 2002—New England 16, Oakland 13, at New England in AFC Divisional Playoff Game; Patriots win toss. Pass returns kickoff 24 yards to New England 34. Patriots drive to Oakland 5. Vinatieri kicks 23-yard field goal at 8:29.

Jan. 11, 2003—Tennessee 34, Pittsburgh 31, at Tennessee in AFC Divisional Playoff Game; Tennessee wins toss. Reed kicks 60 yards. Returned by Simon 21 yards to Tennessee 31. Titans drive to Pittsburgh 8. Nedney's 26-yard field goal is good at 2:15.

Jan. 4, 2004—Green Bay 33, Seattle 27, at Green Bay in NFC Wild Card Game; Seahawks win toss. Morris returns kick to Seattle 33. Seahawks drive to Seattle 42. Rouen's 44-yard punt returned by Chatman to Green Bay 26. Packers drive to Green Bay 31. Bidwell punts 35 yards to Seattle 34. Seahawks drive to Seattle 45. Hasselbeck's pass to Bannister intercepted by Packers' Harris and returned 52 yards for touchdown at 4:25.

Jan. 10, 2004—Carolina 29, St. Louis 23, at St. Louis in NFC Divisional Game; Panthers win toss. Smart returns kick to Carolina 32. Panthers drive to St. Louis 27. Kasay's 45-yard field-goal attempt no good. Rams take over at own 35 and drive to Carolina 35. Wilkins' 53-yard field-goal attempt no good. Panthers take over at Carolina 43, drive to Carolina 47. Sauerbrun punts 40 yards to St. Louis 13. Rams drive to Carolina 38. Bulger's pass intercepted by Manning at Carolina 35. Panthers drive to Carolina 31. First overtime ends. On first play of second overtime, Delhomme passes to Smith for 69-yard touchdown at 15:10.

Jan. 11, 2004—Philadelphia 20, Green Bay 17, at Philadelphia in NFC Divisional Game; Eagles win toss. Thrash returns kick to Philadelphia 28. Eagles drive to Philadelphia 24. Johnson punts 49 yards and Packers start at own 32 after holding penalty. Favre's pass intercepted by Dawkins at Philadelphia 31 and returned to Green Bay 34. Eagles drive to Green Bay 13. Akers kicks 31-yard field goal at 4:48.

NFL POSTSEASON OVERTIME GAMES (BY LENGTH OF GAME)

Date	Game	Length
Dec. 25, 1971	Miami 27, KANSAS CITY 24	82:40
Dec. 23, 1962	Dallas Texans 20, HOUSTON 17	77:54
Jan. 3 1987	CLEVELAND 23, N.Y. Jets 20	77:02
Dec. 24, 1977	Oakland 37, BALTIMORE 31	75:43
Jan. 10, 2004	Carolina 29, ST. LOUIS 23	75:10
Jan 2, 1982	San Diego 41, MIAMI 38	73:52
Dec. 26, 1965	GREEN BAY 13, Baltimore 10	73:39
Jan 17, 1999	Atlanta 30, MINNESOTA 27	71:52
Dec. 30, 2000	MIAMI 23, Indianapolis 17	71:16
Jan 8, 1994	KANSAS CITY 27, Pittsburgh 24	71:03
Jan. 19, 2002	NEW ENGLAND 16, Oakland 13	68:29
Dec. 28, 1958	Baltimore 23, N.Y. GIANTS 17	68:15
Jan. 3, 1988	HOUSTON 23, Seattle 20	68:05
Jan. 11, 1987	Denver 23, CLEVELAND 20	65:38
Jan. 11, 2004	PHILADELPHIA 20, Green Bay 17	64:48
Jan. 4, 2004	GREEN BAY 33, Seattle 27	64:25
Dec. 31, 1989	Pittsburgh 26, HOUSTON 23	63:26
Jan. 3, 1993	BUFFALO 41, Houston 38	63:06
Jan. 11, 2003	TENNESSEE 34, Pittsburgh 31	62:15
Jan. 7, 1990	L.A. Rams 19, N.Y. GIANTS 13	61:06

Home team in CAPS

There have been 20 overtime postseason games dating back to 1958. In 17 cases, both teams have had at least one possession. Last time: 1/11/04, PHILADELPHIA 20, Green Bay 17.

OVERTIME WON-LOST RECORDS, 1974-2003 (REGULAR SEASON)

Team	Win	Loss	Tie	Pct.
AFC				
Baltimore	4	3	1	.563
Buffalo	17	9	0	.654
Cincinnati	14	9	0	.609
Cleveland	13	12	1	.519
Denver	17	12	2	.581
Houston	0	1	0	.000
Indianapolis	11	9	1	.548
Jacksonville	2	2	0	.500
Kansas City	10	11	2	.478
Miami	11	17	1	.397
New England	16	18	0	.471
New York Jets	13	10	2	.560
Oakland	13	16	0	.448
Pittsburgh	15	8	2	.640
San Diego	10	16	0	.385
Tennessee	11	14	0	.440
NFC				
Arizona	16	11	2	.586
Atlanta	9	15	2	.385
Carolina	4	6	0	.400
Chicago	15	14	0	.517
Dallas	12	10	0	.545
Detroit	11	12	1	.479
Green Bay	9	11	4	.458
Minnesota	15	14	2	.516
New Orleans	6	8	0	.429
New York Giants	13	12	2	.519
Philadelphia	10	14	3	.426
St. Louis	8	7	1	.531
San Francisco	12	13	1	.481
Seattle	7	13	0	.350
Tampa Bay	10	13	1	.438
Washington	15	9	1	.620

OVERTIME GAMES BY YEAR (REGULAR SEASON)

2003-23	1995-21	1987-13	1979-12
2002-25*	1994-16	1986-16	1978-11
2001-17	1993-7	1985-10	1977-6
2000-13	1992-10	1984- 9	1976-5
1999-11	1991-15	1983-19	1975-9
1998-7	1990-10	1982- 4	1974-2
1997-17	1989-11	1981-10	
1996-14	1988- 9	1980-13	

**Record*

OVERTIME GAME SUMMARY—1974-2003

There have been 365 overtime games in regular season play since the rule was adopted in 1974 (23 in 2003 season). Breakdown follows:

261(16) times both teams had at least one possession (71.5%)
189(12) times the team which won the toss won the game (51.8%)
160(11) times the team which lost the toss won the game (43.8%)
16 (0) games ended tied (4.4%). Last time: Nov. 10, 2002, Atlanta 34 at Pittsburgh 34.
102 (6) times the team which won the toss drove for winning score (75 FG, 27 TD) (27.9%)
9 (0) times the team which won the toss elected to kick off (4 wins) (2.5%)
255(19) games were decided by a field goal (69.9%)
93 (4) games were decided by a touchdown (25.5%)
1 (0) games were decided by a safety (0.27%)

Note: The number in parentheses represents 2003 Season Total in each category.

MOST OVERTIME GAMES, SEASON

5 Green Bay Packers, 1983
4 Denver Broncos, 1985
Cleveland Browns, 1989
Minnesota Vikings, 1994
Arizona Cardinals, 1995
Minnesota Vikings, 1995
Arizona Cardinals, 1997
San Francisco 49ers, 2001
Atlanta Falcons, 2002
San Diego Chargers, 2002
Carolina Panthers, 2003

LONGEST CONSECUTIVE GAME STREAKS WITHOUT OVERTIME (Current)

55 Jacksonville Jaguars (Last OT Game, 10/29/00 at Dallas)
(Record: 110, St. Louis/Phoenix Cardinals, 12/7/86-12/19/93)

SHORTEST OVERTIME GAMES

0:14 New York Jets 37, BUFFALO 31; 9/8/02
0:16 CHICAGO 37, San Francisco 31; 10/28/01
0:17 NEW ORLEANS 20, Seattle 17; 11/16/97
0:21 Chicago 23, DETROIT 17; 11/27/80
0:30 Baltimore 29, NEW ENGLAND 23; 9/4/83

LONGEST OVERTIME GAMES (ALL POSTSEASON GAMES)

22:40 Miami 27, KANSAS CITY 24; 12/25/71
17:54 Dallas Texans 20, HOUSTON 17; 12/23/62
17:02 CLEVELAND 23, New York Jets 20; 1/3/87
15:43 Oakland 37, BALTIMORE 31; 12/24/77
15:10 Carolina 29, ST. LOUIS 23; 1/10/04

OVERTIME SCORING SUMMARY

255 were decided by a field goal
41 were decided by a touchdown pass
26 were decided by a touchdown run
15 were decided by an interception (Atlanta 40, New Orleans 34, 9/2/79; Atlanta 47, Green Bay 41, 11/27/83; New York Giants 16, Philadelphia 10, 9/29/85; Indianapolis 23, Cleveland 17, 12/10/89; Cleveland 30, San Diego 24, 10/20/91; Kansas City 23, Oakland 17, 9/17/95; New York Giants 27, Arizona 21, 10/8/95; Washington 36, Detroit 30, 10/22/95; Arizona 20, Seattle 14, 10/29/95; Cincinnati 34, Detroit 28, 9/13/98; New York Giants 23, Philadelphia 17, 10/31/99; Chicago 37, San Francisco 31, 10/28/01; Chicago 27, Cleveland 21, 11/4/01; New Orleans 26, Tampa Bay 20, 9/8/02; Atlanta 20, Carolina 14, 12/7/03)
2 were decided on a fake field goal/touchdown pass (Minnesota 22, Chicago 16, 10/16/77; Cleveland 23, Minnesota 17, 12/17/89)
2 were decided by a fumble recovery (Baltimore 29, New England 23, 9/4/83; Denver 36, Seattle 30, 12/19/99)
2 were decided by a kickoff return (Chicago 23, Detroit 17, 11/27/80; New York Jets 37, Buffalo 31, 9/8/02)
1 was decided by a punt return (Kansas City 29, San Diego 23, 10/9/95)
1 was decided on a fake field goal/touchdown run (Los Angeles Rams 27, Minnesota 21, 12/2/79)
1 was decided on a blocked field goal (Denver 30, San Diego 24, 11/17/85)
1 was decided on a blocked field goal/recovery by kicker (Green Bay 12, Chicago 6, 9/7/80)
1 was decided on a blocked field goal/recovery by kicking team (Philadelphia 23, New York Giants 17, 11/20/88)
1 was decided by a safety (Minnesota 23, Los Angeles Rams 21, 11/5/89)
16 ended tied

OVERTIME GAMES

OVERTIME RECORDS

Longest Touchdown Pass

99 Yards — Ron Jaworski to Mike Quick, Philadelphia 23, Atlanta 17 (11/10/85)
82 Yards — Tom Brady to Troy Brown, New England 19, Miami 13 (10/19/03)
76 Yards — Troy Aikman to Raghib Ismail, Dallas 41, Washington 35 (9/12/99)

Longest Touchdown Run

96 Yards — Garrison Hearst, San Francisco 36, New York Jets 30 (9/6/98)
60 Yards — Herschel Walker, Dallas 23, New England 17 (11/15/87)
46 Yards — Michael Vick, Atlanta 30, Minnesota 24 (12/1/02)

Longest Field Goal

53 Yards — Chris Jacke, Green Bay 23, San Francisco 20 (10/4/96)
52 Yards — Mike Cofer, Indianapolis 27, New York Jets 24 (9/10/95)
51 Yards — Greg Davis, New England 23, Indianapolis 20 (10/29/89); Greg Davis, Arizona 20, Pittsburgh 17 (10/30/94); Michael Husted, Tampa Bay 20, Minnesota 17 (10/15/95); Mike Vanderjagt, Indianapolis 23, Denver 20 (11/24/02)

Longest Touchdown Plays

99 Yards — (Pass) Ron Jaworski to Mike Quick, Philadelphia 23, Atlanta 17 (11/10/85)
96 Yards — (Run) Garrison Hearst, San Francisco 36, New York Jets 30 (9/6/98)
96 Yards — (Kickoff return) Chad Morton, New York Jets 37, Buffalo 31 (9/8/02)
95 Yards — (Kickoff return) Dave Williams, Chicago 23, Detroit 17 (11/27/80)
86 Yards — (Punt return) Tamarick Vanover, Kansas City 29, San Diego 23 (10/9/95)

FIRST-ROUND SELECTIONS

If club had no first-round selection, first player drafted is listed with round in parentheses.

ARIZONA CARDINALS

Year Player, College, Position

1936 Jim Lawrence, Texas Christian, B
1937 Ray Buivid, Marquette, B
1938 Jack Robbins, Arkansas, B
1939 Charles (Ki) Aldrich, TCU, C
1940 George Cafego, Tennessee, B
1941 John Kimbrough, Texas A&M, B
1942 Steve Lach, Duke, B
1943 Glenn Dobbs, Tulsa, B
1944 Pat Harder, Wisconsin, B
1945 Charley Trippi, Georgia, B
1946 Dub Jones, Louisiana State, B
1947 DeWitt (Tex) Coulter, Army, T
1948 Jim Spavital, Oklahoma A&M, B
1949 Bill Fischer, Notre Dame, G
1950 Jack Jennings, Ohio State, T (2)
1951 Jerry Groom, Notre Dame, C
1952 Ollie Matson, San Francisco, B
1953 Johnny Olszewski, California, B
1954 Lamar McHan, Arkansas, B
1955 Max Boydston, Oklahoma, E
1956 Joe Childress, Auburn, B
1957 Jerry Tubbs, Oklahoma, C
1958 King Hill, Rice, B
John David Crow, Texas A&M, B
1959 Bill Stacy, Mississippi State, B
1960 George Izo, Notre Dame, QB
1961 Ken Rice, Auburn, T
1962 Fate Echols, Northwestern, DT
Irv Goode, Kentucky, C
1963 Jerry Stovall, Louisiana State, S
Don Brumm, Purdue, DE
1964 Ken Kortas, Louisville, DT
1965 Joe Namath, Alabama, QB
1966 Carl McAdams, Oklahoma, LB
1967 Dave Williams, Washington, WR
1968 MacArthur Lane, Utah State, RB
1969 Roger Wehrli, Missouri, DB
1970 Larry Stegent, Texas A&M, RB
1971 Norm Thompson, Utah, CB
1972 Bobby Moore, Oregon, RB-WR
1973 Dave Butz, Purdue, DT
1974 J.V. Cain, Colorado, TE
1975 Tim Gray, Texas A&M, DB
1976 Mike Dawson, Arizona, DT
1977 Steve Pisarkiewicz, Missouri, QB
1978 Steve Little, Arkansas, K
Ken Greene, Washington State, DB
1979 Ottis Anderson, Miami, RB
1980 Curtis Greer, Michigan, DE
1981 E.J. Junior, Alabama, LB
1982 Luis Sharpe, UCLA, T
1983 Leonard Smith, McNeese St., DB
1984 Clyde Duncan, Tennessee, WR
1985 Freddie Joe Nunn, Mississippi, LB
1986 Anthony Bell, Michigan State, LB
1987 Kelly Stouffer, Colorado State, QB
1988 Ken Harvey, California, LB
1989 Eric Hill, Louisiana State, LB
Joe Wolf, Boston College, G
1990 Anthony Thompson, Indiana, RB (2)
1991 Eric Swann, No College, DE
1992 Tony Sacca, Penn State, QB (2)
1993 Garrison Hearst, Georgia, RB
Ernest Dye, South Carolina, T
1994 Jamir Miller, UCLA, LB
1995 Frank Sanders, Auburn, WR (2)
1996 Simeon Rice, Illinois, DE
1997 Tom Knight, Iowa, DB
1998 Andre Wadsworth, Florida St., DE
1999 David Boston, Ohio State, WR
L.J. Shelton, Eastern Michigan, T
2000 Thomas Jones, Virginia, RB
2001 Leonard Davis, Texas, T
2002 Wendell Bryant, Wisconsin, DT
2003 Bryant Johnson, Penn State, WR
Calvin Pace, Wake Forest, DE
2004 Larry Fitzgerald, Pittsburgh, WR

ATLANTA FALCONS

Year Player, College, Position

1966 Tommy Nobis, Texas, LB
Randy Johnson, Texas A&I, QB
1967 Leo Carroll, San Diego St., DE (2)
1968 Claude Humphrey, Tennessee St., DE
1969 George Kunz, Notre Dame, T
1970 John Small, Citadel, LB
1971 Joe Profit, Northeast Louisiana, RB
1972 Clarence Ellis, Notre Dame, DB
1973 Greg Marx, Notre Dame, DT (2)
1974 Gerald Tinker, Kent State, WR (2)
1975 Steve Bartkowski, California, QB
1976 Bubba Bean, Texas A&M, RB
1977 Warren Bryant, Kentucky, T
Wilson Faumuina, San Jose St., DT
1978 Mike Kenn, Michigan, T
1979 Don Smith, Miami, DE
1980 Junior Miller, Nebraska, TE
1981 Bobby Butler, Florida State, DB
1982 Gerald Riggs, Arizona State, RB
1983 Mike Pitts, Alabama, DE
1984 Rick Bryan, Oklahoma, DT
1985 Bill Fralic, Pittsburgh, T
1986 Tony Casillas, Oklahoma, NT
Tim Green, Syracuse, LB
1987 Chris Miller, Oregon, QB
1988 Aundray Bruce, Auburn, LB
1989 Deion Sanders, Florida State, DB
Shawn Collins, No. Arizona, WR
1990 Steve Broussard, Washington St., RB
1991 Bruce Pickens, Nebraska, DB
Mike Pritchard, Colorado, WR
1992 Bob Whitfield, Stanford, T
Tony Smith, So. Mississippi, RB
1993 Lincoln Kennedy, Washington, T
1994 Bert Emanuel, Rice, WR (2)
1995 Devin Bush, Florida State, DB
1996 Shannon Brown, Alabama, DT (3)
1997 Michael Booker, Nebraska, DB
1998 Keith Brooking, Georgia Tech, LB
1999 Patrick Kerney, Virginia, DE
2000 Travis Claridge, So. California, T (2)
2001 Michael Vick, Virginia Tech, QB
2002 T.J. Duckett, Michigan State, RB
2003 Bryan Scott, Penn State, DB (2)
2004 DeAngelo Hall, Virginia Tech, DB
Michael Jenkins, Ohio State, WR

BALTIMORE RAVENS

Year Player, College, Position

1996 Jonathan Ogden, UCLA, T
Ray Lewis, Miami, LB
1997 Peter Boulware, Florida State, DE
1998 Duane Starks, Miami, DB
1999 Chris McAlister, Arizona, DB
2000 Jamal Lewis, Tennessee, RB
Travis Taylor, Florida, WR
2001 Todd Heap, Arizona State, TE
2002 Ed Reed, Miami, DB
2003 Terrell Suggs, Arizona State, DE
Kyle Boller, California, QB
2004 Dwan Edwards, Oregon St., DT (2)

BUFFALO BILLS

Year Player, College, Position

1960 Richie Lucas, Penn State, QB
1961 Ken Rice, Auburn, T
1962 Ernie Davis, Syracuse, RB
1963 Dave Behrman, Michigan State, C
1964 Carl Eller, Minnesota, DE
1965 Jim Davidson, Ohio State, T
1966 Mike Dennis, Mississippi, RB
1967 John Pitts, Arizona State, S
1968 Haven Moses, San Diego St., WR
1969 O.J. Simpson, So. California, RB
1970 Al Cowlings, So. California, DE
1971 J.D. Hill, Arizona State, WR
1972 Walt Patulski, Notre Dame, DE
1973 Paul Seymour, Michigan, TE
Joe DeLamielleure, Michigan St., G
1974 Reuben Gant, Oklahoma State, TE
1975 Tom Ruud, Nebraska, LB
1976 Mario Clark, Oregon, DB
1977 Phil Dokes, Oklahoma State, DT
1978 Terry Miller, Oklahoma State, RB
1979 Tom Cousineau, Ohio State, LB
Jerry Butler, Clemson, WR
1980 Jim Ritcher, North Carolina St., C
1981 Booker Moore, Penn State, RB
1982 Perry Tuttle, Clemson, WR
1983 Tony Hunter, Notre Dame, TE
Jim Kelly, Miami, QB
1984 Greg Bell, Notre Dame, RB
1985 Bruce Smith, Virginia Tech, DE
Derrick Burroughs, Memphis St., DB
1986 Ronnie Harmon, Iowa, RB
Will Wolford, Vanderbilt, T
1987 Shane Conlan, Penn State, LB
1988 Thurman Thomas, Oklahoma St., RB (2)
1989 Don Beebe, Chadron, Neb., WR (3)
1990 James Williams, Fresno State, DB
1991 Henry Jones, Illinois, DB
1992 John Fina, Arizona, T
1993 Thomas Smith, North Carolina, DB
1994 Jeff Burris, Notre Dame, DB
1995 Ruben Brown, Pittsburgh, G
1996 Eric Moulds, Mississippi St., WR
1997 Antowain Smith, Houston, RB
1998 Sam Cowart, Florida State, LB (2)
1999 Antoine Winfield, Ohio State, DB
2000 Erik Flowers, Arizona State, DE
2001 Nate Clements, Ohio State, DB
2002 Mike Williams, Texas, T
2003 Willis McGahee, Miami, RB
2004 Lee Evans, Wisconsin, WR
J.P. Losman, Tulane, QB

CAROLINA PANTHERS

Year Player, College, Position

1995 Kerry Collins, Penn State, QB
Tyrone Poole, Ft. Valley State, DB
Blake Brockermeyer, Texas, T
1996 Tim Biakabutuka, Michigan, RB

1997 Rae Carruth, Colorado, WR
1998 Jason Peter, Nebraska, DT
1999 Chris Terry, Georgia, T (2)
2000 Rashard Anderson, Jackson St., DB
2001 Dan Morgan, Miami, LB
2002 Julius Peppers, North Carolina, DE
2003 Jordan Gross, Utah, T
2004 Chris Gamble, Ohio State, DB

CHICAGO BEARS

Year Player, College, Position
1936 Joe Stydahar, West Virginia, T
1937 Les McDonald, Nebraska, E
1938 Joe Gray, Oregon State, B
1939 Sid Luckman, Columbia, QB
Bill Osmanski, Holy Cross, B
1940 Clyde (Bulldog) Turner, Hardin-Simmons, C
1941 Tom Harmon, Michigan, B
Norm Standlee, Stanford, B
Don Scott, Ohio State, B
1942 Frankie Albert, Stanford, B
1943 Bob Steber, Missouri, B
1944 Ray Evans, Kansas, B
1945 Don Lund, Michigan, B
1946 Johnny Lujack, Notre Dame, QB
1947 Bob Fenimore, Oklahoma State, B
Don Kindt, Wisconsin, B
1948 Bobby Layne, Texas, QB
Max Bumgardner, Texas, E
1949 Dick Harris, Texas, C
1950 Chuck Hunsinger, Florida, B
Fred Morrison, Ohio State, B
1951 Bob Williams, Notre Dame, B
Billy Stone, Bradley, B
Gene Schroeder, Virginia, E
1952 Jim Dooley, Miami, B
1953 Billy Anderson, Compton (Calif.) J.C., B
1954 Stan Wallace, Illinois, B
1955 Ron Drzewiecki, Marquette, B
1956 Menan (Tex) Schriewer, Texas, E
1957 Earl Leggett, Louisiana State, T
1958 Chuck Howley, West Virginia, G
1959 Don Clark, Ohio State, B
1960 Roger Davis, Syracuse, G
1961 Mike Ditka, Pittsburgh, E
1962 Ronnie Bull, Baylor, RB
1963 Dave Behrman, Michigan State, C
1964 Dick Evey, Tennessee, DT
1965 Dick Butkus, Illinois, LB
Gale Sayers, Kansas, RB
Steve DeLong, Tennessee, T
1966 George Rice, Louisiana State, DT
1967 Loyd Phillips, Arkansas, DE
1968 Mike Hull, Southern California, RB
1969 Rufus Mayes, Ohio State, T
1970 George Farmer, UCLA, WR (3)
1971 Joe Moore, Missouri, RB
1972 Lionel Antoine, Southern Illinois, T
Craig Clemons, Iowa, DB
1973 Wally Chambers, Eastern Kentucky, DE
1974 Waymond Bryant, Tennessee St., LB
Dave Gallagher, Michigan, DT
1975 Walter Payton, Jackson State, RB
1976 Dennis Lick, Wisconsin, T
1977 Ted Albrecht, California, T
1978 Brad Shearer, Texas, DT (3)
1979 Dan Hampton, Arkansas, DT
Al Harris, Arizona State, DE
1980 Otis Wilson, Louisville, LB
1981 Keith Van Horne, So. California, T
1982 Jim McMahon, Brigham Young, QB
1983 Jim Covert, Pittsburgh, T
Willie Gault, Tennessee, WR
1984 Wilber Marshall, Florida, LB
1985 William Perry, Clemson, DT
1986 Neal Anderson, Florida, RB
1987 Jim Harbaugh, Michigan, QB
1988 Brad Muster, Stanford, RB
Wendell Davis, Louisiana St., WR
1989 Donnell Woolford, Clemson, DB
Trace Armstrong, Florida, DE
1990 Mark Carrier, So. California, DB
1991 Stan Thomas, Texas, T
1992 Alonzo Spellman, Ohio State, DE
1993 Curtis Conway, So. California, WR
1994 John Thierry, Alcorn State, DE
1995 Rashaan Salaam, Colorado, RB
1996 Walt Harris, Mississippi State, DB
1997 John Allred, So. California, TE (2)
1998 Curtis Enis, Penn State, RB
1999 Cade McNown, UCLA, QB
2000 Brian Urlacher, New Mexico, LB
2001 David Terrell, Michigan, WR
2002 Marc Colombo, Boston College, T
2003 Michael Haynes, Penn State, DE
Rex Grossman, Florida, QB
2004 Tommie Harris, Oklahoma, DT

CINCINNATI BENGALS

Year Player, College, Position
1968 Bob Johnson, Tennessee, C
1969 Greg Cook, Cincinnati, QB
1970 Mike Reid, Penn State, DT
1971 Vernon Holland, Tennessee St., T
1972 Sherman White, California, DE
1973 Isaac Curtis, San Diego State, WR
1974 Bill Kollar, Montana State, DT
1975 Glenn Cameron, Florida, LB
1976 Billy Brooks, Oklahoma, WR
Archie Griffin, Ohio State, RB
1977 Eddie Edwards, Miami, DT
Wilson Whitley, Houston, DT
Mike Cobb, Michigan State, TE
1978 Ross Browner, Notre Dame, DT
Blair Bush, Washington, C
1979 Jack Thompson, Washington St., QB
Charles Alexander, Louisiana St., RB
1980 Anthony Muñoz, So. California, T
1981 David Verser, Kansas, WR
1982 Glen Collins, Mississippi State, DE
1983 Dave Rimington, Nebraska, C
1984 Ricky Hunley, Arizona, LB
Pete Koch, Maryland, DE
Brian Blados, North Carolina, T
1985 Eddie Brown, Miami, WR
Emanuel King, Alabama, LB
1986 Joe Kelly, Washington, LB
Tim McGee, Tennessee, WR
1987 Jason Buck, Brigham Young, DE
1988 Rickey Dixon, Oklahoma, DB
1989 Eric Ball, UCLA, RB (2)
1990 James Francis, Baylor, LB
1991 Alfred Williams, Colorado, LB
1992 David Klingler, Houston, QB
Darryl Williams, Miami, DB
1993 John Copeland, Alabama, DE
1994 Dan Wilkinson, Ohio State, DT
1995 Ki-Jana Carter, Penn State, RB
1996 Willie Anderson, Auburn, T
1997 Reinard Wilson, Florida State, LB
1998 Takeo Spikes, Auburn, LB
Brian Simmons, North Carolina, LB
1999 Akili Smith, Oregon, QB
2000 Peter Warrick, Florida State, WR
2001 Justin Smith, Missouri, DE
2002 Levi Jones, Arizona State, T
2003 Carson Palmer, Southern California, QB
2004 Chris Perry, Michigan, RB

CLEVELAND BROWNS

Year Player, College, Position
1950 Ken Carpenter, Oregon State, B
1951 Ken Konz, Louisiana State, B
1952 Bert Rechichar, Tennessee, DB
Harry Agganis, Boston U., QB
1953 Doug Atkins, Tennessee, DE
1954 Bobby Garrett, Stanford, QB
John Bauer, Illinois, G
1955 Kurt Burris, Oklahoma, C
1956 Preston Carpenter, Arkansas, B
1957 Jim Brown, Syracuse, RB
1958 Jim Shofner, Texas Christian, DB
1959 Rich Kreitling, Illinois, DE
1960 Jim Houston, Ohio State, DE
1961 Bobby Crespino, Mississippi, TE
1962 Gary Collins, Maryland, WR
Leroy Jackson, Western Illinois, RB
1963 Tom Hutchinson, Kentucky, WR
1964 Paul Warfield, Ohio State, WR
1965 James Garcia, Purdue, T (2)
1966 Milt Morin, Massachusetts, TE
1967 Bob Matheson, Duke, LB
1968 Marvin Upshaw, Trinity, Tex., DT-DE
1969 Ron Johnson, Michigan, RB
1970 Mike Phipps, Purdue, QB
Bob McKay, Texas, T
1971 Clarence Scott, Kansas State, CB
1972 Thom Darden, Michigan, DB
1973 Steve Holden, Arizona State, WR
Pete Adams, Southern California, T
1974 Billy Corbett, Johnson C. Smith, T (2)
1975 Mack Mitchell, Houston, DE
1976 Mike Pruitt, Purdue, RB
1977 Robert Jackson, Texas A&M, LB
1978 Clay Matthews, So. California, LB
Ozzie Newsome, Alabama, TE
1979 Willis Adams, Houston, WR
1980 Charles White, So. California, RB
1981 Hanford Dixon, So. Mississippi, DB
1982 Chip Banks, So. California, LB
1983 Ron Brown, Arizona State, WR (2)
1984 Don Rogers, UCLA, DB
1985 Greg Allen, Florida State, RB (2)
1986 Webster Slaughter, San Diego St., WR (2)
1987 Mike Junkin, Duke, LB
1988 Clifford Charlton, Florida, LB
1989 Eric Metcalf, Texas, RB
1990 Leroy Hoard, Michigan, RB (2)
1991 Eric Turner, UCLA, DB
1992 Tommy Vardell, Stanford, RB
1993 Steve Everitt, Michigan, C
1994 Antonio Langham, Alabama, DB
Derrick Alexander, Michigan, WR
1995 Craig Powell, Ohio State, LB
1999 Tim Couch, Kentucky, QB
2000 Courtney Brown, Penn State, DE
2001 Gerard Warren, Florida, DT
2002 William Green, Boston College, RB
2003 Jeff Faine, Norte Dame, C
2004 Kellen Winslow, Miami, TE

DALLAS COWBOYS

Year Player, College, Position

1960 None
1961 Bob Lilly, Texas Christian, DT
1962 Sonny Gibbs, TCU, QB (2)
1963 Lee Roy Jordan, Alabama, LB
1964 Scott Appleton, Texas, DT
1965 Craig Morton, California, QB
1966 John Niland, Iowa, G
1967 Phil Clark, Northwestern, DB (3)
1968 Dennis Homan, Alabama, WR
1969 Calvin Hill, Yale, RB
1970 Duane Thomas, West Texas St., RB
1971 Tody Smith, So. California, DE
1972 Bill Thomas, Boston College, RB
1973 Billy Joe DuPree, Michigan St., TE
1974 Ed (Too Tall) Jones, Tennessee St., DE
Charley Young, North Carolina St., RB
1975 Randy White, Maryland, LB
Thomas Henderson, Langston, LB
1976 Aaron Kyle, Wyoming, DB
1977 Tony Dorsett, Pittsburgh, RB
1978 Larry Bethea, Michigan State, DE
1979 Robert Shaw, Tennessee, C
1980 Bill Roe, Colorado, LB (3)
1981 Howard Richards, Missouri, T
1982 Rod Hill, Kentucky State, DB
1983 Jim Jeffcoat, Arizona State, DE
1984 Billy Cannon, Jr., Texas A&M, LB
1985 Kevin Brooks, Michigan, DE
1986 Mike Sherrard, UCLA, WR
1987 Danny Noonan, Nebraska, DT
1988 Michael Irvin, Miami, WR
1989 Troy Aikman, UCLA, QB
1990 Emmitt Smith, Florida, RB
1991 Russell Maryland, Miami, DT
Alvin Harper, Tennessee, WR
Kelvin Pritchett, Mississippi, DT
1992 Kevin Smith, Texas A&M, DB
Robert Jones, East Carolina, LB
1993 Kevin Williams, Miami, WR (2)
1994 Shante Carver, Arizona State, DE
1995 Sherman Williams, Alabama, RB (2)
1996 Kavika Pittman, McNeese St., DE (2)
1997 David LaFleur, Louisiana State, TE
1998 Greg Ellis, North Carolina, DE
1999 Ebenezer Ekuban, North Carolina, DE
2000 Dwayne Goodrich, Tennessee, DB (2)
2001 Quincy Carter, Georgia, QB (2)
2002 Roy Williams, Oklahoma, DB
2003 Terence Newman, Kansas State, DB
2004 Julius Jones, RB, Notre Dame (2)

DENVER BRONCOS

Year Player, College, Position

1960 Roger LeClerc, Trinity, Conn., C
1961 Bob Gaiters, New Mexico St., RB
1962 Merlin Olsen, Utah State, DT
1963 Kermit Alexander, UCLA, CB
1964 Bob Brown, Nebraska, T
1965 Dick Butkus, Illinois, LB (2)
1966 Jerry Shay, Purdue, DT
1967 Floyd Little, Syracuse, RB
1968 Curley Culp, Arizona State, DE (2)
1969 Grady Cavness, Texas-El Paso, DB (2)
1970 Bob Anderson, Colorado, RB
1971 Marv Montgomery, So. California, T
1972 Riley Odoms, Houston, TE
1973 Otis Armstrong, Purdue, RB
1974 Randy Gradishar, Ohio State, LB
1975 Louis Wright, San Jose State, DB
1976 Tom Glassic, Virginia, G
1977 Steve Schindler, Boston College, G
1978 Don Latimer, Miami, DT
1979 Kelvin Clark, Nebraska, T
1980 Rulon Jones, Utah State, DE (2)
1981 Dennis Smith, So. California, DB
1982 Gerald Willhite, San Jose St., RB
1983 Chris Hinton, Northwestern, G
1984 Andre Townsend, Mississippi, DE (2)
1985 Steve Sewell, Oklahoma, RB
1986 Jim Juriga, Illinois, T (4)
1987 Ricky Nattiel, Florida, WR
1988 Ted Gregory, Syracuse, NT
1989 Steve Atwater, Arkansas, DB
1990 Alton Montgomery, Houston, DB (2)
1991 Mike Croel, Nebraska, LB
1992 Tommy Maddox, UCLA, QB
1993 Dan Williams, Toledo, DE
1994 Allen Aldridge, Houston, LB (2)
1995 Jamie Brown, Florida A&M, T (4)
1996 John Mobley, Kutztown, LB
1997 Trevor Pryce, Clemson, DT
1998 Marcus Nash, Tennessee, WR
1999 Al Wilson, Tennessee, LB
2000 Deltha O'Neal, California, DB
2001 Willie Middlebrooks, Minnesota, DB
2002 Ashley Lelie, Hawaii, WR
2003 George Foster, Georgia, T
2004 D.J. Williams, Miami, LB

DETROIT LIONS

Year Player, College, Position

1936 Sid Wagner, Michigan State, G
1937 Lloyd Cardwell, Nebraska, B
1938 Alex Wojciechowicz, Fordham, C
1939 John Pingel, Michigan State, B
1940 Doyle Nave, Southern California, B
1941 Jim Thomason, Texas A&M, B
1942 Bob Westfall, Michigan, B
1943 Frank Sinkwich, Georgia, B
1944 Otto Graham, Northwestern, B
1945 Frank Szymanski, Notre Dame, C
1946 Bill Dellastatious, Missouri, B
1947 Glenn Davis, Army, B
1948 Y.A. Tittle, Louisiana State, B
1949 John Rauch, Georgia, B
1950 Leon Hart, Notre Dame, E
Joe Watson, Rice, C
1951 Dick Stanfel, San Francisco, G (2)
1952 Yale Lary, Texas A&M, B (3)
1953 Harley Sewell, Texas, G
1954 Dick Chapman, Rice, T
1955 Dave Middleton, Auburn, B
1956 Hopalong Cassady, Ohio State, B
1957 Bill Glass, Baylor, G
1958 Alex Karras, Iowa, T
1959 Nick Pietrosante, Notre Dame, B
1960 John Robinson, Louisiana State, S
1961 Danny LaRose, Missouri, T (2)
1962 John Hadl, Kansas, QB
1963 Daryl Sanders, Ohio State, T
1964 Pete Beathard, So. California, QB
1965 Tom Nowatzke, Indiana, RB
1966 Nick Eddy, Notre Dame, RB (2)
1967 Mel Farr, UCLA, RB
1968 Greg Landry, Massachusetts, QB
Earl McCullouch, So. California, WR
1969 Altie Taylor, Utah State, RB (2)
1970 Steve Owens, Oklahoma, RB
1971 Bob Bell, Cincinnati, DT
1972 Herb Orvis, Colorado, DE
1973 Ernie Price, Texas A&I, DE
1974 Ed O'Neil, Penn State, LB
1975 Lynn Boden, South Dakota St., G
1976 James Hunter, Grambling, DB
Lawrence Gaines, Wyoming, RB
1977 Walt Williams, New Mexico St., DB (2)
1978 Luther Bradley, Notre Dame, DB
1979 Keith Dorney, Penn State, T
1980 Billy Sims, Oklahoma, RB
1981 Mark Nichols, San Jose State, WR
1982 Jimmy Williams, Nebraska, LB
1983 James Jones, Florida, RB
1984 David Lewis, California, TE
1985 Lomas Brown, Florida, T
1986 Chuck Long, Iowa, QB
1987 Reggie Rogers, Washington, DE
1988 Bennie Blades, Miami, DB
1989 Barry Sanders, Oklahoma St., RB
1990 Andre Ware, Houston, QB
1991 Herman Moore, Virginia, WR
1992 Robert Porcher, South Carolina St., DE
1993 Ryan McNeil, Miami, DB (2)
1994 Johnnie Morton, So. California, WR
1995 Luther Elliss, Utah, DT
1996 Reggie Brown, Texas A&M, LB
Jeff Hartings, Penn State, G
1997 Bryant Westbrook, Texas, DB
1998 Terry Fair, Tennessee, DB
1999 Chris Claiborne, So. California, LB
Aaron Gibson, Wisconsin, T
2000 Stockar McDougle, Oklahoma, T
2001 Jeff Backus, Michigan, T
2002 Joey Harrington, Oregon, QB
2003 Charles Rogers, Michigan State, WR
2004 Roy Williams, Texas, WR
Kevin Jones, Virginia Tech, RB

GREEN BAY PACKERS

Year Player, College, Position

1936 Russ Letlow, San Francisco, G
1937 Eddie Jankowski, Wisconsin, B
1938 Cecil Isbell, Purdue, B
1939 Larry Buhler, Minnesota, B
1940 Harold Van Every, Minnesota, B
1941 George Paskvan, Wisconsin, B
1942 Urban Odson, Minnesota, T
1943 Dick Wildung, Minnesota, T
1944 Merv Pregulman, Michigan, G
1945 Walt Schlinkman, Texas Tech, B
1946 Johnny Strzykalski, Marquette, B
1947 Ernie Case, UCLA, B
1948 Earl (Jug) Girard, Wisconsin, B
1949 Stan Heath, Nevada, B
1950 Clayton Tonnemaker, Minnesota, C
1951 Bob Gain, Kentucky, T
1952 Babe Parilli, Kentucky, QB
1953 Al Carmichael, So. California, B
1954 Art Hunter, Notre Dame, T
Veryl Switzer, Kansas State, B
1955 Tom Bettis, Purdue, G
1956 Jack Losch, Miami, B
1957 Paul Hornung, Notre Dame, B
Ron Kramer, Michigan, E
1958 Dan Currie, Michigan State, C
1959 Randy Duncan, Iowa, B
1960 Tom Moore, Vanderbilt, RB
1961 Herb Adderley, Michigan State, CB
1962 Earl Gros, Louisiana State, RB

1963 Dave Robinson, Penn State, LB
1964 Lloyd Voss, Nebraska, DT
1965 Donny Anderson, Texas Tech, RB
Lawrence Elkins, Baylor, E
1966 Jim Grabowski, Illinois, RB
Gale Gillingham, Minnesota, T
1967 Bob Hyland, Boston College, C
Don Horn, San Diego State, QB
1968 Fred Carr, Texas-El Paso, LB
Bill Lueck, Arizona, G
1969 Rich Moore, Villanova, DT
1970 Mike McCoy, Notre Dame, DT
Rich McGeorge, Elon, TE
1971 John Brockington, Ohio State, RB
1972 Willie Buchanon, San Diego St., DB
Jerry Tagge, Nebraska, QB
1973 Barry Smith, Florida State, WR
1974 Barty Smith, Richmond, RB
1975 Bill Bain, So. California, G (2)
1976 Mark Koncar, Colorado, T
1977 Mike Butler, Kansas, DE
Ezra Johnson, Morris Brown, DE
1978 James Lofton, Stanford, WR
John Anderson, Michigan, LB
1979 Eddie Lee Ivery, Georgia Tech, RB
1980 Bruce Clark, Penn State, DE
George Cumby, Oklahoma, LB
1981 Rich Campbell, California, QB
1982 Ron Hallstrom, Iowa, G
1983 Tim Lewis, Pittsburgh, DB
1984 Alphonso Carreker, Florida St., DE
1985 Ken Ruettgers, So. California, T
1986 Kenneth Davis, TCU, RB (2)
1987 Brent Fullwood, Auburn, RB
1988 Sterling Sharpe, South Carolina, WR
1989 Tony Mandarich, Michigan State, T
1990 Tony Bennett, Mississippi, LB
Darrell Thompson, Minnesota, RB
1991 Vinnie Clark, Ohio State, DB
1992 Terrell Buckley, Florida State, DB
1993 Wayne Simmons, Clemson, LB
George Teague, Alabama, DB
1994 Aaron Taylor, Notre Dame, T
1995 Craig Newsome, Arizona State, DB
1996 John Michels, Southern California, T
1997 Ross Verba, Iowa, T
1998 Vonnie Holliday, North Carolina, DT
1999 Antuan Edwards, Clemson, DB
2000 Bubba Franks, Miami, TE
2001 Jamal Reynolds, Florida State, DE
2002 Javon Walker, Florida State, WR
2003 Nick Barnett, Oregon State, LB
2004 Ahmad Carroll, Arkansas, DB

HOUSTON TEXANS

Year Player, College, Position
2002 David Carr, Fresno State, QB
2003 Andre Johnson, Miami, WR
2004 Dunta Robinson, South Carolina, DB
Jason Babin, Western Michigan, LB

INDIANAPOLIS COLTS

Year Player, College, Position
1953 Billy Vessels, Oklahoma, B
1954 Cotton Davidson, Baylor, B
1955 George Shaw, Oregon, B
Alan Ameche, Wisconsin, FB
1956 Lenny Moore, Penn State, B
1957 Jim Parker, Ohio State, G
1958 Lenny Lyles, Louisville, B
1959 Jackie Burkett, Auburn, C
1960 Ron Mix, Southern California, T
1961 Tom Matte, Ohio State, RB
1962 Wendell Harris, Louisiana State, S
1963 Bob Vogel, Ohio State, T
1964 Marv Woodson, Indiana, CB
1965 Mike Curtis, Duke, LB
1966 Sam Ball, Kentucky, T
1967 Bubba Smith, Michigan State, DT
Jim Detwiler, Michigan, RB
1968 John Williams, Minnesota, G
1969 Eddie Hinton, Oklahoma, WR
1970 Norman Bulaich, Texas Christian, RB
1971 Don McCauley, North Carolina, RB
Leonard Dunlap, North Texas St., DB
1972 Tom Drougas, Oregon, T
1973 Bert Jones, Louisiana State, QB
Joe Ehrmann, Syracuse, DT
1974 John Dutton, Nebraska, DE
Roger Carr, Louisiana Tech, WR
1975 Ken Huff, North Carolina, G
1976 Ken Novak, Purdue, DT
1977 Randy Burke, Kentucky, WR
1978 Reese McCall, Auburn, TE
1979 Barry Krauss, Alabama, LB
1980 Curtis Dickey, Texas A&M, RB
Derrick Hatchett, Texas, DB
1981 Randy McMillan, Pittsburgh, RB
Donnell Thompson, North Carolina, DT
1982 Johnie Cooks, Mississippi St., LB
Art Schlichter, Ohio State, QB
1983 John Elway, Stanford, QB
1984 Leonard Coleman, Vanderbilt, DB
Ron Solt, Maryland, G
1985 Duane Bickett, So. California, LB
1986 Jon Hand, Alabama, DE
1987 Cornelius Bennett, Alabama, LB
1988 Chris Chandler, Washington, QB (3)
1989 Andre Rison, Michigan State, WR
1990 Jeff George, Illinois, QB
1991 Shane Curry, Miami, DE (2)
1992 Steve Emtman, Washington, DT
Quentin Coryatt, Texas A&M, LB
1993 Sean Dawkins, California, WR
1994 Marshall Faulk, San Diego St., RB
Trev Alberts, Nebraska, LB
1995 Ellis Johnson, Florida, DT
1996 Marvin Harrison, Syracuse, WR
1997 Tarik Glenn, California, T
1998 Peyton Manning, Tennessee, QB
1999 Edgerrin James, Miami, RB
2000 Rob Morris, Brigham Young, LB
2001 Reggie Wayne, Miami, WR
2002 Dwight Freeney, Syracuse, DE
2003 Dallas Clark, Iowa, TE
2004 Bob Sanders, Iowa, DB (2)

JACKSONVILLE JAGUARS

Year Player, College, Position
1995 Tony Boselli, Southern California, T
James Stewart, Tennessee, RB
1996 Kevin Hardy, Illinois, LB
1997 Renaldo Wynn, Notre Dame, DT
1998 Fred Taylor, Florida, RB
Donovin Darius, Syracuse, DB
1999 Fernando Bryant, Alabama, DB
2000 R. Jay Soward, So. California, WR
2001 Marcus Stroud, Georgia, DT
2002 John Henderson, Tennessee, DT
2003 Byron Leftwich, Marshall, QB
2004 Reggie Williams, Washington, WR

KANSAS CITY CHIEFS

Year Player, College, Position
1960 Don Meredith, So. Methodist, QB
1961 E.J. Holub, Texas Tech, C
1962 Ronnie Bull, Baylor, RB
1963 Buck Buchanan, Grambling, DT
Ed Budde, Michigan State, G
1964 Pete Beathard, So. California, QB
1965 Gale Sayers, Kansas, RB
1966 Aaron Brown, Minnesota, DE
1967 Gene Trosch, Miami, DE-DT
1968 Mo Moorman, Texas A&M, G
George Daney, Texas-El Paso, G
1969 Jim Marsalis, Tennessee State, CB
1970 Sid Smith, Southern California, T
1971 Elmo Wright, Houston, WR
1972 Jeff Kinney, Nebraska, RB
1973 Gary Butler, Rice, TE (2)
1974 Woody Green, Arizona State, RB
1975 Elmore Stephens, Kentucky, TE (2)
1976 Rod Walters, Iowa, G
1977 Gary Green, Baylor, DB
1978 Art Still, Kentucky, DE
1979 Mike Bell, Colorado State, DE
Steve Fuller, Clemson, QB
1980 Brad Budde, Southern California, G
1981 Willie Scott, South Carolina, TE
1982 Anthony Hancock, Tennessee, WR
1983 Todd Blackledge, Penn State, QB
1984 Bill Maas, Pittsburgh, DT
John Alt, Iowa, T
1985 Ethan Horton, North Carolina, RB
1986 Brian Jozwiak, West Virginia, T
1987 Paul Palmer, Temple, RB
1988 Neil Smith, Nebraska, DE
1989 Derrick Thomas, Alabama, LB
1990 Percy Snow, Michigan State, LB
1991 Harvey Williams, Louisiana St., RB
1992 Dale Carter, Tennessee, DB
1993 Will Shields, Nebraska, G (3)
1994 Greg Hill, Texas A&M, RB
1995 Trezelle Jenkins, Michigan, T
1996 Jerome Woods, Memphis, DB
1997 Tony Gonzalez, California, TE
1998 Victor Riley, Auburn, T
1999 John Tait, Brigham Young, T
2000 Sylvester Morris, Jackson St., WR
2001 Eric Downing, Syracuse, DT (3)
2002 Ryan Sims, North Carolina, DT
2003 Larry Johnson, Penn State, RB
2004 Junior Siavii, Oregon, DT (2)

MIAMI DOLPHINS

Year Player, College, Position
1966 Jim Grabowski, Illinois, RB
Rick Norton, Kentucky, QB
1967 Bob Griese, Purdue, QB
1968 Larry Csonka, Syracuse, RB
Doug Crusan, Indiana, T
1969 Bill Stanfill, Georgia, DE
1970 Jim Mandich, Michigan, TE (2)
1971 Otto Stowe, Iowa State, WR (2)
1972 Mike Kadish, Notre Dame, DT
1973 Chuck Bradley, Oregon, C (2)
1974 Donald Reese, Jackson State, DE
1975 Darryl Carlton, Tampa, T
1976 Larry Gordon, Arizona State, LB
Kim Bokamper, San Jose State, LB

1977 A.J. Duhe, Louisiana State, DT
1978 Guy Benjamin, Stanford, QB (2)
1979 Jon Giesler, Michigan, T
1980 Don McNeal, Alabama, DB
1981 David Overstreet, Oklahoma, RB
1982 Roy Foster, Southern California, G
1983 Dan Marino, Pittsburgh, QB
1984 Jackie Shipp, Oklahoma, LB
1985 Lorenzo Hampton, Florida, RB
1986 John Offerdahl, Western Michigan, LB (2)
1987 John Bosa, Boston College, DE
1988 Eric Kumerow, Ohio State, DE
1989 Sammie Smith, Florida State, RB
Louis Oliver, Florida, DB
1990 Richmond Webb, Texas A&M, T
1991 Randal Hill, Miami, WR
1992 Troy Vincent, Wisconsin, DB
Marco Coleman, Georgia Tech, LB
1993 O.J. McDuffie, Penn State, WR
1994 Tim Bowens, Mississippi, DT
1995 Billy Milner, Houston, T
1996 Daryl Gardener, Baylor, DT
1997 Yatil Green, Miami, WR
1998 John Avery, Mississippi, RB
1999 J.J. Johnson, Mississippi St., RB (2)
2000 Todd Wade, Mississippi, T (2)
2001 Jamar Fletcher, Wisconsin, DB
2002 Seth McKinney, Texas A&M, C (3)
2003 Eddie Moore, Tennessee, LB (2)
2004 Vernon Carey, Miami, T

MINNESOTA VIKINGS

Year Player, College, Position

1961 Tommy Mason, Tulane, RB
1962 Bill Miller, Miami, WR (3)
1963 Jim Dunaway, Mississippi, T
1964 Carl Eller, Minnesota, DE
1965 Jack Snow, Notre Dame, WR
1966 Jerry Shay, Purdue, DT
1967 Clint Jones, Michigan State, RB
Gene Washington, Michigan St., WR
Alan Page, Notre Dame, DT
1968 Ron Yary, Southern California, T
1969 Ed White, California, G (2)
1970 John Ward, Oklahoma State, DT
1971 Leo Hayden, Ohio State, RB
1972 Jeff Siemon, Stanford, LB
1973 Chuck Foreman, Miami, RB
1974 Fred McNeill, UCLA, LB
Steve Riley, Southern California, T
1975 Mark Mullaney, Colorado State, DE
1976 James White, Oklahoma State, DT
1977 Tommy Kramer, Rice, QB
1978 Randy Holloway, Pittsburgh, DE
1979 Ted Brown, North Carolina St., RB
1980 Doug Martin, Washington, DT
1981 Mardye McDole, Mississippi St., WR (2)
1982 Darrin Nelson, Stanford, RB
1983 Joey Browner, So. California, DB
1984 Keith Millard, Washington St., DE
1985 Chris Doleman, Pittsburgh, LB
1986 Gerald Robinson, Auburn, DE
1987 D.J. Dozier, Penn State, RB
1988 Randall McDaniel, Arizona State, G
1989 David Braxton, Wake Forest, LB (2)
1990 Mike Jones, Texas A&M, TE (3)
1991 Carlos Jenkins, Michigan St., LB (3)
1992 Robert Harris, Southern Univ., DE (2)
1993 Robert Smith, Ohio State, RB
1994 DeWayne Washington, N. Carolina St., DB
Todd Steussie, California, T
1995 Derrick Alexander, Florida St., DE
Korey Stringer, Ohio State, T
1996 Duane Clemons, California, DE
1997 Dwayne Rudd, Alabama, LB
1998 Randy Moss, Marshall, WR
1999 Daunte Culpepper, Central Florida, QB
Dimitrius Underwood, Michigan St., DE
2000 Chris Hovan, Boston College, DT
2001 Michael Bennett, Wisconsin, RB
2002 Bryant McKinnie, Miami, T
2003 Kevin Williams, Oklahoma State, DT
2004 Kenechi Udeze, Southern California, DE

NEW ENGLAND PATRIOTS

Year Player, College, Position

1960 Ron Burton, Northwestern, RB
1961 Tommy Mason, Tulane, RB
1962 Gary Collins, Maryland, WR
1963 Art Graham, Boston College, WR
1964 Jack Concannon, Boston College, QB
1965 Jerry Rush, Michigan State, DE
1966 Karl Singer, Purdue, T
1967 John Charles, Purdue, S
1968 Dennis Byrd, North Carolina St., DE
1969 Ron Sellers, Florida State, WR
1970 Phil Olsen, Utah State, DE
1971 Jim Plunkett, Stanford, QB
1972 Tom Reynolds, San Diego St., WR (2)
1973 John Hannah, Alabama, G
Sam Cunningham, So. California, RB
Darryl Stingley, Purdue, WR
1974 Steve Corbett, Boston College, G (2)
1975 Russ Francis, Oregon, TE
1976 Mike Haynes, Arizona State, DB
Pete Brock, Colorado, C
Tim Fox, Ohio State, DB
1977 Raymond Clayborn, Texas, DB
Stanley Morgan, Tennessee, WR
1978 Bob Cryder, Alabama, G
1979 Rick Sanford, South Carolina, DB
1980 Roland James, Tennessee, DB
Vagas Ferguson, Notre Dame, RB
1981 Brian Holloway, Stanford, T
1982 Kenneth Sims, Texas, DT
Lester Williams, Miami, DT
1983 Tony Eason, Illinois, QB
1984 Irving Fryar, Nebraska, WR
1985 Trevor Matich, Brigham Young, C
1986 Reggie Dupard, So. Methodist, RB
1987 Bruce Armstrong, Louisville, T
1988 John Stephens, Northwestern St., La., RB
1989 Hart Lee Dykes, Oklahoma St., WR
1990 Chris Singleton, Arizona, LB
Ray Agnew, North Carolina St., DE
1991 Pat Harlow, Southern California, T
Leonard Russell, Arizona St., RB
1992 Eugene Chung, Virginia Tech, T
1993 Drew Bledsoe, Washington St., QB
1994 Willie McGinest, So. California, DE
1995 Ty Law, Michigan, DB
1996 Terry Glenn, Ohio State, WR
1997 Chris Canty, Kansas State, DB
1998 Robert Edwards, Georgia, RB
Tebucky Jones, Syracuse, DB
1999 Damien Woody, Boston College, C
Andy Katzenmoyer, Ohio State, LB
2000 Adrian Klemm, Hawaii, T (2)
2001 Richard Seymour, Georgia, DT
2002 Daniel Graham, Colorado, TE
2003 Ty Warren, Texas A&M, DT
2004 Vince Wilfork, Miami, DT
Ben Watson, Georgia, TE

NEW ORLEANS SAINTS

Year Player, College, Position

1967 Les Kelley, Alabama, RB
1968 Kevin Hardy, Notre Dame, DE
1969 John Shinners, Xavier, G
1970 Ken Burrough, Texas Southern, WR
1971 Archie Manning, Mississippi, QB
1972 Royce Smith, Georgia, G
1973 Derland Moore, Oklahoma, DE (2)
1974 Rick Middleton, Ohio State, LB
1975 Larry Burton, Purdue, WR
Kurt Schumacher, Ohio State, T
1976 Chuck Muncie, California, RB
1977 Joe Campbell, Maryland, DE
1978 Wes Chandler, Florida, WR
1979 Russell Erxleben, Texas, P-K
1980 Stan Brock, Colorado, T
1981 George Rogers, South Carolina, RB
1982 Lindsay Scott, Georgia, WR
1983 Steve Korte, Arkansas, G (2)
1984 James Geathers, Wichita State, DE
1985 Alvin Toles, Tennessee, LB
1986 Jim Dombrowski, Virginia, T
1987 Shawn Knight, Brigham Young, DT
1988 Craig Heyward, Pittsburgh, RB
1989 Wayne Martin, Arkansas, DE
1990 Renaldo Turnbull, West Virginia, DE
1991 Wesley Carroll, Miami, WR (2)
1992 Vaughn Dunbar, Indiana, RB
1993 Willie Roaf, Louisiana Tech, T
Irv Smith, Notre Dame, TE
1994 Joe Johnson, Louisville, DE
1995 Mark Fields, Washington State, LB
1996 Alex Molden, Oregon, DB
1997 Chris Naeole, Colorado, G
1998 Kyle Turley, San Diego State, T
1999 Ricky Williams, Texas, RB
2000 Darren Howard, Kansas St., DE (2)
2001 Deuce McAllister, Mississippi, RB
2002 Donte' Stallworth, Tennessee, WR
Charles Grant, Georgia, DE
2003 Johnathan Sullivan, Georgia, DT
2004 Will Smith, Ohio State, DE

NEW YORK GIANTS

Year Player, College, Position

1936 Art Lewis, Ohio U., T
1937 Ed Widseth, Minnesota, T
1938 George Karamatic, Gonzaga, B
1939 Walt Neilson, Arizona, B
1940 Grenville Lansdell, So. California, B
1941 George Franck, Minnesota, B
1942 Merle Hapes, Mississippi, B
1943 Steve Filipowicz, Fordham, B
1944 Billy Hillenbrand, Indiana, B
1945 Elmer Barbour, Wake Forest, B
1946 George Connor, Notre Dame, T
1947 Vic Schwall, Northwestern, B
1948 Tony Minisi, Pennsylvania, B
1949 Paul Page, Southern Methodist, B
1950 Travis Tidwell, Auburn, B
1951 Kyle Rote, Southern Methodist, B
Jim Spavital, Oklahoma A&M, B
1952 Frank Gifford, Southern California, B
1953 Bobby Marlow, Alabama, B
1954 Ken Buck, Pacific, C (2)

1955 Joe Heap, Notre Dame, B
1956 Henry Moore, Arkansas, B (2)
1957 Sam DeLuca, South Carolina, T (2)
1958 Phil King, Vanderbilt, B
1959 Lee Grosscup, Utah, B
1960 Lou Cordileone, Clemson, G
1961 Bruce Tarbox, Syracuse, G (2)
1962 Jerry Hillebrand, Colorado, LB
1963 Frank Lasky, Florida, T (2)
1964 Joe Don Looney, Oklahoma, RB
1965 Tucker Frederickson, Auburn, RB
1966 Francis Peay, Missouri, T
1967 Louis Thompson, Alabama, DT (4)
1968 Dick Buzin, Penn State, T (2)
1969 Fred Dryer, San Diego State, DE
1970 Jim Files, Oklahoma, LB
1971 Rocky Thompson, West Texas St., WR
1972 Eldridge Small, Texas A&I, DB
Larry Jacobson, Nebraska, DE
1973 Brad Van Pelt, Michigan St., LB (2)
1974 John Hicks, Ohio State, G
1975 Al Simpson, Colorado State, T (2)
1976 Troy Archer, Colorado, DE
1977 Gary Jeter, Southern California, DT
1978 Gordon King, Stanford, T
1979 Phil Simms, Morehead State, QB
1980 Mark Haynes, Colorado, DB
1981 Lawrence Taylor, North Carolina, LB
1982 Butch Woolfolk, Michigan, RB
1983 Terry Kinard, Clemson, DB
1984 Carl Banks, Michigan State, LB
William Roberts, Ohio State, T
1985 George Adams, Kentucky, RB
1986 Eric Dorsey, Notre Dame, DE
1987 Mark Ingram, Michigan State, WR
1988 Eric Moore, Indiana, T
1989 Brian Williams, Minnesota, C-G
1990 Rodney Hampton, Georgia, RB
1991 Jarrod Bunch, Michigan, RB
1992 Derek Brown, Notre Dame, TE
1993 Michael Strahan, Texas Southern, DE (2)
1994 Thomas Lewis, Indiana, WR
1995 Tyrone Wheatley, Michigan, RB
1996 Cedric Jones, Oklahoma, DE
1997 Ike Hilliard, Florida, WR
1998 Shaun Williams, UCLA, DB
1999 Luke Petitgout, Notre Dame, T
2000 Ron Dayne, Wisconsin, RB
2001 Will Allen, Syracuse, DB
2002 Jeremy Shockey, Miami, TE
2003 William Joseph, Miami, DT
2004 Philip Rivers, North Carolina St., QB

NEW YORK JETS
Year Player, College, Position
1960 George Izo, Notre Dame, QB
1961 Tom Brown, Minnesota, G
1962 Sandy Stephens, Minnesota, QB
1963 Jerry Stovall, Louisiana State, S
1964 Matt Snell, Ohio State, RB
1965 Joe Namath, Alabama, QB
Tom Nowatzke, Indiana, RB
1966 Bill Yearby, Michigan, DT
1967 Paul Seiler, Notre Dame, T
1968 Lee White, Weber State, RB
1969 Dave Foley, Ohio State, T
1970 Steve Tannen, Florida, CB
1971 John Riggins, Kansas, RB
1972 Jerome Barkum, Jackson St., WR
Mike Taylor, Michigan, LB
1973 Burgess Owens, Miami, DB
1974 Carl Barzilauskas, Indiana, DT
1975 Anthony Davis, So. California, RB (2)
1976 Richard Todd, Alabama, QB
1977 Marvin Powell, So. California, T
1978 Chris Ward, Ohio State, T
1979 Marty Lyons, Alabama, DE
1980 Johnny (Lam) Jones, Texas, WR
1981 Freeman McNeil, UCLA, RB
1982 Bob Crable, Notre Dame, LB
1983 Ken O'Brien, Cal-Davis, QB
1984 Russell Carter, So. Methodist, DB
Ron Faurot, Arkansas, DE
1985 Al Toon, Wisconsin, WR
1986 Mike Haight, Iowa, T
1987 Roger Vick, Texas A&M, RB
1988 Dave Cadigan, So. California, T
1989 Jeff Lageman, Virginia, LB
1990 Blair Thomas, Penn State, RB
1991 Browning Nagle, Louisville, QB (2)
1992 Johnny Mitchell, Nebraska, TE
1993 Marvin Jones, Florida State, LB
1994 Aaron Glenn, Texas A&M, DB
1995 Kyle Brady, Penn State, TE
Hugh Douglas, Central St., Ohio, DE
1996 Keyshawn Johnson, So. California, WR
1997 James Farrior, Virginia, LB
1998 Dorian Boose, Washington St., DE (2)
1999 Randy Thomas, Mississippi St., G (2)
2000 Shaun Ellis, Tennessee, DE
John Abraham, South Carolina, LB
Chad Pennington, Marshall, QB
Anthony Becht, West Virginia, TE
2001 Santana Moss, Miami, WR
2002 Bryan Thomas, Ala.-Birmingham, DE
2003 Dewayne Robertson, Kentucky, DT
2004 Jonathan Vilma, Miami, LB

OAKLAND RAIDERS
Year Player, College, Position
1960 Dale Hackbart, Wisconsin, CB
1961 Joe Rutgens, Illinois, DT
1962 Roman Gabriel, North Carolina St., QB
1963 George Wilson, Alabama, RB (6)
1964 Tony Lorick, Arizona State, RB
1965 Harry Schuh, Memphis State, T
1966 Rodger Bird, Kentucky, S
1967 Gene Upshaw, Texas A&I, G
1968 Eldridge Dickey, Tennessee St., QB
1969 Art Thoms, Syracuse, DT
1970 Raymond Chester, Morgan St., TE
1971 Jack Tatum, Ohio State, S
1972 Mike Siani, Villanova, WR
1973 Ray Guy, Southern Mississippi, P
1974 Henry Lawrence, Florida A&M, T
1975 Neal Colzie, Ohio State, DB
1976 Charles Philyaw, Texas Southern, DT (2)
1977 Mike Davis, Colorado, DB (2)
1978 Dave Browning, Washington, DE (2)
1979 Willie Jones, Florida State, DE (2)
1980 Marc Wilson, Brigham Young, QB
1981 Ted Watts, Texas Tech, DB
Curt Marsh, Washington, T
1982 Marcus Allen, So. California, RB
1983 Don Mosebar, So. California, T
1984 Sean Jones, Northeastern, DE (2)
1985 Jessie Hester, Florida State, WR
1986 Bob Buczkowski, Pittsburgh, DE
1987 John Clay, Missouri, T
1988 Tim Brown, Notre Dame, WR
Terry McDaniel, Tennessee, DB
Scott Davis, Illinois, DE
1989 Jeff Francis, Tennessee, QB (6)
1990 Anthony Smith, Arizona, DE
1991 Todd Marinovich, So. California, QB
1992 Chester McGlockton, Clemson, DE
1993 Patrick Bates, Texas A&M, DB
1994 Rob Fredrickson, Michigan St., LB
1995 Napoleon Kaufman, Washington, RB
1996 Rickey Dudley, Ohio State, TE
1997 Darrell Russell, Southern
California, DT
1998 Charles Woodson, Michigan, DB
Mo Collins, Florida, T
1999 Matt Stinchcomb, Georgia, T
2000 Sebastian Janikowski, Florida St., K
2001 Derrick Gibson, Florida State, DB
2002 Phillip Buchanon, Miami, DB
Napoleon Harris, Northwestern, LB
2003 Nnamdi Asomugha, California, DB
Tyler Brayton, Colorado, DE
2004 Robert Gallery, Iowa, T

PHILADELPHIA EAGLES
Year Player, College, Position
1936 Jay Berwanger, Chicago, B
1937 Sam Francis, Nebraska, B
1938 Jim McDonald, Ohio State, B
1939 Davey O'Brien, Texas Christian, B
1940 George McAfee, Duke, B
1941 Art Jones, Richmond, B (2)
1942 Pete Kmetovic, Stanford, B
1943 Joe Muha, Virginia Military, B
1944 Steve Van Buren, Louisiana St., B
1945 John Yonaker, Notre Dame, E
1946 Leo Riggs, Southern California, B
1947 Neill Armstrong, Oklahoma A&M, E
1948 Clyde (Smackover) Scott, Arkansas, B
1949 Chuck Bednarik, Pennsylvania, C
Frank Tripucka, Notre Dame, B
1950 Harry (Bud) Grant, Minnesota, E
1951 Ebert Van Buren, Louisiana St., B
Chet Mutryn, Xavier, B
1952 Johnny Bright, Drake, B
1953 Al Conway, Army, B (2)
1954 Neil Worden, Notre Dame, B
1955 Dick Bielski, Maryland, B
1956 Bob Pellegrini, Maryland, C
1957 Clarence Peaks, Michigan State, B
1958 Walt Kowalczyk, Michigan State, B
1959 J.D. Smith, Rice, T (2)
1960 Ron Burton, Northwestern, RB
1961 Art Baker, Syracuse, RB
1962 Pete Case, Georgia, G (2)
1963 Ed Budde, Michigan State, G
1964 Bob Brown, Nebraska, T
1965 Ray Rissmiller, Georgia, T (2)
1966 Randy Beisler, Indiana, DE
1967 Harry Jones, Arkansas, RB
1968 Tim Rossovich, So. California, DE
1969 Leroy Keyes, Purdue, RB
1970 Steve Zabel, Oklahoma, TE
1971 Richard Harris, Grambling, DE
1972 John Reaves, Florida, QB
1973 Jerry Sisemore, Texas, T
Charle Young, So. California, TE
1974 Mitch Sutton, Kansas, DT (3)
1975 Bill Capraun, Miami, T (7)
1976 Mike Smith, Florida, DE (4)
1977 Skip Sharp, Kansas, DB (5)

1978 Reggie Wilkes, Georgia Tech, LB (3)
1979 Jerry Robinson, UCLA, LB
1980 Roynell Young, Alcorn State, DB
1981 Leonard Mitchell, Houston, DE
1982 Mike Quick, North Carolina St., WR
1983 Michael Haddix, Mississippi St., RB
1984 Kenny Jackson, Penn State, WR
1985 Kevin Allen, Indiana, T
1986 Keith Byars, Ohio State, RB
1987 Jerome Brown, Miami, DT
1988 Keith Jackson, Oklahoma, TE
1989 Jessie Small, Eastern Kentucky, LB (2)
1990 Ben Smith, Georgia, DB
1991 Antone Davis, Tennessee, T
1992 Siran Stacy, Alabama, RB (2)
1993 Lester Holmes, Jackson State, T
Leonard Renfro, Colorado, DT
1994 Bernard Williams, Georgia, T
1995 Mike Mamula, Boston College, DE
1996 Jermane Mayberry, Texas A&M-Kingsville, T
1997 Jon Harris, Virginia, DE
1998 Tra Thomas, Florida State, T
1999 Donovan McNabb, Syracuse, QB
2000 Corey Simon, Florida State, DT
2001 Freddie Mitchell, UCLA, WR
2002 Lito Sheppard, Florida, DB
2003 Jerome McDougle, Miami, DE
2004 Shawn Andrews, Arkansas, T

PITTSBURGH STEELERS

Year Player, College, Position

1936 Bill Shakespeare, Notre Dame, B
1937 Mike Basrak, Duquesne, C
1938 Byron (Whizzer) White, Colorado, B
1939 Bill Patterson, Baylor, B (3)
1940 Kay Eakin, Arkansas, B
1941 Chet Gladchuk, Boston College, C (2)
1942 Bill Dudley, Virginia, B
1943 Bill Daley, Minnesota, B
1944 Johnny Podesto, St. Mary's, Calif., B
1945 Paul Duhart, Florida, B
1946 Felix (Doc) Blanchard, Army, B
1947 Hub Bechtol, Texas, E
1948 Dan Edwards, Georgia, E
1949 Bobby Gage, Clemson, B
1950 Lynn Chandnois, Michigan St., B
1951 Butch Avinger, Alabama, B
1952 Ed Modzelewski, Maryland, B
1953 Ted Marchibroda, St. Bonaventure, B
1954 Johnny Lattner, Notre Dame, B
1955 Frank Varrichione, Notre Dame, T
1956 Gary Glick, Colorado A&M, B
Art Davis, Mississippi State, B
1957 Len Dawson, Purdue, B
1958 Larry Krutko, West Virginia, B (2)
1959 Tom Barnett, Purdue, B (8)
1960 Jack Spikes, Texas Christian, RB
1961 Myron Pottios, Notre Dame, LB (2)
1962 Bob Ferguson, Ohio State, RB
1963 Frank Atkinson, Stanford, T (8)
1964 Paul Martha, Pittsburgh, S
1965 Roy Jefferson, Utah, WR (2)
1966 Dick Leftridge, West Virginia, RB
1967 Don Shy, San Diego State, RB (2)
1968 Mike Taylor, Southern California, T
1969 Joe Greene, North Texas State, DT
1970 Terry Bradshaw, Louisiana Tech, QB
1971 Frank Lewis, Grambling, WR
1972 Franco Harris, Penn State, RB
1973 J.T. Thomas, Florida State, DB
1974 Lynn Swann, So. California, WR
1975 Dave Brown, Michigan, DB
1976 Bennie Cunningham, Clemson, TE
1977 Robin Cole, New Mexico, LB
1978 Ron Johnson, Eastern Michigan, DB
1979 Greg Hawthorne, Baylor, RB
1980 Mark Malone, Arizona State, QB
1981 Keith Gary, Oklahoma, DE
1982 Walter Abercrombie, Baylor, RB
1983 Gabriel Rivera, Texas Tech, DT
1984 Louis Lipps, So. Mississippi, WR
1985 Darryl Sims, Wisconsin, DE
1986 John Rienstra, Temple, G
1987 Rod Woodson, Purdue, DB
1988 Aaron Jones, Eastern Kentucky, DE
1989 Tim Worley, Georgia, RB
Tom Ricketts, Pittsburgh, T
1990 Eric Green, Liberty, TE
1991 Huey Richardson, Florida, DE
1992 Leon Searcy, Miami, T
1993 Deon Figures, Colorado, DB
1994 Charles Johnson, Colorado, WR
1995 Mark Bruener, Washington, TE
1996 Jamain Stephens, North Carolina A&T, T
1997 Chad Scott, Maryland, DB
1998 Alan Faneca, Louisiana State, G
1999 Troy Edwards, Lousiana Tech, WR
2000 Plaxico Burress, Michigan St., WR
2001 Casey Hampton, Texas, DT
2002 Kendall Simmons, Auburn, G
2003 Troy Polamalu, Southern California, DB
2004 Ben Roethlisberger, Miami (OH), QB

ST. LOUIS RAMS

Year Player, College, Position

1937 Johnny Drake, Purdue, B
1938 Corbett Davis, Indiana, B
1939 Parker Hall, Mississippi, B
1940 Ollie Cordill, Rice, B
1941 Rudy Mucha, Washington, C
1942 Jack Wilson, Baylor, B
1943 Mike Holovak, Boston College, B
1944 Tony Butkovich, Illinois, B
1945 Elroy (Crazylegs) Hirsch, Wisconsin, B
1946 Emil Sitko, Notre Dame, B
1947 Herman Wedemeyer, St. Mary's, Calif., B
1948 Tom Keane, West Virginia, B (2)
1949 Bobby Thomason, Virginia Military, B
1950 Ralph Pasquariello, Villanova, B
Stan West, Oklahoma, G
1951 Bud McFadin, Texas, G
1952 Bill Wade, Vanderbilt, QB
Bob Carey, Michigan State, E
1953 Donn Moomaw, UCLA, C
Ed Barker, Washington State, E
1954 Ed Beatty, Cincinnati, C
1955 Larry Morris, Georgia Tech, C
1956 Joe Marconi, West Virginia, B
Charles Horton, Vanderbilt, B
1957 Jon Arnett, Southern California, B
Del Shofner, Baylor, E
1958 Lou Michaels, Kentucky, T
Jim Phillips, Auburn, E
1959 Dick Bass, Pacific, B
Paul Dickson, Baylor, T
1960 Billy Cannon, Louisiana State, RB
1961 Marlin McKeever, So. California, E-LB
1962 Roman Gabriel, North Carolina St., QB
Merlin Olsen, Utah State, DT
1963 Terry Baker, Oregon State, QB
Rufus Guthrie, Georgia Tech, G
1964 Bill Munson, Utah State, QB
1965 Clancy Williams, Washington St., CB
1966 Tom Mack, Michigan, G
1967 Willie Ellison, Texas Southern, RB (2)
1968 Gary Beban, UCLA, QB (2)
1969 Larry Smith, Florida, RB
Jim Seymour, Notre Dame, WR
Bob Klein, Southern California, TE
1970 Jack Reynolds, Tennessee, LB
1971 Isiah Robertson, Southern, LB
Jack Youngblood, Florida, DE
1972 Jim Bertelsen, Texas, RB (2)
1973 Cullen Bryant, Colorado, DB (2)
1974 John Cappelletti, Penn State, RB
1975 Mike Fanning, Notre Dame, DT
Dennis Harrah, Miami, T
Doug France, Ohio State, T
1976 Kevin McLain, Colorado State, LB
1977 Bob Brudzinski, Ohio State, LB
1978 Elvis Peacock, Oklahoma, RB
1979 George Andrews, Nebraska, LB
Kent Hill, Georgia Tech, T
1980 Johnnie Johnson, Texas, DB
1981 Mel Owens, Michigan, LB
1982 Barry Redden, Richmond, RB
1983 Eric Dickerson, So. Methodist, RB
1984 Hal Stephens, East Carolina, DE (5)
1985 Jerry Gray, Texas, DB
1986 Mike Schad, Queen's Univ., Canada, T
1987 Donald Evans, Winston-Salem, DE (2)
1988 Gaston Green, UCLA, RB
Aaron Cox, Arizona State, WR
1989 Bill Hawkins, Miami, DE
Cleveland Gary, Miami, RB
1990 Bern Brostek, Washington, C
1991 Todd Lyght, Notre Dame, DB
1992 Sean Gilbert, Pittsburgh, DE
1993 Jerome Bettis, Notre Dame, RB
1994 Wayne Gandy, Auburn, T
1995 Kevin Carter, Florida, DE
1996 Lawrence Phillips, Nebraska, RB
Eddie Kennison, Louisiana St., WR
1997 Orlando Pace, Ohio State, T
1998 Grant Wistrom, Nebraska, DE
1999 Torry Holt, North Carolina St., WR
2000 Trung Canidate, Arizona, RB
2001 Damione Lewis, Miami, DT
Adam Archuleta, Arizona State, DB
Ryan Pickett, Ohio State, DT
2002 Robert Thomas, UCLA, LB
2003 Jimmy Kennedy, Penn State, DT
2004 Steven Jackson, Oregon State, RB

SAN DIEGO CHARGERS

Year Player, College, Position

1960 Monty Stickles, Notre Dame, E
1961 Earl Faison, Indiana, DE
1962 Bob Ferguson, Ohio State, RB
1963 Walt Sweeney, Syracuse, G
1964 Ted Davis, Georgia Tech, LB
1965 Steve DeLong, Tennessee, DE
1966 Don Davis, Cal St.-Los Angeles, DT
1967 Ron Billingsley, Wyoming, DE
1968 Russ Washington, Missouri, DT
Jimmy Hill, Texas A&I, DB
1969 Marty Domres, Columbia, QB
Bob Babich, Miami, Ohio, LB
1970 Walker Gillette, Richmond, WR
1971 Leon Burns, Long Beach State, RB

1972 Pete Lazetich, Stanford, DE (2)
1973 Johnny Rodgers, Nebraska, WR
1974 Bo Matthews, Colorado, RB
Don Goode, Kansas, LB
1975 Gary Johnson, Grambling, DT
Mike Williams, Louisiana State, DB
1976 Joe Washington, Oklahoma, RB
1977 Bob Rush, Memphis State, C
1978 John Jefferson, Arizona State, WR
1979 Kellen Winslow, Missouri, TE
1980 Ed Luther, San Jose State, QB (4)
1981 James Brooks, Auburn, RB
1982 Hollis Hall, Clemson, DB (7)
1983 Billy Ray Smith, Arkansas, LB
Gary Anderson, Arkansas, WR
Gill Byrd, San Jose State, DB
1984 Mossy Cade, Texas, DB
1985 Jim Lachey, Ohio State, G
1986 Leslie O'Neal, Oklahoma State, DE
James FitzPatrick, So. California, T
1987 Rod Bernstine, Texas A&M, TE
1988 Anthony Miller, Tennessee, WR
1989 Burt Grossman, Pittsburgh, DE
1990 Junior Seau, So. California, LB
1991 Stanley Richard, Texas, DB
1992 Chris Mims, Tennessee, DE
1993 Darrien Gordon, Stanford, DB
1994 Isaac Davis, Arkansas, G (2)
1995 Terrance Shaw, Stephen F. Austin, DB (2)
1996 Bryan Still, Virginia Tech, WR (2)
1997 Freddie Jones, North Carolina, TE (2)
1998 Ryan Leaf, Washington State, QB
1999 Jermaine Fazande, Oklahoma, RB (2)
2000 Rogers Beckett, Marshall, DB (2)
2001 LaDainian Tomlinson, TCU, RB
2002 Quentin Jammer, Texas, DB
2003 Sammy Davis, Texas A&M, DB
2004 Eli Manning, Mississippi, QB

SAN FRANCISCO 49ERS

Year Player, College, Position
1950 Leo Nomellini, Minnesota, T
1951 Y.A. Tittle, Louisiana State, B
1952 Hugh McElhenny, Washington, B
1953 Harry Babcock, Georgia, E
Tom Stolhandske, Texas, E
1954 Bernie Faloney, Maryland, B
1955 Dickie Moegle, Rice, B
1956 Earl Morrall, Michigan State, B
1957 John Brodie, Stanford, B
1958 Jim Pace, Michigan, B
Charlie Krueger, Texas A&M, T
1959 Dave Baker, Oklahoma, B
Dan James, Ohio State, C
1960 Monty Stickles, Notre Dame, E
1961 Jimmy Johnson, UCLA, CB
Bernie Casey, Bowling Green, WR
Bill Kilmer, UCLA, QB
1962 Lance Alworth, Arkansas, WR
1963 Kermit Alexander, UCLA, CB
1964 Dave Parks, Texas Tech, WR
1965 Ken Willard, North Carolina, RB
George Donnelly, Illinois, DB
1966 Stan Hindman, Mississippi, DE
1967 Steve Spurrier, Florida, QB
Cas Banaszek, Northwestern, T
1968 Forrest Blue, Auburn, C
1969 Ted Kwalick, Penn State, TE
Gene Washington, Stanford, WR
1970 Cedrick Hardman, North Texas St., DE
Bruce Taylor, Boston U., DB
1971 Tim Anderson, Ohio State, DB
1972 Terry Beasley, Auburn, WR
1973 Mike Holmes, Texas Southern, DB
1974 Wilbur Jackson, Alabama, RB
Bill Sandifer, UCLA, DT
1975 Jimmy Webb, Mississippi St., DT
1976 Randy Cross, UCLA, C (2)
1977 Elmo Boyd, Eastern Kentucky, WR (3)
1978 Ken MacAfee, Notre Dame, TE
Dan Bunz, Cal St.-Long Beach, LB
1979 James Owens, UCLA, WR (2)
1980 Earl Cooper, Rice, RB
Jim Stuckey, Clemson, DT
1981 Ronnie Lott, So. California, DB
1982 Bubba Paris, Michigan, T (2)
1983 Roger Craig, Nebraska, RB (2)
1984 Todd Shell, Brigham Young, LB
1985 Jerry Rice, Mississippi Valley St., WR
1986 Larry Roberts, Alabama, DE (2)
1987 Harris Barton, North Carolina, T
Terrence Flagler, Clemson, RB
1988 Danny Stubbs, Miami, DE (2)
1989 Keith DeLong, Tennessee, LB
1990 Dexter Carter, Florida State, RB
1991 Ted Washington, Louisville, DT
1992 Dana Hall, Washington, DB
1993 Dana Stubblefield, Kansas, DT
Todd Kelly, Tennessee, DE
1994 Bryant Young, Notre Dame, DT
William Floyd, Florida State, RB
1995 J.J. Stokes, UCLA, WR
1996 Israel Ifeanyi, So.California, DE (2)
1997 Jim Druckenmiller, Virginia Tech, QB
1998 R.W. McQuarters, Oklahoma St., DB
1999 Reggie McGrew, Florida, DT
2000 Julian Peterson, Michigan St., LB
Ahmed Plummer, Ohio State, DB
2001 Andre Carter, California, DE
2002 Mike Rumph, Miami, DB
2003 Kwame Harris, Stanford, T
2004 Rashaun Woods, Oklahoma St., WR

SEATTLE SEAHAWKS

Year Player, College, Position
1976 Steve Niehaus, Notre Dame, DT
1977 Steve August, Tulsa, G
1978 Keith Simpson, Memphis St., DB
1979 Manu Tuiasosopo, UCLA, DT
1980 Jacob Green, Texas A&M, DE
1981 Ken Easley, UCLA, DB
1982 Jeff Bryant, Clemson, DE
1983 Curt Warner, Penn State, RB
1984 Terry Taylor, Southern Illinois, DB
1985 Owen Gill, Iowa, RB (2)
1986 John L. Williams, Florida, RB
1987 Tony Woods, Pittsburgh, LB
1988 Brian Blades, Miami, WR (2)
1989 Andy Heck, Notre Dame, T
1990 Cortez Kennedy, Miami, DT
1991 Dan McGwire, San Diego St., QB
1992 Ray Roberts, Virginia, T
1993 Rick Mirer, Notre Dame, QB
1994 Sam Adams, Texas A&M, DT
1995 Joey Galloway, Ohio State, WR
1996 Pete Kendall, Boston College, T
1997 Shawn Springs, Ohio State, DB
Walter Jones, Florida State, T
1998 Anthony Simmons, Clemson, LB
1999 Lamar King, Saginaw Valley St., DE
2000 Shaun Alexander, Alabama, RB
Chris McIntosh, Wisconsin, T
2001 Koren Robinson, North Carolina St., WR
Steve Hutchinson, Michigan, G
2002 Jerramy Stevens, Washington, TE
2003 Marcus Trufant, Washington State, DB
2004 Marcus Tubbs, Texas, DT

TAMPA BAY BUCCANEERS

Year Player, College, Position
1976 Lee Roy Selmon, Oklahoma, DT
1977 Ricky Bell, Southern California, RB
1978 Doug Williams, Grambling, QB
1979 Greg Roberts, Oklahoma, G (2)
1980 Ray Snell, Wisconsin, G
1981 Hugh Green, Pittsburgh, LB
1982 Sean Farrell, Penn State, G
1983 Randy Grimes, Baylor, C (2)
1984 Keith Browner, So. California, LB (2)
1985 Ron Holmes, Washington, DE
1986 Bo Jackson, Auburn, RB
Roderick Jones, So. Methodist, DB
1987 Vinny Testaverde, Miami, QB
1988 Paul Gruber, Wisconsin, T
1989 Broderick Thomas, Nebraska, LB
1990 Keith McCants, Alabama, LB
1991 Charles McRae, Tennessee, T
1992 Courtney Hawkins, Michigan St., WR (2)
1993 Eric Curry, Alabama, DE
1994 Trent Dilfer, Fresno State, QB
1995 Warren Sapp, Miami, DT
Derrick Brooks, Florida State, LB
1996 Regan Upshaw, California, DE
Marcus Jones, North Carolina, DT
1997 Warrick Dunn, Florida State, RB
Reidel Anthony, Florida, WR
1998 Jacquez Green, Florida, WR (2)
1999 Anthony McFarland, Louisiana St., DT
2000 Cosey Coleman, Tennessee, G (2)
2001 Kenyatta Walker, Florida, T
2002 Marquise Walker, Michigan, WR (3)
2003 Dewayne White, Louisville, DE (2)
2004 Michael Clayton, Louisiana St., WR

TENNESSEE TITANS

Year Player, College, Position
1960 Billy Cannon, Louisiana State, RB
1961 Mike Ditka, Pittsburgh, E
1962 Ray Jacobs, Howard Payne, DT
1963 Danny Brabham, Arkansas, LB
1964 Scott Appleton, Texas, DT
1965 Lawrence Elkins, Baylor, WR
1966 Tommy Nobis, Texas, LB
1967 George Webster, Michigan St., LB
Tom Regner, Notre Dame, G
1968 Mac Haik, Mississippi, WR (2)
1969 Ron Pritchard, Arizona State, LB
1970 Doug Wilkerson, N. Carolina Central, G
1971 Dan Pastorini, Santa Clara, QB
1972 Greg Sampson, Stanford, DE
1973 John Matuszak, Tampa, DE
George Amundson, Iowa State, RB
1974 Steve Manstedt, Nebraska, LB (4)
1975 Robert Brazile, Jackson State, LB
Don Hardeman, Texas A&I, RB
1976 Mike Barber, Louisiana Tech, TE (2)
1977 Morris Towns, Missouri, T
1978 Earl Campbell, Texas, RB
1979 Mike Stensrud, Iowa State, DE (2)
1980 Angelo Fields, Michigan St., T (2)

1981 Michael Holston, Morgan St., WR (3)
1982 Mike Munchak, Penn State, G
1983 Bruce Matthews, So. California, T
1984 Dean Steinkuhler, Nebraska, T
1985 Ray Childress, Texas A&M, DE
Richard Johnson, Wisconsin, DB
1986 Jim Everett, Purdue, QB
1987 Alonzo Highsmith, Miami, RB
Haywood Jeffires, North Carolina St., WR
1988 Lorenzo White, Michigan State, RB
1989 David Williams, Florida, T
1990 Lamar Lathon, Houston, LB
1991 Mike Dumas, Indiana, DB (2)
1992 Eddie Robinson, Alabama St., LB (2)
1993 Brad Hopkins, Illinois, T
1994 Henry Ford, Arkansas, DE
1995 Steve McNair, Alcorn State, QB
1996 Eddie George, Ohio State, RB
1997 Kenny Holmes, Miami, DE
1998 Kevin Dyson, Utah, WR
1999 Jevon Kearse, Florida, DE
2000 Keith Bulluck, Syracuse, LB
2001 Andre Dyson, Utah, DB (2)
2002 Albert Haynesworth, Tennessee, DT
2003 Andre Woolfolk, Oklahoma, DB
2004 Ben Troupe, Florida, TE (2)

WASHINGTON REDSKINS

Year Player, College, Position
1936 Riley Smith, Alabama, B
1937 Sammy Baugh, Texas Christian, B
1938 Andy Farkas, Detroit, B
1939 I.B. Hale, Texas Christian, T
1940 Ed Boell, New York U., B
1941 Forest Evashevski, Michigan, B
1942 Orban (Spec) Sanders, Texas, B
1943 Jack Jenkins, Missouri, B
1944 Mike Micka, Colgate, B
1945 Jim Hardy, Southern California, B
1946 Cal Rossi, UCLA, B*
1947 Cal Rossi, UCLA, B
1948 Harry Gilmer, Alabama, B
Lowell Tew, Alabama, B
1949 Rob Goode, Texas A&M, B
1950 George Thomas, Oklahoma, B
1951 Leon Heath, Oklahoma, B
1952 Larry Isbell, Baylor, B
1953 Jack Scarbath, Maryland, B
1954 Steve Meilinger, Kentucky, E
1955 Ralph Guglielmi, Notre Dame, B
1956 Ed Vereb, Maryland, B
1957 Don Bosseler, Miami, B
1958 Mike Sommer, George Washington, B (2)
1959 Don Allard, Boston College, B
1960 Richie Lucas, Penn State, QB
1961 Norman Snead, Wake Forest, QB
Joe Rutgens, Illinois, DT
1962 Ernie Davis, Syracuse, RB
1963 Pat Richter, Wisconsin, TE
1964 Charley Taylor, Arizona St., RB-WR
1965 Bob Breitenstein, Tulsa, T (2)
1966 Charlie Gogolak, Princeton, K
1967 Ray McDonald, Idaho, RB
1968 Jim Smith, Oregon, DB
1969 Eugene Epps, Texas-El Paso, DB (2)
1970 Bill Bundige, Colorado, DT (2)
1971 Cotton Speyrer, Texas, WR (2)
1972 Moses Denson, Maryland St., RB (8)
1973 Charles Cantrell, Lamar, G (5)
1974 Jon Keyworth, Colorado, TE (6)
1975 Mike Thomas, Nevada-Las Vegas, RB (6)
1976 Mike Hughes, Baylor, G (5)
1977 Duncan McColl, Stanford, DE (4)
1978 Tony Green, Florida, RB (6)
1979 Don Warren, San Diego St., TE (4)
1980 Art Monk, Syracuse, WR
1981 Mark May, Pittsburgh, T
1982 Vernon Dean, San Diego St., DB (2)
1983 Darrell Green, Texas A&I, DB
1984 Bob Slater, Oklahoma, DT (2)
1985 Tory Nixon, San Diego St., DB (2)
1986 Markus Koch, Boise State, DE (2)
1987 Brian Davis, Nebraska, DB (2)
1988 Chip Lohmiller, Minnesota, K (2)
1989 Tracy Rocker, Auburn, DT (3)
1990 Andre Collins, Penn State, LB (2)
1991 Bobby Wilson, Michigan State, DT
1992 Desmond Howard, Michigan, WR
1993 Tom Carter, Notre Dame, DB
1994 Heath Shuler, Tennessee, QB
1995 Michael Westbrook, Colorado, WR
1996 Andre Johnson, Penn State, T
1997 Kenard Lang, Miami, DE
1998 Stephen Alexander, Oklahoma, TE (2)
1999 Champ Bailey, Georgia, DB
2000 LaVar Arrington, Penn State, LB
Chris Samuels, Alabama, T
2001 Rod Gardner, Clemson, WR
2002 Patrick Ramsey, Tulane, QB
2003 Taylor Jacobs, Florida, WR (2)
2004 Sean Taylor, Miami, DB

**Choice lost because of ineligibility*

NUMBER-ONE DRAFT CHOICES

NUMBER-ONE DRAFT CHOICES

Season	Date	Team	Player	Position	College
2004	April 24-25	San Diego	Eli Manning	QB	Mississippi
2003	April 26-27	Cincinnati	Carson Palmer	QB	Southern California
2002	April 20-21	Houston	David Carr	QB	Fresno State
2001	April 21-22	Atlanta	Michael Vick	QB	Virginia Tech
2000	April 15-16	Cleveland	Courtney Brown	DE	Penn State
1999	April 17-18	Cleveland	Tim Couch	QB	Kentucky
1998	April 18-19	Indianapolis	Peyton Manning	QB	Tennessee
1997	April 19-20	St. Louis	Orlando Pace	T	Ohio State
1996	April 20-21	New York Jets	Keyshawn Johnson	WR	Southern California
1995	April 22-23	Cincinnati	Ki-Jana Carter	RB	Penn State
1994	April 24-25	Cincinnati	Dan Wilkinson	DT	Ohio State
1993	April 25-26	New England	Drew Bledsoe	QB	Washington State
1992	April 26-27	Indianapolis	Steve Emtman	DT	Washington
1991	April 21-22	Dallas	Russell Maryland	DT	Miami
1990	April 22-23	Indianapolis	Jeff George	QB	Illinois
1989	April 23-24	Dallas	Troy Aikman	QB	UCLA
1988	April 24-25	Atlanta	Aundray Bruce	LB	Auburn
1987	April 28-29	Tampa Bay	Vinny Testaverde	QB	Miami
1986	April 29-30	Tampa Bay	Bo Jackson	RB	Auburn
1985	April 30-May 1	Buffalo	Bruce Smith	DE	Virginia Tech
1984	May 1-2	New England	Irving Fryar	WR	Nebraska
1983	April 26-27	Baltimore	John Elway	QB	Stanford
1982	April 27-28	New England	Kenneth Sims	DT	Texas
1981	April 28-29	New Orleans	George Rogers	RB	South Carolina
1980	April 29-30	Detroit	Billy Sims	RB	Oklahoma
1979	May 3-4	Buffalo	Tom Cousineau	LB	Ohio State
1978	May 2-3	Houston	Earl Campbell	RB	Texas
1977	May 3-4	Tampa Bay	Ricky Bell	RB	Southern California
1976	April 8-9	Tampa Bay	Lee Roy Selmon	DE	Oklahoma
1975	January 28-29	Atlanta	Steve Bartkowski	QB	California
1974	January 29-30	Dallas	Ed Jones	DE	Tennessee State
1973	January 30-31	Houston	John Matuszak	DE	Tampa
1972	February 1-2	Buffalo	Walt Patulski	DE	Notre Dame
1971	January 28-29	New England	Jim Plunkett	QB	Stanford
1970	January 27-28	Pittsburgh	Terry Bradshaw	QB	Louisiana Tech
1969	January 28-29	Buffalo (AFL)	O.J. Simpson	RB	Southern California
1968	January 30-31	Minnesota	Ron Yary	T	Southern California
1967	March 14	Baltimore	Bubba Smith	DT	Michigan State
1966	November 27, 1965	Atlanta	Tommy Nobis	LB	Texas
	November 28, 1965	Miami (AFL)	Jim Grabowski	RB	Illinois
1965	November 28, 1964	New York Giants	Tucker Frederickson	RB	Auburn
	November 28, 1964	Houston (AFL)	Lawrence Elkins	E	Baylor
1964	December 2, 1963	San Francisco	Dave Parks	E	Texas Tech
	November 30, 1963	Boston (AFL)	Jack Concannon	QB	Boston College
1963	December 3, 1962	Los Angeles	Terry Baker	QB	Oregon State
	December 1, 1962	Kansas City (AFL)	Buck Buchanan	DT	Grambling
1962	December 4, 1961	Washington	Ernie Davis	RB	Syracuse
	December 2, 1961	Oakland (AFL)	Roman Gabriel	QB	North Carolina State
1961	December 27-28, 1960	Minnesota	Tommy Mason	RB	Tulane
	November 23, 1960	Buffalo (AFL)	Ken Rice	G	Auburn
1960	Secret Draft	Los Angeles	Billy Cannon	RB	Louisiana State
	November 22, December 2, 1959	(AFL had no formal first pick)			
1959	December 2, 1958	Green Bay	Randy Duncan	QB	Iowa
1958	December 2, 1957	Chicago Cardinals	King Hill	QB	Rice
1957	November 27, 1956	Green Bay	Paul Hornung	HB	Notre Dame
1956	November 29, 1955	Pittsburgh	Gary Glick	DB	Colorado A&M
1955	January 27-28	Baltimore	George Shaw	QB	Oregon
1954	January 28	Cleveland	Bobby Garrett	QB	Stanford
1953	January 22	San Francisco	Harry Babcock	E	Georgia
1952	January 17	Los Angeles	Bill Wade	QB	Vanderbilt
1951	January 18-19	New York Giants	Kyle Rote	HB	Southern Methodist

Season	Date	Team	Player	Position	College
1950	January 21-22	Detroit	Leon Hart	E	Notre Dame
1949	December 21, 1948	Philadelphia	Chuck Bednarik	C	Pennsylvania
1948	December 19, 1947	Washington	Harry Gilmer	QB	Alabama
1947	December 16, 1946	Chicago Bears	Bob Fenimore	HB	Oklahoma A&M
1946	January 14	Boston	Frank Dancewicz	QB	Notre Dame
1945	April 6	Chicago Cardinals	Charley Trippi	HB	Georgia
1944	April 19	Boston	Angelo Bertelli	QB	Notre Dame
1943	April 8	Detroit	Frank Sinkwich	HB	Georgia
1942	December 22, 1941	Pittsburgh	Bill Dudley	HB	Virginia
1941	December 10, 1940	Chicago Bears	Tom Harmon	HB	Michigan
1940	December 9, 1939	Chicago Cardinals	George Cafego	HB	Tennessee
1939	December 8, 1938	Chicago Cardinals	Ki Aldrich	C	Texas Christian
1938	December 12, 1937	Cleveland	Corbett Davis	FB	Indiana
1937	December 12, 1936	Philadelphia	Sam Francis	FB	Nebraska
1936	February 8	Philadelphia	Jay Berwanger	HB	Chicago

Note: From 1947 through 1958, the first selection in the draft was a Bonus pick, awarded to the winner of a random draw. That club, in turn, forfeited its last-round draft choice. The winner of the Bonus choice was eliminated from future draws. The system was abolished after 1958, by which time all clubs had received a Bonus choice.

ASSOCIATED PRESS NFL AWARDS

THE FOLLOWING AWARDS WERE NAMED BY *ASSOCIATED PRESS* IN BALLOTING BY A NATIONWIDE PANEL OF MEDIA.

NFL MOST VALUABLE PLAYER AWARD

YEAR	PLAYER	POS.	TEAM	ACCOMPLISHMENTS
1957	Jim Brown	RB	Cleveland Browns	Rushed for league-leading 942 yards and added 9 TDs as a rookie.
1958	Gino Marchetti	DE	Baltimore Colts	Leader of defense that permitted league-low 1,291 rushing yards and division-low 203 points.
1959	Charley Conerly	QB	New York Giants	Passed for 14 TDs and only 4 interceptions. Led offense to division-leading 284 points.
1960*	Norm Van Brocklin	QB	Philadelphia Eagles	Guided Eagles to first division title since 1949. Passed for 2,471 yards and 24 TDs.
	Joe Schmidt	LB	Detroit Lions	After 0-3 start, team went 7-2 when he returned from injury. Scored 2 defensive TDs.
1961	Paul Hornung	RB	Green Bay Packers	Led league in scoring for second straight season with 146 points (10 TD, 15 FG, 41 PAT).
1962	Jim Taylor	RB	Green Bay Packers	League rushing champion with 1,474 yards. Scored then all-time record 19 touchdowns.
1963	Y.A. Tittle	QB	New York Giants	Set then all-time season record with 36 TD passes. Guided league's top offense (5,024 yards).
1964	Johnny Unitas	QB	Baltimore Colts	Guided Colts to NFL's best record (12-2) and league's top offensive attack (4,779 yards).
1965	Jim Brown	RB	Cleveland Browns	Leader of NFL's top rushing attack. Led league with 1,544 yards, added 21 total TDs.
1966	Bart Starr	QB	Green Bay Packers	Passed for 14 touchdowns and only 3 interceptions. Led Packers to league-best 12-2 record.
1967	Johnny Unitas	QB	Baltimore Colts	Passed for 3,428 yards and 20 touchdowns. Led Colts to 11-1-2 record.
1968	Earl Morrall	QB	Baltimore Colts	Guided Colts to NFL-best 13-1 record. Led league with 26 touchdown passes.
1969	Roman Gabriel	QB	Los Angeles Rams	Led NFL with 24 touchdown passes. Guided Rams to 11-3 record.
1970	John Brodie	QB	San Francisco 49ers	Took 49ers to first division title. Threw NFL-best 24 TD passes.
1971	Alan Page	DT	Minnesota Vikings	Led defense that allowed NFL-low 139 points. Vikings won fourth straight NFC Central title.
1972	Larry Brown	RB	Washington Redskins	Led conference with 1,216 rushing yards. Redskins had NFC-best 11-3 record.
1973	O.J. Simpson	RB	Buffalo Bills	Rushed for then all-time record 2,003 yards, including three 200-yard performances.
1974	Ken Stabler	QB	Oakland Raiders	Led league with 26 touchdown passes and only 12 interceptions. Raiders had NFL-best 12-2 record.
1975	Fran Tarkenton	QB	Minnesota Vikings	Tied for league-best 12-2 record. Led NFC with 91.7 passer rating.
1976	Bert Jones	QB	Baltimore Colts	Threw 24 touchdowns and only 9 interceptions for 102.5 passer rating.
1977	Walter Payton	RB	Chicago Bears	Rushed for league-leading 1,852 yards and 16 total touchdowns.
1978	Terry Bradshaw	QB	Pittsburgh Steelers	Led Steelers to league-leading 14-2 mark. Set club record with 28 TD passes.
1979	Earl Campbell	RB	Houston Oilers	Led league with 1,697 rushing yards and 19 touchdowns.
1980	Brian Sipe	QB	Cleveland Browns	NFL-best 91.4 passer rating. Set Browns' records with 30 TD passes and 4,132 yards.
1981	Ken Anderson	QB	Cincinnati Bengals	Led Bengals to first division title since 1973. NFL-high 98.5 passer rating.
1982	Mark Moseley	K	Washington Redskins	Converted 20 of 21 FGs. Set then consecutive field-goal record at 23 (including last three in '81).
1983	Joe Theismann	QB	Washington Redskins	Leader of offense that scored then-NFL record 541 points. Redskins had NFL-best 14-2 record.
1984	Dan Marino	QB	Miami Dolphins	Set NFL records with 5,084 yards and 48 TD passes. Led Dolphins to AFC-best 14-2 mark.
1985	Marcus Allen	RB	Los Angeles Raiders	Rushed for league-leading 1,759 yards. Tied for AFC lead with 11 rushing touchdowns.
1986	Lawrence Taylor	LB	New York Giants	Recorded league-high 20.5 sacks, and led Giants' second-ranked defense (297.3).
1987	John Elway	QB	Denver Broncos	In 12 games, passed for 19 TDs and 3,198 yards, including four 300-yard games.
1988	Boomer Esiason	QB	Cincinnati Bengals	Led NFL with 97.4 passer rating. Tied for AFC lead with 28 TD passes.
1989	Joe Montana	QB	San Francisco 49ers	Set then-NFL record with 112.4 passer rating, including 70.2 completion percentage.
1990	Joe Montana	QB	San Francisco 49ers	Led 49ers to league-best 14-2 record. Completed NFC-high 61.7 percent of passes.
1991	Thurman Thomas	RB	Buffalo Bills	Recorded league-high 2,038 yards from scrimmage (1,407 rushing, 631 receiving).

1992	Steve Young	QB	San Francisco 49ers	NFL's top passer with 107.0 rating. Led 49ers to league-best 14-2 record.
1993	Emmitt Smith	RB	Dallas Cowboys	Led league in rushing (1,486 yards) for third straight year despite missing first two games.
1994	Steve Young	QB	San Francisco 49ers	Compiled NFL all-time best 112.8 passer rating. Completed more than 70 percent of his passes.
1995	Brett Favre	QB	Green Bay Packers	Led league with 38 touchdown passes and NFC with 99.5 passer rating.
1996	Brett Favre	QB	Green Bay Packers	Led Packers to top conference record (13-3). Threw NFL-best 39 TD passes.
1997*	Brett Favre	QB	Green Bay Packers	Led league with 35 touchdown passes. Led NFC with 3,867 passing yards.
	Barry Sanders	RB	Detroit Lions	Rushed for all-time second-best 2,053 yards, including record 14 straight 100-yard games.
1998	Terrell Davis	RB	Denver Broncos	Rushed for 2,008 yards and scored league-best 23 total touchdowns.
1999	Kurt Warner	QB	St. Louis Rams	Became the second QB in history to have 40 touchdown passes in a season (41).
2000	Marshall Faulk	RB	St. Louis Rams	Set NFL record with 26 touchdowns and led NFC with 2,189 yards from scrimmage.
2001	Kurt Warner	QB	St. Louis Rams	Led NFL with 4,830 passing yards, 36 touchdowns, 68.7 completion percentage, and 101.4 passer rating.
2002	Rich Gannon	QB	Oakland Raiders	Set single-season records with 10 300-yard passing games and 418 completions, and led NFL with 4,689 passing yards.
2003*	Peyton Manning	QB	Indianapolis Colts	Led NFL with 4,267 passing yards, had AFC-best 29 touchdown passes, and posted 99.0 passer rating.
	Steve McNair	QB	Tennessee Titans	Posted NFL-best 100.4 passer rating, passing for 3,215 yards with 24 touchdowns against 7 interceptions.

Total *Associated Press* NFL MVPs: 50
Two-time Winners: Jim Brown, Brett Favre (3), Joe Montana, Johnny Unitas, Kurt Warner, Steve Young
* The award was shared in 1960, 1997, and 2003.

ASSOCIATED PRESS MVPs WHO WON SUPER BOWL/ NFL CHAMPIONSHIP IN SAME SEASON: 15

1958	Gino Marchetti	Baltimore Colts
1960	Norm Van Brocklin	Philadelphia Eagles
1961	Paul Hornung	Green Bay Packers
1962	Jim Taylor	Green Bay Packers
1966	Bart Starr	Green Bay Packers
1968	Earl Morrall	Baltimore Colts
1978	Terry Bradshaw	Pittsburgh Steelers
1982	Mark Moseley	Washington Redskins
1986	Lawrence Taylor	New York Giants
1989	Joe Montana	San Francisco 49ers
1993	Emmitt Smith	Dallas Cowboys
1994	Steve Young	San Francisco 49ers
1996	Brett Favre	Green Bay Packers
1998	Terrell Davis	Denver Broncos
1999	Kurt Warner	St. Louis Rams

ASSOCIATED PRESS NFL MVP BY POSITION

Quarterback:	31	**Defensive End:**	1
Running Back:	14	**Defensive Tackle:**	1
Linebacker:	2	**Kicker:**	1

ASSOCIATED PRESS MVPs BY TEAM

6 Green Bay Packers
Indianapolis/Baltimore Colts

5 San Francisco 49ers

4 St. Louis/Los Angeles Rams

3 Cleveland Browns
New York Giants
Oakland/Los Angeles Raiders
Washington Redskins

2 Buffalo Bills
Cincinnati Bengals
Denver Broncos
Detroit Lions
Minnesota Vikings

1 Chicago Bears
Dallas Cowboys
Houston Oilers
Miami Dolphins
Philadelphia Eagles
Pittsburgh Steelers
Tennessee Titans

ASSOCIATED PRESS NFL MOST VALUABLE PLAYERS

AP OFFENSIVE PLAYER OF THE YEAR

1973	O.J. Simpson	RB	Buffalo Bills
1974	Ken Stabler	QB	Oakland Raiders
1975	Fran Tarkenton	QB	Minnesota Vikings
1976	Bert Jones	QB	Baltimore Colts
1977	Walter Payton	RB	Chicago Bears
1978	Earl Campbell	RB	Houston Oilers
1979	Earl Campbell	RB	Houston Oilers
1980	Earl Campbell	RB	Houston Oilers
1981	Ken Anderson	QB	Cincinnati Bengals
1982	Dan Fouts	QB	San Diego Chargers
1983	Joe Theismann	QB	Washington Redskins
1984	Dan Marino	QB	Miami Dolphins
1985	Marcus Allen	RB	Los Angeles Raiders
1986	Eric Dickerson	RB	Los Angeles Rams
1987	Jerry Rice	WR	San Francisco 49ers
1988	Roger Criag	RB	San Francisco 49ers
1989	Joe Montana	QB	San Francisco 49ers
1990	Warren Moon	QB	Houston Oilers
1991	Thurman Thomas	RB	Buffalo Bills
1992	Steve Young	QB	San Francisco 49ers
1993	Jerry Rice	WR	San Francisco 49ers
1994	Barry Sanders	RB	Detroit Lions
1995	Brett Favre	QB	Green Bay Packers
1996	Terrell Davis	RB	Denver Broncos
1997	Barry Sanders	RB	Detroit Lions
1998	Terrell Davis	RB	Denver Broncos
1999	Marshall Faulk	RB	St. Louis Rams
2000	Marshall Faulk	RB	St. Louis Rams
2001	Marshall Faulk	RB	St. Louis Rams
2002	Priest Holmes	RB	Kansas City Chiefs
2003	Jamal Lewis	RB	Baltimore Ravens

AP OFFENSIVE ROOKIE OF THE YEAR

1957	Jim Brown	RB	Cleveland Browns
1958	Jimmy Orr	WR	Pittsburgh Steelers
1959	Nick Pietrosante	RB	Detroit Lions
1960	Gail Cogdill	WR	Detroit Lions
1961	Mike Ditka	TE	Chicago Bears
1962	Ron Bull	RB	Chicago Bears
1963	Paul Flatley	WR	Minnesota Vikings
1964	Charley Taylor	WR	Washington Redskins
1965	Gale Sayers	RB	Chicago Bears
1966	Johnny Roland	RB	St. Louis Cardinals
1967	Mel Farr	RB	Detroit Lions
1968	Earl McCullouch	WR	Detroit Lions
1969	Calvin Hill	RB	Dallas Cowboys
1970	Duane Thomas	RB	Dallas Cowboys
1971	John Brockington	RB	Green Bay Packers
1972	Franco Harris	RB	Pittsburgh Steelers
1973	Chuck Foreman	RB	Minnesota Vikings
1974	Don Woods	RB	San Diego Chargers
1975	Mike Thomas	RB	Washington Redskins
1976	Sammy White	WR	Minnesota Vikings
1977	Tony Dorsett	RB	Dallas Cowboys
1978	Earl Campbell	RB	Houston Oilers
1979	Ottis Anderson	RB	St. Louis Cardinals
1980	Billy Sims	RB	Detroit Lions
1981	George Rogers	RB	New Orleans Saints
1982	Marcus Allen	RB	Los Angeles Raiders
1983	Eric Dickerson	RB	Los Angeles Rams
1984	Louis Lipps	WR	Pittsburgh Steelers
1985	Eddie Brown	WR	Cincinnati Bengals
1986	Rueben Mayes	RB	New Orleans Saints
1987	Troy Stradford	RB	Miami Dolphins
1988	John Stephens	RB	New England Patriots
1989	Barry Sanders	RB	Detroit Lions
1990	Emmitt Smith	RB	Dallas Cowboys
1991	Leonard Russell	RB	New England Patriots
1992	Carl Pickens	WR	Cincinnati Bengals
1993	Jerome Bettis	RB	Los Angeles Rams
1994	Marshall Faulk	RB	Indianapolis Colts
1995	Curtis Martin	RB	New England Patriots
1996	Eddie George	RB	Houston Oilers
1997	Warrick Dunn	RB	Tampa Bay Buccaneers
1998	Randy Moss	WR	Minnesota Vikings
1999	Edgerrin James	RB	Indianapolis Colts
2000	Mike Anderson	RB	Denver Broncos
2001	Anthony Thomas	RB	Chicago Bears
2002	Clinton Portis	RB	Denver Broncos
2003	Anquan Boldin	WR	Arizona Cardinals

AP DEFENSIVE PLAYER OF THE YEAR

1971	Alan Page	DT	Minnesota Vikings
1972	Joe Greene	DT	Pittsburgh Steelers
1973	Dick Anderson	S	Miami Dolphins
1974	Joe Greene	DT	Pittsburgh Steelers
1975	Mel Blount	CB	Pittsburgh Steelers
1976	Jack Lambert	LB	Pittsburgh Steelers
1977	Harvey Martin	DE	Dallas Cowboys
1978	Randy Gradishar	LB	Denver Broncos
1979	Lee Roy Selmon	DE	Tampa Bay Buccaneers
1980	Lester Hayes	CB	Oakland Raiders
1981	Lawrence Taylor	LB	New York Giants
1982	Lawrence Taylor	LB	New York Giants
1983	Doug Betters	DE	Miami Dolphins
1984	Kenny Easley	S	Seattle Seahawks
1985	Mike Singletary	LB	Chicago Bears
1986	Lawrence Taylor	LB	New York Giants
1987	Reggie White	DT	Philadelphia Eagles
1988	Mike Singletary	LB	Chicago Bears
1989	Keith Millard	DT	Minnesota Vikings
1990	Bruce Smith	DE	Buffalo Bills
1991	Pat Swilling	LB	New Orleans Saints
1992	Cortez Kennedy	DT	Seattle Seahawks
1993	Rod Woodson	CB	Pittsburgh Steelers
1994	Deion Sanders	CB	San Francisco 49ers
1995	Bryce Paup	LB	Buffalo Bills
1996	Bruce Smith	DE	Buffalo Bills
1997	Dana Stubblefield	DT	San Francisco 49ers
1998	Reggie White	DE	Green Bay Packers
1999	Warren Sapp	DT	Tampa Bay Buccaneers
2000	Ray Lewis	LB	Baltimore Ravens
2001	Michael Strahan	DE	New York Giants
2002	Derrick Brooks	LB	Tampa Bay Buccaneers
2003	Ray Lewis	LB	Baltimore Ravens

AP DEFENSIVE ROOKIE OF THE YEAR

1967	Lem Barney	CB	Detroit Lions
1968	Claude Humphrey	DE	Atlanta Falcons
1969	Joe Greene	DT	Pittsburgh Steelers
1970	Bruce Taylor	CB	San Franicsco 49ers
1971	Isiah Robertson	LB	Los Angeles Rams
1972	Willie Buchanon	CB	Green Bay Packers
1973	Wally Chambers	DT	Chicago Bears
1974	Jack Lambert	LB	Pittsburgh Steelers
1975	Robert Brazile	LB	Houston Oilers
1976	Mike Haynes	S	New England Patriots
1977	A.J. Duhe	DT	Miami Dolphins
1978	Al Baker	DE	Detroit Lions
1979	Jim Haslett	LB	Buffalo Bills
1980*	Buddy Curry	LB	Atlanta Falcons
	Al Richardson	LB	Atlanta Falcons
1981	Lawrence Taylor	LB	New York Giants
1982	Chip Banks	LB	Cleveland Browns
1983	Vernon Maxwell	LB	Baltimore Colts

1984	Bill Maas	NT	Kansas City Chiefs
1985	Duane Bickett	LB	Indianapolis Colts
1986	John Offerdahl	LB	Miami Dolphins
1987	Shane Conlan	LB	Buffalo Bills
1988	Erik McMillon	S	New York Jets
1989	Derrick Thomas	LB	Kansas City Chiefs
1990	Mark Carrier	S	Chicago Bears
1991	Mike Croel	LB	Denver Broncos
1992	Dale Carter	CB	Kansas City Chiefs
1993	Dana Stubblefield	DT	San Francisco 49ers
1994	Tim Bowens	DT	Miami Dolphins
1995	Hugh Douglas	DE	New York Jets
1996	Simeon Rice	DE	Arizona Cardinals
1997	Peter Boulware	LB	Baltimore Ravens
1998	Charles Woodson	CB	Oakland Raiders
1999	Jevon Kearse	DE	Tennessee Titans
2000	Brian Urlacher	LB	Chicago Bears
2001	Kendrell Bell	LB	Pittsburgh Steelers
2002	Julius Peppers	DE	Carolina Panthers
2003	Terrell Suggs	LB	Baltimore Ravens

*The award was shared in 1980.

AP COMEBACK PLAYER OF THE YEAR

1998	Doug Flutie	QB	Buffalo Bills
1999	Bryant Young	DT	San Francisco 49ers
2000	Joe Johnson	DE	New Orleans Saints
2001	Garrison Hearst	RB	San Francisco 49ers
2002	Tommy Maddox	QB	Pittsburgh Steelers
2003	Jon Kitna	QB	Cincinnati Bengals

AP COACH OF THE YEAR

1957	George Wilson	Detroit Lions
1958	Weeb Ewbank	Baltimore Colts
1959	Vince Lombardi	Green Bay Packers
1960	Buck Shaw	Philadelphia Eagles
1961	Allie Sherman	New York Giants
1962	Allie Sherman	New York Giants
1963	George Halas	Chicago Bears
1964	Don Shula	Baltimore Colts
1965	George Halas	Chicago Bears
1966	Tom Landry	Dallas Cowboys
1967*	George Allen	Los Angeles Rams
	Don Shula	Baltimore Colts
1968	Don Shula	Baltimore Colts
1969	Bud Grant	Minnesota Vikings
1970	Paul Brown	Cincinnati Bengals
1971	George Allen	Washington Redskins
1972	Don Shula	Miami Dolphins
1973	Chuck Knox	Los Angeles Rams
1974	Don Coryell	St. Louis Cardinals
1975	Ted Marchibroda	Baltimore Colts
1976	Forrest Gregg	Cleveland Browns
1977	Red Miller	Denver Broncos
1978	Jack Patera	Seattle Seahawks
1979	Jack Pardee	Washington Redskins
1980	Chuck Knox	Buffalo Bills
1981	Bill Walsh	San Francisco 49ers
1982	Joe Gibbs	Washington Redskins
1983	Joe Gibbs	Washington Redskins
1984	Chuck Knox	Seattle Seahawks
1985	Mike Ditka	Chicago Bears
1986	Bill Parcells	New York Giants
1987	Jim Mora	New Orleans Saints
1988	Mike Ditka	Chicago Bears
1989	Lindy Infante	Green Bay Packers
1990	Jimmy Johnson	Dallas Cowboys
1991	Wayne Fontes	Detroit Lions
1992	Bill Cowher	Pittsburgh Steelers
1993	Dan Reeves	New York Giants
1994	Bill Parcells	New England Patriots
1995	Ray Rhodes	Philadelphia Eagles
1996	Dom Capers	Carolina Panthers
1997	Jim Fassel	New York Giants
1998	Dan Reeves	Atlanta Falcons
1999	Dick Vermeil	St. Louis Rams
2000	Jim Haslett	New Orleans Saints
2001	Dick Jauron	Chicago Bears
2002	Andy Reid	Philadelphia Eagles
2003	Bill Belichick	New England Patriots

*The award was shared in 1967.

WALTER PAYTON NFL MAN OF THE YEAR

WALTER PAYTON NFL MAN OF THE YEAR

The Walter Payton NFL Man of the Year Award is the only NFL award that recognizes a player for his community service activities as well as his excellence on the field. Renamed in 1999 for the legendary Chicago Bears Pro Football Hall of Fame running back, the Walter Payton NFL Man of the Year Award has been given annually since 1970.

YEAR	PLAYER	POS.	TEAM
1970	Johnny Unitas	QB	Baltimore Colts
1971	John Hadl	QB	San Diego Chargers
1972	Willie Lanier	LB	Kansas City Chiefs
1973	Len Dawson	QB	Kansas City Chiefs
1974	George Blanda	QB	Oakland Raiders
1975	Ken Anderson	QB	Cincinnati Bengals
1976	Franco Harris	RB	Pittsburgh Steelers
1977	Walter Payton	RB	Chicago Bears
1978	Roger Staubach	QB	Dallas Cowboys
1979	Joe Greene	DT	Pittsburgh Steelers
1980	Harold Carmichael	WR	Philadelphia Eagles
1981	Lynn Swann	WR	Pittsburgh Steelers
1982	Joe Theismann	QB	Washington Redskins
1983	Rolf Benirschke	K	San Diego Chargers
1984	Marty Lyons	T	New York Jets
1985	Dwight Stephenson	C	Miami Dolphins
1986	Reggie Williams	LB	Cincinnati Bengals
1987	Dave Duerson	S	Chicago Bears
1988	Steve Largent	WR	Seattle Seahawks
1989	Warren Moon	QB	Houston Oilers
1990	Mike Singletary	LB	Chicago Bears
1991	Anthony Muñoz	T	Cincinnati Bengals
1992	John Elway	QB	Denver Broncos
1993	Derrick Thomas	LB	Kansas City Chiefs
1994	Junior Seau	LB	San Diego Chargers
1995	Boomer Esiason	QB	New York Jets
1996	Darrell Green	CB	Washington Redskins
1997	Troy Aikman	QB	Dallas Cowboys
1998	Dan Marino	QB	Miami Dolphins
1999	Cris Carter	WR	Minnesota Vikings
2000*	Derrick Brooks	LB	Tampa Bay Buccaneers
	Jim Flanigan	DT	Chicago Bears
2001	Jerome Bettis	RB	Pittsburgh Steelers
2002	Troy Vincent	CB	Philadelphia Eagles
2003	Will Shields	G	Kansas City Chiefs

* The award was shared in 2000.

NFL'S TEN HIGHEST SCORING WEEKENDS

Point Total	Date	Weekend
788	September 5, 8-9, 2002	1st
762	November 10-11, 1996	11th
761	October 16-17, 1983	7th
753	December 8-9, 2002	14th
740	November 29-30, 1998	13th
739	November 23, 26-27, 1995	13th
736	October 25-26, 1987	7th
734	November 19-20, 1995	12th
732	November 9-10, 1980	10th
725	November 24, 27-28, 1983	13th

TOP 10 TELEVISED SPORTS EVENTS OF ALL-TIME

(Based on A.C. Nielsen Figures)

Program	Date	Network	Share	Rating
Super Bowl XVI	1/24/82	CBS	73%	49.1
Super Bowl XVII	1/30/83	NBC	69%	48.6
Winter Olympics	2/23/94	CBS	64%	48.5
Super Bowl XX	1/26/86	NBC	70%	48.3
Super Bowl XII	1/15/78	CBS	67%	47.2
Super Bowl XIII	1/21/79	NBC	74%	47.1
Super Bowl XVIII	1/22/84	CBS	71%	46.4
Super Bowl XIX	1/20/85	ABC	63%	46.4
Super Bowl XIV	1/20/80	CBS	67%	46.3
Super Bowl XXX	1/28/96	NBC	68%	46.0

TEN MOST WATCHED TV PROGRAMS & ESTIMATED TOTAL NUMBER OF VIEWERS

(Based on A.C. Nielsen Figures)

Program	Date	Network	*Total Viewers
Super Bowl XXXVIII	Feb. 1, 2004	CBS	144,400,000
Super Bowl XXXVII	Jan. 26, 2003	ABC	138,900,000
Super Bowl XXX	Jan. 28, 1996	NBC	138,488,000
Super Bowl XXVIII	Jan. 30, 1994	NBC	134,800,000
Super Bowl XXXII	Jan. 25, 1998	NBC	133,400,000
Super Bowl XXVII	Jan. 31, 1993	NBC	133,400,000
Super Bowl XXXVI	Feb. 3, 2002	FOX	131,700,000
Super Bowl XXXV	Jan. 28, 2001	CBS	131,200,000
Super Bowl XXXIV	Jan. 30, 2000	ABC	130,744,800
Super Bowl XXXI	Jan. 26, 1997	FOX	128,900,000

**Watched some portion of the broadcast*

NFL'S TOP FIVE PAID ATTENDANCE TOTALS FOR ALL GAMES

Year	Preseason	Regular Season	Postseason	All Games
2003	3,853,924	16,913,584	805,546	21,573,054
2002	3,889,884	16,833,310	781,944	21,505,138
2000	3,757,231	16,387,289	809,132	20,953,652
1999	3,762,331	16,206,640	793,759	20,762,730
2001	3,656,928	16,166,258	766,905	20,590,091

TEN HIGHEST-RATED ABC *NFL MONDAY NIGHT FOOTBALL* GAMES OF ALL-TIME

(Based on A.C. Nielsen Figures)

Game	Date	Share	Rating
Chicago at Miami	12/2/85	46%	29.6
N.Y. Giants at San Francisco	12/3/90	42%	26.9
Dallas at Washington	10/2/78	43%	26.8
Pittsburgh at San Diego	12/22/80	40%	25.3
Philadelphia at Miami	11/30/81	40%	25.3
Pittsburgh at Houston	12/10/79	40%	25.1
Dallas at Miami	12/17/84	40%	25.1
Pittsburgh at Dallas	9/13/82	42%	24.9
Cincinnati at Oakland	12/6/76	40%	24.7
Dallas at Washington	10/8/73	40%	24.6
Minnesota at Atlanta	11/19/73	40%	24.6

NFL'S TEN BIGGEST SINGLE-GAME ATTENDANCE TOTALS

Date	Site	Game	Teams	Attendance
August 15, 1994	Azteca Stadium	American Bowl (Mexico City)	Cowboys vs. Oilers	112,376
August 17, 1998	Azteca Stadium	American Bowl (Mexico City)	Cowboys vs. Patriots	106,424
August 22, 1947	Soldier Field	College All-Star	Bears vs. All-Stars	105,840
August 4, 1997	Estadio Guillermo Canedo	American Bowl (Mexico City)	Broncos vs. Dolphins	104,629
January 20, 1980	Rose Bowl	Super Bowl XIV	Steelers vs. Rams	103,985
January 30, 1983	Rose Bowl	Super Bowl XVII	Redskins vs. Dolphins	103,667
January 9, 1977	Rose Bowl	Super Bowl XI	Raiders vs. Vikings	103,438
November 10, 1957	L.A. Coliseum	Regular Season	49ers at Rams	102,368
January 25, 1987	Rose Bowl	Super Bowl XXI	Giants vs. Broncos	101,643
August 20, 1948	Soldier Field	College All-Star	Cardinals vs. All-Stars	101,220

PAID ATTENDANCE

NFL'S TOP 10 PAID ATTENDANCE WEEKENDS

Weekend	Games	Attendance
December 27-28, 2003	16	1,106,818
September 4, 7-8, 2003	16	1,095,720
November 23-24, 2003	16	1,087,869
September 15-16, 2002	16	1,081,206
December 7-8, 2003	16	1,078,229
November 24-25, 2002	16	1,078,011
November 27, 30-December 1, 2003	16	1,070,451
September 5, 8-9, 2002	16	1,067,957
November 17-18, 2002	16	1,062,040
November 16-17, 2003	16	1,058,317

NFL'S TOP 10 TEAM SINGLE-SEASON HOME PAID ATTENDANCE TOTALS

Year	Club	Games	Attendance
2003	Washington Redskins	8	667,033
2002	Washington Redskins	8	663,536
2001	Washington Redskins	8	661,970
2000	Washington Redskins	8	656,599
1980	Detroit Lions	8	634,204
1988	Buffalo Bills	8	631,818
1991	Buffalo Bills	8	631,786
1992	Buffalo Bills	8	630,978
1997	Kansas City Chiefs	8	629,763
1999	Kansas City Chiefs	8	629,569

NFL PAID ATTENDANCE

For detailed 2003 attendance, see page 344.

Year	Regular Season			Average	Postseason	Total
2003	#16,913,584	(255 games***)		#66,328	805,546 (12)	#17,719,130
2002	16,833,310	(256 games)		65,755	781,944 (12)	17,615,254
2001	16,166,258	(248 games)		65,187	766,905 (12)	16,933,163
2000	16,387,289	(248 games)		66,078	809,132 (12)	17,196,421
1999	16,206,640	(248 games)		65,349	793,759 (12)	17,000,399
1998	15,364,873	(240 games)		64,020	822,885 (12)	16,187,758
1997	14,967,314	(240 games)		62,364	801,879 (12)	15,769,193
1996	14,612,417	(240 games)		60,885	769,310 (12)	15,381,727
1995	15,043,562	(240 games)		62,682	790,906 (12)	15,834,468
1994	14,030,435	(224 games)		62,636	779,738 (12)	14,810,173
1993	13,966,843	(224 games)		62,352	814,607 (12)	14,781,450
1992	13,828,887	(224 games)		61,736	815,910 (12)	14,644,797
1991	13,841,459	(224 games)		61,792	813,247 (12)	14,654,706
1990	13,959,896	(224 games)		62,321	847,543 (12)	14,807,439
1989	13,625,662	(224 games)		60,829	685,771 (10)	14,311,433
1988	13,539,848	(224 games)		60,446	658,317 (10)	14,198,165
1987	11,406,166	(210 games**)		54,315	656,977 (10)	12,063,143
1986	13,588,551	(224 games)		60,663	734,002 (10)	14,322,553
1985	13,345,047	(224 games)		59,567	710,768 (10)	14,055,815
1984	13,398,112	(224 games)		59,813	665,194 (10)	14,063,306
1983	13,277,222	(224 games)		59,273	675,513 (10)	13,952,735
1982	7,367,438	(126 games*)		58,472	1,033,153 (16)	8,400,591
1981	13,606,990	(224 games)		60,745	637,763 (10)	14,244,753
1980	13,392,230	(224 games)		59,787	624,430 (10)	14,016,660
1979	13,182,039	(224 games)		58,848	630,326 (10)	13,812,365
1978	12,771,800	(224 games)		57,017	624,388 (10)	13,396,188
1977	11,018,632	(196 games)		56,218	534,925 (8)	11,553,557
1976	11,070,543	(196 games)		56,482	492,884 (8)	11,563,427
1975	10,213,193	(182 games)		56,116	475,919 (8)	10,689,112
1974	10,236,322	(182 games)		56,244	438,664 (8)	10,674,986
1973	10,730,933	(182 games)		58,961	525,433 (8)	11,256,366
1972	10,445,827	(182 games)		57,395	483,345 (8)	10,929,172
1971	10,076,035	(182 games)		55,363	483,891 (8)	10,559,926
1970	9,533,333	(182 games)		52,381	458,493 (8)	9,991,826
1969	6,096,127	(112 games)	NFL	54,430	162,279 (3)	6,258,406
	2,843,373	(70 games)	AFL	40,620	167,088 (3)	3,010,461
1968	5,882,313	(112 games)	NFL	52,521	215,902 (3)	6,098,215
	2,635,004	(70 games)	AFL	37,643	114,438 (2)	2,749,442
1967	5,938,924	(112 games)	NFL	53,026	166,208 (3)	6,105,132
	2,295,697	(63 games)	AFL	36,439	53,330 (1)	2,349,027
1966	5,337,044	(105 games)	NFL	50,829	74,152 (1)	5,411,196
	2,160,369	(63 games)	AFL	34,291	42,080 (1)	2,202,449
1965	4,634,021	(98 games)	NFL	47,286	100,304 (2)	4,734,325
	1,782,384	(56 games)	AFL	31,828	30,361 (1)	1,812,745
1964	4,563,049	(98 games)	NFL	46,562	79,544 (1)	4,642,593
	1,447,875	(56 games)	AFL	25,855	40,242 (1)	1,488,117
1963	4,163,643	(98 games)	NFL	42,486	45,801 (1)	4,209,444
	1,208,697	(56 games)	AFL	21,584	63,171 (2)	1,271,868
1962	4,003,421	(98 games)	NFL	40,851	64,892 (1)	4,068,313
	1,147,302	(56 games)	AFL	20,487	37,981 (1)	1,185,283
1961	3,986,159	(98 games)	NFL	40,675	39,029 (1)	4,025,188
	1,002,657	(56 games)	AFL	17,904	29,556 (1)	1,032,213

Year	Regular Season			Average	Postseason	Total
1960	3,128,296	(78 games)	NFL	40,106	67,325 (1)	3,195,621
	926,156	(56 games)	AFL	16,538	32,183 (1)	958,339
1959	3,140,000	(72 games)		43,617	57,545 (1)	3,197,545
1958	3,006,124	(72 games)		41,752	123,659 (2)	3,129,783
1957	2,836,318	(72 games)		39,393	119,579 (2)	2,955,897
1956	2,551,263	(72 games)		35,434	56,836 (1)	2,608,099
1955	2,521,836	(72 games)		35,026	85,693 (1)	2,607,529
1954	2,190,571	(72 games)		30,425	43,827 (1)	2,234,398
1953	2,164,585	(72 games)		30,064	54,577 (1)	2,219,162
1952	2,052,126	(72 games)		28,502	97,507 (2)	2,149,633
1951	1,913,019	(72 games)		26,570	57,522 (1)	1,970,541
1950	1,977,753	(78 games)		25,356	136,647 (3)	2,114,400
1949	1,391,735	(60 games)		23,196	27,980 (1)	1,419,715
1948	1,525,243	(60 games)		25,421	36,309 (1)	1,561,552
1947	1,837,437	(60 games)		30,624	66,268 (2)	1,903,705
1946	1,732,135	(55 games)		31,493	58,346 (1)	1,790,481
1945	1,270,401	(50 games)		25,408	32,178 (1)	1,302,579
1944	1,019,649	(50 games)		20,393	46,016 (1)	1,065,665
1943	969,128	(40 games)		24,228	71,315 (2)	1,040,443
1942	887,920	(55 games)		16,144	36,006 (1)	923,926
1941	1,108,615	(55 games)		20,157	55,870 (2)	1,164,485
1940	1,063,025	(55 games)		19,328	36,034 (1)	1,099,059
1939	1,071,200	(55 games)		19,476	32,279 (1)	1,103,479
1938	937,197	(55 games)		17,040	48,120 (1)	985,317
1937	963,039	(55 games)		17,510	15,878 (1)	978,917
1936	816,007	(54 games)		15,111	29,545 (1)	845,552
1935	638,178	(53 games)		12,041	15,000 (1)	653,178
1934	492,684	(60 games)		8,211	35,059 (1)	527,743

 # Record

**Players' 57-day strike reduced 224-game schedule to 126 games.*

***Players' 24-day strike reduced 224-game schedule to 210 games.*

****The Week 8 Miami at San Diego game is not included. The game was moved to Arizona due to the San Diego wildfires and tickets were distributed at no charge.*

ALL-TIME NFL TEAMS

75TH ANNIVERSARY ALL-TIME TEAM

Chosen by a selection committee of media and league personnel in 1994.

Position	Name	Team(s)	Ht.	Wt.	College
OFFENSE					
QB	Sammy Baugh	Washington Redskins (1937-52)	6-2	180	Texas Christian
QB	Otto Graham	Cleveland Browns (1946-55)	6-1	195	Northwestern
QB	Joe Montana	San Francisco 49ers (1979-92), Kansas City Chiefs (1993-94)	6-2	195	Notre Dame
QB	Johnny Unitas	Baltimore Colts (1956-72), San Diego Chargers (1973)	6-1	195	Louisville
RB	Jim Brown	Cleveland Browns (1957-65)	6-2	232	Syracuse
RB	Marion Motley	Cleveland Browns (1946-53), Pittsburgh Steelers (1955)	6-1	238	Nevada-Reno
RB	Bronko Nagurski	Chicago Bears (1930-37, 1943)	6-2	225	Minnesota
RB	Walter Payton	Chicago Bears (1975-87)	5-10	202	Jackson State
RB	Gale Sayers	Chicago Bears (1965-71)	6-0	200	Kansas
RB	O.J. Simpson	Buffalo Bills (1969-77), San Francisco 49ers (1978-79)	6-1	212	Southern California
RB	Steve Van Buren	Philadelphia Eagles (1944-51)	6-1	200	Louisiana State
WR	Lance Alworth	San Diego Chargers (1962-70), Dallas Cowboys (1971-72)	6-0	184	Arkansas
WR	Raymond Berry	Baltimore Colts (1955-67)	6-2	187	Southern Methodist
WR	Don Hutson	Green Bay Packers (1935-45)	6-1	180	Alabama
WR	Jerry Rice	San Francisco 49ers (1985-2000), Oakland Raiders (2001-present)	6-2	200	Miss. Valley State
TE	Mike Ditka	Chicago Bears (1961-66), Philadelphia Eagles (1967-68), Dallas Cowboys (1969-72)	6-3	225	Pittsburgh
TE	Kellen Winslow	San Diego Chargers (1979-87)	6-5	250	Missouri
T	Roosevelt Brown	New York Giants (1953-65)	6-3	255	Morgan State
T	Forrest Gregg	Green Bay Packers (1956, 1958-70)	6-4	250	Southern Methodist
T	Anthony Muñoz	Cincinnati Bengals (1980-92)	6-6	285	Southern California
G	John Hannah	New England Patriots (1973-85)	6-3	265	Alabama
G	Jim Parker	Baltimore Colts (1957-67)	6-3	273	Ohio State
G	Gene Upshaw	Oakland Raiders (1967-81)	6-5	255	Texas A&I
C	Mel Hein	New York Giants (1931-45)	6-2	225	Washington State
C	Mike Webster	Pittsburgh Steelers (1974-88), Kansas City Chiefs (1989-90)	6-2	250	Wisconsin
DEFENSE					
DE	David (Deacon) Jones	Los Angeles Rams (1961-71), San Diego Chargers (1972-73), Washington Redskins (1974)	6-5	250	Miss. Vocational-South Carolina St.
DE	Gino Marchetti	Dallas Texans (1952), Baltimore Colts (1953-64, 1966)	6-4	245	San Francisco
DE	Reggie White	Philadelphia Eagles (1985-92), Green Bay Packers (1993-1998), Carolina Panthers (2000)	6-5	290	Tennessee
DT	Joe Greene	Pittsburgh Steelers (1969-81)	6-4	260	North Texas State
DT	Bob Lilly	Dallas Cowboys (1961-74)	6-5	260	Texas Christian
DT	Merlin Olsen	Los Angeles Rams (1962-76)	6-5	270	Utah State
LB	Dick Butkus	Chicago Bears (1965-73)	6-3	245	Illinois
LB	Jack Ham	Pittsburgh Steelers (1971-82)	6-1	225	Penn State
LB	Ted Hendricks	Baltimore Colts (1969-73), Green Bay Packers (1974), Oakland/L.A. Raiders (1975-83)	6-7	235	Miami
LB	Jack Lambert	Pittsburgh Steelers (1974-84)	6-4	220	Kent State
LB	Willie Lanier	Kansas City Chiefs (1967-77)	6-1	245	Morgan State
LB	Ray Nitschke	Green Bay Packers (1958-72)	6-3	235	Illinois
LB	Lawrence Taylor	New York Giants (1981-93)	6-3	243	North Carolina
CB	Mel Blount	Pittsburgh Steelers (1970-83)	6-3	205	Southern
CB	Mike Haynes	New England Patriots (1976-82), Los Angeles Raiders (1983-89)	6-2	190	Arizona State
CB	Dick (Night Train) Lane	Los Angeles Rams (1952-53), Chicago Cardinals (1954-59), Detroit Lions (1960-65)	6-2	210	Scottsbluff JC
CB	Rod Woodson	Pittsburgh Steelers (1987-96), San Francisco 49ers (1997), Baltimore Ravens (1998-2001), Oakland Raiders (2002-present)	6-0	200	Purdue
S	Ken Houston	Houston Oilers (1967-72), Washington Redskins (1973-80)	6-3	198	Prairie View A&M
S	Ronnie Lott	San Francisco 49ers (1981-90), Los Angeles Raiders (1991-92), New York Jets (1993-94)	6-0	200	Southern California
S	Larry Wilson	St. Louis Cardinals (1960-72)	6-0	190	Utah
SPECIAL TEAMS					
P	Ray Guy	Oakland/L.A. Raiders (1973-86)	6-3	190	Southern Mississippi
K	Jan Stenerud	Kansas City Chiefs (1967-79), Green Bay Packers (1980-83), Minnesota Vikings (1984-85)	6-2	190	Montana State
PR	Billy (White Shoes) Johnson	Houston Oilers (1974-80), Atlanta Falcons (1982-87), Washington Redskins (1988)	5-9	170	Widener
KR	Gale Sayers	Chicago Bears (1965-71)	6-0	200	Kansas

75TH ANNIVERSARY ALL-TWO-WAY TEAM

Positions	
Quarterback, Defensive Halfback, Punter	Sammy Baugh
Center, Linebacker	Chuck Bednarik
Quarterback, Defensive Halfback, Punter	Earl (Dutch) Clark
Tackle, Defensive Tackle	George Connor
Guard, Defensive Tackle	Danny Fortmann
Center, Defensive Tackle	Mel Hein
Tackle, Defensive Tackle, Punter	Wilbur (Pete) Henry
Back, Defensive Halfback	Bill Hewitt
Fullback, Linebacker, Kicker	Clarke Hinkle
Tackle, Defensive Tackle	Cal Hubbard
End, Defensive Halfback	Don Hutson
Back, Defensive Back	George McAfee
Fullback, Linebacker	Marion Motley
Guard-Tackle, Defensive Tackle	George Musso
Fullback, Linebacker	Bronko Nagurski
Halfback, Defensive Halfback	Ernie Nevers
End, Defensive Back	Pete Pihos
Tackle, Defensive Tackle	Joe Stydahar
Running Back, Defensive Back	Steve Van Buren

50TH ANNIVERSARY TEAM

Chosen by the Hall of Fame Selection Committee in 1969.

Offense

Split End	Don Hutson
Tight End	John Mackey
Tackle	Cal Hubbard
Guard	Jerry Kramer
Center	Chuck Bednarik
Flanker	Elroy Hirsch
Quarterback	Johnny Unitas
Halfback	Jim Thorpe
Halfback	Gale Sayers
Fullback	Jim Brown
Kicker	Lou Groza

Defense

End	Gino Marchetti
Tackle	Leo Nomellini
Linebacker	Ray Nitschke
Cornerback	Dick (Night Train) Lane
Safety	Emlen Tunnell

SUPER BOWL SILVER ANNIVERSARY TEAM

Chosen by the fans in 1990 prior to Super Bowl XXV.

Head Coach Vince Lombardi

Offense

Quarterback	Joe Montana
Running Back	Franco Harris
Running Back	Larry Csonka
Wide Receiver	Lynn Swann
Wide Receiver	Jerry Rice
Tight End	Dave Casper
Tackle	Art Shell
Tackle	Forrest Gregg
Guard	Gene Upshaw
Guard	Jerry Kramer
Center	Mike Webster

Defense

Defensive End	L.C. Greenwood
Defensive End	Ed (Too Tall) Jones
Defensive Tackle	Joe Greene
Defensive Tackle	Randy White
Inside Linebacker	Jack Lambert
Inside Linebacker	Mike Singletary
Outside Linebacker	Jack Ham
Outside Linebacker	Ted Hendricks
Cornerback	Ronnie Lott
Cornerback	Mel Blount
Safety	Donnie Shell
Safety	Willie Wood

Special Teams

Punter	Ray Guy
Kicker	Jan Stenerud
Kick Returner	John Taylor

ALL-TIME NFL TEAMS

All-Decade teams chosen by the Hall of Fame Selection Committee members.

1920s ALL-DECADE TEAM

End	Guy Chamberlin
End	Lavern Dilweg
End	George Halas
Tackle	Ed Healey
Tackle	Wilbur (Pete) Henry
Tackle	Cal Hubbard
Tackle	Steve Owen
Guard	Hunk Anderson
Guard	Walt Kiesling
Guard	Mike Michalske
Center	George Trafton
Quarterback	Jimmy Conzelman
Quarterback	John (Paddy) Driscoll
Halfback	Harold (Red) Grange
Halfback	Joe Guyon
Halfback	Earl (Curly) Lambeau
Halfback	Jim Thorpe
Fullback	Ernie Nevers

1930s ALL-DECADE TEAM

End	Bill Hewitt
End	Don Hutson
End	Wayne Millner
End	Gaynell Tinsley
Tackle	George Christensen
Tackle	Frank Cope
Tackle	Glen (Turk) Edwards
Tackle	Bill Lee
Tackle	Joe Stydahar
Guard	Grover (Ox) Emerson
Guard	Dan Fortmann
Guard	Charles (Buckets) Goldenberg
Guard	Russ Letlow
Center	Mel Hein
Center	George Svendsen
Quarterback	Earl (Dutch) Clark
Quarterback	Arnie Herber
Quarterback	Cecil Isbell
Halfback	Cliff Battles
Halfback	Johnny (Blood) McNally
Halfback	Beattie Feathers
Halfback	Alphonse (Tuffy) Leemans
Halfback	Ken Strong
Fullback	Clarke Hinkle
Fullback	Bronko Nagurski

1940s ALL-DECADE TEAM

End	Jim Benton
End	Jack Ferrante
End	Ken Kavanaugh
End	Dante Lavelli
End	Pete Pihos
End	Mac Speedie
End	Ed Sprinkle
Tackle	Al Blozis
Tackle	George Connor
Tackle	Frank (Bucko) Kilroy
Tackle	Buford (Baby) Ray
Tackle	Vic Sears
Tackle	Al Wistert
Guard	Bruno Banducci
Guard	Bill Edwards
Guard	Garrard (Buster) Ramsey
Guard	Bill Willis
Guard	Len Younce
Center	Charley Brock
Center	Clyde (Bulldog) Turner
Center	Alex Wojciechowicz
Quarterback	Sammy Baugh
Quarterback	Sid Luckman
Quarterback	Bob Waterfield
Halfback	Tony Canadeo
Halfback	Bill Dudley
Halfback	George McAfee
Halfback	Charley Trippi
Halfback	Steve Van Buren
Halfback	Byron (Whizzer) White
Fullback	Pat Harder
Fullback	Marion Motley
Fullback	Bill Osmanski

1950s ALL-DECADE TEAM

Offense

End	Raymond Berry
End	Tom Fears
End	Bobby Walston
Halfback-End	Elroy (Crazylegs) Hirsch
Tackle	Roosevelt Brown
Tackle	Bob St. Clair
Guard	Dick Barwegan
Guard	Jim Parker
Guard	Dick Stanfel
Center	Chuck Bednarik
Quarterback	Otto Graham
Quarterback	Bobby Layne
Quarterback	Norm Van Brocklin
Halfback	Frank Gifford
Halfback	Ollie Matson
Halfback	Hugh McElhenny
Halfback	Lenny Moore
Fullback	Alan Ameche
Fullback	Joe Perry
Kicker	Lou Groza

Defense

End	Len Ford
End	Gino Marchetti
Tackle	Art Donovan
Tackle	Leo Nomellini
Tackle	Ernie Stautner
Linebacker	Joe Fortunato
Linebacker	Bill George
Linebacker	Sam Huff
Linebacker	Joe Schmidt
Halfback	Jack Butler
Halfback	Dick (Night Train) Lane
Safety	Jack Christiansen
Safety	Yale Lary
Safety	Emlen Tunnell

1960s ALL-DECADE TEAM

Offense

Split End	Del Shofner
Split End	Charley Taylor
Flanker	Gary Collins
Flanker	Boyd Dowler
Tight End	John Mackey
Tackle	Bob Brown
Tackle	Forrest Gregg
Tackle	Ralph Neely
Guard	Gene Hickerson
Guard	Jerry Kramer
Guard	Howard Mudd
Center	Jim Ringo
Quarterback	Sonny Jurgensen
Quarterback	Bart Starr
Quarterback	Johnny Unitas
Halfback	John David Crow
Halfback	Paul Hornung
Halfback	Leroy Kelly
Halfback	Gale Sayers
Fullback	Jim Brown
Fullback	Jim Taylor
Kicker	Jim Bakken

Defense

End	Doug Atkins
End	Willie Davis
End	David (Deacon) Jones
Tackle	Alex Karras
Tackle	Bob Lilly
Tackle	Merlin Olsen
Linebacker	Dick Butkus
Linebacker	Larry Morris
Linebacker	Ray Nitschke
Linebacker	Tommy Nobis
Linebacker	Dave Robinson
Cornerback	Herb Adderley
Cornerback	Lem Barney
Cornerback	Bobby Boyd
Safety	Eddie Meador
Safety	Larry Wilson
Safety	Willie Wood
Punter	Don Chandler

1970s ALL-DECADE TEAM

Offense

Wide Receiver	Harold Carmichael
Wide Receiver	Drew Pearson
Wide Receiver	Lynn Swann
Wide Receiver	Paul Warfield
Tight End	Dave Casper
Tight End	Charlie Sanders
Tackle	Dan Dierdorf
Tackle	Art Shell
Tackle	Rayfield Wright
Tackle	Ron Yary
Guard	Joe DeLamielleure
Guard	John Hannah
Guard	Larry Little
Guard	Gene Upshaw
Center	Jim Langer
Center	Mike Webster
Quarterback	Terry Bradshaw
Quarterback	Ken Stabler
Quarterback	Roger Staubach
Running Back	Earl Campbell
Running Back	Franco Harris
Running Back	Walter Payton
Running Back	O.J. Simpson
Kicker	Garo Yepremian

Defense

End	Carl Eller
End	L.C. Greenwood
End	Harvey Martin
End	Jack Youngblood
Tackle	Joe Greene
Tackle	Bob Lilly
Tackle	Merlin Olsen
Tackle	Alan Page
Linebacker	Bobby Bell
Linebacker	Robert Brazile
Linebacker	Dick Butkus
Linebacker	Jack Ham
Linebacker	Ted Hendricks
Linebacker	Jack Lambert
Cornerback	Willie Brown
Cornerback	Jimmy Johnson
Cornerback	Roger Wehrli
Cornerback	Louis Wright
Safety	Dick Anderson
Safety	Cliff Harris
Safety	Ken Houston
Safety	Larry Wilson
Punter	Ray Guy

1980s ALL-DECADE TEAM

Offense

Wide Receiver	Jerry Rice
Wide Receiver	Steve Largent
Wide Receiver	James Lofton
Wide Receiver	Art Monk
Tight End	Kellen Winslow
Tight End	Ozzie Newsome
Tackle	Anthony Munoz
Tackle	Jim Covert
Tackle	Gary Zimmerman
Tackle	Joe Jacoby
Guard	John Hannah
Guard	Russ Grimm
Guard	Bill Fralic
Guard	Mike Munchak
Center	Dwight Stephenson
Center	Mike Webster
Quarterback	Joe Montana
Quarterback	Dan Fouts
Running Back	Walter Payton
Running Back	Eric Dickerson
Running Back	Roger Craig
Running Back	John Riggins

Defense

End	Reggie White
End	Howie Long
End	Lee Roy Selmon
End	Bruce Smith
Tackle	Randy White
Tackle	Dan Hampton
Tackle	Keith Millard
Tackle	Dave Butz
Linebacker	Mike Singletary
Linebacker	Lawrence Taylor
Linebacker	Ted Hendricks
Linebacker	Jack Lambert
Linebacker	Andre Tippett
Linebacker	John Anderson
Linebacker	Carl Banks
Cornerback	Mike Haynes
Cornerback	Mel Blount
Cornerback	Frank Minnifield
Cornerback	Lester Hayes
Safety	Ronnie Lott
Safety	Kenny Easley
Safety	Deron Cherry
Safety	Joey Browner
Safety	Nolan Cromwell

Specialists

Punter	Sean Landeta
Punter	Reggie Roby
Kicker	Morten Andersen
Kicker	Gary Anderson
Kicker	Eddie Murray
Punt Returner	Billy (White Shoes) Johnson
Punt Returner	John Taylor
Kick Returner	Mike Nelms
Kick Returner	Rick Upchurch
Coach	Bill Walsh
Coach	Chuck Noll

1990s ALL-DECADE TEAM

Offense

Wide Receiver	Cris Carter
Wide Receiver	Jerry Rice
Wide Receiver	Tim Brown
Wide Receiver	Michael Irvin
Tight End	Shannon Sharpe
Tight End	Ben Coates
Tackle	William Roaf
Tackle	Gary Zimmerman
Tackle	Tony Boselli
Tackle	Richmond Webb
Guard	Bruce Matthews
Guard	Randall McDaniel
Guard	Larry Allen
Guard	Steve Wisniewski
Center	Dermontti Dawson
Center	Mark Stepnoski
Quarterback	John Elway
Quarterback	Brett Favre
Running Back	Barry Sanders
Running Back	Emmitt Smith
Running Back	Terrell Davis
Running Back	Thurman Thomas

Defense

End	Bruce Smith
End	Reggie White
End	Chris Doleman
End	Neil Smith
Tackle	Cortez Kennedy
Tackle	John Randle
Tackle	Warren Sapp
Tackle	Bryant Young
Linebacker	Kevin Greene
Linebacker	Junior Seau
Linebacker	Derrick Thomas
Linebacker	Cornelius Bennett
Linebacker	Hardy Nickerson
Linebacker	Levon Kirkland
Cornerback	Deion Sanders
Cornerback	Rod Woodson
Cornerback	Darrell Green
Cornerback	Aeneas Williams
Safety	Steve Atwater
Safety	LeRoy Butler
Safety	Carnell Lake
Safety	Ronnie Lott

Specialists

Punter	Darren Bennett
Punter	Sean Landeta
Kicker	Morten Andersen
Kicker	Gary Anderson
Punt Returner	Deion Sanders
Punt Returner	Mel Gray
Kick Returner	Michael Bates
Kick Returner	Mel Gray
Coach	Bill Parcells
Coach	Marv Levy

ALL-TIME NFL TEAMS

ALL-TIME AFL TEAM

Chosen by 1969 AFL Hall of Fame Selection Committee members.

Offense

Flanker	Lance Alworth
End	Don Maynard
Tight End	Fred Arbanas
Tackle	Ron Mix
Tackle	Jim Tyrer
Guard	Ed Budde
Guard	Billy Shaw
Center	Jim Otto
Quarterback	Joe Namath
Running Back	Clem Daniels
Running Back	Paul Lowe

Defense

End	Jerry Mays
End	Gerry Philbin
Tackle	Houston Antwine
Tackle	Tom Sestak
Linebacker	Bobby Bell
Linebacker	George Webster
Linebacker	Nick Buoniconti
Cornerback	Willie Brown
Cornerback	Dave Grayson
Safety	Johnny Robinson
Safety	George Saimes

Special Teams

Kicker	George Blanda
Punter	Jerrel Wilson

ALL-TIME NFL TEAM

Chosen by members of the Hall of Fame Selection Committee in 2000 for the book NFL's Greatest.

Offense

Wide Receiver	Don Hutson
Wide Receiver	Jerry Rice
Tight End	John Mackey
Tackle	Roosevelt Brown
Tackle	Anthony Muñoz
Guard	John Hannah
Guard	Jim Parker
Center	Mike Webster
Quarterback	Johnny Unitas
Running Back	Jim Brown
Running Back	Walter Payton

Defense

End	Deacon Jones
End	Reggie White
Tackle	Joe Greene
Tackle	Bob Lilly
Middle Linebacker	Dick Butkus
Outside Linebacker	Jack Ham
Outside Linebacker	Lawrence Taylor
Cornerback	Mel Blount
Cornerback	Dick (Night Train) Lane
Safety	Ronnie Lott
Safety	Larry Wilson

Special Teams

Kicker	Jan Stenerud
Punter	Ray Guy
Kick Returner	Gale Sayers
Punt Returner	Deion Sanders
Special Teams	Steve Tasker

AFL-NFL 1960-1984 ALL-STAR TEAM

Chosen by the Hall of Fame Selection Committee in 1985.

Offense

Quarterback	Johnny Unitas
Running Back	Jim Brown
Running Back	O.J. Simpson
Wide Receiver	Lance Alworth
Wide Receiver	Raymond Berry
Tight End	Kellen Winslow
Tight End	Forrest Gregg
Tight End	Ron Mix
Guard	Jim Parker
Guard	John Hannah
Center	Jim Otto

Defense

End	Gino Marchetti
End	Willie Davis
Tackle	Bob Lilly
Tackle	Merlin Olsen
Linebacker	Dick Butkus
Linebacker	Jack Lambert
Linebacker	Ray Nitschke
Cornerback	Willie Brown
Cornerback	Dick (Night Train) Lane
Safety	Larry Wilson
Safety	Yale Lary

Special Teams

Punter	Ray Guy
Kicker	Jan Stenerud
Kick Returner	Gale Sayers
Kick Returner	Rick Upchurch

Coach	Don Shula
Coach	Vince Lombardi

Records

Compiled by Elias Sports Bureau

The following records reflect all available official information on the National Football League from its formation in 1920 to date. Also included are all applicable records from the American Football League, 1960-69.

Individuals eligible for Rookie records are players who were in their first season of professional football and had not been on the roster of another professional football team, including teams in other leagues, for any regular-season or postseason games in a previous season. Eligible players, therefore, include those who were under contract to a National Football League club for a previous season but were terminated prior to their club's first regular-season game and not re-signed, or who were placed on Reserve/Injured (or another category of the Reserve List) prior to their club's first regular-season game and were not activated during the rest of the regular season or postseason.

INDIVIDUAL RECORDS

SERVICE

Most Seasons

26 George Blanda, Chi. Bears, 1949, 1950-58; Baltimore, 1950; Houston, 1960-66; Oakland, 1967-1975
22 Morten Andersen, New Orleans, 1982-1994; Atlanta, 1995-2000; N.Y. Giants, 2001; Kansas City, 2002-03
Gary Anderson, Pittsburgh, 1982-1994; Philadelphia, 1995-96; San Francisco, 1997; Minnesota, 1998-2002; Tennessee, 2003
21 Earl Morrall, San Francisco, 1956; Pittsburgh, 1957-58; Detroit, 1958-1964; N.Y. Giants, 1965-67; Baltimore, 1968-1971; Miami, 1972-76

Most Seasons, One Club

20 Jackie Slater, L.A. Rams, 1976-1994; St. Louis, 1995
Darrell Green, Washington, 1983-2002
19 Jim Marshall, Minnesota, 1961-1979
Bruce Matthews, Houston, 1983-1996; Tennessee, 1997-2001
18 Jim Hart, St. Louis, 1966-1983
Jeff Van Note, Atlanta, 1969-1986
Pat Leahy, N.Y. Jets, 1974-1991

Most Games Played, Career

340 George Blanda, Chi. Bears, 1949, 1950-58; Baltimore, 1950; Houston, 1960-66; Oakland, 1967-1975
338 Morten Andersen, New Orleans, 1982-1994; Atlanta, 1995-2000; N.Y. Giants, 2001; Kansas City, 2002-03
Gary Anderson, Pittsburgh, 1982-1994; Philadelphia, 1995-96; San Francisco, 1997; Minnesota, 1998-2002; Tennessee, 2003
296 Bruce Matthews, Houston, 1983-1996; Tennessee, 1997-2001

Most Consecutive Games Played, Career

282 Jim Marshall, Cleveland, 1960; Minnesota, 1961-1979
256 Jeff Feagles, New England, 1988-89; Philadelphia, 1990-93; Arizona, 1994-97; Seattle, 1998-2002; N.Y. Giants, 2003 (current)
248 Morten Andersen, New Orleans, 1987-1994; Atlanta, 1995-2000; N.Y. Giants, 2001; Kansas City, 2002

SCORING

Most Seasons Leading League

5 Don Hutson, Green Bay, 1940-44
Gino Cappelletti, Boston, 1961, 1963-66
3 Earl (Dutch) Clark, Portsmouth, 1932; Detroit, 1935-36
Pat Harder, Chi. Cardinals, 1947-49
Paul Hornung, Green Bay, 1959-1961
2 Jack Manders, Chi. Bears, 1934, 1937
Gordy Soltau, San Francisco, 1952-53
Doak Walker, Detroit, 1950, 1955
Gene Mingo, Denver, 1960, 1962
Jim Turner, N.Y. Jets, 1968-69
Fred Cox, Minnesota, 1969-1970
Chester Marcol, Green Bay, 1972, 1974
John Smith, New England, 1979-1980
Marshall Faulk, St. Louis, 2000-01

Most Consecutive Seasons Leading League

5 Don Hutson, Green Bay, 1940-44
4 Gino Cappelletti, Boston, 1963-66
3 Pat Harder, Chi. Cardinals, 1947-49
Paul Hornung, Green Bay, 1959-1961

POINTS

Most Points, Career

2,346 Gary Anderson, Pittsburgh, 1982-1994; Philadelphia 1995-96; San Francisco, 1997; Minnesota, 1998-2002; Tennessee, 2003 (783-pat, 521-fg)
2,259 Morten Andersen, New Orleans, 1982-1994; Atlanta, 1995-2000; N.Y. Giants, 2001; Kansas City, 2002-03 (753-pat, 502-fg)
2,002 George Blanda, Chi. Bears, 1949, 1950-58; Baltimore, 1950; Houston, 1960-66; Oakland, 1967-1975 (9-td, 943-pat, 335-fg)

Most Points, Season

176 Paul Hornung, Green Bay, 1960 (15-td, 41-pat, 15-fg)
164 Gary Anderson, Minnesota, 1998 (59-pat, 35-fg)
163 Jeff Wilkins, St. Louis, 2003 (46-pat, 39-fg)

Most Points, No Touchdowns, Season

164 Gary Anderson, Minnesota, 1998 (59-pat, 35-fg)
163 Jeff Wilkins, St. Louis, 2003 (46-pat, 39-fg)
161 Mark Moseley, Washington, 1983 (62-pat, 33-fg)

Most Seasons, 100 or More Points

14 Gary Anderson, Pittsburgh, 1982-1994; Philadelphia 1995-96; San Francisco, 1997; Minnesota, 1998-2002; Tennessee, 2003
Morten Andersen, New Orleans, 1982-1994; Atlanta, 1995-2000; N.Y. Giants, 2001; Kansas City, 2002-03
11 Nick Lowery, Kansas City, 1981, 1983-86, 1988-1993
Jason Elam, Denver, 1993-2003
9 Norm Johnson, Seattle, 1983-84, 1986, 1988, 1990; Atlanta, 1993; Pittsburgh, 1995-97
Pete Stoyanovich, Miami, 1990-95; Kansas City, 1997-99

Most Points, Rookie, Season

144 Kevin Butler, Chicago, 1985 (51-pat, 31-fg)
132 Gale Sayers, Chicago, 1965 (22-td)
128 Doak Walker, Detroit, 1950 (11-td, 38-pat, 8-fg)
Chester Marcol, Green Bay, 1972 (29-pat, 33-fg)

Most Points, Game

40 Ernie Nevers, Chi. Cardinals vs. Chi. Bears, Nov. 28, 1929 (6-td, 4-pat)
36 Dub Jones, Cleveland vs. Chi. Bears, Nov. 25, 1951 (6-td)
Gale Sayers, Chicago vs. San Francisco, Dec. 12, 1965 (6-td)
33 Paul Hornung, Green Bay vs. Baltimore, Oct. 8, 1961 (4-td, 6-pat, 1-fg)

Most Consecutive Games Scoring

316 Morten Andersen, New Orleans, 1983-1994; Atlanta, 1995-2000; N.Y. Giants, 2001; Kansas City, 2002-03 (current)
186 Jim Breech, Oakland, 1979; Cincinnati, 1980-1992
172 Jason Elam, Denver, 1993-2003 (current)

TOUCHDOWNS

Most Seasons Leading League

8 Don Hutson, Green Bay, 1935-38, 1941-44
3 Jim Brown, Cleveland, 1958-59, 1963

Lance Alworth, San Diego, 1964-66
Emmitt Smith, Dallas, 1992, 1994-95
2 By many players

Most Consecutive Seasons Leading League
4 Don Hutson, Green Bay, 1935-38, 1941-44
3 Lance Alworth, San Diego, 1964-66
2 By many players

Most Touchdowns, Career
205 Jerry Rice, San Francisco, 1985-2000; Oakland, 2001-03 (10-r, 194-p, 1-ret)
166 Emmitt Smith, Dallas, 1990-2002; Arizona, 2003 (155-r, 11-p)
145 Marcus Allen, L.A. Raiders, 1982-1992; Kansas City, 1993-97 (123-r, 21-p, 1-ret)

Most Touchdowns, Season
27 Priest Holmes, Kansas City, 2003 (27-r)
26 Marshall Faulk, St. Louis, 2000 (18-r, 8-p)
25 Emmitt Smith, Dallas, 1995 (25-r)

Most Touchdowns, Rookie, Season
22 Gale Sayers, Chicago, 1965 (14-r, 6-p, 2-ret)
20 Eric Dickerson, L.A. Rams, 1983 (18-r, 2-p)
17 Randy Moss, Minnesota, 1998 (17-p)
Fred Taylor, Jacksonville, 1998 (14-r, 3-p)
Edgerrin James, Indianapolis, 1999 (13-r, 4-p)
Clinton Portis, Denver, 2002 (15-r, 2-p)

Most Touchdowns, Game
6 Ernie Nevers, Chi. Cardinals vs. Chi. Bears, Nov. 28, 1929 (6-r)
Dub Jones, Cleveland vs. Chi. Bears, Nov. 25, 1951 (4-r, 2-p)
Gale Sayers, Chicago vs. San Francisco, Dec. 12, 1965 (4-r, 1-p, 1-ret)
5 Jimmy Conzelman, Rhode Island vs. Evansville, Oct. 15, 1922 (5-r)
Bob Shaw, Chi. Cardinals vs. Baltimore, Oct. 2, 1950 (5-p)
Jim Brown, Cleveland vs. Baltimore, Nov. 1, 1959 (5-r)
Abner Haynes, Dall. Texans vs. Oakland, Nov. 26, 1961 (4-r, 1-p)
Billy Cannon, Houston vs. N.Y. Titans, Dec. 10, 1961 (3-r, 2-p)
Cookie Gilchrist, Buffalo vs. N.Y. Jets, Dec. 8, 1963 (5-r)
Paul Hornung, Green Bay vs. Baltimore, Dec. 12, 1965 (3-r, 2-p)
Kellen Winslow, San Diego vs. Oakland, Nov. 22, 1981 (5-p)
Jerry Rice, San Francisco vs. Atlanta, Oct. 14, 1990 (5-p)
James Stewart, Jacksonville vs. Philadelphia, Oct. 12, 1997 (5-r)
Shaun Alexander, Seattle vs. Minnesota, Sept. 29, 2002 (4-r, 1-p)
Clinton Portis, Denver vs. Kansas City, Dec. 7, 2003 (5-r)
4 By many players. Last time: Joe Horn, New Orleans vs. N.Y. Giants, Dec. 14, 2003 (4-p)

Most Consecutive Games Scoring Touchdowns
18 Lenny Moore, Baltimore, 1963-65
14 O.J. Simpson, Buffalo, 1975
13 John Riggins, Washington, 1982-83
George Rogers, Washington, 1985-86
Jerry Rice, San Francisco, 1986-87

POINTS AFTER TOUCHDOWN

Most Seasons Leading League
8 George Blanda, Chi. Bears, 1956; Houston, 1961-62; Oakland, 1967-69, 1972, 1974
4 Bob Waterfield, Cleveland, 1945; Los Angeles, 1946, 1950, 1952
3 Earl (Dutch) Clark, Portsmouth, 1932; Detroit, 1935-36 Jack Manders, Chi. Bears, 1933-35
Don Hutson, Green Bay, 1941-42, 1945

Most (Kicking) Points After Touchdown Attempted, Career
959 George Blanda, Chi. Bears, 1949, 1950-58; Baltimore, 1950; Houston, 1960-66; Oakland, 1967-1975
790 Gary Anderson, Pittsburgh, 1982-1994; Philadelphia 1995-96; San Francisco, 1997; Minnesota, 1998-2002; Tennessee, 2003
763 Morten Andersen, New Orleans, 1982-1994; Atlanta, 1995-2000; N.Y. Giants, 2001; Kansas City, 2002-03

Most (Kicking) Points After Touchdown Attempted, Season
70 Uwe von Schamann, Miami, 1984
65 George Blanda, Houston, 1961
64 Jeff Wilkins, St. Louis, 1999

Most (Kicking) Points After Touchdown Attempted, Game
10 Charlie Gogolak, Washington vs. N.Y. Giants, Nov. 27, 1966
9 Pat Harder, Chi. Cardinals vs. N.Y. Giants, Oct. 17, 1948; vs. N.Y. Bulldogs, Nov. 13, 1949
Bob Waterfield, Los Angeles vs. Baltimore, Oct. 22, 1950
Bob Thomas, Chicago vs. Green Bay, Dec. 7, 1980
8 By many players

Most (One-Point) Points After Touchdown, Career
943 George Blanda, Chi. Bears, 1949, 1950-58; Baltimore, 1950; Houston, 1960-66; Oakland, 1967-1975
783 Gary Anderson, Pittsburgh, 1982-1994; Philadelphia 1995-96; San Francisco, 1997; Minnesota, 1998-2002; Tennessee, 2003
753 Morten Andersen, New Orleans, 1982-1994; Atlanta, 1995-2000; N.Y. Giants, 2001; Kansas City, 2002-03

Most (One-Point) Points After Touchdown, Season
66 Uwe von Schamann, Miami, 1984
64 George Blanda, Houston, 1961
Jeff Wilkins, St. Louis, 1999
62 Mark Moseley, Washington, 1983

Most (One-Point) Points After Touchdown, Game
9 Pat Harder, Chi. Cardinals vs. N.Y. Giants, Oct. 17, 1948
Bob Waterfield, Los Angeles vs. Baltimore, Oct. 22, 1950
Charlie Gogolak, Washington vs. N.Y. Giants, Nov. 27, 1966
8 By many players

Most Consecutive (Kicking) Points After Touchdown
371 Jason Elam, Denver, 1993-2002
301 Norm Johnson, Atlanta, 1991-94; Pittsburgh, 1995-98; Philadelphia, 1999
250 Eddie Murray, Detroit, 1988-1991; Kansas City, 1992; Tampa Bay, 1992; Dallas, 1993; Philadelphia, 1994; Washington, 1995; Minnesota, 1997

Highest (Kicking) Points After Touchdown Percentage, Career (200 points after touchdown)
99.57 Mike Vanderjagt, Indianapolis, 1998-2003 (234-233)
99.56 Jason Elam, Denver, 1993-2003 (451-449)
99.43 Tommy Davis, San Francisco, 1959-1969 (350-348)

Most (Kicking) Points After Touchdown, No Misses, Season
64 Jeff Wilkins, St. Louis, 1999
59 Gary Anderson, Minnesota, 1998
58 Jason Elam, Denver, 1998
Jeff Wilkins, St. Louis, 2001

Most (Kicking) Points After Touchdown, No Misses, Game
9 Pat Harder, Chi. Cardinals vs. N.Y. Giants, Oct. 17, 1948
Bob Waterfield, Los Angeles vs. Baltimore, Oct. 22, 1950

8 By many players

Most Two-Point Conversions, Career

Two-point conversions include AFL (1960-69) and NFL (since 1994).

6 Terance Mathis, Atlanta, 1994-2001; Pittsburgh, 2002
5 Cris Carter, Minnesota, 1994-2001; Miami, 2002
Rob Moore, N.Y. Jets, 1994; Arizona, 1995-99
Willie Jackson, Jacksonville, 1995-97; Cincinnati, 1998-99; New Orleans, 2000-01; Washington, 2002
Keenan McCardell, Cleveland, 1994-95; Jacksonville, 1996-2001; Tampa Bay, 2002-03
Marvin Harrison, Indianapolis, 1996-2003
Marcus Pollard, Indianapolis, 1995-2003
Todd Heap, Baltimore, 2001-03
4 Gino Cappelletti, Boston, 1960-69
Jerry Rice, San Francisco, 1994-2000; Oakland, 2001-03
Lamar Smith, Seattle, 1994-97; New Orleans, 1998-99; Miami, 2000-01; Carolina, 2002; New Orleans, 2003
Floyd Turner, Indianapolis, 1994-95; Baltimore, 1996, 1998
Jackie Harris, Tampa Bay, 1994-97; Tennessee, 1998-99; Dallas, 2000-01
Marshall Faulk, Indianapolis, 1994-98; St. Louis, 1999-2003
Frank Sanders, Arizona, 1995-2002; Baltimore, 2003
Hines Ward, Pittsburgh, 1998-2003
Kerry Collins, Carolina, 1995-98; New Orleans, 1998; N.Y. Giants, 1999-2003

Most Two-Point Conversions, Season

4 Todd Heap, Baltimore, 2003
3 Gino Cappelletti, Boston, 1960
Richie Lucas, Buffalo, 1961
Ronnie Harmon, San Diego, 1994
Haywood Jeffires, Houston, 1994
Tom Tupa, Cleveland, 1994
Terance Mathis, Atlanta, 1995
Lamar Smith, Seattle, 1996
Cris Carter, Minnesota, 1997
Terrell Davis, Denver, 1997
James Stewart, Detroit, 2000
Hines Ward, Pittsburgh, 2002
2 By many players

Most Two-Point Conversions, Game

2 Brett Perriman, Detroit vs. Green Bay, Nov. 6, 1994
Michael Jackson, Baltimore vs. New England, Oct. 6, 1996
Terrell Davis, Denver vs. Atlanta, Sept. 28, 1997
Charles Johnson, Pittsburgh vs. Tennessee, Nov. 1, 1998
Marshall Faulk, St. Louis vs. Atlanta, Oct. 15, 2000
Todd Heap, Baltimore vs. Cincinnati, Oct. 19, 2003

FIELD GOALS

Most Seasons Leading League

5 Lou Groza, Cleveland, 1950, 1952-54, 1957
4 Jack Manders, Chi. Bears, 1933-34, 1936-37
Ward Cuff, N.Y. Giants, 1938-39, 1943; Green Bay, 1947
Mark Moseley, Washington, 1976-77, 1979, 1982
3 Bob Waterfield, Los Angeles, 1947, 1949, 1951
Gino Cappelletti, Boston, 1961, 1963-64
Fred Cox, Minnesota, 1965, 1969-1970
Jan Stenerud, Kansas City, 1967, 1970, 1975

Most Consecutive Seasons Leading League

3 Lou Groza, Cleveland, 1952-54
2 Jack Manders, Chi. Bears, 1933-34
Armand Niccolai, Pittsburgh, 1935-36
Jack Manders, Chi. Bears, 1936-37
Ward Cuff, N.Y. Giants, 1938-39
Clark Hinkle, Green Bay, 1940-41
Cliff Patton, Philadelphia, 1948-49
Gino Cappelletti, Boston, 1963-64
Jim Turner, N.Y. Jets, 1968-69
Fred Cox, Minnesota, 1969-1970
Mark Moseley, Washington, 1976-77
Chip Lohmiller, Washington, 1991-92
Pete Stoyanovich, Miami, 1991-92

Most Field Goals Attempted, Career

650 Gary Anderson, Pittsburgh, 1982-1994; Philadelphia 1995-96; San Francisco, 1997; Minnesota, 1998-2002; Tennessee, 2003
637 George Blanda, Chi. Bears, 1949, 1950-58; Baltimore, 1950; Houston, 1960-66; Oakland, 1967-1975
636 Morten Andersen, New Orleans, 1982-1994; Atlanta, 1995-2000; N.Y. Giants, 2001; Kansas City, 2002-03

Most Field Goals Attempted, Season

49 Bruce Gossett, Los Angeles, 1966
Curt Knight, Washington, 1971
48 Chester Marcol, Green Bay, 1972
47 Jim Turner, N.Y. Jets, 1969
David Ray, Los Angeles, 1973
Mark Moseley, Washington, 1983

Most Field Goals Attempted, Game

9 Jim Bakken, St. Louis vs. Pittsburgh, Sept. 24, 1967
8 Lou Michaels, Pittsburgh vs. St. Louis, Dec. 2, 1962
Garo Yepremian, Detroit vs. Minnesota, Nov. 13, 1966
Jim Turner, N.Y. Jets vs. Buffalo, Nov. 3, 1968
Billy Cundiff, Dallas vs. N.Y. Giants, Sept. 15, 2003 (OT)
7 By many players

Most Field Goals, Career

521 Gary Anderson, Pittsburgh, 1982-1994; Philadelphia 1995-96; San Francisco, 1997; Minnesota, 1998-2002; Tennessee, 2003
502 Morten Andersen, New Orleans, 1982-1994; Atlanta, 1995-2000; N.Y. Giants, 2001; Kansas City, 2002-03
383 Nick Lowery, New England, 1978; Kansas City, 1980-1993; N.Y. Jets, 1994-1996

Most Field Goals, Season

39 Olindo Mare, Miami, 1999
Jeff Wilkins, St. Louis, 2003
37 John Kasay, Carolina, 1996
Mike Vanderjagt, Indianapolis, 2003
36 Cary Blanchard, Indianapolis, 1996
Al Del Greco, Tennessee, 1998

Most Field Goals, Rookie, Season

35 Ali Haji-Sheikh, N.Y. Giants, 1983
34 Richie Cunningham, Dallas, 1997
33 Chester Marcol, Green Bay, 1972

Most Field Goals, Game

7 Jim Bakken, St. Louis vs. Pittsburgh, Sept. 24, 1967
Rich Karlis, Minnesota vs. L.A. Rams, Nov. 5, 1989 (OT)
Chris Boniol, Dallas vs. Green Bay, Nov. 18, 1996
Billy Cundiff, Dallas vs. N.Y. Giants, Sept. 15, 2003 (OT)
6 Gino Cappelletti, Boston vs. Denver, Oct. 4, 1964
Garo Yepremian, Detroit vs. Minnesota, Nov. 13, 1966
Jim Turner, N.Y. Jets vs. Buffalo, Nov. 3, 1968
Tom Dempsey, Philadelphia vs. Houston, Nov. 12, 1972
Bobby Howfield, N.Y. Jets vs. New Orleans, Dec. 3, 1972
Jim Bakken, St. Louis vs. Atlanta, Dec. 9, 1973
Joe Danelo, N.Y. Giants vs. Seattle, Oct. 18, 1981
Ray Wersching, San Francisco vs. New Orleans, Oct. 16, 1983
Gary Anderson, Pittsburgh vs. Denver, Oct. 23, 1988

John Carney, San Diego vs. Seattle, Sept. 5, 1993
John Carney, San Diego vs. Houston, Sept. 19, 1993
Doug Pelfrey, Cincinnati vs. Seattle, Nov. 6, 1994 (OT)
Norm Johnson, Atlanta vs. New Orleans, Nov. 13, 1994
Jeff Wilkins, San Francisco vs. Atlanta, Sept. 29, 1996
Steve Christie, Buffalo vs. N.Y. Jets, Oct. 20, 1996
Greg Davis, San Diego vs. Oakland, Oct. 5, 1997
Gary Anderson, Minnesota vs. Baltimore, Dec. 13, 1998
Olindo Mare, Miami vs. New England, Oct. 17, 1999
Jason Hanson, Detroit vs. Minnesota, Oct. 17, 1999
Jeff Reed, Pittsburgh vs. Jacksonville, Dec. 1, 2002

5 By many players

Most Field Goals, One Quarter

4 Garo Yepremian, Detroit vs. Minnesota, Nov. 13, 1966 (second quarter)
Curt Knight, Washington vs. N.Y. Giants, Nov. 15, 1970 (second quarter)
Roger Ruzek, Dallas vs. N.Y. Giants, Nov. 2, 1987 (fourth quarter)
Cary Blanchard, Indianapolis vs. Buffalo, Sept. 21 1997 (second quarter)
Sebastian Janikowski, Oakland vs. Chicago, Oct. 5, 2003 (second quarter)
Jeff Wilkins, St. Louis vs. Baltimore, Nov. 9, 2003 (fourth quarter)

3 By many players

Most Consecutive Games Scoring Field Goals

38 Matt Stover, Baltimore, 1999-2001
31 Fred Cox, Minnesota, 1968-1970
28 Jim Turner, N.Y. Jets, 1970; Denver, 1971-72
Chip Lohmiller, Washington, 1988-1990

Most Consecutive Field Goals

41 Mike Vanderjagt, Indianapolis, 2002-03 (current)
40 Gary Anderson, San Francisco, 1997; Minnesota, 1998
31 Fuad Reveiz, Minnesota, 1994-95

Longest Field Goal

63 Tom Dempsey, New Orleans vs. Detroit, Nov. 8, 1970
Jason Elam, Denver vs. Jacksonville, Oct. 25, 1998
60 Steve Cox, Cleveland vs. Cincinnati, Oct. 21, 1984
Morten Andersen, New Orleans vs. Chicago, Oct. 27, 1991
59 Tony Franklin, Philadelphia vs. Dallas, Nov. 12, 1979
Pete Stoyanovich, Miami vs. N.Y. Jets, Nov. 12, 1989
Steve Christie, Buffalo vs. Miami, Sept. 26, 1993
Morten Andersen, Atlanta vs. San Francisco, Dec. 24, 1995

Highest Field Goal Percentage, Career (100 field goals)

87.88 Mike Vanderjagt, Indianapolis, 1998-2003
82.96 David Akers, Washington, 1998; Philadelphia, 1999-2003
82.35 Olindo Mare, Miami, 1997-2003

Highest Field Goal Percentage, Season (Qualifiers)

100.00 Tony Zendejas, L.A. Rams, 1991 (17-17)
Gary Anderson, Minnesota, 1998 (35-35)
Jeff Wilkins, St. Louis, 2000 (17-17)
Mike Vanderjagt, Indianapolis, 2003 (37-37)
96.43 Chris Boniol, Dallas, 1995 (28-27)
96.30 Norm Johnson, Atlanta, 1993 (27-26)
Pete Stoyanovich, Kansas City, 1997 (27-26)

Most Field Goals, No Misses, Game

7 Rich Karlis, Minnesota vs. L.A. Rams, Nov. 5, 1989 (OT)
Chris Boniol, Dallas vs. Green Bay, Nov. 18, 1996
6 Gino Cappelletti, Boston vs. Denver, Oct. 4, 1964
Joe Danelo, N.Y. Giants vs. Seattle, Oct. 18, 1981
Ray Wersching, San Francisco vs. New Orleans, Oct. 16, 1983
Gary Anderson, Pittsburgh vs. Denver, Oct. 23, 1988
John Carney, San Diego vs. Seattle, Sept. 5, 1993
John Carney, San Diego vs. Houston, Sept. 19, 1993
Doug Pelfrey, Cincinnati vs. Seattle, Nov. 6, 1994 (OT)
Norm Johnson, Atlanta vs. New Orleans, Nov. 13, 1994
Jeff Wilkins, San Francisco vs. Atlanta, Sept. 29, 1996
Greg Davis, San Diego vs. Oakland, Oct. 5, 1997
Gary Anderson, Minnesota vs. Baltimore, Dec. 13, 1998
Olindo Mare, Miami vs. New England, Oct. 17, 1999
Jeff Reed, Pittsburgh vs. Jacksonville, Dec. 1, 2002

5 By many players

Most Field Goals, 50 or More Yards, Career

40 Morten Andersen, New Orleans, 1982-1994; Atlanta, 1995-2000; N.Y. Giants, 2001; Kansas City, 2002-03
31 Jason Elam, Denver, 1993-2003
25 Jason Hanson, Detroit, 1992-2003

Most Field Goals, 50 or More Yards, Season

8 Morten Andersen, Atlanta, 1995
6 Dean Biasucci, Indianapolis, 1988
Chris Jacke, Green Bay, 1993
Tony Zendejas, L.A. Rams, 1993
Mike Vanderjagt, Indianapolis, 1998
5 Fred Steinfort, Denver, 1980
Norm Johnson, Seattle, 1986
Kevin Butler, Chicago, 1993
Jason Elam, Denver, 1995
Cary Blanchard, Indianapolis, 1996
Jason Elam, Denver, 1999
Martín Gramatica, Tampa Bay, 2000, 2002
Paul Edinger, Chicago, 2002

Most Field Goals, 50 or More Yards, Game

3 Morten Andersen, Atlanta vs. New Orleans, Dec. 10, 1995
2 By many players. Last time: Mike Vanderjagt, Indianapolis vs. Denver, Nov. 24, 2002 (OT)

SAFETIES

Most Safeties, Career

4 Ted Hendricks, Baltimore, 1969-1973; Green Bay, 1974; Oakland, 1975-1981; L.A. Raiders, 1982-83
Doug English, Detroit, 1975-79, 1981-85
3 Bill McPeak, Pittsburgh, 1949-1957
Charlie Krueger, San Francisco, 1959-1973
Ernie Stautner, Pittsburgh, 1950-1963
Jim Katcavage, N.Y. Giants, 1956-1968
Roger Brown, Detroit, 1960-66; Los Angeles, 1967-69
Bruce Maher, Detroit, 1960-67; N.Y. Giants, 1968-69
Ron McDole, St. Louis, 1961; Houston, 1962; Buffalo, 1963-1970; Washington, 1971-78
Alan Page, Minnesota, 1967-1978; Chicago, 1979-1981
Lyle Alzado, Denver, 1971-78; Cleveland, 1979-1981; L.A. Raiders, 1982-85
Rulon Jones, Denver, 1980-88
Steve McMichael, New England, 1980; Chicago, 1981-1993; Green Bay, 1994
Kevin Greene, L.A. Rams, 1985-1992; Pittsburgh, 1993-95; Carolina, 1996, 1998-99; San Francisco, 1997
Burt Grossman, San Diego, 1989-1993; Philadelphia, 1994
Eric Swann, Phoenix, 1991-93; Arizona, 1994-99; Carolina, 2000
Dan Saleaumua, Detroit, 1987-88; Kansas City, 1989-1996; Seattle, 1997-98
Derrick Thomas, Kansas City, 1989-1999

Bryant Young, San Francisco, 1994-2003
2 By many players

Most Safeties, Season
2 Tom Nash, Green Bay, 1932
Roger Brown, Detroit, 1962
Ron McDole, Buffalo, 1964
Alan Page, Minnesota, 1971
Fred Dryer, Los Angeles, 1973
Benny Barnes, Dallas, 1973
James Young, Houston, 1977
Doug English, Detroit, 1983
Don Blackmon, New England, 1985
Tim Harris, Green Bay, 1988
Brian Jordan, Atlanta, 1991
Burt Grossman, San Diego, 1992
Rod Stephens, Seattle, 1993
Bryant Young, San Francisco, 1996

Most Safeties, Game
2 Fred Dryer, Los Angeles vs. Green Bay, Oct. 21, 1973

RUSHING

Most Seasons Leading League
8 Jim Brown, Cleveland, 1957-1961, 1963-65
4 Steve Van Buren, Philadelphia, 1945, 1947-49
O.J. Simpson, Buffalo, 1972-73, 1975-76
Eric Dickerson, L.A. Rams, 1983-84, 1986; Indianapolis, 1988
Emmitt Smith, Dallas, 1991-93, 1995
Barry Sanders, Detroit, 1990, 1994, 1996-97
3 Earl Campbell, Houston, 1978-1980

Most Consecutive Seasons Leading League
5 Jim Brown, Cleveland, 1957-1961
3 Steve Van Buren, Philadelphia, 1947-49
Jim Brown, Cleveland, 1963-65
Earl Campbell, Houston, 1978-1980
Emmitt Smith, Dallas, 1991-93
2 Bill Paschal, N.Y. Giants, 1943-44
Joe Perry, San Francisco, 1953-54
Jim Nance, Boston, 1966-67
Leroy Kelly, Cleveland, 1967-68
O.J. Simpson, Buffalo, 1972-73; 1975-76
Eric Dickerson, L.A. Rams, 1983-84
Barry Sanders, Detroit, 1996-97
Edgerrin James, Indianapolis, 1999-2000

ATTEMPTS

Most Seasons Leading League
6 Jim Brown, Cleveland, 1958-59, 1961, 1963-65
4 Steve Van Buren, Philadelphia, 1947-1950
Walter Payton, Chicago, 1976-79
3 Cookie Gilchrist, Buffalo, 1963-64; Denver, 1965
Jim Nance, Boston, 1966-67, 1969
O.J. Simpson, Buffalo, 1973-75
Eric Dickerson, L.A. Rams, 1983, 1986; Indianapolis, 1988
Emmitt Smith, Dallas, 1991, 1994-95

Most Consecutive Seasons Leading League
4 Steve Van Buren, Philadelphia, 1947-1950
Walter Payton, Chicago, 1976-79
3 Jim Brown, Cleveland, 1963-65
Cookie Gilchrist, Buffalo, 1963-64; Denver, 1965
O.J. Simpson, Buffalo, 1973-75
2 By many players

Most Attempts, Career
4,142 Emmitt Smith, Dallas, 1990-2002; Arizona, 2003
3,838 Walter Payton, Chicago, 1975-1987
3,119 Jerome Bettis, L.A. Rams, 1993-94; St. Louis, 1995; Pittsburgh, 1996-2003

Most Attempts, Season
410 Jamal Anderson, Atlanta, 1998
407 James Wilder, Tampa Bay, 1984
404 Eric Dickerson, L.A. Rams, 1986

Most Attempts, Rookie, Season
390 Eric Dickerson, L.A. Rams, 1983
378 George Rogers, New Orleans, 1981
369 Edgerrin James, Indianapolis, 1999

Most Attempts, Game
45 Jamie Morris, Washington vs. Cincinnati, Dec. 17, 1988 (OT)
43 Butch Woolfolk, N.Y. Giants vs. Philadelphia, Nov. 20, 1983
James Wilder, Tampa Bay vs. Green Bay, Sept. 30, 1984 (OT)
Rudi Johnson, Cincinnati vs. Houston, Nov. 9, 2003
42 James Wilder, Tampa Bay vs. Pittsburgh, Oct. 30, 1983
Terrell Davis, Denver vs. Buffalo, Oct. 26, 1997 (OT)
Ricky Williams, Miami vs. Buffalo, Sept. 21, 2003

YARDS GAINED

Most Yards Gained, Career
17,418 Emmitt Smith, Dallas, 1990-2002; Arizona, 2003
16,726 Walter Payton, Chicago, 1975-1987
15,269 Barry Sanders, Detroit, 1989-1998

Most Seasons, 1,000 or More Yards Rushing
11 Emmitt Smith, Dallas, 1991-2001
10 Walter Payton, Chicago, 1976-1981, 1983-86
Barry Sanders, Detroit, 1989-1998
9 Curtis Martin, New England, 1995-97; N.Y. Jets, 1998-2003

Most Consecutive Seasons, 1,000 or More Yards Rushing
11 Emmitt Smith, Dallas, 1991-2001
10 Barry Sanders, Detroit, 1989-1998
9 Curtis Martin, New England, 1995-97; N.Y. Jets, 1998-2003 (current)

Most Yards Gained, Season
2,105 Eric Dickerson, L.A. Rams, 1984
2,066 Jamal Lewis, Baltimore, 2003
2,053 Barry Sanders, Detroit, 1997

Most Yards Gained, Rookie, Season
1,808 Eric Dickerson, L.A. Rams, 1983
1,674 George Rogers, New Orleans, 1981
1,605 Ottis Anderson, St. Louis, 1979

Most Yards Gained, Game
295 Jamal Lewis, Baltimore vs. Cleveland, Sept. 14, 2003
278 Corey Dillon, Cincinnati vs. Denver, Oct. 22, 2000
275 Walter Payton, Chicago vs. Minnesota, Nov. 20, 1977

Most Games, 200 or More Yards Rushing, Career
6 O.J. Simpson, Buffalo, 1969-1977; San Francisco, 1978-79
4 Jim Brown, Cleveland, 1957-1965
Earl Campbell, Houston, 1978-1984; New Orleans, 1984-85
Barry Sanders, Detroit, 1989-1998
LaDainian Tomlinson, San Diego, 2001-03
3 Eric Dickerson, L.A. Rams, 1983-87; Indianapolis, 1987-1991; L.A. Raiders, 1992; Atlanta, 1993
Greg Bell, Buffalo, 1984-87; L.A. Rams, 1987-89; L.A. Raiders, 1990
Terrell Davis, Denver, 1995-2001
Corey Dillon, Cincinnati, 1997-2003
Marshall Faulk, Indianapolis, 1994-98; St. Louis, 1999-2003

Most Games, 200 or More Yards Rushing, Season
4 Earl Campbell, Houston, 1980
3 O.J. Simpson, Buffalo, 1973
2 Jim Brown, Cleveland, 1963

O.J. Simpson, Buffalo, 1976
Walter Payton, Chicago, 1977
Eric Dickerson, L.A. Rams, 1984
Greg Bell, L.A. Rams, 1989
Terrell Davis, Denver, 1997
Barry Sanders, Detroit, 1997
Corey Dillon, Cincinnati, 2000
Marshall Faulk, St. Louis, 2000
LaDainian Tomlinson, San Diego, 2002
Ricky Williams, Miami, 2002
Jamal Lewis, Baltimore, 2003
LaDainian Tomlinson, San Diego, 2003

Most Consecutive Games, 200 or More Yards Rushing
2 O.J. Simpson, Buffalo, 1973, 1976
Earl Campbell, Houston, 1980
Ricky Williams, Miami, 2002

Most Games, 100 or More Yards Rushing, Career
77 Walter Payton, Chicago, 1975-1987
76 Barry Sanders, Detroit, 1989-1998
Emmitt Smith, Dallas, 1990-2002; Arizona, 2003
64 Eric Dickerson, L.A. Rams, 1983-87; Indianapolis, 1987-1991; L.A. Raiders, 1992; Atlanta, 1993

Most Games, 100 or More Yards Rushing, Season
14 Barry Sanders, Detroit, 1997
12 Eric Dickerson, L.A. Rams, 1984
Barry Foster, Pittsburgh, 1992
Jamal Anderson, Atlanta, 1998
Jamal Lewis, Baltimore, 2003
11 O.J. Simpson, Buffalo, 1973
Earl Campbell, Houston, 1979
Marcus Allen, L.A. Raiders, 1985
Eric Dickerson, L.A. Rams, 1986
Emmitt Smith, Dallas, 1995
Terrell Davis, Denver, 1998

Most Consecutive Games, 100 or More Yards Rushing
14 Barry Sanders, Detroit, 1997
11 Marcus Allen, L.A. Raiders, 1985-86
9 Walter Payton, Chicago, 1985
Fred Taylor, Jacksonville, 2000
Deuce McAllister, New Orleans, 2003

Longest Run From Scrimmage
99 Tony Dorsett, Dallas vs. Minnesota, Jan. 3, 1983 (TD)
98 Ahman Green, Green Bay vs. Denver, Dec. 28, 2003 (TD)
97 Andy Uram, Green Bay vs. Chi. Cardinals, Oct. 8, 1939 (TD)
Bob Gage, Pittsburgh vs. Chi. Bears, Dec. 4, 1949 (TD)

AVERAGE GAIN

Highest Average Gain, Career (750 attempts)
6.36 Randall Cunningham, Philadelphia, 1985-1995; Minnesota, 1997-99; Dallas, 2000; Baltimore, 2001 (775-4,928)
5.22 Jim Brown, Cleveland, 1957-1965 (2,359-12,312)
5.14 Eugene (Mercury) Morris, Miami, 1969-1975; San Diego, 1976 (804-4,133)

Highest Average Gain, Season (Qualifiers)
8.44 Beattie Feathers, Chi. Bears, 1934 (119-1,004)
7.98 Randall Cunningham, Philadelphia, 1990 (118-942)
6.88 Michael Vick, Atlanta, 2002 (113-777)

Highest Average Gain, Game (10 attempts)
17.30 Michael Vick, Atlanta vs. Minnesota, Dec. 1, 2002 (OT) (10-173)
17.09 Marion Motley, Cleveland vs. Pittsburgh, Oct. 29, 1950 (11-188)
16.70 Bill Grimes, Green Bay vs. N.Y. Yanks, Oct. 8, 1950 (10-167)

TOUCHDOWNS

Most Seasons Leading League
5 Jim Brown, Cleveland, 1957-59, 1963, 1965
4 Steve Van Buren, Philadelphia, 1945, 1947-49
3 Abner Haynes, Dall. Texans, 1960-62
Cookie Gilchrist, Buffalo, 1962-64
Paul Lowe, L.A. Chargers, 1960; San Diego, 1961, 1965
Leroy Kelly, Cleveland, 1966-68
Emmitt Smith, Dallas, 1992, 1994-95

Most Consecutive Seasons Leading League
3 Steve Van Buren, Philadelphia, 1947-49
Jim Brown, Cleveland, 1957-59
Abner Haynes, Dall. Texans, 1960-62
Cookie Gilchrist, Buffalo, 1962-64
Leroy Kelly, Cleveland, 1966-68

Most Touchdowns, Career
155 Emmitt Smith, Dallas, 1990-2002; Arizona, 2003
123 Marcus Allen, L.A. Raiders, 1982-1992; Kansas City, 1993-97
110 Walter Payton, Chicago, 1975-1987

Most Touchdowns, Season
27 Priest Holmes, Kansas City, 2003
25 Emmitt Smith, Dallas, 1995
24 John Riggins, Washington, 1983

Most Touchdowns, Rookie, Season
18 Eric Dickerson, L.A. Rams, 1983
15 Ickey Woods, Cincinnati, 1988
Mike Anderson, Denver, 2000
Clinton Portis, Denver, 2002
14 Gale Sayers, Chicago, 1965
Barry Sanders, Detroit, 1989
Curtis Martin, New England, 1995
Fred Taylor, Jacksonville, 1998

Most Touchdowns, Game
6 Ernie Nevers, Chi. Cardinals vs. Chi. Bears, Nov. 28, 1929
5 Jimmy Conzelman, Rhode Island vs. Evansville, Oct. 15, 1922
Jim Brown, Cleveland vs. Baltimore, Nov. 1, 1959
Cookie Gilchrist, Buffalo vs. N.Y. Jets, Dec. 8, 1963
James Stewart, Jacksonville vs. Philadelphia, Oct. 12, 1997
Clinton Portis, Denver vs. Kansas City, Dec. 7, 2003
4 By many players

Most Consecutive Games Rushing for Touchdowns
13 John Riggins, Washington, 1982-83
George Rogers, Washington, 1985-86
11 Lenny Moore, Baltimore, 1963-64
Emmitt Smith, Dallas, 1994-95
Emmitt Smith, Dallas, 1995
Priest Holmes, Kansas City, 2002
10 Greg Bell, L.A. Rams, 1988-89
Terry Allen, Washington, 1995-96

PASSING

Most Seasons Leading League
6 Sammy Baugh, Washington, 1937, 1940, 1943, 1945, 1947, 1949
Steve Young San Francisco, 1991-94, 1996-97
4 Len Dawson, Dall. Texans; 1962; Kansas City, 1964, 1966, 1968
Roger Staubach, Dallas, 1971, 1973, 1978-79
Ken Anderson, Cincinnati, 1974-75, 1981-82
3 Arnie Herber, Green Bay, 1932, 1934, 1936
Norm Van Brocklin, Los Angeles, 1950, 1952, 1954
Bart Starr, Green Bay, 1962, 1964, 1966

Most Consecutive Seasons Leading League
4 Steve Young, San Francisco, 1991-94

2 Cecil Isbell, Green Bay, 1941-42
Milt Plum, Cleveland, 1960-61
Ken Anderson, Cincinnati, 1974-75, 1981-82
Roger Staubach, Dallas, 1978-79
Steve Young, San Francisco, 1996-97

PASSER RATING

Highest Passer Rating, Career (1,500 attempts)
97.2 Kurt Warner, St. Louis, 1998-2003
96.8 Steve Young, Tampa Bay, 1985-86; San Francisco, 1987-1999
92.3 Joe Montana, San Francisco, 1979-1990, 1992; Kansas City, 1993-94

Highest Passer Rating, Season (Qualifiers)
112.8 Steve Young, San Francisco, 1994
112.4 Joe Montana, San Francisco, 1989
110.4 Milt Plum, Cleveland, 1960

Highest Passer Rating, Rookie, Season (Qualifiers)
96.0 Dan Marino, Miami, 1983
88.2 Greg Cook, Cincinnati, 1969
84.0 Charlie Conerly, N.Y. Giants, 1948

ATTEMPTS

Most Seasons Leading League
5 Dan Marino, Miami, 1984, 1986, 1988, 1992, 1997
4 Sammy Baugh, Washington, 1937, 1943, 1947-48
Johnny Unitas, Baltimore, 1957, 1959-1961
George Blanda, Chi. Bears, 1953; Houston, 1963-65
3 Arnie Herber, Green Bay, 1932, 1934, 1936
Sonny Jurgensen, Washington, 1966-67, 1969
Drew Bledsoe, New England, 1994-96

Most Consecutive Seasons Leading League
3 Johnny Unitas, Baltimore, 1959-1961
George Blanda, Houston, 1963-65
Drew Bledsoe, New England, 1994-96
2 By many players

Most Passes Attempted, Career
8,358 Dan Marino, Miami, 1983-1999
7,250 John Elway, Denver, 1983-1998
6,823 Warren Moon, Houston, 1984-1993; Minnesota, 1994-96; Seattle, 1997-98; Kansas City, 1999-2000

Most Passes Attempted, Season
691 Drew Bledsoe, New England, 1994
655 Warren Moon, Houston, 1991
636 Drew Bledsoe, New England, 1995

Most Passes Attempted, Rookie, Season
575 Peyton Manning, Indianapolis, 1998
540 Chris Weinke, Carolina, 2001
486 Rick Mirer, Seattle, 1993

Most Passes Attempted, Game
70 Drew Bledsoe, New England vs. Minnesota, Nov. 13, 1994 (OT)
69 Vinny Testaverde, N.Y. Jets vs. Baltimore, Dec. 24, 2000
68 George Blanda, Houston vs. Buffalo, Nov. 1, 1964
Jon Kitna, Cincinnati vs. Pittsburgh, Dec. 30, 2001 (OT)

COMPLETIONS

Most Seasons Leading League
6 Dan Marino, Miami, 1984-86, 1988, 1992, 1997
5 Sammy Baugh, Washington, 1937, 1943, 1945, 1947-48
4 George Blanda, Chi. Bears, 1953; Houston, 1963-65
Sonny Jurgensen, Philadelphia, 1961; Washington, 1966-67, 1969

Most Consecutive Seasons Leading League
3 George Blanda, Houston, 1963-65
Dan Marino, Miami, 1984-86
2 By many players

Most Passes Completed, Career
4,967 Dan Marino, Miami, 1983-1999
4,123 John Elway, Denver, 1983-1998
3,988 Warren Moon, Houston, 1984-1993; Minnesota, 1994-96; Seattle, 1997-98; Kansas City, 1999-2000

Most Passes Completed, Season
418 Rich Gannon, Oakland, 2002
404 Warren Moon, Houston, 1991
400 Drew Bledsoe, New England, 1994

Most Passes Completed, Rookie, Season
326 Peyton Manning, Indianapolis, 1998
293 Chris Weinke, Carolina, 2001
274 Rick Mirer, Seattle, 1993

Most Passes Completed, Game
45 Drew Bledsoe, New England vs. Minnesota, Nov. 13, 1994 (OT)
43 Rich Gannon, Oakland vs. Pittsburgh, Sept. 15, 2002
42 Richard Todd, N.Y. Jets vs. San Francisco, Sept. 21, 1980
Vinny Testaverde, N.Y. Jets vs. Seattle, Dec. 6, 1998

Most Consecutive Passes Completed
22 Joe Montana, San Francisco vs. Cleveland (5), Nov. 29, 1987; vs. Green Bay (17), Dec. 6, 1987
21 Rich Gannon, Oakland vs. Denver, Nov. 11, 2002
20 Ken Anderson, Cincinnati vs. Houston, Jan. 2, 1983
Hugh Millen, Denver vs. L.A. Raiders (7), Dec. 11, 1994; vs. San Francisco (13), Dec. 17, 1994
Steve Young, San Francisco vs. Washington, Nov. 24, 1996

COMPLETION PERCENTAGE

Most Seasons Leading League
8 Len Dawson, Dall. Texans, 1962; Kansas City, 1964-69, 1975
7 Sammy Baugh, Washington, 1940, 1942-43, 1945, 1947-49
5 Joe Montana, San Francisco, 1980-81, 1985, 1987, 1989
Steve Young, San Francisco, 1992, 1994-97

Most Consecutive Seasons Leading League
6 Len Dawson, Kansas City, 1964-69
4 Steve Young, San Francisco, 1994-97
3 Sammy Baugh, Washington, 1947-49
Otto Graham, Cleveland, 1953-55
Milt Plum, Cleveland, 1959-1961
Kurt Warner, St. Louis, 1999-2001

Highest Completion Percentage, Career (1,500 attempts)
66.41 Kurt Warner, St. Louis, 1998-2003 (1,688-1,121)
64.28 Steve Young, Tampa Bay, 1985-86; San Francisco, 1987-1999 (4,149-2,667)
63.24 Joe Montana, San Francisco, 1979-1990, 1992; Kansas City, 1993-94 (5,391-3,409)

Highest Completion Percentage, Season (Qualifiers)
70.55 Ken Anderson, Cincinnati, 1982 (309-218)
70.33 Sammy Baugh, Washington, 1945 (182-128)
70.28 Steve Young, San Francisco, 1994 (461-324)

Highest Completion Percentage, Rookie, Season (Qualifiers)
58.45 Dan Marino, Miami, 1983 (296-173)
57.18 Byron Leftwich, Jacksonville, 2003 (418-239)
57.14 Jim McMahon, Chicago, 1982 (210-120)

Highest Completion Percentage, Game (20 attempts)
91.30 Vinny Testaverde, Cleveland vs. L.A. Rams, Dec. 26, 1993 (23-21)
90.91 Ken Anderson, Cincinnati vs. Pittsburgh, Nov. 10, 1974 (22-20)
90.48 Lynn Dickey, Green Bay vs. New Orleans,

Dec. 13, 1981 (21-19)

YARDS GAINED

Most Seasons Leading League
5 Sonny Jurgensen, Philadelphia, 1961-62; Washington, 1966-67, 1969
Dan Marino, Miami, 1984-86, 1988, 1992
4 Sammy Baugh, Washington, 1937, 1940, 1947-48
Johnny Unitas, Baltimore, 1957, 1959-1960, 1963
Dan Fouts, San Diego, 1979-1982
3 Arnie Herber, Green Bay, 1932, 1934, 1936
Sid Luckman, Chi. Bears, 1943, 1945-46
John Brodie, San Francisco, 1965, 1968, 1970
John Hadl, San Diego, 1965, 1968, 1971
Joe Namath, N.Y. Jets, 1966-67, 1972

Most Consecutive Seasons Leading League
4 Dan Fouts, San Diego, 1979-1982
3 Dan Marino, Miami, 1984-86
2 By many players

Most Yards Gained, Career
61,361 Dan Marino, Miami, 1983-1999
51,475 John Elway, Denver, 1983-1998
49,325 Warren Moon, Houston, 1984-1993; Minnesota, 1994-96; Seattle, 1997-98; Kansas City, 1999-2000

Most Seasons, 3,000 or More Yards Passing
13 Dan Marino, Miami, 1984-1992, 1994-95, 1997-98
12 John Elway, Denver, 1985-1991, 1993-97
Brett Favre, Green Bay, 1992-2003
9 Warren Moon, Houston, 1984,1986, 1989-1991, 1993; Minnesota, 1994-95; Seattle, 1997

Most Yards Gained, Season
5,084 Dan Marino, Miami, 1984
4,830 Kurt Warner, St. Louis, 2001
4,802 Dan Fouts, San Diego, 1981

Most Yards Gained, Rookie, Season
3,739 Peyton Manning, Indianapolis, 1998
2,931 Chris Weinke, Carolina, 2001
2,833 Rick Mirer, Seattle, 1993

Most Yards Gained, Game
554 Norm Van Brocklin, Los Angeles vs. N.Y. Yanks, Sept. 28, 1951
527 Warren Moon, Houston vs. Kansas City, Dec. 16, 1990
522 Boomer Esiason, Arizona vs. Washington, Nov. 10, 1996

Most Games, 400 or More Yards Passing, Career
13 Dan Marino, Miami, 1983-1999
7 Joe Montana, San Francisco, 1979-1990, 1992; Kansas City, 1993-94
Warren Moon, Houston, 1984-1993; Minnesota, 1994-96; Seattle, 1997-98; Kansas City, 1999-2000
6 Dan Fouts, San Diego, 1973-1987
Drew Bledsoe, New England, 1993-2001; Buffalo, 2002-03

Most Games, 400 or More Yards Passing, Season
4 Dan Marino, Miami, 1984
3 Dan Marino, Miami, 1986
2 By many players

Most Consecutive Games, 400 or More Yards Passing
2 Dan Fouts, San Diego, 1982
Dan Marino, Miami, 1984
Phil Simms, N.Y. Giants, 1985

Most Games, 300 or More Yards Passing, Career
63 Dan Marino, Miami, 1983-1999
51 Dan Fouts, San Diego, 1973-1987
49 Warren Moon, Houston, 1984-1993; Minnesota, 1994-96; Seattle, 1997-98; Kansas City, 1999-2000

Most Games, 300 or More Yards Passing, Season
10 Rich Gannon, Oakland, 2002
9 Dan Marino, Miami, 1984
Warren Moon, Houston, 1990
Kurt Warner, St. Louis, 1999
Kurt Warner, St. Louis, 2001
8 Dan Fouts, San Diego, 1980
Kurt Warner, St. Louis, 2000

Most Consecutive Games, 300 or More Yards Passing
6 Steve Young, San Francisco, 1998
Kurt Warner, St. Louis, 2000
Rich Gannon, Oakland, 2002
5 Joe Montana, San Francisco, 1982
Kerry Collins, N.Y. Giants, 2001-02
4 Dan Fouts, San Diego, 1979
Dan Fouts, San Diego, 1980-81
Bill Kenney, Kansas City, 1983
Joe Montana, San Francisco, 1985-86
Joe Montana, San Francisco, 1990
Warren Moon, Houston, 1990
Drew Bledsoe, New England, 1993-94
Kurt Warner, St. Louis, 1999
Brian Griese, Denver, 2002

Longest Pass Completion (All TDs except as noted)
99 Frank Filchock (to Farkas), Washington vs. Pittsburgh, Oct. 15, 1939
George Izo (to Mitchell), Washington vs. Cleveland, Sept. 15, 1963
Karl Sweetan (to Studstill), Detroit vs. Baltimore, Oct. 16, 1966
Sonny Jurgensen (to Allen), Washington vs. Chicago, Sept. 15, 1968
Jim Plunkett (to Branch), L.A. Raiders vs. Washington, Oct. 2, 1983
Ron Jaworski (to Quick), Philadelphia vs. Atlanta, Nov. 10, 1985
Stan Humphries (to Martin), San Diego vs. Seattle, Sept. 18, 1994
Brett Favre (to Brooks), Green Bay vs. Chicago, Sept. 11, 1995
Trent Green (to Boerigter), Kansas City vs. San Diego, Dec. 22, 2002
98 Doug Russell (to Tinsley), Chi. Cardinals vs. Cleveland, Nov. 27, 1938
Ogden Compton (to Lane), Chi. Cardinals vs. Green Bay, Nov. 13, 1955
Bill Wade (to Farrington), Chicago Bears vs. Detroit, Oct. 8, 1961
Jacky Lee (to Dewveall), Houston vs. San Diego, Nov. 25, 1962
Earl Morrall (to Jones), N.Y. Giants vs. Pittsburgh, Sept. 11, 1966
Jim Hart (to Moore), St. Louis vs. Los Angeles, Dec. 10, 1972 (no TD)
Bobby Hebert (to Haynes), Atlanta vs. New Orleans, Sept. 12, 1993
Charlie Batch (to Morton), Detroit vs. Chicago, Oct. 4, 1998
97 Pat Coffee (to Tinsley), Chi. Cardinals vs. Chi. Bears, Dec. 5, 1937
Bobby Layne (to Box), Detroit vs. Green Bay, Nov. 26, 1953
George Shaw (to Tarr), Denver vs. Boston, Sept. 21, 1962
Bernie Kosar (to Slaughter), Cleveland vs. Chicago, Oct. 23, 1989
Steve Young (to Taylor), San Francisco vs. Atlanta, Nov. 3, 1991

AVERAGE GAIN

Most Seasons Leading League

7 Sid Luckman, Chi. Bears, 1939-1943, 1946-47
5 Steve Young, San Francisco, 1991-94, 1997
3 Arnie Herber, Green Bay, 1932, 1934, 1936
Norm Van Brocklin, Los Angeles, 1950, 1952, 1954
Len Dawson, Dall. Texans, 1962; Kansas City, 1966, 1968
Bart Starr, Green Bay, 1966-68
Kurt Warner, St. Louis, 1999-2001

Most Consecutive Seasons Leading League

5 Sid Luckman, Chi. Bears, 1939-1943
4 Steve Young, San Francisco, 1991-94
3 Bart Starr, Green Bay, 1966-68
Kurt Warner, St. Louis, 1999-2001

Highest Average Gain, Career (1,500 attempts)

8.63 Otto Graham, Cleveland, 1950-55 (1,565-13,499)
8.56 Kurt Warner, St. Louis, 1998-2003 (1,688-14,447)
8.42 Sid Luckman, Chi. Bears, 1939-1950 (1,744-14,686)

Highest Average Gain, Season (Qualifiers)

11.17 Tommy O'Connell, Cleveland, 1957 (110-1,229)
10.86 Sid Luckman, Chi. Bears, 1943 (202-2,194)
10.55 Otto Graham, Cleveland, 1953 (258-2,722)

Highest Average Gain, Rookie, Season (Qualifiers)

9.411 Greg Cook, Cincinnati, 1969 (197-1,854)
9.409 Bob Waterfield, Cleveland, 1945 (171-1,609)
8.36 Zeke Bratkowski, Chi. Bears, 1954 (130-1,087)

Highest Average Gain, Game (20 attempts)

18.58 Sammy Baugh, Washington vs. Boston, Oct. 31, 1948 (24-446)
18.50 Johnny Unitas, Baltimore vs. Atlanta, Nov. 12, 1967 (20-370)
17.71 Joe Namath, N.Y. Jets vs. Baltimore, Sept. 24, 1972 (28-496)

TOUCHDOWNS

Most Seasons Leading League

4 Johnny Unitas, Baltimore, 1957-1960
Len Dawson, Dall. Texans, 1962; Kansas City, 1963, 1965-66
Steve Young, San Francisco, 1992-94, 1998
Brett Favre, Green Bay, 1995-97, 2003
3 Arnie Herber, Green Bay, 1932, 1934, 1936
Sid Luckman, Chi. Bears, 1943, 1945-46
Y.A. Tittle, San Francisco, 1955; N.Y. Giants, 1962-63
Dan Marino, Miami, 1984-86
2 By many players

Most Consecutive Seasons Leading League

4 Johnny Unitas, Baltimore, 1957-1960
3 Dan Marino, Miami, 1984-86
Steve Young, San Francisco, 1992-94
Brett Favre, Green Bay, 1995-97
2 By many players

Most Touchdown Passes, Career

420 Dan Marino, Miami, 1983-1999
346 Brett Favre, Atlanta, 1991; Green Bay, 1992-2003
342 Fran Tarkenton, Minnesota, 1961-66, 1972-78; N.Y. Giants, 1967-1971

Most Touchdown Passes, Season

48 Dan Marino, Miami, 1984
44 Dan Marino, Miami, 1986
41 Kurt Warner, St. Louis, 1999

Most Touchdown Passes, Rookie, Season

26 Peyton Manning, Indianapolis, 1998
22 Charlie Conerly, N.Y. Giants, 1948
20 Dan Marino, Miami, 1983

Most Touchdown Passes, Game

7 Sid Luckman, Chi. Bears vs. N.Y. Giants, Nov. 14, 1943
Adrian Burk, Philadelphia vs. Washington, Oct. 17, 1954
George Blanda, Houston vs. N.Y. Titans, Nov. 19, 1961
Y.A. Tittle, N.Y. Giants vs. Washington, Oct. 28, 1962
Joe Kapp, Minnesota vs. Baltimore, Sept. 28, 1969
6 By many players. Last time:
Peyton Manning, Indianapolis vs. New Orleans, Sept. 28, 2003

Most Games, Four or More Touchdown Passes, Career

21 Dan Marino, Miami, 1983-1999
17 Johnny Unitas, Baltimore, 1956-1972; San Diego, 1973
16 Brett Favre, Atlanta, 1991; Green Bay, 1992-2003

Most Games, Four or More Touchdown Passes, Season

6 Dan Marino, Miami, 1984
5 Dan Marino, Miami, 1986
Brett Favre, Green Bay, 1996
4 George Blanda, Houston, 1961
Vince Ferragamo, Los Angeles, 1980
Steve Young, San Francisco, 1994
Randall Cunningham, Minnesota, 1998

Most Consecutive Games, Four or More Touchdown Passes

4 Dan Marino, Miami, 1984
2 By many players

Most Consecutive Games, Touchdown Passes

47 Johnny Unitas, Baltimore, 1956-1960
30 Dan Marino, Miami, 1985-87
28 Dave Krieg, Seattle, 1983-85

HAD INTERCEPTED

Most Consecutive Passes Attempted, None Intercepted

308 Bernie Kosar, Cleveland, 1990-91
294 Bart Starr, Green Bay, 1964-65
279 Jeff George, Indianapolis, 1993; Atlanta, 1994

Most Passes Had Intercepted, Career

277 George Blanda, Chi. Bears, 1949, 1950-58; Baltimore, 1950; Houston, 1960-66; Oakland, 1967-1975
268 John Hadl, San Diego, 1962-1972; Los Angeles, 1973-74; Green Bay, 1974-75; Houston, 1976-77
266 Fran Tarkenton, Minnesota, 1961-66, 1972-78; N.Y. Giants, 1967-1971

Most Passes Had Intercepted, Season

42 George Blanda, Houston, 1962
35 Vinny Testaverde, Tampa Bay, 1988
34 Frank Tripucka, Denver, 1960

Most Passes Had Intercepted, Game

8 Jim Hardy, Chi. Cardinals vs. Philadelphia, Sept. 24, 1950
7 Parker Hall, Cleveland vs. Green Bay, Nov. 8, 1942
Frank Sinkwich, Detroit vs. Green Bay, Oct. 24, 1943
Bob Waterfield, Los Angeles vs. Green Bay, Oct. 17, 1948
Zeke Bratkowski, Chicago vs. Baltimore, Oct. 2, 1960
Tommy Wade, Pittsburgh vs. Philadelphia, Dec. 12, 1965
Ken Stabler, Oakland vs. Denver, Oct. 16, 1977
Steve DeBerg, Tampa Bay vs. San Francisco, Sept. 7, 1986
Ty Detmer, Detroit vs. Cleveland, Sept. 23, 2001
6 By many players

Most Attempts, No Interceptions, Game

70 Drew Bledsoe, New England vs. Minnesota, Nov. 13, 1994 (OT)
63 Rich Gannon, Minnesota vs. New England, Oct. 20, 1991 (OT)
60 Davey O'Brien, Philadelphia vs. Washington, Dec. 1, 1940

LOWEST PERCENTAGE, PASSES HAD INTERCEPTED

Most Seasons Leading League, Lowest Percentage, Passes Had Intercepted

5 Sammy Baugh, Washington, 1940, 1942, 1944-45, 1947
3 Charlie Conerly, N.Y. Giants, 1950, 1956, 1959
Bart Starr, Green Bay, 1962, 1964, 1966
Roger Staubach, Dallas, 1971, 1977, 1979
Ken Anderson, Cincinnati, 1972, 1981-82
Ken O'Brien, N.Y. Jets, 1985, 1987-88
2 By many players

Lowest Percentage, Passes Had Intercepted, Career (1,500 attempts)

2.11 Neil O'Donnell, Pittsburgh, 1991-95; N.Y. Jets, 1996-97; Cincinnati, 1998; Tennessee, 1999-2003 (3,229-68)
2.31 Donovan McNabb, Philadelphia, 1999-2003 (2,117-49)
2.36 Mark Brunell, Green Bay, 1994; Jacksonville, 1995-2003 (3,643-86)

Lowest Percentage, Passes Had Intercepted, Season (Qualifiers)

0.66 Joe Ferguson, Buffalo, 1976 (151-1)
0.90 Steve DeBerg, Kansas City, 1990 (444-4)
1.16 Steve Bartkowski, Atlanta, 1983 (432-5)

Lowest Percentage, Passes Had Intercepted, Rookie, Season (Qualifiers)

1.98 Charlie Batch, Detroit, 1998 (303-6)
2.03 Dan Marino, Miami, 1983 (296-6)
2.10 Gary Wood, N.Y. Giants, 1964 (143-3)

TIMES SACKED

Times Sacked has been compiled since 1963.

Most Times Sacked, Career

516 John Elway, Denver, 1983-1998
494 Dave Krieg, Seattle, 1980-1991; Kansas City, 1992-93; Detroit, 1994; Arizona, 1995; Chicago, 1996; Tennessee, 1997-98
484 Randall Cunningham, Philadelphia, 1985-1995; Minnesota, 1997-99; Dallas, 2000; Baltimore, 2001

Most Times Sacked, Season

76 David Carr, Houston, 2002
72 Randall Cunningham, Philadelphia, 1986
62 Ken O'Brien, N.Y. Jets, 1985
Steve Beuerlein, Carolina, 2000

Most Times Sacked, Game

12 Bert Jones, Baltimore vs. St. Louis, Oct. 26, 1980
Warren Moon, Houston vs. Dallas, Sept. 29, 1985
11 Charley Johnson, St. Louis vs. N.Y. Giants, Nov. 1, 1964
Bart Starr, Green Bay vs. Detroit, Nov. 7, 1965
Jack Kemp, Buffalo vs. Oakland, Oct. 15, 1967
Bob Berry, Atlanta vs. St. Louis, Nov. 24, 1968
Greg Landry, Detroit vs. Dallas, Oct. 6, 1975
Ron Jaworski, Philadelphia vs. St. Louis, Dec. 18, 1983
Paul McDonald, Cleveland vs. Kansas City, Sept. 30, 1984
Archie Manning, Minnesota vs. Chicago, Oct. 28, 1984
Steve Pelluer, Dallas vs. San Diego, Nov. 16, 1986
Randall Cunningham, Philadelphia vs. L.A. Raiders, Nov. 30, 1986 (OT)
David Norrie, N.Y. Jets vs. Dallas, Oct. 4, 1987
Troy Aikman, Dallas vs. Philadelphia, Sept. 15, 1991
Bernie Kosar, Cleveland vs. Indianapolis, Sept. 6, 1992
10 By many players

RECEIVING

Most Seasons Leading League

8 Don Hutson, Green Bay, 1936-37, 1939, 1941-45
5 Lionel Taylor, Denver, 1960-63, 1965
3 Tom Fears, Los Angeles, 1948-1950
Pete Pihos, Philadelphia, 1953-55
Billy Wilson, San Francisco, 1954, 1956-57
Raymond Berry, Baltimore, 1958-1960
Lance Alworth, San Diego, 1966, 1968-69
Sterling Sharpe, Green Bay, 1989, 1992-93

Most Consecutive Seasons Leading League

5 Don Hutson, Green Bay, 1941-45
4 Lionel Taylor, Denver, 1960-63
3 Tom Fears, Los Angeles, 1948-1950
Pete Pihos, Philadelphia, 1953-55
Raymond Berry, Baltimore, 1958-1960

Most Pass Receptions, Career

1,519 Jerry Rice, San Francisco, 1985-2000; Oakland, 2001-03
1,101 Cris Carter, Philadelphia, 1987-89; Minnesota, 1990-2001; Miami, 2002
1,070 Tim Brown, L.A. Raiders, 1988-1994; Oakland, 1995-2003

Most Seasons, 50 or More Pass Receptions

17 Jerry Rice, San Francisco, 1986-1996, 1998-2000; Oakland, 2001-03
13 Andre Reed, Buffalo, 1986-1994, 1996-99
11 Cris Carter, Minnesota, 1991-2001
Tim Brown, L.A. Raiders, 1993-1994; Oakland, 1995-2003
Shannon Sharpe, Denver 1992-98; Baltimore, 2000-01; Denver, 2002-03

Most Pass Receptions, Season

143 Marvin Harrison, Indianapolis, 2002
123 Herman Moore, Detroit, 1995
122 Cris Carter, Minnesota, 1994
Cris Carter, Minnesota, 1995
Jerry Rice, San Francisco, 1995

Most Pass Receptions, Rookie, Season

101 Anquan Boldin, Arizona, 2003
90 Terry Glenn, New England, 1996
83 Earl Cooper, San Francisco, 1980

Most Pass Receptions, Game

20 Terrell Owens, San Francisco vs. Chicago, Dec. 17, 2000
18 Tom Fears, Los Angeles vs. Green Bay, Dec. 3, 1950
17 Clark Gaines, N.Y. Jets vs. San Francisco, Sept. 21, 1980

Most Consecutive Games, Pass Receptions

273 Jerry Rice, San Francisco, 1985-2000; Oakland, 2001-03 (current)
183 Art Monk, Washington, 1983-1993; N.Y. Jets, 1994; Philadelphia, 1995
177 Steve Largent, Seattle, 1977-1989

YARDS GAINED

Most Seasons Leading League

7 Don Hutson, Green Bay, 1936, 1938-39, 1941-44
6 Jerry Rice, San Francisco, 1986, 1989-1990, 1993-95
3 Raymond Berry, Baltimore, 1957, 1959-1960
Lance Alworth, San Diego, 1965-66, 1968

Most Consecutive Seasons Leading League

4 Don Hutson, Green Bay, 1941-44
3 Jerry Rice, San Francisco, 1993-95
2 By many players

Most Yards Gained, Career

22,466 Jerry Rice, San Francisco, 1985-2000; Oakland, 2001-03

14,734 Tim Brown, L.A. Raiders, 1988-1994; Oakland, 1995-2003
14,004 James Lofton, Green Bay, 1978-1986; L.A. Raiders, 1987-88; Buffalo, 1989-1992; L.A. Rams, 1993; Philadelphia, 1993

Most Seasons, 1,000 or More Yards, Pass Receiving
14 Jerry Rice, San Francisco, 1986-1996, 1998; Oakland, 2001-02
9 Tim Brown, L.A. Raiders, 1993-94; Oakland, 1995-2001
8 Steve Largent, Seattle, 1978-1981, 1983-86
Cris Carter, Minnesota, 1993-2000

Most Yards Gained, Season
1,848 Jerry Rice, San Francisco, 1995
1,781 Isaac Bruce, St. Louis, 1995
1,746 Charley Hennigan, Houston, 1961

Most Yards Gained, Rookie, Season
1,473 Bill Groman, Houston, 1960
1,377 Anquan Boldin, Arizona, 2003
1,313 Randy Moss, Minnesota, 1998

Most Yards Gained, Game
336 Willie Anderson, L.A. Rams vs. New Orleans, Nov. 26, 1989 (OT)
309 Stephone Paige, Kansas City vs. San Diego, Dec. 22, 1985
303 Jim Benton, Cleveland vs. Detroit, Nov. 22, 1945

Most Games, 200 or More Yards Pass Receiving, Career
5 Lance Alworth, San Diego, 1962-1970; Dallas, 1971-72
4 Don Hutson, Green Bay, 1935-45
Charley Hennigan, Houston, 1960-66
Jerry Rice, San Francisco, 1985-2000; Oakland, 2001-03
3 Don Maynard, N.Y. Giants, 1958; N.Y. Jets, 1960-1972; St. Louis, 1973
Wes Chandler, New Orleans, 1978-1981; San Diego, 1981-87; San Francisco, 1988
Isaac Bruce, L.A. Rams, 1994; St. Louis, 1995-2003

Most Games, 200 or More Yards Pass Receiving, Season
3 Charley Hennigan, Houston, 1961
2 Don Hutson, Green Bay, 1942
Gene Roberts, N.Y. Giants, 1949
Lance Alworth, San Diego, 1963
Don Maynard, N.Y. Jets, 1968

Most Games, 100 or More Yards Pass Receiving, Career
75 Jerry Rice, San Francisco, 1985-2000; Oakland, 2001-03
50 Don Maynard, N.Y. Giants, 1958; N.Y. Jets, 1960-1972; St. Louis, 1973
47 Michael Irvin, Dallas, 1988-1999

Most Games, 100 or More Yards Pass Receiving, Season
11 Michael Irvin, Dallas, 1995
10 Charley Hennigan, Houston, 1961
Herman Moore, Detroit, 1995
Marvin Harrison, Indianapolis, 2002
Torry Holt, St. Louis, 2003
9 Elroy (Crazylegs) Hirsch, Los Angeles, 1951
Bill Groman, Houston, 1960
Lance Alworth, San Diego, 1965
Don Maynard, N.Y. Jets, 1967
Stanley Morgan, New England, 1986
Mark Carrier, Tampa Bay, 1989
Robert Brooks, Green Bay, 1995
Isaac Bruce, St. Louis, 1995
Jerry Rice, San Francisco, 1995
Marvin Harrison, Indianapolis, 1999
Jimmy Smith, Jacksonville, 1999
David Boston, Arizona, 2001

Most Consecutive Games, 100 or More Yards Pass Receiving
7 Charley Hennigan, Houston, 1961
Michael Irvin, Dallas, 1995
6 Raymond Berry, Baltimore, 1960
Bill Groman, Houston, 1961
Pat Studstill, Detroit, 1966
Isaac Bruce, St. Louis, 1995
5 Elroy (Crazylegs) Hirsch, Los Angeles, 1951
Bob Boyd, Los Angeles, 1954
Terry Barr, Detroit, 1963
Lance Alworth, San Diego, 1966
Don Maynard, N.Y. Jets, 1968-69
Harold Jackson, Philadelphia, 1971-72
Patrick Jeffers, Carolina, 1999

Longest Pass Reception (All TDs except as noted)
99 Andy Farkas (from Filchock), Washington vs. Pittsburgh, Oct. 15, 1939
Bobby Mitchell (from Izo), Washington vs. Cleveland, Sept. 15, 1963
Pat Studstill (from Sweetan), Detroit vs. Baltimore, Oct. 16, 1966
Gerry Allen (from Jurgensen), Washington vs. Chicago, Sept. 15, 1968
Cliff Branch (from Plunkett), L.A. Raiders vs. Washington, Oct. 2, 1983
Mike Quick (from Jaworski), Philadelphia vs. Atlanta, Nov. 10, 1985
Tony Martin (from Humphries), San Diego vs. Seattle, Sept. 18, 1994
Robert Brooks (from Favre), Green Bay vs. Chicago, Sept. 11, 1995
Marc Boerigter (from Green), Kansas City vs. San Diego, Dec. 22, 2002
98 Gaynell Tinsley (from Russell), Chi. Cardinals vs. Cleveland, Nov. 17, 1938
Dick (Night Train) Lane (from Compton), Chi. Cardinals vs. Green Bay, Nov. 13, 1955
John Farrington (from Wade), Chicago vs. Detroit, Oct. 8, 1961
Willard Dewveall (from Lee), Houston vs. San Diego, Nov. 25, 1962
Homer Jones (from Morrall), N.Y. Giants vs. Pittsburgh, Sept. 11, 1966
Bobby Moore (from Hart), St. Louis vs. Los Angeles, Dec. 10, 1972 (no TD)
Michael Haynes (from Hebert), Atlanta vs. New Orleans, Sept. 12, 1993
Johnnie Morton (from Batch), Detroit vs. Chicago, Oct. 4, 1998
97 Gaynell Tinsley (from Coffee), Chi. Cardinals vs. Chi. Bears, Dec. 5, 1937
Cloyce Box (from Layne), Detroit vs. Green Bay, Nov. 26, 1953
Jerry Tarr (from Shaw), Denver vs. Boston, Sept. 21, 1962
Webster Slaughter (from Kosar), Cleveland vs. Chicago, Oct. 23, 1989
John Taylor (from Young), San Francisco vs. Atlanta, Nov. 3, 1991

AVERAGE GAIN

Highest Average Gain, Career (200 receptions)
22.26 Homer Jones, N.Y. Giants, 1964-69; Cleveland, 1970 (224-4,986)
20.83 Buddy Dial, Pittsburgh, 1959-1963; Dallas, 1964-66 (261-5,436)
20.24 Harlon Hill, Chi. Bears, 1954-1961; Pittsburgh, 1962; Detroit, 1962 (233-4,717)

Highest Average Gain, Season (24 receptions)
32.58 Don Currivan, Boston, 1947 (24-782)
31.44 Bucky Pope, Los Angeles, 1964 (25-786)
28.60 Bobby Duckworth, San Diego, 1984 (25-715)

Highest Average Gain, Game (3 receptions)
63.00 Torry Holt, St. Louis vs. Atlanta, Sept. 24, 2000 (3-189)
60.67 Bill Groman, Houston vs. Denver, Nov. 20, 1960 (3-182)
Homer Jones, N.Y. Giants vs. Washington, Dec. 12, 1965 (3-182)
60.33 Don Currivan, Boston vs. Washington, Nov. 30, 1947 (3-181)

TOUCHDOWNS

Most Seasons Leading League
9 Don Hutson, Green Bay, 1935-38, 1940-44
6 Jerry Rice, San Francisco, 1986-87, 1989-1991, 1993
3 Lance Alworth, San Diego, 1964-66
Cris Carter, Minnesota, 1995, 1997, 1999
Randy Moss, Minnesota, 1998, 2000, 2003

Most Consecutive Seasons Leading League
5 Don Hutson, Green Bay, 1940-44
4 Don Hutson, Green Bay, 1935-38
3 Lance Alworth, San Diego, 1964-66
Jerry Rice, San Francisco, 1989-1991

Most Touchdowns, Career
194 Jerry Rice, San Francisco, 1985-2000; Oakland, 2001-03
130 Cris Carter, Philadelphia, 1987-89; Minnesota, 1990-2001; Miami, 2002
100 Steve Largent, Seattle, 1976-1989

Most Touchdowns, Season
22 Jerry Rice, San Francisco, 1987
18 Mark Clayton, Miami, 1984
Sterling Sharpe, Green Bay, 1994
17 Don Hutson, Green Bay, 1942
Elroy (Crazylegs) Hirsch, Los Angeles, 1951
Bill Groman, Houston, 1961
Jerry Rice, San Francisco, 1989
Cris Carter, Minnesota, 1995
Carl Pickens, Cincinnati, 1995
Randy Moss, Minnesota, 1998
Randy Moss, Minnesota, 2003

Most Touchdowns, Rookie, Season
17 Randy Moss, Minnesota, 1998
13 Bill Howton, Green Bay, 1952
John Jefferson, San Diego, 1978
12 Harlon Hill, Chi. Bears, 1954
Bill Groman, Houston, 1960
Mike Ditka, Chicago, 1961
Bob Hayes, Dallas, 1965

Most Touchdowns, Game
5 Bob Shaw, Chi. Cardinals vs. Baltimore, Oct. 2, 1950
Kellen Winslow, San Diego vs. Oakland, Nov. 22, 1981
Jerry Rice, San Francisco vs. Atlanta, Oct. 14, 1990
4 By many players. Last time: Joe Horn, New Orleans vs. N.Y. Giants, Dec. 14, 2003

Most Consecutive Games, Touchdowns
13 Jerry Rice, San Francisco, 1986-87
11 Elroy (Crazylegs) Hirsch, Los Angeles, 1950-51
Buddy Dial, Pittsburgh, 1959-1960
10 Carl Pickens, Cincinnati, 1994-95

YARDS FROM SCRIMMAGE

Most Scrimmage Yards, Career
23,111 Jerry Rice, San Francisco 1985-2000; Oakland, 2001-03
21,264 Walter Payton, Chicago, 1975-1987
20,537 Emmitt Smith, Dallas, 1990-2002; Arizona, 2003

Most Scrimmage Yards, Season
2,429 Marshall Faulk, St. Louis, 1999 (1,381 rush., 1,048 rec.)
2,370 LaDainian Tomlinson, San Diego, 2003 (1,645 rush., 725 rec.)
2,358 Barry Sanders, Detroit, 1997 (2,053 rush., 305 rec.)

Most Scrimmage Yards, Rookie, Season
2,212 Eric Dickerson, L.A. Rams, 1983 (1,808 rush., 404 rec.)
2,139 Edgerrin James, Indianapolis, 1999 (1,553 rush., 586 rec.)
1,924 Billy Sims, Detroit, 1980 (1,303 rush., 621 rec.)

Most Scrimmage Yards, Game
336 Flipper Anderson, L.A. Rams vs. New Orleans, Nov. 26, 1989 (OT) (336 rec.)
330 Billy Cannon, Houston vs. N.Y. Titans, Dec. 10, 1961 (216 rush., 114 rec.)
309 Stephone Paige, Kansas City vs. San Diego, Dec. 22, 1985 (309 rec.)

INTERCEPTIONS BY

Most Seasons Leading League
3 Everson Walls, Dallas, 1981-82, 1985
2 Dick (Night Train) Lane, Los Angeles, 1952; Chi. Cardinals, 1954
Jack Christiansen, Detroit, 1953, 1957
Milt Davis, Baltimore, 1957, 1959
Dick Lynch, N.Y. Giants, 1961, 1963
Johnny Robinson, Kansas City, 1966, 1970
Bill Bradley, Philadelphia, 1971-72
Emmitt Thomas, Kansas City, 1969, 1974
Ronnie Lott, San Francisco, 1986; L.A. Raiders, 1991
Rod Woodson, Baltimore, 1999; Oakland, 2002

Most Interceptions By, Career
81 Paul Krause, Washington, 1964-67; Minnesota, 1968-1979
79 Emlen Tunnell, N.Y. Giants, 1948-1958; Green Bay, 1959-1961
71 Rod Woodson, Pittsburgh, 1987-1996; San Francisco, 1997; Baltimore, 1998-2001; Oakland, 2002-03

Most Interceptions By, Season
14 Dick (Night Train) Lane, Los Angeles, 1952
13 Dan Sandifer, Washington, 1948
Orban (Spec) Sanders, N.Y. Yanks, 1950
Lester Hayes, Oakland, 1980
12 By nine players

Most Interceptions By, Rookie, Season
14 Dick (Night Train) Lane, Los Angeles, 1952
13 Dan Sandifer, Washington, 1948
12 Woodley Lewis, Los Angeles, 1950
Paul Krause, Washington, 1964

Most Interceptions By, Game
4 Sammy Baugh, Washington vs. Detroit, Nov. 14, 1943
Dan Sandifer, Washington vs. Boston, Oct. 31, 1948
Don Doll, Detroit vs. Chi. Cardinals, Oct. 23, 1949
Bob Nussbaumer, Chi. Cardinals vs. N.Y. Bulldogs, Nov. 13, 1949
Russ Craft, Philadelphia vs. Chi. Cardinals, Sept. 24, 1950
Bobby Dillon, Green Bay vs. Detroit, Nov. 26, 1953
Jack Butler, Pittsburgh vs. Washington, Dec. 13, 1953
Austin (Goose) Gonsoulin, Denver vs. Buffalo, Sept. 18, 1960
Jerry Norton, St. Louis vs. Washington, Nov. 20, 1960; vs. Pittsburgh, Nov. 26, 1961
Dave Baker, San Francisco vs. L.A. Rams, Dec. 4, 1960
Bobby Ply, Dall. Texans vs. San Diego, Dec. 16, 1962
Bobby Hunt, Kansas City vs. Houston, Oct. 4, 1964
Willie Brown, Denver vs. N.Y. Jets, Nov. 15, 1964
Dick Anderson, Miami vs. Pittsburgh, Dec. 3, 1973
Willie Buchanon, Green Bay vs. San Diego, Sept. 24, 1978

Deron Cherry, Kansas City vs. Seattle, Sept. 29, 1985
Kwamie Lassiter, Arizona vs. San Diego, Dec. 27, 1998
Deltha O'Neal, Denver vs. Kansas City, Oct. 7, 2001

Most Consecutive Games, Passes Intercepted By

8 Tom Morrow, Oakland, 1962-63
7 Tom Landry, N.Y. Giants, 1950-51
Paul Krause, Washington, 1964
Larry Wilson, St. Louis, 1966
Ben Davis, Cleveland, 1968
6 By many players.
Last time: Brian Russell, Minnesota, 2003

YARDS GAINED

Most Seasons Leading League

2 Dick (Night Train) Lane, Los Angeles, 1952; Chi. Cardinals, 1954
Herb Adderley, Green Bay, 1965, 1969
Dick Anderson, Miami, 1968, 1970

Most Yards Gained, Career

1,483 Rod Woodson, Pittsburgh, 1987-1996; San Francisco, 1997; Baltimore, 1998-2001; Oakland, 2002-03
1,282 Emlen Tunnell, N.Y. Giants, 1948-1958; Green Bay, 1959-1961
1,207 Dick (Night Train) Lane, Los Angeles, 1952-53; Chi. Cardinals, 1954-59; Detroit, 1960-65

Most Yards Gained, Season

349 Charlie McNeil, San Diego, 1961
303 Deion Sanders, San Francisco, 1994
301 Don Doll, Detroit, 1949

Most Yards Gained, Rookie, Season

301 Don Doll, Detroit, 1949
298 Dick (Night Train) Lane, Los Angeles, 1952
275 Woodley Lewis, Los Angeles, 1950

Most Yards Gained, Game

177 Charlie McNeil, San Diego vs. Houston, Sept. 24, 1961
170 Louis Oliver, Miami vs. Buffalo, Oct. 4, 1992
167 Dick Jauron, Detroit vs. Chicago, Nov. 18, 1973

Longest Return (All TDs)

103 Vencie Glenn, San Diego vs. Denver, Nov. 29, 1987
Louis Oliver, Miami vs. Buffalo, Oct. 4, 1992
102 Bob Smith, Detroit vs. Chi. Bears, Nov. 24, 1949
Erich Barnes, N.Y. Giants vs. Dall. Cowboys, Oct. 15, 1961
Gary Barbaro, Kansas City vs. Seattle, Dec. 11, 1977
Louis Breeden, Cincinnati vs. San Diego, Nov. 8, 1981
Eddie Anderson, L.A. Raiders vs. Miami, Dec. 14, 1992
Donald Frank, San Diego vs. L.A. Raiders, Oct. 31, 1993
Artrell Hawkins, Cincinnati vs. Houston, Nov. 3, 2002
101 Richie Petitbon, Chicago vs Los Angeles, Dec. 9, 1962
Henry Carr, N.Y. Giants vs. Los Angeles, Nov. 13, 1966
Tony Greene, Buffalo vs. Kansas City, Oct. 3, 1976
Tom Pridemore, Atlanta vs. San Francisco, Sept. 20, 1981
Bryant Westbrook, Detroit vs. New England, Nov. 23, 2000

TOUCHDOWNS

Most Touchdowns, Career

12 Rod Woodson, Pittsburgh, 1987-1996; San Francisco, 1997; Baltimore, 1998-2001; Oakland, 2002-03
9 Ken Houston, Houston, 1967-1972; Washington, 1973-1980
Aeneas Williams, Phoenix, 1991-93; Arizona, 1994-2000; St. Louis, 2001-03
8 Deion Sanders, Atlanta, 1989-1993; San Francisco, 1994; Dallas, 1995-99; Washington, 2000
Eric Allen, Philadelphia, 1988-1994; New Orleans, 1995-97; Oakland, 1998-2001

Most Touchdowns, Season

4 Ken Houston, Houston, 1971
Jim Kearney, Kansas City, 1972
Eric Allen, Philadelphia, 1993
3 Dick Harris, San Diego, 1961
Dick Lynch, N.Y. Giants, 1963
Herb Adderley, Green Bay, 1965
Lem Barney, Detroit, 1967
Miller Farr, Houston, 1967
Monte Jackson, Los Angeles, 1976
Rod Perry, Los Angeles, 1978
Ronnie Lott, San Francisco, 1981
Lloyd Burruss, Kansas City, 1986
Wayne Haddix, Tampa Bay, 1990
Robert Massey, Phoenix, 1992
Ray Buchanan, Indianapolis, 1994
Deion Sanders, San Francisco, 1994
Mark McMillian, Kansas City, 1997
Otis Smith, N.Y. Jets, 1997
Jimmy Hitchcock, Minnesota, 1998
Eric Allen, Oakland, 2000
Derrick Brooks, Tampa Bay, 2002
2 By many players

Most Touchdowns, Rookie, Season

3 Lem Barney, Detroit, 1967
Ronnie Lott, San Francisco, 1981
2 By many players

Most Touchdowns, Game

2 Bill Blackburn, Chi. Cardinals vs. Boston, Oct. 24, 1948
Dan Sandifer, Washington vs. Boston, Oct. 31, 1948
Bob Franklin, Cleveland vs. Chicago, Dec. 11, 1960
Bill Stacy, St. Louis vs. Dall. Cowboys, Nov. 5, 1961
Jerry Norton, St. Louis vs. Pittsburgh, Nov. 26, 1961
Miller Farr, Houston vs. Buffalo, Dec. 7, 1968
Ken Houston, Houston vs. San Diego, Dec. 19, 1971
Jim Kearney, Kansas City vs. Denver, Oct. 1, 1972
Lemar Parrish, Cincinnati vs. Houston, Dec. 17, 1972
Dick Anderson, Miami vs. Pittsburgh, Dec. 3, 1973
Prentice McCray, New England vs. N.Y. Jets, Nov. 21, 1976
Kenny Johnson, Atlanta vs. Green Bay, Nov. 27, 1983 (OT)
Mike Kozlowski, Miami vs. N.Y. Jets, Dec. 16, 1983
Dave Brown, Seattle vs. Kansas City, Nov. 4, 1984
Lloyd Burruss, Kansas City vs. San Diego, Oct. 19, 1986
Henry Jones, Buffalo vs. Indianapolis, Sept. 20, 1992
Robert Massey, Phoenix vs. Washington, Oct. 4, 1992
Eric Allen, Philadelphia vs. New Orleans, Dec. 26, 1993
Ken Norton, San Francisco vs. St. Louis, Oct. 22, 1995
Otis Smith, N.Y. Jets vs. Tampa Bay, Dec. 14, 1997
Dewayne Washington, Pittsburgh vs. Jacksonville, Nov. 22, 1998
Aaron Glenn, Houston vs. Pittsburgh, Dec. 8, 2002

PUNTING

Most Seasons Leading League

4 Sammy Baugh, Washington, 1940-43
Jerrel Wilson, Kansas City, 1965, 1968, 1972-73
3 Yale Lary, Detroit, 1959, 1961, 1963
Jim Fraser, Denver, 1962-64
Ray Guy, Oakland, 1974-75, 1977
Rohn Stark, Baltimore, 1983; Indianapolis, 1985-86
2 By many players

Most Consecutive Seasons Leading League
4 Sammy Baugh, Washington, 1940-43
3 Jim Fraser, Denver, 1962-64
2 By many players

PUNTS

Most Punts, Career
1,327 Sean Landeta, N.Y. Giants, 1985-1993; L.A. Rams, 1993-94; St. Louis, 1995-96; Tampa Bay, 1997; Green Bay, 1998; Philadelphia, 1999-2002; St. Louis, 2003
1,290 Jeff Feagles, New England, 1988-89; Philadelphia, 1990-93; Arizona, 1994-97; Seattle, 1998-2002; N.Y. Giants, 2003
1,226 Lee Johnson, Houston, 1985-87; Cleveland, 1987-88; Cincinnati, 1988-1998; New England, 1999-2001; Minnesota, 2001; Philadelphia, 2002

Most Punts, Season
114 Bob Parsons, Chicago, 1981
Chad Stanley, Houston, 2002
111 Brad Maynard, N.Y. Giants, 1997
109 John James, Atlanta, 1978

Most Punts, Rookie, Season
111 Brad Maynard, N.Y. Giants, 1997
108 John Teltschik, Philadelphia, 1986
101 Daniel Pope, Kansas City, 1999

Most Punts, Game
16 Leo Araguz, Oakland vs. San Diego, Oct. 11, 1998
15 John Teltschik, Philadelphia vs. N.Y. Giants, Dec. 6, 1987 (OT)
14 Dick Nesbitt, Chi. Cardinals vs. Chi. Bears, Nov. 30, 1933
Keith Molesworth, Chi. Bears vs. Green Bay, Dec. 10, 1933
Sammy Baugh, Washington vs. Philadelphia, Nov. 5, 1939
Carl Kinscherf, N.Y. Giants vs. Detroit, Nov. 7, 1943
George Taliaferro, N.Y. Yanks vs. Los Angeles, Sept. 28, 1951

Longest Punt
98 Steve O'Neal, N.Y. Jets vs. Denver, Sept. 21, 1969
94 Joe Lintzenich, Chi. Bears vs. N.Y. Giants, Nov. 16, 1931
93 Shawn McCarthy, New England vs. Buffalo, Nov. 3, 1991

AVERAGE YARDAGE

Highest Average, Punting, Career (250 punts)
45.69 Shane Lechler, Oakland, 2002-03 (287-13,113)
45.10 Sammy Baugh, Washington, 1937-1952 (338-15,245)
44.68 Tommy Davis, San Francisco, 1959-1969 (511-22,833)

Highest Average, Punting, Season (Qualifiers)
51.40 Sammy Baugh, Washington, 1940 (35-1,799)
48.94 Yale Lary, Detroit, 1963 (35-1,713)
48.73 Sammy Baugh, Washington, 1941 (30-1,462)

Highest Average, Punting, Rookie, Season (Qualifiers)
45.92 Frank Sinkwich, Detroit, 1943 (12-551)
45.91 Shane Lechler, Oakland, 2000 (65-2,984)
45.66 Tommy Davis, San Francisco, 1959 (59-2,694)

Highest Average, Punting, Game (4 punts)
61.75 Bob Cifers, Detroit vs. Chi. Bears, Nov. 24, 1946 (4-247)
61.60 Roy McKay, Green Bay vs. Chi. Cardinals, Oct. 28, 1945 (5-308)
59.50 Darren Bennett, San Diego vs. Pittsburgh, Oct. 1, 1995 (4-238)

PUNTS HAD BLOCKED

Most Consecutive Punts, None Blocked
978 Chris Gardocki, Chicago, 1992-94; Indianapolis, 1995-98; Cleveland, 1999-2003 (current)
762 Bryan Barker, Kansas City, 1993; Philadelphia, 1994; Jacksonville, 1995-2000; Washington, 2001-03 (current)
623 Dave Jennings, N.Y. Giants, 1976-1983

Most Punts Had Blocked, Career
14 Herman Weaver, Detroit, 1970-76; Seattle, 1977-1980
Harry Newsome, Pittsburgh, 1985-89; Minnesota, 1990-93
12 Jerrel Wilson, Kansas City, 1963-1977; New England, 1978
Tom Blanchard, N.Y. Giants, 1971-73; New Orleans, 1974-78; Tampa Bay, 1979-1981
11 David Lee, Baltimore, 1966-1978

Most Punts Had Blocked, Season
6 Harry Newsome, Pittsburgh, 1988
4 Bryan Wagner, Cleveland, 1990
3 By many players

PUNTS INSIDE THE 20

Punts Inside the 20 have been compiled since 1976.

Most Punts Inside the 20, Career
407 Jeff Feagles, New England, 1988-89; Philadelphia, 1990-93; Arizona, 1994-97; Seattle, 1998-2002; N.Y. Giants, 2003
365 Sean Landeta, N.Y. Giants, 1985-1993; L.A. Rams, 1993-94; St. Louis, 1995-96; Tampa Bay, 1997; Green Bay, 1998; Philadelphia, 1999-2002; St. Louis, 2003
318 Lee Johnson, Houston, 1985-87; Cleveland, 1987-88; Cincinnati, 1988-1998; New England, 1999-2001; Minnesota, 2001; Philadelphia, 2002

Most Punts Inside the 20, Season
39 Kyle Richardson, Baltimore, 1999
36 Brad Maynard, Chicago, 2001
Chad Stanley, Houston, 2002
Chad Stanley, Houston, 2003
35 Rich Camarillo, Houston, 1994
Mark Royals, Pittsburgh, 1994
Craig Hentrich, Tennessee, 1999
Kyle Richardson, Baltimore, 2000
Todd Sauerbrun, Carolina, 2001

Most Punts Inside the 20, Game
8 Mark Royals, Pittsburgh vs. Houston, Nov. 6, 1994 (OT)
Bryan Barker, Jacksonville vs. Baltimore, Nov. 14, 1999
7 Josh Miller, Pittsburgh vs. Cincinnati, Dec. 20, 1998
6 By many players

PUNT RETURNS

Most Seasons Leading League
3 Les (Speedy) Duncan, San Diego, 1965-66; Washington, 1971
Rick Upchurch, Denver, 1976, 1978, 1982
2 Dick Christy, N.Y. Titans, 1961-62
Claude Gibson, Oakland, 1963-64
Billy (White Shoes) Johnson, Houston, 1975, 1977
Mel Gray, New Orleans, 1987; Detroit, 1991
Jermaine Lewis, Baltimore, 1997, 2000

PUNT RETURNS

Most Punt Returns, Career
463 Brian Mitchell, Washington, 1990-99; Philadelphia, 2000-02; N.Y. Giants, 2003

351 Eric Metcalf, Cleveland, 1989-1994; Atlanta, 1995-96; San Diego, 1997; Arizona, 1998; Carolina, 1999; Washington, 2001; Green Bay, 2002
349 David Meggett, N.Y. Giants, 1989-1994; New England, 1995-97; N.Y. Jets, 1998

Most Punt Returns, Season
70 Danny Reece, Tampa Bay, 1979
62 Fulton Walker, Miami-L.A. Raiders, 1985
58 J.T. Smith, Kansas City, 1979
Greg Pruitt, L.A. Raiders, 1983
Leo Lewis, Minnesota, 1988
Desmond Howard, Green Bay, 1996

Most Punt Returns, Rookie, Season
57 Lew Barnes, Chicago, 1986
54 James Jones, Dallas, 1980
53 Louis Lipps, Pittsburgh, 1984

Most Punt Returns, Game
11 Eddie Brown, Washington vs. Tampa Bay, Oct. 9, 1977
10 Theo Bell, Pittsburgh vs. Buffalo, Dec. 16, 1979
Mike Nelms, Washington vs. New Orleans, Dec. 26, 1982
Ronnie Harris, New England vs. Pittsburgh, Dec. 5, 1993
9 Rodger Bird, Oakland vs. Denver, Sept. 10, 1967
Ralph McGill, San Francisco vs. Atlanta, Oct. 29, 1972
Ed Podolak, Kansas City vs. San Diego, Nov. 10, 1974
Anthony Leonard, San Francisco vs. New Orleans, Oct. 17, 1976
Butch Johnson, Dallas vs. Buffalo, Nov. 15, 1976
Larry Marshall, Philadelphia vs. Tampa Bay, Sept. 18, 1977
Nesby Glasgow, Baltimore vs. Kansas City, Sept. 2, 1979
Mike Nelms, Washington vs. St. Louis, Dec. 21, 1980
Leon Bright, N.Y. Giants vs. Philadelphia, Dec. 11, 1982
Pete Shaw, N.Y. Giants vs. Philadelphia, Nov. 20, 1983
Cleotha Montgomery, L.A. Raiders vs. Detroit, Dec. 10, 1984
Phil McConkey, N.Y. Giants vs. Philadelphia, Dec. 6, 1987 (OT)
Andre Hastings, Pittsburgh vs. Cleveland, Nov. 13, 1995
Steve Smith, Carolina vs. Detroit, Sept. 15, 2002

FAIR CATCHES

Most Fair Catches, Career
231 Brian Mitchell, Washington, 1990-99; Philadelphia, 2000-02; N.Y. Giants, 2003
150 Tim Brown, L.A. Raiders, 1988-1994; Oakland, 1995-2003
144 Glyn Milburn, Denver, 1993-95; Detroit, 1996-97; Chicago, 1998-2001; San Diego, 2001

Most Fair Catches, Season
33 Brian Mitchell, Philadelphia, 2000
27 Leo Lewis, Minnesota, 1989
26 Eric Guliford, New Orleans, 1997
Glyn Milburn, Detroit, 1997
Glyn Milburn, Chicago, 2000

Most Fair Catches, Game
7 Lem Barney, Detroit vs. Chicago, Nov. 21, 1976
Bobby Morse, Philadelphia vs. Buffalo, Dec. 27, 1987
6 Jake Scott, Miami vs. Buffalo, Dec. 20, 1970
Greg Pruitt, L.A. Raiders vs. Seattle, Oct. 7, 1984
Phil McConkey, San Diego vs. Kansas City, Dec. 17, 1989
Gerald McNeil, Houston vs. Pittsburgh, Sept. 16, 1990
Bobby Engram, Chicago vs. Minnesota, Sept. 15, 1996
Eddie Kennison, New Orleans vs. Baltimore, Dec. 19, 1999
5 By many players

YARDS GAINED

Most Seasons Leading League
3 Alvin Haymond, Baltimore, 1965-66; Los Angeles, 1969
2 Bill Dudley, Pittsburgh, 1942, 1946
Emlen Tunnell, N.Y. Giants, 1951-52
Dick Christy, N.Y. Titans, 1961-62
Claude Gibson, Oakland, 1963-64
Rodger Bird, Oakland, 1966-67
J.T. Smith, Kansas City, 1979-1980
Vai Sikahema, St. Louis, 1986-87
David Meggett, N.Y. Giants, 1989-1990
Tamarick Vanover, Kansas City, 1995, 1999

Most Yards Gained, Career
4,999 Brian Mitchell, Washington, 1990-99; Philadelphia, 2000-02; N.Y. Giants, 2003
3,708 David Meggett, N.Y. Giants, 1989-1994; New England, 1995-97; N.Y. Jets, 1998
3,601 Darrien Gordon, San Diego, 1993-94, 1996; Denver, 1997-98; Oakland, 1999-2000; Atlanta, 2001; Green Bay, 2002

Most Yards Gained, Season
875 Desmond Howard, Green Bay, 1996
692 Fulton Walker, Miami-L.A. Raiders, 1985
666 Greg Pruitt, L.A. Raiders, 1983

Most Yards Gained, Rookie, Season
656 Louis Lipps, Pittsburgh, 1984
655 Neal Colzie, Oakland, 1975
619 Leon Johnson, N.Y. Jets, 1997

Most Yards Gained, Game
207 LeRoy Irvin, Los Angeles vs. Atlanta, Oct. 11, 1981
205 George Atkinson, Oakland vs. Buffalo, Sept. 15, 1968
184 Tom Watkins, Detroit vs. San Francisco, Oct. 6, 1963
Jermaine Lewis, Baltimore vs. Seattle, Dec. 7, 1997

Longest Punt Return (All TDs)
103 Robert Bailey, L.A. Rams vs. New Orleans, Oct. 23, 1994
98 Gil LeFebvre, Cincinnati vs. Brooklyn, Dec. 3, 1933
Charlie West, Minnesota vs. Washington, Nov. 3, 1968
Dennis Morgan, Dallas vs. St. Louis, Oct. 13, 1974
Terance Mathis, N.Y. Jets vs. Dallas, Nov. 4, 1990
97 Greg Pruitt, L.A. Raiders vs. Washington, Oct. 2, 1983

AVERAGE YARDAGE

Highest Average, Career (75 returns)
12.78 George McAfee, Chi. Bears, 1940-41, 1945-1950 (112-1,431)
12.75 Jack Christiansen, Detroit, 1951-58 (85-1,084)
12.55 Claude Gibson, San Diego, 1961-62; Oakland, 1963-65 (110-1,381)

Highest Average, Season (Qualifiers)
23.00 Herb Rich, Baltimore, 1950 (12-276)
21.47 Jack Christiansen, Detroit, 1952 (15-322)
21.28 Dick Christy, N.Y. Titans, 1961 (18-383)

Highest Average, Rookie, Season (Qualifiers)
23.00 Herb Rich, Baltimore, 1950 (12-276)
20.88 Jerry Davis, Chi. Cardinals, 1948 (16-334)
20.73 Frank Sinkwich, Detroit, 1943 (11-228)

Highest Average, Game (3 returns)
51.00 Steve Smith, Carolina vs. Cincinnati, Dec. 8, 2002 (3-153)

47.67 Chuck Latourette, St. Louis vs. New Orleans, Sept. 29, 1968 (3-143)
47.33 Johnny Roland, St. Louis vs. Philadelphia, Oct. 2, 1966 (3-142)

TOUCHDOWNS

Most Touchdowns, Career

10 Eric Metcalf, Cleveland, 1989-1994; Atlanta, 1995-96; San Diego, 1997; Arizona, 1998; Carolina, 1999; Washington, 2001; Green Bay, 2002
9 Brian Mitchell, Washington, 1990-99; Philadelphia 2000-02; N.Y. Giants, 2003
8 Jack Christiansen, Detroit, 1951-58
Rick Upchurch, Denver, 1975-1983
Desmond Howard, Washington, 1992-94; Jacksonville, 1995; Green Bay, 1996, 1999; Oakland, 1997-98; Detroit, 1999-2002

Most Touchdowns, Season

4 Jack Christiansen, Detroit, 1951
Rick Upchurch, Denver, 1976
3 Emlen Tunnell, N.Y. Giants, 1951
Billy (White Shoes) Johnson, Houston, 1975
LeRoy Irvin, Los Angeles, 1981
Desmond Howard, Green Bay, 1996
Darrien Gordon, Denver, 1997
Eric Metcalf, San Diego, 1997
2 By many players

Most Touchdowns, Rookie, Season

4 Jack Christiansen, Detroit, 1951
2 By many players

Most Touchdowns, Game

2 Jack Christiansen, Detroit vs. Los Angeles, Oct. 14, 1951; vs. Green Bay, Nov. 22, 1951
Dick Christy, N.Y. Titans vs. Denver, Sept. 24, 1961
Rick Upchurch, Denver vs. Cleveland, Sept. 26, 1976
LeRoy Irvin, Los Angeles vs. Atlanta, Oct. 11, 1981
Vai Sikahema, St. Louis vs. Tampa Bay, Dec. 21, 1986
Todd Kinchen, L.A. Rams vs. Atlanta, Dec. 27, 1992
Eric Metcalf, Cleveland vs. Pittsburgh, Oct. 24, 1993; San Diego vs. Cincinnati, Nov. 2, 1997
Darrien Gordon, Denver vs. Carolina, Nov. 9, 1997
Jermaine Lewis, Baltimore vs. Seattle, Dec. 7, 1997; Baltimore vs. N.Y. Jets, Dec. 24, 2000
Steve Smith, Carolina vs. Cincinnati, Dec. 8, 2002

KICKOFF RETURNS

Most Seasons Leading League

3 Abe Woodson, San Francisco, 1959, 1962-63
2 Lynn Chandnois, Pittsburgh, 1951-52
Bobby Jancik, Houston, 1962-63
Travis Williams, Green Bay, 1967; Los Angeles, 1971
Mel Gray, Detroit, 1991, 1994
Michael Bates, Carolina, 1996-97

KICKOFF RETURNS

Most Kickoff Returns, Career

607 Brian Mitchell, Washington, 1990-99; Philadelphia 2000-02; N.Y. Giants, 2003
421 Mel Gray, New Orleans, 1986-88; Detroit, 1989-1994; Houston, 1995-96; Tennessee, 1997; Philadelphia, 1997
407 Glyn Milburn, Denver, 1993-95; Detroit, 1996-97; Chicago, 1998-2001; San Diego, 2001

Most Kickoff Returns, Season

82 MarTay Jenkins, Arizona, 2000
73 Josh Scobey, Arizona, 2003
70 Tyrone Hughes, New Orleans, 1996
Michael Lewis, New Orleans, 2002

Most Kickoff Returns, Rookie, Season

73 Josh Scobey, Arizona, 2003
67 Ronney Jenkins, San Diego, 2000
56 Tony Horne, St. Louis, 1998
Steve Smith, Carolina, 2001

Most Kickoff Returns, Game

10 Desmond Howard, Oakland vs. Seattle, Oct. 26, 1997
9 Noland Smith, Kansas City vs. Oakland, Nov. 23, 1967
Dino Hall, Cleveland vs. Pittsburgh, Oct. 7, 1979
Paul Palmer, Kansas City vs. Seattle, Sept. 20, 1987
Eric Metcalf, Atlanta vs. San Francisco, Sept. 29, 1996; vs. St. Louis, Nov. 10, 1996
Michael Bates, Carolina vs. Atlanta, Oct. 4, 1998
Nate Jacquet, Minnesota vs. Philadelphia, Nov. 11, 2001
Ahmad Merritt, Chicago vs. San Francisco, Sept. 7, 2003
Josh Scobey, Arizona vs. Cleveland, Nov. 16, 2003
8 By many players

YARDS GAINED

Most Seasons Leading League

3 Bruce Harper, N.Y. Jets, 1977-79
Tyrone Hughes, New Orleans, 1994-96
2 Marshall Goldberg, Chi. Cardinals, 1941-42
Woodley Lewis, Los Angeles, 1953-54
Al Carmichael, Green Bay, 1956-57
Timmy Brown, Philadelphia, 1961, 1963
Bobby Jancik, Houston, 1963, 1966
Ron Smith, Atlanta, 1966-67

Most Yards Gained, Career

14,014 Brian Mitchell, Washington, 1990-99; Philadelphia, 2000-02; N.Y. Giants, 2003
10,250 Mel Gray, New Orleans, 1986-88; Detroit, 1989-1994; Houston, 1995-96; Tennessee, 1997; Philadelphia, 1997
9,788 Glyn Milburn, Denver, 1993-95; Detroit, 1996-97; Chicago, 1998-2001; San Diego, 2001

Most Yards Gained, Season

2,186 MarTay Jenkins, Arizona, 2000
1,807 Michael Lewis, New Orleans, 2002
1,791 Tyrone Hughes, New Orleans, 1996

Most Yards Gained, Rookie, Season

1,684 Josh Scobey, Arizona, 2003
1,531 Ronney Jenkins, San Diego, 2000
1,431 Steve Smith, Carolina, 2001

Most Yards Gained, Game

304 Tyrone Hughes, New Orleans vs. L.A. Rams, Oct. 23, 1994
294 Wally Triplett, Detroit vs. Los Angeles, Oct. 29, 1950
278 Chad Morton, N.Y. Jets vs. Buffalo, Sept. 8, 2002 (OT)

Longest Kickoff Return (All TDs)

106 Al Carmichael, Green Bay vs. Chi. Bears, Oct. 7, 1956
Noland Smith, Kansas City vs. Denver, Dec. 17, 1967
Roy Green, St. Louis vs. Dallas, Oct. 21, 1979
105 Frank Seno, Chi. Cardinals vs. N.Y. Giants, Oct. 20, 1946
Ollie Matson, Chi. Cardinals vs. Washington, Oct. 14, 1956
Abe Woodson, San Francisco vs. Los Angeles, Nov. 8, 1959
Timmy Brown, Philadelphia vs. Cleveland, Sept. 17, 1961
Jon Arnett, Los Angeles vs. Detroit, Oct. 29, 1961
Eugene (Mercury) Morris, Miami vs. Cincinnati, Sept. 14, 1969
Travis Williams, Los Angeles vs. New Orleans, Dec. 5, 1971
Terry Fair, Detroit vs. Tampa Bay, Sept. 28, 1998

104 By many players

AVERAGE YARDAGE

Highest Average, Career (75 returns)

30.56 Gale Sayers, Chicago, 1965-1971 (91-2,781)
29.57 Lynn Chandnois, Pittsburgh, 1950-56 (92-2,720)
28.69 Abe Woodson, San Francisco, 1958-1964; St. Louis, 1965-66 (193-5,538)

Highest Average, Season (Qualifiers)

41.06 Travis Williams, Green Bay, 1967 (18-739)
37.69 Gale Sayers, Chicago, 1967 (16-603)
35.50 Ollie Matson, Chi. Cardinals, 1958 (14-497)

Highest Average, Rookie, Season (Qualifiers)

41.06 Travis Williams, Green Bay, 1967 (18-739)
33.08 Tom Moore, Green Bay, 1960 (12-397)
32.88 Duriel Harris, Miami, 1976 (17-559)

Highest Average, Game (3 returns)

73.50 Wally Triplett, Detroit vs. Los Angeles, Oct. 29, 1950 (4-294)
67.33 Lenny Lyles, San Francisco vs. Baltimore, Dec. 18, 1960 (3-202)
65.33 Ken Hall, Houston vs. N.Y. Titans, Oct. 23, 1960 (3-196)

TOUCHDOWNS

Most Touchdowns, Career

6 Ollie Matson, Chi. Cardinals, 1952, 1954-58; L.A. Rams, 1959-1962; Detroit, 1963; Philadelphia, 1964
Gale Sayers, Chicago, 1965-1971
Travis Williams, Green Bay, 1967-1970; Los Angeles, 1971
Mel Gray, New Orleans, 1986-88; Detroit, 1989-1994; Houston, 1995-96; Tennessee, 1997; Philadelphia, 1997
5 Bobby Mitchell, Cleveland, 1958-1961; Washington, 1962-68
Abe Woodson, San Francisco, 1958-1964; St. Louis, 1965-66
Timmy Brown, Green Bay, 1959; Philadelphia, 1960-67; Baltimore, 1968
Michael Bates, Seattle, 1993-94; Cleveland, 1995; Carolina, 1996-2000, 2002; Washington, 2001; N.Y. Jets, 2003; Dallas, 2003
4 Cecil Turner, Chicago, 1968-1973
Ron Brown, L.A. Rams, 1984-89, 1991; L.A. Raiders, 1990
Jon Vaughn, New England, 1991-92; Seattle, 1993-94; Kansas City, 1994
Andre Coleman, San Diego, 1994-96; Seattle, 1997; Pittsburgh, 1997-98
Tamarick Vanover, Kansas City, 1995-99, San Diego, 2002
Tony Horne, St. Louis, 1998-2000
Brian Mitchell, Washington, 1990-99; Philadelphia, 2000-02; N.Y. Giants, 2003
Darrick Vaughn, Atlanta, 2000-01; Houston, 2003

Most Touchdowns, Season

4 Travis Williams, Green Bay, 1967
Cecil Turner, Chicago, 1970
3 Verda (Vitamin T) Smith, Los Angeles, 1950
Abe Woodson, San Francisco, 1963
Gale Sayers, Chicago, 1967
Raymond Clayborn, New England, 1977
Ron Brown, L.A. Rams, 1985
Mel Gray, Detroit, 1994
Darrick Vaughn, Atlanta, 2000
2 By many players

Most Touchdowns, Rookie, Season

4 Travis Williams, Green Bay, 1967
3 Raymond Clayborn, New England, 1977
Darrick Vaughn, Atlanta, 2000
2 By many players

Most Touchdowns, Game

2 Timmy Brown, Philadelphia vs. Dallas, Nov. 6, 1966
Travis Williams, Green Bay vs. Cleveland, Nov. 12, 1967
Ron Brown, L.A. Rams vs. Green Bay, Nov. 24, 1985
Tyrone Hughes, New Orleans vs. L.A. Rams, Oct. 23, 1994
Chad Morton, N.Y. Jets vs. Buffalo, Sept. 8, 2002 (OT)

COMBINED KICK RETURNS

Most Combined Kick Returns, Career

1,070 Brian Mitchell, Washington, 1990-99; Philadelphia, 2000-02; N.Y. Giants, 2003 (p-463, k-607)
711 Glyn Milburn, Denver, 1993-95; Detroit, 1996-97; Chicago, 1998-2001; San Diego, 2001 (p-304, k-407)
673 Mel Gray, New Orleans, 1986-88; Detroit, 1989-1994; Houston, 1995-96; Tennessee, 1997; Philadelphia, 1997 (p-252, k-421)

Most Combined Kick Returns, Season

114 Michael Lewis, New Orleans, 2002 (p-44, k-70)
103 Brian Mitchell, Washington, 1998 (p-44, k-59)
102 Glyn Milburn, Detroit, 1997 (p-47, k-55)

Most Combined Kick Returns, Game

13 Stump Mitchell, St. Louis vs. Atlanta, Oct. 18, 1981 (p-6, k-7)
Ronnie Harris, New England vs. Pittsburgh, Dec. 5, 1993 (p-10, k-3)
12 Mel Renfro, Dallas vs. Green Bay, Nov. 29, 1964 (p-4, k-8)
Larry Jones, Washington vs. Dallas, Dec. 13, 1975 (p-6, k-6)
Eddie Brown, Washington vs. Tampa Bay, Oct. 9, 1977 (p-11, k-1)
Nesby Glasgow, Baltimore vs. Denver, Sept. 2, 1979 (p-9, k-3)
Tim Dwight, Atlanta vs. Detroit, Nov. 12, 2000 (p-8, k-4)
11 By many players

YARDS GAINED

Most Yards Returned, Career

19,013 Brian Mitchell, Washington, 1990-99; Philadelphia, 2000-02; N.Y. Giants, 2003 (p-4,999; k-14,014)
13,003 Mel Gray, New Orleans, 1986-88; Detroit, 1989-1994; Houston, 1995-96; Tennessee, 1997; Philadelphia, 1997 (p-2,753; k-10,250)
12,772 Glyn Milburn, Denver, 1993-95; Detroit, 1996-97; Chicago, 1998-2001; San Diego, 2001 (p-2,984; k-9,788)

Most Yards Returned, Season

2,432 Michael Lewis, New Orleans, 2002 (p-625, k-1,807)
2,187 MarTay Jenkins, Arizona, 2000 (p-1, k-2,186)
1,992 Charlie Rogers, Seattle, 2000 (p-363, k-1,629)

Most Yards Returned, Game

347 Tyrone Hughes, New Orleans vs. L.A. Rams, Oct. 23, 1994 (p-43, k-304)
294 Wally Triplett, Detroit vs. Los Angeles, Oct. 29, 1950 (k-294)
Woodley Lewis, Los Angeles vs. Detroit, Oct. 18, 1953 (p-120, k-174)
289 Eddie Payton, Detroit vs. Minnesota, Dec. 17, 1977 (p-105, k-184)

TOUCHDOWNS

Most Touchdowns, Career

13 Brian Mitchell, Washington, 1990-99; Philadelphia, 2000-02; N.Y. Giants, 2003 (p-9, k-4)
12 Eric Metcalf, Cleveland, 1989-1994; Atlanta, 1995-96; San Diego, 1997; Arizona, 1998; Carolina, 1999; Washington, 2001; Green Bay, 2002 (p-10, k-2)
9 Ollie Matson, Chi. Cardinals, 1952, 1954-58; Los Angeles, 1959-1962; Detroit, 1963; Philadelphia, 1964-66 (p-3, k-6)
Mel Gray, New Orleans, 1986-88; Detroit, 1989-1994; Houston, 1995-96; Tennessee, 1997; Philadelphia, 1997 (p-3, k-6)
Deion Sanders, Atlanta, 1989-1993; San Francisco, 1994; Dallas, 1995-99; Washington, 2000 (p-6, k-3)

Most Touchdowns, Season

4 Jack Christiansen, Detroit, 1951 (p-4)
Emlen Tunnell, N.Y. Giants, 1951 (p-3, k-1)
Gale Sayers, Chicago, 1967 (p-1, k-3)
Travis Williams, Green Bay, 1967 (k-4)
Cecil Turner, Chicago, 1970 (k-4)
Billy Johnson, Houston, 1975 (p-3, k-1)
Rick Upchurch, Denver, 1976 (p-4)
Dante Hall, Kansas City, 2003 (p-2, r-2)
3 Verda (Vitamin T) Smith, Los Angeles, 1950 (k-3)
Abe Woodson, San Francisco, 1963 (k-3)
Raymond Clayborn, New England, 1977 (k-3)
Billy Johnson, Houston, 1977 (p-2, k-1)
LeRoy Irvin, Los Angeles, 1981 (p-3)
Ron Brown, L.A. Rams, 1985 (k-3)
Tyrone Hughes, New Orleans, 1993 (p-2, k-1)
Mel Gray, Detroit, 1994 (k-3)
Andre Coleman, San Diego, 1995 (p-2; k-1)
Tamarick Vanover, Kansas City, 1995 (p-1, k-2)
Desmond Howard, Green Bay, 1996 (p-3)
Darrien Gordon, Denver, 1997 (p-3)
Eric Metcalf, San Diego, 1997 (p-3)
Glyn Milburn, Chicago, 1998 (p-2, k-1)
Roell Preston, Green Bay, 1998 (p-2, k-1)
Darrick Vaughn, Atlanta, 2000 (k-3)
Steve Smith, Carolina, 2001 (p-1, k-2)
Michael Lewis, New Orleans, 2002 (p-1, k-2)
Dante Hall, Kansas City, 2002 (p-2, k-1)
2 By many players

Most Touchdowns, Game

2 Jack Christiansen, Detroit vs. Los Angeles, Oct. 14, 1951 (p-2); vs. Green Bay, Nov. 22, 1951 (p-2)
Jim Patton, N.Y. Giants vs. Washington, Oct. 30, 1955 (p-1, k-1)
Bobby Mitchell, Cleveland vs. Philadelphia, Nov. 23, 1958 (p-1, k-1)
Dick Christy, N.Y. Titans vs. Denver, Sept. 24, 1961 (p-2)
Al Frazier, Denver vs. Boston, Dec. 3, 1961 (p-1, k-1)
Timmy Brown, Philadelphia vs. Dallas, Nov. 6, 1966 (k-2)
Travis Williams, Green Bay vs. Cleveland, Nov. 12, 1967 (k-2); vs. Pittsburgh, Nov. 2, 1969 (p-1, k-1)
Gale Sayers, Chicago vs. San Francisco, Dec. 3, 1967 (p-1, k-1)
Rick Upchurch, Denver vs. Cleveland, Sept. 26, 1976 (p-2)
Eddie Payton, Detroit vs. Minnesota, Dec. 17, 1977 (p-1, k-1)
LeRoy Irvin, Los Angeles vs. Atlanta, Oct. 11, 1981 (p-2)
Ron Brown, L.A. Rams vs. Green Bay, Nov. 24, 1985 (k-2)
Vai Sikahema, St. Louis vs. Tampa Bay, Dec. 21, 1986 (p-2)
Todd Kinchen, L.A. Rams vs. Atlanta, Dec. 27, 1992 (p-2)
Eric Metcalf, Cleveland vs. Pittsburgh, Oct. 24, 1993 (p-2); San Diego vs. Cincinnati, Nov. 2, 1997 (p-2)
Tyrone Hughes, New Orleans vs. L.A. Rams, Oct. 23, 1994 (k-2)
Darrien Gordon, Denver vs. Carolina, Nov. 9, 1997 (p-2)
Jermaine Lewis, Baltimore vs. Seattle, Dec. 7, 1997 (p-2); Baltimore vs. N.Y. Jets, Dec. 24, 2000 (p-2)
Chad Morton, N.Y. Jets vs. Buffalo, Sept. 8, 2002 (OT) (k-2)
Michael Lewis, New Orleans vs. Washington, Oct. 13, 2002 (p-1, k-1)
Dante Hall, Kansas City vs. St. Louis, Dec. 8, 2002 (p-1, k-1)
Steve Smith, Carolina vs. Cincinnati, Dec. 8, 2002 (p-2)

FUMBLES

Most Fumbles, Career

161 Warren Moon, Houston, 1984-1993; Minnesota, 1994-96; Seattle, 1997-98; Kansas City, 1999-2000
153 Dave Krieg, Seattle, 1980-1991; Kansas City, 1992-93; Detroit, 1994; Arizona, 1995; Chicago, 1996; Tennessee, 1997-98
137 John Elway, Denver, 1983-1998

Most Fumbles, Season

23 Kerry Collins, N.Y. Giants, 2001
Daunte Culpepper, Minnesota, 2002
21 Tony Banks, St. Louis, 1996
David Carr, Houston, 2002
18 Dave Krieg, Seattle, 1989
Warren Moon, Houston, 1990

Most Fumbles, Game

7 Len Dawson, Kansas City vs. San Diego, Nov. 15, 1964
6 Sam Etcheverry, St. Louis vs. N.Y. Giants, Sept, 17, 1961
Dave Krieg, Seattle vs. Kansas City, Nov. 5, 1989
Brett Favre, Green Bay vs. Tampa Bay, Dec. 7, 1998
Kurt Warner, St. Louis vs. N.Y. Giants, Sept. 7, 2003
5 Paul Christman, Chi. Cardinals vs. Green Bay, Nov. 10, 1946
Charlie Conerly, N.Y. Giants vs. San Francisco, Dec. 1, 1957
Jack Kemp, Buffalo vs. Houston, Oct. 29, 1967
Roman Gabriel, Philadelphia vs. Oakland, Nov. 21, 1976
Randall Cunningham, Philadelphia vs. L.A. Raiders, Nov. 30, 1986 (OT)
Willie Totten, Buffalo vs. Indianapolis, Oct. 4, 1987
Dave Walter, Cincinnati vs. Seattle, Oct. 11, 1987
Dave Krieg, Seattle vs. San Diego, Nov. 25, 1990 (OT)
Andre Ware, Detroit vs. Green Bay, Dec. 6, 1992
Steve Beuerlein, Carolina vs. San Francisco, Nov. 8, 1998
Patrick Ramsey, Washington vs. Green Bay, Oct. 20, 2002

FUMBLES RECOVERED

Most Fumbles Recovered, Career, Own and Opponents'

56 Warren Moon, Houston, 1984-1993; Minnesota, 1994-96; Seattle, 1997-98; Kansas City, 1999-2000 (56 own)
47 Dave Krieg, Seattle, 1980-1991; Kansas City, 1992-93; Detroit, 1994; Arizona, 1995; Chicago, 1996; Tennessee, 1997-98 (47 own)
45 Boomer Esiason, Cincinnati, 1984-1992, 1997; N.Y. Jets, 1993-95; Arizona, 1996 (45 own)

Most Fumbles Recovered, Season, Own and Opponents'

12 David Carr, Houston, 2002 (12 own)
9 Don Hultz, Minnesota, 1963 (9 opp)
Dave Krieg, Seattle, 1989 (9 own)
Brian Griese, Denver, 1999 (9 own)
Jon Kitna, Seattle, 2000 (9 own)
8 Paul Christman, Chi. Cardinals, 1945 (8 own)
Joe Schmidt, Detroit, 1955 (8 opp)
Bill Butler, Minnesota, 1963 (8 own)
Kermit Alexander, San Francisco, 1965 (4 own, 4 opp)
Jack Lambert, Pittsburgh, 1976 (1 own, 7 opp)
Danny White, Dallas, 1981 (8 own)
Dan Marino, Miami, 1988 (7 own, 1 opp)
Tony Banks, St. Louis, 1998 (8 own)

Most Fumbles Recovered, Game, Own and Opponents'

4 Otto Graham, Cleveland vs. N.Y. Giants, Oct. 25, 1953 (4 own)
Sam Etcheverry, St. Louis vs. N.Y. Giants, Sept. 17, 1961 (4 own)
Roman Gabriel, Los Angeles vs. San Francisco, Oct. 12, 1969 (4 own)
Joe Ferguson, Buffalo vs. Miami, Sept. 18, 1977 (4 own)
Randall Cunningham, Philadelphia vs. L.A. Raiders, Nov. 30, 1986 (OT) (4 own)
3 By many players

OWN FUMBLES RECOVERED

Most Own Fumbles Recovered, Career

56 Warren Moon, Houston, 1984-1993; Minnesota, 1994-96; Seattle, 1997-98; Kansas City, 1999-2000
47 Dave Krieg, Seattle, 1980-1991; Kansas City, 1992-93; Detroit, 1994; Arizona, 1995; Chicago, 1996; Tennessee, 1997-98
45 Boomer Esiason, Cincinnati, 1984-1992, 1997; N.Y. Jets, 1993-95; Arizona, 1996

Most Own Fumbles Recovered, Season

12 David Carr, Houston, 2002
9 Dave Krieg, Seattle, 1989
Brian Griese, Denver, 1999
Jon Kitna, Seattle, 2000
8 Paul Christman, Chi. Cardinals, 1945
Bill Butler, Minnesota, 1963
Danny White, Dallas, 1981
Tony Banks, St. Louis, 1998

Most Own Fumbles Recovered, Game

4 Otto Graham, Cleveland vs. N.Y. Giants, Oct. 25, 1953
Sam Etcheverry, St. Louis vs. N.Y. Giants, Sept. 17, 1961
Roman Gabriel, Los Angeles vs. San Francisco, Oct. 12, 1969
Joe Ferguson, Buffalo vs. Miami, Sept. 18, 1977
Randall Cunningham, Philadelphia vs. L.A. Raiders, Nov. 30, 1986 (OT)
3 By many players

OPPONENTS' FUMBLES RECOVERED

Most Opponents' Fumbles Recovered, Career

29 Jim Marshall, Cleveland, 1960; Minnesota, 1961-1979
28 Rickey Jackson, New Orleans, 1981-1993; San Francisco, 1994-95
26 Kevin Greene, L.A. Rams, 1985-1992; Pittsburgh, 1993-95; Carolina, 1996, 1998-99; San Francisco, 1997
Cornelius Bennett, Buffalo, 1987-1995; Atlanta, 1996-98; Indianapolis, 1999-2000

Most Opponents' Fumbles Recovered, Season

9 Don Hultz, Minnesota, 1963
8 Joe Schmidt, Detroit, 1955
7 Alan Page, Minnesota, 1970
Jack Lambert, Pittsburgh, 1976
Ray Childress, Houston, 1988
Rickey Jackson, New Orleans, 1990

Most Opponents' Fumbles Recovered, Game

3 Corwin Clatt, Chi. Cardinals vs. Detroit, Nov. 6, 1949
Vic Sears, Philadelphia vs. Green Bay, Nov. 2, 1952
Ed Beatty, San Francisco vs. Los Angeles, Oct. 7, 1956
Ron Carroll, Houston vs. Cincinnati, Oct. 27, 1974
Maurice Spencer, New Orleans vs. Atlanta, Oct. 10, 1976
Steve Nelson, New England vs. Philadelphia, Oct. 8, 1978
Charles Jackson, Kansas City vs. Pittsburgh, Sept. 6, 1981
Willie Buchanon, San Diego vs. Denver, Sept. 27, 1981
Joey Browner, Minnesota vs. San Francisco, Sept. 8, 1985
Ray Childress, Houston vs. Washington, Oct. 30, 1988
John Thierry, Chicago vs. Houston, Oct. 22, 1995
Stephen Boyd, Detroit vs. Chicago, Oct. 4, 1998
Darryl Williams, Seattle vs. Kansas City, Oct. 4, 1998
Rod Woodson, Oakland vs. Pittsburgh, Sept. 15, 2002
Brian Young, St. Louis vs. Baltimore, Nov. 9, 2003
2 By many players

YARDS RETURNING FUMBLES

Longest Fumble Run (All TDs)

104 Jack Tatum, Oakland vs. Green Bay, Sept. 24, 1972
Aeneas Williams, Arizona vs. Washington, Nov. 5, 2000
102 Travis Davis, Pittsburgh vs. Carolina, Dec. 26, 1999
100 Chris Martin, Kansas City vs. Miami, Oct. 13, 1991

TOUCHDOWNS

Most Touchdowns, Career (Total)

5 Jessie Tuggle, Atlanta, 1987-2000
4 Bill Thompson, Denver, 1969-1981
Derrick Thomas, Kansas City, 1989-1999
Jason Taylor, Miami, 1997-2003
3 By many players

Most Touchdowns, Season (Total)

2 Harold McPhail, Boston, 1934
Harry Ebding, Detroit, 1937
John Morelli, Boston, 1944
Frank Maznicki, Boston, 1947
Fred (Dippy) Evans, Chi. Bears, 1948
Ralph Heywood, Boston, 1948
Art Tait, N.Y. Yanks, 1951
John Dwyer, Los Angeles, 1952
Leo Sugar, Chi. Cardinals, 1957
Doug Cline, Houston, 1961
Jim Bradshaw, Pittsburgh, 1964
Royce Berry, Cincinnati, 1970
Ahmad Rashad, Buffalo, 1974

Tim Gray, Kansas City, 1977
Charles Phillips, Oakland, 1978
Kenny Johnson, Atlanta, 1981
George Martin, N.Y. Giants, 1981
Del Rodgers, Green Bay, 1982
Mike Douglass, Green Bay, 1983
Shelton Robinson, Seattle, 1983
Erik McMillan, N.Y. Jets, 1989
Les Miller, San Diego, 1990
Seth Joyner, Philadelphia, 1991
Robert Goff, New Orleans, 1992
Willie Clay, Detroit, 1993
Tyrone Hughes, New Orleans, 1994
Chad Brown, Seattle, 1997
Marcus Robertson, Tennessee, 1997
Dwayne Rudd, Minnesota, 1998
Keith McKenzie, Green Bay, 1999

Most Touchdowns, Career (Own recovered)
2 Ken Kavanaugh, Chi. Bears, 1940-41, 1945-1950
Mike Ditka, Chicago, 1961-66; Philadelphia, 1967-68; Dallas, 1969-1972
Gail Cogdill, Detroit, 1960-68; Baltimore, 1968; Atlanta, 1969-1970
Ahmad Rashad, St. Louis, 1972-73; Buffalo, 1974; Minnesota, 1976-1982
Jim Mitchell, Atlanta, 1969-1979
Drew Pearson, Dallas, 1973-1983
Del Rodgers, Green Bay, 1982, 1984; San Francisco, 1987-88
Alan Richard, Baltimore, 2001-03

Most Touchdowns, Season (Own recovered)
2 Ahmad Rashad, Buffalo, 1974
Del Rodgers, Green Bay, 1982
1 By many players

Most Touchdowns, Career (Opponents' recovered)
5 Jessie Tuggle, Atlanta, 1987-2000
4 Derrick Thomas, Kansas City, 1989-1999
Jason Taylor, Miami, 1997-2003
3 By many players

Most Touchdowns, Season (Opponents' recovered)
2 Harold McPhail, Boston, 1934
Harry Ebding, Detroit, 1937
John Morelli, Boston, 1944
Frank Maznicki, Boston, 1947
Fred (Dippy) Evans, Chi. Bears, 1948
Ralph Heywood, Boston, 1948
Art Tait, N.Y. Yanks, 1951
John Dwyer, Los Angeles, 1952
Leo Sugar, Chi. Cardinals, 1957
Doug Cline, Houston, 1961
Jim Bradshaw, Pittsburgh, 1964
Royce Berry, Cincinnati, 1970
Tim Gray, Kansas City, 1977
Charles Phillips, Oakland, 1978
Kenny Johnson, Atlanta, 1981
George Martin, N.Y. Giants, 1981
Mike Douglass, Green Bay, 1983
Shelton Robinson, Seattle, 1983
Erik McMillan, N.Y. Jets, 1989
Les Miller, San Diego, 1990
Seth Joyner, Philadelphia, 1991
Robert Goff, New Orleans, 1992
Willie Clay, Detroit, 1993
Tyrone Hughes, New Orleans, 1994
Chad Brown, Seattle, 1997
Marcus Robertson, Tennessee, 1997
Dwayne Rudd, Minnesota, 1998
Keith McKenzie, Green Bay, 1999

Most Touchdowns, Game (Opponents' recovered)
2 Fred (Dippy) Evans, Chi. Bears vs. Washington, Nov. 28, 1948

COMBINED NET YARDS GAINED

Rushing, receiving, interception returns, punt returns, kickoff returns, and fumble returns

Most Seasons Leading League
5 Jim Brown, Cleveland, 1958-1961, 1964
4 Brian Mitchell, Washington, 1994-96, 1998
3 Cliff Battles, Boston, 1932-33; Washington, 1937
Gale Sayers, Chicago, 1965-67
Eric Dickerson, L.A. Rams, 1983-84, 1986
Thurman Thomas, Buffalo, 1989, 1991-92

Most Consecutive Seasons Leading League
4 Jim Brown, Cleveland, 1958-1961
3 Gale Sayers, Chicago, 1965-67
Brian Mitchell, Washington, 1994-96
2 Cliff Battles, Boston, 1932-33
Charley Trippi, Chi. Cardinals, 1948-49
Timmy Brown, Philadelphia, 1962-63
Floyd Little, Denver, 1967-68
James Brooks, San Diego, 1981-82
Eric Dickerson, L.A. Rams, 1983-84
Thurman Thomas, Buffalo, 1991-92

ATTEMPTS

Most Attempts, Career
4,655 Emmitt Smith, Dallas, 1990-2002; Arizona, 2003
4,368 Walter Payton, Chicago, 1975-1987
3,624 Marcus Allen, L.A. Raiders, 1982-1992; Kansas City, 1993-97

Most Attempts, Season
496 James Wilder, Tampa Bay, 1984
455 Eddie George, Tennessee, 2000
451 LaDainian Tomlinson, San Diego, 2002

Most Attempts, Rookie, Season
442 Eric Dickerson, L.A. Rams, 1983
433 Edgerrin James, Indianapolis, 1999
401 Curtis Martin, New England, 1995

Most Attempts, Game
48 James Wilder, Tampa Bay vs. Pittsburgh, Oct. 30, 1983
LaDainian Tomlinson, San Diego vs. Denver, Dec. 1, 2002 (OT)
47 James Wilder, Tampa Bay vs. Green Bay, Sept. 30, 1984 (OT)
Terrell Davis, Denver vs. Buffalo, Oct. 26, 1997 (OT)
46 Gerald Riggs, Atlanta vs. L.A. Rams, Nov. 17, 1985

YARDS GAINED

Most Yards Gained, Career
23,330 Brian Mitchell, Washington, 1990-99; Philadelphia, 2000-02; N.Y. Giants, 2003
23,117 Jerry Rice, San Francisco, 1985-2000; Oakland, 2001-03
21,803 Walter Payton, Chicago, 1975-1987

Most Yards Gained, Season
2,690 Derrick Mason, Tennessee, 2000
2,647 Michael Lewis, New Orleans, 2002
2,535 Lionel James, San Diego, 1985

Most Yards Gained, Rookie, Season
2,317 Tim Brown, L.A. Raiders, 1988
2,272 Gale Sayers, Chicago, 1965
2,212 Eric Dickerson, L.A. Rams, 1983

Most Yards Gained, Game
404 Glyn Milburn, Denver vs. Seattle, Dec. 10, 1995
373 Billy Cannon, Houston vs. N.Y. Titans, Dec. 10, 1961
356 Michael Lewis, New Orleans vs. Washington, Oct. 13, 2002

SACKS

Sacks have been compiled since 1982.

Most Seasons Leading League
2 Mark Gastineau, N.Y. Jets, 1983-84
Reggie White, Philadelphia, 1987-88
Kevin Greene, Pittsburgh, 1994; Carolina, 1996
Michael Strahan, N.Y. Giants, 2001, 2003

Most Sacks, Career
200.0 Bruce Smith, Buffalo, 1985-1999; Washington, 2000-03
198.0 Reggie White, Philadelphia, 1985-1992; Green Bay, 1993-98; Carolina, 2000
160.0 Kevin Greene, L.A. Rams, 1985-1992; Pittsburgh, 1993-95; Carolina, 1996, 1998-99; San Francisco, 1997

Most Sacks, Season
22.5 Michael Strahan, N.Y. Giants, 2001
22.0 Mark Gastineau, N.Y. Jets, 1984
21.0 Reggie White, Philadelphia, 1987
Chris Doleman, Minnesota, 1989

Most Sacks, Rookie, Season
14.5 Jevon Kearse, Tennessee, 1999
13.0 Dwight Freeney, Indianapolis, 2002
12.5 Leslie O'Neal, San Diego, 1986
Simeon Rice, Arizona, 1996

Most Sacks, Game
7.0 Derrick Thomas, Kansas City vs. Seattle, Nov. 11, 1990
6.0 Fred Dean, San Francisco vs. New Orleans, Nov. 13, 1983
Derrick Thomas, Kansas City vs. Oakland, Sept. 6, 1998
5.5 William Gay, Detroit vs. Tampa Bay, Sept. 4, 1983

Most Seasons, 10 or More Sacks
13 Bruce Smith, Buffalo, 1986-1990, 1992-98; Washington, 2000
12 Reggie White, Philadelphia, 1985-1992; Green Bay, 1993, 1995, 1997-98
10 Kevin Greene, L.A. Rams, 1988-1990, 1992; Pittsburgh, 1993-94; Carolina, 1996, 1998-99; San Francisco, 1997

Most Consecutive Seasons, 10 or More Sacks
9 Reggie White, Philadelphia, 1985-1992; Green Bay, 1993
8 John Randle, Minnesota, 1992-99
7 Lawrence Taylor, N.Y. Giants, 1984-1990
Bruce Smith, Buffalo, 1992-98

Most Consecutive Games, Sack
10 Simon Fletcher, Denver, Nov. 15, 1992-Sept. 20, 1993
9 Bruce Smith, Buffalo, Nov. 16, 1986-Oct. 25, 1987
Kevin Greene, San Francisco-Carolina, Dec. 7, 1997-Oct. 18, 1998
8 By many players

MISCELLANEOUS

Longest Return of Missed Field Goal (All TDs)
107 Chris McAlister, Baltimore vs. Denver, Sept. 30, 2002
104 Aaron Glenn, N.Y. Jets vs. Indianapolis, Nov. 15, 1998
101 Al Nelson, Philadelphia vs. Dallas, Sept. 26, 1971

TEAM RECORDS

CHAMPIONSHIPS

Most Seasons League Champion
12 Green Bay, 1929-1931, 1936, 1939, 1944, 1961-62, 1965-67, 1996
9 Chi. Bears, 1921, 1932-33, 1940-41, 1943, 1946, 1963, 1985
6 N.Y. Giants, 1927, 1934, 1938, 1956, 1986, 1990

Most Consecutive Seasons League Champion
3 Green Bay, 1929-1931
Green Bay, 1965-67
2 Canton, 1922-23
Chi. Bears, 1932-33
Chi. Bears, 1940-41
Philadelphia, 1948-49
Detroit, 1952-53
Cleveland, 1954-55
Baltimore, 1958-59
Houston, 1960-61
Green Bay, 1961-62
Buffalo, 1964-65
Miami, 1972-73
Pittsburgh, 1974-75
Pittsburgh, 1978-79
San Francisco, 1988-89
Dallas, 1992-93
Denver, 1997-98

Most Times Finishing First, Regular Season
20 N.Y. Giants, 1927, 1933-35, 1938-39, 1941, 1944, 1946, 1956, 1958-59, 1961-63, 1986, 1989-1990, 1997, 2000
19 Dallas, 1966-1971, 1973, 1976-79, 1981, 1985, 1992-96, 1998
Chi. Bears, 1921, 1932-34, 1937, 1940-43, 1946, 1956, 1963, 1984-88, 1990, 2001
Green Bay, 1929-1931, 1936, 1938-39, 1944, 1960-62, 1965-67, 1972, 1995-97, 2002-03
18 Cle. Browns, 1950-55, 1957, 1964-65, 1967-69, 1971, 1980, 1985-87, 1989
Cleveland/L.A./St. Louis Rams, 1945, 1949-1951, 1955, 1967, 1969, 1973-79, 1985, 1999, 2001, 2003

Most Consecutive Times Finishing First, Regular Season
7 Los Angeles, 1973-79
6 Cleveland, 1950-55
Dallas, 1966-1971
Minnesota, 1973-78
Pittsburgh, 1974-79
5 Oakland, 1972-76
Chicago, 1984-88
San Francisco, 1986-1990
Dallas, 1992-96

GAMES WON

Most Consecutive Games Won
17 Chi. Bears, 1933-34
16 Chi. Bears, 1941-42
Miami, 1971-73
Miami, 1983-84
15 L.A. Chargers/San Diego, 1960-61
San Francisco, 1989-1990

Most Consecutive Games Without Defeat
25 Canton, 1921-23 (won 22, tied 3)
24 Chi. Bears, 1941-43 (won 23, tied 1)
23 Green Bay, 1928-1930 (won 21, tied 2)

Most Games Won, Season
15 San Francisco, 1984
Chicago, 1985
Minnesota, 1998
14 Frankford, 1926
Miami, 1972
Pittsburgh, 1978
Washington, 1983
Miami, 1984
Chicago, 1986
N.Y. Giants, 1986
San Francisco, 1989
San Francisco, 1990

Washington, 1991
San Francisco, 1992
Atlanta, 1998
Denver, 1998
Jacksonville, 1999
St. Louis, 2001
New England, 2003
13 By many teams

Most Consecutive Games Won, Season
14 Miami, 1972
13 Chi. Bears, 1934
Denver, 1998
12 Minnesota, 1969
Chicago, 1985
New England, 2003

Most Consecutive Games Won, Start of Season
14 Miami, 1972, entire season
13 Chi. Bears, 1934, entire season
Denver, 1998
12 Chicago, 1985

Most Consecutive Games Won, End of Season
14 Miami, 1972, entire season
13 Chi. Bears, 1934, entire season
12 New England, 2003

Most Consecutive Games Without Defeat, Season
14 Miami, 1972 (won 14)
13 Chi. Bears, 1926 (won 11, tied 2)
Green Bay, 1929 (won 12, tied 1)
Chi. Bears, 1934 (won 13)
Baltimore, 1967 (won 11, tied 2)
Denver, 1998 (won 13)
12 Canton, 1922 (won 10, tied 2)
Canton, 1923 (won 11, tied 1)
Minnesota, 1969 (won 12)
Chicago, 1985 (won 12)
New England, 2003 (won 12)

Most Consecutive Games Without Defeat, Start of Season
14 Miami, 1972 (won 14), entire season
13 Chi. Bears, 1926 (won 11, tied 2)
Green Bay, 1929 (won 12, tied 1), entire season
Chi. Bears, 1934 (won 13), entire season
Baltimore, 1967 (won 11, tied 2)
Denver, 1998 (won 13)
12 Canton, 1922 (won 10, tied 2), entire season
Canton, 1923 (won 11, tied 1), entire season
Chicago, 1985 (won 12)

Most Consecutive Games Without Defeat, End of Season
14 Miami, 1972 (won 14), entire season
13 Green Bay, 1929 (won 12, tied 1), entire season
Chi. Bears, 1934 (won 13), entire season
12 Canton, 1922 (won 10, tied 2), entire season
Canton, 1923 (won 11, tied 1), entire season
New England, 2003 (won 12)

Most Consecutive Home Games Won
27 Miami, 1971-74
25 Green Bay, 1995-98
24 Denver, 1996-98

Most Consecutive Home Games Without Defeat
30 Green Bay, 1928-1933 (won 27, tied 3)
27 Miami, 1971-74 (won 27)
25 Chi. Bears, 1923-25 (won 19, tied 6)
Green Bay, 1995-98 (won 25)

Most Consecutive Road Games Won
18 San Francisco, 1988-1990
11 L.A. Chargers/San Diego, 1960-61
San Francisco, 1987-88
10 Chi. Bears, 1941-42
Dallas, 1968-69
New Orleans, 1987-88

Most Consecutive Road Games Without Defeat
18 San Francisco, 1988-1990 (won 18)
13 Chi. Bears, 1941-43 (won 12, tied 1)
12 Green Bay, 1928-1930 (won 10, tied 2)

Most Shutout Games Won or Tied, Season
10 Pottsville, 1926 (won 9, tied 1)
N.Y. Giants, 1927 (won 9, tied 1)
9 Akron, 1921 (won 8, tied 1)
Canton, 1922 (won 7, tied 2)
Frankford, 1926 (won 9)
Frankford, 1929 (won 6, tied 3)
8 By many teams

Most Consecutive Shutout Games Won or Tied
13 Akron, 1920-21 (won 10, tied 3)
7 Pottsville, 1926 (won 6, tied 1)
Detroit, 1934 (won 7)
6 Buffalo, 1920-21 (won 5, tied 1)
Frankford, 1926 (won 6)
Detroit, 1926 (won 4, tied 2)
N.Y. Giants, 1926-27 (won 5, tied 1)

GAMES LOST

Most Consecutive Games Lost
26 Tampa Bay, 1976-1977
19 Chi. Cardinals, 1942-43, 1945
Oakland, 1961-62
18 Houston, 1972-73

Most Consecutive Games Without Victory
26 Tampa Bay, 1976-77 (lost 26)
23 Rochester, 1922-25 (lost 21, tied 2)
Washington, 1960-61 (lost 20, tied 3)
19 Dayton, 1927-29 (lost 18, tied 1)
Chi. Cardinals, 1942-43, 1945 (lost 19)
Oakland, 1961-62 (lost 19)

Most Games Lost, Season
15 New Orleans, 1980
Dallas, 1989
New England, 1990
Indianapolis, 1991
N.Y. Jets, 1996
San Diego, 2000
Carolina, 2001
14 By many teams

Most Consecutive Games Lost, Season
15 Carolina, 2001
14 Tampa Bay, 1976
New Orleans, 1980
Baltimore, 1981
New England, 1990
13 Oakland, 1962
Pittsburgh, 1969
Indianapolis, 1986

Most Consecutive Games Lost, Start of Season
14 Tampa Bay, 1976, entire season
New Orleans, 1980
13 Oakland, 1962
Indianapolis, 1986
12 Tampa Bay, 1977
Detroit, 2001

Most Consecutive Games Lost, End of Season
15 Carolina, 2001
14 Tampa Bay, 1976, entire season
New England, 1990
13 Pittsburgh, 1969

Most Consecutive Games Without Victory, Season
15 Carolina, 2001 (lost 15)
14 Tampa Bay, 1976 (lost 14), entire season
New Orleans, 1980 (lost 14)
Baltimore, 1981 (lost 14)
New England, 1990 (lost 14)

13 Washington, 1961 (lost 12, tied 1)
Oakland, 1962 (lost 13)
Pittsburgh, 1969 (lost 13)
Indianapolis, 1986 (lost 13)

Most Consecutive Games Without Victory, Start of Season
14 Tampa Bay, 1976 (lost 14), entire season
New Orleans, 1980 (lost 14)
13 Washington, 1961 (lost 12, tied 1)
Oakland, 1962 (lost 13)
Indianapolis, 1986 (lost 13)
12 Dall. Cowboys, 1960 (lost 11, tied 1), entire season
Tampa Bay, 1977 (lost 12)
Detroit, 2001 (lost 12)

Most Consecutive Games Without Victory, End of Season
15 Carolina, 2001
14 Tampa Bay, 1976, (lost 14), entire season
New England, 1990 (lost 14)
13 Pittsburgh, 1969 (lost 13)

Most Consecutive Home Games Lost
14 Dallas, 1988-89
13 Houston, 1972-73
Tampa Bay, 1976-77
N.Y. Jets, 1995-97
11 Oakland, 1961-62
Los Angeles, 1961-63
Cincinnati, 1998-99

Most Consecutive Home Games Without Victory
14 Dallas, 1988-89 (lost 14)
13 Houston, 1972-73 (lost 13)
Tampa Bay, 1976-77 (lost 13)
N.Y. Jets, 1995-97 (lost 13)
12 Philadelphia, 1936-38 (lost 11, tied 1)

Most Consecutive Road Games Lost
24 Detroit, 2001-03 (current)
23 Houston, 1981-84
22 Buffalo, 1983-86

Most Consecutive Road Games Without Victory
24 Detroit, 2001-03 (lost 24) (current)
23 Houston, 1981-84 (lost 23)
22 Buffalo, 1983-86 (lost 22)

Most Shutout Games Lost or Tied, Season
8 Frankford, 1927 (lost 6, tied 2)
Brooklyn, 1931 (lost 8)
7 Dayton, 1925 (lost 6, tied 1)
Orange, 1929 (lost 4, tied 3)
Frankford, 1931 (lost 6, tied 1)
6 By many teams

Most Consecutive Shutout Games Lost or Tied
8 Rochester, 1922-24 (lost 8)
7 Hammond, 1922-23 (lost 6, tied 1)
6 Providence, 1926-27 (lost 5, tied 1)
Brooklyn, 1942-43 (lost 6)

TIE GAMES

Most Tie Games, Season
6 Chi. Bears, 1932
5 Frankford, 1929
4 Chi. Bears, 1924
Orange, 1929
Portsmouth, 1932

Most Consecutive Tie Games
3 Chi. Bears, 1932
2 By many teams

SCORING

Most Seasons Leading League
10 Chi. Bears, 1932, 1934-35, 1939, 1941-43, 1946-47, 1956
9 San Francisco, 1953, 1965, 1970, 1987, 1989, 1992-95
L.A./St. Louis Rams, 1950-52, 1957, 1967, 1973, 1999-2001
7 Green Bay, 1931, 1936-38, 1961-62, 1996

Most Consecutive Seasons Leading League
4 San Francisco, 1992-1995
3 Green Bay, 1936-38
Chi. Bears, 1941-43
Los Angeles, 1950-52
Oakland, 1967-69
St. Louis, 1999-2001
2 By many teams

POINTS

Most Points, Season
556 Minnesota, 1998
541 Washington, 1983
540 St. Louis, 2000

Fewest Points, Season (Since 1932)
37 Cincinnati/St. Louis, 1934
38 Cincinnati, 1933
Detroit, 1942
51 Pittsburgh, 1934
Philadelphia, 1936

Most Points, Game
72 Washington vs. N.Y. Giants, Nov. 27, 1966
70 Los Angeles vs. Baltimore, Oct. 22, 1950
65 Chi. Cardinals vs. N.Y. Bulldogs, Nov. 13, 1949
Los Angeles vs. Detroit, Oct. 29, 1950

Most Points, Both Teams, Game
113 Washington (72) vs. N.Y. Giants (41), Nov. 27, 1966
101 Oakland (52) vs. Houston (49), Dec. 22, 1963
99 Seattle (51) vs. Kansas City (48), Nov. 27, 1983 (OT)

Fewest Points, Both Teams, Game
0 In many games. Last time: N.Y. Giants vs. Detroit, Nov. 7, 1943

Most Points, Shutout Victory, Game
64 Philadelphia vs. Cincinnati, Nov. 6, 1934
62 Akron vs. Oorang, Oct. 29, 1922
60 Rock Island vs. Evansville, Oct. 15, 1922
Chi. Cardinals vs. Rochester, Oct. 7, 1923

Fewest Points, Shutout Victory, Game
2 Green Bay vs. Chi. Bears, Oct. 16, 1932
Chi. Bears vs. Green Bay, Sept. 18, 1938

Most Points Overcome to Win Game
28 San Francisco vs. New Orleans, Dec. 7, 1980 (OT) (trailed 7-35, won 38-35)
26 Buffalo vs. Indianapolis, Sept., 21, 1997 (trailed 0-26, won 37-35)
25 St. Louis vs. Tampa Bay, Nov. 8, 1987 (trailed 3-28, won 31-28)

Most Points Overcome to Tie Game
31 Denver vs. Buffalo, Nov. 27, 1960 (trailed 7-38, tied 38-38)
28 Los Angeles vs. Philadelphia, Oct. 3, 1948 (trailed 0-28, tied 28-28)

Most Points, Each Half
1st: 49 Green Bay vs. Tampa Bay, Oct. 2, 1983
48 Buffalo vs. Miami, Sept. 18, 1966
45 Green Bay vs. Cleveland, Nov. 12, 1967
Indianapolis vs. Denver, Oct. 31, 1988
Houston vs. Cleveland, Dec. 9, 1990
Seattle vs. Minnesota, Sept. 29, 2002
2nd: 49 Chi. Bears vs. Philadelphia, Nov. 30, 1941
48 Chi. Cardinals vs. Baltimore, Oct. 2, 1950
N.Y. Giants vs. Baltimore, Nov. 19, 1950
45 Cincinnati vs. Houston, Dec. 17, 1972

Most Points, Both Teams, Each Half
1st: 70 Houston (35) vs. Oakland (35), Dec. 22, 1963
62 N.Y. Jets (41) vs. Tampa Bay (21), Nov. 17, 1985
59 St. Louis (31) vs. Philadelphia (28), Dec. 16, 1962

2nd: 65 Washington (38) vs. N.Y. Giants (27), Nov. 27, 1966
62 L.A. Raiders (31) vs. San Diego (31), Jan. 2, 1983
Baltimore (38) vs. Seattle (24), Nov. 23, 2003
58 New England (37) vs. Baltimore (21), Nov. 23, 1980
N.Y. Jets (37) vs. New England (21), Sept. 21, 1987
N.Y. Giants (34) vs. Indianapolis (24), Dec. 22, 2002

Most Points, One Quarter
41 Green Bay vs. Detroit, Oct. 7, 1945 (second quarter)
Los Angeles vs. Detroit, Oct. 29, 1950 (third quarter)
37 Los Angeles vs. Green Bay, Sept. 21, 1980 (second quarter)
35 Chi. Cardinals vs. Boston, Oct. 24, 1948 (third quarter)
Green Bay vs. Cleveland, Nov. 12, 1967 (first quarter)
Green Bay vs. Tampa Bay, Oct. 2, 1983 (second quarter)

Most Points, Both Teams, One Quarter
49 Oakland (28) vs. Houston (21), Dec. 22, 1963 (second quarter)
48 Green Bay (41) vs. Detroit (7), Oct. 7, 1945 (second quarter)
Los Angeles (41) vs. Detroit (7), Oct. 29, 1950 (third quarter)
47 St. Louis (27) vs. Philadelphia (20), Dec. 13, 1964 (second quarter)

Most Points, Each Quarter
1st: 35 Green Bay vs. Cleveland, Nov. 12, 1967
31 Buffalo vs. Kansas City, Sept. 13, 1964
28 By eight teams
2nd: 41 Green Bay vs. Detroit, Oct. 7, 1945
37 Los Angeles vs. Green Bay, Sept. 21, 1980
35 Green Bay vs. Tampa Bay, Oct. 2, 1983
3rd: 41 Los Angeles vs. Detroit, Oct. 29, 1950
35 Chi. Cardinals vs. Boston, Oct. 24, 1948
28 By 10 teams
4th: 31 Oakland vs. Denver, Dec. 17, 1960
Oakland vs. San Diego, Dec. 8, 1963
Atlanta vs. Green Bay, Sept. 13, 1981
30 N.Y. Jets vs. Miami, Oct. 23, 2000
28 By many teams

Most Points, Both Teams, Each Quarter
1st: 42 Green Bay (35) vs. Cleveland (7), Nov. 12, 1967
35 Dall. Texans (21) vs. N.Y. Titans (14), Nov. 11, 1962
Dallas (28) vs. Philadelphia (7), Oct. 19, 1969
Kansas City (21) vs. Seattle (14), Dec. 11, 1977
Detroit (21) vs. L.A. Raiders (14), Dec. 10, 1990
Dallas (21) vs. Atlanta (14), Dec. 22, 1991
34 Los Angeles (21) vs. Baltimore (13), Oct. 22, 1950
Oakland (21) vs. Atlanta (13), Nov. 30, 1975
2nd: 49 Oakland (28) vs. Houston (21), Dec. 22, 1963
48 Green Bay (41) vs. Detroit (7), Oct. 7, 1945
47 St. Louis (27) vs. Philadelphia (20), Dec. 13, 1964
3rd: 48 Los Angeles (41) vs. Detroit (7), Oct. 29, 1950
42 Washington (28) vs. Philadelphia (14), Oct. 1, 1955
41 Green Bay (21) vs. N.Y. Yanks (20), Oct. 8, 1950
4th: 42 Chi. Cardinals (28) vs. Philadelphia (14), Dec. 7, 1947
Green Bay (28) vs. Chi. Bears (14), Nov. 6, 1955
N.Y. Jets (28) vs. Boston (14), Oct. 27, 1968
Pittsburgh (21) vs. Cleveland (21), Oct. 18, 1969
New England (21) vs. Kansas City (21), Sept. 22, 2002
41 Baltimore (27) vs. New England (14), Sept. 18, 1978
New England (27) vs. Baltimore (14), Nov. 23, 1980
40 Chicago (21) vs. Tampa Bay (19), Nov. 19, 1989

Most Consecutive Games Scoring
418 San Francisco, 1977-2003 (current)
274 Cleveland, 1950-1971
218 Dallas, 1970-1985

TOUCHDOWNS

Most Seasons Leading League, Touchdowns
13 Chi. Bears, 1932, 1934-35, 1939, 1941-44, 1946-48, 1956, 1965
7 Dallas, 1966, 1968, 1971, 1973, 1977-78, 1980
San Francisco, 1953, 1970, 1987, 1992-95
L.A./St. Louis Rams, 1949-1952, 1999-2001
6 Oakland, 1967-69, 1972, 1974, 1977
San Diego, 1963, 1965, 1979, 1981-82, 1985
Green Bay, 1932, 1937-38, 1961-62, 1996

Most Consecutive Seasons Leading League, Touchdowns
4 Chi. Bears, 1941-44
Los Angeles, 1949-1952
San Francisco, 1992-95
3 Chi. Bears, 1946-48
Baltimore, 1957-59
Oakland, 1967-69
St. Louis, 1999-2001
2 By many teams

Most Touchdowns, Season
70 Miami, 1984
67 St. Louis, 2000
66 Houston, 1961
San Francisco, 1994
St. Louis, 1999

Fewest Touchdowns, Season (Since 1932)
3 Cincinnati, 1933
4 Cincinnati/St. Louis, 1934
5 Detroit, 1942

Most Touchdowns, Game
10 Philadelphia vs. Cincinnati, Nov. 6, 1934
Los Angeles vs. Baltimore, Oct. 22, 1950
Washington vs. N.Y. Giants, Nov. 27, 1966
9 Chi. Cardinals vs. Rochester, Oct. 7, 1923
Chi. Cardinals vs. N.Y. Giants, Oct. 17, 1948
Chi. Cardinals vs. N.Y. Bulldogs, Nov. 13, 1949
Los Angeles vs. Detroit, Oct. 29, 1950
Pittsburgh vs. N.Y. Giants, Nov. 30, 1952
Chicago vs. San Francisco, Dec. 12, 1965
Chicago vs. Green Bay, Dec. 7, 1980
8 By many teams

Most Touchdowns, Both Teams, Game
16 Washington (10) vs. N.Y. Giants (6), Nov. 27, 1966
14 Chi. Cardinals (9) vs. N.Y. Giants (5), Oct. 17, 1948
Los Angeles (10) vs. Baltimore (4), Oct. 22, 1950
Houston (7) vs. Oakland (7), Dec. 22, 1963
13 New Orleans (7) vs. St. Louis (6), Nov. 2, 1969
Kansas City (7) vs. Seattle (6), Nov. 27, 1983 (OT)
San Diego (8) vs. Pittsburgh (5), Dec. 8, 1985
N.Y. Jets (7) vs. Miami (6), Sept. 21, 1986 (OT)

Most Consecutive Games Scoring Touchdowns
166 Cleveland, 1957-1969
97 Oakland, 1966-1973
Minnesota, 1995-2001
96 Kansas City, 1963-1970

POINTS AFTER TOUCHDOWN

Most (One-Point) Points After Touchdown, Season
66 Miami, 1984
65 Houston, 1961
64 St. Louis, 1999

Fewest (One-Point) Points After Touchdown, Season
2 Chi. Cardinals, 1933
3 Cincinnati, 1933
Pittsburgh, 1934
4 Cincinnati/St. Louis, 1934

Most (One-Point) Points After Touchdown, Game
10 Los Angeles vs. Baltimore, Oct. 22, 1950
9 Chi. Cardinals vs. N.Y. Giants, Oct. 17, 1948
Pittsburgh vs. N.Y. Giants, Nov. 30, 1952

Washington vs. N.Y. Giants, Nov. 27, 1966
8 By many teams

Most (One-Point) Points After Touchdown, Both Teams, Game
14 Chi. Cardinals (9) vs. N.Y. Giants (5), Oct. 17, 1948
Houston (7) vs. Oakland (7), Dec. 22, 1963
Washington (9) vs. N.Y. Giants (5), Nov. 27, 1966
13 Los Angeles (10) vs. Baltimore (3), Oct. 22, 1950
12 In many games

Most Two-Point Conversions, Season
6 Miami, 1994
Minnesota, 1997
5 Arizona, 1995
Baltimore, 1996
Jacksonville, 1996
Chicago, 1997
San Francisco, 1998
Pittsburgh, 2002
4 By many teams

Most Two-Point Conversions, Game
4 St. Louis vs. Atlanta, Oct. 15, 2000
3 Baltimore vs. New England, Oct. 6, 1996
Pittsburgh vs. Tennessee, Nov. 1, 1998
2 By many teams

Most Two-Point Conversions, Both Teams, Game
5 Baltimore (3) vs. New England (2), Oct. 6, 1996
St. Louis (4) vs. Atlanta (1), Oct. 15, 2000
3 Seattle (2) vs. Kansas City (1), Oct. 23, 1994
Minnesota (2) vs. Seattle (1), Nov. 10, 1996
Pittsburgh (3) vs. Tennessee (0), Nov. 1, 1998
2 In many games

FIELD GOALS

Most Seasons Leading League, Field Goals
11 Green Bay, 1935-36, 1940-43, 1946-47, 1955, 1972, 1974
8 Washington, 1945, 1956, 1971, 1976-77, 1979, 1982, 1992
7 N.Y. Giants, 1933, 1937, 1939, 1941, 1944, 1959, 1983
L.A./St. Louis Rams, 1949, 1951, 1958, 1966, 1973, 1978, 2003

Most Consecutive Seasons Leading League, Field Goals
4 Green Bay, 1940-43
3 Cleveland, 1952-54
2 By many teams

Most Field Goals Attempted, Season
49 Los Angeles, 1966
Washington, 1971
48 Green Bay, 1972
47 N.Y. Jets, 1969
Los Angeles, 1973
Washington, 1983

Fewest Field Goals Attempted, Season (Since 1938)
0 Chi. Bears, 1944
2 Cleveland, 1939
Card-Pitt, 1944
Boston, 1946
Chi. Bears, 1947
3 Chi. Bears, 1945
Cleveland, 1945

Most Field Goals Attempted, Game
9 St. Louis vs. Pittsburgh, Sept. 24, 1967
8 Pittsburgh vs. St. Louis, Dec. 2, 1962
Detroit vs. Minnesota, Nov. 13, 1966
N.Y. Jets vs. Buffalo, Nov. 3, 1968
Dallas vs. N.Y. Giants, Sept. 15, 2003 (OT)
7 By many teams

Most Field Goals Attempted, Both Teams, Game
11 St. Louis (6) vs. Pittsburgh (5), Nov. 13, 1966
Washington (6) vs. Chicago (5), Nov. 14, 1971
Green Bay (6) vs. Detroit (5), Sept. 29, 1974
Washington (6) vs. N.Y. Giants (5), Nov. 14, 1976
10 In many games

Most Field Goals, Season
39 Miami, 1999
St. Louis, 2003
37 Carolina, 1996
Indianapolis, 2003
36 Indianapolis, 1996
Tennessee, 1998

Fewest Field Goals, Season (Since 1932)
0 Boston, 1932, 1935
Chi. Cardinals, 1932, 1945
Green Bay, 1932, 1944
N.Y. Giants, 1932
Brooklyn, 1944
Card-Pitt, 1944
Chi. Bears, 1944, 1947
Boston, 1946
Baltimore, 1950
Dallas, 1952

Most Field Goals, Game
7 St. Louis vs. Pittsburgh, Sept. 24, 1967
Minnesota vs. L.A. Rams, Nov. 5, 1989 (OT)
Dallas vs. Green Bay, Nov. 18, 1996
Dallas vs. N.Y. Giants, Sept. 15, 2003 (OT)
6 Boston vs. Denver, Oct. 4, 1964
Detroit vs. Minnesota, Nov. 13, 1966
N.Y. Jets vs. Buffalo, Nov. 3, 1968
Philadelphia vs. Houston, Nov. 12, 1972
N.Y. Jets vs. New Orleans, Dec. 3, 1972
St. Louis vs. Atlanta, Dec. 9, 1973
N.Y. Giants vs. Seattle, Oct. 18, 1981
San Francisco vs. New Orleans, Oct. 16, 1983
Pittsburgh vs. Denver, Oct. 23, 1988
San Diego vs. Seattle, Sept. 5, 1993
San Diego vs. Houston, Sept. 19, 1993
Cincinnati vs. Seattle, Nov. 6, 1994
Atlanta vs. New Orleans, Nov. 13, 1994
San Francisco vs. Atlanta, Sept. 29, 1996
Buffalo vs. N.Y. Jets, Oct. 20, 1996
San Diego vs. Oakland, Oct. 5, 1997
Minnesota vs. Baltimore, Dec. 13, 1998
Detroit vs. Minnesota, Oct. 17, 1999
Miami vs. New England, Oct. 17, 1999
Pittsburgh vs. Jacksonville, Dec. 1, 2002
5 By many teams

Most Field Goals, Both Teams, Game
9 San Diego (5) vs. Kansas City (4), Sept. 29, 1996
Miami (6) vs. New England (3), Oct. 17, 1999
8 Cleveland (4) vs. St. Louis (4), Sept. 20, 1964
Chicago (5) vs. Philadelphia (3), Oct. 20, 1968
Washington (5) vs. Chicago (3), Nov. 14, 1971
Kansas City (5) vs. Buffalo (3), Dec. 19, 1971
Detroit (4) vs. Green Bay (4), Sept. 29, 1974
Cleveland (5) vs. Denver (3), Oct. 19, 1975
New England (4) vs. San Diego (4), Nov. 9, 1975
San Francisco (6) vs. New Orleans (2), Oct. 16, 1983
Seattle (5) vs. L.A. Raiders (3), Dec. 18, 1988
Atlanta (6) vs. New Orleans (2), Nov. 13, 1994
Indianapolis (4) vs. San Diego (4), Nov. 3, 1996
Dallas (7) vs. N.Y. Giants (1), Sept. 15, 2003 (OT)
Oakland (5) vs. Chicago (3), Oct. 5, 2003
7 In many games

Most Consecutive Games Scoring Field Goals
38 Baltimore, 1999-2001
31 Minnesota, 1968-1970
28 Washington, 1988-1990

SAFETIES

Most Safeties, Season

4 Cleveland, 1927
Detroit, 1962
Seattle, 1993
San Francisco, 1996
Tennessee, 1999
3 By many teams

Most Safeties, Game

3 L.A. Rams vs. N.Y. Giants, Sept. 30, 1984
2 N.Y. Giants vs. Pottsville, Oct. 30, 1927
Chi. Bears vs. Pottsville, Nov. 13, 1927
Detroit vs. Brooklyn, Dec. 1, 1935
N.Y. Giants vs. Pittsburgh, Sept. 17, 1950
N.Y. Giants vs. Washington, Nov. 5, 1961
Chicago vs. Pittsburgh, Nov. 9, 1969
Dallas vs. Philadelphia, Nov. 19, 1972
Los Angeles vs. Green Bay, Oct. 21, 1973
Oakland vs. San Diego, Oct. 26, 1975
Denver vs. Seattle, Jan. 2, 1983
New Orleans vs. Cleveland, Sept. 13, 1987
Buffalo vs. Denver, Nov. 8, 1987
San Francisco vs. St. Louis, Sept. 8, 1996
Jacksonville vs. Pittsburgh, Oct. 3, 1999
Minnesota vs. Atlanta, Oct. 5, 2003
Dallas vs. Arizona, Oct. 5, 2003
Buffalo vs. Houston, Nov. 16, 2003

Most Safeties, Both Teams, Game

3 L.A. Rams (3) vs. N.Y. Giants (0), Sept. 30, 1984
2 Chi. Cardinals (1) vs. Frankford (1), Nov. 19, 1927
Chi. Cardinals (1) vs. Cincinnati (1), Nov. 12, 1933
Chi. Bears (1) vs. San Francisco (1), Oct. 19, 1952
Cincinnati (1) vs. Los Angeles (1), Oct. 22, 1972
Chi. Bears (1) vs. San Francisco (1), Sept. 19, 1976
Baltimore (1) vs. Miami (1), Oct. 29, 1978
Atlanta (1) vs. Detroit (1), Oct. 5, 1980
Houston (1) vs. Philadelphia (1), Oct. 2, 1988
Cleveland (1) vs. Seattle (1), Nov. 14, 1993
Arizona (1) vs. Houston (1), Dec. 4, 1994
(Also see previous record)

FIRST DOWNS

Most Seasons Leading League

9 Chi. Bears, 1935, 1939, 1941, 1943, 1945, 1947-49, 1955
7 San Diego, 1965, 1969, 1980-83, 1985
L.A./St. Louis Rams, 1946, 1950-51, 1954, 1957, 1973, 2001
6 San Francisco, 1965, 1987, 1989, 1993-94, 1998

Most Consecutive Seasons Leading League

4 San Diego, 1980-83
3 Chi. Bears, 1947-49
2 By many teams

Most First Downs, Season

387 Miami, 1984
383 Denver, 2000
381 San Francisco, 1998

Fewest First Downs, Season

51 Cincinnati, 1933
64 Pittsburgh, 1935
67 Philadelphia, 1937

Most First Downs, Game

39 N.Y. Jets vs. Miami, Nov. 27, 1988
Washington vs. Detroit, Nov. 4, 1990 (OT)
38 Los Angeles vs. N.Y. Giants, Nov. 13, 1966
37 Green Bay vs. Philadelphia, Nov. 11, 1962

Fewest First Downs, Game

0 N.Y. Giants vs. Green Bay, Oct. 1, 1933
Pittsburgh vs. Boston, Oct. 29, 1933
Philadelphia vs. Detroit, Sept. 20, 1935
N.Y. Giants vs. Washington, Sept. 27, 1942
Denver vs. Houston, Sept. 3, 1966

Most First Downs, Both Teams, Game

64 Seattle (32) vs. Kansas City (32), Nov. 24, 2002
62 San Diego (32) vs. Seattle (30), Sept. 15, 1985
Oakland (31) vs. Kansas City (31), Nov. 5, 2000
59 Miami (31) vs. Buffalo (28), Oct. 9, 1983 (OT)
Seattle (33) vs. Kansas City (26), Nov. 27, 1983 (OT)
N.Y. Jets (32) vs. Miami (27), Sept. 21, 1986 (OT)
N.Y. Jets (39) vs. Miami (20), Nov. 27, 1988
Oakland (31) vs. San Francisco (28), Oct. 8, 2000 (OT)

Fewest First Downs, Both Teams, Game

7 Chi. Cardinals (2) vs. Detroit (5), Sept. 15, 1940
9 Pittsburgh (1) vs. Boston (8), Oct. 27, 1935
Boston (4) vs. Brooklyn (5), Nov. 24, 1935
N.Y. Giants (3) vs. Detroit (6), Nov. 7, 1943
Pittsburgh (4) vs. Chi. Cardinals (5), Nov. 11, 1945
N.Y. Bulldogs (1) vs. Philadelphia (8), Sept. 22, 1949
10 N.Y. Giants (4) vs. Washington (6), Dec. 11, 1960

Most First Downs, Rushing, Season

181 New England, 1978
177 Los Angeles, 1973
176 Chicago, 1985

Fewest First Downs, Rushing, Season

36 Cleveland, 1942
Boston, 1944
39 Brooklyn, 1943
40 Philadelphia, 1940
Detroit, 1945

Most First Downs, Rushing, Game

25 Philadelphia vs. Washington, Dec. 2, 1951
23 St. Louis vs. New Orleans, Oct. 5, 1980
21 Cleveland vs. Philadelphia, Dec. 13, 1959
Green Bay vs. Philadelphia, Nov. 11, 1962
Los Angeles vs. New Orleans, Nov. 25, 1973
Pittsburgh vs. Kansas City, Nov. 7, 1976
New England vs. Denver, Nov. 28, 1976
Oakland vs. Green Bay, Sept. 17, 1978
Buffalo vs. Washington, Nov. 3, 1996
San Francisco vs. Detroit, Dec. 14, 1998

Fewest First Downs, Rushing, Game

0 By many teams. Last time: Pittsburgh vs. Baltimore, Dec. 28, 2003 (OT)

Most First Downs, Rushing, Both Teams, Game

36 Philadelphia (25) vs. Washington (11), Dec. 2, 1951
31 Detroit (18) vs. Washington (13), Sept. 30, 1951
30 Los Angeles (17) vs. Minnesota (13), Nov. 5, 1961
New Orleans (17) vs. Green Bay (13), Sept. 9, 1979
New Orleans (16) vs. San Francisco (14), Nov. 11, 1979
New England (16) vs. Kansas City (14), Oct. 4, 1981

Fewest First Downs, Rushing, Both Teams, Game

1 Oakland (0) vs. Tennessee (1), Sept. 7, 2003
2 Houston (0) vs. Denver (2), Dec. 2, 1962
N.Y. Jets, (1) vs. St. Louis (1), Dec. 3, 1995
Miami (1) vs. San Diego (1), Dec. 19, 1999
New Orleans (0) vs. Baltimore (2), Dec. 19, 1999
3 In many games

Most First Downs, Passing, Season

259 San Diego, 1985
251 Houston, 1990
250 Miami, 1986

Fewest First Downs, Passing, Season

18 Pittsburgh, 1941
23 Brooklyn, 1942
N.Y. Giants, 1944
24 N.Y. Giants, 1943

Most First Downs, Passing, Game

29 N.Y. Giants vs. Cincinnati, Oct. 13, 1985
27 San Diego vs. Seattle, Sept. 15, 1985
26 Miami vs. Cleveland, Dec. 12, 1988

Fewest First Downs, Passing, Game
0 By many teams. Last time: Cleveland vs. Jacksonville, Dec. 3, 2000

Most First Downs, Passing, Both Teams, Game
43 San Diego (23) vs. Cincinnati (20), Dec. 20, 1982
Miami (24) vs. N.Y. Jets (19), Sept. 21, 1986 (OT)
42 San Francisco (22) vs. San Diego (20), Dec. 11, 1982
41 San Diego (27) vs. Seattle (14), Sept. 15, 1985
Miami (26) vs. Cleveland (15), Dec. 12, 1988
Kansas City (23) vs. Oakland (18), Nov. 5, 2000

Fewest First Downs, Passing, Both Teams, Game
0 Brooklyn vs. Pittsburgh, Nov. 29, 1942
1 Green Bay (0) vs. Cleveland (1), Sept. 21, 1941
Pittsburgh (0) vs. Brooklyn (1), Oct. 11, 1942
N.Y. Giants (0) vs. Detroit (1), Nov. 7, 1943
Pittsburgh (0) vs. Chi. Cardinals (1), Nov. 11, 1945
N.Y. Bulldogs (0) vs. Philadelphia (1), Sept. 22, 1949
Chicago (0) vs. Buffalo (1), Oct. 7, 1979
2 In many games

Most First Downs, Penalty, Season
47 Buffalo, 2002
43 Denver, 1994
42 Chicago, 1987

Fewest First Downs, Penalty, Season
2 Brooklyn, 1940
4 Chi. Cardinals, 1940
N.Y. Giants, 1942, 1944
Washington, 1944
Cleveland, 1952
Kansas City, 1969
5 Brooklyn, 1939
Chi. Bears, 1939
Detroit, 1953
Los Angeles, 1953
Houston, 1982

Most First Downs, Penalty, Game
11 Denver vs. Houston, Oct. 6, 1985
9 Chi. Bears vs. Cleveland, Nov. 25, 1951
Baltimore vs. Pittsburgh, Oct. 30, 1977
N.Y. Jets vs. Houston, Sept. 18, 1988
8 Philadelphia vs. Detroit, Dec. 2, 1979
Cincinnati vs. N.Y. Jets, Oct. 6, 1985
Buffalo vs. Houston, Sept. 20, 1987
Houston vs. Atlanta, Sept. 9, 1990
Kansas City vs. L.A. Raiders, Oct. 3, 1993
San Francisco vs. New Orleans, Oct. 11, 1998
Oakland vs. San Francisco, Oct. 8, 2000 (OT)
Philadelphia vs. Chicago, Nov. 3, 2002

Most First Downs, Penalty, Both Teams, Game
12 Buffalo (7) vs. San Francisco (5), Oct. 4, 1998
11 Chi. Bears (9) vs. Cleveland (2), Nov. 25, 1951
Cincinnati (8) vs. N.Y. Jets (3), Oct. 6, 1985
Denver (11) vs. Houston (0), Oct. 6, 1985
Detroit (6) vs. Dallas (5), Nov. 8, 1987
N.Y. Jets (9) vs. Houston (2), Sept. 18, 1988
Kansas City (8) vs. L.A. Raiders (3), Oct. 3, 1993
Detroit (6) vs. San Diego (5), Nov. 11, 1996
Philadelphia (8) vs. Chicago (3), Nov. 3, 2002
10 In many games

NET YARDS GAINED RUSHING AND PASSING

Most Seasons Leading League
12 Chi. Bears, 1932, 1934-35, 1939, 1941-44, 1947, 1949, 1955-56
9 L.A./St. Louis Rams, 1946, 1950-51, 1954, 1957, 1973, 1999-2001
7 San Diego, 1963, 1965, 1980-83, 1985

Most Consecutive Seasons Leading League
4 Chi. Bears, 1941-44
San Diego, 1980-83
3 Baltimore, 1958-1960
Houston, 1960-62
Oakland, 1968-1970
St. Louis, 1999-2001
2 By many teams

Most Yards Gained, Season
7,075 St. Louis, 2000
6,936 Miami, 1984
6,800 San Francisco, 1998

Fewest Yards Gained, Season
1,150 Cincinnati, 1933
1,443 Chi. Cardinals, 1934
1,486 Chi. Cardinals, 1933

Most Yards Gained, Game
735 Los Angeles vs. N.Y. Yanks, Sept. 28, 1951
683 Pittsburgh vs. Chi. Cardinals, Dec. 13, 1958
682 Chi. Bears vs. N.Y. Giants, Nov. 14, 1943

Fewest Yards Gained, Game
–7 Seattle vs. Los Angeles, Nov. 4, 1979
–5 Denver vs. Oakland, Sept. 10, 1967
14 Chi. Cardinals vs. Detroit, Sept. 15, 1940

Most Yards Gained, Both Teams, Game
1,133 Los Angeles (636) vs. N.Y. Yanks (497), Nov. 19, 1950
1,102 San Diego (661) vs. Cincinnati (441), Dec. 20, 1982
1,092 Pittsburgh (645) vs. Atlanta (447), Nov. 10, 2002 (OT)

Fewest Yards Gained, Both Teams, Game
30 Chi. Cardinals (14) vs. Detroit (16), Sept. 15, 1940
136 Chi. Cardinals (50) vs. Green Bay (86), Nov. 18, 1934
154 N.Y. Giants (51) vs. Washington (103), Dec. 11, 1960

Most Consecutive Games, 400 or More Yards Gained
11 San Diego, 1982-83
8 St. Louis, 1999-2000
6 Houston, 1961-62
San Diego, 1981
San Francisco, 1987

Most Consecutive Games, 300 or More Yards Gained
30 Minnesota, 1999-2000
St. Louis, 2000-02
29 Los Angeles, 1949-1951
Minnesota, 2002-03 (current)
26 Miami, 1983-85

RUSHING

Most Seasons Leading League
16 Chi. Bears, 1932, 1934-35, 1939-1942, 1951, 1955-56, 1968, 1977, 1983-86
7 Buffalo, 1962, 1964, 1973, 1975, 1982, 1991-92
6 Cleveland, 1958-59, 1963, 1965-67
San Francisco, 1952-54, 1987, 1998-99

Most Consecutive Seasons Leading League
4 Chi. Bears, 1939-1942
Chi. Bears, 1983-86
3 Detroit, 1936-38
San Francisco, 1952-54
Cleveland, 1965-67
2 By many teams

ATTEMPTS

Most Rushing Attempts, Season
681 Oakland, 1977
674 Chicago, 1984
671 New England, 1978

Fewest Rushing Attempts, Season
211 Philadelphia, 1982
219 San Francisco, 1982
225 Houston, 1982

Most Rushing Attempts, Game
72 Chi. Bears vs. Brooklyn, Oct. 20, 1935
70 Chi. Cardinals vs. Green Bay, Dec. 5, 1948
69 Chi. Cardinals vs. Green Bay, Dec. 6, 1936

Kansas City vs. Cincinnati, Sept. 3, 1978

Fewest Rushing Attempts, Game
6 Chi. Cardinals vs. Boston, Oct. 29, 1933
7 Oakland vs. Buffalo, Oct. 15, 1963
Houston vs. N.Y. Giants, Dec. 8, 1985
Seattle vs. L.A. Raiders, Nov. 17, 1991
Green Bay vs. Miami, Sept. 11, 1994
8 Denver vs. Oakland, Dec. 17, 1960
Buffalo vs. St. Louis, Sept. 9, 1984
Detroit vs. San Francisco, Oct. 20, 1991
Atlanta vs. Detroit, Sept. 5, 1993
St. Louis vs. San Francisco, Nov. 2, 2003

Most Rushing Attempts, Both Teams, Game
108 Chi. Cardinals (70) vs. Green Bay (38), Dec. 5, 1948
105 Oakland (62) vs. Atlanta (43), Nov. 30, 1975 (OT)
104 Chi. Bears (64) vs. Pittsburgh (40), Oct. 18, 1936

Fewest Rushing Attempts, Both Teams, Game
34 Atlanta (12) vs. Houston (22), Dec. 5, 1993
Atlanta (15) vs. San Francisco (19), Dec. 24, 1995
35 Seattle (15) vs. New Orleans (20), Sept. 1, 1991
Oakland (17) vs. Pittsburgh (18), Sept. 15, 2002
36 Houston (15) vs. N.Y. Jets (21), Oct. 13, 1991
St. Louis (16) vs. Detroit (20), Nov. 7, 1999
Detroit (15) vs. Washington (21), Dec. 5, 1999
Tennessee (14) vs. Baltimore (22), Dec. 5, 1999
Tampa Bay (16) vs. St. Louis (20), Sept. 23, 2002
Oakland (14) vs. Denver (22), Nov. 11, 2002

YARDS GAINED

Most Yards Gained Rushing, Season
3,165 New England, 1978
3,088 Buffalo, 1973
2,986 Kansas City, 1978

Fewest Yards Gained Rushing, Season
298 Philadelphia, 1940
467 Detroit, 1946
471 Boston, 1944

Most Yards Gained Rushing, Game
426 Detroit vs. Pittsburgh, Nov. 4, 1934
423 N.Y. Giants vs. Baltimore, Nov. 19, 1950
420 Boston vs. N.Y. Giants, Oct. 8, 1933

Fewest Yards Gained Rushing, Game
–53 Detroit vs. Chi. Cardinals, Oct. 17, 1943
–36 Philadelphia vs. Chi. Bears, Nov. 19, 1939
–33 Phil-Pitt vs. Brooklyn, Oct. 2, 1943

Most Yards Gained Rushing, Both Teams, Game
595 Los Angeles (371) vs. N.Y. Yanks (224), Nov. 18, 1951
574 Chi. Bears (396) vs. Pittsburgh (178), Oct. 10, 1934
558 Boston (420) vs. N.Y. Giants (138), Oct. 8, 1933

Fewest Yards Gained Rushing, Both Teams, Game
–15 Detroit (–53) vs. Chi. Cardinals (38), Oct. 17, 1943
4 Detroit (–10) vs. Chi. Cardinals (14), Sept. 15, 1940
62 L.A. Rams (15) vs. San Francisco (47), Dec. 6, 1964

AVERAGE GAIN

Highest Average Gain, Rushing, Season
5.74 Cleveland, 1963
5.65 San Francisco, 1954
5.56 San Diego, 1963

Lowest Average Gain, Rushing, Season
0.94 Philadelphia, 1940
1.45 Boston, 1944
1.55 Pittsburgh, 1935

TOUCHDOWNS

Most Touchdowns, Rushing, Season
36 Green Bay, 1962
33 Pittsburgh, 1976
32 Kansas City, 2003

Fewest Touchdowns, Rushing, Season
1 Brooklyn, 1934
2 Chi. Cardinals, 1933
Cincinnati, 1933
Pittsburgh, 1934
Philadelphia, 1935
Philadelphia, 1936
Philadelphia, 1937
Philadelphia, 1938
Pittsburgh, 1940
Philadelphia, 1972
N.Y. Jets, 1995
3 By many teams

Most Touchdowns, Rushing, Game
7 Los Angeles vs. Atlanta, Dec. 4, 1976
6 By many teams

Most Touchdowns, Rushing, Both Teams, Game
8 Los Angeles (6) vs. N.Y. Yanks (2), Nov. 18, 1951
Chi. Bears (5) vs. Green Bay (3), Nov. 6, 1955
Denver (5) vs. Kansas City (3), Dec. 7, 2003
7 In many games

PASSING

ATTEMPTS

Most Passes Attempted, Season
709 Minnesota, 1981
699 New England, 1994
686 New England, 1995

Fewest Passes Attempted, Season
102 Cincinnati, 1933
106 Boston, 1933
120 Detroit, 1937

Most Passes Attempted, Game
70 New England vs. Minnesota, Nov. 13, 1994 (OT)
69 N.Y. Jets vs. Baltimore, Dec. 24, 2000
68 Houston vs. Buffalo, Nov 1, 1964
Cincinnati vs. Pittsburgh, Dec. 30, 2001 (OT)

Fewest Passes Attempted, Game
0 Green Bay vs. Portsmouth, Oct. 8, 1933
Detroit vs. Cleveland, Sept. 10, 1937
Pittsburgh vs. Brooklyn, Nov. 16, 1941
Pittsburgh vs. Los Angeles, Nov. 13, 1949
Cleveland vs. Philadelphia, Dec. 3, 1950

Most Passes Attempted, Both Teams, Game
112 New England (70) vs. Minnesota (42), Nov. 13, 1994
104 Miami (55) vs. N.Y. Jets (49), Oct. 18, 1987 (OT)
N.Y. Jets (58) vs. San Francisco (46), Sept. 6, 1998 (OT)
103 Cincinnati (68) vs. Pittsburgh (35), Dec. 30, 2001 (OT)
Seattle (53) vs. San Diego (50), Dec. 29, 2002 (OT)

Fewest Passes Attempted, Both Teams, Game
4 Chi. Cardinals (1) vs. Detroit (3), Nov. 3, 1935
Detroit (0) vs. Cleveland (4), Sept. 10, 1937
6 Chi. Cardinals (2) vs. Detroit (4), Sept. 15, 1940
8 Brooklyn (2) vs. Philadelphia (6), Oct. 1, 1939

COMPLETIONS

Most Passes Completed, Season
432 San Francisco, 1995
418 Oakland, 2002
411 Houston, 1991

Fewest Passes Completed, Season
25 Cincinnati, 1933
33 Boston, 1933
34 Chi. Cardinals, 1934
Detroit, 1934

Most Passes Completed, Game
45 New England vs. Minnesota, Nov. 13, 1994 (OT)
43 Washington vs. Detroit, Nov. 4, 1990 (OT)
Oakland vs. Pittsburgh, Sept. 15, 2002
42 N.Y. Jets vs. San Francisco, Sept. 21, 1980

N.Y. Jets vs. Seattle, Dec. 6, 1998

Fewest Passes Completed, Game
0 By many teams. Last time: Buffalo vs. N.Y. Jets, Sept. 29, 1974

Most Passes Completed, Both Teams, Game
71 New England (45) vs. Minnesota (26), Nov. 13, 1994
68 San Francisco (37) vs. Atlanta (31), Oct. 6, 1985
Denver (34) vs. Oakland (34), Nov. 11, 2002
66 Cincinnati (40) vs. San Diego (26), Dec. 20, 1982

Fewest Passes Completed, Both Teams, Game
1 Chi. Cardinals (0) vs. Philadelphia (1), Nov. 8, 1936
Detroit (0) vs. Cleveland (1), Sept. 10, 1937
Chi. Cardinals (0) vs. Detroit (1), Sept. 15, 1940
Brooklyn (0) vs. Pittsburgh (1), Nov. 29, 1942
2 Chi. Cardinals (0) vs. Detroit (2), Nov. 3, 1935
Buffalo (0) vs. N.Y. Jets (2), Sept. 29, 1974
Chi. Cardinals (0) vs. Green Bay (2), Nov. 18, 1934
3 In seven games

YARDS GAINED

Most Seasons Leading League, Passing Yardage
10 San Diego, 1965, 1968, 1971, 1978-1983, 1985
8 Chi. Bears, 1932, 1939, 1941, 1943, 1945, 1949, 1954, 1964
Washington, 1938, 1940, 1944, 1947-48, 1967, 1974, 1989
7 Houston, 1960-61, 1963-64, 1990-92
L.A./St. Louis Rams, 1946, 1950-51, 1956, 1999-2001

Most Consecutive Seasons Leading League, Passing Yardage
6 San Diego, 1978-1983
4 Green Bay, 1934-37
3 Miami, 1986-88
Houston, 1990-92
St. Louis, 1999-2001

Most Yards Gained, Passing, Season
5,232 St. Louis, 2000
5,018 Miami, 1984
4,870 San Diego, 1985

Fewest Yards Gained, Passing, Season
302 Chi. Cardinals, 1934
357 Cincinnati, 1933
459 Boston, 1934

Most Yards Gained, Passing, Game
554 Los Angeles vs. N.Y. Yanks, Sept. 28, 1951
530 Minnesota vs. Baltimore, Sept. 28, 1969
521 Miami vs. N.Y. Jets, Oct. 23, 1988

Fewest Yards Gained, Passing, Game
–53 Denver vs. Oakland, Sept. 10, 1967
–52 Cincinnati vs. Houston, Oct. 31, 1971
–39 Atlanta vs. San Francisco, Oct. 23, 1976

Most Yards Gained, Passing, Both Teams, Game
884 N.Y. Jets (449) vs. Miami (435), Sept. 21, 1986 (OT)
883 San Diego (486) vs. Cincinnati (397), Dec. 20, 1982
874 Miami (456) vs. New England (418), Sept. 4, 1994

Fewest Yards Gained, Passing, Both Teams, Game
–11 Green Bay (–10) vs. Dallas (–1), Oct. 24, 1965
1 Chi. Cardinals (0) vs. Philadelphia (1), Nov. 8, 1936
7 Brooklyn (0) vs. Pittsburgh (7), Nov. 29, 1942

TIMES SACKED

Most Seasons Leading League, Fewest Times Sacked
10 Miami, 1973, 1982-1990
5 N.Y. Jets, 1965-66, 1968, 1993, 2000
4 San Diego, 1963-64, 1967-68
San Francisco, 1964-65, 1970-71

Most Consecutive Seasons Leading League, Fewest Times Sacked
9 Miami, 1982-1990
3 St. Louis, 1974-76
2 By many teams

Most Times Sacked, Season
104 Philadelphia, 1986
78 Arizona, 1997
76 Houston, 2002

Fewest Times Sacked, Season
7 Miami, 1988
8 San Francisco, 1970
St. Louis, 1975
9 N.Y. Jets, 1966
Washington, 1991

Most Times Sacked, Game
12 Pittsburgh vs. Dallas, Nov. 20, 1966
Baltimore vs. St. Louis, Oct. 26, 1980
Detroit vs. Chicago, Dec. 16, 1984
Houston vs. Dallas, Sept. 29, 1985
11 St. Louis vs. N.Y. Giants, Nov. 1, 1964
Los Angeles vs. Baltimore, Nov. 22, 1964
Denver vs. Buffalo, Dec. 13, 1964
Green Bay vs. Detroit, Nov. 7, 1965
Buffalo vs. Oakland, Oct. 15, 1967
Denver vs. Oakland, Nov. 5, 1967
Atlanta vs. St. Louis, Nov. 24, 1968
Detroit vs. Dallas, Oct. 6, 1975
Philadelphia vs. St. Louis, Dec. 18, 1983
Cleveland vs. Kansas City, Sept. 30, 1984
Minnesota vs. Chicago, Oct. 28, 1984
Atlanta vs. Cleveland, Nov. 18, 1984
Dallas vs. San Diego, Nov. 16, 1986
Philadelphia vs. Detroit, Nov. 16, 1986
Philadelphia vs. L.A. Raiders, Nov. 30, 1986 (OT)
L.A. Raiders vs. Seattle, Dec. 8, 1986
N.Y. Jets vs. Dallas, Oct. 4, 1987
Philadelphia vs. Chicago, Oct. 4, 1987
Dallas vs. Philadelphia, Sept. 15, 1991
Cleveland vs. Indianapolis, Sept. 6, 1992
10 By many teams

Most Times Sacked, Both Teams, Game
18 Green Bay (10) vs. San Diego (8), Sept. 24, 1978
17 Buffalo (10) vs. N.Y. Titans (7), Nov. 23, 1961
Pittsburgh (12) vs. Dallas (5), Nov. 20, 1966
Atlanta (9) vs. Philadelphia (8), Dec. 16, 1984
Philadelphia (11) vs. L.A. Raiders (6), Nov. 30, 1986 (OT)
16 Los Angeles (11) vs. Baltimore (5), Nov. 22, 1964
Buffalo (11) vs. Oakland (5), Oct. 15, 1967

COMPLETION PERCENTAGE

Most Seasons Leading League, Completion Percentage
14 San Francisco, 1952, 1957-58, 1965, 1981, 1983, 1987, 1989, 1992-97
11 Washington, 1937, 1939-1940, 1942-45, 1947-48, 1969-1970
8 Green Bay, 1936, 1941, 1961-62, 1964, 1966, 1968, 1998

Most Consecutive Seasons Leading League, Completion Percentage
6 San Francisco, 1992-97
4 Washington, 1942-45
Kansas City, 1966-69
3 Cleveland, 1953-55
St. Louis, 1999-2001

Highest Completion Percentage, Season
70.65 Cincinnati, 1982 (310-219)
70.25 San Francisco, 1994 (511-359)
70.19 San Francisco, 1989 (483-339)

Lowest Completion Percentage, Season
22.9 Philadelphia, 1936 (170-39)
24.5 Cincinnati, 1933 (102-25)
25.0 Pittsburgh, 1941 (168-42)

TOUCHDOWNS

Most Touchdowns, Passing, Season

49 Miami, 1984
48 Houston, 1961
46 Miami, 1986

Fewest Touchdowns, Passing, Season

0 Cincinnati, 1933
Pittsburgh, 1945
1 Boston, 1932
Boston, 1933
Chi. Cardinals, 1934
Cincinnati/St. Louis, 1934
Detroit, 1942
2 Chi. Cardinals, 1932
Stapleton, 1932
Chi. Cardinals, 1935
Brooklyn, 1936
Pittsburgh, 1942

Most Touchdowns, Passing, Game

7 Chi. Bears vs. N.Y. Giants, Nov. 14, 1943
Philadelphia vs. Washington, Oct. 17, 1954
Houston vs. N.Y. Titans, Nov. 19, 1961
Houston vs. N.Y. Titans, Oct. 14, 1962
N.Y. Giants vs. Washington, Oct. 28, 1962
Minnesota vs. Baltimore, Sept. 28, 1969
San Diego vs. Oakland, Nov. 22, 1981
6 By many teams

Most Touchdowns, Passing, Both Teams, Game

12 New Orleans (6) vs. St. Louis (6), Nov. 2, 1969
11 N.Y. Giants (7) vs. Washington (4), Oct. 28, 1962
Oakland (6) vs. Houston (5), Dec. 22, 1963
10 San Diego (5) vs. Seattle (5), Sept. 15, 1985
Miami (6) vs. N.Y. Jets (4), Sept. 21, 1986 (OT)
San Francisco (6) vs. Atlanta (4), Oct. 14, 1990

PASSES HAD INTERCEPTED

Most Passes Had Intercepted, Season

48 Houston, 1962
45 Denver, 1961
41 Card-Pitt, 1944

Fewest Passes Had Intercepted, Season

5 Cleveland, 1960
Green Bay, 1966
Kansas City, 1990
N.Y. Giants, 1990
6 Green Bay, 1964
St. Louis, 1982
Dallas, 1993
7 Los Angeles, 1969

Most Passes Had Intercepted, Game

9 Detroit vs. Green Bay, Oct. 24, 1943
Pittsburgh vs. Philadelphia, Dec. 12, 1965
8 Green Bay vs. N.Y. Giants, Nov. 21, 1948
Chi. Cardinals vs. Philadelphia, Sept. 24, 1950
N.Y. Yanks vs. N.Y. Giants, Dec. 16, 1951
Denver vs. Houston, Dec. 2, 1962
Chi. Bears vs. Detroit, Sept. 22, 1968
Baltimore vs. N.Y. Jets, Sept. 23, 1973
7 By many teams. Last time: Detroit vs. Cleveland, Sept. 23, 2001

Most Passes Had Intercepted, Both Teams, Game

13 Denver (8) vs. Houston (5), Dec. 2, 1962
11 Philadelphia (7) vs. Boston (4), Nov. 3, 1935
Boston (6) vs. Pittsburgh (5), Dec. 1, 1935
Cleveland (7) vs. Green Bay (4), Oct. 30, 1938
Green Bay (7) vs. Detroit (4), Oct. 20, 1940
Detroit (7) vs. Chi. Bears (4), Nov. 22, 1942
Detroit (7) vs. Cleveland (4), Nov. 26, 1944
Chi. Cardinals (8) vs. Philadelphia (3), Sept. 24, 1950
Washington (7) vs. N.Y. Giants (4), Dec. 8, 1963
Pittsburgh (9) vs. Philadelphia (2), Dec 12, 1965
10 In many games

PUNTING

Most Seasons Leading League (Average Distance)

7 Denver 1962-64, 1966-67, 1982, 1999
6 Washington, 1940-43, 1945, 1958
Kansas City, 1968, 1971-73, 1979, 1984
5 L.A. Rams, 1946, 1949, 1955-56, 1994
Oakland, 1974-75, 1977-78, 2003

Most Consecutive Seasons Leading League (Average Distance)

4 Washington, 1940-43
3 Cleveland, 1950-52
Denver, 1962-64
Kansas City, 1971-73

Most Punts, Season

116 Houston, 2002
114 Chicago, 1981
113 Boston, 1934
Brooklyn, 1934
Dallas, 2002

Fewest Punts, Season

23 San Diego, 1982
31 Cincinnati, 1982
32 Chi. Bears, 1941

Most Punts, Game

17 Chi. Bears vs. Green Bay, Oct. 22, 1933
Cincinnati vs. Pittsburgh, Oct. 22, 1933
16 Cincinnati vs. Portsmouth, Sept. 17, 1933
Chi. Cardinals vs. Chi. Bears, Nov. 30, 1933
Chi. Cardinals vs. Detroit, Sept. 15, 1940
Oakland vs. San Diego, Oct. 11, 1998
15 N.Y. Giants vs. Chi. Bears, Nov. 17, 1935
Philadelphia vs. N.Y. Giants, Dec. 6, 1987 (OT)

Fewest Punts, Game

0 By many teams. Last time:
Miami vs. N.Y. Jets, Dec. 28, 2003

Most Punts, Both Teams, Game

31 Chi. Bears (17) vs. Green Bay (14), Oct. 22, 1933
Cincinnati (17), vs. Pittsburgh (14), Oct. 22, 1933
29 Chi. Cardinals (15) vs. Cincinnati (14), Nov. 12, 1933
Chi. Cardinals (16) vs. Chi. Bears (13), Nov. 30, 1933
Chi. Cardinals (16) vs. Detroit (13), Sept. 15, 1940
28 Philadelphia (14) vs. Washington (14), Nov. 5, 1939

Fewest Punts, Both Teams, Game

0 Buffalo vs. San Francisco, Sept. 13, 1992
1 Baltimore (0) vs. Cleveland (1), Nov. 1, 1959
Dall. Cowboys (0) vs. Cleveland (1), Dec. 3, 1961
Chicago (0) vs. Detroit (1), Oct. 1, 1972
San Francisco (0) vs. N.Y. Giants (1), Oct. 15, 1972
Green Bay (0) vs. Buffalo (1), Dec. 5, 1982
Miami (0) vs. Buffalo (1), Oct. 12, 1986
Green Bay (0) vs. Chicago (1), Dec. 17, 1989
Oakland (0) vs. Seattle (1), Dec. 5, 1999
Tampa Bay (0) vs. Minnesota (1), Oct. 29, 2000
New Orleans (0) vs. San Francisco (1), Oct. 20, 2002
2 In many games

AVERAGE YARDAGE

Highest Average Distance, Punting, Season

47.6 Detroit, 1961 (56-2,664)
47.2 Tennessee, 1998 (69-3,258)
47.0 Carolina, 2001 (94-4,419)

Lowest Average Distance, Punting, Season

32.7 Card-Pitt, 1944 (60-1,964)
33.8 Cincinnati, 1986 (59-1,996)
33.9 Detroit, 1969 (74-2,510)

PUNT RETURNS

Most Seasons Leading League (Average Return)

9 Detroit, 1943-45, 1951-52, 1962, 1966, 1969, 1991
7 Chi. Cardinals/St. Louis, 1948-49, 1955-56, 1959, 1986-87
6 Green Bay, 1950, 1953-54, 1961, 1972, 1996
Dallas/Kansas City, 1960, 1968, 1970, 1979-1980, 2003

Most Consecutive Seasons Leading League (Average Return)

3 Detroit, 1943-45
2 By many teams

Most Punt Returns, Season

71 Pittsburgh, 1976
Tampa Bay, 1979
L.A. Raiders, 1985
67 Pittsburgh, 1974
Los Angeles, 1978
L.A. Raiders, 1984
65 San Francisco, 1976

Fewest Punt Returns, Season

12 Baltimore, 1981
San Diego, 1982
14 Los Angeles, 1961
Philadelphia, 1962
Baltimore, 1982
15 Houston, 1960
Washington, 1960
Oakland, 1961
N.Y. Giants, 1969
Philadelphia, 1973
Kansas City, 1982

Most Punt Returns, Game

12 Philadelphia vs. Cleveland, Dec. 3, 1950
11 Chi. Bears vs. Chi. Cardinals, Oct. 8, 1950
Washington vs. Tampa Bay, Oct. 9, 1977
10 Philadelphia vs. N.Y. Giants, Nov. 26, 1950
Philadelphia vs. Tampa Bay, Sept. 18, 1977
Pittsburgh vs. Buffalo, Dec. 16, 1979
Washington vs. New Orleans, Dec. 26, 1982
Philadelphia vs. Seattle, Dec. 13, 1992 (OT)
New England vs. Pittsburgh, Dec. 5, 1993

Most Punt Returns, Both Teams, Game

17 Philadelphia (12) vs. Cleveland (5), Dec. 3, 1950
16 N.Y. Giants (9) vs. Philadelphia (7), Dec. 12, 1954
Washington (11) vs. Tampa Bay (5), Oct. 9, 1977
Oakland (8) vs. San Diego (8), Oct. 11, 1998
15 Detroit (8) vs. Cleveland (7), Sept. 27, 1942
Los Angeles (8) vs. Baltimore (7), Nov. 27, 1966
Pittsburgh (8) vs. Houston (7), Dec. 1, 1974
Philadelphia (10) vs. Tampa Bay (5), Sept. 18, 1977
Baltimore (9) vs. Kansas City (6), Sept. 2, 1979
Washington (10) vs. New Orleans (5), Dec. 26, 1982
L.A. Raiders (8) vs. Cleveland (7), Nov. 16, 1986

FAIR CATCHES

Most Fair Catches, Season

34 Baltimore, 1971
33 Philadelphia, 2000
32 San Diego, 1969
Oakland, 2001

Fewest Fair Catches, Season

0 San Diego, 1975
New England, 1976
Tampa Bay, 1976
Pittsburgh, 1977
Dallas, 1982
1 Cleveland, 1974
San Francisco, 1975
Kansas City, 1976
St. Louis, 1976
San Diego, 1976
L.A. Rams, 1982
St. Louis, 1982
Tampa Bay, 1982
Arizona, 2001
2 By many teams

Most Fair Catches, Game

7 Minnesota vs. Dallas, Sept. 25, 1966
N.Y. Jets vs. Miami, Nov. 20, 1966
Detroit vs. Chicago, Nov. 21, 1976
Philadelphia vs. Buffalo, Dec. 27, 1987
6 By many teams

YARDS GAINED

Most Yards, Punt Returns, Season

875 Green Bay, 1996
785 L.A. Raiders, 1985
781 Chi. Bears, 1948

Fewest Yards, Punt Returns, Season

27 St. Louis, 1965
35 N.Y. Giants, 1965
37 New England, 1972

Most Yards, Punt Returns, Game

231 Detroit vs. San Francisco, Oct. 6, 1963
225 Oakland vs. Buffalo, Sept. 15, 1968
219 Los Angeles vs. Atlanta, Oct. 11, 1981

Fewest Yards, Punt Returns, Game

-28 Washington vs. Dallas, Dec. 11, 1966
-23 N.Y. Giants vs. Buffalo, Oct. 20, 1975
Pittsburgh vs. Houston, Sept. 20, 1970
-20 New Orleans vs. Pittsburgh, Oct. 20, 1968

Most Yards, Punt Returns, Both Teams, Game

282 Los Angeles (219) vs. Atlanta (63), Oct. 11, 1981
245 Detroit (231) vs. San Francisco (14), Oct. 6, 1963
244 Oakland (225) vs. Buffalo (19), Sept. 15, 1968

Fewest Yards, Punt Returns, Both Teams, Game

-18 Buffalo (-18) vs. Pittsburgh (0), Oct. 29, 1972
-14 Miami (-14) vs. Boston (0), Nov. 30, 1969
Tennessee (-14) vs. New Orleans (0), Sept. 21, 2003
-13 N.Y. Giants (-13) vs. Cleveland (0), Nov. 14, 1965

AVERAGE YARDS RETURNING PUNTS

Highest Average, Punt Returns, Season

20.2 Chi. Bears, 1941 (27-546)
19.1 Chi. Cardinals, 1948 (35-669)
18.2 Chi. Cardinals, 1949 (30-546)

Lowest Average, Punt Returns, Season

1.2 St. Louis, 1965 (23-27)
1.5 N.Y. Giants, 1965 (24-35)
1.7 Washington, 1970 (27-45)

TOUCHDOWNS RETURNING PUNTS

Most Touchdowns, Punt Returns, Season

5 Chi. Cardinals, 1959
4 Chi. Cardinals, 1948
Detroit, 1951
N.Y. Giants, 1951
Denver, 1976
3 Washington, 1941
Detroit, 1952
Pittsburgh, 1952
Houston, 1975
Los Angeles, 1981
Cleveland, 1993
Green Bay, 1996
Denver, 1997
San Diego, 1997

Most Touchdowns, Punt Returns, Game
2 Detroit vs. Los Angeles, Oct. 14, 1951
Detroit vs. Green Bay, Nov. 22, 1951
Chi. Cardinals vs. Pittsburgh, Nov. 1, 1959
Chi. Cardinals vs. N.Y. Giants, Nov. 22, 1959
N.Y. Titans vs. Denver, Sept. 24, 1961
Denver vs. Cleveland, Sept. 26, 1976
Los Angeles vs. Atlanta, Oct. 11, 1981
St. Louis vs. Tampa Bay, Dec. 21, 1986
L.A. Rams vs. Atlanta, Dec. 27, 1992
Cleveland vs. Pittsburgh, Oct. 24, 1993
San Diego vs. Cincinnati, Nov. 2, 1997
Denver vs. Carolina, Nov. 9, 1997
Baltimore vs. Seattle, Dec. 7, 1997
Baltimore vs. N.Y. Jets, Dec. 24, 2000
Oakland vs. Tennessee, Sept. 29, 2002
Carolina vs. Cincinnati, Dec. 8, 2002

Most Touchdowns, Punt Returns, Both Teams, Game
2 Philadelphia (1) vs. Washington (1), Nov. 9, 1952
Kansas City (1) vs. Buffalo (1), Sept. 11, 1966
Baltimore (1) vs. New England (1), Nov. 18, 1979
L.A. Raiders (1) vs. Philadelphia (1), Nov. 30, 1986 (OT)
Cincinnati (1) vs. Green Bay (1), Sept. 20, 1992
Oakland (1) vs. Seattle (1), Nov. 15, 1998
Atlanta (1) vs. Tennessee (1), Nov. 23, 2003
(Also see previous record)

KICKOFF RETURNS

Most Seasons Leading League (Average Return)
8 Washington, 1942, 1947, 1962-63, 1973-74, 1981, 1995
6 Chicago Bears, 1943, 1948, 1958, 1966, 1972, 1985
5 N.Y. Giants, 1944, 1946, 1949, 1951, 1953

Most Consecutive Seasons Leading League (Average Return)
3 Denver, 1965-67
2 By many teams

Most Kickoff Returns, Season
89 Cleveland, 1999
88 New Orleans, 1980
87 Atlanta, 1996
New Orleans, 2001

Fewest Kickoff Returns, Season
17 N.Y. Giants, 1944
20 N.Y. Giants, 1941, 1943
Chi. Bears, 1942
23 Washington, 1942

Most Kickoff Returns, Game
12 N.Y. Giants vs. Washington, Nov. 27, 1966
10 By many teams

Most Kickoff Returns, Both Teams, Game
19 N.Y. Giants (12) vs. Washington (7), Nov. 27, 1966
18 Houston (10) vs. Oakland (8), Dec. 22, 1963
17 Washington (9) vs. Green Bay (8), Oct. 17, 1983
San Diego (9) vs. Pittsburgh (8), Dec. 8, 1985
Detroit (9) vs. Green Bay (8), Nov. 27, 1986
L.A. Raiders (9) vs. Seattle (8), Dec. 18, 1988
Oakland (10) vs. Seattle (7), Oct. 26, 1997
Buffalo (9) vs. Minnesota (8), Sept. 15, 2002 (OT)

YARDS GAINED

Most Yards, Kickoff Returns, Season
2,296 Arizona, 2000
2,039 Detroit, 2002
2,027 New Orleans, 2001

Fewest Yards, Kickoff Returns, Season
282 N.Y. Giants, 1940
381 Green Bay, 1940
424 Chicago, 1963

Most Yards, Kickoff Returns, Game
367 Baltimore vs. Minnesota, Dec. 13, 1998
362 Detroit vs. Los Angeles, Oct. 29, 1950
304 Chi. Bears vs. Green Bay, Nov. 9, 1952
New Orleans vs. L.A. Rams, Oct. 23, 1994

Most Yards, Kickoff Returns, Both Teams, Game
560 Detroit (362) vs. Los Angeles (198), Oct. 29, 1950
511 Baltimore (367) vs. Minnesota (144), Dec. 13, 1998
501 New Orleans (304) vs. L.A. Rams (197), Oct. 23, 1994

AVERAGE YARDAGE

Highest Average, Kickoff Returns, Season
29.4 Chicago, 1972 (52-1,528)
28.9 Pittsburgh, 1952 (39-1,128)
28.2 Washington, 1962 (61-1,720)

Lowest Average, Kickoff Returns, Season
14.7 N.Y. Jets, 1993 (46-675)
15.8 N.Y. Giants, 1993 (32-507)
15.9 Tampa Bay, 1993 (58-922)

TOUCHDOWNS

Most Touchdowns, Kickoff Returns, Season
4 Green Bay, 1967
Chicago, 1970
Detroit, 1994
3 Los Angeles, 1950
Chi. Cardinals, 1954
San Francisco, 1963
Denver, 1966
Chicago, 1967
New England, 1977
L.A. Rams, 1985
Atlanta, 2000
2 By many teams

Most Touchdowns, Kickoff Returns, Game
2 Chi. Bears vs. Green Bay, Sept. 22, 1940
Chi. Bears vs. Green Bay, Nov. 9, 1952
Philadelphia vs. Dallas, Nov. 6, 1966
Green Bay vs. Cleveland, Nov. 12, 1967
L.A. Rams vs. Green Bay, Nov. 24, 1985
New Orleans vs. L.A. Rams, Oct. 23, 1994
Baltimore vs. Minnesota, Dec. 13, 1998
N.Y. Jets vs. Buffalo, Sept. 8, 2002 (OT)

Most Touchdowns, Kickoff Returns, Both Teams, Game
3 Baltimore (2) vs. Minnesota (1), Dec. 13, 1998
2 In many games

FUMBLES

Most Fumbles, Season
56 Chi. Bears, 1938
San Francisco, 1978
54 Philadelphia, 1946
51 New England, 1973

Fewest Fumbles, Season
7 Kansas City, 2002
8 Cleveland, 1959
10 Indianapolis, 1998
Minnesota, 1998

Most Fumbles, Game
10 Phil-Pitt vs. N.Y. Giants, Oct. 9, 1943
Detroit vs. Minnesota, Nov. 12, 1967
Kansas City vs. Houston, Oct. 12, 1969
San Francisco vs. Detroit, Dec. 17, 1978
9 Philadelphia vs. Green Bay, Oct. 13, 1946
Kansas City vs. San Diego, Nov. 15, 1964
N.Y. Giants vs. Buffalo, Oct. 20, 1975
St. Louis vs. Washington, Oct. 25, 1976
San Diego vs. Green Bay, Sept. 24, 1978
Pittsburgh vs. Cincinnati, Oct. 14, 1979

Cleveland vs. Seattle, Dec. 20, 1981
Cleveland vs. Pittsburgh, Dec. 23, 1990
Oakland vs. Seattle, Dec. 22, 1996
8 By many teams

Most Fumbles, Both Teams, Game
14 Washington (8) vs. Pittsburgh (6), Nov. 14, 1937
Chi. Bears (7) vs. Cleveland (7), Nov. 24, 1940
St. Louis (8) vs. N.Y. Giants (6), Sept. 17, 1961
Kansas City (10) vs. Houston (4), Oct. 12, 1969
13 Washington (8) vs. Pittsburgh (5), Nov. 14, 1937
Philadelphia (7) vs. Boston (6), Dec. 8, 1946
N.Y. Giants (7) vs. Washington (6), Nov. 5, 1950
Kansas City (9) vs. San Diego (4), Nov. 15, 1964
Buffalo (7) vs. Denver (6), Dec. 13, 1964
N.Y. Jets (7) vs. Houston (6), Sept. 12, 1965
Cleveland (7) vs. New Orleans (6), Dec. 12, 1971
Houston (8) vs. Pittsburgh (5), Dec. 9, 1973
St. Louis (9) vs. Washington (4), Oct. 25, 1976
Cleveland (9) vs. Seattle (4), Dec. 20, 1981
Green Bay (7) vs. Detroit (6), Oct. 6, 1985
12 In many games

FUMBLES LOST

Most Fumbles Lost, Season
36 Chi. Cardinals, 1959
31 Green Bay, 1952
29 Chi. Cardinals, 1946
Pittsburgh, 1950
Cleveland, 1978

Fewest Fumbles Lost, Season
2 Kansas City, 2002
3 Philadelphia, 1938
Minnesota, 1980
4 San Francisco, 1960
Kansas City, 1982
Minnesota, 1998
Detroit, 2003

Most Fumbles Lost, Game
8 St. Louis vs. Washington, Oct. 25, 1976
Cleveland vs. Pittsburgh, Dec. 23, 1990
7 Cincinnati vs. Buffalo, Nov. 30, 1969
Pittsburgh vs. Cincinnati, Oct. 14, 1979
Cleveland vs. Seattle, Dec. 20, 1981
6 By many teams

FUMBLES RECOVERED

Most Fumbles Recovered, Season, Own and Opponents'
58 Minnesota, 1963 (27 own, 31 opp)
51 Chi. Bears, 1938 (37 own, 14 opp)
San Francisco, 1978 (24 own, 27 opp)
50 Philadelphia, 1987 (23 own, 27 opp)

Fewest Fumbles Recovered, Season, Own and Opponents'
9 San Francisco, 1982 (5 own, 4 opp)
11 Cincinnati, 1982 (5 own, 6 opp)
12 Washington, 1994 (6 own, 6 opp)
Arizona, 1997 (7 own, 5 opp)

Most Fumbles Recovered, Game, Own and Opponents'
10 Denver vs. Buffalo, Dec. 13, 1964 (5 own, 5 opp)
Pittsburgh vs. Houston, Dec. 9, 1973 (5 own, 5 opp)
Washington vs. St. Louis, Oct. 25, 1976 (2 own, 8 opp)
9 St. Louis vs. N.Y. Giants, Sept. 17, 1961 (6 own, 3 opp)
Houston vs. Cincinnati, Oct. 27, 1974 (4 own, 5 opp)
Kansas City vs. Dallas, Nov. 10, 1975 (4 own, 5 opp)
Green Bay vs. Detroit, Oct. 6, 1985 (5 own, 4 opp)
Pittsburgh vs. Cleveland, Dec. 23, 1990 (1 own, 8 opp)
8 By many teams

Most Own Fumbles Recovered, Season
37 Chi. Bears, 1938
28 Pittsburgh, 1987
27 Philadelphia, 1946
Minnesota, 1963

Fewest Own Fumbles Recovered, Season
2 Washington, 1958
Miami, 2000
3 Detroit, 1956
Cleveland, 1959
Houston, 1982
4 By many teams

Most Opponents' Fumbles Recovered, Season
31 Minnesota, 1963
29 Cleveland, 1951
28 Green Bay, 1946
Houston, 1977
Seattle, 1983

Fewest Opponents' Fumbles Recovered, Season
3 Los Angeles, 1974
Green Bay, 1995
4 Philadelphia, 1944
San Francisco, 1982
5 Baltimore, 1982
Arizona, 1997
Baltimore, 1998
Chicago, 2003

Most Opponents' Fumbles Recovered, Game
8 Washington vs. St. Louis, Oct. 25, 1976
Pittsburgh vs. Cleveland, Dec. 23, 1990
7 Buffalo vs. Cincinnati, Nov. 30, 1969
Cincinnati vs. Pittsburgh, Oct. 14, 1979
Seattle vs. Cleveland, Dec. 20, 1981
6 By many teams

TOUCHDOWNS

Most Touchdowns, Fumbles Recovered, Season, Own and Opponents'
5 Chi. Bears, 1942 (1 own, 4 opp)
Los Angeles, 1952 (1 own, 4 opp)
San Francisco, 1965 (1 own, 4 opp)
Oakland, 1978 (2 own, 3 opp)
4 Chi. Bears, 1948 (1 own, 3 opp)
Boston, 1948 (4 opp)
Denver, 1979 (1 own, 3 opp)
Atlanta, 1981 (1 own, 3 opp)
Denver, 1984 (4 opp)
St. Louis, 1987 (4 opp)
Minnesota, 1989 (4 opp)
Atlanta, 1991 (4 opp)
Philadelphia, 1995 (4 opp)
Atlanta, 1998 (4 opp)
New Orleans, 1998 (4 opp)
Kansas City, 1999 (4 opp)
3 By many teams

Most Touchdowns, Own Fumbles Recovered, Season
2 Chi. Bears, 1953
New England, 1973
Buffalo, 1974
Denver, 1975
Oakland, 1978
Green Bay, 1982
New Orleans, 1983
Cleveland, 1986
Green Bay, 1989
Miami, 1996
Buffalo, 2000

Most Touchdowns, Opponents' Fumbles Recovered, Season
4 Detroit, 1937
Chi. Bears, 1942

Boston, 1948
Los Angeles, 1952
San Francisco, 1965
Denver, 1984
St. Louis, 1987
Minnesota, 1989
Atlanta, 1991
Philadelphia, 1995
Atlanta, 1998
New Orleans, 1998
Kansas City, 1999
3 By many teams

Most Touchdowns, Fumbles Recovered, Game, Own and Opponents'
2 By many teams

Most Touchdowns, Fumbles Recovered, Game, Both Teams, Own and Opponents'
3 Detroit (2) vs. Minnesota (1), Dec. 9, 1962 (2 own, 1 opp)
Green Bay (2) vs. Dallas (1), Nov. 29, 1964 (3 opp)
Oakland (2) vs. Buffalo (1), Dec. 24, 1967 (3 opp)
Oakland (2) vs. Philadelphia (1), Sept. 24, 1995 (3 opp)
Tennessee (2) vs. Pittsburgh (1), Jan. 2, 2000 (3 opp)

Most Touchdowns, Own Fumbles Recovered, Game
2 Miami vs. New England, Sept.1, 1996

Most Touchdowns, Opponents' Fumbles Recovered, Game
2 Many times. Last time:
San Diego vs. St. Louis, Nov. 10, 2002

Most Touchdowns, Opponents' Fumbles Recovered, Game, Both Teams
3 Green Bay (2) vs. Dallas (1), Nov. 29, 1964
Oakland (2) vs. Buffalo (1), Dec. 24, 1967
Oakland (2) vs. Philadelphia (1), Sept. 24, 1995
Tennessee (2) vs. Pittsburgh (1), Jan. 2, 2000

TURNOVERS

(Number of times losing the ball on interceptions and fumbles.)

Most Turnovers, Season
63 San Francisco, 1978
58 Chi. Bears, 1947
Pittsburgh, 1950
N.Y. Giants, 1983
57 Green Bay, 1950
Houston, 1962, 1963
Pittsburgh, 1965

Fewest Turnovers, Season
12 Kansas City, 1982
14 N.Y. Giants, 1943
Cleveland, 1959
N.Y. Giants, 1990
15 Dallas, 1998
Jacksonville, 2002
Kansas City, 2002

Most Turnovers, Game
12 Detroit vs. Chi. Bears, Nov. 22, 1942
Chi. Cardinals vs. Philadelphia, Sept. 24, 1950
Pittsburgh vs. Philadelphia, Dec. 12, 1965
11 San Diego vs. Green Bay, Sept. 24, 1978
10 Washington vs. N.Y. Giants, Dec. 4, 1938
Pittsburgh vs. Green Bay, Nov. 23, 1941
Detroit vs. Green Bay, Oct. 24, 1943
Chi. Cardinals vs. Green Bay, Nov. 10, 1946
Chi. Cardinals vs. N.Y. Giants, Nov. 2, 1952
Minnesota vs. Detroit, Dec. 9, 1962
Houston vs. Oakland, Sept. 7, 1963
Washington vs. N.Y. Giants, Dec. 8, 1963
Chicago vs. Detroit, Sept. 22, 1968
St. Louis vs. Washington, Oct. 25, 1976
N.Y. Jets vs. New England, Nov. 21, 1976
San Francisco vs. Dallas, Oct. 12, 1980
Cleveland vs. Seattle, Dec. 20, 1981
Detroit vs. Denver, Oct. 7, 1984

Most Turnovers, Both Teams, Game
17 Detroit (12) vs. Chi. Bears (5), Nov. 22, 1942
Boston (9) vs. Philadelphia (8), Dec. 8, 1946
16 Chi. Cardinals (12) vs. Philadelphia (4), Sept. 24, 1950
Chi. Cardinals (8) vs. Chi. Bears (8), Dec. 7, 1958
Minnesota (10) vs. Detroit (6), Dec. 9, 1962
Houston (9) vs. Kansas City (7), Oct. 12, 1969
15 Philadelphia (8) vs. Chi. Cardinals (7), Oct. 3, 1954
Denver (9) vs. Houston (6), Dec. 2, 1962
Washington (10) vs. N.Y. Giants (5), Dec. 8, 1963
St. Louis (9) vs. Kansas City (6), Oct. 2, 1983

PENALTIES

Most Seasons Leading League, Fewest Penalties
13 Miami, 1968, 1976-1984, 1986, 1990-91
9 Pittsburgh, 1946-47, 1950-52, 1954, 1963, 1965, 1968
7 Boston/New England, 1962, 1964-65, 1973, 1987, 1989, 1993

Most Consecutive Seasons Leading League, Fewest Penalties
9 Miami, 1976-1984
3 Pittsburgh, 1950-52
2 By many teams

Most Seasons Leading League, Most Penalties
16 Chi. Bears, 1941-44, 1946-49, 1951, 1959-1961, 1963, 1965, 1968, 1976
13 Oakland/L.A. Raiders, 1963, 1966, 1968-69, 1975, 1982, 1984, 1991, 1993-96, 2003
7 L.A./St. Louis Rams, 1950, 1952, 1962, 1969, 1978, 1980, 1997

Most Consecutive Seasons Leading League, Most Penalties
4 Chi. Bears, 1941-44, 1946-49
Oakland/L.A. Raiders, 1993-96
3 Chi. Cardinals, 1954-56
Chi. Bears, 1959-1961

Fewest Penalties, Season
19 Detroit, 1937
21 Boston, 1935
24 Philadelphia, 1936

Most Penalties, Season
158 Kansas City, 1998
156 L.A. Raiders, 1994
Oakland, 1996
149 Houston, 1989

Fewest Penalties, Game
0 By many teams. Last time:
Washington vs. Carolina, Nov. 16, 2003

Most Penalties, Game
22 Brooklyn vs. Green Bay, Sept. 17, 1944
Chi. Bears vs. Philadelphia, Nov. 26, 1944
San Francisco vs. Buffalo, Oct. 4, 1998
21 Cleveland vs. Chi. Bears, Nov. 25, 1951
20 Tampa Bay vs. Seattle, Oct. 17, 1976
Oakland vs. Denver, Dec. 15, 1996

Fewest Penalties, Both Teams, Game
0 Brooklyn vs. Pittsburgh, Oct. 28, 1934
Brooklyn vs. Boston, Sept. 28, 1936
Cleveland vs. Chi. Bears, Oct. 9, 1938
Pittsburgh vs. Philadelphia, Nov. 10, 1940

Most Penalties, Both Teams, Game
37 Cleveland (21) vs. Chi. Bears (16), Nov. 25, 1951
35 Tampa Bay (20) vs. Seattle (15), Oct. 17, 1976
34 San Francisco (22) vs. Buffalo (12), Oct. 4, 1998

YARDS PENALIZED

Most Seasons Leading League, Fewest Yards Penalized

13 Miami, 1967-68, 1973, 1977-1984, 1990-91
10 Boston/Washington, 1935, 1953-54, 1956-58, 1970, 1985, 1995, 1997
7 Pittsburgh, 1946-47, 1950, 1952, 1962, 1965, 1968
Boston/New England, 1962, 1964-66, 1987, 1989, 1993

Most Consecutive Seasons Leading League, Fewest Yards Penalized

8 Miami, 1977-1984
3 Washington, 1956-58
Boston, 1964-66
2 By many teams

Most Seasons Leading League, Most Yards Penalized

15 Chi. Bears, 1935, 1937, 1939-1944, 1946-47, 1949, 1951, 1961-62, 1968
12 Oakland/L.A. Raiders, 1963-64, 1968-69, 1975, 1982, 1984, 1991, 1993-94, 1996, 2003
6 Buffalo, 1962, 1967, 1970, 1972, 1981, 1983
Houston, 1961, 1985-86, 1988-1990

Most Consecutive Seasons Leading League, Most Yards Penalized

6 Chi. Bears, 1939-1944
3 Houston, 1988-1990
2 By many teams

Fewest Yards Penalized, Season

139 Detroit, 1937
146 Philadelphia, 1937
159 Philadelphia, 1936

Most Yards Penalized, Season

1,304 Kansas City, 1998
1,274 Oakland, 1969
1,266 Oakland, 1996

Fewest Yards Penalized, Game

0 By many teams. Last time:
Washington vs. Carolina, Nov. 16, 2003

Most Yards Penalized, Game

212 Tennessee vs. Baltimore, Oct. 10, 1999
209 Cleveland vs. Chi. Bears, Nov. 25, 1951
191 Philadelphia vs. Seattle, Dec. 13, 1992 (OT)

Fewest Yards Penalized, Both Teams, Game

0 Brooklyn vs. Pittsburgh, Oct. 28, 1934
Brooklyn vs. Boston, Sept. 28, 1936
Cleveland vs. Chi. Bears, Oct. 9, 1938
Pittsburgh vs. Philadelphia, Nov. 10, 1940

Most Yards Penalized, Both Teams, Game

374 Cleveland (209) vs. Chi. Bears (165), Nov. 25, 1951
310 Tampa Bay (190) vs. Seattle (120), Oct. 17, 1976
309 Green Bay (184) vs. Boston (125), Oct. 21, 1945

DEFENSE

SCORING

Most Seasons Leading League, Fewest Points Allowed

11 N.Y. Giants, 1927, 1935, 1938-39, 1941, 1944, 1958-59, 1961, 1990, 1993
10 Chi. Bears, 1932, 1936-37, 1942, 1948, 1963, 1985-86, 1988, 2001
7 Cleveland, 1951, 1953-57, 1994
Green Bay, 1929, 1935, 1947, 1962, 1965-66, 1996

Most Consecutive Seasons Leading League, Fewest Points Allowed

5 Cleveland, 1953-57
3 Buffalo, 1964-66
Minnesota, 1969-1971
2 By many teams

Fewest Points Allowed, Season (Since 1932)

44 Chi. Bears, 1932
54 Brooklyn, 1933
59 Detroit, 1934

Most Points Allowed, Season

533 Baltimore, 1981
501 N.Y. Giants, 1966
487 New Orleans, 1980

Fewest Touchdowns Allowed, Season (Since 1932)

6 Chi. Bears, 1932
Brooklyn, 1933
7 Detroit, 1934
8 Green Bay, 1932

Most Touchdowns Allowed, Season

68 Baltimore, 1981
66 N.Y. Giants, 1966
63 Baltimore, 1950

FIRST DOWNS

Fewest First Downs Allowed Season

77 Detroit, 1935
79 Boston, 1935
82 Washington, 1937

Most First Downs Allowed, Season

406 Baltimore, 1981
371 Seattle, 1981
368 Cleveland, 1999

Fewest First Downs Allowed, Rushing, Season

35 Chi. Bears, 1942
40 Green Bay, 1939
41 Brooklyn, 1944

Most First Downs Allowed, Rushing, Season

179 Detroit, 1985
178 New Orleans, 1980
175 Seattle, 1981

Fewest First Downs Allowed, Passing, Season

33 Chi. Bears, 1943
34 Pittsburgh, 1941
Washington, 1943
35 Detroit, 1940
Philadelphia, 1940, 1944

Most First Downs Allowed, Passing, Season

230 Atlanta, 1995
227 Kansas City, 2002
221 Detroit, 2002

Fewest First Downs Allowed, Penalty, Season

1 Boston, 1944
3 Philadelphia, 1940
Pittsburgh, 1945
Washington, 1957
4 Cleveland, 1940
Green Bay, 1943
N.Y. Giants, 1943

Most First Downs Allowed, Penalty, Season

56 Kansas City, 1998
48 Houston, 1985
46 Houston, 1986

NET YARDS ALLOWED RUSHING AND PASSING

Most Seasons Leading League, Fewest Yards Allowed

8 Chi. Bears, 1942-43, 1948, 1958, 1963, 1984-86
6 N.Y. Giants, 1938, 1940-41, 1951, 1956, 1959
Philadelphia, 1944-45, 1949, 1953, 1981, 1991
Minnesota, 1969-1970, 1975, 1988-89, 1993
5 Boston/Washington, 1935-37, 1939, 1946

Most Consecutive Seasons Leading League, Fewest Yards Allowed

3 Boston/Washington, 1935-37
Chicago, 1984-86
2 By many teams

Fewest Yards Allowed, Season

1,539 Chi. Cardinals, 1934
1,703 Chi. Bears, 1942

1,789 Brooklyn, 1933

Most Yards Allowed, Season
6,793 Baltimore, 1981
6,403 Green Bay, 1983
6,391 Seattle, 2000

RUSHING

Most Seasons Leading League, Fewest Yards Allowed
10 Chi. Bears, 1937, 1939, 1942, 1946, 1949, 1963, 1984-85, 1987-88
7 Detroit, 1938, 1950, 1952, 1962, 1970, 1980-81
Philadelphia, 1944-45, 1947-48, 1953, 1990-91
Dallas, 1966-69, 1972, 1978, 1992
6 Pittsburgh, 1961, 1976, 1982, 1997, 2001-02

Most Consecutive Seasons Leading League, Fewest Yards Allowed
4 Dallas, 1966-69
2 By many teams

Fewest Yards Allowed, Rushing, Season
519 Chi. Bears, 1942
558 Philadelphia, 1944
762 Pittsburgh, 1982

Most Yards Allowed, Rushing, Season
3,228 Buffalo, 1978
3,106 New Orleans, 1980
3,010 Baltimore, 1978

Fewest Touchdowns Allowed, Rushing, Season
2 Detroit, 1934
Dallas, 1968
Minnesota, 1971
3 By many teams

Most Touchdowns Allowed, Rushing, Season
36 Oakland, 1961
31 N.Y. Giants, 1980
Tampa Bay, 1986
30 Baltimore, 1981

PASSING

Most Seasons Leading League, Fewest Yards Allowed
9 Green Bay, 1947-48, 1962, 1964-68, 1996
7 Washington, 1939, 1942, 1945, 1952-53, 1980, 1985
Philadelphia 1934, 1936, 1940, 1949, 1981, 1991, 1998
6 Chi. Bears, 1938, 1943-44, 1958, 1960, 1963
Minnesota, 1969-1970, 1972, 1975-76, 1989
Pittsburgh, 1941, 1946, 1951, 1955, 1974, 1990

Most Consecutive Seasons Leading League, Fewest Yards Allowed
5 Green Bay, 1964-68
2 By many teams

Fewest Yards Allowed, Passing, Season
545 Philadelphia, 1934
558 Portsmouth, 1933
585 Chi. Cardinals, 1934

Most Yards Allowed, Passing, Season
4,541 Atlanta, 1995
4,389 N.Y. Jets, 1986
4,311 San Diego, 1981

Fewest Touchdowns Allowed, Passing, Season
1 Portsmouth, 1932
Philadelphia, 1934
2 Brooklyn, 1933
Chi. Bears, 1934
3 Chi. Bears, 1932
Green Bay, 1932
Green Bay, 1934
Chi. Bears, 1936
New York, 1939
New York, 1944

Most Touchdowns Allowed, Passing, Season
40 Denver, 1963
38 St. Louis, 1969
37 Washington, 1961
Baltimore, 1981

SACKS

Most Seasons Leading League
5 Oakland/L.A. Raiders, 1966-68, 1982, 1986
4 New England/Boston, 1961, 1963, 1977, 1979
Dallas, 1966, 1968-69, 1978
Dallas/Kansas City, 1960, 1965, 1969, 1990
L.A./St. Louis Rams, 1968, 1970, 1988, 1999
3 San Francisco, 1967, 1972, 1976
N.Y. Giants, 1963, 1985, 1998
New Orleans, 1992, 1997, 2000
Pittsburgh, 1974, 1994, 2001

Most Consecutive Seasons Leading League
3 Oakland, 1966-68
2 Dallas, 1968-69

Most Sacks, Season
72 Chicago, 1984
71 Minnesota, 1989
70 Chicago, 1987

Fewest Sacks, Season
11 Baltimore, 1982
12 Buffalo, 1982
13 Baltimore, 1981

Most Sacks, Game
12 Dallas vs. Pittsburgh, Nov. 20, 1966
St. Louis vs. Baltimore, Oct. 26, 1980
Chicago vs. Detroit, Dec. 16, 1984
Dallas vs. Houston, Sept. 29, 1985
11 N.Y. Giants vs. St. Louis, Nov. 1, 1964
Baltimore vs. Los Angeles, Nov. 22, 1964
Buffalo vs. Denver, Dec. 13, 1964
Detroit vs. Green Bay, Nov. 7, 1965
Oakland vs. Buffalo, Oct. 15, 1967
Oakland vs. Denver, Nov. 5, 1967
St. Louis vs. Atlanta, Nov. 24, 1968
Dallas vs. Detroit, Oct. 6, 1975
St. Louis vs. Philadelphia, Dec. 18, 1983
Kansas City vs. Cleveland, Sept. 30, 1984
Chicago vs. Minnesota, Oct. 28, 1984
Cleveland vs. Atlanta, Nov. 18, 1984
Detroit vs. Philadelphia, Nov. 16, 1986
San Diego vs. Dallas, Nov. 16, 1986
L.A. Raiders vs. Philadelphia, Nov. 30, 1986 (OT)
Seattle vs. L.A. Raiders, Dec. 8, 1986
Chicago vs. Philadelphia, Oct. 4, 1987
Dallas vs. N.Y. Jets, Oct. 4, 1987
Philadelphia vs. Dallas, Sept. 15, 1991
Indianapolis vs. Cleveland, Sept. 6, 1992
10 By many teams

Most Opponents Yards Lost Attempting to Pass, Season
666 Oakland, 1967
583 Chicago, 1984
573 San Francisco, 1976

Fewest Opponents Yards Lost Attempting to Pass, Season
72 Jacksonville, 1995
75 Green Bay, 1956
77 N.Y. Bulldogs, 1949

INTERCEPTIONS BY

Most Seasons Leading League
10 N.Y. Giants, 1933, 1937-39, 1944, 1948, 1951, 1954, 1961, 1997
8 Green Bay, 1940, 1942-43, 1947, 1955, 1957, 1962, 1965

Chi. Bears, 1935-36, 1941-42, 1946, 1963, 1985, 1990
6 Kansas City, 1966-1970, 1974

Most Consecutive Seasons Leading League
5 Kansas City, 1966-1970
3 N.Y. Giants, 1937-39
2 By many teams

Most Passes Intercepted By, Season
49 San Diego, 1961
42 Green Bay, 1943
41 N.Y. Giants, 1951

Fewest Passes Intercepted By, Season
3 Houston, 1982
5 Baltimore, 1982
6 Houston, 1972
St. Louis, 1982
Atlanta, 1996

Most Passes Intercepted By, Game
9 Green Bay vs. Detroit, Oct. 24, 1943
Philadelphia vs. Pittsburgh, Dec. 12, 1965
8 N.Y. Giants vs. Green Bay, Nov. 21, 1948
Philadelphia vs. Chi. Cardinals, Sept. 24, 1950
N.Y. Giants vs. N.Y. Yanks, Dec. 16, 1951
Houston vs. Denver, Dec. 2, 1962
Detroit vs. Chicago, Sept. 22, 1968
N.Y. Jets vs. Baltimore, Sept. 23, 1973
7 By many teams. Last time:
Cleveland vs. Detroit, Sept. 23, 2001

Most Consecutive Games, One or More Interceptions By
46 L.A. Chargers/San Diego, 1960-63
37 Detroit, 1960-63
36 Boston, 1944-47

Most Yards Returning Interceptions, Season
929 San Diego, 1961
712 Los Angeles, 1952
697 Seattle, 1984

Fewest Yards Returning Interceptions, Season
5 Los Angeles, 1959
37 Dallas, 1989
39 Denver, 2003

Most Yards Returning Interceptions, Game
325 Seattle vs. Kansas City, Nov. 4, 1984
314 Los Angeles vs. San Francisco, Oct. 18, 1964
245 Houston vs. N.Y. Jets, Oct. 15, 1967

Most Yards Returning Interceptions, Both Teams, Game
356 Seattle (325) vs. Kansas City (31), Nov. 4, 1984
338 Los Angeles (314) vs. San Francisco (24), Oct. 18, 1964
308 Dallas (182) vs. Los Angeles (126), Nov. 2, 1952

Most Touchdowns, Returning Interceptions, Season
9 San Diego, 1961
8 Seattle, 1998
7 Seattle, 1984
St. Louis, 1999

Most Touchdowns Returning Interceptions, Game
4 Seattle vs. Kansas City, Nov. 4, 1984
3 Baltimore vs. Green Bay, Nov. 5, 1950
Cleveland vs. Chicago, Dec. 11, 1960
Philadelphia vs. Pittsburgh, Dec. 12, 1965
Baltimore vs. Pittsburgh, Sept. 29, 1968
Buffalo vs. N.Y. Jets, Sept. 29, 1968
Houston vs. San Diego, Dec. 19, 1971
Cincinnati vs. Houston, Dec. 17, 1972
Tampa Bay vs. New Orleans, Dec. 11, 1977
2 By many teams

Most Touchdown Returning Interceptions, Both Teams, Game
4 Philadelphia (3) vs. Pittsburgh (1), Dec. 12, 1965
Seattle (4) vs. Kansas City (0), Nov. 4, 1984
3 Los Angeles (2) vs. Detroit (1), Nov. 1, 1953
Cleveland (2) vs. N.Y. Giants (1), Dec. 18, 1960
Pittsburgh (2) vs. Cincinnati (1), Oct. 10, 1983
Kansas City (2) vs. San Diego (1), Oct. 19, 1986
(Also see previous record)

PUNT RETURNS

Fewest Opponents Punt Returns, Season
7 Washington, 1962
San Diego, 1982
10 Buffalo, 1982
11 Boston, 1962

Most Opponents Punt Returns, Season
71 Tampa Bay, 1976, 1977
69 N.Y. Giants, 1953
Cleveland, 2000
68 Cleveland, 1974
Cleveland, 1999

Fewest Yards Allowed, Punt Returns, Season
22 Green Bay, 1967
30 Buffalo, 1982
34 Washington, 1962

Most Yards Allowed, Punt Returns, Season
932 Green Bay, 1949
913 Boston, 1947
906 New Orleans, 1974

Lowest Average Allowed, Punt Returns, Season
1.20 Chi. Cardinals, 1954 (46-55)
1.22 Cleveland, 1959 (32-39)
1.55 Chi. Cardinals, 1953 (44-68)

Highest Average Allowed, Punt Returns, Season
18.6 Green Bay, 1949 (50-932)
18.0 Cleveland, 1977 (31-558)
17.9 Boston, 1960 (20-357)

Most Touchdowns Allowed, Punt Returns, Season
4 New York, 1959
Atlanta, 1992
3 Green Bay, 1949
Chi. Cardinals, 1951
L.A. Rams, 1951, 1994
Washington, 1952
Dallas, 1952
Pittsburgh, 1959, 1993
N.Y. Jets, 1968
Cleveland, 1977
Atlanta, 1986
Tampa Bay, 1986
Arizona, 2002
Cincinnati, 2002
Tennessee, 2002
2 By many teams

KICKOFF RETURNS

Fewest Opponents Kickoff Returns, Season
10 Brooklyn, 1943
13 Denver, 1992
15 Detroit, 1942
Brooklyn, 1944

Most Opponents Kickoff Returns, Season
93 Indianapolis, 2003
91 Washington, 1983
90 Denver, 2000

Fewest Yards Allowed, Kickoff Returns, Season
225 Brooklyn, 1943
254 Denver, 1992
293 Brooklyn, 1944

Most Yards Allowed, Kickoff Returns, Season
2,194 St. Louis, 2001
2,115 St. Louis, 1999
2,045 Kansas City, 1966

Lowest Average Allowed, Kickoff Returns, Season
14.3 Cleveland, 1980 (71-1,018)

14.9 Indianapolis, 1993 (37-551)
15.0 Seattle, 1982 (24-361)

Highest Average Allowed, Kickoff Returns, Season
29.5 N.Y. Jets, 1972 (47-1,386)
29.4 Los Angeles, 1950 (48-1,411)
29.1 New England, 1971 (49-1,427)

Most Touchdowns Allowed, Kickoff Returns, Season
4 Minnesota, 1998
3 Minnesota, 1963, 1970
Dallas, 1966
Detroit, 1980
Pittsburgh, 1986
Buffalo, 1997
Atlanta, 2000
2 By many teams

FUMBLES

Fewest Opponents Fumbles, Season
11 Cleveland, 1956
Baltimore, 1982
Tennessee, 1998
12 Green Bay, 1995
Cincinnati, 1998
13 Los Angeles, 1956
Chicago, 1960
Cleveland, 1963
Cleveland, 1965
Detroit, 1967
San Diego, 1969

Most Opponents Fumbles, Season
50 Minnesota, 1963
San Francisco, 1978
48 N.Y. Giants, 1980
N.Y. Jets, 1986
47 N.Y. Giants, 1977
Seattle, 1984

TURNOVERS

(Number of times losing the ball on interceptions and fumbles.)

Fewest Opponents Turnovers, Season
11 Baltimore, 1982
13 San Francisco, 1982
15 St. Louis, 1982

Most Opponents Turnovers, Season
66 San Diego, 1961
63 Seattle, 1984
61 Washington, 1983

Most Opponents Turnovers, Game
12 Chi. Bears vs. Detroit, Nov. 22, 1942
Philadelphia vs. Chi. Cardinals, Sept. 24, 1950
Philadelphia vs. Pittsburgh, Dec. 12, 1965
11 Green Bay vs. San Diego, Sept. 24, 1978
10 By 14 teams

OUTSTANDING PERFORMERS

1,000 YARDS RUSHING IN A SEASON

Year	Player, Team	Att.	Yards	Avg.	Long	TD
2003	Jamal Lewis, Baltimore[3]	387	2,066	5.3	82	14
	Ahman Green, Green Bay[4]	355	1,883	5.3	98	15
	LaDainian Tomlinson, San Diego[3]	313	1,645	5.3	73	13
	Deuce McAllister, New Orleans[2]	351	1,641	4.7	76	8
	Clinton Portis, Denver[2]	290	1,591	5.5	65	14
	Fred Taylor, Jacksonville[4]	345	1,572	4.6	62	6
	Stephen Davis, Carolina[4]	318	1,444	4.5	40	8
	Shaun Alexander, Seattle[3]	326	1,435	4.4	55	14
	Priest Holmes, Kansas City[4]	320	1,420	4.4	31	27
	Ricky Williams, Miami[4]	392	1,372	3.5	45	9
	Travis Henry, Buffalo[2]	331	1,356	4.1	64	10
	Curtis Martin, N.Y. Jets[9]	323	1,308	4.1	56	2
	Edgerrin James, Indianapolis[3]	310	1,259	4.1	43	11
	Tiki Barber, N.Y. Giants[3]	278	1,216	4.4	27	2
	*Domanick Davis, Houston	238	1,031	4.3	51	8
	Eddie George, Tennessee[7]	312	1,031	3.3	27	5
	Kevan Barlow, San Francisco	201	1,024	5.1	78	6
	Anthony Thomas, Chicago[2]	244	1,024	4.2	67	6
2002	Ricky Williams, Miami[3]	383	1,853	4.8	63	16
	LaDainian Tomlinson, San Diego[2]	372	1,683	4.5	76	14
	Priest Holmes, Kansas City[3]	313	1,615	5.2	56	21
	*Clinton Portis, Denver	273	1,508	5.5	59	15
	Travis Henry, Buffalo	325	1,438	4.4	34	13
	Deuce McAllister, New Orleans	325	1,388	4.3	62	13
	Tiki Barber, N.Y. Giants[2]	304	1,387	4.6	70	11
	Jamal Lewis, Baltimore[2]	308	1,327	4.3	75	6
	Fred Taylor, Jacksonville[3]	287	1,314	4.6	63	8
	Corey Dillon, Cincinnati[6]	314	1,311	4.2	67	7
	Michael Bennett, Minnesota	255	1,296	5.1	85	5
	Ahman Green, Green Bay[3]	286	1,240	4.3	43	7
	Shaun Alexander, Seattle[2]	295	1,175	4.0	58	16
	Eddie George, Tennessee[6]	343	1,165	3.4	35	12
	Curtis Martin, N.Y. Jets[8]	261	1,094	4.2	35	7
	Duce Staley, Philadelphia[3]	269	1,029	3.8	57	5
	James Stewart, Detroit[2]	231	1,021	4.4	56	4
2001	Priest Holmes, Kansas City[2]	327	1,555	4.8	41	8
	Curtis Martin, N.Y. Jets[7]	333	1,513	4.5	47	10
	Stephen Davis, Washington[3]	356	1,432	4.0	32	5
	Ahman Green, Green Bay[2]	304	1,387	4.6	83	9
	Marshall Faulk, St. Louis[7]	260	1,382	5.3	71	12
	Shaun Alexander, Seattle	309	1,318	4.3	88	14
	Corey Dillon, Cincinnati[5]	340	1,315	3.9	96	10
	Ricky Williams, New Orleans[2]	313	1,245	4.0	46	6
	*LaDainian Tomlinson, San Diego	339	1,236	3.6	54	10
	Garrison Hearst, San Francisco[4]	252	1,206	4.8	43	4
	*Anthony Thomas, Chicago	278	1,183	4.3	46	7
	Antowain Smith, New England[2]	287	1,157	4.0	44	12
	*Dominic Rhodes, Indianapolis	233	1,104	4.7	77	9
	Jerome Bettis, Pittsburgh[8]	225	1,072	4.8	48	4
	Emmitt Smith, Dallas[11]	261	1,021	3.9	44	3
2000	Edgerrin James, Indianapolis[2]	387	1,709	4.4	30	13
	Robert Smith, Minnesota[4]	295	1,521	5.2	72	7
	Eddie George, Tennessee[5]	403	1,509	3.7	35	14
	*Mike Anderson, Denver	297	1,487	5.0	80	15
	Corey Dillon, Cincinnati[4]	315	1,435	4.6	80	7
	Fred Taylor, Jacksonville[2]	292	1,399	4.8	71	12
	*Jamal Lewis, Baltimore	309	1,364	4.4	45	6
	Marshall Faulk, St. Louis[6]	253	1,359	5.4	36	18
	Jerome Bettis, Pittsburgh[7]	355	1,341	3.8	30	8
	Stephen Davis, Washington[2]	332	1,318	4.0	50	11
	Ricky Watters, Seattle[7]	278	1,242	4.5	55	7
	Curtis Martin, N.Y. Jets[6]	316	1,204	3.8	55	9
	Emmitt Smith, Dallas[10]	294	1,203	4.1	52	9
	James Stewart, Detroit	339	1,184	3.5	34	10
	Ahman Green, Green Bay	263	1,175	4.5	39	10
	Charlie Garner, San Francisco[2]	258	1,142	4.4	42	7
	Lamar Smith, Miami	309	1,139	3.7	68	14
	Warrick Dunn, Tampa Bay[2]	248	1,133	4.6	70	8

	James Allen, Chicago	290	1,120	3.9	29	2
	Tyrone Wheatley, Oakland	232	1,046	4.5	80	9
	Jamal Anderson, Atlanta[4]	282	1,024	3.6	42	6
	Tiki Barber, N.Y. Giants	213	1,006	4.7	78	8
	Ricky Williams, New Orleans	248	1,000	4.0	26	8
1999	*Edgerrin James, Indianapolis	369	1,553	4.2	72	13
	Curtis Martin, N.Y. Jets[5]	367	1,464	4.0	50	5
	Stephen Davis, Washington	290	1,405	4.8	76	17
	Emmitt Smith, Dallas[9]	329	1,397	4.3	63	11
	Marshall Faulk, St. Louis[5]	253	1,381	5.5	58	7
	Eddie George, Tennessee[4]	320	1,304	4.1	40	9
	Duce Staley, Philadelphia[2]	325	1,273	3.9	29	4
	Charlie Garner, San Francisco	241	1,229	5.1	53	4
	Ricky Watters, Seattle[6]	325	1,210	3.7	45	5
	Corey Dillon, Cincinnati[3]	263	1,200	4.6	50	5
	*Olandis Gary, Denver	276	1,159	4.2	71	7
	Jerome Bettis, Pittsburgh[6]	299	1,091	3.7	35	7
	Dorsey Levens, Green Bay[2]	279	1,034	3.7	36	9
	Robert Smith, Minnesota[3]	221	1,015	4.6	70	2
1998	Terrell Davis, Denver[4]	392	2,008	5.1	70	21
	Jamal Anderson, Atlanta[3]	410	1,846	4.5	48	14
	Garrison Hearst, San Francisco[3]	310	1,570	5.1	96	7
	Barry Sanders, Detroit[10]	343	1,491	4.3	73	4
	Emmitt Smith, Dallas[8]	319	1,332	4.2	32	13
	Marshall Faulk, Indianapolis[4]	324	1,319	4.1	68	6
	Eddie George, Tennessee[3]	348	1,294	3.7	37	5
	Curtis Martin, N.Y. Jets[4]	369	1,287	3.5	60	8
	Ricky Watters, Seattle[5]	319	1,239	3.9	39	9
	*Fred Taylor, Jacksonville	264	1,223	4.6	77	14
	Robert Smith, Minnesota[2]	249	1,187	4.8	74	6
	Jerome Bettis, Pittsburgh[5]	316	1,185	3.8	42	3
	Corey Dillon, Cincinnati[2]	262	1,130	4.3	66	4
	Antowain Smith, Buffalo	300	1,124	3.7	30	8
	*Robert Edwards, New England	291	1,115	3.8	53	9
	Duce Staley, Philadelphia	258	1,065	4.1	64	5
	Gary Brown, N.Y. Giants[2]	247	1,063	4.3	45	5
	Adrian Murrell, Arizona[3]	274	1,042	3.8	32	8
	Warrick Dunn, Tampa Bay	245	1,026	4.2	50	2
	Priest Holmes, Baltimore	233	1,008	4.3	56	7
1997	Barry Sanders, Detroit[9]	335	2,053	6.1	82	11
	Terrell Davis, Denver[3]	369	1,750	4.7	50	15
	Jerome Bettis, Pittsburgh[4]	375	1,665	4.4	34	7
	Dorsey Levens, Green Bay	329	1,435	4.4	52	7
	Eddie George, Tennessee[2]	357	1,399	3.9	30	6
	Napoleon Kaufman, Oakland	272	1,294	4.8	83	6
	Robert Smith, Minnesota	232	1,266	5.5	78	6
	Curtis Martin, New England[3]	274	1,160	4.2	70	4
	*Corey Dillon, Cincinnati	233	1,129	4.8	71	10
	Ricky Watters, Philadelphia[4]	285	1,110	3.9	28	7
	Adrian Murrell, N.Y. Jets[2]	300	1,086	3.6	43	7
	Emmitt Smith, Dallas[7]	261	1,074	4.1	44	4
	Marshall Faulk, Indianapolis[3]	264	1,054	4.0	45	7
	Raymont Harris, Chicago	275	1,033	3.8	68	10
	Garrison Hearst, San Francisco[2]	234	1,019	4.4	51	4
	Jamal Anderson, Atlanta[2]	290	1,002	3.5	39	7
1996	Barry Sanders, Detroit[8]	307	1,553	5.1	54	11
	Terrell Davis, Denver[2]	345	1,538	4.5	71	13
	Jerome Bettis, Pittsburgh[3]	320	1,431	4.5	50	11
	Ricky Watters, Philadelphia[3]	353	1,411	4.0	56	13
	*Eddie George, Houston	335	1,368	4.1	76	8
	Terry Allen, Washington[4]	347	1,353	3.9	49	21
	Adrian Murrell, N.Y. Jets	301	1,249	4.1	78	6
	Emmitt Smith, Dallas[6]	327	1,204	3.7	42	12
	Curtis Martin, New England[2]	316	1,152	3.6	57	14
	Anthony Johnson, Carolina	300	1,120	3.7	29	6
	*Karim Abdul-Jabbar, Miami	307	1,116	3.6	29	11
	Jamal Anderson, Atlanta	232	1,055	4.5	32	5
	Thurman Thomas, Buffalo[8]	281	1,033	3.7	36	8
1995	Emmitt Smith, Dallas[5]	377	1,773	4.7	60	25
	Barry Sanders, Detroit[7]	314	1,500	4.8	75	11

Year	Player, Team	Att.	Yards	Avg.	Long	TD
	*Curtis Martin, New England	368	1,487	4.0	49	14
	Chris Warren, Seattle[4]	310	1,346	4.3	52	15
	Terry Allen, Washington[3]	338	1,309	3.9	28	10
	Ricky Watters, Philadelphia[2]	337	1,273	3.8	57	11
	Errict Rhett, Tampa Bay[2]	332	1,207	3.6	21	11
	Rodney Hampton, N.Y. Giants[5]	306	1,182	3.9	32	10
	*Terrell Davis, Denver	237	1,117	4.7	60	7
	Harvey Williams, Oakland	255	1,114	4.4	60	9
	Craig Heyward, Atlanta	236	1,083	4.6	31	6
	Marshall Faulk, Indianapolis[2]	289	1,078	3.7	40	11
	*Rashaan Salaam, Chicago	296	1,074	3.6	42	10
	Garrison Hearst, Arizona	284	1,070	3.8	38	1
	Edgar Bennett, Green Bay	316	1,067	3.4	23	3
	Thurman Thomas, Buffalo[7]	267	1,005	3.8	49	6
1994	Barry Sanders, Detroit[6]	331	1,883	5.7	85	7
	Chris Warren, Seattle[3]	333	1,545	4.6	41	9
	Emmitt Smith, Dallas[4]	368	1,484	4.0	46	21
	Natrone Means, San Diego	343	1,350	3.9	25	12
	*Marshall Faulk, Indianapolis	314	1,282	4.1	52	11
	Thurman Thomas, Buffalo[6]	287	1,093	3.8	29	7
	Rodney Hampton, N.Y. Giants[4]	327	1,075	3.3	27	6
	Terry Allen, Minnesota[2]	255	1,031	4.0	45	8
	Jerome Bettis, L.A. Rams[2]	319	1,025	3.2	19	3
	*Errict Rhett, Tampa Bay	284	1,011	3.6	27	7
1993	Emmitt Smith, Dallas[3]	283	1,486	5.3	62	9
	*Jerome Bettis, L.A. Rams	294	1,429	4.9	71	7
	Thurman Thomas, Buffalo[5]	355	1,315	3.7	27	6
	Erric Pegram, Atlanta	292	1,185	4.1	29	3
	Barry Sanders, Detroit[5]	243	1,115	4.6	42	3
	Leonard Russell, New England	300	1,088	3.6	21	7
	Rodney Hampton, N.Y. Giants[3]	292	1,077	3.7	20	5
	Chris Warren, Seattle[2]	273	1,072	3.9	45	7
	*Reggie Brooks, Washington	223	1,063	4.8	85	3
	*Ron Moore, Phoenix	263	1,018	3.9	20	9
	Gary Brown, Houston	195	1,002	5.1	26	6
1992	Emmitt Smith, Dallas[2]	373	1,713	4.6	68	18
	Barry Foster, Pittsburgh	390	1,690	4.3	69	11
	Thurman Thomas, Buffalo[4]	312	1,487	4.8	44	9
	Barry Sanders, Detroit[4]	312	1,352	4.3	55	9
	Lorenzo White, Houston	265	1,226	4.6	44	7
	Terry Allen, Minnesota	266	1,201	4.5	51	13
	Reggie Cobb, Tampa Bay	310	1,171	3.8	25	9
	Harold Green, Cincinnati	265	1,170	4.4	53	2
	Rodney Hampton, N.Y. Giants[2]	257	1,141	4.4	63	14
	Cleveland Gary, L.A. Rams	279	1,125	4.0	63	7
	Herschel Walker, Philadelphia[2]	267	1,070	4.0	38	8
	Chris Warren, Seattle	223	1,017	4.6	52	3
	Ricky Watters, San Francisco	206	1,013	4.9	43	9
1991	Emmitt Smith, Dallas	365	1,563	4.3	75	12
	Barry Sanders, Detroit[3]	342	1,548	4.5	69	16
	Thurman Thomas, Buffalo[3]	288	1,407	4.9	33	7
	Rodney Hampton, N.Y. Giants	256	1,059	4.1	44	10
	Earnest Byner, Washington[3]	274	1,048	3.8	32	5
	Gaston Green, Denver	261	1,037	4.0	63	4
	Christian Okoye, Kansas City[2]	225	1,031	4.6	48	9
1990	Barry Sanders, Detroit[2]	255	1,304	5.1	45	13
	Thurman Thomas, Buffalo[2]	271	1,297	4.8	80	11
	Marion Butts, San Diego	265	1,225	4.6	52	8
	Earnest Byner, Washington[2]	297	1,219	4.1	22	6
	Bobby Humphrey, Denver[2]	288	1,202	4.2	37	7
	Neal Anderson, Chicago[3]	260	1,078	4.1	52	10
	Barry Word, Kansas City	204	1,015	5.0	53	4
	James Brooks, Cincinnati[3]	195	1,004	5.1	56	5
1989	Christian Okoye, Kansas City	370	1,480	4.0	59	12
	*Barry Sanders, Detroit	280	1,470	5.3	34	14
	Eric Dickerson, Indianapolis[7]	314	1,311	4.2	21	7
	Neal Anderson, Chicago[2]	274	1,275	4.7	73	11
	Dalton Hilliard, New Orleans	344	1,262	3.7	40	13
	Thurman Thomas, Buffalo	298	1,244	4.2	38	6

	James Brooks, Cincinnati[2]	221	1,239	5.6	65	7
	*Bobby Humphrey, Denver	294	1,151	3.9	40	7
	Greg Bell, L.A. Rams[3]	272	1,137	4.2	47	15
	Roger Craig, San Francisco[3]	271	1,054	3.9	27	6
	Ottis Anderson, N.Y. Giants[6]	325	1,023	3.1	36	14
1988	Eric Dickerson, Indianapolis[6]	388	1,659	4.3	41	14
	Herschel Walker, Dallas	361	1,514	4.2	38	5
	Roger Craig, San Francisco[2]	310	1,502	4.8	46	9
	Greg Bell, L.A. Rams[2]	288	1,212	4.2	44	16
	*John Stephens, New England	297	1,168	3.9	52	4
	Gary Anderson, San Diego	225	1,119	5.0	36	3
	Neal Anderson, Chicago	249	1,106	4.4	80	12
	Joe Morris, N.Y. Giants[3]	307	1,083	3.5	27	5
	*Ickey Woods, Cincinnati	203	1,066	5.3	56	15
	Curt Warner, Seattle[4]	266	1,025	3.9	29	10
	John Settle, Atlanta	232	1,024	4.4	62	7
	Mike Rozier, Houston	251	1,002	4.0	28	10
1987	Charles White, L.A. Rams	324	1,374	4.2	58	11
	Eric Dickerson, L.A. Rams-Indianapolis[5]	283	1,288	4.6	57	6
1986	Eric Dickerson, L.A. Rams[4]	404	1,821	4.5	42	11
	Joe Morris, N.Y. Giants[2]	341	1,516	4.4	54	14
	Curt Warner, Seattle[3]	319	1,481	4.6	60	13
	*Rueben Mayes, New Orleans	286	1,353	4.7	50	8
	Walter Payton, Chicago[10]	321	1,333	4.2	41	8
	Gerald Riggs, Atlanta[3]	343	1,327	3.9	31	9
	George Rogers, Washington[4]	303	1,203	4.0	42	18
	James Brooks, Cincinnati	205	1,087	5.3	56	5
1985	Marcus Allen, L.A. Raiders[3]	390	1,759	4.6	61	11
	Gerald Riggs, Atlanta[2]	397	1,719	4.3	50	10
	Walter Payton, Chicago[9]	324	1,551	4.8	40	9
	Joe Morris, N.Y. Giants	294	1,336	4.5	65	21
	Freeman McNeil, N.Y. Jets[2]	294	1,331	4.5	69	3
	Tony Dorsett, Dallas[8]	305	1,307	4.3	60	7
	James Wilder, Tampa Bay[2]	365	1,300	3.6	28	10
	Eric Dickerson, L.A. Rams[3]	292	1,234	4.2	43	12
	Craig James, New England	263	1,227	4.7	65	5
	Kevin Mack, Cleveland	222	1,104	5.0	61	7
	Curt Warner, Seattle[2]	291	1,094	3.8	38	8
	George Rogers, Washington[3]	231	1,093	4.7	35	7
	Roger Craig, San Francisco	214	1,050	4.9	62	9
	Earnest Jackson, Philadelphia[2]	282	1,028	3.6	59	5
	Stump Mitchell, St. Louis	183	1,006	5.5	64	7
	Earnest Byner, Cleveland	244	1,002	4.1	36	8
1984	Eric Dickerson, L.A. Rams[2]	379	2,105	5.6	66	14
	Walter Payton, Chicago[8]	381	1,684	4.4	72	11
	James Wilder, Tampa Bay	407	1,544	3.8	37	13
	Gerald Riggs, Atlanta	353	1,486	4.2	57	13
	Wendell Tyler, San Francisco[3]	246	1,262	5.1	40	7
	John Riggins, Washington[5]	327	1,239	3.8	24	14
	Tony Dorsett, Dallas[7]	302	1,189	3.9	31	6
	Earnest Jackson, San Diego	296	1,179	4.0	32	8
	Ottis Anderson, St. Louis[5]	289	1,174	4.1	24	6
	Marcus Allen, L.A. Raiders[2]	275	1,168	4.2	52	13
	Sammy Winder, Denver	296	1,153	3.9	24	4
	*Greg Bell, Buffalo	262	1,100	4.2	85	7
	Freeman McNeil, N.Y. Jets	229	1,070	4.7	53	5
1983	*Eric Dickerson, L.A. Rams	390	1,808	4.6	85	18
	William Andrews, Atlanta[4]	331	1,567	4.7	27	7
	*Curt Warner, Seattle	335	1,449	4.3	60	13
	Walter Payton, Chicago[7]	314	1,421	4.5	49	6
	John Riggins, Washington[4]	375	1,347	3.6	44	24
	Tony Dorsett, Dallas[6]	289	1,321	4.6	77	8
	Earl Campbell, Houston[5]	322	1,301	4.0	42	12
	Ottis Anderson, St. Louis[4]	296	1,270	4.3	43	5
	Mike Pruitt, Cleveland[4]	293	1,184	4.0	27	10
	George Rogers, New Orleans[2]	256	1,144	4.5	76	5
	Joe Cribbs, Buffalo[3]	263	1,131	4.3	45	3
	Curtis Dickey, Baltimore	254	1,122	4.4	56	4
	Tony Collins, New England	219	1,049	4.8	50	10
	Billy Sims, Detroit[3]	220	1,040	4.7	41	7

OUTSTANDING PERFORMERS

Year	Player, Team	Att.	Yards	Avg.	Long	TD
	Marcus Allen, L.A. Raiders	266	1,014	3.8	19	9
	Franco Harris, Pittsburgh[8]	279	1,007	3.6	19	5
1981	*George Rogers, New Orleans	378	1,674	4.4	79	13
	Tony Dorsett, Dallas[5]	342	1,646	4.8	75	4
	Billy Sims, Detroit[2]	296	1,437	4.9	51	13
	Wilbert Montgomery, Philadelphia[3]	286	1,402	4.9	41	8
	Ottis Anderson, St. Louis[3]	328	1,376	4.2	28	9
	Earl Campbell, Houston[4]	361	1,376	3.8	43	10
	William Andrews, Atlanta[3]	289	1,301	4.5	29	10
	Walter Payton, Chicago[6]	339	1,222	3.6	39	6
	Chuck Muncie, San Diego[2]	251	1,144	4.6	73	19
	*Joe Delaney, Kansas City	234	1,121	4.8	82	3
	Mike Pruitt, Cleveland[3]	247	1,103	4.5	21	7
	Joe Cribbs, Buffalo[2]	257	1,097	4.3	35	3
	Pete Johnson, Cincinnati	274	1,077	3.9	39	12
	Wendell Tyler, Los Angeles[2]	260	1,074	4.1	69	12
	Ted Brown, Minnesota	274	1,063	3.9	34	6
1980	Earl Campbell, Houston[3]	373	1,934	5.2	55	13
	Walter Payton, Chicago[5]	317	1,460	4.6	69	6
	Ottis Anderson, St. Louis[2]	301	1,352	4.5	52	9
	William Andrews, Atlanta[2]	265	1,308	4.9	33	4
	*Billy Sims, Detroit	313	1,303	4.2	52	13
	Tony Dorsett, Dallas[4]	278	1,185	4.3	56	11
	*Joe Cribbs, Buffalo	306	1,185	3.9	48	11
	Mike Pruitt, Cleveland[2]	249	1,034	4.2	56	6
1979	Earl Campbell, Houston[2]	368	1,697	4.6	61	19
	Walter Payton, Chicago[4]	369	1,610	4.4	43	14
	*Ottis Anderson, St. Louis	331	1,605	4.8	76	8
	Wilbert Montgomery, Philadelphia[2]	338	1,512	4.5	62	9
	Mike Pruitt, Cleveland	264	1,294	4.9	77	9
	Ricky Bell, Tampa Bay	283	1,263	4.5	49	7
	Chuck Muncie, New Orleans	238	1,198	5.0	69	11
	Franco Harris, Pittsburgh[7]	267	1,186	4.4	71	11
	John Riggins, Washington[3]	260	1,153	4.4	66	9
	Wendell Tyler, Los Angeles	218	1,109	5.1	63	9
	Tony Dorsett, Dallas[3]	250	1,107	4.4	41	6
	*William Andrews, Atlanta	239	1,023	4.3	23	3
1978	*Earl Campbell, Houston	302	1,450	4.8	81	13
	Walter Payton, Chicago[3]	333	1,395	4.2	76	11
	Tony Dorsett, Dallas[2]	290	1,325	4.6	63	7
	Delvin Williams, Miami[2]	272	1,258	4.6	58	8
	Wilbert Montgomery, Philadelphia	259	1,220	4.7	47	9
	Terdell Middleton, Green Bay	284	1,116	3.9	76	11
	Franco Harris, Pittsburgh[6]	310	1,082	3.5	37	8
	Mark van Eeghen, Oakland[3]	270	1,080	4.0	34	9
	*Terry Miller, Buffalo	238	1,060	4.5	60	7
	Tony Reed, Kansas City	206	1,053	5.1	62	5
	John Riggins, Washington[2]	248	1,014	4.1	31	5
1977	Walter Payton, Chicago[2]	339	1,852	5.5	73	14
	Mark van Eeghen, Oakland[2]	324	1,273	3.9	27	7
	Lawrence McCutcheon, Los Angeles[4]	294	1,238	4.2	48	7
	Franco Harris, Pittsburgh[5]	300	1,162	3.9	61	11
	Lydell Mitchell, Baltimore[3]	301	1,159	3.9	64	3
	Chuck Foreman, Minnesota[3]	270	1,112	4.1	51	6
	Greg Pruitt, Cleveland[3]	236	1,086	4.6	78	3
	Sam Cunningham, New England	270	1,015	3.8	31	4
	*Tony Dorsett, Dallas	208	1,007	4.8	84	12
1976	O.J. Simpson, Buffalo[5]	290	1,503	5.2	75	8
	Walter Payton, Chicago	311	1,390	4.5	60	13
	Delvin Williams, San Francisco	248	1,203	4.9	80	7
	Lydell Mitchell, Baltimore[2]	289	1,200	4.2	43	5
	Lawrence McCutcheon, Los Angeles[3]	291	1,168	4.0	40	9
	Chuck Foreman, Minnesota[2]	278	1,155	4.2	46	13
	Franco Harris, Pittsburgh[4]	289	1,128	3.9	30	14
	Mike Thomas, Washington	254	1,101	4.3	28	5
	Rocky Bleier, Pittsburgh	220	1,036	4.7	28	5
	Mark van Eeghen, Oakland	233	1,012	4.3	21	3
	Otis Armstrong, Denver[2]	247	1,008	4.1	31	5
	Greg Pruitt, Cleveland[2]	209	1,000	4.8	64	4

1975	O.J. Simpson, Buffalo[4]	329	1,817	5.5	88	16
	Franco Harris, Pittsburgh[3]	262	1,246	4.8	36	10
	Lydell Mitchell, Baltimore	289	1,193	4.1	70	11
	Jim Otis, St. Louis	269	1,076	4.0	30	5
	Chuck Foreman, Minnesota	280	1,070	3.8	31	13
	Greg Pruitt, Cleveland	217	1,067	4.9	50	8
	John Riggins, N.Y. Jets	238	1,005	4.2	42	8
	Dave Hampton, Atlanta	250	1,002	4.0	22	5
1974	Otis Armstrong, Denver	263	1,407	5.3	43	9
	*Don Woods, San Diego	227	1,162	5.1	56	7
	O.J. Simpson, Buffalo[3]	270	1,125	4.2	41	3
	Lawrence McCutcheon, Los Angeles[2]	236	1,109	4.7	23	3
	Franco Harris, Pittsburgh[2]	208	1,006	4.8	54	5
1973	O.J. Simpson, Buffalo[2]	332	2,003	6.0	80	12
	John Brockington, Green Bay[3]	265	1,144	4.3	53	3
	Calvin Hill, Dallas[2]	273	1,142	4.2	21	6
	Lawrence McCutcheon, Los Angeles	210	1,097	5.2	37	2
	Larry Csonka, Miami[3]	219	1,003	4.6	25	5
1972	O.J. Simpson, Buffalo	292	1,251	4.3	94	6
	Larry Brown, Washington[2]	285	1,216	4.3	38	8
	Ron Johnson, N.Y. Giants[2]	298	1,182	4.0	35	9
	Larry Csonka, Miami[2]	213	1,117	5.2	45	6
	Marv Hubbard, Oakland	219	1,100	5.0	39	4
	*Franco Harris, Pittsburgh	188	1,055	5.6	75	10
	Calvin Hill, Dallas	245	1,036	4.2	26	6
	Mike Garrett, San Diego[2]	272	1,031	3.8	41	6
	John Brockington, Green Bay[2]	274	1,027	3.7	30	8
	Eugene (Mercury) Morris, Miami	190	1,000	5.3	33	12
1971	Floyd Little, Denver	284	1,133	4.0	40	6
	*John Brockington, Green Bay	216	1,105	5.1	52	4
	Larry Csonka, Miami	195	1,051	5.4	28	7
	Steve Owens, Detroit	246	1,035	4.2	23	8
	Willie Ellison, Los Angeles	211	1,000	4.7	80	4
1970	Larry Brown, Washington	237	1,125	4.7	75	5
	Ron Johnson, N.Y. Giants	263	1,027	3.9	68	8
1969	Gale Sayers, Chicago[2]	236	1,032	4.4	28	8
1968	Leroy Kelly, Cleveland[3]	248	1,239	5.0	65	16
	*Paul Robinson, Cincinnati	238	1,023	4.3	87	8
1967	Jim Nance, Boston[2]	269	1,216	4.5	53	7
	Leroy Kelly, Cleveland[2]	235	1,205	5.1	42	11
	Hoyle Granger, Houston	236	1,194	5.1	67	6
	Mike Garrett, Kansas City	236	1,087	4.6	58	9
1966	Jim Nance, Boston	299	1,458	4.9	65	11
	Gale Sayers, Chicago	229	1,231	5.4	58	8
	Leroy Kelly, Cleveland	209	1,141	5.5	70	15
	Dick Bass, Los Angeles[2]	248	1,090	4.4	50	8
1965	Jim Brown, Cleveland[7]	289	1,544	5.3	67	17
	Paul Lowe, San Diego[2]	222	1,121	5.0	59	7
1964	Jim Brown, Cleveland[6]	280	1,446	5.2	71	7
	Jim Taylor, Green Bay[5]	235	1,169	5.0	84	12
	John Henry Johnson, Pittsburgh[2]	235	1,048	4.5	45	7
1963	Jim Brown, Cleveland[5]	291	1,863	6.4	80	12
	Clem Daniels, Oakland	215	1,099	5.1	74	3
	Jim Taylor, Green Bay[4]	248	1,018	4.1	40	9
	Paul Lowe, San Diego	177	1,010	5.7	66	8
1962	Jim Taylor, Green Bay[3]	272	1,474	5.4	51	19
	John Henry Johnson, Pittsburgh	251	1,141	4.5	40	7
	Cookie Gilchrist, Buffalo	214	1,096	5.1	44	13
	Abner Haynes, Dall. Texans	221	1,049	4.7	71	13
	Dick Bass, Los Angeles	196	1,033	5.3	57	6
	Charlie Tolar, Houston	244	1,012	4.1	25	7
1961	Jim Brown, Cleveland[4]	305	1,408	4.6	38	8
	Jim Taylor, Green Bay[2]	243	1,307	5.4	53	15
1960	Jim Brown, Cleveland[3]	215	1,257	5.8	71	9
	Jim Taylor, Green Bay	230	1,101	4.8	32	11
	John David Crow, St. Louis	183	1,071	5.9	57	6
1959	Jim Brown, Cleveland[2]	290	1,329	4.6	70	14
	J.D. Smith, San Francisco	207	1,036	5.0	73	10
1958	Jim Brown, Cleveland	257	1,527	5.9	65	17
1956	Rick Casares, Chi. Bears	234	1,126	4.8	68	12

OUTSTANDING PERFORMERS

Year	Player, Team	Att.	Yards	Avg.	Long	TD
1954	Joe Perry, San Francisco[2]	173	1,049	6.1	58	8
1953	Joe Perry, San Francisco	192	1,018	5.3	51	10
1949	Steve Van Buren, Philadelphia[2]	263	1,146	4.4	41	11
	Tony Canadeo, Green Bay	208	1,052	5.1	54	4
1947	Steve Van Buren, Philadelphia	217	1,008	4.6	45	13
1934	*Beattie Feathers, Chi. Bears	119	1,004	8.4	82	8

First season of professional football.

200 YARDS RUSHING IN A GAME

Date	Player, Team, Opponent	Att.	Yards	TD
Dec. 28, 2003	Ahman Green, Green Bay vs. Denver	20	218	2
Dec. 28, 2003	LaDainian Tomlinson, San Diego vs. Oakland	31	243	2
Dec. 21, 2003	Jamal Lewis, Baltimore vs. Cleveland	22	205	2
Dec. 7, 2003	Clinton Portis, Denver vs. Kansas City	22	218	5
Oct. 19, 2003	LaDainian Tomlinson, San Diego vs. Cleveland	26	200	1
Sept. 14, 2003	Jamal Lewis, Baltimore vs. Cleveland	30	295	2
Dec. 29, 2002	*Clinton Portis, Denver vs. Arizona	24	228	2
Dec. 28, 2002	Tiki Barber, N.Y. Giants vs. Philadelphia	32	203	0
Dec. 9, 2002	Ricky Williams, Miami vs. Chicago	31	216	2
Dec. 1, 2002	LaDainian Tomlinson, San Diego vs. Denver	37	220	3
Dec. 1, 2002	Ricky Williams, Miami vs. Buffalo	27	228	2
Sept. 29, 2002	LaDainian Tomlinson, San Diego vs. New England	27	217	2
Dec. 23, 2001	Marshall Faulk, St. Louis vs. Carolina	30	202	2
Nov. 11, 2001	Shaun Alexander, Seattle vs. Oakland	35	266	3
Dec. 24, 2000	Marshall Faulk, St. Louis vs. New Orleans	32	220	2
Dec. 3, 2000	Corey Dillon, Cincinnati vs. Arizona	35	216	1
Dec. 3, 2000	Warrick Dunn, Tampa Bay vs. Dallas	22	210	2
Dec. 3, 2000	*Mike Anderson, Denver vs. New Orleans	37	251	4
Dec. 3, 2000	Curtis Martin, N.Y. Jets vs. Indianapolis	30	203	1
Nov. 19, 2000	Fred Taylor, Jacksonville vs. Pittsburgh	30	234	3
Oct. 22, 2000	Corey Dillon, Cincinnati vs. Denver	22	278	2
Oct. 15, 2000	Marshall Faulk, St. Louis vs. Atlanta	25	208	1
Oct. 15, 2000	Edgerrin James, Indianapolis vs. Seattle	38	219	3
Sept. 24, 2000	Charlie Garner, San Francisco vs. Dallas	36	201	1
Sept. 3, 2000	Duce Staley, Philadelphia vs. Dallas	26	201	1
Nov. 22, 1998	Priest Holmes, Baltimore vs. Cincinnati	36	227	1
Oct. 11, 1998	Terrell Davis, Denver vs Seattle	30	208	1
Dec. 4, 1997	*Corey Dillon, Cincinnati vs. Tennessee	39	246	4
Nov. 23, 1997	Barry Sanders, Detroit vs. Indianapolis	24	216	2
Oct. 26, 1997	Terrell Davis, Denver vs. Buffalo (OT)	42	207	1
Oct. 19, 1997	Napoleon Kaufman, Oakland vs. Denver	28	227	1
Oct. 12, 1997	Barry Sanders, Detroit vs. Tampa Bay	24	215	2
Sept. 21, 1997	Terrell Davis, Denver vs. Cincinnati	27	215	1
Aug. 31, 1997	Eddie George, Tennessee vs. Oakland (OT)	35	216	1
Sept. 22, 1996	LeShon Johnson, Arizona vs. New Orleans	21	214	2
Nov. 13, 1994	Barry Sanders, Detroit vs. Tampa Bay	26	237	0
Dec. 12, 1993	*Jerome Bettis, L.A. Rams vs. New Orleans	28	212	1
Oct. 31, 1993	Emmitt Smith, Dallas vs. Philadelphia	30	237	1
Nov. 24, 1991	Barry Sanders, Detroit vs. Minnesota	23	220	4
Dec. 23, 1990	James Brooks, Cincinnati vs. Houston	20	201	1
Oct. 14, 1990	Barry Word, Kansas City vs. Detroit	18	200	2
Sept. 24, 1990	Thurman Thomas, Buffalo vs. N.Y. Jets	18	214	0
Dec. 24, 1989	Greg Bell, L.A. Rams vs. New England	26	210	1
Sept. 24, 1989	Greg Bell, L.A. Rams vs. Green Bay	28	221	2
Sept. 17, 1989	Gerald Riggs, Washington vs. Philadelphia	29	221	1
Dec. 18, 1988	Gary Anderson, San Diego vs. Kansas City	34	217	1
Nov. 30, 1987	*Bo Jackson, L.A. Raiders vs. Seattle	18	221	2
Nov. 15, 1987	Charles White, L.A. Rams vs. St. Louis	34	213	1
Dec. 7, 1986	Rueben Mayes, New Orleans vs. Miami	28	203	2
Oct. 5, 1986	Eric Dickerson, L.A. Rams vs. Tampa Bay (OT)	30	207	2
Dec. 21, 1985	George Rogers, Washington vs. St. Louis	34	206	1
Dec. 21, 1985	Joe Morris, N.Y. Giants vs. Pittsburgh	36	202	3
Dec. 9, 1984	Eric Dickerson, L.A. Rams vs. Houston	27	215	2
Nov. 18, 1984	*Greg Bell, Buffalo vs. Dallas	27	206	1
Nov. 4, 1984	Eric Dickerson, L.A. Rams vs. St. Louis	21	208	0
Sept. 2, 1984	Gerald Riggs, Atlanta vs. New Orleans	35	202	2
Nov. 27, 1983	*Curt Warner, Seattle vs. Kansas City (OT)	32	207	3
Nov. 6, 1983	James Wilder, Tampa Bay vs. Minnesota	31	219	1
Sept. 18, 1983	Tony Collins, New England vs. N.Y. Jets	23	212	3

Date	Player, Team, Opponent	Att.	Yards	TD
Sept. 4, 1983	George Rogers, New Orleans vs. St. Louis	24	206	2
Dec. 21, 1980	Earl Campbell, Houston vs. Minnesota	29	203	1
Nov. 16, 1980	Earl Campbell, Houston vs. Chicago	31	206	0
Oct. 26, 1980	Earl Campbell, Houston vs. Cincinnati	27	202	2
Oct. 19, 1980	Earl Campbell, Houston vs. Tampa Bay	33	203	0
Nov. 26, 1978	*Terry Miller, Buffalo vs. N.Y. Giants	21	208	2
Dec. 4, 1977	*Tony Dorsett, Dallas vs. Philadelphia	23	206	2
Nov. 20, 1977	Walter Payton, Chicago vs. Minnesota	40	275	1
Oct. 30, 1977	Walter Payton, Chicago vs. Green Bay	23	205	2
Dec. 5, 1976	O.J. Simpson, Buffalo vs. Miami	24	203	1
Nov. 25, 1976	O.J. Simpson, Buffalo vs. Detroit	29	273	2
Oct. 24, 1976	Chuck Foreman, Minnesota vs. Philadelphia	28	200	2
Dec. 14, 1975	Greg Pruitt, Cleveland vs. Kansas City	26	214	3
Sept. 28, 1975	O.J. Simpson, Buffalo vs. Pittsburgh	28	227	1
Dec. 16, 1973	O.J. Simpson, Buffalo vs. N.Y. Jets	34	200	1
Dec. 9, 1973	O.J. Simpson, Buffalo vs. New England	22	219	1
Sept. 16, 1973	O.J. Simpson, Buffalo vs. New England	29	250	2
Dec. 5, 1971	Willie Ellison, Los Angeles vs. New Orleans	26	247	1
Dec. 20, 1970	John (Frenchy) Fuqua, Pittsburgh vs. Philadelphia	20	218	2
Nov. 3, 1968	Gale Sayers, Chicago vs. Green Bay	24	205	0
Oct. 30, 1966	Jim Nance, Boston vs. Oakland	38	208	2
Oct. 10, 1964	John Henry Johnson, Pittsburgh vs. Cleveland	30	200	3
Dec. 8, 1963	Cookie Gilchrist, Buffalo vs. N.Y. Jets	36	243	5
Nov. 3, 1963	Jim Brown, Cleveland vs. Philadelphia	28	223	1
Oct. 20, 1963	Clem Daniels, Oakland vs. N.Y. Jets	27	200	2
Sept. 22, 1963	Jim Brown, Cleveland vs. Dallas	20	232	2
Dec. 10, 1961	Billy Cannon, Houston vs. N.Y. Titans	25	216	3
Nov. 19, 1961	Jim Brown, Cleveland vs. Philadelphia	34	237	4
Dec. 18, 1960	John David Crow, St. Louis vs. Pittsburgh	24	203	0
Nov. 15, 1959	Bobby Mitchell, Cleveland vs. Washington	14	232	3
Nov. 24, 1957	*Jim Brown, Cleveland vs. Los Angeles	31	237	4
Dec. 16, 1956	*Tom Wilson, Los Angeles vs. Green Bay	23	223	0
Nov. 22, 1953	Dan Towler, Los Angeles vs. Baltimore	14	205	1
Nov. 12, 1950	Gene Roberts, N.Y. Giants vs. Chi. Cardinals	26	218	2
Nov. 27, 1949	Steve Van Buren, Philadelphia vs. Pittsburgh	27	205	0
Oct. 8, 1933	Cliff Battles, Boston vs. N.Y. Giants	16	215	1

**First season of professional football.*

TIMES 200 OR MORE

95 times by 62 players…Simpson 6; Brown, Campbell, Sanders, Tomlinson 4; Bell, Davis, Dickerson, Dillon, Faulk 3; Lewis, Payton, Portis, Riggs, Rogers, Williams 2.

4,000 YARDS PASSING IN A SEASON

Year	Player, Team	Att.	Comp.	Pct.	Yards	TD	Int.
2003	Peyton Manning, Indianapolis[5]	566	379	67.0	4,267	29	10
	Trent Green, Kansas City	523	330	63.1	4,039	24	12
2002	Rich Gannon, Oakland	618	418	67.6	4,689	26	10
	Drew Bledsoe, Buffalo[3]	610	375	61.5	4,359	24	15
	Peyton Manning, Indianapolis[4]	591	392	66.3	4,200	27	19
	Kerry Collins, N.Y. Giants	545	335	61.5	4,073	19	14
2001	Kurt Warner, St. Louis[2]	546	375	68.7	4,830	36	22
	Peyton Manning, Indianapolis[3]	547	343	62.7	4,131	26	23
2000	Peyton Manning, Indianapolis[2]	571	357	62.5	4,413	33	15
	Jeff Garcia, San Francisco	561	355	63.3	4,278	31	10
	Elvis Grbac, Kansas City	547	326	59.6	4,169	28	14
1999	Steve Beuerlein, Carolina	571	343	60.1	4,436	36	15
	Kurt Warner, St. Louis	499	325	65.1	4,353	41	13
	Peyton Manning, Indianapolis	533	331	62.1	4,135	26	15
	Brett Favre, Green Bay[3]	595	341	57.3	4,091	22	23
	Brad Johnson, Washington	519	316	60.9	4,005	24	13
1998	Brett Favre, Green Bay[2]	551	347	63.0	4,212	31	23
	Steve Young, San Francisco[2]	517	322	62.3	4,170	36	12
1996	Mark Brunell, Jacksonville	557	353	63.4	4,367	19	20
	Vinny Testaverde, Baltimore	549	325	59.2	4,177	33	19
	Drew Bledsoe, New England[2]	623	373	59.9	4,086	27	15
1995	Brett Favre, Green Bay	570	359	63.0	4,413	38	13
	Scott Mitchell, Detroit	583	346	59.3	4,338	32	12

Year	Player, Team	Att.	Comp.	Pct.	Yards	TD	Int.
	Warren Moon, Minnesota[4]	606	377	62.2	4,228	33	14
	Jeff George, Atlanta	557	336	60.3	4,143	24	11
1994	Drew Bledsoe, New England	691	400	57.9	4,555	25	27
	Dan Marino, Miami[6]	615	385	62.6	4,453	30	17
	Warren Moon, Minnesota[3]	601	371	61.7	4,264	18	19
1993	John Elway, Denver	551	348	63.2	4,030	25	10
	Steve Young, San Francisco	462	314	68.0	4,023	29	16
1992	Dan Marino, Miami[5]	554	330	59.6	4,116	24	16
1991	Warren Moon, Houston[2]	655	404	61.7	4,690	23	21
1990	Warren Moon, Houston	584	362	62.0	4,689	33	13
1989	Don Majkowski, Green Bay	599	353	58.9	4,318	27	20
	Jim Everett, L.A. Rams	518	304	58.7	4,310	29	17
1988	Dan Marino, Miami[4]	606	354	58.4	4,434	28	23
1986	Dan Marino, Miami[3]	623	378	60.7	4,746	44	23
	Jay Schroeder, Washington	541	276	51.0	4,109	22	22
1985	Dan Marino, Miami[2]	567	336	59.3	4,137	30	21
1984	Dan Marino, Miami	564	362	64.2	5,084	48	17
	Neil Lomax, St. Louis	560	345	61.6	4,614	28	16
	Phil Simms, N.Y. Giants	533	286	53.7	4,044	22	18
1983	Lynn Dickey, Green Bay	484	289	59.7	4,458	32	29
	Bill Kenney, Kansas City	603	346	57.4	4,348	24	18
1981	Dan Fouts, San Diego[3]	609	360	59.1	4,802	33	17
1980	Dan Fouts, San Diego[2]	589	348	59.1	4,715	30	24
	Brian Sipe, Cleveland	554	337	60.8	4,132	30	14
1979	Dan Fouts, San Diego	530	332	62.6	4,082	24	24
1967	Joe Namath, N.Y. Jets	491	258	52.5	4,007	26	28

400 YARDS PASSING IN A GAME

Date	Player, Team, Opponent	Att.	Comp.	Yards	TD
Nov. 16, 2003	Peyton Manning, Indianapolis vs. N.Y. Jets	36	27	401	1
Oct. 12, 2003	Trent Green, Kansas City vs. Green Bay (OT)	45	27	400	3
Oct. 12, 2003	Steve McNair, Tennessee vs. Houston	27	18	421	3
Dec. 29, 2002	Matt Hasselbeck, Seattle vs. San Diego (OT)	53	36	449	2
Dec. 1, 2002	Matt Hasselbeck, Seattle vs. San Francisco	55	30	427	3
Nov. 10, 2002	Marc Bulger, St. Louis vs. San Diego	48	36	453	4
Nov. 10, 2002	Tommy Maddox, Pittsburgh vs. Atlanta (OT)	41	28	473	4
Oct. 6, 2002	Drew Bledsoe, Buffalo vs. Oakland	53	32	417	2
Sept. 22, 2002	Tom Brady, New England vs. Kansas City (OT)	54	39	410	4
Sept. 15, 2002	Drew Bledsoe, Buffalo vs. Minnesota (OT)	49	35	463	3
Sept. 15, 2002	Rich Gannon, Oakland vs. Pittsburgh	64	43	403	1
Dec. 30, 2001	Jon Kitna, Cincinnati vs. Pittsburgh	68	35	411	2
Dec. 23, 2001	Chris Chandler, Atlanta vs. Buffalo	40	28	431	2
Nov. 18, 2001	Charlie Batch, Detroit vs. Arizona	62	36	436	3
Nov. 18, 2001	Kurt Warner, St. Louis vs. New England	42	30	401	3
Sept. 23, 2001	Peyton Manning, Indianapolis vs. Buffalo	29	23	421	4
Dec. 24, 2000	Vinny Testaverde, N.Y. Jets vs. Baltimore	69	36	481	2
Dec. 17, 2000	Jeff Garcia, San Francisco vs. Chicago	44	36	402	2
Dec. 3, 2000	Aaron Brooks, New Orleans vs. Denver	48	30	441	2
Nov. 19, 2000	Gus Frerotte, Denver vs. San Diego	58	36	462	5
Nov. 5, 2000	Elvis Grbac, Kansas City vs. Oakland	53	39	504	2
Nov. 5, 2000	Trent Green, St. Louis vs. Carolina	42	29	431	2
Sept. 25, 2000	Peyton Manning, Indianapolis vs. Jacksonville	36	23	440	4
Sept. 4, 2000	Kurt Warner, St. Louis vs. Denver	35	25	441	3
Dec. 26, 1999	Brad Johnson, Washington vs. San Francisco (OT)	47	32	471	2
Dec. 5, 1999	Jeff Garcia, San Francisco vs. Cincinnati	49	33	437	3
Nov. 28, 1999	Jim Harbaugh, San Diego vs. Minnesota	39	25	404	1
Nov. 14, 1999	Jim Miller, Chicago vs. Minnesota (OT)	48	34	422	3
Sept. 26, 1999	Peyton Manning, Indianapolis vs. San Diego	54	29	404	2
Dec. 6, 1998	Vinny Testaverde, N.Y. Jets vs. Seattle	63	42	418	2
Dec. 6, 1998	John Elway, Denver vs. Kansas City	32	22	400	2
Nov. 26, 1998	Troy Aikman, Dallas vs. Minnesota	57	34	455	1
Nov. 23, 1998	Drew Bledsoe, New England vs. Miami	54	28	423	2
Nov. 15, 1998	Jake Plummer, Arizona vs. Dallas	56	31	465	3
Oct. 5, 1998	Randall Cunningham, Minnesota vs. Green Bay	32	20	442	4
Sept. 6, 1998	Glenn Foley, N.Y. Jets vs. San Francisco (OT)	58	30	415	3
Nov. 2, 1997	Tony Banks, St. Louis vs. Atlanta	34	23	401	2
Oct. 26, 1997	Warren Moon, Seattle vs. Oakland	44	28	409	5
Nov. 10, 1996	Boomer Esiason, Arizona vs. Washington (OT)	59	35	522	3
Nov. 3, 1996	Drew Bledsoe, New England vs. Miami	41	30	419	3

Date	Player, Team, Opponent	Att.	Comp.	Yards	TD
Oct. 27, 1996	Vinny Testaverde, Baltimore vs. St. Louis (OT)	51	31	429	3
Oct. 20, 1996	Mark Brunell, Jacksonville vs. St. Louis	52	37	421	0
Sept. 22, 1996	Mark Brunell, Jacksonville vs. New England (OT)	39	23	432	3
Dec. 18, 1995	Steve Young, San Francisco vs. Minnesota	49	30	425	3
Nov. 26, 1995	Dave Krieg, Arizona vs. Atlanta (OT)	43	27	413	4
Nov. 23, 1995	Scott Mitchell, Detroit vs. Minnesota	45	30	410	4
Oct. 1, 1995	Dan Marino, Miami vs. Cincinnati	48	33	450	2
Nov. 20, 1994	Warren Moon, Minnesota vs. N.Y. Jets	50	33	400	2
Nov. 13, 1994	Drew Bledsoe, New England vs. Minnesota (OT)	70	45	426	3
Nov. 6, 1994	Warren Moon, Minnesota vs. New Orleans	57	33	420	3
Sept. 25, 1994	Dan Marino, Miami vs. Minnesota	54	29	431	3
Sept. 4, 1994	Dan Marino, Miami vs. New England (OT)	42	23	473	5
Sept. 4, 1994	Drew Bledsoe, New England vs. Miami (OT)	51	32	421	4
Dec. 19, 1993	Steve Beuerlein, Phoenix vs. Seattle	53	34	431	3
Dec. 5, 1993	Brett Favre, Green Bay vs. Chicago	54	36	402	2
Nov. 28, 1993	Steve Young, San Francisco vs. L.A. Rams	32	26	462	4
Oct. 31, 1993	Jeff Hostetler, L.A. Raiders vs. San Diego	32	20	424	2
Sept. 13, 1992	Steve Young, San Francisco vs. Buffalo	37	26	449	3
Sept. 13, 1992	Jim Kelly, Buffalo vs. San Francisco	33	22	403	3
Nov. 10, 1991	Warren Moon, Houston vs. Dallas (OT)	56	41	432	0
Nov. 10, 1991	Mark Rypien, Washington vs. Atlanta	31	16	442	6
Oct. 13, 1991	Warren Moon, Houston vs. N.Y. Jets	50	35	423	2
Dec. 16, 1990	Warren Moon, Houston vs. Kansas City	45	27	527	3
Nov. 4, 1990	Joe Montana, San Francisco vs. Green Bay	40	25	411	3
Oct. 14, 1990	Joe Montana, San Francisco vs. Atlanta	49	32	476	6
Oct. 7, 1990	Boomer Esiason, Cincinnati vs. L.A. Rams (OT)	45	31	490	3
Dec. 23, 1989	Warren Moon, Houston vs. Cleveland	51	32	414	2
Dec. 11, 1989	Joe Montana, San Francisco vs. L.A. Rams	42	30	458	3
Nov. 26, 1989	Jim Everett, L.A. Rams vs. New Orleans (OT)	51	29	454	1
Nov. 26, 1989	Mark Rypien, Washington vs. Chicago	47	30	401	4
Oct. 2, 1989	Randall Cunningham, Philadelphia vs. Chicago	62	32	401	1
Sept. 24, 1989	Joe Montana, San Francisco vs. Philadelphia	34	25	428	5
Sept. 24, 1989	Dan Marino, Miami vs. N.Y. Jets	55	33	427	3
Sept. 17, 1989	Randall Cunningham, Philadelphia vs. Washington	46	34	447	5
Dec. 18, 1988	Dave Krieg, Seattle vs. L.A. Raiders	32	19	410	4
Dec. 12, 1988	Dan Marino, Miami vs. Cleveland	50	30	404	4
Oct. 23, 1988	Dan Marino, Miami vs. N.Y. Jets	60	35	521	3
Oct. 16, 1988	Vinny Testaverde, Tampa Bay vs. Indianapolis	42	25	469	2
Sept. 11, 1988	Doug Williams, Washington vs. Pittsburgh	52	30	430	2
Nov. 29, 1987	Tom Ramsey, New England vs. Philadelphia	53	34	402	3
Nov. 22, 1987	Boomer Esiason, Cincinnati vs. Pittsburgh	53	30	409	0
Sept. 20, 1987	Neil Lomax, St. Louis vs. San Diego	61	32	457	3
Dec. 21, 1986	Boomer Esiason, Cincinnati vs. N.Y. Jets	30	23	425	5
Dec. 14, 1986	Dan Marino, Miami vs. L.A. Rams (OT)	46	29	403	5
Nov. 23, 1986	Bernie Kosar, Cleveland vs. Pittsburgh (OT)	46	28	414	2
Nov. 17, 1986	Joe Montana, San Francisco vs. Washington	60	33	441	0
Nov. 16, 1986	Dan Marino, Miami vs. Buffalo	54	39	404	4
Nov. 10, 1986	Bernie Kosar, Cleveland vs. Miami	50	32	401	0
Nov. 2, 1986	Tommy Kramer, Minnesota vs. Washington (OT)	35	20	490	4
Nov. 2, 1986	Ken O'Brien, N.Y. Jets vs. Seattle	32	26	431	4
Oct. 27, 1986	Jay Schroeder, Washington vs. N.Y. Giants	40	22	420	1
Oct. 12, 1986	Steve Grogan, New England vs. N.Y. Jets	42	23	401	3
Sept. 21, 1986	Ken O'Brien, N.Y. Jets vs. Miami (OT)	43	29	479	4
Sept. 21, 1986	Dan Marino, Miami vs. N.Y. Jets (OT)	50	30	448	6
Sept. 21, 1986	Tony Eason, New England vs. Seattle	45	26	414	3
Dec. 20, 1985	John Elway, Denver vs. Seattle	42	24	432	1
Nov. 10, 1985	Dan Fouts, San Diego vs. L.A. Raiders (OT)	41	26	436	4
Oct. 13, 1985	Phil Simms, N.Y. Giants vs. Cincinnati	62	40	513	1
Oct. 13, 1985	Dave Krieg, Seattle vs. Atlanta	51	33	405	4
Oct. 6, 1985	Phil Simms, N.Y. Giants vs. Dallas	36	18	432	3
Oct. 6, 1985	Joe Montana, San Francisco vs. Atlanta	57	37	429	5
Sept. 19, 1985	Tommy Kramer, Minnesota vs. Chicago	55	28	436	3
Sept. 15, 1985	Dan Fouts, San Diego vs. Seattle	43	29	440	4
Dec. 16, 1984	Neil Lomax, St. Louis vs. Washington	46	37	468	2
Dec. 9, 1984	Dan Marino, Miami vs. Indianapolis	41	29	404	4
Dec. 2, 1984	Dan Marino, Miami vs. L.A. Raiders	57	35	470	4
Nov. 25, 1984	Dave Krieg, Seattle vs. Denver	44	30	406	3
Nov. 4, 1984	Dan Marino, Miami vs. N.Y. Jets	42	23	422	2
Oct. 21, 1984	Dan Fouts, San Diego vs. L.A. Raiders	45	24	410	3

OUTSTANDING PERFORMERS

Date	Player, Team, Opponent	Att.	Comp.	Yards	TD
Sept. 30, 1984	Dan Marino, Miami vs. St. Louis	36	24	429	3
Sept. 2, 1984	Phil Simms, N.Y. Giants vs. Philadelphia	30	23	409	4
Dec. 11, 1983	Bill Kenney, Kansas City vs. San Diego	41	31	411	4
Nov. 20, 1983	Dave Krieg, Seattle vs. Denver	42	31	418	3
Oct. 9, 1983	Joe Ferguson, Buffalo vs. Miami (OT)	55	38	419	5
Oct. 2, 1983	Joe Theismann, Washington vs. L.A. Raiders	39	23	417	3
Sept. 25, 1983	Richard Todd, N.Y. Jets vs. L.A. Rams (OT)	50	37	446	2
Dec. 26, 1982	Vince Ferragamo, L.A. Rams vs. Chicago	46	30	509	3
Dec. 20, 1982	Dan Fouts, San Diego vs. Cincinnati	40	25	435	1
Dec. 20, 1982	Ken Anderson, Cincinnati vs. San Diego	56	40	416	2
Dec. 11, 1982	Dan Fouts, San Diego vs. San Francisco	48	33	444	5
Nov. 21, 1982	Joe Montana, San Francisco vs. St. Louis	39	26	408	3
Nov. 15, 1981	Steve Bartkowski, Atlanta vs. Pittsburgh	50	33	416	2
Oct. 25, 1981	Brian Sipe, Cleveland vs. Baltimore	41	30	444	4
Oct. 25, 1981	David Woodley, Miami vs. Dallas	37	21	408	3
Oct. 11, 1981	Tommy Kramer, Minnesota vs. San Diego	43	27	444	4
Dec. 14, 1980	Tommy Kramer, Minnesota vs. Cleveland	49	38	456	4
Nov. 16, 1980	Doug Williams, Tampa Bay vs. Minnesota	55	30	486	4
Oct. 19, 1980	Dan Fouts, San Diego vs. N.Y. Giants	41	26	444	3
Oct. 12, 1980	Lynn Dickey, Green Bay vs. Tampa Bay (OT)	51	35	418	1
Sept. 21, 1980	Richard Todd, N.Y. Jets vs. San Francisco	60	42	447	3
Oct. 3, 1976	James Harris, Los Angeles vs. Miami	29	17	436	2
Nov. 17, 1975	Ken Anderson, Cincinnati vs. Buffalo	46	30	447	2
Nov. 18, 1974	Charley Johnson, Denver vs. Kansas City	42	28	445	2
Dec. 11, 1972	Joe Namath, N.Y. Jets vs. Oakland	46	25	403	1
Sept. 24, 1972	Joe Namath, N.Y. Jets vs. Baltimore	28	15	496	6
Dec. 21, 1969	Don Horn, Green Bay vs. St. Louis	31	22	410	5
Sept. 28, 1969	Joe Kapp, Minnesota vs. Baltimore	43	28	449	7
Sept. 9, 1968	Pete Beathard, Houston vs. Kansas City	48	23	413	2
Nov. 26, 1967	Sonny Jurgensen, Washington vs. Cleveland	50	32	418	3
Oct. 1, 1967	Joe Namath, N.Y. Jets vs. Miami	39	23	415	3
Sept. 17, 1967	Johnny Unitas, Baltimore vs. Atlanta	32	22	401	2
Nov. 13, 1966	Don Meredith, Dallas vs. Washington	29	21	406	2
Nov. 28, 1965	Sonny Jurgensen, Washington vs. Dallas	43	26	411	3
Oct. 24, 1965	Fran Tarkenton, Minnesota vs. San Francisco	35	21	407	3
Nov. 1, 1964	Len Dawson, Kansas City vs. Denver	38	23	435	6
Oct. 25, 1964	Cotton Davidson, Oakland vs. Denver	36	23	427	5
Oct. 16, 1964	Babe Parilli, Boston vs. Oakland	47	25	422	4
Dec. 22, 1963	Tom Flores, Oakland vs. Houston	29	17	407	6
Nov. 17, 1963	Norm Snead, Washington vs. Pittsburgh	40	23	424	2
Nov. 10, 1963	Don Meredith, Dallas vs. San Francisco	48	30	460	3
Oct. 13, 1963	Charley Johnson, St. Louis vs. Pittsburgh	41	20	428	2
Dec. 16, 1962	Sonny Jurgensen, Philadelphia vs. St. Louis	34	15	419	5
Nov. 18, 1962	Bill Wade, Chicago vs. Dall. Cowboys	46	28	466	2
Oct. 28, 1962	Y.A. Tittle, N.Y. Giants vs. Washington	39	27	505	7
Sept. 15, 1962	Frank Tripucka, Denver vs. Buffalo	56	29	447	2
Dec. 17, 1961	Sonny Jurgensen, Philadelphia vs. Detroit	42	27	403	3
Nov. 19, 1961	George Blanda, Houston vs. N.Y. Titans	32	20	418	7
Oct. 29, 1961	George Blanda, Houston vs. Buffalo	32	18	464	4
Oct. 29, 1961	Sonny Jurgensen, Philadelphia vs. Washington	41	27	436	3
Oct. 13, 1961	Jacky Lee, Houston vs. Boston	41	27	457	2
Dec. 13, 1958	Bobby Layne, Pittsburgh vs. Chi. Cardinals	49	23	409	2
Nov. 8, 1953	Bobby Thomason, Philadelphia vs. N.Y. Giants	44	22	437	4
Oct. 4, 1952	Otto Graham, Cleveland vs. Pittsburgh	49	21	401	3
Sept. 28, 1951	Norm Van Brocklin, Los Angeles vs. N.Y. Yanks	41	27	554	5
Dec. 11, 1949	Johnny Lujack, Chi. Bears vs. Chi. Cardinals	39	24	468	6
Oct. 31, 1948	Sammy Baugh,Washington vs. Boston	24	17	446	4
Oct. 31, 1948	Jim Hardy, Los Angeles vs. Chi. Cardinals	53	28	406	3
Nov. 14, 1943	Sid Luckman, Chi. Bears vs. N.Y. Giants	32	21	433	7

TIMES 400 OR MORE

168 times by 90 players…Marino 13; Montana, Moon 7; Bledsoe, Fouts 6; Jurgensen, Krieg 5; Esiason, Kramer, Manning, Testaverde 4; Cunningham, Namath, Simms, Young 3; Anderson, Blanda, Brunell, Elway, Garcia, Green, Hasselbeck, Johnson, Kosar, Lomax, Meredith, O'Brien, Rypien, Todd, Warner, Williams 2.

100 PASS RECEPTIONS IN A SEASON

Year	Player, Team	No.	Yards	Avg.	Long	TD
2003	Torry Holt, St. Louis	117	1,696	14.5	48	12
	Randy Moss, Minnesota[2]	111	1,632	14.7	72	17
	*Anquan Boldin, Arizona	101	1,377	13.6	71	8
	LaDainian Tomlinson, San Diego	100	725	7.3	73	4
2002	Marvin Harrison, Indianapolis[4]	143	1,722	12.0	69	11
	Hines Ward, Pittsburgh	112	1,329	11.9	72	12
	Randy Moss, Minnesota	106	1,347	12.7	60	7
	Eric Moulds, Buffalo	100	1,292	12.9	70	10
	Terrell Owens, San Francisco	100	1,300	13.0	76	13
2001	Rod Smith, Denver[2]	113	1,343	11.9	65	11
	Jimmy Smith, Jacksonville[2]	112	1,373	12.3	35	8
	Marvin Harrison, Indianapolis[3]	109	1,524	14.0	68	15
	Keyshawn Johnson, Tampa Bay	106	1,266	11.9	47	1
	Troy Brown, New England	101	1,199	11.9	60	5
	Marty Booker, Chicago	100	1,071	10.7	66	8
2000	Marvin Harrison, Indianapolis[2]	102	1,413	13.9	78	14
	Muhsin Muhammad, Carolina	102	1,183	11.6	36	6
	Ed McCaffrey, Denver	101	1,317	13.0	61	9
	Rod Smith, Denver	100	1,602	16.0	49	8
1999	Jimmy Smith, Jacksonville	116	1,636	14.1	62	6
	Marvin Harrison, Indianapolis	115	1,663	14.5	57	12
1997	Tim Brown, Oakland	104	1,408	13.5	59	5
	Herman Moore, Detroit[3]	104	1,293	12.4	79	8
1996	Jerry Rice, San Francisco[4]	108	1,254	11.6	39	8
	Herman Moore, Detroit[2]	106	1,296	12.2	50	9
	Carl Pickens, Cincinnati	100	1,180	11.8	61	12
1995	Herman Moore, Detroit	123	1,686	13.7	69	14
	Jerry Rice, San Francisco[3]	122	1,848	15.1	81	15
	Cris Carter, Minnesota[2]	122	1,371	11.2	60	17
	Isaac Bruce, St. Louis	119	1,781	15.0	72	13
	Michael Irvin, Dallas	111	1,603	14.4	50	10
	Brett Perriman, Detroit	108	1,488	13.8	91	9
	Eric Metcalf, Atlanta	104	1,189	11.4	62	8
	Robert Brooks, Green Bay	102	1,497	14.7	99	13
	Larry Centers, Arizona	101	962	9.5	32	2
1994	Cris Carter, Minnesota	122	1,256	10.3	65	7
	Jerry Rice, San Francisco[2]	112	1,499	13.4	69	13
	Terance Mathis, Atlanta	111	1,342	12.1	81	11
1993	Sterling Sharpe, Green Bay[2]	112	1,274	11.4	54	11
1992	Sterling Sharpe, Green Bay	108	1,461	13.5	76	13
1991	Haywood Jeffires, Houston	100	1,181	11.8	44	7
1990	Jerry Rice, San Francisco	100	1,502	15.0	64	13
1984	Art Monk, Washington	106	1,372	12.9	72	7
1964	Charley Hennigan, Houston	101	1,546	15.3	53	8
1961	Lionel Taylor, Denver	100	1,176	11.8	52	4

1,000 YARDS PASS RECEIVING IN A SEASON

Year	Player, Team	No.	Yards	Avg.	Long	TD
2003	Torry Holt, St. Louis[4]	117	1,696	14.5	48	12
	Randy Moss, Minnesota[6]	111	1,632	14.7	72	17
	*Anquan Boldin, Arizona	101	1,377	13.6	71	8
	Chad Johnson, Cincinnati[2]	90	1,355	15.1	82	10
	Derrick Mason, Tennessee[3]	95	1,303	13.7	50	8
	Marvin Harrison, Indianapolis[5]	94	1,272	13.5	79	10
	Laveranues Coles, Washington[2]	82	1,204	14.7	64	6
	Keenan McCardell, Tampa Bay[5]	84	1,174	14.0	76	8
	Hines Ward, Pittsburgh[3]	95	1,163	12.2	50	10
	Darrell Jackson, Seattle[2]	68	1,137	16.7	80	9
	Steve Smith, Carolina	88	1,110	12.6	67	7
	Santana Moss, N.Y. Jets	74	1,105	14.9	65	10
	Terrell Owens, San Francisco[5]	80	1,102	13.8	75	9
	Amani Toomer, N.Y. Giants[5]	63	1,057	16.8	77	5
2002	Marvin Harrison, Indianapolis[4]	143	1,722	12.0	69	11
	Randy Moss, Minnesota[5]	106	1,347	12.7	60	7
	Amani Toomer, N.Y. Giants[4]	82	1,343	16.4	82	8
	Hines Ward, Pittsburgh[2]	112	1,329	11.9	72	12
	Plaxico Burress, Pittsburgh[2]	78	1,325	17.0	62	7
	Joe Horn, New Orleans[3]	88	1,312	14.9	63	7

OUTSTANDING PERFORMERS

Year	Player, Team	No.	Yards	Avg.	Long	TD
	Torry Holt, St. Louis[3]	91	1,302	14.3	58	4
	Terrell Owens, San Francisco[4]	100	1,300	13.0	76	13
	Eric Moulds, Buffalo[3]	100	1,292	12.9	70	10
	Laveranues Coles, N.Y. Jets	89	1,264	14.2	43	5
	Peerless Price, Buffalo	94	1,252	13.3	73	9
	Koren Robinson, Seattle	78	1,240	15.9	83	5
	Jerry Rice, Oakland[14]	92	1,211	13.2	75	7
	Marty Booker, Chicago[2]	97	1,189	12.3	54	6
	Chad Johnson, Cincinnati	69	1,166	16.9	72	5
	Keyshawn Johnson, Tampa Bay[4]	76	1,088	14.3	76	5
	Isaac Bruce, St. Louis[6]	79	1,075	13.6	34	7
	Donald Driver, Green Bay	70	1,064	15.2	85	9
	Jimmy Smith, Jacksonville[7]	80	1,027	12.8	47	7
	Rod Smith, Denver[6]	89	1,027	11.5	46	5
	Derrick Mason, Tennessee[2]	79	1,012	12.8	40	5
	Rod Gardner, Washington	71	1,006	14.2	43	8
2001	David Boston, Arizona[2]	98	1,598	16.3	61	8
	Marvin Harrison, Indianapolis[3]	109	1,524	14.0	68	15
	Terrell Owens, San Francisco[3]	93	1,412	15.2	60	16
	Jimmy Smith, Jacksonville[6]	112	1,373	12.3	35	8
	Torry Holt, St. Louis[2]	81	1,363	16.8	51	7
	Rod Smith, Denver[5]	113	1,343	11.9	65	11
	Keyshawn Johnson, Tampa Bay[3]	106	1,266	11.9	47	1
	Joe Horn, New Orleans[2]	83	1,265	15.2	56	9
	Randy Moss, Minnesota[4]	82	1,233	15.0	73	10
	Troy Brown, New England	101	1,199	11.9	60	5
	Tim Brown, Oakland[9]	91	1,165	12.8	46	9
	Johnnie Morton, Detroit[4]	77	1,154	15.0	76	4
	Jerry Rice, Oakland[13]	83	1,139	13.7	40	9
	Derrick Mason, Tennessee	73	1,128	15.5	71	9
	Curtis Conway, San Diego[3]	71	1,125	15.8	72	6
	Keenan McCardell, Jacksonville[4]	93	1,110	11.9	45	6
	Isaac Bruce, St. Louis[5]	64	1,106	17.3	51	6
	Kevin Johnson, Cleveland	84	1,097	13.1	55	9
	Darrell Jackson, Seattle	70	1,081	15.4	64	8
	Marty Booker, Chicago	100	1,071	10.7	66	8
	Qadry Ismail, Baltimore[2]	74	1,059	14.3	77	7
	Amani Toomer, N.Y. Giants[3]	72	1,054	14.6	60	5
	Willie Jackson, New Orleans	81	1,046	12.9	63	5
	Plaxico Burress, Pittsburgh	66	1,008	15.3	43	6
	Hines Ward, Pittsburgh	94	1,003	10.7	34	4
2000	Torry Holt, St. Louis	82	1,635	19.9	85	6
	Rod Smith, Denver[4]	100	1,602	16.0	49	8
	Isaac Bruce, St. Louis[4]	87	1,471	16.9	78	9
	Terrell Owens, San Francisco[2]	97	1,451	15.0	69	13
	Randy Moss, Minnesota[3]	77	1,437	18.7	78	15
	Marvin Harrison, Indianapolis[2]	102	1,413	13.9	78	14
	Derrick Alexander, Kansas City[3]	78	1,391	17.8	81	10
	Joe Horn, New Orleans	94	1,340	14.3	52	8
	Eric Moulds, Buffalo[2]	94	1,326	14.1	52	5
	Ed McCaffrey, Denver[3]	101	1,317	13.0	61	9
	Cris Carter, Minnesota[8]	96	1,274	13.3	53	9
	Jimmy Smith, Jacksonville[5]	91	1,213	13.3	65	8
	Keenan McCardell, Jacksonville[3]	94	1,207	12.8	67	5
	Tony Gonzalez, Kansas City	93	1,203	12.9	39	9
	Muhsin Muhammad, Carolina[2]	102	1,183	11.6	36	6
	David Boston, Arizona	71	1,156	16.3	70	7
	Tim Brown, Oakland[8]	76	1,128	14.8	45	11
	Amani Toomer, N.Y. Giants[2]	78	1,094	14.0	54	7
1999	Marvin Harrison, Indianapolis	115	1,663	14.5	57	12
	Jimmy Smith, Jacksonville[4]	116	1,636	14.1	62	6
	Randy Moss, Minnesota[2]	80	1,413	17.7	67	11
	Marcus Robinson, Chicago	84	1,400	16.7	80	9
	Tim Brown, Oakland[7]	90	1,344	14.9	47	6
	Germane Crowell, Detroit	81	1,338	16.5	77	7
	Muhsin Muhammad, Carolina	96	1,253	13.1	60	8
	Cris Carter, Minnesota[7]	90	1,241	13.8	68	13
	Michael Westbrook, Washington	65	1,191	18.3	65	9
	Amani Toomer, N.Y. Giants	79	1,183	15.0	80	6

	Keyshawn Johnson, N.Y. Jets[2]	89	1,170	13.2	65	8
	Isaac Bruce, St. Louis[3]	77	1,165	15.1	60	12
	Terry Glenn, New England[2]	69	1,147	16.6	67	4
	Albert Connell, Washington	62	1,132	18.3	62	7
	Johnnie Morton, Detroit[3]	80	1,129	14.1	48	5
	Qadry Ismail, Baltimore	68	1,105	16.3	76	6
	Raghib Ismail, Dallas[2]	80	1,097	13.7	76	6
	Patrick Jeffers, Carolina	63	1,082	17.2	88	12
	Antonio Freeman, Green Bay[3]	74	1,074	14.5	51	6
	Bill Schroeder, Green Bay	74	1,051	14.2	51	5
	Marshall Faulk, St. Louis	87	1,048	12.1	57	5
	Tony Martin, Miami[4]	67	1,037	15.5	69	5
	Darnay Scott, Cincinnati	68	1,022	15.0	76	7
	Rod Smith, Denver[3]	79	1,020	12.9	71	4
	Ed McCaffrey, Denver[2]	71	1,018	14.3	78	7
	Terance Mathis, Atlanta[4]	81	1,016	12.5	52	6
1998	Antonio Freeman, Green Bay[2]	84	1,424	17.0	84	14
	Eric Moulds, Buffalo	67	1,368	20.4	84	9
	*Randy Moss, Minnesota	69	1,313	19.0	61	17
	Rod Smith, Denver[2]	86	1,222	14.2	58	6
	Jimmy Smith, Jacksonville[3]	78	1,182	15.2	72	8
	Tony Martin, Atlanta[3]	66	1,181	17.9	62	6
	Jerry Rice, San Francisco[12]	82	1,157	14.1	75	9
	Frank Sanders, Arizona[2]	89	1,145	12.9	42	3
	Terance Mathis, Atlanta[3]	64	1,136	17.8	78	11
	Keyshawn Johnson, N.Y. Jets	83	1,131	13.6	41	10
	Terrell Owens, San Francisco	67	1,097	16.4	79	14
	Wayne Chrebet, N.Y. Jets	75	1,083	14.4	63	8
	Michael Irvin, Dallas[7]	74	1,057	14.3	51	1
	Ed McCaffrey, Denver	64	1,053	16.5	48	10
	O.J. McDuffie, Miami	90	1,050	11.7	61	7
	Joey Galloway, Seattle[3]	65	1,047	16.1	81	10
	Johnnie Morton, Detroit[2]	69	1,028	14.9	98	2
	Raghib Ismail, Carolina	69	1,024	14.8	62	8
	Carl Pickens, Cincinnati[4]	82	1,023	12.5	67	5
	Tim Brown, Oakland[6]	81	1,012	12.5	49	9
	Cris Carter, Minnesota[6]	78	1,011	13.0	54	12
1997	Rob Moore, Arizona[3]	97	1,584	16.3	47	8
	Tim Brown, Oakland[5]	104	1,408	13.5	59	5
	Yancey Thigpen, Pittsburgh[2]	79	1,398	17.7	69	7
	Jimmy Smith, Jacksonville[2]	82	1,324	16.1	75	4
	Irving Fryar, Philadelphia[5]	86	1,316	15.3	72	6
	Herman Moore, Detroit[4]	104	1,293	12.4	79	8
	Antonio Freeman, Green Bay	81	1,243	15.3	58	12
	Michael Irvin, Dallas[6]	75	1,180	15.7	55	9
	Rod Smith, Denver	70	1,180	16.9	78	12
	Keenan McCardell, Jacksonville[2]	85	1,164	13.7	60	5
	Jake Reed, Minnesota[4]	68	1,138	16.7	56	6
	Shannon Sharpe, Denver[3]	72	1,107	15.4	68	3
	Andre Rison, Kansas City[5]	72	1,092	15.2	45	7
	Cris Carter, Minnesota[5]	89	1,069	12.0	43	13
	Johnnie Morton, Detroit	80	1,057	13.2	73	6
	Joey Galloway, Seattle[2]	72	1,049	14.6	53	12
	Frank Sanders, Arizona	75	1,017	13.6	70	4
	Robert Brooks, Green Bay[2]	60	1,010	16.8	48	7
	Derrick Alexander, Baltimore[2]	65	1,009	15.5	92	9
1996	Isaac Bruce, St. Louis[2]	84	1,338	15.9	70	7
	Jake Reed, Minnesota[3]	72	1,320	18.3	82	7
	Herman Moore, Detroit[3]	106	1,296	12.2	50	9
	Jerry Rice, San Francisco[11]	108	1,254	11.6	39	8
	Jimmy Smith, Jacksonville	83	1,244	15.0	62	7
	Michael Jackson, Baltimore	76	1,201	15.8	86	14
	Irving Fryar, Philadelphia[4]	88	1,195	13.6	42	11
	Carl Pickens, Cincinnati[3]	100	1,180	11.8	61	12
	Tony Martin, San Diego[2]	85	1,171	13.8	55	14
	Cris Carter, Minnesota[4]	96	1,163	12.1	43	10
	*Terry Glenn, New England	90	1,132	12.6	37	6
	Keenan McCardell, Jacksonville	85	1,129	13.3	52	3
	Tim Brown, Oakland[4]	90	1,104	12.3	42	9
	Derrick Alexander, Baltimore	62	1,099	17.7	64	9

OUTSTANDING PERFORMERS

Year	Player, Team	No.	Yards	Avg.	Long	TD
	Shannon Sharpe, Denver[2]	80	1,062	13.3	51	10
	Curtis Conway, Chicago[2]	81	1,049	13.0	58	7
	Andre Reed, Buffalo[4]	66	1,036	15.7	67	6
	Brett Perriman, Detroit[2]	94	1,021	10.9	44	5
	Rob Moore, Arizona[2]	58	1,016	17.5	69	4
	Henry Ellard, Washington[7]	52	1,014	19.5	51	2
	Charles Johnson, Pittsburgh	60	1,008	16.8	70	3
1995	Jerry Rice, San Francisco[10]	122	1,848	15.1	81	15
	Isaac Bruce, St. Louis	119	1,781	15.0	72	13
	Herman Moore, Detroit[2]	123	1,686	13.7	69	14
	Michael Irvin, Dallas[5]	111	1,603	14.4	50	10
	Robert Brooks, Green Bay	102	1,497	14.7	99	13
	Brett Perriman, Detroit	108	1,488	13.8	91	9
	Cris Carter, Minnesota[3]	122	1,371	11.2	60	17
	Tim Brown, Oakland[3]	89	1,342	15.1	80	10
	Yancey Thigpen, Pittsburgh	85	1,307	15.4	43	5
	Jeff Graham, Chicago	82	1,301	15.9	51	4
	Carl Pickens, Cincinnati[2]	99	1,234	12.5	68	17
	Tony Martin, San Diego	90	1,224	13.6	51	6
	Eric Metcalf, Atlanta	104	1,189	11.4	62	8
	Jake Reed, Minnesota[2]	72	1,167	16.2	55	9
	Quinn Early, New Orleans	81	1,087	13.4	70	8
	Anthony Miller, Denver[5]	59	1,079	18.3	62	14
	Bert Emanuel, Atlanta	74	1,039	14.0	52	5
	*Joey Galloway, Seattle	67	1,039	15.5	59	7
	Terance Mathis, Atlanta[2]	78	1,039	13.3	54	9
	Curtis Conway, Chicago	62	1,037	16.7	76	12
	Henry Ellard, Washington[6]	56	1,005	17.9	59	5
	Mark Carrier, Carolina[2]	66	1,002	15.2	66	3
	Brian Blades, Seattle[4]	77	1,001	13.0	49	4
1994	Jerry Rice, San Francisco[9]	112	1,499	13.4	69	13
	Henry Ellard, Washington[5]	74	1,397	18.9	73	6
	Terance Mathis, Atlanta	111	1,342	12.1	81	11
	Tim Brown, L.A. Raiders[2]	89	1,309	14.7	77	9
	Andre Reed, Buffalo[2]	90	1,303	14.5	83	8
	Irving Fryar, Miami[3]	73	1,270	17.4	54	7
	Cris Carter, Minnesota[2]	122	1,256	10.3	65	7
	Michael Irvin, Dallas[4]	79	1,241	15.7	65	6
	Jake Reed, Minnesota	85	1,175	13.8	59	4
	Ben Coates, New England	96	1,174	12.2	62	7
	Herman Moore, Detroit	72	1,173	16.3	51	11
	Fred Barnett, Philadelphia[2]	78	1,127	14.4	54	5
	Carl Pickens, Cincinnati	71	1,127	15.9	70	11
	Sterling Sharpe, Green Bay[4]	94	1,119	11.9	49	18
	Anthony Miller, Denver[4]	60	1,107	18.5	76	5
	Andre Rison, Atlanta[3]	81	1,088	13.4	69	8
	Brian Blades, Seattle[3]	81	1,088	13.4	45	4
	Rob Moore, N.Y. Jets	78	1,010	12.9	41	6
	Shannon Sharpe, Denver	87	1,010	11.6	44	4
1993	Jerry Rice, San Francisco[8]	98	1,503	15.3	80	15
	Michael Irvin, Dallas[3]	88	1,330	15.1	61	7
	Sterling Sharpe, Green Bay[4]	112	1,274	11.4	54	11
	Andre Rison, Atlanta[3]	86	1,242	14.4	53	15
	Tim Brown, L.A. Raiders	80	1,180	14.8	71	7
	Anthony Miller, San Diego[3]	84	1,162	13.8	66	7
	Cris Carter, Minnesota	86	1,071	12.5	58	9
	Reggie Langhorne, Indianapolis	85	1,038	12.2	72	3
	Irving Fryar, Miami[2]	64	1,010	15.8	65	5
1992	Sterling Sharpe, Green Bay[3]	108	1,461	13.5	76	13
	Michael Irvin, Dallas[2]	78	1,396	17.9	87	7
	Jerry Rice, San Francisco[7]	84	1,201	14.3	80	10
	Andre Rison, Atlanta[2]	93	1,119	12.0	71	11
	Fred Barnett, Philadelphia	67	1,083	16.2	71	6
	Anthony Miller, San Diego[2]	72	1,060	14.7	67	7
	Eric Martin, New Orleans[3]	68	1,041	15.3	52	5
1991	Michael Irvin, Dallas	93	1,523	16.4	66	8
	Gary Clark, Washington[5]	70	1,340	19.1	82	10
	Jerry Rice, San Francisco[6]	80	1,206	15.1	73	14
	Haywood Jeffires, Houston[2]	100	1,181	11.8	44	7

	Michael Haynes, Atlanta	50	1,122	22.4	80	11
	Andre Reed, Buffalo[2]	81	1,113	13.7	55	10
	Drew Hill, Houston[5]	90	1,109	12.3	61	4
	Mark Duper, Miami[4]	70	1,085	15.5	43	5
	James Lofton, Buffalo[6]	57	1,072	18.8	77	8
	Mark Clayton, Miami[5]	70	1,053	15.0	43	12
	Henry Ellard, L.A. Rams[4]	64	1,052	16.4	38	3
	Art Monk, Washington[5]	71	1,049	14.8	64	8
	Irving Fryar, New England	68	1,014	14.9	56	3
	John Taylor, San Francisco[2]	64	1,011	15.8	97	9
	Brian Blades, Seattle[2]	70	1,003	14.3	52	2
1990	Jerry Rice, San Francisco[5]	100	1,502	15.0	64	13
	Henry Ellard, L.A. Rams[3]	76	1,294	17.0	50	4
	Andre Rison, Atlanta	82	1,208	14.7	75	10
	Gary Clark, Washington[4]	75	1,112	14.8	53	8
	Sterling Sharpe, Green Bay[2]	67	1,105	16.5	76	6
	Willie Anderson, L.A. Rams[2]	51	1,097	21.5	55	4
	Haywood Jeffires, Houston	74	1,048	14.2	87	8
	Stephone Paige, Kansas City	65	1,021	15.7	86	5
	Drew Hill, Houston[4]	74	1,019	13.8	57	5
	Anthony Carter, Minnesota[3]	70	1,008	14.4	56	8
1989	Jerry Rice, San Francisco[4]	82	1,483	18.1	68	17
	Sterling Sharpe, Green Bay	90	1,423	15.8	79	12
	Mark Carrier, Tampa Bay	86	1,422	16.5	78	9
	Henry Ellard, L.A. Rams[2]	70	1,382	19.7	53	8
	Andre Reed, Buffalo	88	1,312	14.9	78	9
	Anthony Miller, San Diego	75	1,252	16.7	69	10
	Webster Slaughter, Cleveland	65	1,236	19.0	97	6
	Gary Clark, Washington[3]	79	1,229	15.6	80	9
	Tim McGee, Cincinnati	65	1,211	18.6	74	8
	Art Monk, Washington[4]	86	1,186	13.8	60	8
	Willie Anderson, L.A. Rams	44	1,146	26.0	78	5
	Ricky Sanders, Washington[2]	80	1,138	14.2	68	4
	Vance Johnson, Denver	76	1,095	14.4	69	7
	Richard Johnson, Detroit	70	1,091	15.6	75	8
	Eric Martin, New Orleans[2]	68	1,090	16.0	53	8
	John Taylor, San Francisco	60	1,077	18.0	95	10
	Mervyn Fernandez, L.A. Raiders	57	1,069	18.8	75	9
	Anthony Carter, Minnesota[2]	65	1,066	16.4	50	4
	Brian Blades, Seattle	77	1,063	13.8	60	5
	Mark Clayton, Miami[4]	64	1,011	15.8	78	9
1988	Henry Ellard, L.A. Rams	86	1,414	16.4	68	10
	Jerry Rice, San Francisco[3]	64	1,306	20.4	96	9
	Eddie Brown, Cincinnati	53	1,273	24.0	86	9
	Anthony Carter, Minnesota	72	1,225	17.0	67	6
	Ricky Sanders, Washington	73	1,148	15.7	55	12
	Drew Hill, Houston[3]	72	1,141	15.8	57	10
	Mark Clayton, Miami[3]	86	1,129	13.1	45	14
	Roy Green, Phoenix[3]	68	1,097	16.1	52	7
	Eric Martin, New Orleans	85	1,083	12.7	40	7
	Al Toon, N.Y. Jets[2]	93	1,067	11.5	42	5
	Bruce Hill, Tampa Bay	58	1,040	17.9	42	9
	Lionel Manuel, N.Y. Giants	65	1,029	15.8	46	4
1987	J.T. Smith, St. Louis[2]	91	1,117	12.3	38	8
	Jerry Rice, San Francisco[2]	65	1,078	16.6	57	22
	Gary Clark, Washington[2]	56	1,066	19.0	84	7
	Carlos Carson, Kansas City[3]	55	1,044	19.0	81	7
1986	Jerry Rice, San Francisco	86	1,570	18.3	66	15
	Stanley Morgan, New England[3]	84	1,491	17.8	44	10
	Mark Duper, Miami[3]	67	1,313	19.6	85	11
	Gary Clark, Washington	74	1,265	17.1	55	7
	Al Toon, N.Y. Jets	85	1,176	13.8	62	8
	Todd Christensen, L.A. Raiders[3]	95	1,153	12.1	35	8
	Mark Clayton, Miami[2]	60	1,150	19.2	68	10
	*Bill Brooks, Indianapolis	65	1,131	17.4	84	8
	Drew Hill, Houston[2]	65	1,112	17.1	81	5
	Steve Largent, Seattle[8]	70	1,070	15.3	38	9
	Art Monk, Washington[3]	73	1,068	14.6	69	4
	*Ernest Givins, Houston	61	1,062	17.4	60	3
	Cris Collinsworth, Cincinnati[4]	62	1,024	16.5	46	10

Year	Player, Team	No.	Yards	Avg.	Long	TD
	Wesley Walker, N.Y. Jets[2]	49	1,016	20.7	83	12
	J.T. Smith, St. Louis	80	1,014	12.7	45	6
	Mark Bavaro, N.Y. Giants	66	1,001	15.2	41	4
1985	Steve Largent, Seattle[7]	79	1,287	16.3	43	6
	Mike Quick, Philadelphia[3]	73	1,247	17.1	99	11
	Art Monk, Washington[2]	91	1,226	13.5	53	2
	Wes Chandler, San Diego[4]	67	1,199	17.9	75	10
	Drew Hill, Houston	64	1,169	18.3	57	9
	James Lofton, Green Bay[5]	69	1,153	16.7	56	4
	Louis Lipps, Pittsburgh	59	1,134	19.2	51	12
	Cris Collinsworth, Cincinnati[3]	65	1,125	17.3	71	5
	Tony Hill, Dallas[3]	74	1,113	15.0	53	7
	Lionel James, San Diego	86	1,027	11.9	67	6
	Roger Craig, San Francisco	92	1,016	11.0	73	6
1984	Roy Green, St. Louis[2]	78	1,555	19.9	83	12
	John Stallworth, Pittsburgh[3]	80	1,395	17.4	51	11
	Mark Clayton, Miami	73	1,389	19.0	65	18
	Art Monk, Washington	106	1,372	12.9	72	7
	James Lofton, Green Bay[4]	62	1,361	22.0	79	7
	Mark Duper, Miami[2]	71	1,306	18.4	80	8
	Steve Watson, Denver[3]	69	1,170	17.0	73	7
	Steve Largent, Seattle[6]	74	1,164	15.7	65	12
	Tim Smith, Houston[2]	69	1,141	16.5	75	4
	Stacey Bailey, Atlanta	67	1,138	17.0	61	6
	Carlos Carson, Kansas City[2]	57	1,078	18.9	57	4
	Mike Quick, Philadelphia[2]	61	1,052	17.2	90	9
	Todd Christensen, L.A. Raiders[2]	80	1,007	12.6	38	7
	Kevin House, Tampa Bay[2]	76	1,005	13.2	55	5
	Ozzie Newsome, Cleveland[2]	89	1,001	11.2	52	5
1983	Mike Quick, Philadelphia	69	1,409	20.4	83	13
	Carlos Carson, Kansas City	80	1,351	16.9	50	7
	James Lofton, Green Bay[3]	58	1,300	22.4	74	8
	Todd Christensen, L.A. Raiders	92	1,247	13.6	45	12
	Roy Green, St. Louis	78	1,227	15.7	71	14
	Charlie Brown, Washington	78	1,225	15.7	75	8
	Tim Smith, Houston	83	1,176	14.2	47	6
	Kellen Winslow, San Diego[3]	88	1,172	13.3	46	8
	Earnest Gray, N.Y. Giants	78	1,139	14.6	62	5
	Steve Watson, Denver[2]	59	1,133	19.2	78	5
	Cris Collinsworth, Cincinnati[2]	66	1,130	17.1	63	5
	Steve Largent, Seattle[5]	72	1,074	14.9	46	11
	Mark Duper, Miami	51	1,003	19.7	85	10
1982	Wes Chandler, San Diego[3]	49	1,032	21.1	66	9
1981	Alfred Jenkins, Atlanta[2]	70	1,358	19.4	67	13
	James Lofton, Green Bay[2]	71	1,294	18.2	75	8
	Steve Watson, Denver	60	1,244	20.7	95	13
	Frank Lewis, Buffalo[2]	70	1,244	17.8	33	4
	Steve Largent, Seattle[4]	75	1,224	16.3	57	9
	Charlie Joiner, San Diego[4]	70	1,188	17.0	57	7
	Kevin House, Tampa Bay	56	1,176	21.0	84	9
	Wes Chandler, N.O.-San Diego[2]	69	1,142	16.6	51	6
	Dwight Clark, San Francisco	85	1,105	13.0	78	4
	John Stallworth, Pittsburgh[2]	63	1,098	17.4	55	5
	Kellen Winslow, San Diego[2]	88	1,075	12.2	67	10
	Pat Tilley, St. Louis	66	1,040	15.8	75	3
	Stanley Morgan, New England[2]	44	1,029	23.4	76	6
	Harold Carmichael, Philadelphia[3]	61	1,028	16.9	85	6
	Freddie Scott, Detroit	53	1,022	19.3	48	5
	*Cris Collinsworth, Cincinnati	67	1,009	15.1	74	8
	Joe Senser, Minnesota	79	1,004	12.7	53	8
	Ozzie Newsome, Cleveland	69	1,002	14.5	62	6
	Sammy White, Minnesota	66	1,001	15.2	53	3
1980	John Jefferson, San Diego[3]	82	1,340	16.3	58	13
	Kellen Winslow, San Diego	89	1,290	14.5	65	9
	James Lofton, Green Bay	71	1,226	17.3	47	4
	Charlie Joiner, San Diego[3]	71	1,132	15.9	51	4
	Ahmad Rashad, Minnesota[2]	69	1,095	15.9	76	5
	Steve Largent, Seattle[3]	66	1,064	16.1	67	6
	Tony Hill, Dallas[2]	60	1,055	17.6	58	8

Year	Player, Team	No.	Yards	Avg.	Long	TD
	Alfred Jenkins, Atlanta	57	1,026	18.0	57	6
1979	Steve Largent, Seattle[2]	66	1,237	18.7	55	9
	John Stallworth, Pittsburgh	70	1,183	16.9	65	8
	Ahmad Rashad, Minnesota	80	1,156	14.5	52	9
	John Jefferson, San Diego[2]	61	1,090	17.9	65	10
	Frank Lewis, Buffalo	54	1,082	20.0	55	2
	Wes Chandler, New Orleans	65	1,069	16.4	85	6
	Tony Hill, Dallas	60	1,062	17.7	75	10
	Drew Pearson, Dallas[2]	55	1,026	18.7	56	8
	Wallace Francis, Atlanta	74	1,013	13.7	42	8
	Harold Jackson, New England[3]	45	1,013	22.5	59	7
	Charlie Joiner, San Diego[2]	72	1,008	14.0	39	4
	Stanley Morgan, New England	44	1,002	22.8	63	12
1978	Wesley Walker, N.Y. Jets	48	1,169	24.4	77	8
	Steve Largent, Seattle	71	1,168	16.5	57	8
	Harold Carmichael, Philadelphia[2]	55	1,072	19.5	56	8
	*John Jefferson, San Diego	56	1,001	17.9	46	13
1976	Roger Carr, Baltimore	43	1,112	25.9	79	11
	Cliff Branch, Oakland[2]	46	1,111	24.2	88	12
	Charlie Joiner, San Diego	50	1,056	21.1	81	7
1975	Ken Burrough, Houston	53	1,063	20.1	77	8
1974	Cliff Branch, Oakland	60	1,092	18.2	67	13
	Drew Pearson, Dallas	62	1,087	17.5	50	2
1973	Harold Carmichael, Philadelphia	67	1,116	16.7	73	9
1972	Harold Jackson, Philadelphia[2]	62	1,048	16.9	77	4
	John Gilliam, Minnesota	47	1,035	22.0	66	7
1971	Otis Taylor, Kansas City[2]	57	1,110	19.5	82	7
1970	Gene Washington, San Francisco	53	1,100	20.8	79	12
	Marlin Briscoe, Buffalo	57	1,036	18.2	48	8
	Dick Gordon, Chicago	71	1,026	14.5	69	13
	Gary Garrison, San Diego[2]	44	1,006	22.9	67	12
1969	Warren Wells, Oakland[2]	47	1,260	26.8	80	14
	Harold Jackson, Philadelphia	65	1,116	17.2	65	9
	Roy Jefferson, Pittsburgh[2]	67	1,079	16.1	63	9
	Dan Abramowicz, New Orleans	73	1,015	13.9	49	7
	Lance Alworth, San Diego[7]	64	1,003	15.7	76	4
1968	Lance Alworth, San Diego[6]	68	1,312	19.3	80	10
	Don Maynard, N.Y. Jets[5]	57	1,297	22.8	87	10
	George Sauer, N.Y. Jets[3]	66	1,141	17.3	43	3
	Warren Wells, Oakland	53	1,137	21.5	94	11
	Gary Garrison, San Diego	52	1,103	21.2	84	10
	Roy Jefferson, Pittsburgh	58	1,074	18.5	62	11
	Paul Warfield, Cleveland	50	1,067	21.3	65	12
	Homer Jones, N.Y. Giants[3]	45	1,057	23.5	84	7
	Fred Biletnikoff, Oakland	61	1,037	17.0	82	6
	Lance Rentzel, Dallas	54	1,009	18.7	65	6
1967	Don Maynard, N.Y. Jets[4]	71	1,434	20.2	75	10
	Ben Hawkins, Philadelphia	59	1,265	21.4	87	10
	Homer Jones, N.Y. Giants[2]	49	1,209	24.7	70	13
	Jackie Smith, St. Louis	56	1,205	21.5	76	9
	George Sauer, N.Y. Jets[2]	75	1,189	15.9	61	6
	Lance Alworth, San Diego[5]	52	1,010	19.4	71	9
1966	Lance Alworth, San Diego[4]	73	1,383	18.9	78	13
	Otis Taylor, Kansas City	58	1,297	22.4	89	8
	Pat Studstill, Detroit	67	1,266	18.9	99	5
	Bob Hayes, Dallas[2]	64	1,232	19.3	95	13
	Charlie Frazier, Houston	57	1,129	19.8	79	12
	Charley Taylor, Washington	72	1,119	15.5	86	12
	George Sauer, N.Y. Jets	63	1,081	17.2	77	5
	Homer Jones, N.Y. Giants	48	1,044	21.8	98	8
	Art Powell, Oakland[5]	53	1,026	19.4	46	11
1965	Lance Alworth, San Diego[3]	69	1,602	23.2	85	14
	Dave Parks, San Francisco	80	1,344	16.8	53	12
	Don Maynard, N.Y. Jets[3]	68	1,218	17.9	56	14
	Pete Retzlaff, Philadelphia	66	1,190	18.0	78	10
	Lionel Taylor, Denver[4]	85	1,131	13.3	63	6
	Tommy McDonald, Los Angeles[3]	67	1,036	15.5	51	9
	*Bob Hayes, Dallas	46	1,003	21.8	82	12
1964	Charley Hennigan, Houston[3]	101	1,546	15.3	53	8
	Art Powell, Oakland[4]	76	1,361	17.9	77	11

OUTSTANDING PERFORMERS

Year	Player, Team	No.	Yards	Avg.	Long	TD
	Lance Alworth, San Diego[2]	61	1,235	20.2	82	13
	Johnny Morris, Chicago	93	1,200	12.9	63	10
	Elbert Dubenion, Buffalo	42	1,139	27.1	72	10
	Terry Barr, Detroit[2]	57	1,030	18.1	58	9
1963	Bobby Mitchell, Washington[2]	69	1,436	20.8	99	7
	Art Powell, Oakland[3]	73	1,304	17.9	85	16
	Buddy Dial, Pittsburgh[2]	60	1,295	21.6	83	9
	Lance Alworth, San Diego	61	1,205	19.8	85	11
	Del Shofner, N.Y. Giants[4]	64	1,181	18.5	70	9
	Lionel Taylor, Denver[3]	78	1,101	14.1	72	10
	Terry Barr, Detroit	66	1,086	16.5	75	13
	Charley Hennigan, Houston[2]	61	1,051	17.2	83	10
	Sonny Randle, St. Louis[2]	51	1,014	19.9	68	12
	Bake Turner, N.Y. Jets	71	1,009	14.2	53	6
1962	Bobby Mitchell, Washington	72	1,384	19.2	81	11
	Sonny Randle, St. Louis	63	1,158	18.4	86	7
	Tommy McDonald, Philadelphia[2]	58	1,146	19.8	60	10
	Del Shofner, N.Y. Giants[3]	53	1,133	21.4	69	12
	Art Powell, N.Y. Titans[2]	64	1,130	17.7	80	8
	Frank Clarke, Dall. Cowboys	47	1,043	22.2	66	14
	Don Maynard, N.Y. Titans[2]	56	1,041	18.6	86	8
1961	Charley Hennigan, Houston	82	1,746	21.3	80	12
	Lionel Taylor, Denver[2]	100	1,176	11.8	52	4
	Bill Groman, Houston[2]	50	1,175	23.5	80	17
	Tommy McDonald, Philadelphia	64	1,144	17.9	66	13
	Del Shofner, N.Y. Giants[2]	68	1,125	16.5	46	11
	Jim Phillips, Los Angeles	78	1,092	14.0	69	5
	*Mike Ditka, Chicago	56	1,076	19.2	76	12
	Dave Kocourek, San Diego	55	1,055	19.2	76	4
	Buddy Dial, Pittsburgh	53	1,047	19.8	88	12
	R.C. Owens, San Francisco	55	1,032	18.8	54	5
1960	*Bill Groman, Houston	72	1,473	20.5	92	12
	Raymond Berry, Baltimore	74	1,298	17.5	70	10
	Don Maynard, N.Y. Titans	72	1,265	17.6	65	6
	Lionel Taylor, Denver	92	1,235	13.4	80	12
	Art Powell, N.Y. Titans	69	1,167	16.9	76	14
1958	Del Shofner, Los Angeles	51	1,097	21.5	92	8
1956	Bill Howton, Green Bay[2]	55	1,188	21.6	66	12
	Harlon Hill, Chi. Bears[2]	47	1,128	24.0	79	11
1954	Bob Boyd, Los Angeles	53	1,212	22.9	80	6
	*Harlon Hill, Chi. Bears	45	1,124	25.0	76	12
1953	Pete Pihos, Philadelphia	63	1,049	16.7	59	10
1952	*Bill Howton, Green Bay	53	1,231	23.2	90	13
1951	Elroy (Crazylegs) Hirsch, Los Angeles	66	1,495	22.7	91	17
1950	Tom Fears, Los Angeles[2]	84	1,116	13.3	53	7
	Cloyce Box, Detroit	50	1,009	20.2	82	11
1949	Bob Mann, Detroit	66	1,014	15.4	64	4
	Tom Fears, Los Angeles	77	1,013	13.2	51	9
1945	Jim Benton, Cleveland	45	1,067	23.7	84	8
1942	Don Hutson, Green Bay	74	1,211	16.4	73	17

**First season of professional football.*

250 YARDS PASS RECEIVING IN A GAME

Date	Player, Team, Opponent	No.	Yards	TD
Nov. 10, 2002	Plaxico Burress, Pittsburgh vs. Atlanta (OT)	9	253	2
Dec. 17, 2000	Terrell Owens, San Francisco vs. Chicago	20	283	1
Sept. 10, 2000	Jimmy Smith, Jacksonville vs. Baltimore	15	291	3
Dec. 12, 1999	Qadry Ismail, Baltimore vs. Pittsburgh	6	258	3
Dec. 18, 1995	Jerry Rice, San Francisco vs. Minnesota	14	289	3
Dec. 11, 1989	John Taylor, San Francisco vs. L.A. Rams	11	286	2
Nov. 26, 1989	Willie Anderson, L.A. Rams vs. New Orleans (OT)	15	336	1
Oct. 18, 1987	Steve Largent, Seattle vs. Detroit	15	261	3
Oct. 4, 1987	Anthony Allen, Washington vs. St. Louis	7	255	3
Dec. 22, 1985	Stephone Paige, Kansas City vs. San Diego	8	309	2
Dec. 20, 1982	Wes Chandler, San Diego vs. Cincinnati	10	260	2
Sept. 23, 1979	*Jerry Butler, Buffalo vs. N.Y. Jets	10	255	4
Nov. 4, 1962	Sonny Randle, St. Louis vs. N.Y. Giants	16	256	1
Oct. 28, 1962	Del Shofner, N.Y. Giants vs. Washington	11	269	1
Oct. 13, 1961	Charley Hennigan, Houston vs. Boston	13	272	1

Date	Player, Team, Opponent	No.	Yards	TD
Oct. 21, 1956	Billy Howton, Green Bay vs. Los Angeles	7	257	2
Dec. 3, 1950	Cloyce Box, Detroit vs. Baltimore	12	302	4
Nov. 22, 1945	Jim Benton, Cleveland vs. Detroit	10	303	1

**First season of professional football.*

2,000 COMBINED NET YARDS GAINED IN A SEASON

Year	Player, Team	Rushing Att.-Yds.	Pass Rec.	Punt Ret.	Kickoff Ret.	Fum. Ret.	Total Yds.
2003	Dante Hall, Kansas City[2]	16-73	40-423	29-472	57-1,478	0-0	142-2,446
	LaDainian Tomlinson, San Diego[2]	313-1,645	100-725	0-0	0-0	2-0	415-2,370
	Jamal Lewis, Baltimore	387-2,066	26-205	0-0	0-0	1-0	414-2,271
	Ahman Green, Green Bay	355-1,883	50-367	0-0	0-0	2-0	407-2,250
	Deuce McAllister, New Orleans	351-1,641	69-516	0-0	0-0	3-(-3)	423-2,154
	Priest Holmes, Kansas City[3]	320-1,420	74-690	0-0	0-0	0-0	394-2,110
2002	Michael Lewis, New Orleans	1-15	8-200	44-625	70-1,807	2-0	125-2,647
	Priest Holmes, Kansas City[2]	313-1,615	70-672	0-0	0-0	0-0	383-2,287
	Ricky Williams, Miami	383-1,853	47-363	0-0	0-0	1-0	431-2,216
	LaDainian Tomlinson, San Diego	372-1,683	79-489	0-0	0-0	0-0	451-2,172
	Dante Hall, Kansas City	11-54	20-322	29-390	57-1,354	1-0	118-2,120
2001	Priest Holmes, Kansas City	327-1,555	62-614	0-0	0-0	0-0	389-2,169
	Marshall Faulk, St. Louis[4]	260-1,382	83-765	0-0	0-0	2-0	345-2,147
	Derrick Mason, Tennessee[2]	0-0	73-1,128	20-128	34-748	1-0	128-2,004
2000	Derrick Mason, Tennessee	1-1	63-895	51-662	42-1,132	1-0	158-2,690
	MarTay Jenkins, Arizona	1-(-4)	17-219	1-1	82-2,186	0-0	101-2,402
	Edgerrin James, Indianapolis[2]	387-1,709	63-594	0-0	0-0	0-0	450-2,303
	Marshall Faulk, St. Louis[3]	253-1,359	81-830	0-0	1-18	2-0	337-2,207
	Tiki Barber, N.Y. Giants	213-1,006	70-719	39-332	1-28	5-0	328-2,085
1999	Marshall Faulk, St. Louis[2]	253-1,381	87-1,048	0-0	0-0	0-0	340-2,429
	*Edgerrin James, Indianapolis	369-1,553	62-586	0-0	0-0	2-0	433-2,139
	*Terrence Wilkins, Indianapolis	1-2	42-565	41-388	51-1,134	1-0	136-2,089
	Glyn Milburn, Chicago[2]	16-102	20-151	30-346	61-1,426	2-0	129-2,025
1998	Brian Mitchell, Washington[4]	39-208	44-306	44-506	59-1,337	0-0	186-2,357
	Marshall Faulk, Indianapolis	324-1,319	86-908	0-0	0-0	2-13	412-2,240
	Terrell Davis, Denver[2]	392-2,008	25-217	0-0	0-0	1-0	418-2,225
	Jamal Anderson, Atlanta	410-1,846	27-319	0-0	0-0	1-0	438-2,165
	Garrison Hearst, San Francisco	310-1,570	39-535	0-0	0-0	1-0	350-2,105
1997	Barry Sanders, Detroit[2]	335-2,053	33-305	0-0	0-0	1-0	369-2,358
	Kevin Williams, Arizona	1-(-2)	20-273	40-462	59-1,458	1-0	121-2,191
	Brian Mitchell, Washington[3]	23-107	36-438	38-442	47-1,094	0-0	144-2,081
	Terrell Davis, Denver	369-1,750	42-287	0-0	0-0	2-(-7)	413-2,030
	Jermaine Lewis, Baltimore	3-35	42-648	28-437	41-905	2-0	116-2,025
1995	Brian Mitchell, Washington[2]	46-301	38-324	25-315	55-1,408	0-0	164-2,348
	Emmitt Smith, Dallas[2]	377-1,773	62-375	0-0	0-0	0-0	439-2,148
	Glyn Milburn, Denver	49-266	22-191	31-354	47-1,269	0-0	149-2,080
	Ernie Mills, Pittsburgh	5-39	39-679	0-0	54-1,306	0-0	98-2,024
1994	Brian Mitchell, Washington	78-311	26-236	32-452	58-1,478	0-0	194-2,477
	Barry Sanders, Detroit	331-1,883	44-283	0-0	0-0	0-0	375-2,166
1992	Thurman Thomas, Buffalo[2]	312-1,487	58-626	0-0	0-0	1-0	371-2,113
	Emmitt Smith, Dallas	373-1,713	59-335	0-0	0-0	1-0	433-2,048
	Barry Foster, Pittsburgh	390-1,690	36-344	0-0	0-0	2-(–20)	428-2,014
1991	Thurman Thomas, Buffalo	288-1,407	62-631	0-0	0-0	0-0	350-2,038
1990	Herschel Walker, Minnesota[2]	184-770	35-315	0-0	44-966	4-0	267-2,051
1988	*Tim Brown, L.A. Raiders	14-50	43-725	49-444	41-1,098	7-0	154-2,317
	Roger Craig, San Francisco[2]	310-1,502	76-534	0-0	2-32	2-0	390-2,068
	Eric Dickerson, Indianapolis[4]	388-1,659	36-377	0-0	0-0	1-0	425-2,036
	Herschel Walker, Dallas	361-1,514	53-505	0-0	0-0	3-0	417-2,019
1986	Eric Dickerson, L.A. Rams[3]	404-1,821	26-205	0-0	0-0	2-0	432-2,026
	Gary Anderson, San Diego	127-442	80-871	25-227	24-482	2-0	258-2,022
1985	Lionel James, San Diego	105-516	86-1,027	25-213	36-779	1-0	253-2,535
	Marcus Allen, L.A. Raiders	380-1,759	67-555	0-0	0-0	2-(–6)	449-2,308
	Roger Craig, San Francisco	214-1,050	92-1,016	0-0	0-0	0-0	306-2,066
	Walter Payton, Chicago[4]	324-1,551	49-483	0-0	0-0	1-0	374-2,034
1984	Eric Dickerson, L.A. Rams[2]	379-2,105	21-139	0-0	0-0	4-15	404-2,259
	James Wilder, Tampa Bay	407-1,544	85-685	0-0	0-0	4-0	496-2,229
	Walter Payton, Chicago[3]	381-1,684	45-368	0-0	0-0	1-0	427-2,052
1983	*Eric Dickerson, L.A. Rams	390-1,808	51-404	0-0	0-0	1-0	442-2,212
	William Andrews, Atlanta[2]	331-1,567	59-609	0-0	0-0	2-0	392-2,176
	Walter Payton, Chicago[2]	314-1,421	53-607	0-0	0-0	2-0	369-2,028
1981	*James Brooks, San Diego	109-525	46-329	22-290	40-949	2-0	219-2,093

OUTSTANDING PERFORMERS

Year	Player, Team	Rushing Att.-Yds.	Pass Rec.	Punt Ret.	Kickoff Ret.	Fum. Ret.	Total Yds.
	William Andrews, Atlanta	289-1,301	81-735	0-0	0-0	0-0	370-2,036
1980	Bruce Harper, N.Y. Jets[2]	45-126	50-634	28-242	49-1,070	3-0	175-2,072
1979	Wilbert Montgomery, Philadephia	338-1,512	41-494	0-0	1-6	2-0	382-2,012
1978	Bruce Harper, N.Y. Jets	58-303	13-196	30-378	55-1,280	1-0	157-2,157
1977	Walter Payton, Chicago	339-1,852	27-269	0-0	2-95	5-0	373-2,216
	Terry Metcalf, St. Louis[3]	149-739	34-403	14-108	32-772	1-0	230-2,022
1975	Terry Metcalf, St. Louis[2]	165-816	43-378	23-285	35-960	2-23	268-2,462
	O.J. Simpson, Buffalo[2]	329-1,817	28-426	0-0	0-0	1-0	358-2,243
1974	Mack Herron, New England	231-824	38-474	35-517	28-629	3-0	335-2,444
	Otis Armstrong, Denver	263-1,407	38-405	0-0	16-386	1-0	318-2,198
	Terry Metcalf, St. Louis	152-718	50-377	26-340	20-623	7-0	255-2,058
1973	O.J. Simpson, Buffalo	332-2,003	6-70	0-0	0-0	0-0	338-2,073
1966	Gale Sayers, Chicago[2]	229-1,231	34-447	6-44	23-718	3-0	295-2,440
	Leroy Kelly, Cleveland	209-1,141	32-366	13-104	19-403	0-0	273-2,014
1965	*Gale Sayers, Chicago	166-867	29-507	16-238	21-660	4-0	236-2,272
1963	Timmy Brown, Philadelphia[2]	192-841	36-487	16-152	33-945	2-3	279-2,428
	Jim Brown, Cleveland	291-1,863	24-268	0-0	0-0	0-0	315-2,131
1962	Timmy Brown, Philadelphia	137-545	52-849	6-81	30-831	4-0	229-2,306
	Dick Christy, N.Y. Titans	114-535	62-538	15-250	38-824	2-0	231-2,147
1961	Billy Cannon, Houston	200-948	43-586	9-70	18-439	2-0	272-2,043
1960	*Abner Haynes, Dallas Texans	156-875	55-576	14-215	19-434	4-0	248-2,100

**First season of professional football.*

300 COMBINED NET YARDS GAINED IN A GAME

Date	Player, Team, Opponent	No.	Yards	TD
Dec. 14, 2003	Derrick Mason, Tennessee vs. Buffalo	21	302	0
Nov. 16, 2003	Jonathan Carter, N.Y. Jets vs. Indianapolis	7	304	2
Dec. 8, 2002	Steve Smith, Carolina vs. Cincinnati	9	313	3
Nov. 24, 2002	Priest Holmes, Kansas City vs. Seattle	30	307	3
Oct. 13, 2002	Michael Lewis, New Orleans vs. Washington	8	356	2
Dec. 24, 1999	Jason Tucker, Dallas vs. New Orleans	13	331	1
Dec. 7, 1997	Jermaine Lewis, Baltimore vs. Seattle	10	308	3
Dec. 25, 1995	Kevin Williams, Dallas vs. Arizona	16	307	2
Dec. 10, 1995	Glyn Milburn, Denver vs. Seattle	33	404	0
Oct. 23, 1994	Tyrone Hughes, New Orleans vs. L.A. Rams	11	347	2
Dec. 11, 1989	John Taylor, San Francisco vs. L.A. Rams	14	321	2
Nov. 26, 1989	Willie Anderson, L.A. Rams vs. New Orleans (OT)	15	336	1
Nov. 28, 1988	*Tim Brown, L.A. Raiders vs. Seattle	12	308	1
Dec. 22, 1985	Stephone Paige, Kansas City vs. San Diego	8	309	2
Nov. 10, 1985	Lionel James, San Diego vs. L.A. Raiders (OT)	23	345	0
Sept. 22, 1985	Lionel James, San Diego vs. Cincinnati	20	316	2
Dec. 21, 1975	*Walter Payton, Chicago vs. New Orleans	32	300	1
Nov. 23, 1975	Greg Pruitt, Cleveland vs. Cincinnati	28	304	2
Nov. 1, 1970	Eugene (Mercury) Morris, Miami vs. Baltimore	17	302	0
Oct. 4, 1970	O.J. Simpson, Buffalo vs. N.Y. Jets	26	303	2
Dec. 6, 1969	Jerry LeVias, Houston vs. N.Y. Jets	18	329	1
Nov. 2, 1969	Travis Williams, Green Bay vs. Pittsburgh	11	314	3
Dec. 18, 1966	Gale Sayers, Chicago vs. Minnesota	20	339	2
Dec. 12, 1965	*Gale Sayers, Chicago vs. San Francisco	17	336	6
Nov. 17, 1963	Gary Ballman, Pittsburgh vs. Washington	12	320	2
Dec. 16, 1962	Timmy Brown, Philadelphia vs. St. Louis	19	341	2
Dec. 10, 1961	Billy Cannon, Houston vs. N.Y. Titans	32	373	5
Nov. 19, 1961	Jim Brown, Cleveland vs. Philadelphia	38	313	4
Dec. 3, 1950	Cloyce Box, Detroit vs. Baltimore	13	302	4
Oct. 29, 1950	Wally Triplett, Detroit vs. Los Angeles	11	331	1
Nov. 22, 1945	Jim Benton, Cleveland vs. Detroit	10	303	1

**First season of professional football.*

2,000 SCRIMMAGE YARDS GAINED IN A SEASON

Year	Player, Team	Att.	Rushing Yards	Receptions	Receiving Yards	Scrimm. Yards
2003	LaDainian Tomlinson, San Diego[2]	313	1,645	100	725	2,370
	Jamal Lewis, Baltimore	387	2,066	26	205	2,271
	Ahman Green, Green Bay	355	1,883	50	367	2,250
	Deuce McAllister, New Orleans	351	1,641	69	516	2,157
	Priest Holmes, Kansas City[3]	320	1,420	74	690	2,110
2002	Priest Holmes, Kansas City[2]	313	1,615	70	672	2,287
	Ricky Williams, Miami	383	1,853	47	363	2,216
	LaDainian Tomlinson, San Diego	372	1,683	79	489	2,172

Year	Player, Team	Att.	Rushing Yards	Receptions	Receiving Yards	Scrimm. Yards
2001	Priest Holmes, Kansas City	327	1,555	62	614	2,169
	Marshall Faulk, St. Louis[4]	260	1,382	83	765	2,147
2000	Edgerrin James, Indianapolis[2]	387	1,709	63	594	2,303
	Marshall Faulk, St. Louis[3]	253	1,359	81	830	2,189
1999	Marshall Faulk, St. Louis[2]	253	1,381	87	1,048	2,429
	*Edgerrin James, Indianapolis	369	1,553	62	586	2,139
1998	Marshall Faulk, Indianapolis	324	1,319	86	908	2,227
	Terrell Davis, Denver[2]	392	2,008	25	217	2,225
	Jamal Anderson, Atlanta	410	1,846	27	319	2,165
	Garrison Hearst, San Francisco	310	1,570	39	535	2,105
1997	Barry Sanders, Detroit[2]	335	2,053	33	305	2,358
	Terrell Davis, Denver	369	1,750	42	287	2,037
1995	Emmitt Smith, Dallas[2]	377	1,773	62	375	2,148
1994	Barry Sanders, Detroit	331	1,883	44	283	2,166
1992	Thurman Thomas, Buffalo[2]	312	1,487	58	626	2,113
	Emmitt Smith, Dallas	373	1,713	59	335	2,048
	Barry Foster, Pittsburgh	390	1,690	36	344	2,034
1991	Thurman Thomas, Buffalo	288	1,407	62	631	2,038
1988	Roger Craig, San Francisco[2]	310	1,502	76	534	2,036
	Eric Dickerson, Indianapolis[4]	388	1,659	36	377	2,036
	Herschel Walker, Dallas	361	1,514	53	505	2,019
1986	Eric Dickerson, L.A. Rams[3]	404	1,821	26	205	2,026
1985	Marcus Allen, L.A. Raiders	380	1,759	67	555	2,314
	Roger Craig, San Francisco	214	1,050	92	1,016	2,066
	Walter Payton, Chicago[4]	324	1,551	49	483	2,034
1984	Eric Dickerson, L. A. Rams[2]	379	2,105	21	139	2,244
	James Wilder, Tampa Bay	407	1,544	85	685	2,229
	Walter Payton, Chicago[3]	381	1,684	45	368	2,052
1983	*Eric Dickerson, L.A. Rams	390	1,808	51	404	2,212
	William Andrews, Atlanta[2]	331	1,567	59	609	2,176
	Walter Payton, Chicago[2]	314	1,421	53	607	2,028
1981	William Andrews, Atlanta	289	1,301	81	735	2,036
1979	Wilbert Montgomery, Philadelphia	338	1,512	41	494	2,006
1977	Walter Payton, Chicago	339	1,852	27	269	2,121
1975	O.J. Simpson, Buffalo[2]	329	1,817	28	426	2,243
1973	O.J. Simpson, Buffalo	332	2,003	6	70	2,073
1963	Jim Brown, Cleveland	91	1,863	24	268	2,131

First season of professional football.

300 COMBINED SCRIMMAGE YARDS GAINED IN A GAME

Date	Player, Team, Opponent	Att.	Yards	TD
Nov. 24, 2002	Priest Holmes, Kansas City vs. Seattle	30	307	3
Nov. 26, 1989	Flipper Anderson, L.A. Rams vs. New Orleans (OT)	15	336	1
Dec. 22, 1985	Stephone Paige, Kansas City vs. San Diego	8	309	2
Dec. 10, 1961	Billy Cannon, Houston vs. N.Y. Titans	30	330	5
Dec. 3, 1950	Cloyce Box, Detroit vs. Baltimore	12	302	4
Nov. 22, 1945	Jim Benton, Cleveland vs. Detroit	10	303	1

TOP 20 SCORERS

Player	Years	TD	FG	PAT	TP
Gary Anderson	22	0	521	783	2,346
Morten Andersen	22	0	502	753	2,259
George Blanda	26	9	335	942	2,002
Norm Johnson	18	0	366	638	1,736
Nick Lowery	18	0	383	562	1,711
Jan Stenerud	19	0	373	580	1,699
Eddie Murray	19	0	352	538	1,594
Al Del Greco	17	0	347	543	1,584
Pat Leahy	18	0	304	558	1,470
Jim Turner	16	1	304	521	1,439
John Carney	16	0	343	404	1,433
Matt Bahr	17	0	300	522	1,422
Mark Moseley	16	0	300	482	1,382
Jim Bakken	17	0	282	534	1,380
Steve Christie	14	0	314	435	1,377
Fred Cox	15	0	282	519	1,365
Matt Stover	13	0	321	401	1,364
Lou Groza	17	1	234	641	1,349

Jason Elam	11	0	288	449	1,313
Jim Breech	14	0	243	517	1,246

TOP 20 TOUCHDOWN SCORERS

Player	Years	Rush	Rec.	Total Returns	TD
Jerry Rice	19	10	194	1	205
Emmitt Smith	14	155	11	0	166
Marcus Allen	16	123	21	1	145
Cris Carter	16	0	130	1	131
Marshal Faulk	10	97	34	0	131
Jim Brown	9	106	20	0	126
Walter Payton	13	110	15	0	125
John Riggins	14	104	12	0	116
Lenny Moore	12	63	48	2	113
Barry Sanders	10	99	10	0	109
Don Hutson	11	3	99	3	105
Tim Brown	16	1	99	4	104
Steve Largent	14	1	100	0	101
Franco Harris	13	91	9	0	100
Eric Dickerson	11	90	6	0	96
Jim Taylor	10	83	10	0	93
Tony Dorsett	12	77	13	1	91
Bobby Mitchell	11	18	65	8	91
Ricky Watters	10	78	13	0	91
Leroy Kelly	10	74	13	3	90
Charley Taylor	13	11	79	0	90

TOP 20 RUSHERS

Player	Years	Att.	Yards	Avg.	Long	TD
Emmitt Smith	14	4,124	17,418	4.2	75	155
Walter Payton	13	3,838	16,726	4.4	76	110
Barry Sanders	10	3,062	15,269	5.0	85	99
Eric Dickerson	11	2,996	13,259	4.4	85	90
Tony Dorsett	12	2,936	12,739	4.3	99	77
Jerome Bettis	11	3,119	12,353	4.0	71	69
Jim Brown	9	2,359	12,312	5.2	80	106
Marcus Allen	16	3,022	12,243	4.1	61	123
Franco Harris	13	2,949	12,120	4.1	75	91
Thurman Thomas	13	2,877	12,074	4.2	80	65
Curtis Martin	9	2,927	11,669	4.0	70	73
John Riggins	14	2,916	11,352	3.9	66	104
O.J. Simpson	11	2,404	11,236	4.7	94	61
Marshall Faulk	10	2,576	11,213	4.4	71	97
Ricky Watters	10	2,622	10,643	4.1	57	78
Ottis Anderson	14	2,562	10,273	4.0	76	81
Eddie George	8	2,733	10,009	3.7	76	64
Earl Campbell	9	2,187	9,407	4.3	81	74
Terry Allen	10	2,152	8,614	4.0	55	73
Jim Taylor	10	1,941	8,597	4.4	84	83

TOP 20 COMBINED YARDS GAINED

Player	Years	Tot.	Rush.	Rec.	Int. Ret.	Punt Ret.	Kickoff Ret.	Fumble Ret.
Brian Mitchell	14	23,330	1,967	2,336	0	4,999	14,014	14
Jerry Rice	19	23,117	645	22,466	0	0	6	0
Walter Payton	13	21,803	16,726	4,538	0	0	539	0
Emmitt Smith	14	20,537	17,418	3,119	0	0	0	0
Tim Brown	16	19,434	190	14,734	0	3,272	1,235	3
Barry Sanders	10	18,308	15,269	2,921	0	0	118	0
Herschel Walker	12	18,168	8,225	4,859	0	0	5,084	0
Marcus Allen	16	17,648	12,243	5,411	0	0	0	-6
Marshall Faulk	10	17,523	11,213	6,274	0	0	18	18
Eric Metcalf	13	17,230	2,392	5,572	0	3,453	5,813	0
Thurman Thomas	13	16,532	12,074	4,458	0	0	0	0
Tony Dorsett	12	16,326	12,739	3,554	0	0	0	54
Henry Ellard	16	15,718	50	13,777	0	1,527	364	0
Irving Fryar	17	15,594	242	12,785	0	2,055	505	7
Jim Brown	9	15,459	12,312	2,499	0	0	648	0
Eric Dickerson	11	15,411	13,259	2,137	0	0	0	15
Glyn Milburn	9	14,911	817	1,322	0	2,984	9,788	0
James Brooks	12	14,910	7,962	3,621	0	565	2,762	0

Ricky Watters	10	14,891	10,643	4,248	0	0	0	0
Curtis Martin	9	14,635	11,669	2,966	0	0	0	0

TOP 20 YARDS FROM SCRIMMAGE

Player	Years	Scrimmage Yards	Rushing Yards	Receiving Yards
Jerry Rice	19	23,111	645	22,466
Walter Payton	13	21,264	16,726	4,538
Emmitt Smith	14	20,537	17,418	3,119
Barry Sanders	10	18,190	15,269	2,921
Marcus Allen	16	17,654	12,243	5,411
Marshall Faulk	10	17,487	11,213	6,274
Thurman Thomas	13	16,532	12,074	4,458
Tony Dorsett	12	16,293	12,739	3,554
Eric Dickerson	11	15,396	13,259	2,137
Tim Brown	16	14,924	190	14,734
Ricky Watters	10	14,891	10,643	4,248
Jim Brown	9	14,811	12,312	2,499
Curtis Martin	9	14,635	11,669	2,966
Franco Harris	13	14,407	12,120	2,287
James Lofton	16	14,250	246	14,004
Cris Carter	16	13,940	41	13,899
Henry Ellard	16	13,827	50	13,777
Jerome Bettis	11	13,716	12,353	1,363
Andre Reed	16	13,698	500	13,198
John Riggins	14	13,442	11,352	2,090

TOP 20 PASSERS

Player	Years	Att.	Comp.	Pct. Comp.	Yards	Avg. Gain	TD	Pct. TD	Int.	Pct. Int.	Rating
Kurt Warner	6	1,688	1,121	66.4	14,447	8.56	102	6.0	65	3.9	97.2
Steve Young	15	4,149	2,667	64.3	33,124	7.98	232	5.6	107	2.6	96.8
Joe Montana	15	5,391	3,409	63.2	40,551	7.52	273	5.1	139	2.6	92.3
Jeff Garcia	5	2,360	1,449	61.4	16,408	6.95	113	4.8	56	2.4	88.3
Peyton Manning	6	3,383	2,128	62.9	24,885	7.36	167	4.9	110	3.3	88.1
Daunte Culpepper	5	1,843	1,160	62.9	13,881	7.53	90	4.9	63	3.4	88.0
Brett Favre	13	6,464	3,960	61.3	45,646	7.06	346	5.4	209	3.2	86.9
Dan Marino	17	8,358	4,967	59.4	61,361	7.34	420	5.0	252	3.0	86.4
Trent Green	6	2,266	1,336	59.0	17,016	7.51	106	4.7	65	2.9	86.1
Tom Brady	4	1,544	955	61.9	10,233	6.63	69	4.5	38	2.5	85.9
Mark Brunell	10	3,643	2,196	60.3	25,793	7.08	144	4.0	86	2.4	85.2
Rich Gannon	15	4,138	2,492	60.2	28,219	6.82	177	4.3	102	2.5	84.7
Jim Kelly	11	4,779	2,874	60.1	35,467	7.42	237	5.0	175	3.7	84.4
Brad Johnson	10	3,401	2,101	61.8	23,239	6.83	140	4.1	95	2.8	84.1
Steve McNair	9	3,180	1,884	59.2	22,637	7.12	132	4.2	83	2.6	84.1
Roger Staubach	11	2,958	1,685	57.0	22,700	7.67	153	5.2	109	3.7	83.4
Brian Griese	6	1,808	1,118	61.8	12,576	6.96	76	4.2	59	3.3	83.0
Neil Lomax	8	3,153	1,817	57.6	22,771	7.22	136	4.3	90	2.9	82.7
Sonny Jurgensen	18	4,262	2,433	57.1	32,224	7.56	255	6.0	189	4.4	82.6
Len Dawson	19	3,741	2,136	57.1	28,711	7.67	239	6.4	183	4.9	82.6

1,500 or more attempts. The passing ratings are based on performance standards established for completion percentage, interception percentage, touchdown percentage, and average gain. Please consult page 364 for more information.

OUTSTANDING PERFORMERS

TOP 20 LEADERS IN PASSES COMPLETED

Dan Marino	4,967
John Elway	4,123
Warren Moon	3,988
Brett Favre	3,960
Fran Tarkenton	3,686
Joe Montana	3,409
Vinny Testaverde	3,334
Dan Fouts	3,297
Drew Bledsoe	3,193
Dave Krieg	3,105
Boomer Esiason	2,969
Troy Aikman	2,898
Steve DeBerg	2,874
Jim Kelly	2,874
Jim Everett	2,841
Johnny Unitas	2,830
Steve Young	2,667
Ken Anderson	2,654
Jim Hart	2,593
Phil Simms	2,576

TOP 20 LEADERS IN PASSING YARDS

Dan Marino	61,361
John Elway	51,475
Warren Moon	49,325
Fran Tarkenton	47,003
Brett Favre	45,646
Dan Fouts	43,040
Vinny Testaverde	40,943
Joe Montana	40,551
Johnny Unitas	40,239
Dave Krieg	38,147
Boomer Esiason	37,920
Drew Bledsoe	36,876
Jim Kelly	35,467
Jim Everett	34,837
Jim Hart	34,665
Steve DeBerg	34,241
John Hadl	33,503
Phil Simms	33,462
Steve Young	33,124
Troy Aikman	32,942

TOP 20 LEADERS IN TOUCHDOWN PASSES

Dan Marino	420
Brett Favre	346
Fran Tarkenton	342
John Elway	300
Warren Moon	291
Johnny Unitas	290
Joe Montana	273
Dave Krieg	261
Sonny Jurgensen	255
Dan Fouts	254
Vinny Testaverde	251
Boomer Esiason	247
John Hadl	244
Len Dawson	239
Jim Kelly	237
George Blanda	236
Steve Young	232
John Brodie	214
Terry Bradshaw	212
Y.A. Tittle	212

TOP 20 LEADERS IN RECEPTION YARDS

Jerry Rice	22,466
Tim Brown	14,734
James Lofton	14,004
Cris Carter	13,899
Henry Ellard	13,777
Andre Reed	13,198
Steve Largent	13,089
Irving Fryar	12,785
Art Monk	12,721
Charlie Joiner	12,146
Michael Irvin	11,904
Don Maynard	11,834
Gary Clark	10,856
Stanley Morgan	10,716
Isaac Bruce	10,461
Harold Jackson	10,372
Lance Alworth	10,266
Andre Rison	10,205
Jimmy Smith	10,092
Marvin Harrison	10,072

TOP 20 PASS RECEIVERS

Player	Years	No.	Yards	Avg.	Long	TD
Jerry Rice	19	1,519	22,466	14.8	96	194
Cris Carter	16	1,101	13,899	12.6	80	130
Tim Brown	16	1,070	14,734	13.8	80	99
Andre Reed	16	951	13,198	13.9	83	87
Art Monk	16	940	12,721	13.5	79	68
Irving Fryar	17	851	12,785	15.0	80	84
Larry Centers	14	827	6,797	8.2	54	28
Steve Largent	14	819	13,089	16.0	74	100
Shannon Sharpe	14	815	10,060	12.3	82	62
Henry Ellard	16	814	13,777	16.9	81	65
James Lofton	16	764	14,004	18.3	80	75
Marvin Harrison	8	759	10,072	13.3	79	83
Michael Irvin	12	750	11,904	15.9	87	65
Charlie Joiner	18	750	12,146	16.2	87	65
Andre Rison	12	743	10,205	13.7	80	84
Keenan McCardell	12	724	9,370	12.9	76	52
Jimmy Smith	10	718	10,092	14.1	75	55
Gary Clark	11	699	10,856	15.5	84	65
Terance Mathis	13	689	8,809	12.8	81	63
Isaac Bruce	10	688	10,461	15.2	80	68

TOP 20 INTERCEPTORS

Player	Years	No.	Yards	Avg.	Long	TD
Paul Krause	16	81	1,185	14.6	81	3
Emlen Tunnell	14	79	1,282	16.2	55	4
Rod Woodson	17	71	1,483	20.9	98	12
Dick (Night Train) Lane	14	68	1,207	17.8	80	5
Ken Riley	15	65	596	9.2	66	5
Ronnie Lott	14	63	730	11.6	83	5
Dave Brown	15	62	698	11.3	90	5
Dick LeBeau	14	62	762	12.3	70	3
Emmitt Thomas	13	58	937	16.2	73	5
Mel Blount	14	57	736	12.9	52	2
Bobby Boyd	9	57	994	17.4	74	4
Eugene Robinson	16	57	762	13.4	49	1
Johnny Robinson	12	57	741	13.0	57	1
Everson Walls	13	57	504	8.8	40	1
Lem Barney	11	56	1,077	19.2	71	7
Pat Fischer	17	56	941	16.8	69	4
Aeneas Williams	13	55	807	14.7	65	9
Eric Allen	14	54	826	15.3	94	8
Willie Brown	16	54	472	8.7	45	2
Darrell Green	20	54	621	11.5	83	6

TOP 20 PUNTERS (MINIMUM 250 PUNTS)

Player	Years	No.	Yards	Avg.	Long	Blk.
Shane Lechler	4	287	13,113	45.7	73	2
Sammy Baugh	16	338	15,245	45.1	85	9
Tommy Davis	11	511	22,833	44.7	82	2
Yale Lary	11	503	22,279	44.3	74	4
Todd Sauerbrun	9	684	30,092	44.0	73	5
Bob Scarpitto	8	283	12,408	43.8	87	4
Horace Gillom	7	385	16,872	43.8	80	5
Darren Bennett	9	771	33,776	43.8	66	3
Jerry Norton	11	358	15,671	43.8	78	2
Dave Lewis	4	285	12,447	43.7	63	0
Tom Rouen	10	723	31,557	43.6	76	9
Greg Montgomery	9	524	22,831	43.6	77	8
Don Chandler	12	660	28,678	43.5	90	4
Rick Tuten	11	741	32,190	43.4	73	2
Rohn Stark	16	1,141	49,471	43.4	72	7
Sean Landeta	19	1,327	57,491	43.3	77	5
Reggie Roby	16	992	42,951	43.3	77	5
Tom Tupa	15	770	33,318	43.3	73	1
Mitch Berger	9	554	23,910	43.2	75	3
Jerrel Wilson	16	1,072	46,139	43.0	72	12

OUTSTANDING PERFORMERS

TOP 20 PUNT RETURNERS (MINIMUM 75 RETURNS)

Player	Years	No.	Yards	Avg.	Long	TD
George McAfee	8	112	1,431	12.8	74	2
Jack Christiansen	8	85	1,084	12.8	89	8
Claude Gibson	5	110	1,381	12.6	85	3
Bill Dudley	9	124	1,515	12.2	96	3
Rick Upchurch	9	248	3,008	12.1	92	8
Desmond Howard	11	244	2,895	11.9	95	8
Dante Hall	4	96	1,134	11.8	93	4
Billy Johnson	14	282	3,317	11.8	87	6
Mack Herron	3	84	982	11.7	66	0
Billy Thompson	13	157	1,814	11.6	60	0
Az-Zahir Hakim	6	131	1,513	11.5	86	3
Darrien Gordon	9	314	3,601	11.5	94	6
Henry Ellard	16	135	1,527	11.3	83	4
Rodger Bird	3	94	1,063	11.3	78	0
Bosh Pritchard	6	95	1,072	11.3	81	2
Jermaine Lewis	8	272	3,055	11.2	89	6
Michael Lewis	3	88	981	11.1	83	1
Terry Metcalf	6	84	936	11.1	69	1
Bob Hayes	11	104	1,158	11.1	90	3
Floyd Little	9	81	893	11.0	72	2

TOP 20 KICKOFF RETURNERS (MINIMUM 75 RETURNS)

Player	Years	No.	Yards	Avg.	Long	TD
Gale Sayers	7	91	2,781	30.6	103	6
Lynn Chandnois	7	92	2,720	29.6	93	3
Abe Woodson	9	193	5,538	28.7	105	5
Buddy Young	6	90	2,514	27.9	104	2
Travis Williams	5	102	2,801	27.5	105	6
Joe Arenas	7	139	3,798	27.3	96	1
Clarence Davis	8	79	2,140	27.1	76	0
Steve Van Buren	8	76	2,030	26.7	98	3
Lenny Lyles	12	81	2,161	26.7	103	3
Mercury Morris	8	111	2,947	26.5	105	3
Bobby Jancik	6	158	4,185	26.5	61	0
Mel Renfro	14	85	2,246	26.4	100	2
Bobby Mitchell	14	102	2,690	26.4	98	5
Ollie Matson	14	143	3,746	26.2	105	6
Alvin Haymond	10	170	4,438	26.1	98	2
Noland Smith	3	82	2,137	26.1	106	1
Al Nelson	9	101	2,625	26.0	78	0
Timmy Brown	11	184	4,781	26.0	105	5
Vic Washington	6	129	3,341	25.9	98	1
Dave Hampton	8	113	2,923	25.9	101	3

TOP 20 LEADERS IN SACKS

Player	*Years	No.
Bruce Smith	19	200.0
Reggie White	15	198.0
Kevin Greene	15	160.0
Chris Doleman	15	150.5
Richard Dent	15	137.5
John Randle	14	137.5
Leslie O'Neal	13	132.5
Lawrence Taylor	12	132.5
Rickey Jackson	14	128.0
Derrick Thomas	11	126.5
Clyde Simmons	15	121.5
Michael Strahan	11	114.0
Sean Jones	13	113.0
Greg Townsend	13	109.5
Pat Swilling	12	107.5
Trace Armstrong	15	106.0
Neil Smith	13	104.5
Jim Jeffcoat	15	102.5
William Fuller	13	100.5
Charles Haley	12	100.5

**Years played since 1982 when sacks became an official statistic.*

POSTSEASON LEADERS

TOP 10 POSTSEASON RUSHERS

Player	Att.	Yards	Avg.	Long	TD
Emmitt Smith	349	1,586	4.5	65	19
Franco Harris	400	1,556	3.9	50	16
Thurman Thomas	339	1,442	4.3	40	16
Tony Dorsett	302	1,383	4.6	53	9
Marcus Allen	267	1,347	5.0	74	11
Terrell Davis	204	1,140	5.6	62	12
John Riggins	251	996	4.0	43	12
Larry Csonka	225	891	4.0	49	9
Chuck Foreman	229	860	3.8	62	7
Roger Craig	208	841	4.0	80	7

TOP 10 POSTSEASON PASSERS

Player	Att.	Comp.	Pct. Comp.	Yards	Avg. Gain	TD	Pct. TD	Int.	Pct. Int.	Rating
Bart Starr	213	130	61.0	1,753	8.23	15	7.0	3	1.4	104.8
Joe Montana	734	460	62.7	5,772	7.86	45	6.1	21	2.9	95.6
Ken Anderson	166	110	66.3	1,321	7.96	9	5.4	6	3.6	93.5
Kurt Warner	268	169	63.1	2,221	8.29	15	5.6	10	3.7	92.3
Joe Theismann	211	128	60.7	1,782	8.45	11	5.2	7	3.3	91.4
Troy Aikman	502	320	63.7	3,849	7.67	23	4.6	17	3.4	88.3
Brett Favre	630	379	60.2	4,686	7.44	33	5.2	22	3.5	86.1
Steve Young	471	292	62.0	3,326	7.06	20	4.2	13	3.5	84.9
Warren Moon	403	259	64.3	2,870	7.12	17	4.2	14	3.5	84.9
Rich Gannon	240	154	64.2	1,691	7.05	11	4.6	9	3.8	84.6

TOP 10 POSTSEASON PASS RECEIVERS

Player	No.	Yards	Avg.	Long	TD
Jerry Rice	151	2,245	14.9	72	22
Micahel Irvin	87	1,315	15.1	53	8
Andre Reed	85	1,229	14.5	72	9
Thurman Thomas	76	672	8.8	27	5
Cliff Branch	73	1,289	17.7	72	5
Fred Biletnikoff	70	1,167	16.7	57	10
Art Monk	69	1,062	15.4	48	7
Drew Pearson	67	1,105	16.5	83	8
Tony Nathan	65	649	10.0	39	2
Cris Carter	63	870	13.8	66	8
Roger Craig	63	606	9.6	40	2

TOP 10 POSTSEASON INTERCEPTION LEADERS

Player	Interceptions
Ronnie Lott	9
Bill Simpson	9
Charlie Waters	9
Lester Hayes	8
Willie Brown	7
Dennis Thurman	7
Bobby Bryant	6
Eric Davis	6
Glen Edwards	6
Darrell Green	6
Cliff Harris	6
Vernon Perry	6
Aeneas Williams	6

TOP 10 POSTSEASON SACK LEADERS

Player	Sacks
Bruce Smith	14.5
Reggie White	12.0
Willie McGinest	11.5
Charles Haley	11.0
Richard Dent	10.5
Trace Armstrong	10.0
Charles Mann	10.0
Tony Tolbert	10.0
Neil Smith	9.5
Jeff Wright	9.0

**Sacks became an official statistic in 1982.*

YEARLY STATISTICAL LEADERS

ANNUAL SCORING LEADERS

Year	Player, Team	TD	FG	PAT	TP
2003	Jeff Wilkins, St. Louis, NFC	0	39	46	163
	Priest Holmes, Kansas City, AFC	27	0	0	162
2002	Priest Holmes, Kansas City, AFC	24	0	0	144
	Jay Feely, Atlanta, NFC	0	32	42	138
2001	Marshall Faulk, St. Louis, NFC	21	0	0	#128
	Mike Vanderjagt, Indianapolis, AFC	0	28	41	125
2000	Marshall Faulk, St. Louis, NFC	26	0	0	##160
	Matt Stover, Baltimore, AFC	0	35	30	135
1999	Mike Vanderjagt, Indianapolis, AFC	0	34	43	145
	Jeff Wilkins, St. Louis, NFC	0	20	64	124
1998	Gary Anderson, Minnesota, NFC	0	35	59	164
	Steve Christie, Buffalo, AFC	0	33	41	140
1997	Mike Hollis, Jacksonville, AFC	0	31	41	134
	Richie Cunningham, Dallas, NFC	0	34	24	126
1996	John Kasay, Carolina, NFC	0	37	34	145
	Cary Blanchard, Indianapolis, AFC	0	36	27	135
1995	Emmitt Smith, Dallas, NFC	25	0	0	150
	Norm Johnson, Pittsburgh, AFC	0	34	39	141
1994	John Carney, San Diego, AFC	0	34	33	135
	Fuad Reveiz, Minnesota, NFC	0	34	30	132
1993	Jeff Jaeger, L.A. Raiders, AFC	0	35	27	132
	Jason Hanson, Detroit, NFC	0	34	28	130
1992	Pete Stoyanovich, Miami, AFC	0	30	34	124
	Morten Andersen, New Orleans, NFC	0	29	33	120
	Chip Lohmiller, Washington, NFC	0	30	30	120
1991	Chip Lohmiller, Washington, NFC	0	31	56	149
	Pete Stoyanovich, Miami, AFC	0	31	28	121
1990	Nick Lowery, Kansas City, AFC	0	34	37	139
	Chip Lohmiller, Washington, NFC	0	30	41	131
1989	Mike Cofer, San Francisco, NFC	0	29	49	136
	*David Treadwell, Denver, AFC	0	27	39	120
1988	Scott Norwood, Buffalo, AFC	0	32	33	129
	Mike Cofer, San Francisco, NFC	0	27	40	121
1987	Jerry Rice, San Francisco, NFC	23	0	0	138
	Jim Breech, Cincinnati, AFC	0	24	25	97
1986	Tony Franklin, New England, AFC	0	32	44	140
	Kevin Butler, Chicago, NFC	0	28	36	120
1985	*Kevin Butler, Chicago, NFC	0	31	51	144
	Gary Anderson, Pittsburgh, AFC	0	33	40	139
1984	Ray Wersching, San Francisco, NFC	0	25	56	131
	Gary Anderson, Pittsburgh, AFC	0	24	45	117
1983	Mark Moseley, Washington, NFC	0	33	62	161
	Gary Anderson, Pittsburgh, AFC	0	27	38	119
1982	*Marcus Allen, L.A. Raiders, AFC	14	0	0	84
	Wendell Tyler, L.A. Rams, NFC	13	0	0	78
1981	Ed Murray, Detroit, NFC	0	25	46	121
	Rafael Septien, Dallas, NFC	0	27	40	121
	Jim Breech, Cincinnati, AFC	0	22	49	115
	Nick Lowery, Kansas City, AFC	0	26	37	115
1980	John Smith, New England, AFC	0	26	51	129
	*Ed Murray, Detroit, NFC	0	27	35	116
1979	John Smith, New England, AFC	0	23	46	115
	Mark Moseley, Washington, NFC	0	25	39	114
1978	*Frank Corral, Los Angeles, NFC	0	29	31	118
	Pat Leahy, N.Y. Jets, AFC	0	22	41	107
1977	Errol Mann, Oakland, AFC	0	20	39	99
	Walter Payton, Chicago, NFC	16	0	0	96
1976	Toni Linhart, Baltimore, AFC	0	20	49	109
	Mark Moseley, Washington, NFC	0	22	31	97
1975	O.J. Simpson, Buffalo, AFC	23	0	0	138
	Chuck Foreman, Minnesota, NFC	22	0	0	132
1974	Chester Marcol, Green Bay, NFC	0	25	19	94
	Roy Gerela, Pittsburgh, AFC	0	20	33	93
1973	David Ray, Los Angeles, NFC	0	30	40	130
	Roy Gerela, Pittsburgh, AFC	0	29	36	123
1972	*Chester Marcol, Green Bay, NFC	0	33	29	128
	Bobby Howfield, N.Y. Jets, AFC	0	27	40	121
1971	Garo Yepremian, Miami, AFC	0	28	33	117

Year	Player, Team	TD	FG	PAT	TP
	Curt Knight, Washington, NFC	0	29	27	114
1970	Fred Cox, Minnesota, NFC	0	30	35	125
	Jan Stenerud, Kansas City, AFC	0	30	26	116
1969	Jim Turner, N.Y. Jets, AFL	0	32	33	129
	Fred Cox, Minnesota, NFL	0	26	43	121
1968	Jim Turner, N.Y. Jets, AFL	0	34	43	145
	Leroy Kelly, Cleveland, NFL	20	0	0	120
1967	Jim Bakken, St. Louis, NFL	0	27	36	117
	George Blanda, Oakland, AFL	0	20	56	116
1966	Gino Cappelletti, Boston, AFL	6	16	35	119
	Bruce Gossett, Los Angeles, NFL	0	28	29	113
1965	*Gale Sayers, Chicago, NFL	22	0	0	132
	Gino Cappelletti, Boston, AFL	9	17	27	132
1964	Gino Cappelletti, Boston, AFL	7	25	36	#155
	Lenny Moore, Baltimore, NFL	20	0	0	120
1963	Gino Cappelletti, Boston, AFL	2	22	35	113
	Don Chandler, N.Y. Giants, NFL	0	18	52	106
1962	Gene Mingo, Denver, AFL	4	27	32	137
	Jim Taylor, Green Bay, NFL	19	0	0	114
1961	Gino Cappelletti, Boston, AFL	8	17	48	147
	Paul Hornung, Green Bay, NFL	10	15	41	146
1960	Paul Hornung, Green Bay, NFL	15	15	41	176
	*Gene Mingo, Denver, AFL	6	18	33	123
1959	Paul Hornung, Green Bay	7	7	31	94
1958	Jim Brown, Cleveland	18	0	0	108
1957	Sam Baker, Washington	1	14	29	77
	Lou Groza, Cleveland	0	15	32	77
1956	Bobby Layne, Detroit	5	12	33	99
1955	Doak Walker, Detroit	7	9	27	96
1954	Bobby Walston, Philadelphia	11	4	36	114
1953	Gordy Soltau, San Francisco	6	10	48	114
1952	Gordy Soltau, San Francisco	7	6	34	94
1951	Elroy (Crazylegs) Hirsch, Los Angeles	17	0	0	102
1950	*Doak Walker, Detroit	11	8	38	128
1949	Pat Harder, Chi. Cardinals	8	3	45	102
	Gene Roberts, N.Y. Giants	17	0	0	102
1948	Pat Harder, Chi. Cardinals	6	7	53	110
1947	Pat Harder, Chi. Cardinals	7	7	39	102
1946	Ted Fritsch, Green Bay	10	9	13	100
1945	Steve Van Buren, Philadelphia	18	0	2	110
1944	Don Hutson, Green Bay	9	0	31	85
1943	Don Hutson, Green Bay	12	3	36	117
1942	Don Hutson, Green Bay	17	1	33	138
1941	Don Hutson, Green Bay	12	1	20	95
1940	Don Hutson, Green Bay	7	0	15	57
1939	Andy Farkas, Washington	11	0	2	68
1938	Clarke Hinkle, Green Bay	7	3	7	58
1937	Jack Manders, Chi. Bears	5	8	15	69
1936	Earl (Dutch) Clark, Detroit	7	4	19	73
1935	Earl (Dutch) Clark, Detroit	6	1	16	55
1934	Jack Manders, Chi. Bears	3	10	31	79
1933	Ken Strong, N.Y. Giants	6	5	13	64
	Glenn Presnell, Portsmouth	6	6	10	64
1932	Earl (Dutch) Clark, Portsmouth	6	3	10	55

**First season of professional football.*
#Cappelletti's total and Faulk's total in 2001 include a two-point conversion.
##Faulk's total in 2000 includes 2 two-point conversions.

ANNUAL TOUCHDOWN LEADERS

Year	Player, Team	TD	Rush	Pass	Ret.
2003	Priest Holmes, Kansas City, AFC	27	27	0	0
	Ahman Green, Green Bay, NFC	20	15	5	0
2002	Priest Holmes, Kansas City, AFC	24	21	3	0
	Shaun Alexander, Seattle, NFC	18	16	2	0
2001	Marshall Faulk, St. Louis, NFC	21	12	9	0
	Shaun Alexander, Seattle, AFC	16	14	2	0
2000	Marshall Faulk, St. Louis, NFC	26	18	8	0
	Edgerrin James, Indianapolis, AFC	18	13	5	0

YEARLY STATISTICAL LEADERS

Year	Player, Team	TD	Rush	Pass	Ret.
1999	Stephen Davis, Washington, NFC	17	17	0	0
	*Edgerrin James, Indianapolis, AFC	17	13	4	0
1998	Terrell Davis, Denver, AFC	23	21	2	0
	*Randy Moss, Minnesota, NFC	17	0	17	0
1997	Karim Abdul-Jabbar, Miami, AFC	16	15	1	0
	Barry Sanders, Detroit, NFC	14	11	3	0
1996	Terry Allen, Washington, NFC	21	21	0	0
	Curtis Martin, New England, AFC	17	14	3	0
1995	Emmitt Smith, Dallas, NFC	25	25	0	0
	Carl Pickens, Cincinnati, AFC	17	0	17	0
1994	Emmitt Smith, Dallas, NFC	22	21	1	0
	*Marshall Faulk, Indianapolis, AFC	12	11	1	0
	Natrone Means, San Diego, AFC	12	12	0	0
1993	Jerry Rice, San Francisco, NFC	16	1	15	0
	Marcus Allen, Kansas City, AFC	15	12	3	0
1992	Emmitt Smith, Dallas, NFC	19	18	1	0
	Thurman Thomas, Buffalo, AFC	12	9	3	0
1991	Barry Sanders, Detroit, NFC	17	16	1	0
	Mark Clayton, Miami, AFC	12	0	12	0
	Thurman Thomas, Buffalo, AFC	12	7	5	0
1990	Barry Sanders, Detroit, NFC	16	13	3	0
	Derrick Fenner, Seattle, AFC	15	14	1	0
1989	Dalton Hilliard, New Orleans, NFC	18	13	5	0
	Christian Okoye, Kansas City, AFC	12	12	0	0
	Thurman Thomas, Buffalo, AFC	12	6	6	0
1988	Greg Bell, L.A. Rams, NFC	18	16	2	0
	Eric Dickerson, Indianapolis, AFC	15	14	1	0
	*Ickey Woods, Cincinnati, AFC	15	15	0	0
1987	Jerry Rice, San Francisco, NFC	23	1	22	0
	Johnny Hector, N.Y. Jets, AFC	11	11	0	0
1986	George Rogers, Washington, NFC	18	18	0	0
	Sammy Winder, Denver, AFC	14	9	5	0
1985	Joe Morris, N.Y. Giants, NFC	21	21	0	0
	Louis Lipps, Pittsburgh, AFC	15	1	12	2
1984	Marcus Allen, L.A. Raiders, AFC	18	13	5	0
	Mark Clayton, Miami, AFC	18	0	18	0
	Eric Dickerson, L.A. Rams, NFC	14	14	0	0
	John Riggins, Washington, NFC	14	14	0	0
1983	John Riggins, Washington, NFC	24	24	0	0
	Pete Johnson, Cincinnati, AFC	14	14	0	0
	*Curt Warner, Seattle, AFC	14	13	1	0
1982	*Marcus Allen, L.A. Raiders, AFC	14	11	3	0
	Wendell Tyler, L.A. Rams, NFC	13	9	4	0
1981	Chuck Muncie, San Diego, AFC	19	19	0	0
	Wendell Tyler, Los Angeles, NFC	17	12	5	0
1980	*Billy Sims, Detroit, NFC	16	13	3	0
	Earl Campbell, Houston, AFC	13	13	0	0
	*Curtis Dickey, Baltimore, AFC	13	11	2	0
	John Jefferson, San Diego, AFC	13	0	13	0
1979	Earl Campbell, Houston, AFC	19	19	0	0
	Walter Payton, Chicago, NFC	16	14	2	0
1978	David Sims, Seattle, AFC	15	14	1	0
	Terdell Middleton, Green Bay, NFC	12	11	1	0
1977	Walter Payton, Chicago, NFC	16	14	2	0
	Nat Moore, Miami, AFC	13	1	12	0
1976	Chuck Foreman, Minnesota, NFC	14	13	1	0
	Franco Harris, Pittsburgh, AFC	14	14	0	0
1975	O.J. Simpson, Buffalo, AFC	23	16	7	0
	Chuck Foreman, Minnesota, NFC	22	13	9	0
1974	Chuck Foreman, Minnesota, NFC	15	9	6	0
	Cliff Branch, Oakland, AFC	13	0	13	0
1973	Larry Brown, Washington, NFC	14	8	6	0
	Floyd Little, Denver, AFC	13	12	1	0
1972	Emerson Boozer, N.Y. Jets, AFC	14	11	3	0
	Ron Johnson, N.Y. Giants, NFC	14	9	5	0
1971	Duane Thomas, Dallas, NFC	13	11	2	0
	Leroy Kelly, Cleveland, AFC	12	10	2	0

Year	Player, Team	TD	Rush	Pass	Ret.
1970	Dick Gordon, Chicago, NFC	13	0	13	0
	MacArthur Lane, St. Louis, NFC	13	11	2	0
	Gary Garrison, San Diego, AFC	12	0	12	0
1969	Warren Wells, Oakland, AFL	14	0	14	0
	Tom Matte, Baltimore, NFL	13	11	2	0
	Lance Rentzel, Dallas, NFL	13	0	12	1
1968	Leroy Kelly, Cleveland, NFL	20	16	4	0
	Warren Wells, Oakland, AFL	12	1	11	0
1967	Homer Jones, N.Y. Giants, NFL	14	1	13	0
	Emerson Boozer, N.Y. Jets, AFL	13	10	3	0
1966	Leroy Kelly, Cleveland, NFL	16	15	1	0
	Dan Reeves, Dallas, NFL	16	8	8	0
	Lance Alworth, San Diego, AFL	13	0	13	0
1965	*Gale Sayers, Chicago, NFL	22	14	6	2
	Lance Alworth, San Diego, AFL	14	0	14	0
	Don Maynard, N.Y. Jets, AFL	14	0	14	0
1964	Lenny Moore, Baltimore, NFL	20	16	3	1
	Lance Alworth, San Diego, AFL	15	2	13	0
1963	Art Powell, Oakland, AFL	16	0	16	0
	Jim Brown, Cleveland, NFL	15	12	3	0
1962	Abner Haynes, Dallas, AFL	19	13	6	0
	Jim Taylor, Green Bay, NFL	19	19	0	0
1961	Bill Groman, Houston, AFL	18	1	17	0
	Jim Taylor, Green Bay, NFL	16	15	1	0
1960	Paul Hornung, Green Bay, NFL	15	13	2	0
	Sonny Randle, St. Louis, NFL	15	0	15	0
	Art Powell, N.Y. Titans, AFL	14	0	14	0
1959	Raymond Berry, Baltimore	14	0	14	0
	Jim Brown, Cleveland	14	14	0	0
1958	Jim Brown, Cleveland	18	17	1	0
1957	Lenny Moore, Baltimore	11	3	7	1
1956	Rick Casares, Chi. Bears	14	12	2	0
1955	*Alan Ameche, Baltimore	9	9	0	0
	Harlon Hill, Chi. Bears	9	0	9	0
1954	*Harlon Hill, Chi. Bears	12	0	12	0
1953	Joseph Perry, San Francisco	13	10	3	0
1952	Cloyce Box, Detroit	15	0	15	0
1951	Elroy (Crazylegs) Hirsch, Los Angeles	17	0	17	0
1950	Bob Shaw, Chi. Cardinals	12	0	12	0
1949	Gene Roberts, N.Y. Giants	17	9	8	0
1948	Mal Kutner, Chi. Cardinals	15	1	14	0
1947	Steve Van Buren, Philadelphia	14	13	0	1
1946	Ted Fritsch, Green Bay	10	9	1	0
1945	Steve Van Buren, Philadelphia	18	15	2	1
1944	Don Hutson, Green Bay	9	0	9	0
	Bill Paschal, N.Y. Giants	9	9	0	0
1943	Don Hutson, Green Bay	12	0	11	1
	*Bill Paschal, N.Y. Giants	12	10	2	0
1942	Don Hutson, Green Bay	17	0	17	0
1941	Don Hutson, Green Bay	12	2	10	0
	George McAfee, Chi. Bears	12	6	3	3
1940	John Drake, Cleveland	9	9	0	0
	Richard Todd, Washington	9	4	4	1
1939	Andrew Farkas, Washington	11	5	5	1
1938	Don Hutson, Green Bay	9	0	9	0
1937	Cliff Battles, Washington	7	5	1	1
	Clarke Hinkle, Green Bay	7	5	2	0
	Don Hutson, Green Bay	7	0	7	0
1936	Don Hutson, Green Bay	9	0	8	1
1935	*Don Hutson, Green Bay	7	0	6	1
1934	*Beattie Feathers, Chi. Bears	9	8	1	0
1933	*Charlie (Buckets) Goldenberg, Green Bay	7	4	1	2
	John (Shipwreck) Kelly, Brooklyn	7	2	3	2
	*Elvin (Kink) Richards, N.Y. Giants	7	4	3	0
1932	Earl (Dutch) Clark, Portsmouth	6	3	3	0
	Red Grange, Chi. Bears	6	3	3	0

**First season of professional football.*

YEARLY STATISTICAL LEADERS

ANNUAL LEADERS—MOST FIELD GOALS MADE

Year	Player, Team	Att.	Made	Pct.
2003	Jeff Wilkins, St. Louis, NFC	42	39	92.9
	Mike Vanderjagt, Indianapolis, AFC	37	37	100.0
2002	Jay Feely, Atlanta, NFC	40	32	80.0
	Martín Gramatica, Tampa Bay, NFC	39	32	82.1
	Adam Vinatieri, New England, AFC	30	27	90.0
2001	Jason Elam, Denver, AFC	36	31	86.1
	*Jay Feely, Atlanta, NFC	37	29	78.4
2000	Matt Stover, Baltimore, AFC	39	35	89.7
	Ryan Longwell, Green Bay, NFC	38	33	86.8
1999	Olindo Mare, Miami, AFC	46	39	84.8
	*Martin Gramatica, Tampa Bay, NFC	32	27	84.4
1998	Al Del Greco, Tennessee, AFC	39	36	92.3
	Gary Anderson, Minnesota, NFC	35	35	100.0
1997	Richie Cunningham, Dallas, NFC	37	34	91.9
	Cary Blanchard, Indianapolis, AFC	41	32	78.1
1996	John Kasay, Carolina, NFC	45	37	82.2
	Cary Blanchard, Indianapolis, AFC	40	36	90.0
1995	Norm Johnson, Pittsburgh, AFC	41	34	82.9
	Morten Andersen, Atlanta, NFC	37	31	83.8
1994	John Carney, San Diego, AFC	38	34	89.5
	Fuad Reveiz, Minnesota, NFC	39	34	87.2
1993	Jeff Jaeger, L.A. Raiders, AFC	44	35	79.5
	Jason Hanson, Detroit, NFC	43	34	79.1
1992	Pete Stoyanovich, Miami, AFC	37	30	81.1
	Chip Lohmiller, Washington, NFC	40	30	75.0
1991	Pete Stoyanovich, Miami, AFC	37	31	83.8
	Chip Lohmiller, Washington, NFC	43	31	72.1
1990	Nick Lowery, Kansas City, AFC	37	34	91.9
	Chip Lohmiller, Washington, NFC	40	30	75.0
1989	Rich Karlis, Minnesota, NFC	39	31	79.5
	*David Treadwell, Denver, AFC	33	27	81.8
1988	Scott Norwood, Buffalo, AFC	37	32	86.5
	Mike Cofer, San Francisco, NFC	38	27	71.1
1987	Morten Andersen, New Orleans, NFC	36	28	77.8
	Dean Biasucci, Indianpolis, AFC	27	24	88.9
	Jim Breech, Cincinnati, AFC	30	24	80.0
1986	Tony Franklin, New England, AFC	41	32	78.0
	Kevin Butler, Chicago, NFC	41	28	68.3
1985	Gary Anderson, Pittsburgh, AFC	42	33	78.6
	Morten Andersen, New Orleans, NFC	35	31	88.6
	*Kevin Butler, Chicago, NFC	37	31	83.8
1984	*Paul McFadden, Philadelphia, NFC	37	30	81.1
	Gary Anderson, Pittsburgh, AFC	32	24	75.0
	Matt Bahr, Cleveland, AFC	32	24	75.0
1983	*Ali-Haji-Sheikh, N.Y. Giants, NFC	42	35	83.3
	*Raul Allegre, Baltimore, AFC	35	30	85.7
1982	Mark Moseley, Washington, NFC	21	20	95.2
	Nick Lowery, Kansas City, AFC	24	19	79.2
1981	Rafael Septien, Dallas, NFC	35	27	77.1
	Nick Lowery, Kansas City, AFC	36	26	72.2
1980	*Ed Murray, Detroit, NFC	42	27	64.3
	John Smith, New England, AFC	34	26	76.5
	Fred Steinfort, Denver, AFC	34	26	76.5
1979	Mark Moseley, Washington, NFC	33	25	75.8
	John Smith, New England, AFC	33	23	69.7
1978	*Frank Corral, Los Angeles, NFC	43	29	67.4
	Pat Leahy, N.Y. Jets, AFC	30	22	73.3
1977	Mark Moseley, Washington, NFC	37	21	56.8
	Errol Mann, Oakland, AFC	28	20	71.4
1976	Mark Moseley, Washington, NFC	34	22	64.7
	Jan Stenerud, Kansas City, AFC	38	21	55.3
1975	Jan Stenerud, Kansas City, AFC	32	22	68.8
	Toni Fritsch, Dallas, NFC	35	22	62.9
1974	Chester Marcol, Green Bay, NFC	39	25	64.1
	Roy Gerela, Pittsburgh, AFC	29	20	69.0
1973	David Ray, Los Angeles, NFC	47	30	63.8
	Roy Gerela, Pittsburgh, AFC	43	29	67.4

Year	Player, Team	Att.	Made	Pct.
1972	*Chester Marcol, Green Bay, NFC	48	33	68.8
	Roy Gerela, Pittsburgh, AFC	41	28	68.3
1971	Curt Knight, Washington, NFC	49	29	59.2
	Garo Yepremian, Miami, AFC	40	28	70.0
1970	Jan Stenerud, Kansas City, AFC	42	30	71.4
	Fred Cox, Minnesota, NFC	46	30	65.2
1969	Jim Turner, N.Y. Jets, AFL	47	32	68.1
	Fred Cox, Minnesota, NFL	37	26	70.3
1968	Jim Turner, N.Y. Jets, AFL	46	34	73.9
	Mac Percival, Chicago, NFL	36	25	69.4
1967	Jim Bakken, St. Louis, NFL	39	27	69.2
	Jan Stenerud, Kansas City, AFL	36	21	58.3
1966	Bruce Gossett, Los Angeles, NFL	49	28	57.1
	Mike Mercer, Oakland-Kansas City, AFL	30	21	70.0
1965	Pete Gogolak, Buffalo, AFL	46	28	60.9
	Fred Cox, Minnesota, NFL	35	23	65.7
1964	Jim Bakken, St. Louis, NFL	38	25	65.8
	Gino Cappelletti, Boston, AFL	39	25	64.1
1963	Jim Martin, Baltimore, NFL	39	24	61.5
	Gino Cappelletti, Boston, AFL	38	22	57.9
1962	Gene Mingo, Denver, AFL	39	27	69.2
	Lou Michaels, Pittsburgh, NFL	42	26	61.9
1961	Steve Myhra, Baltimore, NFL	39	21	53.8
	Gino Cappelletti, Boston, AFL	32	17	53.1
1960	Tommy Davis, San Francisco, NFL	32	19	59.4
	*Gene Mingo, Denver, AFL	28	18	64.3
1959	Pat Summerall, N.Y. Giants	29	20	69.0
1958	Paige Cothren, Los Angeles	25	14	56.0
	*Tom Miner, Pittsburgh	28	14	50.0
1957	Lou Groza, Cleveland	22	15	68.2
1956	Sam Baker, Washington	25	17	68.0
1955	Fred Cone, Green Bay	24	16	66.7
1954	Lou Groza, Cleveland	24	16	66.7
1953	Lou Groza, Cleveland	26	23	88.5
1952	Lou Groza, Cleveland	33	19	57.6
1951	Bob Waterfield, Los Angeles	23	13	56.5
1950	Lou Groza, Cleveland	19	13	68.4
1949	Cliff Patton, Philadelphia	18	9	50.0
	Bob Waterfield, Los Angeles	16	9	56.3
1948	Cliff Patton, Philadelphia	12	8	66.7
1947	Ward Cuff, Green Bay	16	7	43.8
	Pat Harder, Chi. Cardinals	10	7	70.0
	Bob Waterfield, Los Angeles	16	7	43.8
1946	Ted Fritsch, Green Bay	17	9	52.9
1945	Joe Aguirre, Washington	13	7	53.8
1944	Ken Strong, N.Y. Giants	12	6	50.0
1943	Ward Cuff, N.Y. Giants	9	3	33.3
	Don Hutson, Green Bay	5	3	60.0
1942	Bill Daddio, Chi. Cardinals	10	5	50.0
1941	Clarke Hinkle, Green Bay	14	6	42.9
1940	Clarke Hinkle, Green Bay	14	9	64.3
1939	Ward Cuff, N.Y. Giants	16	7	43.8
1938	Ward Cuff, N.Y. Giants	9	5	55.6
	Ralph Kercheval, Brooklyn	13	5	38.5
1937	Jack Manders, Chi. Bears		8	
1936	Jack Manders, Chi. Bears		7	
	Armand Niccolai, Pittsburgh		7	
1935	Armand Niccolai, Pittsburgh		6	
	Bill Smith, Chi. Cardinals		6	
1934	Jack Manders, Chi. Bears		10	
1933	*Jack Manders, Chi. Bears		6	
	Glenn Presnell, Portsmouth		6	
1932	Earl (Dutch) Clark, Portsmouth		3	

**First season of professional football.*

ANNUAL RUSHING LEADERS

Year	Player, Team	Att.	Yards	Avg.	TD
2003	Jamal Lewis, Baltimore, AFC	387	2,066	5.3	14
	Ahman Green, Green Bay, NFC	355	1,883	5.3	15

YEARLY STATISTICAL LEADERS

Year	Player, Team	Att.	Yards	Avg.	TD
2002	Ricky Williams, Miami, AFC	383	1,853	4.8	16
	Deuce McAllister, New Orleans, NFC	325	1,388	4.3	13
2001	Priest Holmes, Kansas City, AFC	327	1,555	4.8	8
	Stephen Davis, Washington, NFC	356	1,432	4.0	5
2000	Edgerrin James, Indianapolis, AFC	387	1,709	4.4	13
	Robert Smith, Minnesota, NFC	295	1,521	5.2	7
1999	*Edgerrin James, Indianapolis, AFC	369	1,553	4.2	13
	Stephen Davis, Washington, NFC	290	1,405	4.8	17
1998	Terrell Davis, Denver, AFC	392	2,008	5.1	21
	Jamal Anderson, Atlanta, NFC	410	1,846	4.5	14
1997	Barry Sanders, Detroit, NFC	335	2,053	6.1	11
	Terrell Davis, Denver, AFC	369	1,750	4.7	15
1996	Barry Sanders, Detroit, NFC	307	1,553	5.1	11
	Terrell Davis, Denver, AFC	345	1,538	4.5	13
1995	Emmitt Smith, Dallas, NFC	377	1,773	4.7	25
	*Curtis Martin, New England, AFC	368	1,487	4.0	14
1994	Barry Sanders, Detroit, NFC	331	1,883	5.7	7
	Chris Warren, Seattle, AFC	333	1,545	4.6	9
1993	Emmitt Smith, Dallas, NFC	283	1,486	5.3	9
	Thurman Thomas, Buffalo, AFC	355	1,315	3.7	6
1992	Emmitt Smith, Dallas, NFC	373	1,713	4.6	18
	Barry Foster, Pittsburgh, AFC	390	1,690	4.3	11
1991	Emmitt Smith, Dallas, NFC	365	1,563	4.3	12
	Thurman Thomas, Buffalo, AFC	288	1,407	4.9	7
1990	Barry Sanders, Detroit, NFC	255	1,304	5.1	13
	Thurman Thomas, Buffalo, AFC	271	1,297	4.8	11
1989	Christian Okoye, Kansas City, AFC	370	1,480	4.0	12
	*Barry Sanders, Detroit, NFC	280	1,470	5.3	14
1988	Eric Dickerson, Indianapolis, AFC	388	1,659	4.3	14
	Herschel Walker, Dallas, NFC	361	1,514	4.2	5
1987	Charles White, L.A. Rams, NFC	324	1,374	4.2	11
	Eric Dickerson, Indianapolis, AFC	223	1,011	4.5	5
1986	Eric Dickerson, L.A. Rams, NFC	404	1,821	4.5	11
	Curt Warner, Seattle, AFC	319	1,481	4.6	13
1985	Marcus Allen, L.A. Raiders, AFC	380	1,759	4.6	11
	Gerald Riggs, Atlanta, NFC	397	1,719	4.3	10
1984	Eric Dickerson, L.A. Rams, NFC	379	2,105	5.6	14
	Earnest Jackson, San Diego, AFC	296	1,179	4.0	8
1983	*Eric Dickerson, L.A. Rams, NFC	390	1,808	4.6	18
	*Curt Warner, Seattle, AFC	335	1,449	4.3	13
1982	Freeman McNeil, N.Y. Jets, AFC	151	786	5.2	6
	Tony Dorsett, Dallas, NFC	177	745	4.2	5
1981	*George Rogers, New Orleans, NFC	378	1,674	4.4	13
	Earl Campbell, Houston, AFC	361	1,376	3.8	10
1980	Earl Campbell, Houston, AFC	373	1,934	5.2	13
	Walter Payton, Chicago, NFC	317	1,460	4.6	6
1979	Earl Campbell, Houston, AFC	368	1,697	4.6	19
	Walter Payton, Chicago, NFC	369	1,610	4.4	14
1978	*Earl Campbell, Houston, AFC	302	1,450	4.8	13
	Walter Payton, Chicago, NFC	333	1,395	4.2	11
1977	Walter Payton, Chicago, NFC	339	1,852	5.5	14
	Mark van Eeghen, Oakland, AFC	324	1,273	3.9	7
1976	O.J. Simpson, Buffalo, AFC	290	1,503	5.2	8
	Walter Payton, Chicago, NFC	311	1,390	4.5	13
1975	O.J. Simpson, Buffalo, AFC	329	1,817	5.5	16
	Jim Otis, St. Louis, NFC	269	1,076	4.0	5
1974	Otis Armstrong, Denver, AFC	263	1,407	5.3	9
	Lawrence McCutcheon, Los Angeles, NFC	236	1,109	4.7	3
1973	O.J. Simpson, Buffalo, AFC	332	2,003	6.0	12
	John Brockington, Green Bay, NFC	265	1,144	4.3	3
1972	O.J. Simpson, Buffalo, AFC	292	1,251	4.3	6
	Larry Brown, Washington, NFC	285	1,216	4.3	8
1971	Floyd Little, Denver, AFC	284	1,133	4.0	6
	*John Brockington, Green Bay, NFC	216	1,105	5.1	4
1970	Larry Brown, Washington, NFC	237	1,125	4.7	5
	Floyd Little, Denver, AFC	209	901	4.3	3
1969	Gale Sayers, Chicago, NFL	236	1,032	4.4	8
	Dickie Post, San Diego, AFL	182	873	4.8	6

Year	Player, Team	Att.	Yards	Avg.	TD
1968	Leroy Kelly, Cleveland, NFL	248	1,239	5.0	16
	*Paul Robinson, Cincinnati, AFL	238	1,023	4.3	8
1967	Jim Nance, Boston, AFL	269	1,216	4.5	7
	Leroy Kelly, Cleveland, NFL	235	1,205	5.1	11
1966	Jim Nance, Boston, AFL	299	1,458	4.9	11
	Gale Sayers, Chicago, NFL	229	1,231	5.4	8
1965	Jim Brown, Cleveland, NFL	289	1,544	5.3	17
	Paul Lowe, San Diego, AFL	222	1,121	5.0	7
1964	Jim Brown, Cleveland, NFL	280	1,446	5.2	7
	Cookie Gilchrist, Buffalo, AFL	230	981	4.3	6
1963	Jim Brown, Cleveland, NFL	291	1,863	6.4	12
	Clem Daniels, Oakland, AFL	215	1,099	5.1	3
1962	Jim Taylor, Green Bay, NFL	272	1,474	5.4	19
	Cookie Gilchrist, Buffalo, AFL	214	1,096	5.1	13
1961	Jim Brown, Cleveland, NFL	305	1,408	4.6	8
	Billy Cannon, Houston, AFL	200	948	4.7	6
1960	Jim Brown, Cleveland, NFL	215	1,257	5.8	9
	*Abner Haynes, Dall. Texans, AFL	156	875	5.6	9
1959	Jim Brown, Cleveland	290	1,329	4.6	14
1958	Jim Brown, Cleveland	257	1,527	5.9	17
1957	*Jim Brown, Cleveland	202	942	4.7	9
1956	Rick Casares, Chi. Bears	234	1,126	4.8	12
1955	*Alan Ameche, Baltimore	213	961	4.5	9
1954	Joe Perry, San Francisco	173	1,049	6.1	8
1953	Joe Perry, San Francisco	192	1,018	5.3	10
1952	Dan Towler, Los Angeles	156	894	5.7	10
1951	Eddie Price, N.Y. Giants	271	971	3.6	7
1950	Marion Motley, Cleveland	140	810	5.8	3
1949	Steve Van Buren, Philadelphia	263	1,146	4.4	11
1948	Steve Van Buren, Philadelphia	201	945	4.7	10
1947	Steve Van Buren, Philadelphia	217	1,008	4.6	13
1946	Bill Dudley, Pittsburgh	146	604	4.1	3
1945	Steve Van Buren, Philadelphia	143	832	5.8	15
1944	Bill Paschal, N.Y. Giants	196	737	3.8	9
1943	*Bill Paschal, N.Y. Giants	147	572	3.9	10
1942	*Bill Dudley, Pittsburgh	162	696	4.3	5
1941	Clarence (Pug) Manders, Brooklyn	111	486	4.4	5
1940	Byron (Whizzer) White, Detroit	146	514	3.5	5
1939	*Bill Osmanski, Chicago	121	699	5.8	7
1938	*Byron (Whizzer) White, Pittsburgh	152	567	3.7	4
1937	Cliff Battles, Washington	216	874	4.0	5
1936	*Alphonse (Tuffy) Leemans, N.Y. Giants	206	830	4.0	2
1935	Doug Russell, Chi. Cardinals	140	499	3.6	0
1934	*Beattie Feathers, Chi. Bears	119	1,004	8.4	8
1933	Jim Musick, Boston	173	809	4.7	5
1932	*Cliff Battles, Boston	148	576	3.9	3

**First season of professional football.*

ANNUAL PASSING LEADERS

(Current rating system implemented in 1973)

Year	Player, Team	Att.	Comp.	Yards	TD	Int.	Rating
2003	Steve McNair, Tennessee, AFC	400	250	3,215	24	7	100.4
	Daunte Culpepper, Minnesota, NFC	454	295	3,479	25	11	96.4
2002	Chad Pennington, N.Y. Jets, AFC	399	275	3,120	22	6	104.2
	Brad Johnson, Tampa Bay, NFC	451	281	3,049	22	6	92.9
2001	Kurt Warner, St. Louis, NFC	546	375	4,830	36	22	101.4
	Rich Gannon, Oakland, AFC	549	361	3,828	27	9	95.5
2000	Brian Griese, Denver, AFC	336	216	2,688	19	4	102.9
	Trent Green, St. Louis, NFC	240	145	2,063	16	5	101.8
1999	Kurt Warner, St. Louis, NFC	499	325	4,353	41	13	109.2
	Peyton Manning, Indianapolis, AFC	533	331	4,135	26	15	90.7
1998	Randall Cunningham, Minnesota, NFC	425	259	3,704	34	10	106.0
	Vinny Testaverde, N.Y. Jets, AFC	421	259	3,256	29	7	101.6
1997	Steve Young, San Francisco, NFC	356	241	3,029	19	6	104.7
	Mark Brunell, Jacksonville, AFC	435	264	3,281	18	7	91.2
1996	Steve Young, San Francisco NFC	316	214	2,410	14	6	97.2
	John Elway, Denver, AFC	466	287	3,328	26	14	89.2
1995	Jim Harbaugh, Indianapolis, AFC	314	200	2,575	17	5	100.7
	Brett Favre, Green Bay, NFC	570	359	4,413	38	13	99.5

YEARLY STATISTICAL LEADERS

Year	Player, Team	Att.	Comp.	Yards	TD	Int.	Rating
1994	Steve Young, San Francisco, NFC	461	324	3,969	35	10	112.8
	Dan Marino, Miami, AFC	615	385	4,453	30	17	89.2
1993	Steve Young, San Francisco, NFC	462	314	4,023	29	16	101.5
	John Elway, Denver, AFC	551	348	4,030	25	10	92.8
1992	Steve Young, San Francisco, NFC	402	268	3,465	25	7	107.0
	Warren Moon, Houston, AFC	346	224	2,521	18	12	89.3
1991	Steve Young, San Francisco, NFC	279	180	2,517	17	8	101.8
	Jim Kelly, Buffalo, AFC	474	304	3,844	33	17	97.6
1990	Jim Kelly, Buffalo, AFC	346	219	2,829	24	9	101.2
	Phil Simms, N.Y. Giants, NFC	311	184	2,284	15	4	92.7
1989	Joe Montana, San Francisco, NFC	386	271	3,521	26	8	112.4
	Boomer Esiason, Cincinnati, AFC	455	258	3,525	28	11	92.1
1988	Boomer Esiason, Cincinnati, AFC	388	223	3,572	28	14	97.4
	Wade Wilson, Minnesota, NFC	332	204	2,746	15	9	91.5
1987	Joe Montana, San Francisco, NFC	398	266	3,054	31	13	102.1
	Bernie Kosar, Cleveland, AFC	389	241	3,033	22	9	95.4
1986	Tommy Kramer, Minnesota, NFC	372	208	3,000	24	10	92.6
	Dan Marino, Miami, AFC	623	378	4,746	44	23	92.5
1985	Ken O'Brien, N.Y. Jets, AFC	488	297	3,888	25	8	96.2
	Joe Montana, San Francisco, NFC	494	303	3,653	27	13	91.3
1984	Dan Marino, Miami, AFC	564	362	5,084	48	17	108.9
	Joe Montana, San Francisco, NFC	432	279	3,630	28	10	102.9
1983	Steve Bartkowski, Atlanta, NFC	432	274	3,167	22	5	97.6
	*Dan Marino, Miami, AFC	296	173	2,210	20	6	96.0
1982	Ken Anderson, Cincinnati, AFC	309	218	2,495	12	9	95.3
	Joe Theismann, Washington, NFC	252	161	2,033	13	9	91.3
1981	Ken Anderson, Cincinnati, AFC	479	300	3,754	29	10	98.4
	Joe Montana, San Francisco, NFC	488	311	3,565	19	12	88.4
1980	Brian Sipe, Cleveland, AFC	554	337	4,132	30	14	91.4
	Ron Jaworski, Philadelphia, NFC	451	257	3,529	27	12	91.0
1979	Roger Staubach, Dallas, NFC	461	267	3,586	27	11	92.3
	Dan Fouts, San Diego, AFC	530	332	4,082	24	24	82.6
1978	Roger Staubach, Dallas, NFC	413	231	3,190	25	16	84.9
	Terry Bradshaw, Pittsburgh, AFC	368	207	2,915	28	20	84.7
1977	Bob Griese, Miami, AFC	307	180	2,252	22	13	87.8
	Roger Staubach, Dallas, NFC	361	210	2,620	18	9	87.0
1976	Ken Stabler, Oakland, AFC	291	194	2,737	27	17	103.4
	James Harris, Los Angeles, NFC	158	91	1,460	8	6	89.6
1975	Ken Anderson, Cincinnati, AFC	377	228	3,169	21	11	93.9
	Fran Tarkenton, Minnesota, NFC	425	273	2,994	25	13	91.8
1974	Ken Anderson, Cincinnati, AFC	328	213	2,667	18	10	95.7
	Sonny Jurgensen, Washington, NFC	167	107	1,185	11	5	94.5
1973	Roger Staubach, Dallas, NFC	286	179	2,428	23	15	94.6
	Ken Stabler, Oakland, AFC	260	163	1,997	14	10	88.3
1972	Norm Snead, N.Y. Giants, NFC	325	196	2,307	17	12	
	Earl Morrall, Miami, AFC	150	83	1,360	11	7	
1971	Roger Staubach, Dallas, NFC	211	126	1,882	15	4	
	Bob Griese, Miami, AFC	263	145	2,089	19	9	
1970	John Brodie, San Francisco, NFC	378	223	2,941	24	10	
	Daryle Lamonica, Oakland, AFC	356	179	2,516	22	15	
1969	Sonny Jurgensen, Washington, NFL	442	274	3,102	22	15	
	*Greg Cook, Cincinnati, AFL	197	106	1,854	15	11	
1968	Len Dawson, Kansas City, AFL	224	131	2,109	17	9	
	Earl Morrall, Baltimore, NFL	317	182	2,909	26	17	
1967	Sonny Jurgensen, Washington, NFL	508	288	3,747	31	16	
	Daryle Lamonica, Oakland, AFL	425	220	3,228	30	20	
1966	Bart Starr, Green Bay, NFL	251	156	2,257	14	3	
	Len Dawson, Kansas City, AFL	284	159	2,527	26	10	
1965	Rudy Bukich, Chicago, NFL	312	176	2,641	20	9	
	John Hadl, San Diego, AFL	348	174	2,798	20	21	
1964	Len Dawson, Kansas City, AFL	354	199	2,879	30	18	
	Bart Starr, Green Bay, NFL	272	163	2,144	15	4	
1963	Y.A. Tittle, N.Y. Giants, NFL	367	221	3,145	36	14	
	Tobin Rote, San Diego, AFL	286	170	2,510	20	17	
1962	Len Dawson, Dallas Texans, AFL	310	189	2,759	29	17	
	Bart Starr, Green Bay, NFL	285	178	2,438	12	9	
1961	George Blanda, Houston, AFL	362	187	3,330	36	22	
	Milt Plum, Cleveland, NFL	302	177	2,416	18	10	

Year	Player, Team	Att.	Comp.	Yards	TD	Int.	Rating
1960	Milt Plum, Cleveland, NFL	250	151	2,297	21	5	
	Jack Kemp, L.A. Chargers, AFL	406	211	3,018	20	25	
1959	Charlie Conerly, N.Y. Giants	194	113	1,706	14	4	
1958	Eddie LeBaron, Washington	145	79	1,365	11	10	
1957	Tommy O'Connell, Cleveland	110	63	1,229	9	8	
1956	Ed Brown, Chicago Bears	168	96	1,667	11	12	
1955	Otto Graham, Cleveland	185	98	1,721	15	8	
1954	Norm Van Brocklin, Los Angeles	260	139	2,637	13	21	
1953	Otto Graham, Cleveland	258	167	2,722	11	9	
1952	Norm Van Brocklin, Los Angeles	205	113	1,736	14	17	
1951	Bob Waterfield, Los Angeles	176	88	1,566	13	10	
1950	Norm Van Brocklin, Los Angeles	233	127	2,061	18	14	
1949	Sammy Baugh, Washington	255	145	1,903	18	14	
1948	Tommy Thompson, Philadelphia	246	141	1,965	25	11	
1947	Sammy Baugh, Washington	354	210	2,938	25	15	
1946	Bob Waterfield, Los Angeles	251	127	1,747	18	17	
1945	Sammy Baugh, Washington	182	128	1,669	11	4	
	Sid Luckman, Chicago Bears	217	117	1,725	14	10	
1944	Frank Filchock, Washington	147	84	1,139	13	9	
1943	Sammy Baugh, Washington	239	133	1,754	23	19	
1942	Cecil Isbell, Green Bay	268	146	2,021	24	14	
1941	Cecil Isbell, Green Bay	206	117	1,479	15	11	
1940	Sammy Baugh, Washington	177	111	1,367	12	10	
1939	*Parker Hall, Cleveland	208	106	1,227	9	13	
1938	Ed Danowski, N.Y. Giants	129	70	848	7	8	
1937	*Sammy Baugh, Washington	171	81	1,127	8	14	
1936	Arnie Herber, Green Bay	173	77	1,239	11	13	
1935	Ed Danowski, N.Y. Giants	113	57	794	10	9	
1934	Arnie Herber, Green Bay	115	42	799	8	12	
1933	*Harry Newman, N.Y. Giants	136	53	973	11	17	
1932	Arnie Herber, Green Bay	101	37	639	9	9	

**First season of professional football.*

ANNUAL PASSING TOUCHDOWN LEADERS

Year	Player, Team	TD
2003	Brett Favre, Green Bay, NFC	32
	Peyton Manning, Indianapolis, AFC	29
2002	Tom Brady, New England, AFC	28
	Aaron Brooks, New Orleans, NFC	27
	Brett Favre, Green Bay, NFC	27
2001	Kurt Warner, St. Louis, NFC	36
	Rich Gannon, Oakland, AFC	27
2000	Daunte Culpepper, Minnesota, NFC	33
	Peyton Manning, Indianapolis, AFC	33
1999	Kurt Warner, St. Louis, NFC	41
	Peyton Manning, Indianapolis, AFC	26
1998	Steve Young, San Francisco, NFC	36
	Vinny Testaverde, N.Y. Jets, AFC	29
1997	Brett Favre, Green Bay, NFC	35
	Jeff George, Oakland, AFC	29
1996	Brett Favre, Green Bay, NFC	39
	Vinny Testaverde, Baltimore, AFC	33
1995	Brett Favre, Green Bay, NFC	38
	Jeff Blake, Cincinnati, AFC	28
1994	Steve Young, San Francisco, NFC	35
	Dan Marino, Miami, AFC	30
1993	Steve Young, San Francisco, NFC	29
	John Elway, Denver, AFC	25
1992	Steve Young, San Francisco, NFC	25
	Dan Marino, Miami, AFC	24
1991	Jim Kelly, Buffalo, AFC	33
	Mark Rypien, Washington, NFC	28
1990	Warren Moon, Houston, AFC	33
	Randall Cunningham, Philadelphia, NFC	30
1989	Jim Everett, L.A. Rams, NFC	29
	Boomer Esiason, Cincinnati, AFC	28
1988	Jim Everett, L.A. Rams, NFC	31
	Boomer Esiason, Cincinnati, AFC	28
	Dan Marino, Miami, AFC	28
1987	Joe Montana, San Francisco, NFC	31
	Dan Marino, Miami, AFC	26
1986	Dan Marino, Miami, AFC	44
	Tommy Kramer, Minnesota, NFC	24
1985	Dan Marino, Miami, AFC	30
	Joe Montana, San Francisco, NFC	27
1984	Dan Marino, Miami, AFC	48
	Neil Lomax, St. Louis, NFC	28
	Joe Montana, San Francisco, NFC	28
1983	Lynn Dickey, Green Bay, NFC	32
	Joe Ferguson, Buffalo, AFC	26
	Brian Sipe, Cleveland, AFC	26
1982	Terry Bradshaw, Pittsburgh, AFC	17
	Dan Fouts, San Diego, AFC	17
	Joe Montana, San Francisco, NFC	17
1981	Dan Fouts, San Diego, AFC	33
	Steve Bartkowski, Atlanta, NFC	30
1980	Steve Bartkowski, Atlanta, NFC	31
	Dan Fouts, San Diego, AFC	30
	Brian Sipe, Cleveland, AFC	30
1979	Steve Grogan, New England, AFC	28
	Brian Sipe, Cleveland, AFC	28
	Roger Staubach, Dallas, NFC	27
1978	Terry Bradshaw, Pittsburgh, AFC	28
	Roger Staubach, Dallas, NFC	25
	Fran Tarkenton, Minnesota, NFC	25
1977	Bob Griese, Miami, AFC	22
	Ron Jaworski, Philadelphia, NFC	18
	Roger Staubach, Dallas, NFC	18
1976	Ken Stabler, Oakland, AFC	27
	Jim Hart, St. Louis, NFC	18
1975	Joe Ferguson, Buffalo, AFC	25
	Fran Tarkenton, Minnesota, NFC	25
1974	Ken Stabler, Oakland, AFC	26
	Jim Hart, St. Louis, NFC	20

YEARLY STATISTICAL LEADERS

Year	Player, Team	TD
1973	Roman Gabriel, Philadelphia, NFC	23
	Roger Staubach, Dallas, NFC	23
	Charley Johnson, Denver, AFC	20
1972	Billy Kilmer, Washington, NFC	19
	Joe Namath, N.Y. Jets, AFC	19
1971	John Hadl, San Diego, AFC	21
	John Brodie, San Francisco, NFC	18
1970	John Brodie, San Francisco, NFC	24
	John Hadl, San Diego, AFC	22
	Daryle Lamonica, Oakland, AFC	22
1969	Daryle Lamonica, Oakland, AFL	34
	Roman Gabriel, Los Angeles, NFL	24
1968	John Hadl, San Diego, AFL	27
	Earl Morrall, Baltimore, NFL	26
1967	Sonny Jurgensen, Washington, NFL	31
	Daryle Lamonica, Oakland, AFL	30
1966	Frank Ryan, Cleveland, NFL	29
	Len Dawson, Kansas City, AFL	26
1965	John Brodie, San Francisco, NFL	30
	Len Dawson, Kansas City, AFL	21
1964	Babe Parilli, Boston, AFL	31
	Frank Ryan, Cleveland, NFL	25
1963	Y.A. Tittle, N.Y. Giants, NFL	36
	Len Dawson, Kansas City, AFL	26
1962	Y.A. Tittle, N.Y. Giants, NFL	33
	Len Dawson, Dallas, AFL	29
1961	George Blanda, Houston, AFL	36
	Sonny Jurgensen, Philadelphia, NFL	32
1960	Al Dorow, N.Y. Titans, AFL	26
	Johnny Unitas, Baltimore, NFL	25
1959	Johnny Unitas, Baltimore	32
1958	Johnny Unitas, Baltimore	19
1957	Johnny Unitas, Baltimore	24
1956	Tobin Rote, Green Bay	18
1955	Tobin Rote, Green Bay	17
	Y.A. Tittle, San Francisco	17
1954	Adrian Burk, Philadelphia	23
1953	Robert Thomason, Philadelphia	21
1952	Jim Finks, Pittsburgh	20
	Otto Graham, Cleveland	20
1951	Bobby Layne, Detroit	26
1950	George Ratterman, N.Y. Yanks	22
1949	Johnny Lujack, Chi. Bears	23
1948	Tommy Thompson, Philadelphia	25
1947	Sammy Baugh, Washington	25
1946	Sid Luckman, Chi. Bears	17
	Bob Waterfield, Los Angeles	17
1945	Sid Luckman, Chi. Bears	14
	*Bob Waterfield, Cleveland	14
1944	Frank Filchock, Washington	13
1943	Sid Luckman, Chi. Bears	28
1942	Cecil Isbell, Green Bay	24
1941	Cecil Isbell, Green Bay	15
1940	Sammy Baugh, Washington	12
1939	Frank Filchock, Washington	11
1938	Bob Monnett, Green Bay	9
1937	Bernie Masterson, Chi. Bears	9
1936	Arnie Herber, Green Bay	11
1935	Ed Danowski, N.Y. Giants	10
1934	Arnie Herber, Green Bay	8
1933	*Harry Newman, N.Y. Giants	11
1932	Arnie Herber, Green Bay	9

**First season of professional football.*

ANNUAL PASS RECEIVING LEADERS

Year	Player, Team	No.	Yards	Avg.	TD
2003	Torry Holt, St. Louis, NFC	117	1,696	14.5	12
	LaDainian Tomlinson, San Diego, AFC	100	725	7.3	4
2002	Marvin Harrison, Indianapolis, AFC	143	1,722	12.0	11
	Randy Moss, Minnesota, NFC	106	1,347	12.7	7
2001	Rod Smith, Denver, AFC	113	1,343	11.9	11
	Keyshawn Johnson, Tampa Bay, NFC	106	1,266	11.9	1
2000	Marvin Harrison, Indianapolis, AFC	102	1,413	13.9	14
	Muhsin Muhammad, Carolina, NFC	102	1,183	11.6	6
1999	Jimmy Smith, Jacksonville, AFC	116	1,636	14.1	6
	Muhsin Muhammad, Carolina, NFC	96	1,253	13.1	8
1998	O.J. McDuffie, Miami, AFC	90	1,050	11.7	7
	Frank Sanders, Arizona, NFC	89	1,145	12.9	3
1997	Tim Brown, Oakland, AFC	104	1,408	13.5	5
	Herman Moore, Detroit, NFC	104	1,293	12.4	8
1996	Jerry Rice, San Francisco, NFC	108	1,254	11.6	8
	Carl Pickens, Cincinnati, AFC	100	1,180	11.8	12
1995	Herman Moore, Detroit, NFC	123	1,686	13.7	14
	Carl Pickens, Cincinnati, AFC	99	1,234	12.5	17
1994	Cris Carter, Minnesota, NFC	122	1,256	10.3	7
	Ben Coates, New England, AFC	96	1,174	12.2	7
1993	Sterling Sharpe, Green Bay, NFC	112	1,274	11.4	11
	Reggie Langhorne, Indianapolis, AFC	85	1,038	12.2	3
1992	Sterling Sharpe, Green Bay, NFC	108	1,461	13.5	13
	Haywood Jeffires, Houston, AFC	90	913	10.1	9
1991	Haywood Jeffires, Houston, AFC	100	1,181	11.8	7
	Michael Irvin, Dallas, NFC	93	1,523	16.4	8
1990	Jerry Rice, San Francisco, NFC	100	1,502	15.0	13
	Haywood Jeffires, Houston, AFC	74	1,048	14.2	8
	Drew Hill, Houston, AFC	74	1,019	13.8	5
1989	Sterling Sharpe, Green Bay, NFC	90	1,423	15.8	12
	Andre Reed, Buffalo, AFC	88	1,312	14.9	9
1988	Al Toon, N.Y. Jets, AFC	93	1,067	11.5	5
	Henry Ellard, L.A. Rams, NFC	86	1,414	16.4	10

Year	Player, Team	No.	Yards	Avg.	TD
1987	J.T. Smith, St. Louis, NFC	91	1,117	12.3	8
	Al Toon, N.Y. Jets, AFC	68	976	14.4	5
1986	Todd Christensen, L.A. Raiders, AFC	95	1,153	12.1	8
	Jerry Rice, San Francisco, NFC	86	1,570	18.3	15
1985	Roger Craig, San Francisco, NFC	92	1,016	11.0	6
	Lionel James, San Diego, AFC	86	1,027	11.9	6
1984	Art Monk, Washington, NFC	106	1,372	12.9	7
	Ozzie Newsome, Cleveland, AFC	89	1,001	11.2	5
1983	Todd Christensen, L.A. Raiders, AFC	92	1,247	13.6	12
	Roy Green, St. Louis, NFC	78	1,227	15.7	14
	Charlie Brown, Washington, NFC	78	1,225	15.7	8
	Earnest Gray, N.Y. Giants, NFC	78	1,139	14.6	5
1982	Dwight Clark, San Francisco, NFC	60	913	15.2	5
	Kellen Winslow, San Diego, AFC	54	721	13.4	6
1981	Kellen Winslow, San Diego, AFC	88	1,075	12.2	10
	Dwight Clark, San Francisco, NFC	85	1,105	13.0	4
1980	Kellen Winslow, San Diego, AFC	89	1,290	14.5	9
	*Earl Cooper, San Francisco, NFC	83	567	6.8	4
1979	Joe Washington, Baltimore, AFC	82	750	9.1	3
	Ahmad Rashad, Minnesota, NFC	80	1,156	14.5	9
1978	Rickey Young, Minnesota, NFC	88	704	8.0	5
	Steve Largent, Seattle, AFC	71	1,168	16.5	8
1977	Lydell Mitchell, Baltimore, AFC	71	620	8.7	4
	Ahmad Rashad, Minnesota, NFC	51	681	13.4	2
1976	MacArthur Lane, Kansas City, AFC	66	686	10.4	1
	Drew Pearson, Dallas, NFC	58	806	13.9	6
1975	Chuck Foreman, Minnesota, NFC	73	691	9.5	9
	Reggie Rucker, Cleveland, AFC	60	770	12.8	3
	Lydell Mitchell, Baltimore, AFC	60	544	9.1	4
1974	Lydell Mitchell, Baltimore, AFC	72	544	7.6	2
	Charles Young, Philadelphia, NFC	63	696	11.0	3
1973	Harold Carmichael, Philadelphia, NFC	67	1,116	16.7	9
	Fred Willis, Houston, AFC	57	371	6.5	1
1972	Harold Jackson, Philadelphia, NFC	62	1,048	16.9	4
	Fred Biletnikoff, Oakland, AFC	58	802	13.8	7
1971	Fred Biletnikoff, Oakland, AFC	61	929	15.2	9
	Bob Tucker, N.Y. Giants, NFC	59	791	13.4	4
1970	Dick Gordon, Chicago, NFC	71	1,026	14.5	13
	Marlin Briscoe, Buffalo, AFC	57	1,036	18.2	8
1969	Dan Abramowicz, New Orleans, NFL	73	1,015	13.9	7
	Lance Alworth, San Diego, AFL	64	1,003	15.7	4
1968	Clifton McNeil, San Francisco, NFL	71	994	14.0	7
	Lance Alworth, San Diego, AFL	68	1,312	19.3	10
1967	George Sauer, N.Y. Jets, AFL	75	1,189	15.9	6
	Charley Taylor, Washington, NFL	70	990	14.1	9
1966	Lance Alworth, San Diego, AFL	73	1,383	18.9	13
	Charley Taylor, Washington, NFL	72	1,119	15.5	12
1965	Lionel Taylor, Denver, AFL	85	1,131	13.3	6
	Dave Parks, San Francisco, NFL	80	1,344	16.8	12
1964	Charley Hennigan, Houston, AFL	101	1,546	15.3	8
	Johnny Morris, Chicago, NFL	93	1,200	12.9	10
1963	Lionel Taylor, Denver, AFL	78	1,101	14.1	10
	Bobby Joe Conrad, St. Louis, NFL	73	967	13.2	10
1962	Lionel Taylor, Denver, AFL	77	908	11.8	4
	Bobby Mitchell, Washington, NFL	72	1,384	19.2	11
1961	Lionel Taylor, Denver, AFL	100	1,176	11.8	4
	Jim (Red) Phillips, Los Angeles, NFL	78	1,092	14.0	5
1960	Lionel Taylor, Denver, AFL	92	1,235	13.4	12
	Raymond Berry, Baltimore, NFL	74	1,298	17.5	10
1959	Raymond Berry, Baltimore	66	959	14.5	14
1958	Raymond Berry, Baltimore	56	794	14.2	9
	Pete Retzlaff, Philadelphia	56	766	13.7	2
1957	Billy Wilson, San Francisco	52	757	14.6	6
1956	Billy Wilson, San Francisco	60	889	14.8	5
1955	Pete Pihos, Philadelphia	62	864	13.9	7
1954	Pete Pihos, Philadelphia	60	872	14.5	10
	Billy Wilson, San Francisco	60	830	13.8	5
1953	Pete Pihos, Philadelphia	63	1,049	16.7	10
1952	Mac Speedie, Cleveland	62	911	14.7	5

YEARLY STATISTICAL LEADERS

Year	Player, Team	No.	Yards	Avg.	TD
1951	Elroy (Crazylegs) Hirsch, Los Angeles	66	1,495	22.7	17
1950	Tom Fears, Los Angeles	84	1,116	13.3	7
1949	Tom Fears, Los Angeles	77	1,013	13.2	9
1948	*Tom Fears, Los Angeles	51	698	13.7	4
1947	Jim Keane, Chi. Bears	64	910	14.2	10
1946	Jim Benton, Los Angeles	63	981	15.6	6
1945	Don Hutson, Green Bay	47	834	17.7	9
1944	Don Hutson, Green Bay	58	866	14.9	9
1943	Don Hutson, Green Bay	47	776	16.5	11
1942	Don Hutson, Green Bay	74	1,211	16.4	17
1941	Don Hutson, Green Bay	58	738	12.7	10
1940	*Don Looney, Philadelphia	58	707	12.2	4
1939	Don Hutson, Green Bay	34	846	24.9	6
1938	Gaynell Tinsley, Chi. Cardinals	41	516	12.6	1
1937	Don Hutson, Green Bay	41	552	13.5	7
1936	Don Hutson, Green Bay	34	536	15.8	8
1935	*Tod Goodwin, N.Y. Giants	26	432	16.6	4
1934	Joe Carter, Philadelphia	16	238	14.9	4
	Morris (Red) Badgro, N.Y. Giants	16	206	12.9	1
1933	John (Shipwreck) Kelly, Brooklyn	22	246	11.2	3
1932	Ray Flaherty, N.Y. Giants	21	350	16.7	3

**First season of professional football.*

ANNUAL PASS RECEIVING LEADERS (YARDS)

Year	Player, Team	No.	Yards	Avg.	TD
2003	Torry Holt, St. Louis, NFC	117	1,696	14.5	12
	Chad Johnson, Cincinnati, AFC	90	1,355	15.1	10
2002	Marvin Harrison, Indianapolis, AFC	143	1,722	12.0	11
	Randy Moss, Minnesota, NFC	106	1,347	12.7	7
2001	David Boston, Arizona, NFC	98	1,598	16.3	8
	Marvin Harrison, Indianapolis, AFC	109	1,524	14.0	15
2000	Torry Holt, St. Louis, NFC	82	1,635	19.9	6
	Rod Smith, Denver, AFC	100	1,602	16.0	8
1999	Marvin Harrison, Indianapolis, AFC	115	1,663	14.5	12
	Randy Moss, Minnesota, NFC	80	1,413	17.7	11
1998	Antonio Freeman, Green Bay, NFC	84	1,424	17.0	14
	Eric Moulds, Buffalo, AFC	67	1,368	20.4	9
1997	Rob Moore, Arizona, NFC	97	1,584	16.3	8
	Tim Brown, Oakland, AFC	104	1,408	13.5	5
1996	Isaac Bruce, St. Louis, NFC	84	1,338	15.9	7
	Jimmy Smith, Jacksonville, AFC	83	1,244	15.0	7
1995	Jerry Rice, San Francisco, NFC	122	1,848	15.1	15
	Tim Brown, Oakland, AFC	89	1,342	15.1	10
1994	Jerry Rice, San Francisco, NFC	112	1,499	13.4	13
	Tim Brown, L.A. Raiders, AFC	89	1,309	14.7	9
1993	Jerry Rice, San Francisco, NFC	98	1,503	15.3	15
	Tim Brown, L.A. Raiders, AFC	80	1,180	14.8	7
1992	Sterling Sharpe, Green Bay, NFC	108	1,461	13.5	13
	Anthony Miller, San Diego, AFC	72	1,060	14.7	7
1991	Michael Irvin, Dallas, NFC	93	1,523	16.4	8
	Haywood Jeffires, Houston, AFC	100	1,181	11.8	7
1990	Jerry Rice, San Francisco, NFC	100	1,502	15.0	13
	Haywood Jeffires, Houston, AFC	74	1,048	14.2	8
1989	Jerry Rice, San Francisco, NFC	82	1,483	18.1	17
	Andre Reed, Buffalo, AFC	88	1,312	14.9	9
1988	Henry Ellard, L.A. Rams, NFC	86	1,414	16.4	10
	Eddie Brown, Cincinnati, AFC	53	1,273	24.0	9
1987	J.T. Smith, St. Louis, NFC	91	1,117	12.3	8
	Carlos Carson, Kansas City, AFC	55	1,044	19.0	7
1986	Jerry Rice, San Francisco, NFC	86	1,570	18.3	15
	Stanley Morgan, New England, AFC	84	1,491	17.8	10
1985	Steve Largent, Seattle, AFC	79	1,287	16.3	6
	Mike Quick, Philadelphia, NFC	73	1,247	17.1	11
1984	Roy Green, St. Louis, NFC	78	1,555	19.9	12
	John Stallworth, Pittsburgh, AFC	80	1,395	17.4	11
1983	Mike Quick, Philadelphia, NFC	69	1,409	20.4	13
	Carlos Carson, Kansas City, AFC	80	1,351	16.9	7
1982	Wes Chandler, San Diego, AFC	49	1,032	21.1	9
	Dwight Clark, San Francisco, NFC	60	913	15.2	5

Year	Player, Team	No.	Yards	Avg.	TD
1981	Alfred Jenkins, Atlanta, NFC	70	1,358	19.4	13
	Frank Lewis, Buffalo, AFC	70	1,244	17.8	4
	Steve Watson, Denver, AFC	60	1,244	20.7	13
1980	John Jefferson, San Diego, AFC	82	1,340	16.3	13
	James Lofton, Green Bay, NFC	71	1,226	17.3	4
1979	Steve Largent, Seattle, AFC	66	1,237	18.7	9
	Ahmad Rashad, Minnesota, NFC	80	1,156	14.5	9
1978	Wesley Walker, N.Y. Jets, AFC	48	1,169	24.4	8
	Harold Carmichael, Philadelphia, NFC	55	1,072	19.5	8
1977	Drew Pearson, Dallas, NFC	48	870	18.1	2
	Ken Burrough, Houston, AFC	43	816	19.0	8
1976	Roger Carr, Baltimore, AFC	43	1,112	25.9	11
	*Sammy White, Minnesota, NFC	51	906	17.8	10
1975	Ken Burrough, Houston, AFC	53	1,063	20.1	8
	Mel Gray, St. Louis, NFC	48	926	19.3	11
1974	Cliff Branch, Oakland, AFC	60	1,092	18.2	13
	Drew Pearson, Dallas, NFC	62	1,087	17.5	2
1973	Harold Carmichael, Philadelphia, NFC	67	1,116	16.7	9
	*Isaac Curtis, Cincinnati, AFC	45	843	18.7	9
1972	Harold Jackson, Philadelphia, NFC	62	1,048	16.9	4
	Rich Caster, N.Y. Jets, AFC	39	833	21.4	10
1971	Otis Taylor, Kansas City, AFC	57	1,110	19.5	7
	Gene Washington, San Francisco, NFC	46	884	19.2	4
1970	Gene Washington, San Francisco, NFC	53	1,100	20.8	12
	Marlin Briscoe, Buffalo, AFC	57	1,036	18.2	8
1969	Warren Wells, Oakland, AFL	47	1,260	26.8	14
	Harold Jackson, Philadelphia, NFL	65	1,116	17.2	9
1968	Lance Alworth, San Diego, AFL	68	1,312	19.3	10
	Roy Jefferson, Pittsburgh, NFL	58	1,074	18.5	11
1967	Don Maynard, N.Y. Jets, AFL	71	1,434	20.3	10
	Ben Hawkins, Philadelphia, NFL	59	1,265	21.4	10
1966	Lance Alworth, San Diego, AFL	73	1,383	18.9	13
	Pat Studstill, Detroit, NFL	67	1,266	18.9	5
1965	Lance Alworth, San Diego, AFL	69	1,602	23.2	14
	Dave Parks, San Francisco, NFL	80	1,344	16.8	12
1964	Charley Hennigan, Houston, AFL	101	1,546	15.3	8
	Johnny Morris, Chicago, NFL	93	1,200	12.9	10
1963	Bobby Mitchell, Washington, NFL	69	1,436	20.8	7
	Art Powell, Oakland, AFL	73	1,304	17.8	16
1962	Bobby Mitchell, Washington, NFL	72	1,384	19.2	11
	Art Powell, N.Y. Titans, AFL	64	1,130	17.6	8
1961	Charley Hennigan, Houston, AFL	82	1,746	21.3	12
	Tommy McDonald, Philadelphia, NFL	64	1,144	17.9	13
1960	*Bill Groman, Houston, AFL	72	1,473	20.5	12
	Raymond Berry, Baltimore, NFL	74	1,298	17.5	10
1959	Raymond Berry, Baltimore	66	959	14.5	14
1958	Del Shofner, Los Angeles	51	1,097	21.5	8
1957	Raymond Berry, Baltimore	47	800	17.0	6
1956	Billy Howton, Green Bay	55	1,188	21.6	12
1955	Pete Pihos, Philadelphia	62	864	13.9	7
1954	Bob Boyd, Los Angeles	53	1,212	22.9	6
1953	Pete Pihos, Philadelphia	63	1,049	16.7	10
1952	*Bill Howton, Green Bay	53	1,231	23.2	13
1951	Elroy (Crazylegs) Hirsch, Los Angeles	66	1,495	22.7	17
1950	Tom Fears, Los Angeles	84	1,116	13.3	7
1949	Bob Mann, Detroit	66	1,014	15.4	4
1948	Mal Kutner, Chi. Cardinals	41	943	23.0	14
1947	Mal Kutner, Chi. Cardinals	43	944	21.9	7
1946	Jim Benton, Los Angeles	63	981	15.5	6
1945	Jim Benton, Cleveland	45	1,067	23.7	8
1944	Don Hutson, Green Bay	58	866	14.6	9
1943	Don Hutson, Green Bay	47	776	16.5	11
1942	Don Hutson, Green Bay	74	1,211	16.4	17
1941	Don Hutson, Green Bay	58	738	12.7	10
1940	*Don Looney, Philadelphia	58	707	12.2	4
1939	Don Hutson, Green Bay	34	846	24.9	6
1938	Don Hutson, Green Bay	32	548	17.1	9
1937	*Gaynell Tinsley, Chi. Cardinals	36	675	18.8	5
1936	Don Hutson, Green Bay	34	526	15.5	8

YEARLY STATISTICAL LEADERS

Year	Player, Team	No.	Yards	Avg.	TD
1935	Charley Malone, Boston	22	433	19.7	2
1934	Harry Ebding, Detroit	9	257	28.6	2
1933	*Paul Moss, Pittsburgh	18	383	21.3	2
1932	Johnny (Blood) McNally, Green Bay	19	326	17.2	3

First season of professional football.

ANNUAL PUNT RETURN LEADERS

Year	Player, Team	No.	Yards	Avg.	Long	TD
2003	Dante Hall, Kansas City, AFC	29	472	16.3	93	2
	Brian Westbrook, Philadelphia, NFC	20	306	15.3	84	2
2002	Jimmy Williams, San Francisco, NFC	20	336	16.8	89	1
	Santana Moss, N.Y. Jets, AFC	25	413	16.5	63	2
2001	Troy Brown, New England, AFC	29	413	14.2	85	2
	Darrien Gordon, Atlanta, NFC	31	437	14.1	74	0
2000	Jermaine Lewis, Baltimore, AFC	36	578	16.1	89	2
	Az-Zahir Hakim, St. Louis, NFC	32	489	15.3	86	1
1999	*Charlie Rogers, Seattle, AFC	22	318	14.5	94	1
	*Mac Cody, Arizona, NFC	32	373	11.7	31	0
1998	Deion Sanders, Dallas, NFC	24	375	15.6	69	2
	Reggie Barlow, Jacksonville, AFC	43	555	12.9	85	1
1997	Jermaine Lewis, Baltimore, AFC	28	437	15.6	89	2
	David Palmer, Minnesota, NFC	34	444	13.1	57	0
1996	Desmond Howard, Green Bay, NFC	58	875	15.1	92	3
	Darrien Gordon, San Diego, AFC	36	537	14.9	81	1
1995	David Palmer, Minnesota, NFC	26	342	13.2	74	1
	Andre Coleman, San Diego, AFC	28	326	11.6	88	1
1994	Brian Mitchell, Washington, NFC	32	452	14.1	78	2
	Darrien Gordon, San Diego, AFC	36	475	13.2	90	2
1993	*Tyrone Hughes, New Orleans, NFC	37	503	13.6	83	2
	Eric Metcalf, Cleveland, AFC	36	464	12.9	91	2
1992	Johnny Bailey, Phoenix, NFC	20	263	13.2	65	0
	Rod Woodson, Pittsburgh, AFC	32	364	11.4	80	1
1991	Mel Gray, Detroit, NFC	25	385	15.4	78	1
	Rod Woodson, Pittsburgh, AFC	28	320	11.4	40	0
1990	Clarence Verdin, Indianapolis, AFC	31	396	12.8	36	0
	*Johnny Bailey, Chicago, NFC	36	399	11.1	95	1
1989	Walter Stanley, Detroit, NFC	36	496	13.8	74	0
	Clarence Verdin, Indianapolis, AFC	23	296	12.9	49	1
1988	John Taylor, San Francisco, NFC	44	556	12.6	95	2
	JoJo Townsell, N.Y. Jets, AFC	35	409	11.7	59	1
1987	Mel Gray, New Orleans, NFC	24	352	14.7	80	0
	Bobby Joe Edmonds, Seattle, AFC	20	251	12.6	40	0
1986	*Bobby Joe Edmonds, Seattle, AFC	34	419	12.3	75	1
	*Vai Sikahema, St. Louis, NFC	43	522	12.1	71	2
1985	Irving Fryar, New England, AFC	37	520	14.1	85	2
	Henry Ellard, L.A. Rams, NFC	37	501	13.5	80	1
1984	Mike Martin, Cincinnati, AFC	24	376	15.7	55	0
	Henry Ellard, L.A. Rams, NFC	30	403	13.4	83	2
1983	*Henry Ellard, L.A. Rams, NFC	16	217	13.6	72	1
	Kirk Springs, N.Y. Jets, AFC	23	287	12.5	76	1
1982	Rick Upchurch, Denver, AFC	15	242	16.1	78	2
	Billy Johnson, Atlanta, NFC	24	273	11.4	71	0
1981	LeRoy Irvin, Los Angeles, NFC	46	615	13.4	84	3
	*James Brooks, San Diego, AFC	22	290	13.2	42	0
1980	J.T. Smith, Kansas City, AFC	40	581	14.5	75	2
	*Kenny Johnson, Atlanta, NFC	23	281	12.2	56	0
1979	John Sciarra, Philadelphia, NFC	16	182	11.4	38	0
	*Tony Nathan, Miami, AFC	28	306	10.9	86	1
1978	Rick Upchurch, Denver, AFC	36	493	13.7	75	1
	Jackie Wallace, Los Angeles, NFC	52	618	11.9	58	0
1977	Billy Johnson, Houston, AFC	35	539	15.4	87	2
	Larry Marshall, Philadelphia, NFC	46	489	10.6	48	0
1976	Rick Upchurch, Denver, AFC	39	536	13.7	92	4
	Eddie Brown, Washington, NFC	48	646	13.5	71	1
1975	Billy Johnson, Houston, AFC	40	612	15.3	83	3
	Terry Metcalf, St. Louis, NFC	23	285	12.4	69	1
1974	Lemar Parrish, Cincinnati, AFC	18	338	18.8	90	2
	Dick Jauron, Detroit, NFC	17	286	16.8	58	0

Year	Player, Team	No.	Yards	Avg.	Long	TD
1973	Bruce Taylor, San Francisco, NFC	15	207	13.8	61	0
	Ron Smith, San Diego, AFC	27	352	13.0	84	2
1972	Ken Ellis, Green Bay, NFC	14	215	15.4	80	1
	Chris Farasopoulos, N.Y. Jets, AFC	17	179	10.5	65	1
1971	Les (Speedy) Duncan, Washington, NFC	22	233	10.6	33	0
	Leroy Kelly, Cleveland, AFC	30	292	9.7	74	0
1970	Ed Podolak, Kansas City, AFC	23	311	13.5	60	0
	*Bruce Taylor, San Francisco, NFC	43	516	12.0	76	0
1969	Alvin Haymond, Los Angeles, NFL	33	435	13.2	52	0
	*Bill Thompson, Denver, AFL	25	288	11.5	40	0
1968	Bob Hayes, Dallas, NFL	15	312	20.8	90	2
	Noland Smith, Kansas City, AFL	18	270	15.0	80	1
1967	Floyd Little, Denver, AFL	16	270	16.9	72	1
	Ben Davis, Cleveland, NFL	18	229	12.7	52	1
1966	Les (Speedy) Duncan, San Diego, AFL	18	238	13.2	81	1
	Johnny Roland, St. Louis, NFL	20	221	11.1	86	1
1965	Leroy Kelly, Cleveland, NFL	17	265	15.6	67	2
	Les (Speedy) Duncan, San Diego, AFL	30	464	15.5	66	2
1964	Bobby Jancik, Houston, AFL	12	220	18.3	82	1
	Tommy Watkins, Detroit, NFL	16	238	14.9	68	2
1963	Dick James, Washington, NFL	16	214	13.4	39	0
	Claude (Hoot) Gibson, Oakland, AFL	26	307	11.8	85	2
1962	Dick Christy, N.Y. Titans, AFL	15	250	16.7	73	2
	Pat Studstill, Detroit, NFL	29	457	15.8	44	0
1961	Dick Christy, N.Y. Titans, AFL	18	383	21.3	70	2
	Willie Wood, Green Bay, NFL	14	225	16.1	72	2
1960	*Abner Haynes, Dall. Texans, AFL	14	215	15.4	46	0
	Abe Woodson, San Francisco, NFL	13	174	13.4	48	0
1959	Johnny Morris, Chi. Bears	14	171	12.2	78	1
1958	Jon Arnett, Los Angeles	18	223	12.4	58	0
1957	Bert Zagers, Washington	14	217	15.5	76	2
1956	Ken Konz, Cleveland	13	187	14.4	65	1
1955	Ollie Matson, Chi. Cardinals	13	245	18.8	78	2
1954	*Veryl Switzer, Green Bay	24	306	12.8	93	1
1953	Charley Trippi, Chi. Cardinals	21	239	11.4	38	0
1952	Jack Christiansen, Detroit	15	322	21.5	79	2
1951	Claude (Buddy) Young, N.Y. Yanks	12	231	19.3	79	1
1950	*Herb Rich, Baltimore	12	276	23.0	86	1
1949	Verda (Vitamin T) Smith, Los Angeles	27	427	15.8	85	1
1948	George McAfee, Chi. Bears	30	417	13.9	60	1
1947	*Walt Slater, Pittsburgh	28	435	15.5	33	0
1946	Bill Dudley, Pittsburgh	27	385	14.3	52	0
1945	*Dave Ryan, Detroit	15	220	14.7	56	0
1944	*Steve Van Buren, Philadelphia	15	230	15.3	55	1
1943	Andy Farkas, Washington	15	168	11.2	33	0
1942	Merlyn Condit, Brooklyn	21	210	10.0	23	0
1941	Byron (Whizzer) White, Detroit	19	262	13.8	64	0

**First season of professional football.*

ANNUAL KICKOFF RETURN LEADERS

Year	Player, Team	No.	Yards	Avg.	Long	TD
2003	Jerry Azumah, Chicago, NFC	41	1,191	29.0	89	2
	*Bethel Johnson, New England, AFC	30	847	28.2	92	1
2002	MarTay Jenkins, Arizona, NFC	20	559	28.0	95	1
	Kevin Faulk, New England, AFC	26	725	27.9	87	2
2001	Ronney Jenkins, San Diego, AFC	58	1,541	26.6	93	2
	*Steve Smith, Carolina, NFC	56	1,431	25.6	99	2
2000	*Darrick Vaughn, Atlanta, NFC	39	1,082	27.7	100	3
	Derrick Mason, Tennessee, AFC	42	1,132	27.0	66	0
1999	Tony Horne, St. Louis, NFC	30	892	29.7	101	2
	Tremain Mack, Cincinnati, AFC	51	1,382	27.1	99	1
1998	*Terry Fair, Detroit, NFC	51	1,428	28.0	105	2
	Corey Harris, Baltimore, AFC	35	965	27.6	95	1
1997	Michael Bates, Carolina, NFC	47	1,281	27.3	56	0
	Aaron Glenn, N.Y. Jets, AFC	28	741	26.5	96	1
1996	Michael Bates, Carolina, NFC	33	998	30.2	93	1
	Tamarick Vanover, Kansas City, AFC	33	854	25.9	97	1
1995	Ron Carpenter, N.Y. Jets, AFC	20	553	27.7	58	0
	Brian Mitchell, Washington, NFC	55	1,408	25.6	59	0

YEARLY STATISTICAL LEADERS

Year	Player, Team	No.	Yards	Avg.	Long	TD
1994	Mel Gray, Detroit, NFC	45	1,276	28.4	102	3
	Randy Baldwin, Cleveland, AFC	28	753	26.9	85	1
1993	Robert Brooks, Green Bay, NFC	23	611	26.6	95	1
	*Raghib Ismail, L.A. Raiders, AFC	25	605	24.2	66	0
1992	Jon Vaughn, New England, AFC	20	564	28.2	100	1
	Deion Sanders, Atlanta, NFC	40	1,067	26.7	99	2
1991	Mel Gray, Detroit, NFC	36	929	25.8	71	0
	Nate Lewis, San Diego, AFC	23	578	25.1	95	1
1990	Kevin Clark, Denver, AFC	20	505	25.3	75	0
	David Meggett, N.Y. Giants, NFC	21	492	23.4	58	0
1989	Rod Woodson, Pittsburgh, AFC	36	982	27.3	84	1
	Mel Gray, Detroit, NFC	24	640	26.7	57	0
1988	*Tim Brown, L.A. Raiders, AFC	41	1,098	26.8	97	1
	Donnie Elder, Tampa Bay, NFC	34	772	22.7	51	0
1987	Sylvester Stamps, Atlanta, NFC	24	660	27.5	97	1
	Paul Palmer, Kansas City, AFC	38	923	24.3	95	2
1986	Dennis Gentry, Chicago, NFC	20	576	28.8	91	1
	Lupe Sanchez, Pittsburgh, AFC	25	591	23.6	64	0
1985	Ron Brown, L.A. Rams, NFC	28	918	32.8	98	3
	Glen Young, Cleveland, AFC	35	898	25.7	63	0
1984	*Bobby Humphery, N.Y. Jets, AFC	22	675	30.7	97	1
	Barry Redden, L.A. Rams, NFC	23	530	23.0	40	0
1983	Fulton Walker, Miami, AFC	36	962	26.7	78	0
	Darrin Nelson, Minnesota, NFC	18	445	24.7	50	0
1982	*Mike Mosley, Buffalo, AFC	18	487	27.1	66	0
	Alvin Hall, Detroit, NFC	16	426	26.6	96	1
1981	Mike Nelms, Washington, NFC	37	1,099	29.7	84	0
	Carl Roaches, Houston, AFC	28	769	27.5	96	1
1980	Horace Ivory, New England, AFC	36	992	27.6	98	1
	Rich Mauti, New Orleans, NFC	31	798	25.7	52	0
1979	Larry Brunson, Oakland, AFC	17	441	25.9	89	0
	Jimmy Edwards, Minnesota, NFC	44	1,103	25.1	83	0
1978	Steve Odom, Green Bay, NFC	25	677	27.1	95	1
	*Keith Wright, Cleveland, AFC	30	789	26.3	86	0
1977	*Raymond Clayborn, New England, AFC	28	869	31.0	101	3
	*Wilbert Montgomery, Philadelphia, NFC	23	619	26.9	99	1
1976	*Duriel Harris, Miami, AFC	17	559	32.9	69	0
	Cullen Bryant, Los Angeles, NFC	16	459	28.7	90	1
1975	*Walter Payton, Chicago, NFC	14	444	31.7	70	0
	Harold Hart, Oakland, AFC	17	518	30.5	102	1
1974	Terry Metcalf, St. Louis, NFC	20	623	31.2	94	1
	Greg Pruitt, Cleveland, AFC	22	606	27.5	88	1
1973	Carl Garrett, Chicago, NFC	16	486	30.4	67	0
	*Wallace Francis, Buffalo, AFC	23	687	29.9	101	2
1972	Ron Smith, Chicago, NFC	30	924	30.8	94	1
	*Bruce Laird, Baltimore, AFC	29	843	29.1	73	0
1971	Travis Williams, Los Angeles, NFC	25	743	29.7	105	1
	Eugene (Mercury) Morris, Miami, AFC	15	423	28.2	94	1
1970	Jim Duncan, Baltimore, AFC	20	707	35.4	99	1
	Cecil Turner, Chicago, NFC	23	752	32.7	96	4
1969	Bobby Williams, Detroit, NFL	17	563	33.1	96	1
	*Bill Thompson, Denver, AFL	18	513	28.5	63	0
1968	Preston Pearson, Baltimore, NFL	15	527	35.1	102	2
	*George Atkinson, Oakland, AFL	32	802	25.1	60	0
1967	*Travis Williams, Green Bay, NFL	18	739	41.1	104	4
	*Zeke Moore, Houston, AFL	14	405	28.9	92	1
1966	Gale Sayers, Chicago, NFL	23	718	31.2	93	2
	*Goldie Sellers, Denver, AFL	19	541	28.5	100	2
1965	Tommy Watkins, Detroit, NFL	17	584	34.4	94	0
	Abner Haynes, Denver, AFL	34	901	26.5	60	0
1964	*Clarence Childs, N.Y. Giants, NFL	34	987	29.0	100	1
	Bo Roberson, Oakland, AFL	36	975	27.1	59	0
1963	Abe Woodson, San Francisco, NFL	29	935	32.2	103	3
	Bobby Jancik, Houston, AFL	45	1,317	29.3	53	0
1962	Abe Woodson, San Francisco, NFL	37	1,157	31.3	79	0
	*Bobby Jancik, Houston, AFL	24	826	30.3	61	0
1961	Dick Bass, Los Angeles, NFL	23	698	30.3	64	0
	*Dave Grayson, Dall. Texans, AFL	16	453	28.3	73	0

Year	Player, Team	No.	Yards	Avg.	Long	TD
1960	*Tom Moore, Green Bay, NFL	12	397	33.1	84	0
	Ken Hall, Houston, AFL	19	594	31.3	104	1
1959	Abe Woodson, San Francisco	13	382	29.4	105	1
1958	Ollie Matson, Chi. Cardinals	14	497	35.5	101	2
1957	*Jon Arnett, Los Angeles	18	504	28.0	98	1
1956	*Tom Wilson, Los Angeles	15	477	31.8	103	1
1955	Al Carmichael, Green Bay	14	418	29.9	100	1
1954	Billy Reynolds, Cleveland	14	413	29.5	51	0
1953	Joe Arenas, San Francisco	16	551	34.4	82	0
1952	Lynn Chandnois, Pittsburgh	17	599	35.2	93	2
1951	Lynn Chandnois, Pittsburgh	12	390	32.5	55	0
1950	Verda (Vitamin T) Smith, Los Angeles	22	742	33.7	97	3
1949	*Don Doll, Detroit	21	536	25.5	56	0
1948	*Joe Scott, N.Y. Giants	20	569	28.5	99	1
1947	Eddie Saenz, Washington	29	797	27.5	94	2
1946	Abe Karnofsky, Boston	21	599	28.5	97	1
1945	Steve Van Buren, Philadelphia	13	373	28.7	98	1
1944	Bob Thurbon, Card.-Pitt.	12	291	24.3	55	0
1943	Ken Heineman, Brooklyn	16	444	27.8	69	0
1942	Marshall Goldberg, Chi. Cardinals	15	393	26.2	95	1
1941	Marshall Goldberg, Chi. Cardinals	12	290	24.2	41	0

First season of professional football.

ANNUAL INTERCEPTION LEADERS

Year	Player, Team	No.	Yards	TD
2003	Tony Parrish, San Francisco, NFC	9	202	0
	Brian Russell, Minnesota, NFC	9	185	0
	Ed Reed, Baltimore, AFC	7	132	1
	Marcus Coleman, Houston, AFC	7	95	0
	Patrick Surtain, Miami, AFC	7	59	0
2002	Rod Woodson, Oakland, AFC	8	225	2
	Brian Kelly, Tampa Bay, NFC	8	68	0
2001	*Anthony Henry, Cleveland, AFC	10	177	1
	Ronde Barber, Tampa Bay, NFC	10	86	1
2000	Darren Sharper, Green Bay, NFC	9	109	0
	Samari Rolle, Tennessee, AFC	7	140	1
	Brian Walker, Miami, AFC	7	80	0
1999	Rod Woodson, Baltimore, AFC	7	195	2
	Sam Madison, Miami, AFC	7	164	1
	James Hasty, Kansas City, AFC	7	98	2
	Donnie Abraham, Tampa Bay, NFC	7	115	2
	Troy Vincent, Philadelphia, NFC	7	91	0
1998	Ty Law, New England, AFC	9	133	1
	Kwamie Lassiter, Arizona, NFC	8	80	0
1997	Ryan McNeil, St. Louis, NFC	9	127	1
	Mark McMillian, Kansas City, AFC	8	274	3
	Darryl Williams, Seattle, AFC	8	172	1
1996	Tyrone Braxton, Denver, AFC	9	128	1
	Keith Lyle, St. Louis, NFC	9	152	0
1995	*Orlando Thomas, Minnesota, NFC	9	108	1
	Willie Williams, Pittsburgh, AFC	7	122	1
1994	Eric Turner, Cleveland, AFC	9	199	1
	Aeneas Williams, Arizona, NFC	9	89	0
1993	Eugene Robinson, Seattle, AFC	9	80	0
	Nate Odomes, Buffalo, AFC	9	65	0
	Deion Sanders, Atlanta, NFC	7	91	0
1992	Henry Jones, Buffalo, AFC	8	263	2
	Audray McMillian, Minnesota, NFC	8	157	2
1991	Ronnie Lott, L.A. Raiders, AFC	8	52	0
	Ray Crockett, Detroit, NFC	6	141	1
	Deion Sanders, Atlanta, NFC	6	119	1
	*Aeneas Williams, Phoenix, NFC	6	60	0
	Tim McKyer, Atlanta, NFC	6	24	0
1990	*Mark Carrier, Chicago, NFC	10	39	0
	Richard Johnson, Houston, AFC	8	100	1
1989	Felix Wright, Cleveland, AFC	9	91	1
	Eric Allen, Philadelphia, NFC	8	38	0
1988	Scott Case, Atlanta, NFC	10	47	0
	Erik McMillan, N.Y. Jets, AFC	8	168	2
1987	Barry Wilburn, Washington, NFC	9	135	1
	Mike Prior, Indianapolis, AFC	6	57	0
	Mark Kelso, Buffalo, AFC	6	25	0
	Keith Bostic, Houston, AFC	6	-14	0
1986	Ronnie Lott, San Francisco, NFC	10	134	1
	Deron Cherry, Kansas City, AFC	9	150	0
1985	Everson Walls, Dallas, NFC	9	31	0
	Albert Lewis, Kansas City, AFC	8	59	0
	Eugene Daniel, Indianapolis, AFC	8	53	0
1984	Ken Easley, Seattle, AFC	10	126	2
	*Tom Flynn, Green Bay, NFC	9	106	0
1983	Mark Murphy, Washington, NFC	9	127	0
	Ken Riley, Cincinnati, AFC	8	89	2
	Vann McElroy, L.A. Raiders, AFC	8	68	0
1982	Everson Walls, Dallas, NFC	7	61	0
	Ken Riley, Cincinnati, AFC	5	88	1
	Bobby Jackson, N.Y Jets, AFC	5	84	1
	Dwayne Woodruff, Pittsburgh, AFC	5	53	0
	Donnie Shell, Pittsburgh, AFC	5	27	0
1981	*Everson Walls, Dallas, NFC	11	133	0
	John Harris, Seattle, AFC	10	155	2
1980	Lester Hayes, Oakland, AFC	13	273	1
	Nolan Cromwell, Los Angeles, NFC	8	140	1
1979	Mike Reinfeldt, Houston, AFC	12	205	0
	Lemar Parrish, Washington, NFC	9	65	0
1978	Thom Darden, Cleveland, AFC	10	200	0
	Ken Stone, St. Louis, NFC	9	139	0
	Willie Buchanon, Green Bay, NFC	9	93	1
1977	Lyle Blackwood, Baltimore, AFC	10	163	0
	Rolland Lawrence, Atlanta, NFC	7	138	0
1976	Monte Jackson, Los Angeles, NFC	10	173	3
	Ken Riley, Cincinnati, AFC	9	141	1
1975	Mel Blount, Pittsburgh, AFC	11	121	0
	Paul Krause, Minnesota, NFC	10	201	0
1974	Emmitt Thomas, Kansas City, AFC	12	214	2
	Ray Brown, Atlanta, NFC	8	164	1
1973	Dick Anderson, Miami, AFC	8	163	2
	Mike Wagner, Pittsburgh, AFC	8	134	0
	Bobby Bryant, Minnesota, NFC	7	105	1
1972	Bill Bradley, Philadelphia, NFC	9	73	0
	Mike Sensibaugh, Kansas City, AFC	8	65	0

Year	Player, Team	No.	Yards	TD
1971	Bill Bradley, Philadelphia, NFC	11	248	0
	Ken Houston, Houston, AFC	9	220	4
1970	Johnny Robinson, Kansas City, AFC	10	155	0
	Dick LeBeau, Detroit, NFC	9	96	0
1969	Mel Renfro, Dallas, NFL	10	118	0
	Emmitt Thomas, Kansas City, AFL	9	146	1
1968	Dave Grayson, Oakland, AFL	10	195	1
	Willie Williams, N.Y. Giants, NFL	10	103	0
1967	Miller Farr, Houston, AFL	10	264	3
	*Lem Barney, Detroit, NFL	10	232	3
	Tom Janik, Buffalo, AFL	10	222	2
	Dave Whitsell, New Orleans, NFL	10	178	2
	Dick Westmoreland, Miami, AFL	10	127	1
1966	Larry Wilson, St. Louis, NFL	10	180	2
	Johnny Robinson, Kansas City, AFL	10	136	1
	Bobby Hunt, Kansas City, AFL	10	113	0
1965	W.K. Hicks, Houston, AFL	9	156	0
	Bobby Boyd, Baltimore, NFL	9	78	1
1964	Dainard Paulson, N.Y. Jets, AFL	12	157	1
	*Paul Krause, Washington, NFL	12	140	1
1963	Fred Glick, Houston, AFL	12	180	1
	Dick Lynch, N.Y. Giants, NFL	9	251	3
	Roosevelt Taylor, Chicago, NFL	9	172	1
1962	Lee Riley, N.Y. Titans, AFL	11	122	0
	Willie Wood, Green Bay, NFL	9	132	0
1961	Billy Atkins, Buffalo, AFL	10	158	0
	Dick Lynch, N.Y. Giants, NFL	9	60	0
1960	*Austin (Goose) Gonsoulin, Denver, AFL	11	98	0
	Dave Baker, San Francisco, NFL	10	96	0
	Jerry Norton, St. Louis, NFL	10	96	0
1959	Dean Derby, Pittsburgh	7	127	0
	Milt Davis, Baltimore	7	119	1
	Don Shinnick, Baltimore	7	70	0
1958	Jim Patton, N.Y. Giants	11	183	0
1957	Milt Davis, Baltimore	10	219	2
	Jack Christiansen, Detroit	10	137	1
	Jack Butler, Pittsburgh	10	85	0
1956	Linden Crow, Chi. Cardinals	11	170	0
1955	Will Sherman, Los Angeles	11	101	0
1954	Dick (Night Train) Lane, Chi. Cardinals	10	181	0
1953	Jack Christiansen, Detroit	12	238	1
1952	*Dick (Night Train) Lane, Los Angeles	14	298	2
1951	Otto Schnellbacher, N.Y. Giants	11	194	2
1950	Orban (Spec) Sanders, N.Y. Yanks	13	199	0
1949	Bob Nussbaumer, Chi. Cardinals	12	157	0
1948	*Dan Sandifer, Washington	13	258	2
1947	Frank Reagan, N.Y. Giants	10	203	0
	Frank Seno, Boston	10	100	0
1946	Bill Dudley, Pittsburgh	10	242	1
1945	Roy Zimmerman, Philadelphia	7	90	0
1944	*Howard Livingston, N.Y. Giants	9	172	1
1943	Sammy Baugh, Washington	11	112	0
1942	Clyde (Bulldog) Turner, Chi. Bears	8	96	1
1941	Marshall Goldberg, Chi. Cardinals	7	54	0
	*Art Jones, Pittsburgh	7	35	0
1940	Clarence (Ace) Parker, Brooklyn	6	146	1
	Kent Ryan, Detroit	6	65	0
	Don Hutson, Green Bay	6	24	0

**First season of professional football.*

ANNUAL PUNTING LEADERS

Year	Player, Team	No.	Avg.	Long
2003	Shane Lechler, Oakland, AFC	96	46.9	73
	Todd Sauerbrun, Carolina, NFC	77	44.6	64
2002	Todd Sauerbrun, Carolina, NFC	104	45.5	67
	Chris Hanson, Jacksonville, AFC	81	44.2	64
2001	Todd Sauerbrun, Carolina, NFC	93	47.5	73
	Shane Lechler, Oakland, AFC	73	46.2	65
2000	Darren Bennett, San Diego, AFC	92	46.2	66
	Mitch Berger, Minnesota, NFC	62	44.7	60
1999	Tom Rouen, Denver, AFC	84	46.5	65
	Mitch Berger, Minnesota, NFC	61	45.4	75
1998	Craig Hentrich, Tennessee, AFC	69	47.2	71
	Mark Royals, New Orleans, NFC	88	45.6	64
1997	Mark Royals, New Orleans, NFC	88	45.9	66
	Tom Tupa, New England, AFC	78	45.8	73
1996	John Kidd, Miami, AFC	78	46.3	63
	Matt Turk, Washington, NFC	75	45.1	63
1995	Rick Tuten, Seattle, AFC	83	45.0	73
	Sean Landeta, St. Louis, NFC	83	44.3	63
1994	Sean Landeta, L.A. Rams, NFC	78	44.8	62
	Jeff Gossett, L.A. Raiders, AFC	77	43.9	65
1993	Greg Montgomery, Houston, AFC	54	45.6	77
	Jim Arnold, Detroit, NFC	72	44.5	68
1992	Greg Montgomery, Houston, AFC	53	46.9	66
	Harry Newsome, Minnesota, NFC	72	45.0	84
1991	Reggie Roby, Miami, AFC	54	45.7	64
	Harry Newsome, Minnesota, AFC	68	45.5	65
1990	Mike Horan, Denver, AFC	58	44.4	67
	Sean Landeta, N.Y. Giants, NFC	75	44.1	67
1989	Rich Camarillo, Phoenix, NFC	76	43.4	58
	Greg Montgomery, Houston, AFC	56	43.3	63
1988	Harry Newsome, Pittsburgh, AFC	65	45.4	62
	Jim Arnold, Detroit, NFC	97	42.4	69
1987	Rick Donnelly, Atlanta, NFC	61	44.0	62
	Ralf Mojsiejenko, San Diego, AFC	67	42.9	57
1986	Rohn Stark, Indianapolis, AFC	76	45.2	63
	Sean Landeta, N.Y. Giants, NFC	79	44.8	61
1985	Rohn Stark, Indianapolis, AFC	78	45.9	68
	*Rick Donnelly, Atlanta, NFC	59	43.6	68
1984	Jim Arnold, Kansas City, AFC	98	44.9	63
	*Brian Hansen, New Orleans, NFC	69	43.8	66
1983	Rohn Stark, Baltimore, AFC	91	45.3	68
	Frank Garcia, Tampa Bay, NFC	95	42.2	64
1982	Luke Prestridge, Denver, AFC	45	45.0	65
	Carl Birdsong, St. Louis, NFC	54	43.8	65
1981	Pat McInally, Cincinnati, AFC	72	45.4	62
	Tom Skladany, Detroit, NFC	64	43.5	74
1980	Dave Jennings, N.Y. Giants, NFC	94	44.8	63
	Luke Prestridge, Denver, AFC	70	43.9	57
1979	*Bob Grupp, Kansas City, AFC	89	43.6	74
	Dave Jennings, N.Y. Giants, NFC	104	42.7	72
1978	Pat McInally, Cincinnati, AFC	91	43.1	65
	*Tom Skladany, Detroit, NFC	86	42.5	63
1977	Ray Guy, Oakland, AFC	59	43.3	74
	Tom Blanchard, New Orleans, NFC	82	42.4	66
1976	Marv Bateman, Buffalo, AFC	86	42.8	78
	John James, Atlanta, NFC	101	42.1	67
1975	Ray Guy, Oakland, AFC	68	43.8	64
	Herman Weaver, Detroit, NFC	80	42.0	61
1974	Ray Guy, Oakland, AFC	74	42.2	66
	Tom Blanchard, New Orleans, NFC	88	42.1	71
1973	Jerrel Wilson, Kansas City, AFC	80	45.5	68
	*Tom Wittum, San Francisco, NFC	79	43.7	62
1972	Jerrel Wilson, Kansas City, AFC	66	44.8	69
	Dave Chapple, Los Angeles, NFC	53	44.2	70
1971	Dave Lewis, Cincinnati, AFC	72	44.8	56
	Tom McNeill, Philadelphia, NFC	73	42.0	64
1970	Dave Lewis, Cincinnati, AFC	79	46.2	63
	*Julian Fagan, New Orleans, NFC	77	42.5	64
1969	David Lee, Baltimore, NFL	57	45.3	66
	Dennis Partee, San Diego, AFL	71	44.6	62
1968	Jerrel Wilson, Kansas City, AFL	63	45.1	70
	Billy Lothridge, Atlanta, NFL	75	44.3	70
1967	Bob Scarpitto, Denver, AFL	105	44.9	73
	Billy Lothridge, Atlanta, NFL	87	43.7	62
1966	Bob Scarpitto, Denver, AFL	76	45.8	70
	*David Lee, Baltimore, NFL	49	45.6	64

Year	Player, Team	No.	Avg.	Long
1965	Gary Collins, Cleveland, NFL	65	46.7	71
	Jerrel Wilson, Kansas City, AFL	69	45.4	64
1964	Bobby Walden, Minnesota, NFL	72	46.4	73
	Jim Fraser, Denver, AFL	73	44.2	67
1963	Yale Lary, Detroit, NFL	35	48.9	73
	Jim Fraser, Denver, AFL	81	44.4	66
1962	Tommy Davis, San Francisco, NFL	48	45.6	82
	Jim Fraser, Denver, AFL	55	43.6	75
1961	Yale Lary, Detroit, NFL	52	48.4	71
	Billy Atkins, Buffalo, AFL	85	44.5	70
1960	Jerry Norton, St. Louis, NFL	39	45.6	62
	*Paul Maguire, L.A. Chargers, AFL	43	40.5	61
1959	Yale Lary, Detroit	45	47.1	67
1958	Sam Baker, Washington	48	45.4	64
1957	Don Chandler, N.Y. Giants	60	44.6	61
1956	Norm Van Brocklin, Los Angeles	48	43.1	72
1955	Norm Van Brocklin, Los Angeles	60	44.6	61
1954	Pat Brady, Pittsburgh	66	43.2	72
1953	Pat Brady, Pittsburgh	80	46.9	64
1952	Horace Gillom, Cleveland	61	45.7	73
1951	Horace Gillom, Cleveland	73	45.5	66
1950	*Fred (Curly) Morrison, Chi. Bears	57	43.3	65
1949	*Mike Boyda, N.Y. Bulldogs	56	44.2	61
1948	Joe Muha, Philadelphia	57	47.3	82
1947	Jack Jacobs, Green Bay	57	43.5	74
1946	Roy McKay, Green Bay	64	42.7	64
1945	Roy McKay, Green Bay	44	41.2	73
1944	Frank Sinkwich, Detroit	45	41.0	73
1943	Sammy Baugh, Washington	50	45.9	81
1942	Sammy Baugh, Washington	37	48.2	74
1941	Sammy Baugh, Washington	30	48.7	75
1940	Sammy Baugh, Washington	35	51.4	85
1939	*Parker Hall, Cleveland	58	40.8	80

First season of professional football.

ANNUAL LEADERS IN SACKS (SINCE 1982)

Year	Player, Team	Sacks
2003	Michael Strahan, N.Y. Giants, NFC	18.5
	Adewale Ogunleye, Miami, AFC	15.0
2002	Jason Taylor, Miami, AFC	18.5
	Simeon Rice, Tampa Bay, NFC	15.5
2001	Michael Strahan, N.Y. Giants, NFC	22.5
	Peter Boulware, Baltimore, AFC	15.0
2000	La'Roi Glover, New Orleans, NFC	17.0
	Trace Armstrong, Miami, AFC	16.5
1999	Kevin Carter, St. Louis, NFC	17.0
	*Jevon Kearse, Tennessee, AFC	14.5
1998	Michael Sinclair, Seattle, AFC	16.5
	Reggie White, Green Bay, NFC	16.0
1997	John Randle, Minnesota, NFC	15.5
	Bruce Smith, Buffalo, AFC	14.0
1996	Kevin Greene, Carolina, NFC	14.5
	Michael McCrary, Seattle, AFC	13.5
	Bruce Smith, Buffalo, AFC	13.5
1995	Bryce Paup, Buffalo, AFC	17.5
	William Fuller, Philadelphia, NFC	13.0
	Wayne Martin, New Orleans, NFC	13.0
1994	Kevin Greene, Pittsburgh, AFC	14.0
	Ken Harvey, Washington, NFC	13.5
	John Randle, Minnesota, NFC	13.5
1993	Neil Smith, Kansas City, AFC	15.0
	Renaldo Turnbull, New Orleans, NFC	13.0
	Reggie White, Green Bay, NFC	13.0
1992	Clyde Simmons, Philadelphia, NFC	19.0
	Leslie O'Neal, San Diego, AFC	17.0
1991	Pat Swilling, New Orleans, NFC	17.0
	William Fuller, Houston, AFC	15.0
1990	Derrick Thomas, Kansas City, AFC	20.0
	Charles Haley, San Francisco, NFC	16.0
1989	Chris Doleman, Minnesota, NFC	21.0
	Lee Williams, San Diego, AFC	14.0
1988	Reggie White, Philadelphia, NFC	18.0
	Greg Townsend, L.A. Raiders, AFC	11.5
1987	Reggie White, Philadelphia, NFC	21.0
	Andre Tippett, New England, AFC	12.5
1986	Lawrence Taylor, N.Y. Giants, NFC	20.5
	Sean Jones, L.A. Raiders, AFC	15.5
1985	Richard Dent, Chicago, NFC	17.0
	Andre Tippett, New England, AFC	16.5
1984	Mark Gastineau, N.Y. Jets, AFC	22.0
	Richard Dent, Chicago, NFC	17.5
1983	Mark Gastineau, N.Y. Jets, AFC	19.0
	Fred Dean, San Francisco, NFC	17.5
1982	Doug Martin, Minnesota, NFC	11.5
	Jesse Baker, Houston, AFC	7.5

First season of professional football.

POINTS SCORED

Year	Team	Points
2003	Kansas City, AFC	484
	St. Louis, NFC	447
2002	Kansas City, AFC	467
	New Orleans, NFC	432
2001	St. Louis, NFC	503
	Indianapolis, AFC	413
2000	St. Louis, NFC	540
	Denver, AFC	485
1999	St. Louis, NFC	526
	Indianapolis, AFC	423
1998	Minnesota, NFC	556
	Denver, AFC	501
1997	Denver, AFC	472
	Green Bay, NFC	422
1996	Green Bay, NFC	456
	New England, AFC	418
1995	San Francisco, NFC	457
	Pittsburgh, AFC	407
1994	San Francisco, NFC	505
	Miami, AFC	389
1993	San Francisco, NFC	473
	Denver, AFC	373
1992	San Francisco, NFC	431
	Buffalo, AFC	381
1991	Washington, NFC	485
	Buffalo, AFC	458
1990	Buffalo, AFC	428
	Philadelphia, NFC	396
1989	San Francisco, NFC	442
	Buffalo, AFC	409
1988	Cincinnati, AFC	448
	L.A. Rams, NFC	407
1987	San Francisco, NFC	459
	Cleveland, AFC	390
1986	Miami, AFC	430
	Minnesota, NFC	398
1985	San Diego, AFC	467
	Chicago, NFC	456
1984	Miami, AFC	513
	San Francisco, NFC	475
1983	Washington, NFC	541
	L.A. Raiders, AFC	442
1982	San Diego, AFC	288
	Dallas, NFC	226
	Green Bay, NFC	226
1981	San Diego, AFC	478
	Atlanta, NFC	426
1980	Dallas, NFC	454
	New England, AFC	441

Year	Team	Points
1979	Pittsburgh, AFC	416
	Dallas, NFC	371
1978	Dallas, NFC	384
	Miami, AFC	372
1977	Oakland, AFC	351
	Dallas, NFC	345
1976	Baltimore, AFC	417
	Los Angeles, NFC	351
1975	Buffalo, AFC	420
	Minnesota, NFC	377
1974	Oakland, AFC	355
	Washington, NFC	320
1973	Los Angeles, NFC	388
	Denver, AFC	354
1972	Miami, AFC	385
	San Francisco, NFC	353
1971	Dallas, NFC	406
	Oakland, AFC	344
1970	San Francisco, NFC	352
	Baltimore, AFC	321
1969	Minnesota, NFL	379
	Oakland, AFL	377
1968	Oakland, AFL	453
	Dallas, NFL	431
1967	Oakland, AFL	468
	Los Angeles, NFL	398
1966	Kansas City, AFL	448
	Dallas, NFL	445
1965	San Francisco, NFL	421
	San Diego, AFL	340
1964	Baltimore, NFL	428
	Buffalo, AFL	400
1963	N.Y. Giants, NFL	448
	San Diego, AFL	399
1962	Green Bay, NFL	415
	Dall. Texans, AFL	389
1961	Houston, AFL	513
	Green Bay, NFL	391
1960	N.Y. Titans, AFL	382
	Cleveland, NFL	362
1959	Baltimore	374
1958	Baltimore	381
1957	Los Angeles	307
1956	Chi. Bears	363
1955	Cleveland	349
1954	Detroit	337
1953	San Francisco	372
1952	Los Angeles	349
1951	Los Angeles	392
1950	Los Angeles	466
1949	Philadelphia	364
1948	Chi. Cardinals	395
1947	Chi. Bears	363
1946	Chi. Bears	289
1945	Philadelphia	272
1944	Philadelphia	267
1943	Chi. Bears	303
1942	Chi. Bears	376
1941	Chi. Bears	396
1940	Washington	245
1939	Chi. Bears	298
1938	Green Bay	223
1937	Green Bay	220
1936	Green Bay	248
1935	Chi. Bears	192
1934	Chi. Bears	286
1933	N.Y. Giants	244
1932	Chi. Bears	160

TOTAL YARDS GAINED

Year	Team	Yards
2003	Minnesota, NFC	6,294
	Kansas City, AFC	5,910
2002	Oakland, AFC	6,237
	Minnesota, NFC	6,192
2001	St. Louis, NFC	6,690
	Indianapolis, AFC	5,955
2000	St. Louis, NFC	7,075
	Denver, AFC	6,554
1999	St. Louis, NFC	6,412
	Indianapolis, AFC	5,726
1998	San Francisco, NFC	6,800
	Denver, AFC	6,092
1997	Denver, AFC	5,872
	Detroit, NFC	5,798
1996	Denver, AFC	5,791
	Philadelphia, NFC	5,627
1995	Detroit, NFC	6,113
	Denver, AFC	6,040
1994	Miami, AFC	6,078
	San Francisco, NFC	6,060
1993	San Francisco, NFC	6,435
	Miami, AFC	5,812
1992	San Francisco, NFC	6,195
	Buffalo, AFC	5,893
1991	Buffalo, AFC	6,252
	San Francisco, NFC	5,858
1990	Houston, AFC	6,222
	San Francisco, NFC	5,895
1989	San Francisco, NFC	6,268
	Cincinnati, AFC	6,101
1988	Cincinnati, AFC	6,057
	San Francisco, NFC	5,900
1987	San Francisco, NFC	5,987
	Denver, AFC	5,624
1986	Cincinnati, AFC	6,490
	San Francisco, NFC	6,082
1985	San Diego, AFC	6,535
	San Francisco, NFC	5,920
1984	Miami, AFC	6,936
	San Francisco, NFC	6,366
1983	San Diego, AFC	6,197
	Green Bay, NFC	6,172
1982	San Diego, AFC	4,048
	San Francisco, NFC	3,242
1981	San Diego, AFC	6,744
	Detroit, NFC	5,933
1980	San Diego, AFC	6,410
	Los Angeles, NFC	6,006
1979	Pittsburgh, AFC	6,258
	Dallas, NFC	5,968
1978	New England, AFC	5,965
	Dallas, NFC	5,959
1977	Dallas, NFC	4,812
	Oakland, AFC	4,736
1976	Baltimore, AFC	5,236
	St. Louis, NFC	5,136
1975	Buffalo, AFC	5,467
	Dallas, NFC	5,025
1974	Dallas, NFC	4,983
	Oakland, AFC	4,718
1973	Los Angeles, NFC	4,906
	Oakland, AFC	4,773
1972	Miami, AFC	5,036
	N.Y. Giants, NFC	4,483
1971	Dallas, NFC	5,035
	San Diego, AFC	4,738
1970	Oakland, AFC	4,829
	San Francisco, NFC	4,503

Year	Team	Yards
1969	Dallas, NFL	5,122
	Oakland, AFL	5,036
1968	Oakland, AFL	5,696
	Dallas, NFL	5,117
1967	N.Y. Jets, AFL	5,152
	Baltimore, NFL	5,008
1966	Dallas, NFL	5,145
	Kansas City, AFL	5,114
1965	San Francisco, NFL	5,270
	San Diego, AFL	5,188
1964	Buffalo, AFL	5,206
	Baltimore, NFL	4,779
1963	San Diego, AFL	5,153
	N.Y. Giants, NFL	5,024
1962	N.Y. Giants, NFL	5,005
	Houston, AFL	4,971
1961	Houston, AFL	6,288
	Philadelphia, NFL	5,112
1960	Houston, AFL	4,936
	Baltimore, NFL	4,245
1959	Baltimore	4,458
1958	Baltimore	4,539
1957	Los Angeles	4,143
1956	Chi. Bears	4,537
1955	Chi. Bears	4,316
1954	Los Angeles	5,187
1953	Philadelphia	4,811
1952	Cleveland	4,352
1951	Los Angeles	5,506
1950	Los Angeles	5,420
1949	Chi. Bears	4,873
1948	Chi. Cardinals	4,705
1947	Chi. Bears	5,053
1946	Los Angeles	3,793
1945	Washington	3,549
1944	Chi. Bears	3,239
1943	Chi. Bears	4,045
1942	Chi. Bears	3,900
1941	Chi. Bears	4,265
1940	Green Bay	3,400
1939	Chi. Bears	3,988
1938	Green Bay	3,037
1937	Green Bay	3,201
1936	Detroit	3,703
1935	Chi. Bears	3,454
1934	Chi. Bears	3,900
1933	N.Y. Giants	2,973
1932	Chi. Bears	2,755

YARDS RUSHING

Year	Team	Yards
2003	Baltimore, AFC	2,674
	Green Bay, NFC	2,558
2002	Minnesota, NFC	2,507
	Miami, AFC	2,502
2001	Pittsburgh, AFC	2,774
	San Francisco, NFC	2,244
2000	Oakland, AFC	2,470
	Minnesota, NFC	2,129
1999	San Francisco, NFC	2,095
	Jacksonville, AFC	2,091
1998	San Francisco, NFC	2,544
	Denver, AFC	2,468
1997	Pittsburgh, AFC	2,479
	Detroit, NFC	2,464
1996	Denver, AFC	2,362
	Washington, NFC	1,910
1995	Kansas City, AFC	2,222
	Dallas, NFC	2,201
1994	Pittsburgh, AFC	2,180
	Detroit, NFC	2,080
1993	N.Y. Giants, NFC	2,210
	Seattle, AFC	2,015
1992	Buffalo, AFC	2,436
	Philadelphia, NFC	2,388
1991	Buffalo, AFC	2,381
	Minnesota, NFC	2,201
1990	Philadelphia, NFC	2,556
	San Diego, AFC	2,257
1989	Cincinnati, AFC	2,483
	Chicago, NFC	2,287
1988	Cincinnati, AFC	2,710
	San Francisco, NFC	2,523
1987	San Francisco, NFC	2,237
	L.A. Raiders, AFC	2,197
1986	Chicago, NFC	2,700
	Cincinnati, AFC	2,533
1985	Chicago, NFC	2,761
	Indianapolis, AFC	2,439
1984	Chicago, NFC	2,974
	N.Y. Jets, AFC	2,189
1983	Chicago, NFC	2,727
	Baltimore, AFC	2,695
1982	Buffalo, AFC	1,371
	Dallas, NFC	1,313
1981	Detroit, NFC	2,795
	Kansas City, AFC	2,633
1980	Los Angeles, NFC	2,799
	Houston, AFC	2,635
1979	N.Y. Jets, AFC	2,646
	St. Louis, NFC	2,582
1978	New England, AFC	3,165
	Dallas, NFC	2,783
1977	Chicago, NFC	2,811
	Oakland, AFC	2,627
1976	Pittsburgh, AFC	2,971
	Los Angeles, NFC	2,528
1975	Buffalo, AFC	2,974
	Dallas, NFC	2,432
1974	Dallas, NFC	2,454
	Pittsburgh, AFC	2,417
1973	Buffalo, AFC	3,088
	Los Angeles, NFC	2,925
1972	Miami, AFC	2,960
	Chicago, NFC	2,360
1971	Miami, AFC	2,429
	Detroit, NFC	2,376
1970	Dallas, NFC	2,300
	Miami, AFC	2,082
1969	Dallas, NFL	2,276
	Kansas City, AFL	2,220
1968	Chicago, NFL	2,377
	Kansas City, AFL	2,227
1967	Cleveland, NFL	2,139
	Houston, AFL	2,122
1966	Kansas City, AFL	2,274
	Cleveland, NFL	2,166
1965	Cleveland, NFL	2,331
	San Diego, AFL	2,085
1964	Green Bay, NFL	2,276
	Buffalo, AFL	2,040
1963	Cleveland, NFL	2,639
	San Diego, AFL	2,203
1962	Buffalo, AFL	2,480
	Green Bay, NFL	2,460
1961	Green Bay, NFL	2,350
	Dall. Texans, AFL	2,189
1960	St. Louis, NFL	2,356

YEARLY STATISTICAL LEADERS

Year	Team	Yards
	Oakland, AFL	2,056
1959	Cleveland	2,149
1958	Cleveland	2,526
1957	Los Angeles	2,142
1956	Chi. Bears	2,468
1955	Chi. Bears	2,388
1954	San Francisco	2,498
1953	San Francisco	2,230
1952	San Francisco	1,905
1951	Chi. Bears	2,408
1950	N.Y. Giants	2,336
1949	Philadelphia	2,607
1948	Chi. Cardinals	2,560
1947	Los Angeles	2,171
1946	Green Bay	1,765
1945	Cleveland	1,714
1944	Philadelphia	1,661
1943	Phil-Pitt	1,730
1942	Chi. Bears	1,881
1941	Chi. Bears	2,263
1940	Chi. Bears	1,818
1939	Chi. Bears	2,043
1938	Detroit	1,893
1937	Detroit	2,074
1936	Detroit	2,885
1935	Chi. Bears	2,096
1934	Chi. Bears	2,847
1933	Boston	2,260
1932	Chi. Bears	1,770

YARDS PASSING

Leadership in this category has been based on net yards since 1952.

Year	Team	Yards
2003	Indianapolis, AFC	4,179
	St. Louis, NFC	3,961
2002	Oakland, AFC	4,475
	St. Louis, NFC	4,154
2001	St. Louis, NFC	4,663
	Indianapolis, AFC	3,989
2000	St. Louis, NFC	5,232
	Indianapolis, AFC	4,282
1999	St. Louis, NFC	4,353
	Indianapolis, AFC	4,066
1998	Minnesota, NFC	4,328
	N.Y. Jets, AFC	3,836
1997	Seattle, AFC	3,959
	Green Bay, NFC	3,705
1996	Jacksonville, AFC	4,110
	Philadelphia, NFC	3,745
1995	San Francisco, NFC	4,608
	Miami, AFC	4,210
1994	New England, AFC	4,444
	Minnesota, NFC	4,324
1993	Miami, AFC	4,353
	San Francisco, NFC	4,302
1992	Houston, AFC	4,029
	San Francisco, NFC	3,880
1991	Houston, AFC	4,621
	San Francisco, NFC	3,997
1990	Houston, AFC	4,805
	San Francisco, NFC	4,177
1989	Washington, NFC	4,349
	Miami, AFC	4,216
1988	Miami, AFC	4,516
	Washington, NFC	4,136
1987	Miami, AFC	3,876
	San Francisco, NFC	3,750
1986	Miami, AFC	4,779
	San Francisco, NFC	4,096
1985	San Diego, AFC	4,870
	Dallas, NFC	3,861
1984	Miami, AFC	5,018
	St. Louis, NFC	4,257
1983	San Diego, AFC	4,661
	Green Bay, NFC	4,365
1982	San Diego, AFC	2,927
	San Francisco, NFC	2,502
1981	San Diego, AFC	4,739
	Minnesota, NFC	4,333
1980	San Diego, AFC	4,531
	Minnesota, NFC	3,688
1979	San Diego, AFC	3,915
	San Francisco, NFC	3,641
1978	San Diego, AFC	3,375
	Minnesota, NFC	3,243
1977	Buffalo, AFC	2,530
	St. Louis, NFC	2,499
1976	Baltimore, AFC	2,933
	Minnesota, NFC	2,855
1975	Cincinnati, AFC	3,241
	Washington, NFC	2,917
1974	Washington, NFC	2,978
	Cincinnati, AFC	2,804
1973	Philadelphia, NFC	2,998
	Denver, AFC	2,519
1972	N.Y. Jets, AFC	2,777
	San Francisco, NFC	2,735
1971	San Diego, AFC	3,134
	Dallas, NFC	2,786
1970	San Francisco, NFC	2,923
	Oakland, AFC	2,865
1969	Oakland, AFL	3,271
	San Francisco, NFL	3,158
1968	San Diego, AFL	3,623
	Dallas, NFL	3,026
1967	N.Y. Jets, AFL	3,845
	Washington, NFL	3,730
1966	N.Y. Jets, AFL	3,464
	Dallas, NFL	3,023
1965	San Francisco, NFL	3,487
	San Diego, AFL	3,103
1964	Houston, AFL	3,527
	Chicago, NFL	2,841
1963	Baltimore, NFL	3,296
	Houston, AFL	3,222
1962	Denver, AFL	3,404
	Philadelphia, NFL	3,385
1961	Houston, AFL	4,392
	Philadelphia, NFL	3,605
1960	Houston, AFL	3,203
	Baltimore, NFL	2,956
1959	Baltimore	2,753
1958	Pittsburgh	2,752
1957	Baltimore	2,388
1956	Los Angeles	2,419
1955	Philadelphia	2,472
1954	Chi. Bears	3,104
1953	Philadelphia	3,089
1952	Cleveland	2,566
1951	Los Angeles	3,296
1950	Los Angeles	3,709
1949	Chi. Bears	3,055
1948	Washington	2,861
1947	Washington	3,336
1946	Los Angeles	2,080
1945	Chi. Bears	1,857
1944	Washington	2,021

Year	Team	Yards
1943	Chi. Bears	2,310
1942	Green Bay	2,407
1941	Chi. Bears	2,002
1940	Washington	1,887
1939	Chi. Bears	1,965
1938	Washington	1,536
1937	Green Bay	1,398
1936	Green Bay	1,629
1935	Green Bay	1,449
1934	Green Bay	1,165
1933	N.Y. Giants	1,348
1932	Chi. Bears	1,013

FEWEST POINTS ALLOWED

Year	Team	Points
2003	New England, AFC	238
	Dallas, NFC	260
2002	Tampa Bay, NFC	196
	Miami, AFC	301
2001	Chicago, NFC	203
	Pittsburgh, AFC	212
2000	Baltimore, AFC	165
	Philadelphia, NFC	245
1999	Jacksonville, AFC	217
	Tampa Bay, NFC	235
1998	Miami, AFC	265
	Dallas, NFC	275
1997	Kansas City, AFC	232
	Tampa Bay, NFC	263
1996	Green Bay, NFC	210
	Pittsburgh, AFC	257
1995	Kansas City, AFC	241
	San Francisco, NFC	258
1994	Cleveland, AFC	204
	Dallas, NFC	248
1993	N.Y. Giants, NFC	205
	Houston, AFC	238
1992	New Orleans, NFC	202
	Pittsburgh, AFC	225
1991	New Orleans, NFC	211
	Denver, AFC	235
1990	N.Y. Giants, NFC	211
	Pittsburgh, AFC	240
1989	Denver, AFC	226
	N.Y. Giants, NFC	252
1988	Chicago, NFC	215
	Buffalo, AFC	237
1987	Indianapolis, AFC	238
	San Francisco, NFC	253
1986	Chicago, NFC	187
	Seattle, AFC	293
1985	Chicago, NFC	198
	N.Y. Jets, AFC	264
1984	San Francisco, NFC	227
	Denver, AFC	241
1983	Miami, AFC	250
	Detroit, NFC	286
1982	Washington, NFC	128
	Miami, AFC	131
1981	Philadelphia, NFC	221
	Miami, AFC	275
1980	Philadelphia, NFC	222
	Houston, AFC	251
1979	Tampa Bay, NFC	237
	San Diego, AFC	246
1978	Pittsburgh, AFC	195
	Dallas, NFC	208
1977	Atlanta, NFC	129
	Denver, AFC	148

Year	Team	Points
1976	Pittsburgh, AFC	138
	Minnesota, NFC	176
1975	Los Angeles, NFC	135
	Pittsburgh, AFC	162
1974	Los Angeles, NFC	181
	Pittsburgh, AFC	189
1973	Miami, AFC	150
	Minnesota, NFC	168
1972	Miami, AFC	171
	Washington, NFC	218
1971	Minnesota, NFC	139
	Baltimore, AFC	140
1970	Minnesota, NFC	143
	Miami, AFC	228
1969	Minnesota, NFL	133
	Kansas City, AFL	177
1968	Baltimore, NFL	144
	Kansas City, AFL	170
1967	Los Angeles, NFL	196
	Houston, AFL	199
1966	Green Bay, NFL	163
	Buffalo, AFL	255
1965	Green Bay, NFL	224
	Buffalo, AFL	226
1964	Baltimore, NFL	225
	Buffalo, AFL	242
1963	Chicago, NFL	144
	San Diego, AFL	255
1962	Green Bay, NFL	148
	Dall. Texans, AFL	233
1961	San Diego, AFL	219
	N.Y. Giants, NFL	220
1960	San Francisco, NFL	205
	Dall. Texans, AFL	253
1959	N.Y. Giants	170
1958	N.Y. Giants	183
1957	Cleveland	172
1956	Cleveland	177
1955	Cleveland	218
1954	Cleveland	162
1953	Cleveland	162
1952	Detroit	192
1951	Cleveland	152
1950	Philadelphia	141
1949	Philadelphia	134
1948	Chi. Bears	151
1947	Green Bay	210
1946	Pittsburgh	117
1945	Washington	121
1944	N.Y. Giants	75
1943	Washington	137
1942	Chi. Bears	84
1941	N.Y. Giants	114
1940	Brooklyn	120
1939	N.Y. Giants	85
1938	N.Y. Giants	79
1937	Chi. Bears	100
1936	Chi. Bears	94
1935	Green Bay	96
	N.Y. Giants	96
1934	Detroit	59
1933	Brooklyn	54
1932	Chi. Bears	44

FEWEST TOTAL YARDS ALLOWED

Year	Team	Yards
2003	Dallas, NFC	4,056
	Buffalo, AFC	4,313

Year	Team	Yards
2002	Tampa Bay, NFC	4,044
	Miami, AFC	4,656
2001	Pittsburgh, AFC	4,137
	St. Louis, NFC	4,471
2000	Tennessee, AFC	3,813
	Washington, NFC	4,474
1999	Buffalo, AFC	4,045
	Tampa Bay, NFC	4,280
1998	San Diego, AFC	4,208
	Tampa Bay, NFC	4,345
1997	San Francisco, NFC	4,013
	Denver, AFC	4,671
1996	Green Bay, NFC	4,156
	Pittsburgh, AFC	4,362
1995	San Francisco, NFC	4,398
	Kansas City, AFC	4,549
1994	Dallas, NFC	4,313
	Pittsburgh, AFC	4,326
1993	Minnesota, NFC	4,406
	Pittsburgh, AFC	4,531
1992	Dallas, NFC	3,931
	Houston, AFC	4,211
1991	Philadelphia, NFC	3,549
	Denver, AFC	4,549
1990	Pittsburgh, AFC	4,115
	N.Y. Giants, NFC	4,206
1989	Minnesota, NFC	4,184
	Kansas City, AFC	4,293
1988	Minnesota, NFC	4,091
	Buffalo, AFC	4,578
1987	San Francisco, NFC	4,095
	Cleveland, AFC	4,264
1986	Chicago, NFC	4,130
	L.A. Raiders, AFC	4,804
1985	Chicago, NFC	4,135
	L.A. Raiders, AFC	4,603
1984	Chicago, NFC	3,863
	Cleveland, AFC	4,641
1983	Cincinnati, AFC	4,327
	New Orleans, NFC	4,691
1982	Miami, AFC	2,312
	Tampa Bay, NFC	2,442
1981	Philadelphia, NFC	4,447
	N.Y. Jets, AFC	4,871
1980	Buffalo, AFC	4,101
	Philadelphia, NFC	4,443
1979	Tampa Bay, NFC	3,949
	Pittsburgh, AFC	4,270
1978	Los Angeles, NFC	3,893
	Pittsburgh, AFC	4,168
1977	Dallas, NFC	3,213
	New England, AFC	3,638
1976	Pittsburgh, AFC	3,323
	San Francisco, NFC	3,562
1975	Minnesota, NFC	3,153
	Oakland, AFC	3,629
1974	Pittsburgh, AFC	3,074
	Washington, NFC	3,285
1973	Los Angeles, NFC	2,951
	Oakland, AFC	3,160
1972	Miami, AFC	3,297
	Green Bay, NFC	3,474
1971	Baltimore, AFC	2,852
	Minnesota, NFC	3,406
1970	Minnesota, NFC	2,803
	N.Y. Jets, AFC	3,655
1969	Minnesota, NFL	2,720
	Kansas City, AFL	3,163
1968	Los Angeles, NFL	3,118
	N.Y. Jets, AFL	3,363
1967	Oakland, AFL	3,294
	Green Bay, NFL	3,300
1966	St. Louis, NFL	3,492
	Oakland, AFL	3,910
1965	San Diego, AFL	3,262
	Detroit, NFL	3,557
1964	Green Bay, NFL	3,179
	Buffalo, AFL	3,878
1963	Chicago, NFL	3,176
	Boston, AFL	3,834
1962	Detroit, NFL	3,217
	Dall. Texans, AFL	3,951
1961	San Diego, AFL	3,726
	Baltimore, NFL	3,782
1960	St. Louis, NFL	3,029
	Buffalo, AFL	3,866
1959	N.Y. Giants	2,843
1958	Chi. Bears	3,066
1957	Pittsburgh	2,791
1956	N.Y. Giants	3,081
1955	Cleveland	2,841
1954	Cleveland	2,658
1953	Philadelphia	2,998
1952	Cleveland	3,075
1951	N.Y. Giants	3,250
1950	Cleveland	3,154
1949	Philadelphia	2,831
1948	Chi. Bears	2,931
1947	Green Bay	3,396
1946	Washington	2,451
1945	Philadelphia	2,073
1944	Philadelphia	1,943
1943	Chi. Bears	2,262
1942	Chi. Bears	1,703
1941	N.Y. Giants	2,368
1940	N.Y. Giants	2,219
1939	Washington	2,116
1938	N.Y. Giants	2,029
1937	Washington	2,123
1936	Boston	2,181
1935	Boston	1,996
1934	Chi. Cardinals	1,539
1933	Brooklyn	1,789

FEWEST RUSHING YARDS ALLOWED

Year	Team	Yards
2003	Tennessee, AFC	1,295
	Dallas, NFC	1,425
2002	Pittsburgh, AFC	1,375
	Tampa Bay, NFC	1,554
2001	Pittsburgh, AFC	1,195
	Chicago, NFC	1,313
2000	Baltimore, AFC	970
	N.Y. Giants, NFC	1,156
1999	St. Louis, NFC	1,189
	Baltimore, AFC	1,231
1998	San Diego, AFC	1,140
	Atlanta, NFC	1,203
1997	Pittsburgh, AFC	1,318
	San Francisco, NFC	1,366
1996	Denver, AFC	1,331
	Green Bay, NFC	1,416
1995	San Francisco, NFC	1,061
	Pittsburgh, AFC	1,321
1994	Minnesota, NFC	1,090
	San Diego, AFC	1,404

Year	Team	Yards
1993	Houston, AFC	1,273
	Minnesota, NFC	1,536
1992	Dallas, NFC	1,244
	Buffalo, AFC	1,395
	San Diego, AFC	1,395
1991	Philadelphia, NFC	1,136
	N.Y. Jets, AFC	1,442
1990	Philadelphia, NFC	1,169
	San Diego, AFC	1,515
1989	New Orleans, NFC	1,326
	Denver, AFC	1,580
1988	Chicago, NFC	1,326
	Houston, AFC	1,592
1987	Chicago, NFC	1,413
	Cleveland, AFC	1,433
1986	N.Y. Giants, NFC	1,284
	Denver, AFC	1,651
1985	Chicago, NFC	1,319
	N.Y. Jets, AFC	1,516
1984	Chicago, NFC	1,377
	Pittsburgh, AFC	1,617
1983	Washington, NFC	1,289
	Cincinnati, AFC	1,499
1982	Pittsburgh, AFC	762
	Detroit, NFC	854
1981	Detroit, NFC	1,623
	Kansas City, AFC	1,747
1980	Detroit, NFC	1,599
	Cincinnati, AFC	1,680
1979	Denver, AFC	1,693
	Tampa Bay, NFC	1,873
1978	Dallas, NFC	1,721
	Pittsburgh, AFC	1,774
1977	Denver, AFC	1,531
	Dallas, NFC	1,651
1976	Pittsburgh, AFC	1,457
	Los Angeles, NFC	1,564
1975	Minnesota, NFC	1,532
	Houston, AFC	1,680
1974	Los Angeles, NFC	1,302
	New England, AFC	1,587
1973	Los Angeles, NFC	1,270
	Oakland, AFC	1,470
1972	Dallas, NFC	1,515
	Miami, AFC	1,548
1971	Baltimore, AFC	1,113
	Dallas, NFC	1,144
1970	Detroit, NFC	1,152
	N.Y. Jets, AFC	1,283
1969	Dallas, NFL	1,050
	Kansas City, AFL	1,091
1968	Dallas, NFL	1,195
	N.Y. Jets, AFL	1,195
1967	Dallas, NFL	1,081
	Oakland, AFL	1,129
1966	Buffalo, AFL	1,051
	Dallas, NFL	1,176
1965	San Diego, AFL	1,094
	Los Angeles, NFL	1,409
1964	Buffalo, AFL	913
	Los Angeles, NFL	1,501
1963	Boston, AFL	1,107
	Chicago, NFL	1,442
1962	Detroit, NFL	1,231
	Dall. Texans, AFL	1,250
1961	Boston, AFL	1,041
	Pittsburgh, NFL	1,463
1960	St. Louis, NFL	1,212
	Dall. Texans, AFL	1,338
1959	N.Y. Giants	1,261
1958	Baltimore	1,291
1957	Baltimore	1,174
1956	N.Y. Giants	1,443
1955	Cleveland	1,189
1954	Cleveland	1,050
1953	Philadelphia	1,117
1952	Detroit	1,145
1951	N.Y. Giants	913
1950	Detroit	1,367
1949	Chi. Bears	1,196
1948	Philadelphia	1,209
1947	Philadelphia	1,329
1946	Chi. Bears	1,060
1945	Philadelphia	817
1944	Philadelphia	558
1943	Phil-Pitt	793
1942	Chi. Bears	519
1941	Washington	1,042
1940	N.Y. Giants	977
1939	Chi. Bears	812
1938	Detroit	1,081
1937	Chi. Bears	933
1936	Boston	1,148
1935	Boston	998
1934	Chi. Cardinals	954
1933	Brooklyn	964

FEWEST PASSING YARDS ALLOWED

Leadership in this category has been based on net yards since 1952.

Year	Team	Yards
2003	Dallas, NFC	2,631
	Buffalo, AFC	2,707
2002	Tampa Bay, NFC	2,490
	Indianapolis, AFC	2,917
2001	Miami, AFC	2,829
	Philadelphia, NFC	2,864
2000	Tennessee, AFC	2,423
	Washington, NFC	2,621
1999	Buffalo, AFC	2,675
	Tampa Bay, NFC	2,873
1998	Philadelphia, NFC	2,720
	Oakland, AFC	2,876
1997	Dallas, NFC	2,522
	Indianapolis, AFC	2,820
1996	Green Bay, NFC	2,740
	Pittsburgh, AFC	2,947
1995	N.Y. Jets, AFC	2,740
	Philadelphia, NFC	2,816
1994	Dallas, NFC	2,752
	Houston, AFC	2,795
1993	New Orleans, NFC	2,606
	Cincinnati, AFC	2,798
1992	New Orleans, NFC	2,470
	Kansas City, AFC	2,537
1991	Philadelphia, NFC	2,413
	Denver, AFC	2,755
1990	Pittsburgh, AFC	2,500
	Dallas, NFC	2,639
1989	Minnesota, NFC	2,501
	Kansas City, AFC	2,527
1988	Kansas City, AFC	2,434
	Minnesota, NFC	2,489
1987	San Francisco, NFC	2,484
	L.A. Raiders, AFC	2,727
1986	St. Louis, NFC	2,637
	New England, AFC	2,978

Year	Team	Yards
1985	Washington, NFC	2,746
	Pittsburgh, AFC	2,783
1984	New Orleans, NFC	2,453
	Cleveland, AFC	2,696
1983	New Orleans, NFC	2,691
	Cincinnati, AFC	2,828
1982	Miami, AFC	1,027
	Tampa Bay, NFC	1,384
1981	Philadelphia, NFC	2,696
	Buffalo, AFC	2,870
1980	Washington, NFC	2,171
	Buffalo, AFC	2,282
1979	Tampa Bay, NFC	2,076
	Buffalo, AFC	2,530
1978	Buffalo, AFC	1,960
	Los Angeles, NFC	2,048
1977	Atlanta, NFC	1,384
	San Diego, AFC	1,725
1976	Minnesota, NFC	1,575
	Cincinnati, AFC	1,758
1975	Minnesota, NFC	1,621
	Cincinnati, AFC	1,729
1974	Pittsburgh, AFC	1,466
	Atlanta, NFC	1,572
1973	Miami, AFC	1,290
	Atlanta, NFC	1,430
1972	Minnesota, NFC	1,699
	Cleveland, AFC	1,736
1971	Atlanta, NFC	1,638
	Baltimore, AFC	1,739
1970	Minnesota, NFC	1,438
	Kansas City, AFC	2,010
1969	Minnesota, NFL	1,631
	Kansas City, AFL	2,072
1968	Houston, AFL	1,671
	Green Bay, NFL	1,796
1967	Green Bay, NFL	1,377
	Buffalo, AFL	1,825
1966	Green Bay, NFL	1,959
	Oakland, AFL	2,118
1965	Green Bay, NFL	1,981
	San Diego, AFL	2,168
1964	Green Bay, NFL	1,647
	San Diego, AFL	2,518
1963	Chicago, NFL	1,734
	Oakland, AFL	2,589
1962	Green Bay, NFL	1,746
	Oakland, AFL	2,306
1961	Baltimore, NFL	1,913
	San Diego, AFL	2,363
1960	Chicago, NFL	1,388
	Buffalo, AFL	2,124
1959	N.Y. Giants	1,582
1958	Chi. Bears	1,769
1957	Cleveland	1,300
1956	Cleveland	1,103
1955	Pittsburgh	1,295
1954	Cleveland	1,608
1953	Washington	1,751
1952	Washington	1,580
1951	Pittsburgh	1,687
1950	Cleveland	1,581
1949	Philadelphia	1,607
1948	Green Bay	1,626
1947	Green Bay	1,790
1946	Pittsburgh	939
1945	Washington	1,121
1944	Chi. Bears	1,052
1943	Chi. Bears	980

Year	Team	Yards
1942	Washington	1,093
1941	Pittsburgh	1,168
1940	Philadelphia	1,012
1939	Washington	1,116
1938	Chi. Bears	897
1937	Detroit	804
1936	Philadelphia	853
1935	Chi. Cardinals	793
1934	Philadelphia	545
1933	Portsmouth	558

Compiled by Elias Sports Bureau

Super Bowl I, 1/15/67	Super Bowl XX, 1/26/86
Super Bowl II, 1/14/68	Super Bowl XXI, 1/25/87
Super Bowl III, 1/12/69	Super Bowl XXII, 1/31/88
Super Bowl IV, 1/11/70	Super Bowl XXIII, 1/22/89
Super Bowl V, 1/17/71	Super Bowl XXIV, 1/28/90
Super Bowl VI, 1/16/72	Super Bowl XXV, 1/27/91
Super Bowl VII, 1/14/73	Super Bowl XXVI, 1/26/92
Super Bowl VIII, 1/13/74	Super Bowl XXVII, 1/31/93
Super Bowl IX, 1/12/75	Super Bowl XXVIII, 1/30/94
Super Bowl X, 1/18/76	Super Bowl XXIX, 1/29/95
Super Bowl XI, 1/9/77	Super Bowl XXX, 1/28/96
Super Bowl XII, 1/15/78	Super Bowl XXXI, 1/26/97
Super Bowl XIII, 1/21/79	Super Bowl XXXII, 1/25/98
Super Bowl XIV, 1/20/80	Super Bowl XXXIII, 1/31/99
Super Bowl XV, 1/25/81	Super Bowl XXXIV, 1/30/00
Super Bowl XVI, 1/24/82	Super Bowl XXXV, 1/28/01
Super Bowl XVII, 1/30/83	Super Bowl XXXVI, 2/3/02
Super Bowl XVIII, 1/22/84	Super Bowl XXXVII, 1/26/03
Super Bowl XIX, 1/20/85	Super Bowl XXXVIII, 2/1/04

INDIVIDUAL RECORDS

SERVICE

Most Games

6 Mike Lodish, Buffalo, XXV-XXVIII; Denver, XXXII-XXXIII
5 Marv Fleming, Green Bay, I-II; Miami, VI-VIII
Larry Cole, Dallas, V-VI, X, XII-XIII
Cliff Harris, Dallas, V-VI, X, XII-XIII
Charles Haley, San Francisco, XXIII-XXIV; Dallas, XXVII-XXVIII, XXX
D.D. Lewis, Dallas, V-VI, X, XII-XIII
Preston Pearson, Baltimore, III; Pittsburgh, IX; Dallas, X, XII-XIII
Charlie Waters, Dallas, V-VI, X, XII-XIII
Rayfield Wright, Dallas, V-VI, X, XII-XIII
Cornelius Bennett, Buffalo, XXV-XXVIII; Atlanta, XXXIII
John Elway, Denver, XXI-XXII, XXIV, XXXII-XXXIII
Glenn Parker, Buffalo, XXV-XXVIII; N.Y. Giants, XXXV
Bill Romanowski, San Francisco, XXIII-XXIV; Denver, XXXII-XXXIII; Oakland, XXXVII
4 By many players

Most Games, Winning Team

5 Charles Haley, San Francisco, XXIII-XXIV; Dallas, XXVII-XXVIII, XXX
4 By many players

Most Games, Coach

6 Don Shula, Baltimore, III; Miami, VI-VIII, XVII, XIX
5 Tom Landry, Dallas, V-VI, X, XII-XIII
4 Bud Grant, Minnesota, IV, VIII-IX, XI
Chuck Noll, Pittsburgh, IX-X, XIII-XIV
Joe Gibbs, Washington, XVII-XVIII, XXII, XXVI
Marv Levy, Buffalo, XXV-XXVIII
Dan Reeves, Denver, XXI-XXII, XXIV; Atlanta, XXXIII

Most Games, Winning Team, Coach

4 Chuck Noll, Pittsburgh, IX-X, XIII-XIV
3 Bill Walsh, San Francisco, XVI, XIX, XXIII
Joe Gibbs, Washington, XVII, XXII, XXVI
2 Vince Lombardi, Green Bay, I-II
Tom Landry, Dallas, VI, XII
Don Shula, Miami, VII-VIII
Tom Flores, Oakland, XV; L.A. Raiders, XVIII
Bill Parcells, N.Y. Giants, XXI, XXV
Jimmy Johnson, Dallas, XXVII-XXVIII
George Seifert, San Francisco, XXIV, XXIX
Mike Shanahan, Denver, XXXII-XXXIII
Bill Belichick, New England, XXXVI, XXXVIII

Most Games, Losing Team, Coach

4 Bud Grant, Minnesota, IV, VIII-IX, XI
Don Shula, Baltimore, III; Miami, VI, XVII, XIX
Marv Levy, Buffalo, XXV-XXVIII
Dan Reeves, Denver, XXI-XXII, XXIV; Atlanta, XXXIII
3 Tom Landry, Dallas, V, X, XIII

SCORING

POINTS

Most Points, Career

48 Jerry Rice, San Francisco-Oakland, 4 games (8-td)
30 Emmitt Smith, Dallas, 3 games (5-td)
24 Franco Harris, Pittsburgh, 4 games (4-td)
Roger Craig, San Francisco, 3 games (4-td)
Thurman Thomas, Buffalo, 4 games (4-td)
John Elway, Denver, 5 games (4-td)

Most Points, Game

18 Roger Craig, San Francisco vs. Miami, XIX (3-td)
Jerry Rice, San Francisco vs. Denver, XXIV (3-td); vs. San Diego, XXIX (3-td)
Ricky Watters, San Francisco vs. San Diego, XXIX (3-td)
Terrell Davis, Denver vs. Green Bay, XXXII (3-td)
15 Don Chandler, Green Bay vs. Oakland, II (3-pat, 4-fg)
14 Ray Wersching, San Francisco vs. Cincinnati, XVI (2-pat, 4-fg)
Kevin Butler, Chicago vs. New England, XX (5-pat, 3-fg)

TOUCHDOWNS

Most Touchdowns, Career

8 Jerry Rice, San Francisco-Oakland, 4 games (8-p)
5 Emmitt Smith, Dallas, 3 games (5-r)
4 Franco Harris, Pittsburgh, 4 games (4-r)
Roger Craig, San Francisco, 3 games (2-r, 2-p)
Thurman Thomas, Buffalo, 4 games (4-r)
John Elway, Denver, 5 games (4-r)

Most Touchdowns, Game

3 Roger Craig, San Francisco vs. Miami, XIX (1-r, 2-p)
Jerry Rice, San Francisco. vs. Denver, XXIV (3-p); vs. San Diego, XXIX (3-p)
Ricky Watters, San Francisco vs. San Diego, XXIX (1-r, 2-p)
Terrell Davis, Denver vs. Green Bay, XXXII (3-r)
2 Max McGee, Green Bay vs. Kansas City, I (2-p)
Elijah Pitts, Green Bay vs. Kansas City, I (2-r)
Bill Miller, Oakland vs. Green Bay, II (2-p)
Larry Csonka, Miami vs. Minnesota, VIII (2-r)
Pete Banaszak, Oakland vs. Minnesota, XI (2-r)
John Stallworth, Pittsburgh vs. Dallas, XIII (2-p)
Franco Harris, Pittsburgh vs. Los Angeles, XIV (2-r)
Cliff Branch, Oakland vs. Philadelphia, XV (2-p)
Dan Ross, Cincinnati vs. San Francisco, XVI (2-p)
Marcus Allen, L.A. Raiders vs. Washington, XVIII (2-r)
Jim McMahon, Chicago vs. New England, XX (2-r)
Ricky Sanders, Washington vs. Denver, XXII (2-p)
Timmy Smith, Washington vs. Denver, XXII (2-r)
Tom Rathman, San Francisco vs. Denver, XXIV (2-r)
Gerald Riggs, Washington vs. Buffalo, XXVI (2-r)
Michael Irvin, Dallas vs. Buffalo, XXVII (2-p)
Emmitt Smith, Dallas vs. Buffalo, XXVIII (2-r)
Emmitt Smith, Dallas vs. Pittsburgh, XXX (2-r)
Antonio Freeman, Green Bay vs. Denver, XXXII (2-p)
Howard Griffith, Denver vs. Atlanta, XXXIII (2-r)
Eddie George, Tennessee vs. St. Louis, XXXIV (2-r)
Keenan McCardell, Tampa Bay vs. Oakland, XXXVII (2-r)
Dwight Smith, Tampa Bay vs. Oakland, XXXVII (2-ret)

POINTS AFTER TOUCHDOWN

Most (One-Point) Points After Touchdown, Career

9 Mike Cofer, San Francisco, 2 games (10 att)
8 Don Chandler, Green Bay, 2 games (8 att)

Roy Gerela, Pittsburgh, 3 games (9 att)
Chris Bahr, Oakland-L.A. Raiders, 2 games (8 att)
Jason Elam, Denver, 2 games (8 att)
Adam Vinatieri, New England, 3 games (8 att)
7 Ray Wersching, San Francisco, 2 games (7 att)
Lin Elliott, Dallas, 1 game (7 att)
Doug Brien, San Francisco, 1 game (7 att)

Most (One-Point) Points After Touchdown, Game
7 Mike Cofer, San Francisco vs. Denver, XXIV (8 att)
Lin Elliott, Dallas vs. Buffalo, XXVII (7 att)
Doug Brien, San Francisco vs. San Diego, XXIX (7 att)
6 Ali Haji-Sheikh, Washington vs. Denver, XXII (6 att)
Martín Gramatica, Tampa Bay vs. Oakland, XXXVII (6 att)
5 Don Chandler, Green Bay vs. Kansas City, I (5 att)
Roy Gerela, Pittsburgh vs. Dallas, XIII (5 att)
Chris Bahr, L.A. Raiders vs. Washington, XVIII (5 att)
Ray Wersching, San Francisco vs. Miami, XIX (5 att)
Kevin Butler, Chicago vs. New England, XX (5 att)

Most Two-Point Conversions, Game
1 Mark Seay, San Diego vs. San Francisco, XXIX
Alfred Pupunu, San Diego vs. San Francisco, XXIX
Mark Chmura, Green Bay vs. New England, XXXI
Kevin Faulk, New England vs. Carolina, XXXVIII

FIELD GOALS

Field Goals Attempted, Career
6 Jim Turner, N.Y. Jets-Denver, 2 games
Roy Gerela, Pittsburgh, 3 games
Rich Karlis, Denver, 2 games
Jeff Wilkins, St. Louis, 2 games
5 Efren Herrera, Dallas, 1 game
Ray Wersching, San Francisco, 2 games
Jason Elam, Denver, 2 games
Adam Vinatieri, New England, 3 games

Most Field Goals Attempted, Game
5 Jim Turner, N.Y. Jets vs. Baltimore, III
Efren Herrera, Dallas vs. Denver, XII
4 Don Chandler, Green Bay vs. Oakland, II
Roy Gerela, Pittsburgh vs. Dallas, X
Ray Wersching, San Francisco vs. Cincinnati, XVI
Rich Karlis, Denver vs. N.Y. Giants, XXI
Mike Cofer, San Francisco vs. Cincinnati, XXIII
Jason Elam, Denver vs. Atlanta, XXXIII
Jeff Wilkins, St. Louis vs. Tennessee, XXXIV

Most Field Goals, Career
5 Ray Wersching, San Francisco, 2 games (5 att)
4 Don Chandler, Green Bay, 2 games (4 att)
Jim Turner, N.Y. Jets-Denver, 2 games (6 att)
Uwe von Schamann, Miami, 2 games (4 att)
Jeff Wilkins, St. Louis, 2 games (6 att)
3 Mike Clark, Dallas, 2 games (3 att)
Jan Stenerud, Kansas City, 1 game (3 att)
Chris Bahr, Oakland-L.A. Raiders, 2 games (4 att)
Mark Moseley, Washington, 2 games (4 att)
Kevin Butler, Chicago, 1 game (3 att)
Rich Karlis, Denver, 2 games (6 att)
Jim Breech, Cincinnati, 2 games (3 att)
Matt Bahr, Pittsburgh-N.Y. Giants, 2 games (3 att)
Chip Lohmiller, Washington, 1 game (3 att)
Steve Christie, Buffalo, 2 games (3 att)
Eddie Murray, Dallas, 1 game (3 att)
Jason Elam, Denver, 2 games (5 att)
Adam Vinatieri, New England, 3 games (5 att)

Most Field Goals, Game
4 Don Chandler, Green Bay vs. Oakland, II
Ray Wersching, San Francisco vs. Cincinnati, XVI
3 Jim Turner, N.Y. Jets vs. Baltimore, III
Jan Stenerud, Kansas City vs. Minnesota, IV
Uwe von Schamann, Miami vs. San Francisco, XIX
Kevin Butler, Chicago vs. New England, XX
Jim Breech, Cincinnati vs. San Francisco, XXIII
Chip Lohmiller, Washington vs. Buffalo, XXVI
Eddie Murray, Dallas vs. Buffalo, XXVIII
Jeff Wilkins, St. Louis vs. Tennessee, XXXIV

Longest Field Goal
54 Steve Christie, Buffalo vs. Dallas, XXVIII
51 Jason Elam, Denver vs. Green Bay, XXXII
50 Jeff Wilkins, St. Louis vs. New England, XXXVI
John Kasay, Carolina vs. New England, XXXVIII

SAFETIES

Most Safeties, Game
1 Dwight White, Pittsburgh vs. Minnesota, IX
Reggie Harrison, Pittsburgh vs. Dallas, X
Henry Waechter, Chicago vs. New England, XX
George Martin, N.Y. Giants vs. Denver, XXI
Bruce Smith, Buffalo vs. N.Y. Giants, XXV

RUSHING

ATTEMPTS

Most Attempts, Career
101 Franco Harris, Pittsburgh, 4 games
70 Emmitt Smith, Dallas, 3 games
64 John Riggins, Washington, 2 games

Most Attempts, Game
38 John Riggins, Washington vs. Miami, XVII
34 Franco Harris, Pittsburgh vs. Minnesota, IX
33 Larry Csonka, Miami vs. Minnesota, VIII

YARDS GAINED

Most Yards Gained, Career
354 Franco Harris, Pittsburgh, 4 games
297 Larry Csonka, Miami, 3 games
289 Emmitt Smith, Dallas, 3 games

Most Yards Gained, Game
204 Timmy Smith, Washington vs. Denver, XXII
191 Marcus Allen, L.A. Raiders vs. Washington, XVIII
166 John Riggins, Washington vs. Miami, XVII

Longest Run From Scrimmage
74 Marcus Allen, L.A. Raiders vs. Washington, XVIII (TD)
58 Tom Matte, Baltimore vs. N.Y. Jets, III
Timmy Smith, Washington vs. Denver, XXII (TD)
49 Larry Csonka, Miami vs. Washington, VII

AVERAGE GAIN

Highest Average Gain, Career (20 attempts)
9.6 Marcus Allen, L.A. Raiders, 1 game (20-191)
9.3 Timmy Smith, Washington, 1 game (22-204)
5.3 Walt Garrison, Dallas, 2 games (26-139)

Highest Average Gain, Game (10 attempts)
10.5 Tom Matte, Baltimore vs. N.Y. Jets, III (11-116)
9.6 Marcus Allen, L.A. Raiders vs. Washington, XVIII (20-191)
9.3 Timmy Smith, Washington vs. Denver, XXII (22-204)

TOUCHDOWNS

Most Touchdowns, Career
5 Emmitt Smith, Dallas, 3 games
4 Franco Harris, Pittsburgh, 4 games
Thurman Thomas, Buffalo, 4 games
John Elway, Denver, 5 games
3 Terrell Davis, Denver, 2 games

Most Touchdowns, Game
3 Terrell Davis, Denver vs. Green Bay, XXXII
2 Elijah Pitts, Green Bay vs. Kansas City, I
Larry Csonka, Miami vs. Minnesota, VIII
Pete Banaszak, Oakland vs. Minnesota, XI
Franco Harris, Pittsburgh vs. Los Angeles, XIV
Marcus Allen, L.A. Raiders vs. Washington, XVIII

Jim McMahon, Chicago vs. New England, XX
Timmy Smith, Washington vs. Denver, XXII
Tom Rathman, San Francisco vs. Denver, XXIV
Gerald Riggs, Washington vs. Buffalo, XXVI
Emmitt Smith, Dallas vs. Buffalo, XXVIII
Emmitt Smith, Dallas vs. Pittsburgh, XXX
Howard Griffith, Denver vs. Atlanta, XXXIII
Eddie George, Tennessee vs. St. Louis, XXXIV

PASSING

PASSER RATING

Highest Passer Rating, Career (40 attempts)

127.8 Joe Montana, San Francisco, 4 games
122.8 Jim Plunkett, Oakland-L.A. Raiders, 2 games
112.8 Terry Bradshaw, Pittsburgh, 4 games

ATTEMPTS

Most Passes Attempted, Career

152 John Elway, Denver, 5 games
145 Jim Kelly, Buffalo, 4 games
122 Joe Montana, San Francisco, 4 games

Most Passes Attempted, Game

58 Jim Kelly, Buffalo vs. Washington, XXVI
50 Dan Marino, Miami vs. San Francisco, XIX
Jim Kelly, Buffalo vs. Dallas, XXVIII
49 Stan Humphries, San Diego vs. San Francisco, XXIX
Neil O'Donnell, Pittsburgh vs. Dallas, XXX

COMPLETIONS

Most Passes Completed, Career

83 Joe Montana, San Francisco, 4 games
81 Jim Kelly, Buffalo, 4 games
76 John Elway, Denver, 5 games

Most Passes Completed, Game

32 Tom Brady, New England vs. Carolina, XXXVIII
31 Jim Kelly, Buffalo vs. Dallas, XXVIII
29 Dan Marino, Miami vs. San Francisco, XIX

Most Consecutive Completions, Game

13 Joe Montana, San Francisco vs. Denver, XXIV
10 Phil Simms, N.Y. Giants vs. Denver, XXI
Troy Aikman, Dallas vs. Pittsburgh, XXX
9 Jim Kelly, Buffalo vs. Dallas, XXVIII
Neil O'Donnell, Pittsburgh vs. Dallas, XXX
Steve McNair, Tennessee vs. St. Louis, XXXIV

COMPLETION PERCENTAGE

Highest Completion Percentage, Career (40 attempts)

70.0 Troy Aikman, Dallas, 3 games, (80-56)
68.0 Joe Montana, San Francisco, 4 games (122-83)
64.0 Tom Brady, New England, 2 games (75-48)

Highest Completion Percentage, Game (20 attempts)

88.0 Phil Simms, N.Y. Giants vs. Denver, XXI (25-22)
75.9 Joe Montana, San Francisco vs. Denver, XXIV (29-22)
73.5 Ken Anderson, Cincinnati vs. San Francisco, XVI (34-25)

YARDS GAINED

Most Yards Gained, Career

1,142 Joe Montana, San Francisco, 4 games
1,128 John Elway, Denver, 5 games
932 Terry Bradshaw, Pittsburgh, 4 games

Most Yards Gained, Game

414 Kurt Warner, St. Louis vs. Tennessee, XXXIV
365 Kurt Warner, St. Louis vs. New England, XXXVI
357 Joe Montana, San Francisco vs. Cincinnati, XXIII

Longest Pass Completion

85 Jake Delhomme (to Muhammad), Carolina vs. New England, XXXVIII (TD)
81 Brett Favre (to Freeman), Green Bay vs. New England, XXXI (TD)
80 Jim Plunkett (to King), Oakland vs. Philadelphia, XV (TD)
Doug Williams (to Sanders), Washington vs. Denver, XXII (TD)
John Elway (to R. Smith), Denver vs. Atlanta, XXXIII (TD)

AVERAGE GAIN

Highest Average Gain, Career (40 attempts)

11.10 Terry Bradshaw, Pittsburgh, 4 games (84-932)
9.62 Bart Starr, Green Bay, 2 games (47-452)
9.41 Jim Plunkett, Oakland-L.A. Raiders, 2 games (46-433)

Highest Average Gain, Game (20 attempts)

14.71 Terry Bradshaw, Pittsburgh vs. Los Angeles, XIV (21-309)
12.80 Jim McMahon, Chicago vs. New England, XX (20-256)
12.43 Jim Plunkett, Oakland vs. Philadelphia, XV (21-261)

TOUCHDOWNS

Most Touchdown Passes, Career

11 Joe Montana, San Francisco, 4 games
9 Terry Bradshaw, Pittsburgh, 4 games
8 Roger Staubach, Dallas, 4 games

Most Touchdown Passes, Game

6 Steve Young, San Francisco vs. San Diego, XXIX
5 Joe Montana, San Francisco vs. Denver, XXIV
4 Terry Bradshaw, Pittsburgh vs. Dallas, XIII
Doug Williams, Washington vs. Denver, XXII
Troy Aikman, Dallas vs. Buffalo, XXVII

HAD INTERCEPTED

Lowest Percentage, Passes Had Intercepted, Career (40 attempts)

0.00 Jim Plunkett, Oakland-L.A. Raiders, 2 games (46-0)
Joe Montana, San Francisco, 4 games (122-0)
1.25 Troy Aikman, Dallas, 3 games (80-1)
1.33 Tom Brady, New England, 2 games (75-1)

Most Attempts, Without Interception, Game

45 Kurt Warner, St. Louis vs. Tennessee, XXXIV
36 Joe Montana, San Francisco vs. Cincinnati, XXIII
Steve Young, San Francisco vs. San Diego, XXIX
Steve McNair, Tennessee vs. St. Louis, XXXIV
35 Joe Montana, San Francisco vs. Miami, XIX

Most Passes Had Intercepted, Career

8 John Elway, Denver, 5 games
7 Craig Morton, Dallas-Denver, 2 games
Jim Kelly, Buffalo, 4 games
6 Fran Tarkenton, Minnesota, 3 games

Most Passes Had Intercepted, Game

5 Rich Gannon, Oakland vs. Tampa Bay, XXXVII
4 Craig Morton, Denver vs. Dallas, XII
Jim Kelly, Buffalo vs. Washington, XXVI
Drew Bledsoe, New England vs. Green Bay, XXXI
Kerry Collins, N.Y. Giants vs. Baltimore, XXXV
3 By ten players

PASS RECEIVING

RECEPTIONS

Most Receptions, Career

33 Jerry Rice, San Francisco-Oakland, 4 games
27 Andre Reed, Buffalo, 4 games
20 Roger Craig, San Francisco, 3 games
Thurman Thomas, Buffalo, 4 games

Most Receptions, Game

11 Dan Ross, Cincinnati vs. San Francisco, XVI
Jerry Rice, San Francisco vs. Cincinnati, XXIII
10 Tony Nathan, Miami vs. San Francisco, XIX
Jerry Rice, San Francisco vs. San Diego, XXIX
Andre Hastings, Pittsburgh vs. Dallas, XXX
Deion Branch, New England vs. Carolina, XXXVIII

9 Ricky Sanders, Washington vs. Denver, XXII
Antonio Freeman, Green Bay vs. Denver, XXXII

YARDS GAINED

Most Yards Gained, Career

589 Jerry Rice, San Francisco-Oakland, 4 games
364 Lynn Swann, Pittsburgh, 4 games
323 Andre Reed, Buffalo, 4 games

Most Yards Gained, Game

215 Jerry Rice, San Francisco vs. Cincinnati, XXIII
193 Ricky Sanders, Washington vs. Denver, XXII
162 Isaac Bruce, St. Louis vs. Tennessee, XXXIV

Longest Reception

85 Muhsin Muhammad (from Delhomme), Carolina vs. New England, XXXVIII
81 Antonio Freeman (from Favre), Green Bay vs. New England, XXXI (TD)
80 Kenny King (from Plunkett), Oakland vs. Philadelphia, XV (TD)
Ricky Sanders (from Williams), Washington vs. Denver, XXII (TD)
Rod Smith (from Elway), Denver vs. Atlanta, XXXIII

AVERAGE GAIN

Highest Average Gain, Career (8 receptions)

24.4 John Stallworth, Pittsburgh, 4 games (11-268)
23.4 Ricky Sanders, Washington, 2 games (10-234)
22.8 Lynn Swann, Pittsburgh, 4 games (16-364)

Highest Average Gain, Game (3 receptions)

40.33 John Stallworth, Pittsburgh vs. Los Angeles, XIV (3-121)
40.25 Lynn Swann, Pittsburgh vs. Dallas, X (4-161)
38.33 John Stallworth, Pittsburgh vs. Dallas, XIII (3-115)

TOUCHDOWNS

Most Touchdowns, Career

8 Jerry Rice, San Francisco-Oakland, 4 games
3 John Stallworth, Pittsburgh, 4 games
Lynn Swann, Pittsburgh, 4 games
Cliff Branch, Oakland-L.A. Raiders, 3 games
Antonio Freeman, Green Bay, 2 games
2 Max McGee, Green Bay, 2 games
Bill Miller, Oakland, 1 game
Butch Johnson, Dallas, 2 games
Dan Ross, Cincinnati, 1 game
Roger Craig, San Francisco, 3 games
Ricky Sanders, Washington, 2 games
John Taylor, San Francisco, 3 games
Gary Clark, Washington, 2 games
Don Beebe, Buffalo-Green Bay, 4 games
Michael Irvin, Dallas, 3 games
Ricky Watters, San Francisco, 1 game
Jay Novacek, Dallas, 3 games
Keenan McCardell, Tampa Bay, 1 game
Ricky Proehl, St. Louis-Carolina, 3 games

Most Touchdowns, Game

3 Jerry Rice, San Francisco vs. Denver, XXIV; vs. San Diego, XXIX
2 Max McGee, Green Bay vs. Kansas City, I
Bill Miller, Oakland vs. Green Bay, II
John Stallworth, Pittsburgh vs. Dallas, XIII
Cliff Branch, Oakland vs. Philadelphia, XV
Dan Ross, Cincinnati vs. San Francisco, XVI
Roger Craig, San Francisco vs. Miami, XIX
Ricky Sanders, Washington vs. Denver, XXII
Michael Irvin, Dallas vs. Buffalo, XXVII
Ricky Watters, San Francisco vs. San Diego, XXIX
Antonio Freeman, Green Bay vs. Denver, XXXII
Keenan McCardell, Tampa Bay vs. Oakland, XXXVII

INTERCEPTIONS BY

Most Interceptions By, Career

3 Chuck Howley, Dallas, 2 games
Rod Martin, Oakland-L.A. Raiders, 2 games
Larry Brown, Dallas, 3 games
2 Randy Beverly, N.Y. Jets, 1 game
Jake Scott, Miami, 3 games
Mike Wagner, Pittsburgh, 3 games
Mel Blount, Pittsburgh, 4 games
Eric Wright, San Francisco, 4 games
Barry Wilburn, Washington, 1 game
Brad Edwards, Washington, 1 game
Thomas Everett, Dallas, 2 games
James Washington, Dallas, 2 games
Darrien Gordon, San Diego-Denver-Oakland, 4 games
Dexter Jackson, Tampa Bay, 1 game
Dwight Smith, Tampa Bay, 1 game

Most Interceptions By, Game

3 Rod Martin, Oakland vs. Philadelphia, XV
2 Randy Beverly, N.Y. Jets vs. Baltimore, III
Chuck Howley, Dallas vs. Baltimore, V
Jake Scott, Miami vs. Washington, VII
Barry Wilburn, Washington vs. Denver, XXII
Brad Edwards, Washington vs. Buffalo, XXVI
Thomas Everett, Dallas vs. Buffalo, XXVII
Larry Brown, Dallas vs. Pittsburgh, XXX
Darrien Gordon, Denver vs. Atlanta, XXXIII
Dexter Jackson, Tampa Bay vs. Oakland, XXXVII
Dwight Smith, Tampa Bay vs. Oakland, XXXVII

YARDS GAINED

Most Yards Gained, Career

108 Darrien Gordon, San Diego-Denver-Oakland, 4 games
94 Dwight Smith, Tampa Bay, 1 game
77 Larry Brown, Dallas, 3 games

Most Yards Gained, Game

108 Darrien Gordon, Denver vs. Atlanta, XXXIII
94 Dwight Smith, Tampa Bay vs. Oakland, XXXVII
77 Larry Brown, Dallas vs. Pittsburgh, XXX

Longest Return

75 Willie Brown, Oakland vs. Minnesota, XI (TD)
60 Herb Adderley, Green Bay vs. Oakland, II (TD)
58 Darrien Gordon, Denver vs. Atlanta, XXXIII

TOUCHDOWNS

Most Touchdowns, Game

2 Dwight Smith, Tampa Bay vs. Oakland, XXXVII
1 Herb Adderley, Green Bay vs. Oakland, II
Willie Brown, Oakland vs. Minnesota, XI
Jack Squirek, L.A. Raiders vs. Washington, XVIII
Reggie Phillips, Chicago vs. New England, XX
Duane Starks, Baltimore vs. N.Y. Giants, XXXV
Ty Law, New England vs. St. Louis, XXXVI
Derrick Brooks, Tampa Bay vs. Oakland, XXXVII

PUNTING

Most Punts, Career

17 Mike Eischeid, Oakland-Minnesota, 3 games
Mike Horan, Denver-St. Louis, 4 games
15 Larry Seiple, Miami, 3 games
14 Ron Widby, Dallas, 2 games
Ray Guy, Oakland-L.A. Raiders, 3 games
Chris Mohr, Buffalo, 3 games
Craig Hentrich, Green Bay-Tennessee, 3 games

Most Punts, Game

11 Brad Maynard, N.Y. Giants vs. Baltimore, XXXV
10 Kyle Richardson, Baltimore vs. N.Y. Giants, XXXV

9 Ron Widby, Dallas vs. Baltimore, V

Longest Punt

63 Lee Johnson, Cincinnati vs. San Francisco, XXIII
62 Rich Camarillo, New England vs. Chicago, XX
61 Jerrel Wilson, Kansas City vs. Green Bay, I

AVERAGE YARDAGE

Highest Average, Punting, Career (10 punts)

46.5 Jerrel Wilson, Kansas City, 2 games (11-511)
43.0 Kyle Richardson, Baltimore, 1 game (10-430)
Tom Tupa, New England-Tampa Bay, 2 games (12-516)
41.9 Ray Guy, Oakland-L.A. Raiders, 3 games (14-587)

Highest Average, Punting, Game (4 punts)

48.8 Bryan Wagner, San Diego vs. San Francisco, XXIX (4-195)
48.5 Jerrel Wilson, Kansas City vs. Minnesota, IV (4-194)
46.3 Jim Miller, San Francisco vs. Cincinnati, XVI (4-185)

PUNT RETURNS

Most Punt Returns, Career

6 Willie Wood, Green Bay, 2 games
Jake Scott, Miami, 3 games
Theo Bell, Pittsburgh, 2 games
Mike Nelms, Washington, 1 game
John Taylor, San Francisco, 3 games
Desmond Howard, Green Bay, 1 game
David Meggett, N.Y. Giants-New England, 2 games
Darrien Gordon, San Diego-Denver-Oakland, 4 games
5 Dana McLemore, San Francisco, 1 game
Troy Brown, New England, 2 games
4 By eight players

Most Punt Returns, Game

6 Mike Nelms, Washington vs. Miami, XVII
Desmond Howard, Green Bay vs. New England, XXXI
5 Willie Wood, Green Bay vs. Oakland, II
Dana McLemore, San Francisco vs. Miami, XIX
4 By eight players

Most Fair Catches, Game

4 Jermaine Lewis, Baltimore vs. N.Y. Giants, XXXV
Karl Williams, Tampa Bay vs. Oakland, XXXVII
3 Ron Gardin, Baltimore vs. Dallas, V
Golden Richards, Dallas vs. Pittsburgh, X
Greg Pruitt, L.A. Raiders vs. Washington, XVIII
Al Edwards, Buffalo vs. N.Y. Giants, XXV
David Meggett, N.Y. Giants vs. Buffalo, XXV

YARDS GAINED

Most Yards Gained, Career

94 John Taylor, San Francisco, 3 games
90 Desmond Howard, Green Bay, 1 game
67 David Meggett, N.Y. Giants-New England, 2 games

Most Yards Gained, Game

90 Desmond Howard, Green Bay vs. New England, XXXI
56 John Taylor, San Francisco vs. Cincinnati, XXIII
52 Mike Nelms, Washington vs. Miami, XXII

Longest Return

45 John Taylor, San Francisco vs. Cincinnati, XXIII
34 Darrell Green, Washington vs. L.A. Raiders, XVIII
Desmond Howard, Green Bay vs. New England, XXXI
Jermaine Lewis, Baltimore vs. N.Y. Giants, XXXV
32 Desmond Howard, Green Bay vs. New England, XXXI

AVERAGE YARDAGE

Highest Average, Career (4 returns)

15.7 John Taylor, San Francisco, 3 games (6-94)
15.0 Desmond Howard, Green Bay, 1 game (6-90)
11.2 David Meggett, N.Y. Giants-New England, 2 games (6-67)

Highest Average, Game (3 returns)

18.7 John Taylor, San Francisco vs. Cincinnati, XXIII (3-56)
15.0 Desmond Howard, Green Bay vs. New England, XXXI (6-90)
12.7 John Taylor, San Francisco vs. Denver, XXIV (3-38)

TOUCHDOWNS

Most Touchdowns, Game

None

KICKOFF RETURNS

Most Kickoff Returns, Career

10 Ken Bell, Denver, 3 games
8 Larry Anderson, Pittsburgh, 2 games
Fulton Walker, Miami, 2 games
Andre Coleman, San Diego, 1 game
Marcus Knight, Oakland, 1 game
7 Preston Pearson, Baltimore-Pittsburgh-Dallas, 5 games
Stephen Starring, New England, 1 game
David Meggett, N.Y. Giants-New England, 2 games

Most Kickoff Returns, Game

8 Andre Coleman, San Diego vs. San Francisco, XXIX
Marcus Knight, Oakland vs. Tampa Bay, XXXVII
7 Stephen Starring, New England vs. Chicago, XX
6 Darren Carrington, Denver vs. San Francisco, XXIV
Antonio Freeman, Green Bay vs. Denver, XXXII
Ron Dixon, N.Y. Giants vs. Baltimore, XXXV

YARDS GAINED

Most Yards Gained, Career

283 Fulton Walker, Miami, 2 games
244 Andre Coleman, San Diego, 1 game
210 Tim Dwight, Atlanta, 1 game

Most Yards Gained, Game

244 Andre Coleman, San Diego vs. San Francisco, XXIX
210 Tim Dwight, Atlanta vs. Denver, XXXIII
190 Fulton Walker, Miami vs. Washington, XVII

Longest Return

99 Desmond Howard, Green Bay vs. New England, XXXI (TD)
98 Fulton Walker, Miami vs. Washington, XVII (TD)
Andre Coleman, San Diego vs. San Francisco, XXIX (TD)
97 Ron Dixon, N.Y. Giants vs. Baltimore, XXXV (TD)

AVERAGE YARDAGE

Highest Average, Career (4 returns)

42.0 Tim Dwight, Atlanta, 1 game (5-210)
38.5 Desmond Howard, Green Bay, 1 game (4-154)
35.4 Fulton Walker, Miami, 2 games (8-283)

Highest Average, Game (3 returns)

47.5 Fulton Walker, Miami vs. Washington, XVII (4-190)
42.0 Tim Dwight, Atlanta vs. Denver, XXXIII (5-210)
38.5 Desmond Howard, Green Bay vs. New England, XXXI (4-154)

TOUCHDOWNS

Most Touchdowns, Game

1 Fulton Walker, Miami vs. Washington, XVII
Stanford Jennings, Cincinnati vs. San Francisco, XXIII
Andre Coleman, San Diego vs. San Francisco, XXIX
Desmond Howard, Green Bay vs. New England, XXXI
Tim Dwight, Atlanta vs. Denver, XXXIII
Ron Dixon, N.Y. Giants vs. Baltimore, XXXV
Jermaine Lewis, Baltimore vs. N.Y. Giants, XXXV

FUMBLES

Most Fumbles, Career

5 Roger Staubach, Dallas, 4 games
4 Jim Kelly, Buffalo, 4 games

3 Franco Harris, Pittsburgh, 4 games
Terry Bradshaw, Pittsburgh, 4 games
John Elway, Denver, 5 games
Frank Reich, Buffalo, 4 games
Thurman Thomas, Buffalo, 4 games

Most Fumbles, Game

3 Roger Staubach, Dallas vs. Pittsburgh, X
Jim Kelly, Buffalo vs. Washington, XXVI
Frank Reich, Buffalo vs. Dallas, XXVII
2 Franco Harris, Pittsburgh vs. Minnesota, IX
Butch Johnson, Dallas vs. Denver, XII
Terry Bradshaw, Pittsburgh vs. Dallas, XIII
Joe Montana, San Francisco vs. Cincinnati, XXIII
John Elway, Denver vs. San Francisco, XXIV
Thurman Thomas, Buffalo vs. Dallas, XXVIII

RECOVERIES

Most Fumbles Recovered, Career

2 Jake Scott, Miami, 3 games (1 own, 1 opp)
Fran Tarkenton, Minnesota, 3 games (2 own)
Franco Harris, Pittsburgh, 4 games (2 own)
Roger Staubach, Dallas, 4 games (2 own)
Bobby Walden, Pittsburgh, 2 games (2 own)
John Fitzgerald, Dallas, 4 games (2 own)
Randy Hughes, Dallas, 3 games (2 opp)
Butch Johnson, Dallas, 2 games (2 own)
Mike Singletary, Chicago, 1 game (2 opp)
John Elway, Denver, 5 games (2 own)
Jimmie Jones, Dallas, 2 games (2 opp)
Kenneth Davis, Buffalo, 4 games (2 own)
Kurt Warner, St. Louis, 2 games (2 own)

Most Fumbles Recovered, Game

2 Jake Scott, Miami vs. Minnesota, VIII (1 own, 1 opp)
Roger Staubach, Dallas vs. Pittsburgh, X (2 own)
Randy Hughes, Dallas vs. Denver, XII (2 opp)
Butch Johnson, Dallas vs. Denver, XII (2 own)
Mike Singletary, Chicago vs. New England, XX (2 opp)
Jimmie Jones, Dallas vs. Buffalo, XXVII (2 opp)

YARDS GAINED

Most Yards Gained, Game

64 Leon Lett, Dallas vs. Buffalo, XXVII (opp)
49 Mike Bass, Washington vs. Miami, VII (opp)
46 James Washington, Dallas vs. Buffalo, XXVIII (opp)

Longest Return

64 Leon Lett, Dallas vs. Buffalo, XXVII
49 Mike Bass, Washington vs. Miami, VII (TD)
46 James Washington, Dallas vs. Buffalo, XXVIII (TD)

TOUCHDOWNS

Most Touchdowns, Game

1 Mike Bass, Washington vs. Miami, VII (opp 49 yds)
Mike Hegman, Dallas vs. Pittsburgh, XIII (opp 37 yds)
Jimmie Jones, Dallas vs. Buffalo, XXVII (opp 2 yds)
Ken Norton, Dallas vs. Buffalo, XXVII (opp 9 yds)
James Washington, Dallas vs. Buffalo, XXVIII (opp 46 yds)

COMBINED NET YARDS GAINED

(Rushing, receiving, interception returns, punt returns, kickoff returns, and fumble returns)

ATTEMPTS

Most Attempts, Career

108 Franco Harris, Pittsburgh, 4 games
81 Emmitt Smith, Dallas, 3 games
72 Roger Craig, San Francisco, 3 games
Thurman Thomas, Buffalo, 4 games

Most Attempts, Game

39 John Riggins, Washington vs. Miami, XVII
35 Franco Harris, Pittsburgh vs. Minnesota, IX
34 Matt Snell, N.Y. Jets vs. Baltimore, III
Emmitt Smith, Dallas vs. Buffalo, XXVIII

YARDS GAINED

Most Yards Gained, Career

604 Jerry Rice, San Francisco-Oakland, 4 games
468 Franco Harris, Pittsburgh, 4 games
410 Roger Craig, San Francisco, 3 games

Most Yards Gained, Game

244 Andre Coleman, San Diego vs. San Francisco, XXIX
Desmond Howard, Green Bay vs. New England, XXXI
235 Ricky Sanders, Washington vs. Denver, XXII
230 Antonio Freeman, Green Bay vs. Denver, XXXII

SACKS

Sacks have been compiled since XVII.

Most Sacks, Career

4.5 Charles Haley, San Francisco-Dallas, 5 games
3.0 Danny Stubbs, San Francisco, 2 games
Leonard Marshall, N.Y. Giants, 2 games
Jeff Wright, Buffalo, 4 games
Reggie White, Green Bay, 2 games
Willie McGinest, New England, 3 games
2.5 Dexter Manley, Washington, 3 games

Most Sacks, Game

3.0 Reggie White, Green Bay vs. New England, XXXI
2.0 Dwaine Board, San Francisco vs. Miami, XIX
Dennis Owens, New England vs. Chicago, XX
Otis Wilson, Chicago vs. New England, XX
Leonard Marshall, N.Y. Giants vs. Denver, XXI
Alvin Walton, Washington vs. Denver, XXII
Charles Haley, San Francisco vs. Cincinnati, XXIII
Danny Stubbs, San Francisco vs. Denver, XXIV
Jeff Wright, Buffalo vs. Dallas, XXVIII
Raylee Johnson, San Diego vs. San Francisco, XXIX
Chad Hennings, Dallas vs. Pittsburgh, XXX
Tedy Bruschi, New England vs. Green Bay, XXXI
Michael McCrary, Baltimore vs. N.Y. Giants, XXXV
Simeon Rice, Tampa Bay vs. Oakland, XXXVII
Mike Vrabel, New England vs. Carolina, XXXVIII

TEAM RECORDS

GAMES, VICTORIES, DEFEATS

Most Games

8 Dallas, V-VI, X, XII-XIII, XXVII-XXVIII, XXX
6 Denver, XII, XXI-XXII, XXIV, XXXII-XXXIII
5 Miami, VI-VIII, XVII, XIX
Washington, VII, XVII-XVIII, XXII, XXVI
San Francisco, XVI, XIX, XXIII-XXIV, XXIX
Pittsburgh, IX-X, XIII-XIV, XXX
Oakland/L.A. Raiders, II, XI, XV, XVIII, XXXVII

Most Consecutive Games

4 Buffalo, XXV-XXVIII
3 Miami, VI-VIII
2 Green Bay, I-II; XXXI-XXXII
Dallas, V-VI; XII-XIII; XXVII-XXVIII
Minnesota, VIII-IX
Pittsburgh, IX-X; XIII-XIV
Washington, XVII-XVIII
Denver, XXI-XXII; XXXII-XXXIII
San Francisco XXIII-XXIV

Most Games Won

5 San Francisco, XVI, XIX, XXIII-XXIV, XXIX
Dallas, VI, XII, XXVII-XXVIII, XXX
4 Pittsburgh, IX-X, XIII-XIV
3 Oakland/L.A. Raiders, XI, XV, XVIII
Washington, XVII, XXII, XXVI
Green Bay, I-II, XXXI

Most Consecutive Games Won
- 2 Green Bay, I-II
  Miami, VII-VIII
  Pittsburgh, IX-X, XIII-XIV
  San Francisco, XXIII-XXIV
  Dallas, XXVII-XXVIII
  Denver, XXXII-XXXIII

Most Games Lost
- 4 Minnesota, IV, VIII-IX, XI
  Denver, XII, XXI-XXII, XXIV
  Buffalo, XXV-XXVIII
- 3 Dallas, V, X, XIII
  Miami, VI, XVII, XIX
- 2 Washington, VII, XVIII
  Cincinnati, XVI, XXIII
  New England, XX, XXXI
  L.A./St. Louis Rams, XIV, XXXVI
  Oakland/L.A. Raiders, II, XXXVII

Most Consecutive Games Lost
- 4 Buffalo, XXV-XXVIII
- 2 Minnesota, VIII-IX
  Denver, XXI-XXII

SCORING

Most Points, Game
- 55 San Francisco vs. Denver, XXIV
- 52 Dallas vs. Buffalo, XXVII
- 49 San Francisco vs. San Diego, XXIX

Fewest Points, Game
- 3 Miami vs. Dallas, VI
- 6 Minnesota vs. Pittsburgh, IX
- 7 By five teams

Most Points, Both Teams, Game
- 75 San Francisco (49) vs. San Diego (26), XXIX
- 69 Dallas (52) vs. Buffalo (17), XXVII
  Tampa Bay (48) vs. Oakland (21), XXXVII
- 66 Pittsburgh (35) vs. Dallas (31), XIII

Fewest Points, Both Teams, Game
- 21 Washington (7) vs. Miami (14), VII
- 22 Minnesota (6) vs. Pittsburgh (16), IX
- 23 Baltimore (7) vs. N.Y. Jets (16), III

Largest Margin of Victory, Game
- 45 San Francisco vs. Denver, XXIV (55-10)
- 36 Chicago vs. New England, XX (46-10)
- 35 Dallas vs. Buffalo, XXVII (52-17)

Most Points, Each Half
- 1st: 35 Washington vs. Denver, XXII
- 2nd: 30 N.Y. Giants vs. Denver, XXI

Most Points, Each Quarter
- 1st: 14 Miami vs. Minnesota, VIII
  Oakland vs. Philadelphia, XV
  Dallas vs. Buffalo, XXVII
  San Francisco vs. San Diego, XXIX
  New England vs. Green Bay, XXXI
- 2nd: 35 Washington vs. Denver, XXII
- 3rd: 21 Chicago vs. New England, XX
- 4th: 21 Dallas vs. Buffalo, XXVII

Most Points, Both Teams, Each Half
- 1st: 45 Washington (35) vs. Denver (10), XXII
- 2nd: 46 Tampa Bay (28) vs. Oakland (18), XXXVII

Fewest Points, Both Teams, Each Half
- 1st: 2 Minnesota (0) vs. Pittsburgh (2), IX
- 2nd: 7 Miami (0) vs. Washington (7), VII
  Denver (0) vs. Washington (7), XXII

Most Points, Both Teams, Each Quarter
- 1st: 24 New England (14) vs. Green Bay (10), XXXI
- 2nd: 35 Washington (35) vs. Denver (0), XXII
- 3rd: 24 Washington (14) vs. Buffalo (10), XXVI
- 4th: 37 Carolina (19) vs. New England (18), XXXVIII

TOUCHDOWNS

Most Touchdowns, Game
- 8 San Francisco vs. Denver, XXIV
- 7 Dallas vs. Buffalo, XXVII
  San Francisco vs. San Diego, XXIX
- 6 Washington vs. Denver, XXII
  Tampa Bay vs. Oakland, XXXVII

Fewest Touchdowns, Game
- 0 Miami vs. Dallas, VI
- 1 By 18 teams

Most Touchdowns, Both Teams, Game
- 10 San Francisco (7) vs. San Diego (3), XXIX
- 9 Pittsburgh (5) vs. Dallas (4), XIII
  San Francisco (8) vs. Denver (1), XXIV
  Dallas (7) vs. Buffalo (2), XXVII
  Tampa Bay (6) vs. Oakland (3), XXXVII
- 8 Carolina (4) vs. New England (4), XXXVIII

Fewest Touchdowns, Both Teams, Game
- 2 Baltimore (1) vs. N.Y. Jets (1), III
- 3 In six games

POINTS AFTER TOUCHDOWN

Most (One-Point) Points After Touchdown, Game
- 7 San Francisco vs. Denver, XXIV
  Dallas vs. Buffalo, XXVII
  San Francisco vs. San Diego, XXIX
- 6 Washington vs. Denver, XXII
  Tampa Bay vs. Oakland, XXXVII
- 5 Green Bay vs. Kansas City, I
  Pittsburgh vs. Dallas, XIII
  L.A. Raiders vs. Washington, XVIII
  San Francisco vs. Miami, XIX
  Chicago vs. New England, XX

Most (One-Point) Points After Touchdown, Both Teams, Game
- 9 Pittsburgh (5) vs. Dallas (4), XIII
  Dallas (7) vs. Buffalo (2), XXVII
- 8 San Francisco (7) vs. Denver (1), XXIV
  San Francisco (7) vs. San Diego (1), XXIX
- 7 Washington (6) vs. Denver (1), XXII
  Washington (4) vs. Buffalo (3), XXVI
  Denver (4) vs. Green Bay (3), XXXII

Fewest (One-Point) Points After Touchdown, Both Teams, Game
- 2 Baltimore (1) vs. N.Y. Jets (1), III
  Baltimore (1) vs. Dallas (1), V
  Minnesota (0) vs. Pittsburgh (2), IX

Most Two-Point Conversions, Game
- 2 San Diego vs. San Francisco, XXIX

Most Two-Point Conversions, Both Teams, Game
- 2 San Diego (2) vs. San Francisco (0), XXIX

FIELD GOALS

Most Field Goals Attempted, Game
- 5 N.Y. Jets vs. Baltimore, III
  Dallas vs. Denver, XII
- 4 Green Bay vs. Oakland, II
  Pittsburgh vs. Dallas, XX
  San Francisco vs. Cincinnati, XVI; XXIII
  Denver vs. N.Y. Giants, XXI
  Denver vs. Atlanta, XXXIII
  St. Louis vs. Tennessee, XXXIV

Most Field Goals Attempted, Both Teams, Game
- 7 N.Y. Jets (5) vs. Baltimore (2), III
  San Francisco (4) vs. Cincinnati (3), XXIII
  St. Louis (4) vs. Tennessee (3), XXXIV
  Denver (4) vs. Atlanta (3), XXXIII
- 6 Dallas (5) vs. Denver (1), XII
- 5 Green Bay (4) vs. Oakland (1), II
  Pittsburgh (4) vs. Dallas (1), X
  Oakland (3) vs. Philadelphia (2), XV
  Denver (4) vs. N.Y. Giants (1), XXI

Dallas (3) vs. Buffalo (2), XXVIII

Fewest Field Goals Attempted, Both Teams, Game

1 Minnesota (0) vs. Miami (1), VIII
San Francisco (0) vs. Denver (1), XXIV
2 Green Bay (0) vs. Kansas City (2), I
Miami (1) vs. Washington (1), VII
Minnesota (1) vs. Pittsburgh (1), IX
Dallas (1) vs. Pittsburgh (1), XIII
Dallas (1) vs. Buffalo (1), XXVII
San Diego (1) vs. San Francisco (1), XXIX
Denver (1) vs. Green Bay (1), XXXII

Most Field Goals, Game

4 Green Bay vs. Oakland, II
San Francisco vs. Cincinnati, XVI
3 N.Y. Jets vs. Baltimore, III
Kansas City vs. Minnesota, IV
Miami vs. San Francisco, XIX
Chicago vs. New England, XX
Cincinnati vs. San Francisco, XXIII
Washington vs. Buffalo, XXVI
Dallas vs. Buffalo, XXVIII
St. Louis vs. Tennessee, XXXIV

Most Field Goals, Both Teams, Game

5 Cincinnati (3) vs. San Francisco (2), XXIII
Dallas (3) vs. Buffalo (2), XXVIII
4 Green Bay (4) vs. Oakland (0), II
San Francisco (4) vs. Cincinnati (0), XVI
Miami (3) vs. San Francisco (1), XIX
Chicago (3) vs. New England (1), XX
Washington (3) vs. Buffalo (1), XXVI
Atlanta (2) vs. Denver (2), XXXIII
St. Louis (3) vs. Tennessee (1), XXXIV
3 In 13 games

Fewest Field Goals, Both Teams, Game

0 Miami vs. Washington, VII
Pittsburgh vs. Minnesota, IX
1 Green Bay (0) vs. Kansas City (1), I
Minnesota (0) vs. Miami (1), VIII
Pittsburgh (0) vs. Dallas (1), XIII
Washington (0) vs. Denver (1), XXII
San Francisco (0) vs. Denver (1), XXIV
San Francisco (0) vs. San Diego (1), XXIX

SAFETIES

Most Safeties, Game

1 Pittsburgh vs. Minnesota, IX; vs. Dallas, X
Chicago vs. New England, XX
N.Y. Giants vs. Denver, XXI
Buffalo vs. N.Y. Giants, XXV

FIRST DOWNS

Most First Downs, Game

31 San Francisco vs. Miami, XIX
29 New England vs. Carolina, XXXVIII
28 San Francisco vs. Denver, XXIV
San Francisco vs. San Diego, XXIX

Fewest First Downs, Game

9 Minnesota vs. Pittsburgh, IX
Miami vs. Washington, XVII
10 Dallas vs. Baltimore, V
Miami vs. Dallas, VI
11 Denver vs. Dallas, XII
N.Y. Giants vs. Baltimore, XXXV
Oakland vs. Tampa Bay, XXXVII

Most First Downs, Both Teams, Game

50 San Francisco (31) vs. Miami (19), XIX
Tennessee (27) vs. St. Louis (23), XXXIV
49 Buffalo (25) vs. Washington (24), XXVI
48 San Francisco (28) vs. San Diego (20), XXIX

Fewest First Downs, Both Teams, Game

24 Dallas (10) vs. Baltimore (14), V
N.Y. Giants (11) vs. Baltimore (13), XXXV
26 Minnesota (9) vs. Pittsburgh (17), IX
27 Pittsburgh (13) vs. Dallas (14), X

RUSHING

Most First Downs, Rushing, Game

16 San Francisco vs. Miami, XIX
15 Dallas vs. Miami, VI
14 Washington vs. Miami, XVII
San Francisco vs. Denver, XXIV
Denver vs. Green Bay, XXXII

Fewest First Downs, Rushing, Game

1 New England vs. Chicago, XX
St. Louis vs. Tennessee, XXXIV
Oakland vs. Tampa Bay, XXXVII
2 Minnesota vs. Kansas City, IV; vs. Pittsburgh, IX;
vs. Oakland, XI
Pittsburgh vs. Dallas, XIII
Miami vs. San Francisco, XIX
N.Y. Giants vs. Baltimore, XXXV
3 Miami vs. Dallas, VI
Philadelphia vs. Oakland, XV
New England vs. Green Bay, XXXI
Carolina vs. New England, XXXVIII

Most First Downs, Rushing, Both Teams, Game

21 Washington (14) vs. Miami (7), XVII
19 Washington (13) vs. Denver (6), XXII
San Francisco (14) vs. Denver (5), XXIV
18 Dallas (15) vs. Miami (3), VI
Miami (13) vs. Minnesota (5), VIII
San Francisco (16) vs. Miami (2), XIX
N.Y. Giants (10) vs. Buffalo (8), XXV
Denver (14) vs. Green Bay (4), XXXII

Fewest First Downs, Rushing, Both Teams, Game

7 Oakland (1) vs. Tampa Bay (6), XXXVII
8 Baltimore (4) vs. Dallas (4), V
Pittsburgh (2) vs. Dallas (6), XIII
N.Y. Giants (2) vs. Baltimore (6), XXXV
9 Philadelphia (3) vs. Oakland (6), XV

PASSING

Most First Downs, Passing, Game

19 New England vs. Carolina, XXXVIII
18 Buffalo vs. Washington, XXVI
St. Louis vs. Tennessee, XXXIV
17 Miami vs. San Francisco, XIX
San Francisco vs. San Diego, XXIX

Fewest First Downs, Passing, Game

1 Denver vs. Dallas, XII
2 Miami vs. Washington, XVII
4 Miami vs. Minnesota, VIII

Most First Downs, Passing, Both Teams, Game

32 Miami (17) vs. San Francisco (15), XIX
31 San Francisco (17) vs. San Diego (14), XXIX
St. Louis (18) vs. Tennessee (13), XXXIV
New England (19) vs. Carolina (12), XXXVIII
30 Buffalo (18) vs. Washington (12), XXVI

Fewest First Downs, Passing, Both Teams, Game

9 Denver (1) vs. Dallas (8), XII
10 Minnesota (5) vs. Pittsburgh (5), IX
11 Dallas (5) vs. Baltimore (6), V
Miami (2) vs. Washington (9), XVII

PENALTY

Most First Downs, Penalty, Game

4 Baltimore vs. Dallas, V
Miami vs. Minnesota, VIII
Cincinnati vs. San Francisco, XVI

Buffalo vs. Dallas, XXVII
St. Louis vs. Tennessee, XXXIV
3 Kansas City vs. Minnesota, IV
Minnesota vs. Oakland, XI
Buffalo vs. Washington, XXVI
Green Bay vs. Denver, XXXII
N.Y. Giants vs. Baltimore, XXXV
St. Louis vs. New England, XXXVI
Tampa Bay vs. Oakland, XXXVII
New England vs. Carolina, XXXVIII

Most First Downs, Penalty, Both Teams, Game
6 Cincinnati (4) vs. San Francisco (2), XVI
St. Louis (4) vs. Tennessee (2), XXXIV
5 Baltimore (4) vs. Dallas (1), V
Miami (4) vs. Minnesota (1), VIII
Buffalo (3) vs. Washington (2), XXVI
Green Bay (3) vs. Denver (2), XXXII
New England (3) vs. Carolina (2), XXXVIII
4 Kansas City (3) vs. Minnesota (1), IV
Buffalo (4) vs. Dallas (0), XXVII
N.Y. Giants (3) vs. Baltimore (1), XXXV
St. Louis (3) vs. New England (1), XXXVI
Tampa Bay (3) vs Oakland (1), XXXVII

Fewest First Downs, Penalty, Both Teams, Game
0 Dallas vs. Miami, VI
Miami vs. Washington, VII
Dallas vs. Pittsburgh, X
Miami vs. San Francisco, XIX
1 Green Bay (0) vs. Kansas City (1), I
Miami (0) vs. Washington (1), XVII
Cincinnati (0) vs. San Francisco (1), XXIII
San Francisco (0) vs. Denver (1), XXIV
Dallas (0) vs. Buffalo (1), XXVIII
Dallas (0) vs. Pittsburgh (1), XXX
Denver (0) vs. Atlanta (1), XXXIII

NET YARDS GAINED RUSHING AND PASSING

Most Yards Gained, Game
602 Washington vs. Denver, XXII
537 San Francisco vs. Miami, XIX
481 New England vs. Carolina, XXXVIII

Fewest Yards Gained, Game
119 Minnesota vs. Pittsburgh, IX
123 New England vs. Chicago, XX
152 N.Y. Giants vs. Baltimore, XXXV

Most Yards Gained, Both Teams, Game
929 Washington (602) vs. Denver (327), XXII
868 New England (481) vs. Carolina (387), XXXVIII
851 San Francisco (537) vs. Miami (314), XIX

Fewest Yards Gained, Both Teams, Game
396 N.Y. Giants (152) vs. Baltimore (244), XXXV
452 Minnesota (119) vs. Pittsburgh (333), IX
481 Washington (228) vs. Miami (253), VII
Denver (156) vs. Dallas (325), XII

RUSHING

ATTEMPTS

Most Attempts, Game
57 Pittsburgh vs. Minnesota, IX
53 Miami vs. Minnesota, VIII
52 Oakland vs. Minnesota, XI
Washington vs. Miami, XVII

Fewest Attempts, Game
9 Miami vs. San Francisco, XIX
11 New England vs. Chicago, XX
Oakland vs. Tampa Bay, XXXVII
13 New England vs. Green Bay, XXXI
St. Louis vs. Tennessee, XXXIV

Most Attempts, Both Teams, Game
81 Washington (52) vs. Miami (29), XVII
78 Pittsburgh (57) vs. Minnesota (21), IX
Oakland (52) vs. Minnesota (26), XI
77 Miami (53) vs. Minnesota (24), VIII
Pittsburgh (46) vs. Dallas (31), X

Fewest Attempts, Both Teams, Game
47 St. Louis (22) vs. New England (25), XXXVI
49 Miami (9) vs. San Francisco (40), XIX
New England (13) vs. Green Bay (36), XXXI
St. Louis (13) vs. Tennessee (36), XXXIV
N.Y. Giants (16) vs. Baltimore (33), XXXV
51 San Diego (19) vs. San Francisco (32), XXIX
Carolina (16) vs. New England (35), XXXVIII

YARDS GAINED

Most Yards Gained, Game
280 Washington vs. Denver, XXII
276 Washington vs. Miami, XVII
266 Oakland vs. Minnesota, XI

Fewest Yards Gained, Game
7 New England vs. Chicago, XX
17 Minnesota vs. Pittsburgh, IX
19 Oakland vs. Tampa Bay, XXXVII

Most Yards Gained, Both Teams, Game
377 Washington (280) vs. Denver (97), XXII
372 Washington (276) vs. Miami (96), XVII
338 N.Y. Giants (172) vs. Buffalo (166), XXV

Fewest Yards Gained, Both Teams, Game
158 New England (43) vs. Green Bay (115), XXXI
159 Dallas (56) vs. Pittsburgh (103), XXX
168 Buffalo (43) vs. Washington (125), XXVI

AVERAGE GAIN

Highest Average Gain, Game
7.00 L.A. Raiders vs. Washington, XVIII (33-231)
Washington vs. Denver, XXII (40-280)
6.64 Buffalo vs. N.Y. Giants, XXV (25-166)
6.22 Baltimore vs. N.Y. Jets, III (23-143)

Lowest Average Gain, Game
0.64 New England vs. Chicago, XX (11-7)
0.81 Minnesota vs. Pittsburgh, IX (21-17)
1.73 Oakland vs. Tampa Bay, XXXVII (11-19)

TOUCHDOWNS

Most Touchdowns, Game
4 Chicago vs. New England, XX
Denver vs. Green Bay, XXXII
3 Green Bay vs. Kansas City, I
Miami vs. Minnesota, VIII
San Francisco vs. Denver, XXIV
Denver vs. Atlanta, XXXIII
2 Oakland vs. Minnesota, XI
Pittsburgh vs. Los Angeles, XIV
L.A. Raiders vs. Washington, XVIII
San Francisco vs. Miami, XIX
N.Y. Giants vs. Denver, XXI
Washington vs. Denver, XXII; vs. Buffalo, XXVI
Buffalo vs. N.Y. Giants, XXV
Dallas vs. Buffalo, XXVIII; vs. Pittsburgh, XXX
Tennessee vs. St. Louis, XXXIV

Fewest Touchdowns, Game
0 By 24 teams

Most Touchdowns, Both Teams, Game
4 Miami (3) vs. Minnesota (1), VIII
Chicago (4) vs. New England (0), XX
San Francisco (3) vs. Denver (1), XXIV
Denver (4) vs. Green Bay (0), XXXII
3 In nine games

Fewest Touchdowns, Both Teams, Game
0 Pittsburgh vs. Dallas, X
Oakland vs. Philadelphia, XV

Cincinnati vs. San Francisco, XXIII
1 In 10 games

PASSING

ATTEMPTS

Most Passes Attempted, Game
59 Buffalo vs. Washington, XXVI
55 San Diego vs. San Francisco, XXIX
50 Miami vs. San Francisco, XIX
Buffalo vs. Dallas, XXVIII

Fewest Passes Attempted, Game
7 Miami vs. Minnesota, VIII
11 Miami vs. Washington, VII
14 Pittsburgh vs. Minnesota, IX

Most Passes Attempted, Both Teams, Game
93 San Diego (55) vs. San Francisco (38), XXIX
92 Buffalo (59) vs. Washington (33), XXVI
85 Miami (50) vs. San Francisco (35), XIX

Fewest Passes Attempted, Both Teams, Game
35 Miami (7) vs. Minnesota (28), VIII
39 Miami (11) vs. Washington (28), VII
40 Pittsburgh (14) vs. Minnesota (26), IX
Miami (17) vs. Washington (23), XVII

COMPLETIONS

Most Passes Completed, Game
32 New England vs. Carolina, XXXVIII
31 Buffalo vs. Dallas, XXVIII
29 Miami vs. San Francisco, XIX
Buffalo vs. Washington, XXVI

Fewest Passes Completed, Game
4 Miami vs. Washington, XVII
6 Miami vs. Minnesota, VIII
8 Miami vs. Washington, VII
Denver vs. Dallas, XII

Most Passes Completed, Both Teams, Game
53 Miami (29) vs. San Francisco (24), XIX
52 San Diego (27) vs. San Francisco (25), XXIX
50 Buffalo (31) vs. Dallas (19), XXVIII

Fewest Passes Completed, Both Teams, Game
19 Miami (4) vs. Washington (15), XVII
20 Pittsburgh (9) vs. Minnesota (11), IX
22 Miami (8) vs. Washington (14), VII

COMPLETION PERCENTAGE

Highest Completion Percentage, Game (20 attempts)
88.0 N.Y. Giants vs. Denver, XXI (25-22)
75.0 San Francisco vs. Denver, XXIV (32-24)
73.5 Cincinnati vs. San Francisco, XVI (34-25)

Lowest Completion Percentage, Game (20 attempts)
32.0 Denver vs. Dallas, XII (25-8)
37.9 Denver vs. San Francisco, XXIV (29-11)
38.5 Denver vs. Washington, XXII (39-15)
N.Y. Giants vs. Baltimore, XXXV (39-15)

YARDS GAINED

Most Yards Gained, Game
407 St. Louis vs. Tennessee, XXXIV
354 New England vs. Carolina, XXXVIII
341 San Francisco vs. Cincinnati, XXIII

Fewest Yards Gained, Game
35 Denver vs. Dallas, XII
63 Miami vs. Minnesota, VIII
69 Miami vs. Washington, VII

Most Yards Gained, Both Teams, Game
649 New England (354) vs. Carolina (295), XXXVIII
615 San Francisco (326) vs. Miami (289), XIX
St. Louis (407) vs. Tennessee (208), XXXIV
603 San Francisco (316) vs. San Diego (287), XXIX

Fewest Yards Gained, Both Teams, Game
156 Miami (69) vs. Washington (87), VII
186 Pittsburgh (84) vs. Minnesota (102), IX
204 Miami (80) vs. Washington (124), XVII

TIMES SACKED

Most Times Sacked, Game
7 Dallas vs. Pittsburgh, X
New England vs. Chicago, XX
6 Kansas City vs. Green Bay, I
Washington vs. L.A. Raiders, XVIII
Denver vs. San Francisco, XXIV
5 Dallas vs. Denver, XII; vs. Pittsburgh, XIII
Cincinnati vs. San Francisco, XVI; XXIII
Denver vs. Washington, XXII
Buffalo vs. Washington, XXVI
Green Bay vs. New England, XXXI
New England vs. Green Bay, XXXI
Oakland vs. Tampa Bay, XXXVII

Fewest Times Sacked, Game
0 Baltimore vs. N.Y. Jets, III; vs. Dallas, V
Minnesota vs. Pittsburgh, IX
Pittsburgh vs. Los Angeles, XIV
Philadelphia vs. Oakland, XV
Washington vs. Buffalo, XXVI
Denver vs. Green Bay, XXXII; vs. Atlanta, XXXIII
Tampa Bay vs. Oakland, XXXVII
New England vs. Carolina, XXXVIII
1 By 13 teams

Most Times Sacked, Both Teams, Game
10 New England (7) vs. Chicago (3), XX
Green Bay (5) vs. New England (5), XXXI
9 Kansas City (6) vs. Green Bay (3), I
Dallas (7) vs. Pittsburgh (2), X
Dallas (5) vs. Denver (4), XII
Dallas (5) vs. Pittsburgh (4), XIII
Cincinnati (5) vs. San Francisco (4), XXIII
8 Washington (6) vs. L.A. Raiders (2), XVIII

Fewest Times Sacked, Both Teams, Game
1 Philadelphia (0) vs. Oakland (1), XV
Denver (0) vs. Green Bay (1), XXXII
2 Baltimore (0) vs. N.Y. Jets (2), III
Baltimore (0) vs. Dallas (2), V
Minnesota (0) vs. Pittsburgh (2), IX
Denver (0) vs. Atlanta (2), XXXIII
3 In five games

TOUCHDOWNS

Most Touchdowns, Game
6 San Francisco vs. San Diego, XXIX
5 San Francisco vs. Denver, XXIV
4 Pittsburgh vs. Dallas, XIII
Washington vs. Denver, XXII
Dallas vs. Buffalo, XXVII

Fewest Touchdowns, Game
0 By 19 teams

Most Touchdowns, Both Teams, Game
7 Pittsburgh (4) vs. Dallas (3), XIII
San Francisco (6) vs. San Diego (1), XXIX
6 Carolina (3) vs. New England (3), XXXVIII
5 Washington (4) vs. Denver (1), XXII
San Francisco (5) vs. Denver (0), XXIV
Dallas (4) vs. Buffalo (1), XXVII

Fewest Touchdowns, Both Teams, Game
0 N.Y. Jets vs. Baltimore, III
Miami vs. Minnesota, VIII
Buffalo vs. Dallas, XXVIII
1 In seven games

INTERCEPTIONS BY

Most Interceptions By, Game

5 Tampa Bay vs. Oakland, XXXVII
4 N.Y. Jets vs. Baltimore, III
Dallas vs. Denver, XII
Washington vs. Buffalo, XXVI
Dallas vs. Buffalo, XXVII
Green Bay vs. New England, XXXI
Baltimore vs. N.Y. Giants, XXXV
3 By 12 teams

Most Interceptions By, Both Teams, Game

6 Baltimore (3) vs. Dallas (3), V
Tampa Bay (5) vs. Oakland (1), XXXVII
5 Washington (4) vs. Buffalo (1), XXVI
4 In 10 games

Fewest Interceptions By, Both Teams, Game

0 Buffalo vs. N.Y. Giants, XXV
St. Louis vs. Tennessee, XXXIV
1 Oakland (0) vs. Green Bay (1), II
Miami (0) vs. Dallas (1), VI
Minnesota (0) vs. Miami (1), VIII
N.Y. Giants (0) vs. Denver (1), XXI
Cincinnati (0) vs. San Francisco (1), XXIII
New England (0) vs. Carolina (1), XXXVIII

YARDS GAINED

Most Yards Gained, Game

172 Tampa Bay vs. Oakland (12), XXXVII
136 Denver vs. Atlanta, XXXIII
95 Miami vs. Washington, VII

Most Yards Gained, Both Teams, Game

184 Tampa Bay (172) vs. Oakland (12), XXXVII
137 Denver (136) vs. Atlanta (1), XXXIII
95 Miami (95) vs. Washington (0), VII

TOUCHDOWNS

Most Touchdowns, Game

3 Tampa Bay vs. Oakland, XXXVII
1 Green Bay vs. Oakland, II
Oakland vs. Minnesota, XI
L.A. Raiders vs. Washington, XVIII
Chicago vs. New England, XX
Baltimore vs. N.Y. Giants, XXXV
New England vs. St. Louis, XXXVI

PUNTING

Most Punts, Game

11 N.Y. Giants vs. Baltimore, XXXV
10 Baltimore vs. N.Y. Giants, XXXV
9 Dallas vs. Baltimore, V

Fewest Punts, Game

1 Atlanta vs. Denver, XXXIII
Denver vs. Atlanta, XXXIII
2 Pittsburgh vs. Los Angeles, XIV
Denver vs. N.Y. Giants, XXI
St. Louis vs. Tennessee, XXXIV
3 By 11 teams

Most Punts, Both Teams, Game

21 N.Y. Giants (11) vs. Baltimore (10), XXXV
15 Washington (8) vs. L.A. Raiders (7), XVIII
New England (8) vs. Green Bay (7), XXXI
13 Dallas (9) vs. Baltimore (4), V
Pittsburgh (7) vs. Minnesota (6), IX

Fewest Punts, Both Teams, Game

2 Atlanta (1) vs. Denver (1), XXXIII
5 Denver (2) vs. N.Y. Giants (3), XXI
St. Louis (2) vs. Tennessee (3), XXXIV
6 Oakland (3) vs. Philadelphia (3), XV

AVERAGE YARDAGE

Highest Average, Game (4 punts)

48.75 San Diego vs. San Francisco, XXIX (4-195)
48.50 Kansas City vs. Minnesota, IV (4-194)
46.25 San Francisco vs. Cincinnati, XVI (4-185)

Lowest Average, Game (4 punts)

31.00 Tampa Bay vs. Oakland, XXXVII (5-155)
31.20 Washington vs. Miami, VII (5-156)
32.38 Washington vs. L.A. Raiders, XVIII (8-259)

PUNT RETURNS

Most Punt Returns, Game

6 Washington vs. Miami, XVII
Green Bay vs. New England, XXXI
5 By seven teams

Fewest Punt Returns, Game

0 Minnesota vs. Miami, VIII
Buffalo vs. N.Y. Giants, XXV
Washington vs. Buffalo, XXVI
Denver vs. Green Bay, XXXII
Green Bay vs. Denver, XXXII
Atlanta vs. Denver, XXXIII
Denver vs. Atlanta, XXXIII
1 By 19 teams

Most Punt Returns, Both Teams, Game

10 Green Bay (6) vs. New England (4), XXXI
9 Pittsburgh (5) vs. Minnesota (4), IX
8 Green Bay (5) vs. Oakland (3), II
Baltimore (5) vs. Dallas (3), V
Washington (6) vs. Miami (2), XVII
N.Y. Giants (5) vs. Baltimore (3), XXXV

Fewest Punt Returns, Both Teams, Game

0 Denver vs. Green Bay, XXXII
Atlanta vs. Denver, XXXIII
2 Dallas (1) vs. Miami (1), VI
Denver (1) vs. N.Y. Giants (1), XXI
Buffalo (0) vs. N.Y. Giants (2), XXV
Buffalo (1) vs. Dallas (1), XXVIII
3 Kansas City (1) vs. Minnesota (2), IV
Minnesota (0) vs. Miami (3), VIII
Washington (1) vs. Denver (2), XXII
Washington (0) vs. Buffalo (3), XXVI
Dallas (1) vs. Pittsburgh (2), XXX
Tennessee (1) vs. St. Louis (2), XXXIV

YARDS GAINED

Most Yards Gained, Game

90 Green Bay vs. New England, XXXI
56 San Francisco vs. Cincinnati, XXIII
52 Washington vs. Miami, XVII

Fewest Yards Gained, Game

–1 Dallas vs. Miami, VI
Tennessee vs. St. Louis, XXXIV
0 By 12 teams

Most Yards Gained, Both Teams, Game

120 Green Bay (90) vs. New England (30), XXXI
80 N.Y. Giants (46) vs. Baltimore (34), XXXV
74 Washington (52) vs. Miami (22), XVII

Fewest Yards Gained, Both Teams, Game

0 Denver vs. Green Bay, XXXII
Atlanta vs. Denver, XXXIII
7 Tennessee (-1) vs. St. Louis (8), XXXIV
9 Washington (0) vs. Bufffalo (9), XXVI

AVERAGE RETURN

Highest Average, Game (3 returns)

18.7 San Francisco vs. Cincinnati, XXIII (3-56)
15.0 Green Bay vs. New England, XXXI (6-90)
12.7 San Francisco vs. Denver, XXIV (3-38)

TOUCHDOWNS
Most Touchdowns, Game
None

KICKOFF RETURNS
Most Kickoff Returns, Game
9 Denver vs. San Francisco, XXIV
Oakland vs. Tampa Bay, XXXVII
8 San Diego vs. San Francisco, XXIX
7 By eight teams
Fewest Kickoff Returns, Game
1 N.Y. Jets vs. Baltimore, III
L.A. Raiders vs. Washington, XVIII
Washington vs. Buffalo, XXVI
2 By eight teams
Most Kickoff Returns, Both Teams, Game
13 Oakland (9) vs. Tampa Bay (4), XXXVII
12 Denver (9) vs. San Francisco (3), XXIV
San Diego (8) vs. San Francisco (4), XXIX
11 Los Angeles (6) vs. Pittsburgh (5), XIV
Miami (7) vs. San Francisco (4), XIX
New England (7) vs. Chicago (4), XX
Green Bay (6) vs. Denver (5), XXXII
Fewest Kickoff Returns, Both Teams, Game
5 N.Y. Jets (1) vs. Baltimore (4), III
Miami (2) vs. Washington (3), VII
Washington (1) vs. Buffalo (4), XXVI
6 In three games

YARDS GAINED
Most Yards Gained, Game
244 San Diego vs. San Francisco, XXIX
227 Atlanta vs. Denver, XXXIII
222 Miami vs. Washington, XVII
Fewest Yards Gained, Game
16 Washington vs. Buffalo, XXVI
17 L.A. Raiders vs. Washington, XVIII
25 N.Y. Jets vs. Baltimore, III
Most Yards Gained, Both Teams, Game
292 San Diego (244) vs. San Francisco (48), XXIX
289 Green Bay (154) vs. New England (135), XXXI
281 N.Y. Giants (170) vs. Baltimore (111), XXXV
Fewest Yards Gained, Both Teams, Game
78 Miami (33) vs. Washington (45), VII
82 Pittsburgh (32) vs. Minnesota (50), IX
92 San Francisco (40) vs. Cincinnati (52), XVI

AVERAGE GAIN
Highest Average, Game (3 returns)
44.0 Cincinnati vs. San Francisco, XXIII (3-132)
38.5 Green Bay vs. New England, XXXI (4-154)
37.0 Miami vs. Washington, XVII (6-222)

TOUCHDOWNS
Most Touchdowns, Game
1 Miami vs. Washington, XVII
Cincinnati vs. San Francisco, XXIII
San Diego vs. San Francisco, XXIX
Green Bay vs. New England, XXXI
Atlanta vs. Denver, XXXIII
Baltimore vs. N.Y. Giants, XXXV
N.Y. Giants vs. Baltimore, XXXV
Most Touchdowns, Both Teams, Game
2 Baltimore (1) vs. N.Y. Giants (1), XXXV

PENALTIES
Most Penalties, Game
12 Dallas vs. Denver, XII
Carolina vs. New England, XXXVIII
10 Dallas vs. Baltimore, V
9 Dallas vs. Pittsburgh, XIII
Green Bay vs. Denver, XXXII
Baltimore vs. N.Y. Giants, XXXV
Fewest Penalties, Game
0 Miami vs. Dallas, VI
Pittsburgh vs. Dallas, X
Denver vs. San Francisco, XXIV
Atlanta vs. Denver, XXXIII
1 Green Bay vs. Oakland, II
Miami vs. Minnesota, VIII; vs. San Francisco, XIX
Buffalo vs. Dallas, XXVIII
2 By six teams
Most Penalties, Both Teams, Game
20 Dallas (12) vs. Denver (8), XII
Carolina (12) vs. New England (8), XXXVIII
16 Cincinnati (8) vs. San Francisco (8), XVI
Green Bay (9) vs. Denver (7), XXXII
15 St. Louis (8) vs. Tennessee (7), XXXIV
Baltimore (9) vs. N.Y. Giants (6), XXXV
Fewest Penalties, Both Teams, Game
2 Pittsburgh (0) vs. Dallas (2), X
3 Miami (0) vs. Dallas (3), VI
Miami (1) vs. San Francisco (2), XIX
4 Denver (0) vs. San Francisco (4), XXIV
Atlanta (0) vs. Denver (4), XXXIII

YARDS PENALIZED
Most Yards Penalized, Game
133 Dallas vs. Baltimore, X
122 Pittsburgh vs. Minnesota, IX
94 Dallas vs. Denver, XII
Fewest Yards Penalized, Game
0 Miami vs. Dallas, VI
Pittsburgh vs. Dallas, X
Denver vs. San Francisco, XXIV
Atlanta vs. Denver, XXXIII
4 Miami vs. Minnesota, VIII
10 Miami vs. San Francisco, XIX
San Francisco vs. Miami, XIX
Buffalo vs. Dallas, XXVIII
Most Yards Penalized, Both Teams, Game
164 Dallas (133) vs. Baltimore (31), V
154 Dallas (94) vs. Denver (60), XII
140 Pittsburgh (122) vs. Minnesota (18), IX
Fewest Yards Penalized, Both Teams, Game
15 Miami (0) vs. Dallas (15), VI
20 Pittsburgh (0) vs. Dallas (20), X
Miami (10) vs. San Francisco (10), XIX
38 Denver (0) vs. San Francisco (38), XXIV

FUMBLES
Most Fumbles, Game
8 Buffalo vs. Dallas, XXVII
6 Dallas vs. Denver, XII
Buffalo vs. Washington, XXVI
5 Baltimore vs. Dallas, V
Fewest Fumbles, Game
0 By 17 teams
Most Fumbles, Both Teams, Game
12 Buffalo (8) vs. Dallas (4), XXVII
10 Dallas (6) vs. Denver (4), XII
8 Dallas (4) vs. Pittsburgh (4), X
Fewest Fumbles, Both Teams, Game
0 Los Angeles vs. Pittsburgh, XIV
Green Bay vs. New England, XXXI
1 Oakland (0) vs. Minnesota (1), XI
Oakland (0) vs. Philadelphia (1), XV
Denver (0) vs. Washington (1), XXII
N.Y. Giants (0) vs. Buffalo (1), XXV
Denver (0) vs. Atlanta (1), XXXIII

2 In eight games

Most Fumbles Lost, Game

5 Buffalo vs. Dallas, XXVII
4 Baltimore vs. Dallas, V
Denver vs. Dallas, XII
New England vs. Chicago, XX
2 In many games

Most Fumbles Lost, Both Teams, Game

7 Buffalo (5) vs. Dallas (2), XXVII
6 Denver (4) vs. Dallas (2), XII
New England (4) vs. Chicago (2), XX
5 Baltimore (4) vs. Dallas (1), V

Fewest Fumbles Lost, Both Teams, Game

0 Green Bay vs. Kansas City, I
Dallas vs. Pittsburgh, X
Los Angeles vs. Pittsburgh, XIV
Denver vs. N.Y. Giants, XXI; vs. Washington, XXII
Buffalo vs. N.Y. Giants, XXV
San Diego vs. San Francisco, XXIX
Dallas vs. Pittsburgh, XXX
Green Bay vs. New England, XXXI
St. Louis vs. Tennessee, XXXIV
Oakland vs. Tampa Bay, XXXVII

Most Fumbles Recovered, Game

8 Dallas vs. Denver, XII (4 own, 4 opp.)
6 Dallas vs. Buffalo, XXVII (1 own, 5 opp.)
5 Chicago vs. New England, XX (1 own, 4 opp.)

TURNOVERS

(Number of times losing the ball on interceptions and fumbles.)

Most Turnovers, Game

9 Buffalo vs. Dallas, XXVII
8 Denver vs. Dallas, XII
7 Baltimore vs. Dallas, V

Fewest Turnovers, Game

0 Green Bay vs. Oakland, II
Miami vs. Minnesota, VIII
Pittsburgh vs. Dallas, X
Oakland vs. Minnesota, XI; vs. Philadelphia, XV
N.Y. Giants vs. Denver, XXI; vs. Buffalo, XXV
San Francisco vs. Denver, XXIV; vs. San Diego, XXIX
Buffalo vs. N.Y. Giants, XXV
Dallas vs. Pittsburgh, XXX
Green Bay vs. New England, XXXI
St. Louis vs. Tennessee, XXXIV
Tennessee vs. St. Louis, XXXIV
Baltimore vs. N.Y. Giants, XXXV
New England vs. St. Louis, XXXVI
1 By many teams

Most Turnovers, Both Teams, Game

11 Baltimore (7) vs. Dallas (4), V
Buffalo (9) vs. Dallas (2), XXVII
10 Denver (8) vs. Dallas (2), XII
8 New England (6) vs. Chicago (2), XX

Fewest Turnovers, Both Teams, Game

0 Buffalo vs. N.Y. Giants, XXV
St. Louis vs. Tennessee, XXXIV
1 N.Y. Giants (0) vs. Denver (1), XXI
2 Green Bay (1) vs. Kansas City (1), I
Miami (0) vs. Minnesota (2), VIII
Cincinnati (1) vs. San Francisco (1), XXIII
Carolina (1) vs. New England (1), XXXVIII

POSTSEASON RECORDS

Compiled by Elias Sports Bureau

Throughout this all-time postseason record section, the following abbreviations are used to indicate various levels of postseason games:

SB Super Bowl (1966 to date)

AFC AFC Championship Game (1970 to date) or AFL Championship Game (1960-69)

NFC NFC Championship Game (1970 to date) or NFL Championship Game (1933-69)

AFC-D AFC Divisional Playoff Game (1970 to date), AFC Second-Round Playoff Game (1982), AFL Inter-Divisional Playoff Game (1969), or special playoff game to break tie for AFL Division Championship (1963, 1968)

NFC-D NFC Divisional Playoff Game (1970 to date), NFC Second-Round Playoff Game (1982), NFL Conference Championship Game (1967-69), or special playoff game to break tie for NFL Division or Conference Championship (1941, 1943, 1947, 1950, 1952, 1957, 1958, 1965)

AFC-FR AFC First-Round Playoff Game (1978 to date)

NFC-FR NFC First-Round Playoff Game (1978 to date)

Year indicates season in which game took place and does not necessarily reflect calendar year.

POSTSEASON GAME COMPOSITE STANDINGS

	W	L	PCT.	PTS.	OP
Baltimore Ravens	5	2	.714	142	73
Carolina Panthers	4	2	.667	140	115
Green Bay Packers	24	13	.649	871	692
San Francisco 49ers	25	17	.595	1,044	853
Washington Redskins*	22	15	.595	778	642
Dallas Cowboys	32	22	.593	1,281	1,008
Oakland Raiders**	25	18	.581	1,028	797
Pittsburgh Steelers	23	17	.575	912	808
New England Patriots#	13	10	.565	443	461
Denver Broncos	16	13	.552	626	698
Miami Dolphins	20	19	.513	780	848
Jacksonville Jaguars	4	4	.500	208	200
Buffalo Bills	14	15	.483	681	658
Chicago Bears	14	15	.483	598	585
Philadelphia Eagles	14	15	.483	531	513
Indianapolis Colts***	12	14	.462	486	537
Tampa Bay Buccaneers	6	7	.462	206	238
Tennessee Titans†	14	17	.452	563	732
St. Louis Rams††	18	23	.439	726	877
New York Jets	7	9	.438	335	315
New York Giants	16	21	.432	647	699
Minnesota Vikings	17	23	.425	779	913
Atlanta Falcons	5	7	.417	241	287
Cincinnati Bengals	5	7	.417	246	257
Detroit Lions	7	10	.412	365	404
Kansas City Chiefs****	8	12	.400	332	422
San Diego Chargers†††	7	11	.389	332	428
Cleveland Browns	11	20	.355	629	728
Seattle Seahawks	3	6	.333	172	192
Arizona Cardinals††††	2	5	.286	122	182
New Orleans Saints	1	5	.167	103	185

* *One game played when franchise was in Boston (lost 21-6).*

** *12 games played when franchise was in Los Angeles (won 6, lost 6, 268 points scored, 224 points allowed).*

*** *15 games played when franchise was in Baltimore (won 8, lost 7, 264 points scored, 262 points allowed).*

**** *One game played when franchise was Dallas Texans (won 20-17).*

\# *Two games played when franchise was in Boston (won 26-8, lost 51-10).*

† *22 games played when franchise was in Houston and known as the Oilers (won 9, lost 13, 371 points scored, 533 points allowed).*

†† *One game played when franchise was in Cleveland (won 15-14), 32 games played when franchise was in Los Angeles (won 12, lost 20, 486 points scored, 683 points allowed).*

††† *One game played when franchise was in Los Angeles (lost 24-16).*

†††† *Two games played when franchise was in Chicago (won 28-21, lost 7-0), three games played when franchise was in St. Louis (lost 30-14, lost 35-23, lost 41-16).*

INDIVIDUAL RECORDS

SERVICE

Most Games, Career

28 Jerry Rice, San Francisco-Oakland (SB 4,NFC 6, AFC 1, NFC-D 11, Afc-D 2, NFC-FR 3, AFC-FR 1)
27 D.D. Lewis, Dallas (SB 5, NFC 9, NFC-D 12, NFC-FR 1)
26 Larry Cole, Dallas (SB 5, NFC 8, NFC-D 12, NFC-FR 1)
Bill Romanowski, San Francisco-Philadelphia-Denver-Oakland (SB 5, NFC 5, AFC 3, NFC-D 6, AFC-D 4, NFC-FR 1, AFC-FR 2)

Most Games, Head Coach

36 Tom Landry, Dallas
Don Shula, Baltimore-Miami
24 Chuck Noll, Pittsburgh
22 Bud Grant, Minnesota

Most Games Won, Head Coach

20 Tom Landry, Dallas
19 Don Shula, Baltimore-Miami
16 Chuck Noll, Pittsburgh
Joe Gibbs, Washington

Most Games Lost, Head Coach

17 Don Shula, Baltimore-Miami
16 Tom Landry, Dallas
12 Bud Grant, Minnesota

SCORING

POINTS

Most Points, Career

153 Gary Anderson, Pittsburgh-Philadelphia-San Francisco-Minnesota-Tennessee, (57-pat, 32-fg)
132 Jerry Rice, San Francisco-Oakland, 28 games (22-td)
126 Thurman Thomas, Buffalo, 21 games (21-td)
Emmitt Smith, Dallas, 17 games (21-td)

Most Points, Game

30 Ricky Watters, NFC-D: San Francisco vs. N.Y. Giants, 1993 (5-td)
19 Pat Harder, NFC-D: Detroit vs. Los Angeles, 1952 (2-td, 4-pat, 1-fg)
Paul Hornung, NFC: Green Bay vs. N.Y. Giants, 1961 (1-td, 4-pat, 3-fg)
18 By many players

Most Consecutive Games Scoring

19 George Blanda, Chi. Bears-Houston-Oakland, 1956-1975
16 Norm Johnson, Seattle-Atlanta-Pittsburgh, 1983-1997
15 Roy Gerela, Houston-Pittsburgh, 1969-1978

TOUCHDOWNS

Most Touchdowns, Career

22 Jerry Rice, San Francisco-Oakland, 28 games (22-p)
21 Thurman Thomas, Buffalo, 21 games (16-r, 5-p)
Emmitt Smith, Dallas, 17 games (19-r, 2-p)
17 Franco Harris, Pittsburgh, 19 games (16-r, 1-p)

Most Touchdowns, Game

5 Ricky Watters, NFC-D: San Francisco vs. N.Y. Giants, 1993 (5-r)
3 Andy Farkas, NFC-D: Washington vs. N.Y. Giants, 1943 (3-r)
Tom Fears, NFC-D: Los Angeles vs. Chi. Bears, 1950 (3-p)
Otto Graham, NFC: Cleveland vs. Detroit, 1954 (3-r)
Gary Collins, NFC: Cleveland vs. Baltimore, 1964 (3-p)

Craig Baynham, NFC-D: Dallas vs. Cleveland, 1967 (2-r, 1-p)
Fred Biletnikoff, AFC-D: Oakland vs. Kansas City, 1968 (3-p)
Tom Matte, NFC: Baltimore vs. Cleveland, 1968 (3-r)
Larry Schreiber, NFC-D: San Francisco vs. Dallas, 1972 (3-r)
Larry Csonka, AFC: Miami vs. Oakland, 1973 (3-r)
Franco Harris, AFC-D: Pittsburgh vs. Buffalo, 1974 (3-r)
Preston Pearson, NFC: Dallas vs. Los Angeles, 1975 (3-p)
Dave Casper, AFC-D: Oakland vs. Baltimore, 1977 (OT) (3-p)
Alvin Garrett, NFC-FR: Washington vs. Detroit, 1982 (3-p)
John Riggins, NFC-D: Washington vs. L.A. Rams, 1983 (3-r)
Roger Craig, SB: San Francisco vs. Miami, 1984 (1-r, 2-p)
Jerry Rice, NFC-D: San Francisco vs. Minnesota, 1988 (3-p)
Jerry Rice, SB: San Francisco vs. Denver, 1989 (3-p)
Kenneth Davis, AFC: Buffalo vs. L.A. Raiders, 1990 (3-r)
Andre Reed, AFC-FR: Buffalo vs. Houston, 1992 (OT) (3-p)
Sterling Sharpe, NFC-FR: Green Bay vs. Detroit, 1993 (3-p)
Napoleon McCallum, AFC-FR: L.A. Raiders vs. Denver, 1993 (3-r)
Thurman Thomas, AFC: Buffalo vs. Kansas City, 1993 (3-r)
William Floyd, NFC-D: San Francisco vs. Chicago, 1994 (3-r)
Ricky Watters, SB: San Francisco vs. San Diego, 1994 (1-r, 2-p)
Jerry Rice, SB: San Francisco vs. San Diego, 1994 (3-p)
Emmitt Smith, NFC: Dallas vs. Green Bay, 1995 (3-r)
Curtis Martin, AFC-D: New England vs. Pittsburgh, 1996 (3-r)
Terrell Davis, SB: Denver vs. Green Bay, 1997 (3-r)
Mario Bates, NFC-D: Arizona vs. Minnesota, 1998 (3-r)
Leroy Hoard, NFC-D: Minnesota vs. Arizona, 1998 (2-r, 1-p)
Willie Jackson, NFC-FR: New Orleans vs. St. Louis, 2000 (3-p)
Amani Toomer, NFC-FR: N.Y. Giants vs. San Francisco, 2002 (3-p)
Shaun Alexander, NFC-FR: Seattle vs. Green Bay, 2003 (OT) (3-r)

Most Consecutive Games Scoring Touchdowns
9 Thurman Thomas, Buffalo, 1992-98
8 John Stallworth, Pittsburgh, 1978-1983
Emmitt Smith, Dallas, 1993-96
7 John Riggins, Washington, 1982-84
Marcus Allen, L.A. Raiders, 1982-85
Terrell Davis, Denver, 1996-98

POINTS AFTER TOUCHDOWN

Most (One-Point) Points After Touchdown, Career
57 Gary Anderson, Pittsburgh-Philadelphia-San Francisco-Minnesota-Tennessee, 22 games (57 att)
49 George Blanda, Chi. Bears-Houston-Oakland, 19 games (49 att)
42 Mike Cofer, San Francisco, 12 games (46 att)

Most (One-Point) Points After Touchdown, Game
8 Lou Groza, NFC: Cleveland vs. Detroit, 1954 (8 att)
Jim Martin, NFC: Detroit vs. Cleveland, 1957 (8 att)
George Blanda, AFC-D: Oakland vs. Houston, 1969 (8 att)
Mike Hollis, AFC-D: Jacksonville vs. Miami, 1999 (8 att)
7 Danny Villanueva, NFC-D: Dallas vs. Cleveland, 1967 (7 att)
Raul Allegre, NFC-D: N.Y. Giants vs. San Francisco, 1986 (7 att)
Mike Cofer, SB: San Francisco vs. Denver, 1989 (8 att)
Lin Elliott, SB: Dallas vs. Buffalo, 1992 (7 att)
Doug Brien, SB: San Francisco vs. San Diego, 1994 (7 att)
Gary Anderson, NFC-FR: Philadelphia vs. Detroit, 1995 (7 att)
Jeff Wilkins, NFC-D: St. Louis vs. Minnesota, 1999 (7 att)
6 George Blair, AFC: San Diego vs. Boston, 1963 (6 att)
Mark Moseley, NFC-D: Washington vs. L.A. Rams, 1983 (6 att)
Uwe von Schamann, AFC: Miami vs. Pittsburgh, 1984 (6 att)
Ali Haji-Sheikh, SB: Washington vs. Denver, 1987 (6 att)
Scott Norwood, AFC: Buffalo vs. L.A. Raiders, 1990 (7 att)
Jeff Jaeger, AFC-FR: L.A. Raiders vs. Denver, 1993 (6 att)
Jason Elam, AFC-FR: Denver vs. Jacksonville, 1997 (6 att)
Jeff Wilkins, NFC-D: St. Louis vs. Green Bay, 2001 (6 att)
Martín Gramatica, SB: Tampa Bay vs. Oakland, 2002 (6 att)

Most (Kicking) Points After Touchdown, No Misses, Career
57 Gary Anderson, Pittsburgh-Philadelphia-San Francisco-Minnesota-Tennessee, 22 games
49 George Blanda, Chi. Bears-Houston-Oakland, 19 games
41 Rafael Septien, L.A. Rams-Dallas, 15 games

Most Two-Point Conversions, Career
2 Terrell Owens, San Francisco, 9 games

Most Two-Point Conversions, Game
2 Terrell Owens, NFC-FR: San Francisco vs. N.Y. Giants, 2002

FIELD GOALS

Most Field Goals Attempted, Career
40 Gary Anderson, Pittsburgh-Philadelphia-San Francisco-Minnesota-Tennessee, 22 games
39 George Blanda, Chi. Bears-Houston-Oakland, 19 games
31 Mark Moseley, Washington-Cleveland, 11 games

Most Field Goals Attempted, Game
6 George Blanda, AFC: Oakland vs. Houston, 1967
David Ray, NFC-D: Los Angeles vs. Dallas, 1973
Mark Moseley, AFC-D: Cleveland vs. N.Y. Jets, 1986 (OT)
Matt Bahr, NFC: N.Y. Giants vs. San Francisco, 1990
Steve Christie, AFC: Buffalo vs. Miami, 1992
Jeff Wilkins, NFC-D: St. Louis vs. Carolina, 2003 (2 OT)
5 By many players

Most Field Goals, Career
32 Gary Anderson, Pittsburgh-Philadelphia-San Francisco-Minnesota-Tennessee, 22 games
22 George Blanda, Chi. Bears-Houston-Oakland, 19 games
Steve Christie, Buffalo, 12 games
21 Matt Bahr, Pittsburgh-Cleveland-N.Y. Giants-New England, 14 games

Most Field Goals, Game
5 Chuck Nelson, NFC-D: Minnesota vs. San Francisco, 1987
Matt Bahr, NFC: N.Y. Giants vs. San Francisco, 1990
Steve Christie, AFC: Buffalo vs. Miami, 1992
Brad Daluiso, NFC-FR: N.Y. Giants vs. Minnesota, 1997
John Kasay, NFC-FR: Carolina vs. Dallas, 2003
Jeff Wilkins, NFC-D: St. Louis vs. Carolina, 2003 (2 OT)
Adam Vinatieri, AFC: New England vs. Indianapolis, 2003
4 Gino Cappelletti, AFC-D: Boston vs. Buffalo, 1963
George Blanda, AFC: Oakland vs. Houston, 1967
Don Chandler, SB: Green Bay vs. Oakland, 1967
Curt Knight, NFC: Washington vs. Dallas, 1972
George Blanda, AFC-D: Oakland vs. Pittsburgh, 1973
Ray Wersching, SB: San Francisco vs. Cincinnati, 1981
Tony Franklin, AFC-FR: New England vs. N.Y. Jets, 1985
Jess Atkinson, NFC-FR: Washington vs. L.A. Rams, 1986
Luis Zendejas, NFC-D: Philadelphia vs. Chicago, 1988
Gary Anderson, AFC-FR: Pittsburgh vs. Houston, 1989 (OT)
Norm Johnson, AFC-D: Pittsburgh vs. Buffalo, 1995
Chris Boniol, NFC-FR: Dallas vs. Minnesota, 1996
John Kasay, NFC-D: Carolina vs. Dallas, 1996
Mike Hollis, AFC-D: Jacksonville vs. New England, 1998
Al Del Greco, AFC-D: Tennessee vs. Indianapolis, 1999
David Akers, NFC-D: Philadelphia vs. Chicago, 2001
3 By many players

Most Consecutive Games Scoring Field Goals
13 Toni Fritsch, Dallas-Houston, 1972-79
9 Kevin Butler, Chicago, 1985-1991
Scott Norwood, Buffalo, 1988-1991
Al Del Greco, Houston-Tennessee, 1991-2000
Morten Andersen, New Orleans-Atlanta-Kansas City, 1987-2003 (current)
Adam Vinatieri, New England, 1997-2003 (current)
8 Mark Moseley, Washington-Cleveland, 1982-86
Rich Karlis, Denver-Minnesota, 1984-89

Steve Christie, Buffalo, 1992-1995
Gary Anderson, Pittsburgh-Philadelphia, 1989-1995
Gary Anderson, San Francisco-Minnesota-Tennessee, 1997-2003 (current)
David Akers, Philadelphia, 2000-03 (current)

Most Consecutive Field Goals
16 Gary Anderson, Pittsburgh-Philadelphia, 1989-1995
15 Rafael Septien, Dallas, 1978-1982
14 Mike Hollis, Jacksonville, 1996-99
John Kasay, Carolina, 1996-2003

Longest Field Goal
58 Pete Stoyanovich, AFC-FR: Miami vs. Kansas City, 1990
54 Ed Murray, NFC-D: Detroit vs. San Francisco, 1983
Steve Christie, SB: Buffalo vs. Dallas, 1993
John Carney, AFC-FR: San Diego vs. Indianapolis, 1995
53 Al Del Greco, AFC-FR: Houston vs. N.Y. Jets, 1991

Highest Field Goal Percentage, Career (10 field goals)
91.7 Martín Gramatica, Tampa Bay, 7 games (12-11)
90.9 Chuck Nelson, L.A. Rams-Minnesota, 6 games (11-10)
88.9 Mike Hollis, Jacksonville, 8 games (18-16)

SAFETIES

Most Safeties, Game
1 Bill Willis, NFC-D: Cleveland vs. N.Y. Giants, 1950
Carl Eller, NFC-D: Minnesota vs. Los Angeles, 1969
George Andrie, NFC-D: Dallas vs. Detroit, 1970
Alan Page, NFC-D: Minnesota vs. Dallas, 1971
Dwight White, SB: Pittsburgh vs. Minnesota, 1974
Reggie Harrison, SB: Pittsburgh vs. Dallas, 1975
Jim Jensen, NFC-D: Dallas vs. Los Angeles, 1976
Ted Washington, AFC: Houston vs. Pittsburgh, 1978
Randy White, NFC-D: Dallas vs. Los Angeles, 1979
Henry Waechter, SB: Chicago vs. New England, 1985
Rulon Jones, AFC-FR: Denver vs. New England, 1986
George Martin, SB: N.Y. Giants vs. Denver, 1986
D.D. Hoggard, AFC: Cleveland vs. Denver, 1987
Bruce Smith, SB: Buffalo vs. N.Y. Giants, 1990
Reggie White, NFC-FR: Philadelphia vs. New Orleans, 1992
Willie Clay, NFC-FR: Detroit vs. Green Bay, 1994
Carnell Lake, AFC-D: Pittsburgh vs. Cleveland, 1994
Reuben Davis, AFC-D: San Diego vs. Miami, 1994
Jevon Kearse, AFC-FR: Tennessee vs. Buffalo, 1999

RUSHING

ATTEMPTS

Most Attempts, Career
400 Franco Harris, Pittsburgh, 19 games
349 Emmitt Smith, Dallas, 17 games
339 Thurman Thomas, Buffalo, 21 games

Most Attempts, Game
40 Lamar Smith, AFC-FR: Miami vs. Indianapolis, 2000 (OT)
38 Ricky Bell, NFC-D: Tampa Bay vs. Philadelphia, 1979
John Riggins, SB: Washington vs. Miami, 1982
37 Lawrence McCutcheon, NFC-D: Los Angeles vs. St. Louis, 1975
John Riggins, NFC-D: Washington vs. Minnesota, 1982

YARDS GAINED

Most Yards Gained, Career
1,586 Emmitt Smith, Dallas, 17 games
1,556 Franco Harris, Pittsburgh, 19 games
1,442 Thurman Thomas, Buffalo, 21 games

Most Yards Gained, Game
248 Eric Dickerson, NFC-D: L.A. Rams vs. Dallas, 1985
209 Lamar Smith, AFC-FR: Miami vs. Indianapolis, 2000 (OT)
206 Keith Lincoln, AFC: San Diego vs. Boston, 1963

Most Games, 100 or More Yards Rushing, Career
7 Emmitt Smith, Dallas, 17 games
Terrell Davis, Denver, 8 games
6 John Riggins, Washington, 9 games
Thurman Thomas, Buffalo, 21 games
5 Franco Harris, Pittsburgh, 19 games
Marcus Allen, L.A. Raiders-Kansas City, 16 games

Most Consecutive Games, 100 or More Yards Rushing
7 Terrell Davis, Denver, 1997-98
6 John Riggins, Washington, 1982-83
4 Thurman Thomas, Buffalo, 1990-91

Longest Run From Scrimmage
90 Fred Taylor, AFC-D: Jacksonville vs. Miami, 1999 (TD)
80 Roger Craig, NFC-D: San Francisco vs. Minnesota, 1988 (TD)
Charlie Garner, AFC-FR: Oakland vs. N.Y. Jets, 2001 (TD)
78 Curtis Martin, AFC-D: New England vs. Pittsburgh, 1996 (TD)

AVERAGE GAIN

Highest Average Gain, Career (100 attempts)
5.59 Terrell Davis, Denver, 8 games (204-1,140)
5.04 Marcus Allen, L.A. Raiders-Kansas City, 16 games (267-1,347)
4.89 Eric Dickerson, L.A. Rams-Indianapolis, 7 games (148-724)

Highest Average Gain, Game (10 attempts)
15.90 Elmer Angsman, NFC: Chi. Cardinals vs. Philadelphia, 1947 (10-159)
15.85 Keith Lincoln, AFC: San Diego vs. Boston, 1963 (13-206)
11.31 Zack Crockett, AFC-FR: Indianapolis vs. San Diego, 1995 (13-147)

TOUCHDOWNS

Most Touchdowns, Career
19 Emmitt Smith, Dallas, 17 games
16 Franco Harris, Pittsburgh, 19 games
Thurman Thomas, Buffalo, 21 games
12 John Riggins, Washington, 9 games
Terrell Davis, Denver, 8 games

Most Touchdowns, Game
5 Ricky Watters, NFC-D: San Francisco vs. N.Y. Giants, 1993
3 Andy Farkas, NFC-D: Washington vs. N.Y. Giants, 1943
Otto Graham, NFC: Cleveland vs. Detroit, 1954
Tom Matte, NFC: Baltimore vs. Cleveland, 1968
Larry Schreiber, NFC-D: San Francisco vs. Dallas, 1972
Larry Csonka, AFC: Miami vs. Oakland, 1973
Franco Harris, AFC-D: Pittsburgh vs. Buffalo, 1974
John Riggins, NFC-D: Washington vs. L.A. Rams, 1983
Kenneth Davis, AFC: Buffalo vs. L.A. Raiders, 1990
Napoleon McCallum, AFC-FR: L.A. Raiders vs. Denver, 1993
Thurman Thomas, AFC: Buffalo vs. Kansas City, 1993
William Floyd, NFC-D: San Francisco vs. Chicago, 1994
Emmitt Smith, NFC: Dallas vs. Green Bay, 1995
Curtis Martin, AFC-D: New England vs. Pittsburgh, 1996
Terrell Davis, SB: Denver vs. Green Bay, 1997
Mario Bates, NFC-D: Arizona vs. Minnesota, 1998
Shaun Alexander, NFC-FR: Seattle vs. Green Bay, 2003 (OT)

Most Consecutive Games Rushing for Touchdowns
8 Emmitt Smith, Dallas, 1993-96
Thurman Thomas, Buffalo, 1992-98
7 John Riggins, Washington, 1982-84
Terrell Davis, Denver, 1996-98
5 Franco Harris, Pittsburgh, 1974-75
Franco Harris, Pittsburgh, 1977-79
Curtis Martin, New England-N.Y. Jets, 1996-98

PASSING

PASSER RATING

Highest Passer Rating, Career (150 attempts)
104.8 Bart Starr, Green Bay, 10 games
95.6 Joe Montana, San Francisco-Kansas City, 23 games
93.5 Ken Anderson, Cincinnati, 6 games

ATTEMPTS

Most Passes Attempted, Career
734 Joe Montana, San Francisco-Kansas City, 23 games

687 Dan Marino, Miami, 18 games
651 John Elway, Denver, 22 games

Most Passes Attempted, Game
65 Steve Young, NFC-D: San Francisco vs. Green Bay, 1995
64 Bernie Kosar, AFC-D: Cleveland vs. N.Y. Jets, 1986 (OT)
Dan Marino, AFC-FR: Miami vs. Buffalo, 1995
58 Jim Kelly, SB: Buffalo vs. Washington, 1991

COMPLETIONS

Most Passes Completed, Career
460 Joe Montana, San Francisco-Kansas City, 23 games
385 Dan Marino, Miami, 18 games
379 Brett Favre, Green Bay, 19 games

Most Passes Completed, Game
36 Warren Moon, AFC-FR: Houston vs. Buffalo, 1992 (OT)
33 Dan Fouts, AFC-D: San Diego vs. Miami, 1981 (OT)
Bernie Kosar, AFC-D: Cleveland vs. N.Y. Jets, 1986 (OT)
Dan Marino, AFC-FR: Miami vs. Buffalo, 1995
32 Neil Lomax, NFC-FR: St. Louis vs. Green Bay, 1982
Danny White, NFC-FR: Dallas vs. L.A. Rams, 1983
Warren Moon, AFC-D: Houston vs. Kansas City, 1993
Neil O'Donnell, AFC: Pittsburgh vs. San Diego, 1994
Steve Young, NFC-D: San Francisco vs. Green Bay, 1995
Tom Brady, AFC-D: New England vs. Oakland, 2001 (OT)
Tom Brady, SB: New England vs. Carolina, 2003

COMPLETION PERCENTAGE

Highest Completion Percentage, Career (150 attempts)
66.3 Ken Anderson, Cincinnati, 6 games (166-110)
64.3 Warren Moon, Houston-Minnesota, 10 games (403-259)
64.2 Rich Gannon, Minnesota-Kanas City-Oakland, 10 games (240-154)

Highest Completion Percentage, Game (15 completions)
88.0 Phil Simms, SB: N.Y. Giants vs. Denver, 1986 (25-22)
86.7 Joe Montana, NFC: San Francisco vs. L.A. Rams, 1989 (30-26)
84.6 Peyton Manning, AFC-FR: Indianapolis vs. Denver, 2003 (26-22)

YARDS GAINED

Most Yards Gained, Career
5,772 Joe Montana, San Francisco-Kansas City, 23 games
4,964 John Elway, Denver, 22 games
4,686 Brett Favre, Green Bay, 19 games

Most Yards Gained, Game
489 Bernie Kosar, AFC-D: Cleveland vs. N.Y. Jets, 1986 (OT)
433 Dan Fouts, AFC-D: San Diego vs. Miami, 1981 (OT)
429 Kelly Holcomb, AFC-FR: Cleveland vs. Pittsburgh, 2002

Most Games, 300 or More Yards Passing, Career
6 Joe Montana, San Francisco-Kansas City, 23 games
5 Dan Fouts, San Diego, 7 games
4 Warren Moon, Houston-Minnesota, 10 games
Troy Aikman, Dallas, 16 games
Dan Marino, Miami, 18 games
John Elway, Denver, 22 games
Kurt Warner, St. Louis, 7 games

Most Consecutive Games, 300 or More Yards Passing
4 Dan Fouts, San Diego, 1979-1981
3 Jim Kelly, Buffalo, 1989-1990
Warren Moon, Houston, 1991-93
2 Daryle Lamonica, Oakland, 1968
Ken Anderson, Cincinnati, 1981-82
Terry Bradshaw, Pittsburgh, 1979-1982
Joe Montana, San Francisco, 1983-84
Dan Marino, Miami, 1984
Troy Aikman, Dallas, 1994
Steve Young, San Francisco, 1994-95
Kurt Warner, St. Louis, 1999-2000
Peyton Manning, Indianapolis, 2003

Longest Pass Completion
96 Trent Dilfer (to Sharpe), AFC: Baltimore vs. Oakland, 2000 (TD)
94 Troy Aikman (to Harper), NFC-D: Dallas vs. Green Bay, 1994 (TD)
93 Daryle Lamonica (to Dubenion), AFC-D: Buffalo vs. Boston, 1963 (TD)

AVERAGE GAIN

Highest Average Gain, Career (150 attempts)
8.45 Joe Theismann, Washington, 10 games (211-1,782)
8.43 Jim Plunkett, Oakland/L.A.Raiders, 10 games (272-2,293)
8.41 Terry Bradshaw, Pittsburgh, 19 games (456-3,833)

Highest Average Gain, Game (20 attempts)
14.71 Terry Bradshaw, SB: Pittsburgh vs. Los Angeles, 1979 (21-309)
14.50 Peyton Manning, AFC-FR: Indianapolis vs. Denver, 2003 (26-377)
13.33 Bob Waterfield, NFC-D: Los Angeles vs. Chi. Bears, 1950 (21-280)

TOUCHDOWNS

Most Touchdown Passes, Career
45 Joe Montana, San Francisco-Kansas City, 23 games
33 Brett Favre, Green Bay, 19 games
32 Dan Marino, Miami, 18 games

Most Touchdown Passes, Game
6 Daryle Lamonica, AFC-D: Oakland vs. Houston, 1969
Steve Young, SB: San Francisco vs. San Diego, 1994
5 Sid Luckman, NFC: Chi. Bears vs. Washington, 1943
Daryle Lamonica, AFC-D: Oakland vs. Kansas City, 1968
Joe Montana, SB: San Francisco vs. Denver, 1989
Kurt Warner, NFC-D: St. Louis vs. Minnesota, 1999
Kerry Collins, NFC: N.Y. Giants vs. Minnesota, 2000
Peyton Manning, AFC-FR: Indianapolis vs. Denver, 2003
4 Otto Graham, NFC: Cleveland vs. Los Angeles, 1950
Tobin Rote, NFC: Detroit vs. Cleveland, 1957
Bart Starr, NFC: Green Bay vs. Dallas, 1966
Ken Stabler, AFC-D: Oakland vs. Miami, 1974
Roger Staubach, NFC: Dallas vs. Los Angeles, 1975
Terry Bradshaw, SB: Pittsburgh vs. Dallas, 1978
Don Strock, AFC-D: Miami vs. San Diego, 1981 (OT)
Lynn Dickey, NFC-FR: Green Bay vs. St. Louis, 1982
Dan Marino, AFC: Miami vs. Pittsburgh, 1984
Phil Simms, NFC-D: N.Y. Giants vs. San Francisco, 1986
Doug Williams, SB: Washington vs. Denver, 1987
Jim Kelly, AFC-D: Buffalo vs. Cleveland, 1989
Joe Montana, NFC-D: San Francisco vs. Minnesota, 1989
Warren Moon, AFC-FR: Houston vs. Buffalo, 1992 (OT)
Frank Reich, AFC-FR: Buffalo vs. Houston, 1992 (OT)
Troy Aikman, SB: Dallas vs. Buffalo, 1992
Jeff George, NFC-D: Minnesota vs. St. Louis, 1999
Aaron Brooks, NFC-FR: New Orleans vs. St. Louis, 2000
Kerry Collins, NFC-FR: N.Y. Giants vs. San Francisco, 2002

Most Consecutive Games, Touchdown Passes
15 Brett Favre, Green Bay, 1995-2003 (current)
13 Dan Marino, Miami, 1983-1995
10 Ken Stabler, Oakland, 1973-77
Joe Montana, San Francisco-Kansas City, 1988-1993

HAD INTERCEPTED

Lowest Percentage, Passes Had Intercepted, Career (150 attempts)
1.35 Tom Brady, New England, 6 games (223-3)
1.41 Bart Starr, Green Bay, 10 games (213-3)
2.15 Phil Simms, N.Y. Giants, 10 games (279-6)

Most Attempts Without Interception, Game
54 Neil O'Donnell, AFC: Pittsburgh vs. San Diego, 1994
48 Warren Moon, AFC-FR: Houston vs. Pittsburgh, 1989 (OT)
Randall Cunningham, NFC: Minnesota vs. Atlanta, 1998 (OT)
47 Daryle Lamonica, AFC: Oakland vs. N.Y. Jets, 1968

Most Passes Had Intercepted, Career
28 Jim Kelly, Buffalo, 17 games

26 Terry Bradshaw, Pittsburgh, 19 games
24 Dan Marino, Miami, 18 games

Most Passes Had Intercepted, Game

6 Frank Filchock, NFC: N.Y. Giants vs. Chi. Bears, 1946
Bobby Layne, NFC: Detroit vs. Cleveland, 1954
Norm Van Brocklin, NFC: Los Angeles vs. Cleveland, 1955
Brett Favre, NFC-D: Green Bay vs. St. Louis, 2001
5 Frank Filchock, NFC: Washington vs. Chi. Bears, 1940
George Blanda, AFC: Houston vs. San Diego, 1961
George Blanda, AFC: Houston vs. Dall. Texans, 1962 (OT)
Y.A. Tittle, NFC: N.Y. Giants vs. Chicago, 1963
Mike Phipps, AFC-D: Cleveland vs. Miami, 1972
Dan Pastorini, AFC: Houston vs. Pittsburgh, 1978
Dan Fouts, AFC-D: San Diego vs. Houston, 1979
Tommy Kramer, NFC-D: Minnesota vs. Philadelphia, 1980
Dan Fouts, AFC-D: San Diego vs. Miami, 1982
Richard Todd, AFC: N.Y. Jets vs Miami, 1982
Gary Danielson, NFC-D: Detroit vs. San Francisco, 1983
Jay Schroeder, AFC: L.A. Raiders vs. Buffalo, 1990
Rich Gannon, SB: Oakland vs. Tampa Bay, 2002
4 By many players

PASS RECEIVING

RECEPTIONS

Most Receptions, Career

151 Jerry Rice, San Francisco-Oakland, 28 games
87 Michael Irvin, Dallas, 16 games
85 Andre Reed, Buffalo, 21 games

Most Receptions, Game

13 Kellen Winslow, AFC-D: San Diego vs. Miami, 1981 (OT)
Thurman Thomas, AFC-D: Buffalo vs. Cleveland, 1989
Shannon Sharpe, AFC-FR: Denver vs. L.A. Raiders, 1993
Chad Morton, NFC-D: New Orleans vs. Minnesota, 2000
12 Raymond Berry, NFC: Baltimore vs. N.Y. Giants, 1958
Michael Irvin, NFC: Dallas vs. San Francisco, 1994
11 Dante Lavelli, NFC: Cleveland vs. Los Angeles, 1950
Dan Ross, SB: Cincinnati vs. San Francisco, 1981
Franco Harris, AFC-FR: Pittsburgh vs. San Diego, 1982
Steve Watson, AFC-D: Denver vs. Pittsburgh, 1984
John L. Williams, AFC-D: Seattle vs. Cincinnati, 1988
Jerry Rice, SB: San Francisco vs. Cincinnati, 1988
Ernest Givins, AFC-FR: Houston vs. Pittsburgh, 1989 (OT)
Amp Lee, NFC-D: Minnesota vs. Chicago, 1994
Jay Novacek, NFC-D: Dallas vs. Green Bay, 1994
O.J. McDuffie, AFC-FR: Miami vs. Buffalo, 1995
Jerry Rice, NFC-C: San Francisco vs. Green Bay, 1995
Hines Ward, AFC-FR: Pittsburgh vs. Cleveland, 2002

Most Consecutive Games, Pass Receptions

28 Jerry Rice, San Francisco-Oakland, 1985-2002 (current)
22 Drew Pearson, Dallas, 1973-1983
18 Paul Warfield, Cleveland-Miami, 1964-1974
Cliff Branch, Oakland/L.A. Raiders, 1974-1983
Thurman Thomas, Buffalo, 1989-1998
Shannon Sharpe, Denver-Baltimore-Denver, 1991-2003 (current)

YARDS GAINED

Most Yards Gained, Career

2,245 Jerry Rice, San Francisco-Oakland, 28 games
1,315 Michael Irvin, Dallas, 16 games
1,289 Cliff Branch, Oakland/L.A. Raiders, 22 games

Most Yards Gained, Game

240 Eric Moulds, AFC-FR: Buffalo vs. Miami, 1998
227 Anthony Carter, NFC-D: Minnesota vs. San Francisco, 1987
215 Jerry Rice, SB: San Francisco vs. Cincinnati, 1988

Most Games, 100 or More Yards Receiving, Career

8 Jerry Rice, San Francisco-Oakland, 28 games
6 Michael Irvin, Dallas, 16 games
5 John Stallworth, Pittsburgh, 18 games
Andre Reed, Buffalo, 21 games

Most Consecutive Games, 100 or More Yards Receiving, Career

3 Tom Fears, Los Angeles, 1950-51
Jerry Rice, San Francisco, 1988-89
Randy Moss, Minnesota, 1999-2000
2 By many players

Longest Reception

96 Shannon Sharpe (from Dilfer), AFC: Baltimore vs. Oakland, 2000 (TD)
94 Alvin Harper (from Aikman), NFC-D: Dallas vs. Green Bay, 1994 (TD)
93 Elbert Dubenion (from Lamonica), AFC-D: Buffalo vs. Boston, 1963 (TD)

AVERAGE GAIN

Highest Average Gain, Career (20 receptions)

27.3 Alvin Harper, Dallas, 10 games (24-655)
23.7 Willie Gault, Chicago-L.A. Raiders, 12 games (21-497)
22.8 Harold Jackson, L.A. Rams-New England-Minnesota-Seattle, 14 games (24-548)

Highest Average Gain, Game (3 receptions)

46.3 Harold Jackson, NFC: Los Angeles vs. Minnesota, 1974 (3-139)
42.7 Billy Cannon, AFC: Houston vs. L.A. Chargers, 1960 (3-128)
42.0 Lenny Moore, NFC: Baltimore vs. N.Y. Giants, 1959 (3-126)

TOUCHDOWNS

Most Touchdowns, Career

22 Jerry Rice, San Francisco-Oakland, 28 games
12 John Stallworth, Pittsburgh, 18 games
10 Fred Biletnikoff, Oakland, 19 games
Antonio Freeman, Green Bay-Philadelphia-Green Bay, 16 games

Most Touchdowns, Game

3 Tom Fears, NFC-D: Los Angeles vs. Chi. Bears, 1950
Gary Collins, NFC: Cleveland vs. Baltimore, 1964
Fred Biletnikoff, AFC-D: Oakland vs. Kansas City, 1968
Preston Pearson, NFC: Dallas vs. Los Angeles, 1975
Dave Casper, AFC-D: Oakland vs. Baltimore, 1977 (OT)
Alvin Garrett, NFC-FR: Washington vs. Detroit, 1982
Jerry Rice, NFC-D: San Francisco vs. Minnesota, 1988
Jerry Rice, SB: San Francisco vs. Denver, 1989
Andre Reed, AFC-FR: Buffalo vs. Houston, 1992 (OT)
Sterling Sharpe, NFC-FR: Green Bay vs. Detroit, 1993
Jerry Rice, SB: San Francisco vs. San Diego, 1994
Willie Jackson, NFC-FR: New Orleans vs. St. Louis, 2000
Amani Toomer, NFC-FR: N.Y. Giants vs. San Francisco, 2002

Most Consecutive Games, Touchdown Passes Caught

8 John Stallworth, Pittsburgh, 1978-1983
5 James Lofton, Green Bay-Buffalo, 1982-1990
Randy Moss, Minnesota, 1998-2000
Antonio Freeman, Green Bay, 1997-2001
4 Lynn Swann, Pittsburgh, 1978-79
Harold Carmichael, Philadelphia, 1978-1980
Fred Solomon, San Francisco, 1983-84
Jerry Rice, San Francisco, 1988-89
John Taylor, San Francisco, 1988-89

INTERCEPTIONS BY

Most Interceptions, Career

9 Charlie Waters, Dallas, 25 games
Bill Simpson, Los Angeles-Buffalo, 11 games
Ronnie Lott, San Francisco-L.A. Raiders, 20 games
8 Lester Hayes, Oakland/L.A. Raiders, 13 games
7 Willie Brown, Oakland, 17 games
Dennis Thurman, Dallas, 14 games

Most Interceptions, Game

4 Vernon Perry, AFC-D: Houston vs. San Diego, 1979
3 Joe Laws, NFC: Green Bay vs. N.Y. Giants, 1944
Charlie Waters, NFC-D: Dallas vs. Chicago, 1977
Rod Martin, SB: Oakland vs. Philadelphia, 1980
Dennis Thurman, NFC-D: Dallas vs. Green Bay, 1982

A.J. Duhe, AFC: Miami vs. N.Y. Jets, 1982
Ty Law, AFC: New England vs. Indianapolis, 2003
Ricky Manning Jr., NFC: Carolina vs. Philadelphia, 2003
2 By many players

Most Consecutive Games, Interceptions
4 Aeneas Williams, Arizona-St. Louis, 1998-2001
3 By many players. Last time:
Duane Starks, Baltimore, 2000-01

YARDS GAINED

Most Yards Gained, Career
196 Willie Brown, Oakland, 17 games
187 Ronnie Lott, San Francisco-L.A.-Raiders, 20 games
160 George Teague, Green Bay-Dallas-Miami-Dallas, 12 games

Most Yards Gained, Game
108 Darrien Gordon, SB: Denver vs. Atlanta, 1998
101 George Teague, NFC-FR: Green Bay vs. Detroit, 1993
98 Darrol Ray, AFC-FR: N.Y. Jets vs. Cincinnati, 1982
Tory James, AFC-D: Oakland vs. Miami, 2000

Longest Return
101 George Teague, NFC-FR: Green Bay vs. Detroit, 1993 (TD)
98 Darrol Ray, AFC-FR: N.Y. Jets vs. Cincinnati, 1982 (TD)
94 LeRoy Irvin, NFC-FR: L.A. Rams vs. Dallas, 1983

TOUCHDOWNS

Most Touchdowns, Career
3 Willie Brown, Oakland, 17 games
2 Lester Hayes, Oakland/L.A. Raiders, 13 games
Ronnie Lott, San Francisco-L.A. Raiders, 20 games
Darrell Green, Washington, 18 games
Melvin Jenkins, Seattle-Detroit, 5 games
George Teague, Green Bay-Dallas-Miami-Dallas, 12 games
Aeneas Williams, Arizona-St. Louis, 6 games
Dwight Smith, Tampa Bay, 4 games

Most Touchdowns, Game
2 Aeneas Williams, NFC-D: St. Louis vs. Green Bay, 2001
Dwight Smith, SB: Tampa Bay vs. Oakland, 2002
1 By many players

PUNTING

Most Punts, Career
111 Ray Guy, Oakland/L.A. Raiders, 22 games
92 Craig Hentrich, Green Bay-Tennessee, 20 games
84 Danny White, Dallas, 18 games
Sean Landeta, N.Y. Giants-Tampa Bay-Green Bay-Philadelphia-St. Louis, 18 games

Most Punts, Game
14 Dave Jennings, AFC-D: N.Y. Jets vs. Cleveland, 1986 (OT)
12 David Lee, AFC-D: Baltimore vs. Oakland, 1977 (OT)
11 Ken Strong, NFC: N.Y. Giants vs. Chi. Bears, 1933
Jim Norton, AFC: Houston vs. Oakland, 1967
Ode Burrell, AFC-D: Houston vs. Oakland, 1969
Dale Hatcher, NFC: L.A. Rams vs. Chicago, 1985
Brad Maynard, SB: N.Y. Giants vs. Baltimore, 2000

Longest Punt
76 Ed Danowski, NFC: N.Y. Giants vs. Detroit, 1935
Mike Horan, AFC: Denver vs. Buffalo, 1991
72 Charlie Conerly, NFC-D: N.Y. Giants vs. Cleveland, 1950
Yale Lary, NFC: Detroit vs. Cleveland, 1953
71 Ray Guy, AFC: Oakland vs. San Diego, 1980

AVERAGE YARDAGE

Highest Average, Career (25 punts)
44.5 Rich Camarillo, New England, 6 games (35-1,559)
44.3 Jeff Feagles, Philadelphia-Seattle, 4 games (26-1,151)
43.4 Jerrel Wilson, Kansas City-New England, 8 games (43-1,866)

Highest Average, Game (4 punts)
56.0 Ray Guy, AFC: Oakland vs. San Diego, 1980 (4-224)
52.5 Sammy Baugh, NFC: Washington vs. Chi. Bears, 1942 (6-315)
52.0 Craig Hentrich, AFC-D: Tennessee vs. Indianapolis, 1999 (5-260)

PUNT RETURNS

Most Punt Returns, Career
34 David Meggett, N.Y. Giants-New England-N.Y. Jets, 13 games
Brian Mitchell, Washington-Philadelphia, 16 games
25 Theo Bell, Pittsburgh-Tampa Bay, 10 games
24 Darrien Gordon, San Diego-Denver-Oakland, 14 games

Most Punt Returns, Game
7 Ron Gardin, AFC-D: Baltimore vs. Cincinnati, 1970
Carl Roaches, AFC-FR: Houston vs. Oakland, 1980
Gerald McNeil, AFC-D: Cleveland vs. N.Y. Jets, 1986 (OT)
Phil McConkey, NFC-D: N.Y. Giants vs. San Francisco, 1986
David Meggett, AFC-D: New England vs. Pittsburgh, 1996
Reggie Barlow, AFC-FR: Jacksonville vs. New England, 1998
6 George McAfee, NFC-D: Chi. Bears vs. Los Angeles, 1950
Eddie Brown, NFC-D: Washington vs. Minnesota, 1976
Theo Bell, AFC: Pittsburgh vs. Houston, 1978
Eddie Brown, NFC: Los Angeles vs. Tampa Bay, 1979
John Sciarra, NFC: Philadelphia vs. Dallas, 1980
Kurt Sohn, AFC: N.Y. Jets vs. Miami, 1982
Mike Nelms, SB: Washington vs. Miami, 1982
Anthony Carter, NFC-FR: Minnesota vs. New Orleans, 1987
Desmond Howard, SB: Green Bay vs. New England, 1996
Nate Jacquet, AFC-FR: Miami vs. Seattle, 1999
Derrick Mason, AFC-FR: Tennessee vs. Baltimore, 2003
Antonio Chatman, AFC-D: Green Bay vs. Philadelphia, 2003
5 By many players

YARDS GAINED

Most Yards Gained, Career
339 Brian Mitchell, Washington-Philadelphia, 16 games
312 David Meggett, N.Y. Giants-New England-N.Y. Jets, 13 games
259 Anthony Carter, Minnesota-Detroit, 9 games

Most Yards Gained, Game
143 Anthony Carter, NFC-FR: Minnesota vs. New Orleans, 1987
141 Bob Hayes, NFC-D: Dallas vs. Cleveland, 1967
117 Desmond Howard, NFC-D: Green Bay vs. San Francisco, 1996

Longest Return
88 Jermaine Lewis, AFC-D: Baltimore vs. Pittsburgh, 2001 (TD)
84 Anthony Carter, NFC-FR: Minnesota vs. New Orleans, 1987 (TD)
81 Hugh Gallarneau, NFC-D: Chi. Bears vs. Green Bay, 1941 (TD)

AVERAGE YARDAGE

Highest Average, Career (10 returns)
15.3 Robert Brooks, Green Bay, 11 games (14-214)
15.2 Anthony Carter, Minnesota-Detroit, 9 games (17-259)
14.3 Antonio Freeman, Green Bay-Philadelphia-Green Bay, 16 games (10-143)

Highest Average Gain, Game (3 returns)
47.0 Bob Hayes, NFC-D: Dallas vs. Cleveland, 1967 (3-141)
33.0 Jermaine Lewis, AFC-D: Baltimore vs. Pittsburgh, 2001 (3-99)
29.0 George (Butch) Byrd, AFC: Buffalo vs. San Diego, 1965 (3-87)

POSTSEASON RECORDS

TOUCHDOWNS

Most Touchdowns

1 Hugh Gallarneau, NFC-D: Chicago Bears vs. Green Bay, 1941
Bosh Pritchard, NFC-D: Philadelphia vs. Pittsburgh, 1947
Charley Trippi, NFC: Chicago Cardinals vs. Philadelphia, 1947
Verda (Vitamin T) Smith, NFC-D: Los Angeles vs. Detroit, 1952
George (Butch) Byrd, AFC: Buffalo vs. San Diego, 1965
Golden Richards, NFC: Dallas vs. Minnesota, 1973
Wes Chandler, AFC-D: San Diego vs. Miami, 1981 (OT)
Shaun Gayle, NFC-D: Chicago vs. N.Y. Giants, 1985
Anthony Carter, NFC-FR: Minnesota vs. New Orleans, 1987
Darrell Green, NFC-D: Washington vs. Chicago, 1987
Antonio Freeman, NFC-FR: Green Bay vs. Atlanta, 1995
Desmond Howard, NFC-D: Green Bay vs. San Francisco, 1996
Jermaine Lewis, AFC-D: Baltimore vs. Pittsburgh, 2001
Troy Brown, AFC: New England vs. Pittsburgh, 2001
Antwaan Randle El, AFC-FR: Pittsburgh vs. Cleveland, 2002

KICKOFF RETURNS

Most Kickoff Returns, Career

36 Brian Mitchell, Washington-Philadelphia, 16 games
31 Kevin Williams, Dallas-Buffalo, 12 games
29 Fulton Walker, Miami-L.A. Raiders, 10 games

Most Kickoff Returns, Game

8 Marc Logan, AFC-D: Miami vs. Buffalo, 1990
Andre Coleman, SB: San Diego vs. San Francisco, 1994
Marcus Knight, SB: Oakland vs. Tampa Bay, 2002
7 Don Bingham, NFC: Chi. Bears vs. N.Y. Giants, 1956
Reggie Brown, NFC-FR: Atlanta vs. Minnesota, 1982
David Verser, AFC-FR: Cincinnati vs. N.Y. Jets, 1982
Del Rodgers, NFC-D: Green Bay vs. Dallas, 1982
Henry Ellard, NFC-D: L.A. Rams vs. Washington, 1983
Stephen Starring, SB: New England vs. Chicago, 1985
Darick Holmes, AFC-D: Buffalo vs. Pittsburgh, 1995
Antonio Freeman, NFC: Green Bay vs. Dallas, 1995
Roell Preston, NFC-FR: Green Bay vs. San Francisco, 1998
Robert Tate, NFC-D: Minnesota vs. St. Louis, 1999
Fred McAfee, NFC-D: New Orleans vs. Minnesota, 2000
Michael Bates, NFC-FR: Dallas vs. Carolina, 2003
Dante Hall, AFC-D: Kansas City vs. Indianapolis, 2003
6 By many players

YARDS GAINED

Most Yards Gained, Career

875 Brian Mitchell, Washington-Philadelphia, 16 games
677 Fulton Walker, Miami-L.A. Raiders, 10 games
632 Kevin Williams, Dallas-Buffalo, 12 games

Most Yards Gained, Game

244 Andre Coleman, SB: San Diego vs. San Francisco, 1994
210 Tim Dwight, SB: Atlanta vs. Denver, 1998
208 Dante Hall, AFC-D: Kansas City vs. Indianapolis, 2003

Longest Return

100 Brian Mitchell, NFC-D: Washington vs. Tampa Bay, 1999 (TD)
99 Desmond Howard, SB: Green Bay vs. New England, 1996 (TD)
98 Fulton Walker, SB: Miami vs. Washington, 1982 (TD)
Andre Coleman, SB: San Diego vs. San Francisco, 1994 (TD)

AVERAGE YARDAGE

Highest Average, Career (10 returns)

34.3 Tim Dwight, Atlanta, 3 games (10-343)
30.1 Carl Garrett, Oakland, 5 games (16-481)
30.0 Reggie Barlow, Jacksonville, 8 games (12-360)

Highest Average, Game (3 returns)

56.7 Les (Speedy) Duncan, NFC-D: Washington vs. San Francisco, 1971 (3-170)
51.3 Ed Podolak, AFC-D: Kansas City vs. Miami, 1971 (OT) (3-154)
49.0 Les (Speedy) Duncan, AFC: San Diego vs. Buffalo, 1964 (3-147)

TOUCHDOWNS

Most Touchdowns, Career

2 Ron Dixon, N.Y. Giants, 4 games
1 By many players

Most Touchdowns, Game

1 Vic Washington, NFC-D: San Francisco vs. Dallas, 1972
Nat Moore, AFC-D: Miami vs. Oakland, 1974
Marshall Johnson, AFC-D: Baltimore vs. Oakland, 1977 (OT)
Fulton Walker, SB: Miami vs. Washington, 1982
Stanford Jennings, SB: Cincinnati vs. San Francisco, 1988
Eric Metcalf, AFC-D: Cleveland vs. Buffalo, 1989
Andre Coleman, SB: San Diego vs. San Francisco, 1994
Desmond Howard, SB: Green Bay vs. New England, 1996
Chuck Levy, NFC: San Franisco vs. Green Bay, 1997
Tim Dwight, SB: Atlanta vs. Denver, 1998
Kevin Dyson, AFC-FR: Tennessee vs. Buffalo, 1999
Charlie Rogers, AFC-FR: Seattle vs. Miami, 1999
Brian Mitchell, NFC-D: Washington vs. Tampa Bay, 1999
Tony Horne, NFC-D: St. Louis vs. Minnesota, 1999
Derrick Mason, AFC: Tennessee vs. Jacksonville, 1999
Ron Dixon, NFC-D: N.Y. Giants vs. Philadelphia, 2000; SB: N.Y. Giants vs. Baltimore, 2000
Jermaine Lewis, SB: Baltimore vs. N.Y. Giants, 2000
Dante Hall, AFC-D: Kansas City vs. Indianapolis, 2003

FUMBLES

Most Fumbles, Career

16 Warren Moon, Houston-Minnesota, 10 games
14 John Elway, Denver, 22 games
13 Tony Dorsett, Dallas, 17 games

Most Fumbles, Game

5 Warren Moon, AFC-D: Houston vs. Kansas City, 1993
4 Brian Sipe, AFC-D: Cleveland vs. Oakland, 1980
Randall Cunningham, NFC-FR: Minnesota vs. N.Y. Giants, 1997
3 By many players

RECOVERIES

Most Own Fumbles Recovered, Career

8 Warren Moon, Houston-Minnesota, 10 games
7 John Elway, Denver, 22 games
6 Jim Kelly, Buffalo, 17 games

Most Opponents' Fumbles Recovered, Career

4 Cliff Harris, Dallas, 21 games
Harvey Martin, Dallas, 22 games
Ted Hendricks, Baltimore-Oakland/L.A. Raiders, 21 games
Alvin Walton, Washington, 9 games
Monte Coleman, Washington, 21 games
Dave Thomas, Dallas-Jacksonville-N.Y. Giants, 13 games
3 Paul Krause, Minnesota, 19 games
Jack Lambert, Pittsburgh, 18 games
Fred Dryer, Los Angeles, 14 games
Charlie Waters, Dallas, 25 games
Jack Ham, Pittsburgh, 16 games
Mike Hegman, Dallas, 16 games
Tom Jackson, Denver, 10 games
Rich Milot, Washington, 13 games
Mike Singletary, Chicago, 12 games
Darryl Grant, Washington, 16 games

Wes Hopkins, Philadelphia, 3 games
Wilber Marshall, Chicago-Washington, 15 games
Tyrone Braxton, Denver-Miami-Denver, 19 games
Neil Smith, Kansas City-Denver, 16 games
Tony Brackens, Jacksonville, 7 games
Phil Hansen, Buffalo, 14 games
Carnell Lake, Pittsburgh-Jacksonville-Baltimore, 17 games
Jason Gildon, Pittsburgh, 13 games
2 By many players

Most Fumbles Recovered, Game, Own and Opponents'
3 Jack Lambert, AFC: Pittsburgh vs. Oakland, 1975 (3 opp)
Ron Jaworski, NFC-FR: Philadelphia vs. N.Y. Giants, 1981 (3 own)
2 By many players

YARDS GAINED
Longest Return
93 Andy Russell, AFC-D: Pittsburgh vs. Baltimore, 1975 (opp, TD)
79 Neil Smith, AFC-D: Denver vs. Miami, 1998 (opp, TD)
64 Leon Lett, SB: Dallas vs. Buffalo, 1992 (opp)

TOUCHDOWNS
Most Touchdowns
1 By many players

COMBINED NET YARDS GAINED
Rushing, receiving, interception returns, punt returns, kickoff returns, and fumble returns.

ATTEMPTS
Most Attempts, Career
454 Franco Harris, Pittsburgh, 19 games
417 Thurman Thomas, Buffalo, 21 games
397 Emmitt Smith, Dallas, 17 games

Most Attempts, Game
43 Lamar Smith, AFC-FR: Miami vs. Indianapolis, 2000 (OT)
42 Curtis Martin, AFC-D: N.Y. Jets vs. Jacksonville, 1998
40 Lawrence McCutcheon, NFC-D: Los Angeles vs. St. Louis, 1975

YARDS GAINED
Most Yards Gained, Career
2,289 Jerry Rice, San Francisco-Oakland, 28 games
2,124 Thurman Thomas, Buffalo, 21 games
2,060 Franco Harris, Pittsburgh, 19 games

Most Yards Gained, Game
350 Ed Podolak, AFC-D: Kansas City vs. Miami, 1971 (OT)
329 Keith Lincoln, AFC: San Diego vs. Boston, 1963
285 Bob Hayes, NFC-D: Dallas vs. Cleveland, 1967

SACKS
Sacks have been compiled since 1982.

Most Sacks, Career
14.5 Bruce Smith, Buffalo, 20 games
12.0 Reggie White, Philadelphia-Green Bay, 19 games
11.5 Willie McGinest, New England, 13 games

Most Sacks, Game
3.5 Rich Milot, NFC-D: Washington vs. Chicago, 1984
Richard Dent, NFC-D: Chicago vs. N.Y. Giants, 1985
3.0 Richard Dent, NFC-D: Chicago vs. Washington, 1984
Garin Veris, AFC-FR: New England vs. N.Y. Jets, 1985
Gary Jeter, NFC-D: L.A. Rams vs. Dallas, 1985
Carl Hairston, AFC-D: Cleveland vs. N.Y. Jets, 1986 (OT)
Charles Mann, NFC-D: Washington vs. Chicago, 1987
Kevin Greene, NFC-FR: L.A. Rams vs. Minnesota, 1988
Greg Townsend, AFC-D: L.A. Raiders vs. Cincinnati, 1990
Wilber Marshall, NFC: Washington vs. Detroit, 1991
Fred Stokes, NFC-FR: Washington vs. Minnesota, 1992
Pierce Holt, NFC-D: San Francisco vs. Washington, 1992
Tony Casillas, NFC: Dallas vs. San Francisco, 1992
Gerald Williams, AFC-FR: Pittsburgh vs. Kansas City, 1993
Chad Brown, AFC-FR: Pittsburgh vs. Indianapolis, 1996
Reggie White, SB: Green Bay vs. New England, 1996
Warren Sapp, NFC-D: Tampa Bay vs. Green Bay, 1997
Trace Armstrong, AFC-FR: Miami vs. Seattle, 1999
Michael McCrary, AFC-FR: Baltimore vs. Denver, 2000
Willie McGinest, AFC-D: New England vs. Tennessee, 2003
2.5 Lyle Alzado, AFC-D: L.A. Raiders vs. Pittsburgh, 1983
Jacob Green, AFC-FR: Seattle vs. L.A. Raiders, 1984
Larry Roberts, NFC-D: San Francisco vs. Minnesota, 1988
Leslie O'Neal, AFC-FR: San Diego vs. Kansas City, 1992
Bruce Smith, AFC-FR: Buffalo vs. Tennessee, 1999
Jarvis Green, AFC: New England vs. Indianapolis, 2003

TEAM RECORDS

GAMES, VICTORIES, DEFEATS
Most Seasons Participating in Postseason Games
27 Dallas, 1966-1973, 1975-1983, 1985, 1991-96, 1998-99, 2003
26 N.Y. Giants, 1933-35, 1938-39, 1941, 1943-44, 1946, 1950, 1956, 1958-59, 1961-63, 1981, 1984-86, 1989-1990, 1993, 1997, 2000, 2002
Cleveland/L.A./St. Louis Rams, 1945, 1949-1952, 1955, 1967, 1969, 1973-1980, 1983-86, 1988-89, 1999-2001, 2003
24 Cleveland, 1950-55, 1957-58, 1964-65, 1967-69, 1971-72, 1980, 1982, 1985-89, 1994, 2002

Most Consecutive Seasons Participating in Postseason Games
9 Dallas, 1975-1983
8 Dallas, 1966-1973
Pittsburgh, 1972-79
Los Angeles, 1973-1980
San Francisco, 1983-1990
7 Houston, 1987-1993
San Francisco, 1992-98

Most Games
54 Dallas, 1966-1973, 1975-1983, 1985, 1991-96, 1998-99, 2003
43 Oakland/L.A. Raiders, 1967-1970, 1972-77, 1980, 1982-85, 1990-91, 1993, 2000-02
42 San Francisco, 1957, 1970-72, 1981, 1983-1990, 1992-98, 2001-02

Most Games Won
32 Dallas, 1967, 1970-73, 1975, 1977-78, 1980-82, 1991-96
25 Oakland/L.A. Raiders, 1967-1970, 1973-77, 1980, 1982-83, 1990, 1993, 2000-02
San Francisco, 1970-71, 1981, 1983-84, 1988-1990, 1992-94, 1996-98, 2002
24 Green Bay, 1936, 1939, 1944, 1961-62, 1965-67, 1982, 1993-97, 2001, 2003

Most Consecutive Games Won
9 Green Bay, 1961-62, 1965-67
7 Pittsburgh, 1974-76
San Francisco, 1988-1990
Dallas, 1992-94
Denver, 1997-98
6 Miami, 1972-73
Pittsburgh, 1978-79
Washington, 1982-83
New England, 2001, 2003 (current)

Most Games Lost
23 Minnesota, 1968-1971, 1973-78, 1980, 1982, 1987-89, 1992-94, 1996-2000
L.A./St. Louis Rams, 1949-1950, 1952, 1955, 1967, 1969, 1973-1980, 1983-86, 1988-89, 2000-01, 2003

22 Dallas, 1966-1970, 1972-73, 1975-76, 1978-1983, 1985, 1991, 1994, 1996, 1998-99, 2003
21 N.Y. Giants, 1993, 1935, 1939, 1941, 1943-44, 1946, 1950, 1958-59, 1961-63, 1981, 1984-85, 1989, 1993, 1997, 2000, 2002

Most Consecutive Games Lost

6 N.Y. Giants, 1939, 1941, 1943-44, 1946, 1950
Cleveland, 1969, 1971-72, 1980, 1982, 1985
Minnesota, 1988-89, 1992-94, 1996
Detroit, 1991, 1993-95, 1997, 1999 (current)
5 N.Y. Giants, 1958-59, 1961-63
Los Angeles, 1952, 1955, 1967, 1969, 1973
Denver, 1977-79, 1983-84
Baltimore/Indianapolis, 1971, 1975-77, 1987
Philadelphia, 1980-81, 1988-1990
Indianapolis, 1995-96, 1999-2000, 2002
Kansas City, 1993-95, 1997, 2003 (current)
Seattle, 1984, 1987-88, 1999, 2003 (current)
4 Washington, 1972-74, 1976
Miami, 1974, 1978-79, 1981
Chi. Cardinals/St. Louis, 1948, 1974-75, 1982
Boston/New England, 1963, 1976, 1978, 1982
New Orleans, 1987, 1990-92
Buffalo, 1995-96, 1998-99 (current)
Dallas, 1996, 1998-99, 2003 (current)

SCORING

Most Points, Game

73 NFC: Chi. Bears vs. Washington, 1940
62 AFC-D: Jacksonville vs. Miami, 1999
59 NFC: Detroit vs. Cleveland, 1957

Most Points, Both Teams, Game

95 NFC-FR: Philadelphia (58) vs. Detroit (37), 1995
86 NFC-D: St. Louis (49) vs. Minnesota (37), 1999
79 AFC-D: San Diego (41) vs. Miami (38), 1981 (OT)
AFC-FR: Buffalo (41) vs. Houston (38), 1992 (OT)

Fewest Points, Both Teams, Game

5 NFC-D: Detroit (0) vs. Dallas (5), 1970
7 NFC: Chi. Cardinals (0) vs. Philadelphia (7), 1948
9 NFC: Tampa Bay (0) vs. Los Angeles (9), 1979

Largest Margin of Victory, Game

73 NFC: Chi. Bears vs. Washington, 1940 (73-0)
55 AFC-D: Jacksonville vs. Miami, 1999 (62-7)
49 AFC-D: Oakland vs. Houston, 1969 (56-7)

Most Points, Shutout Victory, Game

73 NFC: Chi. Bears vs. Washington, 1940
41 NFC: N.Y. Giants vs. Minnesota, 2000
AFC-FR: N.Y. Jets vs. Indianapolis, 2002
38 NFC-D: Dallas vs. Tampa Bay, 1981

Most Points Overcome to Win Game

32 AFC-FR: Buffalo vs. Houston, 1992 (trailed 3-35, won 41-38) (OT)
24 NFC-FR: San Francisco vs. N.Y. Giants, 2002 (trailed 14-38, won 39-38)
20 NFC-D: Detroit vs. San Francisco, 1957 (trailed 7-27, won 31-27)

Most Points, Each Half

1st: 41 AFC: Buffalo vs. L.A. Raiders, 1990
AFC-D: Jacksonville vs. Miami, 1999
38 NFC-D: Washington vs. L.A. Rams, 1983
NFC-FR: Philadelphia vs. Detroit, 1995
35 NFC: Cleveland vs. Detroit, 1954
AFC-D: Oakland vs. Houston, 1969
SB: Washington vs. Denver, 1987
2nd: 45 NFC: Chi. Bears vs. Washington, 1940
35 AFC-FR: Buffalo vs. Houston, 1992
NFC-D: St. Louis vs. Minnesota, 1999
30 SB: N.Y. Giants vs. Denver, 1986
AFC: Cleveland vs. Denver, 1987
NFC-FR: Detroit vs. Philadelphia, 1995

Most Points, Each Quarter

1st: 28 AFC-D: Oakland vs. Houston, 1969
24 AFC-D: San Diego vs. Miami, 1981
AFC-D: Jacksonville vs. Miami, 1999
21 NFC: Chi. Bears vs. Washington, 1940
AFC: San Diego vs. Boston, 1963
AFC-D: Oakland vs. Kansas City, 1968
AFC: Oakland vs. San Diego, 1980
AFC: Buffalo vs. L.A. Raiders, 1990
NFC: San Francisco vs. Dallas, 1994
2nd: 35 SB: Washington vs. Denver, 1987
31 NFC-FR: Philadelphia vs. Detroit, 1995
26 AFC-D: Pittsburgh vs. Buffalo, 1974
3rd: 28 AFC-FR: Buffalo vs. Houston, 1992
26 NFC: Chi. Bears vs. Washington, 1940
21 NFC-D: Dallas vs. Cleveland, 1967
NFC-D: Dallas vs. Tampa Bay, 1981
AFC-D: L.A. Raiders vs. Pittsburgh, 1983
SB: Chicago vs. New England, 1985
NFC-D: N.Y. Giants vs. San Francisco, 1986
AFC: Cleveland vs. Denver, 1987
AFC: Cleveland vs. Denver, 1989
NFC-D: St. Louis vs. Minnesota, 1999
4th: 27 NFC: N.Y. Giants vs. Chi. Bears, 1934
26 NFC-FR: Philadelphia vs. New Orleans, 1992
24 NFC: Baltimore vs. N.Y. Giants, 1959
OT: 6 NFC: Baltimore vs. N.Y. Giants, 1958
AFC-D: Oakland vs. Baltimore, 1977
NFC-D: L.A. Rams vs. N.Y. Giants, 1989
AFC-FR: Miami vs. Indianapolis, 2000
NFC-FR: Green Bay vs. Seattle, 2003
NFC-D: Carolina vs. St. Louis, 2003

TOUCHDOWNS

Most Touchdowns, Game

11 NFC: Chi. Bears vs. Washington, 1940
8 NFC: Cleveland vs. Detroit, 1954
NFC: Detroit vs. Cleveland, 1957
AFC-D: Oakland vs. Houston, 1969
SB: San Francisco vs. Denver, 1989
AFC-D: Jacksonville vs. Miami, 1999
7 AFC: San Diego vs. Boston, 1963
NFC-D: Dallas vs. Cleveland, 1967
NFC-D: N.Y. Giants vs. San Francisco, 1986
AFC: Buffalo vs. L.A. Raiders, 1990
SB: Dallas vs. Buffalo, 1992
SB: San Francisco vs. San Diego, 1994
NFC-FR: Philadelphia vs. Detroit, 1995
NFC-D: St. Louis vs. Minnesota, 1999

Most Touchdowns, Both Teams, Game

12 NFC-FR: Philadelphia (7) vs. Detroit (5), 1995
NFC-D: St. Louis (7) vs. Minnesota (5), 1999
11 NFC: Chi. Bears (11) vs. Washington (0), 1940
10 NFC: Detroit (8) vs. Cleveland (2), 1957
AFC-D: Miami (5) vs. San Diego (5), 1981 (OT)
AFC: Miami (6) vs. Pittsburgh (4), 1984
AFC-FR: Buffalo (5) vs. Houston (5), 1992 (OT)
SB: San Francisco (7) vs. San Diego (3), 1994
NFC-FR: San Francisco (5) vs. N.Y. Giants (5), 2002

Fewest Touchdowns, Both Teams, Game

0 NFC-D: N.Y. Giants vs. Cleveland, 1950
NFC-D: Dallas vs. Detroit, 1970
NFC: Los Angeles vs. Tampa Bay, 1979
1 NFC: Chi. Cardinals (0) vs. Philadelphia (1), 1948
NFC-D: Cleveland (0) vs. N.Y. Giants (1), 1958
AFC: San Diego (0) vs. Houston (1), 1961
AFC-D: N.Y. Jets (0) vs. Kansas City (1), 1969
NFC-D: Green Bay (0) vs. Washington (1), 1972
NFC-FR: New Orleans (0) vs. Chicago (1), 1990
NFC: N.Y. Giants (0) vs. San Francisco (1), 1990

AFC-FR: L.A. Raiders (0) vs. Kansas City (1), 1991
AFC-D: New England (0) vs. Pittsburgh (1), 1997
NFC: Tampa Bay (0) vs. St. Louis (1), 1999
AFC: Oakland (0) vs. Baltimore (1), 2000
2 In many games

POINTS AFTER TOUCHDOWN

Most (One-Point) Points After Touchdown, Game
8 NFC: Cleveland vs. Detroit, 1954
NFC: Detroit vs. Cleveland, 1957
AFC-D: Oakland vs. Houston, 1969
AFC-D: Jacksonville vs. Miami, 1999
7 NFC: Chi. Bears vs. Washington, 1940
NFC-D: Dallas vs. Cleveland, 1967
NFC-D: N.Y. Giants vs. San Francisco, 1986
SB: San Francisco vs. Denver, 1989
SB: Dallas vs. Buffalo, 1992
SB: San Francisco vs. San Diego, 1994
NFC-FR: Philadelphia vs. Detroit, 1995
NFC-D: St. Louis vs. Minnesota, 1999
6 AFC: San Diego vs. Boston, 1963
NFC-D: Washington vs. L.A. Rams, 1983
AFC: Miami vs. Pittsburgh, 1984
SB: Washington vs. Denver, 1987
AFC: Buffalo vs. L.A. Raiders, 1990
AFC-FR: L.A. Raiders vs. Denver, 1993
AFC-FR: Denver vs. Jacksonville, 1997
NFC-D: St. Louis vs. Green Bay, 2001
SB: Tampa Bay vs. Oakland, 2002

Most (One-Point) Points After Touchdown, Both Teams, Game
10 NFC: Detroit (8) vs. Cleveland (2), 1957
AFC-D: Miami (5) vs. San Diego (5), 1981 (OT)
AFC: Miami (6) vs. Pittsburgh (4), 1984
AFC-FR: Buffalo (5) vs. Houston (5), 1992 (OT)
NFC-FR: Philadelphia (7) vs. Detroit (3), 1995
9 In many games

Fewest (One-Point) Points After Touchdown, Both Teams, Game
0 NFC-D: N.Y. Giants vs. Cleveland, 1950
NFC-D: Dallas vs. Detroit, 1970
NFC: Los Angeles vs. Tampa Bay, 1979
NFC: St. Louis vs. Tampa Bay, 1999

Most Two-Point Conversions, Game
2 SB: San Diego vs. San Francisco, 1994
NFC-FR: Detroit vs. Philadelphia, 1995
NFC-FR: San Francisco vs.. N.Y. Giants, 2002
1 By many teams

FIELD GOALS

Most Field Goals, Game
5 NFC-D: Minnesota vs. San Francisco, 1987
NFC: N.Y. Giants vs. San Francisco, 1990
AFC: Buffalo vs. Miami, 1992
NFC-FR: N.Y. Giants vs. Minnesota, 1997
NFC-FR: Carolina vs. Dallas, 2003
NFC-D: St. Louis vs. Carolina, 2003 (2 OT)
AFC: New England vs. Indianapolis, 2003
4 AFC-D: Boston vs. Buffalo, 1963
AFC: Oakland vs. Houston, 1967
SB: Green Bay vs. Oakland, 1967
NFC: Washington vs. Dallas, 1972
AFC-D: Oakland vs. Pittsburgh, 1973
SB: San Francisco vs. Cincinnati, 1981
AFC-FR: New England vs. N.Y. Jets, 1985
NFC-FR: Washington vs. L.A. Rams, 1986
NFC-D: Philadelphia vs. Chicago, 1988
AFC-FR: Pittsburgh vs. Houston, 1989 (OT)
AFC-D: Pittsburgh vs. Buffalo, 1995
NFC-FR: Dallas vs. Minnesota, 1996
NFC-D: Carolina vs. Dallas, 1996
AFC-FR: Jacksonville vs. New England, 1998
AFC-D: Tennessee vs. Indianapolis, 1999
NFC-D: Philadelphia vs. Chicago, 2001
3 By many teams

Most Field Goals, Both Teams, Game
8 NFC-FR: N.Y. Giants (5) vs. Minnesota (3), 1997
NFC-D: St. Louis (5) vs. Carolina (3), 2003 (2 OT)
7 AFC-FR: Pittsburgh (4) vs. Houston (3), 1989 (OT)
NFC: N.Y. Giants (5) vs. San Francisco (2), 1990
NFC-D: Carolina (4) vs. Dallas (3), 1996
AFC-D: Tennessee (4) vs. Indianapolis (3), 1999
6 NFC-D: Minnesota (5) vs. San Francisco (1), 1987
NFC-D: Philadelphia (4) vs. Chicago (2), 1988
AFC: Buffalo (5) vs. Miami (1), 1992
NFC-FR: Carolina (5) vs. Dallas (1), 2003

Most Field Goals Attempted, Game
6 AFC: Oakland vs. Houston, 1967
NFC-D: Los Angeles vs. Dallas, 1973
AFC-D: Cleveland vs. N.Y. Jets, 1986 (OT)
NFC: N.Y. Giants vs. San Francisco, 1990
AFC: Buffalo vs. Miami, 1992
NFC-D: St. Louis vs. Carolina, 2003 (2 OT)
5 By many teams

Most Field Goals Attempted, Both Teams, Game
11 NFC-D: St. Louis (6) vs. Carolina (5), 2003 (2 OT)
9 NFC-D: Philadelphia (5) vs. Chicago (4), 1988
NFC-FR: N.Y. Giants (5) vs. Minnesota (4), 1997
8 NFC-D: Los Angeles (6) vs. Dallas (2), 1973
NFC-D: Detroit (5) vs. San Francisco (3), 1983
AFC-D: Cleveland (6) vs. N.Y. Jets (2), 1986 (OT)
NFC-D: Minnesota (5) vs. San Francisco (3), 1987
AFC-FR: Houston (4) vs. Pittsburgh (4), 1989 (OT)
NFC-FR: Chicago (4) vs. New Orleans (4), 1990
NFC: N.Y. Giants (6) vs. San Francisco (2), 1990

SAFETIES

Most Safeties, Game
1 By many teams

Most Safeties, Both Teams, Game
1 In many games

FIRST DOWNS

Most First Downs, Game
34 AFC-D: San Diego vs. Miami, 1981 (OT)
33 AFC-D: Cleveland vs. N.Y. Jets, 1986 (OT)
31 SB: San Francisco vs. Miami, 1984
NFC-D: San Francisco vs. Minnesota, 1997
NFC: N.Y. Giants vs. Minnesota, 2000

Fewest First Downs, Game
6 NFC: N.Y. Giants vs. Green Bay, 1961
AFC-D: Baltimore vs. Tennessee, 2000
7 NFC: Green Bay vs. Boston, 1936
NFC-D: Pittsburgh vs. Philadelphia, 1947
NFC: Chi. Cardinals vs. Philadelphia, 1948
NFC: Los Angeles vs. Philadelphia, 1949
NFC-D: Cleveland vs. N.Y. Giants, 1958
AFC-D: Cincinnati vs. Baltimore, 1970
NFC-D: Detroit vs. Dallas, 1970
NFC: Tampa Bay vs. Los Angeles, 1979
AFC-D: Baltimore vs. Pittsburgh, 2001
8 By many teams

Most First Downs, Both Teams, Game
59 AFC-D: San Diego (34) vs. Miami (25), 1981 (OT)
55 AFC-FR: San Diego (29) vs. Pittsburgh (26), 1982
54 AFC-FR: Buffalo (28) vs. Miami (26), 1995

Fewest First Downs, Both Teams, Game
15 NFC: Green Bay (7) vs. Boston (8), 1936
19 NFC: N.Y. Giants (9) vs. Green Bay (10), 1939
NFC: Washington (9) vs. Chi. Bears (10), 1942
20 NFC-D: Cleveland (9) vs. N.Y. Giants (11), 1950

RUSHING

Most First Downs, Rushing, Game

19 NFC-FR: Dallas vs. Los Angeles, 1980
18 AFC-D: Miami vs. Cincinnati, 1973
AFC: Miami vs. Oakland, 1973
AFC-D: Pittsburgh vs. Buffalo, 1974
AFC-FR: Buffalo vs. Miami, 1995
AFC-FR: Denver vs. Jacksonville, 1997
17 AFC-D: Cincinnati vs. Seattle, 1988
AFC: Buffalo vs. Kansas City, 1993

Fewest First Downs, Rushing, Game

0 NFC: Los Angeles vs. Philadelphia, 1949
AFC-D: Buffalo vs. Boston, 1963
AFC: Oakland vs. Pittsburgh, 1974
NFC-FR: New Orleans vs. Minnesota, 1987
NFC: L.A. Rams vs. San Francisco, 1989
NFC-D: Chicago vs. N.Y. Giants, 1990
AFC-FR: Indianapolis vs. Pittsburgh, 1996
AFC-FR: Seattle vs. Miami, 1999
AFC-D: Miami vs. Jacksonville, 1999
AFC-D: Miami vs. Oakland, 2000
AFC-D: Baltimore vs. Pittsburgh, 2001
1 By many teams

Most First Downs, Rushing, Both Teams, Game

26 AFC: Buffalo (14) vs. L.A. Raiders (12), 1990
25 NFC-FR: Dallas (19) vs. Los Angeles (6), 1980
23 NFC: Cleveland (15) vs. Detroit (8), 1952
AFC-D: Miami (18) vs. Cincinnati (5), 1973
AFC-D: Pittsburgh (18) vs. Buffalo (5), 1974
AFC-FR: Buffalo (18) vs. Miami (5), 1995

Fewest First Downs, Rushing, Both Teams, Game

2 NFC-FR: New Orleans (1) vs. St. Louis (1), 2000
5 AFC-D: Buffalo (0) vs. Boston (5), 1963
NFC-D: Washington (1) vs. Tampa Bay (4), 1999
AFC-FR: Cleveland (2) vs. Pittsburgh (3), 2002
6 NFC: Green Bay (2) vs. Boston (4), 1936
NFC-D: Baltimore (2) vs. Minnesota (4), 1968
AFC-D: Houston (1) vs. Oakland (5), 1969
AFC-FR: N.Y. Jets (1) vs. Houston (5), 1991
AFC-FR: Denver (1) vs. Baltimore (5), 2000

PASSING

Most First Downs, Passing, Game

24 AFC-FR: Pittsburgh vs. Cleveland, 2002
21 AFC-D: Miami vs. San Diego, 1981 (OT)
AFC-D: San Diego vs. Miami, 1981 (OT)
AFC-D: Cleveland vs. N.Y. Jets, 1986 (OT)
NFC-D: Philadelphia vs. Chicago, 1988
20 NFC-FR: Dallas vs. L.A. Rams, 1983
AFC-D: Buffalo vs. Cleveland, 1989
AFC-FR: Miami vs. Buffalo, 1995
NFC-FR: Detroit vs. Philadelphia, 1995
AFC-FR: San Diego vs. Indianapolis, 1995
NFC-D: Minnesota vs. St. Louis, 1999

Fewest First Downs, Passing, Game

0 NFC: Philadelphia vs. Chi. Cardinals, 1948
1 NFC-D: N.Y. Giants vs. Washington, 1943
NFC: Cleveland vs. Detroit, 1953
SB: Denver vs. Dallas, 1977
2 By many teams

Most First Downs, Passing, Both Teams, Game

42 AFC-D: Miami (21) vs. San Diego (21), 1981 (OT)
AFC-FR: Pittsburgh (24) vs. Cleveland (18), 2002
38 AFC-FR: Pittsburgh (19) vs. San Diego (19), 1982
NFC-D: Minnesota (20) vs. St. Louis (18), 1999
36 NFC: Minnesota (19) vs. Atlanta (17), 1998 (OT)

Fewest First Downs, Passing, Both Teams, Game

2 NFC: Philadelphia (0) vs. Chi. Cardinals (2), 1948
4 NFC-D: Cleveland (2) vs. N.Y. Giants (2), 1950
5 NFC: Detroit (2) vs. N.Y. Giants (3), 1935
NFC: Green Bay (2) vs. N.Y. Giants (3), 1939

PENALTY

Most First Downs, Penalty, Game

7 AFC-D: New England vs. Oakland, 1976
AFC: Tennessee vs. Oakland, 2002
6 AFC-D: Cleveland vs. N.Y. Jets, 1986 (OT)
5 AFC-FR: Cleveland vs. L. A. Raiders, 1982
NFC-D: San Francisco vs. Minnesota, 1997
AFC-FR: Miami vs. Buffalo, 1998
NFC-D: Arizona vs. Minnesota, 1998
AFC: Pittsburgh vs. New England, 2001
AFC-D: Pittsburgh vs. Tennessee, 2002 (OT)

Most First Downs, Penalty, Both Teams, Game

10 AFC: Tennessee (7) vs. Oakland (3), 2002
9 AFC-D: New England (7) vs. Oakland (2), 1976
8 NFC-FR: Atlanta (4) vs. Minnesota (4), 1982
AFC-FR: Miami (5) vs. Buffalo (3), 1998

NET YARDS GAINED RUSHING AND PASSING

Most Yards Gained, Game

610 AFC: San Diego vs. Boston, 1963
602 SB: Washington vs. Denver, 1987
569 AFC: Miami vs. Pittsburgh, 1984

Fewest Yards Gained, Game

86 NFC-D: Cleveland vs. N.Y. Giants, 1958
99 NFC: Chi. Cardinals vs. Philadelphia, 1948
114 NFC-D: N.Y. Giants vs. Washington, 1943
NFC: Minnesota vs. N.Y. Giants, 2000

Most Yards Gained, Both Teams, Game

1,038 AFC-FR: Buffalo (536) vs. Miami (502), 1995
1,036 AFC-D: San Diego (564) vs. Miami (472), 1981 (OT)
1,024 AFC: Miami (569) vs. Pittsburgh (455), 1984

Fewest Yards Gained, Both Teams, Game

331 NFC: Chi. Cardinals (99) vs. Philadelphia (232), 1948
332 NFC-D: N.Y. Giants (150) vs. Cleveland (182), 1950
336 NFC: Boston (116) vs. Green Bay (220), 1936

RUSHING

ATTEMPTS

Most Attempts, Game

65 NFC: Detroit vs. N.Y. Giants, 1935
61 NFC: Philadelphia vs. Los Angeles, 1949
59 AFC: New England vs. Miami, 1985

Fewest Attempts, Game

8 AFC-D: Miami vs. San Diego, 1994
9 SB: Miami vs. San Francisco, 1984
NFC: Minnesota vs. N.Y. Giants, 2000
10 NFC: L.A. Rams vs. San Francisco, 1989
NFC-FR: Atlanta vs. Green Bay, 1995
NFC-FR: Detroit vs. Washington, 1999

Most Attempts, Both Teams, Game

109 NFC: Detroit (65) vs. N.Y. Giants (44), 1935
97 AFC-D: Baltimore (50) vs. Oakland (47), 1977 (OT)
91 NFC: Philadelphia (57) vs. Chi. Cardinals (34), 1948

Fewest Attempts, Both Teams, Game

32 AFC-D: Houston (14) vs. Kansas City (18), 1993
38 NFC-D: Detroit (16) vs. Dallas (22), 1991
39 NFC-FR: Atlanta (10) vs. Green Bay (29), 1995

YARDS GAINED

Most Yards Gained, Game

382 NFC: Chi. Bears vs. Washington, 1940
341 AFC-FR: Buffalo vs. Miami, 1995
338 NFC-FR: Dallas vs. Los Angeles, 1980

Fewest Yards Gained, Game

–4 NFC-FR: Detroit vs. Green Bay, 1994
7 AFC-D: Buffalo vs. Boston, 1963
SB: New England vs. Chicago, 1985
14 AFC-D: Miami vs. Denver, 1998

AFC: N.Y. Jets vs. Denver, 1998

Most Yards Gained, Both Teams, Game

430 NFC-FR: Dallas (338) vs. Los Angeles (92), 1980
426 NFC: Cleveland (227) vs. Detroit (199), 1952
411 AFC-FR: Buffalo (341) vs. Miami (70), 1995

Fewest Yards Gained, Both Teams, Game

77 NFC-FR: Detroit (–4) vs. Green Bay (81), 1994
84 NFC-FR: St. Louis (34) vs. New Orleans (50), 2000
90 AFC-D: Buffalo (7) vs. Boston (83), 1963
NFC-D: Tampa Bay (44) vs. Washington (46), 1999

AVERAGE GAIN

Highest Average Gain, Game

9.94 AFC: San Diego vs. Boston, 1963 (32-318)
9.29 NFC-D: Green Bay vs. Dallas, 1982 (17-158)
7.35 NFC-FR: Dallas vs. Los Angeles, 1980 (46-338)

Lowest Average Gain, Game

– 0.27 NFC-FR: Detroit vs. Green Bay, 1994 (15-(– 4))
0.58 AFC-D: Buffalo vs. Boston, 1963 (12-7)
0.64 SB: New England vs. Chicago, 1985 (11-7)

TOUCHDOWNS

Most Touchdowns, Game

7 NFC: Chi. Bears vs. Washington, 1940
6 NFC-D: San Francisco vs. N.Y. Giants, 1993
5 NFC: Cleveland vs. Detroit, 1954
NFC-D: San Francisco vs. Chicago, 1994
AFC-FR: Pittsburgh vs. Indianapolis, 1996
AFC-FR: Denver vs. Jacksonville, 1997

Most Touchdowns, Both Teams, Game

7 NFC: Chi. Bears (7) vs. Washington (0), 1940
6 NFC: Cleveland (5) vs. Detroit (1), 1954
NFC-D: San Francisco (6) vs. N.Y. Giants (0), 1993
NFC-D: San Francisco (5) vs. Chicago (1), 1994
AFC-FR: Denver (5) vs. Jacksonville (1), 1997
5 NFC: Chi. Cardinals (3) vs. Philadelphia (2), 1947
AFC: San Diego (4) vs. Boston (1), 1963
AFC-D: Cincinnati (3) vs. Buffalo (2), 1981
AFC-FR: Pittsburgh (5) vs. Indianapolis (0), 1996
NFC-D: Arizona (3) vs. Minnesota (2), 1998
NFC-FR: Seattle (3) vs. Green Bay (2), 2003 (OT)

PASSING

ATTEMPTS

Most Attempts, Game

66 AFC-FR: Miami vs. Buffalo, 1995
65 AFC-D: Cleveland vs. N.Y. Jets, 1986 (OT)
NFC-D: San Francisco vs. Green Bay, 1995
61 NFC-FR: Minnesota vs. Chicago, 1994

Fewest Attempts, Game

5 NFC: Detroit vs. N.Y. Giants, 1935
6 AFC: Miami vs. Oakland, 1973
7 SB: Miami vs. Minnesota, 1973

Most Attempts, Both Teams, Game

102 AFC-D: San Diego (54) vs. Miami (48), 1981 (OT)
96 AFC: N.Y. Jets (49) vs. Oakland (47), 1968
95 AFC-D: Cleveland (65) vs. N.Y. Jets (30), 1986 (OT)

Fewest Attempts, Both Teams, Game

18 NFC: Detroit (5) vs. N.Y. Giants (13), 1935
23 NFC: Chi. Cardinals (11) vs. Philadelphia (12), 1948
24 NFC-D: Cleveland (9) vs. N.Y. Giants (15), 1950

COMPLETIONS

Most Completions, Game

36 AFC-FR: Houston vs. Buffalo, 1992 (OT)
34 AFC-D: Cleveland vs. N.Y. Jets, 1986 (OT)
AFC-FR: Miami vs. Buffalo, 1995
33 AFC-D: San Diego vs. Miami, 1981 (OT)
NFC-FR: Minnesota vs. Chicago, 1994

Fewest Completions, Game

2 NFC: Detroit vs. N.Y. Giants, 1935
NFC: Philadelphia vs. Chi. Cardinals, 1948
3 NFC: N.Y. Giants vs. Chi. Bears, 1941
NFC: Green Bay vs. N.Y. Giants, 1944
NFC: Chi. Cardinals vs. Philadelphia, 1947
NFC: Chi. Cardinals vs. Philadelphia, 1948
NFC-D: Cleveland vs. N.Y. Giants, 1950
NFC-D: N.Y. Giants vs. Cleveland, 1950
NFC: Cleveland vs. Detroit, 1953
AFC: Miami vs. Oakland, 1973
4 NFC: N.Y. Giants vs. Detroit, 1935
NFC-D: N.Y. Giants vs. Washington, 1943
NFC-D: Pittsburgh vs. Philadelphia, 1947
NFC-D: Dallas vs. Detroit, 1970
AFC: Miami vs. Baltimore, 1971
SB: Miami vs. Washington, 1982
AFC-FR: Seattle vs. L.A. Raiders, 1984

Most Completions, Both Teams, Game

64 AFC-D: San Diego (33) vs. Miami (31), 1981 (OT)
57 AFC-FR: Houston (36) vs. Buffalo (21), 1992 (OT)
NFC-FR: N.Y. Giants (29) vs. San Francisco (28), 2002
56 NFC-D: Dallas (28) vs. Green Bay (28), 1993
NFC: Minnesota (29) vs. Atlanta (27), 1998 (OT)
NFC-D: Minnesota (29) vs. St. Louis (27), 1999
AFC-FR: Pittsburgh (30) vs. Cleveland (26), 2002

Fewest Completions, Both Teams, Game

5 NFC: Philadelphia (2) vs. Chi. Cardinals (3), 1948
6 NFC: Detroit (2) vs. N.Y. Giants (4), 1935
NFC-D: Cleveland (3) vs. N.Y. Giants (3), 1950
11 NFC: Green Bay (3) vs. N.Y. Giants (8), 1944
NFC-D: Dallas (4) vs. Detroit (7), 1970

COMPLETION PERCENTAGE

Highest Completion Percentage, Game (20 attempts)

88.0 SB: N.Y. Giants vs. Denver, 1986 (25-22)
87.1 NFC: San Francisco vs. L.A. Rams, 1989 (31-27)
83.9 AFC-FR: Indianapolis vs. Denver, 2003

Lowest Completion Percentage, Game (20 attempts)

18.5 NFC: Tampa Bay vs. Los Angeles, 1979 (27-5)
20.0 NFC-D: N.Y. Giants vs. Washington, 1943 (20-4)
25.8 NFC: Chi. Bears vs. Washington, 1937 (31-8)

YARDS GAINED

Most Yards Gained, Game

483 AFC-D: Cleveland vs. N.Y. Jets, 1986 (OT)
435 AFC: Miami vs. Pittsburgh, 1984
432 AFC-FR: Miami vs. Buffalo, 1995

Fewest Yards Gained, Game

3 NFC: Chi. Cardinals vs. Philadelphia, 1948
7 NFC: Philadelphia vs. Chi. Cardinals, 1948
9 NFC-D: N.Y. Giants vs. Cleveland, 1950
NFC: Cleveland vs. Detroit, 1953

Most Yards Gained, Both Teams, Game

809 AFC-D: San Diego (415) vs. Miami (394), 1981 (OT)
762 NFC-D: Minnesota (388) vs. St. Louis (374), 1999
752 AFC-FR: Cleveland (409) vs. Pittsburgh (343), 2002

Fewest Yards Gained, Both Teams, Game

10 NFC: Chi. Cardinals (3) vs. Philadelphia (7), 1948
38 NFC-D: N.Y. Giants (9) vs. Cleveland (29), 1950
102 NFC-D: Dallas (22) vs. Detroit (80), 1970

TIMES SACKED

Most Times Sacked, Game

9 AFC: Kansas City vs. Buffalo, 1966
NFC: Chicago vs. San Francisco, 1984
AFC-D: N.Y. Jets vs. Cleveland, 1986 (OT)
AFC-D: Houston vs. Kansas City, 1993
8 NFC: Green Bay vs. Dallas, 1967
NFC: Minnesota vs. Washington, 1987

NFC-D: Philadelphia vs. Green Bay, 2003 (OT)
7 NFC-D: Dallas vs. Los Angeles, 1973
SB: Dallas vs. Pittsburgh, 1975
AFC-FR: Houston vs. Oakland, 1980
NFC-D: Washington vs. Chicago, 1984
SB: New England vs. Chicago, 1985
AFC-FR: Kansas City vs. San Diego, 1992
AFC-D: Pittsburgh vs. Buffalo, 1992

Most Times Sacked, Both Teams, Game
13 AFC: Kansas City (9) vs. Buffalo (4), 1966
AFC-D: N.Y. Jets (9) vs. Cleveland (4), 1986 (OT)
12 NFC-D: Dallas (7) vs. Los Angeles (5), 1973
NFC-D: Washington (7) vs. Chicago (5), 1984
NFC: Chicago (9) vs. San Francisco (3), 1984
AFC-FR: Kansas City (7) vs. San Diego (5), 1992
11 AFC-D: Houston (9) vs. Kansas City (2), 1993

Fewest Times Sacked, Both Teams, Game
0 AFC-D: Buffalo vs. Pittsburgh, 1974
AFC-FR: Pittsburgh vs. San Diego, 1982
AFC: Miami vs. Pittsburgh, 1984
AFC-D: Buffalo vs. Miami, 1990
AFC-D: Denver vs. Houston, 1991
AFC-FR: Buffalo vs. Miami, 1995
AFC-D: Indianapolis vs. Tennessee, 1999
1 In many games

TOUCHDOWNS

Most Touchdowns, Game
6 AFC-D: Oakland vs. Houston, 1969
SB: San Francisco vs. San Diego, 1994
5 NFC: Chi. Bears vs. Washington, 1943
NFC: Detroit vs. Cleveland, 1957
AFC-D: Oakland vs. Kansas City, 1968
SB: San Francisco vs. Denver, 1989
NFC-D: St. Louis vs. Minnesota, 1999
NFC: N.Y. Giants vs. Minnesota, 2000
AFC-FR: Indianapolis vs. Denver, 2003
4 By many teams

Most Touchdowns, Both Teams, Game
9 NFC-D: St. Louis (5) vs. Minnesota (4), 1999
8 AFC-FR: Buffalo (4) vs. Houston (4), 1992 (OT)
7 NFC: Chi. Bears (5) vs. Washington (2), 1943
AFC-D: Oakland (6) vs. Houston (1), 1969
SB: Pittsburgh (4) vs. Dallas (3), 1978
AFC-D: Miami (4) vs. San Diego (3), 1981 (OT)
AFC: Miami (4) vs. Pittsburgh (3), 1984
AFC-D: Buffalo (4) vs. Cleveland (3), 1989
SB: San Francisco (6) vs. San Diego (1), 1994
NFC-FR: Detroit (4) vs. Philadelphia (3), 1995
NFC-FR: New Orleans (4) vs. St. Louis (3), 2000
NFC-FR: N.Y. Giants (4) vs. San Francisco (3), 2002

INTERCEPTIONS BY

Most Interceptions By, Game
8 NFC: Chi. Bears vs. Washington, 1940
7 NFC: Cleveland vs. Los Angeles, 1955
6 NFC: Green Bay vs. N.Y. Giants, 1939
NFC: Chi. Bears vs. N.Y. Giants, 1946
NFC: Cleveland vs. Detroit, 1954
AFC: San Diego vs. Houston, 1961
AFC: Buffalo vs. L.A. Raiders, 1990
NFC-FR: Philadelphia vs. Detroit, 1995
NFC-D: St. Louis vs. Green Bay, 2001

Most Interceptions By, Both Teams, Game
10 NFC: Cleveland (7) vs. Los Angeles (3), 1955
AFC: San Diego (6) vs. Houston (4), 1961
9 NFC: Green Bay (6) vs. N.Y. Giants (3), 1939
8 NFC: Chi. Bears (8) vs. Washington (0), 1940
NFC: Chi. Bears (6) vs. N.Y. Giants (2), 1946
NFC: Cleveland (6) vs. Detroit (2), 1954

AFC-FR: Buffalo (4) vs. N.Y. Jets (4), 1981
AFC: Miami (5) vs. N.Y. Jets (3), 1982

YARDS GAINED

Most Yards Gained, Game
172 SB: Tampa Bay vs. Oakland, 2002
161 NFC-D: St. Louis vs. Green Bay, 2001
138 AFC-FR: N.Y. Jets vs. Cincinnati, 1982

Most Yards Gained, Both Teams, Game
184 SB: Tampa Bay (172) vs. Oakland (12), 2002
161 NFC-D: St. Louis (161) vs. Green Bay (0), 2001
156 NFC: Green Bay (123) vs. N.Y. Giants (33), 1939

TOUCHDOWNS

Most Touchdowns, Game
3 NFC: Chi. Bears vs. Washington, 1940
NFC-D: St. Louis vs. Green Bay, 2001
SB: Tampa Bay vs Oakland, 2002
2 NFC-D: Los Angeles vs. St. Louis, 1975
NFC-FR: Philadelphia vs. Detroit, 1995
1 In many games

Most Touchdowns, Both Teams, Game
3 NFC: Chi. Bears (3) vs. Washington (0), 1940
NFC-D: St. Louis (3) vs. Green Bay (0), 2001
SB: Tampa Bay (3) vs. Oakland (0), 2002
2 NFC-D: Los Angeles (2) vs. St. Louis(0), 1975
NFC-D: Dallas (1) vs. Green Bay (1), 1982
NFC-D: Minnesota (1) vs. San Francisco (1), 1987
NFC-FR: Detroit (1) vs. Green Bay (1), 1993
NFC-FR: Philadelphia (2) vs. Detroit (0), 1995
AFC-FR: Buffalo (1) vs. Jacksonville (1), 1996
1 In many games

PUNTING

Most Punts, Game
14 AFC-D: N.Y. Jets vs. Cleveland, 1986 (OT)
13 NFC: N.Y. Giants vs. Chi. Bears, 1933
AFC-D: Baltimore vs. Oakland, 1977 (OT)
11 AFC: Houston vs. Oakland, 1967
AFC-D: Houston vs. Oakland, 1969
NFC: L.A. Rams vs. Chicago, 1985
SB: N.Y. Giants vs. Baltimore, 2000

Fewest Punts, Game
0 NFC-FR: St. Louis vs. Green Bay, 1982
AFC-FR: N.Y. Jets vs. Cincinnati, 1982
AFC-FR: Indianapolis vs. Denver, 2003
AFC-D: Kansas City vs. Indianapolis, 2003
AFC-D: Indianapolis vs. Kansas City, 2003
1 By many teams

Most Punts, Both Teams, Game
23 NFC: N.Y. Giants (13) vs. Chi. Bears (10), 1933
22 AFC-D: N.Y. Jets (14) vs. Cleveland (8), 1986 (OT)
21 AFC-D: Baltimore (13) vs. Oakland (8), 1977 (OT)
NFC: L.A. Rams (11) vs. Chicago (10), 1985
SB: N.Y. Giants (11) vs. Baltimore (10), 2000

Fewest Punts, Both Teams, Game
0 AFC-D: Kansas City vs. Indianapolis, 2003
1 NFC-FR: St. Louis (0) vs. Green Bay (1), 1982
2 AFC-FR: N.Y. Jets (0) vs. Cincinnati (2), 1982
SB: Atlanta (1) vs. Denver (1), 1998
AFC-FR: Indianapolis (0) vs. Denver (2), 2003

AVERAGE YARDAGE

Highest Average, Punting, Game (4 punts)
56.0 AFC: Oakland vs. San Diego, 1980
52.5 NFC: Washington vs. Chi. Bears, 1942
52.0 AFC-D: Tennessee vs. Indianapolis, 1999

Lowest Average, Punting, Game (4 punts)
24.9 NFC: Washington vs. Chi. Bears, 1937
25.3 AFC-FR: Pittsburgh vs. Houston, 1989

25.5 NFC: Green Bay vs. N.Y. Giants, 1962

PUNT RETURNS

Most Punt Returns, Game

8 NFC: Green Bay vs. N.Y. Giants, 1944
7 By many teams

Most Punt Returns, Both Teams, Game

13 AFC-FR: Houston (7) vs. Oakland (6), 1980
12 AFC-D: New England (7) vs. Pittsburgh (5), 1996
11 NFC: Green Bay (8) vs. N.Y. Giants (3), 1944
NFC-D: Green Bay (6) vs. Baltimore (5), 1965
AFC-FR: Jacksonville (7) vs. New England (4), 1998

Fewest Punt Returns, Both Teams, Game

0 NFC: Chi. Bears vs. N.Y. Giants, 1941
AFC: Boston vs. San Diego, 1963
NFC-FR: Green Bay vs. St. Louis, 1982
AFC-FR: Houston vs. N.Y. Jets, 1991
AFC-D: Denver vs. Houston, 1991
NFC-D: San Francisco vs. Washington, 1992
SB: Denver vs. Green Bay, 1997
SB: Atlanta vs. Denver, 1998
AFC-FR: Oakland vs. N.Y. Jets, 2001
AFC-D: N.Y. Jets vs. Oakland, 2002
AFC-FR: Denver vs. Indianapolis, 2003
NFC-D: Carolina vs. St. Louis, 2003
AFC-D: Indianapolis vs. Kansas City, 2003
1 In many games

YARDS GAINED

Most Yards Gained, Game

155 NFC-D: Dallas vs. Cleveland, 1967
150 NFC: Chi. Cardinals vs. Philadelphia, 1947
143 NFC-FR: Minnesota vs. New Orleans, 1987

Fewest Yards Gained, Game

–10 NFC: Green Bay vs. Cleveland, 1965
–9 NFC: Dallas vs. Green Bay, 1966
AFC-D: Kansas City vs. Oakland, 1968
–7 NFC-D: San Francisco vs. Atlanta, 1998

Most Yards Gained, Both Teams, Game

166 NFC-D: Dallas (155) vs. Cleveland (11), 1967
AFC-D: Baltimore (99) vs. Pittsburgh (67), 2001
160 NFC: Chi. Cardinals (150) vs. Philadelphia (10), 1947
147 AFC-FR: Pittsburgh (77) vs. Cleveland (70), 2002

Fewest Yards Gained, Both Teams, Game

–9 NFC: Dallas (–9) vs. Green Bay (0), 1966
–6 AFC-D: Miami (–5) vs. Oakland (–1), 1970
–3 NFC-D: San Francisco (–5) vs. Dallas (2), 1972

TOUCHDOWNS

Most Touchdowns, Game

1 By 15 teams

KICKOFF RETURNS

Most Kickoff Returns, Game

10 NFC-D: L.A. Rams vs. Washington, 1983
NFC-FR: Detroit vs. Philadelphia, 1995
9 NFC: Chi. Bears vs. N.Y. Giants, 1956
AFC: Boston vs. San Diego, 1963
AFC: Houston vs. Oakland, 1967
SB: Denver vs. San Francisco, 1989
AFC-D: Miami vs. Buffalo, 1990
AFC: L.A. Raiders vs. Buffalo, 1990
AFC-D: Miami vs. Jacksonville, 1999
SB: Oakland vs. Tampa Bay, 2002
8 By many teams

Most Kickoff Returns, Both Teams, Game

15 AFC-D: Miami (9) vs. Buffalo (6), 1990
14 NFC-FR: Detroit (10) vs. Philadelphia (4), 1995
13 NFC-D: Green Bay (7) vs. Dallas (6), 1982
NFC-FR: Green Bay (7) vs. San Francisco (6), 1998
AFC-FR: N.Y. Jets (8) vs. Oakland (5), 2001
NFC-FR: San Francisco (7) vs. N.Y. Giants (6), 2002
AFC-D: Tennessee (7) vs. Pittsburgh (6), 2002
SB: Oakland (9) vs. Tampa Bay (4), 2002
NFC-FR: Seattle (7) vs. Green Bay (6), 2003 (OT)
AFC-D: Kansas City (7) vs. Indianapolis (6), 2003

Fewest Kickoff Returns, Both Teams, Game

1 NFC: Green Bay (0) vs. Boston (1), 1936
AFC-FR: San Diego (0) vs. Kansas City (1), 1992
2 NFC-D: Los Angeles (0) vs. Chi. Bears (2), 1950
AFC: Houston (0) vs. San Diego (2), 1961
AFC-D: Oakland (1) vs. Pittsburgh (1), 1972
AFC-D: N.Y. Jets (0) vs. L.A. Raiders (2), 1982
AFC: Miami (1) vs. N.Y. Jets (1), 1982
NFC: N.Y. Giants (0) vs. Washington (2), 1986
3 In many games

YARDS GAINED

Most Yards Gained, Game

244 SB: San Diego vs. San Francisco, 1994
227 SB: Atlanta vs. Denver, 1998
225 NFC: Washington vs. Chi. Bears, 1940

Most Yards Gained, Both Teams, Game

379 AFC-D: Baltimore (193) vs. Oakland (186), 1977 (OT)
348 NFC-D: Minnesota (174) vs. St. Louis (174), 1999
322 NFC-D: Green Bay (194) vs. San Francisco (128), 1998

Fewest Yards Gained, Both Teams, Game

5 AFC-FR: San Diego (0) vs. Kansas City (5), 1992
15 NFC: N.Y. Giants (0) vs. Washington (15), 1986
31 NFC-D: Los Angeles (0) vs. Chi. Bears (31), 1950

TOUCHDOWNS

Most Touchdowns, Game

1 NFC-D: San Francisco vs. Dallas, 1972
AFC-D: Miami vs. Oakland, 1974
AFC-D: Baltimore vs. Oakland, 1977 (OT)
SB: Miami vs. Washington, 1982
SB: Cincinnati vs. San Francisco, 1988
AFC-D: Cleveland vs. Buffalo, 1989
SB: San Diego vs. San Francisco, 1994
SB: Green Bay vs. New England, 1996
NFC: San Francisco vs. Green Bay, 1997
SB: Atlanta vs. Denver, 1998
AFC-FR: Tennessee vs. Buffalo, 1999
AFC-FR: Seattle vs. Miami, 1999
NFC-D: Washington vs. Tampa Bay, 1999
NFC-D: St. Louis vs. Minnesota, 1999
AFC: Tennessee vs. Jacksonville, 1999
NFC-D: N.Y. Giants vs. Philadelphia, 2000
SB: Baltimore vs. N.Y. Giants, 2000
SB: N.Y. Giants vs. Baltimore, 2000
AFC-D: Kansas City vs. Indianapolis, 2003

Most Touchdowns, Both Teams, Game

2 SB: Baltimore (1) vs. N.Y. Giants (1), 2000

PENALTIES

Most Penalties, Game

17 AFC-FR: L.A. Raiders vs. Denver, 1993
14 AFC-FR: Oakland vs. Houston, 1980
NFC-D: San Francisco vs. N.Y. Giants, 1981
AFC: Oakland vs. Tennessee, 2002
13 AFC-FR: Houston vs. Cleveland, 1988
AFC-D: Houston vs. Denver, 1991
NFC-D: Arizona vs. Minnesota, 1998
NFC-D: Carolina vs. St. Louis, 2003 (2 OT)

Fewest Penalties, Game

0 NFC: Philadelphia vs. Green Bay, 1960
NFC-D: Detroit vs. Dallas, 1970
AFC-D: Miami vs. Oakland, 1970
SB: Miami vs. Dallas, 1971

NFC-D: Washington vs. Minnesota, 1973
SB: Pittsburgh vs. Dallas, 1975
NFC: San Francisco vs. Chicago, 1988
SB: Denver vs. San Francisco, 1989
AFC-D: L.A. Raiders vs. Cincinnati, 1990
AFC-D: Miami vs. San Diego, 1992
SB: Atlanta vs. Denver, 1998
AFC-FR: N.Y. Jets vs. Oakland, 2001
NFC-FR: Carolina vs. Dallas, 2003
1 By many teams

Most Penalties, Both Teams, Game
27 AFC-FR: L.A. Raiders (17) vs. Denver (10), 1993
22 AFC-FR: Oakland (14) vs. Houston (8), 1980
NFC-D: San Francisco (14) vs. N.Y. Giants (8), 1981
AFC-FR: Houston (13) vs. Cleveland (9), 1988
NFC-D: Arizona (13) vs. Minnesota (9), 1998
21 AFC-D: Oakland (11) vs. New England (10), 1976
AFC: Oakland (14) vs. Tennessee (7), 2002

Fewest Penalties, Both Teams, Game
1 AFC-D: L.A. Raiders (0) vs. Cincinnati (1), 1990
2 NFC: Washington (1) vs. Chi. Bears (1), 1937
NFC-D: Washington (0) vs. Minnesota (2), 1973
SB: Pittsburgh (0) vs. Dallas (2), 1975
NFC-FR: Carolina (0) vs. Dallas (2), 2003
3 AFC: Miami (1) vs. Baltimore (2), 1971
NFC: San Francisco (1) vs. Dallas (2), 1971
SB: Miami (0) vs. Dallas (3), 1971
AFC-D: Pittsburgh (1) vs. Oakland (2), 1972
AFC-D: Miami (1) vs. Cincinnati (2), 1973
SB: Miami (1) vs. San Francisco (2), 1984
NFC: San Francisco (0) vs. Chicago (3), 1988

YARDS PENALIZED

Most Yards Penalized, Game
145 NFC-D: San Francisco vs. N.Y. Giants, 1981
133 SB: Dallas vs. Baltimore, 1970
130 AFC-FR: L.A. Raiders vs. Denver, 1993

Fewest Yards Penalized, Game
0 By many teams

Most Yards Penalized, Both Teams, Game
227 AFC-FR: L.A. Raiders (130) vs. Denver (97), 1993
206 NFC-D: San Francisco (145) vs. N.Y. Giants (61), 1981
201 NFC-FR: Detroit (126) vs. Washington (75), 1999

Fewest Yards Penalized, Both Teams, Game
5 AFC-D: L.A. Raiders (0) vs. Cincinnati (5), 1990
9 NFC-D: Washington (0) vs. Minnesota (9), 1973
11 NFC-FR: Carolina (0) vs. Dallas (11), 2003

FUMBLES

Most Fumbles, Game
8 SB: Buffalo vs. Dallas, 1992
7 AFC-D: Houston vs. Kansas City, 1993
6 By 12 teams

Most Fumbles, Both Teams, Game
12 AFC: Houston (6) vs. Pittsburgh (6), 1978
SB: Buffalo (8) vs. Dallas (4), 1992
10 NFC: Chi. Bears (5) vs. N.Y. Giants (5), 1934
SB: Dallas (6) vs. Denver (4), 1977
AFC: Jacksonville (5) vs. Tennessee (5), 1999
9 NFC-D: San Francisco (6) vs. Detroit (3), 1957
NFC-D: San Francisco (5) vs. Dallas (4), 1972
NFC: Dallas (5) vs. Philadelphia (4), 1980

Most Fumbles Lost, Game
5 SB: Buffalo vs. Dallas, 1992
AFC-D: Miami vs. Jacksonville, 1999
4 NFC: N.Y. Giants vs. Baltimore, 1958 (OT)
AFC: Kansas City vs. Oakland, 1969
SB: Baltimore vs. Dallas, 1970
AFC: Pittsburgh vs. Oakland, 1975
SB: Denver vs. Dallas, 1977
AFC: Houston vs. Pittsburgh, 1978
AFC: Miami vs. New England, 1985
SB: New England vs. Chicago, 1985
NFC-FR: L.A. Rams vs. Washington, 1986
NFC-FR: Minnesota vs. Dallas, 1996
AFC-FR: Buffalo vs. Miami, 1998
AFC: N.Y. Jets vs. Denver, 1998
AFC: Jacksonville vs. Tennessee, 1999
3 By many teams

Fewest Fumbles, Both Teams, Game
0 NFC: Green Bay vs. Cleveland, 1965
AFC-D: Houston vs. San Diego, 1979
NFC-D: Dallas vs. Los Angeles, 1979
SB: Los Angeles vs. Pittsburgh, 1979
AFC-D: Buffalo vs. Cincinnati, 1981
NFC: Minnesota vs. Washington, 1987
NFC-D: San Francisco vs. Washington, 1990
NFC: Dallas vs. Green Bay, 1995
AFC-D: New England vs. Pittsburgh, 1996
SB: Green Bay vs. New England, 1996
AFC-FR: Miami vs. Seattle, 1999
AFC-FR: Miami vs. Indianapolis, 2000 (OT)
AFC-D: Baltimore vs. Tennessee, 2000
1 In many games

RECOVERIES

Most Total Fumbles Recovered, Game
8 SB: Dallas vs. Denver, 1977 (4 own, 4 opp)
7 NFC: Chi. Bears vs. N.Y. Giants, 1934 (5 own, 2 opp)
NFC-D: San Francisco vs. Detroit, 1957 (4 own, 3 opp)
NFC-D: San Francisco vs. Dallas, 1972 (4 own, 3 opp)
AFC: Pittsburgh vs. Houston, 1978 (3 own, 4 opp)
6 AFC: Houston vs. San Diego, 1961 (4 own, 2 opp)
AFC-D: Cleveland vs. Baltimore, 1971 (4 own, 2 opp)
AFC-D: Cleveland vs. Oakland, 1980 (5 own, 1 opp)
NFC: Philadelphia vs. Dallas, 1980 (3 own, 3 opp)
SB: Dallas vs. Buffalo, 1992 (1 own, 5 opp)
NFC-D: Green Bay vs. San Francisco, 1996 (4 own, 2 opp)
AFC: Denver vs. N.Y. Jets, 1998 (2 own, 4 opp)
AFC: Tennessee vs. Jacksonville, 1999 (2 own, 4 opp)

Most Own Fumbles Recovered, Game
5 NFC: Chi. Bears vs. N.Y. Giants, 1934
AFC-D: Cleveland vs. Oakland, 1980
4 By many teams

TOUCHDOWNS

Most Touchdowns, Game
2 SB: Dallas vs. Buffalo, 1992

TURNOVERS

Numbers of times losing the ball on interceptions and fumbles.

Most Turnovers, Game
9 NFC: Washington vs. Chi. Bears, 1940
NFC: Detroit vs. Cleveland, 1954
AFC: Houston vs. Pittsburgh, 1978
SB: Buffalo vs. Dallas, 1992
8 NFC: N.Y. Giants vs. Chi. Bears, 1946
NFC: Los Angeles vs. Cleveland, 1955
NFC: Cleveland vs. Detroit, 1957
SB: Denver vs. Dallas, 1977
NFC-D: Minnesota vs. Philadelphia, 1980
NFC-D: Green Bay vs. St. Louis, 2001
7 In many games

Fewest Turnovers, Game
0 By many teams

Most Turnovers, Both Teams, Game
14 AFC: Houston (9) vs. Pittsburgh (5), 1978
13 NFC: Detroit (9) vs. Cleveland (4), 1954
AFC: Houston (7) vs. San Diego (6), 1961

12 AFC: Pittsburgh (7) vs. Oakland (5), 1975

Fewest Turnovers, Both Teams, Game

0 SB: Buffalo vs. N.Y. Giants, 1990
AFC-FR: Kansas City vs Pittsburgh, 1993 (OT)
NFC-FR: Detroit vs. Green Bay, 1994
AFC-FR: Denver vs. Jacksonville, 1996
SB: St. Louis vs. Tennessee, 1999

1 AFC-D: Baltimore (0) vs. Cincinnati (1), 1970
AFC-D: Pittsburgh (0) vs. Buffalo (1), 1974
AFC: Oakland (0) vs. Pittsburgh (1), 1976
NFC-D: Minnesota (0) vs. Washington (1), 1982
NFC-D: Chicago (0) vs. N.Y. Giants (1), 1985
SB: N.Y. Giants (0) vs. Denver (1), 1986
NFC: Washington (0) vs. Minnesota (1), 1987
AFC-D: Cincinnati (0) vs. L.A. Raiders (1), 1990
NFC: N.Y. Giants (0) vs. San Francisco (1), 1990
NFC-FR: N.Y. Giants (0) vs. Minnesota (1), 1993
AFC-FR: L.A. Raiders (0) vs. Denver (1), 1993
NFC: Dallas (0) vs. San Francisco (1), 1993
AFC: Indianapolis (0) vs. Pittsburgh (1), 1995
NFC-D: San Francisco (0) vs. Minnesota (1), 1997
AFC-D: Indianapolis (0) vs. Tennessee (1), 1999
AFC-FR: Baltimore (0) vs. Denver (1), 2000
AFC-D: Baltimore (0) vs. Tennessee (1), 2000
AFC-D: Oakland (0) vs. New England (1), 2001
NFC-FR: Green Bay (0) vs. Seattle (1), 2003 (OT)
AFC-D: Indianapolis (0) vs. Kansas City (1), 2003

2 In many games

AFC-NFC PRO BOWL RECORDS

Includes records of AFC-NFC Pro Bowls, 1971-2003
Compiled by Elias Sports Bureau

INDIVIDUAL RECORDS

SERVICE

Most Games

12 Randall McDaniel, Minnesota 1990-2000; Tampa Bay 2001
11 *Reggie White, Philadelphia, 1987-1993; Green Bay, 1994, 1996-97, 1999
Junior Seau, San Diego, 1992-2002
Rod Woodson, Pittsburgh, 1990-95, 1997; Baltimore, 2000-02; Oakland, 2003
10 Lawrence Taylor, N.Y. Giants, 1982-1991
Ronnie Lott, San Francisco, 1982-85, 1987-1991; L.A. Raiders 1992
Mike Singletary, Chicago, 1984-1993
**Bruce Matthews, Houston, 1989-1995, 1997; Tennessee, 2000, 2002
***Jerry Rice, San Francisco, 1987-88, 1990-94, 1996, 1999; Oakland, 2003

**Also selected, but did not play, in two additional games*
***Also selected, but did not play, in four additional games*
****Also selected but did not play, in three additional games*

SCORING

POINTS

Most Points, Career

45 Morten Andersen, New Orleans, 1986-89, 1991, 1993; Atlanta, 1996 (15-pat, 10-fg)
30 Jan Stenerud, Kansas City, 1971-72, 1976; Minnesota, 1985 (6-pat, 8-fg)
Jimmy Smith, Jacksonville, 1998-2001 (5-td)
26 Nick Lowery, Kansas City, 1982, 1991, 1993 (5 pat, 7 fg)

Most Points, Game

18 John Brockington, Green Bay, 1973 (3-td)
Mike Alstott, Tampa Bay, 2000 (3-td)
Jimmy Smith, Jacksonville, 2000 (3-td)
Shaun Alexander, Seattle, 2004 (3-td)
15 Garo Yepremian, Miami, 1974 (5-fg)
Jason Hanson, Detroit, 2000 (6-pat, 3-fg)
14 Jan Stenerud, Kansas City, 1972 (2-pat, 4-fg)

TOUCHDOWNS

Most Touchdowns, Career

5 Jimmy Smith, Jacksonville, 1998-2001 (5-p)
4 Mike Alstott, Tampa Bay, 1998-2003 (3-r, 1-p)
Marvin Harrison, Indianapolis, 2000-04 (4-p)
Tony Gonzalez, Kansas City, 2000-01, 2003-04 (4-p)
3 John Brockington, Green Bay, 1972-74 (2-r, 1-p)
Earl Campbell, Houston, 1979-1982, 1984 (3-r)
Chuck Muncie, New Orleans, 1980; San Diego, 1982-83 (3-r)
William Andrews, Atlanta, 1981-84 (1-r, 2-p)
Marcus Allen, L.A. Raiders, 1983, 1985-86, 1988; Kansas City, 1994 (2-r, 1-p)
Cris Carter, Minnesota, 1994-2001 (3-p)
Curtis Martin, New England, 1996-97; N.Y. Jets, 1999, 2002 (2-r, 1-p)
Shaun Alexander, Seattle, 2004 (2-r, 1-p)

Most Touchdowns, Game

3 John Brockington, Green Bay, 1973 (2-r, 1-p)
Mike Alstott, Tampa Bay, 2000 (3-r)
Jimmy Smith, Jacksonville, 2000 (3-p)
Shaun Alexander, Seattle, 2004 (2-r, 1-p)
2 Mel Renfro, Dallas, 1971 (2-ret)
Earl Campbell, Houston, 1980 (2-r)
Chuck Muncie, New Orleans, 1980 (2-r)
William Andrews, Atlanta, 1984 (2-p)
Herschel Walker, Dallas, 1989 (2-r)
Johnny Johnson, Phoenix, 1991 (2-r)
Eric Green, Pittsburgh, 1995 (2-p)
Marvin Harrison, Indianapolis, 2001 (2-p)
Ricky Wiilliams, Miami, 2003 (2-r)

POINTS AFTER TOUCHDOWN

Most Points After Touchdown, Career

15 Morten Andersen, New Orleans, 1986-89, 1991, 1993; Atlanta, 1996 (15 att)
9 Jason Hanson, Detroit, 1998, 2000 (9 att)
8 Jason Elam, Denver, 1996, 1999, 2002 (9 att)

Most Points After Touchdown, Game

7 Mike Vanderjagt, Indianapolis, 2004 (7 att)
6 Ali Haji-Sheikh, N.Y. Giants, 1984 (6 att)
Jason Hanson, Detroit, 2000 (6 att)
Adam Vinatieri, New England, 2003 (6 att)
5 John Carney, San Diego, 1995 (5 att)
Matt Stover, Baltimore, 2001 (5 att)
Jason Elam, Denver, 2002 (5 att)
Jeff Wilkins, St. Louis, 2004 (5 att)

FIELD GOALS

Most Field Goals Attempted, Career

18 Morten Andersen, New Orleans, 1986-89, 1991, 1993; Atlanta, 1996
15 Jan Stenerud, Kansas City, 1971-72, 1976; Minnesota, 1985
10 Nick Lowery, Kansas City, 1982, 1991, 1993

Most Field Goals Attempted, Game

6 Jan Stenerud, Kansas City, 1972
Eddie Murray, Detroit, 1981
Mark Moseley, Washington, 1983
5 Garo Yepremian, Miami, 1974
4 Jan Stenerud, Kansas City, 1976
Nick Lowery, Kansas City, 1991, 1993
Morten Andersen, New Orleans, 1993
Cary Blanchard, Indianapolis, 1997
John Kasay, Carolina, 1997
David Akers, Philadelphia, 2002
Jeff Wilkins, St. Louis, 2004

Most Field Goals, Career

10 Morten Andersen, New Orleans, 1986-89, 1991, 1993; Atlanta, 1996
8 Jan Stenerud, Kansas City, 1971-72, 1976; Minnesota, 1985
7 Nick Lowery, Kansas City, 1982, 1991, 1993

Most Field Goals, Game

5 Garo Yepremian, Miami, 1974 (5 att)
4 Jan Stenerud, Kansas City, 1972 (6 att)
Eddie Murray, Detroit, 1981 (6 att)
3 Nick Lowery, Kansas City, 1991 (4 att)
Nick Lowery, Kansas City, 1993 (4 att)
Jason Elam, Denver, 1999 (3 att)
Jason Hanson, Detroit, 2000 (3 att)
David Akers, Philadelphia, 2002 (4 att)

Longest Field Goal

53 David Akers, Philadelphia, 2003
51 Morten Andersen, New Orleans, 1989
Jason Hanson, Detroit, 2000
49 Fuad Reveiz, Minnesota, 1995
David Akers, Philadelphia, 2002

SAFETIES

Most Safeties, Game

1 Art Still, Kansas City, 1983
Mark Gastineau, N.Y. Jets, 1985
Greg Townsend, L.A. Raiders, 1992

RUSHING

ATTEMPTS

Most Attempts, Career
81 Walter Payton, Chicago, 1977-1981, 1984-87
68 O.J. Simpson, Buffalo, 1973-77
66 Barry Sanders, Detroit, 1990-93, 1995-98

Most Attempts, Game
19 O.J. Simpson, Buffalo, 1974
17 Marv Hubbard, Oakland, 1974
16 O.J. Simpson, Buffalo, 1973
Marcus Allen, L.A. Raiders, 1986

YARDS GAINED

Most Yards Gained, Career
368 Walter Payton, Chicago, 1977-1981, 1984-87
356 O.J. Simpson, Buffalo, 1973-77
271 Marshall Faulk, Indianapolis, 1995-96, 1999; St. Louis, 2000, 2002-03

Most Yards Gained, Game
180 Marshall Faulk, Indianapolis, 1995
127 Chris Warren, Seattle, 1995
112 O. J. Simpson, Buffalo, 1973

Longest Run From Scrimmage
49 Marshall Faulk, Indianapolis, 1995 (TD)
41 Lawrence McCutcheon, Los Angeles, 1976
Natrone Means, San Diego, 1995
Marshall Faulk, Indianapolis, 1995
39 Chris Warren, Seattle, 1994
Priest Holmes, Kansas City, 2002

AVERAGE GAIN

Highest Average Gain, Career (20 attempts)
9.36 Chris Warren, Seattle, 1994-96, (25-234)
6.45 Marshall Faulk, Indianapolis, 1995-96, 1999; St. Louis, 2000, 2002-03 (42-271)
5.81 Marv Hubbard, Oakland, 1972-74 (36-209)

Highest Average Gain, Game (10 attempts)
13.85 Marshall Faulk, Indianapolis, 1995 (13-180)
9.07 Chris Warren, Seattle, 1995 (14-127)
7.00 O.J. Simpson, Buffalo, 1973 (16-112)
Ottis Anderson, St. Louis, 1981 (10-70)

TOUCHDOWNS

Most Touchdowns, Career
3 Earl Campbell, Houston, 1979-1982, 1984
Chuck Muncie, New Orleans, 1980; San Diego, 1982-83
Mike Alstott, Tampa Bay, 1998-2003
2 John Brockington, Green Bay, 1972-74
O.J. Simpson, Buffalo, 1973-77
Walter Payton, Chicago, 1977-1981, 1984-87
Marcus Allen, L.A. Raiders, 1983, 1985-86, 1988; Kansas City, 1994
Herschel Walker, Dallas, 1988-89
Johnny Johnson, Phoenix, 1991
Barry Sanders, Detroit, 1990-93, 1995-98
Curtis Martin, New England, 1996-97; N.Y. Jets, 1999, 2002
Ricky Williams, Miami, 2003
Shaun Alexander, Seattle, 2004

Most Touchdowns, Game
3 Mike Alstott, Tampa Bay, 2000
2 John Brockington, Green Bay, 1973
Earl Campbell, Houston, 1980
Chuck Muncie, New Orleans, 1980
Herschel Walker, Dallas, 1989
Johnny Johnson, Phoenix, 1991
Ricky Williams, Miami, 2003
Shaun Alexander, Seattle, 2004

PASSING

ATTEMPTS

Most Attempts, Career
120 Dan Fouts, San Diego, 1980-84, 1986
101 Steve Young, San Francisco, 1993-96, 1998-99
98 Peyton Manning, Indianapolis, 2000-01, 2003-04

Most Attempts, Game
41 Peyton Manning, Indianapolis, 2004
32 Bill Kenney, Kansas City, 1984
Steve Young, San Francisco, 1993
30 Dan Fouts, San Diego, 1983

COMPLETIONS

Most Completions, Career
63 Dan Fouts, San Diego, 1980-84, 1986
60 Peyton Manning, Indianapolis, 2000-01, 2003-04
48 Steve Young, San Francisco, 1993-96, 1998-99

Most Completions, Game
22 Peyton Manning, Indianapolis, 2004
21 Joe Theismann, Washington, 1984
18 Steve Young, San Francisco, 1993

COMPLETION PERCENTAGE

Highest Completion Percentage, Career (40 attempts)
68.9 Joe Theismann, Washington, 1983-84 (45-31)
67.9 Rich Gannon, Oakland, 2000-03 (53-36)
64.4 Jim Kelly, Buffalo, 1988, 1991-92 (45-29)

Highest Completion Percentage, Game (10 attempts)
90.0 Archie Manning, New Orleans, 1980 (10-9)
85.7 Rich Gannon, Oakland, 2001 (14-12)
80.0 Rich Gannon, Oakland, 2002 (10-8)

YARDS GAINED

Most Yards Gained, Career
890 Dan Fouts, San Diego, 1980-84, 1986
862 Peyton Manning, Indianapolis, 2000-01, 2003-04
614 Steve Young, San Francisco, 1993-96, 1998-99

Most Yards Gained, Game
342 Peyton Manning, Indianapolis, 2004
274 Dan Fouts, San Diego, 1983
270 Peyton Manning, Indianapolis, 2000

Longest Completion
93 Jeff Blake, Cincinnati (to Thigpen, Pittsburgh), 1996 (TD)
90 Steve McNair, Tennessee (to Johnson, Cincinnati), 2004 (TD)
80 Mark Brunell, Jacksonville (to Brown, Oakland), 1997 (TD)

AVERAGE GAIN

Highest Average Gain, Career (40 attempts)
8.80 Peyton Manning, Indianapolis, 2000-01, 2003-04 (98-862)
8.19 Rich Gannon, Oakland, 2000-03 (53-434)
8.12 Brett Favre, Green Bay, 1993-94, 1996-97 (57-463)

Highest Average Gain, Game (10 attempts)
15.27 Randall Cunningham, Philadelphia, 1991 (11-168)
13.70 Rich Gannon, Oakland, 2002 (10-137)
13.00 Brett Favre, Green Bay, 1997 (11-143)

TOUCHDOWNS

Most Touchdowns, Career
8 Peyton Manning, Indianapolis, 2000-01, 2003-04
7 Rich Gannon, Oakland, 2000-03
5 Peyton Manning, Indianapolis, 2000-01, 2003
4 Steve Young, San Francisco, 1993-96, 1998-99
Marc Bulger, St. Louis, 2004

Most Touchdowns, Game
4 Marc Bulger, St. Louis, 2004
3 Joe Theismann, Washington, 1984

Phil Simms, N.Y. Giants, 1986
Peyton Manning, Indianapolis, 2004
2 James Harris, Los Angeles, 1975
Mike Boryla, Philadelphia, 1976
Ken Anderson, Cincinnati, 1977
Jim Kelly, Buffalo, 1991
Mark Rypien, Washington, 1992
Steve Young, San Francisco, 1998
Peyton Manning, Indianapolis, 2000
Rich Gannon, Oakland, 2001
Peyton Manning, Indianapolis, 2001
Rich Gannon, Oakland, 2002
Donovan McNabb, Philadelphia, 2002
Rich Gannon, Oakland, 2003
Brad Johnson, Tampa Bay, 2003

HAD INTERCEPTED

Most Passes Had Intercepted, Career
8 Dan Fouts, San Diego, 1980-84, 1986
6 Jim Hart, St. Louis, 1975-78
5 Ken Stabler, Oakland, 1974-75, 1978
Peyton Manning, Indianapolis, 2000-01, 2003-04

Most Passes Had Intercepted, Game
5 Jim Hart, St. Louis, 1977
4 Ken Stabler, Oakland, 1974
3 Dan Fouts, San Diego, 1986
Mark Rypien, Washington, 1990
Steve Young, San Francisco, 1993
Jim Harbaugh, Indianapolis, 1996
Vinny Testaverde, N.Y. Jets, 1999
Jeff Garcia, San Francisco, 2003

Most Attempts, Without Interception, Game
27 Joe Theismann, Washington, 1984
Phil Simms, N.Y. Giants, 1986
26 John Brodie, San Francisco, 1971
Danny White, Dallas, 1983
23 Dave Krieg, Seattle, 1990

PERCENTAGE, PASSES HAD INTERCEPTED

Lowest Percentage, Passes Had Intercepted, Career (40 attempts)
0.00 Joe Theismann, Washington, 1983-84 (45-0)
1.89 Rich Gannon, Oakland, 2000-03 (53-1)
2.13 Dave Krieg, Seattle, 1985, 1989-1990 (47-1)

PASS RECEIVING

RECEPTIONS

Most Receptions, Career
37 Jerry Rice, San Francisco, 1987-88, 1990-94, 1996, 1999; Oakland, 2003
27 Cris Carter, Minnesota, 1994-2001
24 Marvin Harrison, Indianapolis, 2000-04

Most Receptions, Game
9 Randy Moss, Minnesota, 2000
8 Steve Largent, Seattle, 1986
Michael Irvin, Dallas, 1992
Andre Rison, Atlanta, 1993
Jimmy Smith, Jacksonville, 2000
Marvin Harrison, Indianapolis, 2001
Terrell Owens, San Francisco, 2002
7 John Stallworth, Pittsburgh, 1983
Jerry Rice, San Francisco, 1992
Isaac Bruce, St. Louis, 1997
Keyshawn Johnson, N.Y. Jets, 1999
Randy Moss, Minnesota, 1999
Warrick Dunn, Tampa Bay, 2001
Torry Holt, St. Louis, 2001
Torry Holt, St. Louis, 2004

YARDS GAINED

Most Yards Gained, Career
495 Jerry Rice, San Francisco, 1987-88, 1990-94, 1996, 1999; Oakland, 2003
408 Tim Brown, L.A. Raiders, 1989, 1992, 1994-95; Oakland, 1996-98, 2002
335 Cris Carter, Minnesota, 1994-2001

Most Yards Gained, Game
212 Randy Moss, Minnesota, 2000
156 Chad Johnson, Cincinnati, 2004
137 Tim Brown, Oakland, 1997

Longest Reception
93 Yancey Thigpen, Pittsburgh (from Blake, Cincinnati), 1996 (TD)
90 Chad Johnson, Cincinnati (from McNair, Tennessee), 2004 (TD)
80 Tim Brown, Oakland (from Brunell, Jacksonville), 1997 (TD)

TOUCHDOWNS

Most Touchdowns, Career
5 Jimmy Smith, Jacksonville, 1998-2001
4 Marvin Harrison, Indianapolis, 2000-04
Tony Gonzalez, Kansas City, 2000-01, 2003-04
3 Cris Carter, Minnesota, 1994-2001

Most Touchdowns, Game
3 Jimmy Smith, Jacksonville, 2000
2 William Andrews, Atlanta, 1984
Eric Green, Pittsburgh, 1995
Marvin Harrison, Indianapolis, 2001

INTERCEPTIONS BY

Most Interceptions By, Career
4 Everson Walls, Dallas, 1982-84, 1986
Deion Sanders, Atlanta, 1992-94; San Francisco, 1995; Dallas, 1999
3 Ken Houston, Houston, 1971-73; Washington, 1974-79
Jack Lambert, Pittsburgh, 1976-1984
Ted Hendricks, Baltimore, 1972-74; Green Bay, 1975; Oakland, 1981-82; L.A. Raiders, 1983-84
Mike Haynes, New England, 1978-1981, 1983; L.A. Raiders, 1985-87
Ty Law, New England, 1999, 2002-04
Champ Bailey, Washington, 2001-04
2 By 16 players

Most Interceptions By, Game
2 Mel Blount, Pittsburgh, 1977
Everson Walls, Dallas, 1982, 1983
LeRoy Irvin, L.A. Rams, 1986
David Fulcher, Cincinnati, 1990
Brian Dawkins, Philadelphia, 2000
Rod Woodson, Oakland, 2003

YARDS GAINED

Most Yards Gained, Career
147 Ty Law, New England, 1999, 2002-04
103 Deion Sanders, Atlanta, 1992-94; San Francisco, 1995; Dallas, 1999
88 Rod Woodson, Pittsburgh, 1990-95, 1997; Baltimore, 2000-02; Oakland, 2003

Most Yards Gained, Game
87 Deion Sanders, Dallas, 1999
73 Rod Woodson, Pittsburgh, 1994
67 Ty Law, New England, 1999

Longest Gain
87 Deion Sanders, Dallas, 1999
73 Rod Woodson, Pittsburgh, 1994 (lateral)
67 Ty Law, New England, 1999 (TD)

TOUCHDOWNS

Most Touchdowns, Career

2 Ty Law, New England, 1999, 2002-04
1 By many

Most Touchdowns, Game

1 Bobby Bell, Kansas City, 1973
Nolan Cromwell, L.A. Rams, 1984
Joey Browner, Minnesota, 1986
Jerry Gray, L.A. Rams, 1990
Mike Johnson, Cleveland, 1990
Junior Seau, San Diego, 1993
Ken Harvey, Washington, 1996
Ashley Ambrose, Cincinnati, 1997
Ty Law, New England, 1999
Derrick Brooks, Tampa Bay, 2000
Aeneas Williams, Arizona, 2000
Ray Lewis, Baltimore, 2002
Ty Law, New England, 2003
Dre' Bly, Detroit, 2004

PUNTING

Most Punts, Career

33 Ray Guy, Oakland, 1974-79, 1981
23 Rohn Stark, Indianapolis, 1986-87, 1991, 1993
22 Reggie Roby, Miami, 1985, 1990; Washington, 1995

Most Punts, Game

10 Reggie Roby, Miami, 1985
9 Tom Wittum, San Francisco, 1974
Rohn Stark, Indianapolis, 1987
8 Jerrel Wilson, Kansas City, 1971
Tom Skladany, Detroit, 1982
Reggie Roby, Washington, 1995

Longest Punt

73 Shane Lechler, Oakland, 2002
70 Shane Lechler, Oakland, 2002
64 Tom Wittum, San Francisco, 1974
Darren Bennett, San Diego, 1996

AVERAGE YARDAGE

Highest Average, Career (10 punts)

46.73 Reggie Roby, Miami, 1985, 1990; Washington, 1995 (22-1,028)
45.27 Matt Turk, Washington, 1997-99 (15-679)
45.25 Jerrel Wilson, Kansas City, 1971-73 (16-724)

Highest Average, Game (4 punts)

60.75 Shane Lechler, Oakland, 2002 (4-243)
55.50 Darren Bennett, San Diego, 1996 (4-222)
52.00 Matt Turk, Washington, 1999 (4-208)

PUNT RETURNS

Most Punt Returns, Career

13 Rick Upchurch, Denver, 1977, 1979-1980, 1983
11 Vai Sikahema, St. Louis, 1987-88
Eric Metcalf, Cleveland 1994-95; San Diego 1998
10 Mike Nelms, Washington, 1981-83

Most Punt Returns, Game

7 Vai Sikahema, St. Louis, 1987
6 Henry Ellard, L.A. Rams, 1985
Gerald McNeil, Cleveland, 1988
Eric Metcalf, Cleveland, 1995
5 Rick Upchurch, Denver, 1980
Mike Nelms, Washington, 1981
Carl Roaches, Houston, 1982
Johnny Bailey, Phoenix, 1993

Most Fair Catches, Game

2 Jerry Logan, Baltimore, 1971
Dick Anderson, Miami, 1974
Henry Ellard, L.A. Rams, 1985
Isaac Bruce, St. Louis, 1997
Desmond Howard, Detroit, 2001

YARDS GAINED

Most Yards Gained, Career

183 Billy Johnson, Houston, 1976, 1978; Atlanta, 1984
138 Mel Renfro, Dallas, 1971-72, 1974
Rick Upchurch, Denver, 1977, 1979-1980, 1983
135 Eric Metcalf, Cleveland, 1994-95; San Diego 1998

Most Yards Gained, Game

159 Billy Johnson, Houston, 1976
138 Mel Renfro, Dallas, 1971
117 Wally Henry, Philadelphia, 1980

Longest Punt Return

90 Billy Johnson, Houston, 1976 (TD)
86 Wally Henry, Philadelphia, 1980 (TD)
82 Mel Renfro, Dallas, 1971 (TD)

AVERAGE YARDAGE

Highest Average, Career (4 returns)

22.88 Billy Johnson, Houston, 1976, 1978; Atlanta, 1984 (8-183)
21.50 Tony Green, Washington, 1979 (4-86)
15.67 David Meggett, N.Y. Giants, 1990; New England, 1997

Highest Average, Game (3 returns)

39.75 Billy Johnson, Houston, 1976 (4-159)
39.00 Wally Henry, Philadelphia, 1980 (3-117)
21.50 Tony Green, Washington, 1979 (4-86)

TOUCHDOWNS

Most Touchdowns, Game

2 Mel Renfro, Dallas, 1971
1 Billy Johnson, Houston, 1976
Wally Henry, Philadelphia, 1980

KICKOFF RETURNS

Most Kickoff Returns, Career

17 Michael Bates, Carolina, 1997-2001
14 Mel Gray, Detroit, 1991-92, 1995
11 Eric Metcalf, Cleveland, 1994-95; San Diego, 1998
Derrick Mason, Tennessee, 2001, 2004

Most Kickoff Returns, Game

8 Derrick Mason, Tennessee, 2004
7 Mel Gray, Detroit, 1995
Jerry Azumah, Chicago, 2004
6 Greg Pruitt, L.A. Raiders, 1984
David Meggett, New England, 1997
Michael Bates, Carolina, 1998
Steve Smith, Carolina, 2002

YARDS GAINED

Most Yards Gained, Career

488 Michael Bates, Carolina, 1997-2001
309 Greg Pruitt, Cleveland, 1974-75, 1977-78; L.A. Raiders, 1984
294 Mel Gray, Detroit, 1991-92, 1995

Most Yards Gained, Game

228 Jerry Azumah, Chicago, 2004
217 Michael Lewis, New Orleans, 2003
192 Greg Pruitt, L.A. Raiders, 1984

Longest Kickoff Return

66 Michael Bates, Carolina, 2000
62 Greg Pruitt, L.A. Raiders, 1984
61 Eugene (Mercury) Morris, Miami, 1972

AVERAGE YARDAGE

Highest Average, Career (4 returns)

43.40 Michael Lewis, New Orleans, 2003 (5-217)
35.00 Les (Speedy) Duncan, Washington, 1972 (5-175)
32.57 Jerry Azumah, Chicago, 2004 (7-228)

Highest Average, Game (3 returns)
43.40 Michael Lewis, New Orleans, 2003 (5-217)
42.00 Michael Bates, Carolina, 2000 (4-168)
35.00 Les (Speedy) Duncan, Washington, 1972 (5-175)

TOUCHDOWNS
Most Touchdowns, Game
None

FUMBLES
Most Fumbles, Career
6 Dan Fouts, San Diego, 1980-84, 1986
4 Lawrence McCutcheon, Los Angeles, 1974-78
Franco Harris, Pittsburgh, 1973-76, 1978-1981
Jay Schroeder, Washington, 1987
Vai Sikahema, St. Louis, 1987-88
Trent Green, Kansas City, 2004
3 O.J. Simpson, Buffalo, 1973-77
William Andrews, Atlanta, 1981-84
Joe Montana, San Francisco, 1982, 1984-85, 1988
Walter Payton, Chicago, 1977-1981, 1984-87
Neil Lomax, St. Louis, 1985, 1988
Jim Kelly, Buffalo, 1988, 1991-92
Chris Chandler, Atlanta, 1998-99
Peyton Manning, Indianapolis, 2000-01, 2003-04

Most Fumbles, Game
4 Jay Schroeder, Washington, 1987
Trent Green, Kansas City, 2004
3 Dan Fouts, San Diego, 1982
Vai Sikahema, St. Louis, 1987
2 By 14 players

RECOVERIES
Most Fumbles Recovered, Career
3 Harold Jackson, Philadelphia, 1973; Los Angeles, 1974, 1976, 1978 (3-own)
Dan Fouts, San Diego, 1980-84, 1986 (3-own)
Randy White, Dallas, 1978, 1980-86 (3-opp)
Trent Green, Kansas City, 2004 (3-own)
2 By many players

Most Fumbles Recovered, Game
3 Trent Green, Kansas City, 2004 (3-own)
2 Dick Anderson, Miami, 1974 (1-own, 1-opp)
Harold Jackson, Los Angeles, 1974 (2-own)
Dan Fouts, San Diego, 1982 (2-own)
Joey Browner, Minnesota, 1990 (2-opp)
Jessie Armstead, N.Y. Giants, 1999 (1-own, 1-opp)
Steve Beuerlein, Carolina, 2000 (2-own)

YARDAGE
Longest Fumble Return
83 Art Still, Kansas City, 1985 (TD, opp)
51 Phil Villapiano, Oakland, 1974 (opp)
37 Sam Mills, New Orleans, 1988 (opp)

TOUCHDOWNS
Most Touchdowns, Game
1 Art Still, Kansas City, 1985
Keith Millard, Minnesota, 1990

SACKS
Sacks have been compiled since 1983.

Most Sacks, Career
9.5 Reggie White, Philadelphia, 1987-1993; Green Bay, 1994, 1996-97, 1999
9.0 Howie Long, L.A. Raiders, 1984-88, 1990, 1993-1994
7.5 Bruce Smith, Buffalo, 1988-1991, 1995-96, 1998-99

Most Sacks, Game
4 Mark Gastineau, N.Y. Jets, 1985
Reggie White, Philadelphia, 1987
3 Richard Dent, Chicago, 1985
Bruce Smith, Buffalo, 1991
2.5 Bruce Smith, Buffalo, 1998

TEAM RECORDS

SCORING
Most Points, Game
55 NFC, 2004

Fewest Points, Game
3 AFC, 1984, 1989, 1994

Most Points, Both Teams, Game
107 NFC (55) vs. AFC (52), 2004

Fewest Points, Both Teams, Game
16 NFC (6) vs. AFC (10), 1987

TOUCHDOWNS
Most Touchdowns, Game
7 AFC, 2004
NFC, 2004

Fewest Touchdowns, Game
0 AFC, 1971, 1974, 1984, 1989, 1994
NFC, 1987, 1988

Most Touchdowns, Both Teams, Game
14 AFC (7) vs. NFC (7), 2004

Fewest Touchdowns, Both Teams, Game
1 AFC (0) vs. NFC (1), 1974
NFC (0) vs. AFC (1), 1987
NFC (0) vs. AFC (1), 1988

POINTS AFTER TOUCHDOWN
Most Points After Touchdown, Game
7 AFC, 2004

Most Points After Touchdown, Both Teams, Game
12 AFC (7) vs. NFC (5), 2004

FIELD GOALS
Most Field Goals Attempted, Game
6 AFC, 1972
NFC, 1981, 1983

Most Field Goals Attempted, Both Teams, Game
9 NFC (6) vs. AFC (3), 1983

Most Field Goals, Game
5 AFC, 1974

Most Field Goals, Both Teams, Game
7 AFC (5) vs. NFC (2), 1974

NET YARDS GAINED RUSHING AND PASSING
Most Yards Gained, Game
626 AFC, 2004

Fewest Yards Gained, Game
114 AFC, 1993

Most Yards Gained, Both Teams, Game
1,022 AFC (626) vs. NFC (396), 2004

Fewest Yards Gained, Both Teams, Game
424 AFC (202) vs. NFC (222), 1987

RUSHING
ATTEMPTS
Most Attempts, Game
50 AFC, 1974

Fewest Attempts, Game
9 NFC, 2001

Most Attempts, Both Teams, Game
80 AFC (50) vs. NFC (30), 1974

Fewest Attempts, Both Teams, Game
32 NFC (9) vs. AFC (23), 2001

YARDS GAINED
Most Yards Gained, Game
400 AFC, 1995
Fewest Yards Gained, Game
28 NFC, 1992
Most Yards Gained, Both Teams, Game
441 AFC (400) vs. NFC (41), 1995
Fewest Yards Gained, Both Teams, Game
119 NFC (36) vs. AFC (83), 2001

TOUCHDOWNS
Most Touchdowns, Game
3 NFC, 1989, 1991, 2000
AFC, 1995
Most Touchdowns, Both Teams, Game
4 AFC (2) vs. NFC (2), 1973
AFC (2) vs. NFC (2), 1980

PASSING

ATTEMPTS
Most Attempts, Game
58 NFC, 2002
Fewest Attempts, Game
17 NFC, 1972
Most Attempts, Both Teams, Game
101 NFC (54) vs. AFC (47), 2003
Fewest Attempts, Both Teams, Game
42 NFC (17) vs. AFC (25), 1972

COMPLETIONS
Most Completions, Game
32 NFC, 1993
AFC, 2001
Fewest Completions, Game
7 NFC, 1972, 1982
Most Completions, Both Teams, Game
60 AFC (32) vs. NFC (28), 2001
Fewest Completions, Both Teams, Game
18 NFC (7) vs. AFC (11), 1972

YARDS GAINED
Most Yards Gained, Game
515 AFC, 2004
Fewest Yards Gained, Game
42 NFC, 1982
Most Yards Gained, Both Teams, Game
775 AFC (515) vs. NFC (260), 2004
Fewest Yards Gained, Both Teams, Game
215 NFC (89) vs. AFC (126), 1972

TIMES SACKED
Most Times Sacked, Game
9 NFC, 1985
Fewest Times Sacked, Game
0 AFC, 1998, 1999, 2000, 2003
NFC, 1971, 1997, 2001
Most Times Sacked, Both Teams, Game
17 NFC (9) vs. AFC (8), 1985
Fewest Times Sacked, Both Teams, Game
1 NFC (0) vs. AFC (1), 1997

TOUCHDOWNS
Most Touchdowns, Game
5 AFC, 2004
Most Touchdowns, Both Teams, Game
9 AFC (5) vs. NFC (4), 2004

INTERCEPTIONS BY

Most Interceptions By, Game
6 AFC, 1977, 2003
Most Interceptions By, Both Teams, Game
8 AFC (6) vs. NFC (2), 2003

YARDS GAINED
Most Yards Gained, Game
113 AFC, 2003
Most Yards Gained, Both Teams, Game
172 NFC (102) vs. AFC (70), 1999

TOUCHDOWNS
Most Touchdowns, Game
2 NFC, 2000

PUNTING

Most Punts, Game
10 AFC, 1985
Fewest Punts, Game
0 NFC, 1989
Most Punts, Both Teams, Game
16 AFC (10) vs. NFC (6), 1985
Fewest Punts, Both Teams, Game
4 NFC (1) vs. AFC (3), 1992

PUNT RETURNS

Most Punt Returns, Game
7 NFC, 1985, 1987
AFC, 1995
Fewest Punt Returns, Game
0 AFC, 1984, 1989
Most Punt Returns, Both Teams, Game
11 NFC (7) vs. AFC (4), 1985
Fewest Punt Returns, Both Teams, Game
2 AFC (1) vs. NFC (1), 1996

YARDS GAINED
Most Yards Gained, Game
177 AFC, 1976
Fewest Yards Gained, Game
–1 NFC, 1991
Most Yards Gained, Both Teams, Game
263 AFC (177) vs. NFC (86), 1976
Fewest Yards Gained, Both Teams, Game
16 AFC (0) vs. NFC (16), 1984

TOUCHDOWNS
Most Touchdowns, Game
2 NFC, 1971

KICKOFF RETURNS

Most Kickoff Returns, Game
10 AFC, 2004
Fewest Kickoff Returns, Game
1 NFC, 1971, 1984, 1994
AFC, 1988, 1991
Most Kickoff Returns, Both Teams, Game
18 AFC (10) vs. NFC (8), 2004
Fewest Kickoff Returns, Both Teams, Game
5 NFC (2) vs. AFC (3), 1979
AFC (1) vs. NFC (4), 1988
NFC (2) vs. AFC (3), 1992
NFC (1) vs. AFC (4), 1994

YARDS GAINED
Most Yards Gained, Game
247 NFC, 2004

Fewest Yards Gained, Game
6 NFC, 1971
Most Yards Gained, Both Teams, Game
461 NFC (247) vs. AFC (214), 2004
Fewest Yards Gained, Both Teams, Game
99 NFC (48) vs. AFC (51), 1987

TOUCHDOWNS
Most Touchdowns, Game
None

FUMBLES
Most Fumbles, Game
10 NFC, 1974
Most Fumbles, Both Teams, Game
15 NFC (10) vs. AFC (5), 1974

RECOVERIES
Most Fumbles Recovered, Game
10 NFC, 1974 (6 own, 4 opp)
Most Fumbles Lost, Game
4 AFC, 1974, 1988
NFC, 1974

YARDS GAINED
Most Yards Gained, Game
87 AFC, 1985

TOUCHDOWNS
Most Touchdowns, Game
1 AFC, 1985
NFC, 1990

TURNOVERS
(Number of times losing the ball on interceptions and fumbles.)
Most Turnovers, Game
8 AFC, 1974
Fewest Turnovers, Game
0 AFC, 1991, 1997
NFC, 1991, 1995, 1996, 2001
Most Turnovers, Both Teams, Game
12 AFC (8) vs. NFC (4), 1974
Fewest Turnovers, Both Teams, Game
0 AFC vs. NFC, 1991

Rules

OFFICIALS

2004 NFL ROSTER OF OFFICIALS
Mike Pereira, Director of Officiating
Larry Upson, Director of Officiating Operations

No.	Name	Position	College
66	Anderson, Walt	Referee	Texas
108	Arthur, Gary	Line Judge	Wright State
34	Austin, Gerald	Referee	Western Carolina
26	Baltz, Mark	Head Linesman	Ohio University
72	Banks, Michael	Side Judge	Illinois State
55	Barnes, Tom	Line Judge	Minnesota
32	Bergman, Jeff	Line Judge	Robert Morris
91	Bergman, Jerry	Head Linesman	Robert Morris
7	Blum, Ron	Line Judge	Marin College
109	Boger, Jerome	Line Judge	Morehouse College
18	Boston, Byron	Line Judge	Austin
74	Bowers, Derick	Line Judge	Oklahoma
31	Brown, Chad	Umpire	East Texas State
134	Camp, Ed	Head Linesman	William Paterson
126	Carey, Don	Back Judge	UC Riverside
94	Carey, Mike	Referee	Santa Clara
39	Carlsen, Don	Side Judge	Cal State-Chico
63	Carollo, Bill	Referee	Wisconsin-Milwaukee
11	Carroll, Duke	Field Judge	Ithaca
60	Cavaletto, Gary	Field Judge	Hancock
41	Cheek, Boris	Field Judge	Morgan State
51	Cheffers, Carl	Side Judge	UC Irvine
65	Coleman, Walt	Referee	Arkansas
99	Corrente, Tony	Referee	Cal State-Fullerton
71	Coukart, Ed	Umpire	Northwestern
70	Dawson, Scott	Umpire	Virginia Tech
53	DeFelice, Garth	Umpire	San Diego State
113	Dorkowski, Don	Back Judge	Cal State-Los Angeles
6	Dornan, Kirk	Back Judge	Central Washington
27	Dyer, Lee	Field Judge	Tennessee-Chattanooga
3	Edwards, Scott	Field Judge	Alabama
81	Ellison, Roy	Umpire	Savannah State
61	Ferguson, Keith	Back Judge	San Jose State
64	Ferrell, Dan	Umpire	Cal State-Fullerton
47	Fincken, Tom	Side Judge	Kansas State
133	Freeman, Steve	Back Judge	Mississippi State
80	Gautreaux, Greg	Field Judge	Southwestern Louisiana
19	Green, Scott	Back Judge	Delaware
23	Grier, Johnny	Referee	University of D.C.
49	Hall, Rich	Umpire	Arizona
40	Hannah, Butch	Umpire	Middle Tennessee State
125	Hayes, Laird	Side Judge	Princeton
54	Hayward, George	Head Linesman	Missouri Western
93	Helverson, Scott	Back Judge	Iowa
97	Hill, Tom	Side Judge	Carson-Newman
28	Hittner, Mark	Head Linesman	Pittsburg State
85	Hochuli, Ed	Referee	Texas-El Paso
82	Horton, Buddy	Field Judge	Oregon State
37	Howey, Jim	Back Judge	Erskine College
35	Hussey, John	Line Judge	Idaho State
76	Jenkins, Darrell	Umpire	San Jose State
101	Johnson, Carl	Line Judge	Nicholls State
106	Jury, Al	Field Judge	San Bernardino Valley
86	Kukar, Bernie	Referee	St. John's
103	Lamberth, Jeff	Side Judge	Texas A&M
73	Larrew, Joe	Side Judge	St. Louis University
17	Lawing, Bob	Back Judge	North Carolina State
127	Leavy, Bill	Referee	San Jose State
130	Lewis, Darryll	Line Judge	Dartmouth
98	Lovett, Bill	Field Judge	Maryland
59	Luckett, Phil	Back Judge	Texas-El Paso

Ron Baynes, Supervisor of Officials
Jim Daopoulos, Supervisor of Officials
Neely Dunn, Supervisor of Officials

No.	Name	Position	College
92	Madsen, Carl	Umpire	Washington
77	McAulay, Terry	Referee	Louisiana State
120	McGrath, John	Head Linesman	Kentucky
110	McKinnely, Phil	Head Linesman	UCLA
48	Mello, Jim	Head Linesman	Northeastern
78	Meyer, Greg	Side Judge	TCU
115	Michalek, Tony	Umpire	Indiana
135	Morelli, Pete	Referee	St. Mary's College
20	Nemmers, Larry	Referee	Upper Iowa
124	Paganelli, Carl	Umpire	Michigan State
46	Paganelli, Perry	Back Judge	Hope College
132	Parry, John	Side Judge	Purdue
15	Patterson, Rick	Side Judge	Wofford
9	Perlman, Mark	Line Judge	Salem
10	Phares, Ron	Head Linesman	Virginia Tech
38	Powers, Eddy	Field Judge	Tennessee
5	Quirk, Jim	Umpire	Delaware
83	Reels, Richard	Back Judge	Chicago State
44	Rice, Jeff	Umpire	Northwestern
57	Riveron, Alberto	Side Judge	Miami
121	Rivers, Sanford	Head Linesman	Youngstown State
128	Rose, Larry	Side Judge	Florida
67	Rosenbaum, Doug	Field Judge	Illinois Wesleyan
58	Saracino, Jim	Field Judge	Northern Colorado
21	Schleyer, John	Head Linesman	Millersville
122	Schmitz, Bill	Back Judge	Colorado State
129	Schuster, BIll	Umpire	Alfred
45	Seeman, Jeff	Line Judge	Minnesota
118	Sifferman, Tom	Field Judge	Seattle
30	Slaughter, Gary	Head Linesman	East Texas State
2	Smith, Billy	Back Judge	East Carolina
90	Spanier, Michael	Line Judge	St. Cloud State
8	Spyksma, Bill	Line Judge	South Dakota
24	Stabile, Tom	Head Linesman	Slippery Rock
12	Steed, Greg	Back Judge	Howard
88	Steenson, Scott	Field Judge	North Texas
84	Steinkerchner, Mark	Line Judge	Akron
22	Stelljes, Steve	Head Linesman	Friends University
68	Stephan, Tom	Line Judge	Pittsburg State
114	Steratore, Gene	Field Judge	Kent State
112	Steratore, Tony	Back Judge	California (Penn.)
62	Stewart, Charles	Line Judge	Long Beach State
4	Toole, Doug	Side Judge	Utah State
42	Triplette, Jeff	Referee	Wake Forest
75	Vernatchi, Rob	Side Judge	UC Riverside
36	Veteri, Tony	Head Linesman	Manhattan College
52	Vinovich, Bill	Referee	San Diego
25	Waggoner, Bob	Back Judge	Juniata College
96	Wash, Undrey	Umpire	Texas-Arlington
116	Weatherford, Mike	Side Judge	Oklahoma State
87	Weidner, Paul	Head Linesman	Cincinnati
50	Weir, Mike	Field Judge	Missouri
123	White, Tom	Referee	Temple
43	Wilson, James	Head Linesman	Eastern Kentucky
29	Wilson, Steve	Umpire	Whitworth College
14	Winter, Ron	Referee	Michigan State
89	Wrolstad, Craig	Field Judge	Washington
16	Wyant, David	Side Judge	Virginia
33	Zimmer, Steve	Field Judge	Hofstra

NUMERICAL ROSTER

No.	Name	Position
2	Billy Smith	BJ
3	Scott Edwards	FJ
4	Doug Toole	SJ
5	Jim Quirk	U
6	Kirk Dornan	BJ
7	Ron Blum	LJ
8	Bill Spyksma	LJ
9	Mark Perlman	LJ
10	Ron Phares	HL
11	Duke Carroll	FJ
12	Greg Steed	BJ
14	Ron Winter	R
15	Rick Patterson	SJ
16	David Wyant	SJ
17	Bob Lawing	BJ
18	Byron Boston	LJ
19	Scott Green	BJ
20	Larry Nemmers	R
21	John Schleyer	HL
22	Steve Stelljes	HL
23	Johnny Grier	R
24	Tom Stabile	HL
25	Bob Waggoner	BJ
26	Mark Baltz	HL
27	Lee Dyer	FJ
28	Mark Hittner	HL
29	Steve Wilson	U
30	Gary Slaughter	HL
31	Chad Brown	U
32	Jeff Bergman	LJ
33	Steve Zimmer	FJ
34	Gerry Austin	R
35	John Hussey	LJ
36	Tony Veteri	HL
37	Jim Howey	BJ
38	Eddy Powers	FJ
39	Don Carlsen	SJ
40	Butch Hannah	U
41	Boris Cheek	FJ
42	Jeff Triplette	R
43	James Wilson	HL
44	Jeff Rice	U
45	Jeff Seeman	LJ
46	Perry Paganelli	BJ
47	Tom Fincken	SJ
48	Jim Mello	HL
49	Rich Hall	U
50	Mike Weir	FJ
51	Carl Cheffers	SJ
52	Bill Vinovich	R
53	Garth DeFelice	U
54	George Hayward	HL
55	Tom Barnes	LJ
57	Alberto Riveron	SJ
58	Jim Saracino	FJ
59	Phil Luckett	BJ
60	Gary Cavaletto	FJ
61	Keith Ferguson	BJ
62	Charles Stewart	LJ
63	Bill Carollo	R
64	Dan Ferrell	U
65	Walt Coleman	R
66	Walt Anderson	R
67	Doug Rosenbaum	FJ
68	Tom Stephan	LJ
70	Scott Dawson	U
71	Ed Coukart	U
72	Michael Banks	SJ
73	Joe Larrew	SJ
74	Derick Bowers	LJ
75	Rob Vernatchi	SJ
76	Darrell Jenkins	U
77	Terry McAulay	R
78	Greg Meyer	SJ
80	Greg Gautreaux	FJ
81	Roy Ellison	U
82	Buddy Horton	FJ
83	Richard Reels	BJ
84	Mark Steinkerchner	LJ
85	Ed Hochuli	R
86	Bernie Kukar	R
87	Paul Weidner	HL
88	Scott Steenson	FJ
89	Craig Wrolstad	FJ
90	Michael Spanier	LJ
91	Jerry Bergman	HL
92	Carl Madsen	U
93	Scott Helverson	BJ
94	Mike Carey	R
96	Undrey Wash	U
97	Tom Hill	SJ
98	Bill Lovett	FJ
99	Tony Corrente	R
101	Carl Johnson	LJ
103	Jeff Lamberth	SJ
106	Al Jury	FJ
107	Ron Marinucci	LJ
108	Gary Arthur	LJ
109	Jerome Boger	LJ
110	Phil McKinnely	HL
112	Tony Steratore	BJ
113	Don Dorkowski	BJ
114	Gene Steratore	FJ
115	Tony Michalek	U
116	Mike Weatherford	SJ
118	Tom Sifferman	FJ
120	John McGrath	HL
121	Sanford Rivers	HL
122	Bill Schmitz	BJ
123	Tom White	R
124	Carl Paganelli	U
125	Laird Hayes	SJ
126	Don Carey	BJ
127	Bill Leavy	R
128	Larry Rose	SJ
129	Bill Schuster	U
130	Darryll Lewis	LJ
132	John Parry	SJ
133	Steve Freeman	BJ
134	Ed Camp	HL
135	Pete Morelli	R

2004 OFFICIALS AT A GLANCE

REFEREES

Walt Anderson, No. **66,** Texas, dentist, orthodontics, 9th year.
Gerry Austin, No. **34,** Western Carolina, president, leadership development group, 23rd year.
Mike Carey, No. **94,** Santa Clara, owner, skiing accessories, 15th year.
Bill Carollo, No. **63,** Wisconsin-Milwaukee, marketing executive, 16th year.
Walt Coleman, No. **65,** Arkansas, manager, dairy processor, 16th year.
Tony Corrente, No. **99,** Cal State-Fullerton, educator, 10th year.
Johnny Grier, No. **23,** University of D.C., planning engineer, 24th year.
Ed Hochuli, No. **85,** Texas-El Paso, attorney, 15th year.
Bernie Kukar, No. **86,** St. John's, sales representative, employees benefit plan, 21st year.
Bill Leavy, No. **127,** San Jose State, retired firefighter, 10th year.
Terry McAulay, No. **77,** Louisiana State, senior computer scientist, 7th year.
Pete Morelli, No. **135,** St. Mary's, high school principal, 8th year.
Larry Nemmers, No. **20,** Upper Iowa, motivational speaker, 20th year.
Jeff Triplette, No. **42,** Wake Forest, vice president, world-wide energy company, 9th year.
Bill Vinovich, No. **52,** San Diego, certified public accountant, 4th year.
Tom White, No. **123,** Temple, consultant, 16th year.
Ron Winter, No. **14,** Michigan State, university professor, 10th year.

UMPIRES

Chad Brown, No. **31,** East Texas State, manager, intramural/sports clubs, former NFL player, 13th year.
Ed Coukart, No. **71,** Northwestern, vice-president, commercial bank, 16th year.
Scott Dawson, No. **70,** Virginia Tech, president/owner, commercial construction company, 10th year.
Garth DeFelice, No. **53,** San Diego State, director of distributing, beverage company, 7th year.
Roy Ellison, No. **81,** Savannah State, technical staff member, 2nd year.
Dan Ferrell, No. **64,** Cal State-Fullerton, regional manager, parts distribution and logistics, 2nd year.
Rich Hall, No. **49,** Arizona, custom cabinetry, 1st year.
Butch Hannah, No. **40,** Middle Tennessee State, federal probation officer, 6th year.
Darrell Jenkins, No. **76,** San Jose State, retired, 3rd year.
Carl Madsen, No. **92,** Washington, partner/owner, office furniture dealership, 8th year.
Tony Michalek, No. **115,** Indiana, eurodollar future trader, 3rd year.
Carl Paganelli, No. **124,** Michigan State, federal probation officer, 6th year.
Jim Quirk, No. **5,** Delaware, consultant, 17th year.
Jeff Rice, No. **44,** Northwestern, attorney, 10th year.
Bill Schuster, No. **129,** Alfred, insurance broker, 5th year.
Undrey Wash, No. **96,** Texas-Arlington, claims manager, 5th year.
Steve Wilson, No. **29,** Whitworth College, church administrator, 6th year.

HEAD LINESMEN

Mark Baltz, No. **26,** Ohio University, sales consultant, 16th year.
Jerry Bergman, No. **91,** Robert Morris, sales executive, 3rd year.
Ed Camp, No. **134,** William Paterson, teacher, 5th year.
George Hayward, No. **54,** Missouri Western, vice-president and manager, warehouse company, 14th year.
Mark Hittner, No. **28,** Pittsburg State, investment banker, 8th year.
John McGrath, No. **120,** Kentucky, senior account executive, 3rd year.
Phil McKinnely, No. **110,** UCLA, inventory control, former NFL player, 2nd year.
Jim Mello, No. **48,** Northeastern, facilities management, 1st year.
Ron Phares, No. **10,** Virginia Tech, president, construction company, 20th year.
Sanford Rivers, No. **121,** Youngstown State, university vice-president, 15th year.
John Schleyer, No. **21,** Millersville, medical sales, 15th year.
Gary Slaughter, No. **30,** East Texas State, general manager, 9th year.
Tom Stabile, No. **24,** Slippery Rock, secondary educational administrator, 10th year.
Steve Stelljes, No. **22,** Friends University, business planning manager, 3rd year.
Tony Veteri, No. **36,** Manhattan, director of athletics, 13th year.
Paul Weidner, No. **87,** Cincinnati, marketing manager, 19th year.
James Wilson, No. **43,** Eastern Kentucky, area sales manager, 7th year.

LINE JUDGES

Gary Arthur, No. **108,** Wright State, president, commercial printing company, 8th year.
Tom Barnes, No. **55,** Minnesota, manufacturing representative, 19th year.
Jeff Bergman, No. **32,** Robert Morris, president and chief executive officer, medical services, 13th year.
Ron Blum, No. **7,** Marin College, professional golfer, 20th year.
Jerome Boger, No. **109,** Morehouse College, commercial insurance underwriter, 1st year.
Byron Boston, No. **18,** Austin, tax consultant, 10th year.
Derick Bowers, No. **74,** East Central University, purchasing supervisor, 2nd year.
John Hussey, No. **35,** Idaho State, sales representative, retail logistics group, 3rd year.
Carl Johnson, No. **101,** Nicholls State, district sales manager, 4th year.
Darryll Lewis, No. **130,** Dartmouth, associate professor, 6th year.
Mark Perlman, No. **9,** Salem, teacher, 4th year.
Jeff Seeman, No. **45,** Minnesota, brokerage sales, 3rd year.
Mike Spanier, No. **90,** St. Cloud State, middle school principal, 6th year.
Bill Spyksma, No. **8,** South Dakota, managing partner, marina, 10th year.
Mark Steinkerchner, No. **84,** Akron, vice-president, 11th year.
Tom Stephan, No. **68,** Pittsburg State, business broker, 6th year.
Charles Stewart, No. **62,** Long Beach State, retired human services administrator, 13th year.

FIELD JUDGES

Duke Carroll, No. **11,** Ithaca, insurance sales, 10th year.
Gary Cavaletto, No. **60,** Hancock, general manager, agricultural operations, 2nd year.
Boris Cheek, No. **41,** Morgan State, director of operations and management, 9th year.
Lee Dyer, No. **27,** Tennessee-Chattanooga, sales manager, 2nd year.
Scott Edwards, No. **3,** Alabama, environmental engineer, 6th year.
Greg Gautreaux, No. **80,** Southwestern Louisiana, athletic programs manager, 3rd year.
Buddy Horton, No. **82,** Oregon State, water service worker, 6th year.
Al Jury, No. **106,** San Bernardino Valley, state traffic officer, 27th year.
Bill Lovett, No. **98,** Maryland, managing partner, financial sales, 15th year.
Eddy Powers, No. **38,** Tennessee, sales/design office supply, 3rd year.
Doug Rosenbaum, No. **67,** Illinois Wesleyan, financial advisor, 4th year.
Jim Saracino, No. **58,** Northern Colorado, secondary educator, 10th year.
Tom Sifferman, No. **118,** Seattle, manufacturer's representative, 19th year.
Scott Steenson, No. **88,** North Texas, commercial real estate broker, 14th year.
Gene Steratore, No. **114,** Kent State, co-owner, supply company, 2nd year.
Mike Weir, No. **50,** Missouri, owner, sporting goods store, 3rd year.
Craig Wrolstad, No. **89,** Washington, education, 2nd year.
Steve Zimmer, No. **33,** Hofstra, attorney, 8th year.

SIDE JUDGES

Michael Banks, No. **72,** Illinois State, carpenter foreman, 3rd year.
Don Carlsen, No. **39,** Cal State-Chico, retired county school superintendent, 16th year.
Carl Cheffers, No. **51,** UC Irvine, sales manager, 5th year.
Tom Fincken, No. **47,** Emporia State, retired educational administrator, 21st year.
Laird Hayes, No. **125,** Princeton, professor, physical education & athletics, 10th year.
Tom Hill, No. **97,** Carson Newman, teacher, 6th year.
Jeff Lamberth, No. **103,** Texas A&M, attorney, 3rd year.
Joe Larrew, No. **73,** St. Louis University, attorney, 3rd year.
Greg Meyer, No. **78,** TCU, banker, 3rd year.
John Parry, No. **132,** Purdue, corporate pilot, 5th year.
Rick Patterson, No. **15,** Wofford, banker, 9th year.
Alberto Riveron, No. **57,** Miami, commercial restaurant equipment, 1st year.
Larry Rose, No. **128,** Florida, financial planner, 8th year.
Doug Toole, No. **4,** Utah State, physical therapist, 17th year.
Rob Vernatchi, No. **75,** UC Riverside, enforcement investigator, 1st year.
Mike Weatherford, No. **116,** Oklahoma State, energy trader, 3rd year.
David Wyant, No. **16,** Virginia, consulting engineer, 14th year.

BACK JUDGES

Don Carey, No. **126,** UC Riverside, contract manager, 10th year.
Don Dorkowski, No. **113,** Cal State-Los Angeles, pump manufacturer, 19th year.
Kirk Dornan, No. **6,** Central Washington, purchasing manager, 11th year.
Keith Ferguson, No. **61,** San Jose State, sales, 5th year.
Steve Freeman, No. **133,** Mississippi State, custom home builder, 4th year.
Scott Green, No. **19,** Delaware, vice-president, government relations, 14th year.
Scott Helverson, No. **93,** Iowa, sales, printing and promotions, 2nd year.
Jim Howey, No. **37,** Erskine College, director of adult education, 6th year.
Bob Lawing, No. **17,** North Carolina State, real estate management, 8th year.
Phil Luckett, No. **59,** Texas-El Paso, computer program analyst, federal civil services, 14th year.
Perry Paganelli, No. **46,** Hope College, high school administrator, 7th year.
Richard Reels, No. **83,** Chicago State, director of security, court services, 12th year.
Bill Schmitz, No. **122,** Colorado State, general sales manager, 16th year.
Billy Smith, No. **2,** East Carolina, federal government, 11th year.
Greg Steed, No. **12,** Howard, computer systems analyst, 2nd year.
Tony Steratore, No. **112,** California (Penn.), co-owner, supply company, 5th year.
Bob Waggoner, No. **25,** Juniata College, probation officer, 8th year.

OFFICIAL SIGNALS

1

TOUCHDOWN, FIELD GOAL, or SUCCESSFUL TRY
Both arms extended above head.

2

SAFETY
Palms together above head.

3

FIRST DOWN
Arm pointed toward defensive team's goal.

4

CROWD NOISE, DEAD BALL, or NEUTRAL ZONE ESTABLISHED
One arm above head with an open hand.
With fist closed: **Fourth Down.**

5

BALL ILLEGALLY TOUCHED, KICKED, or BATTED
Fingertips tap both shoulders.

6

TIME OUT
Hands crisscrossed above head.
Same signal followed by placing one hand on top of cap: **Referee's Time Out.**
Same signal followed by arm swung at side: **Touchback.**

7

NO TIME OUT or
TIME IN WITH WHISTLE
Full arm circled to simulate moving clock.

8

DELAY OF GAME
or EXCESS TIME OUT
Folded arms.

9

FALSE START,
ILLEGAL FORMATION, or
KICKOFF or SAFETY KICK
OUT OF BOUNDS or
KICKING TEAM PLAYER
VOLUNTARILY OUT OF BOUNDS
DURING A PUNT
Forearms rotated over and over in front of body.

10

PERSONAL FOUL
One wrist striking the other above head.
Same signal followed by swinging leg:
Roughing the Kicker.
Same signal followed by raised arm swinging forward:
Roughing the Passer.
Same signal followed by grasping facemask: **Major Facemask.**

11

HOLDING
Grasping one wrist, the fist clenched, in front of chest.

12

ILLEGAL USE OF HANDS,
ARMS, or BODY
Grasping one wrist, the hand open and facing forward, in front of chest.

OFFICIAL SIGNALS

13

PENALTY REFUSED, INCOMPLETE PASS, PLAY OVER, or MISSED FIELD GOAL or EXTRA POINT
Hands shifted in horizontal plane.

14

PASS JUGGLED INBOUNDS AND CAUGHT OUT OF BOUNDS
Hands up and down in front of chest (following incomplete pass signal).

15

ILLEGAL FORWARD PASS
One hand waved behind back followed by loss of down signal (23), when appropriate.

16

INTENTIONAL GROUNDING OF PASS
Parallel arms waved in a diagonal plane across body. Followed by loss of down signal (23).

17

INTERFERENCE WITH FORWARD PASS or FAIR CATCH
Hands open and extended forward from shoulders with hands vertical.

18

INVALID FAIR-CATCH SIGNAL
One hand waved above head.

19

INELIGIBLE RECEIVER or INELIGIBLE MEMBER OF KICKING TEAM DOWNFIELD
Right hand touching top of cap.

20

ILLEGAL CONTACT
One open hand extended forward.

21

OFFSIDE, ENCROACHMENT, or NEUTRAL ZONE INFRACTION
Hands on hips.

22

ILLEGAL MOTION AT SNAP
Horizontal arc with one hand.

23

LOSS OF DOWN
Both hands held behind head.

24

INTERLOCKING INTERFERENCE, PUSHING, or HELPING RUNNER
Pushing movement of hands to front with arms downward.

25

TOUCHING A FORWARD PASS or SCRIMMAGE KICK
Diagonal motion of one hand across another.

26

UNSPORTSMANLIKE CONDUCT
Arms outstretched, palms down.

27

ILLEGAL CUT
Hand striking front of thigh.
ILLEGAL BLOCK BELOW THE WAIST
One hand striking front of thigh preceded by personal-foul signal (10).
CHOP BLOCK
Both hands striking side of thighs preceded by personal-foul signal (10).
CLIPPING
One hand striking back of calf preceded by personal-foul signal (10).

28

ILLEGAL CRACKBACK
Strike of an open right hand against the right mid-thigh preceded by personal foul signal (10).

29

PLAYER DISQUALIFIED
Ejection signal.

30

TRIPPING
Repeated action of right foot in back of left heel.

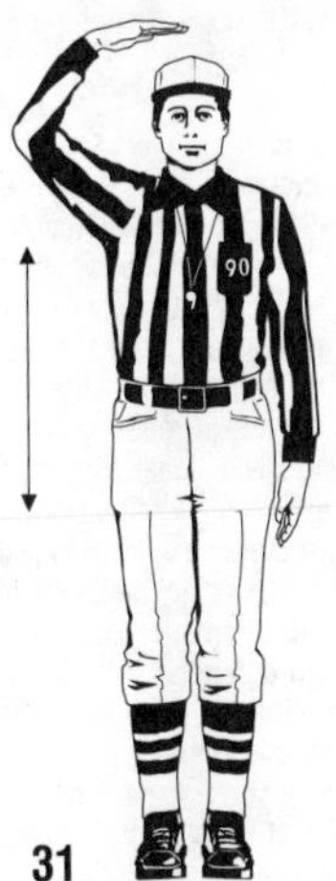

31

UNCATCHABLE FORWARD PASS
Palm of right hand held parallel to ground above head and moved back and forth.

32

TWELVE MEN IN OFFENSIVE HUDDLE or TOO MANY MEN ON THE FIELD
Both hands on top of head.

33

FACEMASK
Grasping facemask with one hand.

34

ILLEGAL SHIFT
Horizontal arcs with two hands.

35

RESET PLAY CLOCK– 25 SECONDS
Pump one arm vertically.

36

RESET PLAY CLOCK– 40 SECONDS
Pump two arms vertically.

NFL DIGEST OF RULES

This Digest of Rules of the National Football League has been prepared to aid players, fans, and members of the press, radio, and television media in their understanding of the game.

It is not meant to be a substitute for the official rule book. In any case of conflict between these explanations and the official rules, the rules always have precedence.

In order to make it easier to coordinate the information in this digest, the topics discussed generally follow the order of the rule book.

OFFICIALS' JURISDICTIONS, POSITIONS, AND DUTIES

Referee—General oversight and control of game. Gives signals for all fouls and is final authority for rule interpretations. Takes a position in backfield 10 to 12 yards behind line of scrimmage, favors right side (if quarterback is right-handed passer). Determines legality of snap, observes deep back(s) for legal motion. On running plays, observes quarterback during and after handoff, remains with him until action has cleared away, then proceeds downfield, checking on runner and contact behind him. When runner is downed, Referee determines forward progress from wing official and, if necessary, adjusts final position of ball.

On pass plays, drops back as quarterback begins to fade back, picks up legality of tackle on Head Linesman's side. Changes to complete concentration on quarterback as defenders approach. Primarily responsible to rule on possible roughing action on passer and if ball becomes loose, rules whether ball is free on a fumble or dead on an incomplete pass. Shares responsibility with Umpire, Linesman, and Line Judge on intentional grounding.

During kicking situations, Referee has primary responsibility to rule on kicker's actions and whether or not any subsequent contact by a defender is legal. During punt plays, Referee's position is parallel to kicker and wide. The Referee will announce on the microphone when each period is ended, penalties, a charged team time out, and when the two-minute warning for each half is reached.

Umpire—Primary responsibilities are to rule on players' conduct and actions on scrimmage line, as well as check on their equipment. Lines up approximately four to five yards downfield, varying position from the outside shoulder of one guard to outside shoulder of opposite guard. Looks for possible false start by offensive linemen. Observes legality of contact by both offensive linemen while blocking and by defensive players while they attempt to ward off blockers. Is prepared to call rule infractions if they occur on offense or defense. Moves forward to line of scrimmage when pass play develops in order to insure that interior linemen do not move illegally downfield. If offensive linemen indicate screen pass is to be attempted, Umpire shifts his attention toward screen side, picks up potential receiver in order to insure that he will legally be permitted to run his pattern and continues to rule on action of blockers. Umpire is to assist in ruling on incomplete or trapped passes when ball is thrown overhead or short. On field goal and try-kick attempts, he will become a second umpire with the Side Judge.

Head Linesman—Primarily responsible for ruling on offside, encroachment, and actions pertaining to scrimmage line prior to or at snap. Takes a position straddling the line of scrimmage. Keys on closest setback on his side of the field. On pass plays, Linesman is responsible to clear his receiver approximately seven yards downfield as he moves to a point five yards beyond the line. Linesman's secondary responsibility is to rule on any illegal action taken by defenders on any delay receiver moving downfield. Has full responsibility for ruling on sideline plays on his side, e.g., pass receiver or runner in or out of bounds. Together with Referee, Linesman is responsible for keeping track of number of downs and is in charge of mechanics of his chain crew in connection with its duties.

Linesman must be prepared to assist in determining forward progress by a runner on play directed toward middle or into his side zone. He, in turn, is to signal Referee or Umpire what forward point ball has reached. Linesman is also responsible to rule on legality of action involving any receiver who approaches his side zone. He is to call pass interference when the infraction occurs and is to rule on legality of blockers and defenders on plays involving ball carriers, whether it is entirely a running play, a combination pass and run, or a play involving a kick. Also assists referee with intentional grounding.

Line Judge—Straddles line of scrimmage on side of field opposite Linesman. Keeps time of game as a backup for official clock operator. However, should official clock malfunction or be operated improperly, the time kept by the Line Judge is official. Along with Linesman is responsible for offside, encroachment, and actions pertaining to scrimmage line prior to or at snap. Line Judge keys on closest setback on his side of field. Line Judge is to observe his receiver until he moves at least seven yards downfield. He then moves toward backfield side, being especially alert to rule on any back in motion and on flight of ball when pass is made (he must rule whether forward or backward). Line Judge has primary responsibility to rule whether or not passer is behind or beyond line of scrimmage when pass is made. He also assists in observing actions by blockers and defenders who are on his side of field. After pass is thrown, Line Judge directs attention toward activities that occur in back of Umpire. During punting situations, Line Judge remains at line of scrimmage to be sure that only the end men move downfield until kick has been made. He also rules whether or not the kick crossed line and then observes action by members of the kicking team who are moving downfield to cover the kick. The Line Judge will advise the Referee when time has expired at the end of each period.

Field Judge—Operates on same side of field as Line Judge, 20 yards deep. Keys on widest receiver on his side. Concentrates on path of end or back, observing legality of his potential block(s) or of actions taken against him. Is prepared to rule from deep position on holding or illegal use of hands by end or back or on defensive infractions committed by player guarding him. Has primary responsibility to make decisions involving sideline on his side of field, e.g., pass receiver or runner in or out of bounds.

Field Judge makes decisions involving catching, recovery, or illegal touching of a loose ball beyond line of scrimmage. Rules on plays involving pass receiver, including legality of catch or pass interference. Assists in covering actions of runner, including blocks by teammates and that of defenders. Rules on blocking during punt returns and, together with Back Judge, rules whether or not field goal and try-kick attempts are successful.

Side Judge—Operates on same side of field as Linesman, 20 yards deep. Keys on widest receiver on his side. Concentrates on path of this receiver, observing legality of his potential block(s) or of actions taken against him. Is prepared to rule from deep position on holding or illegal use of hands by the receiver or on defensive infractions committed by player defending him. Has primary responsibility to make decisions involving sideline on his side of field, e.g., pass receiver or runner in or out of bounds.

Side Judge makes decisions involving catching, recovery, or illegal touching of a loose ball beyond line of scrimmage. Rules on plays involving pass receiver, including legality of catch or pass interference. Assists in covering actions of runner, including blocks by teammates and that of defenders and rules on blocking during punt returns. On field goals and try-kick attempts, he becomes a second umpire.

Back Judge—Takes a position 25 yards downfield. In general, favors the tight end's side of field. Usually keys on tight end, concentrates on his path and observes legality of tight end's potential block(s) or of actions taken against him. Is prepared to rule from deep position on holding or illegal use of hands by end or back or on defensive infractions committed by player defending him.

Back Judge times interval between plays on 40/25-second clock plus intermission between two periods of each half. Makes decisions involving catching, recovery, or illegal touching of a loose ball beyond line of scrimmage. Is responsible to rule on plays involving end line. Calls pass interference, fair-catch infractions, and blocking during kick returns and, together with Field Judge, rules whether or not field goal and try-kick attempts are successful.

DEFINITIONS

1. **Chucking:** Warding off an opponent who is in front of a defender by contacting him with a quick extension of arm or arms, followed by the return of arm(s) to a flexed position, thereby breaking the original contact.
2. **Clipping:** Throwing the body across the back of an opponent's leg or hitting him from the back below the waist while moving up from behind unless the opponent is a runner or the contact is above the knee in close line play.
3. **Close Line Play:** The area between the positions normally occupied by the offensive tackles, extending three yards on each side of the line of scrimmage. It is legal to clip above the knee.
4. **Crackback:** Eligible receivers who take or move to a position more than two yards outside the tackle or a player in a backfielf position may not block an opponent below the waist toward the ball at the snap and within five yards of the line of scrimmage.
5. **Dead Ball:** Ball not in play.
6. **Double Foul:** A foul by each team during the same down.
7. **Down:** The period of action that starts when the ball is put in play and ends when it is dead.
8. **Encroachment:** When a defensive player enters the neutral zone and makes contact with an opponent before the ball is snapped.
9. **Fair Catch:** An unhindered catch of a kick by a member of the receiving team who must raise one arm a full length above his head and wave his arm from side to side while the kick is in flight.
10. **Foul:** Any violation of a playing rule.
11. **Free Kick:** A kickoff or safety kick. It may be a placekick, dropkick, or punt, except a punt may not be used on a kickoff following a touchdown, successful field goal, or to begin each half or overtime period. A tee cannot be used on a fair-catch or safety kick.
12. **Fumble:** The unintentional loss of player possession of the ball.
13. **Game Clock:** Scoreboard game clock.
14. **Impetus:** The action of a player that gives momentum to the ball and sends it into the end zone.
15. **Live Ball:** A ball legally free-kicked or snapped. It continues in play until the down ends.
16. **Loose Ball:** A live ball not in possession of any player.
17. **Muff:** The touching of a loose ball by a player in an unsuccessful attempt to obtain possession.
18. **Neutral Zone:** The space the length of a ball between the two scrimmage lines. The offensive team and defensive team must remain behind their end of the ball.
    Exception: The offensive player who snaps the ball.
19. **Offside:** A player is offside when any part of his body is beyond his scrimmage or free kick line when the ball is snapped or kicked. Exception: Snapper, holder of placekick or kicker.
20. **Own Goal:** The goal a team is defending.
21. **Play Clock:** 40/25 second clock.
22. **Pocket Area:** Applies from a point two yards outside of either offensive tackle and includes the tight end if he drops off the line of scrimmage to pass protect. Pocket extends longitudinally behind the line back to offensive team's own end line. For purposes of intentional grounding, the pocket is considered tackle to tackle.
23. **Possession of a Pass:** When a player controls the ball throughout the act of clearly touching both feet, or any other part of his body other than his hand(s), to the ground inbounds.
24. **Post-Possession Foul:** A foul by the receiving team that occurs after a ball is legally kicked from scrimmage prior to possession changing. The ball must cross the line of scrimmage and the receiving team must retain the kicked ball unless it is part of a double foul.
25. **Punt:** A kick made when a player drops the ball and kicks it while it is in flight.
26. **Safety:** The situation in which the ball is dead on or behind a team's own goal if the impetus comes from a player on that team. Two points are scored for the opposing team.
27. **Shift:** The movement of two or more offensive players at the same time before the snap.
28. **Striking:** The act of swinging, clubbing, or propelling the arm or forearm in contacting an opponent.
29. **Sudden Death:** The continuation of a tied game into sudden death overtime in which the team scoring first (by safety, field goal, or touchdown) wins.
30. **Touchback:** When a ball is dead on or behind a team's own goal line, provided the impetus came from an opponent and provided it is not a touchdown or a missed field goal attempt when the ball was kicked outside the 20-yard line.
31. **Touchdown:** When any part of the ball, legally in possession of a player inbounds, breaks the plane of the opponent's goal line, provided it is not a touchback.
32. **Unsportsmanlike Conduct:** Any act contrary to the generally understood principles of sportsmanship.

SUMMARY OF PENALTIES

Automatic First Down

1. Awarded to offensive team on all <u>defensive fouls</u> with these exceptions:
   (a) Offside.
   (b) Encroachment.
   (c) Delay of game.
   (d) Illegal substitution.
   (e) Excessive time out(s).
   (f) Incidental grasp of facemask.
   (g) Neutral zone infraction.
   (h) Running into the kicker.
   (i) More than 11 players on the field at the snap for either team.

Five Yards

1. Defensive holding or illegal use of hands (automatic first down).
2. Delay of game on offense or defense.
3. Delay of kickoff.
4. Encroachment.
5. Excessive time out(s).
6. False start.
7. Illegal formation.
8. Illegal shift.
9. Illegal motion.
10. Illegal substitution.
11. First onside kickoff out of bounds between goal lines and untouched or last touched by kickers.
12. Invalid fair catch signal.
13. More than 11 players on the field at snap for either team.
14. Less than seven men on offensive line at snap.
15. Offside.
16. Failure to pause one second after shift or huddle.
17. Running into kicker.
18. More than one man in motion at snap.
19. Grasping facemask of the ball carrier or quarterback.
20. Player out of bounds at snap.
21. Ineligible member(s) of kicking team going beyond line of scrimmage before ball is kicked.
22. Illegal return.
23. Failure to report change of eligibility.
24. Neutral zone infraction.

25. Loss of team time out(s) or five-yard penalty on the defense for excessive crowd noise. Offensive team's quarterback can be penalized if he does not make every effort to put the ball in play.
26. Ineligible player downfield during passing down.
27. Second forward pass behind the line.
28. Forward pass is first touched by eligible receiver who has gone out of bounds and returned.
29. Forward pass touches or is caught by an ineligible receiver on or behind line.
30. Forward pass thrown from behind line of scrimmage after ball once crossed the line.
31. Kicking team player voluntarily out of bounds during a punt.
32. Twelve (12) men in the huddle.

Ten Yards

1. Offensive pass interference.
2. Holding, illegal use of hands, arms, or body by offense.
3. Tripping by a member of either team.
4. Helping the runner.
5. Deliberately batting or punching a loose ball.
6. Deliberately kicking a loose ball.
7. Illegal block above the waist.

Fifteen Yards

1. Chop block.
2. Clipping below the waist.
3. Fair catch interference.
4. Illegal crackback block by offense.
5. Piling on.
6. Roughing the kicker.
7. Roughing the passer.
8. Twisting, turning, or pulling an opponent by the facemask.
9. Unnecessary roughness.
10. Unsportsmanlike conduct.
11. Delay of game at start of either half.
12. Illegal low block.
13. A tackler using his helmet to butt, spear, or ram an opponent.
14. Any player who uses the top of his helmet unnecessarily.
15. A punter, placekicker, or holder who simulates being roughed by a defensive player.
16. Leaping.
17. Leverage.
18. Any player who removes his helmet after a play while on the field.
19. Taunting.

Five Yards and Loss of Down (Combination Penalty)

1. Forward pass thrown from beyond line of scrimmage.

Ten Yards and Loss of Down (Combination Penalty)

1. Intentional grounding of forward pass (safety if passer is in own end zone). If foul occurs more than 10 yards behind line, play results in loss of down at spot of foul.

Fifteen Yards and Loss of Coin Toss Option

1. Team's late arrival on the field prior to scheduled kickoff.
2. Captains not appearing for coin toss.

Fifteen Yards (and disqualification if flagrant)

1. Striking opponent with fist.
2. Kicking or kneeing opponent.
3. Striking opponent on head or neck with forearm, elbow, or hands whether or not the initial contact is made below the neck area.
4. Roughing kicker.
5. Roughing passer.
6. Malicious unnecessary roughness.
7. Unsportsmanlike conduct.
8. Palpably unfair act. (Distance penalty determined by the Referee after consultation with other officials.)

Fifteen Yards and Automatic Disqualification

1. Using a helmet (not worn) as a weapon.
2. Striking or purposely shoving a game official.

Suspension From Game For One Down

1. Illegal equipment. (Player may return after one down when legally equipped.)

Touchdown Awarded (Palpably Unfair Act)

1. When Referee determines a palpably unfair act deprived a team of a touchdown. (Example: Player comes off bench and tackles runner apparently en route to touchdown.)

FIELD

1. Sidelines and end lines are out of bounds. The goal line is actually in the end zone. A player with the ball in his possession scores a touchdown when the ball is on, above, or over the goal line.
2. The field is rimmed by a white border, six feet wide, along the sidelines. All of this is out of bounds.
3. The hashmarks (inbound lines) are 70 feet, 9 inches from each sideline.
4. Goal posts must be single-standard type, offset from the end line and painted bright gold. The goal posts must be 18 feet, 6 inches wide and the top face of the crossbar must be 10 feet above the ground. Vertical posts extend at least 30 feet above the crossbar. A ribbon 4 inches by 42 inches long is to be attached to the top of each post. The actual goal is the plane extending indefinitely above the crossbar and between the outer edges of the posts.
5. The field is 360 feet long and 160 feet wide. The end zones are 30 feet deep. The line used in try-for-point plays is two yards out from the goal line.
6. Chain crew members and ball boys must be uniformly identifiable.
7. All clubs must use standardized sideline markers. Pylons must be used for goal line and end line markings.
8. End zone markings and club identification at 50 yard line must be approved by the Commissioner to avoid any confusion as to delineation of goal lines, sidelines, and end lines.

BALL

1. The home club shall have 36 balls for outdoor games and 24 for indoor games available for testing with a pressure gauge by the referee two hours prior to the starting time of the game to meet with League requirements. Twelve (12) new footballs, sealed in a special box and shipped by the manufacturer, will be opened in the officials' locker room two hours prior to the starting time of the game. These balls are to be specially marked with the letter "k" and used exclusively for the kicking game.

COIN TOSS

1. The toss of coin will take place within three minutes of kickoff in center of field. The toss will be called by the visiting captain before the coin is flipped. The winner may choose one of two privileges and the loser gets the other:
   (a) Receive or kick
   (b) Goal his team will defend
2. Immediately prior to the start of the second half, the captains of both teams must inform the officials of their respective choices. The loser of the original coin toss gets first choice.

TIMING

1. The stadium game clock is official. In case it stops or is operating incorrectly, the Line Judge takes over the official timing on the field.
2. Each period is 15 minutes. The intermission between the periods is two minutes. Halftime is 12 minutes, unless otherwise specified.
3. On charged team time outs, the Back Judge starts watch and blows whistle after 1 minute 50 seconds, unless television does not utilize the time for commercial. In this case the length of the time out is reduced to 30 seconds.

4. The Referee will allow necessary time to attend to an injured player, or repair a legal player's equipment.
5. Each team is allowed three time outs each half.
6. Time between plays will be 40 seconds from the end of a given play until the snap of the ball for the next play, or a 25-second interval after certain administrative stoppages and game delays.
7. Clock will start running when ball is snapped following all changes of team possession.
8. With the exception of the last two minutes of the first half and the last five minutes of the second half, the game clock will be restarted following a player going out of bounds on a play from scrimmage, or after declined penalties when appropriate on the referee's signal.
9. Consecutive team time outs can be taken by opposing teams but the length of the second time out will be reduced to 30 seconds.
10. When, in the judgment of the Referee, the level of crowd noise prevents the offense from hearing its signals, he can institute a series of procedures which can result in a loss of team time outs or a five-yard penalty against the defensive team.
11. On kickoff, clock does not start until the ball has been legally touched by player of either team in the field of play.

SUDDEN DEATH

1. The sudden death system of determining the winner shall prevail when score is tied at the end of the regulation playing time of all NFL games. The team scoring first during overtime play shall be the winner and the game automatically ends upon any score (by safety, field goal, or touchdown) or when a score is awarded by Referee for a palpably unfair act.
2. At the end of regulation time the Referee will immediately toss coin at center of field in accordance with rules pertaining to the usual pregame toss. The captain of the visiting team will call the toss prior to the coin being flipped.
3. Following a three-minute intermission after the end of the regulation game, play will be continued in 15-minute periods or until there is a score. There is a two-minute intermission between subsequent periods. The teams change goals at the start of each period. Each team has three time outs per half and all general timing provisions apply as during a regular game. Disqualified players are not allowed to return.
   Exception: In preseason and regular season games there shall be a maximum of 15 minutes of sudden death with two time outs instead of three. General provisions that apply for the fourth quarter will prevail. Try not attempted if touchdown scored.

TIMING IN FINAL TWO MINUTES OF EACH HALF

1. A team cannot buy an excess time out for a penalty. However, a fourth time out is allowed without penalty for an injured player, who must be removed immediately. A fifth time out or more is allowed for an injury and a five-yard penalty is assessed. Additionally, if the clock was running and the score is tied or the team in possession is losing, the ball cannot be put in play for at least 10 seconds on the fourth or more time out. The half or game can end while those 10 seconds are run off on the clock.
2. If the defensive team is behind in the score and commits a foul when it has no time outs left in the final 40 seconds of either half, the offensive team can decline the penalty for the foul and have the time on the clock expire.
3. Fouls that occur in the last five minutes of the fourth quarter as well as the last two minutes of the first half will result in the clock starting on the snap.

TRY

1. After a touchdown, the scoring team is allowed a try during one scrimmage down. The ball may be spotted anywhere between the inbounds lines, two or more yards from the goal line. The successful conversion counts one point by kick; two points for a successful conversion by touchdown; or one point for a safety.
2. The defensive team never can score on a try. As soon as defense gets possession or the kick is blocked or a touchdown is not scored, the try is over.
3. Any distance penalty for fouls committed by the defense that prevent the try from being attempted can be enforced on the succeeding try or succeeding kickoff. Any foul committed on a successful try will result in a distance penalty being assessed on the ensuing kickoff.
4. Only the fumbling player can recover and advance a fumble during a try.

PLAYERS-SUBSTITUTIONS

1. Each team is permitted 11 men on the field at the snap.
2. Unlimited substitution is permitted. However, players may enter the field only when the ball is dead. Players who have been substituted for are not permitted to linger on the field. Such lingering will be interpreted as unsportsmanlike conduct.
3. Players leaving the game must be out of bounds on their own side, clearing the field between the end lines, before a snap or free kick. If player crosses end line leaving field, it is delay of game (five-yard penalty).
4. Offensive substitutes who remain in the game must move onto the field as far as the inside of the field numerals before moving to a wide position.
5. With the exception of the last two minutes of either half, the offensive team, while in the process of substitution or simulated substitution, is prohibited from rushing quickly to the line and snapping the ball with the obvious attempt to cause a defensive foul; i.e., too many men on the field.
6. There never can be 12 or more players in the offensive huddle.

KICKOFF

1. The kickoff shall be from the kicking team's 30-yard line at the start of each half and after a field goal and try. A kickoff is one type of free kick.
2. A one-inch tee may be used (no tee permitted for field goal, safety kick, or try attempt) on a kickoff. The ball is put in play by a placekick.
3. A kickoff may not score a field goal.
4. A kickoff is illegal unless it travels 10 yards OR is touched by the receiving team. Once the ball is touched by the receiving team or has gone 10 yards, it is a free ball. Receivers may recover and advance. Kicking team may recover but NOT advance UNLESS receiver had possession and lost the ball.
5. When a kickoff goes out of bounds between the goal lines without being touched by the receiving team, the ball belongs to the receivers 30 yards from the spot of the kick or at the out-of-bounds spot unless the ball went out-of-bounds the first time an onside kick was attempted. In this case, the kicking team is penalized five yards and the ball must be kicked again.
6. When a kickoff goes out of bounds between the goal lines and is touched last by receiving team, it is receiver's ball at out-of-bounds spot.
7. If the kicking team either illegally kicks off out of bounds or is guilty of a short free kick on two or more consecutive onside kicks, receivers may take possession of the ball at the dead ball spot, out-of-bounds spot, or spot of illegal touch.

SAFETY

1. In addition to a kickoff, the other free kick is a kick after a safety (safety kick). A punt may be used (a punt may not be used on a kickoff).
2. On a safety kick, the team scored upon puts ball in play by a punt, dropkick, or placekick without tee. No score can be

made on a free kick following a safety, even if a series of penalties places team in position. (A field goal can be scored only on a play from scrimmage or a free kick after a fair catch.)

FAIR CATCH KICK

1. After a fair catch, the receiving team has the option to put the ball in play by a snap or a fair catch kick (field goal attempt), with fair catch kick lines established ten yards apart. All general rules apply as for a field goal attempt from scrimmage. The clock starts when the ball is kicked. (No tee permitted.)

FIELD GOAL

1. All field goals attempted (kicker) and missed from beyond the 20-yard line will result in the defensive team taking possession of the ball at the spot of the kick. On any field goal attempted and missed where the spot of the kick is on or inside the 20-yard line, ball will revert to defensive team at the 20-yard line.

SAFETY

1. The important factor in a safety is impetus. Two points are scored for the opposing team when the ball is dead on or behind a team's own goal line if the impetus came from a player on that team.

Examples of Safety:

(a) Blocked punt goes out of kicking team's end zone. Impetus was provided by punting team. The block only changes direction of ball, not impetus.
(b) Ball carrier retreats from field of play into his own end zone and is downed. Ball carrier provides impetus.
(c) Offensive team commits a foul and spot of enforcement is behind its own goal line.
(d) Player on receiving team muffs punt and, trying to get ball, forces or illegally kicks (creating new impetus) it into end zone where it goes out of the end zone or is recovered by a member of the receiving team in the end zone.

Examples of Non-Safety:

(a) Player intercepts a pass with both feet inbounds in the field of play and his momentum carries him into his own end zone. Ball is put in play at spot of interception.
(b) Player intercepts a pass in his own end zone and is downed in the end zone, even after recovering in the end zone. Impetus came from passing team, not from defense. (Touchback)
(c) Player passes from behind his own goal line. Opponent bats down ball in end zone. (Incomplete pass)

MEASURING

1. The forward point of the ball is used when measuring.

POSITION OF PLAYERS AT SNAP

1. Offensive team must have at least seven players on line.
2. Offensive players, not on line, must be at least one yard back at snap.
   (Exception: player who takes snap.)
3. No interior lineman may move abruptly after taking or simulating a three-point stance.
4. No player of either team may enter neutral zone before snap.
5. No player of offensive team may charge or move abruptly, after assuming set position, in such manner as to lead defense to believe snap has started. No player of the defensive team within one yard of the line of scrimmage may make an abrupt movement in an attempt to cause the offense to false start.
6. If a player changes his eligibility, the Referee must alert the defensive captain after player has reported to him.
7. All players of offensive team must be stationary at snap, except one back who may be in motion parallel to scrimmage line or backward (not forward).
8. After a shift or huddle all players on offensive team must come to an absolute stop for at least one second with no movement of hands, feet, head, or swaying of body.
9. Quarterbacks can be called for a false start penalty (five yards) if their actions are judged to be an obvious attempt to draw an opponent offside.
10. Offensive linemen are permitted to interlock legs.

USE OF HANDS, ARMS, AND BODY

1. No player on offense may assist a runner except by blocking for him. There shall be no interlocking interference.
2. A runner may ward off opponents with his hands and arms but no other player on offense may use hands or arms to obstruct an opponent by grasping with hands, pushing, or encircling any part of his body during a block. Hands (open or closed) can be thrust forward to initially contact an opponent on or outside the opponent's frame, but the blocker immediately must work to bring his hands on or inside the frame.
   Note: Pass blocking: Hand(s) thrust forward that slip outside the body of the defender will be legal if blocker immediately worked to bring them back inside. Hand(s) or arm(s) that encircle a defender—i.e., hook an opponent—are to be considered illegal and officials are to call a foul for holding. Blocker cannot use his hands or arms to push from behind, hang onto, or encircle an opponent in a manner that restricts his movement as the play develops.
3. Hands cannot be thrust forward above the frame to contact an opponent on the neck, face or head.
   Note: The frame is defined as the part of the opponent's body below the neck that is presented to the blocker.
4. A defensive player may not tackle or hold an opponent other than a runner. Otherwise, he may use his hands, arms, or body only:
   (a) To defend or protect himself against an obstructing opponent.
   Exception: An eligible receiver is considered to be an obstructing opponent ONLY to a point five yards beyond the line of scrimmage unless the player who receives the snap clearly demonstrates no further intention to pass the ball. Within this five-yard zone, a defensive player may chuck an eligible player in front of him. A defensive player is allowed to maintain continuous and unbroken contact within the five-yard zone until a point when the receiver is even with the defender. The defensive player cannot use his hands or arms to push from behind, hang onto, or encircle an eligible receiver in a manner that restricts movement as the play develops. Beyond this five-yard limitation, a defender may use his hands or arms ONLY to defend or protect himself against impending contact caused by a receiver. In such reaction, the defender may not contact a receiver who attempts to take a path to evade him.
   (b) To push or pull opponent out of the way on line of scrimmage.
   (c) In actual attempt to get at or tackle runner.
   (d) To push or pull opponent out of the way in a legal attempt to recover a loose ball.
   (e) During a legal block on an opponent who is not an eligible pass receiver.
   (f) When legally blocking an eligible pass receiver above the waist.
   Exception: Eligible receivers lined up within two yards of the tackle, whether on or immediately behind the line, may be blocked below the waist at or behind the line of scrimmage. NO eligible receiver may be blocked below the waist after he goes beyond the line. (Illegal cut)

Note: Once the quarterback hands off or pitches the ball to a back, or if the quarterback leaves the pocket area, the restrictions (illegal chuck, illegal cut) on the defensive team relative to the offensive receivers will end, provided the ball is not in the air.

5. A defensive player may not contact an opponent above the shoulders with the palm of his hand except to ward him off on the line. This exception is permitted only if it is not a repeated act against the same opponent during any one contact. In all other cases the palms may be used on head, neck, or face only to ward off or push an opponent in legal attempt to get at the ball.
6. Any offensive player who pretends to possess the ball or to whom a teammate pretends to give the ball may be tackled provided he is crossing his scrimmage line between the ends of a normal tight offensive line.
7. An offensive player who lines up more than two yards outside his own tackle or a player who, at the snap, is in a backfield position and subsequently takes a position more than two yards outside a tackle may not clip an opponent anywhere nor may he contact an opponent below the waist if the blocker is moving toward the ball and if contact is made within an area five yards on either side of the line. (crackback)
8. A player of either team may block at any time provided it is not pass interference, fair catch interference, or unnecessary roughness.
9. A player may not bat or punch:
   (a) A loose ball (in field of play) toward his opponent's goal line or in any direction in either end zone.
   (b) A ball in player possession.
   Note: If there is any question as to whether a defender is stripping or batting a ball in player possession, the official(s) will rule the action as a legal act (stripping the ball).
   Exception: A forward or backward pass may be batted, tipped, or deflected in any direction at any time by either the offense or the defense.
   Note: A pass in flight that is controlled or caught may only be thrown backward, if it is thrown forward it is considered an illegal bat.
10. No player may deliberately kick any ball except as a punt, dropkick, or placekick.

FORWARD PASS

1. A forward pass may be touched or caught by any eligible receiver. All members of the defensive team are eligible. Eligible receivers on the offensive team are players on either end of line (other than center, guard, or tackle) or players at least one yard behind the line at the snap. A T-formation quarterback is not eligible to receive a forward pass during a play from scrimmage.
   Exception: T-formation quarterback becomes eligible if pass is previously touched by an eligible receiver.
2. An offensive team may make only one forward pass during each play from scrimmage (Loss of 5 yards).
3. The passer must be behind his line of scrimmage (Loss of down and five yards, enforced from the spot of pass).
4. Any eligible offensive player may catch a forward pass. If a pass is touched by one eligible offensive player and touched or caught by a second offensive player, pass completion is legal. Further, all offensive players become eligible once a pass is touched by an eligible receiver or any defensive player.
5. The rules concerning a forward pass and ineligible receivers:
   (a) If ball is touched accidentally by an ineligible receiver on or behind his line: loss of five yards.
   (b) If ineligible receiver is illegally downfield: loss of five yards.
   (c) If touched or caught (intentionally or accidentally) by ineligible receiver beyond the line: loss of 5 yards.
6. The player who first controls and continues to maintain control of a pass will be awarded the ball even though his opponent later establishes joint control of the ball.
7. Any forward pass becomes incomplete and ball is dead if:
   (a) Pass hits the ground or goes out of bounds.
   (b) Pass hits the goal post or the crossbar of either team.
8. A forward pass is complete when a receiver clearly possesses the pass and touches the ground with both feet inbounds while in possession of the ball. If a receiver would have landed inbounds with both feet but is carried or pushed out of bounds while maintaining possession of the ball, pass is complete at the out-of-bounds spot.
9. If a personal foul is committed by the defense prior to the completion of a pass, the penalty is 15 yards from the spot where ball becomes dead.
10. If a personal foul is committed by the offense prior to the completion of a pass, the penalty is 15 yards from the previous line of scrimmage.

INTENTIONAL GROUNDING OF FORWARD PASS

1. Intentional grounding of a forward pass is a foul: loss of down and 10 yards from previous spot if passer is in the field of play or loss of down at the spot of the foul if it occurs more than 10 yards behind the line or safety if passer is in his own end zone when ball is released.
2. Intentional grounding will be called when a passer, facing an imminent loss of yardage due to pressure from the defense, throws a forward pass without a realistic chance of completion.
3. Intentional grounding will not be called when a passer, while out of the pocket and facing an imminent loss of yardage, throws a pass that lands at or beyond the line of scrimmage, even if no offensive player(s) have a realistic chance to catch the ball (including if the ball lands out of bounds over the sideline or end line).

PROTECTION OF PASSER

1. By interpretation, a pass begins when the passer—with possession of ball—starts to bring his hand forward. If ball strikes ground after this action has begun, play is ruled an incomplete pass. If passer loses control of ball prior to his bringing his hand forward, play is ruled a fumble.
2. When a passer is holding the ball to pass it forward, any intentional movement forward of his hand starts a forward pass. If a defensive player contacts the passer or the ball after forward movement begins, and the ball leaves the passer's hand, a forward pass is ruled, regardless of where the ball strikes the ground or a player.
3. No defensive player may run into a passer of a legal forward pass after the ball has left his hand (15 yards). The Referee must determine whether opponent had a reasonable chance to stop his momentum during an attempt to block the pass or tackle the passer while he still had the ball.
4. No defensive player who has an unrestricted path to the quarterback may hit him flagrantly in the area of the knee(s) or below when approaching in any direction.
5. Officials are to blow the play dead as soon as the quarterback is clearly in the grasp and control of any tackler, and his safety is in jeopardy.
6. No defensive player may hit the quarterback in the head, face, or neck.

PASS INTERFERENCE

1. There shall be no interference with a forward pass thrown from behind the line. The restriction for the passing team starts with the snap. The restriction on the defensive team starts when the ball leaves the passer's hand. Both restrictions end when the ball is touched by anyone.
2. The penalty for defensive pass interference is an automatic first down at the spot of the foul. If interference is in the end

zone, it is first down for the offense on the defense's 1-yard line. If previous spot was inside the defense's 1-yard line, penalty is half the distance to the goal line.

3. The penalty for offensive pass interference is 10 yards from the previous spot.
4. It is pass interference by either team when any player movement beyond the line of scrimmage significantly hinders the progress of an eligible player of such player's opportunity to catch the ball. Offensive pass interference rules apply from the time the ball is snapped until the ball is touched. Defensive pass interference rules apply from the time the ball is thrown until the ball is touched.

   Actions that constitute defensive pass interference include but are not limited to:
   (a) Contact by a defender who is not playing the ball and such contact restricts the receiver's opportunity to make the catch.
   (b) Playing through the back of a receiver in an attempt to make a play on the ball.
   (c) Grabbing a receiver's arm(s) in such a manner that restricts his opportunity to catch a pass.
   (d) Extending an arm across the body of a receiver thus restricting his ability to catch a pass, regardless of whether the defender is playing the ball.
   (e) Cutting off the path of a receiver by making contact with him without playing the ball.
   (f) Hooking a receiver in an attempt to get to the ball in such a manner that it causes the receiver's body to turn prior to the ball arriving.

   Actions that do not constitute pass interference include but are not limited to:
   (a) Incidental contact by a defender's hands, arms, or body when both players are competing for the ball, or neither player is looking for the ball. If there is any question whether contact is incidental, the ruling shall be no interference.
   (b) Inadvertent tangling of feet when both players are playing the ball or neither player is playing the ball.
   (c) Contact that would normally be considered pass interference, but the ball is clearly uncatchable by the involved players.
   (d) Laying a hand on a receiver that does not restrict the receiver in an attempt to make a play on the ball.
   (e) Contact by a defender who has gained position on a receiver in an attempt to catch the ball.

   Actions that constitute offensive pass interference include but are not limited to:
   (a) Blocking downfield by an offensive player prior to the ball being touched.
   (b) Initiating contact with a defender by shoving or pushing off thus creating a separation in an attempt to catch a pass.
   (c) Driving through a defender who has established a position on the field.

   Actions that do not constitute offensive pass interference include but are not limited to:
   (a) Incidental contact by a receiver's hands, arms, or body when both players are competing for the ball or neither player is looking for the ball.
   (b) Inadvertent touching of feet when both players are playing the ball or neither player is playing the ball.
   (c) Contact that would normally be considered pass interference, but the ball is clearly uncatchable by involved players.

Note 1: If there is any question whether player contact is incidental, the ruling should be no interference.

Note 2: Defensive players have as much right to the path of the ball as eligible offensive players.

Note 3: Pass interference for both teams ends when the pass is touched.

Note 4: There can be no pass interference at or behind the line of scrimmage, but defensive actions such as tackling a receiver can still result in a 5-yard penalty for defensive holding, if accepted.

Note 5: Whenever a team presents an apparent punting formation, defensive pass interference is not to be called for action on the end man on the line of scrimmage, or an eligible receiver behind the line of scrimmage who is aligned or in motion more than one yard outside the end man on the line. Defensive holding, such as tackling a receiver, still can be called and result in a 5-yard penalty and automatic first down from the previous spot, if accepted. Offensive pass interference rules still apply.

BACKWARD PASS

1. Any pass not forward is regarded as a backward pass. A pass parallel to the line is a backward pass. A runner may pass backward at any time.
2. A backward pass that strikes the ground can be recovered and advanced by either team.
3. A backward pass caught in the air can be advanced by either team.
4. A backward pass in flight may not be batted forward by an offensive player.

FUMBLE

1. The distinction between a fumble and a muff should be kept in mind in considering rules about fumbles. A fumble is the loss of player possession of the ball. A muff is the touching of a loose ball by a player in an unsuccessful attempt to obtain possession.
2. A fumble may be advanced by any player on either team regardless of whether recovered before or after ball hits the ground.
3. A fumble that goes forward and out of bounds will return to the fumbling team at the spot of the fumble unless the ball goes out of bounds in the opponent's end zone. In this case, it is a touchback.
4. On a play from scrimmage, if an offensive player fumbles anywhere on the field during fourth down, only the fumbling player is permitted to recover and/or advance the ball. If any player fumbles after the two-minute warning in a half, only the fumbling player is permitted to recover and/or advance the ball. If recovered by any other offensive player, the ball is dead at the spot of the fumble unless it is recovered behind the spot of the fumble. In that case, the ball is dead at the spot of recovery. Any defensive player may recover and/or advance any fumble at any time.
5. A muffed hand-to-hand snap from center is treated as a fumble.

KICKS FROM SCRIMMAGE

1. Any kick from scrimmage must be made from behind the line to be legal.
2. Any punt or missed field goal that touches a goal post is dead.
3. During a kick from scrimmage, only the end men, as eligible receivers on the line of scrimmage at the time of the snap, are permitted to go beyond the line before the ball is kicked.
   Exception: An eligible receiver who, at the snap, is aligned or in motion behind the line and more than one yard outside the end man on his side of the line, clearly making him the outside receiver, replaces that end man as the player eligible to go downfield after the snap. All other members of the kicking team must remain at the line of scrimmage until the ball has been kicked.
4. Any punt that is blocked and does not cross the line of scrimmage can be recovered and advanced by either team. However, if offensive team recovers it must make the yardage necessary for its first down to retain possession if punt was

on fourth down.

5. The kicking team may never advance its own kick even though legal recovery is made beyond the line of scrimmage. Possession only.
6. A member of the receiving team may not run into or rough a kicker who kicks from behind his line unless contact is:
   (a) Incidental to and after he had touched ball in flight.
   (b) Caused by kicker's own motions.
   (c) Occurs during a quick kick, or a kick made after a run behind the line, or after kicker recovers a loose ball on the ground. Ball is loose when kicker muffs snap or snap hits ground.
   (d) Defender is blocked into kicker.
   The penalty for running into the kicker is 5 yards. For roughing the kicker: 15 yards, an automatic first down and disqualification if flagrant.
7. If a member of the kicking team attempting to down the ball on or inside opponent's 5-yard line carries the ball into the end zone, it is a touchback.
8. Fouls during a punt are enforced from the previous spot (line of scrimmage).
   Exception: Illegal touching, fair-catch interference, invalid fair-catch signal, or personal foul (blocking after a fair-catch signal).
9. While the ball is in the air or rolling on the ground following a punt or field-goal attempt and receiving team commits a foul only before or after gaining possession, receiving team will retain possession and will be penalized for its foul.
10. It will be illegal for a defensive player to jump or stand on any player, or be picked up by a teammate or to use a hand or hands on a teammate to gain additional height in an attempt to block a kick (Penalty: 15 yards, unsportsmanlike conduct).
11. A punted ball remains a kicked ball until it is declared dead or in possession of either team.
12. Any member of the punting team may down the ball anywhere in the field of play. However, it is illegal touching (Official's time out and receiver's ball at spot of illegal touching). This foul does not offset any foul by receivers during the down.
13. Defensive team may advance all kicks from scrimmage (including unsuccessful field goal) whether or not ball crosses defensive team's goal line. Rules pertaining to kicks from scrimmage apply until defensive team gains possession.
14. When a team presents a punt formation, defensive pass interference is not to be called for actions on the widest player eligible to go beyond line. Defensive holding may be called.

FAIR CATCH

1. The member of the receiving team must raise one arm a full length above his head and wave it from side to side while kick is in flight. (Failure to give proper sign: receivers' ball five yards behind spot of signal.) **Note:** It is legal for the receiver to shield his eyes from the sun by raising one hand no higher than the helmet.
2. No opponent may interfere with the fair catcher, the ball, or his path to the ball. Penalty: 15 yards from spot of foul and fair catch is awarded.
3. A player who signals for a fair catch is not required to catch the ball. However, if a player signals for a fair catch, he may not block or initiate contact with any player on the kicking team until the ball touches a player. Penalty: snap 15 yards.
4. If ball is touched by member of kicking team in flight, fair catch signal is off and all rules for a kicked ball apply.
5. Any undue advance by a fair catch receiver is delay of game. No specific distance is specified for undue advance as ball is dead at spot of catch. If player comes to a reasonable stop, no penalty. For penalty, five yards.
6. If time expires while ball is in play and a fair catch is awarded, receiving team may choose to extend the period with one fair catch kick down. However, placekicker may not use tee.

FOUL ON LAST PLAY OF HALF OR GAME

1. On a foul by defense on last play of half or game, the down is replayed if penalty is accepted.
2. On a foul by the offense on last play of half or game, the down is not replayed and the play in which the foul is committed is nullified.
   Exception: Fair catch interference, foul following change of possession, illegal touching. No score by offense counts.

SPOT OF ENFORCEMENT OF FOUL

1. There are four basic spots at which a penalty for a foul is enforced:
   (a) Spot of foul: The spot where the foul is committed.
   (b) Previous spot: The spot where the ball was put in play.
   (c) Spot of snap, backward pass or fumble: The spot where the foul occurred or the spot where the penalty is to be enforced.
   (d) Succeeding spot: The spot where the ball next would be put in play if no distance penalty were to be enforced.
   Exception: If foul occurs after a touchdown and before the whistle for a try, succeeding spot is spot of next kickoff.
2. All fouls committed by offensive team behind the line of scrimmage (except in the end zone) shall be penalized from the previous spot. If the foul is in the end zone, it is a safety.
3. When spot of enforcement for fouls involving defensive holding or illegal use of hands by the defense is behind the line of scrimmage, any penalty yardage to be assessed on that play shall be measured from the line if the foul occurred beyond the line.

DOUBLE FOUL

1. If there is a double foul during a down in which there is a change of possession, the team last gaining possession may keep the ball unless its foul was committed prior to the change of possession.
2. If double foul occurs after a change of possession, the defensive team retains the ball at the spot of its foul or dead ball spot.
3. If one of the fouls of a double foul involves disqualification, that player must be removed, but no penalty yardage is to be assessed.
4. If the kickers foul during a kickoff, punt, safety kick, or field-goal attempt before possession changes, the receivers will have the option of replaying the down at the previous spot (offsetting fouls), or keeping the ball after enforcement for its fouls.

PENALTY ENFORCED ON FOLLOWING KICKOFF

1. When a team scores by touchdown, field goal, extra point, or safety and either team commits a personal foul, unsportsmanlike conduct, or obvious unfair act during the down, the penalty will be assessed on the following kickoff.

EMERGENCIES AND UNFAIR ACTS

Emergencies—Policy

The National Football League requires all League personnel, including game officials, League office employees, players, coaches, and other club employees to use best effort to see that each game—preseason, regular season, and postseason—is played to its conclusion. The League recognizes, however, that emergencies may arise that make a game's completion impossible or inadvisable. Such circumstances may include, but are not limited to, severely inclement weather, natural or manmade disaster, power failure, and spectator interference. Games should be suspended, cancelled, postponed, or terminated when circumstances exist such that comencement or continuation of play would pose a threat to the safety of participants or spectators.

Authority of Commissioner's Office

1. Authority to cancel, postpone, or terminate games is vested only in the Commissioner and the League President (other League office representatives and referees may suspend play temporarily; see point No. 3 under this section and point No. 1 under "Authority of Referee" below). The following definitions apply:
   - **Cancel.** To cancel a game is to nullify it either before or after it begins and to make no provision for rescheduling it or for including its score or other performance statistics in League records.
   - **Postpone.** To postpone a game is (a) to defer its starting time to a later date, or (b) to suspend it after play has begun and to make provision to resume at a later date with all scores and other performance statistics up to the point of postponement added to those achieved in the resumed portion of the game.
   - **Terminate.** To terminate a game is to end it short of a full 60 minutes of play, to record it officially as a completed game, and to make no provision to resume it at a later date. The Commissioner or League President may terminate a game in an emergency if, in his opinion, it is reasonable to project that its resumption (a) would not change its ultimate result or (b) would not adversely affect any other interteam competitive issue.
   - **Forfeit.** The Commissioner, (except in cases of disciplinary action; see last section on "Removing Team from Field"), League President, and their representatives, including referees, are not authorized unilaterally to declare forfeits. A forfeit occurs only when a game is not played because of the failure or refusal of *one* team to participate. In that event, the other team, if ready and willing to play, is the winner by a score of 2-0.
2. If an emergency arises that may require cancellation, postponement, or termination (see above), the highest ranking representative from the Commissioner's office working the game in a "control" capacity will consult with the Commissioner, League President, or game-day duty officer designated by the League (by telephone, if that person is not in attendance) concerning such decision. If circumstances warrant, the League representative should also attempt to consult with the weather bureau and with appropriate security personnel of the League, club, stadium, and local authorities. If no representative from the Commissioner's office is working the game in a "control" capacity, the referee will be in charge (see "Authority of Referee" below).
3. In circumstances where safety is of immediate concern, the Commissioner's office representative may, after consulting with the referee, authorize a temporary suspension in play and, if warranted, removal of the participants from the playing field. The representative should be mindful of the safety of spectators, players, game officials, nonplayer personnel in the bench areas, and other field-level personnel such as photographers and cheerleaders.
4. If possible, the League-office representative should consult with authorized representatives of the two participating clubs before any decision involving cancellation, postponement, or termination is made by the Commissioner or League President.
5. If the Commissioner or League President decides to cancel, postpone, or terminate a game, his representative at the game or the game-day duty officer will then determine the method(s) for announcing such decision, e.g., by public-address announcement over referee's wireless microphone, by public-address announcement by home club, or by communication to radio, television, and other news media.

Authority of Referee

1. If a referee determines that an emergency warrants immediate removal of participants from the playing field for safety reasons, he may do so on his own authority. If, however, circumstances allow him the time, he must reach the highest ranking full-time League office representative working at the game in a "control" capacity or the game-day duty officer designated by the League (by telephone, if that person is not in attendance) and discuss the actual or potential emergency with such representative or duty officer. That representative or duty officer then will make the final decision on removal of participants from the field or obtain a decision from the Commissioner or League President.
2. If a referee removes participants from the playing field under No. 1 above, he may order them to their respective bench areas or to their locker rooms, whichever is appropriate in the circumstances.
3. After appropriate consultation under No. 1 above, the referee must advise the two participating head coaches of the nature of the emergency and the action contemplated (if the decision has not yet been reached) or of the final decision.
4. The referee must *not*, before a decision is reached, make an announcement on his microphone concerning the possibility of a cancellation, postponement, or termination unless instructed to do so by an appropriate representative of the Commissioner's office.
5. The referee must *not* discuss a forfeit with head coaches or club personnel and must *not* use that term over the referee's microphone (see definition of *forfeit* under No. 1 of "Authority of Commissioner's Office" above).
6. The referee must *not* assess an unsportsmanlike-conduct penalty on the home team for actions of fans that cause or contribute to an emergency.
7. The referee should be mindful of the safety of not only players and officials, but also of the spectators and other nonparticipants.
8. If an emergency involves spectator interference (for example, nonparticipants on the field or thrown objects), the referee immediately should contact the appropriate club or League representative for additional security assistance, including, if applicable, involvement of the League's security representative(s) assigned to the game.
9. The referee may order the resumption of play when he deems conditions safe for all concerned and, if circumstances warrant, after consultation with appropriate representatives of the Commissioner's office.
10. Under no circumstances is the referee authorized to cancel, postpone, terminate, or declare forfeiture of a game unilaterally.

Procedures for Starting and Resuming Games

Subject to the points of authority listed above, League personnel and referees will be guided by the following procedures for starting and resuming games that are affected by emergencies.

1. If, because of an emergency, a regular-season or postseason game is not started at its scheduled time and cannot be played at any later time that same day, the game nevertheless must be played on a subsequent date to be determined by the Commissioner.
2. If an emergency threatens to occur during the playing of a game (for example, an incoming tropical storm), the starting time of the game will not be moved to an earlier time unless there is clearly sufficient time to make an orderly change.
3. All games that are suspended temporarily and resumed on the same day, and all suspended games that are postponed to a later date, will be resumed at the point of suspension. On suspension, the referee will call timeout and make a record of the following: team possessing the ball, direction in which its offense was headed, position of the ball on the field, down, distance, period, time remaining in the period, and any other pertinent information required for an orderly and equitable resumption of play.
4. For regular-season postponements, the Commissioner will make every effort to set the game for no later than two days

after its originally scheduled date and at the same site. If unable to schedule at the same site, he will select an appropriate alternative site. If it is impossible to schedule the game within two days after its original date, the Commissioner will attempt to schedule it on the Tuesday of the next calendar week. The Commissioner will keep in mind the potential for competitive inequities if one or both of the involved clubs has already been scheduled for a game close to the Tuesday of that week (for example, a Thursday game).

5. For postseason postponements, the Commissioner will make every effort to set the game as soon as possible after its originally scheduled date and at the same site. If unable to schedule at the same site, he will select an appropriate alternative site.
6. Whenever postponement is attributable to negligence by a club, the negligent club is responsible for all home club costs and expenses, including, subject to approval by the Commissioner, gate receipts and television-contract income. [See Section 19.11 (C) of the NFL Constitution and Bylaws.]
7. Each home club is strictly responsible for having the playing surface of its stadium well maintained and suitable for NFL play.

UNFAIR ACTS

Commissioner's Authority

The Commissioner has sole authority to investigate and to take appropriate disciplinary or corrective measures if any club action, nonparticipant interference, or emergency occurs in an NFL game which he deems so unfair or outside the accepted tactics encountered in professional football that such action has a major effect on the result of a game.

No Club Protests

The authority and measures provided for in this section (UNFAIR ACTS) do not constitute a protest machinery for NFL clubs to dispute the result of a game. The Commissioner will conduct an investigation under this section only to review an act or occurrence that he deems so unfair that the result of the game in question may be inequitable to one of the participating teams. The Commissioner will not apply his authority under this section when a club registers a complaint concerning judgmental errors or routine errors of omission by game officials. Games involving such complaints will continue to stand as completed.

Penalties for Unfair Acts

The Commissioner's powers under this section (UNFAIR ACTS) include the imposition of monetary fines and draft choice forfeitures, suspension of persons involved, and, if appropriate, the reversal of a game's result or the rescheduling of a game, either from the beginning or from the point at which the extraordinary act occurred. In the event of rescheduling a game, the Commissioner will be guided by the procedures specified above ("Procedures for Starting and Resuming Games" under EMERGENCIES). In all cases, the Commissioner will conduct a full investigation, including the opportunity for hearings, use of game videotape, and any other procedures he deems appropriate.

REMOVING TEAM FROM FIELD

No player, coach, or other person affiliated with a club may remove that club's team from the field during the playing of any game, including preseason, except at the direction of the referee. Any club violating this rule will be subject to disciplinary action by the Commissioner, including possible game forfeiture and sole liability for financial losses suffered by the opposing club and any other affected member clubs of the League. [See Section 9.1 (E) of the NFL Constitution and Bylaws.]

NATIONAL FOOTBALL LEAGUE, 2004

280 Park Avenue, New York, New York 10017 (212) 450-2000

NFL Internet Network: www.NFL.com

Commissioner: Paul Tagliabue

Executive Vice President/Chief Operating Officer: Roger Goodell

Executive Vice President/Chief Administrative Officer-Counsel: Jeff Pash

Executive Vice President of Labor Relations/Chairman NFLMC: Harold Henderson

Executive Vice President of Communications and Public Affairs: Joe Browne

Executive Vice President of Media/President and Chief Executive Officer of NFL Network: Steve Bornstein